Essentials of

FINANCIAL ACCOUNTING

Information for Business Decisions

Essentials of

FINANCIAL ACCOUNTING

Information for Business Decisions

Seventh Edition

Kermit D. Larson
University of Texas–Austin

Irwin
McGraw-Hill

Boston, Massachusetts   Burr Ridge, Illinios   Dubuque, Iowa
Madison, Wisconsin   New York, New York   San Francisco, California   St. Louis, Missouri

Irwin/McGraw-Hill

A Division of The McGraw·Hill Companies

Previously published as *Financial Accounting.*

ESSENTIALS OF FINANCIAL ACCOUNTING: INFORMATION FOR BUSINESS DECISIONS

4 5 6 7 8 9 0 QD QD 9 0 9

ISBN 0-256-20916-2

Publisher: *Michael W. Junior*
Executive editor: *Jeff Shelstad*
Editorial coordinator: *Martin Quinn*
Marketing manager: *Heather L. Woods*
Project supervisor: *Susan Trentacosti*
Production supervisor: *Bob Lange*
Cover designer: *Kiera Cunningham*
Prepress buyer: *Charlene R. Perez*
Compositor: *York Graphic Services, Inc.*
Typeface: *10.5/12 Times Roman*
Printer: Quebecor Printing Book Group/Dubuque

Library of Congress Cataloging-in-Publication Data

Larson, Kermit D.
　　Essentials of financial accounting: information for business
decisions/Kermit D. Larson—7th ed.
　　　　p.　　cm.—(The Irwin series in undergraduate accounting)
　　Rev. ed. of: Financial accounting.
　　Includes bibliographical references and index.
　　ISBN 0-256-20916-2
　　1. Accounting.　I. Larson, Kermit D. Financial accounting.
II. Title.　III. Series.
HF5635.P974　1997
657—dc21　　　　　　　　　　　　　　　　　96-48062

http://www.mhcollege.com

To Cindy

About the Author

Kermit D. Larson is the Arthur Andersen & Co. Alumni Professor of Accounting Emeritus at The University of Texas at Austin. He served as chairman of the U.T. Department of Accounting and was Visiting Associate Professor at Tulane University. His scholarly articles have been published in a variety of journals, including *The Accounting Review, Journal of Accountancy,* and *Abacus.* He is the author of several books, including *Fundamental Accounting Principles* and *Fundamentals of Financial and Managerial Accounting,* both published by Richard D. Irwin, Inc.

Professor Larson is a member of The American Accounting Association, the Texas Society of CPAs, and the American Institute of CPAs. His activities with the AAA have involved serving as Vice President, as Southwest Regional Vice President, and as chairperson of several committees, including the Committee on Concepts and Standards. He was a member of the committee that planned the first AAA Doctoral Consortium and served as its Director.

Professor Larson's other activities have included serving on the Accounting Accreditation Committee and on the Accounting Standards Committee of the AACSB. He was a member of the Constitutional Drafting Committee of the Federation of Schools of Accountancy and a member of the Commission on Professional Accounting Education. He has been an expert witness on cases involving mergers, antitrust litigation, consolidation criteria, franchise taxes, and expropriation of assets by foreign governments. Professor Larson served on the Board of Directors and Executive Committee of Tekcon, Inc., and on the National Accountant Advisory Board of Safe-Guard Business Systems. In his leisure time, he enjoys skiing and is an avid sailor and golfer.

Preface

Essentials of Financial Accounting introduces students to accounting information, how it is developed, and how it is used to make decisions about corporations and other economic organizations. The text provides an efficient, clear presentation that is student friendly. It supports a variety of teaching approaches and now is very supportive of those who want to emphasize decision making, critical thinking, and communication skills.

MAJOR CHANGES IN THE TEXT

This edition incorporates several major changes. Most notable are the following:

1. A new Chapter 1 explains the relevance of accounting to business decisions and to the future careers of business students. The chapter describes the role of accounting in the context of other organizational functions such as finance, human resources, research and development, production, marketing, and executive management. It also explains the work accountants do, their certifications, and the pervasive importance of ethics in accounting.

2. Corporations are now used in the illustrations and examples throughout the early chapters of the book. Students will find the presentation easy to understand and it is responsive to the requests of many adopters.

3. The text consistently places the student reader in the role of an information user. Thus, selected procedural matters such as the work sheet have been minimized or removed from the body of specific chapters. (Appropriate work sheet coverage is provided in an appendix.)

4. The chapter on merchandising operations has been completely rewritten to focus on perpetual inventory systems. This change reflects the increasing use of perpetual systems. It also shows students more clearly how accounting deals with both the cost and revenue aspects of sales transactions.

5. Chapter 9 includes a new explanation of periodic inventories with a transaction-by-transaction comparison to perpetual systems.

6. Chapter 13 contains new material that describes the differences between "C" corporations, "S" corporations, limited liability companies, partnerships, proprietorships, limited partnerships, and limited liability partnerships.

7. New Progress Check questions are spaced appropriately throughout each chapter with answers provided at the end of the chapter. These review questions get students to stop momentarily and reflect on whether they should spend more time studying a given section of the text before moving on.

8. A new Quick Study category of five-minute exercises is provided after each chapter. Instructors confirm an increasing reliance on shorter problem material for use

as in-class illustrations as well as homework assignments. Undoubtedly, the prospect of solving problems in a short time and the rapid feedback of having done so successfully are motivating factors that lead students to extend their study efforts. We provide at least one Quick Study exercise for each learning objective.

9. A selected number of problems and alternate problems now have requirements that are separated into a *Preparation Component* and an *Analysis Component.* The analysis component typically requires students to consider the financial statement effects of alternative situations and present their analysis in the form of an essay.

10. Each chapter includes a new category of assignments under the heading Critical Thinking: Essays, Problems, and Cases. These include:

   • Analytical Essays.
   • Business Communication Cases.
   • Financial Reporting Problems.
   • Financial Statement Analysis Cases.
   • Managerial Decision Cases.
   • Managerial Analysis Problems.
   • Ethical Issues Essays.

11. A new Concept Tester question, designed as a crossword puzzle, is provided at the end of many chapters. These puzzles motivate students to learn the meaning of the glossary terms and are supported by the working papers.

12. A new opening scenario for each chapter draws on the facts of a real company to identify some of the analysis and decision questions addressed in the chapter. Later in the chapter, one or more references show how the ideas being explained at that point apply to the company that was described in the chapter opening.

13. The entire text reflects a dramatically expanded emphasis on real-world examples that have been carefully selected and integrated into the discussion. Most of these references are accompanied by photos that draw attention to the nature of the business or the specific company used as the example.

14. The book has been carefully redesigned to generate student interest and yet provide a basis for pricing the text in a manner that is responsive to increasing student concerns with the high cost of textbooks.

ADDITIONAL NOTEWORTHY FEATURES

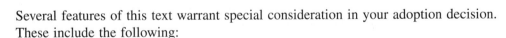

Several features of this text warrant special consideration in your adoption decision. These include the following:

1. In every chapter, the book is now written so that students learn and practice how to use accounting information in making decisions. This shift in focus has been accomplished while maintaining the appropriate goal of showing students how the information is developed. Too often, the importance of this understanding to managers and other nonaccountant decision makers has been overlooked or dismissed. By gaining an introductory understanding of the processes by which accounting information and reports are generated, future decision makers learn the limits of accounting information. They learn to avoid overstating or misinterpreting the information. Thus, they are less apt to confuse such things as book values and market values, accumulated depreciation and spendable funds, or net income and cash inflows.

2. An increasing number of companies routinely convert their receivables into cash without waiting to receive customer payments. In dealing with this modern business practice, this text replaces the traditional discussion of discounting notes receivable with a more general examination of the various ways businesses convert receivables into cash.

3. Streamlined discussions provide clear treatment of topics such as lower of cost or market, retail inventory methods, accelerated depreciation, MACRS, and leases.

4. The text has a uniquely balanced set of asset chapters. In particular, the coverage of Chapter 11 is notable. It completes the asset coverage by discussing natural resources, intangible assets, and long-term investments. The long-term investments portion naturally concludes with a discussion of investments in international operations.

5. Instructors and reviewers have uniformly called for a new commitment to show students the relevance of accounting information and to teach them how to use the information. The text responds to this in a variety of ways. Most obviously, each chapter includes a section under the general heading Using the Information. These sections show students how to calculate, interpret, and use information. In addition, a large number of the assignments require students to analyze and/or interpret the financial statement consequences of various transactions or events.

6. A complete set of Alternate Problems is published in a separate booklet that is available in quantity to adopters.

7. A variety of assignments in each chapter introduce students to the complete financial statements with footnotes and related disclosures for two companies in different industries, Southwest Airlines Co. and Lands' End, Inc.

8. Mark-to-market accounting is a major break from the tradition of historical cost accounting. As a result, the text reflects a special effort to clearly explain it in the contexts of short-term investments, long-term investments, and alternative valuation models.

SUPPLEMENTS THAT SUPPORT THE TEXT

A full set of supplements accompany *Essentials of Financial Accounting*. Additional information about each of them is available from the publisher's representatives. The supplements include:

- *Solutions Manual.*
- *Working Papers.*
- *Study Guide.*
- *Practice Sets.*
- *Test Bank.*
- *Computest.*
- *Teletest.*
- *GLAS (General Ledger Applications Software.).*
- *SPATS (Spreadsheet Applications Template Software).*
- *Tutorial Software.*
- *Solutions Transparencies.*
- *Teaching Transparencies.*
- *Video Library.*
- *Lecture Review Videos.*

ACKNOWL-
EDGMENTS

I appreciate the reviews, suggestions, and encouragement I have received from numerous instructors.

John B. K. Aheto
Pace University

James Biesel
Longview Community College

John C. Borke
University of Wisconsin—Platteville

Rodger Brannan
University of Minnesota—Duluth

Annhenrie Campbell
California State University—Stanislaus

Kenneth L. Coffey
Johnson County Community College

Robert Conway
University of Wisconsin—Platteville

Harvey J. Cooke
Penn Valley Community College

Constance Cooper
University of Cincinnati

David L. Davis
Tallahassee Community College

Diane J. Davis
Indiana University—Purdue/Ft. Wayne

Marvin J. Dittman
Elgin Community College

William J. Engel
Longview Community College

Robert R. Garrett
American River College

Bonnie Givens
Avila College

David Gotlob
Indiana University—Purdue/Ft. Wayne

Maki Ohy Gragg
City College of San Francisco

Duane E. Harper
Johnson County Community College

Charles Hawkins
NW Missouri State University

Linda A. Herrington
Community College of Allegheny County

Sharon J. Huxley
Teikyo Post University

Randy Kidd
Penn Valley Community College

Shirley A. Kleiner
Johnson County Community College

Alvin Koslofsky
San Jose City College

Terrie Kroshus
Inver Hills Community College

Wayne A. Kunert
Inver Hills Community College

Thomas W. Lee
Winona State University

Marie C. Mari
Miami Dade Community College

Linda Spotts Michael
Maple Woods Community College

Barbara Muncaster
Rose State College

Catherine J. Pitts
Highline Community College

Bill Potts
University of Wisconsin—Platteville

Allan M. Rabinowitz
Pace University

Elizabeth Rosa
Allentown College

Richard W. Schneider
Winona State University

Sara Seyedin
Evergreen Valley College

Dennis Stanczak
Indiana University NW

Dick D. Wasson
Southwestern College

Jane G. Wiese
Valencia Community College

In addition, during the last year, several instructors helped us by providing detailed chapter-by-chapter comments and suggestions. For this invaluable service, I want to thank:

Vernon Allen
Central Florida Community College

Stanford Kahn
University of Cincinnati—University College

Angie Kingerski
University of Maryland—Baltimore County

Pat McGowan
University of St. Thomas

Bernard Newman
Pace University

Jerri Tittle
Rose State College

Charles Vawter III
Glendale Community College

Dick D. Wasson
Southwestern College

I am particularly indebted to Paul Miller of The University of Colorado—Colorado Springs, whose previous work and continued counsel have helped shape this edition. Finally, I will always be grateful for the talent and dedication provided by Betsey Jones and Sue Ann Meyer.

Kermit D. Larson

Contents in Brief

Contents

APPENDIXES:

Essentials of

FINANCIAL ACCOUNTING

Information for Business Decisions

Accounting in Business Organizations and Society

	First Year	Second Year	Total
Using Method A:			
Reported income	$40,000	$40,000	$80,000
Allocation to Jarrett and Wilson:			
Jarrett (75% and 50%)	30,000	20,000	50,000
Wilson (25% and 50%)	10,000	20,000	30,000
Using Method B:			
Reported income	$10,000	$70,000	$80,000
Allocation to Jarrett and Wilson:			
Jarrett (75% and 50%)	7,500	35,000	42,500
Wilson (25% and 50%)	2,500	35,000	37,500

*L*isa Jarrett and Brad Wilson are recent graduates of Austin Community College in Austin, Texas. Shortly before they graduated, Jarrett approached Wilson with a proposal to start a new business together. Jarrett's idea was to seek contracts with companies in the Austin area to provide a shuttle service for employees to and from the Austin airport. Jarrett already had received tentative commitments from three companies and had held preliminary discussions with a local bank about a loan for the business. Wilson agreed to join Jarrett and they convinced the bank to give them a loan to purchase a van and cover some of the initial operating expenses. Soon thereafter, Jarrett and Wilson began operations using the business name JW Shuttle.

Jarrett and Wilson agreed that since Jarrett had the original idea and had done a substantial amount of the work to get started, Jarrett should receive 75% and Wilson 25% of any income the business earned during its first year of operations. After the first year, each would receive 50%. The business expanded more rapidly than expected and near the end of the first year, they sought the advice of an accountant to determine how much income had been earned.

The accountant, who is Wilson's close relative, understands that the amount of income reported in the first year depends on the methods used to measure the income. More precisely, the total income for the first two years will include $30,000 that will either be recognized in the first year or the second year, depending on the accounting method used. Based on projections through the end of the second year, the table to the left shows the results of the two alternatives.

After studying Chapter 1, you should be able to:

1. **Describe the types of organizations that use accounting to generate information about their economic activities.**
2. **Describe the main purpose of accounting and, more specifically, its role in an organization of providing information for internal and external parties.**
3. **Describe some benefits that result from the study of accounting, and describe the main fields of accounting and the activities carried on in each field.**
4. **State several reasons for the importance of ethics in accounting.**
5. **Define or explain the words and phrases listed in the chapter glossary.**

What goes on in business and other organizations? How are their economic activities carried out? Who is responsible for them? And, what part does accounting play? This chapter answers these questions and explains why your study of accounting is important even if you are not planning to be an accountant. You also learn about different kinds of accountants and the work they do. Finally, the chapter considers why the role of accounting in society requires giving great importance to ethical issues and behavior.

BUSINESS ORGANIZATIONS

LO 1
Describe the types of organizations that use accounting to generate information about their economic activities.

Most organizations engage in some forms of economic activity. They may collect funds through dues, taxes, contributions, or investments, or by borrowing. Other typical forms of their economic activity include purchasing products and services and perhaps selling products and services. Nearly all of these organizations use accounting to generate information about their economic activity. Many of these organizations are businesses.

Individuals organize and operate businesses as a means of making a livelihood or of increasing their wealth. Thus, businesses are often described as profit-oriented organizations. In general, businesses take one of three alternative legal forms. These are *corporations, single proprietorships,* and *partnerships.* We describe them in the following paragraphs.

Corporations

A **corporation** is a separate legal entity chartered (or *incorporated*) under state or federal laws.[1] The ownership (also called *equity*) of a corporation is divided into units called shares of **stock,** and the individuals or organizations that own these shares are called **shareholders** or **stockholders.** For example, **Pier 1 Imports, Inc.,** is a corporation that had issued 37,617,000 shares of stock as of the close of its 1994 business year. In other words, Pier 1's equity was divided into 37,617,000 units. A stockholder who owned 376,170 shares would own 1% of the company. When a corporation issues only one class of stock, it is called **common stock** or *capital stock.* We discuss other classes of stock in Chapter 13.

A very important characteristic of corporations is that they are recognized under the law as legal entities. In other words, they are legally separate and distinct from their owners. This characteristic means that a corporation is responsible for its own acts and its own debts. As a result, the corporation's stockholders are not

---

[1] A corporation normally can be identified by its name, which includes the word *Corporation, Company,* or *Incorporated* or an abbreviation such as *Corp., Co.,* or *Inc.*

personally liable for these acts and debts. This limited liability feature is a major reason why corporations are able to obtain resources from investors who are not active participants in managing the affairs of the business.

The separate legal status of a corporation also means that it can enter into its own contracts. For example, a corporation can buy, own, and sell property in its own name. It also can sue and be sued in its own name. In short, the separate legal status enables a corporation to conduct its business affairs with all the rights, duties, and responsibilities of a person. Of course, a corporation lacks a physical body and must act through its managers, who are its legal agents.

In addition, the separate legal status of a corporation means that its life is not limited by its owners' lives or by a need for them to remain owners. Thus, a stockholder can sell or transfer shares to another person without affecting the operations of the corporation.

Single Proprietorships and Partnerships

A **single proprietorship,** or **sole proprietorship,** is owned by one person and is not organized under state or federal laws as a corporation. Small retail stores and service enterprises often are operated as single proprietorships. No special legal requirements must be met to start this kind of business. As a result, single proprietorships are the most numerous of all types of businesses.

A **partnership** is owned by two or more people, called *partners.* Like a single proprietorship, no special legal requirements must be met in starting a partnership. All that is required is an agreement between the partners to operate a business together. The agreement can be either oral or written. However, a written partnership agreement may help the partners avoid or resolve later disputes.

In a strict legal sense, single proprietorships and partnerships are not separate from their owners. Thus, for example, a court can order an owner to sell personal assets to pay the debts of a proprietorship or partnership. In fact, an owner's personal assets may have to be sold to satisfy *all* the debts of a proprietorship or a partnership, even if this amount exceeds the owner's equity in the company. This unlimited liability feature of proprietorships and partnerships is sometimes a disadvantage and is an important characteristic to remember.

There are fewer corporations in the United States than proprietorships and partnerships. However, the corporate form of business offers advantages for accumulating and managing capital resources. As a result, corporations control the most economic wealth.

Economic activities such as purchasing or selling various goods and services go on in many different organizations. In addition to businesses, the organizations that use accounting to generate information about their economic activities include a wide variety of government and nonprofit organizations. Consider the following examples:

GOVERNMENT AND NONPROFIT ORGANIZATIONS

Airports	Health departments
Army	Highway departments
Churches	Homeless shelters
Cities	Hospitals
City bus lines	Judicial courts
Civic theaters	Legislatures
Colleges	Libraries
Defense department	Museums
Electric utility departments	Navy
Fraternities	Parks departments

Police departments	School districts
Postal service	Service clubs
Prisons	Treasury department

This list represents a tiny sample of the various government and nonprofit organizations that engage in economic activities. Note that some of these organizations, hospitals for example, might be operated as private, nonprofit organizations, or as governmental units, or as profit-oriented businesses. In any case, all of these organizations use accounting to capture information about their economic activities.

COMMON ACTIVITIES IN BUSINESS, GOVERNMENT, AND NONPROFIT ORGANIZATIONS

Organizations that engage in economic activities may differ in many important ways. They may differ in respect to the products or services they produce, their primary goals, the manner by which they are established, the legal form they take, and the processes by which they are managed. Nevertheless, many of the major activities or functions that are performed in economic organizations are quite similar.

Illustration 1–1 shows the major activities or functions of businesses that manufacture and sell products. Businesses that sell services, such as airlines and express delivery companies, perform very similar activities. So do governmental and nonprofit organizations. The following paragraphs describe these functions in more detail.

Finance

Every organization needs money to operate and grow. Organizations use money to acquire equipment, buildings, vehicles, and financial holdings. The finance function has the task of planning how to obtain money from such sources as payments from customers, loans from banks, and new investments from owners. Government organizations may acquire cash by collecting taxes and fees, while nonprofit organizations may acquire their cash from contributions by donors. In preparing plans, the finance department identifies and evaluates alternative sources of funds. In addition, finance analyzes alternative investment opportunities to identify which to take and which to reject.

Human Resources

All organizations require efforts from people. As a result, employees must be located, screened, hired, trained, compensated, promoted, and counseled. And, they may be released from employment by being retired or laid off. The human resources function is responsible for handling these tasks. In large companies, hundreds of employees may be engaged in looking after the other employees.

Research and Development

All organizations need to find new ways to meet the needs of their customers and others. Thus, research into new technologies and products or services is essential. This may be as simple as testing a new recipe for pizza or as complex as creating a more powerful computer. Once research is completed, the development process uses the new knowledge to design or modify specific products or services. If organizations are to survive, this function is essential.

Production

Many companies produce and then sell goods to their customers. Producing these goods requires planning and coordinating many specific activities. These activities include designing the production process, acquiring materials used in production, and

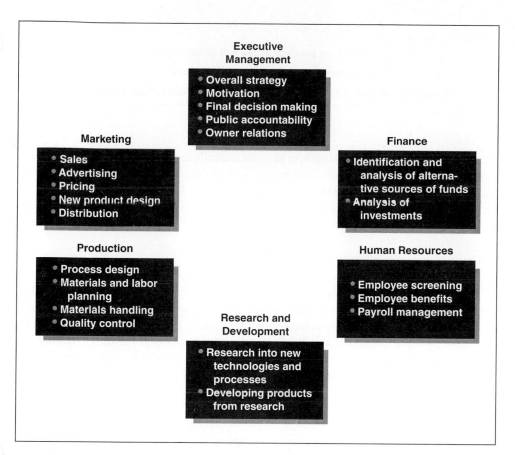

Illustration 1-1
Activities within an Economic
Organization

selecting the workers' skills to be applied. In addition, materials handling systems must be in place to ensure that raw materials and finished goods are delivered on time. Production management also requires paying a great deal of attention to the quality of the goods. Similar activities in retail and service organizations ensure that quality merchandise and services are delivered to consumers.

Marketing

Companies can sell goods and services only if customers are willing to buy them. Marketing provides customers with information about goods and services and encourages their purchase. This includes sales efforts involving direct customer contact and advertising that provides information to large numbers of potential customers. Another activity is setting prices that are low enough to encourage sales and high enough to earn profits. Marketing involves identifying new products that might meet customers' needs and also includes developing systems that distribute products to customers when and where they need them. These activities are sometimes summed up as the four P's of marketing—product, promotion, price, and place.

Executive Management

All organizations must have leadership, vision, and coordination. Long-term strategies need to be established and employees must be motivated to do their best. In addition, major decisions have to be made. These tasks are the duty of the company's executive managers, who also represent the company in dealing with the public. In some companies, the owner or owners carry out the executive management functions. In others, key employees take on these responsibilities. They may be called the president, the chief executive officer, or the chairman of the board of directors. In nonprofit organizations, the top managers often are called executive directors.

Progress Check
(Answers to Progress Checks are provided at the end of the chapter.)

1-1   What are the three general forms of business organization?

1-2   Identify six different activities or functions carried on within most organizations.

ACCOUNTING AND ITS ROLE IN ORGANIZATIONS

LO 2
Describe the main purpose of accounting and, more specifically, its role in an organization of providing information for internal and external parties.

The main purpose of **accounting** is to provide useful information to people who make rational investment, credit, and similar decisions.[2] Nearly all organizations that engage in economic activities use accounting to generate information about their activities. These organizations include profit-oriented businesses, government agencies, and other nonprofit organizations. They may be manufacturers, merchandisers, or service providers.

Because accountants serve decision makers by providing them with financial information that helps them make better decisions, accounting is often described as a service activity. Decision makers who use accounting information include present and potential investors, lenders, managers, suppliers, and customers. Users of accounting information about nonprofit organizations also include the people who donate to or pay taxes to those organizations. Whether you are planning to be an accountant, an employee, a manager in an organization, or an external user of the information, your knowledge of accounting will help you achieve success in your career.

USING ACCOUNTING TO SERVE INTERNAL NEEDS

The internal role of accounting is to serve the organization's various functions by providing information that helps managers complete their tasks. By providing this information, accounting helps the organization reach its overall goals. Illustration 1–2 shows some of the information accounting provides within an organization.

The finance function uses information about actual cash flows as a basis for projecting future cash flows and evaluating past decisions. Human resources can carry out its work more effectively if it has information about the company's employees, including payroll costs. Research and development managers need information about the costs they already have incurred so they can decide whether to continue their projects. Marketing managers also use accounting information, especially reports about the company's sales and its marketing costs.

The production function of a company depends heavily on accounting information to determine whether its operating costs are occurring as expected. In carrying out its work, production operates within a set of *internal controls* designed primarily by the accounting department. In fact, well-managed companies use carefully developed internal control procedures to guide all areas of activity, not just production. To promote efficiency and prevent unauthorized use of the company's resources, these controls specify procedures that must be followed before certain actions can take place. For example, internal controls may require a manager's approval before any materials are moved to the production line. Internal controls also dictate procedures that are necessary to ensure that accounting reports about production activities are dependable and useful. You will learn more about internal control procedures in Chapter 7.

Because executive management has overall responsibility for the organization, it depends heavily on accounting information to understand what is happening. One important set of reports includes the *financial statements*. We explain the content, usefulness, and limits of these statements throughout this book. (Chapter 2 introduces

---

[2] Financial Accounting Standards Board, *Statement of Financial Accounting Concepts No. 1,* "Objectives of Financial Reporting by Business Enterprises" (Norwalk, CT, 1978), par. 34.

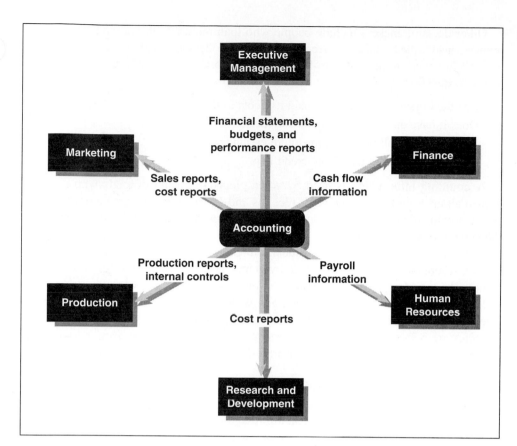

Illustration 1-2
The Internal Role of Accounting

the four primary financial statements.) Executive management also receives and uses budget reports that describe future plans. After events have unfolded, accounting provides performance reports that help managers understand what was done well and where improvements might be made.

Perhaps the most important point to learn at this stage is that accounting activities are not important by themselves. They are important because they provide information that is useful to other parts of the organization.

USING ACCOUNTING TO SERVE EXTERNAL NEEDS

In addition to using accounting information to meet internal needs, organizations use it for reporting to various external groups. For example, these external decision makers include owners not actively involved in managing the business. Owners use information about the company's performance and financial strength to help them determine whether to hold their investments.

In making decisions about an organization, internal and external decision makers generally begin by asking questions. The answers often are based on accounting information. For example, owners and managers use accounting information to help them answer questions like these:

- Are the resources owned by the organization adequate to accomplish its objectives?
- Are the debts it owes excessive in amount?
- How much income is it earning?
- Are the expenses appropriate for the amount of sales?
- Are customers' accounts being collected promptly?

Other decision makers include people who loan money to the organization. These lenders, also called *creditors,* need information to decide whether the company has enough financial strength and profits to pay its debts. For example, they look for answers to questions like these:

- Has the organization promptly paid its debts in the past?
- Does it have the ability to pay its current debts?
- Does it have good prospects for future earnings?
- Should it be granted additional credit now?

Accounting information is used by voters, legislators, and officials who are concerned about a government agency's receipts and expenditures. Contributors to a non-profit organization also use accounting information to understand what happens to their donations.

A company's employees have a special interest in knowing whether an organization represents a stable source of employment. They can use accounting information to help them understand their employer's financial health and performance.

Some government agencies are charged with regulating business activities. They often need financial information to carry out that responsibility. Other government agencies are responsible for collecting income taxes. As you know from personal experience, taxpayers use accounting information to determine how much income they have and how much tax they owe.

We explained earlier that executive management is responsible for an organization's relationships with external decision makers. As the diagram in the margin shows, accounting provides most of the financial information that executive management presents to external decision makers. An objective of this book is to explain the contents and usefulness of the financial statements that are created for these external reporting activities.

Some accounting information is designed to satisfy the needs of a particular external party. For example, information provided to the government for tax calculations may differ significantly from the information in the financial statements. We describe the work of tax accountants later in this chapter.

Progress Check

1-3 The primary function of accounting is to provide financial information: *(a)* to an organization's managers; *(b)* to an organization's creditors; *(c)* that is useful in making rational investment, credit, and similar decisions.

1-4 Accounting's external function is to provide: *(a)* assurance that management has complied with all laws; *(b)* information to users who are not involved in the organization's daily activities; *(c)* information that managers use to control business operations.

WHY STUDY ACCOUNTING?

LO 3
Describe some benefits that result from the study of accounting, and describe the main fields of accounting and the activities carried on in each field.

Because of the wide range of questions that are answered with accounting information, you will almost certainly use accounting in your future career. (In fact, you probably already use some accounting information as a result of having a checking account or credit card.) To use accounting effectively, you need to understand the unique accounting words and terms widely used in business.

You also should understand the concepts and procedures that are followed in generating accounting information. One important benefit of this understanding is that it will make you aware of the limitations of accounting information. For example, much of it is based on estimates instead of precise measurements. By understanding how these estimates are made, you will be able to avoid misinterpreting the information.

Another very good reason for studying accounting is to make it the basis for an interesting and rewarding career. The next section of this chapter describes what accountants do.

The Difference between Accounting and Bookkeeping

Because accounting and bookkeeping both are concerned with financial information and records, some people mistakenly think that they are the same thing. In fact, accounting involves much more than bookkeeping. Although bookkeeping is critical to developing useful accounting information, it is only the clerical part of accounting. That is, **bookkeeping** is the part of accounting that records transactions and other events, either manually or with computers. In contrast, accounting involves analyzing transactions and events, deciding how to report them in financial statements, and interpreting the results. Accounting also involves designing and implementing systems to produce useful reports and to control the operations of an organization. Accounting involves more professional expertise and judgment than bookkeeping because accountants must analyze complex and unusual events.

Whether you want to be an accountant, plan to hold some other position in an organization, or expect to be an investor or creditor, you will benefit by understanding how accounting information is developed. To gain this understanding, we explain some basic bookkeeping practices in the next few chapters. You will use this knowledge to learn how accountants present financial data in useful reports. As your knowledge expands, you will learn how to analyze and interpret this information. Eventually, you will be able to use the reports more effectively because you will understand how the information has been processed.

Accounting and Computers

Since computers first became available in the 1950s, they have spread throughout our everyday lives and the business world. Computers are widely used in accounting because they efficiently store, process, and summarize large quantities of financial data. Furthermore, computers perform these functions quickly with limited operator involvement. Thus, computers reduce the time, effort, and cost of processing data while improving clerical accuracy. As a result of these advantages, most accounting systems are now computerized. Even so, manual accounting systems are still used by a surprisingly large number of small businesses.

To prepare, analyze, and use accounting information in today's world, you need to understand the important role computers play in most accounting systems. In essence, computers are tools that help accountants provide useful information for decision makers. The huge growth in the number and power of computers has greatly changed how accountants and other people work. However, computers have not eliminated the need for people to learn about accounting. A strong demand exists for people who can design accounting systems, supervise their operation, analyze complex transactions, and interpret reports. A strong demand also exists for people who can make good decisions because they clearly understand how accounting information relates to business activities. While computers have taken over many routine tasks, they are not substitutes for qualified people with abilities to generate and use accounting information.

THE TYPES OF ACCOUNTANTS

One way to classify accountants is to identify the kinds of work they perform. In general, accountants work in these three broad fields:

1. Financial accounting.
2. Managerial accounting.
3. Tax accounting.

These fields provide a variety of information to different users. We describe the activities of accountants in these fields later in this chapter.

Another way to classify accountants is to identify the kinds of organizations in which they work. Most accountants are **private accountants.** A private accountant works for a single employer other than government. A large business might employ a hundred or more private accountants, but most companies have fewer.

Many other accountants are **public accountants.** Public accountants provide their services to many different clients. They are called *public accountants* because their services are available to the public. Some public accountants are self-employed. Many others work for public accounting firms that may have thousands of employees or only a few.

Government accountants work for federal, state, or local branches of government. Some government accountants perform accounting services for their own governmental unit. Other government accountants are involved with business regulation. Still others investigate violations of laws.

Accounting is recognized as a profession like law and medicine because it requires special abilities and education and accountants have unique responsibilities. The professional status of an accountant often is indicated by one or more certificates.

The CPA Certificate

Each state in the United States, as well as the District of Columbia, Guam, Puerto Rico, and the Virgin Islands, has an agency that licenses Certified Public Accountants **(CPAs).** The licensing process helps ensure that a high standard of professional service is available to the public. Individuals can legally identify themselves as CPAs only if they hold this license.

To become a licensed CPA, an individual must meet education and experience requirements, pass the CPA examination, and have good ethical character. Most states require a college degree with the equivalent of a major in accounting.

The CPA examination covers topics in financial and managerial accounting, as well as income taxes, auditing, and business law. The uniform two-day examination is given in all states and other jurisdictions every May and November. Although the exam is administered by individual state boards, it is prepared and graded by the American Institute of Certified Public Accountants **(AICPA),** the largest and most influential national professional organization of CPAs.

In addition, many states issue a certificate only after the applicant has one or more years of experience working under the supervision of a CPA. Nearly all states reduce the amount of experience if an applicant has completed a specified amount of coursework beyond the undergraduate degree. Some states do not require any work experience. A few states allow applicants to substitute work experience for part of the formal education requirements.

As early as 1969, the AICPA's governing council took the position that CPAs need at least five years of college education (150 semester hours). This position was supported in 1983 by the National Association of State Boards of Accountancy **(NASBA).** In 1988, the members of the AICPA voted to require all CPAs admitted to the institute after 2000 to have 150 semester hours of college education. More than 30 states have changed their laws to eventually require new CPAs to complete at least 150 semester hours. We expect many more to adopt this requirement.

Other Professional Certificates

Many private accountants hold CPA certificates because they were public accountants earlier in their careers. Some private accountants hold other certificates in addition to or instead of the CPA license. For example, you may want to obtain a Certificate in Management Accounting **(CMA)** or become a Certified Internal Auditor **(CIA).** Holders of these certificates must meet examination, education, and experience requirements similar to those applied to CPAs. Unlike the CPA license, the CMA and CIA certificates are not issued by the government and do not give their holders any legal authority. The CMA is awarded by the Institute of Management Accountants and the CIA is granted by the Institute of Internal Auditors.

THE FIELDS OF ACCOUNTING

Accountants practice in three fields—financial, managerial, and tax accounting. The actual work done by an accountant depends on the field and whether the person is employed in private, public, or government accounting. Illustration 1–3 identifies the specific activities of the three types of accountants within these fields.

Financial Accounting

Financial accounting provides information to decision makers who are not involved in the day-to-day operations of an organization. As we described earlier, these external decision makers include investors, creditors, and others. The information is distributed primarily through general purpose financial statements. Financial statements describe the condition of the organization and the events that happened during the year. Chapter 2 explains the form and contents of financial statements.

The Financial Accounting column of Illustration 1–3 shows that a company's financial statements are prepared by its private accountants. However, many companies issue their financial statements only after an **audit** by independent CPAs.[3] An audit is a thorough check of an organization's accounting systems and records; it is performed to add credibility to the financial statements. For example, banks require audits of the financial statements of companies applying for large loans. Also, federal and state laws require companies to have audits before their securities (stocks and bonds) can be sold to the public. Then, as long as the securities are traded, their annual financial statements must be audited.

To perform an audit, auditors examine the financial statements and the accounting system. Their objective is to decide whether the statements reflect the company's financial position and operating results in agreement with **generally accepted accounting principles (GAAP).** These principles are rules adopted by the accounting profession as guides for measuring and reporting the financial condition and activities of a business. You learn more about GAAP in Chapter 2 and in many of the following chapters.

When an audit is completed, the auditors prepare a report that expresses their professional opinion about the financial statements. The audi-

---

[3] Little or no credibility would be added to the statements if they were audited by a company's own employees.

Illustration 1-3
Activities of Accountants

Types of Accountants	Fields of Accounting		
	Financial Accounting	**Managerial Accounting**	**Tax Accounting**
Private accountants	Preparing financial statements	General accounting Cost accounting Budgeting Internal auditing	Preparing tax returns Planning
Public accountants	Auditing financial statements	Providing management advisory services	Preparing tax returns Planning
Government accountants	Preparing financial statements Reviewing financial reports Writing regulations Assisting companies Investigating violations	General accounting Cost accounting Budgeting Internal auditing	Reviewing tax returns Assisting taxpayers Writing regulations Investigating violations

tors' report must accompany the statements when they are distributed. For an example, find the auditors' report on **Southwest Airlines Co.'s** 1994 financial statements in Appendix E at the end of the book.

As the first column of Illustration 1–3 shows, some government accountants prepare financial statements. These statements describe the financial status of government agencies and results of events occurring during the year. The financial statements of governmental bodies are usually audited by independent CPAs.

Other government accountants are involved with regulating financial accounting practices used by businesses. For example, some accountants work for the Securities and Exchange Commission (**SEC**). Congress created the SEC in 1934 to regulate securities markets, including the flow of information from companies to the public. SEC accountants review companies' financial reports before they are distributed to the public. The purpose of the review is to be sure that the reports comply with the SEC's regulations.

Accountants who work for other regulatory agencies, such as the Federal Trade Commission, may review reports filed by businesses subject to the agencies' authority. Government accountants help write regulations concerning financial accounting. They also help companies understand and comply with them.

As we mentioned briefly, some government accountants investigate possible violations of laws and regulations. For example, accountants who work for the SEC investigate crimes related to securities. Other accountants investigate financial frauds and white-collar crimes in their capacity as agents of the Federal Bureau of Investigation.

Managerial Accounting

The field of managerial accounting involves providing information to an organization's managers. Managerial accounting reports often include much of the same information used in financial accounting. However, managerial accounting reports also include a great deal of information that is not reported outside the company.

Look at the upper and lower sections of the Managerial Accounting column in Illustration 1–3. Notice that private and government accountants have the same four major activities. The middle section of the column shows that public accountants also perform activities related to managerial accounting. These activities are described next.

General Accounting. The task of recording transactions, processing the recorded data, and preparing reports for managers is called **general accounting.** General accounting also includes preparing the financial statements that executive management presents to external users. An organization's own accountants usually design the accounting information system, often with help from public accountants. The general accounting staff is supervised by a chief accounting officer, who is called the **controller.** This title stems from the fact that accounting information is used to control the organization's operations.

Cost Accounting. To plan and control operations, managers need information about the nature of costs incurred. **Cost accounting** is a process of accumulating the information managers need about operating costs. It helps managers identify, measure, and control these costs. Cost accounting may involve accounting for the costs of products, services, or specific activities. Cost accounting information also is useful for evaluating each manager's performance. Large companies usually employ many cost accountants because cost accounting information is so important.

Budgeting. The process of developing formal plans for an organization's future activities is called **budgeting.** One goal of budgeting is to give managers from different areas in the organization a clear understanding of how their activities affect the entire organization. After the budget has been adopted, it provides a basis for evaluating actual performance.

Internal Auditing. Just as auditing by independent CPAs adds credibility to financial statements, many organizations employ individuals as internal auditors. **Internal auditing** adds credibility to reports produced and used within an organization but goes beyond an examination of record-keeping processes. Internal auditors also assess whether managers are following established operating procedures and evaluate the efficiency of operating procedures. Almost all large companies and government agencies employ internal auditors.

Management Advisory Services. Public accountants participate in managerial accounting by providing **management advisory services** to their clients. Independent auditors gain an intimate knowledge of a client's accounting and operating procedures when they conduct their examinations. As a result, auditors are in an excellent position to offer suggestions for improving the company's procedures. Most clients expect these suggestions as a useful by-product of the audit. For example, public accountants often help companies design and install new accounting and internal control systems. This effort includes offering advice on selecting new computer systems. Other advice might relate to budgeting procedures or employee benefit plans.

Tax Accounting

Many taxes raised by federal, state, and city governments are based on the income earned by taxpayers. These taxpayers include both individuals and corporate businesses. The amount of taxes is based on what the laws define to be income. Tax accountants help taxpayers comply with these laws by preparing their tax returns. Another **tax accounting** activity involves planning future transactions to minimize the amount of tax to be paid. The Tax Accounting column of Illustration 1–3 identifies the activities of accountants in this field.

Large companies usually have private accountants who are responsible for preparing tax returns and doing tax planning. However, large companies may consult with public accountants when they need special tax expertise. Most small companies rely on public accountants for their tax work.

Many accountants are employed on the government side of the tax process. For example, the Internal Revenue Service (**IRS**) employs numerous tax accountants. The

IRS has the duty of collecting federal taxes and otherwise enforcing tax laws. Most IRS accountants review tax returns filed by taxpayers. Other IRS accountants offer assistance to taxpayers and help write regulations. Still other IRS accountants investigate possible violations of tax laws.

Summary

The preceding discussion shows how important accounting is for most organizations. Regardless of your career goals, you will surely use accounting information and work with accountants. The discussion also shows the variety of opportunities available if you find accounting to be enjoyable and challenging. Next, we consider the important role of ethics in business and accounting.

Progress Check

1-5 What is the relationship between accounting and bookkeeping?

1-6 The services performed by public accountants generally include: *(a)* income tax services, management advisory services, and independent auditing; *(b)* general accounting, independent auditing, and budgeting; *(c)* government accounting, private accounting, and independent auditing.

1-7 What are the three broad fields of accounting?

1-8 What is the purpose of an audit? Describe what Certified Public Accountants do when they perform an audit.

THE IMPORTANCE OF ETHICS IN ACCOUNTING

LO 4
State several reasons for the importance of ethics in accounting.

As a student, you realize that ethics and ethical behavior are important features of any society. Disappointing stories in the media often remind us how much ethics affect our society. These stories tell us about attempts to defraud the elderly and other vulnerable people, missed child support payments, harassment, misconduct by public figures, bribery of government officials, and the use of insider information for personal gain in the stock market. Events like these make it difficult for people to trust each other. If trust is lacking, our commercial and personal lives are much more complicated, inefficient, and unpleasant.

In this section, we introduce the meaning of ethics in general and describe how ethics affect business and accounting in particular. We discuss ethics at the beginning of this book because business activity is so central to everyone's life and because useful accounting information is so important for business. The purpose of accounting is to provide useful information that can be trusted, which requires that accountants be ethical. How could the users of accounting information rely on it if they could not trust accountants? The need to avoid this difficult situation has prompted the development of special ethics for accountants.

The Meaning of Ethics

Ethics are the "principles that determine the rightness or wrongness of particular acts or activities." Ethics are also "accepted standards of good behavior . . . in a profession or trade."[4] Ethics and laws often coincide, with the result that many unethical actions (such as theft and physical violence) are also illegal. Other actions may not be against the law but are generally recognized as unethical. For example, the crime of perjury (not telling the truth) occurs only if the liar has been put under an oath. However, not telling the truth is nearly always unethical.[5] Because of differences between laws and ethics, we cannot count on laws to keep people ethical.

---

[4] *The New Lexicon Webster's Dictionary of the English Language* (New York: Lexington Publications, Inc., 1989), p. 324.

[5] The usual exceptions to this rule involve protecting another person against harm.

In some cases, a person may face difficulty in deciding whether an action is right or wrong. In these situations, the most ethical choice may be to take a course of action that avoids any doubt about the ethical correctness of the action. For example, financial statement readers would not trust a CPA's report on the statements if the CPA's financial success depended on the success of the reporting company.

Should this prevent an auditor from investing in a client if the investment is only a small part of the auditor's personal wealth? To avoid the question of how much would be too much, ethics rules for auditors forbid any direct investment in their clients' securities, regardless of the amount.[6] Also, auditors cannot accept contingent fees that depend on amounts reported in a client's financial statements.[7] These rules are designed to prevent conflicts of interest or even the possibility that the CPA might appear to lack independence.

Many controversial issues that we face in school, the workplace, or elsewhere have ethical implications. These ethical issues are an unavoidable part of life. However, a commitment to being ethical requires us to think carefully before we act to be certain that we are making ethical choices. Our success in making those choices affects how we feel about ourselves and how others feel about us. In fact, our combined individual choices greatly affect the quality of our entire society and the individual experience that each of us enjoys.

Beyond these general ideas, how do ethics relate to business, and more specifically, how do they relate to accounting?

Ethics in Business

Many people have expressed concern about what they see as low ethical standards in business and government. For example, a survey of more than 1,100 executives, deans of business schools, and members of Congress showed that 94% of the respondents agreed with the statement that "the business community is troubled by ethical problems."[8] However, the survey also showed that the vast majority of the respondents believed high ethical standards are followed by companies that are successful over the long run. This second finding confirms an old saying: "Good ethics is good business." Ethical business practices build trust, which in turn promotes loyalty and productive relationships with customers, suppliers, and employees. As a result, good ethics contribute to a company's reputation and eventually its success.

Because of the important public interest in business ethics, many companies have adopted their own codes of ethics. These codes establish standards for internal activities and for relationships with customers, suppliers, regulators, the public, and even competitors. Companies often use their codes as public statements of their commitment to ethical business practices. More importantly, they serve as guides for employees to follow.

Ethics in Accounting

As we mentioned earlier, ethics are important in accounting because accountants are expected to provide useful information for decision makers. These decisions can have a profound effect on many individuals, businesses, and other institutions. As a result, accountants often face ethical issues as they consider what information should be provided to decision makers. Accountants' choices can affect such things as the amount of money a company pays in taxes or distributes to its stockholders. The information can affect the price that a buyer pays for a business or the amount of compensation paid to a company's managers. Internal information can affect judgments about the

---

[6] *AICPA Code of Professional Conduct,* Rule 101.

[7] *AICPA Code of Professional Conduct,* Rule 301.

[8] Touche Ross & Co., *Ethics in American Business* (New York, 1988), pp. 1–2.

success of a company's specific products or divisions. If inadequate accounting information would cause a successful division to be closed, its employees, customers, and suppliers would be significantly harmed. Accountants need to consider all these effects in deciding what information will be most useful for these important decisions.

In response to the need for guidance for accountants, ethics codes have been adopted and enforced by professional accounting organizations. These include the American Institute of Certified Public Accountants and the Institute of Management Accountants. To keep their codes up to date, these organizations continually monitor their effectiveness and applicability to new ways of operating. The As a Matter of Opinion box presents the views of Herbert Finkston, the director of the AICPA's division of professional ethics, on the importance of ethical behavior for accountants and others.

As an example of an ethical accounting issue, recall the JW Shuttle business described at the beginning of the chapter. This case shows how accounting can affect the allocation of wealth between people. Wilson receives $7,500 more and Jarrett receives $7,500 less if Method B is used instead of Method A.

More information is needed in this case to help Jarrett and Wilson decide which method should be used. However, in explaining the appropriate uses of Method A and Method B, the accountant has an ethical responsibility to be fair to both parties. Knowing that Method B is more favorable to Wilson, the accountant must be careful to avoid giving a biased argument in favor of Method B.

Accountants and managers often face situations that are similar to the JW Shuttle case. For example, many companies pay their managers bonuses based on the amount of income reported. Generally, the managers benefit from the use of accounting alternatives that accelerate the reporting of income. However, those alternatives reduce the money available to invest for the benefit of the owners.

Another ethics issue in accounting involves the confidential nature of the information that accountants deal with in their work. For example, auditors have access to salary records and plans for the future. Their clients could be damaged if the auditors released this information to others. To prevent this, auditors' ethics require them to keep information confidential.[9] In addition, internal accountants are not supposed to use confidential information for personal advantage.[10]

These examples show why accountants, their clients, and the public need ethical guidance and commitment. Guidance provides a basis for knowing which actions to take and commitment provides the courage to do what needs to be done. Guidance also tells clients what they can rightfully expect from their accountants and gives the public a basis for having confidence in financial statements. In fact, the performance of the entire economy depends to a considerable extent on having financial information that is trustworthy.

The Ethical Challenge

As you proceed in your study of accounting, you will encounter many other situations in which ethical issues are raised. We encourage you to explore these issues. We also urge you to remember that accounting must be done ethically if it is to be an effective tool in the service of society. Of all the principles of accounting that you learn from this book, the need for ethics is the most fundamental.

---

[9] *AICPA Code of Professional Conduct,* Rule 301.

[10] *Institute of Management Accountants Standards of Ethical Conduct.*

As a Matter of Opinion

Mr. Finkston received his B.A. in accounting from Brooklyn College and his J.D. from Brooklyn Law School. He is a member of the New York State Bar and was a public accountant early in his career. Since 1979, he has been the Director of the Division of Professional Ethics of the American Institute of CPAs.

The accounting profession has earned high regard because of its ethical standards. Our standards require ethical behavior in our relationships with our clients and our employers. They also require ethical behavior in our dealings with the public and its interests. And, our standards require us to render high-quality professional services. By adhering to the concepts of objectivity, integrity, and independence, and by continued striving for quality, the profession has won a respected place in the entire business community and among the other professions.

As a student of accounting, be aware of the ethical implications of all that you study. As a member of the accounting profession, or any other profession, practice ethics in all that you do. By doing so, you will bring honor to yourself and your profession.

Herbert A. Finkston, CPA

In your own approach to life, you are in control of your ethical standards and the ethical decisions that you make. Each of us is individually free to shape our personal morals. To paraphrase former Supreme Court Chief Justice Earl Warren, it can be said that civilized society "floats on a sea of ethics." It is your choice how you elect to navigate this sea. Do not be misled into thinking that your choice does not matter. Eventually, your choice affects everyone, and that is the ethical challenge each of us faces.

Progress Check

1-9 Both the American Institute of Certified Public Accountants and the Institute of Management Accountants have adopted codes of ethics. Is this true or false?

1-10 Ethical rules prevent CPAs from accepting certain kinds of contingent fees. Is this true or false?

SUMMARY OF THE CHAPTER IN TERMS OF LEARNING OBJECTIVES

LO 1. Describe the types of organizations that use accounting to generate information about their economic activities. Almost all organizations engage in some economic activities and most of them use accounting to generate information about these activities. These organizations include businesses, government agencies, and private, nonprofit organizations. Businesses include sole proprietorships, partnerships, and corporations. A single (or sole) proprietorship is an unincorporated business owned by one individual. A partnership differs from a single proprietorship in that it has more than one owner. Proprietors and partners are personally responsible for the debts of their businesses. A corporation is a separate legal entity. As such, its owners are not personally responsible for its debts.

Many organizations such as hospitals might be operated as private, nonprofit organizations, or as governmental units, or as profit-oriented businesses. Regardless of how they are organized, many involve similar activities or functions. These include executive management, finance, human resources, research and development, production, and marketing.

LO 2. Describe the main purpose of accounting and, more specifically, its role in an organization of providing information for internal and external parties. The main purpose of accounting is to provide useful information to people who make rational investment, credit, and similar decisions. These decision makers include present and potential investors, lenders, and other users. Other users include managers of organizations, suppliers who sell to them, and customers who buy from them. Internally, accounting provides information that managers use in all of the major areas of business activity.

In addition to using accounting information to meet internal needs, organizations also report accounting information to various external parties. These external decision makers include people who invest in the organizations and people who loan money to them. Lenders need information to assess whether the company has enough financial strength and profitability to pay its debts.

LO 3. Describe some benefits that result from the study of accounting, and describe the main fields of accounting and the activities carried on in each field. Accounting information is used by many different groups of people in their decision-making activities. An understanding of accounting information and the processes by which it is produced helps individuals use the information effectively.

Another reason to study accounting is to prepare for a career in accounting. Accountants work in private, public, and government accounting. All three may include working in financial, managerial, and tax accounting. Financial accountants prepare or audit financial statements that are distributed to people who are not involved in day-to-day management. Managerial accountants provide information to people who are involved in day-to-day management. Managerial accounting activities include general accounting, cost accounting, budgeting, internal auditing, and management advisory services. Tax accounting includes preparing tax returns and tax planning.

LO 4. State several reasons for the importance of ethics in accounting. Ethics are principles that determine the rightness or wrongness of particular acts or activities. Ethics also are principles of conduct that govern an individual or a profession. The foundation for trust in business activities is the expectation that people are trustworthy. Ethics are especially important for accounting because users of the information have to trust that it has not been manipulated. Without ethics, accounting information could not be trusted, and economic activity would be much more difficult to accomplish.

GLOSSARY

Accounting a service activity that provides useful information to people who make rational investment, credit, and similar decisions to help them make better decisions. p. 6

AICPA American Institute of Certified Public Accountants, the largest and most influential national professional organization of Certified Public Accountants in the United States. p. 10

Audit a thorough check of an organization's accounting systems and records that adds credibility to financial statements; the specific goal is to determine whether the statements reflect the company's financial position and operating results in agreement with generally accepted accounting principles. p. 11

Bookkeeping the part of accounting that records transactions and other events, either manually or with computers. p. 9

Budgeting the process of developing formal plans for future activities, which then serve as a basis for evaluating actual performance. p. 13

CIA Certified Internal Auditor; a certification that an individual is professionally competent in internal auditing; granted by the Institute of Internal Auditors. p. 11

CMA Certificate in Management Accounting; a certification that an individual is professionally competent in managerial

accounting; awarded by the Institute of Management Accountants. p. 11

Common stock the name given to a corporation's stock when it issues only one kind, or class, of stock. p. 2

Controller the chief accounting officer of an organization. p. 10

Corporation a business chartered, or incorporated, as a separate legal entity under state or federal laws. p. 2

Cost accounting a managerial accounting activity designed to help managers identify, measure, and control operating costs. p. 13

CPA Certified Public Accountant; an accountant who has passed an examination and has met education and experience requirements; CPAs are licensed by state boards to practice public accounting. p. 10

Ethics principles that determine the rightness or wrongness of particular acts or activities; also accepted standards of good behavior in a profession or trade. p. 14.

GAAP the abbreviation for *generally accepted accounting principles.* p. 11

General accounting the task of recording transactions, processing the recorded data, and preparing reports for managers; also includes preparing the financial statements that executive management presents to external users. p. 13

Generally accepted accounting principles rules adopted by the accounting profession as guides for measuring and reporting the financial condition and activities of a business. p. 11

Government accountants accountants employed by federal, state, or local branches of government. p. 10

Internal auditing activity by an organization's employees that includes examining the organization's record-keeping processes, assessing whether managers are following established operating procedures, and evaluating the efficiency of operating procedures. p. 13

IRS Internal Revenue Service; the federal agency that has the duty of collecting federal taxes and otherwise enforcing tax laws. p. 13

Management advisory services the public accounting activity in which suggestions are offered for improving a company's procedures; the suggestions may concern new accounting and internal control systems, new computer systems, budgeting, and employee benefit plans. p. 13

NASBA National Association of State Boards of Accountancy. p. 10

Partnership a business that is owned by two or more people and not organized as a corporation. p. 3

Private accountants accountants who work for a single employer other than the government. p. 10

Public accountants accountants who provide their services to many different clients. p. 10

SEC Securities and Exchange Commission; the federal agency created by Congress in 1934 to regulate securities markets, including the flow of information from companies to the public. p. 12

Shareholders another name for stockholders. p. 2

Single proprietorship a business that is owned by one individual and not organized as a corporation. p. 3

Sole proprietorship another name for a single proprietorship. p. 3

Stock equity of a corporation divided into units called *shares.* p. 2

Stockholders the owners of a corporation; also called *shareholders.* p. 2

Tax accounting the field of accounting that includes preparing tax returns and planning future transactions to minimize the amount of tax; involves private, public, and government accountants. p. 13

QUESTIONS

1. Name some typical examples of organizations that may be organized as profit oriented businesses but also may be organized as government units or as nonprofit organizations.
2. What kinds of accounting information might be useful to those who carry on the marketing activities of a business?
3. What is the main purpose of accounting?
4. Describe the internal role of accounting for organizations.
5. What are three or four questions that business owners might try to answer by looking to accounting information?
6. Since computers are used to process accounting data, why should people study accounting?
7. Why do states license Certified Public Accountants?
8. According to the laws in at least 30 states, how many years of college education will a person need to enter the public accounting profession in the future?
9. Identify the three types of services typically offered by public accountants.
10. What title is frequently used for an organization's chief accounting officer? Why?
11. Identify four managerial accounting activities performed by private and government accountants.
12. Identify two management advisory services typically provided by public accountants.
13. Identify several examples of the types of work performed by government accountants.
14. What do tax accountants do in addition to preparing tax returns?
15. Why is accounting described as a service activity?
16. What ethical issues might accountants face in dealing with confidential information?
17. Identify the CPA firm that audited the financial statements of Lands' End, Inc., in Appendix F at the end of this book.

QUICK STUDY (Five-Minute Exercises)

Organizations use accounting to provide information about their economic activities. Name some examples of these economic activities.

QS 1–1
(LO 1)

Name four types of organizational activity in the general category of marketing. Also, name three types of organizational activity in the general category of executive management.

QS 1–2
(LO 1)

An important responsibility of a company's accounting department is to design and implement internal control procedures for the company. Explain the general purpose and nature of these internal control procedures.

QS 1–3
(LO 2)

QS 1-4
(LO 3)

Name the three fields in which accountants work. Also name three types of accountants which indicate the nature of the organizations in which accountants work.

QS 1-5
(LO 4)

In some situations, an accountant may have to choose between alternative methods of accounting for certain transactions. Explain why these situations may be matters of ethical concern.

EXERCISES

Exercise 1–1
(LO 1)

For each of the following, determine whether the situation refers to a sole proprietorship, partnership, or corporation:

a. The equity of Foster Company is divided into 10,000 shares of stock.

b. Metal Roofing Company is owned by Chris Fisher, who is personally liable for the debts of the business.

c. Jerry Forrentes and Susan Montgomery own Money Services, a company that cashes payroll checks for individuals and provides a variety of personal services. Neither Forrentes nor Montgomery has personal responsibility for the debts of Money Services.

d. Nancy Kerr and Frank Maples own Downtown Runners, a courier service. Both Kerr and Maples are personally liable for the debts of the business.

e. Consulting Services is a business that does not have a separate legal existence apart from the one person who owns it.

f. This is the most numerous of all types of business.

g. Businesses that take this form control the most wealth in the United States.

Exercise 1–2
(LO 2)

Each of the following questions mentions two areas of business activity. The information described in the question probably is used in both of them. Nevertheless, the information is most obviously relevant to one of the areas of activity. Select that area.

a. Which of the following business activities is most likely to use payroll information provided by accounting: marketing or human resources?

b. Which of the following business activities is most likely to use sales report information provided by accounting: marketing or production?

c. Which of the following business activities is most likely to use cash flow information provided by accounting: finance or human resources?

d. Which of the following business activities is most likely to use financial statement, budget, and performance report information provided by accounting: research and development or executive management?

e. Which of the following business activities is most likely to use production report information provided by accounting: finance or production?

Exercise 1–3
(LO 2)

Name at least three types of external decision makers that might use accounting information about a business and describe some of the questions they might seek to answer through their use of accounting information.

Exercise 1–4
(LO 3)

Three broad fields of accounting are:

A. Financial accounting
B. Managerial accounting
C. Tax accounting

For each of the following activities, identify the field of accounting that involves the activity:

___ 1. Auditing financial statements.
___ 2. Planning transactions to minimize the amount of tax to be paid.

__ 3. Cost accounting.

__ 4. Preparing financial statements.

__ 5. Reviewing financial reports to be sure they comply with SEC requirements.

__ 6. Budgeting.

__ 7. Internal auditing.

__ 8. Investigating violations of tax laws.

For each of the following roles, present a brief example of a situation in which ethical considerations would play an important role in guiding your action:

**Exercise 1–5
(LO 4)**

a. You are a student in a class.

b. You are a manager with responsibility for several employees.

c. You are an accountant preparing tax returns for several clients.

d. You are an accountant with audit clients that compete with each other.

Indicate which term is best described by each of the following statements:

**Exercise 1–6
(LO 5)**

A. Audit
B. Controller
C. Cost accounting
D. GAAP
E. Ethics
F. General accounting
G. Budgeting
H. Tax accounting

__ 1. A field of accounting that includes planning future transactions to minimize the amount of tax a company will have to pay.

__ 2. A managerial accounting activity designed to help managers identify, measure, and control operating costs.

__ 3. Principles that determine the rightness or wrongness of particular acts or activities.

__ 4. A thorough check of an organization's accounting system and records that adds credibility to financial statements.

__ 5. The task of recording transactions, processing the recorded data, and preparing reports and financial statements.

__ 6. The chief accounting officer of an organization.

Indicate which term is best described by each of the following statements:

**Exercise 1–7
(LO 5)**

A. Government accountants
B. Internal auditing
C. IRS
D. SEC
E. CIA
F. NASBA
G. Private accountants
H. Public accountants
I. AICPA
J. CMA

__ 1. Activity by an organization's employees that involves examining the organization's record-keeping processes and also assessing whether managers are following established operating procedures and evaluating the efficiency of operating procedures.

__ 2. Accountants who work for a single employer other than the government.

__ 3. The National Association of State Boards of Accountancy.

__ 4. The federal agency that has the duty of collecting federal taxes and otherwise enforcing tax laws.

__ 5. Accountants who provide their services to many different clients.

__ 6. Accountants who are employed by federal, state, or local branches of government.

CRITICAL THINKING: ESSAYS, PROBLEMS, AND CASES

Analytical Essay
(LO 1, 2)

Refer to the discussion of JW Shuttle on the first page of this chapter. Prior to establishing the business, Jarrett and Wilson met with a loan officer of the local bank to discuss obtaining a loan for the business. Assume that you were the loan officer of the bank. Write an essay discussing the kinds of information you would have requested from Jarrett and Wilson. Also, discuss whether the information you would seek, as well as your ultimate loan decision, would be affected by the form of business organization that Jarrett and Wilson selected for JW Shuttle.

Managerial Decision Case
(LO 4)

Assume that you are a partner in a CPA firm with several audit clients. Robert Jones is an employee of your firm who hopes to be promoted to partner. Recently, the management of Shader Company approached Jones to propose that Jones perform an audit of Shader's financial statements. In discussing the fee for the audit, Shader's management suggested a range of fees whereby the amount would depend on the reported profit of Shader Company. The higher the profit, the higher would be the fee. Decide whether your firm should accept a fee arrangement of this nature and describe some of the arguments that support your decision.

CONCEPT TESTER

Test your understanding of the concepts introduced in this chapter by completing the following crossword puzzle.

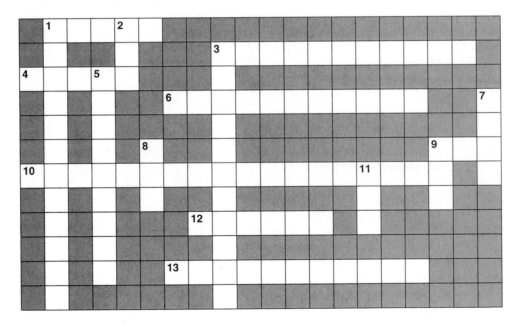

Across Clues

1. Equity of a corporation divided into units called shares.
3. 2 words; the name of a corporation's stock when it issues only one class of stock.
4. The National Association of State Boards of Accountancy.
6. A business owned by two or more people that is not organized as a corporation.
9. A certification that a person is professionally competent in managerial accounting.
10. 2 words; a business owned by one individual that is not organized as a corporation.
12. Principles that determine the rightness or wrongness of particular acts or activities.
13. The part of accounting that records transactions and other events.

Down Clues

1. The owners of a corporation.
2. A certification that a person is professionally competent in internal auditing.
3. A business that is chartered as a separate legal entity under state or federal laws.
5. The process of developing formal plans for future activities.
7. Rules adopted by the accounting profession as guides for reporting financial activities.
8. The federal agency that has the duty of collecting federal taxes and enforcing tax laws.
9. An accountant who is licensed by a state board to practice public accounting.
11. The federal agency that regulates securities markets.

ANSWERS TO PROGRESS CHECKS

1–1 Sole proprietorship, partnership, corporation

1–2 The activities are finance, human resources, research and development, production, marketing, and executive management.

1–3 c

1–4 b

1–5 Bookkeeping is the part of accounting that records transactions and other events, either manually or with computers. Accounting activities are concerned with identifying how transactions and events should be described in financial statements. Accounting activities also involve designing and implementing systems that make it possible to produce useful reports and to control the operations of an organization. Accounting involves more professional expertise and judgment than bookkeeping because accountants must analyze complex and unusual events. Also, accountants must be able to interpret and explain the information in the financial reports.

1–6 a

1–7 The three broad fields of accounting are financial, managerial, and tax accounting.

1–8 The purpose of an audit is to add credibility to financial statements. When performing an audit, CPAs examine financial statements and the accounting records used to prepare them. During the audit, they decide whether the statements reflect the company's financial position and operating results in agreement with generally accepted accounting principles.

1–9 True

1–10 True

Financial Statements and Accounting Principles

*K*aren and Mark Smith recently graduated from Notre Dame University and have accepted employment with different companies in Chicago. Already committed to a long-term savings program, they have been seeking advice about alternative investments. One investment that has been suggested to them is H & R Block, Inc. As customers of H & R Block, the Smiths have used the company's services related to the preparation and filing of income tax returns. After receiving the company's annual report, however, they have learned that H & R Block also owns CompuServe Information Services, which provides communications and information services to personal computer owners. In April 1995, the company acquired SPRY, Inc., a leading provider of Internet products.

Currently, the Smiths are trying to understand the financial information contained in H & R Block's annual report. In fact, they have become so fascinated by the process that they recently enrolled in Accounting Principles I, a course they are taking in the evening at South Suburban College near Chicago.

H & R BLOCK, INC.	Year Ended April 30		
(In thousands)	1996	1995	1994
For the Year:			
Total revenues	$1,679,600	$1,360,318	$1,238,677
Net earnings	177,168	107,259	200,528
At Year-End:			
Total assets	$1,755,841	$1,078,038	$1,074,704
Stockholders' equity	1,039,543	685,865	707,875

LEARNING OBJECTIVES

After studying Chapter 2, you should be able to:

1. **Describe the information presented in financial statements and be able to prepare simple financial statements.**
2. **Explain the accounting principles introduced in the chapter and describe the process by which generally accepted accounting principles are established.**
3. **Analyze business transactions to determine their effects on the accounting equation.**
4. **Analyze a company's performance with the return on equity ratio.**
5. **Define or explain the words and phrases listed in the chapter glossary.**

In this chapter, you learn about the kind of information accountants provide in financial statements to decision makers. Also, we discuss some general principles that guide accountants in developing these statements. This discussion includes identifying some of the organizations that regulate and influence financial accounting. The chapter also shows you how accountants analyze business transactions to generate useful information. This is important for understanding why financial statements are useful. Finally, we explain the return on equity ratio, which you can use in evaluating a company's operating success.

FINANCIAL STATEMENTS

LO 1
Describe the information presented in financial statements and be able to prepare simple financial statements.

As you learned in Chapter 1, accounting is intended to provide useful information to people who make rational investment, credit, and similar decisions.[1] These decision makers include investors, lenders, managers, suppliers, customers, and other interested people. Be sure to read the As a Matter of Opinion box to learn how one decision maker uses accounting information to help him fulfill his responsibilities as a member of a city council.

Many organizations provide accounting information to managers and other decision makers in the form of financial statements. The statements are useful because they describe the organization's financial health and performance in a condensed and highly informative format. Because they give an overall view of the entire organization, financial statements are a good place to start your study of accounting. We begin by looking at the income statement and the balance sheet. This diagram represents the relationship between these two statements:

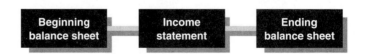

In effect, the income statement for the reporting period links the balance sheets as of the beginning and end of the reporting period.

The Income Statement

Look at the **income statement** in Illustration 2–1. The income statement shows whether the business earned a profit (also called *net income*). A company earns a **net income** if its revenues exceed its expenses. A company incurs a **net loss** if its expenses exceed its revenues. In Illustration 2–1, observe that the income statement does not simply report the amount of net income or net loss. Instead, it lists the types and amounts of the revenues and expenses. As another example, **The Walt Disney Company** classifies the revenues and expenses on its income statement into the fol-

---

[1] Financial Accounting Standards Board, *Statement of Financial Accounting Concepts No. 1,* "Objectives of Financial Reporting by Business Enterprises" (Norwalk, CT, 1978), par. 34.

As a Matter of Opinion

Mr. Garcia earned a BBA degree and has done additional graduate work at The University of Texas at Austin. He has been president of the Austin Chapter of CPAs, president of Austin's Hispanic Chamber of Commerce, and president and trustee of the Austin Independent School District and Austin Community College. He has served on the board of directors of the State Bar of Texas and the board of directors of the Greater Austin Chamber of Commerce.

During my 25-year career in public service, I have served in a variety of both appointed and elected positions. Currently, I am a member of the City Council of Austin, Texas. The council oversees an annual budget of over $1 billion that includes the operation of an airport, an electric utility, a hospital, a general fund, and several other enterprises.

Having a good understanding of accounting has been like having an extra high-powered flashlight that helps me examine and understand the intricacies of this tremendously complex organization.

My accounting education is like a good friend that helps me decipher the many difficult situations we face daily. My accounting experience allows me to quickly understand the full economic impact and effects of proposed transactions and activities. This valuable insight helps me make decisions that hopefully protect and enhance the economic situation of our city and its citizens.

Gustavo L. Garcia, CPA

CLEAR COPY, INC. Income Statement For Month Ended December 31, 19X1		
Revenues:		
Copy services revenue........................		$4,100
Operating expenses:		
Rent expense...........................	$1,000	
Salaries expense........................	700	
Total operating expenses		1,700
Net income		$2,400

Illustration 2–1
Income Statement for Clear Copy, Inc.[2]

---

lowing categories: theme parks, filmed entertainment, and consumer products. This detailed information is more useful for decision making than just a simple profit or loss number.

Revenues are inflows of assets received in exchange for goods or services provided to customers as part of the major or central operations of the business. Revenues also may occur as decreases in liabilities.[3] For now, think of assets as economic resources owned by a business and liabilities as the debts owed by a business. Later, we define these terms more completely.

The income statement in Illustration 2–1 shows that the business of Clear Copy, Inc., earned revenues of $4,100 by providing copy services to customers during the month of December. Examples of revenues for other businesses include sales of products and amounts earned from rent, dividends, and interest.

Expenses are outflows or the using up of assets that occur in the process of delivering goods or rendering services to customers. Expenses also may occur in the

---

[2] Normally, corporations are subject to income taxes. However, to simplify the discussion, we assume no income taxes in the Clear Copy illustrations and in the assignments at the end of the chapter.

[3] Financial Accounting Standards Board, *Statement of Financial Accounting Concepts No. 6,* "Elements of Financial Statements" (Norwalk, CT, 1985), par. 78.

form of increases in liabilities.[4] The income statement in Illustration 2–1 shows that Clear Copy used up some of its assets by paying for rented office space. The $1,000 cost of the space is reported in Illustration 2–1 as rent expense. The business also paid for an employee's services at a cost of $700. This is reported on the income statement as salaries expense.

Notice that the heading in Illustration 2–1 names the business, states that the report is an income statement, and shows the time period covered by the statement. Knowledge of the time period is important for judging if the company's performance is satisfactory. For example, to decide whether Clear Copy's $2,400 net income is satisfactory, you need to know that the business earned the net income during a one-month period.

The Balance Sheet

The purpose of the **balance sheet** is to provide information that helps users understand a company's financial status as of a given date. As a result, the balance sheet often is called the **statement of financial position.** The balance sheet describes financial position by listing the types and dollar amounts of assets, liabilities, and equity of the business. (Equity is the difference between a company's assets and its liabilities.)

Illustration 2–2 presents the balance sheet for Clear Copy as of December 31, 19X1. Unlike the income statement that refers to a period of time, the balance sheet describes conditions that exist at a point in time. Thus, the heading shows the specific date on which the assets and liabilities are identified and measured. The amounts in the balance sheet are stated as of the close of business on that date.

The balance sheet in Illustration 2–2 reports that the company owned three different assets at the close of business on December 31, 19X1. The assets were cash, store supplies, and copy equipment. The total dollar amount for these assets was $38,000. The balance sheet also shows that there were liabilities of $6,200. Stockholders' equity was $31,800. This amount is the difference between the assets and the liabilities.

Notice that the total amounts on the two sides of the balance sheet are equal. This equality is why the statement is called a *balance sheet.* The name also reflects the fact that the statement reports the balances of the assets, liabilities, and equity on a given date.

ASSETS, LIABILITIES, AND EQUITY

In general, the **assets** of a business are the properties or economic resources owned by the business. More precisely, assets are defined as "probable future economic benefits obtained or controlled by a particular entity as a result of past transactions or events."[5] One familiar asset is cash. Another asset consists of amounts owed to the business by its customers for goods and services sold to them on credit. This asset is called **accounts receivable.** In general, individuals who owe amounts to the business are called its **debtors.** Other assets owned by businesses include merchandise held for sale, supplies, equipment, buildings, and land. Assets also can be intangible rights, such as those granted by a patent or copyright.

The **liabilities** of a business are its debts. Liabilities are defined more precisely as "probable future sacrifices of economic benefits arising from present obligations of a particular entity to transfer assets or provide services to other entities in the future as a result of past transactions or events."[6] One common liability consists of amounts

---

[4] Ibid., par. 80.

[5] Financial Accounting Standards Board, *Statement of Financial Accounting Concepts No. 6,* "Elements of Financial Statements" (Norwalk, CT, 1985), par. 25.

[6] Ibid., par. 35.

Illustration 2-2
Balance Sheet for
Clear Copy, Inc.

CLEAR COPY, INC.
Balance Sheet
December 31, 19X1

Assets		Liabilities		
Cash	$ 8,400	Accounts payable		$ 6,200
Store supplies	3,600			
Copy equipment	26,000	**Stockholders' Equity**		
		Contributed capital:		
		Common stock....	$30,000	
		Retained earnings...	1,800	31,800
		Total liabilities and		
Total assets	$38,000	stockholders' equity		$38,000

owed for goods and services bought on credit. This liability is called **accounts payable.** Other liabilities are salaries and wages owed to employees, taxes payable, notes payable, and interest payable.

A liability represents a claim against a business. In general, those who have the right to receive payments from a company are called its **creditors.** From the creditor's viewpoint, a liability is the right to be paid by a business. (In effect, one party's payable is another party's receivable.) If a business fails to pay its debts, the law gives creditors the right to force the sale of its assets to obtain the money to meet their claims. When the assets are sold under these conditions, the creditors are paid first, up to the full amount of their claims, with the remainder (the residual) going to the owners of the business.

Creditors often use a balance sheet to help them decide whether to loan money to a business. They can use the balance sheet to compare the amounts of existing liabilities and assets. A loan is less risky if the liabilities are small in comparison to the assets. There is less risk because there is a larger cushion if the assets are sold for less than the amounts shown on the balance sheet. On the other hand, a loan is more risky if the liabilities are large compared to the assets. The risk is greater because it is more likely that the assets cannot be sold for enough cash to pay all the debts.

Equity is defined as "the residual interest in the assets of an entity that remains after deducting its liabilities."[7] Equity also is called **net assets.** If a business is organized as a corporation, the owners of the business are stockholders and the equity is described as *stockholders' equity.* Since Clear Copy is a corporation, note that the equity heading of the balance sheet in Illustration 2–2 is *stockholders' equity.* Chapter 14 briefly describes the accounting practices used when a business is not organized as a corporation.

As Illustration 2–2 shows, the stockholders' equity of a corporation is divided into two categories. The first category is called **contributed capital** or **paid-in capital.** It represents the assets contributed to the corporation by its stockholders. In the present discussion, the contributed capital of a corporation includes only common stock. In Chapter 14, you will learn about other items that may be reported as part of a corporation's contributed capital.

The second category of a corporation's equity is called *retained earnings.* **Retained earnings** are created by profitable activities. They represent the equity that results from all of the past net incomes earned by the corporation less any net losses and less all dividends. **Dividends** are distributions of assets by the corporation to its stockholders.

---

[7] Ibid., par. 49.

Earlier we defined net income as the difference between revenue and expense for a time period. Net income is also the change in stockholders' equity that occurred during the period as a result of the company's major or central operations. By describing this change, the income statement links the company's balance sheets from the beginning and end of the reporting period.

We use this background on the balance sheet and income statement to explain more about financial accounting. The next sections of the chapter describe the principles that guide financial accounting.

Progress Check
(Answers to Progress Checks are provided at the end of the chapter.)

2-1   Which set of information is reported on an income statement?   *(a)* assets, liabilities, and stockholders' equity;   *(b)* revenues, expenses, and stockholders' equity;   *(c)* assets, liabilities, and net income;   *(d)* revenues, expenses, and net income.

2-2   What do accountants mean by the term *expense?*

2-3   Considering the income statement and the balance sheet, which statement reports conditions at a particular point in time? Which reports activities during a period of time?

GENERALLY ACCEPTED ACCOUNTING PRINCIPLES (GAAP)

LO 2

Explain the accounting principles introduced in the chapter and describe the process by which generally accepted accounting principles are established.

In Chapter 1, we explained that financial accounting practice is governed by a set of rules called *generally accepted accounting principles,* or *GAAP.* To use and interpret financial statements effectively, you need to have a basic understanding of these principles.

A primary purpose of GAAP is to make the information in financial reports relevant, reliable, and comparable. Information that is relevant has the capacity to affect the decisions made by financial statement users. Reliable information is necessary if decision makers are to depend on it. In addition, the information should allow statement users to compare companies. These comparisons are more likely to be useful if all companies use similar practices. GAAP impose limits on the variety of accounting practices that companies can use, thereby making the financial statements more useful.

The Development of GAAP

Prior to the 1930s, GAAP were developed through common usage. In effect, a practice was considered suitable if it was acceptable to most accountants. This history is still reflected in the phrase *generally accepted.* However, as the accounting profession grew and the world of business became more complex, many people were not satisfied with the profession's progress in providing useful information.

The desire for improvement caused many accountants, managers, and government regulators to want more uniformity in practice. Thus, in the 1930s, they began to give authority for defining accepted principles to small groups of experienced professional accountants. Since then, a series of committees or boards have had authority to establish GAAP. In general, the authority of these groups has increased over time. We describe the present arrangement for establishing GAAP later in this chapter.

Broad and Specific Accounting Principles

GAAP include both broad and specific principles. The broad principles describe the basic assumptions and general guidelines that accountants follow in preparing financial statements. The specific principles provide more detailed rules that accountants follow in reporting the results of various business activities. The broad principles stem from observing long-used accounting practices. In contrast, the specific principles are established more often by the rulings of authoritative bodies.

As a user of financial statements, an understanding of both broad and specific principles will give you insight as to what the information means. It also will help you know what the information does not mean, and thereby avoid using it incorrectly. Because the broad principles are especially helpful for learning about accounting, we emphasize them in the early chapters of the book. The broad principles include the following:[8]

	First Introduced	
	Chapter	**Page**
Business entity principle	2	35
Objectivity principle	2	35
Cost principle	2	36
Going-concern principle	2	36
Revenue recognition principle	2	40
Time period principle	4	110
Matching principle	4	111
Materiality principle	8	288
Full-disclosure principle	8	294
Consistency principle	9	323
Conservatism principle	9	356

Specific principles are especially important for understanding individual items in the financial statements. They are described throughout the book as we come to them.

Accounting Principles, Auditing Standards, and Financial Accounting

Generally accepted accounting principles are not natural laws like the laws of physics or other sciences. Instead, GAAP are identified in response to the needs of users and others affected by accounting. Thus, GAAP are subject to change as needs change.

Three groups of people are most directly affected by financial reporting: preparers, auditors, and users. The following diagram shows the relationship between the financial statements and these groups.

Private accountants prepare the financial statements. To give users more confidence in the statements, independent auditors (CPAs) usually examine the financial statements and develop an audit report. The statements and the audit report then are distributed to the users.

Illustration 2–3 expands this diagram to show how accounting principles and auditing standards relate to the financial reporting process. First, in Illustration 2–3, we show

---

[8]In describing these accounting principles, some writers have used different words to mean the same thing. For example, broad principles also have been called *concepts, theories, assumptions,* and *postulates.* We call them *principles,* but don't be confused if you see them called by other names in other books.

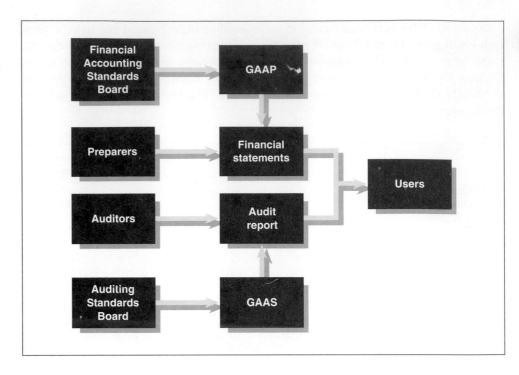

that GAAP are applied in preparing the financial statements. Preparers use GAAP to decide what procedures to follow as they account for business transactions and put the statements together.

Second, in Illustration 2–3, we show that audits are performed in accordance with **generally accepted auditing standards (GAAS).** GAAS are the rules adopted by the accounting profession as guides for conducting audits of financial statements. GAAS tell auditors what they must do in their audits to determine whether the financial statements comply with GAAP.

Applying both GAAP and GAAS assures users that financial statements include relevant, reliable, and comparable information. The audit does not, however, ensure that they can safely invest in or loan to the company. The audit does not reduce the risk that the company's products and services will not be successfully marketed or that other factors could cause it to fail.

HOW ACCOUNTING PRINCIPLES ARE ESTABLISHED

In Illustration 2–3, we also identify the two organizations that are the primary authoritative sources of GAAP and GAAS. The primary authoritative source of GAAP is the Financial Accounting Standards Board **(FASB).** The FASB is a nonprofit organization with seven board members who serve full time. The FASB is located in Norwalk, Connecticut, approximately 50 miles from New York City, and has a 40-member research staff to help identify problems in financial accounting and to find ways to solve them. The board seeks advice from groups affected by GAAP and often holds public hearings for this purpose. In summary, the FASB's job is to improve financial reporting while balancing the interests of the affected groups.[9]

The FASB announces its findings in several different publications. The most important are **Statements of Financial Accounting Standards (SFAS).** These state-

[9] For more detailed information about the board, see Paul B. W. Miller, Rodney J. Redding, and Paul R. Bahnson, *The FASB—The People, the Process, and the Politics,* 3rd ed. (Burr Ridge, IL: Richard D. Irwin, 1994).

ments establish generally accepted accounting principles in the United States and may affect practice in other countries.

The FASB gains its authority from a variety of sources. The most significant source is the Securities and Exchange Commission (SEC). Congress created the SEC in 1934 to regulate securities markets, including the flow of information from companies to the public. When the FASB began operating in 1973, the SEC designated it as the primary authority for establishing GAAP. However, the SEC may overrule the FASB if the SEC thinks doing so will protect the public interest. To date, this authority has been exercised only one time.[10]

The FASB also has authority because it has been endorsed by each of the state boards that license certified public accountants. In auditing financial statements, CPAs confirm that the statements comply with the FASB's rules. The state ethics codes require the CPAs' audit reports to disclose any areas in which the statements fail to comply. If the CPAs fail to report these problems, they may lose their licenses to practice. The AICPA's Code of Professional Conduct includes a similar provision. Also, a member of the AICPA may be expelled from the institute for not objecting to financial statements that fail to comply with FASB rules.

Many other professional organizations support the FASB's process by providing input and by giving financial support through the Financial Accounting Foundation.[11] They include:

- American Accounting Association (**AAA**)—a professional association of individuals, primarily college and university accounting faculty.
- Financial Executives Institute (**FEI**)—a professional association of private accountants.
- Institute of Management Accountants (**IMA**)—a professional association of private accountants, formerly called the *National Association of Accountants*.
- Association for Investment Management and Research (**AIMR**)—a professional association of people who use financial statements in the process of evaluating companies' financial performance.
- Securities Industry Association (**SIA**)—an association of individuals involved with issuing and marketing securities.

These groups boost the Board's credibility by participating in its process for identifying GAAP.

Prior to the FASB, the accounting profession depended on the Accounting Principles Board (**APB**) to identify GAAP. The APB was a special committee of the AICPA, and its members served as unpaid volunteers. The APB issued 31 *Opinions* from 1959 to 1973. These *Opinions* created GAAP, just like the FASB's standards. Many APB *Opinions* remain in effect, and we describe their requirements throughout this book.

Prior to the APB, the accounting profession depended on the Committee on Accounting Procedure (**CAP**) for identifying GAAP. Like the APB, the CAP was a committee of the AICPA with unpaid members. The CAP issued 51 *Accounting Research Bulletins* during its life from 1936 to 1959. Only a few bulletins remain in effect.

The authority for identifying generally accepted auditing standards (GAAS) presently belongs to the Auditing Standards Board (**ASB**). The ASB is a special committee of the AICPA with unpaid volunteer members. The SEC is an important source of the ASB's authority.

---

[10] The SEC overruled the FASB's *Statement of Financial Accounting Standards No. 19* in 1978. This standard concerned accounting for oil and gas producing companies.

[11] Working alongside the FASB is the Governmental Accounting Standards Board (GASB), which identifies special accounting principles to be applied in preparing financial statements for state and local governments. Both the FASB and the GASB operate under the Financial Accounting Foundation.

Pronouncements issued by the FASB, APB, CAP, and ASB define specific GAAP and GAAS. They are available for accountants and users of financial statements in publications issued by the FASB and the AICPA. Many of these principles are described in this book.

INTERNATIONAL ACCOUNTING STANDARDS

In today's world, people in different countries engage in business with each other more easily than in the past. A company in the United States might sell its products all over the world. Another company in Singapore might raise cash by selling stock to American and Japanese investors. At the same time, it might borrow from creditors in Saudi Arabia and Germany.

An increasing number of companies have international operations. For example, **Marriott International, Inc.,** is a United States company with operations in lodging and contract services. Most of the company's operations are in the United States. However, for 1995 alone, the company announced or was scheduled to open properties in Aruba, the Bahamas, Egypt, Lebanon, Puerto Rico, Costa Rica, Ecuador, Germany, Guatemala, Indonesia, Malaysia, Mexico, and Thailand.

Despite this trend toward global business, a major problem exists because each country has its own unique set of acceptable accounting practices. Consider, for example, the Singapore company we described earlier in this section. Should it prepare financial statements that comply with Singapore accounting standards, or with the standards used in the United States, Japan, Saudi Arabia, or Germany? Should it have to prepare five different sets of reports to gain access to financial markets in all five countries?

Accounting organizations from around the world responded to this problem by creating the International Accounting Standards Committee (**IASC**) in 1973. With headquarters in London, the IASC issues *International Accounting Standards* that identify preferred accounting practices and then encourages their worldwide acceptance. By narrowing the range of alternative practices, the IASC hopes to create more harmony among the accounting practices of different countries. If standards could be harmonized, a single set of financial statements could be used by one company in all financial markets.

In many countries, the bodies that set accounting standards have encouraged the IASC to reduce the differences. Both the FASB and the SEC have provided this encouragement and technical assistance. However, the IASC does not have the authority to impose its standards on companies. Although progress has been slow, interest is growing in moving United States GAAP toward the IASC's preferred practices. The authority to make such changes rests with the FASB and the SEC.

Progress Check

2–4   Which body currently establishes generally accepted accounting principles in the United States?   *(a)* the SEC;   *(b)* the U.S. Congress;   *(c)* the FASB;   *(d)* the AICPA;   *(e)* the IASC.

2–5   What is the difference between GAAP and GAAS?

2–6   Are United States companies with operations in foreign countries required to prepare their financial statements according to the rules established by the IASC?

Recall from Chapter 1 that the purpose of accounting is to provide useful information to people who make rational investment, credit, and similar decisions. In fact, this description of the purpose of accounting comes from a major FASB project called the *conceptual framework*. This framework defines several accounting terms that should be understood by financial statement users as well as accountants. For example, we relied on the conceptual framework in preceding discussions when we defined revenues, expenses, assets, liabilities, and equity.

Another purpose of the conceptual framework is to describe the characteristics that make accounting information useful for decisions. Earlier, we referred to the conceptual framework's commonsense ideas that information is useful only if it has both *relevance* and *reliability*.

Now that you have some background on how accounting principles are developed, we can begin to describe some of the broad principles listed on page 31. These broad principles will help you understand financial statements and the procedures used to prepare them.

UNDERSTANDING GENERALLY ACCEPTED ACCOUNTING PRINCIPLES

LO 2
Explain the accounting principles introduced in the chapter and describe the process by which generally accepted accounting principles are established.

Business Entity Principle

Recall from Chapter 1 that corporations have a separate legal existence but single proprietorships and partnerships do not. Nevertheless, the **business entity principle** requires every business to be accounted for separately and distinctly from its owner or owners. The principle applies to all three forms of business. This principle also requires us to account separately for other entities that might be controlled by the same owners. The reason behind this principle is that separate information for each business is relevant to decisions that its users make.

To illustrate, suppose that the owners of a business want to see how well it is doing. To be useful, the financial statements for the business should not mix the owners' personal transactions with the business's transactions. For example, the owners' personal expenses should not be subtracted from the company's revenues on its income statement because they do not contribute to the company's success. Thus, the income statement should not report such things as the owners' personal entertainment and transportation expenses. Otherwise, the company's reported net income would be understated and the business would appear less profitable than it really is.

In summary, a company's reports should not include the personal transactions, assets, and liabilities of its stockholders. Furthermore, the company's reports should not include the transactions, assets, and liabilities of another business. If this principle is not carefully followed, the reported information about the company's financial position and net income is not useful for rational investment and credit decisions.

PRINCIPLE APPLICATION
Business Entity Principle
AT&T Corp. owns about 86% of AT&T Capital Corporation's equity. Nevertheless, AT&T Capital Corporation accounts for its operations as a separate entity and prepares its own financial statements.

Objectivity Principle

The **objectivity principle** requires financial statement information to be supported by evidence other than someone's opinion or imagination. Information would not be reliable if it were based only on what the statement preparer thinks might be true. The preparer might be too optimistic or too pessimistic. In the worst case, an unethical preparer might try to mislead financial statement users by deliberately misrepresenting the truth. The objectivity principle is intended to make financial statements useful by ensuring that they present reliable information.

Cost Principle

The **cost principle** requires financial statement information to be based on costs incurred in business transactions. Sales and purchases are examples of **business transactions.** Business transactions are exchanges of economic consideration between two parties. The consideration may include such things as goods, services, money, or rights to collect money. In applying the cost principle, cost is measured on a cash or cash equivalent basis. If cash is given for an asset or service, the cost of the asset or service is measured as the entire amount of cash paid. If something other than cash is exchanged (such as an old vehicle traded in for a new one), cost is measured as the cash equivalent value of what was given up or of the item received, whichever is more clearly evident.[12]

The *cost principle* is accepted because it puts relevant information in the financial statements. Cost is the amount initially sacrificed to purchase an asset or service. Cost also approximates the market value of the asset or service when it was acquired. Information about the amount sacrificed and the initial market value of what was received is generally thought to be relevant to decisions. Complying with the cost principle provides this information.

In addition, the cost principle is consistent with the *objectivity principle.* Most accountants believe that information based on actual costs is more likely to be objective than information based on estimates of values. For example, reporting purchases of assets and services at cost is more objective than reporting the manager's estimate of their value. Thus, financial statements based on costs are believed to be more reliable because the information is more objective.

To illustrate, suppose that a business pays $50,000 for land used in its operations. The cost principle tells us to record the purchase at $50,000. It would make no difference if the buyer thinks that the land is worth at least $60,000. The cost principle requires the purchase to be recorded at the cost of $50,000. However, you learn in later chapters that, to provide more useful information, objective estimates of value are sometimes reported instead of costs.

Going-Concern Principle

The **going-concern principle** (also called the **continuing-concern principle**) requires financial statements to reflect the assumption that the business will continue operating instead of being closed or sold. Thus, a company's balance sheet does not report the liquidation values of operating assets that are being held for long-term use. Instead, these assets are reported at amounts based on their cost. Many accountants have argued that the going-concern principle leads to reporting relevant information because many decisions about a business are made with the expectation that it will continue to exist in the future.

As a result of applying the cost and going-concern principles, a company's balance sheet seldom describes what the company is worth. Thus, if a company is to be bought or sold, the buyer and seller are well advised to obtain additional information from other sources.[13]

The going-concern principle must be ignored if the company is expected to fail or be liquidated. In these cases, the going-concern principle and the cost principle do not apply. Instead, estimated market values are relevant and costs are not relevant.

---

[12] FASB, *Accounting Standards—Current Text* (Norwalk, CT, 1995), sec. N35.105. First published as *APB Opinion No. 29,* par. 18.

[13] In *SFAS 107,* the FASB established a requirement for supplemental disclosures (in the notes to the financial statements) of the current market values of many assets and liabilities.

Progress Check

2-7   Name and describe two qualities of useful information identified by the FASB's conceptual framework.

2-8   Why are the personal activities of business owners excluded from the financial statements of the owners' business?

2-9   If a company finds a bargain on some equipment worth $40,000 to the company and is able to buy the equipment for $25,000, what amount should be reported for the equipment on the company's balance sheet prepared immediately after the purchase? Which principle governs your answer?

Up to this stage, you have learned that financial statements describe the financial activities of a business. You also know that many of these activities (for example, purchases and sales) involve business transactions. To clearly understand the information in the statements, you need to see how an accounting system captures relevant data from the transactions, classifies and saves it, and then organizes it on the financial statements. We begin to explain this in the next section of the chapter. Our explanation continues through Chapter 5. We start with a simple example.

The beginning point for accounting systems is the definition of *owners' equity* as the difference between an organization's assets and liabilities. This definition can be stated as the following equation:

$$Assets - Liabilities = Owners' \ Equity$$

More specifically, for a corporation:

$$Assets - Liabilities = Stockholders' \ Equity$$

Like any equation, this one can be modified by rearranging the terms. The following modified form of the equation is called the **balance sheet equation:**

$$Assets = Liabilities + Stockholders' \ Equity$$

Because it serves as the basis for financial accounting information, the balance sheet equation also is called the **accounting equation.** The next section shows you how to use this equation to keep track of changes in a company's assets, liabilities, and equity in a way that provides useful information.

USING THE BALANCE SHEET EQUATION TO PROVIDE USEFUL INFORMATION

LO 3
Analyze business transactions to determine their effects on the accounting equation.

THE EFFECTS OF TRANSACTIONS ON THE ACCOUNTING EQUATION

A transaction is an exchange between two parties of such things as goods, services, money, or rights to collect money. Because the two parties exchange assets and liabilities, transactions affect the components of the accounting equation. Importantly, each and every transaction always leaves the equation in balance. That is, the total assets always equal the sum of the liabilities and the equity regardless of what happens in a transaction. We show how this equality is preserved by looking at the transactions of a new small business called Clear Copy, Inc.

Transaction 1.   On December 1, 19X1, Annette Dow, Libby DeShazo, and Richard Tucker formed a new photocopying store that they organized as a corporation. Dow agreed to serve as president of the corporation. The organizers expect the store's primary focus to be on serving business customers who place relatively large orders. Each organizer invested $10,000 cash in the new corporation and received 10,000 shares of its $1 par value common stock. Par value is an arbitrary amount established in the corporation's charter. You will learn more about par values in Chapter 14. Dow deposited the $30,000 in a bank account opened under the name of Clear Copy, Inc.

Illustration 2–4
Changes in the Balance
Sheet Equation Caused by
Asset Purchases for Cash

		Cash	+	Store Supplies	+	Copy Equipment	=	Common Stock	Explanation of Change
		Assets						**Stockholders' Equity**	
(1)		$30,000						$30,000	Investment
(2)		− 2,500		+$2,500					
Bal.		$27,500		$2,500				$30,000	
(3)		−20,000				+$20,000			
Bal.		$ 7,500	+	$2,500	+	$20,000	=	$30,000	

After this event, the cash (an asset) and the stockholders' equity each equal $30,000. As you can see, the accounting equation is in balance:

$$\underbrace{\text{Assets}}_{\text{Cash, \$30,000}} = \underbrace{\text{Stockholders' Equity}}_{\text{Common Stock, \$30,000}}$$

The equation shows that the business has one asset, cash, equal to $30,000. It has no liabilities, and the stockholders' equity in the business is $30,000.

Transactions 2 and 3. In its second business transaction, Clear Copy used $2,500 of its cash to purchase store supplies. In a third transaction, Clear Copy spent $20,000 to buy photocopying equipment. Transactions 2 and 3 were both exchanges of cash for other assets. Neither transaction produced an expense because no value was lost. Instead, the purchases merely changed the form of the assets from cash to supplies and equipment.

The effects of these transactions are shown in bold type in Illustration 2–4. Observe that the decreases in cash are exactly equal to the increases in the store supplies and copy equipment. As a result, the equation remains in balance after each transaction.

Transaction 4. Next, Dow decided that the business needed more store supplies and additional copy equipment. The items to be purchased would have a total cost of $7,100. However, as shown on the last line of the first column in Illustration 2–4, the business had only $7,500 in cash after transaction 3. Because these purchases would use almost all of Clear Copy's cash, Dow arranged to purchase them on credit from Handy Supply Company. That is, Clear Copy took delivery of the items in exchange for a promise to pay for them later. The supplies cost $1,100, the copy equipment cost $6,000, and the total liability to Handy Supply is $7,100.

The effects of this purchase are shown in Illustration 2–5 as transaction 4. Notice that the purchase increased total assets by $7,100 while the company's liabilities (called *accounts payable*) increased by the same amount. The transaction did not create an expense, so the amount of equity remained unchanged from the original $30,000 balance.

Transaction 5. A primary objective of a business is to increase the wealth of its owners. This goal is met when the business produces a profit (also called *net income*). A net income is reflected in the accounting equation as a net increase in stockholders' equity. Clear Copy's method of generating revenues is to sell photocopying services to its customers. The business produces a net income only if its revenues are greater than the expenses incurred in earning them. As you should expect, the process of earning copy services revenues and incurring expenses creates changes in the accounting equation.

We can see how the accounting equation is affected by earning revenues in transaction 5. In this transaction, Clear Copy provided copying services to a customer on

Illustration 2-5 Changes in the Balance Sheet Equation Caused by Asset Purchases on Credit, Revenues Received in Cash, and Expenses Paid in Cash

	Assets			Liabilities		Stockholders' Equity		
	Cash	+ Store Supplies	+ Copy Equipment	= Accounts Payable	+ Common Stock	+ Retained Earnings	Explanation of Change
Bal.	$7,500	$2,500	$20,000		$30,000		
(4)		+1,100	+6,000	+$7,100			
Bal.	$7,500	$3,600	$26,000	$7,100	$30,000		
(5)	+2,200					+2,200	Revenue
Bal.	$9,700	$3,600	$26,000	$7,100	$30,000	$2,200	
(6)	−1,000					−1,000	Expense
Bal.	$8,700	$3,600	$26,000	$7,100	$30,000	$1,200	
(7)	−700					−700	Expense
Bal.	$8,000 +	$3,600 +	$26,000 =	$7,100 +	$30,000 +	$ 500	

December 10 and immediately collected $2,200 cash. Illustration 2–5 shows that this event increased cash by $2,200 and increased retained earnings by $2,200. This increase in equity is identified in the last column as a revenue because it was earned by providing services. This information can be used later to prepare the income statement.

Transactions 6 and 7. Also on December 10, Clear Copy paid $1,000 rent to the owner of the building in which its store is located. Paying this amount allowed Clear Copy to occupy the space for the entire month of December. The effects of this event are shown in Illustration 2–5 as transaction 6. On December 12, Clear Copy paid the $700 salary of the company's only employee. This event is reflected in Illustration 2–5 as transaction 7.

Both transactions 6 and 7 produced expenses for the business. That is, they used up cash for the purpose of providing services to customers. Unlike the asset purchases in transactions 2 and 3, the cash payments in transactions 6 and 7 acquired services. The benefits of these services do not last beyond the end of the month. The equations in Illustration 2–5 show that both transactions reduced cash and the retained earnings component of stockholders' equity. Thus, the accounting equation remains in balance after each event. The last column in Illustration 2–5 shows that these decreases were expenses. This information is useful when the income statement is prepared.

Summary. We said before that a business produces a net income when its revenues exceed its expenses. Net income increases stockholders' equity. If the expenses exceed the revenues, a net loss occurs and equity is decreased. Remember that the amount of net income or loss is not affected by transactions completed between a business and its owners. Thus, the stockholders' initial investment of $30,000 is not income to the business, even though it increased the equity.

To keep things simple, and to emphasize the fact that revenues and expenses produce changes in equity, the illustrations in this chapter add the revenues directly to retained earnings and subtract the expenses directly from retained earnings. In actual practice, however, information about the revenues and expenses is accumulated separately and the amounts are added to or subtracted from retained earnings. We describe more details about this process in Chapters 3, 4, and 5.

Because of the importance of earning revenues for a company's success, we briefly interrupt the description of Clear Copy's transactions to describe the *revenue recognition principle.* This principle guides us in knowing when to report a company's revenue in the income statement.

REVENUE RECOGNITION PRINCIPLE

LO 2
Explain the accounting principles introduced in the chapter and describe the process by which generally accepted accounting principles are established.

PRINCIPLE APPLICATION
Revenue Recognition Principle
MCI Communications Corporation records as revenue the amount of communications services rendered, as measured by the minutes of traffic processed, after deducting an estimate of the traffic that will be neither billed nor collected.

Managers need guidance in deciding when to recognize revenue. (*Recognize* means to record an event for the purpose of reporting its effects in the financial statements.) For example, if revenue is recognized too early, the income statement reports net income sooner than it should and the business looks more profitable than it really is. On the other hand, if the revenue is not recognized on time, the income statement shows lower amounts of revenue and net income than it should and the business looks less profitable than it really is. In either case, the income statement does not provide decision makers with useful information about the company's success.

The question of when revenue should be recognized on the income statement is addressed by the **revenue recognition principle** (also called the **realization principle).** This principle includes three important guidelines:

1. *Revenue should be recognized at the time it is earned.* The whole process of getting ready to provide services, finding customers, convincing them to buy, and providing a service contributes to the earning of revenue. However, the amount of revenue earned at any point in the process usually cannot be determined reliably until the entire process is complete. This does not occur until the business acquires the right to collect the selling price. Therefore, in most cases, revenue should not be recognized on the income statement until the earnings process is essentially complete. For most businesses, the earnings process is completed only when services are rendered or when the seller transfers ownership of goods sold to the buyer. For example, suppose that a customer pays in advance of taking delivery of a good or service. Because the earnings process is not completed, the seller should not recognize any revenue. Instead, the seller must actually complete the earnings process before recognizing the revenue.[14] This practice is known as the *sales basis of revenue recognition.*

2. *The inflow of assets associated with revenue does not have to be in the form of cash.* The most common noncash asset acquired by the seller in a revenue transaction is the customer's promise to pay at a future date. From the seller's point of view, the customer's promise is an account receivable. These transactions, called *credit sales,* occur because it is convenient for the customer to get the goods or services now and pay for them later. (Remember that Clear Copy took advantage of this convenience in transaction 4 when it bought supplies and equipment on credit.) If objective evidence shows that the seller has the right to collect from the customer, the seller should recognize the account receivable as an asset and recognize the revenue. When the cash is collected later, no additional revenue is recognized. Instead, collecting the cash simply changes the form of the asset from a receivable to cash.

3. *The amount of recognized revenue should be measured as the cash received plus the cash equivalent value (fair market value) of any other asset or assets received.* For example, if the transaction creates an account receivable, the seller should recognize revenue equal to the value of the receivable, which usually is equivalent to the amount of cash to be collected.

The footnotes to a company's financial statements should include an explanation of the specific approach to revenue recognition used by the company. For example, **General Motors Corporation** states in its 1994 annual report that "Sales are generally recorded by the Corporation when products are shipped to independent dealers."

---

[14] FASB, *Accounting Standards—Current Text* (Norwalk, CT, 1995), sec. R75.101. First published as *APB Opinion No. 10,* par. 12.

Illustration 2-6 Changes in the Balance Sheet Equation Caused by Noncash Revenues, the Later Receipt of Cash, the Payment of Payables, and Payment of Dividends

	Cash	+	Accounts Receivable	+	Store Supplies	+	Copy Equipment	=	Accounts Payable	+	Common Stock	+	Retained Earnings	Explanation of Change
					Assets				**Liabilities**				**Stockholders' Equity**	
Bal.	$8,000				$3,600		$26,000		$7,100		$30,000		$ 500	
(8)			+$1,900										+1,900	Revenue
Bal.	$8,000		$1,900		$3,600		$26,000		$7,100		$30,000		$2,400	
(9)	+1,900		−1,900											
Bal.	$9,900		$ 0		$3,600		$26,000		$7,100		$30,000		$2,400	
(10)	− 900								− 900					
Bal.	$9,000		$ 0		$3,600		$26,000		$6,200		$30,000		$2,400	
(11)	− 600												− 600	Dividend
Bal.	$8,400	+	$ 0	+	$3,600	+	$26,000	=	$6,200	+	$30,000	+	$1,800	

To show how the revenue recognition principle works, we return to the example of Clear Copy, Inc.

Transactions 8 and 9. Assume that Clear Copy provided copy services for a customer and billed that customer $1,900. This event is identified as transaction 8 in Illustration 2–6. Ten days later, the customer paid Clear Copy the full $1,900 in transaction 9.

Illustration 2–6 shows that transaction 8 created a new asset, the account receivable from the customer. The $1,900 increase in assets produces an equal increase in retained earnings and stockholders' equity. Notice that this increase in equity is identified as a revenue in the last column of Illustration 2–6.

Transaction 9 occurred when the customer in transaction 8 paid the account receivable. This event merely converted the receivable to cash. Because transaction 9 did not increase total assets and did not affect liabilities, equity did not change. Thus, this transaction did not create any new revenue. The revenue was generated when Clear Copy rendered the services, not when the cash was collected. This emphasis on the earning process instead of cash flows reflects the goal of providing useful information in the income statement by applying the *revenue recognition principle*.

Transaction 10. In transaction 10, Clear Copy paid $900 to Handy Supply Company on December 24. The $900 payment relates to the earlier $6,000 purchase of equipment from Handy, leaving $5,100 unpaid. (The $1,100 amount due Handy for the supplies purchase also remains unpaid.) Illustration 2–6 shows that this transaction decreased Clear Copy's cash by $900 and decreased its liability to Handy Supply by the same amount. As a result, stockholders' equity did not change. This event did not create an expense, even though cash flowed out of the company.

Transaction 11. Another type of event, the payment of cash to the stockholders, is identified in Illustration 2–6 as transaction 11. In this case, Clear Copy paid a total of $600 to the stockholders. Recall that payments by a corporation of cash (or other assets) to its stockholders are called *dividends*. In Illustration 2–6, note that this decrease in stockholders' equity is not called an expense. Dividends are not an expense because they do not occur as part of the revenue-generating process of delivering goods or rendering services to customers. Because dividends are not expenses, they are not used to calculate net income. Dividends are sometimes described as distributions of retained earnings.

THE EFFECTS OF ADDITIONAL TRANSACTIONS ON THE ACCOUNTING EQUATION

Illustration 2-7 Changes in the Balance Sheet Equation Caused by Noncash Revenues, the Later Receipt of Cash, the Payment of Payables, and Payment of Dividends

	Cash	+	Accounts Receivable	+	Store Supplies	+	Copy Equipment	=	Accounts Payable	+	Common Stock	+	Retained Earnings	Explanation of Change
					Assets				**Liabilities**		**Stockholders' Equity**			
(1)	$30,000										$30,000			Investment
(2)	− 2,500				+$2,500									
Bal.	$27,500				$2,500						$30,000			
(3)	−20,000						+$20,000							
Bal.	$ 7,500				$2,500		$20,000				$30,000			
(4)					+1,100		+6,000		+$7,100					
Bal.	$ 7,500				$3,600		$26,000		$7,100		$30,000			
(5)	+ 2,200												+$2,200	Revenue
Bal.	$ 9,700				$3,600		$26,000		$7,100		$30,000		$2,200	
(6)	− 1,000												−1,000	Expense
Bal.	$ 8,700				$3,600		$26,000		$7,100		$30,000		$1,200	
(7)	− 700												700	Expense
Bal.	$ 8,000				$3,600		$26,000		$7,100		$30,000		$ 500	
(8)			+$1,900										+1,900	Revenue
Bal.	$ 8,000		$1,900		$3,600		$26,000		$7,100		$30,000		$2,400	
(9)	+ 1,900		−1,900											
Bal.	$ 9,900		$ 0		$3,600		$26,000		$7,100		$30,000		$2,400	
(10)	− 900								− 900					
Bal.	$ 9,000		$ 0		$3,600		$26,000		$6,200		$30,000		$2,400	
(11)	− 600												− 600	Dividend
Bal.	$ 8,400	+	$ 0	+	$3,600	+	$26,000	=	$6,200	+	$30,000	+	$1,800	

Summary. Illustration 2–7 presents the effects of the entire series of 11 transactions for Clear Copy. Take time now to see that the equation remains in balance after each transaction. This is because the effects of each transaction are always in balance. In transactions 1, 5, and 8, total assets and equity increased by equal amounts. In transactions 2, 3, and 9, one asset increased while another decreased by an equal amount. Transaction 4 increased total assets and a liability by equal amounts. In transactions 6, 7, and 11, assets and equity decreased by equal amounts. Finally, transaction 10 decreased an asset and a liability by the same amount. The equality of these effects is central to the working of double entry accounting. You learn more about double entry accounting in the next chapter.

Progress Check

2-10 A new business has the following transactions: (1) stockholders invested $3,600 cash; (2) supplies were purchased for $2,600 cash; (3) services were provided to a customer for $2,300 cash; (4) a salary of $1,000 was paid to an employee; and (5) $3,000 cash was borrowed from the bank. After these transactions, total assets, total liabilities, and total stockholders' equity are: *(a)* $7,900, $5,300, $2,600; *(b)* $7,900, $3,000, $4,900; *(c)* $7,900, $3,000, $3,600.

2-11 Is it possible for a transaction to increase a liability without affecting any asset, other liability, or stockholders' equity? Explain.

Up to this point, you have learned about only two financial statements: the income statement and the balance sheet. GAAP also require companies to include two other statements in their reports. They are the statement of retained earnings[15] and the statement of cash flows.

The following diagram shows how all four financial statements are linked.

UNDERSTANDING MORE ABOUT THE FINANCIAL STATEMENTS

LO 1
Describe the information presented in financial statements and be able to prepare simple financial statements.

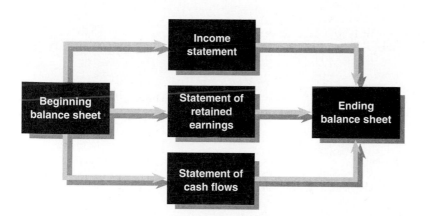

The income statement describes how stockholders' equity changed during the period through the company's income earning activities. The statement of retained earnings reconciles the beginning and ending amounts of retained earnings. The statement of cash flows describes how the amount of cash changed between the beginning and ending balance sheets. The statement of cash flows also describes many of the changes in the company's other assets and liabilities. Thus, most of the company's activities are described by the three statements in the middle, while the balance sheets describe the company's financial position before and after those activities occurred.

The Income Statement

The top section of Illustration 2–8 shows Clear Copy's income statement as it appeared in Illustration 2–1. Now you can see that it is based on the information about revenues and expenses recorded in the retained earnings column in Illustration 2–7.

In the income statement, the copy services revenue of $4,100 resulted from transactions 5 and 8. If the business had earned other kinds of revenues, they would have been listed separately to help users understand more about the company's activities. The income statement then lists the rent and salaries expenses incurred in transactions 6 and 7. The types of expenses are identified to help users form a more complete picture of the events of the time period. Finally, the income statement presents the amount of net income earned during the month.

The Statement of Retained Earnings

The **statement of retained earnings** presents information about what happened to the retained earnings component of stockholders' equity during the reporting period. The statement shows the retained earnings balance at the beginning of the period, the increase (or decrease) that resulted from a net income (or net loss), the decrease that resulted from dividends, and the balance at the end of the period.

---

[15] Many corporations replace the statement of retained earnings with a more comprehensive statement of changes in stockholders' equity. We explain this statement in a later chapter.

Illustration 2-8
Financial Statements for
Clear Copy, Inc.

CLEAR COPY, INC.
Income Statement
For Month Ended December 31, 19X1

Revenues:		
Copy services revenue		$4,100
Operating expenses:		
Rent expense	$1,000	
Salaries expense	700	
Total operating expenses		1,700
Net income		$2,400

CLEAR COPY, INC.
Statement of Retained Earnings
For Month Ended December 31, 19X1

Retained earnings, November 30, 19X1	$ -0-
Plus net income	2,400
Total	$2,400
Less dividends	600
Retained earnings, December 31, 19X1	$1,800

CLEAR COPY, INC.
Balance Sheet
December 31, 19X1

Assets		Liabilities	
Cash	$ 8,400	Accounts payable	$ 6,200
Store supplies	3,600	**Stockholders' Equity**	
Copy equipment	26,000	Contributed capital:	
		Common stock	30,000
		Retained earnings	1,800
		Total liabilities and	
Total assets	$38,000	stockholders' equity	$38,000

The middle section of Illustration 2–8 shows the statement of retained earnings for Clear Copy, Inc. The heading refers to December 19X1 because the statement describes events that happened during that month. The beginning retained earnings balance is stated as of the close of business on November 30. It is zero because the business did not exist before then. An existing business would report the balance as of the end of the prior reporting period. The Clear Copy statement shows the $2,400 of net income earned during the month. This item links the income statement to the statement of retained earnings. The statement also reports $600 of dividends to stockholders and the ending retained earnings balance of $1,800.

The Balance Sheet

The lower section of Illustration 2–8 presents Clear Copy's balance sheet (the same statement appeared in Illustration 2–2). The heading shows that the statement describes the company's financial condition at the close of business on December 31, 19X1.

The left side of the balance sheet lists the company's assets: cash, store supplies, and copy equipment. The right side of the balance sheet shows that the company owes $6,200 on accounts payable. If any other liabilities had existed (such as bank loans), they would have been listed in this section. The equity section shows the $30,000 invested by the stockholders as common stock and shows a retained earnings balance

Illustration 2-9
Statement of Cash Flows
for Clear Copy, Inc.

CLEAR COPY, INC.
Statement of Cash Flows
For Month Ended December 31, 19X1

Cash flows from operating activities:		
Cash received from customers	$ 4,100	
Cash paid for store supplies	(2,500)	
Cash paid for rent	(1,000)	
Cash paid to employee	(700)	
Net cash used by operating activities		$ (100)
Cash flows from investing activities:		
Purchase of copy equipment	$(20,000)	
Net cash used by investing activities		(20,000)
Cash flows from financing activities:		
Cash received from issuing common stock	$ 30,000	
Repayment of debt	(900)	
Dividends paid to stockholders	(600)	
Net cash provided by financing activities		28,500
Net increase in cash		$ 8,400
Cash balance, November 30, 19X1		– 0 –
Cash balance, December 31, 19X1		$ 8,400

of $1,800. Note that this retained earnings balance equals the amount on the last line of the statement of retained earnings. Thus, it links these two statements.

The Statement of Cash Flows

The fourth financial statement is the **statement of cash flows,** which describes where a company's cash came from and where it went during the period. The statement also shows how much cash was on hand at the beginning of the period, and how much was left at the end. This information is important for both internal and external decision makers because a company must manage its cash well if it is going to survive and prosper. For example, **Delta Airlines, Inc.,** had net losses totaling more than $1.3 billion during the three-year period ended June 30, 1994. Nevertheless, Delta avoided bankruptcy by carefully managing its cash through delayed capital spending, borrowing, and issuing additional stock. In 1995, Delta returned to profitability, generating a net income of $408 million.

Cash Flows from Operating Activities. Illustration 2–9 shows Clear Copy's statement of cash flows for December. The first section of the statement shows the amount of cash used by the company's *operating activities*. The $4,100 of cash received from customers equals the total revenues on the income statement only because Clear Copy collected all of its revenues in cash. If some credit sales are not collected, or if credit sales from a prior reporting period are collected, the amount of cash received from customers does not equal the revenues reported on the income statement for the same period.

This first section also lists cash payments for store supplies, rent, and salaries. These cash flows occurred in transactions 2, 6, and 7. Notice that the amounts are in parentheses to indicate that they are subtracted. The amounts for rent and salaries equal the expenses reported on Clear Copy's income statement only because Clear Copy paid cash for the expenses.

The payment for supplies is reported as an operating activity because supplies are expected to be consumed in short-term operations. (We explain this more completely in Chapter 16.) The net outflow from operating activities for December was $100. Decision makers are especially interested in this section of the statement of cash flows because, in the long run, companies must generate cash from their operating activities to stay in existence.

Cash Flows from Investing Activities. The second section of the statement of cash flows describes the cash flows from *investing activities.* In general, investing activities involve buying or selling assets such as land or equipment that are held for long-term use in the business. Clear Copy's only investing activity was the $20,000 purchase of equipment in transaction 3. Notice that no cash flows are reported for transaction 4, which was a credit purchase.

Decision makers are interested in this section of the statement of cash flows because it describes how a company is preparing for the future. If the company is spending cash for productive assets, it should be able to grow. On the other hand, the company might be spending too much on productive assets for its size. The information in the investing section helps decision makers understand what the company has done.

Cash Flows from Financing Activities. The third section of the statement shows the cash flows related to *financing activities.* Financing activities include borrowing cash from creditors and receiving cash by issuing stock. Financing activities also include loan repayments and cash dividends to stockholders. The statement of cash flows in Illustration 2–9 shows that Clear Copy obtained $30,000 from issuing stock in transaction 1. If the business had borrowed cash, the amount would appear here as an increase in cash. Decision makers also are interested in the financing section. The sources of cash used by a company can affect the future. For example, excessive borrowing can burden the company with too much debt and reduce its potential for growth.

The financing activities section of Illustration 2–9 also shows the $900 paid to Handy Supply in transaction 10 and the $600 dividend from transaction 11. The overall effect of the financing activities was a $28,500 net inflow of cash. The information in this section explains why the business did not run out of cash even though it spent $20,000 on assets and used $100 in its operating activities.

The last section of the statement of cash flows shows that the company increased its cash balance by $8,400. Because the company started out with no cash, the ending balance is also $8,400. This final amount links the statement of cash flows to the balance sheet. We present a more detailed explanation of the statement of cash flows in Chapter 16.

Progress Check

2-12   Which of the following is one of the three categories of cash flows that appear on the statement of cash flows?   *(a)* cash receipts from stockholders' investments;   *(b)* cash payments for operating expenses;   *(c)* cash flows from investing activities.

2-13   What financial statement item appears on both the income statement and the statement of retained earnings?

2-14   What financial statement item appears on both the statement of retained earnings and the balance sheet?

USING THE INFORMATION— RETURN ON EQUITY

An important reason for recording and reporting information about a company's assets, liabilities, equity, and net income is to help the owners judge the business venture's relative success compared to other activities or investments. One way to de-

scribe this success is to calculate the **return on equity ratio,** which equals the
amount of income achieved in a period divided by the amount of stockholders' equity. The formula for this ratio is as follows:

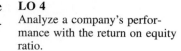

$$\text{Return on equity} = \frac{\text{Net income}}{\text{Beginning stockholders' equity}}$$

Recall from the beginning of this chapter the story of Karen and Mark Smith, who
are considering an investment in **H & R Block, Inc.** In starting to analyze that company, they could use the financial information presented on page 25 to calculate
H & R Block's 1996 return on equity, as follows:

$$\frac{\text{Net earnings}}{\text{Beginning stockholders' equity}} = \frac{\$177,168}{\$685,865} = 25.8\%$$

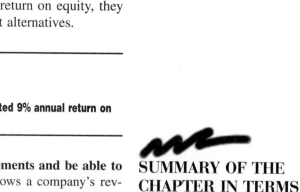

Interpreting the rate of return achieved by a company
requires an understanding of several factors. For example, the rate should be compared with the rates that
could be earned on other kinds of investments.

In the example of Clear Copy, Inc., the financial
statements show that the company earned a return on
equity at the rate of 8.0% for the month of December.
To find this rate, we divide $2,400 of net income by the
$30,000 beginning balance of stockholders' equity.

Clear Copy's rate for December is high compared to
most investments and may appear very appealing, especially for the first month of operations. However, we
have not completely measured the income for the month. Chapters 3 and 4 introduce
additional revenues and expenses, the net effect of which will be to reduce the net income amount shown here.

Furthermore, the earnings of many companies fluctuate widely from one month to
another. Many unusual factors can have a material effect on any one month. Thus,
you get much better information by calculating the return over a longer period such
as one year.

Analysts use historical return on equity statistics as a basis for predicting what the
return is likely to be in the future. In evaluating the expected return on equity, they
compare the rate with the returns provided by other investment alternatives.

Progress Check

2-15 Why might a stockholder calculate the return on equity ratio?

2-16 What should be used as a basis for evaluating whether an expected 9% annual return on
equity is acceptable?

**LO 1. Describe the information presented in financial statements and be able to
prepare simple financial statements.** The income statement shows a company's revenues, expenses, and net income or loss. The balance sheet lists a company's assets, liabilities, and stockholders' equity. The statement of retained earnings shows the effects on
retained earnings from net income or net loss and dividends. The statement of cash flows
shows the changes in cash that resulted from operating, investing, and financing activities. The financial statements are prepared with information about the effects of each
transaction on the accounting equation.

**LO 2. Explain the accounting principles introduced in the chapter and describe
the process by which generally accepted accounting principles are established.**
Accounting principles help accountants produce relevant and reliable information. Among

**SUMMARY OF THE
CHAPTER IN TERMS
OF LEARNING
OBJECTIVES**

others, broad accounting principles include the business entity principle, the objectivity principle, the cost principle, the going-concern principle, and the revenue recognition principle. Specific accounting principles for financial accounting are established in the United States primarily by the Financial Accounting Standards Board (FASB), with oversight by the Securities and Exchange Commission (SEC). Auditing standards are established by the Auditing Standards Board (ASB), a committee of the American Institute of CPAs (AICPA). The International Accounting Standards Committee (IASC) identifies preferred practices and encourages their adoption throughout the world.

LO 3. Analyze business transactions to determine their effects on the accounting equation. The accounting equation states that Assets = Liabilities + Owners' Equity. Business transactions always have at least two effects on the elements in the accounting equation. The equation is always in balance when business transactions are properly recorded.

LO 4. Analyze a company's performance with the return on equity ratio. Return on equity is defined as net income divided by the stockholders' equity at the beginning of the period. The ratio measures the company's performance and is used as a basis for predicting future performance. To evaluate the ratio, analysts compare a company's return on equity with the returns on other alternative investments.

DEMONSTRATION PROBLEM

After several months of planning, Barbara Schmidt started a haircutting business called Cutlery Corporation. The following events occurred during its first month:

a. On August 1, 19X1, Cutlery Corporation issued 18,000 shares of $1 par value common stock to Schmidt in exchange for $3,000 cash and equipment worth $15,000.

b. On August 2, Cutlery paid $600 cash for furniture for the shop.

c. On August 3, Cutlery paid $500 cash to rent space in a strip mall for August.

d. On August 4, the equipment was installed and some additional equipment was purchased on credit for $1,200. This amount is to be repaid in three equal payments at the end of August, September, and October.

e. On August 5, the business opened for business. Receipts from cash sales in the first week and a half of business (ended August 15) were $1,025.

f. On August 17, Cutlery paid $125 wages to an assistant for working during the grand opening.

g. Cash receipts from sales during the second half of August were $1,730.

h. On August 31, Cutlery paid an installment on the account payable.

i. On August 31, Cutlery paid Schmidt a $1,000 salary.

j. On August 31, Cutlery paid a dividend of $900.

Required

1. Arrange the following asset, liability, and stockholders' equity titles in a table similar to the one in Illustration 2-7: Cash; Furniture; Store Equipment; Accounts Payable; Common Stock, $1 Par Value; and Retained Earnings. Show the effects of each transaction on the equation. Explain each of the changes in stockholders' equity.

2. Prepare an income statement for August. Assume no income taxes.

3. Prepare a statement of retained earnings for August.

4. Prepare a balance sheet as of August 31.

5. Prepare a statement of cash flows for August.

6. Determine the return on equity ratio for August.

- Set up a table with the appropriate columns, including a final column for describing the events that affect stockholders' equity.

- Analyze each transaction and show its effects as increases or decreases in the appropriate columns. Be sure that the accounting equation remains in balance after each event.

- To prepare the income statement, find the revenues and expenses in the last column. List those items on the statement, calculate the difference, and label the result as *net income* or *net loss*.

- Use the information in the Explanation of Change column to prepare the statement of retained earnings.

- Use the information on the last row of the table to prepare the balance sheet.

- To prepare the statement of cash flows, include all events listed in the Cash column of the table. Classify each cash flow as operating, investing, or financing. Follow the example in Illustration 2–9.

- Calculate the return on equity by dividing net income by the beginning equity.

Planning the Solution

Solution to Demonstration Problem

1.

	Assets					Liabilities		Stockholders' Equity			
	Cash	+	Furniture	+	Store Equipment	=	Accounts Payable	+	Common Stock	+	Retained Earnings	Explanation of Change
a.	$3,000				$15,000				$18,000			Stock issue
b.	− 600		+ $600									
Bal.	$2,400		$600		$15,000				$18,000			
c.	− 500										− $ 500	Expense
Bal.	$1,900		$600		$15,000				$18,000		− $ 500	
d.					+ 1,200		+ $1,200					
Bal.	$1,900		$600		$16,200		$1,200		$18,000		− $ 500	
e.	+1,025										+ 1,025	Revenue
Bal.	$2,925		$600		$16,200		$1,200		$18,000		$ 525	
f.	− 125										−125	Expense
Bal.	$2,800		$600		$16,200		$1,200		$18,000		$ 400	
g.	+1,730										+ 1,730	Revenue
Bal.	$4,530		$600		$16,200		$1,200		$18,000		$2,130	
h.	− 400						−400					
Bal.	$4,130		$600		$16,200		$ 800		$18,000		$2,130	
i.	−1,000										−1,000	Expense
Bal.	$3,130		$600		$16,200		$ 800		$18,000		$1,130	
j.	− 900										−900	Dividend
Bal.	$2,230	+	$600	+	$16,200	=	$ 800	+	$18,000	+	$ 230	

2.

CUTLERY CORPORATION
Income Statement
For Month Ended August 31, 19X1

Revenues:		
Haircutting services revenue.		$2,755
Operating expenses:		
Rent expense	$ 500	
Salaries expense	1,125	
Total operating expenses		1,625
Net income.		$1,130

3.

CUTLERY CORPORATION
Statement of Retained Earnings
For Month Ended August 31, 19X1

Retained earnings, July 31, 19X1	$ 0
Plus net income	1,130
Total	$1,130
Less dividends to stockholders.	(900)
Retained earnings, August 31, 19X1	$ 230

4.

CUTLERY CORPORATION
Balance Sheet
August 31, 19X1

Assets		Liabilities	
Cash.	$ 2,230	Accounts payable	$ 800
Furniture	600	**Stockholders' Equity**	
Store equipment	16,200	Contributed capital:	
		Common stock, $1 par value	18,000
		Retained earnings	230
		Total liabilities and	
Total assets	$19,030	stockholders' equity	$19,030

5.

CUTLERY CORPORATION
Statement of Cash Flows
For Month Ended August 31, 19X1

Cash flows from operating activities:		
Cash received from customers	$ 2,755	
Cash paid for rent	(500)	
Cash paid for wages	(1,125)	
Net cash provided by operating activities.		$1,130
Cash flows from investing activities:		
Cash paid for furniture.		(600)
Cash flows from financing activities:		
Cash received from issuing common stock	$ 3,000	
Dividend paid to stockholder	(900)	
Repayment of debt	(400)	
Net cash provided by financing activities.		1,700
Net increase in cash		$2,230
Cash balance, July 31, 19X1		0
Cash balance, August 31, 19X1		$2,230

6.

$$\text{Return on equity} = \frac{\text{Net income}}{\text{Beginning stockholders' equity}} = \frac{\$1,130}{\$18,000} = 6.3\%$$

GLOSSARY

AAA the American Accounting Association, a professional association of college and university accounting faculty. p. 33

Accounting equation a description of the relationship between a company's assets, liabilities, and equity; expressed as Assets = Liabilities + Owners' Equity; also called the *balance sheet equation.* p. 37

Accounts payable liabilities created by buying goods and services on credit. p. 29

Accounts receivable assets created by selling goods and services on credit. p. 28

AIMR Association for Investment Management and Research; a professional association of people who use financial statements in the process of evaluating companies' financial performance. p. 33

APB Accounting Principles Board, a former authoritative committee of the AICPA that was responsible for identifying generally accepted accounting principles from 1959 to 1973; predecessor to the FASB. p. 33

ASB Auditing Standards Board; the authoritative committee of the AICPA that identifies generally accepted auditing standards. p. 33

Assets properties or economic resources owned by the business; more precisely, probable future economic benefits obtained or controlled by a particular entity as a result of past transactions or events. p. 28

Balance sheet a financial statement providing information that helps users understand a company's financial status; lists the types and dollar amounts of assets, liabilities, and equity as of a specific date; also called the *statement of financial position.* p. 28

Balance sheet equation another name for the accounting equation. p. 37

Business entity principle the principle that requires every business to be accounted for separately and distinctly from its owner or owners; based on the goal of providing relevant information about the business. p. 35

Business transaction an exchange of economic consideration (such as goods, services, money, or rights to collect money) between two parties. p. 36

CAP Committee on Accounting Procedure; the authoritative body for identifying generally accepted accounting principles from 1936 to 1959. p. 33

Continuing-concern principle another name for the going-concern principle. p. 36

Contributed capital the category of stockholders' equity created by the stockholders' investments. p. 29

Cost principle the accounting principle that requires financial statement information to be based on costs incurred in business transactions; it requires assets and services to be recorded initially at the cash or cash equivalent amount given in exchange. p. 36

Creditors individuals or organizations entitled to receive payments from a company. p. 29

Debtors individuals or organizations that owe amounts to a business. p. 28

Dividends distributions of assets by a corporation to its stockholders. p. 29

Equity the difference between a company's assets and its liabilities; more precisely, the residual interest in the assets of an entity that remains after deducting its liabilities; also called *net assets.* p. 29

Expenses outflows or the using up of assets as a result of the major or central operations of a business; also, liabilities may be increased. p. 27

FASB Financial Accounting Standards Board, the seven-member nonprofit board that currently has the authority to identify generally accepted accounting principles. p. 32

FEI Financial Executives Institute, a professional association of private accountants. p. 33

GAAS the abbreviation for generally accepted auditing standards. p. 32

Generally accepted auditing standards rules adopted by the accounting profession as guides for conducting audits of financial statements. p. 32

Going-concern principle the rule that requires financial statements to reflect the assumption that the business will continue operating instead of being closed or sold, unless evidence shows that it will not continue. p. 36

IASC International Accounting Standards Committee; a committee that attempts to create more harmony among the accounting practices of different countries by identifying preferred practices and encouraging their worldwide acceptance. p. 34

IMA Institute of Management Accountants, a professional association of private accountants, formerly called the *National Association of Accountants.* p. 33

Income statement the financial statement that shows whether the business earned a profit; it lists the types and amounts of the revenues and expenses. p. 26

Liabilities debts owed by a business or organization; probable future sacrifices of economic benefits arising from present obligations of a particular entity to transfer assets or provide services to other entities in the future as a result of past transactions or events. p. 28

Net assets another name for equity. p. 29

Net income the excess of revenues over expenses for a period. p. 26

Net loss the excess of expenses over revenues for a period. p. 26

Objectivity principle the accounting guideline that requires financial statement information to be supported by evidence other than someone's opinion or imagination; objectivity adds to the reliability and usefulness of accounting information. p. 35

Paid-in capital another name for contributed capital. p. 29

Realization principle another name for the *revenue recognition principle.* p. 40

Retained earnings the stockholders' equity that results from all of the past net incomes earned by the corporation less any net losses and less all dividends. p. 29

Return on equity ratio the ratio of net income to beginning stockholders' equity; used to judge a business's success compared to other activities or investments. p. 46

Revenue recognition principle the rule that (1) requires revenue to be recognized at the time it is earned, (2) allows the inflow of assets associated with revenue to be in a form other than cash, and (3) measures the amount of revenue as the cash plus the cash equivalent value of any noncash assets received from customers in exchange for goods or services. p. 40

Revenues inflows of assets received in exchange for goods or services provided to customers as part of the major or central operations of the business; may occur as inflows of assets or decreases in liabilities. p. 27

SIA Securities Industry Association; an association of individuals involved with issuing and marketing securities. p. 33

Statement of cash flows a financial statement that describes where a company's cash came from and where it went during the period; the cash flows are classified as being caused by operating, investing, and financing activities. p. 45

Statement of financial position another name for the balance sheet. p. 28

Statement of retained earnings a financial statement that shows the retained earnings at the beginning of the period, the increase (or decrease) that resulted from a net income (or net loss), the decrease that resulted from dividends, and the balance at the end of the period. p. 43

Statements of Financial Accounting Standards (SFAS) the publications of the FASB that establish new generally accepted accounting principles in the United States. p. 32

QUESTIONS

1. What information is presented in an income statement?
2. What do accountants mean by the term *revenue*?
3. Why does the user of an income statement need to know the time period that it covers?
4. What information is presented in a balance sheet?
5. Define *(a)* assets, *(b)* liabilities, *(c)* equity, and *(d)* net assets.
6. Identify two categories of generally accepted accounting principles.
7. What FASB pronouncements identify generally accepted accounting principles?
8. What does the objectivity principle require for information presented in financial statements? Why?
9. A business shows office stationery on the balance sheet at its $430 cost, although it cannot be sold for more than $10 as scrap paper. Which accounting principle justifies this treatment?
10. Why is the revenue recognition principle needed? What does it require?

11. What events or activities change stockholders' equity?
12. Identify four financial statements that a business presents to its owners and other users.
13. What should a company's return on equity ratio be compared with to evaluate the company's performance?
14. Find the financial statements of Lands' End, Inc., in Appendix F. To what level of significance are the dollar amounts rounded? What time period does the income statement cover?

15. Review the financial statements of Southwest Airlines Co. in Appendix E. What is the amount of total assets reported at December 31, 1994? How much net cash was provided by operating activities during 1994?

QUICK STUDY (Five-Minute Exercises)[16]

QS 2–1
(LO 1)

Name the financial statement on which each of the following items appears:

a.	Office supplies.	*e.*	Office equipment.
b.	Service fees earned.	*f.*	Accounts payable.
c.	Cash received from customers.	*g.*	Repayment of bank loan.
d.	Dividends paid to stockholders.	*h.*	Utilities expense.

QS 2–2
(LO 2)

Identify which broad accounting principle describes most directly each of the following practices:

a. Tracy Regis owns Second-Time-Around Clothing, Inc., and also owns Antique Accents Corp. In having financial statements prepared for the antique store, Regis should be sure that the expense transactions of Second-Time-Around are excluded from the statements.

b. In December 19X1, Classic Coverings received a customer's order to install carpet and tile in a new house that would not be ready for completion until March 19X2. Classic Coverings should record the revenue for the order in March 19X2, not in December 19X1.

c. If $30,000 cash is paid to buy land, the land should be reported on the purchaser's balance sheet at $30,000.

QS 2–3
(LO 3)

Determine the missing amount for each of the following equations:

	Assets	=	Liabilities	+	Owners' Equity
a.	$ 75,000		$ 40,500		?
b.	$300,000		?		$85,500
c.	?		$187,500		$95,400

---

[16] In solving the exercises and problems in this and later chapters, assume no income taxes unless they are specifically mentioned.

Use the accounting equation to determine:

a. The stockholders' equity in a business that has $374,700 of assets and $252,450 of liabilities.

b. The liabilities of a business having $150,900 of assets and $126,000 of stockholders' equity.

c. The assets of a business having $37,650 of liabilities and $112,500 of stockholders' equity.

In its 1994 financial statements, The Boeing Company, which is the largest aerospace company in the United States, reported the following:

Sales and other operating revenues	$21,924 million
Net earnings (net income)	856 million
Total assets	21,463 million
Total beginning-of-year shareholders' equity	8,983 million
Total end-of-year shareholders' equity	9,700 million

Calculate the return on equity.

EXERCISES[17]

The following equation shows the effects of five transactions on the assets, liabilities, and stockholders' equity of Pace Design, Inc. Write short descriptions of the probable nature of each transaction.

Exercise 2–1
Effects of transactions on the accounting equation
(LO 3)

	Cash	+	Accounts Receivable	+	Office Supplies	+	Land	=	Accounts Payable	+	Common Stock	+	Retained Earnings
	$7,500				$2,500		$14,500				$24,500		
a.	−3,000						13,000						
	$4,500				$2,500		$17,500				$24,500		
b.					+400				+$ 400				
	$4,500				$2,900		$17,500		$ 400		$24,500		
c.			+$ 1,050										+$1,050
	$4,500		$ 1,050		$2,900		$17,500		$ 400		$24,500		$1,050
d.	−400								−400				
	$4,100		$ 1,050		$2,900		$17,500		$ 0		$24,500		$1,050
e.	+1,050		−1,050										
	$5,150	+	$ 0	+	$2,900	+	$17,500	=	$ 0	+	$24,500	+	$1,050

Carter Stark began operating a new consulting firm on January 3. The accounting equation showed the following balances after each of the company's first five transactions. Analyze the equations and describe each of the five transactions with their amounts.

Exercise 2–2
Analyzing the accounting equation
(LO 3)

After Trans-action	Cash	+	Accounts Receivable	+	Office Supplies	+	Office Furniture	=	Accounts Payable	+	Common Stock	+	Retained Earnings
a.	$30,000		$ 0		$ 0		$ 0		$ 0		$30,000		
b.	29,000		0		1,750		0		750		30,000		
c.	21,000		0		1,750		8,000		750		30,000		
d.	21,000		2,000		1,750		8,000		750		30,000		$2,000
e.	20,500		2,000		1,750		8,000		750		30,000		1,500

---

[17] In solving the exercises and problems in this and later chapters, assume no income taxes unless they are specifically mentioned.

Exercise 2–3
Determining net income
(LO 1, 3)

A business had the following amounts of assets and liabilities at the beginning and end of a recent year:

	Assets	Liabilities
Beginning of the year	$ 75,000	$30,000
End of the year.	120,000	46,000

Determine the net income earned or net loss incurred by the business during the year under each of the following unrelated assumptions:

a. There were no additional investments in the company by stockholders during the year and no cash dividends were declared.

b. There were no additional investments in the company by stockholders during the year and a $21,000 cash dividend was declared and paid to stockholders.

c. Common stock was issued to investors during the year in exchange for $32,500 cash, but no cash dividends were declared.

d. Common stock was issued to investors during the year in exchange for $25,000 cash and a $21,000 cash dividend was declared and paid on December 31.

Exercise 2–4
The effects of transactions on the accounting equation and return on equity
(LO 3, 4)

Linda Champion began a professional practice on May 1 and plans to prepare financial statements at the end of each month. During May, Champion completed these transactions:

a. The practice issued 12,000 shares of $5 par value common stock to Champion in exchange for $50,000 cash and equipment that had a $10,000 fair market (cash equivalent) value.

b. Paid $1,600 rent for office space for the month.

c. Purchased $12,000 of additional equipment on credit.

d. Completed work for a client and immediately collected $2,000 cash.

e. Completed work for a client and sent a bill for $7,000 to be paid within 30 days.

f. Purchased $8,000 of additional equipment for cash.

g. Paid an assistant $2,400 as wages for the month.

h. Collected $5,000 of the amount owed by the client described in transaction e.

i. Paid for the equipment purchased in transaction c.

Required

Create a table like the one in Illustration 2–7, using the following headings for the columns: Cash; Accounts Receivable; Equipment; Accounts Payable; Common Stock, $5 Par Value; and Retained Earnings. Then, use additions and subtractions to show the effects of the transactions on the elements of the equation. Show new totals after each transaction. Determine the return on equity ratio.

Exercise 2–5
The effects of transactions on the accounting equation
(LO 3)

Following are seven pairs of changes in elements of the accounting equation. Provide an example of a transaction that creates the described effects:

a. Decreases a liability and increases a liability.

b. Increases an asset and decreases an asset.

c. Decreases an asset and decreases equity.

d. Increases a liability and decreases equity.

e. Increases an asset and increases a liability.

f. Increases an asset and increases equity.

g. Decreases an asset and decreases a liability.

Exercise 2–6
Income statement
(LO 1)

On November 1, Joseph Grayson organized a new consulting firm called The Grayson Group, Inc. On November 30, the company's records showed the following items. Use this information to prepare a November income statement for the business.

Cash	$12,000	Cash dividends declared	$ 3,360
Accounts receivable	15,000	Consulting fees earned	15,000
Office supplies	2,250	Rent expense	2,550
Automobiles	36,000	Salaries expense	6,000
Office equipment	28,000	Telephone expense	660
Accounts payable	7,500	Miscellaneous expenses	680
Common stock, $10 par value	84,000		

Use the facts in Exercise 2–6 to prepare a November statement of retained earnings for The Grayson Group, Inc.

Exercise 2–7
Statement of retained earnings
(LO 1)

Use the facts in Exercise 2–6 to prepare a November 30 balance sheet for The Grayson Group, Inc.

Exercise 2–8
Balance sheet
(LO 1)

Match each of these numbered items with the financial statement or statements on which it should be presented. Indicate your answer by writing the letter or letters for the correct statement in the blank space next to each item.

Exercise 2–9
Information in financial statements
(LO 1)

A. Income statement
B. Statement of retained earnings

C. Balance sheet
D. Statement of cash flows

___ 1. Cash received from customers
___ 2. Office supplies
___ 3. Rent expense paid in cash
___ 4. Consulting fees earned
    and received as cash

___ 5.   Accounts payable
___ 6.   Investments by stockholders
___ 7.   Accounts receivable
___ 8.   Cash dividends paid

Calculate the amount of the missing item in each of the following independent cases:

Exercise 2–10
Missing information
(LO 4)

	a	b	c	d
Stockholders' equity, January 1	$ 0	$ 0	$ 0	$ 0
Stockholders' investments during the year	120,000	?	63,000	75,000
Cash dividends paid during the year	?	(54,000)	(30,000)	(31,500)
Net income (loss) for the year	31,500	81,000	(9,000)	?
Stockholders' equity, December 31	102,000	99,000	?	85,500

Match each of these numbered descriptions with the term it best describes. Indicate your answer by writing the letter for the correct principle in the blank space next to each description.

Exercise 2–11
Accounting principles
(LO 2)

A. Broad principle
B. Cost principle
C. Business entity principle
D. Revenue recognition principle

E. Specific principle
F. Objectivity principle
G. Going-concern principle

___ 1. Requires every business to be accounted for separately from its owner or owners.

___ 2. Requires financial statement information to be supported by evidence other than someone's opinion or imagination.

___ 3. Usually created by a pronouncement from an authoritative body.

___ 4. Requires financial statement information to be based on costs incurred in transactions.

___ 5. Derived from long-used accounting practices.

___ 6. Requires financial statements to reflect the assumption that the business will continue operating instead of being closed or sold.

___ 7. Requires revenue to be recorded only when the earnings process is complete.

Exercise 2-12
Return on equity
(LO 4)

Use the information for each of the following independent cases to calculate the company's return on equity:

	a	b	c	d
Beginning equity	$50,000	$800,000	$300,000	$572,800
Net income	10,800	216,000	91,500	177,930

PROBLEMS

Problem 2–1
Analyzing the effects of transactions and calculating return on equity
(LO 3, 4)

Hemphill Enterprises, Inc., incurred the following transactions during its first month of operations:

a. Sold 9,000 shares of $10 par value common stock in exchange for $60,000 cash and office equipment valued at $30,000.

b. Paid $300,000 for a small building to be used as an office. Paid $50,000 in cash and signed a note payable promising to pay the balance over several years.

c. Purchased $4,000 of office supplies for cash.

d. Purchased $36,000 of office equipment on credit.

e. Completed a project on credit and billed the client $4,000 for the work.

f. Paid a local newspaper $1,000 for an announcement that the office had opened.

g. Completed a project for a client and collected $18,000 cash.

h. Made a $2,000 payment on the equipment purchased in transaction d.

i. Received $3,000 from the client described in transaction e.

j. Paid $2,500 cash for the office secretary's wages.

k. Declared and paid a $1,800 cash dividend to stockholders.

Required

Preparation component:

1. Create a table like the one in Illustration 2–7, using the following headings for the columns: Cash; Accounts Receivable; Office Supplies; Office Equipment; Building; Accounts Payable; Notes Payable; Common Stock, $10 Par Value; and Retained Earnings. Leave space for an Explanation column to the right of the Retained Earnings column.

2. Use additions and subtractions to show the transactions' effects on the elements of the equation. Show new totals after each transaction. Also, indicate next to each change in the stockholders' equity whether it was caused by an investment, a revenue, an expense, or a dividend.

CHECK FIGURE:
Net income, $18,500

3. Once you have completed the table, determine the company's net income.

Analysis component:

4. Determine the return on equity. State whether you think the business is a good use of the investors' money if an alternative investment would have returned 12% for the same period.

Problem 2–2
Balance sheet, income statement, and statement of retained earnings
(LO 1, 3)

Resource Consulting, Inc., began operations on April 1 and completed these transactions during the month:

Apr. 1   Issued 12,000 shares of $5 par value common stock in exchange for $60,000 cash.

1   Rented a furnished office and paid $3,200 cash for April's rent.

3   Purchased office supplies for $1,680 cash.

5   Paid $800 cash for the month's cleaning services.

8   Provided consulting services for a client and immediately collected $4,600 cash.

Apr. 12 Provided consulting services for a client on credit, $3,000.

15 Paid $850 cash for an assistant's salary for the first half of the month.

20 Received payment in full for the services provided on April 12.

22 Provided consulting services on credit, $2,800.

23 Purchased additional office supplies on credit, $1,000.

28 Received full payment for the services provided on April 22.

29 Paid for the office supplies purchased on April 23.

30 Purchased advertising for $60 in the local paper. The payment is due May 1.

30 Paid $200 cash for the month's telephone bill.

30 Paid $480 cash for the month's utilities.

30 Paid $850 cash for an assistant's salary for the second half of the month.

30 Purchased insurance protection for the next 12 months (beginning May 1) by paying a $3,000 premium. Because none of this insurance protection had been used up, it was considered to be an asset called Prepaid Insurance.

30 Declared and paid a $1,200 cash dividend to stockholders.

Required

1. Arrange the following asset, liability, and stockholders' equity titles in an equation like Illustration 2-7: Cash; Accounts Receivable; Prepaid Insurance; Office Supplies; Accounts Payable; Common Stock, $5 Par Value; and Retained Earnings. Include an Explanation column for changes in stockholders' equity.

2. Show the effects of the transactions on the elements of the equation by recording increases and decreases in the appropriate columns. Do not determine new totals for the items of the equation after each transaction. Next to each change in stockholders' equity, state whether it was caused by an investment, a revenue, an expense, or a dividend. Determine the final total for each item and verify that the equation is in balance.

3. Prepare an income statement for April, a statement of retained earnings for April, and an April 30 balance sheet.

CHECK FIGURE:
Ending retained earnings balance, $2,760

The accounting records of Goodall Corporation show the following balance sheet accounts as of the end of 19X1 and 19X2:

Problem 2–3
Calculating and interpreting net income, preparing a balance sheet, and calculating return on equity
(LO 1, 3, 4)

	December 31	
	19X1	**19X2**
Cash	$ 52,500	$ 18,750
Accounts receivable	28,500	22,350
Office supplies	4,500	3,300
Trucks	54,000	54,000
Office equipment	138,000	147,000
Building		180,000
Land		45,000
Accounts payable	7,500	37,500
Notes payable		105,000
Common stock, $1 par value	200,000	235,000
Retained earnings	?	?

Late in December 19X2 (just before the amounts in the second column were calculated), Goodall purchased a small office building and moved the business from rented quarters to the new building. The building and the land it occupies cost $225,000. The business paid $120,000 in cash and a note payable was signed for the balance. Goodall had to issue 35,000 shares of $1 par value common stock to enable it to pay the $120,000. The business earned a satisfactory net income during 19X2, which enabled it to pay a $5,000 cash dividend on December 31.

Required

1. Prepare balance sheets for the business as of the end of 19X1 and the end of 19X2. (Remember that stockholders' equity equals the difference between the assets and the liabilities.)
2. By comparing the stockholders' equity amounts from the balance sheets and using the additional information presented in the problem, prepare a calculation to show how much net income was earned by the business during 19X2.
3. Calculate the 19X2 return on equity for the business.

CHECK FIGURE:
Return on equity, 10.3%

Problem 2–4
Analyzing transactions, preparing financial statements, and calculating return on equity
(LO 1, 3, 4)

Frey Electrical, Inc., began operations in November and incurred these transactions during the month:

Nov. 1 Issued 28,000 shares of $2 par value common stock in exchange for $56,000 cash.

1 Rented office space and paid cash for the month's rent of $800.

3 Purchased electrical equipment from an electrician who was going out of business for $14,000 by paying $3,200 in cash and agreeing to pay the balance in six months.

5 Purchased office supplies by paying $900 cash.

6 Completed electrical work and immediately collected $1,000 for doing the work.

8 Purchased $3,800 of office equipment on credit.

15 Completed electrical work on credit in the amount of $4,000.

18 Purchased $500 of office supplies on credit.

20 Paid for the office equipment purchased on November 8.

24 Billed a client $600 for electrial work; the balance is due in 30 days.

28 Received $4,000 for the work completed on November 15.

30 Paid the assistant's salary of $1,200.

30 Paid the monthly utility bills of $440.

30 Declared and paid a $700 cash dividend to common stockholders.

Required

Preparation component:

1. Arrange the following asset, liability, and stockholders' equity titles in an equation like Illustration 2–7: Cash; Accounts Receivable; Office Supplies; Office Equipment; Electrical Equipment; Accounts Payable; Common Stock, $2 Par Value; and Retained Earnings. Leave space for an Explanation column to the right of Retained Earnings.
2. Use additions and subtractions to show the effects of each transaction on the items in the equation. Show new totals after each transaction. Next to each change in stockholders' equity, state whether the change was caused by an investment, a revenue, an expense, or a dividend.

CHECK FIGURE:
Ending retained earnings balance, $2,460

3. Use the increases and decreases in the last column of the equation to prepare an income statement and a statement of retained earnings for the month. Also prepare a balance sheet as of the end of the month.
4. Calculate the return on equity for the month, using the initial investment by stockholders as the beginning balance of equity.

Analysis component:

5. Assume that the investment transaction on November 1 had been 20,000 shares of common stock in exchange for $40,000 instead of 28,000 shares for $56,000, and that Frey obtained the $16,000 difference by borrowing it from a bank. Explain the effect of this change on total assets, total liabilities, stockholders' equity, and return on equity.

The following financial statement information is known about five unrelated companies:

Problem 2–5
Missing information
(LO 1)

	Company A	Company B	Company C	Company D	Company E
December 31, 19X1:					
Assets...............	$45,000	$35,000	$29,000	$80,000	$123,000
Liabilities	23,500	22,500	14,000	38,000	?
December 31, 19X2:					
Assets...............	48,000	41,000	?	125,000	112,500
Liabilities	?	27,500	19,000	64,000	75,000
During 19X2:					
Stockholder investments .	5,000	1,500	7,750	?	4,500
Net income	7,500	?	9,000	12,000	18,000
Dividends	2,500	3,000	3,875	0	9,000

Required

1. Answer the following questions about Company A:
   a. What was the stockholders' equity on December 31, 19X1?
   b. What was the stockholders' equity on December 31, 19X2?
   c. What was the amount of liabilities owed on December 31, 19X2?

2. Answer the following questions about Company B:
   a. What was the stockholders' equity on December 31, 19X1?
   b. What was the stockholders' equity on December 31, 19X2?
   c. What was the net income for 19X2?

3. Calculate the amount of assets owned by Company C on December 31, 19X2.

4. Calculate the amount of stockholder investments in Company D made during 19X2.

5. Calculate the amount of liabilities owed by Company E on December 31, 19X1.

CHECK FIGURE:
Co. C, 12/31/X2 assets, $46,875

Identify how each of the following transactions affects the company's financial statements. For the balance sheet, identify how each transaction affects total assets, total liabilities, and stockholders' equity. For the income statement, identify how each transaction affects net income. For the statement of cash flows, identify how each transaction affects cash flows from operating activities, cash flows from financing activities, and cash flows from investing activities. If there is an increase, place a "+" in the column or columns. If there is a decrease, place a "−" in the column or columns. If there is both an increase and a decrease, place a "+/−" in the column or columns. The line for the first transaction is completed as an example.

Problem 2–6
Identifying the effects of
transactions on the financial
statements
(LO 1, 3)

	Transaction	Total Assets	Total Liab.	Equity	Net Income	Operating	Financing	Investing
		Balance Sheet			**Income Statement**	**Statement of Cash Flows**		
1	Issue common stock for cash	+		+			+	
2	Sell services for cash							
3	Acquire services on credit							
4	Pay wages with cash							
5	Pay cash dividend to common stockholders							
6	Borrow cash with note payable							

		Balance Sheet			Income Statement	Statement of Cash Flows		
	Transaction	Total Assets	Total Liab.	Equity	Net Income	Operating	Financing	Investing
7	Sell services on credit							
8	Buy office equipment for cash							
9	Collect receivable from (7)							
10	Buy asset with note payable							

CRITICAL THINKING: ESSAYS, PROBLEMS, AND CASES

Analytical Essays

AE 2-1
(LO 3)

Review the facts presented in Problem 2–2. Now assume that all of the company's revenue transactions generated cash (that is, none had been made on credit). Also assume that all of the expense and purchase transactions used cash and none were on credit. Describe the differences, if any, these alternate assumptions would create for the income statement, the statement of retained earnings, and the balance sheet. Construct your answer in general terms without stating the actual dollar amounts of each difference. Be certain to explain why each statement would or would not be affected by the changes in the assumptions.

AE 2-2
(LO 2, 3)

Review the facts presented in Problem 2–1 for transactions *e* and *i*. Identify the transaction that creates a revenue and explain your answer. Then explain why the other transaction did not create a revenue. Next, review the facts for transactions *c* and *j*. Identify the transaction that creates an expense for the current reporting period and explain your answer. Finally, explain why the other transaction did not create an expense.

Financial Statement Analysis Case

(LO 1)

Southwest Airlines Co. features low fares and targets both business commuters and leisure travelers. The financial statements and other information from Southwest Airlines's 1994 annual report are included in Appendix E at the end of the book. Use information from that report to answer the following questions:

1. Examine Southwest Airlines's consolidated balance sheet. To what level of significance are the dollar amounts rounded?
2. What is the closing date of Southwest Airlines's most recent annual reporting period?
3. What amount of net income did Southwest Airlines have during 1994?
4. How much cash (and cash equivalents) did the company hold at the end of 1994?
5. What was the net amount of cash provided by the company's operating activities during 1994?
6. Did the company's investing activities for 1994 create a net cash inflow or outflow? What was the amount of the net flow?
7. Compare 1994's results to 1993's results to determine whether the company's total revenues increased or decreased. If so, what was the amount of the increase or decrease?
8. What was the change in the company's net income between 1993 and 1994?
9. What amount was reported as total assets at the end of 1994?
10. Calculate the return on equity that Southwest Airlines achieved in 1994.

Barnes & Noble is the world's largest and fastest growing bookseller. It provides a comfortable and friendly environment for book browsing and purchasing. The company's 1994 annual report showed total revenues of nearly $1,623 million and net earnings of over $25 million. The annual report also included the following information in its footnotes:

Principles Application Problem

(LO 2)

11. Certain relationships and related transactions

Marboro Books Corp., the Company's mail-order subsidiary, leases an office/warehouse from a partnership in which a shareholder of the Company has an interest. The lease term is for 15 years commencing August 1987 and requires annual rental payments of approximately $700,000 plus certain escalations.

Explain why Barnes & Noble might have included these comments in its report. What accounting principle might be compromised by related-party transactions like the lease agreement with Marboro Books Corp.?

CONCEPT TESTER

Test your understanding of the concepts introduced in this chapter by completing the following crossword puzzle.

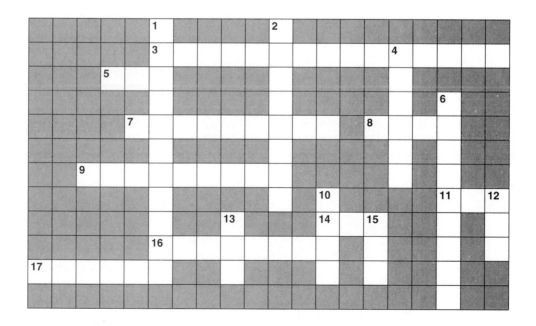

Across Clues

3. 2 words; statement that shows revenues, expenses, and net income or loss.
5. Securities Industry Association.
7. Distributions of assets by a corporaion to its stockholders.
8. Association for Investment Management and Research.
9. 2 words; the excess of revenues over expenses.
11. Institute of Management Accountants.
14. American Accounting Association.
16. Outflows or using up of assets as a result of the major or central operations of a business.
17. Properities or economic resources owned by a business.

Down Clues

1. Debts owed by a business or organization.
2. Inflows of assets received in exchange for goods or services provided to customers.
4. The difference between a company's assets and its liabilities.
6. Individuals or organizations entitled to receive payments from a company.
10. Financial Accounting Standards Board.
12. Auditing Standards Board.
13. Financial Executives Institute.
15. Accounting Principles Board.

ANSWERS TO PROGRESS CHECKS

2–1 *d*

2–2 An expense is an outflow or using up of assets as a result of the major or central operations of a business. An expense also may occur as an increase in liabilities.

2–3 The balance sheet reports conditions at a particular point in time. The income statement reports activities during a time period.

2–4 *c*

2–5 GAAP are the principles that govern the reporting of information in the financial statements. GAAS, on the other hand, are the standards that guide auditors in performing an audit.

2–6 No. The IASC does not have the authority to impose standards. The United States company must comply with the GAAP established by the FASB.

2–7 The FASB's conceptual framework identifies relevance and reliability as two qualities of useful information.

2–8 A company's financial statements present its activities separate from its owners' activities because separate information is necessary for evaluating the company.

2–9 The equipment should be reported at its $25,000 cost, according to the cost principle.

2–10 *b*

2–11 No. If a liability increases, one or more of three other things must happen: an asset increases, or equity decreases, or another liability decreases.

2–12 *c*

2–13 Net income appears on both the income statement and the statement of retained earnings.

2–14 The balance of retained earnings at the end of the period appears on both the statement of retained earnings and the balance sheet.

2–15 A stockholder may use the return on equity ratio to describe the success of the business in a way that can be compared to other investment opportunities.

2–16 An expected return on equity should be evaluated by comparing it with the returns provided by other investment alternatives.

Recording Transactions

*T*o prepare for her business communications class, Karen White spent an afternoon looking through the annual reports section of her school library. She was interested in learning about the information companies present in their annual reports.

One report that caught White's attention was the 1994 Annual Report of Chiquita Brands International, Inc. Chiquita is the largest producer and distributor of bananas in the world. It distributes a wide variety of fresh fruit and vegetables and also markets a variety of processed foods.

As is true in most annual reports, Chiquita's 1994 report includes a letter from the executive officers. White found this Message from the Chairman and President interesting and informative. However, since White had not yet taken an accounting course, she found some of the statements in it hard to understand.

For example, under a Looking Forward heading, one sentence states that "our financial strategy is to de-leverage the balance sheet and lower Chiquita's overall cost of capital." The executive officers indicate that "the prospects for meaningful accomplishment (of this strategy or goal) have been enhanced by completion of Chiquita's investment spending program." White concluded that the investment spending program apparently had caused the company's balance sheet to reflect too much leverage. However, White did not understand exactly what that meant and therefore was confused as to why it might be desirable to de-leverage the balance sheet.

CHIQUITA BRANDS INTERNATIONAL, INC.
(In thousands)

December 31	Total Assets	Total Liabilities	Shareholders' Equity
1994	$2,902,021	$2,257,212	$644,809
1993	2,740,753	2,138,755	601,998
1992	2,880,624	2,205,737	674,887
1991	2,937,344	1,969,419	967,925
1990	1,913,674	1,225,965	687,709

LEARNING OBJECTIVES

After studying Chapter 3, you should be able to:

1. **Describe the events recorded in accounting systems and the importance of source documents and business papers in those systems.**

2. **Describe how accounts are used to record information about the effects of transactions, how code numbers are used to identify each account, and the meaning of the words *debit* and *credit*.**

3. **Describe how debits and credits are used to analyze transactions and record their effects in the accounts.**

4. **Record transactions in a General Journal, describe balance column accounts, and post entries from the journal to the ledger.**

5. **Prepare a trial balance, explain its usefulness, and calculate a company's debt ratio.**

6. **Define or explain the words and phrases listed in the chapter glossary.**

In Chapter 2, you learned how the accounting equation (Assets = Liabilities + Stockholders' Equity) is affected by business transactions. In this chapter, you learn how the effects of transactions are recorded in accounts. All accounting systems, small or large, manual or computerized, use procedures similar to those described in this chapter. No matter how unusual or complicated a business might be, these procedures are the first steps in a process that leads to financial statements.

We begin by describing how source documents provide useful information about transactions. Then, we describe accounts and explain how they are used. Next, we explain debits and credits and use them to show how transactions affect the accounts. With this background in place, we describe the process of recording events in the journal and ledger. The chapter concludes by describing how to use a company's debt ratio to assess risk.

THE ACCOUNTING PROCESS

LO 1
Describe the events recorded in accounting systems and the importance of source documents and business papers in those systems.

Chapter 2 explains that accounting provides useful financial information to decision makers. To generate this information, a company uses an accounting process that analyzes economic events, records the results, and classifies and summarizes the information in reports and financial statements. These reports and statements are provided to individuals who find the information to be useful for making investment, credit, and other decisions about the entity. You can see the overall steps in this process in the flowchart in Illustration 3–1.

Business Transactions and Other Events

Notice that the economic events in Illustration 3–1 consist of business transactions and other events. Recall from Chapter 2 that business transactions are exchanges of economic consideration between two parties. Also, remember that a company's accounting equation is affected by transactions. The accounting process begins by analyzing transactions to determine how they affect the equation. Then, those effects are recorded in accounting records, informally referred to as the *books*. Additional processing steps summarize and classify the effects of all transactions. The process is not complete until it provides useful information to decision makers in financial statements or other reports.

Because business transactions are exchanges between the entity and some other person or organization, they are sometimes called **external transactions.** Other economic events, called **internal transactions,** can affect the accounting equation. These events are not transactions with outside parties. For example, suppose that a company uses a machine in its operations. As the machine is used, its total remaining usefulness decreases. This using up of the machine's economic benefit is an economic event that decreases assets and decreases stockholders' equity.

Illustration 3–1   The Accounting Process

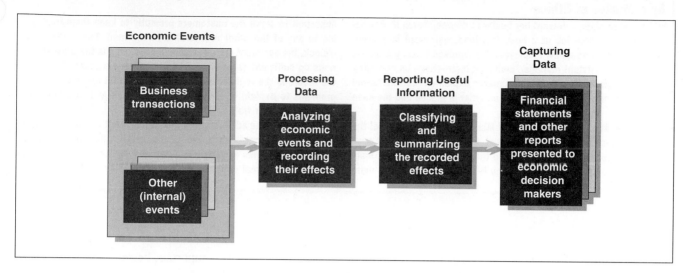

Other events that can affect a company's accounting equation include natural events such as floods that destroy assets and create losses. In a few circumstances, changes in the market values of certain assets are also recorded. Economic events like these are not transactions between the company and other parties. We explain the analysis and recording of these economic events in Chapter 4.

SOURCE DOCUMENTS AND BUSINESS PAPERS

Companies use various documents and other papers when they conduct business. These **business papers** include sales tickets, checks, purchase orders, bills to customers, bills from suppliers, employee earnings records, and bank statements. Business papers are also called **source documents** because they are the source of the information recorded with accounting entries. Source documents may be printed on paper or they may exist only in computer records.

For example, when you buy a pocket calculator on credit, the store prepares at least two copies of a sales ticket. One copy is given to you. Another is sent to the store's accounting department and triggers an entry in the system to record the sale. (In many systems, this copy is sent electronically without a physical document.) Or, if you pay cash for the calculator, the sale is rung up on a cash register that records and stores the amount of each sale.

Some cash registers print the amount of each sale on a paper tape locked inside the register. Most newer registers store the data electronically. In either case, the proper keyboard commands at the end of the day cause the cash register to determine the total cash sales for that day. This total is then used to record the day's sales in the accounting records. These systems are designed to ensure that the accounting records include all transactions. They also help prevent mistakes and theft. The As a Matter of Ethics case on page 66 describes a challenge created by an instruction to overlook these accounting procedures. Read the case and think about what you would do if you were Karen Muñoz.

Both buyers and sellers use sales tickets (also called *invoices*) as source documents. For example, if the new calculator is going to be used in your business, your copy of the invoice is a source document. It provides information to record the purchase in accounting records for your business.

To summarize, business papers are the starting point in the accounting process. These source documents, especially if they are created outside the business, provide objective evidence about transactions and the amounts to be recorded for them. As

PRINCIPLE APPLICATION
Objectivity Principle p. 35
The need for credible source documents is created by the *objectivity principle*. For example, at the end of its 1995 business year, Sizzler International, Inc., reported a Cash balance of $12,220,000. The company's auditors were able to confirm this amount primarily by analyzing the company's bank statements.

you learned in Chapter 2, this type of evidence is important because it makes the reported information more reliable and useful.

Years ago, most accounting systems required pen and ink to manually record and process data about transactions. Today, only very small companies use manual systems. Now, large and small companies use computers to record and process the data. However, you will find it easier to understand the steps in the accounting process by learning to prepare accounting data manually. Despite the differences, the general concepts you learn by studying manual methods apply equally well to computerized accounting systems. More importantly, these concepts help you use financial statements because you understand the source of their information.

Progress Check
(Answers to Progress Checks are provided at the end of the chapter.)

3-1   Which of the following are examples of accounting source documents? *(a)* Journals and ledgers; *(b)* Income statements and balance sheets; *(c)* External transactions and internal transactions; *(d)* Bank statements and sales tickets; *(e)* All of the above.

3-2   What kinds of economic events affect a company's accounting equation?

3-3   Why are business papers called source documents?

RECORDING INFORMATION IN THE ACCOUNTS

LO 2
Describe how accounts are used to record information about the effects of transactions, how code numbers are used to identify each account, and the meaning of the words *debit* and *credit*.

An **account** is a place or location within an accounting system in which the increases and decreases in a specific asset, liability, stockholders' equity, revenue, or expense are recorded and stored. The diagram in Illustration 3–2 shows how the information about the company's events flows into the accounts and from the accounts into the financial statements.

When financial statements (or other reports) are needed, the information is taken from the accounts, summarized, and presented in helpful formats. To display information about a specific item in the statements, a separate account must be maintained for that item. Thus, a company's accounting system includes a separate account for each revenue and expense on the income statement. The system also includes a separate account for each asset, liability, and stockholders' equity item on the balance sheet. In addition, important changes such as dividends are captured in separate accounts. Because each company is different from all others, each has its own unique set of accounts. However, most companies use many accounts that are similar. The following paragraphs describe some commonly used accounts.

Illustration 3-2 The flow of information through the Accounts into the Financial Statements

Information about Events

Accounts	Revenues	Expenses	Retained Earnings	Cash Dividends Declared	Assets	Liabilities	Contributed Capital

Financial Statements	Income Statement	Statement of Retained Earnings	Balance Sheet

Net income → *Ending retained earnings* →

Asset Accounts

Because most companies own the following kinds of assets, their accounting systems include accounts for them.

Cash. Increases and decreases in the amount of cash are recorded in a *Cash* account. A company's cash consists of money, balances in checking accounts, or any document that a bank accepts for deposit. Thus, cash includes coins, currency, checks, and money orders.

Accounts Receivable. Goods and services are often sold to customers in return for promises to pay in the future. These transactions are called *credit sales* or *sales on account.* The promises from the buyers are called the seller's *accounts receivable.* Accounts receivable are increased by new credit sales and are decreased by customer payments. Because a company sends bills to its credit customers, it needs to know the amount currently due from each of them. Therefore, it creates a separate record of each customer's purchases and payments. We describe the system for maintaining these separate records in Chapter 7. For now, how-ever, we can use the simpler practice of recording all increases and decreases in receivables in a single account called *Accounts Receivable.*

The importance of accounts receivable depends on the nature of a company's operations. For example, at the end of its 1994 business year, **Showbiz Pizza Time, Inc.'s** accounts receivable amounted to less than 2% of its total assets. By comparison, **Nike, Inc.'s** accounts receivable amounted to almost 30% of its total assets.

Notes Receivable. A **promissory note** is an unconditional written promise to pay a definite sum of money on demand or on a defined future date (or dates). If a company holds one of these notes signed by another party, it owns a valuable asset. These assets called notes receivable are recorded in a *Notes Receivable* account.

Prepaid Insurance. Insurance contracts provide protection against losses caused by fire, theft, accidents, or other events. Normally, an insurance policy requires the fee (called a *premium*) to be paid in advance, and the protection usually lasts for a year or even as much as three years. As a result, the unused portion of the coverage may be an asset for a substantial time after the premium is paid.

When an insurance premium is paid in advance, the cost is typically recorded in an asset account called *Prepaid Insurance.* When financial statements are prepared later, the expired portion of the insurance cost is removed from the asset account and reported as an expense on the income statement. The unexpired portion remains in the Prepaid Insurance account and is reported on the balance sheet as an asset.

Office Supplies. All companies use office supplies such as computer diskettes, printer ribbons and cartridges, stationery, paper, and pens. These supplies are assets until they are used. When they are consumed, their cost becomes an expense. Increases and decreases in the cost of the assets are recorded in an *Office Supplies* account.

Store Supplies. Many stores keep plastic and paper bags, gift boxes, cartons, and similar items on hand to use in wrapping purchases for their customers. Increases and decreases in the cost of the assets are recorded in a *Store Supplies* account.

Other Prepaid Expenses. When payments are made for assets that are not used until later, the assets are often called **prepaid expenses.** Then, as the economic benefits of the assets are used up, the costs of the assets become expenses. As a practical matter, an asset's cost can be initially recorded as an expense if its benefits will be consumed before the next set of financial statements is prepared. If the asset's benefits will not be used up before the end of the current reporting period, the prepayments are recorded in asset accounts.

Office supplies and store supplies are usually described as prepaid expenses. Other examples of prepaid expenses include prepaid insurance, prepaid rent, and legal or accounting fees paid in advance of receiving the services. To provide useful information, each prepaid expense is typically accounted for in a separate asset account.

Equipment. Virtually all companies own computers, printers, typewriters, desks, chairs, and other equipment that they use in their business. The costs incurred to buy the equipment are recorded in an *Office Equipment* account. The costs of assets used in a store, such as counters, showcases, and cash registers, are recorded in a separate *Store Equipment* account.

Buildings. A building owned by a business provides space for a store, an office, a warehouse, or a factory. Because they produce future benefits, buildings are assets, and their costs are recorded in a *Buildings* account. If several buildings are owned, separate accounts may be used to record the cost incurred in buying each of them.

Land. A *Land* account is used to record the cost of land owned by a business. The cost of land is separated from the cost of buildings located on the land to provide more useful information in the financial statements. Although the land and the buildings may appear to be inseparable and a single asset, the buildings wear out, or *depreciate,* and their costs become expenses. Land does not depreciate, and its cost does not become an expense. Therefore, the costs of the land and the buildings are recorded in separate accounts to simplify accounting for depreciation.

Liability Accounts

Chapter 2 explained that liabilities are present obligations to transfer assets or provide services to other entities in the future. A business may have several different types of liabilities. Therefore, each type is represented by a separate account. The following liability accounts are widely used.

Accounts Payable. When purchases of merchandise, supplies, equipment, or services are made by an oral or implied promise to pay later, the resulting debts are called *accounts payable.* Because it is useful to know the amount owed to each creditor, accounting systems keep separate records about purchases from and the payments to each of them. We describe these individual records in Chapter 8. For now, however, we can use the simpler practice of recording all increases and decreases in payables in a single account called *Accounts Payable.*

Notes Payable. When an entity's promise to pay is formally recognized by having the entity sign a promissory note, the resulting liability is called a *note payable.* Depending on how soon the liability must be repaid, its amount may be recorded in a *Short-Term Notes Payable* account or a *Long-Term Notes Payable* account.

Unearned Revenues. As you learned in Chapter 2, the *revenue recognition principle* requires accountants to report revenues on the income statement only after they are earned. This principle demands careful treatment of transactions in which customers pay in advance for products or services. Because the cash from these transactions is received before the revenues are earned, the seller considers them to be **unearned revenues.** An unearned revenue is a liability that is satisfied by delivering the product or service in the future. Unearned revenues include subscriptions collected in advance by a magazine publisher. For example, **The Reader's Digest Association, Inc.,** reported unearned revenues of $391,700,000 as of June 30, 1995. Other unearned revenues include rent collected in advance by a building owner, and professional or other service fees collected in advance.

When cash is received in advance, the seller records the amount in a liability account such as *Unearned Subscriptions, Unearned Rent,* or *Unearned Professional Fees.* When the products or services are delivered, the earned revenues are transferred to revenue accounts such as *Subscription Fees Earned, Rent Earned,* or *Professional Fees Earned.*

Other Short-Term Liabilities. Other short-term liabilities include wages payable, taxes payable, and interest payable. Each of these debts is normally recorded in a separate liability account. However, if they are not large in amount, one or more of them may be added together and reported as a single amount on the balance sheet. For example, the liabilities section of **La-Z-Boy Chair Company's** balance sheet at the end of its 1995 year included an item called *Other current liabilities,* which amounted to $15,343,000.

Stockholders' Equity, Revenue, Expense, and Cash Dividends Declared Accounts

In Chapter 2, we described four types of transactions that affected stockholders' equity in a corporation. They are (1) investments by stockholders, (2) revenues, (3) expenses, and (4) dividends paid to stockholders. In the illustrations in Chapter 2, investments by stockholders were entered in a column labeled Common Stock. However, the effects of the other three types of transactions—revenues, expenses, and dividends—were all entered in one Retained Earnings column. This procedure showed the effects of transactions on the accounting equation.

When we prepared an income statement and a statement of retained earnings in Chapter 2, we had to analyze the items entered in the Retained Earnings column. Now you can see that such an analysis is not necessary if a separate account is maintained for each type of transaction. We describe these accounts in the following paragraphs.

Common stock. When a corporation issues stock in exchange for assets invested by stockholders, the corporation records the investments in a Common Stock account. The account title may also indicate the par value of the stock. The amounts recorded in this account represent the contributed capital portion of stockholders' equity. In Chapter 13, you learn about additional accounts that are sometimes used to record transactions involving contributed capital.

Revenue and Expense Accounts. Decision makers often want information about the amounts of revenue earned and expenses incurred during the reporting period. A business uses a variety of revenue and expense accounts to provide this information on its income statement. As you might expect, various companies have different kinds of revenues and expenses. Examples of possible revenue accounts are *Sales, Commissions Earned, Professional Fees Earned, Rent Earned,* and *Interest Earned.* Examples of expense accounts are *Advertising Expense, Store Supplies Expense, Office Salaries Expense, Office Supplies Expense, Rent Expense, Utilities Expense,* and *Insurance Expense.*

You can get an idea of the variety of accounts that a company might use by looking at the list of accounts at the back of this book. It lists the accounts you need to solve the exercises and problems in this book.[1]

Cash Dividends Declared. When a corporation earns a net income, the net assets of the business increase. The additional assets may be left in the business with the intent of using them to increase future profits. However, many corporations distribute some of the increased assets to their stockholders. These declarations and payments of dividends reduce both the assets and the retained earnings of the corporation.

To prepare the statement of retained earnings, you need to know the total amount of dividends that were declared during a period. Thus, whenever a corporation declares and pays a dividend, the reduction in retained earnings is recorded in a Cash Dividends Declared account.

Retained Earnings Account. After the revenue, expense, and Cash Dividends Declared account balances are used in preparing the financial statements, these account balances are transferred to a Retained Earnings account. This is done at the end of each period. As a result, the Retained Earnings account balance shows the cumulative effect on stockholders' equity of all past revenues, expenses, and dividend declarations. In Chapter 5, you learn more about the process of transferring the revenue, expense, and Cash Dividends Declared account balances to Retained Earnings.

THE LEDGER AND THE CHART OF ACCOUNTS

Accounts may have different physical forms, depending on the system. In computerized systems, accounts are stored in files on floppy or hard disks. In manual systems, each account may be a separate page in a loose-leaf book or a separate card in a tray of cards. Regardless of their physical form, the collection of all accounts is called the **ledger.** If the accounts are in files on a hard disk, those files are the ledger. If the accounts are pages in a book or cards in a file, the book or file is the ledger. In other words, a ledger is simply a group of accounts.

A company's size affects the number of accounts needed in its accounting system. A small company may get by with as few as 20 or 30 accounts, while a large company may use several thousand. The **chart of accounts** is a list of all accounts used

---

[1]Remember that different companies may use different account titles than the titles in the list. For example, a company might use Interest Revenue instead of Interest Earned or Rental Expense instead of Rent Expense. All that is required is that an account title describe the item it represents.

by a company. The chart also includes an identification number assigned to each account. To be efficient, companies assign their account identification numbers in a systematic manner. For example, a small business might use this numbering system for its accounts:

101–199	Asset accounts
201–299	Liability accounts
301–399	Stockholders' equity accounts
401–499	Revenue accounts
501–699	Operating expense accounts

Although this system provides for 99 asset accounts, a company may not use all of them. The numbers create a three-digit code that conveys information to the company's accountants and bookkeepers. For example, the first digit of the code numbers assigned to the asset accounts is a 1, while the first digit assigned to the liability accounts is a 2, and so on. In each case, the first digit of an account's number reveals whether the account appears on the balance sheet or the income statement. The second and third digits may also relate to the accounts' categories. We describe account numbering systems more completely in the next chapter.

USING T-ACCOUNTS

In its simplest form, an account looks like the letter T:

(Name)	
(Left side)	(Right side)

Because of its shape, this simple form is called a **T-account.** Notice that the T format gives the account a left side, a right side, and a convenient place for its name.

The shape of a T-account provides one side for recording increases in the item and the other side for recording decreases. For example, the following T-account represents Clear Copy's cash account after the transactions in Chapter 2:

Cash			
Investments by stockholders	30,000	Purchase of store supplies	2,500
Copy services revenue earned	2,200	Purchase of copy equipment	20,000
Collection of account receivable	1,900	Payment of rent	1,000
		Payment of salary	700
		Payment of account payable	900
		Payment of dividend	600

Calculating the Balance of an Account

An **account balance** is simply the difference between the increases and decreases recorded in the account. Thus, for example, the balance of an asset account is the cost of that asset on the date the balance is calculated. The balance of a liability account is the amount owed on the date of the balance. Putting the increases on one side of the account and the decreases on the other makes it easy to find an account's balance. To determine the balance, simply find the total increases shown on one side (including the beginning balance), find the total decreases shown on the other side, and then subtract the sum of the decreases from the sum of the increases.

For example, the total increases in Clear Copy's Cash account were $34,100, the total decreases were $25,700, and the account balance is $8,400. This T-account shows how to calculate the $8,400 balance:

Cash

Issued common stock	30,000	Purchase of store supplies	2,500
Copy services revenue earned	2,200	Purchase of copy equipment	20,000
Collection of account receivable	1,900	Payment of rent	1,000
		Payment of salary	700
		Payment of account payable	900
		Payment of dividend	600
Total increases	**34,100**	Total decreases	**25,700**
Less decreases	**−25,700**		
Balance	**8,400**		

Debits and Credits

In accounting terms, the left side of a T-account is called the **debit** side, often abbreviated Dr. The right side is called the **credit** side, abbreviated Cr.[2] To enter amounts on the left side of an account is to *debit* the account. To enter amounts on the right side is to *credit* the account. The difference between the total debits and the total credits in an account is the account balance. When the sum of the debits exceeds the sum of the credits, the account has a debit balance. It has a credit balance when the sum of the credits exceeds the sum of the debits.

From looking at the Cash account, you might think that the terms *debit* and *credit* mean *increase* and *decrease*. That is not correct. Whether a debit is an increase or decrease depends on the type of account. Similarly, whether a credit increases or decreases an account depends on the type of account. In any account, however, a debit and a credit have opposite effects. That is, in an account where a debit is an increase, a credit is a decrease. And, if a debit is a decrease in a particular account, a credit is an increase.

When we work with T-accounts, a debit simply means an entry on the left side and a credit simply means an entry on the right side. For example, notice the way in which the investments by stockholders in Clear Copy are recorded in the Cash and Common Stock accounts:

Cash		Common Stock, $1 Par Value	
Issued stock 30,000			30,000 shares 30,000

Notice that the cash increase is recorded on the left side of the Cash account with a $30,000 debit entry; the corresponding increase in Common Stock is recorded on the right side of the capital account with a $30,000 credit entry. This method of recording the transaction is an essential feature of *double-entry accounting,* which we explain in the next section.

Progress Check

3–4   Which of the following answers properly classifies these commonly used accounts?
(1) Prepaid Rent;   (2) Unearned Fees;   (3) Buildings;   (4) Retained Earnings;   (5) Wages Payable;   (6) Office Supplies.

---

[2]These abbreviations are remnants of 18th-century English bookkeeping practices that used the terms *Debitor* and *Creditor* instead of *debit* and *credit*. These abbreviations use the first and last letters from the words, just as we still do for *Saint* (St.) and *Doctor* (Dr.).

	Assets	Liabilities	Stockholders' Equity
a.	1,6	2,5	3,4
b.	1,3,6	2,5	4
c.	1,3,6	5	2,4

3-5   What are accounts? What is a ledger?

3-6   What determines the quantity and types of accounts used by a company?

3-7   Does debit always mean increase and credit always mean decrease?

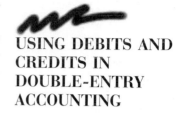

USING DEBITS AND CREDITS IN DOUBLE-ENTRY ACCOUNTING

LO 3
Describe how debits and credits are used to analyze transactions and record their effects in the accounts.

In **double-entry accounting,** every transaction affects and is recorded in at least two accounts. When recording each transaction, *the total amount debited must equal the total amount credited.* Because each transaction is recorded with total debits equal to total credits, the sum of the debits for all entries must equal the sum of the credits for all entries. Furthermore, the sum of the debit account balances in the ledger must equal the sum of the credit account balances. The only reason the sum of the debit balances would not equal the sum of the credit balances would be that an error has occurred. Thus, an important result of double-entry accounting is that many errors are avoided by being sure that the debits and credits for each transaction are equal.

According to traditional double-entry accounting, increases in assets are recorded on the debit side of asset accounts.[3] Why are asset accounts given debit balances? There is no specific reason. The choice is simply a convention that makes it easier for accountants by having all accounting systems work the same way. Then, because asset accounts have debit balances, increases in those balances are recorded with debits and decreases are recorded with credits.

Because asset accounts have debit balances and because debits must equal credits, liability accounts and stockholders' equity accounts must have credit balances. This follows from the logic of the accounting equation (Assets = Liabilities + Stockholders' Equity). Therefore, increases in liability and stockholders' equity accounts are recorded with credit entries. In other words, if asset increases are recorded with debit entries, equal debits and credits for a transaction are possible only if increases in liabilities and stockholders' equity are recorded as credits. To summarize, double-entry accounting systems record increases and decreases in balance sheet accounts as follows:

Assets		=	Liabilities		+	Stockholders' Equity	
Debit for increases	Credit for decreases		Debit for decreases	Credit for increases		Debit for decreases	Credit for increases

The practices shown in these T-accounts can be expressed as the following rules for recording transactions in a double-entry accounting system:

1. Increases in assets are debited to asset accounts; therefore, decreases in assets are recorded with credit entries to asset accounts.

2. Increases in liabilities are credited to liability accounts; therefore, decreases in liabilities are recorded with debit entries to liability accounts.

3. Increases in stockholders' equity are credited to stockholders' equity accounts; therefore, decreases in stockholders' equity are recorded with debit entries to stockholders' equity accounts.

Chapter 2 taught you that stockholders' equity is increased by stockholders' investments and by revenues. You also learned that stockholders' equity is decreased by expenses and by dividends. Therefore, the following rules also apply:

---

[3]These double-entry practices originated in 15th-century Italy and have stood the test of more than 500 years of change and progress in business.

4. Investments in a corporation by its stockholders are credited to Common Stock, which is a contributed capital account and is part of stockholders' equity.

5. Dividends are debited to Cash Dividends Declared, the balance of which is subtracted from the retained earnings portion of stockholders' equity.

6. Revenues are credited to revenue accounts because they increase the retained earnings portion of stockholders' equity. The system should include a separate account for each type of revenue.

7. Expenses are debited to expense accounts because they decrease the retained earnings portion of stockholders' equity. The system should include a separate account for each type of expense.

At this stage, you may find it helpful to memorize these rules. You will use them over and over in the course of your study. Before long, the rules will become second nature to you.

EXAMPLES OF DEBITS AND CREDITS

The following transactions for Clear Copy will help you learn how to apply these debit and credit rules. Study each transaction carefully to be sure that you understand it before you go on to the next one.

Each transaction is numbered so you can identify the transaction's effects on the accounts. You should recognize the first 11 transactions because they were used in Chapter 2 to show how transactions affect the accounting equation. In this chapter, we add five more transactions (numbers 12 through 16) to illustrate different kinds of events.

Before recording a transaction, the bookkeeper first analyzes it to determine what was increased or decreased. Then, the debit and credit rules are applied to decide how to record the increases or decreases. The bookkeeper's analysis of each transaction appear next to the T-accounts. Study each analysis carefully to be sure that you understand the process.

1. On December 1, Clear Copy issued 30,000 shares of its $1 par value common stock in exchange for $30,000.

Cash	
(1) 30,000	

Common Stock, $1 Par Value	
	(1) 30,000

Analysis of the transaction: The transaction increased the company's cash. At the same time, it increased stockholders' equity. Increases in assets are debited and increases in stockholders' equity are credited. Therefore, record the transaction with a debit to Cash and a credit to Common Stock, $1 Par Value, for $30,000.

2. Purchased store supplies by paying $2,500 cash.

Store Supplies	
(2) 2,500	

Cash	
(1) 30,000	(2) 2,500

Analysis of the transaction: The cost of the store supplies is increased by the purchase and cash is decreased. Increases in assets are debited and decreases are credited. Therefore, record the transaction with a debit to Store Supplies and a credit to Cash for $2,500.

3. Purchased copying equipment by paying $20,000 cash.

Copy Equipment	
(3)	20,000

Cash			
(1)	30,000	(2)	2,500
		(3)	20,000

Analysis of the transaction: The cost of the copying equipment is increased and cash is decreased. Increases in assets are debited and decreases are credited. Debit Copy Equipment and credit Cash for $20,000.

4. Purchased $1,100 of store supplies and $6,000 of copying equipment on credit from Handy Supply Company.

Store Supplies	
(2)	2,500
(4)	1,100

Copy Equipment	
(3)	20,000
(4)	6,000

Accounts Payable			
		(4)	7,100

Analysis of the transaction: This transaction increased two assets, store supplies and copy equipment. It also created a new liability. Increases in assets are debits and increases in liabilities are credits. Therefore, debit Store Supplies for $1,100, debit Copy Equipment for $6,000, and credit Accounts Payable for $7,100.

5. Provided copying services to a customer and immediately collected $2,200 cash.

Cash			
(1)	30,000	(2)	2,500
(5)	2,200	(3)	20,000

Copy Services Revenue			
		(5)	2,200

Analysis of the transaction: This revenue transaction increased both assets and stockholders' equity. Increases in assets are debits and increases in stockholders' equity are credits. Revenue accounts are increased with credits because revenues increase stockholders' equity. Therefore, debit Cash $2,200 to record the increase in assets. Credit Copy Services Revenue $2,200 to increase stockholders' equity and to accumulate information for the income statement.

6. Paid $1,000 cash for rent for December.

Rent Expense	
(6)	1,000

Cash			
(1)	30,000	(2)	2,500
(5)	2,200	(3)	20,000
		(6)	1,000

Analysis of the transaction: The cost of renting the store during December is an expense, which decreases stockholders' equity. Because decreases in stockholders' equity are debits, expenses are recorded as debits. Therefore, debit Rent Expense $1,000 to decrease stockholders' equity and to accumulate information for the income statement. Also, credit Cash $1,000 to record the decrease in assets.

7. Paid $700 cash for the employee's salary for the pay period ended on December 12.

Salaries Expense	
(7) 700	

Cash			
(1)	30,000	(2)	2,500
(5)	2,200	(3)	20,000
		(6)	1,000
		(7)	**700**

Analysis of the transaction: The employee's salary is an expense that decreased stockholders' equity. Debit Salaries Expense $700 to decrease stockholders' equity and to accumulate information for the income statement. Also, credit Cash $700 to record the decrease in assets.

8. Completed copying work on credit and billed the customer $1,900 for the services.

Accounts Receivable	
(8) **1,900**	

Copy Services Revenue		
	(5)	2,200
	(8)	**1,900**

Analysis of the transaction: This revenue transaction gave Clear Copy the right to collect $1,900 from the customer. Thus, it increased both assets and stockholders' equity. Therefore, debit Accounts Receivable $1,900 for the increase in assets and credit Copy Services Revenue $1,900 to increase stockholders' equity and to accumulate information for the income statement.

9. The customer paid the $1,900 account receivable created in transaction 8.

Cash			
(1)	30,000	(2)	2,500
(5)	2,200	(3)	20,000
(9)	**1,900**	(6)	1,000
		(7)	700

Accounts Receivable			
(8)	1,900	(9)	**1,900**

Analysis of the transaction: One asset was increased and another decreased. Debit Cash $1,900 to record the increase in cash, and credit Accounts Receivable $1,900 to record the decrease in the account receivable.

10. Paid Handy Supply Company $900 cash on the $7,100 owed for the supplies and equipment purchased on credit in transaction 4.

Accounts Payable			
(10)	**900**	(4)	7,100

Cash			
(1)	30,000	(2)	2,500
(5)	2,200	(3)	20,000
(9)	1,900	(6)	1,000
		(7)	700
		(10)	**900**

Analysis of the transaction: A payment to a creditor decreases an asset and a liability by the same amount. Decreases in liabilities are debited, and decreases in assets are credited. Debit Accounts Payable $900 and credit Cash $900.

11. Declared and paid $600 in dividends to the stockholders.

Cash Dividends Declared	
(11)	600	

Cash			
(1)	30,000	(2)	2,500
(5)	2,200	(3)	20,000
(9)	1,900	(6)	1,000
		(7)	700
		(10)	900
		(11)	600

Analysis of the transaction: This event reduced stockholders' equity and assets by the same amount. Cash Dividends Declared is debited $600 to decrease stockholders' equity and to accumulate information for the statement of retained earnings. Cash is credited $600 to record the asset reduction.

12. Signed a contract with a customer and accepted $3,000 cash in advance of providing any services.

Cash			
(1)	30,000	(2)	2,500
(5)	2,200	(3)	20,000
(9)	1,900	(6)	1,000
(12)	3,000	(7)	700
		(10)	900
		(11)	600

Unearned Copy Services Revenue	
	(12)	3,000

Analysis of the transaction: The $3,000 inflow of cash increased assets but a revenue was not earned. Instead, the transaction creates a liability that will be satisfied by doing the client's copying work in the future. Record the asset increase by debiting Cash for $3,000 and record the liability increase by crediting Unearned Copy Services Revenue for $3,000.

13. Paid $2,400 cash for the premium on a two-year insurance policy.

Prepaid Insurance	
(13)	2,400	

Cash			
(1)	30,000	(2)	2,500
(5)	2,200	(3)	20,000
(9)	1,900	(6)	1,000
(12)	3,000	(7)	700
		(10)	900
		(11)	600
		(13)	2,400

Analysis of the transaction: The advance payment of the insurance premium creates an asset (a prepaid expense) by decreasing another asset. The new asset is recorded with a $2,400 debit to Prepaid Insurance and the payment is recorded with a $2,400 credit to Cash.

14. Paid $120 cash for additional store supplies.
15. Paid $230 cash for the December utilities bill.

16. Paid $700 cash for the employee's salary for two weeks ended December 26.

Store Supplies	
(2)	2,500
(4)	1,100
(14)	**120**

Utilities Expense	
(15)	230

Salaries Expense	
(7)	700
(16)	**700**

Cash			
(1)	30,000	(2)	2,500
(5)	2,200	(3)	20,000
(9)	1,900	(6)	1,000
(12)	3,000	(7)	700
		(10)	900
		(11)	600
		(13)	2,400
		(14)	**120**
		(15)	**230**
		(16)	**700**

Analysis of the transactions: These transactions are similar because each of them decreased cash. They are different from each other because the store supplies are assets while the utilities and employee's salary are expenses. The $120 cost of the supplies should be debited to the Store Supplies asset account, while the $230 for utilities and the $700 salary should be debited to separate expense accounts. Each transaction requires its own credit to Cash.

ACCOUNTS AND THE ACCOUNTING EQUATION

Illustration 3–3 shows the accounts of Clear Copy, Inc., after the 16 transactions have been recorded and the balances computed. The three columns in the illustration relate the accounts to the assets, liabilities, and stockholders' equity elements of the accounting equation. When we take the totals of the balance in each of the three columns, we find that total assets are $40,070 ($7,950 + $0 + $2,400 + $3,720 + $26,000). The total liabilities are $9,200 ($6,200 + $3,000), and the total of the equity accounts is $30,870 ($30,000 − $600 + $4,100 − $1,000 − $1,400 − $230). Thus, the total assets of $40,070 equals the $40,070 sum of the liabilities and the stockholders' equity ($9,200 + $30,870). Cash Dividends Declared and the revenue and expense accounts in the box record the events that change equity; their balances are reported as events on the income statement and statement of retained earnings. Their balances are eventually combined with the balance of the Retained Earnings account to produce the amount of equity reported on the balance sheet. Chapter 5 describes the bookkeeping (closing) process for combining these balances.

Progress Check

3–8 Double-entry accounting requires that:
   a. All transactions that create debits to asset accounts must create credits to liability or stockholders' equity accounts.
   b. A transaction that requires a debit to a liability account must require a credit to an asset account.
   c. Every transaction must be recorded with total debits equal to total credits.

3–9 What kinds of transactions increase stockholders' equity? What kinds decrease stockholders' equity?

3–10 Why are most accounting systems called *double-entry?*

Illustration 3–3   The Ledger for Clear Copy, Inc.

Assets	=	Liabilities	+	Stockholders' Equity

Cash

(1)	30,000	(2)	2,500
(5)	2,200	(3)	20,000
(9)	1,900	(6)	1,000
(12)	3,000	(7)	700
		(10)	900
		(11)	600
		(13)	2,400
		(14)	120
		(15)	230
		(16)	700
Total	37,100	Total	29,150
	−29,150		
Balance	7,950		

Accounts Receivable

(8)	1,900	(9)	1,900

Prepaid Insurance

(13)	2,400	

Store Supplies

(2)	2,500	
(4)	1,100	
(14)	120	
Balance	3,720	

Copy Equipment

(3)	20,000	
(4)	6,000	
Balance	26,000	

Accounts Payable

(10)	900	(4)	7,100
Total	900	Total	7,100
			−900
		Balance	6,200

Unearned Copy Services Revenue

	(12)	3,000

Common Stock, $1 Par Value

	(1)	30,000

Cash Dividends Declared

(11)	600	

Copy Services Revenue

	(5)	2,200
	(8)	1,900
	Bal.	4,100

Rent Expense

(6)	1,000	

Salaries Expense

(7)	700	
(16)	700	
Balance	1,400	

Utilities Expense

(15)	230	

The accounts in this box record increases and decreases in stockholders' equity. Their balances are reported on the income statement or the statement of retained earnings.

$40,070	=	$9,200	+	$30,870

In the preceding pages, we used debits and credits to show how transactions affect accounts. This process of analyzing transactions and recording their effects directly in the accounts is helpful as a learning exercise. However, real accounting systems do not record transactions directly in the accounts. If the bookkeeper recorded the effects directly in the accounts, errors would be easily made and difficult to track down and correct.

To help avoid errors, accounting systems record transactions in a **journal** before recording them in the accounts. This practice provides a complete record of each transaction in one place and links the debits and credits for each transaction. After the debits and credits for each transaction are entered in the journal, they are transferred to the ledger accounts. This two-step process produces useful records for the auditor about a company's transactions. At the same time, the process helps the book-

TRANSACTIONS ARE FIRST RECORDED IN THE JOURNAL

LO 4
Record transactions in a General Journal, describe balance column accounts, and post entries from the journal to the ledger.

80 Chapter 3

Illustration 3–4 The Sequence of Steps in Recording Transactions

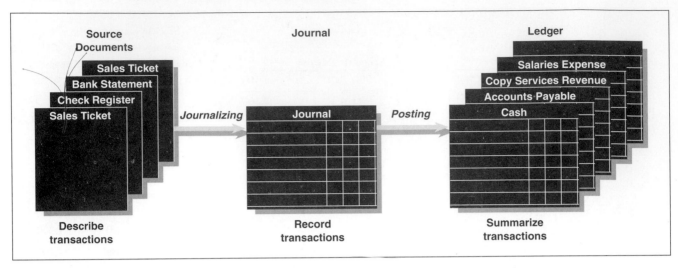

keeper avoid errors. And, if errors are made, the process makes it easier to find and correct them.

The process of recording transactions in a journal is called *journalizing*. The process of transferring journal entry information to the ledger is called **posting.** This sequence of steps is represented in Illustration 3–4. Various source documents provide the evidence that transactions have occurred. Next, these transactions are recorded in the journal. Finally, the journal entries are posted to the ledger. This sequence causes the journal to be called the **book of original entry** while the ledger is sometimes called the **book of final entry.**

The General Journal

The most flexible type of journal is the **General Journal.** The General Journal can be used to record any kind of transaction. A journal entry records this information about each transaction:

1. The transaction's date.
2. The names of the affected accounts.
3. The amount of each debit and credit.
4. An explanation of the transaction.
5. The identifying numbers of the accounts.

Illustration 3–5 shows how the first four transactions for Clear Copy would be recorded in a typical General Journal in a manual system. General Journals used in computerized systems may look like the manual journal page, or they may differ. Regardless of their form or appearance, journals serve the same purpose in every system.

Notice that the fourth entry in Illustration 3–5 uses three accounts to record the credit purchase of store supplies and additional copying equipment. A transaction that affects at least three accounts is recorded in the General Journal with a **compound journal entry.**

Recording Transactions in a General Journal

A bookkeeper follows routine procedures when recording entries in the General Journal. The following steps were used to record the entries in Illustration 3–5. As you read these steps, compare them to the illustration to see how they produced the journal entries:

Illustration 3-5 A General Journal Showing Transactions for Clear Copy, Inc.

			GENERAL JOURNAL				Page 1	
Date			**Account Titles and Explanation**	**PR**	**Debit**		**Credit**	
19X1								
Dec.	1		Cash		30,000	00		
			Common Stock, $1 Par Value				30,000	00
			Issued 30,000 shares to stockholders.					
	2		Store Supplies		2,500	00		
			Cash				2,500	00
			Purchased store supplies for cash.					
	3		Copy Equipment		20,000	00		
			Cash				20,000	00
			Purchased copy equipment for cash.					
	6		Store Supplies		1,100	00		
			Copy Equipment		6,000	00		
			Accounts Payable				7,100	00
			Purchased supplies and equipment on credit.					

1. Enter the year at the top of the first column of the first line on the page.
2. Enter the month on the first line of the journal entry in the first column. (Successive entries in the same month on the same page of the journal would not show the month again.)
3. Enter the day's date for the transaction in the second column on the first line of each entry.
4. Enter the names of the accounts to be debited. The account titles are taken from the chart of accounts and are aligned with the left margin of the Account Titles and Explanation column.
5. Enter the amount debited to each account in the Debit column of the journal on the same line as the account title.
6. Enter the names of the accounts to be credited. The account titles are taken from the chart of accounts and are indented far enough from the left margin of the column to distinguish them from the debited accounts (perhaps as much as an inch).
7. Enter the amount credited to each account in the Credit column of the journal on the same line as the account title.
8. Provide a brief explanation of the transaction to help an auditor or other person understand what happened. The explanation is indented about half as far as the credited account titles to avoid confusing the explanation with either a debit or credit entry. (For clarity, this book italicizes the explanations.)
9. Skip a single line between each journal entry to keep them separate.

Once the journalizing process is completed, the journal entry provides a complete and useful description of the event's effects on the organization.

In a manual system, nothing is entered in the **Posting Reference (PR) column** when a transaction is initially recorded in the journal. As a control over the posting process, the account numbers are not entered until the entries are posted to the ledger. (Because the old word for page was *folio* and because each account used to be a separate page in a book, the Posting Reference column in the journal is occasionally called the *folio column*.)

Computerized Journals. Journals in computerized accounting systems serve the same purpose of providing a complete record of each transaction. In some systems, they even look like the manual journal page in Illustration 3–5. In addition, they may include error-checking routines that ensure the debits in the entry equal the credits. They often provide shortcuts that allow the computer operator to enter account numbers instead of names, or to enter the account names and numbers with pull-down menus or other easy-to-use techniques.

BALANCE COLUMN ACCOUNTS

T-accounts are used in textbooks and accounting classes to show how accounts work. T-accounts are helpful because they allow you to disregard some details and concentrate on the main ideas. Actual accounting systems, however, use **balance column accounts** like the one in Illustration 3–6.

The balance column account format is similar to a T-account because it has columns for entering each debit and credit. It is different because it provides space for the entry's date and any explanation that might be needed. It also has a third column for showing the balance of the account after each entry is posted. As a result, the amount on the last line in this column is the account's current balance. For example, Clear Copy's Cash account in Illustration 3–6 was debited on December 1 for the $30,000 issuance of common stock. As a result, the account had a $30,000 debit balance. The account was then credited on December 2 for $2,500, and its new $27,500 balance was entered in the third column. On December 3, it was credited again, this time for $20,000, and its balance was reduced to $7,500. Finally, the Cash account was debited for $2,200 on December 10, and its balance was increased to $9,700.

When the balance column format is used, the heading of the Balance column does not indicate whether the account has a debit or credit balance. However, this omission should not create any problems because every account has a *normal balance*. The normal balance of each type of account (asset, liability, stockholders' equity, revenue, or expense) is the same as the debit or credit entry used to record an increase in the account. This table shows the normal balances for accounts:

Type of Account	Increases Are Recorded as	Normal Balance
Asset	Debits	Debit
Liability	Credits	Credit
Stockholders' equity:		
Common stock	Credits	Credit
Retained earnings	Credits	Credit
Cash dividends declared	Debits	Debit
Revenue	Credits	Credit
Expense	Debits	Debit

Abnormal Balances. Some unusual events may cause an account to have an abnormal balance. For example, a credit customer might accidentally pay its balance twice, which would give the account receivable a credit balance instead of a zero balance. If an abnormal balance is created, the bookkeeper can identify it by circling the amount or by entering the balance in red or some other nonstandard color. Many com-

Illustration 3–6   The Cash Account for Clear Copy, Inc., in the Balance Column Format

Date			Explanation	PR	Debit		Credit		Balance	
19X1										
Dec.	1			G1	30,000	00			30,000	00
	2			G1			2,500	00	27,500	00
	3			G1			20,000	00	7,500	00
	10			G1	2,200	00			9,700	00

puterized systems automatically provide a code beside the balance, such as *dr.* or *cr.* to identify the kind of balance.

Zero Balances.   If an account has a zero balance, it is customary to indicate that fact by writing zeros or a dash in the Balance column. This practice avoids confusion between a zero balance and an accidentally omitted balance.

POSTING JOURNAL ENTRIES

Illustration 3–4 on page 80 shows that journal entries are posted to the accounts in the ledger. To ensure that the ledger is up to date, journal entries are posted as promptly as possible, which may be daily, weekly, or as time permits. All entries need to be posted before the end of the reporting period to provide the accounts with up-dated balances when the financial statements are prepared.

When posting the entries to the ledger, the bookkeeper copies the debits in the journal entries into the accounts as debits, and copies the journal entry credits into the accounts as credits. The diagram in Illustration 3–7 identifies the six steps used in a manual system to post each debit and credit from the journal entry. Use the diagram to see how these six steps are completed:

For the debit:

1. Find the account that was debited in the journal entry.
2. Enter the date of the journal entry in the account on the next available line for the debit.
3. Write the amount debited in the journal entry in the Debit column of the account.
4. To show where the debit came from, enter the letter *G* and the journal page number in the Posting Reference (PR) column for the account. (The letter *G* shows that the posted entry came from the General Journal. Other journals are identified by their own letters. We discuss other journals in Appendix C at the end of the book.)
5. Calculate and enter the account's new balance in the third column.
6. To show that the posting process is complete, enter the account number in the Posting Reference column on the entry's line in the journal. (If posting is interrupted, the bookkeeper can use the journal's Posting Reference column to take up the process where it was stopped.)

For the credit:
Repeat the six steps. However, the credit amount is entered in the Credit column and has a credit effect on the account balance.

Illustration 3-7 Six Steps for Posting a General Journal Entry to the Ledger.

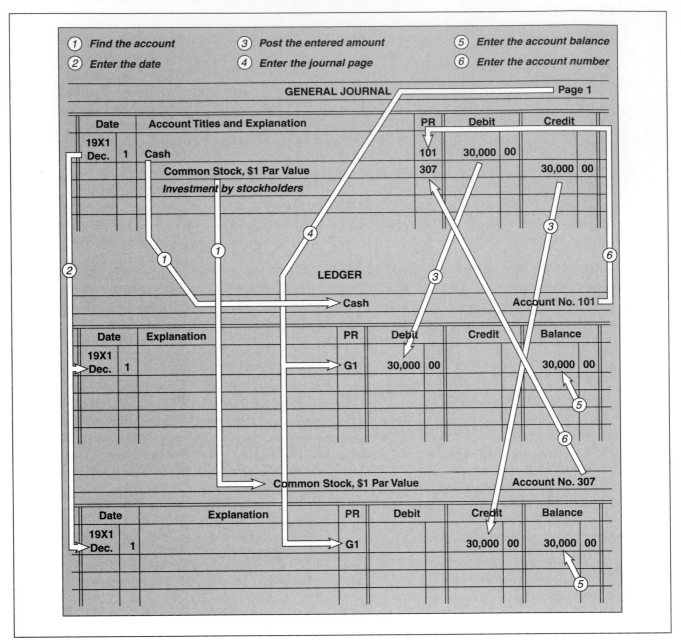

Notice that step 6 in the posting procedure for either the debit or the credit of an entry inserts the account number in the journal's Posting Reference column. This creates a link between the ledger and the journal entry. This link provides a cross-reference that helps the bookkeeper and the auditor trace an amount from one record to the other.

Posting in Computerized Systems. Computerized accounting systems do not require any additional effort by the operator to post the journal entries to the ledger. The programs in the systems are designed to automatically transfer the debit and credit entries from the journal into the database. In effect, the journal entries are posted directly into the accounts in the ledger without any additional steps. Many systems include error-detection routines that test the reasonableness of the journal entry and the account balance when the new entry is recorded.

Progress Check

3-11 When Davis Shipping was incorporated, Brian Davis purchased common stock in exchange for $15,000 cash and land with a fair market value of $23,000. The corporation also assumed responsibility for an $18,000 note payable originally issued to finance the purchase of the land. The journal entry to record this investment consists of: *(a)* one debit and one credit; *(b)* two debits and one credit; *(c)* two debits and two credits; or *(d)* debits that total $38,000 and credits that total $33,000.

3-12 What is a compound journal entry?

3-13 Why are posting reference numbers entered in the journal when entries are posted to the accounts?

PREPARING AND USING THE TRIAL BALANCE

LO 5
Prepare a trial balance, explain its usefulness, and calculate a company's debt ratio.

Recall that a double-entry accounting system records every transaction with equal debits and credits. As a result, the bookkeeper can tell that an error has occurred if the sum of the debit entries in the ledger does not equal the sum of the credit entries. The bookkeeper also knows that an error has occurred if the sum of the debit account balances does not equal the sum of the credit balances.

One purpose for preparing a **trial balance** is to find out if the debit and credit account balances are equal. A trial balance is a summary of the ledger that is a list of the accounts and their balances. The account balances are placed in either the debit or credit column of the trial balance. Illustration 3–8 presents the trial balance for Clear Copy after the 16 entries described earlier in the chapter have been posted to the ledger.

The trial balance also serves as a helpful internal document for preparing the financial statements. The task of preparing the statements is simplified if the accountant can take the account balances from the trial balance instead of looking them up in the ledger. (Chapter 4 describes the statement preparation process in more detail.)

The bookkeeper uses these five steps to prepare a trial balance:

1. Find the balance of each account in the ledger.
2. List each account and place its balance beside it. Debit balances are entered in the Debit column and credit balances are entered in the Credit column. (If an account has a zero balance, it may be included in the trial balance with a zero in the column for its normal balance.)
3. Compute the total of the debit balances.
4. Compute the total of the credit balances.
5. Verify that the sum of the debit balances equals the sum of the credit balances.

The trial balance for Clear Copy in Illustration 3–8 is presented in a typical format. Notice that the total of the debit balances equals the total of the credit balances. If the two totals were not equal, we would know that at least one error had occurred. However, the fact that the two totals are equal does not prove that all errors were avoided.

The Information Provided by a Trial Balance

When a trial balance does not balance (that is, the columns are not equal), we know that at least one error has occurred. The error (or errors) may have occurred during these steps in the accounting process: (1) preparing journal entries, (2) posting journal entries to the ledger, (3) calculating account balances, (4) copying account balances to the trial balance, or (5) totaling the trial balance columns.

If the trial balance does balance, the accounts are likely to be free from errors that create unequal debits and credits. However, bookkeeping accuracy is not assured if the column totals are equal because some errors do not create unequal debits and

Illustration 3–8

CLEAR COPY, INC.
Trial Balance
December 31, 19X1

	Debit	Credit
Cash	$ 7,950	
Accounts receivable	0	
Prepaid insurance	2,400	
Store supplies	3,720	
Copy equipment	26,000	
Accounts payable		$ 6,200
Unearned copy services revenue		3,000
Common stock, $1 par value		30,000
Cash dividends declared	600	
Copy services revenue		4,100
Rent expense	1,000	
Salaries expense	1,400	
Utilities expense	230	
Total	$43,300	$43,300

credits. For example, the bookkeeper may debit a correct amount to the wrong account in preparing the journal entry or in posting a journal entry to the ledger. This error would cause two accounts to have incorrect balances but the trial balance would not be out of balance. Another error would be to record equal debits and credits of an incorrect amount. This error would give the two accounts incorrect balances but would not create unequal debits and credits. As a result, the fact that the trial balance column totals are equal does not prove that all journal entries have been recorded and posted correctly. However, equal totals do suggest that several types of errors probably have not occurred.

Searching for Errors

If the trial balance does not balance, at least one error has occurred. The error (or errors) need to be found and corrected before going on to prepare the financial statements. The search for the error is more efficient if the bookkeeper checks the journalizing, posting, and trial balance preparation steps in reverse order.

First, the bookkeeper should verify that the trial balance columns were correctly added. Second, if that step does not find the error, the bookkeeper should verify that account balances were accurately copied from the ledger. Third, the bookkeeper should check to see if a debit or credit balance was mistakenly listed in the trial balance as a credit or debit. (A clue to this kind of error would be that the difference between the total debits and total credits in the trial balance would equal twice the amount of the incorrectly listed account balance.)

If the error remains undiscovered, the bookkeeper's fourth step is to recalculate each account balance. Then, if the error is not found, it is necessary to verify that each journal entry was properly posted to the accounts. Finally, the only remaining (and least likely) source of the error would be an original journal entry that did not have equal debits and credits.

One frequent error is called a *transposition*. This error occurs when two digits are switched or transposed within a number. For example, a $691 debit in a journal entry may be posted to the ledger as $619. If this happens and it is the only error, the difference between the two trial balance columns is evenly divisible by nine. For example, suppose that a posting error places a $619 debit in an account instead of the journal's correct amount of $691. As a result, the total credits in the trial balance would be larger than the total debits by $72 ($691 − $619). This number is evenly divisible by 9 ($72/9 = 8$). Furthermore, the quotient (8) equals the difference between the two transposed numbers. The number of digits in the quotient also signals the location of the transposition. In this example, the fact that the quotient (8) has only one digit tells us that the transposition occurred in the first digit of the transposed numbers, starting from the right.[4]

Correcting Errors

If errors are discovered in either the journal or the ledger, they need to be corrected to ensure that the financial statements provide useful information. The approach to correcting the records depends on the nature of the errors and when they are discovered.

If an error in a journal entry is discovered before the error is posted, it can be corrected in a manual system by drawing a line through the incorrect information. Then, the correct information can be written above it to create a record of the change for the auditor. (Most computerized systems allow the operator to simply replace the incorrect information.) If a correct amount in the journal was posted incorrectly in the ledger, the bookkeeper can correct it the same way.

If an error in a journal entry is not discovered before it is posted, the correction may have to be done differently. For example, suppose that a journal entry incorrectly debited (or credited) the wrong account. If the journal entry has already been posted to that incorrect account, the bookkeeper generally does not strike through both erroneous entries in the journal and ledger. Instead, the usual practice is to correct the error in the original journal entry by creating another journal entry. This *correcting entry* removes the amount from the wrong account and moves it to the right account. For example, suppose that the bookkeeper recorded a purchase of office supplies with this incorrect debit in the journal entry to the Office Equipment account and then posted it to the accounts in the ledger:

Oct.	14	Office Equipment	1,600.00	
		Cash		1,600.00
		To record the purchase of office supplies.		

As a result of posting this incorrect entry, the Office Supplies account balance is too small (understated) by $1,600 and the Office Equipment account balance is too large (overstated) by the same amount. Three days later, the error is discovered and the following entry is made to correct both account balances:

Oct.	17	Office Supplies	1,600.00	
		Office Equipment		1,600.00
		To record the entry of October 14 that incorrectly		
		debited Office Equipment instead of Office Supplies.		

The credit in the correcting entry cancels the error from the first entry, and the debit correctly records the supplies. The explanation in the correcting entry allows the auditor to know exactly what happened.

Similar correcting entries may be needed in computerized accounting systems. The exact procedure depends on the particular program being used.

---

[4]If the transposition error had posted $961 instead of the correct $691, the difference would have been $270, and the quotient would have been $30 ($270/9). The fact that the quotient has two digits tells us to carefully examine the second digits from the right for a transposition of two numbers with a difference of 3.

OTHER FORMATTING CONVENTIONS

When amounts are entered manually on ruled accounting paper in a journal, ledger, or trial balance, commas are not needed to indicate thousands and decimal points are not needed to separate dollars and cents. However, commas and decimal points are used in financial statements and other reports.

As a matter of convenience, dollar signs are not used in journals and ledgers. However, they do appear in financial statements and other reports, including trial balances. This book follows the practice of putting a dollar sign beside the first amount in each column of numbers and the first amount appearing after a ruled line indicating that an addition or subtraction has been performed. The financial statements in Illustrations 2–8 and 2–9 on pages 44 and 45 demonstrate how dollar signs are used in this book. Different companies use various conventions for dollar signs. For example, dollar signs are used beside only the first and last numbers in the columns in the financial statements for **Southwest Airlines Co.** in Appendix E.

If an amount entered manually in a ledger or a journal consists of even dollars without cents, a convenient shortcut uses a dash in the cents column instead of two zeros. To simplify the illustrations, this book usually shows exact dollar amounts.

Even small companies seldom show decimal points or cents in their financial statements. Normally, the amounts are rounded, perhaps to the nearest dollar but often to a higher level. **Exxon Corporation** is typical of many very large companies in that it rounds its financial statement amounts to the nearest million dollars.

USING THE INFORMATION— THE DEBT RATIO

With so much emphasis in this chapter on bookkeeping activities, it might be easy to temporarily overlook the fact that accounting records are created for the purpose of providing useful information in financial statements. This chapter closes by describing a ratio that users apply to assess a company's risk of failing to pay its debts when they are due.

Almost all companies finance some portion of their assets with liabilities and the remaining portion with equity. A company that finances a relatively large portion of its assets with liabilities is said to have a high degree of financial leverage.

You learn more about financial leverage in Chapter 14. However, you should understand that financial leverage involves risk. Because liabilities must be repaid and also require a company to pay interest, the risk of liabilities is that the company may not be able to make the required payments. In general, the risk is higher if a company is highly leveraged.

One way to evaluate the risk associated with a company's use of liabilities to finance its assets is to calculate and evaluate the **debt ratio.** This ratio describes the relationship between the amounts of the company's iiabilities and assets, as follows:

$$\text{Debt ratio} = \frac{\textbf{Total liabilities}}{\textbf{Total assets}}$$

To see how the debt ratio is applied, consider the example of **Chiquita Brands International, Inc.,** discussed at the beginning of the chapter. Using the data that was presented on page 63, the company's debt ratios at the end of each year from 1990 through 1994 are as follows:

	1994	1993	1992	1991	1990
a. Total liabilities	$2,257,212	$2,138,755	$2,205,737	$1,969,419	$1,225,965
b. Total assets	2,902,021	2,740,753	2,880,624	2,937,344	1,913,674
c. Debt ratio (*a* ÷ *b*)	.778	.780	.766	.670	.641

Evaluating a company's debt ratio depends on several factors such as the nature of its operations, its ability to generate cash flows, the economic conditions at the time, and the industry in which it operates. Thus, it is not possible to say that a specific debt ratio is good for all companies.

However, notice that Chiquita's debt ratio increased each year since 1990. In the company's 1993 annual report, Chiquita's executives said they had adopted a strategy of de-leveraging the company's balance sheet in the future. In other words, they decided that the company's debt ratio had become too high.

To reduce the ratio in the future, they might use the cash provided by profitable operations to repay debt. Also, they might obtain additional money from the owners and use it to repay debt. A third possibility would be to sell some assets and use the proceeds to repay debt.

Progress Check

3-14   Which of the following terms describes a list of all of a company's accounts and their iden-tifying numbers?   *(a)* A journal;   *(b)* A ledger;   *(c)* A trial balance;   *(d)* A source docu-ment;   *(e)* A chart of accounts.

3-15   When are dollar signs used in accounting reports?

3-16   A $4,000 debit to Store Equipment in a journal entry was incorrectly posted to the ledger as a $4,000 credit, and the account had a resulting debit balance of $20,000. What is the effect of the error on the trial balance column totals?

3-17   Which debt ratio implies more risk, ignoring other factors?   *(a)* 6.6;   *(b)* 5.0.

SUMMARY OF THE CHAPTER IN TERMS OF LEARNING OBJECTIVES

LO 1. Describe the events recorded in accounting systems and the importance of source documents and business papers in those systems. Accounting systems record transactions and other events that affect a company's assets, liabilities, and equity. The other events include internal transactions that use up assets or external events that cause the company's assets or liabilities to change. Source documents describe information that is recorded with accounting entries.

LO 2. Describe how accounts are used to record information about the effects of transactions, how code numbers are used to identify each account, and the meaning of the words *debit* and *credit*. An account is a location in which the increases and de-creases in a particular asset, liability, stockholders' equity, revenue, or expense item are recorded and stored. The ledger is the collection of accounts used by an organization. Each account is assigned an identification number based on a code that indicates what kind of account it is. Debits record increases in asset, dividends declared, and expense ac-counts. Credits record decreases in these same accounts. Credits also record increases in liabilities, stockholders' equity, and revenues, while debits record decreases in these accounts.

LO 3. Describe how debits and credits are used to analyze transactions and record their effects in the accounts. To understand how a transaction affects a business, deter-mine what accounts were increased or decreased. Every transaction affects at least two accounts, and the sum of the debits for each transaction equals the sum of the credits. As a result, the effects of business transactions never create an imbalance in the accounting equation (Assets = Liabilities + Stockholders' Equity).

LO 4. Record transactions in a General Journal, describe balance column ac-counts, and post entries from the journal to the ledger. Transactions are first recorded in a journal that provides a record of all their effects in one location. Second, each entry in the journal is posted to the accounts in the ledger. This process places information in the accounts that is used to produce the company's financial statements. Balance column accounts are widely used in accounting systems. These accounts include columns for debit entries, credit entries, and the balance after each entry.

LO 5. Prepare a trial balance, explain its usefulness, and calculate a company's debt ratio. A trial balance is a list of the accounts in the ledger that shows their debit and credit balances in separate columns. The trial balance is a convenient summary of the ledger's contents. It also reveals the existence of some kinds of errors if the sum of the debit account balances does not equal the sum of the credit account balances. A company's debt ratio is the ratio between its total liabilities and total assets. It provides information about the risk a company faces by using liabilities to finance its assets.

DEMONSTRATION PROBLEM

This demonstration problem is based on the same facts as the demonstration problem at the end of Chapter 2. The following events occurred during the first month of a new haircutting business called Cutlery Corporation:

a. On August 1, Cutlery Corporation issued 18,000 shares of $1 par value common stock to Barbara Schmidt in exchange for a cash investment of $3,000 and $15,000 of equipment that she already owned.

b. On August 2, paid $600 cash for furniture for the shop.

c. On August 3, paid $500 cash to rent space in a strip mall for August.

d. On August 4, furnished the shop by installing the old equipment and some new equipment purchased on credit for $1,200. This amount is to be repaid in three equal payments at the end of August, September, and October.

e. On August 5, Cutlery Corporation opened for business. Receipts from cash sales in the first week and a half of business (ended August 15) were $1,025.

f. On August 17, paid $125 wages to an assistant for working during the grand opening.

g. Cash receipts from sales during the second half of August were $1,730.

h. On August 31, paid an installment on the accounts payable.

i. On August 31, paid Barbara Schmidt a $1,000 salary.

j. On August 31, declared and paid a $900 cash dividend.

Required

1. Prepare general journal entries for the preceding transactions.
2. Open the following accounts: Cash, 101; Furniture, 161; Store Equipment, 165; Accounts Payable, 201; Common Stock, $1 Par Value, 307; Cash Dividends Declared, 319; Haircutting Services Revenue, 403; Salaries Expense, 622; Wages Expense, 623; and Rent Expense, 640.
3. Post the journal entries to the ledger accounts.
4. Prepare a trial balance as of August 31.

Planning the Solution

- Analyze each transaction to identify the accounts affected by the transaction and the amount of each effect.
- Use the debit and credit rules to prepare a journal entry for each transaction.
- Post each debit and each credit in the journal entries to the appropriate ledger accounts and cross-reference each amount in the Posting Reference columns in the journal and the accounts.
- Calculate each account balance and list the accounts with their balances on a trial balance.
- Verify that the total debits in the trial balance equal total credits.

1. General journal entries:

Page 1

Date		Account Titles and Explanations	PR	Debit	Credit
Aug.	1	Cash	101	3,000.00	
		Store Equipment	165	15,000.00	
		Common Stock, $1 Par Value	307		18,000.00
		Issued 18,000 shares.			
	2	Furniture	161	600.00	
		Cash	101		600.00
		Purchased furniture for cash.			
	3	Rent Expense	640	500.00	
		Cash	101		500.00
		Paid rent for August.			
	4	Store Equipment	165	1,200.00	
		Accounts Payable	201		1,200.00
		Purchased additional equipment on credit.			
	15	Cash	101	825.00	
		Haircutting Services Revenue	403		825.00
		Cash receipts from ten days of operations.			
	17	Wages Expense	623	125.00	
		Cash	101		125.00
		Paid wages to assistant.			
	31	Cash	101	930.00	
		Haircutting Services Revenue	403		930.00
		Cash receipts from second half of August.			
	31	Accounts Payable	201	400.00	
		Cash	101		400.00
		Paid an installment on accounts payable.			
	31	Salaries Expense	622	1,000.00	
		Cash	101		1,000.00
		Paid Schmidt's salary.			
	31	Cash Dividends Declared	319	900.00	
		Cash	101		900.00
		Declared and paid a cash dividend.			

2. 3. Accounts in the ledger:

Cash   **Account No.** 101

Date		Explanation	PR	Debit	Credit	Balance
Aug.	1		G1	3,000.00		3,000.00
	2		G1		600.00	2,400.00
	3		G1		500.00	1,900.00
	15		G1	1,025.00		2,925.00
	17		G1		125.00	2,800.00
	31		G1	1,730.00		4,530.00
	31		G1		400.00	4,130.00
	31		G1		1,000.00	3,130.00
	31		G1		900.00	2,230.00

Furniture   Account No. 161

Date		Explanation	PR	Debit	Credit	Balance
Aug.	2		G1	600.00		600.00

Store Equipment   Account No. 165

Date		Explanation	PR	Debit	Credit	Balance
Aug.	1		G1	15,000.00		15,000.00
	4		G1	1,200.00		16,200.00

Accounts Payable   Account No. 201

Date		Explanation	PR	Debit	Credit	Balance
Aug.	4		G1		1,200.00	1,200.00
	31		G1	400.00		800.00

Common Stock, $1 Par Value   Account No. 307

Date		Explanation	PR	Debit	Credit	Balance
Aug.	1		G1		18,000.00	18,000.00

Cash Dividends Declared   Account No. 319

Date		Explanation	PR	Debit	Credit	Balance
Aug.	31		G1	900.00		900.00

Haircutting Services Revenue   Account No. 403

Date		Explanation	PR	Debit	Credit	Balance
Aug.	15		G1		1,025.00	1,025.00
	31		G1		1,730.00	2,755.00

Salaries Expense   Account No. 622

Date		Explanation	PR	Debit	Credit	Balance
Aug.	31		G1	1,000.00		1,000.00

Wages Expense   Account No. 623

Date		Explanation	PR	Debit	Credit	Balance
Aug.	17		G1	125.00		125.00

Rent Expense   Account No. 640

Date		Explanation	PR	Debit	Credit	Balance
Aug.	3		G1	500.00		500.00

4.

CUTLERY CORPORATION
Trial Balance
August 31, 19X1

	Debit	Credit
Cash	$ 2,230	
Furniture	600	
Store equipment	16,200	
Accounts payable		$ 800
Common stock, $1 par value		18,000
Cash dividends declared	900	
Haircutting services revenue		2,755
Salaries expense	1,000	
Wages expense	125	
Rent expense	500	
Totals	$21,555	$21,555

GLOSSARY

Account a place or location within an accounting system in which the increases and decreases in a specific asset, liability, stockholders' equity, revenue, or expense are recorded and stored. p. 66

Account balance the difference between the increases (including the beginning balance) and decreases recorded in an account. p. 71

Balance column account an account with debit and credit columns for recording entries and a third column for showing the balance of the account after each entry is posted. p. 82

Book of final entry another name for a ledger. p. 80

Book of original entry another name for a journal. p. 80

Business papers various kinds of documents and other papers that companies use when they conduct their business; sometimes called *source documents*. p. 65

Chart of accounts a list of all accounts used by a company; includes the identification number assigned to each account. p. 70

Compound journal entry a journal entry that affects at least three accounts. p. 80

Credit an entry that decreases asset and expense accounts or increases liability, stockholders' equity, and revenue accounts; recorded on the right side of a T-account. p. 72

Debit an entry that increases asset and expense accounts or decreases liability, stockholders' equity, and revenue accounts; recorded on the left side of a T-account. p. 72

Debt ratio the ratio between a company's total liabilities and total assets; used to describe the risk associated with the company's debts. p. 88

Double-entry accounting an accounting system that records the effects of transactions and other events in at least two accounts with equal debits and credits. p. 73

External transactions exchanges between the entity and some other person or organization. p. 64

General Journal the most flexible type of journal; can be used to record any kind of transaction. p. 80

Internal transactions a term occasionally used to describe economic events that affect an entity's accounting equation but that are not transactions between two parties. p. 64

Journal a record in which the effects of transactions are first recorded; amounts are posted from the journal to the ledger; also called the *book of original entry*. p. 79

Ledger the collection of all accounts used by a business. p. 70

Posting the process of copying journal entry information to the ledger. p. 80

Posting Reference (PR) column a column in journals and accounts used to cross-reference journal and ledger entries. p. 81

Prepaid expenses assets created by payments for economic benefits that are not used until later; as the benefits are used up, the cost of the assets becomes an expense. p. 68

Promissory note an unconditional written promise to pay a definite sum of money on demand or on a defined future date (or dates). p. 67

Source documents another name for business papers; these documents are the source of information recorded with accounting entries. p. 65

T-account a simple account form widely used in accounting education to illustrate how debits and credits work. p. 71

Trial balance a summary of the ledger that lists the accounts and their balances; the total debit balances should equal the total credit balances. p. 85

Unearned revenues liabilities created by cash receipts from customers for products or services they have not yet received; satisfied by delivering the products or services in the future. p. 69

QUESTIONS

1. What are the three fundamental steps in the accounting process?

2. What is the difference between a note receivable and an account receivable?

3. If assets are valuable resources and asset accounts have debit balances, why do expense accounts have debit balances?

4. Why does the bookkeeper prepare a trial balance?

5. Should a transaction be recorded first in a journal or the ledger? Why?

6. Are debits or credits listed first in general journal entries? Are the debits or the credits indented?

7. What kinds of transactions can be recorded in a General Journal?

8. If a wrong amount was journalized and posted to the accounts, how should the error be corrected?

9. Review the 1995 consolidated statement of cash flows for Lands' End, Inc., in Appendix F. What was the total effect on the company's Cash account from the proceeds from short-term and long-term debt? Were these transactions recorded with debits or credits to the Cash account?

10. Review the 1994 consolidated statement of cash flows for Southwest Airlines Co. in Appendix E. What was the total effect on the company's Cash account from the payment of long-term debt and capital lease obligations? Were these transactions recorded with debits or credits to the Cash account?

QUICK STUDY (Five-Minute Exercises)

QS 3–1
(LO 1)

Select the items from the following list that are likely to serve as source documents:

a. Income statement.
b. Trial balance.
c. Telephone bill.
d. Invoice from supplier.
e. Cash Dividends Declared account.
f. Balance sheet.
g. Bank statement.
h. Sales ticket.

QS 3–2
(LO 2)

Indicate the financial statement on which each of the following accounts appears, using IS for income statement, SRE for the statement of retained earnings, and BS for balance sheet:

a. Buildings.
b. Interest Earned.
c. Cash Dividends Declared.
d. Common Stock.
e. Prepaid Insurance.
f. Interest Payable.
g. Accounts Receivable.
h. Salaries Expense.
i. Office Supplies.
j. Repair Services Revenue.

QS 3–3
(LO 3)

Indicate whether a debit or credit is necessary to *decrease* the normal balance of each of the following accounts:

a. Buildings.
b. Interest Earned.
c. Cash Dividends Declared.
d. Common Stock.
e. Prepaid Insurance.
f. Interest Payable.
g. Accounts Receivable.
h. Salaries Expense.
i. Office Supplies.
j. Repair Services Revenue.

QS 3–4
(LO 2, 3)

Identify whether a debit or credit entry would be made to record the indicated change in each of the following accounts:

a. To increase Notes Payable.
b. To decrease Accounts Receivable.
c. To increase Common Stock.
d. To decrease Unearned Fees.
e. To decrease Prepaid Insurance.
f. To decrease Cash.
g. To increase Utilities Expense.
h. To increase Fees Earned.

i. To increase Store Equipment. j. To increase Cash Dividends Declared.

Prepare journal entries for the following transactions:

a. On January 15, a landscaping business issued 10,000 shares of $10 par value common stock in exchange for $60,000 and equipment having a $40,000 fair value.

b. On January 20, purchased office supplies on credit for $340.

c. On January 28, received $5,200 in return for providing landscaping services to a customer.

QS 3–5
(LO 4)

A trial balance has total debits of $21,000 and total credits of $25,500. Which one of the following errors would create this imbalance? Explain.

a A $4,500 debit to Salaries Expense in a journal entry was incorrectly posted to the ledger as a $4,500 credit, leaving the Salaries Expense account with a $750 debit balance.

b. A $2,250 credit to Consulting Fees Earned in a journal entry was incorrectly posted to the ledger as a $2,250 debit, leaving the Consulting Fees Earned account with a $6,300 credit balance.

c. A $2,250 debit to Rent Expense in a journal entry was incorrectly posted to the ledger as a $2,250 credit, leaving the Rent Expense account with a $3,000 debit balance.

QS 3 6
(LO 5)

EXERCISES

Complete the following table by (1) identifying the type of account listed on each line, (2) entering *debit* or *credit* in the blank spaces to identify the kind of entry that would increase or decrease the account balance, and (3) identifying the normal balance of the account.

Exercise 3–1
Increases, decreases, and
normal balances of accounts
(LO 2, 3)

	Account	Type of Account	Increase	Decrease	Normal Balance
a.	Land				
b.	Retained earnings				
c.	Accounts receivable				
d.	Cash dividends declared				
e.	Cash				
f.	Equipment				
g.	Unearned revenue				
h.	Accounts payable				
i.	Postage expense				
j.	Prepaid insurance				
k.	Wages expense				
l.	Fees earned				

Davis & Garret, P.C., recently notified a client that it would have to pay a $48,000 fee for accounting services. Unfortunately, the client did not have enough cash to pay the entire bill. Davis & Garret agreed to accept the following items in full payment: $7,500 cash and computer equipment worth $75,000. The company also had to assume responsibility for a $34,500 note payable related to the equipment. The entry Davis & Garret would make to record this transaction would include which of the following:

a. $34,500 increase in a liability account.

b. $7,500 increase in the Cash account.

c. $7,500 increase in a revenue account.

Exercise 3–2
Analyzing the effects of a
transaction on the accounts
(LO 3)

d. $48,000 increase in the Davis & Garret Retained Earnings account.

e. $48,000 increase in a revenue account.

Exercise 3–3
Recording the effects of transactions directly in T-accounts
(LO 3)

Open the following T-accounts: Cash; Accounts Receivable; Office Supplies; Office Equipment; Accounts Payable; Common Stock, $5 Par Value; Fees Earned; and Rent Expense. Next, record these transactions of the Global Corporation by recording the debit and credit entries directly in the T-accounts. Use the letters beside each transaction to identify the entries. Finally, determine the balance of each account.

a. Issued 2,550 shares of common stock in exchange for $12,750 cash.

b. Purchased $375 of office supplies for cash.

c. Purchased $7,050 of office equipment on credit.

d. Received $1,500 cash as fees for services provided to a customer.

e. Paid for the office equipment purchased in transaction c.

f. Billed a customer $2,700 as fees for services.

g. Paid the monthly rent with $525 cash.

h. Collected $1,125 of the account receivable created in transaction f.

Exercise 3–4
Preparing a trial balance
(LO 5)

After recording the transactions of Exercise 3–3 in T-accounts and calculating the balance of each account, prepare the trial balance for the ledger. Use May 31, 19X1, as the date.

Exercise 3–5
Effects of posting errors on the trial balance
(LO 5)

Complete the following table by filling in the blanks. For each of the listed posting errors, enter in column (1) the amount of the difference that the error would create between the two trial balance columns (show a zero if the columns would balance). If there would be a difference between the two columns, identify in column (2) the trial balance column that would be larger. The answer for the first error is provided as an example.

	Description	(1) Difference between Debit and Credit Columns	(2) Column with the Larger Total
a.	A $2,400 debit to Rent Expense was posted as a $1,590 debit.	$810	credit
b.	A $42,000 debit to Machinery was posted as a debit to Accounts Payable.		
c.	A $4,950 credit to Services Revenue was posted as a $495 credit.		
d.	A $1,440 debit to Store Supplies was not posted at all.		
e.	A $2,250 debit to Prepaid Insurance was posted as a debit to Insurance Expense.		
f.	A $4,050 credit to Cash was posted twice as two credits to the Cash account.		
g.	A $9,900 debit to Cash Dividends Declared was debited to Common Stock.		

Exercise 3–6
Analyzing a trial balance error
(LO 5)

As the bookkeeper for a company, you are disappointed to learn that the column totals in your new trial balance are not equal. After going through a careful analysis, you have discovered only one error. Specifically, the balance of the Office Equipment account has a debit balance of $23,400 on the trial balance. However, you have figured out that a correctly recorded credit purchase of a computer for $5,250 was posted from the journal to the ledger with a $5,250 debit to Office Equipment and another $5,250 debit to Accounts Payable. Answer each of the following questions and present the dollar amount of any misstatement:

a. Is the balance of the Office Equipment account overstated, understated, or correctly stated in the trial balance?

b. Is the balance of the Accounts Payable account overstated, understated, or correctly stated in the trial balance?

c. Is the debit column total of the trial balance overstated, understated, or correctly stated?

d. Is the credit column total of the trial balance overstated, understated, or correctly stated?

e. If the debit column total of the trial balance is $360,000 before correcting the error, what is the total of the credit column?

On January 1, Jan Taylor created a new business called The Party Place, Inc. Near the end of the year, she hired a new bookkeeper without making a careful reference check. As a result, a number of mistakes have been made in preparing the following trial balance:

Exercise 3–7
Preparing a corrected trial balance
(LO 5)

THE PARTY PLACE, INC.
Trial Balance
December 31

	Debit	Credit
Cash	$ 5,500	
Accounts receivable		$ 7,900
Office supplies	2,650	
Office equipment	20,500	
Accounts payable		9,465
Common stock, $1 par value	16,745	
Services revenue		22,350
Wages expense		6,000
Rent expense		4,800
Advertising expense		1,250
Totals	$45,395	$52,340

Taylor's analysis of the situation has uncovered these errors:

a. The sum of the debits in the Cash account is $37,175 and the sum of the credits is $30,540.

b. A $275 payment from a credit customer was posted to Cash but was not posted to Accounts Receivable.

c. A credit purchase of office supplies for $400 was completely unrecorded.

d. A transposition error occurred in copying the balance of the Services Revenue account to the trial balance. The correct amount was $23,250.

Other errors were made in placing account balances in the trial balance columns and in taking the totals of the columns. Use all this information to prepare a correct trial balance.

Use the information in each of the following situations to calculate the unknown amount:

a. During October, Ridgeway Corporation had $97,500 of cash receipts and $101,250 of cash disbursements. The October 31 Cash balance was $16,800. Determine how much cash the company had on hand at the close of business on September 30.

Exercise 3–8
Analyzing account entries and balances
(LO 2, 3)

b. On September 30, Ridgeway had a $97,500 balance in Accounts Receivable. During October, the company collected $88,950 from its credit customers. The October 31 balance in Accounts Receivable was $100,500. Determine the amount of sales on account that occurred in October.

c. Ridgeway had $147,000 of accounts payable on September 30 and $136,500 on October 31. Total purchases on account during October were $270,000. Determine how much cash was paid on accounts payable during October.

Seven transactions were posted to these T-accounts. Provide a short description of each trans-

Exercise 3–9
Analyzing transactions from T-accounts
(LO 2, 3)

action. Include the amounts in your descriptions.
Use the information in the T-accounts in Exercise 3–9 to prepare general journal entries for

	Cash				Automobiles	
(a)	7,000	(b)	3,600	(a)	11,000	
(e)	2,500	(c)	600			
		(f)	2,400			
		(g)	700			

		Accounts Payable	
(f)	2,400	(d)	9,600

	Office Supplies				Common Stock, $1 Par Value	
(c)	600				(a)	23,600
(d)	200					

	Prepaid Insurance			Delivery Services Revenue	
(b)	3,600			(e)	2,500

	Equipment				Gas and Oil Expense	
(a)	5,600			(g)	700	
(d)	9,400					

Exercise 3–10
General journal entries
(LO 4)

the seven transactions. (Omit the account numbers.)

Prepare general journal entries to record the following transactions of PhotoFinish, Inc.

Exercise 3–11
General journal entries
(LO 4)

Aug. 1 Issued 8,000 shares of $5 par value common stock in exchange for $7,500 cash and photography equipment with a fair value of $32,500.

1 Rented a studio, paying $3,000 for the next three months in advance.

5 Purchased office supplies for $1,400 cash.

20 Received $2,650 in photography fees.

31 Paid $875 for August utilities.

Exercise 3–12
T-accounts and the trial balance
(LO 3, 5)

Use the information provided in Exercise 3–11 to prepare an August 31 trial balance for PhotoFinish, Inc. First, open these T-accounts: Cash; Office Supplies; Prepaid Rent; Photography Equipment; Common Stock, $5 Par Value; Photography Fees Earned; and Utilities Expense. Then post the general journal entries to the T-accounts. Finally, prepare the trial balance.

Exercise 3–13
Analyzing and journalizing revenue transactions
(LO 4)

Examine the following transactions and identify those that created revenues for ETS Corporation. Prepare general journal entries to record those transactions and explain why the other transactions did not create revenues.

a. Issued 3,825 shares of $10 par value common stock in exchange for $38,250 cash.

b. Provided $1,350 of services on credit.

c. Received $1,575 cash for services provided to a client.

d. Received $9,150 from a client in payment for services to be provided next year.

e. Received $4,500 from a client in partial payment of an account receivable.

f. Borrowed $150,000 from the bank by signing a promissory note.

Exercise 3–14
Analyzing and journalizing expense transactions
(LO 4)

Examine the following transactions and identify those that created expenses for ETS Corporation. Prepare general journal entries to record those transactions and explain why the other transactions did not create expenses.

a. Paid $14,100 cash for office supplies purchased 30 days previously.

b. Paid the $1,125 salary of the receptionist.

c. Paid $45,000 cash for equipment.
d. Paid utility bill with $930 cash.
e. Paid a $1,050 cash dividend to the stockholders of the corporation.

Calculate the debt ratio for each of the following cases:

Exercise 3–15
Calculating the debt ratio
(LO 5)

Case	Assets	Liabilities	Stockholders' Equity
1	$ 88,500	$11,000	$77,500
2	62,000	46,000	16,000
3	30,500	25,500	5,000
4	145,000	55,000	90,000
5	90,000	30,000	60,000
6	102,500	50,500	52,000

PROBLEMS

Following are business transactions completed by Smith & Peck, P.C., during the month of November:

Problem 3–1
Recording transactions in T-accounts; preparing a trial balance
(LO 2, 3, 5)

a. Issued 11,000 shares of $10 par value common stock in exchange for $80,000 cash and office equipment with a $30,000 fair value.
b. Purchased land and a small office building. The land was worth $30,000, and the building was worth $170,000. The purchase price was paid with $40,000 cash and a long-term note payable for $160,000.
c. Purchased $2,400 of office supplies on credit.
d. Issued 1,800 shares of $10 par value common stock in exchange for Smith's personal automobile, which had a value of $18,000, to be used exclusively in the business.
e. Purchased $6,000 of additional office equipment on credit.
f. Paid $1,500 salary to an assistant.
g. Provided services to a client and collected $6,000 cash.
h. Paid $800 for the month's utilities.
i. Paid account payable created in transaction c.
j. Purchased $20,000 of new office equipment by paying $18,600 cash and trading in old equipment with a recorded cost of $1,400.
k. Completed $5,200 of services for a client. This amount is to be paid within 30 days.
l. Paid $1,500 salary to an assistant.
m. Received $3,800 payment on the receivable created in transaction k.
n. Declared and paid a $6,400 cash dividend to the stockholders.

Required

1. Open the following T-accounts: Cash; Accounts Receivable; Office Supplies; Automobiles; Office Equipment; Building; Land; Accounts Payable; Long-Term Notes Payable; Common Stock, $10 Par Value; Cash Dividends Declared; Fees Earned; Salaries Expense; and Utilities Expense.
2. Record the effects of the listed transactions by entering debits and credits directly in the T-accounts. Use the transaction letters to identify each debit and credit entry.
3. Determine the balance of each account and prepare a trial balance as of November 30.

CHECK FIGURE:
Total debits in trial balance, $305,200

Problem 3–2
Recording transactions in
T-accounts, preparing a trial
balance, and calculating debt
ratio
(LO 2, 3, 5)

Forest Engineering, Inc., completed the following transactions during the month of July:

a. Created the business by issuing 31,200 shares of $5 par value common stock in exchange for $105,000 cash, office equipment with a value of $6,000, and $45,000 of drafting equipment.

b. Purchased land for an office. The land was worth $54,000, which was paid with $5,400 cash and a long-term note payable for $48,600.

c. Purchased a portable building with $75,000 cash and moved it onto the land.

d. Paid $6,000 cash for the premiums on two one-year insurance policies.

e. Completed and delivered a set of plans for a client and collected $5,700 cash.

f. Purchased additional drafting equipment for $22,500. Paid $10,500 cash and signed a long-term note payable for the $12,000 balance.

g. Completed $12,000 of engineering services for a client. This amount is to be paid within 30 days.

h. Purchased $2,250 of additional office equipment on credit.

i. Completed engineering services for $18,000 on credit.

j. Received a bill for rent on equipment that was used on a completed job. The $1,200 rent must be paid within 30 days.

k. Collected $7,200 from the client described in transaction g.

l. Paid $1,500 wages to a drafting assistant.

m. Paid the account payable created in transaction h.

n. Paid $675 cash for some repairs to an item of drafting equipment.

o. Declared and paid a $9,360 cash dividend to the stockholders.

p. Paid $1,500 wages to a drafting assistant.

q. Paid $3,000 cash to advertise in the local newspaper.

Required

1. Open the following T-accounts: Cash; Accounts Receivable; Prepaid Insurance; Office Equipment; Drafting Equipment; Building; Land; Accounts Payable; Long-Term Notes Payable; Common Stock, $5 Par Value; Cash Dividends Declared; Engineering Fees Earned; Wages Expense; Equipment Rental Expense; Advertising Expense; and Repairs Expense.

CHECK FIGURE:
Total debits in trial balance,
$253,500

2. Record the transactions by entering debits and credits directly in the accounts. Use the transaction letters to identify each debit and credit. Prepare a trial balance as of July 31.

3. Calculate the company's debt ratio. Use $236,265 as the ending total assets.

Problem 3–3
Preparing and posting general
journal entries and preparing a
trial balance
(LO 4, 5)

Mendez Corporation completed the following transactions during May:

May 1 Issued 124,000 shares of $1 par value common stock in exchange for $100,000 in cash and office equipment that had a fair value of $24,000.

1 Prepaid $7,200 cash for three months' rent for an office.

2 Made credit purchases of office equipment for $12,000 and office supplies for $2,400.

6 Completed services for a client and immediately received $2,000 cash.

9 Completed an $8,000 project for a client, who will pay within 30 days.

10 Paid the account payable created on May 2.

19 Paid $6,000 cash for the annual premium on an insurance policy.

22 Received $6,400 as partial payment for the work completed on May 9.

25 Completed work for another client for $2,640 on credit.

May 31   Declared and paid a $6,200 cash dividend to the stockholders.

31   Purchased $800 of additional office supplies on credit.

31   Paid $700 for the month's utility bill.

Required

1.   Prepare general journal entries to record the transactions.

2.   Open the following accounts (use the balance column format): Cash (101); Accounts Receivable (106); Office Supplies (124); Prepaid Insurance (128); Prepaid Rent (131); Office Equipment (163); Accounts Payable (201); Common Stock, $1 Par Value (307); Cash Dividends Declared (319); Services Revenue (403); and Utilities Expense (690).

3.   Post the entries to the accounts and enter the balance after each posting.

4.   Prepare a trial balance as of the end of the month.

CHECK FIGURE:
Cash account balance, $73,900

Able Movers, Inc., organized and began operations in July. The company hired Art Platt as a bookkeeper. His accounting and bookkeeping skills are not well polished, and he needs some help gathering information at the end of the month. He recorded the following journal entries during the month:

Problem 3–4
Interpreting journals, posting, and analyzing trial balance errors
(LO 4, 5)

July	1	Cash	60,000.00	
		Trucks	44,000.00	
		Common Stock, $2 Par Value		104,000.00
	2	Office Supplies	1,292.00	
		Cash		1,292.00
	4	Moving Equipment	12,800.00	
		Accounts Payable		12,800.00
	8	Cash	2,000.00	
		Accounts Receivable	10,000.00	
		Moving Fees Earned		12,000.00
	12	Cash	1,600.00	
		Moving Fees Earned		1,600.00
	15	Prepaid Insurance	2,700.00	
		Cash		2,700.00
	21	Cash	10,000.00	
		Accounts Receivable		10,000.00
	23	Accounts Payable	12,800.00	
		Cash		12,800.00
	25	Office Equipment	18,800.00	
		Common Stock, $2 Par Value		18,800.00
	29	Office Supplies	2,908.00	
		Accounts Payable		2,908.00
	31	Cash Dividends Declared	4,912.00	
		Cash		4,912.00
	31	Wages Expense	6,280.00	
		Cash		6,280.00

Based on these entries, Platt prepared the following trial balance:

ABLE MOVERS, INC.
Trial Balance
For Month Ended July 31

Cash	$ 45,616	
Accounts receivable	0	
Office supplies	2,400	
Prepaid insurance	2,700	
Trucks	44,000	
Office equipment	18,800	
Moving equipment		$ 12,800
Accounts payable		29,080
Common stock, $2 par value		122,800
Cash dividends declared	491	
Moving fees earned		13,600
Wages expense	6,280	
Totals	$120,287	$178,280

Required

Preparation component:

Platt remembers something about trial balances and realizes that the preceding one has at least one error. To help him find the mistakes, set up the following balance-column accounts and post the entries to them: Cash (101); Accounts Receivable (106); Office Supplies (124); Prepaid Insurance (128); Trucks (153); Office Equipment (163); Moving Equipment (167); Accounts Payable (201); Common Stock, $2 Par Value (307); Cash Dividends Declared (319); Moving Fees Earned (401); and Wages Expense (623).

Analysis component:

CHECK FIGURE:
Total credits in trial balance,
$139,308

Although Platt's journal entries are correct, he forgot to provide explanations of the events. Analyze each entry and present a reasonable explanation of what happened. Then, prepare a correct trial balance and describe the errors that Platt made.

Problem 3–5
Analyzing account balances
(LO 2, 5)

Young Consulting, Inc., began operations in March and completed seven transactions, including the issuance of 17,000 shares of $1 par value common stock for $17,000 cash. After these transactions, the ledger included the following accounts with their normal balances:

Cash	$26,660
Office supplies	660
Prepaid insurance	3,200
Office equipment	16,500
Accounts payable	16,500
Common stock, $1 par value	17,000
Cash dividends declared	3,740
Consulting fees earned	24,000
Rent expense	6,740

Required

Preparation component:

Prepare a trial balance for the business.

Analysis component:

Analyze the accounts and balances and prepare a list that describes each of the seven most likely transactions and their amounts. Also, present a schedule that shows how the transactions resulted in the $26,660 Cash balance.

SERIAL PROBLEM

(This comprehensive problem starts in this chapter and continues in Chapters 4, 5, and 6. Because of its length, this problem is most easily solved if you use the Working Papers that accompany this text.)

Echo Systems, Inc.

On October 1, 19X1, Mary Graham organized a computer service company called Echo Systems, Inc. Echo is organized as a corporation, with Graham doing consulting services, computer system installations, and custom program development. Graham has adopted the calendar year for reporting, and expects to prepare the company's first set of financial statements as of December 31, 19X1. The initial chart of accounts for the accounting system includes these items:

Account	No.	Account	No.
Cash	101	Common Stock, $10 Par Value	307
Accounts Receivable	106	Cash Dividends Declared	319
Computer Supplies	126	Computer Services Revenue	403
Prepaid Insurance	128	Wages Expense	623
Prepaid Rent	131	Advertising Expense	655
Office Equipment	163	Mileage Expense	676
Computer Equipment	167	Miscellaneous Expenses	677
Accounts Payable	201	Repairs Expense, Computer	684

Required

1. Prepare journal entries to record each of the following transactions for Echo Systems, Inc.
2. Open balance column accounts for the company and post the journal entries to them.

Transactions:

Oct. 1   Issued 7,200 shares of $10 par value common stock to Mary Graham in exchange for $45,000 cash, along with an $18,000 computer system and $9,000 of office equipment.

     2   Rented office space for $1,125 per month and paid the first four months' rent in advance.

     3   Purchased computer supplies on credit for $1,320 from Abbott Office Products.

     5   Paid $2,160 cash for one year's premium on a property and liability insurance policy.

     6   Billed Capital Leasing $3,300 for installing a new computer.

     8   Paid for the computer supplies purchased from Abbott Office Products.

   10   Hired Carly Smith as a part-time assistant for $100 per day, as needed. These wages will be paid once each month.

   12   Billed Capital Leasing another $1,200 for services.

   15   Received $3,300 from Capital Leasing on their account.

   17   Paid $705 to repair computer equipment damaged when moving into the new office.

   20   Paid $1,860 for an advertisement in the local newspaper.

   22   Received $1,200 from Capital Leasing on their account.

   28   Billed Decker Company $3,225 for services.

   31   Paid Carly Smith for seven days' work.

   31   Declared and paid a $3,600 cash dividend on the common stock.

Nov. 1   Reimbursed Mary Graham's business automobile mileage for 1,000 miles at $0.25 per mile.

     2   Received $4,650 cash from Elite Corporation for computer services.

Nov. 5 Purchased $960 of computer supplies from Abbott Office Products.

8 Billed Fostek Co. $4,350 for services.

13 Notified by Alamo Engineering Co. that Echo's bid of $3,750 for an upcoming project was accepted.

18 Received $1,875 from Decker Company against the bill dated October 28.

22 Donated $750 to the United Way in the company's name.

24 Completed work for Alamo Engineering Co. and sent them a bill for $3,750.

25 Sent another bill to Decker Company for the past due amount of $1,350.

28 Reimbursed Mary Graham's business automobile mileage for 1,200 miles at $0.25 per mile.

30 Paid Carly Smith for 14 days' work.

30 Declared and paid a $1,800 cash dividend on the common stock.

CRITICAL THINKING: ESSAYS, PROBLEMS, AND CASES

Analytical Essays

AE 3–1
(LO 3)

Consider the facts in Problem 3–2 and focus on transactions *h* and *o*. Explain how transaction *h* affects the accounting equation differently from transaction *o*. Describe how the effects of transaction *o* would differ if the check had been written to pay the company's property taxes instead of the described purpose.

AE 3–2
(LO 3, 5)

Consider the facts in Problem 3–3 and assume that the following mistakes were made in journalizing and posting the transactions. Explain how each mistake would affect the account balances and the column totals in the trial balance.

a. The May 1 issuance of common stock was recorded correctly in the journal, but the debit to Cash was incorrectly posted to the Cash account as $10,000.

b. The May 6 transaction was incorrectly recorded in the journal as a collection of an account receivable.

c. In recording the May 19 transaction in the journal, the account that should have been debited was credited and the account that should have been credited was debited.

d. The May 31 purchase of office supplies was recorded correctly in the journal, and the debit was correctly posted, but the credit was not posted at all.

e. The $700 payment of the utility bill on May 31 was recorded incorrectly in both accounts in the journal as a $70 payment.

Financial Reporting Problems

FRP 3–1
(LO 2)

Travis McAllister operates a surveying company. For the first few months of the company's life (through April), the accounting records were maintained by an outside bookkeeping service. According to those records, McAllister's Retained Earnings balance was $75,000 as of April 30. To save on expenses, McAllister decided to keep the records himself. He managed to record May's transactions properly, but was a bit rusty when the time came to prepare the financial statements. His first versions of the balance sheet and income statement follow. McAllister is bothered that the company operated at a loss during the month, even though he had been very busy. Using the information contained in the original financial statements, prepare revised statements, including a statement of retained earnings, for the month of May.

MCALLISTER SURVEYING, INC.
Income Statement
May 31

Revenue:

Common stock, $1 par value		$ 3,000
Unearned surveying fees		6,000
Total		$ 9,000

Operating expenses:

Rent expense	$3,100	
Telephone expense	600	
Surveying equipment	5,400	
Advertising expense	3,200	
Utilities expense	300	
Insurance expense	900	
Cash dividends declared	6,000	
Total operating expenses		19,500
Net income (loss)		$(10,500)

MCALLISTER SURVEYING, INC.
Balance Sheet
For Month Ended May 31

Assets		**Liabilities**	
Cash	$ 3,900	Accounts payable	$ 2,400
Accounts receivable	2,700	Surveying fees earned	18,000
Prepaid insurance	1,800	Short-term notes payable	48,000
Prepaid rent	4,200	Total liabilities	$ 68,400
Office supplies	300		
Buildings	81,000		
Land	36,000	**Stockholders' Equity**	
Salaries expense	3,000	Retained earnings	64,500
		Total liabilities and	
Total assets	$132,900	stockholders' equity	$132,900

Aaron Strickland organized his new computer consulting business as a corporation and com- **FRP 3–2**
pleted a number of transactions during June, the first month of operation. He recorded all **(LO 3, 4)**
transactions with double entries in just two accounts, Cash and Income Summary. At the end
of the first month, he asks you to review his records and improve his ledger. Based on the
following information, you should present a compound general journal entry dated June 30 to
show your corrections and improvements.

Cash   Acct. No. 101

Date		Explanation	PR	Debit	Credit	Balance
June	1	Issued 2,400 shares of $5 par value common stock.	G1	12,000		12,000
	1	Purchased computer equipment.	G1		8,400	3,600
	2	Purchased office equipment.	G1		2,000	1,600
	6	Signed short-term note payable to bank.	G1	4,000		5,600
	9	Paid for June office rental.	G1		800	4,800
	12	Received cash for services.	G1	1,200		6,000
	15	Paid wages of assistant.	G1		540	5,460
	25	Received cash for July services.	G1	2,400		7,860
	27	Purchased computer supplies.	G1		400	7,460
	29	Received cash for services.	G1	1,600		9,060
	30	Paid wages of assistant.	G1		460	8,600
	30	Declared and paid cash dividend.	G1		1,800	6,800

Income Summary					Acct. No. 901
Date	Explanation	PR	Debit	Credit	Balance
June 1		G1		12,000	12,000
1		G1	8,400		3,600
2		G1	2,000		1,600
6		G1		4,000	5,600
9		G1	800		4,800
12		G1		1,200	6,000
15		G1	540		5,460
25		G1		2,400	7,860
27		G1	400		7,460
29		G1		1,600	9,060
30		G1	460		8,600
30		G1	1,800		6,800

Financial Statement Analysis Case

(LO 2)

Refer to the financial statements and related information for Southwest Airlines Co. in Appendix E. Find the answers to the following questions by analyzing the information in the report:

1. What three categories of revenues are reported on Southwest Airlines' consolidated statement of income?
2. What five current assets are reported on the company's consolidated balance sheet?
3. What five current liabilities are reported on the balance sheet?
4. What dollar amounts of provisions for income taxes are reported by Southwest Airlines on its income statements for the annual reporting periods ending in 1994 and 1993?
5. During the annual reporting period ended December 31, 1994, how much cash did Southwest Airlines pay in dividends?
6. What is the company's debt ratio at the end of 1994? (Remember that Liabilities = Assets − Stockholders' equity.) How does this compare to the ratio at the end of 1993?

Ethical Issues Essay

Review the As a Matter of Ethics case on page 66. Discuss the nature of the dilemma faced by Karen Muñoz and evaluate the alternative courses of action that she should consider.

CONCEPT TESTER

Test your understanding of the concepts introduced in this chapter by completing the following crossword puzzle.

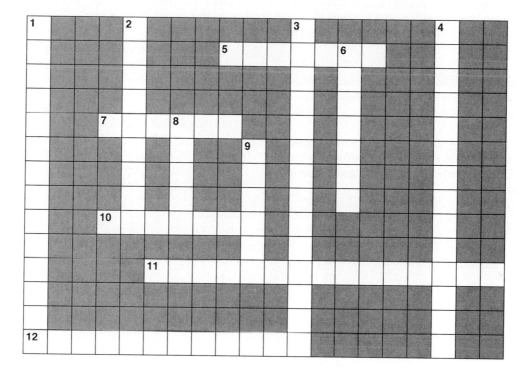

Across Clues

5. A record in which the effects of transactions are first recorded.
7. An entry that decreases an asset or expense or increases a liability, revenue, or equity.
10. The process of copying journal entry information to the ledger.
11. 2 words; liability created by a cash receipt from customers in advance of providing the service.
12. 2 words; a summary of the ledger that lists the accounts and their balances.

Down Clues

1. 2 words; a document that is the source of information recorded with accounting entries.
2. 2 words; the ratio between a company's total liabilities and its total assets.
3. 2 words; an asset created by a payment for benefits that are not used until later.
4. 2 words; an unconditional written promise to pay a definite sum of money on demand or a fixed date.
6. A place in which increases and decreases in a specific financial statement item are stored.
8. An entry that increases an asset or expense or decreases a liability, revenue, or equity.
9. The collection of all the accounts used by a business.

ANSWERS TO PROGRESS CHECKS

3–1 *d*

3–2 A company's accounting equation is affected by external transactions and other economic events sometimes called internal transactions.

3–3 Business papers are called *source documents* because they are the source of information that is recorded with accounting entries.

3–4 *b*

3–5 An account is a place or location in an accounting system in which the increases and decreases in a specific asset, liability, stockholders' equity, revenue, or expense item are recorded and stored. A ledger is a collection of all accounts used by a business.

3–6   A company's size affects the number of accounts needed in its accounting system. The types of accounts used by a business depend on the information the business needs to present in its financial statements.

3–7   No, debit and credit both can mean increase or decrease; the particular meaning in a circumstance depends on the type of account. For example, a debit increases the balance of an expense account but decreases the balance in a revenue account.

3–8   c

3–9   Stockholders' equity is increased by revenues and investments in the corporation. Stockholders' equity is decreased by expenses and cash dividends paid to stockholders.

3–10 The name *double-entry* is used because all transactions affect and are recorded in at least two accounts. There must be at least one debit in one account and at least one credit in another.

3–11 c

3–12 A compound journal entry affects at least three accounts.

3–13 Posting reference numbers are entered in the journal when posting to the ledger as a control over the posting process. They provide a cross-reference that allows the bookkeeper or auditor to trace debits and credits from one record to the other. They also create a place marker in case the posting process is interrupted.

3–14 e

3–15 Dollar signs are used in financial statements and other reports to identify the kind of currency being used in the reports. At a minimum, they are placed beside the first and last numbers in each column. Some companies place dollar signs beside any amount that appears after a ruled line to indicate that an addition or subtraction has taken place.

3–16 The effect of the error is to understate the trial balance's debit column total by $4,000 and overstate the credit column total by $4,000. This results in an $8,000 difference between the two totals.

3–17 a

Adjusting the Accounts and Preparing the Statements

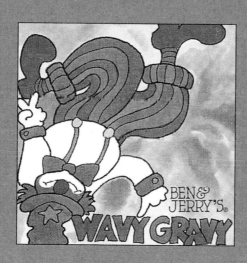

*O*ne day a Ben & Jerry's shareholder came into the company office and said: "Your annual report is great, but the financial statements are impossible to read for people who aren't trained in accounting."

Fran, the chief financial officer, responded: "I guess that's true. It's hard to make financial statements look friendly to nonfinancial people, because they are written in the language of business. That's the definition of accounting—the language of business. If we wrote the front half of the annual report in Martian, most creatures other than Martians wouldn't find that too friendly, either."

"Well can't you do something about it? Can't you just draw some pictures and write some clever things in them so we can understand them better?"

"Not really. The rules called *generally accepted accounting principles* are really specific, to make sure a company presents very clear, standardized information about its finances to its investors. Financial statements have footnotes and a 'management's discussion and analysis' that explain a lot of things about a company's finances. The footnotes and analysis may look imposing, but go ahead and look them over. Relax, have a bowl of Ben & Jerry's and unlock the secrets."

"Well, the language of business is a real secret to me. Help me out. I know the stuff in the front is important. That's one of the reasons why I bought stock. Now I want to learn more about the money side."[1]

BEN & JERRY'S HOMEMADE, INC.
(In thousands)

	Year Ended				
	12/26/94	12/28/93	12/29/92	12/30/91	12/31/90
Net sales	$148,802	$140,328	$131,969	$96,997	$77,024
Net income (loss) .	(1,868)	7,200	6,675	3,739	2,609

[1]Quoted from the "Financial (not so very) Funnies" section of *Ben & Jerry's 1992 Annual Report,* © 1993, Ben & Jerry's Homemade, Inc., Waterbury, VT.

LEARNING OBJECTIVES

After studying Chapter 4, you should be able to:

1. **Explain why financial statements are prepared at the end of regular accounting periods, why the accounts must be adjusted at the end of each period, and why the accrual basis of accounting produces more useful income statements and balance sheets than the cash basis.**
2. **Prepare adjusting entries for prepaid expenses, depreciation, unearned revenues, accrued expenses, and accrued revenues and prepare entries to record cash receipts and cash disbursements related to accrued assets and liabilities.**
3. **Prepare a schedule that includes the unadjusted trial balance, the adjustments, and the adjusted trial balance and use the adjusted trial balance to prepare financial statements.**
4. **Explain why some companies record prepaid and unearned items in income statement accounts and prepare adjusting entries when this procedure is used.**
5. **Calculate the profit margin ratio and describe what it reveals about a company's performance.**
6. **Define or explain the words and phrases listed in the chapter glossary.**

You learned in Chapter 3 that companies use accounting systems to collect information about transactions and other economic events. That chapter showed you how journals and ledgers are used to capture information about external transactions. This chapter explains how the accounting system gathers information about economic events that are not transactions with outside parties. The process involves adjusting the account balances at the end of the reporting period to reflect the economic events that are sometimes called *internal transactions*. As a result, the adjusted accounts contain the amounts to be reported on the financial statements according to generally accepted accounting principles. In addition, the chapter describes the profit margin ratio that decision makers use to assess a company's performance.

ACCOUNTING PERIODS AND FISCAL YEARS

LO 1
Explain why financial statements are prepared at the end of regular accounting periods, why the accounts must be adjusted at the end of each period, and why the accrual basis of accounting produces more useful income statements and balance sheets than the cash basis.

To be useful, information must reach decision makers frequently and promptly. To provide timely information, accounting systems are designed to produce periodic reports at regular intervals. As a result, the accounting process is based on the **time period principle.** According to this principle, an organization's activities are identified with specific time periods, such as a month, a three-month quarter, or a year. Then, financial statements are prepared for each reporting period. The time periods covered by the reports are called **accounting periods.** Most organizations use one year as their primary accounting period. As a result, they prepare annual financial statements. However, nearly all organizations also prepare **interim financial reports** that cover one or three months of activity.

The annual reporting period is not always the same as the calendar year ending December 31. In fact, an organization can adopt a **fiscal year** consisting of any 12 consecutive months. An acceptable variation of this is to adopt an annual reporting period of 52 weeks. For example, look at the consolidated balance sheets of **Lands' End, Inc.,** in Appendix F. The company's 1995 year ended on January 27, while the 1994 year ended on January 28.

Companies that do not experience much seasonal variation in sales volume within the year often choose the calendar year as their fiscal year. For example, the financial statements of **Southwest Airlines Co.** in Appendix E reflect a fiscal year that ends on December 31. On the other hand, companies that experience major seasonal variations in sales often choose a fiscal year that corresponds to their **natural business year.** The natural business year ends when sales activities are at their lowest point during the year. For example, the natural business year for retail stores ends around January 31, af-

ter the Christmas and January selling seasons. As a result, they often start their annual accounting periods on February 1.

During an accounting period, the normal process is to record the economic events that occur in the form of external transactions (with outside parties). After all external transactions are recorded, several accounts in the ledger need to be updated before their balances appear in the financial statements. This need arises from the fact that some economic events remain unrecorded because they did not occur as external transactions.

For example, the costs of some assets expire as time passes. Notice that the third item in the trial balance of Clear Copy, Inc., in Illustration 4–1 is prepaid insurance and that it has a balance of $2,400. This amount is the original cost of the premium for two years of insurance protection beginning on December 1, 19X1. By December 31, 19X1, one month's coverage has been used up, and $2,400 is no longer the cost of the remaining prepaid insurance. Because the coverage costs an average of $100 per month ($2,400/24 months), the Prepaid Insurance account balance should be reduced by that amount. In addition, the income statement should report $100 as insurance expense.

Similarly, the $3,720 balance in the Store Supplies account includes the cost of some supplies that were consumed during December. The cost of these supplies should be reported as an expense of the month. Because of these unrecorded events, the balances of the Prepaid Insurance and Store Supplies accounts should be *adjusted* before they are presented on the December 31 balance sheet.

Another adjustment is necessary because one month of the copy equipment's useful life has expired. In addition, the balances of the Unearned Copy Services Revenue, Copy Services Revenue, and Salaries Expense accounts may need to be adjusted before they appear on the December income statement.

The next section of the chapter explains how the adjusting process is accomplished. As you study the material, remember that our goal is to provide useful information in the financial statements.

The adjusting process is consistent with two accounting principles, the *revenue recognition principle* and the *matching principle.* Chapter 2 explained that the *revenue recognition principle* requires revenue to be reported on the income statement only when it is earned, not before and not after. For most firms, revenue is earned when a service or a product is delivered to the customer. For example, if Clear Copy, Inc., provides copy services to a customer during December, the revenue is earned during December. As a result, it should be reported on the December income statement, even if the customer paid for the services in November or will pay for them in January. One major goal for the adjusting process is to ensure that revenue is reported, or recognized, in the time period when it is earned.

The goal of the **matching principle** is to report expenses on the income statement in the same accounting period as the revenues that were earned as a result of the expenses. For example, assume that a business earns revenues during December while

WHY ARE THE ACCOUNTS ADJUSTED AT THE END OF AN ACCOUNTING PERIOD?

THE ADJUSTING PROCESS

PRINCIPLE APPLICATION
Revenue Recognition Principle,
p. 40
One way IBM Corporation earns revenue is by providing maintenance and services to its customers. It reports these revenues as the services are performed. Revenues on the products it sells are reported when the products are shipped.

Illustration 4-1

CLEAR COPY, INC.
Trial Balance
December 31, 19X1

	Debit	Credit
Cash	$ 7,950	
Accounts receivable	0	
Prepaid insurance	2,400	
Store supplies	3,720	
Copy equipment	26,000	
Accounts payable		$ 6,200
Unearned copy services revenue		3,000
Common stock, $1 par value		30,000
Cash dividends declared	600	
Copy services revenue		4,100
Rent expense	1,000	
Salaries expense	1,400	
Utilities expense	230	
Total	$43,300	$43,300

it operates out of rented store space. According to the *revenue recognition principle,* the business should report its revenues on the December income statement. In earning those revenues, the business incurs rent expense. The *matching principle* tells us that the rent should be reported on the income statement for December, even if the rent was paid in November or will be paid in January. As a result, the rent expense for December is matched with December's revenues. This matching of expenses with revenues is a major goal of the adjusting process.

Matching expenses with revenues often requires a company to predict future events. To use financial statements wisely, you need to understand that they are based on predictions and therefore include measurements that are not precise. For example, **The Walt Disney Company's** 1994 annual report explains that the company allocates film production costs to years based on a ratio of actual revenues to date from the film divided by its predicted total gross revenues.

ACCRUAL BASIS COMPARED WITH CASH BASIS ACCOUNTING

When the adjusting process assigns revenues to the periods in which they are earned and matches expenses with the revenues, the company is using **accrual basis accounting.** The objective of the accrual basis is to report the economic effects of revenues and expenses when they are earned or incurred, not when cash is received or paid.

The alternative to accrual accounting is **cash basis accounting.** Under the cash basis, revenues are recognized when cash is received and expenses are reported when cash is paid. For example, if revenue is earned in December but cash is not received from the customer until January, the cash basis reports the revenue in January. Because revenues are reported when cash is received and expenses are deducted when cash is paid, cash basis net income for a period is the difference between revenues received in cash (called *receipts*) and expenses paid with cash (called *expenditures* or *disbursements*).

Although some small companies use a cash basis for preparing their internal statements and reports, cash-basis income statements and balance sheets are not consistent with generally accepted accounting principles. "Accrual accounting generally provides a better indication of enterprise performance than information about current

Illustration 4–2 Allocating the $2,400 Cost of Insurance Protection for 24 Months Beginning December 1, 19X1

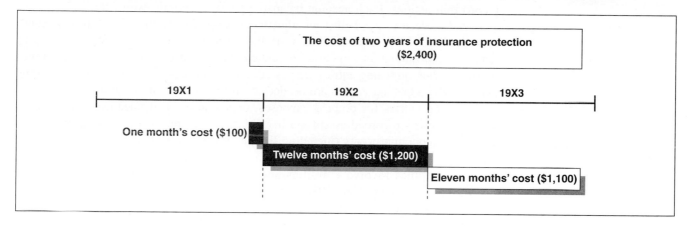

cash receipts and payments."[2] Accrual accounting increases the *comparability* of income statements and balance sheets from one period with those of another period.

For example, Clear Copy paid $2,400 for two years of insurance coverage beginning on December 1. Under accrual accounting, $100 of insurance expense is reported on the December 19X1 income statement. During 19X2, $1,200 of expense will be reported. During 19X3, $1,100 of expense will be reported for the first 11 months of the year. This allocation of the insurance cost among the three fiscal years is represented graphically in Illustration 4–2.

In contrast, a cash basis income statement for December 19X1 would report insurance expense of $2,400. The income statements for 19X2 and 19X3 would not report any insurance expense from this policy. To provide useful information about the company's activities and assets, the accrual basis shows that each of the 24 months had $100 of insurance expense. The balance sheet also reports the remaining unexpired premium as the cost of the prepaid insurance asset. However, the cash basis would never report an asset. In summary, the cash basis information would be less useful for decisions because the reported income for 19X1, 19X2, and 19X3 would not reflect comparable measures of the cost of having insurance in those years.

The accrual basis is generally accepted for external reporting because it produces more useful information. The cash basis is not acceptable for a balance sheet or income statement because it provides incomplete information about assets, liabilities, revenues, and expenses. However, information about cash flows is also useful. That's why GAAP requires companies to report a statement of cash flows.

Progress Check

(Answers to Progress Checks are provided at the end of the chapter.)

4-1 A company's annual reporting period: *(a)* is called the fiscal year; *(b)* always ends at the close of the natural business year; *(c)* always ends at the close of the calendar business year; or *(d)* cannot be divided into shorter interim periods.

4-2 Why do companies prepare interim financial statements?

4-3 Which accounting principles lead most directly to the adjustment process?

4-4 Is the cash basis of accounting consistent with the matching principle?

4-5 On April 1, 19X1, Collins Company paid a $4,800 premium for two years of insurance coverage. Under the cash basis, how much insurance expense will be reported in 19X2?

---

[2]*Statement of Financial Accounting Concepts No. 1,* "Objectives of Financial Reporting by Business Enterprises" (Norwalk, CT, 1978), par. 44.

ADJUSTING SPECIFIC ACCOUNTS

LO 2

Prepare adjusting entries for prepaid expenses, depreciation, unearned revenues, accrued expenses, and accrued revenues and prepare entries to record cash receipts and cash disbursements related to accrued assets and liabilities.

The process of adjusting the accounts is similar to the process used to analyze and record transactions. Each account balance and the economic events that affect it are analyzed to determine whether an adjustment is needed. If an adjustment is needed, an **adjusting entry** is recorded to bring the asset or liability account balance up to date. The adjustment also updates the related expense or revenue account. Like other journal entries, adjusting entries are posted to the accounts. The following paragraphs explain why adjusting entries are needed to provide useful information.

Adjusting entries for prepaid expenses, depreciation, and unearned revenues involve previously recorded assets and liabilities. These entries are made to record the effects of economic events (including the passing of time) that have changed these assets and liabilities. On the other hand, adjusting entries for accrued expenses and accrued revenues involve liabilities and assets that have not yet been recorded. Adjusting entries record the effects of economic events that created these liabilities and assets as well as the related expenses and revenues.

Prepaid Expenses

A prepaid expense is an economic benefit paid for in advance of its use. When it is paid for, the company acquires an asset that will expire or be used up. As the asset is used, its cost becomes an expense.

Prepaid Insurance. For example, recall that Clear Copy paid $2,400 for two years of insurance protection that went into effect on December 1, 19X1. (The allocation of this cost to 19X1, 19X2, and 19X3 is described in Illustration 4–2.) As each day of December went by, some of the benefit of the insurance protection expired, and a portion of the asset's cost became an expense. By December 31, one month's insurance coverage had expired. This expense is measured as $100, which is 1/24 of $2,400. The following adjusting entry records the expense with a debit, and reduces the cost of the asset with a credit to the asset account:

		Adjustment a		
Dec.	31	Insurance Expense	100.00	
		Prepaid Insurance		100.00
		To record the expense created by expired insurance.		

Posting the adjusting entry has the following effect on the accounts:

Prepaid Insurance				Insurance Expense		
Dec. 26	2,400	**Dec. 31**	**100**	**Dec. 31**	**100**	
	− 100					
Balance	2,300					

After the entry is posted, the $100 balance in Insurance Expense and the $2,300 balance in Prepaid Insurance are ready to be presented on the financial statements.

The allocation process in Illustration 4–2 shows that another adjusting entry in 19X2 transfers $1,200 from Prepaid Insurance to Insurance Expense. A third adjusting entry in 19X3 transfers the remaining $1,100 to the expense account.

Store Supplies. Store supplies are another prepaid expense that is adjusted. For example, Clear Copy purchased $3,720 of store supplies in December and used some of them up during the month. Consuming these supplies created an expense equal to their cost. However, the daily consumption of the supplies was not recorded in the accounts because the information was not needed. Due to the fact that the account balances are not presented in financial statements until the end of the month, bookkeeping effort can be reduced by making only one adjusting entry to record the total cost of all supplies consumed in the month.

Because an income statement is to be prepared for December, the cost of the store supplies used during the month needs to be recognized as an expense. To learn the amount used, Clear Copy's employee counts (or, takes an inventory of) the remaining unused supplies. Then, the cost of the remaining supplies is deducted from the cost of the purchased supplies. For example, suppose that Clear Copy finds that $2,670 of supplies remain out of the $3,720 purchased in December. The $1,050 difference between these two amounts is the cost of the consumed supplies. This amount is the month's store supplies expense. This adjusting entry records the expense with a debit and reduces the asset account balance with an equal credit:

		Adjustment b		
Dec.	31	Store Supplies Expense	1,050.00	
		Store Supplies		1,050.00
		To record the expense created by using store supplies.		

Posting the adjusting entry has the following effect on the accounts:

Store Supplies					**Store Supplies Expense**		
Dec. 2	2,500	**Dec. 31**	**1,050**	**Dec. 31**	**1,050**	
6	1,100					
26	120					
Total	3,720	Total	1,050			
	− 1,050					
Balance	2,670					

As a result, the balance of the store supplies account now equals the $2,670 cost revealed by the count of inventory.

Other Prepaid Expenses. Unlike the two previous examples, some prepaid expenses are both acquired and fully used up within a single accounting period. For example, a company may pay monthly rent on the first day of each month. Every month, the payment creates a prepaid expense that fully expires by the end of the month. In these cases, the bookkeeper can ignore the fact that the payment creates an asset and record the payment with a debit to the expense account instead of the asset account. (These practices are described more completely later in the chapter.)

Depreciation

In accounting, the term **plant and equipment** describes tangible long-lived assets that are used to produce or sell goods and services. Examples of plant and equipment are land, buildings, machines, vehicles, and professional libraries. Except for land, plant and equipment assets eventually wear out or otherwise lose their usefulness and value. Therefore, income statements should report the cost of using these assets as expenses during their useful lives. The expense created by allocating the original cost of assets is called **depreciation.** Depreciation expense is recorded with an adjusting entry similar to the entries to record the using up of prepaid expenses. However, the entry is slightly more complicated because a special account is used to record the reduced asset balance.

For example, Clear Copy uses copy equipment to earn revenue. This equipment's cost should be depreciated to provide a complete income statement. Early in December, Clear Copy made two purchases of equipment, one for $20,000 and the other for $6,000. Using information received from the manufacturer and other sources,

Annette Dow predicts that the equipment will have a four-year useful life. Dow also predicts that the company will be able to sell the equipment for $8,000 at the end of the four years. Therefore, the net cost expected to expire over the useful life is $18,000 ($26,000 − $8,000). When this net cost is divided by the 48 months in the asset's predicted life, the result is an average monthly cost of $375 ($18,000/48). This average cost is recorded as depreciation expense for each month with this adjusting entry:

		Adjustment c		
Dec.	31	Depreciation Expense	375.00	
		Accumulated Depreciation, Copy Equipment		375.00
		To record the expense created by using the copying equipment.		

Posting the adjusting entry has the following effect on the accounts:

Copy Equipment				**Depreciation Expense, Copy Equipment**		
Dec. 3	20,000			Dec. 31	375	
6	6,000					
Total	26,000					

Accumulated Depreciation, Copy Equipment		
	Dec. 31	375

After the entry is posted, the Copy Equipment account and its related Accumulated Depreciation, Copy Equipment account together show the December 31 balance sheet amounts for this asset. The Depreciation Expense, Copy Equipment account shows the amount of expense that will appear on the December income statement.

In most cases, a decrease in an asset account is recorded by entering a credit directly in the account. However, note in the illustrated accounts that this procedure is not followed in recording depreciation. Instead, depreciation is recorded in a **contra account.** A contra account's balance is subtracted from a related account's balance to provide more information than simply the net amount. In this example, the contra account is Accumulated Depreciation, Copy Equipment.

Why are contra accounts used to record depreciation? Contra accounts allow balance sheet readers to observe both the original cost of the assets and the estimated amount of depreciation that has been charged to expense in the past. By knowing both the original cost and the accumulated depreciation, decision makers can more completely assess the company's productive capacity and the potential need to replace the assets. For example, Clear Copy's balance sheet shows both the $26,000 original cost of the equipment and the $375 balance in the accumulated depreciation contra account. This information lets statement users see that the equipment is almost new. In contrast, if Clear Copy simply reported the net remaining cost of $25,625, the users would not know whether the equipment is new or so old that it needs immediate replacement.

Note the words *accumulated depreciation* in the title of the contra account. This reflects the fact that this account reports the total amount of depreciation expense recognized in all prior periods since the assets were put into service. For example, the Copy Equipment and the Accumulated Depreciation accounts would look like this on February 28, 19X2, after three monthly adjusting entries:

Copy Equipment			Accumulated Depreciation, Copy Equipment		
Dec. 3	20,000		Dec. 31		375
6	6,000		Jan. 31		375
Total	26,000		Feb. 28		375
			Total		1,125

These account balances would be presented on the February 28 balance sheet as follows

Copy equipment	$26,000
Less accumulated depreciation	1,125
Net	$24,875

Later chapters describe how other contra accounts are used in other situations.

Unearned Revenues

An unearned revenue is a liability that is created when a customer's payment is received in advance of delivering the goods or services. For example, the December 31, 1994, balance sheet of the **New York Times Company** reported a liability for subscriptions in excess of $77 million. This amount was over 17% of the company's total current liabilities.

Clear Copy, Inc., also has unearned revenue. On December 26, the company agreed to provide copying services for a customer for the fixed fee of $1,500 per month. On that day, the customer paid the first two months' fees in advance to cover the period from December 27 to February 26. This entry records the cash receipt:

Dec.	26	Cash	3,000.00	
		Unearned Copy Services Revenue		3,000.00
		Received advance payment for copying services to be provided over two months.		

This advance payment increased cash and created an obligation to do copying work over the next two months. By December 31, the business provided five days' service and earned one-sixth of the $1,500 revenue for the first month. This amount is $250 ($1,500/6). The company also discharged one-twelfth of the total $3,000 liability because five days is one-twelfth of two months. According to the *revenue recognition principle,* the $250 of revenue should appear on the December income statement. Notice that the event that caused the earning of revenue was simply the passage of time. There was no external transaction. The following adjusting entry updates the accounts by reducing the liability and recognizing the earned revenue:

		Adjustment d		
Dec.	31	Unearned Copy Services Revenue	250.00	
		Copy Services Revenue ($1,500/6)		250.00
		Earned revenue that was received in advance.		

The accounts look like this after the entry is posted:

Unearned Copy Services Revenue				Copy Services Revenue		
Dec. 31	**250**	Dec. 26	3,000		Dec. 10	2,200
			− 250		12	1,900
		Balance	2,750		**31**	**250**
					Total	4,350

In effect, the adjusting entry transfers $250 of earned revenue from the liability account to the revenue account.

Accrued Expenses

Most expenses are recorded when they are paid with cash. In making the journal entry to record the transaction, the credit to the Cash account is accompanied by a debit to the expense account. However, because some expenses incurred during the period have not been paid for, they may remain unrecorded at the end of an accounting period. These incurred but unpaid expenses are called **accrued expenses.** One typical example of an accrued expense is the unpaid wages earned by employees for work they have already completed.

Accrued Salaries. For example, Clear Copy's only employee earns $70 per day or $350 for a five-day workweek that begins on Monday and ends on Friday. The employee's salary is paid every two weeks on Friday. On the 12th and the 26th of December, these wages were paid, recorded in the journal, and posted to the ledger. The Salaries Expense and Cash accounts show these entries:

Cash			Salaries Expense	
Dec. 12	700	Dec. 12	700	
26	700	26	700	

DECEMBER 19X1						
S	M	T	W	T	F	S
	1	2	3	4	5	6
7	8	9	10	11	12	13
14	15	16	17	18	19	20
21	22	23	24	25	26	27
28	**29**	**30**	**31**			

The calendar for December 19X1 in the margin shows us that three working days (December 29, 30, and 31) come after the December 26 payday. Thus, the employee earned three days' salary at the close of business on Wednesday, December 31. Because this salary had not been paid, the expense was not recorded. But, the financial statements would be incomplete if they failed to report this additional expense and the liability to the employee for the unpaid salary. Therefore, this adjusting entry should be recorded on December 31 to produce a complete record of the company's expenses and liabilities:

		Adjustment e		
Dec.	31	Salaries Expense	210.00	
		Salaries Payable		210.00
		To record three days' accrued salary (3 × $70).		

After this entry is posted, the Salaries Expense and liability accounts appear as follows:

Salaries Expense			Salaries Payable	
Dec. 12	700		**Dec. 31**	**210**
26	700			
31	**210**			
Total	1,610			

As a result of this entry, $1,610 of salaries expense is reported on the income statement. In addition, the balance sheet reports a $210 liability to the employee.

Accrued Interest Expense. Another typical accrued expense is interest incurred on accounts and notes payable. Interest expense is incurred simply with the passage of time. Therefore, unless interest is paid on the last day of the accounting period, some additional amount will have accrued since the previous payment. A company's financial statements will be incomplete unless this expense and additional liability are recorded. The adjusting entry for interest is similar to the one used to accrue the unpaid salary.

Accrued Revenues

Many revenues are recorded when cash is received from the customer. Other revenues are recorded when goods and services are sold on credit. However, some earned revenues are not recorded until adjusting entries are made at the end of the accounting period. Although these **accrued revenues** are earned, they are unrecorded because the customer has not yet paid for them or the seller has not yet billed the customer. For example, suppose that Clear Copy agreed to provide copying services for a bank at a fixed fee of $2,700 per month. The terms of the agreement call for Clear Copy to provide services from the 12th of December, 19X1, through the 11th of the following month. The bank will pay $2,700 cash to Clear Copy on January 11, 19X2, when the service period is over.

As of December 31, 19X1, 20 days of services have been provided to the bank. However, because Clear Copy has not yet been paid, it has not recorded the earning of the revenue. Because 20 days equal two-thirds of a month, Clear Copy has earned two-thirds of one month's fee, or $1,800 ($2,700 × 2/3). According to the *revenue recognition principle,* this revenue should be reported on the December income statement because it was earned in that month. In addition, the balance sheet should report that the bank owes the company $1,800. Clear Copy makes this adjusting entry to record the effects of the agreement:

			Adjustment f		
Dec.	31	Accounts Receivable		1,800.00	
		Copy Services Revenue			1,800.00
		To record 20 days' accrued revenue.			

The debit to the receivable reflects the fact that the bank owes Clear Copy for the provided services. After this entry is posted, the affected accounts look like this:

Accounts Receivable					**Copy Services Revenue**		
Dec. 12	1,900	Dec. 22	1,900		Dec. 10		2,200
31	**1,800**				12		1,900
Total	3,700	Total	1,900		31		250
	− 1,900				**31**		**1,800**
Balance	1,800				Total		6,150

Accounts receivable are reported on the balance sheet at $1,800, and $6,150 of revenues are reported on the income statement.

Accrued Interest Income. We mentioned earlier that interest is an accrued expense recorded with an adjusting entry. Interest is also an accrued revenue when a company is entitled to receive it from a debtor. If a company has notes or accounts receivable that produce interest income, the bookkeeper records an adjusting entry to recognize any accrued but uncollected interest revenue. The entry also records the interest receivable from the debtor as an asset.

Take time to read the As a Matter of Ethics case. It tells about pressure being applied to an accountant to omit some adjusting entries that are needed to present complete financial statements. Consider the situation and determine what you would do if you were in this accountant's place.

As a Matter of Ethics

Bill Palmer is the accountant for the Crown Company. Just as Palmer was about to prepare adjusting entries to record some accrued expenses at the end of the company's first year, he was called into the company president's office. The president asked about the accrued expenses and then instructed Palmer to not make the adjustments. Although Palmer expressed concern about these instructions, the president said that the expenses should not be reported until next year because they would be paid in January or later.

As Palmer was turning to leave, the president asked how much the current year's revenues would be increased by the purchase order that was recently received from the Fisher Company. Palmer explained that there will be no effect on sales until the next year because Fisher will not take delivery until the middle of January.

The exasperated president pointed out that the order had already been received and Crown was ready to make the delivery. Even though Fisher's order indicated the merchandise should not be delivered until January 15, the president told Palmer to record the sale in December.

Palmer knows that the combination of recording the sales to Fisher Company and not accruing the expenses will have a large effect on the income statement. In fact, it would report a net income instead of a net loss. Palmer is unsure about following the president's instructions. He also wonders how the company's independent auditors would react if they reviewed the statements and records and found that the adjusting entries were not made. What do you think Palmer should do?

Progress Check

4-6 At the end of its 19X1 fiscal year, Corona Company omitted an adjustment to record $200 of accrued service revenues. The effect of the error is to: *(a)* overstate 19X1 net income by $200; *(b)* overstate 19X1 revenues by $200; *(c)* understate total assets by $200; or *(d)* overstate total assets by $200.

4-7 What is a contra account?

4-8 What is an accrued expense? Give an example.

4-9 How does an unearned revenue arise? Give an example of an unearned revenue.

THE ADJUSTED TRIAL BALANCE

LO 3

Prepare a schedule that includes the unadjusted trial balance, the adjustments, and the adjusted trial balance and use the adjusted trial balance to prepare financial statements.

An **unadjusted trial balance** is prepared before adjustments have been recorded. As you might expect, an **adjusted trial balance** uses the account balances after the adjusting entries have been posted to the ledger. In Illustration 4–3, parallel columns show the unadjusted trial balance, the adjustments, and the adjusted trial balance for Clear Copy as of December 31, 19X1. Notice that several new accounts have been added because of the adjusting entries. (The order of the accounts has also been changed to match the order of the account numbers listed at the end of the book.) Also notice that the letters in the Adjustments columns identify the debits and credits that were recorded with adjusting entries presented earlier in the chapter.

PREPARING FINANCIAL STATEMENTS FROM THE ADJUSTED TRIAL BALANCE

Chapter 3 explained that the trial balance summarizes the information in the ledger by showing the account balances. This summary is easier to work with than the entire ledger when preparing financial statements. The accountant uses the adjusted trial balance for this purpose because it includes the balances that should appear in the statements.

Illustration 4–4 shows how Clear Copy's revenue and expense balances are transferred to an income statement. The illustration also shows how to use the net income and the cash dividends declared to prepare a statement of retained earnings.

Illustration 4–5 shows how the asset, liability, and stockholders' equity items are drawn from the adjusted trial balance and arranged on a balance sheet. The balance sheet is prepared last because the retained earnings balance is calculated in the statement of retained earnings.

Illustration 4–3 The Unadjusted Trial Balance, Adjustments, and Adjusted Trial Balance for Clear Copy, Inc., as of December 31, 19X1

	Unadjusted Trial Balance		Adjustments		Adjusted Trial Balance	
Cash	7,950				7,950	
Accounts receivable			(f) 1,800		1,800	
Store supplies	3,720			(b)1,050	2,670	
Prepaid insurance	2,400			(a) 100	2,300	
Copy equipment	26,000				26,000	
Accumulated depreciation, copy equipment				(c) 375		375
Accounts payable		6,200				6,200
Salaries payable				(e) 210		210
Unearned copy services revenue		3,000	(d) 250			2,750
Common stock, 1$ par value		30,000				30,000
Cash dividends declared	600				600	
Copy services revenue		4,100		(d) 250		
				(f)1,800		6,150
Depreciation expense, copy equipment			(c) 375		375	
Salaries expense	1,400		(e) 210		1,610	
Insurance expense			(a) 100		100	
Rent expense	1,000				1,000	
Store supplies expense			(b)1,050		1,050	
Utilities expense	230				230	
Totals	43,300	43,300	3,785	3,785	45,685	45,685

ALTERNATIVE BALANCE SHEET FORMATS

Different companies choose different formats for their balance sheets. For example, the balance sheet in Illustration 2–8 (on p. 44) places the liabilities and stockholders' equity to the right of the assets. This format creates an **account form balance sheet.** If the items are arranged vertically, as shown in Illustration 4–5, the format creates a **report form balance sheet.** Both forms are widely used, and neither is considered more useful than the other.

Progress Check

4–10 The following information has been taken from Jones Corporation's unadjusted and adjusted trial balances:

	Unadjusted		Adjusted	
	Debit	Credit	Debit	Credit
Prepaid insurance	$6,200		$5,900	
Salaries payable				$1,400

The adjusting entries must have included these items: *(a)* a $300 debit to Prepaid Insurance and a $1,400 credit to Salaries Payable; *(b)* a $300 credit to Prepaid Insurance and a $1,400 debit to Salaries Payable; or *(c)* a $300 debit to Insurance Expense and a $1,400 debit to Salaries Expense.

4–11 What types of accounts are taken from the adjusted trial balance to prepare an income statement?

4–12 In preparing financial statements from an adjusted trial balance, which statement is prepared second?

Illustration 4–4 Preparing the Income Statement and the Statement of Retained Earnings

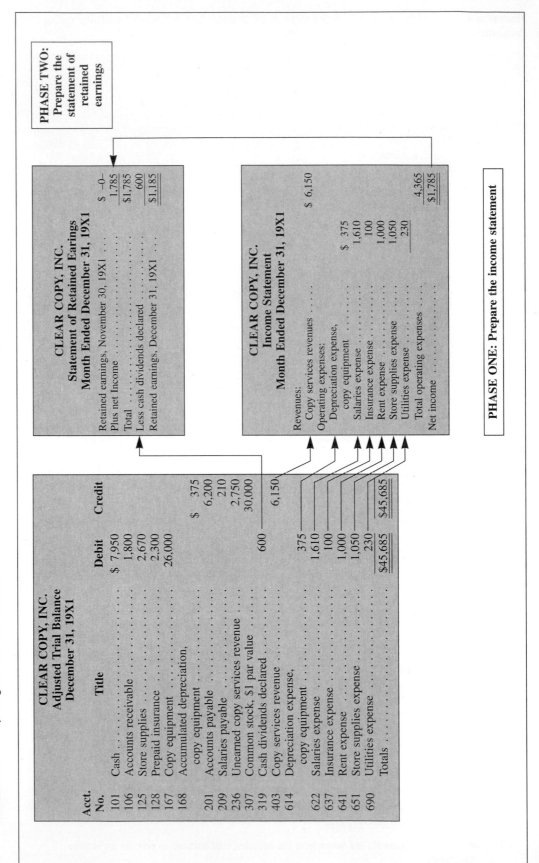

PHASE TWO: Prepare the statement of retained earnings

CLEAR COPY, INC.
Statement of Retained Earnings
Month Ended December 31, 19X1

Retained earnings, November 30, 19X1 . . .	$ -0-
Plus net Income	1,785
Total	$1,785
Less cash dividends declared	600
Retained earnings, December 31, 19X1	$1,185

CLEAR COPY, INC.
Income Statement
Month Ended December 31, 19X1

Revenues:		
Copy services revenues		$ 6,150
Operating expenses:		
Depreciation expense,		
copy equipment	$ 375	
Salaries expense	1,610	
Insurance expense	100	
Rent expense	1,000	
Store supplies expense	1,050	
Utilities expense	230	
Total operating expenses		4,365
Net income		$1,785

CLEAR COPY, INC.
Adjusted Trial Balance
December 31, 19X1

Acct. No.	Title	Debit	Credit
101	Cash	$ 7,950	
106	Accounts receivable	1,800	
125	Store supplies	2,670	
128	Prepaid insurance	2,300	
167	Copy equipment	26,000	
168	Accumulated depreciation,		
	copy equipment		$ 375
201	Accounts payable		6,200
209	Salaries payable		210
236	Unearned copy services revenue . .		2,750
307	Common stock, $1 par value . . .		30,000
319	Cash dividends declared	600	
403	Copy services revenue		6,150
614	Depreciation expense,		
	copy equipment	375	
622	Salaries expense	1,610	
637	Insurance expense	100	
641	Rent expense	1,000	
651	Store supplies expense	1,050	
690	Utilities expense	230	
	Totals	$45,685	$45,685

PHASE ONE: Prepare the income statement

Illustration 4-5 Preparing the Balance Sheet from the Adjusted Trial Balance and the Statement of Retained Earnings

PHASE THREE: Prepare the balance sheet

CLEAR COPY, INC.
Adjusted Trial Balance
December 31, 19X1

Acct. No.	Title	Debit	Credit
101	Cash	$ 7,950	
106	Accounts receivable	1,800	
125	Store supplies	2,670	
128	Prepaid insurance	2,300	
167	Copy equipment	26,000	
168	Accumulated depreciation, copy equipment		$ 375
201	Accounts payable		6,200
209	Salaries payable		210
236	Unearned copy services revenue		2,750
307	Common stock, $1 par value		30,000
319	Cash dividends declared	600	
403	Copy services revenue		6,150
614	Depreciation expense, copy equipment	375	
622	Salaries expense	1,610	
637	Insurance expense	100	
641	Rent expense	1,000	
651	Store supplies expense	1,050	
690	Utilities expense	230	
	Totals	$45,685	$45,685

CLEAR COPY, INC.
Balance Sheet
December 31, 19X1

Assets

Cash		$ 7,950
Accounts receivable		1,800
Store supplies		2,670
Prepaid insurance		2,300
Copy equipment	$26,000	
Less accumulated depreciation	(375)	25,625
Total assets		$40,345

Liabilities

Accounts payable	$ 6,200
Salaries payable	210
Unearned copy services revenue	2,750
Total liabilities	$ 9,160

Stockholders' Equity

Contributed capital:		
Common stock, $1 par value	$30,000	
Retained earnings	1,185	
Total stockholders' equity		31,185
Total liabilities and stockholders' equity		$40,345

From statement of retained earnings (Illustration 4-4)

REMOVING ACCRUED ASSETS AND LIABILITIES FROM THE ACCOUNTS

LO 2

Prepare adjusting entries for prepaid expenses, depreciation, unearned revenues, accrued expenses, and accrued revenues and prepare entries to record cash receipts and cash disbursements related to accrued assets and liabilities.

Revenues that are accrued at the end of an accounting period usually result in cash receipts from customers during the next period. In addition, expenses that were accrued at the end of an accounting period usually result in cash payments during the next period to settle the unpaid liabilities. This section explains how the accrued assets and accrued liabilities are removed from the accounts.

Accrued Expenses

Earlier, Clear Copy, Inc., recorded three days of accrued wages for its employee with this adjusting entry:

Dec.	31	Salaries Expense	210.00	
		Salaries Payable		210.00
		To record three days' accrued salary (3 × $70).		

When the next payday comes on Friday, January 9, the following entry removes the accrued liability and records additional salaries expense for January:

Jan.	9	Salaries Payable (3 days at $70)	210.00	
		Salaries Expense (7 days at $70)	490.00	
		Cash		700.00
		Paid two weeks' salary, including three days' accrued in December.		

The first debit in the January 9 entry records the payment of the liability for the three days' salary accrued on December 31. The second debit records the salary for January's first seven working days (including the New Year's Day holiday) as an expense of the new accounting period. The credit records the total amount of cash paid to the employee.

Accrued Revenues

On December 31, the following adjusting entry was made to record 20 days' accrued revenue earned under Clear Copy's contract with the bank:

Dec.	31	Accounts Receivable	1,800.00	
		Copy Services Revenue		1,800.00
		To record 20 days' accrued revenue.		

When the first month's fee is received on January 11, the company makes the following entry to eliminate the receivable and recognize the revenue earned in January:

Jan.	11	Cash	2,700.00	
		Accounts Receivable		1,800.00
		Copy Services Revenue		900.00
		Received cash for accrued and earned copy services revenue.		

The first credit in the entry records the collection of the receivable. The second credit records the earned revenue.

Progress Check

4-13   On December 31, 19X1, Hall Company recorded $1,600 of accrued salaries. On January 5 (the next payday), salaries of $8,000 were paid. From this you know that: *(a)* the company uses cash basis accounting; *(b)* the January 5 entry includes a $6,400 credit to Cash; or *(c)* the salaries expense assigned to 19X2 is $6,400.

Prepaid Expenses

The previous discussion in this chapter emphasized the fact that prepaid expenses are assets at the time they are purchased. Therefore, at the time of purchase, we recorded prepaid expenses with debits to asset accounts. Then, at the end of the accounting period, adjusting entries transferred the cost that had expired to expense accounts. We also recognized that some prepaid expenses are purchased and will fully expire before the end of the accounting period. In these cases, the accountant can avoid having to make adjusting entries by charging the prepaid items to expense accounts at the time of purchase.

Some companies follow a practice of recording all prepaid expenses with debits to expense accounts. Then, at the end of the accounting period, if any amounts remain unused or unexpired, adjusting entries are made to transfer the cost of the unused portions from the expense accounts to prepaid expense (asset) accounts. This practice is perfectly acceptable. The reported financial statements are exactly the same under either procedure.

To illustrate the differences between the two procedures, recall that on December 26, Clear Copy paid for 24 months of insurance coverage that began on December 1. We recorded that payment with a debit to an asset account but could have recorded a debit to an expense account. The alternatives are:

RECORDING PREPAID AND UNEARNED ITEMS IN INCOME STATEMENT ACCOUNTS

LO 4
Explain why some companies record prepaid and unearned items in income statement accounts and prepare adjusting entries when this procedure is used.

		Payment Recorded as Asset		Payment Recorded as Expense	
Dec.	26 Prepaid Insurance	2,400.00			
	Cash		2,400.00		
	26 Insurance Expense			2,400.00	
	Cash				2,400.00

At the end of the accounting period (December 31), insurance protection for one month has expired. That means $2,400/24 = $100 of the asset expired and became an expense of December. The required adjusting entry depends on how the original payment was recorded. The alternative adjusting entries are:

		Payment Recorded as Asset		Payment Recorded as Expense	
Dec.	31 Insurance Expense	100.00			
	Prepaid Insurance		100.00		
	31 Prepaid Insurance			2,300.00	
	Insurance Expense				2,300.00

When these entries are posted to the accounts, you can see that the two alternative procedures give the same results. Regardless of which procedure is followed, the December 31 adjusted account balances show prepaid insurance of $2,300 and insurance expense of $100.

Payment Recorded as Asset			**Payment Recorded as Expense**		
Prepaid Insurance			**Prepaid Insurance**		
Dec. 26	2,400	Dec. 31 100	Dec. 31	2,300	
	− 100				
Balance	2,300				

Insurance Expense			**Insurance Expense**		
Dec. 31	100		Dec. 26	2,400	Dec. 31 2,300
				− 2,300	
			Balance	100	

To continue the example for another month, assume that on January 1, Clear Copy paid $750 to purchase a second insurance policy. This policy provides protection for three months beginning January 1. Therefore, the total cost of unexpired insurance on January 1 was $2,300 + $750 = $3,050. On January 31, $250 of the second policy's cost (one month's worth) had expired. Since $100 of the first insurance policy and $250 of the second insurance policy expired during January, the adjusting entry on January 31 must be designed to report an insurance expense of $350 and a prepaid insurance asset of $3,050 − $350 = $2,700. Depending on how the original payments were recorded, the alternative adjusting entries are:

		Payment Recorded as Asset		**Payment Recorded as Expense**	
Jan.	31 Insurance Expense	350.00			
	Prepaid Insurance		350.00		
	31 Prepaid Insurance			400.00	
	Insurance Expense				400.00

Note that if the insurance payments are debited to an expense account, the required adjusting entry increases the Prepaid Insurance account balance $400, from $2,300 to $2,700. The credit in the entry reduces the Insurance Expense account debit balance from $750 to $350.

Unearned Revenues

The procedures for recording unearned revenues are similar to those used to record prepaid expenses. Receipts of unearned revenues may be recorded with credits to liability accounts (as described earlier in the chapter) or they may be recorded with credits to revenue accounts. The adjusting entries at the end of the period are different, depending on which procedure is followed. Nevertheless, either procedure is acceptable. The amounts reported in the financial statements are exactly the same, regardless of which procedure is used.

To illustrate the alternative procedures of recording unearned revenues, recall that on December 26, Clear Copy received $3,000 in payment for copying services to be provided over the two-month period beginning December 15. Earlier in the chapter, that receipt was recorded with a credit to a liability account. The alternative would be to record it with a credit to a revenue account. Both alternatives follow:

		Receipt Recorded as a Liability		**Receipt Recorded as a Revenue**	
Dec.	26 Cash	3,000.00			
	Unearned Copy Services Revenue		3,000.00		
	26 Cash			3,000.00	
	Copy Services Revenue . . .				3,000.00

By the end of the accounting period (December 31), Clear Copy had earned $250 of this revenue. That means $250 of the liability had been satisfied. Depending on how the original receipt was recorded, the required adjusting entry is as follows:

		Reciept Recorded as a Liability	Reciept Recorded as a Revenue
Dec.	31 Unearned Copy Services Revenue	250.00	
	Copy Services Revenue		250.00
	31 Copy Services Revenue		2,750.00
	Unearned Copy Services		
	Revenue		2,750.00

After these entries are posted, you can see that the two alternative procedures give the same results. Regardless of which procedure is followed, the December 31 adjusted account balances show unearned copy services revenue of $2,750 and copy services revenue of $250.

Receipt Recorded as a Liability				Receipt Recorded as a Revenue			
Unearned Copy Services Revenue				**Unearned Copy Services Revenue**			
Dec. 31	250	Dec. 26	3,000			Dec. 31	2,750
			− 250				
		Balance	2,750				

Copy Services Revenue				**Copy Services Revenue**			
		Dec. 31	250	Dec. 31	2,250	Dec. 26	3,000
							− 2,750
						Balance	250

Progress Check

4–14   Burr Company records cash receipts of unearned revenues and cash payments of prepaid expenses in balance sheet accounts. Diggs Company records these items in income statement accounts. Explain any difference in the financial statements of the companies that will result from their use of different procedures.

By now, it should be clear that accountants go to great lengths to ensure that a company's financial statements reflect up-to-date information about its assets, liabilities, revenues, and expenses. A primary goal of this effort is to provide information that helps internal and external decision makers evaluate the results achieved in the reporting period. This includes evaluating management's success in generating profits. The information may suggest ways to achieve better results and also helps users predict future results.

In using accounting information to evaluate the results of operations, one widely used ratio relates the company's net income to its sales. The ratio is called the **profit margin** or the **return on sales,** and is calculated with this formula:

$$\text{Profit margin} = \frac{\text{Net income}}{\text{Revenues}}$$

In effect, this ratio measures the average portion of each dollar of revenue that ends up as profit.

USING THE INFORMATION— THE PROFIT MARGIN

LO 5
Calculate the profit margin ratio and describe what it reveals about a company's performance.

Recall from the beginning of the chapter the conversation between the chief financial officer of **Ben & Jerry's Homemade, Inc.,** and a Ben & Jerry's stockholder. The stockholder expressed a desire to learn more about the money side of the company. The company's profit margin is one measure the stockholder might use to evaluate the company's performance. The profit margins during several past years were:

(in thousands)	Year Ended				
	12/26/94	**12/28/93**	**12/29/92**	**12/30/91**	**12/31/90**
Net income	$ (1,868)	$ 7,200	$ 6,675	$ 3,739	$ 2,609
Net sales	148,802	140,328	131,969	96,997	77,024
Profit margin	**(1.3%)**	**5.1%**	**5.1%**	**3.9%**	**3.4%**

Note the positive trend in the company's profit margin prior to 1994. This appeared even more favorable because the company's sales volume increased from a little more than $47.5 million to almost $132 million during the same period of time. In 1994, however, the rate of growth slowed and the company struggled with operating inefficiencies. As a result, the profit margin was a negative 1.3%.

In evaluating Ben & Jerry's profit margin, the negative profit margin in 1994 obviously was not good. Even if we assume that the company returns to the levels of profit margin in previous years, you cannot say that the values are good without making comparisons to other companies. In fact, Ben & Jerry's is a relatively small competitor in the super-premium ice cream industry. As a result of selling in this segment of the market, the company's historical profit margins are higher than those of producers with more standard products. However, the competition from larger super-premium companies keeps Ben & Jerry's from enjoying a higher margin.

In a small company that has only a few stockholders, the stockholders may be active in managing the company. Sometimes the salaries paid by the company to these stockholders, if any, do not reflect the value of their services to the company. Thus, care must be taken in evaluating the profit margins of small, closely held companies.

For example, you may have noticed that Annette Dow, the president of Clear Copy, Inc., does not receive a salary. Therefore, to calculate a reasonable profit margin for the company, you should modify the formula by subtracting the value of Dow's management efforts from the net income. To illustrate, assume that Dow's efforts on behalf of Clear Copy are worth $1,500 per month. Based on this assumption, the company's modified profit margin for December 19X1 should be calculated as follows:

$$\text{Modified profit margin} = \frac{\$1,785 - \$1,500}{\$6,150} = 4.6\%$$

Progress Check

4-15   The profit margin is the ratio between a company's net income and total *(a)* expenses; *(b)* assets; *(c)* liabilities; or *(d)* revenues.

4-16   If a company had a profit margin of 22.5% and net income of $1,012,500, what was the total amount of its revenues for the reporting period?

LO 1. Explain why financial statements are prepared at the end of regular accounting periods, why the accounts must be adjusted at the end of each period, and why the accrual basis of accounting produces more useful income statements and balance sheets than the cash basis. Companies prepare reports once each year. They also prepare interim financial statements because decision makers need information frequently and promptly. Adjusting entries are needed to capture information about unrecorded events that are not external transactions. The revenue recognition principle requires adjustments to ensure that revenue is reported when it is earned. The matching principle requires adjustments to ensure that expenses are reported in the same period as the revenue that was earned as a result of the expenses.

Accrual accounting is preferred to cash basis accounting because accrual accounting reports the economic effects of events when they occur, not when the cash flows happen. In addition to accrual basis financial statements, however, GAAP requires companies to report a statement of cash flows.

LO 2. Prepare adjusting entries for prepaid expenses, depreciation, unearned revenues, accrued expenses, and accrued revenues and prepare entries to record cash receipts and cash disbursements related to accrued assets and liabilities. Adjusting entries are used *(a)* to record expenses when prepaid expenses expire, *(b)* to record depreciation expense as the cost of using plant and equipment assets, *(c)* to record revenues when the company converts unearned revenues to earned revenues, *(d)* to accrue expenses and related liabilities, and *(e)* to accrue revenues and related assets.

Payments of accrued expenses in the next accounting period are recorded with a debit to the accrued liability and may include another debit for any additional expense incurred since the beginning of the new period. When accrued revenues are collected, the entry credits the previously recorded asset (a receivable) and may include another credit for any additional revenue earned during the new period.

LO 3. Prepare a schedule that includes the unadjusted trial balance, the adjustments, and the adjusted trial balance and use the adjusted trial balance to prepare financial statements. The effects of adjustments can be shown in a six-column schedule that presents the unadjusted trial balance in the first two columns, the adjusting entries in the next two columns, and the adjusted trial balance in the final two columns. The adjusted trial balance shows all ledger accounts, including assets, liabilities, revenues, expenses, and stockholders' equity. As a result, it can be used to prepare the income statement, the statement of retained earnings, and the balance sheet.

LO 4. Explain why some companies record prepaid and unearned items in income statement accounts and prepare adjusting entries when this procedure is used. Because many prepaid expenses expire during the same period they are purchased, some companies choose to charge all prepaid expenses to expense accounts at the time they are purchased. When this is done, end-of-period adjusting entries are required to transfer any unexpired amounts from the expense accounts to appropriate asset accounts. Also, unearned revenues may be credited to revenue accounts at the time cash is received. If so, end-of-period adjusting entries are required to transfer any unearned amounts from the revenue accounts to appropriate unearned revenue accounts.

LO 5. Calculate the profit margin ratio and describe what it reveals about a company's performance. The profit margin ratio describes a company's income earning activities by showing the period's net income as a percentage of total revenue. It is found by dividing the reporting period's net income by the revenue for the same period. The ratio can be usefully interpreted only in light of additional facts about the company and its industry.

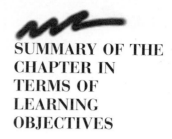

SUMMARY OF THE CHAPTER IN TERMS OF LEARNING OBJECTIVES

DEMONSTRATION PROBLEM

The following information relates to Best Plumbing Corporation on December 31, 19X2. The company uses the calendar year as its annual reporting period. The company initially records prepaid and unearned items in balance sheet accounts.

a. The company's weekly payroll is $2,800, paid every Friday for a five-day workweek. December 31, 19X2, falls on a Wednesday, but the employees will not be paid until Friday, January 2, 19X3.

b. Eighteen months earlier, on July 1, 19X1, the company purchased equipment that cost $10,000 and had no salvage value. Its useful life is predicted to be five years.

c. On October 1, 19X2, the company agreed to work on a new housing project. For installing plumbing in 24 new homes, the company was paid $144,000 in advance. When the $144,000 cash was received on October 1, 19X2, that amount was credited to the Unearned Plumbing Revenue account. Between October 1 and December 31, 19X2, work on 18 homes was completed.

d. On September 1, 19X2, the company purchased a one-year insurance policy for $1,200. The transaction was recorded with a $1,200 debit to Prepaid Insurance.

Required

1. Prepare the adjusting entries needed on December 31, 19X2, to record the previously unrecorded effects of the events.

2. Complete the following table describing the effects of your adjusting entries on the 19X2 income statement and the December 31, 19X2, balance sheet. Use parentheses to indicate a decrease.

Entry	Amount in the Entry	Effect on Net Income	Effect on Total Assets	Effect on Total Liabilities	Effect on Stockholders' Equity
a					
b					
c					
d					

Planning the Solution

- Analyze the information for each situation to determine which accounts need to be updated with an adjustment.
- Calculate the size of each adjustment and prepare the necessary journal entries.
- Show the amount entered by each adjustment in the designated accounts, determine the adjusted balance, and then determine the balance sheet classification that the account falls within.
- Determine each entry's effect on net income for the year and on total assets, total liabilities, and stockholders' equity at the end of the year.

Solution to Demonstration Problem

1. Adjusting journal entries:

a.	Dec.	31	Wages Expense	1,680.00	
			Wages Payable		1,680.00
			To accrue wages for the last three days of the year ($2,800 × 3/5).		
b.	Dec.	31	Depreciation Expense, Equipment	2,000.00	
			Accumulated Depreciation, Equipment		2,000.00
			To record depreciation expense for the full year ($10,000/5 = $2,000).		
c.	Dec.	31	Unearned Plumbing Revenue	108,000.00	
			Plumbing Services Revenue		108,000.00
			To recognize plumbing revenues earned ($144,000 × 18/24).		

d. Dec. 31 Insurance Expense 400.00
                      Prepaid Insurance 400.00
                      To adjust for the expired portion of
                      insurance ($1,200 × 4/12).

2.

Entry	Amount in the Entry	Effect on Net Income	Effect on Total Assets	Effect on Total Liabilities	Effect on Stockholders' Equity
a	$1,680	$1,680	No effect	$1,680	$(1,680)
b	$2,000	$(2,000)	$(2,000)	No effect	$(2,000)
c	$108,000	$108,000	No effect	$(108,000)	$108,000
d	$400	$(400)	$(400)	No effect	$(400)

GLOSSARY

Account form balance sheet a balance sheet that places the liabilities and stockholders' equity to the right of the assets. p. 121.

Accounting period the length of time covered by periodic financial statements and other reports. p. 110

Accrual basis accounting the approach to preparing financial statements based on recognizing revenues when they are earned and matching expenses to those revenues; the basis for generally accepted accounting principles. p. 112

Accrued expenses incurred but unpaid expenses that are recorded during the adjusting process; recorded with a debit to an expense and a credit to a liability. p. 118

Accrued revenues earned but uncollected revenues that are recorded during the adjusting process; recorded with a credit to a revenue and a debit to an asset. p. 119

Adjusted trial balance a trial balance prepared after adjustments have been recorded. p. 120

Adjusting entry a journal entry at the end of an accounting period that recognizes revenues earned or expenses incurred in that period while updating the related liability and asset accounts. p. 114

Cash basis accounting the approach to preparing financial statements based on recognizing revenues when the cash is received and reporting expenses when the cash is paid; not generally accepted. p. 112

Contra account an account the balance of which is subtracted from the balance of a related account so that more complete information than simply the net amount is provided. p. 116

Depreciation the expense created by allocating the cost of plant and equipment to the periods in which they are used; represents the expense of using the assets. p. 115

Fiscal year the 12 consecutive months (or 52 weeks) selected as an organization's annual accounting period. p. 110

Interim financial reports financial reports covering less than one year; usually based on one- or three-month periods. p. 110

Matching principle the broad principle that requires expenses to be reported in the same period as the revenues that were earned as a result of the expenses. p. 111

Natural business year a 12-month period that ends when a company's sales activities are at their lowest point. p. 111

Plant and equipment tangible long-lived assets used to produce goods or services. p. 115

Profit margin the ratio of a company's net income to its revenues; measures the average proportion of each dollar of revenue that ends up as profit. p. 127

Report from balance sheet a balance sheet that places the assets above the liabilities and stockholders' equity. p. 121

Return on sales another name for profit margin. p. 127

Time period principle a broad principle that requires identifying the activities of a business with specific time periods such as months, quarters, or years. p. 110.

Unadjusted trial balance a trial balance prepared before adjustments have been recorded. p. 120

QUESTIONS

1. What type of business is most likely to select a fiscal year that corresponds to the natural business year instead of the calendar year?

2. What kind of assets require adjusting entries to record depreciation?

3. What contra account is used when recording and reporting the effects of depreciation? Why is it used?

4. Where is an unearned revenue reported in the financial statements?

5. What is an accrued revenue? Give an example.

6. What is the difference between the cash and accrual bases of accounting?

7. Where is a prepaid expense reported in the financial statements?

8. Why is the accrual basis of accounting preferred over the cash basis?

9. If a company initially records prepaid expenses with debits to expense accounts, what type of account is debited in the adjusting entries for prepaid expenses?

10. Why might a small, closely held corporation require special procedures in calculating the profit margin?

11. Review the consolidated balance sheets of Lands' End in Appendix F. Assume that all accrued expenses existing at the end of each year are paid within a few months. What was the total amount of expenses that were accrued in the company's adjusting entries as of January 27, 1995?

LANDS' END
DIRECT MERCHANTS

12. Review the consolidated balance sheet of Southwest Airlines Co. presented in Appendix E. As a simplification, assume that the company did not sell any property, plant, and equipment during 1994. How much depreciation was recorded in the adjusting entries at the end of 1994?

QUICK STUDY (Five-Minute Exercises)

QS 4–1
(LO 1)

In its first year of operations, Harris Co. earned $39,000 in revenues and received $33,000 cash from customers. The company incurred expenses of $22,500 but had not paid for $2,250 of them at year-end. In addition, Harris prepaid $3,750 for expenses that would be incurred the next year. Calculate the first year's net income under a cash basis and calculate the first year's net income under an accrual basis.

QS 4–2
(LO 2)

In recording its transactions during the year, Stark Company records prepayments of expenses in asset accounts and receipts of unearned revenues in liability accounts. At the end of its annual accounting period, the company must make three adjusting entries. They are: *(a)* to accrue salaries expense, *(b)* to adjust the Unearned Services Revenue account to recognize earned revenue, and *(c)* to record the earning of services revenue for which cash will be received the following period. For each of these adjusting entries, use the numbers assigned to the following accounts to indicate the correct account to be debited and the correct account to be credited.

1. Prepaid Salaries Expense
2. Cash
3. Salaries Payable
4. Accounts Receivable
5. Salaries Expense
6. Services Revenue Earned
7. Unearned Services Revenue

QS 4–3
(LO 2)

In making adjusting entries at the end of its accounting period, Carter Corp. failed to record $1,400 of insurance premiums that had expired. This cost had been initially debited to the Prepaid Insurance account. The company also failed to record accrued salaries payable of $800. As a result of these oversights, the financial statements for the reporting period will: *(a)* understate assets by $1,400; *(b)* understate expenses by $2,200; *(c)* understate net income by $800; or *(d)* overstate liabilities by $800.

QS 4–4
(LO 3)

The following information has been taken from Shank Company's unadjusted and adjusted trial balances:

	Unadjusted		Adjusted	
	Debit	**Credit**	**Debit**	**Credit**
Prepaid insurance	$3,100		$2,950	
Interest payable				$700

The adjusting entries must have included these items:

a. A $150 debit to Insurance Expense and a $700 debit to Interest Expense.

b. A $150 credit to Prepaid Insurance and a $700 debit to Interest Payable.

c. A $150 debit to Insurance Expense and a $700 debit to Interest Payable.

Foster Company initially records prepaid and unearned items in income statement accounts. In preparing adjusting entries at the end of the company's first accounting period:

QS 4–5
(LO 4)

a. Unpaid salaries will be recorded with a debit to Prepaid Salaries and a credit to Salaries Expense.

b. The cost of unused office supplies will be recorded with a debit to Supplies Expense and a credit to Office Supplies.

c. Unearned fees will be recorded with a debit to Consulting Fees Earned and a credit to Unearned Consulting Fees.

d. Earned but unbilled consulting fees will be recorded with a debit to Unearned Consulting Fees and a credit to Consulting Fees Earned.

e. None of the above is correct.

Revell Corporation had net income of $37,925 and revenue of $390,000 for the year ended December 31, 19X1. Calculate Revell's profit margin.

QS 4–6
(LO 5)

EXERCISES

Prepare adjusting journal entries for the financial statements for the year ended December 31, 19X1, for each of these independent situations. Assume that prepaid expenses are initially recorded in asset accounts.

Exercise 4–1

Adjusting entries for expenses
(LO 2)

a. Depreciation on the company's equipment for 19X1 was estimated to be $16,000.

b. The Prepaid Insurance account had a $7,000 debit balance at December 31, 19X1, before adjusting for the costs of any expired coverage. An analysis of the company's insurance policies showed that $1,040 of unexpired insurance remained in effect.

c. The Office Supplies account had a $300 debit balance on January 1, 19X1; $2,680 of office supplies were purchased during the year; and the December 31, 19X1, account showed that $354 of supplies are on hand.

d. Six months' property taxes are estimated to be $10,800. They have accrued since June 30, 19X1, but are unrecorded and unpaid at December 31, 19X1.

e. The Prepaid Insurance account had a $5,600 debit balance at December 31, 19X1, before adjusting for the costs of any expired coverage. An analysis of the company's insurance policies showed that $4,600 of coverage had expired.

Resource Management, Inc., has five part-time employees, and each earns $100 per day. They are normally paid on Fridays for work completed on Monday through Friday of the same week. They were all paid in full on Friday, December 28, 19X1. The next week, all five of the employees worked only four days because New Year's Day was an unpaid holiday. Show the adjusting entry that would be recorded on Monday, December 31, 19X1, and the journal entry that would be made to record paying the employees' wages on Friday, January 4, 19X2.

Exercise 4–2

Adjusting and subsequent entries for accrued expenses
(LO 2)

Exercise 4–3

Identifying adjusting entries

(LO 2)

In the blank space beside each of these adjusting entries, enter the letter of the explanation that most closely describes the entry:

a.   To record the year's depreciation expense.

b.   To record accrued salaries expense.

c.   To record the year's consumption of a prepaid expense.

d.   To record accrued income.

e.   To record accrued interest expense.

f.   To record the earning of previously unearned income.

___ 1.	Unearned Professional Fees	18,450.00	
	Professional Fees Earned		18,450.00
___ 2.	Interest Receivable	2,700.00	
	Interest Earned		2,700.00
___ 3.	Depreciation Expense	49,500.00	
	Accumulated Depreciation		49,500.00
___ 4.	Salaries Expense	16,400.00	
	Salaries Payable		16,400.00
___ 5.	Interest Expense.............................	3,800.00	
	Interest Payable		3,800.00
___ 6.	Insurance Expense	4,200.00	
	Prepaid Insurance		4,200.00

Exercise 4–4

Missing data in supplies expense calculations

(LO 2)

Determine the missing amounts in each of these four independent situations:

	a.	b.	c.	d.
Supplies on hand—January 1	$ 300	$1,600	$1,360	?
Supplies purchased during the year	2,100	5,400	?	$6,000
Supplies on hand—December 31	750	?	1,840	800
Supplies expense for the year	?	1,300	9,600	6,575

Exercise 4–5

Adjustments and payments of accrued items

(LO 2)

The following three situations require adjusting journal entries to prepare financial statements as of April 30. For each situation, present the adjusting entry and the entry that would be made to record the payment of the accrued liability during May.

a.   The company has a $780,000 note payable that requires 0.8% interest to be paid each month on the 20th of the month. The interest was last paid on April 20 and the next payment is due on May 20.

b.   The total weekly salaries expense for all employees is $9,000. This amount is paid at the end of the day on Friday of each week. April 30 falls on Tuesday of this year, which means that the employees had worked two days since the last payday. The next payday is May 3.

c.   On April 1, the company retained an attorney at a flat monthly fee of $2,500. This amount is payable on the 12th of the following month.

Exercise 4–6

Amounts of cash and accrual basis expenses

(LO 1, 2)

On March 1, 19X1, a company paid a $16,200 premium on a three-year insurance policy for protection beginning on that date. Fill in the blanks in the following table:

	Balance Sheet Asset under the:			Insurance Expense under the:		
	Accrual Basis	Cash Basis			Accrual Basis	Cash Basis
12/31/X1	$_____	$_____	19X1		$_____	$_____
12/31/X2	_____	_____	19X2		_____	_____
12/31/X3	_____	_____	19X3		_____	_____
12/31/X4	_____	_____	19X4		_____	_____
			Total		$_____	$_____

Landmark Properties owns and operates an apartment building and prepares annual financial statements based on a March 31 fiscal year.

Exercise 4–7

Unearned and accrued revenues

(LO 2)

a. The tenants of one of the apartments paid five months' rent in advance on November 1, 19X1. The monthly rental is $1,500 per month. The journal entry credited the Unearned Rent account when the payment was received. No other entry had been recorded prior to March 31, 19X2. Give the adjusting journal entry that should be recorded on March 31, 19X2.

b. On January 1, 19X2, the tenants of another apartment moved in and paid the first month's rent. The $1,350 payment was recorded with a credit to the Rent Earned account. However, the tenants have not paid the rent for February or March. They have agreed to pay it as soon as possible. Give the adjusting journal entry that should be recorded on March 31, 19X2.

c. On April 2, 19X2, the tenants described in part b paid $4,050 rent for February, March, and April. Give the journal entry to record the cash collection.

Following are two income statements for Pemberton Company for the year ended December 31. The left column was prepared before any adjusting entries were recorded and the right column includes the effects of adjusting entries. The company records cash receipts and disbursements related to unearned and prepaid items in balance sheet accounts. Analyze the statements and prepare the adjusting entries that must have been recorded. Thirty percent of the additional fees were earned but not billed and the other 70% were earned by performing services that the customers had paid for in advance.

Exercise 4–8

Identifying the effects of adjusting entries

(LO 2, 3)

PEMBERTON COMPANY
Income Statements
For Year Ended December 31

	Before Adjustments	After Adjustments
Revenues:		
Fees earned	$24,000	$30,000
Commissions earned	42,500	42,500
Total revenues	$66,500	$72,500
Operating expenses:		
Depreciation expense, computers		$ 1,500
Depreciation expense, office furniture . .		1,750
Salaries expense	$12,500	14,950
Insurance expense		1,300
Rent expense	4,500	4,500
Office supplies expense		480
Advertising expense	3,000	3,000
Utilities expense	1,250	1,320
Total operating expenses	$21,250	$28,800
Net income	$45,250	$43,700

Classic Customs, Inc., began operations on December 1. In setting up the bookkeeping procedures, the company decided to debit expense accounts when the company prepays its expenses and to credit revenue accounts when customers pay for services in advance. Prepare journal entries for items a through d and adjusting entries as of December 31 for items e through g:

Exercise 4–9

Adjustments for prepaid items recorded in expense and revenue accounts

(LO 4)

a. Supplies were purchased on December 1 for $3,000.

b. The company prepaid insurance premiums of $1,440 on December 2.

c. On December 15, the company received an advance payment of $12,000 from one customer for remodeling work.

d. On December 28, the company received $3,600 from a second customer for remodeling work to be performed in January.

e.   By counting them on December 31, Classic Customs determined that $1,920 of supplies were on hand.

f.   An analysis of the insurance policies in effect on December 31 showed that $240 of insurance coverage had expired.

g.   As of December 31, only one project had been completed. The $6,300 fee for this particular project had been received in advance.

Exercise 4–10
Alternative procedures for revenues received in advance
(LO 2, 4) ˙

The Pavillion Company experienced the following events and transactions during July:

July 1   Received $2,000 in advance of performing work for Andrew Renking.
       6   Received $8,400 in advance of performing work for Matt Swarbuck.
      12   Completed the job for Andrew Renking.
      18   Received $7,500 in advance of performing work for Drew Sayer.
      27   Completed the job for Matt Swarbuck.
      31   The job for Drew Sayer is still unfinished.

a.   Give journal entries (including any adjusting entry as of the end of the month) to record these events using the procedure of initially crediting the Unearned Fees account when a payment is received from a customer in advance of performing services.

b.   Give journal entries (including any adjusting entry as of the end of the month) to record these events using the procedure of initially crediting the Fees Earned account when a payment is received from a customer in advance of performing services.

c.   Under each method, determine the amount of earned fees that should be reported on the income statement for July and the amount of unearned fees that should appear on the balance sheet as of July 31.

Exercise 4–11
Calculating the profit margin
(LO 5)

Use the following information to calculate the profit margin for each case:

	Net Income	Revenue
a.	$ 3,490	$ 31,620
b.	96,744	394,953
c.	110,204	252,786
d.	55,026	1,350,798
e.	79,264	433,914

PROBLEMS

Problem 4–1
Adjusting and subsequent journal entries
(LO 2)

Garza Corp.'s annual accounting period ends on December 31, 19X2. Garza follows the practice of recording prepaid expenses and unearned revenues in balance sheet accounts. The following information concerns the adjusting entries to be recorded as of that date:

a.   The Office Supplies account started the year with a $3,000 balance. During 19X2, the company purchased supplies at a cost of $12,400, which was added to the Office Supplies account. The inventory of supplies on hand at December 31 had a cost of $2,640.

b.   An analysis of the company's insurance policies provided these facts:

Policy	Date of Purchase	Years of Coverage	Total Cost
1	April 1, 19X1	2	$15,840
2	April 1, 19X2	3	13,068
3	August 1, 19X2	1	2,700

The total premium for each policy was paid in full at the purchase date, and the Prepaid Insurance account was debited for the full cost.

c. The company has 15 employees who earn a total of $2,100 in salaries for every working day. They are paid each Monday for their work in the five-day workweek ending on the preceding Friday. December 31, 19X2, falls on Tuesday, and all 15 employees worked the first two days of the week. Because New Year's Day is a paid holiday, they will be paid salaries for five full days on Monday, January 6, 19X3.

d. The company purchased a building on August 1, 19X2. The building cost $855,000 and is expected to have a $45,000 salvage value at the end of its predicted 30-year life.

e. Because the company is not large enough to occupy the entire building, it arranged to rent some space to a tenant at $2,400 per month, starting on November 1, 19X2. The rent was paid on time on November 1, and the amount received was credited to the Rent Earned account. However, the tenant has not paid the December rent. The company has worked out an agreement with the tenant, who has promised to pay both December's and January's rent in full on January 15. The tenant has agreed not to fall behind again.

f. On November 1, the company also rented space to another tenant for $2,175 per month. The tenant paid five months' rent in advance on that date. The payment was recorded with a credit to the Unearned Rent account.

Required

1. Use the information to prepare adjusting entries as of December 31, 19X2.
2. Prepare journal entries to record the subsequent cash transactions described in parts *c* and *e*.

CHECK FIGURE:
Insurance expense, $12,312

Problem 4–2
Adjusting entries, financial statements, and profit margin
(LO 2, 3, 5)

Southwest Careers, Inc., provides training to individuals who pay tuition directly to the business and also offers extension training to groups in off-site locations. The school's unadjusted trial balance as of December 31, 19X2, follows. Southwest Careers follows the practice of initially recording prepaid expenses and unearned revenues in balance sheet accounts. Facts that require eight adjusting entries on December 31, 19X2, are presented after the trial balance:

SOUTHWEST CAREERS, INC.
Unadjusted Trial Balance

Cash	$ 26,000	
Accounts receivable		
Teaching supplies	10,000	
Prepaid insurance	15,000	
Prepaid rent	2,000	
Professional library	30,000	
Accumulated depreciation, professional library		$ 9,000
Equipment	70,000	
Accumulated depreciation, equipment		16,000
Accounts payable		36,000
Salaries payable		
Unearned extension fees		11,000
Common stock, $1 par value		40,000
Retained earnings		23,600
Cash dividends declared	40,000	
Tuition fees earned		102,000
Extension fees earned		38,000
Depreciation expense, equipment		
Depreciation expense, professional library		
Salaries expense	48,000	
Insurance expense		
Rent expense	22,000	
Teaching supplies expense		
Advertising expense	7,000	
Utilities expense	5,600	
Totals	$275,600	$275,600

Additional facts:

a. An analysis of the company's policies shows that $3,000 of insurance coverage has expired.

b. An inventory shows that teaching supplies costing $2,600 are on hand at the end of the year.

c. The estimated annual depreciation on the equipment is $12,000.

d. The estimated annual depreciation on the professional library is $6,000.

e. The school offers off-campus services for specific employers. On November 1, the company agreed to do a special six-month course for a client. The contract calls for a monthly fee of $2,200, and the client paid the first five months' fees in advance. When the cash was received, the Unearned Extension Fees account was credited.

f. On October 15, the school agreed to teach a four-month class for an individual for $3,000 tuition per month payable at the end of the class. The services have been provided as agreed, and no payment has been received.

g. The school's two employees are paid weekly. As of the end of the year, two days' wages have accrued at the rate of $100 per day for each employee.

h. The balance in the Prepaid Rent account represents the rent for December.

Required

1. Enter the unadjusted trial balance in the first two columns of a six-column table like the one shown in Illustration 4–3.

2. Enter the adjusting entries in the Adjustments columns of the table. Identify the debits and credits of each entry with the letters in the list of additional facts. Complete the adjusted trial balance.

3. Prepare the company's income statement and statement of retained earnings for 19X2 and prepare the balance sheet as of December 31, 19X2.

4. Calculate the company's profit margin for the year.

CHECK FIGURE:
Ending retained earnings balance, $22,100

Problem 4–3
Comparing the unadjusted and adjusted trial balances, preparing financial statements, and calculating profit margin
(LO 2, 3, 5)

In the six-column table for RPE Corporation, on the opposite page, the first two columns contain the unadjusted trial balance for the company as of July 31, 19X2. The last two columns contain the adjusted trial balance as of the same date.

Required

Preparation component:

1. Prepare the company's income statement and the statement of retained earnings for the year ended July 31, 19X2.

2. Prepare the company's balance sheet as of July 31, 19X2.

3. Calculate the company's profit margin for the year.

CHECK FIGURE:
Profit margin, 22%

Analysis component:

4. Analyze the differences between the unadjusted and adjusted trial balances to determine the adjustments that must have been made. Show the results of your analysis by inserting the adjusting journal entries that must have been recorded by the company in the two middle columns. Label each entry with a letter and provide a short description of the purpose for recording it. (Use the Working Papers that accompany the text or recreate the table.)

	Unadjusted Trial Balance		Adjustments		Adjusted Trial Balance	
Cash	$ 27,000				$ 27,000	
Accounts receivable	12,000				22,460	
Office supplies	18,000				3,000	
Prepaid insurance	7,320				4,880	
Office equipment	92,000				92,000	
Accumulated depreciation, office equipment		$ 12,000				$ 18,000
Accounts payable		9,300				10,200
Interest payable						800
Salaries payable						6,600
Unearned consulting fees ..		16,000				14,300
Long-term notes payable ..		44,000				44,000
Common stock, $2 par value		20,000				20,000
Retained earnings		8,420				8,420
Cash dividends declared ...	10,000				10,000	
Consulting fees earned		156,000				168,160
Depreciation expense, office equipment					6,000	
Salaries expense	71,000				77,600	
Interest expense	1,400				2,200	
Insurance expense					2,440	
Rent expense	13,200				13,200	
Office supplies expense ...					15,000	
Advertising expense	13,800				14,700	
Totals	$265,720	$265,720			$290,480	$290,480

Problem 4–4

Accrual basis income

(LO 1, 2)

The records for Urban Landscape Co. were kept on the cash basis instead of the accrual basis. However, the company is now applying for a loan and the bank wants to know what its net income for 19X2 was under generally accepted accounting principles. Here is the income statement for 19X2 under the cash basis:

URBAN LANDSCAPE CO.
Income Statement (Cash Basis)
For Year Ended December 31, 19X2

Revenues	$525,000
Expenses	330,000
Net income	$195,000

This additional information was gathered to help the accountant convert the income statement to the accrual basis:

	As of 12/31/X1	As of 12/31/X2
Accrued revenues	$12,000	$16,500
Unearned revenues ...	66,000	21,000
Accrued expenses	14,700	9,000
Prepaid expenses	27,000	20,700

All prepaid expenses from the beginning of the year were consumed or expired, all unearned revenues from the beginning of the year were earned, and all accrued expenses and revenues from the beginning of the year were paid or collected.

Required

Prepare an accrual basis income statement for this business for 19X2. Provide schedules that explain how you converted from cash revenues and expenses to accrual revenues and expenses.

CHECK FIGURE:
Net income, $243,900

Problem 4–5

Identifying adjusting and subsequent entries

(LO 2)

For these adjusting and transaction entries, enter the letter of the explanation that most closely describes the adjustment or transaction in the blank space beside each entry. (You can use some letters more than once.)

a. To record collection of an unearned revenue.

b. To record the earning of previously unearned income.

c. To record payment of an accrued expense.

d. To record collection of an accrued revenue.

e. To record an accrued expense.

f. To record accrued income.

g. To record the year's consumption of a prepaid expense.

h. To record payment of a prepaid expense.

i. To record the year's depreciation expense.

___	1.	Depreciation Expense	3,000.00	
		Accumulated Depreciation		3,000.00
___	2.	Unearned Professional Fees	2,000.00	
		Professional Fees Earned		2,000.00
___	3.	Rent Expense	1,000.00	
		Prepaid Rent		1,000.00
___	4.	Interest Expense	4,000.00	
		Interest Payable		4,000.00
___	5.	Prepaid Rent	3,500.00	
		Cash		3,500.00
___	6.	Salaries Expense	5,000.00	
		Salaries Payable		5,000.00
___	7.	Insurance Expense	6,000.00	
		Prepaid Insurance		6,000.00
___	8.	Salaries Payable	1,500.00	
		Cash		1,500.00
___	9.	Cash	6,500.00	
		Unearned Professional Fees		6,500.00
___	10.	Cash	9,000.00	
		Interest Receivable		9,000.00
___	11.	Interest Receivable	7,000.00	
		Interest Earned		7,000.00
___	12.	Cash	8,000.00	
		Accounts Receivable		8,000.00

Problem 4–6

Preparing financial statements from the adjusted trial balance and calculating profit margin

(LO 3, 5)

This adjusted trial balance is for Conquest Corp. as of December 31, 19X2:

	Debit	Credit
Cash	$ 22,000	
Accounts receivable	44,000	
Interest receivable	10,000	
Notes receivable (due in 90 days)	160,000	
Office supplies	8,000	
Automobiles	160,000	
Accumulated depreciation, automobiles		$ 42,000
Equipment	130,000	
Accumulated depreciation, equipment		10,000
Land	70,000	
Accounts payable		88,000
Interest payable		12,000
Salaries payable		11,000
Unearned fees		22,000
Long-term notes payable		130,000
Common stock, $5 par value		200,000
Retained earnings		47,800
Dividends	38,000	
Fees earned		420,000
Interest earned		16,000

	Debit	Credit
Depreciation expense, automobiles	18,000	
Depreciation expense, equipment	10,000	
Salaries expense	180,000	
Wages expense	32,000	
Interest expense	24,000	
Office supplies expense	26,000	
Advertising expense	50,000	
Repairs expense, automobiles	16,800	
Total	$998,800	$998,800

Required

1. Use the information in the trial balance to prepare (a) the income statement for the year ended December 31, 19X2; (b) the statement of retained earnings for the year ended December 31, 19X2; and (c) the balance sheet as of December 31, 19X2.

2. Calculate the profit margin for 19X2. Assume that Stella Young is the sole stockholder of Conquest, and that her management contributions, valued at $30,000, are not compensated with a salary. Calculate the modified profit margin for 19X2.

CHECK FIGURE:
Total assets, $552,000

The following events occurred for a company during the last two months of its fiscal year ended December 31:

Problem 4–7

Recording prepaid expenses and unearned revenues

(LO 2, 4)

Nov. 1 Paid $1,500 for future newspaper advertising.

 1 Paid $2,160 for insurance through October 31 of the following year.

 30 Received $3,300 for future services to be provided to a customer.

Dec. 1 Paid $2,700 for the services of a consultant, to be received over the next three months.

 15 Received $7,650 for future services to be provided to a customer.

 31 Of the advertising paid for on November 1, $900 worth had not yet been published by the newspaper.

 31 Part of the insurance paid for on November 1 had expired.

 31 Services worth $1,200 had not yet been provided to the customer who paid on November 30.

 31 One-third of the consulting services paid for on December 1 had been received.

 31 The company had performed $3,000 of the services that the customer had paid for on December 15.

Required

Preparation component:

1. Prepare entries for the above events under the approach that records prepaid expenses as assets and records unearned revenues as liabilities. Also, prepare adjusting entries at the end of the year.

2. Prepare entries under the approach that records prepaid expenses as expenses and records unearned revenues as revenues. Also, prepare adjusting entries at the end of the year.

Analysis component:

3. Explain why the alternative sets of entries in requirements 1 and 2 do not result in different financial statement amounts.

SERIAL PROBLEM

Echo Systems, Inc.

(This comprehensive problem was introduced in Chapter 3 and continues in Chapters 5 and 6. If the Chapter 3 segment has not been completed, the assignment can begin at this point. However, you will need to use the facts presented on pages 103–104 in Chapter 3. Because of its length, this problem is most easily solved if you use the Working Papers that accompany this text.)

After the success of its first two months, Mary Graham has decided to continue operating Echo Systems, Inc. (The transactions that occurred in these months are described in Chapter 3.) Before proceeding into December, Graham adds these new accounts to the chart of accounts for the ledger:

Account	No.
Accumulated Depreciation, Office Equipment	164
Accumulated Depreciation, Computer Equipment	168
Wages Payable	210
Unearned Computer Services Revenue	236
Depreciation Expense, Office Equipment	612
Depreciation Expense, Computer Equipment	613
Insurance Expense	637
Rent Expense	640
Computer Supplies Expense	652

Required

1. Prepare journal entries to record each of the following transactions for Echo Systems, Inc. Post the entries to the accounts in the ledger.
2. Prepare adjusting entries to record the events described on December 31. Post the entries to the accounts in the ledger.
3. Prepare an adjusted trial balance as of December 31, 19X1.
4. Prepare an income statement for the three months ended December 31, 19X1.
5. Prepare a statement of retained earnings for the three months ended December 31, 19X1.
6. Prepare a balance sheet as of December 31, 19X1.

Transactions and other data:

Dec. 2   Paid $1,050 to the Lakeshore Mall for the company's share of mall advertising costs.

3   Paid $600 to repair the company's computer.

4   Received $3,750 from Alamo Engineering Co. for the receivable from the prior month.

10   Paid Carly Smith for six days' work at the rate of $100 per day.

14   Notified by Alamo Engineering Co. that Echo's bid of $6,000 on a proposed project was accepted. Alamo paid an advance of $1,500.

15   Purchased $1,155 of computer supplies on credit from Abbott Office Products.

16   Sent a reminder to Fostek Co. to pay the fee for services originally recorded on November 8.

20   Completed project for Elite Corporation and received $5,625 cash.

22–26 Took the week off for the holidays.

28   Received $2,850 from Fostek Co. on their receivable.

29   Reimbursed Mary Graham's business automobile mileage of 600 miles at $0.25 per mile.

Dec. 31 Declared and paid a $1,800 cash dividend on the common stock.

31 The following information was collected to be used in adjusting entries prior to preparing financial statements for the company's first three months:

a. The December 31 inventory of computer supplies was $720.

b. Three months have passed since the annual insurance premium was paid.

c. As of the end of the year, Carly Smith has not been paid for four days of work at the rate of $100 per day.

d. The computer is expected to have a four-year life with no salvage value.

e. The office equipment is expected to have a three-year life with no salvage value.

f. Prepaid rent for three of the four months has expired.

CRITICAL THINKING: ESSAYS, PROBLEMS, AND CASES

Analytical Essays

Review the information presented in paragraphs c, d, and e of Problem 4–1. Describe how each of the following errors from 19X2 would affect the company's income statements for 19X2 and 19X3 and its balance sheets as of December 31, 19X2, and 19X3 (treat each case as independent from the others). None of the errors were repeated in 19X3, but they remained undiscovered until well into 19X4.

AE 4–1
(LO 1, 2)

1. The company mistakenly recorded the $4,200 of accrued salary expense described in part c as if the amount was only $3,000. However, the employees were paid the correct amount on January 6, 19X3. At that time, the Salaries Payable account was debited for $3,000 and the remainder of the $10,500 payment to the employees was debited to the Salaries Expense account for 19X3.

2. The company failed to record the $11,250 depreciation expense on the building described in part d.

3. The company failed to record the $2,400 of accrued rent income described in part e. Instead, the revenue was recorded on January 15 as income earned in 19X3.

On November 1, 19X1, Capital Company and Hastings Company each paid $12,000 for six months' rent on their offices. Capital recorded its payment with a debit to the Prepaid Rent account. On the other hand, Hastings debited the Rent Expense account for $12,000. Both companies use calendar years as their accounting periods. Describe the differences between the adjusting entries the two companies should make on December 31, 19X1. Be sure to explain how the two companies' different bookkeeping procedures affect the financial statements.

AE 4–2
(LO 1, 2, 4)

Financial Reporting Problems

The 19X1 and 19X2 balance sheets for Hudson Co., Inc., reported the following assets and liabilities:

FRP 4–1
(LO 1, 2)

	19X1	19X2
Accounts receivable	$90,000	$124,000
Prepaid insurance	9,600	7,200
Interest payable	11,500	18,500
Unearned fees	34,000	50,000

The company's records show that the following amounts of cash were spent and received during 19X2:

Cash spent to pay insurance premiums	$ 25,000
Cash spent to pay interest	28,000
Cash received on accounts receivable	240,000
Cash received in advance for fees	216,000

Calculate the amounts to be reported on Hudson Co., Inc.'s 19X2 income statement for (a) insurance expense, (b) interest expense, and (c) total fees earned.

FRP 4–2
(LO 2, 3, 5)

Early in January, Carl Young created a new business called Penco Corp. Young is the sole stockholder of the $5 par value common stock and manager of the company. Unfortunately, Young has not maintained any double-entry accounting records, although all cash receipts and disbursements have been carefully recorded. In addition, all unpaid invoices for the company's expenses and purchases are kept in a file until they are paid. The cash records have been summarized in this schedule:

Cash received:		
Investments by stockholder	$ 96,000	
Services revenue	122,000	
Total		$218,000
Cash paid:		
Office equipment	$ 42,400	
Office supplies	50,000	
Rent	16,800	
Insurance premiums	1,800	
Newspaper advertising	4,000	
Utility bills	3,200	
Employee's wages	16,000	
Total cash payments		134,200
Cash balance as of December 31		$ 83,800

Young wants to know the net income for the first year and the company's financial position at the end of the year. Provide this information by preparing an accrual basis income statement, a statement of retained earnings, and a balance sheet. Also compute the profit margin for the year. Assuming Young's efforts are worth $42,000 per year, compute the modified profit margin.

    The following information will help you: The office equipment was bought in January and is predicted to have a useful life of 10 years, with a $2,400 salvage value. There is an $8,000 unpaid invoice in the file; it is for supplies that have been purchased and received. An inventory shows that $16,400 of supplies are on hand at the end of the year. The office space is rented for $1,200 per month under a five-year lease. The lease contract required Penco to pay the first and the final two months' rents in advance. The insurance premiums acquired two policies on January 2. The first is a one-year policy that cost $1,000, and the second is a two-year policy that cost $800. There are $380 of earned but unpaid wages as of December 31, and customers owe the company $7,500 for services they have received.

Financial Statement Analysis Case

(LO 2, 5)

Refer to the financial statements and related information for Southwest Airlines Co. in Appendix E. Find the answers to the following questions by analyzing the information in the report.

1. What type of balance sheet does Southwest Airlines present?
2. What is the total amount of accrued liabilities at December 31, 1994? Of the total amount of accrued liabilities, what portion is for interest? For vacation pay?
3. What is the total amount of accumulated depreciation as of December 31, 1994?
4. What amount of cash dividends was paid to stockholders?
5. What is the company's profit margin for the years ended 1994 and 1993?

Review the As a Matter of Ethics case on page 120. Describe the ethical dilemma faced by Bill Palmer and describe the alternative courses of action that he might take. Explain how your answer would differ given the following assumptions: *(a)* Palmer knows that the company's financial statements are not going to be audited; *(b)* Palmer knows that the president's bonus depends on the amount of income reported in the first year; and *(c)* Palmer's job depends on complying with the president's wishes.

Ethical Issues Essay

CONCEPT TESTER

Test your understanding of the concepts introduced in this chapter by completing the following crossword puzzle.

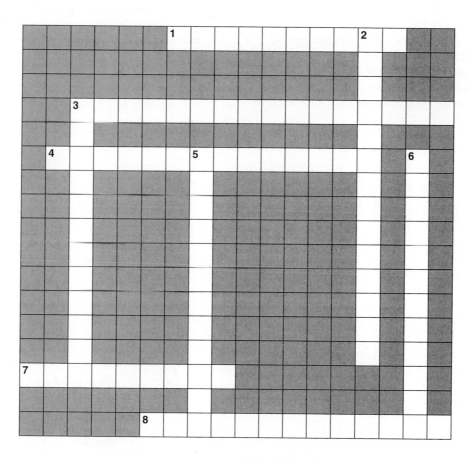

Across Clues

1. 2 words; the 12 months (or 52 weeks) selected as the annual accounting period.
3. 2 words; the length of time covered by periodic financial statements.
4. 2 words; earned but uncollected revenue that is recorded during the adjusting process.
7. 2 words; recognizes revenue when cash is received and expenses when cash is paid.
8. 2 words; an account whose balance is subtracted from a related account.

Down Clues

2. 2 words; an incurred but unpaid expense that is recorded during the adjusting process.
3. 2 words; recognizes revenues when they are earned and matches expenses with those revenues.
5. Expense created by allocating the cost of plant assets to the periods in which they are used.
6. 2 words; net income divided by revenues.

ANSWERS TO PROGRESS CHECKS

4-1   *a*

4-2   Interim financial statements are prepared to provide decision makers information frequently and promptly.

4-3   The revenue recognition principle and the matching principle.

4-4   No, the cash basis is not consistent with the matching principle because it does not always report expenses in the same period as the revenues that were earned as a result of the expenses.

4-5   No expense is reported in 19X2. Under the cash basis, the entire $4,800 is reported as expense in 19X1 when the premium was paid.

4-6   *c*

4-7   The balance of a contra account is subtracted from the balance of a related account so that more complete information than simply the net amount is provided.

4-8   An accrued expense is an incurred expense that is not recorded prior to adjusting entries because it has not been paid. An example is unpaid salaries earned by employees prior to the year-end.

4-9   An unearned revenue arises when cash is received from a customer before the service is provided to the customer. Magazine subscription receipts are an example.

4-10 *c*

4-11 Revenue accounts and expense accounts.

4-12 The statement of retained earnings is prepared second.

4-13 *c*

4-14 As long as adjusting entries are correctly prepared, it does not make any difference whether cash receipts of unearned revenues and cash payments of prepaid expenses are recorded in balance sheet accounts or in income statement accounts. The financial statements of the companies will be the same.

4-15 *d*

4-16 $1,012,500/Revenues = 22.5%. Therefore, total revenues were $4,500,000.

Concluding the Accounting Cycle and Expanding the Balance Sheet

Jay Cochren has been a loyal owner of a Harley-Davidson motorcycle for years and has often thought an investment in the company might be a good thing. To learn more about the company, he obtained a copy of its 1994 annual report. From the report, Cochren learned that the company shipped 95,811 motorcycle units to dealers during 1994. This represented a 17.3% increase over unit shipments in 1993.

The company also has a Transportation Vehicles segment that produces motor homes, other recreational vehicles, and commercial vehicles such as delivery vans and truck bodies. The Transportation Vehicles segment accounts for about 25% of Harley-Davidson's total dollar sales.

Cochren is not very familiar with financial statements but observed that one of the statements lists a variety of assets under a label called "current assets." It also lists several current liabilities. Cochren wonders why these items are separated from the other items on the statement and why they are described as being *current*. Perhaps they are related to each other in some important way.

HARLEY-DAVIDSON, INC.
(in thousands)

	December 31,	
	1994	1993
Assets		
Total current assets	$405,636	$333,758
Total current liabilities	216,278	190,762

LEARNING OBJECTIVES

After studying Chapter 5, you should be able to:

1. **Explain why the temporary accounts are closed at the end of each accounting period and prepare closing entries and a post-closing trial balance for a service business.**
2. **Describe and perform each step in the accounting cycle.**
3. **Define each asset and liability category for the balance sheet and prepare a classified balance sheet.**
4. **Calculate the current ratio and describe what it reveals about a company's financial condition.**
5. **Define or explain the words and phrases listed in the chapter glossary.**

After studying Appendix A at the end of Chapter 5, you should be able to:

6. **Prepare work sheets and reversing entries and explain why they are useful.**

In business since 1903, Harley-Davidson, Inc., realizes the importance of communicating its position through its annual reports. For example, the company used its 1994 annual report to point out the 17.3% increase in motorcycle units shipped to dealers, its record sales and earnings, and the success of its operations overseas. To accurately present this financial picture, a company must have an effective accounting system in place.

This chapter continues your study of the accounting process by describing the concluding procedures that the accountant performs at the end of each reporting period. This includes the closing process that prepares the revenue, expense, and Cash Dividends Declared accounts for the next reporting period and updates the Retained Earnings account. The chapter also explains how accounts can be classified on the balance sheet to provide more useful information. Finally, it describes the current ratio, which is used by decision makers to assess the company's ability to pay its liabilities in the near future.

In Appendix A at the end of the chapter, you learn about optional work sheet and reversing entries that accountants may use. Studying the work sheet allows you to get an overall perspective on the steps in the accounting cycle.

CLOSING ENTRIES

LO 1

Explain why the temporary accounts are closed at the end of each accounting period and prepare closing entries and a post-closing trial balance for a service business.

In Chapter 4, you learned how adjusting entries update the account balances so the financial statements will reflect current information. After the adjusting entries are recorded and the financial statements are prepared, the next step in the accounting cycle is to journalize and post **closing entries.** Closing entries are designed to transfer the end-of-period balances in the revenue, expense, and Cash Dividends Declared accounts to the Retained Earnings account. These entries are necessary because:

1. Revenues increase retained earnings, while expenses and dividends decrease retained earnings.
2. During an accounting period, these increases and decreases are temporarily accumulated in revenue, expense, and the Cash Dividends Declared accounts rather than in the Retained Earnings account.
3. By transferring the effects of revenues, expenses, and dividends from the revenue, expense, and Cash Dividends Declared accounts to the Retained Earnings account, closing entries install the correct end-of-period balance in the Retained Earnings account.
4. Closing entries also cause the revenue, expense, and Cash Dividends Declared accounts to begin the new accounting period with zero balances.

Remember that an income statement reports the revenues earned and expenses incurred during one accounting period and is prepared from information recorded in the

Illustration 5-1

CLEAR COPY, INC.
Adjusted Trial Balance
December 31, 19X1

Cash	$ 7,950	
Accounts receivable	1,800	
Store supplies	2,670	
Prepaid insurance	2,300	
Copy equipment	26,000	
Accumulated depreciation,		
copy equipment		$ 375
Accounts payable		6,200
Salaries payable		210
Unearned copy services revenue		2,750
Common stock, $1 par value		30,000
Cash dividends declared	600	
Copy services revenue		6,150
Depreciation expense,		
copy equipment	375	
Salaries expense	1,610	
Insurance expense	100	
Rent expense	1,000	
Store supplies expense	1,050	
Utilities expense	230	
Totals	$45,685	$45,685

revenue and expense accounts. Also, the statement of retained earnings reports the changes in the Retained Earnings account during one period and uses the information accumulated in the Cash Dividends Declared account. Because the revenue, expense, and Cash Dividends Declared accounts accumulate information for only one period and then must be ready to do the same thing the next period, they must start each period with zero balances.

To close the revenue and expense accounts, the accountant transfers their balances first to a summary account called **Income Summary.** Then, the Income Summary balance, which is the net income or loss, is transferred to the Retained Earnings account. Finally, the accountant transfers the Cash Dividends Declared account balance to the Retained Earnings account. After the closing entries are posted, the revenue, expense, Income Summary, and Cash Dividends Declared accounts have zero balances. Thus, these accounts are said to be closed or cleared.

Recall that Clear Copy, Inc.'s adjusted trial balance on December 31, 19X1, was originally presented in Illustration 4–3. The adjusted trial balance is repeated in Illustration 5–1. Illustration 5–2 uses these adjusted account balances to show the four entries that close Clear Copy, Inc.'s revenue, expense, Income Summary, and Cash Dividends Declared accounts.

Entry 1

The first closing entry transfers the credit balances in the revenue accounts to the Income Summary account. In general journal form, the entry is:

Dec.	31	Copy Services Revenue	6,150.00	
		Income Summary		6,150.00
		* To close the revenue account and create the*		
		* Income Summary account.*		

Illustration 5-2   Closing Entries for Clear Copy, Inc.

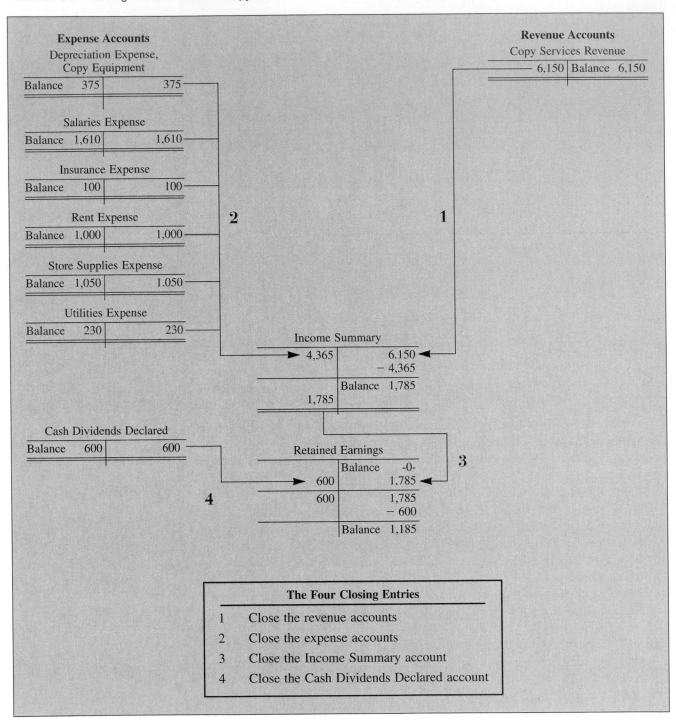

Note that this entry closes the revenue account by giving it a zero balance. If the company had several different revenue accounts, this entry would be a compound entry that included a debit to each of them. This clearing of the accounts allows them to be used to record new revenues in the upcoming year.

The Income Summary account is created especially for the closing process and is used only during that process. The $5,950 credit balance in Income Summary equals the total revenues for the year.

Entry 2

The second closing entry transfers the debit balances in the expense accounts to the Income Summary account. This step concentrates all the expense account debit balances in the Income Summary account. It also closes the expense accounts by giving them zero balances. That allows them to be used to record new expenses in the upcoming year. The second closing entry for Clear Copy is:

Dec.	31	Income Summary	4,365.00	
		Depreciation Expense, Copy Equipment		375.00
		Salaries Expense		1,610.00
		Insurance Expense		100.00
		Rent Expense		1,000.00
		Store Supplies Expense		1,050.00
		Utilities Expense		230.00
		To close the expense accounts.		

Illustration 5–2 shows that posting this entry gives each expense account a zero balance and prepares it to accept entries for expenses in 19X2. The entry also makes the balance of the Income Summary account equal to December's net income of $1,785. In effect, all the debit and credit balances of the expense and revenue accounts have now been concentrated in the Income Summary account.

Entry 3

The third closing entry transfers the balance of the Income Summary account to the Retained Earnings account. This entry closes the Income Summary account and adds the company's net income to Retained Earnings:

Dec.	31	Income Summary	1,785.00	
		Retained Earnings		1,785.00
		To close the Income Summary account.		

After this entry is posted, the Income Summary account has a zero balance. It will continue to have a zero balance until the closing process occurs at the end of the next year. The Retained Earnings account has been increased by the amount of the net income but still does not include the effects of the dividend that occurred in December.

Entry 4

The final closing entry transfers the debit balance of the Cash Dividends Declared account to Retained Earnings. This entry for Clear Copy is:

Dec.	31	Retained Earnings	600.00	
		Cash Dividends Declared		600.00
		To close Cash Dividends Declared.		

This entry gives the Cash Dividends Declared account a zero balance, which allows it to accumulate the next year's distributions to the stockholders. It also reduces the Retained Earnings account balance to the $1,185 amount reported on the balance sheet.

Illustration 5–3
The Adjusted Trial Balance, Closing Entries, and Post-Closing Trial Balance for Clear Copy, Inc.

	Adjusted Trial Balance		Closing Entries		Post-Closing Trial Balance	
Cash	7,950				7,950	
Accounts receivable	1,800				1,800	
Store supplies	2,670				2,670	
Prepaid insurance	2,300				2,300	
Copy equipment	26,000				26,000	
Accumulated depreciation, copy equipment		375				375
Accounts payable		6,200				6,200
Salaries payable		210				210
Unearned copy services revenue		2,750				2,750
Common stock, $1 par value		30,000				30,000
Retained earnings			(4) 600	(3) 1,785		1,185
Cash dividends declared	600			(4) 600		
Copy services revenue		6,150	(1) 6,150			
Depreciation expense, copy equipment	375			(2) 375		
Salaries expense	1,610			(2) 1,610		
Insurance expense	100			(2) 100		
Rent expense	1,000			(2) 1,000		
Store supplies expense	1,050			(2) 1,050		
Utilities expense	230			(2) 230		
Income summary			(2) 4,365	(1) 6,150		
			(3) 1,785			
Totals	45,685	45,685	12,900	12,900	40,720	40,720

SOURCES OF CLOSING ENTRY INFORMATION

The accountant can identify the accounts to be closed and the amounts to be used in the closing entries by referring to the individual revenue, expense, and Cash Dividends Declared accounts in the ledger. If an adjusted trial balance is prepared after the adjusting process, the information for the closing entries is conveniently gathered on the trial balance.

THE POST-CLOSING TRIAL BALANCE

The six-column table in Illustration 5–3 summarizes the effects of the closing process. The first two columns contain the adjusted trial balance with two additional lines for the Income Summary account and one additional line for Retained Earnings. The next two columns present the closing entries, numbered (1) through (4). The last two columns contain the **post-closing trial balance,** which lists the balances of the accounts that were not closed. These accounts represent the company's assets, liabilities, and stockholders' equity as of the end of 19X1. These items and amounts are the same as those presented in the balance sheet in Illustration 4–5.

Instead of preparing the six-column table in Illustration 5–3, the post-closing trial balance is often prepared as a separate two-column table, as in Illustration 5–4. Regardless of the format, the post-closing trial balance is the last step in the annual accounting process.

Permanent (Real) Accounts and Temporary (Nominal) Accounts

Asset, liability, and stockholders' equity accounts are not closed as long as the company continues to own the assets, owe the liabilities, and have stockholders' equity. Because these accounts are not closed, they are called **permanent accounts** or **real accounts.** These accounts are permanent because they describe existing conditions.

Cash	$ 7,950	
Accounts receivable	1,800	
Store supplies	2,670	
Prepaid insurance	2,300	
Copy equipment	26,000	
Accumulated depreciation, copy equipment ..		$ 375
Accounts payable		6,200
Salaries payable		210
Unearned copy services revenue		2,750
Common stock, $1 per value		30,000
Retained earnings		1,185
Totals	$40,720	$40,720

Illustration 5-4
Separate Post-Closing Trial Balance for Clear Copy, Inc.

In contrast, the terms **temporary accounts** or **nominal accounts** describe the revenue, expense, Income Summary, and Cash Dividends Declared accounts. They are temporary because the accounts are opened at the beginning of the year, used to record events, and then closed at the end of the year. They describe nominal events or changes that have occurred rather than conditions that exist at the end of the accounting period.

THE LEDGER FOR CLEAR COPY, INC.

To complete the Clear Copy example, look at Illustration 5–5, the company's entire ledger as of December 31, 19X1. Review the accounts and observe that the temporary accounts (the Cash Dividends Declared account and all accounts with numbers greater than 400) have been closed.

Progress Check
(Answers to Progress Checks are provided at the end of the chapter.)

5-1   When closing entries are prepared:
  a. The accounts for expenses, revenues, and Cash Dividends Declared are closed to the Income Summary account.
  b. The final balance of the Income Summary account equals net income or net loss for the period.
  c. All temporary accounts have zero balances after the process is completed.

5-2   Why are revenue and expense accounts called temporary? Are there any other temporary accounts?

5-3   What accounts are listed on the post-closing trial balance?

Chapters 3, 4, and 5 have described the accounting procedures that are completed during each reporting period. They begin with recording external transactions in the journal and end with preparing the post-closing trial balance. Because these steps are repeated each period, they are often called the **accounting cycle.** In Illustration 5–6, a flow chart shows the steps in order. Steps 1 and 2 take place every day as the company engages in business transactions. The other steps are completed at the end of the accounting period. Notice that steps 4 and 9 are identified as being optional. They are explained in Appendix A at the end of the chapter.

A REVIEW OF THE ACCOUNTING CYCLE

LO 2
Describe and perform each step in the accounting cycle.

Illustration 5–5   The Ledger for Clear Copy, Inc., as of December 31, 19X1 (after adjustments and closing entries have been posted)

Asset Accounts:

Cash   # 101

Date		Expl.	Debit	Credit	Balance
19X1					
Dec.	1		30,000		30,000
	2			2,500	27,500
	3			20,000	7,500
	10		2,200		9,700
	12			1,000	8,700
	12			700	8,000
	22		1,900		9,900
	24			900	9,000
	24			600	8,400
	26		3,000		11,400
	26			2,400	9,000
	26			120	8,880
	26			230	8,650
	26			700	7,950

Store Supplies   # 125

Date		Expl.	Debit	Credit	Balance
19X1					
Dec.	2		2,500		2,500
	6		1,100		3,600
	26		120		3,720
	31			1,050	2,670

Prepaid Insurance   # 128

Date		Expl.	Debit	Credit	Balance
19X1					
Dec.	26		2,400		2,400
	31			100	2,300

Accounts Receivable   # 106

Date		Expl.	Debit	Credit	Balance
19X1					
Dec.	12		1,900		1,900
	22			1,900	0
	31		1,800		1,800

Copy Equipment   # 167

Date		Expl.	Debit	Credit	Balance
19X1					
Dec.	3		20,000		20,000
	6		6,000		26,000

Accumulated Depreciation, Copy Equipment   # 168

Date		Expl.	Debit	Credit	Balance
19X1					
Dec.	31			375	375

Liability and Equity Accounts:

Accounts Payable   # 201

Date		Expl.	Debit	Credit	Balance
19X1					
Dec.	6			7,100	7,100
	24		900		6,200

Common Stock, $1 Par Value   # 301

Date		Expl.	Debit	Credit	Balance
19X1					
Dec.	1			30,000	30,000

Salaries Payable   # 209

Date		Expl.	Debit	Credit	Balance
19X1					
Dec.	31			210	210

Retained Earnings   # 318

Date		Expl.	Debit	Credit	Balance
19X1					
Dec.	31			1,785	1,785
	31		600		1,185

Unearned Copy Services Revenue   # 236

Date		Expl.	Debit	Credit	Balance
19X1					
Dec.	26			3,000	3,000
	31		250		2,750

Cash Dividends Declared   # 319

Date		Expl.	Debit	Credit	Balance
19X1					
Dec.	24		600		600
	31			600	0

Illustration 5–5 *(concluded)*

Revenue and Expense Accounts (including Income Summary):

Copy Services Revenue   # 403

Date		Expl.	Debit	Credit	Balance
19X1					
Dec.	10			2,200	2,200
	12			1,900	4,100
	31			250	4,350
	31			1,800	6,150
	31		5,950		0

Rent Expense   # 641

Date		Expl.	Debit	Credit	Balance
19X1					
Dec.	12		1,000		1,000
	31			1,000	0

Depreciation Expense, Copy Equipment   # 614

Date		Expl.	Debit	Credit	Balance
19X1					
Dec.	31		375		375
	31			375	0

Store Supplies Expense   # 651

Date		Expl.	Debit	Credit	Balance
19X1					
Dec.	31		1,050		1,050
	31			1,050	0

Salaries Expense   # 622

Date		Expl.	Debit	Credit	Balance
19X1					
Dec.	12		700		700
	26		700		1,400
	31		210		1,610
	31			1,610	0

Utilities Expense   # 690

Date		Expl.	Debit	Credit	Balance
19X1					
Dec.	26		230		230
	31			230	0

Insurance Expense   # 637

Date		Expl.	Debit	Credit	Balance
19X1					
Dec.	31		100		100
	31			100	0

Income Summary   # 901

Date		Expl.	Debit	Credit	Balance
19X1					
Dec.	31			6,150	6,150
	31		4,365		1,785
	31		1,785		0

Review Illustration 5–6 on page 157 and the following list of the steps to be sure that you understand how each one helps accountants provide useful information in the financial statements:

Step	Description
1. Journalizing	Analyzing transactions and recording debits and credits in a journal.
2. Posting	Copying the debits and credits from the journal entries to the accounts in the ledger.
3. Preparing the unadjusted trial balance	Summarizing the ledger accounts and partially testing clerical accuracy. (If a work sheet is used, this is done on the work sheet. See Appendix A.)
4. Completing the work sheet (optional—see Appendix A)	Identifying the effects of adjustments on the financial statements before entering them in the ledger and posting them to the accounts; also drafting the adjusted trial balance, extending the adjusted amounts to the appropriate financial statement columns, and determining the size of the net income or net loss.

5. Adjusting the accounts	Identifying necessary adjustments to bring the account balances up to date; journalizing and posting entries to record the adjustments in the accounts.
6. Preparing the financial statements	Using the information on the adjusted trial balance to prepare an income statement, a statement of retained earnings, a balance sheet, and a statement of cash flows. (Techniques for preparing the cash flow statement are described in Chapter 16.)
7. Closing the temporary accounts	Journalizing and posting entries to close the revenue, expense, and Cash Dividends Declared accounts and to update the Retained Earnings account.
8. Preparing the post-closing trial balance	Testing the clerical accuracy of the adjusting and closing procedures.
9. Preparing reversing entries	An optional step. (See Appendix A.)

A Practical Point

Normally, accountants are not able to make all of the adjusting and closing entries on the last day of the fiscal year. Information about the economic events that require adjustments often is not available until after several days or even a few weeks. As a result, the adjusting and closing entries are recorded later but dated as of the last day of the year. This means the financial statements reflect what is known on the date that they are prepared instead of what was known on the financial statement date.

For example, a company might receive a utility bill on January 14 for costs incurred from December 1 through December 31. Upon receiving the bill, the company's accountant records the expense and the payable as of December 31. The income statement for December reflects the full expense and the December 31 balance sheet includes the payable, even though the exact amounts were not actually known on December 31.

Progress Check

5–4   **The steps in the accounting cycle**
     a. **Are concluded by preparing a post-closing trial balance.**
     b. **Are concluded by preparing a balance sheet.**
     c. **Begin with preparing the unadjusted trial balance.**

5–5   **What steps in the accounting cycle are optional?**

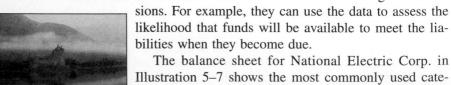

CLASSIFYING BALANCE SHEET ITEMS

LO 3
Define each asset and liability category for the balance sheet and prepare a classified balance sheet.

Up to this point, we have presented only **unclassified balance sheets.** (For example, see Illustration 4–5 on page 123.) However, the information on a balance sheet is more useful if assets and liabilities are classified into relevant groups. Readers of these **classified balance sheets** have more information to use in making their decisions. For example, they can use the data to assess the likelihood that funds will be available to meet the liabilities when they become due.

The balance sheet for National Electric Corp. in Illustration 5–7 shows the most commonly used categories. Assets are classified as (1) current assets, (2) investments, (3) plant and equipment, and (4) intangible assets. Liabilities are either current or long term.

Illustration 5–6 The Accounting Cycle

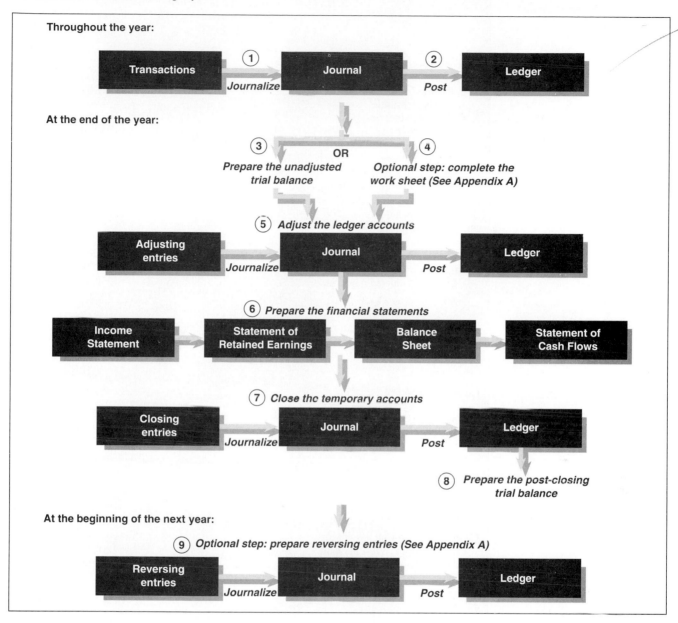

However, all companies do not use the same categories of assets and liabilities on their balance sheets. For example, **Whirlpool's** 1995 balance sheet has only three asset classes: current assets; property and equipment; and other assets.

Current Assets

Current assets are cash and other assets that are reasonably expected to be sold, collected, or consumed within one year or within the normal **operating cycle of the business,** whichever is longer.[1] In addition to cash, current assets typically include short-term investments in marketable securities, accounts receivable, notes receivable, goods expected to be sold to customers (called *merchandise* or *inventory*), and prepaid expenses.

---

[1]FASB, *Accounting Standards—Current Text* (Norwalk, CT, 1995), Sec. B05.105. First published as *Accounting Research Bulletin No. 43,* Chapter 3A, par. 4.

NATIONAL ELECTRIC CORP.
Balance Sheet
December 31, 19X1

Assets

Current assets:

Cash		$ 6,500	
Short-term investments		2,100	
Accounts receivable		4,400	
Notes receivable		1,500	
Merchandise inventory		27,500	
Prepaid expenses		2,400	
Total current assets			$ 44,400

Investments:

Chrysler Corporation common stock		$ 18,000	
Land held for future expansion		48,000	
Total investments			66,000

Plant and equipment:

Store equipment	$ 33,200		
Less accumulated depreciation	8,000	$ 25,200	
Buildings	$170,000		
Less accumulated depreciation	45,000	125,000	
Land		73,200	
Total plant and equipment			223,400

Intangible assets:

Trademark			10,000
Total assets			$343,800

Liabilities

Current liabilities:

Accounts payable		$ 15,300	
Wages payable		3,200	
Notes payable		3,000	
Current portion of long-term liabilities		7,500	
Total current liabilities			$ 29,000

Long-term liabilities:

Notes payable (net of current portion)			150,000
Total liabilities			$179,000

Stockholders' Equity

Contributed capital:

Common stock, $100 par value		$100,000	
Retained earnings		64,800	
Total stockholders' equity			164,800
Total liabilities and stockholders' equity			$343,800

The Operating Cycle. The length of a company's operating cycle depends on its activities. The diagrams in Illustration 5–8 represent the phases of operating cycles for service and merchandising companies. For a company that sells services, the operating cycle is the average time between paying the employees who perform the services and receiving the cash from customers. For a company that sells goods, the operating cycle is the average time between paying for the merchandise and receiving cash from customers.

Most operating cycles are shorter than one year. As a result, most companies use a one-year period in deciding which assets are current. However, a few companies have an operating cycle longer than one year. For example, a company may routinely allow customers to take several years to pay for their purchases. Some producers of beverages and other products allow their products to age for several years. In both

Illustration 5–8   The Phases of Operating Cycles for Companies that Sell Services and Merchandise

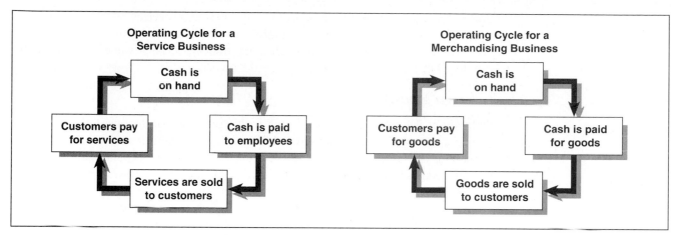

cases, these companies use the longer operating cycle in deciding which assets are current.[2]

Other Details.   The balance sheet in Illustration 5–7 lists current assets first. This practice gives a prominent position to assets that are most easily converted into cash. Items within the current asset category are traditionally listed in the order of how quickly they will be converted to cash. Prepaid expenses are usually listed last because they will not be converted to cash.

A company's individual prepaid expenses are usually small compared to other assets on the balance sheet. As a result, they are often combined and shown as a single item. Thus, it is likely that the prepaid expenses item in Illustration 5–7 includes such things as prepaid insurance, prepaid rent, office supplies, and store supplies.

Investments

The second balance sheet classification is long-term investments. In many cases, notes receivable and investments in stocks and bonds are not current assets because they will be held for more than one year (or one operating cycle). Investments also include land that is not being used in operations because it is held for future expansion. Notice that the short-term investments on the second line in Illustration 5–7 are current assets and are not presented in the investments section. We explain the differences between short- and long-term investments in a later chapter.

Plant and Equipment

In Chapter 4, we described plant and equipment as tangible long-lived assets that are used to produce or sell goods and services. Examples include equipment, vehicles, buildings, and land. Two key phrases in the definition are *long-lived* and *used to produce or sell goods and services*. Although it is tangible and has a long life, land held for future expansion is not a plant asset because it is not used to produce or sell goods and services.

The term *plant and equipment* is often used as a balance sheet caption. Other widely used titles for the same category are *property, plant, and equipment,* or *land, buildings, and equipment*. The order of the listing of the types of plant assets within the category varies among organizations.

---

[2]In these unusual situations, the companies provide supplemental information about their current assets and liabilities to allow users to compare them with other companies.

Intangible Assets

Some assets that are used to produce or sell goods and services do not have a physical form. These assets are called **intangible assets.** Examples of intangible assets are goodwill, patents, trademarks, copyrights, and franchises. Their value comes from the privileges or rights granted to or held by the owner.

Current Liabilities

Obligations due to be paid or liquidated within one year (or the operating cycle, if it is longer) are classified as **current liabilities.** Current liabilities are usually satisfied by paying out current assets. Typical current liabilities are accounts payable, notes payable, wages payable, taxes payable, interest payable, and unearned revenues. Also, any portion of a long-term liability due to be paid within one year (or a longer operating cycle) is a current liability. Illustration 5–7 shows how the current portion of long-term liabilities is usually described on a balance sheet. Unearned revenues are classified as current liabilities because they will be settled by delivering goods or services within the year (or the operating cycle). Different companies present current liabilities in different orders. Generally, the first position goes to the liabilities that will be paid first.

Long-Term Liabilities

The second liability classification consists of **long-term liabilities.** These liabilities are not due to be paid within one year, or the operating cycle. Notes payable and bonds payable are usually long-term liabilities. If a company has both short- and long-term notes payable, it probably uses separate accounts for them in its ledger.

STOCKHOLDERS' EQUITY

As you learned in Chapter 2, the amounts the corporation received when it issued shares to stockholders are classified as contributed capital or paid-in capital. Also, when only one class of stock is issued, it is called *common stock*. Thus, in Illustration 5–7, the $100,000 amount of common stock is the amount originally contributed to the corporation by its stockholders through their purchase of the corporation's stock. The retained earnings portion of stockholders' equity represents the sum of past net incomes less net losses and dividends. In Illustration 5–7, this amount is $64,800.

USING CODE NUMBERS FOR ACCOUNTS

We described a possible three-digit account numbering system in Chapter 3. In these systems, the code number assigned to an account not only identifies the account but also provides information about the account's financial statement category.

In the following simple system, the first digit in an account's number identifies its primary balance sheet or income statement category. For example, account numbers beginning with a 1 are assigned to asset accounts and account numbers beginning with a 2 are assigned to liability accounts. Under this system, the following numbers could be assigned to the accounts of a company that buys and sells merchandise:

101–199	Asset accounts
201–299	Liability accounts
301–399	Stockholders' equity and dividends declared accounts
401–499	Sales or revenue accounts
501–599	Cost of goods sold accounts (These are discussed in Chapter 6.)
601–699	Operating expense accounts
701–799	Accounts that reflect unusual and/or infrequent gains
801–899	Accounts that reflect unusual and/or infrequent losses

In this system, the second digit of each account number identifies its classification within the primary category, as follows:

101–199   Assets
    101–139   Current assets (second digit is 0, 1, 2, or 3)
    141–149   Long-term investments (second digit is 4)
    151–179   Plant assets (second digit is 5, 6, or 7)
    181–189   Natural resources (second digit is 8)
    191–199   Intangible assets (second digit is 9)
201–299   Liabilities
    201–249   Current liabilities (second digit is 0, 1, 2, 3, or 4)
    251–299   Long-term liabilities (second digit is 5, 6, 7, 8, or 9)

Finally, the third digit completes the unique code for each account. For example, specific current asset accounts might be assigned the following numbers:

101–199   Assets
    101–139   Current assets
      101   Cash
      106   Accounts Receivable
      110   Rent Receivable
      128   Prepaid Insurance

An extensive list of accounts using this code is provided at the back of this book.

A three-digit account numbering system may be adequate for many smaller businesses. However, a numbering system for a more complex business might use four, five, or even more digits.

Progress Check

5-6   Which of the following assets should be classified as current assets? Which should be classified as plant and equipment? *(a)* Land used in operating the business; *(b)* Office supplies; *(c)* Receivables from customers due in 10 months; *(d)* Insurance protection for the next nine months; *(e)* Trucks used to provide services to customers; *(f)* Trademarks used in advertising the company's services.

5-7   Identify two examples of assets classified as investments on the balance sheet.

5-8   On a balance sheet, what are the two categories within stockholders' equity?

USING THE INFORMATION— THE CURRENT RATIO

LO 4
Calculate the current ratio and describe what it reveals about a company's financial condition.

Most financial statement users find it helpful to evaluate a company's ability to pay its debts in the near future. This ability affects decisions by suppliers about allowing the company to buy on credit. It affects decisions by banks about lending money to the company and the terms of the loan, including the interest rate, due date, and any assets to be pledged as security against the loan. The ability to pay debts also affects a business manager's decisions about obtaining cash to pay existing debts when they come due.

The **current ratio** is used to evaluate a company's ability to pay its short-term obligations. It is calculated by dividing the current assets by the current liabilities:

$$\text{Current ratio} = \frac{\text{Current assets}}{\text{Current liabilities}}$$

Using the data for **Harley-Davidson, Inc.,** presented at the beginning of the chapter, the current ratios at the end of 1994 and 1993 are calculated as follows:

December 31, 1994:

$$\text{Current ratio} = \frac{\$405,636}{\$216,278} = 1.88$$

December 31, 1993:

$$\text{Current ratio} = \frac{\$333,758}{\$190,762} = 1.75$$

Note that the ratio improved from the end of 1993 to the end of 1994. Both values suggest that the company's short-term obligations could be satisfied with the short-term resources on hand. If the ratio were to be closer to one, the company might expect to face more difficulty in paying the liabilities. However, the company's sales may generate sufficient new cash to pay the liabilities. If the ratio were less than 1, the company would be more likely to have difficulty because its current liabilities would be greater than its current assets.

Progress Check

5-9   Which category of liabilities is used in the calculation of the current ratio?

SUMMARY OF THE CHAPTER IN TERMS OF LEARNING OBJECTIVES

LO 1. Explain why the temporary accounts are closed at the end of each accounting period and prepare closing entries and a post-closing trial balance for a service business. The temporary accounts are closed at the end of each accounting period for two reasons. First, this process updates the Retained Earnings account to include the effects of all economic events recorded for the year. Second, it prepares the revenue, expense, and Cash Dividends Declared accounts for the next reporting period by giving them zero balances. The revenue and expense account balances are initially transferred to the Income Summary account, which is then closed to the Retained Earnings account. Finally, the Cash Dividends Declared account is closed to the Retained Earnings account.

LO 2. Describe and perform each step in the accounting cycle. The accounting cycle consists of eight steps: (1) journalizing external transactions during the period; (2) posting the entries during the period; (3) preparing either an unadjusted trial balance, or; (4) preparing a work sheet (see Appendix A); (5) preparing and posting adjusting entries; (6) preparing the financial statements; (7) preparing and posting closing entries; and (8) preparing the post-closing trial balance. An optional step (9) of preparing reversing entries is explained in Appendix A.

LO 3. Define each asset and liability category for the balance sheet and prepare a classified balance sheet. Classified balance sheets usually report four categories of assets: current assets, investments, plant and equipment, and intangible assets. The two categories of liabilities are current and long term. Stockholders' equity includes contributed capital (the amounts received when stock was issued to stockholders) and retained earnings (the equity from net incomes less net losses and dividends).

LO 4. Calculate the current ratio and describe what it reveals about a company's financial condition. A company's current ratio is used to evaluate its ability to pay its current liabilities out of its current assets. The value of the ratio equals the amount of the current assets divided by the current liabilities.

This six-column table shows the December 31, 19X1, adjusted trial balance of Westside Appliance Repair Company:

DEMONSTRATION PROBLEM

	Adjusted Trial Balance		Closing Entries		Post-Closing Trial Balance	
Cash	83,300					
Notes receivable	60,000					
Prepaid insurance	19,000					
Prepaid rent	5,000					
Equipment	165,000					
Accumulated depreciation, equipment		52,000				
Accounts payable		37,000				
Long-term notes payable		58,000				
Common stock, $10 par value		100,000				
Retained earnings		73,500				
Cash dividends declared	25,000					
Repair services revenue		294,000				
Interest earned		6,500				
Depreciation expense, equipment	26,000					
Wages expense	155,000					
Rent expense	47,000					
Insurance expense	7,000					
Interest expense	4,700					
Income taxes expense	24,000					
Income summary						
Totals	621,000	621,000				

Required

1. Prepare closing entries for Westside Appliance Repair Co.
2. Complete the six-column schedule.
3. Set up a Retained Earnings account and post the closing entries to this account.

- Prepare entries to close the revenue accounts to Income Summary, to close the expense accounts to Income Summary, to close Income Summary to the Retained Earnings account, and to close the Cash Dividends Declared account to the Retained Earnings account.

- Enter the four closing entries in the second pair of columns in the six-column schedule and then extend the balances of the asset and liability accounts to the third pair of columns.

- Enter the post-closing balance of the Retained Earnings account in the last column. Examine the totals of the columns to verify that they are equal.

- Post the third and fourth closing entries to the Retained Earnings account.

Planning the Solution

1.

Solution to Demonstration Problem

Dec.	31	Repair Services Revenue	294,000.00	
		Interest Earned	6,500.00	
		Income Summary		300,500.00
		To close the revenue accounts and create the Income Summary account.		

Dec.	31	Income Summary	263,700.00	
		Depreciation Expense, Equipment		26,000.00
		Wages Expense		155,000.00
		Rent Expense		47,000.00
		Insurance Expense		7,000.00
		Interest Expense		4,700.00
		Income Taxes Expense		24,000.00
		To close the expense accounts.		
	31	Income Summary	36,800.00	
		Retained Earnings		36,800.00
		To close the Income Summary account.		
	31	Retained Earnings	25,000.00	
		Cash Dividends Declared		25,000.00
		To close the Cash Dividends Declared account.		

2.

	Adjusted Trial Balance		Closing Entries		Post-Closing Trial Balance	
Cash	83,300				83,300	
Notes receivable	60,000				60,000	
Prepaid insurance	19,000				19,000	
Prepaid rent	5,000				5,000	
Equipment	165,000				165,000	
Accumulated depreciation, equipment		52,000				52,000
Accounts payable		37,000				37,000
Long-term notes payable		58,000				58,000
Common stock, $10 par value		100,000				100,000
Retained earnings		73,500	(4) 25,000	(3) 36,800		85,300
Cash dividends declared	25,000			(4) 25,000		
Repair services revenue		294,000	(1)294,000			
Interest earned		6,500	(1) 6,500			
Depreciation expense, equipment	26,000			(2) 26,000		
Wages expense	179,000			(2)179,000		
Rent expense	47,000			(2) 47,000		
Insurance expense	7,000			(2) 7,000		
Interest expense	4,700			(2) 4,700		
Income summary			(2)263,700	(1)300,500		
			(3) 36,800			
Totals	621,000	621,000	626,000	626,000	332,300	332,300

3.

Retained Earnings   Account No. 318

Date			Explanation	Debit	Credit	Balance
19X1						
Jan.	1		Beginning balance			73,500.00
Dec.	31		Close Income Summary		36,800.00	110,300.00
	31		Close Cash Dividends Declared	25,000.00		85,300.00

Work Sheets and Reversing Entries

When organizing the information presented in formal reports to internal and external decision makers, accountants prepare numerous analyses and informal documents. These informal documents are important tools for accountants. Traditionally, they are called **working papers.** One widely used working paper is the **work sheet.** Normally, the work sheet is not distributed to decision makers. It is prepared and used by accountants.

USING WORK SHEETS AT THE END OF ACCOUNTING PERIODS

LO 6
Prepare work sheets and reversing entries and explain why they are useful.

Why Study the Work Sheet?

As we stated previously, preparing a work sheet is an optional procedure. When a business has only a few accounts and adjustments, preparing a work sheet is not necessary. Also, computerized accounting systems provide financial statements without first generating a work sheet. Nevertheless, there are several reasons why an understanding of work sheets is helpful:

1. In a manual accounting system involving many accounts and adjustments, the work sheet helps the accountant avoid errors.

2. Studying the work sheet is an effective way for you to see the entire accounting process from beginning to end. In a sense, it gives a bird's-eye view of the process between the occurrence of economic events and the presentation of their effects in financial statements.

3. After a company has tentatively prepared its financial statements, the auditors of the statements often use a work sheet as a basis for planning and organizing the audit. Also, they may use a work sheet to reflect any additional adjustments that appear necessary as a result of the audit.

4. Accountants often use work sheets to prepare interim (monthly or quarterly) financial statements.

5. A modified form of the work sheet sometimes is used to show the effects of proposed transactions.

Where Does the Work Sheet Fit into the Accounting Process?

In practice, the work sheet is an optional step in the accounting process that can simplify the accountant's efforts in preparing financial statements. When a work sheet is used, it is prepared before making the adjusting entries at the end of the reporting period. The work sheet gathers information about the accounts, the needed adjustments, and the financial statements. When it is finished, the work sheet contains information that is recorded in the journal and then presented in the statements.

Illustration A-1   Step One: Entering the Unadjusted Trial Balance for Clear Copy, Inc.

Account Titles	Unadjusted Trial Balance Dr.	Unadjusted Trial Balance Cr.	Adjustments Dr.	Adjustments Cr.	Adjusted Trial Balance Dr.	Adjusted Trial Balance Cr.	Income Statement Dr.	Income Statement Cr.	Statement of Retained Earnings or Balance Sheet Dr.	Statement of Retained Earnings or Balance Sheet Cr.
CLEAR COPY, INC. Work Sheet For Month Ended December 31, 19X1										
Cash	7,950									
Accounts receivable										
Store supplies	3,720									
Prepaid insurance	2,400									
Copy equipment	26,000									
Accumulated depreciation, copy equipment										
Accounts payable		6,200								
Salaries payable										
Unearned copy services revenue		3,000								
Common stock, $1 par value		30,000								
Retained earnings										
Cash dividends declared	600									
Copy services revenue		4,100								
Depreciation expense, copy equipment										
Salaries expense	1,400									
Insurance expense										
Rent expense	1,000									
Store supplies expense										
Utilities expense	230									
Totals	43,300	43,300								

Preparing a Work Sheet

Illustration A–1 shows the multicolumn form used to prepare a work sheet. Note that this form provides two columns each for the unadjusted trial balance, the adjustments, the adjusted trial balance, the income statement, and the statement of retained earnings or balance sheet. A work sheet could contain two separate columns for the statement of retained earnings and two separate columns for the balance sheet. However, because the statement of retained earnings includes only a few items, this usually is not done. Instead, most work sheets provide only two columns for both statements, as Illustration A–1 shows.

Step One. When a work sheet is used, the accountant does not prepare the unadjusted trial balance on a separate form. Instead, the first step in preparing the work sheet is to list the title of every account expected to appear on the company's financial statements. Then, the unadjusted debit or credit balances of the accounts are found in the ledger and recorded in the first two columns. Because these columns serve as the unadjusted trial balance, the totals of the columns should be equal. Illustration A–1 shows Clear Copy, Inc.'s work sheet after completing this first step.

Remember from Chapters 2 through 4 that Clear Copy completed a number of transactions during December 19X1. The unadjusted trial balance in Illustration A–1 reflects the account balances after these December transactions were recorded but *before any adjusting entries were journalized or posted.*

Illustration A–2   Step Two: Entering the Adjustments and Preparing the Adjusted Trial Balance

	Unadjusted Trial Balance		Adjustments		Adjusted Trial Balance		Income Statement		Statement of Retained Earnings or Balance Sheet	
Account Titles	**Dr.**	**Cr.**	**Dr.**	**Cr.**	**Dr.**	**Cr.**	**Dr.**	**Cr.**	**Dr.**	**Cr.**
Cash	7,950				7,950					
Accounts receivable			(f) 1,800		1,800					
Store supplies	3,720			(b) 1,050	2,670					
Prepaid insurance	2,400			(a) 100	2,300					
Copy equipment	26,000				26,000					
Accumulated depreciation, copy equipment				(c) 375		375				
Accounts payable		6,200				6,200				
Salaries payable				(e) 210		210				
Unearned copy services revenue		3,000	(d) 250			2,750				
Common stock, $1 par value		30,000				30,000				
Retained earnings										
Cash dividends declared	600				600					
Copy services revenue		4,100		(d) 250						
				(f) 1,800		6,150				
Depreciation expense, copy equipment			(c) 375		375					
Salaries expense	1,400		(e) 210		1,610					
Insurance expense			(a) 100		100					
Rent expense	1,000				1,000					
Store supplies expense			(b) 1,050		1,050					
Utilities expense	230				230					
Totals	43,300	43,300	3,785	3,785	45,685	45,685				

CLEAR COPY, INC.
Work Sheet
For Month Ended December 31, 19X1

In Illustration A–1, note that a blank line was left after the Copy Services Revenue account. Based on past experience, the accountant may realize that more than one line will be needed to show the adjustments to a particular account. You will see in Illustration A–3 that Copy Services Revenue is an example. Another alternative is to squeeze two adjustments on one line or to combine the effects of two or more adjustments in one amount.

Step Two. The next step in preparing a work sheet is to enter the adjustments in the columns labeled Adjustments, as shown in Illustration A–2. The adjustments shown in Illustration A–2 are the same ones that we discussed in Chapter 4. Notice that an identifying letter relates the debit and credit of each adjustment. After preparing a work sheet, the accountant still has to enter the adjusting entries in the journal and post them to the ledger. At that time, the identifying letters help match correctly the debit and credit of each adjusting entry.

The illustration shows the six adjustments for Clear Copy, Inc., that were explained in Chapter 4:

a.   Expiration of $100 of prepaid insurance.
b.   Consumption of $1,050 of store supplies.
c.   Depreciation of copy equipment by $375.
d.   Earnings of $250 of previously unearned revenue.
e.   Accrual of $210 of salaries owed to the employee.
f.   Accrual of $1,800 of revenue owed by a customer.

In making the adjustments, the accountant may determine that additional accounts need to be inserted on the work sheet. If so, the additional accounts may be inserted below the initial list.

After the adjustments are entered in the Adjustments columns, the columns are totaled and the adjusted trial balance is prepared by combining the adjustments with the unadjusted balances. For example, in Illustration A–2, the Prepaid Insurance account has a $2,400 debit balance in the Unadjusted Trial Balance columns. This $2,400 debit is combined with the $100 credit in the Adjustments columns to give Prepaid Insurance a $2,300 debit in the Adjusted Trial Balance columns. The totals of the Adjusted Trial Balance columns again confirm the equality of the debits and credits.

Step Three. The next step is to sort the adjusted amounts to the proper financial statement columns, as shown in Illustration A–3. Expense items go to the Income Statement Debit column and revenues to the Income Statement Credit column. Assets and Cash Dividends Declared are extended to the Statement of Retained Earnings or Balance Sheet Debit column. Liabilities, Common Stock, and Retained Earnings are sorted to the Statement of Retained Earnings or Balance Sheet Credit column.

Recall that this work sheet relates to the first period of Clear Copy's operations. Thus, the corporation did not have a retained earnings balance at the beginning of the period. As a result, on the Retained Earnings row in Illustration A–3, there was nothing to extend. In later periods, the Retained Earnings account would have a beginning-of-period balance to be extended on the work sheet.

Step Four. After sorting the amounts to the proper columns, the difference between the totals of the Income Statement columns is the net income or loss. The difference is the net income or loss because revenues are entered in the Credit column and expenses in the Debit column. If the Credit column total exceeds the Debit column total, the difference is a net income. If the Debit column total exceeds the Credit column total, the difference is a net loss. In the illustrated work sheet, the Credit column total exceeds the Debit column total, and the result is a $1,785 net income.

After calculating the net income in the Income Statement columns, the accountant adds it to the Statement of Retained Earnings or Balance Sheet Credit column. Because the last two columns include the balance sheet accounts, adding the net income to the last Credit column has the effect of adding it to retained earnings. Had there been a loss, it would have been necessary to add the loss to the last Debit column. In that case, the effect would be to subtract it from retained earnings.

In Illustration A–3, notice that the retained earnings balance on December 31 is not listed. It may be calculated as the beginning balance of $0 plus the $1,785 net income in the last Credit column less the $600 Cash Dividends Declared in the last Debit column.

When the net income or net loss is added to the appropriate Statement of Retained Earnings or Balance Sheet column, the totals of the last two columns should balance. If they do not balance, one or more errors were made in constructing the work sheet. The error or errors may have been mathematical, or an amount may have been sorted to a wrong column.

Although balancing the last two columns is done in an effort to discover errors, the fact that they balance is not proof that the work sheet is free from error. These columns balance even when certain types of errors have been made. For example, if an asset amount is incorrectly carried into the Income Statement Debit column, the columns still balance. Or, if a liability amount is carried into the Income Statement Credit column, the columns still balance. Either error causes the net income amount to be incorrect. But, the columns are in balance.

Illustration A-3   Steps Three and Four: Extending the Adjusted Amounts and Completing The Work Sheet

CLEAR COPY, INC.
Work Sheet
For Month Ended December 31, 19X1

Account Titles	Unadjusted Trial Balance Dr.	Cr.	Adjustments Dr.	Cr.	Adjusted Trial Balance Dr.	Cr.	Income Statement Dr.	Cr.	Statement of Retained Earnings or Balance Sheet Dr.	Cr.
Cash	7,950				7,950				7,950	
Accounts receivable			(f) 1,800		1,800				1,800	
Store supplies	3,720			(b) 1,050	2,670				2,670	
Prepaid insurance	2,400			(a) 100	2,300				2,300	
Copy equipment	26,000				26,000				26,000	
Accumulated depreciation, copy equipment				(c) 375		375				375
Accounts payable		6,200				6,200				6,200
Salaries payable				(e) 210		210				210
Unearned copy services revenue		3,000	(d) 250			2,750				2,750
Common stock, $1 par value		30,000				30,000				30,000
Retained earnings										
Cash dividends declared	600				600				600	
Copy services revenue		4,100		(d) 250 (f) 1,800		6,150		6,150		
Depreciation expense, copy equipment			(c) 375		375		375			
Salaries expense	1,400		(e) 210		1,610		1,610			
Insurance expense			(a) 100		100		100			
Rent expense	1,000				1,000		1,000			
Store supplies expense			(b) 1,050		1,050		1,050			
Utilities expense	230				230		230			
Totals	43,300	43,300	3,785	3,785	45,685	45,685	4,365	6,150	41,320	39,535
Net income							1,785			1,785
Totals							6,150	6,150	41,320	41,320

Preparing Adjusting and Closing Entries from the Work Sheet

Entering the adjustments in the Adjustments columns of a work sheet does not get these adjustments into the ledger accounts. Therefore, after completing the work sheet, adjusting entries like the ones described in Chapter 4 must be entered in the General Journal and posted to the accounts in the ledger. The work sheet makes this easy because its Adjustments columns provide the information for these entries. If adjusting entries are prepared from the information in Illustration A–3, you will see that they are the same adjusting entries we discussed in the last chapter.

The information for the closing entries is also summarized on the work sheet. All of the items in the Income Statement columns must be closed to Income Summary. Then, the net income or net loss shown on the work sheet must be closed to Retained Earnings. Finally, the Cash Dividends Declared balance shown in the last Debit column must be closed to Retained Earnings.

Preparing Financial Statements from the Work Sheet

A work sheet is not a substitute for the financial statements. The work sheet is nothing more than a supporting tool that the accountant uses at the end of an accounting period to help organize the data. However, as soon as it is completed, the accountant uses the information in the work sheet to prepare the financial statements.

Why Use a Work Sheet?

At this point, it should be clear that we ended up with exactly the same financial statements and adjusting entries that we developed in Chapter 4 without using a work sheet. So, why prepare a work sheet?

First, the example in this chapter is greatly simplified. Real companies have many more adjusting entries and accounts than Clear Copy. A work sheet makes it easier to organize all the additional information. As we mentioned earlier, auditors often use work sheets to plan and organize their work. In fact, they may request that a company provide a work sheet showing the adjustments made prior to the audit.

Second, the work sheet can be used to prepare *interim* financial statements without recording the adjusting entries in the journal and ledger. Thus, a company can prepare statements each month or quarter and avoid taking the time to formally journalize and post the adjustments except once at the end of each year. All large companies with publicly traded ownership prepare interim financial reports, usually on a quarterly basis. Some of them, such as **PepsiCo, Inc.,** also include summaries of the past year's quarterly data in their annual reports.

Also, companies may use a work sheet format to show the effects of proposed transactions. In doing this, they enter their adjusted financial statement amounts in the first two columns, arranging them to appear in the form of financial statements. Then, the proposed transactions are inserted in the second two columns. The extended amounts in the last columns show the effects of the proposed transactions on the financial statements. These final columns are called **pro forma statements,** because they show the statements as if the proposed transactions had already occurred.

OPTIONAL REVERSING ENTRIES

Reversing entries are optional entries that relate to accrued assets and liabilities created by adjusting entries at the end of a reporting period. Reversing entries are used for the practical purpose of simplifying a company's bookkeeping process.

Illustration A–4 shows how reversing entries work. The top of the diagram shows the adjusting entry that Clear Copy, Inc., recorded on December 31, 19X1, for the employee's earned but unpaid salary. The entry recorded three days' salary to increase December's total salary expense to $1,610. The entry also recognized a liability of $210. The expense is reported on December's income statement and the expense account is closed. As a result, the ledger on January 1, 19X2, reflects a $210 liability and a zero balance in the Salaries Expense account. At this point, the choice is made between using or not using reversing entries.

Bookkeeping without Reversing Entries

The path down the left side of Illustration A–4 was described in Chapter 4. When the next payday occurs on January 9, the bookkeeper records the payment with a compound entry that debits both the expense and liability accounts. Posting the entry creates a $490 balance in the expense account and reduces the liability account balance to zero because the debt has been settled.

The disadvantage of this approach is the complex entry on January 9. Paying the accrued liability causes the entry to differ from the routine entries made on all other paydays. To construct the proper entry on January 9, the bookkeeper must be informed of the effect of the adjusting entry. Reversing entries overcome this disadvantage.

Illustration A–4 Reversing Entries for Accrued Expenses

Accrue salaries expense on December 31, 19X1

Salaries Expense _____ 210
    Salaries Payable _____ 210

Salaries Expense

Date	Expl.	Debit	Credit	Balance
19X1				
Dec. 12	(7)	700		700
26	(16)	700		1,400
31	(e)	210		1,610

Salaries Payable

Date	Expl.	Debit	Credit	Balance
19X1				
Dec. 31	(e)		210	210

No reversing entry recorded on January 1, 19X2

NO ENTRY

Salaries Expense

Date	Expl.	Debit	Credit	Balance
19X2				

Salaries Payable

Date	Expl.	Debit	Credit	Balance
19X1				
Dec. 31	(e)		210	210
19X2				

Reversing entry recorded on January 1, 19X2

Salaries Payable _____ 210
    Salaries Expense _____ 210

Salaries Expense

Date	Expl.	Debit	Credit	Balance
19X2				
Jan. 1			210	(210)

Salaries Payable

Date	Expl.	Debit	Credit	Balance
19X1				
Dec. 31	(e)		210	210
19X2				
Jan. 1		210		0

Pay the accrued and current salaries on January 9, the first payday in 19X2

Salaries Expense _____ 490
Salaries Payable _____ 210
    Cash _____ 700

Salaries Expense

Date	Expl.	Debit	Credit	Balance
19X2				
Jan. 9		490		490

Salaries Payable

Date	Expl.	Debit	Credit	Balance
19X1				
Dec. 31	(e)		210	210
19X2				
Jan. 9		210		0

Salaries Expense _____ 700
    Cash _____ 700

Salaries Expense

Date	Expl.	Debit	Credit	Balance
19X2				
Jan. 1			210	(210)
Jan. 9		700		490

Salaries Payable

Date	Expl.	Debit	Credit	Balance
19X1				
Dec. 31	(e)		210	210
19X2				
Jan. 1		210		0

Under both approaches, the expense and liability accounts have the same balances after the subsequent payment on January 9:

Salaries Expense _____ $ 490
Salaries Payable _____ $ 0

Bookkeeping with Reversing Entries

The right side of Illustration A–4 shows how a reversing entry on January 1 overcomes the disadvantage of the complex January 9 entry. The reversing entry is the exact opposite of the adjusting entry recorded on December 31. In other words, the Salaries Payable liability is debited for $210, with the result that the account has a zero balance after the entry is posted. Technically, the Salaries Payable account now understates the liability, but no problem exists because financial statements will not be prepared before the liability is settled on January 9.

The credit to the Salaries Expense account is unusual because it gives the account an *abnormal credit balance*. This account's balance also is temporary and does not cause a problem because financial statements will not be prepared before January 9.

As a result of the reversing entry, the January 9 entry to record the payment is simple. Notice that it debits the Salaries Expense account for the full $700 paid. This entry is the same as all other entries made to record 10 days' salary for the employee.

Look next at the accounts on the lower right side of Illustration A–4. After the payment entry is posted, the Salaries Expense account has the $490 balance that it should have to reflect seven days' salary of $70 per day. The zero balance in the Salaries Payable account is now correct. Then, the lower section of the illustration shows that the expense and liability accounts have exactly the same balances whether reversing occurs or not.

As a general rule, adjusting entries that create new asset or new liability accounts are the best candidates for reversing.

Progress Check

A-1 On a work sheet, the $99,400 salaries expense balance was incorrectly extended from the Adjusted Trial Balance column to the Statement of Retained Earnings and Balance Sheet Debit column. As a result of this error:
a. The Adjusted Trial Balance columns will not balance.
b. Revenues on the work sheet will be understated.
c. Net income on the work sheet will be overstated.

A-2 Where does the accountant obtain the amounts entered in the Unadjusted Trial Balance columns of the work sheet?

A-3 What is the advantage of using a work sheet to prepare adjusting entries?

A-4 How are the financial statements affected by the decision to make reversing entries?

SUMMARY OF APPENDIX A IN TERMS OF LEARNING OBJECTIVE

LO 6. Prepare work sheets and reversing entries and explain why they are useful. Accountants often use work sheets at the end of an accounting period in the process of preparing adjusting entries, the adjusted trial balance, and the financial statements. The work sheet is only a tool for accountants and is not distributed to investors or creditors. The work sheet described in this chapter has five pairs of columns for the unadjusted trial balance, the adjustments, the adjusted trial balance, the income statement, and the statement of retained earnings and balance sheet.

Optional reversing entries can be applied to accrued assets and liabilities, including accrued interest earned, accrued interest expense, accrued taxes, and accrued salaries or wages. The goal of reversing entries is to simplify subsequent journal entries. The financial statements are not affected by the choice. Reversing entries are used simply as a matter of convenience in bookkeeping.

GLOSSARY

Accounting cycle eight recurring steps performed each accounting period, starting with recording transactions in the journal and continuing through the post-closing trial balance. p. 153

Classified balance sheet a balance sheet that presents the assets and liabilities in relevant groups. p. 156

Closing entries journal entries recorded at the end of each accounting period to prepare the revenue, expense, and Cash Dividends Declared accounts for the upcoming period and update the Retained Earnings account for the events of the period just finished. p. 148

Current assets cash or other assets that are reasonably expected to be sold, collected, or consumed within one year or within the normal operating cycle of the business, whichever is longer. p. 157

Current liabilities obligations due to be paid or liquidated within one year or the operating cycle, whichever is longer. p. 160

Current ratio a ratio that is used to evaluate a company's ability to pay its short-term obligations, calculated by dividing current assets by current liabilities. p. 161

Income Summary the special account used only in the closing process to temporarily hold the amounts of revenues and expenses before the net difference is added to (or subtracted from) the Retained Earnings account. p. 149

Intangible assets assets without a physical form that are used to produce or sell goods and services; their value comes from the privileges or rights that are granted to or held by the owner. p. 160

Long-term liabilities obligations that are not due to be paid within one year or the operating cycle, whichever is longer. p. 160

Nominal accounts another name for *temporary accounts*. p. 153

Operating cycle of a business the average time between paying cash for employee salaries or merchandise and receiving cash from customers. p. 157

Permanent accounts accounts that are used to describe assets, liabilities, and stockholders' equity; they are not closed as long as the company continues to own the assets, owe the liabilities, or have stockholders' equity; the balances of these accounts appear on the balance sheet. p. 152

Post-closing trial balance a trial balance prepared after the closing entries have been posted; the final step in the accounting cycle. p. 152

Pro forma statements statements that show the effects of the proposed transactions as if the transactions had already occurred. p. 170

Real accounts another name for *permanent accounts*. p. 152

Reversing entries optional entries recorded at the beginning of a new year that prepare the accounts for simplified journal entries subsequent to accrual adjusting entries. p. 170

Temporary accounts accounts that are used to describe revenues, expenses, and cash dividends declared; they are closed at the end of the reporting period. p. 153

Unclassified balance sheet a balance sheet that does not separate the assets and liabilities into categories. p. 156

Work sheet a 10-column spreadsheet used to draft a company's unadjusted trial balance, adjusting entries, adjusted trial balance, and financial statements; an optional step in the accounting process. p. 165

Working papers analyses and other informal reports prepared by accountants when organizing the useful information presented in formal reports to internal and external decision makers. p. 165

The letter ^A *identifies the questions, quick studies, exercises, and problems based on Appendix A at the end of the chapter.*

QUESTIONS

1. What two purposes are accomplished by recording closing entries?
2. What are the four closing entries?
3. What accounts are affected by closing entries? What accounts are not affected?
4. Describe the similarities and differences between adjusting and closing entries.
5. What is the purpose of the Income Summary account?
6. Explain whether an error has occurred if a post-closing trial balance includes a Depreciation Expense, Building account.

7. Refer to the consolidated balance sheet for Southwest Airlines Co. in Appendix E at the end of the book. Assume that during 1994 Southwest Airlines correctly recorded payments for all of the accrued liabilities that were outstanding at the end of 1993. What amount of accrued expenses was recorded in the process of preparing adjustments at the end of 1994?

8. Refer to the financial statements of Lands' End, Inc., in Appendix F at the end of the book. What journal entry was recorded as of January 27, 1995, to close the company's Income Summary account?

LANDS' END
DIRECT MERCHANTS

9. How is an unearned revenue classified on the balance sheet?
10. What classes of assets and liabilities are shown on a typical classified balance sheet?
11. What is a company's operating cycle?

12. What are the characteristics of plant and equipment?
A13. What tasks are performed with the work sheet?
A14. Why are the debit and credit entries in the Adjustments columns of the work sheet identified with letters?
A15. How do reversing entries simplify a company's bookkeeping efforts?
A16. If a company accrued unpaid salaries expense of $500 at the end of a fiscal year, what reversing entry could be made? When would it be made?

QUICK STUDY (Five-Minute Exercises)

QS 5–1
(LO 1)

Jontil Corporation began the current period with a Retained Earnings balance of $14,000. At the end of the period, the company's adjusted account balances include the following temporary accounts with normal balances:

Service fees earned	$35,000
Salaries expense	19,000
Depreciation expense	4,000
Interest earned	3,500
Cash dividends declared	6,000
Utilities expense	2,300

After closing the revenue and expense accounts, what will be the balance of the Income Summary account?
After all of the closing entries are journalized and posted, what will be the balance of the Retained Earnings account?

QS 5–2
(LO 2)

List the following steps of the accounting cycle in the proper order:

a. Preparing the unadjusted trial balance.

b. Preparing the post-closing trial balance.

c. Journalizing and posting adjusting entries.

d. Journalizing and posting closing entries.

e. Preparing the financial statements.

f. Journalizing transactions.

g. Posting the transaction entries.

h. Completing the work sheet.

QS 5–3
(LO 3)

The following are categories on a classified balance sheet:

A. Current assets

B. Investments

C. Property, plant, and equipment

D. Intangible assets

E. Current liabilities

F. Long-term liabilities

For each of the following items, select the letter that identifies the balance sheet category in which the item should appear.

___ 1. Store equipment

___ 2. Wages payable

___ 3. Cash

___ 4. Notes payable (due in three years)

___ 5. Land not currently used in business operations

___ 6. Accounts receivable

___ 7. Trademarks

Calculate Tucker Company's current ratio, given the following information about its assets and liabilities:

**QS 5–4
(LO 4)**

Accounts receivable	$15,000
Accounts payable	10,000
Buildings	42,000
Cash	6,000
Long-term notes payable	20,000
Office supplies	1,800
Prepaid insurance	2,500
Unearned services revenue	4,000

In preparing a work sheet, indicate the financial statement debit column to which a normal balance of each of the following accounts should be extended. Use IS for the Income Statement Debit column and BS for the Statement of Retained Earnings or Balance Sheet Debit column.

**AQS 5–5
(LO 6)**

1. Equipment

2. Cash dividends declared

3. Insurance expense

4. Prepaid insurance

5. Accounts receivable

6. Depreciation expense, equipment

The following information is from the work sheet for Pursley Company as of December 31, 19X1. Using this information, determine the amount of retained earnings that should be reported on the December 31, 19X1, balance sheet.

**AQS 5–6
(LO 6)**

	Income Statement		Statement of Retained Earnings and Balance Sheet	
	Dr.	Cr.	Dr.	Cr.
Retained earnings				65,000
Cash dividends declared			32,000	
Totals	115,000	174,000		

On December 31, 19X1, Yacht Management Co. prepared an adjusting entry for $6,700 of earned but unrecorded management fees. On January 16, 19X2, Ace received $15,500 of management fees which included the fees earned in 19X1. Assuming the company uses reversing entries, prepare the reversing entry and the January 16, 19X2, entry.

**AQS 5–7
(LO 6)**

EXERCISES

The following adjusted trial balance contains the accounts and balances of Painters, Inc., as of December 31, 19X1, the end of its fiscal year:

Exercise 5–1
Closing entries
(LO 1)

No.	Title	Debit	Credit
101	Cash	$18,000	
126	Supplies	12,000	
128	Prepaid insurance	2,000	
167	Equipment	23,000	
168	Accumulated depreciation, equipment		$ 6,500
209	Salaries payable		
307	Common stock, $10 par value		34,000
318	Retained earnings		12,600
319	Cash dividends declared	6,000	
404	Services revenue		36,000
612	Depreciation expense, equipment	2,000	
622	Salaries expense	21,000	
637	Insurance expense	1,500	
640	Rent expense	2,400	
652	Supplies expense	1,200	
	Totals	$89,100	$89,100

Required

Journalize closing entries for the company.

Exercise 5–2
Preparing closing entries and
the post-closing trial balance
(LO 1)

The adjusted trial balance for West Plumbing Co. follows. Prepare a table with two columns under each of the following headings: Adjusted Trial Balance, Closing Entries, and Post-Closing Trial Balance. Complete the table by providing four closing entries and the post-closing trial balance.

No.	Title	Adjusted Trial Balance	
101	Cash	$ 8,200	
106	Accounts receivable	24,000	
153	Trucks	41,000	
154	Accumulated depreciation, trucks		$ 16,500
193	Franchise	30,000	
201	Accounts payable		14,000
209	Salaries payable		3,200
233	Unearned fees		2,600
307	Common stock, $1 par value		40,000
318	Retained earnings		24,500
319	Cash dividends declared	14,400	
401	Plumbing fees earned		79,000
611	Depreciation expense, trucks	11,000	
622	Salaries expense	31,500	
640	Rent expense	12,000	
677	Miscellaneous expenses	7,700	
901	Income summary		
	Totals	$179,800	$179,800

Exercise 5–3
Closing entries
(LO 1)

The following balances of the Retained Earnings and temporary accounts are from High Rider, Inc.'s adjusted trial balance:

	Debit	Credit
Retained earnings		$42,100
Cash dividends declared	$ 7,500	
Services revenue		32,000
Interest earned		5,300
Salaries expense	25,400	
Insurance expense	3,800	
Rental expense	6,400	
Supplies expense	3,100	
Depreciation expense, trucks	10,600	

Required

a. Prepare the closing entries.

b. Determine the amount of retained earnings to be reported on the company's balance sheet.

Open the following T-accounts with the provided balances. Prepare closing journal entries and post them to the accounts.

Exercise 5–4
Preparing and posting closing entries
(LO 1)

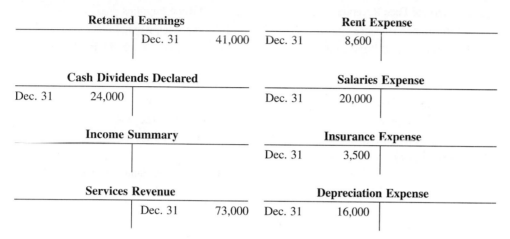

Retained Earnings			Rent Expense		
	Dec. 31	41,000	Dec. 31	8,600	

Cash Dividends Declared			Salaries Expense		
Dec. 31	24,000		Dec. 31	20,000	

Income Summary			Insurance Expense		
			Dec. 31	3,500	

Services Revenue			Depreciation Expense		
	Dec. 31	73,000	Dec. 31	16,000	

Use the following adjusted trial balance of Hanson Trucking Company to prepare a classified balance sheet as of December 31, 19X1.

Exercise 5–5
Preparing a classified balance sheet
(LO 3)

	Debit	Credit
Cash	$ 7,000	
Accounts receivable	16,500	
Office supplies	2,000	
Trucks	170,000	
Accumulated depreciation, trucks		$ 35,000
Land	75,000	
Accounts payable		11,000
Interest payable		3,000
Long-term notes payable		52,000
Common stock, $10 par value		120,000
Retained earnings		41,000
Cash dividends declared	19,000	
Trucking fees earned		128,000
Depreciation expense, trucks	22,500	
Salaries expense	60,000	
Office supplies expense	7,000	
Repairs expense, trucks	11,000	
Total	$390,000	$390,000

Use the information provided in Exercise 5–5 to determine the value of the current ratio as of the balance sheet date.

Exercise 5–6
Calculating the current ratio
(LO 4)

Calculate the current ratio in each of the following cases:

Exercise 5–7
Calculating the current ratio
(LO 4)

	Current Assets	Current Liabilities
Case 1	$ 78,000	$31,000
Case 2	104,000	75,000
Case 3	44,000	48,000
Case 4	84,500	80,600
Case 5	60,000	99,000

^AExercise 5–8
Extending adjusted account
balances on a work sheet
(LO 6)

These accounts are from the Adjusted Trial Balance columns in a company's 10-column work sheet. In the blank space beside each account, write the letter of the appropriate financial statement column to which a normal account balance should be extended.

A.   Debit column for the income statement
B.   Credit column for the income statement
C.   Debit column for the statement of retained earnings and balance sheet
D.   Credit column for the statement of retained earnings and balance sheet

__ 1.	Service Fees Revenue	__ 9.	Office Supplies
__ 2.	Insurance Expense	__ 10.	Accounts Payable
__ 3.	Accumulated Depreciation, Machinery	__ 11.	Common Stock, $1 Par Value
__ 4.	Interest Earned	__ 12.	Wages Payable
__ 5.	Accounts Receivable	__ 13.	Machinery
__ 6.	Rent Expense	__ 14.	Interest Receivable
__ 7.	Depreciation Expense, Machinery	__ 15.	Interest Expense
__ 8.	Cash	__ 16.	Cash Dividends Declared

^AExercise 5–9
Preparing adjusting entries from
work sheet information
(LO 6)

Use the following information from the Adjustments columns of a 10-column work sheet to prepare adjusting journal entries:

		Adjustments	
No.	**Title**	**Debit**	**Credit**
109	Interest receivable	(d) 580	
124	Office supplies		(b) 1,650
128	Prepaid insurance		(a) 900
164	Accumulated depreciation, office equipment		(c) 3,300
209	Salaries payable		(e) 660
409	Interest earned		(d) 580
612	Depreciation expense, office equipment	(c) 3,300	
620	Office salaries expense	(e) 660	
636	Insurance expense, office equipment	(a) 432	
637	Insurance expense, store equipment	(a) 468	
650	Office supplies expense	(b) 1,650	
	Totals	7,090	7,090

^AExercise 5–10
Completing the income
statement columns and
preparing closing entries
(LO 1, 6)

These partially completed Income Statement columns from a 10-column work sheet are for WinSail Rental, Inc. Use the information to determine the amount that should be entered on the net income line of the work sheet. In addition, draft closing entries for the company. The corporation did not pay any dividends.

	Debit	**Credit**
Rent earned		102,000
Salaries expense	45,300	
Insurance expense	6,400	
Dock rental expense	15,000	
Boat supplies expense	3,200	
Depreciation expense, boats	19,500	
Totals		
Net income		
Totals		

The Adjusted Trial Balance columns of a 10-column work sheet for Plummers Corp. follow. Complete the work sheet by extending the account balances into the appropriate financial statement columns and by entering the amount of net income for the reporting period.

^A**Exercise 5–11**
Extending accounts in the work sheet
(LO 6)

No.	Title	Adjusted Trial Balance	
101	Cash	$ 6,000	
106	Accounts receivable	26,200	
153	Trucks	41,000	
154	Accumulated depreciation, trucks		$ 16,500
193	Franchise	30,000	
201	Accounts payable		14,000
209	Salaries payable		3,200
233	Unearned fees		2,600
307	Common stock, $100 par value		20,000
318	Retained earnings		44,500
319	Cash dividends declared	14,400	
401	Plumbing fees earned		79,000
611	Depreciation expense, trucks	5,500	
622	Salaries expense	37,000	
640	Rent expense	12,000	
677	Miscellaneous expenses	7,700	
	Totals	$179,800	$179,800

Breaker Corporation records the prepaid assets and unearned revenues in balance sheet accounts. The following information was used to prepare adjusting entries for Breaker Corporation as of August 31, the end of the company's fiscal year:

^A**Exercise 5–12**
Reversing entries
(LO 6)

a. The company has earned $5,000 of unrecorded service fees.

b. The expired portion of prepaid insurance is $2,700.

c. The earned portion of the Unearned Fees account balance is $1,900.

d. Depreciation expense for the office equipment is $2,300.

e. Employees have earned but have not been paid salaries of $2,400.

Required

Prepare the reversing entries that would simplify the bookkeeping effort for recording subsequent events related to these adjustments.

The following two conditions existed for Maxit Corporation on October 31, 19X1, the end of its fiscal year:

^A**Exercise 5–13**
Reversing entries
(LO 6)

a. Maxit rents a building from its owner for $3,200 per month. By a prearrangement, the company delayed paying October's rent until November 5. On this date, the company paid the rent for both October and November.

b. Maxit rents space in a building it owns to a tenant for $750 per month. By prearrangement, the tenant delayed paying the October rent until November 8. On this date, the tenant paid the rent for both October and November.

Required

1. Prepare the adjusting entries that Maxit should record for these situations as of October 31.

2. Assuming that Maxit does not use reversing entries, prepare journal entries to record Maxit's payment of rent on November 5 and the collection of rent on November 8 from Maxit's tenant.

3. Assuming that Maxit does use reversing entries, prepare those entries and the journal entries to record Maxit's payment of rent on November 5 and the collection of rent on November 8 from Maxit's tenant.

PROBLEMS

Problem 5–1
Closing entries, financial statements, and current ratio
(LO 1, 3, 4)

Bradshaw Repairs Corporation's adjusted trial balance on December 31, 19X2, appeared as follows:

BRADSHAW REPAIRS CORPORATION
Adjusted Trial Balance
December 31, 19X2

No.	Title	Debit	Credit
101	Cash	$ 13,000	
124	Office supplies	1,200	
128	Prepaid insurance	1,950	
167	Equipment	48,000	
168	Accumulated depreciation, equipment		$ 4,000
201	Accounts payable		12,000
210	Wages payable		500
307	Common stock, $0.10 par value		32,000
318	Retained earnings		8,000
319	Cash dividends declared	15,000	
401	Repair fees earned		77,750
612	Depreciation expense, equipment	4,000	
623	Wages expense	36,500	
637	Insurance expense	700	
640	Rent expense	9,600	
650	Office supplies expense	2,600	
690	Utilities expense	1,700	
	Totals	$134,250	$134,250

Required

Preparation component:

CHECK FIGURE: Ending retained earnings, $15,650

1. Prepare an income statement and a statement of retained earnings for the 19X2 year and a classified balance sheet at the end of the year.

2. Enter the adjusted trial balance in the first two columns of a 6-column table that also has columns for closing entries and for a post-closing trial balance. Insert an Income Summary account in the trial balance.

3. Enter the closing entries in the table and prepare journal entries for them.

4. Determine the company's current ratio.

Analysis component:

5. Assume that the adjusted trial balance differs as follows:
   a. None of the $700 insurance expense had expired during the year but instead was a prepayment of future insurance protection.
   b. There were no earned but unpaid wages at the end of the year.
   Describe the changes in the financial statements that would result from these assumptions.

Problem 5–2
Closing entries, financial statements, and ratios
(LO 1, 3, 4)

The adjusted trial balance for Graw, Inc. as of December 31, 19X2, follows:

GRAW, INC.
Adjusted Trial Balance
December 31, 19X2

No.	Title	Debit	Credit
101	Cash	$ 4,000	
104	Short-term investments	22,000	
126	Supplies	7,100	
128	Prepaid insurance	6,000	
167	Equipment	39,000	
168	Accumulated depreciation, equipment		$ 20,000
173	Building	130,000	

174	Accumulated depreciation, building		55,000
183	Land	45,000	
201	Accounts payable		15,500
203	Interest payable		1,500
208	Rent payable		2,500
210	Wages payable		1,500
213	Property taxes payable		800
233	Unearned professional fees		6,500
251	Long-term notes payable		66,000
307	Common stock, $10 par value		50,000
318	Retained earnings		32,700
319	Cash dividends declared	12,000	
401	Professional fees earned		96,000
406	Rent earned		13,000
407	Dividends earned		1,900
409	Interest earned		1,000
606	Depreciation expense, building	10,000	
612	Depreciation expense, equipment	5,000	
623	Wages expense	31,000	
633	Interest expense	4,100	
637	Insurance expense	9,000	
640	Rent expense	12,400	
652	Supplies expense	6,400	
682	Postage expense	3,200	
683	Property taxes expense	4,000	
684	Repairs expense	7,900	
688	Telephone expense	2,200	
690	Utilities expense	3,600	
	Totals	$363,900	$363,900

An analysis of other information reveals that the company is required to make a $6,600 payment on the long-term note payable during 19X3.

Required

1. Present the income statement, statement of retained earnings, and classified balance sheet.

2. Present the closing entries made at the end of the year.

3. Use the information in the financial statements to calculate these ratios:
   a. Return on equity.
   b. Debt ratio.
   c. Profit margin (use total revenues as the denominator).
   d. Current ratio.

CHECK FIGURE: Total assets, $178,100

On June 1, 19X1, three investors created a new travel agency called International Tours, Inc. The company records prepaid and unearned items in balance sheet accounts. These events occurred during the company's first month:

Problem 5–3
Performing the steps in the accounting cycle
(LO 1, 2, 3)

June 1 Issued 600 shares of $100 par value, common stock to the investors in exchange for $20,000 cash and computer equipment worth $40,000.

2 Rented furnished office space by paying $1,700 rent for the first month.

3 Purchased $1,100 of office supplies for cash.

10 Paid $3,600 for the premium on a one-year insurance policy. Insurance coverage began on June 10.

14 Paid $1,800 for two weeks' salaries to employees.

24 Collected $7,900 of commissions from airlines on tickets obtained for customers.

28 Paid another $1,800 for two weeks' salaries.

29 Paid the month's $650 telephone bill.

30 Paid $250 cash to repair the company's computer.

30 Paid $1,500 cash dividends to stockholders.

The company's chart of accounts included these accounts:

101	Cash	405	Commissions Earned
106	Accounts Receivable	612	Depreciation Expense, Computer Equipment
124	Office Supplies	622	Salaries Expense
128	Prepaid Insurance	637	Insurance Expense
167	Computer Equipment	640	Rent Expense
168	Accumulated Depreciation, Computer Equipment	650	Office Supplies Expense
209	Salaries Payable	684	Repairs Expense
307	Common Stock, $100 Par Value	688	Telephone Expense
318	Retained Earnings		
319	Cash Dividends Declared	901	Income Summary

Required

1. Use the balance-column format to create each of the listed accounts.
2. Prepare journal entries to record the transactions for June and post them to the accounts.
3. Prepare an unadjusted trial balance as of June 30.
4. Use the following information to journalize and post adjusting entries for the month:
   a. Two-thirds of one month's insurance coverage was consumed.
   b. There were $700 of office supplies on hand at the end of the month.
   c. Depreciation on the computer equipment was estimated to be $600.
   d. The employees had earned $320 of unpaid and unrecorded salaries.
   e. The company had earned $1,650 of commissions that had not yet been billed.

CHECK FIGURE: Ending Retained Earnings, $330

5. Prepare an income statement, a statement of retained earnings, and a balance sheet.
6. Prepare journal entries to close the temporary accounts and post them to the accounts.
7. Prepare a separate post-closing trial balance.

Problem 5–4
Balance sheet classifications
(LO 4)

In the blank space beside each numbered balance sheet item, enter the letter of its balance sheet classification. If the item should not appear on the balance sheet, enter a z in the blank.

a. Current assets
b. Investments
c. Plant and equipment
d. Intangible assets

e. Current liabilities
f. Long-term liabilities
g. Stockholders' equity

___ 1.	Depreciation expense, trucks	___ 11.	Accumulated depreciation, trucks
___ 2.	Cash dividends declared	___ 12.	Cash
___ 3.	Interest receivable	___ 13.	Building
___ 4.	Utilities payable	___ 14.	Retained earnings
___ 5.	Automobiles	___ 15.	Office equipment
___ 6.	Notes payable—due in three years	___ 16.	Land (used in operations)
___ 7.	Accounts payable	___ 17.	Repairs expense
___ 8.	Prepaid insurance	___ 18.	Prepaid property taxes
___ 9.	Common stock, $5 par value	___ 19.	Current portion of long-term note payable
___ 10.	Unearned services revenue	___ 20.	Investment in Chrysler common stock (long-term holding)

This unadjusted trial balance is for Whiten Construction, Inc., as of the end of its 19X2 fiscal year.

ᴬProblem 5–5

Work sheet, journal entries, financial statements, and current ratio

(LO 1, 3, 4, 6)

WHITEN CONSTRUCTION, INC.
Unadjusted Trial Balance
April 30, 19X2

No.	Title	Debit	Credit
101	Cash	$ 17,500	
126	Supplies	8,900	
128	Prepaid insurance	6,200	
167	Equipment	131,000	
168	Accumulated depreciation, equipment		$ 25,250
201	Accounts payable		5,800
203	Interest payable		
208	Rent payable		
210	Wages payable		
213	Property taxes payable		
251	Long-term notes payable		24,000
307	Common stock, $10 par value		50,000
318	Retained earnings		27,660
319	Cash dividends declared	30,000	
401	Construction fees earned		134,000
612	Depreciation expense, equipment		
623	Wages expense	45,860	
633	Interest expense	2,640	
637	Insurance expense		
640	Rent expense	13,200	
652	Supplies expense		
683	Property taxes expense	4,600	
684	Repairs expense	2,810	
690	Utilities expense	4,000	
	Totals	$266,710	$266,710

Required

Preparation component:

1. Prepare a 10-column work sheet for 19X2, starting with the unadjusted trial balance and including adjustments based on these additional facts:
   a. The inventory of supplies at the end of the year had a cost of $3,200.
   b. The cost of expired insurance for the year is $3,900.
   c. Annual depreciation on the equipment is $8,500.
   d. The April utilities expense of $550 was not included in the trial balance because the bill arrived after it was prepared. The $550 amount owed needs to be recorded.
   e. The company's employees have earned $1,600 of accrued wages.
   f. The lease for the office requires the company to pay total rent for the year ended April 30 equal to 10% of the company's annual revenues. The rent is paid to the building owner with monthly payments of $1,100. If the annual rent exceeds the total monthly payments, the company must pay the excess before May 31. If the total is less than the amount previously paid, the building owner will refund the difference by May 31.
   g. Additional property taxes of $900 have been assessed on the equipment but have not been paid or recorded in the accounts.
   h. The long-term note payable bears interest at 1% per month, which the company is required to pay by the 10th of the following month. The balance of the Interest Expense account equals the amount paid during the past fiscal year. The interest for April has not yet been paid or recorded. In addition, the company is required to make a $5,000 payment on the note on June 30, 19X2.

2. Use the work sheet to journalize the adjusting and closing entries.

3. Prepare an income statement, a statement of retained earnings, and a classified balance sheet. Calculate the company's current ratio.

CHECK FIGURE: Total assets, $120,250

Analysis component:

4. Analyze the following potential errors and describe how each would affect the 10-column work sheet. Explain whether the error is likely to be discovered in completing the work sheet and, if not, the effect of the error on the financial statements.

    a. Assume the adjustment for supplies consumption credited Supplies for $3,200 and debited the same amount to Supplies Expense.

    b. When completing the adjusted trial balance in the work sheet, the $17,500 cash balance was incorrectly entered in the Credit column.

^A**Problem 5–6**
Adjusting, reversing, and subsequent entries
(LO 6)

The unadjusted trial balance for Shooting Ranges, Inc., as of December 31, 19X1, follows:

SHOOTING RANGES, INC.
December 31, 19X1

	Unadjusted Trial Balance	
Cash	$ 13,000	
Accounts receivable		
Supplies	5,500	
Equipment	130,000	
Accumulated depreciation, equipment		$ 25,000
Interest payable		
Salaries payable		
Unearned membership fees		14,000
Notes payable		50,000
Common stock, $50 par value		30,000
Retained earnings		28,250
Cash dividends declared	20,000	
Membership fees earned		53,000
Depreciation expense, equipment		
Salaries expense	28,000	
Interest expense	3,750	
Supplies expense		
Totals	$200,250	$200,250

Required

1. Prepare a six-column table with two columns under each of the following headings: Unadjusted Trial Balance, Adjustments, and Adjusted Trial Balance. Complete the table by entering adjustments that reflect the following information:

    a. As of December 31, employees have earned $900 of unpaid and unrecorded salaries. The next payday is January 4, and the total salaries to be paid is $1,600.

    b. The cost of supplies on hand at December 31 is $2,700.

    c. The note payable requires an interest payment to be made every three months. The amount of unrecorded accrued interest at December 31 is $1,250, and the next payment is due on January 15. This payment will be $1,500.

    d. An analysis of the unearned membership fees shows that $5,600 remains unearned at December 31.

    e. In addition to the membership fees included in the revenue account balance, the company has earned another $9,100 in fees that will be collected on January 21. The company is also expected to collect $8,000 on the same day for new fees earned during January.

    f. Depreciation expense for the year is $12,500.

CHECK FIGURE: Total debits in adjusted trial balance, $224,000

2. Prepare journal entries for the adjustments drafted in the six-column table.

3. Prepare journal entries to reverse the effects of the adjusting entries that involve accruals.

4. Prepare journal entries to record the cash payments and collections that are described for January.

SERIAL PROBLEM

(The first two segments of this comprehensive problem were in Chapters 3 and 4, and the final segment is presented in Chapter 6. If the Chapter 3 and 4 segments have not been completed, the assignment can begin at this point. However, you should use the Working Papers that accompany this text because they reflect the account balances that resulted from posting the entries required in Chapters 3 and 4.)

Echo Systems, Inc.

The transactions of Echo Systems, Inc., for October through December 19X1 have been recorded in the problem segments in Chapters 3 and 4, as well as the year-end adjusting entries. Prior to closing the revenue and expense accounts for 19X1, the accounting system is modified to include the Retained Earnings account and the Income Summary account, which are given the numbers 318 and 901, respectively.

Required

1. Record and post the appropriate closing entries.
2. Prepare a post-closing trial balance.

CHECK FIGURE: Total credits in post-closing trial balance, $78,560.

CRITICAL THINKING: ESSAYS, PROBLEMS, AND CASES

On December 31, 19X1, the Carter Stone Company recorded a $7,500 liability to its employees for wages earned in 19X1 that will be paid on January 5, the first pay day in 19X2. The January payment will also include another $3,750 for wages earned in 19X2. The accountant did not prepare a reversing entry as of January 1, 19X2, but did not inform the bookkeeper about the liability accrued for the wages. As a result, on January 5, the bookkeeper recorded an $11,250 debit to Wages Expense and an $11,250 credit to Cash.

Describe the effects of this error on the financial statements for 19X1. Describe any erroneous account balances that will exist during 19X2. Suggest a reasonable point in time at which the error would be discovered.

^A^Analytical Essay

(LO 6)

As the end of the calendar year is approaching, Controller Karen Harrison is getting the Blackwood Company's accounting department ready to prepare the annual financial statements. One concern is the expense of the services provided by an external consultant under a three-month contract that runs from November 30, 19X1, through February 28, 19X2. The total fee for the contract is based on the hours of the consultant's time, with the result that the total fee is not known.

The controller is concerned that the company's financial statements could not be prepared until March because the amount of consulting expense will not be known until then. To avoid this problem, the controller has asked you to prepare a letter to Keith Hanson, the consultant, that would ask for a progress report by the end of the first week of January. This report would specifically identify the hours and charges that will be billed for Hanson's time in December.

Draft the letter that will be sent to Hanson requesting this information. It will be signed by the controller on December 15, 19X1.

Business Communications Case

(LO 2)

ᴬFinancial Reporting Problem

(LO 2, 6)

The following balance sheet was prepared at the end of the company's fiscal year:

TUNES TO GO, INC.
Balance Sheet
December 31, 19X2

Assets

Current assets:		
Cash		$ 9,500
Office supplies		2,500
Prepaid insurance		1,600
Total current assets		$13,600
Plant and equipment:		
Automobiles	$32,000	
Accumulated depreciation, automobiles	(12,000)	$20,000
Office equipment	$35,000	
Accumulated depreciation, office equipment	(8,500)	26,500
Total plant and equipment		$46,500
Total assets		$60,100

Liabilities

Current liabilities:		
Accounts payable		$ 4,100
Interest payable		500
Salaries payable		900
Unearned fees		2,100
Total current liabilities		$ 7,600
Long-term liabilities:		
Long-term notes payable		40,000
Total liabilities		$47,600

Stockholders' Equity

Contributed capital:		
Common stock, $100 par value	$10,000	
Retained earnings	2,500	12,500
Total liabilities and stockholders' equity		$60,100

The company's accountant also prepared and posted the following adjusting and closing entries:

Dec.	31	Insurance Expense	700.00	
		Prepaid Insurance		700.00
		To record consumed insurance coverage.		
	31	Office Supplies Expense	3,800.00	
		Office Supplies		3,800.00
		To record consumed office supplies.		
	31	Depreciation Expense, Automobiles	4,500.00	
		Accumulated Depreciation, Automobiles		4,500.00
		To record depreciation on automobiles.		
	31	Depreciation Expense, Office Equipment	2,500.00	
		Accumulated Depreciation, Office Equipment		2,500.00
		To record depreciation on equipment.		
	31	Unearned Fees	700.00	
		Fees Earned		700.00
		To record earning of fees paid in advance.		
	31	Salaries Expense	900.00	
		Salaries Payable		900.00
		To record accrued salaries.		
	31	Interest Expense	500.00	
		Interest Payable		500.00
		To record accrued interest expense.		
	31	Fees Earned	58,000.00	
		Income Summary		58,000.00
		To close the revenue account and open the		
		Income Summary account.		

Dec.	31	Income Summary	44,660.00	
		Depreciation Expense, Automobiles		4,500.00
		Depreciation Expense, Office Equipment		2,500.00
		Salaries Expense		18,600.00
		Interest Expense		3,500.00
		Insurance Expense		700.00
		Rent Expense		7,800.00
		Office Supplies Expense		3,800.00
		Gas, Oil, and Repairs Expense		2,150.00
		Telephone Expense		1,110.00
		To close the expense accounts.		
	31	Income Summary	13,340.00	
		Retained Earnings		13,340.00
		To close the Income Summary account.		
	31	Retained Earnings	12,000.00	
		Cash Dividends Declared		12,000.00
		To close the Cash Dividends Declared account.		

Use the information in the balance sheet and the journal entries to complete a 10-column work sheet. (The five steps should be completed in reverse order.)

Review the consolidated balance sheet for Southwest Airlines Co. in Appendix E at the end of this book. Assume that a ledger account exists for each item in the balance sheet and prepare a post-closing trial balance for the company as of December 31, 1994. For simplicity, the amounts in the trial balance can be stated in thousands of dollars as they are presented in the balance sheet.

Financial Statement Analysis Case

(LO 1, 4)

Calculate the company's current ratios at the end of 1994 and 1993 and comment on any change.

COMPREHENSIVE PROBLEM

Following is the unadjusted trial balance of Texas Plumbing and Heating, Inc., as of November 30, 19X2. The company records prepaid and unearned items in balance sheet accounts. The account balances include the effects of transactions during the first 11 months of the year.

Texas Plumbing and Heating, Inc.

(Review of Chapters 2–5 plus Appendix A)

TEXAS PLUMBING AND HEATING, INC.
Unadjusted Trial Balance
November 30, 19X2

No.	Account	Debit	Credit
101	Cash	$ 18,500	
124	Office supplies	8,400	
126	Repair supplies	86,000	
128	Prepaid insurance	2,400	
153	Trucks	72,000	
154	Accumulated depreciation, trucks		$ 30,000
173	Building	195,000	
174	Accumulated depreciation, building		42,000
201	Accounts payable		16,500
210	Wages payable		
233	Unearned heating fees		3,700
307	Common stock, $10 par value		100,000
318	Retained earnings		71,600
319	Cash dividends declared	25,000	
401	Plumbing fees earned		176,000
402	Heating fees earned		102,000
606	Depreciation expense, building		
611	Depreciation expense, trucks		
623	Wages expense	67,000	
637	Insurance expense		
650	Office supplies expense		
652	Repair supplies expense		
669	Gas, oil, and repairs expense	16,500	
672	General and administrative expenses	51,000	
	Totals	$541,800	$541,800

188   Chapter 5

The following transactions occurred during December 19X2:

Dec. 2   Received $1,400 for completed heating work.
      5   Paid $7,400 on accounts payable.
      6   Paid $3,600 insurance premium in advance.
      7   Received $3,200 cash for plumbing work completed.
      10 Purchased $2,500 of repair supplies on credit.
      14 Paid $2,800 for wages earned December 1 to 14.
      17 Purchased $350 of office supplies on credit.
      21 Received $3,200 cash for plumbing work completed and $9,000 cash for heating work.
      24 Paid $1,230 for truck repairs related to an accident.
      28 Paid $2,800 for wages earned December 15 to 28.
      30 Received $1,600 cash for plumbing work completed and $2,300 cash for heating work.

Required

1. Use the balance column format to create the accounts listed in the November 30 trial balance and the Income Summary account. Enter the unadjusted November 30 balances in the accounts.
2. Journalize and post journal entries to record the transactions for December.
3. Prepare a 10-column work sheet as of December 31. Start by entering the unadjusted balances from the accounts as of that date. Continue by entering adjustments for the following items and then complete the rest of the work sheet.
    a. At the end of the year, the office supplies inventory was $1,730.
    b. At the end of the year, the repair supplies inventory was $9,900.
    c. At the end of the year, the unexpired portion of the prepaid insurance was $3,200.
    d. Annual depreciation on the trucks was $15,000.
    e. Annual depreciation on the building was $9,500.
    f. At the end of the year, the employees had earned $1,990 in accrued wages.
    g. At the end of the year, the balance of unearned heating fees was $500.
4. Prepare adjusting journal entries and post them to the accounts.
5. Prepare an income statement and a statement of retained earnings for 19X2 and a balance sheet as of December 31, 19X2.
6. Prepare closing journal entries and post them to the accounts.
7. Prepare a post-closing trial balance.
8. Calculate the following ratios:
    a. Return on equity.
    b. Profit margin.

ANSWERS TO PROGRESS CHECKS

5–1 c

5–2 Revenue and expense accounts are called temporary because they are opened and closed every reporting period. The Income Summary and Cash Dividends Declared accounts are also temporary accounts.

5–3 Permanent accounts are listed on the post-closing trial balance. These accounts include the asset, liability, and stockholders' equity accounts.

5–4 a

5–5 Optional steps in the accounting cycle include preparing a work sheet and preparing reversing entries.

5–6 Current assets: b, c, d.
     Plant and equipment: a, e.

5–7 Investment in common stock, Land held for future expansion.

5–8 Contributed capital and retained earnings.

5–9 Current liabilities.

A–1 *c*

A–2 The amounts in the Unadjusted Trial Balance columns are taken from the account balances in the ledger.

A–3 The work sheet offers the advantage of providing on one page all of the necessary information to make the adjusting entries.

A–4 The financial statements are unchanged by the choice between using or not using reversing entries.

Accounting for Merchandising Activities

*J.*C. Penney Company, Inc., is a major retailer that has department stores in all 50 states and Puerto Rico. The primary products sold by the company include family apparel, shoes, jewelry, accessories, and home furnishings.

J.C. Penney uses a fiscal year of 52 weeks that ends in late January. The company describes its annual accounting period that ended on January 28, 1995, as the 1994 year. During the five-year period ending on January 28, 1995, the products the company owned for the purpose of reselling them to customers increased from $2,897 million to $3,876 million. During the same period, the receivables held by the company (primarily from customers) increased from $4,303 million to $5,159 million. Thus, at the end of the 1994 year, the company's assets included $9,035 million ($3,876 million + $5,159 million) of products it held for sale and receivables. This amounted to nearly 56% of its total assets.

Many financial statement readers are interested in evaluating the effects of these large holdings of products and receivables on the company's ability to meet its current debt obligations. How might this issue be evaluated?

J.C. PENNEY COMPANY, INC.
(in millions)

	End of Year	
	1994	1993
Current assets:		
Cash and short-term investments	$ 261	$ 173
Receivables, net	5,159	4,679
Merchandise inventories	3,876	3,545
Prepaid expenses	172	168
Total current assets	$9,468	$8,565
Total current liabilities	$4,481	$3,883

LEARNING OBJECTIVES

After studying Chapter 6, you should be able to:

1. **Describe merchandising activities, the unique aspects of a merchandising company's financial statements, and the difference between periodic and perpetual inventory systems.**

2. **Using a perpetual inventory system, analyze and record transactions involving merchandise purchases, purchase discounts, purchase returns and allowances, and transportation-in.**

3. **Using a perpetual inventory system, analyze and record transactions involving merchandise sales, sales discounts, and sales returns and allowances and explain the use of debit and credit memoranda.**

4. **Prepare the adjusting and closing entries for a merchandising company that uses a perpetual inventory system and describe the flow of information through the Merchandise Inventory and Cost of Goods Sold accounts.**

5. **Describe the alternative income statement formats used by businesses and explain the use of the acid-test ratio as an indicator of a company's liquidity.**

6. **Define or explain the words and phrases in the chapter glossary.**

This chapter introduces some of the business and accounting practices used by companies that engage in merchandising activities. These companies buy goods and then resell them to customers. This chapter shows how the financial statements describe the special transactions and assets related to these activities. In particular, you will learn about the additional financial statement elements created by merchandising activities. To help you understand where the information comes from, we describe how accountants close the accounts of merchandising companies and design income statements.

THE NATURE OF MERCHANDISING ACTIVITIES

LO 1
Describe merchandising activities, the unique aspects of a merchandising company's financial statements, and the difference between periodic and perpetual inventory systems.

The focus of the previous chapters in this book was on the development of financial statements for companies that provide services to their customers. Examples of service companies include **Greyhound Lines Inc., Merrill Lynch & Co., Inc., America West Airlines, Inc., Avis, Inc.,** and **Marriott International Inc.** In return for services provided to its customers, a service company receives commissions, fares, or fees as revenue. Its net income for a reporting period is the difference between its revenues and the operating expenses incurred in providing the services.

In contrast, a merchandising company earns net income by buying and selling **merchandise,** which consists of goods that the company acquires for the purpose of reselling them to customers.[1] Examples of merchandising companies include **CompUSA, Inc., Kmart Corporation,** and **J.C. Penney Company.**

Income Statements for Merchandising Companies

To achieve a net income, the revenue from selling the merchandise needs to exceed not only the cost of the merchandise sold to customers but also the company's other operating expenses for the reporting period. The accounting term for the revenues

---

[1]A merchandising company can be either a wholesaler or a retailer. Wholesalers buy goods from manufacturers and sell them to retailers or other wholesalers. Retailers buy goods from wholesalers and sell them to individual customers.

Illustration 6-1
Income Statement for a
Merchandising Company

MEGAMART, INC.
Condensed Income Statement
For Year Ended December 31, 19X2

Net sales	$314,700
Cost of goods sold	(230,400)
Gross profit from sales	$ 84,300
Total other expenses	(71,400)
Net income	$ 12,900

from selling merchandise is *sales* and the term used to describe the expense of buying and preparing the merchandise is *cost of goods sold.*[2] The company's other expenses are often called *operating expenses.*

In Illustration 6–1, the condensed income statement for MegaMart, Inc., shows you how these three elements of net income are related to each other. The statement indicates that MegaMart sold goods to its customers for $314,700. The company acquired those goods at a total cost of $230,400. As a result, it earned $84,300 of **gross profit,** which is the difference between the net sales and the cost of goods sold. In addition, the company incurred $71,400 of other expenses and achieved $12,900 of net income for the year.

Balance Sheets for Merchandising Companies

A merchandising company's balance sheet includes an additional element that is not on the balance sheet of a service company. That element is a current asset called **merchandise inventory.** This asset consists of goods the company owns on the balance sheet date and holds for the purpose of selling to its customers. For example, in Illustration 6–2, the classified balance sheet for MegaMart, Inc., reports merchandise inventory of $21,000. The cost of this asset includes the cost incurred to buy the goods, ship them to the store, and otherwise make them ready for sale. Even though they also have inventories of supplies, many companies simply refer to merchandise on hand as *inventory.*

The next sections of the chapter provide more information about these unique elements of the financial statements for merchandising companies.

MEASURING INVENTORY AND COST OF GOODS SOLD

Keep in mind that a merchandising company's income statement includes the item called *cost of goods sold* and its balance sheet includes a current asset called *inventory.* The amount of the cost of goods sold is the cost of the merchandise that was sold to customers during the period. The amount of the asset on the balance sheet equals the cost of the inventory on hand at the end of the period.

Two different inventory accounting systems may be used to collect information about the cost of goods sold and the cost of the inventory on hand. The two systems are called *perpetual* and *periodic.* They are described in the following paragraphs.

Periodic Inventory Systems

Under **periodic inventory systems,** a company does not continuously update its records to reflect the quantity and cost of goods on hand or sold. Instead, the company simply records the cost of new merchandise in a temporary *Purchases* account.

---

[2]Cost of goods sold is often described as one of the operating expenses. Also, many service companies use the word *sales* in their income statements to describe their revenues.

Illustration 6–2
Classified Balance Sheet for
a Merchandising Company

MEGAMART, INC.
Balance Sheet
December 31, 19X2

Assets

Current assets:			
Cash		$ 8,200	
Accounts receivable		11,200	
Merchandise inventory		21,000	
Prepaid expenses		1,100	
Total current assets			$41,500
Plant and equipment:			
Office equipment	$ 4,200		
Less accumulated depreciation	1,400	$ 2,800	
Store equipment	$30,000		
Less accumulated depreciation	6,000	24,000	
Total plant and equipment			26,800
Total assets			$68,300

Liabilities

Current liabilities:		
Accounts payable	$16,000	
Salaries payable	800	
Total liabilities		$16,800

Stockholders' Equity

Contributed capital:			
Common stock, $100 par value		$25,000	
Retained earnings		26,500	51,500
Total liabilities and stockholders' equity			$68,300

When merchandise is sold, the revenue is recorded but the cost of the merchandise that was sold is not recorded as an expense. When financial statements are prepared, the company takes a *physical inventory* by counting the quantities of merchandise on hand. The total cost is determined by relating the quantities to records that show each item's original cost. This total cost is then used to determine the cost of goods sold.

Traditionally, periodic systems were used by companies such as drug and department stores that sold large quantities of low-valued items. Without computers and scanners, it was not feasible for accounting systems to track such small items as toothpaste, pain killers, clothing, and housewares through the inventory and into the customers' hands.

Perpetual Inventory Systems

As suggested by their name, **perpetual inventory systems** provide a continuous record of the amount of inventory on hand. This perpetual record is maintained by adding the cost of each newly purchased item to the inventory account and subtracting the cost of each sold item from the account. When an item is sold, its cost is recorded in the Cost of Goods Sold account. Users of perpetual systems can determine the cost of merchandise on hand by looking at the balance of the inventory account. They can also determine the cost of goods sold thus far during the period by referring to the Cost of Goods Sold account.

Before computers were used widely, perpetual systems were generally used only by businesses that made a limited number of sales each day, such as automobile dealers or major appliance stores. Because there were relatively few transactions, the perpetual accounting system could be operated efficiently. However, the availability of improved technology has greatly increased the number of companies that use perpetual systems.

Because perpetual inventory systems provide more timely information to managers and are now widely used, our focus in the rest of this chapter is on perpetual systems. Periodic systems are described more completely in Chapter 9.

Progress Check
(Answers to Progress Checks are provided at the end of the chapter.)

6–1 Which of the following items is not unique to the financial statements of merchandising companies? *(a)* Cost of goods sold; *(b)* Accounts receivable; *(c)* Gross profit; *(d)* Merchandise inventory.

6–2 What is a merchandising company's gross profit?

6–3 Which inventory system has had expanded use as a result of the increased availability of computers and related technology?

RECORDING THE COST OF PURCHASED MERCHANDISE IN PERPETUAL INVENTORY SYSTEMS

LO 2
Using a perpetual inventory system, analyze and record transactions involving merchandise purchases, purchase discounts, purchase returns and allowances, and transportation-in.

Under a perpetual inventory system, the cost of merchandise bought for resale is debited to the Merchandise Inventory asset account. For example, MegaMart records a $1,200 cash purchase of merchandise on November 2 with this entry:

Nov.	2	Merchandise Inventory	1,200.00	
		Cash		1,200.00
		Purchased merchandise for cash.		

To determine the net cost of purchased merchandise, the price must be adjusted for the effects of: (1) any discounts granted to the purchaser by the seller; (2) any returns and allowances for unsatisfactory items received from the supplier; and (3) any freight costs paid by the buyer to get the goods into the buyer's inventory. The following paragraphs explain how these items affect the recorded cost of merchandise purchases.

Trade Discounts

When a manufacturer or wholesaler prepares a catalog of the items it offers for sale, each item is given a **list price,** which is also called a *catalog price.* The list price generally is not the intended selling price of the item. Instead, the intended selling price equals the list price reduced by a given percentage called a **trade discount.**

The amount of the trade discount usually depends on whether the buyer is a wholesaler, a retailer, or the final consumer. For example, a wholesaler that buys large quantities is granted a larger discount than a retailer that buys smaller quantities. Regardless of its amount, a trade discount is a reduction in a list price that is applied to determine the actual selling price of the goods to a customer.

Trade discounts are commonly used by manufacturers and wholesalers to change selling prices without republishing their catalogs. When the seller wants to change the selling prices, it can notify its customers merely by sending them a new set of trade discounts to apply to the catalog prices.

Because a list price is not intended to reflect the negotiated value of merchandise, the buyer does not enter the list price and the trade discount in its accounts. Instead, the buyer records the net amount of the list price less the trade discount. For example, recall the previous entry to record a purchase of merchandise by MegaMart. In that transaction, MegaMart received a 40% trade discount in purchasing an item listed in the seller's catalog at $2,000. Thus, the purchase price was $1,200, which is [$2,000 − (40% × $2,000)].

Purchase Discounts

When goods are purchased on credit, the expected amounts and dates of future payments need to be clearly stated to avoid misunderstandings. The **credit terms** for a purchase describe the amounts and timing of payments that the buyer agrees to make in the future. The specific terms usually reflect the ordinary practices in the industry. For example, in one industry, purchasers might expect terms that require payment within 10 days after the end of the month in which the purchase occurred. These credit terms would be stated on sales invoices or tickets as "n/10 EOM," with the abbreviation **EOM** standing for "end of the month." In another industry, invoices may normally be due and payable 30 calendar days after the invoice date. These terms are abbreviated as "n/30," and the 30-day period is called the **credit period.**

When the credit period is long, the seller often grants a **cash discount** if the customer pays promptly. From the perspective of the buyer, the cash discount is called a **purchase discount.** From the perspective of the seller, it is called a *sales discount.* If cash discounts for early payment are granted, they are described in the credit terms on the invoice. For example, the terms of 2/10, n/60 mean that a 60-day credit period passes before full payment is due. However, to encourage early payment, the seller allows the buyer to deduct 2% of the invoice amount from the payment if it is made within 10 days of the invoice date. The **discount period** is the period in which the reduced payment can be made.

To illustrate a buyer's accounting for purchase discounts, assume that MegaMart's previous purchase of merchandise for $1,200 had been a credit purchase with terms of 2/10, n/30. MegaMart's entry to record the purchase would have been:

Nov.	2	Merchandise Inventory	1,200.00	
		Accounts Payable		1,200.00
		Purchased merchandise on credit, invoice dated		
		November 2, terms 2/10, n/30.		

Now assume that MegaMart takes advantage of the discount and pays the amount due on November 12. This entry records the payment:

Nov.	12	Accounts Payable	1,200.00	
		Merchandise Inventory (2% × $1,200)		24.00
		Cash		1,176.00
		Paid for the purchase of November 2 less the discount.		

As a result of this entry, the following Merchandise Inventory account reflects the net cost of the merchandise purchased and the Accounts Payable account shows that the debt has been satisfied.

Merchandise Inventory				Accounts Payable			
Nov. 2	1,200	Nov. 12	24	Nov. 12	1,200	Nov. 2	1,200
Balance	1,176						

A Cash Management Technique

Failure to pay within the discount period is usually quite expensive. For example, if MegaMart did not pay within 10 days, it would delay the payment by only 20 more days. This delay would cost an additional 2%. As a result, most buyers attempt to take advantage of their purchase discount opportunities.

AS A MATTER OF ETHICS

Renee Fleck was recently hired by Mid-Mart, a medium-size retailing company that purchases most of its merchandise on credit. She overlapped on the new job for several days with the outgoing employee in her position, Martin Hull, so that he could help her learn the ropes.

One of Fleck's responsibilities is to see that the payables are paid promptly to maintain the company's credit standing with its suppliers and to take advantage of all cash discounts. Hull told Fleck that the current system has accomplished both goals easily and has also made another contribution to the company's profits. He explained that the computer system has been programmed to prepare checks for amounts net of the cash discounts. Even though the checks are dated as of the last day of the discount period, they are not mailed until five days later. Because the accounts are always paid, the company has had virtually no trouble with its suppliers. "It's simple," Hull explained to Fleck. "We get the free use of the cash for an extra five days, and who's going to complain? Even when somebody does, we just blame the computer system and the people in the mail room."

A few days later, Hull had departed and Fleck assumed her new duties. The first invoice that she examined had a 10-day discount period on a $10,000 purchase. The transaction occurred on April 9 subject to terms of 2/10, n/30. Fleck had to decide whether she should mail the $9,800 check on April 19 or wait until the 24th.

To ensure that discounts are not missed, most companies set up a system to pay all invoices within the discount period. Furthermore, careful cash management ensures that no invoice is paid until the last day of the discount period. A helpful technique for reaching both of these goals is to file each invoice in such a way that it automatically comes up for payment on the last day of its discount period. For example, a simple manual system uses 31 folders, one for each day in the month. After an invoice is recorded in the journal, it is placed in the file folder for the last day of its discount period. Thus, if the last day of an invoice's discount period is November 12, it is filed in folder number 12. Then, the invoice and any other invoices in the same folder are removed and paid on November 12. Computerized systems can accomplish the same result by using a code that identifies the last date in the discount period. When that date is reached, the computer automatically provides a reminder that the account should be paid.

Read the As a Matter of Ethics case and consider what you would do if you were faced with the situation it describes.

Purchase Returns and Allowances

Sometimes, merchandise received from a supplier is not acceptable and must be returned. When this occurs the Merchandise Inventory account must be updated to reflect the return. For example, assume that on November 15, MegaMart returned some of the merchandise, originally purchased on November 2, because it was defective. If the recorded cost of the defective merchandise is $300, MegaMart records the return with this entry:

Nov.	15	Accounts Payable	300.00	
		Merchandise Inventory		300.00
		Returned defective merchandise.		

Depending on MegaMart's agreement with its supplier, the supplier will either refund the $300 to MegaMart or offset the $300 against MegaMart's next purchase from the supplier.

Instead of returning defective merchandise, the purchaser may keep imperfect but marketable merchandise because the supplier grants an allowance, which is a reduction in the purchase price. The purchaser's entry to record such an allowance is the same as if the merchandise had been returned.

Discounts and Returned Merchandise

If part of a shipment of goods is returned within the discount period, the buyer can take the discount only on the remaining balance of the invoice. For example, suppose that MegaMart is offered a 2% cash discount on $5,000 of merchandise. Two days later, the company returns $800 of the goods before the invoice is paid. When the liability is paid within the discount period, MegaMart can take the 2% discount only on the $4,200 balance. Thus, the discount is $84 (2% × $4,200) and the cash payment must be $4,116 ($4,200 − $84).

Transportation Costs

Depending on the terms negotiated with its suppliers, a company may be responsible for paying the shipping costs for transporting the acquired goods to its own place of business. These costs, which are called *transportation-in* or *freight-in costs,* are necessary to make the goods ready for sale. Therefore, the cost principle requires including them in the cost of purchased merchandise. To illustrate, the following entry records a $75 freight charge for incoming merchandise:

PRINCIPLE APPLICATION
Cost Principle, p. 36
CompUSA Inc.'s 1995 annual report disclosed that the company had 86 stores in 41 metropolitan areas across the United States. When the company purchases merchandise from a vendor and then distributes it among these stores, the cost of shipping the merchandise to the stores should be included in the costs of the store inventories according to the cost principle.

Nov.	24	Merchandise Inventory	75.00	
		Cash		75.00
		Paid freight charges on purchased merchandise.		

Transportation-in costs are very different from the costs of shipping goods to customers. Transportation-in costs are included in the cost of merchandise inventory whereas the costs of shipping goods to customers are not. The costs of shipping goods to customers are recorded in a Delivery Expense account and reported as a selling expense. These delivery expenses are sometimes described as *freight-out.*

Identifying Ownership Responsibilities and Risks

When a merchandise transaction is planned, the buyer and seller need to establish which party will be responsible for paying any freight costs and which will bear the risk of loss during transit.

The basic issue to be negotiated is the point at which ownership is transferred from the buyer to the seller. The place of the transfer is called the **FOB** point, which is the abbreviation for the phrase, *free on board.* The meaning of different FOB points is explained by the diagram in Illustration 6–3.

Under an *FOB shipping point* agreement (also called *FOB factory*), the buyer accepts ownership at the seller's place of business. As a result, the buyer is responsible for paying the shipping costs and bears the risk of damage or loss while the goods are in transit. In addition, the goods are part of the buyer's inventory while they are in transit because the buyer already owns them.

Alternatively, an *FOB destination* agreement causes ownership of the goods to pass at the buyer's place of business. If so, the seller is responsible for paying the shipping charges and bears the risk of damage or loss in transit. Furthermore, the seller should not record the sales revenue until the goods arrive at the destination because the transaction is not complete before that point in time.

Compaq Computer Corporation originally shipped all of its products under FOB factory agreements. However, customers' shipping companies proved to be undependable in picking up shipments at scheduled times and caused backups at the plant, missed deliveries, and disappointed end users. The company changed its agreements to FOB destination and cleared up these problems.

Illustration 6–3 Identifying Ownership Responsibilities and Risk

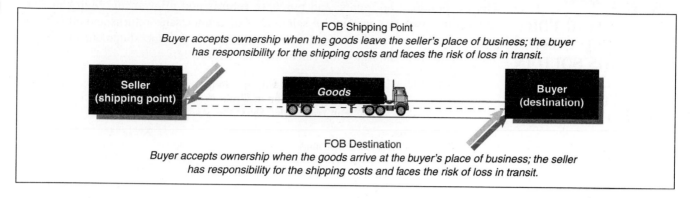

FOB Shipping Point
Buyer accepts ownership when the goods leave the seller's place of business; the buyer has responsibility for the shipping costs and faces the risk of loss in transit.

Seller (shipping point)

Goods

Buyer (destination)

FOB Destination
Buyer accepts ownership when the goods arrive at the buyer's place of business; the seller has responsibility for the shipping costs and faces the risk of loss in transit.

Accumulating Information about Purchase Discounts, Returns and Allowances, and Transportation-In

Recall from the previous sections that purchase discounts, purchase returns and allowances, and transportation-in are all included in determining the cost of merchandise inventory. After recording purchases (net of trade discounts) as debits to Merchandise Inventory, purchase discounts, returns, and allowances are credited to Merchandise Inventory. In addition, transportation-in is debited to Merchandise Inventory. For example, the following calculation shows how these costs were combined in MegaMart's Merchandise Inventory account during 19X2:

MEGAMART, INC. Calculating the Net Cost of Goods Purchased For Year Ended December 31, 19X2	
Purchases	$235,800
Less: Purchase discounts	(4,200)
Purchase returns and allowances	(1,500)
Add transportation-in	2,300
Net cost of goods purchased	$232,400

As a result of combining all of these cost elements in the Merchandise Inventory account, the account reflects the net cost of the purchased merchandise according to the *cost principle.* Also, recall that the Merchandise Inventory account is updated after each transaction that affects the cost of merchandise. Later, we explain how the account also is updated each time merchandise is sold to customers. These timely updates of the Merchandise Inventory account reflect the essence of a perpetual inventory system.

One problem with the system as it has been described so far is that it does not provide separate records for total purchases, total purchase discounts, total purchase returns and allowances, and total transportation-in. Managers need this information to evaluate and control each of these cost elements. Many companies collect this detailed information in supplementary records. Chapter 8 explains the process by which supplementary records of this nature can be maintained.

Progress Check

6–4 How long are the credit and discount periods under credit terms of 2/10, n/60?

6–5 Which of the following items is subtracted from the list price of merchandise to determine the actual sales price? *(a)* Freight-in; *(b)* Trade discount; *(c)* Purchase discount; *(d)* Purchase return and/or allowance.

6–6 What is the meaning of the abbreviation *FOB?* What is the meaning of the term *FOB destination?*

ACCOUNTING FOR SALES AND COST OF GOODS SOLD IN A PERPETUAL INVENTORY SYSTEM

LO 3

Using a perpetual inventory system, analyze and record transactions involving merchandise sales, sales discounts, and sales returns and allowances and explain the use of debit and credit memoranda.

We just explained how companies that buy merchandise for resale account for purchases, purchase discounts, and purchase returns and allowances. Merchandising companies also must account for sales, sales discounts, sales returns and allowances, and cost of goods sold. A merchandising company's income statement may report these items as in the following calculation for MegaMart:

MEGAMART, INC. Calculation of Gross Profit For Year Ended December 31, 19X2		
Sales		$321,000
Less: Sales discounts	$4,300	
Sales returns and allowances . .	2,000	6,300
Net sales		$314,700
Cost of goods sold		(230,400)
Gross profit		$ 84,300

In the following sections, we explain how the information in this calculation is derived from the transactions that involve sales, sales discounts, and sales returns and allowances.

Accounting for Sales Transactions

From a merchandise seller's point of view, each sales transaction involves two related components. One component is the revenue that occurs in the form of receiving an asset from the customer. The other component is the expense that occurs in the form of transferring merchandise to the customer. Accounting for a sales transaction should capture information about both of these components.

The sales transactions of most merchandise companies include sales for cash and sales on credit. Whether a sale is for cash or on credit, recording the transaction requires two entries, one for the revenue component and one for the expense component. For example, assume that on November 3, MegaMart sold merchandise for $1,200 on credit. The following entry records the revenue component of the transaction:

Nov.	3	Accounts Receivable	1,200.00	
		Sales		1,200.00
		Sold merchandise on credit.		

This entry records the increase in the company's assets in the form of the account receivable and records the revenue from the credit sale.[3] If the sale had been for cash, the debit would have been to Cash instead of Accounts Receivable.

Now assume that the cost of the merchandise MegaMart sold on November 3 was $800. In a perpetual inventory system, the entry to record the expense component of the sales transaction is:

Nov.	3	Cost of Goods Sold	800.00	
		Merchandise Inventory		800.00
		To record the cost of Nov. 3 sale.		

As a result of making an entry like this each time a sale occurs, the Merchandise Inventory account continues to reflect the cost of the remaining merchandise on hand.

---

[3]Chapter 8 describes how stores account for sales to customers who use third-party credit cards, such as those issued by banks.

Sales Discounts

When goods are sold on credit, the expected amounts and dates of future payments need to be clearly stated to avoid misunderstandings. As we explained previously, the credit terms may include a discount to encourage early payment. Companies that grant cash discounts to customers refer to those discounts as **sales discounts.** Such sales discounts may benefit the seller by resulting in less delay before cash is received. In addition, prompt payments reduce future efforts and costs of billing customers.

At the time of a credit sale, the seller does not know that the customer will pay within the discount period and take advantage of a cash discount. As a result, the discount is usually not recorded until the customer pays within the discount period. For example, suppose that MegaMart, Inc., completed a credit sale on November 12 at a gross selling price of $100, subject to terms of 2/10, n/60. This entry records the sale:

Nov.	12	Accounts Receivable	100.00	
		Sales		100.00
		Sold merchandise under terms of 2/10, n/60.		

Even though the customer may pay less than the gross price, the entry records the receivable and the revenue as if the full amount will be collected.

In fact, the customer has two alternatives. One option is to wait 60 days until January 11 and pay the full $100. If this is done, MegaMart records the collection as follows:

Jan.	11	Cash	100.00	
		Accounts Receivable		100.00
		Collected account receivable.		

The customer's other option is to pay $98 within a 10-day period that runs through November 22. If the customer pays on November 22, MegaMart records the collection with this entry:

Nov.	22	Cash	98.00	
		Sales Discounts	2.00	
		Accounts Receivable		100.00
		Received payment for the November 12 sale less the discount.		

Because management needs to monitor the amount of sales discounts to assess their effectiveness and their cost, they are recorded in a *contra-revenue* account called Sales Discounts. The balance of this account is deducted from the balance of the Sales account when calculating the company's net sales. Although information about the amount of discounts is useful internally, it is seldom reported on income statements distributed to external decision makers.

Sales Returns and Allowances

Most companies allow customers to return merchandise for a full refund. If a customer keeps the goods because they are damaged but still usable, the customer may be granted a reduced selling price. When this is done, the price reduction is called a sales *allowance.* Whether merchandise is returned or a price reduction is granted, returns and allowances involve dissatisfied customers and the possibility of lost future sales. To monitor the extent of these problems, managers need information about actual returns and allowances. Thus, many accounting systems record the revenue reduction from returns and allowances in a separate contra-revenue account.

For example, recall MegaMart's sale of merchandise on November 3. As recorded in the previous entries, that merchandise was sold for $1,200 and had cost $800. Now assume that on November 6, the customer returned part of the merchandise. The returned items had been sold for $400 and had cost $300. The following entry records the reduction in revenue resulting from the refund:

Nov.	6	Sales Returns and Allowances	400.00	
		Accounts Receivable		400.00
		Customer returned merchandise.		

MegaMart could record the refund with a debit to the Sales account. However, although this would provide the same measure of net sales, it would not provide information that the manager can use to monitor the refunds and allowances. By using the Sales Returns and Allowances contra account, the information is readily available. To simplify the reports provided to external decision makers, published income statements usually omit this detail and present only the amount of net sales.

Now assume that the merchandise returned to MegaMart was not defective and could be resold to another customer. Thus, MegaMart returned the goods to its inventory. As a result, the following entry is necessary to restore the cost to the Merchandise Inventory account:

Nov.	6	Merchandise Inventory	300.00	
		Cost of Goods Sold		300.00
		Returned goods to inventory.		

Sometimes, when a customer returns defective merchandise, the seller may discard the returned items. If this is done, the cost of the returned merchandise should not be restored to the Merchandise Inventory account. Instead, most companies leave the cost of the defective goods in the Cost of Goods Sold account.[4]

Now assume that the merchandise MegaMart sold on November 3 was defective but the customer decided to keep it because MegaMart granted the customer a price reduction of $150. In this case, the only entry MegaMart must make is to record the revenue reduction, as follows:

Nov.	6	Sales Returns and Allowances	150.00	
		Accounts Receivable		150.00
		To record price reduction.		

DEBIT AND CREDIT MEMORANDA

Buyers and sellers often find that they need to adjust the amount that is owed between them. For example, purchased merchandise may not meet specifications, unordered goods may be received, different quantities may be received than were ordered and billed, and billing errors may occur.

---

[4]If managers want to monitor the cost of defective merchandise, a better approach is to remove the cost from Cost of Goods Sold and charge it to a Loss from Defective Merchandise account.

Illustration 6–4 The Use of Debit and Credit Memoranda

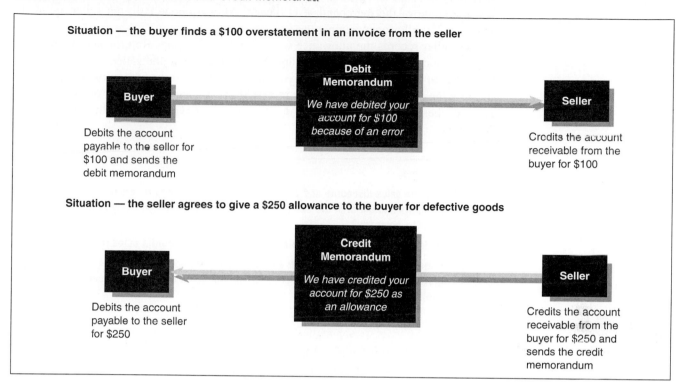

In some cases, the original balance can be adjusted by the buyer without a negotiation. For example, a seller may make an error on an invoice. If the buying company discovers the error, it can make its own adjustment and notify the seller by sending a **debit memorandum** or a **credit memorandum.** A debit memorandum is a business document that informs the recipient that the sender has *debited* the account receivable or payable. It provides the notification with words like these: "We have debited your account," followed by the amount and an explanation. On the other hand, a credit memorandum informs the recipient that the sender has credited the receivable or payable. See Illustration 6–4 for two situations that involve these documents.

The debit memorandum in Illustration 6–4 is based on a case in which a buyer initially records an invoice as an account payable and later discovers an error by the seller that overstated the total bill by $100. The buyer corrects the balance of its liability and formally notifies the seller of the mistake with a debit memorandum reading: "We have debited your account for $100 because of an error." Additional information is provided about the invoice, its date, and the nature of the error. The buyer sends a *debit* memorandum because the correction debits the account payable to reduce its balance. The buyer's debit to the payable is offset by a credit to the asset account for the purchased goods.

When the seller receives its copy of the debit memorandum, it records a *credit* to the buyer's account receivable to reduce its balance. An equal debit is recorded in the Sales account. The seller does not use a contra account because the adjustment was created by an error.

In other situations, an adjustment can be made only after negotiations between the buyer and the seller. For example, suppose that a buyer claims that some merchandise does not meet specifications. The amount of the allowance to be given by the seller can be determined only after discussion. Assume that a buyer accepts delivery of merchandise and records the transaction with a $750 debit to the Merchandise

Inventory account and an equal credit to Accounts Payable. Later, the buyer discovers that some of the merchandise is flawed. After a phone call, the seller agrees to grant a $250 allowance against the original purchase price.

The seller records the allowance with a debit to the Sales Returns and Allowances contra account and a credit to Accounts Receivable. Then, the seller formally notifies the buyer of the allowance with a credit memorandum. A *credit* memorandum is used because the adjustment credited the receivable to reduce its balance. When the buyer receives the credit memorandum, it debits Accounts Payable and credits Merchandise Inventory.

Progress Check

6–7 Why are sales discounts and sales returns and allowances recorded in contra-revenue accounts instead of in the Sales account? Is this information likely to be reported outside the company?

6–8 Under what conditions are two entries necessary to record a sales return?

6–9 If merchandise is sold on credit and the seller later notifies the buyer that the seller is granting the buyer a price reduction, would the seller send a credit memorandum or a debit memorandum?

ADJUSTING ENTRIES FOR MERCHANDISING COMPANIES

LO 4

Prepare the adjusting and closing entries for a merchandising company that uses a perpetual inventory system and describe the flow of information through the Merchandise Inventory and Cost of Goods Sold accounts.

Most of the adjusting entries made by companies that sell services and companies that sell merchandise are the same. They include adjustments for prepaid expenses, accrued expenses, unearned revenues, and accrued revenues.

A merchandising company that uses a perpetual inventory system may be required to make one additional adjustment. That entry updates the Merchandise Inventory account to reflect any losses of merchandise. Merchandising companies lose merchandise in a variety of ways, including shoplifting and deterioration while an item is on the shelf or in the warehouse. These losses are called **shrinkage.**

Even though a perpetual inventory system tracks all goods as they move into and out of the company, a perpetual system is not able to directly measure shrinkage. However, the accountant can calculate shrinkage by comparing a physical count of the inventory with recorded quantities. Normally, a physical count is performed at least annually to correct the Merchandise Inventory account. Assuming the correction is not abnormally large, most companies record the adjustment by charging the amount of the shrinkage to Cost of Goods Sold.

For example, assume that at the end of the 19X2 year, MegaMart's Merchandise Inventory account had a balance of $21,250 and a physical count of the inventory disclosed that only $21,000 remained on hand. The following adjusting entry records the $250 shrinkage:

Dec.	31	Cost of Goods Sold	250.00	
		Merchandise Inventory		250.00
		To adjust for $250 shrinkage disclosed by physical count of inventory.		

CLOSING ENTRIES FOR MERCHANDISING COMPANIES

When a merchandising company uses a perpetual inventory system, the closing entries are similar to those made by service companies. The only differences involve closing the temporary accounts that relate to merchandising activities.

To illustrate the closing process, assume that MegaMart, Inc.'s adjusted trial balance at the end of 19X2 includes the accounts shown in Illustration 6–5.

Cash	$ 8,200	
Accounts receivable	11,200	
Merchandise inventory	21,000	
Office supplies	550	
Store supplies	250	
Prepaid insurance	300	
Office equipment	4,200	
Accumulated depreciation, office equipment ..		$ 1,400
Store equipment	30,000	
Accumulated depreciation, store equipment ...		6,000
Accounts payable		16,000
Salaries payable		800
Common stock, $100 par value		25,000
Retained earnings		17,600
Cash dividends declared	4,000	
Sales		321,000
Sales discounts	4,300	
Sales returns and allowances	2,000	
Cost of goods sold	230,400	
Depreciation expense, store equipment	3,000	
Depreciation expense, office equipment	700	
Office salaries expense	25,300	
Sales salaries expense	18,500	
Insurance expense	600	
Rent expense, office space	900	
Rent expense, selling space	8,100	
Office supplies expense	1,800	
Store supplies expense	1,200	
Advertising expense	2,700	
Income taxes expense	8,600	
Totals	$387,800	$387,800

Illustration 6–5
Adjusted Trial Balance for MegaMart, Inc., at December 31, 19X2

The trial balance includes these unique accounts for merchandising activities: Merchandise Inventory, Sales, Sales Discounts, Sales Returns and Allowances, and Cost of Goods Sold. Their presence in the ledger causes the four closing entries to be slightly different from the ones described in Chapter 5.

Entry 1—Close the Temporary Accounts that Have Credit Balances

The first entry closes the temporary accounts that have credit balances. MegaMart has only one temporary account with a credit balance, which is closed with this entry:

Dec.	31	Sales	321,000.00	
		Income Summary		321,000.00
		To close temporary accounts with credit balances.		

Posting this entry gives a zero balance to the Sales account and opens the Income Summary account.

Entry 2—Close the Temporary Accounts that Have Debit Balances

The second entry closes the temporary accounts that have debit balances, including Cost of Goods Sold, Sales Discounts, and Sales Returns and Allowances. It also establishes the amount of net income as the balance in the Income Summary account. The second closing entry for MegaMart is:

Dec.	31	Income Summary	308,100.00	
		Sales Discounts		**4,300.00**
		Sales Returns and Allowances		**2,000.00**
		Cost of Goods Sold		**230,400.00**
		Depreciation Expense, Store Equipment		3,000.00
		Depreciation Expense, Office Equipment		700.00
		Office Salaries Expense		25,300.00
		Sales Salaries Expense		18,500.00
		Insurance Expense		600.00
		Rent Expense, Office Space		900.00
		Rent Expense, Selling Space		8,100.00
		Office Supplies Expense		1,800.00
		Store Supplies Expense		1,200.00
		Advertising Expense		2,700.00
		Income Taxes Expense		8,600.00
		To close temporary accounts with debit balances.		

Entry 3—Close Income Summary to Retained Earnings

The third closing entry for a merchandising company is the same as the third closing entry for a service company. It closes the Income Summary account and updates the balance of the Retained Earnings account. The third closing entry for MegaMart is:

Dec.	31	Income Summary	12,900.00	
		Retained Earnings		12,900.00
		To close the Income Summary account.		

Recall from Illustration 6–1 on page 193 that the $12,900 amount in the entry is the net income reported on the income statement.

Entry 4—Close the Cash Dividends Declared Account to Retained Earnings

The fourth closing entry for a merchandising company is the same as the fourth closing entry for a service company. It closes the Cash Dividends Declared account and reduces the Retained Earnings balance to the amount shown on the balance sheet. The fourth closing entry for MegaMart is:

Dec.	31	Retained Earnings	4,000.00	
		Cash Dividends Declared		4,000.00
		To close the Cash Dividends Declared account.		

When this entry is posted, all the temporary accounts are cleared and ready to record events in 19X3. In addition, the Retained Earnings account has been fully updated to reflect the events of 19X2.

RELATIONSHIP BETWEEN PURCHASES, INVENTORY, AND COST OF GOODS SOLD

Illustration 6–6 summarizes the relationship between purchases, inventory, and cost of goods sold. As explained previously, the net cost of purchases takes into account trade discounts, any purchase discounts granted, and purchase returns and allowances. In a perpetual inventory system, these elements of the net cost of purchases are col-

Illustration 6-6 Relationship between Purchases, Inventory, and Cost of Goods Sold

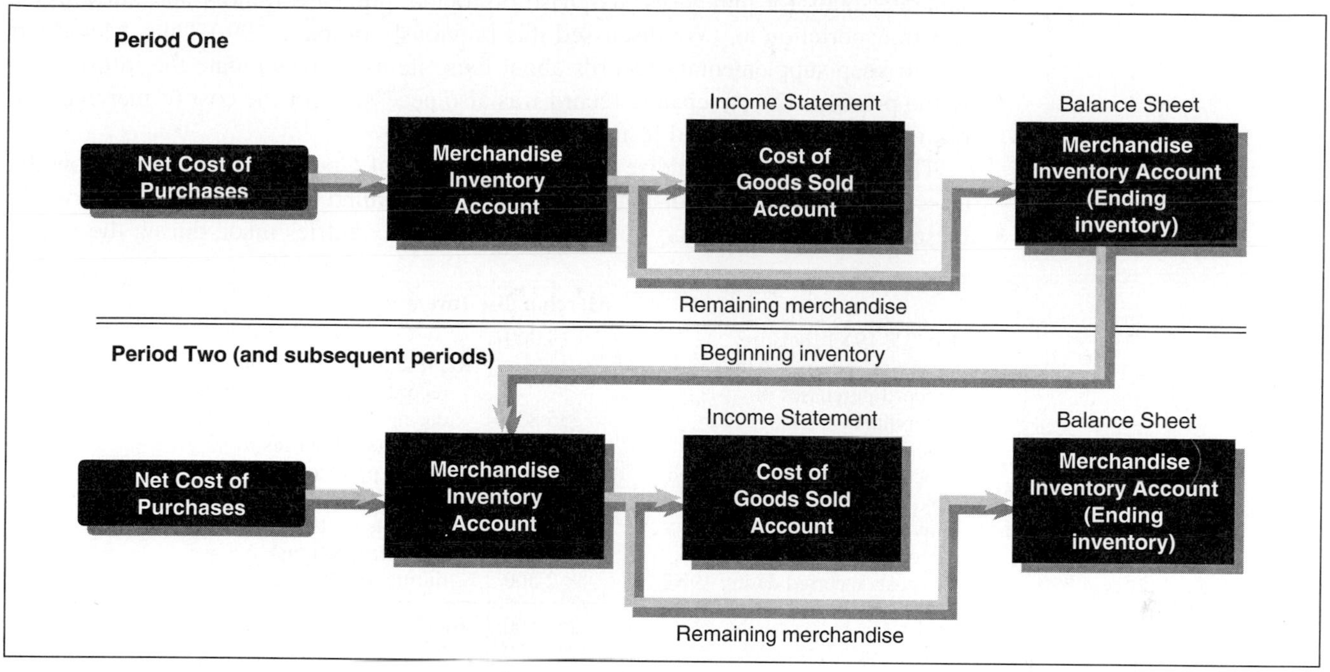

lected in the Merchandise Inventory account. Then, as each sale occurs, the cost of the items sold is transferred to the Cost of Goods Sold account, which is reported on the income statement. Illustration 6–6 shows the net effect of these transfers after taking into account any returns of merchandise by customers. The remaining balance in the Merchandise Inventory account is reported in the balance sheet at the end of the period.

In Illustration 6–6, notice that the Merchandise Inventory account balance at the end of period one is the amount of the beginning inventory in period two. The sequence of events during period two (and every period thereafter) is the same as during period one. The cost of each purchase is added to the Merchandise Inventory account and the cost of each sale is transferred from Merchandise Inventory to Cost of Goods Sold. At the end of the period, the remaining Merchandise Inventory balance is reported on the balance sheet.

To clarify how merchandising transactions affect the Merchandise Inventory and Cost of Goods Sold accounts, assume that MegaMart's merchandising activities during 19X2 included the following:

EFFECTS OF MERCHANDISE ACTIVITIES ON MERCHANDISE INVENTORY AND COST OF GOODS SOLD

Total cost of merchandise purchases	$235,800
Total cost of freight to bring merchandise to MegaMart's store	2,300
Total amount of purchase discounts MegaMart received from making payments within the discount periods	4,200
Total amount of refunds and credit granted to MegaMart as a result of purchase returns and allowances	1,500
Total cost of merchandise sold to customers	231,550
Total cost of merchandise returned by customers and restored to MegaMart's inventory	1,400
Total cost of inventory shrinkage determined by physical count of inventory at year-end	250
In addition, assume that MegaMart's ending inventory on December 31, 19X1 was	19,000

Recall that the perpetual inventory system described in this chapter does not provide separate totals for purchases, purchase discounts, purchase returns and allowances, and transportation-in. (We discussed this previously on page 199.) Thus, MegaMart had to keep supplementary records about these items to accumulate the information in the previous list. A separate record was also necessary for the cost of merchandise returned by customers and restored in inventory.

The following Merchandise Inventory and Cost of Goods Sold accounts show the effects of these merchandising activities. Keep in mind that most of the entries in these accounts are summary representations of many entries made during the year.

Merchandise Inventory

Dec. 31, 19X1, balance	19,000		
Represents all entries to record purchases of merchandise	235,800	Represents all entries to record purchase discounts during 19X2	4,200
Represents all entries to record merchandise returned by customers and restored to inventory during 19X2	1,400	Represents all entries to record purchase returns and allowances during 19X2	1,500
Represents all transportation-in costs incurred during 19X2 ..	2,300	Represents cost of all sales transactions during 19X2	231,550
Total	258,500	Total	237,250
	−237,250		
Dec. 31, 19X2 unadjusted balance .	21,250		
		Dec. 31 Shrinkage	250
Total	21,250	Total	250
	−250		
Dec. 31, 19X2 adjusted balance ...	21,000		

Cost of Goods Sold

Represents all entries to record the cost component of all sales transactions	231,550	Represents all entries to record merchandise returned by customers and restored to inventory during 19X2	1,400
Inventory shrinkage recorded in December 31, 19X2, adjusting entry	250		
Total			231,800
	−1,400		
Balance (before closing)	230,400		

Notice that the Cost of Goods Sold balance of $230,400 is the amount reported in the income statement (see Illustration 6–1). In addition, the Merchandise Inventory balance of $21,000 is the amount reported as a current asset in the balance sheet (see Illustration 6–2). These amounts also appear in the adjusted trial balance (see Illustration 6–6).

Progress Check

6-10 If a merchandising company uses a perpetual inventory system, why might it be necessary to correct the Merchandise Inventory balance with an adjusting entry?

6-11 What temporary accounts would you expect to find in a merchandising business but not in a service business?

6-12 How many closing entries would normally be made by a merchandising company?

Illustration 6–7
Classified, Multiple-Step
Income Statement for
Internal Use

MEGAMART, INC.
Income Statement
For Year Ended December 31, 19X2

Sales			$321,000
Less: Sales discounts		$ 4,300	
Sales returns and allowances		2,000	6,300
Net sales			$314,700
Cost of goods sold:			
Merchandise inventory, December 31, 19X1		$ 19,000	
Purchases	$235,800		
Less: Purchase discounts	(4,200)		
Purchase returns and allowances	(1,500)		
Add transportation-in	2,300		
Net cost of goods purchased		232,400	
Goods available for sale		$251,400	
Merchandise inventory, December 31, 19X2		21,000	
Cost of goods sold			230,400
Gross profit from sales			$ 84,300
Operating expenses:			
Selling expenses:			
Depreciation expense, store equipment	$ 3,000		
Sales salaries expense	18,500		
Rent expense, selling space	8,100		
Store supplies expense	1,200		
Advertising expense	2,700		
Total selling expenses		$33,500	
General and administrative expenses:			
Depreciation expense, office equipment	$ 700		
Office salaries expense	25,300		
Insurance expense	600		
Rent expense, office space	900		
Office supplies expense	1,800		
Total general and administrative expenses		29,300	
Total operating expenses			62,800
Income from operations			$ 21,500
Less income taxes expense			8,600
Net income			$ 12,900

ALTERNATIVE INCOME STATEMENT FORMATS

LO 5
Describe the alternative income
statement formats used by businesses and explain the use of
the acid-test ratio as an indicator of a company's liquidity.

Generally accepted accounting principles do not require companies to use exactly the same financial statement formats. In fact, practice shows that many different formats are used. This section of the chapter describes several possible formats that MegaMart, Inc., could use for its income statement.

Classified, Multiple-Step Income Statements for Internal Use

In Illustration 6–7, we present a **classified income statement** that would probably be distributed only to the company's managers because of the details that it includes. Notice that the statement shows detailed calculations of net sales and cost of goods sold. Also, operating expenses are classified as selling expenses or as general and administrative expenses. This format is also called a **multiple-step income statement** because it shows several intermediate totals between sales and net income. The sales section is the same as the calculation presented earlier in the chapter. The cost of goods sold section assumes that MegaMart has maintained supplementary records on purchases, purchase discounts, purchase returns and allowances, and transportation-in. The difference between the net sales and cost of goods sold is the gross profit for the year.

Also notice that the operating expenses section classifies the expenses into two categories. **Selling expenses** include the expenses of promoting sales through displaying and advertising the merchandise, making sales, and delivering goods to customers. **General and administrative expenses** support the overall operations of a business and include the expenses of activities such as accounting, human resource management, and financial management.

Some expenses may be divided between categories because they contribute to both activities. For example, Illustration 6–7 reflects the fact that MegaMart, Inc., divided the total rent expense of $9,000 for its store building between the two categories. Ninety percent ($8,100) was selling expense and the remaining 10% ($900) was general and administrative expense.[5] The cost allocation should reflect an economic relationship between the prorated amounts and the activities. For example, the allocation in this case could be based on relative rental values.

In Illustration 6–7, note that the result of subtracting operating expenses from gross profit is called *income from operations*. Then, income taxes expense is subtracted from income from operations to obtain net income.

Multiple-Step Income Statements for External Use

Illustration 6–8 shows a multiple-step format that is sometimes used in external reports. In comparing Illustrations 6–8 and 6–7, notice that Illustration 6–8 leaves out the detailed calculations of net sales and cost of goods sold. Also, the selling expenses have been combined with the general and administrative expenses. This more con-

densed presentation is typical in statements that are published for the use of external parties.

Even more condensed formats are frequently used. For example, the income statement for **Lands' End, Inc.,** in Appendix F presents only a single line item called *selling, general and administrative expenses*. However, the annual report also provides management's discussion and analysis of these expenses.

Single-Step Income Statements

Another widely used format is a **single-step income statement** like the one shown in Illustration 6–9 for MegaMart. This simpler format includes cost of goods sold as an operating expense and presents only one intermediate total for total expenses. Also, the operating expenses are highly summarized.

In practice, many companies use formats that combine some of the features of both the single- and multiple-step statements. As long as the income statement elements are presented logically, management can choose the format that it wants to use.[6]

The statement of retained earnings and statement of cash flows are designed the same way for merchandising companies and service companies.

---

[5]These expenses can be recorded in a single account or in two separate accounts. If they are recorded in one account, the accountant allocates its balance between the two expenses when preparing the statements.

[6]Later chapters describe other possible elements, such as extraordinary gains and losses, that must be presented in specified locations on the income statement.

Illustration 6-8
Multiple-Step Income
Statement for External Use

MEGAMART, INC.
Income Statement
For Year Ended December 31, 19X2

Net sales		$314,700
Cost of goods sold		230,400
Gross profit from sales		$ 84,300
Operating expenses:		
Depreciation expense	$ 3,700	
Salaries expense	43,800	
Rent expense	9,000	
Insurance expense	600	
Supplies expense	3,000	
Advertising expense	2,700	
Total operating expenses		62,800
Income from operations		$ 21,500
Less income taxes expense		8,600
Net income		$ 12,900

Illustration 6-9
Single-Step Income
Statement

MEGAMART, INC.
Income Statement
For Year Ended December 31, 19X2

Net sales		$314,700
Cost of goods sold	$230,400	
Selling expenses	33,500	
General and administrative expenses	29,300	
Income taxes expense	8,600	
Total expenses		301,800
Net income		$ 12,900

You have learned in this chapter that a company's current assets may include a merchandise inventory. Thus, you can understand that a major part of a company's current assets may not be immediately available for paying its existing liabilities. The inventory must be sold and the resulting accounts receivable must be collected before cash is available. As a result, the current ratio (which we described in Chapter 5) may not be an adequate indicator of a company's ability to pay its current liabilities.

Another measure that financial statement users often use to evaluate a company's ability to settle its current debts with its existing assets is the **acid-test ratio.** The acid-test ratio is similar to the current ratio but differs because it excludes the less liquid current assets. The acid-test ratio is calculated just like the current ratio except that its numerator omits inventory and prepaid expenses. The remaining current assets (cash, short-term investments, and receivables) are called the company's *quick assets.* The formula for the ratio is:

$$\text{Acid-test ratio} = \frac{\text{Quick assets}}{\text{Current liabilities}}$$

Recall the discussion of **J.C. Penney Company** at the beginning of the chapter. The acid-test ratios for J.C. Penney are computed as follows:

**USING THE
INFORMATION—
THE ACID-TEST
RATIO**

	End of Year	
Acid-Test Ratios	**1994**	**1993**
($261 + $5,159)/$4,481	1.2	
($173 + $4,679)/$3,883		1.2

In contrast, the current ratios (current assets/current liabilities) for J.C. Penney have these values:

Current Ratios	End of Year 1994	1993
$9,468/$4,481	2.1	
$8,565/$3,883		2.2

A traditional rule of thumb is that an acid-test ratio value of at least 1.0 suggests the company is not likely to face a liquidity crisis in the near future. However, a value less than 1.0 may not be threatening if the company can generate enough cash from sales or the accounts payable are not due until later in the year. On the other hand, a value more than 1.0 may hide a liquidity crisis if the payables are due at once but the receivables will not be collected until late in the year. These possibilities reinforce the point that a single ratio is seldom enough to reach a conclusion as to strength or weakness. However, it can identify areas that the analyst should look into more deeply.

Progress Check

6-13   Which income statement format shows the detailed calculations of net sales and cost of goods sold? Which format does not present any intermediate totals (other than total expenses)?

6-14   Which assets are defined as quick assets for the purpose of calculating the acid-test ratio? *(a)* Cash, short-term investments, and prepaid expenses; *(b)* Merchandise inventory and prepaid expenses; *(c)* Merchandise inventory and short-term investments; *(d)* Cash, short-term investments, and receivables.

6-15   Which ratio is a more strict test of a company's ability to meet its obligations in the very near future, the acid-test ratio or the current ratio?

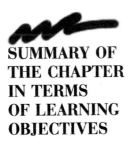

SUMMARY OF THE CHAPTER IN TERMS OF LEARNING OBJECTIVES

LO 1. Describe merchandising activities, the unique aspects of a merchandising company's financial statements, and the difference between periodic and perpetual inventory systems. The operations of merchandising companies involve buying goods and reselling them. On a merchandiser's income statement, the difference between sales and cost of goods sold is called gross profit. The current asset section of a merchandising company's balance sheet includes merchandise inventory.

A perpetual inventory system continuously tracks the cost of goods on hand and the cost of goods sold. A periodic system merely accumulates the cost of goods purchased during the period and does not determine the amount of inventory on hand or the cost of goods sold until the end of the period.

LO 2. Using a perpetual inventory system, analyze and record transactions involving merchandise purchases, purchase discounts, purchase returns and allowances, and transportation-in. In a perpetual inventory system, purchases net of trade discounts are debited to the Merchandise Inventory account. Purchase discounts and purchase returns and allowances are credited to Merchandise Inventory and transportation-in costs are debited to Merchandise Inventory. Some companies keep supplementary records to accumulate information about the total amounts of purchases, purchase discounts, purchase returns and allowances, and transportation-in.

LO 3. Using a perpetual inventory system, analyze and record transactions involving merchandise sales, sales discounts, and sales returns and allowances and explain the use of debit and credit memoranda. The seller of merchandise records the sale at the list price less any trade discount. In addition, the cost of the items sold is transferred from Merchandise Inventory to Cost of Goods Sold. The refunds or credits given to customers for unsatisfactory merchandise are debited to Sales Returns and Allowances, which is a contra account to Sales. If merchandise is returned and restored to the inventory, the cost of the merchandise is removed from Cost of Goods Sold and transferred back to Merchandise Inventory. When cash discounts from the sales price are offered and the customers pay within the discount period, the seller debits the discounts to Sales Discounts, a contra account to Sales.

Debit and credit memoranda are documents sent between buyers and sellers to communicate the fact that the sender is either debiting or crediting the account of the recipient.

LO 4. Prepare the adjusting and closing entries for a merchandising company that uses a perpetual inventory system and describe the flow of information through the Merchandise Inventory and Cost of Goods Sold accounts. When a perpetual inventory system is used, merchandise companies may be required to make an adjusting entry for inventory shrinkage, which is determined by comparing a physical count of inventory with the Merchandise Inventory account balance. Normally, the shrinkage is charged to Cost of Goods Sold. Temporary accounts of merchandising companies include Sales, Sales Discounts, Sales Returns and Allowances, and Cost of Goods Sold. All of these are closed in Income Summary.

The net cost of merchandise purchases flows into the Merchandise Inventory and from there to Cost of Goods Sold. The remaining Merchandise Inventory balance is reported on the balance sheet and becomes the beginning inventory of the next period.

LO 5. Describe the alternative income statement formats used by businesses and explain the use of the acid-test ratio as an indicator of a company's liquidity. Classified income statements for internal use show more details, including the calculations of net sales and the cost of goods sold. They also present expenses in categories that reflect different activities. Income statements that are published for the use of external parties may be multiple-step or single-step statements. In either case, they typically present the information in a condensed form.

The acid-test ratio is used to assess a company's ability to pay its current liabilities with its existing quick assets (cash, short-term investments, and receivables). The costs of the merchandise inventory and prepaid expenses are not included in the numerator. A ratio that is equal to or greater than one is usually considered to be adequate.

DEMONSTRATION PROBLEM

Use the following adjusted trial balance and additional information to complete the requirements:

IOWA ANTIQUES, INCORPORATED
Adjusted Trial Balance
December 31, 19X2

Cash	$ 19,000	
Merchandise inventory	50,000	
Store supplies	1,000	
Equipment	44,600	
Accumulated depreciation, equipment		$ 16,500
Accounts payable		8,000
Salaries payable		1,000
Common stock, $5 par value		40,000
Retained earnings		29,000
Cash dividends declared	8,000	
Sales		325,000
Sales discounts	6,000	
Sales returns and allowances	5,000	
Cost of goods sold	148,000	
Depreciation expense, store equipment	4,000	
Depreciation expense, office equipment	1,500	
Sales salaries expense	28,000	
Office salaries expense	32,000	
Insurance expense	12,000	
Rent expense (70% is store, 30% is office)	24,000	
Store supplies expense	6,000	
Advertising expense	21,000	
Income taxes expense	9,400	
Totals	$419,500	$419,500

Iowa Antiques's supplementary records for 19X2 indicate the following merchandising activities:

Purchases	$140,000
Purchase discounts	3,500
Purchase returns and allowances	2,600
Transportation-in	4,000

Required

1. Calculate the December 31, 19X1, Merchandise Inventory balance.
2. Present a single-step income statement for 19X2 similar to the one in Illustration 6–9.
3. Prepare a 19X2 classified, multiple-step income statement for internal use.
4. Prepare closing entries.

Planning the Solution

- Calculate the cost of goods available for sale and the net cost of goods purchased. Then, subtract the net cost of goods purchased from the cost of goods available for sale to determine the December 31, 19X1, Merchandise Inventory balance.
- To prepare the single-step income statement, begin with the net sales. Then, list and subtract the operating expenses.
- Calculate net sales. Then, to calculate cost of goods sold, add the net cost of goods purchased for the year to the beginning inventory and subtract the cost of the ending inventory. Subtract cost of goods sold from net sales to get gross profit. Then, classify the operating expenses as selling expenses and general administrative expenses. Finally, subtract income taxes expense to get net income.
- The first closing entry debits all temporary accounts with credit balances and opens the Income Summary account. The second closing entry credits all temporary accounts with debit balances. The third entry closes the Income Summary account to Retained Earnings, and the fourth closing entry closes Cash Dividends Declared to Retained Earnings.

Solution to Demonstration Problem

1.

December 31, 19X2, inventory		$ 50,000
Cost of goods sold		148,000
Cost of goods available for sale		$198,000
Purchases	$140,000	
Less: Purchase discounts	(2,600)	
Purchase returns and allowances	(3,500)	
Add transportation-in	4,000	
Less net cost of goods purchased		137,900
Merchandise inventory, December 31, 19X1		$ 60,100

2. Single-step income statement

IOWA ANTIQUES, INCORPORATED
Income Statement
For Year Ended December 31, 19X2

Net sales		$314,000
Operating expenses:		
Cost of goods sold	$148,000	
Selling expenses	75,800	
General and administrative expenses	52,700	
Income taxes expense	9,400	285,900
Net income		$ 28,100

3. Classified, multiple-step income statement

IOWA ANTIQUES, INCORPORATED
Income Statement
For Year Ended December 31, 19X2

Sales			$325,000
Less: Sales discounts		$ 6,000	
Sales returns and allowances		5,000	11,000
Net sales			$314,000
Cost of goods sold:			
Merchandise inventory, December 31, 19X1		$ 60,100	
Purchases	$140,000		
Less: Purchase discounts	(3,500)		
Purchase returns and allowances	(2,600)		
Add transportation-in	4,000		
Net cost of goods purchased		137,900	
Goods available for sale		$198,000	
Merchandise inventory, December 31, 19X2		50,000	
Cost of goods sold			148,000
Gross profit from sales			$166,000
Operating expenses:			
Selling expenses:			
Depreciation expense, store equipment	$ 4,000		
Sales salaries expense	28,000		
Rent expense, selling space	16,800		
Store supplies expense	6,000		
Advertising expense	21,000		
Total selling expenses		$ 75,800	
General and administrative expenses:			
Depreciation expense, office equipment	$ 1,500		
Office salaries expense	32,000		
Insurance expense	12,000		
Rent expense, office space	7,200		
Total general and administrative expenses		52,700	
Total operating expenses			128,500
Income from operations			$ 37,500
Less income taxes expense			9,400
Net income			$ 28,100

4.

Dec.	31	Sales	325,000.00	
		Income Summary		325,000.00
		To close temporary accounts with credit balances.		
	31	Income Summary	296,900.00	
		Sales Discounts		6,000.00
		Sales Returns and Allowances		5,000.00
		Cost of Goods Sold		148,000.00
		Depreciation Expense, Store Equipment		4,000.00
		Depreciation Expense, Office Equipment		1,500.00
		Sales Salaries Expense		28,000.00
		Office Salaries Expense		32,000.00
		Insurance Expense		12,000.00
		Rent Expense		24,000.00
		Store Supplies Expense		6,000.00
		Advertising Expense		21,000.00
		Income Taxes Expense		9,400.00
		To close temporary accounts with debit balances.		
	31	Income Summary	28,100.00	
		Retained Earnings		28,100.00
		To close the Income Summary account.		
	31	Retained Earnings	8,000.00	
		Cash Dividends Declared		8,000.00
		To close the Cash Dividends Declared account.		

GLOSSARY

Acid-test ratio a ratio used to assess the company's ability to settle its current debts with its existing assets; it is the ratio between a company's quick assets (cash, short-term investments, and receivables) and its current liabilities. p. 211

Cash discount a reduction in the price of merchandise that is granted by a seller to a purchaser in exchange for the purchaser's making payment within a specified period of time called the *discount period*. p. 196

Classified income statement an income statement format that classifies items in significant groups and shows detailed calculations of sales and cost of goods sold. p. 209

Credit memorandum a notification that the sender has entered a credit in the recipient's account maintained by the sender. p. 203

Credit period the time period that can pass before a customer's payment is due. p. 196

Credit terms the description of the amounts and timing of payments that a buyer agrees to make in the future. p. 196

Debit memorandum a notification that the sender has entered a debit in the recipient's account maintained by the sender. p. 203

Discount period the time period in which a cash discount is available. p. 196

EOM the abbreviation for *end-of-month;* used to describe credit terms for some transactions. p. 196

FOB the abbreviation for *free on board;* the designated point at which ownership of goods passes to the buyer; FOB shipping point (or factory) means that the buyer pays the shipping costs and FOB destination means that the seller pays the shipping costs. p. 198

General and administrative expenses expenses that support the overall operations of a business and include the expenses of such activities as providing accounting services, human resource management, and financial management. p. 210

Gross profit the difference between net sales and the cost of goods sold. p. 193

List price the price of an item before any trade discount is deducted. p. 195

Merchandise goods acquired for the purpose of reselling them to customers. p. 192

Merchandise inventory goods a company owns on any given date and holds for the purpose of selling them to its customers. p. 193

Multiple-step income statement an income statement format that shows several intermediate totals between sales and net income. p. 209

Periodic inventory system a method of accounting that records the cost of inventory purchased but does not track the quantity on hand or sold to customers; the records are updated at the end of each period to reflect the results of physical counts of the items on hand. p. 193

Perpetual inventory system a method of accounting that maintains continuous records of the cost of inventory on hand and the cost of goods sold. p. 194

Purchase discount a term used by a purchaser to describe a cash discount granted to the purchaser for paying within the discount period. p. 196

Sales discount a term used by a seller to describe a cash discount granted to customers for paying within the discount period. p. 201

Selling expenses the expenses of promoting sales by displaying and advertising the merchandise, making sales, and delivering goods to customers. p. 210

Shrinkage inventory losses that occur as a result of shoplifting or deterioration. p. 204

Single–step income statement an income statement format that does not present intermediate totals other than total expenses. p. 210

Trade discount a reduction below a list or catalog price that is negotiated in setting the selling price of goods. p. 195

QUESTIONS

1. What items appear in the financial statements of merchandising companies but not in the statements of service companies?
2. Explain how a business can earn a gross profit on its sales and still have a net loss.
3. Why would a company offer a cash discount?
4. What is the difference between a sales discount and a purchase discount?
5. Distinguish between cash discounts and trade discounts. Is the amount of a trade discount on purchased merchandise recorded in the Purchase Discounts account?
6. How does a company that uses a perpetual inventory system determine the amount of inventory shrinkage?
7. Why would a company's manager be concerned about the quantity of its purchase returns if its suppliers allow unlimited returns?
8. Does the sender of a debit memorandum record a debit or a credit in the account of the recipient? Which does the recipient record?
9. What is the difference between single-step and multiple-step income statement formats?
10. In comparing the accounts of a merchandising company with those of a service company, what additional accounts would the merchandising company be likely to use, assuming it employs a perpetual inventory system?
11. Refer to the income statement for Lands' End, Inc., in

Appendix F at the end of the book. What term is used instead of cost of goods sold? Does the company present a detailed calculation of the cost of goods sold?

12. Refer to the income statement for Southwest Airlines Co. in Appendix E. Does the company report an amount of gross profit? Why?

QUICK STUDY (Five-Minute Exercises)

Which system of accounting for merchandise inventory

QS 6–1
(LO 1)

a. Requires a physical count of inventory to determine the amount of inventory to report on the balance sheet?

b. Records the cost of goods sold each time a sales transaction occurs?

c. Provides more timely information to managers?

d. Was traditionally used by companies such as drug and department stores that sold large quantities of low-valued items?

Prepare journal entries to record each of the following transactions of a merchandising company. Show any supporting calculations.

QS 6–2
(LO 2)

Mar. 5 Purchased 500 units of product with a list price of $5 per unit. The purchaser was granted a trade discount of 20% and the terms of the sale were 2/10, n/60.

Mar. 7 Returned 50 defective units from the March 5 purchase and received full credit.

Mar. 15 Paid the amount due resulting from the March 5 purchase, less the return on March 7.

Prepare journal entries to record each of the following transactions of a merchandising company. Show any supporting calculations.

QS 6–3
(LO 3)

Apr. 1 Sold merchandise for $2,000, granting the customer terms of 2/10, EOM. The cost of the merchandise was $1,400.

Apr. 4 The customer in the April 1 sale returned merchandise and received credit for $500. The merchandise, which had cost $350, was returned to inventory.

Apr. 11 Received payment for the amount due resulting from the April 1 sale, less the return on April 4.

Bee Company's ledger on July 31, the end of the fiscal year, includes the following accounts which have normal balances:

QS 6–4
(LO 4)

Merchandise inventory	$ 34,800
Common stock, $10 par value	50,000
Retained earnings	65,300
Cash dividends declared	4,000
Sales	157,200
Sales discounts	1,700
Sales returns and allowances	3,500
Cost of goods sold	102,000
Depreciation expense	7,300
Salaries expense	29,500
Miscellaneous expenses	2,000

A physical count of the inventory discloses that the cost of the merchandise on hand is $32,900. Prepare the entry to record this information.

QS 6–5
(LO 4)

Refer to QS 6–4 and prepare the entries to close the income statement accounts. Do not forget to take into consideration the entry that was made to solve QS 6–4.

QS 6–6
(LO 5)

Calculate net sales and gross profit in each of the following situations:

	a	b	c	d
Sales	$130,000	$512,000	$35,700	$245,700
Sales discounts	4,200	16,500	400	3,500
Sales returns and allowances	17,000	5,000	5,000	700
Cost of goods sold	76,600	326,700	21,300	125,900

QS 6–7
(LO 5)

Use the following information to calculate the acid-test ratio:

Cash	$1,200
Accounts receivable	2,700
Inventory	5,000
Prepaid expenses	600
Accounts payable	4,750
Other current liabilities	950

EXERCISES

Exercise 6–1
Merchandising terms
(LO 1, 2, 3)

Insert the letter for each term in the blank space beside the definition that it most closely matches:

A. Cash discount   E. FOB shipping point   H. Purchase discount

B. Credit period   F. Gross profit   I. Sales discount

C. Discount period   G. Merchandise inventory   J. Trade discount

D. FOB destination

___ 1. An agreement that ownership of goods is transferred at the buyer's place of business.

___ 2. The time period in which a cash discount is available.

___ 3. The difference between net sales and the cost of goods sold.

___ 4. A reduction in a receivable or payable that is granted if it is paid within the discount period.

___ 5. A purchaser's description of a cash discount received from a supplier of goods.

___ 6. An agreement that ownership of goods is transferred at the seller's place of business.

___ 7. A reduction below a list or catalog price that is negotiated in setting the selling price of goods.

___ 8. A seller's description of a cash discount granted to customers in return for early payment.

___ 9. The time period that can pass before a customer's payment is due.

___ 10. The goods that a company owns and expects to sell to its customers.

Exercise 6–2
Recording journal entries for
merchandise transactions
(LO 2)

Prepare journal entries to record the following transactions for a retail store:

Mar. 2   Purchased merchandise from Blanton Company under the following terms: $3,600 invoice price, 2/15, n/60, FOB factory.

3   Paid $200 for shipping charges on the purchase of March 2.

4   Returned to Blanton Company unacceptable merchandise that had an invoice price of $600.

17   Sent a check to Blanton Company for the March 2 purchase, net of the discount and the returned merchandise.

Mar. 18   Purchased merchandise from Fleming Corp. under the following terms: $7,500 invoice price, 2/10, n/30, FOB destination.

21   After brief negotiations, received from Fleming Corp. a $2,100 allowance on the purchase of March 18.

28   Sent a check to Fleming Corp. paying for the March 18 purchase, net of the discount and the allowance.

On May 11, Wilson Inc. accepted delivery of $30,000 of merchandise it purchased for resale. With the merchandise was an invoice dated May 11, with terms of 3/10, n/90, FOB Hostel Corporation's factory. The cost of the goods to Hostel was $20,000. When the goods were delivered, Wilson paid $335 to Express Shipping Service for the delivery charges on the merchandise. The next day, Wilson returned $1,200 of goods to the seller, who received them one day later and restored them to inventory. The returned goods had cost Hostel $800. On May 20, Wilson mailed a check to Hostel Corporation for the amount owed on that date. It was received the following day.

Exercise 6–3
Analyzing and recording merchandise transactions and returns
(LO 2, 3)

Required

a.   Present the journal entries that Wilson Inc. should record for these transactions.

b.   Present the journal entries that Hostel Corporation should record for these transactions.

Sundown Corp. purchased merchandise for resale from Raintree Inc. with an invoice price of $22,000 and credit terms of 3/10, n/60. The merchandise had cost Raintree $15,000. Sundown paid within the discount period.

Exercise 6–4
Analyzing and recording merchandise transactions and discounts
(LO 2, 3)

Required

a.   Prepare the entries that the purchaser should record for the purchase and payment.

b.   Prepare the entries that the seller should record for the sale and collection.

c.   Assume that the buyer borrowed enough cash to pay the balance on the last day of the discount period at an annual interest rate of 8% and paid it back on the last day of the credit period. Calculate how much the buyer saved by following this strategy. (Use a 365-day year.)

Determine each of the missing numbers in the following situations:

Exercise 6–5
Cost of goods sold calculations
(LO 5)

	a	b	c
Purchases	$90,000	$40,000	$30,500
Purchase discounts	4,000	?	650
Purchase returns and allowances	3,000	1,500	1,100
Transportation-in	?	3,500	4,000
Beginning inventory	7,000	?	9,000
Cost of goods purchased	89,400	39,500	?
Ending inventory	4,400	7,500	?
Cost of goods sold	?	41,600	34,130

Friar Corporation's ledger and supplementary records at the end of the period disclose the following information:

Exercise 6–6
Calculating expenses and cost of goods sold
(LO 1, 5)

Sales	$340,000
Sales discounts	5,500
Sales returns	14,000
Beginning inventory	30,000
Purchases	175,000
Purchase discounts	3,600
Purchase returns and allowances	6,000
Transportation-in	11,000
Gross profit from sales	145,000
Net income	65,000

Required

Calculate the *(a)* total operating expenses, *(b)* cost of goods sold, and *(c)* ending inventory.

Exercise 6–7
Calculating expenses and income
(LO 1, 5)

Fill in the blanks in the following income statements. Identify any losses by putting the amount in parentheses.

	a	b	c	d	e
Sales	$60,000	$42,500	$36,000	$?	$23,600
Cost of goods sold:					
Beginning inventory	$ 6,000	$17,050	$ 7,500	$ 7,000	$ 2,560
Purchases	36,000	?	?	32,000	5,600
Ending inventory	?	(2,700)	(9,000)	(6,600)	?
Cost of goods sold	$34,050	$15,900	$?	$?	$ 5,600
Gross profit	$?	$?	$ 3,750	$45,600	$?
Expenses	9,000	10,650	12,150	2,600	6,000
Net income (loss)	$?	$15,950	$(8,400)	$43,000	$?

Exercise 6–8
Sales returns and allowances
(LO 3)

Travis Parts, Inc., was organized on June 1, 19X1, and made its first purchase of merchandise on June 3. The purchase was for 1,000 units of Product X at a price of $10 per unit. On June 5, Travis sold 600 of the units for $14 per unit to Decker Co. Terms of the sale were 2/10, n/60. Prepare entries to record the sale and each of the following independent alternatives:

a. On June 7, Decker returned 100 units because they did not fit the customer's needs. Travis restored the units to its inventory.

b. Decker discovered that 100 units were damaged but of some use. Therefore, Decker kept the units. Travis sent Decker a credit memorandum for $600 to compensate for the damage.

c. Decker returned 100 defective units and Travis concluded that the units could not be resold. As a result, Travis discarded the units.

Exercise 6–9
Purchase returns and allowances
(LO 2)

Refer to Exercise 6–8 and prepare the appropriate journal entries on the books of Decker Co. to record the purchase and each of the three independent alternatives presented. Assume that Decker is a retailer and purchased the units for resale.

Exercise 6–10
Effects of merchandising activities on the accounts
(LO 4)

The following items summarize Transeer, Inc.'s merchandising activities during 19X2. Set up T-accounts for Merchandise Inventory and Cost of Goods Sold. Then record the summarized activities directly in the accounts and calculate the account balances.

Cost of merchandise transferred to customers in sales transactions	$186,000
Merchandise inventory balance, December 31, 19X1 ..	27,000
Purchases of merchandise	190,500
Shrinkage determined on December 31, 19X2	700
Transportation-in	1,900
Cost of merchandise returned by customers and restored to inventory	2,200
Purchase discounts	1,600
Purchase returns and allowances	4,100

Exercise 6–11
Adjusting and closing entries
(LO 4)

The following list includes selected real accounts and all of the temporary accounts taken from the December 31, 19X1, unadjusted trial balance of Vintner, Inc. Use the information in these columns to journalize adjusting and closing entries.

	Debit	Credit
Merchandise inventory	$ 28,000	
Prepaid selling expenses	5,000	
Cash dividends declared	1,800	
Sales		$429,000
Sales returns and allowances	16,500	
Sales discounts	4,000	

	Debit	Credit
Cost of goods sold	211,000	
Sales salaries expense	47,000	
Utilities expense	14,000	
Selling expenses	35,000	
Administrative expenses	95,000	

Additional information: Accrued sales salaries amount to $1,600. Prepaid selling expenses of $2,000 have expired. A physical count of merchandise inventory discloses $27,450 of goods on hand.

Calculate the current and acid-test ratios in each the following cases:

Exercise 6–12
Acid-test ratio
(LO 5)

	Case X	Case Y	Case Z
Cash	$ 800	$ 910	$1,100
Short-term investments			500
Receivables		990	800
Inventory	2,000	1,000	4,000
Prepaid expenses	1,200	600	900
Total current assets	$4,000	$3,500	$7,300
Current liabilities	$2,200	$1,100	$3,650

PROBLEMS

Prepare general journal entries to record the following transactions of Belton, Incorporated. (Use a separate account for each receivable and payable; for example, record the purchase on July 1 in Accounts Payable—Jones Company.)

Problem 6–1
Journal entries for merchandising activities
(LO 1, 2, 3)

July 1   Purchased merchandise from Jones Company for $6,000 under credit terms of 1/15, n/30, FOB factory.

2   Sold merchandise to Terra Co. for $800 under credit terms of 2/10, n/60, FOB shipping point. The merchandise had cost $500.

3   Paid $100 for freight charges on the purchase of July 1.

8   Sold merchandise that cost $1,200 for $1,600 cash.

9   Purchased merchandise from Keene Co. for $2,300 under credit terms of 2/15, n/60, FOB destination.

12   Received a $200 credit memorandum acknowledging the return of merchandise purchased on July 9.

13   Received the balance due from Terra Co. for the credit sale dated July 2, net of the discount.

16   Paid the balance due to Jones Company within the discount period.

19   Sold merchandise that cost $900 to Urban Co. for $1,250 under credit terms of 2/10, n/60, FOB shipping point.

21   Issued a $150 credit memorandum to Urban Co. for an allowance on goods sold on July 19.

22   Received a debit memorandum from Urban Co. for an error that overstated the total invoice by $50.

24   Paid Keene Co. the balance due after deducting the discount.

30   Received the balance due from Urban Co. for the credit sale dated July 19, net of the discount.

31   Sold merchandise that cost $3,200 to Terra Co. for $5,000 under credit terms of 2/10, n/60, FOB shipping point.

Problem 6–2
Journal entries for merchandising activities
(LO 1, 2, 3)

Prepare general journal entries to record the following transactions of Hanifin Corp. (Use a separate account for each receivable and payable; for example, record the purchase on August 1 in Accounts Payable—Dickson Company.)

Aug. 1 Purchased merchandise from Dickson Company for $6,000 under credit terms of 1/10, n/30, FOB destination.

4 At Dickson's request, paid $100 for freight charges on the August 1 purchase, reducing the amount owed to Dickson.

5 Sold merchandise to Griften Corp. for $4,200 under credit terms of 2/10, n/60, FOB destination. The merchandise had cost $3,000.

8 Purchased merchandise from Kendall Corporation for $5,300 under credit terms of 1/10, n/45, FOB shipping point, plus $240 shipping charges. The invoice showed that at Hanifin's request, Kendall had paid $240 shipping charges and added that amount to the bill.

9 Paid $120 shipping charges related to the August 5 sale to Griften Corp.

10 Griften returned merchandise from the August 5 sale that had cost $500 and been sold for $700. The merchandise was restored to inventory.

12 After negotiations with Kendall Corporation concerning problems with the merchandise purchased on August 8, received a credit memorandum from Kendall granting a price reduction of $800.

15 Received balance due from Griften Corp. for the August 5 sale less the return on August 10.

18 Paid the amount due Kendall Corporation for the August 8 purchase less the price reduction granted.

19 Sold merchandise to Farley, Inc., for $3,600 under credit terms of 1/10, n/30, FOB shipping point. The merchandise had cost $2,500.

22 Farley, Inc., requested a price reduction on the August 19 sale because the merchandise did not meet specifications. Sent Farley a credit memorandum for $600 to resolve the issue.

29 Received Farley, Inc.'s payment of the amount due from the August 19 purchase.

30 Paid Dickson Company the amount due from the August 1 purchase.

Problem 6–3
Income statement calculations and formats
(LO 2, 3, 5)

The following amounts appeared on Davison Company's adjusted trial balance as of October 31, 19X2, the end of its fiscal year:

	Debit	Credit
Merchandise inventory	$ 31,000	
Other assets	128,400	
Liabilities		$ 35,000
Common stock, $10 par value		50,000
Retained earnings		67,650
Cash dividends declared	16,000	
Sales		212,000
Sales discounts	3,250	
Sales returns and allowances	14,000	
Cost of goods sold	82,600	
Sales salaries expense	29,000	
Rent expense, selling space	10,000	
Store supplies expense	2,500	
Advertising expense	18,000	
Office salaries expense	16,500	
Rent expense, office space	2,600	
Office supplies expense	800	
Income taxes expense	10,000	
Totals	$364,650	$364,650

On October 31, 19X1, the company's merchandise inventory amounted to $25,000. Supplementary records of merchandising activities during the 19X2 year disclosed the following:

Purchases	$91,000
Purchase discounts	1,900
Purchase returns and allowances	4,400
Transportation-in	3,900

Required

1. Calculate the company's net sales for the year.
2. Calculate the company's cost of goods purchased for the year.
3. Prepare a classified, multiple-step income statement for internal use (see Illustration 6–7) that lists the company's net sales, cost of goods sold, and gross profit, as well as the components and amounts of selling expenses and general and administrative expenses.
4. Present a condensed single-step income statement that lists these expenses: cost of goods sold, selling expenses, and general and administrative expenses.

CHECK FIGURE:
Part 4, total expenses, $172,000

Use the data for Davison Company in Problem 6–3 to meet the following requirements:

Problem 6–4
Closing entries and interpreting information about discounts and returns
(LO 2, 3, 4)

Required

Preparation component:

1. Prepare closing entries for the company as of October 31.

Analysis component:

2. All of the company's purchases were made on credit and the suppliers uniformly offer a 3% sales discount. Does it appear that the company's cash management system is accomplishing the goal of taking all available discounts? Explain.

3. In prior years, the company has experienced a 4% return rate on its sales, which means that approximately 4% of its gross sales were for items that were eventually returned outright or that caused the company to grant allowances to customers. How does this year's record compare to prior years' results?

CHECK FIGURE:
Second closing entry: debit to Income Summary, $189,250

The following unadjusted trial balance was prepared at the end of the fiscal year for Tinker Sales Company:

Problem 6–5
Adjusting entries, income statements, and acid-test ratio
(LO 4, 5)

TINKER SALES COMPANY
Unadjusted Trial Balance
July 31, 19X2

Cash	$ 4,200	
Merchandise inventory	11,500	
Store supplies	4,800	
Prepaid insurance	2,300	
Store equipment	41,900	
Accumulated depreciation, store equipment		$ 15,000
Accounts payable		9,000
Common stock, $1 par value		25,000
Retained earnings		10,200
Cash dividends declared	3,200	
Sales		104,000
Sales discounts	1,000	
Sales returns and allowances	2,000	
Cost of goods sold	37,400	
Depreciation expense, store equipment		
Salaries expense	31,000	
Insurance expense		
Rent expense	14,000	
Store supplies expense		
Advertising expense	8,800	
Income taxes expense	1,100	
Totals	$163,200	$163,200

Rent and salaries expense are equally divided between the selling and general and administrative functions.

Required

1. Prepare adjusting journal entries for the following:
   a. Store supplies on hand at year-end amount to $1,650.
   b. Expired insurance, an administrative expense, for the year is $1,500.
   c. Depreciation expense, a selling expense, for the year is $1,400.
   d. A physical count of the ending merchandise inventory shows $11,100 of goods on hand.

2. Prepare a multiple-step income statement for external users (see Illustration 6–8).

3. Prepare a single-step income statement that would be provided to external users (see Illustration 6–9).

CHECK FIGURE:
Part 3, total expenses, $98,750

4. Compute the company's current and acid-test ratios as of July 31, 19X2.

SERIAL PROBLEM

Echo Systems, Inc.

(The first three segments of this comprehensive problem were presented in Chapters 3, 4, and 5. If those segments have not been completed, the assignment can begin at this point. However, you should use the Working Papers that accompany this text because they reflect the account balances that resulted from posting the entries required in Chapters 3, 4, and 5.)

Earlier segments of this problem have described how Mary Graham created Echo Systems, Inc., on October 1, 19X1. The company has been successful, and its list of customers has started to grow. To accommodate the growth, the accounting system is ready to be modified to set up separate accounts for each customer. The following list of customers includes the account number used for each account and any balance as of the end of 19X1. Graham decided to add a fourth digit with a decimal point to the 106 account number that had been used for the single Accounts Receivable account. This modification allows the existing chart of accounts to continue being used. The list also shows the balances that two customers owed as of December 31, 19X1:

Account	No.	Dec. 31 Balance
Alamo Engineering Co.	106.1	
Buckman Services	106.2	
Capital Leasing	106.3	
Decker Co.	106.4	$1,350
Elite Corporation	106.5	
Fostek Co.	106.6	$1,500
Grandview Co.	106.7	
Hacienda, Inc.	106.8	
Images, Inc.	106.9	

In response to frequent requests from customers, Graham has decided to begin selling computer software. The company will extend credit terms of 1/10, n/30 to customers who purchase merchandise. No cash discount will be available on consulting fees. The following additional accounts were added to the General Ledger to allow the system to account for the company's new merchandising activities:

Account	No.
Merchandise Inventory	119
Sales	413
Sales Discounts	414
Sales Returns and Allowances	415
Cost of Goods Sold	502

Because the accounting system does not use reversing entries, all revenue and expense accounts have zero balances as of January 1, 19X2.

Required

1. Prepare journal entries to record each of the following transactions for Echo Systems, Inc.

2. Post the journal entries to the accounts in the company's General Ledger. (Use asset, liability, and equity accounts that start with balances as of December 31, 19X1.)

2. Prepare a six-column table similar to Illustration 4–3 that presents the unadjusted trial balance, the March 31 adjustments, and the adjusted trial balance. Do not prepare closing entries and do not journalize the adjusting entries or post them to the ledger.

4. Prepare an interim income statement for the three months ended March 31, 19X2. Use a single-step format like the one in Illustration 6–9. List all expenses without differentiating between selling expenses and general and administrative expenses.

5. Prepare an interim statement of retained earnings for the three months ended March 31, 19X2.

6. Prepare an interim balance sheet as of March 31, 19X2.

Transactions:

Jan. 4 Paid Carly Smith for five days at the rate of $100 per day, including one day in addition to the four unpaid days from the prior year.

5 Mary Graham invested an additional $24,000 cash in the business in exchange for 2,400 shares of $10 par value common stock.

7 Purchased $5,600 of merchandise from Shephard Corp. with terms of 1/10, n/30, FOB shipping point.

9 Received $1,500 from Fostek Co. as final payment on its account.

11 Completed five-day project for Alamo Engineering Co. and billed them $4,500, which is the total price of $6,000 less the advance payment of $1,500.

13 Sold merchandise with a retail value of $4,200 and a cost of $3,360 to Elite Corporation with terms of 1/10, n/30, FOB shipping point.

15 Paid $700 for freight charges on the merchandise purchased on January 7.

16 Received $3,000 cash from Grandview Co. for computer services.

17 Paid Shephard Corp. for the purchase on January 7, net of the discount.

20 Elite Corporation returned $400 of defective merchandise from its purchase on January 13. The returned merchandise, which had a cost of $320, was discarded.

22 Received the balance due from Elite Corporation net of the discount and the credit for the returned merchandise.

24 Returned defective merchandise to Shephard Corp. and accepted credit against future purchases. Its cost, net of the discount, was $396.

26 Purchased $8,000 of merchandise from Shephard Corp. with terms of 1/10, n/30, FOB destination.

26 Sold merchandise with a cost of $4,640 for $5,800 on credit to Hacienda, Inc.

29 Received a $396 credit memo from Shephard Corp. concerning the merchandise returned on January 24.

31 Paid Carly Smith for 10 days' work at $100 per day.

Feb. 1 Paid $3,375 to the Lakeshore Mall for another three months' rent in advance.

3 Paid Shephard Corp. for the balance due, net of the cash discount, less the $396 amount in the credit memo.

5 Paid $800 to the local newspaper for advertising.

11 Received the balance due from Alamo Engineering Co. for fees billed on January 11.

15 Declared and paid a $4,800 cash dividend on the common stock.

23 Sold merchandise with a cost of $2,560 for $3,200 on credit to Grandview Co.

26 Paid Carly Smith for eight days' work at $100 per day.

27 Reimbursed Mary Graham's business automobile mileage for 600 miles at $0.25 per mile.

Mar. 8 Purchased $2,400 of computer supplies from Abbott Office Products on credit.

9 Received the balance due from Grandview Co. for merchandise sold on February 23.

11 Repaired the company's computer at the cost of $860.

16 Received $4,260 cash from Images, Inc., for computing services.

19 Paid the full amount due to Abbott Office Products, including amounts created on December 15 and March 8.

24 Billed Capital Leasing for $5,900 of computing services.

25 Sold merchandise with a cost of $1,002 for $1,800 on credit to Buckman Services.

30 Sold merchandise with a cost of $1,100 for $2,220 on credit to Decker Company.

31 Reimbursed Mary Graham's business automobile mileage for 400 miles at $0.25 per mile.

Information for the March 31 adjustments and financial statements:

a. The March 31 inventory of computer supplies is $2,115.

b. Three more months have passed since the company purchased the annual insurance policy at the cost of $2,160.

c. Carly Smith has not been paid for 7 days of work.

d. Three months have passed since any prepaid rent cost has been transferred to expense. The monthly rent is $1,125.

e. Depreciation on the computer for January through March is $1,500.

f. Depreciation on the office equipment for January through March is $750.

g. The March 31 inventory of merchandise is $980.

CRITICAL THINKING: ESSAYS, PROBLEMS, AND CASES

Analytical Essays

AE 6–1
(LO 1)

Briefly explain why a company's manager would want the accounting system to record a customer's return of unsatisfactory goods in the Sales Returns and Allowances account instead of the Sales account. In addition, explain whether the information would be useful for external decision makers.

AE 6–2
(LO 2)

A retail company recently completed taking a physical count of the ending merchandise inventory to use in preparing adjusting entries. In determining the cost of the counted inventory, company employees failed to consider that $2,000 of incoming goods had been shipped by a supplier on December 31 under an FOB factory agreement. These goods had been recorded in Merchandise Inventory as a purchase, but they were not included in the physical count because they were not on hand. Explain how this overlooked fact would affect the company's financial statements and these ratios: return on equity, debt ratio, current ratio, profit margin, and acid-test ratio.

Korner Store, Inc., has operated for several years but has never used an accrual accounting system. To have more useful information, the company has engaged you to help prepare an income statement for 19X2. Based on data that you have gathered from the cash basis accounting system and other documents, you have been able to prepare the following balance sheets as of the beginning and end of 19X2:

Financial Reporting Problem
(LO 1, 2, 3, 4)

	December 31	
	19X1	**19X2**
Cash	$ 15,400	$ 36,350
Accounts receivable	18,900	26,500
Merchandise inventory	39,300	33,000
Equipment (net of depreciation)	76,000	60,000
Total assets	$149,600	$155,850
Accounts payable	$ 27,300	$ 36,550
Wages payable	2,200	2,400
Common stock, $50 par value	75,000	75,000
Retained earnings	45,100	41,900
Total liabilities and stockholders' equity . .	$149,600	$155,850

The store's cash records also provided the following facts for 19X2:

Amount collected on accounts receivable . .	$337,500
Payments for:	
Accounts payable	196,150
Employees' wages	47,500
All other operating expenses	33,600
Cash dividends declared	39,300

You have determined that all merchandise purchases and sales were made on credit, and that no equipment was either purchased or sold during the year.

Use the preceding information to calculate the amounts of the company's sales, cost of goods purchased, cost of goods sold, depreciation expense, and wages expense for 19X2. Then, prepare a multiple-step income statement that shows the company's gross profit.

Financial Statement Analysis Cases

Calculate the current and acid-test ratios for each of these three cases, and comment on your findings.

FSAC 6–1
(LO 5)

	Case A	Case B	Case C
Current assets:			
Cash	$ 600	$3,300	$ 400
Short-term investments	1,600	2,700	600
Accounts receivable	3,200	3,100	1,200
Interest receivable	300	1,000	0
Merchandise inventory	4,400	1,300	7,600
Office supplies	500	600	1,200
Prepaid insurance	1,300	700	1,100
Prepaid rent	800	0	600
Current liabilities:			
Accounts payable	$1,400	$2,600	$4,100
Interest payable	400	900	300
Salaries payable	900	1,000	800
Notes payable	2,900	1,100	400

FSAC 6–2
(LO 1, 5)

Use the financial statements for Lands' End, Inc., in Appendix F at the end of the book to find the answers to these questions:

a. Assume that the amounts reported for inventories and cost of sales were all purchased ready for resale and then calculate the net cost of goods purchased during the fiscal year ended January 27, 1995.

b. Calculate the current and acid-test ratios as of the end of the fiscal years ended January 27, 1995, and January 28, 1994. Comment on what you find.

Ethical Issues Essay

Describe the problem faced by Renee Fleck in the As a Matter of Ethics case on page 197 and evaluate her alternative courses of action.

CONCEPT TESTER

Test your understanding of the concepts introduced in this chapter by completing the following crossword puzzle.

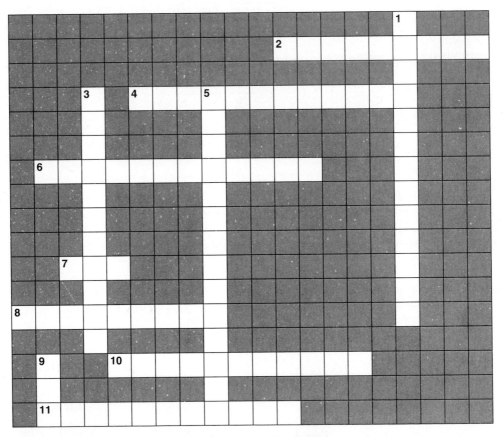

Across Clues

2. 2 words; the price of an item before any trade discount is deducted.
4. 2 words; the time after a sale that can pass before a customer's payment is due.
6. 2 words; a price reduction granted in return for early payment.
7. The abbreviation for free on board.
8. Inventory losses that occur as a result of shoplifting or deterioration.
10. 2 words; description of the amounts and timing of payments that a buyer agrees to make.
11. Goods acquired for the purpose of reselling them to customers.

Down Clues

1. 2 words; a reduction below a list price that is used to set the selling price of goods.
3. 2 words; the difference between net sales and cost of goods sold.
5. 2 words; the time after a sale in which a cash discount is available.
9. The abbreviation for end-of-month.

ANSWERS TO PROGRESS CHECKS

6–1   *b*

6–2   Gross profit is the difference between net sales and cost of goods sold.

6–3   The perpetual inventory system.

6–4   Under credit terms of 2/10, n/60, the credit period is 60 days and the discount period is 10 days.

6–5   *b*

6–6   FOB means free on board. The term *FOB destination* means that the seller does not transfer ownership of the goods to the buyer until they arrive at the buyer's place of business. Thus, the seller is responsible for paying the shipping charges and bears the risk of damage during shipment.

6–7   Keeping sales discounts and sales returns and allowances separate from sales makes useful information readily available to managers for internal monitoring and decision making. This information is not likely to be reported outside the company because it would not be useful for external decision makers.

6–8   When a customer returns merchandise and the seller restores the merchandise to inventory, two entries are necessary. One entry records the revenue reduction and credits the customer's account. The other entry debits inventory and reduces cost of goods sold.

6–9   A credit memorandum.

6–10   The Merchandise Inventory balance may need to be corrected to reflect shrinkage.

6–11   Sales, Sales Discounts, Sales Returns and Allowances, and Cost of Goods Sold.

6–12   Four.

6–13   The classified income statement; the single-step income statement.

6–14   *d*

6–15   The acid-test ratio.

CHAPTER 7

Accounting for Cash

Robert, left, and Susanna Scaretta, owners of Revere Armored Inc., arriving at Federal court on Long Island for their arraignment. (*The New York Times*, May 14, 1993.)

*W*hite-collar crimes continue to increase in the United States causing substantial financial loss. In some cases, these crimes have been devastating enough to cause bankruptcy. Many of them apparently could have been prevented if the victims had used appropriate procedures to protect their assets.

In the infamous Revere Armoured Inc. case, federal prosecutors concluded that the fraud involved up to $45 million in bank funds. The banks involved in the case placed their cash in the custodianship of Revere and overlooked the red flags that should have prompted an audit.[1] In a second case involving a $60,000 embezzlement from a church, an analysis of the facts attributed the fraud to the governing board's lack of basic accounting knowledge. In a third case, police arrested a bookkeeper who allegedly embezzled at least $600,000 from seven small businesses in Southern California.

Other news reports indicate that a wide range of business entities—medical offices, travel agencies, retail operations, utility companies, and major unions—are victims of substantial embezzlement. In addition, accounting literature indicates that small businesses and not-for-profit organizations often have weak internal control structures that leave them vulnerable to embezzlement.

It is management's responsibility to set up policies and procedures to ensure the safeguarding of business assets, including cash. To do so, management and employees of organizations should understand and be able to apply the basic principles of internal control.

[1] *The New York Times*, July 11, 1994, p. A9.

LEARNING OBJECTIVES

After studying Chapter 7, you should be able to:

1. **Explain the concept of liquidity and the difference between cash and cash equivalents.**
2. **Explain why internal control procedures are needed in a large organization and state the broad principles of internal control.**
3. **Describe internal control procedures used to protect cash received from cash sales, cash received through the mail, and cash disbursements.**
4. **Explain the operation of a petty cash fund and be able to prepare journal entries to record petty cash fund transactions.**
5. **Explain why the bank balance and the book balance of cash should be reconciled and be able to prepare a reconciliation.**
6. **Explain how recording invoices at net amounts helps gain control over cash discounts taken and calculate days' sales uncollected.**
7. **Define or explain the words and phrases listed in the chapter glossary.**

Cash is an asset that every business owns and uses. Most organizations own at least some assets known as *cash equivalents,* which are very similar to cash. In studying this chapter, you will learn the general principles of internal control and the specific principles that guide businesses in managing and accounting for cash. If these internal control principles had been followed by the victims described on the previous page, many of the entities might have been saved from financial loss.

The chapter shows you how to establish and use a petty cash fund and how to reconcile a checking account. Also, you will learn a method of accounting for purchases that helps management determine whether cash discounts on purchases are being lost and, if so, how much has been lost.

CASH, CASH EQUIVALENTS, AND THE CONCEPT OF LIQUIDITY

LO 1

Explain the concept of liquidity and the difference between cash and cash equivalents.

In previous chapters, you learned that a company can own many different kinds of assets such as accounts receivable, merchandise inventory, equipment, buildings, and land. These assets all have value, but most of them are not easily used as a means of payment when buying other assets, acquiring services, or paying off liabilities. Usually, cash must be used as the method of payment. Another way to state this is to say that cash is more *liquid* than these other assets.

In more general terms, the **liquidity** of an asset refers to how easily the asset can be converted into other types of assets or be used to buy services or satisfy obligations. All assets can be evaluated in terms of their relative liquidity. Assets such as cash are said to be **liquid assets** because they can be converted easily into other types of assets or used to buy services or pay liabilities.

As you know, a company needs more than valuable assets to stay in business. That is, the company must own some liquid assets so that bills are paid on time and purchases can be made for cash when necessary.

For financial accounting, the asset *cash* includes not only currency and coins but also amounts on deposit in bank accounts, including checking accounts (sometimes called *demand deposits*) and some savings accounts (also called *time deposits*). In addition, cash includes items that are acceptable for deposit in those accounts, especially customers' checks made payable to the company.

To increase their return, many companies invest their idle cash balances in assets called **cash equivalents.** These assets are short-term, highly liquid investments that satisfy two criteria:

1. The investment must be readily convertible to a known amount of cash.
2. The investment must be sufficiently close to its maturity date so that its market value is relatively insensitive to interest rate changes.

In general, only investments purchased within three months of their maturity dates satisfy these criteria.[2] Examples of cash equivalents include short-term investments in U.S. treasury bills, commercial paper (short-term corporate notes payable), and money market funds.

Because cash equivalents are so similar to cash, most companies combine them with cash as a single item on the balance sheet. For example, **Chrysler Corporation**'s balance sheet on December 31, 1994, reported the following:

Cash and cash equivalents	$4,972 (million)

As another example, **Mattel Inc.**'s December 31, 1993, balance sheet does not mention cash equivalents. It simply reports cash with a balance of $239,100,000 on its December 31, 1994, balance sheet. However, Mattel discloses the following in a footnote:

> Cash includes cash equivalents. Highly liquid investments with maturities of three months or less when purchased are considered to be cash equivalents. Because of the short maturities of these instruments, the carrying amount is a reasonable estimate of fair value.

As you would expect, cash is an important asset for every business. Because cash is so important, companies need to be careful about keeping track of it. They also need to carefully control access to cash by employees and others who might want to take it for their own use. A good accounting system supports both goals. It can keep track of how much cash is on hand, and it helps control who has access to the cash. Because of the special importance of cash, this chapter describes the practices companies follow to account for and protect cash.

The importance of accounting for cash and cash equivalents is highlighted by the fact that a complete set of financial statements includes a statement of cash flows. That statement identifies the types of activities that caused changes in cash and cash equivalents. You learn more about that statement in Chapter 16.

Progress Check
(Answers to Progress Checks are provided at the end of the chapter.)

7-1   Why does a company need to own liquid assets?

7-2   Why does a company own cash equivalent assets in addition to cash?

7-3   Which of the following assets should be classified as a cash equivalent? *(a)* Land purchased as an investment; *(b)* Accounts receivable; *(c)* Common stock purchased as a short-term investment; *(d)* A 90-day Treasury bill issued by the U.S. Government.

In a small business, the manager often controls the entire operation through personal supervision and direct participation in all its activities. For example, he or she commonly buys all the assets and services used in the business. The manager also hires and supervises all employees, negotiates all contracts, and signs all checks. As a re-

INTERNAL CONTROL

LO 2
Explain why internal control procedures are needed in a large organization and state the broad principles of internal control.

---

[2]FASB, *Accounting Standards—Current Text* (Norwalk, CT, 1995), sec. C25.106. First published in *Statement of Financial Accounting Standards No. 95,* par. 8.

sult, the manager knows from personal contact and observation whether the business actually received the assets and services for which the checks were written. However, as a business grows, it becomes increasingly difficult to maintain this close personal contact. At some point, the manager must delegate responsibilities and rely on formal procedures rather than personal contact in controlling the operations of the business.

The procedures a company uses to control its operations make up its **internal control system.** A properly designed internal control system encourages adherence to prescribed managerial policies. In doing so, it promotes efficient operations and protects the assets from waste, fraud, and theft. The system also helps ensure that accurate and reliable accounting data are produced.

Specific internal control procedures vary from company to company and depend on such factors as the nature of the business and its size. However, the same broad principles of internal control apply to all companies. These broad principles are:

1. Clearly establish responsibilities.
2. Maintain adequate records.
3. Insure assets and bond employees.
4. Separate record-keeping and custody over assets.
5. Divide responsibility for related transactions.
6. Use mechanical devices whenever feasible.
7. Perform regular and independent reviews.

We discuss these seven principles in the following paragraphs. Throughout, we describe how various internal control procedures prevent fraud and theft. Remember, however, that these procedures are needed to ensure that the accounting records are complete and accurate.

Clearly Establish Responsibilities

To have good internal control, responsibility for each task must be clearly established and assigned to one person. When responsibility is not clearly spelled out, it is difficult to determine who is at fault when something goes wrong. For example, if two sales clerks share access to the same cash register and there is a shortage, it may not be possible to tell which clerk is at fault. Neither can prove that he or she did not cause the shortage. To prevent this problem, one clerk should be given responsibility for making all change. Alternately, the business can use a register with separate cash drawers for each operator.

Maintain Adequate Records

A good record-keeping system helps protect assets and ensures that employees follow prescribed procedures. Reliable records are also a source of information that management uses to monitor the operations of the business. For example, if detailed records of manufacturing equipment and tools are maintained, items are unlikely to be lost or otherwise disappear without any discrepancy being noticed. As another example, expenses and other expenditures are less likely to be debited to the wrong accounts if a comprehensive chart of accounts is established and followed carefully. If the chart is not in place or is not used correctly, management may never discover that some expenses are excessive.

Numerous preprinted forms and internal business papers should be designed and properly used to maintain good internal control. For example, if sales slips are properly designed, sales personnel can record the needed information efficiently without errors or delays to customers. And, if all sales slips are prenumbered and controlled, each salesperson can be held responsible for the sales slips issued to him or her. As a result, a salesperson is not able to pocket cash by making a sale and destroying the sales slip. Computerized point-of-sale systems can achieve the same control results.

Insure Assets and Bond Key Employees

Assets should be covered by adequate casualty insurance, and employees who handle cash and negotiable assets should be bonded. An employee is said to be *bonded* when the company purchases an insurance policy, or a bond, against losses from theft by that employee. Bonding clearly reduces the loss suffered by a theft. It also tends to discourage theft because bonded employees know that an impersonal bonding company must be dealt with when a theft is discovered.

Separate Record-Keeping and Custody over Assets

A fundamental principle of internal control is that the person who has access to or is otherwise responsible for an asset should not maintain the accounting record for that asset. When this principle is followed, the custodian of an asset, knowing that a record of the asset is being kept by another person, is not as likely to misplace, steal, or waste the asset. And, the record-keeper, who does not have access to the asset, has no reason to falsify the record. As a result, two people would have to agree to commit a fraud (called *collusion*) if the asset were to be stolen and the theft concealed in the records. Because collusion is necessary to commit the fraud, it is less likely to happen.

Divide Responsibility for Related Transactions

Responsibility for a transaction or a series of related transactions should be divided between individuals or departments so that the work of one acts as a check on the other. However, this principle does not call for duplication of work. Each employee or department should perform an unduplicated portion.

For example, responsibility for placing orders, receiving the merchandise, and paying the vendors should not be given to one individual or department. Doing so creates a situation in which mistakes and perhaps fraud are more likely to occur. Having a different person check incoming goods for quality and quantity may encourage more care and attention to detail than having it done by the person who placed the order. And, designating a third person to approve the payment of the invoice offers additional protection against error and fraud. Finally, giving a fourth person the authority to actually write checks adds another measure of protection.

Use Mechanical Devices Whenever Feasible

Cash registers, check protectors, time clocks, and mechanical counters are examples of control devices that should be used whenever feasible. A cash register with a locked-in tape makes a record of each cash sale. A check protector perforates the amount of a check into its face and makes it difficult to change the amount. A time clock registers the exact time an employee arrives on the job and the exact time the employee departs. Using mechanical change and currency counters is faster and more accurate than counting by hand and reduces the possibility of loss.

Perform Regular and Independent Reviews

Even a well-designed internal control system has a tendency to deteriorate as time passes. Changes in personnel and computer equipment present opportunities for shortcuts and other omissions. The stress of time pressures tends to bring about the same results. Thus, regular reviews of internal control systems are needed to be sure that the standard procedures are being followed. Where possible, these reviews should be performed by internal auditors who are not directly involved in operations. From their independent perspective, internal auditors can evaluate the overall efficiency of operations as well as the effectiveness of the internal control system.

Many companies also have audits by independent auditors who are CPAs. After testing the company's financial records, the CPAs give an opinion as to whether the company's financial statements are presented fairly in accordance with generally accepted accounting principles. However, before CPAs decide on how much testing they must do, they evaluate the effectiveness of the internal control system. When making their evaluation, they can find areas for improvement and offer suggestions.

In the **Revere Armoured Inc.** case cited in the opening scenario, if the banks that placed their cash in Revere's custodianship had periodically sent auditors to conduct a joint audit, the fraud could have been avoided. Instead, the audits for each bank were not coordinated, and Revere was able to avoid discovery by moving funds from one bank vault to another.

COMPUTERS AND INTERNAL CONTROL

The broad principles of internal control should be followed for both manual and computerized accounting systems. However, computers have several important effects on internal control. Perhaps the most obvious is that computers provide rapid access to large quantities of information. As a result, management's ability to monitor and control business operations can be greatly improved.

Computers Reduce Processing Errors

Computers reduce the number of errors in processing information. Once the data are entered correctly, the possibility of mechanical and mathematical errors is largely eliminated. On the other hand, data entry errors may occur because the process of entering data may be more complex in a computerized system. Also, the lack of human involvement in later processing may cause data entry errors to go undiscovered.

Computers Allow More Extensive Testing of Records

The regular review and audit of computerized records can include more extensive testing because information can be accessed so rapidly. To reduce costs when manual methods are used, managers may select only small samples of data to test. But, when computers are used, large samples or even complete data files can be reviewed and analyzed.

Computerized Systems May Limit Hard Evidence of Processing Steps

Because many data processing steps are performed by the computer, fewer items of documentary evidence may be available for review. However, computer systems can create additional evidence by recording more information such as who made entries and even when they were made. And, the computer can be programmed to require the use of passwords before making entries so that access to the system is limited. Therefore, internal control may depend more on reviews of the design and operation of the computerized processing system and less on reviews of the documents left behind by the system.

Separation of Duties Must Be Maintained

Because computerized systems are so efficient, companies often need fewer employees. This savings carries the risk that the separation of critical responsibilities may not be maintained. In addition, companies that use computers need employees with special skills to program and operate them. The duties of such employees must be controlled to minimize undetected errors and the risk of fraud. For example, better control is maintained if the person who designs and programs the system does not serve as the operator. Also, control over programs and files related to cash receipts and disbursements should be separated. To prevent fraud, check-writing activities should not be controlled by the computer operator. However, achieving a suitable separation of duties can be especially difficult in small companies that have only a few employees.

Recall from the first page of the chapter the **Revere Armoured Inc.** case in which $600,000 was embezzled from seven small businesses in Southern California. The bookkeeper in that case was responsible for making deposits and handling computerized general ledger records. Although other employees prepared and verified deposit slips, the bookkeeper replaced the slips as he took deposits to the bank. Manipulation of computerized records hid shortfalls that he pocketed.

Progress Check

7-4 **The broad principles of internal control require that:**

   a. Responsibility for a series of related transactions (such as placing orders for, receiving, and paying for merchandise) should be given to one person so that responsibility is clearly assigned.

   b. Responsibility for specific tasks should be shared by more than one employee so that one serves as a check on the other.

   c. Employees who handle cash and negotiable assets should be bonded.

7-5 **What are some of the effects of computers on internal control?**

INTERNAL CONTROL FOR CASH

LO 3
Describe internal control procedures used to protect cash received from cash sales, cash received through the mail, and cash disbursements.

Now that we have covered the principles of good internal control in general, it is helpful to see how they are applied to cash, the most liquid of all assets. A good system of internal control for cash should provide adequate procedures for protecting both cash receipts and cash disbursements. In the procedures, three basic guidelines should always be observed:

1. Duties should be separated so that people responsible for actually handling cash are not responsible for keeping the cash records.
2. All cash receipts should be deposited in the bank, intact, each day.
3. All cash payments should be made by check.

The reason for the first principle is that a division of duties helps avoid errors. It also requires two or more people to collude if cash is to be embezzled (stolen) and the theft concealed in the accounting records. One reason for the second guideline is that the daily deposit of all receipts produces a timely independent test of the accuracy of the count of the cash received and the deposit. It also helps prevent loss or theft and keeps an employee from personally using the money for a few days before depositing it.

Finally, if all payments are made by check, the bank records provide an independent description of cash disbursements. This arrangement also tends to prevent thefts of cash. (One exception to this principle allows small disbursements of currency and coins to be made from a petty cash fund. Petty cash funds are discussed later in this chapter.) Note especially that the daily intact depositing of receipts and making disbursements by check allows you to use the bank records as a separate and external record of essentially all cash transactions. Later in the chapter, you learn how to use bank records to confirm the accuracy of your own records.

The exact procedures used to achieve control over cash vary from company to company. They depend on such factors as company size, number of employees, the volume of cash transactions, and the sources of cash. Therefore, the procedures described in the following paragraphs illustrate many but not all situations.

Cash from Cash Sales

Cash sales should be recorded on a cash register at the time of each sale. To help ensure that correct amounts are entered, each register should be placed so that customers can read the amounts displayed. Also, clerks should be required to ring up each sale before wrapping the merchandise and should give the customer a receipt. Finally, each cash register should be designed to provide a permanent, locked-in record of each transaction. In some systems, the register is directly connected to a computer. The computer is programmed to accept cash register transactions and enter them in the accounting records. In other cases, the register simply prints a record of each transaction on a paper tape locked inside the register.

We stated earlier that custody over cash should be separated from record-keeping for cash. For cash sales, this separation begins with the cash register. The salesclerk who has access to the cash in the register should not have access to its locked-in record. At the end of each day, the salesclerk should count the cash in the register, record the result, and turn over the cash and this record of the count to an employee in the cashier's office. The employee in the cashier's office, like the salesclerk, has access to the cash and should not have access to the computerized accounting records (or the register tape). A third employee, preferably from the accounting department, examines the computerized record of register transactions (or the register tape) and compares its total with the cash receipts reported by the cashier's office. The computer record (or register tape) becomes the basis for the journal entry to record cash sales. Note that the accounting department employee has access to the records for cash but does not have access to the actual cash. The salesclerk and the employee from the cashier's office have access to the cash but not to the accounting records. Thus, their accuracy is automatically checked, and none of them can make a mistake or divert any cash without the difference being revealed.

Cash Received through the Mail

Control of cash that comes in through the mail begins with the person who opens the mail. Preferably, two people should be present when the mail is opened. One should make a list (in triplicate) of the money received. The list should record each sender's name, the amount, and the purpose for which the money was sent. One copy is sent with the money to the cashier. A second copy goes to the accounting department. A third copy is kept by the clerk who opened the mail. The cashier deposits the money in the bank, and the bookkeeper records the amounts received in the accounting records. Then, when the bank balance is reconciled by another person (this process is discussed later in the chapter), errors or fraud by the clerk, the cashier, or the bookkeeper are detected. They will be detected because the bank's record of the amount of cash deposited and the records of three people must agree. Note how this arrangement makes errors and fraud nearly impossible, unless the employees enter into collusion. If the clerk does not report all receipts accurately, the customers will question their account balances. If the cashier does not deposit all receipts intact, the bank balance does not agree with the bookkeeper's cash balance. The bookkeeper and the person who reconciles the bank balance do not have access to cash and, therefore, have no opportunity to divert any to themselves. Thus, undetected errors and fraud are made highly unlikely.

Cash Disbursements

The previous discussions clearly show the importance of gaining control over cash from sales and cash received through the mail. Most large embezzlements, however, are actually accomplished through payments of fictitious invoices. Therefore, controlling cash disbursements is perhaps even more critical than controlling cash receipts.

As described earlier, the key to controlling cash disbursements is to require all expenditures to be made by check, except very small payments from petty cash. And, if authority to sign checks is assigned to some person other than the business owner, that person should not have access to the accounting records. This separation of duties helps prevent an employee from concealing fraudulent disbursements in the accounting records.

In a small business, the manager usually signs checks and normally knows from personal contact that the items being paid for were actually received. However, this arrangement is impossible in a larger business. Instead, internal control procedures must be substituted for personal contact. The procedures are designed to assure the check signer that the obligations to be paid were properly incurred and should be paid. Often these controls are achieved through a voucher system.

THE VOUCHER SYSTEM AND CONTROL

A **voucher system** is a set of procedures designed to control the incurrence of obligations and disbursements of cash. This kind of system:

1. Establishes procedures for incurring obligations that result in cash disbursements, such as permitting only authorized individuals to make purchase commitments.
2. Provides established procedures for verifying, approving, and recording these obligations.
3. Permits checks to be issued only in payment of properly verified, approved, and recorded obligations.
4. Requires that every obligation be recorded at the time it is incurred and that every purchase be treated as an independent transaction, complete in itself.

A good voucher system produces these results for every transaction, even if several purchases are made from the same company during a month or other billing period.

When a voucher system is used, control over cash disbursements begins as soon as the company incurs an obligation that will result in cash being paid out. A key factor in making the system work is that only specified departments and individuals are authorized to incur such obligations. Managers should also limit the kind of obligations that each department or individual can incur. For example, in a large retail store, only a specially created purchasing department should be authorized to incur obligations through merchandise purchases. In addition, the procedures for purchasing, receiving, and paying for merchandise should be divided among several departments. These departments include the one that originally requested the purchase, the purchasing department, the receiving department, and the accounting department. To coordinate and control the responsibilities of these departments, several different business papers are used. Illustration 7–1 shows how these papers are accumulated in a **voucher.** A voucher is an internal business paper that is used to accumulate other papers and information needed to control the disbursement of cash and to ensure that the transaction is properly recorded. The following explanation of each paper going into the voucher will show you how companies use this system to gain control over cash disbursements for merchandise purchases.

Purchase Requisition

In a large retail store, department managers generally are not allowed to place orders directly with suppliers. If each manager could deal directly with suppliers, the amount of merchandise purchased and the resulting liabilities would not be well controlled. Therefore, to gain control over purchases and the resulting liabilities, department managers are usually required to place all orders through the purchasing department.

When merchandise is needed, the department managers inform the purchasing department of their needs by preparing and signing a **purchase requisition.** On the requisition, the manager lists the merchandise needed by the department and requests that it be purchased. Two copies of the purchase requisition are sent to the purchasing department. The manager of the requisitioning department (identified in Illustration 7–1 as Department A) keeps a third copy as a backup. The purchasing department sends one copy to the accounting department. When it is received, the accounting department creates a new voucher.

Purchase Order

A **purchase order** is a business paper used by the purchasing department to place an order with the seller, or **vendor,** which usually is a manufacturer or wholesaler. The purchase order authorizes the vendor to ship the ordered merchandise at the stated price and terms.

When the purchasing department receives a purchase requisition, it prepares at least four copies of a purchase order. The copies are distributed as follows:

> **Copy 1** is sent to the vendor as a request to purchase and as authority to ship the merchandise.
>
> **Copy 2,** with a copy of the purchase requisition attached, is sent to the accounting department, where it is used in approving the payment of the invoice for the purchase; this copy is shown in Illustration 7–1.
>
> **Copy 3** is sent to the department originally issuing the requisition to inform its manager that the action has been taken.
>
> **Copy 4** is retained on file by the purchasing department.

Invoice

An **invoice** is an itemized statement of goods prepared by the vendor that lists the customer's name, the items sold, the sales prices, and the terms of sale. In effect, the invoice is the bill sent to the buyer by the seller. (From the vendor's point of view, it is a *sales invoice.*) The vendor sends the invoice to the buyer, or **vendee,** who treats it as a *purchase invoice.* On receiving a purchase order, the vendor ships the ordered merchandise to the buyer and mails a copy of the invoice that covers the shipment. The goods are delivered to the buyer's receiving department and the invoice is sent directly to the buyer's accounting department, where it is placed in the voucher. Illustration 7–1 also presents this document flow.

Receiving Report

Most large companies maintain a special department that receives all merchandise or other purchased assets. When each shipment arrives, this receiving department counts the goods and checks them for damage and agreement with the purchase order. Then, it prepares four or more copies of a **receiving report.** This report is a form used within the business to notify the appropriate persons that ordered goods were received and to describe the quantities and condition of the goods. As shown in Illustration 7–1, one copy is sent to the accounting department and placed in the voucher. Copies are also sent to the original requisitioning department and the purchasing department to notify them that the goods have arrived. The receiving department retains a copy in its files.

Invoice Approval Form

After the receiving report arrives, the accounting department should have copies of these papers on file in the voucher:

Illustration 7-1 The Accumulation of Documents in the Voucher

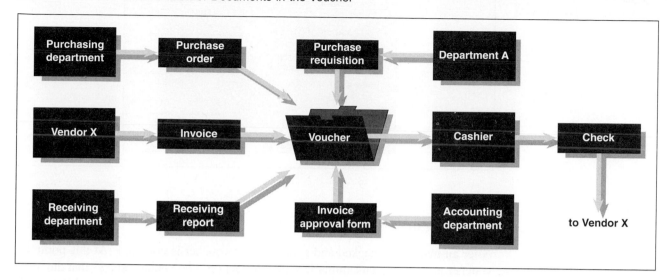

1. The *purchase requisition* listing the items to be ordered.
2. The *purchase order* listing the merchandise that was actually ordered.
3. The *invoice* showing the quantity, description, price, and total cost of the goods shipped by the seller.
4. The *receiving report* listing the quantity and condition of the items actually received by the buyer.

With the information on these papers, the accounting department is in a position to make an entry recording the purchase and to approve its eventual payment before the end of the discount period. In approving the invoice for payment, the accounting department checks and compares the information on all the papers. To facilitate the checking procedure and to ensure that no step is omitted, the department commonly uses an **invoice approval form.** (See Illustration 7–2.) This form is a document on which the accounting department notes that it has performed each step in the process of checking an invoice and approving it for recording and payment. An invoice approval form may be a separate business paper that is filed in the voucher or it may be preprinted on the voucher. It may also be stamped on the invoice. For clarity, the flowchart in Illustration 7–1 shows the form as a separate document.

As each step in the checking procedure is finished, the clerk initials the invoice approval form and records the current date. Initials in each space on the form indicate that the following administrative actions have been taken:

1. **Requisition check** . . . . The items on the invoice were actually requisitioned, as shown on the copy of the purchase requisition.

2. **Purchase order check** . . . . The items on the invoice were actually ordered, as shown on the copy of the purchase order.

3. **Receiving report check** . . . . The items on the invoice were actually received, as shown on the copy of the receiving report.

4. **Invoice check:**
   Price approval . . . . The invoice prices are stated as agreed with the vendor.

   Calculations . . . . The invoice has no mathematical errors.

   Terms . . . . The terms are stated as agreed with the vendor.

Illustration 7-2
An Invoice Approval Form

	By	Date
Purchase order number	_____	_____
Requisition check	_____	_____
Purchase order check	_____	_____
Receiving report check	_____	_____
Invoice check:		
Price approval	_____	_____
Calculations	_____	_____
Terms	_____	_____
Approved for payment	_____	_____

The Voucher

After an invoice is checked and approved, the voucher is complete. At this point, the voucher is a record that summarizes the transaction. The voucher shows that the transaction has been certified as correct and authorizes its recording as an obligation of the buyer. The voucher also contains approval for paying the obligation on the appropriate date. Of course, the actual physical form used for vouchers varies substantially from company to company. In general, they are designed so that the invoice and other documents from which they are prepared are placed inside the voucher, which is often a folder. The information printed on the inside of a typical voucher is shown in Illustration 7–3, and the information on the outside is shown in Illustration 7–4.

The preparation of a voucher requires a clerk to enter the specified information in the proper blanks. The information is taken from the invoice and all the supporting documents filed inside the voucher. Once the steps are completed, the voucher is sent to the appropriate authorized individual (sometimes called the *auditor*), who completes one final review of the information, approves the accounts and amounts to be debited (called the *accounting distribution*), and approves the voucher for recording.

After a voucher is approved and recorded, it is filed until its due date, when it is sent to the cashier's office for payment. Here, the person responsible for issuing checks relies on the approved voucher and its signed supporting documents as proof that the obligation was properly incurred and should be paid. As described earlier, the purchase requisition and purchase order attached to the voucher confirm that the purchase was authorized. The receiving report shows that the items were received, and the invoice approval form verifies that the invoice was checked for errors. As a result, there is little chance for error. There is even less chance for fraud without collusion, unless all the documents and signatures are forged.

THE VOUCHER SYSTEM AND EXPENSES

Under a voucher system, obligations should be approved for payment and recorded as liabilities as soon as possible after they are incurred. As shown in the example, this practice should be followed for all purchases. It should also be followed for all expenses. For example, when a company receives a monthly telephone bill, the charges (especially long-distance calls) should be examined for accuracy. A voucher should be prepared, and the telephone bill should be filed inside the voucher. The voucher is then recorded with a journal entry. If the amount is due at once, a check should be issued. Otherwise, the voucher should be filed for payment on the due date.

The requirement that vouchers be prepared for expenses as they are incurred helps ensure that every expense payment is approved only when adequate information is available. However, invoices or bills for such things as equipment repairs are sometimes not received until weeks after the work is done. If no records of the repairs exist, it may be difficult to determine whether the invoice or bill correctly states the

Illustration 7-3
Inside of a Voucher

NORTHWEST SUPPLY COMPANY   Voucher No. _93–767_
Eugene, Oregon

Date _____ Oct. 1, 19X1 _____

Pay to _____ A. B. Seay Wholesale Company _____

City _____ Salem _____   State _____ Oregon _____

For the following: (attach all invoices and supporting papers)

Date of Invoice	Terms	Invoice Number and Other Details	Amount
Sept. 30, 19X1	2/10, n/60	Invoice No. C-11750 Less discount Net amount payable	800.00 16.00 784.00

Payment approved

_____ N. O. Neal _____
Auditor

Illustration 7-4
Outside of a Voucher

Voucher No. _93–767_

ACCOUNTING DISTRIBUTION

Account Debited	Amount
Purchases	800.00
Transportation-In	
Store Supplies	
Office Supplies	
Sales Salaries	
Other	
Total Vouch. Pay. Cr.	800.00

Due date _____ October 10, 19X1 _____

Pay to _____ A. B. Seay Wholesale Company _____
City _____ Salem _____
State _____ Oregon _____

Summary of charges:
Total charges _____ 800.00 _____
Discount _____ 16.00 _____
Net payment _____ 784.00 _____

Record of payment:
Paid _____
Check No. _____

amount owed. Also, if no records exist, it may be possible for a dishonest employee to arrange with an outsider for more than one payment of an obligation, or for payment of excessive amounts, or for payment for goods and services not received. A properly functioning voucher system helps prevent all of these undesirable results.

Progress Check

7-6 Regarding internal control procedures for cash receipts:
  a. All cash disbursements, other than from petty cash, should be made by check.
  b. An accounting employee should count the cash received from sales and promptly deposit the receipts.
  c. Mail containing cash receipts should be opened by an accounting employee who is responsible for recording and depositing the receipts.

7-7 Do all companies need a voucher system? At what approximate point in a company's growth would you recommend installing a voucher system?

THE PETTY CASH FUND

LO 4
Explain the operation of a petty cash fund and be able to prepare journal entries to record petty cash fund transactions.

A basic principle for controlling cash disbursements requires that all disbursements be made by check. However, an exception to this rule is made for *petty cash disbursements*. Every business must make many small payments for items such as postage, express charges, repairs, and small items of supplies. If firms made such payments by check, they would end up writing many checks for small amounts. This arrangement would be both time-consuming and expensive. Therefore, to avoid writing checks for small amounts, a business should establish a petty cash fund and use the money in this fund to make payments like those listed earlier.

Establishing a petty cash fund requires estimating the total amount of small payments likely to be made during a short period such as a month. Then, a check is drawn by the company cashier's office for an amount slightly in excess of this estimate. This check is recorded with a debit to the Petty Cash account (an asset) and a credit to Cash. The check is cashed, and the currency is turned over to a member of the office staff designated as the *petty cashier*. This person is responsible for the safekeeping of the cash, for making payments from this fund, and for keeping accurate records.

The petty cashier should keep the petty cash in a locked box in a safe place. As each disbursement is made, the person receiving payment signs a *petty cash receipt* (see Illustration 7–5). The receipt is then placed in the petty cashbox with the remaining money. Under this system, the sum of all the receipts plus the remaining cash should always equal the amount of the fund. For example, a $100 petty cash fund could have (a) $100 in cash, (b) $80 in cash and $20 in receipts, or (c) $10 in cash and $90 in receipts. Notice that each disbursement reduces the cash and increases the sum of the receipts in the petty cashbox. When the cash is nearly gone, the fund should be reimbursed.

To reimburse the fund, the petty cashier presents the receipts to the company cashier. The company cashier stamps all receipts *paid* so that they cannot be reused, retains them, and gives the petty cashier a check for their sum. When this check is cashed and the proceeds returned to the cashbox, the money in the box is restored to its original amount, and the fund is ready to begin a new cycle of operations.

At the time a check is written to reimburse the petty cash fund, the petty cashier should sort the paid receipts according to the type of expense or other accounts to be debited in recording payments from the fund. Each group is then totaled, and the totals are used in making the entry to record the reimbursement.

ILLUSTRATION OF A PETTY CASH FUND

To avoid writing numerous checks for small amounts, a company established a petty cash fund on November 1, designating one of its office clerks, Carl Burns, as petty cashier. A $75 check was drawn, cashed, and the proceeds turned over to Burns. The following entry recorded the check:

Nov.	1	Petty Cash	75.00	
		Cash		75.00
		Established a petty cash fund.		

Notice that this entry transfers $75 from the regular Cash account to the Petty Cash account. After the petty cash fund is established, the Petty Cash account is not debited or credited again unless the size of the total fund is changed. For example, the fund should be increased if it is being exhausted and reimbursed too frequently.

Illustration 7-5
A Petty Cash Receipt

```
No. ___ -1- ___                                              $ ___10.00___

                    RECEIVED OF PETTY CASH

                                          Date ___Nov. 2___ 19 _X1_

For ___Washing windows_____

    _____

    Charge to_____Miscellaneous Expenses_____

    _____

    Approved by                    Received by
    CaB                            Bob Jone

    TOPS-Form 3008
```

Another entry like the preceding one would be made to record an increase in the size of the fund. That is, there would be a debit to Petty Cash and credit to Cash for the amount of the increase. If the fund is too large, some of the money in the fund should be redeposited in the checking account. Such a reduction in the fund is recorded with a debit to Cash and a credit to Petty Cash.

During November, Carl Burns, the petty cashier, made several payments from the petty cash fund. Each time, he asked the person who received payment to sign a receipt. On November 27, after making a $26.50 payment for repairs to an office computer, Burns noticed that only $3.70 cash remained in the fund. Therefore, he summarized and totaled the petty cash receipts as shown in Illustration 7–6. Then, he gave the summary and the petty cash receipts to the company cashier in exchange for a $71.30 check to reimburse the fund. Burns cashed the check, put the $71.30 proceeds in the petty cashbox, and then was ready to make additional payments from the fund. The reimbursing check is recorded with the following journal entry:

Nov.	27	Miscellaneous Expenses	46.50	
		Transportation-In	15.05	
		Delivery Expense	5.00	
		Office Supplies	4.75	
		Cash		71.30
		Reimbursed petty cash.		

Information for this entry came from the petty cashier's summary of payments. Note that the debits in the entry record the petty cash payments. Even if the petty cash fund is not low on funds at the end of an accounting period, it may be reimbursed at that time to record the expenses in the proper period. Otherwise, the financial statements show an overstated petty cash asset and understated expenses or assets that were paid for out of petty cash. (Of course, the amounts involved are seldom if ever significant to users of the financial statements.)

Illustration 7-6
Summary of Petty Cash
Payments

Miscellaneous expenses:		
Nov. 2, washing windows	$10.00	
Nov. 17, washing windows	10.00	
Nov. 27, computer repairs	26.50	$46.50
Transportation-in:		
Nov. 5, delivery of merchandise purchased ...	$ 6.75	
Nov. 20, delivery of merchandise purchased ..	8.30	15.05
Delivery expense:		
Nov. 18, customer's package delivered		5.00
Office supplies:		
Nov. 15, purchased office supplies		4.75
Total		$71.30

CASH OVER AND SHORT

Sometimes, a petty cashier fails to get a receipt for a payment. Then, when the fund is reimbursed, he or she may forget the purpose of the expenditure. This mistake causes the fund to be short. If, for whatever reason, the petty cash fund is short at reimbursement time, the shortage is recorded as an expense in the reimbursing entry with a debit to the **Cash Over and Short account.** This account is an income statement account that records the income effects of cash overages and cash shortages arising from omitted petty cash receipts and from errors in making change.

Errors in making change are discovered when there are differences between the cash in a cash register and the record of the amount of cash sales. Even though a cashier is careful, some customers may be given too much or too little change. As a result, at the end of a day, the actual cash from a cash register may not equal the cash sales rung up. For example, assume that a cash register shows cash sales of $550 but the actual count of cash in the register is $555. The entry to record the cash sales and the overage would be:

Nov.	23	Cash	555.00	
		Cash Over and Short		5.00
		Sales		550.00
		Day's cash sales and overage.		

On the other hand, if there were a shortage of cash in the register on the next day, the entry to record cash sales and the shortage would look like the following:

Nov.	24	Cash	621.00	
		Cash Over and Short	4.00	
		Sales		625.00
		Day's cash sales and shortage.		

Because customers are more likely to dispute being shortchanged, the Cash Over and Short account usually has a debit balance by the end of the accounting period. Because it is a debit, this balance represents an expense. This expense may be shown on the income statement as a separate item in the general and administrative expense section. Or, because the amount is usually small, you can combine it with other small expenses and report them as a single item called *miscellaneous expenses*. If Cash Over and Short has a credit balance at the end of the period, it usually is shown on the income statement as part of *miscellaneous revenues*.

Progress Check

7-8 Why are some cash payments made from a petty cash fund?

7-9 Why should a petty cash fund be reimbursed at the end of an accounting period?

7-10 What are two results of reimbursing the petty cash fund?

RECONCILING THE BANK BALANCE

LO 5
Explain why the bank balance and the book balance of cash should be reconciled and be able to prepare a reconciliation.

At least once every month, banks send depositors bank statements that show the activity in their accounts during the month. Different banks use a variety of formats for their bank statements. However, all of them include the following items of information in one place or another:

1. The balance of the depositor's account at the beginning of the month.
2. Deposits and any other amounts added to the account during the month.
3. Checks and any other amounts deducted from the account during the month.
4. The account balance at the end of the month.

Of course, all this information is presented as it appears in the bank's records. Examine Illustration 7–7, an example of a typical bank statement, to find the four items just listed.

Note that section A of Illustration 7–7 summarizes the changes in the account. Section B lists specific debits and credits to the account (other than canceled checks). Section C lists all paid checks in numerical order, and section D shows the daily account balances.

Enclosed with the monthly statement are the depositor's **canceled checks** and any debit or credit memoranda that have affected the account. Canceled checks are checks that the bank has paid and deducted from the customer's account during the month. Additional deductions that may appear on the bank statement for an individual include withdrawals through automatic teller machines (ATM withdrawals) and periodic payments arranged in advance by the depositor.[3] Other deductions from the depositor's account may include service charges and fees assessed by the bank, customers' checks deposited that prove to be uncollectible, and corrections of previous errors. Except for the service charges, the bank notifies the depositor of the deduction in each case with a debit memorandum at the time that the bank reduces the balance. For completeness, a copy of each debit memorandum is usually sent with the monthly statement.[4]

In addition to deposits made by the depositor, the bank may add amounts to the depositor's account. Examples of additions would be amounts the bank has collected

---

[3]Because of the need to make all disbursements by check, most business checking accounts do not allow ATM withdrawals.

[4]A depositor's account is a liability on the bank's records. Thus, a deposit increases the account balance, and the bank records it with a *credit* to the account. Debit memos from the bank produce *credits* on the depositor's books, and credit memos lead to *debits*.

Illustration 7-7 A Typical Bank Statement

First National Bank P.O. BOX 1727 AUSTIN, TEXAS 78767 512/473-4343

VALLEY COMPANY
1300 FALCON LEDGE
AUSTIN, TEXAS 78746

ACCOUNT NUMBER	DATE OF THIS STATEMENT	DATE OF LAST STATEMENT	PAGE NO.
494 504 2	10/31/X5	9/30/X5	1

A
BALANCE OF PREVIOUS STATEMENT ON 9/30/X5	1,609.58
5 DEPOSITS AND OTHER CREDITS TOTALING	1,155.00
10 CHECKS AND OTHER DEBITS TOTALING	723.00
SERVICE CHARGE AMOUNT	.00
INTEREST AMOUNT AT 5.2500%	8.42
CURRENT BALANCE AS OF THIS STATEMENT	2,050.00
AVERAGE BALANCE AS OF THIS STATEMENT	1,924.95
TOTAL INTEREST PAID TO DATE	124.00

B
CHECKING ACCOUNT TRANSACTIONS

DATE	AMOUNT	TRANSACTION DESCRIPTION
10/02	240.00 +	DEPOSIT
10/09	180.00 +	DEPOSIT
10/12	23.00 −	CHARGE FOR PRINTING NEW CHECKS
10/15	100.00 +	DEPOSIT
10/16	150.00 +	DEPOSIT
10/23	485.00 +	NOTE COLLECTION LESS FEE
10/25	30.00 −	NSF CHECK AND NSF CHARGE
10/31	8.42 +	INTEREST PAID

C
DATE	CHECK NO	AMOUNT	DATE	CHECK NO	AMOUNT
10/03	119	55.00	10/16	123	25.00
10/19	120	200.00	10/23	125*	10.00
10/10	121	120.00	10/26	127*	50.00
10/14	122	75.00	10/29	128	135.00

*INDICATES A SKIP IN CHECK NUMBER SEQUENCE

D
DAILY BALANCE SUMMARY

DATE	BALANCE	DATE	BALANCE	DATE	BALANCE
10/01	1,609.58	10/12	1,831.58	10/23	2,256.58
10/02	1,849.58	10/14	1,756.58	10/25	2,226.58
10/03	1,794.58	10/15	1,856.58	10/26	2,176.58
10/09	1,974.58	10/16	1,981.58	10/29	2,041.58
10/10	1,854.58	10/19	1,781.58	10/31	2,050.00

FOR QUESTIONS ON DIRECT DEPOSITS, PLEASE CALL 473-4522, BETWEEN 9:00–4:00 MONDAY-FRIDAY OR WRITE P.O. BOX 1727, AUSTIN, TEXAS 78767.

on behalf of the depositor and corrections of previous errors. Credit memoranda notify the depositor of all additions when they are first recorded. For completeness, a copy of each credit memorandum may be sent with the monthly statement.

Another item commonly added to the bank balance on the statement is interest earned by the depositor. Many checking accounts pay the depositor interest based on the average cash balance maintained in the account. The bank calculates the amount of interest earned and credits it to the depositor's account each month. In Illustration 7–7, note that the bank credited $8.42 of interest to the account of Valley Company. (The methods used to calculate interest are discussed in the next chapter.)

When the business deposits all receipts intact and when all payments (other than petty cash payments) are drawn from the checking account, the bank statement is a device for proving the accuracy of the depositor's cash records. The test of the accuracy begins by preparing a **bank reconciliation.** This analysis explains the difference between the balance of a checking account in the depositor's records and the balance on the bank statement.

Need for Reconciling the Bank Balance

For virtually all checking accounts, the balance on the bank statement does not agree with the balance in the depositor's accounting records. Therefore, to prove the accuracy of both the depositor's records and those of the bank, you must *reconcile* the two balances. In other words, you must explain or account for the differences between them.

Numerous factors cause the bank statement balance to differ from the depositor's book balance. Some are:

1. **Outstanding checks.** These checks were written (or drawn) by the depositor, deducted on the depositor's records, and sent to the payees. However, they did not reach the bank for payment and deduction before the statement date.

2. **Unrecorded deposits.** Companies often make deposits at the end of each business day, after the bank is closed. These deposits made in the bank's night depository are not recorded by the bank until the next business day. Therefore, a deposit placed in the night depository on the last day of the month cannot appear on the bank statement for that month. In addition, deposits mailed to the bank toward the end of the month may be in transit and unrecorded when the statement is prepared.

3. **Charges for uncollectible items and for service.** Occasionally, a company deposits a customer's check that bounces, or turns out to be uncollectible. Usually, this is because the balance in the customer's account is not large enough to cover the check. In these cases, the check is called a nonsufficient funds (NSF) check. In other situations, the customer's account has been closed. In processing deposited checks, the bank credits the depositor's account for the full amount. Later, when the bank learns that the check is uncollectible, it debits (reduces) the depositor's account for the amount of the check. Also, the bank may charge the depositor a fee for processing the uncollectible check. At the same time, the bank notifies the depositor of each deduction by mailing a debit memorandum. Although each deduction should be recorded by the depositor on the day the debit memorandum is received, sometimes an entry is not made until the bank reconciliation is prepared.

   Other charges to a depositor's account that a bank might report on the bank statement include the printing of new checks. Also, the bank may assess a monthly service charge for maintaining the account. Notification of these charges is *not* provided until the statement is mailed.

4. **Credits for collections and for interest.** Banks sometimes act as collection agents for their depositors by collecting promissory notes and other items. When the bank collects an item, it deducts a fee and adds the net proceeds to the depositor's account. At the same time, it sends a credit memorandum to notify the depositor of the transaction. As soon as the memorandum is received, it should be recorded by the depositor. However, these items may remain unrecorded until the time of the bank reconciliation.

   Many bank accounts earn interest on the average cash balance in the account during the month. If an account earns interest, the bank statement includes a credit for the amount earned during the past month. Notification of earned interest is provided only by the bank statement.

5. **Errors.** Regardless of care and systems of internal control for automatic error detection, both banks and depositors make errors. Errors by the bank may not be discovered until the depositor completes the bank reconciliation. Also, the depositor's errors often are not discovered until the balance is reconciled.

Steps in Reconciling the Bank Balance

To obtain the benefits of separated duties, an employee who does not handle cash receipts, process checks, or maintain cash records should prepare the bank reconciliation. In preparing to reconcile the balance, this employee must gather information from the bank statement and from other sources in the records. The person who performs the reconciliation must do the following:

- Compare the deposits listed on the bank statement with the deposits shown in the accounting records. Identify any discrepancies and determine which is correct. Make a list of any errors or unrecorded deposits.

- Examine all other credits on the bank statement and determine whether each was recorded in the books. These items include collections by the bank, correction of previous bank statement errors, and interest earned by the depositor. List any unrecorded items.

- Compare the canceled checks listed on the bank statement with the actual checks returned with the statement. For each check, make sure that the correct amount was deducted by the bank and that the returned check was properly charged to the company's account. List any discrepancies or errors.

- Compare the canceled checks listed on the bank statement with the checks recorded in the books. (To make this process easier, the bank statement normally lists canceled checks in numerical order.) Prepare a list of any outstanding checks.

- Although an individual may occasionally write a check and fail to record it in the books, companies with reasonable internal controls rarely if ever write a check without recording it. Nevertheless, prepare a list of any canceled checks unrecorded in the books.

- Determine whether any outstanding checks listed on the previous month's bank reconciliation are not included in the canceled checks listed on the bank statement. Prepare a list of any of these checks that remain outstanding at the end of the current month. Send this list to the cashier's office for follow-up with the payees to see if the checks were actually received.

- Examine all other debits to the account shown on the bank statement and determine whether each was recorded in the books. These include bank charges for newly printed checks, NSF checks, and monthly service charges. List those not yet recorded.

When this information has been gathered, the employee can complete the reconciliation like the one in Illustration 7–8 by using these steps:

1. Start with the bank balance of the cash account.
2. Identify and list any unrecorded deposits and any bank errors that understated the bank balance. Add them to the bank balance.
3. Identify and list any outstanding checks and any bank errors that overstated the bank balance. Subtract them from the bank balance.
4. Compute the adjusted balance. This amount is also called the correct, or reconciled, balance.
5. Start with the book balance of the cash account.
6. Identify and list any unrecorded credit memoranda from the bank (perhaps for the proceeds of a collected note), interest earned, and any errors that understated the balance. Add them to the book balance.
7. Identify and list any unrecorded debit memoranda from the bank (perhaps for an NSF check from a customer), service charges, and any errors that overstated the book balance. Subtract them from the book balance.
8. Compute the reconciled balance. This is also the correct balance.
9. Verify that the two adjusted balances from steps 4 and 8 are equal. If so, they are reconciled. If not, check for mathematical accuracy and for any missing data.

When the reconciliation is complete, the employee should send a copy to the accounting department so that any needed journal entries can be recorded. For example, entries are needed to record any unrecorded debit and credit memoranda and any

Illustration 7-8
A Typical Bank Reconciliation

VALLEY COMPANY
Bank Reconciliation
October 31, 19X5

①Bank statement balance	$2,050.00	⑤Book balance		$1,404.58
②Add:		⑥Add:		
Deposit of 10/31	145.00	Proceeds of note less		
		collection fee	$ 485.00	
		Interest earned	8.42	
		Total	$ 493.42	
Total	$2,195.00	Total		$1,898.00
③Deduct:		⑦Deduct:		
Outstanding checks:		NSF check plus service		
No. 124	$ 150.00	charge	$ 30.00	
No. 126	200.00	Check printing charge	23.00	
Total	$ 350.00	Total	$ 53.00	
④Reconciled balance	$1,845.00	⑧Reconciled balance		$1,845.00

⑨The two balances both equal $1,845.00.

ILLUSTRATION OF A BANK RECONCILIATION

of the company's mistakes. Another copy should go to the cashier's office, especially if the bank has made an error that needs to be corrected.

We can illustrate a bank reconciliation by preparing one for Valley Company as of October 31. In preparing to reconcile the bank account, the Valley Company employee gathered the following facts:

- The bank balance shown on the bank statement was $2,050.

- The cash balance according to the accounting records was $1,404.58.

- A $145 deposit was placed in the bank's night depository on October 31 and was unrecorded by the bank when the bank statement was mailed.

- Enclosed with the bank statement was a copy of a credit memorandum showing that the bank had collected a note receivable for the company on October 23. The note's proceeds of $500 (less a $15 collection fee) were credited to the company's account. This credit memorandum had not been recorded by the company.

- The bank statement also showed a credit of $8.42 for interest earned on the average cash balance in the account. Because there had been no prior notification of this item, it had not been recorded on the company's books.

- A comparison of canceled checks with the company's books showed that two checks were outstanding — No. 124 for $150 and No. 126 for $200.

- Other debits on the bank statement that had not been previously recorded on the books included (a) a $23 charge for checks printed by the bank; and (b) an NSF (nonsufficient funds) check for $20 plus the related processing fee of $10. The NSF check had been received from a customer, Frank Green, on October 16 and had been included in that day's deposit.

Illustration 7–8 shows the bank reconciliation that reflects these items. The numbers in the circles beside the various parts of the reconciliation correspond to the numbers of the steps listed earlier.

Preparing a bank reconciliation helps locate any errors made by either the bank or the depositor. It also identifies unrecorded items that should be recorded on the company's books. For example, in Valley Company's reconciliation, the adjusted balance of $1,845.00 is the correct balance as of October 31, 19X5. However, at that date, Valley Company's accounting records show a $1,404.58 balance. Therefore, journal entries must be made to increase the book balance to the correct balance. This process requires four entries. The first is:

Nov.	2	Cash	485.00	
		Collection Expense	15.00	
		Notes Receivable		500.00
		To record the collection fee and proceeds of a note collected by the bank.		

This entry records the net proceeds of Valley Company's note receivable that had been collected by the bank, the expense of having the bank perform that service, and the reduction in the Notes Receivable account.

The second entry records the interest credited to Valley Company's account by the bank:

Nov.	2	Cash	8.42	
		Interest Earned		8.42
		To record interest earned on the average cash balance maintained in the checking account.		

Interest earned is a revenue, and the entry recognizes both the revenue and the related increase in Cash.

The third entry records the NSF check that was returned as uncollectible. The $20 check was received from Green in payment of his account and deposited. The bank charged $10 for handling the NSF check and deducted $30 from Valley Company's account. Therefore, the company must reverse the entry made when the check was received and also record the $10 processing fee:

Nov.	2	Accounts Receivable—Frank Green	30.00	
		Cash		30.00
		To charge Frank Green's account for his NSF check and for the bank's fee.		

This entry reflects the fact that Valley Company followed customary business practice and added the NSF $10 fee to Green's account. Thus, it will try to collect the entire $30 from Green.

The fourth entry debits Miscellaneous Expenses for the check printing charge. The entry is:

Nov.	2	Miscellaneous Expenses	23.00	
		Cash		23.00
		Check printing charge.		

After these entries are recorded, the balance of cash is increased to the correct amount of $1,845.00 ($1,404.58 + $485.00 + $8.42 − $30.00 − $23.00).

Progress Check

7-11 What is a bank statement?

7-12 What is the meaning of the phrase to *reconcile a bank balance*?

7-13 Why should you reconcile the bank statement balance of cash and the depositor's book balance of cash?

7-14   **List items that commonly affect the bank side of a reconciliation and indicate if the items are added or subtracted.**

7-15   **List items that commonly affect the book side of a reconciliation and indicate if the items are added or subtracted.**

Internal control principles apply to every phase of a company's operations including merchandise purchases, sales, cash receipts, cash disbursements, and owning and operating plant assets. Many of these procedures are discussed in later chapters. At this point, we consider a way that a company can gain more control over *purchase discounts*.

Recall that entries such as the following have recorded the receipt and payment of an invoice for a purchase of merchandise:

OTHER INTERNAL CONTROL PROCEDURES

LO 6
Explain how recording invoices at net amounts helps gain control over cash discounts taken and calculate days' sales uncollected.

Oct.	2	Merchandise Inventory	1,000.00	
		Accounts Payable		1,000.00
		Purchased merchandise, terms 2/10, n/60.		
	12	Accounts Payable	1,000.00	
		Merchandise Inventory		20.00
		Cash		980.00
		Paid the invoice of October 2.		

These entries reflect the **gross method of recording purchases;** that is, the invoice was recorded at its gross amount of $1,000 before considering the cash discount. Many companies record invoices in this way. However, the **net method of recording purchases** records invoices at their *net* amounts (after cash discounts). This method is widely thought to provide more useful information to management.

To illustrate the net method, assume that a company purchases merchandise with a $1,000 invoice price and terms of 2/10, n/60. On receiving the goods, the purchasing company deducted the offered $20 discount from the gross amount and recorded the purchase at the $980 net amount:

Oct.	2	Merchandise Inventory	980.00	
		Accounts Payable		980.00
		Purchased merchandise on credit.		

If the invoice for this purchase is paid within the discount period, the entry to record the payment debits Accounts Payable and credits Cash for $980. However, if payment is not made within the discount period and the discount is *lost,* an entry such as the following must be made either before or when the invoice is paid:

Dec.	1	Discounts Lost	20.00	
		Accounts Payable		20.00
		To record the discount lost.		

A check for the full $1,000 invoice amount is then written, recorded, and mailed to the creditor.[5]

---

[5] Alternatively, the lost discount can be recorded with the late payment in a single entry.

Advantage of the Net Method

When invoices are recorded at *gross* amounts, the amount of discounts taken is deducted from the balance of the Merchandise Inventory account. However, the amount of any lost discounts does not appear in any account or on the income statement. Therefore, lost discounts may not come to the attention of management.

On the other hand, when purchases are recorded at *net* amounts, the amount of discounts taken does not appear on the income statement. Instead, an expense for **discounts lost** is brought to management's attention through its appearance on the income statement as an operating expense.

Recording invoices at their net amounts supplies management with useful information about the amount of discounts missed through oversight, carelessness, or some other reason. Thus, this practice gives management better control over the people responsible for paying bills on time so that cash discounts can be taken. When the accounts record the fact that discounts are missed, someone has to explain why. As a result, it is likely that fewer discounts are lost through carelessness.

USING THE INFORMATION— DAYS' SALES UNCOLLECTED

Many companies attract customers by selling to them on credit. As a result, cash flows from customers are postponed until the accounts receivable are collected. To evaluate the liquidity of a company's assets, investors want to know how quickly the company converts its accounts receivable into cash. One way financial statement users evaluate the liquidity of the receivables is to look at the **days' sales uncollected.** This is calculated by taking the ratio between the present balance of receivables and the credit sales over the preceding year and then multiplying by the number of days in the year. Because the amount of credit sales usually is not reported, net sales is typically used in the calculation. Thus, the formula for the calculation is:

$$\text{Days' sales uncollected} = \frac{\text{Accounts receivable}}{\text{Net sales}} \times 365$$

For example, MegaMart, Inc., (see p. 194) had accounts receivable of $11,200 at the end of 19X2 and net sales of $314,700 (see page 209) for the year. By dividing $11,200 by $314,700, we find that the receivables balance represents 3.56% of the year's sales. Because there are 365 days in a year, the $11,200 balance is 3.56% of 365 days of sales, or 13 days of sales.

The number of days' sales uncollected is used as an estimate of how much time is likely to pass before cash receipts from credit sales equal the amount of the existing accounts receivable. In evaluating this number, financial statement users should compare it to days' sales uncollected calculations for other companies in the same industry. In addition, they may make comparisons between the current and prior periods. To illustrate such a comparison, selected data from the annual reports of two toy manufacturing companies are used to compute days' sales uncollected:

(in thousands)	TYCO TOYS, INC. (1994)	MATTEL, INC. (1994)
Accounts receivable	$\dfrac{\$211,400}{\$753,098} \times 365$	$\dfrac{\$762,024}{\$3,205,025} \times 365$
Net sales		
Days' sales uncollected	102 days	87 days

If **Tyco Toys, Inc.'s** management made the preceding comparison, the resulting figures might motivate them to investigate how this compares to last year and how they could improve this ratio. Continuation of a financially sound business requires continuous monitoring of the liquidity of the firm's assets.

Progress Check

7-16 When invoices are recorded at net amounts:
   a. The amount of purchase discounts taken is not recorded in a separate account.
   b. Purchase discounts taken are recorded in a Purchase Discounts account.
   c. The cash expenditures for purchases will always be less than if the invoices are recorded at gross amounts.

7-17 Why is the days' sales uncollected calculation usually based on net sales instead of credit sales?

LO 1. Explain the concept of liquidity and the difference between cash and cash equivalents. The liquidity of an asset refers to how easily the asset can be converted into other types of assets or used to buy services or satisfy obligations. Cash is the most liquid asset. To increase their return, companies may invest their idle cash balances in cash equivalents. These investments are readily convertible to a known amount of cash and are purchased so close to their maturity date that their market values are relatively insensitive to interest rate changes.

LO 2. Explain why internal control procedures are needed in a large organization and state the broad principles of internal control. Internal control systems are designed to encourage adherence to prescribed managerial policies. In doing so, they promote efficient operations and protect assets against theft or misuse. They also help ensure that accurate and reliable accounting data are produced. Principles of good internal control include establishing clear responsibilities, maintaining adequate records, insuring assets and bonding employees, separating record-keeping and custody of assets, dividing responsibilities for related transactions, using mechanical devices whenever feasible, and performing regular independent reviews of internal control practices.

LO 3. Describe internal control procedures used to protect cash received from cash sales, cash received through the mail, and cash disbursements. To maintain control over cash, custody must be separated from record-keeping for cash. All cash receipts should be deposited intact in the bank on a daily basis, and all payments (except for minor petty cash payments) should be made by check. A voucher system helps maintain control over cash disbursements by ensuring that payments are made only after full documentation and approval.

LO 4. Explain the operation of a petty cash fund and be able to prepare journal entries to record petty cash transactions. The petty cashier, who should be a responsible employee, makes small payments from the petty cash fund and obtains signed receipts for the payments. The Petty Cash account is debited when the fund is established or increased in size. Petty cash disbursements are recorded with a credit to Cash whenever the fund is replenished.

LO 5. Explain why the bank balance and the book balance of cash should be reconciled and be able to prepare a reconciliation. A bank reconciliation is produced to prove the accuracy of the depositor's and the bank's records. In completing the reconciliation, the bank statement balance is adjusted for such items as outstanding checks and unrecorded deposits made on or before the bank statement date but not reflected on the statement. The depositor's cash account balance is adjusted to the correct balance. The difference arises from such items as service charges, collections the bank has made for the depositor, and interest earned on the average checking account balance.

LO 6. Explain how recording invoices at net amounts helps gain control over cash discounts taken and calculate days' sales uncollected. When the net method of recording invoices is used, missed cash discounts are reported as an expense in the income statement. In contrast, when the gross method is used, discounts taken are reported as reductions in the cost of the purchased goods. Therefore, the net method directs management's attention to instances where the company failed to take advantage of discounts. In evaluating the liquidity of a company, financial statement users may calculate days' sales uncollected.

SUMMARY OF THE CHAPTER IN TERMS OF LEARNING OBJECTIVES

**DEMONSTRATION
PROBLEM**

Set up a table with the following headings for a bank reconciliation as of September 30:

Bank Balance		Book Balance			Not Shown on the Reconcil- iation
Add	Deduct	Add	Deduct	Must Adjust	

For each item that follows, place an *x* in the appropriate columns to indicate whether the item should be added to or deducted from the book or bank balance, or whether it should not appear on the reconciliation. If the book balance is to be adjusted, place a *Dr.* or *Cr.* in the Must Adjust column to indicate whether the Cash balance should be debited or credited.

1. Interest earned on the account.
2. Deposit made on September 30 after the bank was closed.
3. Checks outstanding on August 31 that cleared the bank in September.
4. NSF check from customer returned on September 15 but not recorded by the company.
5. Checks written and mailed to payees on September 30.
6. Deposit made on September 5 that was processed on September 8.
7. Bank service charge.
8. Checks written and mailed to payees on October 5.
9. Checks written by another depositor but charged against the company's account.
10. Principal and interest collected by the bank but not recorded by the company.
11. Special charge for collection of note in No. 10 on company's behalf.
12. Check written against the account and cleared by the bank; erroneously omitted by the bookkeeper.

Planning the Solution

- Examine each item to determine whether it affects the book balance or the bank balance.
- If it acts to increase the balance, place an *x* in the Add column. If it acts to decrease the balance, place an *x* in the Deduct column.
- If the item increases or decreases the book balance, enter a *Dr.* or *Cr.* in the adjustment column.
- If the item does not affect either balance, place an *x* in the Not Shown on the Reconciliation column.

*Solution to
Demonstration
Problem*

	Bank Balance		Book Balance			Not Shown on the Reconcil- iation
	Add	Deduct	Add	Deduct	Must Adjust	
1. Interest earned on the account.			×		Dr.	
2. Deposit made on September 30 after the bank was closed.	×					
3. Checks outstanding on August 31 that cleared the bank in September.						×
4. NSF check from customer returned on September 15 but not recorded by the company.				×	Cr.	

	Bank Balance		Book Balance			Not Shown on the Reconciliation
	Add	Deduct	Add	Deduct	Must Adjust	
5. Checks written and mailed to payees on September 30.		×				
6. Deposit made on September 5 that was processed on September 8.						
7. Bank service charge.				×	Cr	×
8. Checks written and mailed to payees on October 5.						×
9. Check written by another depositor but charged against the company's account.	×					
10. Principal and interest collected by the bank but not recorded by the company.			×		Dr.	
11. Special charge for collection of note in No. 10 on company's behalf.				×	Cr.	
12. Check written against the account and cleared by the bank; erroneously omitted by the bookkeeper.				×	Cr.	

GLOSSARY

Bank reconciliation an analysis that explains the difference between the balance of a checking account shown in the depositor's records and the balance shown on the bank statement. p. 248

Canceled checks checks that the bank has paid and deducted from the customer's account during the month. p. 247

Cash equivalents temporary investments readily convertible to a known amount of cash that are insensitive to interest rate changes; normally purchased within three months of their maturity dates. p. 232

Cash Over and Short account an income statement account used to record cash overages and cash shortages arising from omitted petty cash receipts and from errors in making change. p. 246

Days' sales uncollected the number of days of average credit sales volume accumulated in the accounts receivable balance, calculated as the product of 365 times the ratio of the accounts receivable balance divided by credit (or net) sales. p. 254

Discounts lost an expense resulting from failing to take advantage of cash discounts on purchases. p. 254

Gross method of recording purchases a method of recording purchases at the full invoice price without deducting any cash discounts. p. 253

Internal control system procedures adopted by a business to encourage adherence to prescribed managerial policies; in doing so, the system also promotes operational efficiencies and protects the business assets from waste, fraud, and theft, and helps ensure that accurate and reliable accounting data are produced. p. 234

Invoice an itemized statement prepared by the vendor that lists the customer's name, the items sold, the sales prices, and the terms of sale. p. 240

Invoice approval form a document on which the accounting department notes that it has performed each step in the process of checking an invoice and approving it for recording and payment. p. 241

Liquid asset an asset such as cash that is easily converted into other types of assets or used to buy services or pay liabilities. p. 232

Liquidity a characteristic of an asset that refers to how easily the asset can be converted into another type of asset or used to buy services or satisfy obligations. p. 232

Net method of recording purchases a method of recording purchases at the full invoice price less any cash discounts. p. 253

Outstanding checks checks that were written (or drawn) by the depositor, deducted on the depositor's records, and sent to the payees; however, they had not reached the bank for payment and deduction before the statement date. p. 249

Purchase order a business paper used by the purchasing department to place an order with the vendor; authorizes the vendor to ship the ordered merchandise at the stated price and terms. p. 240

Purchase requisition a business paper used to request that the Purchasing Department buy the needed merchandise or other items. p. 240

Receiving report a form used within the business to notify the appropriate persons that ordered goods were received and to describe the quantities and condition of the goods. p. 240

Vendee the buyer or purchaser of goods or services. p. 240

Vendor the seller of goods or services, usually a manufacturer or wholesaler. p. 240

Voucher an internal business paper used to accumulate other papers and information needed to control the disbursement of cash and to ensure that the transaction is properly recorded. p. 239

Voucher system a set of procedures designed to control the incurrence of obligations and disbursements of cash. p. 239

QUESTIONS

1. Which of the following assets is most liquid and which is least liquid; merchandise inventory, building, accounts receivable, cash?
2. List the seven broad principles of internal control.
3. Why should the person who keeps the record of an asset not be the person responsible for custody of the asset?
4. Internal control procedures are important in every business, but at what stage in the development of a business do they become critical?
5. Why should responsibility for a sequence of related transactions be divided among different departments or individuals?
6. Why should all receipts be deposited intact on the day of receipt?
7. When merchandise is purchased for a large store, why are department managers not permitted to deal directly with suppliers?
8. What is a petty cash receipt? Who signs a petty cash receipt?

9. Southwest Airlines Co.'s consolidated statement of cash flows (see Appendix E) describes the changes in cash and cash equivalents that occurred during the year ended December 31, 1994. What amount was provided by (or used in) investing activities and what amount was provided by (or used in) financing activities?

10. Refer to the Lands' End, Inc. financial statements in Appendix F. What was the difference in the number of days' sales uncollected on January 27, 1995, and January 28, 1994?

QUICK STUDY (Five-Minute Exercises)

QS 7–1
(LO 1)

What is the difference between the terms *liquidity* and *cash equivalent?*

QS 7–2
(LO 2)

a. What is the main objective of internal control and how is it accomplished?
b. Why should record-keeping for assets be separated from custody over the assets?

QS 7–3
(LO 3)

In a good system of internal control for cash that provides adequate procedures for protecting both cash receipts and cash disbursements, three basic guidelines should always be observed. What are these guidelines?

QS 7–4
(LO 4)

a. The petty cash fund of the Wee Ones Agency was established at $75. At the end of the month, the fund contained $12.74 and had the following receipts: film rentals, $19.40; refreshments for meetings, $22.81 (both expenditures to be classified as Entertainment Expense); postage, $6.95; and printing, $13.10. Prepare the journal entries to record (a) the establishment of the fund and (b) the reimbursement at the end of the month.
b. Explain when the Petty Cash account would be credited in a journal entry.

a. Identify whether each of the following items affects the bank or book side of the reconciliation and indicate if the amount represents an addition or a subtraction:

    (1) Unrecorded deposits.
    (2) Interest on average monthly balance.
    (3) Credit memos.
    (4) Bank service charges.
    (5) Outstanding checks.
    (6) Debit memos.
    (7) NSF checks.

b. Which of the previous items require a journal entry?

QS 7–5
(LO 5)

Which accounting method uses a Discounts Lost account and what is the advantage of this method?

QS 7–6
(LO 6)

Refer to Southwest Airlines Co.'s financial statements in Appendix E. What was the difference in the number of days' sales uncollected in 1994 and 1993? According to this ratio analysis, is Southwest Airlines' collection of receivables improving? Explain your answer.

QS 7–7
(LO 6)

EXERCISES

Lombard Company is a young business that has grown rapidly. The company's bookkeeper, who was hired two years ago, left town suddenly after the company's manager discovered that a great deal of money had disappeared over the past 18 months. An audit disclosed that the bookkeeper had written and signed several checks made payable to the bookkeeper's brother and then recorded the checks as salaries expense. The brother, who cashed the checks but had never worked for the company, left town with the bookkeeper. As a result, the company incurred an uninsured loss of $84,000.

    Evaluate Lombard Company's internal control system and indicate which principles of internal control appear to have been ignored in this situation.

Exercise 7–1
Analyzing internal control
(LO 2)

What internal control procedures would you recommend in each of the following situations?

a. A concession company has one employee who sells T-shirts and sunglasses at the beach. Each day, the employee is given enough shirts and sunglasses to last through the day and enough cash to make change. The money is kept in a box at the stand.

b. An antique store has one employee who is given cash and sent to garage sales each weekend. The employee pays cash for merchandise to be resold at the antique store.

Exercise 7–2
Recommending internal control procedures
(LO 2, 3)

Some of Fannin Corporation's cash receipts from customers are sent to the company in the mail. Fannin's bookkeeper opens the letters and deposits the cash received each day. What internal control problem is inherent in this arrangement? What changes would you recommend?

Exercise 7–3
Internal control over cash receipts
(LO 2)

Eanes, Inc., established a $200 petty cash fund on January 1. One week later, on January 8, the fund contained $27.50 in cash and receipts for these expenditures: postage, $64.00; transportation-in (merchandise inventory), $19.00; store supplies, $36.50; and miscellaneous expenses, $53.00.

    Prepare the journal entries to *(a)* establish the fund on January 1 and *(b)* reimburse it on January 8. Now assume that the fund was not only reimbursed on January 8 but also increased to $500 because it was exhausted so quickly. *(c)* Give the entry to reimburse the fund and increase it to $500.

Exercise 7–4
Petty cash fund
(LO 4)

Exercise 7–5
Petty cash fund
(LO 4)

Brady Corp. established a $400 petty cash fund on September 9. On September 30, the fund had $164.25 in cash and receipts for these expenditures: transportation-in (merchandise inventory), $32.45; office supplies, $113.55; and miscellaneous expenses, $87.60. The petty cashier could not account for the $2.15 shortage in the fund. Prepare (a) the September 9 entry to establish the fund and (b) the September 30 entry to reimburse the fund and reduce it to $300.

Exercise 7–6
Bank reconciliation
(LO 5)

Medline Service Co. deposits all receipts intact on the day received and makes all payments by check. On July 31, 19X1, after all posting was completed, its Cash account showed a $11,352 debit balance. However, Medline's July 31 bank statement showed only $10,332 on deposit in the bank on that day. Prepare a bank reconciliation for Medline, using the following information:

a.   Outstanding checks, $1,713.

b.   Included with the July canceled checks returned by the bank was an $18 debit memorandum for bank services.

c.   Check No. 919, returned with the canceled checks, was correctly drawn for $489 in payment of the utility bill and was paid by the bank on July 15. However, it had been recorded with a debit to Utilities Expense and a credit to Cash as though it were for $498.

d.   The July 31 cash receipts, $2,724, were placed in the bank's night depository after banking hours on that date and were unrecorded by the bank at the time the July bank statement was prepared.

Exercise 7–7
Adjusting entries resulting from bank reconciliation
(LO 5)

Give the journal entries that Medline Service Co. should make as a result of having prepared the bank reconciliation in the previous exercise.

Exercise 7–8
Completion of bank reconciliation
(LO 5)

Complete the following bank reconciliation by filling in the missing amounts:

JAMBOREE ENTERPRISES
Bank Reconciliation
November 30, 19X1

Bank statement balance	$38,520		Book balance of cash	$?	
Add:			Add:		
Deposit of November 30 . .	$17,150		Collection of note	$30,000	
Bank error	?		Interest earned	900	
Total	$?		Total	$?	
Total	$55,830		Total	$47,280	
Deduct:			Deduct:		
Outstanding checks	?		NSF check	$ 1,100	
			Recording error	?	
			Service charge	40	
			Total	$?	
Reconciled balance	$46,020		Reconciled balance	$?	

Exercise 7–9
Recording invoices at gross or net amounts
(LO 6)

Peltier's Imports, Inc., had the following transactions during the month of May. Prepare entries to record the transactions assuming Peltier's records invoices (a) at gross amounts and (b) at net amounts.

May   2   Received merchandise purchased at a $2,016 invoice price, invoice dated April 29, terms 2/10, n/30.

       10   Received a $416 credit memorandum (invoice price) for merchandise received on May 2 and returned for credit.

       17   Received merchandise purchased at a $4,480 invoice price, invoice dated May 16, terms 2/10, n/30.

May 26 Paid for the merchandise received on May 17, less the discount.

28 Paid for the merchandise received on May 2. Payment was delayed because the invoice was mistakenly filed for payment today. This error caused the discount to be lost. The filing error occurred after the credit memorandum received on May 10 was attached to the invoice dated April 29.

Federated Merchandise Co. reported net sales for 19X1 and 19X2 of $565,000 and $647,000. The end-of-year balances of accounts receivable were December 31, 19X1, $51,000; and December 31, 19X2, $83,000. Calculate the days' sales uncollected at the end of each year and describe any changes in the apparent liquidity of the company's receivables.

Exercise 7–10
Liquidity of accounts receivable
(LO 6)

PROBLEMS

Palladium Art Gallery completed the following petty cash transactions during February of the current year:

Problem 7–1
Establishing, reimbursing, and increasing the petty cash fund
(LO 4)

Feb. 2 Drew a $300 check, cashed it, and gave the proceeds and the petty cash box to Nick Reed, the petty cashier.

5 Purchased paper for the copier, $10.13.

9 Paid $22.50 COD charges on merchandise purchased for resale.

12 Paid $9.95 postage to express mail a contract to a client.

14 Reimbursed Gina Barton, the manager of the business, $58.00 for business car mileage.

20 Purchased stationery, $77.76.

23 Paid a courier $18.00 to deliver merchandise sold to a customer.

25 Paid $15.10 COD charges on merchandise purchased for resale.

28 Paid $64.00 for stamps.

28 Reed sorted the petty cash receipts by accounts affected and exchanged them for a check to reimburse the fund for expenditures. However, there was only $21.23 in cash in the fund, and he could not account for the shortage. In addition, the size of the petty cash fund was increased to $400.

Required

1. Prepare a journal entry to record establishing the petty cash fund.
2. Prepare a summary of petty cash payments that has these categories: delivery expense, mileage expense, postage expense, transportation-in (merchandise inventory), and office supplies. Sort the payments into the appropriate categories and total the expenditures in each category.
3. Prepare the journal entry to record the reimbursement and the increase of the fund.

CHECK FIGURE: February 28, Cash, $378.77 Cr.

El Gatto, Inc., has only a General Journal in its accounting system and uses it to record all transactions. However, the company recently set up a petty cash fund to facilitate payments of small items. The following petty cash transactions were noted by the petty cashier as occurring during April (the last month of the company's fiscal year):

Problem 7–2
Petty cash fund; reimbursement and analysis of errors
(LO 4)

Apr. 1 Received a company check for $250 to establish the petty cash fund.

15 Received a company check to replenish the fund for the following expenditures made since April 1 and to increase the fund to $450.

    a.   Paid $78 for janitorial service.

    b.   Purchased office supplies for $63.68.

    c.   Purchased postage stamps for $43.50.

    d.   Paid $57.15 to *The County Crier* for an advertisement in the newspaper.

    e.   Discovered that $11.15 remained in the petty cash box.

Apr. 30   The petty cashier noted that $293.39 remained in the fund and decided that the April 15 increase in the fund was too large. Therefore, a company check was drawn to replenish the fund for the following expenditures made since April 15 and to reduce the fund to $400.

    f.   Purchased office supplies for $48.36.

    g.   Reimbursed office manager for business mileage, $28.50.

    h.   Paid $39.75 COD delivery charges on merchandise purchased for resale.

Required

Preparation component:

CHECK FIGURE: Cash credits: April 15, $438.85; April 30, $106.61

1.   Prepare journal entries to record the establishment of the fund on April 1 and its replenishments on April 15 and on April 30.

Analysis component:

2.   Explain how the company's financial statements would be affected if the petty cash fund is not replenished and no entry is made on April 30. (Hint: The amount of office supplies that appears on a balance sheet is determined by a physical count of the supplies on hand.)

Problem 7–3
Preparation of bank reconciliation and recording adjustments
(LO 5)

The following information was available to reconcile Archdale Corporation's book balance of cash with its bank statement balance as of October 31, 19X1:

    a.   After all posting was completed on October 31, the company's Cash account had a $26,193 debit balance, but its bank statement showed a $28,020 balance.

    b.   Checks No. 3031 for $1,380 and No. 3040 for $552 were outstanding on the September 30 bank reconciliation. Check No. 3040 was returned with the October canceled checks, but Check No. 3031 was not. It was also found that Check No. 3065 for $336 and Check No. 3069 for $2,148, both drawn in October, were not among the canceled checks returned with the statement.

    c.   In comparing the canceled checks returned by the bank with the entries in the accounting records, it was found that Check No. 3056 for the October rent was correctly drawn for $1,250 but was erroneously entered in the accounting records as $1,230.

    d.   A credit memorandum enclosed with the bank statement indicated that the bank had collected a $9,000 noninterest-bearing note for Archdale, deducted a $45 collection fee, and credited the remainder to the account. This event was not recorded by Archdale before receiving the statement.

    e.   A debit memorandum for $805 listed a $795 NSF check plus a $10 NSF charge. The check had been received from a customer, Jefferson Tyler. Archdale had not recorded this bounced check before receiving the statement.

    f.   Also enclosed with the statement was a $15 debit memorandum for bank services. It had not been recorded because no previous notification had been received.

    g.   The October 31 cash receipts, $10,152, were placed in the bank's night depository after banking hours on that date and this amount did not appear on the bank statement.

Required

Preparation component:

1. Prepare a bank reconciliation for the company as of October 31, 19X1.

2. Prepare the general journal entries necessary to bring the company's book balance of cash into conformity with the reconciled balance.

Analysis component:

3. Assume that an October 31, 19X1, bank reconciliation for the company has already been prepared and some of the items were treated incorrectly in preparing the reconciliation. For each of the following errors, explain the effect of the error on: (1) the final balance that was calculated by adjusting the bank statement balance, and (2) the final balance that was calculated by adjusting the Cash account balance.
   a. The company's Cash account balance of $26,193 was listed on the reconciliation as $26,139.
   b. The bank's collection of a $9,000 note less the $45 collection fee was added to the bank statement balance.

CHECK FIGURE: Reconciled balance, $34,308.00

Walburg Company reconciled its bank and book statement balances of cash on August 31 and showed two checks outstanding at that time, No. 5888 for $1,038.05 and No. 5893 for $484.25. The following information was available for the September 30, 19X1, reconciliation:

Problem 7–4
Preparation of bank reconciliation and recording adjustments **(LO 5)**

From the September 30 bank statement:

BALANCE OF PREVIOUS STATEMENT ON 08/31/X1	16,800.45
6 DEPOSITS AND OTHER CREDITS TOTALING	11,182.85
9 CHECKS AND OTHER DEBITS TOTALING	9,620.05
CURRENT BALANCE AS OF 09/30/X1	18,363.25

CHECKING ACCOUNT TRANSACTIONS

DATE	AMOUNT	TRANSACTION DESCRIPTION ....
09/05	1,103.75+	Deposit
09/12	2,226.90+	Deposit
09/17	588.25−	NSF check
09/21	4,093.00+	Deposit
09/25	2,351.70+	Deposit
09/30	22.50+	Interest
09/30	1,385.00+	Credit memorandum

DATE ..	CHECK NO ..	AMOUNT	DATE ..	CHECK NO ..	AMOUNT
09/03	5888	1,038.05	09/22	5904	2,080.00
09/07	5901*	1,824.25	09/20	5905	937.00
09/04	5902	731.90	09/28	5907*	213.85
09/22	5903	399.10	09/29	5909*	1,807.65

*Indicates a skip in check sequence.

From Walburg Company's accounting records:

	Cash Receipts Deposited				Cash Disbursements	
Date		**Cash Debit**		**Check No.**		**Cash Credit**
Sept. 5		1,103.75		5901		1,824.25
12		2,226.90		5902		731.90
21		4,093.00		5903		399.10
25		2,351.70		5904		2,050.00
30		1,582.75		5905		937.00
		11,358.10		5906		859.30
				5907		213.85
				5908		276.00
				5909		1,807.65
						9,099.05

	Cash				Account No. 101	
Date	Explanation	PR	Debit	Credit	Balance	
Aug. 31	Balance				15,278.45	
Sept. 30	Total receipts	R12	11,358.10		26,636.55	
30	Total disbursements	D23		9,099.05	17,537.50	

Check No. 5904 was correctly drawn for $2,080 to pay for computer equipment; however, the bookkeeper misread the amount and entered it in the accounting records with a debit to Computer Equipment and a credit to Cash as though it were for $2,050.

The NSF check was originally received from a customer, Delia Hahn, in payment of her account. Its return was not recorded when the bank first notified the company. The credit memorandum resulted from the collection of a $1,400 note for Walburg Company by the bank. The bank had deducted a $15 collection fee. The collection has not been recorded.

Required

Preparation component:

CHECK FIGURE: Reconciled balance, $18,326.75

1. Prepare a September 30 bank reconciliation for the company.
2. Prepare the general journal entries needed to adjust the book balance of cash to the reconciled balance.

Analysis component:

3. The preceding bank statement discloses three places where the canceled checks returned with the bank statement are not numbered sequentially. In other words, some of the prenumbered checks in the sequence are missing. Several possible situations would explain why the canceled checks returned with a bank statement might not be numbered sequentially. Describe three situations, each of which is a possible explanation of why the canceled checks returned with a bank statement are not numbered sequentially.

CRITICAL THINKING: ESSAYS, PROBLEMS, AND CASES

Analytical Essay

(LO 2)

Pioneer Manufacturing Co. has enjoyed rapid growth since it was created several years ago. Last year, for example, its sales exceeded $10 million. However, its purchasing procedures have not kept pace with its growth. A plant supervisor or department head who needs raw materials, plant assets, or supplies telephones a request to the purchasing department manager. The purchasing department manager then prepares a purchase order in duplicate, sends one copy to the company selling the goods, and keeps the other copy in the files. When the seller's invoice is received, it is sent directly to the purchasing department. When the goods arrive, receiving department personnel count and inspect the items and prepare only one copy of a receiving report, which is then sent to the purchasing department. The purchasing department manager attaches the receiving report and the file copy of the purchase order to the invoice. If all is in order, the invoice is stamped *approved for payment* and signed by the purchasing department manager. The invoice and its supporting documents are then sent to the accounting department to be recorded and filed until due. On its due date, the invoice and its supporting documents are sent to the office of the company treasurer and a check is prepared and mailed. The number of the check is entered on the invoice, and the invoice is sent to the accounting department for an entry to record its payment.

Do Pioneer's procedures make it fairly easy for someone in the company to initiate the payment of fictitious invoices by the company? If so, who is most likely to commit the fraud and what would that person have to do to receive payment of a fictitious invoice? What changes should be made in the company's purchasing procedures, and why should each change be made?

On June 9, Raceway Auto Parts received Joshua Brand's check number 815, dated June 8, in the amount of $973. The check was to pay for merchandise Brand had purchased on May 10. The merchandise was shipped from Raceway's shop at 2005 American Road, Cleveland, Ohio 44143, to Brand's home at 10500 Market Street, Akron, Ohio 44332. On June 10, Raceway's cashier deposited the check in the company's bank account. The bank returned the check to Raceway with the June 30 bank statement. Also included was a debit memorandum indicating that Brand's check was returned for nonsufficient funds, and the bank was charging Raceway a $15 NSF processing fee. Immediately after reconciling the bank statement on July 3, Frances Ford, Raceway's accountant, asks you to write a letter for her signature using the company's letterhead stationery. Your letter to Brand should explain the amount owed and request prompt payment.

Business Communications Case

(LO 5)

For this problem, turn to the financial statements of Southwest Airlines Co. in Appendix E. Use the information presented in the financial statements to answer these questions:

1. For both 1994 and 1993, determine the total amount of cash and cash equivalents that Southwest Airlines held at the end of the year. Determine the percentage that this amount represents of total current assets, total current liabilities, total stockholders' equity, and total assets.
2. For both 1994 and 1993, determine the total amount of cash, cash equivalents, and accounts receivable that Southwest Airlines held at the end of the year. Determine the percentage that this amount represents of total current assets, total current liabilities, total stockholders' equity, and total assets.
3. For 1994, use the information in the consolidated statement of cash flows to determine the percentage change between the beginning of the year and end of the year holding of cash and cash equivalents.
4. What was the number of days' sales uncollected at the end of 1994 and at the end of 1993?

Financial Statement Analysis Case

(LO 1, 6)

Review the As a Matter of Ethics case on page 247. Discuss the nature of the problem faced by Nancy Tucker and evaluate the alternative courses of action she should consider.

Ethical Issues Essay

CONCEPT TESTER

Test your understanding of the concepts introduced in this chapter by completing the following crossword puzzle.

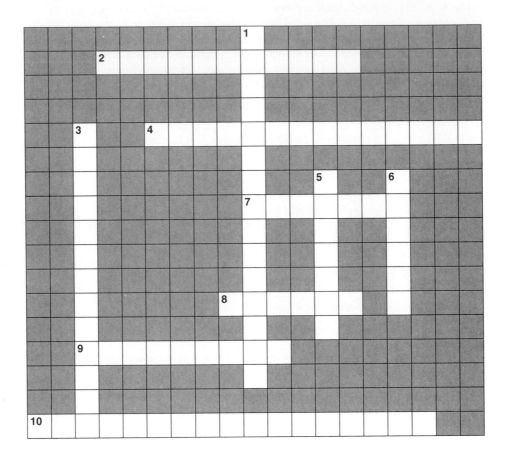

Across Clues

2. 2 words; an asset that is easily converted into other types of assets or used to buy services.
4. 2 words; checks that the bank has paid and deducted from the customer's account.
7. A vendor's statement that lists the customer, items sold, sales prices, and terms of sale.
8. The buyer or purchaser of goods or services.
9. Asset characteristic; refers to how quickly the asset can be used to pay for other assets.
10. 2 words; checks sent to payees but not yet returned to and paid by the bank.

Down Clues

1. 2 words; liquid investments that can be converted to a known amount of cash, usually within three months.
3. 2 words; an expense resulting from failing to take advantage of purchase discounts.
5. An internal document used to accumulate information and control cash disbursements.
6. The seller of goods or services.

ANSWERS TO PROGRESS CHECKS

7–1 A company needs to own liquid assets to be able to acquire other assets, buy services, and pay its obligations.

7–2 A company owns cash equivalents because they earn more income than does cash.

7–3 *d*

7–4 *c*

7–5 Computers reduce processing errors, allow more extensive testing of records, tend to limit the amount of hard evidence of processing steps that is available, and highlight the importance of maintaining a separation of duties.

7–6 *a*

7–7 Not necessarily. A voucher system should be used when the manager can no longer control the purchasing procedures through personal supervision and direct participation in the activities of the business.

7–8 If all cash payments were made by check, numerous checks for small amounts would be written. Because this practice would be expensive and often would take too long, a petty cash fund is established to avoid writing checks for small amounts.

7–9 If the petty cash fund is not reimbursed at the end of an accounting period, the transactions for which petty cash expenditures were made are unrecorded in the accounts and the asset petty cash is overstated. However, these amounts are seldom large enough to affect the financial statements.

7–10 When the petty cash fund is reimbursed, the petty cash transactions are recorded in the accounts. The reimbursement also allows the fund to continue being used for its intended purpose.

7–11 A bank statement is a report prepared by the bank that describes the activity in a depositor's account.

7–12 To reconcile a bank balance means to explain the difference between the cash balance in the depositor's accounting records and the balance on the bank statement.

7–13 The purpose of the bank reconciliation is to determine if any errors have been made by the bank or by the depositor and to determine if the bank has completed any transactions affecting the depositor's account that the depositor has not recorded.

7–14
Outstanding checks	subtracted
Unrecorded deposits	added

7–15
Bank service charges	subtracted
Debit memos	subtracted
NSF checks	subtracted
Interest earned	added
Credit memos	added

7–16 *a*

7–17 The calculation is based on net sales because the amount of credit sales normally is not known by statement readers.

Short-Term Investments and Receivables

*P*epsiCo, Inc., an internationally known manufacturer of soft drinks, reported having sales in 1994 of over $28.4 billion. In the information from the company's balance sheet that follows, note that PepsiCo's short-term investments and accounts and notes receivable represent 63% of the firm's total current assets (23% + 40%). Sound financial management of these assets is vital to ensure future liquidity and growth potential. Accounting for these highly liquid assets provides important information to help managers assess the risk and success of their decisions regarding these assets. Economic conditions causing many businesses and consumers to take longer to pay their bills and an increasing amount of defaults due to bankruptcies have made receivables management a top priority today.

PEPSICO, INC.
(in millions)
December 31, 1994

Current Assets		
Cash and cash equivalents	$ 330.7	7%
Short-term investments	1,157.4	23
Accounts and notes receivable, less $150.6 allowance	2,050.9	40
Inventories	970.0	19
Prepaid expenses, taxes and other current assets	563.2	11
Total current assets	$5,072.2	100%

LEARNING OBJECTIVES

After studying Chapter 8, you should be able to:

1. **Prepare journal entries to account for short-term investments and explain how fair (market) value gains and losses on such investments are reported.**
2. **Prepare entries to account for credit card sales.**
3. **Prepare entries to account for transactions with credit customers, including accounting for bad debts under the allowance method and the direct write-off method.**
4. **Calculate the interest on promissory notes and prepare entries to record the receipt of promissory notes and their payment or dishonor.**
5. **Explain how receivables can be converted into cash before they are due and calculate accounts receivable turnover.**
6. **Define or explain the words and phrases listed in the chapter glossary.**

The focus of the prior chapter was on accounting for cash, the most liquid of all assets. This chapter continues the discussion of liquid assets by focusing on short-term investments, accounts receivable, and short-term notes receivable. You will learn about current business trends relating to receivables and about new accounting regulations for short-term investments. You will then be better able to understand and use the financial statement information related to these current assets.

Because companies use cash to acquire assets and to pay expenses and obligations, good managers plan to maintain a cash balance large enough to meet expected payments plus some surplus for unexpected needs. Also, idle cash balances may exist during some months of each year because of seasonal fluctuations in sales volume. Rather than leave these idle cash balances in checking accounts that pay little or no interest, most companies invest them in securities that earn higher returns.

SHORT-TERM INVESTMENTS

LO 1
Prepare journal entries to account for short-term investments and explain how fair (market) value gains and losses on such investments are reported.

Recall from Chapter 7 that cash equivalents are investments that can be easily converted into a known amount of cash; generally, they mature no more than three months after purchase. Some investments of idle cash balances do not meet these criteria of cash equivalents but, nevertheless, are classified as current assets. Although these **short-term investments** or **temporary investments** do not qualify as cash equivalents, they serve a similar purpose. Like cash equivalents, short-term investments can be converted into cash easily and are an available source of cash to satisfy the needs of current operations. Management usually expects to convert them into cash within one year or the current operating cycle of the business, whichever is longer.[1]

Short-term investments may be made in the form of government or corporate debt

obligations (called *debt securities*) or in the form of stock (called *equity securities*). Some short-term investments in debt securities mature within one year or the current operating cycle of the business and will be held until they mature. Other securities that do not mature in the short term can be classified as current assets only if they are marketable. In other words, the reporting company must be able to sell them without excessive delays.

In the notes to their financial statements, companies usually give their definition of cash equivalents and short-term investments. **Texas Instruments, Incorporated,** for example, includes this note:

---

[1]FASB, *Accounting Standards—Current Text* (Norwalk, CT, 1995), sec. B05.105. First published as *Accounting Research Bulletin No. 43*, chap. 3A, par. 4.

Debt securities with original maturities within three months are considered cash equivalents. Debt securities with original maturities beyond three months have remaining maturities within 13 months and are considered short-term investments.

When short-term investments are purchased, they should be recorded at cost. For example, assume that on January 10 Alpha Company purchased Ford Motor Company's short-term notes payable for $40,000. Alpha's entry to record the transaction is

Jan.	10	Short-Term Investments	40,000.00	
		Cash		40,000.00
		Bought $40,000 of Ford Motor Company notes due May 10.		

Assume that these notes mature on May 10 and that the cash proceeds are $40,000 plus $1,200 interest. When the receipt is recorded, this entry credits the interest to a revenue account:

May	10	Cash	41,200.00	
		Short-Term Investments		40,000.00
		Interest Earned		1,200.00
		Received cash proceeds from matured notes.		

To determine the cost of an investment, you must include any commissions paid. For example, assume that on June 2, 19X1, Bailey Company purchased 1,000 shares of Xerox Corporation common stock as a short-term investment. The purchase price was 70⅛ ($70.125 per share) plus a $625 broker's commission. The entry to record the transaction is[2]

June	2	Short-Term Investments	70,750.00	
		Cash		70,750.00
		Bought 1,000 shares of Xerox stock at 70⅛ plus $625 broker's commission.		

Notice that the commission is not recorded in a separate account.

When cash dividends are received on stock held as a short-term investment, they are credited to a revenue account, as follows:

Dec.	12	Cash	1,000.00	
		Dividends Earned		1,000.00
		Received dividend of $1 per share on 1,000 shares of Xerox stock.		

Reporting Short-Term Investments in the Financial Statements

In past years, companies reported their short-term investments at the lower of cost or market value. The losses on reducing cost to market value were subtracted in the calculation of net income on the income statement. Recently, however, these reporting requirements have changed.

---

[2]Stock prices are quoted on stock exchanges on the basis of dollars and ⅛ dollars per share. For example, a stock quoted at 23⅛ sold for $23.125 per share and one quoted at 36½ sold for $36.50 per share.

In 1993, the FASB issued a new standard that requires companies to report most short-term investments at their fair (market) values.[3] The exact requirements of the standard vary, depending on whether the investments are classified as (1) investments in securities held to maturity, (2) investments in trading securities, or (3) investments in securities available for sale.

Short-Term Investments in Securities Held to Maturity

If a company has the positive intent and ability to hold investments in debt securities until they mature, the investments are classified as **investments in securities held to maturity.**[4] For example, in the summary of significant accounting policies in the notes to their 1994 financial statements, **International Dairy Queen, Inc.,** stated:

> Management determines the appropriate classification of debt securities at the time of purchase and reevaluates such designation as of each balance sheet date. Debt securities are classified as held-to-maturity because the Company has the positive intent and ability to hold such securities to maturity.

As we mentioned earlier, these investments cannot qualify as current assets unless their maturity dates fall within one year or the current operating cycle of the business. Short-term investments in debt securities (that will be) held until maturity are reported at cost.

Short-Term Investments in Trading Securities

Some short-term investments in securities are actively managed. In other words, frequent purchases and sales generally are made with the objective of generating profits on short-term changes in price. Most often, such investments are made by financial institutions such as banks or insurance companies. The FASB notes that these **investments in trading securities** are bought principally for the purpose of selling them in the near term.

According to *SFAS 115,* companies must report investments in trading securities at their fair (market) values. The related gains and losses of fair (market) value are reported on the income statement as part of net income or loss.

Short-Term Investments in Securities Available for Sale

Investments in securities available for sale include all securities investments that do not qualify as investments in trading securities or as investments in securities held to maturity. Securities available for sale are purchased to earn interest, dividends, and perhaps increases in market value. They are not actively managed like trading securities. Many industrial and commercial companies have short-term investments in securities available for sale.

As in the case of trading securities, *SFAS 115* requires companies to adjust the reported amount of securities available for sale to reflect all changes in fair value. Unlike trading securities, however, the fair value gains and losses on securities available for sale are not reported on the income statement. Instead, they are reported in the equity section of the balance sheet.

---

[3]FASB, "Accounting for Certain Investments in Debt and Equity Securities," *Statement of Financial Accounting Standards No. 115* (Norwalk, CT, 1995). The requirements of *SFAS 115* also apply to long-term investments in debt and marketable equity securities. You will learn more about this in Chapter 11.

[4]Ibid., par. 7.

For example, assume that Bailey Company did not have any short-term investments prior to its purchase of the Xerox stock on June 2, 19X1. Later during 19X1, Bailey purchased two other short-term investments. Assume that all three are classified as securities available for sale. On December 31, 19X1, the cost and fair values of these securities are:

Short Term Investments in Securities Available for Sale on December 31, 19X1	Costs	Fair (Market) Values
Sears, Roebuck & Co. common stock	$ 42,600	$ 43,500
Chrysler Corporation notes payable	30,500	30,200
Xerox Corporation common stock	70,750	78,250
Total	$143,850	$151,950

The difference between the $143,850 cost and the $151,950 fair (market) value amounts to a $8,100 gain in fair value. Because the amount of the gain has not yet been confirmed by the sale of the security, accountants describe this gain as an **unrealized holding gain.** The following entry records the gain:

Dec.	31	Short-Term Investments, Fair Value Adjustment	8,100.00	
		Unrealized Holding Gain (Loss)		8,100.00
		To reflect fair values of short-term investments in securities available for sale.		

After posting this entry, the cost and fair value adjustment of the short-term investments appear in the accounts as follows:

Short-term investments	$143,850
Short-term investments, fair value adjustment	8,100
Total	$151,950

Note that the cost of the investments is maintained in one account and the adjustment to fair values is recorded in a separate account. Keeping the Short-Term Investments account at cost facilitates calculating realized gains or losses that must be recorded when securities are sold.

Depending on whether the fair value adjustment account has a debit or credit balance, it is added to or subtracted from the cost to determine the fair value amount reported on the balance sheet. Bailey's December 31, 19X1, balance sheet includes the following:

Assets

Current assets:
Cash and cash equivalents	$ xx,xxx
Short-term investments	151,950
Accounts receivable	xxx,xxx

Stockholders' Equity

Common stock	$xxx,xxx
Retained earnings	xxx,xxx
Unrealized holding gain on securities held for sale	8,100
Total stockholders' equity	$xxx,xxx

Notice that the unrealized holding gain is reported as a separate item in the stockholders' equity section. It is not reported on the income statement and is not closed. If the fair value of the securities available for sale had been less than cost, the **unrealized holding loss** would have appeared in stockholders' equity as a deduction. When a short-term investment in securities available for sale is sold, the cash proceeds from the sale are compared with the cost of the investment to determine the *realized* gain or loss. This realized gain or loss is reported on the income statement and closed as part of the net income or loss.

For example, assume that on May 14, 19X2, Bailey sold its investment in Xerox common stock for $81,000. The entry to record the sale is

May	14	Cash	81,000.00	
		Short-Term Investments		70,750.00
		Gain on Sale of Short-Term Investments		10,250.00
		To record sale of Xerox common stock.		

Note that the realized gain is calculated by comparing the proceeds with cost, not with the previously reported fair value of the stock. Then, at the next balance sheet date, the unrealized gain or loss account is adjusted so the securities available for sale are reported at their new fair values.

For example, assume that Bailey did not buy or sell any other securities during 19X2. As a result, the securities available for sale on December 31, 19X2, include the Sears common stock and the Chrysler notes payable. The costs and December 31, 19X2, fair values of these securities are as follows:

Short-Term Investments in Securities Available for Sale on December 31, 19X2	Costs	Fair (Market) Values
Sears common stock	$42,600	$41,200
Chrysler notes payable	30,500	29,900
Total	$73,100	$71,100

Recall the December 31, 19X1, entry that recorded the $8,100 excess of fair values over costs. That entry gave the Short-Term Investments, Fair Value Adjustment account a debit balance of $8,100 and gave the Unrealized Holding Gain (Loss) account a credit balance of $8,100. On December 31, 19X2, these account balances must be revised to show that the $73,100 costs exceed the $71,100 fair values by $2,000. The required adjustments are calculated as follows:

	Short-Term Investments, Fair Value Adjustment	Unrealized Holding Gain (Loss)
Existing balances	$ 8,100 Debit	$ 8,100 Credit
Required balances, December 31, 19X2	2,000 Credit	2,000 Debit
Necessary adjustment	$10,100 Credit	$10,100 Debit

The following adjusting entry updates the account balances:

Dec.	31	Unrealized Holding Gain (Loss)	10,100.00	
		Short-Term Investments, Fair Value Adjustment		10,100.00
		To reflect fair values of short-term investments		
		in securities held for sale.		

Progress Check

(Answers to Progress Checks are provided at the end of the chapter.)

8–1   How are securities held to maturity reported on the balance sheet—at cost or fair (market) values? How are investments in trading securities reported?

8–2   On what statement are unrealized holding gains and losses on investments in securities available for sale reported?

8–3   Where are unrealized holding gains and losses on investments in trading securities reported?

In addition to cash, cash equivalents, and short-term investments, the liquid assets of a business include receivables that result from credit sales to customers. In the following sections, we discuss the procedures to account for sales when customers use credit cards issued by banks or credit card companies. Then, we focus on accounting for credit sales when a business grants credit directly to its customers. This situation requires the company (1) to maintain a separate account receivable for each customer and (2) to account for bad debts that result from credit sales. In addition, we discuss how to account for notes receivable, many of which arise from extending credit to customers.

CREDIT SALES AND RECEIVABLES

Many customers use credit cards such as Visa, MasterCard, or American Express to charge purchases from various businesses. This practice gives the customers the ability to make purchases without carrying cash or writing checks. It also allows them to defer their payments to the credit card company. Further, once credit is established with the credit card company, the customer does not have to open an account with each store. Finally, customers who use credit cards can make single monthly payments instead of several to different creditors.

There are good reasons why businesses allow customers to use credit cards instead of maintaining their own accounts receivable. First, the business does not have to evaluate the credit standing of each customer or make decisions about who should get credit and how much. Second, the business avoids the risk of extending credit to customers who cannot or do not pay. Instead, this risk is faced by the credit card company. Third, the business typically receives cash from the credit card company sooner than it would if it granted credit directly to its customers. Fourth, a variety of credit

CREDIT CARD SALES

LO 2
Prepare entries to account for credit card sales.

options for customers offers a potential increase in sales volume. **Sears, Roebuck & Co.,** one of the nation's largest credit providers among retailers, historically offered credit only to customers using a SearsCharge card. As the 1994 annual report notes in the following management discussion, this policy changed in 1993:

Through an aggressive in-store acquisition program, Sears opened 5.7 million new SearsCharge accounts in 1994, surpassing the previous record established in 1993. SearsCharge increased its share of Sears retail sales even as the company expanded the payment options available to its customers with the acceptance in 1993 of VISA, MasterCard, and American Express in addition to the Discover Card.

In dealing with some credit cards, usually those issued by banks, the business deposits a copy of each credit card sales receipt in its bank account just like it deposits a customer's check. Thus, the business receives a credit to its checking account without delay. Other credit cards require the business to send a copy of each receipt to the credit card company. Until payment is received, the business has an account receivable from the credit card company. In return for the services provided by the credit card company, a business pays a fee ranging from 2% to 5% of credit card sales. This charge is deducted from the credit to the checking account or the cash payment to the business.

The procedures used in accounting for credit card sales depend on whether cash is received immediately on deposit or is delayed until paid by the credit card company. If cash is received immediately, the entry to record $100 of credit card sales with a 4% fee is:

Jan.	25	Cash	96.00	
		Credit Card Expense	4.00	
		Sales		100.00
		To record credit card sales less a 4% credit card expense.		

If the business must send the receipts to the credit card company and wait for payment, this entry on the date of the sales records them:

Jan.	25	Accounts Receivable, Credit Card Company	100.00	
		Sales		100.00
		To record credit card sales.		

When cash is received from the credit card company, the entry to record the receipt and the deduction of the fee is:

Feb.	10	Cash	96.00	
		Credit Card Expense	4.00	
		Accounts Receivable—Credit Card Co.		100.00
		To record cash receipt less 4% credit card expense.		

In the last two entries, notice that the credit card expense was not recorded until cash was received from the credit card company. This practice is merely a matter of convenience. By following this procedure, the business avoids having to calculate and record the credit card expense each time sales are recorded. Instead, the expense related to many sales can be calculated once and recorded when cash is received. However, the *matching principle* requires reporting credit card expense in the same period as the sale. Therefore, if the sale and the cash receipt occur in different periods, the accountant must accrue and report the credit card expense in the period of the sale by using an adjusting entry at the end of the year. For example, this year-end adjustment accrues $24 of credit card expense on a $600 receivable that the credit card company has not yet paid:

Dec.	31	Credit Card Expense	24.00	
		Accounts Receivable—Credit Card Company		24.00
		To accrue credit card expense that is unrecorded at the end of the year.		

The following entry records the cash collection in January:

Jan.	5	Cash	576.00	
		Accounts Receivable—Credit Card Company		576.00
		To record collection of the amount due from Credit Card Company.		

Some firms report credit card expense in the income statement as a type of discount that is deducted from sales to get net sales. Other companies classify it as a selling expense or even as an administrative expense. Arguments can be made for all three alternatives but there is little practical difference in the result.

Progress Check

8–4 In recording credit card sales, when do you debit Accounts Receivable and when do you debit Cash?

8–5 When are credit card expenses recorded in situations where sales receipts must be accumulated before they can be sent to the credit card company? When are these expenses incurred?

8–6 If payment for a credit card sale has not been received by the end of the accounting period, how do you account for the credit card expense associated with that sale?

PRINCIPLE APPLICATION
Matching Principle, p. 111
In 1994, J. C. Penney Company had retail sales of $20,380 million. In addition to bad debt expenses, the credit costs the company matched with these revenues included operating expenses and third-party credit costs of $270 million.

MAINTAINING A SEPARATE ACCOUNT FOR EACH CREDIT CUSTOMER

LO 3
Prepare entries to account for transactions with credit customers, including accounting for bad debts under the allowance method and the direct write-off method.

In previous chapters, we recorded credit sales by debiting a single Accounts Receivable account. However, a business with more than one credit customer must design its accounting system to show how much each customer has purchased, how much each customer has paid, and how much each customer still owes. This information provides the basis for sending bills to the customers. To have this information on hand, businesses that extend credit directly to their customers must maintain a separate account receivable for each of them.

One possible way of keeping a separate account for each customer would be to include all of these accounts in the same ledger that contains the financial statement accounts. However, this approach is usually not used because there are too many customers. Instead, the **General Ledger,** which is the ledger that contains the financial statement accounts, has only a single Accounts Receivable account. In addition, a supplementary record is established in which a separate account is maintained for each customer. This supplementary record is the **Accounts Receivable Ledger.**

Illustration 8-1 The Accounts Receivable Account and the Accounts Receivable Ledger

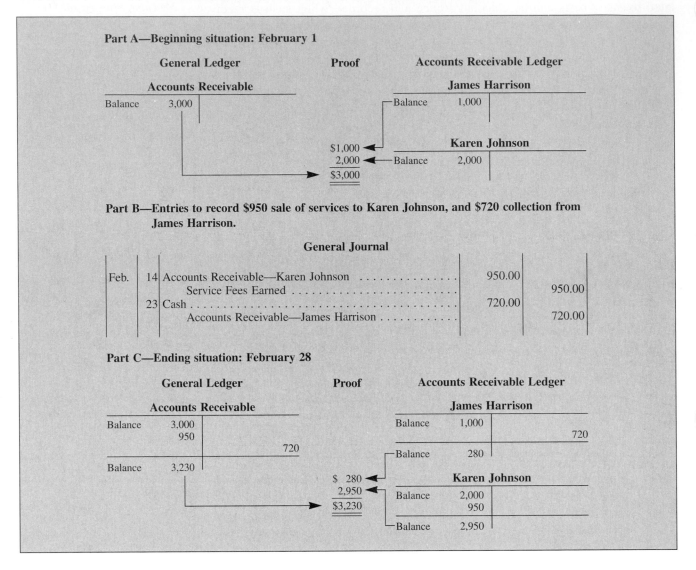

Illustration 8–1 shows the relationship between the Accounts Receivable account in the General Ledger and the individual customer accounts in the Accounts Receivable Ledger. In Part A of Illustration 8–1, notice that the $3,000 sum of the two balances in the Accounts Receivable Ledger is equal to the balance of the Accounts Receivable account in the General Ledger as of February 1. To maintain this relationship, each time that credit sales are posted with a debit to the Accounts Receivable account in the General Ledger, they are also posted with debits to the appropriate customer accounts in the Accounts Receivable Ledger. Also, cash receipts from credit customers must be posted with credits to both the Accounts Receivable account in the General Ledger and to the appropriate customer accounts.

Part B shows the general journal entry to record a credit sale of services on February 14 to customer Karen Johnson. It also shows the entry to record the collection of $720 from James Harrison.

Part C presents the general ledger account and the Accounts Receivable Ledger as of February 28. Notice how the General Ledger account shows the effects of the sale and the collection and the resulting balance of $3,230. The same events are reflected in the accounts for the two customers: Harrison now has a balance of only $280, and

Johnson owes $2,950. The $3,230 sum of their accounts equals the debit balance of the General Ledger account.

Note that posting debits or credits to Accounts Receivable twice does not violate the requirement that debits equal credits. The equality of debits and credits is maintained *in the General Ledger.* The Accounts Receivable Ledger is simply a supplementary record that provides detailed information concerning each customer.

Because the balance in the Accounts Receivable account is always equal to the sum of the balances in the customers' accounts, the Accounts Receivable account is said to control the Accounts Receivable Ledger and is an example of a **controlling account.** And, the Accounts Receivable Ledger is an example of a supplementary record that is controlled by an account in the General Ledger; this kind of supplementary record is called a **subsidiary ledger.**

The Accounts Receivable account and the Accounts Receivable Ledger are not the only examples of controlling accounts and subsidiary ledgers. Most companies buy on credit from several suppliers and must use a controlling account and subsidiary ledger for accounts payable. Another example might be an Office Equipment account that would control a subsidiary ledger in which the cost of each item of equipment is recorded in a separate account.

BAD DEBTS

When a company grants credit to its customers, there usually are a few who do not pay what they promised. The accounts of such customers are called **bad debts.** These bad debt amounts that cannot be collected are an expense of selling on credit.

You might ask why merchants sell on credit if it is likely that some of the accounts prove to be uncollectible. The answer is that they believe granting credit will increase revenues and profits. They are willing to incur bad debt losses if the net effect is to increase sales and profits. Therefore, bad debt losses are an expense of selling on credit that is incurred to increase sales.

The reporting of bad debts expense on the income statement is governed by the *matching principle.* This principle requires that the expenses from bad debts be reported in the same accounting period as the revenues they helped produce.

PRINCIPLE APPLICATION
Matching Principle, p. 111
In a note to their 1995 financial statements, Pier 1 Imports explained that bad debts expense for the period is netted against revenues generated by credit sales (finance charges) and charged as a selling, general, and administrative expense.

Managers realize that some portion of credit sales result in bad debts. However, the fact that a specific credit sale will not be collected does not become apparent until later. If a customer fails to pay within the credit period, most businesses send out several repeat billings and make other efforts to collect. Usually, they do not accept the fact that the customer is not going to pay until every reasonable means of collection has been exhausted. In many cases, this point may not be reached until one or more accounting periods after the period in which the sale was made. Thus, matching this expense with the revenue it produced requires the company to estimate its unknown amount at the end of the year. The **allowance method of accounting for bad debts** accomplishes this matching of bad debts expense with revenues.

MATCHING BAD DEBT EXPENSES WITH SALES

ALLOWANCE METHOD OF ACCOUNTING FOR BAD DEBTS

At the end of each accounting period, the allowance method of accounting for bad debts requires estimating the total bad debts expected to result from the period's sales. An allowance is then provided for the loss. This method has two advantages: (1) the expense is charged to the period in which the revenue is recognized; and (2) the accounts receivable are reported on the balance sheet at the estimated amount of cash to be collected.

Recording the Estimated Bad Debts Expense

Under the allowance method of accounting for bad debts, bad debts expense is estimated at the end of each accounting period and recorded with an adjusting entry. For example, assume that Fritz Company had credit sales of $300,000 during the first year of its operations. At the end of the year, $20,000 remains uncollected. Based on the experience of similar businesses, Fritz Company estimates that $1,500 of accounts receivable will be uncollectible. This estimated expense is recorded with the following adjusting entry:

Dec.	31	Bad Debts Expense	1,500.00	
		Allowance for Doubtful Accounts		1,500.00
		To record the estimated bad debts.		

The debit in this entry causes the expense to appear on the income statement of the year in which the sales were made. As a result, the estimated $1,500 expense of selling on credit is matched with the $300,000 revenue it helped produce.

Note that the credit of the entry is to a contra account called **Allowance for Doubtful Accounts.** A contra account must be used because at the time of the adjusting entry, the accountant does not know which customers will not pay. Therefore, because specific bad accounts are not identifiable at the time of the adjusting entry, they cannot be removed from the subsidiary Accounts Receivable Ledger. Because the customer accounts are left in the subsidiary ledger, the controlling account for Accounts Receivable cannot be reduced. Instead, the Allowance for Doubtful Accounts account *must* be credited.

Bad Debts in the Accounts and in the Financial Statements

The process of evaluating customers and approving them for credit usually is not assigned to the selling department of a business. Otherwise, given the primary objective of increasing sales, the selling department might not use good judgment in approving customers for credit. Because the sales department is not responsible for granting credit, it should not be held responsible for bad debts expense. Therefore, bad debts expense often appears on the income statement as an administrative expense rather than a selling expense.

Recall from the previous example that Fritz Company has $20,000 of outstanding accounts receivable at the end of its first year of operations. Thus, after the bad debts adjusting entry is posted, the company's Accounts Receivable and Allowance for Doubtful Accounts show these balances:

Accounts Receivable		Allowance for Doubtful Accounts	
Dec. 31 20,000		Dec. 31 1,500	

The Allowance for Doubtful Accounts credit balance of $1,500 has the effect of reducing accounts receivable (net of the allowance) to their estimated **realizable value.** The term *realizable value* means the expected proceeds from converting the assets into cash. Although $20,000 is legally owed to Fritz Company by all of its customers, only $18,500 is likely to be realized in cash collections from customers.

When the balance sheet is prepared, the allowance for doubtful accounts is subtracted from the accounts receivable to show the amount expected to be realized from the accounts. For example, this information could be reported as follows:

Current assets:		
Cash and cash equivalents		$11,300
Short-term investments, at fair		
market value (cost is $16,200)		14,500
Accounts receivable	$20,000	
Less allowance for doubtful accounts	(1,500)	18,500
Merchandise inventory		52,700
Prepaid expenses		1,100
Total current assets		$98,100

In this example, compare the presentations of short-term investments and accounts receivable, and note that contra accounts are subtracted in both cases. Even though the contra account to the Short-Term Investments account is not shown on the statement, you can easily determine that its balance is $1,700 by comparing the $16,200 cost with the $14,500 net amount. Sometimes, the contra account to Accounts Receivable is presented in a similar fashion, as follows:

Accounts receivable (net of $1,500 estimated	
uncollectible accounts)	$18,500

Writing Off a Bad Debt

When specific accounts are identified as uncollectible, they are written off against the Allowance for Doubtful Accounts. For example, after spending a year trying to collect from Jack Vale, the Fritz Company finally decided that his $100 account was uncollectible and made the following entry to write it off:

Jan.	23	Allowance for Doubtful Accounts	100.00	
		Accounts Receivable—Jack Vale		100.00
		To write off an uncollectible account.		

Posting the credit of the entry to the Accounts Receivable account removes the amount of the bad debt from the controlling account. Posting it to the Jack Vale account removes the amount of the bad debt from the subsidiary ledger. By removing it from the subsidiary ledger, Fritz Company avoids the cost of sending additional bills to Vale. After the entry is posted, the general ledger accounts appear as follows:

Accounts Receivable				Allowance for Doubtful Accounts		
Dec. 31	20,000				Dec. 31	1,500
		Jan. 23	100	Jan. 23	100	

Notice two aspects of the entry and the accounts. First, although bad debts are an expense of selling on credit, the allowance account is debited in the write-off. The expense account is not debited. The expense account is not debited because the estimated expense was previously recorded at the end of the period in which the sale occurred. At that time, the expense was estimated and recorded with an adjusting entry.

Second, although the write-off removed the amount of the account receivable from the ledgers, it did not affect the estimated realizable value of Fritz Company's net accounts receivable, as the following tabulation shows:

	Before	After
Accounts receivable	$20,000	$19,900
Less allowance for doubtful accounts	1,500	1,400
Estimated realizable accounts receivable	$18,500	$18,500

Thus, neither total assets nor net income are affected by the decision to write off a specific account. However, both total assets and net income are affected by the recognition of the year's bad debts expense in the adjusting entry. Again, a primary purpose of writing off a specific account is to avoid the cost of additional collection efforts.

Bad Debt Recoveries

When a customer fails to pay and the account is written off, his or her credit standing is jeopardized. Therefore, the customer may choose to voluntarily pay all or part of the amount owed after the account is written off as uncollectible. This payment helps restore the credit standing. Thus, when this event happens, it should be recorded in the customer's subsidiary account where the information will be retained for use in future credit evaluations.

When a company collects an account that was previously written off, it makes two journal entries. The first reverses the original write-off and reinstates the customer's account. The second entry records the collection of the reinstated account. For example, assume that on August 15 Jack Vale pays in full the account that Fritz Company had previously written off. The entries to record the bad debt recovery are:

Aug.	15	Accounts Receivable—Jack Vale	100.00	
		Allowance for Doubtful Accounts		100.00
		To reinstate the account of Jack Vale written off on January 23.		
	15	Cash	100.00	
		Accounts Receivable—Jack Vale		100.00
		Received full payment of account.		

In this case, Jack Vale paid the entire amount previously written off. In other situations, the customer may pay only a portion of the amount owed. The question then arises of whether the entire balance of the account should be returned to accounts receivable or just the amount paid. The answer is a matter of judgment. If you believe the customer will later pay in full, the entire amount owed should be returned. However, only the amount paid should be returned if you believe that no more will be collected.

Progress Check

8-7 In meeting the requirements of the matching principle, why must bad debts expenses be estimated?

8-8 What term describes the balance sheet valuation of accounts receivable less the allowance for doubtful accounts?

8-9 Why is estimated bad debts expense credited to a contra account rather than to the Accounts Receivable controlling account?

As you already learned, the allowance method of accounting for bad debts requires an adjusting entry at the end of each accounting period to record management's estimate of the bad debts expense for the period. That entry takes the following form:

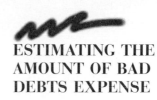

ESTIMATING THE AMOUNT OF BAD DEBTS EXPENSE

Dec.	31	Bad Debts Expense	????	
		Allowance for Doubtful Accounts		????
		To record the estimated bad debts.		

How does a business determine the amount to record in this entry? There are two alternative approaches. One focuses on the income statement relationship between bad debts expense and sales. The other focuses on the balance sheet relationship between accounts receivable and allowance for doubtful accounts. Both alternatives require a careful analysis of past experience.

Estimating Bad Debts by Focusing on the Income Statement

The income statement approach to estimating bad debts is based on the idea that some particular percentage of a company's credit sales for the period will become uncollectible.[5] Hence, in the income statement, the amount of bad debts expense should equal that amount.

For example, suppose that Baker Company had credit sales of $400,000 in 19X2. Based on past experience and the experience of similar companies, Baker Company estimates that 0.6% of credit sales will be uncollectible. Using this prediction, Baker Company can expect $2,400 of bad debts expense to result from the year's sales ($400,000 × 0.006 = $2,400). The adjusting entry to record this estimated expense is:

Dec.	31	Bad Debts Expense	2,400.00	
		Allowance for Doubtful Accounts		2,400.00
		To record the estimated bad debts.		

This entry does not mean the December 31, 19X2, balance in Allowance for Doubtful Accounts will be $2,400. A $2,400 balance would occur only if the account had a zero balance immediately prior to posting the adjusting entry. For several reasons, however, the unadjusted balance of Allowance for Doubtful Accounts is not likely to be zero.

First, unless Baker Company was created during the current year, the Allowance for Doubtful Accounts would have had a credit balance at the beginning of the year. The beginning-of-year credit balance would have resulted from entries made in past years to record estimated bad debts expense and to write off uncollectible accounts. The cumulative effect of these entries would show up as a credit balance at the beginning of the current year.

Second, because bad debts expense must be estimated each year, the total amount of expense recorded in past years is not likely to equal the amounts that were written off as uncollectible. Although annual expense estimates are based on past experience, some residual difference between recorded expenses and amounts written off should be expected to show up in the unadjusted Allowance for Doubtful Accounts balance.

---

[5]Note that the factor to be considered is *credit* sales. Naturally, cash sales do not produce bad debts, and they generally should not be used in the calculation. However, if cash sales are relatively small compared to credit sales, there is no practical difference in the result.

Third, some of the amounts written off as uncollectible during the current year probably relate to credit sales made during the current year. These debits affect the unadjusted Allowance for Doubtful Accounts balance. In fact, they may cause the account to have a debit balance prior to posting the adjusting entry for bad debts expense.

For these reasons, you should not expect the Allowance for Doubtful Accounts to have an unadjusted balance of zero at the end of the year. As we stated earlier, this means that the adjusted balance reported on the balance sheet normally does not equal the amount of expense reported on the income statement.

Remember that expressing bad debts expense as a percentage of sales is an estimate based on past experience. As new experience is gained over time, the percentage used may appear to have been too large or too small. When this happens, a different rate should be used in future periods.

Estimating Bad Debts by Focusing on the Balance Sheet

The balance sheet approach to estimating bad debts is based on the idea that some portion of the end-of-period accounts receivable balance will not be collected. From this point of view, the goal of the bad debts adjusting entry is to make the Allowance for Doubtful Accounts balance equal to the portion of outstanding accounts receivable estimated to be uncollectible. To obtain this required balance in the Allowance for Doubtful Accounts account, simply compare its balance before the adjustment with the required balance. The difference between the two is debited to Bad Debts Expense and credited to Allowance for Doubtful Accounts. Estimating the required balance of the allowance account can be done in two ways: (1) by using the simplified approach and (2) by aging the accounts receivable.

The Simplified Balance Sheet Approach. Using the simplified balance sheet approach, a company estimates that a certain percentage of its outstanding receivables will prove to be uncollectible. This estimated percentage is based on past experience and the experience of similar companies. It also may be affected by current conditions such as recent prosperity or economic difficulties faced by the firm's customers. Then, the total dollar amount of all outstanding receivables is multiplied by the estimated percentage to determine the estimated dollar amount of uncollectible accounts. This amount must appear in the balance sheet as the balance of the Allowance for Doubtful Accounts. To put this balance in the account, you must prepare an adjusting entry that debits Bad Debts Expense and credits Allowance for Doubtful Accounts. The amount of the adjustment is the amount necessary to provide the required balance in Allowance for Doubtful Accounts.

For example, assume that Baker Company (of the previous illustration) has $50,000 of outstanding accounts receivable on December 31, 19X2. Past experience suggests that 5% of the outstanding receivables are uncollectible. Thus, after the adjusting entry is posted, the Allowance for Doubtful Accounts should have a $2,500 credit balance (5% of $50,000). Assume that before the adjustment the account appears as follows:

Allowance for Doubtful Accounts

		Dec. 31, 19X1, balance	2,000
Feb. 6	800		
July 10	600		
Nov. 20	400		
		Unadjusted balance	200

The $2,000 beginning balance appeared on the December 31, 19X1, balance sheet. During 19X2, accounts of specific customers were written off on February 6, July 10, and November 20. As a result, the account has a $200 credit balance prior to the

December 31, 19X2, adjustment. The adjusting entry to give the allowance the required $2,500 balance is:

Dec.	31	Bad Debts Expense	2,300.00	
		Allowance for Doubtful Accounts		2,300.00
		To record the estimated bad debts.		

After this entry is posted, the allowance has a $2,500 credit balance, as shown here:

Allowance for Doubtful Accounts

			Dec. 31, 19X1, balance	2,000
Feb. 6	800			
July 10	600			
Nov. 20	400			
			Unadjusted balance	200
			Dec. 31	2,300
			Dec. 31, 19X2, balance	2,500

Aging Accounts Receivable. Both the income statement approach and the simplified balance sheet approach use knowledge gained from *past* experience to estimate the amount of bad debts expense. Another balance sheet approach produces a more refined estimate based on past experience and on information about current conditions.

This method involves **aging of accounts receivable.** Under this method, each account receivable is examined in the process of estimating the amount that is uncollectible. Specifically, the receivables are classified by how long they have been outstanding. Then, estimates of uncollectible amounts are made under the assumption that the longer an amount is outstanding, the more likely it will be uncollectible.

To age the accounts receivable outstanding at the end of the period, you must examine each account and classify the outstanding amounts by how much time has passed since they were created. The selection of the classes to be used depends on the judgment of each company's management. However, the classes are often based on 30-day (or one month) periods. After the outstanding amounts have been classified (or aged), past experience is used to estimate a percentage of each class that will become uncollectible. These percentages are applied to the amounts in the classes to determine the required balance of the Allowance for Doubtful Accounts. The calculation is completed by setting up a schedule like the one in Illustration 8–2 for Baker Company.

In Illustration 8–2, notice that each customer's account is listed with its total balance. Then, each balance is allocated to five categories based on the age of the unpaid charges that make up the balance. (In computerized systems, this allocation is done automatically.) When all accounts have been aged, the amounts in each category are totaled and multiplied by the estimated percentage of uncollectible accounts for each category. The reasonableness of the percentages used must be reviewed regularly and frequently reflect reactions to the state of the economy. The following excerpt from the management discussion in the 1994 annual report of **Sears, Roebuck & Co.** illustrates this point:

> The provision for uncollectible accounts was 18.2% lower than 1993 due to favorable customer receivable write-off trends. Despite the improvement in write-offs, delinquencies trended upward in the fourth quarter of 1994 and the Group re-

Illustration 8-2 Estimating Bad Debts by Aging the Accounts

BAKER COMPANY
Schedule of Accounts Receivable by Age
December 31, 19X2

Customer's Name	Total	Not Due	1 to 30 Days Past Due	31 to 60 Days Past Due	61 to 90 Days Past Due	Over 90 Days Past Due
Charles Abbot	$ 450.00	$ 450.00				
Frank Allen	710.00			$ 710.00		
George Arden	500.00	300.00	$ 200.00			
Paul Baum	740.00				$ 100.00	$ 640.00
ZZ Services	1,000.00	810.00	190.00			
Totals	$49,900.00	$37,000.00	$6,500.00	$3,500.00	$1,900.00	$1,000.00
Rate		× 2%	× 5%	× 10%	× 25%	× 40%
Estimated uncollectible accounts . . .	$ 2,290.00	$ 740.00	$ 325.00	$ 350.00	$ 475.00	$ 400.00

sponded by increasing its collection staff and implementing additional collection strategies. In 1993, the provision for uncollectible accounts declined 8.9% primarily due to a decline in customer bankruptcies.

For example, in Illustration 8–2, Baker Company is owed $3,500 that is 31 to 60 days past due. Baker's management estimates that 10% of the amounts in this age category will not be collected. Thus, the dollar amount of uncollectible accounts in this category is $350 ($3,500 × 10%). The total in the first column tells us that the adjusted balance in Baker Company's Allowance for Doubtful Accounts should be $2,290 ($740 + $325 + $350 + $475 + $400). Because the allowance has an unadjusted credit balance of $200, the aging of accounts receivable approach requires the following change in its balance:

Unadjusted balance	$ 200 credit
Required balance	2,290 credit
Required adjustment	$2,090 credit

As a result, Baker should record the following adjusting entry:

Dec.	31	Bad Debts Expense	2,090.00	
		Allowance for Doubtful Accounts		2,090.00
		To record the estimated bad debts.		

For instructional purposes, suppose that Baker's allowance had an unadjusted *debit* balance of $500. In this case, the calculation of the adjustment amount and the entry would be:

Unadjusted balance	$ 500 debit
Required balance	2,290 credit
Required adjustment	$2,790 credit

Dec.	31	Bad Debts Expense	2,790.00	
		Allowance for Doubtful Accounts		2,790.00
		To record the estimated bad debts.		

Recall from page 283 that when the income statement approach was used, Baker's bad debts expense for 19X2 was estimated to be $2,400. When the simplified balance sheet approach was used (see page 284), the estimate was $2,300. And when aging of accounts receivable was used the first time, the estimate was $2,090. Do not be surprised that the amounts are different; after all, each approach is only an estimate of what will prove to be true. However, the aging of accounts receivable is based on a more detailed examination of specific outstanding accounts and is usually the most reliable.[6]

DIRECT WRITE-OFF METHOD OF ACCOUNTING FOR BAD DEBTS

The allowance method of accounting for bad debts satisfies the requirements of the *matching principle.* Therefore, it is the method that should be used in most cases. However, another method may be suitable under certain limited circumstances. Under this **direct write-off method of accounting for bad debts,** no attempt is made to estimate uncollectible accounts or bad debts expense at the end of each period. In fact, no adjusting entry is made. Instead, bad debts expense is recorded when specific accounts are written off as uncollectible. For example, note the following entry to write off a $52 uncollectible account:

Nov.	23	Bad Debts Expense	52.00	
		Accounts Receivable—Dale Hall		52.00
		To write off the uncollectible account		
		under the direct write-off method.		

The debit of the entry charges the uncollectible amount directly to the current year's Bad Debts Expense account. The credit removes the balance of the account from the subsidiary ledger and from the controlling account.

If an account previously written off directly to Bad Debts Expense is later collected in full, the following entries record the recovery:

Mar.	11	Accounts Receivable—Dale Hall	52.00	
		Bad Debts Expense		52.00
		To reinstate the account of Dale Hall		
		previously written off.		
	11	Cash	52.00	
		Accounts Receivable—Dale Hall		52.00
		In full payment of account.		

Sometimes an amount previously written off directly to Bad Debts Expense is recovered in the year following the write-off. If there is no balance in the Bad Debts Expense account from previous write-offs and no other write-offs are expected, the credit portion of the entry recording the recovery can be made to a Bad Debt Recoveries revenue account.

---

[6]In many cases, the aging analysis is supplemented with information about specific customers that allows management to decide whether those accounts should be classified as uncollectible. This information often is supplied by the sales and credit department managers.

The direct write-off method usually mismatches revenues and expenses. The mismatch occurs because bad debts expense is not recorded until an account becomes uncollectible, which often does not occur during the same period as the credit sale. Despite this weakness, the direct write-off method may be used when a company's bad debts expenses are very small in relation to other financial statement items such as total sales and net income. In such cases, the direct write-off method is justified by the *materiality principle,* which we explain next.

THE MATERIALITY PRINCIPLE

The basic idea of the **materiality principle** is that the requirements of accounting principles may be ignored if the effect on the financial statements is unimportant to their users. In other words, failure to follow the requirements of an accounting principle is acceptable when the failure does not produce an error or misstatement large enough to influence a financial statement reader's judgment of a given situation.

INSTALLMENT ACCOUNTS AND NOTES RECEIVABLE

Many companies allow their credit customers to make periodic payments over several months. When this is done, the selling company's assets may be in the form of **installment accounts receivable** or notes receivable. As is true for other accounts receivable, the evidence behind installment accounts receivable includes sales slips or invoices that describe the sales transactions. A note receivable, on the other hand, is a written document that promises payment and is signed by the customer. In either case, when payments are made over several months or if the credit period is long, the customer is usually charged interest. Although installment accounts and notes receivable may have credit periods of more than one year, they should be classified as current assets if the company regularly offers customers such terms.

Generally, creditors prefer notes receivable over accounts receivable when the credit period is long and the receivable relates to a single sale for a fairly large amount. Notes also can replace accounts receivable when customers ask for additional time to pay their past-due accounts. In these situations, creditors prefer notes to accounts receivable for legal reasons. If a lawsuit is needed to collect from a customer, a note represents a clear written acknowledgment by the debtor of the debt, its amount, and its terms.

Progress Check

D & C Boutiques International estimated that based on an aging of accounts receivable, $6,142 would be uncollectible. The year-end 12/31/X1 balance of the allowance account is a credit of $440.

8-10   Prepare the year-end adjusting entry.

8-11   Using the following information, prepare the appropriate journal entries.
   January 10, 19X2:   The $300 account of customer Felix Arthur was determined uncollectible.
   April 12, 19X2:   Felix Arthur paid the account that was determined uncollectible on January 10, 19X2.

PROMISSORY NOTES

LO 4
Calculate the interest on promissory notes and prepare entries to record the receipt of promissory notes and their payment or dishonor.

A **promissory note** is an unconditional written promise to pay a definite sum of money on demand or at a fixed or determinable future date. In the promissory note shown in Illustration 8–3, Hugo Brown promises to pay Frank Tomlinson or to his order (that is, according to Tomlinson's instructions) a definite sum of money ($1,000), called the **principal of the note** at a fixed future date (April 8, 19X1). As the one who signed the note and promised to pay it at maturity, Hugo Brown is the **maker**

Illustration 8–3
A Promissory Note

$1,000.00	Eugene, Oregon	March 9, 19X1

Thirty days _____ after date _____ I _____ promise to pay to

the order of _____ Frank Tomlinson _____

One thousand and no / 100 - dollars

for value received with interest at _____ 12% _____

payable at _____ First National Bank of Eugene, Oregon _____

_____ Hugo Brown _____

of the note. As the person to whom the note is payable, Frank Tomlinson is the **payee of the note.** To Hugo Brown, the illustrated note is a liability called a *note payable.* To Frank Tomlinson, the same note is an asset called a *note receivable.*

The Hugo Brown note bears **interest** at 12%. Interest is the charge assessed for the use of money. To a borrower, interest is an expense. To a lender, it is a revenue. The rate of interest that a note bears is stated on the note.

Calculating Interest

Unless otherwise stated, the rate of interest on a note is the rate charged for the use of the principal for one year. The formula for calculating interest is:

$$\begin{array}{c}\text{Principal} \\ \text{of the} \\ \text{note}\end{array} \times \begin{array}{c}\text{Annual} \\ \text{rate of} \\ \text{interest}\end{array} \times \begin{array}{c}\text{Time of the} \\ \text{note expressed} \\ \text{in years}\end{array} = \text{Interest}$$

For example, interest on a $1,000, 12%, six-month note is calculated as:

$$\$1,000 \times 12\% \times \frac{6}{12} = \$60$$

The **maturity date of a note** is the day on which the note (principal and interest) must be repaid. Many notes mature in less than a full year, and the period covered by them is often expressed in days. When the time of a note is expressed in days, the maturity date is the specified number of days after the note's date. As a simple example, a one-day note dated June 15 matures and is due on June 16. Also, a 90-day note dated July 10 matures on October 8. This October 8 due date is calculated as follows:

Number of days in July	31
Minus the date of the note	10
Gives the number of days the note runs in July	21
Add the number of days in August	31
Add the number of days in September	30
Total through September 30	82
Days in October needed to equal the 90-day time of the	
note, also the maturity date of the note (October 8)	8
Total time the note runs in days	90

In other situations, the period of a note is expressed in months. In these cases, the note matures and is payable in the month of its maturity on the same day of the month as its original date. For example, a three-month note dated July 10 is payable on October 10.

To simplify interest calculations for notes that have periods expressed in days, a common practice has been to treat a year as having just 360 days. Although this practice is not applied as frequently as it used to be, we use it in this book to make it easier for you to work the exercises and problems assigned by your instructor. We also assume a 360-day year in the following discussion. Suppose, for example, that there is a 90-day, 12%, $1,000 note. The amount of interest is calculated as follows:

$$\text{Interest} = \text{Principal} \times \text{Rate} \times \frac{\text{Exact days}}{360}$$

or

$$\text{Interest} = \$1,000 \times 12\% \times \frac{90}{360} = \$30$$

Recording the Receipt of a Note

To simplify record-keeping, notes receivable are usually recorded in a single Notes Receivable account. Only one account is needed because the individual original notes are on hand. Therefore, the maker, rate of interest, due date, and other information may be learned by examining each note.[7]

When a company receives a note at the time of a sale, an entry such as this one is recorded:

Dec.	5	Notes Receivable	650.00	
		Sales		650.00
		Sold merchandise in exchange for a six-month, 9% note.		

A business also may accept a note from an overdue customer as a way of granting a time extension on the past-due account receivable. When this happens, the business may collect part of the past-due balance in cash. This partial payment forces a concession from the customer, reduces the customer's debt (and the seller's risk), and produces a note for a smaller amount. For example, Symplex Company agrees to accept $232 in cash and a $600, 60-day, 15% note from Joseph Cook to settle his $832 past-due account. Symplex makes the following entry to record the receipt of the cash and note:

Oct.	5	Cash	232.00	
		Notes Receivable	600.00	
		Accounts Receivable—Joseph Cook		832.00
		Received cash and a note in settlement of an account.		

When Cook pays the note on the due date, Symplex records the receipt as follows:

Dec.	4	Cash	615.00	
		Notes Receivable		600.00
		Interest Earned		15.00
		Collected the Joseph Cook note including interest of $600 ×		
		15% × 60/360.		

---

[7]If the company holds a large number of notes, it may be more efficient to set up a controlling account and a subsidiary ledger.

Dishonored Notes Receivable

Sometimes, the maker of a note is not able to pay the note at maturity. When a note's maker is unable or refuses to pay at maturity, the note is said to be dishonored. This act of **dishonoring a note** does not relieve the maker of the obligation to pay. Furthermore, the payee should use every legitimate means to collect. However, collection may require lengthy legal proceedings.

The usual practice is to have the balance of the Notes Receivable account show only the amount of notes that have not matured. Therefore, when a note is dishonored, the accountant removes the amount of the note from the Notes Receivable account and charges it back to an account receivable from its maker. To illustrate, Symplex Company holds an $800, 12%, 60-day note of George Hart. At maturity, Hart dishonors the note. To remove the dishonored note from the Notes Receivable account, the company makes the following entry:

Oct.	14	Accounts Receivable—George Hart	816.00	
		Interest Earned		16.00
		Notes Receivable		800.00
		To charge the account of George Hart for his dishonored note including interest of $800 × 12% × 60/360.		

Charging a dishonored note back to the account of its maker serves two purposes. First, it removes the amount of the note from the Notes Receivable account, leaving in the account only notes that have not matured. It also records the dishonored note in the maker's account. The second purpose is important. If the maker of the dishonored note again applies for credit in the future, his or her account will show all past dealings, including the dishonored note. Restoring the account also reminds the business to continue collection efforts.

Note that Hart owes both the principal and the interest. Therefore, the entry records the full amount owed in Hart's account and credits the interest to Interest Earned. This procedure assures that the interest will be included in future efforts to collect from Hart.

End-of-Period Adjustments

When notes receivable are outstanding at the end of an accounting period, the accrued interest should be calculated and recorded. This procedure recognizes the interest revenue when it is earned and recognizes the additional asset owned by the note's holder. For example, on December 16, Perry Company accepted a $3,000, 60-day, 12% note from a customer in granting an extension on a past-due account. When the company's accounting period ends on December 31, $15 of interest will have accrued on this note ($3,000 × 12% × 15/360). The following adjusting entry records this revenue:

Dec.	31	Interest Receivable	15.00	
		Interest Earned		15.00
		To record accrued interest.		

The adjusting entry causes the interest earned to appear on the income statement of the period in which it was earned. It also causes the interest receivable to appear on the balance sheet as a current asset.

Collecting Interest Previously Accrued

When the note is collected, Perry Company's entry to record the cash receipt is:

Feb.	14	Cash	3,060.00	
		Interest Earned		45.00
		Interest Receivable		15.00
		Notes Receivable		3,000.00
		Received payment of a note and its interest.		

Observe that the entry's credit to Interest Receivable records collection of the interest accrued at the end of the previous period. Only the $45 of interest earned between January 1 and February 14 is recorded as revenue.

Progress Check

8-12 White Corporation purchased $7,000 of merchandise from Stamford Company on December 16, 19X1. Stamford accepted White's $7,000, 90-day, 12% note as payment. Assuming Stamford's annual accounting period ends on December 31 and it does not make reversing entries, prepare entries for Stamford Company on December 16, 19X1, and December 31, 19X1.

8-13 Based on the facts in 8-12, prepare the March 16, 19X2, entry assuming White dishonors the note.

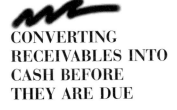

CONVERTING RECEIVABLES INTO CASH BEFORE THEY ARE DUE

LO 5
Explain how receivables can be converted into cash before they are due and calculate accounts receivable turnover.

Many companies grant credit to customers and then hold the receivables until they are paid by the customers. However, some companies convert receivables into cash without waiting until they are due. This is done either by selling the receivables or by using them as security for a loan. In certain industries such as textiles and furniture, this has been a common practice for years. More recently, the practice has spread to other industries, in particular the apparel industry. More small businesses are using sale of receivables as a source of cash, especially those selling to other businesses and government agencies that often delay payment.

Selling Accounts Receivable

A business may sell its accounts receivable to a finance company or bank. The buyer, which is called a *factor,* charges the seller a *factoring fee* and then collects the receivables as they come due. By incurring the factoring fee cost, the seller receives the cash earlier and passes the risk of bad debts to the factor. The seller also avoids the cost of billing and accounting for the receivables.

For example, assume that a business sells $20,000 of its accounts receivable and is charged a 2% factoring fee. The seller records the sale with the following entry:

Aug.	15	Cash	19,600.00	
		Factoring Fee Expense	400.00	
		Accounts Receivable		20,000.00
		Sold accounts receivable for cash, less a 2% factoring fee.		

Factoring has become big business today. **CIT Group/Commercial Services,** the factoring firm with the largest volume in recent years, posted a 7.6% increase in volume to $3.738 billion in the first half of 1993. It is interesting to note that 90% of the factoring industry's business comes from textile and apparel businesses.

Pledging Accounts Receivable as Security for a Loan

When a business borrows money and pledges its accounts receivable as security for the loan, the business records the loan with an entry such as the following:

Aug.	20	Cash	35,000.00	
		Notes Payable		35,000.00
		Borrowed money on a note secured by the pledge of accounts receivable.		

Under the pledging arrangement, the risk of bad debts is not transferred to the lender. The borrower retains ownership of the receivables. However, if the borrower defaults on the loan, the creditor has the right to be paid from the cash receipts as the accounts receivable are collected.

Because pledged receivables are committed as security for a loan from a particular creditor, the borrower's financial statements should disclose the fact that accounts receivable have been pledged. For example, the following footnote to the financial statements provides the necessary information: "Accounts receivable in the amount of $40,000 are pledged as security for a $35,000 note payable to Western National Bank."

Discounting Notes Receivable

Notes receivable also can be converted into cash before they mature, usually by discounting the notes receivable at a bank. For example, if a company discounts a $50,000 note receivable at a cost of $700, it records the discounting with the following entry:

Aug.	25	Cash	49,300.00	
		Interest Expense	700.00	
		Notes Receivable		50,000.00
		Discounted a note receivable.		

Notes receivable may be discounted with recourse or without recourse. If a note is discounted with recourse and the original maker of the note fails to pay the bank when the note matures, the original payee of the note must pay. Thus, a company that discounts a note with recourse has a contingent liability until the bank is paid. A **contingent liability** is an obligation to make a future payment if, and only if, an uncertain future event actually occurs. The company should disclose the contingent liability in its financial statements with a footnote such as: "The company is contingently liable for a $50,000 note receivable discounted with recourse."

In the preceding entry, notice the debit to Interest Expense. This indicates that the discounting transaction is understood to be a loan. In some cases, discounting a note with recourse is considered to be a sale.[8] When the transaction is a sale, the debit should be to Loss on Sale of Notes instead of to Interest Expense.

When a note is discounted *without recourse,* the bank assumes the risk of a bad debt loss and the original payee does not have a contingent liability. A note discounted without recourse is clearly understood to be sold.

Accounting Trends and Techniques, an annual survey of accounting practices followed in 600 stockholders' reports, shows that 125 of the companies surveyed in 1994 disclosed either the sale of receivables or the pledging of receivables as collateral. The following footnote from **Pitney Bowes, Inc.'s** annual report illustrates disclosure of substantial receivables sold with recourse:

> The company has sold net finance receivables with varying amounts of recourse in privately-placed transactions with third-party investors. The uncollected principal balance of receivables sold and residual guarantee contracts totaled $275.2 million and $379.8 million at December 31, 1994 and 1993, respectively. These contracts are supported by the underlying equipment value and credit worthiness of customers. Adequate provisions have been made for sold receivables which may be uncollectible.

FULL-DISCLOSURE PRINCIPLE

The disclosure of contingent liabilities in footnotes is consistent with the **full-disclosure principle.** This principle requires financial statements (including the footnotes) to present all relevant information about the operations and financial position of the entity. A company should report any facts important enough to affect a statement reader's evaluation of the company's operations, financial position, or cash flows. This principle does not require companies to report excessive detail. It simply means that significant information should not be withheld and that enough information should be provided to make the reports understandable. Examples of items that are reported to satisfy the full-disclosure principle include contingent liabilities, long-term commitments under contracts, and accounting methods used.

Contingent Liabilities. In addition to discounted notes, a company should disclose any items for which the company is contingently liable. Examples are possible additional tax assessments, debts of other parties that the company has guaranteed, and unresolved lawsuits against the company. Information about these facts helps

users predict events that might affect the company. In October of 1994, *The Wall Street Journal* reported: "Pennzoil said it agreed to pay the IRS $454 million in back taxes and interest to resolve a claim stemming from its 1988 settlement with Texaco." Those that had a financial interest in **Pennzoil Company** were aware of this potential tax liability because, following GAAP requirements, Pennzoil made the following disclosure in the footnotes to their 1993 annual report:

> In January 1994, Pennzoil received a letter and examination report from the District Director of the IRS that proposes a tax deficiency based on an audit of Pennzoil's 1988 federal income tax return. The examination report proposes two principal adjustments with which Pennzoil disagrees . . . The proposed tax defi-

---

[8]The criteria for deciding whether discounting with recourse is a loan or a sale are explained in more advanced accounting courses.

ciency relating to this proposed adjustment is $550.9 million, net of available off-sets. Pennzoil estimates that the additional after-tax interest on this proposed deficiency would be approximately $234.3 million as of December 31, 1993.

Long-Term Commitments under Contracts. A company should disclose that it has signed a long-term lease requiring material annual payments, even though the obligation does not appear in the accounts. Also, a company should reveal that it has pledged certain of its assets as security for loans. These facts show statement readers that the company has restricted its flexibility.

Accounting Methods Used. When more than one accounting method can be applied, a company must describe the one it uses, especially when the choice can materially affect reported net income.[9] For example, a company must describe the methods it uses to account for inventory and depreciation. (These methods are explained in future chapters.) This information helps users understand how the company determines its net income.

In Chapter 7, you learned how to calculate *days' sales uncollected,* which provides information about the short-term liquidity of a company. In evaluating short-term liquidity, you also may want to calculate **accounts receivable turnover.** The formula for this ratio is:

USING THE INFORMATION— ACCOUNTS RECEIVABLE TURNOVER

$$\text{Accounts receivable turnover} = \frac{\text{Net sales}}{\text{Average accounts receivable}}$$

Recall that days' sales uncollected relates to the accounts receivable balance at the end of the year. In contrast, notice that the denominator in the turnover formula is the average accounts receivable balance during the year. The average is often calculated as:

$$\frac{\text{(The beginning balance + The ending balance)}}{2}$$

This method of estimating the average balance provides a useful result if the seasonal changes in the accounts receivable balances during the year are not too large.

Accounts receivable turnover indicates how often the company converted its average accounts receivable balance into cash during the year. Thus, a turnover of 12 suggests that the average accounts receivable balance was converted into cash 12 times during the year.

Accounts receivable turnover also provides useful information for evaluating how efficient management has been in granting credit to produce revenues. A ratio that is high in comparison with competing companies suggests that management should consider using more liberal credit terms to increase sales. A low ratio suggests that management should consider less liberal credit terms and more aggressive collection efforts to avoid an excessive investment in accounts receivable. The following data was extracted from the annual reports of competing companies to illustrate the calculations and comparisons:

Dell Computer Corporation
(Year ended January 29, 1995—In thousands)

$$\text{Accounts receivable turnover} = \frac{\$3,475,343}{(\$537,974 + \$410,774)/2} = 7.3 \text{ times}$$

---

[9]FASB, *Accounting Standards—Current Text* (Norwalk, CT, 1995), sec. A10.105. First published as *APB Opinion No. 22,* pars. 12, 13.

Compaq Computer Corporation
(Year ended December 31, 1994—In millions)

$$\text{Accounts receivable turnover} = \frac{\$10,866}{(\$2,287 + \$1,377)/2} = 5.9 \text{ times}$$

Progress Check

8-14   A garment manufacturer is short of cash but has substantial accounts receivable. What alternatives are available for gaining cash from the accounts receivable prior to receiving payments from the credit customers? Show the entry that would be made for each alternative.

8-15   Calculate Mattel, Inc.'s accounts receivable turnover for 1994 based on the following information:

(In thousands)	1994	1993
Accounts receivable	762,024	580,313
Total current assets	1,543,523	1,470,750
Net sales	3,205,025	2,704,448
Net income	255,832	117,208

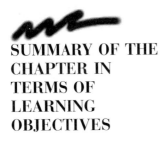

SUMMARY OF THE CHAPTER IN TERMS OF LEARNING OBJECTIVES

LO 1. Prepare journal entries to account for short-term investments and explain how fair (market) value gains and losses on such investments are reported. Short-term investments are recorded at cost; dividends and interest on the investments are recorded in appropriate income statement accounts. On the balance sheet, investments in securities held to maturity are reported at cost; investments in trading securities and securities available for sale are reported at their fair values. Unrealized gains and losses on trading securities are included in income, but unrealized gains and losses on securities available for sale are reported as a separate stockholders' equity item.

LO 2. Prepare entries to account for credit card sales. When credit card receipts are deposited in a bank account, the credit card expense is recorded at the time of the deposit. When credit card receipts must be submitted to the credit card company for payment, Accounts Receivable is debited for the sales amount. Then, credit card expense is recorded when cash is received from the credit card company. However, any unrecorded credit card expense should be accrued at the end of each accounting period.

LO 3. Prepare entries to account for transactions with credit customers, including accounting for bad debts under the allowance method and the direct write-off method. Under the allowance method, bad debts expense is recorded with an adjustment at the end of each accounting period that debits the expense and credits the Allowance for Doubtful Accounts. The amount of the adjustment is determined by focusing on either (*a*) the income statement relationship between bad debts expense and credit sales or (*b*) the balance sheet relationship between accounts receivable and the Allowance for Doubtful Accounts. The latter approach may involve using a simple percentage relationship or aging the accounts. Uncollectible accounts are written off with a debit to the Allowance for Doubtful Accounts. The direct write-off method charges Bad Debts Expense when accounts are written off as uncollectible. This method is suitable only when the amount of bad debts expense is immaterial.

LO 4. Calculate the interest on promissory notes and prepare entries to record the receipt of promissory notes and their payment or dishonor. Interest rates are typically stated in annual terms. When a note's time to maturity is more or less than one year, the amount of interest on the note must be determined by expressing the time as a fraction of one year and multiplying the note's principal by that fraction and the annual interest rate. Dishonored notes are credited to Notes Receivable and debited to Accounts Receivable and to the account of the maker.

LO 5. Explain how receivables can be converted into cash before they are due and calculate accounts receivable turnover. To obtain cash from receivables before they are due, a company may sell accounts receivable to a factor, who charges a factoring fee. Also, a company may borrow money by signing a note payable that is secured by pledging the accounts receivable. Notes receivable may be discounted at a bank, with or without recourse. The full-disclosure principle requires companies to disclose the amount of accounts receivable that have been pledged and the contingent liability for notes discounted with recourse.

DEMONSTRATION PROBLEM

Garden Company had the following transactions during 19X2:

May 8	Purchased 300 shares of Federal Express common stock as a short-term investment in a security available for sale. The cost of $40 per share plus $975 in broker's commissions was paid in cash.
July 14	Wrote off a $750 account receivable arising from a sale several months ago. (Garden Company uses the allowance method.)
Aug. 15	Accepted a $2,000 down payment and a $10,000 note receivable from a customer in exchange for an inventory item that normally sells for $12,000. The note was dated August 15, bears 12% interest, and matures in six months.
Sept. 2	Sold 100 shares of Federal Express stock at $47 per share and continued to hold the other 200 shares. The broker's commission on the sale was $225.
Sept. 15	Received $9,850 in return for discounting without recourse the $10,000 note (dated August 15) at the local bank.
Dec. 2	Purchased 400 shares of McDonald's Corp. stock for $60 per share plus $1,600 in commissions. The stock is to be held as a short-term investment in a security available for sale.

Required

1. Prepare journal entries to record these transactions on the books of Garden Company.
2. Prepare adjusting journal entries as of December 31, 19X2, for the following items (assume 19X2 is the first year of operations):
   a. The market prices of the equity securities held by Garden Company are: $48 per share for the Federal Express stock and $55 per share for the McDonald's stock.
   b. Bad debts expense is estimated by an aging of accounts receivable. The unadjusted balance of the Allowance for Doubtful Accounts account is a $1,000 debit, while the required balance is estimated to be a $20,400 credit.

Planning the Solution

- Examine each item to determine which accounts are affected and produce the needed journal entries.
- With respect to the year-end adjustments, adjust stock investments to fair value and record the bad debts expense.

Solution to Demonstration Problem

1.

May	8	Short-Term Investments	12,975.00	
		Cash		12,975.00
		Purchased 300 shares of Federal Express. Cost is (300 × $40) + $975.		
July	14	Allowance for Doubtful Accounts	750.00	
		Accounts Receivable		750.00
		Wrote off an uncollectible account.		

Aug.	15	Cash	2,000.00	
		Notes Receivable	10,000.00	
		Sales		12,000.00
		Sold merchandise to customer for $2,000 cash and $10,000 note receivable.		
Sept.	2	Cash	4,475.00	
		Gain on Sale of Investment		150.00
		Short-Term Investments		4,325.00
		Sold 100 shares of Federal Express for $47 per share less a $225 commission. The original cost is ($12,975 × ($12,975 100/300).		
	15	Cash	9,850.00	
		Loss on Sale of Notes	150.00	
		Notes Receivable		10,000.00
		Discounted note receivable dated August 15.		
Dec.	2	Short-Term Investments	25,600.00	
		Cash		25,600.00
		Purchased 400 shares of McDonald's for $60 per share plus $1,600 in commissions.		

2.

Dec.	31	Short-Term Investments, Fair Value Adjustment	2,650.00	
		Unrealized Holding Gain (Loss)		2,650.00
		To reflect fair values of short-term investments in securities available for sale.		

Short-Term Investments in Securities Available for Sale	Shares	Cost per Share	Total Cost	Market Value per Share	Total Market Value	Difference
Federal Express	200	$43.25	$ 8,650	$48.00	$ 9,600	
McDonald's	400	64.00	25,600	55.00	22,000	
Total			$34,250		$31,600	$2,650

	31	Bad Debts Expense	21,400.00	
		Allowance for Doubtful Accounts		21,400.00
		To adjust the allowance account from $1,000 debit balance to $20,400 credit balance.		

GLOSSARY

Accounts Receivable Ledger a supplementary record (also called a *subsidiary ledger*) having an account for each customer. p. 277

Accounts receivable turnover a measure of how long it takes a company to collect its accounts, calculated by dividing credit sales (or net sales) by the average accounts receivable balance. p. 295

Aging accounts receivable a process of classifying accounts receivable in terms of how long they have been out-

standing for the purpose of estimating the amount of uncollectible accounts. p. 285

Allowance for Doubtful Accounts a contra asset account with a balance equal to the estimated amount of accounts receivable that will be uncollectible. p. 280

Allowance method of accounting for bad debts an accounting procedure that (1) estimates and reports bad debts expense from credit sales during the period of the sales and (2) reports accounts receivable at the amount of cash proceeds that is expected from their collection (their estimated realizable value). p. 279

Bad debts accounts receivable from customers that are not collected; the amount is an expense of selling on credit. p. 279

Contingent liability an obligation to make a future payment if, and only if, an uncertain future event actually occurs. p. 293

Controlling account a general ledger account with a balance that is always equal to the sum of the balances in a related subsidiary ledger. p. 279

Direct write-off method of accounting for bad debts a method that makes no attempt to estimate uncollectible accounts or bad debts expense at the end of each period; instead, when an account is found to be uncollectible, it is written off directly to Bad Debts Expense; this method is generally considered to be inferior to the allowance method. p. 287

Dishonoring a note failure by a promissory note's maker to pay the amount due at maturity. p. 291

Full-disclosure principle the accounting principle that requires financial statements (including the footnotes) to contain all relevant information about the operations and financial position of the entity; it also requires that the information be presented in an understandable manner. p. 294

General Ledger the ledger that contains all the financial statement accounts of an organization. p. 277

Installment accounts receivable accounts receivable that allow the customer to make periodic payments over several months and that typically earn interest for the seller. p. 288

Interest the charge assessed for the use of money. p. 289

Investments in securities available for sale investments in debt and equity securities that do not qualify as investments in trading securities or as investments in securities held to maturity. p. 272

Investments in securities held to maturity investments in debt securities that the owner positively intends to hold and has the ability to hold until maturity. p. 272

Investments in trading securities investments in debt and equity securities that the owner actively manages, so that frequent purchases and sales generally are made with the objective of generating profits on short-term differences in price. p. 272

Maker of a note one who signs a note and promises to pay it at maturity. p. 289

Materiality principle the idea that the requirements of an accounting principle may be ignored if the effect on the financial statements is unimportant to their users. p. 288

Maturity date of a note the date on which a note and any interest are due and payable. p. 289

Payee of a note the one to whom a promissory note is made payable. p. 289

Principal of a note the amount that the signer of a promissory note agrees to pay back when it matures, not including the interest. p. 288

Promissory note an unconditional written promise to pay a definite sum of money on demand or at a fixed or determinable future date. p. 288

Realizable value the expected proceeds from converting assets into cash. p. 280

Short-term investments investments that can be converted into cash quickly (but less quickly than cash equivalents) and that management intends to sell as a source of cash to satisfy the needs of current operations; short-term investments include such things as government or corporate debt obligations and marketable equity securities. p. 270

Subsidiary ledger a collection of accounts (other than general ledger accounts) that contains the details underlying the balance of a controlling account in the General Ledger. p. 279

Temporary investments another name for short-term investments. p. 270

Unrealized holding gain an increase in the fair (market) value of a security that has not yet been confirmed by the sale of the security. p. 273

Unrealized holding loss a decrease in the fair (market) value of a security that has not yet been confirmed by the sale of the security. p. 274

QUESTIONS

1. Under what conditions should investments be classified as current assets?
2. If a short-term investment in securities held for sale cost $6,780 and was sold for $7,500, how should the difference between the two amounts be recorded?
3. On a balance sheet, what valuation must be reported for short-term investments in trading securities?
4. If a company purchases short-term investments in securities available for sale for the first time, and their fair (market) values fall below cost, what account is credited for the amount of the unrealized loss?
5. For which category of short-term investments are unrealized holding gains included in earnings and reported on the income statement?
6. How do businesses benefit from allowing their customers to use credit cards?
7. Explain why writing off a bad debt against the allowance account does not reduce the estimated realizable value of a company's accounts receivable.
8. Why does the Bad Debts Expense account usually not have the same adjusted balance as the Allowance for Doubtful Accounts?
9. Why does the direct write-off method of accounting for bad debts commonly fail to match revenues and expenses?
10. What is the essence of the accounting principle of materiality?
11. Why might a business prefer a note receivable to an account receivable?

12. In its 1995 annual report, Apple Computer, Inc., shows cash and cash equivalents of $756,000,000 and short-term investments of $196,000,000 on its consolidated balance sheet as of September 29, 1995. Considering the fact that both of these items are current assets, why are they reported separately?

QUICK STUDY (Five-Minute Exercises)

QS 8–1
(LO 1)

On April 18, Kimmell Industries, Inc., made a short-term investment in 200 shares of Computer Links common stock. The intent is to actively manage these stocks. The purchase price was 42½ and the broker's fee was $350. On June 30, Kimmell received $2 per share in dividends. Prepare the April 18 and June 30 journal entries.

QS 8–2
(LO 1)

During this year, Rose Consulting Group acquired short-term investment securities at a cost of $35,000. These securities were classified as available for sale. At December 31 year-end, these securities had a market (fair) value of $29,000.

a. Prepare the necessary year-end adjustment.

b. Explain how each account used in requirement a would affect or be reported in the financial statements.

QS 8–3
(LO 2)

Journalize the following transactions:

a. Sold $10,000 in merchandise on Mastercard credit cards. The sales receipts were deposited in our business account. Mastercard charges us a 5% fee.

b. Sold $3,000 on miscellaneous credit cards. Cash will be received within 10 days and a 4% fee will be charged.

QS 8–4
(LO 3)

Foster Corporation uses the allowance method to account for uncollectibles. On October 31, they wrote off a $1,000 account of a customer, Gwen Rowe. On December 9, they received a $200 payment from Rowe.

a. Make the appropriate entry or entries for October 31.

b. Make the appropriate entry or entries for December 9.

QS 8–5
(LO 3)

Duncan Company's year-end trial balance shows accounts receivable of $89,000, allowance for doubtful accounts of $500 (credit), and sales of $270,000. Uncollectibles are estimated to be 1.5% of outstanding accounts receivable.

a. Prepare the December 31 year-end adjustment.

b. What amount would have been used in the year-end adjustment if the allowance account had a year-end debit balance of $200?

c. Assume the same facts, except that Duncan estimates uncollectibles as 1% of sales. What amount would be used in the adjustment?

QS 8–6
(LO 4)

On August 2, 19X1, SLM, Inc., received a $5,500, 90-day, 12% note from customer Will Carr as payment on his account. Prepare the August 2 and maturity date entries, assuming the note is honored by Carr.

QS 8–7
(LO 4)

Seaver Company's December 31 year-end trial balance shows an $8,000 balance in Notes Receivable. This balance is from one note dated December 1, with a period of 45 days and 9% interest. Prepare the December 31 and maturity date entries, assuming the note is honored.

QS 8–8
(LO 5)

The following facts were extracted from the comparative balance sheets of Ernest Blue, P.C.:

	19X2	19X1
Accounts receivable	$152,900	$133,700
Sales (net)	754,200	810,600

Compute the accounts receivable turnover for 19X2.

EXERCISES

Prepare general journal entries to record the following transactions involving the short-term investments of Morton Financial Corp., all of which occurred during 19X1:

a. On February 15, paid $150,000 to purchase $150,000 of American General's 90-day short-term notes payable, which are dated February 15 and pay 10% interest.

b. On March 22, bought 700 shares of Royal Industries common stock at 25½ plus a $250 brokerage fee.

c. On May 16, received a check from American General in payment of the principal and 90 days' interest on the notes purchased in transaction a.

d. On July 30, paid $50,000 to purchase $50,000 of OMB Electronics' 8% notes payable, dated July 30, 19X1, and due January 30, 19X2.

e. On September 1, received a $0.50 per share cash dividend on the Royal Industries common stock purchased in transaction b.

f. On October 8, sold 350 shares of Royal Industries common stock for $32 per share, less a $175 brokerage fee.

g. On October 30, received a check from OMB Electronics for three months' interest on the notes purchased in transaction d.

Exercise 8–1
Transactions involving short-term investments
(LO 1)

On December 31, 19X1, Style, Inc., held the following short-term investments in securities available for sale:

	Cost	Fair Value
Nintendo Co. common stock	$68,900	$75,300
Atlantic Richfield Co. bonds payable	24,500	22,800
Kellogg Company notes payable	50,000	47,200
McDonald's Corp. common stock	91,400	86,600

Style, Inc., had no short-term investments prior to 19X1. Prepare the December 31 adjusting entry to record the change in fair value of the investments.

Exercise 8–2
Recording fair values of short-term investments
(LO 1)

Columbian Company's annual accounting period ends on December 31. The total cost and fair (market) value of the company's short-term investments in securities available for sale were as follows:

	Total Cost	Total Fair Value
Short-term investments in securities available for sale:		
On December 31, 19X1	$79,483	$72,556
On December 31, 19X2	85,120	90,271

Prepare Columbian's December 31, 19X2, adjusting entry to update the fair values of the short-term investments.

Exercise 8–3
Adjusting the short-term investment accounts to reflect changes in fair value
(LO 1)

Aston Corporation allows customers to use two credit cards in charging purchases. With the OmniCard, Aston receives an immediate credit when it deposits sales receipts in its checking account. OmniCard assesses a 4% service charge for credit card sales. The second credit card that Aston accepts is Colonial Bank Card. Aston sends its accumulated receipts to Colonial Bank on a weekly basis and is paid by Colonial approximately 10 days later. Colonial Bank charges 2% of sales for using its card. Prepare entries in journal form to record the following credit card transactions of Aston Corporation:

Apr. 6 Sold merchandise for $9,200, accepting the customers' OmniCards. At the end of the day, the OmniCard receipts were deposited in Aston's account at the bank.

   10 Sold merchandise for $310, accepting the customer's Colonial Bank Card.

   17 Mailed $5,480 of credit card receipts to Colonial Bank, requesting payment.

   28 Received Colonial Bank's check for the April 17 billing, less the normal service charge.

Exercise 8–4
Credit card transactions
(LO 2)

Exercise 8–5
Subsidiary ledger accounts
(LO 3)

Jenkins, Inc., recorded the following transactions during November 19X1:

Nov.	3	Accounts Receivable—ABC Shop	4,417.00	
		Sales		4,417.00
	8	Accounts Receivable—Colt Enterprises	1,250.00	
		Sales		1,250.00
	11	Accounts Receivable—Red McKenzie	733.00	
		Sales		733.00
	19	Sales Returns and Allowances	189.00	
		Accounts Receivable—Red McKenzie		189.00
	28	Accounts Receivable—ABC Shop	2,606.00	
		Sales		2,606.00

Required

1. Open a General Ledger having T-accounts for Accounts Receivable, Sales, and Sales Returns and Allowances. Also, open a subsidiary Accounts Receivable Ledger having a T-account for each customer. Post the preceding entries to the general ledger accounts and the customer accounts.
2. List the balances of the accounts in the subsidiary ledger, total the balances, and compare the total with the balance of the Accounts Receivable controlling account.

Exercise 8–6
Allowance for doubtful accounts
(LO 3)

At the end of its annual accounting period, Bali Company estimated its bad debts as one-half of 1% of its $875,000 of credit sales made during the year. On December 31, Bali made an addition to its Allowance for Doubtful Accounts equal to that amount. On the following February 1, management decided the $420 account of Catherine Hicks was uncollectible and wrote it off as a bad debt. Four months later, on June 5, Hicks unexpectedly paid the amount previously written off. Give the journal entries required to record these events.

Exercise 8–7
Bad debts expense
(LO 3)

At the end of each year, Deutch Supply Co. uses the simplified balance sheet approach to estimate bad debts. On December 31, 19X1, it has outstanding accounts receivable of $53,000 and estimates that 4% will be uncollectible. Give the entry to record bad debts expense for 19X1 (a) under the assumption that the Allowance for Doubtful Accounts has a $915 credit balance before the adjustment and (b) under the assumption that the Allowance for Doubtful Accounts has a $1,332 debit balance before the adjustment.

Exercise 8–8
Dishonor of a note
(LO 4)

Prepare journal entries to record these transactions:

Mar. 21   Accepted a $3,100, six-month, 10% note dated today from Bradley Brooks in granting a time extension on his past-due account.

Sept. 21   Brooks dishonored his note when presented for payment.

Dec. 31   After exhausting all legal means of collection, wrote off Brooks' account against the Allowance for Doubtful Accounts.

Exercise 8–9
Selling and pledging accounts receivable
(LO 5)

On July 31, Konrad International had $125,900 of accounts receivable. Prepare journal entries to record the following August transactions. Also, prepare any footnotes to the August 31 financial statements that should be reported as a result of these transactions.

Aug. 2   Sold merchandise to customers on credit, $6,295.

7   Sold $18,770 of accounts receivable to Fidelity Bank. Fidelity charges a 1.5% fee.

15   Received payments from customers, $3,436.

25   Borrowed $10,000 from Fidelity Bank, pledging $14,000 of accounts receivable as security for the loan.

The following information is from the financial statements of Whimsy, Inc.:

	19X3	19X2	19X1
Net sales	$305,000	$236,000	$288,000
Accounts receivable (December 31)	22,900	20,700	17,400

Calculate Whimsy's accounts receivable turnover for 19X2 and 19X3. Compare the two results and give a possible explanation for any significant change.

Exercise 8–10
Accounts receivable turnover
(LO 5)

PROBLEMS

Checkers, Inc., had no short-term investments prior to 19X1 but had the following transactions involving short-term investments in securities available for sale during 19X1:

Problem 8–1
Accounting for short-term investments
(LO 1)

Mar. 16   Purchased 3,000 shares of Diamond Shamrock, Inc., common stock at 22¼ plus a $1,948 brokerage fee.

Apr. 1   Paid $100,000 to buy 90-day U.S. Treasury bills, $100,000 principal amount, 5%, dated April 1.

June 7   Purchased 1,800 shares of PepsiCo, Inc., common stock at 49½ plus a $1,235 brokerage fee.

20   Purchased 700 shares of Xerox Corp. common stock at 15¾ plus a $466 brokerage fee.

July 3   Received a check for the principal and accrued interest on the U.S. Treasury bills that matured on June 30.

15   Received a $0.95 per share cash dividend on the Diamond Shamrock common shares.

28   Sold 1,500 shares of Diamond Shamrock common stock at 26 less a $912 brokerage fee.

Sept. 1   Received a $2.10 per share cash dividend on the PepsiCo common shares.

Dec. 15   Received a $1.35 per share cash dividend on the remaining Diamond Shamrock common shares owned.

31   Received a $1.60 per share cash dividend on the PepsiCo common shares.

On December 31, 19X1, the market prices of the securities held by Checkers, Inc., were: Diamond Shamrock, 29½; PepsiCo, 51⅜; and Xerox, 16¾.

Required

Preparation component:

1.   Prepare journal entries to record the preceding transactions.

2.   Prepare a schedule to compare the cost and fair (market) values of Checkers' short-term investments in securities available for sale.

3.   Prepare an adjusting entry, if necessary, to record the fair value adjustment of the short-term investments.

CHECK FIGURE:
Unrealized holding gain (loss), $12,275 Cr.

Analysis component:

4.   Explain the balance sheet presentation of the fair value adjustment.

5.   How did the short-term investments of Checkers, Inc., affect the reported profitability for the year and the final equity figure?

Accessories Unlimited allows a few customers to make purchases on credit. Other customers may use either of two credit cards. Express Bank deducts a 3% service charge for sales on its credit card but credits the checking accounts of its commercial customers immediately when

Problem 8–2
Credit sales and credit card sales
(LO 2)

credit card receipts are deposited. Accessories Unlimited deposits the Express Bank credit card receipts at the close of each business day.

When customers use UniCharge credit cards, Accessories Unlimited accumulates the receipts for several days before submitting them to UniCharge for payment. UniCharge deducts a 2% service charge and usually pays within one week of being billed. Accessories Unlimited completed the following transactions during the month of May:

May 4   Sold merchandise on credit to Anne Bismarck for $565. (The terms of all credit sales are 2/15, n/30, and all sales are recorded at the gross price.)

5   Sold merchandise for $5,934 to customers who used their Express Bank credit cards. Sold merchandise for $4,876 to customers who used their UniCharge cards.

8   Sold merchandise for $3,213 to customers who used their UniCharge credit cards.

10   The UniCharge card receipts accumulated since May 5 were submitted to the credit card company for payment.

13   Wrote off the account of Mandy Duke against Allowance for Doubtful Accounts. The $329 balance in Duke's account stemmed from a credit sale in October of last year.

17   Received the amount due from UniCharge.

18   Received Bismarck's check paying for the purchase of May 4.

Required

Prepare journal entries to record the preceding transactions and events.

Problem 8–3
Estimating bad debts expense
(LO 3)

On December 31, 19X1, SysComm Corporation's records showed the following results for the year:

Cash sales	$1,803,750
Credit sales	3,534,000

In addition, the unadjusted trial balance included the following items:

Accounts receivable	$1,070,100 debit
Allowance for doubtful accounts	15,750 debit

Required

1. Prepare the adjusting entry needed in SysComm's books to recognize bad debts under each of the following independent assumptions:

CHECK FIGURE:
Bad debts expense (1a),
$70,680 Dr.

   a.   Bad debts are estimated to be 2% of credit sales.
   b.   Bad debts are estimated to be 1% of total sales.
   c.   An analysis suggests that 5% of outstanding accounts receivable on December 31, 19X1, will become uncollectible.

2. Show how Accounts Receivable and the Allowance for Doubtful Accounts would appear on the December 31, 19X1, balance sheet given the facts in requirement 1a.

3. Show how Accounts Receivable and the Allowance for Doubtful Accounts would appear on the December 31, 19X1, balance sheet given the facts in requirement 1c.

Problem 8–4
Aging accounts receivable
(LO 3)

Jewell, Inc., had credit sales of $2.6 million in 19X1. On December 31, 19X1, the company's Allowance for Doubtful Accounts had a credit balance of $13,400. The accountant for Jewell has prepared a schedule of the December 31, 19X1, accounts receivable by age and, on the basis of past experience, has estimated the percentage of the receivables in each age category that will become uncollectible. This information is summarized as follows:

December 31, 19X1 Accounts Receivable	Age of Accounts Receivable	Expected Percentage Uncollectible
$730,000	Not due (under 30 days)	1.25%
354,000	1 to 30 days past due	2.00
76,000	31 to 60 days past due	6.50
48,000	61 to 90 days past due	32.75
12,000	Over 90 days past due	68.00

Required

Preparation component:

1. Calculate the amount that should appear in the December 31, 19X1, balance sheet as the allowance for doubtful accounts.
2. Prepare the journal entry to record bad debts expense for 19X1.

Analysis component:

3. On June 30, 19X2, Jewell, Inc., concluded that a customer's $3,750 receivable (created in 19X1) was uncollectible and that the account should be written off. What effect will this action have on Jewell's 19X2 net income? Explain your answer.

Harrell Industries began operations on January 1, 19X1. During the next two years, the company completed a number of transactions involving credit sales, accounts receivable collections, and bad debts. These transactions are summarized as follows:

Problem 8–5
Recording accounts receivable transactions and bad debt adjustments
(LO 3)

19X1
a. Sold merchandise on credit for $1,144,500, terms n/30.
b. Wrote off uncollectible accounts receivable in the amount of $17,270.
c. Received cash of $667,100 in payment of outstanding accounts receivable.
d. In adjusting the accounts on December 31, concluded that 1.5% of the outstanding accounts receivable would become uncollectible.

19X2
e. Sold merchandise on credit for $1,423,800, terms n/30.
f. Wrote off uncollectible accounts receivable in the amount of $26,880.
g. Received cash of $1,103,900 in payment of outstanding accounts receivable.
h. In adjusting the accounts on December 31, concluded that 1.5% of the outstanding accounts receivable would become uncollectible.

Required

Prepare journal entries to record Harrell's 19X1 and 19X2 summarized transactions and the adjusting entries to record bad debts expense at the end of each year.

Following are transactions of The Perry-Finch Company:

Problem 8–6
Analysis and journalizing of notes receivable transactions
(LO 4, 5)

19X1
Dec. 16 Accepted a $9,600, 60-day, 9% note dated this day in granting Hal Krueger a time extension on his past-due account.
31 Made an adjusting entry to record the accrued interest on the Krueger note.
31 Closed the Interest Earned account.

19X2
Feb. 14 Received Krueger's payment for the principal and interest on the note dated December 16.
Mar. 2 Accepted a $5,120, 10%, 90-day note dated this day in granting a time extension on the past-due account of ARC Company.
17 Accepted a $1,600, 30-day, 9% note dated this day in granting Penny Bobek a time extension on her past-due account.
Apr. 16 Bobek dishonored her note when presented for payment.
21 Discounted, with recourse, the ARC Company note at BancFirst at a cost of $50. The transaction was considered to be a loan.
June 2 Received notice from BancFirst that ARC Company defaulted on the note due May 31. Paid the bank the principal plus interest due on the note. (Hint: Create an account receivable for the maturity value of the note.)

July 16 Received payment from ARC Company for the maturity value of its dishonored note plus interest for 45 days beyond maturity at 10%.

Aug. 7 Accepted a $5,440, 90-day, 12% note dated this day in granting a time extension on the past-due account of Mertz & Ivy.

Sept. 3 Accepted a $2,080, 60-day, 10% note dated this day in granting Cecile Duval a time extension on her past-due account.

      18 Discounted, without recourse, the Duval note at BancFirst at a cost of $25.

Nov. 5 Received payment of principal plus interest from Mertz & Ivy for the note of August 7.

Dec. 1 Wrote off the Penny Bobek account against Allowance for Doubtful Accounts.

Required

Preparation component:

Prepare journal entries to record Perry-Finch's transactions.

Analysis component:

What reporting is necessary when a business discounts notes receivable with recourse and these notes have not reached maturity by the end of the fiscal period? Explain the reason for this requirement and what accounting principle is being satisfied.

Problem 8–7
Entries and fair value adjustments for short-term investments
(LO 1)

Franklin Security, Inc., has relatively large idle cash balances and invests them in common stocks that it holds available for sale. Following is a series of events and other facts relevant to the short-term investment activity of the company:

19X1

Jan. 20 Purchased 900 shares of Johnson & Johnson at 18¾ plus a $590 commission.

Feb. 9 Purchased 2,200 shares of Sony Corp. at 46⅞ plus a $2,578 commission.

Oct. 12 Purchased 500 shares of Mattel, Inc., at 55½ plus an $832 commission.

Dec. 31 These per share market values were known for the stocks in the portfolio: Johnson & Johnson, 20⅜; Mattel, 57¼; Sony, 39.

19X2

Apr. 15 Sold 900 shares of Johnson & Johnson at 21¾ less a $685 commission.

July 5 Sold 500 shares of Mattel at 49⅛ less a $491 commission.

      22 Purchased 1,600 shares of Sara Lee Corp. at 36¼ plus a $1,740 commission.

Aug. 19 Purchased 1,800 shares of Eastman Kodak Company at 28 plus a $1,260 commission.

Dec. 31 These per share market values were known for the stocks in the portfolio: Kodak, 31¾; Sara Lee, 30; Sony, 36½.

19X3

Feb. 27 Purchased 3,400 shares of Microsoft Corp. at 23⅝ plus a $1,606 commission.

Mar. 3 Sold 1,600 shares of Sara Lee at 31¼ less a $1,750 commission.

June 21 Sold 2,200 shares of Sony at 40 less a $2,640 commission.

      30 Purchased 1,200 shares of The Black & Decker Corp. at 47½ plus a $1,995 commission.

Nov. 1 Sold 1,800 shares of Eastman Kodak at 42¾ less a $2,309 commission.

Dec. 31 These per share market values were known for the stocks in the portfolio: Black & Decker, 56½; Microsoft, 28.

Required

CHECK FIGURE:
12/31/X3 Short-Term Investments, Fair Value Adjustments, $53,727 Dr.

1. Prepare journal entries to record the events and any year-end adjustments needed to record the fair values of the short-term investments.

2. Prepare a schedule that shows the total cost, total fair value adjustment, and total fair value of the investments at the end of each year.

3. For each year, prepare a schedule that shows the realized gains and losses included in earnings and the total unrealized gain or loss at the end of each year.

CRITICAL THINKING: ESSAYS, PROBLEMS, AND CASES

Analytical Essays

The Whitney Corporation did not own any short-term investments prior to 19X2. After purchasing some short-term investments in 19X2, the company's accountant made the following December 31, 19X2, adjusting entry:

AE 8–1
(LO 1)

Dec.	31	Short-Term Investments, Fair Value Adjustment	12,500.00	
		Holding Gain (Loss)		12,500.00
		To record fair value of short-term investments		
		in securities available for sale.		

When Whitney's accountant reviewed the year-end adjustments with an office manager of the company, the accountant commented that the adjustment shown above might have been different if the company had owned short-term investments on December 31, 19X1. The office manager thought the accountant must be confused. The manager said that the December 31, 19X2, adjustment was supposed to record a gain that occurred during 19X2, and therefore should not be affected by any events that occurred during 19X1.

Required

Explain why the accountant's comment is correct.

Review the facts about SysComm Corporation in Problem 8–3.

AE 8–2
(LO 3)

Required

1. Recall that Allowance for Doubtful Accounts is a contra asset account. Nevertheless, SysComm's unadjusted trial balance shows that this account has a $15,750 debit balance. Explain how this contra asset account could have a debit balance.
2. In Problem 8–3, requirement 1c indicates that 5% of the outstanding accounts receivable ($1,070,100 × 5% = $53,505) will become uncollectible. Given this conclusion, explain why the adjusting entry should not include a $53,505 credit to Accounts Receivable.

As the accountant for Stephenson Distributing, Inc., you recently attended a sales managers' meeting devoted to a discussion of the company's credit policies. At the meeting, you reported that bad debts expense for the past year was estimated to be $59,000 and accounts receivable at the end of the year amounted to $1,750,000 less a $43,000 allowance for doubtful accounts. Sylvia Greco, one of the sales managers, expressed confusion over the fact that bad debts expense and the allowance for doubtful accounts were different amounts. To save time at the meeting, you agreed to discuss the matter with Greco after the meeting.

    Because the meeting lasted longer than expected, Greco had to leave early to catch a plane back to her sales district. As a result, you need to write a memorandum to her explaining why a difference in bad debts expense and the allowance for doubtful accounts is not unusual. (Assume that the company estimates bad debts expense to be 2% of sales.)

**Business
Communications
Case**

(LO 3)

Rappaport Industries has been in business for six years and has used the direct write-off method of accounting for bad debts. The following information is available from the accounting records for the first five years:

**Financial Reporting
Problem**

(LO 3)

	19X5	19X4	19X3	19X2	19X1
Sales	$5,158,900	$2,691,000	$5,980,000	$7,834,000	$2,185,000
Net income	773,250	402,500	897,460	1,171,810	327,070
Bad debts written off during year	38,460	50,300	132,180	32,350	5,890
Bad debts by year of sale* .	58,790	33,570	82,210	90,720	29,400

*Results from classifying bad debt losses so that the losses appear in the same years as the sales that produced them. For example, the $58,790 for 19X5 includes $28,750 of bad debts that became uncollectible during 19X6.

You are the manager of Rappaport Industries and want to change the method of accounting for bad debts from the direct write-off method to the allowance method. Glenn Rochelle, the president of the company, feels this is not necessary.

Required

1. Prepare a five-year schedule for Rochelle showing:
   a. Net income if bad debts expense is defined to be bad debts by year of sale.
   b. The dollar amount of difference between net income using the direct write-off method and the answer to requirement *a*.
   c. The answer to requirement *b* as a percentage of the answer to requirement *a*.
   d. Bad debts by year of sale as a percentage of sales.
   e. Bad debts written off during the year as a percentage of sales.
2. Use the schedule to support your argument for using the allowance method to account for bad debts.

Financial Statement Analysis Case

(LO 1, 5)

Refer to the financial statements and related disclosures from Southwest Airlines Co.'s 1994 annual report in Appendix E. Based on your examination of this information, answer the following:

1. Southwest Airlines' most liquid assets include "cash and cash equivalents" and "accounts receivable." What total amount of those assets did the company have on December 31, 1994?
2. Express Southwest Airlines' total liquid assets as of December 31, 1994, (as previously defined) as a percentage of current liabilities. Do the same for December 31, 1993. Comment on the company's ability to satisfy current liabilities at the end of 1994 as compared to the end of 1993.
3. What criteria did Southwest Airlines use to classify items as cash equivalents?
4. Calculate Southwest Airlines' accounts receivable turnover for 1994.

ANSWERS TO PROGRESS CHECKS

8-1 Securities held to maturity are reported at cost; investments in trading securities are reported at fair (market) value.

8-2 The equity section of the balance sheet.

8-3 The income statement.

8-4 If cash is received as soon as copies of credit card sales receipts are deposited in the bank, the business debits Cash at the time of the sale. If the business does not receive payment until after it submits the receipts to the credit card company, it debits Accounts Receivable at the time of the sale.

8-5 The credit card expenses are *recorded* when the cash is received from the credit card company; however, they are *incurred* at the time of the related sales.

8-6 An adjusting entry must be made to satisfy the matching principle. The credit card expense must be reported in the same period as the sale.

8-7 Bad debts expense must be matched with the sales that gave rise to the accounts receivable. This requires that companies estimate bad debts before they learn which accounts are uncollectible.

8–8 Realizable value.

8–9 The estimated amount of bad debts expense cannot be credited to the Accounts Receivable account because the specific customer accounts that will prove uncollectible cannot be identified and removed from the subsidiary Accounts Receivable Ledger. If the controlling account were credited directly, its balance would not equal the sum of the subsidiary account balances.

8–10

19X1				
Dec.	31	Bad Debts Expense	5,702.00	
		Allowance for Doubtful Accounts		5,702.00

8–11

19X2				
Jan.	10	Allowance for Doubtful Accounts	300.00	
		Accounts Receivable—Felix Arthur		300.00
Apr.	12	Accounts Receivable—Felix Arthur	300.00	
		Allowance for Doubtful Accounts		300.00
	12	Cash	300.00	
		Accounts Receivable—Felix Arthur		300.00

8–12

19X1				
Dec.	16	Notes Receivable	7,000.00	
		Sales		7,000.00
		(90 day, 12% note)		
	31	Interest Receivable	35.00	
		Interest Earned		35.00
		($7,000 × 12% × 15/360)		

8–13

19X2				
Mar.	16	Accounts Receivable—White Corp.	7,210.00	
		Interest Earned		175.00
		Interest Receivable		35.00
		Notes Receivable		7,000.00

8–14 Alternatives are (1) selling their accounts receivable to a factor, and (2) pledging the accounts receivable as security for a loan. The entries to record these transactions would take the following form:

(1)　Cash
　　　Factoring Fee Expense
　　　　　Accounts Receivable
(2)　Cash
　　　　　Notes Payable

8–15 Accounts receivable turnover

$$= \frac{3,205,025}{(762,024 + 580,313)/2}$$

$$= 4.78 \text{ times}$$

Inventories and Cost of Goods Sold

*C*an the choice of an accounting method affect the amount of income or loss that a company reports? Often the choice of one acceptable accounting approach over another can have a dramatic impact on net income. To illustrate, in 1994 Mobil Corporation changed the method it used to account for inventory and disclosed that the change caused a $680 million charge against revenues. The following information was extracted from the news release prepared by Mobil. Note that Mobil's change in accounting method (principle) for inventory required that the company restate its results from a net income of $733 million to $53 million for the first six months of 1994.

NEWS RELEASE:

FAIRFAX, VA. July 29—Mobil Corporation announced today that it is making a change in its method of applying the lower-of-cost-or-market test for crude oil and product inventories. Accordingly, it will reduce previously reported first quarter 1994, and therefore year-to-date, net income by a $680 million after-tax, noncash charge. This inventory accounting change was adopted by Mobil at its board meeting today. . . The previously reported 1994 first quarter and estimated six months net income will be restated as follows (in millions of dollars):

	Three Months Ended March 31, 1994	Six Months Ended June 30, 1994 Estimated
Net income as previously reported	$ 535	$ 733
Cumulative effect of change in accounting principle	(680)	(680)
Restated net income (loss)	$(145)	$ 53

LEARNING OBJECTIVES

After studying Chapter 9, you should be able to:

1. Explain the difference between periodic and perpetual inventory systems and prepare entries to record merchandise transactions using a periodic system.
2. Describe how the cost of ending inventory is determined, explain how it affects the financial statements, and calculate the cost of an inventory based on *(a)* specific invoice prices, *(b)* weighted-average cost, *(c)* FIFO, and *(d)* LIFO.
3. Explain the effect of an inventory error on the financial statements of the current and succeeding years.
4. Calculate the lower-of-cost-or-market amount of an inventory.
5. Use the retail method and the gross profit method to estimate an inventory and calculate merchandise turnover and days' stock on hand.
6. Define or explain the words and phrases listed in the chapter glossary.

The operations of merchandising businesses involve the purchase and resale of tangible goods. In Chapter 6, when we first introduced the topic of accounting for merchandisers, we explained how perpetual inventory systems are used to account for merchandise inventory. In this chapter, we begin by explaining periodic inventory systems, which some companies use instead of perpetual systems. Increased availability of computers and scanners has allowed many firms to switch from periodic to perpetual systems. Nevertheless, a large number of firms continue to use periodic systems for some or all of their inventories.

Later in the chapter, we examine the methods businesses use at the end of each period to assign dollar amounts to merchandise inventory and to cost of goods sold. The principles and procedures that we explain in this chapter are used in department stores, grocery stores, and other businesses that purchase goods for resale. Since these procedures affect the reported amounts of income, assets, and equity, understanding the fundamental concepts of inventory accounting will enhance your ability to use and interpret financial statements.

PERIODIC INVENTORY SYSTEMS

LO 1

Explain the difference between periodic and perpetual inventory systems and prepare entries to record merchandise transactions using a periodic system.

Recall from Chapter 6 that under a perpetual system, the Merchandise Inventory account is updated after each purchase and each sale. At the same time, the Cost of Goods Sold account is updated after each sale so that during the period the account balance reflects the period's total cost of goods sold to date.

By comparison, under a periodic inventory system, the Merchandise Inventory account is updated only once each accounting period, at the end of the period. Throughout the next period, the Merchandise Inventory balance remains unchanged, thereby reflecting the beginning inventory balance until it is updated once again at the end of the period. In addition, in a periodic inventory system, cost of goods sold is not recorded as each sale occurs. Instead, the total cost of goods sold during the period is calculated at the end of the period.

Recording Merchandise Transactions

Recall that under a perpetual system, each purchase, purchase return and allowance, purchase discount, and transportation-in transaction is recorded in the Merchandise Inventory account. Under a periodic system, a separate temporary account is established for each of these items. Then, at the end of the period, each of these temporary accounts is closed and the Merchandise Inventory account is updated. To illustrate these differences, we use parallel columns to show the typical journal entries made under periodic and perpetual inventory systems.

Purchases. Assume that on May 1, Blay, Inc., purchased merchandise on credit for $5,000, with terms of 2/10, n/60. Blay's entry to record the purchase under each system is:

Periodic			Perpetual		
Purchases	5,000		Merchandise Inventory	5,000	
Accounts Payable		5,000	Accounts Payable		5,000

Notice the periodic system uses a temporary Purchases account. It accumulates the cost of all purchase transactions during the period.

Purchase Returns and Allowances. Now assume that Blay returned $500 of the merchandise from the previous purchase and received credit. Blay's entry to record the return is:

Periodic			Perpetual		
Accounts Payable	500		Accounts Payable	500	
Purchase Returns and			Merchandise Inventory .		500
Allowances		500			

This entry would be exactly the same if Blay had been granted a price reduction (allowance) instead of returning the merchandise. In the periodic system, the temporary Purchase Returns and Allowances account accumulates the cost of all returns and allowances transactions during the period.

Purchase Discounts. When Blay paid the supplier for the previous purchase within the discount period, the required payment was ($5,000 − $500) × 98% = $4,410. The following entry records the payment:

Periodic			Perpetual		
Accounts Payable	4,500		Accounts Payable	4,500	
Purchase Discounts		90	Merchandise Inventory .		90
Cash		4,410	Cash		4,410

If the payment had been delayed until after the discount period expired, the entry under both methods would simply debit Accounts Payable and credit Cash for $4,500.

Transportation-In. Assume that Blay paid $300 freight charges to bring merchandise to its store. In the periodic system, the cost is charged to a temporary Transportation-In account. The recording entry is:

Periodic			Perpetual		
Transportation-In	300		Merchandise Inventory	300	
Cash		300	Cash		300

Sales. Assume that Blay sold merchandise on credit for $3,000 and that Blay's cost of the merchandise was $2,000. The entries to record the sale are:

Periodic			Perpetual		
Accounts Receivable	3,000		Accounts Receivable	3,000	
Sales		3,000	Sales		3,000
			Cost of Goods Sold	2,000	
			Merchandise Inventory .		2,000

Note that under the periodic system the cost of goods sold is not recorded at the time of sale. Later, we show how the periodic system calculates total cost of goods sold at the end of the period.

Sales Returns. Now assume that the customer in the previous transaction returned merchandise that had cost Blay $400 and been sold to the customer for $600. Blay restored the merchandise to inventory and records the return as follows:

Periodic			**Perpetual**		
Sales Returns and Allowances .	600		Sales Returns and Allowances .	600	
Accounts Receivable . . .		600	Accounts Receivable . . .		600
			Merchandise Inventory	400	
			Cost of Goods Sold . . .		400

Notice that the periodic system records only the revenue reduction.

Adjusting and Closing Entries

To illustrate the differences in the adjusting and closing entries, assume that Blay, Inc.'s unadjusted trial balances at the end of the period under each of the alternative methods are as shown in Illustration 9–1.

In Illustration 9–1, notice that the Merchandise Inventory balance is $8,000 under the periodic system and $12,500 under the perpetual system. Because the periodic system does not revise the Merchandise Inventory balance during the period, the $8,000 amount is the beginning inventory. The $12,500 balance under the perpetual system is the recorded ending inventory before adjusting for any inventory shrinkage.

Assume that a physical count of inventory taken at the end of the period disclosed $12,200 of merchandise on hand. Thus, inventory shrinkage was $12,500 − $12,200 = $300. Illustration 9–2 shows the adjusting and closing entries under the two systems.

Notice that the periodic system does not require an adjusting entry to record the inventory shrinkage. Instead, the periodic system adds the ending inventory of $12,200 to the Merchandise Inventory account in the first closing entry, and removes the $8,000 beginning inventory balance from the account in the second closing entry.

By updating Merchandise Inventory and closing Purchases, Purchase Returns and Allowances, Purchase Discounts, and Transportation-In, the periodic system transfers the cost of goods sold amount to Income Summary. Look at the periodic side of Illustration 9–2 and notice that the boldface items have the following effects on Income Summary:

Credited to Income Summary in the first closing entry:	
Merchandise inventory	$12,200
Purchase returns and allowances	3,700
Purchase discounts	600
Debited to Income Summary in the second closing entry:	
Merchandise inventory	(8,000)
Purchases	(36,000)
Transportation-in	(900)
Net effect on Income Summary	$28,400)

This $28,400 effect on Income Summary is the cost of goods sold amount, as the following calculation confirms:

Illustration 9–1   Comparison of Unadjusted Trial Balances—Periodic and Perpetual

Periodic			Perpetual		
Cash	$ 4,000		Cash	$ 4,000	
Accounts receivable	7,000		Accounts receivable	7,000	
Other assets	10,000		Other assets	10,000	
Merchandise inventory	**8,000**		**Merchandise inventory**	**12,500**	
Common stock		10,000	Common stock		$10,000
Retained earnings		15,000	Retained earnings		15,000
Sales		60,000	Sales		60,000
Sales returns and allowances	1,800		Sales returns and allowances	1,800	
Purchases	**36,000**				
Purchase returns and allowances		**3,700**			
Purchase discounts		**600**			
Transportation-in	**900**		Cost of goods sold	28,100	
Other expenses	21,600		Other expenses	21,600	
Totals	$89,300	$89,300	Totals	$85,000	$85,000

Illustration 9–2   Comparison of Adjusting and Closing Entries—Periodic and Perpetual

Periodic			Perpetual		
Adjusting entries:			*Adjusting entries:*		
			Cost of Goods Sold	300	
			Merchandise Inventory		300
Closing entries:			*Closing entries:*		
Sales	60,000		Sales	60,000	
Merchandise Inventory	**12,200**		Income Summary		60,000
Purchase Returns and Allowances	**3,700**				
Purchase Discounts	**600**				
Income Summary		76,500			
Income Summary	68,300		Income Summary	51,800	
Sales Returns and Allowances		1,800	Sales Returns and Allowances		1,800
Merchandise Inventory		**8,000**	Cost of Goods Sold		28,400
Purchases		**36,000**	Other Expenses		21,600
Transportation-In		**900**			
Other Expenses		21,600			
Income Summary	8,200		Income Summary	8,200	
Retained Earnings		8,200	Retained Earnings		8,200

Beginning inventory		$ 8,000
Purchases	$36,000	
Less purchase returns and allowances	(3,700)	
Less purchase discounts	(600)	
Plus transportation-in	900	
Net cost of goods purchased		32,600
Cost of goods available for sale		$40,600
Less ending inventory		(12,200)
Cost of goods sold		$28,400

Thus, the periodic system transfers the cost of goods sold expense to the Income Summary account but does not use a Cost of Goods Sold account.

Notice that the periodic system does not measure shrinkage. All this system does is determine the cost of goods available for sale, subtract the cost of the ending inventory, and define the difference as cost of goods sold. In fact, this difference is the cost of goods that have disappeared, which includes the cost of goods sold plus shrinkage.

The Adjusting Entry Approach to Recording the Change in the Merchandise Inventory Account

In the previous discussion of the periodic system, the change in the Merchandise Inventory account was recorded in the process of making closing entries. This closing entry approach is widely used in practice. However, an alternative approach is also widely used. The alternative is to record the change in the Merchandise Inventory account with adjusting entries. After these adjusting entries are made, the first two closing entries do not include changes in the Merchandise Inventory account.

This adjusting entry approach is preferred by some accountants. It is also used by many computerized accounting systems that do not allow the Merchandise Inventory account (a permanent account) to be changed in the closing process.

The Adjusting Entries. Under the adjusting entry approach to the periodic system, Blay removes the beginning balance from the Merchandise Inventory account by recording this adjusting entry at the end of 19X2:

Dec.	31	Income Summary	8,000.00	
		Merchandise Inventory		8,000.00
		To remove the beginning balance from the Merchandise Inventory account.		

A second adjusting entry produces the correct ending balance in the Merchandise Inventory account:

Dec.	31	Merchandise Inventory	12,200.00	
		Income Summary		12,200.00
		To insert the correct ending balance into the Merchandise Inventory account.		

After these entries are posted, the Merchandise Inventory account has a $12,200 debit balance. In addition, the Income Summary account has a $4,200 credit balance.

The Closing Entries. If the two adjusting entries for inventory are used, the closing entries differ only by not including the Merchandise Inventory account. Thus, Blay records the following two closing entries under the adjusting entry approach:

Dec.	31	Sales	60,000.00	
		Purchase Returns and Allowances	3,700.00	
		Purchase Discounts	600.00	
		Income Summary		64,300.00
		To close temporary accounts with credit balances.		
Dec.	31	Income Summary	60,300.00	
		Sales Returns and Allowances		1,800.00
		Purchases		36,000.00
		Transportation-In		900.00
		Other Expenses		21,600.00
		To close temporary accounts with debit balances.		

The entry to close Income Summary is the same as in Illustration 9–2. However, in the adjusting entry approach, the $8,200 net income results from four previous entries instead of two:

Dec.	31	Income Summary	8,200.00	
		Retained Earnings		8,200.00
		To close the Income Summary account.		

Progress Check
(Answers to Progress Checks are provided at the end of the chapter.)

9–1   What account is used in a perpetual inventory system but not in a periodic system?

9–2   Which of the following accounts are temporary accounts? *(a)* Merchandise Inventory; *(b)* Purchases; *(c)* Transportation-In.

9–3   In a periodic inventory system, which of the following statements is true?
   a. A sale of merchandise requires two entries, one to record the revenue and one to record the cost of goods sold.
   b. A separate Cost of Goods Sold account is used.
   c. The Merchandise Inventory account balance reflects the amount of merchandise on hand only at the end of the period.

9–4   How is the cost of goods sold determined under a periodic inventory accounting system?

9–5   Will the reported amounts of ending inventory and net income differ if the adjusting entry approach to recording the change in inventory is used instead of the closing entry approach?

MATCHING MERCHANDISE COSTS WITH REVENUES

LO 2
Describe how the cost of ending inventory is determined, explain how it affects the financial statements, and calculate the cost of an inventory based on *(a)* specific invoice prices, *(b)* weighted-average cost, *(c)* FIFO, and *(d)* LIFO.

Accounting for inventories affects both the balance sheet and the income statement. However, "the major objective [in accounting for the goods in the inventory] is the matching of appropriate **costs** against revenues in order that there may be a proper determination of the realized income."[1] We first discussed the *matching principle* in Chapter 4 (p. 111). For inventories, it involves deciding how much of the cost of the goods available for sale during a period should be deducted from the period's revenue and how much should be carried forward as inventory to be matched against a future period's revenue.

In a periodic inventory system, when the cost of goods available for sale is allocated between cost of goods sold and ending inventory, the key problem is assigning a cost to the ending inventory. Remember, however, that by assigning a cost to the ending inventory, you are also determining cost of goods sold. This is true because the ending inventory is subtracted from the cost of goods available for sale to determine cost of goods sold.

Items to Include in Merchandise Inventory

The merchandise inventory of a business includes all goods owned by the business and held for sale, regardless of where the goods may be located at the time inventory is counted. In applying this rule, most items present no problem. All that is required is to see that all items are counted, that nothing is omitted, and that nothing is counted more than once. However, goods in transit, goods sold but not delivered, goods on consignment, and obsolete and damaged goods require special attention.

---

[1]FASB, *Accounting Standards—Current Text* (Norwalk, CT, 1995), sec. I78.104. First published as *Accounting Research Bulletin No. 43,* chap. 4, par. 4.

Should merchandise be included in the inventory of a business if the goods are in transit from a supplier to a business on the date the business takes an inventory? The answer to this question depends on whether the rights and risks of ownership have passed from the supplier to the purchaser. If ownership has passed to the purchaser, they should be included in the purchaser's inventory. If the buyer is responsible for paying the freight charges, ownership usually passes as soon as the goods are loaded on the means of transportation. (As mentioned in Chapter 6, the terms would be FOB the seller's factory or warehouse.) On the other hand, if the seller is to pay the freight charges, ownership passes when the goods arrive at their destination (FOB destination).

Goods on consignment are goods shipped by their owner (known as the **consignor**) to another person or firm (called the **consignee**) who is to sell the goods for the owner. Consigned goods belong to the consignor and should appear on the consignor's inventory. For example, **Score Board Inc.** pays sports celebrities such as Shaquille O'Neal and Joe DiMaggio to sign memorabilia. The autographed baseballs, jerseys, photos, and so on, are then offered to the shopping networks on consignment as well as sold through catalogs and dealers.

Damaged goods and deteriorated or obsolete goods should not be counted in the inventory if they are not salable. If such goods can be sold at a reduced price, they should be included in the inventory at a conservative estimate of their **net realizable value** (sales price less the cost of making the sale). Thus, the accounting period in which the goods deteriorated, were damaged, or became obsolete suffers the resultant loss.

Elements of Merchandise Cost

As applied to merchandise, cost means the sum of the expenditures and charges directly or indirectly incurred in bringing an article to its existing condition and location.[2] Therefore, the cost of an inventory item includes the invoice price, less any discount, plus any additional or incidental costs necessary to put the item into place and condition for sale. The additional costs may include import duties, transportation-in, storage, insurance, and any other related costs such as those incurred during an aging process (for example, the aging of wine).

All of these costs should be included in the cost of merchandise. When calculating the cost of a merchandise inventory, however, some concerns do not include the incidental costs of acquiring merchandise. They price the inventory on the basis of invoice prices only. As a result, the incidental costs are allocated to cost of goods sold during the period in which they are incurred.

In theory, a share of each incidental cost should be assigned to every unit purchased. This causes a portion of each to be carried forward in the inventory to be matched against the revenue of the period in which the inventory is sold. However, the effort of computing costs on such a precise basis may outweigh the benefit from the extra accuracy. Therefore, many businesses take advantage of the *materiality principle* and charge such costs to cost of goods sold.

Taking an Ending Inventory

When a physical inventory is taken at the end of the period, the dollar amount of the inventory is determined as follows: count the units of each product on hand, multiply the count for each product by its cost per unit, and add the costs for all products.

PRINCIPLE APPLICATION
Materiality Principle, p. 288
In 1994, Colgate-Palmolive Company reported net sales of $7,587.9 million, cost of sales of $3,913.3 million, and net income of $580.2 million. End-of-year inventories were $713.9 million and total assets were $6,142.4 million. Consider whether a $1 million or $10 million error in allocating a cost between inventory and cost of goods sold could be ignored under the materiality principle. (In general, determining whether an amount is material is a matter of professional judgment.)

---

[2]Ibid., sec. I78.402. First published as *Accounting Research Bulletin No. 43,* ch. 4, par. 5.

Illustration 9–3   Inventory Tickets Used to Tag Inventory Items as They Are Counted

INVENTORY TICKET NO. _786_   Quantity counted _____

Item _____   Sales price $ _____

Counted by _____   Cost price $ _____

Checked by _____   Purchase date _____

In making the count, items are less likely to be counted twice or omitted from the count if you use prenumbered **inventory tickets** like the one in Illustration 9–3.

Before beginning the inventory count, a sufficient number of the tickets, at least one for each product on hand, is issued to the employees who make the count. Next, the employees count the quantity of each product. From the count and the price tag attached to the merchandise, the required inventory tickets are filled in and attached to the counted items. By the time the count is completed, inventory tickets should have been attached to all counted items. After checking for uncounted items, the employees remove the tickets and send them to the accounting department. To ensure that no ticket is lost or left attached to merchandise, the accounting department verifies that all the prenumbered tickets issued have been returned.

In the accounting department, the unit and cost data on the tickets are aggregated by multiplying the number of units of each product by its unit cost. This gives the dollar amount of each product in the inventory and the total for all the products is the dollar total of the inventory.

Progress Check

9–6   Which accounting principle most directly governs the allocation of cost of goods available for sale between the ending inventory and cost of goods sold?

9–7   If Campbell sells goods to Thompson, FOB Campbell's factory, and the goods are still in transit from Campbell to Thompson, which company should include the goods in its inventory?

9–8   Kramer Gallery purchased an original painting for $11,400. Additional costs incurred in obtaining and offering the artwork for sale included $130 for transportation-in, $150 for import duties, $100 for insurance during shipment, $180 for advertising costs, $400 for framing, and $800 for sales salaries. In calculating the cost of inventory, what total cost should be assigned to the painting? (a) $11,400; (b) $11,530; (c) $11,780; (d) $12,180.

ASSIGNING COSTS TO INVENTORY ITEMS

One of the major issues in accounting for merchandise involves determining the unit cost amounts that will be assigned to items in the inventory. When all units are purchased at the same unit cost, this process is easy. However, when identical items were purchased at different costs, a problem arises as to which costs apply to the ending inventory and which apply to the goods sold. There are four commonly used methods of assigning costs to goods in the ending inventory and to goods sold. They are

320   Chapter 9

(1) specific invoice prices; (2) weighted-average cost; (3) first-in, first-out; and (4) last-in, first-out. All four methods are generally accepted.

To illustrate the four methods, assume that a company has 12 units of Product X on hand at the end of its annual accounting period. Also, assume that the inventory at the beginning of the year and the purchases during the year were as follows:

Jan. 1	Beginning inventory	10 units @ $100 =	$1,000
Mar. 13	Purchased	15 units @ $108 =	1,620
Aug. 17	Purchased	20 units @ $120 =	2,400
Nov. 10	Purchased	10 units @ $125 =	1,250
Total	....	55 units	$6,270

Specific Invoice Prices

When each item in an inventory can be clearly related to a specific purchase and its invoice, **specific invoice inventory pricing** may be used to assign costs. For example, assume that 6 of the 12 unsold units of Product X were from the November purchase and 6 were from the August purchase. With this information, specific invoice prices can be used to assign costs to the ending inventory and to goods sold as follows:

Total cost of 55 units available for sale		$6,270
Less ending inventory priced by means of specific invoices:		
6 units from the November purchase at $125 each	$750	
6 units from the August purchase at $120 each	720	
12 units in the ending inventory		1,470
Cost of goods sold		$4,800

Weighted Average

When using **weighted-average inventory pricing,** the accountant multiplies the per unit costs of the beginning inventory and of each purchase by the number of units in the beginning inventory and each purchase. Then, the total of these amounts is divided by the total number of units available for sale to find the weighted-average cost per unit as follows:

10 units @ $100 =	$1,000
15 units @ $108 =	1,620
20 units @ $120 =	2,400
10 units @ $125 =	1,250
55	$6,270

$6,270/55 = $114 weighted-average cost per unit

After determining the weighted-average cost per unit, the accountant uses it to assign costs to the inventory and to the units sold as follows:

Total cost of 55 units available for sale	$6,270
Less ending inventory priced on a weighted-average cost basis: 12 units at $114 each	1,368
Cost of goods sold	$4,902

First-In, First-Out

First-in, first-out inventory pricing (FIFO) assumes the items in the beginning inventory are sold first. Additional sales are assumed to come in the order in which they were purchased. Thus, the costs of the last items received are assigned to the ending inventory, and the remaining costs are assigned to goods sold. For example, when first-in, first-out is used, the costs of Product X are assigned to the inventory and goods sold as follows:

Total cost of 55 units available for sale		$6,270
Less ending inventory priced on a basis of FIFO:		
10 units from the November purchase at $125 each	$1,250	
2 units from the August purchase at $120 each	240	
12 units in the ending inventory		1,490
Cost of goods sold		$4,780

Understand that FIFO is acceptable whether or not the physical flow of goods actually follows a first-in, first-out pattern. The physical flow of products depends on the nature of the product and the way the products are stored. If a product is perishable (for example, fresh tomatoes), the business attempts to sell them in a first-in, first-out pattern. Other products, for example, bolts or screws kept in a large bin, may tend to be sold on a last-in, first-out basis. In either case, the FIFO method of allocating cost may be used.

Last-In, First-Out

Under the **last-in, first-out inventory pricing (LIFO)** method, the costs of the last goods received are charged to cost of goods sold and matched with revenue from sales. Again, this method is acceptable even though the physical flow of goods may not be on a last-in, first-out basis.

One argument for the use of LIFO is based on the fact that a going concern must replace the inventory items it sells. When goods are sold, replacements are purchased. Thus, a sale causes the replacement of goods. From this point of view, a correct matching of costs with revenues would be to match replacement costs with the sales that made replacements necessary. Although the costs of the most recent purchases are not quite the same as replacement costs, they usually are close approximations of replacement costs. Because LIFO assigns the most recent purchase costs to the income statement, LIFO (compared to FIFO or weighted average) comes closest to matching replacement costs with revenues.

Under LIFO, costs are assigned to the 12 remaining units of Product X and to the goods sold as follows:

Total cost of 55 units available for sale		$6,270
Less ending inventory priced on a basis of LIFO:		
10 units in the beginning inventory at $100 each	$1,000	
2 units from the March purchase at $108 each	216	
12 units in the ending inventory		1,216
Cost of goods sold		$5,054

Notice that when LIFO is used to match costs and revenues, the ending inventory cost is the cost of the oldest 12 units.

Comparison of Methods

In a stable market where prices remain unchanged, the choice of an inventory pricing method is not important. When prices are unchanged over a period of time, all methods give the same cost figures. However, in a changing market where prices are rising or falling, each method may give a different result. These differences are shown in Illustration 9–4, where we assume that Product X sales were $6,000 and operating expenses were $500.

In Illustration 9–4, note the differences that resulted from the choice of an inventory pricing method. Because purchase prices were rising throughout the period, FIFO resulted in the lowest cost of goods sold, the highest gross profit, and the highest net income. On the other hand, LIFO resulted in the highest cost of goods

sold, the lowest gross profit, and the lowest net income. As you would expect, the results of using the weighted-average method fall between FIFO and LIFO. The results of using specific invoice prices depend entirely on which units were actually sold.

Some companies' financial statements indicate what the difference would be if another method were used. For example, footnote 4 in **Ford Motor Company's** 1994 annual report states:

Inventories are stated at the lower of cost or market. The cost of most U.S. inventories is determined by the last-in, first-out ("LIFO") method. The cost of the remaining inventories is determined primarily by the first-in, first-out ("FIFO") method.

If the FIFO method had been used instead of the LIFO method, inventories would have been $1,383 million and $1,342 million higher than reported at December 31, 1994, and 1993, respectively.

Each of the four pricing methods is generally accepted, and arguments can be made for using each. One argument is that specific invoice prices exactly match costs and revenues. It is clearly the most appropriate method when each unit of product has unique features that affect the cost of that particular unit. However, this method may not be practical except for relatively high-priced items when just a few units are kept in stock and sold. Weighted-average costs tend to smooth out price fluctuations. FIFO provides an inventory valuation on the balance sheet that most closely approximates current replacement cost. LIFO causes the last costs incurred to be assigned to cost of goods sold. Therefore, it results in a better matching of current costs with revenues on the income statement.

Because the choice of an inventory pricing method often has material effects on the financial statements, the choice of a method should be disclosed in the footnotes to the statements. This information is important to an understanding of the statements and is required by the *full-disclosure principle.*[3]

Tax Effect of LIFO

The income statements in Illustration 9–4 are assumed to be those of a corporation. Therefore, the income statements include income taxes expense (at an assumed rate of 30%). Note that a tax advantage was gained by using LIFO because purchase prices were rising. This advantage arises because LIFO assigns the largest dollar amounts to cost of goods sold when purchase prices are increasing. As a result, the

---

[3]Ibid., sec. A10.105, 106. First published as *APB Opinion No. 22,* pars. 12, 13.

	Specific Invoice Prices	Weighted Average	FIFO	LIFO
Sales	$6,000	$6,000	$6,000	$6,000
Cost of goods sold:				
Merchandise inventory, January 1	$1,000	$1,000	$1,000	$1,000
Purchases	5,270	5,270	5,270	5,270
Cost of goods available for sale	$6,270	$6,270	$6,270	$6,270
Merchandise inventory, December 31	1,470	1,368	1,490	1,216
Cost of goods sold	$4,800	$4,902	$4,780	$5,054
Gross profit	$1,200	$1,098	$1,220	$ 946
Operating expenses	500	500	500	500
Income before taxes	$ 700	$ 598	$ 720	$ 446
Income taxes expense (30%)	210	179	216	134
Net income	$ 490	$ 419	$ 504	$ 312

Illustration 9–4
The Income Statement Effects of Alternative Inventory Pricing Methods

smallest income is reported when LIFO is used. This in turn results in the smallest income taxes expense.

The Consistency Principle

Because the choice of an inventory pricing method can have a material effect on the financial statements, some companies might be inclined to make a new choice each year. Their objective would be to select whichever method would result in the most favorable financial statements. If this were allowed, however, readers of financial statements would find it extremely difficult to compare the company's financial statements from one year to the next. If income increased, the reader would have difficulty deciding whether the increase resulted from more successful operations or from the change in the accounting method. The **consistency principle** is used to avoid this problem.

The *consistency principle* requires that a company use the same accounting methods period after period, so that the financial statements of succeeding periods will be comparable.[4] The *consistency principle* is not limited just to inventory pricing methods. Whenever a company must choose between alternative accounting methods, consistency requires that the company continue to use the selected method period after period. As a result, a reader of a company's financial statements may assume that in keeping its records and in preparing its statements, the company used the same procedures employed in previous years. Only on the basis of this assumption can meaningful comparisons be made of the data in a company's statements year after year.

The consistency principle does not require a company to use one inventory valuation method exclusively. It can use different methods to value different categories of inventory. For example, **Texaco, Inc.,** includes the following note to its 1994 financial statements:

> Virtually all inventories of crude oil, petroleum products, and petrochemicals are stated at cost, determined on the last-in, first-out (LIFO) method. Other merchan-

---

[4]FASB, *Statement of Financial Accounting Concepts No. 2,* "Qualitative Characteristics of Accounting Information" (Norwalk, CT, 1980), par. 120.

dise inventories are stated at cost, determined on the first-in, first-out (FIFO) method. Materials and supplies are stated at average cost. Inventories are valued at the lower of cost or market.

In achieving comparability, the *consistency principle* does not mean that a company can never change from one accounting method to another. Rather, if a company justifies a different acceptable method or procedure as an improvement in financial reporting, a change may be made. However, when such a change is made, the *full-disclosure principle* requires that the nature of the change, justification for the change, and the effect of the change on net income be disclosed in footnotes to the statements.[5]

Progress Check

9-9   A company with the following beginning inventory and purchases ended the period with 30 units on hand:

	Units	Unit Cost
Beginning Inventory	100	10
Purchases #1	40	12
#2	20	14

a. Determine the ending inventory using FIFO.
b. Determine cost of goods sold using LIFO.

9-10   In a period of rising costs and prices, which method (LIFO or FIFO) reports the higher net income?

9-11   In a period of rising costs and prices, what effect will LIFO as compared to FIFO have on the balance sheet?

INVENTORY ERRORS

LO 3
Explain the effect of an inventory error on the financial statements of the current and succeeding years.

Companies must be especially careful in taking the end-of-period inventory. If an error is made, it will cause misstatements in cost of goods sold, gross profit, net income, current assets, and stockholders' equity. Also, the ending inventory of one period is the beginning inventory of the next. Therefore, the error will carry forward and cause misstatements in the succeeding period's cost of goods sold, gross profit, and net income. Furthermore, since the amount involved in an inventory often is large, the misstatements can materially reduce the usefulness of the financial statements.

To illustrate the effects of an inventory error, assume that in each of the years 19X1, 19X2, and 19X3, a company had $100,000 in sales. If the company maintained a $20,000 inventory throughout the period and made $60,000 in purchases in each of the years, its cost of goods sold each year was $60,000 and its annual gross profit was $40,000. However, assume the company incorrectly calculated its December 31, 19X1, inventory at $16,000 rather than $20,000. Note the effects of the error in Illustration 9–5.

Observe in Illustration 9–5 that the $4,000 understatement of the December 31, 19X1, inventory caused a $4,000 overstatement in 19X1 cost of goods sold and a $4,000 understatement in gross profit. To keep the example simple, we will ignore income taxes, in which case the error also understates net income by $4,000. Also, because the ending inventory of 19X1 became the beginning inventory of 19X2, the error caused an understatement in the 19X2 cost of goods sold and a $4,000 overstatement in gross profit and net income. However, by 19X3 the error had no effect.

---

[5]FASB, *Accounting Standards—Current Text* (Norwalk, CT, 1995), sec. A06.113. First published as *APB Opinion No. 20*, par. 17.

Illustration 9-5 Effects of Inventory Errors—Periodic Inventory System

	19X1		19X2		19X3	
Sales		$100,000		$100,000		$100,000
Cost of goods sold:						
Beginning inventory	$20,000		$16,000*		$20,000	
Purchases	60,000		60,000		60,000	
Goods for sale	$80,000		$76,000		$80,000	
Ending inventory	16,000*		20,000		20,000	
Cost of goods sold		64,000		56,000		60,000
Gross profit		$ 36,000		$ 44,000		$ 40,000
Other expenses		–0–		–0–		–0–
Net income		$ 36,000		$ 44,000		$ 40,000

*Should have been $20,000.

In Illustration 9–5, the December 31, 19X1, inventory is understated. Had it been overstated, it would have caused opposite results—the 19X1 net income would have been overstated and the 19X2 income understated.

Because an inventory error causes an offsetting error in the next period, it is sometimes said to be self-correcting. Thus, you might be inclined to think that they are not serious. Do not make this mistake. Management, creditors, and owners base many important decisions on fluctuations in reported net income. Therefore, inventory errors must be avoided.

Progress Check

9-12 Falk Company maintains its inventory records on a periodic basis. In making the physical count of inventory at 19X1 year-end, an error was made that overstated the 19X1 ending inventory by $10,000. Will this error cause cost of goods sold to be over- or understated in 19X1? In 19X2? By how much?

As we have discussed, the cost of the ending inventory is determined by using one of the four pricing methods (FIFO, LIFO, weighted average, or specific invoice prices). However, the cost of the inventory is not necessarily the amount reported on the balance sheet. Generally accepted accounting principles require that the inventory be reported at market value whenever market is lower than cost. Thus, merchandise inventory is shown on the balance sheet at the **lower of cost or market (LCM).**

Market Normally Means Replacement Cost

In applying lower of cost or market (LCM) to merchandise inventories, what do accountants mean by the term *market?* In this situation, market does not mean the expected sales price. Instead, market normally means *replacement cost.*[6] That is the price a company would pay if it bought new items to replace those in its inventory.

The theory underlying LCM is that when the sales price of merchandise falls, the replacement cost also is likely to fall. The decline from the previously incurred cost to replacement cost represents a loss of value that should be recognized when the loss occurs. This is accomplished at the end of the period by writing the ending merchandise down from cost to replacement cost.

LOWER OF COST OR MARKET

LO 4
Calculate the lower-of-cost-or-market amount of an inventory.

---

[6]Exceptions to the normal definition of market as replacement cost are explained in more advanced accounting courses.

Product	Units on Hand	Per Unit Cost	Per Unit Replacement Cost	Total Cost	Total Replacement Cost	Lower of Cost or Replacement Cost
X	20	$8	$7	$160	$140	$140
Y	10	5	6	50	60	50
Z	5	9	7	45	35	35
Total cost originally incurred				$255		
LCM (applied to whole inventory)					$235	
LCM (applied to each product)						$225

PRINCIPLE APPLICATION
Full-Disclosure Principle, p. 294
The Home Depot states in Note 1 to its 1994 financial statements that: "Inventories are stated at the lower of cost (first-in, first-out) or market, as determined by the retail inventory method."

Note that when LCM is applied to the whole inventory, the total is $235, which is $20 lower than the $255 cost. And when the method is applied separately to each product, the sum is only $225. In general, a company may apply LCM three different ways:

1. LCM may be applied separately to each product.
2. LCM may be applied to major categories of products.
3. If the products are not too different, LCM may be applied to the inventory as a whole.

Recall that the opening of the chapter discussed **Mobil Corporation's** decision to change the method it uses to determine the LCM of its inventories. The company's news release did not explain exactly how the LCM method was changed, but it did indicate the effect of the change on net income. Following the *full-disclosure principle,* Mobil will repeat this information in its financial statements.

THE CONSERVATISM PRINCIPLE

Generally accepted accounting principles require writing inventory down to market when market is less than cost. On the other hand, inventory generally cannot be written up to market when market exceeds cost. If writing inventory down to market is justified, why not also write inventory up to market? What is the reason for this apparent inconsistency?

The reason is that the gain from a market value increase is not realized until a sales transaction provides verifiable evidence of the amount of the gain. But why, then, are inventories written down when market is below cost?

Accountants often justify the lower-of-cost-or-market rule by citing the **conservatism principle.** This principle attempts to guide the accountant in uncertain situations where amounts must be estimated. In general terms, it implies that when "two estimates of amounts to be received or paid in the future are about equally likely, . . . the less optimistic" should be used.[7] Because the value of inventory is uncertain, writing the inventory down when its market value falls is clearly the less optimistic estimate of the inventory's value to the company.

---

[7]FASB, *Statement of Financial Accounting Concepts No. 2* (Norwalk, CT, 1980) par. 95.

Progress Check

9-13 A company's ending inventory includes the following items:

Product	Units on Hand	Unit Cost	Market Value per Unit
A	20	$ 6	$ 5
B	40	9	8
C	10	12	15

The inventory's lower of cost or market, applied separately to each product, is:
(a) $520; (b) $540; (c) $570; (d) $600.

THE RETAIL METHOD OF ESTIMATING INVENTORIES

LO 5
Use the retail method and the gross profit method to estimate an inventory and calculate merchandise turnover and days' stock on hand.

Most companies prepare financial statements on a quarterly or monthly basis. These monthly or quarterly statements are called **interim statements** because they are prepared between the regular year-end statements. The cost of goods sold information that is necessary to prepare interim statements is readily available if a perpetual inventory system is used. However, a periodic system requires a physical inventory to determine cost of goods sold. To avoid the time-consuming and expensive process of taking a physical inventory each month or quarter, some companies use the **retail inventory method** to estimate cost of goods sold and ending inventory. Then, they take a physical inventory at the end of each year. Other companies also use the retail inventory method to prepare the year-end statements. However, all companies should take a physical inventory at least once each year to correct any errors or shortages.

Estimating an Ending Inventory by the Retail Method

When the retail method is used to estimate an inventory, the company's records must show the amount of inventory it had at the beginning of the period both at *cost* and at *retail*. You already understand the cost of an inventory. The retail amount of an inventory is simply the dollar amount of the inventory at the marked selling prices of the inventory items.

In addition to the beginning inventory, the accounting records must show the net amount of goods purchased during the period both at cost and at retail. This is the balance of the Purchases account less returns, allowances, and discounts. Also, the records must show the amount of net sales at retail. With this information, you estimate the ending inventory as follows:

Step 1: Compute the amount of goods available for sale during the period both at cost and at retail.

Step 2: Divide the goods available at cost by the goods available at retail to obtain a **retail method cost ratio.**

Step 3: Deduct sales (at retail) from goods available for sale (at retail) to determine the ending inventory at retail.

Step 4: Multiply the ending inventory at retail by the cost ratio to reduce the inventory to a cost basis.

Look at Illustration 9–6 to see these calculations.

This is the essence of Illustration 9–6: (1) The company had $100,000 of goods (at marked selling prices) for sale during the period. (2) The cost of these goods was 60% of their $100,000 marked retail sales value. (3) The company's records (its Sales account) showed that $70,000 of these goods were sold, leaving $30,000 (retail value) of unsold merchandise in the ending inventory. (4) Since cost in this store is 60% of retail, the estimated cost of this ending inventory is $18,000.

An ending inventory calculated as in Illustration 9–6 is an estimate arrived at by deducting sales (goods sold) from goods available for sale. As we said before, this method may be used for interim statements or even for year-end statements.

Illustration 9–6
Calculating the Ending
Inventory Cost by the Retail
Method

		At Cost	At Retail
Step 1:	Goods available for sale:		
	Beginning inventory	$20,500	$ 34,500
	Net purchases	39,500	65,500
	Goods available for sale	$60,000	$100,000
Step 2:	Cost ratio: ($60,000/$100,000) × 100 = 60%		
Step 3:	Deduct net sales at retail		70,000
	Ending inventory at retail		$ 30,000
Step 4:	Ending inventory at cost ($30,000 × 60%)	$18,000	

Nevertheless, a store must take a physical count of the inventory at least once each year to correct any errors or shortages.

Using the Retail Method to Reduce a Physical Inventory to Cost

In retail stores, items for sale normally have price tags attached that show selling prices. So, when a store takes a physical inventory, it commonly takes the inventory at the marked selling prices of the items on hand. It then reduces the dollar total of this inventory to a cost basis by applying its cost ratio. It does this because the selling prices are readily available and the application of the cost ratio eliminates the need to look up the invoice price of each item on hand.

For example, assume that the company in Illustration 9–6 estimates its inventory by the retail method and takes a physical inventory at the marked selling prices of the goods. Also assume that the total retail amount of this physical inventory is $29,600. The company can calculate the cost for this inventory simply by applying its cost ratio to the inventory total as follows:

$$\$29,600 \times 60\% = \$17,760$$

The $17,760 cost figure for this company's ending physical inventory is a satisfactory figure for year-end statement purposes. It is also acceptable to the Internal Revenue Service for tax purposes.

Inventory Shortage

An inventory determined as in Illustration 9–6 is an estimate of the amount of goods on hand. Since it is determined by deducting sales from goods for sale, it does not reveal any shrinkage due to breakage, loss, or theft. However, you can estimate the amount of shrinkage by comparing the inventory as calculated in Illustration 9–6 with the amount that results from taking a physical inventory.

For example, in Illustration 9–6, we estimated that the ending inventory at retail was $30,000. Then, we assumed that this same company took a physical inventory and counted only $29,600 of merchandise on hand (at retail). Therefore, the company must have had an inventory shortage at retail of $30,000 − $29,600 = $400. Stated in terms of cost, the shortage is $400 × 60% = $240.

GROSS PROFIT METHOD OF ESTIMATING INVENTORIES

Sometimes, a business that does not use a perpetual inventory system or the retail method may need to estimate the cost of its inventory. For example, if the inventory is destroyed by fire or is stolen, the business must estimate the inventory so that it can file a claim with its insurance company. In cases such as this, the cost of the inventory can be estimated by the **gross profit method.** With this method, the historical relationship between cost of goods sold and sales is applied to sales of the current period as a way of estimating cost of goods sold during the current period. Then,

Illustration 9–7
The Gross Profit Method
of Estimating Inventory

Goods available for sale:		
Inventory, January 1, 19X1		$12,000
Net purchases	$20,000	
Add transportation-in	500	20,500
Goods available for sale		$32,500
Less estimated cost of goods sold:		
Sales	$31,500	
Less sales returns	(1,500)	
Net sales	$30,000	
Estimated cost of goods sold (70% × $30,000)		(21,000)
Estimated March 27 inventory and inventory loss		$11,500

cost of goods sold is subtracted from the cost of goods available for sale to get the estimated cost of the ending inventory.

To use the gross profit method, several items of accounting information must be available. These include information about the normal gross profit margin or rate, the cost of the beginning inventory, the cost of net purchases, transportation-in, and the amount of sales and sales returns.

For example, assume that the inventory of a company was totally destroyed by a fire on March 27, 19X1. The company's average gross profit rate during the past five years has been 30% of net sales. On the date of the fire, the company's accounts showed the following balances:

Sales	$31,500
Sales returns	1,500
Inventory, January 1, 19X1	12,000
Net purchases	20,000
Transportation-in	500

With this information, the gross profit method may be used to estimate the company's inventory loss. To apply the gross profit method, the first step is to recognize that whatever portion of each dollar of net sales was gross profit, the remaining portion was cost of goods sold. Thus, if the company's gross profit rate averages 30%, then 30% of each net sales dollar was gross profit, and 70% was cost of goods sold. In Illustration 9–7, we show how the 70% is used to estimate the inventory that was lost.

To understand Illustration 9–7, recall that an ending inventory is normally subtracted from goods available for sale to determine the cost of goods sold. Then, observe in Illustration 9–7 that the opposite subtraction is made. Estimated cost of goods sold is subtracted from goods available for sale to determine the estimated ending inventory.

As we mentioned, the gross profit method is often used to estimate the amount of an insurance claim. Accountants also use this method to see if an inventory amount determined by management's physical count of the items on hand is reasonable.

USING THE INFORMATION— MERCHANDISE TURNOVER AND DAYS' STOCK ON HAND

In prior chapters, we explained some ratios that you can use to evaluate a company's short-term liquidity. These ratios include the current ratio, the acid-test ratio, days' sales uncollected, and accounts receivable turnover. A company's ability to pay its short-term obligations also depends on how rapidly it sells its merchandise inventory. To evaluate this, you may calculate **merchandise turnover.** The formula for this ratio is:

$$\text{Merchandise turnover} = \frac{\text{Cost of goods sold}}{\text{Average merchandise inventory}}$$

In this ratio, the average merchandise inventory is usually calculated by adding the beginning and ending inventory amounts and dividing the total by two. However, if the company's sales vary by season of the year, you may want to take an average of the inventory amounts at the end of each quarter.

Analysts use merchandise turnover in evaluating short-term liquidity. In addition, they may use it to assess whether management is doing a good job of controlling the amount of inventory kept on hand. A ratio that is high compared to the ratios of competing companies may indicate that the amount of merchandise held in inventory is too low. As a result, sales may be lost because customers are unable to find what they want. A ratio that is low compared to other companies may indicate an inefficient use of assets. In other words, the company may be holding more merchandise than is needed to support its sales volume.

Earlier in the chapter, we explained how the choice of an inventory costing method (such as FIFO, weighted average, or LIFO) affects the reported amounts of inventory and cost of goods sold. The choice of an inventory costing method also affects the calculated amount of merchandise turnover. Therefore, comparing the merchandise turnover ratios of different companies may be misleading unless they use the same costing method.

Another inventory statistic used to evaluate the liquidity of the merchandise inventory is **days' stock on hand.** This is similar to the days' sales uncollected measure described in Chapter 7. The formula for days' stock on hand is:

$$\text{Days' stock on hand} = \frac{\text{Ending inventory}}{\text{Cost of goods sold}} \times 365$$

Notice the difference in the focus of merchandise turnover and days' stock on hand. Merchandise turnover is an average that occurred during an accounting period. By comparison, the focus of days' stock on hand is on the end-of-period inventory. Days' stock on hand is an estimate of how many days it will take to convert the inventory on hand at the end of the period into accounts receivable or cash.

Nike, Inc.'s 1995 annual report states that "the company places strong emphasis on inventory management..." The following data from Nike's 1995 financial statements show that merchandise turnover increased from 4.3 during 1994 to 5.2 during 1995. Nevertheless, days' stock on hand increased from 74.5 days at the end of 1994 to 80.2 days at the end of 1995.

Year ended May 31:	1995	1994	1993
Cost of goods sold	$2,865,280	$2,301,423	
Ending merchandise inventory	629,742	470,023	$592,986

Merchandise turnover:

1995: $$\frac{\$2,865,280}{(\$629,742 + \$470,023)/2} = 5.2 \text{ times}$$

1994: $$\frac{\$2,301,423}{(\$470,023 + \$592,986)/2} = 4.3 \text{ times}$$

Days' stock on hand:

1995: $$\frac{\$629,742}{\$2,865,280} \times 365 = 80.2 \text{ days}$$

1994: $$\frac{\$470,023}{\$2,301,423} \times 365 = 74.5 \text{ days}$$

Progress Check

9-14 The following data relates to Taylor Company's inventory during the year:

	Cost	Retail
Beginning inventory	$324,000	$530,000
Purchases	204,000	348,000
Purchase returns	9,000	13,000
Sales		320,000

Using the retail method, the estimated cost of the ending inventory is: *(a)* $545,000; *(b)* $324,200; *(c)* $333,200; *(d)* $314,000; *(e)* $327,000.

9-15 Which ratio refers to end-of-period data only: merchandise turnover or days' stock on hand?

SUMMARY OF THE CHAPTER IN TERMS OF LEARNING OBJECTIVES

LO 1. Explain the difference between periodic and perpetual inventory systems and prepare entries to record merchandise transactions using a periodic system. Unlike a perpetual inventory system in which the Merchandise Inventory account is updated for each purchase and sale, the periodic system updates the account only at the end of each accounting period. Also, purchases, and purchase returns and allowances, purchase discounts, and transportation-in are recorded in separate temporary accounts. Then, at the end of the period, these accounts are closed and Merchandise Inventory is updated. The amount of cost of goods sold is accumulated in the Income Summary account without using a separate Cost of Goods Sold account.

LO 2. Describe how the cost of ending inventory is determined, explain how it affects the financial statements, and calculate the cost of an inventory based on *(a)* specific invoice prices, *(b)* weighted-average cost, *(c)* FIFO, and *(d)* LIFO. The allocation of the cost of goods available for sale between cost of goods sold and ending inventory is an accounting application of the *matching principle*. Merchandise inventory should include all goods that are owned by the business and held for resale. This includes items the business has placed on consignment with other parties but excludes items that the business has taken on consignment from other parties. The cost of merchandise includes not only the invoice price less any discounts but also any additional or incidental costs incurred to put the merchandise into place and condition for sale.

When specific invoice prices are used to price an inventory, each item in the inventory is identified and the cost of the item is determined by referring to the item's purchase invoice. With weighted-average cost, the total cost of the beginning inventory and of purchases is divided by the total number of units available to determine the weighted-average cost per unit. Multiplying this cost by the number of units in the ending inventory yields the cost of the inventory. FIFO prices the ending inventory based on the assumption that the first units purchased are the first units sold. LIFO is based on the assumption that the last units purchased are the first units sold. All of these methods are acceptable.

LO 3. Explain the effect of an inventory error on the financial statements of the current and succeeding years. An error in counting the ending inventory affects assets (inventory), net income (cost of goods sold), and stockholders' equity. Since the ending inventory is the beginning inventory of the next period, an error at the end of one period affects the cost of goods sold and the net income of the next period. These next period effects offset the financial statement effects in the previous period.

LO 4. Calculate the lower-of-cost-or-market amount of an inventory. When lower of cost or market is applied to merchandise inventory, market usually means replacement cost. Lower of cost or market may be applied separately to each product, to major categories of products, or to the merchandise inventory as a whole.

LO 5. Use the retail method and the gross profit method to estimate an inventory and calculate merchandise turnover and days' stock on hand. When the retail method is used, sales are subtracted from the retail amount of goods available for sale to determine the ending inventory at retail. This is multiplied by the cost ratio to reduce the inventory amount to cost. To calculate the cost ratio, divide the cost of goods available by the retail value of goods available.

With the gross profit method, multiply sales by (1 − the gross profit rate) to estimate cost of goods sold. Then, subtract the answer from the cost of goods available for sale to estimate the cost of the ending inventory.

Analysts use merchandise turnover and days' stock on hand in evaluating a company's short-term liquidity. They also use merchandise turnover to evaluate whether the amount of merchandise kept in inventory is too high or too low.

DEMONSTRATION PROBLEM

Tale Company uses a periodic inventory system and had the following beginning inventory and purchases during 19X1:

		Item X	
Date		Units	Unit Cost
1/1	Inventory	400	$14
3/10	Purchase	200	15
5/9	Purchase	300	16
9/22	Purchase	250	20
11/28	Purchase	100	21

At December 31, 19X1, there were 550 units of X on hand.

Required

1. Using the preceding information, apply FIFO inventory pricing and calculate the cost of goods available for sale in 19X1, the ending inventory, and the cost of goods sold.

2. In preparing the financial statements for 19X1, the bookkeeper was instructed to use FIFO but failed to do so and computed the cost of goods sold according to LIFO. Determine the size of the misstatement of 19X1's income from this error. Also determine the effect of the error on the 19X2 income. Assume no income taxes.

Planning the Solution

*   Multiply the units of each purchase and the beginning inventory by the appropriate unit costs to determine the total costs. Then, calculate the cost of goods available for sale.

*   For FIFO, calculate the ending inventory by multiplying the units on hand by the unit costs of the latest purchases. Then, subtract the ending inventory from the cost of goods available for sale.

*   For LIFO, calculate the ending inventory by multiplying the units on hand by the unit costs of the beginning inventory and the earliest purchases. Then, subtract the total ending inventory from the cost of goods available for sale.

*   Compare the ending 19X1 inventory amounts under FIFO and LIFO to determine the misstatement of 19X1 income that resulted from using LIFO. The 19X2 and 19X1 errors are equal in amount but have opposite effects.

Solution to Demonstration Problem

1. FIFO basis:

1/1 inventory (400 @ $14)		$ 5,600
Purchases:		
3/10 purchase (200 @ $15)	$3,000	
5/9 purchase (300 @ $16)	4,800	
9/22 purchase (250 @ $20)	5,000	
11/28 purchase (100 @ $21)	2,100	14,900
Cost of goods available for sale		$20,500
Ending inventory at FIFO cost:		
11/28 purchase (100 @ $21)	$2,100	
9/22 purchase (250 @ $20)	5,000	
5/9 purchase (200 @ $16)	3,200	
FIFO cost of ending inventory		10,300
Cost of goods sold		$10,200

2. LIFO basis:

Cost of goods available for sale		$20,500
Ending inventory at LIFO cost:		
1/1 inventory (400 @ $14)	$5,600	
3/10 purchase (150 @ $15)	2,250	
LIFO cost of ending inventory		7,850
Cost of goods sold		$12,650

If LIFO was mistakenly used when FIFO should have been used, cost of goods sold in 19X1 would be overstated by $2,450, which is the difference between the FIFO and LIFO amounts of ending inventory. Income would be understated in 19X1 by $2,450. In 19X2, income would be overstated by $2,450 because of the understatement of the beginning inventory.

GLOSSARY

Conservatism principle the accounting principle that guides accountants to select the less optimistic estimate when two estimates of amounts to be received or paid are about equally likely. p. 326

Consignee one who receives and holds goods owned by another party for the purpose of selling the goods for the owner. p. 318

Consignor an owner of goods who ships them to another party who will then sell the goods for the owner. p. 318

Consistency principle the accounting requirement that a company use the same accounting methods period after period so that the financial statements of succeeding periods will be comparable. p. 323

Days' stock on hand an estimate of how many days it will take to convert the inventory on hand at the end of the period into accounts receivable or cash; calculated by dividing the ending inventory by cost of goods sold and multiplying the result by 365. p. 330

First-in, first-out inventory pricing (FIFO) the pricing of an inventory under the assumption that the first items received were the first items sold. p. 321

Gross profit method a procedure for estimating an ending inventory in which the past gross profit rate is used to estimate cost of goods sold, which is then subtracted from the cost of goods available for sale to determine the estimated ending inventory. p. 328

Interim statements monthly or quarterly financial statements prepared in between the regular year-end statements. p. 327

Inventory ticket a form attached to the counted items in the process of taking a physical inventory. p. 319

Last-in, first-out inventory pricing (LIFO) the pricing of an inventory under the assumption that the last items received were the first items sold. p. 321

Lower of cost or market (LCM) the required method of reporting merchandise inventory in the balance sheet, in which market is normally defined as replacement cost on the date of the balance sheet. p. 325

Merchandise turnover the number of times a company's average inventory was sold during an accounting period, calculated by dividing cost of goods sold by the average merchandise inventory balance. p. 329

Net realizable value the expected sales price of an item less any additional costs to sell. p. 318

Retail inventory method a method for estimating an ending inventory based on the ratio of the amount of goods for sale at cost to the amount of goods for sale at marked selling prices. p. 327

Retail method cost ratio the ratio of goods available for sale at cost to goods available for sale at retail prices. p. 327

Specific invoice inventory pricing the pricing of an inventory where the purchase invoice of each item in the ending inventory is identified and used to determine the cost assigned to the inventory. p. 320

Weighted-average inventory pricing an inventory pricing system in which the unit prices of the beginning inventory and of each purchase are weighted by the number of units in the beginning inventory and each purchase. The total of these amounts is then divided by the total number of units available for sale to find the unit cost of the ending inventory and of the units that were sold. p. 320

QUESTIONS

1. What accounts are used in a periodic inventory system but not in a perpetual inventory system?
2. What is meant when it is said that inventory errors correct themselves?
3. If inventory errors correct themselves, why be concerned when such errors are made?
4. Where is merchandise inventory disclosed in the financial statements?

5. Why are incidental costs often ignored in pricing an inventory? Under what accounting principle is this permitted?

6. Give the meanings of the following when applied to inventory: *(a)* FIFO; *(b)* LIFO; and *(c)* cost.

7. If prices are falling, will the LIFO or the FIFO method of inventory valuation result in the lower cost of goods sold?

8. May a company change its inventory pricing method each accounting period?

9. Does the accounting principle of consistency preclude any changes from one accounting method to another?

10. What effect does the full-disclosure principle have if a company changes from one acceptable accounting method to another?

11. What guidance for accountants is provided by the principle of conservatism?

12. What is the usual meaning of the word *market* as it is used in determining the lower of cost or market for merchandise inventory?

13. Refer to Lands' End, Inc.'s financial statements in Appendix F. On January 27, 1995, what percentage of Lands' End's current assets was represented by inventory?

LANDS' END
DIRECT MERCHANTS

QUICK STUDY (Five-Minute Exercises)

QS 9–1
(LO 1)

Journalize the following transactions for Metro Distributing, Inc., under the periodic inventory system:

Feb. 4   Purchased and received 50 cases of soda for $9 per case, FOB destination.

13   Sold 10 cases of soda on account for $12 per case.

21   Returned 15 cases of soda to supplier.

QS 9–2
(LO 1)

Sanborn Corp. uses a periodic inventory system and the closing entry approach to updating the Merchandise Inventory account. Given the following accounts with normal year-end balances, prepare the closing entry that transfers the income statement accounts with debit balances to Income Summary.

Merchandise inventory	$ 34,800
Common stock, $10 par value	50,000
Retained earnings	65,300
Cash dividends declared	4,000
Sales	157,200
Sales returns and allowances	3,500
Sales discounts	1,700
Purchases	102,000
Purchase returns and allowances	8,100
Purchase discounts	2,000
Transportation-in	5,400
Depreciation expense	7,300
Salaries expense	29,500
Miscellaneous expenses	1,900

A physical count of the inventory discloses that the cost of the merchandise on hand is $22,900.

QS 9–3
(LO 1)

Refer to the information presented in QS 9–2. Now assume that Sanborn Corp. uses the adjusting entry approach to update the Merchandise Inventory account. Prepare the closing entry that transfers the income statement accounts with debit balances to Income Summary.

QS 9–4
(LO 2)

Crafts and More, Inc., a distributor of handmade gifts, operates out of owner Scott Arlen's home. At the end of the accounting period, Arlen tells us he has 1,500 units of products in his basement, 30 of which were damaged by water leaks and cannot be sold. He also has another 250 units in his van, ready to deliver to fill a customer order, terms FOB destination, and another 70 units out on consignment to a friend who owns a stationery store. How many units should be included in the end-of-period inventory?

QS 9–5
(LO 2)

Rigby & Son, antique dealers, purchased the contents of an estate for a bulk bid price of $37,500. The terms of the purchase were FOB shipping point, and the cost of transporting the goods to Rigby & Son's warehouse was $1,200. Rigby & Son insured the shipment at a cost of $150. Prior to placing the goods in the store, they cleaned and refurbished some merchandise at a cost of $490 for labor and parts. Determine the cost of the inventory acquired in the purchase of the estate's contents.

A company had the following beginning inventory and purchases during January for a particular item. What is the cost of the 140 units that remain in the ending inventory, assuming *(a)* FIFO, *(b)* LIFO, and *(c)* weighted average? (Round numbers to the nearest cent.)

QS 9–6
(LO 2)

	Units	Unit Cost
Beginning inventory on January 1 . .	310	$3.00
Purchase on January 9	75	3.20
Purchase on January 25	100	3.35

Identify the inventory costing method most closely related to each of the following statements, assuming a period of rising costs:

QS 9–7
(LO 2)

a. Matches recent costs against revenue.

b. Provides a tax advantage.

c. Understates current value of inventory on a balance sheet.

d. Results in a balance sheet inventory closest to replacement costs.

e. Is best because each unit of product has unique features that affect cost.

The Weston Corporation maintains its inventory records on a periodic basis. In taking a physical inventory at the end of 19X1, certain units were counted twice. Explain how this error affects the following: *(a)* 19X1 cost of goods sold, *(b)* 19X1 gross profit, *(c)* 19X1 net income, *(d)* 19X2 net income, *(e)* the combined two-year income, and *(f)* income in years after 19X2.

QS 9–8
(LO 3)

Thrifty Trading Co. has the following products in its ending inventory:

QS 9–9
(LO 4)

Product	Quantity	Cost	Market
Aprons	9	$6.00	$5.50
Bottles	12	3.50	4.25
Candles	25	8.00	7.00

Calculate lower of cost or market *(a)* for the inventory as a whole and *(b)* applied separately to each product.

The inventory of Bell Department Store was destroyed by a fire on September 10, 19X1. The following 19X1 data were found in the accounting records:

QS 9–10
(LO 5)

Jan. 1 inventory	$180,000
Jan. 1–Sept. 10 purchases (net)	$342,000
Jan. 1–Sept. 10 sales	$675,000
19X1 estimated gross profit rate	42%

Determine the cost of the inventory destroyed in the fire.

Using Lands' End, Inc.'s financial statements in Appendix F, calculate the days' stock on hand on January 27, 1995. (Round your answer to a whole number.)

QS 9–11
(LO 5)

EXERCISES

Devoe Supply Corp. had 80 units of a product that cost $23.00 per unit in its beginning inventory on January 1, 19X1. Prepare general journal entries to record the following 19X1 transactions for Devoe, assuming a periodic inventory system and the closing entry approach.

Exercise 9–1
Periodic inventory system
(LO 1)

Mar. 12   Purchased on credit 200 units of the product at $26.00 per unit.

19   Returned 40 defective units from the March 12 purchase to the supplier.

July 6 Purchased for cash 120 units of the product at $25.00 per unit.

Oct. 20 Sold 150 units of merchandise for cash at a price of $37.00 per unit.

Dec. 31 Prepare entries to close the revenue and expense accounts to Income Summary. Assume there are no revenues or expenses other than those that result from the transactions described in this exercise. A physical count of inventory at the end of the period disclosed $5,300 of merchandise on hand.

Exercise 9–2
Calculating gross profit
(LO 1)

The following accounts and balances are taken from the year-end adjusted trial balance of Vintage Stores, Inc.

	Debit	Credit
Merchandise inventory	$ 28,000	
Sales		$425,000
Sales returns and allowances	16,500	
Sales discounts	4,000	
Purchases	240,000	
Purchase returns and allowances		18,000
Purchase discounts		2,000
Transportation-in	6,000	
Selling expenses	35,000	
General and administrative expenses	95,000	
Cash dividends declared	25,000	

The count of the ending inventory shows that its cost is $37,000.

Required

Calculate the company's net sales, cost of goods sold, and gross profit.

Exercise 9–3
Periodic inventory system; closing entry approach
(LO 1)

Refer to the facts provided in Exercise 9–2 and assume the company uses the closing entry approach to update its inventory account. Prepare the closing entries for this company and post the entries to a balance column account for Merchandise Inventory that includes the beginning balance.

Exercise 9–4
Periodic inventory system; adjusting entry approach
(LO 1)

Assume that the company in Exercise 9–2 uses the adjusting entry approach to update its inventory account. Prepare adjusting and closing journal entries for this company and post them to a balance column account for Merchandise Inventory that includes the beginning balance.

Exercise 9–5
Alternative cost flow assumptions, periodic inventory system
(LO 2)

Paddington Gifts, Inc., made purchases of a particular product in the current year as follows:

Jan. 1	Beginning inventory	120 units @ $3.00 =	$ 360
Mar. 7	Purchased	250 units @ $2.80 =	700
July 28	Purchased	500 units @ $2.50 =	1,250
Oct. 3	Purchased	450 units @ $2.30 =	1,035
Dec. 19	Purchased	100 units @ $2.05 =	205
	Total	1,420 units	$3,550

Required

The business uses a periodic inventory system, and the ending inventory consists of 150 units, 50 from each of the last three purchases. Determine the share of the $3,550 cost of the units for sale that should be assigned to the ending inventory and to goods sold under each of the following: *(a)* costs are assigned on the basis of specific invoice prices, *(b)* costs are assigned on a weighted-average cost basis, *(c)* costs are assigned on the basis of FIFO, and *(d)* costs are assigned on the basis of LIFO. Assuming the company has enough income to require that it pay income taxes, which method provides a current tax advantage?

Jasper & Williams, Inc., made purchases of a particular product in the current year as follows:

Jan. 1	Beginning inventory	120 units @ $2.00 =	$ 240
Mar. 7	Purchased	250 units @ $2.30 =	575
July 28	Purchased	500 units @ $2.50 =	1,250
Oct. 3	Purchased	450 units @ $2.80 =	1,260
Dec. 19	Purchased	100 units @ $2.96 =	296
	Total	1,420 units	$3,621

Required

The company uses a periodic inventory system, and the ending inventory consists of 150 units, 50 from each of the last three purchases. Determine the share of the $3,621 cost of the units for sale that should be assigned to the ending inventory and to goods sold under each of the following: (a) costs are assigned on the basis of specific invoice prices, (b) costs are assigned on a weighted-average cost basis, (c) costs are assigned on the basis of FIFO, and (d) costs are assigned on the basis of LIFO. Assuming the company has enough income to require that it pay income taxes, which method provides a current tax advantage?

Assume that The John Henry Corporation had $900,000 of sales during each of three consecutive years, and it purchased merchandise costing $500,000 during each of the years. It also maintained a $200,000 inventory from the beginning to the end of the three-year period. However, in accounting under a periodic inventory system, it made an error at the end of year 1 that caused its ending year 1 inventory to appear on its statements at $180,000 rather than the correct $200,000.

Required

1. State the actual amount of the company's gross profit in each of the years.
2. Prepare a comparative income statement like Illustration 9–5 to show the effect of this error on the company's cost of goods sold and gross profit in year 1, year 2, and year 3.

Showtime Company's ending inventory includes the following items:

Product	Units on Hand	Unit Cost	Replacement Cost per Unit
BB	22	$50	$54
FM	15	78	72
MB	36	95	91
SL	40	36	36

Replacement cost is determined to be the best measure of market. Calculate lower of cost or market for the inventory (a) as a whole and (b) applied separately to each product.

During 19X1, Harmony, Inc., sold $130,000 of merchandise at marked retail prices. At the end of 19X1, the following information was available from its records:

	At Cost	At Retail
Beginning inventory	$31,900	$64,200
Net purchases	57,810	98,400

Use the retail method to estimate Harmony's 19X1 ending inventory at cost.

Assume that in addition to estimating its ending inventory by the retail method, Harmony, Inc., of Exercise 9–9 also took a physical inventory at the marked selling prices of the inventory items at the end of 19X1. Assume further that the total of this physical inventory at marked selling prices was $27,300. Then, (a) determine the amount of this inventory at cost and (b) determine Harmony's 19X1 inventory shrinkage from breakage, theft, or other causes at retail and at cost.

Exercise 9–10
Reducing physical inventory
to cost—retail method
(LO 5)

Exercise 9–11
Estimating ending inventory—
gross profit method
(LO 5)

On January 1, The Parts Store had a $450,000 inventory at cost. During the first quarter of the year, it purchased $1,590,000 of merchandise, returned $23,100, and paid freight charges on purchased merchandise totaling $37,600. During the past several years, the store's gross profit on sales has averaged 30%. Under the assumption the store had $2,000,000 of sales during the first quarter of the year, use the gross profit method to estimate its inventory at the end of the first quarter.

Exercise 9–12
Merchandise turnover and days'
stock on hand
(LO 5)

From the following information for Russo Merchandising Co., calculate merchandise turnover for 19X3 and 19X2 and days' stock on hand at December 31, 19X3 and 19X2. (Round answers to one decimal place.)

	19X3	19X2	19X1
Cost of goods sold	$643,825	$426,650	$391,300
Inventory (December 31)	96,400	86,750	91,500

Comment on Russo's efficiency in using its assets to support increasing sales from 19X2 to 19X3.

PROBLEMS

Problem 9–1
Alternative cost flows—
periodic system
(LO 2)

Mill House Corporation began 19X1 with 20,000 units of Product X in its inventory that cost $15 each, and it made successive purchases of the product as follows:

Mar. 7	28,000 units @ $18 each
May 25	30,000 units @ $22 each
Aug. 1	20,000 units @ $24 each
Nov. 10	33,000 units @ $27 each

The company uses a periodic inventory system. On December 31, 19X1, a physical count disclosed that 35,000 units of Product X remained in inventory.

Required

1. Prepare a calculation showing the number and total cost of the units available for sale during 19X1.

CHECK FIGURE:
Cost of goods sold (FIFO):
$1,896,000

2. Prepare calculations showing the amounts that should be assigned to the 19X1 ending inventory and to cost of goods sold, assuming (a) a FIFO basis, (b) a LIFO basis, and (c) a weighted-average cost basis.

Problem 9–2
Income statement comparisons
and cost flow assumptions
(LO 2)

Green Jeans, Inc., sold 5,500 units of its product at $45 per unit during 19X1. Incurring operating expenses of $6 per unit in selling the units, it began the year with and made successive purchases of the product as follows:

January 1 beginning inventory	600 units @ $18.00 per unit
Purchases:	
February 20	1,500 units @ $19.00 per unit
May 16	700 units @ $20.00 per unit
October 3	400 units @ $21.00 per unit
December 11	3,300 units @ $22.00 per unit
	6,500 units

Required

Preparation component:

CHECK FIGURE:
Net income (LIFO), $69,020

1. Prepare a comparative income statement for the company, showing in adjacent columns the net incomes earned from the sale of the product, assuming the company uses a periodic inventory system and prices its ending inventory on the basis of: (a) FIFO, (b) LIFO, and (c) weighted-average cost. Assume an income tax rate of 30%.

Analysis component:

2. How would the results of the three alternatives change if Green Jeans had been experiencing declining prices in the acquisition of additional inventory?

3. What specific advantages and disadvantages are offered by using LIFO and by using FIFO, assuming the cost trends given at the beginning of this problem?

Shockley Corp. keeps its inventory records on a periodic basis. The following amounts were reported in the company's financial statements:

Problem 9–3
Analysis of inventory errors
(LO 3)

**Financial Statements for
Year Ended December 31,**

	19X1	19X2	19X3
(a) Cost of goods sold	$ 715,000	$ 847,000	$ 770,000
(b) Net income	220,000	275,000	231,000
(c) Total current assets	1,155,000	1,265,000	1,100,000
(d) Stockholders' equity ...	1,287,000	1,430,000	1,232,000

In making the physical counts of inventory, the following errors were made:

Inventory on December 31, 19X1	Understated $66,000
Inventory on December 31, 19X2	Overstated $30,000

Required

Preparation component:

1. For each of the preceding financial statement items—*(a), (b), (c),* and *(d)*—prepare a schedule similar to the following and show the adjustments that would have been necessary to correct the reported amounts.

	19X1	19X2	19X3
Cost of goods sold:			
Reported	_____	_____	_____
Adjustments: 12/31/X1 error	_____	_____	_____
12/31/X2 error	_____	_____	_____
Corrected	======	======	======

Analysis component:

2. What is the error in the aggregate net income for the three-year period that resulted from the inventory errors? Explain why this result occurs. Also explain why the understatement of inventory by $66,000 at the end of 19X1 resulted in an understatement of equity by the same amount that year.

The following information pertains to the physical inventory of Electronics Unlimited taken at December 31:

Problem 9–4
Lower of cost or market
(LO 4)

		Per Unit	
Product	Units on Hand	Cost	Replacement Cost
Audio equipment:			
Receivers	335	$ 90	$ 98
CD players	250	111	100
Cassette decks	316	86	95
Turntables	194	52	41
Video equipment:			
Televisions	470	150	125
VCRs	281	93	84
Video cameras	202	310	322
Car audio equipment:			
Cassette radios	175	70	84
CD radios	160	97	105

Required

Calculate the lower of cost or market *(a)* for the inventory as a whole, *(b)* for the inventory by major category, and *(c)* for the inventory, applied separately to each product.

Problem 9–5
Retail inventory method
(LO 5)

The records of Basics, Inc., provided the following information for the year ended December 31:

	At Cost	At Retail
January 1 beginning inventory	$ 471,350	$ 927,150
Purchases	3,328,830	6,398,700
Purchase returns	52,800	119,350
Sales		5,495,700
Sales returns		44,600

Required

1. Prepare an estimate of the company's year-end inventory by the retail method.

2. Under the assumption the company took a year-end physical inventory at marked selling prices that totaled $1,675,800, prepare a schedule showing the store's loss from theft or other cause at cost and at retail.

Problem 9–6
Gross profit method
(LO 5)

Walker Corporation wants to prepare interim financial statements for the first quarter of 19X1. The company uses a periodic inventory system but would like to avoid making a physical count of inventory. During the last five years, the company's gross profit rate has averaged 35%. The following information for the year's first quarter is available from its records:

January 1 beginning inventory	$ 300,260
Purchases	945,200
Purchase returns	13,050
Transportation-in	6,900
Sales	1,191,150
Sales returns	9,450

Required

Use the gross profit method to prepare an estimate of the company's March 31 inventory.

CRITICAL THINKING: ESSAYS, PROBLEMS, AND CASES

Analytical Essay

(LO 2)

Closefit Furniture uses a periodic inventory system to account for its merchandise. Describe what effect, if any, the following independent errors would have on Closefit's financial statements for 19X2 and 19X3:

a. Goods held on consignment by Closefit were included in its December 31, 19X2, inventory.

b. Merchandise stored in one of Closefit's warehouses was double counted in the inventory taken on December 31, 19X1.

c. Closefit purchased and received merchandise in December 19X2 but did not record the purchase until 19X3. (Assume payment for the merchandise was not due until January 19X3.)

Financial Reporting Problems

FRP 9–1
(LO 2)

The Dow Chemical Company is the fifth largest chemical company in the world, with annual sales of more than $20 billion. The company provides chemicals, plastics, energy, agricultural products, consumer goods, and environmental services to customers in almost all countries around the world. In the company's 1995 annual report, the footnotes to the financial statements included the following:

Inventories

The amounts of reserve required to reduce inventories from the first-in, first-out (FIFO) basis to the last-in, first-out (LIFO) basis on December 31, 1995 and 1994, were $66 [million] and $119 [million], respectively. The inventories that were valued on a LIFO basis represented 34 and 35 percent of the total inventories on December 31, 1995 and 1994, respectively.

A reduction of certain inventories resulted in the liquidation of some quantities of LIFO inventory, which increased pretax income by $8 [million] in 1995 and $16 [million] in 1994, and decreased pretax income by $18 [million] in 1993.

Courtesy of Dow Chemical Company

Discuss the financial statement effects of experiencing a reduction in inventory when LIFO is used and explain how this applies to Dow Chemical.

The Times Mirror Company is a media and information company that does business in three principal areas: print media, professional information and book publishing, and electronic media. Times Mirror uses the FIFO method for books and certain finished products and LIFO for newsprint, paper, and certain other inventories. The 1994 annual report of Times Mirror included the following footnote to its financial statements:

FRP 9–2 (LO 2)

Note G—Inventories

Inventories consist of the following (in thousands):

	December 31	
	1994	1993
Newsprint, paper, and other raw materials	$ 33,789	$ 39,066
Books and other finished products	94,290	94,675
Work-in-process	24,938	27,510
	$153,017	$161,251

Inventories determined on the last-in, first-out method were $21,946,000 and $26,994,000 at December 31, 1994 and 1993, respectively, and would have been higher by $9,825,000 in 1994 and $8,232,000 in 1993 had the first-in, first-out method (which approximates current cost) been used exclusively.

Courtesy of Times Mirror Company

Times Mirror reported a net income of $173,117,000 in 1994. Retained earnings on December 31, 1994, was $1,720,725,000. If Times Mirror had used FIFO for all of its inventories, what would the total inventories reported on December 31, 1994, and December 31, 1993, have been? Assuming the average income tax rate applicable to the company was 30% in all past years, what would have been reported as the 1994 net income if FIFO had been used for all inventories? What would have been the balance of retained earnings on December 31, 1994? Comment on Times Mirror's policy of using FIFO for some inventories and LIFO for other inventories in light of the consistency principle.

Refer to the financial statements and related disclosures from Lands' End, Inc.'s 1995 annual report in Appendix F. Based on your examination of this information, answer the following:

Financial Statement Analysis Case

(LO 2, 5)

1. What was the total amount of inventories held as current assets by Lands' End on January 27, 1995? On January 28, 1994?

2. Inventories represented what percentage of total assets on January 27, 1995? On January 28, 1994?

3. Comment on the relative size of inventories Lands' End holds compared to other types of assets.

4. What method did Lands' End use to determine the inventory amounts reported on its balance sheet?

5. Calculate merchandise turnover for fiscal year 1995 and days' stock on hand on January 27, 1995. (Use cost of sales for cost of goods sold.)

CONCEPT TESTER

Test your understanding of the concepts introduced in this chapter by completing the following crossword puzzle.

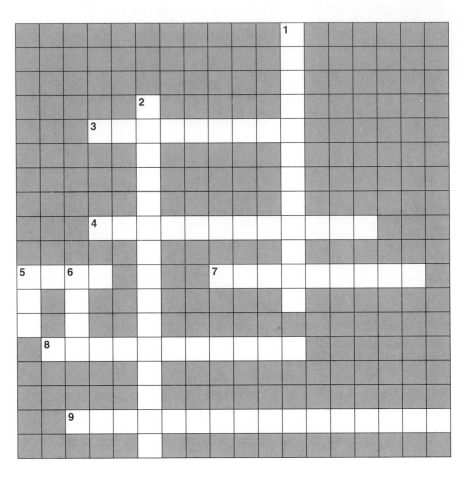

Across Clues

3. One who holds goods owned by another party for the purpose of selling the goods.
4. 2 words; method of estimating inventory that relates cost and retail price of goods available.
5. Inventory pricing method that assumes last goods purchased are the first to be sold.
7. The owner of goods held by another party for the purpose of selling them.
8. Principle that requires a firm to use the same accounting methods period after period.
9. 2 words; a monthly or quarterly financial statement.

Down Clues

1. Principle that guides accountants to select the less optimistic estimate.
2. 2 words; a form attached to the counted items in the process of taking an inventory.
5. The method of reporting merchandise at the lower of cost or market value.
6. Inventory pricing method that assumes the first items purchased are the first to be sold.

ANSWERS TO PROGRESS CHECKS

9–1 Cost of Goods Sold.

9–2 Purchases and Transportation-In.

9–3 *c*

9–4 Under a periodic inventory system, the cost of goods sold is determined at the end of an accounting period by adding the net cost of goods purchased to the beginning inventory and subtracting the ending inventory.

9–5 Both approaches will report the same ending inventory and net income.

9–6 The matching principle.

9–7 Thompson.

9–8 *d.* $11,400 + $130 + $150 + $100 + $400 = $12,180

9–9 *a.* (20 × $14) + (10 × $12) = $400

      b. (20 × $14) + (40 × $12) + (70 × $10) = $1,460

9–10 FIFO. LIFO results in a higher cost of goods sold and therefore a lower gross profit, which carries through to a lower net income.

9–11 LIFO will result in a smaller inventory figure on the balance sheet, as compared to FIFO which will result in an inventory figure that is close to current replacement costs.

9–12 The cost of goods sold will be understated by $10,000 in 19X1 and overstated by $10,000 in 19X2.

9–13 *b.* $(20 \times \$5) + (40 \times \$8) + (10 \times \$12) = \$540$

9–14 *e.* $\dfrac{\$324,000 + \$204,000 - \$9,000}{\$530,000 + \$348,000 - \$13,000} = 60\%$

$[(\$530,000 + \$348,000 - \$13,000) - \$320,000] \times 60\% = \$327,000$

9–15 Days' stock on hand.

CHAPTER 10

Plant and Equipment

*C*oca-Cola Bottling Co. Consolidated intensified the fruit drink wars in 1994 when it announced that it had invested $150 million to expand production of its Fruitopia beverage by purchasing additional plants in Waco, Texas, and Northampton, Massachusetts, and by upgrading bottling lines in existing production facilities. The information below from the company's 1994 annual report provides a basis for understanding the magnitude of the plant asset investment. As an analyst from Solomon Brothers said: "This shows that Coca-Cola is serious about Fruitopia. The $150 million investment is half of Coca-Cola's domestic capital expenditure budget." (*New York Times,* November 11, 1994, p. D4.)

COCA-COLA BOTTLING CO. CONSOLIDATED
CONSOLIDATED BALANCE SHEETS
(In thousands)

ASSETS	January 1, 1995
Property, plant and equipment, at cost	$327,052
Less: Accumulated depreciation and amortization	141,419
Property, plant and equipment, net	$185,633

LEARNING OBJECTIVES

After studying Chapter 10, you should be able to:

1. **Describe the differences between plant assets and other kinds of assets and calculate the cost and record the purchase of plant assets.**

2. **Explain depreciation accounting (including the reasons for depreciation), calculate depreciation by the straight-line and units-of-production methods, and calculate depreciation after revising the estimated useful life of an asset.**

3. **Describe the use of accelerated depreciation for financial accounting and tax accounting purposes and calculate accelerated depreciation under (a) the declining-balance method and (b) the Modified Accelerated Cost Recovery System.**

4. **Describe the difference between revenue and capital expenditures and account properly for costs such as repairs and betterments incurred after the original purchase of plant assets.**

5. **Prepare entries to account for the disposal or exchange of plant assets and explain the use of total asset turnover in evaluating a company's efficiency in using its assets.**

6. **Define or explain the words and phrases listed in the chapter glossary.**

The focus of this chapter is long-term, tangible assets used in the operation of a business. These plant assets represent a major category of investment by businesses. Recent financial press predictions call for an increase in spending related to plant assets. For example, in the **Sony Corporation** annual report for the year ended March 31, 1995, management made the following statement: "Capital expenditures during the year under review increased 27.9% to… $2,817 million. The largest single item included was approximately… $449 million for expanding semiconductor facilities. In the fiscal year ending March 31, 1996, Sony intends to further increase its capital expenditures."

As another example, **Wendy's International Inc.'s** 1994 annual report indicated that the company had made capital expenditures of $142 million during the year. The report indicated current plans "to open or have under construction about 400 new Wendy's restaurants in 1995, of which approximately 120 will be company-operated. Capital expenditures could total as much as $170 million in 1995."

Learning fundamental concepts of accounting for plant and equipment will enable you to recognize the direct financial statement impact of business activities like those described for Coca-Cola, Sony, and Wendy's. In studying this chapter, you will learn what distinguishes plant and equipment from other types of assets, how to determine their cost, and how companies allocate their costs to the periods that benefit from their use.

PLANT ASSETS COMPARED TO OTHER TYPES OF ASSETS

Tangible assets that are used in the production or sale of other assets or services and that have a useful life longer than one accounting period are called *plant assets*. In the past, such assets were often described as *fixed assets*. However, more descriptive terms such as *plant and equipment* or perhaps *property, plant, and equipment* are now used.

The main difference between plant assets and merchandise is that plant assets are held for use while merchandise is held for sale. For example, a business that buys a computer for the purpose of reselling it should report the computer on the balance sheet as merchandise inventory. If the same retailer owns another computer that is used to account for business operations and to prepare reports, it is classified as plant and equipment.

The characteristic that distinguishes plant assets from current assets is the length of their useful lives. For example, supplies are usually consumed within a short time after they are placed in use. Thus, their cost is assigned to the single period in which they are used. By comparison, plant assets have longer useful lives that extend over more than one accounting period. As the usefulness of plant assets expires over these periods, their cost must be allocated among them. This allocation should be accomplished in a systematic and rational manner.[1]

Plant assets are also different than the items that are reported on the balance sheet as long-term investments. Although both are held for more than one accounting period, long-term investments are not used in the primary operations of the business. For example, land that is held for future expansion is classified as a long-term investment. On the other hand, land on which the company's factory is located is a plant asset. In addition, standby equipment held for use in case of a breakdown or during peak periods of production is a plant asset. However, equipment that is removed from service and held for sale is no longer considered a plant asset.

LO 1
Describe the differences between plant assets and other kinds of assets and calculate the cost and record the purchase of plant assets.

COST OF A PLANT ASSET

When a plant asset is purchased, it should be recorded at cost. This cost includes all normal and reasonable expenditures necessary to get the asset in place and ready to use. For example, the cost of a factory machine includes its invoice price, less any cash discount for early payment, plus freight, unpacking, and assembling costs. The cost of an asset also includes the costs of installing a machine before placing it in service. Examples are the costs to build a concrete base or foundation for a machine, to provide electrical connections, and to adjust the machine before using it in operations.

An expenditure cannot be charged to and reported as part of the cost of a plant asset unless the expenditure is reasonable and necessary. For example, if a machine is damaged by being dropped during unpacking, the repairs should not be added to its cost. Instead, they should be charged to an expense account. Also, a fine paid for moving a heavy machine on city streets without proper permits is not part of the cost of the machine. However, if proper permits are obtained, their cost is included in the cost of the asset. Sometimes, costs in addition to the purchase price are incurred to modify or customize a new plant asset. These items should be charged to the asset's cost.

When a plant asset is constructed by a business for its own use, cost includes material and labor costs plus a reasonable amount of indirect overhead costs such as the costs of heat, lights, power, and depreciation on the machinery used to construct the asset. Cost also includes design fees, building permits, and insurance during construction. However, insurance costs for coverage after the asset has been placed in service are an operating expense.

When land is purchased for a building site, its cost includes the total amount paid for the land, including any real estate commissions. Its cost also includes fees for insuring the title, legal fees, and any accrued property taxes paid by the purchaser.

---

[1]See FASB, *Statement of Financial Accounting Concepts No. 6,* "Elements of Financial Statements of Business Enterprises" (Norwalk, CT, 1985), par. 149.

Payments for surveying, clearing, grading, draining, and landscaping also are included in the cost of land. Other costs of land include assessments by the local government, whether incurred at the time of purchase or later, for such things as installing streets, sewers, and sidewalks. These assessments are included because they add a more or less permanent value to the land.

Land purchased as a building site may have an old building that must be removed. In such cases, the total purchase price should be charged to the Land account. Also, the cost of removing the old building, less any amounts recovered through the sale of salvaged materials, should be charged to the Land account.

Because land has an unlimited life and is not consumed when it is used, it is not subject to depreciation. However, **land improvements** such as parking lot surfaces, fences, and lighting systems have limited useful lives. Although these costs increase the usefulness of the land, they must be charged to separate Land Improvement accounts so that they can be depreciated. Of course, a separate Building account must be charged for the costs of purchasing or constructing a building that will be used as a plant asset.

Land, land improvements, and buildings often are purchased in a single transaction for a lump-sum price. When this occurs, the accountant must allocate the cost of the purchase among the different types of assets, based on their relative market values. These market values may be estimated by appraisal or by using the tax-assessed valuations of the assets.

For example, assume that a company pays $90,000 cash to acquire land appraised at $30,000, land improvements appraised at $10,000, and a building appraised at $60,000. The $90,000 cost is allocated on the basis of appraised values as follows:

	Appraised Value	Percentage of Total	Apportioned Cost
Land	$ 30,000	30%	$27,000
Land improvements	10,000	10	9,000
Building	60,000	60	54,000
Totals	$100,000	100%	$90,000

Progress Check

(Answers to Progress Checks are provided at the end of the chapter.)

10–1 Identify the asset classification for *(a)* office supplies, *(b)* office equipment, *(c)* merchandise, *(d)* land held for future expansion, *(e)* trucks used in operations.

10–2 Identify the account charged for each of the following expenditures: *(a)* the purchase price of a vacant lot and *(b)* the cost of paving that vacant lot.

10–3 What amount should be recorded as the cost of a new production machine, given the following items related to the machine: gross purchase price, $700,000; sales tax, $49,000; purchase discount taken, $21,000; freight to move machine to plant, $3,500; assembly costs, $3,000; cost of foundation for machine, $2,500; cost of spare parts to be used in maintaining the machine, $4,200?

Because plant assets are purchased for use, you can think of a plant asset as a quantity of usefulness that contributes to the operations of the business throughout the service life of the asset. And, because the life of any plant asset (other than land) is limited, this quantity of usefulness expires as the asset is used. This expiration of a plant asset's quantity of usefulness is generally described as *depreciation.* In accounting, this term describes the process of allocating and charging the cost of the usefulness to the accounting periods that benefit from the asset's use.

For example, when a company buys an automobile for use as a plant asset, it acquires a quantity of usefulness in the sense that it obtains a quantity of transportation. The total cost of the transportation is the cost of the car less the expected proceeds to be received when the car is sold or traded in at the end of its service life. This net cost must be allocated to the accounting periods that benefit from the car's use. In other words, the asset's cost must be depreciated. Note that the depreciation process does not measure the decline in the car's market value each period. Nor does it measure the physical deterioration of the car each period. Under generally accepted accounting principles, depreciation is a process of allocating a plant asset's cost to income statements of the years in which it is used.

Because depreciation represents the cost of using a plant asset, you should not begin recording depreciation charges until the asset is actually put to use providing services or producing products.

NATURE OF DEPRECIATION

LO 2
Explain depreciation accounting (including the reasons for depreciation), calculate depreciation by the straight-line and units-of-production methods, and calculate depreciation after revising the estimated useful life of an asset.

The **service life** of a plant asset is the length of time it will be used in the operations of the business. This service life (or useful life) may not be as long as the asset's potential life. For example, although computers have a potential life of six to eight years, a company may plan to trade in its old computers for new ones every three years. In this case, the computers have a three-year service life. Therefore, this company should charge the cost of the computers (less their expected trade-in value) to depreciation expense over this three-year period.

Several factors often make the service life of a plant asset hard to predict. Wear and tear from use determine the service life of many assets. However, two additional factors, **inadequacy** and **obsolescence,** need to be considered.

When a business grows more rapidly than anticipated, the capacity of the assets may become too limited for the productive demands of the business. As this happens, the assets become inadequate. Obsolescence, like inadequacy, is hard to anticipate because the timing of new inventions and improvements normally cannot be predicted. Yet, new inventions and improvements may cause a company to discard an obsolete asset long before it wears out.

Many times a company is able to predict the service life of a new asset based on the company's past experience with similar assets. In other cases, when it has no experience with a particular type of asset, a company must depend on the experience of others or on engineering studies and judgment.

In its 1993 annual report, **Microsoft Corporation** disclosed the following information regarding its depreciation procedures:

SERVICE (USEFUL) LIFE OF A PLANT ASSET

Property, plant, and equipment is stated at cost and depreciated using the straight-line method over the following estimated useful lives:

Buildings	30 years
Leasehold improvements	Lease term
Computer equipment and other . . .	3–5 years

SALVAGE VALUE

The total amount of depreciation that should be taken over an asset's service life is the asset's cost minus its estimated salvage value. The **salvage value** of a plant asset is the amount that you expect to receive from selling the asset at the end of its life. If you expect an asset to be traded in on a new asset, the salvage value is the expected trade-in value.

Sometimes, a company must incur additional costs to dispose of plant assets. For example, a company may plan to clean and paint an old machine before offering it for sale. In this case, the estimated salvage value is the expected proceeds from the sale of the asset less the cleaning and painting costs.

ALLOCATING DEPRECIATION

Many depreciation methods for allocating a plant asset's total cost among the several accounting periods in its service life have been suggested and used in the past. However, at present, most companies use the *straight-line method* of depreciation in their financial accounting records for presentation in their financial statements. Some types of assets are depreciated according to the *units-of-production method.* We explain these two methods next and then consider some *accelerated depreciation* methods.

Straight-Line Method

Straight-line depreciation charges the same amount of expense to each year of the asset's life. To determine the annual expense, the total cost to be depreciated over the asset's life is calculated by first subtracting the asset's estimated salvage value from its cost. This total amount to be depreciated is then divided by the estimated number of accounting periods in the asset's service life.

For example, if an asset costs $7,000, has an estimated service life of five years, and has an estimated $2,000 salvage value, its depreciation per year by the straight-line method is $1,000. This amount is calculated as follows:

$$\frac{\text{Cost} - \text{Salvage}}{\text{Service life in years}} = \frac{\$7,000 - \$2,000}{5 \text{ years}} = \$1,000 \text{ per year}$$

If this asset is purchased on December 31, 19X1, and used throughout its predicted service life of five years, the straight-line method will allocate an equal amount of depreciation to each of those years (19X2 through 19X6). The left graph in Illustration 10–1 shows that this $1,000 per year amount will be reported each year as an expense. The right graph shows the amount that will be reported on each of the six balance sheets that will be produced while the company actually owns the asset. This **book value** of the asset is its original cost less accumulated depreciation. The book

value goes down by $1,000 each year. Both graphs show why this method is called *straight-line.*

Although most companies use straight-line depreciation, other methods are common in certain industries. For example, **Boise Cascade Corporation** uses the units-of-production method in nearly all of its facilities that manufacture paper and wood products.

Units-of-Production Method

The purpose of recording depreciation is to provide relevant information about the cost of consuming an asset's usefulness. In general, this means that each accounting period an asset is used should be charged with a fair share of its cost. The straight-line method charges an equal share to each period. If plant assets are used about the same amount in each accounting period, this method produces a reasonable result.

Illustration 10-1 The Financial Statement Effects of Straight-Line Depreciation

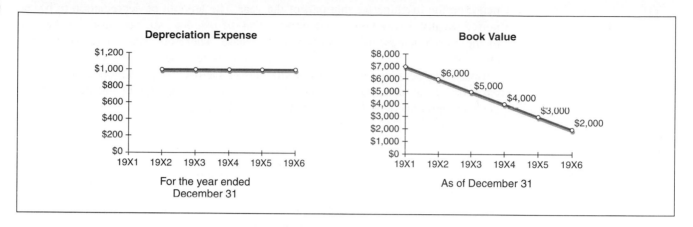

However, the use of some plant assets varies greatly from one accounting period to another. For example, a contractor may use a particular piece of construction equipment for a month and then not use it again for a few months.

Because the use of such equipment varies from period to period, the units-of-production depreciation method may provide a better matching of expenses with revenues than straight-line depreciation. Under **units-of-production depreciation,** the cost of an asset minus its estimated salvage value is divided by the total number of units that management predicts it will produce during its service life. Units of production may be expressed as units of product or in any other unit of measure such as hours of use or miles driven. In effect, this method computes the amount of depreciation per unit of service provided by the asset. Then, the amount of depreciation taken in an accounting period is determined by multiplying the units produced in that period by the depreciation per unit.

For example, a truck that cost $24,000 has a predicted salvage value of $4,000 and an estimated service life of 125,000 miles. The depreciation per mile, or the depreciation per unit of service, is $0.16, which is calculated as follows:

$$\text{Depreciation per unit of production} = \frac{\text{Cost} - \text{Salvage value}}{\text{Predicted units of production}}$$

$$= \frac{\$24,000 - \$4,000}{125,000 \text{ miles}}$$

$$= \$0.16 \text{ per mile}$$

If the truck is driven 20,000 miles during its first year, depreciation for the first year is $3,200 (20,000 miles at $0.16 per mile). If the truck is driven 15,000 miles in the second year, depreciation for the second year is 15,000 miles times $0.16 per mile, or $2,400.

DEPRECIATION FOR PARTIAL YEARS

Of course, plant assets may be purchased or disposed of at any time during the year. When an asset is purchased (or disposed of) at some time other than the beginning or end of an accounting period, depreciation must be recorded for part of a year. Otherwise, the year of purchase or the year of disposal is not charged with its share of the asset's depreciation.

For example, assume that a machine was purchased and placed in service on October 8, 19X1, and that the annual accounting period ends on December 31. The machine cost $4,600; it has an estimated service life of five years and an estimated salvage value of $600. Because the machine was purchased and used nearly three months during 19X1, the annual income statement should reflect depreciation expense on the machine for that part of the year. The amount of depreciation to be reported usually is based on the assumption that the machine was purchased on the first of the month nearest the actual date of purchase. Therefore, since the purchase occurred on October 8, three months' depreciation is recorded on December 31. If the purchase had been on October 16 or later during October, depreciation would be calculated as if the purchase had been on November 1. Using straight-line depreciation, the three months' depreciation of $200 is calculated as follows:

$$\frac{\$4,600 - \$600}{5} \times \frac{3}{12} = \$200$$

A similar calculation is necessary when the disposal of an asset occurs during a year. For example, suppose that the preceding asset is sold on June 24, 19X6. On the date of the disposal, depreciation should be recognized. The partial year's depreciation, calculated to the nearest whole month, is:

$$\frac{\$4,600 - \$600}{5} \times \frac{6}{12} = \$400$$

DEPRECIATION ON THE BALANCE SHEET

In presenting information about the plant assets of a business, both the cost and accumulated depreciation of plant assets should be reported. For example, **Apple Computer, Inc.'s** balance sheet at the close of its 1995 fiscal year included the following:

(Dollars in millions)	1995	1994
Property, plant, and equipment:		
Land and buildings	$ 504	$ 484
Machinery and equipment	638	573
Office furniture and equipment	145	158
Leasehold improvements	205	237
	$1,492	$1,452
Accumulated depreciation and amortization ...	(781)	(785)
Net property, plant, and equipment	$ 711	$ 667

PRINCIPLE APPLICATION
Full-Disclosure Principle,
p. 294
In the footnotes to its 1995 financial statements, Sara Lee Corporation states: "Property is stated at cost, and depreciation is computed using principally the straight-line method at annual rates of 2% to 20% for buildings and improvements, and 4% to 33% for machinery and equipment."

Notice that Apple reported only the total amount of accumulated depreciation and amortization for all plant and equipment. This is the usual practice in published financial statements. In fact, many companies show plant and equipment on one line with the net amount of cost less accumulated depreciation. When this is done, however, the amount of accumulated depreciation is disclosed in a footnote. To satisfy the *full-disclosure principle*, companies also describe the depreciation method or methods used.[2] Usually, they do this in a footnote.

Reporting both the cost and the accumulated depreciation of plant assets may help balance sheet readers compare the status of different companies. For example, a company that holds assets having an original cost of $50,000 and accumulated depreciation of $40,000 may be in a quite different situation than another company with new

---
[2]FASB, *Accounting Standards—Current Text* (Norwalk, CT, 1995), sec. D40.101. First published as *APB Opinion No. 12,* par. 5.

assets that cost $10,000. Although the net undepreciated cost is the same in both cases, the first company may have more productive capacity available but probably is facing the need to replace its older assets. These differences are not conveyed if the balance sheets report only the $10,000 book values.

From the discussion so far, you should recognize that depreciation is a process of cost allocation rather than valuation. Plant assets are reported on balance sheets at their remaining undepreciated costs (book value), not at market values.

Some people argue that financial statements should report the market value of plant assets. However, this practice has not gained general acceptance. Instead, most accountants believe that financial statements should be based on the *going-concern principle* described in Chapter 2. This principle states that, unless there is adequate evidence to the contrary, the accountant should assume the company will continue in business. This leads to a related assumption that plant assets will be held and used long enough to recover their original cost through the sale of products and services. Therefore, since the plant assets will not be sold, their market values are not reported in the financial statements. Instead, the assets are carried on the balance sheet at cost less accumulated depreciation. This is the remaining portion of the original cost that is expected to be recovered in future periods.

Inexperienced financial statement readers may make the mistake of thinking that the accumulated depreciation shown on a balance sheet represents funds accumulated to buy new assets when the presently owned assets must be replaced. However, you know that accumulated depreciation is a contra account with a credit balance that cannot be used to buy anything. If a business has funds available to buy assets, the funds are shown on the balance sheet as liquid assets such as *Cash,* not as accumulated depreciation.

REVISING DEPRECIATION RATES

Because the calculation of depreciation must be based on an asset's *predicted* useful life, depreciation expense is an estimate. Therefore, during the life of an asset, new information may indicate that the original prediction of useful life was inaccurate. If your estimate of an asset's useful life changes, what should be done? The answer is to use the new estimate of the remaining useful life to calculate depreciation in the future. In other words, revise the estimate of annual depreciation expense in the future by spreading the remaining cost to be depreciated over the revised remaining useful life. This approach should be followed whether the depreciation method is straight-line, units-of-production, or some other method.

For example, assume that a machine was purchased seven years ago at a cost of $10,500. At that time, the machine was predicted to have a 10-year life with a $500 salvage value. Therefore, it was depreciated by the straight-line method at the rate of $1,000 per year [($10,500 − $500)/10 = $1,000]. At the beginning of the asset's eighth year, its book value is $3,500, calculated as follows:

Cost	$10,500
Less seven years' accumulated depreciation ...	7,000
Book value	$ 3,500

At the beginning of its eighth year, the predicted number of years remaining in the useful life is changed from three to five years. The estimated salvage value is also changed to $300. Depreciation for each of the machine's five remaining years should be calculated as follows:

$$\frac{\text{Book value} - \text{Revised salvage value}}{\text{Revised remaining useful life}} = \frac{\$3,500 - \$300}{5 \text{ years}} = \$640 \text{ per year}$$

Thus, $640 of depreciation should be recorded for the machine at the end of the eighth and each remaining year in its useful life.

Because this asset was depreciated at the rate of $1,000 per year for the first seven years, you might contend that depreciation expense was overstated during the first seven years. While that view may have merit, accountants have concluded that past years' financial statements generally should not be restated to reflect facts that were not known when the statements were originally prepared.

A revision of the predicted useful life of a plant asset is an example of a **change in an accounting estimate.** Such changes result "from new information or subsequent developments and accordingly from better insight or improved judgment."[3] Generally accepted accounting principles require that changes in accounting estimates, such as a change in estimated useful life or salvage value, be reflected only in future financial statements, not by modifying past statements.

Progress Check

10–4   For accounting purposes, what is the meaning of the term *depreciation*?

10–5   Clandestine Gift Shop purchased a new machine for $96,000 on January 1, 19X1. Its predicted useful life is five years or 100,000 units of product, and salvage value is $8,000. During 19X1, 10,000 units of product were produced. Find the book value of the machine on December 31, 19X1, assuming *(a)* straight-line depreciation and *(b)* units-of-production depreciation.

10–6   In early January of 19X1, Betty's Brownies acquired mixing equipment at a cost of $3,800. The company estimated that this equipment would be used for three years and then have a salvage value of $200. Early in 19X3, they changed the estimate to a four-year life with no residual value. Assuming straight-line depreciation, how much will be reported as depreciation on this equipment for the year ended 19X3?

ACCELERATED DEPRECIATION

LO 3
Describe the use of accelerated depreciation for financial accounting and tax accounting purposes and calculate accelerated depreciation under (*a*) the declining-balance method and (*b*) the Modified Accelerated Cost Recovery System.

An annual survey of 600 industrial companies indicates that straight-line is the most widely used method of depreciation. However, note in the following table that **accelerated depreciation** methods were used 12% of the time in 1995.

	Depreciation Methods Used	
	1994	**1993**
Straight-line	80%	80%
An accelerated method	12	13
Units-of-production	7	6
Other	1	1
Total	100%	100%

Source: *Accounting Trends & Techniques,* Copyright © 1995 (1994) by American Institute of Certified Public Accountants, Inc., Table 3–13, p. 386.

Accelerated depreciation methods produce larger depreciation charges during the early years of an asset's life and smaller charges in the later years. Although more than one accelerated method is used in financial reporting, the most commonly used is the declining-balance method.

---

[3]FASB, *Accounting Standards—Current Text* (Norwalk, CT, 1995), sec. A35.104 and sec. A06.130. First published as *APB Opinion No. 20*, par. 13 and par. 31.

As a Matter of Ethics

Fascar Company has struggled financially for more than two years. The economic situation surrounding the company has been depressed and there are no signs of improvement for at least two more years. As a result, net income has been almost zero, and the future seems bleak.

The operations of Fascar require major investments in equipment. As a result, depreciation is a large factor in the calculation of income. Because competition in Fascar's industry normally has required frequent replacements of equipment, the equipment has been depreciated over only three years. However, Fascar's presi-

dent has recently instructed Sue Ann Meyer, the company's accountant, to revise the estimated useful lives of existing equipment to six years and to use a six-year life on new equipment.

Meyer suspects that the president's instruction is motivated by a desire to improve the reported income of the company. In trying to determine whether to follow the president's instructions, Meyer is torn between her loyalty to her employer and her responsibility to the public, the stockholders, and others who use the company's financial statements. She also wonders what the independent CPA who audits the financial statements will think about the change.

Declining-Balance Method

Under **declining-balance depreciation,** a depreciation rate of up to twice the straight-line rate is applied each year to the book value of the asset at the beginning of the year. Because the book value *declines* each year, the amount of depreciation gets smaller each year.

When the depreciation rate used is twice the straight-line rate, the method is called the *double-declining-balance method.* To use the double-declining-balance method: (1) calculate the straight-line depreciation rate for the asset; (2) double it; and (3) calculate depreciation expense for the year by applying this rate to the asset's book value at the beginning of that year. Note that the salvage value is not used in the calculation.

For example, assume that the double-declining-balance method is used to calculate depreciation on a new $10,000 asset; it has an estimated life of five years and an estimated salvage value of $1,000. The steps to follow are:

1. Divide 100% by five years to determine the straight-line annual depreciation rate of 20% per year.
2. Double this 20% rate to get a declining balance rate of 40% per year.
3. Calculate the annual depreciation charges as shown in the following table:

Year	Beginning Book Value	Annual Depreciation (40% of Book Value)*	Accumulated Depreciation at the Year-End	Ending Book Value ($10,000 Cost Less Accumulated Depreciation)
First	$10,000	$4,000	$4,000	$6,000
Second	6,000	2,400	6,400	3,600
Third	3,600	1,440	7,840	2,160
Fourth	2,160	864	8,704	1,296
Fifth	1,296	296*	9,000	1,000
Total		$9,000		

*Fifth year depreciation is $1,296 − $1,000 = $296.

In the fifth year of the table, notice that the annual depreciation of $296 for the fifth year does not equal 40% × $1,296, or $518.40. Instead, the $296 was calculated by subtracting the $1,000 salvage value from the $1,296 book value at the beginning of the fifth year. This was done because, according to generally accepted accounting principles, an asset should not be depreciated below its salvage value. If the declining-balance procedure had been applied in the fifth year, the $518.40 of annual depreciation would have reduced the ending book value to $777.60, which is less than the $1,000 estimated salvage value.

Earlier in the chapter we discussed the calculation of a partial year's depreciation when the straight-line method is used. Recall that when an asset is purchased (or disposed of) at some time other than the end of an accounting period, depreciation must be recorded for part of a year. Declining-balance depreciation does not complicate this calculation. For example, if depreciation must be calculated for three months, the annual amount of depreciation is simply multiplied by 3/12. So, if an asset that cost $10,000 is purchased three months before the end of the year and the annual declining-balance depreciation rate is 20%, depreciation for the last three months is $10,000 × 20% × 3/12 = $500.

Accelerated Depreciation for Tax Purposes

Some people fail to understand why the records a company keeps for financial accounting purposes may be different from the records it keeps for tax accounting purposes. Some may even suspect fraud when they hear there are differences between the two sets of records. In fact, differences between the two are normal and to be expected. Accelerated depreciation provides an example of this.

Many companies prefer to use accelerated depreciation for the purpose of calculating their taxable income. Accelerated methods reduce taxable income in the early years of an asset's life and increase taxable income in the later years. The effect of this is to defer income tax payments. Taxes are decreased in the early years and increased in the later years.

Beginning in 1981, a United States federal income tax law installed new rules for depreciating assets. Those rules were revised beginning in 1987 and are now called the **Modified Accelerated Cost Recovery System (MACRS).** MACRS allows straight-line depreciation and for most kinds of property also provides an accelerated method. MACRS separates depreciable assets purchased after December 31, 1986, into eight different types or classes. These include 3-year, 5-year, 7-year, 10-year, 15-year, 20-year, 27½-year, 31½-year, and 39-year classes. For example, computer equipment and general-purpose, heavy trucks are in the five-year class while office furniture is in the seven-year class.

When calculating depreciation for tax purposes, salvage values are ignored. Also, depreciation methods for personal property are based on the assumption that the asset is purchased halfway through the year and sold or retired halfway through the year. This *half-year convention* is required regardless of when the asset was actually purchased or sold.[4]

To simplify accelerated calculations under MACRS, the Internal Revenue Service provides a table for each class of assets. The tables show the percentage of original cost to be deducted as depreciation on each year's tax return. For example, Illustration 10–2 shows the accelerated depreciation rates for the three-year, five-year, and seven-year classes. In the table, note that it takes four years to fully depreciate the assets in the three-year class. Also, it takes six years to depreciate the assets in the five-year class, and eight years to depreciate the assets in the seven-year class. This happens because the half-year convention provides one-half of one year's depreciation during the first year and one-half of one year's depreciation during the last year.

Remember that the half-year convention also applies to straight-line depreciation under MACRS. Thus, under straight-line, it also takes four years to fully depreciate an asset in the three-year class.

---

[4]Under certain conditions, a half-quarter convention must be used. Depreciation methods for real property are based on a half-month convention.

	Asset Classes		
Year	Three-Year	Five-Year	Seven-Year
1	33.33%	20.00%	14.29%
2	44.45	32.00	24.49
3	14.81	19.20	17.49
4	7.41	11.52	12.49
5		11.52	8.93
6		5.76	8.92
7			8.93
8			4.46
Total	100.00%	100.00%	100.00%

As an example of how MACRS is applied, assume an asset in the five-year class (for example, a general-purpose, heavy truck) is purchased in 19X1 at a cost of $10,000. In the following table, the second column shows the MACRS accelerated rates for assets in the five-year class, which includes the truck. The remaining columns in the table show the effects of applying accelerated depreciation under MACRS to the $10,000 truck:

Year	MACRS Accelerated Depreciation Rate	Beginning Tax Basis	(Depreciation Rate × $10,000)	Ending Tax Basis
19X1	20.00%	$10,000	$2,000	$8,000
19X2	32.00	8,000	3,200	4,800
19X3	19.20	4,800	1,920	2,880
19X4	11.52	2,880	1,152	1,728
19X5	11.52	1,728	1,152	576
19X6	5.76	576	576	0
Total	100.00%			

While MACRS is now required for tax purposes, MACRS is not consistent with *generally accepted accounting principles.* It is not consistent because it allocates depreciation over an arbitrary period that usually is much shorter than the estimated service life of the asset. For example, general-purpose, heavy trucks in the 5-year class normally have useful lives of up to 10 years. Even when straight-line depreciation is used under MACRS, acceleration occurs because the length of life assumed for tax purposes is shorter than the expected service life of the asset. As a result, companies typically have to keep one set of depreciation records for tax purposes and another set for financial accounting purposes.

Progress Check

10-7   On January 1, 19X1, Temperware Industries paid $77,000 to purchase office furniture having an estimated salvage value of $14,000. The furniture has an estimated service life of 10 years, but it is in the 7-year class for tax purposes. What is the 19X1 depreciation on the furniture using (1) the double-declining-balance method for financial accounting purposes and (2) the straight-line method under MACRS with the half-year convention?

REVENUE AND CAPITAL EXPENDITURES

LO 4
Describe the difference between revenue and capital expenditures and account properly for costs such as repairs and betterments incurred after the original purchase of plant assets.

By this time, you have learned that some expenditures are recorded as expenses right away while others are recorded as assets with expenses coming later. After a plant asset is acquired and put into service, additional expenditures may be incurred to operate, maintain, repair, and improve it. In recording these additional expenditures, the accountant must decide whether they should be debited to expense accounts or asset accounts. The issue is whether more useful information is provided by reporting these expenditures as current expenses or by adding them to the plant asset's cost and depreciating them over its remaining useful life.

Expenditures that are recorded as expenses and deducted from revenues on the current period's income statement are called **revenue expenditures.** They are reported on the income statement because they do not provide material benefits in future periods. Examples of revenue expenditures that relate to plant assets are supplies, fuel, lubricants, and electrical power.

In contrast to revenue expenditures, **capital expenditures** produce economic benefits that do not fully expire before the end of the current period. Because they are debited to asset accounts and reported on the balance sheet, they are also called **balance sheet expenditures.** Capital expenditures increase or improve the kind or amount of service that an asset provides.

Because the information in the financial statements is affected for several years by the choice made between recording costs as revenue expenditures or as capital expenditures, managers must be careful in deciding how to classify them. In making these decisions, it is helpful to identify the costs as ordinary repairs, extraordinary repairs, betterments, or purchases of assets with low costs.

Ordinary Repairs

Ordinary repairs are made to keep an asset in normal, good operating condition. These expenditures are necessary if an asset is to provide its expected level of service over its estimated useful life. However, ordinary repairs do not extend the useful life beyond the original estimate and do not increase the productivity of the asset beyond the levels originally estimated. For example, machines must be cleaned, lubricated, and adjusted, and small parts must be replaced when they wear out. These

ordinary repairs typically are made every year, and accountants treat them as *revenue expenditures.* Thus, their costs should be reported on the current income statement as expenses.

Consistent with the guidelines given here, **America West Airlines, Inc.,** expenses routine maintenance and repairs as incurred. In addition, the cost of scheduled airframe and engine overhauls is capitalized because such expenditures are expected to benefit future periods.

Extraordinary Repairs

In contrast to ordinary repairs that keep a plant asset in its normal, good operating condition, **extraordinary repairs** extend the asset's service life beyond the original estimate. Because they benefit future periods, the costs of extraordinary repairs are *capital expenditures.* They may be debited to the asset account. However, by tradition, they are debited to the repaired asset's accumulated depreciation account to show that they restore the effects of past years' depreciation. For example, a machine was purchased for $8,000 and depreciated under the assumption it would last eight years and have no salvage value. At the beginning of the machine's seventh year, when the machine's book value is $2,000, it is given a major overhaul at a cost of

$2,100. The overhaul extends the machine's estimated useful life three years. Thus, the company now predicts that the machine will be used for five more years. The $2,100 cost of the extraordinary repair should be recorded as follows:

Jan.	12	Accumulated Depreciation, Machinery	2,100.00	
		Cash		2,100.00
		To record extraordinary repairs.		

This entry increases the book value of the asset from $2,000 to $4,100. For the remaining five years of the asset's life, depreciation should be based on this new book value. The effects of the extraordinary repairs are as follows:

	Before	Extraordinary Repair	After
Original cost	$ 8,000		$ 8,000
Accumulated depreciation	(6,000)	$2,100	(3,900)
Book value	$ 2,000		$ 4,100
Annual depreciation expense for remaining years ($4,100/5 years)			$ 820

Notice that because the $2,100 cost of the extraordinary repairs is included in the $4,100 book value, it is depreciated over the asset's remaining life of five years.

Betterments

A **betterment** (or an improvement) occurs when a plant asset is modified to make it more efficient or productive. A betterment often involves adding a component to an asset or replacing one of its old components with an improved or superior component. While a betterment makes an asset more productive, it may not increase the asset's useful life. For example, replacing the manual controls on a machine with automatic controls reduces future labor costs. But, the machine still wears out just as fast as it would have with the manual controls.

A betterment benefits future periods and should be debited to the asset account as a capital expenditure. Then, the new book value (less salvage) should be depreciated over the remaining service life of the asset. For example, suppose that a company paid $80,000 for a machine with an eight-year service life and no salvage value. On January 2, after three years and $30,000 of depreciation, it adds an automatic control system to the machine at a cost of $18,000. As a result, the company's labor cost to operate the machine in future periods will be reduced. The cost of the betterment is added to the Machinery account with this entry:

Jan.	2	Machinery	18,000.00	
		Cash		18,000.00
		To record the installation of the automatic control system.		

At this point, the remaining cost to be depreciated is $80,000 + $18,000 − $30,000 = $68,000. Because five years remain in the useful life, the annual depreciation expense hereafter will be $13,600 per year ($68,000/5 years).

Plant Assets with Low Costs

Even with the help of computers, keeping individual plant asset records can be expensive. Therefore, many companies do not keep detailed records for assets that cost less than some minimum amount such as $50 or $100. Instead, they treat the acquisition as a revenue expenditure and charge the cost directly to an expense account at the time of purchase. As long as the amounts are small, this practice is acceptable under the *materiality principle.* That is, treating these capital expenditures as revenue expenditures is unlikely to mislead a user of the financial statements.

In its 1994 annual report, **Coca-Cola Bottling Co. Consolidated** discloses the following aspects of its accounting policies related to plant assets:

Property, plant and equipment are recorded at cost and depreciated using the straight-line method over the estimated useful lives of the assets. Additions and major replacements or betterments are added to the assets at cost. Maintenance and repair costs and minor replacements are charged to expense when incurred. When assets are replaced or otherwise disposed of, the cost and accumulated depreciation are removed from the accounts, and the gain or loss, if any, is reflected in income.

Progress Check

10-8   At the beginning of the fifth year of a machine's estimated six-year useful life, the machine was completely overhauled and its estimated useful life was extended to nine years in total. The machine originally cost $108,000, and the overhaul cost was $12,000. Prepare the journal entry to record the cost of the overhaul.

10-9   What is the difference between revenue expenditures and capital expenditures and how should they be recorded?

10-10   What is a betterment? How should a betterment to a machine be recorded?

PLANT ASSET DISPOSALS

LO 5
Prepare entries to account for the disposal or exchange of plant assets and explain the use of total asset turnover in evaluating a company's efficiency in using its assets.

A variety of events might lead to the disposal of plant assets. Some assets wear out or become obsolete. Other assets may be sold because of changing business plans. Sometimes an asset is discarded or sold because it is damaged by a fire or other accident. Regardless of what leads to a disposal, the journal entry or entries related to the disposal should:

1.   Record depreciation expense up to the date of the disposal and bring the accumulated depreciation account up to date.
2.   Remove the asset and accumulated depreciation account balances that relate to the disposal.
3.   Record any cash received or paid as a result of the disposal.
4.   Record any gain or loss that results from comparing the book value of the asset with the cash received or paid as a result of the disposal.

For example, assume a machine that cost $9,000 was totally destroyed in a fire on June 25. Accumulated depreciation at the end of the previous year was $3,000 and unrecorded depreciation for the first six months of the current year is $500. The following entry brings the accumulated depreciation account up to date:

June	25	Depreciation Expense	500.00	
		Accumulated Depreciation, Machinery		500.00
		To record depreciation up to the date of the fire.		

Assume the owner of the machine carried insurance against fire losses and received a $4,400 cash settlement for the loss. The following entry records the loss of the machine and the cash settlement:

June	25	Cash	4,400.00	
		Loss on Fire[5]	1,100.00	
		Accumulated Depreciation, Machinery	3,500.00	
		Machinery		9,000.00
		To record the destruction of machinery, the receipt		
		of insurance settlement, and the net loss resulting		
		from the fire.		

Notice that the two entries accomplish all four of the necessary changes that occurred as a result of the asset disposal. Of course, an asset disposal might involve a gain instead of a loss. Also, a disposal might involve a cash payment instead of a receipt. Regardless of the specific facts, entries similar to these must be made so the income statement shows any gain or loss resulting from the disposal and the balance sheet reflects the necessary changes in the asset and accumulated depreciation accounts.

In recent years, many corporations have restructured and downsized their operations. These activities frequently involve disposing of plant assets. For example, as part of its restructuring, **Woolworth Corporation** sold approximately 120 of its Woolco discount stores to Wal-Mart stores. At the same time, Woolworth planned to continue expanding in the area of specialty operations such as Foot Locker, Northern Reflections, and Accessory Lady. The disposition of the Woolco stores resulted in a $168 million loss that was charged against revenues and contributed to a $495 million reported net loss. It is also interesting to note that the disposition of the Woolco stores generated net cash of approximately $200 million.

EXCHANGING PLANT ASSETS

Many plant assets are sold for cash when they are retired from use. Others, such as machinery, automobiles, and office equipment, are commonly exchanged for new assets. In a typical exchange of assets, a trade-in allowance is received on the old asset, and any balance is paid in cash.

Accounting for the exchange of nonmonetary assets depends on whether the old and the new assets are similar in the functions they perform. For example, trading an old truck for a new truck is an exchange of similar assets. An example of exchanging dissimilar assets would be trading a parcel of land for a truck.

Exchanges of Dissimilar Assets

If a company exchanges a plant asset for another asset that is *dissimilar* in use or purpose, any gain or loss on the exchange must be recorded. The gain or loss can be de-

---

[5]Note that the recorded loss of $1,100 probably does not equal the economic loss from the fire. The economic loss depends on the difference between the cost of replacing the asset and any insurance settlement. A difference between this economic loss and the reported loss arises from the fact that the accounting records do not attempt to reflect the replacement value of plant assets.

termined by comparing the book value of the assets given up with the fair market value of the assets received. For example, assume that a company exchanges an old machine plus $16,500 cash for some merchandise inventory. The old machine originally cost $18,000 and had accumulated depreciation of $15,000 at the time of the exchange. Also assume that the fair market value of the merchandise received in the exchange was $21,000. This entry would record the exchange:

Jan.	5	Merchandise Inventory (or Purchases)	21,000.00	
		Accumulated Depreciation, Machinery	15,000.00	
		Machinery		18,000.00
		Cash		16,500.00
		Gain on Exchange of Assets		1,500.00
		Exchanged old machine and cash for merchandise inventory.		

Note that the book value of the assets given up totaled $19,500, which included $16,500 cash plus $3,000 ($18,000 − $15,000) for the machine. Because the merchandise had a fair market value of $21,000, the entry recorded a gain of $1,500 ($21,000 − $19,500).

Another way to calculate the gain or loss is to compare the machine's book value with the trade-in allowance granted for the machine. Since the fair market value of the merchandise was $21,000 and the cash paid was $16,500, the trade-in allowance granted for the machine was $4,500. The difference between the machine's $3,000 book value and the $4,500 trade-in allowance equals the $1,500 gain on the exchange.

Exchanges of Similar Assets

In general, accounting for exchanges of similar assets depends on whether the book value of the asset given up is less or more than the trade-in allowance received for the asset.[6] When the trade-in allowance is less than the book value, the difference is recognized as a loss. However, when the trade-in allowance is more than the book value, no gain is recognized.

Recognition of a Loss. To illustrate the recognition of a loss on an exchange of similar assets, assume the machine that cost $18,000 and has accumulated depreciation of $15,000 is traded in on a similar but new machine. The new machine has a $21,000 cash price, and a $1,000 trade-in allowance is received. The $20,000 balance of the cost is paid in cash. Under these assumptions, the book value of the old machine and the loss on the exchange are calculated as follows:

Cost of old machine	$18,000
Less accumulated depreciation	15,000
Book value	$ 3,000
Less trade-in allowance	1,000
Loss on exchange	$ 2,000

---

[6]These general rules apply to exchanges of similar assets when the exchange includes a cash payment or when no cash is received or paid. The accounting is more complex when the exchange involves a cash receipt. Such cases are explained in more advanced accounting texts. See FASB, *Accounting Standards—Current Text* (Norwalk, CT, 1995), sec. N35.109. First published as *APB Opinion No. 29,* par. 22.

The entry to record this exchange transaction is:

Jan.	5	Machinery	21,000.00	
		Loss on Exchange of Machinery	2,000.00	
		Accumulated Depreciation, Machinery	15,000.00	
		Machinery		18,000.00
		Cash		20,000.00
		Exchanged old machine and cash for a similar machine.		

The $21,000 debit to Machinery puts the new machine in the accounts at its cash price. The debit to Loss on Exchange of Machinery records the loss. The old machine is removed from the accounts with the $15,000 debit to Accumulated Depreciation and the $18,000 credit to Machinery.

Nonrecognition of a Gain. When similar assets are exchanged and the trade-in allowance of the asset given up is more than its book value, the difference between the trade-in allowance and the book value may be perceived as a gain. However, generally accepted accounting principles do not allow the recognition of this gain. Instead, the new asset is recorded at the sum of the old asset's book value plus any cash paid.

For example, assume that the exchange for the $21,000 machine in the previous section involved a trade-in allowance of $4,500 instead of $1,000. As a result, the balance to be paid in cash is only $16,500. Since the $4,500 trade-in allowance exceeds the $3,000 book value of the old asset, the difference is a gain. However, you cannot recognize the gain in the accounts. Rather, it is absorbed into the cost of the new machine, which is calculated as follows:

Cost of old machine	$18,000
Less accumulated depreciation	15,000
Book value of old machine	$ 3,000
Cash given in the exchange	16,500
Cost recorded for the new machine	$19,500

The following entry records the exchange:

Jan.	5	Machinery	19,500.00	
		Accumulated Depreciation, Machinery	15,000.00	
		Machinery		18,000.00
		Cash		16,500.00
		Exchanged old machine and cash for a similar but new machine.		

Observe that the $19,500 recorded for the new machine equals its cash price less the unrecognized $1,500 gain on the exchange ($21,000 − $1,500 = $19,500). In other words, the $1,500 gain was absorbed into the amount at which the new machine was recorded. The $19,500 is the *cost basis* of the new machine and is the amount used to calculate its depreciation and/or any gain or loss on its sale.

In summary, when similar plant assets are exchanged and there is a cash payment, losses are recognized but gains are not recognized. This rule is based on the opinion that "revenue [or a gain] should not be recognized merely because one productive asset is substituted for a similar productive asset but rather should be considered to flow from the production and sale of the goods or services to which the substituted productive asset is committed."[7] As a result, the effect of a gain is delayed. In future income statements, the gain appears in the form of smaller depreciation charges or perhaps as a gain on the sale of the asset. In the previous example, depreciation calculated on the recorded $19,500 cost basis of the new machine is smaller than it would be if it was based on the machine's $21,000 cash price.

USING THE INFORMATION— TOTAL ASSET TURNOVER

We have not yet discussed all of the different assets a business might own. Nevertheless, you can see from this and previous chapters that a company's assets are usually very important factors in determining the company's ability to earn profits. Managers spend a great deal of time and energy deciding which assets a company should acquire, how much should be acquired, and how the assets can be used most efficiently. Outside investors and other financial statement readers also are interested in evaluating whether a company uses its assets efficiently.

One way to describe the efficiency of a company's use of its assets is to calculate **total asset turnover.** The formula for this calculation is:

$$\text{Total asset turnover} = \frac{\text{Net sales}}{\text{Average total assets}}$$

This calculation can be performed regardless of the type of company being evaluated. It can be applied to manufacturing and merchandising companies, and also service companies. The numerator, net sales, represents all operating revenues generated by the company. Average total assets is often approximated by averaging the total assets at the beginning of the year with total assets at the end of the year.

For example, suppose that a company with total assets of $9,650,000 at the beginning of the year and $10,850,000 at the end of the year generated sales of $44,000,000 during the year. The company's total asset turnover for the year is calculated as follows:

$$\text{Total asset turnover} = \frac{\$44,000,000}{(\$9,650,000 + \$10,850,000)/2} = 4.3$$

Thus, in describing the efficiency of the company in using its assets to generate sales, we can say that it turned its assets over 4.3 times during the year. Or, we might say that each $1.00 of assets produced $4.30 of sales during the year.

As is true for other financial ratios, a company's total asset turnover is meaningful only when compared to the results in other years and of similar companies. Interpreting the total asset turnover also requires that users understand the company's

operations. Some operations are capital intensive, meaning that a relatively large amount must be invested in assets to generate sales. This suggests a relatively low total asset turnover. On the other hand, if operations are labor intensive, sales are generated more by the efforts of people than the use of assets. Thus, we would expect a higher total asset turnover.

Fortune magazine conducts an annual Corporate Reputations Survey, in which more than 10,000 senior executives, outside directors, and financial analysts are asked to rate the 10 largest companies in their own industries. In 1994, **Rubbermaid Incorporated** was se-

---

[7]APB, "Accounting for Nonmonetary Transactions," *APB Opinion No. 29* (New York: AICPA, May 1973), par. 16.

lected as the most admired corporation in America. The participants in the survey rank companies on eight attributes of reputation, one of which is "use of corporate assets." Rubbermaid's total asset turnover in 1994 was:

$$\text{Total asset turnover} = \frac{\$2,169,354,000}{(\$1,709,180,000 + \$1,513,124,000)/2} = 1.35$$

Progress Check

10-11   Melanie Co. acquired equipment on January 10, 19X1, at a cost of $42,000. Straight-line depreciation was used assuming a five-year life and $7,000 salvage value. On June 27, 19X2, the company decided to change their manufacturing methods and sold this equipment for $32,000. Prepare the appropriate entry or entries for June 27, 19X2.

10-12   Standard Company traded an old truck for a new one. The original cost of the old truck was $30,000, and its accumulated depreciation at the time of the trade was $23,400. The new truck had a cash price of $45,000. Prepare entries to record the trade assuming Standard received   (a) a $3,000 trade-in allowance or   (b) a $7,000 trade-in allowance.

10-13   Using the annual report for Land's End, Inc., in Appendix F, calculate the total asset turnover for the year ended January 27, 1995.

LO 1. Describe the differences between plant assets and other kinds of assets and calculate the cost and record the purchase of plant assets. Plant assets are tangible items that have a useful life longer than one accounting period. Plant assets are not held for sale but are used in the production or sale of other assets or services. The cost of plant assets includes all normal and reasonable expenditures necessary to get the assets in place and ready to use. The cost of a lump-sum purchase should be allocated among the individual assets based on their relative market values.

LO 2. Explain depreciation accounting (including the reasons for depreciation), calculate depreciation by the straight-line and units-of-production methods, and calculate depreciation after revising the estimated useful life of an asset. The cost of plant assets that have limited service lives must be allocated to the accounting periods that benefit from their use. The straight-line method of depreciation divides the cost minus salvage value by the number of periods in the service life of the asset to determine the depreciation expense of each period. The units-of-production method divides the cost minus salvage value by the estimated number of units the asset will produce to determine the depreciation per unit. If the estimated useful life of a plant asset is changed, the remaining cost to be depreciated is spread over the remaining (revised) useful life of the asset.

LO 3. Describe the use of accelerated depreciation for financial accounting and tax accounting purposes and calculate accelerated depreciation under (a) the declining-balance method and (b) the Modified Accelerated Cost Recovery System. Accelerated depreciation methods such as the declining-balance method are acceptable for financial accounting purposes if they are based on realistic estimates of useful life. However, they are not widely used at the present time. The Modified Accelerated Cost Recovery System (MACRS), which is used for tax purposes, is not based on realistic estimates of useful life. Thus, MACRS is not acceptable for financial accounting purposes.

SUMMARY OF THE CHAPTER IN TERMS OF LEARNING OBJECTIVES

LO 4. Describe the difference between revenue and capital expenditures and account properly for costs such as repairs and betterments incurred after the original purchase of plant assets. The benefit of revenue expenditures expires during the current period. Thus, revenue expenditures are debited to expense accounts and matched with current revenues. Capital expenditures are debited to asset accounts because they benefit future periods. Ordinary repairs are revenue expenditures. Examples of capital expenditures include extraordinary repairs and betterments. Amounts paid for assets with low costs are technically capital expenditures but can be treated as revenue expenditures if they are not material.

LO 5. Prepare entries to account for the disposal or exchange of plant assets and explain the use of total asset turnover in evaluating a company's efficiency in using its assets. When a plant asset is discarded or sold, the cost and accumulated depreciation are removed from the accounts. Any cash proceeds are recorded and compared to the asset's book value to determine gain or loss. When nonmonetary assets are exchanged and they are dissimilar, the new asset is recorded at its fair value, and either a gain or a loss on disposal is recognized. When similar assets are exchanged, losses are recognized but gains are not. Instead, the new asset account is debited for the book value of the old asset plus any cash paid. Total asset turnover measures the efficiency of a company's use of its assets to generate sales.

DEMONSTRATION PROBLEM

On July 14, 19X1, Tulsa Company paid $600,000 to acquire a fully equipped factory. The purchase included the following:

Asset	Appraised Value	Estimated Salvage Value	Estimated Service Life	Depreciation Method
Land	$160,000			Not depreciated
Land improvements	80,000	$ -0-	10 years	Straight line
Building	320,000	100,000	10 years	Double-declining balance
Machinery	240,000	20,000	10,000 units	Units of production*
Total	$800,000			

*The machinery was used to produce 700 units in 19X1 and 1,800 units in 19X2.

Required

1. Allocate the total $600,000 cost among the separate assets.
2. Calculate the 19X1 (six months) and 19X2 depreciation expense for each type of asset and calculate the total each year for all assets.

Planning the Solution

*   Complete a three-column worksheet showing these amounts for each asset: appraised value, percentage of total value, and allocated cost.
*   Using the allocated costs, compute the amount of depreciation for 19X1 (only one-half year) and 19X2 for each asset. Then, summarize those calculations in a table showing the total depreciation for each year.

Solution to Demonstration Problem

1. Allocation of total cost among the assets:

Asset	Appraised Value	Percentage of Total Value	Allocated Cost
Land	$160,000	20%	$120,000
Land improvements	80,000	10	60,000
Building	320,000	40	240,000
Machinery	240,000	30	180,000
Total	$800,000	100%	$600,000

2. Depreciation for each asset:

Land Improvements:

Cost	$60,000
Salvage value	-0-
Net cost	$60,000
Service life	10 years
Annual expense ($60,000/10)	$6,000
19X1 depreciation ($6,000 × 6/12)	$3,000
19X2 depreciation	$6,000

Building:

Straight-line rate = 100%/10 = 10%
Double-declining-balance rate = 10% × 2 = 20%

19X1 depreciation ($240,000 × 20% × 6/12)	$24,000
19X2 depreciation [($240,000 − $24,000) × 20%]	$43,200

Machinery:

Cost	$180,000
Salvage value	20,000
Net cost	$160,000
Total expected units	10,000
Expected cost per unit ($160,000/10,000)	$ 16

Year	Units × Unit Cost	Depreciation
19X1	700 × $16	$11,200
19X2	1,800 × $16	28,800

Total depreciation expense:

	19X2	19X1
Land improvements	$ 6,000	$ 3,000
Building	43,200	24,000
Machinery	28,800	11,200
Total	$78,000	$38,200

GLOSSARY

Accelerated depreciation depreciation methods that produce larger depreciation charges during the early years of an asset's life and smaller charges in the later years. p. 354

Balance sheet expenditure another name for capital expenditure. p. 358

Betterment a modification to an asset to make it more efficient, usually by replacing one of its components with an improved or superior component. p. 359

Book value the amount assigned to an item in the accounting records and in the financial statements; for a plant asset, book value is its original cost less accumulated depreciation. p. 350

Capital expenditure an expenditure that produces economic benefits that do not fully expire before the end of the current period; because it creates or adds to existing assets, it should appear on the balance sheet as the cost of an asset. Also called a *balance sheet expenditure*. p. 358

Change in an accounting estimate a change in a calculated amount used in the financial statements that results from new

information or subsequent developments and from better insight or improved judgment. p. 354

Declining-balance depreciation a depreciation method in which a plant asset's depreciation charge for the period is determined by applying a constant depreciation rate (up to twice the straight-line rate) each year to the asset's book value at the beginning of the year. p. 355

Extraordinary repairs major repairs that extend the service life of a plant asset beyond original expectations; treated as a capital expenditure. p. 358

Inadequacy a condition in which the capacity of plant assets becomes too small for the productive demands of the business. p. 349

Land improvements assets that increase the usefulness of land but that have a limited useful life and are subject to depreciation. p. 348

Modified Accelerated Cost Recovery System (MACRS) the system of depreciation required by federal income tax law for assets placed in service after 1986. p. 356

Obsolescence a condition in which, because of new inventions and improvements, a plant asset can no longer be used to produce goods or services with a competitive advantage. p. 349

Ordinary repairs repairs made to keep a plant asset in normal, good operating condition; treated as a revenue expenditure. p. 358

Revenue expenditure an expenditure that should appear on the current income statement as an expense and be deducted from the period's revenues because it does not provide a material benefit in future periods. p. 358

Salvage value the amount that management predicts will be recovered at the end of a plant asset's service life through a sale or as a trade-in allowance on the purchase of a new asset. p. 350

Service life the length of time in which a plant asset will be used in the operations of the business. p. 349

Straight-line depreciation a method that allocates an equal portion of the total depreciation for a plant asset (cost minus salvage) to each accounting period in its service life. p. 350

Total asset turnover a measure of how efficiently a company uses its assets to generate sales; calculated by dividing net sales by average total assets. p. 364

Units-of-production depreciation a method that allocates an equal portion of the total depreciation for a plant asset (cost minus salvage) to each unit of product or service that it produces, or on a similar basis, such as hours of use or miles driven. p.351

QUESTIONS

1. What characteristics of a plant asset make it different from other assets?
2. What is the balance sheet classification of land held for future expansion? Why is the land not classified as a plant asset?
3. In general, what is included in the cost of a plant asset?
4. What is the difference between land and land improvements?
5. Does the balance of the account, Accumulated Depreciation, Machinery, represent funds accumulated to replace the machinery when it wears out? What does the balance of Accumulated Depreciation represent?
6. Why is the Modified Accelerated Cost Recovery System not generally accepted for financial accounting purposes?
7. What is the difference between ordinary repairs and extraordinary repairs and how should they be recorded?
8. What accounting principle justifies charging the $75 cost of a plant asset immediately to an expense account?
9. What are some of the events that might lead to the disposal of a plant asset?
10. Should a gain on an exchange of plant assets be recorded?
11. How is total asset turnover calculated? Why would a financial statement user be interested in calculating total asset turnover?
12. Refer to the consolidated balance sheets for Southwest Airlines in Appendix E. What phrase does Southwest Airlines use to describe its plant assets? What is the book value of plant assets as of December 31, 1994, and December 31, 1993?

QUICK STUDY (Five-Minute Exercises)

QS 10–1 (LO 1) Explain the difference between (a) plant assets and current assets; (b) plant assets and inventory; and (c) plant assets and long-term investments.

QS 10–2 (LO 1) Starbuck Lanes installed automatic score-keeping equipment. The electrical work required to prepare for the installation was $18,000. The invoice price of the equipment was $180,000. Additional costs were $3,000 for delivery and $12,600, sales tax. During the installation, a component of the equipment was damaged because it was carelessly left on a lane and hit by the automatic lane cleaning machine during a daily maintenance run. The cost of repairing the component was $2,250. What is the cost of the automatic score-keeping equipment?

QS 10–3 (LO 2) On January 2, 19X1, Crossfire acquired sound equipment for concert performances at a cost of $55,900. The rock band estimated they would use this equipment for four years, during which time they anticipated performing about 12 concerts. They estimated that at that point they could sell the equipment for $1,900. During 19X1, the band performed four concerts. Calculate the 19X1 depreciation using (a) the straight-line method and (b) the units-of-production method.

QS 10–4 (LO 2) Refer to the facts in QS 10–3. Assume that Crossfire chose straight-line depreciation but recognized during the second year that due to concert bookings beyond expectations, this equipment would only last a total of three years. The salvage value would remain unchanged. Calculate the revised depreciation for the second year and the third year.

A fleet of refrigerated delivery trucks acquired on January 5, 19X1, at a cost of $930,000 had an estimated useful life of eight years and an estimated salvage value of $150,000. Calculate the 19X1 depreciation under (a) the double-declining-balance method for financial accounting purposes and (b) the accelerated method under MACRS with the half-year convention for tax purposes. (MACRS classifies this asset in a five-year category.)

QS 10–5
(LO 3)

a. Classify the following expenditures as revenue or capital expenditures:
    (1) The cost of annual tune-ups for delivery trucks.
    (2) The cost of replacing a compressor for a meatpacking firm's refrigeration system that extends the estimated life of the system four years, $30,000.
    (3) The cost of $220,000 for an addition of a new wing on an office building.
    (4) The monthly replacement cost of filters on an air conditioning system, $175.
b. Prepare the journal entry to record (2) and (3).

QS 10–6
(LO 4)

Spectrum Flooring owned an automobile with a $15,000 cost and $13,500 accumulated depreciation. In a transaction with a neighboring computer retailer, Spectrum exchanged this auto for a computer with a fair market value of $4,500. Spectrum was required to pay an additional $3,750 cash. Prepare the entry to record this transaction for Spectrum.

QS 10–7
(LO 5)

Mayes Corp. owns an industrial machine that cost $38,400 and has been depreciated $20,400. Mayes exchanged the machine for a newer model that has a fair value of $48,000. Record the exchange assuming a trade-in allowance of (a) $32,000 and then (b) $24,000.

QS 10–8
(LO 5)

Eastman Kodak Company reported the following facts in its 1994 annual report: net sales of $13,557 million for 1994 and $12,670 million for 1993; total end-of-year assets of $14,968 million for 1994 and $18,810 million for 1993. Calculate the total asset turnover for 1994.

QS 10–9
(LO 5)

EXERCISES

Santiago Co. purchased a machine for $11,500, terms 2/10, n/60, FOB shipping point. The seller prepaid the freight charges, $260, adding the amount to the invoice and bringing its total to $11,760. The machine required a special steel mounting and power connections costing $795, and another $375 was paid to assemble the machine and get it into operation. In moving the machine onto its steel mounting, it was dropped and damaged. The repairs cost $190. Later, $30 of raw materials were consumed in adjusting the machine so that it would produce a satisfactory product. The adjustments were normal for this type of machine and were not the result of the damage. However, the items produced while the adjustments were being made were not sellable. Prepare a calculation to show the cost of this machine for accounting purposes. (Assume Santiago pays for the purchase within the discount period.)

Exercise 10–1
Cost of a plant asset
(LO 1)

Horizon Company paid $368,250 for real estate plus $19,600 in closing costs. The real estate included land appraised at $166,320; land improvements appraised at $55,440; and a building appraised at $174,240. Prepare a calculation showing the allocation of the total cost among the three purchased assets and present the journal entry to record the purchase.

Exercise 10–2
Lump-sum purchase of plant assets
(LO 1)

After planning to build a new plant, Monarch Manufacturing purchased a large lot on which a small building was located. The negotiated purchase price for this real estate was $225,000 for the lot plus $120,000 for the building. The company paid $34,500 to have the old building torn down and $51,000 for landscaping the lot. Finally, it paid $1,440,000 in construction costs, which included the cost of a new building plus $85,500 for lighting and paving a parking lot next to the building. Present a single journal entry to record the costs incurred by Monarch, all of which were paid in cash.

Exercise 10–3
Recording costs of real estate
(LO 1)

Exercise 10–4
Alternative depreciation methods
(LO 2, 3)

Barrow Company installed a computerized machine in its factory at a cost of $42,300. The machine's useful life was estimated at 10 years, or 363,000 units of product, with a $6,000 trade-in value. During its second year, the machine produced 35,000 units of product. Determine the machine's second-year depreciation under the (a) straight-line, (b) units-of-production, and (c) double-declining-balance methods.

Exercise 10–5
Alternative depreciation methods; partial year's depreciation
(LO 2, 3)

On April 1, 19X1, Rodgers Backhoe Co. purchased a trencher for $250,000. The machine was expected to last five years and have a salvage value of $25,000. Calculate depreciation expense for 19X2, using (a) the straight-line method and (b) the double-declining-balance method.

Exercise 10–6
Revising depreciation rates
(LO 2)

BodySmart Fitness Club used straight-line depreciation for a machine that cost $21,750, under the assumption it would have a four-year life and a $2,250 trade-in value. After two years, BodySmart determined that the machine still had three more years of remaining useful life, after which it would have an estimated $1,800 trade-in value. (a) Calculate the machine's book value at the end of its second year. (b) Calculate the amount of depreciation to be charged during each of the remaining years in the machine's revised useful life.

Exercise 10–7
Income statement effects of alternative depreciation methods
(LO 2, 3)

Shamrock Enterprises recently paid $235,200 for equipment that will last five years and have a salvage value of $52,500. By using the machine in its operations for five years, the company expects to earn $85,500 annually, after deducting all expenses except depreciation. Present a schedule showing income before depreciation, depreciation expense, and net income for each year and the total amounts for the five-year period, assuming (a) straight-line depreciation and (b) double-declining-balance depreciation.

Exercise 10–8
MACRS depreciation
(LO 2, 3)

In January 19X1, Labtech purchased computer equipment for $147,000. The equipment will be used in research and development activities for four years and then sold at an estimated salvage value of $30,000. The equipment is in the five-year class for tax purposes, and the half-year convention is required. Prepare schedules showing the depreciation under MACRS for each year's tax return, assuming (a) straight-line depreciation and (b) accelerated depreciation. (To calculate accelerated depreciation, use the MACRS rates shown in Illustration 10–2.)

Exercise 10–9
Ordinary repairs, extraordinary repairs, and betterments
(LO 4)

Archer Company paid $262,500 for equipment that was expected to last four years and have a salvage value of $30,000. Prepare journal entries to record the following costs related to the equipment:

a. During the second year of the equipment's life, $21,000 cash was paid for a new component that was expected to increase the equipment's productivity by 10% each year.

b. During the third year, $5,250 cash was paid for repairs necessary to keep the equipment in good working order.

c. During the fourth year, $13,950 was paid for repairs that were expected to increase the service life of the equipment from four to six years.

Exercise 10–10
Extraordinary repairs
(LO 4)

Flemming Corp. owns a building that appeared on its balance sheet at the end of last year at its original $561,000 cost less $420,750 accumulated depreciation. The building has been depreciated on a straight-line basis under the assumption that it would have a 20-year life and no salvage value. During the first week in January of the current year, major structural repairs were completed on the building at a cost of $67,200. The repairs did not increase the building's capacity, but they did extend its expected life for 7 years beyond the 20 years originally estimated.

a. Determine the building's age as of the end of last year.

b. Give the entry to record the repairs, which were paid with cash.

c. Determine the book value of the building after the repairs were recorded.

d. Give the entry to record the current year's depreciation.

Levy, Inc., purchased and installed a machine on January 1, 19X1, at a total cost of $92,750. Straight-line depreciation was taken each year for four years, based on the assumption of a seven-year life and no salvage value. The machine was disposed of on July 1, 19X5, during its fifth year of service. Present the entries to record the partial year's depreciation on July 1, 19X5, and to record the disposal under each of the following unrelated assumptions: *(a)* the machine was sold for $35,000 cash; and *(b)* Levy received an insurance settlement of $30,000 resulting from the total destruction of the machine in a fire.

Exercise 10–11
Partial year's depreciation; disposal of plant asset
(LO 2, 5)

Greenbelt Construction traded in an old tractor for a new tractor, receiving a $28,000 trade-in allowance and paying the remaining $82,000 in cash. The old tractor cost $95,000, and straight-line depreciation of $52,500 had been recorded under the assumption that it would last eight years and have an $11,000 salvage value. Answer the following questions:

a. What was the book value of the old tractor?

b. What is the loss on the exchange?

c. What amount should be debited to the new Tractor account?

Exercise 10–12
Exchanging plant assets
(LO 5)

On January 2, 19X1, Hammond Service Co. disposed of a machine that cost $42,000 and had been depreciated $22,625. Present the journal entries to record the disposal under each of the following unrelated assumptions:

a. The machine was sold for $16,250 cash.

b. The machine was traded in on a new machine of like purpose having a $58,500 cash price. A $20,000 trade-in allowance was received, and the balance was paid in cash.

c. A $15,000 trade-in allowance was received for the machine on a new machine of like purpose having a $58,500 cash price. The balance was paid in cash.

d. The machine was traded for vacant land adjacent to the shop to be used as a parking lot. The land had a fair value of $37,500, and Hammond paid $12,500 cash in addition to giving the seller the machine.

Exercise 10–13
Recording plant asset disposal or exchange
(LO 5)

Atherton Corp. reported net sales of $4,862,000 for 19X2 and $7,542,000 for 19X3. End-of-year balances for total assets were: 19X1, $1,586,000; 19X2, $1,700,000; and 19X3, $1,882,000. Calculate Atherton's total asset turnover for 19X2 and 19X3 and comment on the corporation's efficiency in the use of its assets.

Exercise 10–14
Evaluating efficient use of assets
(LO 5)

PROBLEMS

In 19X1, Lightscapes paid $2,800,000 for a tract of land and two buildings on it. The plan was to demolish Building One and build a new store in its place. Building Two was to be used as a company office and was appraised at a value of $641,300, with a useful life of 20 years and an $80,000 salvage value. A lighted parking lot near Building One had improvements (Land Improvements One) valued at $408,100 that were expected to last another 14 years and have no salvage value. Without considering the buildings or improvements, the tract of land was estimated to have a value of $1,865,600. Lightscapes incurred the following additional costs:

Problem 10–1
Real estate costs; partial year's depreciation
(LO 1, 2)

Cost to demolish Building One	$ 422,600
Cost of additional landscaping	167,200
Cost to construct new building (Building Three), having a useful life of 25 years and a $390,100 salvage value	2,019,000
Cost of new land improvements near Building Two (Land Improvements Two) which have a 20-year useful life and no salvage value	158,000

Required

1. Prepare a schedule having the following column headings: Land, Building Two, Building Three, Land Improvements One, and Land Improvements Two. Allocate the costs incurred by Lightscapes to the appropriate columns and total each column.

2. Prepare a single journal entry dated March 31 to record all the incurred costs, assuming they were paid in cash on that date.

3. Using the straight-line method, prepare December 31 adjusting entries to record depreciation for the nine months of 19X1 during which the assets were in use.

CHECK FIGURE:
Accum. Depreciation, Land Improvements Two, $5,925

Problem 10–2
Plant asset costs; partial year's depreciation; alternative methods, including MACRS
(LO 1, 2, 3)

Gunner Construction recently negotiated a lump-sum purchase of several assets from a company that was going out of business. The purchase was completed on March 1, 19X1, at a total cash price of $787,500 and included a building, land, certain land improvements, and 12 vehicles. The estimated market values of the assets were: building, $408,000; land, $289,000; land improvements, $42,500; and vehicles, $110,500. The company's fiscal year ends on December 31.

Required

Preparation component:

1. Prepare a schedule to allocate the lump-sum purchase price to the separate assets that were purchased. Also present the journal entry to record the purchase.

2. Calculate the 19X1 depreciation expense on the building using the straight-line method, assuming a 15-year life and a $25,650 salvage value.

3. Calculate the 19X1 depreciation expense on the land improvements assuming a five-year life and double-declining-balance depreciation.

4. The vehicles are in the five-year class for tax purposes but are expected to last seven years and have a salvage value of $14,700. Prepare a schedule showing each year's depreciation for the vehicles under MACRS, assuming (a) straight-line and (b) accelerated depreciation. (To calculate accelerated depreciation, use the MACRS rates in Illustration 10–2.)

CHECK FIGURE:
19X1, depreciation expense on land improvements, $13,125

Analysis component:

5. Defend or refute this statement: Accelerated depreciation results in lower taxes over the life of the asset.

Problem 10–3
Alternative depreciation methods; partial year's depreciation; disposal of plant asset
(LO 2, 3, 5)

Part 1. A machine that cost $210,000, with a four-year life and an estimated $20,000 salvage value, was installed in Casablanca Company's factory on January 1. The factory manager estimated that the machine would produce 475,000 units of product during its life. It actually produced the following units: year 1, 121,400; year 2, 122,400; year 3, 119,600; and year 4, 118,200. Note the total number of units produced by the end of year 4 exceeded the original estimate. Nevertheless, the machine should not be depreciated below the estimated salvage value.

Required

Prepare a form with the following column headings:

Year	Straight Line	Units of Production	Double-Declining Balance

CHECK FIGURE:
Year 4, units-of-production depreciation expense, $44,640

Then show the depreciation for each year and the total depreciation for the machine under each depreciation method.

Part 2. Casablanca purchased a used machine for $167,000 on January 2. It was repaired the next day at a cost of $3,420 and installed on a new platform that cost $1,080. The company predicted that the machine would be used for six years and would then have a $14,600 salvage value. Depreciation was to be charged on a straight-line basis. A full year's depreciation was charged on December 31, the end of the first year of the machine's use. On September 30 of its sixth year in service, it was retired.

Required

1. Prepare journal entries to record the purchase of the machine, the cost of repairing it, and the installation. Assume that cash was paid.

2. Prepare entries to record depreciation on the machine on December 31 of its first year and on September 30 in the year of its disposal.

3. Prepare entries to record the retirement of the machine under each of the following unrelated assumptions: *(a)* it was sold for $13,500; *(b)* it was sold for $36,000; and *(c)* it was destroyed in a fire and the insurance company paid $24,000 in full settlement of the loss claim.

Crenshaw Contractors completed these transactions involving the purchase and operation of heavy equipment:

19X1

July 1   Paid $255,440 cash for a new front-end loader, plus $15,200 in state sales tax and $2,500 for transportation charges. The loader was estimated to have a four-year life and a $34,740 salvage value.

Oct. 2   Paid $3,660 to enclose the cab and install air conditioning in the loader. This increased the estimated salvage value of the loader by $1,110.

Dec. 31   Recorded straight-line depreciation on the loader.

19X2

Feb. 17   Paid $920 to repair the loader after the operator backed it into a tree.

June 30   Paid $4,500 to overhaul the loader's engine. As a result, the estimated useful life of the loader was increased by two years.

Dec. 31   Recorded straight-line depreciation on the loader.

Required

Prepare journal entries to record the transactions.

Problem 10–4
Partial year's depreciation; revising depreciation rates; revenue and capital expenditures
(LO 2, 3, 4)

CHECK FIGURE:
12/31/19X2, Accum. Depr., Heavy Equipment, $48,674

ACT, Inc., completed the following transactions involving delivery trucks:

19X1

Mar. 26   Paid cash for a new delivery truck, $19,415 plus $1,165 state sales tax. The truck was estimated to have a five-year life and a $3,000 trade-in value.

Dec. 31   Recorded straight-line depreciation on the truck.

19X2

Dec. 31   Recorded straight-line depreciation on the truck. However, due to new information obtained earlier in the year, the original estimated service life of the truck was changed from five years to four years, and the original estimated trade-in value was increased to $3,500.

19X3

July 7   Traded in the old truck and paid $13,565 in cash for a new truck. The new truck was estimated to have a six-year life and a $3,125 trade-in value. The invoice for the exchange showed these items:

Problem 10–5
Partial year's depreciation; revising depreciation rates; exchanging plant assets
(LO 2, 3, 5)

Price of the new truck	$22,550
Trade-in allowance granted on the old truck	(9,750)
Balance of purchase price	$12,800
State sales tax	765
Total paid in cash	$13,565

Dec. 31   Recorded straight-line depreciation on the new truck.

CHECK FIGURE:
July 7, 19X3, Loss on Exchange of Delivery Trucks, $1,527

Required

Prepare journal entries to record the transactions.

Problem 10–6
Partial year's depreciation; alternative methods; disposal of plant assets
(LO 2, 3, 5)

Wallingford Co. completed the following transactions involving machinery:

Machine No. 15–50 was purchased for cash on May 4, 19X1, at an installed cost of $158,700. Its useful life was estimated to be six years with a $12,900 trade-in value. Straight-line depreciation was recorded for the machine at the end of 19X1, 19X2, and 19X3. On April 27, 19X4, it was traded for Machine No. 17–95, a similar asset with an installed cash price of $185,700. A trade-in allowance of $90,330 was received for Machine No. 15–50, and the balance was paid in cash.

Machine No. 17–95's life was predicted to be four years with a $24,600 trade-in value. Double-declining-balance depreciation on this machine was recorded each December 31. On December 31, 19X5, it was traded for Machine No. BT–311, which was a dissimilar asset with an installed cash price of $537,000. A trade-in allowance of $81,000 was received for Machine No. 17–95, and the balance was paid in cash.

It was estimated that Machine No. BT–311 would produce 600,000 units of product during its five-year useful life, after which it would have a $105,000 trade-in value. Units-of-production depreciation was recorded for the machine for 19X5, a period in which it produced 93,000 units of product. Between January 1, 19X6, and August 24, 19X8, the machine produced 324,000 more units. On the latter date, it was sold for $243,600.

Required

CHECK FIGURE:
11/5/X5 Gain on Sale of Machinery, $20,610.

Prepare journal entries to record: (a) the purchase of each machine, (b) the depreciation expense recorded on the first December 31 of each machine's life, and (c) the disposal of each machine. (Only one entry is needed to record the exchange of one machine for another.)

CRITICAL THINKING: ESSAYS, PROBLEMS, AND CASES

Analytical Essay

(LO 4)

It is January 2, 19X2, and you have just been hired as an accountant for Bosworth Manufacturing. The previous accountant brought the accounting records up to date through December 31, 19X1, the end of the fiscal year, including the year-end adjusting entries. In reviewing the entries made last year, you discover the following three items:

a.   An expenditure to have a factory machine reconditioned by the manufacturer so it would last three years longer than originally estimated was recorded as a debit to Repairs Expense, Machinery.

b.   The lubrication of factory machinery was recorded as a debit to Machinery.

c.   The installation of a security system for the building was recorded as a debit to Building. The new system allowed the company to reduce the number of security guards.

Required

For each of the three items, explain why you think a correction is or is not necessary. Also, describe any correcting entry that should be made.

While examining the accounting records of Katz Company on December 15, 19X5, you discover two 19X5 entries that appear questionable. The first entry recorded the cash proceeds from an insurance settlement as follows:

Apr.	30	Cash	58,000.00	
		Loss on Fire	9,200.00	
		Accumulated Depreciation, Machinery	50,400.00	
		Machinery		117,600.00
		Received payment of fire loss claim.		

Your investigation shows that this entry was made to record the receipt of an insurance company's $58,000 check to settle a claim resulting from the destruction of a machine in a small fire on April 2, 19X5. The machine originally cost $117,600 and was put into operation on January 3, 19X2. It was depreciated on a straight-line basis for three years, under the assumptions that it would have a seven-year life and no salvage value. During the first week of January 19X5, the machine was overhauled at a cost of $8,400, which was debited to Repairs Expense. The overhaul did not increase the machine's capacity or its salvage value. However, it was expected that the overhaul would lengthen the machine's service life two years beyond the seven originally expected.

The second entry that appears questionable was made to record the receipt of a check from selling a portion of a tract of land. The land was adjacent to the company's plant and had been purchased the year before. It cost $210,000, and another $36,000 was paid for clearing and grading it. Both amounts had been debited to the Land account. The land was to be used for storing finished products but, sometime after the grading was completed, it became obvious the company did not need the entire tract. Katz received an offer from a purchaser to buy the north section for $189,100 or the south section for $120,900. The company decided to sell the north section and recorded the receipt of the purchaser's check with the following entry:

Nov.	16	Cash	189,100.00	
		Land		189,100.00
		Sold unneeded land.		

Required

Write a memo to the company's Corrections File describing any errors made in recording these transactions. Since the Corrections File is used in making the year-end adjusting journal entries, show the entry or entries needed to correct each error described in your memo.

Riverside Company temporarily recorded the costs of a new plant in a single account called Land and Buildings. Now, management has asked you to examine this account and prepare any necessary entries to correct the account balances. In doing so, you find the following debits and credits to the account:

Debits

Jan.	2	Cost of land and building acquired for new plant site	$1,128,000
	5	Attorney's fee for title search	3,000
	19	Cost of demolishing old building on plant site	75,000
	31	Nine months' liability and fire insurance during construction	12,150
Sept.	30	Payment to building contractor on completion	1,638,000
Oct.	3	Architect's fee for new building	50,400
	5	City assessment for street improvements	84,000
	24	Cost of landscaping new plant site	21,000
			$3,011,550

Credits

Jan.	23	Proceeds from sale of salvaged materials from old building	$ 15,800
Oct.	2	Refund of one month's liability and fire insurance premium	1,350
Dec.	31	Depreciation at 2-1/2% per year	18,716
			$ 35,866
		Debit balance	$2,975,684

An account called Depreciation Expense, Land and Buildings was debited in recording the $18,716 of depreciation. Your investigation suggests that 40 years is a reasonable life expectancy for a building of the type involved and that an assumption of zero salvage value is reasonable.

To summarize your analysis, set up a schedule with columns headed Date, Description, Total Amount, Land, Buildings, and Other Accounts. Next, enter the items found in the Land and Buildings account on the schedule, distributing the amounts to the proper columns. Show credits on the schedule by enclosing the amounts in parentheses. Also, draft any required correcting entry or entries, under the assumption that the accounts have not been closed.

Financial Statement Analysis Case

(LO 1, 2)

Refer to the annual report for Southwest Airlines Co. in Appendix E. Give particular attention to the balance sheet, statement of income, and notes to financial statements before answering the following questions:

1. What percentage of the original cost of Southwest Airlines's property and equipment remains to be depreciated as of December 31, 1994, and 1993? (Assume the assets have no salvage value.)

2. What method of depreciation does Southwest Airlines use in depreciating its flight equipment and its ground property and equipment?

3. What was the net change in total property and equipment (before depreciation) during the year ended December 31, 1994? What was the amount of cash generated by (or used for) investment in property and equipment during the year ended December 31, 1993? What is one possible explanation for the difference between these two amounts?

4. Calculate Southwest Airlines's total asset turnover for the year ended December 31, 1994.

Ethical Issues Essay

Review the As a Matter of Ethics case on page 355 and write a short essay discussing the situation faced by Sue Ann Meyer. Include a discussion of the alternative courses of action available to Meyer and indicate how you think she should deal with the situation.

CONCEPT TESTER

Test your understanding of the concepts introduced in this chapter by completing the following crossword puzzle.

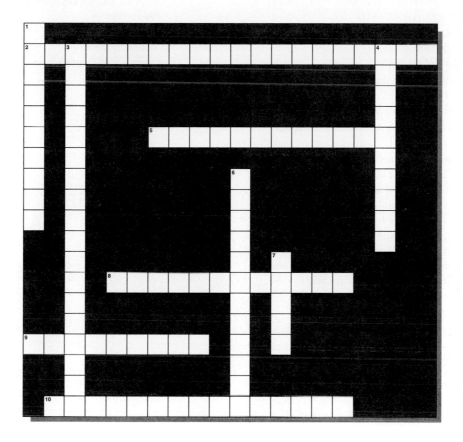

Across Clues

2. Two words; major repairs that extend the service life of a plant asset.
5. Two words; depreciation method that allocates an equal amount to each period.
8. Two words; the expected amount to be recovered at the end of an asset's life.
9. Two words; the original cost of an asset less the accumulated depreciation.
10. Two words; repairs made to keep an asset in normal, good operating condition.

Down Clues

1. A cost incurred to make an asset more efficient.
3. Three words; a measure of how efficiently a company uses its assets.
4. A condition in which the capacity of an asset becomes too small for the demands of the business.
6. A condition in which an asset has lost its usefulness because of new inventions and improvements.
7. Acronym for the depreciation method required under the tax law.

ANSWERS TO PROGRESS CHECKS

10–1 (a) office supplies—current assets
(b) office equipment—plant assets
(c) merchandise—current assets
(d) land held for future expansion—long-term investments
(e) trucks used in operations—plant assets

10–2 (a) Land
(b) Land Improvements

10–3 $700,000 + $49,000 − $21,000 + $3,500 + $3,000 + $2,500 = $737,000

10–4 Depreciation is a process of allocating and charging the cost of plant assets to the accounting periods that benefit from the assets' use.

10–5 (*a*) Book value using straight-line depreciation:
$96,000 − [($96,000 − $8,000)/5] = $78,400
(*b*) Book value using units of production:
$96,000 − [($96,000 − $8,000) ×
(10,000/100,000)] = $87,200

10–6 ($3,800 − $200)/3 = $1,200
$1,200 × 2 = $2,400
($3,800 − $2,400)/2 = $700

10–7 Double-declining-balance depreciation: $77,000 ×
(10% × 2) = $15,400
Straight-line MACRS: ($77,000/7) × 1/2 = $5,500

10–8 Accumulated Depreciation, Machinery . . 12,000
    Cash   12,000

10–9 A revenue expenditure benefits only the current period and should be charged to expense of the current period. A capital expenditure has a benefit that extends beyond the end of the current period and should be charged to an asset.

10–10 A betterment involves modifying an existing plant asset to make it more efficient, usually by replacing part of the asset with an improved or superior part. A betterment should be debited to the improved machine's account.

10–11 Depreciation Expense 3,500
    Accumulated Depreciation   3,500

Cash 32,000
Accumulated Depreciation 10,500
    Gain on Sale of Equipment   500
    Equipment   42,000

10–12 (*a*) Truck 45,000
    Loss on Trade-In 3,600
    Accumulated Depreciation 23,400
        Truck   30,000
        Cash   42,000
(*b*) Truck 44,600
    Accumulated Depreciation 23,400
        Truck   30,000
        Cash   38,000

10–13 Total asset turnover:
$$\frac{\$992,106,000}{(\$297,612,000 + \$273,830,000)/2} = 3.5 \text{ times}$$

Natural Resources, Intangible Assets, and Long-Term Investments

THE FAR SIDE   By GARY LARSON

"Well, shoot. I just can't figure it out.
I'm movin' over 500 doughnuts a day,
but I'm still just barely squeakin' by."

*T*he question posed in *The New York Times's* business section (October 17, 1994) was "What, exactly, lies beyond 'The Far Side'?" when cartoonist Gary Larson announced that he planned to stop drawing the widely popular cartoon in January of 1995. Analysts anticipated that the $500 million merchandising empire related to "Far Side" would be shaken by his move.

Manufacturers had invested huge sums for the rights to manufacture "Far Side" products such as books, calendars, greeting cards, mugs, and T-shirts. Without the newspaper exposure of this cartoon, demand for these products would drop. The manufacturers of "Far Side" products would probably experience a dramatic reduction in related revenues in the years to come. Other financial disclosures by these firms also might be affected.

LEARNING OBJECTIVES

After studying Chapter 11, you should be able to:

1. **Identify assets that should be classified as natural resources or as intangible assets and prepare entries to account for them, including entries to record depletion and amortization.**

2. **State the criteria for classifying assets as long-term investments and describe the categories of securities that are classified as long-term investments.**

3. **Describe the methods used to report long-term securities investments in the financial statements.**

4. **Describe the primary accounting problems of having investments in international operations and prepare entries to account for sales to foreign customers.**

5. **Explain the use of return on total assets in evaluating a company's efficiency in using its assets.**

6. **Define or explain the words and phrases listed in the chapter glossary.**

In Chapters 7 through 10, you learned about current assets and plant assets. This chapter concludes the focus on assets with a discussion of natural resources, intangible assets, and long-term investments. Natural resources and intangible assets may be particularly important in evaluating the future prospects of some companies. For example, the rights to manufacture "Far Side" products are intangible assets of the companies that purchased these rights from the cartoon's creator or the copyright owner. Gary Larson's decision to lay down his pen no doubt would have an impact on the amounts reported for these assets.

Many companies make long-term investments in assets such as real estate and debt and equity securities issued by other companies. Also, an increasing number of companies invest in foreign countries or have international operations. The financial statement effects of these investments are often very important. As a result, your study of these topics in this chapter will enrich your ability to understand and interpret financial reports.

NATURAL RESOURCES

LO 1
Identify assets that should be classified as natural resources or as intangible assets and prepare entries to account for them, including entries to record depletion and amortization.

Natural resources include such things as standing timber, mineral deposits, and oil reserves. Because they are physically consumed when they are used, they are known as *wasting assets*. In their natural state, they represent inventories of raw materials that will be converted into a product by cutting, mining, or pumping. However, until the

conversion takes place, they are noncurrent assets and appear on a balance sheet under captions such as Timberlands, Mineral deposits, or Oil reserves. Sometimes, this caption appears under the property, plant, and equipment category of assets and sometimes it is a separate category. **Aluminum Company of America** combines its natural resources with other fixed assets in one balance sheet item called *Properties, plants and equipment.* However, a note to the financial statements provides more detailed information by separating the total into the following categories: land and land rights, including mines; structures; machinery and equipment; and construction work in progress.

Natural resources are initially recorded at cost. Like the cost of plant assets, the cost of natural resources is allocated to the periods in which they are consumed. The cost created by consuming the usefulness of natural resources is called **depletion**. On the balance sheet, natural resources are shown at cost less *accumulated depletion*. The amount by which such assets are depleted each year by cutting, mining, or pumping is usually calculated on a units-of-production basis. For example, **Exxon Corporation** uses the units-of-production method to amortize the costs of discovering and operating its oil wells.

To illustrate the units-of-production method, assume that a mineral deposit has an estimated 500,000 tons of available ore and is purchased for $500,000. The units-of-production depletion charge per ton of ore mined is $1. Thus, if 85,000 tons are mined and sold during the first year, the depletion charge for the year of $85,000 is recorded as follows:

Dec.	31	Depletion Expense, Mineral Deposit	85,000.00	
		Accumulated Depletion, Mineral Deposit		85,000.00
		To record depletion of the mineral deposit.		

On the balance sheet prepared at the end of the first year, the mineral deposit should appear at its $500,000 cost less accumulated depletion of $85,000. Because the 85,000 tons of ore were sold during the year, the entire $85,000 depletion charge is reported on the income statement. However, if a portion of the ore had remained unsold at year-end, the depletion cost related to the unsold ore should be carried forward on the balance sheet as part of the cost of the unsold ore inventory, which is a current asset.

The conversion of natural resources through mining, cutting, or pumping often requires the use of machinery and buildings. Because the usefulness of these assets is related to the depletion of the natural resource, their costs should be depreciated over the life of the natural resource in proportion to the annual depletion charges. In other words, depreciation should be calculated using the units-of-production method. For example, if a machine is installed in a mine and one-eighth of the mine's ore is mined and sold during a year, one-eighth of the machine's cost (less salvage value) should be charged to depreciation expense.

INTANGIBLE ASSETS

Some assets represent certain legal rights and economic relationships beneficial to the owner. Because they have no physical existence, they are called **intangible assets.** Patents, copyrights, leaseholds, leasehold improvements, goodwill, and trademarks are intangible assets. We discuss each of these intangible items in more detail in the following sections. Although notes and accounts receivable are also intangible in nature, they are not used to produce products or provide services. Therefore, they are not listed on the balance sheet as intangible assets; instead, they are classified as current assets or investments.

When an intangible asset is purchased, it is recorded at cost. Thereafter, its cost must be systematically written off to expense over its estimated useful life through the process of **amortization.** Generally accepted accounting principles require that the amortization period for an intangible asset be 40 years or less.[1] Companies often disclose the amortization periods they apply to their intangibles. For example, **Corning Incorporated's** 1994 annual

---

[1]FASB, *Accounting Standards—Current Text* (Norwalk, CT, 1995), sec. I60.110. First published as *APB Opinion No. 17,* par. 29.

report discloses that it amortizes goodwill over a maximum of 40 years and other intangible assets over a maximum of 15 years.

Amortization of intangible assets is similar to depreciation of plant assets and depletion of natural resources in that all three are processes of cost allocation. However, only the straight-line method can be used for amortizing intangibles unless the reporting company can demonstrate that another method is more appropriate. Also, while the effects of depreciation and depletion on the assets are recorded in a contra account (Accumulated Depreciation or Accumulated Depletion), amortization is usually credited directly to the intangible asset account. As a result, the full original cost of intangible assets generally is not reported on the balance sheet. Instead, only the remaining amount of unamortized cost is reported.

Normally, intangible assets are shown in a separate section of the balance sheet that follows immediately after plant and equipment. However, not all companies follow this tradition. The following paragraphs describe several specific intangible assets.

Patents

The federal government grants patents to encourage the invention of new machines, mechanical devices, and production processes. A **patent** gives its owner the exclusive right to manufacture and sell a patented machine or device, or to use a process, for 17 years. When patent rights are purchased, the cost of acquiring the rights is debited to an account called *Patents.* Also, if the owner engages in lawsuits to defend a patent, the cost of the lawsuits should be debited to the Patents account. However, the costs of research and development leading to a new patent are not debited to an asset account.[2]

Although a patent gives its owner exclusive rights to the patented device or process for 17 years, the cost of the patent should be amortized over its predicted useful life, which might be less than the full 17 years. For example, if a patent that cost $25,000 has an estimated useful life of 10 years, the owner makes the following adjusting entry at the end of each of those years to write off one-tenth of its cost:

Dec.	31	Amortization Expense, Patents	2,500.00	
		Patents		2,500.00
		To write off patent costs over the expected 10-year life.		

The entry's debit causes $2,500 of patent costs to appear on the income statement as one of the costs of the product manufactured and sold under the protection of the patent. Note that we have followed the convention of crediting the Patents account rather than a contra account.

Copyrights

A copyright is granted by the federal government or by international agreement. In most cases, a **copyright** gives its owner the exclusive right to publish and sell a musical, literary, or artistic work during the life of the composer, author, or artist and for 50 years thereafter. Most copyrights have value for a much shorter time, and their costs should be amortized over the shorter period. Often, the only identifiable cost of a copyright is the fee paid to the Copyright Office. If this fee is not material, it may be charged directly to an expense account. Otherwise, the copyright costs should be

---

[2]FASB, *Accounting Standards—Current Text* (Norwalk, CT, 1995), sec. R50.108. First published as *Statement of Financial Accounting Standards No. 2,* par. 12.

capitalized (recorded as a capital expenditure), and the periodic amortization of a copyright should be debited to an account called *Amortization Expense, Copyrights.*

Leaseholds

Property is rented under a contract called a **lease.** The person or company that owns the property and grants the lease is called the **lessor.** The person or company that secures the right to possess and use the property is called the **lessee.** The rights granted to the lessee by the lessor under the lease are called a **leasehold.** A leasehold is an intangible asset for the lessee.

Some leases require no advance payment from the lessee but do require monthly rent payments. In such cases, a Leasehold account is not needed and the monthly payments are debited to a Rent Expense account. Sometimes, a long-term lease requires the lessee to pay the final year's rent in advance when the lease is signed. If so, the lessee records the advance payment with a debit to its Leasehold asset account. Because the usefulness of the advance payment is not consumed until the final year is reached, the Leasehold account balance remains intact until that year. At that time, the balance is transferred to Rent Expense.[3]

Often, a long-term lease gains value because the current rental rates for similar property increase while the required payments under the lease remain constant. In such cases, the increase in value of the lease is not reported on the lessee's balance sheet since no extra cost was incurred to acquire it. However, if the property is subleased and the new tenant makes a cash payment to the original lessee for the rights under the old lease, the new tenant should debit the payment to a Leasehold account. Then, the balance of the Leasehold account should be amortized to Rent Expense over the remaining life of the lease.

To appreciate how the changing value of a lease can affect business decisions, consider La Côte Basque, one of the world's most esteemed and historic restaurants located in New York City. Late in 1994, La Côte Basque sold the two years remaining on its lease to The Walt Disney Company. La Côte Basque knew that it would not be able to renew the lease when it expired because Disney had negotiated a long-term lease of the property with the building owner, The Coca-Cola Company. La Côte Basque had been operating in this location for 36 years but could not compete with the rental fees being offered by Disney. The inevitability of nonrenewal prompted the restaurant to sell the remainder of its lease for a sizable amount and attempt to relocate sooner rather than later.

Leasehold Improvements

Long-term leases often require the lessee to pay for any alterations or improvements to the leased property, such as new partitions and store fronts. Normally, the costs of these **leasehold improvements** are debited to an account called *Leasehold Improvements.* Also, since the improvements become part of the property and revert to the lessor at the end of the lease, the lessee must amortize the cost of the improvements over the life of the lease or the life of the improvements, whichever is shorter. The amortization entry commonly debits Rent Expense and credits Leasehold Improvements.

Goodwill

The term **goodwill** has a special meaning in accounting. In theory, a business has an intangible asset called goodwill when its rate of expected future earnings is greater

---

[3]Some long-term leases give the lessee essentially the same rights as a purchaser and result in tangible assets and liabilities reported by the lessee. Chapter 12 describes these leases.

than the rate of earnings normally realized in its industry. Above-average earnings and the existence of theoretical goodwill may be demonstrated with the following information about Companies A and B, both of which are in the same industry:

	Company A	Company B
Net assets (other than goodwill)	$100,000	$100,000
Normal rate of return in this industry . .	10%	10%
Normal return on net assets	$ 10,000	$ 10,000
Expected net income	10,000	15,000
Expected earnings above average	$ -0-	$ 5,000

Company B is expected to have an above-average earnings rate compared to its industry and, therefore, is said to have goodwill. This goodwill may be the result of excellent customer relations, the location of the business, the quality and uniqueness of its products, monopolistic market advantages, a superior management and work force, or a combination of these and other factors.[4] Consequently, a potential investor would be willing to pay more for Company B than for Company A. Thus, goodwill is theoretically an asset that has value.

Normally, goodwill is purchased only when an entire business operation is acquired. In determining the purchase price of a business, the buyer and seller may estimate the amount of goodwill in several different ways. If the business is expected to have $5,000 each year in above-average earnings, its goodwill may be valued at, say, four times its above-average earnings, or $20,000. Or, if the $5,000 is expected to continue indefinitely, they may think of it as a return on an investment at a given rate of return, say, 10%. In this case, the estimated amount of goodwill is $5,000/10% = $50,000. However, in the final analysis, the value of goodwill is confirmed only by the price the seller is willing to accept and the buyer is willing to pay.

To keep financial statement information from being too subjective, accountants have agreed that goodwill should not be recorded unless it is purchased. The amount

of goodwill is measured by subtracting the fair market value of the purchased business's net assets (excluding goodwill) from the purchase price. In many business acquisitions, goodwill represents a major component of total cost. For example, **Procter & Gamble Company's** purchase of Revlon, Inc.'s worldwide Max Factor and Betrix lines of cosmetics for $1,025 million (net of cash acquired) included goodwill and other intangibles of $927 million.

Like other intangible assets, goodwill must be amortized on a straight-line basis over its estimated useful life. However, estimating the useful life of goodwill is very difficult and highly arbitrary in most situations. As a result, you can expect to find companies reporting amortization expense for goodwill based on an estimated useful life of 5 years upward, but not more than 40 years.

Trademarks and Trade Names

Companies often adopt unique symbols or select unique names that they use in marketing their products. Sometimes, the ownership and exclusive right to use such a **trademark** or **trade name** can be established simply by demonstrating that one com-

---

[4]Of course, the value of the location may be reflected in a higher cost for the land owned and used by the company.

As A Matter of Fact

Intangible Assets Disclosed	Number of Companies			
	1994	**1993**	**1992**	**1991**
Goodwill recognized in a business combination	395	385	383	381
Patents, patent rights	62	69	62	59
Trademarks, brand names, copyrights	52	51	50	48
Noncompete covenants	27	26	21	18
Licenses, franchises, memberships	19	19	17	17
Technology	15	15	13	13
Customer lists	13	9	13	11
Other—described	40	32	29	31

Excerpted with permission from *Accounting Trends & Techniques,* Annual Survey of Accounting Practices Followed in 600 Stockholders' Reports, Forty-Nineth Edition, Copyright © 1995 by American Institute of Certified Public Accountants, Inc., Table 2–17, p. 210.

pany has used the trademark or trade name before other businesses. However, ownership generally can be established more definitely by registering the trademark or trade name at the U.S. Patent Office. The cost of developing, maintaining, or enhancing the value of a trademark or trade name, perhaps through advertising, should be charged to expense in the period or periods incurred. However, if a trademark or trade name is purchased, the purchase cost should be debited to an asset account and amortized over time.

Amortization of Intangibles

Some intangibles, such as patents, copyrights, and leaseholds, have limited useful lives that are determined by law, contract, or the nature of the asset. Other intangibles, such as goodwill, trademarks, and trade names, have lives that cannot be clearly determined. In general, the cost of intangible assets should be amortized over the periods expected to be benefited by their use, which in no case is longer than their legal existence. However, as we stated earlier, generally accepted accounting principles require that the amortization period of intangible assets never be longer than 40 years. This limitation applies even if the life of the asset (for example, goodwill) may continue indefinitely into the future.

Progress Check
(Answers to the Progress Checks are provided at the end of the chapter.)

11-1 Give an example of an intangible asset and of a natural resource.

11-2 Prospect Mining Company paid $650,000 for an ore deposit. The deposit had an estimated 325,000 tons of ore that would be fully mined during the next 10 years. During the current year, 91,000 tons were mined, processed, and sold. What is the amount of depletion for the year?

11-3 On January 6, 19X1, Fun-4-U Toy Company paid $120,000 for a patent with a 17-year legal life to produce a toy that is expected to be marketable for about 3 years. Prepare the entries necessary to record the acquisition and the December 31, 19X1, adjustment.

CLASSIFYING INVESTMENTS

LO 2
State the criteria for classifying securities investments as long-term investments and describe the categories of securities that are reported as long-term investments.

In Chapter 8, you learned how to account for short-term investments in debt and equity securities. (We encourage you to review pages 270–275 before you study this section.) Recall that short-term investments are current assets; they are expected to be converted into cash within one year or the current operating cycle of the business, whichever is longer. In general, short-term investments are held as "an investment of cash available for current operations."[5] They either mature within one year or the current operating cycle or are easily sold and therefore qualify as being *marketable*.

Securities investments that do not qualify as current assets are called **long-term investments.** Long-term investments include investments in bonds and stocks that are not marketable or that, although marketable, are not intended to serve as a ready source of cash. Long-term investments also include funds earmarked for a special purpose, such as bond sinking funds, and land or other assets owned but not used in the regular operations of the business. In general, these assets are reported on the balance sheet in a separate *Long-term investments* section.

Recall from Chapter 8 that accounting for short-term investments depends on whether the investments are in (1) trading securities, (2) debt securities held to maturity, or (3) debt and equity securities available for sale. Investments in trading securities always are short-term investments; they are reported as current assets. The other two types of investments may be long-term or short-term.

In Illustration 11–1, the boxes on the left side show the different long-term investments in securities. Note that they include (1) debt securities held to maturity, (2) debt and equity securities available for sale, (3) equity securities that give the investor a significant influence over the investee, and (4) equity securities that give the investor control over the investee. We discuss each of these types of investments in the following sections.

Progress Check

11-4   What types of assets are classified as long-term investments?

11-5   Under what conditions should a stock investment be classified on the balance sheet as a long-term investment?

LONG-TERM INVESTMENTS IN SECURITIES

LO 3
Describe the methods used to report long-term securities investments in the financial statements.

Much of what you learned about short-term investments in Chapter 8 also applies to long-term investments. For example, at the time of purchase, investments are recorded at cost, which includes any commissions or brokerage fees paid to make the purchase. After the purchase, the accounting treatment depends on the type of investment.

Investments in Debt Securities Held to Maturity

Debt securities held to maturity may be short-term or long-term investments. In either case, the owner must have the positive intent and the ability to hold the securities until they mature.[6] At the time of purchase, these investments are recorded at cost. Then, interest revenue is recorded as it accrues.

The cost of an investment in debt securities may be more or less than the maturity value of the securities. When the investment is long-term, any difference between cost and maturity value must be amortized over the remaining life of the security. Chapter 12 explains the process of amortizing this difference. In this chapter, however, we assume that the costs of debt investments equal their maturity values.

---

[5]FASB, *Accounting Standards—Current Text* (Norwalk, CT, 1995), sec. B05.105. Previously published in *Accounting Research Bulletin No. 43*, ch. 3, sec. A, par. 4.

[6]FASB, "Accounting for Certain Investments in Debt and Equity Securities," *Statement of Accounting Standards No. 115* (Norwalk, CT, 1995), par. 6.

Illustration 11-1 Accounting for Long-Term Investments in Securities

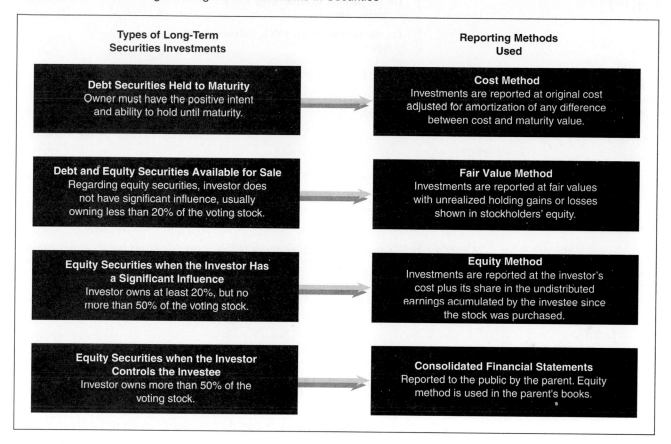

For example, on August 31, 19X1, Francis, Inc., paid $29,500 plus a brokerage fee of $500 to buy $30,000 par value of Candice Corp.'s 7% bonds payable. The bonds pay interest semiannually on August 31 and February 28. The amount of each payment is $30,000 \times 7\% \times 6/12 = $1,050. Francis has the positive intent to hold the bonds until they mature on August 31, 19X3. The following entry records the purchase:

19X1				
Aug.	31	Investment in Candice Corp. Bonds	30,000.00	
		Cash		30,000.00
		Purchased bonds to be held to maturity.		

On December 31, 19X1, at the end of its accounting period, Francis accrues interest receivable with the following entry:

Dec.	31	Interest Receivable	700.00	
		Interest Earned		700.00
		$1,050 \times 4/6 = $700.		

In this entry, the $700 represents 4/6 of the semiannual cash receipt for interest. As a result of these entries, Francis's financial statements for 19X1 show the following items:

On the income statement for 19X1:

Interest earned . . . . $ 700

On the December 31, 19X1, balance sheet:

Assets:

Long-term investments:

Investment in Candice Corp. bonds . . $30,000

On February 28, 19X2, Francis records the receipt of interest with the following entry:

19X2				
Feb.	28	Cash	1,050.00	
		Interest Receivable		700.00
		Interest Earned		350.00
		Received 6 months' interest on Candice Corp. bonds.		

When the bonds mature, this entry records the proceeds from the matured bonds:

19X3				
Aug.	31	Cash	30,000.00	
		Investment in Candice Corp. Bonds		30,000.00
		Received cash from matured bonds.		

Investments in Securities Available for Sale

On the left side of Illustration 11–1, notice that only the top two boxes include debt securities. In other words, debt securities that do not qualify as securities held to maturity are classified as securities available for sale. In the second box on the left side of Illustration 11–1, you can see that securities available for sale also include certain equity securities. To be included in this group of long-term investments, the investor in equity securities must not have a significant influence over the investee. Normally, this means that the investor owns less than 20% of the investee corporation's voting stock.[7]

Debt Securities Available for Sale. Accounting for debt securities available for sale is similar to debt securities held to maturity. At the time of purchase, the debt securities are recorded at cost. Then, interest is recorded as it accrues.

For example, assume that in the previous discussion, the bonds purchased by Francis, Inc., were not classified as debt securities held to maturity. Instead, assume they were securities available for sale. In other words, assume that Francis did not necessarily intend to hold the bonds to maturity. The previous entries to record the purchase of the bonds on August 31, the accrual of interest on December 31, 19X1, and the receipt of interest on February 28, 19X2, would be exactly the same. If Francis were to sell the bonds before they mature, any gain or loss realized on the sale would be reported in the income statement.

The only difference between debt securities held to maturity and debt securities available for sale involves the amount reported on the balance sheet. Debt securities held to maturity are reported at cost (adjusted for the amortized amount of any difference between cost and maturity value). Debt securities available for sale are reported at their fair value. We explain this more completely after discussing equity securities available for sale.

---

[7]The 20% limit is not an absolute rule. Other factors may overrule. FASB, *Accounting Standards—Current Text* (Norwalk, CT, 1995), sec. I82.107–108. First published in *FASB Interpretation No. 35,* pars. 3–4.

Equity Securities Available for Sale. Chapter 8 (pages 272–274) explained the procedures of accounting for short-term investments in equity securities available for sale. These same procedures are used for long-term investments. At the time of purchase, the investments are recorded at cost. As dividends are received, they are credited to Dividends Earned and reported in the income statement. When the shares are sold, the proceeds from the sale are compared with the cost of the investment and any gain or loss realized on the sale is reported in the income statement.

Continuing with Francis, Inc., assume that on October 10, 19X1, Francis purchased 1,000 shares of Intex Corp.'s common stock at their par value of $86,000. The following entry records the purchase:

Oct.	10	Investment in Intex Corp. Common Stock	86,000.00	
		Cash		86,000.00
		Purchased 1,000 shares.		

On November 2, Francis received a $1,720 quarterly dividend on the Intex shares. The following entry records the receipt:

Nov.	2	Cash	1,720.00	
		Dividends Earned		1,720.00
		Received dividend of $1.72 per share.		

On December 20, Francis sold 500 of the Intex shares for $45,000, and records the sale with the following entry:

Dec.	20	Cash	45,000.00	
		Investment in Intex Corp. Common Stock		43,000.00
		Gain on Sale of Long-Term Investment		2,000.00
		$86,000/2 = $43,000		

Reporting the Fair Values of Securities Available for Sale. On the balance sheet, long-term investments in securities available for sale are reported at their fair values. This includes both debt and equity securities. Unrealized holding gains (losses) are reported as a separate item in the equity section.

For example, assume that Francis had no prior investments in securities available for sale, other than the bonds purchased on August 31 and the stock purchased on October 10. The following table shows the book values and fair values of these investments on December 31, 19X1:

	Book Value	Fair (Market) Value
Candice Corp. bonds payable	$30,000	$29,050
Intex Corp. common stock, 500 shares . . .	43,000	45,500
Total	$73,000	$74,550

The entry to record the fair value of the investments is:

Dec.	31	Long-Term Investments, Fair Value Adjustment	1,550.00	
		Unrealized Holding Gain (Loss)		1,550.00
		To record change in fair value of securities available		
		for sale.		

In preparing Francis's December 31, 19X1, balance sheet, the cost of the investments normally would be combined with the balance in the Long-Term Investments, Fair Value Adjustment account and reported as a single amount. Thus, Francis's balance sheet would include the following items:

Assets:
    Long-term investments:
        Securities available for sale (at fair value) $74,550
Stockholders' equity:
    Common stock   xxx
    Retained earnings   xxx
    Unrealized holding gain   1,550

Investment in Equity Securities; Investor Has a Significant Influence or Has Control

Sometimes, an investor buys a large block of a corporation's voting stock and is able to exercise a significant influence over the investee corporation. An investor who owns 20% or more of a corporation's voting stock is normally presumed to have a significant influence over the investee. There may be cases, however, where the accountant concludes that the 20% test of significant influence should be overruled by other, more persuasive, evidence.

An investor who owns more than 50% of a corporation's voting stock can dominate all of the other stockholders in electing the corporation's board of directors. Thus, the investor usually has control over the investee corporation's management.[8]

As we stated earlier, the method of accounting for a stock investment depends on the relationship between the investor and the investee. In studying Illustration 11–1, note that if the investor has a significant influence, the *equity method* of accounting and reporting is used. Finally, if the investor controls the investee, the investor uses the equity method in its records but reports *consolidated financial statements* to the public. We discuss the equity method and consolidated statements in the following sections.

The Equity Method of Accounting for Common Stock Investments

If a common stock investor has significant influence over the investee, the **equity method** of accounting for the investment must be used. When the stock is acquired, the investor records the purchase at cost. For example, on January 1, 19X1, Gordon Company purchased 3,000 shares (30%) of JWM, Inc., common stock for a total cost of $70,650. This entry records the purchase on Gordon's books:

Jan.	1	Investment in JWM Common Stock	70,650.00	
		Cash		70,650.00
		Purchased 3,000 shares.		

Under the equity method, the earnings of the investee corporation not only increase the investee's net assets but also increase the investor's equity claims against the investee's assets. Therefore, when the investee closes its books and reports the amount of its earnings, the investor takes up its share of those earnings in its investment account. For example, assume that JWM reported net income of $20,000 for 19X1. Gordon's entry to record its 30% share of these earnings is:

---

[8]Ibid., sec. C51.102. First published in *Statement of Financial Accounting Standards No. 94,* par. 13.

Dec.	31	Investment in JWM Common Stock	6,000.00	
		Earnings from Investment in JWM, Inc.		6,000.00
		To record 30% equity in investee's earnings		
		of $20,000.		

The debit records the increase in Gordon Company's equity in JWM. The credit causes 30% of JWM's net income to appear on Gordon Company's income statement as earnings from the investment. As with any other revenue, Gordon closes the earnings to Income Summary.

If the investee corporation incurs a net loss instead of a net income, the investor records its share of the loss and reduces (credits) its investment account. Then, the investor closes the loss to Income Summary.

Under the equity method, the receipt of cash dividends is not recorded as revenue because the investor has already recorded its share of the earnings reported by the investee. Instead, dividends received from the investee simply convert the form of the investor's asset from a stock investment to cash. Thus, the equity method records dividends as a reduction in the balance of the investment account.

For example, assume that JWM declared and paid $10,000 in cash dividends on its common stock. Gordon's entry to record its 30% share of these dividends, which it received on January 9, 19X2, is:

Jan.	9	Cash	3,000.00	
		Investment in JWM Common Stock		3,000.00
		To record receipt of 30% of the $10,000 dividend		
		paid by JWM, Inc.		

Thus, when the equity method is used, the carrying value of a common stock investment equals the cost of the investment plus the investor's equity in the *undistributed* earnings of the investee. For example, after the preceding transactions are recorded on the books of Gordon Company, the investment account appears as follows:

Investment in JWM Common Stock

Date		Explanation	Debit	Credit	Balance
19X1					
Jan.	1	Investment	70,650		70,650
Dec.	31	Share of earnings	6,000		76,650
19X2					
Jan.	9	Share of dividend		3,000	73,650

If Gordon prepared a balance sheet on January 9, the investment in JWM would be reported as $73,650. This is the original cost of the investment, plus Gordon's equity in JWM's earnings since the date of purchase, less Gordon's equity in JWM's dividends since the date of purchase.

When an equity method stock investment is sold, the gain or loss on the sale is determined by comparing the proceeds from the sale with the carrying value (book value) of the investment on the date of sale. For example, suppose that Gordon Company sold its JWM stock for $80,000 on January 10, 19X2. The entry to record the sale is:

Jan.	10	Cash	80,000.00	
		Investment in JWM Common Stock		73,650.00
		Gain on Sale of Investments		6,350.00
		Sold 3,000 shares of stock for $80,000.		

Investments That Require Consolidated Financial Statements

Corporations often own stock in and may even control other corporations. For example, if Par Company owns more than 50% of the voting stock of Sub Company, Par Company can elect Sub Company's board of directors and thus control its activities and resources. The controlling corporation, Par Company, is known as the **parent company** and Sub Company is called a **subsidiary.**

Many large companies are parents with subsidiaries. For example, **PepsiCo, Inc.** is the parent of several subsidiaries, including Taco Bell, Pizza Hut, Kentucky Fried Chicken, and Frito-Lay.

When a corporation owns all the outstanding stock of a subsidiary, it can take over the subsidiary's assets, cancel the subsidiary's stock, and merge the subsidiary into the parent company. However, there often are financial, legal, and tax advantages if a large business is operated as a parent corporation that controls one or more subsidiary corporations. In fact, many large companies are parent corporations that own one or more subsidiaries.

When a business operates as a parent company with subsidiaries, separate accounting records are maintained by each corporation. From a legal viewpoint, the parent and each subsidiary are still separate entities with all the rights, duties, and responsibilities of individual corporations. However, investors in the parent company indirectly are investors in the subsidiaries. To evaluate their investments, parent company investors must consider the financial status and operations of the subsidiaries as well as the parent. This information is provided in **consolidated financial statements.**

Consolidated statements show the financial position, the results of operations, and the cash flows of all corporations under the parent's control, including the subsidiaries. These statements are prepared as if the business is organized as a single company. Although the parent uses the equity method in its accounts, the investment account is not reported on the parent's financial statements. Instead, the individual assets and liabilities of the affiliated companies are combined on a single balance sheet. Also, their revenues and expenses are combined on a single income statement and their cash flows are combined on a single statement of cash flows. More detailed explanations of consolidated statements are included in advanced accounting courses.

Progress Check

11-6   What are the similarities and differences in accounting for long-term investments in debt securities that are held to maturity and those that are available for sale?

11-7   What are the three categories of long-term equity investments? Describe the criteria for each category and the method used to account for each.

INVESTMENTS IN INTERNATIONAL OPERATIONS

LO 4

Describe the primary accounting problems of having investments in international operations and prepare entries to account for sales to foreign customers.

In today's complex world, many companies conduct business activities in more than one country. In fact, the operations of some large corporations involve so many different countries that they are called **multinational businesses.** The problems of managing and accounting for companies that have international operations can be very complex. Because of this complexity, the following pages present only a brief discussion. A more detailed study of these issues is reserved for advanced business courses.

Two primary problems in accounting for international operations occur because businesses with transactions in more than one country have to deal with more than one currency. These two problems are (1) accounting for sales or purchases denominated in a foreign currency and (2) preparing consolidated financial statements with foreign subsidiaries. To simplify the discussion of these problems, we assume that the companies have a base of operations in the United States and prepare their financial statements in the U.S. dollar. Hence, the **reporting currency** of such firms is the U.S. dollar.

Exchange Rates between Currencies

Active markets for the purchase and sale of foreign currencies exist all over the world. In these markets, U.S. dollars can be exchanged for Canadian dollars, British pounds, French francs, Japanese yen, or other currencies. The price of one currency stated in terms of another currency is called a **foreign exchange rate.** For example, assume that the current exchange rate for British pounds and U.S. dollars was $1.7515 on January 31, 19X1. This rate means that one pound could have been acquired for $1.7515. On the same day, assume that the exchange rate between German marks and U.S. dollars was $0.5321. This number means that one mark could be purchased for $0.5321. Foreign exchange rates fluctuate daily (or even hourly) in accordance with the changing supply and demand for each currency and expectations about future events.

Sales or Purchases Denominated in a Foreign Currency

When a U.S. company makes a credit sale to a foreign customer, a special problem can arise in accounting for the sale and the account receivable. If the sales terms require the foreign customer's payment to be in U.S. dollars, no special accounting problem arises. But if the terms of the sale state that payment is to be made in a foreign currency, the U.S. company must go through special steps to account for the sale and the account receivable.

For example, suppose that a U.S. company, the Boston Company, makes a credit sale to London Outfitters, a British company. The sale occurs on December 12, 19X1, and the price is £10,000, which is due on February 10, 19X2. Naturally, Boston Company keeps its accounting records in U.S. dollars. Therefore, to record the sale, Boston Company must translate the sales price from pounds to dollars. This is done using the current exchange rate on the date of the sale. Assuming that the current exchange rate on December 12 is $1.80, Boston records the sale as follows:

Dec.	12	Accounts Receivable—London Outfitters	18,000.00	
		Sales (10,000 × $1.80)		18,000.00
		To record a sale at £10,000, when the exchange rate		
		equals $1.80.		

Now, assume that Boston Company prepares annual financial statements on December 31, 19X1. On that date, the current exchange rate has increased to $1.84. Therefore, the current dollar value of Boston Company's receivable is $18,400 (10,000 × $1.84). This amount is now $400 greater than the amount originally recorded on December 12. According to generally accepted accounting principles, the receivable must be reported in the balance sheet at its current dollar value. Hence, Boston Company must make the following entry to record the increase in the dollar value of the receivable:

Dec.	31	Accounts Receivable—London Outfitters	400.00	
		Foreign Exchange Gain or Loss		400.00
		To record the effects of the increased value of the		
		British pound on our receivable.		

The Foreign Exchange Gain or Loss is closed to the Income Summary account and reported on the income statement.[9]

Assume that Boston Company receives London Outfitters' payment of £10,000 on February 10, and immediately exchanges the pounds for U.S. dollars. On this date, the exchange rate for pounds has declined to $1.78. Therefore, Boston Company receives only $17,800 (10,000 × $1.78). The firm records the receipt and the loss associated with the decline in the exchange rate as follows:

Feb.	10	Cash	17,800.00	
		Foreign Exchange Gain or Loss	600.00	
		Accounts Receivable—London Outfitters		18,400.00
		Received foreign currency payment of account and		
		converted it into dollars.		

Accounting for credit purchases from a foreign supplier is similar to the previous example of a credit sale to a foreign customer. If the U.S. company is required to make a payment in a foreign currency, the account payable must be translated into dollars before the U.S. company can record it. Then, if the exchange rate changes, the U.S. company must recognize an exchange gain or loss at any intervening balance sheet date and at the payment date.

Consolidated Statements with Foreign Subsidiaries

A second problem of accounting for international operations involves the preparation of consolidated financial statements when the parent company has one or more foreign subsidiaries. For example, suppose that a U.S. company owns a controlling interest in a French subsidiary. The reporting currency of the U.S. parent is the dollar. However, the French subsidiary maintains its financial records in francs. Before preparing consolidated statements, the parent must translate financial statements of the French company into U.S. dollars. After the translation is completed, the preparation of consolidated statements is not any different than for any other subsidiary.[10]

The procedures for translating a foreign subsidiary's account balances depend on the nature of the subsidiary's operations. In simple terms, the general process requires the parent company to select appropriate foreign exchange rates and then to apply those rates to the account balances of the foreign subsidiary.

Progress Check

11-8   If a U.S. company makes a credit sale of merchandise to a French customer and the sales terms require payment in francs:
  a. The U.S. company will incur an exchange loss if the foreign exchange rate between francs and dollars increases from $0.189 at the date of sale to $0.199 at the date the account is settled.
  b. The French company may eventually have to record an exchange gain or loss.
  c. The U.S. company may be required to record an exchange gain or loss on the date of the sale.
  d. None of the above is correct.

---

[9]Ibid., sec. F60.122. First published as FASB, *Statement of Financial Accounting Standards No. 52,* par. 15.

[10]The problem grows much more complicated when the accounts of the French subsidiary are maintained in accordance with the French version of GAAP. The French statements must be converted to U.S. GAAP before the consolidation can be completed.

After studying this and the previous chapters, you have learned about all of the important classes of assets that businesses own. Recall from Chapter 10 that in evaluating the efficiency of a company in using its assets, a ratio that is often calculated and reviewed is total asset turnover. Another ratio that provides information about a company's efficiency in using its assets is **return on total assets.** You can calculate the return on total assets with this formula:

$$\text{Return on total assets} = \frac{\text{Net income}}{\text{Average total assets}}$$

USING THE INFORMATION— RETURN ON TOTAL ASSETS

LO 5
Explain the use of return on total assets in evaluating a company's efficiency in using its assets.

For example, **Reebok International, Ltd.,** a worldwide distributor of sports and fitness products, earned a net income of $254,478,000 during 1994. At the beginning of 1994, Reebok had total assets of $1,391,711,000, and at the end of the year total assets were $1,649,461,000. If the average total assets owned during the year is approximated by averaging the beginning and ending asset balances, Reebok's return on total assets for 1994 was:

$$\text{Return on total assets} = \frac{\$254,478,000}{(\$1,391,711,000 + \$1,649,461,000)/2} = 16.7\%$$

As we have seen for other ratios, a company's return on total assets should be compared with past performance and with the ratios of similar companies. In addition, you must be careful not to place too much importance on the evaluation of any single ratio. For past performance comparisons, Reebok's return on total assets and total asset turnover over a six year period were as follows:

Year	Return on Total Assets	Total Asset Turnover
1994	16.7%	2.2
1993	16.3	2.1
1992	8.3	2.2
1991	16.7	1.9
1990	13.9	1.7
1989	15.8	1.6

Notice that the change in return on total assets suggests that the company's efficiency in using its assets improved. Also, the total asset turnover improved.

To compare Reebok to a similar company, consider the fact that **Nike, Inc.,** reported a 14.5% return on assets for the year ended May 31, 1995. A more general basis for comparison would be the average return on assets for manufacturers of athletic footwear. Industry averages such as this are provided by Dun & Bradstreet's *Industry Norms and Key Ratios.*

Progress Check

11-9 A company had net income of $140,000 for 19X1 and $100,000 for 19X2. At December 31, 19X1 and 19X2, total assets reported were $800,000 and $900,000, respectively. What was the return on total assets for 19X2?

SUMMARY OF THE CHAPTER IN TERMS OF LEARNING OBJECTIVES

LO 1. Identify assets that should be classified as natural resources or as intangible assets and prepare entries to account for them, including entries to record depletion and amortization. The cost of a natural resource is recorded in an asset account. Then, depletion of the natural resource is recorded by allocating the cost to expense according to a units-of-production basis. The depletion is credited to an accumulated depletion account. Intangible assets are recorded at the cost incurred to purchase the assets. The allocation of intangible asset cost to expense is done on a straight-line basis and is called *amortization.* Normally, amortization is recorded with credits made directly to the asset account instead of a contra account.

LO 2. State the criteria for classifying assets as long-term investments and describe the categories of securities that are classified as long-term investments. Securities investments are classified as current assets if they are held as a source of cash to be used in current operations and if they mature within one year or the current operating cycle of the business or are marketable. All other investments in securities are long-term investments, which also include assets held for a special purpose and not used in operations.

Long-term investments in securities are classified in four groups: *(a)* debt securities held to maturity, *(b)* debt and equity securities available for sale, *(c)* equity securities when the investor has a significant influence over the investee, and *(d)* equity securities when the investor controls the investee.

LO 3. Describe the methods used to report long-term securities investments in the financial statements. Debt held to maturity is reported at its original cost adjusted for amortization of any difference between cost and maturity value. Debt and equity securities available for sale are reported at their fair values with unrealized gains or losses shown in the stockholders' equity section of the balance sheet. Gains and losses realized on the sale of the investments are reported in the income statement.

The equity method is used if the investor has a significant influence over the investee. This situation usually exists when the investor owns 20% or more of the investee's voting stock. If an investor owns more than 50% of another corporation's voting stock and controls the investee, the investor's financial reports are prepared on a consolidated basis.

Under the equity method, the investor records its share of the investee's earnings with a debit to the investment account and a credit to a revenue account. Dividends received satisfy the investor's equity claims, and reduce the investment account balance.

LO 4. Describe the primary accounting problems of having investments in international operations and prepare entries to account for sales to foreign customers. If a U.S. company makes a credit sale to a foreign customer and the sales terms call for payment with a foreign currency, the company must translate the foreign currency into dollars to record the receivable. If the exchange rate changes before payment is received, foreign exchange gains or losses are recognized in the year in which they occur. The same treatment is used if a U.S. company makes a credit purchase from a foreign supplier and is required to make payment in a foreign currency. Also, if a U.S. company has a foreign subsidiary that maintains its accounts in a foreign currency, the account balances must be translated into dollars before they can be consolidated with the parent's accounts.

LO 5. Explain the use of return on total assets in evaluating a company's efficiency in using its assets. Return on total assets is used along with other ratios such as total asset turnover to evaluate the efficiency of a company in using its assets. Return on total assets is usually calculated as the annual net income divided by the average amount of total assets.

The following transactions relate to Brown Company's long-term investment activities during 19X1 and 19X2. Brown did not own any long-term investments prior to 19X1. Show the appropriate journal entries and the portions of each year's balance sheet and income statement that describe these transactions.

DEMONSTRATION PROBLEM

19X1

Sept. 9 Purchased 1,000 shares of Packard, Inc., common stock for $80,000 cash. These shares represent 30% of Packard's outstanding shares.

Oct. 2 Purchased 2,000 shares of AT&T common stock for $60,000 cash. These shares represent less than a 1% ownership in AT&T.

17 Purchased as a long-term investment 1,000 shares of Apple Computer common stock for $40,000 cash. These shares are less than 1% of Apple's outstanding shares.

Nov. 1 Received $5,000 cash dividend from Packard.

30 Received $3,000 cash dividend from AT&T.

Dec. 15 Received $1,400 cash dividend from Apple.

31 Packard's 19X1 net income was $70,000.

31 Market values for the investments in marketable equity securities are Packard, $84,000; AT&T, $48,000; and Apple Computer, $45,000.

31 After closing the accounts, selected account balances on Brown Company's books are:

> Common stock $500,000
> Retained earnings 350,000

19X2

Jan. 1 Packard, Inc., was taken over by other investors, and Brown sold its shares for $108,000 cash.

May 30 Received $3,100 cash dividend from AT&T.

June 15 Received $1,600 cash dividend from Apple.

Aug. 17 Sold the AT&T stock for $52,000 cash.

19 Purchased 2,000 shares of Coca-Cola common stock for $50,000 as a long-term investment. The stock represents less than a 5% ownership in Coca-Cola.

Dec. 15 Received $1,800 cash dividend from Apple.

31 Market values of the investments in marketable equity securities are Apple, $39,000 and Coca-Cola, $48,000.

31 After closing the accounts, selected account balances on Brown Company's books are:

> Common stock $500,000
> Retained earnings 410,000

- Account for the investment in Packard under the equity method.
- Account for the investments in AT&T, Apple, and Coca-Cola as long-term investments in securities available for sale.
- Prepare the information for the two balance sheets by including the appropriate assets and stockholders' equity accounts.

Planning the Solution

Journal entries during 19X1:

Solution to Demonstration Problem

Sept.	9	Investment in Packard Common Stock	80,000.00	
		Cash		80,000.00
		Acquired 1,000 shares representing a 30% equity in Packard, Inc.		

Oct.	2	Investment in AT&T Common Stock	60,000.00	
		Cash		60,000.00
		Acquired 2,000 shares as a long-term investment		
		in securities available for sale.		
	17	Investment in Apple Common Stock	40,000.00	
		Cash		40,000.00
		Acquired 1,000 shares as a long-term investment		
		in securities available for sale.		
Nov.	1	Cash	5,000.00	
		Investment in Packard Common Stock		5,000.00
		Received dividend from Packard, Inc.		
	30	Cash	3,000.00	
		Dividends Earned		3,000.00
		Received dividend from AT&T.		
Dec.	15	Cash	1,400.00	
		Dividends Earned		1,400.00
		Received dividend from Apple.		
	31	Investment in Packard Common Stock	21,000.00	
		Earnings from Investment in Packard		21,000.00
		To record our 30% share of Packard's annual		
		earnings of $70,000.		
	31	Unrealized Holding Gain (Loss)	7,000.00	
		Long-Term Investments, Fair Value Adjustment		7,000.00
		To record change in fair value of securities		
		available for sale.		

	Cost	Fair (Market) Value
AT&T	$ 60,000	$48,000
Apple	40,000	45,000
Total	$100,000	$93,000

Required credit balance of Long-Term Investments, Fair Value Adjustment account ($100,000 − $93,000)	$ 7,000
Existing balance	-0-
Necessary credit	$ 7,000

December 31, 19X1, balance sheet items:

Assets

Long-term investments:		
Securities available for sale (at fair value)	$93,000	
Investment in Packard, Inc.	96,000	
Total		$189,000

Stockholders' Equity

Common stock	$500,000
Retained earnings	350,000
Unrealized holding gain (loss)	(7,000)

Income statement items for the year ended December 31, 19X1:

Dividends earned	$ 4,400
Earnings from equity method investment	21,000

Jan.	1	Cash		108,000.00	
		Investment in Packard Common Stock			96,000.00
		Gain on Sale of Investments			12,000.00
		Sold 1,000 shares for cash.			
May	30	Cash		3,100.00	
		Dividends Earned			3,100.00
		Received dividend from AT&T.			
June	15	Cash		1,600.00	
		Dividends Earned			1,600.00
		Received dividend from Apple.			
Aug.	17	Cash		52,000.00	
		Loss on Sale of Investments		8,000.00	
		Investment in AT&T Common Stock			60,000.00
		Sold 2,000 shares for cash.			
	19	Investment in Coca-Cola Common Stock		50,000.00	
		Cash			50,000.00
		Acquired 2,000 shares as a long-term investment			
		in securities available for sale.			
Dec.	15	Cash		1,800.00	
		Dividends Earned			1,800.00
		Received dividend from Apple.			
	31	Long-Term Investments, Fair Value Adjustment		4,000.00	
		Unrealized Holding Gain (Loss)			4,000.00
		To record change in fair value of securities			
		available for sale			

	Cost	Fair (Market) Value
Apple..	$40,000	$39,000
Coca-Cola	50,000	48,000
Total	$90,000	$87,000

Required credit balance of Long-Term Investments, Fair Value Adjustment account ($90,000 − $87,000)	$ 3,000
Existing credit balance..	7,000
Necessary debit	$ 4,000

December 31, 19X2, balance sheet items:

Assets

Long-term investments:	
Securities available for sale (fair value)	$87,000

Stockholders' Equity

Common stock...	$500,000
Retained earnings	410,000
Unrealized holding gain (loss)............................	(3,000)

Income statement items for the year ended December 31, 19X2:

Dividends earned..	$ 6,500
Gain on sale of investments...............................	12,000
Loss on sale of investments	(8,000)

GLOSSARY

Amortization the process of systematically writing off the cost of an intangible asset to expense over its estimated useful life. p. 381

Consolidated financial statements financial statements that show the results of all operations under the parent's control, including those of any subsidiaries; assets and liabilities of all affiliated companies are combined on a single balance sheet, revenues and expenses are combined on a single income statement, and cash flows are combined on a single statement of cash flows as though the business were in fact a single company. p. 392

Copyright an exclusive right granted by the federal government or by international agreement to publish and sell a musical, literary, or artistic work for a period of years. p. 382

Depletion the cost created by consuming the usefulness of natural resources. p. 380

Equity method an accounting method used when the investor has influence over the investee; the investment account is initially debited for cost and then is increased to reflect the investor's share of the investee's earnings and decreased to reflect the investor's receipt of dividends paid by the investee. p. 390

Foreign exchange rate the price of one currency stated in terms of another currency. p. 393

Goodwill an intangible asset of a business that represents future earnings greater than the average in its industry; recognized in the financial statements only when a business is acquired at a price in excess of the fair market value of its net assets (excluding goodwill). p. 383

Intangible asset an asset representing certain legal rights and economic relationships; it has no physical existence but is beneficial to the owner. p. 381

Lease a contract under which the owner of property (the lessor) grants to a lessee the right to use the property. p. 383

Leasehold the rights granted to a lessee by the lessor under the terms of a lease contract. p. 383

Leasehold improvements improvements to leased property made and paid for by the lessee. p. 383

Lessee the individual or company that acquires the right to use property under the terms of a lease. p. 383

Lessor the individual or company that owns property to be used by a lessee under the terms of a lease. p. 383

Long-term investments investments in stocks and bonds that are not marketable or, if marketable, are not intended to be a ready source of cash in case of need; also funds earmarked for a special purpose, such as bond sinking funds, and land or other assets not used in regular operations. p. 386

Multinational business a company that operates in a large number of different countries. p. 392

Parent company a corporation that owns a controlling interest in another corporation (more than 50% of the voting stock is required). p. 392

Patent exclusive right granted by the federal government to manufacture and sell a patented machine or device, or to use a process, for 17 years. p. 382

Reporting currency the currency in which a company presents its financial statements. p. 393

Return on total assets a measure of a company's operating efficiency, calculated by expressing net income as a percentage of average total assets. p. 395

Subsidiary a corporation that is controlled by another corporation (the parent) because the parent owns more than 50% of the subsidiary's voting stock. p. 392

Trademark a unique symbol used by a company in marketing its products or services. p. 384

Trade name a unique name used by a company in marketing its products or services. p. 384

QUESTIONS

1. What is the name for the process of allocating the cost of natural resources to expense as the natural resources are used?
2. What are the characteristics of an intangible asset?
3. Is the declining-balance method an acceptable means of calculating depletion of natural resources?
4. What general procedures are followed in accounting for intangible assets?
5. When does a business have goodwill? Under what conditions can goodwill appear in a company's balance sheet?
6. X Company bought an established business and paid for goodwill. If X Company plans to incur substantial advertising and promotional costs each year to maintain the value of the goodwill, must the company also amortize the goodwill?
7. In accounting for common stock investments, when should the equity method be used?
8. Under what circumstances would a company prepare consolidated financial statements?
9. Under what circumstances are long-term investments in debt securities reported at their original cost adjusted for amortization of any difference between cost and maturity value?
10. What are two basic problems of accounting for international operations?
11. If a U.S. company makes a credit sale to a foreign customer and the customer is required to make payment in U.S. dollars, can the U.S. company have an exchange gain or loss as a result of the sale?

12. A U.S. company makes a credit sale to a foreign customer, and the customer is required to make payment in a foreign currency. The foreign exchange rate was $1.40 on the date of the sale and is $1.30 on the date the customer pays the receivable. Will the U.S. company record an exchange gain or an exchange loss?

13. Refer to Lands' End, Inc.'s 1995 annual report in Appendix F. What is the net amount of intangible assets as of January 27, 1995? According to the footnote on signifi-

cant accounting policies, what is the primary component of intangibles?

LANDS' END
DIRECT MERCHANTS

14. Refer to the financial statements of Southwest Airlines Co. in Appendix E. Calculate the company's return on total assets for 1994.

SOUTHWEST

QUICK STUDY (Five-Minute Exercises)

Boise Industries acquired an ore mine at a cost of $1,300,000. It was necessary to incur $200,000 to access the mine. The mine is estimated to hold 500,000 tons of ore and the estimated value of the land after the ore is removed is $150,000.

**QS 11–1
(LO 1)**

a. Prepare the entry to record the acquisition.

b. Prepare the year-end adjusting entry assuming that 90,000 tons of ore were removed from the mine this year.

Which of the following assets should be reported on the balance sheet as intangible assets? Which should be reported as natural resources? (a) leasehold, (b) salt mine, (c) building, (d) oil well, (e) trademark.

**QS 11–2
(LO 1)**

On January 4 of the current year, Amber's Boutique incurred a $95,000 cost to modernize its store. The improvements included new floors, lighting, and shelving for the merchandise. It was estimated that these improvements would last for 10 years. Amber's leases its retail space and has eight years remaining on the lease. Prepare the entry to record the modernization and the adjusting entry at the end of the current year.

**QS 11–3
(LO 1)**

Which of the following are true of long-term investments?

**QS 11–4
(LO 2)**

a. They are held as an investment of cash available for current operations.

b. They may include debt securities held to maturity.

c. They may include bonds and stocks that are not intended to serve as a ready source of cash.

d. They may include funds earmarked for a special purpose, such as bond sinking funds.

e. They may include investments in trading securities.

f. They are easily sold and therefore qualify as being marketable.

g. They may include debt and equity securities available for sale.

On February 1, 19X1, Tom LeJeune purchased 6% bonds issued by Aberdeen Utilities Corp. at a cost of $30,000, which equals their par value. The bonds pay interest semiannually on July 31 and January 31. Prepare the entries to record the July 31 receipt of interest and the December 31 accrual.

**QS 11–5
(LO 3)**

On May 20, 19X1, Castle, Inc., paid $750,000 to acquire 25,000 (10%) of S&P Corp.'s outstanding common shares as a long-term investment. On August 5, 19X3, Castle sold half of the shares for $475,000. What method should be used to account for this stock investment? Prepare entries to record the acquisition of the stock and the stock sale.

**QS 11–6
(LO 3)**

QS 11–7
(LO 3)

Assume the same facts as in QS 11–6, except assume that the stock acquired represented 40% of S&P Corp.'s outstanding stock. Also assume that S&P Corp. paid a $125,000 dividend on November 1, 19X1, and reported a net income of $550,000 for 19X1. Prepare the entry to record the receipt of the dividend and the year-end adjustment of the investment account.

QS 11–8
(LO 4)

On March 1, 19X1, a U.S. company made a sale with credit terms requiring payment in 30 days to a German company, Bittner Corp. The amount of the sale was 20,000 marks. Assuming the exchange rate between German marks and U.S. dollars was $0.6811 on March 1 and $0.6985 on March 31, prepare the entries to record the sale and the cash receipt on March 31.

QS 11–9
(LO 5)

How is the return on total assets calculated? What does this ratio evaluate?

EXERCISES

Exercise 11–1
Depletion of natural resources
(LO 1)

On April 2, 19X1, Cascade Mining Co. paid $3,633,750 for an ore deposit containing 1,425,000 tons. The company also installed machinery in the mine that cost $171,000, had an estimated seven-year life with no salvage value, and was capable of removing all the ore in six years. The machine will be abandoned when the ore is completely mined. Cascade began operations on May 1, 19X1, and mined and sold 156,200 tons of ore during the remaining eight months of the year. Give the December 31, 19X1, entries to record the depletion of the ore deposit and the depreciation of the mining machinery.

Exercise 11–2
Amortization of intangible assets
(LO 1)

The Falstaff Gallery purchased the copyright on an oil painting for $236,700 on January 1, 19X1. The copyright legally protects its owner for 19 more years. However, the company plans to market and sell prints of the original for only 12 years. Prepare journal entries to record the purchase of the copyright and the annual amortization of the copyright on December 31, 19X1.

Exercise 11–3
Estimating goodwill
(LO 1)

Corey Boyd has devoted years to developing a profitable business that earns an attractive return. Boyd is now considering the possibility of selling the business and is attempting to estimate the value of the goodwill in the business. The fair value of the net assets of the business (excluding goodwill) is $437,000, and in a typical year net income is about $85,000. Most businesses of this type are expected to earn a return of about 10% on net assets. Estimate the value of the goodwill assuming *(a)* the value is equal to 10 times the excess earnings above average, and *(b)* the value can be found by capitalizing the excess earnings above average at a rate of 8%.

Exercise 11–4
Classifying stock investments; recording fair values
(LO 2, 3)

During 19X1, GeoMass Corporation's investments in securities included five items. These securities, with their December 31, 19X1, market values, are as follows:

a. Weller Company bonds payable: $418,500 cost; $455,000 market value. GeoMass positively intends and is able to hold these bonds until they mature in 19X6.

b. Baybridge common stock: 29,500 shares; $332,450 cost; $361,375 market value. GeoMass owns 32% of Baybridge's voting stock and has a significant influence over Baybridge.

c. Carrollton common stock: 12,000 shares; $169,750 cost; $183,000 market value. The goal of this investment, which amounts to 3% of Carrollton's outstanding shares, is to earn dividends over the next few years.

d. Zetech common stock: 3,500 shares; $95,300 cost; $93,625 market value. The goal of this investment is an expected increase in market value of the stock over the next three to five years. Zetech has 30,000 common shares outstanding.

e. Flavius common stock: 16,300 shares; $102,860 cost; $109,210 market value. This stock is marketable and is held as an investment of cash available for operations.

State whether each of these investments should be classified as a current asset or as a long-term investment. Also, for each of the long-term items, indicate in which of the four types of long-term investments the item should be classified. Then, prepare a journal entry dated December 31, 19X1, to record the fair value of the long-term investments in securities available for sale. Assume that GeoMass had no long-term investments prior to 19X1.

Vallejo Services, Inc., began operations in 19X1 and regularly makes long-term investments in securities available for sale. The total cost and fair value of these investments at the end of several years were:

Exercise 11–5
Investments in securities available for sale
(LO 3)

	Cost	Market Value
On December 31, 19X1	$374,000	$362,560
On December 31, 19X2	426,900	453,200
On December 31, 19X3	580,700	686,450
On December 31, 19X4	875,500	778,800

Prepare journal entries to record the fair value of Vallejo's investments at the end of each year.

Prepare general journal entries to record the following events on the books of Kedgewick Corp.:

Exercise 11–6
Stock investment transactions; equity method
(LO 3)

19X1

Jan. 2 Purchased 30,000 shares of Lintex Co. common stock for $204,000 plus a broker's fee of $3,480. Lintex has 90,000 shares of common stock outstanding and has acknowledged the fact that its policies will be significantly influenced by Kedgewick.

Sept. 1 Lintex declared and paid a cash dividend of $3.10 per share.

Dec. 31 Lintex announced that net income for the year amounted to $624,900.

19X2

June 1 Lintex declared and paid a cash dividend of $3.60 per share.

Dec. 31 Lintex announced that net income for the year amounted to $699,750.

    31 Kedgewick sold 10,000 shares of Lintex for $162,500.

On May 8, 19X1, Jefferson, Inc. (a U.S. company) made a credit sale to Devereaux (a French company). The terms of the sale required Devereaux to pay 800,000 francs on February 10, 19X2. Jefferson prepares quarterly financial statements on March 31, June 30, September 30, and December 31. The foreign exchange rates for francs during the time the receivable was outstanding were:

Exercise 11–7
Receivables denominated in a foreign currency
(LO 4)

May 8, 19X1	$0.1984
June 30, 19X1	0.2013
September 30, 19X1	0.2029
December 31, 19X1	0.1996
February 10, 19X2	0.2047

Calculate the foreign exchange gain or loss that Jefferson should report on each of its quarterly income statements during the last three quarters of 19X1 and the first quarter of 19X2. Also calculate the amount that should be reported on Jefferson's balance sheets at the end of the last three quarters of 19X1.

Red Rover of New York sells its products to customers in the United States and in Great Britain. On December 16, 19X1, Red Rover sold merchandise on credit to Bronson Ltd. of London, England, at a price of 17,000 pounds. The exchange rate on that day for 1 pound was $1.5238. On December 31, 19X1, when Red Rover prepared its financial statements, the exchange rate was 1 pound for $1.4990. Bronson paid its bill in full on January 15, 19X2, at

Exercise 11–8
Foreign currency transactions
(LO 4)

which time the exchange rate was 1 pound for $1.5156. Red Rover immediately exchanged the 17,000 pounds for U.S. dollars. Prepare journal entries on December 16, December 31, and January 15, to account for the sale and account receivable on Red Rover's books.

Exercise 11–9
Return on total assets
(LO 5)

The following information is available from the financial statements of Rawhide Industries:

	19X1	19X2	19X3
Total assets, December 31	$190,000	$320,000	$750,000
Net income	28,200	36,400	58,300

Calculate Rawhide's return on total assets for 19X2 and 19X3. (Round answers to one decimal place.) Comment on the company's efficiency in using its assets in 19X2 and 19X3.

PROBLEMS

Problem 11–1
Intangible assets and natural resources
(LO 1)

Part 1. In 19X1, The Pullman Corporation leased space in a building for 15 years. The lease contract calls for annual rental payments of $70,000 to be made on each July 1 throughout the life of the lease and also provides that the lessee must pay for all additions and improvements to the leased property. In 19X6, Pullman decided to sublease the space to Kidman & Associates, Inc., for the remaining 10 years of the lease. On June 20, 19X6, Kidman paid $185,000 to Pullman for the right to sublease the space and agreed to assume the obligation to pay the $70,000 annual rent to the building owner beginning July 1, 19X6. After taking possession of the leased space, Kidman paid for improving the office portion of the leased space at a cost of $129,840. The improvements were paid for on July 5, 19X6, and are estimated to have a life equal to the 16 years remaining in the life of the building.

Required

Prepare entries for Kidman to record (a) its payment to Pullman for the right to sublease the building space, (b) its payment of the 19X6 annual rent to the building owner, and (c) its payment for the office improvements. Also, prepare the adjusting entries required at the end of 19X6 to amortize (d) a proper share of the $185,000 cost of the sublease and (e) a proper share of the office improvements.

Part 2. On July 3 of the current year, Jackson Mining Co. paid $4,836,000 for land estimated to contain 7.8 million tons of recoverable ore of a valuable mineral. It installed machinery costing $390,000, which had a 10-year life and no salvage value, and was capable of exhausting the ore deposit in eight years. The machinery was paid for on July 25, nine days before mining operations began. The company removed 400,000 tons of ore during the first five months of operations.

Required

Preparation component:

Prepare entries to record (a) the purchase of the land, (b) the installation of the machinery, (c) the first five months' depletion under the assumption that the land will be valueless after the ore is mined, and (d) the first five months' depreciation on the machinery, which will be abandoned after the ore is fully mined.

CHECK FIGURE:
Depletion Expense, $248,000

Analysis component:

Describe the similarities and differences in amortization, depletion, and depreciation.

Problem 11–2
Goodwill
(LO 1)

American Rental Corp., an equipment rental business, has the following balance sheet on December 31, 19X1:

Cash	$ 93,930
Equipment	678,800
Accumulated depreciation, equipment	(271,500)
Buildings	340,000
Accumulated depreciation, buildings	(182,400)
Land	93,000
Total assets	$751,830
Accounts payable	$ 18,650
Long-term note payable	337,250
Common stock, $20 par value	200,000
Retained earnings	195,930
Total liabilities and stockholders' equity	$751,830

In this industry, earnings average 20% of stockholders' equity. American Rental, however, is expected to earn $100,000 annually. The balance sheet amounts are reasonable estimates of fair market values for all assets except goodwill, which does not appear on the financial statement. In negotiations to sell the business, American Rental has proposed that goodwill should be measured by capitalizing the amount of above-average earnings at a rate of 15%. On the other hand, the potential buyer thinks that goodwill should be valued at five times the amount of earnings above the average for the industry.

Required

1. Calculate the amount of goodwill proposed by American Rental.

2. Calculate the amount of goodwill according to the potential buyer.

3. Suppose that the buyer purchases the business for the amount of the net assets reported on the December 31, 19X1, balance sheet plus the amount proposed by American Rental for the goodwill. If the amount of expected earnings (before amortization of goodwill) is obtained the first year, and the goodwill is amortized over the longest permissible time period, what amount of net income will be reported for the first year after the business is purchased?

4. What rate of return on the buyer's investment does the first year's net income represent?

CHECK FIGURE:
Goodwill, $138,760 or $104,070

Hammerman Steel Works was organized on January 4, 19X1. The following investment transactions and events subsequently occurred:

Problem 11–3
Accounting for stock investments
(LO 3)

19X1

Jan. 5   Hammerman purchased 30,000 shares (20%) of Falcon International's outstanding common stock for $780,000.

Oct. 23   Falcon declared and paid a cash dividend of $1.60 per share.

Dec. 31   Falcon announced that its net income for 19X1 was $582,000. Market value of the stock was $27.75 per share.

19X2

Oct. 15   Falcon declared and paid a cash dividend of $1.30 per share.

Dec. 31   Falcon announced that its net income for 19X2 was $738,000. Market value of the stock was $30.45 per share.

19X3

Jan. 2   Hammerman sold all of its investment in Falcon for $947,000 cash.

Part 1. Assume that Hammerman has a significant influence over Falcon because it owns 20% of the stock.

Required

1. Give the entries to record the preceding events in Hammerman's books.

2. Calculate the carrying value per share of Hammerman's investment as reflected in the investment account on January 1, 19X3.

3. Calculate the change in Hammerman's equity from January 5, 19X1, through January 2, 19X3, resulting from its investment in Falcon.

CHECK FIGURE:
Carrying value per share,
$31.90

Part 2. Assume that even though Hammerman owns 20% of Falcon's outstanding stock, a thorough investigation of the surrounding circumstances indicates that it does not have a significant influence over the investee.

Required

1. Give the entries to record the preceding events in Hammerman's books. Also prepare an entry dated January 2, 19X3, to remove any balances related to the fair value adjustment.
2. Calculate the cost per share of Hammerman's investment as reflected in the investment account on January 1, 19X3.
3. Calculate the change in Hammerman's equity from January 5, 19X1, through January 2, 19X3, resulting from its investment in Falcon.

Problem 11–4
Accounting for long-term investments
(LO 2, 3)

Decker Manufacturing Co.'s long-term investment portfolio at December 31, 19X1, consisted of the following:

Securities Available for Sale	Cost	Fair (Market) Value
80,000 shares of Company A common stock	$1,070,600	$ 980,000
14,000 shares of Company B common stock	318,750	308,000
35,000 shares of Company C common stock	1,325,500	1,281,875

Decker had the following long-term investment transactions during 19X2:

Jan. 29   Sold 7,000 shares of Company B common stock for $158,375 less a brokerage fee of $3,100.

Apr. 17   Purchased 20,000 shares of Company W common stock for $395,000 plus a brokerage fee of $6,800. The shares represent a 30% ownership in Company W.

July 6   Purchased 9,000 shares of Company X common stock for $253,125 plus a brokerage fee of $3,500. The shares represent a 10% ownership in Company X.

Aug. 22   Purchased 100,000 shares of Company Y common stock for $750,000 plus a brokerage fee of $8,200. The shares represent a 51% ownership in Company Y.

Nov. 13   Purchased 17,000 shares of Company Z common stock for $533,800 plus a brokerage fee of $6,900. The shares represent a 5% ownership in Company Z.

Dec. 9   Sold 80,000 shares of Company A common stock for $1,030,000 less a brokerage fee of $8,200.

The fair (market) values of Decker's investments at December 31, 19X2, are: B, $162,750; C, $1,220,625; W, $382,500; X, $236,250; Y, $1,062,500; Z, $557,600.

Required

1. Determine what amount should be reported on Decker's December 31, 19X2, balance sheet for its investments in equity securities available for sale.
2. Prepare a December 31, 19X2, adjusting entry, if necessary, to record the fair value adjustment of the long-term investments in securities available for sale.
3. What amount of gain or loss on those transactions relating to securities available for sale should be reported on Decker's December 31, 19X2, income statement?

CHECK FIGURE:
Unrealized Holding Gain (Loss), $40,000 Cr.

Problem 11–5
Foreign currency transactions
(LO 4)

Savannah, Inc., is a U.S. corporation that has customers in several foreign countries. Following are some of Savannah's 19X1 and 19X2 transactions:

19X1

Apr. 8   Sold merchandise to Salinas & Sons of Mexico for $7,938 cash. The exchange rate for pesos was $0.1323.

July 21   Sold merchandise on credit to Sumitomo Corp. located in Japan. The price of 1.5 million yen was to be paid 120 days from the date of sale. The exchange rate for yen was $0.009646 on this date.

Oct. 14   Sold merchandise for 19,000 pounds to Smithers Ltd. of Great Britain, payment in full to be received in 90 days. The exchange rate for pounds was $1.5181.

Nov. 18   Received Sumitomo's payment for its purchase of July 21, and exchanged the yen for dollars. The current foreign exchange rate for yen was $0.009575.

Dec. 20   Sold merchandise for 17,000 marks to Schmidt Haus of Germany, payment in full to be received in 30 days. On this day, the foreign exchange rate for marks was $0.6852.

     31   Prepared adjusting entries to recognize exchange gains or losses on the annual financial statements. Rates for exchanging foreign currencies on this day included the following:

Pesos (Mexico)	$0.1335
Yen (Japan)	0.009551
Pounds (Britain)	1.5235
Marks (Germany)	0.6807

19X2

Jan. 12   Received full payment from Smithers for the sale of October 14 and immediately exchanged the pounds for dollars. The exchange rate for pounds was $1.5314.

     19   Received Schmidt Haus's full payment for the sale of December 20 and immediately exchanged the marks for dollars. The exchange rate for marks was $0.6771.

Required

Preparation component:

1. Prepare general journal entries to account for these transactions on Savannah's books.
2. Calculate the foreign exchange gain or loss to be reported on Savannah's 19X1 income statement.

Analysis component:

3. What actions might Savannah consider to reduce its risk of foreign exchange gains or losses?

CHECK FIGURE:
19X1 total foreign exchange loss, $80.40

CRITICAL THINKING: ESSAYS, PROBLEMS, AND CASES

On March 1, The Hobart Corporation purchased 7,500 shares of TP&L Utilities common stock for $22 per share, or $165,000. Hobart's purchase represents a 25% ownership in TP&L. Hobart did not own any investments prior to the TP&L stock purchase. TP&L did not declare any dividends on its common stock during the year, and on December 31 reported a net loss of $34,000. The market value of the TP&L stock on December 31 was $24 per share. Hobart's accountant made the following adjusting entry to update the account balances for the investment in TP&L:

Analytical Essay
(LO 3)

Dec.	31	Long-Term Investments, Fair Value Adjustment	15,000.00	
		Unrealized Holding Gain (Loss)		15,000.00
		(7,500 × $24) − $165,000 = $15,000		

     Describe the method that Hobart's accountant apparently used to account for the investment in TP&L. Explain why this method is incorrect and identify the correct method. Without providing specific amounts, describe what impact the accountant's error had on Hobart's financial statements.

Business Communications Case

(LO 2, 3)

You are the accountant for Jackson Company. The president of the company, Abel Terrio, has finished reviewing the financial statements you prepared for 19X3 and questions the $6,000 loss reported on the company's sale of its investment in the common stock of Blackhawk Industries.

Jackson acquired 50,000 shares of Blackhawk's outstanding common stock on December 31, 19X1, at a cost of $500,000. This stock purchase represented a 40% interest in Blackhawk. The 19X2 income statement showed that the investments made by Jackson proved to be very profitable and that the earnings from all investments were $126,000. On January 3, 19X3, Jackson Company sold the Blackhawk stock for $575,000. Blackhawk did not pay any dividends during 19X2 and reported a net income of $202,500 for the year.

Terrio believes that because the purchase price of the Blackhawk stock was $500,000, and it was sold for $575,000, the 19X3 income statement should report a $75,000 gain on the sale.

Draft a memo to Terrio explaining why the $6,000 loss on the sale of the Blackhawk stock is correctly reported.

Managerial Analysis Problem

(A review problem)

Star, Inc., is considering buying either Elan Corp. or Verve Corp., similar businesses that acquired their equipment and began operating four years ago. In evaluating the two companies, Star has determined that they have not used the same accounting procedures, so their financial statements are not comparable. Over the past four years, Elan has reported an average annual net income of $316,500 and Verve has reported $406,700. The current balance sheets of the two companies show the following:

	Elan Corp.	Verve Corp.
Cash	$ 210,400	$ 231,040
Accounts receivable	1,555,610	1,723,500
Allowance for doubtful accounts	(91,200)	0
Merchandise inventory	2,029,120	2,665,300
Office equipment	794,880	673,270
Accumulated depreciation, office equipment	(469,298)	(269,308)
Total assets	$4,029,512	$5,023,802
Total liabilities	$1,882,880	$2,253,970

Elan has used the allowance method of accounting for bad debts and Verve has used the direct write-off method. An examination of each company's accounts revealed that only $48,000 of Elan's accounts are probably uncollectible and that Verve's estimated uncollectible accounts total $85,000.

Because Verve uses FIFO, its ending inventory amounts approximate replacement cost. However, Elan uses LIFO. As a result, Elan's current inventory is reported $190,000 below replacement cost.

In taking depreciation for the past four years, both companies have assumed 10-year lives and no salvage value for their equipment. However, Elan has used double-declining-balance depreciation, while Verve has used straight-line. Star believes that straight-line depreciation results in reporting equipment on the balance sheet at its approximate fair market value.

Star is willing to pay fair market value for the net assets (including goodwill) of either business. Star estimates goodwill to be three times the average annual earnings in excess of 12% of the fair market value of the net tangible assets (assets, other than goodwill, minus liabilities).

Required

Prepare the following schedules: (a) the net tangible assets of each company at fair market values assessed by Star; (b) the revised net incomes of the companies based on adjusted amounts of bad debts expense, FIFO inventories, and straight-line depreciation; (c) the calculation of each company's goodwill; and (d) the maximum purchase price Star would pay for each business, if it assumed the liabilities of the purchased business. (Note: Round all calculations to the nearest dollar.)

Financial Statement Analysis Case

(LO 1, 4, 5)

Examine Lands' End, Inc.'s financial statements and supplemental information in Appendix F and answer the following questions:

1. Are Lands' End's financial statements consolidated? How can you tell?
2. Does Lands' End have more than one subsidiary? How can you tell?

3. Does Lands' End have any foreign operations? How can you tell?

4. Is there a foreign exchange gain or loss on the income statement (consolidated statement of operations)? Describe what you find or do not find.

5. What intangible assets does Lands' End own? What is the time period that Lands' End is using to amortize its intangibles?

6. Calculate Lands' End's return on total assets for the year ended January 27, 1995.

CONCEPT TESTER

Test your understanding of the concepts introduced in this chapter by completing the following crossword puzzle.

Across Clues

1. A unique symbol used by a company in marketing its products or services.

4. The individual or company that acquires the right to use property under a lease.

6. Exclusive right granted by government to manufacture and sell a device or use a process.

9. 2 words; A valuable legal right or economic relationship that has no physical existence.

10. 3 words; the price of one currency stated in terms of another currency.

12. 2 words; a unique name used by a company in marketing its products or services.

13. An exclusive right granted by the government to sell a musical, literary, or artistic work.

Down Clues

2. The cost created by consuming the usefulness of natural resources.

3. 2 words; the currency in which a company presents its financial statements.

5. A corporation that is controlled by another corporation (the parent).

7. The individual or company that owns property to be used by a lessee under a lease.

8. An intangible asset that represents future earnings greater than average.

11. A contract under which the owner of property grants a lessee the right to use the property.

ANSWERS TO PROGRESS CHECKS

11–1 Some possible answers:

  Intangible assets:

  Patents

  Copyrights

  Leaseholds

  Leasehold Improvements

  Goodwill

  Trademarks

  Exclusive Licenses

  Natural Resources:

  Timberlands

  Mineral Deposits

  Oil Reserves

11–2 $650,000 \times (91,000/325,000) = $182,000

11–3

Jan.	6	Patents	120,000.00	
		Cash		120,000.00
Dec.	31	Amortization Expense	40,000.00	
		Patents		40,000.00

  $120,000/3 = $40,000

11–4 Long-term investments include funds earmarked for a special purpose, bonds and stocks that do not meet the test of a current asset, and other assets that are not used in the regular operations of the business.

11–5 A stock investment is classified as a long-term investment if it is not marketable or, if marketable, it is not held as an available source of cash to meet the needs of current operations.

11–6 Debt securities held to maturity and debt securities available for sale are recorded at cost and interest on both is accrued as earned. However, only securities held to maturity require amortizing the difference between cost and maturity value. In addition, only securities available for sale require end-of-period adjustments to fair market value.

11–7 Long-term equity investments are placed in the following three categories and accounted for using the method indicated:

  a. Noninfluential holding (less than 20% of outstanding stock)—Fair Value Method.

  b. Significantly influential holding (20% to 50% of outstanding stock)—Equity Method.

  c. Controlling holding (more than 50%)—Consolidated Statements.

11–8 *d*

11–9 ($800,000 + $900,000)/2 = $850,000

  $100,000/$850,000 = 11.8%

Current and Long-Term Liabilities

*S*afeway Inc. is one of the world's largest food retailers. At the end of its 1994 year, Safeway operated 1,062 stores in the United States and Canada. The company's 1994 annual report appears to indicate that Safeway has successfully emerged from a very difficult period of losses. At the end of its 1990 year, total stockholders' equity was a negative $183.4 million (a deficit). In other words, total liabilities exceeded total assets by $183.4 million. This situation improved each year until, at the end of 1994, total stockholders' equity was a positive $643.8 million.

C. A. Smith is considering investing in Safeway. In evaluating Safeway's financial condition, Smith is confused about the nature of the company's liabilities. The balance sheet reports four different categories of liabilities, and the differences between these categories are not clear to Smith.

SAFEWAY INC. AND SUBSIDIARIES
(In millions)

	Year-End 1994	Year-End 1993
Current liabilities:		
Current maturities of notes and debentures	$ 152.5	$ 188.6
Current obligations under capital leases	19.3	19.3
Accounts payable	1,012.1	880.5
Accrued salaries and wages	223.6	216.3
Other accrued liabilities	416.1	369.1
Total current liabilities	$1,823.6	$1,673.8
Long-term debt:		
Notes and debentures	$1,849.5	$2,287.7
Obligations under capital leases	174.8	193.6
Total long-term debt	$2,024.3	$2,481.3
Deferred income taxes	128.3	145.5
Accrued claims and other liabilities	402.1	391.2
Total liabilities	$4,378.3	$4,691.8

LEARNING OBJECTIVES

After studying Chapter 12, you should be able to:

1. **Define liabilities, explain the difference between current and long-term liabilities, and describe the uncertainties related to some liabilities.**
2. **Describe how accountants record and report estimated liabilities such as warranties and income taxes and how they report contingent liabilities.**
3. **Describe payroll expenses and liabilities and prepare journal entries to account for them.**
4. **Describe how accountants record and report short-term notes payable.**
5. **Explain and calculate the present value of an amount to be paid at a future date and the present value of a series of equal amounts to be paid at future dates.**
6. **Describe how accountants use present value concepts in accounting for long-term notes and how liabilities may result from leasing assets.**
7. **Calculate the number of times a company earns its fixed interest charges and describe what it reveals about a company's situation.**
8. **Define or explain the words and phrases listed in the chapter glossary.**

Previous chapters have described liabilities for accounts payable, notes payable, wages payable, and unearned revenues. In this chapter, you will learn about liabilities arising from warranties, income taxes, borrowing, asset purchases, leases, and payrolls. We also describe contingent liabilities and the important concept of present value. As you study this chapter, you will learn how accountants define, classify, and measure liabilities for the purpose of reporting useful information about them.

DEFINING AND CLASSIFYING LIABILITIES

LO 1

Define liabilities, explain the difference between current and long-term liabilities, and describe the uncertainties related to some liabilities.

In general, a liability means that because of a past event, a business has a present obligation to make a future payment. More precisely, liabilities are probable future payments of assets or services that an entity is presently obligated to make as a result of past transactions or events.[1] As shown in the diagram, this definition involves three dimensions in time:

- The company is obligated in the present
- To pay out assets or deliver services in the future
- Because of an event in the past

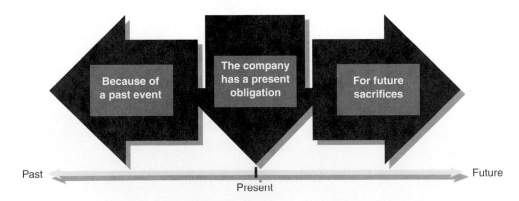

This definition also tells us that liabilities do not include all expected future payments. For example, suppose that a company expects to pay wages to its employees in the coming months. These future payments are not liabilities because the company is not presently obligated to pay them. The company is not presently obligated because the employees have not yet earned the future wages. In other words, no past

---

[1]Financial Accounting Standards Board, *Statement of Financial Accounting Concepts No. 6,* "Elements of Financial Statements" (Norwalk, CT, 1985), par. 35.

transaction has resulted in a present obligation. The liabilities will be created in the future only when the employees actually perform the work.

Current and Long-Term Liabilities

Information about liabilities is more useful when the balance sheet identifies the liabilities as current and long-term. *Current liabilities* are expected to be paid by using existing current assets or creating other current liabilities.[2] Current liabilities are due within one year or the company's operating cycle, whichever is longer. Typical current liabilities include accounts payable, short-term notes payable, wages payable, warranty liabilities, lease liabilities, payroll and other taxes payable, and unearned revenues.

The specific current liabilities reported by a company depend on the nature of its operations. For example, the 1993 balance sheet for **Southern Company** (an electric utility) reports more than $100 million in its current liabilities for customer deposits. As another example, **US West, Inc.'s** 1994 balance sheet included a $337 million liability for the current portion of restructuring charges.

Obligations that are not expected to be paid within one year (or a longer operating cycle) should be classified as *long-term liabilities*. Typical long-term liabilities include long-term notes payable, warranty liabilities, lease liabilities, and bonds payable. On the balance sheet, these may be presented in a single long-term liabilities section. However, many companies show them as two or more items such as *long-term debt* and *other liabilities*. For example, the liabilities of **Safeway Inc.,** on page 411 include long-term debt, deferred income taxes, and accrued claims and other liabilities. All of these are reported below current liabilities and are understood to be noncurrent (long-term) liabilities.

Some kinds of liabilities may be either current or long term. A specific debt is assigned to a category on the basis of how soon it will be paid. In fact, a single liability is divided between the two categories if the company expects to make payments in both the near and more distant future. For example, recall the liabilities of **Safeway Inc.** Notice that the first two current liabilities represent the current portions of the two items listed as long-term debt.

A few liabilities do not have a fixed due date because they are payable on the creditor's demand. They are reported as current liabilities because they may have to be paid within the year or a longer operating cycle.

Three important questions concerning liabilities are: Who must be paid? When is payment due? How much is to be paid? In many situations, the answers to these three questions are determined at the time the liability is incurred. For example, assume that Coleman Company has an account payable for precisely $100, payable on August 15, 19X1, to R. L. Tucker. There is no uncertainty about any of the questions. The company knows who to pay, when to pay, and how much to pay. Other types of liabilities may be uncertain with respect to one or more of the three questions.

UNCERTAIN ASPECTS OF SOME LIABILITIES

---

[2]FASB, *Accounting Standards—Current Text* (Norwalk, CT, 1995), sec. B05.402. First published as *Accounting Research Bulletin No. 43*, Ch. 3A, par. 7.

When the Identity of the Creditor Is Uncertain. Some liabilities have uncertainty about who will be paid. For example, a corporation's board of directors creates a liability with a known amount when it declares a dividend payable to the stockholders. Because the dividend will be paid to the investors who actually own stock on a specified future date, the recipients are not known with certainty until that date. Despite this uncertainty, the corporation has a liability that is reported on the balance sheet.

When the Due Date Is Uncertain. In other situations, a company may have an obligation of a known amount to a known creditor but not know exactly when the debt must be settled. For example, a copy services company may accept fees in advance from a customer who expects to need copies later. Thus, the copy service company has a liability that will be settled by providing services at an unknown future date. Even though this uncertainty exists, the company's balance sheet is complete only if it includes this liability to its customer. (These obligations are reported as current liabilities because they may have to be settled in the short term.)

When the Amount Is Uncertain. In addition, a company may know that an obligation exists but may not know exactly how much will be required to settle it. For example, a company uses electrical power every day but is billed only after the meter has been read. The cost has been incurred and the liability has been created, even though the bill has not been received. As a result, a liability to the power company is reported with an estimated amount if the balance sheet is prepared before the bill arrives.

Progress Check
(Answers to Progress Checks are provided at the end of the chapter.)

12–1   What is a liability?

12–2   Is every expected future payment a liability?

12–3   If a liability is payable in 15 months, should it be classified as current or long term?

ESTIMATED LIABILITIES

LO 2
Describe how accountants record and report estimated liabilities such as warranties and income taxes and how they report contingent liabilities.

PRINCIPLE APPLICATION
Full-Disclosure Principle,
p. 294
At the end of its 1994 year, General Motors Corporation reported that the $42,867.3 million of other liabilities and deferred credits reported on its balance sheet included $13,290.2 million for warranties, dealer and customer allowances, claims, and discounts.

An obligation of uncertain amount that can be reasonably estimated is called an **estimated liability.** A common example of an estimated liability involves warranties offered by a seller. Other estimated liabilities are created for contracts to provide future services, income taxes, property taxes, and employee benefits such as pensions and health care.

Warranty Liabilities

An estimated liability is created when a company sells products covered by a warranty. In effect, a **warranty** obligates the seller or manufacturer to pay for replacing or repairing the product when it breaks or otherwise fails to perform within a specified period. For example, a used car might be sold with a warranty that covers parts and labor.

To comply with the *full-disclosure* and the *matching principles,* the seller must report the expense of providing a warranty during the same period as the revenue from the sales of the product. The seller also must report the obligation under the warranty as a liability, even though it is uncertain about the existence, amount, payee, and date of its future sacrifices. The seller's warranty obligation does not require payments unless the products break and are returned for repairs. Nonetheless, future payments are probable, and the amount of the liability can be estimated using the company's past experience with warranties.

For example, suppose that a dealer sells a used car for $8,000 on December 1, 19X1, with a one-year or 12,000-mile warranty that covers repair parts and labor charges. Experience shows that the warranty expense averages about 4% of a car's selling price. In this case, the expense is expected to be $320 ($8,000 × 4%). The dealer records the expense and liability with this entry:

19X1				
Dec.	1	Warranty Expense	320.00	
		Estimated Warranty Liability		320.00
		To record the warranty expense and liability at 4% of		
		the selling price.		

Alternatively, this entry can be made as an end-of-period adjustment. Either way, it causes the expense to be reported on the 19X1 income statement. It also causes the warranty liability to appear on the balance sheet for December 31, 19X1.

Now, suppose that the customer returns the car for warranty repairs on January 9, 19X2. The dealer performs the work by replacing parts that cost $90 and using labor at a cost of $110. This entry records the partial settlement of the estimated warranty liability:

19X2				
Jan.	9	Estimated Warranty Liability	200.00	
		Auto Parts Inventory		90.00
		Cash		110.00

Notice that this entry does not record any additional expense in 19X2. Instead, the entry reduces the balance of the estimated warranty liability. The warranty expense was already recorded in 19X1, the year the car was sold under the warranty.

What happens if the total warranty costs actually turn out to be more or less than the predicted $320? In fact, some difference is highly likely for any particular car. Over the long term, management should monitor the actual warranty costs to see whether the 4% rate provides useful information. If actual experience reveals a large difference, the rate should be modified for future sales.

Income Tax Liabilities

Corporations are subject to income taxes and must estimate the amount of their income tax liability when they prepare interim financial statements. We explain this process in the following paragraphs. Then, in the next section, we discuss deferred income tax liabilities that arise from temporary differences between GAAP and income tax rules.

Income tax expense for a corporation creates a liability that exists until payments are made to the government. Because the taxes are created by the process of earning income, a liability is incurred as soon as the income is earned. However, the taxes must be paid quarterly under federal regulations.

For example, suppose that Foster, Inc., prepares monthly financial statements. Based on the income earned in January, the company estimates that it owes income taxes of $12,100. The following adjusting entry records the estimate:

Jan.	31	Income Taxes Expense	12,100.00	
		Income Taxes Payable		12,100.00
		Accrued income tax expense and liability based on the		
		estimated income for the month of January.		

The liability is adjusted each month until the first quarterly payment is made. Assuming the taxes for the first three months total $50,000, the following entry records the payment:

Apr.	10	Income Taxes Payable	50,000.00	
		Cash		50,000.00
		Paid the quarterly income taxes based on the estimated income for the first quarter of the year.		

The process of accruing and then paying the taxes continues throughout the year. However, by the time the annual financial statements are prepared at the end of the year, the company's accountant knows the amount of income that has been earned and the actual amount of income taxes that must be paid. This information allows the accountant to update the expense and liability accounts.

For example, suppose that Foster, Inc.'s accounts include a $22,000 credit balance in the Income Taxes Liability account at December 31, 19X1. Information about the company's income for the year shows that the actual liability should be $33,500. This entry records the additional expense and liability:

Dec.	31	Income Taxes Expense	11,500.00	
		Income Taxes Payable		11,500.00
		To record additional tax expense and liability.		

The liability will be settled when the company makes its final quarterly payment early in 19X2.

Deferred Income Tax Liabilities

Another special type of income tax liability may be incurred when the amount of income before taxes reported on a corporation's income statement is not the same as the amount of income reported on its income tax return. These differences arise because income tax laws define income differently than GAAP.[3]

Some of the differences between the tax law and GAAP are temporary. These *temporary differences* arise when the tax return and the income statement report a revenue or expense in different years. As an example, for tax purposes, companies are often able to deduct higher amounts of depreciation in the early years of an asset's life and smaller amounts in the later years. On their income statements, they often report an equal amount of depreciation expense in each year. Thus, in the early years, depreciation for tax purposes is more than depreciation expense on the income statement. Then, in the later years, depreciation for tax purposes is less than depreciation expense on the income statement.

When there are temporary differences between taxable income on the tax return and income before taxes on the income statement, GAAP requires corporations to calculate income tax expense based on the income reported on the income statement. In the previous example involving depreciation, the result is that the income tax expense reported in the early years is more than the amount of income tax payable. This difference is called a **deferred income tax liability.**

For example, assume that after making and recording its quarterly income tax payments, a company determines at the end of the year that an additional $25,000 of in-

---

[3]The differences between the tax laws and GAAP arise because Congress uses the tax law to generate receipts, stimulate the economy, and otherwise influence behavior. GAAP, on the other hand, are intended to provide financial information that is useful for decision making.

come tax expense should be recorded. It also determines that only $21,000 is currently due and $4,000 is deferred to future years. The following entry records the end-of-year adjustment:

Dec.	31	Income Taxes Expense	25,000.00	
		Income Taxes Payable		21,000.00
		Deferred Income Tax Liability		4,000.00
		To record tax expense and deferred tax liability.		

In this entry, the credit to Income Taxes Payable represents the amount that is currently due to be paid. The credit to Deferred Income Tax Liability represents the tax payments that are deferred until future years when the temporary difference reverses.

Many companies report deferred income tax liabilities. For example, **Ford Motor Company's** December 31, 1994, balance sheet shows that Ford had a deferred income tax liability of $2,958 million.

In some circumstances, temporary differences may cause a company to pay income taxes before they are reported on the income statement as expense. If so, the company usually reports a *deferred income tax asset* on its balance sheet that is similar to a prepaid expense. For example, **The Clorox Company's** June 30, 1996, balance sheet reported deferred income taxes of $10,987,000 as a current asset.

Progress Check

12-4   Estimated liabilities would include an obligation to pay:
   a. An uncertain but reasonably estimated amount to a specific person on a specific date.
   b. A known amount to a specific person on an uncertain due date.
   c. A known amount to an uncertain person on a known due date.
   d. All of the above.

12-5   An automobile was sold for $15,000 on June 1, 19X1, with a one-year warranty that covers parts and labor. Based on past experience, warranty expense is estimated at 1.5% of the selling price. On March 1, 19X2, the customer returned the car for warranty repairs that used replacement parts at a cost of $75 and labor at a cost of $60. The amount that should be recorded as warranty expense at the time of the March 1 repairs is: (a) $0;   (b) $60;   (c) $75;   (d) $135;   (e) $225.

12-6   Why would a corporation accrue an income tax liability for interim reports?

Sometimes, past transactions have the effect of requiring a future payment only if some uncertain future event takes place. If the likelihood that the uncertain future event will occur is remote, the company is not required to report a liability in the statements or the footnotes. However, if the uncertain future event is probable and the amount of the payment can be reasonably estimated, the company is required to report the payment as a liability.[4]

CONTINGENT LIABILITIES

LO 2

Describe how accountants record and report estimated liabilities such as warranties and income taxes and how they report contingent liabilities.

---

[4]FASB, *Accounting Standards—Current Text* (Norwalk, CT, 1995), sec. C59.105. First published as *FASB Statement No. 5*, par. 8.

Contingent liabilities involve situations that fall between these two extremes. In one situation, the uncertain future event is probable but the amount of the payment cannot be reasonably estimated. In the other, the uncertain future event is not probable but has a reasonable possibility of occurring. These contingent liabilities are not recorded in the books as liabilities. However, the *full-disclosure principle* requires disclosure of contingent liabilities in the financial statements or in the footnotes.

Distinguishing between Liabilities and Contingent Liabilities?

Contingent liabilities become definite obligations only if some previously uncertain event actually takes place. For example, a typical contingent liability is a discounted note receivable that becomes a definite obligation only if the original signer of the note fails to pay it at maturity. We discussed this example in Chapter 8.

Does a product warranty create a liability or a contingent liability? A product warranty requires service or payment only if the product fails and the customer returns it for service. These conditions make it appear to be like a contingent liability. However, the contingent obligation should be recorded in the books as a liability if the occurrence of the future contingency is probable and if the amount of the liability can be reasonably estimated. Product warranties are usually recorded as liabilities because (1) the failure of some percentage of the sold products is probable, and (2) past experience allows the seller to develop a reasonable estimate of the amount to be paid.

Other Examples of Contingent Liabilities

Potential Legal Claims. In today's legal environment, many companies find themselves being sued for damages for a variety of reasons. The accounting question is this: Should the defendant recognize a liability on the balance sheet or disclose a contingent liability in the footnotes while a lawsuit is outstanding and not yet settled? The answer is that the potential claim should be recorded as a liability only if a payment for damages is probable and the amount can be reasonably estimated. If the potential claim cannot be reasonably estimated or is less than probable but is reasonably possible, it should be described as a contingent liability.

Debt Guarantees. Sometimes a company will guarantee the payment of a debt owed by a supplier, customer, or other company. Usually, the guarantor describes the guarantee in the financial statement footnotes as a contingent liability. However, if it is probable that the original debtor will default, the guarantor needs to record and report the guarantee as a liability.

Other Uncertainties

All companies and other organizations face major uncertainties from future economic events, such as natural disasters and the development of new competing products. If these events do occur, they may destroy the company's assets or drive it out of business. However, these uncertainties are not liabilities because they are future events that are not a result of past transactions. Financial statements are not useful if they include speculation about possible effects of events that have not yet occurred.

Be sure to read the comment by Diana Scott in As a Matter of Opinion. She discusses additional liabilities that companies may need to describe in the future if accounting principles are changed.

As a Matter of Opinion

Diana Scott is a graduate of Wittenberg University. She worked for Price Waterhouse in its national office in New York before joining the FASB staff as a project manager in 1985. After leaving that position in 1991, she joined the management consulting firm of Towers Perrin in Chicago, where she is an accounting and financial consultant in the Technical Services Group.

Over the past several years, accountants have begun to pay much more attention to the potential future payments that businesses may be obligated to make as a result of current operations. A good example involves the promises of employers to pay health care benefits for their retired employees. Prior to the FASB's standard on this topic *(SFAS 106)*, companies generally did not report this obligation except by reporting an expense for actual payments they had already made. The standard requires them to provide information about their obligations and to recognize the expenses for probable future payments.

Are there other obligations that we presently ignore but someday may have to recognize as liabilities? I would not be surprised. One that comes to mind is potential claims from injuries to product users. Some juries have given large awards many years after a product was sold. Another possible liability is the cost of cleaning up toxic wastes discarded before anyone was aware of the danger.

Nobody can say whether these particular examples will eventually result in new liabilities or disclosures. But, I have no doubt that accounting will continue to evolve in response to an increasing emphasis on the obligations of doing business responsibly.

Diana Scott

Progress Check

12-7 A future payment should be reported as a liability on a company's balance sheet if the payment is contingent on a future event that:
   a. Is not probable but is reasonably possible and the amount of the payment cannot be reasonably estimated.
   b. Is probable and the amount of the payment can be reasonably estimated.
   c. Is not probable but the amount of the payment is known.

12-8 Under what circumstances should a future payment be reported in the financial statements as a contingent liability?

Most liabilities arise in situations with little uncertainty. The procedures used to account for these debts are described in the following sections of the chapter. The topics include:

- Payroll liabilities.
- Short-term notes payable.
- Long-term notes payable.
- Lease liabilities.

In addition, we discuss the present value calculations that accountants use when accounting for long-term liabilities and interest expense.

ACCOUNTING FOR KNOWN LIABILITIES

An employer typically incurs several expenses and liabilities as a result of having employees. The expenses and liabilities arise from the salaries or wages earned by employees, from employee benefits, and from payroll taxes levied on the employer. These items are discussed in the next sections. In addition, you can learn more about payroll reports, records, and procedures by studying Appendix C at the end of the book.

PAYROLL LIABILITIES

(LO 3)
Describe payroll expenses and liabilities and prepare journal entries to account for them.

FICA Taxes on Employees

The federal Social Security system provides qualified workers who retire at age 62 with monthly cash payments for the rest of their lives. The retirees also receive *Medicare benefits* beginning at age 65. In addition, the system provides monthly payments to deceased workers' surviving families who qualify for the assistance. These benefits are paid with **FICA taxes** collected under the Federal Insurance Contributions Act. The taxes for retirees and survivors are often called *Social Security taxes* to distinguish them from *Medicare taxes.*

Among other things, the law requires employers to withhold FICA taxes from each employee's salary or wages paid on each payday. The two components of these taxes for Social Security and Medicare are calculated separately. In 1996, the amount withheld from each employee's pay for Social Security was 6.2% of the first $62,700 earned by the employee in the calendar year. The Medicare tax was 1.45% of all wages earned by the employee.

Employers are required to promptly pay the withheld taxes to the Internal Revenue Service. Substantial penalties can be levied against those who fail to turn the withheld taxes over to the IRS on time. Until all these taxes are paid, they are included in the employers' current liabilities.

Employees' Federal Income Tax Withholdings

With very few exceptions, employers must withhold an amount of federal income tax from each employee's paycheck. The amount withheld is determined from tables published by the IRS. The amount depends on the employee's annual earnings rate and the number of *withholding allowances* claimed by the employee. Employees can claim allowances for themselves and their dependents. They also can claim additional allowances if they anticipate major reductions in their taxable income for medical expenses or other deductible items. The income taxes withheld from employees must be paid promptly to the IRS. Until they are paid, withholdings are reported as a current liability on the employer's balance sheet.

Other Withholdings from Wages

In addition to Social Security, Medicare, and income taxes, employers may withhold other amounts from employees' earnings according to their instructions. These withholdings may include amounts for charitable contributions, medical insurance premiums, investment purchases, and union dues. Until they are paid, these withholdings are current liabilities of employers.

Recording Payroll Expenses and Other Withholdings

Employers must accrue the payroll expenses and liabilities at the end of each pay period. As an example, this entry shows a typical entry to accrue the payroll:

Jan.	31	Salaries Expense	2,000.00	
		FICA Taxes Payable		153.00
		Employees' Federal Income Taxes Payable		213.00
		Employees' Medical Insurance Payable		85.00
		Employees' Union Dues Payable		25.00
		Accrued Payroll Payable		1,524.00
		To record the payroll for the pay period ended		
		January 31.		

The debit to Salaries Expense records the fact that the company's employees earned gross salaries of $2,000. The first four credits record liabilities that the employer owes on behalf of its employees for their FICA taxes, income taxes, medical insurance, and union dues. The credit to the Accrued Payroll Payable account records the $1,524 net pay that the employees will receive from the $2,000 that they earned.

When employees are actually paid, another entry (or a series of entries) is required to record the checks actually written and distributed. To record the payments, Accrued Payroll Payable is debited and Cash is credited.

EMPLOYER'S PAYROLL TAXES

In addition to the taxes assessed on the employees, employers must pay other taxes. They include FICA and unemployment taxes.

Employer's FICA Tax

Employers must pay FICA taxes equal in amount to the FICA taxes withheld from their employees. An employer's tax is credited to the same FICA Taxes Payable account used to record the FICA taxes withheld from the employees. The debit is recorded in a Payroll Taxes Expense account.

Federal and State Unemployment Taxes

The federal government participates with the states in a joint federal-state unemployment insurance program. Under this joint program, each state administers its own program. These programs provide unemployment benefits to covered workers. The federal government approves the state programs and pays a portion of their administrative expenses.

The Federal Unemployment Tax (FUTA). Employers are subject to a federal unemployment tax on wages paid to their employees. In 1995, the Federal Unemployment Tax Act (called *FUTA*) required employers to pay a tax of as much as 6.2% of the first $7,000 in salary or wages paid to each employee. However, the federal tax can be reduced by a credit of up to 5.4% for taxes paid to a state program. As a result, the net federal unemployment tax is normally only 0.8%.

State Unemployment Insurance Taxes (SUTA). All states support their unemployment insurance programs by placing a payroll tax on employers. In most states, the basic rate is 5.4% of the first $7,000 paid each employee. However, the employer's experience in creating or avoiding unemployment is described in a **merit rating** assigned by the state. A good rating is based on high stability and allows the employer to pay less than the basic 5.4% rate. A history of high turnover or seasonal hiring and layoffs may cause the employer to pay more.

A favorable merit rating may offer important cash savings. For example, an employer with 100 employees who each earn $7,000 or more per year would save $34,300 annually if it received a merit rating that reduced the rate from 5.4% to 0.5%. It would pay $37,800 at the 5.4% rate, but only $3,500 at the 0.5% rate.

Recording the Employer's Payroll Taxes

The employer's payroll taxes are an additional expense above the salaries earned by the employees. As a result, these taxes are usually recorded in a journal entry separate from the one recording the basic payroll expense and withholding liabilities.

For example, assume that the previously recorded $2,000 salaries expense was earned by employees who have earned less than $7,000 so far in the year. Also, assume that the federal unemployment tax rate was 0.8% and that the state unemployment tax rate was 5.4%.

The FICA portion of the employer's tax expense is $153, which equals 7.65% (6.2% + 1.45%) of the $2,000 gross pay. The state unemployment (SUTA) taxes are $108, which is 5.4% of the $2,000 gross pay. The federal unemployment (FUTA) taxes are $16, which is 0.8% of $2,000. This entry records the employer's payroll tax expense and the related liabilities:

Jan.	31	Payroll Taxes Expense	277.00	
		FICA Taxes Payable		153.00
		State Unemployment Taxes Payable		108.00
		Federal Unemployment Taxes Payable		16.00
		To record payroll taxes.		

EMPLOYEE BENEFITS

In addition to salaries and wages earned by employees and payroll taxes paid by employers, many companies provide a variety of **employee benefits.** For example, an employer may pay all or part of the premiums for medical, dental, life, and disability insurance. Many employers also contribute to pension plans or offer special stock purchase plans for their employees.

By the time that payroll taxes and employee benefits costs are added to the employees' basic earnings, employers often find that their total payroll cost exceeds the employees' gross earnings by 25% or more. The following paragraphs describe two specific employee benefits.

Employer Contributions to Insurance and Pension Plans

The entries that record employee benefit costs are similar to the entries for payroll taxes. Returning to the previous example, suppose that the employer agreed to pay an amount for medical insurance equal to the $85 withheld from the employees' paychecks and to contribute an additional 10% of the employees' $2,000 gross salary to a retirement program. This entry would record these benefits:

Jan.	7	Employee Benefits Expense	285.00	
		Employees' Medical Insurance Payable		85.00
		Employees' Retirement Program Payable		200.00
		To record employee benefits.		

Vacation Pay

Another widely offered benefit is paid vacations. For example, many employees earn 2 weeks' vacation by working 50 weeks. This benefit increases the employer's payroll expenses above their apparent amount because the employees are paid for 50 weeks of work over the 52 weeks in the year. Although the total annual salary is the same, the cost per week worked is greater than the amount paid per week. For example, suppose that an employee is paid $20,800 for 52 weeks of employment but works only 50 weeks. The weekly salary expense to the employer is $416 ($20,800/50 weeks) instead of the $400 paid weekly to the employee ($20,800/52 weeks). The $16 difference between these two amounts is recorded as salary expense and a liability for vacation pay. When the employee actually takes vacation, the employer reduces the vacation pay liability and does not record additional expense.

Progress Check

12-9   Midtown Repairs pays its one employee $3,000 per month. The company's net FUTA rate is 0.8% on the first $7,000 earned by the employee, the SUTA rate is 4.0% on the first $7,000, the Social Security tax rate is 6.2% of the first $61,200, and the Medicare tax rate is 1.45% of all amounts earned by the employee. The entry to record the company's payroll taxes for March would include a total expense of: *(a)* $277.50; *(b)* $293.50; *(c)* $373.50; *(d)* $1,120.50; *(e)* $4,093.20.

12-10   Indicate whether the employer or the employee pays each of these taxes: *(a)* FICA taxes; *(b)* FUTA taxes; *(c)* SUTA taxes; and *(d)* Withheld income taxes.

SHORT-TERM NOTES PAYABLE

LO 4
Describe how accountants record and report short-term notes payable.

A short-term note payable may be created when a company purchases merchandise on credit and then extends the credit period by signing a note that replaces the account. Short-term notes payable also arise when money is borrowed from a bank.

Note Given to Extend a Credit Period

In some cases, a company may create a note payable to replace an account payable. For example, a creditor may ask that an interest-bearing note be substituted for an account that does not bear interest. In other situations, the borrower's weak financial condition may encourage the creditor to obtain a note and close the account to ensure that additional credit sales are not made to this customer.

For example, assume that on August 23, Broke Company asks to extend its past-due $600 account payable to Smart Company. After some negotiations, Smart agrees to accept $100 cash and a 60-day, 12%, $500 note payable to replace the account payable. The accountant for Broke records the substitution with this entry:

Aug.	23	Accounts Payable—Smart Company	600.00	
		Cash		100.00
		Notes Payable		500.00
		Paid $100 cash and gave a 60-day, 12% note to extend		
		the due date on the account.		

Notice that signing the note does not pay off the debt. Instead, the debt's form is merely changed from an account to a note payable. Smart Company may prefer to have the note because it earns interest and because it provides reliable documentation of the debt's existence, term, and amount.

When the note becomes due, Broke will pay the note and interest by giving Smart a check for $510 and then record the payment with this entry:

Oct.	22	Notes Payable	500.00	
		Interest Expense	10.00	
		Cash		510.00
		Paid note with interest ($500 × 12% × 60/360).		

Note that the interest expense is calculated by multiplying the principal of the note by the original rate for the fraction of the year the note was outstanding.

Borrowing from a Bank

When making a loan, a bank typically requires the borrower to sign a promissory note. When the note matures, the borrower pays back a larger amount. The difference between the two amounts is *interest*. In many situations, the note states that the signer of the note promises to pay the *principal* (the amount borrowed) plus the interest. If so, the *face value* of the note equals the principal.

In other situations, the bank may have the borrower sign a note with a face value that includes both the principal and the interest. In these cases, the signer of the note borrows less than the note's face value. The difference between the borrowed amount and the note's face value is interest. Because the borrowed amount is less than the face value, the difference is sometimes called the **discount on note payable.** To illustrate these two kinds of loans, assume that Robin Goode borrows $2,000 from a bank on behalf of the Goode Company. The loan is made on September 30 and will be repaid in 60 days. It has a 12% annual interest rate.

Face Value Equals the Amount Borrowed. Suppose that the bank requires Goode to sign a loan with a face value equal to the borrowed $2,000. If so, the note will include the following phrase: "I promise to pay $2,000 plus interest at 12% 60 days after September 30." The Goode Company records the increase in cash and the new liability with this entry:

Sept.	30	Cash	2,000.00	
		Notes Payable		2,000.00
		Borrowed cash with a 60-day, 12% note.		

When the note and interest are paid 60 days later, Goode records the event with this entry:

Nov.	29	Notes Payable	2,000.00	
		Interest Expense	40.00	
		Cash		2,040.00
		Paid note with interest ($2,000 × 12% × 60/360).		

Face Value Equals the Amount Borrowed and the Interest. If Goode's bank wishes, it may draw up a note that includes the 12% interest in its face value. If so, the note contains the following promise: "I promise to pay $2,040 60 days after September 30." Notice that the note does not refer to the rate that was used to compute the $40 of interest included in the $2,040 face value. In all other respects, the note is exactly the same. However, the lack of a stated rate of interest sometimes causes an agreement like this one to be called a **noninterest-bearing note.** In fact, this widely used term is not precise because the note does bear interest, which is included in the face value.

When the face value of the note includes principal and interest, Goode could record the debt with an entry exactly like the previous September 30 entry. However, the more typical practice is to credit Notes Payable for the face value of the note and record the discount in a contra account. The following entry takes this approach:

Sept.	30	Cash	2,000.00	
		Discount on Notes Payable	40.00	
		Notes Payable		2,040.00
		Borrowed cash with a 60-day, 12% note		
		(Discount = $2,000 × 12% × 60/360).		

The Discount on Notes Payable account is contra to the Notes Payable account. If a balance sheet is prepared on September 30, the $40 discount is subtracted from the $2,040 balance in the Notes Payable account to reflect the $2,000 net amount borrowed.

When the note matures 60 days later on November 29, the entry to record Goode's $2,040 payment to the bank is:

Nov.	29	Notes Payable	2,040.00	
		Interest Expense	40.00	
		Cash		2,040.00
		Discount on Notes Payable		40.00
		Paid note with interest.		

If the end of an accounting period falls between the signing of a note payable and its maturity date, the *matching principle* requires the accountant to record the accrued but unpaid interest on the note. For example, suppose that Robin Goode borrowed $2,000 on December 16, 19X1, instead of September 30. The 60-day note matures on February 14, 19X2. Because the company's fiscal year ends on December 31, the accountant records interest expense for the 15 days in December. The entries depend on the form of the note.

ADJUSTMENTS AT THE END OF THE REPORTING PERIOD

Face Value Equals the Amount Borrowed. If the note's face value equals the amount borrowed, the accrued interest is charged to expense and credited to an Interest Payable account. To illustrate, assume that the $2,000 note signed by Goode on December 16 bears 12% interest. Because 15 out of the 60 days covered by the note have elapsed by December 31, one-fourth (15 days/60 days) of the $40 total interest is an expense of 19X1. Goode records this expense with the following adjusting entry at the end of 19X1:

19X1				
Dec.	31	Interest Expense	10.00	
		Interest Payable		10.00
		To record accrued interest on note payable		
		($2,000 × 12% × 15/360).		

When the note matures on February 14, Goode records this entry:

19X2				
Feb.	14	Interest Expense ($2,000 × 12% × 45/360)	30.00	
		Interest Payable	10.00	
		Notes Payable	2,000.00	
		Cash		2,040.00
		Paid note with interest.		

The entry recognizes the 45 days of interest expense for 19X2 and removes the balances of the two liability accounts.

Face Value Equals the Amount Borrowed and the Interest. Now assume that the face value of the note includes the interest. For example, assume that Goode signed a $2,040 noninterest-bearing note on December 15. In recording the note, Goode credited the $2,040 face value of the note to Notes Payable and debited the $40 discount to a contra account. This adjusting entry is needed to record the accrual of 15 days of interest at the end of 19X1:

Dec.	31	Interest Expense	10.00	
		Discount on Notes Payable		10.00
		To record accrued interest on note payable		
		($2,000 × 12% × 15/360).		

Observe that the accrued interest is not credited to Interest Payable. Instead, the entry reduces the balance of the contra account from $40 to $30. As a result, it increases the net liability to $2,010 ($2,040 − $30).

When the note matures, the following entry accrues the interest expense for the last 45 days of the note and records its payment:

19X2					
Feb.	14	Interest Expense	30.00		
		Notes Payable	2,040.00		
		Discount on Notes Payable		30.00	
		Cash		2,040.00	
		Paid note with interest ($2,000 × 12% × 45/360).			

Progress Check

12-11   Why would a creditor want a past-due account to be replaced by a note?

12-12   A company borrows money for six months by signing a $1,050 note payable. In recording the transaction, the company's bookkeeper correctly debited $50 to Discount on Notes Payable. How much was borrowed? What annual rate of interest was charged?

LONG-TERM LIABILITIES

In addition to current liabilities, companies often have liabilities that are repaid after one year (or a longer operating cycle). These *long-term liabilities* can arise when money is borrowed from a bank or when a note is issued to buy an asset. A long-term liability also may be created when a company enters into a multiyear lease agreement that is similar to buying the asset. Each of these liability arrangements is described in this chapter. In addition, large companies often borrow money by issuing *bonds* to a number of creditors. These securities are usually long-term liabilities that exist as long as 30 years or more. Accounting for bonds is described in Chapter 13.

Because of the extended lives of long-term liabilities, accounting for them is often more complicated than accounting for short-term liabilities. In particular, the accountant may need to apply present value techniques to measure a long-term liability when it is created and to assign interest expense to each of the years in the liability's life.

PRESENT VALUE CONCEPTS

LO 5

Explain and calculate the present value of an amount to be paid at a future date and the present value of a series of equal amounts to be paid at future dates.

Information based on the concept of **present value** enters into many financing and investing decisions. It also enters into accounting for liabilities resulting from those decisions. Therefore, an understanding of present value is important for all business students.

Because this chapter focuses on liabilities, we explain present value concepts by referring to future cash outflows, payables, and interest expense. However, the same concepts also apply to future cash inflows, receivables, and interest income. The most fundamental present value concept is based on the idea that an amount of cash to be paid (or received) in the future has less value now than the same amount of cash to be paid (or received) today.

For example, $1 to be paid one year from now has a present value that is less than $1. To see why this is true, assume that $0.9259 is borrowed for one year at 8% interest. The amount of interest that will be incurred is $0.9259 × 8% = $0.0741. When the $0.0741 interest is added to the $0.9259, the sum equals the $1 payment that is necessary to repay the debt with interest, as shown here:

Amount borrowed	$0.9259
Interest for one year at 8%	0.0741
Total debt after one year	$1.0000

In this example, the $0.9259 borrowed amount is the present value of the $1 future payment. To state the concept more generally, a borrowed amount is the present value of a future payment if the borrowed amount generates interest at a given rate and the future payment will repay the debt with interest.[5]

To carry this example of present value further, assume that the $1 payment is to be made after two years and the 8% interest is to be compounded annually. Compounding means that interest during the second period is based on the sum of the amount borrowed plus the interest accrued during the first period. In other words, the second period's interest is 8% multiplied by the sum of the original amount borrowed plus the interest earned during the first period.

In this example, where $1 is to be paid back after two years, the amount that can be borrowed (the present value) is $0.8573. The following calculation shows why $0.8573 is the present value:

Amount borrowed during first year	$0.8573
Interest during first year ($0.8573 × 8%)	0.0686
Amount borrowed during second year	$0.9259
Interest during second year ($0.9259 × 8%) . .	0.0741
Total debt after one year	$1.0000

Notice that the first year's interest is added to the principal amount borrowed so that the second year's interest is based on $0.9259.[6]

Present Value Tables

The present value of $1 to be paid after a number of periods in the future can be calculated by using this formula: $1/(1 + i)^n$. The symbol i in the equation is the interest rate per period and n is the number of periods until the future payment must be made. For example, the present value of $1 to be paid after two periods at 8% is $1/(1.08)^2$, which equals $0.8573.

Although you can use this formula to find present values, other techniques are available. For example, many electronic calculators are preprogrammed to find present values. You can also use a **present value table** that shows present values computed with the formula at various interest rates for different time periods. In fact, many students find it helpful to learn how to make the calculations with the tables, and then move on to use calculators when they become comfortable with present value concepts.

Table 12–1 shows present values of a future payment of $1 for up to 10 periods at five different interest rates. The present values in the table have been rounded to four decimal places.[7] (This table is taken from a larger and more complete table in Appendix D at the end of the book.)

---

[5]Exactly the same analysis applies to an investment. If $0.9259 is invested at 8%, it will generate $0.0741 interest revenue in one year, thereby amounting to a $1 receipt of principal and interest.

[6]Benjamin Franklin is said to have described compounding with this expression: "The money money makes makes more money."

[7]Four decimal places are sufficient for the applications described in this book. Other situations may require more precision.

Table 12-1
Present Value of $1

Periods	Rate				
	2%	4%	6%	8%	10%
1	0.9804	0.9615	0.9434	0.9259	0.9091
2	0.9612	0.9246	0.8900	0.8573	0.8264
3	0.9423	0.8890	0.8396	0.7938	0.7513
4	0.9238	0.8548	0.7921	0.7350	0.6830
5	0.9057	0.8219	0.7473	0.6806	0.6209
6	0.8880	0.7903	0.7050	0.6302	0.5645
7	0.8706	0.7599	0.6651	0.5835	0.5132
8	0.8535	0.7307	0.6274	0.5403	0.4665
9	0.8368	0.7026	0.5919	0.5002	0.4241
10	0.8203	0.6756	0.5584	0.4632	0.3855

To use this table, notice that the first value in the 8% column in Table 12–1 is 0.9259. We used this value in the previous section as the present value of $1 at 8%. Go down one row in the same 8% column to find the present value of $1 discounted at 8% for two years. You should find the value of 0.8573 that we used in the second example. This value means that $0.8573 is the present value of the obligation to pay $1 after two periods, discounted at 8% per period.

Using a Present Value Table

To demonstrate how an accountant can measure a liability by using a present value table like Table 12–1, assume that a company plans to borrow cash and then repay it as follows:

To be paid back after one year	$ 2,000
To be paid back after two years	3,000
To be paid back after three years	5,000
Total to be paid back	$10,000

If the company will have to pay 10% interest on this loan, how much will it be able to borrow? The answer is that it can borrow the present value of the three future payments, discounted at 10%. This is calculated in Illustration 12–1 with values from Table 12–1. The illustration shows that the company can borrow $8,054 at 10% in exchange for its promise to make the three payments at the scheduled dates.

Present Values of Annuities

The $8,054 present value of the loan in Illustration 12–1 is the sum of the present values of the three different payments. If the expected cash flows for a liability are not equal, their combined present value must be found by calculating each of their individual present values. In other cases, a loan may create an **annuity;** this is a series of equal payments occurring at equal time intervals. The present value of an annuity can be found with fewer calculations.

For example, suppose that a company can repay a 6% loan by making a $5,000 payment at the end of each year for the next four years. The amount to be borrowed under this loan equals the present value of the four payments discounted at 6%. The present value is calculated in Illustration 12–2 by multiplying each payment by the appropriate value from Table 12–1. The illustration shows that the company can borrow $17,326 under these terms.

Because the series of $5,000 payments is an annuity, the accountant can determine the present value with either of two shortcuts. As shown in the third column of Illustration 12–2, the total of the present values of $1 at 6% for 1 through 4 periods

Years from Now	Expected Payments	Present Value of $1 at 10%	Present Value of Expected Payments
1	$2,000	0.9091	$1,818
2	3,000	0.8264	2,479
3	5,000	0.7513	3,757
Total present value of the payments . . .			$8,054

Illustration 12-1
Finding the Present Value of a Series of Unequal Payments

Years from Now	Expected Payments	Present Value of $1 at 6%	Present Value of Expected Payments
1	$5,000	0.9434	$ 4,717
2	5,000	0.8900	4,450
3	5,000	0.8396	4,198
4	5,000	0.7921	3,961
Total		3.4651	$17,326

Illustration 12-2
Finding the Present Value of a Series of Equal Payments (an Annuity) by Discounting Each Payment

equals 3.4651. One shortcut multiplies this total of 3.4651 by the $5,000 annual payment to get the combined present value of $17,326. This shortcut requires only one multiplication instead of four.

The second shortcut uses an *annuity table* such as Table 12–2.[8] (Table 12–2 is taken from a more complete table in Appendix D at the end of the book.) Instead of having to take the sum of the individual present values from Table 12–1, you can go directly to the annuity table to find the present (table) value that relates to a specific number of payments and a specific interest rate. Then, you multiply this table value by the amount of the payment to find the present value of all the payments in the annuity.

To continue the example, the second shortcut proceeds as follows: Enter Table 12–2 on the row for four payments and go across until you reach the column for 6%, where we find the value of 3.4651. This amount equals the present value of an annuity with four payments of $1, discounted at 6%. Then, multiply 3.4651 times $5,000 to get the $17,326 present value of the annuity.

In the previous examples, the interest rates were applied to periods of one year. However, in many situations, interest is compounded over shorter periods. For example, the interest rate on bonds is usually described as an annual rate but the interest is actually paid every six months. As a result, the present value of the interest payments to be received from these bonds must be based on interest periods that are six months long.

COMPOUNDING PERIODS SHORTER THAN A YEAR

---

[8]The formula for finding the table values is: $\dfrac{1 - \dfrac{1}{(1 + i)^n}}{i}$

However, the present values in Table 12–2 can be found by adding the values of the individual payments in Table 12–1. (Because the tables show only four decimal places, there are some ±0.0001 rounding differences between them.)

Table 12–2
Present Value of
an Annuity of $1

Payments	Rate				
	2%	**4%**	**6%**	**8%**	**10%**
1	0.9804	0.9615	0.9434	0.9259	0.9091
2	1.9416	1.8861	1.8334	1.7833	1.7355
3	2.8839	2.7751	2.6730	2.5771	2.4869
4	3.8077	3.6299	3.4651	3.3121	3.1699
5	4.7135	4.4518	4.2124	3.9927	3.7908
6	5.6014	5.2421	4.9173	4.6229	4.3553
7	6.4720	6.0021	5.5824	5.2064	4.8684
8	7.3255	6.7327	6.2098	5.7466	5.3349
9	8.1622	7.4353	6.8017	6.2469	5.7590
10	8.9826	8.1109	7.3601	6.7101	6.1446

To illustrate a calculation based on six-month interest periods, suppose that a borrower wants to know the present value of a series of 10 $4,000 semiannual payments to be made over five years. These payments are to be discounted with an *annual* interest rate of 8%. Although the interest rate is described as an annual rate of 8%, it is actually a rate of 4% per six-month interest period. To find the present value of the series of $4,000 payments, enter Table 12–2 on row 10 and go across to the 4% column. The table value is 8.1109, and the present value of the annuity is $32,444 (8.1109 × $4,000).

Study Appendix D at the end of the book to learn more about present value concepts. The appendix includes more complete present value tables and provides future value tables. It also includes exercises that will help you understand discounting.

Progress Check

12-13 A company enters into an agreement to make four annual payments of $1,000 each, starting one year from now. The annual interest rate is 8%. The present value of these four payments is: *(a)* $2,923; *(b)* $2,940; *(c)* $3,312; *(d)* $4,000; *(e)* $6,733.

12-14 Suppose that a company has an option to pay either $10,000 after one year or $5,000 after six months and another $5,000 after one year. Which choice always has the smaller present value?

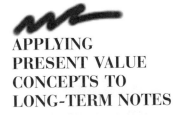

APPLYING PRESENT VALUE CONCEPTS TO LONG-TERM NOTES

LO 6
Describe how accountants use present value concepts in accounting for long-term notes and how liabilities may result from leasing assets.

Earlier in the chapter, we stated that accountants use present value concepts to measure liabilities and to assign or allocate interest expense to each reporting period in a liability's life. In doing this, the liability is initially measured as the present value of the future payments. Over the life of the note, the amount of interest allocated to each period equals the product of multiplying the original interest rate by the balance of the liability at the beginning of the period. The balance at any point in time equals the original balance plus any allocated interest less any payments.[9]

Interest-Bearing Notes that Require a Single Payment

Suppose that a company buys equipment on January 2 with a fair market value of $45,000 by issuing an 8%, three-year note. If the 8% interest is at the prevailing market rate, the face value of the note should be $45,000. The buyer records the purchase with this entry:

---

[9]The liability's balance at any date also equals the present value of all remaining future payments, discounted at the original interest rate.

Illustration 12-3 Allocation of Interest on a Note with All Interest Paid at Maturity

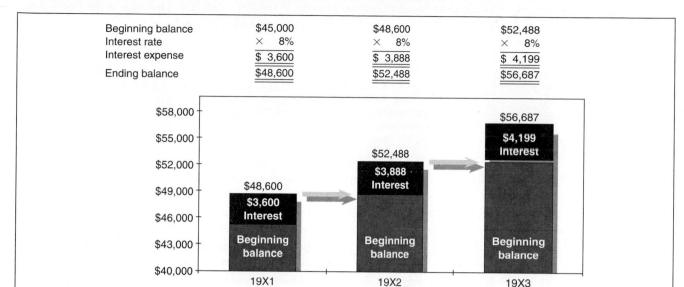

Beginning balance	$45,000	$48,600	$52,488
Interest rate	× 8%	× 8%	× 8%
Interest expense	$ 3,600	$ 3,888	$ 4,199
Ending balance	$48,600	$52,488	$56,687

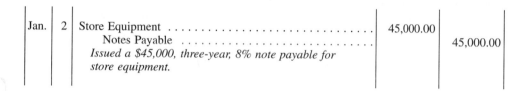

Jan.	2	Store Equipment	45,000.00	
		Notes Payable		45,000.00
		Issued a $45,000, three-year, 8% note payable for		
		store equipment.		

Over the life of the note, the issuer reports annual interest expense equal to the original interest rate times each year's beginning balance for the liability. Illustration 12–3 shows the interest allocation. Note that the interest is allocated by multiplying each year's beginning balance by the original 8% interest rate. Then, the interest is added to the beginning balance to find the ending balance, which then becomes the next year's beginning balance. Because the balance grows through compounding, the amount of interest allocated to each year increases over the life of the note. The final ending balance of $56,687 equals the original $45,000 borrowed plus the total interest of $11,687.

Noninterest-Bearing Notes

Earlier in the chapter, we described so-called noninterest-bearing notes, which include the interest in their initial face values. When a noninterest-bearing note is used to purchase an asset, the note's face value is greater than the asset's fair value. As a result, the asset and the note should be recorded at the asset's fair value or at the note's fair value, whichever is more clearly determinable.[10] The note's fair value can be estimated by finding the present value of its payments discounted at the market interest rate when it was issued.

For example, suppose that Harborg Company buys machinery on January 2, 19X1, by issuing a noninterest-bearing, five-year, $10,000 note payable. The company's managers conclude that their estimate of the asset's fair value is less reliable than is the current 10% interest rate available to the company.

When the note is issued, its fair value equals the present value of the $10,000 payment due after five years, discounted at 10%. Table 12–1 shows us that the present

---

[10]FASB, *Accounting Standards—Current Text* (Norwalk, CT, 1995), sec. I69.105. First published as *APB Opinion No. 21*, par. 12.

value of 1 discounted at 10% for five years is 0.6209. Thus, the present (fair) value of the note is calculated as $10,000 \times 0.6209 = $6,209$. This also is the implied fair value of the asset. The following entry records the purchase:

19X1				
Jan.	2	Machinery	6,209.00	
		Discount on Notes Payable	3,791.00	
		Long-Term Notes Payable		10,000.00
		Exchanged a five-year noninterest-bearing note for a machine.		

By recording the maturity value in one account and the discount in a contra account, the entry follows the typical approach of recording a noninterest-bearing note. In the entry, the $3,791 debit to Discount on Notes Payable equals the total amount of interest that must be allocated to the five years in the note's life.

In Illustration 12–4, we calculate each year's interest and show the effect of the allocation on the discount and the net liability. The net liability balance grows over the five years until it reaches the maturity amount of $10,000. Note also that the discount balance decreases to $0 after five years. Because the discount is gradually reduced to zero, this process is often referred to as *amortizing the discount.*

Notice that the process of calculating each year's interest is the same as it was in the previous discussion of interest-bearing notes that require a single payment. The net liability balance at the beginning of each year is multiplied by the 10% interest rate to determine the interest for the year.

The first year's interest and reduction of the discount are recorded when the accountant makes this year-end adjusting entry:

19X1				
Dec.	31	Interest Expense	621.00	
		Discount on Notes Payable		621.00
		To record interest expense accrued on a noninterest-bearing note.		

Similar entries are recorded at the end of each year until the balance of the discount account equals $0 and the net liability balance equals $10,000.

When the note matures on January 2, 19X6, the issuer records the payment with this entry:

19X6				
Jan.	2	Long-Term Notes Payable	10,000.00	
		Cash		10,000.00
		Paid noninterest-bearing note.		

LIABILITIES FROM LEASING

As an alternative to purchasing property, companies can lease it by agreeing to make a series of rental payments to the property owner, who is called the *lessor.* Because a lease gives the property's user (called the *lessee*) exclusive control over the property's usefulness, the lessee can use it to earn revenues. In addition, a lease creates a liability if it has essentially the same effect as purchasing the asset on credit.

According to the generally accepted accounting principles described in *Statement of Financial Accounting Standards No. 13,* the lessee's financial statements must report a leased asset and a lease liability if the lease qualifies as a capital lease. The essence of a **capital lease** is that the lease agreement gives the lessee the risks and benefits normally associated with ownership. In general, a capital lease covers a number of years and creates a long-term liability that is paid off with a series of equal

Illustration 12-4 Allocating Interest Expense over the Life of a Noninterest-bearing Note

	19X1	19X2	19X3	19X4	19X5
Beginning balance	$6,209	$6,830	$7,513	$8,264	$ 9,090
Interest rate	× 10%	× 10%	× 10%	× 10%	× 10%
Interest expense	$ 621	$ 683	$ 751	$ 826	$ 910*
Ending balance	$6,830	$7,513	$8,264	$9,090	$10,000

*Adjusted for rounding.

payments. For example, **Federal Express Corporation** reported that its capital leases for equipment and facilities covered assets with a cost of $513 million and a book value of $183 million as of May 31, 1994. The leases also involved liabilities of $199 million.

When a capital lease is created, the lessee recognizes a leased asset and depreciates it over its useful life. The lessee also recognizes a lease liability and allocates interest expense to the years in the lease. The interest allocation process is the same as we have seen for notes payable.

Leases that are not capital leases are called **operating leases.** With an operating lease, the lessee does not report the lease as an asset. The lessee's income statement reports rent expense and does not report either interest or depreciation expense.

Intermediate accounting textbooks describe more details about the characteristics of leases that cause them to be accounted for as capital or operating. They also describe financial accounting practices used by the lessor and lessee for capital leases.

Progress Check

12-15   On January 1, 19X1, Fairview Co. signed a $6,000 three-year note payable bearing 6% annual interest. The original principal and all interest are to be paid on December 31, 19X3. The interest will compound every year. How much interest should be allocated to 19X2? *(a)* $0; *(b)* $360; *(c)* $381.60; *(d)* $404.50.

12-16   Suppose that a company promises to pay a lender $4,000 at the end of four years. If the annual interest rate is 8% and the interest is included in the $4,000, what is the amount that the company originally borrowed?

12-17   Which one of the following requires the lessee to record a liability? *(a)* Operating lease; *(b)* Lessor; *(c)* Contingent liability; *(d)* Capital lease.

Chapter 12

USING THE INFORMATION— TIMES FIXED INTEREST CHARGES EARNED

LO 7

Calculate the number of times a company earns its fixed interest charges and describe what it reveals about a company's situation.

A company incurs interest expense when it issues notes or bonds and when it enters into capital leases. Many of these liabilities are long-term obligations that are likely to remain outstanding for a substantial period of time even if the company experiences a decline in sales. As a result, interest expense is often viewed as a fixed cost. That is, the amount of interest is not likely to fluctuate much as a result of changes in sales volume.

Although fixed costs can be advantageous when a company is growing, they create the risk that the company might not be able to pay them if sales decline. The following example shows a company's results for the current year and two possible outcomes for the next year:

	Current Year	Next Year	
		If Sales Increase	If Sales Decrease
Sales	$600,000	$900,000	$300,000
Expenses (75% of sales)	450,000	675,000	225,000
Income before interest	$150,000	$225,000	$ 75,000
Interest expense (fixed)	60,000	60,000	60,000
Net income	$ 90,000	$165,000	$ 15,000

As we show in the table, expenses other than interest are projected to stay at 75% of sales. In contrast, the interest is expected to remain at $60,000 per year. Note in the second column that the company's income would nearly double if its sales increased by 50%. However, the company's profits would fall drastically if the sales decreased by 50%. These numbers show that a company's risk is affected by the amount of fixed interest charges that it incurs each year.

The risk created by these fixed expenses can be described numerically with the **times fixed interest charges earned** ratio. You can use the following formula to find the ratio:

$$\text{Times fixed interest charges earned} = \frac{\text{Income before interest}}{\text{Interest expense}}$$

For this company's current year, the income before interest is $150,000. Therefore, the ratio is $150,000/$60,000, which equals 2.5 times. This result suggests that the company faces a relatively low degree of risk. Its sales would have to go down by a large amount before the company would not be able to cover its interest expenses. This condition should provide comfort to the company's creditors and its owners.

Care must be taken in calculating the times fixed interest charges earned ratio for a corporation. Because interest is deducted in determining taxable income, the numerator for a corporation can be expressed as follows:

Income before interest = Net income + Interest expense + Income taxes expense

The times fixed interest charges earned ratio is best interpreted in light of information about the variability of the company's net income before interest. If this amount is stable from year to year or is growing, the company can afford to take on some of the risk created by borrowing. However, if the company's income before interest varies greatly from year to year, fixed interest charges can increase the risk that the owner will not earn a return or that the company will be unable to pay the interest.

Progress Check

12-18 The times fixed interest charges earned ratio:
   a. Equals interest expense divided by net income.
   b. Takes on a larger value as the amount of fixed interest charges gets larger.
   c. Is best interpreted in light of information about the variability of the company's net income before interest.

12-19 Two companies each have net income after interest of $100,000. First Company has fixed interest charges of $200,000 and Second Company has fixed interest charges of $40,000. Which one is in a more risky situation in terms of being affected by a drop in sales?

SUMMARY OF THE CHAPTER IN TERMS OF LEARNING OBJECTIVES

LO 1. Define liabilities, explain the difference between current and long-term liabilities, and describe the uncertainties related to some liabilities. Liabilities are probable future payments of assets or services that an entity is presently obligated to make as a result of past events. Current liabilities are due within one year or one operating cycle, whichever is longer. All other liabilities are long-term liabilities. Potential uncertainties about a liability include the identity of the creditor, the due date, and the amount to be paid.

LO 2. Describe how accountants record and report estimated liabilities such as warranties and income taxes and how they report contingent liabilities. If an uncertain future payment depends on a probable future event and the amount can be reasonably estimated, the payment should be reported as a liability. The future payment must be described as a contingent liability if *(a)* the future event is reasonably possible but not probable, or *(b)* the event is probable but the amount of the payment cannot be reasonably estimated.

Liabilities for warranties and income taxes are recorded with estimated amounts to be paid. This practice recognizes the expenses in the time period that they are incurred. Deferred income tax liabilities are recognized if temporary differences between GAAP and tax rules result in recording more income tax expense than the amount to be currently paid.

LO 3. Describe payroll expenses and liabilities and prepare journal entries to account for them. An employer's payroll expenses include gross earnings of the employees, additional employee benefits, and payroll taxes levied against the employer. Payroll liabilities include the net pay of employees, amounts withheld from the employees' wages, employee benefits, and the employer's payroll taxes. Payroll taxes are assessed for Social Security, Medicare, and unemployment programs.

LO 4. Describe how accountants record and report short-term notes payable. Short-term notes payable may be interest-bearing, in which case the face value of the note equals the amount borrowed and the note specifies a rate of interest to be paid until maturity. Noninterest-bearing notes include interest in their face value; thus, the face value equals the amount to be paid when the note matures.

LO 5. Explain and calculate the present value of an amount to be paid at a future date and the present value of a series of equal amounts to be paid at future dates. The primary present value concept is that today's value of an amount of cash to be paid or received in the future is less than today's value of the same amount of cash to be paid or received today. Another present value concept is that interest is compounded, which means that the interest is added to the balance and used to determine interest for succeeding periods. An annuity is a series of equal payments occurring at equal time intervals.

LO 6. Describe how accountants use present value concepts in accounting for long-term notes and how liabilities may result from leasing assets. Accountants may use present value concepts to determine the fair value of assets purchased in return for issuing debt. They also use present value concepts to allocate interest expense among the periods in a note's life by multiplying the note's beginning-of-period balance by the original interest rate. Noninterest-bearing notes are normally recorded with a discount account that is contra to the liability account. The balance of the discount account is amortized in the process of recognizing interest expense over the note's life.

Leases are an alternative to purchases as a means of gaining the use of assets. Capital leases give the lessee essentially the same risks and potential rewards as ownership. As a result, the leases and related lease obligations are recorded as assets and liabilities. Other leases, which are called operating leases, involve recording rent expense as the asset is used.

LO 7. Calculate the number of times a company earns its fixed interest charges and describe what it reveals about a company's situation. Times fixed interest charges earned is calculated by dividing a company's net income before interest by the amount of fixed interest charges incurred. This ratio describes the cushion that exists to protect the company's ability to pay interest and earn a profit for its owners against declines in its sales.

DEMONSTRATION PROBLEM

The following series of transactions and other events took place at the Kern Company during its calendar reporting year. Describe their effects on the financial statements by presenting the journal entries described in each situation.

a.   Throughout September 19X1, Kern sold $140,000 of merchandise that was covered by a 180-day warranty. Prior experience shows that the costs of fulfilling the warranty will equal 5% of the sales revenue. Calculate September's warranty expense and the increase in the warranty liability and show how it would be recorded with a September 30 adjusting entry. Also show the journal entry that would be made on October 8 to record an expenditure of $300 cash to provide warranty service on an item sold in September.

b.   On October 12, Kern arranged with a supplier to replace an overdue $10,000 account payable by paying $2,500 cash and signing a note for the remainder. The note matured in 90 days and had a 12% interest rate. Show the entries that would be recorded on October 12, December 31, and January 10, 19X2 (when the note matures).

c.   Kern acquired a machine on December 1 by giving a $60,000 noninterest-bearing note due in one year. The market rate of interest for this type of debt was 10%. Show the entries that would be made when the note is created as of December 31, 19X1, and at maturity on December 1, 19X2.

Planning the Solution

•   For *(a)*, compute the warranty expense for September and record it with an estimated liability. Record the October expenditure as a decrease in the liability.

•   For *(b)*, eliminate the liability for the account payable and create the liability for the note payable. Calculate the interest expense for the 80 days that the note is outstanding in 19X1 and record it as an additional liability. Record the payment of the note, being sure to include the interest for the 10 days in 19X2.

•   For *(c)*, measure the cost of the machinery by finding the present value of the $60,000 cash expected to be paid when the note matures. Record the note at its face value and use a contra-liability account to record the discount. Accrue 30 days' interest at December 31 by reducing the discount account. At maturity, the journal entry should record additional interest expense for 19X2, eliminate the note payable account balance, and eliminate the discount account balance.

Solution to Demonstration Problem

a.   Warranty expense = 5% × $140,000 = $7,000

Sept.	30	Warranty Expense	7,000.00	
		Estimated Warranty Liability		7,000.00
		To record warranty expense and liability at 5% of sales for the month.		
Oct.	8	Estimated Warranty Liability	300.00	
		Cash		300.00
		To record the cost of the warranty service.		

b. Interest expense for 19X1 = 12% × $7,500 × 80/360 = $200
    Interest expense for 19X2 = 12% × $7,500 × 10/360 = $25

Oct.	12	Accounts Payable	10,000.00	
		Notes Payable		7,500.00
		Cash		2,500.00
		Paid $2,500 cash and gave a 90-day, 12% note		
		to extend the due date on the account.		
Dec.	31	Interest Expense	200.00	
		Interest Payable		200.00
		To accrue interest on note payable.		
Jan.	10	Interest Expense	25.00	
		Interest Payable	200.00	
		Notes Payable	7,500.00	
		Cash		7,725.00
		Paid note with interest, including accrued		
		interest payable.		

c. Cost of the asset = Present value of the note
    Present value of the note = $60,000 × Table 12–1 value for $n = 1$ and $i = 10\%$
    Present value of the note = $60,000 × 0.9091 = $54,546
    Discount on the note = $60,000 − $54,546 = $5,454

Dec.	1	Machinery	54,546.00	
		Discount on Notes Payable	5,454.00	
		Notes Payable		60,000.00
		Exchanged a one-year, noninterest-bearing note		
		for a machine.		

Interest expense for 19X1 = 10% × $54,546 × 30/360 = $455
Interest expense for 19X2 = $5,454 − $455 = $4,999

Dec.	31	Interest Expense	455.00	
		Discount on Notes Payable		455.00
		To accrue interest on noninterest-bearing		
		note payable.		
19X2				
Dec.	1	Interest Expense	4,999.00	
		Notes Payable	60,000.00	
		Cash		60,000.00
		Discount on Notes Payable		4,999.00
		Paid noninterest-bearing note payable.		

GLOSSARY

Annuity a series of equal payments occurring at equal time intervals. p. 428

Capital lease a lease that gives the lessee the risks and benefits normally associated with ownership. p. 432

Deferred income tax liability payments of income taxes that are deferred until future years because of temporary differences between GAAP and tax rules. p. 416

Discount on note payable the difference between the face value of a noninterest-bearing note payable and the amount borrowed; represents interest that will be paid on the note over its life. p. 424

Employee benefits additional compensation paid to or on behalf of employees, such as premiums for medical, dental, life, and disability insurance, contributions to pension plans, and vacations. p. 422

Estimated liability an obligation that is reported as a liability even though the amount to be paid is uncertain. p. 414

FICA taxes taxes assessed on both employers and employees under the Federal Insurance Contributions Act; these taxes fund Social Security and Medicare programs. p. 420

Merit rating a rating assigned to an employer by a state according to the employer's past record for creating or not creating unemployment; a higher rating produces a lower unemployment tax rate. p. 421

Noninterest-bearing note a note that does not have a stated rate of interest; the interest is included in the face value of the note. p. 424

Operating lease a lease that is not a capital lease. p. 433

Present value the amount that can be invested (borrowed) at a given interest rate to generate a total future investment (debt) that will equal the amount of a specified future receipt (payment). p. 426

Present value table a table that shows the present values of an amount to be received when discounted at various interest rates for various periods of time, or the present values of a series of equal payments to be received for a varying number of periods when discounted at various interest rates. p. 427

Times fixed interest charges earned the ratio of a company's income before interest divided by the amount of interest charges; used to evaluate the risk of being committed to make interest payments when income varies. p. 434

Warranty an agreement that obligates the seller or manufacturer to repair or replace a product that fails to perform properly within a specified period. p. 414

QUESTIONS

1. What is the difference between a current and a long-term liability?
2. What is an estimated liability?
3. What are the three important questions concerning the certainty of liabilities?
4. Suppose that a company has a facility located in an area where disastrous weather conditions often occur. Should it report a probable loss from a future disaster as a liability on its balance sheet? Why?
5. Why are warranty liabilities usually recognized on the balance sheet as liabilities even when they are uncertain?
6. What is an employer's unemployment merit rating? Why are these ratings assigned to employers?
7. What factors affect the present value of a future $2,000 payment?

8. How would a lease create an asset and a liability for the lessee?
9. Examine Southwest Airlines Co.'s consolidated balance sheet in Appendix E. How much of the company's long-term debt is due to be paid during 1995?

10. Find the footnote on leases following the financial statements of Southwest Airlines Co. in Appendix E. What is the total minimum amount of capital lease payments in future years?

QUICK STUDY (Five-Minute Exercises)

QS 12–1
(LO 1)

Which of the following items would normally be classified as a current liability for a company that has a 15-month operating cycle?

   a. Salaries payable.

   b. A note payable due in 18 months.

   c. Bonds payable that mature in two years.

   d. A note payable due in 11 months.

   e. The portion of a long-term note that is due to be paid in 15 months.

QS 12–2
(LO 2)

On September 11, Valentine's Department Store sold a lawn mower for $400 with a one-year warranty that covers parts and labor. Warranty expense was estimated at 5% of sales. On July 24, the mower was brought in for repairs covered under the warranty requiring $15 in parts and $20 of labor. Prepare the July 24 journal entry to record the warranty repairs.

Yeager, Inc., has five employees, each of whom earns $2,600 per month. FICA taxes are 7.65% of gross pay. FUTA taxes are 0.8% and SUTA taxes are 2.8% of the first $7,000 paid to each employee. Prepare the March 31 journal entry to record March payroll taxes expense.

**QS 12–3
(LO 3)**

On November 7, 19X1, the Eggemeyer Corporation borrowed $150,000 and signed a 90-day, 8% note payable with a face value of $150,000.

**QS 12–4
(LO 4)**

a. Calculate the accrued interest payable on December 31.

b. Present the journal entry to record the paying of the note at maturity.

Determine the amount that can be borrowed under each of the following circumstances:

**QS 12–5
(LO 5)**

a. A promise to pay $90,000 in seven years at an interest rate of 6%.

b. An agreement made on February 1, 19X1, to make three payments of $20,000 on February 1 of 19X2, 19X3, and 19X4. The annual interest rate was 10%.

On January 1, 19X1, The Deitrich Company borrowed $75,000 in exchange for an interest-bearing note. The note plus compounded interest at an annual rate of 8% is due on December 31, 19X3. Determine the amount that Deitrich will pay on the due date. (Round to the nearest dollar.)

**QS 12–6
(LO 6)**

Calculate the times fixed interest charges earned for a company that has income after interest expense and before taxes of $1,575,500 and interest expense of $137,000.

**QS 12–7
(LO 7)**

EXERCISES

The following list of items might appear as liabilities on the balance sheet of a company that has a two-month operating cycle. Identify the proper classification of each item. In the space beside each item write a *C* if it is a current liability, an *L* if it is a long-term liability, or an *N* if it is not a liability.

Exercise 12–1
Classifying liabilities
(LO 1)

—— a.   Income taxes payable.

—— b.   Notes receivable in 30 days.

—— c.   Mortgage payable (payments due in the next 12 months).

—— d.   Notes payable in 6 to 12 months.

—— e.   Bonds payable (mature in 5 years).

—— f.   Notes payable in 13 to 24 months.

—— g.   Wages payable.

—— h.   Accounts receivable.

—— i.   Notes payable in 120 days.

—— j.   Mortgage payable (payments due after the next 12 months).

Mikado, Inc., sold a copier with a cost of $3,800 and a two-year parts and labor warranty to a customer on August 16, 19X1, for $5,500 cash. Mikado uses the perpetual system to account for inventories. Based on prior experience, Mikado expects to eventually incur warranty costs equal to 4% of this selling price. The liability expense is recorded with an adjusting entry at the end of the year. On November 22, 19X2, the copier required on-site repairs that were completed the same day. The cost of the repairs consisted of $69 for the materials taken from the parts inventory and $130 of labor that was fully paid with cash. These were the only repairs required in 19X2 for this copier.

Exercise 12–2
Warranty expense and liability
(LO 2)

a. How much warranty expense should the company report in 19X1 for this copier?

b. How much is the warranty liability for this copier as of December 31, 19X1?

c. How much warranty expense should the company report in 19X2 for this copier?

d. How much is the warranty liability for this copier as of December 31, 19X2?

e. Show the journal entries that would be made to record (1) the sale; (2) the adjustment on December 31, 19X1, to record the warranty expense; and (3) the repairs that occurred in November 19X2.

Exercise 12–3
Accounting for income taxes
(LO 2)

Constructo Company prepares interim financial statements each month. As part of the process, estimated income taxes are accrued each month for 30% of the current month's net income. The estimated income taxes are paid in the first month of each quarter for the amount accrued in the prior quarter. These facts are known about the last quarter of 19X1:

a.   October net income $27,900
     November net income   18,200
     December net income   32,700

b.   After the tax return was completed in early January, the accountant determined that the Income Taxes Payable account balance should be $29,100 on December 31.

Required

1.   Determine the amount of the adjustment needed on December 31 to produce the proper ending balance in the Income Taxes Payable account.

2.   Present the journal entries to record the adjustment to the Income Taxes Payable account and to record the January 15 payment of the fourth-quarter taxes.

Exercise 12–4
Payroll taxes
(LO 3)

Natkin Co. has a single employee on its payroll. The employee and the company are subject to the following taxes:

Tax	Rate	Applied to
FICA—Social Security	6.20%	First $65,000
FICA—Medicare	1.50	Gross pay
FUTA	0.80	First $7,000
SUTA	2.90	First $7,000

Compute the amounts of the four taxes for Natkin on the employee's gross earnings for September under each of these three independent situations:

	Gross Pay through August	Gross Pay for September
a.	$ 6,400	$ 800
b.	18,200	2,100
c.	60,600	7,900

Exercise 12–5
Payroll tax journal entries
(LO 3)

Using the data in requirement a of Exercise 12–4, prepare September 30 journal entries to record the gross earnings and withholdings for the employee and the company's payroll taxes. The employee's withheld income taxes are $90.

Exercise 12–6
Interest-bearing and noninterest-bearing notes payable
(LO 4)

Portable Systems, Inc., borrowed $94,000 on May 15, 19X1, for 60 days at 12% interest by signing a note.

a.   On what date will this note mature?

b.   How much interest expense is created by this note? (Assume a 360-day year.)

c.   Suppose that the face value of the note equals the principal of the loan. Show the general journal entries to record issuing the note and paying it at maturity.

d.   Suppose that the face value of the note includes both the principal of the loan and the interest to be paid at maturity. Show the general journal entries to record issuing the note and paying it at maturity.

Exercise 12–7
Interest-bearing and noninterest-bearing short-term notes payable with year-end adjustments
(LO 4)

Accura Corp. borrowed $150,000 on November 1, 19X1, for 90 days at 9% interest by signing a note.

a.   On what date will this note mature?

b.   How much interest expense is created by this note in 19X1? (Assume a 360-day year.)

c.   How much interest expense is created by this note in 19X2? (Assume a 360-day year.)

d.   Suppose that the face value of the note equals the principal of the loan. Show the general journal entries to record issuing the note, to accrue interest at the end of 19X1, and to record paying the note at maturity.

e. Suppose that the face value of the note includes both the principal of the loan and the interest to be paid at maturity. Show the general journal entries to record issuing the note, to accrue interest at the end of 19X1, and to record paying the note at maturity.

As of January 1, 19X1, a company has agreed to pay $20,000 in three years. If the annual interest rate is 10%, determine how much cash the company can borrow with this promise. Present a three-column table that shows the beginning balance, interest, and ending balance for 19X1, 19X2, and 19X3. (Round interest amounts to the nearest dollar.)

Exercise 12–8
Present value of a future payment and accumulated interest
(LO 5)

Find the amount of money that can be borrowed with each of the following promises:

Exercise 12–9
Present value of liabilities
(LO 5)

	Future Payment	**Number of Years**	**Interest Rate**
a.	$40,000	3	4%
b.	75,000	7	8
c.	52,000	9	10%
d.	18,000	2	4
e.	63,000	8	6
f.	89,000	5	2

C&H Monument Company recently borrowed money and agreed to pay it back with a series of six annual payments of $5,000 each. C&H subsequently borrowed more money and agreed to pay it back with a series of four annual payments of $7,500 each. The annual interest rate for both loans was 6%.

Exercise 12–10
Present value of annuities
(LO 5)

a. Use Table 12–1 to find the present value of these two annuities. (Round all amounts to the nearest dollar.)

b. Use Table 12–2 to find the present value of these two annuities.

Otto, Inc., borrowed cash on April 30, 19X1, by promising to make four payments of $13,000 each on November 1, 19X1, May 1, 19X2, November 1, 19X2, and May 1, 19X3.

Exercise 12–11
Semiannual compounding
(LO 5)

a. How much cash was Otto able to borrow if the interest rate was 8%, compounded semiannually?

b. How much cash was Otto able to borrow if the interest rate was 12%, compounded semiannually?

c. How much cash was Otto able to borrow if the interest rate was 16%, compounded semiannually?

Hauser Corp. purchased some equipment on June 15 that had a purchase price of $22,000. Show the journal entry to record the purchase under these three separate assumptions:

Exercise 12–12
Asset purchase in exchange for a note
(LO 6)

a. The company paid cash for the full purchase price.

b. The company gave an interest-bearing note for the full purchase price.

c. The company gave a noninterest-bearing one-year note for $23,980.

On December 31, 19X1, The Dumond Corporation purchased land by issuing a noninterest-bearing note for $65,000. The fair market value of the land was not reliably known, but the company knew that the market interest rate for the note was 4%. The note matures in three years on January 1, 19X5.

Exercise 12–13
Asset purchase in exchange for a noninterest-bearing note
(LO 6)

a. What is the present value of the note at the time of the purchase?

b. What is the initial balance of the discount on the note payable?

c. Prepare a table that shows the amount of interest that will be allocated to each of the three years in the note's life and the ending balance of the new liability for each year.

d. Prepare a table that determines the ending balance of the discount on the note for each of the three years.

Exercise 12–14
Journal entries for a
noninterest-bearing note
(LO 6)

Use the data in Exercise 12–13 to prepare journal entries for these dates:

a.   December 31, 19X1 (land purchase).

b.   December 31, 19X2 (accrual entry).

c.   December 31, 19X3 (accrual entry).

d.   December 31, 19X4 (accrual entry).

e.   January 1, 19X5 (the payment of the note).

Exercise 12–15
Times fixed interest charges
earned
(LO 7)

Use the following information to compute times fixed interest charges earned:

	Net Income or (Loss)	Interest Expense
a.	$140,000	$48,000
b.	140,000	15,000
c.	140,000	8,000
d.	265,000	12,000
e.	79,000	12,000
f.	(4,000)	12,000

PROBLEMS

Problem 12–1
Estimated product warranty
liabilities
(LO 2)

On October 29, 19X1, Sharp Products, Inc., began to buy and resell electric razors for $80 each. Sharp uses the perpetual method to account for inventories. The razors are covered under a warranty that requires the company to replace any nonworking razor within 90 days. When a razor is returned, the company simply throws it away and mails a new one from inventory to the customer. The company's cost for a new razor is $18. The manufacturer has advised the company to expect warranty costs to equal 7% of the total sales. These events occurred in 19X1 and 19X2:

19X1

Nov. 11   Sold 75 razors for $6,000 cash.

   30   Recognized warranty expense for November with an adjusting entry.

Dec. 9   Replaced 15 razors that were returned under the warranty.

   16   Sold 210 razors for $16,800 cash.

   29   Replaced 30 razors that were returned under the warranty.

   31   Recognized warranty expense for December with an adjusting entry.

19X2

Jan. 5   Sold 130 razors for $10,400 cash.

   17   Replaced 50 razors that were returned under the warranty.

   31   Recognized warranty expense for January with an adjusting entry.

Required

1.   How much warranty expense should be reported for November and December 19X1?

2.   How much warranty expense should be reported for January 19X2?

3.   What is the balance of the estimated warranty liability as of December 31, 19X1?

4.   What is the balance of the estimated warranty liability as of January 31, 19X2?

5.   Prepare journal entries to record the transactions and adjustments.

CHECK FIGURE:
12/31/X1 estimated liability balance, $786

Problem 12–2
Transactions with short-term
notes payable
(LO 4)

The Langley Company entered into the following transactions involving short-term liabilities during 19X1 and 19X2:

19X1

Apr. 20   Purchased merchandise on credit from Franken, Inc., for $38,500. The terms were 1/10, n/30. Assume Franken uses a perpetual inventory system.

May 19   Replaced the account payable to Franken with a 90-day note bearing 9% annual interest. Langley paid $8,500 cash, with the result that the balance of the note was $30,000.

July   8   Borrowed $60,000 from Bank of the North by signing an interest-bearing note for $60,000. The annual interest rate was 10%, and the note has a 120-day terms.

?   Paid the note to Franken, Inc., at maturity.

?   Paid the note to Bank of the North at Maturity.

Nov. 28   Borrowed $21,000 from Crockett Bank by signing a noninterest-bearing note for $21,280 that matures in 60 days. (This amount is based on an 8% interest rate.)

Dec. 31   Recorded an adjusting entry for the accrual of interest on the note to Crockett Bank.

19X2

?   Paid the note to Crockett Bank at maturity.

Required

1.   Determine the maturity dates of the three notes just described.

2.   Determine the interest due at maturity for the three notes. (Assume a 360-day year.)

3.   Determine the interest to be recorded in the adjusting entry at the end of 19X1.

4.   Determine the interest to be recorded in 19X2.

5.   Present journal entries for all the preceding events and adjustments.

CHECK FIGURE:
Total interest for Crockett Bank note, $280

Legal Consultants, Inc., pays its employees every week. The employees' gross earnings are subject to these taxes:

Problem 12–3
Payroll costs, withholdings, and taxes
(LO 3)

	Rate	Applied To
FICA—Social Security	6.25%	First $62,000
FICA—Medicare	1.50	Gross pay
FUTA	0.80	First $7,000
SUTA	2.15	First $7,000

The company is preparing its payroll calculations for the week ended August 25. The payroll records show the following information for the company's four employees:

		This Week	
Name	Gross Pay Through 8/18	Gross Pay	Withholding Tax
Rose	$61,200	$1,800	$252
Chad	29,700	900	99
Mona	6,750	450	54
Jody	1,050	400	36

In addition to the gross pay, the company and each employee pay one-half of the weekly health insurance premium of $32. The company also contributes 8% of each employee's gross earnings to a pension fund.

Required

Use this information to calculate the following for the week ended August 25 (round all amounts to the nearest cent):

1.   Each employee's FICA withholdings for Social Security.

2.   Each employee's FICA withholdings for Medicare.

3.   The employer's FICA taxes for Social Security.

4.   The employer's FICA taxes for Medicare.

5.   The employer's FUTA taxes.

6.   The employer's SUTA taxes.

7.   Each employee's take-home pay.

8.   The employer's total payroll-related expense for each employee.

CHECK FIGURE:
Total take-home pay, $2,832.37

Problem 12–4
Present values of alternative liabilities
(LO 5, 6)

Big Sky Company is negotiating the purchase of a new building. The seller has offered Big Sky the following three payment plans:

Plan A: $75,000 cash to be paid now.

Plan B: $90,000 cash to be paid after two years.

Plan C: $44,000 cash to be paid at the end of each of the next two years.

The market interest rate is 10% at this time.

Required

1. Use the market interest rate to determine the present value of each of the three alternative payment plans.
2. Show the journal entry Big Sky would make to record the acquisition under each of the three plans. (Assume that the note's face value would include all interest to be paid.)
3. Identify the plan that creates the lowest cost for Big Sky.
4. Assume that Plan B is adopted and the present value of the cash flows is used as the building's cost. Determine the amount of interest expense that will be reported in each of the two years in the note's life.

Problem 12–5
Exchanging a noninterest-bearing note for a plant asset
(LO 6)

On January 1, 19X1, Graphite Industries acquired an item of equipment by issuing a $35,000 noninterest-bearing five-year note that will be due on December 31, 19X5. A reliable cash price for the equipment was not readily available. The market annual rate of interest for similar notes was 8% on the day of the exchange.

Required

(Round all amounts to the nearest dollar.)

1. Determine the initial net liability created by issuing this note.
2. Present a table showing the calculation of the amount of interest expense allocated to each year the note is outstanding and the carrying amount of the net liability at the end of each of those years.
3. Present a table that shows the balance of the discount at the end of each year the note is outstanding.
4. Prepare general journal entries to record the purchase of the equipment, the accrual of interest expense at the end of 19X1 and 19X2, and the accrual of interest expense and the payment of the note on December 31, 19X5. Assume that the note's face value includes all interest to be paid.
5. Show how the note should be presented on the balance sheet as of December 31, 19X3.

Problem 12–6
Times fixed interest charges earned
(LO 7)

Here are condensed income statements for two unrelated companies:

Foxtrot Corp.		**Tango Corp.**	
Sales	$500,000	Sales	$500,000
Variable expenses (80%)	400,000	Variable expenses (60%)	300,000
Net income before interest	$100,000	Net income before interest	$200,000
Interest (fixed)	30,000	Interest (fixed)	130,000
Net income	$ 70,000	Net income	$ 70,000

Required

Preparation component:

1. What is the times fixed interest charges earned for Foxtrot Corp.?
2. What is the times fixed interest charges earned for Tango Corp.?
3. What happens to each company's net income if sales increase by 30%?
4. What happens to each company's net income if sales increase by 50%?
5. What happens to each company's net income if sales increase by 80%?
6. What happens to each company's net income if sales decrease by 10%?

7. What happens to each company's net income if sales decrease by 20%?

8. What happens to each company's net income if sales decrease by 40%?

Analysis component:

9. Comment on what you observe in relation to the fixed cost strategies of the two companies and the ratio values you calculated in Parts 1 and 2.

CRITICAL THINKING: ESSAYS, PROBLEMS, AND CASES

Analytical Essays

This problem requires you to demonstrate your understanding of noninterest-bearing notes, interest allocation, and present values by explaining how it would be possible to use incomplete information to discover other facts about a loan. Suppose that a company borrowed some cash on January 1, 19X1, with a four-year noninterest-bearing note payable. A year later, on December 31, 19X1, you know only these two items of information:

AE 12–1
(LO 6)

a. The net liability (net of the remaining discount) as of December 31, 19X1.

b. The interest expense reported for the year ended December 31, 19X1.

Write brief explanations of the calculations you would make to identify the following additional facts about the loan:

1. The amount borrowed on January 1, 19X1.

2. The market interest rate on January 1, 19X1.

3. The amount of interest that will be reported for 19X2.

After a long analysis, the manager of Ramsey, Inc., has decided to acquire an automobile through a long-term noncancellable lease instead of buying it outright. Under the terms of the lease, Ramsey must make regular monthly payments throughout the four-year term of the lease and provide for all the operating costs including gas, insurance, and repairs. At the end of the lease, the lessor will simply give Ramsey the legal title to the auto. Give reasons why Ramsey should account for the lease as if it is essentially a purchase.

AE 12–2
(LO 6)

All 75 regular employees of The Back Yard, Inc., earn at least $7,000 per year. The company operates in a state with a maximum SUTA tax rate of 5.4% on the first $7,000 gross wages of each employee. The company's excellent record has earned a merit rating that reduces its SUTA rate to 2.5%.

Management Decision Case
(LO 3)

The company has recently received an order for a line of smoker/grills from a chain of discount stores. The order should be very profitable and probably will be repeated each year for at least three or four years. The company can produce the grills with its present production facility, but it will have to add 15 more workers for four weeks at 40 hours per week to make the grills and pack them for shipment.

The company is considering two different approaches to getting the workers. That is, it can either go through a local temporary employment service (called Personnel Power) or actually hire them as employees and then lay them off after four weeks. The Back Yard would pay Personnel Power $13.50 per hour for each worker, and Personnel Power would pay their wages and all payroll taxes and benefits. Alternatively, The Back Yard would pay its new employees a wage rate of $9.00 per hour, plus these additional payroll taxes: FICA taxes, 7.8%; FUTA tax, 0.8%; and SUTA tax, 4.0%. The SUTA rate would jump to 4.5% because the company would receive a less favorable merit rating from the state because of the unemployment claims it would create by laying off the workers every year. This higher rate would apply to all of the company's employees. In addition, The Back Yard would provide health care insurance to these employees at the rate of $18 per employee per week.

Compare the total costs under the two alternatives to determine whether The Back Yard should use the services of Personnel Power or hire the additional workers it needs. Provide a complete analysis and explanation.

Business Communications Case

(LO 2)

Norma Yagerhofer is the new manager of accounting and finance for a medium-size manufacturing company. Now that the end of the year is approaching, her problem is determining whether and how to describe some of the company's contingencies in the financial statements. The general manager, Jonas Perlman, raised objections to two specific contingencies in Yagerhofer's preliminary proposal.

First, Perlman objected to the proposal to report nothing about a patent infringement suit that the company has filed against a competitor. The manager's written comment on this proposal was, "We KNOW that we have them cold on this one! There is no way that we're not going to win a very large settlement!"

Second, Perlman objected to Yagerhofer's proposal to recognize an expense and a liability for warranty service on units of a new product that was just introduced in the company's fourth quarter. His scribbled comment on this point was, "There is no way that we can estimate this warranty cost. Besides, we don't owe anybody anything until the products break down and are returned for service. Let's just report an expense if and when we do the repairs."

Develop a short written response for Yagerhofer to send to Perlman addressing his objections in a one-page memorandum dated December 21.

Financial Statement Analysis Case

(LO 1, 2, 6, 7)

Answer the following questions by using the information in the financial statements and footnotes for Lands' End, Inc., that appear in Appendix F at the end of the book:

1. Examine the company's consolidated balance sheet to find the amount of long-term debt on January 27, 1995, and on January 28, 1994. How much is the current portion of long-term debt on these same dates?

2. Calculate times fixed interest charges earned for the years ended January 27, 1995, and comment on Lands' End's ability to cover its interest expense.

3. Does the footnote on leases provide information that allows the reader to determine whether the company has entered into any operating or capital leases?

4. What evidence would you look for as an indication that the company has any temporary differences between the income reported on the income statement and the income reported on its tax return? Can you find any evidence of these differences for Lands' End?

CONCEPT TESTER

Test your understanding of the concepts introduced in this chapter by completing the following crossword puzzle.

Across Clues

3. 2 words; an employer's rating that reflects the employer's past record for creating unemployment.
6. 2 words; an obligation reported as a liability even though the amount to be paid is uncertain.
7. A series of equal payments occurring at equal time intervals.
8. 2 words; compensation to or on behalf of employees in addition to their wages or salaries.
9. 2 words; a lease that gives the lessee the risks and benefits normally related to ownership.

Down Clues

1. 2 words; taxes assessed under the Federal Insurance Contributions Act.
2. 2 words; an amount that, if invested now, will generate a specified future receipt.
4. 2 words; a lease that is not a capital lease.
5. An obligation of a seller or manufacturer to repair or replace products that fail.

COMPREHENSIVE PROBLEM

Aardvark Exterminators, Inc.
(Review of Chapters 1–12)

Aardvark Exterminators, Inc., provides pest control services and sells extermination products manufactured by other companies. The following six-column table contains the company's unadjusted trial balance as of December 31, 19X4.

AARDVARK EXTERMINATORS, INC.
Six-Column Table
December 31, 19X4

	Unadjusted Trial Balance		Adjustments		Adjusted Trial Balance	
Cash	$ 17,000					
Accounts receivable	4,000					
Allowance for doubtful accounts		$ 828				
Merchandise inventory	13,000					
Trucks	32,000					
Accum. depreciation, trucks		0				
Equipment	45,000					
Accum. depreciation equipment		12,200				
Accounts payable		5,000				
Estimated warranty liability		1,500				
Unearned extermination services revenue		0				
Long-term notes payable		15,000				
Discount on notes payable	3,974					
Common stock, $1 par value		20,000				
Retained earnings		39,600				
Cash dividends declared	10,000					
Extermination services revenue		60,000				
Interest earned		872				
Sales		75,000				
Purchases	45,000					
Deprec. expense, trucks	0					
Deprec. expense, equipment	0					
Wages expense	35,000					
Interest expense	0					
Rent expense	9,000					
Bad debts expense	0					
Miscellaneous expenses	1,226					
Repairs expense	8,000					
Utilities expense	6,800					
Warranty expense	0					
Totals	$230,000	$230,000				

The following information applies to the company and its situation at the end of the year:

a. The bank reconciliation as of December 31, 19X4, includes these facts:

Balance per bank	$15,100
Balance per books	17,000
Outstanding checks	1,800
Deposit in transit	2,450
Interest earned	52
Service charges (miscellaneous expense)	15

Included with the bank statement was a canceled check that the company had failed to record. (This information allows you to determine the amount of the check, which was a payment of an account payable.)

b. An examination of customers' accounts shows that accounts totaling $679 should be written off as uncollectible. In addition, it has been determined that the ending balance of the Allowance for Doubtful Accounts account should be $700.

c. A truck was purchased and placed in service on July 1, 19X4. Its cost is being depreciated with the straight-line method using these facts and predictions:

Original cost	$32,000
Expected salvage value	8,000
Useful life (years)	4

d. Two items of equipment (a sprayer and an injector) were purchased and put into service early in January 19X2. Their costs are being depreciated with the straight-line method using these facts and predictions:

	Sprayer	Injector
Original cost	$27,000	$18,000
Expected salvage value	3,000	2,500
Useful life (years)	8	5

e. On August 1, 19X4, the company was paid $3,840 in advance to provide monthly service on an apartment complex for one year. The company began providing the services in August. When the cash was received, the full amount was credited to the Extermination Services Revenue account.

f. The company offers a warranty for all of the products it sells. The expected cost of providing warranty service is 2.5% of sales. No warranty expense has been recorded for 19X4. All costs of servicing products under the warranties in 19X4 were properly debited to the liability account.

g. The $15,000 long-term note is a five-year, noninterest-bearing note that was given to First National Bank on December 31, 19X2. The market interest rate on the date of the loan was 8%.

h. The ending inventory of merchandise was counted and determined to have a cost of $11,700. (Note that Aardvark's unadjusted trial balance includes a Purchases account. Thus, you know that Aardvark uses a periodic inventory system.)

Required

1. Use the preceding information to determine the amounts of the following items:
   a. The correct ending balance of Cash and the amount of the omitted check.
   b. The adjustment needed to obtain the correct ending balance of the Allowance for Doubtful Accounts.
   c. The annual depreciation expense for the truck that was acquired during the year (calculated to the nearest month).
   d. The annual depreciation expense for the two items of equipment that were used during the year.
   e. The correct ending balances of the Extermination Services Revenue and Unearned Extermination Services Revenue accounts.
   f. The correct ending balances of the accounts for Warranty Expense and Estimated Warranty Liability.
   g. The correct ending balances of the accounts for Interest Expense and Discount on Notes Payable. (Round amounts to nearest whole dollar.)
   h. The cost of goods sold for the year.

2. Use the results of requirement 1 to complete the six-column table by first entering the appropriate adjustments for items a through g and then completing the adjusted trial balance columns. (Hint: Item b requires two entries.)

3. Present general journal entries to record the adjustments entered on the six-column table. Assume that Aardvark uses the closing entry approach to account for changes in Merchandise Inventory.

4. Present a single-step income statement, a statement of retained earnings, and a classified balance sheet.

ANSWERS TO PROGRESS CHECKS

12–1 Liabilities are probable future payments of assets or services that an entity is presently obligated to make as a result of past transactions or events.

12–2 No, an expected future payment is not a liability unless an existing obligation was created by a past event or transaction.

12–3 In most cases, a liability due in 15 months should be classified as long term. However, it should be classified as a current liability if the company's operating cycle is at least 15 months long.

12–4 *a*

12–5 *a*

12–6 A corporation would accrue an income tax liability for its interim financial statements because income tax expense is incurred when income is earned, not just at the end of the year.

12–7 *b*

12–8 A future payment should be reported as a contingent liability if *(a)* the uncertain future event is probable but the amount of the payment cannot be reasonably estimated, and *(b)* the uncertain future event is not probable but has a reasonable possibility of occurring.

12–9 *a.* $1,000(.008 + .04) + $3,000(.062 + .0145) = $277.50

12–10 *a.* FICA taxes are paid by both the employee and the employer.

  b. FUTA taxes are paid by the employer.

  c. SUTA taxes are paid by the employer.

  d. Withheld income taxes are paid by the employee.

12–11 A creditor might want to have a note payable instead of an account payable in order to *(a)* start charging interest and/or *(b)* have positive evidence of the debt and its terms.

12–12 The amount borrowed was $1,000 ($1,050 − $50). The rate of interest was 5% ($50/$1,000) for six months, which is an annual rate of 10%.

12–13 *c.* 3.3121 × $1,000 = $3,312

12–14 The option of paying $10,000 after a year always has a lower present value. In effect, it postpones paying the first $5,000 by six months. As a result, the delayed payment is always less.

12–15 *c.* [$6,000 + ($6,000 × .06)] × .06 = $381.60

12–16 $4,000 × 0.7350 = $2,940

12–17 *d*

12–18 *c*

12–19 The risk can be described by the ratio that shows the number of times the fixed interest charges are covered by the net income *before* interest. The ratio for First company is only 1.5 [($100,000 + $200,000)/$200,000], while the ratio for Second company is 3.5 [($100,000 + $40,000)/$40,000]. This analysis shows that First Company is more susceptible to the risk of incurring a loss if its sales decline.

CHAPTER 13

Installment Notes Payable and Bonds

L. A. Gear Inc. designs, develops, and markets a broad range of athletic and lifestyle footwear for adults and children. Its innovative products include lighted shoes sold under the names of *L. A. LIGHTS*™ and *Light Gear*™. Based on industry estimates, the company is one of the largest marketers of branded athletic footwear in the United States.

Nevertheless, during the four-year period of 1991 through 1994, L. A. Gear experienced substantial net losses that resulted from reduced sales. Fiscal year net losses were $66,200,000 in 1991, $71,901,000 in 1992, $32,513,000 in 1993, and $22,195,000 in 1994. In an attempt to regain profitability, the company initiated a long-term restructuring plan late in 1991. That effort, which continued throughout the 1994 year, included a program of international expansion. Primarily to finance that effort, the company issued $50 million of bonds payable during December of 1992. These bonds were described on the company's November 30, 1994, balance sheet as 7 3/4% convertible subordinated debentures due 2002.

L. A. GEAR INC.

(in thousands)	1994	1993	1992	1991
Net sales	$415,966	$398,358	$430,194	$619,175
Net income (loss)	(22,195)	(32,513)	(71,901)	(66,200)
Total assets	224,463	254,613	250,144	327,751
Convertible subordinated debentures	50,000	50,000	—	—
Shareholders' equity	18,149	46,797	87,451	131,715

LEARNING OBJECTIVES

After studying Chapter 13, you should be able to:

1. **Calculate the payments on an installment note payable and describe their effects on the financial statements.**
2. **Describe the various characteristics of different types of bonds and prepare entries to record bond issuances and retirements.**
3. **Estimate the price of bonds issued at a discount and describe their effects on the issuer's financial statements.**
4. **Estimate the price of bonds issued at a premium and describe their effects on the issuer's financial statements.**
5. **Calculate and describe how to use the ratio of pledged assets to secured liabilities.**
6. **Define or explain the words and phrases listed in the chapter glossary.**

In Chapter 12, you learned that some notes payable require a single payment on the date the note matures. In those cases, the single payment includes the borrowed amount plus interest. You also learned about other notes requiring a series of payments that include interest plus a part of the principal. We begin this chapter with a more complete discussion of these installment notes. Then, we turn to bonds, which are securities issued by corporations and government bodies. The discussion explains the nature of bonds such as the convertible subordinated debentures issued by **L.A. Gear.**

INSTALLMENT NOTES PAYABLE

LO 1
Calculate the payments on an installment note payable and describe their effects on the financial statements.

When an *installment note* is used to borrow money, the borrower records the note with an entry similar to the one used for a single-payment note. That is, the increase in cash is recorded with a debit and the increase in the liability is recorded with a credit to Notes Payable. For example, suppose that a company borrows $60,000 by signing an 8% installment note that requires six annual payments. The borrower records the note as follows:

19X1				
Dec.	31	Cash	60,000.00	
		Notes Payable		60,000.00
		Borrowed $60,000 by signing an 8% installment note.		

Installment notes like this one require the borrower to pay back the debt with a series of periodic payments. Usually, each payment includes all interest expense that has accrued up to the date of the payment plus some portion of the original amount borrowed (the *principal*). Installment notes generally specify one of two alternative payment patterns. Some notes require payments that include interest and equal amounts of principal while other notes simply call for equal payments.

Installment Notes with Payments of Accrued Interest and Equal Amounts of Principal

Installment note agreements requiring payments of accrued interest plus equal amounts of principal create cash flows that decrease in size over the life of the note. This pattern occurs because each payment reduces the liability's principal balance, with the result that the following period's interest expense is reduced. The next payment is smaller because the amount of interest is reduced. For example, suppose the $60,000, 8% note that we just recorded requires the borrower to make six payments at the end of each year equal to the accrued interest plus $10,000 of principal.

Illustration 13–1 Installment Note with Payments of Accrued Interest and Equal Amounts of Principal

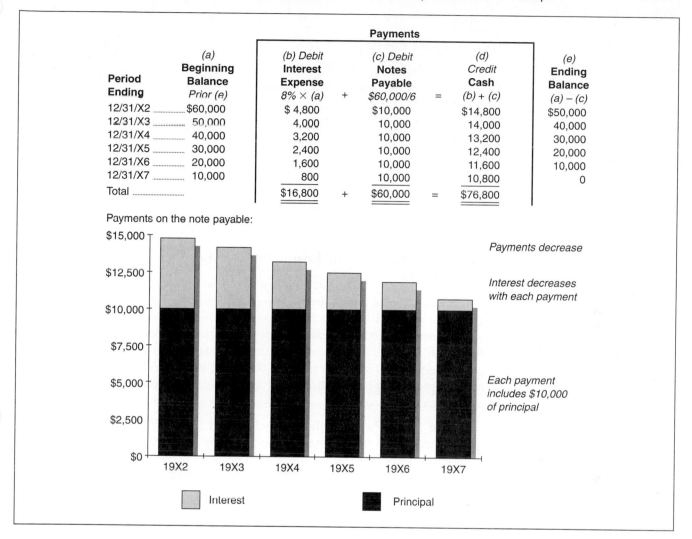

Period Ending	(a) Beginning Balance Prior (e)	(b) Debit Interest Expense 8% × (a)	+	(c) Debit Notes Payable $60,000/6	=	(d) Credit Cash (b) + (c)	(e) Ending Balance (a) − (c)
12/31/X2	$60,000	$ 4,800		$10,000		$14,800	$50,000
12/31/X3	50,000	4,000		10,000		14,000	40,000
12/31/X4	40,000	3,200		10,000		13,200	30,000
12/31/X5	30,000	2,400		10,000		12,400	20,000
12/31/X6	20,000	1,600		10,000		11,600	10,000
12/31/X7	10,000	800		10,000		10,800	0
Total		$16,800	+	$60,000	=	$76,800	

We describe the payments, interest, and changes in the balance of this note in Illustration 13–1. Column *a* of the illustration contains the beginning balance of the note. Columns *b*, *c*, and *d* describe each cash payment and how it is divided between interest and principal. Column *b* calculates the interest expense that accrues during each year at 8% of the beginning balance. Column *c* shows the portion of the payment applied to principal. It shows that each payment reduces the liability with a $10,000 debit to the Notes Payable account. Column *d* calculates each annual payment, which consists of the interest in column *b* plus $10,000. (Notice that the credit to the Cash account equals the sum of the debits to the expense and the liability accounts.) Finally, column *e* shows the ending balance of the liability, which equals the beginning balance in column *a* minus the principal portion of the payment in column *c*. Over the life of the note, the table shows that the total interest expense is $16,800 and the total reduction in principal is $60,000. Thus, the total cash payments are $76,800.

The graph in the lower section of Illustration 13–1 shows these three points: (1) the total payment gets smaller as the loan balance is reduced, (2) the amount of interest included in each payment gets steadily smaller, and (3) the amount of principal in each payment remains constant at $10,000.

The borrower records the effects of the first two payments with these entries:

19X2					
Dec.	31	Interest Expense	4,800.00		
		Notes Payable	10,000.00		
		Cash		14,800.00	
		To record first installment payment.			
19X3					
Dec.	31	Interest Expense	4,000.00		
		Notes Payable	10,000.00		
		Cash		14,000.00	
		To record second installment payment.			

After all six payments are recorded, the balance of the Notes Payable account for the note is eliminated.

Installment Notes with Equal Payments

In contrast to the previous pattern, many installment notes require the borrower to make a series of equal payments. These payments consist of changing amounts of interest and principal. To demonstrate this type of note, assume that a $60,000 note requires the borrower to make a series of six equal payments of $12,979 at the end of each year. Illustration 13–2 shows the effects of making the payments on this note. (The payments are $12,979 because $60,000 is the present value of an annuity of six annual payments of $12,979, discounted at 8%. We show you how to make this calculation later in this section.)

Allocating Each Payment between Interest and Principal. Each payment of $12,979 includes both interest and principal. Look at Illustration 13–2 to see how an accountant allocates the total amount of each payment between interest and principal.

The table is essentially the same as the table in Illustration 13–1. Again, column *a* shows the liability's beginning balance for each year. Column *b* presents the interest that accrues each year at 8% of the beginning balance. Column *c* calculates the change in the principal of the liability caused by each payment. The debit to the liability account in this column is the difference between the total payment in column *d* and the interest expense in column *b*. Finally, column *e* presents the ending balance after each payment is made.

Even though all six payments are equal, the amount of interest decreases each year because the balance of the liability gets smaller. Then, because the amount of interest gets smaller, the amount of the payment applied to the principal gets larger. This effect is presented graphically in Illustration 13–2. Because the tables in Illustrations 13–1 and 13–2 show how the principal balance is reduced (or amortized) by the periodic payments, they are often referred to as *installment note amortization schedules.*[1]

The bookkeeper records the effects of the first two payments with these journal entries:

19X2					
Dec.	31	Interest Expense	4,800.00		
		Notes Payable	8,179.00		
		Cash		12,979.00	
		To record first installment payment.			

---

[1]Many business calculators are programmed to make these amortization calculations for annuities.

Illustration 13-2 Installment Note with Equal Payments

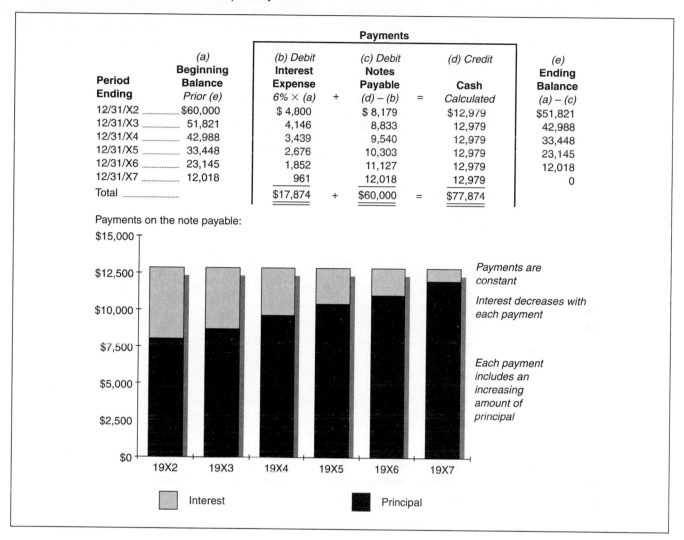

Period Ending	(a) Beginning Balance Prior (e)	Payments			(e) Ending Balance (a) – (c)
		(b) Debit Interest Expense 6% × (a) +	(c) Debit Notes Payable (d) – (b) =	(d) Credit Cash Calculated	
12/31/X2	$60,000	$ 4,800	$ 8,179	$12,979	$51,821
12/31/X3	51,821	4,146	8,833	12,979	42,988
12/31/X4	42,988	3,439	9,540	12,979	33,448
12/31/X5	33,448	2,676	10,303	12,979	23,145
12/31/X6	23,145	1,852	11,127	12,979	12,018
12/31/X7	12,018	961	12,018	12,979	0
Total		$17,874 +	$60,000 =	$77,874	

Payments on the note payable:

Payments are constant

Interest decreases with each payment

Each payment includes an increasing amount of principal

☐ Interest   ■ Principal

19X3					
Dec.	31	Interest Expense	4,146.00		
		Notes Payable	8,833.00		
		Cash		12,979.00	
		To record second installment payment.			

The amounts in these entries come from the table in Illustration 13–2. The borrower would record similar entries for each of the remaining payments. Over the six years, the Notes Payable account balance will be eliminated.

To be sure that you understand the differences between the two payment patterns, compare the numbers and graphs in Illustrations 13–1 and 13–2. Notice that the series of equal payments leads to a greater amount of interest expense over the life of the note. This result occurs because the first three payments in Illustration 13–2 are smaller and thus do not reduce the principal as quickly as the first three payments in Illustration 13–1.

Calculating the Equal Periodic Payments on an Installment Note. In the previous example, we simply gave you the size of the equal annual payments on the installment note. Now, we show you how to calculate the size of the payment.

When a note requires a series of equal payments, you can calculate the size of each payment with a present value table for an annuity such as Table 13–2 on page 475.[2] To make the calculation with the table, start with this equation:

$$\text{Payment} \times \text{Annuity table value} = \text{Present value of the annuity}$$

Then, modify the equation to get this version:

$$\text{Payment} = \frac{\text{Present value of the annuity}}{\text{Annuity table value}}$$

Because the balance of an installment note equals the present value of the series of payments, the equation can again be modified to become this formula:

$$\text{Payment} = \frac{\text{Note balance}}{\text{Annuity table value}}$$

For this example, the initial note balance is $60,000. The annuity table value in the formula is based on the note's interest rate and the number of payments. The interest rate is 8% and there are six payments. Therefore, enter Table 13–2 on the sixth row and go across to the 8% column, where you will find the value of 4.6229. These numbers now can be substituted into the formula to find the payment:

$$\text{Payment} = \frac{\$60,000}{4.6229} = \$12,979$$

This formula can be used for all installment notes that require equal periodic payments.[3]

Progress Check
(Answers to Progress Checks are provided at the end of the chapter.)

13–1   Which of the following is true for an installment note that requires a series of equal payments?
   a. The payments consist of an increasing amount of interest and a decreasing amount of principal.
   b. The payments consist of changing amounts of principal, but the interest portion of the payment remains constant.
   c. The payments consist of a decreasing amount of interest and an increasing amount of principal.

13–2   How is the interest portion of an installment note payment calculated?

13–3   When a borrower records an interest payment on an installment note, how are the balance sheet and income statement affected?

BORROWING BY ISSUING BONDS

LO 2
Describe the various characteristics of different types of bonds and prepare entries to record bond issuances and retirements.

Business corporations often borrow money by issuing bonds.[4] A **bond** is a written promise to pay interest at a stated annual rate and to make a final payment of an amount identified on the bond as the **par value of the bond.** Most bonds require the borrower to pay the interest semiannually. The par value of the bonds (also known as

---

[2]Appendix D provides present value tables that include additional interest rates and additional periods (or payments). You should use them to solve the exercises and problems at the end of the chapter.

[3]Business calculators also can be used to find the size of the payments.

[4]Bonds are also issued by nonprofit corporations, as well as the federal government and other governmental units, such as cities, states, and school districts. Although the examples in this chapter deal with business situations, all issuers use the same practices to account for their bonds.

	Plan A Don't Expand	Plan B Increase Equity	Plan C Issue Bonds
Income before interest	$ 100,000	$ 225,000	$ 225,000
Interest			(50,000)
Net income	$ 100,000	$ 225,000	$ 175,000
Equity	$1,000,000	$1,500,000	$1,000,000
Return on equity	10.0%	15.0%	17.5%

Illustration 13–3
Financing with Bonds or Stock

the *face amount*) is paid at a specified future date called the *maturity date of the bonds*. The amount of interest that must be paid each year is determined by multiplying the par value of the bonds by the stated rate of interest established when the bonds were issued.

Differences between Notes Payable and Bonds

When a business borrows money by signing a note payable, the money is generally obtained from a single lender, such as a bank. In contrast, a group of bonds (often called a *bond issue*) typically consists of a large number of bonds, usually in denominations of $1,000, that are sold to many different lenders. After bonds are originally issued, they often are bought and sold by these investors. Thus, any particular bond may actually be owned by a number of people before it matures.

Differences between Stocks and Bonds

Stocks and bonds are different types of securities. A share of stock represents an ownership right in the corporation. For example, a person who owns 1,000 of a corporation's 10,000 outstanding shares controls one-tenth of the total stockholders' equity. On the other hand, if a person owns a $1,000, 11%, 20-year bond, the bondholder has a receivable from the issuer. The bond owner has the right to receive 11% interest ($110) each year that the bond is outstanding and $1,000 when the bond matures 20 years after its issue date. The issuing company is obligated to make these payments and thus has a liability to the bondholder.

ADVANTAGES OF ISSUING BONDS

Companies that issue bonds are usually trying to increase their rate of return on equity. For example, assume a company that has $1 million of equity is considering spending $500,000 to expand its capacity. Management predicts that the $500,000 will allow the company to earn an additional $125,000 of income before paying any interest. The managers are considering three possible plans. Under Plan A, the expansion will not occur. Under Plan B, the expansion will occur, and the needed funds will be obtained from the owners. Under Plan C, the company will sell $500,000 worth of bonds that pay 10% annual interest ($50,000). Illustration 13–3 shows how the plans would affect the company's net income, equity, and return on equity.

Analysis of the alternatives in the illustration shows that the owners will enjoy a greater rate of return and be better off if the expansion is made and if the funds are obtained by issuing the bonds. Even though the projected total income under Plan C would be smaller than Plan B's income, the rate of return on the equity would be larger because there would be less equity. This result occurs whenever the expected rate of return from the new assets is greater than the rate of interest on the bonds. In addition, issuing bonds allows the current owner or owners of a business to remain in control of the company.

CHARACTERISTICS OF BONDS

Over the years, financial experts have created many different kinds of bonds with various characteristics. We describe some of the more common features of bonds in the following paragraphs.

Serial Bonds

Some companies issue several groups of bonds that mature at different dates. As a result, the bonds are repaid gradually over a number of years. Because these bonds mature in series, they are called **serial bonds.** For example, $1 million of serial bonds might mature at the rate of $100,000 each year from 6 to 15 years after the bonds were issued. There would be 10 groups (or series) of bonds of $100,000 each. One series would mature after six years, another after seven years, and another each successive year until the final series is repaid.

Sinking Fund Bonds

As an alternative to serial bonds, **sinking fund bonds** all mature on the same date. To reduce some of the risk for owners, these bonds require the issuer to create a *sinking fund,* which is a separate pool of assets used only to retire the bonds at maturity. In effect, the issuer must start to set aside the cash to pay off the bonds long before they mature.

Convertible Bonds

Some companies issue **convertible bonds** that can be exchanged by the bondholders for a fixed number of shares of the issuing company's common stock. These bonds offer issuers the advantage that they might be settled without paying back the cash initially borrowed. Convertible bonds also offer the bondholders the potential to participate in future increases in the market value of the stock. However, if the stock does not appreciate, the bondholders continue to receive periodic interest and will receive the par value when the bond matures. In most cases, the bondholders can decide whether and when to convert the bonds to stock. However, the issuer can force conversion by exercising an option to buy the bonds back at a price less than the market value of the stock.

Registered Bonds and Bearer Bonds

A company that issues **registered bonds** keeps a record of the names and addresses of the bonds' owners. Then, over the life of the bonds, the company makes interest payments by sending checks to these registered owners. When one investor sells a bond to another investor, the issuer must be notified of the change. Registered bonds offer the issuer the practical advantage of not having to actually issue bond certificates to the investors. This arrangement also protects investors against loss or theft of the bonds.

Unregistered bonds are called **bearer bonds** because they are payable to whoever holds them (the *bearer*). Since there may be no record of sales or exchanges, the holder of a bearer bond is presumed to be its rightful owner. As a result, lost or stolen bonds are difficult to replace.

Many bearer bonds are also **coupon bonds.** This term reflects the fact that interest coupons are attached to each bond. Each coupon matures on a specific interest payment date. The owner detaches each coupon when it matures and presents it to a bank or broker for collection. At maturity, the owner follows the same process and presents the bond certificates to a bank or broker. Because there is no readily available record of who actually receives the interest, the income tax law discourages companies from issuing new coupon bonds.

Secured Bonds and Debentures

When bonds are secured, specific assets of the issuing company are pledged (or *mortgaged*) as collateral. This arrangement gives the bondholders additional protection against default by the issuer. If the issuing company fails to pay the interest or maturity value, the secured bondholders can demand that the collateral be sold and the proceeds used to repay the debt.

In contrast to secured bonds, unsecured bonds are potentially more risky because they are supported by only the issuer's general credit standing. Unsecured bonds also are called **debentures.** Because of the greater risk of default, a company generally must be financially strong to successfully issue debentures at a favorable rate of interest.

Sometimes, companies issue debentures that rank below certain other unsecured liabilities of the company. Debentures such as this are called *subordinated debentures.* Recall from the discussion at the beginning of the chapter that **L.A. Gear Inc.** issued subordinated debentures. In a liquidation, the subordinated debentures would not be repaid until the claims of the more senior, unsecured liabilities were first satisfied.

Bond Market Values

Bonds are securities and can be easily traded between investors. Because they are bought and sold in the market, they have a market value. As a matter of convenience, bond market values are expressed as a percentage of their face value. For example, a company's bonds might be trading at 103½, which means that they can be bought or sold for 103.5% of their par value. If other bonds are trading at 95, they can be bought or sold at 95% of their par value.

THE PROCESS OF ISSUING BONDS

When a company issues bonds, it normally sells them to an investment firm called an *underwriter.* In turn, the underwriter resells the bonds to the public. In some situations, the issuer may sell the bonds directly to investors as the cash is needed.

The legal document that identifies the rights and obligations of the bondholders and the issuer is called the **bond indenture.** In effect, the bond indenture is the legal contract between the issuer and the bondholders. Although the practice is less common today, each bondholder may receive an actual bond certificate as evidence of the company's debt. However, most companies reduce their costs by not issuing certificates to registered bondholders.

If the underwriter sells the bonds to a large number of investors, the bondholders' interests are represented and protected by a *trustee.* The trustee monitors the issuer to ensure that it complies with the obligations in the bond indenture. Most trustees are large banks or trust companies.

Accounting for the Issuance of Bonds

Before bonds are issued, the terms of the indenture are drawn up and accepted by the trustee. If the bonds are to be offered to the general public by the underwriter, they must be registered with the Securities and Exchange Commission (SEC), which means that the issuer must provide extensive financial information in special reports.

For example, suppose that the Barnes Company receives authorization from the SEC to issue $800,000 of 9%, 20-year bonds dated January 1, 1996, that are due on

December 31, 2015. They will pay interest semiannually on each June 30 and December 31. After the bond indenture is accepted by the trustee on behalf of the bondholders, all or a portion of the bonds may be sold to the underwriter. If all the bonds are sold at their par value, Barnes Company makes this entry to record the sale:

1996					
Jan.	1	Cash	800,000.00	
		Bonds Payable		800,000.00
		Sold bonds at par.		

This entry reflects the fact that the company's cash and long-term liabilities are increased.

Six months later, the first semiannual interest payment is made, and Barnes records the payment with this entry:

1996					
June	30	Interest Expense	36,000.00	
		Cash		36,000.00
		Paid semiannual interest on bonds.		
		(9% × $800,000 × 1/2).		

When the bonds mature 20 years later, Barnes Company will record its payment of the maturity value with the following entry:

2015					
Dec.	31	Bonds Payable	800,000.00	
		Cash		800,000.00
		Paid bonds at maturity.		

SELLING BONDS BETWEEN INTEREST DATES

Like the previous example, many bonds are sold on their original issue date. However, circumstances may cause a company to actually sell some of the bonds later. If so, it is likely that the selling date will fall between interest payment dates. When this happens, the purchasers normally pay the issuer the purchase price plus any interest accrued since the issue date or the preceding interest payment date. This accrued interest is then refunded to the purchasers on the next interest date. For example, assume that the Fields Company sold $100,000 of its 9% bonds at par on March 1, 19X1, which was two months after the original issue date. The interest on the bonds is payable semiannually on each June 30 and December 31. Because two months have passed, the issuer collects two months' interest from the buyer at the time of the sale. This amount is $1,500 ($100,000 × 9% × 2/12). This situation is represented by the following diagram:

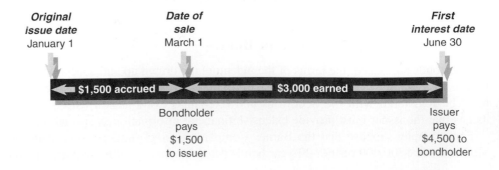

Original issue date	*Date of sale*	*First interest date*
January 1	March 1	June 30

← $1,500 accrued → | ← $3,000 earned →

| | Bondholder pays $1,500 to issuer | Issuer pays $4,500 to bondholder |

The issuer's entry to record the sale is:

Mar.	1	Cash	101,500.00	
		Interest Payable		1,500.00
		Bonds Payable		100,000.00
		Sold $100,000 of bonds with two months' accrued interest.		

Note that the liabilities for the interest and the bonds are recorded in separate accounts.

When the June 30 semiannual interest date arrives, the issuer pays a full six months' interest of $4,500 ($100,000 × 9% × 1/2) to the bondholder. This payment includes the four months' interest of $3,000 earned by the bondholder from March 1 to June 30 plus the refund of the two months' accrued interest collected by the issuer when the bonds were sold. The issuer's entry to record this first payment is:

June	30	Interest Payable	1,500.00	
		Interest Expense	3,000.00	
		Cash		4,500.00
		Paid semiannual interest on the bonds.		

The practice of collecting and then refunding the accrued interest with the next interest payment may seem like a roundabout way to do business. However, it greatly simplifies the bond issuer's administrative efforts. To understand this point, suppose that a company sells bonds on 15 or 20 different dates between the original issue date and the first interest payment date. If the issuer did not collect the accrued interest from the buyers, it would have to pay different amounts of cash to each of them in accordance with how much time had passed since they purchased their bonds. To make the correct payments, the issuer would have to keep detailed records of the purchasers and the dates on which they bought their bonds. Issuers avoid this extra record-keeping by having each buyer pay the accrued interest at the time of purchase. Then, the company pays full six months' interest to all purchasers, regardless of when they bought the bonds.

BOND INTEREST RATES

The interest rate to be paid by the issuer of bonds is specified in the indenture and on the bond certificates. Because it is stated in the indenture, this rate is called the **contract rate** of the bonds. (This rate also is known as the *coupon rate,* the *stated rate,* or the *nominal rate.*) The amount of interest to be paid each year is determined by multiplying the par value of the bonds by the contract rate. The contract rate is usually stated on an annual basis, even if the interest is to be paid semiannually. For example, suppose that a company issues a $1,000, 8% bond that pays interest semiannually. As a result, the annual interest of $80 (8% × $1,000) will be paid in two semiannual payments of $40 each.

Although the contract rate sets the amount of interest that the issuer pays in *cash,* the contract rate is not necessarily the rate of interest *expense* actually incurred by the issuer. In fact, the interest expense depends on the market value of the issuer's bonds, which depends on the purchasers' opinions about the risk of lending to the issuer. This perceived risk (as well as the supply of and demand for bonds) is reflected in the market rate for bond interest. The **market rate** is the consensus rate that borrowers are willing to pay and that lenders are willing to earn at the level of risk inherent in the bonds. This rate changes often (even daily) in response to changes in the supply of and demand for bonds. The market rate tends to go up when the demand for bonds decreases or the supply increases. The rate tends to go down when the supply of bonds decreases or the demand increases.

Because many factors affect the bond market, various companies face different interest rates for their bonds. The market rate for a specific set of bonds depends on the level of risk investors assign to them. As the level of risk increases, the rate increases. Market rates also are affected by the length of the bonds' life. Long-term bonds generally have higher rates because they are more risky.

Many bond issuers offer a contract rate of interest equal to the rate they expect the market to demand as of the bonds' issuance date. If the contract and market rates are equal, the bonds sell at their par value. However, if the contract and market rates are not equal, the bonds are not sold at their par value. Instead, they are sold at a *premium* above their par value or at a *discount* below their par value. Observe the relationship between the interest rates and the issue price of the bonds' values in this table:

When the contract rate is		The bond sells
Above the market rate	⇒	At a *premium*
At the market rate	⇒	At *par value*
Below the market rate	⇒	At a *discount*

Over the last two decades, some companies have issued *zero-coupon bonds* that do not provide any periodic interest payments. Because this contract rate of 0% is always below the market rate, these bonds are always issued at prices less than their face values.

Progress Check

13-4 Unsecured bonds that are backed only by the issuer's general credit standing are called: *(a)* Serial bonds; *(b)* Debentures; *(c)* Registered bonds; *(d)* Convertible bonds; *(e)* Bearer bonds.

13-5 How do you calculate the amount of interest a bond issuer will pay each year?

13-6 On May 1, a company sold 9% bonds with a $500,000 par value that pay semiannual interest on each January 1 and July 1. The bonds were sold at par value plus interest accrued since January 1. The bond issuer's entry to record the first semiannual interest payment on July 1 should include: *(a)* A debit to Interest Payable for $15,000; *(b)* A debit to Interest Expense for $22,500; *(c)* A credit to Interest Payable for $7,500.

13-7 When the contract rate is above the market rate, do the bonds sell at a premium or a discount? Do the purchasers pay more or less than the par value of the bonds?

BONDS SOLD AT A DISCOUNT

LO 3
Estimate the price of bonds issued at a discount and describe their effects on the issuer's financial statements.

As we described in the previous section, a **discount on bonds payable** arises when a company issues bonds with a contract rate less than the market rate. The expected issue price of the bonds can be found by calculating the *present value* of the expected cash flows, discounted at the market rate of interest.

To illustrate, assume that a company offers to issue bonds with a $100,000 par value, an 8% annual contract rate, and a five-year life. Also assume that the market rate of interest for this company's bonds is 10%.[5] In exchange for the purchase price received from the buyers, these bonds obligate the issuer to pay out two different future cash flows:

1. $100,000 at the end of the bonds' five-year life.
2. $4,000 (4% × $100,000) at the end of each six-month interest period throughout the five-year life of the bonds.

---

[5]The spread between the contract rate and the market rate of interest on a new bond issue is seldom more than a fraction of a percent. However, we use a difference of 2% here to emphasize the effects.

To estimate the bonds' issue price, use the market rate of interest to calculate the present value of the future cash flows. Using an annuity table of present values, you must work with *semiannual* compounding periods. Thus, the annual market rate of 10% is changed to the semiannual rate of 5%. Likewise, the five-year life of the bonds is changed to 10 semiannual periods.

The actual calculation requires two steps: (1) find the present value of the $100,000 maturity payment and (2) find the present value of the annuity of 10 payments of $4,000 each.

The present values can be found by using Table 13–1 (on page 475) for the single maturity payment and Table 13–2 for the annuity. To complete the first step, enter Table 13–1 on row 10 and go across to the 5% column. The table value is 0.6139. Second, enter Table 13–2 on row 10 and go across to the 5% column, where the table value is 7.7217. This schedule shows the results when you multiply the cash flow amounts by the table values and add them together:

Cash Flow	Table	Table Value	Amount	Present Value
Par value	13–1	0.6139	$100,000	$61,390
Interest (annuity)	13–2	7.7217	4,000	30,887
Total				$92,277

If 5% is the appropriate semiannual interest rate for the bonds in the current market, the maximum price that informed buyers would offer for the bonds is $92,277. This amount is also the minimum price that the issuer would accept.

If the issuer accepts $92,277 cash for its bonds on the original issue date of December 31, 19X1, it records the event with this entry:

19X1				
Dec.	31	Cash	92,277.00	
		Discount on Bonds Payable	7,723.00	
		Bonds Payable		100,000.00
		Sold bonds at a discount on the original issue date.		

This entry causes the bonds to appear in the long-term liability section of the issuer's balance sheet as follows:

Long-term liabilities:
Bonds payable, 8%, due December 31, 19X6 . . . . $100,000
Less discount 7,723 $92,277

This presentation shows that the discount is deducted from the par value of the bonds to produce the **carrying amount** of the bonds payable. As we saw regarding notes payable in the last chapter, the carrying amount is the net amount at which the bonds are reflected on the balance sheet.

Allocating Interest and Amortizing the Discount

In the previous example, the issuer received $92,277 for its bonds and will pay the bondholders $100,000 after five years have passed. Because the $7,723 discount is eventually paid to the bondholders at maturity, it is part of the cost of using the $92,277 for five years. This table shows that the total interest cost of $47,723 is the difference between the amount repaid and the amount borrowed:

Amount repaid:	
Ten payments of $4,000	$ 40,000
Maturity amount	100,000
Total repaid	$140,000
Less amount borrowed	(92,277)
Total interest expense	$ 47,723

The total expense also equals the sum of the 10 cash payments and the discount:

Ten payments of $4,000	$ 40,000
Plus discount	7,723
Total interest expense	$ 47,723

In describing these bonds and the interest expense, the issuer's accountant must accomplish two things. First, the total interest expense of $47,723 must be allocated among the 10 six-month periods in the bonds' life. Second, the carrying value of the bonds must be updated for each balance sheet. Two alternative methods accomplish these objectives. They are the straight-line and the interest methods of allocating interest. Because the process involves reducing the original discount on the bonds over the life of the bonds, it is also called *amortizing the bond discount*.

Straight-Line Method. The **straight-line method** of allocating the interest is the simpler of the two methods. This method allocates an equal portion of the total interest expense to each of the six-month interest periods.

In applying the straight-line method to the present example, the accountant divides the five years' total expense of $47,723 by 10 (the number of semiannual periods in the bonds' life). The result is $4,772 per period.[6] The same number can be found by dividing the $7,723 original discount by 10. That result is $772, which is the amount of discount to be amortized in each interest period. When the $772 of amortized discount is added to the $4,000 cash payment, the total interest expense for each six-month period is $4,772.

When the semiannual cash payment is made, the issuer uses the following entry to record the interest expense and update the balance of the bond liability:

19X2					
June	30	Interest Expense	4,772.00	
		Discount on Bonds Payable		772.00
		Cash		4,000.00
		To record six months' interest and discount amortization.		

Note that the $772 credit to the Discount on Bonds Payable account actually *increases* the bonds' carrying value. The increase comes about by *decreasing* the balance of the contra account that is subtracted from the Bonds Payable account.

As an example of this, **Chiquita Brands International's** 1994 annual report disclosed debentures with a par value of $250,000,000 and a contract rate of 9⅝%. A footnote explained that the bonds had an "imputed interest rate of 9.8%"

---

[6]For simplicity, all calculations have been rounded to the nearest whole dollar. Use the same practice when solving the exercises and problems at the end of the chapter.

Illustration 13-4 Allocating Interest Expense and Amortizing the Bond Discount with the Straight-Line Method

			Payments			
	(a)	(b)	(c)		(d)	(e)
Period Ending	Beginning Balance	Debit Interest Expense	Credit Discount on Bonds		Credit Cash	Ending Balance
	Prior (e)	$47,723/10	$7,723/10		4% × $100,000	(a) + (c)
6/30/X2	$92,277	$ 4,772	$ 772		$ 4,000	$ 93,049
12/31/X2	93,049	4,772	772		4,000	93,821
6/30/X3	93,821	4,772	772		4,000	94,593
12/31/X3	94,593	4,772	772		4,000	95,365
6/30/X4	95,365	4,772	772		4,000	96,137
12/31/X4	96,137	4,772	772		4,000	96,909
6/30/X5	96,909	4,772	772		4,000	97,681
12/31/X5	97,681	4,772	772		4,000	98,453
6/30/X6	98,453	4,772	772		4,000	99,225
12/31/X6	99,225	4,775*	775		4,000	100,000
Total		$47,723	= $7,723	+	$40,000	

*Adjusted for rounding.

and "unamortized discount of $2,632,000 and $2,805,000" at the end of 1994 and 1993, respectively. The carrying value was $247,368,000 at the end of 1994 and $247,195,000 at the end of 1993. Thus, the unamortized discount decreased by $173,000 and the carrying value of the bonds increased by exactly the same amount.

Illustration 13–4 presents a table similar to the amortization tables that you have studied for notes payable. It shows how the interest expense is allocated among the 10 six-month periods in the bonds' life. It also shows how amortizing the bond discount causes the balance of the net liability to increase until it reaches $100,000 at the end of the bonds' life. Notice the following points as you analyze Illustration 13–4:

1. The $92,277 beginning balance in column *a* equals the cash received from selling the bonds. It also equals the $100,000 face amount of the bonds less the initial $7,723 discount from selling the bonds for less than par.

2. The semiannual interest expense of $4,772 in column *b* for each row equals the amount obtained by dividing the total expense of $47,723 by 10.

3. The credit to the Discount on Bonds Payable account in column *c* equals one-tenth of the total discount of $7,723.

4. The $4,000 interest payment in column *d* is the result of multiplying the $100,000 par value of the bonds by the 4% semiannual contract rate of interest.

5. The ending balance in column *e* equals the beginning balance in column *a* plus the $772 discount amortization in column *c*. This ending balance then becomes the beginning balance on the next row in the table.

6. The balance in column *e* continues to grow each period by the $772 of discount amortization until it finally equals the par value of the bonds when they mature.

The three payment columns show that the company incurs a $4,772 interest expense each period but pays only $4,000. The $772 unpaid portion of the expense is appropriately added to the balance of the liability. It is added to the liability by being taken from the contra account balance. This table shows you how the balance of the discount is partially amortized every six months until it is eliminated:

Period Ending	Beginning Discount Balance	Amount Amortized	Ending Discount Balance
6/30/X2	$7,723	$ (772)	$6,951
12/31/X2	6,951	(772)	6,179
6/30/X3	6,179	(772)	5,407
12/31/X3	5,407	(772)	4,635
6/30/X4	4,635	(772)	3,863
12/31/X4	3,863	(772)	3,091
6/30/X5	3,091	(772)	2,319
12/31/X5	2,319	(772)	1,547
6/30/X6	1,547	(772)	775
12/31/X6	775	(775)	0
Total		$(7,723)	

Interest Method. Straight-line allocations of interest used to be widely applied in practice. However, generally accepted accounting principles now allow the straight-line method to be used only if the results do not differ materially from those obtained by using the **interest method** to allocate the interest over the life of the bonds.[7]

The interest method is exactly the same process for allocating interest that you first learned in Chapter 12 for notes payable. Interest expense for a period is found by multiplying the balance of the liability at the beginning of that period by the original market interest rate.

In Illustration 13–5, we present an amortization table for our example. The key difference between Illustrations 13–4 and 13–5 lies in the calculation of the interest expense in column *b*. Instead of assigning an equal amount of interest to each interest period, the interest method assigns an increasing amount of interest over the bonds' life because the balance of the liability increases over the five years. The interest expense in column *b* equals the original 5% market interest rate times the balance of the liability at the beginning of each period. Notice that both methods allocate the same $47,723 of total expense among the five years, but with different patterns.

The amount of discount amortized in any period is the difference between the interest expense in column *b* and the cash payment in column *d*. In effect, the accrued but unpaid portion of the interest expense in column *c* is added to the net liability in column *a* to get the ending balance in column *e*.

In the following table, you can see how the balance of the discount is amortized by the interest method until it reaches zero:

Period Ending	Beginning Discount Balance	Amount Amortized	Ending Discount Balance
6/30/X2	$7,723	$ (614)	$7,109
12/31/X2	7,109	(645)	6,464
6/30/X3	6,464	(677)	5,787
12/31/X3	5,787	(711)	5,076
6/30/X4	5,076	(746)	4,330
12/31/X4	4,330	(784)	3,546
6/30/X5	3,546	(823)	2,723
12/31/X5	2,723	(864)	1,859
6/30/X6	1,859	(907)	952
12/31/X6	952	(952)	0
Total		$(7,723)	

---

[7]FASB, *Accounting Standards—Current Text* (Norwalk, CT, 1995), sec. I69.108. First published in *APB Opinion No. 21*, par. 15.

Illustration 13–5 Allocating Interest Expense and Amortizing the Bond Discount with the Interest Method

	(a)	(b)		(c)		(d)	(e)
				Payments			
Period Ending	**Beginning Balance** *Prior (e)*	**Debit Interest Expense** *5% × (a)*	=	**Credit Discount on Bonds** *(b) − (d)*	+	**Credit Cash** *4% × $100,000*	**Ending Balance** *(a) + (c)*
6/30/X2	$92,277	$ 4,614		$ 614		$ 4,000	$ 92,891
12/31/X2	92,891	4,645		645		4,000	93,536
6/30/X3	93,536	4,677		677		4,000	94,213
12/31/X3	94,213	4,711		711		4,000	94,924
6/30/X4	94,924	4,746		746		4,000	95,670
12/31/X4	95,670	4,784		784		4,000	96,454
6/30/X5	96,454	4,823		823		4,000	97,277
12/31/X5	97,277	4,864		864		4,000	98,141
6/30/X6	98,141	4,907		907		4,000	99,048
12/31/X6	99,048	4,952		952		4,000	100,000
Total		$47,723	=	$7,723	+	$40,000	

Except for the differences in the amounts, journal entries that record the expense and update the liability balance are the same under the interest method and the straight-line method. For example, the entry to record the interest payment at the end of the first interest period is:

19X2				
June	30	Interest Expense	4,614.00	
		Discount on Bonds Payable		614.00
		Cash		4,000.00
		To record six months' interest and discount amortization.		

The accountant uses the numbers in Illustration 13–5 to make similar entries throughout the five-year life of the bonds.

Comparing the Straight-Line and Interest Methods. With this background in place, we can now look more closely at the differences between the straight-line and interest methods of allocating interest among the periods in the bonds' life. In Illustration 13–6, the two graphs illustrate the differences for bonds issued at a discount.

The horizontal line in the first graph in Illustration 13–6 represents the amounts of interest expense reported each period under the straight-line method. The upward sloping line represents the increasing amounts of interest reported under the interest method. The amounts increase because the constant 5% rate is applied to the growing balance of the liability.

The horizontal line in the second graph represents the constant rate of 5% that the interest method uses to determine the interest expense for every six-month period. The downward sloping line represents the changing interest rates produced by the straight-line method when the bond is issued at a discount. The interest rates decrease each period because the amount of interest expense remains constant while the balance of the liability increases.

The interest method is preferred over the straight-line method because it provides a more reasonable description of the growth of the liability and the amount of interest expense incurred each period. As we mentioned, the straight-line method can be

Illustration 13-6 Comparing the Straight-Line and Interest Methods of Allocating Interest on a Bond Sold at a Discount

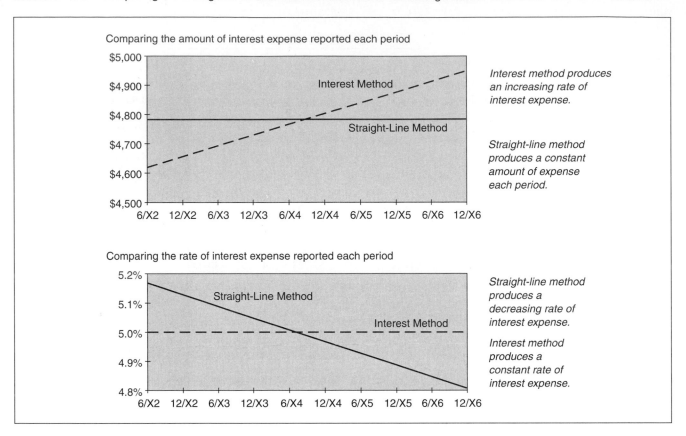

used only if the results do not differ materially from those obtained by using the interest method.

Progress Check

A company recently issued a group of five-year, 6% bonds with a $100,000 par value. The interest is to be paid semiannually, and the market interest rate was 8% on the issue date. Use this information to answer the following questions:

13-8   What is the bonds' selling price? *(a)* $100,000; *(b)* $92,393; *(c)* $91,893; *(d)* $100,321; *(e)* $92,016.

13-9   What is the journal entry to record the sale?

13-10   What is the amount of interest expense recorded at the time of the first semiannual cash payment *(a)* using the straight-line method of allocating interest and *(b)* using the interest method of allocating interest?

BONDS SOLD AT A PREMIUM

LO 4
Estimate the price of bonds issued at a premium and describe their effects on the issuer's financial statements.

When bonds carry a contract interest rate that is greater than the market rate, the bonds sell at a price greater than the par value and the difference between the par and market values is called the **premium on bonds.** In effect, buyers bid up the price of the bonds until it reaches the level that creates the current market rate of interest. As we explained for the discount situation, this premium market price can be estimated by finding the present value of the expected cash flows from the bonds at the market interest rate.

For example, assume that a company decides to issue bonds with a $100,000 par value, a 12% annual contract rate, and a five-year life. On the issue date, the market interest rate for the bonds is only 10%. Thus, potential buyers of these bonds bid up their market price until the effective rate equals the market rate. To estimate this price, we use the 5% semiannual market rate to find the present value of the expected cash flows. The cash flows consist of:

1. $100,000 at the end of the bonds' five-year life.
2. $6,000 (6% × $100,000) at the end of each six-month interest period throughout the five-year life of the bonds.

The present values can be found by using Table 13–1 (page 475) for the single maturity payment and Table 13–2 for the annuity. To complete the first step, enter Table 13–1 on row 10 and go across to the 5% column. The table value is 0.6139. Second, enter Table 13–2 on row 10 and go across to the 5% column, where the table value is 7.7217. Finally, use these table values to reduce the future cash flows to their present value. This schedule shows the results when you multiply the cash flow amounts by the table values and add them together:

Cash Flow	Table	Table Value	Amount	Present Value
Par value	13–1	0.6139	$100,000	$ 61,390
Interest (annuity)	13–2	7.7217	6,000	46,330
Total				$107,720

If 5% is the appropriate semiannual interest rate for the bonds in the current market, the maximum price that informed buyers would offer for the bonds is $107,720. This amount is also the minimum price that the issuer would accept.

If the issuer does accept $107,720 cash for its bonds on the original issue date of December 31, 19X1, it records the event with this entry:

19X1				
Dec.	31	Cash	107,720.00	
		Premium on Bonds Payable		7,720.00
		Bonds Payable		100,000.00
		Sold bonds at a premium on the original issue date.		

This entry causes the bonds to appear in the long-term liability section of the issuer's balance sheet as follows:

Long-term liabilities:		
Bonds payable, 8%, due December 31, 19X6	$100,000	
Plus premium	7,720	$107,720

This presentation shows that the premium is added to the par value of the bonds to produce their carrying amount.

Allocating Interest Expense and Amortizing the Premium

Over the life of these premium bonds, the issuer pays back $160,000, which consists of the 10 periodic interest payments of $6,000 plus the $100,000 par value. Because it borrowed $107,720, the total interest expense will be $52,280. This table shows the calculation:

Illustration 13-7 Allocating Interest Expense and Amortizing the Bond Premium with the Interest Method

	(a)	(b) Debit Interest Expense	(c) Debit Premium on Bonds		(d)	(e)
			Payments			
Period Ending	Beginning Balance *Prior (e)*	**Expense** *5% × (a)*	+ **on Bonds** = *(d) − (b)*		**Credit Cash** *6% × $100,000*	**Ending Balance** *(a) − (c)*
6/30/X2	$107,720	$ 5,386	$ 614		$ 6,000	$107,106
12/31/X2	107,106	5,355	645		6,000	106,461
6/30/X3	106,461	5,323	677		6,000	105,784
12/31/X3	105,784	5,289	711		6,000	105,073
6/30/X4	105,073	5,254	746		6,000	104,327
12/31/X4	104,327	5,216	784		6,000	103,543
6/30/X5	103,543	5,177	823		6,000	102,720
12/31/X5	102,720	5,136	864		6,000	101,856
6/30/X6	101,856	5,093	907		6,000	100,949
12/31/X6	100,949	5,051*	949		6,000	100,000
Total		$52,280	+ $7,720	=	$60,000	

*Adjusted for rounding.

Amount repaid:	
Ten payments of $6,000	$ 60,000
Maturity amount	100,000
Total repaid	$160,000
Less amount borrowed	(107,720)
Total interest expense	$ 52,280

The following calculation confirms that the total expense also equals the difference between the 10 cash payments and the premium:

Ten payments of $6,000	$ 60,000
Less premium	(7,720)
Total interest expense	$ 52,280

The premium is subtracted because it will not be paid to the bondholders when the bonds mature.

This total interest expense can be allocated over the 10 semiannual periods with either the straight-line or the interest method. Because the interest method is preferred, it is the only one illustrated for these bonds. Illustration 13–7 shows an amortization schedule for the bonds using this method.

Again, column *a* of the illustration shows the beginning balance, and column *b* shows the amount of expense at 5% of the beginning balance. But, the amount of cash paid out in column *d* is larger than the expense because the payment is based on the higher 6% contract rate. As a result, the excess payment over the expense reduces the principal. These amounts are shown in column *c*. Finally, column *e* shows the new ending balance after the amortized premium in column *c* is deducted from the beginning balance in column *a*.

The following table shows how the premium is reduced by the amortization process over the life of the bonds:

Period Ending	Beginning Premium Balance	Amount Amortized	Ending Premium Balance
6/30/X2	$7,720	$ (614)	$7,106
12/31/X2	7,106	(645)	6,461
6/30/X3	6,461	(677)	5,784
12/31/X3	5,784	(711)	5,073
6/30/X4	5,073	(746)	4,327
12/31/X4	4,327	(784)	3,543
6/30/X5	3,543	(823)	2,720
12/31/X5	2,720	(864)	1,856
6/30/X6	1,856	(907)	949
12/31/X6	949	(949)	0
Total		$(7,720)	

The effect of premium amortization on interest expense and on the liability can be seen in this journal entry on June 30, 19X2, when the issuer makes the first semiannual interest payment:

19X2				
June	30	Interest Expense	5,386.00	
		Premium on Bonds Payable	614.00	
		Cash		6,000.00
		To record six months' interest and premium amortization.		

Similar entries are recorded at each payment date until the bonds mature at the end of 19X6. However, the interest method causes the company to report decreasing amounts of interest expense and increasing amounts of premium amortization.

ACCOUNTING FOR ACCRUED INTEREST EXPENSE

If a bond's interest period does not coincide with the issuing company's accounting period, an adjusting entry is necessary to recognize the interest expense that has accrued since the most recent interest payment. For example, assume that the bonds described in Illustration 13–7 were issued on September 1, 19X1, instead of December 31, 19X1. As a result, four months' interest (and premium amortization) accrue before the end of the 19X1 calendar year. Because the reporting period ends on that date, an adjusting entry is needed to capture this information about the bonds.

Interest for the four months ended December 31, 19X1, equals $3,591, which is 4/6 of the first six months' interest of $5,386. The premium amortization is $409, which is 4/6 of the first six months' amortization of $614. The sum of the interest expense and the amortization is $4,000 ($3,591 + $409), which also equals 4/6 of the $6,000 cash payment that is due on March 1, 19X2. The accountant records these effects with this adjusting entry:

19X2				
Dec.	31	Interest Expense	3,591.00	
		Premium on Bonds Payable	409.00	
		Interest Payable		4,000.00
		To record four months' accrued interest and premium		
		amortization.		

Similar entries are made on each December 31 throughout the five-year life of the bonds.

When the $6,000 cash payment occurs on the next interest date, the journal entry recognizes the interest expense and amortization for January and February of 19X2 and eliminates the interest payable liability created by the adjusting entry. For this example, the accountant makes the following entry to record the payment on March 1, 19X2:

19X2					
Mar.	1	Interest Payable	4,000.00	
		Interest Expense ($5,386 × 2/6)	1,795.00	
		Premium on Bonds Payable ($614 × 2/6)	205.00	
		Cash		6,000.00
		To record two months' interest and amortization and eliminate the accrued interest liability.		

The interest payments made each September are recorded normally because the entire six-month interest period is included within a single fiscal year.

Progress Check

On December 31, 19X1, Cello Corporation issued 16%, 10-year bonds with a par value of $100,000. Interest is paid on June 30 and December 31. The bonds were sold to yield a 14% annual market rate of interest. Use this information to solve the following:

13-11   What is the selling price of the bonds?

13-12   Using the interest method of allocating interest expense, Cello would record the second interest payment (on December 31, 19X2) with a debit to Premium on Bonds Payable in the amount of: *(a)* $7,470; *(b)* $7,741; *(c)* $259; *(d)* $530; *(e)* $277.

13-13   How would the bonds appear in the long-term liability section of Cello's balance sheet as of December 31, 19X2?

RETIRING BONDS PAYABLE

LO 2
Describe the various characteristics of different types of bonds and prepare entries to record bond issuances and retirements.

For various reasons, companies may want to retire some or all of their bonds prior to maturity. For example, if market interest rates decline significantly, a company may wish to replace old high-interest debt obligations with new lower interest debt. Many companies reserve the right to retire bonds early by issuing **callable bonds.** This means the bond indenture gives the issuing company an option to *call* the bonds before they mature by paying the par value plus a *call premium* to the bondholders. When interest rates were high in the 1980s, **AT&T Corporation** and many other companies issued callable bonds. When market rates dropped dramatically in the early 1990s, many of these bonds were called and retired.

Even if a specific bond issue is not callable, the issuer may be able to retire its bonds by repurchasing them on the open market at the current market price. Whether bonds are called or repurchased, the issuer is unlikely to pay a price that equals the bonds' carrying value. In a repurchase, this is because a bond's market value changes as the market interest rate changes.

If there is a difference between the bonds' carrying value and the amount paid in a bond retirement transaction, the issuer must record a gain or loss equal to the difference.[8] For example, a few years ago, **Mattel Inc.** redeemed debentures that had a principal amount of $99.1 million, paying 105.9% of par. The write-off of unamor-

---

[8]Any material gain or loss from retiring bonds or other debt must be reported on the debtor's income statement as an extraordinary gain or loss. FASB, *Accounting Standards—Current Text* (Norwalk, CT, 1995), sec. D14.105. First published in *FASB Statement of Financial Accounting Standards No. 4,* par. 8.

tized discount associated with the debt together with the early redemption premium resulted in an extraordinary charge of $4.5 million, net of an income tax benefit of $2.6 million.

As another example, assume that a company issued callable bonds with a par value of $100,000. The call option required the issuer to pay a call premium of $3,000 to the bondholders in addition to the par value. Also assume that immediately after a June 30 interest payment, the bonds had a carrying value of $104,500. Then, on July 1, the issuer called all of the bonds and paid $103,000 to the bondholders. The issuer must recognize a $1,500 gain as a result of the difference between the bonds' carrying value of $104,500 and the retirement price of $103,000. This entry records the bond retirement:

July	1	Bonds Payable	100,000.00	
		Premium on Bonds Payable	4,500.00	
		Gain on Retirement of Bonds		1,500.00
		Cash		103,000.00
		To record the retirement of bonds.		

Although a company generally must call all of its bonds when it exercises a call option, it may retire as many or as few bonds as it desires through open market transactions. If it retires less than the entire set of bonds, it recognizes a gain or loss for the difference between the carrying value of those bonds and the amount paid to acquire them.

MORTGAGES AS SECURITY FOR BONDS AND NOTES

Earlier in this chapter, we said that some bonds are secured by collateral agreements, while others, called *debentures,* are not secured. These risk-reducing arrangements also are widely used for notes payable, including car and home loans. Unsecured bonds and notes are more risky because the issuer's obligation to pay interest and principal has the same priority as all other unsecured liabilities in the event of bankruptcy. If the company's financial troubles leave it unable to pay its debts in full, the unsecured creditors (including the holders of debentures) lose a proportion or all of their balances.

Thus, a company's ability to borrow money with or without collateral agreements depends on its credit rating. In many cases, debt financing is simply unavailable if the borrower cannot provide security to the creditors with a collateral agreement. Even if unsecured loans are available, the creditors are likely to charge a higher rate of interest to compensate for the additional risk. To borrow the funds at a more economical rate, many notes payable and bonds are secured by collateral agreements called *mortgages.*

A **mortgage** is a legal agreement that helps protect a lender if a borrower fails to make the required payments on a note payable or on bonds payable. A mortgage gives the lender the right to be paid out of the cash proceeds from the sale of the borrower's specific assets identified in the mortgage.

A separate legal document, called the *mortgage contract,* describes the terms of a mortgage. The mortgage contract is given to the lender who accepts a note payable or to the trustee for the bondholders. Mortgage contracts usually require a borrower to pay all property taxes on the mortgaged assets, to maintain them properly, and to carry adequate insurance against fire and other types of losses. These requirements are designed to keep the property from losing value and thus avoid diminishing the lender's security. Importantly, mortgage contracts grant the lender the right to *fore-close* on the property if the borrower fails to pay in accordance with the terms of the debt agreement. If a foreclosure occurs, a court either orders the property to be sold or simply grants legal title of the mortgaged property to the lender. If the property is sold, the proceeds are first applied to court costs and then to the claims of the mortgage holder. If there are any additional proceeds, the borrower is entitled to receive them. However, this cash is subject to any claims from the company's unsecured creditors.

Given the relevance of information about a company's security agreements with its lenders, the footnotes to the financial statements may describe the amounts of assets pledged as security against liabilities. The next section describes a ratio that can be used to assess a borrower's situation with respect to its security agreements.

Progress Check

13-14   Six years ago, a company issued $500,000 of 6%, 8-year bonds at a price of 95. The current carrying value is $493,750. The company retired 50% of the bonds by buying them on the open market at a price of 102 1/2. What is the amount of gain or loss on retirement of the bonds?

13-15   A mortgage is:
   a. A promissory note that requires the borrower to make a series of payments consisting of interest and principal.
   b. A legal agreement that protects a lender by giving the lender the right to be paid out of the cash proceeds from the sale of specific assets owned by the borrower.
   c. A company's long-term liability that requires periodic payments of interest and a final payment of its par value when it matures.

USING THE INFORMATION— PLEDGED ASSETS TO SECURED LIABILITIES

LO 5
Calculate and describe how to use the ratio of pledged assets to secured liabilities.

As you have learned in this chapter, creditors can reduce their risk with agreements that can force borrowers to sell specific assets to settle overdue debts. Investors who consider buying a company's secured debt obligations need to determine whether the pledged assets of the debtor provide adequate security. One method of evaluating this is to calculate the ratio of **pledged assets to secured liabilities.** This is calculated by dividing the book value of the company's assets pledged as collateral by the book value of the liabilities secured by these collateral agreements:

$$\text{Pledged assets to secured liabilities} = \frac{\text{Book value of pledged assets}}{\text{Book value of secured liabilities}}$$

For example, suppose a company has assets with a book value of $2,300,000 that are pledged against loans with a balance of $1,000,000. The ratio is $2,300,000/$1,000,000 = 2.3 to 1. Although there are no hard and fast guidelines for interpreting the values of this ratio, 2.3 to 1 may be sufficiently high to provide the existing secured creditors with some comfort that the debts are safely covered by the assets.

The pledging of assets for the benefit of secured creditors also affects unsecured creditors. As an increasing portion of the assets are pledged, the unsecured creditors are less likely to receive a full repayment. In evaluating their position, unsecured creditors may gain some information from the ratio of pledged assets to secured creditors. For two reasons, an unusually large ratio may suggest that the unsecured creditors are at risk. First, secured creditors may have demanded an unusually large ratio because the value of the assets in liquidation is low. Second, the secured creditors may perceive that the ability of the company to meet its obligations from operating cash flows is weak.

In using this ratio, a creditor must be aware that the reported book value of the company's assets is unlikely to reflect their fair value. Thus, creditors would have better information if they could determine the assets' current market value and then use it in the ratio instead of book value. Major creditors may be able to get this information directly by asking the borrower to provide recent appraisals or other evidence of the assets' fair value. Other creditors may not have this option. In addition, using the ratio requires knowledge about the amounts of secured liabilities and pledged assets. This information may or may not be clearly identified in the financial statements.

Progress Check

13-16   At the end of 19X3, A to Z Company has $350,000 of unsecured liabilities and $575,000 of secured liabilities. The book value of pledged assets is $1,265,000. Calculate the ratio of pledged assets to secured liabilities.

13-17   Would the secured creditors or the unsecured creditors be more concerned if A to Z's ratio of pledged assets to secured liabilities was 1.7 to 1 the previous year?

PRESENT VALUE TABLES

Table 13–1
Present Value of $1

Periods	Rate							
	3%	4%	5%	6%	7%	8%	10%	12%
1	0.9709	0.9615	0.9524	0.9434	0.9346	0.9259	0.9091	0.8929
2	0.9426	0.9246	0.9070	0.8900	0.8734	0.8573	0.8264	0.7972
3	0.9151	0.8890	0.8638	0.8396	0.8163	0.7938	0.7513	0.7118
4	0.8885	0.8548	0.8227	0.7921	0.7629	0.7350	0.6830	0.6355
5	0.8626	0.8219	0.7835	0.7473	0.7130	0.6806	0.6209	0.5674
6	0.8375	0.7903	0.7462	0.7050	0.6663	0.6302	0.5645	0.5066
7	0.8131	0.7599	0.7107	0.6651	0.6227	0.5835	0.5132	0.4523
8	0.7894	0.7307	0.6768	0.6274	0.5820	0.5403	0.4665	0.4039
9	0.7664	0.7026	0.6446	0.5919	0.5439	0.5002	0.4241	0.3606
10	0.7441	0.6756	0.6139	0.5584	0.5083	0.4632	0.3855	0.3220
20	0.5537	0.4564	0.3769	0.3118	0.2584	0.2145	0.1486	0.1037
30	0.4120	0.3083	0.2314	0.1741	0.1314	0.0994	0.0573	0.0334

Table 13–2
Present Value of an Annuity of $1

Payments	Rate							
	3%	4%	5%	6%	7%	8%	10%	12%
1	0.9709	0.9615	0.9524	0.9434	0.9346	0.9259	0.9091	0.8929
2	1.9135	1.8861	1.8594	1.8334	1.8080	1.7833	1.7355	1.6901
3	2.8286	2.7751	2.7232	2.6730	2.6243	2.5771	2.4869	2.4018
4	3.7171	3.6299	3.5460	3.4651	3.3872	3.3121	3.1699	3.0373
5	4.5797	4.4518	4.3295	4.2124	4.1002	3.9927	3.7908	3.6048
6	5.4172	5.2421	5.0757	4.9173	4.7665	4.6229	4.3553	4.1114
7	6.2303	6.0021	5.7864	5.5824	5.3893	5.2064	4.8684	4.5638
8	7.0197	6.7327	6.4632	6.2098	5.9713	5.7466	5.3349	4.9676
9	7.7861	7.4353	7.1078	6.8017	6.5152	6.2469	5.7590	5.3282
10	8.5302	8.1109	7.7217	7.3601	7.0236	6.7101	6.1446	5.6502
20	14.8775	13.5903	12.4622	11.4699	10.5940	9.8181	8.5136	7.4694
30	19.6004	17.2920	15.3725	13.7648	12.4090	11.2578	9.4269	8.0552

SUMMARY OF THE CHAPTER IN TERMS OF LEARNING OBJECTIVES

LO 1. Calculate the payments on an installment note payable and describe their effects on the financial statements. Typical installment notes require one of two alternative payment patterns: (1) payments that include interest plus equal amounts of principal or (2) equal payments. In either case, interest is allocated to each period in a note's life by multiplying the carrying value by the original interest rate. If a note is repaid with equal payments, the payment's size is found by dividing the borrowed amount by the annuity table value for the interest rate and the number of payments.

LO 2. Describe the various characteristics of different types of bonds and prepare entries to record bond issuances and retirements. Bonds usually are issued to many investors. Serial bonds mature at different points in time. Companies that issue sinking fund bonds must accumulate a fund of assets to use to pay out the par value of the bonds at the maturity date. Convertible bonds can be exchanged by the bondholders for shares of the issuing company's stock. When bonds are registered, each bondholder's name and address is recorded by the issuing company. In contrast, bearer bonds are payable to whoever holds the bonds.

Some bonds are secured by mortgages on the issuer's assets while other bonds, called *debentures,* are unsecured. When bonds are sold between interest dates, the accrued interest is collected from the purchasers, who then are refunded that amount on the next interest payment date. Bonds can be retired early by the issuer by exercising a call option or by purchases on the open market. The issuer must recognize a gain or loss for the difference between the amount paid out and the bonds' carrying value.

LO 3. Estimate the price of bonds issued at a discount and describe their effects on the issuer's financial statements. The cash paid to bondholders on semiannual interest payment dates is calculated as one-half of the result of multiplying the par value of the bonds by their contract interest rate. The market value of a bond can be estimated by using the market interest rate to find the present values of the interest payments and the par value. Bonds are issued at a discount when the contract rate is less than the market rate. Then, the issuer records the issuance with a credit to the Bonds Payable account for the par value and a debit to Discount on Bonds Payable. The amount of interest assigned to each interest period can be allocated with the straight-line method if the result is not materially different from the results of applying the interest method. The interest method assigns interest to a period by multiplying the beginning carrying value by the original market interest rate.

LO 4. Estimate the price of bonds issued at a premium and describe their effects on the issuer's financial statements. Bonds are issued at a premium when the contract rate is higher than the market interest rate. The issuer records the premium in a supplemental account. The balance of this account is reduced over the life of the bonds through the interest allocation process.

LO 5. Calculate and describe how to use the ratio of pledged assets to secured liabilities. Secured and unsecured creditors are both concerned about the relationship between the amounts of assets owned by the debtor and the amounts of secured liabilities. The secured creditors are safer when the ratio of pledged assets to secured liabilities is larger, while the risks of unsecured creditors may be increased in this circumstance.

DEMONSTRATION PROBLEM

The Staley Tile Company patented and successfully test-marketed a new product. However, to expand its ability to produce and market the product, the company needed to raise $800,000 of additional financing. On January 1, 19X1, the company borrowed the money under these arrangements:

a. Staley signed a $400,000, 10% installment note that will be repaid with five equal annual installments. The payments will be made on December 31 of 19X1 through 19X5.

b. Staley issued five-year bonds with a par value of $400,000. The bonds have a 12% annual contract rate and pay interest on June 30 and December 31. The annual market interest rate for the bonds was 10% on January 1, 19X1.

Required

1. For the installment note, *(a)* calculate the size of each payment, *(b)* prepare an amortization table, and *(c)* present the entry for the first payment.

2. For the bonds, *(a)* estimate the issue price of the bonds; *(b)* present the January 1, 19X1, entry to record issuing the bonds; *(c)* prepare an amortization table using the interest method; *(d)* present the June 30, 19X1, entry to record the first payment of interest; and *(e)* present an entry to record retiring the bonds at the call price of $416,000 on January 1, 19X3.

- For the installment note, divide the borrowed amount by the annuity table factor (from Table 13–2 on page 475) for 10% and five payments. Prepare a table similar to Illustration 13–2 and use the numbers in the first line for the entry.

- For the bonds, estimate the issue price by using the market rate to find the present values of the bonds' cash flows. Then, use this result to record issuing the bonds. Next, develop an amortization table like Illustration 13–7, and use it to get the numbers that you need for the journal entry. Finally, use the table to find the carrying value as of the date of the retirement of the bonds that you need for the journal entry.

Planning the Solution

Solution to Demonstration Problem

Part 1:

Payment = Note balance/Table value = $400,000/3.7908 = $105,519
Table value is for 5 payments and an interest rate of 10%.

				Payments				
		(a)	(b) Debit		(c) Debit		(d)	(e)
Period Ending		Beginning Balance	Interest Expense	+	Notes Payable	=	Credit Cash	Ending Balance
19X1		$400,000	$ 40,000		$ 65,519		$105,519	$334,481
19X2		334,481	33,448		72,071		105,519	262,410
19X3		262,410	26,241		79,278		105,519	183,132
19X4		183,132	18,313		87,206		105,519	95,926
19X5		95,926	9,593		95,926		105,519	0
Total			$127,595		$400,000		$527,595	

19X1				
Dec.	31	Interest Expense	40,000.00	
		Notes Payable	65,519.00	
		Cash		105,519.00
		To record first installment payment.		

Part 2:

Estimated issue price of the bonds:

Cash Flow	Table	Table Value	Amount	Present Value
Par value	13–1	0.6139	$400,000	$245,560
Interest (annuity)	13–2	7.7217	24,000	185,321
Total				$430,881

Table value is for 10 payments and an interest rate of 5%.

19X1				
Jan.	1	Cash	430,881.00	
		Premium on Bonds Payable		30,881.00
		Bonds Payable		400,000.00
		Sold bonds at a premium.		

	(a)	Payments			(e)
Period Ending	Beginning Balance	(b) Debit Interest Expense	(c) Debit Premium on Bonds	(d) Credit Cash	Ending Balance
	Prior (e)	5% × (a)	(d) − (b)	6% × $400,000	(a) − (c)
6/30/X1	$430,881	$ 21,544	$ 2,456	$ 24,000	$428,425
12/31/X1	428,425	21,421	2,579	24,000	425,846
6/30/X2	425,846	21,292	2,708	24,000	423,138
12/31/X2	423,138	21,157	2,843	24,000	420,295
6/30/X3	420,295	21,015	2,985	24,000	417,310
12/31/X3	417,310	20,866	3,134	24,000	414,176
6/30/X4	414,176	20,709	3,291	24,000	410,885
12/31/X4	410,885	20,544	3,456	24,000	407,429
6/30/X5	407,429	20,371	3,629	24,000	403,800
12/31/X5	403,800	20,200*	3,800	24,000	400,000
Total		$209,119	$30,881	$240,000	

*Adjusted for rounding.

19X1				
June	30	Interest Expense	21,544.00	
		Premium on Bonds Payable	2,456.00	
		Cash		24,000.00
		Paid semiannual interest on the bonds.		

19X3				
Jan.	1	Bonds Payable	400,000.00	
		Premium on Bonds Payable	20,295.00	
		Cash		416,000.00
		Gain on Retirement of Bonds		4,295.00
		To record the retirement of bonds (carrying value determined as of December 31, 19X2).		

GLOSSARY

Bearer bonds bonds that are made payable to whoever holds them (called the *bearer*); these bonds are not registered. p. 458

Bond a company's long-term liability that requires periodic payments of interest and final payment of its par value when it matures; usually issued in denominations of $1,000. p. 456

Bond indenture the contract between the bond issuer and the bondholders; it identifies the rights and obligations of the parties. p. 459

Callable bonds bonds that give the issuer an option of retiring them before they mature. p. 472

Carrying amount the net amount at which bonds are reflected on the balance sheet; equals the par value of the bonds less any unamortized discount or plus any unamortized premium. p. 463

Contract rate the interest rate specified in the bond indenture; it is multiplied by the par value of the bonds to determine the amount of interest to be paid each year. p. 461

Convertible bonds bonds that can be exchanged by the bondholders for a fixed number of shares of the issuing company's common stock. p. 458

Coupon bonds bonds that have interest coupons attached to their certificates; the bondholders detach the coupons when they mature and present them to a bank for collection. p. 458

Debentures unsecured bonds that are supported by only the general credit standing of the issuer. p. 459

Discount on bonds payable the difference between the par value of a bond and its lower issue price or paying amount; arises when the contract rate is lower than the market rate. p. 462

Installment note promissory note that requires the borrower to make a series of payments consisting of interest and principal. p. 452

Interest method (interest allocation) a method that allocates interest expense to a reporting period by multiplying the beginning paying value by the original market interest rate. p. 466

Market rate the consensus interest rate that borrowers are willing to pay and that lenders are willing to earn at the level of risk inherent in the bonds. p. 461

Mortgage a legal agreement that protects a lender by giving the lender the right to be paid out of the cash proceeds from the sale of the borrower's specific assets identified in the mortgage. p. 473

Par value of a bond the amount that the bond issuer agrees to pay at maturity and the amount on which interest payments are based; also called the *face amount*. p. 456

Pledged assets to secured liabilities the ratio of the book value of a company's pledged assets to the book value of its secured liabilities. p. 474

Premium on bonds the difference between the par value of a bond and its higher issue price or paying amount; arises when the contract rate is higher than the market rate. p. 468

Registered bonds bonds owned by investors whose names and addresses are recorded by the issuing company; the interest payments are made with checks to the bondholders. p. 458

Serial bonds bonds that mature at different dates with the result that the entire debt is repaid gradually over a number of years. p. 458

Sinking fund bonds bonds that require the issuing company to make deposits to a separate pool of assets; the bondholders are repaid at maturity from the assets in this pool. p. 458

Straight-line method (interest allocation) a method that allocates an equal amount of interest to each accounting period in the life of bonds. p. 464

QUESTIONS

1. Describe two alternative payment patterns for installment notes.
2. What is the difference between notes payable and bonds payable?
3. What is the primary difference between a share of stock and a bond?
4. What is the main advantage of issuing bonds instead of obtaining funds from the company's owners?
5. What is a bond indenture? What provisions are usually included in an indenture?
6. What are the duties of a trustee for bondholders?
7. Why does a company that issues bonds between interest dates collect accrued interest from the bonds' purchasers?
8. What are the *contract* and *market interest rates* for bonds?
9. What factors affect the market interest rates for bonds?
10. If you know the par value of bonds, the contract rate, and the market interest rate, how can you estimate the market value of the bonds?

11. Does the straight-line or interest method produce an allocation of interest that creates a constant rate of interest over a bond's life? Explain your answer.
12. What is the cash price of a $2,000 bond that is sold at 98¼? What is the cash price of a $6,000 bond that is sold at 101½?
13. Explain why unsecured creditors should be alarmed when the pledged assets to secured liabilities ratio for a borrower has grown substantially.
14. Refer to the annual report for Lands' End, Inc., presented in Appendix F. Is there any indication that the company has issued bonds?

QUICK STUDY (Five-Minute Exercises)

New West Corp. borrowed $170,000 from a bank and signed an installment note that calls for five annual payments of equal size, with the first payment due one year after the note was signed. Use Table 13–2 on page 475 to calculate the size of the annual payment for each of the following annual interest rates: *a.* 4%, *b.* 8%, *c.* 12%.

QS 13–1
(LO 1)

QS 13–2
(LO 2)

Match the following terms and phrases by entering the letter of the phrase that best describes each term in the blank next to the term.

____	debentures	____	sinking fund bonds
____	bearer bonds	____	serial bonds
____	registered bonds	____	secured bonds
____	bond indenture	____	convertible bonds

   a.   Issuer records the bondholders' names and addresses.
   b.   Unsecured; backed only by the issuer's general credit standing.
   c.   Varying maturity dates.
   d.   Identifies the rights and responsibilities of the issuer and bondholders.
   e.   Can be exchanged for shares of the issuer's common stock.
   f.   Unregistered; interest is paid to whoever possesses them.
   g.   Issuer maintains a separate pool of assets from which bondholders are paid at maturity.
   h.   Specific assets of the issuer are mortgaged as collateral.

QS 13–3
(LO 3)

Lyndon Industries issued 8%, 10-year bonds with a par value of $350,000 and semiannual interest payments. On the issue date, the annual market rate of interest for the bonds was 10%, and they sold for $306,386. The straight-line method is used to allocate the interest.

   a.   What is the total amount of interest expense that will be recognized over the life of the bonds?
   b.   What is the amount of interest expense recorded on the first interest payment date?

QS 13–4
(LO 4)

Top Notch, Inc., issued 10%, 15-year bonds with a par value of $120,000 and semiannual interest payments. On the issue date, the annual market rate of interest for the bonds was 8%, and they sold for $140,748. The interest method is used to allocate the interest.
   a.   What is the total amount of interest expense that will be recognized over the life of the bonds?
   b.   What is the amount of interest expense recorded on the first interest payment date?

QS 13–5
(LO 5)

Use the following information to compute the ratio of pledged assets to secured liabilities for both companies:

	Delta Co.	Sigma Co.
Pledged assets	$387,000	$172,000
Total assets	550,000	490,000
Secured liabilities	163,000	158,000
Unsecured liabilities	266,000	390,000

EXERCISES

When solving the following exercises, round all dollar amounts to the nearest whole dollar. Also assume that none of the companies use reversing entries.

Exercise 13–1
Installment note with payments of accrued interest and equal amounts of principal
(LO 1)

On December 31, 19X1, JMS, Inc., borrowed $25,000 by signing a four-year, 7% installment note. The note requires annual payments of accrued interest and equal amounts of principal on December 31 of each year from 19X2 through 19X5.

   a.   How much principal will be included in each of the four payments?
   b.   Prepare an amortization table for this installment note like the one presented in Illustration 13–1 on page 453.

Exercise 13–2
Journal entries for an installment note with payments of accrued interest and equal amounts of principal
(LO 1)

Use the data in Exercise 13–1 to prepare journal entries that JMS, Inc., would make to record the loan on December 31, 19X1, and the four payments starting on December 31, 19X2, through the final payment on December 31, 19X5.

On December 31, 19X1, Volks Corp. borrowed $25,000 by signing a four-year, 7% installment note. The note requires four equal payments of accrued interest and principal on December 31 of each year from 19X2 through 19X5.

a. Calculate the size of each of the four equal payments.

b. Prepare an amortization table for this installment note like the one presented in Illustration 13–2 on page 455.

Exercise 13–3
Installment note with equal payments
(LO 1)

Use the data in Exercise 13–3 to prepare journal entries that Volks Corp. would make to record the loan on December 31, 19X1, and the four payments starting on December 31, 19X2, through the final payment on December 31, 19X5.

Exercise 13–4
Journal entries for an installment note with equal payments
(LO 1)

On January 1, 19X1, Maverick Enterprises issued bonds dated January 1, 19X1. The bonds have a $1,700,000 par value, mature in 20 years, and pay 9% interest semiannually on June 30 and December 31. The bonds were sold to investors at their par value.

a. How much interest will Maverick pay to the holders of these bonds every six months?

b. Show the journal entries that Maverick would make to record (1) the issuance of the bonds on January 1, 19X1; (2) the first interest payment on June 30, 19X1; and (3) the second interest payment on December 31, 19X1.

Exercise 13–5
Journal entries for bond issuance and interest payments
(LO 2)

On May 1, 19X1, Maverick Enterprises issued bonds dated January 1, 19X1. The bonds have a $1,700,000 par value, mature in 20 years, and pay 9% interest semiannually on June 30 and December 31. The bonds were sold to investors at their par value plus the four months' interest that had accrued since the original issue date.

a. How much accrued interest was paid to Maverick by the purchasers of these bonds on May 1, 19X1?

b. Show the journal entries that Maverick would make to record (1) the issuance of the bonds on May 1, 19X1; (2) the first interest payment on June 30, 19X1; and (3) the second interest payment on December 31, 19X1.

Exercise 13–6
Journal entries for bond issuance with accrued interest
(LO 2)

The Kloss Company issued bonds with a par value of $600,000 on their initial issue date. The bonds mature in 10 years and pay 6% annual interest in two semiannual payments. On the issue date, the annual market rate of interest for the bonds turned out to be 8%.

a. What is the size of the semiannual interest payment for these bonds?

b. How many semiannual interest payments will be made on these bonds over their life?

c. Use the information about the interest rates to decide whether the bonds were issued at par, a discount, or a premium.

d. Estimate the market value of the bonds as of the date they were issued.

e. Present the journal entry that would be made to record the bonds' issuance.

Exercise 13–7
Calculating the present value of a bond and recording the issuance
(LO 2, 3)

Bailey's, Inc., issued bonds with a par value of $90,000 on January 1, 19X2. The annual contract rate on the bonds is 8%, and the interest is paid semiannually. The bonds mature after three years. The annual market interest rate at the date of issuance was 10%, and the bonds were sold for $85,431.

a. What is the amount of the original discount on these bonds?

b. How much total interest expense will be recognized over the life of these bonds?

c. Present an amortization table like Illustration 13–4 on page 465 for these bonds; use the straight-line method of allocating the interest and amortizing the discount.

Exercise 13–8
Straight-line allocation of interest for bonds sold at a discount
(LO 3)

Exercise 13–9
Interest method allocation of interest for bonds sold at a discount
(LO 3)

Profitt Corporation issued bonds with a par value of $250,000 on January 1, 19X2. The annual contract rate on the bonds is 9%, and the interest is paid semiannually. The bonds mature after three years. The annual market interest rate at the date of issuance was 12%, and the bonds were sold for $231,570.

a. What is the amount of the original discount on these bonds?

b. How much total interest expense will be recognized over the life of these bonds?

c. Present an amortization table like Illustration 13–5 on page 467 for these bonds; use the interest method of allocating the interest and amortizing the discount.

Exercise 13–10
Calculating the present value of a bond and recording the issuance
(LO 2, 4)

Innovention, Inc., issued bonds with a par value of $75,000 on their initial issue date. The bonds mature in five years and pay 10% annual interest in two semiannual payments. On the issue date, the annual market rate of interest for the bonds turned out to be 8%.

a. What is the size of the semiannual interest payment for these bonds?

b. How many semiannual interest payments will be made on these bonds over their life?

c. Use the information about the interest rates to decide whether the bonds were issued at par, a discount, or a premium.

d. Estimate the market value of the bonds as of the date they were issued.

e. Present the journal entry that would be made to record the bonds' issuance.

Exercise 13–11
Interest method allocation of interest for bonds sold at a premium
(LO 4)

Great Plains Power Company issued bonds with a par value of $800,000 on January 1, 19X2. The annual contract rate on the bonds was 13%, and the interest is paid semiannually. The bonds mature after three years. The annual market interest rate at the date of issuance was 12%, and the bonds were sold for $819,700.

a. What is the amount of the original premium on these bonds?

b. How much total interest expense will be recognized over the life of these bonds?

c. Present an amortization table like Illustration 13–7 on page 470 for these bonds; use the interest method of allocating the interest and amortizing the premium.

Exercise 13–12
Retiring bonds payable
(LO 2, 3)

On January 1, 19X1, AeroFab, Inc., issued $350,000 of 10%, 15-year bonds at a price of 97¾. Six years later, on January 1, 19X7, the corporation retired 20% of these bonds by buying them on the open market at 104½. All interest had been properly accounted for and paid through December 31, 19X6, the day before the purchase. The straight-line method was used to allocate the interest and amortize the original discount.

a. How much money did the company receive when it first issued the entire group of bonds?

b. How large was the original discount on the entire group of bonds?

c. How much amortization did the company record on the entire group of bonds between January 1, 19X1, and December 31, 19X6?

d. What was the carrying value of the entire group of bonds as of the close of business on December 31, 19X6? What was the carrying value of the retired bonds on this date?

e. How much money did the company pay on January 1, 19X7, to purchase the bonds that it retired?

f. What is the amount of the gain or loss from retiring the bonds?

g. Provide the general journal entry that the company would make to record the retirement of the bonds.

Exercise 13–13
Straight-line amortization table and accrued interest
(LO 2, 3)

Piccolo Corp. issued bonds with a par value of $50,000 and a four-year life on June 1, 19X1. The contract interest rate is 7%. The bonds pay interest on November 30 and May 31. They were issued at a price of $47,974.

a. Prepare an amortization table for these bonds that covers their entire life. Use the straight-line method of allocating interest.

b. Show the journal entries that the issuer would make to record the first two interest payments and to accrue interest as of December 31, 19X1.

PROBLEMS

*When solving the following problems, round all dollar amounts to the nearest whole dollar.
Also assume that none of the companies use reversing entries.*

On October 31, 19X1, Borghese Ltd. borrowed $400,000 from a bank by signing a five-year installment note bearing interest at 8%. The terms of the note require equal payments each year on October 31.

Problem 13–1
Installment notes
(LO 1)

Required

1. Calculate the size of each installment payment. (Use Table 13–2 on page 455.)
2. Complete an installment note amortization schedule for this note similar to Illustration 13–2 on page 455.
3. Present the journal entries that Borghese would make to record accrued interest as of December 31, 19X1 (the end of the annual reporting period) and the first payment on the note.
4. Now assume that the note does not require equal payments but does require four payments that include accrued interest and an equal amount of principal in each payment. Complete an installment note amortization schedule for this note similar to Illustration 13–1 on page 453. Present the journal entries that Borghese would make to record accrued interest as of December 31, 19X1 (the end of the annual reporting period) and the first payment on the note.

CHECK FIGURE:
Part 2, interest for period ending 10/31/X5, $14,292

Abbey Research, Inc., issued bonds on January 1, 19X1, that pay interest semiannually on June 30 and December 31. The par value of the bonds is $20,000, the annual contract rate is 10%, and the bonds mature in ten years.

Problem 13–2
Calculating bond prices and recording issuances with journal entries
(LO 2, 3, 4)

Required

For each of these three situations, *(a)* determine the issue price of the bonds and *(b)* show the journal entry that would record the issuance.

1. The market interest rate at the date of issuance was 8%.
2. The market interest rate at the date of issuance was 10%.
3. The market interest rate at the date of issuance was 12%.

CHECK FIGURE:
Part 1, premium, $2,718

The Scofield Corporation issued $2,000,000 of bonds that pay 6% annual interest with two semiannual payments. The date of issuance was January 1, 19X1, and the interest is paid on June 30 and December 31. The bonds mature after 15 years and were issued at the price of $1,728,224.

Problem 13–3
Straight-line method of allocating interest and amortizing a bond discount
(LO 2, 3)

Required

1. Prepare a general journal entry to record the issuance of the bonds.
2. Determine the total interest expense that will be recognized over the life of these bonds.
3. Prepare the first four lines of an amortization table like Illustration 13–4 based on the straight-line method of allocating the interest.
4. Prepare the first four lines of a separate table that shows the beginning balance of the discount, the amount of straight-line amortization of the discount, and the ending balance.
5. Present the journal entries that Scofield would make to record the first two interest payments.

CHECK FIGURE:
Total interest expense, $2,071,776

Evans Materials Corp. issued $650,000 of bonds that pay 5% annual interest with two semiannual payments. The date of issuance was January 1, 19X1, and the interest is paid on June 30 and December 31. The bonds mature after four years and were issued at the price of $584,361. The market interest rate was 8%.

Problem 13–4
Interest method of allocating bond interest and amortizing a bond discount
(LO 2, 3)

Required

Preparation component:

1. Prepare a general journal entry to record the issuance of the bonds.

2. Determine the total interest expense that will be recognized over the life of these bonds.

3. Prepare the first four lines of an amortization table like Illustration 13–5 based on the interest method.

4. Prepare the first four lines of a separate table that shows the beginning balance of the discount, the amount of interest method amortization of the discount, and the ending balance.

5. Present the journal entries that Evans would make to record the first two interest payments.

Analysis component:

6. Now assume that the market interest rate on January 1, 19X1, was 4% instead of 8%. Without presenting any specific numbers, describe how this change would affect the amounts presented on the Evans's financial statements.

Problem 13–5
Interest method of amortizing
bond interest, amortizing bond
premium, and retiring bonds
(LO 2, 4)

Phantom Industries issued $90,000 of bonds that pay 11% annual interest with two semiannual payments. The date of issuance was January 1, 19X1, and the interest is paid on June 30 and December 31. The bonds mature after three years and were issued at the price of $92,283. The market interest rate was 10%.

Required

1. Prepare a general journal entry to record the issuance of the bonds.

2. Determine the total interest expense that will be recognized over the life of these bonds.

3. Prepare the first four lines of an amortization table like Illustration 13–7 based on the interest method.

4. Prepare the first four lines of a separate table that shows the beginning balance of the premium, the amount of interest method amortization of the premium, and the ending balance.

5. Present the journal entries that Phantom would make to record the first two interest payments.

6. Present the journal entry that would be made to record the retirement of these bonds on December 31, 19X2, at a price of $98.

Problem 13–6
Bond premium amortization and
finding the present value of
remaining cash flows
(LO 3, 4)

Ford Products, Inc., issued bonds with a par value of $500,000 and a five-year life on January 1, 19X1. The bonds pay interest on June 30 and December 31. The contract interest rate is 6.5%. The bonds were issued at a price of $510,666. The market interest rate was 6% on the original issue date.

Required

1. Prepare an amortization table for these bonds that covers their entire life. Use the interest method.

2. Show the journal entries that Ford Products would make to record the first two interest payments.

3. Use the original market interest rate to calculate the present value of the remaining cash flows for these bonds as of December 31, 19X3. Compare your answer with the amount shown on the amortization table as the balance for that date and explain your findings.

On January 1, 19X2, Dailey Company issued at par 11%, four-year bonds with a $135,000 par value. The bonds are secured by a mortgage that specifies assets totaling $225,000 as collateral. On the same date, Weekley Company issued at par 11%, four-year bonds with a par value of $60,000. Weekley is securing its bonds with a mortgage that includes $150,000 of pledged assets. Following is December 31, 19X1, balance sheet information for both companies:

	Dailey Co.	**Weekley Co.**
Total assets	$900,000*	$450,000†
Liabilities:		
Secured	$210,000	$ 75,000
Unsecured	150,000	165,000
Stockholders' equity	540,000	210,000
Total liabilities and		
stockholders' equity . . .	$900,000	$450,000
Footnote	*43% pledged	†55% pledged

Required

Preparation component:

1. Calculate the ratio of pledged assets to secured liabilities for each company after January 1, 19X2.

Analysis component:

2. Which company's bonds appear to offer the best security? What other information might be helpful in evaluating the risk of the bonds?

CRITICAL THINKING: ESSAYS, PROBLEMS, AND CASES

When solving the following, round all dollar amounts to the nearest whole dollar.

An unsecured major creditor of Telstar Corporation has been monitoring the company's financing activities. Two years before, the ratio of its pledged assets to secured liabilities had been 1.7. One year ago, the ratio had climbed to 2.3, and the most recent financial report shows that the ratio value is now 3.1. Briefly describe what this trend may indicate about the company's activities, specifically from the point of view of this creditor.

Longhorn Industrial Corp. is planning major additions to its operating capacity and needs approximately $600,000 to finance the expansion. The company has been considering three alternative proposals for issuing bonds that pay annual interest over the nine years in their lives. The alternatives are:

Plan A: Issue $600,000 of 6% bonds.

Plan B: Issue $675,000 of 5% bonds.

Plan C: Issue $540,000 of 7% bonds.

The market rate of interest for all of these bonds is expected to be 6%.

Required

1. For each plan, calculate:
   a. The expected cash proceeds from issuing the bonds.
   b. The expected annual cash outflow for interest.
   c. The expected interest expense for the first year. (Use the interest method to amortize bond premium or discount.)
   d. The amount that must be paid at maturity.
2. Which plans have the smallest and largest cash demands on the company prior to the final payment at maturity? Which plans require the smallest and largest payments at maturity?

Financial Reporting Problem

(LO 2, 3)

Rowley & Schram, Inc., issued $1,000,000 of zero-coupon bonds on January 1, 19X1. These bonds are scheduled to mature seven years later on December 31, 19X7. Under the terms of the bond agreement, the company will pay out $1,000,000 to the bondholders on the maturity date without making any periodic interest payments. The market rate of interest for these bonds was 7% when they were issued.

Required

1. Estimate the amount of cash that Rowley & Schram received when it issued these bonds (assume annual compounding).
2. Present the journal entry that the company's accountant would use to record the issuance of these bonds.
3. Calculate the total amount of interest expense that will be incurred over the life of the bonds.
4. Prepare an amortization table, using the interest method, that shows the amount of interest expense that will be allocated to each year in the bonds' life.
5. Present the journal entry that Rowley & Schram's accountant would use to record the interest expense from these bonds for the year ended December 31, 19X1.

Financial Statement Analysis Case

(LO 1)

Use the financial statements and the footnotes for Southwest Airlines Co. in Appendix E to answer the following questions:

a. Has Southwest Airlines issued any bonds or long-term notes payable?
b. How often is interest paid on the long-term notes payable?
c. Are the notes payable secured or unsecured?
d. How much cash was paid during 1994 to satisfy long-term debt and capital lease obligations?
e. Did Southwest Airlines issue any new long-term debt during 1994?

ANSWERS TO PROGRESS CHECKS

13–1 *c*

13–2 The interest portion of an installment payment equals the beginning balance for the period multiplied by the original interest rate.

13–3 On the balance sheet, the balances of the liability and cash are decreased. On the income statement, interest expense is increased.

13–4 *b*

13–5 Multiply the par value of the bonds by the contract rate of interest.

13–6 *a*

13–7 The bonds sell at a premium, and the purchasers pay more than the par value of the bonds.

13–8 *c.* (Present values of $100,000 and a semiannual annuity of $3,000, both at 4% for 10 semiannual periods.)

13–9 Cash 91,893.00
    Discount on Bonds Payable . . 8,107.00
        Bonds Payable 100,000.00

13–10 *a.* $3,811 (Total interest equal to $38,107, or 10 payments of $3,000 plus the $8,107 discount, divided by 10 periods.)
    b. $3,676 (Beginning balance of $91,893 times 4% market interest rate.)

13–11 $110,592 (Present value of $100,000 plus the semiannual annuity of $8,000, both at 7% for 20 semiannual periods.)

13–12 *e.* (On 6/30/X2: $110,592 × 7% = $7,741 interest expense; $8,000 − $7,741 = $259 premium amortization; $110,592 − $259 = $110,333 ending balance. On 12/31/X2: $110,333 × 7% = $7,723 interest expense; $8,000 − $7,723 = $277 premium amortization.)

13–13 Bonds payable, 16%, due
    December 31, 19X0 . . . . $100,000
    Plus premium 10,056* $110,056

    *Beginning premium balance of $10,592 less $259 and $277 amortized on 6/30/X2 and 12/31/X2.

13–14 $9,375 loss (Difference between repurchase price of $256,250 [50% of ($500,000 × 102.5%)] and carrying value of $246,875 [50% of $493,750].)

13–15 *b*

13–16 2.2 to 1 ($1,265,000/$575,000)

13–17 Unsecured creditors. They may be less likely to receive full repayment if the portion of assets pledged increases.

CHAPTER 14

Corporations, Proprietorships, and Partnerships

*B*ecause his father worked for Mobil Corporation for 30 years until retirement, Barry Foster has been interested in the company since childhood. He has always been impressed by the fact that Mobil has paid dividends every year since 1902. It has operations in more than 100 countries involving oil and gas, petrochemicals, plastics, mining, and land development. In 1993, these operations generated total revenues in excess of $63 billion.

Late in 1994, Foster began to examine the company's dividend record more closely. In doing so, he noted that during the 10-year period from 1983 to 1993, dividends to common stock increased from $2.00 per share to $3.25 per share. Dividends in 1994 were running at a rate that would accumulate to $3.40 per share. In attempting to evaluate the company, Foster also gathered information about several other companies. However, he was unsure about how to compare them.

| Company | Common Dividend Per Share | | November 1994 |
	1994*	1993	Stock Price
Mobil Corporation	$3.40	$3.25	$82 1/4
Minnesota Mining & Manufacturing Co.	1.76	1.66	53 1/4
Texaco Inc.	3.20	3.20	60 7/8
AT&T Corp.	1.32	1.32	54
GAP, Inc.	0.48	0.38	37 7/8
Microsoft Corp.	0	0	64 1/2

*Estimated 1994 amounts.

LEARNING OBJECTIVES

After studying Chapter 14, you should be able to:

1.   Explain the unique characteristics of the corporate form of business.
2.   Record the issuance of par value stock and no-par stock with or without a stated value and explain the concept of minimum legal capital.
3.   Record transactions that involve dividends and stock subscriptions and explain the effects of stock subscriptions on the balance sheet.
4.   State the differences between common and preferred stock and allocate dividends between the common and preferred stock of a corporation.
5.   Describe convertible preferred stock and explain the meaning of the par value, call price, market value, and book value of corporate stock.
6.   Explain the legal status of a proprietorship, prepare entries to account for the owner's equity of a proprietorship, and prepare a statement of changes in owner's equity.
7.   Explain the characteristics of partnerships, account for the equity of partners, and describe several organizations that mix the characteristics of corporations and partnerships.
8.   Calculate dividend yield and describe its meaning.
9.   Define or explain the words and phrases listed in the chapter glossary.

Of the three common types of business organizations (corporations, proprietorships, and partnerships), corporations are fewest in number. However, they transact more business than the other two combined. Large businesses like **Mobil Corporation** are almost all corporations. In the United States, the dollar sales volume of corporations is approximately nine times the combined sales of unincorporated businesses. Thus, from an overall economic point of view, corporations are clearly the most important form of business organization.

As you study this chapter you will learn about the organization and operation of corporations and more about the procedures used to account for them. You will also learn about proprietorships and partnerships. Your understanding of these three forms of business organizations will allow us to briefly consider several variations of them. The variations include limited partnerships, limited liability partnerships, "S" corporations, and limited liability companies.

CORPORATIONS

CHARACTERISTICS OF CORPORATIONS

LO 1
Explain the unique characteristics of the corporate form of business.

Corporations have become the dominant type of business because of the advantages created by their unique characteristics. We describe these characteristics in the following sections.

Corporations Are Separate Legal Entities

A corporation is a separate legal entity. As a separate entity, a corporation conducts its affairs with the same rights, duties, and responsibilities as a person. However, because it is not a real person, a corporation can act only through its agents, who are its officers and managers.

Stockholders Are Not Liable for the Corporation's Debts

Because a corporation is a separate legal entity, it is responsible for its own acts and its own debts. Its shareholders are not liable for either. From the viewpoint of an investor, this lack of stockholders' liability is, perhaps, the most important advantage of the corporate form of business.

Ownership Rights of Corporations Are Easily Transferred

The ownership of a corporation is represented by shares of stock that, in general, are easily bought or sold. Also, the transfer of shares from one stockholder to another usually has no effect on the corporation or its operations.[1] Many companies have thousands or even millions of their shares bought and sold every day through major stock exchanges located throughout the world. For example, *The Wall Street Journal* reported that on  May 23, 1996, 1,382,000 shares of **American Express Company** stock were traded on the New York Stock Exchange.

Corporations Have Continuity of Life

A corporation's life may continue indefinitely because it is not tied to the physical lives of its owners. In some cases, a corporation's life may be initially limited by the laws of the state of its incorporation. However, the corporation's charter can be renewed and its life extended when the stated time expires. Thus, a corporation may have a perpetual life as long as it continues to be successful.

Stockholders Are Not Agents of the Corporation

As we previously stated, a corporation acts through its agents, who are the officers or managers of the corporation. Stockholders who are not officers or managers of the corporation do not have the power to bind the corporation to contracts. Instead, stockholders participate in the affairs of the corporation only by voting in the stockholders' meetings.

Ease of Capital Accumulation

Buying stock in a corporation often is more attractive to investors than investing in other forms of business. Stock investments are attractive because: (1) stockholders are not liable for the corporation's actions and debts, (2) stock usually can be transferred easily, (3) the life of the corporation is not limited, and (4) stockholders are not agents of the corporation. These advantages make it possible for some corporations to accumulate large amounts of capital from the combined investments of many stockholders. In a sense, a corporation's capacity for raising capital is limited only by its ability to convince investors that it can use their funds profitably.

Governmental Regulation of Corporations

Corporations are created by fulfilling the requirements of a state's incorporation laws. These laws subject a corporation to state regulation and control. Single proprietorships and partnerships may escape some of these regulations. In addition, they may avoid having to file some governmental reports required of corporations.

Taxation of Corporations

Corporations are subject to the same property and payroll taxes as single proprietorships and partnerships. In addition, corporations are subject to taxes that are not levied on either of the other two. The most burdensome of these are federal and state

---

[1]However, a transfer of ownership can create significant effects if it brings about a change in who controls the company's activities.

income taxes that together may take 40% or more of a corporation's pretax income. However, the tax burden does not end there. The income of a corporation is taxed twice, first as income of the corporation and again as personal income to the stockholders when cash is distributed to them as dividends. This differs from single proprietorships and partnerships, which are not subject to income taxes as business units. Their income is taxed only as the personal income of their owners. (Later in the chapter, we describe "S" corporations, which have the same tax status as partnerships.)

The tax situation of a corporation is generally viewed as a disadvantage. However, in some cases, it can work to the advantage of stockholders because corporation and individual tax rates are progressive. That is, higher levels of income are taxed at higher rates and lower levels of income are taxed at lower rates. Therefore, taxes may be saved or at least delayed if a large amount of income is divided among two or more tax-paying entities. Thus, a person who has a large personal income and pays taxes at a high rate may benefit if some of the income is earned by a corporation that person owns, as long as the corporation avoids paying dividends. By not paying dividends, the corporation's income is taxed only once at the lower corporate rate, at least temporarily until dividends are paid.

ORGANIZING A CORPORATION

A corporation is created by securing a charter from a state government. The requirements that must be met to be chartered vary among the states. Usually, a charter application must be signed by the subscribers to the prospective corporation's stock (such persons are called the *incorporators* or *promoters*). Then, the application must be filed with the appropriate state official. When it is properly completed and all fees are paid, the charter is issued and the corporation is formed. The subscribers then purchase the corporation's stock, meet as stockholders, and elect a board of directors. The directors are responsible for guiding the company's business affairs.

ORGANIZATION COSTS

The costs of organizing a corporation, such as legal fees, promoters' fees, and amounts paid to secure a charter, are called **organization costs.** On the corporation's books, these costs are debited to an asset account called Organization Costs. In a sense, this intangible asset benefits the corporation throughout its life. Thus, you could argue that the cost should be amortized over the life of the corporation, which may be unlimited. However, generally accepted accounting principles require any intangible asset to be amortized over a period that is no longer than 40 years.[2]

Income tax rules permit a corporation to write off organization costs as a tax deduction over a minimum of five years. Thus, to make record-keeping simple, many corporations use a five-year amortization period for financial statement purposes. Although the five-year period is arbitrary, it is widely used in practice. Because organization costs usually are not material in amount, the *materiality principle* also supports the arbitrarily short amortization period.

MANAGEMENT OF A CORPORATION

All corporations do not have the same organizational structures. However, the ultimate control of a corporation rests with its stockholders. This control is exercised indirectly through the election of the board of directors. Individual stockholders' rights to participate in management begin and end with a vote in the stockholders' meetings, where each of them has one vote for each share of stock owned.

Normally, a corporation holds a stockholders' meeting once each year to elect directors and transact other business as required by the corporation's bylaws. A group

---

[2]FASB, *Accounting Standards—Current Text* (Norwalk, CT, 1995), sec. I60.110. First published in *APB Opinion No. 17,* par. 29.

of stockholders that owns or controls the votes of 50% plus one share of a corporation's stock can easily elect the board and thereby control the corporation. However, in many companies, very few stockholders attend the annual meeting or even care about getting involved in the voting process. As a result, a much smaller percentage may be able to dominate the election of board members.

Stockholders who do not attend stockholders' meetings must be given an opportunity to delegate their voting rights to an agent. A stockholder does this by signing a document called a **proxy** that gives a designated agent the right to vote the stock. Prior to a stockholders' meeting, a corporation's board of directors typically mails to each stockholder an announcement of the meeting and a proxy that names the existing board chairperson as the voting agent of the stockholder. The announcement asks the stockholder to sign and return the proxy.

A corporation's board of directors is responsible for and has final authority for managing the corporation's activities. However, it can act only as a collective body. An individual director has no power to transact corporate business. Although the board has final authority, it usually limits its actions to establishing broad policy. Day-to-day direction of corporate business is delegated to executive officers appointed by the board.

Traditionally, the chief executive officer (CEO) of the corporation is the president. Under the president, several vice presidents may be assigned specific areas of management responsibility, such as finance, production, and marketing. In addition, the corporation secretary keeps the minutes of the meetings of the stockholders and directors and ensures that all legal responsibilities are fulfilled. In a small corporation, the secretary is also responsible for keeping a record of the stockholders and the changing amounts of their stock interest.

Many corporations have a different structure in which the chairperson of the board of directors is also the chief executive officer. With this arrangement, the president is usually designated the chief operating officer (COO), and the rest of the structure is essentially the same.

STOCK CERTIFICATES AND THE TRANSFER OF STOCK

When investors buy a corporation's stock, they may receive a stock certificate as proof that they purchased the shares.[3] In many corporations, only one certificate is issued for each block of stock purchased. This certificate may be for any number of shares.

When selling shares of a corporation, a stockholder completes and signs a transfer endorsement on the back of the certificate and sends it to the corporation's secretary or the transfer agent. The secretary or agent cancels and files the old certificate, and issues a new certificate to the new stockholder. If the old certificate represents more shares than were sold, the corporation issues two new certificates. One certificate goes to the new stockholder for the sold shares and the other to the original stockholder for the remaining unsold shares.

Many stockholders have their shares held in the name of their stock brokerage. When this is done, the corporation's secretary or registrar keeps a record of who owns the shares but the stockholders do not receive stock certificates.

Registrar and Transfer Agent

If a corporation's stock is traded on a major stock exchange, the corporation must have a *registrar* and a *transfer agent.* The registrar keeps the stockholder records and prepares official lists of stockholders for stockholders' meetings and for dividend payments. The transfer agent facilitates purchases and sales of shares by receiving and is-

---

[3]The issuance of certificates is less common than it used to be. Instead, many stockholders maintain accounts with the corporation or their stockbrokers and never receive certificates.

suing certificates as necessary. Registrars and transfer agents usually are large banks or trust companies that have the computer facilities and staff to carry out this kind of work.

Progress Check
(Answers to Progress Checks are provided at the end of the chapter.)

14-1   Which of the following is not a characteristic of the corporate form of business? *(a)* Ease of capital accumulation;   *(b)* Stockholders are liable for corporate debts; *(c)* Ownership rights are easily transferred.

14-2   Why is the income of a corporation said to be taxed twice?

14-3   What is a proxy?

AUTHORIZATION AND ISSUANCE OF STOCK

LO 2
Record the issuance of par value stock and no-par stock with or without a stated value and explain the concept of minimum legal capital.

When a corporation is organized, its charter authorizes it to issue a specified number of shares of stock. If all of the authorized shares have the same rights and characteristics, the stock is called **common stock.** However, a corporation may be authorized to issue more than one class of stock, including different classes of common stock and preferred stock. (We discuss preferred stock later in this chapter.) For example, **American Greetings Corporation** has two types of common stock outstanding. Class A stock has 1 vote per share and Class B stock has 10 votes per share.

Because a corporation cannot issue more than the number of shares authorized in its charter, its founders usually obtain authorization to issue more shares than they plan to sell when the company is first organized. By doing so, the corporation avoids having to get the state's approval to sell more shares when additional capital is needed

to finance an expansion of the business. A corporation's balance sheet (or footnotes) usually discloses the number of shares authorized as well as the number of shares issued. Typically, these facts are reported in the stockholders' equity section of the statement. For example, **Southwest Airlines Co.'s** balance sheet in Appendix E shows this information:

	(in thousands)	
	1994	**1993**
Common stock, $1.00 par value: 500,000,000 shares authorized; 143,255,795 shares issued in 1994 and 142,756,308 shares in 1993	$143,256	$142,756

Sale of Stock for Cash

When stock is sold for cash and immediately issued, an entry like the following is made to record the sale and issuance:

June	5	Cash	300,000.00	
		Common Stock, $10 Par Value		300,000.00
		Sold at par and issued 30,000 shares of $10 par value common stock.		

Exchanging Stock for Noncash Assets

A corporation may accept assets other than cash in exchange for its stock. In the process, the corporation also may assume some liabilities, such as a mortgage on some of the property. The following entry records a transaction like this:

June	10	Machinery	10,000.00	
		Buildings	65,000.00	
		Land	15,000.00	
		Long-Term Notes Payable		50,000.00
		Common Stock, $10 Par Value		40,000.00
		Exchanged 4,000 shares of $10 par value common stock		
		for machinery, buildings, and land.		

This entry records the acquired assets and the new liability at their fair market values as of the date of the transaction. It also records the difference between the combined fair values of the assets and the liability as an increase in stockholders' equity. If reliable fair values for the assets and liabilities cannot be determined, the fair market value of the stock may be used to estimate their values.

A corporation also may give shares of its stock to its promoters in exchange for their services in organizing the company. In this case, the corporation receives the intangible asset of being organized in exchange for its stock. The company records this transaction as follows:

June	5	Organization Costs	5,000.00	
		Common Stock, $10 Par Value		5,000.00
		Gave the promoters 500 shares of $10 par value common		
		stock in exchange for their services in organizing		
		the corporation.		

PAR VALUE AND MINIMUM LEGAL CAPITAL

Many stocks have a **par value,** which is an arbitrary value assigned to the stock when it is authorized. A corporation may choose to issue stock with a par value of any amount. For example, **Sara Lee Corporation's** common stock has a par value of $1.33⅓. Widely used par values are $100, $25, $10, $5, $1, and $0.01. When a corporation issues par value stock, the par value is printed on each certificate and used in accounting for the stock.

In many states, the par value of a corporation's stock also establishes the **minimum legal capital** for the corporation. Laws that establish minimum legal capital normally require stockholders to invest assets equal in value to at least that amount. Usually, the minimum legal capital is defined as the par value of the issued stock. In other words, persons who buy stock from a corporation must give the corporation assets equal in value to at least the par value of the stock or be subject to making up the difference later. For example, if a corporation issues 1,000 shares of $100 par value stock, the minimum legal capital of the corporation is $100,000. Minimum legal capital requirements also make it illegal to pay any dividends if they will reduce the stockholders' equity below the minimum amount.

The requirements for minimum legal capital are intended to protect the creditors of a corporation. Because a corporation's creditors cannot demand payment from the personal assets of the stockholders, the assets of the corporation are all that is available to satisfy the creditors' claims. To protect a corporation's creditors under these conditions, the minimum legal capital requirement limits a corporation's ability to distribute its assets to its stockholders. The idea is that assets equal to the amount of minimum legal capital cannot be paid to the stockholders unless all creditor claims are paid first.

Because par value determines the amount of minimum legal capital in many states, it is traditionally used in accounting for the part of stockholders' equity derived from the issuance of stock. However, par value does not establish a stock's market value or the price at which a corporation must issue the stock. If purchasers are willing to pay more, a corporation may sell and issue its stock at a price above par.

STOCK PREMIUMS AND DISCOUNTS

Premiums on Stock

When a corporation sells its stock at a price above the par value, the stock is said to be issued at a premium. For example, if a corporation sells and issues its $10 par value common stock at $12 per share, the stock is sold at a $2 per share premium. A **premium on stock** is an amount in excess of par paid by the purchasers of newly issued stock. It is not a revenue and does not appear on the income statement. Rather, a premium is reported on the balance sheet as part of the stockholders' investment.

In accounting for stock sold at a price greater than its par value, the premium is recorded separately from the par value and is called *contributed capital in excess of par value*. For example, assume that a corporation sells and issues 10,000 shares of its $10 par value common stock for cash at $12 per share. The sale is recorded as follows:

Dec.	1	Cash	120,000.00	
		Common Stock, $10 Par Value		100,000.00
		Contributed Capital in Excess of		
		Par Value, Common Stock		20,000.00
		Sold and issued 10,000 shares of $10 par value		
		common stock at $12 per share.		

When a balance sheet is prepared, any contributed capital in excess of par value is added to the par value of the stock in the equity section, as shown in the following example:

Stockholders' Equity	
Common stock, $10 par value, 25,000 shares	
authorized, 20,000 shares issued and outstanding	$200,000
Contributed capital in excess of par value, common stock .	30,000
Total contributed capital	$230,000
Retained earnings	82,400
Total stockholders' equity	$312,400

Discounts on Stock

If stock is issued at a price below par value, the difference between par and the issue price is called a **discount on stock.** Most states prohibit the issuance of stock at a discount because the stockholders would be investing less than minimum legal capital. In states that allow stock to be issued at a discount, its purchasers usually become contingently liable to the corporation's creditors for the amount of the discount. Therefore, stock is seldom issued at a discount. However, if stock is issued at less than par, the discount is not an expense and does not appear on the income statement. Rather, the amount of the discount is debited to a discount account that is contra to the common stock account. The balance of the discount account is subtracted from the par value of the stock on the balance sheet.

NO-PAR STOCK

At one time, all stocks were required to have a par value. Today, nearly all states permit the issuance of stocks that do not have a par value. The primary advantage of **no-par stock** is that it may be issued at any price without having a discount liability attached. Also, printing a par value of, say, $100 on a stock certificate may cause an inexperienced person to think that the share must be worth $100. Therefore, eliminating par value may encourage a closer analysis of the factors that give a stock value. These factors include such things as expected future earnings and dividends, and prospects for the economy as a whole.

In some states, the entire proceeds from the sale of no-par stock becomes minimum legal capital. In this case, the entire proceeds are credited to a no-par stock account. For example, if a corporation issues 1,000 shares of no-par stock at $42 per share, the transaction is recorded like this:

Oct.	20	Cash	42,000.00	
		Common Stock, No-Par		42,000.00
		Sold and issued 1,000 shares of no-par common stock		
		at $42 per share.		

In other states, the board of directors of a corporation places a **stated value** on its no-par stock. The stated value becomes the minimum legal capital and is credited to the no-par stock account. If the stock is issued at an amount in excess of stated value, the excess is credited to Contributed Capital in Excess of Stated Value, No-Par Common Stock. For example, suppose that a corporation issues 1,000 shares of no-par common stock with a stated value of $25 per share for cash of $42 per share. The transaction is recorded as follows:

Oct.	20	Cash	42,000.00	
		Common Stock, No-Par		25,000.00
		Contributed Capital in Excess of		
		Stated Value, No-Par Common Stock		17,000.00
		Sold 1,000 shares of no-par stock having a $25 per		
		share stated value at $42 per share.		

Progress Check

14–4 A company issued 7,000 shares of its $10 par value common stock in exchange for equipment valued at $105,000. The entry to record the transaction would include a credit to: *(a)* Contributed Capital in Excess of Par Value, Common Stock for $35,000; *(b)* Retained Earnings for $35,000; *(c)* Common Stock, $10 Par Value for $105,000.

14–5 What is a stock premium?

14–6 Who is intended to be protected by minimum legal capital?

SALE OF STOCK THROUGH SUBSCRIPTIONS

LO 3
Record transactions that involve dividends and stock subscriptions and explain the effects of stock subscriptions on the balance sheet.

Usually, stock is sold for cash and immediately issued. However, corporations sometimes sell stock through **stock subscriptions.** For example, when a new corporation is formed, the organizers may realize that the new business has limited immediate needs for cash but will need additional capital in the future. To get the corporation started on a sound footing, the organizers may sell the stock to investors who agree to contribute some cash now and to make additional contributions in the future. When stock is sold through subscriptions, the investor agrees to buy a certain number of the shares at a specified price. The agreement also states when payments are to be made.

To illustrate the sale of stock through subscriptions, assume that Northgate Corporation accepted subscriptions on May 6 to 5,000 shares of its $10 par value common stock at $12 per share. The subscription contracts called for a 10% down payment with the balance to be paid in two equal installments due after three and six months. Northgate records the subscriptions with the following entry:

May	6	Subscriptions Receivable, Common Stock	60,000.00	
		Common Stock Subscribed		50,000.00
		Contributed Capital in Excess of Par		
		Value, Common Stock		10,000.00
		Accepted subscriptions to 5,000 shares of $10 par value		
		common stock at $12 per share.		

At the time that subscriptions are accepted, the firm debits the Subscriptions Receivable account for the sum of the stock's par value and premium. This is the total amount the subscribers agreed to pay. Notice that the *Common Stock Subscribed* account (an equity) is credited for par value and that the premium is credited to Contributed Capital in Excess of Par Value, Common Stock.

The receivables are converted into cash when the subscribers pay for their stock. And, when all the payments are received, the subscribed stock is issued. Northgate records the receipt of the down payment and the two installment payments with these entries:

May	6	Cash	6,000.00	
		Subscriptions Receivable, Common Stock		6,000.00
		Collected 10% down payments on the common stock		
		subscriptions.		
Aug.	6	Cash	27,000.00	
		Subscriptions Receivable, Common Stock		27,000.00
		Collected the first installment payments on the common		
		stock subscriptions.		
Nov.	6	Cash	27,000.00	
		Subscriptions Receivable, Common Stock		27,000.00
		Collected the second installment payments on the		
		common stock subscriptions.		

In this case, the down payments accompanied the subscriptions. Therefore, the accountant could have combined the May 6 entries to record the subscriptions and the down payments as follows:

May	6	Cash	6,000.00	
		Subscriptions Receivable, Common Stock	54,000.00	
		Common Stock Subscribed		50,000.00
		Contributed Capital in Excess of Par		
		Value, Common Stock		10,000.00
		Accepted subscriptions to 5,000 shares of $10 par value		
		common stock at $12 per share and received down		
		payments of 10% of the subscription price.		

When stock is sold through subscriptions, the stock usually is not issued until the subscriptions are paid in full. Also, if dividends are declared before subscribed stock has been issued, the dividends go only to the holders of outstanding shares, not to the subscribers. However, as soon as the subscriptions are paid, the stock is issued. The entry to record the issuance of the Northgate common stock is as follows:

Nov	6	Common Stock Subscribed	50,000.00	
		Common Stock, $10 Par Value		50,000.00
		Issued 5,000 shares of common stock sold through subscriptions.		

Subscriptions are usually collected in full, but not always. Sometimes, a subscriber fails to pay the agreed amount. When this default happens, the subscription contract is canceled. If the subscriber has made a partial payment on the contract, the amount may be refunded. Or, the company may issue a smaller amount of stock with a fair value equal to the partial payment. Or, the state law may allow the subscriber's partial payment to be kept by the corporation to compensate it for any damages.

Subscribed Stock and Subscriptions Receivable on the Balance Sheet

If a corporation prepares a balance sheet after accepting subscriptions to its stock but before the stock is issued, the accountant must decide how to report the subscribed stock and the stock subscriptions receivable. The subscribed stock represents stockholders' equity. Thus, it is reported as part of contributed capital.

You might expect that stock subscriptions receivable would be reported as assets, but they are not. The ability of corporations to demand that stock subscribers pay their subscriptions is often questionable. As a result, stock subscriptions receivable are subtracted from contributed capital on the balance sheet.

The following contributed capital section of a balance sheet shows how to report common stock subscribed and subscriptions receivable:

Common stock, $10 par value, 25,000 shares authorized, 20,000 shares issued and outstanding	$200,000
Common stock subscribed, 5,000 shares	50,000
Total common stock issued and subscribed	$250,000
Contributed capital in excess of par value, common stock	40,000
Less subscriptions receivable, common stock	(15,000)
Total contributed capital	$275,000

CORPORATE DIVIDENDS

Many corporations pay cash dividends to their stockholders in regular amounts at regular dates. These cash flows provide a return to the investors and usually affect the stock's market value. In previous discussions, we have assumed that dividends are declared and paid at the same time. Now we should recognize that dividends are typically declared on one date and paid on a later date. Three dates are involved in the process of declaring dividends.

The day the directors vote to pay a dividend is called the **date of declaration.** Stockholders receive a dividend only if the directors formally vote to declare one. By declaring a dividend, the directors create a legal liability of the corporation to its stockholders.

In its declaration, the directors specify a future date on which the persons listed in the corporation's records are identified as those who will receive the dividend. In most cases, this **date of record** follows the date of declaration by at least two weeks. Persons who buy stock in time to be recorded as stockholders on the date of record will receive the dividend.

The declaration by the board of directors also specifies a **date of payment,** which follows the date of record by enough time to allow the corporation to prepare checks payable to the stockholders. If a balance sheet is prepared between the date of declaration and the date of payment, the liability for the dividend is reported as a current liability.

Accounting for Dividends

Because the act of declaring a dividend creates a liability for the corporation, the accountant needs to record the new obligation. This entry would be recorded if the directors of a company with 5,000 outstanding shares declare a $1 per share dividend on January 9, payable on February 1:

Jan.	9	Cash Dividends Declared	5,000.00	
		Common Dividend Payable		5,000.00
		Declared a $1 per share cash dividend on the common stock.		

Recall that Cash Dividends Declared is a temporary account that accumulates information about the total dividends declared during the reporting period. It is not an expense account. The credited account describes the corporation's liability to its stockholders.

No entry is needed at the date of record. And on the payment date, the following entry records the settlement of the liability and the reduction of the cash balance:

Feb.	1	Common Dividend Payable	5,000.00	
		Cash		5,000.00
		Paid the $1 per share cash dividend to the common stockholders.		

At the end of the annual reporting period, the balance of the Cash Dividends Declared account is closed to Retained Earnings. For example, if the company declared four quarterly dividends of $5,000, the account has a $20,000 balance at the end of the year, and the accountant makes this closing entry:

Dec.	31	Retained Earnings	20,000.00	
		Cash Dividends Declared		20,000.00
		To close the Cash Dividends Declared account.		

If one of the declared dividends remains unpaid on December 31, this closing entry is still recorded because the act of declaration reduces retained earnings. The liability account continues to have a balance until the dividends are paid, and its amount is presented on the December 31 balance sheet.

Deficits and Dividends

A corporation with a debit balance of retained earnings is said to have a **deficit.** A deficit arises when a company incurs cumulative losses and pays dividends greater than the cumulative profits earned in other years. A deficit is deducted on a corporation's balance sheet, as in this example:

Stockholders' Equity

Common stock, $10 par value, 5,000 shares authorized and outstanding	$50,000
Deduct retained earnings deficit	(6,000)
Total stockholders' equity	$44,000

In most states, a corporation with a deficit is not allowed to pay a cash dividend to its stockholders. This legal restriction is designed to protect the creditors of the corporation by preventing the distribution of assets to stockholders at a time when the company is in financial difficulty.

Progress Check

14-7 Siskel Co. accepted subscriptions for 9,000 shares of $10 par value common stock at $48 per share. A 10% down payment was made on the date of the contract, the balance to be paid in full in six months. The entries to record receipt of the final balance and the issuance of the stock would include a credit to: *(a)* Subscriptions Receivable, Common Stock for $432,000; *(b)* Common Stock Subscribed for $432,000; *(c)* Common Stock, $10 Par Value for $90,000.

14-8 How is the Common Stock Subscribed account classified on the balance sheet?

14-9 In accounting for cash dividends that have been declared but not paid, the Cash Dividends Declared account is: *(a)* Reported on the balance sheet as a liability; *(b)* Closed to Income Summary; *(c)* Closed to Retained Earnings.

14-10 What three dates are normally involved in the declaration and payment of a cash dividend?

When investors buy a corporation's common stock, they acquire all the *specific* rights granted by the corporation's charter to its common stockholders. They also acquire the *general* rights granted stockholders by the laws of the state in which the company is incorporated. State laws vary, but common stockholders usually have the following general rights:

1. The right to vote at stockholders' meetings.
2. The right to sell or otherwise dispose of their stock.
3. The right of first opportunity to purchase any additional shares of common stock issued by the corporation. This right is called the common stockholders' **preemptive right.** It gives stockholders the opportunity to protect their proportionate interest in the corporation. For example, a stockholder who owns 25% of a corporation's common stock has the first opportunity to buy 25% of any new common stock issued. This arrangement enables the stockholder to maintain a 25% interest.
4. The right to share equally with other common stockholders in any dividends, with the result that each common share receives the same amount.
5. The right to share equally in any assets that remain after creditors are paid when the corporation is liquidated, with the result that each common share receives the same amount.

In addition, stockholders have the right to receive timely reports that describe the corporation's financial position and the results of its activities.

RIGHTS OF COMMON STOCKHOLDERS

LO 4
State the differences between common and preferred stock and allocate dividends between the common and preferred stock of a corporation.

PREFERRED STOCK

As mentioned earlier in this chapter, a corporation may be authorized to issue more than one kind or class of stock. If two classes of common stock are issued, the primary difference between them often is only a matter of voting rights. However, some companies issue two classes of stock with one class being a **preferred stock** and the other class being a common stock.

Preferred stock often has a par value but, like common stock, may be sold at a price that differs from par. Separate contributed capital accounts are used to record the issuance of preferred stock. For example, if 50 shares of preferred stock with a $100 par value are issued for $6,000 cash, the entry is:

June	1	Cash	6,000.00	
		Preferred Stock		5,000.00
		Contributed Capital in Excess of Par		
		Value, Preferred Stock		1,000.00
		Issued preferred stock for cash.		

The term *preferred* is used because the preferred shares have a higher priority (or senior status) relative to common shares in one or more ways. These typically include a preference for receiving dividends and a preference in the distribution of assets if the corporation is liquidated.

In addition to the preferences it receives, preferred stock carries all the rights of common stock, unless they are nullified in the corporation's charter. For example, most preferred stock does not have the right to vote.

Preferred Dividends

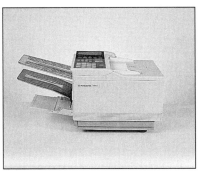

A preference for dividends gives preferred stockholders the right to receive their dividends before the common stockholders receive a dividend. In other words, a dividend cannot be paid to common stockholders unless preferred stockholders also receive one. The amount of dividends that the preferred stockholders must receive is usually expressed as a dollar amount per share or as a percentage applied to the par value. For example, the December 31, 1993, balance sheet of **Pitney Bowes, Inc.** showed that the company had 4%, $50 par value, preferred stock outstanding. These shares required the company to pay quarterly dividends of $0.50 per share (an annual rate of $2 or 4% of par) before the common shareholders could receive a dividend.

A preference for dividends does not, however, grant an absolute right to dividends. If the board of directors does not declare a dividend, neither the preferred nor the common stockholders receive one.

Cumulative and Noncumulative Preferred Stock

Most preferred stock is **cumulative** but some is **noncumulative.** For noncumulative, the right to receive dividends is forfeited in any year that the dividends are not declared. When preferred stock is cumulative and the board of directors fails to declare a dividend to the preferred stockholders, the unpaid dividend is called a **dividend in arrears.** The accumulation of dividends in arrears on cumulative preferred stock does not guarantee that they will be paid. However, the cumulative preferred stockholders must be paid both the current dividend and all dividends in arrears before any dividend can be paid to the common stockholders.

To show the difference between cumulative and noncumulative preferred stock, assume that a corporation's outstanding stock includes 1,000 shares of $100 par, 9% preferred stock and 4,000 shares of $50 par, common stock. During 19X1, the first year of the corporation's operations, the board of directors declared cash dividends of $5,000. During 19X2, it declared $42,000. The allocations of the total dividends are as follows:

	Preferred	Common
Assuming noncumulative preferred:		
19X1	$ 5,000	$ 0
19X2:		
First: current preferred dividend	$ 9,000	
Remainder to common		$33,000
* * * *		
Assuming cumulative preferred:		
19X1	$ 5,000	$ 0
19X2:		
First: dividends in arrears	$ 4,000	
Next: current preferred dividend	9,000	
Remainder to common		$29,000
Totals	$13,000	$29,000

Notice that the allocation of the 19X2 dividends depends on whether the preferred stock is noncumulative or cumulative. With noncumulative preferred stock, the preferred stockholders never receive the $4,000 that was skipped in 19X1. However, when the preferred stock is cumulative, the $4,000 in arrears is paid in 19X2 before the common stockholders receive a dividend.

Disclosure of Dividends in Arrears in the Financial Statements

Dividends are not like interest expense, which is incurred as time passes and therefore must be accrued. A liability for a dividend does not come into existence until the dividend is declared by the board of directors. Thus, if a preferred dividend date passes and the corporation's board fails to declare the dividend on its cumulative preferred stock, the dividend in arrears is not a liability. However, when preparing the financial statements, the *full-disclosure principle* requires the corporation to report the amount of preferred dividends in arrears as of the balance sheet date. Normally, this information is given in a footnote.

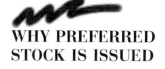

WHY PREFERRED STOCK IS ISSUED

A corporation might issue preferred stock for several reasons. One reason is to raise capital without sacrificing control of the corporation. For example, suppose that the organizers of a business have $100,000 cash to invest but wish to organize a corporation that needs $200,000 of capital to get off to a good start. If they sold $200,000 worth of common stock, they would have only 50% control and would have to negotiate extensively with the other stockholders in making policy. However, if they issue $100,000 worth of common stock to themselves and can sell outsiders $100,000 of 8%, cumulative preferred stock that has no voting rights, they can retain control of the corporation.

A second reason for issuing preferred stock is to boost the return earned by the common stockholders. Using the previous example to illustrate, suppose that the corporation's organizers expect the new company to earn an annual after-tax income of $24,000. If they sell and issue $200,000 worth of common stock, this income produces a 12% return on the $200,000 of common stockholders' equity. However, if they issue $100,000 of 8% preferred stock to the outsiders and $100,000 of common stock to themselves, their own return increases to 16% per year, as shown here:

Net after-tax income	$24,000
Less preferred dividends at 8%	(8,000)
Balance to common stockholders (equal to 16% on their $100,000 investment)	$16,000

In this case, the common stockholders earn 16% because the assets contributed by the preferred stockholders are invested to earn $12,000 while the preferred dividend payments amount to only $8,000.

The use of preferred stock to increase the return to common stockholders is an example of **financial leverage.** Whenever the dividend rate on preferred stock is less than the rate that the corporation earns on its assets, the effect of issuing preferred stock is to increase (or *lever*) the rate earned by common stockholders. Financial leverage also occurs when debt is issued and the interest rate paid on it is less than the rate earned from using the assets the creditors loaned to the corporation.

There are other reasons for issuing preferred stock. For example, a corporation's preferred stock may appeal to some investors who believe that its common stock is too risky or that the dividend rate on the common stock will be too low. Also, if a corporation's management wants to issue common stock but believes the current market price for the common stock is too low, the corporation may issue preferred stock that is convertible into common stock. If and when the price of the common stock increases, the preferred stockholders can convert their shares into common shares.

Participating Preferred Stock—A Defense against Hostile Takeovers

The dividends on most preferred stocks are limited to a maximum amount each year. The maximum is defined as a stated percentage of the stock's par value or as a specific dollar amount per share. Once the preferred stockholders receive this amount, the common stockholders receive any and all additional dividends. Preferred stocks that have this limitation are said to be *nonparticipating.*

In addition to the typical nonparticipating preferred stock, many corporations are authorized to issue **participating preferred stock.** This unique kind of preferred stock is designed to share with the common stockholders in any additional dividends paid in excess of the stated percentage dividend on the preferred.

Although many corporations are authorized to issue participating preferred stock, the shares are rarely issued. That is, companies obtain authorization to issue the shares even though management does not expect to ever sell them. They do this to defend against a *takeover* of the corporation by an unfriendly investor (or a group of investors) who would buy enough voting common stock to gain control over operations. Using terminology from spy novels, the financial world refers to this kind of a plan as a *poison pill* that the company will swallow if it is threatened with capture by an enemy.

A typical poison pill works as follows: The persons who own a corporation's common stock on a given date are granted the right to purchase a large amount of participating preferred stock at a very low price. This right to purchase the preferred shares is not transferable. Thus, if stockholders sell their common shares, the buyers do not gain the right to purchase preferred shares. In addition, the right to purchase preferred shares can only be exercised if the board of directors identifies a buyer of a large block of common shares as an unfriendly buyer.

If an unfriendly investor buys a large block of common shares (which does not have the right to purchase participating preferred shares), the board can issue the preferred shares at a very low price to the remaining common shareholders who retained the right to purchase. When the preferred stock is issued, future dividends will be divided between the preferred shares and the common shares. This transfers some of the value of the common shares to the preferred shares. As a result, the stock owned by the unfriendly buyer loses much of its value and is worth much less than the buyer's cost. The ultimate effect is to eliminate the potential benefit of attempting a hostile takeover.

Progress Check

14-11   In what ways may preferred stock have priority over common stock?

14-12   Increasing the return to common stockholders by including preferred stock in the capital structure is an example of: *(a)* Financial leverage; *(b)* Cumulative earnings; *(c)* Dividends in arrears.

14-13   MBI Corp. has 9,000 shares of $50 par value, 10% cumulative and nonparticipating preferred stock and 27,000 shares of $10 par value common stock issued and outstanding. No dividends have been declared for the past two years, but during the current year, MBI declares a $288,000 dividend. The amount to be paid to common shareholders is: *(a)* $243,000; *(b)* $153,000; *(c)* $135,000.

As we just mentioned, an issue of preferred stock can be made more attractive to some investors by giving them the right to exchange the preferred shares for a fixed number of common shares. **Convertible preferred stock** offers investors a higher potential return than does nonconvertible preferred stock. If the company prospers and its common stock increases in value, the convertible preferred stockholders can share in the prosperity by converting their preferred stock into the more valuable common stock. Conversion is at the option of the investors and therefore does not occur unless it is to their advantage. (The investors can enjoy the results of the increased value of the common stock without converting the preferred stock because the preferred stock's market value reflects the change in the common stock's value.)

CONVERTIBLE PREFERRED STOCK

LO 5
Explain convertible preferred stock and describe the meaning of the par value, call price, market value, and book value of corporate stock.

In addition to a par value, stocks may have a *call price,* a *market value,* and a *book value.*

STOCK VALUES

Call Price of Callable Preferred Stock

Some issues of preferred stock are callable. This means that the issuing corporation has the right to retire the **callable preferred stock** by paying a specified amount to the preferred stockholders. The amount that must be paid to call and retire a preferred share is its **call price** or *redemption value.* This amount is set at the time the stock is issued. Normally, the call price includes the par value of the stock plus a premium that provides the stockholders with some additional return on their investment. When the issuing corporation calls and retires a preferred stock, it must pay not only the call price but also any dividends in arrears.

Market Value

The market value of a share of stock is the price at which it can be bought or sold. Market values are influenced by a wide variety of factors including expected future earnings, dividends, and events in the economy at large. Market values of frequently traded stocks are reported daily in newspapers such as *The Wall Street Journal.* The

Illustration 14–1
Stockholders' Equity
with Preferred
and Common Stock

Stockholders' Equity		
Preferred stock, $100 par value, 7% cumulative, 2,000 shares authorized, 1,000 shares issued and outstanding	$100,000	
Contributed capital in excess of par value, preferred stock	5,000	
Total capital contributed by preferred stockholders		$105,000
Common stock, $25 par value, 12,000 shares authorized, 10,000 shares issued and outstanding	$250,000	
Contributed capital in excess of par value, common stock	10,000	
Total capital contributed by common stockholders		260,000
Total contributed capital		$365,000
Retained earnings		82,000
Total stockholders' equity		$447,000

market values of stocks that are not actively traded can be more difficult to determine. Analysts use a variety of techniques to estimate the value of such stocks, and most of these techniques use accounting information as an important input to the valuation process.

Book Value

The **book value of a share of stock** equals the share's portion of the stockholders' equity as it is recorded in the company's accounts. If a corporation has only common stock, the book value per share equals the total stockholders' equity divided by the number of outstanding shares. For example, if a company has 10,000 outstanding shares and total stockholders' equity of $285,000, the stock's book value is $28.50 per share ($285,000/10,000 shares).

Computing the book value of stock is more complex when both common and preferred shares are outstanding. To calculate the book values of each class of stock, you begin by allocating the total stockholders' equity between the two classes. The preferred stockholders' portion equals the preferred stock's call price (or par value if the preferred is not callable) plus any cumulative dividends in arrears. Then allocate the remaining stockholders' equity to the common shares. To determine the book value per share of preferred, divide the portion of stockholders' equity assigned to preferred by the number of preferred shares outstanding. Similarly, the book value per share of common is the stockholders' equity assigned to common divided by the number of outstanding common shares. For example, assume a corporation has the stockholders' equity as shown in Illustration 14–1.

If the preferred stock is callable at $108 per share and two years of cumulative preferred dividends are in arrears, the book values of the corporation's shares are calculated as follows:

Total stockholders' equity		$ 447,000
Less equity applicable to preferred shares:		
Call price (1,000 × $108)	$108,000	
Cumulative dividends in arrears ($100,000 × 7% × 2)	14,000	(122,000)
Equity applicable to common shares		$ 325,000
Book value of preferred shares ($122,000/1,000)		$122.00
Book value of common shares ($325,000/10,000)		$ 32.50

In their annual reports to shareholders, corporations sometimes report the increase in the book value of their shares that has occurred during a year. Also, book value may have significance in contracts. For example, a stockholder may enter into a contract to sell shares at their book value at some future date. However, remember that book value normally does not approximate market value. For example, the book value per share of **Anheuser-Busch Companies, Inc.'s** common stock on December 31, 1994, was $17.16. This is significantly lower than its market value, which ranged from $47⅜ to $55⅜ during 1994.

Similarly, book value should not be confused with the liquidation value of a stock. If a corporation is liquidated, its assets probably will sell at prices that are quite different from the amounts at which they are carried on the books.

Progress Check

14-14   Potter Co.'s outstanding stock includes 1,000 shares of $90 par value cumulative preferred stock and 12,000 shares of $20 par value common stock. The call price of the preferred stock is $90 and dividends of $18,000 are in arrears. Total stockholders' equity is $630,000. What is the book value per share of the common shares?

14-15   The price at which a share of stock can be bought or sold is the: *(a)* Call price; *(b)* Redemption value; *(c)* Market value.

PROPRIETORSHIPS

Recall from Chapter 1 that a proprietorship (sometimes called a *single proprietorship* or *sole proprietorship*) is a business that is owned by one person and is not organized as a corporation. In the law, a proprietorship is not a separate entity; it does not exist apart from the owner. In other words, a proprietorship is no more than a collection of business activities carried on by an individual person.

Because a proprietorship is not recognized in the law as a separate entity, it is not subject to income taxes. Instead, the income is taxed as personal income of the owner. This is done whether the owner withdraws cash from the business or not.

Because a proprietorship is not legally separate from its owner, the owner is personally responsible for the liabilities of the proprietorship. This means that the personal assets of the owner are available to satisfy the claims of the business creditors.

Although a proprietorship is not a legal entity, managing a proprietorship requires accounting information about the activities, assets, and related liabilities of the business as if it were a separate entity. Thus, the accounting records and financial statements for a proprietorship are based on the assumption that the business is a separate entity. (See the discussion of the *business entity principle* in Chapter 2, page 35).

Accounting for a proprietorship and for a corporation are the same except in regard to owners' equity. In a proprietorship, contributed capital and retained earnings are not recorded in separate accounts. Instead, all of the owner's equity is recorded in a single *capital account.* For example, assume Lisa Dow started a consulting business and invested $10,000 cash in the business. The entry to record the investment on the books of the proprietorship is:

LO 6
Explain the legal status of a proprietorship, prepare entries to account for the owner's equity of a proprietorship, and prepare a statement of changes in owner's equity.

UNLIMITED LIABILITY OF THE PROPRIETOR

ACCOUNTING FOR PROPRIETORSHIPS

Jan.	1	Cash	10,000.00	
		Lisa Dow, Capital		10,000.00
		To record owner's investment.		

When the owner of a proprietorship withdraws cash from the business, the withdrawal is recorded in a special *withdrawals* account that is similar to a corporation's Cash Dividends Declared account. For example, assume that Dow withdrew $7,000 from the business for personal use. The entry to record the withdrawal is:

Nov.	1	Lisa Dow, Withdrawals	7,000.00	
		Cash		7,000.00
		To record owner's cash withdrawal.		

Now assume that Dow's first year of operations resulted in a net income of $12,000 which appears as a credit balance in the Income Summary account. The following entry closes the Income Summary account:

Dec.	31	Income Summary	12,000.00	
		Lisa Dow, Capital		12,000.00
		To close Income Summary.		

Then, the withdrawals account is closed with the following entry:

Dec.	31	Lisa Dow, Capital	7,000.00	
		Lisa Dow, Withdrawals		7,000.00
		To close the withdrawals account.		

The changes in the owner's capital account during an accounting period are reported on a financial statement called a statement of changes in owner's equity. This statement for Dow's consulting business appears as follows:

LISA DOW, CONSULTANT
Statement of Changes in Owner's Equity
For Year Ended December 31, 19X1

Lisa Dow, capital, January 1, 19X1		$ -0-
Plus: Investments by owner	$10,000	
Net income	12,000	22,000
Total		$22,000
Less withdrawals by owner		7,000
Lisa Dow, capital, December 31, 19X1		$15,000

On the balance sheet for a proprietorship, the owner's equity section includes a single item—the capital account balance of the owner. For example, the December 31 balance sheet for Dow's consulting business would include the following:

Owner's Equity

Lisa Dow, capital $15,000

Progress Check

14–16 In accounting for a proprietorship, which of the following is not true?
  a. Cash taken from the business for the personal use of the owner should be debited to the owner's withdrawals account.
  b. The owner's investments of assets in the business should be credited to the owner's capital account.
  c. In making closing entries, an Income Summary balance that represents a net loss should be credited to the owner's capital account.

14–17 Is a proprietorship subject to income taxes?

PARTNERSHIPS

A **partnership** can be defined as *an unincorporated association of two or more persons to carry on a business for profit as co-owners.* Many businesses, such as small retail and service businesses, are organized as partnerships. Also, many professional practitioners—including physicians, lawyers, and certified public accountants—have traditionally organized their practices as partnerships.

LO 7
Explain the characteristics of partnerships, account for the equity of partners, and describe several organizations that mix the characteristics of corporations and partnerships.

CHARACTERISTICS OF GENERAL PARTNERSHIPS

A partnership is a voluntary association between the partners. All that is required to form a partnership is that two or more legally competent people (that is, people who are of age and of sound mental capacity) must agree to be partners. Their agreement becomes a **partnership contract.** Although it should be in writing, the contract is binding even if it is only expressed orally.[4]

The life of a partnership is always limited. Death, bankruptcy, or anything that takes away the ability of one of the partners to enter into or fulfill a contract automatically ends a partnership. In addition, a partnership may be terminated at will by any one of the partners.

Partnerships in which all of the partners have mutual agency and unlimited liability are called **general partnerships.** Before agreeing to join a general partnership, you should understand clearly the income tax status of a partnership and the meaning of mutual agency and unlimited liability.

Income Tax Status

Partnerships have the same tax status as proprietorships; that is, partnerships are not subject to taxes on their income. Instead, the income (or loss) of a partnership is allocated to the partners according to the partnership agreement and thereby included in the process of determining the taxable income of each partner. The allocation of partnership income or loss is done each year whether or not cash is distributed to the partners.

Mutual Agency

In a general partnership, the relationship between the partners involves **mutual agency.** Under normal circumstances, every partner is a fully authorized agent of the partnership. As its agent, a partner can commit or bind the partnership to any contract that is within the apparent scope of the partnership's business. For example, a

---

[4]In some cases, courts have ruled that partnerships have been created by the actions of the partners, even when there was no expressed agreement to form a partnership.

partner in a merchandising business can sign contracts that bind the partnership to buy merchandise, lease a store building, borrow money, or hire employees. These activities are all within the scope of the business of a merchandising firm. On the other hand, a partner in a law firm, acting alone, cannot bind his or her partners to a contract to buy merchandise for resale or rent a retail store building. These actions are not within the normal scope of a law firm's business.

Partners may agree to limit the power of any one or more of the partners to negotiate certain contracts for the partnership. Such an agreement is binding on the partners and on outsiders who know that it exists. However, it is not binding on outsiders who do not know that it exists. Outsiders who are not aware of the agreement have the right to assume that each partner has normal agency powers for the partnership.

Because mutual agency exposes all partners to the risk of unwise actions by any one partner, people should carefully evaluate potential partners before agreeing to join a partnership. The importance of this advice is underscored by the fact that most partnerships are also characterized by unlimited liability.

Unlimited Liability of Partners

When a general partnership cannot pay its debts, the creditors normally can satisfy their claims from the *personal* assets of the partners. Also, if some partners do not have enough assets to meet their share of the partnership's debts, the creditors can turn to the assets of the remaining partners who are able to pay. Because partners may be called on to pay all the debts of the partnership, each partner is said to have **unlimited liability** for the partnership's debts. Mutual agency and unlimited liability are the main reasons why most partnerships have only a few members.

PARTNERSHIP ACCOUNTING

Accounting for a partnership does not differ from accounting for a proprietorship except for transactions that directly affect the partners' equity. Because ownership rights in a partnership are divided among the partners, partnership accounting:

- Uses a capital account for each partner.
- Uses a withdrawals account for each partner.
- Allocates net incomes or losses to the partners according to the provisions of the partnership agreement.

When partners invest in a partnership, their capital accounts are credited for the invested amounts. Partners' withdrawals of assets are debited to their withdrawals accounts. In closing the accounts at the end of the year, the partners' capital accounts are credited or debited for their shares of the net income or loss. Finally, the withdrawals account of each partner is closed to that partner's capital account. These closing procedures are like those used for a single proprietorship. The only difference is that separate capital and withdrawals accounts are maintained for each partner.

NATURE OF PARTNERSHIP EARNINGS

Because they are its owners, partners are not employees of the partnership. If partners devote their time and services to the affairs of their partnership, they are understood to do so for profit, not for salary. Therefore, when the partners calculate the net income of a partnership, salaries to the partners are not deducted as expenses on the income statement. However, when the net income or loss of the partnership is allocated among the partners, the partners may agree to base part of the allocation on salary allowances that reflect the relative values of service provided by the partners.

Partners are also understood to have invested in a partnership for profit, not for interest. Nevertheless, partners may agree that the division of partnership earnings should include a return based on their invested capital. For example, if one partner contributes five times as much capital as another, it is only fair that this fact be considered when earnings are allocated among the partners. Thus, a partnership agreement may provide for interest allowances based on the partners' capital balances. Like salary allowances, interest allowances are not expenses to be reported on the income statement.

DIVISION OF EARNINGS

In the absence of a contrary agreement, the law states that the income or loss of a partnership should be shared equally by the partners. However, partners may agree to any method of sharing. If they agree on how they will share income but say nothing about losses, then losses are shared in the same way as income.

Several methods of sharing partnership earnings can be used. Three frequently used methods divide earnings: (1) on a stated fractional basis, (2) in the ratio of capital investments, or (3) using salary and interest allowances and any remainder in a fixed ratio.

Earnings Allocated on a Stated Fractional Basis

An easy way to divide partnership earnings is to give each partner a fraction of the total. All that is necessary is for the partners to agree on the fractional share that each will receive. For example, assume that the partnership agreement of B. A. Jones and S. A. Meyer states that Jones will receive two-thirds and Meyer will receive one-third of the partnership earnings. If the partnership's net income is $30,000, the earnings are allocated to the partners and the Income Summary account is closed with the following entry:

Dec.	31	Income Summary	30,000.00	
		B. A. Jones, Capital		20,000.00
		S. A. Meyer, Capital		10,000.00
		To close the Income Summary account and allocate		
		the earnings.		

When earnings are shared on a fractional basis, the fractions may reflect the relative capital investments of the partners. For example, suppose that B. Donner and H. Flack formed a partnership and agreed to share earnings in the ratio of their investments. Because Donner invested $50,000 and Flack invested $30,000, Donner will receive five-eighths of the earnings ($50,000/$80,000) while Flack will receive three-eighths of the earnings ($30,000/$80,000).

Salaries and Interest as Aids in Sharing

As we have mentioned, the service contributions and capital contributions of the partners often are not equal. If the service contributions are not equal, salary allowances can compensate for the differences. Or, when capital contributions are not equal, interest allowances can compensate for the unequal investments. When both investment and service contributions are unequal, the allocation of net incomes and losses may include both interest and salary allowances.

For example, in Kathy Stanley and David Breck's new partnership, Stanley is to provide services that they agree are worth an annual salary of $36,000. Breck is less experienced in the business, so his service contribution is worth only $24,000. Also, Stanley will invest $30,000 in the business and Breck will invest $10,000. To compensate Stanley and Breck fairly in light of the differences in their service and capital contributions, they agree to share incomes or losses as follows:

1. Annual salary allowances of $36,000 to Stanley and $24,000 to Breck.
2. Interest allowances equal to 10% of each partner's beginning-of-year capital balance.
3. The remaining balance of income or loss is to be shared equally.

Note that the provisions for salaries and interest in this partnership agreement are called *allowances*. These allowances are not reported on the income statement as salaries and interest expense. They are only a means of splitting up the net income or net loss of the partnership.

Under the Stanley and Breck partnership agreement, a first year's net income of $70,000 is shared as shown in Illustration 14–2. Notice that Stanley gets $42,000, or 60% of the income, while Breck gets $28,000, or 40%.

In Illustration 14–2, notice that the $70,000 net income exceeds the salary and interest allowances of the partners. However, the method of sharing agreed to by Stanley and Breck must be followed even if the net income is smaller than the salary and interest allowances. For example, if the first year's net income was $50,000, it would be allocated to the partners as shown in Illustration 14–3. Notice that this circumstance provides Stanley with 64% of the total income, while Breck gets only 36%.

A net loss would be shared by Stanley and Breck in the same manner as the $50,000 net income. The only difference is that the income-and-loss-sharing procedure would begin with a negative amount of income because of the net loss. After the salary and interest allowances, the remaining balance to be allocated equally would then be a larger negative amount.

ORGANIZATIONS THAT MIX THE CHARACTERISTICS OF CORPORATIONS AND PARTNERSHIPS

Sometimes, neither a corporation nor a general partnership satisfies the needs of business organizers. As a result, lawmakers have developed a number of hybrid organizations that combine the characteristics of corporations and partnerships in various ways. We briefly introduce several of these organizational forms in the following paragraphs.

Limited Partnerships

In a general partnership, all of the partners have unlimited liability. Sometimes, however, individuals who want to invest in a partnership are not willing to accept the risk of unlimited liability. Their needs may be met by using a **limited partnership** which must include in its name the words "Limited Partnership," or "Ltd.," or "L.P." A lim-

Illustration 14–2
Sharing Income When Income Exceeds Salary and Interest Allowances

	Share to Stanley	Share to Breck	Income to be Allocated
Total net income			$70,000
Allocated as salary allowances:			
Stanley	$36,000		
Breck		$24,000	
Total allocated as salary allowances			60,000
Balance of income after salary allowances . .			$10,000
Allocated as interest:			
Stanley (10% on $30,000)	3,000		
Breck (10% on $10,000)		1,000	
Total allocated as interest			4,000
Balance of income after salary and interest allowances			$ 6,000
Balance allocated equally:			
Stanley	3,000		
Breck		3,000	
Total allocated equally			6,000
Balance of income			$ 0
Shares of the partners	$42,000	$28,000	
Percentages of total net income	60%	40%	

	Share to Stanley	Share to Breck	Income to be Allocated
Total net income			$ 50,000
Allocated as salary allowances:			
Stanley	$36,000		
Breck		$24,000	
Total allocated as salary allowances			60,000
Balance of income after salary allowances ..			$(10,000)
Allocated as interest:			
Stanley (10% on $30,000)	3,000		
Breck (10% on $10,000)		1,000	
Total allocated as interest			4,000
Balance of income after salary and			
interest allowances			$(14,000)
Balance allocated equally:			
Stanley	(7,000)		
Breck		(7,000)	
Total allocated equally			(14,000)
Balance of income			$ 0
Shares of the partners	$32,000	$18,000	
Percentages of total net income	64%	36%	

Illustration 14–3
Sharing Income When Interest and Salary Allowances Exceed Income

ited partnership has two classes of partners, general and limited. At least one partner must be a **general partner** who assumes unlimited liability for the debts of the partnership. The **limited partners** have no personal liability beyond the amounts they invest in the business. A limited partnership is managed by the general partner(s). The limited partners have no active role except for major decisions specified in the partnership agreement. A limited partnership agreement is likely to specify unique procedures for allocating incomes and losses between the general and limited partners. Otherwise, the same accounting procedures are used for a limited partnership and a general partnership.

Limited Liability Partnerships

Another form of partnership that an increasing number of states are allowing professionals such as lawyers and accountants to use is the **limited liability partnership** which is identified in its name by including the words "Limited Liability Partnership" or by "L.L.P." This type of partnership is designed to protect innocent partners from malpractice or negligence claims that result from the acts of another partner. When a partner provides service that results in a malpractice claim, that partner has personal liability for the claim. The remaining partners who were not responsible for the actions that resulted in the claim are not personally liable for the claim. In most states, however, all partners have personal liability for other partnership debts. Accounting for a limited liability partnership is the same as for a general partnership.

"S" Corporations

Some corporations that have 35 or fewer shareholders can elect to be treated like a partnership for income tax purposes. These companies are called Sub-Chapter S or simply **"S" corporations.** This distinguishes them from all other corporations, which are called Sub-Chapter C or simply **"C" corporations.** "S" corporations provide stockholders with the same limited liability feature as "C" corporations.

An "S" corporation does not pay income taxes. If stockholders work for an "S" corporation, their salaries are treated as expenses of the corporation and the remaining income or loss of the corporation is allocated to the stockholders for inclusion on their tax returns. Except for the need of "C" corporations to account for income tax expenses and liabilities, the accounting procedures are the same for both "S" and "C" corporations.

Limited Liability Companies

The newest form of business organization is the **limited liability company.** The names of these businesses normally include the words "Limited Liability Company" or one of several alternative abbreviations such as "Ltd.," "Co.," "L.L.C.," or "L.C." This form of business has some features like a corporation and some like a limited partnership. All of the owners, who are called members, are protected with the same limited liability feature as provided by corporations. However, unlike the "S" corporation, ownership is not limited to 35 members. While limited partners cannot actively participate in the management of a limited partnership, the members of a limited liability company can assume an active management role. Usually, but not always, a limited liability company does not have the continuity of life normally associated with a corporation.

For income tax purposes, the IRS may classify a limited liability company as a partnership or as a corporation. The classification depends on factors such as whether the members' equity interests are freely transferable and whether the company has continuity of life.

A limited liability company's accounting system must be designed to help management comply with the dictates of the articles of organization and company regulations adopted by the members. In addition, the accounting system must provide adequate information to support the company's compliance with state and federal laws including taxation. To accomplish these objectives, the system may have some of the features normally associated with corporate accounting and others normally associated with partnership accounting. For example, depending on the articles of organization and company regulations, the allocation of income between members may be similar to a corporation or a partnership.

Progress Check

14-18 A partnership is automatically terminated in the event: *(a)* The partnership agreement is not in writing; *(b)* A partner dies; *(c)* A partner exercises mutual agency.

14-19 Mixon and Reed form a partnership by contributing $70,000 and $35,000, respectively. They agree to an interest allowance equal to 10% of each partner's capital balance at the beginning of the year with the remaining income to be shared equally. Allocate the first-year net income of $40,000 to the partners.

14-20 What does the term *unlimited liability* mean when it is applied to a general partnership?

14-21 Which of the following forms of business organization does not provide limited liability to all of its owners: *(a)* "C" corporation; *(b)* "S" corporation; *(c)* Limited liability company; *(d)* Limited partnership?

USING THE INFORMATION—DIVIDEND YIELD

LO 8
Calculate dividend yield and describe its meaning.

Investors buy shares of a company's stock in anticipation of receiving a return from cash dividends and from increases in the stock's value. Stocks that pay large dividends on a regular basis are sometimes called *income stocks.* They are attractive to investors who want dependable cash flows from their investments. In contrast, other stocks pay few or no dividends but are still attractive to investors because they expect the market value of the stocks to increase rapidly. The stocks of companies that do not distribute cash but use it to finance rapid expansion are often called *growth stocks.*

One way to evaluate whether a company stock should be viewed as an income stock or growth stock is to examine the **dividend yield.** The following formula shows that this ratio is a rate of return based on the annual cash dividends and the stock's market value:

$$\text{Dividend yield} = \frac{\text{Annual cash dividends per share}}{\text{Market value per share}}$$

Dividend yield may be calculated on a historical basis using the prior year's actual dividends or on an expected basis. For example, recall from the first page of this chapter the discussion of Mobil Corporation and the dividend and stock price information for several companies. The dividend yields for those companies were as follows:

Company	Common Dividend Per Share		November 1994 Stock Price	Dividend Yield	
	1994*	1993		1994*	1993
Mobil Corporation	$3.40	$3.25	$82¼	4.1%	4.0%
Minnesota Mining & Mfg. Co.	1.76	1.66	53¼	3.3	3.1
Texaco Inc.	3.20	3.20	60⅞	5.3	5.3
AT&T Corp.	1.32	1.32	54	2.4	2.4
GAP, Inc.	0.48	0.38	37⅞	1.3	1.0
Microsoft Corp.	0	0	64½	—	—

*Estimated 1994 amounts.

An investor can compare these dividend yields to evaluate the relative importance of dividends to the prices of the stocks. Current dividends obviously have no impact on **Microsoft Corp.'s** stock price and very little impact on the **GAP, Inc.'s** stock price. The values of these two stocks must stem from expected increases in their stock prices (and the eventual dividends that may be paid).

On the other hand, **Mobil Corporation** and **Texaco Inc.** pay substantial dividends of 4.0 to 5.3%. These are less than one would expect from investments in corporate debt securities but still high enough to conclude that dividends are a very important factor in establishing their stock prices.

Although income stocks tend to have relatively stable market values, their values can vary substantially in anticipation of changes in the company's ability to pay future dividends or changes in rates of returns on other available investments. Thus, investors should examine much more information in addition to the dividend yield before deciding to buy, sell, or keep a stock.

Progress Check

14–22 Which of the following produces an expected dividend yield of 10% for common stock?

   a. Dividends of $100,000 are expected to be paid next year and expected net income is $1,000,000.

   b. Dividends of $50,000 were paid during the prior year and net income was $500,000.

   c. Dividends of $2 per share are expected to be paid next year and the current market value of the stock is $20 per share.

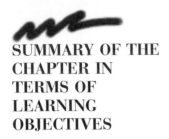

SUMMARY OF THE CHAPTER IN TERMS OF LEARNING OBJECTIVES

LO 1. Explain the unique characteristics of the corporate form of business. Corporations are separate legal entities. As such, their stockholders are not liable for the corporate debts. Stocks issued by corporations are easily transferred between stockholders, and the life of corporations does not end with the incapacity or death of a stockholder. A corporation acts through its agents, who are its officers and managers, not its stockholders. Corporations tend to be closely regulated by government and are subject to income taxes.

LO 2. Record the issuance of par value stock and no-par stock with or without a stated value and explain the concept of minimum legal capital. When stock is issued, the par or stated value is credited to the stock account and any excess is credited to a separate contributed capital account. If the stock has no par or stated value, the entire proceeds are credited to the stock account. Stockholders must contribute assets equal to the minimum legal capital of a corporation or be potentially liable for the deficiency. And, as long as any liabilities remain unpaid, the minimum legal capital cannot be paid to stockholders.

LO 3. Record transactions that involve dividends and stock subscriptions and explain the effects of stock subscriptions on the balance sheet. If a corporation sells stock through subscriptions, the unpaid portion is recorded as a receivable, and the subscribers' equity is recorded in contributed capital accounts. The balance of the Common Stock Subscribed account is transferred to the Common Stock account when the shares are issued, which normally occurs after all payments are received. Three dates are involved when cash dividends are distributed to stockholders. The board of directors binds the company to pay the dividend on the date of declaration. The recipients of the dividend are identified on the date of record. The cash is paid to the stockholders on the date of payment.

LO 4. State the differences between common and preferred stock and allocate dividends between the common and preferred stock of a corporation. Preferred stock has a priority (or senior status) relative to common stock in one or more ways. Usually, common stockholders cannot be paid dividends unless a specified amount of dividends also is paid to preferred shareholders. Preferred stock also may have a priority status if the corporation is liquidated. The dividend preference for most preferred stocks is cumulative. Many companies are authorized to issue participating preferred stocks as a poison pill against hostile takeovers.

LO 5. Describe convertible preferred stock and explain the meaning of the par value, call price, market value, and book value of corporate stock. Convertible preferred stock can be exchanged by its holders for common stock. If preferred stock is callable, the amount that must be paid to retire the stock is its call price plus any dividends in arrears. Market value is the price that a stock commands when it is bought or sold. The book value of preferred stock is any dividends in arrears plus its par value or, if it is callable, its call price. The remaining stockholders' equity is divided by the number of outstanding common shares to determine the book value per share of the common stock.

LO 6. Explain the legal status of a proprietorship, prepare entries to account for the owner's equity of a proprietorship, and prepare a statement of changes in owner's equity. Proprietorships are not separate legal entities but are treated as separate entities for accounting purposes. The owner's equity of a proprietorship is recorded in a single capital account, and withdrawals are recorded in a withdrawals account that is closed to the capital account at the end of each period. A statement of changes in owner's equity shows the change in the owner's capital account balance during a period that resulted from investments and withdrawals by the owner and from the net income or loss.

LO 7. Explain the characteristics of partnerships, account for the equity of partners, and describe several organizations that mix the characteristics of corporations and partnerships. General partnerships are not subject to income taxes. In addition, each partner can bind a partnership to contracts that are within the normal scope of the business and each partner has unlimited liability for the debts of the partnership. A partnership agreement should specify the method for allocating the partnership's net income or loss among the partners. This allocation may be done on a fractional basis, or it may use salary and interest allowances to compensate partners for differences in their service and capital contributions. Organizations that combine the characteristics of partnerships and corporations in differing ways include limited partnerships, limited liability partnerships, "S" corporations, and limited liability companies.

LO 8. Calculate dividend yield and describe its meaning. The dividend yield is the ratio between a stock's annual dividends per share and its market value per share. It describes the rate of return provided to the stockholders from the company's dividends. The yield can be compared with the rates of return offered by other kinds of investments to determine whether the stock should be viewed as an income or growth stock.

DEMONSTRATION PROBLEM

Barton Corporation was created on January 1, 19X1. The following transactions relating to stockholders' equity occurred during the first two years of the company's operations. Prepare the journal entries to record these transactions. Also prepare the balance sheet presentation of the organization costs, liabilities, and stockholders' equity as of December 31, 19X1, and December 31, 19X2. Include appropriate footnotes.

19X1

Jan. 1 Authorized the issuance of 2 million shares of $5 par value common stock and 100,000 shares of $100 par value preferred stock. The preferred stock pays a 10% annual dividend and is cumulative.

1 Issued 200,000 shares of common stock for cash at $12 per share.

1 Issued 100,000 shares of common stock in exchange for a building valued at $820,000 and merchandise inventory valued at $380,000.

1 Accepted subscriptions for 150,000 shares of common stock at $12 per share. The subscribers made no down payments, and the full purchase price was due on April 1, 19X1.

1 Paid a cash reimbursement to the company's founders for $100,000 of organization costs; these costs are to be amortized over 10 years.

1 Issued 12,000 shares of preferred stock for cash at $110 per share.

Apr. 1 Collected the full subscription price for the January 1 common stock and issued the stock.

Dec. 31 The Income Summary account for 19X1 had a $125,000 credit balance before being closed to Retained Earnings; no dividends were declared on either the common or preferred stocks.

19X2

June 4 Issued 100,000 shares of common stock for cash at $15 per share.

Dec. 10 Declared dividends payable on January 10, 19X3, as follows:

> To preferred stockholders for 19X1 . . . . $120,000
> To preferred stockholders for 19X2 120,000
> To common stockholders for 19X2 300,000

31 The Income Summary account for 19X2 had a $1 million credit balance before being closed to Retained Earnings.

Planning the Solution

- Record journal entries for the events in 19X1 and 19X2.
- Close the accounts related to retained earnings at the end of each year.
- Determine the balances for the 19X1 and 19X2 balance sheets, including the following amounts to use in the balance sheet and the accompanying note:
  a. The number of shares issued.
  b. The amount of dividends in arrears.
  c. The unamortized balance of organization costs.
  Prepare the specified portions of the 19X1 and 19X2 balance sheets.

Solution to Demonstration Problem

19X1				
Jan.	1	Cash	2,400,000.00	
		Common Stock		1,000,000.00
		Contributed Capital in Excess of		
		Par Value, Common Stock		1,400,000.00
		Issued 200,000 shares of common stock.		
	1	Building	820,000.00	
		Merchandise Inventory	380,000.00	
		Common Stock		500,000.00
		Contributed Capital in Excess of		
		Par Value, Common Stock		700,000.00
		Issued 100,000 shares of common stock.		
	1	Subscriptions Receivable	1,800,000.00	
		Common Stock Subscribed		750,000.00
		Contributed Capital in Excess of		
		Par Value, Common Stock		1,050,000.00
		Accepted subscriptions for 150,000 shares		
		of common stock.		
	1	Organization Costs	100,000.00	
		Cash		100,000.00
		Reimbursed the founders for organization costs.		
	1	Cash	1,320,000.00	
		Preferred Stock		1,200,000.00
		Contributed Capital in Excess of		
		Par Value, Preferred Stock		120,000.00
		Issued 12,000 shares of preferred stock.		
Apr.	1	Cash	1,800,000.00	
		Subscriptions Receivable		1,800,000.00
		Collected balance due on subscribed common stock.		
	1	Common Stock Subscribed	750,000.00	
		Common Stock		750,000.00
		Issued 150,000 shares of subscribed common stock.		
Dec.	31	Income Summary	125,000.00	
		Retained Earnings		125,000.00
		To close the Income Summary account and update		
		Retained Earnings.		
19X2				
June	4	Cash	1,500,000.00	
		Common Stock		500,000.00
		Contributed Capital in Excess of		
		Par Value, Common Stock		1,000,000.00
		Issued 100,000 shares of common stock.		
Dec.	10	Cash Dividends Declared	540,000.00	
		Common Dividend Payable		300,000.00
		Preferred Dividend Payable		240,000.00
		Declared current dividends and dividends in arrears		
		to common and preferred stockholders, payable on		
		January 10, 19X3.		
	31	Income Summary	1,000,000.00	
		Retained Earnings		1,000,000.00
		To close the Income Summary account and update		
		Retained Earnings.		
	31	Retained Earnings	540,000.00	
		Cash Dividends Declared		540,000.00
		To close the Cash Dividends Declared account.		

Balance sheet presentations:

	As of December 31,	
	19X1	19X2
Assets		
Organization costs	$ 90,000	$ 80,000
Liabilities		
Common dividend payable		$ 300,000
Preferred dividend payable		240,000
Total liabilities		$ 540,000
Stockholders' Equity		
Contributed capital:		
Preferred stock, $100 par value, 10% cumulative dividends, 100,000 shares authorized, 12,000 shares issued and outstanding . .	$1,200,000	$1,200,000
Contributed capital in excess of par value, preferred stock	120,000	120,000
Total capital contributed by preferred stockholders	$1,320,000	$1,320,000
Common stock, $5 par value, 2,000,000 shares authorized, 450,000 shares issued and outstanding in 19X1, and 550,000 shares in 19X2	$2,250,000	$2,750,000
Contributed capital in excess of par value, common stock	3,150,000	4,150,000
Total capital contributed by common stockholders	$5,400,000	$6,900,000
Total contributed capital	$6,720,000	$8,220,000
Retained earnings (See Note 1)	125,000	585,000
Total stockholders' equity	$6,845,000	$8,805,000

Note 1: As of December 31, 19X1, there were $120,000 of dividends in arrears on the preferred stock.

GLOSSARY

Book value of a share of stock one share's portion of the stockholders' equity recorded in the accounts. p. 504

"C" corporation a corporation that does not qualify for and elect to be treated like a partnership for income tax purposes and therefore is subject to income taxes. p. 511

Call price of preferred stock the amount that must be paid to call and retire a preferred share. p. 503

Callable preferred stock preferred stock that the issuing corporation, at its option, may retire by paying a specified amount (the call price) to the preferred stockholders plus any dividends in arrears. p. 503

Common stock stock of a corporation that has only one class of stock, or if there is more than one class, the class that has no preferences over the corporation's other classes of stock. p. 492

Convertible preferred stock a preferred stock that can be exchanged for shares of the issuing corporation's common stock at the option of the preferred stockholder. p. 503

Cumulative preferred stock preferred stock on which undeclared dividends accumulate until they are paid; common

stockholders cannot receive a dividend until all cumulative dividends have been paid. p. 500

Date of declaration the date on which a corporation's board of directors votes to pay a dividend; the dividend becomes a liability on this date. p. 497

Date of payment the date on which a corporation actually disburses a cash dividend directly to the stockholders. p. 498

Date of record the date on which the corporation's records are examined to identify the stockholders who will receive a dividend. p. 498

Deficit a debit balance in the Retained Earnings account; this situation arises when a company's cumulative losses and dividends are greater than the cumulative profits earned in other years. p. 498

Discount on stock the difference between the par value of stock and its issue price when it is issued at a price below par value. p. 494

Dividend in arrears an unpaid dividend on cumulative preferred stock; it must be paid before any regular dividends on the preferred stock and before any dividends on the common stock. p. 500

Dividend yield a company's annual cash dividends per share divided by the market value per share. p. 513

Financial leverage the achievement of an increased return on common stock by paying dividends on preferred stock or interest on debt at a rate that is less than the rate of return earned with the assets invested in the corporation by the preferred stockholders or creditors. p. 502

General partner a partner who assumes unlimited liability for the debts of the partnership; also, the general partner in a limited partnership is responsible for its management. p. 511

General partnership a partnership in which all partners have mutual agency and unlimited liability for partnership debts. p. 507

Limited liability company an unincorporated form of business organization that provides limited liability to its members (owners), that may allow members to actively participate in management, and that generally does not have continuity of life. p. 512

Limited liability partnership a partnership in which each partner is not personally liable for malpractice or negligence claims unless the partner was responsible for providing the service that resulted in the claim. p. 5110

Limited partners partners who have no personal liability for debts of the partnership beyond the amounts they have invested in the partnership. p. 511

Limited partnership a partnership that has two classes of partners, limited partners and general partners. p. 510

Minimum legal capital an amount of assets defined by state law that stockholders must invest and leave invested in a corporation; this provision is intended to protect the creditors of the corporation. p. 493

Mutual agency the legal relationship among the partners whereby each partner is an agent of the partnership and is able to bind the partnership to contracts within the apparent scope of the partnership's business. p. 507

Noncumulative preferred stock a preferred stock on which the right to receive dividends is forfeited for any year that the dividends are not declared. p. 500

No-par stock a class of stock that does not have a par value; no-par stock can be issued at any price without creating a discount liability. p. 495

Organization costs the costs of bringing a corporation into existence, including legal fees, promoters' fees, and amounts paid to the state to secure the charter. p. 490

Participating preferred stock preferred stock that gives its owners the right to share in dividends in excess of the stated percentage or amount. p. 502

Partnership an unincorporated association of two or more persons to carry on a business for profit as co-owners. p. 507

Partnership contract the agreement between partners that sets forth the terms under which the affairs of the partnership will be conducted. p. 507

Par value an arbitrary value assigned to a share of stock when the stock is authorized. p. 493

Preemptive right the right of common stockholders to protect their proportionate interest in a corporation by having the first opportunity to buy additional shares of common stock issued by the corporation. p. 499

Preferred stock stock that gives its owners a priority status over common stockholders in one or more ways, such as the payment of dividends or the distribution of assets on liquidation. p. 500

Premium on stock the difference between the par value of stock and its issue price when it is issued at a price above par value. p. 494

Proxy a legal document that gives an agent of a stockholder the power to exercise the voting rights of that stockholder's shares. p. 491

"S" Corporation a corporation with 35 or fewer shareholders that elects to be treated like a partnership for income tax purposes. p. 511

Stated value of no-par stock an arbitrary amount assigned to no-par stock by the corporation's board of directors; this amount is credited to the no-par stock account when the stock is issued. p. 495

Stock subscription a contractual commitment by an investor to purchase unissued shares of stock and become a stockholder. p. 496

Unlimited liability of partners the legal relationship among general partners that makes each of them responsible for paying all the debts of the partnership if the other partners are unable to pay their shares. p. 508

QUESTIONS

1. Who is responsible for directing the affairs of a corporation?
2. What are organization costs? List several examples of these costs.
3. How are organization costs classified on the balance sheet?
4. What are the duties and responsibilities of a corporation's registrar and transfer agent?
5. List the general rights of common stockholders.
6. What is the preemptive right of common stockholders?
7. What is the main advantage of no-par stock?
8. What is the difference between the par value and the call price of a share of stock?
9. Why would an investor find convertible preferred stock attractive?

10. Who are personally liable for the debts of their business—the owners of proprietorships or the general partners in limited partnerships?

11. Which has the income tax status of a partnership, a "C" corporation or an "S" corporation?

12. Kurt and Ellen are partners in operating a store. Without consulting Kurt, Ellen contracts to purchase merchandise for the store. Kurt contends that he did not authorize the order and refuses to take delivery. Is the partnership obligated to pay? Why or why not?

13. Would your answer to Question 12 differ if Kurt and Ellen were partners in a public accounting firm?

14. Examine the balance sheet for Lands' End, Inc. in Appendix F at the end of the book and determine the classes of stock that the company has issued.

LANDS' END
DIRECT MERCHANTS

15. Refer to the financial statements for Southwest Airlines Co. in Appendix E at the end of the book and calculate the dividend yield for 1994. Use the 4th quarter high sales price in your calculation.

QUICK STUDY (Five-Minute Exercises)

Of the following statements, which are true for the "C" corporation form of business?

**QS 14–1
(LO 1)**

a. Capital often is more easily accumulated than with other forms of organization.

b. It has a limited life.

c. Owners have unlimited liability for corporate debts.

d. Distributed income is taxed twice in normal circumstances.

e. It is a separate legal entity.

f. Ownership rights cannot be easily transferred.

g. Owners are not agents of the corporation.

On February 1, Excel Corporation issued 37,500 shares of $5 par value common stock for $252,000 cash. Present the entry to record this transaction.

**QS 14–2
(LO 2)**

On May 12, Dayton Company accepted subscriptions to 18,000 shares of $1 par value common stock at $10 per share. A 20% down payment was made on this date with the remainder to be paid in six months. Prepare an entry to record this transaction.

**QS 14–3
(LO 3)**

Holden Company's stockholders' equity includes 75,000 shares of $5 par value, 8%, cumulative preferred stock and 200,000 shares of $1 par value common stock. Holden did not declare any dividends during the prior year and now declares and pays a $108,000 cash dividend. Determine the amount distributed to each class of stockholders.

**QS 14–4
(LO 4)**

Prepare journal entries to record the following transactions for Desmond Corporation:

**QS 14–5
(LO 4)**

Apr. 15 Declared a $48,000 cash dividend payable to common stockholders.

June 30 Paid the dividend declared on April 15.

Dec. 31 Closed the Cash Dividends Declared account.

The stockholders' equity section of Courtland Company's balance sheet follows:

**QS 14–6
(LO 5)**

Stockholders' Equity

Preferred stock, 5% cumulative, $10 par value, 10,000 shares authorized, issued and outstanding	$100,000
Common stock, $5 par value, 100,000 shares authorized, 75,000 shares issued and outstanding	375,000
Retained earnings	445,000
Total stockholders' equity	$920,000

The call price of the preferred stock is $30 and one year's dividends are in arrears. Determine the book value per share of the common stock.

QS 14–7
(LO 6)

On May 5, 19X1, Cynthia Young opened a checking account for a new proprietorship business called Pyramid Designs and contributed $44,000 cash, land valued at $35,000, and a building valued at $325,000. Young also expected the business to assume responsibility for the $40,000 long-term note payable associated with the land and building. On November 3, Young withdrew cash of $16,000 for personal use. After closing the revenue and expense accounts on December 31, the Income Summary account had a credit balance of $39,500. Present general journal entries to record the initial investment, the cash withdrawal, and the December 31 closing of the withdrawals and Income Summary accounts.

QS 14–8
(LO 6)

Refer to the facts presented in QS 14–7. Present a statement of changes in owner's equity for the year.

QS 14–9
(LO 7)

Roger Bussey and Art Beery are partners in a business they started two years ago. The partnership agreement states that Bussey should receive a salary allowance of $30,000 and that Beery should receive $40,000. Any remaining income or loss is to be shared equally. Determine each partner's share of the current year's net income of $104,000.

QS 14–10
(LO 8)

Cornerstone Company expects to pay out a $2.10 per share cash dividend next year on its common stock. The current market price per share is $28.50. Calculate the expected dividend yield on the Cornerstone stock.

EXERCISES

Exercise 14–1
Recording stock issuances
(LO 2)

Present the general journal entries that an accountant would prepare to record the following issuances of stock in three different situations:

a. Two thousand shares of no-par common stock are issued to the corporation's promoters in exchange for their efforts in creating it. Their efforts are estimated to be worth $30,000, and the stock has no stated value.

b. Two thousand shares of no-par common stock are issued to the corporation's promoters in exchange for their efforts in creating it. Their efforts are estimated to be worth $30,000, and the stock has a $1 per share stated value.

c. Four thousand shares of $10 par value common stock are issued for $70,000 cash.

Exercise 14–2
Accounting for par and no-par stock issuances
(LO 2)

Hanson, Inc., issued 6,000 shares of its common stock for $144,000 cash on February 2. Present the journal entries that the company's accountant would use to record this event under each of the following situations:

a. The stock has no par or stated value.

b. The stock has a $20 par value.

c. The stock has a stated value of $8 per share.

Exercise 14–3
Interpreting journal entries for stock issuances and subscriptions
(LO 2, 3)

Each of these entries was recently recorded by a different corporation. Provide an explanation for the event or transaction described by each entry.

a.

Apr.	1	Cash	60,000.00	
		Common Stock, No-Par		60,000.00

b.

Apr.	3	Organization Costs	90,000.00	
		Common Stock, No-Par		66,000.00
		Contributed Capital in Excess of		
		Stated Value, No-Par Common Stock		24,000.00

c.

Apr.	2	Cash	100,000.00	
		Subscriptions Receivable, Common Stock	300,000.00	
		Common Stock Subscribed		240,000.00
		Contributed Capital in Excess of		
		Par Value, Common Stock		160,000.00

d.

Apr.	5	Merchandise Inventory	90,000.00	
		Machinery	130,000.00	
		Notes Payable		144,000.00
		Common Stock, $25 Par Value		40,000.00
		Contributed Capital in Excess of		
		Par Value, Common Stock		36,000.00

On October 31, Apex Corp. accepted subscriptions at $38 per share for 8,000 shares of its $20 par value common stock. The subscriptions called for 40% of the subscription price to be paid as a down payment with the balance due on December 31. Show the journal entries that the company's accountant would make to record these three events:

Exercise 14–4
Stock subscriptions
(LO 3)

a. Accepting the subscriptions and the down payments.

b. Receiving the balance of the subscriptions on the due date.

c. Issuing the stock on the same date.

The outstanding stock of Lipscomb includes 40,000 shares of noncumulative preferred stock with a $10 par value and a 7.5% dividend rate, as well as 100,000 shares of common stock with a $1 par value. During its first four years of operation, the corporation declared and paid the following total amounts of dividends:

Exercise 14–5
Dividends on common and noncumulative preferred stock
(LO 4)

19X1	$ 10,000
19X2	24,000
19X3	100,000
19X4	196,000

Determine the amount of dividends paid in each year to each class of stockholders. Also determine the total dividends paid to each class in the four years combined.

Use the data in Exercise 14–5 to determine the amount of dividends paid in each year to each class of stockholders, assuming that the preferred stock is cumulative. Also determine the total dividends paid to each class in the four years combined.

Exercise 14–6
Dividends on common and cumulative preferred stock
(LO 4)

An individual entrepreneur is planning to start a new business and needs $312,500 of start-up capital. This person has $250,000 in personal assets that can be invested and thus needs to raise another $62,500 in cash. The founder will buy 5,000 shares of common stock for $250,000 and has two alternative plans for raising the additional cash. One plan is to sell 1,250 shares of common stock to one or more other investors for $62,500 cash. The second is to sell 625 shares of cumulative preferred stock to one or more investors for $62,500 cash (this stock has a $100 par value, an annual 8% dividend rate, and would be issued at par).

Exercise 14–7
Using preferred stock to create leverage
(LO 4)

1. If the business is expected to earn $45,000 of after-tax net income in the first year, what rate of return on beginning equity will the founder earn under each alternative? Which of the two plans will provide the higher return to the founder?

2. If the business is expected to earn $10,500 of after-tax net income in the first year, what rate of return on beginning equity will the founder earn under each alternative? Which of the two plans will provide the higher return to the founder?

Exercise 14–8
Identifying characteristics of
preferred stock
(LO 4, 5)

Match each of the numbered descriptions with the characteristic of preferred stock that it best describes. Indicate your answer by writing the letter for the correct characteristic in the blank space next to each description.

A. Callable
B. Convertible
C. Cumulative

D. Noncumulative
E. Nonparticipating
F. Participating

___ 1.   The holders of the stock can exchange it for shares of common stock.
___ 2.   The issuing corporation can retire the stock by paying a prearranged price.
___ 3.   The holders of the stock are entitled to receive dividends in excess of the stated rate under some conditions.

___ 4.   The holders of the stock are not entitled to receive dividends in excess of the stated rate.
___ 5.   The holders of the stock lose any dividends that are not declared.
___ 6.   The holders of the stock are entitled to receive current and all past dividends before common stockholders receive any dividends.

Exercise 14–9
Characteristics of corporations
and partnerships
(LO 1, 7)

Next to the following list of eight general characteristics of business organizations, write a brief description of how each characteristic applies to "C" corporations and general partnerships.

		"C" Corporations	General Partnerships
1.	Life		
2.	Owners' liability		
3.	Legal status		
4.	Tax status of income		
5.	Owners' authority		
6.	Ease of formation		
7.	Transferability of ownership		
8.	Ability to raise large amounts of capital		

Exercise 14–10
Comparative entries for
partnership and corporation
(LO 1, 7)

Sandra Hemp and Stanley Abbott created a new business on July 7 when they each invested $120,000 cash in the company. On December 1, they decided that they would each receive $30,000 of the company's cash as a distribution. The checks were prepared and given to Hemp and Abbott on December 15. On December 31, the company's accountant determined that the company's net income was $88,000.

1.   Assume that this company is a general partnership and present the journal entries that the accountant would make to record these events: (a) investments by the owners, (b) the cash distribution to the owners, and (c) the closing of the Income Summary and the owners' withdrawals accounts, assuming they share the income equally.

2.   Assume that this company is a corporation and present the journal entries that the accountant would make to record these events: (a) investments by the owners, (b) the cash distribution to the owners, and (c) the closing of the Income Summary and dividends accounts. When the company was created, each owner acquired 4,000 shares of $25 par value common stock.

The balance sheet for Kuhn Corp. includes the following information:

Stockholders' Equity

Preferred stock, 6% cumulative, $25 par value, $30 call price, 5,000 shares issued and outstanding	$125,000
Common stock, $10 par value, 40,000 shares issued and outstanding	400,000
Retained earnings	267,500
Total stockholders' equity	$792,500

Determine the book value per share of the preferred and common stock under these two situations:

a.   No preferred dividends are in arrears.

b.   Three years of preferred dividends are in arrears.

Marlow and Devoe began a partnership by investing $60,000 and $40,000, respectively. During its first year, the partnership earned $20,000. Show how the partnership's income would be allocated to the partners in each of the following situations:

a.   The partners did not establish a method of sharing income.

b.   The partners agreed to share incomes and losses in proportion to their initial investments.

c.   The partners agreed to share incomes and losses with a $9,000 per year salary allowance to Marlow, a $5,000 per year salary allowance to Devoe, 8% interest on their initial investments, and the balance equally.

Calculate the dividend yield for each of these situations:

	Annual Dividend per Share	Stock's Market Price per Share
a.	$15.00	$216.00
b.	12.00	128.00
c.	6.00	61.00
d.	1.20	86.00
e.	11.00	130.00
f.	2.00	50.00

PROBLEMS

On June 1, Hinton Corporation received authorization to issue up to 60,000 shares of $10 par value preferred stock that pays a 9% cumulative dividend. The company also is authorized to issue up to 300,000 shares of common stock that has no par value; however, the board of directors established a $2 stated value for this stock. The company then completed these transactions over the next three months:

June 9   Accepted subscriptions to 45,000 shares of common stock at $5 per share. The subscribers each made down payments of 30% of the subscription price. The balance is due on August 9.

23   Issued 3,000 shares of common stock to the corporation's promoters for their services in organizing the corporation. The board valued the services at $15,000.

30   Accepted subscriptions to 12,000 shares of preferred stock at $12 per share. The subscribers each made down payments of 40% of the subscription price. The balance is due on August 30.

Aug. 9   Collected the balance due on the June 9 common stock subscriptions and issued the shares.

Aug. 15   Accepted subscriptions to 7,500 shares of preferred stock at $14 per share. The subscribers each made down payments of 40% of the subscription price. The balance is due on October 15.

30   Collected the balance due on the June 30 preferred stock subscriptions and issued the shares.

At the end of August, the balance of retained earnings is $48,000.

Required

Use the information about the transactions to prepare the stockholders' equity section of the company's balance sheet as of August 31. (Note: You will find it useful to prepare journal entries for the transactions to help you process the data.)

CHECK FIGURE:
Total equity, $537,000

Problem 14–2
Stockholders' equity transactions
(LO 2, 3, 5, 8)

Precision Products, Inc., was chartered at the beginning of the year and engaged in a number of transactions. The following journal entries affected its stockholders' equity during its first year of operations:

a.	Cash	150,000.00	
	Common Stock, $25 Par Value		125,000.00
	Contributed Capital in Excess of Par Value, Common Stock		25,000.00
b.	Organization Costs	75,000.00	
	Common Stock, $25 Par Value		62,500.00
	Contributed Capital in Excess of Par Value, Common Stock		12,500.00
c.	Cash	21,500.00	
	Accounts Receivable	7,500.00	
	Office Equipment	10,750.00	
	Building	30,000.00	
	Accounts Payable		11,000.00
	Notes Payable		18,750.00
	Common Stock, $25 Par Value		25,000.00
	Contributed Capital in Excess of Par Value, Common Stock		15,000.00
d.	Cash	60,000.00	
	Common Stock, $25 Par Value		37,500.00
	Contributed Capital in Excess of Par Value, Common Stock		22,500.00
e.	Cash Dividends Declared	7,500.00	
	Common Dividend Payable		7,500.00
f.	Common Dividend Payable	7,500.00	
	Cash		7,500.00

g.   Income Summary 30,000.00
          Retained Earnings 30,000.00

h.   Retained Earnings 7,500.00
          Cash Dividends Declared 7,500.00

Required

1.   Provide explanations for the journal entries.
2.   Prepare answers for the following questions:
      a.   What is the net income for the year?
      b.   How many shares of common stock are outstanding?
      c.   What is the minimum legal capital?
      d.   What is the total contributed capital?
      e.   What is the total retained earnings?
      f.   What is the total stockholders' equity?
      g.   What is the book value per share of the common stock at the end of the year?
      h.   The dividend yield on this stock is 2%. Expected dividends for the upcoming year
            are $1 per share. What is the stock's current market value?
      i.   The market interest rate on bonds ranges from 8 to 10%. Does the value of this
            company's stock appear to be based on income or growth?

CHECK FIGURE:
Part 2f: total equity, $347,500

Odyssey, Inc., has 10,000 outstanding shares of $100 par value, 5% preferred stock and 80,000
shares of $1 par value common stock. During the last seven-year period, the company paid out
the following total amounts in dividends to its preferred and common stockholders:

Problem 14–3
Allocating dividends between
preferred and common stock
(LO 4)

19X1	....	$ 10,000
19X2	....	22,000
19X3	....	45,000
19X4	....	130,000
19X5	....	36,000
19X6	....	70,000
19X7	....	90,000

No dividends were in arrears for years prior to 19X1.

Required

1.   Determine the amounts of dividends paid to the two classes of stock in each year and
      for all seven years combined under these two assumptions:
      a.   The preferred stock is noncumulative.
      b.   The preferred stock is cumulative.
2.   Comment on the difference between the answers to requirement 1.

CHECK FIGURE:
Part 1b: total to common,
$53,000

Segura Corporation's common stock is currently selling on a stock exchange at $170 per share,
and a recent balance sheet shows the following information:

Problem 14–4
Calculating book values
(LO 5)

Stockholders' Equity

Preferred stock, 5%, $? par value, 1,000 shares
    authorized, issued, and outstanding $100,000
Common stock, $? par value, 4,000 shares authorized,
    issued, and outstanding   160,000
Retained earnings   300,000
Total stockholders' equity $560,000

Required

Preparation component:

1. What is the market value of the corporation's common stock?
2. What are the par values of the preferred stock and the common stock?

CHECK FIGURE:
Part 4: book value of common,
$112.50

3. If no dividends are in arrears, what are the book values per share of the preferred stock and the common stock?
4. If two years' preferred dividends are in arrears, what are the book values per share of the preferred stock and the common stock?
5. If two years' preferred dividends are in arrears and the preferred stock is callable at $110 per share, what are the book values per share of the preferred stock and the common stock?

Analysis component:

6. What are some factors that may contribute to the difference between the book value of common stock and its market value?

Problem 14–5
Allocating partnership income
(LO 7)

Schlemmer, Torres, and Urban created a partnership and invested $21,000, $41,500, and $37,500, respectively, at the beginning of the year. During its first year, the partnership achieved a net income of $39,000. Schlemmer, Torres, and Urban each withdrew $7,500 cash from the partnership on December 31.

Required

Preparation component:

1. Prepare schedules that show how the partners would allocate the partnership's net income among themselves under each of the following agreements:
   a. The partners divide the income equally.
   b. The partners share the income in proportion to their initial investments.

CHECK FIGURE:
Part 1c: income to Torres,
$10,820

   c. The partners agree to provide annual salary allowances of $15,000 to Schlemmer, $6,500 to Torres, and $6,500 to Urban, and 8% interest allowances on the partners' initial investments. Any remaining income (or deficit) is to be shared equally.
2. Prepare a schedule that shows the equity balances of each of the three partners as of the end of the year under agreement *c.*

Analysis component:

3. For each of the partnership agreements in requirement 1, describe a probable situation that would result in the partners agreeing that the agreement was a fair allocation of future earnings.

CRITICAL THINKING: ESSAYS, PROBLEMS, AND CASES

Richard Davenport and Gary Payne want to create a new software development business. Each of them can contribute fairly large amounts of capital. However, they know that the business will need additional equity capital from other investors after its first year. With respect to their individual activities, they are both planning to devote full-time effort to getting the first products out the door within the year. They plan to hire three employees initially and expect to distribute a substantial amount of cash every year for their personal expenses. Davenport has proposed organizing the business as a general partnership, but Payne thinks that a corporation offers more advantages. They have asked you to prepare a brief analysis that supports choosing the corporate form. What main points would you include in your analysis?

Analytical Essay

(LO 1, 7)

For a number of years, Jennifer Reyes and Carrie Platt have operated a retailing company called Communications Network. They organized the company as a partnership and have shared income and losses in a 2:3 ratio. (Reyes gets 40% while Platt gets 60%.) Because the business is growing beyond their ability to keep up with it, they have agreed to accept a third person, Harold Nolen, into the business. Part of the new arrangement involves creating a new corporation, called Communications Network, Inc. The corporate charter authorizes 100,000 shares of $10 par value common stock. The deal requires three steps. First, the partners must settle up the old business by revaluing the assets to their fair market values and dividing the previously unrecognized gains and losses. Second, the partnership must transfer its assets and liabilities to the corporation, which will issue shares to the partners in exchange for their equity in the partnership. The shares will be considered to be worth $10 each when the exchange is made. Third, Nolen will pay $10 cash for all authorized shares not issued to the former partners. You have been engaged to help the three phases of the deal go smoothly.

The following spreadsheet has been developed to help you accomplish the first phase of modifying the partnership's accounts to reflect the fair market values for the assets and to modify the partners' equity balances:

Financial Reporting Problem

(LO 2, 7)

COMMUNICATIONS NETWORK
Account Modification Spreadsheet
July 31

Accounts	Unmodified Trial Balance	(a)	(b)	(c)	(d)	(e)	Modified Trial Balance
Debits:							
Cash	42,000						
Accounts receivable	62,000						
Merchandise inventory	300,000	(50,000)					
Store equipment	256,000						
Buildings	560,000						
Land	174,000						
Total	1,394,000						
Credits:							
Allowance for doubtful accounts	(6,000)						
Accumulated depreciation, equipment	(96,000)						
Accumulated depreciation, buildings	(164,000)						
Accounts payable	(64,000)						
Notes payable	(344,000)						
Reyes, capital	(320,000)	20,000					
Platt, capital	(400,000)		30,000				
Total	(1,394,000)						

Numbers in parentheses are credits.

The partners have agreed that the following modifications need to be included in the first phase (they will divide any gains and losses from the changes in recorded value according to their regular income and loss ratio):

a. The merchandise inventory is to be written down to its fair value of $250,000.

b. An account receivable from a customer for $2,000 is known to be uncollectible and will be written off against the allowance for doubtful accounts.

c. After writing off that account, the allowance for doubtful accounts will be adjusted to 5% of the gross accounts receivable.

d. The net recorded value of the store equipment will be decreased to $130,000 by increasing the balance of the accumulated depreciation account.

e. The gross recorded value of the building is to be increased to its replacement cost of $720,000. At the same time, the balance of the accumulated depreciation account is to be adjusted to equal 25% of the replacement cost to represent the fact that the building's fair market value is 75% of its replacement cost.

Your first task is to complete the spreadsheet by entering the effects of each of the five modifications as debits and credits to the affected accounts. The first items have been entered in the spreadsheet as an example. You should provide supporting calculations as needed. Second, determine how many shares each partner is entitled to receive in exchange for the partner's equity. Third, determine how many shares Nolen will purchase for cash. Fourth, present the journal entries that the corporation will use to record the issuance of the shares to all three stockholders. Finally, present a balance sheet for the corporation immediately after the transactions are completed (the notes payable are due within 90 days).

Financial Statement Analysis Cases

FSAC 14–1
(LO 4)

Having received a large lump sum of severance pay, Joe Bolton is thinking about investing the money in one of two securities, either Koehn Development Corporation common stock or the preferred stock issued by Littlefield Company. The companies manufacture similar products and compete in the same market, and both have been operating about the same length of time—four years for Koehn and three years for Littlefield. The two companies also have similar amounts of stockholders' equity, as shown here:

Koehn Development Corporation

Common stock, $1 par value, 400,000 shares authorized, 250,000 shares issued and outstanding	$250,000
Retained earnings	410,000
Total stockholders' equity	$660,000

Littlefield Company

Preferred stock, $50 par value, 6% cumulative, 3,000 shares authorized, issued, and outstanding	$150,000*
Common stock, $20 par value, 25,000 shares authorized, issued, and outstanding	500,000
Retained earnings	30,000
Total stockholders' equity	$680,000

*The current and two prior years' dividends are in arrears on the preferred stock.

Koehn Development Corporation did not pay a dividend on its common stock during its first year's operations; however, it has paid a cash dividend of $0.09 per share in each of the past three years. The stock is currently selling for $3.00 per share. In contrast, the preferred stock of Littlefield Company is selling for $45 per share. Bolton has expressed a leaning for the preferred stock as an investment because it appears to be a bargain at $5 below par value and $14 below book value. Besides, Bolton has told you, "The dividends are guaranteed because it is a preferred stock." Bolton also believes that the common stock of Koehn is overpriced at 14% above book value and 200% above par value, while it is paying only a $0.09 per share dividend. In conclusion, Bolton asks how anyone could prefer a common stock yielding only 3% to a preferred stock that is supposed to pay 6%.

1. Is the preferred stock of Littlefield Company actually selling at $14 below its book value, and is the common stock of Koehn Development Corporation actually selling at 14% above book value and 200% above par?

2. Analyze the stockholders' equity sections and express your opinion of the two stocks as investments by describing some of the factors Bolton should consider in choosing between them.

Use the information provided in the financial statements of Southwest Airlines Co. and the footnotes in Appendix E to answer the following questions:

**FSAC 14–2
(LO 3, 4, 5, 8)**

1. Does it appear that Southwest Airlines has been authorized to issue any preferred stock?

2. How many shares of common stock have been authorized? How many have been issued as of December 31, 1994?

3. What is the par value of the common stock? What is its book value at December 31, 1994?

4. Are any shares of common stock subscribed? Are there any shares that cannot be issued to the public because they have been promised to others?

5. What was the highest market value of the stock during 1994? What was the lowest?

6. Did Southwest Airlines declare any dividends on its capital stock during 1994? If so, how large were the dividends (in total and per share)?

ANSWERS TO PROGRESS CHECKS

14–1 *b*

14–2 A corporation must pay taxes on its income and its stockholders must pay personal income taxes on dividends received from the corporation.

14–3 A proxy is a legal document used to transfer a stockholder's right to vote to another person.

14–4 *a*

14–5 A stock premium is an amount in excess of par paid by purchasers of newly issued stock.

14–6 Creditors of the corporation are intended to be protected by minimum legal capital.

14–7 *c*

14–8 Common Stock Subscribed is classified as contributed capital in the stockholders' equity section of the balance sheet.

14–9 *c*

14–10 The three dates are the date of declaration, the date of record, and the date of payment.

14–11 Typically, preferred stock has a preference in receiving dividends and in the distribution of assets in the case of a company's liquidation.

14–12 *a*

14–13 *b*

Total dividend	$288,000
To preferred shareholders	135,000*
Remainder to common shareholders	$153,000

*9,000 × $50 × .10 × 3 = $135,000

14–14

Total stockholders' equity		$630,000
Less equity applicable to preferred shares:		
Call price (1,000 × $90)	$90,000	
Dividends in arrears	18,000	108,000
Equity applicable to common shares		$522,000
Book value of common shares ($522,000/12,000)		$ 43.50

14–15 *c*

14–16 *c*

14–17 No. Because a single proprietorship is not a separate legal entity, income of the business is the owner's personal income and is taxed as such.

14–18 *b*

14–19

	Mixon	Reed	Income to be Allocated
Total net income			$40,000
Allocated as interest	$ 7,000	$ 3,500	10,500
Remaining balance			$29,500
Balance allocated equally	14,750	14,750	29,500
Remaining balance			$ -0-
Shares of partners	$21,750	$18,250	

14–20 Unlimited liability means that the creditors of a partnership have the right to require each partner to be personally responsible for all partnership debts.

14–21 *d*

14–22 *c*

CHAPTER 15

Additional Corporate Transactions; Reporting Income and Retained Earnings; Earnings per Share

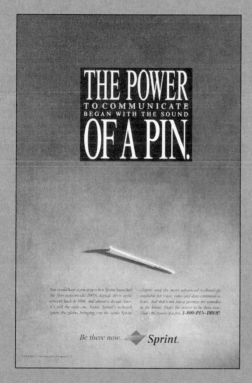

*S*print Corporation is a diversified telecommunications company that provides global voice, data, and video conferencing services and related products. The company's 1994 annual report stated that income from continuing operations decreased slightly from $496.1 million in 1992 to $480.6 million in 1993, and then increased to $883.7 million in 1994. During the same three years, the earnings applicable to common stock declined significantly from $499.3 million in 1992 to $52.1 million in 1993, and then increased to $888.0 million in 1994.

Considering the sharp differences in these trends, a common stockholder might wonder how to assess the company's future prospects. How might Sprint describe the results in its financial statements? In addition to the items in the following table, what information would you look for to help evaluate the company's ability to provide a return to its stockholders?

SPRINT CORPORATION (in millions)	1993	1992	1991
Net operating revenues	$11,367.8	$10,420.3	$9,933.3
Income from continuing operations	480.6	496.1	472.7
Net income	54.9	502.8	520.2
Preferred stock dividends	(2.8)	(3.5)	(4.1)
Earnings applicable to common stock	52.1	499.3	516.1

LEARNING OBJECTIVES

After studying Chapter 15, you should be able to:

1. **Describe stock dividends and stock splits and explain their effects on a corporation's assets and stockholders' equity.**
2. **Record purchases and sales of treasury stock and retirements of stock and describe their effects on stockholders' equity. Also, describe restrictions and appropriations of retained earnings and explain how they are described in financial reports.**
3. **Explain how to report the income effects of discontinued segments, extraordinary items, changes in accounting principles and estimates, and prior period adjustments.**
4. **Calculate earnings per share for companies with simple capital structures and explain the difference between primary and fully diluted earnings per share.**
5. **Calculate the price-earnings ratio and describe its meaning.**
6. **Define or explain the words and phrases listed in the chapter glossary.**

Corporations often enter into special financing transactions that involve changes in stockholders' equity. The first section of this chapter explains several of these transactions, including stock dividends, stock splits, and transactions involving the company's own stock. The second section of the chapter expands your understanding of financial statements by explaining how information about income and retained earnings is classified and reported. The third section explains how corporations report earnings per share. Understanding these topics will help you interpret and use financial statements. In fact, the discussion in this chapter helps clarify some of the reporting issues implied by the previous discussion of **Sprint Corporation.**

CORPORATE DIVIDENDS AND OTHER STOCK TRANSACTIONS

In Chapter 2, we briefly described a corporation's retained earnings as the stockholders' equity that is created by the company's profitable activities. It is equal to the total cumulative amount of the reported net income less any net losses and dividends declared since the company started operating. In effect, retained earnings are the stockholders' residual interest in the corporation that was not created by their investments. Information about retained earnings is helpful to investors and other users of financial statements for predicting future cash flows for dividends and other events.

RETAINED EARNINGS AND DIVIDENDS

LO 1
Describe stock dividends and stock splits and explain their effects on a corporation's assets and stockholders' equity.

Most state laws allow a corporation to pay cash dividends if retained earnings exist. However, in addition to retained earnings, a corporation must have enough cash to pay the dividend. And, even if there is sufficient cash and retained earnings, the directors may decide against declaring a dividend because the cash is needed in the business. Although cash may be paid out in dividends, companies also keep some cash in reserve to meet emergencies, to take advantage of unexpected opportunities, or to avoid having to borrow for future expansion.

Chapter 14 described how cash dividends are recorded in the accounts. The declaration of a dividend reduces the retained earnings and creates a current liability to the stockholders. On the date of record, the recipients of the dividend are identified, but no entry is recorded in the accounts. On the date of payment, cash is sent to the qualifying stockholders and the liability is removed from the books.

Generally, the Cash Dividends Declared account is closed to the Retained Earnings account. However, in limited circumstances, some state laws allow cash dividends to be paid as a return of capital contributed by the stockholders. If so, the Cash Dividends Declared account is closed with a debit entry to one of the contributed capital accounts instead of Retained Earnings. Because these dividends return part of the original investment to the stockholders, they are often called **liquidating dividends.** They usually occur when the company is completing a major downsizing, perhaps in preparation for a merger or even dissolution. In most cases, the equity that originated from the par or stated value of the outstanding stock cannot be used as a basis for liquidating dividends until all creditors have been paid. This situation normally occurs only when the corporation is actually going out of business.

DIVIDENDS BASED ON CONTRIBUTED CAPITAL

Sometimes, a corporation's directors may declare a **stock dividend.** This means the company distributes additional shares of its own stock to its stockholders without receiving any payment in return. Stock dividends and cash dividends are very different. A cash dividend reduces the corporation's assets and stockholders' equity, and a stock dividend does neither. A stock dividend simply transfers some equity from retained earnings into contributed capital.

STOCK DIVIDENDS

Why Stock Dividends Are Distributed

If stock dividends do not affect assets or total stockholders' equity, why are they declared and distributed? Directors can use stock dividends to keep the market value of the stock affordable. For example, if a profitable corporation grows but does not pay cash dividends, the price of its common stock increases in anticipation of continued growth and future dividends. Eventually, the price of a share may become so high that it discourages some investors from buying the stock. Thus, the corporation may declare stock dividends to increase the number of outstanding shares and thereby keep the per share price of its stock low enough to be attractive to smaller investors.

Another reason for declaring a stock dividend is to provide tangible evidence of management's confidence that the company is doing well. The stock dividend may substitute for a cash dividend, thereby saving cash that can be used to expand the business.

The Effect of Stock Dividends on Stockholders' Equity Accounts

Although a stock dividend does not affect the corporation's assets or total stockholders' equity, it does affect the components of stockholders' equity. This effect is recorded by transferring part of the retained earnings to the contributed capital accounts. Because this treatment increases the company's contributed capital, it is often described as *capitalizing* retained earnings.

If a corporation declares a **small stock dividend,** accounting principles require it to capitalize retained earnings equal to the market value of the shares to be distributed. This practice is based on the concept that a small stock dividend is likely to be perceived as similar to a cash dividend because it has a small impact on the price of the stock. A dividend is considered small if it is less than or equal to 25% of the previously outstanding shares.

A **large stock dividend,** one that distributes more than 25% of the outstanding shares before the dividend, is likely to have a noticeable effect on the stock's market price per share. It is not likely to be perceived as a substitute for a cash dividend. Therefore, a large stock dividend is recorded by capitalizing an amount of retained earnings only to the minimum required by the state law governing the corporation. In most cases, the law requires capitalizing retained earnings equal to the par or stated value of the shares.

For example, assume that Northwest Corporation's stockholders' equity consists of the following amounts just before the declaration of a stock dividend:

NORTHWEST CORPORATION
Stockholders' Equity
December 31, 19X1

Common stock, $10 par value, 15,000 shares authorized, 10,000 shares issued and outstanding	$100,000
Contributed capital in excess of par value, common stock ..	8,000
Total contributed capital	$108,000
Retained earnings	35,000
Total stockholders' equity	$143,000

Recording a Small Stock Dividend

To illustrate how a small stock dividend is recorded, let's assume that the directors of Northwest Corporation declare a 10% stock dividend on December 31. The 1,000 dividend shares (10% of the 10,000 outstanding shares) are to be distributed on January 20 to the January 15 stockholders of record.

If the market value of Northwest Corporation's stock on December 31 is $15 per share, the dividend declaration is recorded with this entry:

Dec.	31	Stock Dividends Declared	15,000.00	
		Common Stock Dividend Distributable		10,000.00
		Contributed Capital in Excess of Par Value, Common Stock		5,000.00
		To record the declaration of a 1,000-share common stock dividend.		

The debit is recorded in the temporary account called Stock Dividends Declared. This account serves the same purpose as the Cash Dividends Declared account described in the preceding chapter. A complete chart of accounts includes separate accounts for cash and stock dividends because the financial statements must report stock and cash dividends as separate events. If stock dividends are not frequently declared, a company can get by without a separate account for Stock Dividends Declared. Instead, it can record the debit directly to Retained Earnings. This approach is acceptable as long as the information is reported correctly in the financial statements.

In the previous entry, the first credit puts the par value of the dividend shares in a contributed capital account called Common Stock Dividend Distributable. This account balance exists only until the shares are actually issued. The second credit records the premium on the dividend shares at this time, even though the shares have not yet been issued. This account is the same one that is used for all other issuances at an amount more than par value.

As part of the year-end closing process, the accountant for Northwest Corporation closes the Stock Dividends Declared account to Retained Earnings with this entry:

Dec.	31	Retained Earnings	15,000.00	
		Stock Dividends Declared		15,000.00
		To close the Stock Dividends Declared account.		

Illustration 15–1
The Effect of Northwest
Corporation's 10%
Stock Dividend

Before the 10% stock dividend
Stockholders' equity:

Common stock (10,000 shares)	$100,000
Contributed capital in excess of par value, common stock	8,000
Retained earnings	35,000
Total stockholders' equity	$143,000

Book value per share = $143,000/10,000 shares = $14.30
Book value of Johnson's 200 shares = $14.30 × 200 = $2,860

After the 10% stock dividend
Stockholders' equity:

Common stock (11,000 shares)	$110,000
Contributed capital in excess of par value, common stock	13,000
Retained earnings	20,000
Total stockholders' equity	$143,000

Book value per share = $143,000/11,000 shares = $13.00
Book value of Johnson's 220 shares = $13 × 220 = $2,860

On January 20, the company distributes the new shares to the stockholders and records the event with this entry:

Jan.	20	Common Stock Dividend Distributable	10,000.00	
		Common Stock		10,000.00
		To record the distribution of a 1,000-share common stock dividend.		

The combined effect of these three entries is the transfer (or capitalization) of $15,000 of retained earnings to contributed capital. The amount of capitalized retained earnings equals the market value of the 1,000 issued shares ($15 × 1,000 shares).

This example demonstrates that a stock dividend has no effect on the corporation's assets or total stockholders' equity. Nor does the dividend affect the percentage of the company owned by individual stockholders. For example, assume that Pat Johnson owned 200 shares of Northwest Corporation's stock prior to the 10% stock dividend. When the corporation sent each stockholder one new share for each 10 shares held, Johnson received 20 new shares (10% × 200 shares).

Looking at Illustration 15–1, you can see what the 10% stock dividend does to Northwest Corporation's total contributed capital and retained earnings. Note that nothing happens to the total book value of Johnson's shares. Before the stock dividend, Johnson owned 2% of the corporation's stock, which is 200 of the 10,000 outstanding shares. The book value of this holding was $2,860 (2% × $143,000, or 200 × $14.30 per share). After the dividend, Johnson holds 220 shares, but the holding still equals 2% of the 11,000 shares now outstanding. The book value is still $2,860 (2% × $143,000, or 220 × $13.00 per share). In other words, the only change in Johnson's 2% investment is that now it is represented by 220 shares instead of 200 shares. Also, the only effect on the stockholders' equity is a transfer of $15,000 from retained earnings to contributed capital. There is no change in the corporation's total assets, in its total equity, or in the percentage of equity owned by Johnson. Of course, Johnson's main concern is whether the 220 shares are now worth more than the 200 shares used to be.

Stock Dividends on the Balance Sheet

Because a stock dividend does not reduce the corporation's assets, it is never a liability on a balance sheet prepared between the declaration and distribution dates. Instead, the amount of any declared but undistributed stock dividend appears on the balance sheet as a component of the contributed capital in the stockholders' equity section. For example, the stockholders' equity of Northwest Corporation looks like this just after the 10% stock dividend is declared on December 31:

NORTHWEST CORPORATION
Stockholders' Equity
December 31, 19X1

Common stock, $10 par value, 15,000 shares authorized, 10,000 shares issued and outstanding	$100,000
Common stock dividend distributable, 1,000 shares	10,000
Total common stock issued and to be issued	$110,000
Contributed capital in excess of par value, common stock .	13,000
Total contributed capital	$123,000
Retained earnings	20,000
Total stockholders' equity	$143,000

This updated section of the balance sheet is changed in three ways. First, the amount of equity attributed to the common stock increased from $100,000 to $110,000 because 1,000 additional shares are ready to be issued. Second, the contributed capital in excess of par increased by $5,000, which equals the excess of the $15 per share market value over the $10 per share par value for the 1,000 shares. Finally, the balance of retained earnings decreased by $15,000 from the predividend amount of $35,000 to $20,000.

Recording a Large Stock Dividend

When a stock dividend exceeds 25% of the outstanding shares, the corporation capitalizes retained earnings equal to the minimum amount required by the law. Usually, that is the par or stated value of the newly issued shares. For example, suppose on December 31 Northwest Corporation's board declared a 30% stock dividend instead of 10%. Because the dividend is greater than the arbitrary limit of 25%, it is considered to be large. As a result, only the par value of the new 3,000 shares is capitalized. Thus, the company would record the declaration with this entry:

Dec.	31	Stock Dividends Declared	30,000.00	
		Common Stock Dividend Distributable		30,000.00
		To record the declaration of a 3,000-share stock dividend at par value.		

This entry causes the company's retained earnings to be decreased by the $30,000 par value of the dividend shares. It also causes the company's contributed capital to increase by the same amount.

STOCK SPLITS

Recall that one goal for stock dividends is to reduce the stock's market price. Stock dividends divide the company into a larger number of smaller pieces. The total value of the company is unchanged, but the price of each new share is smaller. The same result can be accomplished through a stock split. When a **stock split** occurs, the corporation calls in its outstanding shares and issues two or more new shares in exchange for each of the old ones.[1]

Suppose that a company has 100,000 outstanding shares of $20 par value common stock that have a current market value of $88 per share. The market value can be cut in half by a two-for-one split. The split replaces the 100,000 $20 par value shares with 200,000 $10 par value shares that have a market value in the neighborhood of $44 per share.

Splits can be accomplished at any ratio, including two-for-one, three-for-one, or even higher. In fact, it is possible for the ratio to be less than one-to-one, causing stockholders to end up with fewer shares. These **reverse stock splits** are intended to increase the stock's market price per share.

A stock split does not affect the total stockholders' equity reported on the balance sheet. It also does not affect a stockholder's percentage interest in the corporation. The contributed capital and Retained Earnings accounts are unchanged by a split, and no journal entry is made. The only effect on the accounts is a change in the account title used for the common stock. The earlier example described a two-for-one split for a $20 par value stock. After the split, the account name would be changed to Common Stock, $10 Par Value. Although nothing else changes in the accounts, the disclosures about the stock on the balance sheet are changed to reflect the additional outstanding shares and the revised par value per share.

In recent years, the difference between stock splits and large stock dividends has become blurred in practice. Many companies report stock splits in their financial statements without calling in the original shares and changing the par value of the common stock. The "split" in effect issues additional shares to the stockholders by capitalizing retained earnings and/or transferring other contributed capital to Common Stock. This practice avoids a great deal of the administrative cost that would be incurred by splitting the stock. For example, **Harley-Davidson, Inc.,** declared a 2-for-1 stock split in 1994 in the form of a 100% stock dividend by transferring additional paid-in capital to common stock.

Progress Check

(Answers to Progress Checks are provided at the end of the chapter.)

15-1   Which of the following statements is correct?

    a. A large stock dividend is recorded by capitalizing retained earnings equal to the market value of the distributable shares.

    b. Stock dividends and stock splits have the same effect on the total assets and retained earnings of the issuing corporation.

    c. A stock dividend does not transfer corporate assets to the stockholders but does require that retained earnings be capitalized.

15-2   What distinguishes a large stock dividend from a small stock dividend?

15-3   When accounting for a small stock dividend, what amount of retained earnings should be capitalized?

TREASURY STOCK

LO 2

Record purchases and sales of treasury stock and retirements of stock and describe their effects on stockholders' equity. Also, describe restrictions and appropriations of retained earnings and explain how they are described in financial reports.

For a variety of reasons, corporations often acquire shares of their own stock. They may use the shares to acquire control of other corporations. Sometimes, they repurchase shares to avoid a hostile takeover by an investor seeking control of the company. Many buy shares and reissue them to employees as compensation. For exam-

---

[1]To reduce the administrative cost, most splits are accomplished by simply issuing new certificates to the stockholders for the additional shares they are entitled to receive. The stockholders do not have to turn in the old certificates.

As a Matter of Ethics

Falcon Corporation's board of directors and officers have been planning the agenda for the corporation's 19X1 annual stockholders' meeting. The first item considered by the directors and officers was whether to report a large government contract that Falcon has just signed. Although this contract will significantly increase income and cash flows in 19X1 and beyond, management saw no need to reveal the news at the stockholders' meeting. "After all," one officer said, "the meeting is intended to be the forum for describing the past year's activities, not the plans for the next year."

After agreeing not to mention the contract, the group moved on to the next topic for the stockholders' meeting. This topic was a motion for the stockholders to approve a compensation plan award-ing managers options to acquire large quantities of shares over the next several years. According to the plan, the managers will have a three-year option to buy shares at a fixed price that equals the market value of the stock as measured 30 days after the upcoming stockholders' meeting. In other words, the managers will be able to buy stock in 19X2, 19X3, or 19X4 by paying the 19X1 market value. Obviously, if the stock increases in value over the next several years, the managers will realize large profits without having to invest any cash. The financial vice president asked the group whether they should reconsider the decision about the government contract in light of its possible relevance to the vote on the stock option plan.

ple, **Hewlett-Packard Company** reports that it has a stock repurchase program to meet future employee stock plan requirements. In 1995, the company purchased 10,395,000 shares under this program.

Less frequently, a corporation may buy a large number of shares to maintain a suitable market for the stock. This practice is widely used when many stock prices have lost a great deal of market value very quickly. By buying the shares, corporations help their stockholders get a better price and bring more stability to the market.

Regardless of the reason for their acquisition, a corporation's reacquired shares are called **treasury stock.** In many respects, treasury stock is similar to unissued stock. Neither unissued nor treasury stock is an asset of the corporation. Neither receive cash or stock dividends, and no one can exercise the vote attached to the shares. However, treasury stock does have one potentially significant difference from unissued stock. If treasury stock was originally issued at its par value or higher, the company can resell the stock at less than par without having the buyers incur a discount liability.

In addition, treasury stock purchases require management to exercise ethical sensitivity. Corporate funds are being paid to specific stockholders instead of all stockholders. As a result, managers must be careful to be sure that the purchase is in the best interest of all the stockholders. These concerns cause most companies to be very open with their stockholders about their treasury stock and other activities related to stock. Read As a Matter of Ethics on this page and consider whether Falcon Corporation's management is showing proper consideration for its stockholders.

PURCHASING TREASURY STOCK

The act of purchasing treasury stock reduces the corporation's assets and stockholders' equity by equal amounts.[2] This effect is illustrated by the two balance sheets of Curry Corporation in Illustrations 15–2 and 15–3. The first balance sheet shows the account balances on April 30, 19X1, before a treasury stock purchase. The second balance sheet shows the account balances after the company purchased 1,000 of its own shares for $11,500 cash.

---

[2]This text discusses the *cost method* of accounting for treasury stock; it is the most widely used. The *par value* method is discussed in more advanced accounting courses.

Illustration 15-2 Curry Corporation's Balance Sheet Prior to the Purchase of Treasury Stock

CURRY CORPORATION
Balance Sheet
April 30, 19X1

Assets		Stockholders' Equity	
Cash	$ 30,000	Contributed capital:	
Other assets	95,000	Common stock, $10 par value, authorized and issued 10,000 shares	$100,000
		Retained earnings	25,000
Total assets	$125,000	Total stockholders' equity	$125,000

Illustration 15-3 Curry Corporation's Balance Sheet Immediately After Purchasing Treasury Stock

CURRY CORPORATION
Balance Sheet
April 30, 19X1

Assets		Stockholders' Equity	
Cash	$ 18,500	Contributed capital:	
Other assets	95,000	Common stock, $10 par value, authorized and issued 10,000 shares, of which 1,000 are in the treasury	$100,000
		Retained earnings, of which $11,500 is restricted by the purchase of treasury stock	25,000
		Total	$125,000
		Less cost of treasury stock	(11,500)
Total assets	$113,500	Total stockholders' equity	$113,500

This entry records the purchase of the 1,000 shares:

May	1	Treasury Stock, Common	11,500.00	
		Cash		11,500.00
		Purchased 1,000 shares of treasury stock at $11.50 per share.		

The entry reduces the stockholders' equity by debiting the Treasury Stock account, which is *contra* to equity. To see the effects of the transaction, look at the balance sheet in Illustration 15–3.

Notice that the purchase reduces the company's cash, total assets, and total equity by $11,500. The equity reduction is reflected on the balance sheet by deducting the cost of the treasury stock in the equity section. The purchase does not reduce the balance of either the Common Stock account or the Retained Earnings account. However, two disclosures in this section describe the effects of the transaction. First, the statement tells the reader that 1,000 of the issued shares are in the treasury of the corporation. Thus, only 9,000 shares are outstanding. Second, the purchase has placed a restriction on the company's retained earnings. This restriction is described in the next section.

Restricting Retained Earnings by the Purchase of Treasury Stock

Cash dividends and purchases of treasury stock have a similar effect on a corporation's assets and stockholders' equity. That is, they both transfer corporate cash to stockholders and reduce assets and equity. Therefore, most states restrict the amount of cash dividends and treasury stock purchases to the amount of retained earnings.

Unlike a cash dividend, a treasury stock purchase does not directly reduce the balance of the Retained Earnings account. However, the corporation should disclose any statutory restrictions on retained earnings. Thus, the balance sheet in Illustration 15–3 identifies the amount of the **restricted retained earnings** created by the treasury stock purchase. In many cases, the restriction is described in a footnote to the financial statements. In addition to this restriction, other limits on dividends may be established by statute and by contract.

Appropriated Retained Earnings

In contrast to statutory or contractual retained earnings restrictions, a corporation's directors may voluntarily limit dividends because of a special need for cash, such as to purchase new facilities. When the directors do this, management usually explains in a letter attached to the financial statements why dividends have not been declared. However, they may notify the stockholders and other financial statement users of this change in policy by setting up an amount of **appropriated retained earnings.** These appropriations are strictly voluntary and nonbinding. They serve only to notify the statement readers of the directors' decision to not pay out cash.

REISSUING TREASURY STOCK

Treasury stock may be reissued by selling it at cost, above cost, or below cost. If it is reissued by being sold at its cost, the entry is the opposite of the entry that was made to record the purchase.

If treasury stock is sold for more than cost, the amount received in excess of cost is credited to a special account called Contributed Capital, Treasury Stock Transactions. For example, if Curry Corporation receives $12 cash per share for 500 treasury shares originally purchased at $11.50 per share, the accountant records the transaction with the following entry:

June	3	Cash	6,000.00	
		Treasury Stock, Common		5,750.00
		Contributed Capital, Treasury Stock Transactions		250.00
		Received $12 per share for 500 treasury shares that		
		cost $11.50 per share.		

Notice that the company does not report a gain from this transaction.

When treasury stock is sold at less than its cost, the entry to record the sale depends on whether there is a credit balance in the Contributed Capital, Treasury Stock Transactions account. If there is no balance, the excess of cost over the sales price is debited to Retained Earnings. However, if the contributed capital account has a credit balance, the excess of the cost over the sales price is debited for an amount up to the balance in that account. When the credit balance in the contributed capital account is eliminated, any remaining difference between the cost and the selling price is debited to Retained Earnings.

For example, if Curry Corporation sells its remaining 500 shares of treasury stock at $10 per share, the company's equity is reduced by $750 (500 shares × $1.50 per share excess of cost over selling price). The reissuance is recorded with this entry:

July	10	Cash	5,000.00	
		Contributed Capital, Treasury Stock Transactions	250.00	
		Retained Earnings	500.00	
		Treasury Stock, Common		5,750.00
		Received $10 per share for 500 treasury shares		
		that cost $11.50 per share.		

This entry eliminates the $250 credit balance in the contributed capital account created on June 3 and then reduces the Retained Earnings balance by the remaining $500 of the excess of the cost over the selling price. Thus, the purchase and reissuance of the treasury shares caused Curry Corporation to incur a $500 decrease in retained earnings and total stockholders' equity. Notice that the company does not report a loss from this transaction.

RETIRING STOCK

Instead of acquiring treasury stock with the intent of reissuing it in the future, a corporation may simply purchase its own stock and retire it. It cancels the shares, which become the same as unissued stock. For example, a few years ago, **Wm. Wrigley Jr. Company** reported in the notes to its financial statements that "the Board of Directors adopted a resolution retiring the entire balance of shares of Common Stock held in the corporate treasury at that time and all subsequent acquisitions to the extent not required for issuance [under the company's management Incentive Plan]." Like purchases of treasury stock, purchases and retirements of stock are permissible under state laws only if they do not jeopardize the best interests of creditors and other stockholders.

When stock is purchased for retirement, the accountant must remove all the contributed capital amounts related to the retired shares. If the purchase price for the shares exceeds the net amount removed from contributed capital, the excess is debited to Retained Earnings. On the other hand, if the purchase price is less than the net amount removed from contributed capital, the difference is credited to a special contributed capital account.

For example, assume that The Carolina Corporation originally issued its $10 par value common stock at $12 per share. As a result, the $2 per share premium was credited to the Contributed Capital in Excess of Par Value, Common Stock account. When the corporation purchased and retired 1,000 shares of this stock at $12 per share on April 12, it recorded the effects of this event with this entry:

Apr.	12	Common Stock	10,000.00	
		Contributed Capital in Excess of Par Value, Common		
		Stock	2,000.00	
		Cash		12,000.00
		Purchased and retired 1,000 shares of common stock		
		at $12 per share.		

This entry restores the accounts to the balances that they would have had if the stock had never been issued.

On the other hand, if the corporation paid only $11 per share instead of $12, the retirement causes equity to increase by $1 per share, the difference between cost and the original issuance price. This increase in equity is recorded as follows:

Apr.	12	Common Stock	10,000.00	
		Contributed Capital in Excess of Par Value, Common		
		Stock	2,000.00	
		Cash		11,000.00
		Contributed Capital from the Retirement of		
		Common Stock		1,000.00
		Purchased and retired 1,000 shares of common stock		
		at $11 per share.		

Even though this transaction increased equity, the amount is not a gain. The concept underlying this treatment is that transactions in a corporation's own stock cannot affect income or increase retained earnings.

The same idea governs the accounting for a retirement accomplished with a purchase price that is greater than the stock's original issuance price. For example, suppose that The Carolina Corporation retired 1,000 shares of its stock at $15 per share, which is $3 per share greater than the $12 original issue price. This entry would be used to account for the event:

Apr.	12	Common Stock	10,000.00	
		Contributed Capital in Excess of Par Value,		
		Common Stock	2,000.00	
		Retained Earnings	3,000.00	
		Cash		15,000.00
		Purchased and retired 1,000 shares of common stock		
		at $15 per share.		

Even though this transaction decreased equity, the $3 per share is not a loss. In this case, the $3,000 is debited to Retained Earnings. If there had been a credit balance in a contributed capital account related to retirements, it would have been debited up to the amount of its balance.

All three retirement examples reduced the company's assets and equity by the amount paid for the stock. However, no income effects are recognized. The only effects on equity are recorded in the contributed capital and Retained Earnings accounts.

Progress Check

15–4   A corporation's purchase of treasury stock: *(a)* Has no effect on total assets; *(b)* Reduces total assets and total stockholders' equity by equal amounts; *(c)* Is recorded with a debit to Retained Earnings.

15–5   Southern Co. purchased shares of Northern Corp. Should these shares be classified as treasury stock by either company?

15–6   How does treasury stock affect the number of authorized, issued, and outstanding shares of stock?

15–7   When a corporation purchases treasury stock: *(a)* Retained earnings is restricted by the amount paid for the stock; *(b)* It is recorded with a credit to Appropriated Retained Earnings; *(c)* It is always retired.

REPORTING INCOME AND RETAINED EARNINGS INFORMATION

When a company's only revenue and expense transactions are created by routine, continuing operations, a single-step income statement is adequate for describing the results of its activities. This format shows the revenues followed by a list of operating expenses and the net income. In today's complex business world, however, activities often include many income related events that are not part of a company's continuing and otherwise normal activities.

The accountant's goal is to provide useful information in a format that helps the statement users understand the past-period events and predict future-period results. To see how this goal is accomplished, look at the income statement in Illustration 15–4. Notice that the income statement is separated into five different sections.

Section 1 of the income statement shows the revenues, expenses, and income generated by the company's continuing operations. This portion looks like the single-step income statement that we first discussed in Chapter 6. Income statement users rely on the information in this section to develop predictions of what will happen in the future. As such, this section usually contains the most important information in the income statement. Previous chapters have explained the nature of the items and measures included in income from continuing operations.

Most large companies have several different lines of business and deal with different groups of customers. For example, **International Business Machines** not only produces and sells computer hardware and software but also delivers system design and repair services. Information about these segments of the business is of particular interest to users of the company's financial statements. According to GAAP, a **segment of a business** is a component of a company's operations that serves a particular line of business or class of customers. A segment has assets, activities, and financial results of operations that can be distinguished from other parts of the business. Large companies with operations in different segments are required to provide supplemental footnote information about each of their major segments.

Reporting Income Statement Information about Discontinued Segments

When a company incurs a gain or loss from selling or closing down a segment, the gain or loss must be reported in a separate section of the income statement.[3] Section 2 of the income statement in Illustration 15–4 includes this information. Note that the income from operating the discontinued segment prior to its disposal also is reported in section 2. When the income statement presents the results of several years side by side, it is necessary to go back and restate the prior years' results to separate out the revenues and expenses of the discontinued segment.

Separate information about a discontinued segment can be useful on its own. However, the primary purpose of reporting the gains or losses from discontinued operations separately is to more clearly present the results of continuing operations. The effect is to provide useful information for predicting the income that will be earned by the segments that continue to operate in the future.

LO 3
Explain how to report the income effects of discontinued segments, extraordinary items, changes in accounting principles and estimates, and prior period adjustments.

CONTINUING OPERATIONS

DISCONTINUED SEGMENTS

---

[3]FASB, *Accounting Standards—Current Text* (Norwalk, CT, 1995), sec. I13.105. Originally published as *APB Opinion No. 30*, par. 8.

Illustration 15-4 Income Statement for a Corporation

CONNELLY CORPORATION
Income Statement
For Year Ended December 31, 19X4

①	Net sales		$8,440,000
	Gain on sale of equipment		38,000
	Total		$8,478,000
	Expenses:		
	Cost of goods sold	$5,950,000	
	Depreciation expense	35,000	
	Other selling, general, and administrative expenses	515,000	
	Interest expense	20,000	
	Income taxes expense	595,500	
	Total expenses		(7,115,500)
	Unusual loss on relocating a plant		(45,000)
	Infrequent gain on sale of surplus land		72,000
	Income from continuing operations		$1,389,500
	Discontinued segment:		
②	Income from operating Division A (net of $180,000 income taxes)	$ 420,000	
	Loss on disposal of Division A (net of $66,000 tax benefit)	(154,000)	266,000
	Income before extraordinary items and cumulative effect of a change in accounting principle		$1,655,500
	Extraordinary items:		
③	Gain on sale of unused land condemned by the state for a highway interchange(net of $61,200 income taxes)	$ 142,800	
	Loss from earthquake damage (net of $270,000 income tax benefit)	(630,000)	(487,200)
	Cumulative effect of a change in accounting principle:		
④	Effect on prior years' income (through December 31, 19X3) of changing to a different depreciation method (net of $24,000 income taxes)		56,000
	Net income		$1,224,300
	Earnings per common share (200,000 outstanding shares):		
⑤	Income from continuing operations		$ 6.95
	Discontinued operations		1.33
	Income before extraordinary items and cumulative effect of a change in accounting principle		$ 8.28
	Extraordinary items		(2.44)
	Cumulative effect of a change in accounting principle		0.28
	Net income		$ 6.12

Distinguishing the Results of Operating a Discontinued Segment from the Gain or Loss on Disposal

Section 2 of Illustration 15–4 reports both the income from operating the discontinued Division A during the year and the loss that occurred from disposing of the division's assets. The income tax effects of operating and disposing of the segment are also disclosed in section 2. As a result, the tax effects related to the discontinued segment are separated from the presentation of continuing operations in section 1. If the tax effects of the discontinued segment were not separated from the continuing operations, the result would not be as useful.

This discussion presents only a highly summarized description of the requirements for reporting the results of discontinued segments. The details are covered in more advanced accounting courses.

EXTRAORDINARY ITEMS

Section 3 of the income statement in Illustration 15–4 reports extraordinary gains and losses that occurred during the year. **Extraordinary gains and losses** are both unusual and infrequent. An **unusual gain or loss** is abnormal or otherwise unrelated to the ordinary activities and environment of the business. An **infrequent gain or loss** is not expected to occur again in the company's operating environment.[4] Reporting extraordinary items in a separate category makes it easier for users to predict what will happen in the future, apart from these extraordinary events.

In light of these definitions of *unusual* and *infrequent*, very few items qualify as extraordinary gains or losses by meeting both criteria. For example, none of the following events are considered extraordinary:

1. Write-downs or write-offs of assets, unless the change in value is caused by a major unusual and infrequent calamity, a condemning or expropriating of property by a domestic or foreign government, or a prohibition against using the assets under a newly enacted law.

2. Gains or losses from exchanging foreign currencies or translating account balances expressed in one currency into another currency.

3. Gains and losses from disposing of a business segment.

4. Effects of a labor action, including one against the company, its competitors, or its major suppliers.

5. Adjustment of accruals on long-term contracts.[5]

Gains or losses that are neither unusual nor infrequent are reported as part of the results of continuing operations. Gains or losses that are either unusual or infrequent but not both are not extraordinary. These items are listed on the income statement in the continuing operations section below the regular revenues, expenses, gains, and losses. For example, **Duracell International, Inc.'s** 1993 income statement reported a $65 million charge for restructuring. The charge related to organizational integration and streamlining, including the closure of a Brazilian manufacturing facility and upgrading global manufacturing capabilities.

Section 1 of Illustration 15–4 includes a "Gain on sale of equipment" that is neither unusual nor infrequent with the revenues. However, an unusual loss and an infrequent gain are reported at the end of the section. The proper classification of these items is not always clear without carefully examining the circumstances.

In addition, GAAP require a few items to be reported as extraordinary gains or losses, even if they do not otherwise meet the normal criteria. For example, *FASB Statement No. 4* requires a gain or loss from retiring debt to be reported as extraordinary. Thus, in 1994, **Chiquita Brands International, Inc.** reported an extraordinary loss of $22,840,000 from the retirement of debt.

---

[4]Ibid., sec. I17.107. Originally published as *APB Opinion No. 30,* par. 20.

[5]Ibid., sec. I17.110. Originally published as *APB Opinion No. 30,* par. 23.

**CHANGES IN
ACCOUNTING
PRINCIPLES**

In general, the *consistency principle* requires a company to continue applying a specific accounting method or principle once it is chosen. (In this context, the term *accounting principles* describes accounting methods, such as FIFO and straight-line depreciation.) However, a company may change from one acceptable accounting principle to another as long as it justifies the change as an improvement in the information provided in its financial statements. In addition, companies often change accounting principles when they adopt new standards issued by the FASB.

When a company changes accounting principles, it usually affects the amount of reported income in more than one way. For example, let's consider Connelly Corporation's income statement in Illustration 15–4. The company purchased its only depreciable asset early in 19X1 for $320,000. The asset has a $40,000 salvage value and has been depreciated with the double-declining-balance method for three of the eight years in its predicted useful life. (This company is subject to a 30% income tax rate.) During 19X4, the company decided that its income statement would be more useful if the annual depreciation were calculated with the straight-line method instead of double-declining balance.

In Illustration 15–5, we compare the results of applying the two depreciation methods to the first three years in the asset's service life and show how the company would determine what to report on its 19X4 income statement. The table shows that the accelerated method caused $185,000 of depreciation to be allocated to 19X1 through 19X3. If the straight-line method had been used from the beginning, only $105,000 of depreciation would have been allocated to those years. To give the accounts the balances that they would have had under the straight-line method, the company needs to decrease accumulated depreciation for this asset by the $80,000 gross difference. Offsetting this debit is a credit of $24,000 (30% × $80,000) to a deferred income tax liability for additional taxes to be paid in the future. The remaining $56,000 is the resulting credit to equity created by this change. Because the change increases equity, the company adds it to the income for the year in which the change is made effective.

Reporting Requirements for Changes in Accounting Principles

The income statement in Illustration 15–4 on page 544 shows the acceptable method of reporting the effects of a change in accounting principles by Connelly Corporation. Section 1 of the income statement includes $35,000 of depreciation expense for the current year. This amount is shown in the straight-line method column for 19X4 in Illustration 15–5. Thus, the income for the year of the change is based on the new accounting principle. The annual depreciation of $35,000 also will be used in 19X5 through 19X8. In Illustration 15–5, we calculate the $56,000 catch-up adjustment reported in section 4 of the income statement in Illustration 15–4. This item is the cumulative effect of the change in accounting principle.

In many cases, the cumulative effect may be millions or even billions of dollars. Many large companies reported cumulative effects when they changed their accounting for employees' benefits other than pensions. These changes were made because the FASB implemented *Statement No. 106.* For example, **Deere & Company** reported a $1,095 million reduction in net income when it first applied *Statement No. 106* in 1993.

In addition to the information in the financial statements, two points about the change should be explained: First, a footnote should describe the change and why it is an improvement over the old principle. Second, the

Illustration 15-5 Calculating the Cumulative Effect of a Change in Accounting Principle

Years prior to change:	Double-Declining Depreciation Amount	Straight-Line Depreciation Amount	Pre-Tax Difference	Tax Rate	After-Tax Cumulative Effect
19X1	$ 80,000	$ 35,000	$45,000		
19X2	60,000	35,000	25,000		
19X3	45,000	35,000	10,000		
Subtotal	$185,000	$105,000	$80,000	30%	$56,000[†]
Year of change:					
19X4	$ 33,750	35,000*			
Years after change:					
19X5		35,000			
19X6		35,000			
19X7		35,000			
19X8		35,000			

*Reported on the 19X4 income statement as depreciation expense.
[†]Reported on the 19X4 income statement as the cumulative adjustment for differences in the three years prior to the change in 19X4, net of $24,000 additional taxes to be paid (30% × $80,000).

footnote should describe what 19X4's income would have been under the old method if the change had not occurred. For the example in Illustration 15–5, the footnote would reveal that leaving the method unchanged would have resulted in 19X4 depreciation of $33,750 under the double-declining method instead of $35,000 under the straight-line method. This footnoted amount appears in Illustration 15–5 as the declining-balance depreciation for 19X4.

Section 5 of Illustration 15–4 provides detailed information about earnings per share results for the year. This information is included on the face of the income statement in accordance with GAAP. This section is more complete than the minimum reporting requirements to show the possible categories companies can and often do report. A later section of the chapter explains the basic procedures to compute earnings per share.

EARNINGS PER SHARE SECTION OF THE INCOME STATEMENT

PRIOR PERIOD ADJUSTMENTS FOR CORRECTING MATERIAL ERRORS

Companies do not report the effect of a prior period adjustment on their current income statements. Instead, prior period adjustments appear in the statement of retained earnings (or the statement of changes in stockholders' equity), net of any income tax effects. **Prior period adjustments** modify the beginning balance of retained earnings for events occurring prior to the earliest year described in the financial statements. Under GAAP, prior period adjustments only record the effects of correcting material errors in earlier years. These errors include arithmetic mistakes, using unacceptable accounting principles, or failing to consider relevant facts.[6] An error would occur if an accountant mistakenly omits depreciation, applies an unacceptable depreciation method, or overlooks important facts in predicting an asset's useful life. For example, assume that the accountant for Connelly Corporation failed to detect an error in

---

[6]Ibid., sec. A35.104. Originally published as *APB Opinion No. 20,* par. 13.

a 19X2 journal entry for the purchase of land incorrectly debited to an expense account. This statement of retained earnings includes a prior period adjustment to correct this error discovered in 19X4:

CONNELLY CORPORATION
Statement of Retained Earnings
For Year Ended December 31, 19X4

Retained earnings, December 31, 19X3, as previously stated . . .	$4,745,000
Prior period adjustment:	
Cost of land incorrectly charged to expense	
(net of $63,000 income taxes)	147,000
Retained earnings, December 31, 19X3, as adjusted	$4,892,000
Plus net income	1,162,500
Less cash dividends declared	(240,000)
Retained earnings, December 31, 19X4	$5,814,500

CHANGES IN ACCOUNTING ESTIMATES

Many of the items disclosed in financial statements are based on estimates and predictions. Future events are certain to reveal that some of these estimates and predictions were inaccurate, even though they were based on the best data available at the time. Because these inaccuracies are not the result of mistakes, they are not considered to be accounting errors. Thus, any corrections of these estimates are not reported as prior period adjustments. Instead, they are **changes in accounting estimates.** For example, depreciation is based on predicted useful lives and salvage values. As new information becomes available, it may be used to change the predictions and modify the amounts reported as depreciation expense. Unlike changes in accounting principles, changes in accounting estimates are not accounted for with cumulative catch-up adjustments. Instead, the revised estimates are applied in determining revenues and expenses for the current and future periods. In Chapter 10, we explained one common change in an accounting estimate when we discussed revising depreciation rates.

STATEMENT OF CHANGES IN STOCKHOLDERS' EQUITY

Most corporations actually do not present a separate statement of retained earnings. Instead, they provide a **statement of changes in stockholders' equity** that lists the beginning and ending balances of each equity account and describes all the changes that occurred during the year. For example, **Albertson's Inc.,** which operates a large chain of retail food-drug stores, presents this information in a format that provides a column for each component of equity and uses the rows to describe the events of the year. (See Illustration 15–6.) Notice that the company acquired treasury stock in the year ended February 3, 1994, and then either reissued or retired all the shares. The statement also indicates a stock split, but the credit to the Common Stock account reveals it was actually a 100% stock dividend. (For reasons not explained in the report, the dividend was recorded with a partial transfer of contributed capital in excess of par to the Common Stock account.)

Progress Check

15–8   Which of the following is an extraordinary item? *(a)* A settlement paid to a customer injured while using the company's product; *(b)* A loss from damages to a plant caused by a meteorite; *(c)* A loss from selling old equipment.

Illustration 15–6

ALBERTSON'S INC.
Consolidated Stockholders' Equity
(in thousands, except per share data)

	Common Stock $1.00 Par Value	Capital in Excess of Par	Retained Earnings	Treasury Stock	Total
Balance at January 30, 1992	$132,131	$ 718	$1,066,603		$1,199,452
Exercise of stock options	199	1,475			4,390
Tax benefits related to					
stock options		2,716			
Cash dividends, $0.32 per share			(84,631)	(84,631)	
Net earnings			269,217		269,217
Balance at January 28, 1993	$132,330	$ 4,909	$1,251,189		$1,388,428
Exercise of stock options	245	1,700			4,483
Tax benefits related to					
stock options		2,538			
Purchase treasury shares				$(517,526)	(517,526)
Issue treasury shares		19,615		244,912	264,527
Retire treasury shares	(5,788)	(25,010)	(241,816)	272,614	
Two-for-one stock split	126,620	(1,635)	(124,985)		
Other			953		953
Cash dividends, $0.36 per share			(91,167)		(91,167)
Net earnings			339,681		339,681
Balance at February 3, 1994	$253,407	$ 2,117	$1,133,855		$1,389,379
Exercise of stock options	577	5,120			5,697
Tax benefits related to					
stock options		4,085			4,085
Cash dividends, $0.44 per share			(111,633)		(111,633)
Net earnings			400,365		400,365
Balance at February 2, 1995	$253,984	$11,322	$1,422,587		$1,687,893

Courtesy of Albertson's Inc.

15–9 Identify the four possible major sections of the income statement that might appear below income from continuing operations.

15–10 A company that used FIFO for the past 15 years has decided to switch to LIFO. The effect of this event on past years' net income should be: *(a)* Reported as a prior period adjustment to retained earnings; *(b)* Ignored as it is a change in an accounting estimate; *(c)* Reported on the current year's income statement.

EARNINGS PER SHARE

Among the most widely quoted items of accounting information is **earnings per share.** This number represents the amount of income earned by each share of a corporation's common stock. Because of the importance and widespread use of earnings per share numbers, accountants have developed detailed guidelines for calculating it. One important factor that shapes the presentation of earnings per share is the company's capital structure, which can be either simple or complex.

LO 4

Calculate earnings per share for companies with simple capital structures and explain the difference between primary and fully diluted earnings per share.

COMPANIES WITH SIMPLE CAPITAL STRUCTURES

Earnings per share calculations can be simple or complicated, depending on a company's situation. The calculations are not difficult for a company with a **simple capital structure** because it has only common stock and perhaps nonconvertible preferred stock outstanding. That is, a simple capital structure cannot include any options or rights to purchase common stock or any preferred stocks or bonds that are convertible into common stock.

Calculating Earnings per Share When the Number of Common Shares Does Not Change

The earnings per share calculation is simple if: (1) a company has only common stock and nonconvertible preferred stock outstanding and (2) the number of outstanding common shares does not change during the period. In this situation, the calculation involves determining the amount of the net income that is available to the common stockholders and dividing it by the number of common shares. The amount of income available to the common stockholders is the year's net income less any dividends declared or accumulated on the preferred stock. (If the preferred stock is cumulative, the current year's dividend must be subtracted even if it was not declared.) The following formula applies:

$$\text{Earnings per share} = \frac{\text{Net income} - \text{Preferred dividends}}{\text{Outstanding common shares}}$$

For example, assume that Blackwell Company earned $40,000 net income in 19X1 and declared dividends of $7,500 on its noncumulative preferred stock. The company had 5,000 common shares outstanding throughout the entire year. Thus:

$$\text{Earnings per share} = \frac{\$40,000 - \$7,500}{5,000 \text{ shares}} = \$6.50$$

The calculation is more complex if the number of outstanding shares changes during the year. The number of shares outstanding may change for a variety of reasons such as sales of additional shares, purchases of treasury stock, and stock dividends or splits.

Finding the Denominator When a Company Sells or Purchases Common Shares

If a company sells additional shares or purchases treasury shares during the year, the denominator of the formula is the weighted-average number of outstanding shares. The idea behind this change is to produce an average amount of earnings accruing to the average number of shares outstanding during the year the income was earned.

For example, suppose that Blackwell Company earned $40,000 in 19X2 and declared preferred dividends of $7,500. As a result, the earnings available to the common stock are again $32,500. Also assume that Blackwell sold 4,000 additional common shares on July 1, 19X2, and purchased 3,000 treasury shares on November 1, 19X2. As a result, 5,000 shares were outstanding for six months, 9,000 shares were outstanding for four months, and 6,000 shares were outstanding for two months. We calculate the weighted-average number of shares outstanding as follows:

Time Period	Outstanding Shares	Fraction of Year	Weighted Average
January–June	5,000	6/12	2,500
July–October	9,000	4/12	3,000
November–December	6,000	2/12	1,000
Weighted-average outstanding shares			6,500

Using the weighted-average number of common shares outstanding for Blackwell, the earnings per share calculation is:

$$\text{Earnings per share} = \frac{\$40,000 - \$7,500}{6,500 \text{ shares}} = \$5.00$$

Blackwell reports this number at the bottom of its 19X2 income statement.

Adjusting the Denominator for Stock Splits and Stock Dividends

The number of outstanding shares can also be affected by a stock split or stock dividend during the year. These events do not bring in any additional assets; thus, they do not affect the company's ability to produce earnings for the common stockholders. In effect, the earnings for the year are simply spread out over a larger number of shares. As a result, in calculating the weighted-average number of shares outstanding, stock splits and stock dividends are not treated like stock sales and purchases.

When a stock split or stock dividend occurs, the number of shares that were outstanding earlier in the year are retroactively restated to reflect the effects of the stock split or dividend as if it occurred at the beginning of the year. For example, reconsider the Blackwell Company example and assume that the stock transactions in 19X2 included a two-for-one stock split on December 1. This split caused the percentage ownership of each share to be cut in half while doubling the number of outstanding shares. The situation is described by this table:

Time Period	Original Shares	Effect of Split	Post-Split Shares
January–June	5,000	2	10,000
July–October	9,000	2	18,000
November	6,000	2	12,000

Then, the numbers in the third column can be inserted into the weighted-average calculation for the new shares:

Time Period	Post-Split Shares	Fraction of Year	Weighted Average
January–June	10,000	6/12	5,000
July–October	18,000	4/12	6,000
November–December	12,000	2/12	2,000
Weighted–average outstanding shares			13,000

The Blackwell Company's earnings per share for 19X2 under this set of assumptions are:

$$\text{Earnings per share} = \frac{\$40,000 - \$7,500}{13,000 \text{ shares}} = \$2.50$$

The same sort of modification is used when stock dividends occur. For example, if the two-for-one stock split had been a 10% stock dividend, the numbers of old outstanding shares would have been multiplied by 1.1 instead of two.

COMPANIES WITH COMPLEX CAPITAL STRUCTURES

Companies with **complex capital structures** have outstanding options or rights to purchase common stock and/or securities such as bonds or preferred stock that are convertible into common stock. Earnings per share calculations for companies with complex capital structures are more complicated. Often, such companies must pre-

sent two types of earnings per share calculations. One is called **primary earnings per share,** and the other is called **fully diluted earnings per share.** For example, in its fiscal year ended January 28, 1995, **J. C. Penney Company, Inc.,** reported primary earnings per share of $4.29 and fully diluted earnings per share of $4.05.

Suppose that a corporation has convertible preferred stock outstanding throughout the current year. However, consider what the effects would have been if the preferred shares had been converted at the beginning of the year. The result of this assumed conversion would have been to increase the number of common shares outstanding and to reduce preferred dividends. The net result may have been to reduce earnings per share or to increase earnings per share. When the assumed conversion of a security reduces earnings per share, the security is said to be **dilutive;** those that increase earnings per share are **antidilutive.**

Primary Earnings per Share

Based on detailed rules, convertible securities are evaluated at the time they are issued.[7] If eventual conversion appears highly probable, the convertible security is called a **common stock equivalent.** Primary earnings per share is calculated as if dilutive common stock equivalents had already been converted at the beginning of the period.

Fully Diluted Earnings per Share

Common stock equivalents have terms that make their eventual conversion very probable. Other convertible securities are less apt to be converted. Nevertheless, if we assume those securities were converted at the beginning of the period, the effect may be to reduce earnings per share; in other words, the assumed conversion may have a dilutive effect. Fully diluted earnings per share is calculated as if all dilutive securities had already been converted.

PRESENTING EARNINGS PER SHARE ON THE INCOME STATEMENT

Because information about earnings per share is important, corporations must report it on the face of their income statements. Furthermore, they usually report the amount of earnings per share for net income and each of the four subcategories of income (continuing operations, discontinued segments, extraordinary items, and the effect of

accounting principle changes). Illustration 15–4 on page 544 shows Connelly Corporation's earnings per share in section 5.

Even though GAAP is flexible in regard to where some earnings per share information should be reported, many companies present all the details in one place for the convenience of the financial statement users. Illustration 15–7 provides real earnings per share presentations by **Sprint Corporation** and **Colgate-Palmolive Company.** Sprint shows the per-share effects of the various components of its income for three fiscal years. Colgate-Palmolive shows the primary and fully diluted results for the same three years.

---

[7]FASB, *Accounting Standards—Current Text* (Norwalk, CT, 1995), sec. E09.122–127. First published as *APB Opinion No. 15,* par. 31, 33, 35–37. Also see FASB, *Statement of Financial Accounting Standards No. 85* (March 1985), par. 2.

As a Matter of Fact

In January 1996, the FASB issued a proposal to simplify earnings per share calculations and bring the United States in line with practices used in other countries. The proposal is to replace primary EPS with a number called *basic EPS*. Basic EPS ignores potential dilution and is calculated by dividing income available to common stockholders by the weighted-average number of common shares outstanding. Companies with complex capital structures would also present a *diluted EPS*, which is calculated much the same as fully diluted earnings per share.

SPRINT CORPORATION
Showing multiple components:

	1994	1993	1992
Earnings per common share			
Continuing operations	$2.53	$1.39	$1.46
Discontinued operations	0.02	(0.04)	
Extraordinary item		(0.08)	(0.05)
Cumulative effect of changes in			
accounting principles		(1.12)	0.07
Total	$2.55	$0.15	$1.48

COLGATE-PALMOLIVE COMPANY
Showing primary and fully diluted results:

	1994	1993	1992
Earnings per common share, primary			
Income before changes in accounting . . .	$ 3.82	$3.38	$2.92
Cumulative effect on prior years of			
accounting changes		(2.30)	
Net income	$ 3.82	$1.08	$2.92
Earnings per common share, fully diluted			
Income before changes in accounting . . .	$ 3.56	$3.15	$2.74
Cumulative effect on prior years of			
accounting changes		(2.10)	
Net income	$ 3.56	$1.05	$2.74

Courtesy of Sprint Corporation and Colgate-Palmolive Company.

Illustration 15–7
Reporting Earnings per Share on the Income Statement

Progress Check

15-11   During 19X1, FDI Co. had net income of $250,000 and paid preferred dividends of $70,000. On January 1, the company had 25,000 outstanding common shares and purchased 5,000 treasury shares on July 1. 19X1 earnings per share is: *(a)* $8.00; *(b)* $9.00; *(c)* $10.00.

15-12   How are stock splits and stock dividends treated in calculating the weighted-average number of outstanding common shares?

15-13   What two sets of earnings per share results are reported for a company with a complex capital structure?

USING THE INFORMATION— THE PRICE-EARNINGS RATIO

LO 5
Calculate the price-earnings ratio and describe its meaning.

You learned in Chapter 14 that a stock's market value is largely affected by the stream of future dividends expected to be paid out to stockholders. Market value is also affected by expected future changes in value. By comparing the company's earnings per share and its market price per share, investors and other decision makers can obtain information about the stock market's apparent expectations for growth in future earnings, dividends, and market values.

Although it would be possible to make this comparison as a rate of return by dividing the earnings per share by the market price per share, the ratio has traditionally been turned upside-down and calculated as the **price-earnings ratio.** Thus, this ratio is found by dividing the stock's market price by the earnings per share, as shown in this formula:

$$\text{Price-earnings ratio} = \frac{\text{Market value per share}}{\text{Earnings per share}}$$

The ratio may be calculated using the earnings per share reported in the past period. However, analysts often calculate the ratio based on the expected earnings per share for the next period. Suppose, for example, that the stock's current market price is $100 per share and that its next year's earnings are expected to be $8 per share. Its price-earnings ratio (often abbreviated as the PE ratio) is found as $100/$8, which is 12.5.

As a general rule, stocks with higher PE ratios (generally greater than 12 to 15) are considered more likely to be overpriced while stocks with lower PE ratios (generally less than 5 to 8) are considered more likely to be underpriced. Thus, some investors prefer to sell or avoid buying stocks with high PE ratios while they prefer to buy or hold stocks that have low PE ratios. Investment decisions are not quite that simple, however, because a stock with a high PE ratio may prove to be a good investment if its earnings increase rapidly. On the other hand, a stock with a low PE ratio may prove to be a low performer. Although the price-earnings ratio is clearly important for investment decisions, it is only one piece of information that investors should consider.

Progress Check

15–14 Calculate the price-earnings ratio for a company with earnings per share of $4.25 and stock with a market value of $34.00.

15–15 Two companies in the same industry face similar levels of risk, have nearly the same level of earnings, and are expected to continue their historical record of paying $1.50 annual dividends per share. Yet, one of the companies has a PE ratio of 6 while the other has a PE ratio of 10. Which company does the market apparently expect to have a higher future growth rate in earnings?

SUMMARY OF THE CHAPTER IN TERMS OF LEARNING OBJECTIVES

LO 1. Describe stock dividends and stock splits and explain their effects on a corporation's assets and stockholders' equity. In contrast to cash dividends, stock dividends do not transfer corporate assets to stockholders. Stock dividends and stock splits do not affect assets, total stockholders' equity, or the equity attributed to each stockholder. Small stock dividends ($\leq 25\%$) are recorded by capitalizing retained earnings equal to the market value of the distributed shares. Large stock dividends ($>25\%$) are recorded by capitalizing retained earnings equal to the par or stated value of the issued shares. Stock splits are not recorded through journal entries but should lead to changing the account title for the common stock if it includes the par or stated value.

LO 2. Record purchases and sales of treasury stock and retirements of stock and describe their effects on stockholders' equity. Also, describe restrictions and appropriations of retained earnings and explain how they are described in financial reports. When outstanding treasury shares are repurchased by the corporation that issued them, the cost of the shares is debited to Treasury Stock. Its balance is subtracted from total stockholders' equity in the balance sheet. When treasury stock is later reissued, the amount of any proceeds in excess of cost is credited to Contributed Capital, Treasury Stock Transactions. If the proceeds are less than cost, the difference is debited to Contributed Capital, Treasury Stock Transactions to the extent a credit balance exists in that account. Any remaining amount is debited to Retained Earnings.

Most states limit dividends and treasury stock purchases to the amount of retained earnings. Companies also enter into contracts that may limit the amount of dividends, even though the companies have both the cash and the retained earnings to pay them. Corporations may voluntarily appropriate retained earnings to inform stockholders why dividends are not larger. Often, however, this information is expressed in a letter to the stockholders.

LO 3. Explain how to report the income effects of discontinued segments, extraordinary items, changes in accounting principles and estimates, and prior period adjustments. If a company has decided to discontinue a segment, the income effects of operating and disposing of the segment are separately reported on the income statement below income from continuing operations. Extraordinary gains or losses also are separated from continuing operations and reported lower in the income statement. A similar treatment is required for the cumulative effects of changes in accounting principles. Prior period adjustments for error corrections are not reported on the income statement but appear on the retained earnings statement or the statement of changes in stockholders' equity. Changes in accounting estimates arise when new information shows the old estimates to be inaccurate. If an accounting estimate is changed, the firm uses the new estimate to calculate income in the current and future periods.

LO 4. Calculate earnings per share for companies with simple capital structures and explain the difference between primary and fully diluted earnings per share. The outstanding securities of companies with simple capital structures do not include any securities that are convertible into common stock. These companies calculate earnings per share by dividing net income (less any preferred dividends) by the weighted-average number of outstanding common shares. Companies with complex capital structures have issued securities that are convertible into common stock. These companies often have to report both primary earnings per share and fully diluted earnings per share.

LO 5. Calculate the price-earnings ratio and describe its meaning. The price-earnings ratio of a common stock is closely watched by investors and other decision makers. The ratio is calculated by dividing the current market value per share by earnings per share. A high ratio may suggest that a stock is overvalued while a low ratio may suggest that a stock is undervalued. However, selecting stocks to buy or sell requires a great deal more information.

DEMONSTRATION PROBLEM

The Precision Company began 19X1 with the following balances in its stockholders' equity accounts:

Common stock, $10 par, 500,000 shares authorized, 200,000 shares issued and outstanding	$2,000,000
Contributed capital in excess of par	1,000,000
Retained earnings	5,000,000
Total	$8,000,000

All of the outstanding stock was issued for $15 when the company was created.

Part 1

Prepare journal entries to account for the following transactions during 19X1:

Mar. 31 Declared a 20% stock dividend. The market value of the stock was $18 per share.

Apr. 15 Distributed the stock dividend declared on March 31.

June 30 Purchased 30,000 shares of treasury stock at $20 per share.

Aug. 31 Sold 20,000 treasury shares at $26 per share.

Nov. 30 Purchased and retired 50,000 shares at $24 per share.

Part 2

Use the following information to prepare an income statement for 19X1, including earnings per share results for each category of income.

Cumulative effect of a change in depreciation method (net of tax benefit)	$ (136,500)
Expenses related to continuing operations	(2,072,500)
Extraordinary gain on debt retirement (net of tax)	182,000
Gain on disposal of discontinued segment's assets (net of tax)	29,000
Gain on sale of stock investment	400,000
Loss from operating discontinued segment (net of tax benefit)	(120,000)
Income taxes on income from continuing operations	(225,000)
Prior period adjustment for error (net of tax benefit)	(75,000)
Sales	4,140,000
Infrequent loss	(650,000)

Planning the Solution

- Decide whether the stock dividend is a small or large dividend. Then, analyze each event to determine the accounts affected and the appropriate amounts to be recorded.

- Based on the shares of outstanding stock at the beginning of the year and the transactions during the year, calculate the weighted-average number of outstanding shares for the year.

- Assign each of the listed items to an appropriate income statement category.

- Prepare an income statement similar to Illustration 15–4, including appropriate earnings per share results.

Solution to Demonstration Problem

Part 1

Mar.	31	Stock Dividends Declared	720,000.00	
		Common Stock Dividend Distributable		400,000.00
		Contributed Capital in Excess of Par Value,		
		Common Stock		320,000.00
		Declared a small stock dividend of 20% or 40,000		
		shares; market value is $18 per share.		
Apr.	15	Common Stock Dividend Distributable	400,000.00	
		Common Stock		400,000.00
		Distributed 40,000 shares of common stock.		
June	30	Treasury Stock, Common	600,000.00	
		Cash		600,000.00
		Purchased 30,000 shares of common stock at $20 per		
		share.		
Aug.	31	Cash	520,000.00	
		Treasury Stock, Common		400,000.00
		Contributed Capital, Treasury Stock Transactions		120,000.00
		Sold 20,000 shares of treasury stock at $26 per share.		
Nov.	30	Common Stock	500,000.00	
		Contributed Capital in Excess of Par Value, Common		
		Stock	250,000.00	
		Retained Earnings	450,000.00	
		Cash		1,200,000.00
		Purchased and retired 50,000 shares at $24 per share.		

Part 2

Calculating the weighted average of outstanding shares:

Time Period	Original Shares	Effect of Dividend	Post-Dividend Shares
January–April 15	200,000	1.2	240,000

Time Period	Post-Dividend Shares	Fraction of Year	Weighted Average
January–June	240,000	6/12	120,000
July–August	210,000	2/12	35,000
September–November	230,000	3/12	57,500
December	180,000	1/12	15,000
Weighted-average outstanding shares			227,500

THE PRECISION COMPANY
Income Statement
For Year Ended December 31, 19X1

Sales		$4,140,000
Expenses		(2,072,500)
Income taxes		(225,000)
Gain on sale of stock investment		400,000
Infrequent loss		(650,000)
Income from continuing operations		$1,592,500
Discontinued operations:		
Loss from operating discontinued segment (net of tax benefit)	$ (120,000)	
Gain on disposal of discontinued segment's assets (net of tax)	29,000	
Loss from discontinued segment		(91,000)
Income before extraordinary items and cumulative effect of a change in accounting principle		$1,501,500
Extraordinary items:		
Extraordinary gain on debt retirement (net of tax)		182,000
Cumulative effect of a change in accounting principle:		
Cumulative effect of a change in depreciation method (net of tax benefit)		(136,500)
Net income		$1,547,000
Earnings per share (227,500 average shares outstanding):		
Income from continuing operations		$ 7.00
Loss from discontinued segment		(0.40)
Income before extraordinary gain and cumulative effect of change in accounting principle		$ 6.60
Extraordinary gain		0.80
Cumulative effect of change in accounting principle		(0.60)
Net income		$ 6.80

GLOSSARY

Antidilutive securities securities the assumed conversion of which has the effect of increasing earnings per share. p. 552

Appropriated retained earnings retained earnings that are voluntarily restricted as a way of informing stockholders that dividends will not be paid. p. 540

Changes in accounting estimates modifications to previous estimates or predictions about future events and outcomes, such as salvage values and the useful lives of operating assets. p. 548

Common stock equivalent a convertible or exercisable se-curity the eventual conversion of which is highly probable. p. 552

Complex capital structure a capital structure that includes outstanding rights or options to purchase common stock or securities that are convertible into common stock. p. 551

Dilutive securities securities the assumed conversion of which has the effect of decreasing earnings per share. p. 552

Earnings per share the amount of income earned by each share of a company's common stock. p. 549

Extraordinary gain or loss a gain or loss that is reported separate from continuing operations because it is both un-usual and infrequent. p. 545

Fully diluted earnings per share earnings per share calcu-lated as if all dilutive securities had already been converted. p. 552

Infrequent gain or loss a gain or loss that is not expected to occur again, given the operating environment of the busi-ness. p. 545

Large stock dividend a stock dividend that is more than 25% of the corporation's previously outstanding shares. p. 533

Liquidating dividends distributions of corporate assets as a dividend that returns part of the original investment to the stockholders; these distributions are charged to contributed capital accounts. p. 533

Price-earnings ratio the ratio between a company's current market value and its earnings per share; used to gain under-standing of the market's expectations for the stock. p. 554

Primary earnings per share earnings per share calculated as if dilutive common stock equivalents had already been converted or exercised. p. 552

Prior period adjustment a correction of an error in a previ-ous year that is reported in the statement of retained earnings. p. 547

Restricted retained earnings retained earnings that are not available for dividends because of legal or contractual limita-tions. p. 540

Reverse stock split an act by a corporation to call in its

stock and replace each share with less than one new share. p. 537

Segment of a business a component of a company's opera-tions that serves a particular line of business or class of cus-tomers and that has assets, activities, and financial results of operations that can be distinguished from other parts of the business. p. 543

Simple capital structure a capital structure that consists of no more than common stock and nonconvertible preferred stock; it cannot include any options or rights to purchase common stock or any convertible preferred stocks or bonds. p. 550

Small stock dividend a stock dividend that is 25% or less of the corporation's previously outstanding shares. p. 533

Statement of changes in stockholders' equity a financial statement that lists the beginning and ending balances of each equity account and describes all the changes that occurred during the year. p. 548

Stock dividend a corporation's distribution of its own stock to its stockholders without receiving any payment in return. p. 533

Stock split an act by a corporation to call in its stock and replace each share with more than one new share. p. 536

Treasury stock stock that was reacquired and is still held by the issuing corporation. p. 538

Unusual gain or loss a gain or loss that is abnormal or oth-erwise unrelated to the ordinary activities and environment of the business. p. 545

QUESTIONS

1. Why is the term *liquidating dividend* used to describe cash dividends that are debited against contributed capital ac-counts?

2. What effects does declaring a stock dividend have on the corporation's assets, liabilities, and total stockholders' eq-uity? What effects does the distribution of the stock have?

3. What is the difference between a stock dividend and a stock split?

4. Courts have determined that a stock dividend is not taxable income to stockholders. What concept justifies this deci-sion?

5. How does the purchase of treasury stock affect the pur-chaser's assets and total stockholders' equity?

6. Why do state laws place limits on purchases of treasury stock?

7. Where on the income statement would a company report an abnormal gain that is not expected to occur more often than once every two years?

8. After taking five years' straight-line depreciation expense for an asset that was expected to have an eight-year useful

life, a company decided that the asset would last another six years. Is this decision a change in accounting principle? How would the financial statements describe this change?

9. How are earnings per share results calculated for a corpora-tion with a simple capital structure?

10. Refer to the financial statements for Lands' End, Inc., in Appendix F at the end of the book. What is the number of shares of treasury stock owned by Lands' End at January 27, 1995? What amount was paid to purchase treasury stock during the year ended January 27, 1995?

LANDS' END
DIRECT MERCHANTS

11. Refer to the 1994 financial statements for Southwest Airlines Co. in Appendix E. Calculate the price-earnings ra-tio using the high sales price for the 4th quarter of 1994.

QUICK STUDY (Five-Minute Exercises)

The stockholders' equity section of Jamestown Co.'s balance sheet as of April 1 follows:

QS 15–1
(LO 1)

Common stock, $5 par value, 375,000 shares	
authorized, 150,000 shares issued and outstanding ...	$ 750,000
Contributed capital in excess of par value, common stock ..	352,500
Total contributed capital	$1,102,500
Retained earnings	633,000
Total stockholders' equity	$1,735,500

On April 1, Jamestown declares and distributes a 10% stock dividend. The market value of the stock on this date is $25. Prepare the stockholders' equity section for Jamestown immediately following the stock dividend.

On May 3, Nicholson Corp. purchased 3,000 shares of its own stock for $27,000. On November 4, Nicholson reissued 750 shares of the treasury stock for $7,080. Prepare the November 4 journal entry Nicholson should make to record the sale of the treasury stock.

QS 15–2
(LO 2)

Answer the questions about each of the following items related to a company's activities for the year:

QS 15–3
(LO 3)

a. After using an expected useful life of seven years and no salvage value to depreciate its office equipment over the preceding three years, the company decided early this year that the equipment will last only two more years. How should the effects of this decision be reported in the current financial statements?

b. In reviewing the notes payable files, it was discovered that last year the company reported the entire amount of a payment on an installment note payable as interest expense. The mistake had a material effect on the amount of income in the prior year. How should the correction be reported in the current year financial statements?

On January 1, Harrell Company had 150,000 shares of common stock issued and outstanding. On April 1, it purchased 12,000 treasury shares and on June 2, declared a 20% stock dividend. Calculate Harrell's weighted-average outstanding shares for the year.

QS 15–4
(LO 4)

Calculate a company's price-earnings ratio if its common stock has a market value of $30.75 per share and if its earnings per share is $4.10.

QS 15–5
(LO 5)

EXERCISES

The stockholders' equity of Brinkman Motors, Inc., on February 5 consisted of the following:

Exercise 15–1
Stock dividends and per share values
(LO 1)

Common stock, $25 par value, 150,000 shares	
authorized, 60,000 shares issued and outstanding	$1,500,000
Contributed capital in excess of par value, common stock ..	525,000
Total contributed capital	$2,025,000
Retained earnings	675,000
Total stockholders' equity	$2,700,000

On February 5, the stock's market value was $40. On that date, the directors declared a 20% stock dividend distributable on February 28 to the February 15 stockholders of record. The stock's market value was $37 on March 2.

Required

1. Prepare entries to record the dividend declaration and distribution.
2. One stockholder owned 750 shares on February 5. Calculate the per share and total book values of the investor's shares immediately before and after the dividend on February 5.
3. Calculate the total market values of the investor's shares as of February 5 and March 2.

Exercise 15–2
Stock dividends and splits
(LO 1)

On June 30, 19X1, Woodward Corporation's common stock was selling for $31 per share and the following information appeared in the stockholders' equity section of its balance sheet as of that date:

Common stock, $10 par value, 60,000 shares authorized, 25,000 shares issued and outstanding	$250,000
Contributed capital in excess of par value, common stock ..	100,000
Total contributed capital	$350,000
Retained earnings	330,000
Total stockholders' equity	$680,000

Required

1. Assume that the company declares and immediately distributes a 100% stock dividend. The event is recorded by capitalizing the required minimum amount of retained earnings. Answer these questions about the stockholders' equity as it exists after issuing the new shares:
   a. What is the retained earnings balance?
   b. What is the total amount of stockholders' equity?
   c. How many shares are outstanding?

2. Assume that the company implements a two-for-one stock split instead of the stock dividend. Answer these questions about the stockholders' equity as it exists after issuing the new shares:
   a. What is the retained earnings balance?
   b. What is the total amount of stockholders' equity?
   c. How many shares are outstanding?

3. Briefly explain the difference, if any, that an investor would experience if new shares are distributed under a large dividend or a stock split.

Exercise 15–3
Reporting a treasury stock purchase
(LO 2)

On October 10, the stockholders' equity section of the balance sheet for Affiliated Systems, Inc., included this information:

Stockholders' Equity

Contributed capital:	
Common stock, $10 par value, 36,000 shares authorized, issued, and outstanding	$360,000
Contributed capital in excess of par value, common stock .	108,000
Total contributed capital	$468,000
Retained earnings	432,000
Total stockholders' equity	$900,000

On the next day, the corporation purchased 4,500 shares of treasury stock at $30 per share. Present the stockholders' equity section as it would appear immediately after the purchase.

Exercise 15–4
Journal entries for treasury stock transactions
(LO 2)

Use the information in Exercise 15–3 to develop the accountant's journal entries to record these events for Affiliated Systems, Inc.:

1. The purchase of the treasury shares on October 11.

2. The sale of 1,200 treasury shares on November 1 for cash at $36 per share.

3. The sale of all the remaining treasury shares on November 25 for cash at $25 per share.

Exercise 15–5
Journal entries for stock retirements
(LO 2)

This information appeared in the stockholders' equity section of Lamar Corp.'s balance sheet as of December 31, 19X1:

Common stock, $5 par value, 20,000 shares authorized, 7,500 shares issued and outstanding	$ 37,500
Contributed capital in excess of par value, common stock ..	82,500
Total contributed capital	$120,000
Retained earnings	95,000
Total stockholders' equity	$215,000

On January 1, 19X2, the company purchased and retired 400 shares of common stock.

1. Determine the average amount of contributed capital per share of outstanding stock.
2. Prepare the journal entries to record the retirement under the following separate situations:
    a.   The stock was purchased for $10 per share.
    b.   The stock was purchased for $16 per share.
    c.   The stock was purchased for $25 per share.

During 19X1, Burks Merchandise, Inc., sold its interest in a chain of wholesale outlets. This sale took the company out of the wholesaling business completely. The company still operates its retail outlets. Following is a lettered list of sections of an income statement:

Exercise 15–6
Income statement categories
(LO 3)

A. Income from continuing operations
B. Income from operating a discontinued segment
C. Gain or loss from disposing of a discontinued segment
D. Extraordinary gain or loss
E. Cumulative effect of a change in accounting principle

Indicate where each of the nine income-related items for the company would appear on the 19X1 income statement by writing the letter of the appropriate section in the blank beside each item.

		Debit	Credit
___ 1.	Depreciation expense	$262,500	
___ 2.	Gain on sale of wholesale segment (net of tax)		$ 675,000
___ 3.	Loss from operating wholesale segment (net of tax)	555,000	
___ 4.	Salaries expense	540,000	
___ 5.	Sales		2,700,000
___ 6.	Gain on state's condemnation of company property (net of tax)		330,000
___ 7.	Cost of goods sold	1,380,000	
___ 8.	Effect of change from declining-balance to straight-line depreciation (net of tax)		135,000
___ 9.	Income taxes expense	207,000	

Use the data for Burks Merchandise, Inc., in Exercise 15–6 to present the income statement for 19X1.

Exercise 15–7
Income statement presentation
(LO 3)

American Home Company put an asset in service on January 1, 19X1. Its cost was $225,000, its predicted service life was six years, and its expected salvage value was $22,500. The company decided to use double-declining-balance depreciation and recorded these amounts of depreciation expense in the first two years of the asset's life:

Exercise 15–8
Accounting for a change in accounting principle
(LO 3)

$$
\begin{array}{ll}
19X1 \ \dots\dots\dots\dots\dots\dots\dots\dots\dots & \$75,000 \\
19X2 \ \dots\dots\dots\dots\dots\dots\dots\dots\dots & 50,000
\end{array}
$$

The scheduled depreciation expense for 19X3 was $33,250. After consulting with the company's auditors, management decided to change to straight-line depreciation in 19X3, without changing either the predicted service life or salvage value. Under this system, the annual depreciation expense for all years in the asset's life would be $33,750. The company faces a 35% income tax rate.

1. Prepare a table like Illustration 15–5 that deals with this situation.
2. How much depreciation expense will be reported on the company's income statement for this asset in 19X3 and in each of the remaining years of the asset's life?
3. What amount will be reported on the company's 19X3 income statement as the after-tax cumulative effect of the change?

Exercise 15–9
Weighted-average shares
outstanding and earnings per
share
(LO 4)

A company reported $1,350,000 of net income for 19X1. It also declared $195,000 of dividends on preferred stock for the same year. At the beginning of 19X1, the company had 270,000 outstanding shares of common stock. These two events changed the number of outstanding shares during the year:

Apr. 30   Sold 180,000 common shares for cash.
Oct. 31   Purchased 108,000 shares of common stock for the treasury.

a. What is the amount of net income available to the common stockholders?
b. What is the weighted-average number of shares of common stock for the year?
c. What is the earnings per share for the year?

Exercise 15–10
Weighted-average shares
outstanding and earnings per
share
(LO 4)

A company reported $480,000 of net income for 19X1. It also declared $65,000 of dividends on preferred stock for the same year. At the beginning of 19X1, the company had 50,000 outstanding shares of common stock. These three events changed the number of outstanding shares during the year:

June 1   Sold 30,000 common shares for cash.
Aug. 31   Purchased 13,000 shares of common stock for the treasury.
Oct. 1   Completed a three-for-one stock split.

a. What is the amount of net income available to the common stockholders?
b. What is the weighted-average number of shares of common stock for the year?
c. What is the earnings per share for the year?

Exercise 15–11
Computing the price-earnings
ratio
(LO 5)

Use the following information to calculate the price-earnings ratio for each case:

	Earnings per Share	Market Value per Share
a.	$ 10.00	$166.00
b.	9.00	86.00
c.	6.50	90.00
d.	1.50	36.00
e.	36.00	240.00

Exercise 15–12
Identifying corporate capital
structure terms
(LO 6)

Match each of the numbered definitions with the term it best defines. Indicate your answer by writing the letter for the correct term in the blank space next to each description.

A. Common stock equivalent
B. Extraordinary gain or loss
C. Large stock dividend
D. Reverse stock split
E. Small stock dividend
F. Stock split
G. Treasury stock

___ 1. Gain or loss that is reported separate from continuing operations because it is both unusual and infrequent.
___ 2. Stock that was reacquired and is still held by the issuing corporation.
___ 3. Stock dividend that is more than 25% of the corporation's previously outstanding shares.
___ 4. Action by a corporation to call in its stock and replace each share with less than one new share.
___ 5. Convertible or exercisable security the eventual conversion of which is highly probable.
___ 6. Action by a corporation to call in its stock and replace each share with more than one new share.
___ 7. Stock dividend that is 25% or less of the corporation's previously outstanding shares.

PROBLEMS

The balance sheet for Livingstone Corp. reported the following components of stockholders' equity on December 31, 19X1:

Problem 15–1
Treasury stock transactions and stock dividends
(LO 1, 2)

Common stock, $10 par value, 50,000 shares authorized, 20,000 shares issued and outstanding	$200,000
Contributed capital in excess of par value, common stock	30,000
Retained earnings	135,000
Total stockholders' equity	$365,000

The company completed these transactions during 19X2:

Jan. 4 Purchased 2,000 shares of treasury stock at $20.00 cash per share.

Feb. 28 The directors declared a $1.50 per share cash dividend payable on March 31 to the March 10 stockholders of record.

Mar. 31 Paid the dividend declared on February 28.

July 6 Sold 750 of the treasury shares at $24.00 per share.

Aug. 22 Sold 1,250 of the treasury shares at $17.00 per share.

Dec. 5 The directors declared a $1.60 per share cash dividend payable on January 4, 19X3, to the December 20 stockholders of record. They also declared a 20% stock dividend distributable on January 4, 19X3, to the December 20 stockholders of record. The market value of the stock was $25.00 per share.

31 Closed the $194,000 credit balance in the Income Summary account to Retained Earnings.

31 Closed the Cash Dividends Declared and Stock Dividends Declared accounts.

Required

1. Prepare general journal entries to record the transactions and closings for 19X2.
2. Prepare a statement of retained earnings for 19X2.
3. Prepare the stockholders' equity section of the company's balance sheet as of December 31, 19X2.

CHECK FIGURE:
Retained earnings, Dec. 31, 19X2, $169,250

At September 30, the end of the third quarter for Granger Co., Inc., these balances existed in its stockholders' equity accounts:

Problem 15–2
Describing equity changes with journal entries and account balances
(LO 1)

Common stock, $12 par value	$720,000
Contributed capital in excess of par value . . .	180,000
Retained earnings	640,000

Over the next three months, the following journal entries were recorded in the company's equity accounts:

Oct.	2	Cash Dividends Declared	120,000.00	
		Common Dividend Payable		120,000.00
	25	Common Dividend Payable	120,000.00	
		Cash		120,000.00
	31	Stock Dividends Declared	150,000.00	
		Common Stock Dividend Distributable		72,000.00
		Contributed Capital in Excess of Par Value, Common Stock		78,000.00
Nov.	5	Common Stock Dividend Distributable	72,000.00	
		Common Stock, $12 Par Value		72,000.00
Dec.	1	Memo—change the title of the common stock account to reflect the new par value of $4 per share.		
	31	Income Summary	420,000.00	
		Retained Earnings		420,000.00
	31	Retained Earnings	270,000.00	
		Cash Dividends Declared		120,000.00
		Stock Dividends Declared		150,000.00

Required

1. Provide explanations for each of the journal entries.
2. Complete the following table showing the balances of the company's equity accounts (including the dividends declared accounts) at each of the indicated dates:

	Oct. 2	Oct. 25	Oct. 31	Nov. 5	Dec. 1	Dec. 31
Common stock	$_____	$_____	$_____	$_____	$_____	$_____
Stock dividend distributable	_____	_____	_____	_____	_____	_____
Contributed capital in excess of par	_____	_____	_____	_____	_____	_____
Retained earnings	_____	_____	_____	_____	_____	_____
Less:						
Cash dividends declared	_____	_____	_____	_____	_____	_____
Stock dividends declared	_____	_____	_____	_____	_____	_____
Combined balances of equity accounts ..	$_____	$_____	$_____	$_____	$_____	$_____

Problem 15–3
Changes in retained earnings
(LO 1, 2)

The equity sections from the 19X1 and 19X2 balance sheets of TRP Corporation appeared as follows:

Stockholders' Equity
(As of December 31, 19X1)

Common stock, $4 par value, 50,000 shares authorized, 20,000 shares issued and outstanding	$ 80,000
Contributed capital in excess of par value, common stock	60,000
Total contributed capital	$140,000
Retained earnings	160,000
Total stockholders' equity	$300,000

Stockholders' Equity
(As of December 31, 19X2)

Common stock, $4 par value, 50,000 shares authorized, 23,700 shares issued, 1,500 in the treasury	$ 94,800
Contributed capital in excess of par value, common stock	89,600
Total contributed capital	$184,400
Retained earnings ($15,000 restricted)	200,000
Total	$384,400
Less cost of treasury stock	(15,000)
Total stockholders' equity	$369,400

The following events occurred during 19X2:

Jan. 5   A $0.50 per share cash dividend was declared, and the date of record was five days later.

Mar. 20   The treasury stock was purchased.

Apr. 5   A $0.50 per share cash dividend was declared, and the date of record was five days later.

July 5   A $0.50 per share cash dividend was declared, and the date of record was five days later.

     31   A 20% stock dividend was declared when the market value was $12.00 per share.

Aug. 14   The dividend shares were issued.

Oct. 5   A $0.50 per share cash dividend was declared, and the date of record was five days later.

Required

1. How many shares were outstanding on each of the cash dividend dates?
2. How large were each of the four cash dividends?
3. How large was the capitalization of retained earnings for the stock dividend?
4. What was the price per share paid for the treasury stock?
5. How much income did the company achieve during 19X2?

The following table shows the balances from various accounts in the adjusted trial balance for Depew Corp. as of December 31, 19X1:

Problem 15–4
Presenting items in an income statement
(LO 3)

		Debit	Credit
a.	Interest earned		$ 12,000
b.	Depreciation expense, equipment	$ 36,000	
c.	Loss on sale of office equipment	24,750	
d.	Accounts payable		42,000
e.	Other operating expenses	97,500	
f.	Accumulated depreciation, equipment		73,500
g.	Gain from settling a lawsuit		42,000
h.	Cumulative effect of change in accounting principle (pre-tax)	63,000	
i.	Accumulated depreciation, buildings		163,500
j.	Loss from operating a discontinued segment (pre-tax)	19,500	
k.	Gain on early settlement of debt (pre-tax)		28,500
l.	Sales		970,500
m.	Depreciation expense, buildings	54,000	
n.	Correction of overstatement of prior year's sales (pre-tax)	15,000	
o.	Gain on sale of discontinued segment's assets (pre-tax)		33,000
p.	Loss from settling a lawsuit	24,000	
q.	Income taxes expense	?	
r.	Cost of goods sold	487,500	

Required

Answer each of these questions by providing detailed schedules:

1. Assuming that the company's income tax rate is 30%, what are the tax effects and after-tax measures of the items labeled as pre-tax?

2. What is the amount of the company's income from continuing operations before income taxes? What is the amount of the company's income taxes expense? What is the amount of the company's income from continuing operations?

3. What is the amount of after-tax income associated with the discontinued segment?

4. What is the amount of income before extraordinary items and the cumulative effect of the change in principle?

5. What is the amount of net income for the year?

CHECK FIGURE:
Net income, $195,825

On January 1, 19X1, Pohl, Inc., purchased some equipment. Its cost was $600,000 and it was expected to have a salvage value of $30,000 at the end of its five-year useful life. Depreciation was allocated to 19X1, 19X2, and 19X3 with the declining-balance method at twice the straight-line rate. Early in 19X4, the company concluded that changing to the straight-line method would produce more useful financial statements because it would be consistent with the practices of other firms in the industry.

Problem 15–5
Changes in accounting principles
(LO 3)

Required

Preparation component:

1. Do generally accepted accounting principles allow Pohl, Inc., to change depreciation methods in 19X4?

2. Prepare a schedule that shows the amount of depreciation expense allocated to 19X1 through 19X3 under the declining-balance method.

3. Prepare a schedule that shows the amount of depreciation expense that would have been allocated to 19X1 through 19X3 under the straight-line method.

4. Combine the information from your answers to requirements 2 and 3 in a table like Illustration 15–5 that computes the before- and after-tax cumulative effects of the change. The company's income tax rate is 30%. (For simplicity, round your answers to the nearest dollar.)

CHECK FIGURE:
After-tax cumulative effect,
$89,880

5. How should the cumulative effect be reported by the company? Does the cumulative effect increase or decrease net income?

6. How much depreciation expense will be reported on the income statement for 19X4?

Analysis component:

7. Assume that Pohl, Inc., makes the mistake of treating the change in depreciation methods as a change in an accounting estimate. Using your answers from requirements 2, 3, and 4, describe the effect this error would have on the 19X4 financial statements.

Problem 15–6
Earnings per share calculations and presentation
(LO 4)

The income statements for Tennison, Inc., presented the following information when they were first published in 19X2, 19X3, and 19X4:

	19X2	19X3	19X4
Sales	$370,000	$425,000	$412,500
Expenses	232,500	260,000	245,500
Income from continuing operations	$137,500	$165,000	$167,000
Loss on discontinued segment	(52,500)		
Income before extraordinary items	$ 85,000	$165,000	$167,000
Extraordinary gain (loss)		33,000	(70,000)
Net income	$ 85,000	$198,000	$ 97,000

The company also experienced some changes in the number of outstanding shares through the following events:

Outstanding shares on December 31, 19X1	40,000
19X2:	
Treasury stock purchase on April 1	−4,000
Issuance of new shares on June 30	+12,000
10% stock dividend on October 1	+4,800
Outstanding shares on December 31, 19X2	52,800
19X3:	
Issuance of new shares on July 1	+16,000
Treasury stock purchase on November 1	−4,800
Outstanding shares on December 31, 19X3	64,000
19X4:	
Issuance of new shares on August 1	+20,000
Treasury stock purchase on September 1	−4,000
Three-for-one split on October 1	+160,000
Outstanding shares on December 31, 19X4	240,000

Required

Preparation component:

1. Calculate the weighted average of the outstanding common shares as of the end of 19X2.

2. Calculate the 19X2 earnings per share amounts to report on the 19X2 income statement for income from continuing operations, loss on discontinued segment, and net income.

3. Calculate the weighted average of the outstanding common shares as of the end of 19X3.

CHECK FIGURE:
19X3 earnings per share for net income, $3.30

4. Calculate the 19X3 earnings per share amounts to report on the 19X3 income statement for income from continuing operations, the extraordinary gain, and net income.

5. Calculate the weighted average of the outstanding common shares as of the end of 19X4.

6. Calculate the 19X4 earnings per share amounts to report on the 19X4 income statement for income from continuing operations, the extraordinary loss, and net income.

Analysis component:

7. Write a brief explanation of how you would use the earnings per share statistics from requirement 6 to estimate earnings per share for 19X5.

CRITICAL THINKING: ESSAYS, PROBLEMS, AND CASES

Analytical Essays

As of December 31, the balance sheet for Trammel Corporation provided this information about the stockholders' equity:

AE 15–1
(LO 1)

Common stock, $10 par value, 25,000 shares authorized, 15,000 shares issued and outstanding	$150,000	
Contributed capital in excess of par value, common stock . .	75,000	
Retained earnings	250,000	
Total stockholders' equity	$475,000	

The company's board of directors wants to decrease the market value of the company's outstanding stock from its current level of $50 per share by increasing the number of outstanding shares from 15,000 to 30,000. They are considering a choice between a two-for-one stock split and a 100% stock dividend.

Required

Write a short essay describing the difference between the two alternatives in terms of:

1. Their effects on the market value of the stock.
2. How they would be recorded in the accounts.
3. Their effects on the balance sheet.

The bookkeeper for Haywood Corporation, who has almost finished preparing the 19X1 financial statements, has come to you for some advice. This draft of the balance sheet accurately describes the company's stockholders' equity situation:

AE 15–2
(LO 4)

Preferred stock, $80 par value, 5%, cumulative, 5,000 shares authorized, 3,000 shares issued and outstanding	$240,000
Common stock, $1 par value, 25,000 shares authorized, 18,000 shares issued and outstanding	18,000
Contributed capital in excess of par value, common stock	130,000
Retained earnings	62,500
Total stockholders' equity	$450,500

The net income for 19X1 has been correctly measured as $125,000, and the accounts show that no cash dividends were declared on the preferred or common stock. In fact, the only stock transaction that occurred during the year was the sale of 1,500 shares of common stock on May 1, 19X1. The bookkeeper has tentatively calculated earnings per share as follows:

$$\frac{\text{Net income}}{\text{Outstanding common plus preferred as of Dec. 31}} = \frac{\$125,000}{18,000 + 3,000} = \$5.95$$

Required

1. Describe any errors that you find in the calculation of earnings per share and specify the corrections that should be made.
2. Explain how the calculation would be different if the preferred stock is not cumulative and if the additional common shares had been issued through a stock dividend instead of a sale.

Financial Reporting Problems

FRP 15–1
(LO 1, 2)

On January 1, 19X1, Calvon, Inc., had the following balances in its stockholders' equity accounts:

Common stock	$375,000
Contributed capital in excess of par value, common stock ..	75,000
Retained earnings	325,000
Total	$775,000

The company was authorized to issue 50,000 shares but had issued only 12,500 shares as of January 1, 19X1. The par value per share was $30. The common stock had the following book values per share as of December 31:

19X1	$70.00
19X2	30.00
19X3	36.00

At the end of each year, the company paid the following dividends per share:

19X1	$3.50
19X2	1.00
19X3	2.00

On March 1, 19X1, the company declared a 20% stock dividend. The market value of the shares was $40 per share. On August 10, 19X2, the stockholders approved a three-for-one split by increasing the number of authorized shares and reducing the par value per share. On April 5, 19X3, the company purchased 5,000 shares of treasury stock at the price of $50 per share.

Required

Use the preceding facts to find the following information (present your work in appropriate schedules):

1. Determine the par value per share of common stock as of the end of 19X1, 19X2, and 19X3.
2. Determine the number of authorized, issued, and outstanding shares as of the end of 19X1, 19X2, and 19X3.
3. Determine the total par value of the issued shares as of the end of 19X1, 19X2, and 19X3.
4. Determine the balance of contributed capital in excess of par as of the end of 19X1, 19X2, and 19X3.
5. Use the book value per share to determine the total stockholders' equity at the end of 19X1, 19X2, and 19X3.
6. Determine the total amount of retained earnings as of the end of 19X1, 19X2, and 19X3.
7. Use the answer to requirement 6 and information about the dividends to determine the amount of net income reported in 19X1, 19X2, and 19X3.

Finally, use the information to complete this table:

	1/1/X1	12/31/X1	12/31/X2	12/31/X3
Common stock:				
Par value per share	____	____	____	____
Authorized shares	____	____	____	____
Issued shares	____	____	____	____
Treasury shares	____	____	____	____
Outstanding shares	____	____	____	____
Account balances:				
Common stock	____	____	____	____
Contributed capital in				
excess of par	____	____	____	____
Retained earnings	____	____	____	____
Total	____	____	____	____
Less treasury stock	____	____	____	____
Total stockholders' equity	____	____	____	____

Over the last three years, Jarman, Inc., has experienced the following income results (all numbers are rounded to the nearest thousand dollars):

FRP 15–2
(LO 3)

	19X1	19X2	19X3
Revenues	$27,500	$29,750	$36,500
Expenses	(17,500)	(19,750)	(19,250)
Gains	8,000	6,000	0
Losses	(3,000)	(4,750)	(9,750)
Net income	$15,000	$11,250	$ 7,500

Part 1

Use the information to develop a general prediction of the company's net income for 19X4.

Part 2

A closer analysis of the information shows that the company discontinued a segment of its operations in 19X3. The company's accountant has determined that the discontinued segment produced the following amounts of income:

	19X1	19X2	19X3
Revenues	$17,500	$6,500	$4,000
Expenses	(12,500)	(12,500)	(10,000)
Gains		1,000	
Losses	(3,000)	(3,750)	(5,250)
Loss on disposal of segment assets			(3,000)

Use the information to calculate the company's income without the discontinued segment and then develop a general prediction of the company's net income for 19X4.

Part 3

A more in-depth analysis of the company's activity reveals that the company experienced these extraordinary items during the three years when it retired some of its debts before their scheduled maturity dates:

	19X1	19X2	19X3
Extraordinary gain	$5,500	$5,000	
Extraordinary loss			$(4,250)

Use the information to calculate the company's income from continuing operations and to develop a general prediction of the company's net income for 19X4.

The financial statements and footnotes from Southwest Airlines Co.'s 1994 annual report are presented in Appendix E at the end of the book. Use that information to answer the following questions:

**Financial Statement
Analysis Case**

(LO 1, 2, 3, 4)

1. Does Southwest Airlines have a simple or complex capital structure?
2. What was Southwest Airlines's earnings per share for income before any cumulative effect of accounting changes in 1994? How does this figure compare with the results for 1993?
3. What was the dollar amount of cash dividends declared during 1994?
4. What was the dollar amount of cash dividends paid during 1994? How does this number compare with the dividends declared?
5. What is the par value of the common stock?
6. How many shares of common stock were outstanding at the end of 1994?
7. Does Southwest Airlines own shares of treasury stock?
8. Did Southwest Airlines have any extraordinary gains or losses during 1994?
9. Did Southwest Airlines have any gains or losses on the disposal of a business segment during 1994?

Ethical Issues Essay   Review the As a Matter of Ethics case on page 538 and discuss the ethical implications of the directors' tentative decision to avoid announcing Falcon Corporation's new government contract. What actions would you take if you were the financial vice president?

CONCEPT TESTER

Test your understanding of the concepts introduced in this chapter by completing the following crossword puzzle.

Across Clues

2. Three words; the calling in of stock to replace each share with less than one new share.
4. Two words; a distribution of shares to stockholders without receiving anything in return.
5. Two words; securities the assumed conversion of which decreases earnings per share.
7. Two words; stock that was reacquired and is still held by the issuing corporation.
8. Two words; a gain that is both infrequent and unusual.

Down Clues

1. Two words; replacing each share of a corporation's stock with more than one new share.
3. Three words; the amount of income earned by each share of a corporation's stock.
6. Two words; a gain that is not expected to occur again, given the environment of the business.

ANSWERS TO PROGRESS CHECKS

15–1 *c*

15–2 A small stock dividend is 25% or less of the previous oustanding shares. A large stock dividend is greater than 25%.

15–3 Retained earnings equal to the market value of the distributable shares should be capitalized.

15–4 *b*

15–5 No. The shares are an investment for Southern Co. and issued outstanding shares for Northern Corp.

15–6 Treasury stock does not affect the number of both authorized and issued shares. It reduces the amount of outstanding shares.

15–7 *a*

15–8 *b*

15–9 The four major sections are discontinued segments, extraordinary items, cumulative effects of changes in accounting principles, and earnings per share.

15–10 *c*

15–11 *a*

Weighted average shares: $(25,000 \times 6/12) + (20,000 \times 6/12) = 22,500$

Earnings per share: $(\$250,000 - \$70,000)/22,500 = \$8.00$

15–12 The number of shares previously outstanding are retroactively restated to reflect the stock split or stock dividend as if it occurred at the beginning of the year.

15–13 The two sets are primary earnings per share and fully diluted earnings per share.

15–14 $\$34.00/\$4.25 = \$8.00$

15–15 The company with the higher PE ratio of 10.

Reporting and Using Cash Flows in Decision Making

*F*inancial news reports indicate that Hollywood studios and other corporations in the entertainment industries have been battling to take over television studios. In 1994, for example, *The Wall Street Journal* described a widespread rumor that The Walt Disney Company considered bidding to acquire NBC. Supposedly, the initial offer being considered was $5 billion. Why might Disney have been interested? Cash flow! The networks' libraries of TV episodes are considered to be major prizes in winning acquisitions. Episodes of "Home Improvement," a successful sitcom owned by The Walt Disney Company, are selling for $3.4 million an episode, and Paramount Pictures' production of "Seinfeld" is expected to sell for $2 to $3 million per episode! (*The Wall Street Journal*, Sept. 9, 1994, p. R4)

As the following excerpts from Disney's annual reports show, the company's cash position declined substantially from 1991 through 1994. Under these circumstances, management must pay particular attention to cash inflows and outflows.

THE WALT DISNEY COMPANY—CONSOLIDATED STATEMENTS OF CASH FLOW
(in millions)

Year ended September 30	1994	1993	1992	1991
Increase (Decrease) in Cash and Cash Equivalents ...	$(176.1)	$(401.8)	$(121.3)	$ 66.3
Cash and Cash Equivalents, Beginning of Year	363.0	764.8	886.1	819.8
Cash and Cash Equivalents, End of Year	$ 186.9	$ 363.0	$ 764.8	$886.1

LEARNING OBJECTIVES

After studying Chapter 16, you should be able to:

1. **Explain why cash flow information is important to decision making and describe the information in a statement of cash flows and the methods used to disclose noncash investing and financing activities.**

2. **Calculate cash inflows and outflows by inspecting the noncash account balances and prepare a statement of cash flows using the direct method.**

3. **Calculate the net cash provided or used by operating activities according to the indirect method and prepare the statement of cash flows.**

4. **Prepare a working paper for a statement of cash flows so that the net cash flow from operating activities is calculated by the indirect method.**

5. **Define or explain the words or phrases listed in the chapter glossary.**

Up to this point in your study of accounting, profitability may have seemed to be the sole focus of business managers. Profits certainly are important to business success. However, a business cannot achieve or maintain profitability without carefully managing its cash. Cash is the lifeblood of a business enterprise. In a sense, cash is the fuel that keeps a business moving forward.

Managers and external parties such as investors and creditors pay close attention to a company's cash position and the events and transactions causing that position to change. Information about these events and transactions is reported in a financial statement called the **statement of cash flows.** By studying this chapter, you will learn how to prepare and interpret a statement of cash flows. You will also begin to appreciate the importance of cash flow information as the basis for projecting future cash flows and making a variety of decisions.

WHY CASH FLOW INFORMATION IS IMPORTANT

LO 1
Explain why cash flow information is important to decision making and describe the information in a statement of cash flows and the methods used to disclose noncash investing and financing

Information about cash flows can influence decision makers in many ways. For example, if a company's regular operations bring in more cash than they use, investors will value the company higher than if property and equipment must be sold to finance operations. Information about cash flows can help creditors decide whether a company will have enough cash to pay its existing debts as they mature. And, investors, creditors, managers, and other users of financial statements use cash flow information to evaluate a company's ability to meet unexpected obligations. Cash flow information is used by decision makers outside as well as inside the firm to evaluate a company's ability to take advantage of new business opportunities that may arise. Managers within a company use cash flow information to plan day-to-day operating activities and make long-term investment decisions.

An example of how careful analysis and management of cash flows can lead to improved financial stability is **R. H. Macy & Company's** dramatic turn-around. The company obtained temporary protection from the bankruptcy court in January 1992 and desperately needed to improve its cash flows. Management did so by engaging in aggressive cost-cutting measures. As a result of this effort, Macy's cash inflow rose to $210 million in its fiscal year ended July 1993 from a negative cash flow of $38.9 million in fiscal 1992. This improvement allowed Macy's to meet its obligations and probably influenced its combination with **Federated Department Stores.** [1]

---

[1] Stephanie Strom, "Cost Curbs Help Macy's Cut Losses," *The New York Times,* October 29, 1993, Business section, p. 1.

The story of **W. T. Grant Co.** is a classic example of why cash flow information should be considered in predicting a firm's future stability and performance. From 1970 to 1973, Grant was reporting net income of more than $40 million per year. At the same time, it was experiencing an alarming decrease in cash provided by operations. Net cash *outflow* exceeded $90 million by 1973.[2] In spite of its earnings performance, Grant went bankrupt within a few years.

The W. T. Grant investors who relied solely on earnings per share figures in the early 1970s were unpleasantly surprised. In more recent years, investors generally have learned to evaluate cash flows as well as income statement and balance sheet information as they make their investment decisions.[3]

The importance of cash flow information to decision makers has directly influenced the thinking of accounting authorities. For example, the FASB's objectives of financial reporting clearly reflect the importance of cash flow information. The FASB stated that financial statements should include information about:

- How a business obtains and spends cash.
- Its borrowing and repayment activities.
- The sale and repurchase of its ownership securities.
- Dividend payments and other distributions to its owners.
- Other factors affecting a company's liquidity or solvency.[4]

To accomplish these objectives, a financial statement is needed to summarize, classify, and report the periodic cash inflows and outflows of a business. This information is provided in a statement of cash flows.

STATEMENT OF CASH FLOWS

In November 1987, the FASB issued *Statement of Financial Accounting Standards No. 95,* "Statement of Cash Flows." This standard requires businesses to include a statement of cash flows in all financial reports that contain both a balance sheet and an income statement. The purpose of this statement is to present information about a company's cash receipts and disbursements during the reporting period.

Illustration 16–1 is a diagram of the information reported in a statement of cash flows. The illustration shows three categories of cash flows: cash flows from operating activities, cash flows from investing activities, and cash flows from financing activities. Both inflows and outflows are included within each category. Because all cash inflows and outflows are reported, the statement reconciles the beginning-of-period and end-of-period balances of cash plus cash equivalents.

Direct Method of Presenting Cash Flows from Operating Activities

When preparing a statement of cash flows, you can calculate the net cash provided (or used) by operating activities two different ways. One is the **direct method of calculating net cash provided (or used) by operating activities.** The other is the in-

---

[2]James Largay and Clyde Stickney, "Cash Flow, Ratio Analysis and the W. T. Grant Company Bankruptcy," *Financial Analysts Journal,* July–August 1980, pp. 51–56.

[3]Marc J. Epstein and Moses L. Pava, "How Useful Is the Statement of Cash Flows," *Management Accounting,* July 1992.

[4]FASB, *Statement of Financial Accounting Concepts No. 1,* "Objectives of Financial Reporting by Business Enterprises" (Norwalk, CT, 1978), par. 49.

direct method. When using the direct method, you separately list each major class of operating cash receipts (for example, cash received from customers) and each major class of cash payments (such as payments for merchandise). Then, you subtract the payments from the receipts to determine the net cash provided (or used) by operating activities.

Indirect Method of Presenting Cash Flows from Operating Activities

The **indirect method of calculating net cash provided (or used) by operating activities** is not as informative as the direct method. The indirect method is not as informative because it does not disclose the individual categories of cash inflows and outflows from operating activities. Instead, the indirect method discloses only the net cash provided (or used) by operating activities.

When using the indirect method, list net income first. Next, adjust it for items that are necessary to reconcile net income to the net cash provided (or used) by operating activities. For example, in the calculation of net income, we subtract depreciation expense. However, depreciation expense does not involve a current cash payment. Therefore, add depreciation expense back to net income in the process of reconciling net income to the net cash provided (or used) by operating activities.

The direct method is most informative and is the method that the FASB recommends. However, most companies use the indirect method in spite of the FASB's recommendation. By learning the direct method first, you will find the indirect method easier to understand. Also, managers use the direct method to predict future cash requirements and cash availability. Thus, we explain the direct method next.

The Format of the Statement of Cash Flows (Direct Method)

Illustration 16–2 shows the statement of cash flows for Grover Company. Notice that the major classes of cash inflows and cash outflows are listed separately in the operating activities section of the statement. This is the format of the direct method. The operating cash outflows are subtracted from the operating cash inflows to determine the net cash provided (or used) by operating activities.

Illustration 16-1 Categories of Information in the Statement of Cash Flows

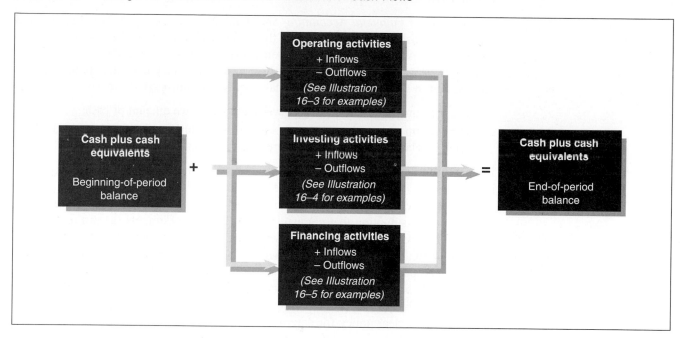

Illustration 16-2
Statement of Cash Flows
(Direct Method)

GROVER COMPANY
Statement of Cash Flows
For Year Ended December 31, 19X2

Cash flows from operating activities:		
Cash received from customers	$570,000	
Cash paid for merchandise	(319,000)	
Cash paid for wages and other operating expenses . .	(218,000)	
Cash paid for interest	(8,000)	
Cash paid for taxes	(5,000)	
Net cash provided by operating activities		$ 20,000
Cash flows from investing activities:		
Cash received from sale of plant assets	$ 12,000	
Cash paid for purchase of plant assets	(10,000)	
Net cash provided by investing activities		2,000
Cash flows from financing activities:		
Cash received from issuing stock	$ 15,000	
Cash paid to retire bonds	(18,000)	
Cash paid for dividends	(14,000)	
Net cash used in financing activities		(17,000)
Net increase in cash		$ 5,000
Cash balance at beginning of 19X2		12,000
Cash balance at end of 19X2		$ 17,000

Also observe in Illustration 16–2 the other two categories of cash flows reported on the statement of cash flows. In both categories—investing activities and financing activities—we subtract the cash outflows from the cash inflows to determine the net cash provided (or used).

Compare the statement in Illustration 16–2 with the chart in Illustration 16–1. Notice that the beginning and ending balances are called *cash plus cash equivalents* in Illustration 16–1. However, in Illustration 16–2, the beginning and ending balances refer only to *cash*. The balances in Illustration 16–2 are called *cash* because Grover Company does not own any cash equivalents.

Cash and Cash Equivalents

In *Statement of Financial Accounting Standards No. 95,* the FASB concluded that a statement of cash flows should explain the difference between the beginning and ending balances of cash and cash equivalents. Prior to this new standard, cash equivalents were generally understood to be short-term, temporary investments of cash. As you learned in Chapter 7, however, a cash equivalent must satisfy these two criteria:

1. The investment must be readily convertible to a known amount of cash.
2. The investment must be sufficiently close to its maturity date so that its market value is relatively insensitive to interest rate changes.

In general, only investments purchased within three months of their maturity dates satisfy these criteria.[5]

The idea of classifying short-term, highly liquid investments as cash equivalents is based on the assumption that companies make these investments to earn a return on idle cash balances. Sometimes, however, items that meet the criteria of cash equivalents are not held as temporary investments of idle cash balances. For example, an investment company that specializes in the purchase and sale of securities may buy cash equivalents as part of its investing strategy. Companies that have such investments are allowed to exclude them from the cash equivalents category. However, the companies must develop a clear policy for determining which items to include and which to exclude. These policies must be disclosed in the footnotes to the financial statements and must be followed consistently from period to period.

CLASSIFYING CASH TRANSACTIONS

On a statement of cash flows, cash and cash equivalents are treated as a single item. In other words, the statement reports the changes in cash plus cash equivalents. Therefore, cash payments to purchase cash equivalents and cash receipts from selling cash equivalents do not appear on the statement. All other cash receipts and payments are classified and reported on the statement as operating, investing, or financing activities. Within each category, individual cash receipts and payments are summarized in a manner that clearly describes the general nature of the company's cash transactions. Then, the summarized cash receipts and payments within each category are netted against each other. A category provides a net cash inflow if the receipts in the category exceed the payments. And, if the payments in a category exceed the receipts, the category is a net cash outflow during the period.

Operating Activities

Look at the cash flows classified as **operating activities** in Illustration 16–2. Notice that operating activities generally include transactions that relate to the calculation of net income. However, some income statement items are not related to operating activities. We discuss these items later.

As disclosed in a statement of cash flows, operating activities involve the production or purchase of merchandise and the sale of goods and services to customers. Operating activities also include expenditures that relate to administering the business. In fact, cash flows from operating activities include all cash flows from transactions that are not defined as investing or financing activities. Illustration 16–3 shows typical cash inflows and outflows from operating activities.

---

[5]FASB, *Accounting Standards—Current Text* (Norwalk, CT, 1995), sec. C25.106. First published in *Statement of Financial Accounting Standards No. 95,* par. 8.

Cash Inflows	**Cash Outflows**
Cash sales to customers.	Payments to employees for salaries and wages.
Cash collections from credit customers.	Payments to suppliers of goods and services.
Receipts of cash dividends from stock investments in other entities.	Payments to government agencies for taxes, fines, and penalties.
Receipts of interest payments.	Interest payments, net of amounts capitalized.
Refunds from suppliers.	Cash refunds to customers.
Cash collected from a lawsuit.	Contributions to charities.

Illustration 16–3
Cash Flows from Operating Activities

Cash Inflows	**Cash Outflows**
Proceeds from selling productive assets (for example, land, buildings, equipment, natural resources, and intangible assets).	Payments to purchase property, plant, and equipment or other productive assets (excluding merchandise inventory).
Proceeds from selling investments in the equity securities of other companies.	Payments to acquire equity securities of other companies.
Proceeds from selling investments in the debt securities of other entities, except cash equivalents.	Payments to acquire debt securities of other entities, except cash equivalents.
Proceeds from collecting the principal amount of loans.	Payments in the form of loans made to other parties.
Proceeds from the sale (discounting) of loans made by the enterprise.	

Illustration 16–4
Cash Flows from Investing Activities

Investing Activities

Transactions that involve making and collecting loans or that involve purchasing and selling plant assets, other productive assets, or investments (other than cash equivalents) are called **investing activities.** Usually, investing activities involve the purchase or sale of assets classified on the balance sheet as plant and equipment, intangible assets, or long-term investments. However, the purchase and sale of short-term investments other than cash equivalents are also investing activities. Illustration 16–4 shows examples of cash flows from investing activities.

The fourth type of receipt listed in Illustration 16–4 involves proceeds from collecting the principal amount of loans. Regarding this item, carefully examine any cash receipts that relate to notes receivable. If the notes resulted from sales to customers, classify the cash receipts as operating activities. Use this classification even if the notes are long-term notes. But, if a company loans money to other parties, classify the cash receipts from collecting the principal of the loans as inflows from investing activities. Nevertheless, the FASB concluded that collections of interest are not investing activities. Instead, they are reported as operating activities.

Illustration 16-5
Cash Flows from Financing
Activities

Cash Inflows	**Cash Outflows**
Proceeds from issuing equity securities (e.g., common and preferred stock).	Payments of dividends and other distributions to owners.
	Payments to purchase treasury stock.
Proceeds from issuing bonds and notes payable.	Repayments of cash loans.
Proceeds from other short- or long-term borrowing transactions.	Payments of the principal amounts involved in long-term credit arrangements.

Financing Activities

The **financing activities** of a business include transactions with its owners and transactions with its creditors to borrow money or to repay the principal amounts of loans. Financing activities include borrowing and repaying both short-term loans and long-term debt. However, cash payments to settle credit purchases of merchandise, whether on account or by note, are operating activities. Payments of interest expense are also operating activities. Illustration 16–5 shows examples of cash flows from financing activities.

NONCASH INVESTING AND FINANCING ACTIVITIES

Some important investing and financing activities do not involve cash receipts or payments during the current period. For example, a company might purchase land and buildings and finance 100% of the purchase by giving a long-term note payable. Although this transaction clearly involves both investing and financing activities, we do not report it in the current period's statement of cash flows because it does not involve a cash inflow or outflow.

Other investing and financing activities may involve some cash receipt or payment as well as giving or receiving other types of consideration. For example, suppose you purchase machinery for $12,000 by paying cash of $5,000 and trading in old machinery that has a market value of $7,000. In this case, the statement of cash flows reports only the $5,000 cash outflow for the purchase of machinery. As a result, this $12,000 investing transaction is only partially described in the statement of cash flows.

The noncash portions of investing and financing activities should *not* be reported in the statement of cash flows. However, they are important events that should be disclosed. To accomplish this disclosure, a company may describe its noncash investing and financing activities in a footnote or a separate schedule. Illustration 16–6 shows an example of how a company might disclose its noncash investing and financing activities.

In Illustration 16–6, notice that the last item describes an exchange of machinery including both the cash and noncash aspects of this transaction. The $5,000 cash payment is reported in Decco Company's statement of cash flows as an investing activity. Nevertheless, the description of noncash investing and financing activities includes both the cash and noncash aspects of the transaction.

Examples of transactions that must be disclosed as noncash investing and financing activities include the following:

- The retirement of debt securities by issuing equity securities.
- The conversion of preferred stock to common stock.
- The leasing of assets in a transaction that qualifies as a capital lease.
- The purchase of long-term assets by issuing a note payable to the seller.
- The exchange of a noncash asset for other noncash assets.
- The purchase of noncash assets by issuing equity or debt securities.

The company issued 1,000 shares of common stock for the purchase of land and buildings with fair values of $5,000 and $15,000, respectively.

The company entered into a capital lease obligation of $12,000 for new computer equipment.

The company exchanged old machinery with a fair value of $7,000 and a book value of $8,000 for new machinery valued at $12,000. The balance of $5,000 was paid in cash.

Illustration 16–6
Decco Company—Footnote Describing Noncash Investing and Financing Activities

Progress Check
(Answers to Progress Checks are provided at the end of the chapter.)

16–1   Does a statement of cash flows disclose payments of cash to purchase cash equivalents? Does it disclose receipts of cash from the liquidation of cash equivalents?

16–2   What are the categories of cash flows reported separately on the statement of cash flows?

16–3   Concerning the direct and indirect methods of presenting cash flows from operating activities, which is most informative? Which is used most often in practice?

16–4   Identify the category for each of the following cash flow activities: *(a)* purchase of equipment for cash; *(b)* payment of wages; *(c)* sale of common stock; *(d)* receipt of cash dividends on stock investment; *(e)* collection from customers; *(f)* issuance of bonds for cash.

The information you need to prepare a statement of cash flows comes from a variety of sources. These include comparative balance sheets at the beginning and the end of the accounting period, an income statement for the period, and a careful analysis of each noncash balance sheet account in the general ledger. However, because cash inflows and cash outflows are to be reported, you might wonder why we do not focus our attention on the Cash account. For the moment, we should at least consider this approach.

PREPARING A STATEMENT OF CASH FLOWS

LO 2
Calculate cash inflows and outflows by inspecting the noncash account balances and prepare a statement of cash flows using the direct method.

Analyzing the Cash Account

All of a company's cash receipts and cash payments are recorded in the Cash account in the General Ledger. Therefore, the Cash account would seem to be the logical place to look for information about cash flows from operating, investing, and financing activities. To demonstrate, review this summarized Cash account of Grover Company:

Summarized Cash Account

Balance, 12/31/X1	12,000		
Receipts from customers	570,000	Payments for merchandise	319,000
Proceeds from sale of plant assets	12,000	Payments for wages and other operating expenses	218,000
Proceeds from stock issuance	15,000	Interest payments	8,000
		Tax payments	5,000
		Payments for purchase of plant assets	10,000
		Payments to retire bonds	18,000
		Dividend payments	14,000
Balance, 12/31/X2	17,000		

In this account, the individual cash transactions are already summarized in terms of major types of receipts and payments. For example, the account has only one debit entry for the total receipts from all customers. All that remains is to determine whether each type of cash inflow or outflow is an operating, investing, or financing

Illustration 16-7   Why an Analysis of the Noncash Accounts Explains the Change in Cash

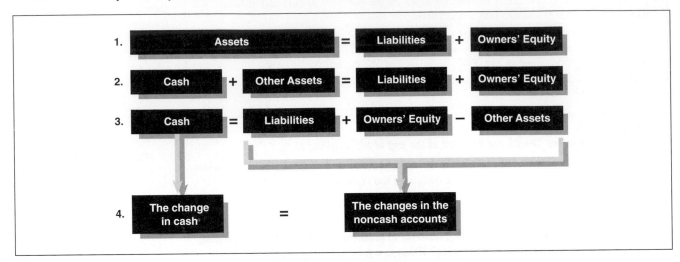

activity and then place it in its proper category on the statement of cash flows. The completed statement of cash flows appears in Illustration 16–2 on page 577.

While an analysis of the Cash account may appear to be an easy way to prepare a statement of cash flows, it has two serious drawbacks. First, most companies have so many individual cash receipts and disbursements that it is not practical to review them all. Imagine what a problem this analysis would present for IBM, General Motors, Kodak, or Exxon, or even for a relatively small business. Second, the Cash account usually does not contain a description of each cash transaction. Therefore, even though the Cash account shows the amount of each debit and credit, you generally cannot determine the type of transaction by looking at the Cash account. Thus, the Cash account does not readily provide the information you need to prepare a statement of cash flows. To obtain the necessary information, you must analyze the changes in the noncash accounts.

Analyzing Noncash Accounts to Determine Cash Flows

When a company records cash inflows and outflows with debits and credits to the Cash account, it also records credits and debits in other accounts. Some of these accounts are balance sheet accounts. Others are revenue and expense accounts that are closed to Retained Earnings, a balance sheet account. As a result, all cash transactions eventually affect noncash balance sheet accounts. Therefore, we can determine the nature of the cash inflows and outflows by examining the changes in the noncash balance sheet accounts. Illustration 16–7 shows this important relationship between the Cash account and the noncash balance sheet accounts.

In Illustration 16–7, notice that the balance sheet equation labeled (1) is expanded in (2) so that cash is separated from the other assets. Then, the equation is rearranged in (3) so that cash is set equal to the sum of the liability and equity accounts less the noncash asset accounts. The illustration then points out in (4) that changes in one side of the equation (cash) must be equal to the changes in the other side (noncash accounts). Equation (4) shows that you can fully explain the changes in cash by analyzing the changes in liabilities, owners' equity, and noncash assets.

This overall process has another advantage. The examination of each noncash account also identifies any noncash investing and financing activities that occurred during the period. As you learned earlier, these noncash items must be disclosed, but not on the statement of cash flows.

When beginning to analyze the changes in the noncash balance sheet accounts, recall that Retained Earnings is affected by revenues, expenses, and dividend declara-

Illustration 16–8   Analysis of the Noncash Accounts Explains the Change in Cash

Income Statement Items	Related Balance Sheet Accounts	Possible Cash Flow Effects
Sales	Accounts receivable	Cash receipts from customers
Cost of goods sold	Merchandise inventory, accounts payable	Cash payments to suppliers
Depreciation expense	Accumulated depreciation	None
Operating expense	Prepaid expenses, accrued liabilities	Cash payments for operating expenses
Gain or loss on sale of plant assets	Plant assets, accumulated depreciation, notes receivable	Cash receipts from sale of plant assets
Gain or loss on retirement of bonds payable	Bonds payable, premium or discount on bonds payable	Cash payments for retirement of bonds

tions. Therefore, look at the income statement accounts to help explain the change in Retained Earnings. In fact, the income statement accounts provide important information that relates to the changes in several balance sheet accounts.

Illustration 16–8 summarizes some of these relationships between income statement accounts, balance sheet accounts, and possible cash flows. For example, to determine the cash receipts from customers during a period, adjust the amount of sales revenue for the increase or decrease in Accounts Receivable.[6] If the Accounts Receivable balance did not change, the cash collected from customers is equal to sales revenue. On the other hand, if the Accounts Receivable balance decreased, cash collections must have been equal to sales revenue *plus* the reduction in Accounts Receivable. And, if the Accounts Receivable balance increased, the cash collected from customers must have been equal to Sales *less* the increase in Accounts Receivable.

By analyzing all noncash balance sheet accounts and related income statement accounts in this fashion, you can obtain the necessary information for a statement of cash flows. Next, we illustrate this process by examining the noncash accounts of Grover Company.

---

[6]This introductory explanation assumes that there is no bad debts expense. However, if bad debts occur and are written off directly to Accounts Receivable, the change in the Accounts Receivable balance will be due in part to the write-off. The remaining change results from credit sales and from cash receipts. This chapter does not discuss the allowance method of accounting for bad debts since it would make the analysis unnecessarily complex at this time.

**GROVER
COMPANY—A
COMPREHENSIVE
EXAMPLE**

Grover Company's December 31, 19X1, and 19X2, balance sheets and its 19X2 income statement are presented in Illustration 16–9. Our objective is to prepare a statement of cash flows that explains the $5,000 increase in cash, based on these financial statements and this additional information about the 19X2 transactions:

a. All accounts payable balances resulted from merchandise purchases.

b. Plant assets that cost $70,000 were purchased by paying $10,000 cash and issuing $60,000 of bonds payable to the seller.

c. Plant assets with an original cost of $30,000 and accumulated depreciation of $12,000 were sold for $12,000 cash. The result was a $6,000 loss.

d. The proceeds from issuing 3,000 shares of common stock were $15,000.

e. The $16,000 gain on the retirement of bonds resulted from paying $18,000 to retire bonds that had a book value of $34,000.

f. Cash dividends of $14,000 were declared and paid.

Operating Activities

We begin the analysis by calculating the cash flows from operating activities. In general, this process involves adjusting the income statement items that relate to operating activities for changes in their related balance sheet accounts.

Cash Received from Customers. The calculation of cash receipts from customers begins with sales revenue. If all sales are for cash, the amount of cash received from customers is equal to sales. However, when sales are on account, you must adjust the amount of sales revenue for the change in Accounts Receivable.

In Illustration 16–9, look at the Accounts Receivable balances on December 31, 19X1, and 19X2. The beginning balance was $40,000, and the ending balance was $60,000. The income statement shows that sales revenue was $590,000. With this information, you can reconstruct the Accounts Receivable account and determine the amount of cash received from customers, as follows:

Accounts Receivable			
Balance, 12/31/X1	40,000		
Sales, 19X2	590,000	Collections =	**570,000**
Balance, 12/31/X2	60,000		

This account shows that the balance of Accounts Receivable increased from $40,000 to $60,000. It also shows that cash receipts from customers are $570,000, which is equal to sales of $590,000 plus the $40,000 beginning balance less the $60,000 ending balance. This calculation can be restated in more general terms like this:

Cash received from customers = Sales − Increase in accounts receivable

And, if the balance of Accounts Receivable decreases, the calculation is:

Cash received from customers = Sales + Decrease in accounts receivable

Now turn back to Illustration 16–2 on page 577. Note that the $570,000 of cash Grover Company received from customers appears on the statement of cash flows as a cash inflow from operating activities.

Cash Payments for Merchandise. The calculation of cash payments for merchandise begins with cost of goods sold and merchandise inventory. For a moment, suppose that all merchandise purchases are for cash and that the ending balance of Merchandise Inventory is unchanged from the beginning balance. In this case, the total cash paid for merchandise equals the cost of goods sold. However, this case is not

Illustration 16-9
Financial Statements

GROVER COMPANY
Balance Sheet
December 31, 19X2 and 19X1

	19X2		19X1	
Assets				
Current assets:				
Cash		$ 17,000		$ 12,000
Accounts receivable		60,000		40,000
Merchandise inventory		84,000		70,000
Prepaid expenses		6,000		4,000
Total current assets		$167,000		$126,000
Long-term assets:				
Plant assets	$250,000		$210,000	
Less accumulated depreciation	60,000	190,000	48,000	162,000
Total assets		$357,000		$288,000
Liabilities				
Current liabilities:				
Accounts payable		$ 35,000		$ 40,000
Interest payable		3,000		4,000
Income taxes payable		22,000		12,000
Total current liabilities		$ 60,000		$ 56,000
Long-term liabilities:				
Bonds payable		90,000		64,000
Total liabilities		$150,000		$120,000
Stockholders' Equity				
Contributed capital:				
Common stock, $5 par value	$ 95,000		$ 80,000	
Retained earnings	112,000		88,000	
Total stockholders' equity		207,000		168,000
Total liabilities and stockholders' equity		$357,000		$288,000

GROVER COMPANY
Income Statement
For Year Ended December 31, 19X2

Sales		$590,000
Cost of goods sold	$300,000	
Wages and other operating expenses ..	216,000	
Interest expense	7,000	
Income taxes expense	15,000	
Depreciation expense	24,000	(562,000)
Loss on sale of plant assets		(6,000)
Gain on retirement of debt		16,000
Net income		$ 38,000

typical. Usually, you expect some change in a company's Merchandise Inventory balance during a period. Also, purchases of merchandise usually are made on account, causing some change in the Accounts Payable balance.

When the balances of Merchandise Inventory and Accounts Payable change, you must adjust cost of goods sold for the changes in these accounts to determine the cash payments for merchandise. This adjustment has two steps. First, combine the change in the balance of Merchandise Inventory with cost of goods sold to determine the cost of purchases during the period. Second, combine the change in the balance of Accounts Payable with the cost of purchases to determine the total cash payments to suppliers of merchandise.

Consider again the Grover Company example. Begin by combining the reported amount of cost of goods sold ($300,000) with the Merchandise Inventory beginning balance ($70,000) and with the ending balance ($84,000) to determine the amount that was purchased during the period. To accomplish this, reconstruct the Merchandise Inventory account as follows:

Merchandise Inventory

Balance, 12/31/X1	70,000		
Purchases =	**314,000**	Cost of goods sold	300,000
Balance, 12/31/X2	84,000		

This account shows that we add the $14,000 increase in merchandise inventory to cost of goods sold of $300,000 to get purchases of $314,000.

To determine the cash paid for merchandise, you adjust purchases for the change in accounts payable. This can be done by reconstructing the Accounts Payable account as follows:

Accounts Payable

		Balance, 12/31/X1	40,000
Payments =	**319,000**	Purchases	314,000
		Balance, 12/31/X2	35,000

In this account, purchases of $314,000 plus a beginning balance of $40,000 less the ending balance of $35,000 equals cash payments of $319,000. In other words, purchases of $314,000 plus the $5,000 decrease in accounts payable equals cash payments of $319,000.

To summarize the adjustments to cost of goods sold that are necessary to calculate cash payments for merchandise:

$$\text{Purchases} = \text{Cost of goods sold} \begin{bmatrix} + \text{ Increase in merchandise inventory} \\ or \\ - \text{ Decrease in merchandise inventory} \end{bmatrix}$$

And,

$$\text{Cash payments for merchandise} = \text{Purchases} \begin{bmatrix} + \text{ Decrease in accounts payable} \\ or \\ - \text{ Increase in accounts payable} \end{bmatrix}$$

Now, look at Illustration 16–2 on page 577. Notice that Grover Company's payments of $319,000 for merchandise are reported on the statement of cash flows as a cash outflow for operating activities.

Cash Payments for Wages and Other Operating Expenses. Grover Company's income statement shows wages and other operating expenses of $216,000 (see Illustration 16–9 on page 585). To determine the amount of cash paid during the period for wages and other operating expenses, we need to combine this amount with the changes in any related balance sheet accounts. In Grover Company's beginning and ending balance sheets in Illustration 16–9, you must look for prepaid expenses and any accrued liabilities that relate to wages and other operating expenses. In this example, the balance sheets show that Grover Company has prepaid expenses but does not have any accrued liabilities. Thus, the adjustment to the expense item is limited to the change in prepaid expenses. The amount of the adjustment can be determined by assuming that all cash payments of wages and other operating expenses were originally debited to Prepaid Expenses. With this assumption, we can reconstruct the Prepaid Expenses account as follows:

Prepaid Expenses			
Balance, 12/31/X1	4,000		
Payments –	**218,000**	Wages and other	
		operating expenses	216,000
Balance, 12/31/X2	6,000		

This account shows that prepaid expenses increased by $2,000 during the period. Therefore, the cash payments for wages and other operating expenses were $2,000 greater than the reported expense. Thus, the amount paid for wages and other operating expenses is $216,000 plus $2,000, or $218,000.

In reconstructing the Prepaid Expenses account, we assumed that all cash payments for wages and operating expenses were debited to Prepaid Expenses. However, this assumption does not have to be true for the analysis to work. If cash payments were debited directly to the expense account, the total amount of cash payments would be the same. In other words, the cash paid for operating expenses still equals the $216,000 expense plus the $2,000 increase in prepaid expenses.

On the other hand, if Grover Company's balance sheets had shown accrued liabilities, we would have to adjust the expense for the change in those accrued liabilities. In general terms, the calculation is as follows:

$$
\begin{array}{c}
\text{Cash paid for} \\
\text{wages and other} \\
\text{operating} \\
\text{expenses}
\end{array}
=
\begin{array}{c}
\text{Wages and} \\
\text{other} \\
\text{operating} \\
\text{expenses}
\end{array}
\left[
\begin{array}{c}
+ \text{ Increase in prepaid} \\
\text{expenses} \\
or \\
- \text{ Decrease in prepaid} \\
\text{expenses}
\end{array}
\right]
\left[
\begin{array}{c}
+ \text{ Decrease in accrued} \\
\text{liabilities} \\
or \\
- \text{ Increase in accrued} \\
\text{liabilities}
\end{array}
\right]
$$

Payments for Interest and Taxes. Grover Company's remaining operating cash flows involve cash payments for interest and for taxes. The analysis of these items is similar because both require adjustments for changes in related liability accounts. Grover Company's income statement shows interest expense of $7,000 and income taxes expense of $15,000. To calculate the related cash payments, adjust interest expense for the change in interest payable and adjust income taxes expense for the change in income taxes payable. These calculations are accomplished by reconstructing the liability accounts as follows:

Interest Payable					Income Taxes Payable			
		Balance, 12/31/X1	4,000				Balance, 12/31/X1	12,000
Interest paid =	**8,000**	Interest expense	7,000	**Income taxes paid** =	**5,000**		Income taxes expense	15,000
		Balance, 12/31/X2	3,000				Balance, 12/31/X2	22,000

These reconstructed accounts show that interest payments were $8,000 and income tax payments were $5,000. The general form of each calculation is:

$$
\text{Cash payment} = \text{Expense}
\left[
\begin{array}{c}
+ \text{ Decrease in related payable} \\
or \\
- \text{ Increase in related payable}
\end{array}
\right]
$$

Both of these cash payments appear as operating items on Grover Company's statement of cash flows in Illustration 16–2 on page 577.

Investing Activities

Investing activities usually involve transactions that affect long-term assets. Recall from the information provided about Grover Company's transactions that the company purchased and also sold plant assets. Both of these transactions are investing activities.

Purchase of Plant Assets. Grover Company purchased plant assets that cost $70,000 by issuing $60,000 in bonds payable to the seller and paying the $10,000 balance in cash. The $10,000 payment is reported as a cash outflow on the statement of cash flows (see Illustration 16–2). Also, because $60,000 of the purchase was financed by issuing bonds payable, this transaction involves noncash investing and financing activities. It might be described in a footnote as follows:

Noncash investing and financing activities:	
Purchased plant assets	$70,000
Issued bonds payable to finance purchase . .	60,000
Balance paid in cash	$10,000

Sale of Plant Assets. Grover Company sold plant assets that cost $30,000 when they had accumulated depreciation of $12,000. The result of the sale was a loss of $6,000 and a cash receipt of $12,000. This cash receipt is reported in the statement of cash flows as a cash inflow from investing activities (see Illustration 16–2).

Recall from Grover Company's income statement that depreciation expense was $24,000. Depreciation does not use or provide cash. Note, however, the effects of depreciation expense, the plant asset purchase, and the plant asset sale on the Plant Assets and Accumulated Depreciation accounts. These accounts are reconstructed as follows:

Plant Assets			
Balance, 12/31/X1	210,000		
Purchase	70,000	Sale	30,000
Balance, 12/31/X2	250,000		

Accumulated Depreciation, Plant Assets			
		Balance, 12/31/X1	48,000
Sale	12,000	Depreciation expense	24,000
		Balance, 12/31/X2	60,000

The beginning and ending balances of these accounts were taken from Grover Company's balance sheets (Illustration 16–9). Reconstructing the accounts shows that the beginning and ending balances of both accounts are completely reconciled by the purchase, the sale, and the depreciation expense. Therefore, we did not omit any of the investing activities that relate to plant assets.

Financing Activities

Financing activities usually relate to a company's long-term debt and stockholders' equity accounts. In the information about Grover Company, four transactions involved financing activities. We already discussed one of these, the $60,000 issuance of bonds payable to purchase plant assets, as a noncash investing and financing activity. The remaining three transactions were the retirement of bonds, the issuance of common stock, and the payment of cash dividends.

Payment to Retire Bonds Payable. Grover Company's December 31, 19X1, balance sheet showed total bonds payable of $64,000. Included within this beginning balance for 19X2 were bonds with a carrying value of $34,000 that were retired for an $18,000 cash payment during the year. The income statement reports the $16,000 difference as a gain. The statement of cash flows shows the $18,000 payment as a cash outflow for financing activities (see Illustration 16–2 on page 577).

Notice that the beginning and ending balances of Bonds Payable are reconciled by the $60,000 issuance of new bonds and the retirement of $34,000 of old bonds. The following reconstructed Bonds Payable account shows the results of these activities:

Bonds Payable

		Balance, 12/31/X1	64,000
Retired bonds	34,000	Issued bonds	60,000
		Balance, 12/31/X2	90,000

Receipt from Common Stock Issuance. During 19X2, Grover Company issued 3,000 shares of common stock at par for $5 per share. This $15,000 cash receipt is reported on the statement of cash flows as a financing activity. Look at the December 31, 19X1 and 19X2, balance sheets in Illustration 16–9. Notice that the Common Stock account balance increased from $80,000 at the end of 19X1 to $95,000 at the end of 19X2. Thus, the $15,000 stock issue explains the change in the Common Stock account.

Payment of Cash Dividends. According to the facts provided about Grover Company's transactions, it paid cash dividends of $14,000 during 19X2. This payment is reported as a cash outflow for financing activities. Also, note that the effects of this $14,000 payment and the reported net income of $38,000 fully reconcile the beginning and ending balances of Retained Earnings. This is shown in the reconstructed Retained Earnings account that follows:

Retained Earnings

		Balance, 12/31/X1	88,000
Cash dividend	14,000	Net income	38,000
		Balance, 12/31/X2	112,000

We have described all of Grover Company's cash inflows and outflows and one noncash investing and financing transaction. In the process of making these analyses, we reconciled the changes in all of the noncash balance sheet accounts. The change in the Cash account is reconciled by the statement of cash flows, as seen in Illustration 16–2 on page 577.

Progress Check

16-5   Net sales during a period were $590,000, beginning accounts receivable were $120,000, and ending accounts receivable were $90,000. What amount was collected from customers during the period?

16-6   The Merchandise Inventory account balance decreased during a period from a beginning balance of $32,000 to an ending balance of $28,000. Cost of goods sold for the period was $168,000. If the Accounts Payable balance increased $2,400 during the period, what was the amount of cash paid for merchandise?

16-7   Hargrave Inc. reports wages and other operating expenses incurred totaled $112,000. At the end of last year, prepaid expenses totaled $1,200, and this year the balance was $4,200. The current balance sheet does show wages payable of $5,600, whereas last year's did not show any accrued liabilities. How much was paid for wages and other operating expenses this year?

16-8   Equipment that cost $80,000 and had accumulated depreciation of $30,000 was sold at a loss of $10,000. What was the cash receipt from the sale? In what category of the statement of cash flows should it be reported?

RECONCILING NET INCOME TO NET CASH PROVIDED (OR USED) BY OPERATING ACTIVITIES

As you learned earlier, the FASB recommends that the operating activities section of the statement of cash flows be prepared according to the direct method. Under this method, the statement reports each major class of cash inflows and outflows from operating activities. *However, when the direct method is used, the FASB also requires that companies disclose a reconciliation of net income to the net cash provided (or used) by operating activities.* This reconciliation is precisely what is accomplished by the *indirect* method of calculating the net cash provided (or used) by operating activities. We explain the indirect method next.

THE INDIRECT METHOD OF CALCULATING NET CASH PROVIDED (OR USED) BY OPERATING ACTIVITIES

LO 3

Calculate the net cash provided or used by operating activities according to the indirect method and prepare the statement of cash flows.

When using the indirect method, list net income first. Then, adjust net income to reconcile its amount to the net amount of cash provided (or used) by operating activities. To see the results of the indirect method, look at Illustration 16–10. This illustration shows Grover Company's statement of cash flows with the reconciliation of net income to the net cash provided by operating activities.

In Illustration 16–10, notice that the net cash provided by operating activities is $20,000. This is the same amount that was reported on the statement of cash flows (direct method) in Illustration 16–2 on page 577. However, these illustrations show entirely different ways of calculating the $20,000 net cash inflow. Under the direct method in Illustration 16–2, we subtracted major classes of operating cash outflows from major classes of cash inflows. By comparison, we include none of the individual cash inflows or cash outflows under the indirect method used in Illustration 16–10. Instead, we modify net income to exclude those amounts included in the determination of net income but not involved in operating cash inflows or outflows during the period. Net income also is modified to include operating cash inflows and outflows not recorded as revenues and expenses.

Illustration 16–10 shows three types of adjustments to net income. The adjustments grouped under section (1) are for changes in noncash current assets and current liabilities that relate to operating activities. Adjustment (2) is for an income statement item that relates to operating activities but that did not involve a cash inflow or outflow during the period. The adjustments grouped under (3) eliminate gains and losses that resulted from investing and financing activities. These gains and losses do not relate to operating activities.

ADJUSTMENTS FOR CHANGES IN CURRENT ASSETS AND CURRENT LIABILITIES

To help you understand why adjustments for changes in noncash current assets and current liabilities are part of the reconciliation process, we use the transactions of a very simple company as an example. Assume that Simple Company's income statement shows only two items, as follows:

Sales	$20,000
Operating expenses	(12,000)
Net income	$ 8,000

For a moment, assume that all of Simple Company's sales and operating expenses are for cash. The company has no current assets other than cash and has no current liabilities. Given these assumptions, the net cash provided by operating activities during the period is $8,000, which is the cash received from customers less the cash paid for operating expenses.

Illustration 16-10
Statement of Cash Flows
(Indirect Method)

GROVER COMPANY
Statement of Cash Flows
For Year Ended December 31, 19X2

Cash flows from operating activities:		
Net income	$ 38,000	
Adjustments to reconcile net income to net		
cash provided by operating activities:		
(1) Increase in accounts receivable	(20,000)	
Increase in merchandise inventory	(14,000)	
Increase in prepaid expenses	(2,000)	
Decrease in accounts payable	(5,000)	
Decrease in interest payable	(1,000)	
Increase in income taxes payable	10,000	
(2) Depreciation expense	24,000	
(3) Loss on sale of plant assets	6,000	
Gain on retirement of bonds	(16,000)	
Net cash provided by operating activities		$ 20,000
Cash flows from investing activities:		
Cash received from sale of plant assets	$ 12,000	
Cash paid for purchase of plant assets	(10,000)	
Net cash provided by investing activities		2,000
Cash flows from financing activities:		
Cash received from issuing stock	$ 15,000	
Cash paid to retire bonds	(18,000)	
Cash paid for dividends	(14,000)	
Net cash used in financing activities		(17,000)
Net increase in cash		$ 5,000
Cash balance at beginning of 19X2		12,000
Cash balance at end of 19X2		$ 17,000

Adjustments for Changes in Noncash Current Assets

Now assume that Simple Company's sales are on account. Also assume that its Accounts Receivable balance was $2,000 at the beginning of the year and $2,500 at the end of the year. Under these assumptions, cash receipts from customers equal sales of $20,000 minus the $500 increase in Accounts Receivable, or $19,500. Therefore, using the *direct* method, the net cash provided by operating activities is $7,500 ($19,500 − $12,000).

When the *indirect* method is used to calculate the net cash flow, net income of $8,000 is adjusted for the $500 increase in Accounts Receivable to get $7,500 as the net amount of cash provided by operating activities. Both calculations are as follows:

Direct Method:	
Receipts from customers ($20,000 − $500)	$19,500
Payments for operating expenses	(12,000)
Cash provided (or used) by operating activities	$ 7,500
Indirect Method:	
Net income	$8,000
Less the increase in accounts receivable	(500)
Cash provided (or used) by operating activities	$7,500

Notice that the direct method calculation subtracts the increase in Accounts Receivable from Sales, while the indirect method calculation subtracts the increase in Accounts Receivable from net income.

As another example, assume instead that the Accounts Receivable balance decreased from $2,000 to $1,200. Under this assumption, cash receipts from customers equal sales of $20,000 plus the $800 decrease in Accounts Receivable, or $20,800. By the direct method, the net cash provided by operating activities is $8,800 ($20,800 − $12,000). And, when the indirect method is used, the $800 decrease in Accounts Receivable is *added* to the $8,000 net income to get $8,800 net cash provided by operating activities.

When the indirect method is used, adjustments like those for Accounts Receivable are required for all noncash current assets related to operating activities. When a noncash current asset increases, part of the cash derived from operating activities is used to pay for the increase. This leaves a smaller amount as the net cash inflow. Therefore, when you calculate the net cash inflow using the indirect method, subtract the noncash current asset increase from net income. But, when a noncash current asset decreases, additional cash is produced, and you should add this amount to net income. These modifications of income for changes in current assets related to operating activities are as follows:

Net income
Add: Decreases in current assets
Subtract: Increases in current assets
Net cash provided (or used) by operating activities

Adjustments for Changes in Current Liabilities

To illustrate the adjustments for changes in current liabilities, return to the original assumptions about Simple Company. Sales of $20,000 are for cash, and operating expenses are $12,000. However, assume now that Simple Company has Interest Payable as its only current liability. Also assume that the beginning-of-year balance in Interest Payable was $500 and the end-of-year balance was $900. This increase means that the operating expenses of $12,000 were $400 larger than the amount paid in cash during the period. Therefore, the cash payments for operating expenses were only $11,600, or ($12,000 − $400). Under these assumptions, the direct method calculation of net cash provided by operating activities is $8,400, or $20,000 receipts from customers less $11,600 payments for expenses. The indirect method calculation of $8,400 is net income of $8,000 plus the $400 increase in Interest Payable.

Alternatively, if the Interest Payable balance decreased, for example by $300, the cash outflow for operating expenses would have been the $12,000 expense plus the $300 liability decrease, or $12,300. Then, the direct calculation of net cash flow is $20,000 − $12,300 = $7,700. The indirect calculation is $8,000 − $300 = $7,700. In other words, when using the indirect method, subtract a *decrease* in Interest Payable from net income.

Using the indirect method requires adjustments like those for Interest Payable for all current liabilities related to operating activities. When a current liability decreases, part of the cash derived from operating activities pays for the decrease. Therefore, subtract the decrease from net income to determine the remaining net cash inflow. And, when a current liability increases, it finances some operating expenses. In other words, cash was not used to pay for the expense and the liability increase must be *added* to net income when you calculate cash provided by operating activities. These adjustments for changes in current liabilities related to operating activities are:

Net income
Add: Increases in current liabilities
Subtract: Decreases in current liabilities
Net cash provided (or used) by operating activities

One way to remember how to make these modifications to net income is to observe that a *debit* change in a noncash current asset or a current liability is *subtracted* from net income. And, a *credit* change in a noncash current asset or a current liability is *added* to net income.

Adjustments for Operating Items That Do Not Provide or Use Cash

Some operating items that appear on an income statement do not provide or use cash during the current period. One example is depreciation. Other examples are amortization of intangible assets, depletion of natural resources, and bad debts expense.

Record these expenses with debits to expense accounts and credits to noncash accounts. They reduce net income but do not require cash outflows during the period. Therefore, when adjustments to net income are made under the indirect method, add these noncash expenses back to net income.

In addition to noncash expenses such as depreciation, net income may include some revenues that do not provide cash inflows during the current period. An example is equity method earnings from a stock investment in another entity (see Chapter 11). If net income includes revenues that do not provide cash inflows, subtract the revenues from net income in the process of reconciling net income to the net cash provided by operating activities.

The indirect method adjustments for expenses and revenues that do not provide or use cash during the current period are as follows:

Net income
Add: Expenses that do not use cash
Subtract: Revenues that do not provide cash
Net cash provided (or used) by operating activities

Adjustments for Nonoperating Items

Some income statement items are not related to the operating activities of the company. These gains and losses result from investing and financing activities. Examples are gains or losses on the sale of plant assets and gains or losses on the retirement of bonds payable.

Remember that the indirect method reconciles net income to the net cash provided (or used) by operating activities. Therefore, net income must be modified to exclude gains and losses created by investing and financing activities. In making the modifications under the indirect method, subtract gains from financing and investing activities from net income and add losses back to net income:

Net income
Add: Losses from investing or financing activities
Subtract: Gains from investing or financing activities
Net cash provided (or used) by operating activities

Progress Check

16-9   Determine the net cash provided (or used) by operating activities based on the following data:

Net income	$74,900
Decrease in accounts receivable	4,600
Increase in inventory	11,700
Decrease in accounts payable	1,000
Loss on sale of equipment	3,400
Payment of dividends	21,500

16-10   Why are expenses such as depreciation and amortization of goodwill added to net income when cash flow from operating activities is calculated by the indirect method?

16-11   A company reports a net income of $15,000 that includes a $3,000 gain on the sale of plant assets. Why is this gain subtracted from net income in calculating cash flow from operating activities according to the indirect method?

APPLYING THE INDIRECT METHOD TO GROVER COMPANY

LO 4
Prepare a working paper for a statement of cash flows so that the net cash flow from operating activities is calculated by the indirect method.

Determining the net cash flows provided (or used) by operating activities according to the indirect method requires balance sheets at the beginning and end of the period, the current period's income statement, and other information about selected transactions. Illustration 16–9 on page 585 shows the income statement and balance sheet information for Grover Company. Based on this information, Illustration 16–10 presents the indirect method of reconciling net income to net cash provided by operating activities.

Preparing the Indirect Method Working Paper

When a company has a large number of accounts and many operating, investing, and financing transactions, the analysis of noncash accounts can be difficult and confusing. In these situations, a working paper can help organize the information you need to prepare a statement of cash flows. A working paper also makes it easier to check the accuracy of your work.

In addition to Grover Company's comparative balance sheets and income statement presented in Illustration 16–9, the information needed to prepare the working paper follows. The letters identifying each item of information also cross reference related debits and credits in the working paper.

a.   Net income was $38,000.

b.   Accounts receivable increased by $20,000.

c.   Merchandise inventory increased by $14,000.

d.   Prepaid expenses increased by $2,000.

e.   Accounts payable decreased by $5,000.

f.   Interest payable decreased by $1,000.

g.   Income taxes payable increased by $10,000.

h.   Depreciation expense was $24,000.

i.   Loss on sale of plant assets was $6,000; assets that cost $30,000 with accumulated depreciation of $12,000 were sold for $12,000 cash.

j.   Gain on retirement of bonds was $16,000; bonds with a book value of $34,000 were retired with a cash payment of $18,000.

k.   Plant assets that cost $70,000 were purchased; the payment consisted of $10,000 cash and issuing $60,000 of bonds payable.

l.   Sold 3,000 shares of common stock for $15,000.

m.   Paid cash dividends of $14,000.

Illustration 16–11

<table>
<tr>
<th colspan="6" style="text-align:center">GROVER COMPANY
Working Paper for Statement of Cash Flows (Indirect Method)
For Year Ended December 31, 19X2</th>
</tr>
<tr>
<th></th>
<th>December
31, 19X1</th>
<th colspan="2">Analysis of Changes</th>
<th>December
31, 19X2</th>
</tr>
<tr>
<th></th>
<th></th>
<th>Debit</th>
<th>Credit</th>
<th></th>
</tr>
<tr>
<td colspan="5">Balance sheet—debits:</td>
</tr>
<tr>
<td>Cash ....</td>
<td>12,000</td>
<td></td>
<td></td>
<td>17,000</td>
</tr>
<tr>
<td>Accounts receivable ....</td>
<td>40,000</td>
<td>(b) 20,000</td>
<td></td>
<td>60,000</td>
</tr>
<tr>
<td>Merchandise inventory ....</td>
<td>70,000</td>
<td>(c) 14,000</td>
<td></td>
<td>84,000</td>
</tr>
<tr>
<td>Prepaid expenses ....</td>
<td>4,000</td>
<td>(d) 2,000</td>
<td></td>
<td>6,000</td>
</tr>
<tr>
<td>Plant assets ....</td>
<td>210,000</td>
<td>(k1) 70,000</td>
<td>(i) 30,000</td>
<td>250,000</td>
</tr>
<tr>
<td></td>
<td>336,000</td>
<td></td>
<td></td>
<td>417,000</td>
</tr>
<tr>
<td colspan="5">Balance sheet—credits:</td>
</tr>
<tr>
<td>Accumulated depreciation ....</td>
<td>48,000</td>
<td>(i) 12,000</td>
<td>(h) 24,000</td>
<td>60,000</td>
</tr>
<tr>
<td>Accounts payable ....</td>
<td>40,000</td>
<td>(e) 5,000</td>
<td></td>
<td>35,000</td>
</tr>
<tr>
<td>Interest payable ....</td>
<td>4,000</td>
<td>(f) 1,000</td>
<td></td>
<td>3,000</td>
</tr>
<tr>
<td>Income taxes payable ....</td>
<td>12,000</td>
<td></td>
<td>(g) 10,000</td>
<td>22,000</td>
</tr>
<tr>
<td>Bonds payable ....</td>
<td>64,000</td>
<td>(j) 34,000</td>
<td>(k2) 60,000</td>
<td>90,000</td>
</tr>
<tr>
<td>Common stock, $5 par value ......</td>
<td>80,000</td>
<td></td>
<td>(l) 15,000</td>
<td>95,000</td>
</tr>
<tr>
<td>Retained earnings ....</td>
<td>88,000</td>
<td>(m) 14,000</td>
<td>(a) 38,000</td>
<td>112,000</td>
</tr>
<tr>
<td></td>
<td>336,000</td>
<td></td>
<td></td>
<td>417,000</td>
</tr>
<tr>
<td colspan="5">Statement of cash flows:</td>
</tr>
<tr>
<td>Operating activities:</td>
<td></td>
<td></td>
<td></td>
<td></td>
</tr>
<tr>
<td>Net income ....</td>
<td></td>
<td>(a) 38,000</td>
<td></td>
<td></td>
</tr>
<tr>
<td>Increase in accounts receivable ...</td>
<td></td>
<td></td>
<td>(b) 20,000</td>
<td></td>
</tr>
<tr>
<td>Increase in merchandise inventory .</td>
<td></td>
<td></td>
<td>(c) 14,000</td>
<td></td>
</tr>
<tr>
<td>Increase in prepaid expenses .....</td>
<td></td>
<td></td>
<td>(d) 2,000</td>
<td></td>
</tr>
<tr>
<td>Decrease in accounts payable ....</td>
<td></td>
<td></td>
<td>(e) 5,000</td>
<td></td>
</tr>
<tr>
<td>Decrease in interest payable .....</td>
<td></td>
<td></td>
<td>(f) 1,000</td>
<td></td>
</tr>
<tr>
<td>Increase in income taxes payable ..</td>
<td></td>
<td>(g) 10,000</td>
<td></td>
<td></td>
</tr>
<tr>
<td>Depreciation expense ....</td>
<td></td>
<td>(h) 24,000</td>
<td></td>
<td></td>
</tr>
<tr>
<td>Loss on sale of plant assets ......</td>
<td></td>
<td>(i) 6,000</td>
<td></td>
<td></td>
</tr>
<tr>
<td>Gain on retirement of bonds .....</td>
<td></td>
<td></td>
<td>(j) 16,000</td>
<td></td>
</tr>
<tr>
<td>Investing activities:</td>
<td></td>
<td></td>
<td></td>
<td></td>
</tr>
<tr>
<td>Receipts from sale of plant assets .</td>
<td></td>
<td>(i) 12,000</td>
<td></td>
<td></td>
</tr>
<tr>
<td>Payment for purchase of plant assets .</td>
<td></td>
<td></td>
<td>(k1) 10,000</td>
<td></td>
</tr>
<tr>
<td>Financing activities:</td>
<td></td>
<td></td>
<td></td>
<td></td>
</tr>
<tr>
<td>Payments to retire bonds ....</td>
<td></td>
<td></td>
<td>(j) 18,000</td>
<td></td>
</tr>
<tr>
<td>Receipts from issuing stock ......</td>
<td></td>
<td>(l) 15,000</td>
<td></td>
<td></td>
</tr>
<tr>
<td>Payments of dividends ....</td>
<td></td>
<td></td>
<td>(m) 14,000</td>
<td></td>
</tr>
<tr>
<td>Noncash investing and financing
activities:</td>
<td></td>
<td></td>
<td></td>
<td></td>
</tr>
<tr>
<td>Purchase of plant assets
financed by bonds ....</td>
<td></td>
<td>(k2) 60,000</td>
<td>(k1) 60,000</td>
<td></td>
</tr>
<tr>
<td></td>
<td></td>
<td>337,000</td>
<td>337,000</td>
<td></td>
</tr>
</table>

Illustration 16–11 shows the indirect method working paper for Grover Company. Notice that the beginning and ending balance sheets are recorded on the working paper. Following the balance sheets, we enter information in the Analysis of Changes columns about cash flows from operating, investing, and financing activities and about noncash investing and financing activities. Note that the working paper does not reconstruct the income statement. Instead, net income is entered as the first item used in computing the amount of cash flows from operating activities.

Entering the Analysis of Changes on the Working Paper

After the balance sheets are entered, we recommend using the following sequence of procedures to complete the working paper:

1. Enter net income as an operating cash inflow (a debit) and as a credit to Retained Earnings.

2. In the Statement of Cash Flows section, adjustments to net income are entered as debits if they increase cash inflows and as credits if they decrease cash inflows. Following this rule, adjust net income for the change in each noncash current asset and current liability related to operating activities. For each adjustment to net income, the offsetting debit or credit should reconcile the beginning and ending balances of a current asset or current liability.

3. Enter the adjustments to net income for income statement items, such as depreciation, that did not provide or use cash during the period. For each adjustment, the offsetting debit or credit should help reconcile a noncash balance sheet account.

4. Adjust net income to eliminate any gains or losses from investing and financing activities. Because the cash associated with a gain must be excluded from operating activities, the gain is entered as a credit in the operating activities section. On the other hand, losses are entered with debits. For each of these adjustments, the related debits and/or credits help reconcile balance sheet accounts and also involve entries to show the cash flow from investing or financing activities.

5. After reviewing any unreconciled balance sheet accounts and related information, enter the reconciling entries for all remaining investing and financing activities. These include items such as purchases of plant assets, issuances of long-term debt, sales of capital stock, and dividend payments. Some of these may require entries in the noncash investing and financing activities section of the working paper.

6. Confirm the accuracy of your work by totaling the Analysis of Changes columns and by determining that the change in each balance sheet account has been explained.

For Grover Company, these steps were performed in Illustration 16–11:

Step	Entries
1	(a)
2	(b) through (g)
3	(h)
4	(i) through (j)
5	(k) through (m)

Because adjustments *i*, *j*, and *k* are more complex, we show them in the following debit and credit format. This format is similar to the one used for general journal entries, except that the changes in the Cash account are identified as sources or uses of cash.

i.	Loss from sale of plant assets	6,000.00	
	Accumulated depreciation	12,000.00	
	Receipt from sale of plant assets (Source of cash)	12,000.00	
	Plant assets		30,000.00
	To describe the sale of plant assets.		
j.	Bonds payable	34,000.00	
	Payments to retire bonds (Use of cash)		18,000.00
	Gain on retirement of bonds		16,000.00
	To describe the retirement of bonds.		

k1.	Plant assets	70,000.00		
	Payment to purchase plant assets (Use of cash)		10,000.00	
	Purchase of plant assets financed by bonds		60,000.00	
	To describe the purchase of plant assets, the cash payment, and the use of noncash financing.			
k2.	Purchase of plant assets financed by bonds	60,000.00		
	Bonds payable		60,000.00	
	To show the issuance of bonds payable to finance the purchase of plant assets.			

Progress Check

16-12 In preparing a working paper for a statement of cash flows with the cash flows from operating activities reported according to the indirect method, which of the following is true?

    a. A decrease in accounts receivable is analyzed with a debit in the Statement of Cash Flows section and a credit in the Balance Sheet section.

    b. A cash dividend paid is analyzed with a debit to Retained Earnings and a credit in the Investing Activities section.

    c. The analysis of a cash payment to retire bonds payable at a loss would require one debit and two credits.

    d. Depreciation expense would not require analysis on the working paper because there is no cash inflow or outflow.

USING THE INFORMATION— CASH FLOWS

LO 1
Explain why cash flow information is important to decision making and describe the information in a statement of cash flows and the methods used to disclose noncash investing and financing activities.

Numerous ratios are used to analyze income statement and balance sheet data. By comparison, ratios related to the statement of cash flows are not widely used.[7] Only one ratio of that nature, cash flow per share, has received much attention. Some financial analysts use that ratio, usually calculated as net income adjusted for noncash items such as depreciation and amortization. Currently, however, the FASB does not allow reporting cash flow per share, apparently because it might be misinterpreted as a measure of earnings performance.

Mary Garza (As a Matter of Opinion, page 576) typifies the attitude of most managers when she emphasizes the importance of understanding and predicting cash flows. Many business decisions are based on cash flow evaluations. For example, creditors evaluate a company's ability to generate cash before deciding whether to loan money to the company. Investors often make similar evaluations before they buy a company's stock. In making these evaluations, cash flows from investing and financing activities are considered. However, special attention is given to the company's ability to generate cash flows from its operations. The cash flows statement facilitates this by separating the investing and financing activity cash flows from the operating cash flows.

To see the importance of identifying cash flows as operating, investing, and financing activities, consider the following three companies. Assume they operate in the same industry and have been in business for several years.

---

[7]To consider some suggested cash flow ratios, see Don E. Giacomino and David E. Mielke, "Cash Flows: Another Approach to Ratio Analysis," *Journal of Accountancy,* March 1993.

	First Company	Second Company	Third Company
Cash provided (used) by operating activities	$90,000	$40,000	$(24,000)
Cash provided (used) by investing activities:			
Proceeds from sale of operating assets			26,000
Purchase of operating assets	(48,000)	(25,000)	
Cash provided (used) by financing activities:			
Proceeds from issuance of debt			13,000
Repayment of debt	(27,000)		
Net increase (decrease) in cash	$15,000	$15,000	$ 15,000

Each of the three companies generated a $15,000 net increase in cash. Their means of accomplishing this, however, were very different. First Company's operating activities provided $90,000, which allowed the company to purchase additional operating assets for $48,000 and repay $27,000 of debt. By comparison, Second Company's operating activities provided only $40,000, enabling it to purchase only $25,000 of operating assets. By comparison, Third Company's net cash increase was obtained only by selling operating assets and incurring additional debt; operating activities resulted in a net cash outflow of $24,000.

The implication of this comparison is that First Company is more capable of generating cash to meet its future obligations than is Second Company; and Third Company is least capable. This evaluation is, of course, tentative and may be contradicted by other information.

Managers analyze cash flows in making a variety of short-term decisions. In deciding whether borrowing will be necessary, managers use the procedures you learned in this chapter to predict cash flows for the next period or periods. These short-term planning situations also may lead to decisions about investing idle cash balances. Another example is deciding whether a customer's offer to buy a product at a reduced price should be accepted or rejected.

Long-term decisions involving new investments usually require detailed cash flow predictions. Companies must estimate cash inflows and outflows over the life of the investment, often extending many years into the future. Other decisions that require cash flow information include deciding whether a product should be manufactured by the company or purchased from an outside supplier and whether a product or a department should be eliminated or retained.

Progress Check

16-13 Refer to the consolidated statements of cash flows for Lands' End, Inc., in Appendix F. What type and amount of investing activities took place during the year ended January 27, 1995? What was the largest source of cash to finance these activities?

SUMMARY OF THE CHAPTER IN TERMS OF LEARNING OBJECTIVES

LO 1. Explain why cash flow information is important to decision making and describe the information in a statement of cash flows and the methods used to disclose noncash investing and financing activities. Many decisions involve evaluating cash flows. Examples are investor and creditor decisions to invest in or loan money to a company. The evaluations include paying attention to the activities that provide or use cash. Managers evaluate cash flows in deciding whether borrowing is necessary, whether cash balances should be invested, and in a variety of other short-term and long-term decisions.

The statement of cash flows reports cash receipts and disbursements as operating, investing, or financing activities. Operating activities include transactions related to producing or purchasing merchandise, selling goods and services to customers, and performing administrative functions. Investing activities include purchases and sales of noncurrent assets and short-term investments that are not cash equivalents. Financing activities include transactions with owners and transactions to borrow or repay the principal amounts of long-term and short-term debt.

For external reporting, a company must supplement its statement of cash flows with a description of its noncash investing and financing activities. Two examples of these activities are the retirement of debt obligations by issuing equity securities and the exchange of a note payable for plant assets.

LO 2. Calculate cash inflows and outflows by inspecting the noncash account balances and prepare a statement of cash flows using the direct method. To identify the cash receipts and cash payments, analyze the changes in the noncash balance sheet accounts created by income statement transactions and other events. For example, the amount of cash collected from customers is calculated by modifying sales revenues for the change in accounts receivable. Also, cash paid for interest is calculated by adjusting interest expense for the change in interest payable.

In using the direct method to report the net cash provided (or used) by operating activities, major classes of operating cash inflows and outflows are separately disclosed. Then, operating cash outflows are subtracted from operating cash inflows to derive the net inflow or outflow from operating activities. This method is encouraged by the FASB but is not required. Company managers generally use the direct method to predict future cash inflows and outflows.

LO 3. Calculate the net cash provided or used by operating activities according to the indirect method and prepare the statement of cash flows. In using the indirect method to calculate the net cash provided (or used) by operating activities, first list the net income and then modify it for these three types of events: (1) changes in noncash current assets and current liabilities related to operating activities, (2) revenues and expenses that did not provide or use cash, and (3) gains and losses from investing and financing activities. If using the direct method, report the reconciliation between net income and net cash provided (or used) by operating activities on a separate schedule.

LO 4. Prepare a working paper for a statement of cash flows so that the net cash flow from operating activities is calculated by the indirect method. To prepare an indirect method working paper, first enter the beginning and ending balances of the balance sheet accounts in columns 1 and 4. Then, establish the three sections of the statement of cash flows. Net income is entered as the first item in the operating activities section. Then, adjust the net income for events (*a*) through (*c*) identified in the preceding paragraph. This process reconciles the changes in the noncash current assets and current liabilities related to operations. Reconcile any remaining balance sheet account changes and report their cash effects in the appropriate sections. Enter noncash investing and financing activities at the bottom of the working paper.

DEMONSTRATION PROBLEM

The following summarized journal entries show the total debits and credits to the Pyramid Corporation's Cash account during 19X2. Use the information to prepare a statement of cash flows for 19X2. The cash provided (or used) by operating activities should be presented according to the direct method. In the statement, identify the entry that records each item of cash flow. Assume that the beginning balance of cash was $133,200.

a.	Cash	1,440,000.00		
	Common Stock, $10 Par Value		360,000.00	
	Contributed Capital in Excess of Par Value,			
	Common Stock		1,080,000.00	
	Issued common stock for cash.			
b.	Cash	2,400,000.00		
	Notes Payable		2,400,000.00	
	Borrowed cash with a note payable.			

c.	Purchases	480,000.00	
	Cash		480,000.00
	Purchased merchandise for cash.		
d.	Accounts Payable	1,200,000.00	
	Cash		1,200,000.00
	Paid for credit purchases of merchandise.		
e.	Wages Expense	600,000.00	
	Cash		600,000.00
	Paid wages to employees.		
f.	Rent Expense	420,000.00	
	Cash		420,000.00
	Paid rent for buildings.		
g.	Cash	3,000,000.00	
	Sales		3,000,000.00
	Made cash sales to customers.		
h.	Cash	1,800,000.00	
	Accounts Receivable		1,800,000.00
	Collected accounts from credit customers.		
i.	Machinery	2,136,000.00	
	Cash		2,136,000.00
	Purchased machinery for cash.		
j.	Investments	2,160,000.00	
	Cash		2,160,000.00
	Purchased investments for cash.		
k.	Interest Expense	216,000.00	
	Notes Payable	384,000.00	
	Cash		600,000.00
	Paid notes and accrued interest.		
l.	Cash	206,400.00	
	Dividends Earned		206,400.00
	Collected dividends from investments.		
m.	Cash	210,000.00	
	Loss on Sale of Investments	30,000.00	
	Investments		240,000.00
	Sold investments for cash.		
n.	Cash	720,000.00	
	Accumulated Depreciation, Machinery	420,000.00	
	Machinery		960,000.00
	Gain on Sale of Machinery		180,000.00
	Sold machinery for cash.		
o.	Common Dividend Payable	510,000.00	
	Cash		510,000.00
	Paid cash dividends to stockholders.		
p.	Income Taxes Payable	480,000.00	
	Cash		480,000.00
	Paid income taxes owed for the year.		
q.	Treasury Stock, Common	228,000.00	
	Cash		228,000.00
	Acquired treasury stock for cash.		

Planning the Solution

- Prepare a blank statement of cash flows with sections for operating, investing, and financing activities.

- Examine each journal entry to determine whether it describes an operating, investing, or financing activity and whether it describes an inflow or outflow of cash.

- Enter the cash effects of the entry in the appropriate section of the statement, being sure to combine similar events, including c and d, as well as g and h. For entry k, identify the portions of the cash flow that should be assigned to operating and financing activities.
- Total each section of the statement, determine the total change in cash, and add the beginning balance to get the ending balance.

PYRAMID CORPORATION
Statement of Cash Flows
For Year Ended December 31, 19X2

Solution to Demonstration Problem

Cash flows from operating activities:			
g,h.	Cash received from customers	$ 4,800,000	
l.	Cash received as dividends	206,400	
c,d.	Cash paid for merchandise	(1,680,000)	
e.	Cash paid for wages	(600,000)	
f.	Cash paid for rent	(420,000)	
k.	Cash paid for interest	(216,000)	
p.	Cash paid for taxes	(480,000)	
	Net cash provided by operating activities		$ 1,610,400
Cash flows from investing activities:			
i.	Cash paid for purchases of machinery	$(2,136,000)	
j.	Cash paid for purchases of investments	(2,160,000)	
m.	Cash received from sale of investments	210,000	
n.	Cash received from sale of machinery	720,000	
	Net cash used in investing activities		(3,366,000)
Cash flows from financing activities:			
a.	Cash received from issuing stock	$ 1,440,000	
b.	Cash received from borrowing	2,400,000	
k.	Cash paid for repayment of note payable	(384,000)	
o.	Cash paid for dividends	(510,000)	
q.	Cash paid for purchases of treasury stock	(228,000)	
	Net cash provided by financing activities		2,718,000
Net increase in cash			$ 962,400
Beginning balance of cash			133,200
Ending balance of cash			$ 1,095,600

GLOSSARY

Direct method of calculating net cash provided (or used) by operating activities a calculation of the net cash provided or used by operating activities that lists the major classes of operating cash receipts, such as receipts from customers, and subtracts the major classes of operating cash disbursements, such as cash paid for merchandise. p. 575

Financing activities transactions with the owners of a business or transactions with its creditors to borrow money or to repay the principal amounts of loans. p. 580

Indirect method of calculating net cash provided (or used) by operating activities a calculation that begins with net income and then adjusts the net income amount by adding and subtracting items that are necessary to reconcile net income to the net cash provided or used by operating activities. p. 576

Investing activities transactions that involve making and collecting loans or that involve purchasing and selling plant assets, other productive assets, or investments other than cash equivalents. p. 579

Operating activities activities that involve the production or purchase of merchandise and the sale of goods and services to customers, including expenditures related to administering the business. p. 578

Statement of cash flows a financial statement that reports the cash inflows and outflows for an accounting period and that classifies those cash flows as operating activities, investing activities, and financing activities. p. 574

QUESTIONS

1. What are some examples of items reported on a statement of cash flows as investing activities?
2. What are some examples of items reported on a statement of cash flows as financing activities?
3. When a statement of cash flows is prepared by the direct method, what are some examples of items reported as cash flows from operating activities?

4. If a corporation pays cash dividends, where on the corporation's statement of cash flows should the payment be reported?

5. A company purchases land for $100,000, paying $20,000 cash and borrowing the remainder on a long-term note payable. How should this transaction be reported on a statement of cash flows?

6. What is the direct method of reporting cash flows from operating activities?

7. What is the indirect method of reporting cash flows from operating activities?

8. Is depreciation a source of cash?

9. On June 3, a company borrowed $50,000 by giving its bank a 60-day, interest-bearing note. On the statement of cash flows, where should this item be reported?

10. If a company reports a net income for the year, is it possible for the company to show a net cash outflow from operating activities? Explain your answer.

11. Refer to Lands' End, Inc.'s consolidated statement of cash flows shown in Appendix F. (*a*) Which method was used to calculate net cash provided by operating activities? (*b*) Although the consolidated balance sheet shows that there was an increase in receivables from fiscal year 1994 to fiscal year 1995, why were receivables subtracted rather than added in the calculation of net cash provided by operating activities during the year ended January 27, 1995?

QUICK STUDY (Five-Minute Exercises)

QS 16–1
(LO 1)

Describe the content of a statement of cash flows.

QS 16–2
(LO 1)

Classify the following cash flows as operating, investing, or financing activities:

1. Issued common stock for cash.
2. Received interest on investment.
3. Paid interest on outstanding bonds.
4. Sold delivery equipment at a loss.
5. Paid property taxes on the company offices.
6. Collected proceeds from sale of long-term investments.
7. Received payments from customers.
8. Paid wages.
9. Purchased merchandise for cash.
10. Paid dividends.

QS 16–3
(LO 1)

List three examples of transactions that are noncash financing and investing transactions.

QS 16–4
(LO 2)

Use the following information in QS 16–4 through QS 16–9.

BRIGHTWELL CO., INC.
Comparative Balance Sheet

Assets	19X2	19X1
Cash	$ 95,800	$ 25,000
Accounts receivable (net)	42,000	52,000
Inventory	86,800	96,800
Prepaid expenses	6,400	5,200
Furniture	110,000	120,000
Accumulated depreciation, furniture	(18,000)	(10,000)
Total assets	$323,000	$289,000

Liabilities and Stockholders' Equity		
Accounts payable	$ 16,000	$ 22,000
Wages payable	10,000	6,000
Income taxes payable	2,400	3,600
Notes payable (long-term)	30,000	70,000
Common stock, $5 par value	230,000	180,000
Retained earnings	34,600	7,400
Total liabilities and stockholders' equity	$323,000	$289,000

BRIGHTWELL CO., INC.
Income Statement
For Year Ended June 30, 19X2

Sales		$468,000
Cost of goods sold		312,000
Gross profit		$156,000
Operating expenses:		
Depreciation expense	$38,600	
Other expenses	57,000	
Total operating expenses		95,600
Net income from operations		$ 60,400
Income taxes		24,600
Net income		$ 35,800

How much cash was received from customers during 19X2?

Refer to the facts in QS 16–4. How much cash was paid for merchandise during 19X2?

QS 16–5
(LO 2)

Refer to the facts in QS 16–4. How much cash was paid for operating expenses during 19X2?

QS 16–6
(LO 2)

Refer to the facts in QS 16–4 and assume furniture that cost $54,000 was sold at its book value and all furniture acquisitions were for cash. What was the cash inflow related to the sale of furniture?

QS 16–7
(LO 2)

Refer to the facts in QS 16–4 and assume that all stock was issued for cash. How much cash was disbursed for dividends?

QS 16–8
(LO 2)

Refer to the facts in QS 16–4. Using the indirect method, calculate cash provided or used from operating activities.

QS 16–9
(LO 3)

When a working paper for a statement of cash flows is prepared, all changes in noncash balance sheet accounts are accounted for on the working paper. Explain why this occurs.

QS 16–10
(LO 4)

EXERCISES

The following events occurred during the year. Assuming that the company uses the direct method of reporting cash provided by operating activities, indicate the proper accounting treatment for each event by placing an *x* in the appropriate column.

Exercise 16–1
Classifying transactions on statement of cash flows (direct method)
(LO 1)

		Statement of Cash Flows			Footnote Describing Noncash Investing and Financing Activities	Not Reported on Statement or in Footnote
		Operating Activities	Investing Activities	Financing Activities		
a.	Borrowed cash from the bank by signing a nine-month note payable.	_____	_____	_____	_____	_____
b.	Paid cash to purchase a patent.	_____	_____	_____	_____	_____
c.	A six-month note receivable was accepted in exchange for a building that had been used in operations.	_____	_____	_____	_____	_____
d.	Long-term bonds payable were retired by issuing common stock.	_____	_____	_____	_____	_____
e.	Recorded depreciation expense on all plant assets.	_____	_____	_____	_____	_____
f.	A cash dividend that was declared in a previous period was paid in the current period.	_____	_____	_____	_____	_____
g.	Surplus merchandise inventory was sold for cash.	_____	_____	_____	_____	_____

Exercise 16–2
Organizing the statement of
cash flows and supporting
footnote
(LO 1)

Use the following information about the 19X2 cash flows of Ulrich Company to prepare a statement of cash flows using the direct method and a footnote describing noncash investing and financing activities.

Cash and cash equivalents balance, December 31, 19X1 ..	$ 25,000
Cash and cash equivalents balance, December 31, 19X2 ..	70,000
Cash received as interest	2,500
Cash paid for salaries	72,500
Bonds payable retired by issuing common stock	
(there was no gain or loss on the retirement)	187,500
Cash paid to retire long-term notes payable	125,000
Cash received from sale of equipment	61,250
Cash borrowed on six-month note payable	25,000
Land purchased and financed by long-term note payable ..	106,250
Cash paid for store equipment	23,750
Cash dividends paid	15,000
Cash paid for other expenses	40,000
Cash received from customers	485,000
Cash paid for merchandise	252,500

Exercise 16–3
Calculating cash flows
(LO 2)

In each of the following cases, use the information provided about the 19X1 operations of Milwood Company to calculate the indicated cash flow:

Case A: Calculate cash paid for salaries:

Salaries expense	$ 51,000
Salaries payable, January 1	3,150
Salaries payable, December 31	3,750

Case B: Calculate cash received from customers:

Sales revenue	$510,000
Accounts receivable, January 1	25,200
Accounts receivable, December 31	34,800

Case C: Calculate cash paid for insurance:

Insurance expense	$ 68,400
Prepaid insurance, January 1	11,400
Prepaid insurance, December 31	17,100

Exercise 16–4
Calculating cash flows
(LO 2)

In each of the following cases, use the information provided about the 19X1 operations of Roche Company to calculate the indicated cash flow:

Case A: Calculate cash received from interest:

Interest revenue	$ 34,000
Interest receivable, January 1	3,000
Interest receivable, December 31	3,600

Case B: Calculate cash paid for rent:

Rent expense	$ 40,800
Rent payable, January 1	8,800
Rent payable, December 31	7,200

Case C: Calculate cash paid for merchandise:

Cost of goods sold	$528,000
Merchandise inventory, January 1	159,600
Accounts payable, January 1	67,800
Merchandise inventory, December 31	131,400
Accounts payable, December 31	84,000

Exercise 16–5
Cash flows from operating
activities (direct method)
(LO 2)

Use the following income statement and information about changes in noncash current assets and current liabilities to present the cash flows from operating activities using the direct method:

RYLANDER COMPANY
Income Statement
For Year Ended December 31, 19X1

Sales		$1,818,000
Cost of goods sold		891,000
Gross profit from sales		$ 927,000
Operating expenses:		
Salaries expense	$248,535	
Depreciation expense	43,200	
Rent expense	48,600	
Amortization expense, patents	5,400	
Utilities expense	19,125	364,860
Total		$ 562,140
Gain on sale of equipment		7,200
Net income		$ 569,340

Changes in current asset and current liability accounts during the year, all of which related to operating activities, were as follows:

Accounts receivable	$40,500 increase
Merchandise inventory	27,000 increase
Accounts payable	13,500 decrease
Salaries payable	4,500 decrease

Refer to the information about Rylander Company presented in Exercise 16–5. Use the indirect method and calculate the cash provided (or used) by operating activities.

Exercise 16–6
Cash flows from operating activities (indirect method)
(LO 3)

Eden Company's 19X1 income statement showed the following: net income, $364,000; depreciation expense, $45,000; amortization expense, $8,200; and gain on sale of plant assets, $7,000. An examination of the company's current assets and current liabilities showed that the following changes occurred because of operating activities: accounts receivable decreased $18,100; merchandise inventory decreased $52,000; prepaid expenses increased $3,700; accounts payable decreased $9,200; other payables increased $1,400. Use the indirect method to calculate the cash flow from operating activities.

Exercise 16–7
Cash flows from operating activities (indirect method)
(LO 3)

The following events occurred during the year. Assuming that the company uses the indirect method of reporting cash provided by operating activities, indicate the proper accounting treatment for each event listed below by placing an *x* in the appropriate column.

Exercise 16–8
Classifying transactions on statement of cash flows (indirect method)
(LO 3)

		Statement of Cash Flows			Footnote Describing Noncash Investing and Financing Activities	Not Reported on Statement or in Footnote
		Operating Activities	Investing Activities	Financing Activities		
a.	Sold plant equipment at a loss.	___	___	___	___	___
b.	Recorded depreciation expense.	___	___	___	___	___
c.	Income taxes payable increased by 15% from prior year.	___	___	___	___	___
d.	Declared and paid a cash dividend.	___	___	___	___	___
e.	Paid cash to purchase merchandise inventory.	___	___	___	___	___
f.	Land for a new plant was purchased by issuing common stock.	___	___	___	___	___
g.	Accounts receivable decreased during the year.	___	___	___	___	___

PROBLEMS

Problem 16–1
Statement of cash flows (direct method)
(LO 1, 2)

Infinity Corporation's 19X2 and 19X1 balance sheets carried the following items:

	December 31	
Debits	**19X2**	**19X1**
Cash	$ 174,000	$ 117,000
Accounts receivable	93,000	81,000
Merchandise inventory	609,000	534,000
Equipment	333,000	297,000
Totals	$1,209,000	$1,029,000
Credits		
Accumulated depreciation, equipment	$ 156,000	$ 102,000
Accounts payable	69,000	96,000
Income taxes payable	27,000	24,000
Common stock, $2 par value	582,000	558,000
Contributed capital in excess of par value, common stock	198,000	162,000
Retained earnings	177,000	87,000
Totals	$1,209,000	$1,029,000

An examination of the company's activities during 19X2, including the income statement, shows the following:

a.	Sales (all on credit)		$1,992,000
b.	Credits to Accounts Receivable during the period were receipts from customers.		
c.	Cost of goods sold		$1,194,000
d.	Purchases of merchandise were on credit.		
e.	Debits to Accounts Payable during the period resulted from payments for merchandise.		
f.	Depreciation expense	54,000	
g.	Other operating expenses (paid with cash)	501,000	
h.	Income taxes expense	42,000	1,791,000
i.	The only decreases in Income Taxes Payable were payments of taxes.		
j.	Net income		$ 201,000
k.	Equipment was purchased for $36,000 cash.		
l.	Twelve thousand shares of stock were issued for cash at $5 per share.		
m.	The company declared and paid $111,000 of cash dividends during the year.		

CHECK FIGURE:
Net cash provided by operating activities, $144,000

Required

Prepare a statement of cash flows that reports the cash inflows and outflows from operating activities according to the direct method. Show your supporting calculations.

Problem 16–2
Statement of cash flows (indirect method)
(LO 3)

Refer to Infinity Corporation's balance sheets presented in Problem 16–1. The additional information about the company's activities during 19X2 is restated as follows:

a. Net income was $201,000.

b. Accounts receivable increased.

c. Merchandise inventory increased.

d. Accounts payable decreased.

e. Income taxes payable increased.

f. Depreciation expense was $54,000.

g. Equipment was purchased for $36,000 cash.

h. Twelve thousand shares of stock were issued for cash at $5 per share.

i. The company declared and paid $111,000 of cash dividends during the year.

Required

Prepare a statement of cash flows that reports the cash inflows and outflows from operating activities according to the indirect method.

CHECK FIGURE:
Net cash provided by operating activities, $144,000

Refer to the facts about Infinity Corporation presented in Problem 16–1 and Problem 16–2.

Problem 16–3
Cash flows working paper (indirect method)
(LO 4)

Required

Prepare a statement of cash flows working paper that follows the indirect method of calculating cash flows from operating activities. Identify the debits and credits in the Analysis of Changes columns with letters that correspond to the list in Problem 16–2.

CHECK FIGURE:
Analysis of Changes column totals, $579,000

Comptex Company's 19X2 and 19X1 balance sheets included the following items:

Problem 16–4
Statement of cash flows (direct method)
(LO 1, 2)

	December 31	
Debits	**19X2**	**19X1**
Cash	$ 53,875	$ 76,625
Accounts receivable	65,000	49,625
Merchandise inventory	273,750	252,500
Prepaid expenses	5,375	6,250
Equipment	159,500	110,000
Totals	$557,500	$495,000
Credits		
Accumulated depreciation, equipment	$ 34,625	$ 44,000
Accounts payable	88,125	116,625
Short-term notes payable	10,000	6,250
Long-term notes payable	93,750	53,750
Common stock, $5 par value	168,750	156,250
Contributed capital in excess of		
par value, common stock	32,500	
Retained earnings	129,750	118,125
Totals	$557,500	$495,000

Additional information about the 19X2 activities of the company is as follows:

a. Sales revenue, all on credit $496,250
b. Credits to Accounts Receivable during the period were receipts from customers.
c. Cost of goods sold $250,000
d. All merchandise purchases were on credit.
e. Debits to Accounts Payable during the period resulted from payments to creditors.
f. Depreciation expense 18,750
g. Other expenses 136,500
h. The other expenses were paid in advance and were initially debited to Prepaid Expenses.
i. Income taxes expense (paid with cash) 12,125
j. Loss on sale of equipment 5,125   422,500
   The equipment cost $46,875, was depreciated by $28,125, and was sold for $13,625.
k. Net income .... $ 73,750
l. Equipment that cost $96,375 was purchased by paying cash of $25,000 and by signing a long-term note payable for the balance.
m. Borrowed $3,750 by signing a short-term note payable.
n. Paid $31,375 to reduce a long-term note payable.
o. Issued 2,500 shares of common stock for cash at $18 per share.
p. Declared and paid cash dividends of $62,125.

Required

Preparation component:

1. Prepare a statement of cash flows that reports the cash inflows and outflows from operating activities according to the direct method. Show your supporting calculations. Also prepare a footnote describing noncash investing and financing activities.

Analysis component:

2. Analyze and discuss the information contained in your answer to requirement 1, giving special attention to the wisdom of the dividend payment.

Problem 16–5
Statement of cash flows (indirect method)
(LO 3)

Refer to Comptex Company's balance sheets presented in Problem 16–4. The additional information about the company's activities during 19X2 is restated as follows:

a. Net income was $73,750.

b. Accounts receivable increased.

c. Merchandise inventory increased.

d. Prepaid expenses decreased.

e. Accounts payable decreased.

f. Depreciation expense was $18,750.

g. Equipment that cost $46,875 with accumulated depreciation of $28,125 was sold for $13,625 cash, which caused a loss of $5,125.

h. Equipment that cost $96,375 was purchased by paying cash of $25,000 and *(i)* by signing a long-term note payable for the balance.

j. Borrowed $3,750 by signing a short-term note payable.

k. Paid $31,375 to reduce a long-term note payable.

l. Issued 2,500 shares of common stock for cash at $18 per share.

m. Declared and paid cash dividends of $62,125.

Required

Prepare a statement of cash flows that reports the cash inflows and outflows from operating activities according to the indirect method.

Problem 16–6
Cash flows working paper (indirect method)
(LO 4)

Refer to the facts about Comptex Company presented in Problem 16–4 and Problem 16–5.

Required

Prepare a statement of cash flows working paper that follows the indirect method of calculating cash flows from operating activities. Identify the debits and credits in the Analysis of Changes columns with letters that correspond to the list for the company presented in Problem 16–5.

CRITICAL THINKING: ESSAYS, PROBLEMS, AND CASES

Analytical Essays

AE 16–1
(LO 2)

Write a brief essay explaining why, in preparing a statement of cash flows according to the direct method, it is generally better to determine the changes in cash by analyzing the changes in the noncash accounts rather than by examining the Cash account directly. You should include in your essay an explanation of why the changes in cash for the period equal the changes in the noncash balance sheet accounts.

The following items might be found on a working paper for a statement of cash flows. Write a brief essay describing where each item appears on a working paper for a statement of cash flows according to the indirect method. Also describe the nature of any debits and/or credits that should be entered in the Analysis of Changes columns next to each item, and any balancing entries.

AE 16–2
(LO 4)

a. Payment for purchase of plant assets.

b. Accounts receivable.

c. Depreciation expense.

Umlauf Company's 19X2 statement of cash flows appeared as follows:

Financial Reporting Problem

(LO 2)

Cash flows from operating activities:		
Cash received from customers	$451,800	
Cash paid for merchandise	(236,775)	
Cash paid for other operating expenses	(122,250)	
Cash paid for income taxes	(13,050)	
Net cash provided by operating activities		$79,725
Cash flows from investing activities:		
Cash received from sale of office equipment	$ 6,975	
Cash paid for store equipment	(10,500)	
Net cash used in investing activities		(3,525)
Cash flows from financing activities:		
Cash paid to retire bonds payable	$ (38,325)	
Cash paid for dividends	(18,750)	
Net cash used in financing activities		(57,075)
Net increase in cash		$19,125
Cash balance at beginning of year		23,925
Cash balance at end of year		$43,050

Umlauf's beginning and ending balance sheets were as follows:

	December 31	
	19X2	**19X1**
Debits		
Cash	$ 43,050	$ 23,925
Accounts receivable	34,125	39,825
Merchandise inventory	156,000	146,475
Prepaid expenses	3,600	1,650
Equipment	135,825	146,700
Totals	$372,600	$358,575
Credits		
Accumulated depreciation, equipment	$ 61,950	$ 47,550
Accounts payable	28,800	33,750
Income taxes payable	5,100	4,425
Dividends payable	-0-	4,500
Bonds payable	-0-	37,500
Common stock, $10 par value	168,750	168,750
Retained earnings	108,000	62,100
Totals	$372,600	$358,575

An examination of the company's statements and accounts showed:

a. All sales were made on credit.

b. All merchandise purchases were on credit.

c. Accounts Payable balances resulted from merchandise purchases.

d. Prepaid expenses relate to other operating expenses.

e. Equipment that cost $21,375 with accumulated depreciation of $11,100 was sold for cash.

f. Equipment was purchased for cash.

g. The change in the balance of Accumulated Depreciation resulted from depreciation expense and from the sale of equipment.

h. The change in the balance of Retained Earnings resulted from dividend declarations and net income.

Required

Present Umlauf's income statement for 19X2. Show your supporting calculations.

Financial Statement Analysis Case

(LO 1, 3)

Look in Appendix E at the end of the book to find Southwest Airlines Co.'s statement of cash flows. Based on your examination of that statement, answer the following questions:

1. Was Southwest Airlines Co.'s statement of cash flows prepared according to the direct method or the indirect method?

2. During each of the fiscal years 1994, 1993, and 1992, was the cash provided by operating activities more or less than the cash paid for dividends?

3. What was the largest item in reconciling the difference between net income and cash flow from operating activities in 1994?

4. Describe the major cash inflows and outflows from investing and financing activities during 1994.

5. The $648,000 change in other current assets on the 1994 statement of cash flows represents the net decrease resulting from a decrease in prepaid expenses and other current assets less an increase in inventories of parts and supplies, at cost. Why was this net decrease added rather than subtracted in the calculation of net cash provided by operating activities?

ANSWERS TO PROGRESS CHECKS

16-1 No. The statement of cash flows reports changes in the sum of cash plus cash equivalents. It does not report transfers between cash and cash equivalents.

16-2 The three categories of cash inflows and outflows are operating activities, investing activities, and financing activities.

16-3 The direct method is most informative. The indirect method is used most often.

16-4 a. Investing

b. Operating

c. Financing

d. Operating

e. Operating

f. Financing

16-5 $590,000 + ($120,000 − $90,000) = $620,000

16-6 $168,000 − ($32,000 − $28,000) − $2,400 = $161,600

16-7 $112,000 + ($4,200 − $1,200) − $5,600 = $109,400

16-8 $80,000 − $30,000 − $10,000 = $40,000

The $40,000 cash receipt should be reported as an investment activity.

16-9 $74,900 + $4,600 − $11,700 − $1,000 + $3,400 = $70,200

16-10 In the calculation of net income, expenses such as depreciation and amortization are subtracted because these expenses do not require current cash outflows. Therefore, adding these expenses back to net income eliminates noncash items from the net income number, converting it to a cash basis.

16-11 In the process of reconciling net income to net cash provided (or used) by operating activities, a gain on the sale of plant assets is subtracted from net income because a sale of plant assets is not an operating activity; it is an investing activity.

16-12 a

16-13 Investing activities during the year ended January 27, 1995, used net cash of $31,346,000. Cash outflows that contributed to this are described as cash paid for capital additions and businesses acquired, $31,365,000; the other investing activity was proceeds from sales of fixed assets, $19,000. The largest source of cash to finance these activities was $32,575,000 obtained from operating activities.

Analyzing Financial Statements

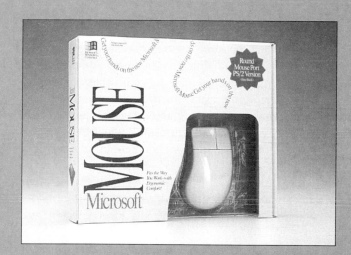

A group of high-tech wizards have a vision and a desire to create a computer software corporation. In their enthusiasm, they have told a few potential investors that their proposed company was likely to be so successful it would rival the current giants in the industry. Microsoft Corporation was named as an example of what the new venture was likely to become. The investors were quite familiar with the history of Microsoft and suggested that the wizards might be wise to be a little more moderate in their expectations. When the wizards disagreed, the investors pointed out that Microsoft was formed in 1975 and by 1995 had revenues of $5.9 billion.

In concluding the conversation, the investors gave the wizards a copy of Microsoft's 1995 annual report and suggested that they study it carefully to see if it really represented a goal they could achieve.

MICROSOFT CORPORATION
(In millions, except earnings per share)

	Year Ended June 30				
	1995	1994	1993	1992	1991
Net revenues	$5,937	$4,649	$3,753	$2,759	$1,843
Net income	1,453	1,146	953	708	463
Earnings per share	2.32	1.88	1.57	1.20	0.82
Total assets	7,210	5,363	3,805	2,640	1,644
Stockholders' equity	5,333	4,450	3,242	2,193	1,351

LEARNING OBJECTIVES

After studying Chapter 17 you should be able to:

1. Explain the relationship between financial reporting and general purpose financial statements.
2. Describe, prepare, and interpret comparative financial statements and common-size comparative statements.
3. Calculate and explain the interpretation of the ratios, turnovers, and rates of return used to evaluate *(a)* short-term liquidity, *(b)* long-term risk and capital structure, and *(c)* operating efficiency and profitability.
4. State the limitations associated with using financial statement ratios and the sources from which standards for comparison may be obtained.
5. Define or explain the words and phrases listed in the chapter glossary.

Chapter 17 demonstrates how to use the information in financial statements to evaluate the activities and financial status of a business. By explaining how you can relate the numbers in financial statements to each other, this chapter expands your ability to interpret the ratios we described in previous chapters.

FINANCIAL REPORTING

LO 1
Explain the relationship between financial reporting and general purpose financial statements.

Many people receive and analyze financial information about business firms. These people include managers, employees, directors, customers, suppliers, current and potential owners, current and potential lenders, brokers, regulatory authorities, lawyers, economists, labor unions, financial advisors, and financial analysts. Some of these, such as managers and some regulatory agencies, are able to gain access to specialized financial reports that meet their specific interests. However, the others must rely on the general purpose financial statements that companies publish periodically. **General purpose financial statements** include the (1) income statement, (2) balance sheet, (3) statement of changes in stockholders' equity (or statement of retained earnings), (4) statement of cash flows, and (5) footnotes related to the statements.

Financial reporting is intended to provide useful information to investors, creditors, and others for making investment, credit, and similar decisions. The information should help the users assess the amounts, timing, and uncertainty of prospective cash inflows and outflows.

Financial reporting includes communicating through a variety of means in addition to the financial statements. Some examples are reports filed with the Securities  and Exchange Commission, news releases, and management letters or analyses included in annual reports. For an example, in Appendix E look at the section of **Southwest Airlines Co.'s** annual report called Management's Discussion and Analysis of Financial Condition and Results of Operations.

Progress Check
(Answers to Progress Checks are provided at the end of the chapter.)

17-1   Who are the intended users of general purpose financial statements?

17-2   What statements are usually included in the general purpose financial statements published by corporations?

COMPARATIVE STATEMENTS

LO 2
Describe, prepare, and interpret comparative financial statements and common-size comparative statements.

In analyzing financial information, individual items usually are not very revealing. However, important relationships exist between items and groups of items. As a result, financial statement analysis involves identifying and describing relationships between items and groups of items and changes in those items.

You can see changes in financial statement items more clearly when amounts for two or more successive accounting periods are placed side by side in columns on a

Illustration 17–1

MICROSOFT CORPORATION
Comparative Balance Sheet
June 30, 1995, and June 30, 1994
(in millions)

	June 30 1995	June 30 1994	Amount of Increase or (Decrease) during 1995	Percentage Increase or (Decrease) during 1995
Assets				
Current assets:				
Cash and short-term investments	$4,750	$3,614	$1,136	31.4
Accounts receivable, net of allowances of $139 and $92	581	475	106	22.3
Inventories	88	102	(14)	(13.7)
Other	201	121	80	66.1
Total current assets	$5,620	$4,312	$1,308	30.3
Property, plant, and equipment—net	1,192	930	262	28.2
Other assets	398	121	277	228.9
Total assets	$7,210	$5,363	$1,847	34.4
Liabilities and Stockholders' Equity				
Current liabilities:				
Accounts payable	$ 563	$ 324	$ 239	73.8
Accrued compensation	130	96	34	35.4
Income taxes payable	410	305	105	34.4
Other	244	188	56	29.8
Total current liabilities	$1,347	$ 913	$ 434	47.5
Minority interest	125	—	125	—
Put warrants	405	—	405	—
Stockholders' equity:				
Common stock and paid-in capital— shares authorized 2,000; issued and outstanding 581 and 588	2,005	1,500	505	33.7
Retained earnings	3,328	2,950	378	12.8
Total stockholders' equity	$5,333	$4,450	$ 883	19.8
Total liabilities and stockholders' equity	$7,210	$5,363	$1,847	34.4

single statement. Statements prepared in this manner are called **comparative statements.** Each financial statement can be presented in this comparative format.

In its simplest form, a comparative balance sheet consists of the amounts from two or more successive balance sheet dates arranged side by side. However, the usefulness of the statement can be improved by also showing each item's dollar amount of change and percentage change. When this is done, large dollar or percentage changes are more readily apparent. Illustration 17–1 shows this type of comparative balance sheet for Microsoft Corporation.

A comparative income statement is prepared in the same way. Amounts for two or more successive periods are placed side by side, with dollar and percentage changes in additional columns. Look at Illustration 17–2 to see **Microsoft Corporation's** comparative income statement.

Illustration 17-2

MICROSOFT CORPORATION
Comparative Income Statement
For Years Ended June 30, 1995 and 1994
(in millions)

	Years Ended June 30		Amount of Increase or (Decrease) during 1995	Percentage Increase or (Decrease) during 1995
	1995	1994		
Net revenues...........................	$5,937	$4,649	$1,288	27.7
Operating expenses:				
Cost of revenues	$ 877	$ 763	$ 114	14.9
Research and development	860	610	250	41.0
Sales and marketing	1,895	1,384	511	36.9
General and administrative	267	166	101	60.8
Total operating expenses	$3,899	$2,923	$ 976	33.4
Operating income	$2,038	$1,726	$ 312	18.1
Interest income—net	191	102	89	87.3
Noncontinuing items*	(46)	(90)	(44)	(48.9)
Other expenses*	(16)	(16)	0	0
Income before income taxes	$2,167	$1,722	$ 445	25.8
Provision for income taxes	714	576	138	24.0
Net income	$1,453	$1,146	$ 307	26.8
Earnings per share	$ 2.32	$ 1.88	$ 0.44	23.4
Weighted-average shares outstanding	627	610		

*On these lines, the (46), (90), and the two (16)s are shown in parentheses because they represent expenses that are subtracted in the calculation of income. The (44) is in parentheses because the Noncontinuing items decreased from 90 to 46. In the third column, the expense decrease (44) must be added to the $312 and $89 increases in operating income and interest income to reconcile the $445 increase in Income before income taxes.

Calculating Percentage Increases and Decreases

To calculate the percentage increases and decreases on comparative statements, divide the dollar increase or decrease of an item by the amount shown for the item in the base year. If no amount is shown in the base year, or if the base year amount is negative (such as a net loss), a percentage increase or decrease cannot be calculated.

In this text, percentages and ratios typically are rounded to one or two decimal places. However, there is no uniform practice on this matter. In general, percentages should be carried out far enough to be meaningful. They should not be carried out so far that the important relationships become lost in the length of the numbers.

Analyzing and Interpreting Comparative Statements

In analyzing comparative data, study any items that show significant dollar or percentage changes. Then, try to identify the reasons for each change and, if possible, determine whether they are favorable or unfavorable. For example, in Illustration 17–1, the first item, "Cash and short-term investments," shows a $1,136 million increase (31.4%). To a large extent, this may be explained by the increase in three other items: the $405 million increase in "Put warrants," the $505 million increase in "Common stock and paid-in capital" and the $378 million increase in "Retained earnings."

Note that **Microsoft Corporation's** current liabilities increased by $434 million. In light of this, the $1,136 million increase in "Cash and short-term investments" might appear to be an excessive investment in highly liquid assets that usually earn a low return. However, the company's very strong and liquid financial position indicates an outstanding ability to respond to new opportunities such as the acquisition of other companies.

Now look at the comparative income statement for Microsoft in Illustration 17–2. Microsoft's rapid growth is reflected by its 27.7% increase in net revenues. In fact, we should point out that the growth in 1995 continued a very strong trend established in prior years. (Later, we present data showing that net revenues in 1995 were 322% of net revenues in 1991.) Perhaps the most fundamental reason for this is the company's commitment to research and development. Note that research and development expenses were $860 million in 1995, up $610 million from 1994.

Most of the income statement items (except "Noncontinuing items" and "Other expenses") reflect the company's rapid growth. The increases ranged from 14.9 to 87.3%. Especially note the large $511 million, or 36.9%, increase in "Sales and marketing." This suggests the company's leadership and strong response to competition in the software industry. Although the dollar increase in "Interest income—net" was only $89 million, this amounted to an 87.3% increase. This is consistent with the large increase in cash and short-term investments reported on the balance sheet.

Trend Percentages

Trend percentages (also known as *index numbers*) can be used to describe changes that have occurred from one period to the next. They also are used to compare data that cover a number of years. To calculate trend percentages:

1. Select a base year and assign each item on the base year statement a weight of 100%.
2. Express each item from the statements for the other years as a percentage of its base year amount. To determine these percentages, divide the amounts in the non-base years by the amount of the item in the base year.

For example, consider the following data for Microsoft Corporation:

	1995	1994	1993	1992	1991
Net revenues	$5,937	$4,649	$3,753	$2,759	$1,843
Cost of revenues	877	763	633	467	362
Gross profit	$5,060	$3,886	$3,120	$2,292	$1,481

Using 1991 as the base year, we calculate the trend percentages for each year by dividing the dollar amounts in each year by the 1991 dollar amounts. When the percentages are calculated, the trends for these items appear as follows:

	1995	1994	1993	1992	1991
Net revenues	322.1%	252.3%	203.6%	149.7%	100%
Cost of revenues ..	242.3	210.8	174.9	129.0	100
Gross profit	341.7	262.4	210.7	154.8	100

Illustration 17-3 Trend Lines Showing Percentage Changes in Net Revenues, Cost of Revenues, and Gross Profit

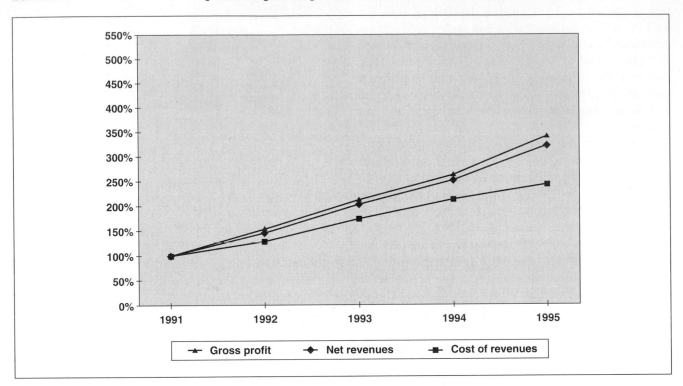

Illustration 17–3 presents the same data in a graph. A graph can help you identify trends and detect changes in their strength or direction. For example, note that the gross profit line and the net revenues line were essentially straight from 1991 to 1994 but bent slightly upward from 1994 to 1995. In other words, the rates of increase were basically unchanged from 1991 to 1994 but improved slightly from 1994 to 1995.

A graph also may help you identify and understand the relationships between items. For example, the graph in Illustration 17–3 shows that through 1995, cost of revenues increased at a rate that was somewhat less than the increase in net revenues. Further, the differing trends in these two items had a clear effect on the percentage changes in gross profit. That is, gross profit increased each year at a faster rate than net revenues or cost of revenues.

The analysis of financial statement items also may include the relationships between items on different financial statements. For example, note the following comparison of Microsoft's total assets and net revenues:

	1995	1991	1995 Amount as a Percentage of 1991
Net revenues	$5,937	$1,843	322.1%
Total assets (fiscal year-end)	7,210	1,644	438.6

The rate of increase in total assets was even larger than the increase in net revenues. Was this change favorable? We cannot say for sure. It might suggest that the company is no longer able to use its assets as efficiently as in earlier years. On the other hand, it might mean that the company is poised for even greater growth in future years. Financial statement analysis often leads the analyst to ask questions, without providing one clear answer.

Illustration 17-4

	June 30		Common-Size Percentages	
	1995	1994	1995	1994
MICROSOFT CORPORATION				

MICROSOFT CORPORATION
Common-Size Comparative Balance Sheet
June 30, 1995, and June 30, 1994
(in millions)

	June 30		Common-Size Percentages	
	1995	1994	1995	1994
Assets				
Current assets:				
Cash and short-term investments	$4,750	$3,614	65.9	67.4
Accounts receivable, net of				
allowances of $139 and $92	581	475	8.1	8.9
Inventories	88	102	1.2	1.9
Other	201	121	2.8	2.3
Total current assets	$5,620	$4,312	78.0*	80.4†
Property, plant, and equipment—net	1,192	930	16.5	17.3
Other assets	398	121	5.5	2.3
Total assets	$7,210	$5,363	100.0	100.0
Liabilities and Stockholders' Equity				
Current liabilities:				
Accounts payable	$ 563	$ 324	7.8	6.0
Accrued compensation	130	96	1.8	1.8
Income taxes payable	410	305	5.7	5.7
Other	244	188	3.4	3.5
Total current liabilities	$1,347	$ 913	18.7	17.0
Minority interest	125		1.7	
Put warrants	405	—	5.6	
Stockholders' equity:				
Common stock and paid-in capital—				
shares authorized 2,000; issued and				
outstanding 581 and 588	$2,005	$1,500	27.8	28.0
Retained earnings	3,328	2,950	46.2	55.0
Total stockholders' equity	$5,333	$4,450	74.0	83.0
Total liabilities and stockholders' equity ..	$7,210	$5,363	100.0	100.0

*Adjusted for rounding.
†Does not foot due to rounding.

Common-Size Comparative Statements

Although the comparative statements illustrated so far show how each item has changed over time, they do not emphasize the relative importance of each item. Changes in the relative importance of each financial statement item are shown more clearly by **common-size comparative statements.**

In common-size statements, each item is expressed as a percentage of a *base amount.* For a common-size balance sheet, the base amount is usually the amount of total assets. This total is assigned a value of 100%. (Of course, the total amount of liabilities plus stockholders' equity also equals 100%.) Then, each asset, liability, and stockholders' equity item is shown as a percentage of total assets (or total liabilities plus stockholders' equity). If you present a company's successive balance sheets in this way, changes in the mixture of the assets or liabilities and equity are more readily apparent.

For example, look at the common-size comparative balance sheet for Microsoft in Illustration 17–4. Note that Cash and short-term investments amounted to 67.4% of

Illustration 17–5

MICROSOFT CORPORATION
Common-Size Comparative Income Statement
For Years Ended June 30, 1995 and 1994
(in millions)

	Years Ended June 30		Common-Size Percentages	
	1995	1994	1995	1994
Net revenues	$5,937	$4,649	100.0	100.0
Operating expenses:				
Cost of revenues	$ 877	$ 763	14.8	16.4
Research and development	860	610	14.5	13.1
Sales and marketing	1,895	1,384	31.9	29.8
General and administrative	267	166	4.5	3.6
Total operating expenses	$3,899	$2,923	65.7	62.9
Operating income	$2,038	$1,726	34.3	37.1
Interest income—net	191	102	3.2	2.2
Noncontinuing items	(46)	(90)	(0.8)	(1.9)
Other expenses	(16)	(16)	(0.3)	(0.3)
Income before income taxes	$2,167	$1,722	36.5*	37.0*
Provision for income taxes	714	576	12.0	12.4
Net income	$1,453	$1,146	24.5	24.7*
Earnings per share	$ 2.32	$ 1.88		
Weighted-average shares outstanding	627	610		

*Does not foot due to rounding.

total assets at the end of the 1994 fiscal year. By comparison, they were 65.9% of total assets at the end of 1995.

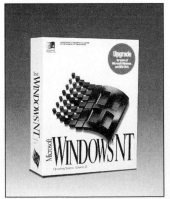

In producing a common-size income statement, the amount of net sales is usually the base amount and is assigned a value of 100%. Then, each statement item appears as a percentage of net sales. If you think of the 100% sales amount as representing one sales dollar, the remaining items show how each sales dollar was distributed among costs, expenses, and profit. For example, the comparative income statement in Illustration 17–5 shows that for each dollar of **Microsoft's** net revenue during 1995, research and development expenses amounted to 14.5 cents. In 1994, research and development consumed 13.1 cents of each sales dollar.

Common-size percentages help the analyst see any potentially important changes in a company's expenses. For Microsoft, the relative size of each expense changed very little from 1994 to 1995.

Many corporate annual reports include graphic presentations such as those in Illustration 17–6 from Microsoft's 1995 Annual Report. The bar charts in the illustration show the revenues generated by each of the company's sales channels. The OEM chart in the illustration refers to original equipment manufacturers.

Illustration 17-6   Bar-Chart Presentations of Sales Channels, Microsoft Corporation

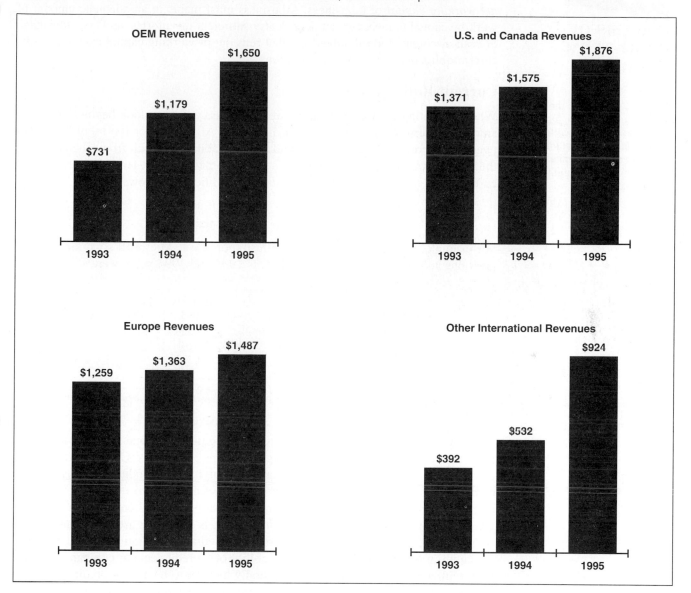

Progress Check

17-3   On common-size comparative statements, which of the following is true?   *(a)* Each item is expressed as a percentage of a base amount.   *(b)* Total assets is assigned a value of 100%.   *(c)* Amounts from two or more successive periods are placed side by side.   *(d)* All of the above are true.

17-4   What is the difference between the percentages shown on a comparative income statement and those shown on a common-size comparative income statement?

17-5   Trend percentages: *(a)* Are shown on the comparative income statement and balance sheet;   *(b)* Are shown on common-size comparative statements; or   *(c)* Are also known as index numbers.

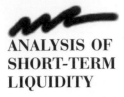

ANALYSIS OF SHORT-TERM LIQUIDITY

LO 3
Calculate and explain the interpretation of the ratios, turnovers, and rates of return used to evaluate *(a)* short-term liquidity, *(b)* long-term risk and capital structure, and *(c)* operating efficiency and profitability.

The amount of current assets less current liabilities is called the **working capital** or *net working capital* of a business. A business must maintain an adequate amount of working capital to meet current debts, carry sufficient inventories, and take advantage of cash discounts. Indeed, a business that runs out of working capital cannot meet its current obligations or continue operations.

Current Ratio

When evaluating the working capital of a business, you must look beyond the dollar amount of current assets less current liabilities. Also consider the relationship between the amounts of current assets and current liabilities. Recall from Chapter 5 that the *current ratio* describes a company's ability to pay its short-term obligations. The current ratio relates current assets to current liabilities, as follows:

$$\text{Current ratio} = \frac{\text{Current assets}}{\text{Current liabilities}}$$

For example, using the information in Illustration 17–1, Microsoft's working capital positions and current ratios at the end of its 1995 and 1994 years were:

(In millions)	June 30, 1995	June 30, 1994
Current assets	$5,620	$4,312
Current liabilities	1,347	913
Working capital	$4,273	$3,399
Current ratio:		
$5,620/$1,347	4.2 to 1	
$4,312/$913		4.7 to 1

A high current ratio generally indicates a strong position because a high ratio suggests the company is capable of meeting its current obligations. On the other hand, a company might have a current ratio that is too high. This condition means that the company has invested too much in current assets compared to its needs. Normally, current assets do not generate very much additional revenue. Therefore, if a company invests too much in current assets, the investment is not being used efficiently.

Years ago, bankers and other creditors often used a current ratio of 2 to 1 as a rule of thumb in evaluating the debt-paying ability of a credit-seeking company. A company with a 2 to 1 current ratio was generally thought to be a good credit risk in the short run. However, most lenders realize that the 2 to 1 rule of thumb is not a good test of debt-paying ability. Whether a company's current ratio is good or bad depends on at least three factors:

1. The nature of the company's business.
2. The composition of its current assets.
3. The turnover rate for some of its current assets.

Whether a company's current ratio is adequate depends on the nature of its business. A service company that has no inventories other than supplies and that grants little or no credit may be able to operate on a current ratio of less than 1 to 1 if its sales generate enough cash to pay its current liabilities on time. On the other hand, a company that sells high-fashion clothing or furniture may occasionally misjudge customer demand. If this happens, the company's inventory may not generate as much cash as expected. A company that faces risks like these may need a current ratio of much more than 2 to 1 to protect its liquidity.

Therefore, when you study the adequacy of working capital, consider the type of business under review. Before you decide that a company's current ratio is too low or too high, compare the company's current ratio with ratios of other successful companies in the same industry. Another important source of insight is to observe how the ratio has changed over time.

Keep in mind that the current ratio can be affected by a company's choice of an inventory flow assumption. For example, a company that uses LIFO tends to report a smaller amount of current assets than if it uses FIFO. Therefore, consider the underlying factors before deciding that a given current ratio is acceptable.

Also consider the composition of a company's current assets when you evaluate its working capital position. Cash and short-term investments are more liquid than accounts and notes receivable. And, short-term receivables normally are more liquid than merchandise inventory. Cash can be used to pay current debts at once. But, accounts receivable and merchandise inventory must be converted into cash before payments can be made. Therefore, an excessive amount of receivables and inventory could weaken the company's ability to pay its current liabilities.

One way to take the composition of current assets into account is to evaluate the acid-test ratio. We discuss this next; then, we examine the turnover rates for receivables and inventories.

Acid-Test Ratio

Recall from Chapter 6 that an easily calculated check on current asset composition is the *acid-test ratio,* also called the *quick ratio.* Quick assets are cash, short-term investments, accounts receivable, and notes receivable. These are the most liquid types of current assets. Calculate the ratio as follows:

$$\text{Acid-test ratio} = \frac{\text{Quick assets}}{\text{Current liabilities}}$$

Using the information in Illustration 17–1, we calculate Microsoft's acid-test ratios as follows:

(In millions)	June 30, 1995	June 30, 1994
Cash and short-term investments . .	$4,750	$3,614
Accounts receivable, net of allowances	581	475
Total quick assets	$5,331	$4,089
Current liabilities	$1,347	$ 913
Acid-test ratio:		
$5,331/$1,347	4.0 to 1	
$4,089/$913		4.5 to 1

A traditional rule of thumb for an acceptable acid-test ratio is 1 to 1. However, as is true for all financial ratios, you should be skeptical about rules of thumb. The working capital requirements of a company are also affected by how frequently the company converts its current assets into cash. Thus, a careful analysis of a company's short-term liquidity should include additional analyses of its receivables and inventories.

Accounts Receivable Turnover

One way to measure how frequently a company converts its receivables into cash is to calculate the *accounts receivable turnover.* As you learned in Chapter 8, this is calculated as follows:

$$\text{Accounts receivable turnover} = \frac{\text{Net sales}}{\text{Average accounts receivable}}$$

Although this ratio is widely known as accounts receivable turnover, all short-term receivables from customers normally are included in the denominator. Thus, if a company has short-term notes receivable, those balances should be included with the accounts receivable. In the numerator, the calculation would be more precise if credit sales were used. Usually, however, net sales is used because information about credit sales is not available.

Applying the formula to Microsoft's 1995 fiscal year results, the company's accounts receivable turnover was:

$$\frac{\$5,937}{(\$581 + \$475)/2} = 11.2 \text{ times}$$

If accounts receivable are collected quickly, the accounts receivable turnover is high. In general, this is favorable because it means that the company does not have to commit large amounts of capital to accounts receivable. However, an accounts receivable turnover may be too high. This might occur when credit terms are so restrictive they negatively affect sales volume.

Sometimes, the ending accounts receivable balance can substitute for the average balance in calculating accounts receivable turnover. This is acceptable if the effect is not significant. Also, some analysts prefer using gross accounts receivable before subtracting the allowance for doubtful accounts. However, balance sheets may report only the net amount of accounts receivable.

Days' Sales Uncollected

Accounts receivable turnover is only one way to measure how frequently a company collects its accounts. Another method is to calculate the *days' sales uncollected,* which we defined in Chapter 7 as:

$$\text{Days' sales uncollected} = \frac{\text{Accounts receivable}}{\text{Net sales}} \times 365$$

Although this formula takes the usual approach of placing accounts receivable in the numerator, short-term notes receivable from customers should be included. To illustrate, we refer to the information about Microsoft in Illustrations 17–1 and 17–2. The days' sales uncollected on June 30, 1995, was:

$$\frac{\$581}{\$5,937} \times 365 = 35.7 \text{ days}$$

Days' sales uncollected has more meaning if you know the credit terms. A rule of thumb is that days' sales uncollected: *(a)* should not exceed one and one-third times the days in the credit period, if discounts are not offered; or *(b)* should not exceed one and one-third times the days in its discount period, if discounts are offered.

Turnover of Merchandise Inventory

Working capital requirements also are affected by how long a company holds merchandise inventory before selling it. This effect can be measured by calculating *merchandise turnover,* which we defined in Chapter 9 as:

$$\text{Merchandise turnover} = \frac{\text{Cost of goods sold}}{\text{Average merchandise inventory}}$$

Using the cost of revenues and inventories information in Illustrations 17–1 and 17–2, we calculate Microsoft's merchandise turnover during 1995 as follows (cost of goods sold is called *cost of revenues* on Microsoft's income statement):

$$\frac{\$877}{(\$88 + \$102)/2} = 9.2 \text{ times}$$

In this calculation, the average inventory was estimated by averaging the beginning and the ending inventories for 1995. In case the beginning and ending inventories do not represent the amount normally on hand, an average of the quarterly inventories may be used, if that is available.

From a working capital point of view, a company with a high turnover requires a smaller investment in inventory than one that produces the same sales with a low turnover. On the other hand, the merchandise turnover may be too high if a company keeps such a small inventory that sales volume is restricted.

Days' Stock on Hand

Recall from Chapter 9 that *days' stock on hand* is another means of evaluating the liquidity of a company's inventory. It relates to inventory in a similar fashion as days' sales uncollected relates to receivables. The calculation is:

$$\text{Days' stock on hand} = \frac{\text{Ending inventory}}{\text{Cost of goods sold}} \times 365$$

Applying the formula to Microsoft's 1995 information, we calculate days' stock on hand as:

$$\frac{\$88}{\$877} \times 365 = 36.6 \text{ days}$$

Assuming the particular products in inventory are those customers demand, the formula estimates that the inventory will be converted into receivables (or cash) in 36.6 days. If all of **Microsoft's** sales were credit sales, the conversion of inventory to receivables in 36.6 days plus the conversion of receivables to cash in 35.7 days would suggest that the inventory would be converted into cash in about 72 days (36.6 + 35.7 approx. ≅ 72.3).

Progress Check

17-6   The following is taken from the 12/31/X2 balance sheet of Paff Company: cash, $820,000; accounts receivable, $240,000; inventories, $470,000; plant and equipment, $910,000; accounts payable, $350,000; and income taxes payable, $180,000. Calculate the *(a)* current ratio and *(b)* acid-test ratio.

17-7   On 12/31/X1, Paff Company (see Progress Check 17-6) had accounts receivable of $290,000 and inventories of $530,000. Also, during 19X2, net sales amounted to $2,500,000 and cost of goods sold was $750,000. Calculate the *(a)* accounts receivable turnover, *(b)* days' sales uncollected, *(c)* merchandise turnover, and *(d)* days' stock on hand.

An analysis of working capital evaluates the short-term liquidity of the company. However, analysts also are interested in a company's ability to meet its obligations and provide security to its creditors over the long run. Indicators of this ability include *debt* and *equity* ratios, the relationship between *pledged assets and secured liabilities,* and the company's capacity to earn *sufficient income to pay its fixed interest charges.*

ANALYSIS OF LONG-TERM RISK AND CAPITAL STRUCTURE

LO 3
Calculate and explain the interpretation of the ratios, turnovers, and rates of return used to evaluate *(a)* short-term liquidity, *(b)* long-term risk and capital structure, and *(c)* operating efficiency and profitability.

Debt and Equity Ratios

Financial analysts are always interested in the portion of a company's assets contributed by its owners and the portion contributed by creditors. This relationship is described by the debt ratio you learned about in Chapter 3. Recall that the debt ratio expresses total liabilities as a percentage of total assets. The **equity ratio** provides complementary information by expressing total stockholders' equity as a percentage of total assets.

Microsoft Corporation's June 30, 1995, balance sheet includes two items that require special consideration. They are minority interest of $125 million and put warrants of $405 million. These items are explained in more advanced courses. However, in calculating debt and equity ratios, they may be recognized by calculating a separate percentage for each one. The following calculations show this approach:

	June 30, 1995	Percentages
Total liabilities (all short-term)	$1,347	18.7%
Minority interest	125	1.7
Put warrants	405	5.6
Total stockholders' equity	5,333	80.0
Total liabilities and stockholders' equity	$7,210	100.0%

Microsoft's financial statements reflect very little debt compared to most companies. It has no long-term liabilities, and at the end of the 1995 year, its current liabilities provide only 18.7% of the total assets. In general, a company is less risky if it has only a small amount of debt in its capital structure. The larger the portion provided by stockholders, the more losses can be absorbed by stockholders before the remaining assets become inadequate to satisfy the claims of creditors.

From the stockholders' point of view, however, including debt in the capital structure of a company may be desirable, so long as the risk is not too great. If a business can earn a return on borrowed capital that is higher than the cost of borrowing, the difference represents increased income to stockholders. Because debt can have the effect of increasing the return to stockholders, the inclusion of debt is sometimes described as *financial leverage*. Companies are said to be highly leveraged if a large portion of their assets is financed by debt.

Pledged Assets to Secured Liabilities

In Chapter 13, we explained how to use the ratio of pledged assets to secured liabilities to evaluate the risk of nonpayment faced by secured creditors. Recall that the ratio also may provide information of interest to unsecured creditors. The ratio is calculated as follows:

$$\text{Pledged assets to secured liabilities} = \frac{\text{Book value of pledged assets}}{\text{Secured liabilities}}$$

Regardless of how helpful this ratio might be in evaluating the risk faced by creditors, the information needed to calculate the ratio is seldom presented in published financial statements. Thus, it is used primarily by persons who have the ability to obtain the information directly from the company managers.

The usual rule-of-thumb minimum value for this ratio is 2 to 1. However, the ratio needs careful interpretation because it is based on the book value of the pledged assets. As you know, book values are not intended to reflect the amount that would be received for the assets in a liquidation sale. Also, the long-term earning ability of the company with pledged assets may be more important than the value of the pledged assets. Creditors prefer that a debtor be able to pay with cash generated by operating activities rather than with cash obtained by liquidating assets.

Times Fixed Interest Charges Earned

As you learned in Chapter 12, the *times fixed interest charges earned* ratio is often calculated to describe the security of the return offered to creditors. The amount of income before the deduction of interest charges and income taxes is the amount available to pay the interest charges. Calculate the ratio as follows:

$$\text{Times fixed interest charges earned} = \frac{\text{Income before interest and income taxes}}{\text{Interest expense}}$$

The larger this ratio, the greater the security for the lenders. A rule of thumb for this statistic is that creditors are reasonably safe if the company earns its fixed interest charges two or more times each year. Look in Illustration 17–2 and observe that Microsoft did not report interest expense as a separate item. Apparently interest expense is not material; probably it is offset against interest income which is reported as "Interest income—net." Also recall from Illustration 17–1 that Microsoft did not have any long-term debt. Furthermore, few if any of the company's current liabilities would be likely to generate interest expense. As a result, we are not able to calculate a times fixed interest charges earned ratio for Microsoft. Yet, we should again recognize that there appears to be little risk for Microsoft's creditors.

ANALYSIS OF OPERATING EFFICIENCY AND PROFITABILITY

Financial analysts are especially interested in the ability of a company to use its assets efficiently to produce profits for its owners and thus to provide cash flows to them. Several ratios are available to help you evaluate operating efficiency and profitability.

Profit Margin

The operating efficiency of a company can be expressed in two components. The first is the company's *profit margin*. As you learned in Chapter 4, this ratio describes a company's ability to earn a net income from sales. It is measured by expressing net income as a percentage of revenues. For example, we can use the information in Illustration 17–2 to calculate **Microsoft's** 1995 profit margin as follows:

$$\text{Profit margin} = \frac{\text{Net income}}{\text{Revenues}} = \frac{\$1,453}{\$5,937} = 24.5\%$$

To evaluate the profit margin of a company, consider the nature of the industry in which the company operates. For example, a publishing company might be expected to have a profit margin between 10% and 15%, while a retail supermarket might have a normal profit margin of 1% or 2%.

Total Asset Turnover

The second component of operating efficiency is *total asset turnover*, which describes the ability of the company to use its assets to generate sales. In Chapter 10, you learned to calculate this ratio as follows:

$$\text{Total asset turnover} = \frac{\text{Net sales}}{\text{Average total assets}}$$

In calculating Microsoft's total asset turnover for 1995, we follow the usual practice of averaging the total assets at the beginning and the end of the year. Taking the information from Illustrations 17–1 and 17–2, the calculation is:

$$\frac{\$5,937}{(\$7,210 + \$5,363)/2} = .944 \text{ times}^*$$

*Carried to three decimal places to avoid later rounding error.

Both profit margin and total asset turnover describe the two basic components of operating efficiency. However, they also evaluate management performance because the management of a company is fundamentally responsible for its operating efficiency.

Return on Total Assets

Because operating efficiency has two basic components (profit margin and total asset turnover), analysts frequently calculate a summary measure of these components. This summary measure is the *return on total assets* that we discussed in Chapter 11. Recall that the calculation is:

$$\text{Return on total assets} = \frac{\text{Net income}}{\text{Average total assets}}$$

Applying this to Microsoft's 1995 year, we calculate return on total assets as:

$$\frac{\$1,453}{(\$7,210 + \$5,363)/2} = 23.1\%$$

Microsoft's 23.1% return on total assets appears very favorable compared to most businesses. However, you should make comparisons with competing companies and alternative investment opportunities before reaching a final conclusion. Also, you should evaluate the trend in the rates of return earned by the company in recent years.

Earlier, we said that the return on total assets summarizes the two components of operating efficiency—profit margin and total asset turnover. The following calculation shows the relationship between these three measures. Notice that both profit margin and total asset turnover contribute to overall operating efficiency, as measured by return on total assets.

Profit margin	×	Total asset turnover	=	Return on total assets
$\dfrac{\text{Net income}}{\text{Net sales}}$	×	$\dfrac{\text{Net sales}}{\text{Average total assets}}$	=	$\dfrac{\text{Net income}}{\text{Average total assets}}$

For Microsoft Corporation:

24.5%	×	.944	=	23.1%

Return on Common Stockholders' Equity

Perhaps the most important reason for operating a business is to earn a net income for its owners. The *return on common stockholders' equity* measures the success of a business in reaching this goal. In Chapter 2, we simplified this calculation by basing it on the beginning balance of stockholders' equity. However, many companies have frequent transactions that involve issuing and perhaps repurchasing stock during each year. Thus, you should allow for these events by calculating the return based on the average stockholders' equity, as follows:

$$\text{Return on common stockholders' equity} = \frac{\text{Net income} - \text{Preferred dividends}}{\text{Average common stockholders' equity}}$$

Recall from Illustration 17–1 that Microsoft did not have any preferred stock outstanding. As a result, we determine Microsoft's 1995 return as follows:

$$\frac{\$1,453}{(\$5,333 + \$4,450)/2} = 29.7\%$$

When preferred stock is outstanding, the denominator in the calculation should be the book value of the common stock. In the numerator, the dividends on cumulative preferred stock must be subtracted whether they were declared or are in arrears. If the preferred is not cumulative, the dividends are subtracted only if declared.

Price-Earnings Ratio

Recall from Chapter 15 that the *price-earnings ratio* is calculated as follows:

$$\text{Price-earnings ratio} = \frac{\text{Market price per share}}{\text{Earnings per share}}$$

Sometimes, the predicted earnings per share for the next period is used in the denominator of the calculation. Other times, the reported earnings per share for the most recent period is used. In either case, the ratio is an indicator of the future growth of and risk related to the company's earnings as perceived by investors who establish the market price of the stock.

During 1995, the market price of Microsoft's common stock ranged from a low of $58.25 to a high of $109.25. Using the $2.32 earnings per share that was reported after the year-end, the price-earnings ratios for the low and the high were:

$$\text{Low:} \qquad \frac{\$58.25}{\$2.32} = 25.1$$

$$\text{High:} \qquad \frac{\$109.25}{\$2.32} = 47.1$$

Microsoft's price-earnings ratios are much higher than for most companies. No doubt, Microsoft's high ratios reflect the expectation of investors that the company would continue to grow at a much higher rate than most companies.

Dividend Yield

As you learned in Chapter 14, *dividend yield* is a statistic used to compare the dividend-paying performance of different investment alternatives. The formula is:

$$\text{Dividend yield} = \frac{\text{Annual dividends per share}}{\text{Market price per share}}$$

Some companies may not declare dividends because they need the cash in the business. For example, Microsoft's 1995 Annual Report stated that the company had not declared any dividends.

Progress Check

17-8 Which ratio describes the security of the return offered to creditors? *(a)* Debt ratio; *(b)* Equity ratio; *(c)* Times fixed interest charges earned; *(d)* Pledged assets to secured liabilities.

17-9 Which ratio measures the success of a business in earning net income for its owners? *(a)* Profit margin; *(b)* Return on common stockholders' equity; *(c)* Price-earnings ratio; *(d)* Dividend yield.

17-10 If BK Company has net sales of $8,500,000, net income of $945,000, and total asset turnover of 1.8 times, what is BK's return on total assets?

REVIEW OF FINANCIAL STATEMENT RATIOS AND STATISTICS FOR ANALYSIS

To evaluate short-term liquidity, use these ratios:

$$\text{Current ratio} = \frac{\text{Current assets}}{\text{Current liabilities}}$$

$$\text{Acid-test ratio} = \frac{\text{Cash} + \text{Short-term investments} + \text{Current receivables}}{\text{Current liabilities}}$$

$$\text{Accounts receivable turnover} = \frac{\text{Net sales}}{\text{Average accounts receivable}}$$

$$\text{Days' sales uncollected} = \frac{\text{Accounts receivable}}{\text{Net sales}} \times 365$$

$$\text{Merchandise turnover} = \frac{\text{Cost of goods sold}}{\text{Average merchandise inventory}}$$

$$\text{Days' stock on hand} = \frac{\text{Ending inventory}}{\text{Cost of goods sold}} \times 365$$

To evaluate long-term risk and capital structure, use these ratios:

$$\text{Debt ratio} = \frac{\text{Total liabilities}}{\text{Total assets}}$$

$$\text{Equity ratio} = \frac{\text{Total stockholders' equity}}{\text{Total assets}}$$

$$\text{Pledged assets to secured liabilities} = \frac{\text{Book value of pledged assets}}{\text{Secured liabilities}}$$

$$\text{Times fixed interest charges earned} = \frac{\text{Income before interest and taxes}}{\text{Interest expense}}$$

To evaluate operating efficiency and profitability, use these ratios:

$$\text{Profit margin} = \frac{\text{Net income}}{\text{Net sales}}$$

$$\text{Total asset turnover} = \frac{\text{Net sales}}{\text{Average total assets}}$$

$$\text{Return on total assets} = \frac{\text{Net income}}{\text{Average total assets}}$$

$$\text{Return on common stockholders' equity} = \frac{\text{Net income} - \text{Preferred dividends}}{\text{Average common stockholders' equity}}$$

$$\text{Price-earnings ratio} = \frac{\text{Market price per common share}}{\text{Earnings per share}}$$

$$\text{Dividend yield} = \frac{\text{Annual dividends per share}}{\text{Market price per share}}$$

STANDARDS OF COMPARISON

LO 4
State the limitations associated with using financial statement ratios and the sources from which standards for comparison may be obtained.

After computing ratios and turnovers in the process of analyzing financial statements, you have to decide whether the calculated amounts suggest good, bad, or merely average performance by the company. To make these judgments, you must have some bases for comparison. The following are possibilities:

1. An experienced analyst may compare the ratios and turnovers of the company under review with *subjective* standards acquired from past experiences.

2. For purposes of comparison, an analyst may calculate the ratios and turnovers of a selected group of competing companies in the same *industry*.

3. *Published* ratios and turnovers (such as those provided by Dun & Bradstreet) may be used for comparison.

4. Some local and national trade associations gather data from their members and publish *standard* or *average* ratios for their trade or industry. When available, these data can give the analyst a useful basis for comparison.

5. *Rule-of-thumb* standards can be used as a basis for comparison.

Of these five standards, the ratios and turnovers of a selected group of competing companies normally are the best bases for comparison. Rule-of-thumb standards should be applied with great care and then only if they seem reasonable in light of past experience and the industry's norms.

Progress Check

17-11 Which of the following would not be used as a basis for comparison when analyzing ratios and turnovers? *(a)* Companies in different industries; *(b)* Subjective standards from past experience; *(c)* Rule-of-thumb standards; *(d)* Averages within a trade or industry.

17-12 Which of the typical bases of comparison is usually best?

SUMMARY OF THE CHAPTER IN TERMS OF LEARNING OBJECTIVES

LO 1. Explain the relationship between financial reporting and general purpose financial statements. Financial reporting is intended to provide information that is useful to investors, creditors, and others in making investment, credit, and similar decisions. The information is communicated in a variety of ways, including general purpose financial statements. These statements normally include an income statement, balance sheet, statement of changes in stockholders' equity or statement of retained earnings, statement of cash flows, and the related footnotes.

LO 2. Describe, prepare, and interpret comparative financial statements and common-size comparative statements. Comparative financial statements show amounts for two or more successive periods, sometimes with the changes in the items disclosed in absolute and percentage terms. In common-size statements, each item is expressed as a percentage of a base amount. The base amount for the balance sheet is usually total assets, and the base amount for the income statement is usually net sales.

LO 3. Calculate and explain the interpretation of the ratios, turnovers, and rates of return used to evaluate *(a)* **short-term liquidity,** *(b)* **long-term risk and capital structure, and** *(c)* **operating efficiency and profitability.** To evaluate the short-term liquidity of a company, calculate a current ratio, an acid-test ratio, the accounts receivable turnover, the days' sales uncollected, the merchandise turnover, and the days' stock on hand.

In evaluating the long-term risk and capital structure of a company, calculate debt and equity ratios, pledged assets to secured liabilities, and the number of times fixed interest charges were earned.

In evaluating operating efficiency and profitability, calculate profit margin, total asset turnover, return on total assets, and return on common stockholders' equity. Other statistics used to evaluate the profitability of alternative investments include the price-earnings ratio and the dividend yield.

LO 4. State the limitations associated with using financial statement ratios and the sources from which standards for comparison may be obtained. In deciding whether financial statement ratio values are satisfactory, too high, or too low, you must have some bases for comparison. These bases may come from past experience and personal judgment, from ratios of similar companies, or from ratios published by trade associations or other public sources. Traditional rules-of-thumb should be applied with great care and only if they seem reasonable in light of past experience.

DEMONSTRATION PROBLEM

Use the financial statements of Precision Company to satisfy the following requirements:

1. Prepare a comparative income statement showing the percentage increase or decrease for 19X2 over 19X1.

2. Prepare a common-size comparative balance sheet for 19X2 and 19X1.

3. Compute the following ratios as of December 31, 19X2, or for the year ended December 31, 19X2:

   a. Current ratio
   b. Acid-test ratiosecured liabilities
   c. Accounts receivable turnover.
   d. Days' sales uncollected
   e. Merchandise turnover
   f. Debt ratio

   g. Pledged assets to secured liabilities
   h. Times fixed interest charges earned
   i. Profit margin
   j. Total asset turnover
   k. Return on total assets
   l. Return on common stockholders' equity

PRECISION COMPANY
Comparative Income Statement
For Years Ended December 31, 19X2 and 19X1

	19X2	19X1
Sales	$2,486,000	$2,075,000
Cost of goods sold	1,523,000	1,222,000
Gross profit from sales	$ 963,000	$ 853,000
Operating expenses:		
Advertising expense	$ 145,000	$ 100,000
Sales salaries expense	240,000	280,000
Office salaries expense	165,000	200,000
Insurance expense	100,000	45,000
Supplies expense	26,000	35,000
Depreciation expense	85,000	75,000
Miscellaneous expenses	17,000	15,000
Total operating expenses	$ 778,000	$ 750,000
Operating income	$ 185,000	$ 103,000
Less interest expense	44,000	46,000
Income before taxes	$ 141,000	$ 57,000
Income taxes	47,000	19,000
Net income	$ 94,000	$ 38,000
Earnings per share	$ 0.99	$ 0.40

PRECISION COMPANY
Comparative Balance Sheet
December 31, 19X2, and December 31, 19X1

	19X2	19X1
Assets		
Current assets:		
Cash	$ 79,000	$ 42,000
Short-term investments	65,000	96,000
Accounts receivable (net)	120,000	100,000
Merchandise inventory	250,000	265,000
Total current assets	$ 514,000	$ 503,000
Plant and equipment:		
Store equipment (net)	$ 400,000	$ 350,000
Office equipment (net)	45,000	50,000
Buildings (net)	625,000	675,000
Land	100,000	100,000
Total plant and equipment	$1,170,000	$1,175,000
Total assets	$1,684,000	$1,678,000

	19X2	19X1
Liabilities		
Current liabilities:		
Accounts payable	$ 164,000	$ 190,000
Short-term notes payable	75,000	90,000
Taxes payable	26,000	12,000
Total current liabilities	$ 265,000	$ 292,000
Long-term liabilities:		
Notes payable (secured by		
mortgage on building and land) .	400,000	420,000
Total liabilities	$ 665,000	$ 712,000
Stockholders' Equity		
Contributed capital:		
Common stock, $5 par value	$ 475,000	$ 475,000
Retained earnings	544,000	491,000
Total stockholders' equity	$1,019,000	$ 966,000
Total liabilities and		
stockholders' equity	$1,684,000	$1,678,000

Planning the Solution

- Set up a four-column income statement; enter the 19X2 and 19X1 amounts in the first two columns and then enter the dollar change in the third column and the percentage change from 19X1 in the fourth column.

- Set up a four-column balance sheet; enter the 19X2 and 19X1 amounts in the first two columns and then compute and enter the amount of each item as a percentage of total assets.

- Compute the given ratios using the provided numbers; be sure to use the average of the beginning and ending amounts where appropriate.

Solution to Demonstration Problem

1.

PRECISION COMPANY
Comparative Income Statement
For Years Ended December 31, 19X2 and 19X1

	19X2	19X1	Increase (Decrease) in 19X2 Amount	Percent
Sales	$2,486,000	$2,075,000	$411,000	19.8%
Cost of goods sold	1,523,000	1,222,000	301,000	24.6
Gross profit from sales	$ 963,000	$ 853,000	$110,000	12.9
Operating expenses:				
Advertising expense	$ 145,000	$ 100,000	$ 45,000	45.0
Sales salaries expense	240,000	280,000	(40,000)	(14.3)
Office salaries expense	165,000	200,000	(35,000)	(17.5)
Insurance expense	100,000	45,000	55,000	122.2
Supplies expense	26,000	35,000	(9,000)	(25.7)
Depreciation expense	85,000	75,000	10,000	13.3
Miscellaneous expenses	17,000	15,000	2,000	13.3
Total operating expenses	$ 778,000	$ 750,000	$ 28,000	3.7
Operating income	$ 185,000	$ 103,000	$ 82,000	79.6
Less interest expense	44,000	46,000	(2,000)	(4.3)
Income before taxes	$ 141,000	$ 57,000	$ 84,000	147.4
Income taxes	47,000	19,000	28,000	147.4
Net income	$ 94,000	$ 38,000	$ 56,000	147.4
Earnings per share	$ 0.99	$ 0.40	$ 0.59	147.5

2.
PRECISION COMPANY
Common-Size, Comparative Balance Sheet
December 31, 19X2, and December 31, 19X1

	December 31		Common-Size Percentages	
	19X2	19X1	19X2*	19X1*
Assets				
Current assets:				
Cash	$ 79,000	$ 42,000	4.7%	2.5%
Short-term investments	65,000	96,000	3.9	5.7
Accounts receivable (net)	120,000	100,000	7.1	6.0
Merchandise inventory	250,000	265,000	14.8	15.8
Total current assets	$ 514,000	$ 503,000	30.5	30.0
Plant and equipment:				
Store equipment (net)	$ 400,000	$ 350,000	23.8	20.9
Office equipment (net)	45,000	50,000	2.7	3.0
Buildings (net)	625,000	675,000	37.1	40.2
Land	100,000	100,000	5.9	6.0
Total plant and equipment	$1,170,000	$1,175,000	69.5	70.0
Total assets	$1,684,000	$1,678,000	100.0	100.0
Liabilities				
Current liabilities:				
Accounts payable	$ 164,000	$ 190,000	9.7	11.3
Short-term notes payable	75,000	90,000	4.5	5.4
Taxes payable	26,000	12,000	1.5	0.7
Total current liabilities	$ 265,000	$ 292,000	15.7	17.4
Long-term liabilities:				
Notes payable (secured by mortgage on building and land)	400,000	420,000	23.8	25.0
Total liabilities	$ 665,000	$ 712,000	39.4	42.4
Stockholders' Equity				
Contributed capital:				
Common stock, $5 par value	$ 475,000	$ 475,000	28.2	28.3
Retained earnings	544,000	491,000	32.3	29.3
Total stockholders' equity	$1,019,000	$ 966,000	60.5	57.6
Total liabilities and equity	$1,684,000	$1,678,000	100.0	100.0

*Columns may not foot due to rounding.

3. **Ratios for 19X2:**

   a. Current ratio: $514,000/$265,000 = 1.9 to 1

   b. Acid-test ratio: ($79,000 + $65,000 + $120,000)/$265,000 = 1.0 to 1

   c. Average receivables: ($120,000 + $100,000)/2 = $110,000
      Accounts receivable turnover: $2,486,000/$110,000 = 22.6 times

   d. Days' sales uncollected: ($120,000/$2,486,000) × 365 = 17.6 days

   e. Average inventory: ($250,000 + $265,000)/2 = $257,500
      Merchandise turnover: $1,523,000/$257,500 = 5.9 times

   f. Debt ratio: $665,000/$1,684,000 = 39.5%

   g. Pledged assets to secured liabilities:
      ($625,000 + $100,000)/$400,000 = 1.8 to 1

   h. Times fixed interest charges earned: $185,000/$44,000 = 4.2 times

   i. Profit margin: $94,000/$2,486,000 = 3.8%

   j. Average total assets: ($1,684,000 + $1,678,000)/2 = $1,681,000
      Total asset turnover: $2,486,000/$1,681,000 = 1.48 times

   k. Return on total assets: $94,000/$1,681,000 = 5.6%
      or 3.8% × 1.48 = 5.6%

   l. Average total equity: ($1,019,000 + $966,000)/2 = $992,500
      Return on common stockholders' equity: $94,000/$992,500 = 9.5%

GLOSSARY

Common-size comparative statements comparative financial statements in which each amount is expressed as a percentage of a base amount. In the balance sheet, the amount of total assets is usually selected as the base amount and is expressed as 100%. In the income statement, net sales is usually selected as the base amount. p. 617

Comparative statement a financial statement with data for two or more successive accounting periods placed in columns side by side, sometimes with changes shown in dollar amounts and percentages. p. 613

Equity ratio the portion of total assets provided by stockholders' equity, calculated as stockholders' equity divided by total assets. p. 624

Financial reporting the process of providing information that is useful to investors, creditors, and others in making investment, credit, and similar decisions. p. 612

General purpose financial statements statements published periodically for use by a wide variety of interested parties; include the income statement, balance sheet, statement of changes in stockholders' equity (or statement of retained earnings), statement of cash flows, and related footnotes. p. 612

Working capital current assets minus current liabilities. p. 620

QUESTIONS

1. Explain the difference between financial reporting and financial statements.
2. What is the difference between comparative financial statements and common-size comparative statements?
3. Which items are usually assigned a value of 100% on a common-size comparative balance sheet and a common-size comparative income statement?
4. Why is working capital given special attention in the process of analyzing balance sheets?
5. What are three factors that would influence your decision as to whether a company's current ratio is good or bad?
6. Suggest several reasons why a 2 to 1 current ratio may not be adequate for a particular company.
7. What does a relatively high accounts receivable turnover indicate about a company's short-term liquidity?
8. What is the significance of the number of days' sales uncollected?
9. Why does merchandise turnover provide information about a company's short-term liquidity?
10. Why is the capital structure of a company, as measured by

debt and equity ratios, of importance to financial statement analysts?
11. Why must the ratio of pledged assets to secured liabilities be interpreted with caution?
12. Why would a company's return on total assets be different from its return on common stockholders' equity?
13. What ratios would you calculate for the purpose of evaluating management performance?
14. Using the financial statements for Lands' End in Appendix F, calculate Lands' End's return on total assets for the fiscal year ended January 27, 1995.

LANDS' END DIRECT MERCHANTS

15. Refer to the financial statements for Southwest Airlines Co. in Appendix E. Calculate Southwest Airlines's equity ratio as of December 31, 1994.

QUICK STUDY (Five-Minute Exercises)

Which of the following items are means of accomplishing the objective of financial reporting but are not included within general purpose financial statements? *(a)* Income statements. *(b)* Company news releases. *(c)* Balance sheets. *(d)* Certain reports filed with the Securities and Exchange Commission. *(e)* Statements of cash flows. *(f)* Management discussions and analyses of financial performance.

QS 17–1 (LO 1)

Given the following information for Heffington Corporation, determine *(a)* the common-size percentages for gross profit from sales and *(b)* the trend percentages for net sales, using 19X1 as the base year.

QS 17–2 (LO 2)

	19X2	19X1
Net sales	$201,600	$114,800
Cost of goods sold	109,200	60,200

QS 17–3
(LO 3)

a. Which two short-term liquidity ratios measure how frequently a company collects its accounts?

b. Which two terms are used to describe the difference between current assets and current liabilities?

c. Which two ratios are the basic components in measuring a company's operating efficiency? Which ratio summarizes these two components?

QS 17–4
(LO 4)

What are five possible bases of comparison you can use when analyzing financial statement ratios? Which of these is generally considered to be the most useful? Which one is least likely to provide a good basis for comparison?

EXERCISES

Exercise 17–1
Calculating trend percentages
(LO 2)

Calculate trend percentages for the following items, using 19X0 as the base year. Then, state whether the situation shown by the trends appears to be favorable or unfavorable.

	19X4	19X3	19X2	19X1	19X0
Sales	$283,880	$271,800	$253,680	$235,560	$151,000
Cost of goods sold	129,200	123,080	116,280	107,440	68,000
Accounts receivable	19,100	18,300	17,400	16,200	10,000

Exercise 17–2
Reporting percentage changes
(LO 2)

Where possible, calculate percentages of increase and decrease for the following:

	19X2	19X1
Short-term investments	$217,800	$165,000
Accounts receivable	42,120	48,000
Notes payable	57,000	-0-

Exercise 17–3
Calculating common-size percentages
(LO 2)

Express the following income statement information in common-size percentages and assess whether the situation is favorable or unfavorable.

HARBISON CORPORATION
Comparative Income Statement
For Years Ended December 31, 19X2, and 19X1

	19X2	19X1
Sales	$720,000	$535,000
Cost of goods sold	475,200	280,340
Gross profit from sales	$244,800	$254,660
Operating expenses	151,200	103,790
Net income	$ 93,600	$150,870

Exercise 17–4
Evaluating short-term liquidity
(LO 3)

Mixon Company's December 31 balance sheets included the following data:

	19X3	19X2	19X1
Cash	$ 30,800	$ 35,625	$ 36,800
Accounts receivable, net	88,500	62,500	49,200
Merchandise inventory	111,500	82,500	53,000
Prepaid expenses	9,700	9,375	4,000
Plant assets, net	277,500	255,000	229,500
Total assets	$518,000	$445,000	$372,500
Accounts payable	$128,900	$ 75,250	$ 49,250
Long-term notes payable secured by mortgages on plant assets	97,500	102,500	82,500
Common stock, $10 par value	162,500	162,500	162,500
Retained earnings	129,100	104,750	78,250
Total liabilities and stockholders' equity	$518,000	$445,000	$372,500

Required

Compare the short-term liquidity positions of the company at the end of 19X3, 19X2, and 19X1 by calculating: *(a)* the current ratio and *(b)* the acid-test ratio. Comment on any changes that occurred.

Refer to the information in Exercise 17–4 about Mixon Company. The company's income statements for the years ended December 31, 19X3, and 19X2 included the following data:

Exercise 17–5
Evaluating short-term liquidity
(LO 3)

	19X3	19X2
Sales	$672,500	$530,000
Cost of goods sold	$410,225	$344,500
Other operating expenses	208,550	133,980
Interest expense	11,100	12,300
Income taxes	8,525	7,845
Total costs and expenses	$638,400	$498,625
Net income	$ 34,100	$ 31,375
Earnings per share	$ 2.10	$ 1.93

Required

For the years ended December 31, 19X3, and 19X2, assume all sales were on credit and calculate the following: *(a)* days' sales uncollected, *(b)* accounts receivable turnover, *(c)* merchandise turnover, and *(d)* days' stock on hand. Comment on any changes that occurred from 19X2 to 19X3.

Refer to the information in Exercises 17–4 and 17–5 about Mixon Company. Compare the long-term risk and capital structure positions of the company at the end of 19X3 and 19X2 by calculating the following ratios: *(a)* debt and equity ratios, *(b)* pledged assets to secured liabilities, and *(c)* times fixed interest charges earned. Comment on any changes that occurred.

Exercise 17–6
Evaluating long-term risk and
capital structure
(LO 3)

Refer to the financial statements of Mixon Company presented in Exercises 17–4 and 17–5. Evaluate the operating efficiency and profitability of the company by calculating the following: *(a)* profit margin, *(b)* total asset turnover, and *(c)* return on total assets. Comment on any changes that occurred.

Exercise 17–7
Evaluating operating efficiency
and profitability
(LO 3)

Refer to the financial statements of Mixon Company presented in Exercises 17–4 and 17–5. This additional information about the company is known:

Exercise 17–8
Evaluating profitability
(LO 3)

Common stock market price, December 31, 19X3	$15.00
Common stock market price, December 31, 19X2	14.00
Annual cash dividends per share in 19X3	.30
Annual cash dividends per share in 19X2	.15

Required

To evaluate the profitability of the company, calculate the following for 19X3 and 19X2: *(a)* return on common stockholders' equity, *(b)* price = earnings ratio on December 31, and *(c)* dividend yield.

Common-size and trend percentages for a company's sales, cost of goods sold, and expenses follow:

Exercise 17–9
Determining income effects
from common-size and trend
percentages
(LO 2)

	Common-Size Percentages			Trend Percentages		
	19X3	19X2	19X1	19X3	19X2	19X1
Sales	100.0%	100.0%	100.0%	104.4%	103.2%	100.0%
Cost of goods sold	62.4	60.9	58.1	102.0	100.1	100.0
Expenses	14.3	13.8	14.1	94.0	90.0	100.0

Required

Determine whether the company's net income increased, decreased, or remained unchanged during this three-year period.

PROBLEMS

Problem 17–1
Calculating ratios and
percentages
(LO 2, 3)

The condensed statements of Thornhill Company follow:

THORNHILL COMPANY
Comparative Income Statement
For Years Ended December 31, 19X3, 19X2, and 19X1
($000)

	19X3	19X2	19X1
Sales	$444,000	$340,000	$236,000
Cost of goods sold	267,288	212,500	151,040
Gross profit from sales	$176,712	$127,500	$ 84,960
Selling expenses	$ 62,694	$ 46,920	$ 31,152
Administrative expenses	40,137	29,920	19,470
Total expenses	$102,831	$ 76,840	$ 50,622
Income before taxes	$ 73,881	$ 50,660	$ 34,338
State and federal income taxes	13,764	10,370	6,962
Net income	$ 60,117	$ 40,290	$ 27,376

THORNHILL COMPANY
Comparative Balance Sheet
December 31, 19X3, 19X2, and 19X1
($000)

	19X3	19X2	19X1
Assets			
Current assets	$ 48,480	$ 37,924	$ 50,648
Long-term investments	-0-	500	3,720
Plant and equipment	90,000	96,000	57,000
Total assets	$138,480	$134,424	$111,368
Liabilities and Stockholders' Equity			
Current liabilities	$ 20,200	$ 19,960	$ 19,480
Common stock	72,000	72,000	54,000
Other contributed capital	9,000	9,000	6,000
Retained earnings	37,280	33,464	31,888
Total liabilities and stockholders' equity	$138,480	$134,424	$111,368

Required

Preparation component:

CHECK FIGURE:
19X3, total assets, 124.34

1. Calculate each year's current ratio.
2. Express the income statement data in common-size percentages.
3. Express the balance sheet data in trend percentages with 19X1 as the base year.

Analysis component:

4. Comment on any significant relationships revealed by the ratios and percentages.

Problem 17–2
Calculation and analysis of
trend percentages
(LO 2)

The condensed comparative statements of Cohorn Company follow:

COHORN COMPANY
Comparative Income Statement
For Years Ended December 31, 19X7–19X1
($000)

	19X7	19X6	19X5	19X4	19X3	19X2	19X1
Sales	$1,594	$1,396	$1,270	$1,164	$1,086	$1,010	$828
Cost of goods sold	1,146	932	802	702	652	610	486
Gross profit from sales	$ 448	$ 464	$ 468	$ 462	$ 434	$ 400	$342
Operating expenses	340	266	244	180	156	154	128
Net income	$ 108	$ 198	$ 224	$ 282	$ 278	$ 246	$214

COHORN COMPANY
Comparative Balance Sheet
December 31, 19X7–19X1
($000)

	19X7	19X6	19X5	19X4	19X3	19X2	19X1
Assets							
Cash	$ 68	$ 88	$ 92	$ 94	$ 98	$ 96	$ 99
Accounts receivable, net ...	480	504	456	350	308	292	206
Merchandise inventory	1,738	1,264	1,104	932	836	710	515
Other current assets	46	42	24	44	38	38	19
Long-term investments	0	0	0	136	136	136	136
Plant and equipment, net ...	2,120	2,114	1,852	1,044	1,078	960	825
Total assets	$4,452	$4,012	$3,528	$2,600	$2,494	$2,232	$1,800
Liabilities and Equity							
Current liabilities	$1,120	$ 942	$ 618	$ 514	$ 446	$ 422	$ 272
Long-term liabilities	1,194	1,040	1,012	470	480	520	390
Common stock	1,000	1,000	1,000	840	840	640	640
Other contributed capital ...	250	250	250	180	180	160	160
Retained earnings	888	780	648	596	548	490	338
Total liabilities and equity ..	$4,452	$4,012	$3,528	$2,600	$2,494	$2,232	$1,800

Required

Preparation component:

1. Calculate trend percentages for the items of the statements using 19X1 as the base year.

CHECK FIGURE:
19X7 total assets, 247.3

Analysis component:

2. Analyze and comment on the situation shown in the statements.

The 19X2 financial statements of Hoffman Corporation follow:

Problem 17–3
Calculation of financial
statement ratios
(LO 3)

HOFFMAN CORPORATION
Income Statement
For Year Ended December 31, 19X2

Sales		$348,600
Cost of goods sold:		
Merchandise inventory, December 31, 19X1 .	$ 32,400	
Purchases	227,900	
Goods available for sale	$260,300	
Merchandise inventory, December 31, 19X2 .	31,150	
Cost of goods sold		229,150
Gross profit from sales		$119,450
Operating expenses		52,500
Operating income		$ 66,950
Interest expense		3,100
Income before taxes		$ 63,850
Income taxes		15,800
Net income		$ 48,050

HOFFMAN CORPORATION
Balance Sheet
December 31, 19X2

Assets		Liabilities and Stockholders' Equity	
Cash	$ 9,000	Accounts payable	$ 16,500
Short-term investments	7,400	Accrued wages payable	2,200
Accounts receivable, net	28,200	Income taxes payable	2,300
Notes receivable (trade)	3,500	Long-term note payable,	
Merchandise inventory	31,150	secured by mortgage on	
Prepaid expenses	1,650	plant assets	62,400
Plant assets, net	152,300	Common stock, $1 par value ...	90,000
		Retained earnings	59,800
		Total liabilities and	
Total assets	$233,200	stockholders' equity	$233,200

Assume that all sales were on credit. On the December 31, 19X1, balance sheet, the assets totaled $182,400, common stock was $90,000, and retained earnings amounted to $31,300.

Required

Calculate the following: *(a)* current ratio, *(b)* acid-test ratio, *(c)* days' sales uncollected, *(d)* merchandise turnover, *(e)* days' stock on hand, *(f)* ratio of pledged assets to secured liabilities, *(g)* times fixed interest charges earned, *(h)* profit margin, *(i)* total asset turnover, *(j)* return on total assets, and *(k)* return on common stockholders' equity.

Problem 17–4
Comparative analysis of financial statement ratios
(LO 3)

Two companies that compete in the same industry are being evaluated by a bank that can lend money to only one of them. Summary information from the financial statements of the two companies follows:

	Datatech Company	Sigma Company
Data from the current year-end balance sheets:		
Assets		
Cash	$ 18,500	$ 33,000
Accounts receivable	36,400	56,400
Notes receivable (trade)	8,100	6,200
Merchandise inventory	83,440	131,500
Prepaid expenses	4,000	5,950
Plant and equipment, net	284,000	303,400
Total assets	$434,440	$536,450
Liabilities and Stockholders' Equity		
Current liabilities	$ 60,340	$ 92,300
Long-term notes payable	79,800	100,000
Common stock, $5 par value	175,000	205,000
Retained earnings	119,300	139,150
Total liabilities and		
stockholders' equity	$434,440	$536,450
Data from the current year's income statements:		
Sales	$660,000	$780,200
Cost of goods sold	485,100	532,500
Interest expense	6,900	11,000
Income tax expense	12,800	19,300
Net income	67,770	105,000
Earnings per share	$1.94	$2.56
Beginning-of-year data:		
Accounts receivable, net	$ 28,800	$ 53,200
Notes receivable	0	0
Merchandise inventory	54,600	106,400
Total assets	388,000	372,500
Common stock, $5 par value	175,000	205,000
Retained earnings	94,300	90,600

Required

1. Calculate the current ratio, acid-test ratio, accounts (including notes) receivable turnover, merchandise turnover, days' stock on hand, and days' sales uncollected for the two companies. Then, identify the company that you consider to be the better short-term credit risk and explain why.
2. Calculate the profit margin, total asset turnover, return on total assets, and return on common stockholders' equity for the two companies. Assuming that each company paid cash dividends of $1.50 per share and each company's stock can be purchased at $25 per share, calculate their price-earnings ratios and dividend yields. Also, identify which company's stock you would recommend as the better investment and explain why.

Providence Corporation began the month of May with $650,000 of current assets, a current ratio of 2.5 to 1, and an acid-test ratio of 1.1 to 1. During the month, it completed the following transactions:

Problem 17–5
Analysis of working capital
(LO 3)

May 2   Bought $75,000 of merchandise on account. (The company uses a perpetual inventory system.)

8   Sold merchandise that cost $58,000 for $103,000.

10   Collected a $19,000 account receivable.

15   Paid a $21,000 account payable.

17   Wrote off a $3,000 bad debt against the Allowance for Doubtful Accounts account.

22   Declared a $1 per share cash dividend on the 40,000 shares of outstanding common stock.

26   Paid the dividend declared on May 22.

27   Borrowed $75,000 by giving the bank a 30-day, 10% note.

28   Borrowed $90,000 by signing a long-term secured note.

29   Used the $175,000 proceeds of the notes to buy additional machinery.

Required

Prepare a schedule showing Providence's current ratio, acid-test ratio, and working capital after each of the transactions. Round calculations to two decimal places.

CHECK FIGURE:
May 29 working capital, $310,000

CRITICAL THINKING: ESSAYS, PROBLEMS, AND CASES

Analytical Essays

Huff Company and Mesa Company are similar firms that operate within the same industry. The following information is available:

AE 17–1
(LO 3)

	Huff			Mesa		
	19X3	**19X2**	**19X1**	**19X3**	**19X2**	**19X1**
Current ratio	1.6	1.7	2.0	3.1	2.6	1.8
Acid-test ratio	.9	1.0	1.1	2.7	2.4	1.5
Accounts receivable turnover .	29.5	24.2	28.2	15.4	14.2	15.0
Merchandise turnover	23.2	20.9	16.1	13.5	12.0	11.6
Working capital	$60,000	$48,000	$42,000	$121,000	$93,000	$68,000

Required

Write a brief essay comparing Huff and Mesa based on the preceding information. Your discussion should include their relative ability to meet current obligations and to use current assets efficiently.

AE 17–2
(LO 3)

Kampa Company and Arbor Company are similar firms that operate within the same industry. Arbor began operations in 19X7 and Kampa in 19X1. In 19X9, both companies paid 7% interest to creditors. The following information is available:

	Kampa Company			Arbor Company		
	19X9	**19X8**	**19X7**	**19X9**	**19X8**	**19X7**
Total asset turnover . . .	3.0	2.7	2.9	1.6	1.4	1.1
Return on total assets . .	8.9	9.5	8.7	5.8	5.5	5.2
Profit margin	2.3	2.4	2.2	2.7	2.9	2.8
Sales	$400,000	$370,000	$386,000	$200,000	$160,000	$100,000

Required

Write a brief essay comparing Kampa and Arbor based on the preceding information. Your discussion should include their relative ability to use assets efficiently to produce profits. Also comment on their relative success in employing financial leverage in 19X9.

Financial Statement Analysis Cases

FSAC 17–1
(LO 2, 3)

In your position as controller of Tallman Company, you are responsible for keeping the board of directors informed about the financial activities and status of the company. In preparing for the next board meeting, you have calculated the following ratios, turnovers, and percentages to enable you to answer questions:

	19X6	19X5	19X4
Sales trend	147.00	135.00	100.00
Selling expenses to net sales	10.1%	14.0%	15.6%
Sales to plant assets	3.8 to 1	3.6 to 1	3.3 to 1
Current ratio	2.9 to 1	2.7 to 1	2.4 to 1
Acid-test ratio	1.1 to 1	1.4 to 1	1.5 to 1
Merchandise turnover	7.8 times	9.0 times	10.2 times
Accounts receivable turnover	7.0 times	7.7 times	8.5 times
Total asset turnover	2.9 times	2.9 times	3.3 times
Return on total assets	9.1%	9.7%	10.4%
Return on stockholders' equity	9.75%	11.50%	12.25%
Profit margin	3.6%	3.8%	4.0%

Required

Using the preceding data, answer each of the following questions and explain your answers:

a. Is it becoming easier for the company to meet its current debts on time and to take advantage of cash discounts?

b. Is the company collecting its accounts receivable more rapidly?

c. Is the company's investment in accounts receivable decreasing?

d. Are dollars invested in inventory increasing?

e. Is the company's investment in plant assets increasing?

f. Is the stockholders' investment becoming more profitable?

g. Is the company using its assets efficiently?

h. Did the dollar amount of selling expenses decrease during the three-year period?

FSAC 17–2
(LO 2, 3)

Refer to the financial statements of Southwest Airlines Co. in Appendix E to answer the following questions:

a. Using 1992 as the base year, calculate trend percentages for 1992–1994 for the total operating revenues, total operating expenses, operating income, and net income.

b. Calculate common-size percentages for 1994 and 1993 for the following categories of assets: total current assets; property, plant, and equipment, net of depreciation; and other assets.

c. Calculate the high and low price-earnings ratio for 1994.

d. Calculate the dividend yield for 1994 using the high stock price for the year.

e. Calculate the debt and equity ratios for 1994.

ANSWERS TO PROGRESS CHECKS

17–1 General purpose financial statements are intended for the large variety of users who are interested in receiving financial information about a business but who do not have the ability to require the company to prepare specialized financial reports designed to meet their specific interests.

17–2 General purpose financial statements include the income statement, balance sheet, statement of changes in stockholders' equity (or statement of retained earnings), and statement of cash flows, plus footnotes related to the statements.

17–3 *d*

17–4 Percentages on a comparative income statement show the increase or decrease in each item from one period to the next. On a common-size comparative income statement, each item is shown as a percentage of net sales for a specific period.

17–5 *c*

17–6 *a* ($820,000 + $240,000 + $470,000)/($350,000 + $180,000) = 2.9 to 1

b ($820,000 + $240,000)/($350,000 + $180,000) = 2 to 1

17–7 *a* $2,500,000/[($290,000 + $240,000)/2] = 9.43 times

b ($240,000/$2,500,000) × 365 = 35 days

c $750,000/[($530,000 + $470,000)/2] = 1.5 times

d ($470,000/$750,000) × 365 = 228.7 days

17–8 *c*

17–9 *b*

17–10 Profit margin × Total asset turnover = Return on total assets ($945,000/$8,500,000) × 1.8 = 20%

17–11 *a*

17–12 The ratios and turnovers of a selected group of competing companies.

Six appendixes supplement the regular topical coverage of *Financial Accounting*. Appendix A appears after Chapter 5. Appendixes B through F are presented in this section of the text. The appendixes are as follows:

A   Work Sheets and Reversing Entries (Chapter 5)

B   Accounting Principles, the FASB's Conceptual Framework, and Alternative Valuation Methods

C   Special Journals (Assign after Chapter 9)

D   Present and Future Values: An Expansion

E   Financial Statements and Related Disclosures from Southwest Airlines Co.'s 1994 Annual Report

F   Financial Statements and Related Disclosures from Lands' End, Inc.'s 1995 Annual Report

Accounting Principles, the FASB's Conceptual Framework, and Alternative Valuation Methods

After studying Appendix B, you should be able to:

1. Explain the difference between descriptive concepts and prescriptive concepts and the difference between bottom-up and top-down approaches to the development of accounting concepts.

2. Describe the major components in the FASB's conceptual framework.

3. Explain why conventional financial statements fail to adequately account for price changes.

4. Use a price index to restate historical cost/nominal dollar costs into constant purchasing power amounts and to calculate purchasing power gains and losses.

5. Explain the current cost approach to valuation, including its effects on the income statement and balance sheet.

6. Explain the current selling price approach to valuation.

7. Define or explain the words and phrases listed in the appendix glossary.

LEARNING OBJECTIVES

Accounting principles or concepts are not laws of nature. They are broad ideas developed as a way of *describing* current accounting practices and *prescribing* new and improved practices. In studying Appendix B, you will learn about some new accounting concepts that the FASB developed in an effort to guide future changes and improvements in accounting. You also will learn about some major alternatives to the historical cost measurements reported in conventional financial statements. Studying these alternatives will help you understand the nature of the information that is contained in conventional statements. In addition, it will help you grasp the meaning of new reporting practices that may occur in future years.

ACCOUNTING PRINCIPLES AND THE FASB'S CONCEPTUAL FRAMEWORK

DESCRIPTIVE AND PRESCRIPTIVE ACCOUNTING CONCEPTS

LO 1
Explain the difference between descriptive concepts and prescriptive concepts and the difference between bottom up and top-down approaches to the development of accounting concepts.

To fully understand the importance of financial accounting concepts or principles, you must realize that they serve two purposes. First, they provide general descriptions of existing accounting practices. In doing this, concepts and principles serve as guidelines that help you learn about accounting. Thus, after learning how the concepts or principles are applied in a few situations, you develop the ability to apply them in different situations. This is easier and more effective than memorizing a very long list of specific practices.

Second, these concepts or principles help accountants analyze unfamiliar situations and develop procedures to account for those situations. This purpose is especially important for the Financial Accounting Standards Board (FASB), which is charged with developing uniform practices for financial reporting in the United States and with improving the quality of such reporting.

In prior chapters, we defined and illustrated several important accounting principles. These principles, which follow, describe in general terms the practices currently used by accountants.

Generally Accepted Principles

Business entity principle
Conservatism principle
Consistency principle
Cost principle
Full-disclosure principle
Going-concern principle
Matching principle
Materiality principle
Objectivity principle
Revenue recognition principle
Time period principle

To help you learn accounting, we first listed these principles in Chapter 2 (p. 31) and have referred to them frequently in later chapters. Although these ideas are labeled *principles,* in this discussion we use the term *concepts* to include both these principles as well as other general rules developed by the FASB. The FASB also uses the word *concepts* in this general manner.

The preceding concepts are useful for teaching and learning about accounting practice and are helpful for dealing with some unfamiliar transactions. As business practices have evolved in recent years, however, these concepts have become less useful as guides for accountants to follow in dealing with new and different types of transactions. This problem has occurred because the concepts are intended to provide general descriptions of current accounting practices. In other words, they describe what accountants currently do; they do not necessarily describe what accountants should do. Also, since these concepts do not identify weaknesses in accounting practices, they do not lead to major changes or improvements in accounting practices.

Because the FASB is charged with improving financial reporting, its first members decided that a new set of concepts should be developed. They also decided that the new set of concepts should not merely *describe* what was being done under current practice. Instead, the new concepts should *prescribe* what ought to be done to make

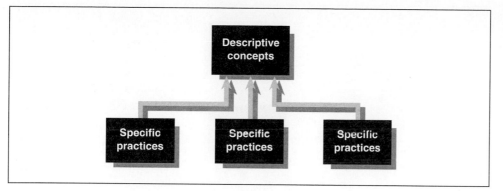

things better. The project to develop a new set of prescriptive concepts was initiated in 1973 and quickly became known as the FASB's *conceptual framework project.*

However, before we examine the concepts developed by the FASB, we need to look more closely at the differences between descriptive and prescriptive uses of accounting concepts.

THE PROCESSES OF DEVELOPING DESCRIPTIVE AND PRESCRIPTIVE ACCOUNTING CONCEPTS

Sets of concepts differ in how they are developed and used. In general, when concepts are intended to describe current practice, they are developed by looking at accepted specific practices and then making some general rules to encompass them. This bottom-up approach is diagrammed in Illustration B–1, which shows the arrows going from the practices to the concepts. The outcome of the process is a set of general rules that summarize practice and that can be used for education and for solving some new problems. For example, this approach leads to the concept that asset purchases are recorded at cost. However, these kinds of concepts often fail to show how new problems should be solved. To continue the example, the concept that assets are recorded at cost does not provide much direct guidance for situations in which assets have no cost because they are donated to a company by a local government. Further, because these concepts are based on the presumption that current practices are adequate, they do not lead to the development of new and improved accounting methods. To continue the example, the concept that assets are initially recorded at cost does not encourage asking the question of whether they should always be carried at that amount.

In contrast, if concepts are intended to *prescribe* improvements in accounting practices, they are likely to be designed by a top-down approach (Illustration B–2). Note that the top-down approach starts with broad accounting objectives. The process then generates broad concepts about the types of information that should be reported. Finally, these concepts should lead to specific practices that ought to be used. The advantage of this approach is that the concepts are good for solving new problems and evaluating old answers; its disadvantage is that the concepts may not be very descriptive of current practice. In fact, the suggested practices may not be in current use.

Since the FASB uses accounting concepts to prescribe accounting practices, the Board used a top-down approach to develop its conceptual framework. The Board's concepts are not necessarily more correct than the previously developed concepts. However, the new concepts are intended to provide better guidelines for developing new and improved accounting practices. The Board has stated that it will use them as a basis for its future actions and already has used them to justify important changes in financial reporting.

Illustration B–2
A "Top-Down" Process of
Developing Prescriptive
Accounting Concepts

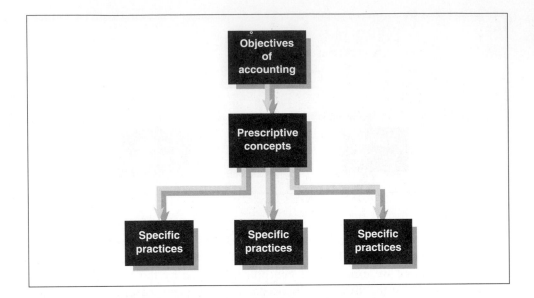

Progress Check
(Answers to Progress Checks are provided at the end of the appendix.)

B–1   The FASB's conceptual framework is intended to:
    a. Provide a historical analysis of accounting practice.
    b. Describe current accounting practice.
    c. Provide concepts that are prescriptive of what should be done in accounting
       practice.

B–2   What is the starting point in a top-down approach to developing accounting concepts?

B–3   What is the starting point in a bottom-up approach to developing accounting concepts?

**THE FASB'S
CONCEPTUAL
FRAMEWORK**

LO 2
Describe the major components
in the FASB's conceptual
framework.

The FASB's approach to developing its conceptual framework is diagrammed in Illustration B–3. Between 1978 and 1985, the Board issued six *Statements of Financial Accounting Concepts (SFAC)*. These concepts statements are not the same as the FASB's *Statement of Financial Accounting Standards (SFAS)*. The *SFAS*s are authoritative statements of generally accepted accounting principles that must be followed. The *SFAC*s are guidelines the Board uses in developing new standards. Accountants are not required to follow the *SFAC*s in practice.

The Objectives of Financial Reporting

The FASB's first *Statement of Financial Accounting Concepts (SFAC 1)* identified the broad objectives of financial reporting (Illustration B–3). The first and most general objective stated in *SFAC 1* is to "provide information that is useful to present and potential investors and creditors and other users in making rational investment, credit, and similar decisions."[1] From this beginning point in *SFAC 1*, the Board expressed other more specific objectives. These objectives recognize (1) that financial reporting should help users predict future cash flows and (2) that information about a company's resources and obligations is useful in making such predictions. All the con-

---

1 FASB, *Statement of Financial Accounting Concepts No. 1*, "Objectives of Financial Reporting by Business Enterprises" (Norwalk, CT, 1978), par. 34.

As a Matter of Opinion

Mr. Beresford graduated from the University of Southern California in 1961 with a B.A. degree in accounting. After working 10 years in the Los Angeles office of Ernst & Ernst (now Ernst & Young), he was assigned to that firm's national office and made a partner. In 1987, he was appointed to the Financial Accounting Standards Board and named as its chairman. In 1991, he was reappointed for a second term, which will expire in 1997. Among his honors is the designation as the Beta Alpha Psi "Accountant of the Year" for 1988.

When the conceptual framework was being created, some thought that it would provide immediate answers for standard-setting issues. However, it could never do that all by itself. Rather, the framework is a tool that helps the FASB do its job.

Because getting to right answers depends on asking the right questions, I've come to realize that perhaps the most critical part of the standard-setting process is identifying and stating the issues properly. That's exactly what the conceptual framework helps us do by providing us with common objectives and terms. In effect, the conceptual framework brings discipline to those who participate in the standard-setting process. This discipline helps the Board to ask the right questions. It also helps other participants comment on our projects in a more consistent manner.

Although all Board members might not agree which answer to a question is best, the odds are much higher that the best answer will be among the alternatives that we consider if we ask the right questions. As a result, we are more likely to ultimately adopt the best answer.

Dennis R. Beresford, C.P.A.

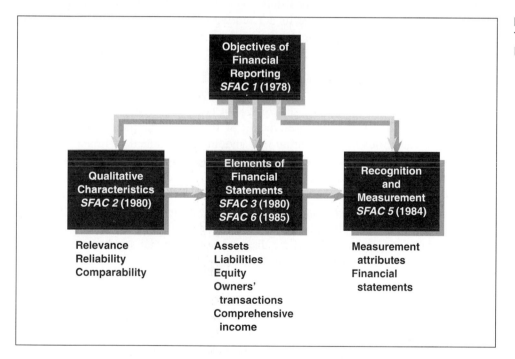

Illustration B-3
The FASB's Conceptual Framework

cepts in the conceptual framework are intended to be consistent with these general objectives. Of course, present accounting practice already provides information about a company's resources and obligations. Thus, although the conceptual framework is intended to be prescriptive of new and improved practices, the concepts in the framework are also descriptive of many current practices.

The Qualities of Useful Information

Illustration B–3 shows that the next step is the conceptual framework project was to identify the qualities (or qualitative characteristics) that financial information should have if it is to be useful in decision making. The Board discussed the fact that information can be useful only if it is understandable to users. However, the users are assumed to have the training, experience, and motivation to analyze financial reports. With this decision, the Board indicated that financial reporting should not try to meet the needs of unsophisticated or other casual report users.

In *SFAC 2,* the FASB said that information is useful if it is (1) relevant, (2) reliable, and (3) comparable. Information is *relevant* if it can make a difference in a decision. Information has this quality when it helps users predict the future or evaluate the past and is received in time to affect their decisions.

Information is *reliable* if users can depend on it to be free from bias and error. Reliable information is verifiable and faithfully represents what is supposed to be described. In addition, users can depend on information only if it is neutral. This means that the rules used to produce information should not be designed to lead users to accept or reject any specific decision alternative.

Information is *comparable* if users can use it to identify differences and similarities between companies. Comparability is possible only if companies follow uniform practices. However, even if all companies uniformly follow the same practices, comparable reports do not result if the practices are not appropriate. For example, comparable information would not be provided if all companies were to ignore the useful lives of their assets and depreciate all assets over two years.

Comparability also requires consistency (see Chapter 9, page 323), which means that a company should not change its accounting practices unless the change is justified as a reporting improvement. Another important concept discussed in *SFAC 2* is materiality (see Chapter 8, page 288).

Elements of Financial Statements

Illustration B–3 shows that another important step in developing the conceptual framework was to determine the elements of financial statements. This involved defining the categories of information that should be contained in financial reports. The Board's discussion of financial statement elements includes definitions of important elements such as assets, liabilities, equity, revenues, expenses, gains and losses. In earlier chapters, we referred to many of these definitions when we explained various accounting procedures. The Board's pronouncement on financial statement elements was first published in 1980 as *SFAC 3.* In 1985, *SFAC 3* was replaced by *SFAC 6,* which modified the discussion of financial statement elements to include several elements for not-for-profit accounting entities.[2]

Recognition and Measurement

In *SFAC 5,* "Recognition and Measurement in Financial Statements of Business Enterprises," the FASB established concepts for deciding (1) when items should be presented (or recognized) in the financial statements and (2) how to assign numbers to (or measure) those items. In general, the Board concluded that items should be recognized in the financial statements if they meet the following criteria:

a. *Definitions.* The item meets the definition of an element of financial statements.
b. *Measurability.* It has a relevant attribute measurable with sufficient reliability.
c. *Relevance.* The information about it is capable of making a difference in user decisions.
d. *Reliability.* The information is representationally faithful, verifiable, and neutral.

---

[2] Among the six *Statements of Financial Accounting Concepts* issued by the FASB, one *(SFAC 4)* is directed toward accounting by not-for-profit organizations. Although *SFAC 4* is important, it is beyond the scope of this course.

The question of how items should be measured raises the fundamental question of whether financial statements should be based on cost or on value. Since this question is quite controversial, the Board's discussion of this issue is more descriptive of current practice than it is prescriptive of new measurement methods.

In *SFAC 5,* the Board stated that a full set of financial statements should show:

1. Financial position at the end of the period.
2. Earnings for the period. (This concept is very similar to the concept of net income used in current practice.)
3. Comprehensive income for the period. (This new concept is broader than earnings and includes all changes in owners' equity other than those that resulted from transactions with the owners. Some changes in asset values are included in this concept but are excluded from earnings.)
4. Cash flows during the period.
5. Investments by and distributions to owners during the period.

We should note that *SFAC 5* was the first official pronouncement to call for the presentation of a statement of cash flows. The statement of cash flows is now required under *SFAS 95,* which was issued two years after *SFAC 5.*

Progress Check

B-4 That a business should be consistent from year to year in its accounting practices most directly relates to the FASB's concept that information reported in financial statements should be: *(a)* relevant; *(b)* material; *(c)* reliable; or *(d)* comparable.

B-5 What are the characteristics of accounting information that make it reliable?

B-6 What is the meaning of the phase *elements of financial statements?*

ALTERNATIVE ACCOUNTING VALUATION SYSTEMS

All accountants agree that conventional financial statements provide useful information for making economic decisions. However, many accountants also believe that conventional financial statements fail to adequately account for the impact of changing prices. Sometimes, this makes the statements misleading. That is, the statements may imply certain facts that are inconsistent with the real state of affairs. As a result, the information in the statements may lead decision makers to make decisions inconsistent with their objectives.

CONVENTIONAL FINANCIAL STATEMENTS FAIL TO ACCOUNT FOR PRICE CHANGES

LO 3
Explain why conventional financial statements fail to adequately account for price changes.

Failure to Account for Price Changes on the Balance Sheet

In what ways do conventional financial statements fail to account for changing prices? The general problem is that transactions are recorded in terms of the historical number of dollars paid. Usually, these amounts are not adjusted even though subsequent price changes may dramatically change the value of the purchased items.[3] For example, Old Company purchased 10 acres of land for $25,000. Then, at the end of each accounting period, Old Company presented a balance sheet showing "Land . . . $25,000." Six years later, after price increases of 97%, New Company purchased

---

[3] An exception to this general rule is the reporting of certain investments in debt and equity securities at their fair (market) values. This exception is explained in Chapters 8 and 11.

10 acres of land that was next to and nearly identical to Old Company's land. New Company paid $49,250 for the land. Comparing the conventional balance sheets of the two companies reveals the following balances:

	Old Company	New Company
Land	$25,000	$49,250

Without knowing the details that led to these balances, a statement reader is likely to conclude that either New Company has more land than Old Company or that New Company's land is more valuable. In reality, both companies own 10 acres that are of equal value. The entire difference between the prices paid by the two companies is explained by the 97% price increase between the two purchase dates. That is, $25,000 \times 1.97 = $49,250.

Failure to Account for Price Changes on the Income Statement

The failure of conventional financial statements to adequately account for changing prices also shows up in the income statement. For example, assume that in the previous example, the companies purchased machines instead of land. Also, assume that the machines of Old Company and New Company are identical except for age; both are being depreciated on a straight-line basis over a 10-year period with no salvage value. As a result, the annual income statements of the two companies show the following:

	Old Company	New Company
Depreciation expense, machinery	$2,500	$4,925

Although assets of equal value are being depreciated, the income statements show depreciation expense for New Company that is 97% higher than Old Company's. This is inconsistent with the fact that both companies own identical machines affected by the same depreciation factors. Furthermore, although Old Company appears more profitable, it must pay more income taxes due to the apparent extra profits. Also, if Old Company's selling prices are linked to its costs, it may not recover the full replacement cost of its machinery through the sale of its products.

VALUATION ALTERNATIVES TO CONVENTIONAL MEASUREMENTS OF COST

There are three basic alternatives to the historical cost measurements presented in conventional financial statements without adjustment for changing prices. These alternatives are:

1. Historical costs adjusted for changes in the general price level.
2. Current replacement cost valuations.
3. Current selling price valuations.

We discuss each of these in the remaining sections of Appendix B.

Progress Check

B-7   The following selected information is from the conventional balance sheets of A Company and B Company:

	A Company	B Company
Cash	$ 24,000	$ 40,000
Equipment, net	96,000	102,200
Land	130,000	157,800
Total assets	$250,000	$300,000

Based on this information, which of the following statements is true?

a. Company B's assets are worth $50,000 more than Company A's assets.

b. If Company A and Company B own identical tracts of land, Company B must have purchased its land at a later date than Company A.

c. The relative values of Company A's and Company B's assets cannot be determined from this conventional balance sheet information.

ADJUSTING HISTORICAL COSTS FOR GENERAL PRICE LEVEL CHANGES

LO 4
Use a price index to restate historical cost/nominal dollar costs into constant purchasing power amounts and to calculate purchasing power gains and losses.

One alternative to conventional financial statements is to restate dollar amounts of cost incurred in earlier years for changes in the general price level. In other words, a specific dollar amount of cost in a previous year can be restated as the number of dollars that would have been expended if the cost had been paid with dollars that have the current amount of purchasing power.

For example, assume the following general price index for December of 19X1 through 19X7:

Year	Price Index
19X1	92.5
19X2	100.0
19X3	109.5
19X4	123.7
19X5	135.0
19X6	150.0
19X7	168.0

Then, assume that a firm purchased assets for $1,000 in December 19X1 and purchased assets for $1,500 in December 19X2. The 19X1 cost of $1,000 correctly states the number of monetary units (dollars) expended in 19X1. Also, the 19X2 cost of $1,500 correctly states the number of monetary units expended in 19X2. However, in a very important way, the 19X1 monetary units do not mean the same thing as the 19X2 monetary units. A dollar (one monetary unit) in 19X1 represents a different amount of purchasing power than a dollar in 19X2. Both of these dollars represent different amounts of purchasing power than a dollar in 19X7.

To communicate the total amount of purchasing power given up for the assets, the historical number of monetary units must be restated in dollars with the same amount of purchasing power. For example, the total amount of cost incurred during 19X1 and 19X2 may be stated in the purchasing power of 19X2 dollars, or stated in the purchasing power of 19X7 dollars. These calculations are presented in Illustration B–4.

Conventional financial statements disclose revenues, expenses, assets, liabilities, and owners' equity in the historical monetary units exchanged when the transactions occurred. As such, they are sometimes called **historical cost/nominal dollar financial statements.** This emphasizes the difference between conventional statements and historical cost/constant purchasing power statements. **Historical cost/constant purchasing power accounting** uses a general price index to restate the dollar amounts on conventional financial statements into amounts that represent current general purchasing power.

The same principles for determining depreciation expense, cost of goods sold, accruals of revenue, and so forth, apply to both historical cost/nominal dollar statements

Illustration B-4   Expressing Costs in Constant Purchasing Power

Year Cost Was Incurred	Monetary Units Expended (a)	Price Index Factor for Adjustment to 19X2 Dollars (b)	Historical Cost Stated in 19X2 Dollars (a × b = c)	Price Index Factor for Adjustment to 19X7 Dollars (d)	Historical Cost Stated in 19X7 Dollars (c × d)
19X1	$1,000	100/92.5 = 1.08108	$1,081	168/100 = 1.68000	$1,816*
19X2	1,500		1,500	168/100 = 1.68000	2,520
Total cost	$2,500		$2,581		$4,336

*An alternative calculation is $1,000 × (168.0/92.5) = $1,816.

and historical cost/constant purchasing power statements. The same generally accepted accounting principles apply to both. The only difference between the two is that constant purchasing power statements reflect adjustments for general price level changes and nominal dollar statements do not.

The Impact of General Price Changes on Monetary Items

Some assets and liabilities are defined as monetary items. **Monetary assets** represent money or claims to receive a fixed amount of money. **Monetary liabilities** are obligations that are fixed in terms of the amount owed. The number of dollars to be received or paid does not change even though the purchasing power of the dollar may change. Examples of monetary items include cash, accounts receivable, accounts payable, and notes payable.

Because the amount of money that will be received or paid is fixed, a monetary item is not adjusted for general price level changes on a historical cost/constant purchasing power balance sheet. For example, assume that $800 in cash was owned at the end of 19X2. Regardless of how the price level has changed since the cash was acquired, the amount to be reported on the December 31, 19X2, historical cost/constant purchasing power balance sheet is $800.

Although monetary items are not adjusted on the balance sheet, they do involve special risks. When the general price level changes, monetary items create **purchasing power gains and losses.** Owning monetary assets during a period of inflation results in a loss of purchasing power. Owing monetary liabilities during a period of inflation results in a gain of purchasing power. During a period of deflation, the effects are just the opposite. Monetary assets result in purchasing power gains and monetary liabilities result in purchasing power losses.

For example, assume that a company has a cash balance of $800 on December 31, 19X2, which resulted from the following:

Cash balance, December 31, 19X1	$ 200
Cash receipts, assumed to have been received uniformly throughout the year	1,500
Cash disbursements, assumed to have been made uniformly throughout the year	(900)
Cash balance, December 31, 19X2	$ 800

Also assume that the general price index was 150.0 at the end of 19X1; that it averaged 160.0 throughout 19X3; and was 168.0 at the end of that year. As the price level increased throughout 19X2, the purchasing power of the cash declined. To calculate the loss during the year, the beginning cash balance and each receipt or disbursement must be adjusted for price changes to the end of the year. Then, the adjusted balance is compared with the actual balance to determine the loss. The calculation is as follows:

	Nominal Dollar Amounts	Price Index Factor for Restatement to December 31, 19X2	Restated to December 31, 19X2	Gain or (Loss)
Beginning balance..........	$ 200	168.0/150.0 = 1.12000	$ 224	
Receipts	1,500	168.0/160.0 = 1.05000	1,575	
Disbursements.............	(900)	168.0/160.0 = 1.05000	(945)	
Ending balance, adjusted			$ 854	
Enging balance, actual.......	$ 800		(800)	
Purchasing power loss				$(54)

Stated in terms of general purchasing power at year-end, the beginning cash balance plus receipts less disbursements was $854. Since the company has only $800 on hand, the $54 difference is a loss of general purchasing power.

In the preceding calculation, note that we adjusted the receipts and disbursements from the *average* price level during the year (160.0) to the ending price level (168.0). Because we assumed the receipts and disbursements occurred uniformly throughout the year, we used the average price level to approximate the price level at the time each receipt and disbursement took place. If receipts and disbursements do not occur uniformly, then we must separately adjust each receipt and each disbursement from the price level at the time of the receipt or disbursement to the price level at year-end.

The calculation of purchasing power gains and losses that result from owing monetary liabilities is the same as it is for monetary assets. Assume, for example, that a note payable for $300 was outstanding on December 31, 19X1, when the price index was 150.0. On April 5, 19X2, when the price index was 157.0, a $700 increase in the note resulted in a $1,000 balance that remained outstanding throughout the rest of 19X2. On December 31, 19X2, the price index was 168.0. On the historical cost/constant purchasing power balance sheet for December 31, 19X2, the note payable is reported at $1,000. The purchasing power gain or loss during 19X2 is calculated as follows:

	Nominal Dollar Amounts	Price Index Factor for Restatement to December 31, 19X2	Restated to December 31, 19X2	Gain or (Loss)
Beginning balance..........	$ 300	168.0/150.0 = 1.120	$ 336	
April 5 increase............	700	168.0/157.0 = 1.070	749	
Ending balance, adjusted			$1,085	
Enging balance, actual.......	$1,000		(1,000)	
Purchasing power gain.......				$85

Stated in terms of general purchasing power at year-end, the amount borrowed was $1,085. Since the company can pay the note with $1,000, the $85 difference is a gain in general purchasing power earned by the firm.

To determine a company's total purchasing power gain or loss during a year, the accountant must analyze each monetary asset and each monetary liability. The final gain or loss is then described as the *purchasing power gain (or loss) on net monetary items owned or owed.*

The Impact of General Price Changes on Nonmonetary Items

Nonmonetary items include stockholders' equity and all assets and liabilities that are not fixed in terms of the number of monetary units to be received or paid. Land, equipment, intangible assets, and many product warranty liabilities are examples of nonmonetary items. The prices of **nonmonetary assets** tend to increase or decrease over time as the general price level increases or decreases. Similarly, the amounts needed to satisfy **nonmonetary liabilities** tend to change with changes in the general price level.

To reflect these changes on historical cost/constant purchasing power balance sheets, nonmonetary items are adjusted for price level changes that occur after the items were acquired. For example, assume that $500 was invested in land (a nonmonetary asset) at the end of 19X1, and the investment was still held at the end of 19X7. During this time, the general price index increased from 92.5 to 168.0. The historical cost/constant purchasing power balance sheets would disclose the following amounts:

Asset	December 31, 19X1 Historical Cost/Constant Purchasing Power Balance Sheet (a)	Price Index Factor for Adjustment to December 31, 19X7 (b)	December 31, 19X7, Historical Cost/Constant Purchasing Power Balance Sheet (a × b)
Land	$500	168.0/92.5 = 1.81622	$908

The $908 shown as the investment in land at the end of 19X7 reflects the same amount of general purchasing power as $500 at the end of 19X1. Thus, no change in general purchasing power is recognized from holding the land.

Illustration B–5 summarizes the impact of general price level changes on monetary and nonmonetary items. The illustration shows which items require adjustments to prepare a historical cost/constant purchasing power balance sheet. It also shows which items generate purchasing power gains and losses that are recognized on a constant purchasing power income statement.

Progress Check

B-8 Foster Company purchased 150 acres of land for $100,000 in 19X1 when the general price index was 125.0. In December 19X4, the general price index was 150.0. What amount should be reported for the land on the 19X4 historical cost/constant purchasing power balance sheet?

B-9 Refer to Progress Check B-8. Should any purchasing power gain or loss pertaining to the land be reported on the 19X4 historical cost/constant purchasing power income statement?

CURRENT COST VALUATIONS

LO 5
Explain the current cost approach to valuation, including its effects on the income statement and balance sheet.

As we said before, all prices do not change at the same rate. In fact, when the general price level is rising, some specific prices may be falling. If this were not so, and if all prices changed at the same rate, then historical cost/constant purchasing power accounting would report current values on the financial statements.

For example, suppose that a company purchased land for $50,000 on January 1, 19X1, when the general price index was 135.0. Then, the price level increased until December 19X2, when the price index was 168.0. A historical cost/constant purchasing power balance sheet for this company on December 31, 19X2, would report the land at $50,000 × 168.0/135.0 = $62,222. If all prices increased at the same rate during that period, the market value of the land would have increased from $50,000 to $62,222, and the company's historical cost/constant purchasing power balance sheet would coincidentally disclose the land at its current value.

Illustration B-5   Reporting the Effects of Price Changes on Monetary and Nonmonetary Items

Financial Statement Item	When the General Price Level Rises (Inflation)		When the General Price Level Falls (Deflation)	
	Balance Sheet Adjustment Required	Income Statement Gain or Loss	Balance Sheet Adjustment Required	Income Statement Gain or Loss
Monetary assets	No	Loss	No	Gain
Nonmonetary assets	Yes	None	Yes	None
Monetary liabilities	No	Gain	No	Loss
Nonmonetary equities and liabilities	Yes	None	Yes	None

Because all prices do not change at the same rate, however, the current value of the land may differ substantially from the historical cost/constant dollar amount of $62,222. For example, assume that the company had the land appraised and determined that its current value on December 31, 19X2, was $80,000. The difference between the original purchase price of $50,000 and the current value of $80,000 is explained as follows:

Total change	$80,000 − $50,000 = $30,000
Adjustment for general price level increase	$62,222 − $50,000 = 12,222
General purchasing power gain (unrealized)	$80,000 − $62,222 = $17,778

In this case, the historical cost/constant purchasing power balance sheet would report land at $62,222, which is $17,778 ($80,000 − $62,222) less than its current value. This illustrates an important fact about historical cost/constant purchasing power accounting; it does not attempt to report current value. Rather, historical cost/constant purchasing power accounting restates original transaction prices into equivalent amounts of current, *general* purchasing power. The balance sheets display current values only if current, *specific* purchasing power is the basis of valuation.

Current Costs on the Income Statement

When the current cost approach to accounting is used, the reported amount of each expense, or **current cost**, is the number of dollars that would have been needed at the time the expense was incurred to acquire the consumed resources. For example, assume that the annual sales of a company included an item sold in May for $1,500. The item had been acquired on January 1 for $500. Also, suppose that in May, at the time of the sale, the cost to replace this item was $700. Then, the annual current cost income statement would show sales of $1,500 less cost of goods sold of $700. In other words, when an asset is acquired and then held for a time before it expires, the historical cost of the asset usually is different from its current cost at the time it expires. Current cost accounting measures the amount of expense as the cost to replace the asset at the time the asset expires or is sold.

The result of measuring expenses in current costs is that revenue is matched with the current (at the time of the sale) cost of the resources used to earn the revenue. Thus, operating profit is not greater than zero unless revenues are large enough to replace all of the resources consumed in the process of producing those revenues. Those who argue for current costs believe that operating profit measured in this fashion provides an improved basis for evaluating the effectiveness of operating activities.

Current Costs on the Balance Sheet

On the balance sheet, current cost accounting reports assets at the amounts that would have to be paid to purchase them as of the balance sheet date. Liabilities are reported at the amounts that would have to be paid to satisfy the liabilities as of the balance sheet date. Note that this valuation basis is similar to historical cost/constant purchasing power accounting in that a distinction exists between monetary and nonmonetary assets and liabilities. Monetary assets and liabilities are fixed in amount regardless of price changes. Therefore, monetary items are not adjusted for price changes. All of the nonmonetary items, however, must be evaluated at each balance sheet date to determine the best estimate of current cost.

For a moment, think about the large variety of assets reported on balance sheets. Given that there are so many different assets, you should not be surprised that accountants have difficulty obtaining reliable estimates of current costs. In some cases, they use price indexes that relate to specific categories of assets. Such specific price indexes may provide the most reliable source of current cost information. In other cases, when an asset is not new and has been partially depreciated, accountants may estimate its current cost by determining the cost to acquire a similar but new asset. Depreciation on the old asset is then based on the current cost of the new asset. Clearly, the accountant's professional judgment is an important factor in developing current cost data.

Progress Check

B-10   **On a balance sheet prepared under the current cost approach to accounting:**
   a. Monetary items are not adjusted for price changes.
   b. Nonmonetary items are restated to reflect general price level changes.
   c. Monetary items are restated to reflect general price level changes.

B-11   **Describe the meaning of *operating profit* under a current cost accounting system.**

CURRENT SELLING PRICE VALUATIONS

LO 6
Explain the current selling price approach to valuation.

In the previous discussion, you learned that conventional financial statements generally report historical costs in nominal dollars. That is, adjustments usually are not made for price changes. We also explained how accountants use a general price level index to adjust the nominal dollar amounts to measure the historical costs in terms of a constant purchasing power. Next, we discussed the alternative of reporting current (replacement) costs in the financial statements.

The final alternative to be considered is the reporting of assets (and liabilities) at current selling prices. On the balance sheet, this means assets would be reported at the amounts that would be received if the assets were sold. Similarly, liabilities would be reported at the amounts that would have to be paid to settle or eliminate the liabilities. The financial press describes this selling price approach to valuation as "mark to market" accounting.

The argument for reporting the current selling prices of assets is based on the idea that the alternative to owning an asset is to sell it. Thus, the sacrifice a business makes to hold an asset is the amount it would receive if the asset were sold. Further, the benefit derived from owing a liability is the amount the business avoids paying by not eliminating the liability. If these current selling prices are reported on the balance sheet, the stockholders' equity represents the net amount of cash that would be realized by liquidating the business. This net liquidation value is the amount that could be invested in other projects if the business were liquidated. Therefore, one can argue that net liquidation value is the most relevant basis for evaluating whether the income the company earns is enough to justify remaining in business.

Some proponents of the current selling price approach believe that it should be applied to assets but not to liabilities. Others argue that it applies equally well to both. Still others believe that it should be applied only to assets held for sale. They would not apply it to assets held for use in the business.

A related issue is whether to report the adjustments to selling price as gains and losses in the income statement. Some businesses, especially banks, argue that reporting such gains or losses causes excessive fluctuations in their reported net incomes. As an alternative to reporting the gains or losses on the income statement, they may be shown in stockholders' equity on the balance sheet as "unrealized gains and losses."

As Chapters 8 and 11 explain, a very recent pronouncement by the FASB *(SFAS 115)* requires companies to use the selling price approach to valuation for some assets. Investments in trading securities are reported at their fair (market) values, with the related changes in fair values reported on the income statement. Investments in securities available for sale are also reported at their fair values, but the related changes in fair values are not reported on the income statement. Instead, they are reported as part of stockholders' equity.

Progress Check

B-12 **If current selling price valuations were used to account for the assets and liabilities of a business:**
   a. **Gains and losses from changing market values would not be recorded.**
   b. **Losses from changing market values would be recorded but not gains.**
   c. **The accounting system might be described as mark-to-market accounting.**

B-13 **What is meant by the current selling price valuation of a liability?**

LO 1. Explain the difference between descriptive concepts and prescriptive concepts and the difference between bottom-up and top-down approaches to the development of accounting concepts. Some accounting concepts provide general descriptions of current accounting practices and are most useful in learning about accounting. Other accounting concepts prescribe the practices accountants should follow. These prescriptive concepts are most useful in developing accounting procedures for new types of transactions and making improvements in accounting practice. A bottom-up approach to developing concepts begins by examining the practices currently in use. Then, concepts are developed that provide general descriptions of those practices. In contrast, a top-down approach begins by stating the objectives of accounting. From these objectives, concepts are developed that prescribe the types of accounting practices accountants should follow.

LO 2. Describe the major components in the FASB's conceptual framework. The FASB's conceptual framework begins with *SFAC 1* by stating the broad objectives of financial reporting. Next, *SFAC 2* identifies the qualitative characteristics accounting information should possess. The elements contained in financial reports are defined in *SFAC 6* and the recognition and measurement criteria to be used are identified in *SFAC 5*.

LO 3. Explain why conventional financial statements fail to adequately account for price changes. Conventional financial statements report transactions in terms of the historical number of dollars received or paid. Therefore, the statements are not adjusted to reflect general price level changes or changes in the specific prices of the items reported.

LO 4. Use a price index to restate historical cost/nominal dollar costs into constant purchasing power amounts and to calculate purchasing power gains and losses. To restate a historical cost/nominal dollar cost in constant purchasing power terms, multiply the nominal dollar cost by a factor that represents the change in the general price

SUMMARY OF THE APPENDIX IN TERMS OF LEARNING OBJECTIVES

level since the cost was incurred. On the balance sheet, monetary assets and liabilities should not be adjusted for changes in prices. However, purchasing power gains or losses result from holding monetary assets and owing monetary liabilities during a period of general price changes.

LO 5. Explain the current cost approach to valuation, including its effects on the income statement and balance sheet. Current costs on the balance sheet are the dollar amounts that would be spent to purchase the assets at the balance sheet date. On the income statement, current costs are the dollar amounts that would be necessary to acquire the consumed assets on the date they were consumed.

LO 6. Explain the current selling price approach to valuation. Reporting current selling prices of assets and liabilities is supported by those who believe the balance sheet should show the net cost of not selling the assets and settling the liabilities. Some argue for applying selling price valuations to all assets and liabilities, or to marketable investments and marketable liabilities only, or to assets only. The related gains and losses may be reported on the income statement, but some would show them as unrealized stockholders' equity items on the balance sheet. The FASB's *SFAS 115* requires companies to use the selling price approach in reporting certain securities investments.

GLOSSARY

Current cost in general, the cost that would be required to acquire (or replace) an asset or service at the present time. On the income statement, the numbers of dollars that would be required, at the time the expense is incurred, to acquire the resources consumed. On the balance sheet, the amounts that would have to be paid to replace the assets or satisfy the liabilities as of the balance sheet date. p. 657

Historical cost/constant purchasing power accounting an accounting system that adjusts historical cost/nominal dollar financial statements for changes in the general purchasing power of the dollar. p. 653

Historical cost/nominal dollar financial statements conventional financial statements that disclose revenues, expenses, assets, liabilities, and owners' equity in terms of the historical monetary units exchanged at the time the transactions occurred. p. 653

Monetary assets money or claims to receive a fixed amount of money; the number of dollars to be received does not

change regardless of changes in the purchasing power of the dollar. p. 654

Monetary liabilities fixed amounts that are owed; the number of dollars to be paid does not change regardless of changes in the general price level. p. 654

Nonmonetary assets assets that are not claims to a fixed number of monetary units, the prices of which therefore tend to fluctuate with changes in the general price level. p. 656

Nonmonetary liabilities obligations that are not fixed in terms of the number of monetary units needed to satisfy them and that therefore tend to fluctuate in amount with changes in the general price level. p. 656

Purchasing power gains or losses the gains or losses that result from holding monetary assets and/or owing monetary liabilities during a period in which the general price level changes. p. 654

QUESTIONS

1. Can a concept be used descriptively and prescriptively?

2. Explain the difference between the FASB's *Statements of Financial Accounting Concepts* and the *Statements of Financial Accounting Standards.*

3. Which three qualitative characteristics of accounting information did the FASB identify as being necessary if the information is to be useful?

4. What is implied by saying that financial information should have the qualitative characteristic of relevance?

5. What are the four criteria an item should satisfy to be recognized in the financial statements?

6. Some people argue that conventional financial statements fail to adequately account for inflation. What general problem with conventional financial statements generates this argument?

7. What is the fundamental difference in the adjustments made under current cost accounting and under historical cost/constant purchasing power accounting?

8. What are historical cost/nominal dollar financial statements?

9. What is the difference between monetary and nonmonetary assets?

EXERCISES

A company's plant and equipment consisted of land purchased in late 19X1 for $690,000, machinery purchased in late 19X4 for $247,000, and a building purchased in late 19X6 for $315,000. Values of the general price index for December of 19X1 through 19X8 are as follows:

19X1	100.0
19X2	105.2
19X3	109.8
19X4	118.0
19X5	126.0
19X6	132.5
19X7	137.7
19X8	145.0

Exercise B–1
Adjusting costs for historical cost/constant purchasing power statements
(LO 4)

Required

1. Assuming the preceding price index adequately represents end-of-year price levels, calculate the amount of each asset's cost that would be shown on a historical cost/constant purchasing power balance sheet for (a) December 31, 19X7, and (b) December 31, 19X8. Ignore any accumulated depreciation. (Round calculations to three decimals.)
2. Would the historical cost/constant purchasing power income statement for 19X8 disclose any purchasing power gain or loss as a consequence of holding these assets? If so, how much?

Determine whether the following are monetary or nonmonetary items.

1. Computer equipment.
2. Retained earnings.
3. Prepaid rent.
4. Notes payable.
5. Merchandise inventory.
6. Copyrights.
7. Savings accounts.
8. Common stock.
9. Product warranties liability.
10. Wages payable.
11. Contributed capital in excess of par value, common stock.
12. Accounts receivable.
13. Goodwill.
14. Prepaid insurance.

Exercise B–2
Classifying monetary and nonmonetary items
(LO 4)

A company purchased land in 19X1 at a cost of $580,000 and in 19X2 at a cost of $737,000. What is the current cost of these land purchases in (a) 19X3 and (b) 19X4, given the following specific price index for land costs? (Round calculations to three decimals.)

19X1	103.6
19X2	100.0
19X3	110.9
19X4	114.2

Exercise B–3
Calculating amounts for current cost statements
(LO 5)

Exercise B–4
Calculating general purchasing power gain or loss
(LO 4)

Calculate the general purchasing power gain or loss in 19X2 given the following information (round calculations to three decimals):

Time Period	Price Index
December 19X1	98.0
Average during 19X2	103.1
December 19X2	107.5

a. The cash balance on December 31, 19X1, was $52,000. During 19X2, cash sales occurred uniformly throughout the year and amounted to $316,000. Payments of expenses also occurred evenly throughout the year and amounted to $221,000. Accounts payable of $15,800 were paid in December.

b. Accounts payable amounted to $33,000 on December 31, 19X1. Additional accounts payable amounting to $64,000 were recorded evenly throughout 19X2. The only payment of accounts during the year was $15,800 in late December.

PROBLEMS

Problem B–1
Adjusting costs to historical cost/constant purchasing power amounts
(LO 4)

MacLennan Corporation purchased machinery for $110,000 on December 31, 19X1. It expected the equipment to last five years and to have no salvage value; straight-line depreciation was to be used. It sold the equipment on December 31, 19X5, for $27,000. End-of-year general price index numbers were as follows:

19X1	109.4
19X2	117.0
19X3	121.7
19X4	129.2
19X5	136.0

Required

(Round answers to the nearest whole dollar.)

1. What should be presented for the machinery and accumulated depreciation on a historical cost/constant purchasing power balance sheet dated December 31, 19X4? Hint: Depreciation is the total amount of cost that has been allocated to expense. Therefore, the price index number that is used to adjust the nominal dollar cost of the asset should also be used to adjust the nominal dollar amount of depreciation.

2. How much depreciation expense should be shown on the historical cost/constant purchasing power income statement for 19X4?

3. How much depreciation expense should be shown on the historical cost/constant purchasing power income statement for 19X5?

4. How much gain on the sale of the machinery should be reported on the historical cost/nominal dollar income statement for 19X5?

CHECK FIGURE:
Purchasing power loss, $349

5. After adjusting the machinery's cost and accumulated depreciation to the end-of-19X5 price level, how much gain in (loss of) purchasing power was realized on the sale of the machinery?

Problem B–2
Calculating purchasing power gain or loss
(LO 4)

CRP, Inc., had three monetary items during 19X2: cash, accounts receivable, and accounts payable. The changes in these items during the year were as follows:

Cash:
Beginning balance	$ 35,200
Cash proceeds from sale of equipment (in May 19X2)	20,400
Cash receipts from customers (spread evenly throughout the year)	143,700
Payments of accounts payable (spread evenly throughout the year)	(109,800)
Dividends declared and paid in July 19X2	(17,000)
Payments of other cash expenses during August 19X2 .	(31,100)
Ending balance	$ 41,400

Accounts receivable:

Beginning balance	$ 37,500
Sales to customers (spread evenly throughout the year)	150,200
Cash receipts from customers (spread evenly throughout the year)	(143,700)
Ending balance	$ 44,000

Accounts payable:

Beginning balance	$ 46,100
Merchandise purchases (spread evenly throughout the year)	92,600
Special purchase December 31, 19X2	19,000
Payments of accounts payable (spread evenly throughout the year)	(109,800)
Ending balance	$ 47,900

General price index numbers at the end of 19X1 and during 19X2 are as follows:

December 19X1	128.2
January 19X2	132.0
May 19X2	139.7
July 19X2	146.4
August 19X2	150.0
December 19X2	162.9
Average for 19X2	149.3

Required

Calculate the general purchasing power gain or loss experienced by CRP, Inc., in 19X2. (Round answers to the nearest whole dollar.)

CHECK FIGURE:
Net purchasing power loss, $11,244

The Deitrich Company purchased a tract of land for $450,000 in 19X1, when the general price index was 138.6. At the same time, a price index for land values in the area of Deitrich's tract was 144.3. In 19X2, when the general price index was 145.8 and the specific price index for land was 154.0, Deitrich bought another tract of land for $238,000. In late 19X7, the general price index is 168.4 and the price index for land values is 185.2.

Problem B–3
Historical cost/nominal dollars, historical cost/constant purchasing power, and current costs
(LO 4, 5)

Required

Preparation component:

(Round answers to the nearest whole dollar.)

1. In preparing a balance sheet at the end of 19X7, show the amount that should be reported for land based on:

   a. Historical cost/nominal dollars.

   b. Historical cost/constant purchasing power

   c. Current costs.

CHECK FIGURE:
Total 19X7 current cost, $863,765

Analysis component:

2. In Deitrich's December 19X7 meeting of the board of directors, one director insists that Deitrich has earned a gain in purchasing power as a result of owning the land. A second director argues that there could not have been a purchasing power gain or loss since land is a nonmonetary asset. Which director do you think is correct? Explain your answer.

CRITICAL THINKING: ESSAYS, PROBLEMS, AND CASES

Write a brief essay that explains the difference between descriptive and prescriptive concepts and that explains why the FASB's conceptual framework is designed to be prescriptive. Also discuss the question of whether specific concepts can be both descriptive and prescriptive.

Analytical Essay

(LO 1, 2)

ANSWERS TO PROGRESS CHECKS

B–1 *c*

B–2 A top-down approach to developing accounting concepts begins by identifying appropriate objectives of accounting reports.

B–3 A bottom-up approach to developing accounting concepts starts by examining existing accounting practices and determining the general features that characterize those procedures.

B–4 *d*

B–5 To have the qualitative characteristic of being reliable, accounting information should be free from bias and error, should be verifiable, should faithfully represent what is supposed to be described, and should be neutral.

B–6 The elements of financial statements are the objects and events that financial statements should describe; for example, assets, liabilities, revenues, and expenses.

B–7 *c*

B–8 $100,000 \times (150/125) = \$120,000$

B–9 No. Land is a nonmonetary asset and therefore no purchasing power gain or loss is generated.

B–10 *a*

B–11 Operating profit is measured as revenues less the current (at the time of sale) cost of the resources that were used to earn those revenues.

B–12 *c*

B–13 The current selling price of a liability is the amount that would have to be paid to settle or eliminate the liability.

APPENDIX C

Special Journals

LEARNING OBJECTIVES

After studying Appendix C, you should be able to:

1. Explain how special journals save posting labor and journalize and post transactions when special journals are used.
2. Define or explain the words and phrases listed in the appendix glossary.

Even in small businesses, the quantity of data that is processed through the accounting system is large. As a result, the accounting system should be designed so that the data can be processed efficiently. This appendix explains some general procedures and techniques that you can use with a manual accounting system to efficiently process data. Computerized systems often involve the same components but, of course, the specific procedures used by the bookkeeper are different.[1]

The General Journal is a flexible journal in which you can record any transaction. However, each debit and credit entered in a General Journal must be individually posted. As a result, a firm that uses a General Journal to record all the transactions of its business requires much time and labor to post the individual debits and credits.

One way to reduce the writing and the posting labor is to divide the transactions of a business into groups of similar transactions and to provide a separate **special journal** for recording the transactions in each group. For example, most of the transactions of a merchandising business fall into four groups: sales on credit, purchases on credit, cash receipts, and cash disbursements. When a special journal is provided for each group, the journals are:

1. A Sales Journal for recording credit sales.
2. A Purchases Journal for recording credit purchases.
3. A Cash Receipts Journal for recording cash receipts.
4. A Cash Disbursements Journal for recording cash payments.
5. A General Journal for the miscellaneous transactions not recorded in the special journals and also for adjusting, closing, and correcting entries.

The following illustrations show how special journals save time in journalizing and posting transactions. They do this by providing special columns for accumulating the debits and credits of similar transactions. These journals allow you to post the amounts entered in the special columns as column totals rather than as individual amounts. For example, you can save posting labor if you record credit sales for a month in a Sales Journal like the one at the top of Illustration C–1.

REDUCING WRITING AND POSTING LABOR

LO 1
Explain how special journals save posting labor and journalize and post transactions when special journals are used.

---

[1]This appendix illustrates special journals that are designed for use with a periodic inventory system. Thus, students should study Chapter 9 prior to this appendix. The use of special journals with a perpetual inventory system would allow transaction-by-transaction updating of subsidiary inventory records. However, the general ledger would be updated on a periodic basis.

Illustration C-1   Posting from the Sales Journal

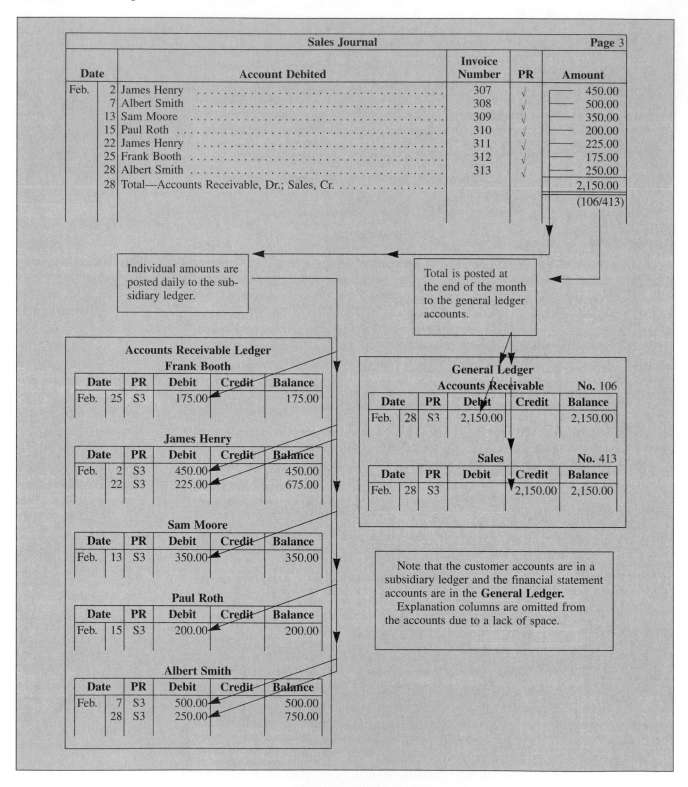

The Sales Journal in Illustration C–1 and the other special journals shown in this appendix are intended for use with a periodic inventory system, which is explained in Chapter 9. Notice that the Sales Journal is designed to record the revenue aspect of sales transactions but not the cost of goods sold. Under a periodic system, the cost of goods sold is determined at the end of the period. If a perpetual inventory system were used, the Sales Journal would include a separate column for recording the cost of goods sold.

As Illustration C–1 shows, credit sales are not posted to the general ledger accounts until the end of the month. Then, the accountant calculates the total sales for the month and posts the total as one debit to Accounts Receivable and as one credit to Sales. Only seven sales are recorded in the illustrated journal. However, if you assume the 7 sales represent 700 sales, you can better appreciate the posting labor saved by making only one debit to Accounts Receivable and one credit to Sales.

The special journal in Illustration C–1 is also called a **columnar journal** because it has columns for recording the date, the customer's name, the invoice number, and the amount of each credit sale. Only credit sales are recorded in it, and they are recorded daily with the information about each sale placed on a separate line. Normally, the information is taken from a copy of the sales ticket or invoice prepared at the time of the sale. However, before discussing the journal further, you need to understand the role played by subsidiary ledgers.

POSTING THE SALES JOURNAL

When customer accounts are maintained in a subsidiary ledger, a Sales Journal is posted as shown in Illustration C–1. The individual sales recorded in the Sales Journal are posted each day to the proper customer accounts in the Accounts Receivable Ledger. These daily postings keep the customer accounts up-to-date. This is important in granting credit because the person responsible for granting credit should know the amount the credit-seeking customer currently owes. The source of this information is the customer's account; if the account is not up-to-date, an incorrect decision may be made.

Note the check marks in the Sales Journal's Posting Reference column. They indicate that the sales recorded in the journal were individually posted to the customer accounts in the Accounts Receivable Ledger. Check marks rather than account numbers are used because customer accounts may not be numbered. When the accounts are not numbered, they are arranged alphabetically in the Accounts Receivable Ledger so they can be located easily.

In addition to the daily postings to customer accounts, the Sales Journal's Amount column is totaled at the end of the month. Then, the total is debited to Accounts Receivable and credited to Sales. The credit records the month's revenue from charge sales. The debit records the resulting increase in accounts receivable.

IDENTIFYING POSTED AMOUNTS

When posting several journals to ledger accounts, you should indicate in the Posting Reference column before each posted amount the journal and the page number of the journal from which the amount was posted. Indicate the journal by using its initial. Thus, items posted from the Cash Disbursements Journal carry the initial *D* before their journal page numbers in the Posting Reference columns. Likewise, items from the Cash Receipts Journal carry the letter *R*. Those from the Sales Journal carry the initial *S*. Items from the Purchases Journal carry the initial *P*, and from the General Journal, the letter *G*.

CASH RECEIPTS JOURNAL

A Cash Receipts Journal that is designed to save labor through posting column totals must be a multicolumn journal. A multicolumn journal is necessary because different accounts are credited when cash is received from different sources. For example, the cash receipts of a store normally fall into three groups: (1) cash from credit customers in payment of their accounts, (2) cash from cash sales, and (3) cash from other sources. Note in Illustration C–2 that a special column is provided for the credits that result when cash is received from each of these sources.

Cash from Credit Customers

When a Cash Receipts Journal similar to the one in Illustration C–2 is used to record cash received in payment of a customer's account, the customer's name is entered in the journal's Account Credited column. The amount credited to the customer's account is entered in the Accounts Receivable Credit column, and the debits to Sales Discounts and Cash are entered in the journal's last two columns.

Look at the Accounts Receivable Credit column. First, observe that this column contains only credits to customer accounts. Second, the individual credits are posted daily to the customer accounts in the subsidiary Accounts Receivable Ledger. Third, the column total is posted at the end of the month as a credit to the Accounts Receivable controlling account. This is the normal recording and posting procedure when using special journals and controlling accounts with subsidiary ledgers. After transactions are entered in a special journal, the individual amounts are posted to the subsidiary ledger accounts and the column totals are posted to the general ledger accounts.

Cash Sales

After cash sales are entered on one or more cash registers and totaled at the end of each day, the daily total is recorded with a debit to Cash and a credit to Sales. When using a Cash Receipts Journal like Illustration C–2, the debits to Cash are entered in the Cash Debit column, and the credits in a special column headed Sales Credit. By using a separate Sales Credit column, the bookkeeper can post the total cash sales for a month as a single amount, the column total. (Although cash sales are normally journalized daily based on the cash register reading, cash sales are journalized only once each week in Illustration C–2 to shorten the illustration.)

At the time they record daily cash sales in the Cash Receipts Journal, some bookkeepers, as in Illustration C–2, place a check mark in the Posting Reference (PR) column to indicate that no amount is individually posted from that line of the journal. Other bookkeepers use a double check (✓✓) to distinguish amounts that are not posted to customer accounts from amounts that are posted.

Miscellaneous Receipts of Cash

Most cash receipts are from collections of accounts receivable and from cash sales. However, other sources of cash include borrowing money from a bank or selling unneeded assets. The Other Accounts Credit column is for receipts that do not occur often enough to warrant a separate column. In most companies, the items entered in this column are few and are posted to a variety of general ledger accounts. As a result, postings are less apt to be omitted if these items are posted daily.

The Cash Receipts Journal's Posting Reference column is used only for daily postings from the Other Accounts and Accounts Receivable columns. The account numbers in the Posting Reference column indicate items that were posted to general ledger accounts. The check marks indicate either that an item (like a day's cash sales) was not posted or that an item was posted to the subsidiary Accounts Receivable Ledger.

Month-End Postings

At the end of the month, the amounts in the Accounts Receivable, Sales, Sales Discounts, and Cash columns of the Cash Receipts Journal are posted as column to-

Illustration C–2   Posting from the Cash Receipts Journal

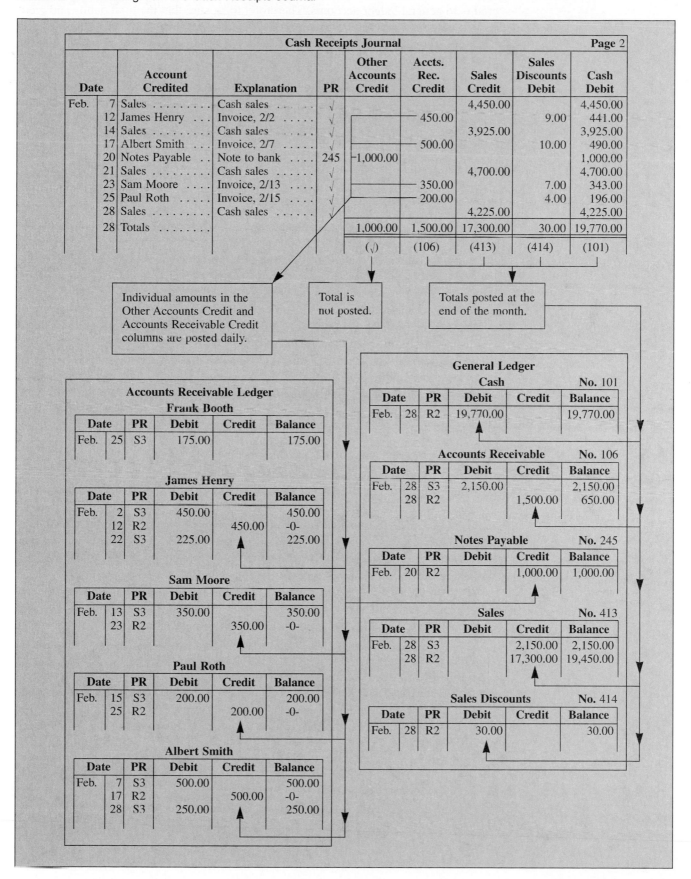

tals. However, the transactions recorded in any journal must result in equal debits and credits to general ledger accounts. Therefore, to be sure that the total debits and credits in a columnar journal are equal, the bookkeeper must *crossfoot* the column totals before posting them. To *foot* a column of numbers is to add it. To crossfoot, add the debit column totals and add the credit column totals; then compare the two sums for equality. For Illustration C–2, the two sums appear as follows:

Debit Columns		Credit Columns	
Sales discounts debit	$ 30	Other accounts credit	$ 1,000
Cash debit	19,770	Accounts receivable credit	1,500
		Sales credit	17,300
Total	$19,800	Total	$19,800

After crossfooting the journal to confirm that debits equal credits, the bookkeeper posts the totals of the last four columns as indicated in each column heading. Because the individual items in the Other Accounts column are posted daily, the column total is not posted. In Illustration C–2, note the check mark below the Other Accounts column. The check mark indicates that the column total was not posted. The account numbers of the accounts to which the remaining column totals were posted are in parentheses below each column.

Posting items daily from the Other Accounts column with a delayed posting of the offsetting items in the Cash column (total) causes the General Ledger to be out of balance during the month. However, this does not matter because posting the Cash column total causes the offsetting amounts to reach the General Ledger before the trial balance is prepared.

PURCHASES JOURNAL

A Purchases Journal with one money column can be used to record purchases of merchandise on credit. However, a Purchases Journal usually is more useful if it is a multicolumn journal in which all credit purchases on account are recorded. Such a journal may have columns similar to those in Illustration C–3. In the illustrated journal, the invoice date and terms together indicate the date on which payment for each purchase is due. The Accounts Payable Credit column is used to record the amounts credited to each creditor's account. These amounts are posted daily to the individual creditor accounts in a subsidiary Accounts Payable Ledger.

In Illustration C–3, note that each line of the Account column shows the subsidiary ledger account that should be posted for the amount in the Accounts Payable Credit column. The Account column also shows the general ledger account to be debited when a purchase involves an amount recorded in the Other Accounts Debit column.

In this illustration, note the separate column provided for purchases of office supplies on credit. A separate column such as this is useful whenever several transactions involve debits to a particular account. The Other Accounts Debit column in Illustration C–3 allows the Purchases Journal to be used for all purchase transactions involving credits to Accounts Payable. The individual amounts in the Other Accounts Debit column typically are posted daily to the indicated general ledger accounts.

Illustration C-3   Posting from the Purchases Journal

Purchases Journal									Page 1

Date		Account	Date of Invoice	Terms	PR	Purchases Debit	Office Supplies Debit	Other Accounts Debit	Accounts Payable Credit
Feb.	3	Horn Supply Co.	2/2	n/30	√	275.00	75.00		350.00
	5	Acme Mfg. Co.	2/5	2/10,n/30	√	200.00			200.00
	13	Wycoff & Co.	2/10	2/10,n/30	√	150.00			150.00
	20	Smith & Co.	2/18	2/10,n/30	√	300.00			300.00
	25	Acme Mfg. Co.	2/24	2/10,n/30	√	100.00			100.00
	28	Store Supplies/HAG Co.	2/28	n/30	125/√	125.00	25.00	75.00	225.00
	28	Totals				1,150.00	100.00	75.00	1,325.00
						(505)	(124)	(√)	(201)

These totals are posted at the end of the month.

Individual amounts in the Other Accounts Debit and Accounts Payable Credit columns are posted daily.

General Ledger

Office Supplies   No. 124

Date		PR	Debit	Credit	Balance
Feb.	28	P1	100.00		100.00

Store Supplies   No. 125

Date		PR	Debit	Credit	Balance
Feb.	28	P1	75.00		75.00

Accounts Payable   No. 201

Date		PR	Debit	Credit	Balance
Feb.	28	P1		1,325.00	1,325.00

Purchases   No. 505

Date		PR	Debit	Credit	Balance
Feb.	28	P1	1,150.00		1,150.00

Accounts Payable Ledger

Acme Mfg. Company

Date		PR	Debit	Credit	Balance
Feb.	5	P1		200.00	200.00
	25	P1		100.00	300.00

HAG Company

Date		PR	Debit	Credit	Balance
Feb.	28	P1		225.00	225.00

Horn Supply Company

Date		PR	Debit	Credit	Balance
Feb.	3	P1		350.00	350.00

Smith & Company

Date		PR	Debit	Credit	Balance
Feb.	20	P1		300.00	300.00

Wycoff & Company

Date		PR	Debit	Credit	Balance
Feb.	13	P1		150.00	150.00

At the end of the month, all of the column totals except the Other Accounts Debit column are posted to the appropriate general ledger accounts. After this is done, the balance in the Accounts Payable controlling account should equal the sum of the account balances in the subsidiary Accounts Payable Ledger.

THE CASH DISBURSEMENTS JOURNAL OR CHECK REGISTER

The Cash Disbursements Journal, like the Cash Receipts Journal, has columns so that you can post repetitive debits and credits in column totals. The repetitive cash payments involve debits to the Accounts Payable controlling account and credits to both Purchase Discounts and Cash. Most companies usually purchase merchandise on credit. Therefore, a Purchases column is not needed. Instead, the occasional cash purchase is recorded as shown on line 2 of Illustration C–4.

Observe that the illustrated journal has a column headed Check Number (Ck. No.). To gain control over cash disbursements, all payments except for very small amounts should be made by check. The checks should be prenumbered by the printer and should be entered in the journal in numerical order with each check's number in the column headed Ck. No. This makes it possible to scan the numbers in the column for omitted checks. When a Cash Disbursements Journal has a column for check numbers, it is often called a **Check Register.**

The individual amounts in the Other Accounts Debit column of a Cash Disbursements Journal are normally posted to the appropriate general ledger accounts on a daily basis. The individual amounts in the Accounts Payable Debit column are also posted daily to the named creditors' accounts in the subsidiary Accounts Payable Ledger. At the end of the month, the bookkeeper crossfoots the column totals and posts the Accounts Payable Debit column total to the Accounts Payable controlling account. Then, the Purchase Discounts Credit column total is posted to the Purchase Discounts account and the Cash Credit column total is posted to the Cash account. The Other Accounts column total is not posted.

SALES TAXES

Many cities and states require retailers to collect sales taxes from their customers and to periodically remit these taxes to the city or state treasurer. When using a columnar Sales Journal, you can have a record of the taxes collected by adding special columns in the journal as shown in Illustration C–5.

As we described earlier in the chapter, the column totals of a Sales Journal are typically posted at the end of each month. This, of course, includes crediting the Sales Taxes Payable account for the total of the Sales Taxes Payable column. The individual amounts in the Accounts Receivable column are posted daily to the customer accounts in the Accounts Receivable Ledger. The individual amounts in the Sales Taxes Payable and Sales columns are not posted.

A business that collects sales taxes on its cash sales may use a special Sales Taxes Payable column in its Cash Receipts Journal.

SALES INVOICES AS A SALES JOURNAL

To save labor, some retailers avoid using Sales Journals for credit sales. Instead, they post each sales invoice total directly to the customer's account in the subsidiary Accounts Receivable Ledger. Then, they place copies of the invoices in numerical order in a binder. At the end of the month, they total all the invoices of that month and make a general journal entry to debit Accounts Receivable and credit Sales for the total. In effect, the bound invoice copies act as a Sales Journal. Such a procedure is known as direct posting of sales invoices.

Illustration C–4 Posting from the Cash Disbursements Journal

Cash Disbursements Journal — Page 2

Date	Ch. No.	Payee	Account Debited	PR	Other Accounts Debit	Accounts Payable Debit	Purchase Discounts Credit	Cash Credit
Feb. 3	105	L. & N. Railroad	Transportation-In	508	15.00			15.00
12	106	East Sales Co.	Purchases	505	25.00			25.00
15	107	Acme Mfg. Co.	Acme Mfg. Co	√		200.00	4.00	196.00
15	108	Jerry Hale	Salaries Expense ...	622	250.00			250.00
20	109	Wycoff & Co.	Wycoff & Co.	√		150.00	3.00	147.00
28	110	Smith & Co.	Smith & Co.	√		300.00	6.00	294.00
28		Totals			290.00	650.00	13.00	927.00
					(√)	(201)	(506)	(101)

Individual amounts in the Other Accounts Debit column and Accounts Payable Debit column are posted daily.

Totals posted at the end of the month.

Accounts Payable Ledger

Acme Mfg. Company

Date	PR	Debit	Credit	Balance
Feb. 5	P1		200.00	200.00
15	D2	200.00		-0-
25	P1		100.00	100.00

HAG Company

Date	PR	Debit	Credit	Balance
Feb. 28	P1		225.00	225.00

Horn Supply Company

Date	PR	Debit	Credit	Balance
Feb. 3	P1		350.00	350.00

Smith & Company

Date	PR	Debit	Credit	Balance
Feb. 20	P1		300.00	300.00
28	D2	300.00		-0-

Wycoff & Company

Date	PR	Debit	Credit	Balance
Feb. 13	P1		150.00	150.00
20	D2	150.00		-0-

General Ledger

Cash — No. 101

Date	PR	Debit	Credit	Balance
Feb. 28	R2	19,770.00		19,770.00
28	D2		927.00	18,843.00

Accounts Payable — No. 201

Date	PR	Debit	Credit	Balance
Feb. 28	P1		1,325.00	1,325.00
28	D2	650.00		675.00

Purchases — No. 505

Date	PR	Debit	Credit	Balance
Feb. 12	D2	25.00		25.00
28	P1	1,150.00		1,175.00

Purchase Discounts — No. 506

Date	PR	Debit	Credit	Balance
Feb. 28	D2		13.00	13.00

Transportation-In — No. 508

Date	PR	Debit	Credit	Balance
Feb. 3	D2	15.00		15.00

Salaries Expense — No. 622

Date	PR	Debit	Credit	Balance
Feb. 15	D2	250.00		250.00

Illustration C-5   A Sales Journal with a Column for Sales Taxes Payable

Sales Journal						
Date	Account Debited	Invoice Number	PR	Accounts Receivable Debit	Sales Taxes Payable Credit	Sales Credit
Dec. 1	D. R. Horn	7-1698		103.00	3.00	100.00

SALES RETURNS

A business that has only a few sales returns may record them in a General Journal with an entry like the following:

Oct.	17	Sales Returns and Allowances	415	17.50	
		Accounts Receivable—George Ball	106/✓		17.50
		Customer returned merchandise.			

    The debit of the entry is posted to the Sales Returns and Allowances account. The credit is posted to both the Accounts Receivable controlling account and to the customer's account. Note the account number and the check mark, 106/✓, in the PR column on the credit line. This indicates that both the Accounts Receivable controlling account in the General Ledger and the George Ball account in the Accounts Receivable Ledger were credited for $17.50. Both were credited because the balance of the controlling account in the General Ledger will not equal the sum of the customer account balances in the subsidiary ledger unless both are credited.

    A company with a large number of sales returns can save posting labor by recording them in a special Sales Returns and Allowances Journal similar to Illustration C–6. Note that this is in keeping with the idea that a company can design and use a special journal for any group of similar transactions if there are enough transactions to warrant the journal. When using a Sales Returns and Allowances Journal to record returns, the amounts in the journal are posted daily to the customers' accounts. Then, at the end of the month, the journal total is posted as a debit to Sales Returns and Allowances and as a credit to Accounts Receivable.

GENERAL JOURNAL ENTRIES

When special journals are used, a General Journal is always necessary for adjusting, closing, and correcting entries and for a few transactions that cannot be recorded in the special journals. Some of these transactions are purchase returns, purchases of plant assets financed by notes payable, and if a Sales Returns and Allowances Journal is not provided, sales returns.

Progress Check
(Answers to Progress Checks are provided at the end of the appendix.)

C-1   **When special journals are used:**
     a. **A General Journal is not used.**
     b. **All cash payments by check are recorded in the Cash Disbursements Journal.**
     c. **All purchase transactions are recorded in the Purchases Journal.**
     d. **All sales transactions are recorded in the Sales Journal.**

Illustration C–6

		Sales Returns and Allowances Journal						
Date		Account Credited	Explanation	Credit Memo No.	PR	Amount		
Oct.	7	Robert Moore	Defective merchandise	203	√	10.00		
	14	James Warren	Defective merchandise	204	√	12.00		
	18	T. M. Jones	Not ordered	205	√	6.00		
	23	Sam Smith	Defective merchandise	206	√	18.00		
	31	Sales Returns and Allowances, Dr.; Accts. Receivable, Cr.				46.00		
						(415/106)		

C–2 Why does a columnar journal save posting labor?

C–3 If sales taxes must be recorded and special journals are used:
  a. The sales taxes must be recorded in the General Journal.
  b. A separate column for sales taxes should be included in the Cash Disbursements Journal.
  c. A separate column for sales taxes should be included in the Cash Receipts Journal and the Sales Journal.
  d. A special Sales Taxes Journal should be used.

C–4 What is meant by "direct posting of sales invoices"?

C–5 If a company uses special journals for sales, purchases, cash receipts, and cash disbursements, why does it need a General Journal?

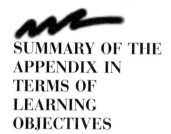

SUMMARY OF THE APPENDIX IN TERMS OF LEARNING OBJECTIVES

LO 1. Explain how special journals save posting labor and journalize and post transactions when special journals are used. Columnar journals are designed so that repetitive debits or credits are entered in separate columns. A typical set of special journals includes a Sales Journal, a Purchases Journal, a Cash Receipts Journal, and a Cash Disbursements Journal (or Check Register). Any transactions that cannot be entered in the special journals are entered in the General Journal.

To record sales taxes, the Sales Journal and the Cash Receipts Journal should include a separate Sales Taxes Payable column. When sales invoices substitute for a Sales Journal, the customer accounts in the Accounts Receivable Ledger are posted directly from the sales invoices. Copies of the invoices for each month are then bound and totaled as a basis for recording the sales in the General Ledger. Sales returns and allowances may be recorded in the General Journal, or a special journal for sales returns and allowances may be used.

GLOSSARY

Check Register a book of original entry for recording cash payments by check.

Columnar journal a book of original entry having columns, each of which is designated as the place for entering specific data about each transaction of a group of similar transactions.

General Ledger the ledger that contains the financial statement accounts of a business.

Special journal a book of original entry that is designed and used for recording only a specified type of transaction.

QUESTIONS

1. When special journals are used, separate special journals normally are used to record each of four different types of transactions. What are these four types of transactions?

2. Why should sales to and receipts of cash from credit customers be recorded and posted daily?

3. Both credits to customer accounts and credits to miscellaneous accounts are individually posted from a Cash Receipts Journal similar to the one in Illustration C–2. Why not put both kinds of credits in the same column and thus save journal space?

4. What procedures allow copies of a company's sales invoices to be used as a Sales Journal?

5. When a general journal entry is used to record a returned credit sale, the credit of the entry must be posted twice. Does this cause the trial balance to be out of balance? Why or why not?

6. How can you identify the journal from which a particular amount in a ledger account was posted?

QUICK STUDY (Five-Minute Exercises)

QS C–1
(LO 1)

Sampson Iron Works uses a Sales Journal, a Purchases Journal, a Cash Receipts Journal, a Cash Disbursements Journal, and a General Journal. Sampson recently completed the following transactions. List the transaction letters and next to each letter give the name of the journal in which the transaction should be recorded.

  a. Sold merchandise on credit.
  b. Purchased shop supplies on credit.
  c. Paid an employee's salary.
  d. Paid a creditor.
  e. Purchased merchandise on credit.
  f. Borrowed money from the bank.
  g. Sold merchandise for cash.

QS C–2
(LO 1)

Nautical Books, Inc., uses a Sales Journal, a Purchases Journal, a Cash Receipts Journal, a Cash Disbursements Journal, and a General Journal. The following transactions occurred during the month of November. Journalize the November transactions that should be recorded in the General Journal.

Nov. 2 Purchased merchandise on credit for $2,900 from the Ringdol Co., terms 2/10, n/30.

  12 The majority stockholder contributed an automobile worth $15,000 to the business in exchange for 1,500 shares of the company's $10 par value, common stock.

  16 Sold merchandise on credit to R. Wyder for $1,100, terms n/30.

  19 R. Wyder returned $150 of merchandise originally purchased on November 16.

  28 Returned $170 of defective merchandise to the Ringdol Co. from the November 2 purchase.

EXERCISES

Exercise C–1
The Sales Journal
(LO 1)

Spindle Corporation uses a Sales Journal, a Purchases Journal, a Cash Receipts Journal, a Cash Disbursements Journal, and a General Journal. The following transactions occurred during the month of February:

Feb. 2 Sold merchandise to S. Mayer for $450 cash, Invoice No. 5703.

  5 Purchased merchandise on credit from Camp Corp., $2,300.

  7 Sold merchandise to J. Eason for $1,150, terms 2/10, n/30, Invoice No. 5704.

8 Borrowed $8,000 by giving a note to the bank.

12 Sold merchandise to P. Lathan for $320, terms n/30, Invoice No. 5705.

16 Received $1,127 from J. Eason to pay for the purchase of February 7.

19 Sold used store equipment to Whiten, Inc., for $900.

25 Sold merchandise to S. Summers for $550, terms n/30, Invoice No. 5706.

Required

On a sheet of notebook paper, draw a Sales Journal like the one that appears in Illustration C–1. Journalize the February transactions that should be recorded in the Sales Journal.

SeaMap Company uses a Sales Journal, a Purchases Journal, a Cash Receipts Journal, a Cash Disbursements Journal, and a General Journal. The following transactions occurred during the month of September:

Exercise C–2
The Cash Receipts Journal
(LO 1)

Sept. 3 Purchased merchandise on credit for $3,100 from Pacer Co.

7 Sold merchandise on credit to J. Namal for $900, subject to an $18 sales discount if paid by the end of the month.

9 Borrowed $2,750 by giving a note to the bank.

13 Issued 350 shares of $100 par value common stock in exchange for $3,500.

18 Sold merchandise to B. Baird for $230 cash.

22 Paid Pacer Co. $3,100 for the merchandise purchased on September 3.

27 Received $882 from J. Namal in payment of the September 7 purchase.

30 Paid salaries of $1,600.

Required

On a sheet of notebook paper, draw a multicolumn Cash Receipts Journal like the one that appears in Illustration C–2. Journalize the September transactions that should be recorded in the Cash Receipts Journal.

Chem Corp. uses a Sales Journal, a Purchases Journal, a Cash Receipts Journal, a Cash Disbursements Journal, and a General Journal. The following transactions occurred during the month of July:

Exercise C–3
The Purchases Journal
(LO 1)

July 1 Purchased merchandise on credit for $8,100 from Angler, Inc., terms n/30.

8 Sold merchandise on credit to B. Harren for $1,500, subject to a $30 sales discount if paid by the end of the month.

10 Issued 40 shares of $50 par value common stock in exchange for $2,000 cash.

14 Purchased store supplies from Steck Company on credit for $240, terms n/30.

17 Purchased office supplies on credit from Marten Company for $260, terms n/30.

24 Sold merchandise to W. Winger for $630 cash.

28 Purchased store supplies from Hadley's for $90 cash.

29 Paid Angler, Inc., $8,100 for the merchandise purchased on July 1.

Required

On a sheet of notebook paper, draw a multicolumn Purchases Journal like the one that appears in Illustration C–3. Journalize the July transactions that should be recorded in the Purchases Journal.

Aeron Supply uses a Sales Journal, a Purchases Journal, a Cash Receipts Journal, a Cash Disbursements Journal, and a General Journal. The following transactions occurred during the month of March:

Exercise C–4
The Cash Disbursements Journal
(LO 1)

Mar. 3   Purchased merchandise for $2,750 on credit from Pace, Inc., terms 2/10, n/30.

9   Issued Check No. 210 to Narlin Corp. to buy store supplies for $450.

12   Sold merchandise on credit to K. Camp for $670, terms n/30.

17   Issued Check No. 211 for $1,500 to repay a note payable to City Bank.

20   Purchased merchandise for $3,500 on credit from LeBaron, terms 2/10, n/30.

29   Issued Check No. 212 to LeBaron to pay the amount due for the purchase of March 20, less the discount.

31   Paid salary of $1,700 to E. Brandon by issuing Check No. 213.

31   Issued Check No. 214 to Pace, Inc., to pay the amount due for the purchase of March 3.

Required

On a sheet of notebook paper, draw a multicolumn Cash Disbursements Journal like the one that appears in Illustration C–4. Journalize the March transactions that should be recorded in the Cash Disbursements Journal.

Exercise C–5
Special journal transactions
(LO 1)

Simon Pharmacy uses the following journals: Sales Journal, Purchases Journal, Cash Receipts Journal, Cash Disbursements Journal, and General Journal. On June 5, Simon purchased merchandise priced at $12,000, subject to credit terms of 2/10, n/30. On June 14, the pharmacy paid the net amount due. However, in journalizing the payment, the bookkeeper debited Accounts Payable for $12,000 and failed to record the cash discount. Cash was credited for the actual amount paid. In what journals would the June 5 and the June 14 transactions have been recorded? What procedure is likely to discover the error in journalizing the June 14 transaction?

Exercise C–6
Posting to subsidiary ledger accounts
(LO 1)

At the end of May, the Sales Journal of Camper Goods appeared as follows:

Sales Journal

Date		Account Debited	Invoice Number	PR	Amount
May	6	Brad Smithers	190		2,880.00
	10	Dan Holland	191		1,940.00
	17	Sanders Farrell	192		850.00
	25	Dan Holland	193		340.00
	31	Total			6,010.00

Camper had also recorded the return of merchandise with the following entry:

May	20	Sales Returns and Allowances	250.00	
		Accounts Receivable—Sanders Farrell		250.00
		Customer returned merchandise.		

Required

1. On a sheet of notebook paper, open a subsidiary Accounts Receivable Ledger that has a T-account for each customer listed in the Sales Journal. Post to the customer accounts the entries in the Sales Journal and any portion of the general journal entry that affects a customer's account.

2. Open a General Ledger that has T-accounts for Accounts Receivable, Sales, and Sales Returns and Allowances. Post the Sales Journal and any portion of the general journal entry that affects these accounts.

3. Prepare a list or schedule of the accounts in the subsidiary Accounts Receivable Ledger and add their balances to show that the total equals the balance in the Accounts Receivable controlling account.

Following are the condensed journals of Tipper Trophies. The journal column headings are incomplete in that they do not indicate whether the columns are debit or credit columns.

Exercise C–7
Posting from special journals and subsidiary ledgers to T-accounts.
(LO 1)

Sales Journal

Account	Amount
Jack Hertz	3,700
Trudy Stone	8,400
Dave Waylon	1,000
Total	13,100

Purchases Journal

Account	Amount
Grass Corp.	5,400
Sulter, Inc.	4,500
McGrew Company	1,700
Total	11,600

General Journal

...	..	Sales Returns and Allowances	300.00	
		Accounts Receivable—Jack Hertz		300.00
	..	Accounts Payable—Grass Corp.	750.00	
		Purchase Returns and Allowances		750.00

Cash Receipts Journal

Account	Other Accounts	Accounts Receivable	Sales	Sales Discounts	Cash
Jack Hertz		3,400		68	3,332
Sales			2,250		2,250
Notes Payable	4,500				4,500
Sales			625		625
Trudy Stone		8,400		168	8,232
Store Equipment	500				500
Totals	5,000	11,800	2,875	236	19,439

Cash Disbursements Journal

Account	Other Accounts	Accounts Payable	Purchase Discounts	Cash
Prepaid Insurance	850			850
Sulter, Inc.		4,500	135	4,365
Grass Corp.		4,650	93	4,557
Store Equipment	1,750			1,750
Totals	2,600	9,150	228	11,522

Required

1. Prepare T-accounts on notebook paper for the following general ledger and subsidiary ledger accounts. Separate the accounts of each ledger group as follows:

General Ledger Accounts
Cash
Accounts Receivable
Prepaid Insurance
Store Equipment
Accounts Payable
Notes Payable
Sales
Sales Discounts
Sales Returns and Allowances
Purchases
Purchase Discounts
Purchase Returns and Allowances

Accounts Receivable Ledger Accounts
Jack Hertz
Trudy Stone
Dave Waylon

Accounts Payable Ledger Accounts
McGrew Company
Grass Corp.
Sulter, Inc.

2.   Without referring to any of the illustrations in the chapter that show complete column headings for the journals, post the journals to the proper T-accounts.

COMPREHENSIVE PROBLEM

Alpine Corporation
(LO 1)

(If the Working Papers that accompany this text are not available, omit this comprehensive problem.)

Assume it is Monday, May 1, the first business day of the month, and you have just been hired as the accountant for Alpine Corporation, which operates with monthly accounting periods. All of the company's accounting work has been completed through the end of April and its ledgers show April 30 balances. During your first month on the job, you record the following transactions:

May   1   Issued Check No. 3410 to S&M Management Co. in payment of the May rent, $3,710. (Use two lines to record the transaction. Charge 80% of the rent to Rent Expense, Selling Space and the balance to Rent Expense, Office Space.)

2   Sold merchandise on credit to Essex Company, Invoice No. 8785, $6,100. (The terms of all credit sales are 2/10, n/30.)

2   Issued a $175 credit memorandum to Nabors, Inc., for defective merchandise sold on April 28 and returned for credit. The total selling price (gross) was $4,725.

3   Received a $798 credit memorandum from Parkay Products for merchandise received on April 29 and returned for credit.

4   Purchased on credit from Thompson Supply Co.: merchandise, $37,072; store supplies, $574; and office supplies, $83. Invoice dated May 4, terms n/10 EOM.

5   Received payment from Nabors, Inc., for the remaining balance from the sale of April 28 less the May 2 return and the discount.

8   Issued Check No. 3411 to Parkay Products to pay for the $7,098 of merchandise received on April 29 less the May 3 return and a 2% discount.

9   Sold store supplies to the merchant next door at cost for cash, $350.

10   Purchased office equipment on credit from Thompson Supply Co., invoice dated May 10, terms n/10 EOM, $4,074.

11   Received payment from Essex Company for the May 2 sale less the discount.

11   Received merchandise and an invoice dated May 10, terms 2/10, n/30, from Gale, Inc., $8,800.

12   Received an $854 credit memorandum from Thompson Supply Co. for defective office equipment received on May 10 and returned for credit.

15   Issued Check No. 3412, payable to Payroll, in payment of sales salaries, $5,320, and office salaries, $3,150. Cashed the check and paid the employees.

15   Cash sales for the first half of the month, $59,220. (Such sales are normally recorded daily. They are recorded only twice in this problem to reduce the repetitive entries.)

15   *Post to the customer and creditor accounts. Also, post individual items that are not included in column totals at the end of the month to the general ledger accounts. (Such items are normally posted daily, but you are asked to post them only twice each month because they are few in number.)*

16   Sold merchandise on credit to Essex Company, Invoice No. 8786, $3,990.

17   Received merchandise and an invoice dated May 14, terms 2/10, n/60, from Chandler Corp., $13,650.

19   Issued Check No. 3413 to Gale, Inc., in payment of its May 10 invoice less the discount.

22   Sold merchandise to Oscar Services, Invoice No. 8787, $6,850, terms 2/10, m/60.

23 Issued Check No. 3414 to Chandler Corp. in payment of its May 14 invoice less the discount.

24 Purchased on credit from Thompson Supply Co.: merchandise, $8,120; store supplies, $630; and office supplies, $280. Invoice dated May 24, terms n/10 EOM.

25 Received merchandise and an invoice dated May 23, terms 2/10, n/30, from Parkay Products, $3,080.

26 Sold merchandise on credit to Deaver Corp., Invoice No. 8788, $14,210.

26 Issued Check No. 3415 to Trinity Power in payment of the April electric bill, $1,283.

29 Declared and paid a $7,000 cash dividend to Clint Barry, the sole stockholder of Alpine Corporation, using Check No. 3416.

30 Received payment from Oscar Services for the May 22 sale less the discount.

30 Issued Check No. 3417, payable to Payroll, in payment of sales salaries, $5,320, and office salaries, $3,150. Cashed the check and paid the employees.

31 Cash sales for the last half of the month were $66,052.

31 *Post to the customer and creditor accounts. Also, post individual items that are not included in column totals at the end of the month to the general ledger accounts.*

31 Foot and crossfoot the journals and make the month-end postings.

Required

1. Enter the transactions in the appropriate journals and post when instructed to do so. Use a periodic inventory system.

2. Prepare a trial balance in the Trial Balance columns of the provided work sheet form and complete the work sheet using the following information. (Assume Alpine uses the closing entry approach to record the change in the Merchandise Inventory account.)
    a. Expired insurance, $553.
    b. Ending store supplies inventory, $2,632.
    c. Ending office supplies inventory, $504.
    d. Estimated depreciation of store equipment, $567.
    e. Estimated depreciation of office equipment, $329.
    f. Ending merchandise inventory, $176,400.

3. Prepare a May multiple-step classified income statement, a May statement of retained earnings, and a May 31 classified balance sheet.

4. Prepare and post adjusting and closing entries.

5. Prepare a post-closing trial balance. Also prepare a list of the Accounts Receivable Ledger accounts and a list of the Accounts Payable Ledger accounts. Total the balances of each to confirm that the totals equal the balances in the controlling accounts.

ANSWERS TO PROGRESS CHECKS

C–1 *b*

C–2 Columnar journals allow you to accumulate repetitive debits and credits and post them as column totals rather than as individual amounts.

C–3 *b*

C–4 This refers to the procedure of using copies of sales invoices as a Sales Journal. Each invoice total is posted directly to the customer's account, and all the invoices are totaled at month-end for posting to the General Ledger accounts.

C–5 The General Journal would still be needed for adjusting, closing, and correcting entries, and for miscellaneous transactions such as sales returns, purchase returns, and plant asset purchases.

Present and Future Values: An Expansion

After studying Appendix D, you should be able to:

1. **Explain what is meant by the present value of a single amount and the present value of an annuity and be able to use tables to solve present value problems.**
2. **Explain what is meant by the future value of a single amount and the future value of an annuity and be able to use tables to solve future value problems.**

The concept of present value is introduced and applied to accounting problems in Chapters 12 and 13. This appendix is designed to supplement those presentations with additional discussion, more complete tables, and additional homework exercises. In studying this appendix, you also learn about the concept of future value.

PRESENT VALUE OF A SINGLE AMOUNT

LO 1
Explain what is meant by the present value of a single amount and the present value of an annuity and be able to use tables to solve present value problems.

The present value of a single amount to be received or paid at some future date may be expressed as:

$$p = \frac{f}{(1 + i)^n}$$

where

p = present value
f = future value
i = rate of interest per period
n = number of periods

For example, assume that $2.20 is to be received one period from now. It would be useful to know how much must be invested now, for one period, at an interest rate of 10% to provide $2.20. We can calculate that amount with this formula:

$$p = \frac{f}{(1 + i)^n} = \frac{\$2.20}{(1 + .10)^1} = \$2.00$$

Alternatively, we can use the formula to find how much must be invested for two periods at 10% to provide $2.42:

$$p = \frac{f}{(1 + i)^n} = \frac{\$2.42}{(1 + .10)^2} = \$2.00$$

Note that the number of periods (n) does not have to be expressed in years. Any period of time such as a day, a month, a quarter, or a year may be used. However, whatever period is used, the interest rate (i) must be compounded for the same period. Thus, if a problem expresses n in months, and i equals 12% per year, then of the amount invested at the beginning of each month is earned during that month and added to the investment. Thus, the interest is compounded monthly.

A present value table shows present values for a variety of interest rates (i) and a variety of numbers of periods (n). Each present value is based on the assumption that the future value (f) is 1. The formula used to construct a table of present values of a single future amount is:

$$p = \frac{1}{(1 + i)^n}$$

Table D–1 on page 688 is a table of present values of a single future amount and is often called a *present value of 1 table*.

Progress Check

(Answers to Progress Checks are provided at the end of the appendix.)

D-1   Lamar Company is considering an investment that will yield $70,000 after six years. If Lamar requires an 8% return, how much should it be willing to pay for the investment?

The following formula for the present value of a single amount can be modified to become the formula for the future value of a single amount with a simple step:

$$p = \frac{f}{(1 + i)^n}$$

Multiplying both sides of the equation by $(1 + i)^n$, the result is:

$$f = p \times (1 + i)^n$$

For example, we can use this formula to determine that $2.00 invested for one period at an interest rate of 10% will increase to a future value of $2.20:

$$f = p \times (1 + i)^n$$
$$= \$2.00 \times (1 + .10)^1$$
$$= \$2.20$$

Alternatively, assume that $2.00 will remain invested for three periods at 10%. The $2.662 amount that will be received after three periods is calculated with the formula as follows:

$$f = p \times (1 + i)^n$$
$$= \$2.00 \times (1 + .10)^3$$
$$= \$2.662$$

A future value table shows future values for a variety of interest rates (i) and a variety of number of periods (n). Each future value is based on the assumption that the present value (p) is 1. Thus, the formula used to construct a table of future values of a single amount is:

$$f = (1 + i)^n$$

Table D–2 on page 689 is a table of future values of a single amount and is often called a *future value of 1 table*.

In Table D–2, look at the row where $n = 0$ and observe that the future value is 1 for all interest rates because no interest is earned.

Observe that a table showing the present values of 1 and a table showing the future values of 1 contain exactly the same information because both tables are based on the same equation. As you have seen, this equation:

$$p = \frac{f}{(1 + i)^n}$$

FUTURE VALUE OF A SINGLE AMOUNT

LO 2
Explain what is meant by the future value of a single amount and the future value of an annuity and be able to use tables to solve future value problems.

is nothing more than a reformulation of:

$$f = p \times (1 + i)^n$$

Both tables reflect the same four variables, p, f, i, and n. Therefore, any problem that can be solved with one of the two tables can also be solved with the other table.

For example, suppose that a person invests $100 for five years and expects to earn 12% per year. How much should the person receive after five years? To solve the problem using Table D–2, find the future value of 1, five periods from now, compounded at 12%. In the table, $f = 1.7623$. Thus, the amount to be accumulated over five years is $176.23 ($100 $\times$ 1.7623).

Table D–1 shows that the present value of 1, discounted five periods at 12% is 0.5674. Recall that the relationship between present value and future value may be expressed as:

$$p = \frac{f}{(1 + i)^n}$$

This formula can be restated as:

$$p = f \times \frac{1}{(1 + i)^n}$$

In turn, it can be restated as:

$$f = \frac{p}{\dfrac{1}{(1 + i)^n}}$$

Because we know from Table D–1 that $1/(1 + i)^n$ equals 0.5674, the future value of $100 invested for 5 periods at 12% is:

$$f = \frac{\$100}{0.5674} = \$176.24$$

In summary, the future value can be found two ways. First, we can multiply the amount invested by the future value found in Table D–2. Second, we can divide the amount invested by the present value found in Table D–1. As you can see in this problem, immaterial differences can occur between these two methods through rounding.

Progress Check

D–2   On May 9, Cindy Huber was notified that she had won $150,000 in a sweepstakes. She decided to deposit the money in a savings account that yields an 8% annual rate of interest and plans on quitting her job when the account equals $299,850. How many years will it be before Cindy is able to quit working? *(a)* 2; *(b)* 8; *(c)* 9.

PRESENT VALUE OF AN ANNUITY

LO 1
Explain what is meant by the present value of a single amount and the present value of an annuity and be able to use tables to solve present value problems.

An annuity is a series of equal payments occurring at equal intervals, such as three annual payments of $100 each. The present value of an annuity is defined as the present value of the payments one period prior to the first payment. Graphically, this annuity and its present value (p) may be represented as follows:

$$\quad\quad\quad \$100 \quad\quad \$100 \quad\quad \$100$$

$$p$$

One way to calculate the present value of this annuity finds the present value of each payment with the formula and adds them together. For this example, assuming an interest rate of 15%, the calculation is:

$$p = \frac{\$100}{(1 + .15)^1} + \frac{\$100}{(1 + .15)^2} + \frac{\$100}{(1 + .15)^3} = \$228.32$$

Another way calculates the present value of the annuity by using Table D–1 to compute the present value of each payment and then takes their sum:

First payment: $p = \$100 \times 0.8696 = \$\ 86.96$
Second payment: $p = \$100 \times 0.7561 = \ \ \ \ 75.61$
Third payment: $p = \$100 \times 0.6575 = \ \ \underline{\ \ \ 65.75}$
Total: $p = \underline{\$228.32}$

We can also use Table D–1 to solve the problem by first adding the table values for the three payments and then multiplying this sum by the $100 amount of each payment:

From Table D–1: $i = 15\%, n = 1, p = \ \ 0.8696$
                            $i = 15\%, n = 2, p = \ \ 0.7561$
                            $i = 15\%, n = 3, p = \ \ \underline{0.6575}$
                                                    $\underline{2.2832}$

$$2.2832 \times \$100 = \underline{\$228.32}$$

An easier way to solve the problem uses a different table that shows the present values of annuities like Table D–3 on page 690, which is often called a *present value of an annuity of 1* table. Look in Table D–3 on the row where $n = 3$ and $i = 15\%$ and observe that the present value is 2.2832. Thus, the present value of an annuity of 1 for three periods, discounted at 15%, is 2.2832.

Although a formula is used to construct a table showing the present values of an annuity, you can construct one by adding the amounts in a present value of 1 table.[1] Examine Table D–1 and Table D–3 to confirm that the following numbers were drawn from those tables.

From Table D–1		From Table D–3	
$i = 8\%, n = 1$	0.9259		
$i = 8\%, n = 2$	0.8573		
$i = 8\%, n = 3$	0.7938		
$i = 8\%, n = 4$	0.7350		
Total	3.3120	$i = 8\%, n = 4$	3.3121

The minor difference in the results occurs only because the numbers in the tables have been rounded.

In addition to the preceding methods, you can use preprogrammed business calculators and spreadsheet computer programs to find the present value of annuities.

Progress Check

D–3   Smith & Company is considering an investment that would pay $10,000 every six months for three years. The first payment would be received in six months. If Smith & Company requires an annual return of 8%, they should be willing to invest no more than: (a) $25,771; (b) $46,229; (c) $52,421.

---

[1] The formula for the present value of an annuity of 1 is:

$$p = \frac{1 - \frac{1}{(1 + i)^n}}{i}$$

FUTURE VALUE OF AN ANNUITY

LO 2
Explain what is meant by the future value of a single amount and the future value of an annuity and be able to use tables to solve problems that involve future values.

Just as an annuity has a present value, it also has a future value. The future value of an annuity is the accumulated value of the annuity payments and interest as of the date of the final payment. Consider the earlier annuity of three annual payments of $100. The points in time at which the present value (p) and the future value (f) occur are shown below:

$$\$100 \qquad \$100 \qquad \$100$$
$$p \qquad\qquad\qquad\qquad\qquad f$$

Note that the first payment is made two periods prior to the point at which the future value is determined. Therefore, for the first payment $n = 2$. For the second payment, $n = 1$. Since the third payment occurs on the future value date, $n = 0$.

One way to calculate the future value of this annuity uses the formula to find the future value of each payment and adds them together. Assuming an interest rate of 15%, the calculation is:

$$f = \$100 \times (1 + .15)^2 + \$100 \times (1 + .15)^1 + \$100 \times (1 + .15)^0 = \$347.25$$

Another way calculates the future value of the annuity by using Table D–2 to find the sum of the future values of each payment:

First payment:	$f = \$100 \times 1.3225 = \$132.25$
Second payment:	$f = \$100 \times 1.1500 = 115.00$
Third payment:	$f = \$100 \times 1.0000 = 100.00$
Total:	$f = \underline{\$347.25}$

A third approach adds the future values of three payments of 1 and multiplies the sum by $100:

From Table D–2:
$$i = 15\%, n = 2, f = 1.3225$$
$$i = 15\%, n = 1, f = 1.1500$$
$$i = 15\%, n = 0, f = \underline{1.0000}$$
$$\text{Sum} = \underline{3.4725}$$
$$\text{Future value} = 3.4725 \times \$100 = \underline{\$347.25}$$

A fourth and easier way to solve the problem uses a table that shows the future values of annuities, often called a *future value of an annuity of 1* table. Table D–4 on page 691 is such a table. Note in Table D–4 that when $n = 1$, the future values are equal to 1 $(f = 1)$ for all rates of interest because the annuity consists of only one payment and the future value is determined on the date of the payment. Thus, the future value equals the payment.

Although a formula is used to construct a table showing the future values of an annuity of 1, you can construct one by adding together the amount in a future value of 1 table like Table D–2.[2] Examine Table D–2 and Table D–4 to confirm that the following numbers were drawn from those tables.

From Table D–2		**From Table D–4**	
$i = 8\%, n = 0$	1.0000		
$i = 8\%, n = 1$	1.0800		
$i = 8\%, n = 2$	1.1664		
$i = 8\%, n = 3$	1.2597		
Total	4.5061	$i = 8\%, n = 4$	4.5061

Minor differences may occur because the numbers in the tables have been rounded.

---

[2]The formula for the future value of an annuity of 1 is:

$$f = \frac{(1 + i)^n - 1}{i}$$

You can also use business calculators and spreadsheet computer programs to find the future values of annuities.

Observe that the future value in Table D–2 is 1.0000 when $n = 0$ but the future value in Table D–4 is 1.0000 when $n = 1$. Why does this apparent contradiction arise? When $n = 0$ in Table D–2, the future value is determined on the date that the single payment occurs. Thus, no interest is earned and the future value equals the payment. However, Table D–4 describes annuities with equal payments occurring each period. When $n = 1$, the annuity has only one payment, and its future value also equals 1 on the date of its final and only payment.

Progress Check

D–4 Syntel Company invests $45,000 per year for five years at 12%. Calculate the value of the investment at the end of five years.

SUMMARY OF THE APPENDIX IN TERMS OF LEARNING OBJECTIVES

LO 1. Explain what is meant by the present value of a single amount and the present value of an annuity and be able to use tables to solve present value problems. The present value of a single amount to be received at a future date is the amount that could be invested now at the specified interest rate to yield that future value. The present value of an annuity is the amount that could be invested now at the specified interest rate to yield that series of equal periodic payments. Present value tables and business calculators simplify calculating present values.

LO 2. Explain what is meant by the future value of a single amount and the future value of an annuity and be able to use tables to solve future value problems. The future value of a single amount invested at a specified rate of interest is the amount that would accumulate at a future date. The future value of an annuity to be invested at a specified rate of interest is the amount that would accumulate at the date of the final equal periodic payment. Future value tables and business calculators simplify calculating future values.

Table D-1   Present Value of 1 Due in *n* Periods

							Rate					
Periods	**1%**	**2%**	**3%**	**4%**	**5%**	**6%**	**7%**	**8%**	**9%**	**10%**	**12%**	**15%**
1	0.9901	0.9804	0.9709	0.9615	0.9524	0.9434	0.9346	0.9259	0.9174	0.9091	0.8929	0.8696
2	0.9803	0.9612	0.9426	0.9246	0.9070	0.8900	0.8734	0.8573	0.8417	0.8264	0.7972	0.7561
3	0.9706	0.9423	0.9151	0.8890	0.8638	0.8396	0.8163	0.7938	0.7722	0.7513	0.7118	0.6575
4	0.9610	0.9238	0.8885	0.8548	0.8227	0.7921	0.7629	0.7350	0.7084	0.6830	0.6355	0.5718
5	0.9515	0.9057	0.8626	0.8219	0.7835	0.7473	0.7130	0.6806	0.6499	0.6209	0.5674	0.4972
6	0.9420	0.8880	0.8375	0.7903	0.7462	0.7050	0.6663	0.6302	0.5963	0.5645	0.5066	0.4323
7	0.9327	0.8706	0.8131	0.7599	0.7107	0.6651	0.6227	0.5835	0.5470	0.5132	0.4523	0.3759
8	0.9235	0.8535	0.7894	0.7307	0.6768	0.6274	0.5820	0.5403	0.5019	0.4665	0.4039	0.3269
9	0.9143	0.8368	0.7664	0.7026	0.6446	0.5919	0.5439	0.5002	0.4604	0.4241	0.3606	0.2843
10	0.9053	0.8203	0.7441	0.6756	0.6139	0.5584	0.5083	0.4632	0.4224	0.3855	0.3220	0.2472
11	0.8963	0.8043	0.7224	0.6496	0.5847	0.5268	0.4751	0.4289	0.3875	0.3505	0.2875	0.2149
12	0.8874	0.7885	0.7014	0.6246	0.5568	0.4970	0.4440	0.3971	0.3555	0.3186	0.2567	0.1869
13	0.8787	0.7730	0.6810	0.6006	0.5303	0.4688	0.4150	0.3677	0.3262	0.2897	0.2292	0.1625
14	0.8700	0.7579	0.6611	0.5775	0.5051	0.4423	0.3878	0.3405	0.2992	0.2633	0.2046	0.1413
15	0.8613	0.7430	0.6419	0.5553	0.4810	0.4173	0.3624	0.3152	0.2745	0.2394	0.1827	0.1229
16	0.8528	0.7284	0.6232	0.5339	0.4581	0.3936	0.3387	0.2919	0.2519	0.2176	0.1631	0.1069
17	0.8444	0.7142	0.6050	0.5134	0.4363	0.3714	0.3166	0.2703	0.2311	0.1978	0.1456	0.0929
18	0.8360	0.7002	0.5874	0.4936	0.4155	0.3503	0.2959	0.2502	0.2120	0.1799	0.1300	0.0808
19	0.8277	0.6864	0.5703	0.4746	0.3957	0.3305	0.2765	0.2317	0.1945	0.1635	0.1161	0.0703
20	0.8195	0.6730	0.5537	0.4564	0.3769	0.3118	0.2584	0.2145	0.1784	0.1486	0.1037	0.0611
25	0.7798	0.6095	0.4776	0.3751	0.2953	0.2330	0.1842	0.1460	0.1160	0.0923	0.0588	0.0304
30	0.7419	0.5521	0.4120	0.3083	0.2314	0.1741	0.1314	0.0994	0.0754	0.0573	0.0334	0.0151
35	0.7059	0.5000	0.3554	0.2534	0.1813	0.1301	0.0937	0.0676	0.0490	0.0356	0.0189	0.0075
40	0.6717	0.4529	0.3066	0.2083	0.1420	0.0972	0.0668	0.0460	0.0318	0.0221	0.0107	0.0037

Table D-2 Future Value of 1 Due in *n* Periods

	Rate											
Periods	**1%**	**2%**	**3%**	**4%**	**5%**	**6%**	**7%**	**8%**	**9%**	**10%**	**12%**	**15%**
0	1.0000	1.0000	1.0000	1.0000	1.0000	1.0000	1.0000	1.0000	1.0000	1.0000	1.0000	1.0000
1	1.0100	1.0200	1.0300	1.0400	1.0500	1.0600	1.0700	1.0800	1.0900	1.1000	1.1200	1.1500
2	1.0201	1.0404	1.0609	1.0816	1.1025	1.1236	1.1449	1.1664	1.1881	1.2100	1.2544	1.3225
3	1.0303	1.0612	1.0927	1.1249	1.1576	1.1910	1.2250	1.2597	1.2950	1.3310	1.4049	1.5209
4	1.0406	1.0824	1.1255	1.1699	1.2155	1.2625	1.3108	1.3605	1.4116	1.4641	1.5735	1.7490
5	1.0510	1.1041	1.1593	1.2167	1.2763	1.3382	1.4026	1.4693	1.5386	1.6105	1.7623	2.0114
6	1.0615	1.1262	1.1941	1.2653	1.3401	1.4185	1.5007	1.5869	1.6771	1.7716	1.9738	2.3131
7	1.0721	1.1487	1.2299	1.3159	1.4071	1.5036	1.6058	1.7138	1.8280	1.9487	2.2107	2.6600
8	1.0829	1.1717	1.2668	1.3686	1.4775	1.5938	1.7182	1.8509	1.9926	2.1436	2.4760	3.0590
9	1.0937	1.1951	1.3048	1.4233	1.5513	1.6895	1.8385	1.9990	2.1719	2.3579	2.7731	3.5179
10	1.1046	1.2190	1.3439	1.4802	1.6289	1.7908	1.9672	2.1589	2.3674	2.5937	3.1058	4.0456
11	1.1157	1.2434	1.3842	1.5395	1.7103	1.8983	2.1049	2.3316	2.5804	2.8531	3.4785	4.6524
12	1.1268	1.2682	1.4258	1.6010	1.7959	2.0122	2.2522	2.5182	2.8127	3.1384	3.8960	5.3503
13	1.1381	1.2936	1.4685	1.6651	1.8856	2.1329	2.4098	2.7196	3.0658	3.4523	4.3635	6.1528
14	1.1495	1.3195	1.5126	1.7317	1.9799	2.2609	2.5785	2.9372	3.3417	3.7975	4.8871	7.0757
15	1.1610	1.3459	1.5580	1.8009	2.0789	2.3966	2.7590	3.1722	3.6425	4.1772	5.4736	8.1371
16	1.1726	1.3728	1.6047	1.8730	2.1829	2.5404	2.9522	3.4259	3.9703	4.5950	6.1304	9.3576
17	1.1843	1.4002	1.6528	1.9479	2.2920	2.6928	3.1588	3.7000	4.3276	5.0545	6.8660	10.7613
18	1.1961	1.4282	1.7024	2.0258	2.4066	2.8543	3.3799	3.9960	4.7171	5.5599	7.6900	12.3755
19	1.2081	1.4568	1.7535	2.1068	2.5270	3.0256	3.6165	4.3157	5.1417	6.1159	8.6128	14.2318
20	1.2202	1.4859	1.8061	2.1911	2.6533	3.2071	3.8697	4.6610	5.6044	6.7275	9.6463	16.3665
25	1.2824	1.6406	2.0938	2.6658	3.3864	4.2919	5.4274	6.8485	8.6231	10.8347	17.0001	32.9190
30	1.3478	1.8114	2.4273	3.2434	4.3219	5.7435	7.6123	10.0627	13.2677	17.4494	29.9599	66.2118
35	1.4166	1.9999	2.8139	3.9461	5.5160	7.6861	10.6766	14.7853	20.4140	28.1024	52.7996	133.176
40	1.4889	2.2080	3.2620	4.8010	7.0400	10.2857	14.9745	21.7245	31.4094	45.2593	93.0510	267.864

Table D–3   Present Value of an Annuity of 1 per Period

						Rate						
Periods	**1%**	**2%**	**3%**	**4%**	**5%**	**6%**	**7%**	**8%**	**9%**	**10%**	**12%**	**15%**
1	0.9901	0.9804	0.9709	0.9615	0.9524	0.9434	0.9346	0.9259	0.9174	0.9091	0.8929	0.8696
2	1.9704	1.9416	1.9135	1.8861	1.8594	1.8334	1.8080	1.7833	1.7591	1.7355	1.6901	1.6257
3	2.9410	2.8839	2.8286	2.7751	2.7232	2.6730	2.6243	2.5771	2.5313	2.4869	2.4018	2.2832
4	3.9020	3.8077	3.7171	3.6299	3.5460	3.4651	3.3872	3.3121	3.2397	3.1699	3.0373	2.8550
5	4.8534	4.7135	4.5797	4.4518	4.3295	4.2124	4.1002	3.9927	3.8897	3.7908	3.6048	3.3522
6	5.7955	5.6014	5.4172	5.2421	5.0757	4.9173	4.7665	4.6229	4.4859	4.3553	4.1114	3.7845
7	6.7282	6.4720	6.2303	6.0021	5.7864	5.5824	5.3893	5.2064	5.0330	4.8684	4.5638	4.1604
8	7.6517	7.3255	7.0197	6.7327	6.4632	6.2098	5.9713	5.7466	5.5348	5.3349	4.9676	4.4873
9	8.5660	8.1622	7.7861	7.4353	7.1078	6.8017	6.5152	6.2469	5.9952	5.7590	5.3282	4.7716
10	9.4713	8.9826	8.5302	8.1109	7.7217	7.3601	7.0236	6.7101	6.4177	6.1446	5.6502	5.0188
11	10.3676	9.7868	9.2526	8.7605	8.3064	7.8869	7.4987	7.1390	6.8052	6.4951	5.9377	5.2337
12	11.2551	10.5753	9.9540	9.3851	8.8633	8.3838	7.9427	7.5361	7.1607	6.8137	6.1944	5.4206
13	12.1337	11.3484	10.6350	9.9856	9.3936	8.8527	8.3577	7.9038	7.4869	7.1034	6.4235	5.5831
14	13.0037	12.1062	11.2961	10.5631	9.8986	9.2950	8.7455	8.2442	7.7862	7.3667	6.6282	5.7245
15	13.8651	12.8493	11.9379	11.1184	10.3797	9.7122	9.1079	8.5595	8.0607	7.6061	6.8109	5.8474
16	14.7179	13.5777	12.5611	11.6523	10.8378	10.1059	9.4466	8.8514	8.3126	7.8237	6.9740	5.9542
17	15.5623	14.2919	13.1661	12.1657	11.2741	10.4773	9.7632	9.1216	8.5436	8.0216	7.1196	6.0472
18	16.3983	14.9920	13.7535	12.6593	11.6896	10.8276	10.0591	9.3719	8.7556	8.2014	7.2497	6.1280
19	17.2260	15.6785	14.3238	13.1339	12.0853	11.1581	10.3356	9.6036	8.9501	8.3649	7.3658	6.1982
20	18.0456	16.3514	14.8775	13.5903	12.4622	11.4699	10.5940	9.8181	9.1285	8.5136	7.4694	6.2593
25	22.0232	19.5235	17.4131	15.6221	14.0939	12.7834	11.6536	10.6748	9.8226	9.0770	7.8431	6.4641
30	25.8077	22.3965	19.6004	17.2920	15.3725	13.7648	12.4090	11.2578	10.2737	9.4269	8.0552	6.5660
35	29.4086	24.9986	21.4872	18.6646	16.3742	14.4982	12.9477	11.6546	10.5668	9.6442	8.1755	6.6166
40	32.8347	27.3555	23.1148	19.7928	17.1591	15.0463	13.3317	11.9246	10.7574	9.7791	8.2438	6.6418

Table D-4 Future Value of an Annuity of 1 per Period

						Rate						
Periods	**1%**	**2%**	**3%**	**4%**	**5%**	**6%**	**7%**	**8%**	**9%**	**10%**	**12%**	**15%**
1	1.0000	1.0000	1.0000	1.0000	1.0000	1.0000	1.0000	1.0000	1.0000	1.0000	1.0000	1.0000
2	2.0100	2.0200	2.0300	2.0400	2.0500	2.0600	2.0700	2.0800	2.0900	2.1000	2.1200	2.1500
3	3.0301	3.0604	3.0909	3.1216	3.1525	3.1836	3.2149	3.2464	3.2781	3.3100	3.3744	3.4725
4	4.0604	4.1216	4.1836	4.2465	4.3101	4.3746	4.4399	4.5061	4.5731	4.6410	4.7793	4.9934
5	5.1010	5.2040	5.3091	5.4163	5.5256	5.6371	5.7507	5.8666	5.9847	6.1051	6.3528	6.7424
6	6.1520	6.3081	6.4684	6.6330	6.8019	6.9753	7.1533	7.3359	7.5233	7.7156	8.1152	8.7537
7	7.2135	7.4343	7.6625	7.8983	8.1420	8.3938	8.6540	8.9228	9.2004	9.4872	10.0890	11.0668
8	8.2857	8.5830	8.8923	9.2142	9.5491	9.8975	10.2598	10.6366	11.0285	11.4359	12.2997	13.7268
9	9.3685	9.7546	10.1591	10.5828	11.0266	11.4913	11.9780	12.4876	13.0210	13.5795	14.7757	16.7858
10	10.4622	10.9497	11.4639	12.0061	12.5779	13.1808	13.8164	14.4866	15.1929	15.9374	17.5487	20.3037
11	11.5668	12.1687	12.8078	13.4864	14.2068	14.9716	15.7836	16.6455	17.5603	18.5312	20.6546	24.3493
12	12.6825	13.4121	14.1920	15.0258	15.9171	16.8699	17.8885	18.9771	20.1407	21.3843	24.1331	29.0017
13	13.8093	14.6803	15.6178	16.6268	17.7130	18.8821	20.1406	21.4953	22.9534	24.5227	28.0291	34.3519
14	14.9474	15.9739	17.0863	18.2919	19.5986	21.0151	22.5505	24.2149	26.0192	27.9750	32.3926	40.5047
15	16.0969	17.2934	18.5989	20.0236	21.5786	23.2760	25.1290	27.1521	29.3609	31.7725	37.2797	47.5804
16	17.2579	18.6393	20.1569	21.8245	23.6575	25.6725	27.8881	30.3243	33.0034	35.9497	42.7533	55.7175
17	18.4304	20.0121	21.7616	23.6975	25.8404	28.2129	30.8402	33.7502	36.9737	40.5447	48.8837	65.0751
18	19.6147	21.4123	23.4144	25.6454	28.1324	30.9057	33.9990	37.4502	41.3013	45.5992	55.7497	75.8364
19	20.8109	22.8406	25.1169	27.6712	30.5390	33.7600	37.3790	41.4463	46.0185	51.1591	63.4397	88.2118
20	22.0190	24.2974	26.8704	29.7781	33.0660	36.7856	40.9955	45.7620	51.1601	57.2750	72.0524	102.444
25	28.2432	32.0303	36.4593	41.6459	47.7271	54.8645	63.2490	73.1059	84.7009	98.3471	133.334	212.793
30	34.7849	40.5681	47.5754	56.0849	66.4388	79.0582	94.4608	113.283	136.308	164.494	241.333	434.745
35	41.6603	49.9945	60.4621	73.6522	90.3203	111.435	138.237	172.317	215.711	271.024	431.663	881.170
40	48.8864	60.4020	75.4013	95.0255	120.800	154.762	199.635	259.057	337.882	442.593	767.091	1,779.09

EXERCISES

Exercise D–1
Present value of an amount
(LO 1)

Flaherty Corp. is considering an investment which, if paid for immediately, is expected to return $140,000 five years hence. If Flaherty demands a 9% return, how much will it be willing to pay for this investment?

Exercise D–2
Future value of an amount
(LO 2)

CII, Inc., invested $630,000 in a project expected to earn a 12% annual rate of return. The earnings will be reinvested in the project each year until the entire investment is liquidated 10 years hence. What will the cash proceeds be when the project is liquidated?

Exercise D–3
Present value of an annuity
(LO 1)

Beene Distributing is considering a contract that will return $150,000 annually at the end of each year for six years. If Beene demands an annual return of 7% and pays for the investment immediately, how much should it be willing to pay?

Exercise D–4
Future value of an annuity
(LO 2)

Claire Fitch is planning to begin an individual retirement program in which she will invest $1,500 annually at the end of each year. Fitch plans to retire after making 30 annual investments in a program that earns a return of 10%. What will be the value of the program on the date of the last investment?

Exercise D–5
Interest rate on an investment
(LO 1)

Ken Francis has been offered the possibility of investing $0.2745 for 15 years, after which he will be paid $1. What annual rate of interest will Francis earn? (Use Table D–1 to find the answer.)

Exercise D–6
Number of periods of an
investment
(LO 1)

Megan Brink has been offered the possibility of investing $0.6651. The investment will earn 6% per year and will return Brink $1 at the end of the investment. How many years must Brink wait to receive the $1? (Use Table D–1 to find the answer.)

Exercise D–7
Number of periods of an
investment
(LO 2)

Bill Thompson expects to invest $1 at 12% and, at the end of the investment, receive $9.6463. How many years will elapse before Thompson receives the payment? (Use Table D–2 to find the answer.)

Exercise D–8
Interest rate on an investment
(LO 2)

Ed Summers expects to invest $1 for 25 years, after which he will receive $10.8347. What rate of interest will Summers earn? (Use Table D–2 to find the answer.)

Exercise D–9
Interest rate on an investment
(LO 1)

Betsey Jones expects an immediate investment of $5.7466 to return $1 annually for 8 years, with the first payment to be received in one year. What rate of interest will Jones earn? (Use Table D–3 to find the answer.)

Exercise D–10
Number of periods of an
investment
(LO 1)

Keith Riggins expects an investment of $8.2014 to return $1 annually for several years. If Riggins is to earn a return of 10%, how many annual payments must he receive? (Use Table D–3 to find the answer.)

Exercise D–11
Interest rate on an investment
(LO 2)

Steve Algoe expects to invest $1 annually for 40 years and have an accumulated value of $154.762 on the date of the last investment. If this occurs, what rate of interest will Algoe earn? (Use Table D–4 to find the answer.)

Exercise D–12
Number of periods of an
investment
(LO 2)

Katherine Beckwith expects to invest $1 annually in a fund that will earn 8%. How many annual investments must Beckwith make to accumulate $30.3243 on the date of the last investment? (Use Table D–4 to find the answer.)

Sam Weber financed a new automobile by paying $6,500 cash and agreeing to make 40 monthly payments of $500 each, the first payment to be made one month after the purchase. The loan was said to bear interest at an annual rate of 12%. What was the cost of the automobile?

Exercise D–13
Present value of an annuity
(LO 1)

Mark Welsch deposited $7,200 in a savings account that earns interest at an annual rate of 8%, compounded quarterly. The $7,200 plus earned interest must remain in the account 10 years before it can be withdrawn. How much money will be in the account at the end of the 10 years?

Exercise D–14
Future value of an amount
(LO 2)

Kelly Malone plans to have $50 withheld from her monthly paycheck and deposited in a savings account that earns 12% annually, compounded monthly. If Malone continues with her plan for 2½ years, how much will be accumulated in the account on the date of the last deposit?

Exercise D–15
Future value of an annuity
(LO 2)

Spiller Corp. plans to issue 10%, 15-year, $500,000 par value bonds payable that pay interest semiannually on June 30 and December 31. The bonds are dated December 31, 19X1, and are to be issued on that date. If the market rate of interest for the bonds is 8% on the date of issue, what will be the cash proceeds from the bond issue?

Exercise D–16
Present value of bonds
(LO 1)

Starr Company has decided to establish a fund that will be used 10 years hence to replace an aging productive facility. The company will make an initial contribution of $100,000 to the fund and plans to make quarterly contributions of $50,000 beginning in three months. The fund is expected to earn 12%, compounded quarterly. What will be the value of the fund 10 years hence?

Exercise D–17
Future value of an amount plus an annuity
(LO 2)

McAdams Company expects to earn 10% per year on an investment that will pay $606,773 six years hence. Use Table D–2 to calculate the present value of the investment.

Exercise D–18
Present value of an amount
(LO 1)

Catten, Inc., invests $163,170 at 7% per year for nine years. Use Table D–1 to calculate the future value of the investment nine years hence.

Exercise D–19
Future value of an amount
(LO 2)

ANSWERS TO PROGRESS CHECKS

D–1 $70,000 × 0.6302 = $44,114

D–2   *c* $299,850/$150,000 = 1.9990
      Table D–2 shows this value for 9 years at 8%.

D–3   *c* $10,000 × 5.2421 = $52,421

D–4 $45,000 × 6.3528 = $285,876

Financial Statements and Related Disclosures from Southwest Airlines Co.'s 1994 Annual Report

Ⓜ️ANAGEMENT'S DISCUSSION AND ANALYSIS OF FINANCIAL CONDITION AND RESULTS OF OPERATIONS

INDUSTRY CONDITIONS

The 1990s have been devastating financially for the domestic passenger airline industry, with Southwest as the sole exception among larger carriers. Since 1990, the industry has been shrinking and we have been expanding. We are now carrying more than twice the number of passengers annually than in 1990, an annualized growth rate of 21 percent. In 1993, with the advent of Continental Lite and plans laid for the United Shuttle, the competitive trend away from Southwest began to reverse. In 1994, in the face of our own aggressive expansion, we experienced a massive increase of new competitive service from United, Continental, Reno, and TWA. We also were negatively impacted by the industry's use of persistent fare sales during the fourth quarter, which occurred at a time when we were aggressively converting Morris Air Corporation (Morris) to Southwest's operations and were experiencing operating difficulties of our own in reservations and revenue management. The result was a 47 percent decline in earnings in fourth quarter 1994 as compared to fourth quarter 1993. Many of the operational issues that surfaced during fourth quarter 1994 have been, or will soon be, addressed, most notably reservations capacity. However, some of their effects will carry over into the first two quarters of 1995, and, further, we cannot predict the actions of our competitors.

In response to these increasing competitive pressures, we implemented several measures. However, we face significantly more competition than we did a year ago, which may also continue to adversely affect comparisons to 1994 quarterly performances, particularly in first half 1995.

As compared to year ago levels, load factors and passenger revenue yields are currently down (the consolidated load factor for January 1995 was 57.8 percent, compared with 63.1 percent for the same month of a year ago). Our expectation is that this trend will continue at least during first half 1995. As expected, the integration of Morris into Southwest during 1994, which included 21 aircraft and seven new cities, resulted in our immediate competitive presence in the northwestern region of the U.S. and Salt Lake City. However, these new markets, which are in the development stage and, therefore, understandably low-yielding, will need to improve for overall yields to compare favorably to year ago levels. While there is no way to predict precisely how fast these markets will develop, we are encouraged by the pace thus far. We have also been encouraged with Customer acceptance of recent price increases, which may improve yield comparisons.

From an operating cost perspective, we have been pleased with recent favorable trends versus year ago levels, including fuel prices. Our goal is to continue this trend in 1995, despite our basic lack of control over fuel prices. Significant cost reduction opportunities lie in distribution costs. Ticketless travel, the new SABRE Basic Booking Request, our enhanced Ticket By Mail product, and expanded reservations operations should all combine to help reduce distribution costs. During 1995, we currently plan to add twenty-seven 737-300 aircraft to our fleet and one new city, Omaha, Nebraska, to our route system, which will allow us to focus on strengthening our existing route system.

RESULTS OF OPERATIONS

1994 COMPARED WITH 1993 The Company's consolidated net income for 1994 was $179.3 million ($1.22 per share), as compared to the corresponding 1993 amount (before the cumulative effect of accounting changes) of $154.3 million ($1.05 per share), an increase of 16.2 percent. The increase in earnings was primarily attributable to an increase in operating income of 8.5 percent and a decrease in other expenses (nonoperating) of 46.9 percent.

OPERATING REVENUES Consolidated operating revenues increased by 12.9 percent in 1994 to $2,591.9 million, compared to $2,296.7 million for 1993. This increase in 1994 operating revenues was derived from a 12.7 percent increase in passenger revenues. Revenue passenger miles (RPMs) increased 14.8 percent in 1994, compared to a 16.8 percent increase in available seat miles (ASMs), resulting in a decrease in load factor from 68.4 percent in 1993 to 67.3 percent in 1994. The 1994 ASM growth resulted from the addition of 21 aircraft during 1994.

Freight revenues in 1994 were $54.4 million, compared to $42.9 million in 1993. The 26.9 percent increase in freight revenues exceeded the 16.8 percent increase in ASMs for the same period primarily due to increased air freight volumes and United States mail services.

OPERATING EXPENSES Consolidated operating expenses for 1994 were $2,275.2 million, compared to $2,004.7 million in 1993, an increase of 13.5 percent, compared to the 16.8 percent increase in ASMs. On a per-ASM basis, operating expenses (excluding 1993 merger expenses) decreased 2.3 percent in 1994. The primary factors contributing to this decrease were an 8.8 percent decrease in average jet fuel cost per gallon and lower agency commission costs, offset by increased aircraft rentals.

Operating expenses per ASM for 1994 and 1993 (excluding 1993 merger expenses) were as follows:

OPERATING EXPENSES PER ASM

	1994	1993	INCREASE (DECREASE)	PERCENT CHANGE
Salaries, wages, and benefits	2.13¢	2.12¢	.01¢	.5%
Profitsharing and Employee savings plans	.22	.21	.01	4.8
Fuel and oil	1.00	1.11	(.11)	(9.9)
Maintenance materials and repairs	.59	.59	-	-
Agency commissions	.47	.53	(.06)	(11.3)
Aircraft rentals	.42	.39	.03	7.7
Landing fees and other rentals	.46	.47	(.01)	(2.1)
Depreciation	.43	.44	(.01)	(2.3)
Other	1.36	1.39	(.03)	(2.2)
Total	7.08¢	7.25¢	(.17)¢	(2.3)%

Salaries, wages, and benefits per ASM increased only .5 percent in 1994. This increase resulted from a 3.0 percent increase in average salary and benefits cost per Employee, partially offset by slower average headcount growth, which increased only 13.8 percent in 1994 versus the 1994 capacity (ASM) increase of 16.8 percent. The majority of the increase in average salary and benefits cost related to increased health benefits and workers' compensation costs. Employee productivity improved from 2,633 passengers handled per Employee in 1993 to 2,676 in 1994.

Profitsharing and Employee savings plan expenses per ASM increased 4.8 percent in 1994. The increase is primarily the result of increased matching contributions to Employee savings plans resulting from increased Employee participation and higher matching rates in 1994 for Flight Attendants and Customer Service Employees under their respective collective bargaining agreements.

Fuel and oil expenses per ASM decreased 9.9 percent in 1994, primarily due to an 8.8 percent reduction in the average jet fuel cost per gallon from 1993. Jet fuel prices remained relatively stable throughout 1994, with quarterly averages ranging from $0.51 to $0.56 per gallon. Since yearend, fuel prices have averaged approximately $0.54 per gallon.

In August 1993, the Revenue Reconciliation Act of 1993 was enacted, which, among other things, included an increase of 4.3 cents per gallon in transportation fuel tax, which becomes effective September 30, 1995, for jet fuel used in commercial aviation. This additional fuel tax will increase fuel expenses approximately $7.5 million in fourth quarter 1995.

Maintenance materials and repairs per ASM was unchanged in 1994 compared to 1993.

Agency commissions per ASM decreased 11.3 percent due to a lower mix of travel agency sales and lower 1994 passenger revenue per ASM. The lower travel agency sales mix resulted from 1994 enhancements to Southwest's ticket delivery systems for direct Customers, as described below.

In response to actions taken by our competitor-owned reservations systems, we reduced our operating costs and enhanced our ticket delivery systems by developing our own Southwest Airlines Air Travel ("SWAT") system allowing high-volume travel agents direct access to reservations; introduced overnight ticket delivery for travel agents; reduced to three the number of advance days reservations required for overnight delivery of tickets to consumers (Ticket By Mail); developed our own Ticketless system, which was rolled out system-wide on January 31, 1995; and subscribed to a new level of service with SABRE that will automate the booking process for SABRE travel agencies effective May 1, 1995. We also continue to actively pursue other cost-effective solutions for automating non-SABRE travel agency bookings.

Aircraft rentals per ASM increased 7.7 percent in 1994. The increase primarily resulted from a third quarter 1994 sale/leaseback transaction involving ten new 737-300 aircraft and a lease of three used aircraft under long-term operating leases. At December 31, 1994, 44.7 percent of the Company's fleet was subject to operating leases, compared to 43.3 percent at December 31, 1993.

Other operating expenses per ASM decreased 2.2 percent in 1994 compared to 1993. The overall decrease is primarily attributable to operating efficiencies resulting from the transition of Morris operational functions to Southwest, primarily contract services which decreased $8.8 million (24.4 percent per ASM), offset by an increase in advertising costs of $24.1 million (22.9 percent per ASM) primarily associated with the start-up of seven new cities and new competitive pressures in 1994.

OTHER "Other expenses (income)" included interest expense, interest income, and nonoperating gains and losses. Interest expense decreased $5.1 million in 1994 due to the March 1, 1993 redemption of $100 million senior unsecured Notes due 1996 and the repayment of approximately $54.0 million of Morris long-term debt during first quarter 1994. Capitalized interest increased $8.6 million in 1994 as a result of higher levels of advance payments on aircraft compared to 1993. Interest income for 1994 decreased $1.9 million primarily due to lower cash balances available for short-term investment.

INCOME TAXES The provision for income taxes decreased in 1994 as a percentage of income before taxes, including cumulative effect of accounting changes, to 40.1 percent from 40.6 percent in 1993. The 1993 rate was higher due to deferred tax adjustments in 1993 related to the 1993 increase in the federal corporate income tax rate from 34 percent to 35 percent (see Note 11 to the Consolidated Financial Statements). This was offset by increased 1994 effective state income tax rates.

1993 COMPARED WITH 1992 Prior to 1993, Morris operated as a charter carrier. In 1993, Morris began operating as a FAR 121 Certificated Air Carrier, or scheduled service carrier, consistent with Southwest. For comparability from 1993 to 1992, the statistical and operating data for 1992 are based on scheduled passenger service only (i.e., Southwest). Accordingly, RPMs and ASMs for 1992 relate only to scheduled carrier operations.

The Company's consolidated income for the year 1993 was $154.3 million ($1.05 per share), before the cumulative effect of accounting changes, compared to pro forma consolidated income of $97.4 million ($.68 per share) for 1992, an increase of 58.4 percent. The increase in earnings was primarily attributable to an increase in operating income of 50.7 percent and was achieved despite an increase in the federal income tax rate, which increased the provision for income taxes $6.5 million, or $.04 per share.

OPERATING REVENUES Consolidated operating revenues increased by 27.4 percent in 1993 to $2,296.7 million. Operating revenue per ASM for scheduled service carrier operations increased in 1993 to $.0835 from $.0789 in 1992. The increase in consolidated operating revenues was primarily related to a 36.5 percent increase in passenger revenues, which accounted for 96.5 percent of total operating revenues in 1993 versus 90.1 percent in 1992.

Consolidated RPMs increased 36.6 percent in 1993, which exceeded the 28.8 percent increase in ASMs, resulting in an increase in the load factor from 64.5 percent to 68.4 percent. The 1993 ASM increase resulted from the conversion of the Morris system from charter to scheduled service and the addition of 16 aircraft to the Southwest fleet. The additional 16 Southwest aircraft were primarily used to expand California, St. Louis, and Chicago markets and to initiate service from Louisville, Baltimore, and San Jose.

Freight revenues increased in 1993 to $42.9 million from $33.1 million in 1992. The 29.6 percent increase in freight revenues exceeded the 28.8 percent ASM increase primarily due to further expansion of United States mail services and increased freight marketing programs.

Charter and other revenues decreased in 1993 from 1992 on a consolidated basis as Morris converted its operations in 1993 to scheduled service from charter operations. In 1993, consistent with the beginning of scheduled carrier service, Morris revenues were primarily derived from scheduled operations and, accordingly, classified as "passenger" revenues. Morris charter revenues totaled $117.8 million in 1992.

OPERATING EXPENSES Consolidated operating expenses increased 24.6 percent to $2,004.7 million from $1,609.2 million in 1992. The primary factors contributing to the increase were the 28.8 percent increase in ASMs; increased contributions to profitsharing and Employee savings plans; higher agency commissions; higher aircraft rentals; and increased maintenance costs.

On a consolidated basis, the Company incurred $10.8 million of one-time merger expenses in connection with the December 1993 Morris acquisition. These expenses included $1.9 million of various professional fees; $4.7 million for disposal of duplicate or incompatible property and equipment; and $4.2 million for Employee relocation and severance costs related to elimination of duplicate or incompatible operations. As required for financial reporting purposes, these expenses have been reported as operating expenses.

Salaries, wages, and benefits per ASM decreased 2.3 percent in 1993. Excluding the effects of Morris, Southwest's cost per ASM for salaries, wages, and benefits increased .9 percent from 1992 to 1993. This increase resulted from a 2.2 percent increase in salaries and wages, offset by a 5.0 percent decrease in health benefit and workers' compensation costs per ASM. Headcount for Southwest increased 17.0 percent in 1993, slightly more than the 15.9 percent increase in ASMs. However, Employee productivity improved to 2,633 passengers handled per Employee in 1993 from 2,597 in 1992.

Morris contracted out all ground handling services, which are included in "other operating expenses." Consequently, salaries, wages, and benefits on a per-ASM basis are considerably lower for Morris than for Southwest contributing to the decrease in consolidated salaries, wages, and benefits per ASM.

Profitsharing and Employee savings plan expenses per ASM increased 16.7 percent in 1993. The increase was primarily the result of higher earnings in 1993. For additional information, see Note 10 to the Consolidated Financial Statements.

Fuel and oil expenses per ASM decreased 2.6 percent in 1993 due to a 2.7 percent reduction in the average cost per gallon of jet fuel from 1992. Jet fuel prices remained relatively stable throughout 1993, continuing the trend which began in 1992, with quarterly averages ranging from $0.57 to $0.63 per gallon.

Maintenance materials and repairs per ASM increased 5.4 percent in 1993. This increase was primarily the result of higher airframe component repairs and higher amortization of capitalized scheduled airframe overhauls.

Agency commissions per ASM increased 6.0 percent in 1993 primarily due to increased passenger revenues per ASM.

Aircraft rentals per ASM increased 30.0 percent in 1993. The increase was primarily attributable to the expansion of Morris scheduled operations, which leased 18 of its 21 aircraft, 11 of which were leased in 1993. Additionally, the increase partially resulted from the sale/leaseback financing by Southwest, since late 1992, of seven 737-300 aircraft with long-term operating leases. Also in 1993, Southwest leased one used 737-300 aircraft under a long-term operating lease and one used 737-200 aircraft under a short-term operating lease.

Depreciation expense per ASM decreased 8.5 percent in 1993 due to the expansion of Morris, which, as stated above, consisted primarily of a leased aircraft fleet.

Other operating expenses per ASM increased 13.8 percent from 1992 to 1993. This increase is primarily the result of higher usage of contract services at Morris. As previously discussed, Morris contracted for all ground handling service, along with various other services that are handled internally at Southwest.

OTHER "Other" expenses (income)" included interest expense, interest income, and nonoperating gains and losses. Interest expense, net of capitalized interest, decreased 7.0 percent in 1993 due to the March 1, 1993 early redemption of $100 million in senior unsecured 9% Notes due 1996. See Note 6 to the Consolidated Financial Statements for further information. Net nonoperating losses in 1993 resulted from the write-down of certain internal system development costs and the settlement of certain employment related litigation for $1.7 million.

INCOME TAXES The provision for income taxes increased in 1993, as a percentage of income before income taxes and cumulative effect of accounting changes, to 40.6 percent from pro forma 38.1 percent in 1992. The increase was primarily the result of the increase in the federal income tax rate. See Note 11 to the Consolidated Financial Statements for further information.

LIQUIDITY AND CAPITAL RESOURCES

Cash provided from operations was $412.7 million in 1994, compared to $392.7 million in 1993. During 1994, additional funds of $315.0 million were generated from the sale and leaseback of ten new 737-300 aircraft subject to long-term operating leases (increasing total commitments for operating leases by $619.0 million).

During 1994, capital expenditures of $788.6 million were primarily for the purchase of 18 new 737-300 aircraft, one used 737-300 aircraft previously leased by Morris, and progress payments for future aircraft deliveries. At December 31, 1994, capital commitments of the Company consisted primarily of scheduled aircraft acquisitions.

As of January 1995, Southwest had one-hundred-sixteen 737s on firm order, including twenty-five to be delivered in 1995, with options to purchase another seventy-four. Aggregate funding required for firm commitments approximated $3,042.7 million through the year 2001 of which $602.6 million related to 1995. See Note 4 to the Consolidated Financial Statements for further information.

The Company recently completed the construction of a $10.0 million reservation center in Little Rock, Arkansas, which began accepting calls on January 24, 1995, and announced that it will build an additional reservation center in Oklahoma City, scheduled to open in second quarter 1995. Total estimated cost of the new Oklahoma City reservation center is approximately $10.0 million.

As of December 31, 1994 and since 1990, the Company had authority from its Board of Directors to purchase 3,750,000 shares of its common stock from time-to-time on the open market. No shares have been purchased since 1990.

The Company has various options available to meet its capital and operating commitments, including cash on hand at December 31, 1994 of $174.5 million, internally generated funds, and a revolving credit line with a group of banks of up to $300 million (none of which had been drawn at December 31, 1994). In addition, the Company will also consider various borrowing or leasing options to maximize earnings and supplement cash requirements.

The Company currently has outstanding shelf registrations for the issuance of $100 million senior unsecured notes and $98 million pass-through certificates relating to sale/leaseback transactions. The Company presently intends to utilize these sources of financing during 1995.

Cash provided from operations was $392.7 million in 1993 as compared to $282.1 million in 1992. During 1993, additional funds of $90.0 million were generated from the sale and leaseback of three new 737-300 aircraft subject to long-term operating leases (increasing total commitments for operating leases by $145.0 million). Morris also generated $17.8 million from certain bank borrowings. These proceeds were primarily used to finance aircraft-related capital expenditures and to provide working capital.

CONSOLIDATED BALANCE SHEET

(in thousands except share and per share amounts)

	DECEMBER 31,	
	1994	1993
ASSETS		
Current assets:		
Cash and cash equivalents	$ 174,538	$ 295,571
Accounts receivable	75,692	70,484
Inventories of parts and supplies, at cost	37,565	31,707
Deferred income taxes (Note 11)	9,822	10,475
Prepaid expenses and other current assets	17,281	23,787
Total current assets	314,898	432,024
Property and equipment, at cost (Notes 3, 4, and 7):		
Flight equipment	2,564,551	2,257,809
Ground property and equipment	384,501	329,605
Deposits on flight equipment purchase contracts	393,749	242,230
	3,342,801	2,829,644
Less allowance for depreciation	837,838	688,280
	2,504,963	2,141,364
Other assets	3,210	2,649
	$ 2,823,071	$ 2,576,037
LIABILITIES AND STOCKHOLDERS' EQUITY		
Current liabilities:		
Accounts payable	$ 117,599	$ 94,040
Accrued liabilities (Note 5)	288,979	265,333
Air traffic liability	106,139	96,146
Income taxes payable		7,025
Current maturities of long-term debt	9,553	16,068
Total current liabilities	522,270	478,612
Long-term debt less current maturities (Note 6)	583,071	639,136
Deferred income taxes (Note 11)	232,850	183,616
Deferred gains from sale and leaseback of aircraft	217,677	199,362
Other deferred liabilities	28,497	21,292
Commitments and contingencies (Notes 4, 7, and 11)		
Stockholders' equity (Notes 8 and 9):		
Common stock, $1.00 par value: 500,000,000 shares authorized;		
143,255,795 shares issued and outstanding in 1994 and 142,756,308 shares in 1993	143,256	142,756
Capital in excess of par value	151,746	141,168
Retained earnings	943,704	770,095
Total stockholders' equity	1,238,706	1,054,019
	$ 2,823,071	$ 2,576,037

See accompanying notes.

CONSOLIDATED STATEMENT OF INCOME

(in thousands except per share amounts)

	YEARS ENDED DECEMBER 31,		
	1994	1993	1992
OPERATING REVENUES:			
Passenger	$ 2,497,765	$ 2,216,342	$ 1,623,828
Freight	54,419	42,897	33,088
Charter and other	39,749	37,434	146,063
Total operating revenues	2,591,933	2,296,673	1,802,979
OPERATING EXPENSES:			
Salaries, wages, and benefits (Note 10)	756,023	641,747	512,983
Fuel and oil	319,552	304,424	257,481
Maintenance materials and repairs	190,308	163,395	122,561
Agency commissions	151,247	144,941	113,504
Aircraft rentals	132,992	107,885	77,472
Landing fees and other rentals	148,107	129,222	105,929
Depreciation	139,045	119,338	101,976
Other operating expenses	437,950	382,945	317,269
Merger expenses (Note 2)		10,803	
Total operating expenses	2,275,224	2,004,700	1,609,175
OPERATING INCOME	316,709	291,973	193,804
OTHER EXPENSES (INCOME):			
Interest expense	53,368	58,460	59,084
Capitalized interest	(26,323)	(17,770)	(15,350)
Interest income	(9,166)	(11,093)	(10,672)
Nonoperating (gains) losses, net	(693)	2,739	3,299
Total other expenses	17,186	32,336	36,361
INCOME BEFORE INCOME TAXES AND CUMULATIVE EFFECT OF ACCOUNTING CHANGES	299,523	259,637	157,443
PROVISION FOR INCOME TAXES (NOTE 11)	120,192	105,353	55,816
INCOME BEFORE CUMULATIVE EFFECT OF ACCOUNTING CHANGES	179,331	154,284	101,627
CUMULATIVE EFFECT OF ACCOUNTING CHANGES (NOTE 3)		15,259	12,538
NET INCOME	$ 179,331	$ 169,543	$ 114,165
PER SHARE AMOUNTS (NOTES 3, 8, AND 12):			
Income before cumulative effect of accounting changes	$ 1.22	$ 1.05	$ .71
Cumulative effect of accounting changes	-	.10	.09
Net income	$ 1.22	$ 1.15	$ .80

See accompanying notes.

C ONSOLIDATED STATEMENT OF STOCKHOLDERS' EQUITY

(in thousands except per share amounts)   *Years ended December 31, 1994, 1993, and 1992*

	COMMON STOCK	CAPITAL IN EXCESS OF PAR VALUE	RETAINED EARNINGS	TREASURY STOCK	TOTAL
Balance at December 31, 1991	$ 45,265	$ 79,240	$ 515,885	$ (4,597)	$ 635,793
Public common stock offering (Note 8)	2,328	82,094	-	2,524	86,946
Conversion of debentures (Note 6)	1,371	34,678	-	-	36,049
Two-for-one stock split (Note 8)	46,180	(46,180)	-	-	-
Sale (retirement) of treasury stock, pooled company	(307)	60	-	1,434	1,187
Issuance of common and treasury stock upon exercise of executive stock options and pursuant to Employee stock option and purchase plans and related tax benefit (Note 9)	156	3,359	-	553	4,068
Sale of preferred stock, pooled company (Note 2)	1,054	13,584	-	-	14,638
Cash dividends, $.03533 per share	-	-	(4,890)	-	(4,890)
Cash distributions of pooled company (Note 2)	-	-	(5,388)	-	(5,388)
Reclassification of retained earnings, pooled company (Note 2)	-	13,844	(13,844)	-	-
Reinstatement of deferred taxes, pooled company (Note 2)	-	(3,032)	-	-	(3,032)
Net income - 1992	-	-	114,165	-	114,165
Balance at December 31, 1992	96,047	177,647	605,928	(86)	879,536
Three-for-two stock split (Note 8)	46,325	(46,325)	-	-	-
Issuance of common and treasury stock upon exercise of executive stock options and pursuant to Employee stock option and purchase plans and related tax benefit (Note 9)	384	9,846	-	86	10,316
Cash dividends, $.03867 per share	-	-	(5,376)	-	(5,376)
Net income - 1993	-	-	169,543	-	169,543
Balance at December 31, 1993	142,756	141,168	770,095	-	1,054,019
Issuance of common stock upon exercise of executive stock options and pursuant to Employee stock option and purchase plans and related tax benefit (Note 9)	500	10,578	-	-	11,078
Cash dividends, $.04000 per share	-	-	(5,722)	-	(5,722)
Net income - 1994	-	-	179,331	-	179,331
Balance at December 31, 1994	**$143,256**	**$151,746**	**$943,704**	**$ -**	**$1,238,706**

See accompanying notes.

Ⓒ ONSOLIDATED STATEMENT OF CASH FLOWS

(in thousands)

	YEARS ENDED DECEMBER 31,		
	1994	1993	1992
CASH FLOWS FROM OPERATING ACTIVITIES:			
Net income	$ 179,331	$ 169,543	$ 114,165
Cumulative effect of accounting changes (Note 3)	-	(15,259)	(12,538)
Income before cumulative effect of accounting changes	179,331	154,284	101,627
Adjustments to reconcile net income to cash provided by operating activities:			
Depreciation	139,045	119,338	101,976
Deferred income taxes	49,887	53,200	21,260
Amortization of deferred gains on sale and leaseback of aircraft	(30,341)	(32,509)	(32,719)
Amortization of scheduled airframe overhauls	14,216	11,630	6,930
Changes in certain assets and liabilities:			
Increase in accounts receivable	(5,208)	(14,253)	(7,440)
Decrease (increase) in other current assets	648	(9,641)	(12,000)
Increase in accounts payable and accrued liabilities	52,679	67,585	65,706
Increase in air traffic liability	9,993	30,212	18,602
Increase (decrease) in other current liabilities	(4,690)	2,393	12,179
Other	7,106	10,440	5,978
Net cash provided by operating activities	412,666	392,679	282,099
CASH FLOWS FROM INVESTING ACTIVITIES:			
Purchases of property and equipment	(788,649)	(524,169)	(432,528)
Net cash used in investing activities	(788,649)	(524,169)	(432,528)
CASH FLOWS FROM FINANCING ACTIVITIES:			
Issuance of long-term debt	-	17,810	113,827
Proceeds from public common stock offering (Note 8)	-	-	86,946
Proceeds from aircraft sale and leaseback transactions	315,000	90,000	120,000
Proceeds from sale of preferred stock, pooled company	-	-	14,638
Payment of long-term debt and capital lease obligations	(63,071)	(120,098)	(10,358)
Payment of cash dividends	(5,722)	(5,376)	(4,890)
Cash distributions of pooled company (Note 2)	-	-	(5,388)
Proceeds from Employee stock plans	8,743	6,743	3,517
Other	-	(7)	802
Net cash provided by (used in) financing activities	254,950	(10,928)	319,094
NET INCREASE (DECREASE) IN CASH AND CASH EQUIVALENTS	(121,033)	(142,418)	168,665
CASH AND CASH EQUIVALENTS AT BEGINNING OF PERIOD	295,571	437,989	269,324
CASH AND CASH EQUIVALENTS AT END OF PERIOD	$ 174,538	$ 295,571	$ 437,989
CASH PAYMENTS FOR:			
Interest, net of amount capitalized	$ 26,598	$ 43,161	$ 39,936
Income taxes	80,461	45,292	27,728

See accompanying notes.

NOTES TO CONSOLIDATED FINANCIAL STATEMENTS

December 31, 1994

1. SUMMARY OF SIGNIFICANT ACCOUNTING POLICIES

BASIS OF PRESENTATION The consolidated financial statements include the accounts of Southwest Airlines Co. (Southwest) and its wholly owned subsidiaries (the Company). All significant intercompany balances and transactions have been eliminated. Certain prior year amounts have been reclassified for comparison purposes.

CASH AND CASH EQUIVALENTS Cash equivalents consist of investment grade commercial paper issued by major financial institutions that are highly liquid and have original maturity dates of three months or less. Cash and cash equivalents are carried at cost, which approximates market value.

INVENTORIES Inventories of flight equipment expendable parts, materials, and supplies are carried at average cost. These items are charged to expense when issued for use.

PROPERTY AND EQUIPMENT Depreciation is provided by the straight-line method to residual values over periods ranging from 15 to 20 years for flight equipment (see Note 3) and 3 to 30 years for ground property and equipment. Property under capital leases and related obligations are recorded at an amount equal to the present value of future minimum lease payments computed on the basis of the lessee's incremental borrowing rate or, when known, the interest rate implicit in the lease. Amortization of property under capital leases is on a straight-line basis over the lease term and is included in depreciation expense.

AIRCRAFT AND ENGINE MAINTENANCE The cost of engine overhauls and routine maintenance costs for aircraft and engine maintenance are charged to maintenance expense as incurred. Scheduled airframe overhaul costs are capitalized at amounts not to exceed the fair market value of the related aircraft and amortized over the estimated periods benefited, presently 8 years. Modifications that significantly enhance the operating performance or extend the useful lives of aircraft or engines are capitalized and amortized over the remaining life of the asset.

REVENUE RECOGNITION Passenger revenue is recognized when the transportation is provided. Tickets sold but not yet used are included in "Air traffic liability."

FREQUENT FLYER AWARDS The Company accrues the estimated incremental cost of providing free travel awards earned under its Company Club Frequent Flyer program.

ADVERTISING The Company expenses the production costs of advertising as incurred. Advertising expense for the years ended December 31, 1994, 1993, and 1992 was $79,475,000, $55,344,000, and $42,068,000, respectively.

2. ACQUISITION

On December 31, 1993, Southwest exchanged 3,574,656 newly issued shares of its common stock for all of the outstanding stock of Morris Air Corporation (Morris), a low-fare commercial/charter air carrier based in Salt Lake City. The acquisition was accounted for as a pooling of interests and, accordingly, the Company's consolidated financial statements were restated to include the accounts and operations of Morris for all periods prior to the acquisition.

Prior to 1993, Morris was treated as an S-Corporation for federal and state income tax purposes under applicable provisions of the Internal Revenue Code and various state tax laws. Therefore, no provision for income taxes was made prior to 1993. Morris made regular cash distributions to its shareholders sufficient to meet their tax liabilities. Upon termination of S-Corporation status on December 31, 1992, the undistributed S-Corporation retained earnings were reclassified to capital in excess of par value. Additionally, Morris established $3,032,000 of deferred income taxes for the cumulative differences in the timing of reporting certain items for financial statement and income tax purposes. These deferred taxes related primarily to depreciation. The establishment of deferred taxes was offset by a reduction of capital in excess of par value.

Merger expenses of $10,803,000 relating to the merger of Southwest and Morris have been included in 1993 operating expenses as required for financial reporting purposes; however, these expenses have been separately reported as "merger expenses" to reflect the impact of the nonrecurring expenses on operating results. Included in these one-time costs resulting from the merger were $1,900,000 of various professional fees; $4,703,000 for disposal of duplicate or incompatible property and equipment; and $4,200,000 for Employee relocation and severance costs related to elimination of duplicate or incompatible operations. During 1994, the integration of Morris into Southwest was substantially completed, including the disposal of incompatible property and equipment and settlement of Employee relocation and severance costs.

3. ACCOUNTING CHANGES

INCOME TAXES Effective January 1, 1993, the Company adopted Statement of Financial Accounting Standards No. 109, "Accounting for Income Taxes" (SFAS 109). As a result of adopting SFAS 109, the Company recorded deferred tax assets of $6,977,000 and reduced deferred tax liabilities by $9,048,000 at January 1, 1993, which resulted in an increase to the Company's 1993 net income of $16,025,000 ($.11 per share) for the cumulative effect of the accounting change.

POSTRETIREMENT BENEFITS Effective January 1, 1993, the Company adopted Statement of Financial Accounting Standards No. 106, "Employers' Accounting for Postretirement Benefits Other Than Pensions" (SFAS 106). The cumulative effect of this change in accounting method at January 1, 1993 reduced 1993 net income by $766,000 (net of benefit from income taxes of $469,000) or $.01 per share. The effect of adopting SFAS 106 on 1993 income before cumulative effect of accounting changes was not material.

SCHEDULED AIRFRAME OVERHAULS Prior to January 1, 1992, the Company expensed scheduled airframe overhaul costs as incurred. This practice was adopted at a time when costs were relatively constant from year to year and consistent with the growth of the fleet.

Given the significant growth of the Company's fleet and the Company's 1991 modification of its airframe overhaul maintenance program with the Federal Aviation Administration (FAA), Southwest changed its method of accounting for scheduled airframe overhauls costs from the direct expense method to that of capitalizing and amortizing the costs over the periods benefited. The Company believes this method is preferable because it results in charges to expense that are consistent with the growth in the fleet; improves financial reporting; and better matches revenues and expenses.

For the year ended December 31, 1992, the Company recognized approximately $6,900,000 in amortization of airframe overhaul expense. Had the direct expense method been used to provide for scheduled airframe overhaul costs during the year ended December 31, 1992, income before cumulative effect of accounting change would have been reduced by approximately $9,800,000 (net of provision for income taxes and profitsharing of approximately $8,800,000), or approximately $.07 per share.

This change in accounting principle had the effect of a one-time adjustment increasing net income for the year ended December 31, 1992 by approximately $12,538,000 (net of provision for income taxes and profitsharing of approximately $11,500,000).

CHANGE IN ACCOUNTING ESTIMATE Effective January 1, 1992, the Company revised the estimated useful lives of its 737-200 aircraft from 15 years to 15-19 years. This change was the result of the Company's assessment of the remaining useful lives of its 737-200 aircraft following the recent promulgation of rules by the FAA for the phase out of Stage 2 aircraft by December 31, 1999. The effect of this change was to reduce depreciation expense approximately $3,680,000, or $.03 per share, for the year ended December 31, 1992.

4. COMMITMENTS

The Company's contractual purchase commitments consist primarily of scheduled aircraft acquisitions. Twenty-five 737-300 aircraft are scheduled for delivery in 1995, 18 in 1996, and ten in 1997. Four 737-700s are scheduled for delivery in 1997, 16 in 1998, 16 in 1999, 15 in 2000, and 12 in 2001. In addition, the Company has options to purchase up to eleven 737-300s in 1997 and up to sixty-three 737-700s during 1998-2004. The Company has the option, which must be exercised two years prior to the contractual delivery date, to substitute 737-400s or 737-500s for the 737-300s to be delivered during 1997 and 737-600s or 737-800s for the 737-700s delivered subsequent to 1999. Aggregate funding needed for these commitments was approximately $3,042.7 million, subject to adjustments for inflation, due as follows: $602.6 million in 1995, $489.5 million in 1996, $447.8 million in 1997, $445.4 million in 1998, $452.9 million in 1999, $366.0 million in 2000, and $238.5 million in 2001. In addition, the Company has an agreement in principle to lease two used 737-300 aircraft in 1995.

The Company uses jet fuel fixed price swap arrangements to hedge its exposure to price fluctuations on approximately 5 percent of its annual fuel requirements. As of December 31, 1994, the Company had jet fuel swap agreements with broker-dealers to exchange monthly payments on notional quantities amounting to 2,100,000 gallons per month, over the ensuing three months. Under the swap agreements, the Company pays or receives the difference between the daily average jet fuel price and a fixed price of approximately $.518 per gallon. Gains and losses on such transactions are recorded as adjustments to fuel expense and have been insignificant. Although the agreements expose the Company to credit loss in the event of nonperformance by the other parties to the agreements, the Company does not anticipate such nonperformance.

5. ACCRUED LIABILITIES

(in thousands)

	1994	1993
Aircraft rentals	$ 67,407	$ 55,459
Profitsharing and savings plans (Note 10)	53,512	45,691
Aircraft maintenance costs	37,330	37,853
Vacation pay	31,801	26,781
Taxes, other than income	25,001	19,183
Interest	20,270	21,311
Merger expenses	-	8,527
Other	53,658	50,528
	$ 288,979	$ 265,333

6. LONG-TERM DEBT

(in thousands)

	1994	1993
9 ¼% Notes due 1998	$ 100,000	$ 100,000
9.4% Notes due 2001	100,000	100,000
8 ¾% Notes due 2003	100,000	100,000
7 ⅞% Notes due 2007	100,000	100,000
Capital leases (Note 7)	195,756	204,904
Secured notes payable to financial institutions, repaid in 1994	-	53,950
Industrial Revenue Bonds, repaid in 1994	-	375
Other	435	13
	596,191	659,242
Less current maturities	9,553	16,068
Less debt discount	3,567	4,038
	$ 583,071	$ 639,136

On March 1, 1993, the Company redeemed the $100 million in senior unsecured 9% Notes due March 1, 1996, issued in March 1986. The Notes were redeemed at par plus accrued interest.

On September 9, 1992, Southwest issued $100 million of senior unsecured 7 ⅞% Notes due September 1, 2007. Interest is payable semi-annually on March 1 and September 1. The Notes are not redeemable prior to maturity.

During 1991, the Company issued $100 million of senior unsecured 9 ¼% Notes, $100 million of senior unsecured 9.4% Notes, and $100 million of senior unsecured 8 ¾% Notes due February 15, 1998, July 1, 2001, and October 15, 2003, respectively. Interest on the Notes is payable semi-annually. The Notes are not redeemable by the Company prior to maturity.

The fair values, based on quoted market prices, of these Notes at December 31, 1994, were as follows (in thousands):

9 ¼% Notes due 1998	$ 102,000
9.4% Notes due 2001	103,820
8 ¾% Notes due 2003	100,670
7 ⅞% Notes due 2007	93,070

In 1992, certain Convertible Subordinated Debentures issued by Southwest Airlines Eurofinance N.V. were redeemed. The principal amount of $35,000,000 was converted into 1,370,902 shares (unadjusted for the 1993 and 1992 stock splits) of Southwest's common stock at the conversion price of $25.53 per share plus accrued interest. The conversion was primarily a noncash transaction and, therefore, was excluded from the Statement of Cash Flows.

In addition to the credit facilities described above, Southwest has an unsecured Bank Credit Agreement with a group of domestic banks that permits Southwest to borrow through December 14, 1996 on a revolving credit basis up to $300 million. Interest rates on borrowings under the Credit Agreement can be, at the option of Southwest, the agent bank's prime rate, .30% over LIBOR, or .50% over domestic certificate of deposit rates. The commitment fee is 0.1875% per annum. There were no outstanding borrowings under this Agreement at December 31, 1994 or 1993.

7. LEASES

Total rental expense for operating leases charged to operations in 1994, 1993, and 1992 was $198,987,000, $167,303,000, and $125,835,000, respectively. The majority of the Company's terminal operations space, as well as 89 aircraft, were under operating leases. The amounts applicable to capital leases included in property and equipment were (in thousands):

	1994	1993
Flight equipment	$ 233,324	$ 232,853
Less accumulated amortization	88,656	74,234
	$ 144,668	$ 158,619

Future minimum lease payments under capital leases and noncancelable operating leases, with initial or remaining terms in excess of one year, at December 31, 1994, were (in thousands):

	CAPITAL LEASES	OPERATING LEASES
1995	$ 26,282	$ 176,439
1996	28,897	178,253
1997	26,843	168,132
1998	32,903	148,017
1999	20,999	137,845
After 1999	191,096	1,559,478
Total minimum lease payments	327,020	$ 2,368,164
Less amount representing interest	131,264	
Present value of minimum lease payments	195,756	
Less current portion	9,542	
Long-term portion	$ 186,214	

The aircraft leases can generally be renewed at rates, based on fair market value at the end of the lease term, for one to five years. Most aircraft leases have purchase options at or near the end of the lease term at fair market value, but generally not to exceed a stated percentage of the lessor's defined cost of the aircraft.

8. COMMON STOCK

At December 31, 1994, the Company had common stock reserved for issuance pursuant to Employee stock benefit plans (12,009,293 shares) and upon exercise of rights pursuant to the Common Stock Rights Agreement (Agreement), as amended (155,265,088 shares).

Pursuant to the Agreement, each outstanding share of the Company's common stock is accompanied by one common share purchase right (Right). Each Right entitles its holder to purchase one share of common stock at an exercise price of $16.67 and is exercisable only in the event of a proposed takeover, as defined by the Agreement. The Company may redeem the Rights at $.0111 per Right prior to the time that 20 percent of the common stock has been acquired by a person or group. If the Company is acquired or if certain self-dealing transactions occur, as defined in the Agreement, each Right will entitle its holder to purchase for $16.67 that number of the acquiring company's or the Company's common shares, as provided in the Agreement, having a market value of two times the exercise price of the Right. The Rights will expire no later than July 30, 1996.

On May 19, 1993, the Company's Board of Directors declared a three-for-two stock split, distributing 46,325,147 shares on July 15, 1993. On May 20, 1992, the Company's Board of Directors declared a two-for-one stock split, distributing 46,180,531 shares on July 15, 1992.

In February 1992, the Company sold 2,500,000 shares (unadjusted for the subsequent 1993 and 1992 stock splits) of its common stock (2,327,892 new shares and 172,108 shares from treasury) in a public offering. Net proceeds from the sale of approximately $86,946,000 were added to the working capital of the Company for general corporate purposes, including the acquisition of aircraft and related equipment.

9. STOCK PLANS

In May 1991, the Company's stockholders approved the Incentive Stock Option Plan and the Non-Qualified Stock Option Plan. Under the Incentive Stock Option Plan, options to purchase a maximum of 9,000,000 shares of Southwest common stock may be granted to key Employees. Under the Non-Qualified Stock Option Plan, options to purchase up to 750,000 shares of Southwest common stock may be granted to key Employees and non-employee directors. Under each plan, the option price per share may not be less than the fair market value of a share on the date the option is granted and the maximum term of an option may not exceed 10 years.

Information regarding the stock option plans is summarized below:

	INCENTIVE PLAN	NON-QUALIFIED PLAN
Outstanding December 31, 1991	3,948,957	282,825
Granted	430,974	97,950
Exercised	(251,817)	(4,350)
Surrendered	(111,210)	(1,800)
Outstanding December 31, 1992	4,016,904	374,625
Granted	724,646	22,512
Exercised	*(198,285)	**(94,810)
Surrendered	(230,978)	(1,050)
Outstanding December 31, 1993	4,312,287	301,277
Granted	794,714	63,918
Exercised	(190,159)	(9,940)
Surrendered	(104,880)	-
Outstanding December 31, 1994	**4,811,962**	**355,255**

Exercisable		
1994	**572,244**	**163,936**
1993	314,322	108,509
1992	198,474	142,575

Available for granting in future periods:		
1994	**3,447,694**	**279,165**
1993	4,137,528	343,083
1992	4,631,196	364,545

Average price of exercised options:		
1994	**$8.23**	**$7.85**
1993	$7.14	$7.37
1992	$6.10	$11.36

*Includes 108,113 pre-split shares and 36,115 post-split shares, of which 5,476 pre-split shares and 72 post-split shares were issued from treasury.

**Includes 12,740 pre-split shares and 75,700 post-split shares.

The exercise price of outstanding options ranged from $6.02 to $37.44 in 1994, $6.02 to $19.71 in 1993, and $6.02 to $12.06 in 1992.

In 1991, the Company's stockholders also approved the Employee Stock Purchase Plan that provides for the sale of common stock to Employees of the Company at a price equal to 90% of the market value at the end of each purchase period. Common stock purchases are paid for through periodic payroll deductions. Participants under the plan received 290,054 shares in 1994, 182,459 shares (59,442 pre-split shares and 93,296 post-split shares) in 1993 and 166,436 shares in 1992 at average prices of $24.98, $25.25, and $12.89, respectively.

At December 31, 1994, 1993, and 1992, 1,489,753, 1,504,753, and 1,512,252 options to purchase the Company's common stock were also outstanding related to employment contracts with the Company's president and chief executive officer. Exercise prices range from $1.00 to $11.33 per share. Options for 15,000 shares, 7,500 shares (5,000 pre-split shares, of which 968 shares were issued from treasury), and 22,500 shares were exercised in 1994, 1993, and 1992, respectively.

Effective January 12, 1995, the Company adopted, pursuant to a collective bargaining agreement between the Company and the Southwest Airlines Pilots' Association (SWAPA), the 1995 SWAPA Non-Qualified Stock Option Plan (SWAPA Plan). Under the terms of the SWAPA Plan, 18,000,000 common shares have been reserved for issuance. An initial grant of approximately 14.5 million shares was made on the effective date at an option price of $20.00 per share. On September 1 of each year of the agreement, commencing September 1, 1996, additional options will be granted to Pilots that became eligible during that year at an option price equal to the fair market value of the common stock of the Company on the date of grant plus 5 percent. Options vest in ten annual increments of 10 percent and must be exercised prior to January 31, 2007, or within a specified time upon retirement or termination. In the event that SWAPA exercises its option to make the collective bargaining agreement amendable on September 1, 1999, any unexercised options will be canceled on December 1, 1999.

10. EMPLOYEE PROFITSHARING AND SAVINGS PLANS

Substantially all of Southwest's Employees are members of the Southwest Airlines Co. Profitsharing Plan (the Plan). Total profitsharing expense charged to operations in 1994, 1993, and 1992 was $52,782,000, $44,959,000, and $26,363,000, respectively. The Company also elected to contribute $3,605,000 in 1992 as a result of an accounting change (see Note 3).

The Company sponsors Employee savings plans under Section 401(k) of the Internal Revenue Code. The plans cover substantially all full-time Employees. The amount of matching contributions varies by

Employee group. Company contributions generally vest over five years with credit for prior years' service granted. Company matching contributions expensed in 1994, 1993, and 1992 were $19,817,000, $13,986,000, and $11,611,000, respectively.

11. INCOME TAXES

Effective January 1, 1993, the Company changed its method of accounting for income taxes from the deferred method to the liability method as required by SFAS 109 (see Note 3).

Under SFAS 109, deferred income taxes reflect the net tax effects of temporary differences between the carrying amounts of assets and liabilities for financial reporting purposes and the amounts used for income tax purposes. The components of deferred tax assets and liabilities at December 31, 1994, and 1993 are as follows (in thousands):

	1994	1993
Deferred tax liabilities:		
Accelerated depreciation	$343,585	$299,195
Scheduled airframe overhauls	23,966	21,512
Other	55,953	45,734
Total deferred tax liabilities	423,504	366,441
Deferred tax assets:		
Deferred gains from sale and leaseback of aircraft	95,602	87,358
Capital and operating leases	38,240	33,637
Alternative minimum tax credit carry forward	22,778	32,122
Other	43,856	40,183
Total deferred tax assets	200,476	193,300
Net deferred tax liability	$223,028	$173,141

In August 1993, the Revenue Reconciliation Act of 1993 (the "1993 Act") was enacted, which contains numerous provision changes including an increase in the federal corporate income tax rate from 34 percent to 35 percent effective January 1, 1993. As a result, the Company recognized approximately $4.0 million of additional expense in 1993 related to deferred tax liabilities existing on January 1, 1993.

The provision for income taxes before the cumulative effect of accounting changes is comprised of the following (in thousands):

	LIABILITY METHOD		DEFERRED METHOD
	1994	1993	1992
Current:			
Federal	$59,603	$46,744	$30,586
State	10,702	5,409	3,970
Total current	70,305	52,153	34,556
Deferred:			
Federal	46,470	48,524	18,144
State	3,417	4,676	3,116
Total deferred	49,887	53,200	21,260
	$120,192	$105,353	$55,816

The components of the provision for deferred income taxes as reported under the previous method of accounting for the year ended December 31, 1992 were as follows (in thousands):

	1992
Depreciation	$ 27,947
Deferred gains on sale\leasebacks	(4,275)
Scheduled airframe overhauls	6,336
Vacation pay	(1,220)
Alternative minimum tax	(10,645)
Other, net	3,117
	$21,260

In January 1994, Southwest received an examination report from the Internal Revenue Service proposing certain adjustments to Southwest's income tax returns for 1987 and 1988. The adjustments relate to certain types of aircraft financings consummated by Southwest, as well as other members of the aviation industry during that time period. Southwest intends to vigorously protest the adjustments proposed with which it does not agree. The industry's difference with the IRS involves complex issues of law and fact that are likely to take a substantial period of time to resolve. Management believes that final resolution of such protest will not have a materially adverse effect upon the results of operations of Southwest.

The effective tax rate on income before cumulative effect of accounting changes differed from the federal income tax statutory rate for the following reasons (in thousands):

	LIABILITY METHOD	DEFERRED METHOD	
	1994	1993	1992
Tax at statutory U.S. tax rates	**$104,833**	$ 90,873	$ 53,531
Less amount associated with S-Corporation earnings of Morris (Note 2)	-	-	(3,607)
	104,833	90,873	49,924
Nondeductible items	**3,689**	1,361	1,131
State income taxes, net of federal benefit	**9,177**	6,632	5,124
Effect of increase in U.S. statutory rates	-	3,957	-
Other, net	**2,493**	2,530	(363)
Total income tax provision	**$120,192**	$ 105,353	$ 55,816

12. NET INCOME PER COMMON AND COMMON EQUIVALENT SHARE

Net income per common and common equivalent share is computed based on the weighted average number of common and common equivalent shares outstanding (147,305,374 in 1994, 147,144,568 in 1993, and 142,945,890 in 1992). Fully diluted earnings per share have not been presented as the fully dilutive effect of shares issuable upon the exercise of options under the Company's Stock Option Plans or conversion of Convertible Subordinated Debentures is anti-dilutive or is not material.

REPORT OF ERNST & YOUNG LLP INDEPENDENT AUDITORS

THE BOARD OF DIRECTORS AND SHAREHOLDERS
SOUTHWEST AIRLINES CO.

We have audited the accompanying consolidated balance sheets of Southwest Airlines Co. as of December 31, 1994 and 1993, and the related consolidated statements of income, stockholders' equity, and cash flows for each of the three years in the period ended December 31, 1994. These financial statements are the responsibility of the Company's management. Our responsibility is to express an opinion on these financial statements based on our audits.

We conducted our audits in accordance with generally accepted auditing standards. Those standards require that we plan and perform the audit to obtain reasonable assurance about whether the financial statements are free of material misstatement. An audit includes examining, on a test basis, evidence supporting the amounts and disclosures in the financial statements. An audit also includes assessing the accounting principles used and significant estimates made by management, as well as evaluating the overall financial statement presentation. We believe that our audits provide a reasonable basis for our opinion.

In our opinion, the financial statements referred to above present fairly, in all material respects, the consolidated financial position of Southwest Airlines Co. at December 31, 1994 and 1993, and the consolidated results of its operations and its cash flows for each of the three years in the period ended December 31, 1994, in conformity with generally accepted accounting principles.

As discussed in Note 3, during 1993, the Company changed its method of accounting for income taxes and postretirement benefits. Also as discussed in Note 3, during 1992, the Company changed its method of accounting for scheduled airframe overhauls.

Ernst + Young LLP

Dallas, Texas
January 26, 1995

S O U T H W E S T   A I R L I N E S   C O.

QUARTERLY FINANCIAL DATA (UNAUDITED)

(in thousands except per share amounts)

| 1994 | THREE MONTHS ENDED | | | |
	MARCH 31	JUNE 30	SEPT. 30	DEC. 31
Operating revenues	$619,412	$661,056	$685,289	$626,176
Operating income	76,046	101,834	101,710	37,119
Income before income taxes	69,538	97,156	97,128	35,701
Net income	41,847	58,522	58,619	20,343
Net income per common and common equivalent share	.28	.40	.40	.14

| 1993 | THREE MONTHS ENDED | | | |
	MARCH 31	JUNE 30	SEPT. 30	DEC. 31
Operating revenues	$498,943	$568,251	$620,918	$608,561
Operating income	48,784	75,812	95,820	71,557
Income before income taxes	40,393 [1]	68,241	86,214	64,789
Net income	24,933 [1]	42,149	48,833	38,369
Net income per common and common equivalent share	.17	.29	.33	.26

[1] Excludes cumulative effect of accounting changes

S O U T H W E S T   A I R L I N E S   C O.

COMMON STOCK PRICE RANGES AND DIVIDENDS

Southwest's common stock is listed on the New York Stock Exchange and is traded under the symbol LUV. The high and low sales prices of the common stock on the Composite Tape and the quarterly dividends per share, as adjusted for the July 1993 three-for-two stock split, were:

PERIOD	DIVIDENDS	HIGH	LOW
1994			
1st Quarter	$.01000	$39.00	$31.25
2nd Quarter	.01000	34.38	24.13
3rd Quarter	.01000	29.63	21.63
4th Quarter	.01000	23.63	15.50
1993			
1st Quarter	$.00933	$25.17	$18.17
2nd Quarter	.00933	30.00	22.17
3rd Quarter	.01000	37.63	28.00
4th Quarter	.01000	37.63	29.88

TEN YEAR SUMMARY

SELECTED CONSOLIDATED FINANCIAL DATA [1]

(in thousands except per share amounts)	1994	1993	1992	1991
Operating revenues:				
Passenger	$ 2,497,765	$ 2,216,342	$ 1,623,828	$ 1,267,897
Freight	54,419	42,897	33,088	26,428
Charter and other	39,749	37,434	146,063	84,961
Total operating revenues	2,591,933	2,296,673	1,802,979	1,379,286
Operating expenses	2,275,224	2,004,700	1,609,175	1,306,675
Operating income	316,709	291,973	193,804	72,611
Other expenses (income), net	17,186	32,336	36,361	18,725
Income before income taxes	299,523	259,637	157,443	53,886
Provision for income taxes [3]	120,192	105,353	60,058	20,738
Net income [3]	$ 179,331	$ 154,284 [4]	$ 97,385 [5]	$ 33,148
Income per common and common equivalent share [3]	$1.22	$1.05 [4]	$.68 [5]	$.25
Cash dividends per common share	$.04000	$.03867	$.03533	$.03333
Total assets	$ 2,823,071	$ 2,576,037	$ 2,368,856	$ 1,854,331
Long-term debt	$ 583,071	$ 639,136	$ 735,754	$ 617,434
Stockholders' equity	$ 1,238,706	$ 1,054,019	$ 879,536	$ 635,793

CONSOLIDATED FINANCIAL RATIOS [1]

	1994	1993	1992	1991
Return on average total assets	6.6%	6.2% [4]	4.6% [5]	2.0%
Return on average stockholders' equity	15.6%	16.0% [4]	12.9% [5]	5.3%
Debt as a percentage of invested capital	32.0%	37.7%	45.5%	49.3%

CONSOLIDATED OPERATING STATISTICS [2]

	1994	1993	1992	1991
Revenue passengers carried	42,742,602 [13]	36,955,221 [13]	27,839,284	22,669,942
RPMs (000s)	21,611,266	18,827,288	13,787,005	11,296,183
ASMs (000s)	32,123,974	27,511,000	21,366,642	18,491,003
Load factor	67.3%	68.4%	64.5%	61.1%
Average length of passenger haul	506	509	495	498
Trips flown	624,476	546,297	438,184	382,752
Average passenger fare	$58.44	$59.97	$58.33	$55.93
Passenger revenue yield per RPM	11.56¢	11.77¢	11.78¢	11.22¢
Operating revenue yield per ASM	8.07¢	8.35¢	7.89¢	7.10¢
Operating expenses per ASM	7.08¢	7.25¢ [14]	7.03¢	6.76¢
Fuel cost per gallon (average)	53.92¢	59.15¢	60.82¢	65.69¢
Number of Employees at yearend	16,818	15,175	11,397	9,778
Size of fleet at yearend [15]	199	178	141	124

(1) The Selected Consolidated Financial Data and Consolidated Financial Ratios for 1992 through 1989 have been restated to include the financial results of Morris. Years prior to 1989 were immaterial for restatement purposes

(2) Prior to 1993, Morris operated as a charter carrier; therefore, no Morris statistics are included for these years

(3) Pro forma assuming Morris, an S-Corporation prior to 1993, was taxed at statutory rates

(4) Excludes cumulative effect of accounting changes of $15.3 million ($.10 per share)

(5) Excludes cumulative effect of accounting change of $12.5 million ($.09 per share)

(6) Includes $2.6 million gains on sales of aircraft and $3.1 million from the sale of certain financial assets

(7) Includes $10.8 million gains on sales of aircraft, $5.9 million from the sale of certain financial assets, and $2.3 million from the settlement of a contingency

(8) Includes $5.6 million gains on sales of aircraft and $3.6 million from the sale of certain financial assets

	1990	1989	1988	1987	1986	1985 [12]
	$ 1,144,421	$ 973,568	$ 828,343	$ 751,649	$ 742,287	$ 656,689
	22,196	18,771	14,433	13,428	13,621	13,643
	70,659	65,390	17,658	13,251	12,882	9,340
	1,237,276	1,057,729	860,434	778,328	768,790	679,672
	1,150,015	955,689	774,454	747,881	679,827	601,148
	87,261	102,040	85,980	30,447 [9]	88,963	78,524
	(6,827) [6]	(13,696) [7]	620 [8]	1,374 [10]	23,517 [11]	17,740
	80,434	115,736	85,360	29,073	65,446	60,784
	29,829	41,231	27,408	8,918	15,411	13,506
	$ 50,605	$ 74,505	$ 57,952	$ 20,155	$ 50,035	$ 47,278
	$.39	$.54	$.41	$.14	$.34	$.34
	$.03223	$.03110	$.02943	$.02890	$.02890	$.02890
	$ 1,480,813	$ 1,423,298	$ 1,308,389	$ 1,042,640	$ 1,061,419	$ 1,002,403
	$ 327,553	$ 354,150	$ 369,541	$ 251,130	$ 339,069	$ 381,308
	$ 607,294	$ 591,794	$ 567,375	$ 514,278	$ 511,850	$ 466,004
	3.5%	5.5%	5.1%	1.9%	4.8%	5.6%
	8.4%	12.9%	10.8%	4.0%	10.3%	11.4%
	35.0%	37.4%	39.4%	32.8%	39.8%	45.0%
	19,830,941	17,958,263	14,876,582	13,503,242	13,637,515	12,651,239
	9,958,940	9,281,992	7,676,257	7,789,376	7,388,401	5,971,400
	16,411,115	14,796,732	13,309,044	13,331,055	12,574,484	9,884,526
	60.7%	62.7%	57.7%	58.4%	58.8%	60.4%
	502	517	516	577	542	472
	338,108	304,673	274,859	270,559	262,082	230,227
	$57.71	$54.21	$55.68	$55.66	$54.43	$51.91
	11.49¢	10.49¢	10.79¢	9.65¢	10.05¢	11.00¢
	7.23¢	6.86¢	6.47¢	5.84¢	6.11¢	6.88¢
	6.73¢	6.20¢	5.82¢	5.61¢	5.41¢	6.08¢
	77.89¢	59.46¢	51.37¢	54.31¢	51.42¢	78.17¢
	8,620	7,760	6,467	5,765	5,819	5,271
	106	94	85	75	79	70

(9) Includes TranStar's results through June 30, 1987

(10) Includes $10.1 million net gains from the discontinuance of TranStar's operations and $4.3 million from the sale of certain financial assets

(11) Includes a gain of $4 million from the sale of aircraft delivery positions

(12) Includes the accounts of TranStar since June 30, 1985

(13) Includes certain estimates for Morris

(14) Excludes merger expenses of $10.8 million

(15) Includes leased aircraft

Financial Statements and Related Disclosures from Lands' End, Inc.'s 1995 Annual Report

Management's Discussion and Analysis

Results of operations for fiscal 1995, compared with fiscal 1994

Consolidated statements of operations presented as a percentage of net sales:

For the period ended	January 27, 1995	January 28, 1994	January 29, 1993
Net sales	100.0%	100.0%	100.0%
Cost of sales	57.3	58.9	58.2
Gross profit	42.7	41.1	41.8
Selling, general and administrative expenses	36.3	33.0	34.2
Reserve for anticipated sale of subsidiary	0.4	–	–
Income from operations	6.0	8.1	7.6
Interest expense	(0.2)	–	(0.2)
Other income (expense)	0.2	(0.1)	–
Income before income taxes and cumulative effect of change in accounting	6.0	8.0	7.4
Income tax provision	2.4	3.1	2.8
Net income before cumulative effect of change in accounting	3.6	4.9	4.6
Cumulative effect of change in accounting for income taxes	–	0.1	–
Net income	3.6%	5.0%	4.6%

Net sales increased 14 percent to $992 million in fiscal 1995, compared with $870 million in fiscal 1994. The increase was primarily due to improved customer reaction to the catalogs and a 23 percent increase in the number of regular and specialty catalogs mailed, from 155 million to 191 million in fiscal 1995. About half of the increase in net sales in fiscal 1995 came from the company's regular monthly catalogs, prospector catalogs and specialty catalogs in the United States. Specialty catalogs include the Kids catalog, featuring children's clothing; Coming Home, a catalog focusing on products for bed and bath; Beyond Buttondowns, a men's tailored clothing and accessories catalog; and the Textures catalog, featuring tailored clothing for women. In addition, over 30 percent of the sales increase was attributed to the strong sales growth from the company's international businesses as well as from two new businesses, The Territory Ahead and Corporate Sales.

The company ended the year with inventory of $169 million, up 13 percent from fiscal 1994 ending inventory of $150 million. Higher inventory levels throughout the year resulted in higher interest expense, but enabled the company to ship nearly 88 percent of items ordered by customers at the time the order was placed, compared with 85 percent for fiscal 1994.

Gross profit increased
Gross profit increased 18 percent to $423 million in fiscal 1995, compared with $357 million in fiscal 1994, primarily due to the 14 percent increase in consolidated net sales as well as to the increase in gross profit margin. As a percentage of net sales, gross profit rose to 42.7 percent in fiscal 1995, compared with 41.1 percent in fiscal 1994. The increase in gross profit margin was mainly due to lower merchandise costs from improvements in domestic and offshore sourcing, partially offset by steeper markdowns of liquidated merchandise. Liquidation of out-of-season and overstocked merchandise was about 10 percent of net sales in each of the last two years.

Costs on inventory purchases increased approximately 0.1 percent in fiscal 1995, compared to 0.8 percent in fiscal 1994. The impact of inflation continues to be low for the merchandise purchased by the company.

Selling, general and administrative expenses
Selling, general and administrative (SG&A) expenses rose 25 percent in fiscal 1995 to $360 million, from $287 million in fiscal 1994, principally due to the 14 percent increase in net sales. Associated with higher sales were advertising expenses (attributed to customer prospecting and increased catalog mailings), fixed expenses (due to investment spending in international and new businesses) and increased variable expenses (primarily due to higher payroll and shipping and handling costs). The costs of producing and mailing catalogs represented about 45 percent of total SG&A in fiscal 1995 and in fiscal 1994.

As a percentage of sales, SG&A increased to 36.3 percent in fiscal 1995 from 33.0 percent in fiscal 1994. The rise in the SG&A ratio was primarily due to the company's investment spending to develop international and new businesses, to expand customer acquisition programs in anticipation of the 1995 postal rate and paper price increases, to enhance its customer service by offering two-day UPS delivery service, and to upgrade its information systems.

Management's Discussion and Analysis

The company continues to invest in the expansion of its international businesses and the development of new catalog businesses. These efforts are expected to continue to have a negative impact on the SG&A ratio.

Depreciation and amortization expense was up 24 percent from the prior year, to $10.3 million. Rental expense was up 19 percent to total $8.6 million, primarily due to increased computer hardware and building rentals.

Increased utilization of credit lines

Higher inventory levels for the majority of the year resulted in more borrowing and higher interest expense throughout the year. In addition, the company purchased approximately $28 million in treasury stock and spent $27 million in capital expenditures. The company's lines of credit peaked at $106 million in October 1994, compared with a peak of $54 million in the prior year. At January 27, 1995, the company had short-term debt outstanding for a subsidiary of $7.5 million and no long-term debt outstanding.

Net income decreased

Net income was $36.1 million, down 17 percent from the $43.7 million the company earned in fiscal 1994. Earnings per common share for the year just ended were $1.03, compared with $1.22 per share in the prior year.

As previously announced, during the fourth quarter of fiscal 1995, the company set up a reserve for the anticipated sale of its subsidiary, MontBell America, Inc., that reduced net income by $2.1 million, or $0.06 per share. During the first quarter of fiscal 1994, the company adopted Statement of Financial Accounting Standards No. 109, "Accounting for Income Taxes," which added $1.3 million of income, or $0.04 per share, to the results for fiscal 1994. Without the effect of these two factors, net income for fiscal 1995 was $38.2 million, or $1.09 per share, compared with $42.4 million, or $1.18 per share, in fiscal 1994. (All per share amounts have been adjusted to reflect the two-for-one stock split declared in May 1994.)

Results of operations for fiscal 1994, compared with fiscal 1993

Net sales increased 19 percent to $870 million in fiscal 1994, compared with $734 million in fiscal 1993. The increase was primarily due to improved customer reaction to the catalogs and an increase in the number of regular and specialty catalogs mailed from 136 million to 155 million in fiscal 1994. About half of the net sales increase came from the main monthly catalogs and prospector catalogs, principally due to a better customer reaction to these catalogs. Other significant sources of the sales growth were four additional issues of specialty catalogs, the acquisition of a majority interest in The Territory Ahead, a California-based catalog company, and growth in our U.K. subsidiary. Specialty catalogs include the Kids catalog, featuring children's clothing; Coming Home, a catalog focusing on products for bed and bath; Beyond Buttondowns, a men's tailored clothing and accessories catalog; and the new Textures catalog, featuring tailored clothing for women.

Inventory at the end of fiscal 1994 totaled $150 million, a 41 percent increase from fiscal 1993 ending inventory of $106 million. At the end of fiscal 1993, the company had 14 percent lower inventory than at the end of fiscal 1992 when inventory totaled $123 million. The company believes that the fiscal 1993 year-end inventory level was lower than needed to offer the service it attempts to give its customers and contributed to the lower than planned service levels, especially in spring of 1993. For the year, the company was able to ship about 85 percent of items ordered by customers at the time of order placement, compared with 87 percent in fiscal 1993.

Gross profit

Gross profit increased 17 percent from $306 million in fiscal 1993 to $357 million in fiscal 1994, primarily due to the 19 percent increase in consolidated net sales, partially offset by the decrease in the gross profit margin. As a percentage of net sales, gross profit decreased from 41.8 percent in fiscal 1993 to 41.1 percent in fiscal 1994, principally due to lower initial markups and steeper markdowns on liquidated merchandise. This was somewhat offset by a favorable

Management's Discussion and Analysis

mix of full-price sales. Liquidation of out-of-season and overstocked merchandise at reduced prices totaled approximately 10 percent of total net sales in fiscal 1994 compared with 11 percent in fiscal 1993.

Costs on inventory purchases increased approximately 0.8 percent in fiscal 1994, compared with 1.1 percent in fiscal 1993.

Selling, general and administrative expenses
Selling, general and administrative expenses increased 14 percent to $287.0 million from $250.7 million in fiscal 1993, principally due to increases in fixed operating expenses, operating expenses associated with higher sales and increases in catalog mailings.

The SG&A ratio declined from 34.2 percent in fiscal 1993 to 33.0 percent in fiscal 1994. The decrease in the ratio was primarily a result of lower catalog production expenses and relatively higher sales demand generated by the catalogs. This was partially offset by higher variable expenses due to increased package delivery costs and slightly lower first-time fulfillment, as well as somewhat higher fixed expenses. A portion of the shipping cost was offset by an increase in shipping charges to customers.

Historically, the cost of producing and mailing catalogs represents about half of total SG&A. In fiscal 1994, that portion relating to catalogs was lower due to savings in printing and lower paper costs.

Depreciation and amortization expense was up 5 percent from the prior year, to $8.3 million. Rental expense was up 15 percent to $7.3 million, primarily due to increased computer hardware and software rentals.

Interest expense
Interest expense on lines of credit was down in fiscal 1994 due to lower borrowing levels throughout the fiscal year. Inventory carried for the first five months of the year was significantly lower, resulting in less borrowing in the first half of the year. The increased level of profits and cash in the second half of the year held borrowing in check, despite rising inventory levels and capital spending increases. The lines of credit peaked at $54 million in October 1993 compared with a peak of $55 million in the prior year. At January 28, 1994, the company had no short-term debt outstanding and had $40,000 of long-term debt related to the land purchase in Reedsburg, Wisconsin.

Net income
During the first quarter of fiscal 1994, the Company adopted Statement of Financial Accounting Standards No. 109, "Accounting for Income Taxes," which added $1.3 million of net income, or $0.04 per share, to the results in fiscal 1994. Before the cumulative effect of such accounting change, net income in fiscal 1994 rose about 27 percent to $42.4 million, or $1.18 per share, compared with $33.5 million, or $0.92 per share, for the similar period in the prior year.

With the inclusion of the cumulative effect of this accounting change, net income increased 31 percent in fiscal 1994 to $43.7 million, from $33.5 million in fiscal 1993. Earnings per common share increased to $1.22 from $0.92 in the prior year. (All per share amounts have been adjusted to reflect the two-for-one stock split declared in May 1994.)

The Christmas season is our busiest

The company's business is highly seasonal. The fall/winter season, which the company regards as a five-month period ending in December, includes the peak selling season during the Thanksgiving and Christmas holidays in the company's fourth quarter. In the longer spring/summer season, orders are fewer and the merchandise offered generally has lower unit selling prices than products offered in the fall/winter season. As a result, net sales are usually substantially greater in the fall/winter season and SG&A as a percentage of net sales is usually higher in the spring/summer season. In addition, as the company continues to refine its marketing efforts by experimenting with the timing of its catalog mailings, quarterly results may fluctuate.

Nearly 40 percent of our annual sales and over 60 percent of our before-tax profit came in the final three months (November, December and January) of fiscal years 1995 and 1994.

Management's Discussion and Analysis

Liquidity and capital resources

To date, the bulk of the company's working capital needs have been met through funds generated from operations and from short-term bank loans. The company's principal need for working capital has been to meet peak inventory requirements associated with its seasonal sales pattern. In addition, the company's resources have been used to make asset additions, purchase treasury stock, pay cash dividends to shareholders, and acquire new businesses.

During fiscal 1995, the board of directors evaluated its dividend practice whereby it had paid an annual dividend of 20 cents per share (10 cents post-split) for the past seven years. In light of the company's intent to buy back additional shares, the board determined that the current practice was no longer desirable and payment of a cash dividend is not planned for the foreseeable future.

The company continues to explore investment opportunities arising from the expansion of its international businesses, the development of new businesses and the acquisition of existing businesses. While this investment spending has had a negative impact on earnings, it is not expected to have a material effect on liquidity.

At January 27, 1995, the company had unsecured domestic credit facilities totaling $110 million, all of which was unused. The company also maintains foreign credit lines for use in foreign operations totaling the equivalent of approximately $20 million, of which $7.5 million was used at January 27, 1995. The company has a separate $20 million bank facility available to fund treasury stock purchases and capital expenditures. This facility runs through December 31, 1995.

Since June 1989, the company's board of directors has authorized the company from time to time to purchase a total of 8.2 million shares of treasury stock, of which 6.2 million shares have been purchased as of January 27, 1995. The company purchased 1.4 million shares (reflecting the two-for-one stock split) of treasury stock in fiscal year ended January 27, 1995. On a pre-split basis, the company purchased 0.1 million and 0.7 million shares of treasury stock in fiscal years ended January 28, 1994, and January 29, 1993, respectively. The total cost of the purchases was $28.0 million, $2.9 million and $21.0 million for fiscal 1995, 1994 and 1993, respectively.

Capital investment

Capital investment was about $27 million in fiscal 1995. Major projects included construction of a second distribution center in Reedsburg, Wisconsin, new computer hardware and software, and material handling equipment.

In the coming year, we plan to invest about $28 million in capital improvements. Major projects will include new computer hardware and software, initial construction of a new office building in Dodgeville, Wisconsin, and material handling equipment. We believe our cash flow from operations and borrowings under our credit facilities will provide adequate resources to meet our capital requirements and operational needs for the foreseeable future.

Catalog mailing costs and paper prices will rise in fiscal 1996

Effective January 1995, United States Postal Service third-class mailing rates increased 14 percent for third-class mailings, which is the rate assigned for the company's catalog mailings. In addition, beginning in late 1994, paper prices have also risen. At this point, the company can not determine the exact increase for fiscal 1996, but estimates that the total increase in paper prices for the full fiscal year will be in excess of 25 percent. The company expects the increases in postage and paper prices will add at least $15 million to our cost of printing, producing and mailing catalogs to our customers.

While many of these increases will have to be absorbed as a rise in the cost of doing business, the company is evaluating various ways to reduce the impact of these increased costs. The company believes it will be difficult to make changes significant enough to fully offset these expenses.

Possible future changes

Congress has from time to time considered proposals that would require mail order companies to collect and remit sales and use tax in states where the company does not have a physical presence. As it is anticipated that the change, if adopted, will be applied prospectively, the company believes there would be no material impact on financial results.

Consolidated Statements of Operations

(In thousands, except per share data)	For the period ended		
	January 27, 1995	January 28, 1994	January 29, 1993
Net sales	$992,106	$869,975	$733,623
Cost of sales	568,634	512,521	427,292
Gross profit	423,472	357,454	306,331
Selling, general and administrative expenses	360,147	287,044	250,737
Reserve for anticipated sale of subsidiary	3,500	–	–
Income from operations	59,825	70,410	55,594
Other income (expense):			
Interest expense	(1,769)	(359)	(1,330)
Interest income	307	346	266
Other	1,300	(527)	(497)
Total other expense, net	(162)	(540)	(1,561)
Income before income taxes and cumulative effect of change in accounting	59,663	69,870	54,033
Income tax provision	23,567	27,441	20,533
Net income before cumulative effect of change in accounting	36,096	42,429	33,500
Cumulative effect of change in accounting for income taxes	–	1,300	–
Net income	$ 36,096	$ 43,729	$ 33,500
Net income per share before cumulative effect of change in accounting	$ 1.03	$ 1.18	$ 0.92
Cumulative effect of change in accounting	–	0.04	–
Net income per share	$ 1.03	$ 1.22	$ 0.92

The accompanying notes to consolidated financial statements are an integral part of these consolidated statements.

Consolidated Balance Sheets

(In thousands)	January 27, 1995	January 28, 1994
Assets		
Current assets:		
Cash and cash equivalents	$ 5,426	$ 21,569
Receivables	4,459	3,644
Inventory	168,652	149,688
Prepaid expenses	11,219	11,787
Deferred income tax benefit	8,412	5,588
Total current assets	198,168	192,276
Property, plant and equipment, at cost:		
Land and buildings	69,798	60,866
Fixtures and equipment	74,745	57,769
Leasehold improvements	1,862	1,346
Total property, plant and equipment	146,405	119,981
Less–accumulated depreciation and amortization	49,414	40,290
Property, plant and equipment, net	96,991	79,691
Intangibles, net	2,453	1,863
Total assets	$297,612	$273,830
Liabilities and shareholders' investment		
Current liabilities:		
Lines of credit	$ 7,539	$ —
Current maturities of long-term debt	40	40
Accounts payable	52,762	54,855
Reserve for returns	5,011	3,907
Accrued liabilities	25,952	17,443
Accrued profit sharing	1,679	2,276
Income taxes payable	9,727	12,528
Total current liabilities	102,710	91,049
Long-term debt, less current maturities	—	40
Deferred income taxes	5,379	5,200
Long-term liabilities	395	256
Shareholders' investment:		
Common stock, 40,221 and 20,110 shares issued, respectively	402	201
Donated capital	8,400	8,400
Paid-in capital	25,817	24,888
Deferred compensation	(1,421)	(2,001)
Currency translation adjustments	284	246
Retained earnings	229,554	193,460
Treasury stock, 5,395 and 2,154 shares at cost, respectively	(73,908)	(47,909)
Total shareholders' investment	189,128	177,285
Total liabilities and shareholders' investment	$297,612	$273,830

The accompanying notes to consolidated financial statements are an integral part of these consolidated balance sheets.

Consolidated Statements of Shareholders' Investment

	For the period ended		
(In thousands)	January 27, 1995	January 28, 1994	January 29, 1993
Common Stock			
Beginning balance	$ 201	$ 201	$ 201
Two-for-one stock split	201	–	–
Ending balance	$ 402	$ 201	$ 201
Donated Capital Balance	$ 8,400	$ 8,400	$ 8,400
Paid-in Capital			
Beginning balance	$ 24,888	$ 24,857	$ 23,782
Tax benefit of stock options exercised	1,130	31	1,075
Two-for-one stock split	(201)	–	–
Ending balance	$ 25,817	$ 24,888	$ 24,857
Deferred Compensation			
Beginning balance	$ (2,001)	$ (1,680)	$ (886)
Issuance of treasury stock	–	(564)	(985)
Amortization of deferred compensation	580	243	191
Ending balance	$ (1,421)	$ (2,001)	$ (1,680)
Foreign Currency Translation			
Beginning balance	$ 246	$ –	$ –
Adjustment for the year	38	246	–
Ending balance	$ 284	$ 246	$ –
Retained Earnings			
Beginning balance	$193,460	$153,324	$123,418
Net income	36,096	43,729	33,500
Cash dividends paid	–	(3,592)	(3,589)
Issuance of treasury stock	(2)	(1)	(5)
Ending balance	$229,554	$193,460	$153,324
Treasury Stock			
Beginning balance	$ (47,909)	$ (45,714)	$ (28,283)
Purchase of treasury stock	(27,979)	(2,861)	(20,972)
Issuance of treasury stock	1,980	666	3,541
Ending balance	$ (73,908)	$ (47,909)	$ (45,714)
Total Stockholders' Equity	$189,128	$177,285	$139,388

The accompanying notes to consolidated financial statements are an integral part of these consolidated statements.

Consolidated Statements of Cash Flows

(In thousands)	For the period ended		
	January 27, 1995	January 28, 1994	January 29, 1993
Cash flows (used for) from operating activities:			
Net income before cumulative effect of change in accounting	**$ 36,096**	$ 42,429	$ 33,500
Adjustments to reconcile net income to net cash flows from operating activities–			
Depreciation and amortization	**10,311**	8,286	7,900
Deferred compensation expense	**580**	243	191
Deferred income taxes	**(2,645)**	(1,684)	(612)
Loss on sales of fixed assets	**145**	684	931
Changes in current assets and liabilities excluding the effects of acquisitions:			
Receivables	**(264)**	(3,179)	365
Inventory	**(16,544)**	(41,769)	16,501
Prepaid expenses	**597**	(5,715)	999
Accounts payable	**(2,093)**	16,765	8,625
Reserve for returns	**1,104**	(98)	552
Accrued liabilities	**8,509**	3,701	(260)
Accrued profit sharing	**(597)**	642	400
Income taxes payable	**(2,801)**	1,570	(1,868)
Other	**177**	502	–
Net cash flows from operating activities	**32,575**	22,377	67,224
Cash flows (used for) from investing activities:			
Cash paid for capital additions and businesses acquired	**(31,365)**	(17,392)	(8,591)
Proceeds from sales of fixed assets	**19**	71	15
Net cash flows used for investing activities	**(31,346)**	(17,321)	(8,576)
Cash flows (used for) from financing activities:			
Proceeds from short-term and long-term debt	**7,539**	80	–
Payment of short-term and long-term debt	**(40)**	–	(16,349)
Tax effect of exercise of stock options	**1,130**	31	1,075
Purchases of treasury stock	**(27,979)**	(2,861)	(20,972)
Issuance of treasury stock	**1,978**	101	2,551
Cash dividends paid to common shareholders	**–**	(3,592)	(3,589)
Net cash flows used for financing activities	**(17,372)**	(6,241)	(37,284)
Net increase (decrease) in cash and cash equivalents	**(16,143)**	(1,185)	21,364
Beginning cash and cash equivalents	**21,569**	22,754	1,390
Ending cash and cash equivalents	**$ 5,426**	$ 21,569	$ 22,754
Supplemental cash flow disclosures:			
Interest paid	**$ 2,828**	$ 364	$ 1,315
Income taxes paid	**27,595**	27,475	21,905

The accompanying notes to consolidated financial statements are an integral part of these consolidated statements.

Notes to Consolidated Financial Statements

Note 1. Summary of significant accounting policies

Nature of business

Lands' End, Inc., (the company) is a direct marketer of traditionally styled apparel, domestics (primarily bedding and bath items), soft luggage, and other products.

Principles of consolidation

The consolidated financial statements include the accounts of the company and its subsidiaries after elimination of intercompany accounts and transactions.

Year-end

The company's fiscal year is comprised of 52–53 weeks ending on the Friday closest to January 31. Fiscal 1995 ended on January 27, 1995, fiscal 1994 ended on January 28, 1994, and fiscal 1993 ended on January 29, 1993. Fiscal 1996 will be a 53-week year ending on February 2, 1996. The additional week will be added in the fourth quarter of fiscal 1996.

Fair values of financial instruments

The fair value of financial instruments does not materially differ from their carrying values.

Inventory

Inventory, primarily merchandise held for sale, is stated at last-in, first-out (LIFO) cost, which is lower than market. If the first-in, first-out (FIFO) method of accounting for inventory had been used, inventory would have been approximately $18.9 million and $19.1 million higher than reported at January 27, 1995, and January 28, 1994, respectively.

Catalog costs

Prepaid expenses primarily consist of catalog production and mailing costs that have not yet been fully amortized over the expected revenue stream, which is approximately three months from the date catalogs are mailed. The company's reporting of such advertising costs is in conformance with the provisions of the AICPA Statement of Position No. 93-7, "Reporting on Advertising Costs," which will become effective for the company in fiscal 1996.

Depreciation and amortization

Depreciation expense is calculated using the straight-line method over the estimated useful lives of the assets, which are 20 to 30 years for buildings and land improvements and 5 to 10 years for leasehold improvements and furniture, fixtures, equipment, and software. The company provides one-half year of depreciation in the year of addition and retirement.

Intangibles

Intangible assets consist primarily of goodwill, the excess of cost over the fair market value of net assets of a business purchased. Goodwill is being amortized over 40 years on a straight-line basis. Other intangibles are amortized over a shorter life. Total accumulated amortization of these intangibles was $0.3 million and $0.1 million at January 27, 1995, and January 28, 1994, respectively.

Net income per share

Net income per share is computed by dividing net income by the weighted average number of common shares outstanding during each period. After the two-for-one stock split, the weighted average common shares outstanding were 35.2 million, 35.9 million and 36.3 million (See Note 2) for fiscal years 1995, 1994 and 1993, respectively. Common stock equivalents include awards, grants and stock options issued by the company. The common stock equivalents do not significantly dilute basic earnings per share.

Reserve for losses on customer returns

At the time of sale, the company provides a reserve equal to the gross profit on projected merchandise returns, based on its prior returns experience.

Financial instruments with off-balance-sheet risk

The company is party to financial instruments with off-balance-sheet risk in the normal course of business to reduce its exposure to fluctuations in foreign currency exchange rates and to meet financing needs.

The company enters into forward exchange contracts to hedge anticipated foreign currency transactions during the upcoming seasons. The purpose of the company's foreign currency hedging activities is to protect the company from the risk that the eventual dollar cash flows resulting from these transactions will be adversely affected by changes in exchange rates. At January 27, 1995, the company had forward exchange contracts, maturing through January 1996, to sell approximately 243.1 million yen and to purchase approximately 119.1 million yen and 5.0 million Canadian dollars. There were no material deferred gains or losses related to the outstanding forward exchange contracts as of January 27, 1995.

Notes to Consolidated Financial Statements

The company also uses import letters of credit to purchase foreign-sourced merchandise. The letters of credit are primarily U.S. dollar-denominated and are issued through third-party financial institutions to guarantee payment for such merchandise within agreed upon time periods. At January 27, 1995, the company had outstanding letters of credit of approximately $18.9 million, all of which had expiration dates of less than 1 year.

The counterparty to the financial instruments discussed above is primarily one large financial institution; management believes the risk of counterparty nonperformance on these financial instruments is not significant.

Foreign currency translation
Financial statements of the foreign subsidiaries are translated into U.S. dollars in accordance with the provisions of Statement of Financial Accounting Standards (SFAS) No. 52. Foreign currency transaction gains were $0.8 million in fiscal 1995. Foreign currency gains and losses for fiscal 1994 and fiscal 1993 were not material.

Postretirement benefits
The company does not currently provide any postretirement benefits for employees other than profit sharing.

Reclassifications
Certain financial statement amounts have been reclassified to be consistent with the fiscal 1995 presentation.

Note 2. Shareholders' investment

Two-for-one stock split
In May 1994, the company declared a two-for-one split (effected as a stock dividend) in the company's common stock. The stock split resulted in an increase in the stated capital of the company from $201,103 to $402,206 with a corresponding reduction in paid-in capital. This has been reflected retroactively in the earnings per share calculations presented.

Capital stock
Pursuant to shareholder approval in May 1994, the company increased its authorized common stock from 30 million shares of $0.01 par value common stock to 160 million shares. Also, the company is authorized to issue 5 million shares of preferred stock, $0.01 par value. The company's board of directors has the authority to issue shares and to fix dividend, voting and conversion rights, redemption provisions, liquidation preferences, and other rights and restrictions of the preferred stock.

Treasury stock
In May 1994, the company's board of directors authorized the additional purchase of 1.0 million shares of the company's common stock, increasing the total shares that have been authorized for purchase since June 1989 from 3.1 million to 4.1 million. After the two-for-one stock split, this number increased from 4.1 million shares to 8.2 million. After the effect of the stock split a total of 6.2 million, 4.8 million and 4.6 million shares had been purchased as of January 27, 1995, January 28, 1994, and January 29, 1993, respectively.

Treasury stock summary:

For the period ended	January 27, 1995	January 28, 1994	January 29, 1993
Beginning balance	2,154,235	2,082,035	1,638,840
Two-for-one stock split	2,154,235		
Purchase of stock	1,380,502	89,800	680,195
Issuance of stock	(294,000)	(17,600)	(237,000)
Ending balance	5,394,972	2,154,235	2,082,035

Stock awards and grants
The shareholders of the company have approved the company's restricted stock award plan. Under the provisions of the plan, a committee of the company's board of directors may award shares of the company's common stock to its officers and key employees. Such shares vest over a ten-year period on a straight-line basis from the date of the award.

In addition, the company granted shares of its common stock to individuals as an inducement to enter the employ of the company.

After the effect of the two-for-one stock split, the following table reflects the activity under the stock award and stock grant plans:

	Awards	Grants
Balance at January 31, 1992	97,120	22,000
Prior years vested	(9,800)	(8,000)
Adjusted balance at January 31, 1992	87,320	14,000
Granted	74,000	–
Forfeited	–	–
Vested	(20,000)	(2,000)
Balance at January 29, 1993	141,320	12,000
Granted	27,200	–
Forfeited	(3,600)	–
Vested	(15,760)	(2,000)
Balance at January 28, 1994	149,160	10,000
Granted	–	–
Forfeited	(15,940)	(10,000)
Vested	(17,860)	–
Balance at January 27, 1995	115,360	–

Notes to Consolidated Financial Statements

The granting of these awards and grants has been recorded as deferred compensation based on the fair market value of the shares at the date of grant. Compensation expense under these plans is recorded as shares vest.

Stock options

Pursuant to shareholder approval in May 1994, the company increased from 1.00 million to 1.25 million the number of shares of common stock, either authorized and unissued shares or treasury shares, that may be issued pursuant to the exercise of options granted under the company's stock option plan. After the two-for-one stock split, the shares increased from 1.25 million to 2.50 million. Options are granted at the discretion of a committee of the company's board of directors to officers and key employees of the company. No option may have an exercise price less than the fair market value per share of the common stock at the date of grant.

After the effect of the two-for-one stock split, activity under the stock option plan is as follows:

	Options	Average Exercise Price	Vested Options
Balance at January 31, 1992	1,380,000	$ 8.57	180,000
Granted	80,000	$13.96	
Exercised	(400,000)	$ 6.38	
Balance at January 29, 1993	1,060,000	$ 9.81	216,000
Granted	637,200	$19.12	
Exercised	(8,000)	$12.69	
Balance at January 28, 1994	1,689,200	$13.31	340,000
Granted	–	–	
Exercised	(294,000)	$ 6.72	
Forfeited	(928,800)	$15.27	
Balance at January 27, 1995	466,400	$13.56	195,480

The above options currently outstanding vest over a five-year period from the date of grant. The outstanding options expire as follows:

2000	100,000
2001	72,000
2002	60,000
2003	234,400
	466,400

Note 3. Income taxes

Effective January 30, 1993, the company adopted SFAS No. 109, "Accounting for Income Taxes." The cumulative effect of adopting the standard was recorded as a change in accounting principle in the first quarter of fiscal 1994 with an increase to net income of $1.3 million or $0.04 per common share.

The components of the provision for income taxes for each of the periods presented are as follows (in thousands):

Period ended	January 27, 1995	January 28, 1994	January 29, 1993
Current:			
Federal	$22,154	$24,607	$17,800
State	4,058	4,518	3,345
Deferred	(2,645)	(1,684)	(612)
	$23,567	$27,441	$20,533

The difference between income taxes at the statutory federal income tax rate of 35 percent for fiscal 1995 and fiscal 1994 and 34 percent for fiscal 1993 and income tax reported in the statements of operations is as follows (in thousands):

Period ended	January 27, 1995	January 28, 1994	January 29, 1993
Tax at statutory federal tax rate	$20,882	$24,421	$18,371
State income taxes, net of federal benefit	2,156	2,818	2,043
Future tax benefits not recognized under SFAS No. 96	–	–	67
Other	529	202	52
	$23,567	$27,441	$20,533

Notes to Consolidated Financial Statements

Temporary differences that give rise to deferred tax assets and liabilities as of January 27, 1995, and January 28, 1994, are as follows (in thousands):

	Current Deferred Tax Benefit		Long-term Deferred Tax Liabilities	
	Jan. 27, 1995	Jan. 28, 1994	Jan. 27, 1995	Jan. 28, 1994
Catalog advertising	$(1,539)	$(1,988)	$ –	$ –
Inventory	7,052	5,585	–	–
Employee benefits	1,243	673	–	–
Reserve for returns	1,406	482	–	–
Depreciation	–	–	5,379	5,200
Foreign operating loss carryforwards	–	–	(807)	(933)
Valuation allowance	–	–	807	933
Other	250	836	–	–
Total	$ 8,412	$ 5,588	$ 5,379	$ 5,200

The valuation allowance required under SFAS No. 109 has been established for the deferred income tax benefits related to certain subsidiary loss carryforwards, which may not be realized.

Prior to January 30, 1993, the company followed the provisions of SFAS No. 96, "Accounting for Income Taxes." The components of the deferred tax provision are as follows (in thousands):

Period ended	January 29, 1993
Depreciation	$(255)
Inventory	(255)
Other	(102)
Deferred tax provision	$(612)

Note 4. Lines of credit

The company has unsecured domestic lines of credit with various banks totaling $110 million. There were no amounts outstanding at January 27, 1995 and January 28, 1994.

In addition, the company has unsecured lines of credit with foreign banks totaling the equivalent of $20 million for a wholly-owned foreign subsidiary. There was $7.5 million outstanding at January 27, 1995, at interest rates averaging 3.0 percent.

Note 5. Long-term debt

There was no long-term debt as of January 27, 1995, compared to $40,000 outstanding as of January 28, 1994.

The company has an agreement that expires December 31, 1995, with a bank for a $20 million credit facility available to fund treasury stock purchases and capital expenditures. The company is currently in compliance with all lending conditions and covenants related to this debt facility.

Note 6. Leases

The company leases store and office space and equipment under various leasing arrangements. The leases are accounted for as operating leases. Total rental expense under these leases was $8.6 million, $7.3 million and $6.3 million for the years ended January 27, 1995, January 28, 1994, and January 29, 1993, respectively.

Total future fiscal year commitments under these leases as of January 27, 1995, are as follows (in thousands):

1996	$ 8,842
1997	7,870
1998	5,545
1999	3,557
2000	2,613
After 2000	3,773
	$32,200

Note 7. Retirement plan

The company has a retirement plan that covers most regular employees and provides for annual contributions at the discretion of the board of directors. Also included in the plan is a 401(k) feature that allows employees to make contributions and the company matches a portion of those contributions. Total expense provided under this plan was $3.5 million, $3.7 million and $1.6 million for the years ended January 27, 1995, January 28, 1994, and January 29, 1993, respectively.

Notes to Consolidated Financial Statements

Note 8. Acquisitions and anticipated disposition

In July 1994, the company formed a wholly-owned subsidiary that acquired the marketing rights and assets of MontBell America, Inc., which designs, develops and distributes premier technical outdoor clothing and equipment through the wholesale channel to outdoor specialty stores, primarily in the United States.

In February 1995, the company announced its intention to sell its wholly-owned subsidiary MontBell America, Inc. The financial statements reflect an after-tax charge of $2.1 million as of January 27, 1995.

In March 1993, the company purchased a majority interest in a catalog company, The Territory Ahead. Merchandise offered in the catalog consists of private label sportswear, accessories and luggage. Beginning in 2003, the minority shareholders have the option to require the company to purchase their shares, and the company will have the option to require the minority shareholders to sell their shares in The Territory Ahead. The price per share would be based on the fair market value of The Territory Ahead.

Results of operations of MontBell America, Inc., and The Territory Ahead were not material to the company, and as a result, no pro forma data is presented. The transactions were accounted for using the purchase method. The excess of the purchase price over the fair value of net assets was recorded as goodwill. The operating results of MontBell America, Inc., and The Territory Ahead are included in the consolidated financial statements of the company from their respective dates of acquisition.

Note 9. Consolidated Quarterly Analysis (unaudited)

(In thousands, except per share data)	Fiscal 1995				Fiscal 1994			
	1st Qtr.	2nd Qtr.	3rd Qtr.	4th Qtr.	1st Qtr.	2nd Qtr.	3rd Qtr.	4th Qtr.
Net sales	$187,012	$179,833	$246,209	$379,052	$156,256	$151,076	$215,133	$347,510
Gross profit	79,718	77,324	100,176	166,254	64,173	62,686	87,513	143,082
Pretax income	8,058	5,651	6,331	39,623	6,857	5,918	13,117	43,978
Net income before cumulative effect of change in accounting	4,878	3,413	3,833	23,972	4,250	3,554	7,976	26,649
Net income per share before cumulative effect of change in accounting	$ 0.14	$ 0.10	$ 0.11	$ 0.69	$ 0.12	$ 0.10	$ 0.22	$ 0.74
Net income	$ 4,878	$ 3,413	$ 3,833	$ 23,972	$ 5,550	$ 3,554	$ 7,976	$ 26,649
Net income per share	$ 0.14	$ 0.10	$ 0.11	$ 0.69	$ 0.16	$ 0.10	$ 0.22	$ 0.74
Cash dividends	–	–	–	–	–	–	–	$ 3,592
Cash dividends per share	–	–	–	–	–	–	–	$ 0.10
Common shares outstanding	35,791	34,893	34,879	34,875	35,954	35,924	35,922	35,912
Market price of shares outstanding:								
market high	27¾	24¹⁄₁₆	20½	19	14¹⁵⁄₁₆	16¼	22¼	24⅞
market low	22⅝	17⅜	16⅞	13	11⅝	13½	14⁹⁄₁₆	20½

*Responsibility for Consolidated
Financial Statements*

*Report of Independent
Public Accountants*

The management of Lands' End, Inc. and its subsidiaries has the responsibility for preparing the accompanying financial statements and for their integrity and objectivity. The statements were prepared in accordance with generally accepted accounting principles applied on a consistent basis. The consolidated financial statements include amounts that are based on management's best estimates and judgments. Management also prepared the other information in the annual report and is responsible for its accuracy and consistency with the consolidated financial statements.

The company's consolidated financial statements have been audited by Arthur Andersen LLP, independent certified public accountants. Management has made available to Arthur Andersen LLP all the company's financial records and related data, as well as the minutes of stockholders' and directors' meetings. Furthermore, management believes that all representations made to Arthur Andersen LLP during its audit were valid and appropriate.

Management of the company has established and maintains a system of internal control that provides for appropriate division of responsibility, reasonable assurance as to the integrity and reliability of the consolidated financial statements, the protection of assets from unauthorized use or disposition, the prevention and detection of fraudulent financial reporting, and the maintenance of an active program of internal audits. Management believes that, as of January 27, 1995, the company's system of internal control is adequate to accomplish the objectives discussed herein.

Two directors of the company, not members of management, serve as the audit committee of the board of directors and are the principal means through which the board supervises the performance of the financial reporting duties of management. The audit committee meets with management, the internal audit staff and the company's independent auditors to review the results of the audits of the company and to discuss plans for future audits. At these meetings, the audit committee also meets privately with the internal audit staff and the independent auditors to assure its free access to them.

Michael J. Smith
Chief Executive Officer

Stephen A. Orum
Chief Financial Officer

*To the Board of Directors and Shareholders of
Lands' End, Inc.:*

We have audited the accompanying consolidated balance sheets of LANDS' END, INC. (a Delaware corporation) and its subsidiaries as of January 27, 1995, and January 28, 1994, and the related consolidated statements of operations, shareholders' investment and cash flows for each of the three years in the period ended January 27, 1995. These financial statements are the responsibility of the company's management. Our responsibility is to express an opinion on these financial statements based on our audits.

We conducted our audits in accordance with generally accepted auditing standards. Those standards require that we plan and perform the audit to obtain reasonable assurance about whether the financial statements are free of material misstatement. An audit includes examining, on a test basis, evidence supporting the amounts and disclosures in the financial statements. An audit also includes assessing the accounting principles used and significant estimates made by management, as well as evaluating the overall financial statement presentation. We believe that our audits provide a reasonable basis for our opinion.

In our opinion, the financial statements referred to above present fairly, in all material respects, the financial position of Lands' End, Inc. and subsidiaries as of January 27, 1995, and January 28, 1994, and the results of their operations and their cash flows for each of the three years in the period ended January 27, 1995, in conformity with generally accepted accounting principles.

As explained in the notes to the consolidated financial statements, effective January 30, 1993, the company changed its method of accounting for income taxes.

Arthur Andersen LLP

Arthur Andersen LLP
Milwaukee, Wisconsin
March 3, 1995

Ten-Year Consolidated Financial Summary (unaudited)

The following selected financial data have been derived from the company's consolidated financial statements, which, except pro forma amounts, have been audited by Arthur Andersen LLP, independent public accountants. The information set forth below should be read in conjunction with "Management's Discussion and Analysis" and the consolidated financial statements and notes thereto included elsewhere herein.

(In thousands, except per share data)	1995	1994[2]	1993
Income statement data:			
Net sales	$992,106	$869,975	$733,623
Pretax income	59,663	69,870	54,033
Percent to net sales	6.0%	8.0%	7.4%
Net income before cumulative effect of change in accounting	36,096	42,429	33,500
Cumulative effect of change in accounting	–	1,300	–
Net income	36,096	43,729	33,500
Net income (pro forma for 1986 and 1987)	36,096	43,729	33,500
Per share of common stock:[1]			
Net income per share before cumulative effect of change in accounting	$ 1.03	$ 1.18	$ 0.92
Cumulative effect of change in accounting	–	0.04	–
Net income per share	$ 1.03	$ 1.22	$ 0.92
Cash dividends per share	–	$ 0.10	$ 0.10
Common shares outstanding	34,826	35,912	36,056
Balance sheet data:			
Current assets	$198,168	$192,276	$137,531
Current liabilities	102,710	91,049	67,315
Property, plant, equipment and intangibles, net	99,444	81,554	74,272
Total assets	297,612	273,830	211,803
Noncurrent liabilities	5,774	5,496	5,100
Shareholders' investment	189,128	177,285	139,388
Other data:			
Net working capital	$ 95,458	$101,227	$ 70,216
Capital expenditures	27,005	16,958	9,965
Depreciation and amortization expense	10,311	8,286	7,900
Return on average shareholder's investment	20%	28%	25%
Return on average assets	13%	18%	16%
Debt/equity ratio	–	–	–

(1) Net income per share (pro forma for 1986 and 1987) was computed after giving retroactive effect to the 108-for-one stock split in August 1986, the two-for-one stock split in August 1987, the two-for-one stock split in May 1994, and assuming the shares sold in the October 1986 initial public offering were issued at the beginning of fiscal 1986.

(2) Effective January 30, 1993, the Company adopted Statement of Financial Accounting Standards (SFAS) No. 109, "Accounting for Income Taxes," which was recorded as a change in accounting principle at the beginning of fiscal 1994 with an increase to net income of $1.3 million or $0.04 per share.

	Fiscal year						
	1992	1991	1990	1989	1988[3]	1987[4]	1986
	$683,427	$601,991	$544,850	$454,644	$335,740	$264,896	$226,575
	47,492	24,943	47,270	52,142	38,328	28,486	21,584
	7.0%	4.1%	8.7%	11.4%	11.4%	10.7%	9.5%
	28,732	14,743	29,071	32,282	22,120	18,650	21,584
	–	–	–	–	685	–	–
	28,732	14,743	29,071	32,282	22,805	18,650	21,584
	28,732	14,743	29,071	32,282	22,805	14,605	11,270
	$ 0.77	$ 0.38	$ 0.73	$ 0.81	$ 0.56	$ 0.37	$ 0.28
	–	–	–	–	0.01	–	–
	$ 0.77	$ 0.38	$ 0.73	$ 0.81	$ 0.57	$ 0.37	$ 0.28
	$ 0.10	$ 0.10	$ 0.10	$ 0.10	$ 0.10	–	–
	36,944	38,436	39,762	40,080	40,080	40,080	39,920
	$131,273	$107,824	$ 99,714	$103,681	$ 78,256	$ 57,660	$ 35,687
	74,548	60,774	43,915	51,530	38,860	32,920	18,002
	74,527	77,576	67,218	47,471	28,723	26,822	19,841
	205,800	185,400	166,932	151,152	106,979	84,482	55,528
	4,620	7,800	8,413	7,674	11,445	13,685	10,321
	126,632	116,826	114,604	91,948	56,674	37,877	27,205
	$ 56,725	$ 47,050	$ 55,799	$ 52,151	$ 39,396	$ 24,740	$ 17,685
	5,347	17,682	25,160	15,872	5,862	9,603	6,483
	7,428	7,041	5,251	3,916	3,185	2,576	1,867
	23%	13%	28%	43%	48%	45%	48%
	15%	8%	18%	25%	24%	21%	22%
	1%	3%	4%	7%	15%	28%	38%

(3) In the fourth quarter of fiscal 1988, the company elected early adoption of the provisions of SFAS No. 96, "Accounting for Income Taxes," as recommended by the Financial Accounting Standards Board. The effect of the change for the year was to increase net income $715,000 including the cumulative effect of $685,000 or $0.01 per common share which was reflected in the first quarter.

(4) The company has been subject to corporate income taxes since October 6, 1986. For earlier periods shown, the company elected to be treated as an S Corporation and accordingly was not subject to corporate income taxes. The net income and net income per share for such periods reflect a pro forma tax provision as if the company had been subject to corporate income taxes.

Comprehensive List of Accounts Used in Exercises and Problems

Current Assets

101	Cash
102	Petty cash
103	Cash equivalents
104	Short-term investments
105	Short-term investments, fair value adjustment
106	Accounts receivable
107	Allowance for doubtful accounts
108	Legal fees receivable
109	Interest receivable
110	Rent receivable
111	Notes receivable
115	Subscriptions receivable, common stock
116	Subscriptions receivable, preferred stock
119	Merchandise inventory
120	_____ inventory
121	_____ inventory
124	Office supplies
125	Store supplies
126	_____ supplies
128	Prepaid insurance
129	Prepaid interest
131	Prepaid rent

Long-Term Investments

141	Investment in _____ stock
142	Investment in _____ bonds
143	Long-term investments, fair value adjustment
144	Investment in _____
145	Bond sinking fund

Plant Assets

151	Automobiles
152	Accumulated depreciation, automobiles
153	Trucks
154	Accumulated depreciation, trucks
155	Boats
156	Accumulated depreciation, boats
157	Professional library
158	Accumulated depreciation, professional library
159	Law library
160	Accumulated depreciation, law library
161	Furniture
162	Accumulated depreciation, furniture
163	Office equipment
164	Accumulated depreciation, office equipment
165	Store equipment
166	Accumulated depreciation, store equipment
167	_____ equipment
168	Accumulated depreciation, _____ equipment
169	Machinery
170	Accumulated depreciation, machinery
173	Building _____
174	Accumulated depreciation, building _____
175	Building _____
176	Accumulated depreciation, building _____
179	Land improvements _____
180	Accumulated depreciation, land improvements _____
181	Land improvements _____
182	Accumulated depreciation, land improvements _____
183	Land

Natural Resources

185   Mineral deposit
186   Accumulated depletion, mineral deposit

Intangible Assets

191   Patents
192   Leasehold
193   Franchise
194   Copyrights
195   Leasehold improvements
196   Organization costs

Current Liabilities

201   Accounts payable
202   Insurance payable
203   Interest payable
204   Legal fees payable
207   Office salaries payable
208   Rent payable
209   Salaries payable
210   Wages payable
211   Accrued payroll payable
213   Property taxes payable
214   Estimated warranty liability
215   Income taxes payable
216   Common dividend payable
217   Preferred dividend payable
218   State unemployment taxes payable
219   Employees' federal income taxes payable
221   Employees' medical insurance payable
222   Employees' retirement program payable
223   Employees' union dues payable
224   Federal unemployment taxes payable
225   FICA taxes payable
226   Estimated vacation pay liability

Unearned Revenues

230   Unearned consulting fees
231   Unearned legal fees
232   Unearned property management fees
233   Unearned _____ fees
234   Unearned _____
235   Unearned janitorial revenue
236   Unearned _____ revenue
238   Unearned rent _____

Notes Payable

240   Short-term notes payable
241   Discount on short-term notes payable
245   Notes payable
251   Long-term notes payable
252   Discount on notes payable

Long-Term Liabilities

253   Long-term lease liability
255   Bonds payable
256   Discount on bonds payable
257   Premium on bonds payable
258   Deferred income tax liability

Owners' Equity

301   _____, capital
302   _____, withdrawals
303   _____, capital
304   _____, withdrawals
305   _____, capital
306   _____, withdrawals

Corporate Contributed Capital

307   Common stock, $_____ par value
308   Common stock, no par
309   Common stock subscribed
310   Common stock dividend distributable
311   Contributed capital in excess of par value, common stock
312   Contributed capital in excess of stated value, no-par common stock
313   Contributed capital from the retirement of common stock
314   Contributed capital, treasury stock transactions
315   Preferred stock
316   Contributed capital in excess of par value, preferred stock
317   Preferred stock subscribed

Retained Earnings

318   Retained earnings
319   Cash dividends declared
320   Stock dividends declared

Other Owners' Equity

321   Treasury stock, common
322   Unrealized holding gain (loss)

Revenues

401   _____ fees earned
402   _____ fees earned
403   _____ services revenue
404   _____ services revenue
405   Commissions earned
406   Rent earned
407   Dividends earned
408   Earnings from investment in _____
409   Interest earned
410   Sinking fund earnings
413   Sales
414   Sales discounts
415   Sales returns and allowances

Cost of Goods Sold Items

502   Cost of goods sold

505   Purchases
506   Purchase discounts
507   Purchase returns and allowances
508   Transportation-in

Expenses

Depletion, Amortization, and Depreciation Expenses

601   Amortization expense, _____
602   Amortization expense, _____
603   Depletion expense, _____
604   Depreciation expense, boats
605   Depreciation expense, automobiles
606   Depreciation expense, building _____
607   Depreciation expense, building _____
608   Depreciation expense, land improvements _____
609   Depreciation expense, land improvements _____
610   Depreciation expense, law library
611   Depreciation expense, trucks
612   Depreciation expense, _____ equipment
613   Depreciation expense, _____ equipment
614   Depreciation expense, _____
615   Depreciation expense, _____

Employee Related Expenses

620   Office salaries expense
621   Sales salaries expense
622   Salaries expense
623   _____ wages expense
624   Employees' benefits expense
625   Payroll taxes expense

Financial Expenses

630   Cash over and short
631   Discounts lost
632   Factoring fee expense
633   Interest expense

Insurance Expenses

635   Insurance expense, delivery equipment
636   Insurance expense, office equipment
637   Insurance expense, _____

Rental Expenses

640   Rent expense
641   Rent expense, office space
642   Rent expense, selling space
643   Press rental expense
644   Truck rental expense
645   _____ rental expense

Supplies Expense

650   Office supplies expense
651   Store supplies expense
652   _____ supplies expense
653   _____ supplies expense

Miscellaneous Expenses

655   Advertising expense
656   Bad debts expense
657   Blueprinting expense
658   Boat expense
659   Collection expense
661   Concessions expense
662   Credit card expense
663   Delivery expense
664   Dumping expense
667   Equipment expense
668   Food and drinks expense
669   Gas, oil, and repairs expense
671   Gas and oil expense
672   General and administrative expense
673   Janitorial expense
674   Legal fees expense
676   Mileage expense
677   Miscellaneous expenses
678   Mower and tools expense
679   Operating expense
681   Permits expense
682   Postage expense
683   Property taxes expense
684   Repairs expense, _____
685   Repairs expense, _____
687   Selling expense
688   Telephone expense
689   Travel and entertainment expense
690   Utilities expense
691   Warranty expense
695   Income taxes expense

Gains and Losses

701   Gain on retirement of bonds
702   Gain on sale of machinery
703   Gain on sale of short-term investments
704   Gain on sale of trucks
705   Gain on _____
706   Foreign exchange gain or loss
801   Loss on disposal of machinery
802   Loss on exchange of equipment
803   Loss on exchange of _____
804   Loss on sale of notes
805   Loss on retirement of bonds
806   Loss on sale of investments
807   Loss on sale of machinery
808   Loss on sale of _____
809   Loss on _____

Clearing Accounts

901   Income summary
902   Manufacturing summary

Photo Credits

Chapter 10

Page 345	©Nicholas Communications
Page 346	Courtesy of Sony Electronics Inc.
Page 346	Courtesy of Wendy's International, Inc.
Page 349	Courtesy of Microsoft Corp.
Page 350	Courtesy of Boise Cascade Corporation
Page 352	©Nicholas Communications
Page 358	Courtesy of America West Airlines
Page 360	©Nicholas Communications
Page 364	Courtesy of Rubbermaid Incorporated

Chapter 11

Page 379	THE FAR SIDE ©1985 FARWORKS, INC./Dist. By UNIVERSAL PRESS SYNDICATE. Reprinted with permission. All rights reserved.
Page 380	Courtesy of Aluminum Company of America
Page 381	Courtesy of the Exxon Corporation
Page 381	Photo courtesy of Corning Inc., Corning, NY
Page 384	©Nicholas Communications
Page 392	Courtesy, PepsiCo, Inc. ©1993
Page 395	Courtesy of Reebok International Ltd.
Page 395	Reprinted with permission of NIKE, Inc.

Chapter 12

Page 411	Courtesy of Safeway Inc.
Page 413	©Fotopic: MGA/Photri
Page 413	Courtesy of Safeway, Inc.
Page 417	Courtesy of Ford Motor Company
Page 417	Courtesy of The Clorox Company
Page 433	Courtesy of Federal Express Corporation

Chapter 13

Page 451	Courtesy of L.A. Gear
Page 459	©Nicholas Communications
Page 464	Courtesy of Chiquita Brands International, Inc.

Page 472	©AdPhoto: MGA/Photri, Inc.
Page 473	Photo ©1994 Mattel, Inc. Used with permission.

Chapter 14

Page 487	Courtesy of Mobil Oil Corporation
Page 489	©Nicholas Communications
Page 493	Courtesy of Sara Lee Corporation
Page 500	Courtesy of Pitney Bowes, Inc.

Chapter 15

Page 531	Courtesy of J. Walter Thompson U.S.A., Inc., on behalf of Sprint
Page 538	Photo courtesy of Hewlett-Packard Company
Page 543	Courtesy of International Business Machines Corporation. Unauthorized use not permitted.
Page 545	©Nicholas Communications
Page 545	Courtesy of Chiquita Brands International, Inc.
Page 546	Courtesy of Deere & Company
Page 548	©Albertson's, Inc. 1994. All rights reserved.
Page 552	Courtesy of J.C. Penney Company, Inc.
Page 552	©Richard Alcom/Courtesy of Colgate Palmolive Company

Chapter 16

Page 573	©Photofest
Page 574	Courtesy of R.H. Macy & Company
Page 575	©The New York Times

Chapter 17

Page 611	Courtesy of Microsoft Corp.
Page 613	Courtesy of Microsoft Corp.
Page 615	Courtesy of Microsoft Corp.
Page 618	Courtesy of Microsoft Corp.
Page 623	Courtesy of Microsoft Corp.
Page 625	Courtesy of Microsoft Corp.

Index

ELEMENTS OF DEMOCRATIC GOVERNMENT

Elements of
Democratic Government

FOURTH EDITION,
REVISED AND ENLARGED

J. A. Corry

THE PRINCIPAL
QUEEN'S UNIVERSITY

Henry J. Abraham

PROFESSOR OF POLITICAL SCIENCE
UNIVERSITY OF PENNSYLVANIA

NEW YORK   OXFORD UNIVERSITY PRESS   1964

Preface to the Fourth Edition

The revision presented in this fourth edition follows the general scheme of the third. In addition to necessary updating, approximately 20–25 per cent of the materials of the preceding edition have been thoroughly rewritten. This rewriting for the most part has been occasioned by the advent of the Fifth French Republic; to a lesser extent there have been significant changes in the other Western democracies and in the Soviet Union. Thus several chapters, notably V, VIII, IX, X, XII, XIII, XIV, XV, XVII, and XIX have been extensively revised; two of these have been retitled; several charts and tables have been added. Wherever we thought it appropriate, we adopted pertinent illustrations taken from states other than the ones of main concern in the book—for example, West Germany in connection with federalism and legislatures. But we have not been current at the expense of depth. Acting upon several suggestions, we have appended the constitutions of the United States, France, and the Soviet Union. In addition to the basic bibliography at the end of the book, lists of suggested references for further reading now follow each chapter.

Once again we wish to express our appreciation to the many colleagues whose helpful suggestions have done so much to make this a better book. In particular, we wish to thank Professor Benjamin E. Lippincott of the University of Minnesota, Professor Charles A. McCoy of Temple University, Professors Philip E. Jacob, Jewell Cass Phillips, and Alvin Z. Rubinstein of the University of Pennsylvania, Professor Garold W. Thumm of Bates College, and Professor Clifton E. Wilson of the University of Arizona. Mrs. Helen S. White typed the manuscript with her usual patience and competence, and our research assistants, Peter B. Harkins, Rocco D'Amico, and Andrea Pilch were always cheerfully helpful. The authors, of course, assume full responsibility for all deficiencies.

Kingston, Ontario   J. A. CORRY
Wynnewood, Pennsylvania   HENRY J. ABRAHAM
December 1963

Preface to the Third Edition

This book expresses the views of two teachers on the way to begin the study of government with students who are—or should be—seriously concerned about liberal democracy. At the beginning, the basic political ideals of liberal democracy and of the modern dictatorships are sketched and contrasted. Thereafter, the bulk of the book is taken up with an elementary description and comparison of the structure and working of government in the United States and Great Britain. Wherever reference to the government and politics of France seems likely to sharpen appreciation of American and British political institutions or to throw light on the fundamental problems of liberal democracy, the relevant features of French government and politics are introduced.

As the institutions and practices of these three leading democracies are described chapter by chapter, their relation to the essential activating ideals is discussed and some analysis of the problem of harmonizing ideals and action is offered. In every chapter where effective contrast seems possible, the relevant institutions of the Soviet Union are sketched and their relation to basic Communist theory is noted. In this way, an effort is made to contrast liberal democratic theory and practice with the theory and practice of Communist dictatorship as represented by the Soviet Union. The book thus has a concern for political theory and analysis on which descriptive works on government often lay little or no stress, and it also has a concreteness of reference that is often lacking in introductory textbooks on political science.

It is designed to direct the student's attention to the questions being asked everywhere about democratic institutions and practices, and to provide sufficient description of the structure and operation of three leading democratic governments to enable him to see the significance of the questions and some of the considerations to be taken into account in looking for answers to them. Thus the great issue of the relation of democratic institutions and practices to democratic ideals occupies the forefront if not the bulk of the discussion. Within this frame of reference, the great expansion of the activities of democratic governments is sketched and analyzed. The significance of this expansion as a response to democratic ideals is considered, and the impact of the greatly expanded functions of government on democratic institutions and practices is kept constantly within the focus of attention.

The great expansion of governmental activities has made the structure of all governments, including the democratic, much more complex. If the introductory course in government is concentrated on the detail of a single government, the trees are always getting in the way of the student's view of the forest. While study of the full detail cannot be shirked if a sure understanding is finally to be reached, it is open to question how far this can be achieved in an introductory course. There is something to be said for trying to concentrate on fundamentals. If there are some fundamentals of democratic government, they are more likely to emerge into clear view from a study of the basic institutions of three governments than from the study of one.

Also, the challenge of the dictatorships and the rapidly changing scope of government in the democracies have led to a reconsideration of democratic creed and practice. In the last thirty years or so, a large literature devoted to such reconsideration has appeared, scattered through many books and journals. The questioning that produced the literature also exists in the student mind, and suggests a course that might serve as an elementary introduction to the literature.

This book has been prepared for a course that would try to emphasize fundamentals and, at the same time, make constant reference to practice. For the student who takes only one course in government, such a course provides an introduction to the great continuing debate about democracy, enabling him, if he is so minded, to follow the debate intelligently on his own account. For the student who intends to take further courses in government, it also furnishes some criteria, of a tentative nature at least, for sorting and judging the detail met in close study of particular governments. The advantages of this method entail some skimping of detailed description of the governments in question and some sketchiness in the analysis of the underlying problems. It has seemed preferable, however, to present a unifying theme and a framework of analysis in the text, and to leave the supplementing of detail, and the critical examination and further development of the analysis, to lectures in the classroom. The steps in analysis and the connectedness of things are presented to the student more precisely and in more durable form than his notes or memory of lectures are likely to supply.

The attempt to define the connection between democratic ideals and democratic institutions, and to give an analysis of the impact of greatly expanded governmental functions on liberal democratic government, has led to numerous generalizations. With many of these, there will be fairly general agreement. Others are conclusions on matters that are widely debated, and will meet with some dissent. Rather than suspend judgment on numerous disputed points in an introductory survey, we have frequently ventured conclusions. We have tried, however, not to be dogmatic, and to give reasons for our conclusions. The conclusions, of course, are no better than the reasons given in their support.

This book was originally written at the end of World War II and was published in 1946 under the title, *Democratic Government and Politics.* In 1947, a revised and enlarged edition was published by the Oxford University Press under the present title. It was prepared at a time when everyone was disposed to hope that the democracies would be able to give their main attention to their own internal problems under conditions of international peace assured by the United Nations. Because this was a fit and decent hope not yet proved illusory, it was thought appropriate to concentrate on democracy as a form of government and to elucidate the subject by an elementary comparison of the governments of the leading democracies, with only incidental reference to the Soviet Union and other modern dictatorships.

By 1950, when the second American edition was prepared, the hopes for a world of settled peace seemed to have little foundation, and only the sanguine will be sure they have a better basis in 1958. The gulf between East and West yawns with thermonuclear menace. The gulf itself, we recognize, is, in large measure, caused by sharply differing conceptions of what the purposes of government and the state are.

In these circumstances, some shift in emphasis in the instruction of the beginning students is needed. Domestic politics cannot now claim to monopolize his attention. The tension between East and West must have some share of it.

Accordingly in the second, and again in the present third, edition significant adjustments of focus have been made. These adjustments have been noted above, with one exception: the insertion of a final chapter on the relations of sovereign states in order to help the student to get some grasp of the tragic dilemma of international politics. This latter topic is not easy to integrate with the other material in the book, but an effort has been made to draw revealing contrasts between *domestic politics* within the cohering frame of an ordered government and an abiding law, and *international politics* in a state system where both government and law exist only in embryo, if at all.

The revision presented in this edition follows closely the general scheme of the last preceding one. Within this scheme, two main modifications have been made. First, systematic comparisons between the government of France and the governments of the United States and Britain have been introduced, thus making explicit the significance of a multiple-party system and of markedly different constitutional tradition on the workings of democracy. Second, some rearrangements of material within chapters, and considerable changes in the sequences of chapters, have been made. In the arrangement of chapters, the book has been moved much closer to what may perhaps be called the standard sequence. The chapters on Federalism and Local Government have been moved from the end of the book to its early part. The chapters dealing with the formation of opinion, the organization of the electorate, and fundamental civil rights now all precede the chapters which discuss the executive, the legislature, and the judiciary. To give coherence to this re-arrangement, some shifting of material from one chapter to another, and some rewriting, have been undertaken.

Whether re-arranged or not, all chapters of the book have been brought up to date by recording relevant changes in the government and politics of the countries dealt with, and by including, wherever possible, additional illustrations drawn from recent events. In particular, all sections on American government have been strengthened by more detailed discussion and added illustrations. For greater ease of reference, many new headings and sub-headings have been introduced throughout the text.

The main burden of preparing this edition has been carried by Professor Henry J. Abraham, who heads the basic courses in Political Science at the University of Pennsylvania, and who signs this preface as co-author. It is hoped that the results of our collaboration will recommend themselves to those whose interest in earlier editions encouraged us to undertake this revision.

At the request of the publisher, the following persons submitted critical analyses of the second American edition: Mr. Warner Moss, Professor of

Government at William and Mary College, Mr. Marbury B. Ogle, Jr., Professor of Government at Purdue University, and Mr. Benjamin E. Lippincott, Professor of Political Science at the University of Minnesota. The manuscript of this revision has been read, either in its entirety or in part by Mr. Guy H. Dodge, Professor of Political Science at Brown University, Mr. John W. Chapman, Assistant Professor of Government at Smith College, and Mr. Charles Gilbert, Assistant Professor of Political Science at Swarthmore College. In their many comments and suggestions, obscurities and defects of analysis came to light, which we have endeavored to repair. We wish to thank them for the help they have given us. We also wish to express our appreciation to Professors G. Edward Janosik and Garold W. Thumm of the Department of Political Science at the University of Pennsylvania, whose constant critical vigilance aided us greatly in the preparation of material for this revision, and to Miss Yolanda C. Legnini, Registrar of the Graduate Division of the Wharton School of Finance and Commerce, for typing the entire manuscript. Such errors and defects as remain after all this help are, of course, our own.

Kingston, Ontario   J. A. CORRY
Philadelphia, Pennsylvania   HENRY J. ABRAHAM
January 1958

Contents

ELEMENTS OF DEMOCRATIC GOVERNMENT

I

The Study of Government

If each of us were solitary and self-sufficient, each could rule himself, and would have no need to control the actions of others, or to be controlled for the sake of others. There would be no need of *government,* which in its simplest and most superficial appearance is the ruling of some aspects of our conduct by others for the sake of others. Nor would we have to concern ourselves with *politics,* which is a term for a particular set of processes by which we try to bring the actions of others under the control of government, or try to divert or modify the application of government to ourselves.

SOCIETY, STATE, AND GOVERNMENT

SOCIETY AND GOVERNMENT

However, we are neither solitary nor self-sufficient. Man is a social creature. To flourish or even to survive in isolation from his fellows, he would have to be an utterly different creature from what he is. All history testifies to his need for *society.* We cannot alter this verdict, nor would we want to do so. The child could not survive to become the man without the family. The man could not flourish without easing the burden of securing food, clothing, and shelter through co-operation with others. If each of us had to produce unaided with our hands all our material needs, we should lead a barren and precarious existence. In economic co-operation with others, we produce wealth and not merely subsistence.

3

The Need for Society. Without society, there would never be the rich heritage of art and literature and practical knowledge needed to improve man's estate. It is only by living in society that a cultural heritage can be transmitted from one generation to another. If each had to learn for himself the hard way about everything, we should never know or enjoy very much. Then, beyond all the selfish calculations about what a good bargain society is for the individual, there is the need for fellowship. Where one man seeks his own company in solitude, thousands of men want to be with their fellows for purposes that run all the way from religious communion to idle gossip.

WHAT IS SOCIETY? Society, as the term is used here, is not a name for an agglomeration of people like a public meeting or the residents of the United States. Nor is it a name for particular groups of persons organized for some purpose, such as the Society of Friends or the Society To Maintain Public Decency. Such groups are called associations, or simply groups. Society is a term for designating the entire network of social relationships between individuals, whether within or without groups, between groups, or between individuals and groups. Thus the total of social relationships in the United States constitutes American society. The word *community* will be used here from time to time in a similar sense to mean the totality of any group, whether it be the people of the United States, or of a particular state, county, or city. The context will always have to be kept in mind to make clear whether it is the national community or some lesser community that is being discussed.

ORDER AND REGULARITY. We enter into varied and innumerable relationships with our fellows expecting advantages and satisfactions of various kinds. If these expectations are not always to be frustrated, there must be some order and regularity in the behavior of those participating. It is true that much of the attraction of a game is suspense about the result, an unpredictable element depending on chance or skill. But the game loses all point if there are no rules, or if everybody plays according to different rules. Even a game of chance is spoiled if somebody cheats. The social relationships that constitute society depend on some minimum of order and regularity.

Economic co-operation in the factory will not satisfy expectations unless the workers come and go at fixed hours, work co-operatively, and accept such direction as is needed for the common task. The same is true of the family, the church, the club, the school. Relationships must be based on some kind of order, must exhibit a pattern that can be relied upon. While no one wants social relationships to have the faultless regularity of a machine, each must know, within limits, what to expect of others, and these expectations must not be too often disappointed. Men must live in society in order to live at all.

The Need for Government. This conclusion is indisputable, but it does not of itself prove the need for government and politics. A multitude of social relationships follow an orderly pattern which has been established and maintained without any obvious control being exercised by anybody over anybody, or at least without any control being exercised by governments. Many of our social relationships are established by custom and maintained by habit. The elementary courtesy of waiting our turn, exemplified at a high level of perfection by the English queue, rests on custom and habit. So do most relationships of family life. Other social relationships are based on conscious and deliberate agreement. Clubs and associations are formed and the terms of association are agreed on by the members. Of course, there is control and direction exercised by the parents in the one instance and by the officers of the club in the other. But the control is voluntarily accepted for the most part; the co-operation is spontaneous. Much of our life in society is ordered in these ways. It is even conceivable that all social relationships might be ordered on the bases of custom, habit, and agreement, that we might learn to do voluntarily all that is needed to ensure the satisfactions of social life and thus make government and politics unnecessary.

While this is conceivable, it seems most unlikely. The history of human societies is a history of conflict as well as of voluntary co-operation. Unruly elements seem deeply rooted in human nature. Children quarrel over the terms of their play and fight for the possession of toys. These dispositions, however moderated and disciplined by social life, continue in grown-ups. The established social relationships are always frustrating to many people, and frustration leads to aggressive and unpredictable behavior. Modern psychology pictures us all as potential aggressors because life can never give any of us all we are capable of demanding.

MAINTENANCE OF PUBLIC ORDER. Even if most of us are pacific and co-operative, the violent and unpredictable behavior of a few is capable of disappointing most of the expectations of social life. Voluntary co-operation rests on confidence, and fear dissolves confidence. A few thugs and burglars operating without restraint can disrupt social relationships and paralyze the social life of a community. So there must be an organization to maintain order and suppress violence through the possession, and use where necessary, of coercive restraining power. This organization, in its concrete tangible form, is government. The primary and indispensable function of government is to ensure a firm framework of public order within which men can order their social life on the bases of habit, custom, and agreement. Ordinarily, it does this by making laws forbidding acts that imperil public order and restraining those who break the law, by force if necessary.

It is not enough for the effective maintenance of public order merely to support custom and habit and the established ways of society. A community that sets itself against all change is static, asserting that the old ways cannot be improved upon. The communities with whose governments this book is primarily concerned are dynamic, bent on progress and improvement. That means acceptance of the principle of change in social relationships, but not necessarily any agreement on what, when, or how. The process of social change is infinitely complex, but its main features are a matter of everyday observation. We have already noted that many people feel frustrated in their established social relationships. There are always individuals and groups bent on particular changes while other individuals and groups resist. This leads to friction and conflict, which if not moderated by some external authority may disrupt public order just as seriously as the activities of thugs and burglars.

GOVERNMENT AND SOCIAL CHANGE. Much of the adjustment of this kind of conflict can be—and is—carried through by voluntary agreement of the individuals and groups affected. However, where society consists of the relationships of tens of millions of people spread over a great territory like the United States, it is too complex for adequate adjustment to be made by voluntary agreement. An example may be taken from the economic field. If Pennsylvania coal miners are granted a change which gives them higher wages and shorter hours of work, such a change does not merely affect them and their employers. It affects all householders and all industries that use their coal, and ultimately it affects all the consumers of goods produced by those industries. It affects everyone in the United States, and people in other countries as well. If the attempt to get higher wages and shorter hours involves a prolonged strike in the coal-mining industry, again everyone is affected. It is not possible, even with the best will in the world, for all the groups and individuals affected to adjust such a conflict by general voluntary agreement. At every turn, one will find that changes in the relationships of particular persons and groups have repercussions on many other persons and groups as well. These latter need some agency that speaks for them and protects their interest in the outcome of the conflict.

Here is another great function of government: presiding over the struggle for social change of whatever kind. Its main purpose here is to ensure that the struggle does not imperil public order. Higher prices for coal are embarrassing and annoying to many but are not likely to endanger public order, unless the rise in price is astronomical. On the other hand, prolonged strikes in the coal industry will paralyze industry and transportation and threaten public order, and government will be required to intervene to protect it. It is through the government that society, threatened by failure of a supply of coal or by any other conflict between individuals and groups, can bring pressure for a solution of the conflict and dictate and enforce its terms if necessary. The very fact of the reserve power of government always overhanging the scene disposes the parties to the conflict to find a solution.

GOVERNMENT AND POLITICS. If we are to live in society with some assurance that it will not be disrupted by individual and group agressions, government is necessary. Its essential function determines its character. It is an organization for controlling human action, mainly through the enforcing of rules, by sheer physical force if necessary. Present-day governments carry on many activities which seem to have little or no connection with making and enforcing rules of conduct, just as a drugstore handles many lines besides drugs. But to understand the essential character of government and the prevailing attitude of individuals and groups toward it, it is necessary to keep its essential function always in mind. Politics is a term for describing the varied methods by which individuals and groups try to move government to stop conduct that is disturbing public order, to compel the settlement of some conflict that is threatening public order, to enforce some social change they want, or to refrain from enforcing some social change they dislike.

Besides the danger of disruption from within, a society is exposed to attack from without, and this will continue until war has been eliminated from human affairs. Society has to take steps to protect itself from external enemies. The example of the countries that have been overrun by war in the last fifty years vividly illustrates this need. Government is a necessary agent for meeting this need through the maintenance of military and naval establishments. It is the organization to which the control and application of naked force is given whether in relation to internal or external matters.

STATE AND GOVERNMENT

When rules enforced by government restrain us from doing things we want to do, we tend to regard it as an alien force imposed on us from the outside. We actually see some few men who form the government, for the time being, apply its power to control the conduct of other men. However, government is not alien and external to society. It is an essential instrument of men in society for ensuring an adequate measure of stability in society. There must be order, dictated by government decree if need be. In times past, men have supported absolute governments over which they themselves had no control because these governments ensured order. They have even regarded absolute monarchs as gifts from God for this indispensable service.

But government does not undertake to define all social relationships by law; it does not try to dictate terms of all social co-operation by government decree. That would scarcely be possible. In any event, it is not necessary, because men always want to be together in society and they exert themselves to find ways to make it possible, such as custom, habit, and voluntary agreement. Because these alone do not suffice, they support government as well to act at critical points and at critical times. All have an interest in seeing that government does its essential job. When it is doing that, it acts for us all in furtherance of common interests and common purposes.

The State as a Mutual Insurance Association. In effect, what we do, at least in democratic countries like the United States, Britain, and France, is to become members of a compulsory mutual insurance association to insure one another against external enemies who would ravage us by war, against private aggression within society, and against disruption of social relationships by individual and group conflict. The taxes we pay are the premiums paid for protection by this kind of insurance. This association is called the state.

It is an association for limited, specific purposes and works by methods appropriate to those purposes. If we want to associate for other purposes, such as religious worship, business, or recreation, we join quite different kinds of associations which work by quite different methods. Every association consisting of large numbers of persons must have a constitution prescribing how it is to act and who is to act for it in protecting the common interests and carrying out the common purposes of its members. The association that is the state has a constitution prescribing the organs of the state and the methods for selecting persons through whom these organs find expression. These organs and persons constitute the government about which we have been talking.

The state is the expression of one aspect of society. The government as a whole is the organ of the state and thus an instrument of society. The government at any moment has concrete and tangible form; we can hear its

Gov't is organ of state and instrument. of society.

voice, and we can see members of Congress, judges, and government officials. The state is always an abstraction, a sign, or a shorthand term for bringing into the focus of attention the discussion of the preceding pages. It denotes the *order* aspect of society. It points to unseen but important realities behind the concrete manifestations of government, helping to clarify our understanding of the place of government in society.

DEFINITION OF STATE. Many definitions of the state, varying in their emphasis, have been attempted—some 145 are available today. But the one which best provides the emphasis wanted here may be quoted and given some comment:

> The state is an association, which, acting through law as promulgated by a government endowed to this end with coercive power, maintains within a community territorially demarcated the universal external conditions of social order.[1]

The state is concerned with order in a given territory. Its rule is universal in that territory. Everyone there must obey the law of the state, and only the government or its delegates are entitled to apply physical coercion. The monopoly of coercive power wielded by the state is called *sovereignty*. Membership of the state depends on the constitution and is at least as extensive as the right to vote. One cannot escape from the laws of the state and the control of the government merely by resigning one's membership. Indeed, the only effective way to resign is to take up membership in another state. Even then, unless one moves physically from the territory of the state in question, one remains subject to its control. The state does not create all social order by its coercive apparatus. Much of the order found in society is spontaneous. The primary concern of the state is with the outward conditions needed to nourish the inward impulses for orderly social relationships.

The State as a Promoter of Common Interests. All persons have a common interest in social order. In this matter, the state can act for all its members with their approval. In fact, wherever its members discover a common interest or a common purpose, the state can appropriately act to protect that common interest and promote that common purpose. So the state can be defined, rather more widely than in the foregoing definition, as an association for promoting the common interests and common purposes of its members. We should always remember, however, that it is the guardianship of social order that gives the state its special and unique characteristics, and

[1] R. M. MacIver, *The Modern State* (Oxford: Clarendon Press, 1926), p. 22.

that most common interests are related, in one way or another, to the maintenance of social order.

The world is divided territorially among a number of states. The definition of the state quoted here is not valid in all its terms for all the states of the present day, nor for many of the states that have existed in the past. We shall see later why this is so. It is, however, correct for those states which have democratic governments, and the primary concern of this book is with democratic states and governments.

Strictly speaking, then, the definition is a description of a particular kind of state as it now exists. It does not purport to explain the essential character of all states that have ever existed. Nor does it purport to explain the historical origin of the state. Historically, the state always arises in response to a need for order. But its first manifestations rarely take the form of an association. It has generally begun as an organization of naked power controlled by a small imperious clique imposing order on its people as *subjects*—i.e. as being under its authority, dominion, and control, exploiting them harshly at the same time, and refusing them their role in the state as *citizens*—i.e. as members of the political community. The definition is valid only for states that have been tamed and made directly responsible to the people on whose behalf order is being provided.

SOCIETY, STATE, AND GOVERNMENT: SUMMATION

To sum up this preliminary discussion, society is the total of social relationships within the given area of the earth's surface on which attention is focused. The state is one particular constellation of social relationships, men associating together to provide the indispensable conditions of public order. The state is therefore *less* than society; it is an instrument of society for its purposes. The government is the concrete embodiment of the state, consisting of organs and persons who carry out the purposes of the state. For democratic countries at any rate, the government at any particular moment is less than the state. It is the agent of the association that directs and controls it.

It is necessary here, however, to anticipate a possible confusion about the use of the term *government*. The word is widely used, and will be used here, in two different senses. *First,* it is used in a narrow sense, as when we speak of the government of the day. It is common to speak of Prime Minister Macmillan's Government in Britain. In this sense, one could speak of President

Kennedy's Government, meaning President Kennedy's Administration. The narrow meaning designates the executive branch of government, which will be described in Chapters XIII and XIV. *Second,* the word is used in a general inclusive sense to denote the whole set of institutions through which some command and others obey. It is in this wide sense that the word is employed in the title of this book, or when we speak of the study of government, ideals of government, forms of government, and so on. In a particular sense in this book, it may not be immediately obvious in which sense the word is used. The context as a whole, however, will make it clear and the reader must attend to the context to avoid confusion.

WHY STUDY GOVERNMENT?

Government affects almost every aspect of our lives. We have already seen that it ensures for us the advantages and satisfactions of life in society. Properly designed and used, it can nourish the highest level of civilization. Clumsily and ignorantly managed, it can lead—and often has led—men to think it is intolerable because of the burdens it puts upon them. It always takes from us in taxes money for which we have infinite uses of our own. It can block our most cherished designs and suppress us ruthlessly if we pursue them in the face of its interdict. It can require us to sacrifice our lives in war. Normally, we can only escape it by submitting to another government somewhere else in the world, which may deal with us still more harshly and summarily. If we want to know anything about our world, if we want to know what we can plan for or expect in the future, we must try to understand government.

The Challenge of Citizenship. In democratic countries, we enjoy the privileges of citizenship. Through voting in elections and through other methods to be discussed later, the citizens who are members of the state collectively decide in broad outline what government will do and how it will behave. The actions of citizens are decisive, as much by their ignorance and inattention as by their understanding and sustained interest. The man who fails to vote is also helping to decide. It is broadly true in a democracy that we get the government we deserve. If it is bad, the first step for each of us is to deserve better by earnest effort to understand and to influence what government does.

CITIZENSHIP A RESPONSIBILITY. Citizenship is more than an opportunity: it is also a responsibility. There have always been critics of democracy, government under the control of the many, who were sure it could not endure permanently because the mass of citizens would not live up to the high responsibilities it entails. It is not necessary, or even possible, for every citizen to understand the nature and problems of government. But democracy will certainly be a failure unless there comes forward voluntarily in each generation a large number of citizens prepared to give the time and thought necessary to the understanding of government, and then to participate actively in political life. By the attitude we take toward this responsibility we decide the fate of democracy.

Hitherto there has not been nearly enough well-informed participation by the citizens of democratic countries. Too many have assumed that they could have the advantages of 'government of the people, for the people, and by the people' without themselves taking up the responsibilities it involves. The men who struggled from the eighteenth century onward to secure the right of participation for all would have found this most difficult to understand. They and their forebears had had a long experience as subjects of states whose governments they could not control, or even persuade to listen to them. The frustrations and humiliations of this condition led them to think that full citizenship, the right of participation in the state, was the greatest gift that could be made to man, and that men who had it would cherish it and exercise it fully.

Democratic Government on Trial. They, who knew the unpleasantness of the alternatives, would have deemed it incredible that the privileges and responsibilities of citizenship should be taken lightly. We of the West, who have enjoyed for a long time the right of participation in the state, have let the unpleasantness of the alternatives fade from our minds and have taken the responsibilities of citizenship lightly. In large measure, we have done this because of the enormous success of democracy in the latter part of the nineteenth century and in the early years of the twentieth. For a time, democracy seemed almost certain to sweep the world and to become the prevailing, if not the universal, form of government. In these circumstances, it was easy to take it for granted and forget the unpleasantness of the alternatives.

However, ever since the end of World War I, the grisly episodes of dictatorship in Nazi Germany and Fascist Italy and the established Communist dictatorships in Russia and Eastern Europe have warned us that the alternatives are very real and very unpleasant. We cannot take democracy for granted. If democratic government is to maintain itself as a genuine alternative to dictatorship, it must be able to draw deeply on the informed under-standing and vigorous participation of a large number of its citizens. This gives a special urgency to the study of democratic government.

Democratic government has not fulfilled all the high hopes of those who first established it in the modern world. It is even probable that some of these hopes were naïve and not capable of full realization. Some of the indifference of citizens toward their privileges and responsibilities may be due to dis-illusionment. The purpose of this book is to reveal the essential characteristics of democratic government, as experience seems to show them to be, by de-scribing and comparing in broad outline the governments of the United States and Britain, and, to a much lesser extent, France, and providing a sharp contrast by sketching some of the main features of government in a modern dictatorship, the Soviet Union. Note will be taken of the defects and limitations democratic government has so far exhibited, especially in the two great countries that have practiced it most successfully and continuously. An effort will be made to show what it does achieve despite its defects and limitations, and to suggest what we can fairly expect it to accomplish.

WAYS OF STUDYING GOVERNMENT

It will help to make clear the scope and limitations of this book if we look briefly at the different ways in which state and government, or particular aspects of them, can be studied. Enough has been said already to show that state and government are very complex, as complex as the total sum of social relationships with which they are in one way or another concerned. Even if one wants to understand state and government completely, one cannot study all aspects of them at once. It is necessary to isolate particular aspects or branches of the study, and focus intensively on each one separately, hoping later to combine these separate pieces of learning in a fuller understanding. Also, particular persons may be interested in one aspect of government and not in another. There have come to be a number of different branches, or foci of interest, in the study of government. Yet the first and most funda-mental thing to note is the distinction between a study of what government actually is and does in any one or several countries, and a study of what government ought to be and ought to do. The difference is one between fact and theory. The focus of interest of each is different, and the method of study appropriate to each is different.

Government as It Is. For instance, one can study the government of the

United States as it actually is, read its Constitution and its laws, learn how the legislature is composed and how it makes laws, fix in one's mind how the executive, the courts, and the civil service are organized. This is a study of existing structure and machinery, and is not very revealing in itself. The next necessary step to understanding the government of the United States is to observe how men act in relation to their government, whether as private citizens or as part of the government. Here one studies the behavior of men in political parties, in elections, in pressure groups, in their dealings with various branches of the government, in trying to get the government to do this, or not to do that. This is the study of political behavior, the dynamics of government, which has received increasing emphasis in recent years, particularly from political scientists.

The examination of structure and dynamics together constitutes the study of the government of the United States, or American Government. But interest is not exhausted and understanding is incomplete with the mere collection of facts. As particular facts are turned up and recorded, the student will ask how this came to be. The Constitution of the United States makes no mention of or provision for political parties. Yet political parties are facts of undeniably first-rate importance in the government of the United States. Why did political parties develop? Why are there two, and not three or more? For that matter, why did Congress pass one particular law and not another? The questions that can be asked are almost endless. Asking them assumes that the facts in question have causes that can be identified. If these causes can be identified, understanding is deepened.

So the study of a particular government to be meaningful must go beyond the collection of facts to inquire into the meaning or significance of facts. This involves analysis, an attempt to discover the relation, if any, between one fact, or set of facts, and another. However, both the description of the facts and their analysis are concerned with seeing and understanding what government actually is in the United States.

This focus of interest and this method can be applied to one government after another, or to two or more in combination. There is a special advantage in comparing side by side two or more governments which have at the same time both marked similarities and striking differences. For example, Britain and the United States have had two-party systems that are similar in a general way, and yet show very striking differences in their detailed structure and working. What accounts for the similarities and for the differences? Some comment will be offered on this question later. We may note now that such comparison tends to sharpen the analysis of cause and effect, and thus improves the understanding of the essentials of both governments. Study conducted on these lines is known as Comparative Government.

Government as It Ought To Be. Then there is the study of government as it ought to be, the search for standards for judging the rightness or wrongness of particular governments as they actually exist and work. Presumably life has a purpose or purposes, and government, if it makes any sense at all, must be an instrument of these purposes. What are the ideals or goals at which we should aim? Is government necessary to help toward these goals? If so, in what way can government help or hinder; what should it do? When should it bring its sovereignty to bear on individuals, and when should it refrain? Who should be allowed to participate in government? How best can government be organized to achieve the purposes we have decided it should pursue?

These and similar questions have been asked again and again since the beginnings of government. Academic philosophers have asked them as academic questions, and tried to find answers for them. Both philosophers and ordinary men have asked them as agonizingly practical questions when they were trying to decide whether it was their duty to obey their government, or to resist it when they themselves thought what it was doing was wrong. There is an immense literature recording what men in the Western world have thought on these questions in the last 2,500 or more years. The study of this record, and original thought on these questions, with a view to finding answers to the problems of our own times is called Political Philosophy or Political Theory. The conclusions drawn from such a study may lead one to deny the rightness of one's own government and to demand that it be changed.

In every stable society there are widely held beliefs or ideals of what government should be; these exercise a pervasive and powerful influence on the structure and working of government in that society. There is a democratic political theory that seeks to justify democratic government and also to determine the uses to which a democratic government will be put. A study of the governments of the United States and Britain that ignored the ideals that have largely determined the present structure and press constantly on the daily working of these two governments would be incomplete. Accordingly, the next chapter attempts to outline democratic political ideals. By way of contrast it will, in turn, be followed by one dealing with the beliefs that have motivated some modern dictatorships. Succeeding chapters will try to show in what ways the structure and working of the governments of the United States and Britain are responses to the democratic ideals. France, which possesses a related but rather different type of governmental structure —and evidently a less predictably stable one—will be treated wherever appropriate, as will certain other governments from time to time.

Cause and Effect Relationships in Government. There is a third approach to the study of government and politics which is concerned not only with understanding what is but also with predicting what will be. It does not focus on the issue of what men should do in government and politics, but on what their fundamental human nature will lead them to do in specific sets of circumstances. We are all given to predictions of this kind in every field of human activity. We say that certain things cannot be done because they are against human nature, or that particular kinds of behavior are inevitable, given human nature. Such forecasts are based on the assumption that human nature, or at least certain elements in it, is constant, and does not change from person to person and from time to time. Public opinion polls take a sample composed of the opinions of a few thousand people and on this basis predict how millions will vote. The predictions are not inevitably right, but they are always based on an assumption of constancy in human nature and human behavior.

Predicting. The interest in prediction is always present in the study of government, as distinct from the study of political philosophy. Whenever we say that political facts A and B in combination cause political event C, we are asserting cause and effect relationships which are the basis of all prediction. It will be suggested later that the fact of political parties, and of at least some of the behavior of men in parties, is the inevitable outcome of human nature in a certain kind of political and social circumstance. To say, as is sometimes said, that the President of the United States should have the power to dissolve Congress and call a new congressional election at any time instead of having fixed election dates, as at present, assumes that political behavior reacting to these changed circumstances would bring predictable beneficial results.

Despite a spate of new methods and techniques, our power of prediction in politics is markedly defective, partly because of the complexity of both human nature and of the circumstances and conditions to which human nature reacts. Also, we have not been able to determine how far men are conditioned by their nature and by circumstances, and how far each is free to direct his actions by conscious and deliberate aim. Presumably they are in some measure conditioned, or there would be no sense in talking about cause and effect or in trying to make any predictions, in human affairs. Presumably they are in some measure free to choose, or there would be no point at all in the thousands of years of talk about what government ought to do or ought not to do. To talk in this way assumes that men are free, to some degree at least, to decide how their government shall be organized and what it shall do. But we do not know where the line between determinism and free will really lies.

DATA FOR PREDICTION IN POLITICS. The science of psychology is trying to discover how far human behavior can be predicted. Psychologists amass great bodies of data from which they draw generalizations about how men can be expected to act in certain defined sets of circumstances. This method can be, and is being increasingly applied to the study of political behavior in elections, in the relations between political leaders and followers, and so on. There may some day be a reliable science of political behavior, but at present it is still in its early, although distinctly promising, stages.

Materials for attempting predictions in the field of government and politics can be drawn from history as well as from psychology. History gives us a long record of the vicissitudes of states and governments. In the course of history, there have been many states and governments, and we know a good deal about how they arose, how they developed and flourished, how they were torn by civil war or revolution, how they fell, or how they have endured for varying lengths of time. By a study of this record, we may be able to discern constantly recurring patterns in history according to which states rise, thrive, and fall.[2] To take specific examples, it has been urged, on the basis of historical record, that men have always been ruled by an elite, a small governing class, which always makes its will prevail whatever the forms of government, and further, that they always will be so ruled.[3] A fascinating study of a number of political revolutions in the past shows them all going through several remarkably similar stages,[4] tempting one to predict that future revolutions will also go through these same stages. Communism claims the warrant of history for its predictions about the outcome of our times, although not resting its case by any means on history alone.[5]

Political Science as Prediction. A study that finds laws by which to predict

[2] Arnold J. Toynbee, *A Study of History,* abridgment of vols. I-VI by D. C. Somervell (New York: Oxford University Press, 1946).

[3] James Burnham, *The Machiavellians* (New York: The John Day Co., 1943).

[4] Crane Brinton, *The Anatomy of Revolution* (London: Allen and Unwin, 1939).

[5] See Chapter III, *infra.*

what will happen in politics in carefully defined sets of circumstances differs markedly from both the study of Government and the study of Political Theory, and is appropriately called Political Science. *Science* is here used in the sense of a body of knowledge that enables us to make accurate predictions on the analogy of the natural sciences, notably physics and chemistry. The identifying mark of these two sciences is the power of prediction.

To talk of Political Science in this sense is somewhat pretentious, because in the present state of knowledge our ability to predict the course of political events is very limited indeed. One has only to ask how much reliable forecast there is in one decade of the major political events of the next decade. We think that careful analysis has given us some insight into causal relationships in government and politics, and the patient intensive study of political behavior will no doubt give us further and deeper insights. At present, however, political science in this strict sense has not advanced very far. It represents an aspiration to a deeper knowledge of political forces rather than any substantial body of reliable generalizations. Yet there is little doubt that political scientists would like to find laws of political activity as certain as the law of gravity.

Political Science as Systematic Study of Government. The term Political Science is more often used in a wider and looser sense to cover the entire study of government and politics in whatever aspect and by any of the methods outlined above. Very often, a college course in Political Science will cover a general description of forms of government, of constitutions and different organs of government, an analysis of the state as an aspect of society, and a consideration of theoretical views on what governments ought to be and ought to do. In this wider sense, the identifying mark of *science* is in the methods of study used: painstaking accuracy in observation and in collection of facts and systematic analysis by close logical reasoning. Defined in this way, any comprehensive, verifiable, and systematic body of knowledge about a specified area of inquiry may be called a science.

In this sense there is a *political* science, and this book at least attempts to be scientific. When, as often happens, universities and colleges put the label Political Science on one or more of their courses in government and politics, they are generally using *science* in this sense. Much of the argument and difference of opinion on whether the study of government is, or can be, a science turns on sharply different definitions of what is a science. It is only when the narrow definition is accepted that a serious issue arises. There is nothing to be gained by pursuing that particular issue further here.

If anyone is to satisfy his own mind as to whether the study of government is, or can be, a science, he must first of all master the existing body of knowledge about government and politics—the science and the art. This book is at most an introduction to a part of that body of knowledge. Then he would need to learn what history and psychology and several other branches of systematic knowledge tell us about human behavior in the past and in the present. With that knowledge, he will be fully aware of the difficulties of deciding. Without it, he cannot make any useful judgment on the issue. As in everything else, one must begin at the beginning.

The purpose here is to make a beginning with one particular kind of government, democratic government, trying to make clear in an elementary way what its essential features are, how it works, and how it is related to the ideals it is supposed to be furthering. Before going ahead, however, a brief survey of forms of government may help to set the stage.

FORMS OF GOVERNMENT

Even in the most primitive societies, government exists in some rudimentary form. There are always leaders who exercise authority, patriarchs or priests if not kings, politicians, or dictators. Government in every society has distinctive characteristics, and as a society develops and changes, government usually passes through several transformations. History is a rich storehouse of forms and types of government, which political thinkers ever since the time of the Greeks have been trying to classify.

Aristotle's Classification. There are many different classifications of government, none of which has been generally accepted as satisfactory. In these circumstances, it would merely be confusing to the beginning student to enumerate and discuss them. It will be worthwhile, however, to discuss briefly one famous classification, an adaptation of that made by Aristotle in his study of the Greek city-states. It is still perhaps more widely accepted than any other, and it illustrates sufficiently the difficulty of classifying different kinds of governments.

The criterion used by this classification for distinguishing types of governments is the number of persons who rule or share the ruling power. Where one person governs, the government is a *monarchy*. Where rule is shared by a relatively small section of the population, the government is an *aristocracy*. Where control of government is vested in the citizens generally, the government is a *democracy*. Accordingly, every government is either a monarchy, an aristocracy, or a democracy.

It should be pointed out that this is both an adaptation and a simplification of Aristotle's classification. It is an adaptation because some of the terms used had not the same meaning for him as for later classifiers. Democracy, for example, meant to him something approaching mob rule and was a perversion of a good form of government, which he called *polity*. His term polity meant something pretty close to what we would call democracy. It is a simplification because Aristotle's classification identified at least six forms of government, some of which were true forms, or models, while others were recurring perversions of these models, i.e., *tyranny, oligarchy,* and *ochlocracy.* He also noted the occurrence of a variety of mixed forms. There have been, of course, many variations on Aristotle's classification, but most of them treat monarchy, aristocracy, and democracy as the basic forms.

DIFFICULTY IN APPLICATION. The difficulty about this threefold classification lies in its application. In one sense, British government is a monarchy. In strict constitutional law, the monarch is the ruler. The ministers who exercise the powers of government derive their formal authority from the monarch and cannot act without it. Relying on this aspect of the British constitution, some have concluded that the British government is a monarchy—a limited monarchy, it is true, but still a monarchy.

However, as we shall see, a large part of the British constitution is made up of *customary rules* which settle the way in which the formal legal powers of the king are to be exercised. These customary rules have been closely adhered to for over a century and they give the monarch only a negligible influence over the appointment of his ministers and the powers they exercise. Briefly, they provide that the monarch must choose ministers who have—and can hold—the confidence of Parliament, and that he must accept their advice. The House of Commons, the effective part of Parliament, is made up of the elected representatives of the electorate, which, in turn, comprises the whole body of adult citizens. On these grounds, many classify British government as a democracy.

If substance rather than shadowy forms is to be the criterion, the British form of government is a democracy, and a highly effective one as matters go in an imperfect world. When we brush aside forms to follow substance, we often encounter serious difficulties in applying a certain classification. To return to the concept of monarchy, for example, when as has often happened, the monarch shares his rule with his mistresses, is the government still a monarchy? More important, no monarchy has ever been able to maintain its rule without the support of at least a small group or class in the community. These do not give their support without sharing in, or imposing limitations on, the powers of the monarch. There are *republics*—e.g., modern Egypt and Ghana—where the forms clearly point to democracy but the practice points equivocally to rule by one or a few, and not to rule by the many. The Communist case against the democracies of the present day is that they are masked oligarchies in which the relatively small owning capitalist class is the effective ruler. An attempt to classify according to the inward practice rather than the outward forms often raises difficult questions and interminable debate on what the realities are.

COMBINED FORMS. The governments of all but the most primitive societies are complex institutions and they cannot be sorted neatly into simple categories. Almost all of them reveal some combination or two or more of the three forms. Some governments combine monarchic and aristocratic elements; others combine aristocratic and democratic, and so on. Attempts at classification are important for the scientific study of government in general, but discussion of these attempts cannot usefully precede careful, detailed study of particular governments.

Those who tried to classify governments as either monarchies, aristocracies, or democracies then proceeded to discuss the merits and demerits of each. By the end of the nineteenth century this discussion had become largely academic. Democracy, defined as rule by the many and marked by wide extensions of the franchise, had triumphed in the Western world. Whether it was the best form of government or not, there was no prospect of a return to aristocratic or monarchial rule.

Dictatorships. If this conclusion needed any confirmation, it was provided by events between the two World Wars. A new form of government—or a very old form of government in a new dress—appeared in Europe. As a result of revolutions in Russia in 1917, in Italy in 1922, and in Germany in 1933, the three most notorious modern dictatorships were established. Somewhat similar forms of rule were set up in Turkey, Poland, Spain, and other countries, such as those of Latin America. Since World War II, dictatorships more or less on the Russian model have been set up in Europe in Rumania, Bulgaria, Hungary, Yugoslavia, Albania, Poland, and Czechoslovakia. Most of these regimes have reviled the existing democracies but have paid them the compliment of regarding them as a serious rival form of government. Monarchy and aristocracy, as the world had hitherto understood these terms, they have dismissed with a shrug of contempt.

Although the three leading modern dictatorships mentioned above are worlds apart in many respects, they have certain striking similarities, particularly in their methods of gaining and maintaining power. These methods were so successful that aspiring revolutionaries are bound to continue to copy them in the future. Where democracy proves to be an inadequate form of government, it seems almost certain to be succeeded by the modern type of dictatorship.

A *Significant Distinction.* World War II was quite accurately represented as a titanic struggle between two forms of government, democracy and Fascist dictatorship. Although the democracies and the Communist dictatorship in Russia were allies in the war, they fell into distrust and bitter rivalry as soon as their common enemy had been overcome. Their fundamental beliefs about government and politics are sharply opposed. They now confront each other 'in a posture of war' in every part of the world. *The only classification of forms of government which seems at all closely related to current realities is that which distinguishes between democracy and dictatorship.* (However, one distinguished observer has inclined to the view that the essential difference is really between non-aggressive and aggressive states.[6])

Dictatorship has been spreading through the world in the past generation, replacing some democratic governments and threatening others. Superficially, it appears as a new form of government in the Western world, threatening the older established democratic forms. But in the perspective of history, democracy, as we know it today, is a newer and rarer form than monarchy, aristocracy, or dictatorship. The human race has had a much wider and longer experience of government imposed by one or a few than it has had of democratic self-government.

EARLY FORMS OF GOVERNMENT

Pre-Christian. Before the Christian era the prevailing form of government over an extensive territory was the despotic empire. For several thousand years, the Middle East, or large parts of it, was ruled successively by the Assyrian, Egyptian, Babylonian, and Persian empires, headed by kings who

---

[6] William Ebenstein, *Today's Isms,* 3rd ed. (Englewood Cliffs, N.J.: Prentice-Hall, 1961), pp. 80–88.

were believed to be gods or demigods as well as kings. They maintained a precarious kind of order throughout their dominions, and demanded crushing taxes and tributes in return. Apart from the dubious public order they provided, they did little for their people, who lived in fear of the tax-gatherer. Their polyglot subjects had no participation in or control over the government. The short-lived empire of Alexander the Great was of this kind.

City-States. In the millennium before Christ many small city-states grew up in the Mediterranean basin, the most famous of which were Athens and Rome. Initially at any rate, their territories were always small, limited to a few square miles. In the course of their histories, they ran the gamut of the forms of government, from monarchy to aristocracy to democracy to dictatorship. The democratic phases were very short in contrast to the duration of the other phases. During their brief appearance, however, the Greek and Roman democracies gave to the world the idea of free and equal citizenship.

Rome. At the dawn of the Christian era the Roman Republic was transformed into the Roman Empire, the greatest and longest-lived empire the Western world has known. It extended citizenship to all subject people of the Empire, and it ruled the known world for four hundred years. However, there were no effective institutional devices by which the citizens could participate in government and control the Empire. The power of the emperor became absolute, and the very office of Emperor became the plaything of the praetorian guard in Rome, who set up and tore down the emperors at will. There was nothing democratic about the forms of government under the Roman Empire.

Dark Ages. The Empire disintegrated in Western Europe in the fifth century of the Christian era. Civilization collapsed and government itself almost disappeared for about 500 years in the Dark Ages that followed. What government there was certainly was not democratic. In the Middle Ages (roughly A.D. 900 to A.D. 1500) Western Europe revived under the feudal system. In its political aspects, *feudalism* was an extremely decentralized form of government. Europe was broken up into thousands of little principalities, many of which would not make a large farm by modern standards. The feudal lord both owned the principality, or farm, and provided the government for his tenants and serfs. There were some elements of popular participation in feudal government, but it was everywhere predominantly monarchical or aristocratic in essential form.

Middle Ages. Throughout the Middle Ages, individual feudal lords and their descendants steadily expanded their holdings by a variety of methods, and the more successful of them finally set themselves up as kings. In this way, a number of large territories were each brought under the sway of a single central government. The process of consolidation first brought the kingdoms of England, France, Spain, Austria, and so on, into existence, and then continued until all the modern states of Europe as we have known them were established. But the final consolidation of Germany and Italy was not completed until after the middle of the nineteenth century.

Modernity. By the end of the fifteenth century feudalism had lost its vigor, and rule by a monarch was becoming the typical form of government in Europe. The Middle Ages came to an end and the modern era began. From the sixteenth to the nineteenth centuries most of Europe was ruled by absolute monarchs who treated their people as subjects rather than as citizens. Indeed, the Czar of Russia, the German Kaiser, and the Austrian Emperor continued to claim almost absolute power until they were all overwhelmed in World War I.

There democracy had triumphed. It seemed to reign supreme. Let us look at it now through a basic and forthright examination of its varied *modis operandi* in theory and practice—its ideals and ideas, its proved accomplishments and those that still remain expectations.

SUGGESTED REFERENCES FOR FURTHER READING

Brecht, A., *Political Theory: The Foundations of 20th Century Political Thought* (Princeton, 1959).

Burns, E. McN., *Ideas in Conflict* (Norton, 1961).

Butler, D. B., *The Study of Political Behaviour* (Hutchinson, 1958).

Catlin, G. E. G., *Systematic Politics* (U. of Toronto, 1962).

Charlesworth, J. C. (Ed.), *The Limits of Behavioralism in Political Science* (The Annals, 1962).

————, *Mathematics and the Social Sciences* (The Annals, 1963).

Crick, B., *The American Science of Politics: Its Opinions and Conditions* (Berkeley, 1959).

Dahl, R. A., *Modern Political Analysis* (Prentice-Hall, 1963).

Easton, D., *The Political System* (Knopf, 1953).

Froman, L. A., *People and Politics* (Prentice-Hall, 1962).

Heckscher, G., *The Study of Comparative Government and Politics* (Allen & Unwin, 1957).

Hyman, H. H., *Political Socialization: A Study in the Psychology of Political Behavior* (Free Press, 1959).

Hyneman, C. S., *The Study of Politics: The Present State of American Political Science* (U. of Illinois, 1959).

Lindsay, A. D., *The Modern Democratic State* (Oxford, 1947).

Lipset, S. M., *Political Man: The Social Bases of Politics* (Doubleday, 1959).

MacIver, R. M., *The Web of Government* (Macmillan, 1947).

————, *The Modern State* (Clarendon Press, 1926).

Macridis, R., *The Study of Comparative Government* (Doubleday, 1959).

Merriam, C., *Systematic Politics* (U. of Chicago, 1945).

Mitchell, W. C., *The American Polity* (Free Press, 1962).

Parsons, T., E. Shils, *et al.* (Eds.), *Theories of Society* (Free Press, 1962).

Ranney, A. (Ed.), *Essays on the Behavioral Study of Politics* (U. of Illinois, 1962).

Sabine, G. H., *A History of Political Theory*, 3rd ed. (Holt, Rinehart, & Winston, 1961).

Storing, H. J. (Ed.), *Essays on the Scientific Study of Politics* (Holt, Rinehart, & Winston, 1962).

Strauss, L. and J. Cropsey (Eds.), *History of Political Philosophy* (Rand McNally, 1963).

Ulmer, S. S. (Ed.), *Introductory Readings in Political Behavior* (Rand McNally, 1961).

UNESCO, *Contemporary Political Science: A Survey of Methods, Research & Teaching* (UNESCO, 1950).

Van Dyke, V., *Political Science: A Philosophical Analysis* (Stanford, 1960).

Verney, D. V., *The Analysis of Political Systems* (Free Press, 1960).

Voegelin, E., *The New Science of Politics: An Introduction* (U. of Chicago, 1952).

Wallas, G., *Human Nature in Politics,* new ed. (U. of Nebraska, 1962).

Young, R. (Ed.), *Approaches to the Study of Politics* (Northwestern, 1958).

II

Basic Assumptions of Democracy

INTRODUCTORY

What Is It? Looked at from the point of view of popular understanding, the word democracy provides a fascinating paradox. Few terms are so widely and favorably used by the people of the free world and at the same time mean so many different things to them. Lip-service to democracy is almost universal, even while it is being misunderstood and often betrayed in practice. Even Communist and other dictatorships use it widely and boastfully as a 'sop' to the people—e.g. the 'People's Democracies' of Russia's Eastern European satellites; Egypt's President Nasser's 'Presidential Democracy'; Ghana's President Kwame Nkrumah's 'Guided Democracy.' Yet the people of the United States, France, Britain, the Lowlands, and Scandinavia, among others, are devoted to its dimly perceived principles, and would fight for them again —as they have fought in the past—even without being clear as to what they were fighting for in specific terms.

DOUBTS. 'Make the world safe for democracy' was a famous slogan of the war effort of the Woodrow Wilson Administration. It was a noble rallying-cry, yet many who were willing to push that effort through to a finish were puzzled about exactly what democracy meant, especially since one of the Allies, Czarist Russia, was evidently fighting to preserve autocracy! During the Second World War, a war that was also fought for democracy, the government of the United States, for one, organized an extensive educational service to answer the oft-voiced query, 'What are we fighting for?' With very few exceptions, the questioners did not ask in a defeatist way; after all, more than anything else, they wanted to lick the 'Krauts' and the 'Japs'; and they would praise democracy in their interminable discussions or 'gripe-sessions.' Because they had been raised in a democratic climate and, for the most part, had not experienced the evils of dictatorship, they were neither articulate about democracy nor fully conscious of its meaning. They were inarticulate because they had absorbed a lot of understanding through the pores of the skin, as it were, but had never been forced to think about it. To many, *democracy* simply—and touchingly—meant a return to family and friends; to others, a chance-to-get-even-with those so-and-so officers and non-commissioned officers in civilian life; to still others, plainly no more than release from the bondage of military service. Probably for all of them, the now famous definition of democracy, written by E. B. White, an editor of *The New Yorker,* in response to a war-time query by the Writers' War Board, best expressed their innermost feelings:

> Surely the Board knows what democracy is. It is the line that forms on the right. It is the don't shove. It is the hole in the stuffed shirt through which the sawdust slowly trickles; it is the dent in the high hat. Democracy is the recurrent suspicion that more than half the people are right more than half the time. It is the feeling of privacy in the voting booths, the feeling of communion in the libraries, the feeling of vitality everywhere. Democracy is a letter to the editor. Democracy is the score at the beginning of the ninth. It is an idea which hasn't been disproved yet, a song the words of which have not gone bad. It's the mustard on the hot dog and the cream in the rationed coffee. Democracy is a request from a War Board, in the middle of a morning in the middle of a war, wanting to know what democracy is.[1]

Difficult Frame of Reference. In part, at least, the aforementioned uncertainties about meaning may be traced to the fact that the term *democracy* is so often used in almost the same breath to describe an *ideal* as well as a form of *government.* It is both—and it is neither: *It is pre-eminently a manner of governing and of being governed.* The basic authority is vested in the people; indeed, this is the literal meaning of the Greek *demos* (people) and *kratos* (authority) from which the term is derived.

FUNDAMENTALS. With that in mind it is, however, possible to discern certain *ideals,* i.e. fundamental aims for which we have fought, on which there is

[1] 'Notes and Comments' from 'The Talk of the Town,' *The New Yorker,* February 3, 1943.

a large measure of agreement, and which constitute the deeper meaning of democracy. Without raising questions of order of importance, these are:

> Respect for Individual Personality   Justice
> Individual Freedom   Rule by Law
> Belief in Rationality   Constitutionalism
> Equality

We shall now examine each of these basic beliefs on which the practice of democracy rests. In reading and thinking about them, the student of government should always remember some essential points: First, no one can run his life in any orderly or meaningful way without a set of values, a system of ends, or ideals, to guide him in deciding what to do next. Second, if people are to live peacefully together in society and not always at cross purposes, there must be some agreement on the values, the ends, and ideals that our life in society is supposed to serve. Third, most of us cling to a set of values by sheer habit, habit inculcated by the family, the school, and the church in our formative years. That is why soldiers and others often find they cannot give any articulate account of the principles by which they live. Fourth, the ideals we share in common set standards for governments. If we are going to be governed with our own consent and approval, there must be some congruence between what the government is doing and what seems good to the governed. Fifth, these ideals of government, as they are called, are often vague and general. We cannot get everyone to acknowledge that they are true in any absolute sense, and it is often hard to decide how to apply them in particular sets of circumstances.

Democratic Ideals and Sources. Our concern here is with the deeply imbedded beliefs that support and justify present-day democratic government, and with the rejection of those beliefs that have brought modern dictatorships to the fore. Understandably, there are significant differences in emphasis in the ideals actually honored in the different democratic states, and the modern dictators vary in the raucousness of their repudiation of Western thought. Yet there is a common core of values that supports all functioning Western democracies; and there is a basic similarity in the negations of the dictatorships.

This common core has been shaped through a long period of history. The beginnings of the Western tradition from which Britain and the United States derive their ideals of government can be traced to Greek political thought five centuries before the Christian era. Significant features of it come from Hebrew thought introduced into the West by Christianity. The Western tradition began to take distinctive shape with the mingling of Graeco-Roman and Hebraic-Christian elements in the later days of the Roman Empire. The fusing of these elements went on in Western Europe for a thousand years before the beginning of the modern age, and produced a remarkable synthesis in the political thought of the Middle Ages.

The modern age ushered in by the Renaissance and Reformation rejected the medieval synthesis and went back again to the classical age of Greece and Rome and to earlier Christianity for inspiration. Another four hundred years of thought and reflection went into the formulation of the democratic ideal as we know it in the West today. While the formulation is different and distinctive, it was not made out of whole cloth. In large measure, it is another synthesis achieved by reworking ideas long current in Western thought. Because of the great emphasis it puts on individual liberty, it is most accurately described as the *liberal democratic ideal*.

FUNDAMENTALS OF DEMOCRATIC BELIEF

A brief sketch cannot do justice to a synthesis that rests on two thousand years of thought and reflection. It can only attempt to state the essentials, ignoring many of the qualifications and refinements of statement needed for precision. Unfortunately, a bald statement of essentials lumps together a number of beliefs that seem on superficial appearance and in everyday unreflective experience to be mutually contradictory. Democrats believe in individual freedom and in social order, in individual freedom and social equality. Yet it often appears that the demands of one can only be met at the expense of the other.

(1) *Respect for Individual Personality*. It is not possible here to phrase a reconciliation of these beliefs. Actually, that reconciliation is one of the perennial and never-ending tasks of democratic politics. But it is necessary to see how a reconciliation is possible. The possibility exists because not all the various ends, purposes, values, and objectives cherished by democratic society are regarded as having equal rank or worth. Some are held because they are thought to contribute to the achieving of still other higher ends. Thus we believe in freedom and social equality not for themselves alone but rather because they are both needed in varying proportion to create the best environment for the development of individual personality.

A wide range of individual freedom enables some to get rich while others remain poor, thus producing sharp social inequalities. Intervening in this situation for the purpose of enforcing some measure of equality would limit individual freedom. The clash between the claims of individual freedom and social equality can be resolved by asking what combination of freedom and equality is needed to promote the purpose that is higher than either of them, namely, the full and rich development of individual personality.

If all other values are subordinate to the claims of individual personality, then it is the superior value, the highest of the democratic ideals. But why should it be the ultimate? Should not our highest aim be to do the will of God, or to serve Truth and Goodness? The ideals of democratic government, that is, government controlled by the people for their purposes, must be widely accepted and believed by the people or those ideals cannot, by definition, be democratic. Respect for individual personality is the maximum on which it has been possible to get widespread agreement. If we say our highest ideal is to do the will of God, that raises the question of what God's will is. If we say our highest ideal is to serve Truth and make it prevail, that raises the question of what Truth is. Answers to these questions will turn on religious or philosophical views about the nature of the universe and man's place in it. And when we ask what is the final scheme of things and man's place in it, we meet divergent answers and hot dispute. We are in the midst of the controversies of the ages and beyond the area in which general agreement is possible in our present state of knowledge.

DISAGREEMENT ON COSMIC ULTIMATES. We cannot frame or hold a common ideal at all if we must first agree about questions on which there is no present prospect of agreement. It is not an accident that all the functioning democracies are committed to religious toleration. Also, it is of the highest significance that modern democracy did not begin to develop and flourish until the commitment on religious toleration was made. For it is in the sphere of religious belief that views on first and last things find passionate and diverse expression. In taking religion out of politics, three assumptions vital to modern democracy were made.

First, by virtue of their common humanity, men have enough common interests and can find a sufficient basis of common beliefs to found a system of order without having to be committed to dogmatic answers to all the ultimates. Second, the profoundest need of all men is for self-expression (in selfless as well as self-regarding forms); all the various interests they struggle to defend and promote are means to that end. Third, they can agree to concede to others the claim to personality that they make for themselves on the ground that, given mutual trust and confidence, this is the best way to protect their own most cherished claims and promote their own deepest needs, including their need for fellowship with others of their fellow-men.

From the point of view of democracy, the highest value, *the ultimate for politics,* is the liberation of and respect for individual personality. In the cosmic sense, there are other values to which men may make personal commitments. For example, the Communist thinks himself to be in possession of a cosmic truth, a final purpose toward which all creation moves, and which he wants to see vindicated through political action at whatever cost to individual men and women right here and now. But from the point of view of democracy, government is a mundane affair, primarily concerned with a framework of order which will serve the concrete needs and interests of an earth-bound humanity. If men will make the adjustments necessary to secure firmly for one another these needs and interests, they are freed in their persons for the pursuit of the various forms of excellence that seem good to them. If one's vision is solitary, he can hitch his wagon to the star of his choice. If he finds others of like mind, they can go forward in voluntary and satisfying fellowship. If the vision fades for some, they need go no further. But when government is harnessed to a cosmic purpose, all are required to go in the same wagon to the same star, willy-nilly.

THE PURSUIT OF HIGHER VALUES. Making individual personality the ultimate value for politics does not deny the existence of other higher values for individual or group activity. On the contrary, it frees men to pursue them. If the highest value is to glorify God, God is best glorified by willing servants who submit freely to His demands as they see them. If the highest value is Truth, it must be discovered by individual minds free of constraint, building on the insights of other free minds. Truth, it is said, will set us free, but we must be free to search for it in the first place. And if Truth is to prevail throughout the world, it must suffuse individual personalities with a sense of its imperative. Belief cannot be coerced; it must be freely given.

Nor does individual personality as an ultimate value for politics deny that, in the final analysis, belief in the value of individual personality must rest on some view of cosmic ultimates, framed in religious or philosophical terms. It merely reiterates that we are far from any agreement on ultimate truth. For example, Christians affirm that belief in the importance of individual personality and in the related values of individual freedom, responsibility, and equality depends on acceptance of the Christian view of man and the universe; positivists deny it, and skeptics beg leave to doubt. All that is affirmed here is that democracy has been made a going concern in Britain and the United States with individual personality as the ultimate for politics, and has managed, over a long period, to get a common loyalty both from those who profess ignorance or doubt about cosmic ultimates and from those who claim to know the final answers but differ about what they are.

What we apprehend of these values, whether it be Goodness, Truth, or Beauty, is crystallized for us by the religious, intellectual, and artistic expression of individual personalities. It is true that individuals give diverse, and often conflicting, interpretations of these values. If it is recognized that each has a right to his own view as long as he respects the equal right of others to their views, competitive expression in these matters enriches our lives. To put it another way, art, literature, and science are debased, and the artist and scientist are defiled, when they conform slavishly to the dictates of a government which claims to be the final authority on first and last things. So the fundamental goal of democratic politics is the securing of the conditions needed for the realization of individual potentialities. Since it makes stupendous demands on human nature, perhaps this goal can never be fully achieved. Yet it is the pursuit of this goal that gives meaning to political life in the democracies.

STOIC AND CHRISTIAN EMPHASIS ON PERSONALITY. In committing itself to the value of individual personality, democracy is carrying forward one of the most persistent themes of the Western tradition. Before the Christian era, the Stoic philosophers in Greece asserted the brotherhood of men, the claims of a common humanity that makes us all members of one another. They urged the duty of the individual to realize Truth and Goodness in his own life, to enlighten the understanding of his fellows by precept and example, and to attest his faith in human dignity by succoring the unfortunate. It is difficult to overestimate the contributions of the Stoics, who broke away from antiquity, and whose works attained their culmination in the writings of Cicero and Seneca.

The central features of the Christian message are the infinite worth of the individual soul, the denial of all distinctions of rank or place, and the redemption of mankind through pity and love. Christianity asserted too the awful responsibility of the individual to God, and the necessity of rendering an account of his stewardship at the Last Judgment. In the final balance of the soul, duty to an earthly king would not be an excuse for failing in the service of God. While Christianity admits that Caesar is entitled to his due, it is not Caesar who sits at the Last Judgment. Religious duty has a higher claim than any earthly authority.

Translated into secular terms, the Christian emphasis on the unique value of the individual soul expresses itself as a profound concern for human personality. The imperative of love for one's neighbor and the denial of social distinctions issue in a demand for the creation of the conditions of self-realization for all, for rough equality of opportunity. The overriding duty to supernatural authority expresses itself in a demand for the limitation of the power of governments so as to ensure to the individual a sphere of private judgment in which his conscience is his guide. Conscience speaks peremptorily but with a different voice to different people. This accounts for much of the bewildering differences of opinion in democratic politics.

Thus the ideal of democracy, although stated in secular terms, has a powerful religious sanction for its main tenets. There is much of the passion that religious feeling evokes in the support ardent democrats give to the claims of personality. There is much of Christian compassion in the demand for a large measure of social equality. Christian belief in the responsibility of the individual to God gives strong support to the claim for individual freedom.

(2) *Individual Freedom.* At later points in this book we shall be concerned with the political significance of the claim for individual freedom and private judgment and the consequent proliferation of diverse opinions. At present we are concerned with the ideals on which there is a large measure of agreement, verging on a religious dogma. In so far as there is a persistent enduring ideal, it is respect for personality. Liberty and equality are also democratic ideals but they are honored when they sub-serve the claims of personality, and limited and qualified in so far as they do not contribute to this purpose. The claims of personality provide the criterion for testing the validity of all other ideals in the political sphere.

INDIVIDUAL PERSONALITY AND FREEDOM. Individual freedom or liberty is the necessary condition for the realization of the potentialities of personality. The sheltered, protected person, like the slave whose choices are made for him by others, is likely to be a colorless, starved, and even weak personality. It is the making of moral choices in which we assess the alternatives and then have to abide the consequences of the decision that develops character and makes life rich and meaningful. The long struggle for individual freedom arose from the claims of ever larger numbers of men seeking to secure for themselves this means to the enrichment of their lives.

It must be added at once that the ideal of respect for personality does not support and justify *every* claim for freedom. *It justifies only that freedom which is exercised responsibly, which respects the equal claims of other personalities to the conditions of self-realization.* The criminal laws express a thousand limitations on the freedoms of those who are disposed to disregard the claims of others. As we have already pointed out, some basic order and physical security from violence is at once seen to be necessary if we are to live in society and enjoy the enrichment of our lives that society makes possible. More controversially, if the freedom of the businessman or the laborer or the farmer to do as he likes with his own property or service can be shown, in present-day conditions, to blight and frustrate the lives of many people, there is a case for its limitation. The ideal of freedom is therefore not an absolute, not an end in itself, but rather a means to the liberation of personality and justified only to the degree that it serves that purpose. This, of course, is the key to the reconciliation of the rival claims of freedom and order.

INDIVIDUAL FREEDOM AND COMPETITIVE STRIVING. Where there are millions of individuals, each bent on securing and defending his claims to self-realization, there is bound to be continual competitive striving and collision. The peaceful harmonizing of freedom and order may seem an impossible task. It is impossible if each thinks only of himself without regard to the claims of others, and blindly refuses to consider the mutual benefits of participation in a society inspired by mutual respect. But the democratic ideal postulates a decent respect for others, an admission that each must exercise his freedom responsibly, and a willingness at least to discuss the validity of his claims and to refer them to some tribunal for settlement. It permits each to argue his case tenaciously, yet counsels him to concede something to the reasonable claims of others reasonably put forward. If this attitude were not widely held, the widespread discussion that goes on in newspapers and legislatures and on election platforms would never take place. Men who are not prepared at some point to contemplate concessions will not be willing to debate. The very fact of debate implies a willingness to 'listen to reason,' and a recognition by the participants that they will have to moderate their demands if these are shown in discussion to be inconsistent with some generally accepted principle.

(3) *Belief in Rationality.* The democratic ideal assumes, in other words, that man is a *rational being,* capable of finding principles of action and sub-

ordinating private desires to those principles. This assumption is of basic importance. If men will not 'listen to reason,' democracy cannot be an enduring form of government. The conflicting aims and interests of numerous individuals cannot be arbitrated and harmonized by discussion and debate unless there are generally accepted rules to decide who wins the debate. The simplest and most obvious of these rules is that the majority carries the day. But the bare principle of majority rule is just as irrational as the proposition that might is right. We choose ballots—and the process of discussion involved therein—rather than bullets because the former make room for rational procedures. For example, in discussion of rival claims, it is common to ask each claimant what he would expect to get if he were in the other's shoes. This is an appeal to a principle, the principle of equality of treatment for all who stand in the same position.

In a society where there is mutual respect for individual personality, men have some confidence that when the majority is making up its mind the appeal to principles will not go entirely unheeded. To be more specific, there is some confidence that when a case is shown to rest on erroneous statements of fact, it will be discredited; that when it is shown to conflict with some widely accepted principle, it will be held to be a bad case. On the other hand, there is some confidence that when a case rests on proved facts and accepted principle, it will be given favorable consideration.

Of course, none of us shows full respect for facts and logic all the time. Some men are always immune to reason; and there are times when emotional appeals seem almost to drive reason from the field. Men are also creatures of feeling and not mere logical machines. But the peaceful interplay of free personalities requires a substantial measure of rationality. The democratic ideal therefore has to assume that, through effort, men can move from the plane of feeling to the plane of reason, there to talk out their differences and settle them on some basis of principle.

(4) *Equality*. Another vital democratic ideal is equality. Just as in the case of individual freedom, there is the widest possible divergence of interpretation on what this ideal requires. Some democrats interpret it narrowly, saying it requires only equality before the law and equal political rights in voting. At the other extreme, it is held by some to require social and economic equality, putting everyone on the same level of income and obliterating all social distinctions. Much of the struggle in contemporary democratic politics is concerned with this issue.

Every attempt to define the ideal of equality with precision raises the problem of harmonizing it with the ideal of liberty. It is obvious that men are not equal in natural endowment, whether it be health or stature or intelligence. As George Orwell obliquely stated, 'all men are born equal, but some are born more equal than others!' So, if they are left free to make of themselves what their inborn capacities make possible, they will turn out to be unequal in artistic perception, intellectual accomplishment, economic status, and what not. Accordingly, an attempt to enforce a dead level of economic and social status would involve the sharpest of restrictions on individual freedom. Even if the emphasis is on pulling the weaker up, a uniform level can only be reached by holding the stronger down. On the other hand, the lifting of all restrictions on individual liberty would mean, in practical effect, the abandoning of the ideal of equality. How are liberty and equality to be reconciled?

LIBERTY AND EQUALITY. They are to be reconciled by remembering that both liberty and equality are subordinate means to the end of releasing the potentialities of individual personality on the widest possible scale. The development of a rich variety of personalities requires a large measure of liberty and forbids all attempts to impose a dead level of social and economic equality. On the other hand, if men are to live together with mutual respect and harmonize their differences by peaceful discussion, they must be able to meet on some plane of equality. For the purposes of discussion, they must treat one another as if they were equal. Even in the midst of differences in natural endowment and in social and economic position, the assumption of equality for the purpose of discussion need not be a fiction. The Christian and Stoic doctrines of the brotherhood of man, if strongly held, dwarf all differences between men. Differences of natural endowment and of social position can become almost irrelevant if men have a sufficiently keen appreciation of what they have in common.

However, we know that, for most of us, the consciousness of brotherhood needs to be buttressed by the sharing of common experience. The antagonism that exists between classes even in democratic countries clearly illustrates this point. So also does the fact that there is more give and take within nations than between nations. Where there are wide distinctions of economic status and social position, the feelings of superiority and inferiority that emerge make discussion between the two extremes almost impossible. It is highly unlikely that the depressed poor will be able to debate on anything like equal terms with the very rich. Even with good will, the experience of life of the two groups is so different that they can scarcely understand each other. They belong to different worlds and cannot find enough common ground for discussion.

EQUALITY OF OPPORTUNITY. The convention of equality, vitally necessary for the purposes of discussion, can scarcely be maintained where social and economic inequalities are so great as to be a standing refutation of it. Discussion moves most easily in a society where these inequalities are kept within bounds. Under the impulsion of the ideal of equality, democratic societies have been moving steadily to reduce existing social and economic inequalities. In this movement, the aim has not been to reach a flat level of economic equality but rather to create a rough equality of opportunity so that each individual, no matter how circumscribed his origins, may by his efforts bring his innate capacities to fruition. Phrased in this way, the ideals of liberty and equality can be reconciled in the service of personality. The actual reconciliation at a particular time and place has to be worked out through discussion in the political process.

LEGAL AND POLITICAL EQUALITY. To sum up, the ideal of equality has insisted that men are politically equal, that all citizens are equally entitled to take part in political life, to exercise the franchise, to run for and hold office. It has insisted that individuals shall be equal before the law, that when the general law confers rights or imposes duties, these rights and duties shall extend to all; or conversely, that the law shall not confer special privileges on particular individuals or groups—such as exempting all-American football stars from the law of assault and battery. For the rest, the emphasis has not been on an enforced flat level of actual equality but on a liberating equality of opportunity.

(5) *Justice*. No account of the ideals of government would be even superficially adequate without some discussion of the ideal of justice. Those who struggled to establish democratic government in the world and those who have struggled to improve it have been inspired by a quest for justice. Indeed, Western political thought for more than two thousand years can be represented as a ceaseless effort to define justice so that governments and other social arrangements could be directed toward achieving it. Every form of government we have known has been defended on the ground that its rule was just, and has also been attacked because it maintained intolerable injustice. There has always been a universal human yearning for justice.

JUSTICE AS VAGUE IDEAL. Yet despite the protracted debate about justice, no general and lasting agreement on a definition of justice has been reached. To take only the question of the distribution of economic rewards: some have tried to show that justice requires payment according to merit, while others have insisted that the standard must be payment according to need, leaving, be it noted, both merit and need still to be defined. Still others have urged standards of justice as diverse as equality of incomes, on the one hand, and what the market will bear, on the other. Equally divergent and clashing views are held on what justice requires in social relationships outside the economic field. One can almost say that each has his own private dream of a just society, and that dream defines justice for him. Just as men disagree about Truth, Beauty, and Goodness, so they disagree about Justice. Yet a common ideal requires agreement rather than disagreement.

JUSTICE AND FREEDOM. However, it is not possible to dismiss the discussion of justice in this way. From the time of Aristotle there has been a persistent tendency to define justice as some kind of a proportion between merits on the one hand, and rewards and recognition on the other. For example, Justinian in his codification of Roman Law in A.D. 525 defined justice for the legal system *as the giving to every man his due.* Even this, of course, remains vague, for it presupposes a recognizable standard for weighing merit and assessing rewards.

Men are not satisfied to get merely what some authority external to themselves thinks they deserve. Hence the establishing of merit in a way that will be accepted as just requires men to be free to try to prove their own valuation of themselves as correct. Equally, since one man's meat is another man's poison, they must be free to say what they regard as fitting reward or recognition. If what wage-workers really want is a share in the control of their working conditions, the demand cannot be met conclusively by merely raising their wages. In other words, *justice as a democratic ideal is in part included under the ideal of freedom.*

JUSTICE AND EQUALITY. The notion of justice as a proportion also implies equality in the sense that persons of equal merit should get equal reward and recognition. Phrased in this general and comprehensive way, the ideal of justice almost comes to a nice refining of the ideal of equality. If governments were asked to enforce justice in this comprehensive sense, some authority would have to be set up that would decide exactly what each was worth and what each should get. But where the dominating political ideal is the liberation of personality, men will not agree to this, and the ideal of justice so phrased would be a profoundly disrupting force rather than a unifying ideal.

As was suggested earlier, the political ideal of democracy is not the vindication of cosmic truth. Neither is it the vindication of some conception of exquisite and exact justice, to be enforced though the heavens fall. Its primary concern is rather the establishment of order and security adequate for the free development of personality. It expresses a faith that once men are secure in their persons they will learn to treat one another with respect and even become friends. Friends do not need to demand justice of one another because that—and more—is freely given without the asking.

JUSTICE AS IMPARTIAL LAW IMPARTIALLY ADMINISTERED. But none of this can come to pass without a solid framework of order and security. Moreover, in this vital sphere, all should be treated equally. We all need the protection that order affords, and therefore we must all be made to observe its requirements. These can only be met by measuring every action against standards laid down in advance by law. The law should be general, playing no favorites and laying down reciprocal rights and duties for all. If it exempts some from the duties it imposes on others, it creates privilege. If the judge, in applying a general law, excuses some but not others from the obligations it imposes, he creates favoritism.

When Justinian said justice aimed to give every man his due, he was declaring against legal privilege and against favoritism in applying the law. It is highly significant that when we think today about an impartial law being impartially applied, we talk about the administration of justice. The most specific meaning given to justice in the Western tradition is justice according to law, which in the main means *equality before the law*. Here the elusive notion of justice as a proportion between merits and deserts is brought down to earth. All merit equal treatment in the vital sphere of order and security protected by law. Also, as we have seen, it is now widely believed that all merit some rough equality of opportunity.

(6) *Rule by Law*. The ideal of an impartial law impartially administered is, of course, conceived as a buttress to individual personality. No one can have any security for his claims as a person, no one can plan his life or take the risk of the responsibility for his own actions, unless he knows what he has a right to try to do and what demands others can effectively make on him. But if he is forearmed with this knowledge he has a chart for his voyage. He can anchor his personality firmly with the cords of the law. Yet no one can expect to have charts and anchorage supplied solely for his

convenience. Each must submit to law for the benefit of others embarked on the adventure of life. Realizing the potentialities of personality requires freedom, but always freedom under law.

To have to submit to capricious and forcible interference is an indignity as well as a frustration. In submitting to the law, however, one submits to a principle which makes equal demands on all. In this there is no indignity, and only such frustration of individual desires as is equally suffered by others for the sake of an ordered society.

LAW AS CURB ON RULERS. The individual needs to know the limits of his rights and duties in relation to his fellow citizens and in relation to his government. There is little point in being free from the caprice of private persons if one remains subject to unlimited and unpredictable demands by the government. There is no essential difference between being bullied by a bully and being bullied by a policeman, a customs official, or an income-tax inspector. Capricious action by a government can be far more oppressive than capricious action by private persons, because governments have far more power, a longer reach, and much greater resources for persecution.

In view of this, the good life is not to be secured by finding a wise ruler and then blindly obeying whatever orders he thinks good for his subjects. Rather, it is to be secured through obedience to a law that defines clearly what the government as well as private persons can and cannot do. Five centuries before the Christian era, Aristotle explained why it was better for the citizens to be ruled by a fixed law than by the imponderable wisdom of even a wise and just ruler. Ever since then Western political thought has been developing and strengthening this conviction. The ideal of rule by law, of 'a government of laws and not of men,' has been one of the strongest beliefs in the democratic creed. It is an absolutely essential one.

(7) *Constitutionalism.* Closely related to the ideal of rule by law is the ideal of constitutionalism—of which much more will be said later. Starting from the conviction that governmental action should be in accordance with law carefully laid down beforehand, it holds that the best way to accomplish this is to establish a fundamental law, a constitution, that defines the organs of government, prescribes how they shall function, and outlines the basic relationships between government and the private citizen. Government is then denied the power to change this fundamental law, except by carefully circumscribed method, and is required to observe its terms. Actually, of course, constitutionalism is a means for achieving the ideal of rule by law. But in the democratic world, the constitution—be it written, unwritten, or

mixed—has become a symbol around which men who are in disagreement on other points can be rallied. A special sanctity attaches to the constitution, and a special revulsion to unconstitutional actions or proposals.

It is worthwhile to note how deep the roots of constitutionalism are in Western culture. Greek political thought was profoundly concerned with the notion of a constitution which would regularize the actions of government, but it did not put especial emphasis on the rights of individuals against governments. Strong emphasis on this point was supplied by Stoic and Christian thought. The Stoic philosophers worked out a conception of a law of nature unconditionally binding on all men at all times in all places, because it expressed the permanent demands of their innermost nature. That is to say, it was thought of as a fundamental law binding on rulers and ruled alike. Christian thought asserts that God rules the world and that the commandments He gives His creatures form the Divine law. Rulers should obey this fundamental law as part of their duty to God. Moreover, individuals cannot render to God that which is God's if Caesar is allowed to use his power to prevent them from doing so. Government therefore must be limited by a law higher than any commands it makes. Secular and religious elements in the Western tradition combine to support rule by law and constitutionalism. To trace the Bill of Rights and other constitutional guarantees of the Constitution of the United States, for example, to their sources in human thought, would take us back to Stoic philosophy and basic Christian doctrine. It may be well to do so from time to time!

DISAGREEMENTS DESPITE COMMON IDEALS

It has been said that these seven fundamentals of democratic belief represent the motivating political ideals of democracy. It cannot be said, however, that they are engraved on the heart of every citizen of a democracy! There are always substantial numbers who are little moved by ideals of any kind. Even those who acknowledge these ideals do not always give automatic and undivided loyalty to them, just as professing Christians do not always live up to the high professions of their faith. Moreover, since the ideals all celebrate the importance of individual personality, they quite naturally invite individual self-expression. Individuals earnestly bent on developing and expressing their inherent capacities will often find it difficult to draw the fine line between legitimate expression of themselves and unwarranted interference with the claims of others for opportunities to realize their capacities. Indeed, the line is so difficult to draw that some serious thinkers in every age have deemed it impossible and have urged the necessity of authoritarian government to keep everyone in his place.

What Should Government Do To Realize the Ideals? Most important of all, these ideals are vague and do not lay down specific rules for harmonizing the infinity of conflicting claims that may easily arise. What should the government do in specific terms to encourage the widest possible realization of individual capacities? At what point does individual freedom become disruptive of order and thus require limitation? How far can the government go in trying to redress grave social inequalities without shackling initiative and destroying incentive? Rules of thumb cannot be laid down for these or for a thousand other issues because almost everything depends on the social and economic circumstances of the time when and the place where the question arises. The ideals provide us only with a goal. They tell us little about the means of reaching or approaching it.

To be still more specific, does the industrial factory and wage system where the many spend their working day under the direction of a few frustrate the personalities of the many? And if it does, what alternative organization of the complex division of labor will be at once less frustrating and also compatible with the maintenance of the conditions of freedom? If a partial answer to this question is the compulsory recognition of trade unions and compulsory collective bargaining, at what point, if at all, does the power of the trade union to withhold labor in a strategic industry imperil social order and deny the reasonable expectations of consumers and workers in other sectors of industry? A comprehensive system of social security helps to redress social and economic inequalities, promotes equality of opportunity, and ensures basic necessities to exposed groups in the community. At what point, if at all, does the security thus provided reduce incentives in the recipients? At what point does the high taxation necessary to finance such measures seriously reduce initiative and enterprise in the taxpayer?

These and many others are questions on which honest men differ. They differ although all may well be equally agreed on the political ideals of democracy and all equally anxious to direct the actions of government to these ideals. Such questions cannot be answered with the convincing assurance that supports the solution of a problem in mathematics. The answers will turn partly on questions of fact, on which it is always very hard to get adequate evidence, and partly on estimates of how human beings will behave in given circumstances. In many matters that vex our present politics, it is impossible to say with certainty and to get general agreement on what to do.

The Clash of Interests and Convictions. Here then are the reasons why, despite broad general agreement on goals, there is so much diversity of opinion, confusion of counsel, and cross-purposes in action in democratic life. The ideals postulate freedom and therefore diversity: they welcome self-expression. Yet we must co-operate to satisfy our need for society, and to preserve and improve the conditions for a further approach to the ideals. Co-operation in politics, in deciding what shall be undertaken and enforced in the name of all, runs into a considerable measure of indifference, a good deal of individual selfishness, honest ignorance of the effects of our actions on the legitimate claims of others, and *honest disagreement about what can or should be done.*

This last presents peculiar difficulties. Men of high purpose who hold strongly to ideals generally also have strong opinions on how to achieve them. Conscience is thus brought into play and sharpens the clash when disagreement is discovered. For example, Christians who feel a profound responsibility for making the will of God manifest in history find a special urgency in many political issues. It leads some to press passionately for the extension of governmental action, and others to press passionately against encroachment by government on the sphere of private judgment.

Agreed Procedures for Dealing with Disagreements. What prevents this diversity of immediate aims and confusion of counsel from disrupting democratic society and degenerating into violence? The widespread acceptance of common ideals helps to dispose men to study together the reasons why they differ on means. It is here that the agreement on certain procedures for handling differences is of vital importance to democracy.

First, there is the agreement that when the state acts, it must act through law (or, as in Britain, universally accepted custom) laid down beforehand in accordance with procedures established in the constitution. Individuals and groups who object to a proposed law should always have a chance to protest and state their objections before coercive state action is taken.

Second, there is the agreement, resting on mutual respect, that differences must be submitted to discussion and debate. Indeed, the process of law-making always involves debate in the legislature; and it often involves long preliminary discussion in innumerable groups, in the press and on the radio, within political party organizations, and between parties on election platforms.

Third, there is the assumption that one's fellows are, within limits, rational beings and will submit their differences to the tests of fact and of logic. There are always two sides to a story. Discussion undertaken in a reasonable and accommodating spirit is likely to be fruitful, revealing some common middle ground on which, admittedly, no one gets his own way entirely but every one gets some concession in reward for cogent facts and argument and for his reasonable attitude.

Fourth, there is the agreement to conclude the debate at some stage by taking a vote, and then to abide by the decision of the majority. The good loser is an essential phenomenon of democracy as well as of sports. Minorities agree to accept majority decision because they have reason to hope that majority decision, reached after a fair hearing in a reasonable spirit, will incorporate some concessions to their points of view, and because they know they can always raise the issue again when circumstances seem favorable. The case of the minorities is not finally defeated by an adverse vote, but rather adjourned for further hearing.

Fundamentally, the democratic political process is one of discussion, accommodation, and compromise. Many persons of imperious, inflexible temperament dislike it and resist it. But as long as the great majority insist on submission to the procedures just outlined, the democratic political process is reasonably secure against disintegration from within.

THE PLACE OF THE STATE IN DEMOCRATIC IDEALS

Given these ideals of government, it can be seen why the state is thought of as an association for securing the common interests and promoting the common purposes of the individuals who are its members. Since the principal point of general agreement and common purpose among the members is liberation of individual personality through individual freedom, the genuinely shared interests and purposes cover only a small part of the interests and purposes entertained and pursued by the members. The greater, and the more cherished, part of human activity must go on outside the state in the area of freedom it is designed to secure. Moreover, the only way to find out what is genuinely shared is through discussion and vote of the members. Even then, the inherent diversity of views noted above compels *continuous compromise in deciding on the scope of action for the state.* Two conclusions follow.

Government: Means not End. FIRST, the state is an instrument of its members. The government, meaning the men who direct the activities of the state at a given time, cannot assert that it has exalted purposes beyond the criticism and understanding of its members. The state cannot be set up as an end in itself. Even when it calls on individuals to sacrifice their lives in a war, the sacrifice is justified only on the ground that it is necessary to protect the society without which individuals cannot realize any of their purposes. That is to say, the supreme demand that the state can make is for the securing of a common interest in maintenance of the society, and it rests on the tragic fact noted by Mr. Justice Holmes—that societies are founded on the death of men.

SECOND, because of its restriction to common purposes, it cannot be an instrument through which particular individuals and groups realize *all* their purposes. Each has to share the state with others. Because the state has to do something for everybody, it cannot be all things to anybody. No one can expect to bend it to the comprehensive service of his particular purposes.

At the same time, men will give their best only to purposes which they, for whatever reason, find good. This is the essential significance of free personality. It follows that men cannot hope to realize their loftiest aims through the state. While the state is necessary for social life, and therefore an aid to the realization of our fondest dreams, we have to find the principal meaning of our lives outside of it.

So the state is not an exalted communion in which men lose themselves gladly and spend themselves prodigally. That calls for spontaneity, and there is little spontaneous enthusiasm left after the processes of discussion and compromise necessary for defining the sphere of state action have been carried through. Discussion consumes time and delays decision. The compromises reached seem, to many, to be tainted with mediocrity. Decisions reached by compromises are rarely executed with single-minded devotion.

The state therefore does not inspire reverence and unthinking obedience. It may evoke respect, and even affection, but it is the affection a man has for a tool that serves his purpose. When a tool begins to turn in his hand or does him injury rather than service, he does not submit to its imperfections but turns critically to remedy its defects and dangers. So shall we consider the state as long as we are moved by the ideals of government sketched above.

Remoteness of the Modern State. The state is also too remote from the lives of most men for them to find in it the principal meaning of existence. Modern states number their citizens in tens of millions dispersed over a great area. This is true even in Britain and France, small as they are by present-day standards. The only active and direct participation of most citizens is in periodic elections. Even with the present wide range of state activities, most citizens have little active contact with the state. Most of them never see Congress or Parliament in action, never see even the outsides of the buildings in Washington, London, or Paris, where the great decisions are taken and administration is carried on.

There is, of course, wider and more sustained participation in state and municipal government, but even there only a tiny fraction of the citizen body gives much of its effort to the work of government. If all had to find the deepest significance of life in the association that is the state, they would lead intolerably barren existences.

Contrast with the Ancient City-State. If the state is small in numbers and area, fellowship in it may have a larger meaning for the citizen. In the city-state of ancient Athens, where the citizens were few, lived cheek by jowl in relative freedom from economic pressure through the use of slave labor, and participated directly and frequently in political life, citizenship came closer to being a full-time job. In those conditions, more things were shared in common and the state was the active supervisor of the common life. The city had an official religion. To put it in our terms, church and state were one. The combined political and religious regulations and ceremonies pervaded almost every aspect of the citizen's life. In this respect, the city-state of Athens resembled the early New England town meeting, which undertook not only the political functions of order and general security but also the supervision of morals and religious observances. Thus the reflective minds of Athens were led to say, in effect, that the purpose of the state was to teach men how to live the good life.

Just as a school which opens the windows of the world for the growing mind can absorb almost the whole life of the adolescent, so the Athenian might be expected to find his life and work as a citizen almost completely absorbing. There was an intimacy in the Greek city-state which made it more like a close-knit family than like the United States of America. Just as a family bound together by loyalty and affection and sharing a common household can often provide the greatest satisfaction for its members, so it could be claimed that fellowship in the city-state was the transfiguring experience for individuals.

Of course, whatever the values of this close fellowship, it had its costs as well. The citizen was so busy participating in politics, submitting to the routine of custom and the regimen of religious observance, that he had little time to be himself. A powerful, almost fierce, communal spirit demanded a high degree of conformity from individuals. Even Socrates, the symbol of liberated intelligence, paid his respects to the gods of the city.

Whether or not this fellowship was worth the price, the choice is not open to the citizen of the modern state. The modern state is too remote from him. While it is well adapted to caring for interests that are common to all, it is not able to meet the particular diverse needs to which the family, for example, can minister. The state can build vast armies for the common defense and equip the soldier adequately for that purpose. But it has the greatest difficulty in catering to the diverse needs of soldiers as individual human beings.

The Importance of Voluntary Association. Yet men need fellowship almost as much as they need their individuality. They cannot realize their individuality except through society. If association in the state cannot supply fellowship, it must be found in other ways. Where the ideals supporting democratic government have been accepted, it has been found through voluntary association. The interests of personality cannot be served at all without allowing like-minded individuals to club together for common purposes. As we shall see in detail later, freedom of association is one of the principal freedoms derived from the democratic ideals of government and supported by constitutional guarantees.

Historically, the critical step was taken when religious toleration was accepted. Its acceptance meant that each was entitled to his own views on religious questions, and to join with others of similar views to establish a communion of their own. In other words, the church became a voluntary association providing both freedom and fellowship. Once freedom of association was conceded in the field of religion, there was no reason for withholding it in any other field of legitimate human activity. An ever-growing number of voluntary groups came into existence, each to further purposes shared in common by its members.

Because each association is devoted to some end that seems good to its members, it helps to give meaning to the lives of the members and in return gets some of their loyalty and allegiance. Particular groups can spend themselves on objectives that seem trivial or even reprehensible to outsiders as long as their activities do not imperil the common interest in public order and general security. They can move faster to their objectives because there is relatively little diversity of views among the members to be discussed and compromised. The dissenters can always resign from the voluntary association whereas they cannot resign from association in the state except by leaving the country. Freedom and fellowship are reconciled through the voluntary association.

THE RISE OF DEMOCRACY

A Glance into History. In the preceding chapter we looked briefly at the origin and the rise of the state as we know it today. We must now examine briefly the development of democracy.

Democracy in the city-states of the ancient world was a short interlude in the long record of government by one or a few. Modern democracy, as we shall see, is sharply different from ancient democracy, particularly in its ambitious application to an enormous territory and to tens of millions of population. This kind of democracy is entirely new in the world. Its effective establishment dates from about the middle of the nineteenth century. We have had little more than a century of experience with it, while other forms of government, in various manifestations, have lasted thousands of years.

Absolute monarchy had never really established itself in Britain. The attempts of the Stuart kings so to assert themselves were defeated in the seventeenth century. From then until the Great Reform Act of 1832, which extended the franchise to the propertied middle classes, Britain was ruled by a landed aristocracy. Universal-manhood franchise was not reached in Britain until 1884. The American Revolution in the late eighteenth century was a popular revolution, but manhood franchise was not fully realized in the United States until about 1840. Similarly, the aspirations for democracy expressed in the French Revolution at the end of the eighteenth century were not actually attained until after the middle of the nineteenth century.

Once established, however, modern democracy spread very quickly. Monarchic and aristocratic governments were everywhere giving way before it in the years preceding World War I. President Wilson represented World War I as a struggle 'to make the world safe for democracy' against monarchical and aristocratic reaction. Victory in this struggle was interpreted as the final victory of democracy over the older forms of government. All new governments established in Europe after that war (excepting always the Soviet Union) were set up under thoroughly democratic constitutions. Yet no sooner did its victory seem assured and complete than a pronounced reaction set in against democracy. This reaction has given us the modern dictatorships.

Reaction against Democracy. So far, the actual replacing of democratic government by dictatorship in our day has been in countries where democracy was entirely new, as in Weimar Germany, in Guinea, or Ghana; or insecurely based, as in Italy or undermined by agents of the Soviet Union, as in Czechoslovakia. Democracy has never been voluntarily abandoned by countries in which it had been *efficiently* established. The desperate eagerness of the leaders of the Soviet Union and of the eastern European countries now under Communist dictatorship to prove that their governments are genuinely 'democratic' shows that the popular aspiration for democracy is still very strong.

But in actual fact democracy has failed to work in many of the countries in which it has been tried. Even in the countries where it has been longest established and works best, the events of the last fifty years have made many wonder if it will be as transitory in the modern world as it was in the ancient world. Why have its prospects declined so rapidly? Why does it work in some countries and not in others? Under what conditions can it be expected to work, and under what conditions it is likely to fail?

The first step in trying to find answers for these questions is to examine the structure and operation of democratic government in countries where it has worked best. Of the larger countries in the world, the United States and Britain have had the longest and most successful experience in democratic government. It was in these countries that religious toleration was first and most firmly established. Together with France, the Lowlands, Switzerland, and the Scandinavian lands, they have the strongest hold on democratic ideals, and they certainly have given the widest application to, and found the most effective guarantees for, individual freedom. Study of the governments of the three largest among these countries should throw light on the essential elements of democratic government and indicate at least some of the conditions in which it can be expected to work successfully.

Contrasts in Ancient and Modern Democracy. Even if an exact definition of democracy as a form of government is difficult to frame, certain common features of the democracies of Britain and the United States, for example, are readily perceived. They have little in common with the democracies Aristotle studied. He was concerned with the Greek city-states, societies within the area of a county and with the population of a smallish city, of which only a minority were citizens entitled to take part in government. The modern democracies have an enormous territory and millions in population. Substantially all who live in the territory are citizens and almost all adult citizens enjoy full political rights.

The ancient democracies were *direct democracies*. Each citizen participated directly in making laws, and could expect to come to public office from time to time by lot or rotation. The democracies to be discussed here are called *representative democracies,* because the common form of participation of the citizen in the control of government is in voting for representatives who govern on his behalf. Other significant ways of influencing the government are open to the citizens generally and are exercised by some, but the periodic election of representatives is the principal and decisive method the many have for enforcing their rule.

There are a host of other differences between the characters of the ancient and modern democracies. Also, of course, the environment, economic, social, and cultural, is entirely different. However much the liberal democratic ideals owe to the political theory of the Greek city-state, they are a modern formulation profoundly influenced by Stoic and Christian thought, which did not make its impact on the world until after the decline of the Greek city-state. Thus little would be gained in trying to compare governments which are not at all comparable. It is true that the closer we approach the fundamental problems of modern democracy the more relevant become the reflections on democracy of the ancient political thinkers. Some patterns of political behavior appear to be repeated throughout the ages. Still, we cannot approach these fundamental problems until some appreciation of the concrete institutions and actual working of modern democracy has been gained.

THE CONSTITUTIONAL TRADITION OF MODERN DEMOCRACY

Basic Influences. The structure of democratic governments has been given a special bias by certain beliefs that came into the Western world with the Renaissance. Briefly, these beliefs, which are an important part of the democratic ideals we have been discussing, exalt the individual and depreciate—sometimes excessively—the collective restraints which society puts upon him through custom, law, and government. They are deeply influenced by the Christian insistence that there is a higher law than the law of the state, whether it be the dictates of an organized church or the promptings of private conscience. The claims of a church can sometimes be so imperious as to threaten public order, and private conscience sometimes leads us to an outrageous disregard of others. These beliefs do not reject all restraints. They recognize the necessity of some minimum of government. We all have impulses which must be restrained, and we are never sure when our own inhibitions, our limited understanding of the claims of others to an equal freedom, and our desire to be thought well of by our fellows will need to be supplemented by the threat, or by the actual use, of the organized force of the community. So there must be government and it must have the ultimate power to apply direct coercion to individuals.

Power. This power to apply force must be a monopoly, because to allow two or more independent centers of coercive power in a community is to create the conditions for civil war. But according to these beliefs, such a monopoly has grave dangers. The obverse of a belief in the importance of the individual is a fear of government which unless controlled can crush him—and more often than not has done so. Government, though necessary, is potentially one of the greatest evils. Like fire, it is a good servant and a bad master. And it is always potentially master because of its monopoly of naked force. What prevents the government of the day from using the army and the police to enforce on us its conception of our own good is the knowledge that its power is contingent and may be taken away at the next election, and the further knowledge that if it pursues its own whims in these matters it will soon find itself violating the law which binds the government as well as the citizens.

Leaders. It will be quickly and properly objected that the Hoovers and the Trumans, the Edens and the Attlees, the Mendès-Frances, and the Spaaks, are not the clay from which dictators can be swiftly moulded. This is equally true of the Roosevelts and the Churchills, although, of course, the leaders the democracies call up in a crisis are likely to have some of the qualities of resolute leadership which undoubtedly mark the crisis-born dictators. Here it is necessary to remember that a system of government attracts and chooses as its leaders the type of men temperamentally suited to work within its limitations. It is extremely unlikely that any of these men would ever have come to power in a dictatorship—not even de Gaulle, who may with reason be viewed as an autocrat, but not as a dictator. On the other hand, the Nazi bosses in Germany were drawn to politics and encouraged to pursue power by violent means because of the prizes, congenial to their taste, which control of the government offered. Four years before Hitler came to power in Germany, the devices for assuring that government should remain servant and not master had ceased to work, and the country was governed by executive decree. That is to say, the riches of the earth lay open to those who could somehow get control of the government. Whenever this happens, the power-hungry, the ruthless, the doctrinaire zealots, who want to impose their conception of the good life on everybody, are all attracted to politics as the bees to the flowers. But where the people are determined that government shall be servant and not master and the machinery of government is constructed to that end, the imperious are little attracted to politics and do not get far even when they try.

Government as Servant. So in approaching the study of democratic governments, the centuries-long tradition of government as servant must be kept to the fore and the machinery of government understood as a means to that end. This draws attention at once to the constitution, which provides for the structure and the control of government. The democratic constitution, be it written, unwritten, or mixed, is a body of fundamental rules which the government of the day cannot change of its own free will, and which is, at the same time, a censor of governmental actions. The constitution gives sanctity to the law, which cannot be changed without the consent of the legislature, and also provides that the government and its agents must obey the law or expose themselves to punishment through the courts.

Constitutionalism. It follows that the democratic constitution is not merely a set of rules by which the people are governed; it is also a device by which the people govern their rulers, by which they ensure that the state remains an instrument for furthering genuine common interests. It is true, of course, that many details of the constitution are neutral on this point. Whether or not women have the vote, whether the life of the legislature is five years or two, whether judges hold office for life or must retire at the age of seventy, are questions that matter little from this point of view. But the main features of the democratic constitution are designed to ensure that those who exercise the powers of government shall act with a sense of responsibility. *The phenomenon of a government conforming to the dictates of a settled constitution is known as constitutionalism.* The democracies to be considered here are called constitutional democracies. Their governments are constitutional governments.

The dictatorships have no constitutions in the sense of meaningful bodies of rules that limit and control what the government can do. What passes for a constitution is either no more than a set of rules for the division of the work of the government or mere window-dressing. Every large organization must have rules for internal management, even if there are no rules for imposing external control upon it. Otherwise, civil servants would not know what to do in their day's work and would be falling over one another all the time. But these rules for internal housekeeping are in no way a restraint upon the dictatorial rulers. They can change them all by decree just as a business corporation can change the rules by which it manages its own affairs or as the owner of a slave plantation could reshuffle the tasks of his slaves. As far as governmental forms are concerned, power is utterly concentrated. The one abiding rule is authority from the top downward, obedience from the bottom upward. Constitutionalism does not exist in the dictatorships. This is true of the Soviet Union as well as the others, past or present. An elaborate Constitution was adopted in the Soviet Union in 1936. Despite claims that it guarantees to its citizens a greater range of rights than any other constitution, it has never been an effective restriction on the power of the small group, the oligarchy, that runs the Soviet Union. The governments of the dictatorships are not constitutional governments.

Democratic countries also must divide the work of government for the sake of efficiency. There is a geographical distribution which delegates certain powers to municipalities while the residue of powers is kept in the hands of the central government. Sometimes this distribution is made more complex by introducing a third and intermediate level of government, as in the federal systems where state governments have exclusive control of a wide range of matters. At each level of government there is always a functional division, generally identified as legislative, executive, and judicial, with still more elaborate division or departmentalization within the executive branch. Such divisions of work, whether geographic or functional, invite disagreement and cross-purposes, and therefore every constitution must define the relations between the different levels and functions so as to limit friction and provide an assured means of breaking deadlocks.

However, these divisions, though necessary for efficiency, are not solely directed to that purpose. In the democracies, they are designed for, and contribute in considerable measure to, preventing the concentration of power in the hands of a few. The legislature is a check on the executive; the judges are independent and commonly are sharp critics of the executive. They cannot be said even to be always sympathetic to the legislature. In a federal system, the state governments are a check on the federal government, and the existence of municipal governments sets limits to the ambitions of state governments.

In the dictatorships, such division of authority as exists does not serve this purpose at all. The concentration of power at the apex is utter and complete. In Germany, for example, the Nazis destroyed the federal system, eliminating the separate states. They destroyed the autonomy of the municipalities, giving them over to the charge of Nazi party bosses. The legislature was a complete farce without power, and the judges were the tools of the leaders. We shall see later that the divisions of authority in the government of the Soviet Union come to the same thing. In the light of this contrast, the squabbling that goes on within and between governments in a democratic country ceases to look entirely deplorable.

LIBERALISM AND DEMOCRACY

It might be concluded from the emphasis of this contrast that the democratic peoples are so much in fear of government as such that they would deny it any significant range of power, holding that the best government is the one that governs least. The men who framed the American Constitution and those who laid down the main lines of the modern British constitution after the expulsion of the Stuart kings in 1688 were much of this mind. However, they were not democrats. They believed in constitutional government and a wide range of individual liberty but not in the control of government by the many. They believed rather that the franchise should be restricted to the upper and middle ranks of the population. They feared that extension of the franchise to the ignorant masses would result in the destruction of all liberty.

British government in the eighteenth century was an aristocracy, and the relatively few who controlled it often confused their own narrow interests with the public interest. But they did banish arbitrary government from Britain, and a by-product of their success was a large measure of civil liberty for individuals. Continental European admirers of Britain in the eighteenth century constantly spoke of it as a land where men were secure in their persons and property from arbitrary governmental action and could think and express themselves freely. It is true that men could still be impressed into the service of the navy against their will, and that Roman Catholics and dissenters from the doctrines of the Church of England were subject to disabilities on the ground of religion. These and other restrictions were deviations from the liberal ideal. Yet, in comparison with earlier times and other countries, the British constitution of the eighteenth century provided a striking vindication of individual liberty. British government, which operated within the strict confines of the constitution, could be fairly described as liberal government.

One of the grounds of complaint that lay behind the American Revolution was that British subjects in America were denied liberties which British subjects were accorded at home. Accordingly, steps were taken in the American Constitution, and in the first ten amendments thereto in 1791, to secure the content of these and other liberties for American citizens. Without attempting a complete catalogue, we should note that the Constitution contains guarantees against arbitrary interference with person or property and specifically assures freedom of religion, freedom of speech, freedom of the press, and freedom of peaceable assembly. The framers put themselves on record as unqualified believers in liberal government. Yet few of them believed in democracy when defined as adult male suffrage.

Adult male suffrage, subject to certain minor qualifications which need not concern us here, was adopted in Britain and the United States in the course of the nineteenth century. It was won by convinced democrats, relying on the freedom to discuss and agitate afforded by liberal constitutional government. These convinced democrats were also convinced liberals and individualists, who asked little of government except that it should protect individuals in the widest possible freedom of action. They wanted manhood suffrage because they thought this was the only way to ensure permanently that government would not restrict freedom in the interests of a narrow class. Thus democracy in Britain and North America inherited beliefs in individual liberty and constitutional government, and made them a central part of its own creed. In the beginning, it feared government as such, and thought of manhood suffrage as an additional device for keeping it under control. The principle of *laisser faire,* the belief that government should be confined to a very narrow sphere of action, was a dogma of first importance through the greater part of the nineteenth century.

Therefore, the governments of Britain and the United States are appropriately described as *liberal democratic governments.* Those who have lived under them and have had no experience of other regimes think, if common speech is any index to belief, that they are sufficiently described as democratic governments, assuming that liberty and democracy inevitably go arm in arm. However, we have just seen that it is possible to conceive of, and to maintain for a time at least, governments which are liberal without being fully democratic. In the strict meaning of words, democracy means merely rule by the many. And it is always possible to have a democracy in which there is little respect for individual liberty. Some of the ancient democracies degenerated into mob rule. Mobs are composed of large numbers who do not behave liberally or constitutionally. There is always some danger of intolerant majorities denying liberty to individuals and minority groups that have aroused their hostility. The record of democracy in the United States and Britain is by no means free of blemishes of this kind.

It can be said with assurance that the principal check on intolerant majorities is the widespread mutual respect engendered in men, despite their differences, by the liberal democratic ideal. The modern dictatorships have not been lacking in certain democratic elements because the dictators have gone to great pains to secure, by one means or another, mass support for their rule. These masses often behaved like mobs, and Mussolini and Hitler encouraged them so to behave. Yet there is no denying that these dictators had extensive popular support, however secured.

Whatever the democratic element in the dictatorships, they have not been liberal any more than they have been constitutional. On every hand the individual is subordinated to some overriding purpose, relentlessly pushed, if not entirely conceived, by the leaders. We know what Mussolini and Hitler thought about freedom for individuals. The Communist dictatorship in the Soviet Union scorns bourgeois liberty as found in the liberal democracies on the ground that it is merely the liberty of the few to exploit the many. It holds forth the promise of a larger liberty—which liberals must acknowledge as a noble ideal—but thus far it has not delivered any significant installments on account.

DEMOCRACY AND THE POPULAR WILL

Whether liberal or not, a government is not democratic unless it responds to the will of the people. With the broadening of the franchise, government in Britain and the United States did so respond, making laws in accordance with the aspirations of the newly enfranchised groups. After manhood franchise had been achieved and people had got some confidence that government was an instrument they could use for their purposes, some of the earlier fear of government as a necessary but regrettable evil began to disappear. At the same time, a variety of circumstances, which will be considered later, suggested a good many purposes that governments could be used to further. The belief in *laisser faire* began rapidly to decline and democratic electorates loaded the government—their servant—with new tasks, new powers, and new obligations until ancient despots might well envy democratic governments their range of authority.

The steadily accelerating tendency to call on government for solutions to any and every social problem, as described earlier, is perhaps the most remarkable social phenomenon of our time. The rapid growth of government action was well under way by 1900. It was accelerated by World War I, it slackened in the 'twenties, gathered speed again in the long depression of the 'thirties, and came, during World War II, almost to match the scope of governmental functions in the dictatorships. While government activities have fallen away from this peak in the United States, and to a lesser extent in Britain and France, there is no likelihood of a return to the 1939 level. (Indeed, the exigencies of defense will require a considerable expansion of governmental action over an indefinite period.) The vast majority of the people no longer show any great fear of government, and there is widespread confidence in the power of the electorate to control and direct its operations.

This raises another important distinction between democracy and dictatorship. In a dictatorship, the leader and a small clique around him decide what government shall do. They are able to act with great rapidity and often with a high degree of consistency, because there are only a few minds to be made up. In a democracy, the ultimate decision about what the government is to do rests with the millions composing the widely scattered electorate. Cumbersome machinery that consumes a great deal of time and effort is necessary for consulting the wishes of the sovereign electorate. More important still, it is exceedingly difficult for millions of people to come to a common mind or a majority decision about anything. When one considers how long a small committee can debate before coming to any agreement about the simplest matters, it is astonishing that the electorate ever manages to agree on instructions to its government. When it is realized how many things democratic governments do nowadays, it is understandable why the will of the people is not always manifest in what is done. What needs explaining is how the electorate is able to transmit coherent instructions to the government at all.

Democracy inherited its devices for restraining governments from the presumptuous abuse of power. It did not, however, inherit its mechanisms for eliciting and transmitting to the government the positive measures it wants to see carried out. It had to create them, feeling its way by trial and error. The chief of these mechanisms is the organized system of political parties. Its workings are far from giving general satisfaction—but a great deal of the dissatisfaction with political parties and with democracy arises from a failure to understand the difficulty of what is being attempted.

Two Principal Themes. The main body of this book has two principal themes. *First,* the need for restraints on government as such, and the instruments by which democratic peoples have maintained these restraints. *Second,* the problem of deciding, in a democracy, what the government is to do in the name of all, and the instruments through which the authentic voice of the electorate is to be heard and translated into action. The two themes cannot always be discussed separately, because the same instrument is often used for both purposes. For example, the legislature is both a check and a spur to government. And, as we shall see, when the electorate wishes to spur the government on to a more positive program of action, it must often be willing to slacken the reins by which government is checked.

In fact, democratic constitutions have been considerably modified in the last sixty or seventy years to allow government to carry out the widening activities it is expected to perform. The adaptation has gone so far that some will challenge the accuracy of the description of democratic constitutions given here. They will say that democratic constitutions are no longer to be understood as devices for restraining governments but rather as instruments for carrying out the will of the people, for ensuring that government does what electoral majorities want it to do. Furthermore, they will contend that any portion of the constitution which does not promote this purpose is outmoded and should be changed forthwith. In other words, where the liberal democrat once sought freedom *from* government, his recent quest has been to seek freedom *through* government! Who, then, is or was the true liberal, Herbert Hoover or Franklin D. Roosevelt? For the past forty or so years, a great debate has been raging in democratic countries over this question.[2]

[2] In this connection, the battle of terminologies involving the concepts of 'liberal' and 'conservative' has hardly been either helpful or enlightening. The terms connote different things to different people and depending upon the times in which one lives, it would appear to be more fashionable (and politically profitable!) to be one rather than the other. Thus, during the heyday of the New Deal in America it was *de rigueur* to be a 'liberal'; in the late 'fifties and early 'sixties, however, to be a 'conservative' was far more 'respectable.' It is clear that much depends upon interpretation and—to use Al Smith's happy phrase—whose ox is gored. Is a 'liberal' one who defends and upholds the Bill of Rights against society's encroachment or is

Some of the considerations bearing on it will be brought out later. First, however, we must sharpen contrasts by addressing ourselves to the basic assumptions of dictatorship.

Suggested References for Further Reading

Becker, C., *Modern Democracy* (Yale, 1941).
Bowle, J., *Western Political Thought* (Oxford, 1948).
Brinton, C., *Ideas and Men* (Prentice-Hall, 1950).
Cahn, E., *The Predicament of Democratic Man* (Macmillan, 1961).
Dahl, R. A., *A Preface to Democratic Theory* (U. of Chicago, 1956).
Ebenstein, W., *Today's Isms,* 3rd ed. (Prentice-Hall, 1960).
Heald, M. M., *A Free Society* (Philosophical Lib., 1953).
Ilbert, Sir C., *Parliament: Its History, Constitution, and Practice* (Oxford, 1950).
Mason, A. T., *Free Government in the Making,* rev. ed. (Oxford, 1956).
Mayo, H. B., *Introduction to Democratic Theory* (Oxford, 1960).
Mill, J. S., *On Liberty and Considerations on Representative Government* (Oxford, 1933).
Montgomery, J. D., *Forced To Be Free* (U. of Chicago, 1957).
Niebuhr, R., *The Children of Light and the Children of Darkness* (Scribner, 1944).
Pennock, J. R., *Liberal Democracy: Its Merits and Prospects* (Rinehart, 1950).
Riemer, N., *The Revival of Democratic Theory* (Appleton-Century-Crofts, 1962).
Ross, A., *Why Democracy?* (Harvard, 1952).
Salvadori, M., *Liberal Democracy* (Doubleday, 1957).
Schattschneider, E. E., *The Semisovereign People: A Realist's View of Democracy in America* (Holt, Rinehart, and Winston, 1961).
Spitz, D., *Democracy and the Challenge of Power* (Columbia, 1958).
Stamps, N. L., *Why Democracies Fail* (Notre Dame, 1957).
Stapleton, L., *The Design of Democracy* (Oxford, 1949).
Watkins, F., *The Political Tradition of the West* (Harvard, 1948).

---

he a 'conservative'? Is it the conservative who still believes in *laisser faire,* or is he a 'liberal'? Or perhaps he is a 'reactionary.' The supporters of the two statesmen named above would give rather different responses! Senator Joseph R. McCarthy of Wisconsin was called a 'conservative' by many, 'radical' by many others. (No one seriously called him 'liberal.') One aspect is certain: man's views change with and generally adapt themselves to the unfolding of events. Labels confuse the issue—unless they are accompanied by meaningful data and objective reflection.

III

Basic Assumptions of Dictatorship

GENERAL BACKGROUND

The Modern Dictatorships. Dictatorship is not a new concept in the language of government and politics. At times of crisis in the ancient Roman Republic, immense—although not quite absolute—power was often put in the hands of a single man, a dictator. But his rule was limited to a very short period of time and was subject to some other limits and restraints as well. The powers of the dictator came automatically to an end and the normal agencies of republican rule were restored. Modern dictatorships, on the other hand, are forms of absolute rule and are not subject to any predetermined limits of time or subject matter.

TYRANNY. While the modern dictatorships are quite unlike the old Roman institution from which the name is derived, they are not entirely new phenomena. One of the ancient forms of government was known as tyranny. At many times and places in the world of the Greek city-states, the government fell into the hands of tyrants. Originally, the word *tyrant* meant merely ruler, and there were good and bad tyrants just as there have been good and bad kings. However, the word gradually came to be a term of abuse used to describe a despotic ruler who seized power by fraud or force, often with the support of the submerged masses of the population. Thus Plato described tyranny as the worst form of government and as the most probable outcome of democracy, which he was disposed to regard as an unworkable form of government. Aristotle regarded tyranny as a perversion of monarchy, the tyrant as a ruler who ruled by demagogic tricks rather than by the kingly virtues of wisdom and forbearance. It is the latter form of government which modern dictatorship most resembles.

Modern dictators are usually persons of obscure origin whose first political successes were in the leadership of crowds. They seize power by unconstitutional means, exercise it in despotic fashion, and, at the same time, go to extraordinary lengths to persuade the masses to support them. To read Aristotle's account of how tyrants maintain their power, one would think he had been studying at first hand the actual methods of Mussolini and Hitler.[1] The way in which these two men and their associates exploited the weaknesses of the faltering democracies of Italy and Germany gives a somber significance to Plato's account of how democracy can degenerate into tyranny.[2]

We have already noted that the three great modern dictatorships are markedly different in many ways. The description just given above is not a wholly accurate statement of the origins of the Communist dictatorship in Russia. It overthrew a degenerate monarchy rather than a degenerate democracy, and the most striking native quality of Lenin and Stalin was not the leadership of crowds. But the methods of exercising and maintaining power are substantially the same for all three.

Therefore, for the purpose of making broad contrasts with democracy, all modern dictatorships can be grouped together. Whether imposed by a single tyrant or by a small group of imperious leaders, dictatorship is necessarily fiercely anti-democratic. Of course, there are sharp practical as well as theoretical differences between communism on the one hand and fascism on the other. There are important distinctions to be made between a Hitler, a Mussolini, a Stalin—and for that matter, between him and Khrushchev— a Peron, a Franco, and a Nasser. But when all is said and done, dictatorship is essentially a negation of liberal democratic ideals. It rejects, in varying degree, the democratic cornerstones of respect for individual personality, personal freedoms, belief in rationality, equality, justice, rule by law, and constitutionalism.

A BASIC POINT. One very important distinction between democracy and dictatorship, if not the basic one, has been best phrased by a wit with no

---

[1] Aristotle, *Politics*, bk. v, ch. viii.
[2] *The Republic of Plato,* tr. by Francis Cornford (New York: Oxford University Press, 1945), pp. 287–96.

pretense to learned scholarship. *In the democracies, he said, what is not forbidden is permitted, while in the dictatorships, what is not forbidden is compulsory.* That is to say, the democracies have been regimes of freedom. In the main, government in democracies has been concerned to forbid and punish various forms of serious anti-social conduct and not to command a precise pattern of behavior on all matters. Murder and wife-beating are forbidden. On the other hand, no one is ordered by the government to love his neighbor as himself or to produce ten children for the glory of the state. Even where the government commands people to do precise and specific things, such as sending their children to school or submitting to compulsory vaccination, the professed object is to enlarge the freedom of the individual.

Government in the dictatorships not only has forbidden a wide range of actions, but has also limited severely individual free choice by ordering many of the details of life from the cradle to the grave. While these minute regulations are explained to the individual as being for the welfare of society and for his own good, they enforce on him the dictator's conception of that good, and prevent him very largely from following his own. In effect, the regimentation is for the glory of the small ruling group, or, at any rate, for something other than the enlargement of the life of individual citizens.

The War of Ideas Between Democracy and Dictatorship. For almost fifty years the world has been convulsed by the antagonism between democracy and dictatorship. The first phase culminated in World War II when Fascist Italy and Nazi Germany went down before a coalition of democratic powers and the Soviet Union. In the second phase, now still very much in progress, Communist Russia—with Communist China ominously in the wings—is ranged against the Western democracies in the 'cold war.' The antagonism between democracies and dictatorships is deep-rooted.

This antagonism has always rested partly on a conflict of material interest, but it is also a conflict of ideas. The cold war at present involves a good deal of maneuvering for strategic advantage but it is essentially a war of ideas, a battle for men's minds. The Soviet Union tries to win converts in the democracies. The democracies have often despaired of making contact with minds behind the Iron Curtain, yet they are deeply aware of the need to try, and they have done so.

There was also, of course, a bitter antagonism between Fascist Italy and Nazi Germany on the one hand, and Communist Russia on the other.

Even today, the most abusive epithet in the great arsenal of Communist invective is 'Fascist.' But again we must note that all three have been remarkably alike in the means they employ and substantially at one in their negations of Western democratic political ideals.

FASCISM AND NAZISM

Philosophic Negations. The Fascist and Nazi philosophies, in so far as ideals of government are concerned, consisted almost entirely of negations. Devoted Fascists and Nazis would, of course, deny that statement or consider its emphasis on ideals quite irrelevant. Italy's Fascists would probably point to such 'positive' accomplishments as Mussolini's brave conquest of the powerful Ethiopians and to the fact that *Il Duce* made the trains run on time! The Nazis would obviously speak in nostalgic terms of the resurrection of *das Reich* and its subsequent aggressive spread over most of Central Europe, and of such internal achievements as Hitler's handsome *Autobahnen* —so helpful to the victory-bent Allies in 1944–45. Why bother with 'ideals' when the material results achieved were so attractive!

SPECIFICS. Nevertheless, a glance into historical evidence clearly shows that widespread resentment, frustration, and despair in both Italy and Germany, arising out of the national humiliation of World War I and its consequences, coupled with severe economic depression and the weakness of existing political institutions, led to disillusionment with democracy and rejection of the Western tradition, without bringing any alternative constructive system of ideas. Moreover, the Fascist and Nazi dictatorships have run their course, and such positive ideas as they embodied are most unlikely to be resurrected in the same form again. Of course, Fascist and Nazi attitudes can still be found, but they no longer seem to dominate many minds. For present purposes, then, our attention will be focused on the philosophic negations. These may be grouped into five general categories:

(1) Contempt for Individual Personality.
(2) Denial of Rationality of Man.
(3) Society and State over the Individual.
(4) The Rule of the Elite.
(5) Denial of Freedom and Equality.

(1) *Contempt for Individual Personality.* The fundamental negation of the Fascists and Nazis is the denial of individual personality as the ultimate for politics. Indeed, these creeds went to the point of denying that the individual, as such, has any significance at all except as means to ends beyond and above him. In part, this view rests on a low estimate of human nature. The great mass of individuals are engrossed in their private lives and are utterly lacking in any conception of the public interest. They live on an emotional level, in continual conflict over squalid selfish aims. If one waits for people of this quality to conceive and carry through great projects, no grand, heroic achievement is possible. The Fascist and Nazi movements had their substantial share of impatient visionaries with vague designs for human betterment who could not wait for a slow, fumbling humanity to realize the vision. It is not difficult, but fatally easy, to despise and even hate people who cannot live up to the plans you have made for them.

Mussolini, the Fascist dictator of Italy, scoffed at public opinion, and one of his favorite epithets for the people was 'mud.' In *Mein Kampf,* the Nazi Bible, Hitler stated bluntly his estimate of human beings. Individually they were ignoramuses and incompetents, collectively a rabble, marked by indolence, stupidity, and cowardice. Individuals are therefore to be regarded as means and not as ends in themselves.

(2) *Denial of Rationality of Man.* This comes out most clearly in the attitude of Hitler and Mussolini toward persuasion in the political process. The democratic ideal assumes the rationality of man. On this assumption, the individual has a claim to be persuaded by reasonable arguments before he gives his consent and support. However many democratic politicians fall short of this in practice by appealing to the passions of their listeners, they all pay lip-service to logic and truth. Hitler and Mussolini paid no such tribute. On the contrary, they paid tribute to falsehood, holding that the more audacious the lie the more likely that it would be believed. For example, in *Mein Kampf,* Hitler blatantly called for resort to the big lie, contending that the greater and more persistent the falsehood the more its likelihood of success! This theory was widely accepted by his countrymen during his regime, despite the fact that the crudity of this and other types of propaganda was an insult to the intelligence of listeners.

Hitler and Mussolini's appeals to the people were not fireside chats: they were mass spectacles in which music, color, ritual, symbols, the atmosphere of church and theater, combined with hypnotic suggestion to overwhelm the minds of the listeners. The heckler, who pricked pretentious bubbles with a question or ribald comment, was brutally silenced. Questioning provoked violence rather than discussion. Indeed, it was unsafe not to applaud. It was best to turn off the mind.

This shows better than anything else the Fascist and Nazi contempt for individual personality. It shows too their unqualified denial of the rationality of man. The success of their methods suggests that there is much truth in their estimate of the susceptibility of men to emotional appeal. There is, in fact, independent evidence from the science of psychology to show that the democratic ideal has underestimated the irrational factors in human nature. This may be acknowledged while pointing to a still further lesson to be learned from the Fascist and Nazi episodes.

The dignity of the individual cannot survive this unqualified denial of his rationality. If he cannot be appealed to on the basis of facts and reasoning, he has to be appealed to on the vague grounds of sentiment and feeling, where obscurantists and liars have an overwhelming advantage. If these will not suffice, he has to be bludgeoned by force. The democratic ideal is compelled to hold to the faith that the individual can be persuaded—and further educated—to take thought about how to settle the terms of his common life with others in society.

(3) *Society and State over the Individual.* If the Fascists and the Nazis denied the value of individual personality, what goal did they ask men to strive for? They asserted the unqualified pre-eminence of society over the individual. The Italian Fascists put it bluntly: 'Society is the end, individuals the means, and its whole life consists in using individuals as instruments for its social ends.' Equally categorical statements abound in Nazi literature. The individual was to realize himself by submerging himself in loyal unquestioning service and boundless sacrifice for society.

Society, for them, was identical with the state. Their one unvarying appeal was to a strident jingoistic nationalism. Mussolini was always promising to revive the glories of the Roman Empire. Hitler's supreme aim was to rouse the German nation to a sense of its so-called racial superiority, and of its world mission consequent on that superiority. Literally, the two dictators demanded that every Italian and German submit himself to severe military discipline for the achievement of these ends. Their watchwords were authority and obedience. No more than any other military commander did they propose to let the private soldiers discuss and decide the plan of campaign.

Three highly important consequences follow from what has been said so far. *First,* grandiose schemes of this kind require concerted effort on a grand scale. The state was the only agency that could undertake the comprehensive co-ordination needed. Hence the state became supreme, in the name of society. Mussolini gave the formula: 'Everything in the state, nothing against the state, nothing outside the state.' Hitler was generally careful to insist that the state was only an instrument in the service of the Germanic Folk. But in practice, the Nazi state was infinitely more imperious than the Fascist state.

This brings us to the *second consequence*. Vague goals like the welfare of society or a world mission do not define any specific program of action. It is still necessary for someone to decide step by step in great detail what to do. If individuals here and now do not matter, the welfare of society has nothing to do with them. If they are lazy, stupid, and self-centered, they are incapable of entertaining a heroic design—let alone of thinking clearly and systematically about the means of promoting it. So the Fascists and the Nazis rejected majority rule by elected representatives in a legislature. The effect of this was to relieve the state from all responsibility to the people. It followed inevitably that the decisions leading to action had to be taken by the state without reference to what the body of citizens might think were common interests or common purposes. The state decided in its utter discretion what were the desirable social ends, what was the world mission, and how to set about them.

But who or what, it may be asked, is the state here? Obviously, it is no longer what adherence to democratic ideals makes it, an association of the people in a given territory for furthering the interest they share in common. Here we reach the *third consequence*. The state becomes identical with the small group of persons who control its power and operate its machinery. State, government, and movement become one and the same thing.

(4) *The Rule of the Elite*. Political power is concentrated in the hands of a small elite, an oligarchy—and those they gather around them. And this, as all Fascist and Nazi literature insists, is as it should be. 'World history is made by minorities.' They alone have the vision, the courage, and the relentless will to struggle against the inertia of the masses, to inspire them with their vision and example, and to drive them when they will not be led. In their eyes the elite alone have the right to rule!

Only one comment on these arrogant claims is needed here. Having elevated themselves so far above their fellows, beyond the reach of responsibility, the leaders can pursue their visions. But having no obligation to listen to anyone or to win consent through rational discussion, they have no way of knowing whether their visions are anything but bad dreams. They have nothing but their own powers of self-criticism—a scarce commodity among visionaries, prophets, and crusaders—to keep them from confusing their private prejudices, hatreds, and ambitions with the great social ends, always vague and undefined, by which they justify their irrespon sible power. The sordid realities of the Fascist and Nazi regimes are not at all surprising. They merely confirm the ancient wisdom that *no man is good enough to be trusted with absolute power.*

(5) *Denial of Freedom and Equality.* The remaining negations of democratic ideals by the Fascists and Nazis can now be stated quickly. Having denied the worth of individual personality, they could find no value in individual freedom. Mussolini sneered at the 'putrescent corpse of the Goddess of Liberty.' Hitler talked much about freedom, but it was freedom for the German nation at the expense of freedom for individual Germans. Individual freedom could not be claimed against the state. It existed only in so far as the state allowed it to exist.

The contempt of the Fascists and Nazis for individuals in general and their glorification of the elite were, in substance, a denial of human equality. The dictators saw clearly the facts of inequality but lacked the deeper sense of the brotherhood of man which is needed to reduce the significance of the more obvious natural and social inequalities. Denying the need for discussion and debate, they had no reason to treat men as if they were equal.

On the contrary, they glorified inequality. 'Fascism,' said Mussolini, 'asserts the irremediable and fertile and beneficial inequality of men.' The Nazi creed of inherent Nordic [3] racial superiority denied the right of Jews to be citizens. Cross-breeding between Germans and Jews produced 'bastards,' an inferior group that had to be eliminated. Furthermore, the aristocratic principle which identifies superior and inferior races also distinguishes between superior and inferior persons within the master race, 'putting the heads above the masses and subjecting the masses to the heads.' In Nazi and Fascist practice, the consequences of these views were fully worked out in the abolition of equality in political and civil rights.

The Totalitarian State. In conclusion, the Fascist and Nazi negation of democratic ideals was categorical and complete. As a result, the individual becomes defenseless before the state. In the place of a state with limited functions, which he as a citizen helps to define, he is faced with a state that

[3] The true 'Nordic' was characterized as tall, blond, blue-eyed, athletic, and handsome. Yet Hitler, the Nordic *Führer,* was short, dark, brown-eyed, unathletic, and unattractive.

undertakes to organize every aspect of his existence when and how it likes. He no longer has a realm of freedom in which he can realize his potentialities outside the state. He has to find the meaning of life in abject surrender and unquestioning obedience. The state is all, the totality, and hence the Fascist and Nazi states were called totalitarian. In place of the ideals of Liberty, Equality, and Fraternity that inspired the French Revolution and the succeeding democratic age, they put Responsibility, Discipline, and Hierarchy.

Fascism and Nazism Contrasted. Fascism and Nazism are commonly classified as one and the same. Broadly speaking, this is logically permissible, especially when employed as a basis of comparison with communism. Fundamentally, both these 'isms' come under the general heading of *fascism,* a term derived from the Italian *fascio,* i.e., a political group or club that served as the early instrumentality for Mussolini's gathering of support and power.[4] *Fascism,* if a definition still be needed after the aforesaid description, may be viewed as the *totalitarian organization of government and society by a single-party dictatorship, intensely nationalist, racist, militarist, and imperialist.* Mussolini and his onetime student and admirer, Hitler—who later grew to despise and ridicule his teacher—merely differed in the degree of application of fascist doctrines. This was partly due to the different types of people with whom each dictator dealt and to the different soils in which fascism found its roots. For a variety of reasons the German soil proved to be considerably more fertile!

Enough has been said in the preceding sections of this chapter to indicate clearly the many similarities between the two types of fascism. A few of the differences are worth noting; however, born of circumstantial expediency, they were not so much differences of principle as of degree.

(1) RELIGION. Whereas the Nazis soon commenced to battle with the Church, and openly denied the need for religious adherence according to traditional beliefs, one of the early steps taken by Mussolini's regime was to enter into a *concordat* with the Vatican. In essence this agreement—known as the Lateran Pact of 1929—meant 'you leave me alone and I shall leave you alone.' Both parties to the *concordat* adhered to it faithfully, although it frequently proved to be an uneasy truce, especially in the realm of the education of Italy's youth.[5]

---

[4] Literally *fascio* means a 'bundle'—commonly a bundle of sticks or wood bound together, thus symbolizing unity of purpose.

[5] For a pertinent discussion, see Richard A. Webster, *Fascism in Italy. The Cross and the Fasces: Christian Democracy and Fascism in Italy* (Stanford: Stanford University Press, 1960).

Hitler, on the other hand, did everything in his power to undermine the authority and influence of both the Protestant and Catholic Church in Germany, even to the extent of establishing a National Church (*Reichskirche*). He, too, had entered a *concordat* with the Vatican in 1933, but he failed to respect it, and Pope Pius XI renounced it in 1937. Although Hitler intimidated many officials and members of the traditional churches, he did not succeed in raising his National Church to a position of omnipotence. Moreover, some of his most effective opposition, however limited, came from such religious leaders as the Bavarian Cardinal Faulhaber and the Prussian Pastor Niemöller—not so much because they necessarily disagreed with Hitler's over-all policies for the German state, but because he interfered with their authority. Cardinal Faulhaber proved to be especially courageous in his opposition, aided indirectly by Rome. Pastor Niemöller, although a dedicated militaristic and nationalistic German, was ultimately sent to a concentration camp.

(2) ANTI-SEMITISM. Undoubtedly the most sordid aspect of the Nazi regime was its racist philosophy, which ultimately culminated in the systematic liquidation of the Jews. Italy's fascist regime made life uneasy and frequently unpleasant for its Jewish citizens, but it did not actively molest them in any extreme sense. Indeed, anti-Semitism was originally no part of Italian fascism; it was 'borrowed' from the Nazis, who finally compelled its adoption.

Viewing the German Jews as 'aliens,' as 'foreigners,' and above all as *non-Aryan,* the Nazis, on the other hand, determined upon their ultimate eradication. This despite the fact that the German Jews had been completely assimilated into the stream of German life and culture, had lived there for centuries prior to the existence of the German state and participated in its creation and development, and numbered but 600,000—scarcely *1 per cent* of the population! However, as a defenseless and generally well-to-do minority, they provided an ideal scapegoat—a basic requirement in dictatorships. The Nazis began their anti-Semitic campaign modestly enough in 1933, but by 1939 they had resolved upon *die entgültige Lösung:* annihilation of all Jews. Any German Jew who had not managed to escape by 1941 was doomed to extermination in one of the dread concentration and extermination camps. Six million European Jews had been thus murdered when Nazi Germany collapsed in 1945.

(3) BRUTALITY. While Mussolini's fascism enforced its own reign of fear through a total suppression of civil liberties by the devices of concentration

camps, a secret police, and spies, it could not match the extreme brutality practiced by the Nazis. The barbarism of such concentration camps as Buchenwald, Dachau, Bergen-Belsen, and Auschwitz represent bestiality on a scale hitherto unknown. Nor could the Italian secret police compete in infamy with the dreaded *Gestapo,* the Secret State Police—a term that has become synonymous with ruthlessness, lawlessness, and terror. Nothing the Italian Fascists did equaled the orgies of murder and torture conducted by their Nazi allies.

(4) ADULATION OF THE LEADER. *Il Duce* had his faithful retinue, his cohorts, and organizations that were blindly loyal to him. He could command the attention of crowds and regale them with the splendor of his regime. Yet the adulation paid to Mussolini was more or less superficial; Italians feared and accepted him as their leader—for indeed he personified Italy's fascism— but their homage was a far cry from the rousing, fanatical allegiance tendered Germany's *Führer* by his masses. Hitler was accorded a devotion that was as blind and unquestioning as it was frightening. 'Heil Hitler' was akin to a charismatic message, one that the *Führer* was able to manipulate as he pleased. He had a profound effect on the German masses.

(5) IDEOLOGY. Mussolini's fascism was devoid of any clear-cut, positive philosophy. It had a highly opportunistic flavor about it. The ideological cement holding the party members was negligible; it simply served as a means to the end of subordination of the individual to the state. The people were compelled to serve the state, and they did—but unlike their fascist German cousins they hardly knew why. As one observer well put it, 'The totalitarianism of the Italian Fascists was shallow and specious. It did not penetrate the life or the thought of the people.'[6] It was simply a fact that took place.

The Nazi brand of fascism, however, was characterized by an extreme form of dogmatism. Dictator and state were identified with the notion of the *Volksgeist*—the spirit of the people. This *Volksgeist* was effectively represented as a personification of German purity and triumph, a triumph over the impurities of the enemies of the Nazi *Reich,* enemies that included such 'devils' as Jews, foreigners, international bankers, socialists, Communists, free-masons, democrats, humanitarians, individualists. The *Volksgeist,* inherent in the purity and greatness of the Aryan race, and incarnated in the German state, became Nazidom's successful gospel. At once incomprehen-

---

[6] R. M. MacIver, *The Web of Government* (New York: The Macmillan Company, 1947), p. 247.

sible and attractive, it provided a watchful Jehovah for the chosen people of the *Vaterland*.

COMMUNISM

COMMUNIST IDEALS OF GOVERNMENT

The ideals professed by the Soviet Union must be discussed more fully. They are now competing with the democratic ideals for men's allegiance all over the world. The Communist ideals were not hastily thrown together to justify power-hungry men in doing what they had already done or determined to do anyway. The Communist Bible is the writings of Karl Marx. He died in 1883, and his theories were anxiously worked over for almost fifty years after his death by a large body of disciples before attempts to put them into practice began in Russia in 1917. Furthermore, for Karl Marx and many of his followers, Communist theory was not a negation of the basic ideals of the Western tradition but rather, in their view, the necessary means to their full realization. Any examination of Communist ideas must begin with Marx.

DEMOCRATIC IDEAL AND ECONOMIC REALITY. Marx was a German philosopher deeply influenced by the Western political tradition. In his youth, he shared with most of the young intellectuals of his time an enthusiasm for the ideals of the French Revolution. But he quite early became acutely conscious of the immense gap between these ideals and the political and social realities of the time. In the Europe of his day, the masses of peasants and urban workers were sunk in degrading poverty, entirely dependent, so it seemed, on the whims of the large landowners and of the capitalists, the owners of commercial and industrial establishments. Formal slavery did not exist but the practical condition of the masses was little improvement on serfdom.

The struggle for a bare existence was so exhausting that the great bulk of the lower ranks of the people had no opportunity to realize whatever possibilities they may have had as individuals. Even in Britain, where individual liberty had been formally acknowledged for over a century, countless thousands of lives were being blighted by the horrors of the early factory system. Theories about the essential dignity of the human person seemed a travesty in the light of these facts. Fired by a genuine passion for human dignity and freedom. Marx set out to discover why things were as they were and how they could be changed.

He concluded that the cause of the plight of the masses was economic. Living on the verge of destitution, one cannot be a person, one cannot have the freedom to do anything or be anything. But the means of production on which the masses had to rely for any improvement in their condition were private property in the hands of landowners and capitalists who did not give them enough in the form of wages or other return to make meaningful freedom possible. More than that, the owning classes took advantage of their superior position in the social structure to exploit their workers.

THE DESTINY OF MAN. Evidence to support these conclusions was easily found in Europe in the middle of the nineteenth century, as it can still be found in parts of Europe and elsewhere. But it would take a considerable knowledge of early-nineteenth-century German philosophy to explain the larger and more general conclusions Marx reached after he saw the importance of economic factors in social life. He concluded, in effect, that this economic exploitation had always been inevitable and also that it was fated to pass entirely away. Mankind, having lived thus far in the 'realm of necessity,' plagued by the economic struggle, would move in the near future into the 'realm of freedom,' where the exploitation of man by man would cease.

Starting from certain highly abstract formulations in German philosophy, he developed an all-embracing philosophy of history to show how all creation moves in a predestined direction. He worked out a theory of social development comparable in certain ways to Darwin's theory of biological development. But while Darwin limited himself to explaining the course of evolution in the past, Marx undertook to show the course of evolution of human society in the future. It was as if Darwin, after showing how the apes came down out of the trees and became men, had gone on to demonstrate that men would now, at the next stage, sprout wings and become angels. The vitally important part about Marx was his prediction of the future.

COMMUNISM IN THEORY

(1) *The Theory of Economic Determinism.* Attempts to sketch briefly a philosophy of history generally end in misrepresentation. Having noted that danger, we may look at Marx's destiny of mankind under three headings.

First, there is the theory of economic determinism. The known ways and means of meeting material needs such as food, clothing, and shelter at any given time determine all significant aspects of social and political organization. If these 'forces of production,' as they are called, are to be fully employed, certain relationships between the different members of society must be established. Those with the know-how must direct the productive effort, and all others must be subordinated to them.

ECONOMIC CAUSES OF CLASS DIVISIONS. The drive to satisfy material needs is so strong that it forces the division of men into economic classes. The significant classes are the directing class, whose dominance has generally been enforced by its taking over the means of production and distribution as its private property, and the servile classes, who are controlled by the directing class. The directing class always comes, sooner or later, to systematic exploitation of the servile classes. The most important fact about any society is the economic class structure.

With the discovery of new resources and new techniques of production, there always comes, sooner or later, a radical change in the mode of production which forces a change in economic organization and a new alignment of economic classes. The *feudal aristocracy* formed the dominant exploiting class in the days of self-sufficient agriculture in the Middle Ages. With improvements in the means of transportation and arts of navigation, and with the discovery of the New World and its new resources, the feudal lords had to give way to the merchants, traders, and adventurers, who alone could organize an economy based primarily on specialization of labor and widespread exchange of goods. At first, they formed a new class, the *middle class,* midway between lords and serfs. With the coming of the Industrial Revolution and the developing factory system, the middle class was enlarged and consolidated in the *capitalist class,* also known as the *bourgeoisie.* With the drawing of the peasantry from the countryside into the factories in rapidly growing urban centers, an entirely new dependent and exploited class, the urban industrial wage-worker, came into existence. Marx identified the capitalists (bourgeoisie) and the *urban proletariat* (the industrial working class) as the two significant classes for our time.

THE STATE. But economic organization determines all other aspects of social and political organization. To ensure the dominant and directing class their control of the forces of production and to prevent revolts by the exploited classes, a *policing organization* is necessary. This is the state, and this is its indispensable function. The state, according to Marx and Engels is not an association for furthering the common interests of the citizens as a whole: 'It is an executive committee for managing the affairs of the bourgeoisie as a whole.' The laws enforced by the state and all significant aspects of political life are direct consequences of the form of economic organization.

IDEALS A REFLECTION OF ECONOMIC INTERESTS. This is only a small part of the story. The ideals of government that hold sway at a particular time arise also from economic sources. The dominant theory about what government should and should not do is always the one that protects the interests of the exploiting class. On this analysis, Marx would say that the decisive feature of the democratic values discussed earlier was the emphasis on freedom. He would say that the significant thing about this ideal of freedom was that it upheld the freedom of the capitalist to do as he liked with his property, i.e. *to continue the exploitation of the working class.* And he would go on to say that this discussion completely misrepresents the relationship of ideals to action when it treats the ideals or values as determining what the state shall and shall not do.

The state always does whatever is necessary to protect the position of the dominant economic class. In their main aspects, democratic ideals are a sort of reflex of the economic system, a set of elaborate afterthoughts that justifies the rule of the capitalist class. The stress on human equality and on the essential worth and dignity of individual personality is merely hocuspocus for hoodwinking the exploited masses and persuading them to accept their subordinate role. When it was pointed out that many democratic values are rooted in religious beliefs, Marx made his famous retort that 'religion is the opiate of the people.' It too is cunningly adapted to keeping the people quiet. The dominant religion at any time is also a reflex of the economic structure.

To put it briefly, Marx banished God from the scheme of things and put 'the forces of production' in His place as the final cause. The Calvinist interpretation of Christianity pictured an all-wise and all-powerful God who governed the universe in every detail. He left men no freedom of action but determined even before their birth whether they were to be saved or damned. This was the doctrine of predestination. Marx also believed in a predestination in which everything is preordained by the forces of production. Men are the pawns of these forces which determine not only what men shall do but also what they shall believe. This is the theory of economic determinism.

(2) *The Theory of Class Conflict.* Second, there is the theory of class conflict. The forces of production divide society into dominant and subordinate classes, into exploiters and exploited, between which there is unceasing and irreconcilable antagonism. There are no common interests uniting all men in society. *There are only conflicting class interests.* The significant classes for our era are the capitalist owners of the means of production and distribution, and the urban industrial proletariat which must sell its labor and work for a wage in order to live. Their antagonism is illustrated by the need of the capitalist to buy labor as cheaply as possible, and the need of the proletariat to sell labor as dearly as possible.

Each class develops a set of beliefs and values which justifies its place in the economic structure—or its aspirations to a better place. Marx thought he was expressing the theory appropriate to the aspirations of the proletariat. The capitalist class justifies itself by reference to democratic ideals which, of course, were formulated and won widespread adherence in the period of its dominance. These are the ideas which the forces of production predestined the capitalist class to believe.

Generally speaking, the members of this class and its adherents sincerely believe in democratic values, and also believe that private property in the means of production and distribution is the best way to a further realization of these values. For these and other reasons, the capitalist class refuses to give up its privileged position, and it will fight the aspirations of the proletariat to the bitter end. *If the proletariat is to realize its aspirations, it must be prepared to overthrow the capitalist class by violence.* This is the theory of class conflict, which denies that there are, or can be, any common interests or common values, any common ground on which men can meet to compose their differences, as long as they are divided into economic classes. The division and the conflict can be ended only by bringing into existence a classless society.

(3) *The Theory of Dialectical Materialism.* If the rule of the capitalists has been predestined by the forces of production, what hope of ousting them can be entertained? This brings us to the *third* heading for discussion, the theory of dialectical materialism. Dialectical materialism is the core of Marx's philosophy of history. The materialism involved in substituting 'the forces of production' for God is obvious enough. *The dialectic can be described for present purposes as an inner mechanism of the material world which ensures the full working out of economic and social change.* Through the ceaseless contention of rival economic classes, it brings new economic and social

arrangements into existence in somewhat the same way as logical argument, or dialectical dispute, between opposing sides in a debate often opens up new truth. In a cunning way, it even makes the capitalist class create the conditions which will ultimately destroy it.

Freedom of individual economic enterprise brought the Industrial Revolution. To reap the full benefits of the Industrial Revolution, the capitalist class had to create the factory system and ultimately the mass-production system. For this purpose, they drew the peasants to the towns and created the urban proletariat. Production on the assembly line in the great factory is an intensely co-operative kind of work, and the capitalist system trained the workers to co-operative action. Incidentally, the workers learned also to co-operate in resisting the efforts of the capitalists to exploit them.

In response to their economic needs, the industrial workers created the great trade-union movement which is almost entirely a development of the period of capitalist dominance. The trade unions are one of the principal means by which the workers are disciplined in co-operative action. Over many years the capitalists fought the trade-union movement bitterly but they were unable to crush it. Thus, even against their own will and efforts they are led to provide the conditions for their own downfall.

THE NEMESIS OF THE PROFIT MOTIVE. The only effective motive the capitalist class can bring to the processes of production is the desire for private profit and gain. This drives the capitalists to suppress competition among themselves and to combine in monopolies. But the effect of monopoly in their hands is restrictive; it thwarts the potentialities of the great productive equipment they themselves brought into existence. To realize these potentialities, it is necessary to abolish private property and the profit motive, and to give unrestricted scope to co-operative impulses and techniques. The only class which has been trained to exploit co-operative production to the full is the industrial proletariat. God, that is to say, 'the forces of production,' will not be mocked. The very forces which once gave mastery to the capitalistic class must now confer it on the proletariat. The industrial working class is destined to become the vanguard of progress. This is the outcome thought to be guaranteed by the theory of dialectical materialism.

Freedom and Equality in the Classless Society

The Dictatorship of the Proletariat. As his own theories show, Marx did not expect the capitalist class to recognize that it was headed for the dustbin.

He anticipated rather that the capitalists would use every means, including the repressive power of the state, to maintain their position. There was no reason to expect they could be ousted by measures short of revolution. The proletariat could not count on being able to take up its historic role without the use of violence. To protect itself against counter-revolution by the capitalists and to construct the new socialist society, *the proletariat would find it necessary to set up and maintain during a transitional period a dictatorship of the proletariat.* In reality, this would be a new kind of state for protecting the interests of the proletariat and for liquidating capitalist remnants. One might have expected, again on Marx's own theories, that it would continue indefinitely as the 'executive committee' of the new governing class.

The Classless Society. But Marx expected the capitalist system in its last days to drive almost everyone except a few great capitalists and their hangers-on into the exploited proletariat. Thus he envisaged something new in history once the threat of capitalist counter-revolution had been removed by liquidating the capitalists. He predicted *the emergence at long last of a classless society.* Since there would no longer be a submerged class or classes to exploit, there could not be an exploiting class. With the disappearance of economic classes, there would no longer be anything to divide men in bitterness and conflict. In place of irreconcilable class interests, there would be at last a genuine and all-absorbing common interest in raising co-operative production to the highest possible level for the benefit of all. Like many other creators of Utopias, he looked to see men live together like one happy family.

The State 'Withers Away.' If the sole cause of contention among men is economic and that cause is removed, the problem of maintaining public order and security is solved. The state and government no longer have any reason for existence. As Engels, Marx's collaborator, said, *the state withers away,* and 'the government of persons is replaced by the administration of things and the direction of the process of production.' Also, the study of government and politics fades from the college curriculum. It becomes as dead as a dead language. In Lenin's own words: 'From the moment all members of society, or even only the vast majority, have learned to administer the state *themselves* . . . the *necessity* of observing the simple, fundamental rules of human intercourse will very soon become a *habit.'* [7]

The Age of Communism. The long, sad record of the exploitation of man by man will then be closed and the violation of human dignity through poverty, oppression, and violence will cease. That is to say, freedom will at

[7] *State and Revolution* (Moscow: Foreign Languages Publishing House, 1948), pp. 160–62.

last become meaningful because there will no longer be a dominant class whose freedom rests by necessity on the exploitation of subordinate classes, and no longer subordinate classes whose freedom is thwarted by the necessities of the economic system. Mankind moves from the 'realm of necessity' into the 'realm of freedom.' Marx's ideal of freedom and equality is realized in the age of communism, where, as he phrased it, *everyone contributes to society according to his capacities and receives according to his needs.*

In chart form, the movement to communism would thus traverse the following path:

Stage 1. Exploitation of All by the Feudal Aristocracy.
Stage 2. Overthrow of the Feudal Aristocracy by the Middle Class, i.e. the Capitalists, the Bourgeoisie.
Stage 3. Exploitation of the Urban Proletariat by the Capitalists.
Stage 4. Overthrow of the Capitalists by the Proletariat.
Stage 5. Temporary Dictatorship of the Proletariat.
Stage 6. Emergence of the Classless Society.
Stage 7. The State Withers Away.

COMMUNISM IN PRACTICE

The above represents the merest outline of Marx's philosophy, popularly known now as communism. Main emphasis here has been put on the economic and political implications. It should be noted, however, that Marx thought he had found the key for explaining every significant aspect of human society. Not only economics and politics but art, literature, science, philosophy, religion, all are to be explained and understood in terms of economic classes and the dialectic. A body of doctrine which uses one key to unlock all mysteries is a religion. In that sense, communism has become a religion to Marx's followers. This goes far to explain their untiring zeal, their sacrificial devotion, their dogmatism and intolerance.

Revolution. As already noted, Marx's doctrines were systematically developed by his followers, especially by Lenin, into what is known as Marxism-Leninism, or communism. Just as interpreters of the Bible claim always to be faithful to the sacred text, so Marx's followers have claimed never to have added to or diminished a word of what Marx has said. Just as in the interpretation of the Scriptures, there has been endless dispute about what Marx really meant. In particular, his followers have disagreed on whether Marx believed that revolution would be necessary to oust the capitalists and bring the proletariat into its own. There are passages in Marx's writings which suggest that he had not ruled out the possibility of a peaceful transition. However, the main trend of his arguments and most of his explicit statements support the interpretation that revolution will be necessary—one that has also been supported by the successful practitioners of today's Marxism-Leninism, the masters of the Soviet Union, the Communist party in the Soviet Union and in the other countries that now have Communist governments. It is they who make Communist ideas a power in the world, and they who determine what communism means today.

However, soon after he had attained complete power Nikita Khrushchev began to talk repeatedly about the possibility of a peaceful transition from capitalism to communism, confidently expressing the belief that 'we will bury you.' Indeed, the text of the Party Draft Program of July 30, 1961, delivered by Khrushchev himself at the 22nd Party Congress, contains this passage: 'Peaceful co-existence of the Socialist and capitalist countries is an objective necessity for the development of human society.' This pronunciamento, which thus became Communist party dogma in the Soviet Union and for its allies, soon engendered a battle of words with the Chinese Communists, with the leader of the latter, Mao Tse-tung, and his followers accusing the Soviet Union of having betrayed orthodox Marxism-Leninism. Of course, it is not at all clear whether this change in the Bible is more than soothing double talk to help in the efforts of the Soviet Union to relax somewhat the tensions of the cold war.

The revolutionary wing of the Russian followers of Marx, led by Lenin and Trotsky, seized power in Russia in 1917 and proclaimed the dictatorship of the proletariat. The social and economic system they set up cannot be discussed here. For the moment, it is sufficient to say that although the capitalists in Russia were always few and were fully liquidated forty years ago, *the state has not withered away and the 'government of persons' is still an active enterprise.* Something will be said later about the continuing dictatorship in the Soviet Union as a form of government. Here the focus of interest is in the ideas behind government.

Negations. It was said earlier that Communist thought in practice rejects the Western political tradition in the same way as did Fascist and Nazi doctrine. These negations are nowhere bluntly stated in Communist doctrine; indeed, it affirms the same fundamental values as the Western tradition and promises the full realization of them in the future. The negations arise from certain consequences and tendencies in the Communist creed which must now be stated.

'Democratic Ideals an Illusion in a Class-Divided Society.' First, in so far as Communists are loyal to their doctrine, they cannot give any allegiance to democratic values as these are understood in the Western world until the exploiting capitalist class is overthrown and the proletariat has come to power. Before the revolution, before the emergence of the classless society, freedom, equality, and justice are meaningless terms. To labor for the realization of these values within the framework of a society made up of conflicting economic classes is to pursue a phantom.

Bernard Shaw, who understood Communist *theory* sympathetically, once said that democracy was a big balloon put aloft to attract the gaping attention of the populace while the exploiting class picked their pockets. That is to say, working for these ideals is merely playing the capitalist game of keeping the masses quiet and submissive. It distracts attention from the vital task of undermining the old system and making way for the new. For this purpose, class antagonisms must be heightened, not lessened. Improving the lot of the masses within the capitalist society tends to lessen antagonisms. For the sake of the future, it is necessary to forget about the values of human personality here and now.

If Communists are loyal to their creed, the important unit is not the individual, but the economic class which is the instrument of destiny. The worth of individuals and the treatment to be accorded them is determined by their class affiliation. Those with capitalist mentality are obstacles stubbornly blocking the new world that awaits its birth. They are in the way and must be removed like any other rubbish that gets in the way.

The proletariat is the vanguard of the new society, the expendable soldiers important now as means and not as ends in themselves. In fact, of course, many members of the proletariat are deaf and inert to the call of destiny. How long must the 'realm of freedom' wait for them to respond? After all, at this stage of history, they are merely means; the class structure prevents them from realizing themselves as persons. In the outcome, the temptation to drive the masses when they will not be led is almost as strong for Communists as it was for Nazis and Fascists.

'NO UNIFYING COMMON INTEREST IN A CLASS-DIVIDED SOCIETY.' *Second,* if the real interests are always class interests in a class-divided society, and if these interests are irreconcilable, it follows that all discussion aimed at composing these diverse interests is useless. Any agreement that might be reached is certain to violate the interests of one or other of both classes and will have to be broken if economic classes are to perform their inevitable role in history. Actually, on Communist theory, genuine agreement is impossible. It is impossible to convince the capitalist that his part on the stage of history is finished, because his economic interest, his membership in his class, determines his beliefs. Blinded by class interests, he cannot see the truth.

Equally, no Communist can agree with propositions put forward by persons of capitalist mentality because he knows in advance that, however plausible they appear on the surface, they must be fallacious and perverse. Discussion and debate will never reveal a common interest which men can agree to pursue together because no such common interest exists. In a class-divided society, there are only capitalist interests and capitalist truth, proletarian interests and proletarian truth, and never the twain shall meet!

Whatever the view about the rationality of man in the classless society of the future, Communist theory denies the possibility of rational discussion in a society divided into economic classes. Men do not think freely and make up their minds on the basis of logic and evidence. Their thinking is just a reflex induced in them by their role in the economic system. This too leads to the denial of the worth of human personality. Individuals cannot treat one another with mutual respect unless there is some common ground of experience and values on which to meet to discuss and compose differences.

RELIGIOUS INTOLERANCE OF COMMUNISM. *Third,* the Communist thinks he has grasped the inner meaning of the world, the final truth about man and society. Communism is thus a kind of 'religion.' Its adherents are so utterly certain of their truth and so intoxicated with the beatific vision of the kingdom of heaven that they become an easy prey to religious intolerance. Their first loyalty is to the truth that will ultimately bring all men to salvation and freedom. Their first duty is to make that truth prevail. The sacred word of Marx says the inevitable way is through intolerance, conflict, and violence. Their impatience with the willful obstructors, the lazy who do not care, and the blind who cannot or will not see, becomes almost unendurable. Consequently, there is a strong tendency to ruthlessness, a disposition to regard the great end as justifying any means. This will not surprise anyone who recalls how the rack and the stake were used in the name of Christian love and charity until the lesson of religious toleration was learned. The democratic ideals are inextricably bound up with religious toleration. Religious intolerance of whatever kind is an utter negation of them.

Procedures Opposed to Theory. The result of these consequences and tendencies in Communist theory is to subordinate individuals to the claims of society, the classless society of the future, just as Fascist and Nazi theory subordinated individuals to the existing Italian and German society. Because all three theories lack respect for individual dignity here and now, the rejection of democratic ideals goes point for point the same. *In Communist theory, individual freedom is not for the present but for the future.* Thus far, wherever Communists have come to power, inequalities that rest on distinctions of economic class have usually been abolished, although the U.S.S.R. has lately introduced a number of obvious modifications of this practice. Thus special privileges have been given to such groups as farmers, plant and farm managers, military and party leaders, intellectuals, scientists, and artists. Professor William Ebenstein sees four distinguishable social classes, with a steadily widening income gap between them: (1) Top government officials, party leaders, military officers, industrial executives, scientists, artists, and writers —totaling *circa* one million families. (2) Intermediary ranks of civilian and military officials, collective farm managers, and some skilled industrial workers and technicians—about two to three million families. (3) The bulk of the population, the workers, and peasants—approximately forty million families. (4) Slave laborers and other disadvantaged persons.[8]

At any rate, a multitude of regulations has been made either to enforce social equality or to recognize the merits of particular groups, without regard for the claims of individual freedom. *The essential feature of this equality is an equal subjection to an all-powerful government.* The one kind of equality that is fundamental in the democratic ideals, equality before the law, is rejected more or less. However, as will be explained more fully in the chapters on civil rights and the judiciary, since Stalin's death and particularly since 1955 under Khrushchev there has been a good deal of talk in government circles about 'Soviet legality.' The 1957–58 law on the judiciary and a liberalized criminal code adopted soon thereafter stress that concept repeatedly. How much all this really means remains to be seen—although it would be a mistake not to recognize some distinct differences between the days of Khrushchev and those of Stalin. An informed and realistic glance at the Soviet Union more than a decade after the latter's death does reveal some of significance.

Changes. The old dictator's legacy still lies heavily on Russia, and the cold war is turned on and off more or less at pleasure. But Khrushchev has given

[8] William Ebenstein, *Today's Isms,* 3rd ed. (Englewood Cliffs, N. J.: Prentice-Hall, 1961), p. 53.

evidence that, up to a point, he is sensitive to world opinion; he has made himself more available to the world; he has roundly and repeatedly condemned the excesses of Stalin's era; much of the erstwhile police terror has disappeared from the lives of millions of Russians; he has given some evidence that deviation from the party line does not necessarily invite liquidation (although it may well result in banishment from public life and oblivion); he has opened his country to tourists (but still denies travel abroad to all but a carefully selected handful of his own countrymen); cultural exchanges have been promoted; and sundry material concessions—even Western jazz!—have been made to the now also comfort-craving Soviet citizenry. But, of course, notwithstanding these very real changes and much talk of co-existence, Khrushchev continues a confirmed enemy of the liberal democracies and their capitalist or quasi-capitalist systems.

ELITISM. Thus it remains true that under Communist rule a small elite, those who have the vision and the hard determination, seizes control of the machinery of government and exercises unlimited power over individuals. This involves the rejection of majority rule in any meaningful sense, the rejection of constitutionalism, of rule by law, of the procedures that ensure meaningful discussion and peaceful accommodation of conflicting interests in the democracies. These ideals and procedures are denied for the sake of getting into power and establishing the dictatorship of the proletariat. Once in power, the elite resists all attempts to limit its power, and the dictatorship *of* the proletariat becomes dictatorship *over* the proletariat. As Milovan Djilas, once a fervent Communist, and a comrade of Stalin and Tito, demonstrated so well in his *The New Class*,[9] a book smuggled out of Yugoslavia in two parts in 1957, Communist rule is essentially a despotism in which a relatively small group that has monopolized all levers of power feeds parasitically on the fruits of the labor of the great mass of the citizenry.

ENDURING DICTATORSHIP. This seems to be the conclusion to be drawn from the course of events in the Soviet Union. Almost five decades after the Revolution, the Soviet Union has not yet realized the realm of freedom. As we shall see in detail later, and despite official assurances of impending future events, the state has not withered away, but has grown to monstrous proportions. The state in the Soviet Union under communism is as totalitarian as the Fascist or Nazi states, although there are highly significant differences between it and the now defunct German and Italian variety—including differences in origin, philosophy, appeal, dogma, application, and execution.

[9] Milovan Djilas, *The New Class* (New York: Frederick A. Praeger, 1957).

Marx and some of his disciples may well have been moved by a generous passion for humanity. But they adopted a theory and a set of procedures which inevitably frustrate the high ideal.

This underlines an important lesson which could be illustrated in many ways. Ideals may come to nothing unless the means appropriate to their realization are chosen and carefully observed. Procedures are almost as important as the ideals themselves. The means used to reach an end cannot be divorced from the end desired. Much of the discussion in this book will be focused on the procedures by which the democracies of the United States, Britain, and France have been trying, however inadequately, to realize the democratic ideals.

Suggested References for Further Reading

Almond, G. A., *The Appeals of Communism* (Princeton, 1954).

Anderson, T. (Ed.), *Masters of Russian Marxism* (Appleton-Century-Crofts, 1963).

Arendt, H., *The Origins of Totalitarianism*, 2nd ed. (Meridian, 1958).

——, *On Revolution* (Viking, 1963).

——, *Eichmann in Jerusalem* (Viking, 1963).

Borkenau, F., *European Communism* (Harper, 1953).

Cohen, C. (Ed.), *Communism, Fascism, and Democracy: The Theoretical Foundations* (Random House, 1962).

Daniels, R. V., *The Nature of Communism* (Random House, 1962).

Deakin, F. W., *The Brutal Friendship: Mussolini, Hitler and the Fall of Italian Fascism* (Harper and Row, 1963).

Djilas, M., *The New Class* (Praeger, 1957).

Ebenstein, W., *The German Record* (Rinehart, 1945).

Fermi, L., *Mussolini* (U. of Chicago, 1961).

Friedrich, C. J., and Z. K. Brzezinski, *Totalitarian Dictatorship and Autocracy* (Praeger, 1961).

Fromm, E., *Escape from Freedom* (Rinehart, 1941).

Germino, D. L., *The Italian Fascist Party in Power* (U. of Minnesota, 1959).

Golob, E. E., *The Isms: A History and Evaluation* (Harper, 1954).

Hilberg, R., *The Destruction of the European Jews* (Quadrangle, 1961).

Hitler, A., *Mein Kampf* (Stackpole, 1939).

Kelsen, H., *The Political Theory of Bolshevism* (U. of California, 1949).

Lenin, V. I., *State and Revolution* (International, 1939).

——, *Imperialism* (International, 1939).

Marx, K., *Das Kapital* (Moore, 1939).

Marx, K., and F. Engels, *The Communist Manifesto* (Appleton-Century, 1955).

Mayo, H. B., *Introduction to Marxist Theory* (Oxford, 1960).

Mills, C. W., *The Marxists* (Dell, 1962).

Neumann, F., *Behemoth: The Structure and Practice of National Socialism, 1933–1944,* 2nd ed. (Oxford, 1944).

Reitlinger, G., *The S.S.: Alibi of a Nation* (Viking, 1959).

Shirer, W. L., *The Rise & Fall of the Third Reich* (Simon & Schuster, 1961).

Solzhenitsyn, A., *One Day in the Life of Ivan Denisovich* (Praeger and Dutton, 1963).

Spitz, D., *Patterns of Anti-Democratic Thought* (Macmillan, 1949).

Stalin, J., *Foundations of Leninism* (International, 1939).

Tetens, T. H., *The New Germany and the Old Nazis* (Random House, 1961).

Webster, R. A., *Fascism in Italy. The Cross and the Fasces: Christian Democracy and Fascism in Italy* (Stanford, 1960).

IV

Constitutions and the Separation of Powers

CONSTITUTIONS

The governments of the United States, Britain, and France are constitutional governments and, as was shown in Chapter II, they are thus marked by constitutionalism—the essential attribute of a government conforming to the dictates of a settled constitution. It is necessary first to look at the constitutions within which these countries work. But we cannot accept a view, which was quite general not so long ago, that a description of the constitution is about all an intelligent person needs to know about a government. We now realize that a constitution is merely the skeleton or essential frame of orderly government—although it is clearly based upon the fundamental concept of *restraints* upon government. The constitution provides for the establishment of and defines the chief organs of government. It outlines the relation between these organs and the citizen, between the state and the individual. Being concerned mainly with the pedigree of governmental organs and the relationship between them, it does not create the government or make it work. By itself, it is inert and lifeless. Only when clothed with flesh and blood—human passions and active agents—does it begin to win friends and enemies and influence people.

We learn very little about a government merely by examining its skeletal structure. We have to study the complex functional system installed in it, and also the hopes, fears, aims, and prejudices, the fundamental drives and conflicts of the individuals and groups whose actions influence the government of the day and in turn provoke governmental action. We must go beyond anatomy to physiology and psychology—vastly more difficult subjects.

Frame or Chassis. The figure may be varied. The constitution is the frame or chassis in which the working engine of government is set. Within a certain tolerance, the type and structure of the engine can be modified without changing the frame. A constitution generally will accommodate a considerable adaptation of the working mechanisms of government. The engine itself will not run without fuel. Human needs and dreams are the fuel on which governments run, and what governments do depends to a large degree on the tangled motives of politicians and on the foibles and cross-purposes, as well as the agreements, of the individuals and groups making up society.

While much always depends on the intelligence and skill of the operators, the structure of the engine nevertheless determines what can be used as fuel. Liberal democratic government will not run on the aspirations of a multitude of would-be dictators. It requires, among other things, a tolerant mentality of its people.

On the other hand, the frame within which the working engine of government is set determines the ways in which the power generated can be transmitted, and the kind of operations to which it can be effectively harnessed. A liberal democratic constitution is not a very good frame for transmitting power for twentieth-century wars. Nor, for that matter, was it for nineteenth-century wars, as Abraham Lincoln showed by ignoring the Constitution in a number of ways—although the United States Supreme Court under Mr. Chief Justice Roger B. Taney took a dim view of at least two of these aberrations.[1] So much improvising for the purpose of war organization is necessary that one can almost say the constitution is temporarily set aside. Most motor vehicles do not lend themselves to amphibious operations, and a constitution of the liberal-democratic type is not designed for traveling at high speed to the new Utopia.

In the study of a particular government, therefore, we have to examine the frame or constitution, to see the essential design. We must also study the working mechanism of government within the constitution. We have to take account of the character of the people and the beliefs and wants on which the government feeds, which calls for an understanding of human nature in

[1] See *Ex parte Merryman,* Fed. Cases, No. 9, 487 (1861) and *Ex parte Milligan,* 4 Wall. 2 (1866).

general and also of the unique qualities of the particular society in question. The government of a people, like the history of that people, is the study of a lifetime. Whatever introductory simplifications may be resorted to, the inherent complexity of the subject must be emphasized.

Contradictions. This suggests why all sorts of contradictory statements can be validly made about government. For example, many close observers of liberal democratic governments have described them and their operations as enforcing the will of the people. On the other hand, many searching critics have described them as tools of an economic oligarchy—instruments for maintaining the rule of the capitalist class. Exponents of both these views are competent and honest and they can both marshal impressive evidence to support them. The truth is that so great a variety of forces and motives enter into government in the twentieth century, and the response of government to these is so complex, that a plausible case for a great many propositions can be made out. No one key will unlock the mysteries of government and we must always beware of thinking we know more than we really do. Alexis de Tocqueville wisely admonished us in 1831 that there is 'nothing absolute in the theoretical value of political institutions,' and that their 'efficiency depends almost always on the original circumstances and the social conditions of the people to whom they are applied.'

If, in his initial approach to government, the student tries to comprehend it in all its complexity, he will be completely baffled. A play-by-play description of what goes on in the national capital on a single day would convince him that he should stick to a tidy subject like mathematics. Difficult subjects can be handled only by taking one at a time the elements involved. One can begin with the anatomy of government—the framework to be found in the constitution. That will occupy the attention of the present chapter and much of the succeeding chapters. At the next level of difficulty, one can isolate the organs and agencies of government and see how they function within the framework. Finally, one can consider how far this functioning is a response to the environment in which government operates, to what extent government action reflects the interplay of the social forces of the community. In the later chapters, some consideration, inevitably incomplete, will be given to the physiology of government and to the reaction of the organs to the environment.[2]

---

[2] The use of the biological analogy must not be taken to suggest that biological laws are in any way applicable to the state. As the analogy becomes more forced in later pages, this will probably become sufficiently obvious.

WHERE TO LOOK FOR THE CONSTITUTION

In the United States. The American Revolution was a fairly clean break with the past and the Americans obtained a written constitution from it. But they did not write on an entirely clean slate. Both in what they accepted and in what they rejected they were decisively influenced by their heritage. British and French political thought played a considerable role. The remarkably short constitution—a document of only five thousand words whose reading time would not alarm the devotee of the popular magazine—is not, however, by any means the whole of the United States Constitution of today. In order to make the paper constitution work in practice and to adapt it to the American scene, much improvising has had to be effected.

HOW THE UNITED STATES CONSTITUTION HAS GROWN. (1) Twenty-four *formal amendments* have been adopted, the last one in 1964. (2) With the passage of time, many *customs and usages,* for which there is no warrant in the written text and which it would take a substantial volume to describe, have acquired an importance and sanctity scarcely less than that of the Constitution itself. The President's cabinet, his power of dismissal of most, but not all, officials who serve under him, and the highly significant role of political parties are just three illustrations of that aspect of constitutional growth.

Then (3), the very terseness of the Constitution left a number of fundamental gaps that have been filled by *Acts of Congress.* Into that category fall, for example, the basic structure of the federal courts—only the Supreme Court is mentioned in the Constitution—and the creation of the ten great executive departments. (4) *Executive action* has played another vital role in constitutional development, particularly, but certainly not exclusively, in foreign affairs. The broad interpretation of the war powers by such assertive Presidents as Lincoln, Theodore Roosevelt, Wilson, and Franklin Roosevelt come to mind at once.

Finally (5), and perhaps most significantly, the *Supreme Court of the United States,* which in a very real sense has the last word on the Constitution, has added a wealth of meaning to many of the clipped phrases of the written document. For example, in *McCulloch* v. *Maryland,*[3] a case presumably known to every high school student, the Court held in 1819 that some matters not expressly mentioned in the Constitution are necessarily implied. As a result, no conceivable effort of imagination would suffice to gather

[3] 4 Wheaton 316.

from the written text what all these years of interpretation have made it mean. It takes hundreds of pages to describe even summarily the contribution of the Supreme Court! Thus there is at least some warrant for the frequent jibe that 'the Constitution is what the Supreme Court says it is'—a crass over-simplification of a complex matter, but one that was publicly used even by the then ex-Associate Justice and future Chief Justice of the U.S. Supreme Court, Mr. Charles Evans Hughes.

In Britain. The British constitution is always said to be unwritten. This is not to say that it has nowhere found expression in the printed word, but rather that the principles and detailed rules of the constitution have never been collected together in a formal document solemnly adopted at a specific date. The British people have never made a sharp revolutionary break with their past. Freedom—and everything else political in nature—has slowly broadened down from precedent to precedent. The present-day constitution which has been worked out over centuries by trial and error, comprises five major elements: (1) great basic documents; (2) statutes; (3) common law; (4) judicial decisions; and (5) custom. What endures is what has been found workable. Magna Carta of A.D. 1215, although overrated in popular oratory, is the earliest, and still a significant, *great basic document* of the constitution. The Petition of Right of 1628, the Bill of Rights of 1689, the Act of Settlement of 1701, the great Reform Act of 1832, are others of prime importance. In terms of bulk, the greater part of the constitution is to be found in the form of *statutes* enacted by Parliament. Almost all the momentous changes of the past century have been thus brought about, e.g. the extension of the franchise, the method of elections, and the defining of rights and duties of public officials.

Many basic principles, however, rest on the *common law,* that vast body of English law based on custom and reshaped to new needs by succeeding generations of judges. The principles that rest on the common law have to be evolved, laboriously, out of the *decisions of the courts* in particular disputes. Finally, a considerable and important portion of the constitution has no other basis than comparatively recent *custom.* The conventions of the constitution, as these are called, concern mainly the relation of the cabinet to Parliament, ensuring that the government is always carried on conformably to the will of the majority in Parliament. Thus a first-hand exploration of the British constitution would take one through ancient charters, scores of statutes, hundreds of judicial decisions, and finally into the biographies and correspondence of statesmen, which often provide the only written evidence for the conventions of the constitution. Its elusiveness is excused by saying it is unwritten. Hence the literal-minded who want everything in precise black-and-white throw up their hands and say, 'The British constitution! There's no such thing!'

In France. After a series of simple, flexible constitutions, including the piecemeal resort to the three 'constitutional laws' of 1875, the framers of the Constitution of the Fifth French Republic—appropriately known as the 'de Gaulle Constitution'—produced a comprehensive document in 1958 that is tantamount to a written constitution. However, unlike the written Constitution of the United States, that of France would seem to depend for its successful functioning more or less on the degree of sympathy accorded to its provisions by the Chief Executive. If this appears to be a glib oversimplification, it must be remembered that—to all intents and purposes—the Constitution of the Fifth Republic has been what de Gaulle has said it is, although there does exist a formal amendment procedure and the Constitutional Council as well as the *conseil d'état* are, at least theoretically, empowered to interpret it within prescribed limits. On the other hand, the current French Constitution represents far more of a legal *document* than does the constitution of its neighbor across the English Channel.

This sketch indicates the sources and some of the range and variety of constitutional provisions in three democratic states. It also suggests that if a search for the essential elements of a constitution is not to lose itself in a welter of confusing materials, some categories to help in classification and analysis will have to be adopted. Just as the amateur botanist, lacking a principle of classification, wanders among the flowers and gets only the impression that nature is wonderful, so the student of government without categories for sorting out his material decides that the subject is incomprehensible.

THE SEPARATION OF POWERS

Threefold. The distinctive feature of government is the exercise of power by some men over other men, and a classification of the kinds of power thus exercised, though artificial to a degree, aids understanding. At the simplest level of discussion, a familiar classification, as old as Aristotle, is available for use. There are, it is said, three distinct kinds of governmental power: legislative, executive, and judicial. *Legislative power* consists in making laws, general rules of conduct supplementing or replacing some of the older rules based on custom or unwritten law. *Executive power* consists in the executing or carrying out of laws and the carrying on of the manifold public activities and services, the daily drudgery which exhausts the civil servant. *Judicial power* consists in interpreting laws or, more concretely, deciding in the event of dispute what specific acts are permitted or required or forbidden in execution of the law.

Montesquieu. While it is impossible thus to classify all the varied powers exercised by modern governments, these categories will serve for immediate purposes. The Baron de Montesquieu, a French jurist and philosopher of the mid-eighteenth century, adopted this classification and made himself famous by arguing that the secret of civil liberty lay in the separation of these powers, in the reserving of each type of power to different persons or bodies of persons. One man or group of men should exercise substantially all legislative power and at the same time have no extensive share in or control over executive or judicial power. Men will always push what power they have to the limit; and if those who make the laws also enforce them, they can tyrannize over their fellows. The result will be the same if either executive and judicial, or legislative and judicial, power is joined in the hands of the same persons. No one body of men, according to this argument, can be trusted with the monopoly of force possessed by government.

According to Montesquieu, assurance that government shall be servant and not master depends on the separation of powers. This, he argued, is the essence of an effective constitution. He thought he discerned a proof of his argument in the British constitution of the eighteenth century. Britain enjoyed individual liberty, while on the Continent, where absolute monarchs had gathered all power into their hands, no one had any sure tenure of freedom. He saw the independent status of the judges in Britain, ensured by the Act of Settlement of 1701. He saw in Parliament a legislative authority independent of the executive, and he thought he saw in the monarch, his advisers, and servants an independent executive authority. He was in substantial error on this last point, but the British constitution did conform to the classification and there was *then* some measure of separation of powers.

The Americans could not find the civil and political liberty they wanted under the British constitution in the days of George III. Yet they were deeply impressed with Montesquieu's analysis, if not with the particular proof he offered. They were the more impressed because John Locke, the philosopher of constitutionalism, had pointed to a similar conclusion. Moreover, the conservative-minded fathers of the American Constitution feared excesses of popularly elected legislatures as much as they feared a powerful executive. Accordingly, they set out to fashion a new government composed of three powers, each of which would be separate and, at the same time, a check on the others. So whatever of enduring wisdom there is in the separation of powers, it is a principle closely associated with the rise and spread of modern constitutional government. The constitutions of the modern world which have tried to hold governments strictly to account have relied heavily on the British and American models. This is reason enough for using Montesquieu's doctrine for preliminary analysis. Its value can be more justly assessed at a later stage.

THE CONSTITUTION OF THE UNITED STATES

Although only a part of the Constitution of the United States is now to be found in the written document and in its twenty-four formal amendments, it is still the most basic part, and attention will, for the present, be directed primarily to the written document. In looking at it, one must always remember that it is an instrument establishing a new national government and it takes the constitutions of the separate states of the Union almost completely for granted. For the most part, too, it takes for granted the main principles of the common law that the colonists imported from Britain and adapted to their use, and from which some significant features of the American constitutional system are derived. With the Revolution, the thirteen states modified or repudiated their charters as British colonies. Before 1789 most of them had adopted republican written constitutions. These constitutions, as since revised and added to by the admission of thirty-seven new states, form an important part of the American constitutional system. But their bulk forbids discussion here and, in any event, on the more fundamental questions they are faithfully paralleled by the Constitution of 1789.

Federalism. The more important principles of the Constitution may now be sketched. The first is its *federal character* arising from the preservation of the integrity and substantial independence of the separate states. The thirteen states that had made the Revolution had need of unity if they were to protect their nascent republicanism in a world of powerful monarchies. Yet they were not prepared at all to submerge themselves in a new state giving all authority to a single central government. The result was a compromise federal system in which a new national government was to have certain specific powers in aid of the broad general objectives stated in the preamble, viz. 'establish justice, insure domestic tranquillity, provide for the common defence, promote the general welfare, and secure the blessings of liberty.' The separate states, on the other hand, as Amendment X adopted in 1791 makes clear, were to continue to exercise such authority as was not specifically granted to the national government (viz. declare war), expressly prohibited to the states (viz. coin money), or withdrawn from the reach of all governments (viz. *ex post facto* laws). Most of the written Constitution is taken up with defining the new national authority and distributing powers between it and the states.

Limited Government. The second principle is that of *limited government.* Whereas the supreme legislative power under the British constitution can regulate every aspect of social life, the American Constitution tried to put certain claims of individuals that were thought to be sacred human rights beyond the reach of Congress. It limited the area of human affairs over which the federal government, and in some cases the states, could exercise power. This sprang, in part, from the eighteenth-century doctrines about the natural rights of man, so prominent in the French Revolution and in the revolutionary constitutions in France. In part, it sprang from the more earthy concern of the conservative framers of the Constitution who feared the radical ferment stirred up by the American Revolution.

CONSTITUTION AND BILL OF RIGHTS. These general limitations on government are to be found principally in the original Constitution of 1789 and in the first ten amendments, adopted in 1791 and generally known as the Bill of Rights. Some of them take the form of abstract *natural rights.* For example, Congress is forbidden to interfere with freedom of religion, of speech, of the press, of petition and of peaceable assembly.[4] Other provisions strike at particular abuses, the usual weapons of arbitrary governments, such as general search warrants, bills of attainder, and *ex post facto* (retroactive penal) laws.[5] Still others sought to preserve against encroaching governments particular institutional procedures that had been useful in the English and American struggles for liberty, such as habeas corpus [6] and trial by jury.[7]

Most of these and numerous other limitations are expressly applicable only to the federal government and do not bind the state governments. Of those mentioned above, only the prohibitions against bills of attainder and *ex post*

---

[4] Constitution of the United States, Amendment I.
[5] Ibid. Art. I, sect. 9, and Amendment IV.
[6] Ibid. Art. I, sect. 9.
[7] Ibid. Amendments V, VI, and VII.

facto laws thus apply to *both* levels of government.[8] However, since most of the state constitutions, in their own bills of rights, go as far as or farther than the federal Constitution in imposing limitations, it is substantially correct to think of all these restrictions as being generally applicable. By gradual judicial interpretation of the due process and equal protection of the laws clauses in the Fourteenth Amendment, which applies to the states, many, but not all, of the limitations in the Bill of Rights have become also effective against the fifty states.[9] Notable exceptions are the guarantees of indictment by grand jury and trial by jury.

'DUE PROCESS.' The most famous of all these restrictive provisions is one imposed by the federal Constitution on state and federal governments alike. The *Fifth* Amendment forbids the *federal* government, and the *Fourteenth* Amendment forbids the *states,* to 'deprive any person of life, liberty, or property, without due process of law.' The phrase 'due process of law' can be traced back into the early history of English law and is reminiscent of the tone of Magna Carta, which stipulated that free men should not be proceeded against except in accordance with the law of the land. The Petition of Right, in which the English Parliament in 1628 petitioned Charles I to respect the rights of his subjects, used the two phrases, 'the law of the land,' and 'due process of law,' interchangeably. The Declaration of Independence pronounced 'life, liberty, and the pursuit of happiness' to be inalienable rights. The exact phrase used in the Constitution, however, comes from John Locke, the philosopher of constitutionalism, who declared 'life, liberty, and property' to be fundamental natural rights of man. But the past fame of these phrases pales before the notoriety they have gained in the American Constitution. The Supreme Court of the United States has been deeply divided over their meaning and this in turn has aroused sharp political debate throughout the country. These deceptively simple phrases have been storm centers of controversy over the last hundred years.

STATE GOVERNMENTS. Some restrictions were laid upon the *state governments only.* In the turbulent period during and after the Revolutionary War, the legislatures of many of the states had been enacting laws that impaired the rights of creditors under existing contracts and/or made the almost worthless paper currency legal tender for payment of debts. It is said that harassed creditors often took to the woods to evade their vindictive and relentless

---

[8] Ibid. Art. 1, sect. 10.
[9] See Mr. Justice Cardozo's opinion for the Supreme Court in *Palko* v. *Connecticut*, 302 U.S. 319 (1937).

debtors who sought to pay them off in inflated currency. Accordingly, the framers of the Constitution, among whom the creditor interest was well represented, inserted clauses providing that no state should pass any 'law impairing the obligation of contracts,' and forbidding states to coin money, emit bills of credit, or make anything but gold or silver legal tender.[10]

These are some of the more important of the clauses illustrating the principle of limited government. In Britain, by contrast, Parliament could lawfully enact each and all of these measures forbidden in the United States. It has not done so. Britain has been no less free of legislative tyranny than the United States. The effective guarantee is not found in a written constitution but in the settled constitutional habit of the British people, of which Parliament is itself an expression. Thus far it has been reasonably adequate. There has not been any significant agitation for written constitutional guarantees against the power of Parliament.

Separation of Powers. The third fundamental principle is the *separation of powers.* The Constitution of 1789 takes Montesquieu's classification for granted. Without defining the nature of the three powers in any way, the first three articles of the document assign legislative, executive, and judicial power to three separate organs. Article I provides that all legislative powers granted therein shall be vested in Congress; Article II that the executive power shall be vested in the President; Article III that the judicial power shall be vested in one Supreme Court and in such inferior courts as Congress may establish. It is also stipulated that no member of Congress shall, during his term in Congress, be appointed to any civil office, and that no person holding any such office shall be a member of Congress. Thus no one can share in the exercise of more than one of the three powers at the same time. Neither the President, nor his cabinet, nor any executive officer can be a member of Congress. The executive power of the United States is exercised not by a committee of the legislature responsible to the legislature, as in Britain, but by an independently elected President aided by such advisers outside Congress as he sees fit to consult. The President is required to keep Congress informed of the state of the Union, to advise it about the administration of national affairs, and to recommend such legislation as he thinks necessary. He has power, in certain circumstances, to convene Congress and to fix a date for its adjournment, but beyond this he is not expected to shape or participate in its deliberations.

The judiciary is appointed by the President with the advice and consent of

[10] Ibid. Art. 1, sect. 10.

the Senate. But once appointed, they hold office during 'good behavior,' which really means for life. Congress cannot intimidate them by reducing their salaries during their continuance in office. Congress alone can remove them, but only through impeachment (by the House) for and conviction (by the Senate) of a serious offense. It would appear that the powers of government are parceled out among the three organs and kept separate by the unscalable walls of the Constitution. In the United States, Montesquieu's principle received its fullest expression.

CHECKS AND BALANCES. Each of the three organs was to have a will of its own and as little ability as possible to influence the choice of the personnel who exercise the other two powers. Still, the framers feared the popularly elected legislatures which had run riot in the Revolutionary period, and they still feared a strong executive who might get it in his head to be a king. It was thought that dividing Congress into two houses, each to be elected by a different method and for different periods, would tend to divide and moderate the legislative will. By providing for indirect election of the President, that office would be shielded from demagogues who notoriously abuse even the widest mandate.

It was thought advisable to have still further checks on power, and this abundance of caution led the framers to introduce some qualifications on the clear-cut separation of powers. Bills and certain resolutions passed by a majority of the two houses of Congress require the approval of the President in order to become law and can only be made law over his veto by a two-thirds vote of both branches. The President was given some share in legislative power. The President, Vice-President, and other executive officers can be removed from office by impeachment in the House and conviction in the Senate, thus giving the Senate some judicial power. The declaration of war, an executive act, can only be made by Congress. The Senate shares with the President the powers of treaty-making and the appointment of high officials, also executive acts. While the President and Senate appoint the federal judges, the Senate can remove them by conviction on impeachment—which has occurred in four cases. The constitution of all courts inferior to the Supreme Court is confided to Congress. These *checks and balances,* as they are called, were not set up to knit the three powers together for concerted action but rather to ensure, in the words of *The Federalist,* No. 51, that the 'several constituent parts [of the government] may by their mutual relations, be the means of keeping each other in their proper place.'

To those who do not know the history of the disorder of the Revolutionary period, the predominantly conservative temper of the framers, and the emphasis put by the prevailing political philosophy of the time on the natural rights of individuals and on the natural propensity of government to tyranny, much of this will seem not merely abundance but excess of caution. Indeed, there is no doubt that the separation of powers and checks and balances have had unfortunate effects on American government; on the other hand, there is doubt whether this complex scheme would have worked at all but for the rise of mediating institutions not contemplated by the authors of the Constitution. Yet the various effects of the scheme on the operation of government, and the important modifications that custom has brought about, largely through the rise of political parties to all-pervasive influence, must be left for succeeding chapters. Meanwhile these words of Mr. Justice Brandeis may be noted: 'The doctrine of the separation of powers was adopted by the Convention of 1787, not to promote efficiency but to preclude the exercise of arbitrary power. The purpose was, not to avoid friction, but, by means of the inevitable friction incident to the distribution of the governmental powers among three departments to save the people from autocracy.' [11]

Judicial Review. The last of the important features of the American Constitution to be sketched here is *judicial review,* the power of any court to hold unconstitutional and hence unenforceable any law, any official action based upon it, and any illegal action by a public official that it deems—upon careful, normally painstaking reflection and in line with the taught traditions of the law as wall as judicial self-restraint—to be in conflict with the Constitution. In other words, in invoking the power of judicial review to be discussed more fully in Chapter XV—a court applies the *superior* of two laws: in the United States, the Constitution.

Of course, the courts cannot range across the statute book on their own motion, slaying legislation at will. But when, in a dispute between parties properly brought before them, the decision is found to turn on the terms of some act of a legislature, the judges—state and inferior federal as well as Supreme Court—may inquire whether the legislation is contrary to state or federal constitutions, and if so, the party relying on its terms will fail through the ensuing declaration of unconstitutionality. An act of a state legislature may be struck down on the ground that it could only be enacted by Congress, or vice versa, and is thus a violation of the federal principle. A statute may be attacked before the courts on the ground that it violates one or the other of the two 'due process of law' clauses, or some other fundamental guarantee,

[11] *Myers* v. *U.S., 272 U.S. 52 (1926).

and thus infringes the principle of limited government. An act of Congress may be challenged on the ground that it violates the principle of the separation of powers. Indeed, any legislative act that in their judgment is prohibited by the Constitution may be held invalid by the courts.

This is in the sharpest contrast with the treatment of legislation in the British courts. They may *interpret* an act of Parliament, but they can never question the power of Parliament to do anything that Parliament has manifestly done. The Rule of Law in Britain means no more than the enforcement as law of what Parliament has said: The Rule of Law in the United States means also the enforcement of the 'higher law' of the Constitution against both the legislature and the executive.

Nor do the French courts possess the power of judicial review of legislation *per se*. However, since its creation by the de Gaulle Constitution of 1958, the *Constitutional Council (conseil constitutionnel)*, consisting of all ex-Presidents of France plus nine distinguished personages, of whom three each are selected by the President of the Republic and the heads of the two houses of Parliament, has been clothed with *limited* authority to safeguard the Constitution. It has the power to declare unconstitutional all *organic* laws and standing orders of Parliament, all of which must be submitted to it prior to their promulgation. It may also strike down *ordinary* laws, treaties, and protocols, but only if these have been *voluntarily* referred to it by the President or Parliament. Furthermore, it possesses certain supervisory powers over national elections and referenda. But it is not really a *court*; it lies outside of both the ordinary and administrative judicial systems of the government (similar, but not the same, extra-judicial bodies exist, among other places, in Austria, Italy, and West Germany); it cannot itself initiate action in constitutional cases; and neither private individuals nor groups are able to challenge the constitutionality of a law although, as will be fully explained in Chapter XVII, the citizens of France may turn to the administrative courts, headed by the Council of State *(conseil d'état)* for the redress of grievances involving members of the executive branch of the government.

An Implied Power

Strangely enough, this power of the United States courts is not explicitly stated in the Constitution. But there is persuasive evidence that between twenty-five and thirty-two of the forty delegates to the Constitutional Convention, Anti-Federalists as well as Federalists, favored it—although for quite different reasons—who, with less than a handful of dissenters, in effect concurred in the pronouncement by Gouverneur Morris of Pennsylvania that the courts should decline to give the weight of law to 'a direct violation of the Constitution.' So prominent a framer as Alexander Hamilton, in No. 78 of *The Federalist* papers, clearly envisaged it and called for its acceptance as an essential element of the Constitution.[12] Moreover, it is noteworthy as a matter of historical fact that the British Privy Council had *established* judicial review over acts passed by the colonial legislatures, and that between 1789 and 1803 the courts in ten of the states had *exercised* that power. Thus, it is one of the powers that the Supreme Court has ever since Mr. Chief Justice Marshall's historic decision in *Marbury* v. *Madison* in 1803[13] held to be necessarily implied from that provision of Article VI of the Constitution known as the 'supremacy clause,' (a) that the Constitution and the laws of Congress made in pursuance thereof and all treaties made under the authority of the United States shall be the supreme law of the land, and (b) that 'the judges in every State shall be bound thereby, anything in the Constitution or laws of any State to the contrary, notwithstanding.' The necessity of the implication has continued to be challenged but, in any event, custom has made judicial review as much a part of the Constitution as if it were explicit in the document. Hundreds of laws, state and federal, chiefly the former, have been held unconstitutional by the judiciary. In this censorship of legislation, of course, the Supreme Court, being the highest court of appeal, has the last word. But it does not resort to the weapon of judicial review lightly: As of the end of its 1962–63 term, it had held unconstitutional 91 provisions of 85 federal laws and 700 state laws.[14]

Congress acting alone has no power to amend the Constitution. The framers made formal amendment extremely difficult. Noting the difficulty and rarity of amendments, many have said that it is the Constitution that is supreme in the United States. Others, noting the relative ease with which the Supreme Court has from time to time found unsuspected meanings in the clauses of the Constitution, have said that it is its nine justices who are supreme. Still others, seeing the numerous cases in which the ruling interpretation given by

[12] 'Limitations [to the legislative authority] can be preserved in practice in no other way than through the medium of courts of justice, whose duty it must be to declare all acts contrary to the manifest tenor of the Constitution void. Without this, all the reservations of particular rights or privileges would amount to nothing.'

[13] 1 Cranch 13.

[14] For a complete table of the former as well as an extensive discussion of the problem, see Henry J. Abraham, *The Judicial Process* (New York: Oxford University Press, 1962), chs. vii and viii.

the Supreme Court rests on the narrow majority of five judges for and four against, make still more disturbing comments. Such remarks are significant, but no simple statement will uncover the locus of supreme power in the United States. As a matter of form, supreme power rests with the bodies that Article V of the Constitution authorizes to make amendments. But, as we have seen, thus far relatively little of the amending and developing of the Constitution has been carried out in this way.

Leading Principles of the British Constitution

Very early in British constitutional history, the powers of government exercised by the Norman and Angevin monarchs began to be differentiated along lines resembling the threefold classification, and distinct organs for their exercise emerged. The Great Council, composed of the great feudal lords and meeting three times a year, 'advised' the monarch largely by trying to set limits to royal action, as in Magna Carta. With the addition of representatives from the counties and boroughs, the Great Council developed into Parliament. The redress of grievances and the imposition of limitations on the monarch took the form of laws enacted with the consent of the king.

Apart from the Great Council, the monarch was advised by an inner council composed of his trusted lieutenants, the heads of an embryonic civil service only slowly differentiated from the monarch's personal household. This inner council, generally called the Curia Regis, carried on all the executive work of government, doing the will of the monarch everywhere except where blocked by the Great Council. As government business increased, several groups of these officials specialized in settling disputes and interpreting the law applicable to them. At first, they were merely committees of the Curia Regis but after developing an organization and procedure of their own, they became distinct and separate courts of law, although until 1701 the judges still held office at the monarch's pleasure. Within the Curia Regis itself, increasing size brought the need for a small executive committee—hence the Privy Council, close to the monarch. The Privy Council became the real executive council, and even today the *formal* authority of the cabinet derives from their being sworn 'of the Privy Council.'

Thus distinct legislative, executive, and judicial organs took shape. It would, however, be misleading to suggest that the judges never made laws and that the legislature and executive always refrained from judging, and wrong to think that each organ had a well-marked sphere of authority in which it was separate and independent. In part at any rate, the struggle between Parliament and the Stuarts arose out of the indefiniteness of the relationship between these organs, which was only cleared up by the constitutional settlement after the Revolution of 1688. The judges once appointed were made independent of the executive. It was settled that only Parliament could change the law or make a new law such as the levying of a tax—which, in effect, made Parliament supreme. The power of governing the country subject to the limitations thus imposed by law, the administration of the colonies, and the conduct of foreign relations remained with the monarch and his advisers appointed by him. It took most of the eighteenth century to establish beyond question the rule that the monarch must choose ministers who enjoy the confidence of Parliament. Montesquieu can be excused for thinking in 1748 that the executive was separate and independent.

The Supremacy of Parliament. But there has been no excuse in the last hundred years for anyone's thinking that the British constitution exhibits a sharp separation of powers. Its basic principle is the supremacy of Parliament. The British courts do not possess the power of judicial review. Any and every law passed by Parliament is constitutional. It has been said that Parliament can do anything except make a man a woman. This is an understatement! If Parliament were to declare that henceforth women were to be treated in all respects as if they were men, the executive and the courts would be obliged so to treat them, even in the face of nature. Women would then have to be called up under the military service law hitherto applicable only to men. Obviously, this means that Parliament can turn absurdities into laws and can work its will on the other two organs of government. It could pass a law dismissing all servants of the Crown and taking into its own hands the entire executive power. It could abolish the judiciary. So it can enlarge or diminish at pleasure the sphere of the executive and judiciary. It can—as it has increasingly done in the last eighty years—delegate law-making powers from itself to the executive. There is no ban on law-making by the executive if only Parliament will authorize it. It can—and does with great frequency—take the power of interpreting particular laws away from the judiciary and give it to the executive.

Of course, as long as the House of Commons, which is the effective part of Parliament, represents the electorate and depends on it for re-election, there are many things it will not dream of doing. There is, in practice, a considerable separation of powers, although there are no formal constitutional provisions ensuring its close observance. If we look at the strict legal forms of the constitution alone, Parliament can change any law by majority vote, and it can change the constitution in the same way. But the British constitution is largely made up of custom and convention which often seem to nullify the legal forms. Constitutionalism and the constitutional practices on which it rests are preserved in Britain by custom and the deeply conservative habit of the British people. They resist rapid and drastic change. They believe in limits on governmental power and those who represent them in Parliament have not been allowed to forget it. As we shall see later, drastic constitutional change is not ordinarily undertaken by Parliament until the proposed change has been made a direct issue in a general election.

Fusion of Powers. The electorate, however, has not insisted on a sharp separation of legislature and executive. It has rather approved an intimate connection and interdependence between them. The executive is directly responsible to Parliament. The ministry, composed of some sixty ministers, heads the various departments of government and directs all the energies and activities of the civil service. A varying number of the more important ministers, generally about twenty, composes the cabinet. Since the cabinet—and the other ministers also—must have seats in Parliament, it is, in reality, a committee of Parliament for the executive management of the nation's affairs. When this committee loses the confidence of the House of Commons, it must either abandon the direction of affairs of state and resign, or seek a dissolution of Parliament in the hope that a newly elected House of Commons will give it renewed confidence. In formal constitutional theory, at any rate, the executive is dependent on Parliament. The cabinet is, in Bagehot's words, a buckle, a hyphen, a combining committee, for ensuring harmony between the detailed execution of the laws by the civil service and the will of the majority in Parliament. The executive and legislative powers are not separated but almost completely fused.

The judges are appointed by the monarch on the advice of his ministers; the appointment is for life and during good behavior. With the exception of county court and magistrate court judges, who are removable for cause by the Lord Chancellor, they can be removed only by an address of both Houses of Parliament. Because of a high standard of judicial rectitude and impartiality, this power has almost never been used and the judicial power has enjoyed a high degree of independence. It must be remembered, however, that Parliament has the power to declare that any and every interpretation of law made by the judges is wrong and, by an amendment, to substitute its own authoritative interpretation. Also, Parliament may take from the courts the power of interpreting particular laws.

Although there is no formal separation of powers, it would be incorrect to think that these organs do not act as some check on one another. The heads of the civil service sometimes find obstacles to doing what Parliament wants to do. The courts not infrequently interpret the laws to mean something different from what Parliament intended and the executive hoped. Even the majority in Parliament that supports the cabinet is sometimes reluctant to support particular ministers. The significant fact is that if Parliament really makes up its mind, nothing can stand in its way.

The Rule of Law. There is another fundamental principle of the British constitution called the Rule of Law. Although its exact significance is a matter of much debate, it is clearly of critical importance. The Rule of Law means, at least, that all actions of government must conform to the law and an individual cannot be prejudiced in person or property by the government or anyone else except in accordance with existing law. It has commonly been thought that, in addition, officials had to justify their actions by the law generally applicable to all citizens before the established judiciary, which is free of all suggestion of executive influence.

A century ago there was much more warrant for this last proposition than there is today. For a long time now, Parliament has been granting to officials special powers to take action not justified under the ordinary law, and it has been limiting the right of the citizen to have the actions of officials scrutinized by the judicial power. Yet there has been no general removal of officials from judicial surveillance, and it remains true in most cases that anyone who asserts that he has been wronged by the action of a government official can bring that official before the courts of law to answer for his conduct. The official may justify himself by pointing to an Act of Parliament that gives him a special privilege to do what he has done. But he cannot turn aside the complaint merely by asserting an exalted official status and an inscrutable executive expediency in what he has done. The state can throw away the conscript's life but it cannot conscript him in the first instance on the plea of high policy or public expedience, except as supported by a law sanctioned by Parliament. The Rule of Law, although qualified today by the grant of special powers to officials, remains an indispensable instrument for ensuring that government remains servant.

Parliament, being supreme, could abolish the Rule of Law tomorrow. As long as Parliament is concerned to keep the executive under control, it is unlikely to do so. Yet the fact that the Rule of Law does not now mean what it meant a hundred years ago indicates that *the really fundamental principle of the British constitution is the supremacy of Parliament.* Or, as has been stated elsewhere, it is not entirely a caricature to describe the British constitution as no more than the current notion of politicians about proper conduct.[15]

The Constitution of France

The constitutions of France's Third Republic and Fourth Republic resembled Britain's in their emphasis upon legislative supremacy and the fusion of powers. But it was not until that of the so-called October Constitution of 1946 of the Fourth Republic that the French resorted to a formal, written document roughly along the lines of the Constitution of the United States, complete with titles (chapters), articles, and a preamble that enumerated a group of civil rights. The Third Republic had adopted a constitution in 1875 that consisted of just *three* briefly stated constitutional laws, around which that most enduring of all of France's late republics functioned for sixty-five years.[16] However, the Constitution of the Fifth Republic, commonly known as the *de Gaulle Constitution of 1958*, although retaining the disciplined written form of its immediate predecessor, has departed from French republican tradition by prescribing a system of government based upon the concept of a strong executive and a weak legislature, coupled with the doctrine of the separation of powers. Like the Constitution of the United States, the de Gaulle Constitution is relatively brief, concise, and elastic—and, as will be pointed out in greater detail in later chapters, has been made even more elastic by the assertiveness and personality of the powerful first President of the French Fifth Republic, General Charles de Gaulle.

Executive Supremacy. Drafted primarily by one of de Gaulle's most intimate advisers, Michel Debré, who became its first Premier from 1958 to 1962—and, incidentally, established the all-time record for republican premiers of three years and three months in office—the 1958 Constitution lodges predominant authority in the executive branch. In theory the executive power is divided between the President and the Premier, who is chosen by the Presi-

[15] David E. Butler, *The Study of Political Behaviour* (London: Hutchinson & Co., 1958), p. 17.
[16] First, a 'Law on the Organization of the Senate'; second, a 'Law on the Organization of the Public Powers'; and third, a 'Law on the Relation of the Public Powers.'

dent and then becomes responsible to Parliament. But it is far less of a meaningful responsibility than that of the earlier republics, especially since the Constitution divides the law- and/or rule-making power between Parliament and the Premier and his cabinet. This division *a fortiori* works to the advantage of the executive since the Constitution spells out limitations upon this power solely for the legislature!

Yet under the new system it is clearly the President who has the upper hand because of an enormous reserve of power, which reaches its zenith when exercised under Article 16. This fountainhead of extraordinary power authorizes the President to assume virtually dictatorial powers 'when the institutions of the Republic, the independence of the nation, the integrity of its territory or the fulfillment of its international commitments are threatened in a grave and immediate manner and when the regular functioning of the constitutional governmental authorities is interrupted.' Under these circumstances, having informed the nation of the impending steps, and upon consultation with the Premier, the Constitutional Council, and the heads of the two branches of Parliament—which may not be dissolved during the application of Article 16—the President 'shall take the measures commanded by these circumstances.' Thus, de Gaulle invoked Article 16 after the attempted military insurrection in Algeria in April 1961.

Separation of Powers. Under the earlier French republics, fusion rather than separation of powers existed between the executive and the legislative branches of government in the native land of Montesquieu. Then the members of the ministry were members of Parliament—although this was not so absolute a requirement as it was and still is across the Channel. In the same sense as in Britain, the French cabinet or ministry was a committee of Parliament for the execution of laws and the supervision of administration, and the titular chief of state who then existed—though also called President of the Republic—possessed only slightly more power than the British monarch. Parliament was all-powerful; in contrast to Britain's House of Commons it could be dissolved only with the greatest of difficulty; it toppled one government after another almost in the manner of a game of bowling.

All this has been changed. Stripped of most of its law-making powers; its effective authority to overthrow cabinets drastically reduced; ridiculed and despised by the President of the Republic, whose power of dissolution is now a real one, the French Parliament, once the undoubted center of gravity of power in France and probably the strongest legislature in the free world of the twentieth century, has been reduced to little more than at worst a debating society and at best a second-rate, frustrated power. Furthermore, a strict separation rather than fusion of powers now governs the relationship between executive and legislature, with no member of one being permitted to hold office under the other (although civil servants may take a 'leave of absence' from their job to serve in Parliament). As has already been indicated in some detail earlier in this chapter, no *bona fide* power of judicial review exists in France, other than the severely circumscribed review function inherent in the duties and powers of the Constitutional Council. But access to that body is limited and depends upon the President or Parliament for voluntary referral of constitutional questions except in the restricted area of organic laws and standing orders of Parliament. Indeed, although of some significance, the Constitutional Council—despite an occasional 'no' to the President—has developed less as an independent judicial organ than as an arm of the chief executive.

Codified Law. A unique feature of the French Constitution is that law is still based chiefly upon the Napoleonic codes. Unlike the largely judge-made law of Britain and the United States, French law is primarily statutory; it is written law, and the judges consider themselves bound thereby. There is far less resort to precedent than in the English-speaking lands. The professional French judges are appointed by the High Council of the Judiciary and the Minister of Justice (theoretically by the President of the Republic), chiefly as a result of special competitive examinations and of four years' attendance at the new (1959) *Center of Judicial Studies* (to be described later). They are removable 'for misconduct in office'—in a sense they are a branch of the civil service, although the de Gaulle Constitution in effect asserts that they are 'irremovable.' They apply and interpret the codified law of the land under a Constitution that has placed a premium upon domination by the President of *la patrie*.

AMENDMENT OF CONSTITUTIONS

So far we have considered constitutions as if they were frozen and static, imposing a rigid frame within which the powers of government are exercised. Obviously a high degree of stability in a constitution is necessary, because order and security depend, in part, on the predictability of what governments can do or can be required to do. On the other hand, only a static, caste-ridden society could tolerate an unchanging constitution. As long as social change, or progress, continues, it is vital that a constitution should respond to decisive social transformations. A too rigid constitution may stifle or distort the direction of change. At the other extreme, the forces dammed back by it may gather enough power to break it by revolutionary means. As an alternative to violence there is stealth. A constitution may be evaded by pretending it does not apply to a particular situation or even by pretending it is not there. If the pretense is accepted for a considerable time without effective protest, it amounts to an unacknowledged change in the constitution. It is important, therefore, to see both what formal methods of amendment, if any, constitutions specifically provide for, and what types of informal amendments, changes by stealth, have been employed.

Formal Amendment. As the British Parliament is utterly supreme, it follows that it can change the constitution as it sees fit. An ordinary law passed by a simple majority suffices to make the profoundest constitutional change. However, the recently developed doctrine of the electoral *mandate,* to be considered later, is an important modification imposed by *custom* on this sweeping power of Parliament.

FRANCE. Title XIV of the Constitution of the Fifth Republic prescribes a fairly simple mode of amendment, with the initiative in the hands of either the President of the Republic, upon the suggestion of the Premier, or of the members of Parliament. To become part of the basic document, an amendment must then be adopted in identical language by both chambers of Parliament *and* ratified by a popular referendum, or—if the President of the Republic so determines—by a three-fifths majority of the two chambers meeting in joint session. No amendments may be proposed 'when the integrity of the territory is in danger,' and the Constitution is emphatic on the point that the 'republican form of government shall not be subjected to amendment.'

As was pre-eminently true of its predecessor, the Fifth Republic has not seen many attempted amendments of its Constitution. And as long as the present trend toward the centripetal presidency continues, it is not likely that legislative action in this sphere will either be attempted or successful. Indeed, in October 1962, over the objections of both the Constitutional Council and the Council of State, President de Gaulle ignored Title XIV, deliberately and (with obvious glee) publicly by-passed a frustrated and angry legislature, and, in violation of the Constitution, submitted directly to the people in a referendum the question of whether future presidents should be chosen by direct popular vote. Parliament revolted, bringing down Premier Pompidou's government by a vote of censure, but President de Gaulle—

though obliged to dissolve the National Assembly and to call a new election —proceeded with his plan for the referendum. The voters subsequently approved the desired change by a *oui* vote of 61 per cent of the responses, the smallest favorable margin of any referendum during Charles de Gaulle's regime. To the charge that he had violated the Constitution, the President countered with the query "How can I violate the Constitution in going to the very fountainhead of its authority, the people of France?" Nonetheless, he had, of course, infringed its terms.

THE UNITED STATES. Article V of the United States Constitution defines the amending procedure—one fairly simple on paper, yet difficult to use effectively. There are two ways of proposing and two of ratifying a constitutional amendment. These methods may be used interchangeably, as the following diagram demonstrates:

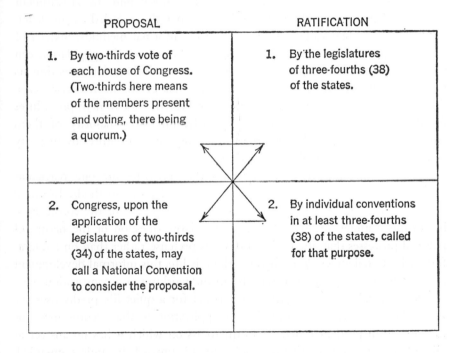

PROPOSAL	RATIFICATION
1. By two-thirds vote of each house of Congress. (Two-thirds here means of the members present and voting, there being a quorum.)	1. By the legislatures of three-fourths (38) of the states.
2. Congress, upon the application of the legislatures of two-thirds (34) of the states, may call a National Convention to consider the proposal.	2. By individual conventions in at least three-fourths (38) of the states, called for that purpose.

Thus far twenty-nine amendments have been proposed by Congress, none by the states. Of these twenty-nine proposals, twenty four have been ratified and four were rejected. One, the no-longer-needed child labor amendment, has been before the states for ratification since 1924, Congress having failed to specify a time limit. All except the Twenty-first Amendment were ratified by the state legislature method. That one, which repealed the 'Prohibition' Amendment (the Eighteenth), was ratified by conventions in three-fourths of the states in eight-and-a-half months. The haste was almost indecent!

The difficulty of formal amendment is thus fairly obvious. If one can judge from experience since the Civil War, it takes about a quarter-century of agitation to get an amendment launched with any hope of success, and the issue must be one that can be dramatized so as to arouse widespread popular interest and feeling. Forbiddingly technical matters, whatever their importance, will scarcely ever muster the necessary support. There were some who thought it would be impossible to repeal the Eighteenth Amendment, even though every man, woman, and child carried his own flask. However, the issue turned out to be one of broad popular appeal and the amendment went through quickly. The Constitution is generally regarded as much too rigid and most changes have been worked by informal methods. Sixteen of the thinly populated states with less than 10 per cent of the population can block an amendment. Although thousands of resolutions for amendments have been introduced in Congress, Congress has given the necessary two-thirds majority only to the twenty-nine, as indicated. Amendment procedures for the fifty state constitutions vary greatly, but in a majority of them amendments are required to be prepared by the state legislatures by majority vote and ratified by popular referendum.

Informal Amendment. A constitution that provides for one particular method of amendment by implication forbids all other methods. Informal amendment is, therefore, a paradox. It is a development of the constitution by unconstitutional means. This raises the large question of the nature of political processes that often rely on devious pretense rather than on straightforward rational attack. Yet wherever there is life, this informal development of the constitution goes on ceaselessly. In the working of a constitution, new problems are always being met. The instinct for a quiet life predisposes the men who are working it to modify its application to the circumstances, or to read into it particular answers to questions on which it has no answer at all, rather than to cry out that the constitution is unworkable unless amended. But the process of patching, stretching, and twisting goes on until it finally becomes clear to everyone that a change has come about and has been generally accepted. The individual men who begin and carry along piecemeal adjustments often do not appreciate their creative role or perceive the general direction of their labors. Like the polyps on the coral reef, they work silently below the surface, building atolls and islands and archipelagoes of which they never dreamed.

AMENDMENT BY CUSTOM. Informal amendment comes about chiefly through custom or judicial decision, although, as already noted, both legislative and executive interpretation also play significant roles. Custom is much more widespread in its operation because it works more silently over longer periods. Notable examples are the conventions or customs of the British constitution that enforce the responsibility of the cabinet to the House of Commons. For centuries the monarch chose whom he would as his advisers and ministers. But it has been clear for over a hundred years that ministers who lose the confidence of the House of Commons must either resign or secure a dissolution of Parliament, hoping to find renewed support in a newly elected House of Commons. In effect, the monarch must now choose as his ministers person who can carry the House of Commons. The various conventions that ensure the workability of cabinet government have been worked out slowly over many years.

We have already stated that the power of Parliament to amend the British constitution has been qualified by the convention that requires Parliament to have a 'mandate' from the electorate for making any fundamental constitutional change. This convention is a very recent one, resting almost entirely on the practice of the last sixty years. But it gets its real authority from an inner logic. If Parliament were to use its undoubted power to make any law whatsoever to force through unpopular and drastic changes in the constitution, it would be soundly punished by the electorate at the first opportunity. Thus it is the part of wisdom for Parliament to refer all proposals for drastic change to the electorate at a general election. Like all constitutional changes resting on custom, its limits are hard to define. How does one identify changes so fundamental as to require a 'mandate'? In 1937 the Public Order Act in Britain put some very substantial restrictions on freedom of assembly. One might have thought this was a fundamental constitutional question, yet no mandate from the electorate was sought.

It is also difficult to know when a decisive change has been effected by custom. Up until 1940 no President of the United States had ever been even nominated for a full third term of office, although some observers of the American scene would designate Grover Cleveland and/or Theodore Roosevelt as 'third-termers.' It was generally said that custom had made a third term unconstitutional. Yet President Franklin D. Roosevelt sought and obtained a third term in 1940 *and a fourth term* in 1944. Did this mean there was no rule against a third term or was it merely an application of the maxim, *inter arma leges silent?* Of course, this particular issue is now settled by the Twenty-second Amendment which forbids *election* of the same person for more than two terms, although a person succeeding to the presidency with less than two years of the unexpired term remaining may serve a total of ten years.

The method of election of the President of the United States is a striking instance of a decisive change brought about by crystallization of usage. The Constitution provides for indirect election of the President through a body of electors. Through the operation of the political party system, these electors are now chosen by popular means and are pledged to cast their votes for the presidential candidates put forward by their respective parties. Indeed, the political parties themselves in the three countries, although their activities are now in some instances regulated by formal legal rules, are extra-constitutional growths depending on custom.

AMENDMENT BY JUDICIAL DECISION. The other method of informal change is judicial decision. In Britain and the United States the judges are required to interpret the constitution when it is in issue in disputes coming before them. He who interprets authoritatively sets the measure of the law, be it constitutional or otherwise. In both these countries part of the constitution is found in the common law, which is derived entirely from judicial decision and which is subtly modified thereby. The judges also interpret statutes, many of which may be said to be part of the constitution; but they do not interpret those conventions of the constitution that depend on modern custom.

In the United States, as has already been demonstrated earlier in this chapter, for over a hundred and sixty years the Supreme Court has had to be continuously deciding what the brief and often vague phrases of the written document mean in relation to the development of a continental domain by a restless and almost inexhaustibly resourceful people. A little reflection on the movement and variety of American life and especially the transformations of the last century will show that the judges could not possibly find all the answers in the short written document. It now takes volumes to do justice to the meanings that the Supreme Court has read into it.

Two illustrations, in brief and inadequate form, must suffice here. Article I, section 8, clause 3, of the Constitution gives Congress power 'to regulate commerce with foreign nations and among the several states . . .' Commerce that is not interstate, but *intra-state*, was to be regulated, if at all, by the state legislatures. The river-boat, pack-horse, and wagon-freight days of 1789 have given way to the age of steamships, railways, motorized road transports, and airliners; local industries serving a local market have been replaced by prodigious enterprises making products shipped to every state in the Union. How much of this activity is interstate commerce? Who would know from an examination of the words alone that an insurance company that insures clients who live in other states is *not* engaging in interstate commerce,[17] whereas the transportation of lottery tickets across state lines *is* interstate commerce [18] and therefore subject to regulation by Congress?

The Constitution does not say expressly that Congress has power to regulate trusts and combines as affecting interstate commerce, but the Supreme Court has held that Congress may do so.[19] On the other hand, in 1918, the Supreme Court decided that Congress could not forbid or regulate child labor as used in making goods that go into interstate commerce.[20] In 1941 it overruled this decision [21] and Congress can now regulate child labor in such circumstances. This is why it can be said, and with some show of reason, that the Constitution means what the Supreme Court says it means. It now takes a sizable book to explain fully what the interstate commerce clause means.

Adopted in 1868, the Fourteenth Amendment forbade the states to 'deprive any person of life, liberty or property without due process of law.' The primary purpose of the amendment was to protect the newly enfranchised Negroes in the Southern states in the exercise of their newly acquired political and civil rights. The amendment was not vigorously used for this purpose, but for forty years the Supreme Court interpreted it as forbidding a variety of efforts by state legislatures to regulate various aspects of economic life on the ground that legislation interfering with economic freedom, except when obviously a police or health measure, was a deprivation of liberty or property, or both, without due process of law. For example, statutes fixing maximum hours of work and minimum wages for employed persons were, for a

---

[17] The Supreme Court so decided in 1869 in *Paul* v. *Virginia*, 8 Wall. 168. But in 1944, in *United States* v. *South-Eastern Underwriters Association*, 322 U.S. 533, it held that such an insurance company *is* engaging in interstate commerce. The 1944 decision stands today as a clear illustration of how the Supreme Court modifies the Constitution.

[18] *Champion* v. *Ames*, 188 U.S. 321 (1903).

[19] *United States* vs. *Northern Securities Co.*, 193 U.S. 197 (1904).

[20] *Hammer* v. *Dagenhart*, 247 U.S. 251 (1918).

[21] *United States* v. *Darby*, 312 U.S. 100 (1941).

time, held to be unconstitutional deprivations of liberty.[22] The *due process* clause was bent to the service of *laisser faire,* the doctrine that government should leave business alone. In recent years, however, with a considerable change in the personnel of the Supreme Court, there has been a marked retreat from this position [23] and a restoration of emphasis on the protection of minorities from attacks on their political and civil rights. The fifty years—roughly from 1885 until 1936—the Supreme Court spent in protecting the freedom of economic enterprise from the more controversial forms of state interference may turn out to have been no more than an episode in constitutional development. In any event, it is a striking illustration of amendment by judicial interpretation.

This discussion does not pretend to be an outline of the constitutions under review or even a comparison of all their salient points. It gives no clue at all in regard to how governments actually operate within these constitutions. It merely marks a number of points of departure and tries to cut a few exploratory paths through the jungle that modern government presents to the student. All classifications and categories are tentative, to be tested with increasing knowledge as that comes from further elaboration of detail. It is hoped that it reveals the inadequacy of engineering and biological analogies. The constitution is a framework constructed for a conscious purpose, but it is one that is constantly being revised and modified by a process that bears an analogy to growth. It is the bony structure or anatomy of government, but it is modified at times by deliberate purposeful intelligence, and here the tempting analogy is mechanics and not biology. The application of other possible analogies would show that a constitution is *sui generis.*

FASCIST AND NAZI SUBVERSION OF CONSTITUTIONS

Both Italy, before the coming of the Fascist dictatorship under Mussolini in 1922, and Germany, before the coming of the Nazi dictatorship under Hitler in 1933, had theoretically democratic forms of government under

---

[22] In 1905, in *Lochner* v. *New York,* 198 U.S. 45, the Supreme Court held—over one of Mr. Justice Holmes' most famous dissents ('The Fourteenth Amendment does not enact Mr. Herbert Spencer's *Social Statics* . . .')—a New York statute fixing maximum hours of work in bakeries to be unconstitutional on this ground. For a similar decision on the constitutionality of minimum-wage legislation, see *Adkins* v. *Children's Hospital,* 261 U.S. 525 (1923).

[23] For example, the Supreme Court overruled its earlier decisions on minimum-wage laws in *West Coast Hotel Co.* v. *Parrish,* 300 U.S. 379 (1937).

written constitutions. Without expressly repealing these constitutions, the dictatorships, in both countries, overrode the constitutions and ignored their terms almost completely. This was accomplished by enlarging the powers of the executive until it was the only effective organ of government and giving it power to make any law it wished by executive decree. In each case, the dictator and the chosen few he gathered round him constituted the executive. The judges continued to be appointed by the executive, but they lost their security of tenure. They held office at the pleasure of, and could be dismissed by, the executive at any time if their decisions did not conform to that body's wishes.

Both the Nazi and Fascist dictatorships recognized a distinction between legislative, executive, and judicial power and maintained, as a matter of form, distinct organs for the exercise of each kind of power. The principle of the separation of powers, however, was denied and therefore exercised no restricting influence on governmental organization. As we shall see later, supreme power was concentrated in the executive. Under the dictatorships, neither Italy nor Germany had any constitution in the sense of a body of rules that restricted and confined the power of the government in any way.

THE SOVIET CONSTITUTION

Unlike the United States, Britain, and France, the Soviet Union has had a very limited experience with constitutions. The first Constitution of Czarist Russia was not introduced until the early years of the twentieth century, and it was overwhelmed by revolution in 1917 without ever having worked effectively. From the Communist revolution of 1917 to 1936 the Soviet Union had two constitutions, but during this period the Communist party was still consolidating its control over the country, and the government was frankly a dictatorship. The present Constitution, widely proclaimed by Communists as 'the most democratic constitution in the world,' was adopted in 1936. As constitutions go, it is brand-new, and there is as yet no special sanctity of age attached to its terms. Its provisions are by-passed with an abandon and amended with a frequency and casualness that is surprising to the Western observer to whom a constitution is something fixed and permanent.

Economic Relationships Defined. The most characteristic feature distinguishing the Soviet Constitution from its Western counterparts is its attempt to define economic relationships within the Soviet Union, which is described as 'a socialist state of workers and peasants.' The constitutions of Britain, France, and the United States leave economic relationships to be defined by ordinary law or, more often, by voluntary arrangements between the parties concerned. Communist theory holds, however, that the economic relationships within a particular society determine all its important human relationships. Consequently the essentials of the economic system must be set out in the Constitution.

The Constitution recites the overthrow of the power of the landlords and capitalists, and proclaims the elimination of the exploitation of man by man. It declares the abolition of private ownership of the means of production and the establishment of socialist ownership of them. It then provides that the economic life of the Soviet Union shall be determined and directed by a national economic plan under the control of the state. It declares the principle for distribution of incomes: 'From each according to his ability, to each according to his work.'[24] However, if we leave aside the clauses relating to economic matters, the Soviet Constitutions reads much like the liberal democratic constitutions we have just been outlining.

A Federal State. Like the United States, and unlike unitary Britain and France, the Soviet Union is a federal state. The Constitution provides for fifteen Soviet Socialist Republics, generally known as Union Republics, whose position is somewhat like that of the states of the United States. These constituent units make up the Union of Soviet Socialist Republics (U.S.S.R.) and are in turn divided into smaller areas of descending importance and size: autonomous republics, autonomous regions, and national areas. The peoples of the Soviet Union belong to numerous nations, or ethnic groups, and speak numerous languages. The Soviet Constitution thus purports to assure each national group a high degree of cultural autonomy in the administration of local affairs, and the preservation of the national tongue through its use in the schools, government offices, and courts of law of the Union Republics and their subdivisions. Soviet federalism and its illusory nature are more fully discussed in Chapter VI. Be it noted here that on paper the Soviet Union is a federal state with enumerated powers vested in a central government and residual powers—the remaining powers not specifically granted the government of the U.S.S.R.—left in the hands of the authorities of the republics, regions, and areas.[25]

The Legislature Formally Supreme. After declaring that all power belongs

---

[24] See, generally, Constitution of the U.S.S.R., ch. I.
[25] Ibid. ch. II.

to the working people as represented by their *soviets*,[26] or councils,[27] the Constitution states that 'the legislative power of the U.S.S.R. is exercised exclusively by the Supreme Soviet of the U.S.S.R.'[28] This body, the Soviet legislature, is composed of two chambers—the Soviet of the Union (lower) and the Soviet of the Nationalities (upper)—chosen on the basis of universal, equal, and direct suffrage by secret ballot, and is theoretically comparable to Congress or the British Parliament. The Supreme Soviet, and it alone, has the power to amend the Constitution by a two-thirds majority in both chambers.[29] The highest executive authority in the Soviet Union is the Council of Ministers. It is both appointed by and responsible to the Supreme Soviet.[30] The highest judicial authority is the Supreme Court of the U.S.S.R. The judges who compose it are elected by the Supreme Soviet for five years.[31] Thus the legislature is formally supreme as in Britain. The American principle of a rigid separation of powers finds no place in the Soviet Constitution.

Bill of Rights. On the other hand, like the Constitution of the United States and of that of the Fourth and Fifth French Republics, but unlike that of Britain, the Soviet Constitution contains a bill of rights.[32] Among other things, it guarantees to the citizen freedom of the person, speech, press, religion, and assembly. However, these rights are stated generally as belonging to the citizen and are not explicitly phrased as limitations on the power of the government. In practice this has turned out to be highly significant: the rights have turned out to be hollow; practice has made them a mockery. The Constitution does not establish effectively the principle of limited government. In effect, the government of the Soviet Union is an unlimited government, a fact quite openly admitted by Khrushchev in his famous speech regarding the post-1934 *Stalin* 'era of the cult of the individual.'

Supremacy of the Communist Party in Practice. The provisions of the Soviet Constitution will be discussed in greater detail later. Here, however, it is necessary to explain why the Soviet Union is governed by an all-powerful, autocratic government, when the Constitution contains most of the guarantees and provides for all the essential machinery of democratic government. It has already been suggested that there may be a wide difference between

---

[26] Ibid. Art. 3.
[27] *Soviet* is the Russian word for *council*.
[28] Constitution of the U.S.S.R., Art. 32.
[29] Ibid. Art. 146.
[30] Ibid. Arts. 64–70.
[31] Ibid. Arts. 102–5.
[32] See generally, ibid. ch. x.

the forms and the actual working of constitutions; that a constitution is only a frame for government; and that how a government operates in its frame, or indeed, whether it operates within the frame at all, depends on the beliefs that are held about the purpose and functions of government, on the capacity of the people for the art of government, and on the whole economic and social environment. The forms may provide an ideal framework for the operation of a certain type of government, but the substance, the actual working performance of government, may be entirely different from what the forms would lead one to expect.

No better example of this can be found, in modern times, than the Soviet Constitution. It is like a blueprint for a magnificent building of a particular functional design, which was never built because of the lack of the materials and the skilled workers needed for that particular kind of construction. Whether the architects of the Soviet Constitution ever intended to build a government conforming faithfully to their blueprint is, of course, a different matter, which cannot be known with any certainty.

In Chapter III, it was shown that the Communists consider the state to be a tool in the hands of the dominant social class. The Soviet state, therefore, was set up in the first place as a state of workers and peasants and presumably embodied the interests of the rural and urban proletariat, although it was actually headed by an elite from the intellectual class. In recent years, Soviet leaders claim, the enemies of the working class have been eliminated and consequently the state now embodies the interests of all the people in the U.S.S.R. But the Communists in the Soviet Union believe that the vigorous leadership needed to further these interests can best be provided by a relatively small group of workers and peasants—the Communist party—which is the vanguard and the leader of the proletariat. We must therefore look to the Communist party in order to understand the practice of Soviet government.

Linking of Party and Government. The Communist party, the only political association tolerated in the Soviet Union, is a tightly controlled, highly centralized 'state' within the Soviet state. Its organization parallels the organization of the Soviet government; each legislative and executive organ of the government is complemented by a party organ whose area of concern coincides with that of the corresponding government organ. Thus, the local soviets (or councils), the organs of government at what we would call the municipal level, are paralleled by the local organizations of the Communist party. So it goes at each level until, at the very top, the Council of Ministers of the U.S.S.R. is paralleled by the Central Committee of the party, and particularly by its two most powerful subcommittees, the *Presidium* of the Central Committee—formerly known as the Political Bureau (*Politbureau*)—and the *Secretariat*. All important decisions on public policy are first decided by one or another of the important subcommittees of the Central Committee of the party, and then transmitted to the appropriate organs of government for action. The transmitting is relatively easy because the key members of the government are almost always leading members of the party hierarchy. From 1941 until his death in 1953, Stalin, for instance, was both the Secretary-General of the Central Committee of the Communist party and the Chairman of the Council of Ministers or cabinet (until 1946 known as the Council of People's Commissars). Frequently decrees issued by the Supreme Soviet and decisions and ordinances of the Council of Ministers are signed by high party officials as well as by the appropriate officers of the government. In practice, most decisions of the highest party organs have the force of law even before they are ratified by the Supreme Soviet.

THE OMNIPOTENCE OF THE COMMUNIST PARTY. The Communist party not only controls the machinery of the state, it dominates all other associations and organizations. That has led some to characterize the Communist party as an *interlocking directorate* which supervises and centralizes all organized activities in the Soviet Union,[33] and as the 'key to the functioning of the Soviet system.'[34] An understanding of the Soviet Constitution and of Soviet government and politics, therefore, requires above all an appreciation of the place of the Communist party in the Soviet Union.

The Constitution is misleading because, while it defines the organs of government and their functions, it does not specify in detail the role of the Communist party in the government. All the Constitution says about the Communist party is that it is 'the vanguard of the working people in their struggle to build communist society and is the leading core of all organizations of the working people, both public and state.'[35] Soviet government gets its essential character not from the formal terms of the Constitution but from the fact that *it is controlled and directed at every point by a small group, the leaders of the Communist party*. It thus earns the label of dictatorship in spite of the Constitution.

[33] Samuel N. Harper and Ronald Thompson, *The Government of the Soviet Union*, 2nd ed. (New York: D. Van Nostrand Co., 1949), p. 56.
[34] John N. Hazard, *The Soviet System of Government*, 2nd ed. (Chicago: The University of Chicago Press, 1960), p. 12.
[35] Constitution of the U.S.S.R., Art. 126. See also Art. 141.

Suggested References for Further Reading

Amery, L., *Thoughts on the Constitution* (Oxford, 1953).

Bagehot, W., *The English Constitution,* 2nd ed. (Oxford, 1936).

Black, C. L., Jr., *The People and the Court: Judicial Review in a Democracy* (Macmillan, 1960).

Corwin, E. S., *The Constitution and What It Means Today,* 12th ed. (Princeton, 1958).

———, *Constitutional Revolution, Ltd.* (Claremont Colleges, 1941).

Crosskey, W. W., *Politics and the Constitution in the History of United States* (U. of Chicago, 1953).

Dicey, A. V., *Introduction to the Study of the Law of the Constitution,* 10th ed. (Macmillan, 1961).

Greaves, H. R. G., *The British Constitution,* 3rd ed. (Allen & Unwin, 1955).

Jackson, R. H., *The Struggle for Judicial Supremacy* (Knopf, 1941).

Jennings, Sir W. I., *The Law and the Constitution,* 5th ed. (U. of London, 1959).

Kelly, A. H., and W. A. Harbison, *The American Constitution,* 3rd ed. (Norton, 1963).

Laski, H. J., *Reflections on the Constitution* (Viking, 1951).

Livingston, W. S., *Federalism and Constitutional Change* (Oxford, 1956).

McBain, H. L., *The Living Constitution* (Macmillan, 1928).

McIlwain, C. H., *Constitutionalism, Ancient and Modern* (Cornell, 1947).

Pickles, W., *The French Constitution of October 4th, 1958* (Stevens, 1960).

Pritchett, H. C., *The American Constitution* (McGraw-Hill, 1959).

Stannard, H., *The Two Constitutions: A Comparative Study of British and American Constitutional Systems* (Van Nostrand, 1949).

Swisher, C. B., *American Constitutional Development,* rev. ed. (Houghton Mifflin, 1956).

Vanderbilt, A. T., *The Doctrine of Separation of Powers and Its Present-Day Significance* (U. of Nebraska, 1953).

Wheare, K. C., *Modern Constitutions* (Oxford, 1951).

———, *The Constitutional Structure of the Commonwealth* (Oxford, 1961).

Whiting, K. R., *The Soviet Union Today: A Concise Handbook* (Praeger, 1962).

Wright, G., *The Reshaping of French Democracy* (Reynal & Hitchcock, 1948).

Zurcher, A. J., *Constitutions and Constitutional Trends Since World War II,* 2nd ed. (New York U., 1955).

V

The Scope of Modern Government

The main lines of the British and American constitutions were laid down in the eighteenth century (those of the French in the nineteenth). Prominent among the factors determining those lines was the view taken about what it was either possible or desirable for government to do. The role government can play in human affairs is physically limited by the means of transport and communication and by the productiveness of the economic system. And the role government ought to play within the limits of the physically possible is determined by the views of the politically powerful of the time and place.

In the eighteenth century modern developments in transport and communication had hardly begun, and the modern industrial economy that has so increased productivity was still in embryo. There were many serious physical limits to governmental action from which we have now been freed. Also, the dominant Anglo-American political thought of the eighteenth century favored individual liberty of action with corresponding restrictions on governmental action. Thus these constitutions did not envisage government's taking on a wide range of functions.

In the first half of the nineteenth century the means of transport and communications were greatly improved and extended, and there was an enormous increase in economic productivity. The inescapable limitations on the range of governmental action were greatly diminished, and governments did take on some new functions. But the political theory of *laisser faire*—literally 'let do' or 'let make'—the theory that government ought to be restricted to a very narrow sphere of operation, steadily gained strength and reached its zenith about 1860. The amazing material progress of the time was generally attributed to the abandonment of government regulation in economic and social matters.

LAISSER FAIRE AND ITS DECLINE

The Negative State. Generally speaking, the *laisser faire* philosophy held that government should restrict itself to protection of the community from external enemies, maintenance of internal order, and a few great essential public works. Maintenance of order may involve much or little. *Laisser faire* interpreted it narrowly, calling it the police function and invoking only the technique of the criminal law. By general laws, the legislature was to forbid those forms of conduct that are disruptive of order and then rely on the policeman and the courts to punish law-breakers. Faced with the certainty of detection and punishment, all but a few would be deterred from anti-social behavior. There would be enough jails—an example of essential public works—to look after the incorrigibles. Within the limits thus imposed, individuals were to be free to direct their energies as they saw fit. Of course, contracts freely entered upon must be kept. The judiciary was to award damages for the breach thereof, and also for a variety of minor transgressions, known as *torts,* not serious enough from a public point of view to merit the proscriptions of the criminal law.

Therefore, public works and military establishment apart, government was to be mainly occupied in making general laws applicable to everybody and enforcing the judgments of the courts on transgressions as they appeared. The state, as thus envisaged, has been aptly described as *the negative state,* imposing restraints at the margins of socially permissible conduct. The believers in *laisser faire,* including even Adam Smith, never were able to restrict the operations of government to the narrow sphere prescribed by their beliefs. But they had a profound influence on the scope of government action throughout the greater part of the nineteenth century. The negative state was not merely an academic theory; it was largely realized in the scope and character of nineteenth-century governments.

Government Intervention in the Economy. After the middle of the nineteenth century, however, a combination of forces steadily undermined the *laisser faire* tradition. Except in Britain, where free trade ruled until 1931, important sections of the business community wanted—and got—government intervention in the form of *tariffs* to aid industrial development. In continental Europe, agriculture as well got tariffs to protect it against the competition of cheap wheat from America. The shift of population from rural isolation to rapidly growing industrial cities brought many new social problems. Elementary education became a necessity; public health measures had to be improved. Later it was seen, for example, that a system of employment exchanges was necessary to give necessary mobility to labor. These are only a few examples of the services necessary to an industrial society that the government has been asked to provide or to supervise.

With increasing economic specialization and further minute division of labor, the social structure became more complex and individuals became less able to control the factors affecting their destiny and more dependent on the actions of others that they could not control. The self-sufficient farmer of earlier times, who produced his own food and most of the other necessities of life, was mainly dependent on the weather, and it did not occur to him that the government could do much about it. The highly specialized farmer of today is dependent on distant markets for his income, and on other specialized producers for many of the necessities of life. The industrial wage earner is dependent on markets too, and also on a multitude of decisions made by his employer and others.

The farmers and workers as individuals cannot control these factors any more than they can control the weather; but it is at least plausible for them to think that the government, which has the longest reach of any agency in the community, can do something to control them. Accordingly, they, and many other groups as well, are disposed to appeal to government. On the whole these appeals have met with considerable success. Economic and social interdependence gives an impetus to government intervention.

Rise of the Social Conscience. Moreover, it was gradually realized that unrestricted individual enterprise did not necessarily bring about the degree of social justice it had been expected to. While wealth and productivity increased at an astonishing pace, a large section of the population was still condemned to grinding poverty and/or acute insecurity. At the same time, competition proved an inadequate regulator in various branches of industry. Large-scale organization produced monopolistic features in industry where entrenched interests levied toll on the public.

Interest in trust-busting and social reform grew up in an atmosphere of the new and experimental trial-and-error approach toward social and political problems, often called *pragmatism,* which prompted two types of governmental measures. First, regulations of various kinds, ranging from factory legislation requiring safety devices in factories to fixing of rates and standards of service for railway companies, were imposed by governments on industry. Government was to regulate industry so as to ensure operation in the public interest. Second, an attempt was made to reduce the glaring inequalities of income and improve the security of the less fortunate members of society through social services or social security measures such as health insurance, unemployment insurance, and old-age pensions. These measures, differing in scope and application, are administered and financially supported by the various governments. Through taxation, income is taken from the taxpayer and transferred to the recipients of these services. The movement toward social security and regulation of business was greatly accelerated by the extension of the franchise to the adult male population in the nineteenth century, and to adult women in the twentieth. The mass of the people had no firm conviction that *laisser faire* was an advantage to them; yet they did see the advantages to be had from social services. Politicians quickly learned the connection between votes and the services desired by large groups in the population.

Special Privileges for All. Once significant breaches were made in the principle of *laisser faire,* its inhibiting power was greatly diminished, and finally it almost disappeared as an influence on public policy. Government had proved amenable to popular control through a democratically elected legislature. Government provided valuable services and there seemed to be no reason why it should not be used to correct all kinds of maladjustments. Britain and the United States had been the great strongholds of *laisser faire,* but by 1939, even in them, almost every significant social group was getting some service or privilege from the government.

In 1840 it had been agreed that the job of government was through general laws to maintain equal rights for all before the law and special privileges for none. Before 1930 the cynics had coined a new slogan, 'special privileges for all and equal rights for none.' For many years socialists have urged that governments must go still further and plan and manage the economic system as a whole, rather than merely intervene at particular points as they were doing prior to the outbreak of war in 1939. During World War II we saw this done, although not with the measure of public ownership socialists desire. What the future scope of government functions will be is impossible to say, but they are quite unlikely to decline to the 1939 level. For present purposes it will be sufficiently revealing to indicate something of how matters stood at that date and to take general note of post-war developments.

The war period also revealed too, in a striking way, how the sheer physical limitations on government action have declined. Transport and communications are now so highly developed that central governments can overcome the handicaps of time and space sufficiently to direct the energies of half a continent. And productivity is now so great that government can absorb for its purposes, including war, well over half the national income and still leave the civilian population a tolerable standard of living. Big spending by government, even to the point of deficit spending, has now become the rule rather than the exception. The following table indicates relative expenditures for the social welfare and national defense sectors in 1962:

COMPARATIVE NATIONAL EXPENDITURES FOR SOCIAL WELFARE
AND NATIONAL DEFENSE IN 1962*

COUNTRY	SOCIAL WELFARE	NATIONAL DEFENSE
Denmark	D.KR. 5,645,000,000	D.KR. 1,300,000,000
France	N.F. 12,378,000,000	N.F. 19,187,000,000
Germany	D.MK. 15,800,000,000 (1960)	D.MK. 9,400,000,000
Great Britain	£ 3,679,000,000	£ 1,675,000,000
Norway	N.KR. 838,937,300	N.KR. 1,285,850,000
Sweden	S.KR. 4,478,621,000 (1960–61)	S.KR. 2,737,744,000 (1960–61)
Switzerland	$87,200,000 (1960)	$214,800,000 (1960)
United States	$10,280,000,000†	$51,212,000,000

* Unless otherwise indicated figures are for fiscal 1962.
† Includes outlays for Veterans Administration and Department of Health, Education and Welfare.

The Positive State. The negative state is now only a memory and we are faced with what is called, by contrast, the *positive state,* also variously called the *social state* and the *welfare state.* The government is not merely imposing restraints; it is acting positively to accomplish a wide range of purposes. In peacetime it is charged with attaining a minimum standard of education, with ensuring public health, with guaranteeing individuals security against a wide range of misfortunes, and with regulating the major facets of economic life in the public interest. In war it must direct all the activities of the population; it must keep the common goal in sight and improvise methods of reaching it. It must do for the nation what the plantation owner did for his estate. This task requires vast resources of energy, foresight, and initiative, which, in the negative state, were largely supplied by individuals operating on their own account. But even before World War II, government was carrying on a great many activities of vital importance to the community.

It has been difficult to adapt constitutions framed on the assumptions of the negative state to the demands of the positive state. In fact, the fighting of two World Wars required the temporary suspension of these constitutions at least in part. The purpose of the separation of powers, for example, was to secure effective restraints on government at the expense of efficiency. When efficiency becomes the prime consideration, the separation of powers is an embarrassment. The tripartite separation of powers, while it may have been an adequate instrument of analysis a hundred years ago, is defective for an understanding of the complex operations of government today. It is widely contended that these *laisser-faire* constitutions are outmoded and will have to be very substantially revised. And it is also urged in many quarters that simple analyses, such as those outlined in Chapter IV, do not get us at all close to the realities of present-day government. This argument will be assessed in later chapters. Here we must sketch in outline the tasks that governments are now called on to perform.

THE NEWER FUNCTIONS OF GOVERNMENT

The broad patterns of government functions in Britain and the United States are strikingly similar. Britain, with a more mature industrial system, has moved faster and further in the provision of social security, but the United States has been catching up rapidly in recent years. On the other hand, government in North America has been called on to assist in opening up the resources of a new continent—an activity for which there has been no scope in Britain. It has not merely been a matter of building canals, roads, and railways. Governments have assisted and encouraged agriculture, mining, and lumbering in a great variety of ways. The trend now, of course, is toward conservation and more efficient use of natural resources, and there is more similarity of pattern in this respect than formerly. In Britain there is a distribution of tasks between central and municipal governments. In the United States, federalism requires a three-way distribution among federal, state, and municipal. Attention here is focused on the activities of central governments, including state but not municipal. No attempt will be made at this stage to distinguish state and federal functions.

In view of the similarity of pattern it will be adequate to sketch the newer activities of central governments in a general way without attempting a separate catalogue for each country. While some of the specific functions pointed to may not be carried on in both Britain and the United States, other functions comparable to them are almost certain to exist and the general impression will be reasonably accurate for both. Space does not permit treatment of this intriguing problem in, for example, France or the Scandinavian countries, which are so experienced in the field. In a general way, however, they fit the pattern of the expanding role of government in America and Britain, with France's policies more closely identifiable with the former and those of the Scandinavian lands with the latter.

REGULATION OF BUSINESS

Regulation of business is either of a broad pervasive character affecting business generally or of a more specific kind affecting directly only particular kinds of trade or business. *General* regulation of business is accomplished by tariffs, anti-monopoly laws, and control of currency and credit.

Tariffs. Tariffs are now much more than the fixing of import duties and the policing of borders to ensure their collection. The government is charged with delicate and frequent adjustment of tariff schedules to the end that native industries shall not be driven out of business by the dumping of cheap foreign goods on the domestic market. Government must be continually collecting and revising statistics on the cost of production of domestic industries, because this knowledge is necessary for intelligent adjustment of the tariff to the end desired. In this way the government substantially protects investment in established industry and gives the employed worker in these industries at least the illusion that his livelihood is also being protected. The tariff has a powerful influence in determining what industries, and what enterprises within an industry, shall be established or maintained.

THE COMMON MARKET. But tariff regulation today has to be considered in an entirely new set of economic conditions. The world has rapidly organized itself into five major trading areas—the Common Market, the United States, the Communist bloc, the Commonwealth, and Latin America. Newest of these is the Common Market of Europe, which at this writing (Autumn 1963) included the original six, geographically joined, member nations of France, West Germany, Italy, Belgium, the Netherlands, and Luxembourg, plus some 'associate members.' In accordance with the Treaty of Rome of 1958, the Common Market—a popular term for the European Economic Community (EEC)—determined to merge the economies of the six member nations into one; establish free trade among all; and set up a common tariff wall around them. Thus trade in the Common Market area would be as easy as trade among any six states of the United States. It has proved so successful that the initial time schedule, adopted to bring about these goals gradually by 1970, had been advanced by several years and fruition in the foreseeable future seems possible, with the possible exception of the vexatious agricultural problem.

The United States met the trade issue by a complete change of tariff policy. With the passing of the New Frontier's 1962 Tariff Bill, the President now possessed power to reduce tariffs on world imports as much as 50 per cent over a five-year period and to eliminate tariffs entirely on certain manufactured goods. Many believe this 'new and bold instrument of American trade policy' to be President Kennedy's greatest legislative achievement, since the bill would put America on equal bargaining grounds with the Common Market and other world economic blocs, and also mark the end of the United States's historical protectionist policy. To counter the effect on industries and labor, the legislation provided for federal aid to adversely affected segments. This new trade policy was designed not only to raise United States industrial production and employment but also to achieve more permanent ties with the nations of the world, particularly the underprivileged.

Britain, on the other hand, found herself confronted with infinitely greater difficulties because of her obligations toward the Commonwealth of Nations, her traditional policies of aloofness and independence from the Continent, and her own characteristic agricultural and industrial complex. But by 1962, if not earlier, Britain realized her salvation lay with the Common Market and thus applied for membership—a move heartily seconded by the United States and by Britain's trading partners in the rather loosely organized European Free Trade Association (E.F.T.A.), consisting of Denmark, Norway, Sweden, Switzerland, Portugal, and Austria. However, Britain's membership application was flatly rejected in 1963 by President de Gaulle of France, after many long months of negotiations—over the objections of most, if not all, of the other five member-nations of the E.E.C., who desired full and immediate membership for Britain. Although Britain had demanded certain concessions on behalf of the Commonwealth and particularly the agricultural interests, the main—some would say the sole—reason for France's veto was evidently de Gaulle's fear that Britain would dominate the Common Market and, moreover, expose it to increasing American influence.

Monetary. Expansion or contraction of business is determined by a great variety of factors. One of the most powerful is the interest rate, the cost of borrowing money to carry on business. This is primarily fixed by the banks as the main lending institutions. The banks are subject to close supervision and inspection by government. Thus, central banks—the Federal Reserve System in the United States and the once-private Bank of England in Britain—control the banking and credit business. The central bank has powers that enable it to exert a crucial influence on the lending policy of the banks. And whether or not the central bank is directly a department of government, the government in the long run sets its general policies. Moreover, the government, either directly or through the central bank, determines the rate at which the domestic currency shall be exchanged for foreign currency. In this way, apart altogether from tariffs, the trend of imports—and exports—can be modified and the outflow of gold regulated. This in turn has profound effects on the economy as a whole. To maintain sound business conditions the central bank, and departments of government associated with its work, must constantly be gathering statistics on domestic and international trade and conducting research continually into their significance in order to know how to used their powers intelligently.

Anti-Trust. A third general kind of regulation of business, as exemplified in the United States by the Sherman and Clayton Anti-Trust Acts of 1890 and 1914, respectively, and their offshoots, is aimed at trade combinations, trusts, and monopolies in the production and distribution of goods and services. It seeks to dissolve those combinations whose activities are clearly detrimental to the public interest,[1] and to prevent particular unfair trade practices by trade associations that otherwise are thought to serve legitimate purposes. For example, price-fixing in violation of the Robinson-Patman Act came under sharp attack in the 1960 indictment of twenty-nine of the largest American electrical firms, leading to a total of $2,000,000 in fines and jail terms of thirty days for seven company executives. Increasingly the government has also eyed mergers[2] and divisions of markets violative of the Sherman Act. In order to keep track of trade agreements and monopolistic

[1] In 1957 one of the most interesting of recent U.S. Supreme Court decisions was handed down in the case of *U.S.* v. *du Pont,* 353 U.S. 586. In a 4:2 opinion, the Court ruled that E. I. duPont de Nemours & Co. was in violation of the anti-trust laws by holding 23 per cent of the stock of General Motors Corporation. The ruling was based on a finding that this stock ownership gave du Pont a preference with General Motors in the market for automotive finishes and fabrics.

[2] See *Brown Shoe Co.* v. *U.S.,* 370 U.S. 294 (1962), in which the Supreme Court denied Brown the right to merge with the G. R. Kinney Co., a large retail shoe outlet, holding that in Section 7 of the Clayton Act—aimed at corporate mergers—Congress had intended to curb 'in their incipience [any] tendencies toward concentration in industry.'

practices in various industries and estimate their effect as well as to secure the evidence necessary for prosecuting offending combinations, government must maintain a staff of economists and accountants continuously engaged in investigation and research. In the United States, the administration and enforcement of the anti-trust laws are in the hands of the Federal Trade Commission, an independent regulatory commission created by Congress in 1914, and the U. S. Department of Justice.[3]

Utilities. Various trades and types of business have been singled out for more specific regulation. The most important group are public utilities, those industries producing an essential service for the public but which, for one reason or another, have a tendency to monopoly with its attendant evils. All transport and communication enterprises are in this class: railways, tramways, motor transport, air transport, shipping, telegraph, telephone, television and radio. The gas, water, and electric power industries also fall into this class. A great variety of regulations that cannot be detailed here are imposed on them by government.

In the United States those public-utility enterprises whose business has the character of interstate commerce are regulated by the federal government. Thus the road, rail, and water-transport utilities fall to the Interstate Commerce Commission, the oldest independent regulatory commission, created in 1887; the telegraph, telephone, television, and radio industries to the Federal Communications Commission (1934); air transport to the Civil Aeronautics Authority (1938); and the electric power utilities to the Federal Power Commission (1920). The public utilities that operate entirely in one state are usually regulated by public utility commissions set up by the several state governments under their *police power.*

Generally speaking, no one can enter any one of these businesses, which are legally viewed as 'affected with a public interest,' without getting a license or a certificate—the 'certificate of public convenience and necessity' —acknowledging that additional facilities in the industry are needed for the public convenience. Rates to be charged and extent and quality of the service to be rendered are subject to governmental control. These rates cannot be fixed without taking into account the rates of return that particular enterprises are to be allowed to earn for their owners. Just what constitutes a proper rate of return has proved to be a difficult problem, indeed, to the

[3] The Sherman Act is administered by the Anti-Trust Division of the Justice Department, headed by an Assistant Attorney General, and the Clayton Act, by the same body and the F.T.C.

American courts; but recent cases seem to indicate that—beyond certain basic standards of 'fair value'—they are disposed to leave the matter to the regulatory authorities.[4] In the transportation businesses a great many regulations are concerned with safety: licensing of pilots and airfields, the load line on ships and licensing of masters and pilots, inspection of brakes, speed limits, size and weight of loads, level crossings, and the like. It will not do for a government to make haphazard decisions on these matters. It obviously must have at its command a great array of economic, accounting, and engineering talent in order to decide on rates of return, rates to be charged to the public, standards of service, and safety measures. And the job cannot be done once and for all. As costs fluctuate, adjustments must be made in the rates to be charged. Technical advances will call for repeated revision of the standards of service and safety.

Financial Enterprises. The financial enterprises of insurance, trust, and loan companies are subject to close government supervision designed to ensure fair dealing and safeguard their financial position. They must secure an annual license and often are required to make deposits with the government covering a portion of their obligations to their clients. They must make annual returns describing their operations and undergo annual inspection by government officials. If their financial practices have been reckless or their financial status becomes seriously impaired, their licenses may be modified or cancelled.

Charters and Securities. Before a corporation can be formed to conduct any enterprise, the promoters must secure a *charter,* or grant of incorporation, from government.[5] All corporations which, on incorporation or during reorganization, wish to sell an issue of securities to the public, are required to make a fair disclosure of the facts relevant to the enterprise. Through refusal to authorize particular issues of securities, and through regulation of brokers and stock exchanges, governments try to prevent reckless and fraudulent misrepresentation in the issue and sale of corporate securities. In several states of the United States *blue-sky* laws, largely ineffective, establish some such structure of regulation. The most effective regulation of

---

[4] See the decisions of the United States Supreme Court in *Smyth* v. *Ames,* 169 U.S. 466 (1898); *Driscoll* v. *Edison Light and Power Co.,* 307 U.S. 104 (1939); *Federal Power Commission* v. *Natural Gas Pipeline Co.,* 315 U.S. 575 (1942); *Federal Power Commission* v. *Hope Natural Gas Co.,* 320 U.S. 591 (1944); and *Phillips Petroleum Co.* v. *State of Wisconsin,* 347 U.S. 672 (1954).

[5] In the United States, private corporations are normally chartered by state governments. An interesting exception is the now wholly privately-owned National Space Communication Corporation, chartered by the federal government in 1962.

incorporations and flotations of securities is imposed through the laws passed by Congress and administered by the Securities and Exchange Commission, created in 1934.

Scores of other kinds of businesses are subjected to license and inspection, generally for police, health, safety, or 'welfare' purposes. The regulations involved need not be described, for by and large they do not profoundly affect the economic life of the community, and do not require the accumulation of records, the marshaling and interpreting of statistics, or the intricate economic and engineering knowledge needed for the working of the more far-reaching controls already described.

Regulation of Employer-Employee Relations. The bringing of large numbers of workers into factories or shops to work under contract for an employer or manager has raised many acute social and economic problems with which governments have tried to deal. Government officials frame—and enforce through periodic inspection—factory, shop, and mine regulations designed to ensure safe and sanitary working conditions and to regulate hours of work and working conditions, especially, but not exclusively, for women and children. Government administers an insurance scheme—left to the states in America—whereby employers are compelled to provide compensation and rehabilitation for their injured workers whatever the cause of the injury may have been. The burden of industrial accidents and industrial diseases, which used to fall mainly on the worker and his family, has been turned through government action into a cost of production that falls on the purchasers of the products of industry.

Minimum wages and maximum hours are fixed by government in considerable detail for most industries in Britain and in the United States. In the latter such regulations were limited, in the main, to the employment of women and children until the passage of the Fair Labor Standards Act of 1938. Prior thereto all federal and many state wage laws for adult males were held to be unconstitutional deprivations of liberty without due process of law. In both countries, government enforces an immigration policy that limits the entrance of foreign workers to compete for jobs with the native-born. There are governmental measures in support of the unionization of labor and collective bargaining. In the United States the National Labor Relations Board, established by Congress in the Wagner Act of 1935, as amended by the Taft-Hartley Act of 1947 and the Landrum-Griffin Act of 1959, actively promotes collective bargaining. Government also provides a conciliation service for mediating in industrial disputes and, in some vital industries, e.g. railroads, it insists on a public investigation and strenuous effort at settlement before a strike or lockout can be called. In this connection too, subsequent statutes, especially the Taft-Hartley Act, effected several changes in the Wagner Act, despite heavy labor opposition.

Government is thus involved in a continuous study of wages, costs of living, standards of living, the trade cycle, industrial diseases, and safety devices. If it is to perform adequately the functions it has undertaken, it must be steadily revising its regulations in the light of accumulating knowledge and changing conditions, and it must put drive and energy into its inspection to detect, punish, and prevent evasions.

Government Economic Enterprises. In some industries, government tries to get a simple solution of the complex problems of business and labor regulation by direct government ownership and operation. Where not so long ago there was only the post office, there are now a number of comparable enterprises owned and managed by the government. Apart altogether from the ownership of waterworks, gasworks, transit systems, electric power plants by municipalities, and liquor distribution systems, central governments in one or both countries own and operate air lines, railways, canals, coal mines, telegraph, telephone, television, and radio transmission systems, and hydo-electric power systems. While governments have undertaken a much wider range of economic enterprises in Britain than in the United States, the Tennessee Valley Authority in the latter is the most diversified government enterprise to be found in either country.[6]

In such undertakings, government sets out to make itself a model employer as well as a model producer and distributor of goods and services. To do this, it has to wrestle with the same problems—except for the payment of heavy taxes—that plague private enterprise and that call for sympathy and imagination. It has to find the energy and resourcefulness, which alone make any enterprise efficient, and it has to find them without the incentives of profit and the spur of competition that have done much to maintain healthy vigor in private enterprise. When government goes into business, business methods have to be carried over into government. These methods are not the methods of the policeman and the judge. Here perhaps more than anywhere else the requirements of the positive state are made clear.

Agriculture. Particularly in the United States, government now takes

---

[6] For a brief description of the T.V.A. and a comparative discussion of government ownership, see Henry J. Abraham, *Government as Entrepreneur and Social Servant* (Washington: Public Affairs Press, 1956).

the lead in promoting the application of science to agriculture. Most of the measures take the form of free services to farmers, relatively few of them are police regulations. The most important of the latter type are regulations for control of animal diseases and plant pests, giving the government powers of inspection, quarantine, and wholesale destruction of plants and animals to check the spread of such threats to agriculture. The effort spreads out as far as the control of commercial poisons offered to combat pests [7] and to the supervision of nurseries that distribute stock. Alongside these powers goes continuous research into the origins and causes of, and the means of controlling, plant pests and animal diseases. For example, decades of research have been put into the development of strains of wheat that will resist rust and the sawfly.

SERVICES. This however, is only a small fraction of governmental research into agricultural matters. Attempts are made to improve every breed of agricultural product, whether plant or animal. The search for champion hens and champion cows, longer bacon pigs, longer ears of corn, and smaller *petits pois,* never ends. Experimental farms and stations—such as the huge farm at Beltsville, Maryland—carry this work into field and laboratory and explore the methods of culture best suited to particular environments. Soil surveys discover soil deficiencies and aid in other extensive governmental efforts to deal with drought, erosion, water conservation, and new methods of irrigation.

Improved methods are of little value unless widely adopted, and education of the farmer is pushed in various ways by illustration stations, extension services, agricultural fairs, county agents, and a barrage of bulletins. Increased production needs wider and better markets. Government tries to find new markets at home and abroad and provides a marketing and intelligence service that analyzes market trends and possibilities. Reliable grades and honest packaging are important aids to marketing. Government now requires that most agricultural products going outside a local market should be sold according to specified grades and in standard packages, and it devises the specifications and employs an inspectorate to see that the regulations are obeyed. Continuous research must go into the establishment and improvement of grades if they are to have their maximum usefulness.

SUPPORTS. The middleman who markets farm produce has always drawn

[7] For an intriguingly controversial treatment of pest control in America see the prize-winning book by Rachel Carson, *Silent Spring* (Boston: Houghton Mifflin Co., 1962).

the wrath of the farmer. Government now intervenes at many points in the marketing process on his behalf. It imposes regulations on stockyards, and on commodity exchanges such as the grain exchange. It puts its influence and authority behind schemes for co-operative marketing and purchasing, and for stabilization of prices and production of a number of agricultural products. For example, in the United States, the Agricultural Adjustment Act of 1938, as amended, attempted, by an intricate and controversial set of measures covering the six principal agricultural products—wheat, cotton, corn, tobacco, rice, and peanuts (facetiously called the 'Holy Six')—to limit acreage, fix marketing quotas, and facilitate the storage of surpluses. The purpose was both to maintain prices and, by an intricate *parity* system, to ensure growers something like an annual average decent purchasing power in good years and bad. It supports, if it does not enforce, efforts to limit acreage and thus to maintain prices, but the surplus problem remains an enormous— and, as some contend, scandalous—burden on the national budget. In both the United States and Britain the law of supply and demand is challenged by the laws of the government in fixing the price and regulating the distribution of fluid milk in urban areas.

The range and variety of government activity in relation to agriculture defy summary description. Enough has been said to afford further illustration that government provides many valuable services and privileges to different groups in the community, and that effective provision of these services makes demands on governmental organization and personnel that were never dreamed of in the days of the negative state.

Public Health. Public health has long been a charge of government, but measures to promote it remained rudimentary until the scientific discoveries of the last century revealed the causes of a great variety of diseases and the necessary means to control them. They remained relatively unimportant until urban concentration and rapid means of transport changed entirely the problem of public health. Since that time, health services of a range and variety comparable to the activities noted in the last section have been developed. The bulk of these are still carried out by the municipal governments, but central governments exercise close control and supervision over the municipal health agencies. Sanitation measures must meet government standards and every municipality must maintain a public health organization that meets certain minimum specifications. These standards are enforced by frequent inspection. Furthermore, governments enforce many precautions against the spread of infectious diseases, and the outbreak of an epidemic brings extraordinary powers of the central government into action.

SERVICES. Government makes available a great many health services for local governments and for individuals. Diagnostic clinics and laboratories aid in the discovery, analysis, and identification of disease. Vaccines and serums, such as the Salk anti-poliomyelitis vaccine, are sponsored and distributed in mass vaccination programs. Research is carried on in the fields of sanitary engineering, preventive medicine and air pollution. The United States Public Health Service maintains seven National Institutes of Health in Bethesda, Maryland, which conduct research on major diseases, including heart, cancer, and mental illness. Statistics are collected and studied, and a program of public education in health matters is advanced by demonstrations, exhibits, bulletins, lectures, and motion pictures.

Besides making grants to aid in the building and maintenance of general hospitals, government provides special clinics and hospitals for those suffering from particular diseases such as tuberculosis, and for the mentally ill and mentally defective. Special health services are given to school children and special attention to maternal and child welfare. Then, of course, there is the matter of compulsory national health insurance like that adopted by Britain in 1948. Its National Health Service entitles every inhabitant to full medical care, the cost of which is met predominantly from public funds. Congress, however, has been very reluctant to legislate health insurance in the United States, largely due to the militant lobbying of the American Medical Association and those opposed to the increase in social security taxes that would accompany such a measure. The Kerr-Mills Act of 1960 does provide medical care for the needy aged, if the state concerned participates in the program, but attempts by the Kennedy Administration to enact the so-called Medicare plan for all elderly citizens under social security had met with repeated defeat as of this writing (Autumn 1963).

OTHERS. Pure-food and drug laws establish standards of quality designed to prevent dangerous adulteration and misrepresentation of food and drugs. Samples offered for sale are collected and analyzed; frequent inspections of food-processing and manufacturing plants are made; and standard programs of testing and reporting are required before a new drug can be put on the market. Government inspectors are permanently installed in the canning and meat-packing plants. The sale of patent medicines and narcotic drugs is subject to regulation. Thus, in 1962, the U. S. Pure Food and Drug Administration was able to prevent the sale of thalidomide, a drug which was strongly and correctly suspected of causing deformed babies. Numerous other interventions in the field of public health could be cited.

Social Security. Governmental research into the incidence and causes of disease proved the close connection between poverty and ill-health and was thus one of the prime causes of the demand that government should supplement charitable relief of poverty. In Britain the relief of the chronically poor has recently become a responsibility of the central government. But in the United States the poor remain, as they have been for centuries, chiefly the responsibility of municipal governments and philanthropy—with increasing exceptions, such as President Kennedy's food stamp program. Central governments have, however, undertaken to insure individuals against misfortune arising from many other causes. Sometimes the technique is that of compulsory insurance, requiring employers—and in two states, Alabama and New Jersey, the employees—to contribute to a fund that the government supplements, as in the case of insurance against unemployment. Sometimes it takes the form of outright grants from the public treasury, as in the case of allowances to unwed, deserted, or widowed mothers, assistance for needy and neglected children, and relief to unemployed workers not covered by unemployment insurance. France, as well as some other countries, goes as far as to give a governmental family allowance to each family unit according to the number of children!

But whether through compulsory insurance or through outright assistance, government comes to the aid of the aged, the blind, and other classes of needy persons, as well as the ones mentioned above. With its later amendments, the United States Social Security Act of 1935 is a comprehensive measure designed to provide a measure of security against the more serious kinds of distress partly through the direct action of the federal government, partly through encouragement of and financial assistance to the state governments, and partly through compulsory contributions by individuals concerned. Government also maintains employment services that assist workers in search of jobs.

Public Housing. Government has heavily subsidized public housing and slum clearance in Britain, France, and the Scandinavian lands for a long time. In the United States it used to be chiefly a matter for local redevelopment authorities. But since the New Deal days, because the vast problems involved have become financially and politically almost impossible for the lower levels of government, the federal government has found it increasingly necessary to grant larger amounts of money for housing development. The federally subsidized projects normally consist of slum clearance, neighborhood renovation, conservation of existing housing, minority group housing, and low-interest, government-insured loan funds.

Education. Although elementary and secondary education is primarily a function of state and local governments, its vital importance in a democracy has led central governments in most countries to pay increasing attention to it. Grants in aid of elementary, secondary, and vocational education by the central government in Britain and by the state governments in the United States have increased steadily. Along with the increase in grants, these governments have extended greatly their control over the local education authorities. To exercise their control intelligently, they must give sustained attention to the varied problems of the educational system, which, viewed as a whole, is a huge undertaking. In the United States the federal government has shown a serious interest in education, and major direct federal grants in aid thereof loomed as a distinct possibility, although not a probability, in 1963. These would be in addition to the well-established loans as well as grants to colleges and universities—sometimes operated as state institutions—and their students, such as those under the National Defense Education Act of 1958. The federal Office of Education in the Department of Health, Education and Welfare not only provides certain specific grants, largely for vocational education, but also makes surveys of existing educational facilities, conducts research in certain educational problems, and offers advice to the local and state authorities concerned with education. Two major barriers to major outright federal aid to secondary and elementary schools have been the question whether such aid should also be extended to parochial schools, and what governmental controls, if any, should be imposed.

Highways. Most central governments in Europe are responsible for the highway systems of their countries. Responsibility for highways in the United States, however, was chiefly left to the states. But of late Congress has appropriated huge amounts of money for a 41,000-mile major inter-state highway system to be completed in 1972. Money for this project is provided in part by taxes on the tire and truck industries and by federal fuel taxes, in addition to general funding. Appropriations are then made to the state from a highway trust fund. Under this recent arrangement, the states contribute but 10 per cent to the costs of the roads within their boundaries and do the actual construction contracting and maintenance. The national government is interested in highways for several reasons. First, America's highways are vastly overcrowded. The time is fast approaching when every family will have one car and possibly two. Second, new roads stimulate the economy of the nation by the work provided in building them and from the fact that they will connect every major industrial center in the United States, thus boosting the trucking as well as the tourist industry. Third, these highways provide a major link in national defense mobilization plans for evacuation routes as well as faster routes for moving equipment and men. With the increased number of vehicles everywhere, government must prevent its highways from becoming obsolete or face internal strangulation.

Conservation of Natural Resources. Public health and social security measures are aimed at conservation of human resources. In recent years in the United States there has been a steadily growing substantial effort by the government to conserve dwindling natural resources. Much of the work of the Departments of Agriculture and the Interior is devoted to stemming the loss of America's natural resources. Restrictions on the taking of fish and game have been tightened and steps toward enforcing a more careful timber-cutting policy have been taken. Fish and game are also ravaged by disease, while fire and insects are the heaviest users of the forest. Forest protection services have been established by government and, at the same time, re-forestation projects are being launched, pollution of rivers and streams is being curbed. Fish hatcheries, wild-life sanctuaries, and national forests are government enterprises. Strenuous government action is being taken to restore the lands ravaged by drought and erosion.

Such measures are not likely to bring significant results unless action is guided by scientific knowledge. So intensification of research goes hand in hand with preventive and restorative action. Even then, the co-operation of the public must be enlisted as government takes up the role of educator and propagandist for conservation. Conservation is no longer a matter of sprinkling the country with a few fish and game wardens. It requires a dozen different kinds of scientists and research laboratories, a large field service staffed by men with highly specialized training for their jobs, a diverse apparatus for fighting fires and insects, for reforestation, and assisting nature to multiply. In another direction, it develops into a large project of public education.

Efforts at conservation in Britain have generally met with considerable success. When conservation bills protecting wildlife and forests are put before Parliament they receive almost no opposition and are quickly passed. The British are proud and protective of their natural realm. Almost every British town has its bird sanctuary or wildlife preserve, and hunting is well regulated to provide some of the best sporting grounds in the world. Most natural resources have come under nationalization plans; thus, the government takes a direct and expedient interest in its coal mines and other resources.

The United States has the largest national park system in the world, and new units are gradually added from time to time. However, federal appropriation of lands for restricted use is often vehemently opposed by private interests, such as cattle, lumber, and mining concerns. Other natural resources, especially minerals, receive varying degrees of government attention, ranging from complete control over uranium and allied fissionable materials to polite attention to the gaping holes of strip-mining operations.

Other Functions and the Post-war Trend. This is a comprehensive but by no means an exhaustive enumeration. The public works that governments maintain or subsidize go far beyond those contemplated by the *laisser faire* tradition. The taxes now levied by governments are not limited to the amounts required by them to finance their direct expenditures. The central government levies taxes and makes grants to the states, or whatever the subdivisions may be called, to assist the latter in carrying out their extensive functions. State governments, in turn, levy taxes in order to make equalizing grants to municipalities of disparate financial capacity, so that all municipalities can maintain a certain minimum level of services. In this way, as well as by direct social security measures, governments are engaged in an extensive compulsory redistribution of the national income.

Each of the functions of government enumerated here is a matter of common knowledge, although few perhaps realize the grand sweep of the operations as a whole. In the main, these are the activities that governments in the United States and Britain and their allies carried on at the outbreak of World War II, and almost none of them was carried on a century earlier. For the purpose of prosecuting the war all these governments went very much further with a great range of activities designed to meet the emergency. Since the end of the war in 1945 a common pattern in new government functions is hard to find. The United States liquidated most of its wartime emergency activities very quickly in an effort to return to the pre-war situation. Britain, much more badly shaken by the war, maintained many of the wartime functions of government, and may continue some of them indefinitely. Moreover, a Labour government came to power in 1945, with a socialist program most of which could only be carried out by large extensions of government action. When the Conservatives returned to power in 1951, they halted but, with the exception of the 'denationalization' of the steel industry, did not reverse that program—although they did sell back to private persons all the road transport for which they could obtain reasonable bids. The Korean crisis of 1950 and the dark shadow of the cold war compelled both countries, however, to reintroduce a number of wartime controls.

In both Britain and the United States, as we have seen, there has thus been an extension of activity in the provision of public housing, health, social security, and in regulation of agricultural prices, with Britain going much further than the United States in housing, health, and social security. Both countries have necessarily undertaken public ownership and development of atomic energy. Both governments are committed, as far as solemn statements of high policy can commit them, to the maintenance of a high level of employment and purchasing power.

Planning for Prosperity. This last is the most important development common to both countries. Governmental planning for war purposes after 1938–39 quickly ended the depression conditions of the early and mid-'thirties and brought an unprecedented level of employment and production. Public opinion came easily, perhaps too easily, to the conclusion that if governments could make and carry out effective economic planning for war, they could do it for peace as well. This conception, if it is to be carried out with vigor and effect, requires a new strategy to be adopted by governments in relation to all their activities. The piecemeal and sporadic intervention of the last sixty years designed to deal with particular maladjustments in a limited way will no longer be enough. Government will have to undertake a large measure of continuous, co-ordinated over-all planning of all its activities with a view to maintaining the economic life of the nation at a high level.

UNITED STATES. The federal Employment Act of 1946 which defines this policy for the United States set up a Council of Economic Advisers to make continuous surveys of the whole economy and to report thereon to the President. The President, in turn, makes an annual report to Congress on the 'economic state of the nation,' along with recommendations for legislative action designed to maintain a high level of employment and purchasing power. It is too early to say how well the government of the United States will be able to discharge this responsibility, and how much governmental activity of a new kind it will involve. That there has been an increase in the latter is clear. However, both in the United States and in Britain the dislocations caused by World War II and the present requirements for national defense, accentuated by the seemingly permanent tension between the Western world and the Soviet Union, obscure the situation.

BRITAIN. The socialist government of Britain took this particular responsibility seriously. It was not alarmed by the prospects of comprehensive economic planning by governments, a policy which socialists have been advocating for at least a generation. It regarded economic planning as an essential part of the program of socialization it pressed between 1945 and 1951. During that period, the nationalization of the electric power industry, which had been in progress for many years, was completed. Rail, motor, and air transport, gas enterprises, and the iron and steel industry were all taken into public ownership. The coal mines and the central bank, the Bank of England, were nationalized in the same way. As has already been noted, when the Conservatives returned to power in 1951 they halted but, with the exception of the 'denationalization' of the steel industry and parts of road transport, did not reverse the socialist trend in Britain.

It was said at the outset, and specific examples have emphasized the point, that in the United States some of these activities are carried on by the federal government and some by the state governments. Always to have specified throughout which are federal and which are state activities would have required a digression to examine the federal distribution of powers in the Constitution. The two chapters following will discuss this subject and describe the impact on the federal system of the great growth in the functions of both federal and state governments.

No judgment is expressed here on the wisdom or unwisdom of any of these governmental activities, and little has been said about the causes that underlie their introduction. Obviously, however, almost all of them are responses to problems that needed to be met somehow. Whether they should have been met in these particular ways, or indeed by governmental action at all, is deliberately left an open question. Some conclusions may suggest themselves later, but for the moment these activities are facts that shape the structure and profoundly influence the operations of government and therefore must be accepted and kept in mind at every turn.[8]

[8] For some examples of 'planning' and the 'positive state' in several modern democracies see Wilfrid Fleisher, *Sweden: The Welfare State* (New York: The John Day Co., 1956); Arnold A. Rogow, *The Labor Government and British Industry, 1945–1951* (Ithaca: Cornell University Press, 1956); M. Einaudi, M. Bye, and E. Possi, *Nationalization in France and Italy* (Ithaca: Cornell University Press, 1956); and Marshall E. Dimock, *The New American Political Economy* (New York: Harper and Row, 1963).

INDIVIDUALISTS AND SOCIALISTS

There has been no lack of judgments about the wisdom or unwisdom of the growth of government activities. All the while there have been wide discussion and controversy about the appropriate range of government action, in the course of which almost every conceivable judgment one way or the other has been made. The focus of the controversy is on the relationship of government and business, or economic life, although wider issues are always involved.

The Range of Opinions. On the question of the relations of government and business there are generally four distinct bodies of opinion. The division is not entirely clear-cut because within each group there are often widely divergent views, and the classifications should be viewed in that light.

EXTREME INDIVIDUALISTS. First, there are the *extreme individualists* who are almost anarchists in believing that government is inherently evil. They hold to *laisser faire*. Economic enterprise should be almost entirely free of government control. But *laisser faire* is dead, if we can judge from the record of the preceding pages, and its supporters are voices crying in the wilderness.

MODERATE INDIVIDUALISTS. Second, there are the *moderate individualists,* most of whom approve, reluctantly or otherwise, of almost all the activities of government undertaken in Britain, the United States, and elsewhere in the West up until World War II. They are the group whose policy has been reflected in the action of these governments in the first sixty years of the century. They are least moved by doctrinaire theories, and counsel a tentative, experimental attitude toward the question of the appropriate functions of the state.

EVOLUTIONARY SOCIALISTS. Third, there are the *evolutionary socialists* who advocate a gradual transition from capitalism to socialism through the piecemeal transfer of the major industries from private ownership to public ownership, where they would be, directly or indirectly, under the control of the government. They are somewhat doctrinaire in thinking that political democracy, government of the people by the people, must somehow bring in its train economic democracy, the operation of the economic system not only for the benefit of the people but by the people, or at any rate by their chosen agents rather than by private owners, or capitalists. But they do point to the stubborn tendency of private industry to combine in ever larger units in fewer and fewer hands. They argue that these concentrations of power in private hands are just as destructive of democracy in the long run as is the monopoly of governmental power in the hands of kings and aristocrats. Because of their undoubted loyalty to democracy they are also called *democratic socialists.*

Democratic socialists accept Marx's prediction of the trend to monopoly and agree with him in expecting it to have dire consequences. But they do not follow him in the further contention that the grip of monopoly capitalism will almost certainly have to be broken by violence. On the contrary, they believe that the capitalists can be compelled to submit to the will of the people through the peaceful processes of democratic politics. Consequently, they see no need to wipe out every vestige of private ownership in the means of production. They are prepared to leave substantial sectors of relatively small industry in private hands.

The vital need, as they see it, is to transfer the great public utilities in the transport and communication field, the massive financial and commercial institutions, and the heavy industries like coal and iron and steel, from private hands to public ownership. It is in this sector that private monopoly is so pervasive and menacing because of the enormous power it puts in a few hands. In fact, this body of opinion has tended in recent years to trim its demands for socialization because it has been realized, first, that many of the vexing problems of the economic system are not solved by nationalization, and second, that there are grave dangers in the state's running everything. Nevertheless, this body of opinion wants government action to go far beyond the scope outlined above. It is not satisfied with government regulation of the economic system. It wants a large measure of public ownership and operation.

The Labour party in Britain, which formed the British Government from 1945 until 1951, is largely, but not entirely, composed of people of this mind. As we have just seen, the Labour party carried through a piecemeal socialization of key industries in Britain until it gave way to the Conservatives in 1951. Thus far the democratic socialists seem to have been right in rejecting Marx's program of violent overthrow of the capitalist system. There is little evidence in Britain that the big capitalists felt able, or seriously disposed to try, to resist socialization by violent non-democratic means. The really critical problems continue to be how to run these industries efficiently now that they have been socialized, how to restore the incentives for production that moved both owners and workers under private ownership.

It should be noted here that not only the British socialists but their colleagues throughout most of Western Europe have begun to advocate a slowing, if not outright abandonment, of nationalization or socialization of *additional* key industries. This is especially true of the Scandinavian countries, where almost the entire emphasis by the social-democratic governments in this sphere has been to provide social security and welfare services for the people. And the 1959 manifesto of the West German Social Democratic party went so far as to repudiate officially the basic tenet of state ownership of the means of production.

COMMUNISTS. Fourth, there are the *Communists,* the revolutionary socialists in the Marxist tradition. As we have seen in Chapter III, they believe that all capitalists must be destroyed, root and branch, and the means of production fully socialized. They think this is necessary in order to free society from the festering bitterness and conflict of class struggle, and to release the full potentialities of the productive system. Their literature has always suggested in vague terms that the management of industry in the classless society would be carried on by the voluntary co-operation of all workers whether by hand or brain. Their practice thus far in the Soviet Union is quite the contrary. The state, which is in the hands of a relatively few, plans and directs the entire productive system. No private person can hire the labor of others in production. They have even socialized agriculture. The state has become the sole employer and substantially all economic life is directed by the government. As far as realities, as distinct from forms, go, it would not be misleading to describe the system as state capitalism. Whether or not the productive system is run for the benefit of the people, it is certainly not run primarily by the people in voluntary co-operation. This is not 'the realm of freedom,' whatever else it may be.

MODERATE INDIVIDUALISTS v. MODERATE SOCIALISTS

Setting communist theory and practice aside, it is important to see that the disagreements among the other three groups are about means rather than ends. The individualists, whether moderate or extreme, and the democratic socialists are mostly agreed in wanting to prepare the social ground in which human personality can grow to its fullest flowering. They are even agreed that a wide range of individual freedom is necessary for that purpose. They differ on the questions of how much freedom is necessary, how far economic freedom is necessary to the maintenance of other freedoms such as freedom of expression and occupation, how far we can go in enlarging the power of the state without making it our master.

Democratic Socialist Views. The democratic socialists think that economic freedom as it now exists, say in the United States, sours the social soil and dwarfs the lives of countless people. On the one hand, the economic freedom which is largely concentrated in the hands of the owners of the means of production is much greater than is needed for the purposes of individual self-realization. It is, in fact, the power to control a large part of the lives of those who work for them for wages. It is more power than they are able to use wisely with due respect for the claims of others for self-realization.

On the other hand, the economic freedom formally conceded to everybody to dispose of his time and labor as he sees fit is illusory and unreal for large sections of the population. The freedom of the working man to choose his occupation has little meaning if over an extended period he cannot get a job at all. Even when he has a job, he is a hired tool, generally employed in routine operations which he had no share in planning and has no power to modify. He lacks a sense of creative and free participation. He is, they insist, almost a slave of the complex process in which he is enmeshed.

In place of these two unsatisfactory kinds of economic freedom, the democratic socialists want gradually to introduce a large measure of ordered planning in economic matters. The planning of economic life will end many of the frustrations of unemployment, strikes, lockouts. It will greatly increase productivity and provide more goods, amenities, and leisure with which to draw out a rich variety of personal achievement in cultural and other fields. By diminishing economic freedom, more freedom of better quality can be assured in other aspects of social life. Moreover, the worker in a publicly owned industry is a part of the public, and therefore a part owner. He will have a sense of sharing in the work and purpose of the industry that is now denied him. He will participate much more than he does now in controlling the conditions under which he works.

Democratic socialists think that social and economic inequality is a major cause of frustration of human possibilities. They are prepared to limit individual freedom in various fields for the sake of greater equality. Thus the socialization of industry is aimed at the elimination of profits and the raising of wages. Furthermore, they demand heavy taxation to maintain comprehensive social security measures, thus leveling income. In Britain today, for example, it is extremely rare for anyone to have a net income the equivalent after taxation of more than $15,000 a year.

Democratic socialists doubt the capacity of democratic government to regulate private monopolies successfully in the public interest, but are confident that it can devise successful means of running public monopolies. As ardent democrats, they believe that the will of the people can control and direct the state even in the massive task of running the key industries of the country. Thus they see no reason to fear the state. They do not believe that economic freedom, the dispersion of ownership in many hands—and it is in many hands despite the features of monopoly—has any significant relation to the other freedoms that they think are more important.

The individualists, on the other hand, think freedom is the main buttress of human personality. The extreme individualists think that those who cannot thrive on freedom are dead losses anyway, and that there is no sense in sending good money after bad. They recognize, of course, that all freedom depends on a framework of order and security and they approve the criminal law which restricts the 'freedom' of the criminally-minded and by that very fact enlarges the freedom of everybody else. But it is hard to convince them that the need for order and security goes much beyond the protection afforded by the criminal law.

Moderate Individualist Views. The moderate individualists are less sure that freedom always serves the interests of personality. For example, whatever the effect of unemployment insurance, maximum hours and minimum wage laws, and factory legislation may be on individual freedom, they see these measures as justifiable, or even necessary, protection to the human claims of industrial workers. But when it comes to widespread public ownership of economic enterprise, they pause. They suspect strongly that there is some close connection between economic freedom and individual freedom in other fields. They remember that absolute monarchy in Europe between the sixteenth and nineteenth centuries went hand in hand with detailed control and direction of economic life by the state. They remember that the triumph of liberal democracy in the nineteenth century was achieved in a period when there was very wide freedom of economic enterprise, and that its triumph was greatest in those countries where the state had least to do with economic life. They cannot forget that the Fascist, Nazi, and Communist dictatorships, which denied all forms of individual freedom in our own day, also took over decisive direction of economic matters.

Independently of this kind of evidence, moderate individualists still fear the state because they think all great concentrations of power tend to override the claims of individuals to live their own lives. For that matter, they fear the concentration of economic power in private hands. They approve the increase of governmental power mainly as a counterpoise to big business, for the purpose of regulating and limiting monopolistic tendencies. They hope to achieve a balance in some kind of mixed economy composed of some private ownership, some public ownership, some governmental economic planning, and considerable governmental regulation of private enterprise. They think extensive socialization of industry would tip the scales too far.

The moderate individualists have difficulty in seeing how the electorate can control the operation of great publicly owned industries through the ballot box. They are not sure that the people could ever reach a united will on matters as complex as the operation of an industry. They are not convinced that the average industrial worker will find much more creative satisfaction in working for a mammoth public enterprise than for General Motors. It would appear, for example, that public ownership of the railways and the coal mines in Britain has not worked any great transformation in labor-management relations in these industries.

Moderate individualists agree with democratic socialists on the dangers of gross social and economic inequality. They support substantial social security measures as a means of narrowing inequalities and providing rough equality of opportunity. But their recipe for enriching human personality has more freedom and less equality than that of the democratic socialist.

Means and Ends. The controversy between the individualists and the democratic socialists is largely one of *means.* One in fundamental purposes, they differ in their judgments on human psychology, the lessons of history, the possibilities of directing the economic system through the political process, and a hundred other complex questions that cannot be discussed here. These questions are debated, and will continue to be debated, on the assumption that the discovery of more facts, a better knowledge of psychology and of political processes, will bring some measure of agreement. The continuing experiment in Britain with socialism is bound to produce persuasive evidence one way or the other on many points. The important point to notice here is that adherence to liberal democratic ideals and democratic procedures compels this kind of discussion about the appropriate range of state action.

The actual merits of the many issues debated between individualists and socialists cannot be discussed here. Many of the considerations involved are too complex for satisfactory discussion in the early stages of the study of government. The present purpose is to describe and analyze the machinery and processes of liberal democratic government. Whatever action government undertakes, it has to be carried out by this machinery and these processes. Is the machine suitably designed, or can it be adapted, for the purpose of running a socialist economy under democratic control?

One further significant comment should be made. While the extension of government activities of the last sixty or so years has been somewhat influenced by the highly technical and theoretical arguments of individualists and socialists on the subject, it does not appear to have been primarily determined by them. It has followed rather a tentative experimental course. Social and economic maladjustments occur and persist. After a time, government is moved to take action about them. The action taken does not proceed so much from theoretical convictions as from the pressure of various elements in the electorate that, for one reason or another, want something done about the maladjustment. The action taken is always tentative. It is later modified, or even abandoned, in the light of the results it seems to have obtained.

THE NEW FUNCTIONS AND THE WILL OF THE PEOPLE

One argument sometimes made in support of the new range of activities should be given attention. All these projects were launched by governments that were supported by a legislative majority, and almost all of them have survived changes of government and reversals of party fortunes. So, it is often argued, they have the support of a majority of the people and from them there is no appeal in a democracy. If plebiscites were taken on particular measures separately one by one, however, it is doubtful how many of them would find majority support. Generally speaking, the truth is that many of these activities directly benefit particular individuals and groups and, in an immediate material sense at any rate, place a burden on other individuals and groups.

Social security measures benefit the recipients and are a burden to the taxpayers. A new customs duty benefits some industries and some groups of workers at the expense of the rest of the community. When price supports and other services are provided for agriculture, they must be paid for by the taxpayer. A workmen's compensation scheme benefits industrial workers, and the cost of it is passed on to the purchasers of the goods and services they produce. It may be that, in each case, there are general benefits to the community as a whole that are shared even by those on whom the burden immediately falls. But these benefits are indirect and difficult to trace and establish. Outside those who think they will be directly prejudiced or advantaged by a particular measure, very few members of the public pay attention to it and, of those, only a fraction attempts the intricate calculations necessary to trace out the effects of the measure.

The Push and Pull of Interests. Thus, in relation to almost any proposed new activity of government, there is an active interested minority pushing for it, supported less strongly by a larger group that thinks social justice or economic efficiency will be served by it. There is an active interested minority opposed to it, passively supported by a larger group that vaguely objects. In most cases, unless the measure is very widespread in its obvious effects or has been effectively dramatized by supporters or opponents, the great mass of the electorate is sufficiently neutral not to take a stand either way. Minorities are often able to get measures in their favor, not because of active support of a majority of the electorate, but because the majority in the legislature think it is a good thing and that, on balance, it will mean more gain than loss in electoral support.

This analysis does not apply to every new function of government, and even where it is applicable it does not begin to do justice to the complexity of the forces behind legislative action. More will be said about it later. At present, we are concerned only with its general significance, namely, that modern legislation is greatly influenced, and often determined, by the push and pull of interest groups. Economic specialization has created almost innumerable groups, each with a special economic interest. Ease of transport and communication has enabled the like-minded across the country to seek one another out and form associations on the basis of their special interest. A thousand religious, philanthropic, cultural, economic, and recreational associations flourish, and they all have purposes that can be promoted by one kind of government action and impeded by another.

The twentieth-century phenomenon of governments undertaking activities for the benefit of special groups is partly due to the ubiquity of special interests and partly the cause of further strengthening of these group interests. They thrive on the benefits they can get from the government for their members and on the defense they can put up against legislation prejudicial to their interests. The voluntary association catering to the diverse needs of individuals is an indispensable feature of liberal democratic society. Once the principle of *laisser faire* was abandoned, it was inevitable that a great variety of voluntary associations should try to advance the interests of their members by bringing pressure on the government.

Normally, most individuals identify themselves more closely with their own special interests—they may belong to any number of different interest groups—than with the general common interest of the community. The immediate loyalties are continuous and intense, the wider loyalties and interests are tenuous and only spasmodically cross the threshold of attention. What the genuine common interest is at any one time has to be clarified by discussion. The industrial worker, the manufacturer, the farmer see much more clearly the advantages of a rise in their money income as producers than they do their corresponding disadvantages as consumers.

There should be no need to illustrate this point. During the war, when the most obvious and vital of general community interests were at stake, we saw producer groups of every kind demanding legislation that would maintain or raise their income despite the patent fact that, to win the war, the general standard of living had to be lowered. This is not due to a callous indifference to the general interest but to the greater immediacy and clarity of our special interest and to the difficulty of comprehending that our narrow advantage may be at variance with the general interest. So, much of the extension of government activity in the twentieth century comes not from a widespread general conviction that the public interest will be served thereby, but from the demands that interest groups, in combination or competition, press upon the government and the legislature.

AGGRANDIZEMENT OF THE EXECUTIVE

One other general result of great significance involved in the burgeoning of government activities must be attended to here. The positive state and the nature of the tasks it undertakes have aggrandized the executive branch of government. Two cases in point may be cited here.

Illustrations. For example, seventy years ago the law, as given content by judicial application of common law principles or as enacted by the legislature, defined in general terms the circumstances under which an employee could recover damages from his employer for injury suffered in the course of his employment. If he suffered injury and the employer denied responsibility, the employee had to bring an action in the courts, where a judge decided the issue and awarded the damages, if any. Whatever damages he got, he then spent either in paying his doctor or by having a day at the races as he saw fit. The executive had no part in the process at all unless the employer refused to pay the damages the court had awarded.

WORKMEN'S COMPENSATION TODAY. The result is entirely different with the present-day workmen's compensation laws, already briefly described. The legislature has outlined in a general way a scheme of compulsory insurance against industrial accident and disease, requiring a fund to be built up by contributions from employers. The carrying out and enforcing of this law is given to an executive agency, a Workmen's Compensation Board or Industrial Accidents Commission. Injured employees make claims to the board, which has substantial discretion as to liability and amount. The courts have no longer any extensive functions in this field. The executive agency is instructed to devote the amount awarded to the rehabilitation of the worker. It is expended on maintenance of his family, medical expenses, and retraining for a new job as the board sees fit.

The agency also has important preventive powers. It can order the use of safety devices in a factory and it can increase the premium payable by employers with a bad record of accidents. This involves not only a field force of inspectors going from place to place but also the compilation of statistics, an engineering branch, and a staff for research into the causes and incidence of industrial accident and disease. The agency soon knows more about industrial accidents than anyone else and therefore can contribute more ideas for the amendment and improvement of the workmen's compensation laws than the legislature.

Moreover, its statistics and its researches show that the health conditions of the worker outside the factory, his education and training, even his biological inheritance, are important factors in the incidence of industrial accident and disease. That is to say, an executive agency that wants to do a really effective job will be pressing constantly for an extension of its powers, and if it were not checked by the legislature it might soon bring public health, education, and eugenics within its purview. As it is, the administration of the workmen's compensation fund brings a significant enlargement of the executive, including an inspectorate, a claims division, medical advisers, a social welfare service, and a research bureau as well as many routine and clerical workers. This agency speaks with great authority on its operations, and its voice is likely to be heard in favor of rather than against an enlargement of its powers.

REGULATION OF PUBLIC UTILITIES. This matter is so important that, even at the risk of boredom, another illustration must be given. Not so long ago the regulation of public utilities, those essential industries enjoying for one reason or another monopoly advantages, was left to the legislature and the judiciary. The law provided merely that railway, telegraph, telephone, and electric power companies must provide reasonable services to the public and must not charge unreasonable rates. Anyone who was aggrieved by the rates or service had to bring an action in the courts asking for a decision that the rate charged him was too high or the service given him inadequate. Now the legislature makes provision for an executive agency, a transport commission, or a public utilities commission.

Aggrieved persons apply to this agency and not to the courts. It determines rates in great detail. To do this, it has to decide what is a *reasonable return* on the investment of the public utility company. It is thus necessary to decide what the investment shall be taken to be, the nominal capital, the actual value of the assets committed to the adventure—i.e. ruling out *watered stock* —their replacement value, or the amount that prudent men would have invested in this particular enterprise. Allowances for depreciation and obsolescence have to be calculated. The commission lays down precise regulations about standards of service. A railway may be required to run more trains, or more cars per train, or forbidden to discontinue particular trains. An electric utility may be required to step up its voltage or entend its lines. This involves finding a very nice balance between public needs in the way of service and the ability of the company to furnish them. New capital seeking entrance to the industry must satisfy the commission that it is in the public interest that the industry should expand, a judgment that calls for a great range of knowledge. This executive agency must go deeply into the economics of the industry, the financial history of particular companies, and relate these to what it is thought the public needs, i.e. the public interest. Expert staffs of economists and accountants are needed.

Moreover, safety is an element in reasonable service, particularly in the transport utilities. The agency must develop regulations regarding the safety measures to be taken. The devising and improving of these regulations and the enforcement of them require an inspectorate and an engineering staff always at work surveying existing facilities in the industry, investigating accidents, and testing new safety devices.

Here again, a large staff is built up; its activities give it unique knowledge about the public utility industry and reveal new ways in which it can improve its regulation by extending the scope of its control. Its experience is always suggesting changes in the laws for the regulation of public utilities and thus it has great, and often decisive, influence when the legislature comes to amend the law.

A Consequence of the Positive State. In almost all the functions of government outlined in this chapter, similar enlargements of the executive have taken place. The New Deal alone in the United States swelled the civil service by some 350,000 persons. The large staffs that carry out the intricate detail of these tasks of government are generally referred to as the administrative, and some have described this as a fourth power alongside the legislature, executive, and judiciary. In fact, it is a part of the executive although it has swollen that power out of all recognition and radically changed its character. Where the executive formerly was something of an automaton carrying out the dictates of legislatures and courts, it now does a great deal of detailed legislating on its own in the course of administration; it is a powerful influence in the determining of legislative policy; and it has everywhere encroached on the judiciary. Its size and the scope of its operations have created a new problem of internal management. How is the President of the United States to co-ordinate and direct the energies of almost three million civil servants in the employ of the federal government? No matter what problem of present-day government is under consideration, it will be found to have been intensified, if not entirely created, by the remarkable developments we have been considering.

This great service and regulatory apparatus called the administrative is also known, in terms of alarm or contempt, as the *bureaucracy*. It is not always understood that it is the necessary concomitant of the positive state. Most people approve of some or other of these new functions of government and almost all castigate bureaucracy, associating it with those activities of government of which they disapprove. But the general effect of the great extension of state action on government, and particularly on democratic government, has never been adequately explored. Later chapters will indicate trends and suggest probabilities.

Suggested References for Further Reading

Abraham, H. J., *Government as Entrepreneur and Social Servant* (Public Affairs Press, 1956).

Anshon, M., and F. D. Wormuth, *Private Enterprise and Public Policy* (Macmillan, 1954).

Bauer, R. A., I. de Sola Pool, and L. A. Dexter, *American Business and Public Policy: The Politics of Foreign Trade* (Atherton, 1963).

Beard, C. A., *The Economic Basis of Politics* (Knopf, 1945).

Carson, R., *Silent Spring* (Houghton Mifflin, 1962).

Chester, D. N., *The Nationalized Industries*, 2nd ed. (Allen & Unwin, 1951).

Childs, M. W., *Sweden: The Middle Way*, rev. ed. (Yale, 1961).

Christenson, R. M., *The Brannan Plan* (U. of Michigan, 1959).

Corry, J. A., *Growth of Government Activities Since Confederation* (King's Printer, 1940).

Cotter, C. P., *Government and Private Enterprise* (Holt, Rinehart, & Winston, 1960).

Davenport, R. W., *U.S.A.: The Permanent Revolution* (Prentice-Hall, 1951).

Dimock, M. E., *The New American Political Economy* (Harper & Row, 1963).

Einaudi, M., M. Bye, and E. Possi, *Nationalization in France and Italy* (Cornell, 1956).

Finer, H., *Road to Reaction* (Little, Brown, 1945).

Galbraith, J. K., *The Affluent Society* (Houghton Mifflin, 1958).

Hanson, A. H., *Parliament and Public Ownership* (Oxford, 1961).

Hayek, F., *The Road to Serfdom* (U. of Chicago, 1944).

Hubbard, P. J., *Origins of the T.V.A.: The Muscle Shoals Controversy* (Vanderbilt, 1961).

Lindsey, A., *Socialized Medicine in England and Wales: The National Health Service, 1948–1961* (U. of N. Carolina, 1962).

Reagan, M. D., *The Managed Economy* (Oxford, 1963).

Roberts, E., *One River—Seven States* (U. of Tennessee, 1955).

Robson, W. A., *Nationalized Industries* (Oxford, 1952).

Rogow, A., *The Labor Government and British Industry, 1945–1951* (Cornell, 1956).

Schumpeter, P. A., *Capitalism, Socialism, and Democracy*, 3rd ed. (Harper, 1950).

Schwartz, H., *Russia's Soviet Economy*, 2nd ed. (Prentice-Hall, 1955).

Sutton, F. X. (Ed.), *The American Business Creed* (Harvard, 1956).

Voorhis, J., *American Cooperatives* (Harper, 1962).

Wildavsky, A., *Dixon-Yates: A Study in Power Politics* (Yale, 1961).

Witte, E. E., *The Development of the Social Security Act* (U. of Wisconsin, 1962).

VI

Federalism

BASIC ARRANGEMENTS AND CONSIDERATIONS

1. Confederate. There are many ways in which separate political communities can come together for common purposes. When several states confer together and agree on a common course of action in certain specified circumstances, such as resistance to a common enemy, they are bound together by *treaty or alliance.* When they go one step further and set up a more or less permanent body of delegates or ambassadors to make detailed recommendations for carrying out the treaty or implementing the alliance, their association together is called a *confederation.* Such was the Congress finally set up by the American colonies in 1781 under the Articles of Confederation of 1777 to fight the war against Britain. In a confederation, the common central body

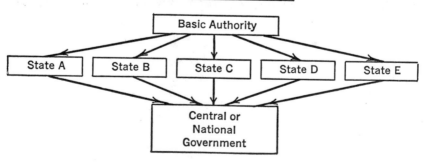

CONFEDERATE STRUCTURE

is merely a committee for deliberating and advising the separate members. It has no meaningful power over the separate states in the association or over the citizens of these states. A confederation is little more than a 'firm league of friendship,' from which the member states have a right to withdraw. In a way, today's United Nations resembles a form of 'confederation.'

2. *Federal.* The next further step is to give irrevocably to the common central body some portion of the authority hitherto exercised by each of the member states on its own account. When this is done, the central body becomes a government with power to act independently of its own volition and not merely a council of ambassadors. A new state comes into existence to which the citizens of the member states owe an allegiance and a duty of obedience. Such are the United States of America brought into existence by the Constitution of 1789 and the Dominion of Canada created in 1867. Other current examples of important federal governments are the Republic of Switzerland, the Commonwealth of Australia, and the Federal Republic of West Germany, as established by their constitutions of 1848, 1900, and 1949, respectively. Such unions are *federal unions or federations.* The member states or provinces are joined together not by treaty but by a written *constitution* from which they have no right to withdraw. It is a marriage and not merely a casual alliance.

FEDERAL STRUCTURE

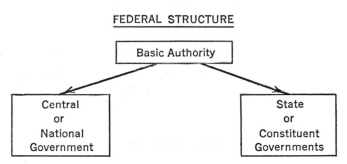

Yet, at the beginning at least, a federal union is merely a marriage of convenience—a practical businesslike arrangement with no sentimental nonsense. The parties insist on retaining their distinct identities and personalities; they do not become one flesh. Of course, with the passing of time and the running of a common household, the marriage of convenience may be transformed into the kind of marriage that is made in heaven, where the identities of the several states are merged in an indissolubly united nation.

3. *Unitary.* If and when this happens, the desire for a genuinely inde-

pendent status in the several participating states will probably disappear. If so, conditions will be ripe for the last step in political unification, the disappearance of autonomous units and the reposing of all final governmental authority in a single central government. This is called the *unitary state,* of which Great Britain, incorporating the once independent communities of England, Wales, and Scotland, and France, incorporating Normandy, Brittany, Provence, and so forth, are leading examples.

UNITARY STRUCTURE

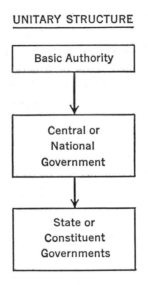

There are still far more unitary states in the world today than any other, although the federal idea has become increasingly popular.

FEDERALISM

Why? Why do separate political communities when uniting together sometimes prefer a federal to a unitary form of government? A federal system is always a compromise between two distinct, and sometimes conflicting, sets of political forces. *First,* there are the pressing common interests and purposes shared by the several states. The American colonies on the Atlantic seaboard had just won their independence from Britain and wanted to secure themselves against the assaults of any European imperialism. The British colonies in North America in 1867 feared the aggrandizement of the United

States, which had emerged from the Civil War as a great military power. Such interests and purposes, among others, can only be protected by presenting a united front.

Second, there is the desire of each of the uniting communities to maintain its identity and a large measure of independence. In part, this desire springs from the same mysterious sources as national pride and national exclusiveness. Robert E. Lee, offered the command of the Northern Army at the outbreak of the Civil War, refused it, saying he could not draw sword against his native state, Virginia. His first allegiance was to Virginia and not to the United States. In part, the desire springs from very practical considerations. The conditions of life and the character of the people as moulded by history and the physical environment vary greatly in the states contemplating union. Just because the unitary form works well in Britain does certainly not mean that it would work well in the United States.

No government that fails to take account of these differences will ever be regarded as satisfactory. A government that is locally controlled is far more sensitive to the factors of uniqueness than is a central national government, which is far away and preoccupied with more general issues. The desire to limit the reach of a distant government is the main reason for a federal system. Without the urgent common interests, there would, of course, be no union at all. But with no insistence on a guaranteed sphere of independence for each of the uniting communities, there would be no reason for a partial union—no case at all for a federal form of government.

Defined. Federalism, therefore, is a dual form of government, based on a territorial and functional division of powers, calculated to reconcile unity with diversity. It provides for a common government for common purposes, generally called the federal, or national, government. In the beginning, the common purposes mostly relate to external matters. The aim is to have a common policy vis-à-vis the rest of the world. The federal scheme also provides for the continuance of the governments of the several states, provinces, or *Laender* in the federation, preserving for them, against the world and against the common government they have set up, control of most matters of internal policy. *The most important aspect of a federal system, then, is the distribution of powers and authority between the common government on the one hand, and the state governments on the other.* To set at rest all later questioning of what this distribution really is, it is written into the Constitution or Basic Law. This distribution of powers firmly established in a written constitution is the distinctive feature of federalism and makes many aspects of politics and government in the United States markedly different from those of Britain and France, both unitary states. Therefore, in discussing federalism, Britain and France cannot be used for purposes of contrast.

There are a number of other federal systems with which comparisons might be made. Limiting the choice to those genuinely within the liberal democratic tradition, there are only Australia, Canada, and Switzerland, plus a very recent entry, West Germany. Australia and Switzerland are both remote, and are products of distinctive environments which would require much explanation. West Germany has had but brief opportunity to see its system in action, nor has Germany had much experience with the liberal tradition! Canada, however, is close at hand and subject to a continental North American environment similar to that of the United States. Consequently, our chief interest here lies with federalism as it exists in Canada and the United States, with sporadic references to the interesting German system.

SCOPE OF COMPARISON. The Dominion of Canada was set up in 1867 by federating the British colonies that remained, or grew up, in North America after the American Revolution. Its Constitution was laid down by a statute of the British Parliament, the British North America Act. Within this framework, only rarely amended, a distinctive federal system has developed. It has managed to hold together in peace, if not in complete harmony, the English-speaking Protestants and the French-speaking Roman Catholics, the two great groups of which the Canadian people are composed. In recent years Canada has undergone rapid industrialization and there has been a great increase in the activities of government, the same factors that have complicated the working of federalism in the United States. The principal features of these two federations will be compared, with occasional allusions to other federal countries. In a concluding section, something will be said briefly about a quite different kind of 'federalism,' that found in the Soviet Union.

Significant Difference. But prior to embarking upon the comparison it is of the utmost importance to point out that, in a very real sense, federalism is a point on a continuum reaching from complete isolation to complete absorption, neither of which is ever found in the actual life of actual states. As Aristotle might have said, there is no such thing as federalism; there are only federal states—states reflecting the federal principle. Hence, the federal idea— defined again recently by Governor Rockefeller of New York as 'a concept of government by which a sovereign people, for their greater protection and Progress, yield a portion of their sovereignty to a political system that has more than one center of sovereign power, energy and creativity'[1]—features dramatic differences. West German federalism is hardly of the same stripe as the Canadian or American, and its pre-Hitler predecessor was always dominated by one of its constituent parts—usually Prussia, sometimes Bavaria. Again, the cantons of Switzerland enjoy significantly more independent power than do the constituent governments of most other federal states. For example, in the areas of 'public economy' and 'police regulation' they are constitutionally permitted to make agreements or compacts with foreign powers—although these must be brought to the attention of the national authorities. Yet an authority on that stable federal state speaks of a tremendous increase in the central government's power, even more than in the United States![2] The federal arrangements of India and Brazil are again utterly different—all underscoring the essential point that when we speak of federal states it is contrast rather than comparison that dominates.

The Federal Distribution of Powers

In the United States. In considering the federal systems of the United States and Canada, the distribution of powers set out in the respective constitutions must be looked at first. It has already been noted in Chapter IV that the Constitution of the United States *limits* the powers of all governments and puts certain matters beyond the reach of either the state or federal government. These matters are said to be *reserved to the people.* We shall leave these aside in order that some of the more important features of the distribution may be pointed out. Certain specified powers are *expressly granted to the national government.* Moreover, it is authorized, in what is known as the 'elastic' or *implied powers* clause,[3] to make such laws 'as are necessary and proper for carrying into effect' the powers expressly granted— a power of far-reaching significance. Some powers are, of course, *expressly forbidden* to the national government.[4] While the Constitution *expressly prohibits the exercise of certain powers by the states,*[5] it nowhere *enumerates*

[1] Nelson A. Rockefeller, 'The Future of Federalism,' The Godkin Lectures, Harvard University, February 1962.

[2] George A. Codding, Jr., *The Federal Government of Switzerland* (Boston: Houghton Mifflin, 1961), ch. iii, *passim.*

[3] Art. i, sect. 8, par. 18.

[4] See Art. i, sect. 9, and the several Amendments.

[5] These prohibitions are found in Art. i, sect. 10, and in Amendments xiii, xiv, xv, xix, and xxiv.

the powers of the states. As Amendment X makes clear, they hold the residue of powers remaining *after* the grants to the national governments, the express prohibitions to the states, and the reservations to the people are accounted for.

Article I, section 8, enumerates the principal powers granted to the United States.[6] Many of these powers relate, directly or indirectly, to external matters: the raising and supporting of armies and navies, the declaring and prosecuting of wars, the regulation of commerce with foreign nations. In internal matters, the powers of the United States were mostly restricted to the promotion of internal trade and interstate commerce. It was necessary to guard against the states' erecting tariff barriers against one another. Accordingly, in addition to an express prohibition of the levying of duties on imports by the states,[7] the federal government was given power to regulate commerce among the several states. The *interstate commerce clause,* as it is called, has been the basis of much of the great extension of federal power through judicial interpretation. To a somewhat lesser extent this is also true of the *taxing* power.

Because a common currency and a common standard of weights and measures were needed to promote internal trade and commerce, the federal government was authorized to coin money and to fix its value, and to fix the standards of weights and measures. The powers to establish post offices and post roads, and to grant patents and copyrights, were, in part, aimed at the same purpose of facilitating commerce. The only clause that *might be* thought to have wide general application in internal matters is the one authorizing the federal government 'to provide . . . for the general welfare of the United States.' But the context in which it appears in Article I, section 8, makes it doubtful whether any extensive power was intended to be granted thereby, and the Supreme Court has refused to recognize the existence of any such sweeping power.[8] It appears not as an independent grant of power but as one of the purposes for which the federal government may levy taxes and spend the funds thus raised.

A few powers, known as concurrent powers, are *shared by both state and federal governments:* the levying of taxes, the borrowing of money, and the establishment of courts. Because the powers of the states are in the form of an unspecified residue, no enumeration would be likely to state them ex-

---

[6] Others of significance vis-à-vis the states are granted in Art. IV, sect. 1, 3, and 4, and in Amendments, XIII, XIV, XV, and XIX.

[7] See Art. I, sect. 10.

[8] For a well-known example, see the interesting and controversial opinions in *U.S.* v. *Butler,* 297 U.S. I (1936).

haustively. The making and altering of the criminal law and the laws of marriage and divorce are merely well-known instances of the power of the states to make diverse laws as they see fit. In fact, as far as the *written* Constitution goes, the states appear to be the important authorities on most aspects of property, intra-state trade and commerce, and personal relationships. At least so one would infer from a reading of section 8 of Article I and Amendment X—but in the light of present-day realities such a conclusion would be an oversimplification at best. The reader must also keep in mind the significance of the Supremacy Clause of the Constitution—Article VI—as explained in Chapter IV, above.

In Canada. When the terms of union of the British colonies in North America were under discussion in the 1860's, seventy-five years of experience under the federal Constitution of the United States were available for guidance. This experience had just culminated in a civil war that threatened to destroy the Union. The immediate, if not the underlying, cause of the Civil War had been the claim by the southern states of the right to withdraw from the Union. Because the powers of the federal government were specific powers that could be interpreted as having been delegated to it by the states, the seceding states claimed the right to withdraw the delegation.

The framers of the Canadian federation wanted to make it clear from the beginning that such a claim had no semblance of right in the Canadian federation. Indeed, some of them did not want a federal system at all but a unitary state with all authority in one national central government. So the British North America Act of 1867, the statute of the British Parliament that established the Canadian federal system, tried to limit and qualify the independence of the provinces more sharply than the American Constitution had limited the states. It was provided that the Lieutenant-Governors, the formal heads of the provincial governments, should be appointed by the federal government and that they should have the power to 'reserve' provincial legislation for the pleasure of the federal cabinet.[9] Also, the federal cabinet was given power to 'disallow' within one year any laws enacted by the provincial legislatures.[10] Most important, the opening paragraph of section 91 of the Act, which authorizes the Dominion Parliament 'to make laws for the peace, order and good government of Canada' on all matters not ex-

---

[9] British North America Act, sect. 58–60, and sect. 57 as extended by sect. 90.

[10] Ibid., sect. 56 as extended by sect. 90. This power is distinct from, and not to be confused with, the much narrower power of the courts to declare null and void acts of the provincial legislatures that purport to deal with matters reserved to the Dominion Parliament under sect. 91.

clusively reserved to the provincial legislatures, was intended to make it clear that the *residuary powers,* the powers not expressly conferred on either Dominion or province, *rested with the Dominion,* and that the provinces were to have certain specified powers (set out in section 92) and no more. All these provisions were calculated to show that the Dominion did not derive its powers from delegation by the provinces. No room was left for the provinces to argue that their independent status included the right to withdraw from the union.

Powers that the Dominion was to exercise exclusively were set out in section 91. The twenty-nine headings in this section, which purport to be illustrative only and not a definitive statement of the scope of Dominion power, covered a wider range of matters than the corresponding list of federal powers in the Constitution of the United States. They covered such aspects of external relations as a British dependency could expect to control on its own account. They went further than the Constitution of the United States in conferring authority over commercial matters on the federal government. In addition to currency and coinage, they included the power to regulate banking, bills of exchange, interest, and legal tender. Furthermore, in authorizing the Dominion to make laws for 'the regulation of trade and commerce,' they seemed to confer a wide power of regulating business and commerce. By an exception to section 92.10, the Dominion was given wide control over the transportation and communications industries. By section 121, the provincial legislatures were forbidden to interfere with freedom of trade between the different provinces. Reflection on these and other powers enumerated in section 91 indicates that the Dominion was intended to have a wider authority in relation to economic life than the federal government in the United States.

Experience in the United States had shown that it was extremely unsatisfactory for the separate states to have exclusive control over the criminal law (except for federal crimes) and over marriage and divorce. Accordingly, these matters, excluding the forms of the marriage ceremony, which were left for provincial determination, were put in the sole control of the Dominion. On the other hand, whether for sufficient reasons or not, the framers wished to avoid duplication of judicial institutions found in the United States, and accordingly the power to constitute courts for the enforcement of both Dominion and provincial law was given to the provinces.[11]

Concurrent powers to levy taxes and borrow money were conferred on

[11] Ibid. sect. 92.14.

both the provinces and the Dominion. In addition, concurrent powers over agriculture and immigration were provided for in section 95.

This contrast is by no means an exhaustive discussion of the distribution of powers between the Dominion and the provinces. It is designed mainly to show that the framers intended, in the light of American experience, to strengthen the Dominion vis-à-vis the provinces. But, in social and economic matters, what men plan and what ensues are often quite different things. Both these constitutions have been interpreted by the courts on almost innumerable occasions since their adoption and it would be difficult for anyone, looking only at the text of the constitutions, to realize that they mean what the courts have declared them to mean.

Judicial Interpretation of the Distribution of Powers

United States. Except for one significant reversal of the general trend in the years immediately before the Civil War—in the famous *Dred Scott* case [12]—the Supreme Court of the United States has steadily enlarged the powers of the federal government by interpretations given in disputes coming before it, although it did balk for several years on some of the more ambitious New Deal measures of the mid-'thirties. By 1963, federal authority had been stretched to the point where it could employ more than two and one-half million civil servants on its legitimate concerns. The Supreme Court, aided by the arbitrament of arms in the Civil War, has confirmed the indissolubility of the Union and enormously strengthened the position of the federal government vis-à-vis the states. Largely, but not entirely, through a liberal interpretation of the federal taxing power, the *elastic clause,* and the interstate commerce clause, Congress has been given an extremely wide power to regulate trade and commerce and economic life.

The President's Commission on Intergovernmental Relations, which in 1955 completed an exhaustive study of the current operation of federalism in the United States—the first official undertaking of this kind since the Constitutional Convention of 1787—took note of this trend in judicial interpretation as follows: '. . . under present judicial interpretations of the Constitution, especially of the spending power and the commerce clause, the boundaries of possible national action are more and more subject to determination by legislative action. In brief, the policy-making authorities of the National Government are for most purposes the arbiters of the federal

[12] 19 How. 393 (1857).

system.'[13] In other words, the Supreme Court would no longer seem to be a major factor in preserving the *federal system*. This, of course, makes the scope of state power depend in large measure on the self-restraint of the national government.

Canada. Judicial interpretation of the distribution of powers in the Canadian Constitution has gone in the *opposite* direction. Until 1949, when the Supreme Court of Canada in Ottawa became the final court of appeal, for constitutional and other cases, the final authority for judicial interpretation of the Canadian Constitution had been the Privy Council in London. The decisions of the Privy Council over a period of fifty years almost denuded of meaning the general, or residuary, clause contained in the opening paragraph of section 91, except for periods of great national emergency. It is by reliance on this clause in time of war that the Dominion substantially supersedes the provincial governments. In times of peace, however, the Dominion has been denied any substantial power under it. Thus the peacetime powers of the Dominion are almost wholly restricted to the matters specifically enumerated in section 91. Even here, the most general clause, 'regulation of trade and commerce,' has been very narrowly interpreted. Most laws for regulating economic life, such as the manner in which particular trades and industries conduct their business, have been held to be beyond the power of the Dominion and to be solely reserved to the provinces under section 92.13, 'property and civil rights in the province.' Legislation providing for social services and social insurance has also been held to be a matter for the provinces under property and civil rights.

Indeed, section 92.13 has been so widely interpreted, and the general clause of section 91 so narrowly construed, that it can now be said, without any great exaggeration, that *the residuary power rests with the provinces and not with the Dominion*. The Privy Council and its successor have magnified the provinces, while the Supreme Court of the United States has magnified the federal government. Although the Privy Council and the Canadian Supreme Court have confirmed the provinces in a wide range of powers, they have never said anything to support the right of the provinces to withdraw from the Confederation. Nor has any province ever seriously claimed it. The high-water mark of provincialism is the claim frequently made in some quarters that the Confederation is a compact between the provinces and cannot be modified without the consent of all the provinces.

---

[13] *The Commission on Intergovernmental Relations: A Report to the President for Transmittal to the Congress* (Washington, D.C.: U.S. Government Printing Office, 1955), p. 59.

It must not be thought, however, that the activities of the Dominion government today are less numerous and important than they were in, say, 1875. On the contrary, they are vastly greater, having grown steadily since the beginning of the twentieth century. The Dominion did not attempt, in the early years of the federation, to exercise all the powers that section 91 conferred on it. It was only when it began, from about 1900 on, to expand its activities that it ran into restrictive interpretations by the Privy Council. The decisions of the highest courts have not prevented the Dominion from enlarging its activities but they have been progressively hampering as the demands for Dominion action have grown. The Dominion could not have carried out during the depression of the 1930's measures comparable to the New Deal in the United States because the British North America Act, as interpreted by the Privy Council, reserved most of such powers to the provinces. The activities of the Dominion government have grown, but not to the extent to those of the federal government in the United States.[14]

A Note on West Germany. A summary word about the post-World War II experience of West Germany with federalism may be in order here. The compromises that resulted in the Basic Law of 1948 (*Grundgesetz*) reflect the Weimar pattern to some extent, but a genuine effort was made to limit the central government more in certain areas, including financial matters, and to increase the power of the *Laender* by making 'their' national house of Parliament, the upper house (*Bundesrat*), more influential. The latter consists of ministers from the *Laender*. Most novel—and perhaps most significant of all, although such a verdict must await the passage of time—was the adoption of the Constitutional Court (*Bundesverfassungsgericht*), patterned somewhat upon the United States Supreme Court. Endowed with the role of arbiter of the Constitution, this novel German tribunal not only can decide the constitutionality of legislative and executive-administrative acts, but also basic questions of constitutional interpretation that might arise (and indeed have done so) between the *Laender* and the central government as well as between the branches of the latter. To the surprise of a number of qualified observers, it has been an assertive as well as busy court, indeed, one that did not hesitate in one important instance—concerning Chancellor Adenauer's efforts to break the *Laender's* control over radio and television—to uphold the Democratic Socialist-led *Laender* and declared the stern Chancellor's ac-

[14] See *Report of the Royal Commission on Dominion-Provincial Relations* (Ottawa: King's Printer, 1940), vol. 1, pp. 247–59. This volume consists largely of a history of Canadian federalism.

tion of instituting a nation-wide federal T.V. network unconstitutional.[15] Significantly, it based its decision on Article 30 of the Constitution, which states that functions not assigned to the federal government remain under the jurisdiction of the *Laender*.

Further to the realm of division of powers, the 1948 Constitution gives to the upper house of Parliament an absolute veto in matters 'affecting the balance of the federal system' and a suspensive one in all other federal legislation. It has proved to be an able and effective defender of the interest of the *Laender* in the legislative process. The central government has *exclusive* legislative powers in eleven fields, including defense, foreign affairs, and railroads; and it has concurrent powers with the *Laender* in twenty-three, among others, comprising, civil and criminal law, anti-trust, labor, and agricultural regulation. As already indicated, all powers not specified in the Constitution are referred to the *Laender*—among these being education, religious and other cultural affairs, plus police and local government administration.

Although this brief sketch of West German federalism [16] may have given an impression of an arrangement of a prerogative-studded well-entrenched '*Laender*-rights' system, such an impression would fail to take cognizance of the not surprising fact of federal life that applies to West Germany as well as to Canada, the United States, Switzerland, and all other federal states: An unmistakable, and in all probability irreversible, trend toward centralization of powers in the hands of the national government.

FEDERALISM AND THE UNIFIED NATIONAL ECONOMY

The essential feature of a federal system is the co-existence of two governments with authority over the same territory and the same persons. Each of these governments is independent of the other. Each has a sphere in which it alone can rule and cannot be overruled by the other. At the launching of the two main federal systems under discussion, it was thought that the sphere of the federal government, on the one hand, and the sphere of the state and provincial governments, on the other, could easily be kept separate, that each of the governments would operate in an almost watertight compartment. The matters committed to the federal government were few and appeared not to

---

[15] *Entscheidungen des Bundesverfassungsgericht,* XII (February 28, 1961).
[16] See Gerard Braunthal, 'Federalism in Germany: The Broadcasting Controversy,' 24 *The Journal of Politics* 545–61 (1962).

bear very directly on life in the different states and provinces.[17] The latter would control their own destinies without serious clash with one another or with the federal authority.

But this expectation, too, has been falsified by events. The Civil War in the United States revealed how the states could become dissatisfied with the policies of one another's governments, and how one group of states could become so incensed with the policies of the federal government as to secede from the Union. No subsequent issue in either country has threatened a civil war, but it has become more difficult, with each succeeding decade, for each government in the federation to carry on in isolation. There is an ever growing number of interstate and federal-state co-operative arrangements. These arrangements, or the lack of them, are often attended by bickering and quarreling between the different governments. To overcome the squabbling, the states are counseled either to have more and better co-operation, or to hand over further powers to the federal government so that one government will have control of the whole matter at issue. If present-day federalism is to be understood, it is necessary to see how this has come about.

Revolution in Transport and Communications. The American federation was founded when the Industrial Revolution was just beginning, and the Canadian Dominion was established before the full consequences of the Industrial Revolution had become apparent. To take only one aspect of it, the revolution in transportation and communications was still to come in 1789, and it was still in its early stages in 1867. In these circumstances, the states were of necessity very largely insulated compartments. People lived, not by buying and selling in distant markets beyond the boundaries of their own state, but by producing practically all their needs either on the family farm or in the local community close to home.

Agriculture was still the basic industry and principally concerned with local markets. The manufacturing industries were still small and mainly occupied in supplying a local demand. Strict accuracy would compel many important qualifications on the description just given. Intercolonial and foreign trade was important on the Atlantic seaboard in 1789 and in the remaining British colonies in North America in 1867, but it had not yet changed the general pattern of economic and social life. At the time the American federations were being launched, most of the states were relatively self-contained.

[17] Henceforth, in this chapter, the word *state* is to be understood to include *province,* unless the context indicates otherwise.

When there was security from foreign aggression, events in the sister states and in other parts of the world had but a limited impact on each state. Federal union aimed at providing security from foreign intervention and did so successfully. With the principal conditions of life determined within their own boundaries, the states could have a genuine independence. There followed in each case a golden age of states' rights and provincial autonomy.

All the while, however, the onrushing economic transformation of the modern world was preparing the decline of this golden age. Free trade within the federation, improved transportation facilities, and rapid industrial and commercial expansion led to economic integration within the federation. In the place of the largely self-contained economies of the separate units in the federation, there grew a single unified national economy. *Independence gave way to interdependence.* Today, if farmers in the agricultural states cannot sell their produce profitably, workmen in the predominantly manufacturing states suffer unemployment, companies fail to pay their expected annual dividends, mortgage payments due to persons in still other states go into arrears. The order of dependence of such events on one another will vary, but it is at least clear that events that take place in one part of the federation have an impact in every other part. In fact, each of the states has become part of a larger whole with no direct power over what happens to the whole.[18]

Effects of Growing Government Activities. This momentous development does not of itself alone bring the several governments in the federation into closer contact, co-operation, or conflict. It was not the mere fact of the development of a world economy in the nineteenth century that brought national governments into conflict and war in the twentieth century. It was rather the fact of the people demanding, whether for adequate reasons or not, that their national governments should intervene in economic and social matters that turned economic rivalries into political conflicts.

So, within the federation, if governmental functions had remained limited to those of the mid-nineteenth century, the several governments would not always be coming across one another's paths as they are today. But they have not been so limited, as will be seen in detail in later chapters. It is the *immense increase in governmental activities* that produces intergovernmental disputes, demands for better co-operation between them, and arguments for

[18] For a superb, analytical enumeration of the changes that took place in the United States between 1789 and 1942, see William Anderson, 'Federalism—Then and Now,' *State Government* XVI (May 1943), 107–12.

enlarging the powers of the federal government, the government whose arm has the longest reach.

Each government working within the sphere assigned to it by the constitution takes action that has repercussions in the spheres of the others. The federal government through its control of tariffs and currency and credit can affect economic conditions in each of the member states. There is scarcely any action it can take on these matters nowadays that does not affect some states favorably and others adversely. This was always true to some extent, but it is more marked now than ever before. On the other hand, the actions taken, or neglected to be taken, by one or all of the states may affect profoundly the matters with which the federal government has to deal. Thus the inability and/or unwillingness of the states to finance a road-building program commensurate with traffic volume compelled the United States Congress in 1956 to pass a mammoth multi-billion, fifteen-year, 41,000-mile road network project known as the National Interstate Highway System. The states were required to pay merely 10 per cent of the cost.

Equally, action taken by one state government may affect some or all of the sister states. Government regulations covering the grading and marketing of produce in the state almost inevitably affect the trade of other states. Laws passed by one state to relieve debt-ridden farmers in that state affect creditor interests in other states. Moreover, there are many matters on which the government of one state cannot hope to take effective action because some of the factors are beyond its control. If one state makes a levy on the industries within its boundaries for the maintenance of a particular health insurance fund, for instance, it takes the risk that industries will shun it in favor of other states which do not follow suit, and where, therefore, the costs of production are lower. If the federal government is restricting credit, state governments cannot hope to take successful measures for expanding production and employment.

Conflict and Co-operation within the Federal System. An excellent illustration of the need for interstate and state-federal co-operation is afforded by the predicament in which the oil-producing industry and the oil-producing states of the United States found themselves in the early 1930's. The great bulk of the oil production of the country comes from the wells in some half a dozen states,[19] whence most of it flows in interstate commerce to the markets

[19] Texas, Louisiana, California, Oklahoma, Wyoming, New Mexico, and Kansas. Smaller quantities are produced in Illinois, Mississippi, Colorado, Montana, Utah, Arkansas, North Dakota, and Nebraska.

in the other states. Between 1926 and 1931 immensely rich new oil fields were opened and production increased at a fantastic rate. With the onset of the depression at the turn of the decade, the demand for oil failed signally to keep pace with production, and the oil-producing industry suffered a catastrophic decline in prices and consequent cut-throat competition. Each state was faced with the additional problem of conserving an irreplaceable natural resource, which was being wasted by overproduction.

Under the Constitution, the regulation of the production of oil—but not its interstate shipment—is a question for the state governments. A state legislature could pass—and several of the legislatures in the major oil-producing states had passed prior to 1930—laws limiting and pro-rating production. But two serious difficulties faced states acting singly and alone. First, oil wells were tapped illegally and the product boot-legged into interstate commerce where control over it could only be exercised by the federal government. Second, it was futile for any one state to impose effective restrictions if the other major oil-producing states failed to act effectively in the same way. The producers in that state would be faced with disastrously low prices in their markets in other states as well as limited in the quantities they could produce and ship.

Complex co-operative arrangements were devised which brought a measure of stability into the oil-producing industry, even if they did not solve the larger problem of wise and effective conservation. Six of the major producing states entered into an interstate compact to restrict the production and marketing of oil. They relied largely on a federal government agency, the Bureau of Mines, to estimate demand and to suggest production quotas for the major oil fields. With these as a basis for discussion, the co-operating states reached agreements on quotas and implemented them by state laws. Congress then enacted a federal law forbidding the transportation in interstate commerce of oil produced and shipped in contravention of state laws.[20] The oil-producing industry is, in many respects, unique, and the severity of the crisis it underwent was due to a fortuitous combination of circumstances. Yet, other illustrations can be given to show that federations are pushed to expedients of this kind under the conditions of a complex interdependent economy.

Interstate Trade Barriers. Another instance of the difficulties that beset the unified national economy in the federation is the rise of trade barriers be-

[20] Cf. Joseph E. Kallenbach, *Federal Coöperation with the States under the Commerce Clause* (Ann Arbor: University of Michigan Press, 1942), pp. 325-31.

tween the states. These trade barriers are facilitated, although not entirely caused by, the extending regulation of economic life by state governments. They run counter to one of the basic purposes of federal union. As already noted, one of the primary aims of the federal unions of the United States and Canada was to create a great free-trade area, and both constitutions con tain provisions forbidding the states to erect barriers against the trade of other states.

In recent years, particularly in the depression decade 1930–39, state govern-ments in both countries resorted to a variety of devices designed to protect home producers against competition from producers in other states. In considerable measure it was a phenomenon of the depression. To the extent that the national economy failed to work satisfactorily, the states were tempted to try to find viable state economies within their own boundaries. The movement assumed much more significant proportions in the United States than in Canada. Much of the Canadian population is found in clusters in relatively small areas, and many of the clusters are separated by great distances and geographical barriers, which limit interprovincial trade. Furthermore, Canada has concentrated a large part of its economic efforts on production of a few products for the international market. Interprovincial trade in Canada is not nearly as significant as interstate trade in the United States, and there is correspondingly less temptation to seek palliatives for economic distress by interstate trade barriers. Illustration is therefore drawn from the experience of the United States.

RESTRICTIONS. The hampering restrictions employed by the states take a multitude of forms. The frank levying of imports or duties on goods coming from other states is forbidden by the Constitution, and therefore barriers to trade have to be masked under the guise of laws that the states have power to enact. One of the most common has been the use of the state taxing power to levy higher rates of taxes on imported products than on native products, or to apply special taxes on non-resident persons or corporations doing busi-ness in the state. For example, some states with an important dairy industry have tried in this way to limit the sale of oleomargarine manufactured in other states. Many states impose a discriminatory tax on imported liquors. Some states impose special taxes on chain stores and higher license fees on dealers who handle imported products.

All states maintain a variety of laws generally acknowledged to be necessary for the protection of 'public health and safety.' Many states have framed and/or administered these regulations in such a way as to discriminate against imports from other states. Laws requiring the inspection of milk and dairy herds have been applied so as to exclude milk produced in other states. Laws providing for inspection of and, if necessary, quarantine on plants, fruit, nursery stock, and livestock to prevent the spread of pests and disease have also been applied at times so as to exclude imports from other states. Economic protection masquerades as biological protection. State laws requiring the grading and labeling of products to protect purchasers against fraud or inferior quality have been framed or applied in such a manner as to prejudice imports from other states.

Sometimes the discrimination thought to be involved in the administration of such laws is largely imaginary or unavoidable. In any event, many of the trade barriers erected in the states have originated as retaliatory measures against discriminations, real or imagined. There has been much mutual re-crimination between states over laws of this kind, something that tends to spread into other aspects of their relationships.

Those discussed above are but a few of the many kinds of trade restrictions that have been employed by some or other of the states from time to time. Some of the devices employed are no doubt unconstitutional and can be—and have been—attacked in the courts, with varying degrees of success.[21] Others can be curbed by Congress acting under the interstate commerce clause of the Constitution—in the realm of labor regulation, for one. But states acting singly cannot deal with the situation. It was regarded as suffi-ciently serious to bring representatives of most of the states together in the National Conference on Interstate Trade Barriers in 1939. Following the Conference, the states made a co-operative attack on the abuse and suc-ceeded in halting the movement toward still more irritating trade barriers and in securing the repeal of some of those already existing.[22] The experience with trade barriers provides another illustration of the way in which the states in a federal system fall foul of one another nowadays, and of the need for vigilant co-operative action.

There are many matters in which all governments should act in concert and unison. Failure to do so causes friction and inefficiency. To take a Canadian example, the Dominion government and its agencies control rail-

[21] For example, see *Mintz* v. *Baldwin,* 289 U.S. 346 (1933)—upheld; but *Minnesota* v. *Barber,* 136 U.S. 313 (1890)—struck down.
[22] On the general subject of trade barriers, see F. Eugene Melder, 'Trade Barriers between States,' *Annals of the American Academy of Political and Social Science,* ccvii (1940), 54–61. This volume of the *Annals* contains a number of articles bearing on the subject matter of the present chapter.

way rates and also meet the deficit on the operations of the publicly owned Canadian National Railways. The Canadian National Railways carry about half the total Canadian railway traffic, and in normal times the deficits on its operations are substantial. The provinces build the highways and determine, through motor licenses and gasoline tax, the conditions on which motor carriers can use them. For the past three decades or more the provinces have, in effect, been subsidizing motor carriers by failing to tax them heavily enough to cover their proportionate share of the cost of construction and upkeep of highways. Motor carriers take advantage of the low costs of operation to take business away from the railways and thus to increase the deficits on, and the necessary Dominion government subsidies to, the Canadian National Railways. Such a situation argues for a single co-ordinated policy of regulating all transportation by rail or road. This can be had only in one of two ways. Either all governments must co-operate closely in the matter, or all authority over the regulations of these forms of transport must be transferred to the federal government.

METHODS OF CONSULTATION AND CO-OPERATION

Methods and organs of consultation and co-operation have been developing over a period of years in both the United States and Canada. In Canada they are still in rudimentary form, going little beyond informal consultation between governments and government officials and occasional Dominion-provincial conferences on critical issues. The conferences often come to little because the governments have not established secretariats to accumulate and analyze data and to prepare for the work of the conferences. Delegates who come to conferences inadequately briefed on the matters to be settled hesitate to agree on anything because they are not in a position to estimate the consequences of any agreement they might make. The United States has gone further in developing methods and organs of consultation; but even here a crying need exists for more knowledge about the facts concerning the number and nature of intergovernmental relationships and the sources and extent of the frictions that appear.

The Interstate Compact. One method for co-operation between the states in the United States is the interstate compact. Article I, section 10, by implication authorizes the states, with the consent of Congress, to make compacts with and among each other. For half a century now, the compact has been used with reasonable success in dealing with matters that can be settled once for all, or for long periods of time, and do not require frequent reconsideration in the light of changing circumstances. By far the greater number of the approximately seventy interstate compacts, entered into since the end of World War II, have dealt with boundary disputes, the regulation of boundary waters, interstate rivers, harbors, and bridges and highways speeding violations. The giant Port of New York Authority, created by action of the legislatures of New York and New Jersey in 1921, and now staffed by 4500 employees, is one of the most successful examples of such an interstate compact.[23] One out of every four of the 13,500,000 residents of the port district of New York City, Northern New Jersey, and environs is supported, directly or indirectly, by the waterborne commerce handled in the huge port area, and about 14,000,000 overseas and domestic air travelers use the Authority's three airports. In 1963 the Authority operated a total of 24 bridges, tunnels, piers, air, truck, train, and other terminals. At the end of the preceding fiscal year its investment in these was circa $1250 million, with an equity in these facilities of approximately $600 million.

Uniform State Laws. There are numerous bodies in the United States devoting some or all of their efforts to securing uniformity in state laws on particular topics. Of these, the National Conference of Commissioners on Uniform State Laws has perhaps the longest record of sustained activity. The members of the Conference are, in a sense, representatives of state governments, and they have agreed upon and drafted many uniform laws on various subjects, which they then recommend to state legislatures. Many states have adopted one or more of these laws, but few such laws have been adopted in all states. The greatest success has been achieved with laws that are interpreted and enforced by the judiciary, laws relating to such matters as negotiable instruments, warehouse receipts, sale of goods, and court procedure. There has been much less success in getting uniformity in laws that require extensive use of the administrative process in their enforcement, i.e. in their interpretation and application by the executive branch.

In any event, where use of the administrative process is involved, it is not sufficient to get state legislatures to adopt uniform laws. Where officials have

---

[23] Others among the better-known interstate agencies, established by interstate compacts, are: the Pecos River Commission; the Atlantic States Fisheries Commission; the Ohio River Valley Water Sanitary Commission; the Interstate Oil Compact Commission; the Delaware River Basin Commission; and the Southern Regional Educational Board. See Richard H. Leach and Redding H. Sugg, Jr., *The Administration of Interstate Compacts* (Baton Rouge: Louisiana State University Press, 1959).

a discretionary power to make rules and decisions and are relied on generally for enforcement, administration sets the measure of the law. Neither uniformity nor effective co-operation can be had without frequent consultation between state executives, or at least between those state officials concerned with particular subjects such as the regulation of insurance companies. Numerous associations of state officials such as the National Association of Supervisors of State Banking, The National Convention of Insurance Commissioners, and The American Association of Motor Vehicle Administrators have been formed to discuss the common or related problems of their members. These associations have made some progress in interstate co-operation at the administrative level, subject always to the limits imposed by political considerations.

Council of State Governments. Because both administrative and political considerations are always involved and must be considered together, the most hopeful development in interstate co-operation is the Council of State Governments organized in 1935. A General Assembly of the Council composed of delegates representing both state legislatures and executives meets every second year to discuss both legislative and administrative questions. The Council has established a secretariat which is continuously engaged in research and in the publication of bulletins on the problems of state governments. The Council has also been successful in persuading most of the states to establish permanent commissions on interstate co-operation. From time to time the Council calls conferences on particular problems. The National Conference on Interstate Trade Barriers referred to above was so called. The Conference, and the influence of the commissions on interstate co-operation, were effective in checking the alarming growth of trade barriers.

The movement has gone on to promote the establishment of interstate commissions on particular subjects of common concern. These commissions are composed of representatives of the states that have agreed to co-operate in searching for a solution. While such interstate commissions are still few in number, they have made considerable progress in dealing with the matters they have attacked. Outstanding examples are the Interstate Commission on Conflicting Taxation, which has eliminated some of the confusion in state tax laws and procedures, and the Interstate Commission on Crime, which has tried to secure interstate co-operation in the enforcement of the criminal law of the several states.

These are some of the methods being used to get uniform or co-operative action by the states.[24] The vigor and success of the work of the Council of State Governments show that there is still a determination to make federalism work and still resourcefulness in finding ways and means. By bringing the states together to find solutions for common problems without abdicating to the federal government, the Council has established a counterpoise to the strong centralizing tendencies of the day.

Federal-State Co-operation. Illustrations have already been given to show that, in some matters, interstate co-operation is not enough. Federal-state co-operation is also needed. It is often found that power to regulate some particular aspect of economic life is divided by the Constitution between the federal and the state governments. Unless the governments concerned agree on legislation and administration, there is likely to be confusion and conflict in the regulation. To give precise illustrations would require exposition of the complexities of the distribution of powers under the Constitution as interpreted by the courts. It will suffice here to indicate some of the methods of federal-state co-operation in use in the United States,[25] many of which have been used to a lesser degree in Canada. It must be remembered that in neither country has the co-operation achieved been adequate to the growing need.

Federal statutes sometimes adopt the relevant provisions of state law as the federal law to be applied in that state. The so-called *fair trade laws* represent an example, resulting in the Miller-Tydings and McGuire Acts of 1937 and 1952, respectively. State laws often adopt the relevant provisions of federal laws or regulations in the same way. In the New Deal era, and later in World War II, many state laws were enacted to facilitate federal laws and policies for promoting economic recovery and the war effort, respectively. Federal and state administrative agencies and officials have co-operated in such fields as railway regulation, vehicular traffic, and enforcement of food and drug legislation. Sometimes attempts are made to fuse the administration of federal and state laws on a particular matter by making state officials federal agents for administering the federal part of the activity, and vice versa.

CO-OPERATIVE FEDERALISM. The full range of the devices of interstate and federal-state co-operation, of which examples have been given here, is some-

---

[24] For more extended treatments of interstate co-operation, see, among others, W. Brooke Graves, *American State Government,* 4th ed. (Boston: D. C. Heath Co., 1953), ch. xxiv.

[25] For detailed discussion, see Kallenbach, op. cit.; Graves, loc. cit. ch. xxv; and the *Report of the Commission on Intergovernmental Relations,* op. cit.

times described as the new co-operative federalism in contrast to the older federalism, in which state and federal governments went their own separate ways on most matters. The meshing of governmental action so far secured in this way is admitted to be inadequate, but its further development and improvement are put forward as the only alternative to massive centralization under the federal government. There is little doubt that this is true. The great increase in the activities of governments is the main cause of the need for intensive intergovernmental co-operation, and there is certainly no reason to expect a decline in the functions of government. So, if co-operative action does not prove to be adequate in particular fields, the alternative is to confer full authority in such fields on the federal government. Because the Canadian provinces could not get together for concerted action in establishing provincial unemployment insurance schemes, they finally accepted an amendment to the British North America Act transferring full constitutional authority over this subject to the Dominion. Some are disposed to think that co-operative federalism is subject to so many frictions and paralyzing delays as to put very severe limits on its development.

It is plausible to think that if a single government is put in control of a particular subject, it will be able to work out a unified, coherent policy. Reasons will be suggested later for thinking that this is too optimistic a view if wholesale centralization were resorted to, and that therefore the utmost effort should be put into making co-operative devices effective. It must be stated, however, that steady co-operation of all or most of the governments in the federation over an extended period is very difficult to maintain. Ultimately, all co-operative enterprises of governments are political matters and cannot be shielded from the impact of politics. Each government, whether state or federal, necessarily responds to the view of the public interest held by the ruling political party or by the combinations of interests that for the time being have the preponderant influence in the councils of governments. Different parties and different combinations of interests may hold power in the different governments at the same time. Diverging conceptions of the public interest are likely to pull some of the meshing gears apart from time to time.

THE TREND TOWARD CENTRALIZATION

Because the fields in which the various governments in the federation come across one another are now so numerous, and because difficulties, delays, and uncertainties always beset co-operative action, some have concluded that federalism is almost obsolete. Because the separate states no longer have an independent economic life of their own, conditions beyond their control may at any time make their independence a sham. When this happens, they become dependent on the federal government. Whether or not this is correct, it is at least clear that the unified national economy in the conditions of widespread governmental activity and regulation tends toward political centralization.

Acting by themselves, the states could do little to overcome the serious depression of the 1930's. In the depths of the economic crisis, almost everyone, both in the United States and Canada, looked to the federal governments, echoing Will Rogers' admonition to the President to do *something*—'even if it is only to burn the White House!' [26] The New Deal brought a tremendous upsurge of federal government action in the United States. The national government thus undertook large new activities or greatly expanded its former activities in relation to such matters as transport, public utilities, banking and credit, stock and commodity exchanges, labor-capital relations, agricultural production, drought relief, housing, social security, and conservation. Some of the functions undertaken were later abandoned, but the balance have every appearance of being permanent additions to the work of the federal government—regardless of which of the two major parties happens to be in power at any given time.

Government Regulation. The persistent centralizing movement could be halted if we could reverse the trend toward ever-greater governmental functions. But the present-day conviction is that business and social life generally must be extensively regulated by governments. When business is organized on a nation-wide scale with many concerns operating in every state, and when labor unions are national, if not international, in scope, the argument for nation-wide regulation of business and labor-capital relations is very strong. Such facts as these reveal the significance of the enlarged interpretation of federal powers by the Supreme Court of the United States— and by Congress, for that matter. It is a response to a need that is felt in Canada as well.

Centralizing Tendencies in Public Finance. Another urge to centralization is found in public finance. Here again the reasons are the same: the unification of the economy and the multiplying of governmental functions. In both

[26] Quoted by Ernest S. Griffith, *The Impasse of Democracy* (New York: Harrison-Hilton, 1939), p. 13.

Canada and the United States many of the most expensive of the new functions of government were allotted to the states by the distribution of powers in the constitutions. For example, highways, education, and the bulk of the social services were conceived to be their responsibilities. But at the same time it was thought to be contrary to the interests of the country as a whole that there should be wide disparities in the number and quality of these services in the several states.

Inequalities between States. Unfortunately, the capacities of the different states to raise the revenues needed to maintain these services at a uniform level vary greatly. Some can maintain a high level of services at moderate rates of taxation while others cannot do so even at very high rates of taxation. That is because some states have prospered while others remain chronically poor relations. In most cases the plight of the latter is largely due to the poverty or lack of variety of their natural resources. Their condition is aggravated, however, by centralizing tendencies in the economic system.

Within the free trade area that the federation maintains, industry and commerce tend to locate in the areas richest in wealth and resources. In 1962, for example, the four states of the Middle Atlantic Region of the United States—New York, New Jersey, Pennsylvania, and Delaware—earned 24 per cent of the nation's income. Manufacturing gravitates to the areas with the best resources of raw materials, industrial skill, and power in form of coal or electricity. Yet the manufacturing industries distribute their products to, and draw their profits from, all parts of the country. The number of products that are nationally advertised is an index of the scope of this business. A similar centralization occurs in the distribution of products. Chain stores and mail-order houses with head offices in a particular state do a nation-wide business, drawing to one point profits that formerly were made and kept by local merchants all over the country. Also, the financial institutions—banks, insurance firms, and trust and loan companies—located in particular areas do business in all areas.

The net result is the pooling of wealth in the states already blessed by nature with rich resources or strategic position, enabling the governments of these states to tap the pools by corporation tax, income tax, and inheritance and estate taxes, while the other state governments are denied comparable access to them. Thus the difficulties of the poorer states in finding tax revenues to support all the activities expected of them are intensified.

Federal Grants-in-Aid. There is one government, however, that has ready access by taxation to all pools of wealth in the country, wherever found. That, of course, is the federal, or national, government. The poorer states, which find it difficult to finance their activities, and other interests that want a high level of government services, are tempted to argue that they have an inherent right to be 'taken care of' by the national government. When that government has collected large funds, so goes the argument of the poorer states, it should either *make grants to the several states,* enabling each of them to maintain the desired level of government services, *or it should itself take over from the states* the more costly functions of government and administer them.

CONSEQUENCES. When either course is adopted, it enhances the importance of the federal government and diminishes the autonomy and independence of the state governments. It is almost inevitable that some federal control will accompany the grants, as well as assistance and co-operation. If the sums are large in amount, as they usually must be to accomplish their purpose, the authority that takes the odium of collecting them is unlikely to give a completely free hand to other authorities in spending them. Control is usually secured by earmarking the grants for specific purposes such as highways, airport and hospital construction, public health services, old-age pensions, child benefit, or unemployment relief. To earn the grant the state governments must comply with the specifications laid down by the federal government covering the particular activity that is being aided.[27] Techniques for federal supervision include periodic reports, audits, and inspections, in addition to the basic specifications.

In the United States and Canada such *grants-in-aid,* as they are called, have been in use for many years, aiding various activities carried on by the state and provincial governments.[28] At the end of 1961 federal grants in the United States made up about 18.5 per cent of the total revenues of the state governments! These ranged all the way from 7.2 per cent in New Jersey to 39.8 per cent in Alaska! From a total of $5.5 *million* in 1915, federal grants-in-aid to the states had risen to $6.5 *billion* in 1962. There were times in Canada in the 1930's when the federal grants-in-aid comprised approximately one-third of the provincial revenues. In some measure then, depending on their amount, these grants require the state governments to dance to the tune of

[27] See the *Report of the Commission on Intergovernmental Relations,* op. cit. ch. v, and *Federal Grants-in-Aid:* Report of the Committee on Federal Grants-in-Aid (Chicago: Council of State Governments, 1949).
[28] In Canada these grants-in-aid are not to be confused with the unconditional Dominion subsidies to the provinces provided for by the British North America Act, sect. 118.

the federal government, which selects the pieces to be played and prescribes the tempo and manner of execution.

ALLOCATION OF GRANTS-IN-AID. This is not a serious interference with state independence as long as the aided activities are only a few of those in which the state governments are engaged. However, grants-in-aid have not thus far been signally successful in reducing the disparities between the financial positions of the various state governments. Generally speaking, the principles on which the amounts of grants allocated to the several states are calculated do not provide sufficiently for discrimination in favor of the poorer states. Common forms are the *proportionate* grants under which the more a state can afford to spend of its own on the particular service, the more federal assistance it will secure. The poorer states can rarely resist the offer of a proportionate grant and they divert some of their revenues from unaided to aided services in order to earn the federal grant. State budgets thus are often distorted. However, the 1956 highway construction bill provided for a 90 per cent federal grant, with the states' contributions limited to a mere 10 per cent.

A strong body of opinion exists which presses for the other alternative— that of transferring some of the costly functions now performed by state governments to the federal government to be administered as well as financed by it. Such a course eases the financial difficulties of the governments of the poorer states, and puts them in a better position to carry the functions that remain to them. In the past thirty years it has been followed in the allocation of sole responsibility for several of the new social security measures to the federal government. In so far as it is followed, it adds to the power and prestige of the federal government. But when in 1958 President Eisenhower proposed to abandon some federal government programs, notably in the financing of vocational education, in return for a 60 per cent cut of the federal tax 'take' on telephone charges, the vast majority of the states objected vehemently.

THE TAX CREDIT DEVICE. The fiscal powers of the federal government are not entirely centralizing in tendency. The difficulties in the way of any one state's undertaking to provide unemployment compensation have already been noted. By the use of a device known as the *tax credit,* the federal government in the United States was able to remove this difficulty. Under the Unemployment Compensation sector of the Social Security Act of 1935, Congress levied a tax on the payrolls of all employers in certain specified industries across the country. It also provided that by far the greater part of this tax would be rebated to employers in those states which established an unemployment compensation scheme complying with certain federal requirements.

In effect, a state that refused to set up such a scheme would be heavily penalized for its refusal, and all states quickly adopted unemployment compensation laws. While this is almost dictation by the federal government to states that did not want to provide unemployment compensation, it is, at the same time, an enabling provision for those that wanted to do so but were restrained by the lack of assurance that other states would do likewise. The capacity of some states to meet what they consider to be serious problems can be enlarged by use of the fiscal powers of the federal government.

Some of the conditions attached to federal grants-in-aid may have a similar long-run influence. When a federal grant to assist a particular state activity is made on the condition—as it is under the Social Security Act of 1935— that the state officials who administer the activity have certain qualifications and be appointed by merit, improvements in state administration are likely to result. Federal guidance and leadership such as has developed in the social security program in the United States, of which more will be said in a subsequent chapter, may help state governments to help themselves.

Centralization by Constitutional Amendment? Yet the net result of the tendencies in public finance, as in economic and social regulation, is to aggrandize the federal governments at the expense of the states. If these tendencies continue, and if they accelerate as they have in the past fifty years, the maintenance of a genuine federal system with its separate and exclusive spheres of governmental power may become impossible. In fact, there are numerous reasons for caution in supporting or acquiescing in these tendencies, which will be considered later. For the moment, it is important to remember that this centralization cannot take place merely because an electoral majority, and Congress or Parliament, happen in be in favor of it. In many cases the written constitution stands in the way, ensuring to the separate states the sphere of power that they presently possess. Certain proposals for enlarging the power and responsibilities of the federal government require amendments to the constitution, and such amendments are not easily carried through. There are always elements in the community that resist, even if they are no more than the state and provincial politicians who do not want to see the range of matters under their direct control narrowed. The slogans *states' rights* and *provincial autonomy* continue to have a strong ring—even if they are of doubtful substance.

Is Federalism Obsolete?

Need for Concerted Action. It has been suggested already that in some quarters federalism is regarded as obsolete. In many of the problems with which governments are expected to deal, no one government in the federation can act effectively alone. The attempt to act in concert involves so much discussion and delay that many problems are not met at all. What each government does affects the conditions facing the others. They often work at cross-purposes and this adds to the friction. Politicians are not above using the distribution of powers to evade responsibility. To get elected to one of the legislatures in the federation they promise to do things that the Constitution reserves to other legislatures, and then try to excuse themselves by blaming the Constitution or the other governments in the federation. Therefore it is urged that no re-allocation of powers will sufficiently moderate the friction, the frustration, and the evasion of responsibility. Those who hold to this view want the states to be abolished.

Claims of Expensive Duplication. Associated with this conclusion are others who hold that there is a great deal of overlapping and duplication among the several governments, adding unjustifiably to the ever-mounting cost of government. They point to the fact that federal departments of labor, agriculture, health, and so on are duplicated by state and provincial departments of the same name. They say that a country that has to support eleven or fifty-one governments is ridiculously overgoverned and that an immense reduction of government expenditures could be had by abandoning federalism altogether.

Whatever may be the case for abandoning federalism in favor of a unitary state, it cannot be rested on this latter ground. The numerous departments of labor, agriculture, and health are not mainly engaged in duplicating one another's efforts. Some duplication there is, but its cost is negligible relative to the total expenditures of all governments in the federation. At any rate, this was the considered conclusion of the Sirois Commission in Canada, which made a careful investigation of the charges of duplication and overlapping in the several governments in Canada.[29] The Commission on Intergovernmental Relations came to a similar conclusion in the United States in 1955.[30]

[29] *Report of the Royal Commission on Dominion-Provincial Relations,* 1940, vol. ii, p. 183.
[30] *The Report of the Commission on Intergovernmental Relations,* op. cit. Introduction and Part i.

Furthermore, the sums that would be saved by abolishing state and provincial governments are such a small fraction of total expenditures of governments in the federation that it would not be worth the upheaval involved. The reason for this is that the cost of upkeep of legislatures, of the internal housekeeping of government departments, and of the salaries of civil servants is but a small part of the current expenditures of governments nowadays. The great outlays of state governments are in regulating community life and in providing expensive services demanded by the public. The only really effective way to lower the cost of government is to abolish some of its numerous activities. As long as these activities are to be maintained, the abolition of ten or fifty legislatures and governmental establishments would not give any very substantial relief to the taxpayer.

The Lessons of War. The question of whether the sprawling, poorly co-ordinated federal system is now obsolete, a mastodon blundering about in a streamlined age, is not so easily answered. The first consideration to be kept constantly in mind is that the prime cause of the present confusion in federal systems is the greatly augmented scope of governmental action. If governmental management of the life of the people in peacetime had stayed at the level reached in World War II, there is little doubt that federalism would be obsolete. The federal governments ran the war and decided almost everything connected with it.

The state governments remained in a condition of suspended animation with no substantial sphere of independent initiative. They continued to perform most of the functions they had performed at the outbreak of war and cooperated in the war effort, but decisions at Washington and Ottawa left them little independent choice concerning what they would do. Peacetime governmental operations of wartime magnitude would equally have to be directed by a single central government. State and provincial governments might remain as agents for carrying out the decisions of the federal governments, but they would cease to be principles operating on their own account.

The Continuing Diversity of a Continental Country. However, if governmental activities can be stabilized at somewhere around their immediate prewar scope, there is still a great deal to be said for a federal system. The United States and Canada each cover half a continent. Few of the successful unitary states have covered an area greater than that covered by one of the larger states or provinces. Britain's 94,000 square miles, for example, correspond to the area of Oregon; France's 212,000 to Manitoba. It is extremely difficult for a single government to carry out a wide range of activities over half a continent and carry them on effectively.

The difficulty does not arise merely from the size of the territory; in fact, modern means of transport and communication are overcoming the physical limitations of time and distance. It arises rather out of the *diversity of conditions* that mark the different parts of a continental country. It was pointed out early in the chapter that the conditions of life and the character of the people vary in the different states at the time of union. These differences are lessened as a common life is shared within the union over a considerable period of time, but they still remain highly significant.

REGIONALISM. The significant differences have become, in most instances, *regional* rather than state or provincial in character. It would not be contended that present-day differences between the conditions of life in New Hampshire and Vermont, Georgia and Alabama, New Brunswick and Nova Scotia, Alberta and Saskatchewan are very marked. But there are distinctive differences between the New England region and the deep south, between the maritime region and the prairie region in Canada. The United States and Canada are made up of a number of distinct regions. The people in each of these regions have common problems and a common outlook on many matters, and their problems and outlook differ markedly from those which form the identifying characteristics of other regions. This is the point made by those who argue in the United States for the amalgamation of groups of states under a smaller number of regional governments. They are not arguing against federalism *per se,* but for a drastic revision of its territorial pattern.[31]

It may be that some such revision will prove to be necessary if federalism is to be rescued from its present difficulties. However, there is no large support for it at present and no agreement at all on what states, or parts of states, should be combined in the new regions. Only one thing is obvious: provinces like Quebec, which, as they stand, are distinct cultural entities, would have to remain as they are. Whatever the outcome of suggestions of this kind, the important point for present purposes is the continuing diversity of conditions in a continental country.

Federalism: Ideals and Facts. Attempting to please all factions interested in the maintenance and preservation of the federal structure in the United

---

[31] For example, see William Yandell Elliott, *The Need for Constitutional Reform* (New York: McGraw-Hill, 1935), pp. 191–8.

States, the Commission on Intergovernmental Relations viewed the problems of federalism in the light of these ideals in 1955:

> Leave to private initiative all the functions that citizens can perform privately; use the level of government closest to the community for all public functions it can handle; utilize co-operative intergovernmental arrangements where appropriate to attain economical performance and popular approval; reserve national action for residual participation where State and local governments are not fully adequate, and for the continuing responsibilities that only the National Government can undertake.[32]

But the naked facts are that it has been the national government that has had to deliver the 'goods,' time and time again. No matter how well-intentioned the several component parts may have been, they have frequently been incapable of performance.

This is by no means astonishing. In No. 17 of *The Federalist* papers, one of his many shrewdly analytical pieces of political practice and theory, Alexander Hamilton went to the heart of the matter some 175 years ago:

> Upon the same principle that a man is more attached to his family than to his neighborhood, to his neighborhood than to the community at large, the people of each State would be apt to feel a stronger bias towards their local governments than towards their government of the Union; unless the force of that principle should be destroyed by a much better administration of the latter.

Broadly speaking, in a very real sense the Commission on Intergovernmental Relations was primarily confronted with the twentieth-century facts of life adverted to in Hamilton's last sentence.

DECENTRALIZATION THROUGH FEDERALISM

If a continental country like the United States or Canada were ruled by a single central government, that government would not be able to adjust all the laws it would have to make and administer to the varying conditions of the different regions. Laws—and even rules and regulations made under them—have to be framed in general terms. When we discuss the civil service we shall see that, under democratic government at least, there is a general

[32] *The Report of the Commission on Intergovernmental Relations,* op. cit. p. 6.

insistence that laws should be administered uniformly with very little discretionary adaptation to special circumstances. There are deep underlying reasons for this characteristic of administration.

In fact, uniformity of law and uniform enforcement of it are highly desirable as long as the laws are aimed merely at generally acknowledged anti-social conduct. The definition of murder and its prescribed punishment should be the same everywhere and should be enforced impartially. But when government is regulating everyday life in great detail, diversity of rule and application to meet special circumstances is necessary. This is the reason for the development of the administrative process, which, as will be demonstrated later, imposes a considerable strain on the constitutional safeguards of liberal democracy.

Traffic codes, old-age pensions, the content of the public-school curriculum should vary according to the general standard of living and the cultural and economic conditions of different areas. If general laws on these and a multitude of other matters were enacted and enforced uniformly across the country, there would be deep dissatisfaction over them almost everywhere. Uniformity in these circumstances is sterile, or disrupting, or both.

The reason for adopting federalism in the first place was to arrest the reach of a distant government that is not trusted to take account of unique circumstances in different areas. As long as the federation with its autonomous states continues to exist, the legislatures of these states adapt the laws, partially at least, to the special circumstances of particular areas. Consequently there is less need to rely on the administrative process and less strain on the constitutional safeguards than there would be if one central legislature made all the laws for the country.

Half a continent cannot be governed by a highly centralized machine in Ottawa or Washington. It would be necessary to try to decentralize administration by establishing regional offices under the direction of officials with discretion to adjust the laws to regional conditions. If any proof of this is required, it is to be found in the growing recognition in Britain, a unitary country, of the need for regional authorities that will stand midway between the municipal governments and the central government. Cautious experiments in this direction were begun during World War II.

If such expedients are desirable in a tight little island like Britain with a homogeneous population and no great diversity of conditions, they would be inevitable under the continental conditions of government in North America. If the decentralization of government which federalism provides were abandoned, it would become immediately necessary to try to restore it in another form by setting up regional branches of the national government.

Excessive Rigidity a Weakness of Centralization. The difficulty is, that as long as governments are kept under control by the governed, there must be fairly narrow limits to discretionary adaptation of laws to special circumstances. The regional branches to which the central government would delegate some discretionary power could not be given enough discretion to make adequate adjustment. They could not begin to respond to the unique aspects of life in a particular region as fully as do the present state governments, each of which must follow the temper of its own particular electorate and does not need to concern itself with what is being done in other parts of the country except in a limited range of matters.

The inability of the regional offices of the national government to adjust uniform nation-wide laws to varying regional conditions is not the only difficulty. Many problems with which governments are expected to deal are peculiar to a particular region and do not require action on a national scale. The national government would either deal with these inadequately or ignore them entirely.

There are even now some matters over which federal governments have sole authority but which are of prime importance in only one or two states. For example, the Dominion Parliament in Canada has exclusive authority over seacoast fisheries. This is necessary because seacoast fisheries involve international negotiation and treaties that the national government alone can undertake. However, the only provinces with a vital interest in seacoast fisheries, in the sense that they are a basis of livelihood of a substantial part of the population, are Newfoundland, Nova Scotia, and British Columbia. The latter two have complained sharply that the Dominion government neglects the fisheries and misunderstands the problems of the industry.

In the past, at any rate, there has been much substance in the complaint. If one compares the range of services provided for agriculture and the amount of scientific knowledge brought to bear on agricultural problems by the Dominion with what the Dominion has done to assist the development of the fishing industry, the disparity is so marked as to require explanation. There are a number of explanations, but most of them turn on one central consideration: Agriculture is an important industry in every province and can claim at every stage a livelier interest and a larger sympathy at Ottawa than fisheries. What is a vital concern in all provinces will always have a prior claim to that which is of serious interest to one or two provinces only.

Farmers will always have more votes in Dominion elections than fisher-men.

Such a priority is not, in general, a just ground for criticism. But the fact that it exists, and is likely to continue to exist, does suggest that there should be, in a country of great diversities, state—or regional—governments Wher ever possible these governments should have control over matters of unique concern to their own areas and should have a substantial sphere of independent action. Where this is so, the electorates to which the governments are responsible will see to it that vital regional interests are not neglected. Energies will be harnessed to the tasks in hand and not exhausted in futile efforts to get distant governments to do what needs to be done.

So while there are some spheres in which federalism is inefficient, there are more in which decentralized autonomous governments are necessary to efficiency. On these grounds alone it might be concluded that federalism is not obsolete, although particular federal systems may badly need revision. The principal consideration in favor of federalism, however, has not yet been stated.

Federalism and Democracy

In Canada and the United States, with their marked sectional differences, it is extremely doubtful whether democratic government could be maintained at all except through the device of federalism. Democracy has been defined as government by consent. Probably the greatest problem in a democracy is to construct electoral majorities that can agree on what the government should do—a problem that has plagued the unitary governments of continental Europe more or less incessantly. The problem grows more acute as the number of decisions to be made in the political arenas increases. If all these decisions had to be made in the national arena, so many diverging sectional interests would be brought face to face on so many issues that it would be impossible to get a majority in the electorate or in the legislature that would agree on how all these issues were to be dealt with. Federal, or national, politics in the United States and Canada have been immensely simplified by the fact of a number of lesser political arenas, the states and provinces, in which a great many issues are settled without ever rising to the level of national politics at all.

Reconciling Unity and Diversity. It is not merely, or even mainly, that political squabbles are decentralized in the 'insulated chambers' of the states.

A lot of little fights may be as serious as one big one. The great triumph of federalism is that many matters that would cause the sharpest conflict if they were thrown into national politics cause little dissension when dealt with separately in each state. Federalism enables many regional interests and idiosyncrasies to have their own way in their own areas without ever facing the necessity of reconciliation with other regional interests. Individuals identify themselves with particular regional interests and find in them a satisfying expression of many facets of their personalities. *Federalism is a device for combining unity and diversity in accordance with the requirements of liberal democratic ideals.* (But, of course, there are liberal democracies that have a *unitary* form—e.g., Britain and France—and dictatorships that, at least in theory, have a *federal* form—e.g., the Soviet Union.)

Even as things stand at present in America the clash of sectional interests in Congress is very marked. It helps greatly to explain why Congress often cannot reach a majority decision on what should be done in the national interest without *logrolling*—i.e. the famous practice of 'you vote for me and I'll vote for you.' If everything that is done by government in the United States had to be determined by Congress, Congress would exhibit far less unity of purpose than it does now—and that is little enough at times!

In Canada, the Dominion Parliament and government have been much blamed in the recent past for their failure to deal vigorously with serious matters such as the great depression of the 1930's. Their vacillation was not due merely to the constitutional limitations on the Dominion. It arose in part from the fact that deep cleavages among the Canadian people prevented them from producing electoral majorities that would support vigorous measures of a specific nature.

The clearest concrete illustration appears in the course of events in Canada in time of war. Twentieth-century wars are national enterprises which require the national government to regulate the most intimate details of life. Under the pressure of war, Canada, for the time being, almost becomes a unitary state. But even the fear of a common enemy is not enough to overcome the basic cultural diversity in the country. Most English-speaking Canadians rise almost spontaneously to support full participation in a war in which Britain is imperiled. French-speaking Quebec, on the other hand, is more deeply isolationist in basic feeling than the Middle West in the United States has ever been. Quebec and the rest of the country cannot go along together in prosecuting a total war without disagreements that threaten to create irreconcilable factions. Separatist movements spring from the fact that, in time of war, the common government asks everybody to agree about everything.

Abolition of the federal system would make what has been an expedient of war an everyday necessity. This would be disruptive in the extreme. While the war lasts, a number of divergencies of sectional interests are kept in check only by a recognition of the overwhelming necessity of presenting a common front to the enemy. Once the war is over, the check ceases to operate. If it were not for the federal system in Canada these divergencies would clash in the national political arena and convulse the country as does the conscription issue in time of war.

POLITICAL PARTIES. As we shall presently have occasion to point out, in the United States the national political parties are actually federations of state parties. National political parties in Canada are in a remarkably similar way federations of provincial parties. Each national party appeals to and gets support from persons and groups of diverse interests and attitudes across the country. Each manages to hold its heterogeneous following together because, up until now, national politics have been concerned principally with matters of general interest throughout the country and do not go to the heart of matters on which regional interests and attitudes diverge sharply. These latter matters are mostly within the purview of state and provincial politics. If, however, it were necessary within each national party to come to agreement on these divisive matters, the national parties would scarcely hold together. There is thus some ground for suggesting that the two-party system in national politics in the United States and Canada has been made possible by federalism and that if federalism goes, it will go too. If, as may properly be contended, democracy and the two-party system are closely related, it would follow that democracy and federalism also have intimate connections in countries of continental extent.

These are some of the reasons for suggesting a close connection between federalism and democracy. However, they fall short of conclusive proof. In any political situation, the factors involved are so numerous and so hard to estimate that all arguments and conclusions must be taken with a grain of salt. On the other hand, there does not appear to be any adequate ground for thinking that federalism is obsolete. It seems advisable to continue patching up the federal system. Any satisfactory patching, however, is likely to involve an increase in the powers of the federal government. There are a number of pressing problems of nation-wide scope that can only be dealt with adequately by action on a national scale.

Political Unification of Continental Areas. Also, when we say that people have come to think of themselves as Americans or Canadians as well as citizens of particular states or provinces, we mean that they have become conscious of sharing a wider range of common interests with all their fellow citizens throughout the country. It is natural that they should look to the national government to protect and further these interests.

As nationalism grows in strength, the particularism that marks the early stages of a federal system diminishes. But this point also must not be pressed too far. There is no agreement on how far nationalism has overcome particularism in the United States and Canada. In so far as history affords any guide, it suggests that the creation of genuinely united nations out of heterogeneous populations is a long, slow process.

CONTRASTS. Those who look at the record of the federal systems of the United States and Canada floundering in the difficulties over the past fifty years are often impatient with the long, slow process. Whether they are watching the exasperating disagreements of Dominion-Provincial conferences in Canada, or the confusion and seeming purposelessness of the United States Congress, they often make a comparison with the tidy system of government in Britain. They are inclined to forget, however, that *Britain is a small homogeneous country with a national unity matured over many hundreds of years,* and therefore not at all comparable with the continental diversity of the United States and Canada. The perspective would be corrected if a contrast were made with the continent of Europe as a whole, which has frequently dealt with continental political problems by the wasteful and inefficient processes of war. Alongside Europe, the federations of the United States and Canada seem not only tidy but also triumphs of civilized efficiency. Such untidiness as they exhibit is due to the fact that each is struggling with the political unification of a continental area.

The existence of numerous state and provincial governments in the United States and Canada gives to government, as a whole, a different character from that of Britain, and raises a number of special types of political problems from which British politics is free.

Another revealing contrast is that with the so-called federal system of the Soviet Union. The Soviet Union also governs a vast continental area. But Soviet federalism is a mask behind which lurks a centralized despotism— the time-honored method of ruling great imperial domains. The domain of the United States of America is of imperial magnitude. No one would claim that it has done full justice to the aspirations of all its areas and minorities. Indeed, a good case could be made for Professor Franz L. Neumann's contention that—by leaving the individual to the diverse and sometimes tender mercies of fifty different police systems, applying a variety of procedural and substantive standards except in those areas of freedom that have been 'nationalized' by the Supreme Court—'. . . the federal system may have speeded up inroads into the civil liberties rather than protecting them.'[33] The system has, however, done something unique in history for a state of this size. Save for one breakdown in the Civil War, it has made internal peace and order in its domain compatible with an extraordinary freedom for individuals and voluntary associations. As Mr. Justice Cardozo of the U. S. Supreme Court once put the matter, 'the Constitution was framed upon the theory that the peoples of the several states must sink or swim together, and that in the long run prosperity and salvation are in union and not in division.'[34] Canada has done the same on a smaller scale for a shorter time but under the added handicap of having to hold together English-speaking Protestants and French-speaking Roman Catholics, two large groups with widely divergent outlooks and aspirations.[35] Only peoples firmly attached to liberal democratic values could have done this. They could not have done it without the procedural device of federalism. The Soviet Union has maintained internal peace and order in its domain, but has done it at the expense of individual and group freedom.

Soviet Federalism

The Soviet Union is declared in the Constitution to be a voluntary federal union of a number of separate socialist republics, known as the Union of Soviet Socialist Republics. The government of the Union, which will be sketched briefly in succeeding chapters, is thus designed to be a common, or federal, government for common purposes, and these purposes are set out in the Constitution. There are fifteen union republics, hereafter called states, each of which has a separate government authorized to deal with all matters not specifically conferred on the federal government.[36]

[33] 'Federalism and Freedom: A Critique,' in Arthur W. Macmahon (Ed.), *Federalism Mature and Emergent* (Garden City, N. Y.: Doubleday & Co., 1955), p. 48.
[34] *Baldwin* v. *G. A. F. Seelig, Inc.,* 294 U.S. 511 (1935).
[35] To cite a petty case in point: in June 1962 the Roman Catholic school board of Trois Rivières, Quebec, returned a bill submitted in English by a Toronto electrical appliance firm. The board said that it was its policy to buy only from companies that submitted their accounts in French! (*The New York Times,* June 11, 1962.)
[36] Constitution of the U.S.S.R., Art. 13.

The Distribution of Powers. The powers expressly conferred on the federal government are very wide. They include the power to organize military defense against foreign enemies, decide the issues of war and peace, and determine the substance of foreign policy. Closely related to these functions is the power of 'safeguarding the security of the state' [37] against internal enemies. In a Communist system, the government with the longest reach must control the economy. The federal government accordingly has the power to administer the banks, control currency and credit, operate the transport and communications system and all other economic enterprises of national importance—whatever these may be. It has power to lay down the basic principles in education, public health, labor legislation, and the use of natural resources. It alone is empowered to allocate the taxes and revenues that are to be used to operate the state and local governments.[38] The budget for the entire country is thus drawn up by the central government!

These are the more important federal powers. Obviously they are much wider than the powers granted the federal government in the constitutions of the other major federalist countries we have discussed or mentioned, the United States, Canada, Australia, Switzerland, and West Germany.

The states in the Soviet Union have the residue of powers not specifically conferred on the federal government, and the Constitution declares that these powers shall be exercised independently by each state.[39] On paper, each state has the right to enter into diplomatic relations with foreign states and to establish its own military organization. Moreover, each is expressly given the right to secede from the U.S.S.R.[40]

Neither the American states or the Canadian provinces, nor any of the other subdivisions of the federal governments we have mentioned, have the power to enter into diplomatic relations with foreign nations or to secede. On the surface, therefore, the states of the Soviet Union appear to have a large degree of autonomy. And it is true that in *cultural* matters, such as the use of the native language and other native customs, there has been a very substantial autonomy. But aside from these cultural matters, the autonomy of the several states has been largely illusory, and Soviet federalism has little resemblance to the federalism of the United States and Canada and that of

[37] Ibid. Art. 14(i).
[38] See ibid. Art. 14, for the enumerated powers of the federal government.
[39] Ibid. Art. 15.
[40] Ibid. Art. 17.

the other major federal powers. Some of the reasons for this judgment may be briefly stated.

Illusory Nature of Soviet Federalism. First, the powers of the federal government of the U.S.S.R. are very wide, and many of them extremely vague, thus affording possibilities of expansion by interpretation. The distribution of powers is not interpreted by an impartial court, as—in varying degree— in the United States and Canada, Australia, and West Germany, *but by the federal government itself, and by those who, in practice, control the federal government, the leaders of the Communist party.* Moreover, the party dominates the governments of the fifteen states and ensures their subordination within the system—in the way it subordinates all other organization. The participation of the states in foreign policy and military activity is regulated by the directing principles laid down by the federal government.

Second, the formal right of secession given by the Constitution is denied in practice. Separatist agitation within the several states has been interpreted by the Soviet courts as a dangerous form of counter-revolutionary activity threatening the security of the Soviet state which the federal government is specifically authorized to safeguard. Also, as already noted, the federal government has the function of allocating the revenues on which the state governments depend for their operations. The power of the purse can be used, where it is so desired, to control the activities of the state.

Third, the federal government determines the economic plan and supervises its execution. Since the economic plan involves regulation and adjustment of almost every aspect of life, and the carrying out of the plan is the first imperative of Soviet life, the area in which the several states can have any assurance of being able to pursue independent policies of their own without regard to the dictates of the federal government is very small.

It should be added, however, that to make such extensive government action effective in a country of the size of the Soviet Union, there must be a high degree of administrative decentralization. So the governments of the several states—and other lesser governmental bodies as well—exercise wide authority in a great variety of matters and have a good deal of discretion in executing this authority—as long as their policies and decisions are in harmony with the general policy of the federal government and the top leaders of the party. The state governments, however, are essentially instruments for carrying out that general policy. Soviet federalism is not, in any significant sense, a mitigation of the overwhelming concentration of power at the top.

Changes. In 1957, Nikita S. Khrushchev, the Communist party boss, announced an over-all gradual revision of the Soviet system of industrial management. The plan, as adopted, divided the Russian Republic (R.S.F.S.R.), largest in the Soviet Union, into seventy economic units. The Ukraine was made up of eleven regions; Uzbekistan of four; Kazakhistan of nine; and the eleven other union republics each constituted a separate economic region. Economic councils were established in each of the 105 new industrial management regions—later reduced at first to 101 and, late in 1962, still further to forty—to direct industrial production and construction. The governments of the fifteen union republics have been given broader control over industrial planning and financing than ever before, aided by 'workers' advisory committees.' Some of the industrial and arms ministries at the national level were abolished and replaced by 'state technological committees'; others were 'drastically reorganized,' evidently a continuing process.

However, Khrushchev made quite clear that the central Soviet government was not relinquishing its key controls over the industrial system. The changes represented as much a 're' as a 'de' centralization. Central control is thus exercised by the *State Planning Commission,* which lays out annual and seven-year 'programs of economic development.' Ultimate financial power has been retained in Moscow. It is the central government that channels surpluses from rich areas into underdeveloped ones. Heavy and defense industries are being kept under centralized control—and these account for more than half of Soviet industrial output. In other words, while significant decentralization has been under way ever since 1957, overriding control still rests at the top, although evidently in altered form.

SUGGESTED REFERENCES FOR FURTHER READING

Anderson, W., *Intergovernmental Relations in Review* (U. of Minnesota, 1960).
———, C. Penniman, and E. W. Weidner, *Government in the Fifty States* (Holt, Rinehart, and Winston, 1960).
Beloff, M., *The American Federal Government* (Oxford, 1959).
Bowie, R. R., and C. J. Friedrich, *Studies in Federalism* (Little, Brown, 1954).
Codding, G. A., Jr., *The Federal Government of Switzerland* (Houghton Mifflin, 1961).
Commission on Intergovernmental Relations, *A Report to the President for Transmittal to the Congress* (U. S. Government Printing Office, 1955).
Dawson, R. M., *Democratic Government of Canada* (U. of Minnesota, 1949).
Elazar, D. J., *The American Partnership* (U. of Chicago, 1963).
Fesler, J. W., *Area and Administration* (U. of Alabama, 1949).
Gavit, B. C., *The Commerce Clause of the United States Constitution* (Principia, 1946).

Golay, J. F., *The Founding of the Federal Republic of Germany* (U. of Chicago, 1958).

Goldwin, R. A. (Ed.), *A Nation of States* (Rand McNally, 1963).

Graves, W. B. (Ed.), *Major Problems in State Constitutional Revision* (Public Adm. Sv., 1961).

Hicks, U. R., F. G. Carnell, *et al., Federalism and Economic Growth in Underdeveloped Countries* (Oxford, 1961).

Hutchins, R. M., *Two Faces of Federalism* (Center for the Study of Democratic Institutions, 1961).

Kallenbach, J. E., *Federal Coöperation with the States under the Commerce Clause* (U. of Michigan, 1942).

Leach, R. H., and R. H. Sugg, *The Administration of Interstate Compacts* (Louisiana State U., 1959).

Livingston, W. S., *Federalism and Constitutional Change* (Oxford, 1956).

Macmahon, A. W. (Ed.), *Federalism: Mature and Emergent* (Doubleday, 1955).

McWhinney, E., *Comparative Federalism: States' Rights and National Power* (U. of Toronto, 1962).

Morley, F., *Freedom and Federalism* (Regnery, 1959).

Pound, R., C. H. McIlwain, and R. F. Nichols, *Federalism as a Democratic Process* (Rutgers, 1942).

Report of the Royal Commission on Dominion-Provincial Relations, Bk. I (King's Printer, 1940).

Rockefeller, N. A., *The Future of Federalism* (Harvard, 1962).

Vile, M. J. C., *The Structure of American Federalism* (Oxford, 1961).

Wells, R. H., *The States in West German Federalism* (Bookman, 1961).

Wheare, K. C., *Federal Government,* 3rd ed. (Oxford, 1953).

White, L. D., *The States and the Nation* (Louisiana State U., 1953).

VII

Local Government

Up to this point we have been considering central governments that rule a wide territory operating from a single center or capital. Even the state governments in a federal system are central governments in this sense. It will be convenient here to refer to all central governments of whatever kind as *senior governments,* thus distinguishing them from a very numerous group of subordinate, or junior, governments, each of which has a limited authority in a very narrow locality.

Central governments have never been able to carry on all the activities wanted of government. They have been compelled to rely on a network of *local governments* which in the aggregate can scarcely be said to be of lesser importance than the senior governments. *Municipal* government, as it is generally called in the United States, touches the lives of more people at more points than do the senior governments. The character of local government and its relation to the senior governments are important factors affecting the working of government as a whole in any country.

STATUS

ANGLO-AMERICAN LOCAL GOVERNMENT

Subordinate Government. The place of local government in the constitutional framework must be considered first. Local government is subordinate government. The city or the county, unlike the states in a federation, has no assured sphere of autonomy that the constitution protects.[1] At any time a law passed by the appropriate legislature may abolish local government, or modify or take away some of the powers exercised by it. The whole structure of local government in Britain has been created by statute, and so has most of local government in the United States. Many state constitutions in the latter, however, contain provisions relating to the structure of local government, and it has been urged that to be useful, municipal 'home rule,' for one should be based upon self-executing constitutional provisions rather than statutes. Without such statutory and/or constitutional provisions, the government of the city, town, county, or township could not exist legally. It would have no power to require citizens to pay taxes or shovel snow off their sidewalks, and no duty to maintain and repair roads and lighting and sewage systems. These statutes prescribe in abundant detail how local governments are to be set up, how they are to operate, and what powers and duties they are to have.

Thus, as far as the constitution is concerned, the local governments remain subject to the control of the legislature of the appropriate senior governments. They have a sphere of operation in which they can do as they like only because a discretion has been conferred on them by statute. The ordinances made by the municipal council are merely delegated or subordinate legislation and subject to controls and limitations by the senior government. For example, if the statutorily created city council makes a by-law requiring the banks to lend money to the needy at 3 per cent interest, no bank need obey the by-law and the courts would, upon challenge, declare it to be invalid. The matters on which the city council has power to make laws are set out in detail in statutes of the legislature, and thus far regulation of banks and rates of interest has never been among them.

In Britain, the local governments derive their authority from, and the limits of their powers are marked out by, Parliament. In the United States, the Constitution assigns local government exclusively to the states. Clauses that assign powers to the federal authority are silent on this subject, and therefore the power to create local governments and to exercise control over

---

[1] This statement is subject to some qualification in the United States, where about one-third of the states have amended their constitutions to provide a defined sphere of 'home rule' for the municipalities in the state. In these states the legislature cannot intervene in this sphere without first getting the 'home rule' amendment of the constitution repealed—a difficult but not impossible task.

them is reserved to the states. The federal government has no *direct* power over the municipalities. They are the creatures of the state.[2]

The Tradition of Local Autonomy. The dependent and subordinate position assigned to local government by the constitution tends to obscure one fundamentally important fact. Local government in the Anglo-American world is *self-government.* There is a long tradition that local governments are not to be district offices of the senior government but institutions through which local affairs are run by local people. For centuries in Britain local government was run by a self-perpetuating local oligarchy. The country squires as justices of the peace governed the county.

This system was introduced in the American colonies, but it never became rooted there. Local government was rapidly democratized in America; and in the course of the nineteenth century in Britain the justices of the peace were replaced by elected councils chosen by a local electorate and responsible to it. Local democracy is now so firmly established in popular estimation that no legislature would think of using its constitutional powers to abridge it seriously. Local government has a wide sphere of autonomy guaranteed by political considerations and not by the constitution.

So the statutes that prescribe the areas and kinds of local government, and the extent of their power, invariably provide for the election of a local governing body or council by residents of the area. The councils are responsible to their electorate and, generally speaking, to no other political authority. Of course, if corruption has been practiced in municipal elections, an action can be brought in the courts to unseat the councilors involved. If the council exceeds its powers or fails to carry out duties imposed on it by law, redress can be sought through judicial proceedings.

It is only in very unusual circumstances, such as a default in payment on municipal bonds, that the senior government can remove the local council or dictate to it what it shall do. It is true also that there are a number of specific matters, to be discussed later, in which the senior government has some power of supervision over local governments. Although these powers are steadily increasing they are still relatively few and, generally speaking, the autonomy of local governments can only be interfered with by the appropriate legislature's amending statutes that define the constitutions of the local governments.

[2] In this chapter, *senior government,* in the singular, refers to the state governments in the United States or to the central government in Britain.

CONTRASTS BETWEEN CONTINENTAL EUROPEAN AND ANGLO-AMERICAN LOCAL GOVERNMENT

The practical autonomy of local government within the sphere marked out for it is regarded in Britain and the United States as part of the natural order and therefore as scarcely requiring comment. It is by no means inevitable, however, as the very difficult status of local government in continental Europe shows. Generally speaking—there are significant exceptions—the countries of continental Europe have no tradition of autonomy in local goevrnment. The absolute monarchies established strong central authority over local government. In the late nineteenth and early twentieth centuries there was a trend toward municipal self-government in Europe. The coming of dictatorships reversed the trend in many countries and made local government more than ever an instrument of the central authority. The relationship of central and local government in France affords a fair illustration of the general situation in Europe before the rise of dictatorships.

Centralization in France. A department of the central government, the Ministry of the Interior, has as its special care the governing of the interior, the local areas of France. In some matters such as education, administration is entirely in the hands of the Minister of the Interior. The teachers are employees of the central government and the school is as much under its direction as is the local post office. In other matters, such as police, locally elected authorities participate to some extent, but the powers of central direction are so strong as to leave only a shadow of local autonomy. Local police chiefs are appointed by the central government and may receive binding instructions from that source at any time. In still other matters, locally elected authorities have what appears on the surface to be a wide power to govern. Even here, however, the agents of the central government exercise continuous supervision and, on all major questions, bend local government to the desires of the Ministry of the Interior.

UNITS OF LOCAL GOVERNMENT. The four main divisions of local government in France are the *department* (*département*), roughly comparable to the county in Anglo-American countries; the *arrondissement,* a subdivision of the department; the *canton,* a subdivision of the arrondissement; and the *commune,* which may be a rural area, a village, a town, or a city. In 1963, there were 90 departments, 281 arrondissements, 3,028 cantons, and 38,014 communes. But the only really important units, those which have standing as 'legal persons,' are the department and the commune.

THE DEPARTMENT. The legislative authority of the department is a *council* elected by manhood suffrage. However, the council is far from having unrestricted powers of law-making for its locality. The power of the purse is the best test of a legislature's authority; yet while the department's council must pass the budget of expenditures, the central government in Paris has wide powers to say what it shall and shall not contain.

Nor has the council the pre-eminence over the executive that we might expect a legislature to possess. Although he is not formally the chief executive officer of the department, the *prefect,* its titular head, is the key figure in French local government and administration. He is usually an experienced administrator, but his appointment is regarded as political, complete loyalty to the Minister of the Interior being essential. As the *agent* of the national government, the prefect is a sort of resident administrative supervisor of the department. This includes supervision of the work of the elected council in any area of national concern—a power known as *tutelle administrative* (administrative guardianship), which compromises the right to dissolve 'illegal' council meetings. If stubborn disputes arise between the prefect and the council of the department, they are resolved by the Minister of the Interior, who may remove the prefect or even, in certain circumstances, dissolve the council and call a new election. There does exist a *formal* executive head of the department, the *president.* He is elected by the members of the council from its own numbers for a three-year term of office—but the prefect obviously sits at the center of power.

Laws passed by the French Parliament confine the council of the department to a very narrow sphere, and it is the prefect who is expected to see that it does not act outside this sphere. So when local aspirations as expressed by the council conflict with the policy of the central government, the prefect has to remember that *his masters are in Paris and not in the locality.* Clearly, then, the department is an administrative area of the central government rather than a unit of effective self-government.

THE COMMUNE. Within each department there is a varying number of communes, large and small. Each commune has a locally elected municipal council with power to make laws relating to local matters. The council chooses one of its members as *mayor* and he is the chief executive of the commune. Once chosen, however, the mayor—who enjoys considerably more power and prestige than the departmental president—becomes substantially independent of the council. It cannot dismiss him or directly control him in the work of administration. In an important sense, the mayor, too, is an agent of the central government. In matters relating to finance, police, and public health, for example, his main function is to enforce decrees of the central government. Under the doctrine of *tutelle administrative,* he is in many other matters subject to close supervision by the prefect, who can suspend or remove him if he fails to carry out instructions from above.

The council of the commune has a wider sphere of local independence than the council of the department. In the last sixty years its power to make ordinances, or laws, has been gradually extended. But the range of its independent action is in no way comparable to that enjoyed by municipal councils in Anglo-American countries. In all genuinely important fields of local government its decisions are subject to modification by the prefect under certain circumstances. In particular, its freedom in matters of finance is very sharply limited. When recalcitrant councils resist that tutelage, the prefect can suspend them or recommend their dissolution.

Although the French system of local government provides for participation of locally elected councils, centralization is its most striking feature. Its character is not seriously misrepresented by charting it in the familiar hierarchical form. At the apex stands the Minister of Interior, a member of the cabinet in the national government, from whom orders go to the prefects at the departmental level. The prefect, in turn, passes on edicts and instructions to the mayors who govern the communes at the base of the pyramid. (As already indicated, there are two other intermediate units of French local government, but they have no genuine significance and need not be considered here.) Local government in most European countries before the era of dictatorships closely resembled the French system. One of the few notable exceptions is Switzerland, where local government has consistently employed a remarkable degree of autonomy.

Anglo-American Decentralization. Local government in Britain and in the United States presents the sharpest contrast to these centralized systems. It is *decentralized.* Within the wide sphere of operations guaranteed to them by law, the locally elected councils govern according to their interpretation of the desires of the often apathetic local electorate. The next election presumably determines whether they have interpreted local opinion on local demands and needs correctly or not.

Not only do municipal councils make what laws they think fit; they also appoint and control the officers who enforce these laws and carry on the work of daily administration—although there are significant departures from this principle in the United States, to be explained later. While there is a steadily growing number of matters in which the senior government prescribes minimum standards that local governments must observe, local governments are not obliged to placate officials of the senior government at every turn. It is true, however, that in some states the governor or a state department head has been given power to remove certain kinds of local officials in certain specified circumstances. No matter how dark a view the senior government takes of the behavior of particular locally elected councils, it cannot suspend or dissolve them. If the council has exceeded its powers or violated the law, the remedy, in almost all cases, is an action in the courts. The only other course generally open to the senior government is to ask the legislature to amend the general law relating to local government. But it hesitates to sponsor such a measure because that will bring it into collision with a general public inclination toward autonomous local self-government.

GEOGRAPHICAL AREAS AND AUTHORITIES IN ANGLO-AMERICAN LOCAL GOVERNMENT

Areas. Local government requires the division of the country into areas, each with a separate authority or government. The number, type, and configuration of these areas vary in each country. What these areas are depends partly on past history and partly on the needs and purposes of the present. The *county* has been a unit of government in Britain since early times, and it was transplanted to North America in colonial times. The county or its equivalent, called 'parish' in Louisiana and 'borough' in Alaska, is found almost everywhere [3] because of the pervasiveness of rural conditions in our past. There may also be smaller rural subdivisions of the county: the *township* in the United States, and the *rural district* in Britain. These are now too small, either in area or in population, for many purposes, and their importance is declining.

There have always been units of urban government as well. The ancient English *boroughs* have a long history of local autonomy. The *cities* and *towns* of more recent origin in both countries have been more or less com-

[3] Rhode Island and Connecticut *abandoned* the county as a unit of government, the latter in 1959; but the other forty-eight states in the United States are holding the line, Alaska having entered the Union in 1959 without counties.

pletely separated from the counties or townships in which they lie and have been given charters of self-government. A few great metropolitan centers in each country are special areas with distinctive forms of government, such as Greater London, and the 'Metro' of Dade County, Florida (Miami) which extends to more than twenty-six municipalities and unincorporated areas, comprising 2,054 square miles with a population of one million! In the United States, the configuration of the rural units and the names given them vary from state to state. Nothing would be gained by attempting detailed description and comparison.

Conditions and needs of rural government differ sharply from those of urban government, and every metropolitan area is in some measure unique. Accordingly, the governmental institutions are more or less adjusted to the differences and there is very little of a common pattern of local government even within a single country. The one great common characteristic has already been discussed: These units are all local democracies practicing a wide measure of self-government in a specified list of matters.

Authorities. In Britain there are very few exceptions to the general authority of the county or city council in local matters. In the United States, however, there are numerous special areas for special purposes, with separately elected governing bodies. These areas may or may not coincide with the boundaries of the town, city, or county. The most typical example is the *school district* for the purpose of education, with its board of trustees or board of education. In addition, in the cities and town in many states, particular matters are often withdrawn from the jurisdiction of the general council and placed under the authority of special bodies like boards of health, police commissions, and public-utilities commissions.

The questions whether there shall be special authorities for particular purposes, and if so, how they shall be chosen, are not left to local choice. They depend on the state legislation that establishes the structure of local government and defines its functions. *Local government, it must be remembered, is subordinate government and cannot frame or alter its own constitution.*[4]

[4] In some states of the United States the state legislatures authorize alternative forms of structure and organization among which localities are free to choose. Four identifiable charters exist: (1) those provided by *special* acts of the state legislature; (2) those provided by *general* laws of the state; (3) optional or *'à la carte'* charters for municipalities; and (4) home rule. Cf. Jewell Cass Phillips, *Municipal Government and Administration in America* (New York: The Macmillan Co., 1960), p. 75 *et seq.* Also, even where state legislation does not offer alternatives, a particular city or county may take the initiative in *proposing* modifications in its charter for the approval of the state legislature, and of its own citizens in a popular referendum.

ELECTED COUNCILS. Something will be said later about the significance of these special local authorities. At present, it is necessary to look at the characteristics of the general government of local areas. The legislative authority of the city, town, or county is always an *elected council* chosen by substantially adult suffrage. Although there are some matters in which the local electorate may, or must, participate in the law-making process by a popular referendum, all laws relating to local affairs require an ordinance by the council. The council also has some control over the executive and administration.

STRUCTURE

LOCAL GOVERNMENT IN BRITAIN

Council in Control. In Britain, this aforementioned control is complete. The council, which is elected for a three-year period, is the executive as well as the legislature, the cabinet as well as the parliament. While the central legislature relies on one small executive committee for all purposes (the cabinet), the local legislatures set up separate executive committees for finance, public works, parks, public welfare, and so on. Each member of the council has a share in the control of one or more branches of administration. Each committee of the council occupies a position comparable to that of the minister in charge of a department of the central government. Indeed, if the chairman of a committee is vigorous and skillful, he may run the committee and thus be the equivalent of a minister.

Each committee has a general oversight of administration but does not itself do the work of daily administration. It relies on a body of appointed civic officials and employees, which is very numerous in great cities and almost nonexistent in rural districts. In a large city the committees of council, like the ministers of large departments of the central government, must rely very heavily on their senior civic employees, restricting themselves to the larger questions of policy. In the smaller units of local governments where the affairs to be managed are few and relatively simple, the committees can—and often do—direct the activity of civic employees in some detail.

The point to be stressed here is that the municipal civil service, be it large or small, is responsible to a committee of the council, and through it to the council itself. The council not only makes the laws, either directly or indirectly through senior officials under its control, but it also enforces by-laws, hires and fires, purchases supplies, lets contracts, and generally conducts civic housekeeping.

Co-ordination. In the senior government of Britain the cabinet co-ordinates the work of the several executive departments, ensuring a degree of harmony in administration as a whole. In local governments, where each branch of administration is under the supervision of a distinct committee or council, there is need for co-ordination to prevent confusion and cross-purposes. The problem is not a serious one until the urban form of government is reached. In cities it is met more or less effectively in a number of ways.

COMMITTEES. The fact of interlocking membership in the various committees helps each committee keep track of what the others are doing. Frequently the finance committee is made up of chairmen of other committees just as in the senior governments administration is integrated through financial control. Furthermore, the committees have no power to make decisions on questions of policy, which must always be settled finally by the council as a whole. That is to say, the council itself performs many of the co-ordinating functions of the cabinet in the senior governments. Finally, in the larger cities, administration is too burdensome and complex for the committees to interfere much in its detail. This is the opportunity of appointed city officials to exercise a good deal of guidance and authority in administration. In many instances the city clerk assumes functions approaching those of a general manager.

The Mayor. This description makes no reference to the office of mayor, which is found in all British cities. The mayor is the first citizen or chief magistrate of his city, but these are formal titles and do not confer on him any specific governmental functions. Like the monarch, he has the influence of an exalted position but no significant power. He is not popularly elected but is chosen annually by the council, generally from among themselves. Apart from being chairman of the council, he is largely a figurehead gracing ceremonial occasions. The real authority both in legislation and administration is the *council.*

LOCAL GOVERNMENT IN THE UNITED STATES

In the United States up to the middle of the nineteenth century, the formal organization of municipal government closely resembled the British pattern just described. Legislative and executive authority were concentrated in the council. The mayors of the cities were mostly figureheads, although they were popularly elected and not appointed officers. Two strong sets of influences of the mid-nineteenth century led the state legislatures to introduce the separation of powers into local government and put the executive and legislative powers in different hands.

Influence of Ultra-Democratic Ideas. First, 'government of the people, by the people, and for the people' was interpreted in the United States as requiring that, wherever possible, those who exercised powers of government should be directly *elected*. Accordingly, provision was made for direct election of mayors as well as of many of the chief officials of the counties and cities. Clerks, treasurers, auditors, assessors, and others, who in Britain are appointed by the municipal council, came to be directly elected by the voters in American municipalities. These officers who control a large part of local administration got a direct mandate from the local electorate and became directly responsible to it.

DIFFUSION OF CONTROL. The control of administration was thus largely taken away from the council, and responsibility for administration was diffused among a number of elected officials. The same impulses led to the establishment and direct election of numerous distinct local boards, comparable in nature to the school boards already mentioned. Power in local affairs was widely diffused instead of being concentrated in a single elected council. While the trend in this direction has been largely reversed in the twentieth century, direct election of many administrative officers and boards is still the rule in most counties and in many of the smaller cities in the United States.

FREQUENCY OF ELECTIONS. Furthermore, ultra-democratic ideas also suggested that the more often elected representatives had to go to the people, the closer the control the people would be able to exercise over their government. So annual election of councilmen and other officials came to be the rule in the late nineteenth and early twentieth centuries. However, there has been a strong reaction against this practice in recent years. One-year terms of office are much less common than formerly. In most cities, mayors are now elected for either two or four years. Some councils are still elected annually, but a majority of them are now chosen for periods running from two to four years.

Influence of Separation of Powers. The second set of influences was derived from the examples set by the federal and state constitutions. In these constitutions the separation of powers set the executive apart from the legislature, and made it necessary to have the chief executive independently elected. It was plausible to think that a principle that is sound for the nation and the several states must also be valid for the municipality. That is to say, if presidents and governors are directly elected and given wide powers to exercise independently of the legislature, so should mayors. Mayors ceased to be largely figureheads and became elected chief executives with independent powers. They were given a suspensive or even full veto on ordinances passed by the council, the power to hire and fire civic employees, and so on. The extent to which mayors have to get confirmation of their executive decisions by the council varies from state to state.

We have already seen how the separation of powers weakens authority and divides responsibility in the federal government of the United States. It has had similar, even more unsatisfactory, results in local government, and about the beginning of the twentieth century a pronounced reaction against it developed.

Reactions against Separation of Powers. For a variety of reasons associated with the rapid growth and heterogeneous population of American cities, local government in the second half of the nineteenth century in the United States was marked by many evils and abuses. One contributing factor was the division of legislative and executive authority and the diffusion of responsibility among many elected officials. In the last quarter of the century there was a rising insistence on drastic reform, and a number of advances toward better local government. Shortly after 1900 the attention of reformers was turned toward the structure of local government itself.

NEW PLANS. Since then, two principal revisions of the general organization of local government known as the *commission* plan and the *council-manager,* or *city-manager,* plan have been adopted by many municipalities. Reorganization of local government in accordance with these plans has made almost no, or at best very little, progress in the rural counties or in cities of more than half a million population. The counties still adhere mainly to the system of many elected officials and widely diffused authority, and most large cities are still governed by some variant of the mayor-council plan. But many of the medium-sized and smaller cities in the United States have gone over to either the commission or council-manager scheme of local government.

1. *The 'Strong' Mayor-Council Plan.* Before speaking more particularly about the commission and the council- or city-manager schemes, it should

be said that the mayor-council form of government—sometimes called the burgess-council—is being rapidly transformed in one city after another, largely by *strengthening the position of the mayor*. This is done by raising the mayor from a mere figurehead—as he is under the 'Weak' Mayor-Council plan—to a chief executive with control over most, if not all, of the administrative departments of the city government, i.e. a 'Strong' Mayor. Under the latter system, the heads of most, if not all, of the departments cease to be elected and are appointed and removed by the mayor. They work under his control and supervision, and he is often given a predominant influence in finance. Moreover, he is frequently armed with a veto over legislation passed by the council. It is being widely recognized that efficiency and responsibility in administration cannot be secured adequately under the older practice of diffusion of authority. In 1963, of the twenty-one largest cities in the United States (all over 500,000 inhabitants), all except Dallas, San Antonio, San Diego, Cincinnati, and Washington, D. C., had the 'Strong' Mayor-Council type of government.

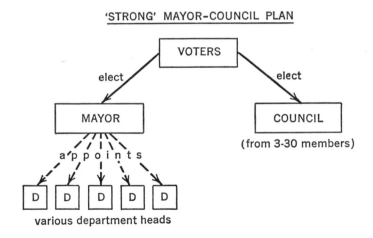

2. *The Commission Plan.* Under the commission plan—which originated in Galveston, Texas, as a direct result of the catastrophic tidal wave and flood of 1900, with which its mayor-council government was unable to deal effectively—a small commission, or council, of from three to seven members is elected for a term of two or four years. With the exception of the still retained school board, as a rule no other officials or boards are normally elected by the voters. One of the commissioners is chosen, either by the

commissioners themselves or by popular vote, to act as chairman or mayor, but he is rarely given any significant independent powers. The commissioners give full time to their work and are paid relatively substantial salaries. All authority and power, both legislative and executive, is concentrated in the commission.

FUSION OF POWER. The separation of powers and the diffusion of authority are eliminated. As a legislative body, the commission enacts by-laws, levies taxes, and appropriates money to the items of expenditure. The day-to-day work of administering the affairs of the city is divided among a number of departments, such as finance, works, health, and safety. There are usually an equal number of commissioners and departments so that each commissioner, in addition to being a legislator, is the executive head of a department, directing all its operations.

This structure might be expected to produce the substance of cabinet government: a small executive linking together the legislature and the administration, and concerting among themselves a unified policy both for the legislature and for the separate departments of administration. In practice, however, it has not worked that way. Collective responsibility, which is a vital feature of cabinet government, is lacking.

DIFFUSION OF RESPONSIBILITY. Each commissioner regards himself as having a distinct mandate from the people for two or four years, and he tends to concentrate his attention on his own department. The commissioners also tend to give too much attention to the detail of their departments instead of leaving it to expert permanent officials, and too little attention to co-operative co-ordination of the varied business of the city as a whole. When, as too often happens, each commissioner fights for his own department, the executive does not work as a team, and administrative rivalries weaken the deliberations of the legislature. Lacking a strong, vigilant opposition in the legislature, there is nothing to compel the commissioners to hang together or hang separately.

DECLINE. While commission government was an advance on the forms of organization it superseded, the defects noted, among others, have brought a considerable decline in recent years. In 1917, a total of 36 per cent of all local governments used it; but by 1963 scarcely 9 per cent (over 5,000) did. Memphis was among the few prominent cities still adhering to it. Some cities that abandoned it—e.g. Jersey City—adopted or returned to the separation of powers between council and mayor, often giving the mayor a stronger position than before. Others have adopted the council-manager, or city-manager, plan, which is the currently favored plan for reorganizing city government.

COMMISSION PLAN

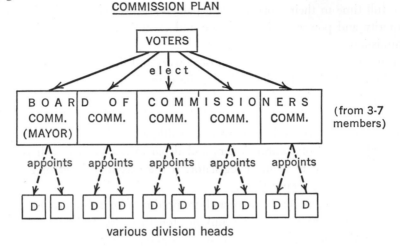

various division heads

3. *The Council- or City-Manager Plan.* The council- or city-manager plan corresponds closely to the commission plan up to the point where responsibility for the day-to-day direction and control of administration is reached. All governing power and responsibility, both legislative and executive, are vested in a small elected council, but the members of the council do not become the active heads of the administrative departments. Instead, *the council appoints a city manager who is directly responsible to the council for executing the laws and managing all the affairs of the city.* The council, or the electorate, elects a mayor, who is the presiding officer of the council and represents the city on ceremonial occasions. The closest parallel is the business corporation. The electorate are the shareholders in the city corporation; the council is the elected board of directors; and the latter appoints a general manager—commonly on a contractual basis—who is operating head of the administration.

THE MANAGER. The line that is drawn is not between legislative and executive, but between the making of policy and the carrying out of policy in detail, or administration. The council makes the ordinances, votes the budget, and has general surveillance over administration. The manager puts the council's decisions into effect. He is a professionally trained governmental expert, usually hired from *outside* of the local area he is to serve, and presumed to be divorced from all political ties and motivations. He advises the council on all matters of detail, such as drafting a proposed budget, appoints and removes all heads of departments and, subject in most cases to civil service regulations, hires and fires the municipal employees. Where the council gets a good manager and can restrain itself from interfering with him in matters of detail, this scheme helps cities to build up a competent expert civil service and to get effective co-ordination of administration. Although these conditions are not always satisfied, the council-manager plan has had a large measure of success. In 1963 some 38 per cent of the cities used it, including, San Diego, San Antonio, Cincinnati, Kansas City, and Dallas. It is generally on the increase in America, especially in small and medium-sized cities, but also in counties and townships.

COUNCIL–OR CITY–MANAGER PLAN

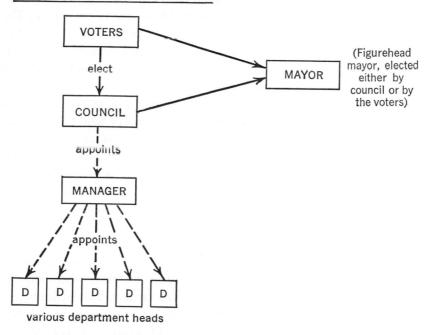

various department heads

Independent 'ad hoc' Boards. About two-thirds of American cities still maintain a more or less marked separation of powers between mayor and council. In these cities, however, the mayor and council are not always the sole authorities in matters of local government. We have noted that the autonomous school district is found in most areas of local government. Schools are controlled by independently elected school boards and not by the council elected for general purposes of local government. Also, in many cities—and in many counties as well—there are other special *ad hoc* authorities, frequently elected but sometimes appointed by the governor or other state officials.

SPECIAL DISTRICTS. Sometimes the physical boundaries of the authority of these bodies coincide with the boundary of the city or county, and sometimes they combine several areas of local government for a particular purpose. For example, there are often *special districts* combining two or more municipalities for the purpose of roads, parks, health, fire protection, and water supply as well as for schools. Wherever a special district is created for the exercise of a particular function of local government, an authority independent of mayor or council, or both, is generally created also.

BOARDS. In addition, there are numerous instances where distinct agencies for exercising particular functions within a city or county are set up. The most common are boards of financial control and police commissions. The former usually consist of the mayor and a small board elected by the voters at large. The latter are often appointed by the state government without reference to the wishes of the local council or local electors.

Such *ad hoc* authorities, where they exist, cause still more diffusion of authority and responsibility in local government. Except where their object is to combine two or more counties and/or cities so as to give a larger unit of administration for such services as roads, water supply, or public health, all the criticisms of the separation of powers between the mayor and the council are valid against them also.

The most important of the original impulses for establishing *ad hoc* independent boards was disgust with the elected municipal council. In the last half of the nineteenth century, American local government suffered greatly from corruption and boss rule. Political machines often controlled municipal elections and used local government for their own purposes rather than for the good government of the municipality. The establishment of independently elected boards for the exercise of particular functions was intended to take those functions out of politics. However, there is little hope of curbing machine politics merely by multiplying elections. If the function in question is an important one, the machine politicians will turn their hand to controlling the elections to the board. The *ad hoc* boards have been extremely unsatisfactory, and the present tendency is toward their elimination.

In addition, the withdrawal of important functions from the control of the council lowers the power and prestige of the council. This, in turn, lowers the caliber of men who seek election to the council, thus providing a fallacious reason for taking still more powers away from the council. Able, public-spirited men are not likely to be willing to give their time and effort to local government unless they see the possibility of solid accomplishment. The surest way to attract them is to concentrate the powers of local government in the general council. This is what has been done in Britain, and British local government, where there is less diffusion of authority, is markedly more efficient than American local government.

PRACTICE AND THEORY

FUNCTIONS OF LOCAL GOVERNMENT

Although the institution of local self-government is common to Britain and the United States, it is evident that there are marked differences in structure and organization. In this same way, a broad similarity exists in the kind of functions performed by local government in both countries, and there are very considerable variations in the detailed scope of the functions undertaken. Even within the same country or state, the scope of the functions of rural and urban government differs greatly. The functions of rural governments are very few while, generally speaking, the larger the city, the more things its government undertakes. It would be burdensome and confusing to list the numerous functions and note the differences. However, if we are to grasp the pressing problems of local government today, it is necessary to see the general character of the functions performed.

Aim. The principal purpose of local government is to provide through collective action a number of services that the citizen, standing alone, cannot secure for himself as well or at all. But local governments have never been left free to undertake anything and everything that a majority of the citizens approve. Local governments can only do the things they have been authorized or required to do by the legislature of the appropriate senior government. The statutes enumerate the functions of local government and limit the action of each municipality to its own area.

THREE CLASSES. The functions fall into three broad classes. First, there are the *protectice services* of police, public safety as in fire protection, public health, and sanitation. Second, there are certain *physical services or facilities,* of which roads, streets, and bridges are the best examples. The public utilities such as light, gas, water, power, and transport, which are increasingly owned and operated by municipalities, fall in the same group.[5] Third, there are what may be broadly described as the *welfare services,* such as education, libraries, parks and other recreation facilities, hospitals, and the care of those for whom some public provision has to be made because of poverty, advanced age, or other defect.

Increasing Cost of Functions. Just as in the case of the senior governments, functions are always changing in scope and emphasis. In local government too, the trend of activity has been sharply upward, particularly in urban areas. The coming of the automobile compelled much greater outlays on roads, streets, and highways. The demand for better education, and education on a wider scale, has imposed steadily rising costs. Greater emphasis on preventive medicine and sanitation measures has raised expenditures on public health. Disturbed economic conditions, with consequent poverty and unemployment combined with an insistence that such distress be relieved at public expense, have multiplied several times the cost of welfare services since the turn of the century. Other expenditures also have tended to rise.

TAXES. The steady, persistent rise in per capita expenditures of local governments over the last century has created a serious problem in municipal finance. Expenditures are always more easily boosted than revenues. But local governments are in a peculiarly difficult position because much the greater part of the revenues they themselves raise comes from a single source, a tax on land values. Municipalities try to increase their revenues by other kinds of taxes, and by imposing licenses and collecting fees of various kinds. In the United States, state governments often share with the local governments the proceeds of taxes on, for example, income, gasoline, and sales. These shared taxes, as they are called, are levied and collected by the state governments, and part of the proceeds are distributed to the local governments, generally without strings attached. Lately, several municipalities in the United States have been granted power by the states to tax income and/or sales directly. Thus New York City now has a city sales tax, Philadelphia a city income tax, and local sales taxes are widely prevalent in California. While local governments are relying increasingly on these other sources of revenue, their combined yield is almost everywhere considerably less than the proceeds of the tax on land values.

---

[5] In 1960, municipalities in Pennsylvania, for example, owned 440 waterworks, 228 operated directly by municipal governments and 212 controlled by authorities; 39 ran electrical systems; a few had gasworks; many provided sewage, garbage, and refuse disposal services. (*Horizons,* 9, May 1962.)

As local expenditures rise, the tax on land values must also rise. This brings an unfortunate tendency into operation. Other factors such as the general level of economic activity remaining constant, sharply rising taxes on real property will depreciate land values, so that local governments are often trying to get more and more revenue from a source that shrinks from and with their every advance.

Furthermore, land values are very sensitive to economic conditions, following the downward swing of depressions and showing the most marked depreciation in the areas hardest hit by economic decline. Unfortunately for local government, the costs of welfare services in particular mount in periods of depression, rising most sharply in the most depressed areas. Thus revenues are hardest to come by when and where they are most needed. Plenty of statistical proof of this predicament could be given, but it is sufficient to recall that many municipalities were bankrupted by the long depression of the 1930's. And even in the best of times there is a marked disparity in the financial capacity of different municipalities to maintain a standard level of services.

THE 'EXPLODING METROPOLIS'

A word must be said here about an ever-increasing problem of mid-twentieth century local government—the 'exploding metropolis' or 'megalopolis.' The increasing size of metropolitan centers of population, including suburban areas as well as cities, has not only compounded the economic and political problems of these urban regions but, in some instances, the situation has reached the crisis stage. More and more cities proper are becoming 'service centers' for outlying areas, with the more prosperous elements of the population moving outside the city's borders, leaving the latter area in large measure to a heavy concentration of the less well-to-do, the underprivileged, and the migrant. The exodus from the cities has not, however, solved the population squeeze, for, increasingly, less open spaces remain and, no matter what their inhabitants may call the outlying areas, they are in fact becoming extensions of the cities. Without too much exaggeration we may speak, for instance, of one huge 'megalopolis' extending from Portland, Maine, to Richmond, Virginia—or certainly from Boston, Massachusetts, to Washington, D. C.

These facts of metropolitan local government have brought with them a frightening number of governmental problems in a host of fields. To mention but a few: ever increasing demand for services; enormous transit traffic and parking difficulties; air pollution; slum clearance; staggering housing problems; recreational needs; insufficient water supply; population mobility; and a crying need for effective planning. Moreover, these and other problems are accompanied by such difficulties as fragmented and pro-liferated units of local government; harassment by the state government; tax inequalities; mal-representation in the state legislature; population shifts and 'ghettos.' It would require a chapter, if not a book, to do justice to these problems that face the 'exploding metropolis.' Suffice it to note them here and to point to the desperate need for solutions—for no matter how strong the traditional sentimental attachment to rural areas may be, today urban centers represent the heart of healthy and effective local government. Already they are compelled to turn more and more to the national govern-ment for aid. If the several states of the United States are to keep their historic relationship to local government, they must recognize the plight of the metropolitan areas where two-thirds of the entire population of the nation now reside.

RELATIONSHIPS BETWEEN LOCAL AND SENIOR GOVERNMENTS

Shifts of Functions. One way of easing the difficulties of the local govern-ments is for the senior governments, which have access to more diversified sources of revenue and can expand their revenues more easily, to take over some of the more onerous functions of the local governments. A num-ber of functions have been thus transferred in recent years. In Britain, distress arising from unemployment, poverty, ill-health, and old age is now solely relieved by the central government. In the United States, a number of welfare problems, which formerly imposed, in one way or another, heavy charges on the funds of local governments, have been taken over by the national or state governments. Thus senior governments now provide unemployment insurance and aid to the aged, the blind, needy mothers, and dependent children, hence giving local governments appreciable relief from the burden of welfare services that would otherwise have fallen on them.

Compulsory Services and Standards. Alongside this movement and in some respects antedating it is another more complex development. The legislatures of senior governments have enacted laws that impose sub-stantial, uncontrollable expenditures on local governments, limiting their ability to retrench in the face of declining revenues. Local governments are required to provide certain services and to keep them at a level of quality determined on by the senior government. Elementary education is free to the child, but it is compulsory on the local government. Local governments are required by law to maintain a wide variety of sanitary facilities and public-health precautions. In a host of other matters, some important and some trivial, central governments require local governments to perform specified duties, to employ officials of recognized qualifications, and so on. In Britain, where this development has gone furthest, there are relatively few functions of local government in which the senior government does not impose some minimum standards of obligatory services.

The reasons for the intervention of the central government, whether convincing or not in particular instances, are clear enough. There is thought to be a national interest in maintaining a minimum level of such services as education and public health all across the country. Areas of illiterary and unchecked disease are menaces to the whole society. Yet for various and excellent reasons, these services are not likely to be as well managed and administered by the senior governments as by the local governments. On the other hand, many, if not all, local governments are hard pressed financially to maintain the standard insisted on by the senior government.

Grants-in-Aid. Accordingly, the imposition of standards has been accompanied by grants of money from the senior governments to the local authorities. For example, compulsory free education is almost everywhere assisted by grants, which have risen in amount as the required standards have risen. In Britain, where the senior government imposes many standards, about one-third of the annual current expenditures of all local governments were being met by grants from the Treasury at the outbreak of World War II. During World War II the proportion increased to one-half. Since 1945 the costs of poor relief, maintenance of hospitals, and medical care have been lifted from the local governments by Parliament, and some new obligations imposed. In 1948 the whole system of grants-in-aid was revised in an effort to come closer to equalizing the disparate financial resources of different local governments. The proportion is now slightly more than one-half.

As we have already noted in connection with federalism, such grants ease the financial position of local governments, but they also limit their independence. The senior government defines in detailed regulations the standard of achievement it expects in particular services, and it usually employs inspectors to check on performance. Serious failure to comply with the regulations may involve a cut in the grant. The central department of education establishes curricula and tests the product of the schools by periodic examination. The recurring visits of its inspectors are a feature of school life. Similar techniques are used in other municipal services whose standards the senior governments want to raise.

Expert Guidance and Services. There is a great deal more to the intervention of the senior government than the drafting of regulations and the prying of inspectors. The departments of the senior government give the local authorities needed encouragement and valuable expert advice. The department of education tries to keep abreast of new movements and new needs in education, and to interpret these to the local school authorities. The senior government provides a number of services for the local authorities that no one of them could provide for itself. Vaccines and serums, diagnostic clinics, and laboratory analysis are provided free of charge. Research in preventive medicine and sanitary engineering is carried on, and the results are available to all local governments. A great work of education in public health is carried on by bulletins, demonstrations, and exhibits. In Britain, this development has gone so far in so many fields that the complex relationships of the central and local governments can best be described as a *partnership* in providing and improving the services supplied by local government.

UNITED STATES. Nothing comparable to this partnership has yet emerged in the relationships of senior and local governments in the United States. North America did not have to face the complexities of crowded urban industrial conditions as early as did Britain, and is only now slowly adjusting itself to them. The United States has not developed the art of local government to the point it has reached in Britain. Municipal civil services, generally speaking, are not nearly as good in quality. Many units of local government are too small, either in area or population, to be effective units of administration for the present-day services required of local government. Little has been accomplished in the way of enlarging these areas. As a consequence of these factors and the financial difficulties of local governments, there has been a tendency in the United States to take particular services entirely away from local governments and make them solely a responsibility of state or national governments. The tendency has been most marked in public-welfare services and in the construction and maintenance of highways.

Whether this is a desirable trend or not, it is the existence of federalism with its intermediate level of government that makes it possible. It would be fantastic for the central government in Britain to think of taking over and administering any significant number of the services that local governments supply. It is not so fantastic in the United States, where the administration of these services can be distributed among fifty governments. Federalism can be employed not only for decentralization but also for a modified centralization.

The Trend Toward Centralization. Here we come again upon a persistent trend of present-day politics, the drive toward centralization. In discussing federalism, it was noted that a rising demand for the states to undertake more expensive functions had created a tendency to centralize more powers in the hands of the federal government. We now see that the pressure for more governmental services at the muncipal level has had similar results. The parallel is remarkably close. In each case, general financial weakness of the governments at the lower level and their widely disparate capacity for maintaining the desired services lead to outright centralization of particular services, and to grants-in-aid and extensive control over other services by the government at the higher level. At this writing (Autumn 1963), it seems but a question of time until a federal Department of Urban Affairs is established by the United States.

Decline of Local Autonomy. Through the convergence of a number of different influences, Anglo American local self-government has substantially less formal autonomy and independence than it had one hundred years ago, or even at the turn of the century. There are some who think that the trend we have been examining threatens to take the 'self' out of local self-government. It is difficult to estimate the seriousness of this threat, but no doubt a good deal depends on the vigor and intelligence shown by local democracy. If local governments are determined to understand the complexities of their present-day functions and to improve their civil services sufficiently to meet their problems, central control and supervision and central-local collaboration may help rather than hinder them in surviving. Certainly local governments need the knowledge, advice, and suggestion which senior governments can supply, and which many local governments cannot easily secure by their unaided efforts.

The probable effect of the growing central control of local government is an important question because it seems likely that vigorous local self-government is necessary to the maintenance of democracy in national politics and government. In a general way, the history of democratic experiments in the last hundred years tends to confirm this conjecture. Democracy has had the greatest stability and the highest measure of success in the countries with strong systems of local self-government. On the other hand, in continental Europe, the countries with centralized systems of local government or relatively weaker institutions of local self-government have most easily fallen prey to dictatorships. Of course, these may be accidental coincidences not in any significant way linked as cause and effect. There are, however, some very plausible reasons for thinking there is a great deal more to it than mere coincidence.

LOCAL GOVERNMENT AND DEMOCRACY

In the Anglo-American tradition local self-government has long been credited with contributing greatly to the working of democracy. Two of the commonest arguments may be looked at first. It is often said that experience on a municipal council is valuable elementary training for budding statesmen and politicians. By being faithful in small things, the municipal councilor learns to handle great affairs when he is called by the electorate to service in national or state politics. Second, the mass of citizens get an indispensable political education through discussion of lively local issues and participation in frequent local elections. Such experience helps them to grasp national issues and to exercise their franchise wisely in national politics.

Essential Links. These two contentions are valid as far as they go, but they are far from revealing the essential links between local self-government and democracy. Indeed, they tend to obscure these links because they tacitly assume that it is national and state politics alone which really matter in a democracy, and that local government is merely a training center, and not even a junior league, in the game of politics.

We miss the essence of democracy if we think of it mainly as something practiced by statesmen in a distant capital and forget that it consists of an attitude of mind toward, and a method of dealing with, all the stresses and strains of living together in a society. If local quarrels were always settled by discussion at the local level, and if local communities put their best efforts into making adjustments that are tolerable to all members of the community, there would be less need to tremble at the mention of dictators.

Unfortunately, we have a weakness for big things. The newspapers, which generally give us the kind of news we want, give us exciting front-page accounts of the dramatic events of national and international politics, while the tiresome wrangles of local politicians are often decently buried under the small headings on an inside page. We do not want to listen to John Smith in a radio discussion on some issue of local government. Rather we want to listen to President Kennedy or Prime Minister Macmillan, to hear what the big men are doing about big things. We give too large a share of our attention to these distant exciting events which we cannot adequately understand and on which, therefore, we often cannot make useful judgments. On the other hand we tend to be fascinated—and revolted—by local scandals!

Need for Participation. The ideal of political democracy demands intelligent, responsible participation by the people in the choice of those who govern and in the approval of the policies by which they are to govern. Intelligent participation requires that the citizen be able to judge the character and qualifications of those who ask for his vote, and to understand the platforms he is asked to support or reject. Responsible participation requires that the citizen, as he votes, should realize that his vote affects the public welfare, that the public welfare will suffer the consequences of his errors in judgment and that he must, therefore, watch his elected representatives and the working out of programs in practice so as to rectify errors at the earliest possible moment. In the subsequent discussion of national government and politics in these pages, numerous reasons will be given for thinking that at present we cannot come at all close to this ideal in the national or state political arena. *The ideal can, however, be much more closely approached in local government and politics, and that is why democracy, like charity, begins at home.*

Some approach to the ideal of intelligent, responsible participation is made in all municipalities where self-government has not degenerated into boss rule. The definite decline of 'boss rule' in a majority of the large American cities augurs well for the future. The citizen sees with his own eyes how the men he has elected behave. He can see whether the policies being followed by his local government work well or ill. It is possible for people, even as they go about their own work, to keep track of their local government.

Remoteness of National and State Politics. It is much more difficult to keep track of national or state politics. More often than not, voters do not know the candidates between whom they must choose. Moreover, many of the issues in state and national politics are hopelessly abstract to the average citizen; they do not arise out of things that have come concretely to his attention and about which he has knowledge. He does not understand the jugglery by which the budget is balanced, he does not understand the cases for and against the manipulation of currency and credit. Most people are wearied by the parade of statistics marshaled for and against particular governmental policies, and bewildered by the seemingly convincing, yet inconsistent, arguments put up on particular points by the opposing candidates and parties.

It must be acknowledged, of course, that the same difficulties arise in the local politics of large cities. There are numerous cities in the United States whose affairs equal or surpass in complexity those of the smaller states. But the difficulties are not as all-pervasive in local as in national or state politics. Even in the great cities, most of the work and the problems of local government come within the range of the average citizen's knowledge and understanding. He may not, in fact, attend closely to them. All that is urged here is that if he did attend closely, he would, on the whole, be better able to make a useful judgment in local than in state or national politics. Public apathy may well be *the* central issue of the problems of local government.

The behavior of political parties provides some support for the general contention made here. In national and state politics, to a greater extent than in local politics, they try not to burden the voter too much with reams of facts and statistics. They try to help him to make up his mind easily by finding simple issues which will appeal to his feelings and which do not require sustained attention. Hence, national and state elections tend, rather more than municipal elections, to emphasize emotional appeals, and so to fall seriously short of the ideal of intelligent responsible participation.

It is not suggested that such elections are solely what has been called registrations of emotions. There are generally some tests of a rational character, applicable to some, at least, of the claims of a political party for support, which the voter can apply fairly easily. Not uncommonly too, some moral issue is at stake, and on it the average man's judgment is likely to be as good as anyone's. Yet no one can have failed to note the frequency of cries about fearsome bogies such as a *creeping bureaucracy,* the *strangling octopus* of socialism, or the *insidious poison* of fascism. And there can be little doubt that the greater the powers exercised by senior governments, the more various and complex election issues become, the less the voter is able to understand, and the more he is thrown back on his emotions.

When a senior government is conducting operations of great magnitude and complexity, how is the voter to know whether it deserves support in the next election—whether it is doing well or ill? For the most part, its record cannot be fairly judged merely by the effects of its policies on the life of any particular voter or his neighborhood. If a rational judgment is to be made on its record, it must be judged by the way its policies have worked all across the country—statistics again. For these statistics the voter is at the mercy of the politicians, the writers in the newspapers, the speakers on the radio, about whose integrity and capacity the voter generally knows little or nothing.

NEED FOR EDUCATION. This is not a criticism of the average citizen nor is it a criticism of the political parties. Until the electorate is much more highly educated and possessed of a great deal of leisure that they can devote to the understanding of political issues, it is hard to see how it could be otherwise. It is a criticism of the assumption that local self-government is just a training ground for democracy that is to be practiced elsewhere. It suggests that, for a long time to come, intelligent, responsible citizenship should find its best and most effective expression in local self-government. At the same time, it is not part of the present argument that local governments are always better run and better controlled than are senior governments. Often they are not. All that is said is that the obstacles in the way are less formidable.

The fact that intelligent, responsible citizenship is hard to achieve in national and state politics must not be allowed to obscure its importance or to lessen efforts to achieve it in those fields. There are a great many matters that cannot be dealt with at all by local governments and so must be entrusted to the senior governments. The recent experience with dictatorship in Europe shows clearly that if democracy fails at the national level of government, it automatically disappears at the local level. The conclusion to be drawn from the fact that democracy can be most effectively practiced at the local level is that as many matters as possible should be reserved for the decision of local governments. Every increase of centralization, even when it is unavoidable, puts heavier burdens on the citizens' capacity to understand what is going on and to control it.

Decentralization and Political Unity. This brings us to an important reason for linking democracy with local self-government, which has already been discussed in the chapter on federalism. It was urged there that the decentralization afforded by a federal system reduces the number of disputed matters that have to be settled in the national political arena, thus making it much easier to get majorities that can agree on what the national government should be doing.

The same argument applies point for point to the still greater decentralization provided by local self-government, and it need not be restated at length here. It is sufficient to say that the more closely the senior governments can be restricted to the general common interests that unite the citizens, the greater will be national unity and the less will be the danger that the two-party system will be splintered into a multiple-party system. One of the best ways of so restricting the senior government is to arrange for local demands and local needs that vary widely to be met by a response to these demands and needs by local governments.

EXPERIENCE OF FRANCE. The experience of the French Republics with their highly centralized local government tends to support the position just stated. It has already been explained how almost all important decisions in the sphere of local government are decided either by the Ministry of the Interior in Paris or by one of its agents in the field. When local matters cannot be decided at home, the main job of each member of the legislature is to represent his constituency at the point where the decisions are made. A great part of the time of the French member of the legislature is taken up with lobbying at the Ministry of the Interior in the interests of his locality.

A frequent combination of professions in French life is that of mayor and member of Parliament. To be a successful mayor, one needs to have close connections with, and some influence over, the Ministry of the Interior. The most effective connection is membership in Parliament. A leading example was the revered Edouard Herriot, perennial Mayor of Lyons, and a prominent officer and member of Parliament for forty years. At each election in the years before the debacle of 1940 at any rate, from fifty to eighty mayors were elected to the lower house—then the Chamber of Deputies—where they formed a powerful mayors' bloc primarily concerned with putting pressure on the Department of the Interior. The Fourth Republic's upper house—the Council of the Republic—contained 107 mayors in 1958. The Senate of the Fifth Republic has seen a continuation of the practice. Every member of Parliament, whether a mayor or not, has a great many chores to do at the Ministry of the Interior. According to the constitutional forms, the central government controls and directs local affairs. In actual practice, local affairs and interests invade the central government, hoping to control its decisions.

French localities must think of their own interests, and they must send to the legislature men who will be determined champions of local needs and interests. If the local water supply is not adequate and more up-to-date facilities cannot be purchased without the consent of the Department of the Interior, it is inevitable that a high proportion of parish pump politicians will go to the legislature. A Parliament with its gaze thus introverted has not enough interest in, time for, or understanding of, broad questions of the national interest.

Politicians biased in favor of local interests find it extremely difficult to find common ground on which to have national political parties united in a common view of the national interest—which was one of the chief reasons for de Gaulle's downgrading of the legislature under the Constitution of 1958. This, it may be suggested, was one of the roots of the multiple-party system in France, although by no means the only one. Localism has always played too important a part in French national politics. Countries with vigorous systems of local self-government are freed of such distractions.

Centralization and the Coup d'état. One other and rather different aspect of the significance of local self-government may be selected for attention. In most countries of continental Europe, such as France, Germany, and Italy, for example, a central department of the interior has had a large measure of control over local government. Usually this includes pretty complete control of the local police forces. Unlike the local police in the Anglo-American system, the *gendarmerie* are virtually agents of the central governments in the localities, taking orders from the center. Thus control of the department of the interior was one of the great prizes for which Nazi and Fascist parties contended when they were fighting their way to power.

NAZI GERMANY. For example, the first government in which Hitler participated in Germany was a coalition of his Nazi party with the Nationalist party, each party getting half the posts in the cabinet. But in that cabinet, Hitler's lieutenants, Göring and Frick, got control of both the Prussian and Reich ministries of the interior, which gave them leverage on the local governments and control of the police across the country. They were thus enabled to fasten their grip on the country in an incredibly short time. This helps somewhat to explain how the Nazis, who never got 40 per cent of the total vote in a *free* election, were able to carry through a revolution without firing a shot—except, of course, the shots of the local police acting under their orders.

A highly centralized system of local government eases the task of a would-be dictator, while local self-government helps to assure its people against the sudden *coup d'état*. Even where there is no immediate need to guard against such eventualities, an effective system of local self-government acts as a counterpoise to the senior government or governments. All forms of human organization tend to expand and aggrandize themselves unless and until checked by stronger forces. It is therefore extremely important, at a time when the powers of central governments are expanding very rapidly, to have active, energetic local centers of political life that are determined to retain a sphere of independence for themselves.

On occasion, indeed, they may resist the central government too strongly, clinging doggedly to powers they can no longer exercise effectively. We must always reckon with the bad which the good often carries with it. The point to be remembered is that the senior governments, which are in ultimate control of the weapons of coercion in the society, are checked not only by legislatures, electorates, and courts but also by independent local governments in which many men of modest ambition find an outlet for their energies and their desire to render public service. These men can be counted on to resist centralizing pretensions and to compel those who urge more centralization to prove its necessity to the hilt.

Evaluation. These are some of the reasons for thinking there is a close connection between local self-government and liberal democratic senior governments. Still others could be given. The fact that dictators always destroy the autonomy of local government also suggests a connection. It does not follow, however, that local self-government will continue to bolster liberal democracy in the twentieth century unless it is substantially modified and improved.

Financial weakness and the necessity for governments to possess technical scientific knowledge are not the only factors in the movement to shift the responsibility for certain services from the local to the senior governments. Many units of local government, particularly rural ones, are too small to carry some of the newer functions of government. The civil services of most American municipalities are not of a sufficiently high quality to perform many municipal functions efficiently. As the things that local governments are expected to do become more numerous and complex, a considerable overhauling of municipal organization is imperative.

LOCAL GOVERNMENT UNDER DICTATORSHIP

If dictators were to exercise close control over all other features of government and social organization and leave local governments a larger sphere of autonomy, all the accumulated dissatisfactions with their repressive rule would express themselves in the sphere of local government. Centers of resistance to the dictatorship would soon be built up at the local level all across the country. So the dictators cannot afford to ignore local government. Once serious shackling of free expression in politics is undertaken, it has to be extended to cover every point where significant clusters of resistance might gather. Furthermore, comprehensive regulation of the lives of people, such as modern dictatorship tries to enforce, has to be carried out in large part through the agency of local governments which touch the lives of more people at more points than does any senior government. Genuine local autonomy would be intolerable.

In Germany and Italy. The Nazi and Fascist dictatorships co-ordinated local government as they co-ordinated everything else. Popular election of local councils was abolished and local governments were committed to party bosses who were responsible to the central government and the party leadership and not to the people of the local community. As in France, local government in Germany and Italy had always been subject to a large degree of direction and supervision by a department of the central government, the ministry of the interior. Under the dictators, it was completely subjected to the central government, which might intervene at any time in any way.

In the Soviet Union. Local government in the Soviet Union is not referred to as 'local government' but as 'local agents of state power,' thus suggesting that there is no truly autonomous area in which it can operate. It is made to respond to the federal government and the top party leaders by somewhat different methods in the Soviet Union, which is divided into territorial administrative units. Government policy is carried out in these administrative units under the supervision of the hierarchy of *soviets,* the governing bodies consisting of representatives of workers, soldiers, and peasants, which will be described in a later chapter. Strictly speaking, it is only the soviets of cities and villages which correspond to Anglo-American local governments, but in a sense the whole area of government *below* the supreme soviets of the union republics can be considered as falling within the category of local government.[6] It should be remembered, of course, that some of these administrative units are larger than many American states.

The tight Communist party control over the nomination of candidates, to be described subsequently, settles the election of local soviets. They are elected for two-year terms by universal suffrage. They 'direct the work of the organs of administration subordinate to them, ensure the maintenance of public order, the observance of the laws and the protection of the rights

[6] See Constitution of the U.S.S.R., ch. XII, for the main provisions relating to local government.

of the citizens, direct local economic and cultural affairs and draw up the local budgets.'[7] These tasks can be carried out by the local soviets only 'within the limits of the powers vested in them by the laws of the U.S.S.R. and of the Union Republic'[8]—and one of these limits is the lack of the power to tax!

CHIEF CONTRASTS. Two main characteristics distinguish Soviet from Anglo-American local government. *First*, the scope of its jurisdiction is considerably wider. Local soviets are not only charged with the administration of local services such as public health, education, and highways, but also must supervise all other locally situated enterprises of the Soviet state, such as factories and retail stores. *Second*, Soviet local government lacks, in practice, the autonomy which gives Anglo-American local government so important a place in democratic politics. Like everything else in the Soviet Union, activities of 'the local organs of state power' are controlled very tightly by the Communist party. The system of local government is yet another means of permitting the party leaders to dominate every aspect of life in the Soviet Union. The maintenance of autonomous local government is essential to the forces of liberal democracy in its continuing struggle against totalitarian government.

SUGGESTED REFERENCES FOR FURTHER READING

Adrian, C. R., *Governing Urban America*, 2nd ed. (McGraw-Hill, 1961).
Anderson, W. (Ed.), *Local Government in Europe* (Appleton-Century, 1937).
Banfield, E. C., and J. Q. Wilson, *City Politics* (Harvard, 1963).
Chapman, B., *French Local Government* (Allen & Unwin, 1953).
Clarke, J. J., *Outlines of Local Government in the United Kingdom,* 17th ed. (Pitman & Sons, 1954).
Dahl, R. A., *Who Governs? Democracy and Power in an American City* (Yale, 1961).
Finer, H., *English Local Government,* 6th ed. (Methuen, 1960).
Gottman, J., *Megalopolis* (20th Century Fund, 1961).
Granik, D., *Management of the Industrial Firm in the U.S.S.R.* (Columbia, 1952).
Greer, S., *Governing the Metropolis* (Wiley, 1962).
Gulick, L. H., *The Metropolitan Problem & American Ideas* (Knopf, 1962).
Jackson, W. E., *Local Government in England and Wales* (Houghton Mifflin, 1945).
Jewel, M. E., *The State Legislative Politics and Practice* (Random House, 1962).
Lockard, D., *The Politics of State and Local Government* (Macmillan, 1963).

[7] Ibid. Art. 97.
[8] Ibid. Art. 98.

Kammerer, G. M. *et al., City Managers in Politics* (U. of Florida, 1962).

Morlan, R. L., *Capitol, Courthouse and City Hall,* 2nd ed. (Houghton Mifflin, 1960).

Phillips, J. C., *State and Local Government in America* (American Book, 1954).

——, *Municipal Government & Administration* (Macmillan, 1960).

Rossi, P., and R. A. Dentler, *The Politics of Urban Renewal* (Free Press, 1961).

Sayre, W. S., and H. Kaufman, *Governing New York City* (Russell Sage, 1960).

Simon, R., *Local Councils and the Citizen* (Stevens, 1948).

Studenski, P., and P. R. Mort, *Centralized v. Decentralized Government in Relation to Democracy* (Columbia, 1941).

Vernon, R., *Metropolis, 1985* (Harvard, 1960).

Warren, J. H., *The English Local Government System,* 5th ed. (Allen & Unwin, 1957).

Williams, O. P., and C. R. Adams, *Four Cities: A Study in Comparative Policy-Making* (U. of Pennsylvania, 1963).

Wood, R. C., *1400 Governments: The Political Economy of the New York Metropolitan Region* (Harvard, 1961).

Zeller, B., *American State Legislatures* (Crowell, 1954).

VIII

Civil Rights and Liberties

It will be recalled from the discussion in Chapter II that liberal democratic ideas affirm the essential worth and dignity of every human being. The ultimate aim of democratic politics is to provide the necessary conditions for the fullest and widest realization of human personality. The principal conditions are two: *First,* there is the indispensable framework of order and general security which government exists to provide for society. Government provides it by the making and enforcing of laws to which all must equally submit. To be secure in his own person, each must be prepared to help to maintain the same security for others through equal laws equally enforced. The *second* condition is individual freedom, within the limits imposed by the need for order, to make of ourselves what we can out of our abilities and our own unique experience of life. These two conditions can be summed up as *freedom under law.*

When the law marks out a defined area of freedom for individuals and provides a means by which individuals can protect themselves in the exercise of freedom in that area, it can be said to create rights. Each individual then has a right to that area of freedom. However, if the constant aim is to foster and protect human personality, certain kinds of freedom are more important than others, so important in fact that they are basic to the whole enterprise. The principal of these are freedom of religion, freedom of expression, freedom of the person, and freedom of public meeting.[1] In the Anglo-

[1] On this point, see Mr. Justice Cardozo's majority opinion in the celebrated case of *Palko* v. *Connecticut,* 302 U.S. 319 (1937).

American world, a number of these basic freedoms have long been accorded a special emphasis and a special protection which will be discussed in this chapter. They have been variously called fundamental freedoms, civil liberties, or civil rights.

FREEDOM UNDER LAW

Freedom under law is an ideal, a goal to be strived for. To make it effective in our political and social life, both freedom and law have to be defined with some precision and reconciled in the interests of personality. The process of adjustment of the two goes on endlessly, and the precise terms of reconciliation vary from time to time. The changing scope of government activities has made continuous adjustment of the boundary between them in the last seventy years. Where to draw the line between the two has been one of the most vexatious problems of our times. To define this boundary with precision in the United States or Britain, and thus to learn in full detail the scope of individual rights of all kinds, one would have to make an extensive study of the whole legal system.

For Individuals. Liberal democracy approaches the mutual adjustment of freedom and law with a leaning toward freedom. As we have already seen it is broadly correct to say that in a liberal democracy *conduct which is not forbidden by law is permitted.* The common law, which is unwritten or customary law, chiefly made by judges, and which is still a large part of the law in the United States and Britain, has a bias toward individual freedom. But it also circumscribes freedom; witness the criminal law—defining offenses committed against the safety and order of the state—which in Britain is still largely common law, increasingly less so in the United States. Statutory law—written and codified law, made by the legislature—is a rapidly growing part of the law, and it also often puts limits on what individuals are free to do. Between them, common law and statutory law define the entire area of individual freedom, largely by the negative process of saying what one may *not* do.

AGAINST OTHER INDIVIDUALS. If individuals break these laws and thereby infringe on the rights and freedoms of other individuals, they are exposed to actions in the courts. If X makes a slanderous statement about Y, he infringes on Y's right to his good name, and may be sued in court by Y for damages by way of compensation. If X puts his statement about Y in writing, the latter can sue for libel.[2] If he obstructs a public highway so as to prevent others from its lawful usage, he interferes with a lawful freedom of those persons, and the courts will, on proper presentation of a charge, impose a penalty for creating a public nuisance. Where mutual respect and the fear of damages or penalty are not enough to make particular individuals respect the lawful claims of others, the courts are open to give redress. In this way, the law protects individuals against wrongful interference by other individuals. It should not be assumed, however, that this protection is foolproof. Indeed, a good case may be made for the position that more civil rights and liberties are violated by private persons against their peers than by free government against its citizenry.

AGAINST GOVERNMENT. But individuals need to be protected against the government as well as against their fellows as private persons. A legislature with power to make the laws and an executive with overwhelming force at its command have effective and alarming power to restrict individual freedom. The men who laid the main lines of the modern British and United States constitutions had had bitter experience with arbitrary governments. One of their most anxious concerns was to limit the power that governments could exercise over individuals.

Accordingly, they selected for special emphasis a number of freedoms thought to be vital to the interests of personality. In Britain, this emphasis led immediately to the Bill of Rights of 1689, a solemn Act of Parliament that curbed sharply the powers of the executive branch of government, and to a genuinely independent judiciary free of executive pressure. Also, it led immediately to a strong affirmation of the Rule of Law, which subjected public officials of all kinds to the same rules of law and to the same courts as private individuals. Then, over the years, it led to an extraordinarily powerful public opinion in favor of these vital freedoms, and opposed to Parliament's restricting them by legislation. In the United States, this emphasis led to the Bill of Rights and other clauses in the Constitution, and to the various bills of rights in the state constitutions, thus protecting individuals in their exercise of certain rights and freedoms from interference by governments.

---

[2] In a much-publicized comment in 1962, Mr. Justice Black expressed the opinion that the First Amendment to the U. S. Constitution in effect forbids all damage suits for libel and slander, since it provides: 'Congress shall make no law . . . abridging freedom of speech or of the press.' His is, however, obviously a minority point of view, based on his absolutist position vis-à-vis the First Amendment.

RIGHTS AND LIBERTIES. The rights and freedoms so protected by constitutional provisions in the United States are generally described as *civil rights*. Substantially the same rights and freedoms are also protected in Britain—there simply called *civil liberties*—by common law or statute against executive interference, and by a strong public opinion against legislative interference. Civil liberties or civil rights are to be distinguished from all the other rights and freedoms that individuals may enjoy under law because they are specially buttressed in one way or another *against violation by governments*.

Civil and Political Rights Distinguished. Civil rights,[3] as they will be normally called here, are to be distinguished from political rights. *Political rights* are those which give the adult citizen the right to the franchise, qualify him to hold public office, and entitle him to direct participation in political life. They are now restricted to persons who are citizens,[4] and full recognition of political rights has lagged behind the recognition of civil rights, both in Britain and the United States. *Civil rights,* on the other hand, are rights which protect the individual against political interference in the private sphere of life. Of course, political rights cannot be exercised effectively without at least some of the civil rights: freedom of speech, freedom of the press, and freedom of peaceable assembly. But the civil rights were never thought to be dependent on political rights or on political democracy for their validity. They are not restricted to citizens [5]—the United States Constitution contains many references to 'persons' and 'people'—but are conceded, generally speaking, as rights to which a man is entitled because of his human person-

---

[3] Civil *rights* has acquired a very special meaning in Canada through the use of it to describe a particular area of provincial legislative power in Sec. 92.13 of the British North America Act. As used there, the term civil rights is primarily concerned with *private law,* the legal relationships between person and person in private life. The rights and liberties treated herein are exclusively in the field of *public law,* which defines the relationships between the government and private persons. Cf. Ch. XV, *infra* and, particularly, J. A. Corry and J. E. Hodgetts, *Democratic Government and Politics,* 3rd ed. rev. (Toronto: University of Toronto Press, 1959).

[4] Aliens were permitted to vote in the State of Arkansas as late as 1926.

[5] Space does not permit a discussion of citizenship and its fascinating problems. Suffice it to note here that, broadly speaking, citizenship may be acquired either by birth or naturalization, and that it is determined throughout the world on the basis of two different legal principles, *jus sanguinis* and *jus soli,* i.e. based upon 'blood' or 'soil,' respectively. Most continental European countries adhere to the former, whereas most English-speaking lands follow the latter. Thus, in the United Kingdom all persons born there and subject to its jurisdiction are British citizens. In the United States the Fourteenth Amendment to the Constitution states that 'all persons born or naturalized in the United States, and subject to the jurisdiction thereof, are citizens of the United States and of the State wherein they reside.' There are various exceptions to these rules, but the basic concepts govern.

ality. Indeed, for a long time they were thought to be inherent in man by virtue of his nature—inalienable endowments from his Creator, as Thomas Jefferson said in the Declaration of Independence—and to rest upon the universal laws of nature as first expounded by the Stoic philosophers.

Civil Rights: Substantive and Procedural. The fundamental civil rights, as already suggested, are freedom of religion, freedom of the person, freedom of speech and of the press, and freedom of peaceable assembly. They are all expressly conferred by the Constitution of the United States, and the scope of the limitations they place on government will be discussed later. They are all generally recognized and asserted in Britain. They are *substantive rights*. But solemn declarations and lip-service do not alone guarantee their effectiveness in practice. The Constituent Assembly of the first French Republic issued its resounding Declaration of the Rights of Man, but this did not prevent the Reign of Terror three years later, an episode in which the fundamental freedoms were trampled underfoot. Ways and means of assuring their effectiveness are also needed.

The most important of these ways and means is *fair trial without undue delay*. Declarations of basic liberties will be of little avail if the government can make arrests on trumped-up charges, and holds its victims without trial or get them convicted in an unfair trial. The first requirement for a fair trial is a judiciary independent of direct control by the government. Other basic requirements are trial by jury, the rights of the accused to know the specific charge against himself, to confront his accusers in open court, not to be compelled to incriminate himself and to have the assistance of a lawyer for his defense. To prevent undue delay in his being brought to trial, there must be a procedure to compel either early trial or speedy release of the accused, such as is provided by habeas corpus. All these *procedural rights* are conferred by the Constitution of the United States—although not always repeated on every point and with equal strength in the constitutions of all of the several states—and are equally guaranteed by common law or statute in Britain.

There are besides a number of weapons that governments bent on persecuting individuals commonly use. They make *ex post facto* laws—retroactive *penal* legislation—which turn into crimes acts committed before the law was passed. They make arrests or search persons and places just in the hope of turning something up, acting on the authority of a general warrant. They require excessive bail from those they have taken into custody. The Bill of Rights in Britain outlaws excessive bail, the common law forbids general warrants, and *ex post facto* legislation would outrage public opinion. The Constitution of the United States outlaws all three abuses. Thus, the protection of individual civil rights or liberties against encroachment by governments is further strengthened.

TWO KINDS OF CIVIL RIGHTS. So there are really two kinds of civil rights. First, there are the essential freedoms that men want for their own sake; these are the *substantive* civil rights. Second, there are the means that the Anglo-American genius for practical political devices has established for making them effective; these are the *procedural* civil rights. Everyone hopes he will never need them. No doubt there is less need for some of them now that political democracy has established a large measure of mutual confidence between government and people. But there is no complete assurance that democratic majorities will always refrain from oppressing minorities, either in the public or the private sphere, and every criminal trial that arouses public passions reminds us that the struggle for fairness of trial is never over.

More will be said later about the scope and significance of some of these civil rights. Immediately, it is important to see how they are guaranteed to the individual in the two leading democracies. The method of guarantee is far more complex in the United States than in Britain; hence we shall look at the simpler British situation first.

CIVIL RIGHTS IN BRITAIN

Parliament is supreme in Britain. There is no authority that stands above it and no provision of the constitution it cannot change by majority vote. The only limitation on its power is the customary one of requiring a 'mandate'—in a sense, instructions—from the people in an election before carrying through a serious constitutional change. The strongest formal guarantee available for civil rights is an act of Parliament—which Parliament could change tomorrow. The English *Bill of Rights of 1689,* from which all American bills of rights borrow, takes the form of an act of Parliament subject to change or repeal by a majority vote of Parliament. Equally, of course, any rights that depend on the common law can be altered by Parliament. No declaration of rights, however solemn, lies beyond its reach.

No Formal Statement. Perhaps for this reason the British people have never made a comprehensive formal statement of their civil rights. The Bill of Rights itself is mostly concerned with the detail of grievances against the Stuart kings in their high-handed conduct of the executive branch of government, and does not purport to give a general guarantee of the important civil rights of today. Nothing is said in it in any direct way about freedom of religion, freedom of the press, or freedom of assembly. It does provide a guarantee of freedom of speech, but only for debates in Parliament. There is no other comparable document in which guarantees of civil rights in Britain can be found. In the main, they have to be spelled out of the common law, which permits what it does not forbid. In the seventeenth-century struggle against the Stuarts, Englishmen appealed to the common law as the basis of their liberties. It still remains the principal source of British civil rights.

Freedom of Speech. The exact nature of British civil rights can be made clear by considering more closely the right of freedom of speech. It is nowhere expressly stated as it is in the First Amendment to the Constitution of the United States. It rests rather on the general proposition that what is not forbidden by the common law or by statute is permitted—and protected. To define it, it is necessary to see what kinds of speech or writing entail adverse legal consequences for the utterer.

LEGAL LIMITATIONS. In the first place, the common law, as modified by statute, sets itself against *libel* and *slander.* Any speech or writing which makes false statements injurious to the reputation of any person is a wrong against that person—slander when spoken, libel when written—and gives him a right to sue for damages. Second, *blasphemy* is a criminal offense, and so is the writing and publishing of indecent or obscene literature. The exact definitions of these offenses do not matter here. It is enough to notice that they place some limits on freedom of expression in the interests of religious sensibilities and sexual morality.

Third, and most important for present purposes, *seditious utterances* are offenses against the criminal law. Seditious libel is broadly defined as 'the use of words tending to arouse hatred or contempt for any of the institutions of government, advocating changes in Church or State other than by lawful means, or raising discontent or ill-will among the populace.'[6] It would be very difficult to carry on vigorous political discussion without committing a technical offense under this law. Not only Communists arguing for revolution, but democratic socialists persuading the poor that existing society is unfair to them, and members of Her Majesty's Loyal Opposition, doing their best to show that the government of the day is stupid and inept, could be

[6] Hiram M. Stout, *British Government* (New York: Oxford University Press, 1953), p. 40.

charged almost daily under this law; and its literal meaning is broad enough to justify conviction. In fact, however, trials for sedition are extremely rare and occur only when there is incitement to immediate violence and revolt.

There are various other limitations on freedom of speech and expression. There are special statutory penalties for trying to arouse disaffection among the police and the armed forces. Dramatic productions, motion pictures, and radio scripts are subject to a relatively mild censorship. This list is not exhaustive, but it covers the main restrictions on freedom of expression.

WHAT IS LEFT? Freedom of speech is what is left after these restrictions and limitations on expression. To be more precise, *the individual has a right to say whatever the courts will allow him to say with impunity.* For it is only in the courts that action can be taken against him for what he has said. The Rule of Law requires the government to act according to law. Officials cannot detain a person or inflict a penalty on him for what he has said on some vague ground that it is unwise, not in the public interest, or unfair to the government. They can only lay a charge against him in the courts alleging violation of a specific law.

Other Basic Freedoms. Freedom of the person is secured in the same way. The common law, supplemented by statute, defines the offenses for which a man may be convicted and imprisoned. The law also authorizes the detention of the mentally unbalanced in institutions. But the sane man who keeps clear of the criminal law has a right to personal freedom. Anyone, of course, may find himself arrested on suspicion of a crime. But here again the law defines carefully the lawful power of police or others to arrest, and the right of the suspect to be released on bail pending trial. On very serious charges like that of treason—an overt act aimed at the overthrow of government, betrayal to the enemy—bail is not allowed. However, if the person arrested is not formally charged and tried for some specific offense, he can secure his release on *habeas corpus,* a proceeding in which the court, often within a period of from forty-eight to seventy-two hours, will order his jailer to release him at once unless the jailer shows that he is lawfully detained under a specific law. The Rule of Law comes into play here also. Police, jailers, and other officials who exceed their lawful powers of arrest and detention are personally liable to actions for damages for assault, false arrest, and false imprisonment. Independent courts and procedures ensuring fair trial are also necessary to make the right of personal freedom effective.

Of the freedoms of religion, press, and assembly, it is enough to say here that freedom of the press has substantially the same protection as freedom of speech and expression; that a wide right of public meeting for all lawful purposes is recognized; and that everyone is free to hold such religious convictions and practice such religious observances as he will. It is true that the Church of England is an established state church, but the right of dissent is fully recognized and there are no longer any civil or political disabilities attached to dissent. The same formula applies to all the basic freedoms. The government cannot penalize anyone for his conduct or hamper him in his actions unless he violates a specific law.

How Civil Rights Are Guaranteed

It must be said again that all civil rights are at the mercy of Parliament—which does, on occasion, limit them. For example, in 1936 Parliament passed the Public Order Act, which limited somewhat the right of public procession and meeting. The occasion was the recurring street-fights between Fascists and Communists, as they tried to break up one another's meetings, thus threatening the most basic of all conditions: order and general security. Also, in time of war, Parliament authorizes a degree of censorship of expression, and of detention without trial of persons suspected of enemy association. But in time of peace, the majority in Parliament always shows a tender and alert regard for basic civil rights. Moreover, as we have just seen, the law against sedition is not enforced nearly as drastically as its terms would justify. That is to say, the executive, the government of the day, which decides whether or not to launch criminal prosecutions against alleged offenders, lets slip almost all its opportunities for pressing charges of sedition. It limits itself almost entirely to prosecuting incitements to immediate violence and to attempts to undermine the loyalty of the armed forces and the police.

Best Record. What is the reason for this forbearance of the executive and majority in Parliament? Why has Britain had, without formal constitutional guarantees, the best record in the world for protecting civil rights? Why is there much more freedom of expressing opinions than a literal interpretation of the existing law allows? The answers to all these questions are the same: *The British people as a whole have an intense attachment to individual freedom.* If the majority party in Parliament were to push through laws sharply restricting civil rights, it would have to expect defeat at the next election. Equally, if the government undertook widespread prosecutions to enforce the letter of the sedition laws, it would arouse formidable protest. Action of either kind might so undermine confidence in the government of the day as to force an immediate election. Moreover, trials for sedition must take place before a jury. Juries are much more concerned with public opinion than with the strict letter of the law, and any attempt by the government to use the sedition laws against its political opponents would be likely to be frustrated by acquittals.

The British concern for civil liberties expresses itself in the crisis of war as well as in time of peace. When war broke out in 1939, Parliament gave wide emergency powers to the executive. Section 18B of the Defence Regulations of 1939, enacted under these powers, authorized the detention without trial of persons suspected of enemy or hostile associations. Several persons, including a member of Parliament, were thus held in prison. When France fell in 1940 before the Nazi tidal wave, there were in Britain some thousands of German refugees who had fled from Nazi Germany before 1939. There was little doubt that most of these were anti-Nazi and therefore trustworthy, but there was equally no certainty that a considerable number of them were not carefully planted Nazi agents. There was no quick, sure way to tell one from the other. Faced with imminent invasion when treachery from within would have been fatal, the government detained most of these German refugees. As they were not known to have committed any offense, they could not be brought to trial; so they were interned without trial.

Importance of Public Opinion. Even in this desperate situation, when Britain stood alone with the world crumbling about her, British passion for fair play and individual liberty would not be stilled. In Parliament and out, the government was subjected to mounting criticism (unlike the situation involving the 1942 evacuation of 111,000 Japanese-Americans from the West Coast of the United States—70,000 of whom had been born in the United States—which evoked but little criticism until after the war). The government finally agreed to establish independent advisory committees to screen the persons detained and to advise on their continued detention or release. Over a period of time, these advisory committees investigated the authenticity of the German refugees who had been detained, and recommended the release of the great majority of them. In most instances, the government followed the recommendation of the advisory committees. The attachment to civil liberties is both sincere and profound, and it finds an eloquent champion in the legislative branch—which is not where the average American would look for defense of his civil liberties: he would first turn to the independent judiciary and its power of judicial review.

RESPECT FOR PRECEDENT. The main reason for this unfailing public opinion in support of civil rights is fairly clear. The British people have lived so long together that they have a deep trust in one another. They feel assured that their fellows will not be roused to precipitate action by the glitter of new ideas. Further, their respect for precedent is enormous. The British are ruled, to an irritating degree, by *custom*. It has even been suggested that the British are able to enjoy such wide civil rights because in much of their lives they submit voluntarily to the dictatorship of custom. However that may be, the customs by which they live are permeated with conceptions of fair play and mutual respect.

Notions of fair play and mutual respect rest upon belief in the supreme importance of human personality. So the final basis for civil rights in Britain is the liberal democratic ideals. As long as these ideals are widely held and ensure the unity of a people, they afford a better guarantee than the express guarantees of a written constitution. For a written constitution, in the long run, is no stronger than the fundamental beliefs of the people who live under it.

CIVIL RIGHTS IN THE UNITED STATES

In the United States, there are two lines of legal defense of civil rights against governments. The first line is substantially the same as in Britain. What is not forbidden by law is permitted. The main differences are in the details of what is forbidden, and in the fact that *state as well as federal laws* have to be taken into account in discovering what is forbidden. Also, the Rule of Law or the supremacy of law, as it is more often called, is a vital principle in the United States. Except where expressly authorized by law to the contrary, government officials must answer according to the ordinary law in the ordinary courts. Independent courts are available to test the question whether an official has infringed the rights of individuals as these are defined either by common law or by the statute law of a legislature. This line of defense is a protection of considerable importance.

In the Written Constitution. But there is a second and more formidable line of defense in the federal and state constitutions. As we have already seen, certain specific civil rights, both substantive and procedural, are written into these constitutions, and thus put beyond the reach of legislatures and executives. Some of the civil rights guaranteed in the federal Constitution are asserted against the federal government only—such as the contents of the first eight amendments; some against state governments only—such as the guarantee of the equal protection of the law; and some against both federal and state—such as *ex post facto* laws and bills of attainder. The state constitutions also contain bills of rights, which usually repeat, and often go beyond, the provisions of the federal Constitution guaranteeing civil rights— but in practice frequently fail to provide the same degree of effective protection as the federal sphere.

The principle of limited government in this context means that laws enacted in violation of these guarantees to the prejudice of civil rights are unconstitutional, and the courts will, upon proper challenge, so declare them. Official action infringing civil rights in pursuance of an unconstitutional statute is itself unconstitutional and the courts will so hold. Before valid legislation cutting away these civil rights could be passed, it would be necessary to amend the Constitution, or constitutions as the case may be, so as to take away the protection they afford. Unlike the situation in Britain, a mere legislative majority cannot cut down the *letter* of guaranteed civil rights— although it can attack their spirit.

PROTECTION AGAINST GOVERNMENT ONLY. The various bills of rights in the American constitutions extend to all persons and not merely to citizens. *But they protect civil rights only against governments and not against private persons or organizations.* If hoodlums break up religious services in a church, the remedy is not an appeal to the First Amendment of the United States Constitution, but to the ordinary law relating to assault, trespass, and public nuisance. American history presents persuasive evidence that on the scale of regard for civil rights, the federal government ranks first, the state governments second, and individuals last.

GENERAL TERMS. Many of the civil rights guaranteed in the federal and state constitutions are stated in general terms without any express qualification. They are not, however, to be regarded as absolute. The substantive rights of freedom of religion, speech, press, petition, and assembly set out in the First Amendment, for example, cannot be pressed to the point where they disrupt the indispensable public order and general security that government must provide if it is to be at all useful. It would be almost correct to say that the Supreme Court has inserted the word 'reasonable' as a qualification on these rights in its interpretation of them. But, in recent years the Supreme Court has put a very high value on the importance of these five freedoms for a liberal democratic society, and may well be expected to strike down statutes that purport to qualify them, unless it is convinced that the qualification is clearly necessary for the preservation of public order. The Court—albeit sometimes by the narrowest of margins—has generally accorded the First Amendment somewhat of a 'preferred' status in the scale of constitutional values.

More will be said on the limits of these rights later. At the moment the important function of the courts, particularly the Supreme Court of the United States, in defining and safeguarding civil rights must be stressed. There are limitations on these rights, and the Supreme Court, subject to reversal by Congress or constitutional amendment, or by its own change-of-mind, has the final word on what they are. Some of them are obvious and occasion no disagreement. As Mr. Justice Holmes once pointed out in what has become a classic statement of the problem, no one has the right falsely to shout 'fire' in a crowded theater.[7] Others are much harder to define, and may even vary from time to time. Much will always depend on the personal outlook of the judges, how strongly they are dedicated to the liberal democratic values, and how much faith they have in the reasonableness of their fellow men.

Nonetheless, in this at once fascinating and vexatious area many judges are quite consistent and predictable. For example, Justices Hugo Black and William O. Douglas, since their appointment to the highest bench in 1937 and 1939, respectively, could almost *always* be found on the side of the individual *versus* the state. Mr. Justice Felix Frankfurter, on the other hand, while embracing similar values personally, became an outspoken advocate of judicial self-restraint during his long tenure from 1938 to 1962, and drew the line more often than not on behalf of *the state,* believing that, on balance, judicial restraint was by far the better part of wisdom and, indeed, required by the role and position of the Court. It is precisely the 'drawing of the line' which is so fundamental and so difficult in the relationship between the rights of the individual and those of society. The first of the guarantees mentioned in Article I of the Bill of Rights affords a poignant illustration.

FREEDOM OF RELIGION IN THE UNITED STATES

To turn now to that most important of the guarantees, the First Amendment of the Constitution begins with the provision that 'Congress shall make no law respecting an establishment of religion, or prohibiting the free exer-

[7] *Schenck* v. *U.S.,* 249 U.S. 47 (1919), at 52.

cise thereof.' Judicial interpretations of the clause of the Fourteenth Amendment, which forbids the states to deprive any person of 'life, liberty or property without due process of law,' have held that the 'liberty' thus protected against the states includes the five freedoms of the First Amendment.[8] So neither Congress nor state legislatures can set up a state church or interfere with the freedom of the individual to worship God in his own way.

The deepest feelings and the strongest convictions of individuals are expressed in their religion. It sums up their judgment of the inner meaning of their lives, and of their relationship to the cosmic scheme of things. The religious system to which each adheres, even when it takes the form of saying there is no God, is the citadel of his personality.

No State Religion. As long as it was believed that unity of religion was the indispensable foundation of political order, the state prescribed an official religion and required everyone to conform. Dissenters, who always appear when there is any freedom to think at all, were required to assert beliefs they did not hold and were persecuted for holding unorthodox beliefs. The final indignity to the individual is to deny him the right to hold and express his innermost convictions. The only escape for the dissenters from this humiliation was to seize the government and turn the tables on their persecutors. So persecution on the one side was matched by seditious conspiracy on the other. In this kind of atmosphere, government by consent and peaceful adjustment of differences is impossible. This is why liberal democracy could not come into existence until religious toleration had been accepted. It was necessary first to see that men have enough in common to support a common system of public order without having to agree on all items of religious faith. This discovery was first made by left-wing Puritans in England and America, such as John Locke and Roger Williams. Freedom of religion is a fundamental necessity for liberal democracy.

Caesar and God. It should not be thought, however, that it is easy to reconcile the imperative claims of public order and freedom of religion. Deep religious convictions demand more than verbal expression and ceremonial practice: they urge the believer to act on them. A faith that does not inspire action is scarcely a faith at all. Moreover, religious leaders have a tendency to imperialism; they want truth to prevail. But there is a definite limit to the freedom of individuals that can be allowed in the interest of

---

[8] See, among others, *Fiske* v. *Kansas*, 274 U.S. 380 (1927)—speech; *Near* v. *Minnesota*, 283 U.S. 697 (1931)—press; *DeJonge* v. *Oregon*, 299 U.S. 353 (1937)—assembly and petition; *Hamilton* v. *Regents of the University of California*, 293 U.S. 245 (1934)—religion.

public order. The difficulty is, as Mr. Justice Roberts put it well, that freedom of religion embraces two concepts—freedom to believe and freedom to act. 'The first is absolute but in the nature of things, the second cannot be. Conduct remains subject to regulation for the protection of society.'[9] The defining of what belongs to Caesar and what to God is a difficult and seemingly endless process. It accounts for much of the diversity of opinions and actions in a liberal democracy.

Two Aspects of the Clause. For the sake of constitutional interpretation, we should distinguish between the first and second parts of the opening clause of the First Amendment. Although the Supreme Court has been inclined to lean over backwards in defense of religious liberty, its role in the area of separation of Church and State—the first part of the clause—has lent itself to considerably more controversy than in the second.

(1) 'CONGRESS SHALL MAKE NO LAW RESPECTING AN ESTABLISHMENT OF RELIGION.' What does this phrase mean? What does it forbid? References to history seem to intensify rather than solve the riddle! In general, the Court has held it to forbid governmental favoritism for any *particular* religion, and—probably, but not certainly—any considerable amount of direct *general* aid to *all* religions. Yet it has not viewed as a violation of the principle of separation of Church and State the general-tax-exemption granted to church-owned property or property simply used for religious functions. Nor has it rejected the long-standing practice of *federal grants* for free lunches for parochial and private schools as well as public schools; nor those to war veterans to attend any institution of higher learning of their choice; nor the use of general *public* funds for the use of chaplains in legislatures and in the armed services. But the Supreme Court has gone beyond the rather broad exemptions just cited, and has upheld certain federal, state, and local governmental practices in the face of allegations that they constitute breaches in what Jefferson termed the 'wall of separation between Church and State' including the expenditure of public funds to furnish non-sectarian textbooks to Louisiana parochial and private schools as well as public schools—on the grounds that such 'public purpose' gifts of texts benefit the *child* rather than religion.[10] Yet in 1962 the Court *refused* to review an Oregon Supreme Court decision *banning* state loans of textbooks to pupils of parochial schools as a violation of the Oregon Constitution.* In its most striking decision in

---

[9] *Cantwell* v. *Connecticut*, 310 U.S. 296 (1940).

[10] *Cochran* v. *Louisiana State Board of Education*, 281 U.S. 370 (1930). See also *Bradfield* v. *Roberts*, 175 U.S. 291 (1899) and *Quick Bear* v. *Leupp*, 210 U.S. 50 (1908).

* *Dickman* v. *School District, Oregon City*, 371 U.S. 823.

this particular field, Mr. Justice Black, speaking for a Court which split 5:4 on the issue, upheld the right of authorities of Ewing Township, New Jersey, to provide free bus transportation to children attending parochial as well as public schools.[11] Here again the 'child benefit' theory was the key factor in the Court's decision.

A related, thorny problem has been the constitutionality of *released time,* an arrangement whereby children attending public schools are 'released' from them at stated times in order to attend religious classes. In the most famous released-time case on record, the issue was a practice of the Board of Education in Champaign, Illinois, whereby privately selected religious instructors were permitted to teach religion *during the school day, on the public school premises,* to students whose parents had signed 'request cards,' with the school authorities keeping attendance records in the same manner as for any other class. In an 8:1 decision, rendered by Mr. Justice Black—and received with considerable hostility by the public at large—the Court held the practice to be unconstitutional on the grounds that:

> . . . here not only are the State's tax-supported public school buildings used for the dissemination of religious doctrines. The State also affords sectarian groups an invaluable aid in that it helps to provide pupils for their religious classes through use of the State's compulsory public school machinery. This is not separation of Church and State.[12]

However, the Court rendered a contrary decision in a New York City released time case four years later. Although the program was essentially like that in Champaign, religious instruction was given *outside* the public school buildings in facilities provided by the various religious groups. While expressly refusing to overrule the Champaign decision, Mr. Justice Douglas contended for the majority that the difference inherent in the administration of New York City's law sufficed to save the program, and added that there is 'no constitutional requirement which makes it necessary for government to be hostile to religion. . . .' But the author of Champaign and Ewing Township majority decisions, Mr. Justice Black, here dissented sharply—as did Justices Frankfurter and Jackson—on the grounds that 'ex-

---

[11] *Everson* v. *Board of Education,* 330 U.S. 1 (1947). Fifteen years later, Mr. Justice Douglas, who was among the majority here, announced from the bench that he thought *Everson* had been wrongly decided. State courts have handed down decisions in favor of both sides.
[12] *Illinois ex rel. McCollum* v. *Board of Education,* 333 U.S. 203 (1948), at 212. See Vashti C. McCollum, *One Woman's Fight* (Boston: Beacon Press, 1961).

cept for the use of the school buildings in Illinois, there is no difference between the systems that I even consider worthy of mention.'[13]

Yet no decision in this delicate realm of conscience fanned the flames of public passion as much as did the Supreme Court's 1962 verdict in the famous 'New York Prayer Case.' With only Mr. Justice Potter Stewart in dissent, the Court there struck down as a violation of the principle of separation of Church and State an official 22-word non-denominational prayer, drafted by the New York State Board of Regents and recommended for reading aloud by the state's teachers and by the children in each classroom at the start of every day in the public schools. Writing for the decisive majority, Mr. Justice Black put into focus the manifold and perhaps non-solvable problems of personal commitments and majority-minority line-drawing that continue to bedevil the religious-constitutional controversy:

> It is neither sacrilegious nor antireligious to say that each separate government in this country should stay out of the business of writing or sanctioning official prayers and leave that purely religious function to the people themselves and to those the people choose to look to for religious guidance.[14]

(2) '. . . OR PROHIBITING THE FREE EXERCISE THEREOF.' The phrase means what it says: Congress—and by interpretation the states—may not interfere with the sacred right to act in accordance with one's religious belief. But this right is not absolute. For example, the Court upheld a congressional statute proscribing the practice or advocacy of polygamy against the challenge by Mormons that it infringed upon their religious freedom;[15] it denied the claim that it includes the right to exhibit poisonous snakes in church;[16] and it saw no violation of religious freedom in state 'blue laws.'[17] On the other hand, parents are not obliged to send their children to public schools, if they prefer a parochial institution;[18] a state may not require a declaration of belief in God as a qualification for public office;[19] and in

---

[13] *Zorach* v. *Clauson*, 343 U.S. 306 (1952), 314–15.

[14] *Engel* v. *Vitale*, 370 U.S. 421. The Court's 8:1 decision, just one year later, that no State or locality may require recitation of the Lord's Prayer or Bible verses in public schools was almost anticlimactic (*Abington Township* v. *Schempp* and *Murray* v. *Curlett*, 374 U.S. 203, 1963).

[15] *Reynolds* v. *U.S.*, 98 U.S. 145 (1878).

[16] *Lawson* v. *Commonwealth*, 291 Ky. 437; 164 S.W. 2d 972 (1942).

[17] See *McGowan* v. *Maryland*, 366 U.S. 420 (1961); *Two Guys from Harrison-Allentown, Inc.*, 366 U.S. 582 (1961); *Braunfeld* v. *Brown*, 366 U.S. 599 (1961); and *Gallagher* v. *Crown Kosher Market*, 366 U.S. 617 (1961).

[18] *Pierce* v. *Society of Sisters*, 268 U.S. 510 (1925).

[19] *Torcaso* v. *Watkins*, 367 U.S. 488 (1961).

1946 the Court reversed two decisions of long standing and admitted to citizenship a Canadian Seventh Day Adventist whose religious beliefs prevented him from bearing arms, but who declared his readiness to serve in the armed forces as a non-combatant.[20]

A long series of cases involving the Jehovah's Witnesses, a militantly evangelical minority religion, serves to emphasize the post-1937 Court's addiction to liberal interpretations of freedom of religion. In the twenty-five years from 1938 to 1963, of sixty-five cases before the Court the Witnesses won fifty-seven.[21] In the most celebrated of these cases—after initially holding that public school pupils could be forced to salute the flag of the United States, despite their claim that to do so would be to 'behold a graven image' in violation of religious beliefs [22]—the Court *reversed* itself less than three years later and struck down a West Virginia compulsory flag salute statute. Speaking for a new majority of six, Mr. Justice Jackson here made an observation that has been frequently quoted:

> . . . Those who begin coercive elimination of dissent soon find themselves exterminating dissenters. Compulsory unification of opinion achieves only the unanimity of the graveyard.[23]

FREEDOM OF SPEECH AND PRESS

The First Amendment to the Constitution of the United States forbids Congress—and now by judicial interpretation the several states—to make any law 'abridging the freedom of speech or of the press.' This guarantee covers both speech and writing in every form and would be more accurately described as *freedom of expression*. Again, the right it protects is not absolute. Common and statutory law impose much the same limitations as in Britain.

Legislative Restrictions. Legislatures in the United States have ample

---

[20] *Girouard* v. *U.S.*, 328 U.S. 61 (1946). Cf. *U.S.* v. *Schwimmer*, 279 U.S. 644 (1929) and *U.S.* v. *MacIntosh*, 283 U.S. 605 (1931). In deference to religious objections to military service, Congress now permits bona fide conscientious objectors to serve a period of time equivalent to that required by the draft in work contributing to the 'national health, safety, or interest,' in lieu of induction.

[21] Cf. *Lovell* v. *City of Griffin*, 303 U.S. 444 (1938); *Cantwell* v. *Connecticut*, 310 U.S. 296 (1940); *Marsh* v. *Alabama*, 326 U.S. 501 (1946); *Tucker* v. *Texas*, 326 U.S. 517 (1946); and *Murdock* v. *Pennsylvania*, 319 U.S. 105 (1943).

[22] *Minersville School District* v. *Gobitis*, 310 U.S. 586 (1940).

[23] *West Virginia State Board of Education* v. *Barnette*, 319 U.S. 624 (1943). On the same day the Court also invalidated a Mississippi statute that made it unlawful to urge people, on religious grounds, not to salute the flag. (*Taylor* v. *Mississippi*, 319 U.S. 583.)

power to make laws curbing seditious utterances or providing against sub-version generally. Congress and the various state legislatures, especially during periods of national emergency, have enacted such laws increasingly since the end of World War II—chiefly as a reaction to and fear of the tactics employed by Communist Russia and its agents.

THE COURT'S ATTITUDE. The Supreme Court has not always applied a uniform test in deciding the validity of such legislation. It has acknowledged that restrictions on speech which would not be justified in time of peace may be justified when the nation is at war.[24] For a long time the prevailing view of the Court was that utterances which had a 'bad tendency' to undermine the belief of Americans in the rightness of their form of government and their established way of life were not entitled to the protection of the First Amendment. But in recent years—with lapses—the Court has shown much more anxious concern for freedom of expression. Its prevailing view in these recent years has been that the only utterances that can lawfully be curbed are those which threaten paramount public interests, 'not doubtfully and remotely but by clear and present danger.'[25] Yet what constitutes a 'clear and present danger'?

The Clear and Present Danger Doctrine. As it was first conceived and spelled out by Justices Holmes and Brandeis in the *Schenck* case in 1919,[26] the 'clear and present danger' doctrine was intended by its authors to draw the all-important line between freedom of expression and the right of the state to guard itself against subversion. Mr. Justice Holmes, in holding for a unanimous Court that the defendant could *not* with impunity agitate for disobedience of the Draft Act of 1917, in the face of a prohibition to the contrary contained in the Espionage Act of 1917, attempted to find and define that line as follows:

> . . . We admit that in many places and in ordinary times the defendants in saying all that was said . . . would have been within their constitutional rights. But the character of every act *depends upon the circumstances* in which it was done . . . The most stringent protection of free speech would not protect a man in *falsely* shouting fire in a theatre and causing a panic. It does not even protect a man from an injunction against uttering words that have all the effects of force . . . The ques-

[24] *Schenck* vs. *U.S.*, 47 (1919).
[25] *Thomas* v. *Collins*, 323 U.S. 516 (1944).
[26] Loc. cit. Some students of the doctrine would credit Judge Learned Hand with an important assist, if not the initial idea, in the creation of the doctrine. See Robert S. Lancaster, 'Judge Hand's Free Speech Problem,' *Vanderbilt Law Review* 10 (February 1957), 301.

tion in every case is whether the *words used are used in such circumstances and are of such a nature as to create a clear and present danger
that they will bring about the substantive evils that Congress has a right
to prevent.* It is a question of proximity and degree.[27]

Yet the enigmatic nature of this 'clear and present danger' test is illustrated
when only six years later a majority of seven held one Benjamin Gitlow's
speeches and publications against the New York State Criminal Anarchy
Act to be in violation of that law, despite his reliance on the guarantees of
freedom of expression under the First and Fourteenth Amendments.[28] Although the Court did not apply the 'clear and present danger' doctrine per
se—for obviously no such danger was created by Gitlow's action—it spoke
of a 'bad tendency' to bring about such results. There were two dissenters:
Justices Holmes and Brandeis—who had already had occasion to disagree
with their brethren on this issue a mere six months after *Schenck*[29]—distinguished this case from *Schenck* chiefly because of the absence of war. Brandeis
seized on an early opportunity to refine and expand their doctrine, with
Holmes's support, when he wrote in a concurring opinion that 'No danger
flowing from speech can be deemed clear and present, *unless* the incidence
of the evil apprehended is so *imminent* that it may fall before there is full
opportunity for discussion.' [30]

PROBLEMS OF INTERPRETATION. Ever since the 'clear and present danger'
doctrine was devised its interpretation has thus troubled the Court. On the
one hand, it has modified the doctrine by its collateral adoption of the 'bad
tendency' test; on the other, it has seen the need to be mindful of the right
of freedom of expression, especially in the face of the congressional and public tendency to be restrictive, even intolerant, of unpopular views in troubled
times.

As a result, either or both tests have been employed in various cases, and
the court has frequently been split—sometimes 5:4—in their application.
Usually, the 'clear and present danger' plus 'imminence' test has been invoked by those justices who feel obligated, under the Constitution, to express a preference for free speech, while the 'bad tendency' test has been
invoked by those who are more strongly inclined to look with favor upon
the discretion of legislatures in the face of threats to national security.

To cite only a few examples of this great problem of drawing the line,

---

[27] *Schenck* v. *U.S.*, op. cit. 52. (Italics supplied.)
[28] *Gitlow* v. *New York*, 268 U.S. 252 (1925).
[29] *Abrams* v. *U.S.*, 250 U.S. 216 (1919).
[30] *Whitney* v. *California*, 274 U.S. 357 (1927). (Italics supplied.)

the Court, by a 5:4 vote, *voided* as an abridgment of freedom of speech a Lockport, New York, ordinance which forbade the use of sound trucks in public except with the advance permission of the chief of police,[31] but *upheld,* also by a 5:4 vote, a Trenton, New Jersey, ordinance prohibiting the use on its city streets of sound trucks emitting 'loud and raucous noises.' The 'switch-vote' by Mr. Chief Justice Vinson was apparently based upon the different wording of the two statutes, which raises the interesting question how sound trucks can be anything but 'loud and raucous.'[32] In another seemingly contradictory set of decisions, the Court *voided* 8:1 the disorderly conduct conviction of a sidewalk speaker under a New York City ordinance deemed to constitute unlawful prior censorship,[33] but—on the same day—it *upheld* 6:3 Syracuse, New York, police in arresting a sidewalk speaker espousing unpopular causes for 'disorderly conduct'—faced with unrest and threatening movements in a crowd that had gathered about him.[34] Lack of space does not permit additional illustrations; suffice it to reiterate the significance and difficulty of the problem of how to reconcile the freedom of individual expression with the safety of the state—once more we see the problem of the 'line.' But something more must be said about the particularly involved and topical problem of the constitutionality of present-day legislative attempts to guard against subversive Communist talk and activity, especially on the national level.

Anti-Communist Legislation. While many states have enacted legislation in this area attention here is directed toward the three major federal statutes:

(1) THE SMITH ACT OF 1940 makes it a crime knowingly to advocate the overthrow of the government by force or violence; or to help organize a society that engages in such advocacy; or knowingly to become a member of it; or to conspire with others to commit any of the first three offenses.

The most important case involving the Communist conspiracy problem was based on the Smith Act. In 1951 the Supreme Court, in a 6:2 decision, upheld its constitutionality in the famous Dennis case.[35] Eleven top leaders of the Communist Party, U.S.A., had been indicted and found guilty of a conspiracy to teach and advocate the overthrow of the government by force and violence, and of conspiring to organize the Communist party to teach

---

[31] *Saia* v. *New York,* 334 U.S. 558 (1948).
[32] *Kovacs* v. *Cooper,* 336 U.S. 77 (1949).
[33] *Kunz* v. *New York,* 340 U.S. 290 (1951).
[34] *Feiner* v. *New York,* 340 U.S. 315 (1951). See also *Beauharnais* v. *Illinois,* 343 U.S. 250 (1952) and *Burstyn* v. *Wilson,* 343 U.S. 495 (1952).
[35] *Dennis* v. *U.S.,* 341 U.S. 494 (1951).

and advocate the same. Their appeal to the Supreme Court raised the free speech issue.

In sustaining the Smith Act, Mr. Chief Justice Vinson's majority opinion invoked the 'clear and present danger' doctrine in relation to the *conspiratorial nature* of the defendants' activities. But in so doing he disregarded the imminence test and replaced it with the test of 'probability,' adapting the following excerpt from Chief Justice Learned Hand's decision in the United States Court of Appeals—the court immediately below the United States Supreme Court:

> . . . (courts) in each case . . . must ask whether the gravity of the evil, *discounted by its improbability,* justifies such invasion of free speech as is necessary to avoid the danger.[36]

Chief Justice Vinson contended:

> . . . The formation by [the convicted persons] of such a highly organized conspiracy, with rigidly disciplined members subject to call when the leaders . . . felt that the time had come for action, coupled with the inflammable nature of world conditions, similar uprisings in other countries and the touch-and-go nature of our relations with countries with whom [the convicted persons] were in the very least ideologically attuned, convince us that their convictions were justified on this score.[37]

But—in addition to two separate concurring opinions by Justices Frankfurter and Jackson—there were two passionate dissents by Justices Black and Douglas who *denied* the existence of a danger either 'clear or present' enough to justify this limitation of freedom of expression and argued for 'full and free discussion even of ideas we hate.' Mr. Justice Black closed his opinion with the observation that:

> Public opinion being what it now is, few will protest the conviction of these Communist petitioners. There is hope, however, that in calmer times, when present pressures, passions, and fears subside, this or some later Court will restore the First Amendment liberties to the high preferred place where they belong in a free society.[38]

There is little doubt that the 'bad tendency' test had been reintroduced— some would find a new test, that of 'grave and probable.' In the eyes of the Court majority—applauded by the country at large—the gravity of the evil obviated, or at least decreased, the necessity for 'clarity and imminence.'

[36] Ibid. citing 183F. 2d, at 212. (Italics supplied.)
[37] Ibid. at 510–511 ff.
[38] Ibid. at 590.

By June 17, 1957, the federal government had obtained 145 indictments and 89 convictions under the Smith Act. But on that date the Supreme Court, with only Mr. Justice Clark dissenting, gave an amended interpretation to the Smith Act and limited its application in the *Yates* case.[39] Writing for the majority, Mr. Justice Harlan narrowed the meaning of the term 'to organize' and drew a clear distinction between the statement of a *philosophical belief* and the *advocacy of an illegal action*. The Smith Act stood, but the federal government would no longer be able to punish members of the Communist party for *expressing a mere belief* in the violent overthrow of the government. It would have to *prove* that individuals on trial for violating the Smith Act actually intended to overthrow the government by force and violence now or in the future, or to persuade others to attempt to do so, and the language employed must be 'calculated to incite to action'—thus reintroducing the clarity, if not the imminence, requirement.

Almost as if to rectify the adverse public reaction to the *Yates* decision, a 5:4 decision by the Court four years later upheld the so-called membership clause of the Smith Act, holding that a person who was a 'knowing, active' member of a subversive group, and who personally had a 'specific intent to bring about violent overthrow,' was convictable.[40] But in a companion case, with Mr. Justice Harlan switching, the Court ruled that the government had not met the above requirements for conviction and must thus release the petitioner.[41] Again, we see the vexatious balancing problem!

(2) THE INTERNAL SECURITY (MC CARRAN) ACT OF 1950, passed over President Truman's veto, requires all 'Communist-action' and 'Communist-front' groups to register with the government, to provide lists of their membership and financial records, and to label all mail as 'Communist.' Members of such groups are among other things, barred from receiving passports and from working for the government or in defense industry. The Act established a Subversive Activities Control Board to determine what organizations are subject to the registration requirements. It also provided for presidential authority to intern any 'suspected persons' upon a declaration of war. In the first significant ruling involving the Act, the Supreme Court held 5:4 in 1961 that the registration requirement did not violate the First Amendment by forced disclosure of members' names.[42] In thus upholding the S.A.C.B.'s order to the Communist Party, U.S.A., to register, the Court did not reach

[39] *Yates et al.* v. *United States,* 354 U.S. 298 (1957).
[40] *Scales* v. *United States,* 367 U.S. 203 (1961).
[41] *Noto* v. *United States,* 367 U.S. 290 (1961).
[42] *Communist Party* v. *Subversive Activities Control Board,* 367 U.S. 1.

any of the other constitutional questions involved, such as the matter of self-incrimination under the Fifth Amendment.

(3) THE COMMUNIST CONTROL ACT OF 1954, passed in the last days of the 83rd Congress, seems to outlaw the Communist party, but whether it actually does so is uncertain. The law specifically provides that the Communist party shall not be 'entitled to any of the rights, privileges and immunities attendant upon legal bodies created under the jurisdiction of the laws of the United States or any subdivision thereof.' And any person who 'knowingly and wilfully becomes or remains a member' of the Communist party is specifically made subject to the Internal Security Act of 1950. No case challenging the constitutionality of the Act had reached the Supreme Court at this writing. (Autumn 1963)

The Position of the Communist Party Today. The language of the majority in the *Dennis* case makes it clear that the decisive facts were *the conspiring and advocating,* as a part of a tightly organized plan for revolutionary action, controlled by the convicted persons themselves, and held at the service of the Soviet Union. The Court expressly said the conviction could not have been upheld if the convicted persons had done 'no more than pursue peaceful studies and discussions or teaching and advocacy *in the realm of ideas.'* Thus, the upholding of the Smith Act in the *Dennis* case appears to be on the ground that it struck at a course of systematic preparation for the realm of action and not at discussion in the realm of ideas; and the *Yates* case, decided six years later, seems to determine that mere advocacy, *without calculated incitement* to action, is not a crime under the Smith Act.

The current legal position of a Communist party member might be described in sum as follows: If the party refuses to register under the Internal Security Act, and the member does not register himself, he is subject to prosecution. If he does register, his mere membership may be legal, but his privileges as a citizen are sharply restricted, and he may be in constant danger of prosecution as 'a knowing, active member' of or a conspirator in a party advocating violent overthrow of the government.

DRAWING THE LINE: CIVIL RIGHTS AND LIBERTIES IN DANGEROUS TIMES

The basis of civil rights or liberties is a tolerant acceptance of diversity and individual differences. Their natural habitat is in those countries where liberal democratic ideas have inculcated a deep mutual respect among men, despite their differences. As we have seen, there is no place for civil liberties in dictatorial regimes. In the free lands of the West, zealous partisans of the Communist, Nazi, and Fascist regimes have made full use of civil rights to denounce liberal democratic ideals and to try to undermine liberal democratic institutions, in preparation for dosing them with their own nostrums. Of course, if these anti-democratic adherents were once able to get control of the government, whether through peaceful or violent means, they would immediately destroy all civil rights. At any rate, this has been the case in all countries where they have secured control. The creeds and the practice of modern dictatorship and the threat they make to liberal democratic societies have led to strong demands for reconsidering the whole philosophy of civil rights. Its heart is freedom of expression, whether the spoken word or the written word.

Should Freedom of Speech Be Restricted? Many who are seriously concerned in defending civil rights balk at defending them for those who will not admit a reciprocal obligation to defend them for others. Tolerance, they say, must not be extended to the intolerant; freedom must not be allowed to be used to destroy freedom. On what ground can freedom of expression be claimed now by those who will destroy it when they have the power? What principle of fair play is it that requires the acceptance of players who will not play according to the rules?

Further to this issue, it is pointed out that the theory and practice of civil rights were developed mainly in the Anglo-American communities. During the latter part of the nineteenth century these communities established themselves so firmly in the world that the possibility of serious civil disaffection or menacing foreign aggression almost disappeared from the consciousness of their people. They came to regard public order as almost impregnable, something that could be taken for granted. It was easy and even desirable in those circumstances to urge civil rights in almost unqualified terms. It was easy to insist that everyone should be allowed to talk though the heavens fall, when nobody believed there was any serious risk that they would fall.

JEFFERSON. This serene confidence is perhaps best illustrated by Thomas Jefferson in his first inaugural address as President of the United States in 1801 when he said: 'If there be any among us who wish to dissolve this union, or change its republican form, let them stand undisturbed as monuments of the safety with which error of opinion may be tolerated where reason is left free to combat it.' Anyone making such a statement today might run the risk of being called before a legislative committee investigating subversive activities.

Assumptions in the Defense of Free Speech. The most important point about Jefferson's statement is its assumptions, what it takes for granted. First, it assumes that most men are rational, that they will support what reason shows to be right and true. Second, it assumes the rightness of the union of the American states on a republican basis. It therefore concludes that public order and political unity are impregnable as long as there is freedom of speech. Likewise, John Milton, one of Jefferson's spiritual ancestors in seventeenth-century England, urged in his *Areopagitica* that truth and falsehood be allowed to grapple, for 'who ever knew Truth put to the worse, in a free and open encounter?'

Something must be said about these assumptions. It is clear that freedom of expression and discussion will accomplish little unless most of the participants in it are deeply concerned with truth and are prepared to follow the argument wherever it goes, and to modify their convictions as the amassing of evidence and the unfolding of logic make their positions untenable. They must be genuine seekers with a sense of curiosity and wonder that is continually refreshed by the flow of discussion. They must be listeners as well as talkers, respectful of what the other side has to say. If, on the other hand, both sides in debate have dogmatic beliefs that will not yield to any demonstration, if they are seeking to convince but unwilling to be convinced, if they are ready to falsify the evidence to gain their point, freedom of speech will drive them further apart instead of bringing them closer together. If the mass of men were as irrational as the Fascists and Nazis said they are, the faith in reason and in freedom of expression would be entirely misplaced. Actually, of course, the experience of the British and American liberal democracies in particular shows that there are conditions in which the faith is justified. The basic problem is to identify these conditions.

Before the members of a society can make fruitful use of freedom of speech, they must be conscious of some underlying unity that transcends difference of opinion. They must believe in one another's reasonableness and have a common loyalty to the pursuit of truth. They must have some measure of agreement on what amounts to proof of the truth of an assertion. If they differ seriously on this point, discussion will not bring them closer together. To be specific, if economic classes can see only their own class interests, there will be one proof which convinces a capitalist and another proof which convinces a proletarian, but no common standard of proof to umpire discussion. A game without generally accepted rules soon ceases to be a game.

BASIS FOR CONFIDENCE. If men are as deeply divided in a society made up of economic classes as the prevailing interpretation of Marxist theory says they are, there is no basis for Jefferson's confidence that public order and political unity will stand the shocks that freedom of speech involves. The real basis of Jefferson's confidence, as applied to the United States of his day, was the belief that Americans were united in support of the ideals he had stated in the Declaration of Independence, and that they would always uphold a union dedicated to the pursuit of these ideals. There can be no other basis for confidence today. Widespread and firm belief in the liberal democratic ideals is the condition on which freedom of expression is constructive rather than disruptive.

Dangers of Division on Fundamentals. It is possible to see now why some sincere defenders of freedom of speech want to deny it to Communists and the holders of other authoritarian creeds that deny the liberal democratic ideals and reject, either expressly or by implication, the rationality of man. They cannot enter into the fellowship of free men because they use freedom of speech destructively rather than constructively.

MILTON AND LOCKE. The argument for denial can be made even clearer by looking briefly at John Milton and John Locke, the two great champions of religious toleration in seventeenth-century England. Milton, arguing for the right to print and publish without license from the government, limited his claim for toleration to those of the Protestant faith, to those who accepted the Scriptures as the final standard of proof and of revealed truth. He expressly excluded Roman Catholics because they recognized in the institutionalized authority of their Church another standard of proof and of truth. In its acceptance of the Scriptures, the Protestant group was united on fundamentals and thus able to discuss constructively. John Locke also excluded Roman Catholics because they denied any obligation to keep faith with heretics. That is to say, they were not comprehended within a unity that transcended differences of opinion. He excluded atheists because they cannot be bound by an oath, and hence cannot be contained by any obligation to society. He excluded also those 'who give themselves up to the protection and service of another prince,' giving as an example Mohammedans —although he was actually referring to Roman Catholics.

CIVIL RIGHTS AND LIBERTIES

J. S. MILL. Milton and Locke, living in the commotion and strife of seventeenth-century England, restricted freedom of expression to those they thought could be trusted to use it constructively. Ardent believers in freedom of thought and speech, they did not think public order was sufficiently secure to allow freedom of speech to those who would try to undermine it. When we come to John Stuart Mill, who lived in the security and peace of mid-nineteenth-century England, we find him arguing for freedom of expression in almost absolute terms. He brushed aside the suggestion that society needs to be protected against subversive and disloyal speech, insisting instead that *it is the individual who needs to be protected against society*. He did not propose discrimination against Roman Catholics because, in his day, their loyalty to their church no longer was in active conflict with their loyalty to Britain. The limitations he proposed on freedom of expression would cover libel, slander, and inflammatory incitements to immediate violence, but little else. 'All mankind has no right to silence a single dissenter,' he urged in his celebrated *On Liberty*, and 'all silencing of discussion is an assumption of infallibility.'

TODAY. Returning to the present situation, we find the whole world convulsed with the clash of rival systems of ideas that threaten war and imperil the security of nation states. Within Britain, the United States, and other western democracies today there are active groups—particularly Communists —that reject the existing basis of public order and are determined to undermine and overthrow it by force if necessary. In these circumstances it is not surprising that many find more affinity with Milton and Locke than with Jefferson and Mill. We have lost some of the serene confidence that Jefferson and Mill had in the impregnability of tolerant liberal societies. In Germany and Italy, we saw freedom of expression destroyed by electorates voting repressive regimes into power. We are alarmed by the danger of a division on fundamentals such as existed between the Protestants and Catholics in seventeenth-century England. In those Communists who take orders from Moscow, we face again the problem of those 'who give themselves up to the protection and service of another prince.' What is to be said concerning the argument that freedom of expression should be denied to those who cannot be counted on to observe the rules of the game?

The Justification of Freedom of Speech. In the first place, as we have seen at some length, the right to free speech is not absolute. The maintenance of public order and security comes first. That is the justification of laws forbidding speech which is a 'clear and present' or 'grave and probable' danger to public order. In the second place, what constitutes such a danger will vary according to circumstances—peace, war, or 'cold war.' It has already been suggested that this is substantially the ground of the decision of the Supreme Court upholding the constitutionality of the Smith Act. The critical case for discussion is whether to forbid disloyal and subversive talk that aims *at present* only to undermine belief in the rightness of the liberal democratic order as a preparation for its overthrow by force *at some future time.*

THE TEST. The test a liberal democracy should apply to this issue is clear enough. *Will the forbidding of such talk further or hamper the realization of liberal democratic ideals?* No doubt subversive propaganda wins some converts. Every such convert is a loss. No society can look with complacency on the weakening of belief in its unifying ideals It is still pertinent, however, to ask why its members are converted.

Most of them are converted to a belief in violent solutions because of some rankling sense of injustice, a conviction of the deep inadequacy of existing society. This sense of injustice may be justified or not in particular instances, but it is at least clear that the liberal democratic societies under discussion here have still not succeeded in ensuring adequate opportunity for self-realization of all their people. As long as this remains true there will be the discontented, prepared to contemplate rebellion. The only effective way to cope with them is to moderate or remove the discontent by education, remedial laws, or other community action.

It is easy to make laws that impose punishment for subversive propaganda. But in the circumstances just outlined, this will not stop it. It will continue underground. Moreover, repression sharpens the sense of injustice and provides an added argument for desperate measures. There is no doubt at all that the loyalty of the mass of men to liberal democracy has been greatly strengthened by the right to freedom of expression. They have felt that they have a stake in a society that allows them to express the passion they feel about their deepest grievances. Thus repressive laws are likely to fail in their immediate purpose of maintaining loyalty.

The Dangers in Repression. The gravest danger in repression is that it excuses the liberal democrat from arguing the case for his ideals and for the highly developed procedures for pursuing them. Because he is not openly confronted by the arguments against them, he is not constantly reminding himself and his fellows of the case in favor of them. The surest way to keep beliefs fresh and strong is to exercise them in debate against the strongest criticism of them that can be made. We then know at any moment why we believe what we believe.

FALSE SENSE OF SECURITY. Repression would give us, for a time, a false sense of security. We would not be outraged daily by hearing ideas we hate. Because social discontent did not break out in violent expression, we would tell ourselves that there were no serious social maladjustments to be met. We would develop a superficial sense of well-being and fail to brace ourselves, in either knowledge or morale, for the kind of problems we have to meet. This is a sort of 'aspirin therapy.' We take two or three tablets five or six times a day and have no way of knowing whether or not we have any aches and pains to which we should be attending.

Freedom for rebellious and revolutionary utterance is a safety valve that gives warning of the existence of dangerous pressures in society. The only effective way to fight the contagion of disloyalty is to get at its causes. A society that descends to repressive measures is losing faith in its ability to win and keep loyalty. This is bound to be fatal. Authoritarian regimes can continue indefinitely even if they are out of touch with the problems and thoughts of their people. Liberal democracy lives only in the hearts of its citizens. If it cannot be kept alive there by free discussion, it certainly cannot be kept alive by repression. Judge Learned Hand stated it aptly in his 'I-Am-An-American-Day' speech in Central Park in New York in 1944: 'Liberty lies in the hearts of men and women; when it dies there no constitution, or law, no court can save it; no constitution, no law nor court can even do much to help it. While it lies there it needs no constitution, no law, no court to save it.'

It would be hard to defend freedom of speech as a sacred personal right of those who will deny it to others if they get a chance. But the merit or lack of merit of the particular claimant is not the issue. The issue is what to do in order to maintain and further the unifying ideals. The answer suggested here is that little or nothing will be accomplished and much will be lost by banning the subversive *speech* of even professed revolutionaries.

This theoretical discussion deals only with the question of what a person should be allowed to say if he can find listeners. It is not concerned with the question of what forum, if any, should be made available for opinions we agree to tolerate. It has nothing to do with the question of dismissal from government employment for radical opinions. These are distinct problems that cannot be discussed here [43] except to say that a government not only is

[43] Cf. Chapter xvi, *infra*, for such a discussion, especially pp. 626 ff.

entitled to be sure of the loyalty of its civil servants, but also has a duty to its people to do so. The big question is how to make sure without unfairly prejudicing the position and prospects of the persons whose loyalty, while not disproved, is doubtful.

FREEDOM OF THE PERSON AND OF MEETING

In the United States, as in Britain, a person has the right to be free of physical restraint in going about any activity he pleases, as long as it is not forbidden by law. In addition, this freedom of the person is further protected by a number of guarantees in federal and state constitutions. To describe the exact scope of them all would require an essay on constitutional law. The most important of them are as follows:

Freedom of the Person. The Thirteenth Amendment of the United States Constitution forbids slavery and involuntary servitude, 'except as a punishment of crime whereof the party shall have been duly convicted.' It was adopted expressly for the purpose of outlawing Negro slavery, but it is equally a protection for all. No legislature can enact laws subjecting persons to servitude, and private persons cannot exact forced labor of anyone. The Fifth Amendment forbids Congress, and the Fourteenth Amendment forbids the states, among other things, to 'deprive any person of life, liberty, or property, without due process of law.' More will be said about these due process clauses later—they are important buttresses of freedom of the person.

The Fourth Amendment and similar clauses in the state constitutions affirm 'the right of the people to be secure in their persons, houses, papers and effects, against unreasonable searches and seizures. . . .'

General warrants are outlawed and, subject to certain exceptions carefully limited by judicial interpretation, no person can be arrested and no person or place searched except upon a warrant sworn out before a judicial officer '*particularly* describing the place to be searched, and the persons or things to be seized.' The main purpose served by 'unreasonable searches and seizures' is to compel the person, in effect, to give self-incriminating evidence. The chief purpose of the Amendment then is to prevent self-incrimination *before* trial. Among several others, the Fifth Amendment contains a provision that no person shall be 'compelled in any criminal case to be a witness against himself.' This 'self-incrimination' clause, frequently invoked by persons holding unpopular beliefs as well as by transgressors of the laws, has prompted enactments of so-called immunity bath statutes. The Immunity

Act of 1954, for one, which permits the federal government to *compel* testimony of witnesses in 'national security' cases in return for a grant of immunity from prosecution, was upheld by a divided Supreme Court against right of silence claims in 1956.[44]

Anyone who has been arrested must either be charged with a criminal offense and given a fair and speedy trial, or be released. The procedural safeguards of this right contained in common law and statute are much the same in their terms as those found in Britain and will be more fully described later. The arrested person has also, however, the second line of defense in the Constitution. Among other things, the Constitution of the United States—in Article I and in Amendments V to VIII inclusive—forbids excessive bail; guarantees: *habeas corpus;* public jury trial in *all criminal* cases and in civil cases in which the value in controversy exceeds twenty dollars; the right of the accused to know the charges against him, to have counsel, and to confront the witnesses against him in open court. On the last point, serious problems have arisen in connection with the government's use of Federal Bureau of Investigation files in criminal prosecutions. Since the data contained in F.B.I. files are considered confidential, defense attorneys, unlike government attorneys, were unable to peruse them until the middle of 1957, when the Supreme Court ruled /.1 that the government could have its choice of producing F.B.I. reports forming the basis of testimony of witnesses in criminal trials, or of dismissing the case.[45] Congress subsequently passed legislation to protect the F.B.I.'s files from indiscriminate 'rummaging' by defendants; but the bill preserves the right of the defense to examine statements of government witnesses that the trial judge rules to be relevant to a pending case.

Broadly speaking, legislatures have no power to take away the procedural rights enumerated above, which are designed to ensure that no one will linger in prison without trial and that no will be convicted without a fair trial. But it must be noticed again here that the presence of many of these guarantees are *not automatically* incumbent upon the states, unless they are among those 'carried over' to the due process clause of the Fourteenth Amendment by judicial decision, or unless they are contained in the state's bill of rights—which they usually, but not always, are.

Freedoms of Meeting and Petition. The First Amendment forbids Congress, and the Fourteenth, as interpreted, forbids the states, to abridge 'the

[44] *Ullman* v. *U.S.,* 350 U.S. 422.
[45] *U.S.* v. *Jencks,* 353 U.S. 657.

rights of the people peaceably to assemble, and to petition the government for redress of grievances.' The right of petition is not so important now as in 1791, because a Congress widely representative of the people is steadily engaged in making laws for the redress of grievances. However, organized pressure groups are continually petitioning the government as well as lobbying Congress, and they have a constitutional right to do so. The right of peaceable assembly is of vital importance for the working of the democratic political processes of discussion. It is also essential to the life of voluntary groups, which are necessary features of liberal democracy. Without the right to meet freely and spontaneously to discuss concerted action, voluntary associations could scarcely exist, and political parties could not perform their functions of promoting discussion and organizing the electorate.

This constitutional right is subject to two principal limitations. First, the assembly must be peaceable. Unruly and turbulent meetings that threaten a breach of the peace do not enjoy its protection. Second, those who want to meet must find a lawful place to meet. They cannot assemble on private property without the consent of the owner or tenant, and they have no right to obstruct traffic or passage in public places. Municipal governments through their ordinances, and local police acting under authority of those ordinances, have considerable, but ill-defined, power to regulate the place and conduct of meetings of any size in the interests of local convenience and order. In actual practice, many such ordinances and much local police action put unconstitutional obstacles in the way of meetings of unpopular groups. As Mr. Justice Frankfurter once put it well: 'The safeguards of liberty have frequently been forged in cases involving not very nice people.' Of course, the Court can deal only with cases or controversies that properly come before it—of which more will be said in Chapter XV.

CIVIL RIGHTS AND DUE PROCESS OF LAW

Procedural and Substantive Protection. As already noted, the Fifth Amendment forbids Congress, and the Fourteenth Amendment forbids the state legislatures, to 'deprive any person of life, liberty, or property, without due process of law.' Even a detailed analysis of the decisions of the Supreme Court on these clauses would not reveal a clear, precise meaning for them. Therefore, what can be said about them in a short space must be put very generally.

PROCEDURAL. First, 'due process of law' affords a *procedural* protection. It guarantees fairness of trial, not only in criminal trials but also in any and every judicial or semi-judicial proceeding in which the rights of persons are *officially* determined. It does not, however, require in civil proceedings all the elaborate constitutional apparatus for criminal trials already discussed. *The standard is the general one of fairness.* As a minimum, any legal body that officially determines private rights must be duly constituted to deal with the case in hand, must give adequate notice in advance to the parties affected, and must give a fair hearing to those whose rights are at stake. The due process clauses deny to governments the power to filch away private rights by hole-and-corner methods. Coerced confessions and deliberately 'stacked' juries are in this category.

SUBSTANTIVE. Second, the due process clauses limit the *substance* of the laws enacted by legislatures as well as the procedures for enforcing them. Because what has not hitherto been forbidden by law is permitted, almost all laws that are made regulate some aspect of a private claim to liberty or property. Legislatures exist, in part, to make laws regulating human relationships, but the Supreme Court has insisted that a legislature in so regulating must not impose 'unreasonable, arbitrary, or capricious' restrictions. For example, a compulsory sterilization statute applicable to inmates of State of Virginia-supported institutions who have been found to be afflicted with 'an *hereditary* form of insanity, idiocy, imbecility, feeble-mindedness, or epilepsy' was sustained 8:1—'three generations of imbeciles are enough,' ruled Mr. Justice Holmes, '. . . the principle that sustains compulsory vaccination is broad enough to cover cutting the Fallopian tubes . . .'[46] But a similar Oklahoma sterilization law made applicable to convicted triple criminal offenders, whose crimes amounted to felonies involving 'moral turpitude,' was voided as a violation of the equal protection of the laws clause of the Fourteenth Amendment on the grounds that the classification of 'criminal' was 'too loose for so serious a business,'[47] especially since it *included* larceny by fraud—Skinner had stolen three chickens—but *excluded* embezzlement. There is a limit on the kind of laws regulating liberty and property that a legislature can make.

Scope of Due Process of Law. Third, judicial opinion on what is 'un-

---

[46] *Buck* v. *Bell*, 274 U.S. 200 (1927). Carrie Buck was a 17-year-old feeble-minded inmate of a state institution—whose mother was also a feeble-minded inmate there—who had given birth to an allegedly mentally deficient child just before her admission to the institution. (One of the Buck arguments in court was that the statute applied only to the mentally deficient persons confined to state institutions and not 'to the multitude outside.')
[47] *Skinner* v. *Oklahoma*, 316 U.S. 535 (1942).

reasonable, arbitrary, or capricious' varies from judge to judge, from time to time, and from place to place. Mr. Justice Frankfurter, for one, viewed 'due process of law' as a concept 'compounded by history, reason, the past course of decisions, and stout confidence in the democratic faith which we profess.' [48] Broadly speaking, without going at length into the detail of decisions made by the courts, there are two schools of thought. Some judges are prepared to impose their view of what is reasonable on the legislature, while others assume that the legislature has its fair share of reasonable men and therefore give the legislature the benefit of any lingering doubt in their own minds about the reasonableness of a particular law.

One very important illustration of the changing views on the substantive requirements of due process may be given. Until the second quarter of this century, and even into the 'thirties, the Supreme Court was strongly disposed to hold unreasonable, and therefore unconstitutional as a violation of substantive due process, any legislation that restricted freedom of contract or the use men were to be allowed to make of their private property. In their decisions they came close to saying that the Constitution guaranteed the freedom of capitalist enterprise and the maintenance of large elements of *laisser faire* in economic life. The best-known cases were those already discussed in Chapters IV and V holding minimum wage and hour laws an unconstitutional violation of personal liberty,[49] but there were many others of similar tenor.

With a change in the personnel of the Supreme Court, the earlier decisions on minimum wage and hour laws were reversed in 1937 and 1941.[50] Since then, laws regulating economic life, restricting freedom of contract, and putting various kinds of shackles on freedom of enterprise have generally been upheld. It is almost true now to say that economic interests must make their reckoning with the legislatures without protection from the Fifth and Fourteenth Amendments. The emphasis of the Supreme Court now is not on economic freedom, but on the more intimate personal freedoms guaranteed by the Bill of Rights, and particularly the First Amendment.

[48] *Joint Anti-Fascist Refugee Committee* v. *McGrath*, 341 U.S. 123 (1951).
[49] Cf. *Hammer* v. *Dagenhart*, 247 U.S. 251 (1918); *Lochner* v. *New York*, 198 U.S. 45 (1905); and *Adkins* v. *Children's Hospital*, 261 U.S. 525 (1923).
[50] Cf. *West Coast Hotel Co.* v. *Parrish*, 300 U.S. 379 (1937) and *United States* v. *Darby Lumber Co.*, 312 U.S. 100 (1941).

Effectiveness of Constitutional Guarantees

There are still other clauses of the United States Constitution affording protection for civil rights, but the principal ones have been discussed sufficiently to show the scope and character of the guarantees of individual freedom against encroachment by the government. How useful these guarantees are to individuals depends, of course, on how well they are observed and enforced. They may be flouted by legislatures and government officials, and if they are redress can only be had by bringing allegations of infringement before the courts, and securing loyal enforcement of them by the latter. Even then, the courts cannot enforce the Constitution in every corner of the United States single-handed. As has been wisely said with particular reference to the maintenance of freedom of speech, 'Nine men in Washington cannot hold a nation to ideals which it is determined to betray.' [51]

Actually, there has been substantial, but by no means wholesale, infringement of some guaranteed civil rights. Congress and many state legislatures have from time to time made, and executives have enforced, laws infringing the constitutional guarantee of freedom of speech, for one. We have alluded to some of these above. It has often been impossible to secure fair trial for Negroes on criminal charges, and it has not always been possible to secure fair trial for widely detested accused persons. Unpopular groups have repeatedly found they could not exercise their right of peaceable assembly because local police or mayors put obstacles in their way. Officials charged with enforcing the criminal law have frequently violated the provisions of the Fourth Amendment outlawing unreasonable searches and seizures. Even when arrests have been lawfully made, the police in many jurisdictions often use 'third degree' methods to extract incriminating evidence from the persons in custody.[52] Other instances could be readily given.[53] In recent years, however, the Supreme Court has given increasingly close scrutiny to alleged

[51] T. R. Powell, quoted in Z. Chafee, *Free Speech in the United States,* rev. ed. (Cambridge: Harvard University Press, 1954), p. x.

[52] Evidence so secured cannot be used directly in a criminal prosecution of the person from whom it is extracted, but the police can use it as a *clue* leading to other evidence that connects the accused with the crime; e.g. they find the loot in the place where the suspected burglar says he put it.

[53] Cf. the annual *Report* of the United States Commission on Civil Rights (Washington, D.C.: U.S. Government Printing Office), 1959 ff. See also David Fellman, *The Defendant's Rights* (New York: Holt, Rinehart, & Winston, Inc., 1958).

violations of due process in criminal proceedings, and the states have thus frequently seen their convictions reversed on appeal.

Consequences of the Melting Pot. Generally speaking, despite constitutional guarantees, civil rights have *not* been as well protected in the United States as in Britain. The fundamental explanation is a simple one. The United States is a young country still creating a national tradition and only slowly absorbing into itself an extraordinarily heterogeneous population. There is still much suspicion and hostility between groups of diverse origins and customary ways of life. Much of the worry about disloyalty is due to a feeling of insecurity about persons of foreign origin who—or so goes the argument—may not yet have been wholly won over to the American way of life. To put it in the terms of the earlier discussion about Britain, the American people have not lived together long enough for mutual trust and mutual respect to permeate the entire society. In so far as these are lacking, the difficulty of ensuring respect for the civil rights of all is correspondingly greater.

IMPORTANCE OF CONSTITUTIONAL GUARANTEES. This explanation underlines the immense importance of the constitutional guarantees in the United States. Where moral censure of every infringement of civil rights is not swift and sure, the second line of defense provided by the Constitution is vital. In the first place, persons belonging to hard-pressed minorities can usually get their civil rights vindicated and proclaimed *if* they are able to fight the issue through the courts. Second, the Constitution is a never-ceasing educator in tolerance and fair play. Third, it is a promise and a pledge for the future, counseling patience. As long as the Constitution stands and Americans continue to affirm their loyalty to it, those whose civil rights are ill-protected now still have reason to hope. The limited appeal that communism has had for the Negro is probably due in part to a belief that Americans will not perpetually be able to reconcile the generally inferior condition in which the Negro still finds himself with loyalty to the constitutional guarantees of civil rights and to liberal democratic ideals. Indeed, important changes in his position have been taking place progressively since the end of World War II.

Continuing Concern for Civil Rights. In fact, the Constitution is the American conscience. It does not always prevent intolerant and arbitrary action by legislatures and officials. But its promptings never cease, and so far the American people have always ultimately repented of unconstitutional excesses, repudiated the leaders associated with these lapses, and repealed most of the offending legislation. Every generation has produced large numbers of staunch defenders of civil rights whose devotion renews the pledges of the Constitution. When viewed in this larger perspective and remembering the heterogeneous turmoil of the United States, the achievement has been remarkable, giving still larger promise for the future.

This promise is illustrated by the widespread concern in recent years over ways and means of improving the protection of civil rights. There are several reasons for this concern. First, the constitutional guarantees discussed above are *guarantees against governments only*. Intimidation and violence in one form or another by private persons and groups of persons are much greater threats to civil rights than actual violations by governments. Second, the question of how far there is any legal remedy for infringements by private persons depends on existing federal and state law. It depends on whether the existing laws make it a criminal offense or authorize a civil suit for damages when private persons infringe the civil rights guaranteed in the Constitution. Where violence or intimidation is used, existing law does provide a remedy, but there are subtler means of violation where no such remedy exists. Third, whether the violation is by a government or a private person, punishment or redress has to be sought in the courts. For this, a person needs financial resources, good legal advice, and the co-operation of the law-enforcement officials. Many lack the knowledge or the means to enforce their rights, and co-operation of the law-enforcement officials is not always easily secured.

Enforcement of Civil Rights as a Government Activity. Considerations of this kind led to the establishment of a Civil Rights Section under President Roosevelt's Attorney General, later Supreme Court Justice, Frank Murphy, in the federal Department of Justice in 1939. Its function was to give 'aggressive protection to the fundamental rights inherent in a free people.' To this end, it was to direct, supervise, and conduct prosecutions of violations of the provisions of the Constitution and Acts of Congress guaranteeing civil rights. The Constitution provides a shield for protection of civil rights *against* the government. The Civil Rights Section was to provide a sword for protection of civil rights *by* the government *against private persons*. Despite handicaps of a very small staff and the vagueness of the laws at its command for enforcement, the Civil Rights Section did much to clarify the law, improve techniques of enforcement, push prosecution, and draw wider public attention to the problem.

'TO SECURE THESE RIGHTS.' In 1946 President Truman appointed a Committee on Civil Rights to investigate the need for additional legislation and for other more effective procedures for protecting civil rights. While asserting that civil rights were being better enforced than ever before, the Committee found an alarming amount of violation in 1947. In its Report, *To Secure These Rights,* it made many recommendations designed chiefly to ascertain that every violation of a civil right by private persons would be a criminal offense. The enforcement of civil rights was to become a new and vigorous government activity on an extended scale. Like all proposals for extending government activity, this one had a political background and became focused in a political issue. President Truman committed himself to the implementing of the Report as far as federal action could do so. Because a number of proposals were aimed at improving the status of the Negro, there came the 'Dixiecrat' revolt in the Democratic party. Although President Truman made the matter an issue in the 1948 presidential elections and won resoundingly, he was subsequently unable to get Congress to enact these proposals for the protection of civil rights. President Eisenhower's initial bills suffered a similar fate.

CIVIL RIGHTS ACTS OF 1957, 1960, AND 1964. The last day of its 1957 session, however, Congress finally did pass a civil rights bill—the first major enactment of such legislation since the Reconstruction era following the Civil War. The much watered-down compromise measure created a Federal Civil Rights Commission with *subpoena* powers; established a special Civil Rights Division within the Department of Justice; and empowered federal prosecution to obtain federal injunctions—with or without the consent of the victim—against actual or threatened interference with the right to vote. The 1957 Act proved to be generally weak and ineffective, but that of 1960 provided a considerable improvement. Although not as far-reaching as many wanted, it has given promise of being a significant piece of legislation chiefly because in an elaborate provision for appointment of federal 'voting referees,' it reaches toward the heart of full citizenship for all—the right to vote free from discrimination. The bill authorizes federal district courts, through appointment of these 'referees,' to enroll qualified voters for *all* state as well as federal elections in areas where local officials have systematically denied them the right to register or to vote. And it enables the federal Department of Justice to file suit to bring this result about. Negro leaders have regarded this machinery as too slow, costly, and cumbersome, but it has been a workable and not ineffective device.[54] The much more far-reaching 1964 Civil

[54] Some four dozen such suits had been brought by the Autumn of 1963.

Rights Act was being heavily debated by Congress as this book went to press in the early fall of 1963.[55]

ENFORCEMENT. The hesitant attitude of Congress underlines the basic inherent difficulty. Despite the Constitution, racial and religious prejudices are still potent forces in many parts of the United States, and Congress reflects local and sectional feeling. Even if civil rights were fully 'nationalized' and federal laws and federal agencies amply provided for enforcing them, enforcement would run into many of the difficulties experienced in trying to enforce the prohibition laws, as has been amply demonstrated since 1954 by the resistance the Supreme Court's decisions in the various segregation cases have encountered.

The difficulty is to get law-enforcement officers to prosecute and juries to convict. State action in a democracy cannot get very far in advance of the sentiments and prejudices of large sections of the people. If it does, it outrages those sections and threatens political unity which is the basis of all hope for the future. For full enforcement of the civil rights of all, there must be all-embracing mutual trust and mutual respect. Government, of course, can do many things to promote trust and respect, yet it cannot be a substitute for the slow, hard process of education. Mutual respect cannot be legislated into existence; it must come by leavening. But leadership by responsible public officials is crucial at all stages.

RACIAL DISCRIMINATION

The same reflections apply for the most part to the common practice of racial discrimination generally. The most striking illustrations are still found in segregation laws and practices resulting in separate accommodations for Negroes and whites, although these are receding increasingly, chiefly as a result of federal pressure.

Racial Segregation Problems. The abolition of slavery and the adoption of the Fourteenth Amendment helped to bring about major interracial problems between the Negroes and the whites. Because of the Negroes' predominant concentration in Southern and Border states,[55] particularly in the former, where in certain areas Negroes outnumber whites, the core of the attendant difficulties of relationship has been concentrated there. In

---

[55] After a 75-day Southern filibuster in the Senate, which was finally terminated by a 79:21 closure vote, the Act became law on July 2, 1964, the Senate having approved it by a vote of 73:27, the House 289:126.

1900 almost 90 per cent of American Negroes lived in the Southern states; by 1963 the figure had declined to 57 per cent. Discrimination against Negroes was prevalent both on a private and a public level. Thus, public authorities—state and municipal legislative bodies—enacted measures either permitting or requiring segregation on busses, streetcars, taxi-cabs, railroads, in waiting rooms, comfort stations, at drinking fountains, in public schools, state colleges and universities, at sporting events, on beaches, in bath houses, swimming pools, parks, on golf courses, in court-house cafeterias, theaters, hotels, restaurants, and other similar *public* or quasi-public facilities. *Private* groups and individuals acted to deny Negroes access to social clubs, fraternities and sororities, private schools, colleges and universities, churches, hospitals, hotels, restaurants, theaters, movies, bowling alleys, swimming pools, drinking fountains, bath houses, sporting events, comfort stations, and employment, among others.

'SEPARATE BUT EQUAL.' While there was little the Negroes could do to combat *private* discrimination, they soon began to battle *public* discrimination in the courts. They chiefly relied upon the Fourteenth Amendment's 'due process' and 'equal protection of the laws' clauses—their ultimate success coming with a firm reliance upon the latter, especially in recent years. But, initially, their efforts seemed doomed to failure, for in 1896 the Supreme Court handed down its famous 'separate but equal' doctrine in the celebrated case of *Plessy v. Ferguson*.[56] At issue was a Louisiana statute requiring segregation of all *intra*-state railway carriers, but at the same time requiring these to provide 'equal but separate accommodations for the white and colored races.' Its 7:1 decision, written for the Court by Mr. Justice Henry B. Brown, a Yale graduate from Michigan, upheld the statute as a reasonable exercise of the state's police power against the challenge that it violated the 'equal protection of the laws' clause of the Fourteenth Amendment. Mr. Justice John Marshall Harlan's—a former slaveholder from Kentucky—often-quoted lone dissent, at once angry and eloquent, did not become majority opinion until almost sixty years later: *'The Constitution is color-blind,* and neither knows nor tolerates classes among citizens.'[57]

The 'separate but equal' doctrine, arising out of the *Plessy* case, remained the law of the land until 1954. Segregation continued to be practiced in the areas and facilities listed above in more than one-third of the American states and in the District of Columbia. But, as the years went by, the 'separate but

[56] 163 U.S. 537.
[57] Ibid. at 559 (Italics supplied.)

equal' doctrine came increasingly under legal attack. Time and again the Supreme Court struck down certain practices by the states as not being 'equal' in facilities, without however going so far as to hold the doctrine itself unconstitutional.

CHIPPING AT THE DOCTRINE. Commencing at the graduate level of *higher education,* the Court began to order particular state universities to admit individual qualified Negroes, or else arrange for truly 'equal' facilities. The state law schools in Missouri and Oklahoma [58] were the first to be so ordered. But in 1950, in a similar case arising in Texas, the Court found the so-called 'equal' law school for Negroes to be inferior, hence constituting a denial of the equal protection of the laws of that state to Negroes.[59] By 1957 the Supreme Court had made it quite clear that there was no longer any right to limit admissions to state-operated colleges on the basis of color or race. While there is still considerable resistance, especially in those states with large numbers of Negroes in their population, more and more Negroes—although they still constitute a small number—are now attending desegregated graduate and professional schools in every state of the South. To achieve that, however, it required the federal troop-enforced bloodshed-accompanied admission of James Meredith to the University of Mississippi in the fall of 1962; the similarly-enforced but peaceful entry of three Negroes to the University of Alabama in 1963; and the admission of Harvey Gantt to Clemson University in South Carolina, also in 1963.

During this time the executive branch of the federal government and the Supreme Court had become involved in segregation battles in other areas. The chipping away at the 'separate but equal' doctrine continued. Thus, President Truman, in 1948, issued a tersely worded order outlawing segregation in the *armed forces;* by 1955 the 'color line' had been abolished in all branches of the military services. President Eisenhower established the Commission on Fair Employment Opportunities. In the realm of *restrictive housing covenants,* the Court held these to be legal but *unenforceable* in either federal or state courts.[60] In 1962, President Kennedy issued an order

---

[58] *Missouri ex rel. Gaines* v. *Canada,* 305 U.S. 337 (1938) and *Sipuel* v. *Board of Regents of the University of Oklahoma,* 332 U.S. 631 (1948). (Actually, the first court-enforced admission of a Negro came in 1936, when the Maryland Court of Appeals ordered Donald Murray admitted to the University of Maryland Law School.) See also the important decision in *McLaurin* v. *Oklahoma State Regents for Higher Education,* 339 U.S. 637. (Oklahoma had admitted McLaurin but compelled him to sit away from the students; at a separate table in the cafeteria; and to study at a special desk in the library.)

[59] *Sweatt* v. *Painter,* 339 U.S. 629 (1950).

[60] *Shelley* v. *Kraemer,* 334 U.S. 1 (1948); *Hurd* v. *Hodge,* 334 U.S. 24 (1948); and *Barrows* v. *Jackson,* 346 U.S. 249 (1953).

banning discrimination in federally constructed or supported housing. Regarding *recreational facilities,* the Court, in a series of cases following close on the heels of the public school cases, affirmed lower federal court decisions that struck down state statutes permitting legal segregation in court house cafeterias, in restaurants, in city-owned parking garages, in *public* parks, on *public* bathing beaches or in *public* swimming pools, at sporting events, on *public* golf links, and similar facilities.[61] *Private* facilities were not affected, of course, in the absence of local anti-discrimination (F.E.P.C.) laws, but the courts rejected as an unconstitutional dodge attempts to make public facilities 'private' by leasing them to private operators.[62]

Transportation facilities also felt the new policies of government and Supreme Court. A Virginia segregation law, applied to interstate busses, fell in 1946.[63] In 1950, segregation on interstate trains was outlawed, first by a Supreme Court decision [64]—then by the Interstate Commerce Commission, which particularly referred to sleeping cars and dining cars. Late in 1955 the I.C.C. went all the way by ordering the cessation of all racial segregation on interstate busses and trains and their public waiting rooms in stations and terminals. That particular cycle was completed when, late in 1956 and early in 1957, federal district court judges in Alabama, Florida, and Louisiana held state segregation laws on *public intra-state* busses to be violations of the 'equal protection of the laws' clause of the Fourteenth Amendment. In a series of decisions since then, the Supreme Court went further by striking down segregation statutorily permitted or mandated in railroad and bus terminals, airports, and their waiting rooms and restaurants, no matter whether these service facilities were publicly or privately operated.[65] The "equal access" sections of the Civil Rights Bill of 1963 endeavored to strike a fatal blow at discrimination in services and facilities of most establishments engaged in interstate commerce.

THE PUBLIC SCHOOL SEGREGATION CASES. Many, if not all, of the sweeping orders and decisions outlined briefly above came about as a direct, or indirect,

---

[61] For examples, see *Dawson* v. *Mayor and City Council of Baltimore City,* 350 U.S. 877 (1955); *Holmes* v. *City of Atlanta,* 350 U.S. 879 (1955); *City of Petersburg et al.* v. *Alsup et al.,* 353 U.S. 922 (1957); *Casey* v. *Plummer,* 353 U.S. 924 (1957); *State Athletic Commission* v. *Dorsey,* 359 U.S. 533 (1959); *Burton* v. *Wilmington Parking Authority,* 365 U.S. 175 (1961); *Watson* v. *Memphis,* 373 U.S. 526 (1963).

[62] Cf. *Derrington* v. *Plummer,* 240 F. 2d 922 (1957).

[63] *Morgan* v. *Virginia,* 328 U.S. 373 (1946).

[64] *Henderson* v. *U.S.,* 333 U.S. 816 (1950).

[65] Cf. *Boynton* v. *Virginia,* 364 U.S. 454 (1960); *Turner* v. *Memphis,* 369 U.S. 350 (1962); and *Bailey* v. *Patterson,* 369 U.S. 31 (1962).

result of the most significant decision in the realm of segregation handed down by the Court since *Plessy* v. *Ferguson* in 1896: On May 17, 1954, a *unanimous* Supreme Court, after deliberating almost two years, struck down the 'separate but equal' doctrine in an historic decision.[66] Speaking for his Court, Mr. Chief Justice Warren held segregation in the public schools to be a violation of the 'equal protection of the laws' clause of the Fourteenth Amendment per se, concluding:

> . . . in the field of public education the doctrine of 'separate but equal' has no place. Separate educational facilities are inherently unequal. . . .

Fully aware of the bombshell-like effect this decision would have upon the South, and of the many real problems involved in compliance, the Court delayed issuing an enforcement order for one year. But on May 31, 1955, it ordered the end of compulsory segregation, charging local authorities with responsibility for compliance under the scrutiny of the nearest federal District Court in the affected area. It directed these courts to order 'a prompt and reasonable start,' but clearly left the door open for consideration of peculiar local problems. However, there was no mistaking its requirement of full and relatively prompt compliance 'with all deliberate speed' in each state.[67]

COMPLIANCE. While the District of Columbia, under direct federal control, integrated its public schools immediately in the fall of 1954, the response in the affected states—in this as well as many of the other fields we have been discussing here—ran the gamut from bowing to the inevitable in more or less good faith, through reasonably delayed action, to absolute refusal to obey —even reaching the stage of outright defiance, at one time or another, accompanied by flurries of violence, in Arkansas, Virginia, South Carolina, Georgia, Florida, Louisiana, Alabama, and Mississippi.[68] Many subterfuges were

---

[66] *Brown* v. *Board of Education of Topeka*, 347 U.S. 483 (1954) and *Bolling* v. *Sharpe*, 347 U.S. 497 (1954).
[67] *Brown* v. *Board of Education of Topeka et al.*, 349 U.S. 294 (1955).
[68] In the fall of 1957 Governor Faubus of Arkansas called out the National Guard in order to prevent scheduled public school integration in Little Rock. When enjoined by a federal district court from continued interference, he removed the Guard. Riots and disorders ensued, compelling President Eisenhower to federalize the Arkansas Guard and to dispatch federal troops to re-establish law and order, thus allowing integration to proceed. In the fall of 1962, it took 25,000 federal troops to overcome the opposition of Mississippi, led by its Governor, Ross Barnett, to enforce the court-ordered admission of Negro James Meredith to that State University; two lives were lost; scores were wounded; an all-night pitched battle was fought. And troops were needed to overcome Alabama Governor George Wallace's opposition to desegregation of his State University.

adopted by these and others, including the closing of all public schools, such as in Prince Edward County, Virginia. Some 170 state segregation laws were enacted since May 1954. Public feeling thus continued to run high indeed over what the whites in the affected states regard as a threat to their way of life and to the right of the states to govern themselves. Not for many a year had the Supreme Court been under such heavy attack by so large and so vocal a segment of the population. But a start, certainly, has been made toward desegregation and eradication of some of the discriminatory public school practices in the South and the Border, especially in the larger and more cosmopolitan cities. Roughly 15.6 per cent of the school districts in the seventeen Southern and Border states had been desegregated by the beginning of the 1963 Autumn term, with 7.8 per cent of the total Negro school population attending 'mixed' classes. Especially the six Border states have traveled far on the road toward compliance; a beginning however limited, has been made in Tennessee, Arkansas, Florida, Texas, and North Carolina; and an even more limited one in Georgia and Louisiana. But faced with the hostility by what at present still seems to be a sizable majority of their citizens, and a disposition by local officials to flout the Court, most of the states of the 'Old South' are still a long way from more than token submission to the hated edict. Many legal battles undoubtedly lie ahead. Customs that have stood for generations are not altered easily. Yet when the schools and colleges opened in September 1963, only one 'hard core' state remained completely untouched by public school integration: Mississippi, and it had at least one instance at the college level.

Moreover, the Supreme Court made quite clear in 1963 that its *Brown* decision 'never contemplated that the concept of "deliberate speed" would countenance indefinite delay in elimination of racial barriers in schools, let alone other public facilities not involving the same physical problems or comparable conditions . . . The basic guarantees of our Constitution,' wrote Mr. Justice Goldberg for the unanimous Court, 'are warrants for the here and now.' [69]

General Problems of Discrimination. The various segregation problems just discussed are the most obvious examples of discrimination. But throughout the country there is frequent discrimination in employment practices and in access to private housing and places of public accommodation. A few of these practices violate the constitutional guarantees of civil rights as presently interpreted, but most of them are not contrary to existing laws, being

[69] *Watson* v. *Memphis,* 373 U.S. 526.

in the area of economic and other freedoms granted to individuals to keep clear of associations they do not like.

'STATE ACTION' AND 'SIT-INS'. Here, too, it becomes a matter of 'balancing,' of drawing lines—lines between liberty and equality, between what is and what is not *state action* which becomes violative of constitutional rights if applied in a discriminatory manner. A pertinent illustration is the vexatious problem caused by the increasingly militant so-called 'sit-in,' 'stand-in,' or 'wade-in' demonstrations by Negroes in private establishments in the South, whose owners have refused to serve them. Here, then, the line becomes not merely one between the right of peaceable assembly and that of serving those whom one wishes to serve but, more pointedly, it raises the issue of whether the policeman, called by the proprietor of the establishment to eject the 'sit-ins,' represents the kind of 'state action' forbidden by the Fourteenth Amendment. Understandably not eager to meet this extremely difficult and delicate issue, the Supreme Court, initially refused to meet the constitutional issue; instead, addressing itself to the specific circumstances of each occurrence, it held in several cases that no 'breach of the peace' or 'trespass' on the part of the 'sit-ins' had taken place. Thus in effect the Court reversed their convictions without reaching the 'state action' issue at all.[70] But in the Spring of 1963 it did come to grips with the basic problem. Throwing out the conviction of lunch-counter demonstrators in four Southern states, it declared it to be clearly unconstitutional for a state or any of its officials *to require segregation either by statute or official policy.*[71] Yet it reserved for later judgment the important issue of *private* segregation—which raises the intriguing question of private propertarian rights!

F.E.P.C. LAWS. President Truman's Committee on Civil Rights had recommended legislative and executive action by state and federal governments against discriminatory practices generally. Led by New York, thirty-four states and many major cities by the autumn of 1963 had enacted so-called fair employment practices laws, commonly known by the letters F.E.P.C. with Kentucky and Maryland joining the ranks in 1963 as the first of the Border and Southern states to adopt either a F.E.P.C. or 'equal accommodations' statute. These commonly prohibit discriminatory practices by employers, labor unions, and employment agencies against any employed or employment-seeking person because of race, color, creed, religion, or national origin. Equal accommodation statutes, such as Maryland's, prohibit refusal of

70 Cf. *Garner* v. *Louisiana,* 368 U.S. 157 (1961); *Taylor* v. *Louisiana,* 369 U.S. 350 (1962).
71 *Peterson* v. *Greenville,* 373 U.S. 244.

service in places of public accommodation, e.g. restaurants and hotels. But, generally speaking, there still are very wide differences of opinion on what can be done by legislation in these fields. Laws of this kind obviously create immense problems of enforcement. Governments have found it hard enough to enforce minimum-wage and maximum-hours laws. How are they to supervise effectively the hiring and firing practices of a multitude of employers and the patronage practices of storekeepers, restaurateurs, and innkeepers? Some strong supporters of civil rights are opposed to such laws on the ground that prejudice and discrimination cannot be prevented by law. The whole question of how to deal with religious and racial discrimination is a disputed matter of public policy and no fair statement of the arguments pro and con can be made in a short space.

Conclusion. One thing, however, can be said. Discriminatory practices, particularly in employment and in access to public health services and public education facilities, are a *pro tanto* denial of the liberal democratic ideal of rough equality of opportunity. Despite widespread discrimination, the strength of that ideal is manifest in most of the varied government activities described in Chapter V, particularly in the large social security programs designed to promote equality. Indeed, the whole development of the positive state is an assertion that the negative approach to civil rights is not enough. Civil rights as discussed in this chapter are negative, aimed at securing freedom from outside restraint. But without positive aids and supports, the freedom of the individual in a complex society may be largely illusory. This is commonly expressed by saying that what is needed is freedom *for,* and not merely freedom *from,* something. Freedom for the realization of the possibilities of human personality requires health, education, and fair opportunities of employment—and many of these are being obtained *through* government.

The strength of this conviction in the world today is further illustrated by the Universal Declaration of Human Rights adopted by the General Assembly of the United Nations in 1948. Significantly, it recites the same liberal democratic ideals that have been stressed here, and it proclaims as universal human rights the substance of the civil rights guaranteed by the Constitution of the United States. However, it then goes on to declare that everyone has a right to social security, education, just and favorable conditions of work, and 'a standard of living adequate for the health and well-being of himself and his family. . . .' These are aspirations easier to phrase than to realize in the life of a society, but they show the strength of current demands for equality of opportunity. Further, the Declaration imposes some kind of moral obligation on the members of the United Nations to live up to it. However this is to be accomplished, by positive government action, by changing the hearts of men, or by both, pressure for what is called positive freedom seems likely to continue. It is in this context that racial and religious discrimination must be considered.

DICTATORSHIPS AND CIVIL RIGHTS

FASCIST AND NAZI DESTRUCTION OF CIVIL RIGHTS

It is not necessary to say much about the status of civil rights of individuals under Fascist and Nazi rule in Italy and Germany. We have already seen that Fascist and Nazi theory glorified the nation, exalted the claims of society as interpreted by the state, and had no respect for the claims of individual personality. Individuals had their significance in being means to the great social ends pursued by the government. Obstruction by individuals asserting their rights against the government was not to be tolerated.

Fascist. Before Mussolini came to power in 1922, Italy had a constitution modeled on that of Britain, recognizing the sovereignty of the legislature. The Fascist party, in control of Parliament, secured the passage of laws giving the executive power to make laws by decree. By use of that decree power, the executive destroyed freedom of speech, subjected the press and radio to close government control, and made the right of public meeting, and of association subject to license by the government. Decrees were passed creating a number of political crimes which, in effect, forbade every criticism of the government.

For example, under these decrees, a person committed a crime if he came to be regarded by 'public opinion' as a person 'dangerous to the national order of the State.' A secret police was set up to ferret out persons suspected of political crimes. On arrest, such suspects were tried by a special tribunal composed of army officers—who were sworn to obey the government—under a procedure that lacked almost all the safeguards afforded accused persons in the United States and Britain.

Nazi. The Nazis came to power in Germany in 1933 in an election under the Weimar Constitution, a thoroughly liberal democratic constitution, which contained a bill of rights designed to guarantee the principal civil rights. It also contained a clause authorizing the executive to rule by decree in an emergency. By the use of this emergency power, the Nazis quickly overrode the Constitution. One of their earliest executive decrees abolished the civil rights of freedom of the person, speech, press, assembly, and association. They made any breach of 'healthy public sentiment' a crime. They established a rigid censorship and destroyed the independence of the judiciary. They set up a secret police system, the *Gestapo,* and the infamous concentration camps, already discussed in Chapter III.

Although the Nazis had made the courts subservient to them, they rarely troubled to use the judicial process on those who were thought to be politically dangerous. Thousands of Germans were bundled off to concentration camps to be tortured, killed, or to languish indefinitely, without having had a trial at all. No one had any rights he could hope to maintain against the government.

By these methods an apparatus of terror was established in both countries which ensured the docility of the great bulk of the population. The few, and they were truly very few in number, who had the courage to think of resisting the government could not agitate openly. They were compelled to go into underground subversive movements. Civil rights were entirely destroyed.

CIVIL RIGHTS IN THE SOVIET UNION

Civil Rights According to the Constitution. Many of the civil rights guaranteed to individuals in Britain and the United States are contained in Chapter X of the Soviet Constitution. Here are set down the rights usually associated with liberal democratic states and generally thought to be repudiated in the dictatorships: freedom of speech, of the press, of assembly, of street processions and demonstrations, and of religious worship. The Constitution also guarantees the inviolability of the person and of the homes of citizens, and the privacy of correspondence.[72] Like the civil rights in the liberal democracies, these rights are negative. They are designed to protect the individual *from* interference by the state or by other individuals.

The Soviet Constitution, however, goes beyond the liberal democratic constitutions in declaring some positive rights designed to give the citizen freedom *for* realizing his potentialities. It was noted earlier that the Universal Declaration of Human Rights emphasizes certain positive economic and social rights. The clauses containing these positive rights were, in fact, included in the United Nations' Declaration partly because of the insistence of the delegates of the Soviet Union and other Communist countries on the

[72] Constitution of the U.S.S.R., Arts. 124, 125, 127–8.

commission that drafted the Declaration. In demanding that the positive freedoms be included, the Communist delegates were urging the example of the Soviet Constitution, which *expressly promises* to every Soviet citizen the right to employment, rest and leisure, maintenance in old age and in sickness and disability, and the right to education.

For his part, the Soviet citizen must abide by the Constitution, observe the laws, 'maintain labor discipline,' honestly perform public duties, and 'respect the rules of socialist intercourse.' [73] He must also 'safeguard and fortify public, socialist property.' [74] His duties are not limited, as are the duties of individuals in the United States, France, and Britain, to the obligation to respect the precisely defined rights of other individuals. They extend far beyond that to include vague, general duties to society which the ruling authorities interpret for him as they see fit.

Denial of Civil Rights in Practice. It has been seen earlier that the facts of Soviet government frequently fail to correspond to the blueprint of the Soviet Constitution. This chapter has suggested that constitutional provisions alone do not guarantee civil rights or liberties. To be effective, these provisions must be enforced by an independent judiciary. The Soviet Union does not meet this requirement. First, the judiciary, like all other institutions of the Soviet government, is dominated by the Communist party. All judges in the Soviet Union are either members of the party, or non-members whose sympathies with the party are strong enough to warrant their appointment or election as judges approved by the party. Consequently the Soviet judiciary is not an effective check *on the government* in its dealings with individuals.

Second, Soviet practice indicates that the Soviet leaders do not think primarily about the essential worth and dignity of every human being. They think primarily about the interests of society as they understand those interests, and they assume that the interests of the individual are identical with their conception of the interests of society. The Soviet state embodies its conception of the interests of society, and consequently no Soviet citizen can assert his individuality when such assertion clashes with government policy as defined by the leaders. *Regardless of what is proclaimed in the Constitution, the Soviet leaders will not suffer the civil rights of the citizens to operate as a restriction on the actions of the government.* The Soviet citizen has no assurance that the interpretation of the law and the Constitution will remain constant and protect him against an overly zealous government.

[73] Ibid. Art. 130.
[74] Ibid. Art. 131.

The Apparatus of Tyranny. In Chapter XV, which describes the Soviet judiciary in some detail, the office of the Procurator-General—a type of supervising prosecutor—will be shown to be, in effect, a check on the Soviet judiciary. The Procurator-General, who, in practice, is responsible only to the Communist party, is empowered to supervise the activities of the Soviet judges, officials, and private citizens. He has yet another power, however—one which helps to explain why the civil rights guaranteed in the Constitution do not ensure the Soviet citizen anything like the degree of freedom enjoyed by individuals in the United States and Britain. Article 127 of the Soviet Constitution states that 'citizens of the U.S.S.R. are guaranteed inviolability of the person; no person may be placed under arrest except by decision of a court *or with the sanction of a procurator.*' [75] This enables the procurator to by-pass the courts.

Since Stalin's death, however, a series of new codes of criminal procedure have been adopted which supposedly 'liberalize' the judicial safeguards of the citizen by placing the burden of proof on the prosecution instead of the defendant. Among the much-heralded reforms of the 1958 Code, for example, is the right to counsel and a prohibition against unlawful arrest and detention and coerced confessions. But there is, of course, still no writ of *habeas corpus* procedure, and during the procurator's investigation of the case detention may be continued. Moreover, 'political' or 'counter-revolutionary' crimes fall, in effect, into a separate category.

POLITICAL CRIMES. In practice, the procurator's powers to abrogate the rights of freedom of the person guaranteed by the Constitution are invoked in cases involving *political crimes,* especially if the accused is deemed 'socially dangerous.' It is impossible to state precisely what constitutes a political crime in the Soviet Union. It is very nearly correct to say that any action of the Soviet citizen which is considered by the Communist party to be contrary to the public interest can be considered as a political crime by the procurator. Thus the manager of a factory who does not meet the production quota set for him by the state planning organization can be accused of sabotage. As a result of this wide interpretation of 'political crime,' a large area of human relationships is potentially taken out of the control of the courts of law.

THE K.G.B. The procurator's orders are carried out by the political police, the K.G.B., or Committee of State Security—an organization with no counterpart in Britain, France, and the United States—which is subordinated to

[75] Authors' italics.

the Council of Ministers. In practice, its authority covers the whole area of political crimes, i.e. any action which is held to be dangerous to the welfare of the Soviet Union, but its powers are a far cry from those of its predecessors, the M.V.D., O.G.P.U., and N.K.V.D., which reached their apogee of dread police-state power under Stalin.

It need not be stressed that the leaders of the Communist party control the K.G.B., and that they do not hesitate to use its machinery against anyone whose conduct they dislike or whose activities might challenge their leadership. Despite much recent talk about 'Soviet legality' since Stalin's demise and Khrushchev's assumption of power, the guarantees of civil rights in the Soviet Constitution are relatively meaningless because the essential procedures—a clearly defined and precisely limited criminal law, confinement of official action by the Rule of Law, *habeas corpus,* impartial courts, and assurance of fair trial—are lacking. Such is the cloth from which dictatorship is cut.

Having made that essential point, we should not, however, ignore the fact that there developed a very real difference between the world of the Stalin of 1953 and that of the Khrushchev of a decade later. To the citizens of the Soviet Union of the latter era, the police state practices of the days of Stalin and Beria had been replaced by less stringent, much less terrifying methods. Terror had not been forsaken, of course—as indeed it cannot be in a dictatorship—but it had become both less crude and less widespread. How long this diminution of extreme oppression would last no one could safely foretell; yet many informed persons do not expect early resumption of the terror that blanketed the Soviet Union under the reign of Stalin.

SUGGESTED REFERENCES FOR FURTHER READING

Abernathy, G., *The Right of Assembly and Association* (U. of So. Carolina, 1961).
Aikin, C., *The Negro Votes* (Chandler, 1962).
Allport, G. W., *The Nature of Prejudice* (Doubleday, 1960).
Ashmore, H. S., *An Epitaph for Dixie* (Norton, 1957).
Barth, A., *The Price of Liberty* (Viking, 1962).
Burlingame, R., *The Sixth Column* (Lippincott, 1962).
Castberg, *Freedom of Speech in the West* (Oceana, 1960).
Chafee, Z., Jr., *The Blessings of Liberty* (Lippincott, 1956).
Clark, T. D., *The Emerging South* (Oxford, 1961).
Cook, J. G., *The Segregationists* (Appleton-Century-Crofts, 1962).

Cushman, R. E., *Civil Liberties in the United States* (Cornell, 1956).

Dash, S., R. Schwartz, and R. E. Knowlton, *The Eavesdroppers* (Rutgers, 1959).

Douglas, W. O., *The Right of the People* (Doubleday, 1958).

Draper, T., *The Roots of American Communism* (Viking, 1957).

Dykeman, W., and J. Stokely, *Neither Black nor White* (Rinehart, 1957).

Fellman, D., *The Defendant's Rights* (Rinehart, 1958).

Franklin, J. H., *From Slavery to Freedom: A History of American Negroes,* 2nd ed. rev. and enl. (Knopf, 1956).

Gellhorn, W., *American Rights: The Constitution in Action* (Macmillan, 1960).

Griswold, E. N., *The Fifth Amendment Today* (Harvard, 1955).

Harris, R. J., *The Quest for Equality: The Constitution, Congress, and the Supreme Court* (Louisiana State U., 1960).

Holcombe, A. N., *Human Rights in the Modern World* (New York University, 1949).

Hook, S., *The Paradoxes of Freedom* (Berkeley, 1962).

Johnson, G. W., *Peril and Promise: An Inquiry Into Freedom of the Press* (Harper, 1958).

Kidd, R., *British Liberty in Danger* (Lawrence, 1942).

Kirchheimer, O., *Political Justice: the Use of Legal Procedure for Political Ends* (Princeton, 1961).

Konvitz, M. R., *Fundamental Liberties of a Free People: Religion, Speech, Press, Assembly* (Cornell, 1957).

MacIver, R. M., *Academic Freedom in Our Time* (Columbia, 1955).

Mason, A. T., *Security Through Freedom* (Cornell, 1955).

Meiklejohn, A., *Free Speech and Its Relation to Self-Government* (Harper, 1948).

Myrdal, G., *An American Dilemma: The Negro Problem and Modern Democracy,* rev. and enl. (Harper, 1962).

O'Brian, J. L., *National Security and Individual Freedom* (Harvard, 1955).

Odegard, P. H., *Religion and Politics* (Oceana, 1960).

Paul, J. C. N., and M. L. Schwartz, *Federal Censorship: Obscenity in the Mail* (Free Press, 1961).

Pfeffer, L., *Church, State and Freedom* (Beacon, 1953).

Powell, T., *The School Bus Law: A Case Study in Education, Religion, and Politics* (Wesleyan, 1961).

Preston, W., Jr., *Aliens and Dissenters* (Harvard, 1963).

Rice, C. E., *Freedom of Association* (New York U., 1963).

Rosen, H. and D., *But Not Next Door* (Obolensky, 1962).

Sibley, M. Q., and P. E. Jacob, *Conscription of Conscience: The American State and the Conscientious Objector, 1940–1947* (Cornell, 1952).

Sowle, C. R. (Ed.), *Police Power and Individual Freedom: The Quest for Balance* (Aldine, 1962).

Stokes, A. P., *Church and State in the United States* (Harper, 1950).

Stouffer, S. A., *Communism, Conformity, and Civil Liberties* (Doubleday, 1955).

Tawney, R. E., *Equality,* 5th ed. (Putnam's, 1961).

Vose, C. E., *Caucasians Only: The Supreme Court, the N.A.A.C.P., and the Restrictive Covenant Clauses* (Berkeley, 1959).

Wilson, H. H., and H. Glickman, *The Problem of Internal Security in Great Britain, 1948–1953* (Doubleday, 1954).

Woodward, C. V., *The Strange Career of Jim Crow,* rev. ed. (Oxford, 1957).

Ziegler, B. M., *Desegregation and the Supreme Court* (Heath, 1958).

IX

Political Parties

The growing democratization of government in the nineteenth century was everywhere accompanied by the rapid development and intensive organization of nation-wide political parties. Put in its simplest terms, a political party is a voluntary association aiming to get control of the government by filling elective offices in the government with its members. Individuals are drawn into the association because they have similar views on the general lines of policy they would have government pursue. Because of the diversity of views on most subjects in a democracy, two or more political parties have always developed wherever democracy has flourished. Invariably, the first step of dictators in destroying democratic government has been to forbid all political parties but one—their own. There is ample reason for suspecting that political parties are somehow essential to the working of democratic government.

It is, however, far too important a matter to be left in the realm of reasonable conjecture. This is particularly true because many people of genuinely democratic instinct are deeply hostile to the party system and are convinced that most of the troubles of democratic countries are due to the spirit of faction which competing parties foster and promote. Thus they still agree with the fears voiced by Madison in *The Federalist* No. 10, almost two centuries ago. An attempt must be made to lay bare the connection between liberal democratic governments and political parties.

Two Types of Democratic Party-Systems. However they may vary between specific countries, two basic patterns exist in the operation of political parties in modern democracies, the *two-party* and the *multi-party* system. From the time of division of sentiment in Britain—between those in favor of and those opposed to the monarch—political parties in English-speaking lands have, in the main, adhered to the two-party system. This tradition is imbedded in the United States, Canada, Australia, New Zealand, and of course Britain.

Conversely, political parties on the European continent have generally followed a multi-party pattern. France, Italy, the Lowlands, and West Germany are leading examples. Constitutional government and political parties did not really appear in these states until the nineteenth century, when the economic and social forces created by the Industrial Revolution aided the splintering of European politics.

POLITICAL PARTIES IN A DEMOCRACY

FUNCTIONS

Whether in two-party or multi-party systems, political parties in modern democracies have assumed certain functions in pursuit of their aim of getting control of the government. Even though each party is moved primarily by partisan objectives, the party system within which it works performs indispensable services in making democracy a workable form of government. To see what these services are requires some attention to the facts of political life, particularly to the prevailing condition of the electorate.

Adult Suffrage. The fundamental fact is *adult suffrage*—although there still exist certain restrictions on the privilege to vote, and women were not fully enfranchised in the United States, Britain, and France until 1920, 1928, and 1946, respectively. In the United States, where the minimum qualifications are fixed by state laws, restrictions vary from state to state. In some, a significant number of adults is excluded from voting by a variety of devices, ranging from the obvious—residence, registration, and literacy requirements —to the more subtle—'understanding' clauses and 'interpretation' tests. Legal tests in the courts have resulted in the banning of the more blatantly unconstitutional devices, e.g. the 'white primary'[1] and the 'grandfather clause.'[2]

But generally speaking, almost every adult[3] who is so inclined, and is

[1] *Smith* v. *Allwright,* 321 U.S. 649 (1944).
[2] *Guinn* v. *U.S.,* 238 U.S. 347 (1915).
[3] Citizens of the states of Georgia, Kentucky, Alaska, and Hawaii are elegible to vote at 18, 18, 19, and 20 years of age, respectively.

willing to comply with minimum requirements, has a vote at his disposal to add to the total from which the will of the people for some common action or program has to emerge. Unfortunately, the people are far from finding spontaneous agreement, or even spontaneous majorities, on what ought to be done. The important basic assumption made here about the prevailing condition of the electorate is that, given the freedom of thought, expression, and association which has marked the liberal democracies, individuals and groups produce a great variety of opinions on political as well as other matters. If ten men are asked what should be done to save the country, there will be several opinions: soften the banks, abolish trade unions, forbid the sale of goods on credit, teach religion in the schools. Even when patterns of partial agreement are found, such as the socializing of certain means of production and distribution, a little further inquiry reveals a multitude of counsel about the pace of advance toward, and the means for reaching, the desired end. Socialists have quarreled bitterly for two generations and broken into a dozen camps over the question of means. The electorate, even after years of education by political parties, is still a mass of various opinions looking for salvation in different directions.

Selecting Candidates for Office. Left to themselves, how would the voters in a constituency pick a representative to the legislature and instruct him on what should be done there to further the common interest? How would candidates be selected to run for office in the first place? At worst each voter would vote for himself and his own panacea. At best there would be numerous candidates, and one of them supported by a small faction that had agreed momentarily to back him would get more votes than any other candidate. Only in the rarest circumstances would any candidate get a majority of all votes or any majority opinion emerge on what should be done to further the public interest. The members of the legislature, thus chosen by haphazard and temporary combinations in each constituency across the country, would themselves be of various opinions, and their accomplishments in the legislature less constructive and more disillusioning than at present.

Providing Alternatives. The two-party system does to this incoherent electorate what the magnet does to the iron filings—it organizes the voters around two poles, orients them in relation to specific alternative programs of political action. Under it the parties select programs, more or less clearly outlined, and choose candidates; and if one party has a majority in the legislature it proceeds with its program. Without the parties, there would be no stable majority in a legislature, and without the support of an enduring majority it would be impossible to maintain steady drive behind a program for even a month, let alone three or four years. When government performs so many important functions, such a situation would be serious indeed.

Self-Maintenance. Hence an important obligation placed upon political parties is self-maintenance. No legal compulsion for their operation exists in the United States—where the widespread mistrust of parties voiced in the Constitutional Convention prevented any mention of them in the Constitution—, Britain, or France. It is circumscribed almost entirely by custom and does not depend upon compliance with constitutional or statutory law. Only the will of thousands of citizens wishing to make a career or an avocation of politics, or considering political activity the most effective means of securing or protecting certain standards, enables political parties to perpetuate themselves from generation to generation.

It is commonly believed that party motivation is predominantly personal and selfish, but the evidence indicates that a considerable share of political activity stems from idealistic motivations. Skeptics to the contrary, the faithful, dogged support of minority parties in regions perpetually dominated by a strong majority party indicates that many people labor for a party simply because they hold it worth supporting—and their support remains constant despite the unlikelihood of material reward.

Each major political party, even in a multi-party system, primarily sets itself to the task of constructing a majority in the legislature. Party politicians— except those who are members of minor, doctrinaire parties, such as the persistent Prohibition party in the United States—are not, and cannot be, crusaders, men of single-minded passionate purpose who drive straight to the realization of their ideals. They are not even generally the inventors of the ideas they expound. In the aptest phrase yet applied to them, they are brokers of ideas.[4]

Brokers of Ideas. They are that because they are middlemen who select from all the ideas pressing for recognition as public policy those they think can be shaped to have the widest appeal and, through their party organization, they try to sell a carefully sifted and edited selection of these ideas— their program—to enough members of the electorate to produce a majority in the legislature.

It puts the activities of the politician at their lowest to say that he seeks to gain power and a livelihood through traffic in the beliefs and ideas of others.

[4] A. Lawrence Lowell, *Public Opinion and Popular Government,* rev. ed. (New York: Longmans, Green, 1914), ch. v.

It is well to see things at their starkest. In fact, most politicians have their own conception of the common interest that they would like to see carried out. That is impossible without power, and power has been dispersed among a numerous electorate. It can only be concentrated in a democratic way by massing votes behind leaders and a program. The party politician, unlike some others, has learned about the facts of life; he knows, as another happy phrase has put it, that votes are not delivered by the stork. Voters have to be attracted and organized. Only when this has been done by nation-wide effort and co-operation of many politicians can any one of them hope to make some of his view of the common good come true. And then he can never hope to realize more than a fraction of it politically. For to get the co-operation of other politicians whose view of the common good differs somewhat from his, each has to give hostages. Each has to give up some portion of the good he sees to make room for some of the good that others see.

When the politicians united in a party come to appeal for the votes of a vast electorate, the program has to set aside much that the politicians personally think desirable in order to accommodate something of the diverse goods held dear by the members of the electorate, and by the organized interest groups within the electorate. In so far as the initial assumption of a radical diversity of opinion in the electorate stands, it is clear that the wider the appeal, the lower will be the highest common factor on which united action can take place.

THE NEED FOR ACCOMMODATION. Perhaps the simplest illustration of the necessity for such accommodation is to be found in Canadian politics. The people of the Province of Quebec are overwhelmingly French-speaking and Roman Catholic, French in social structure and culture; they constitute about one-quarter of the population of Canada. Therefore, it is only rarely that a political party can win power without getting substantial support in Quebec. But Quebec opinion on what the Dominion Parliament should be instructed to do for the common good shows marked divergences from the lines of policy for which majorities can be found in the rest of Canada. Accordingly, political parties must modify their programs to find a compromise that will produce a nation-wide majority. This compromise will be something that neither Quebec nor the rest of the country would fight for if each were going its own way.

It is not the fact of Quebec alone that makes this process necessary, although the French-English diversity provides its most striking illustration. The process is at work in every election district in Canada, Britain, and the

United States. The use of this technique of accommodation is, in varying degree, a skill required of democratic politicians everywhere. Britain, with greater social homogeneity than Canada or the United States, gets on with less watering down of programs of political action, but is far from avoiding it entirely.

In the United States, both the Republican party and the Democratic party have drawn traditional support from different regions and diverse interest groups, and both have framed their electoral appeals to attract votes from almost all sections and interest groups. Thus, in Clinton Rossiter's phrase, they become the 'peacemakers of the American community.' The Democratic party has first to compromise within itself to hold together the conservative-minded agricultural and business interests of its Southern wing and the more radically inclined elements of its traditional support among labor and liberal elements in the urban industrial North. Then, to win a majority, it has to woo the predominantly agricultural West, whose interests differ markedly from those of both Southern and Northern Democrats. The Republican party has won its greatest successes as an alliance of Northern and Northeastern business interests, professionals generally, and Western farmers.

The political combinations involved are much more complex than this statement indicates, and their patterns have changed sporadically. The main point, however, is that *both parties appeal to almost all sections and classes.* A notable exception was the Republican party as it first took shape in the 1850's. It was entirely a combination of Northern interests. Its first victory in 1860 did not take account of Southern interests and demands. Its failure to find a nation-wide basis of compromise was one of the chief factors that led to the Civil War.

Party politicians, therefore, are brokers in another sense. They are always arranging deals between different sections of opinion, finding compromises that 'split the difference,' and thus concentrating votes behind the program of their political party. As long as the sovereign electorate is of numerous diverse opinions, this is the only way majorities can be constructed and power gained to push through any political program in a democracy.

Creating Majorities. It may be objected that the argument proves too much. If opinion were naturally so diverse, the parties could never herd the bulk of the electorate into one or other of two camps. In fact, this is precisely what the democratic politicians of many states of continental Europe—such as pre-Fifth Republic France—were always unable to do, and parties there have tended to become more instead of less numerous. In Britain and the United

States a two-party system was established while the electorate was still small in numbers and politics was, much more than now, a game between the 'ins' and the 'outs.' Large sections of the electorate become habituated to allegiance to one or other of the two parties and become deeply attached to its leaders and traditions.

WEAKNESS OF THIRD PARTIES IN THE UNITED STATES AND BRITAIN. Once the two-party system was firmly established, a number of factors discouraged the setting up of additional parties. Everyone has had cause to remark the plausibility of the politicians. Their programs are devised with generally recognized problems in mind. Their arguments seem convincing to an electorate that knows little about the nature of those problems and has given little attention to the ways of meeting them. Most people find that after earning their daily bread and keeping track of the adventures of their favorite motion-picture stars, they have little time for the serious study of politics. Their interest and conviction are not strong enough to make them launch new parties unless there is a pronounced failure of the established parties to meet obvious and urgent problems.

The voter who has not time to study politics has not time to start an organization to promote his views. If his vote is to count at all, he must attach himself to one of the vote-gathering organizations already in the field with some prospect of winning. He is the more disposed to do this because everyone likes to put his money on the winning team. Third, or minor, parties are launched from time to time, but unless they rapidly come within striking distance of a majority, their support soon falls away. To create new parties is costly and often runs into technical difficulties, such as the need of obtaining a sufficient number of petitions from specified areas of the country. The older parties are deeply entrenched in the community. Their organizations are alert to thwart or undermine the competition of any new political party that emerges. Not infrequently this is done by adopting an attractive aspect of the new party's program. Other factors that have supported the two-party system in the past will be considered in different connections.

The first essential function of the party system then is to organize voters into majorities behind platforms and leaders. The voters get alternatives from which to choose, and the electorate can reward the party that appears to be deserving and be sure that both parties will strive to merit reward. This is the only way in which a numerous electorate can exercise effectively the power that democratic theory assigns to it. Also, as earlier discussion shows, the parties by their activity in the legislature contribute to the political education of the electorate. They turn talk into legislation, and legislation into concrete regulation and services through administration.

Opposing Majorities. Another function of political parties is apparent in the legislative body, where the party out of power, the out-party—or *coalition* of out-parties in multiple-party systems—acts as an agent of restraint on the party or parties in office. The minority may adopt tactics of criticism and/or obstruction of actions taken by the majority. A more positive policy might involve co-operation with the majority on some issues but opposition on others, so that differences might be exploited at the next election. The most formal and most responsible example of opposition is found in Britain. There the minority party is referred to as 'Her Majesty's Loyal Opposition,' and has official standing as such. Through debates in the House of Commons and the daily question period, in which members of the House of Commons ask searching questions of the government, the British Opposition compels the majority to justify, and occasionally even to modify, its actions.

The Opposition, or out-party, in the United States has not customarily shown the same degree of responsibility as has its British counterpart. One reason is that the differences between the two major American parties here are far more blurred. Another reason is, as Hugh Gaitskell, when Leader of the Opposition in Britain, once remarked, that under the American system of separation of powers the *real* opposition is not so much the out-party as it is the *Congress* itself, as an institution of government—a checkmate, however negative or non-constructive it may be.

Concentrating Responsibility. By concentrating votes for themselves, the political parties concentrate responsibility on themselves. It would be difficult to exaggerate the importance of this. A majority party has power to implement its promises, to meet problems as they arise, and to administer laws wisely and fairly. In so far as it is judged in the sequel to have failed, there is no doubt who is responsible and who is to be punished. The people can bring home responsibility to a determinate group of individuals.

If there were no parties and a crisis arose that was not appropriately met, everybody would be equally responsible; i.e. nobody would be responsible. If there were only one party, the responsibility would be clear but it could not be brought home because there would be no alternative government. And the chief defect of the multiple-party system, to be discussed presently, is that in the shifting coalitions it involves, responsibility is blurred and the electorate can scarcely determine where it lies. The two-party system does not enable the sovereign electorate to govern the country, but it does enable it to *choose* and rule its masters and to make government responsible. Those who know the history of government among men will not be disposed to belittle this achievement.

CONSTRUCTING MAJORITIES IN A MASS ELECTORATE

Yet the everyday spectacle of party politics rouses widespread disgust and distaste. To many—and not only to Charles de Gaulle—politicians are the lowest form of life, and all appreciate Artemus Ward's recommendation of himself, saying, 'I am not a politician and all my other habits are good.' In part, this disgust is due to a failure to understand why the democratic politician does not summarily enforce the opinions of the critic and have done with it. In great measure, however, it is a reaction to certain unsavory aspects of political life. The indictment against parties must be heard and a verdict considered and given.

The unsavory features arise mainly from the fact of widespread suffrage, although it must not be inferred from this that politics had a better smell when the franchise was limited to the well-born. It had a different odor, but by no means a better one. In politics, men are always trying to get their hands on the instruments of legalized coercion and on the sweets of office. It is therefore the most ill-disguised struggle for power short of open war, and is likely to be unmannerly and sometimes unscrupulous. Politics is also the arena where passionately held views clash and men are tempted to make the end justify the means. It is rash to think that the political process can ever be turned wholly to sweetness and light.

Burke's Definition. In eighteenth-century England, when the franchise was narrow and gentlemen were born to politics, there was little evidence of the existence of parties outside the legislature. In Parliament itself, the members of the parties made their deals in secret caucus and the only outward evidence of these were the principles the members expounded. It was in these circumstances that Edmund Burke framed his famous definition of a political party as 'a body of men united, for promoting by their joint endeavours the national interest, on some particular principle on which they are all agreed.' [5] Of course, the parties tried to extend their membership and influence to the constituencies in the hope of altering or maintaining the complexion of

[5] *The Works of the Right Honourable Edmund Burke* (Boston: Wells and Lilly, 1826), p. 426.

Parliament at the next election. But the candidate often knew all the voters personally, and in any event could canvass them all himself. Elaborate party organization was unnecessary under these circumstances.

All this has been changed by universal suffrage. Where the voters in a constituency numbered dozens or hundreds, they now number tens of thousands and hundreds of thousands. The candidates cannot personally canvass more than a few of them. Yet their votes are necessary for victory. The party must come to the aid of its candidate with money and scores of tireless workers. For there is much to be done as an election approaches. The voters must be harangued and canvassed. Wavering voters must have the issues at stake specially explained to them. Campaign literature must be prepared and widely distributed. Space in the newspapers and time on the radio must be arranged and paid for. Transportation must be provided to carry the eager and the not-so-eager voters to the polls.

The Need for Organization. An organization that does all this efficiently cannot be thrown together on the eve of an election. It becomes necessary to maintain permanent party committees in each constituency. Nor is this enough. The parties carry on nation-wide campaigns on a national platform and the greatest possible number of seats must be won. A central organization for over-all direction is necessary for maximum results. Local party organizations are sometimes slack and need coaching and encouragement. Doubtful constituencies are the sectors where the front breaks, and the central organization must mobilize strategic reserves. Research is undertaken in problems of public policy, and party speakers across the country are supplied with facts, arguments, and statistics.

The most important work of the central organization, however, is not in fighting this election but in planning the next one. Therefore, it should be a permanent organization with a substantial permanent staff. The platform of the party—no matter how flagrantly it may be disregarded after the election ('We will take it out and read it from time to time,' [6] a remark by House Minority Leader Charles Halleck in 1961, is symptomatic)—must have the widest possible appeal, and it must not be settled on until the contours of opinion in the constituencies have been plotted. The central organization collects much of the data that the leaders must take into account in drafting the program. It gives attention to alternative plans of campaign and to the strategy and tactics appropriate to each. It keeps in touch with constituency

[6] Quoted by James MacGregor Burns, *The Deadlock of Democracy: Four-Party Politics in America* (Englewood Cliffs, N.J.: Prentice-Hall, 1963), p. 255.

organizations, bolstering their morale, explaining the government's policy if the party happens to be in power, and the government's lack of policy if the party is in opposition. Analogies are always misleading, but it comes close to being the directing brain of the party.

The vigor of the central party organizations is much stronger in Britain, where they attend to all the matters described and others as well. In the United States, the national central party organizations are but pale reflections of the picture drawn here. That is because the strongest and most effective party organizations are the state or local organizations. In many of the states central party organizations perform more or less effectively most of the functions described above. It must be clearly understood as a primary lesson of American politics that the locus of power within each party lies at the state or local, *not* at the national, level.

The Need for Funds. In any case, permanent central and constituency organizations are necessities if the parties are to make the most of the possibilities. The maintaining of these organizations and the fighting of periodic elections are a heavy expense to the parties. One of the heaviest items of expense in an election is the provision of thousands of workers to help garner in the vote, and for this reason parties have found it necessary to rely heavily on unpaid volunteer workers who help for the sake of the party. Money is the root of much evil in political parties, as elsewhere. The parties find it too cramping, if not impossible, to finance their operations through the small contributions of a large number of party supporters and much easier to get large contributions from relatively few people.

This philanthropy is not always pure, and there are lively expectations, if not tacit understandings, of favors to come when the party gets into power. Wealth alone is certainly not decisive in nominations or elections, but there is little doubt that it helps in handling the rigorous demands that politics in the United States, especially, imposes on candidates. Also, it is found that volunteer workers are more numerous and zealous if the party can give concrete recognition of their services. The loyal workers who do the party drudgery are often aspirants for favors that will be in the gift of the party when it is victorious. The party cannot be successful without a vigorous organization, and organization depends on benefactors and loyal workers.

Fighting To Win. Party organization has other disillusioning features. All organization has a tendency to fall under the control of a few. The organization tends to become autonomous, to exist for its own sake and for the satisfactions it provides for its active personnel, even at the expense of its principles and original purpose. Most of the supporters of the party have little interest in humdrum matters of organization, and their attention to party affairs subsides between elections. Party organization in the constituency falls normally into the hands of an interested few who try to control it. The national party leaders naturally have a commanding influence in the national organization.

These local and central leaders, along with the permanently employed officials of the party, come to regard the organization as important for its own sake. Since the organization flourishes on victory and languishes in defeat, principles tend to become subordinated to success at the polls. The benefactors and the party workers often make a similar judgment. The former often show how much they care about the principles of the party by making contributions to *both* parties, sometimes the same amount. The party workers and those benefactors who bet on the nose of their horse cannot be rewarded without victory. Furthermore, the sheer delight of battle stirs everyone connected with the parties to put victory first. There have been times when these influences made the party system primarily a struggle between the ins and the outs. The only safeguard against this degeneration at any time is some minimum of intelligence and interest on the part of the electorate.

There is clear support of this estimate in the search of the parties for issues that will capture the vote. Since neither party can escape the necessity of encouraging one section of opinion to expect some things that, if stressed too much, will repel other sections of opinion, each party looks for red herrings to draw across the trail, specious issues that divert the public and force the other party to a less favorable battleground. Such maneuvers can only be prevented by a public that knows too much to let itself be deceived.

DISHONESTY? Two of the counts in the indictment against the party system used to be fraud in the buying of votes and the stuffing of ballot boxes. Election laws have been tightened up, voting machines have replaced the paper ballot in many instances, and party managers have lost a good deal of their interest in such piecemeal methods. Improvements in the art and media of propaganda make it easier to attempt wholesale stampedes of voters, and bribery now tends generally to take the form of promising large sections of the population benefits from the public treasury.

REWARDS. After the election has been won by such methods, those who have deserved well of the party are rewarded. The benefactors who have earned a reward may be given profitable government contracts, improved social security legislation, and other advantages. Some of the party workers get government jobs, often through the dismissal of employees of the government who were just learning how to do their work reasonably well. The patronage or spoils system has many unfortunate effects, which are too well known to need discussion. It must be acknowledged, however, that the worst excesses of the spoils system have now been curbed by reasonably effective reforms—with some glaring exceptions. Moreover, like it or not, patronage is the oil that keeps the party machine running.

A Serious Charge. Thus it is claimed that the parties are run by small cliques of politicians who take pains to exclude men of better will than themselves from influence in party councils or in framing the party platform. They, so continues the charge, deceive the public and frustrate the will of the people for better government. They saddle the public with incompetent servants and use their control of the government to enrich themselves, their friends, and their supporters.

A VERDICT ON PARTIES

If a verdict has to be given on the charges summed up in the last paragraph, it will be neither 'guilty' nor 'not guilty,' but 'greatly exaggerated.' Occasional politicians enrich themselves at the public expense, but most of them live and die poor. Corrupt bargains with benefactors are fewer than is generally supposed. Many men give large sums to their party without expectation of a concrete return, although it would not be correct to say that party policy has been unmindful of the source of contributions to party funds. Loyal workers are rewarded with jobs wherever possible, but the critics of this practice have rarely taken adequate account of the difficulty of finding alternative sources of energy for running the party organizations.

Facts of Political Life. The hard fact is that the parties need funds and workers for their indispensable function of organizing the electorate. Job-seekers are the bane of the politicians' existence, and there is nothing more welcome than utterly voluntary service to the party. It is equally certain that they would prefer to get party funds that entailed no obligation. These have not come forward in sufficient volume from the rank and file of the supporters of the parties, and they have received but little supplement from those who rebuke the politicians for making what shift they can.

It cannot be emphasized too much that the party organizations in a democracy are flexible and necessarily responsible to currents of opinion. Those who are sure that party practices outrage common decency can dedicate themselves to reform of those practices. The obstacles they face are nothing compared to those that vital social movements have overcome in the past.

It is true that a small group of leaders tries to control the party, but that is a general feature of all human organization, certainly not limited to political parties. Men of good will are not excluded from party councils, but they often exclude themselves because they are too inflexible to make the compromises essential to the gathering of votes. The parties do not frustrate the will of the people, because it is only rarely that even a transient majority of the people is genuinely of one mind about a specific political problem. The parties deceive the public, but so do propagandists of every kind. The deception does not often arise from cynicism but rather from zest for the game itself, a general human trait. It may be said generally in conclusion that *the evils in the party system are not peculiar to it but are the outcome of general human frailties.* Indeed, it is hard to see how the parties that must woo the electorate with success can do other than reflect its virtues and its vices. Perhaps it is people as much as institutions that need to be reformed.

These charges and this verdict have been general and make no allowance for the considerable differences in the party system in different countries. Nor do they take account of differences between the parties in the same country. In the last ninety years, at any rate, the spoils system and unsavory bargains with party benefactors have been much more common in the United States than in Britain or France. Moreover, many of the charges leveled at the party system are much less applicable to the newer third and fourth parties—the parties of protest.

These latter parties are maintained by a generous idealism that finances the party and supplies the workers for the sake of the cause. The supporters of these parties, doctrinaire and otherwise, assure us that it is because they appeal to the best rather than to the worst in people. This is not the whole reason. As long as these third parties are a long way from power, it is easy for them to be pure. No one tempts them with donations in return for favors and concessions at public expense. The party workers work hard because until they approach the threshold of power it is possible for each to believe that the party will bring his ideals to fruition. It is only when it becomes necessary to please everyone in order to catch and retain votes that the sickening compromises begin and the disillusionment that saps enthusiasm among the supporters of the older parties sets in.

PARTIES AND PEACEFUL CHANGE OF GOVERNMENT

As long as we adhere to the rule that ultimate power rests with a diffused electorate, political parties are necessary to frame issues and bring public opinion to a focus. However, political parties, two or more in number, perform other even more fundamental functions for democracy. They make peaceful change of government possible and thus eliminate the necessity for the armed *coup d'état* as a means of changing government, and the counter-necessity of ruling by force and terror to prevent such a *coup d'état*. A glance at two striking episodes in the Nazi and Soviet dictatorships will help to make this clear.

It has already been noted that the Soviet Union permits only one party, the Communist party. Some description of this one-party system will be given later in this chapter. Likewise, in Germany under the Nazis, the Nazi party was the only party allowed to exist and participate in the processes of government.

Purges in the One-Party State. In June 1934, the Nazi party in Germany purged itself of scores of prominent members of the party by shooting them down under the pretense that they were resisting arrest. Between 1936 and 1938 there were repeated purges in the Communist party in Russia. Several dozens of the old distinguished members of the party who suffered imprisonment and exile for the sake of the revolution against the Czarist regime were tried for treason and either executed or imprisoned. In each case these actions were the result of a serious split in the party.

NAZI GERMANY. The Nazi party had in it many genuine socialists who wanted to make the party the instrument of out-and-out socialism. In order to win power, however, Hitler had made infamous bargains with anti-socialist elements that he had found expedient to honor for a considerable time after gaining power. The socialist wing, including a minority of important leaders, regarded this as a betrayal of their hopes and of the promises that had been made them. Although the exact circumstances and sequence of events are not clear, it seems that this group was threatening to contest Hitler's leadership of the party when Hitler struck first.

SOVIET RUSSIA. There is also confusion as to what happened in Russia. The accused were charged with and convicted of conspiring with Germany and Japan to overthrow the Russian government. If they did so conspire, it is clear that the conspiracy was the consequence of a conviction that Stalin had betrayed the revolution. For years there had been a widening rift in the party between those who held with Stalin that a strong socialist state must first be established in Russia before trying to convert the rest of the world, and those who sympathized with Trotsky's view that Stalin's policy was bound to fail and that it was necessary to get on with world-wide revolution without a day's delay. In other words, they disagreed profoundly over the means by which the desired end, world-wide socialism, could be reached.

There are strong reasons for thinking that such purges are a periodic necessity in the one-party system, as is demonstrated by the events of the 1950s in Russia, for one. Whether or not they will require bloodshed depends on how deeply and passionately the leaders are divided and how determined both factions are to make their will prevail. But purges of some sort are necessary where free elections are not used to settle disputes over government policy. For to set up a one-party system is to say that there is only one right way to govern the country and that the way is clear and unmistakable. If there were any reasonable doubt, the sensible thing to do would be to allow two or more parties and let them experiment in turn with their solutions to the country's problems. The one party monopolizes all political activity and it can entertain only one policy. Any man with political ambitions or with strong views on what the government ought to be doing must get into the party and try to work his way to influence and authority.

Nazis and Communists, like other people, are of diverse opinions. There is disagreement over policy within the party. When neither group can convince the other and neither will give in, the single party has, in fact, split into two parties. The peaceful way out is to allow the dissenting minority to secede openly and set up party organs of its own, and then to agree to let the people arbitrate this and any subsequent conflict between them, awarding control of the government to the group that wins the confidence of the electorate for the time being. The alternating governments of the democracies are made possible only by the unflinching and unhesitating acceptance of the convention that the party in power always accepts the verdict of the polls.

One-Party State Solution. The frank adoption of this solution is barred in the one-party state because the zealots who set it up are agreed on one thing at least: *they know* what government policy should be and there is nothing for the public to arbitrate. How could it be otherwise with men who think they have perceived the only valid goals of human life and society? It is a betrayal of their vision to allow the perverse and the stupid to organize against them. Nothing will be gained and everything may be lost by reasoning and discussing with the obstructors, who, if they had any reason or good will in them, would have seen the light long ago. For such as these, the zealots have only a burning impatience and contempt. So they destroy without a qualm all organization that might talk or act against their views.

Men who are willing to obliterate all other parties but their own generally will not shrink from obliterating opposition elements within the party. It becomes a question of which faction will shoot first. There is no ground for thinking that Hitler enjoyed shooting old friends who had shared his struggle, or that Stalin found any satisfaction in the judicial liquidation of comrades with whom he had fought and suffered for an ideal. The logic of the one-party system compels such a course of action from time to time.

The Democratic Alternative to Purges. So, when it is asked whether the country can afford to have half its able leaders always obstructing in opposition, the real issue is whether they are more useful there than in the cemetery. The shooting of old friends would not necessarily be bad for the body politic if there were any assurance that those quick on the draw somehow have also the better political opinions. There is no evidence that this is an index to statesmanship.

TESTING OF POLICIES. The prime advantage of the two-or-more-party system is that it applies the only rational test of statesmanship, the testing of policies through their practical application. The public will support one party for a while and then another. Each party experiments with its ideas while in power, and if the results are satisfactory the opposing party acknowledges it by continuing the measure after they come to power. In the past, at any rate, relatively little legislation has been repealed on a change of government. This fact is of great importance. It suggests strongly that the liberal democratic processes of discussion are effective means of enlarging the area of agreement among men and confirming their sense of unity, if they have the patience to thresh out their differences on terms of mutual respect.

TRIAL AND ERROR. Those who come to politics with white-hot convictions will always be impatient with government by trial and error. Before they reject it, they might well examine the alternative and ask whether they wish to put their faith to the test of violence. For violence not only degrades the personalities of those on whom it is practiced. It also destroys the basis of mutual trust and respect on which the pursuit of liberal democratic ideals depends. Those who admit that there may be reasonable differences of opinion on how best to further these ideals will find merit in the open, flexible system. Those who lay store by constitutionalism will cling to the party system because alternating governments are the effective device for keeping power contingent. The people can govern their rulers and hold them responsible only as long as they can dismiss them and find at once a workable alternative government.

TYPES OF DEMOCRATIC PARTY SYSTEMS

At the beginning of this chapter it was explained that two basic main types of democratic party systems exist: two-party and multi-party. The former, in turn, may again be divided into those with and those without tight party discipline—Britain and the United States, respectively. We shall now examine these several systems.

BRITISH TWO-PARTY GOVERNMENT

The evolution of political parties in Britain has produced a system of strongly disciplined national parties, in which the individual political leader, regardless of his eminence, must forgo a certain amount of individuality. The two-party tradition and a unitary form of government have combined to place the location of political power on the *national* rather than on local or state level—the precise reverse of the situation in the United States.

Organization of Control. Despite one victory and several respectable 'also-ran' showings in bi-elections in the early 1960s, it seems probable now that the Liberal party in Britain is doomed to minor party status—although there are some who predict a three-party system. But in the last general elections in 1959, Liberals polled only 5.9 per cent of the popular vote and obtained but six seats in Commons, since then augmented by the one mentioned. In any case, Liberal and Conservative organizations are so similar in pattern that a description of one will serve for the other. Also, the organization of the Labour party steadily grows more like that of the others.[7] It will be sufficient to note a few salient divergences. The basic unit in all three parties is the local constituency organization, composed of all those who formally join the party and maintain their membership. The active and effective part of the local association is the small executive committee, which, in turn, is very

---

[7] On this point and others to follow see the excellent study of Britain's parties by Robert T. McKenzie, *British Political Parties* (New York: St. Martin's Press, 1955), *passim.*

powerfully influenced by its secretary and a paid party agent, whose job it is to win the constituency in the election.

CENTRAL OFFICE. The local associations are in each case united in a national union, which maintains a central party office and holds an annual conference made up of delegates from the constituency organizations. The conference elects a national executive committee, which directs the work of the central office. The central office is an over-all directing and co-ordinating agency, devoted to the planning and winning of elections. In theory, the conference is a representative party legislature for establishing the policy of the party. But it has come under the powerful influence of its executive committee and the permanent staff of the central office. The central office works in the closest relation with the party's leader in Parliament, by whom the party program is drafted with the help of the chairman of the executive committee and the chief official of the central office. Headquarters rarely fails to get this draft approved by the annual conference of the party.

LEADER OF PARTY. Nor does the conference choose the leader of the party. He is chosen by those members of the party who are in Parliament. As he is their leader in the critical party struggles in Parliament, it is most desirable that he should be their choice. Equally, those who lead the party in Parliament, and who have, or will have, the responsibility of making and enforcing government policy, are sternly set against having the annual conference saddle them with a policy that is impracticable or impossible of application. This helps to explain the centralized party machine. The natural tendency toward oligarchy in human organization and the inherent logic of responsible cabinet government both contribute to it.

LABOUR PARTY AND TRADE UNIONS. The main divergences of the Labour party from this pattern of organization arise from the *connection of the party with the trade unions*. Trade unions and local trades councils, as well as individuals, are members of the party and thus entitled to distinct representation in local and national organization. The local party agent is often a trade union official. Because the trade unions are powerful principalities within the party, the central organization cannot dominate the party so fully. The annual Labour party conference discusses party policy more fruitfully. Yet the conference cannot force a policy on the parliamentary group of the party. After all the debate is over, the latter must approve the policy before it becomes official, and they are simply not bound by statements of policy laid down by the conference. The parliamentary group also chooses the person who is to lead them in Parliament. His position is somewhat less secure than that of the leader of the Conservative party, because unlike the latter he must be re-elected each session when the party is out of power, and he has thus no automatic right to be Prime Minister when the party comes to power.

APPROVAL OF CANDIDATES. As part of their duties in planning and executing election campaigns, the central organizations insist that every candidate who represents the party be approved by them, and they make judgments on his orthodoxy in cases where doubt arises. Central party officials often want seats in Parliament, and these—and others—are recommended to the local associations. It is very rarely, however, that the central office will try to force a candidate on a local committee determined to pick its own, although the central office may refuse its imprimatur to a particular choice. Ancillary to its principal duties, the central office carries on research in the problems of government, grinds out party literature, manages the party funds, and nurses the party press. It is active continuously and not merely at election time.

CAMPAIGN FUNDS. Much less is known in detail about the sources of campaign funds in Britain than in America—in part because in Britain their expenditure is governmentally regulated so much more successfully. The two older parties rely mainly on substantial contributions from men of substance. Explicit bargains for a *quid pro quo* are not common, partly because of a high standard of political morality, partly because unlike governments in North America, British governments have not had vast natural resources to give away and have not been subsidizing desirable private economic enterprises such as railways. However, titles of honor have been a significant substitute for railway concessions, timber limits, and tariff increases. The parties exploit social snobbery instead of the natural resources of the country. The Labour party, for obvious reasons, has had little part in such traffic. It has drawn its funds in small amounts from a vast body of supporters, particularly through the trade unions.

REWARDS. The merit system of appointment to the civil service covers most government jobs and it is loyally and honestly applied. There is therefore very little room for operation of the spoils system. The patronage appointments do not begin to provide rewards for doing the drudgery of the party. In so far as voluntary workers do not come forward in sufficient numbers, they must be paid a wage. Here the Labour party has an advantage because it has the largest reserve of crusading enthusiasm. On the other hand, it is at a disadvantage on election day because fewer of its supporters can supply automobiles to take the voters to the polls.

British Party Discipline. As has already been pointed out, candidates are normally chosen by the local party associations. But since localism is not strong in national politics in Britain, and the candidate need not be a resident in the constituency he hopes to represent in the House of Commons, the central party organization strongly influences the choice and often actually provides the candidate.

CHOOSING CANDIDATES. In choosing a candidate, each party in Britain is careful to pick, among other things, a sound party man, one who is loyal to the leadership and principles of the party. In recommending its candidate to the constituency, each party always justifies him by reference to the statesmanlike leadership and sound platform of the party. The candidate himself modestly subordinates to this praise of his party his own claim to merit and preferment. He dwells on its past record, its present promises, the integrity of its leaders, and the wisdom of their policies. He might well repeat the self-depreciation of the hymn, 'Nothing in my hand I bring.' It is assumed throughout that the voting is not merely, or even mainly, to choose a person to represent the constituency but to get the verdict of the voters on the party, its leaders, and its platform.

STRONG PARTY DISCIPLINE IN PARLIAMENT. There have been normally only two significant political parties and one or the other of them gets its members elected to a majority of the seats in the House of Commons. The executive, the cabinet, is chosen from the leaders of the majority party. The rank and file of this majority party respond to its leaders and present a united front on almost all issues. The making of laws and other important decisions in the House of Commons are decisions of the majority party under persuasion and pressure by the cabinet. Often, particular members of Parliament belonging to the majority party are personally opposed, more or less strongly, to the line their party proposes to take. Yet they almost invariably vote for the party line.

All this is common knowledge, but its far-reaching significance is not always grasped. Members of Parliament are often chided for meekly following their party when public opinion in their constituencies is strongly opposed to the line the majority party is following. It is forgotten that the member never held himself to be individually responsible as a mouthpiece for his constituents but rather professed always to be the loyal member of a party. The party takes the responsibility for the man and for the platform, and the constituency is invited to make its reckoning with the party—which, of course, it can effectively do by rejecting the candidate of this particular party at the next election. The political parties have planted themselves between the electorate and the legislature. Moreover, the bulk of the electorate shows its approval of this by voting for a party, for a party leader, and for a party platform rather than for an individual candidate.

SOME CASE STUDIES. It would be both foolish and futile for a political party to invite responsibility in this way unless there was a prospect of power to make good its promises. Actually, if a well-disciplined party wins a majority of the seats in a legislature where decisions are taken by majority vote, it has the power to carry out its promises. To make that power good, it must keep its members in line—as the Government or as the Opposition. In the role of the latter, for example, the Labour party expelled five 'left wing' members from its parliamentary party in March 1961 for having forced a vote against the Government on appropriations for the armed forces, despite Labour's expressly adopted policy to the contrary. As a result, the five M.P.s remained in the Labour party, but were no longer considered members of its official representation in the House of Commons, and henceforth sat as Independent Labourites.

The imposition of party discipline even on the 'back bencher'—the member with little effective power in the party—is complete and enforceable. Members of the majority party are expected to support the cabinet, no matter what their personal reservations concerning the proposal at issue. In 1944, when a Government education bill was reported to the floor by the committee in charge, Thelma Cazalet Keir, a Conservative member of Parliament, proposed an amendment providing equal pay for men and women teachers. The President of the Board of Education, who represented the cabinet, opposed the amendment. But Mrs. Keir was able to rally feminist support to the amendment, and it passed by a vote of 117 to 116, with many of the then 625 members of the House of Commons choosing to vote neither against the Government nor against women. On the following day, however, Prime Minister Churchill declared the issue one of confidence in the Government, whereupon support for the amendment dwindled, the number of persons participating in the vote doubled—and Mrs. Keir's proposal fell victim to party discipline. Among those who 'toed the line'—Mrs. Keir!

A more recent illustration is the Opposition move in December 1956 to censure the Eden Conservative Government over the Suez invasion debacle of six weeks earlier. Although under heavy attack by members of its own party—albeit in part for quite different reasons—the Government prevailed by a vote of 327 to 260. Its subsequent own motion expressing approval of its conduct passed 312 to 260, with fifteen 'right wing' Conservatives abstaining. And, again, in 1963 the Macmillan Conservative Government scored a decisive 333 to 227 victory on the touchy European Common Market issue.

THE PARTY WHIPS. In Britain, each party in the House of Commons has a number of party whips, members of the party whose function it is to maintain close liaison between the leaders of the party and its rank and file. The party whips move constantly among the party members in the House of Commons, sounding opinion among them, informing them of the matters which must be decided, and mobilizing them for a vote when a decision is about to be taken in the House. The jobs of the whips is to ensure the united front of the party and to bring to the attention of the party leadership not only breaches of party loyalty but also any serious murmurs of the rank and file against the policies of the leaders.

The whips try to placate and persuade disgruntled members. If, despite this, members vote against their party on serious issues, they will almost certainly not be nominated as candidates for their party at the next election. These methods of ensuring support generally suffice. Almost all bills introduced in the House of Commons are part of a unified program of the majority party, which gets disciplined support from the members of that party. Moreover, the majority party compels the House of Commons to work to an exacting time-table and to accept an order of priority of business that the party deems essential to the fulfillment of the responsibility it has accepted. It thus controls all significant action in the House of Commons. There are, however, some rare occasions when 'free votes' are authorized and the whips are 'taken off.'

PARTY POLICY AND THE VOTER. Of course, the member of Parliament, of whatever party, keeps in close touch with his constituents and always furthers their interests where he can do so consistently with the party line. The really vital communication is not between the member and his constituents as individuals. It is between him, the local association of his party, and the central organization of his party, and takes the form of a steady flow of information, advice, explanation, and expostulation. If the intelligence thus coming in from all parts of the country indicates that the current party line should be modified, it is not revised through open desertion of it by members of the party in debate in the House of Commons. The revision is made unobtrusively in secret conclave of the parliamentary leaders of the party, where the sensitive antennae of the party organization that reach into all parts of the country register the shifts of opinion that must be heeded.

The British voter accepts this concept of party discipline, and thus eases the task of the party leaders who expect conformity from their parliamentary delegations. The virtual absence of members without party affiliation in the House of Commons is testimony that, in a very real sense, the voters as well as the party expect and impose discipline. In four recent general elections only six independent candidates gained seats in the House of Commons—none in 1950, three in 1951, two in 1955, and one in 1959. With very few exceptions it has proved necessary to run under a party label in order to obtain decisive popular support. The British elector, though he casts his ballot for a representative from a single-member district, in effect votes for *party* rather than *person*—which is the reverse of the custom of American voters. He votes for a national program, rather than for any candidate's personal version thereof, and he therefore expects his representative in Parliament to co-operate with his party's leaders.

BEHIND THE SCENES. In fact, the central organizations of the parties in Britain are so effective in registering the state of opinion in the constituencies that it is rarely necessary for them to hold a caucus, or conference, of the members of the party in the House of Commons to debate an adjustment of party policy. Normally, informal consultation between the party whips and the rank and file of party members in the House suffices to work out the party line. It is in these informal consultations, and occasionally in secret caucus, that the substance of party policy is hammered out in Britain. Quietly behind the scenes and not in open debate in the legislature, members of Parliament show what independence and courage they have. In party caucus or in discussion with party whips, facts ably argued and convictions powerfully expressed may change opinion and alter the party line. Any such alteration is to ensure that virtually all members will support their party in the voting in the House of Commons. In this way, party discipline is made effective, the majority party controls the House of Commons, and hence carries out the bulk of the promises it has made to the electorate.

UNITED STATES TWO-PARTY GOVERNMENT

Location of Control. It is impossible to give a simple description of party organization in the United States. Parties perform their functions in each of the fifty states as well as in national politics, and the necessity for linking state and federal party activity fosters complexity. Although the Republican and Democratic parties are national parties, the state is, for each of them, the vital unit of organization, and the structure of each party varies from state to state.

FREQUENT ELECTIONS. Furthermore, there are more elections in the United States than in any other country. In the national field, there is a presidential election every four years and congressional elections every two years at fixed

FORMAL STRUCTURE OF THE TWO MAJOR
POLITICAL PARTIES IN THE UNITED STATES*

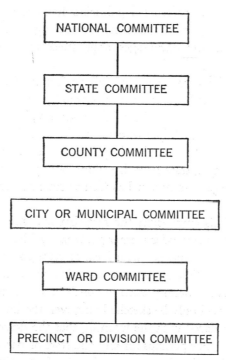

*Although this basic pattern exists throughout the country for both parties, its nomenclature varies at times at the lower levels, and the city or municipal committee is often omitted.

dates. At state elections, generally held at the same time as the national elections, the voters must choose a governor and a state legislature. In addition, many state and municipal executive and administrative posts, which in Britain are filled by appointment, are elective offices in the United States. Also, in almost all states the law now requires each party to hold at least some direct primaries—preliminary elections within the party—for the purpose of choosing party committees, party candidates, and even delegates to conventions that will choose candidates. There is almost always an election in the offing for which preparation must be made.

PARTY MACHINES. The numerous elections and the state-national division account in large part for the hyper-organized condition of political parties and for the large numbers of professional politicians in the United States. Here, more than in any other democratic country, there is justification for calling party organization a *machine,* because of its intricate articulation and smooth efficiency. The professional politician handles the machine with a sure and delicate touch, and the necessity for making the machine work well and almost continuously encourages apprenticeship in the profession of politics.

Yet this organization stops short of full perfection. Despite the fact that the principal popular excitement is over national issues and national elections, party organization at the national level is temporary, haphazard, and almost entirely lacking in the discipline revealed at the state level. Party organization and activity are much regulated by law, but these laws are almost all state laws. For example, state laws determine how party candidates to Congress and party delegates to national as well as state nominating conventions shall be chosen.

ORGANIZATIONS. This emphasizes the fact that *it is the state and local organizations of the parties which are significant.* Although we are mainly concerned with national and not with local or state government, it is necessary to give close attention to the state organization of the political parties. Fortunately, there is a general pattern to which both parties conform in most states. The pattern will only be sketched and even the little that will be said about it must be prefaced with the warning that the description will not be fully accurate for all, nor perhaps for any one state or party.

Local Organization. The lowest general unit of organization of the party is the local committee of the city, town, or township, formally chosen by the interested supporters of the party in a party caucus or primary. The members of these committees are all active party workers, many of whom hold municipal office or jobs in the state government when their party is in power. In the larger cities, organization goes further down into the *wards* and the polling subdivisions, usually called *precincts*. The ward and precinct committees are often dominated by ward leaders and precinct captains, and the more important of these figures find their way into the city organization of the party.

In the larger cities, city organization is generally, but not inevitably, linked directly with state organization of the party. In the smaller centers of population, the local committee is subordinate to the county committee, which is formally chosen by a county convention or primary. Still higher stands the state central committee, chosen through a primary election or by a convention to which delegates from the constituencies go. One can count on finding the more important of the local committeemen on the state committee.

BOSSES OLD AND NEW. It would be hazardous to say how far this formal organization, much regulated by law, represents reality. The situation varies from state to state and often differs as between the two parties in the same state. In some of the larger cities, the party that is in the ascendant is controlled by a city boss who may hold no office in the party at all. Largely because of ever-increasing governmental social welfare services, more and more city bosses are steadily losing their power—the Skeffingtons [8] have had to give away to government as provider of relief—but they are still a factor in American politics. In the past, they had found the best soil for their growth in those cities with a large non-English speaking, foreign-born population. These masses were generally poor and always in need of the elementary necessities of life. They were ignorant of American institutions and ways of life and thus frequent violators of laws and regulations. They were utterly bewildered by the complexities of the political system in which they were asked to participate.

In these circumstances, the city bosses were those who proved to be the best friends of the harassed immigrant and his family, who reasoned that those who could spice concrete assistance in time of need with human sympathy and consideration were to be trusted to give sound advice in political as well as social matters. Unfortunately, such assistance must be financed somehow. A man who can swing numerous votes has political power and can use it to tap the public treasury through various kinds of graft and corruption. The more votes he controls, the greater his leverage on the treasury; and the greater his financial resources, the more voters who appreciate his qualities and his advice on politics. There are many sordid aspects of the power of bosses; these are well enough known without enumeration, while the mitigating, if not redeeming, facts are not so widely appreciated. In any event, the present concern is with the key to the power of the bosses.

The boss who gets together a large following in this way becomes a king-

[8] Skeffington is the Boston political boss, patterned on James Curley, in Edwin O'Connor's *The Last Hurrah* (Boston: Little, Brown, 1956).

maker, if not a king. Without necessarily holding any official party position, he can often determine the make-up of local party committees through his control of the deciding votes in party caucuses and primaries, and he is a power to be reckoned with in the state party machine.

Control by bosses was never, and is not now, limited to cities with large populations of foreign origin. Indeed, the foreign-born no longer constitute an especially numerous group; the days of large-scale immigration terminated with World War I. But every community still has its indigents who, for one reason or another, are ineligible for public assistance. Also there are many who are perplexed by the intricacies of American politics. Organization is always affected by a tendency to oligarchy, and the special features of American politics already noted feed the tendency. Another contributing factor is the extensive patronage system, the number of jobs that politicians in office can give away. United States Senators, who control the federated patronage for their states, have now and then used this and other levers to become the state bosses of their party. Thus Senator Harry F. Byrd of Virginia has dominated that state's politics completely since 1925. While state bosses have been rare, county bosses have not been uncommon.

Even where power in the party is not gathered into a single hand, the most prominent and skillful of the local party leaders generally have a large enough following to get themselves chosen for the state central committee, and that following often enables them to decide who shall be elected to the local and county committees. Thus, power does not always go with the titles to authority and, even where it does, it is often secured by manipulation rather than by the chaste methods prescribed by the democratic ideal. It must suffice to say that the realities are often very different from what the forms would indicate.

A SIGNIFICANT CHANGE. The aforegoing discussion on bosses could prove to be easily misleading, however. The days of the legendary city and/or state bosses, of Tweed, Crocker, Murphy, Penrose, Vare, Hague, Prendergast, and Crump, are gone—never to return. Some reasonable facsimilies may well, as indicated, still linger, and some of the old-style machines still persist in a few—predominantly small—cities. But even there it is at least questionable whether they will outlive their present operators. A new style of 'boss' has arisen—a Dewey or a LaGuardia, a West or a Hartsfield, who are very much their own 'bosses,' and whom the electorate can both respect and support.

Moreover, in many areas of the land the 'political club,' the 'do-it-yourself' movement for voters, the new 'amateur politician' has replaced the old boss.

To a considerable extent, the 'coffee-stained' room is supplanting the 'smoke-filled' room. The passing of the immigrant, the expansion of the middle class, the exodus to the suburbs, the rise in the general educational level, the increasing urbanization of the countryside—all these have combined to bring about a new style of politics which, in the words of a National Chairman of the Democratic party, in a sense has begun to make of an increasing number of citizens their own precinct workers.[9]

Perhaps it is still a bit unrealistic and premature to say so, but Leo Egan may yet turn out to be prophet as well as analyst with his contention that 'in modern society, the political boss of old is being replaced by the expert in public relations, by the people who can create illusions and translate the intricacies of government into simple, understandable general principles, by those who know how to manipulate symbols.'[10]

State Organization. The state central committee, or the person or persons who control it, exercises functions and imposes discipline much as the central office and the parliamentary leaders of the party do in Britain. The party platform for the state is ordinarily made by a party convention composed of delegates from the localities. The central committee influences the choice of delegates and guides them in their deliberations. Candidates are chosen by conventions or in party primaries over which the central committees have a varying influence. The central committee plans the campaign, raises the necessary funds, and supervises the work of the local committees in striving for victory.

It is also active in national, as distinct from state, politics. It must see to it that party delegates to the presidential nominating convention are chosen by convention or direct primary as the law requires. It must conduct direct primaries for choosing the party candidates for Congress. And in the presidential and congressional elections, much of the work of carrying on the campaign, although not so much of its planning, falls to the state central committees. In a good many, although certainly not in all states, party organization is thus highly centralized, generally strongly disciplined, and extremely efficient in converting a heterogeneous electorate into party majorities.

National Organization. After the complexities of the state organization of the parties, their national organization is simple. It can almost be said that there is no permanent national organization but only a succession of tempo-

---

[9] Stephen A. Mitchell, *Elm St. Politics* (New York: Oceana Publications, 1959).
[10] 'The Political Boss: Going, Going—,' *The New York Times Magazine,* January 8, 1961, p. 22.

rary committees for fighting presidential elections every four years. It is true that, for the biennial congressional elections, the party caucuses in the House of Representatives and the Senate pick campaign committees, but these committees do not run the congressional elections. Their activities mainly consist in co-operating with the state party committees.

NATIONAL COMMITTEE. Thus the chief national organization is the national committee, nominally picked by the national convention that every four years chooses a party candidate for the presidency. This national committee consists of one man and one woman from each state, territory, possession, and the District of Columbia.[11] The national convention ratifies the nominations made by the state party organizations. The national committee plans the presidential election, collects a huge campaign fund, and—to a greater or lesser degree—co-ordinates the nation-wide party effort to elect a President. Once the debris of the presidential election is cleared away, the national committee lapses into quietude and customarily rallies only once—when it issues a call for another presidential nominating convention some three years later. In recent years, however, both parties have maintained permanent headquarters and staffs in Washington. Although these staffs are greatly reduced in size after an election, they do carry on some research to aid members of the parties in Congress, beat the propaganda drums, and help in various ways with the continuing problem of party organization.

NATIONAL CHAIRMAN. The chairman of the national committee is the personal choice of the presidential candidate of the party, because he is chiefly responsible for managing the candidate's campaign. The national committee under his direction plans the larger strategy, deciding which are the doubtful states into which money, speakers, and propaganda must be poured. However, the national chairman is scarcely a commander in chief who passes orders to the field commanders, the state party leaders. These latter are remarkably independent, like the leaders of well-organized guerrilla bands, and the authority the chairman can exercise over them depends much more on his personality and his infectious energy and enthusiasm than on his position. One of the most successful of these was James A. Farley, President Franklin D. Roosevelt's shrewd, personable, and ambitious Democratic national chairman from 1932 to 1940. If the party wins the presidency the

---

[11] This is so of the Democrats, but not of the Republicans. A few years ago the latter provided for additional 'bonus members,' in the persons of the *state chairman,* for all those states that had voted for the Republican presidential nominee in the past election, or elected a Republican governor of a state, or chosen a majority of Republicans for the state's seats in the Congress.

incumbent national chairman is often appointed Postmaster General of the United States. His replacement, also selected by the President, is likely to remain active as the national party instrument for distributing patronage and implementing pre-election arrangements.

The effective authority of the national committee is limited to the presidential campaign. The committee pays little attention to the concurrent congressional elections beyond making available a portion of its campaign funds for use in them. It does not frame the national platform of the party nor share directly in the choice of the party candidate for President. These functions are performed by the presidential nominating convention, composed of delegates chosen by the state party organizations, either in primaries or conventions or both, in accordance with state law. The national organizations of the American parties do not carry on planning and research between elections on the same scale as do the central organizations of the British parties.

The Lack of Discipline. It is common to represent any elaborate organization as a pyramid rising from its base on the local organization to the apex of national authority. Such a figure for the American party system would show the chairman of the national committee at the apex and the ward and precinct committees at the base. However, if the pyramid is to represent the realities of authority, the apex must be cut off at the state level. *Below* this level, party discipline is generally sharp and effective. *But there is little discipline imposed, or imposable, on the state organizations from above.* The party that wins the presidency finds that it cannot escape some responsibility for the policy of the national government and thus must accord leadership to the President. The President, armed with this authority and the control of patronage, is a power to be reckoned with in his party, but when he has tried to use his power to purge the party of rebellious elements he has almost always failed. Even so popular and powerful a President as Franklin D. Roosevelt failed in his attempt to 'purge' certain congressional candidates, chiefly from the South, in 1938.[12]

At most, the primacy of the President is a temporary situation in the party. On his retirement or defeat, the state leaders will be again without superiors. Generally, authority flows from the state leaders upward as well as down-

---

[12] These 'purges' comprised three representatives and nine senators. All were re-elected except eight-term Representative John O'Connor of New York. The leading spokesman in Washington for Tammany Hall, O'Connor had opposed and blocked many New Deal measures in his capacity as Chairman of the House Committee on Rules. F.D.R. succeeded in having him defeated for the Democratic nomination; O'Connor then obtained the Republican nomination but lost the election.

ward. The presidential candidate and the national platform of the party are the results of bargains between them.

The national party conventions in the United States—referred to as 'America's Zoo' by some British observers—are, it is universally agreed, like nothing else on earth. They normally end with impressive demonstrations of party unity and solidarity. However, the way to that happy conclusion is marked by sharp struggles over the platform, subtle maneuvers by state delegations over the nomination, and much secret horse-trading. If these features are studied, it will be seen that the national convention also resembles an international conference in which separate nations haggle over a treaty of friendship or alliance.

CONSEQUENCE OF FEDERALISM. The fact is that the federal system, which leaves the states a large measure of autonomy, has provided even more autonomy for state party organization. The great sections of the country have varying interests that it is the business of each political party to try to reconcile. The national committee of the party is somewhat like a gathering of sovereigns, a congress of ambassadors. Thus the national party platforms and the presidential candidates of both parties are compromises dictated by this necessity. *The national party is a loose confederation of the state parties.* This is one reason why national party organization is a temporary coalition of the state parties for winning the presidency and the spoils of office that go with it. The American national party is essentially a coalition—not a hierarchy.

SEPARATION OF POWERS. Another reason is the separation of powers enforced by the Constitution. This division of authority works against the emergence of well-disciplined, permanently organized, national parties. As we have seen, the President is the national leader of his party for the time being. If he is a strong personality and an astute mediator between factions in his party, he exerts a unifying influence on it. But the separation of powers limits his effectiveness. If the executive were closely linked to the legislature as in Britain and the President had the power to dissolve the legislature, the members of his party in Congress would be much more disposed to work with him in trying to ensure discipline in their party, and the opposition party would have to meet this attempt at concentration of power with a comparable attempt. However, when they are so disposed, the parties do *at times* serve as an effective 'bridge' to the separation of powers.

WEAK DISCIPLINE IN CONGRESS. As matters stand, in sharp contrast to Britain, party discipline in the United States Congress is weak, indeed. Well-established custom has made it an inflexible requirement that candidates for election to Congress must reside in the election district they seek to represent. The candidates are almost all chosen in direct party primaries, preliminary elections within each political party to decide who shall be the party candidate. This device was adopted in most of the states between 1900 and 1910 to reduce the influence of party organization, as distinct from that of the rank and file of the party, in the choice of candidates. Whatever the influence of local and state party organizations in the primaries may be, the central organizations of the national parties have never controlled nominations to Congress and have rarely had any significant influence on the choice of candidates. Localism has always been extremely strong in this matter.

As a result, the personalities of those seeking nomination, and their personal attitudes on questions of keen local and sectional concern, rather than their firm stand on the generalities of the platform of their national party, are always highly important and generally decisive. The member of Congress, once elected, is as much a representative of a locality as he is of a national political party, and is, of course, strongly aware of his sectional interest. Lacking any effective counteracting pressure, the members of Congress are the unruly levies of sectionalism rather than the disciplined troops of national parties standing for national policies. So the members of the parties in Congress resist party discipline at the national level for most purposes except the distribution of patronage. As a well-known party independent, Democratic Senator Byrd of Virginia put the matter, 'I recognize no control over my votes by any influence [outside Virginia], including the National Democratic Convention and a caucus of my Democratic colleagues in the Senate.' [13]

It follows that the national parties in the United States do not and cannot take the heavy responsibilities for candidates and for the enforcement of party platforms that British parties accept. The central organization of the national parties in America do not maintain direct and continuous contact with the election districts. Liaison between the parties in the legislature and the districts is primarily furnished by the individual members of Congress, each of whom tries to gauge the drift of opinion in his district.

Factional Parties Within and Without the Major Parties. But something else must be set forth at this juncture, something which has been both indicated and implied by the discussion of the federal nature of the two

[13] *The New York Times,* December 6, 1960.

major American parties and the resultant weak party discipline in Congress. First of all, there is frequently more difference in political philosophy and attitude on public issues among various members of one party than between them and members of the opposite party. Civil rights legislation and fiscal policy are cases in point. Second, except on matters of organization of Congress, each party is composed in effect of several identifiable 'segments' or 'multiple sub-divisions'—at least on certain issues. Thus, one may well contend that there are at least three Democratic legislative parties, classifiable as follows in the 87th Congress: (1) those who came from Southern and Border one-party states; (2) those who represented districts dominated by Northern urban political machines; (3) those who were elected from the so-called 'swing districts' of the North and West. Similarly, again using the 87th Congress, there are at least three Republican parties: (1) those from the economically conservative suburban regions of the large industrial centers; (2) those from the traditionally 'rock-ribbed' Republican centers of strength in agricultural and small-town sectors in New England and the Midwest; (3) and those from the 'swing districts' of the North and West. These groups are not, of course, always constant in their allegiance and policy, nor do they form necessarily predictable 'blocs' on all issues. But they are broadly identifiable, and they readily serve as an exclamation mark to the obvious absence of party discipline and to the so significant over-all heterogeneity of the United States.

Third, and going beyond intra-congressional party problems, a good case can be made for the contention advanced by Professor James MacGregor Burns that, to all intents and purposes, the machinery of the American political process, as seen through the political parties, is essentially a four-party pattern. According to this conception, the Democratic and Republican parties are each divided into *congressional* and *presidential* structures, 'with all the elements that comprise the American type of party.' Burns sees these institutionally and ideologically diverse four parties as: the Roosevelt-Truman-Stevenson-Kennedy presidential Democrats; (2) the Willkie-Dewey-Eisenhower-Rockefeller presidential Republicans; (3) the John Garner-Howard Smith-Harry Byrd-John McClellan congressional Democrats; and (4) the Allen Treadway-Robert Taft-Charles Halleck congressional Republicans. Burns views the two 'presidential' parties as generally internationalist, as favoring activist government, and as being concerned with 'broad way-of-life' issues; whereas he sees the two 'congressional' parties as essentially dedicated to 'bread-and-butter' economic issues and, through their joint control of legislative machinery, devoted to blocking the presidential parties.[14] Although the analysis is perhaps somewhat oversimplified, it contains considerable merit and comes close to the facts of life of the two major American political parties.

Party Machinery in Congress. Each party has its own organization within Congress for getting within its own ranks what agreement and discipline it can. The members of each party in Congress meet in caucus, or party conference, from time to time. In recent years, the caucus has not often been used for deciding the party line on issues of proposed legislation because even though its decisions are theoretically binding, if adopted by two-thirds of the members, in practice they can be easily evaded by individual members on grounds of 'conscience' and 'promises to constituents.' Its principal importance now is in dealing with matters of the internal organization of Congress and issues of party tactics in the political maneuvering within Congress. The nominee of the majority party caucus is assured of election to the post of Speaker of the House of Representatives. The caucus of the majority party also appoints a steering and/or policy committee for each chamber, which is usually headed by the floor leader who commands the party forces on the floor of the chamber. Subject to the rules of legislative procedure, which will be discussed later, the steering or policy committee takes the responsibility for pushing through legislation, determining the priority of measures, and limiting debate. It has, however, much less control over the actual terms of the laws it pushes through than has the leadership of the majority party in Britain.

The minority party also appoints a strategy committee and a floor leader for its party in each chamber. Each party has party whips whose functions are similar to those in Britain. But they are less effective than whips in Britain in securing party regularity in voting because on many matters there are no generally agreed party lines. On many bills in Congress, discussion and voting do not follow party lines at all. On other bills, one or both parties seek a united front for or against, but it often cannot be secured or maintained.

Breaches of party discipline cannot be punished by preventing the selection of the culprit as candidate of the party at the next election because the national parties have no control over selection of candidates. As we have seen, so many excuses have been recognized as justifying a member in flouting the majority decisions of his party caucus that the caucus has virtually

[14] *The Deadlock of Democracy*, op. cit., ch. 10, especially pp. 257–64.

ceased to be a means of securing party regularity on controversial issues. Of course, the leaders of the parties in Congress have a number of means of persuasion they can employ, and according as these are effective, the strength of party discipline in Congress varies from party to party and from time to time. But even at its highest, it falls *far, far short* of that enforced in the British House of Commons.

Platform Implementation. Another reason for the lack of consistency in the policies of the national parties in the United States is the fact that the framing of the party platform and the implementing of it rests in each party with different groups of men. The party platform is determined by the delegates to the presidential nominating convention. The implementing of the platform depends on the action of the men who are elected to Congress on the party ticket. In these circumstances, consistency in the framing and executing of party policy is extremely difficult to achieve and maintain. 'I'll tell you something about the Democratic campaign platform,' once commented the beloved, long-time Speaker of the House of Representatives, Sam Rayburn of Texas: 'Congress determines the platform!' [15] What he meant to convey was that promises are fine for campaigns, but that Congress ultimately decides which planks to throw away and which to endeavor to write into law—with the President as a powerful factor in the program.

It is true that sectionalism is nurtured by the state party leaders who can often make and unmake members of Congress. The power wielded by these leaders would largely disappear if party leadership were centralized at the national level as in Britain. On these grounds, it is sometimes argued that the elimination of local and state party bosses would open the way to disciplined national parties. However, sectionalism is something more than a racket organized and maintained by party bosses at the state level. It is inherent in the variety of life in a country of continental sweep. Even if state party leadership were always secured in a fully democratic way, it would still give expression to sectional interests, although probably not as strongly as at present.

Patronage and Campaign Funds. A great deal could be said about campaign funds and patronage in the American party system, but the abuses are sufficiently notorious to need little description. The most important thing that can be said is that the abuses are by no means the universal practice. The patronage appointment of public officials, or the spoils

[15] *The Philadelphia Evening Bulletin,* January 17, 1961.

system, is more widespread than in any other democratic country. However, it is being steadily diminished by extension of the merit system, and there have always been volunteer workers who do not ask or expect reward.

FUNDS. The campaign funds of the parties are not mainly raised by contributions from the rank and file of their supporters although both major parties have redoubled their efforts toward that end. Exception must be made, however, for the practice of openly or covertly assessing the party supporters who have received government jobs through the good offices of the party. The main reliance is still on substantial contributions from business interests, legitimate or otherwise, and from men of means who often, but by no means always, expect something in return. The fact that governments in the United States have always been promoting the economic development and management of a great country in sundry ways has ensured extremely close relations between business and government. It has not been unknown for campaign managers frankly to solicit contributions from businessmen on the ground that these were policies of insurance on their businesses, and many businessmen take out insurance with both parties. Of course, labor and agriculture, as well as other interests, are being increasingly solicited for contributions with an eye toward mutual benefits.

ATTEMPTED REGULATION. State legislatures, and to some extent Congress, have tried to regulate campaign funds by law. The most frequent provisions are aimed at securing publicity concerning the source and use of party revenues, forbidding contributions by corporations, banks, and labor unions and compulsory assessment of office-holders, forbidding certain kinds of expenditures, and limiting the amounts to be spent by candidates. Most of the provisions of these largely unrealistic and visionary laws are easily and consistently evaded, and there is no adequate inspection or other machinery for enforcement. The chief value of these laws is to interest the public in the questions of where the money comes from and where it goes. But there remains a crying need for the adoption of workable, realistic, enforceable legislation on all levels of government.[16]

If the rank and file of the supporters of a political party could, of their own resources, precipitate a majority opinion on men and measures, the party bosses and wire-pullers would get short shrift. But it is only rarely that they can. Yet a candidate must be chosen and a platform adopted. This is what gives the wire-pullers their opportunity. It also reveals their function.

---

[16] See, for example, Report of the President's Commission on Campaign Costs, *Financing Presidential Campaigns* (Washington, D. C.: U. S. Government Printing Office, 1962).

They act as catalysts, always ready to precipitate, by seeming legerdemain, a majority opinion on particular issues facing the party. Under present conditions, to a greater or lesser extent this will continue until such a time, if ever, a politically educated, enlightened, and articulate electorate takes over the reins.

Some Consequences of the Present System. In a somber essay on the role of the political process in free society, Professor Stephen K. Bailey cited five chief, and very disturbing, consequences of the present amorphous and decentralized conditions of the two major parties in the United States: (1) a government by 'fits and starts,' featuring a lack of co-ordination between the executive and the legislature; (2) an inordinate amount of power in the hands of 'parochial groups' in Congress; (3) a tendency for congressional compromise to favor minority rather than majority interests; (4) as a result of the latter, an 'increasing danger of public cynicism and apathy toward the Congress'; and (5) discouragement and dissipation of sorely needed public criticism of foreign as well as domestic policy.[17] Considerably more will be said regarding the implications of these charges on governmental machinery in subsequent chapters, but there is no doubt that Bailey's indictment is both potent and realistic. Few will gainsay the pressing need for and wisdom of improvements. Yet the sobering fact remains that, notwithstanding its evils and weaknesses, the so often exasperating American party system has served the country well in its prosperous and steadfast growth toward maturity and leadership among the free nations of the world.

FRENCH MULTI-PARTY GOVERNMENT

So far only two-party systems have been discussed. But *multiple* parties have been common throughout the Western democracies on the European continent, from France to the Lowlands, to Scandinavia, to West Germany, and Italy. Most of the social, political, and economic factors rooted in history, which account for multiple parties all over Europe, are found in France, along with some that are peculiarly her own. The France of the pre-de Gaulle Republic days still provides the best illustration of the system of multi-party government in action. But it must be noted that highly significant changes have taken place in the impact of the French party system upon government since 1958, although it is unquestionably still a multi-party system.

[17] *The Condition of Our Political Parties* (New York: The Fund for the Republic, 1959), pp. 4 ff.

Cleavages. Few states could experience a cataclysm on the scale of the French Revolution without disrupting consequences on its political future. The historic battle against the Catholic Church, and the prolonged struggle for political freedom against the absolute monarchy, are examples of issues that still stir up division in France, even as they did long ago; only their accent and degree differ. The relatively small working class, the socially conservative and politically radical peasantry, the small businessman who feels forever wronged, all militate against the homogeneity necessary for constructive compromise and the two-party system. Reforms for the worker were ever countered by the peasant and the *petit-bourgeois,* who did not want government at all—and therefore refused to pay for it. The *Poujadists,* who won 11.5 per cent of the popular vote in the 1956 parliamentary elections and obtained 51 seats in the National Assembly—the lower branch of the legislature, formerly known as the Chamber of Deputies—were composed almost entirely of petty-bourgeois tax rebels. The Poujadist platform had but one truly important plank: a refusal to pay taxes! It took a de Gaulle and a new Constitution to knock political heads together—but it is a brave man, indeed, who would safely predict events *après* de Gaulle!

Little Party Discipline. The economic, social, and religious cleavages of the past have been perpetuated in one way or another. The parties themselves have been split within themselves on many issues, and the 'centrist' parties, in particular, have been unable to enforce discipline. To find such discipline in parties, the observer had to look to the extreme wings of the political scale, such as the *Poujadists* on the extreme right, and the monolithic *Communists* on the extreme left. The birth of the powerful new de Gaullist *U.N.R.* (*L'Union pour la Nouvelle République*) in 1958 added a new dimension of discipline. Together with its ally, the *Independents,* it has succeeded in establishing a coalition that had failed but once as of 1963 —when the U.N.R., lacking a majority, stood alone with de Gaulle in the presidential referendum controversy of the fall of 1962 and did not have sufficient votes to stave off the Government defeat and fall on a motion of censure. But the new parliamentary elections brought the U.N.R. more seats than any one party had ever gained in French parliamentary history: 229 of 465, within easy reach of the desired majority, which was readily obtained by virtue of a coalition with the much-shrunken Independents. But the balance of the French political parties can rarely count on solid support from their nominal followers. For example, members of the *Radical Socialist* party, with solid support in their own districts, would desert their party in the National Assembly, either to form a new wing of their own or to join another parliamentary *bloc* or *groupement* of parties.

Yet the voter, far from being disturbed over this lack of discipline, seemed actually to expect it. He looked upon his representative more or less as a personal delegate, who would, however, speak and cast his vote in Parliament in accordance with his own conscience, in an entirely independent fashion, flouting, if not entirely repudiating, orders from every political party or group. The chief reasons for this attitude are to be found in the historic cleavages, to which we referred above.

THE REVOLUTION. The revolutionary tradition itself, still something more than a memory, breeds both the liberal and the reactionary. For the hundred years following 1789, a fundamental division in French politics was that between the monarchists and the republicans. While this schism has subsided, of course, there remain a good many Frenchmen who cannot quite bring themselves to accept either the Republic or its symbols. If they do not yearn for the Bourbons, they have a nostalgia for Bonaparte and the Empire. Although de Gaulle, filled with disdain for political parties, regarded his U.N.R. as a non-partisan *mouvement,* designed to appeal to all sections of the population, it quickly evolved into a party of conservatism, with much appeal to those who advocate 'strong government' and glorify nationalism and the state. These characteristics, plus its leader's constant attacks upon pressure groups and sectional interests, have caused some observers of the post-World War II French political scene to see in the U.N.R. elements of a neo-monarchist movement. But any conclusions must await de Gaulle's departure from the scene.

RELIGION. Religion, as a political issue, antedates the French Revolution. Inevitably, the Catholic Church, with its emphasis on custom, tradition, and caution in political matters, became allied with the monarchy. The resultant alliance created a deep-rooted and often violent anti-clericalism among the supporters of the republics. When at the end of the nineteenth century the hierarchy of the Catholic Church became allied with the anti-Dreyfus forces, popular feeling eventually pushed through some extreme legislation to reduce Church influence throughout French society. Still fundamental in today's French politics, the religious issue is one of the primary differences, for example, between the clerical *M.R.P.* (the Catholic Popular Republicans) and the anti-clerical *S.F.I.O.* (the Socialists), although these two parties hold similar economic views. Indeed, there is evidence that the Socialists are more anti-clerical than pro-socialist!

FEAR OF A STRONG EXECUTIVE. The experience of absolute monarchy and two Bonapartist Empires created an almost pathological fear of a strong executive. This fear hovered over all attempts to make the executive branch of the government a more effective instrument—until the country, frightened and frustrated by the Algerian crisis, resolved to entrust de Gaulle with the necessary power. One of the reasons for the still large size of the *Communist* party in France today was its early attack upon the strong-executive creed of the de Gaullist movement. The Communists, together with the Socialists, clamored loudly for reposing absolute authority in the legislature. Although they failed to persuade the people to ratify the first proposed post-war constitution, which provided for a very weak executive and a very strong legislature, they did succeed in re-establishing the obsession against a strong head of government, which was embodied in the Constitution of the Fourth Republic.

ECONOMICS. The popularization of socialism in France took place around the turn of the present century, and created additional differences between capitalists who support a free economy—with a minimum of taxes—and socialists who in varying degree believe in a managed economy—also with a minimum of taxes. In contemporary France this issue remains current, although it is obscured by the fact that many Frenchmen support leftist parties for reasons other than a desire for economic revision—such as tradition and anti-clericalism. A similar anomaly is seen, for instance, in the French political party that bears the fierce label *Radical Socialist,* but which actually represents those citizens who seek an economy relatively free of government control. Therefore it is not socialist at all in the sense of the word as it is used today, and it is radical only in the sense in which the British Liberal party and the American Republican party of the nineteenth century were radical.

Parties in the Legislature. The multiplicity of French parties is easily illustrated by referring to the results of the last parliamentary elections of the late Fourth Republic, which took place in January 1956. The National Assembly then elected contained members from nineteen different political parties! Only the *Communist* party and its allies attained as much as one-quarter of the popular vote, 25.6 per cent, to be exact, which netted them 145 of the 627 seats in the National Assembly. The *Socialist* party was next with 15 per cent of the total vote and 88 seats. Only two other parties received 10 per cent or more of the popular vote, the *Poujadists,* with 11.4, and the *M.R.P.,* with exactly 10.

The balance of the seats were distributed among fifteen other parties, several of which usually—but not always—combined for purposes of passing legislation or helping to form governments. Thus, the *Rally of the Republican Left,* the *Radical Socialists* and their allies, gathered 13.6 per cent of the popular vote and 71 seats, and the combined *Independent Republican, Peasant,* and *dissident de Gaullist* splinter parties won 14.1 per cent of the vote and 94 seats in the Assembly.

To complicate matters some twenty-five deputies had no discernible party association, except when they chose to affiliate themselves *ad hoc* with various parties; and twenty deputies held views so distinctive that even temporary affiliation was almost impossible.

DIFFICULTY OF FORMING GOVERNMENTS. With almost two dozen parties dividing the available seats in the National Assembly, and with only the extremist parties on either wing of the multiple political spectrum providing any semblance of party discipline, it is hardly surprising that it proved to be extremely difficult to form a government and even more difficult to maintain one in office. Fourth (and Third) Republic French governments were usually based on coalitions of center parties and groups. The area of the Chamber of the National Assembly occupied by the center parties was popularly known as the 'swamp.' The term described well the spectacle of deputies floating from the fringe of one party to an adjoining—or even a non-adjoining—group, unhampered by party allegiance or party loyalty in constant disagreement on the need for and aim of legislation. This is no foundation for an enduring government. It is thus not astonishing that between the liberation in 1945 and the death of the Fourth Republic in 1958 France had twenty-five different cabinets averaging a life-span of less than six months in office. This contrasted with an average of almost four years for the British cabinets.

WEAK EXECUTIVE. The problem of forming and maintaining a government was enhanced by the French obsession, however justified, against a strong executive branch. With Louis XIV, Napoleon Bonaparte, and Louis Napoleon in mind, the framers of the Fourth French Republic's Constitution placed severe strictures upon the authority of the chief executive, with the result that the French President enjoyed hardly more power than the British Queen.

STRONG LEGISLATURE. Not even trusting in these safeguards against a 'strong man,' the uneasy French constitutional framers of 1946 thus made their Prime Minister and cabinet subservient to the National Assembly.

The legislative branch alone possessed supreme authority, was a law unto itself, exposed to few, if any, of the limitations imposed either upon the Congress of the United States or the British House of Commons. A provision in the Constitution of the Fourth French Republic permitted the President to dissolve the Assembly—under severely limited circumstances. These circumstances arose only once in the history of the Fourth Republic, so the National Assembly was not effectively confined. Furthermore, the extreme parties of the left and the right made it more or less of a habit to vote *against* the coalition ministry in power. They could afford to do so, for they realized that they would not very likely be called upon to form a new government. Ministries thus came and went, but the Assembly customarily lived out its allotted five-year term. Only two governments of the twelve-year life of the Fourth Republic, those headed by MM. Queuille and Mollet, lasted more than twelve months, the former almost thirteen, the latter sixteen.

Coalition Government. The essential function of compromise in democratic government occurs under the two-party system at political conventions and conferences as well as in the legislative chamber. However, in the Third and Fourth Republics in France compromise existed solely in the legislature. The matched distribution of strength among the more important of the multiple French parties necessitated coalition governments, in which no group actually renounced, or even substantially modified, its objectives. It follows, then, that compromise, not having taken place in the selection of candidates or in the construction of a party platform, had to be accomplished in the National Assembly. The accommodations, made by several parties or party groupings in the formation of a ministry, became strained by issues unforeseen when the ministry was formed, and by the personal animosities of the leaders within the coalition. An illustration of the latter was the much-publicized personality clash between three leaders of the Radical Socialists, MM. Faure, Mayer, and Mendès-France, which raged at the very time when that party was an important component of the coalition governments of 1952–55. With the forcing of a cabinet crisis, by dropping some ministers, and adding others, a temporary adjustment was made. The adjustment lasted only as long as coalition leaders and individual members were disposed to suffer it.

The Role of Parties in the Third and Fourth Republics of France. The French parties then, too, performed a semblance of the functions required of political organizations in democratic government, but the results were strikingly unlike those of the two-party system. The French voter was faced with a choice of candidates and policies so broad as to be sometimes meaningless—not necesarily to him, but to the political process. It must be granted that the parties did act as restraints upon each other. The moderate, centrist parties formed the ministries and furnished the Premiers, while the extremist parties waited in a state of continual hopefulness, to unite with dissidents from the moderate groups and overthrow the reigning coalition, often referred to as the Third Force. This, briefly, was the history of the multi-party system in France until de Gaulle's Fifth Republic was established.

Under the Fifth Republic. As has been amply indicated, France, even under its new Fifth Republic, still has a multi-party system. But it is a blunted system, indeed—some have even suggested that an obituary is in order, President de Gaulle having smashed it in the name of unity and efficacy! [18] This would appear to be an oversimplification, and an obituary may well be somewhat premature. Any prospective orator ought at least to await the events of a few post-de Gaulle years. The old cleavages are not done away with so readily; they may have been merely submerged or suppressed in the face of de Gaulle's personal rule.

On the other hand, de Gaulle, who never entered upon the slightest effort to disguise his disdain for *les partis politiques,* made quite clear what they could expect from him. When Parliament had toppled the Pompidou Government as a result of de Gaulle's presidential referendum move, he unloosened a withering attack upon the parties late in 1962. Four times in that speech he characterized them as 'the parties of former times.' The voters, he said, clearly disavowed the parties when they voted, in the face of nearly universal party—and, he might have added, legal—opposition, for his proposal for popular election of future presidents of France. His tone indicated clearly that he had no intention of using conciliatory tactics with the parties if the impending legislative elections would produce an anti-Gaullist or non-Gaullist National Assembly—making quite clear that he was not only prepared, but eager, for a head-on clash with the party regime. The President did, however, acknowledge both that political parties contained individuals of merit in their ranks and that they had the capacity for 'espousing and serving still divers currents of opinion, private interests, local wishes.' [19]

[18] See, for example, Philip M. Williams and Martin Harrison, *De Gaulle's Republic* (New York: Longmans, Green & Co., 1960).
[19] *The New York Times,* November 8, 1962.

The Elections of 1962 and the Future. As we know, the elections, far from bringing an anti- or non-Gaullist National Assembly, gave de Gaulle a smashing victory. The 229 orthodox Gaullists elected under the U.N.R. label fell just four votes short of an absolute majority of the 465 seats! At no time in modern French history had any single political party obtained more than 25 per cent of the total vote—the U.N.R. received 32 per cent. Never before had any single party come so close to commanding an absolute majority. Thus, for the first time in the history of French Republican institutions a single parliamentary party—the combined U.N.R. and individual deputies committed to it—would now hold such a majority—in fact one totaling 261. To the opposition parties this was a severe jolt, indeed. Nonetheless, they were certainly not extinguished. The Socialists garnered 71 seats; the Radicals and allied center groups 38; the moderate Catholic Popular Republicans (*M.R.P.*) 27; the Communists 41 (although still 22 per cent of the popular vote); and the non-Gaullist Independents 30.

The results appeared to give promise of the following developments: *First,* the formation of a true majority party on the wreckage of the unstable coalitions of old that had governed France for almost a century—a denouement that held at least some promise of a presidential system of government. *Second,* if the above-mentioned vanquished centrist, moderate, and non-Communist left among the surviving parties were to have any meaningful hope for the retention of a political future, they would now have to give some serious thoughts to a united political party grouping in order to contest the forthcoming presidential elections in December 1965. Some have already suggested the formation of a 'unified, non-doctrinaire *labor* party' to combat both the U.N.R. and the Communists.

In any event, barring totally unexpected developments, President de Gaulle and his cabinet, headed by Premier Georges Pompidou, would now be able to look forward to the luxury of at least three years of presumably uninterrupted power during which the new governmental system of the Fifth Republic could be consolidated.

MULTIPLE PARTIES IN OTHER WESTERN DEMOCRACIES

Space does not permit a discussion of the operation of the multi-party system in other countries. It suffices to note here that it was at its worst in the Third and Fourth Republics of France. It has shown relatively more stability in Belgium and Holland, and even more in West Germany, but there, too, and particularly in the two Lowlands, governments have been compelled to function as coalitions more often than not. Especially since the death of its post-war leader, Alcide de Gasperi, in 1954, Italy has been severely troubled by its multiple parties, approaching the chaos of pre-de Gaulle France, for the Italians have never succeeded in developing two *major* democratic parties as, for example, have England and—perhaps—West Germany. Multi-party democracy rarely works unless one party is in itself strong enough to govern.

Scandinavia. On the other hand, it has provided stable government in the three Scandinavian countries of Denmark, Norway, and Sweden. There, however, the numerically strongest party—almost always the Social Democrats since the end of World War II—has customarily, as a matter of tradition and accommodation, encountered little, if any, difficulty, in obtaining agreement with one or two of the smaller parties to form a government together, thus emerging as a two-party coalition in a multi-party system. In politically stable Denmark, for example, the Social Democrats (*socialdemokrater*) have polled between 32.8 per cent and 42.1 per cent of the votes in every election since 1945, constituting in each instance a clear plurality but not a majority. Thus coalition government was in order which, after the parliamentary election of 1957, for example, resulted in a three-party coalition, consisting of the Social Democrats (39.4 per cent of the vote and 70 seats in Parliament), the Radicals (7.8 per cent and 14), and the Single Taxers (5.3 per cent and 9). In 1960, the Social Democrats obtained 42.1 per cent of the popular vote and 77 seats and, with the aid of two 'non-political' members of Parliament from Greenland, plus again the Radicals (5.8 per cent and 11) readily succeeded in controlling a majority of the votes in the *folketing*, thereby achieving their basic purpose in parliamentary government—the construction of majorities.[20]

Conclusion on Democratic Political Parties

In conclusion, the scope of the foregoing treatment of political parties should be restated. Attention has been concentrated almost entirely on the functions of political parties in a democracy, and on the organization that parties have worked out for fulfilling these functions. It has been urged that the only practicable method so far discovered for eliciting the will of

[20] For a good discussion of Danish politics, see Poul Meyer, *Politik* (Copenhagen: Nyt Nordisk Forlag Arnold Busck, 1959), chs. 3–17.

the people as a whole is to have political parties compete for the support of the electorate. This is the essential function of political parties. They cannot perform the function without extensive and intricate organization.

It is difficult to energize a football team by pointing out the broad social functions of sport and recreation. The team needs a more immediate concrete objective, the winning of the next game. Party organization also needs an immediate objective, the winning of the next election. Many of those who are active in party organization regard it as primarily, if not solely, an instrument for gaining power. The immediate objective necessarily looms large in party calculations, a fact that can best be appreciated by looking at the scale and character of party organization.

Much of the criticism of political parties, and of democratic government, arises from the belief that both parties and government are the playthings of small cliques of rival politicians. In any assessment of democratic government and politics, it is necessary to attend to criticisms of this kind. A complete investigation of such charges would take us far afield, but the first step is to describe party organization with a view to seeing who exercises power in it, who makes the effective decisions, and under what limitations and controls. These questions are not easy to answer, but at least it has been seen that whatever power small groups may exercise in political parties from time to time, their power is always contingent, can be undermined, and therefore must be used with both eyes on the electorate.

As already pointed out, concentration on the functions and organization of political parties in the United States, France, and Britain leaves aside much that is necessary to an understanding of the political parties in the three countries. From the point of view of the politics of a particular country, the policies for which the parties stand are of primary significance. But these policies cannot be understood without reviewing political history and the vicissitudes of party fortunes, explaining the social and economic structure, and outlining the current politics of the country in question. While some reference to these matters was absolutely essential to an understanding of the multi-party system in France, a similar treatment could not be undertaken for Britain and the United States.

The Two Indispensable Services of Parties. This discussion can be summed up by saying that at least until human nature is greatly changed and education and knowledge are greatly improved and extended, the party system will perform two indispensable functions for a democracy. *First,* it enables the sovereign electorate to participate in the operation of government.

Second, it makes constitutionalism and ultimate control of government by the electorate possible by enabling the people to change their masters when they see fit to do so.

THE ONE-PARTY SYSTEM IN THE DICTATORSHIPS

The essential function of political parties in the liberal democracies is the creation of majorities through competition for support of the electorate. The parties offer a choice between platforms, or at least between sets of politicians, one or a grouping of which is to be entrusted with the task of governing until the next election. As we have seen, democratic government rests on a foundation of party politics. Party politics has to be justified on the ground that the public interest, over the long run, can best be determined by competition between parties rather than by the dictates of one set of permanently established rulers whose decisions cannot be questioned in any way.

The modern dictatorships deny that the public interest can best be determined by the competition of parties for the votes of the electorate. Fascist and Nazi theory denied that the mass of individuals composing the electorate had any adequate conception of the public interest. To them, the bulk of the people were ignorant, short-sighted, and engrossed in private concerns; they lacked the vision, energy, and courage needed for participation in government. The Fascists and Nazis accordingly scorned the notion of allowing electoral majorities or coalitions to determine the public interest. Communist theory reached the same conclusion by a different line of reasoning which will be examined later. As already pointed out, this conclusion is inevitable for men who are convinced that they know exactly what government should do, and how to do it. In their view, what is wanted of the masses is not decision but discipline.

Repudiation of Competition. So all three dictatorships repudiated the system of competitive political parties. In its place they put the *one-party system,* making it impossible for opposition to the government to combine in an opposing political party and compete for the favor of the electorate. The Fascist party became the sole party in Italy, the Nazi party in Germany, and the Communist party in the Soviet Union. Attempts to organize opposing political parties became serious criminal offenses.

Discipline, not Decision. The essential function of this one party is not to elicit decisions from the mass electorate on the big issues of politics, but to ensure discipline and obedience among the people. In its organization and its methods, it is more like an army than a political party. In fact, the Fascist party originally called itself 'a militia in the service of the nation.' To perform its function, it needs a large membership drawn from every city, town, and hamlet in the country. The Italian Fascist party, with the lowest membership of the three, had, at the peak, around two million members. Yet membership was not open to all by any means. It was restricted to those who, it was thought, could be counted on to give loyal and unquestioning devotion to the leaders and their ideas. On the other hand, the Nazi party under Hitler was very large. So confident were the Nazis of their ability to cow and control the Germans that few 'Aryans' were able to remain outside the party or one of its many affiliates. There was, however, a relatively small party-elite, composed of the most trusted and most fanatical Nazis—the dreaded, black-shirted S.S.

Essential Functions. The essential function of the one party is carried out in various ways. First, the party controls all elections to ensure that only reliable people come into positions of prominence. Second, it carries the message and doctrines of the leaders to every person and group that can be reached. It interprets the policy and actions of the government so that everyone sees them in the most favourable light. Third, it maintains an espionage and censorship service for the government on every street corner, if not in every house, reporting the rebellious, silencing the disgruntled, and reproaching the unenthusiastic. Fourth, it busies itself at very point in helping to enforce the endless regulations of the government.

Nazi and Fascist Organization. Both the Fascist and the Nazi parties used the Communist party—to be outlined presently—as a model in their organization, eliminating its elective features and substituting more pronounced elements of military discipline. Both of them have been wiped out, and it is enough to say of them here that, in each instance, the local, district, and regional leaders of the party were not elected from below but appointed from above and that the national organizations, dominated by the Duce and the Fuehrer and their associates, commanded the party somewhat in the way army headquarters commands an army. The Fascist and Nazi rulers militarized the life of Italy and Germany, turning men into obedient soldiers rather than consulting them as responsible citizens. It may be suggested that this is the inevitable outcome of a denial of the value of individual personality.

A Note on Other One-Party Systems. Before proceeding to the discussion of the Communist party, it should be noted, however, that the phenomenon of the one-party system is neither confined to the three dictatorships here at issue nor necessarily even to dictatorships. Regarding its presence in other dictatorships or pre- or non-democratic states of various hue and stripe, if we merely confined ourselves to the Africa of 1962, all of the following states, which became independent since World War II, had either a single or a thoroughly dominant political party at the end of that year, which provided a modicum of cohesion for the states involved: Algeria, Ghana, Guinea, the Ivory Coast, Liberia, Senegal, Tanganyika, Togo, and Tunisia.[21]

Moreover, as is obvious to every student of the political party system of the democratic United States of America, a one-party system has existed, or exists now, in various parts of that free country. Although there are increasingly healthy signs of perceptible, however slow, movements away from traditional one-party control, such control is as apparent as it has been traditional for Democrats in the rural Deep South and for Republicans in portions of rural and small-town upper New England and segments of the rural Midwest, to give but a few pertinent illustrations. However, of course no equation of these one-party systems with those present dictatorships is intended—for the differences are crucial, indeed.[22]

THE COMMUNIST PARTY IN THE SOVIET UNION

The Communist party is, in effect, the only party allowed in the Soviet Union. It has a monopoly on all political activity. Article 126 of the Constitution of the U.S.S.R. states that

> the most active and politically conscious citizens in the ranks of the working class, working peasants, and working intelligentsia, voluntarily unite in the Communist Party of the Soviet Union, which is the vanguard of the working people in their struggle to build communist society, and is the leading core of all organizations of the working people, both public and state.

The Communist party therefore differs very markedly from the political parties of the United States, Britain, and France. It is the aim of the

[21] See Gwendolyn M. Carter (Ed.), *African One-Party States* (Ithaca: Cornell University Press, 1962).
[22] For an illuminating discussion of one- and two-party control in the several states, see V. O. Key, *Politics, Parties, and Pressure Groups*, 4th ed. (New York: Thomas Y. Crowell Co., 1958), ch. 11.

Western democratic parties to build up as large a membership as possible, for political power in a liberal democratic state depends on the numerical strength of a party's following, and a large membership tends to bring a large following at the polls. The Communist party in the Soviet Union, on the other hand, has limited its membership to a relatively small number of citizens, roughly nine million in 1962, who have been compelled to undergo a lengthy period of apprenticeship, and have passed through various stages of party discipline. The Young Communist League (*Komsomol*), which provides a source for future members, had about twenty million. (In 1905, a dozen years before it seized power, the party had but 8500 members; still only 23,000 in 1917.)

The Communist party dominates virtually all organizations in the Soviet Union. Its power is not derived from its numerical strength but from the key position that its members hold in the legislative and executive organs of the state, in the trade unions, and in all other authorized associations, and from the zeal with which they work as the chosen instruments of destiny. According to its present rules, the Communist party is defined as 'a voluntary militant union of Communists, holding the same views, formed of the people of the working class, the working peasantry and the working intelligentsia.'

Party Organization. The party is highly organized throughout the Soviet Union. Party cells everywhere keep a watchful eye on all agencies of the state, on all economic enterprises and all public institutions. At the lowest level of the party organization are the 'primary party organs'—also known as 'cells'—which exist in workshops, factories, offices, farms, and army units, or parts thereof. These cells are formed wherever there are three or more party members. Aside from carrying out the general work of the party, the party rules state that these organs, which meet monthly, 'have the right to exercise control over the activities of the management of their particular enterprise.'

The *primary organization* elects an executive committee, and a secretary who is, in effect, the head of the local party organization. They also appoint delegates to the higher party organ, which is the *city or district conference.* That conference meets only once a year, and elects a city or district committee, which holds monthly meetings and in turn elects an executive bureau and a secretariat. The party pyramid corresponds throughout to the *territorial units* into which the Soviet Union is divided. Above the city or district conferences and other intermediate territorial units are *republican congresses*,[23] corresponding roughly to state party organizations in the United States. The republican congresses of the party are composed of delegates from the party organizations at the lower levels. These congresses meet every eighteen months to elect small executive committees and also to choose delegates to the *All-Union Communist Party Congress*, which is, in form at least, the highest policy-making body in the party.

Until 1925, the All-Union Communist Party Congress met annually, but it is now convened at longer intervals, normally every three or four years. Usually several thousand delegates and alternates participate in the Congress —4400 at the Twenty-Second in October 1961—making effective discussion impossible. The most important task of the All-Union Party Congress is to elect the *Central Committee* of the party. This is a body of about 175 members and 155 alternates (non-voting) who form the executive committee of the Congress and who meet three or four times a year. Even so, this executive committee obviously does not meet often enough to be a serious factor in the shaping of party policy. It is largely a forum for prominent functionaries, although under Khrushchev it was drawn into some important policy debates, e.g. the clash involving the so-called 'anti-party' group in 1957 [24] and policy toward Yugoslavia two years earlier.

The Locus of Power. It is the Central Committee, however, which elects the three most important party bureaus, or committees that, in fact, run party affairs. In accordance with the new party rules of 1952 and 1953, as amended in 1956, 1959, and 1961, the Central Committee establishes the *Presidium of the Central Committee* for political work; the *Secretariat of the Central Committee,* headed by the Party Secretary, for current work of an organizational-executive nature; and the *Party Control Committee,* for the carrying out, and ensuring obedience to, party decisions. These three bureaus form the summit of the party pyramid, and their members are its all-powerful leaders. By virtue of the party's strategic position in the Soviet Union, they are also the leaders of the Soviet state, the trade unions, the army, and

[23] A republican congress is the highest party organ in the particular republics, or states, of which the Soviet federal union is composed. There are, of course, intermediate levels of party organization between the city and district conferences and the republican congress, which need not be outlined in a bare sketch of party organization, but which may be seen on the chart, *infra.*

[24] It was here that Khrushchev scored his dramatic victory over Malenkov, Molotov, and Kaganovich, despite an initial 7:4 adverse vote in the Presidium. Aided by Marshal Zhukov, who used his planes to rush important members of the Central Committee to Moscow, Khrushchev successfully appealed to the Central Committee which reversed the Presidium vote. Later, Khrushchev nonetheless banished Zhukov!

all other important organizations. Of these three party bodies, the Presidium and the Secretariat are the more influential.

THE PARTY'S SECRETARY-GENERAL (FIRST SECRETARY). During Stalin's regime, the Secretary-General of the Central Committee—now known as the First Secretary—who is, in effect, the Secretary-General of the Communist party, was the most powerful individual in the party, and consequently in the state. It is revealing that Stalin (and Khrushchev) achieved his position of undisputed leadership in the Soviet Union by occupying the position of Secretary-General of the Communist party, and not by winning the office of Prime Minister. Stalin did not assume the latter position until 1941, long after he had established his position as the Soviet dictator.

The Communist leader's power in the government, then, is derived from his position in the party; but it does not automatically follow that, as happened to be true of Stalin, the First Secretary of the Communist Party is also its most powerful individual. Whereas Mussolini and Hitler were demagogues and rose to power from the streets and the rostrum, Stalin and Khrushchev rose to power through the party. The Soviet concept of leadership is one of collective leadership. The leading party organs discussed here are committees making collective decisions. Despite the way Stalin was built up in the public imagination as the living symbol of the party and the spiritual heir of the Communist prophets, Marx and Lenin, we do not know whether his work was always law in these committees. He had immense influence, and perhaps overwhelming influence in most matters, but serious students of Soviet politics doubt whether the other members of the Secretariat and Presidium—which was known as the *Politbureau* during his day—were merely yes-men. Some observers thought that they shared Stalin's power as well as his confidence.[25] On the other hand, Khrushchev's revelations at the Twentieth Party Congress in 1956, and subsequent Congresses, make Stalin look a formidable tyrant, indeed.

All that can be said with assurance is that decisive power is concentrated in the above-mentioned committees of the Communist party. Although it is true that none of the Communist leaders since Stalin's death has been able to wield as much personal power as he did, and that they have been part of a ruling oligarchy—a *Kollektivnost,* as the Russians call it—Khrushchev had certainly emerged as the top man in that oligarchy by 1958. He became both the dominant single individual in the Soviet Union and the leading

[25] See, for example, Julian Towster, *Political Power in the U.S.S.R., 1917–1947* (New York: Oxford University Press, 1948), p. 392.

theoretician of the Marxist world. The passing of Stalin, a powerful personality, changed the power structure. But since his death there has been no change in the disciplinary requirements of the Communist party.

STRUCTURE OF THE COMMUNIST PARTY, U.S.S.R. (1963)

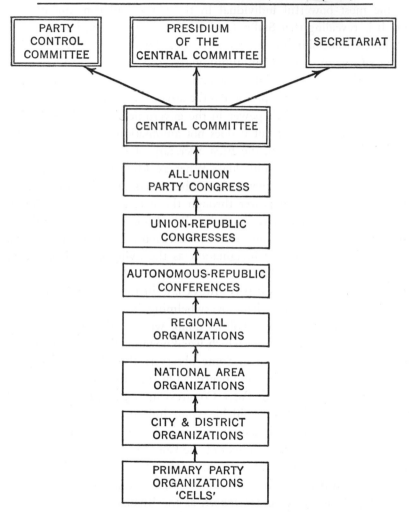

Inner Control. The Presidium, the party's senior brain-trust and policy maker, holds several meetings weekly. The Secretariat, the party's nerve center to determine upon directives to the many subordinate units throughout the organization, meets daily. It is divided into an unknown number of 'sections,' e.g. culture, foreign affairs, education, 'agitation and propaganda.'[26] In 1963, the Presidium consisted of twelve full and six alternate or candidate members; the Secretariat had nine members, four of whom[27] were also in the Presidium. Here at last we come to the bodies that are small enough and meet often enough for full discussion, rapid decision, and vigorous action.

These few men who form the Secretariat and the Presidium control the party and the government. Whatever there is of free discussion of political principles and public policy in the Soviet Union goes on among them; for their decisions are accepted without question and without debate, not only by the Central Committee, the All-Union Party Congress, and the lower organs of the Communist party, but also by the various organs of the government—the Council of Ministers, the Supreme Soviet, its Presidium, and the whole pyramid of soviets.

Monopolistic and Monolithic Nature of the Party. The tremendous power of the handful of top Communist leaders is derived from two facts. First, the Communist party is *monopolistic.* It does not have to moderate its policy and its actions because of a fear that a rival party will win the majority of the electorate in the next election. Second, it is *monolithic* in its internal structure; it is made of one piece, and any serious division of opinion, any splintering or fragmentation within the party, is immediately suppressed. We have already noted the purges in the Soviet Union by which splinters are ejected from the body of the Communist party. The leaders of the party are all-powerful because their party is the 'one and only' party in the state. There is no alternative party that the electorate can put in power. At the same time it is the 'one and united' party because it suppresses ruthlessly all internal dissension within it.

The system of 'democratic centralism,' already mentioned in the discussion of local government, applies as much to the party as it does to the soviets. In a limited way, the lower organs of the party take part in the process of party deliberation and in the process of government. They can send information upward to the higher levels of the party pyramid, and they receive orders and directives from the top, which they must try to implement. The lower levels of the party pyramid provide a vast network of supervision of

[26] See the excellent article by Max Frankel, 'The Communist Party's "Elite" and How They Run the Soviet,' *The New York Times Magazine,* May 29, 1960.
[27] Khrushchev, Koslov, Kuusinen, and Suslov.

the activities of the state agencies, whether they be government offices or industrial enterprises.

Limitations on Party Discussion. The most important decisions, setting the major objectives and goals of government action, and thus molding every aspect of Soviet life, are made in the highest party councils, the Secretariat and the Presidium of the Central Committee. *They are absolutely binding on all members of the party.* The key postion of the members of the party in the Soviet state enables them to explain these decisions to the soviets, the trade unions and other associations, and to spur these bodies on to achieve the objectives set by the decisions. Open opposition to party decisions thus reached is unthinkable in the Soviet Union. Discussion is allowed only on the means of reaching major objectives and never on the rightness of the objectives themselves. Moreover, discussion is allowed only until the party leadership comes to a decision on the means to be used in reaching the settled objectives. As soon as a party decision is made on any matter, all further criticism is branded as 'factionalism' or 'deviationalism,' the two cardinal sins in the Communist creed.

The reasons for this blind acceptance of the dictates of a small group of party leaders must be sought in Communist theory. It will be recalled that Marx believed in a sort of economic predestination. He held that his method of dialectical materialism would reveal, through the analysis of economic forces, the cause and effect relationship of all phenomena, and the course and direction which future events would take. His method, which is sometimes referred to as 'scientific socialism,' was taken over by the Communist party in the Soviet Union, where it is being used, with modifications introduced by Lenin and Stalin, in the process of reaching the major decisions on public policy. It is thought that this science, properly applied by those who understand it, shows clearly what a Communist government should do, and how to do it.

The leaders of the party, as the most competent and able members of the vanguard of the proletariat, are best suited to subject the problems of the day to Marxist analysis. Once they have reached their 'scientific' conclusions, discussion is superfluous, for their findings are accurate, like the verified solution of a mathematical problem. To go on discussing a question after the incontestably right answer to it has been found is a waste of time and consequently is unproductive labor. Unproductive labor is anti-social and, therefore, inimical to the best interests of the proletariat and of the Soviet Union. With this attitude on the futility of discussion of public policy once an issue has been decided by the leaders, it is not surprising that party government in the Soviet Union is something totally different from party government in a liberal democratic state. In Britain and the United States public policy is formulated by the interplay of various interests through the medium of two principal political parties, in other Western lands usually through coalitions of parties. In the Soviet Union it is defined at the top of the party hierarchy, and the main purpose of the widespread party organization is to make sure that the orders of the leaders are carried out by every citizen.[28]

SUGGESTED REFERENCES FOR FURTHER READING

Abraham, H. J., *Compulsory Voting* (Public Affairs Press, 1955).
Agar, H., *The Price of Union* (Houghton Mifflin, 1950).
Bailey, S. K., *Political Parties and the Party System in Britain* (Praeger, 1952).
Barron, R., *Parties and Politics in Modern France* (Public Affairs Press, 1959).
Bullit, S., *To Be a Politican* (Doubleday, 1962).
Burns, J. MacG., *The Deadlock of Democracy: Four-Party Politics in America* (Prentice-Hall, 1963).
Campbell, A., P. E. Converse, W. E. Miller, and D. E. Stokes, *The American Voter* (Wiley, 1960).
Carter, G. M., *African One-Party States* (Cornell, 1962).
David, P. J., R. T. Goldman, and R. C. Bain, *The Politics of National Party Conventions* (Brookings, 1960).
Duverger, M., *Political Parties: Their Organization and Activity in the Modern States,* 2nd ed. (Wiley, 1959).
Flynn, E. J., *You're the Boss* (Viking, 1947).
Gwyn, W. B., *Democracy and the Cost of Politics in Britain* (Oxford, 1962).
Heard, A., *The Costs of Democracy* (U. of North Carolina, 1960).
Herring, P., *The Politics of Democracy: American Parties in Action* (Rinehart, 1947).
Hesseltine, W. B., *The Rise and Fall of Third Parties* (Public Affairs Press, 1948).
Holcombe, A. N., *Our More Perfect Union* (Harvard, 1950).
Key, V. O., *American State Politics* (Knopf, 1956).
———, *Southern Politics* (Knopf, 1949).
Lasswell, H. D., *Politics: Who Gets What, When, How* (McGraw-Hill, 1936).
Leites, N., *On the Game of Politics in France* (Stanford, 1959).
Lubell, S., *The Future of American Politics,* 2nd ed. rev. (Anchor, 1956).
McKenzie, R. T., *British Political Parties* (St. Martin's, 1955).
Merriam, C. E., and H. F. Gosnell, *Non-Voting* (U. of Chicago, 1924).
Meyer, F. S., *The Moulding of Communists: The Training of the Communist Cadre* (Harcourt, Brace, 1962).

[28] See pp. 435–8, *infra,* for a discussion of nominations, elections, and representation in the Soviet Union.

Michels, R., *Political Parties* (Jarrold, 1915).

Milbraith, L., *The Washington Lobbyists* (Rand McNally, 1963).

Mitchell, S. A., *Elm St. Politics* (Oceana, 1959).

Neumann, S. (Ed.), *Modern Political Parties* (U. of Chicago, 1956).

O'Connor, E., *The Last Hurrah* (Little, Brown, 1956).

Panter-Brick, K., *The Single Party* (Oxford, 1963).

Ranney, A., *The Doctrine of Responsible Party Government* (U. of Illinois, 1954).

Rossiter, Clinton, *Parties and Politics in America* (Cornell, 1960).

Schapiro, L., *The Communist Party of the Soviet Union* (Random House, 1960).

Schattschneider, E. E., *Party Government* (Rinehart, 1942).

Taylor, O. R., *The Fourth Republic of France: Constitution and Political Parties* (Royal Institute, 1951).

Tingsten, H., *Political Behavior* (P. S. King, 1937).

Turner, J., *Party and Constituency: Pressures on Congress* (Johns Hopkins, 1951).

Wallas, G., *Human Nature in Politics,* rev. ed., introd. by A. L. Rowse (U. of Nebraska, 1962).

White, T. H., *The Making of the President* (Atheneum, 1961).

Williams, P., *Politics in Post-War France,* 2nd ed. (Longmans, Green, 1958).

X

Interest Groups and Public Opinion

A number of considerations touched on in earlier chapters must now be drawn together. In particular, it is necessary to recall what we said in Chapter II about some of the consequences of accepting the liberal democratic ideals of government. Man, as Aristotle said, is a social animal. Men need fellowship with one another almost as much as they need their individuality. In the great modern nations they cannot find this fellowship in the state because it is too remote and impersonal. At any rate, they cannot find it in the liberal democratic state, because it is mainly limited to the purposes that all share in common. They must seek it in *voluntary associations* which cater to the diverse interests of free personality. Those who share a particular skill, experience, or outlook on life will always respond to one another if they are given the chance. Thus *interest groups* are born.

A Definition. Modern democracy has provided very wide freedom of association, and the ease of transport and communication makes it possible for persons with common or similar interests, experience, and outlook to organize on a national and even international scale; thus, for example, we have the American Cancer Society and the National Education Association, and the International Political Science Association and the Rotary International. The result has been a spontaneous group life without parallel in history. Great hotels in the center of networks of transportation are rarely free from the raucous fraternity of conventions. These interest groups are of a great variety and are not limited, as discussion sometimes seems to suggest, to those that share a common interest based on the intense economic specialization of the modern world—witness the heterogeneous war veterans' groups, for example. There are many types of interest groups, but, as used in this text, *'interest group' means any organized group that, on the basis of one or more shared attitudes, makes certain claims upon other groups in society*.[1]

Organized Group Activity. Although economic interest groups are of special, and perhaps even fateful, significance when government reaches out to regulate many aspects of economic life, they are not necessarily the most active and powerful among organized groups—the type of groups with which we deal here. Activity depends more on intensity of conviction, and this is often strongest in crusading fraternities with no economic axe to grind, such as the Anti-Saloon League. The power of any group, in democratic politics at any rate, depends on the degree of vigor and single-mindedness it exhibits, and on numbers. Other things being equal, the bodies with the largest membership are likely to be the most effective because they can muster the most votes. Thus war veterans' organizations, in so far as they can agree on what they want—usually bigger and better bonuses and pensions and hospital care—are extremely powerful, although not organized around a common economic interest or function. On the other hand, such numerically small, but wealthy, well-organized, and homogeneous interest groups as the American Medical Association and the American Petroleum Institute, for instance, have been extremely effective.

Of the economic interest groups, one might hazard that agricultural associations, trade unions, and business associations will exert the strongest push and pull on public policy in the future. An organization of consumers that naturally includes everyone would overtop all other economic interest groups. But for reasons already suggested, the consumer interest is extremely difficult to harness into an effective organization. The most successful form of consumers' organization has been the consumers' co-operatives. The importance of this movement, in giving concrete expression to common interests shared, but not adequately realized, by producer groups of diverse and often conflicting special interests, is frequently overlooked.

[1] In essence, this is the definition coined by Professor David B. Truman in his expert work on the subject, *The Governmental Process* (New York: Alfred A. Knopf, 1951), pp. 33–7.

INFLUENCE AND PRESSURE

LOBBYING: PRO AND CON

Moreover, the widening range of governmental action affects most of the organized interests in ways that they think favorable or adverse. Every time the government intervenes in economic or social matters, it sets going a chain of consequences which affects the welfare of a number of groups. Organized interests think that their aims and purposes can be advanced or retarded by legislation. Because they actively press their claims upon institutions of government, they are often known as *political* interest groups. Thus, at every session of the legislature, legislation is proposed which some groups want to support and others want to defeat or modify.

It must also be remembered that most laws do not become settled issues merely because a majority in the legislature approves them. Most modern legislation requires continuous administration to accomplish its purposes. Unlike the law of gravity, it is not self-enforcing. To fit the law to the almost infinite variety of situations, the government is given substantial discretionary power by the legislature. The complexity of the conditions that government undertakes to regulate are such as to make it impossible for the government to know fully what it is about, unless it can draw on the knowledge and experience of the interests affected. Day-to-day administration is of even more vital concern to the interest groups than the enactment of the legislation itself.

Lobbying. These are the circumstances underlying the demand for representation of interests in some way that will connect the affected interests directly with the process of government, and not limit their communication to what can be expressed in voting for a candidate in a territorial constituency once in two or three or four years. Unable to take a hand directly in the making of laws and their administration, they have consequently resorted to influence and pressure, familiarly known as *lobbying*. The term itself has a long history, with the word appearing first in the English language about the middle of the sixteenth century. It was derived from the Latin *lobium,* a monastic walk or cloister. Lobbying is the most notorious, but not the only, method by which group interests of various kinds communicate with the government. These methods will be discussed here and in a later chapter dealing with the administrative process. First, however, some cognizance must be taken of the widespread view that lobbying and kindred practices are inevitably sinister.

CON. Lobbying of the executive and the legislative branches of the government by interest groups arouses much indignation and alarm, some of which is clearly justified because lobbying interests have sometimes stooped to bribery and corruption. Also, the clandestine character of much lobbying and the means employed by some interests arouse natural suspicion. Backstairs influence always smells of intrigue and is objectionable in method if not in content. The average citizen, who has no one to lobby for him, is angered by the ease with which organized interests maintain close and intimate connection with government, and he comes to the common-sense conclusion that the practice would not be continued unless it paid dividends. Undoubtedly, organized interests get results from their contact with government, often at the expense of unorganized interests. For example, the price controls established by the United States government during the war were quickly liquidated at the end of the war because of heavy pressure from manufacturing and other business interests, although there is strong ground for thinking that a majority of the American people favored continuance of price control for a further period. Another illustration in the United States has been the continued success of oil and gas interests in obtaining and maintaining favorable action by governmental bodies in the face of almost constant consumer protests—causing one student of the field to conclude that the petroleum industry constitutes a private government which seeks to utilize public government to promote its goals of greater economic power and larger profits.[2] However this may be, the largely unorganized consumer interests always pay for the services that government provides for producer groups.

PRO. These and other points form the case against lobbying. But the real question is whether the practice should be suppressed or encouraged to become more respectable. As long as it is thought to be wholly evil, consultation between government and the interests will rely greatly on backstairs methods. If consultation is recognized as legitimate and even necessary, and required to be carried on openly, it will very likely become as respectable as general community opinion demands. Moreover, the answer to the pressure of selfish interests may be counter-pressure of other interests with diverse aims. One of the pillars of the democratic way of life is freedom of association, and the answer to organization of special interests is counter-organiza-

[2] Robert Engler, *The Politics of Oil* (New York: The Macmillan Co., 1961).

tion. The only thing preventing any significant social interest, economic or otherwise, from enjoying consultation with the government is lack of energy and initiative to organize for that purpose. Everyone who has leverage on a bloc of votes can get himself heard by democratic governments.

Lobbying and the Popular Will. Objections to lobbying, however, go beyond these immediate considerations. The truth is that the practice is a denial of certain widely held beliefs about democracy. These beliefs are that the people, free of oppression by arbitrary governments and privileged classes, all want the same things of government. They want government to act for the good of all and not for any narrow, selfish purpose. That is to say, the sovereign people are essentially devoted to the public good, and the will of the people, if not corrupted or deflected, unerringly concentrates in a general will, a unified will for the good of all. Somehow—it was never very clear how—the people in electing representatives to the legislature informed them of the content of the general will and infused them with a sense of its imperative. It was believed that a legislature so chosen and insulated from all outside influence, except the mandate of the voters at the polls, would produce in its legislation the highest possible expression of the common good. Therefore, it was wrong for any individual or group to rush to the capital and try to explain the bearing of things to the government. Either they had the presumption to think they had some private revelation of the common good, or they were trying to nourish a special interest at the expense of the public interest. Such beliefs are not always clearly articulated, but unqualified objections by democrats to consultation between government and the interests of which society is composed must rest on the assumption that the will of the people makes it sufficiently clear what should be done for the common good.

Earlier discussion has indicated that this picture of a people wholly absorbed in the public good as distinct from the private good, and of a general will, an agreed conception of the common good arising from that absorption, is untrue to the facts. If it were true, there would be no more room for political parties than for lobbying. People are not absorbed in public questions, and it is difficult to see how the mass of citizens in a modern democracy could ever give more than a minor fraction of their time to them. The citizens of the Greek city-state had leisure based on slavery, for this absorption. Moreover, if the diverse interests of free personality cannot find their principal expression in the sprawling modern territorial state, the citizen must largely be absorbed in concerns that lie outside the specific sphere of government.

WHAT IS THE PUBLIC INTEREST? The true public interest does not spring, fully formed, from the hearts of the people. It may be that a supreme being standing above the struggles of life, or that men who are able to eliminate all passion from their deliberations, could perceive *the* public interest purged of all contamination from narrow special interests. But men who can achieve such detachment are rare, and divine revelations of the common good vouchsafed to men appear to be various, and are far from bringing them to a consensus. It is true that most of the members of the community, or nation, will whatever is necessary to preserve the community and to realize the shared ideals, but that will often lacks specific content. While it enables us to agree to resist a foreign aggressor, it does not tell us how to do it or at whose expense. No more does it tell us what laws to make on a given day in peacetime.

FINDING A FORMULA. Therefore, as a practical matter of deciding what government is to do in the common or public interest, the choice is between meek submission to some dictated formula, and a formulation, always partial and incomplete, that emerges from the competition, clash, and compromise of a great variety of individual and group interests. A democracy must choose the latter because it has its origin and main justification in this diversity. The question that then faces us is: How can a government insulated from all contact with the varied interests of men, except what the members of the legislature bring to it, relate the common good to the particular 'goods' that men pursue? Does the common good consist of a partly informed guess of the government at the general will of the people, or in arbitration between interests in the light of all the data that can be discovered from whatever source? If the latter is even partly correct, government must make contact with all interests that are strong enough to make their voices heard.

DIVERSE GROUP INTERESTS AND DEMOCRACY

This analysis is far from doing justice to all the factors involved. It needs to be modified by recalling what was said in Chapter II about the unifying influence of liberal democratic ideals. There is a large measure of agreement about the higher goals of political action. Much of the competitive striving between groups is concerned with exploring means of giving fuller expression to the claims of personality. Also, this analysis leaves aside what we said in the preceding chapter about the important role of political leadership in finding the compromises that reconcile unity and diversity amid the clash of interests, and thus attract the support of majorities. It perhaps suggests by its emphasis that *all* organized interests are narrowly selfish interests, which of course is not true.

Many organized groups find their binding common interest in being their weaker brothers' keepers. Britain, France, and the United States have active associations for penal reform, birth control, child welfare, seaman's welfare, world peace, and prevention of cruelty to animals. Thus, Britain has its Council for Preservation of Rural England, its League for Endowment of Motherhood, and so on. Comparable examples in the United States are the Women's Christian Temperance Union, the American Eugenics Society, and the Society To Maintain Public Decency. France has its equivalent of the Women's Christian Temperance Union and the Society for the Prevention of Cruelty to Animals.

A Check on Extremism. The analysis certainly suggests that interest groups are more single-minded than they really are. Few people find full expression of themselves in one interest, and thus most of those who share a particular interest are reluctant to push it to the limit because that would jeopardize other interests they cherish. The organized farmers—except those mainly or solely engaged in dairying and stock-raising—are interested in a high price for grain. If this were their only interest, they would push for unlimited manufacture and sale of liquor so as to assure a greater demand for their grain. In fact, however, most of them feel they have a stake in a temperate, or even an abstemious society, and this moderates the agricultural lobby. A study of the membership of any interest group would show that almost every member has other—indeed, clashing and competing—interests that moderate his support of this particular interest. Sometimes they even *contradict* it, such as the American Legionnaire clamoring for a federal bonus, who, at the same time, is a member of the Pruning Knife League and clamoring for reduced taxes. The multiplying of interests not only enriches life but also provides an automatic check on extremism. A peaceful society becomes possible—although not guaranteed—through a delicate equilibrium of interests without demanding the agreement of everybody on everything.

It should be clear from these considerations that we have only scratched the surface of the question of the place of interest groups in a democracy. It might be argued, at least for the sake of argument, that what has been called democracy in the last hundred years could never have flourished if there had been on every issue the manifest general will which many yearn for. A society in agreement in detail as to what was right would have muzzled the cranks, throttled discussion, and trampled on minorities, exhibiting all the earmarks of a totalitarian regime and impoverishing life for the sake of a few hard and fast conceptions of what was good.

A Balance of Power. Government by discussion and peaceful adjustment of differences finds its significance in the fact of numerous diverse interests. Each interest is convinced of its own worth and therefore determined to survive and thrive. Being unable—and also unwilling—to ensure its position through a domination of all other interests, it is compelled to seek accommodations with some of these interests and, as James Madison foresaw in *The Federalist,* No. 10, through a series of shifting combinations try to prevent any one interest from dominating all the others. As has already been pointed out, most members of the diverse interest groups want to preserve the community. They thus recognize the necessity of eventual accommodation between diverse groups.

This digression is a luxury of which we can afford only a taste. It does tend to confirm the suggestion that the existence and lively activity of interest groups are closely connected with democracy. At any rate, democratic government has always been involved in maintaining an equilibrium between groups. This has never been an easy task, and it requires the continuous services of a number of highly skilled politicians searching for accommodations that will attract majority support. Thus democracy is not something that can be won today and guaranteed for posterity. It is always on trial. The trial becomes increasingly severe as government activities expand and affect more and more deeply the welfare of an ever larger number of interest groups.

The previous chapter has indicated, and so will others to follow, that the job of appeasing interests by giving them privileges that are immediately, if not ultimately, at the expense of others, has a divisive rather than a unifying tendency, and it becomes harder to mobilize majorities that will accept all these activities as contributions to the common good or the public interest. One of the big problems with interest groups is that what they *really* want is influence in a few important places of public policy—they seek power without responsibility. Yet whether government activity declines or continues to expand, democratic governments must mediate between interests. The mediating will be most successful if done in the light of all the available information, including that tendered by the interests themselves.

FACTORS AFFECTING LOBBYING

In the United States. Much more is generally known about the activities of interest groups, or—as they are often and appropriately called—*pressure groups,* in the United States than elsewhere. There are many reasons for the great quantity of data available on the United States. It is a country where extensive advantage has been taken of freedom of association. No other government has to take account of so wide a range of diversity of interests, most of them organized. In no other country do pressure groups so openly approach the government. Lawmaking is a free-for-all. Indeed, the legislative process in America today is primarily an arena for combat among private organizations. The majority party does not monopolize the defining of public policy, and the executive does not monopolize the drafting of an authoritative legislative program. Laws are made by Congress and its numerous committees, which are always open to suggestion and afford hearings to interested parties. Accordingly, an organized interest can hope to influence legislation by lobbying individual congressmen and by putting its case before the appropriate congressional committees. 'Lobbying,' as long-time Congressman Celler (D.-N.Y.) once wrote, 'is the sum of all communicated influences—both direct and indirect—on legislators concerning legislation. It is indispensable to effective lawmaking which, in a democracy, is always the product of compromise.' [3] But, of course, a pressure group also can, and does, approach members of the executive branch, members of the so-called independent regulatory commissions and agencies—of late a particularly fruitful point of contact.

In Britain. In Britain, where the cabinet formulates policy and party discipline ensures its adoption in substantially the form proposed, interest groups cannot hope to get far by lobbying individual members of Parliament or by urging their case on parliamentary committees. These avenues of influence are not entirely neglected, but the most important representations must be made directly or indirectly to the cabinet. Little is publicly known of what goes on when the cabinet receives delegations or written representations, and still less can be said certainly of their influence on the cabinet's final decision. Equally little is known of what takes place in secret party caucus where the

[3] Emanuel Celler, 'Pressure Groups in Congress,' *The Annals of the American Academy of Political and Social Science,* 319 (September 1958), 1.

cabinet has to clear serious modifications and adjustments of policy with its supporters. Thus interest groups work more unobtrusively and with less publicity than in the United States. Where the party and the cabinet insist on making policy and have to take full responsibility for it, there is less candor in acknowledging the pressure and influence of interest groups. Also, sporadic congressional investigations of lobbying in the United States have brought a good deal of information to light and encouraged further private investigation and research.

So we know that pressure groups are at work in Britain and that they do influence legislation, but the influence is hard to measure. In the United States it is often possible to describe provisions of a particular law in terms of a compromise between numerous groups that lobbied openly on both sides. In Britain, on the surface at any rate, the law represents the agreed policy of majority party and cabinet.

In France. The position of interest groups in France is again different. Given the multi-party system under the Third and Fourth Republics, there was a natural tendency for political parties and interest groups to coalesce organizationally. Many of the numerous French political parties resembled interest groups; for while they were able to bring a certain amount of influence to bear upon governmental action, they never possessed the kind of effective power of decision which lodges in the majority party, or indirectly even in the opposition party, in a two-party system—regardless of whether the latter be of the disciplined or the undisciplined variety. On the other hand, the French multi-party organization provided direct representation in the legislature to the various interests through the elective process. Very often, the leaders of the French interest groups were themselves elected to public office as leaders of the political parties and thus directly represented a particular interest for which these parties might stand—or, indeed, of which they were often frankly composed, e.g. the aforementioned *Poujadist* party, whose sole aim was to perpetuate non-payment of taxes, or at least to make the tax-collector's life miserable.

However, it would be quite erroneous to assume that all attempts to bring pressure in France were exerted upon the parties directly. Throughout the country, influential business, labor, artisan, and agrarian interest groups operated, chiefly on the local level, and attempted to influence not only the representatives of the party to which they belonged but any member of the National Assembly and the executive who might be within reach. The nineteen specialized committees of the former provided ideal bridgeheads for interest group activities. Moreover, there existed the—still surviving—National Economic Council, which was supposed to advise the National Assembly on 'economic' matters—except on the all-important budget! Bereft of actual power, and regarded with suspicion by both interest groups and legislators, it consisted of representatives of segments of the French economy, e.g. workers, farmers, industrial groups, co-operatives, civil servants, and so forth.

UNDER THE FIFTH REPUBLIC. The revolution wrought by the assumption of power by de Gaulle under the 1958 Constitution did not, of course, pass over the French interest groups. The shift of the center of gravity of governmental power from the legislature to the executive, led by a President who regarded all pressure groups as egotistical as well as unrepresentative, drastically diminished their importance in the governmental process. Committed to what he viewed as a fight against 'all intermediate forces which cut the people of the nation off from the public authorities,' de Gaulle thus determined to ignore them, more or less. Gone are the days when the group interests could readily force ministers to come to them to gain approval of legislative plans. Now the ministers are in the driver's seat, backed by a powerful chief executive and supported by a government with majority party support in Parliament. Gone, too, are the convenient National Assembly Committee beachheads—now that they are transformed into six generalized committees against the backdrop of a legislature seriously curtailed in its powers. The National Economic Council, now a 229-member body, composed of some twenty-five or thirty 'economic and social interest groups,' still exists in revised form—as will be pointed out more fully in Chapters XI and XVII—and de Gaulle has, in fact, promised to raise it to a prominent position, but at this writing (Autumn 1963) it is still little more than an advisory body.

The French pressure groups still have important links and connections with the legislature, but they are weakened ones, indeed. Hence they have sought their salvation in combined action, always a tenuous tool in the interest group game. On two occasions in 1961, and one in 1963, however, sensing widespread popular support, they resorted to a seldom-employed but dramatically effective tool: the general strike—that of the teachers, farmers, and coal miners. In these instances, the government ultimately acquiesced to the demands, realizing the popularity of the issues and the power of the groups concerned. Short of such drastic measures there is no question that the immediate influence of individual interest groups suffered a keen blow with the onset of the de Gaulle regime.

INTEREST GROUPS IN ACTION

IN THE UNITED STATES

It is impossible to say precisely how many organized group interests are in active contact with the national government at Washington. Not all register with the government, as they are supposed to do. Certainly the number runs into thousands. Hundreds of different groups maintain offices in Washington. However, many of these organizations are not really effective, neither recognized by congressmen as being genuinely representative of the interests concerned, nor possessed of sufficient voting strength and propaganda power to compel anxious consideration. While all the groups with offices in Washington maintain a representative to look after their interests, only the larger and stronger groups are equipped with all the modern means of research and propaganda. They also employ professional *lobbyists,* or legislative agents as they prefer to be called, and pay them highly for their services. In 1963 alone, some four hundred national organizations maintained a thousand such lobbyists in the capital, well versed in the intricacies of legislative procedure, at home in the labyrinths of administration, and reeking with plausibility. They are generally journalists, ex-civil servants, lawyers, ex-members of Congress—the latter being deemed especially desirable because they have access to the floor of Congress.

The Range of Organized Interests. The groups that exert pressure in Washington are organized to promote a bewildering variety of purposes. It would be difficult to classify them in a limited number of categories. Without attempting to do so, it may be said that the more powerful groups are trade associations (representing industrial and commercial interests), organized labor, agrarian interests, professional associations, the bureaucracy, foreign policy associations, national women's organizations, various reform leagues, and a number of veterans, patriotic, ethnic, and religious organizations.

BUSINESS AND AGRICULTURE. Perhaps the most broadly inclusive and effective of the commercial and industrial organizations are the United States Chamber of Commerce and the National Association of Manufacturers, which in 1906 formed the National Industrial Council to supply expert lobbying against labor legislation, and later participated in setting up the Department of Commerce and other agencies in the federal government. Agricultural interests have found powerful and effective expression in many groups, notably the influential American Farm Bureau Federation, which has held the 'farm bloc' together in Congress; the National Grange; and the National Farmers' Union, the smallest, but the most militant in recent years in its fight for large-scale legislative action in aid of agriculture.

LABOR. The three principal groups representing organized labor are: the recently created 15 million-member A.F.L.-C.I.O., a merger of the American Federation of Labor (which played an active and influential role in the formulation and enactment of legislation concerning employers' liability and workmen's compensation) and the Congress of Industrial Organizations; the four Railroad Brotherhoods which, among other things, secured the passage of the Adamson Act of 1916 providing for an eight-hour day for railway workers; and third, the United Mine Workers, long under the colorful leadership of John L. Lewis.

PROFESSIONAL. The professional organizations are generally not as powerful as the above-mentioned economic interests, because they often lack the financial resources of the business groups and the numbers of the labor and agricultural associations. But they do possess an asset of prime importance in public affairs, namely, technical knowledge, and the prestige related thereto. This knowledge enables them to exert considerable influence upon legislators and administrators and the public. For example, the very active American Medical Association, with a membership of some 200,000, was especially influential in securing the adoption of the pure food and drug laws. It has exerted pressure *for* the reorganization of the health activities of the national government and *against* social insurance laws, particularly those providing for health insurance. In 1949 alone, with a per capita assessment of twenty-five dollars, it collected two million dollars from its members to fight—with success—President Truman's proposal for compulsory national health insurance. Another professional organization, the huge National Education Association, has long pushed plans for a separate federal Department of Education, and has favored such reforms as a law prohibiting profits on the manufacture and sale of munitions, a law providing for unemployment insurance, a federal child-labor law, and laws for the protection of freedom of speech for teachers in the classroom. The 100,000-member American Bar Association plays an important role in judicial staffing and legislation—indeed, its lawyers are active and evident throughout the government.

WOMEN. The women's organizations, particularly the General Federation of Women's Clubs and the League of Women Voters, have brought a large and influential opinion to bear in favor of measures for the censorship of books, magazines, and movies, and have campaigned for better homes, conservation, civil service reform, equality for women, prohibition enforcement, education, social legislation, Americanization, and international co-operation for peace. In many of these agitations, they have co-operated with other reformist groups found in the United States. Of these, perhaps the most outstanding in the whole history of pressure groups was the Anti-Saloon League of the organized churches, which was largely responsible for the enactment of temperance legislation from 1893 on, and often drafted such legislation.

ETHNIC. The associations for promoting the interests of different ethnic groups in the United States are not usually as well organized as the economic and professional groups, but they do exert considerable political pressure from time to time. There are approximately one hundred and eighty of these ethnic organizations. On domestic issues, they press for simplification of electoral procedures and for increased immigration from the countries of their origin. In the field of foreign policy, they strive for good relations between the United States and their countries of origin. After World War I, the pressure of American Poles, Czechs, and Yugoslavs on President Wilson's administration influenced the creation of new states in Central Europe. The German-American *Bund* and a number of Irish organizations tried to prevent the entry of the United States into World War II.

RACIAL. The interests of the Negroes are championed primarily by the National Association for the Advancement of Colored People, the Urban League, and the Congress of Racial Equality (CORE). With increasing success, they have opposed racial discrimination in all walks of life, and have pressed for integration generally, for fair treatment of Negroes in the courts and at the polls, for their appointment to more public offices.

RELIGIOUS. Some of the principal religious organizations of national scope are the National Council of Churches in Christ (U.S.A.), which speaks for several, but not all, influential Protestant groups; the National Catholic Welfare Conference and the Legion of Decency, examples of the unified and well-disciplined Roman Catholic groups; and several Jewish interest groups which, like the Protestant groups, are considerably less united and disciplined —even on the question of Israel—than are their Catholic counterparts. The various religious groups are actively interested, often on different sides, in public policy relating to education, marriage and divorce laws, birth control, literary and motion picture censorship, prohibition, diplomatic representation at the Vatican, and so on.

OTHERS. The above represent only a sample of the manifold interest groups that are active. Every segment of American society has its group or groups—

and we cannot leave this discussion without at least mentioning the influential veterans' organizations, such as the American Legion and the Veterans of Foreign Wars. They are constantly in the public eye, either in behalf of legislation beneficial to the millions of veterans and their dependents or in the role of watchdogs of Americanism.

Looking at the extraordinary range of interests represented by organizations in Washington and noting their frank, persistent, and widespread legislative activity, observers have often described them as a third House of Congress, operating outside the Constitution, but not lacking effectiveness on that account. They do not limit their activities to national government and politics but work in a similar way in state and local government and politics. It is important to remember that pressure groups do not neglect any government that has power to affect their interests.

Techniques of Pressure. These interest groups conduct their campaigns on several fronts. They try to influence congressional nominations and elections. They maintain direct contact with, and apply pressure on, members of Congress and also on members of the executive—sometimes even the judiciary. They pour out propaganda in the hope of influencing public opinion. But it must be remembered that American pressure groups operate *outside* the political party structure as such, although some of their leaders may be individually active as party officials. A vital distinction between a political party and a pressure group is that the former is primarily interested in obtaining office, whereas the latter's chief concern is to influence the personnel *in* office—regardless of party labels.

INFLUENCING ELECTIONS. Pressure groups often act on the theory that simpler and more effective control over legislation is to be had by securing the nomination and election of friendly legislators than by attempting to influence them after they are elected. It does not matter whether candidates or prospective candidates are Democrats or Republicans; they are supported or opposed according to their stand on the questions in which the particular lobby is interested. Those who aspire to Congress are questioned on their views and, if willing to give pre-election promises, are given support in the campaign in various ways, including money contributions to the candidates' campaign funds. Both the 'wets' and the 'drys' in the struggle over prohibition supported candidates financially. Big business, which is often long on money and short in numerical voting strength, commonly contributes to the campaign funds of particular candidates and sometimes even to *opposing* candidates in order to 'promote' good will.

It should be noted that this traffic is encouraged by the lack of clear, precise party programs and the weakness of party discipline. If the parties had clear, firm policies, the promise of a candidate to support the special claims of a pressure group would not be worth buying. If the central party organization had, as in Britain, a virtual veto on the candidacy of particular aspirants, the tools of special interests would have great difficulty in getting a nomination. The weakness of the national parties is the opportunity of diverse interests of every kind.

If an interest group has a large, relatively unified, membership, its delivery of effective support in an election campaign is simpler. If it is well organized and able to persuade its members how to vote, it can bring heavy pressure to bear in any constituency where it has significant voting strength. The A.F.L.-C.I.O., like its unhyphenated predecessors, because of the size and compactness of its membership has been very successful, especially since the 1930's, in ensuring the election of particular candidates friendly to labor and in defeating hostile candidates. Labor's Committee on Political Education (C.O.P.E.), which grew out of the old C.I.O.'s Political Action Committee, endeavors to mobilize the labor vote behind candidates who adhere to labor's objectives. The American Farm Bureau Federation has also had signal success in influencing elections. The Bureau keeps a close check on the legislative record of congressmen from agricultural constituencies and brings that record to the attention of voters at the next election.

Alone or in combination with other groups, interests in America can ensure the election of a number of favorably disposed congressmen who will form a bloc in Congress, supporting what the interests want with little regard for party lines or party platforms. If these legislators do not live up to their promises, they are marked for defeat at the next election. However, this is not enough. Countless pressures from all directions play on all congressmen, and it is necessary to supply sympathizers with data and to counteract other pressures. The lobbies maintain offices in Washington because they want to be close to Congress to express their views directly on all measures that interest them, and to maintain contact with such members of Congress as they hope to impress.

LOBBYING CONGRESS. The oldest form of direct pressure on legislators is the social lobby, which still persists, although its results are generally thought to be meager. Members of Congress are often wined and dined by legislative agents just for the sake of getting acquainted. New members particularly are singled out, and the lobbies—among which members of administrative agencies and foreign interests must also be mentioned—do much to make them feel at home in Washington. But members of Congress cannot be bought for the price of a meal or a cocktail or two, and there is no attempt to do so. The purpose is to establish friendly relations as a prelude to feeding the legislator with information and persuasive arguments.

It has already been pointed out that legislators today are inadequately informed on most of the subjects with which they have to deal. Devices for supplying them with accurate data are lacking, or inadequate, and busy lawmakers cannot do more than a fraction of their own research. But lobbyists on both sides of almost every question are well supplied with information and eager to impart it. They are the chief source of information pro and con on many issues, although by no means all, that come before Congress. The members of Congress whose minds are already made up can draw supporting data and arguments from the source. Those who are in doubt and conscious of their ignorance can be fairly sure that they will get much of the relevant data and arguments by listening to all sides of the story from the interest groups concerned. Naturally, the information is biased, but some of the truth always emerges from the clash of opposites.

The real work of legislation, as will be seen, is done in congressional standing committees and their sub-committees, and therefore lobbyists take special pains to 'educate' members of the committees whose field of work affects them. The committees hold hearings at which they invite evidence from all the interests concerned in a particular bill. These hearings often have a good deal of resemblance to the proceedings of a court, with lobbyists appearing as counsel and witnesses on both sides and members of the committee acting as judge and jury. Of course, the committees are expected to gather information from all possible sources, and officials from the government departments make an appearance to put governmental data and points of view at the disposal of the committee. The evidence of officials may not be wholly impartial either, but it will correct many of the exaggerations and partial truths of the pressure groups.

The well-organized groups go to great pains to convince congressmen that their constituents are solidly behind the group demands. They persuade their own members and prominent citizens who are sympathetic to their point of view to shower congressmen with letters, telegrams, memorials, and resolutions urging the legislators to vote for or against particular measures. Even though the opinions expressed in the 'form letters' often used are clearly inspired by interest groups, most congressmen cannot afford to ignore them *completely,* because the senders may have espoused the opinion expressed in them. Such organizations as the Chamber of Commerce, the Farm Bureau Federation, and the A.F.L.-C.I.O., with their huge memberships, can pour an avalanche of letters and resolutions on legislative bodies.

Professional associations can also make an impressive showing. When the highly unified, wealthy, and ably marshaled American Medical Association—supported by some 200,000 doctors, organized locally into about 2000 county units—asks its members to write, and to persuade their friends and patients to write, to their representatives in Washington—who also have doctors—a heavy mail can be anticipated. In 1949–50, the A.M.A. engaged the well-known public relations firm of Whitaker & Baxter at a fee of $100,000 for its successful campaign against the Truman compulsory health insurance bill. Other similar victories came in subsequent years. The U.S. Savings and Loan League, rated one of the country's most resourceful and influential lobbies, was largely responsible for inspiring a massive letter-writing campaign in 1962 against the Kennedy Administration's measure for the withholding of taxes on interest and dividends. The victorious campaign generated hundreds of thousands of letters to senators after the House had passed the bill—in part insinuating that the advocated withholding constituted a new tax, which was simply untrue. The Senate subsequently deleted the provision and the House failed to fight for it in the joint conference committee that ultimately met to iron out differences in the parent measure dealing with other tax provisions.

LOBBYING OFFICIALS. Pressure groups not only inspire and support the legislation they favor but often draft it and present it to congressional committees. They also maintain direct contact with the administration which, through its discretionary powers, can do much to help or harm the interests of the various groups. How to work your way through the bureaucratic maze at Washington to the official who can and will deal with your problem, instead of referring you to someone else, is a distinct branch of learning, and all the important pressure groups employ experts who have made this province of knowledge their own. They negotiate with officials, investigate administrative practices, especially those of the independent regulatory commissions—an often ideal contact for interest groups[4]—and inform officials

---

[4] The Ethical Practices Sub-Committee of the Senate Committee on Labor and Public Welfare of the 82d Congress, 1st Session (1951), charged that '. . . [these commissions] tend to become the servants rather than the governors of the industries which they regulate . . .' (at p. 60).

of the point of view of their groups on such practices. This is an extremely important part of the work of pressure groups, and it will be considered in more detail when the administrative process is discussed in Chapter XVII.

Even the presumably neutral judiciary is not free from being lobbied, although such efforts are of more subtle nature. Judges are variously praised, condemned, and their opinions 'analyzed' by interested groups. The latter often ask for permission to file a brief *amicus curiae* ('friend of the court'), to present their point of view on behalf of their favored litigant. Also, interests frequently take a hand in confirmation battles of 'controversial' judicial nominees. Thus various conservative business and nationalist groups heatedly opposed, though ultimately unsuccessfully, President Wilson's nomination of Louis Brandeis as an Associate Justice of the United States Supreme Court and attempted to block his confirmation by the Senate. Negro and labor groups did succeed in preventing the confirmation of John J. Parker of North Carolina, who had been nominated to the bench by President Hoover.[5]

MOULDING PUBLIC OPINION. Finally, pressure groups try to mould public opinion. The surest guarantee of success is to convince a large section of the electorate of the justice of their group's claims. Almost every channel of communication is used to proclaim the gospel of the group to the public. Speeches are prepared for sympathetic members of Congress. Books and pamphlets pour out in a steady stream. High-powered advertising and public relations firms are increasingly hired. Special articles and news releases are supplied to the press. Radio and television are used, and motion pictures are not neglected. Speakers are supplied to churches, schools, luncheon clubs, and public forums. When the public utility industry was trying to discredit public ownership of public utilities, it not only used all these common methods of trying to influence public opinion, but also tried to mould the educational system to its purposes. It made extensive efforts to eliminate public school textbooks that spoke favorably of public ownership, and supplied the schools with hundreds of thousands of specially prepared booklets. It endowed public utility research bureaus in universities, which were expected to find facts supporting its views. The grand scope of its activities is indicated by the fact that in one year it sponsored more than 10,000 addresses, which were heard by an estimated 1,500,000 people.

Many other illustrations of these grandiose activities could readily be cited.

---

[5] On these matters generally, see Henry J. Abraham, *The Judicial Process: An Introductory Analysis of the Courts of the United States, Britain, and France* (New York: Oxford University Press, 1962).

For example, the National Association of Manufacturers spends more than two million dollars annually for advertising and publishes four periodicals. The American Petroleum Institute has in recent years spent fifty million dollars per year for general public relations! In connection with its above-mentioned battle against compulsory national health insurance, the American Medical Association, within one year, distributed some 65,000,000 pieces of campaign literature, presenting its views of the proposed legislation. Further, its public relations firm arranged for the printing and distribution of roughly 75,000 appealing picture posters of *The Doctor,* with the caption 'Keep Politics Out of This Picture.' These are just some illustrations of the type of techniques used widely by many interest groups today.

Most pressure groups, of course, work on a much smaller educational program, and few of them think it worth while to try to work through schools and universities, because they want quick results on current issues. But they are all anxious within the limits of their resources to influence public opinion.[6]

Regulation of Lobbying. It has been argued at length here that as long as government is expected to carry on its present wide range of functions affecting the welfare of interest groups, close contact between the interests and government is legitimate and even necessary. That does not mean that all the methods used by pressure groups should be approved or even tolerated. Bribery and corruption have long been offenses against the criminal law. The problem of dealing with such methods is one of detection and punishment. Sinister influences in elections are already outlawed in most states but, as has already been noted, these laws are not effectively enforced. Often they are very difficult to enforce.

In regard to non-criminal methods of persuasion and propaganda brought to bear on Congress, public officials, and public opinion by interest groups, believers in democracy—which is, at bottom, government by persuasion—will find it difficult to distinguish between forms of persuasion that are legitimate and those that are not. The important issue at stake arises out of other distinctions, the distinction between interests that are effectively organized for pressure and those that are not, and perhaps the distinction between those interests with lavish funds and those without. This last is doubtful because

---

[6] As reported, according to law, the ten biggest-spending lobbies in the nation's capital in 1961 were, in order: American Medical Association; American Farm Bureau; American Legion; U.S. Savings and Loan League; National Committee for Insurance Taxation; National Farmers Union; National Housing Conference; American Trucking Associations, Inc.; International Brotherhood of Teamsters. (*The New York Times Magazine,* August 19, 1962.)

small financial resources can often be compensated for by organization and numerical voting strength. The problem is how to protect the unorganized interests, and specifically in the economic field, how to organize the *general consumer interest* to counterbalance the whole range of producer interests. Aside from the difficulty of defining what is evil in the genuinely persuasive practices of pressure groups, the really forbidding difficulty is that of enforcing any law that might be made.

REGULATION OF LOBBYING ACT OF 1946. These considerations help to explain why, despite many years of agitation for the regulation of lobbying by law, and the frequent introduction of bills and resolutions in Congress for that purpose, no law on the subject was enacted by Congress until 1946. As part of the 1946 legislation for the reorganization of Congress, provision was made for the quarterly registration of lobbyists with Congress; the disclosure of the source of their employment; the amount of their compensation; the nature and amount of their expenditure; and the specific aim of their lobbying. The terms of the law are restricted to 'professional lobbyists' who try 'directly' to influence Congress or its committees, or whose 'principal purpose' is to do so. Therefore the law does not cover persons who limit their pressure to the executive or judicial branch of the federal government, or any organized association whose officers do its lobbying 'incidentally' to carrying on the general purposes of the association. The vagueness and difficulties of interpretation are obvious—and there is no enforcement agency! While almost 7000 persons have registered under the law, this registration is not, because of the law's vagueness, a reliable index to the number of persons who, at one time or other, bring the pressure of organized groups to bear on the government of the United States.

The purpose of the law is to identify the source of pressures and to make it a matter of public knowledge who is paid for doing what, and how much. The reliance is on *publicity*, a weapon not to be underestimated in a democracy. Significantly, there is no attempt to distinguish between the methods used by lobbyists, forbidding some and regulating others. It is a matter of the greatest difficulty to get sufficient agreement on what should be forbidden and what should be permitted.[7]

---

[7] To cite some examples of state legislation on this point: in Texas and Louisiana a person is guilty of wrongful lobbying if he privately or secretly attempts to influence a legislator 'except by appealing to his reason.' In Oklahoma a paid lobbyist is guilty if he 'privately attempts to influence the act or vote of any member of the legislature on measures before the latter.' In Georgia and Tennessee lobbying is defined as 'any personal solicitation of any member of the General Assembly . . . not addressed solely to the judgment.'

QUESTIONS OF CONSTITUTIONALITY. Yet even the vague, loosely drawn, and generally deemed ineffective, Regulation of Lobbying Act of 1946 has been repeatedly attacked as an unconstitutional abridgment of the freedoms of speech and petition of the First Amendment and a violation of the due process of law clause of the Fifth Amendment. Lower federal courts have held some sections of the Act constitutional and some, such as the vital registration section, unconstitutional. The first Supreme Court test came in 1953, in which the Court upheld the Act but, at the same time, dealt it a blow by holding that the term 'lobbying activities' meant only *direct* representation before Congress, its members, or its committees, *not indirect* attempts to exert influence through the community.[8] One year later, the Court, five to three, upheld the Act in a second major challenge, but re-iterated that it covered only *'direct communication* with members of Congress on pending or proposed federal legislation.' And the Court further narrowed the scope of the Act by distinguishing between 'solicitation, spending, or receiving' and 'merely spending'—the latter not compelling disclosure.[9] De-livering the majority opinion, Mr. Chief Justice Warren rejected, however, the sweeping contentions of violations of due process of law, freedom of speech, press, and petition, and pointed out that Congress had every right to know 'who is being hired, who is putting up the money, and how much.'[10] The dissenters viewed the Act as unconstitutional on its face because of vagueness and indefiniteness.

Alarm about Lobbying. In the eyes of the public, lobbying has become much more respectable. Less is heard nowadays about outright corruption and backstairs intrigue. The relation between lobbying and the complex functions of government is better understood, and the operations of most of the more effective pressure groups are increasingly conducted in the open. Yet, even if some of the moral stigma has been removed, genuine alarm about the total effect of the activities of pressure groups on the national gov-ernment has perhaps increased rather than diminished.

Largely as a result of the increased governmental activities of the New Deal and World War II, the number of interest groups operating in Wash-ington has increased at a very rapid rate. Their pressure on government has become more pervasive and continuous. There is much fear that their push and pull will rob Congress of any sense of national purpose, and make it

[8] *United States* v. *Rumely,* 345 U.S. 41 (1953).
[9] *United States* v. *Harriss,* 347 U.S. 612 (1954). (Italics supplied.)
[10] Ibid.

mainly an instrument for registering the resultant of all the dispersive influences brought to bear on it. For example, the tactics used by the natural
gas lobby in 1956, in behalf of a bill to exempt producers of natural gas from
direct federal regulation, caused such a national outcry that President Eisenhower vetoed the measure, although he had initially supported it. His disapproval came in the wake of disclosure by Senator Francis Case, Republican
of South Dakota, that an oil company had attempted to contribute $2500 to
his re-election campaign in the hope of influencing his vote on the bill.

The indicated popular fear is by no means groundless. As we shall see
later in this text, Congress has generally found it difficult to reach and maintain a coherent, consistent view of national policy. The persistent lobbying
of many powerful groups with divergent demands increases the difficulty.
As it was demonstrated in Chapter IX, the chief cause of the difficulty under
the federal system in America is the failure of the national parties to develop
clear-cut specific programs and firm party discipline. The majority is potentially in a position to control Congress and to resist the demands of interest
groups, but it generally lacks a firm comprehensive program which it can
agree to enforce in the national interest. If this is correct, enactment of repressive laws against lobbying is not likely to accomplish much. What is
needed are party lines that do not falter or break before the thrusts of interest groups. Such party lines do exist in Britain, and although the phenomenon
of organized interest groups is comparable to that found in the United
States, the activities of these groups do not cause nearly so much alarm.

Interest Groups in Britain

In Britain, there are hundreds of organized interests taking the form of
business, labor, professional, agricultural, reform, philanthropic, and other
associations. In the range of interests thus served, if not in total numbers of
organizations, the British phenomenon is comparable to that of the United
States. On the economic side alone, there are hundreds of associations
representing commercial, manufacturing, transport, shipping, agricultural,
mining, and financial interests. Most of these are in turn linked together in
a few great national federations like the Federation of British Industries,
the Association of British Chambers of Commerce, the National Union of
Manufacturers, and the National Farmers' Union. The numerous labor
unions—which in 1960 totaled 183, containing almost 10 million of the
20 million labor force—have a common organ in the General Council of

the Trades Union Congress (T.U.C.), to which all but one million of the trade unionists belong.

No one of these large federations speaks with a single voice except on a few matters of broad general concern. On many if not most specific issues, the associations in a particular federation will speak discordantly. Professional and philanthropic interests are highly organized, often with national headquarters established close to the governing departments in Whitehall and to Parliament at Westminster. Important among them, for instance, are the British Medical Association and the National Union of Teachers, both of which speak for close to 90 per cent of their respective practitioners. Their purpose in every case is to advance the interests of their members and this generally involves the securing of legislative favors. As we saw in Chapter VII, the numerous associations of municipal governments and municipal government officials, headed by the 185,000-member National and Local Government Officers Association, are among the most effective pressure groups in Britain. And, of course, there are the usual civic, recreational, cultural, and educational organizations as well as some of the typically British 'special social sectional associations,' such as the two million-member Automobile Association and Royal Automobile Club, the Pedestrians' Association, and the Cyclists' Union.

The Techniques of Pressure. For reasons to be more fully discussed later, the working of party government with the cabinet in the driver's seat defeats attempts by interest groups to influence policy through winning over individual members of Parliament. The interests do on occasion try to influence the choice of candidates in particular constituencies, and to exact pledges from candidates by promising support or threatening opposition. Generally speaking, they cannot influence the choice of candidates because the local party associations know they must choose good party men. And the candidate, once in the field, must resist all pressure groups which would bind him to action contrary to the party line. So he refuses to give pledges. In Parliament, members almost always vote with their party. The interests cannot break its grip nor are they allowed to appear before parliamentary committees to press their views. Another important consideration here is that these committees, as will be seen in later chapters, are generalized, as in France, rather than specialized, as in the United States, and thus do not represent a fertile point of 'contact.'

WITHIN AND THROUGH THE POLITICAL PARTIES. The interests therefore must work within and through the parties instead of outside and against them.

While many groups remain outwardly non-partisan, some associate themselves directly with one or other party. The trade unions led the van in forming the Labour party and still constitute its main strength. The bulk of the election expenses of Labour candidates is provided by the trade unions associated in the Trades Union Congress. A Labour government is therefore particularly sensitive to the claims of organized labor. In 1960, eighty trade unions were officially associated with the Labour party.

Although no interest groups are similarly 'affiliated' with the Conservative party, the great organizations of employers, industry, trade, commerce, and farming must be regarded as aligned with the Conservatives.[11] For example, the National Farmers' Union gives a measure of support to the Conservative party. Not only was its president himself chosen and elected as a Conservative candidate in 1935, but he was also a member of a standing committee which later examined and reported favorably on a bill to assist the livestock industry. Without committing themselves fully, the aforementioned groups are thus generally sympathetic to the Conservative, or occasionally the Liberal, rather than to the Labour party, and they often endorse candidates. On the other hand, among the professional associations, the National Union of Teachers and the British Medical Association, for example, pledge support of one or more candidates sympathetic to them, but they are strictly non-partisan.

The mere fact that an interest group manages to smuggle a number of its sympathizers into Parliament under the cloak of one or other of the parties does not, of course, ensure it any great influence. Private members, standing alone, are quite insignificant, as the time afforded and the treatment given to private members' bills clearly shows. Most of the legislation sought by interests involves the expenditure of money, and private members cannot introduce such measures at all. If a private member's bill is unopposed in the House, as bills sponsored by the Royal Society for Prevention of Cruelty to Animals generally are, it may go through easily. But most private members' bills meet opposition, which means they must be debated. The time allotted for such debates is very short and only a few private members' bills ever reach the discussion stage. Finally, the cabinet has to be persuaded; the civil servants on whom the cabinet relies have to be convinced. Consequently, it is something of an occasion when a private member's bill actually becomes law.

[11] On this point, as well as on British pressure groups generally, see the excellent works by S. E. Finer, *Anonymous Empire* (London: Pall Mall, 1959) and J. D. Stewart, *British Pressure Groups* (Oxford: Clarendon Press, 1959).

CONCENTRATION ON THE CABINET. The interests seek to introduce bills through private members mainly for the purpose of getting publicity and building up an agitation that will persuade the government to act. *The interests know they must persuade the cabinet.* They also know that the cabinet is extremely susceptible to the temper of public opinion and of opinion in the House. So they supply members of the House with their literature, and encourage their sympathizers in the House to proselytize and initiate questions and debates bearing on the claims of the group.

This indirect pressure on the cabinet is not the most important activity of interest groups. All the great organized interests are also in close and almost continuous contact with particular ministers and with the cabinet, presenting their facts and urging their point of view. They often appoint a committee to make direct representations to the cabinet or to a particular department of the government. They watch all legislative proposals, and before a bill adverse to their interests goes to Parliament they make strong representations against it to the cabinet.

Interests Consulted. The cabinet, to ensure itself as much as possible against opposition in the House, generally consults all the organized interests concerned while the bill is being drafted. For example, when the bills for nationalizing the coal mines, air lines, and railways were being drafted, the Labour Government consulted both management and trade unions in these industries. Representations are heard on both sides, the criticisms made are subjected to examination by experts, and adjustments and concessions are made by the cabinet as far as it finds it possible to do so. After the legislation is enacted, the interests are generally represented on an advisory committee which is associated with the government department administering the legislation. The committee makes suggestions and criticisms, which often lead to substantial amendment of the legislation at a later date. The cabinet is continually mediating between a great range of interests, each of which claims to be representative of the public interest. It tries to find accommodations that are acceptable or tolerable to the interests concerned but that still enable it to carry out the pledges of the party.

When extremely contentious issues arise, on which the government wants fuller knowledge of facts before committing itself, a royal commission of inquiry, such as the Royal Commission on the Press in the 1940's and 1950's, to which a number of persons who know and can speak for the major affected interests are appointed, is often set up. These bodies perform a function somewhat similar to that of congressional committees in the United

States when they afford public hearings for the various interests on some legislative proposal. If the commission can produce a unanimous report, the government has some ground for hoping that the interest groups will accept its proposals.

A CASE STUDY. In any case, the interests are again consulted by the government before the government frames its bill on the recommendations of the commission. For example, the Minister of Transport submitted the Report of the Royal Commission on Transport of 1931 for comment and criticism to five local government associations, fifteen transport associations, four motoring associations, four trade unions, the Association of British Chambers of Commerce, the Federation of British Industries, and the Mansion House Association on Transport, and the National Federation of Iron and Steel Manufacturers. These interests could not agree. The railway companies and the road transport associations were far apart, as might be expected. The Minister was not yet prepared to state a policy of his own for action by the cabinet and Parliament. He called a conference of representatives of the interests in conflict, which did agree on a proposal, although the road transport associations still refused to accept it. In the end, the Road and Rail Traffic Bill produced by the government diverged somewhat from the recommendations of the Commission and also from the proposal of the conference. This illustrates the kind of negotiation that generally precedes the introduction of complex and controversial legislation into the House of Commons.

Important though organized interests are in the initiation of legislative proposals, their importance as critics of such proposals is even greater. As soon as a bill is published, the cabinet and appropriate government departments get representations from all interests that conceive themselves to be affected. It is often impossible to consult all interests before a bill is drafted. Those that were not consulted, and those that were but are still dissatisfied, urge their views as strongly as they can. If representations to the government are not effective, the interests then circularize the members of Parliament and get sympathetic members to urge their friends to protest. If the issue is one on which a general public opinion might be raised, that too is tried. A combination of these tactics is sometimes effective. To take only a few instances, the Incitement to Disaffection Bill of 1934 and the Population Bill of 1937 were very substantially altered by the government, and the operation of the Teachers' Superannuation Bill of 1956 and the Rent Bill of 1957 were postponed because of widespread dissatisfaction with them in the House of Commons. Organized interests had a considerable part in fostering this dissatisfaction. The objective of interest groups in Britain is always to convince the cabinet or the department concerned that proposed legislation should be passed, amended, or rejected.[12] They have a large share in shaping legislation, although it is not as important a share as in the United States and is achieved by different means.

INTEREST GROUPS IN FRANCE

According to Article 3 of the now superseded French Constitution of 1946, 'national sovereignty belongs to the French people. No section of the people nor any individual may assume its exercise.' This provision had been intended to preserve the fiction of a *direct* relationship between citizens and state in France and, at least on paper, perpetuated the general hostility of French constitutional and political theory to the existence of pressure groups. Charles de Gaulle, under his Constitution of 1958—and outside of it—has brought a real measure of actuality to the fiction as well as to the theory! Interest groups do still exist in France, of course, but as has already been demonstrated at some length earlier in this chapter, the dramatic shift in the core of governmental power from the legislature to the executive has brought about a major diminution in the influence of the French pressure groups. Nonetheless, they remain a factor to be reckoned with, and something more must be said about them here.

The Range of Organized Interests. Pressure groups as such have always been and are now less numerous in France than in Britain and the United States, but—when they are identifiable as organized interests at all—they fall into several major categories: [13]

BUSINESS. Large business concerns, primarily France's most powerful corporations, are organized in the *Confédération Nationale du Patronat Français* (C.N.P.F.), which is dominated by big steel, textile, and chemical firms. It resembles the National Association of Manufacturers in the United States in influence if not in structural organization. Small business, shopkeepers, the

---

[12] Sir W. Ivor Jennings, *Parliament,* 2nd ed. (Cambridge: Cambridge University Press, 1957), ch. VII. The sketch above of pressure groups in Britain is largely drawn from this volume. For more detailed data regarding the 'consultation' procedure between ministries and interests, see J. D. Stewart, op. cit.

[13] For two good treatments of this subject, upon which this discussion has chiefly relied, see Bernard E. Brown, 'Pressure Politics in France,' *The Journal of Politics,* XVIII (1956), 702–19, and George E. Lavan, 'Political Pressures by Interest Groups in France,' in Henry W. Ehrmann (Ed.), *Interest Groups on Four Continents* (Pittsburgh: University of Pittsburgh Press, 1958), pp. 60–95.

professions, and artisans are organized in the *Confédération Générale des Petites et Moyennes Entreprises* (P.M.E.), theoretically a branch of the C.N.P.F., yet actually not only autonomous but quite distrustful of its 'big brother.' It claims a membership of some 2.5 million and, as the spokesman of 'family enterprise' in France, has much popular backing. Pierre Poujade's now defunct right-wing political party grew out of one segment of the P.M.E.'s membership.

AGRICULTURE. The six million French farmers are organized in seven major interest groups, headed by the *Fédération Nationale des Syndicats d'Exploitants Agricoles* (F.N.S.E.A.) with about two million members. Their obvious goal is approximately the same as that of farm pressure groups everywhere: higher prices, subsidies, lower taxes, and other special farm legislation. A highly influential segment of the population, the French farmers' organizations suffer from a typically French malady—disunity and division among themselves. However, some of their efforts have met with signal success. Probably the outstanding example is the sugar-beet subsidy program, which has been a steady drain on the French treasury, with little, if any, relief in sight. The beet growers have been able to maintain their preferred treatment by 'log-rolling' with the grapegrowers, the distillers, and the many retailers of alcoholic products. Their newspaper, *Le Betteravier Français,* boasts of representing a 'huge organization, whose aim is to defend the beet growers' interests day in and day out, to the best of its ability, *vis-à-vis* industry as well as *vis-à-vis* the public authority.' [14]

LABOR. Labor unions, though badly split in France, also carry on the customary lobbying activities, headed by the well-known 1,700,000-member Communist-led *Confédération Générale du Travail* (C.G.T.). Other important unions are the Catholic *Confédération Français des Travailleurs Chrétiens* (C.F.T.C.) with about 750,000 members, and the Socialist-led 400,000-member *Confédération Générale du Travail-Force Ouvrière* (C.G.T.-F.O.). Each union acts as an intermediary between its members and government departments in social security matters, for example. Labor's pressure is applied to the parties, deputies, and administrators alike. In general, however, the French labor unions have been considerably less successful in their lobbying activities than their American and British counterparts.

OTHERS. A few others among the French interest groups should be men-

[14] *Le Betteravier Français,* February 1956. For a particularly pertinent discussion on this industry, see B. E. Brown, 'Alcohol and Politics in France,' *American Political Science Review* 51 (December 1957), 976–94.

tioned. There are family associations that lobby for social welfare legislation; clerical groups whose chief interest is state aid to parochial and private schools; veterans' associations *en masse*—there were fifty-four in 1963—headed by the influential three-million-member *Union Française des Associations de Combattants et de Victimes de la Guerre* (U.F.A.C.). Of the democratic states here discussed, France, having suffered most from wars, has by far the largest proportionate number of war victims and veterans. It is only natural that these 8,500,000 should attempt to obtain favorable treatment.

The Techniques of Pressure. As already stated, the main weapon of the French interest groups, which was the once so effective liaison with political parties, sometimes even outright transformation into a party, suffered a stunning blow with the advent of the Fifth Republic. There is still a natural tendency for farmers, for example, to ally themselves with the Independents and other parties of the Center and Right; for business to look toward the Center and the Right; for labor to exert pressure upon the parties on the political left. Furthermore, all major interest groups still have some liaison with individual deputies, who sometimes are officers of the interest groups themselves. For example, several Communist, Socialist, and Popular Republican deputies are leaders of the French labor unions and many influential businessmen have been elected to Parliament as Gaullists, Independents, and Radicals. On the other hand, it is obvious that certain pressure groups, the home distillers, for one, continue to make almost a fetish of repeatedly claiming 'complete independence of political parties'[15]—a notion so dear to de Gaulle. All of the interests, however, now must and do look to the Gaullist majority for their bounty—and, as has been repeatedly stated, that bounty is no longer the legislature's to give but must come from the fountainhead of all meaningful power in the Fifth Republic, the executive. The latter cannot, of course, ignore the interests—a lesson brought home with the two successful general strikes of 1961—but the executive is now his own boss and decision-maker: no longer must he worry about and mollify the legislature as the interests' 'representatives' except in a very marginal and perhaps psychological sense.

Summation. In the United States, Britain, and France, the interests seek to be heard, not only on what laws should be made, but also on how the laws should be administered and enforced. In fact, as will be shown in detail later, they are as closely connected with the process of administration as with lawmaking. The various interests that make up modern society have found

[15] Cf. A. Lyantey, in *Le Bouilleur de France*, April–May 1956.

means of access to government which ensure that their knowledge, experience, and point of view will not be overlooked. The arguments for proportional and occupational representation, to be discussed in the next chapter, have been met in Britain and the United States by arrangements that, although by no means free of abuses, are less dangerous to democratic institutions. It should also be clear that the present-day phenomenon of assertive pressure groups arises largely from the wide range of governmental functions, and that it is only in this context that the significance of lobbying and kindred practices can be appreciated.

In a democracy, the political parties must seek, at least ostensibly, to represent all groups and classes in order to obtain the necessary majorities. This is the ideal of democratic government—the representation of all—but behind it group adjustment goes on. Rather than abolish political interest groups, they can be accepted as natural in a political democracy. Of course, they have a significant influence on the actions of both executive and legislature. They supplement the activities of political parties in moulding the exercise of both legislative and executive power. Neither of these two branches of government operates in a vacuum.

When all is said and done, we may safely return to the sage statement by Arthur F. Bentley, over half a century ago, in his classic, *The Process of Government,* that '. . . governments are but the interest groupings wrestling with one another.' [16]

THE DICTATORSHIPS AND VOLUNTARY ASSOCIATIONS

Liberal democracy has been marked by a wide freedom of association. Because the state could not be all things to all men, the human need for fellowship and for extensive social co-operation has been met by voluntary association outside the state and free of interference by government, as long as the association restricts itself to lawful purposes. Many of these associations turn into pressure groups trying to influence government. A striking feature common to the phases of totalitarian dictatorship in Germany and Italy, and to Communist rule in the Soviet Union, is the destruction of the independent organization of group interests and associations. Dictatorship exalts the state, insists that men must find their meaning in the service of the state, and forbids them to have any loyalties outside the state. Dictators do not want the

[16] *The Process of Government: A Study of Social Pressures* (Chicago: University of Chicago Press, 1908), p. 307.

government to be diverted or distracted in its sublime mission by narrow selfish interests. Pressure groups, as such, are abolished.

With the elimination of capitalism in the Soviet Union, most of the diverse economic interests associated with it also disappeared. According to socialist theory, the abolition of profit and private property automatically dissolved the diversity of economic interests and replaced it with one common interest, the maximum productivity of the economy as a whole. Consequently, the leaders of the Soviet Union believe that there can be no clash of economic interests in the Soviet Union because all capitalists have been eliminated, and the methods of obtaining maximum productivity have been determined by scientific socialism. In the absence of private competition, the government is free from the obnoxious pressure of groups whose aim is to derive private gain from government policies.

The trade unions, being workers' organizations whose strengthening had been one of the slogans of the Revolution, were continued. However, as we shall see presently, they came entirely under the control of the Communist party and lost their freedom meaningfully to agitate and exert independent pressure on the government. Similarly all other associations that are allowed to exist in the Soviet Union are strictly controlled or specifically tolerated by the party and the government.

Nazi and Fascist Control of Associations. In totalitarian Germany and Italy, the dictators did not tear down the existing social and economic structure with its wide diversity of organized group interests. Rather they reconstructed the jumble of divergent group interests by sternly co-ordinating each of them with the aims of party and government. By pressure and compulsion, associations representing group interests were persuaded to elect as their officers party members or party sympathizers. The associations ceased to be independent organizations lobbying the government; they became instruments by which the government enforced its drastic policies on the groups of which the nation was composed. Under party leadership and control, many groups of the type discussed in this chapter became more highly organized than ever before, and the government delegated to them wide powers of self-government. However, it was not genuine self-government. The associations lost their autonomy and vitality and became merely administrative departments of the government for executing its policy. A good example was the abolition of the independent German trade unions and their state-compelled 'fusion' into the state-supervised *Arbeitsfront,* to which all workers, and most employers in trade and industry, were forced to belong.

The workers were completely regimented, with the Nazi government determining wages (low), hours (12 daily), and even the place and type of occupation.

Modern totalitarian dictatorships cannot tolerate independent group life. It has already been pointed out that political parties in the democracies are, in large measure, combinations of group interests. If the dictators allowed groups their independence, many of them would combine to oppose the government. That is to say, opposing political parties would, in fact, be formed despite the ban on them. Therefore, the organized groups had either to be liquidated, or co-ordinated and knit into the governmental structure. Groups that had objectives the dictators did not like were liquidated. All others were turned into instruments of the totalitarian purposes of the dictators.

Group Interests in the Soviet Union

The Trade Unions. The trade unions in the Soviet Union have been made to serve the totalitarian purposes of the government. They are completely dominated by the Communist party. Most of the trade union leaders are high party officials, and the unions are mainly used to enforce the policies of party and government. For many years, the Soviet trade union chief was Lazar Kaganovich, until his expulsion by Khrushchev in 1957 one of the most powerful members of the party 'elite.' Trade unions are no longer independent bodies seeking primarily to improve the lot of their members; they are rather mass organizations whose main function is to discipline the labor force and press it into enthusiastic service of the state. If the trade unions are to be used effectively for this purpose, it is necessary to have most of the industrial working force inside the unions. While membership in a union is theoretically voluntary, a worker suffers serious disadvantages in remaining outside, and about 90 per cent of the workers are now members.

In 1933, to popularize their then announced new role of 'assisting management in increasing production,' the trade unions took over some essentially governmental functions, administering social insurance funds, arranging holidays and cultural programs, and supervising certain activities in the factories such as control over safety devices. In this way, they became, in effect, executive agencies of the government. Obviously, they cannot act as private pressure groups seeking to further the special interests of their members.

Today Soviet trade unions promote extensive social and cultural activities among the workers and engage in collective bargaining on a nation-wide scale. However, collective bargaining in the Soviet Union is not at all what it is in Britain, France, or the United States. Because the capitalists, the enemies of the workers, have been eliminated, the traditional function of the trade union, the protection of the workers from the capitalist exploiters, no longer exists. So, collective bargaining is carried out on the assumption that labor and the socialist managers of industry have identical interests: maximum production at minimum cost. The total wages fund is fixed by the government in its general economic plan, and collective bargaining merely determines how that fund shall be divided among the workers.

Other Associations. The trade unions are only one of many organized groups in the Soviet Union. Others represent the professional or recreational interests of sections of the population. There are the various co-operatives, some interested in agricultural production, others in the co-operative building and management of dwellings, etc.; youth organizations, groups interested in sports; technical and scientific organizations, such as the Academy of Science of the Soviet Union; and cultural organizations. The activities of all these groups are controlled by the Communist party. Its aim is to harness the group membership into loyal and persevering work for the state, and the groups are expected to conform to these standards.

In the early days of Communist rule in Russia, for instance, a group of writers with common literary interests formed the Pan-Russian Union of Writers. During the bitter struggle between Trotsky and Stalin, this group was sympathetic to Trotsky. Stalin was instrumental in setting up a rival group, the Russian Association of Proletarian Writers (RAPP). Stalin's victory over Trotsky led to the elimination of the older association, largely through giving control of the publishing houses to the newer association, and through the activities of the secret police. Then, in the middle 'thirties, RAPP displeased the leadership of the party and a new association, the Union of Soviet Writers, was founded to take its place. All associations of whatever kind are controlled in the same way. None is permitted to organize without state authorization.

Pressure from Within. The government runs the economic system and supervises social and cultural life. Because there is very little of Soviet society outside the government, it is hard to exert pressure on the government from the outside. However, the push and pull of diverse interests is not wholly eliminated. The innumerable state organizations, government departments, state trusts for running particular industries, state banks, state trading companies, planning agencies, and so on, compete with one another for favored treatment by the masters at the top of the pinnacle.

The managers of the various branches of Soviet industry develop a pride in their projects and have a vested interest in expanding their particular enterprises. The numerous planners themselves have pet projects the success of which seems to them vital for the welfare of the Communist society. So within the government itself, there is a wide division of interest and opinion, and therefore much devious lobbying of those who have the power to decide. However, these various interests cannot organize independently of the government and they must be cautious about the kind and intensity of pressure they exert. Indeed, what goes on is a kind of 'palace politics,' comparable to the rivalry of the courtiers for the favors of an absolute monarch.

PUBLIC OPINION

Democratic government has been defined as government in accordance with the will of the people. The people, in this sense, means the electorate, which, in the countries in question, embraces almost the entire adult population. Taken literally, government in accordance with the will of the electorate means that every member of the electorate must be consulted and must agree before a democratic government can embark on a significant line of policy.

It is clear that this is not so. Democratic legislatures often pass, and democratic executives often enforce, legislation that was not in issue at the last election. Nor does the succeeding election always bring a specific verdict of the electorate on such legislation. Even when it does, the enforcement of the legislation in the interim may have had far-reaching consequences which cannot be undone. Also, it has been remarked again and again that the electorate when it is consulted is never unanimous. There is always some dissent in some section of the electorate on whatever proposal is made for government action.

GOVERNMENT BY PUBLIC OPINION

If the familiar definition of democratic government quoted above is to correspond to realities, two qualifications must be introduced. First, government in accordance with the will of the people cannot be taken to mean consultation on every act of government. Rather it must be taken to mean that periodically each member of the electorate is enabled to state his preference between the candidates and announced policies of two or more political parties. In casting his vote, he may be deciding on the announced policy of parties for the future, on the past record of the parties in and out of power, on the personalities of the candidates, or on some combination of these factors. It would be impossible to discover what factors were decisive for each voter. But this very uncertainty disposes the political parties to take care of their present record, their future program, and the candidates they sponsor. Pronounced attitudes in the electorate have an enormous influence on the behavior of the political parties, either directly or indirectly. Where a crisis of obviously large significance for the community sharply divides the political parties, rouses prolonged debate, and over-shadows other less critical issues, the electorate is certain to get a chance to express itself very directly on the critical question in the next election. If a majority of the electorate is opposed to the policy of the party presently in control of the government, it can change its rulers and bring to power another group of politicians with a policy more to its liking.

This brings us to the second qualification: government in accordance with the will of the people means at most that it is the will of a majority that prevails on controversial questions. Sometimes, as we saw earlier in this chapter, it is merely the will of a vocal, influential, and/or well-organized minority. The fact that there is a controversy ensures that some portion of the electorate will be dissatisfied with any decision taken. The will of the people is not necessarily the will of all. Even then, the majorities are mustered only occasionally, and say their say on only a small fraction of the specific decisions that are taken in the name of government.

The Electorate's Influence. What has just been said refers only to the influence and control exerted by the electorate through elections. However, in earlier chapters we have seen that the influence of the electorate is not limited to voting in elections. Between elections, the political parties are always looking forward to the next election, searching for methods and measures that will be popular, and trying to avoid policies that will be unpopular. Party organization, especially in Britain, and particular politicians everywhere, are constantly seeking to plumb opinion in the country. At the same time, they are attempting to influence the development of opinion. Speeches in the legislature and by the executive—whatever the medium employed—are addressed to the country. Political leaders find many other occasions for utterance designed to enlighten, placate, or mould opinion. Elections are intermittent dramatic interventions by the electorate. Between elections, the democratic electorate maintains constant pressure on its rulers through what is generally called *public opinion*.

Those who are impressed with the effectiveness of this pressure, both in influencing the conduct of government between elections and in shaping the issues and selecting the political leadership for the next election, describe democracy as government by public opinion. The democratic governments chiefly discussed in this text respond to public opinion, but the nature and, particularly, the rapidity of the response differ considerably among them.

Interest Groups and Public Opinion. However, as we concluded earlier, as a practical matter in a democracy, public policy, the decision of what government is to do, always emerges from the competition, clash, and compromise of a great variety of individual and group interests, with important roles assigned to both political leadership and public opinion—no matter how vague and fluctuating the latter may be. It follows, then, that a basic concern of all interest groups is the character and the nature of the opinions that exist in a given community. No organized group, no group leader, can engage in the luxury of being indifferent to public opinion, regardless of whether such opinion is manifested in the full-fledged members of the interest group itself; in the 'hangers-on'—Professor Truman calls them the 'fellow-travelers'; [17] in the unorganized mass which may or may not be neutral or indifferent; or in the hostile element of society.

DEFINING PUBLIC OPINION

Few concepts are quite as hazy as that of *public opinion*. As a distinguished observer of the field, Professor V. O. Key, once put it: 'To speak with precision of public opinion is a task not unlike coming to grips with the Holy Grail.' Some attempt at definition is therefore necessary.

What It Is Not. It seems to be easier to find some agreement on what it is *not*. No serious present-day student of politics would, for example, still defend the centuries'-old proverb, *vox populi, vox dei*. It is hardly that! Indirectly, popular control over governmental policy does exist in a democracy, but on a host of matters a substantial segment of the people has no well-thought out opinion at all, and either 'go along' or 'don't care'—so long as a

[17] Truman, *The Governmental Process*, ch. VI.

particular policy does not obviously affect them personally. Thus, it should also be apparent that public opinion is by no means necessarily over-all *majority* opinion, for, as we have already shown, there may be many, varying 'public opinions,' and it may be difficult, indeed, to find a true majority opinion—short of a desire for peace and a belief in God. Yet opinions will usually differ sharply on how to obtain or retain the first and on the form the second should take.

What It Is. If, as many commentators on public opinion prefer,[18] we separate *public* from *opinion* for the purpose of analysis, we note that *'public'* refers to a 'group'; it is synonymous with 'group.' It is *a* group which is giving attention in any way to a given issue—a government subsidy on tobacco, for example. It follows logically that there may be several divisions within the group on the issue of subsidizing tobacco—those for, those against, those in-between, and so forth.

'*Opinion*,' in turn, is the *expression* of an attitude on the controversial issue, point, or proposition of subsidizing tobacco. And *public opinion, then, consists of the aggregate of the opinions* (on the government subsidy) *of individuals making up the public under discussion.* It includes only those opinions relevant to the issue or situation that defines them as public, not *all* the opinions held by that set of individuals.[19]

Two important points should be noted about this definition. First, it asserts that there are as many publics as there are issues. Second, that public opinion consists of an aggregate of views which may be divergent and clashing, which at any rate do not all point one way. According to this definition, public opinion need not be the opinion of a clear majority of the electorate. Nor does the definition require one to believe that on every public issue a clear-cut majority opinion can always be created by opinion.

CONSENSUS. Of course, in any community that is united at all, there must be matters on which it really is united. In genuinely democratic countries, at any rate, there are always some fundamental beliefs that almost all approve —however few these may be, as recent research in the United States has shown. This is called *consensus,* and for the three countries discussed here roughly corresponds with the liberal democratic ideals outlined in Chapter II. These ideals, the consensus, are scarcely open to any debate at all because

---

[18] See Truman, op. cit. pp. 218–20; John Dewey, *The Public and Its Problems* (New York: Henry Holt, 1927), pp. 12–17; and William Albig, *Modern Public Opinion* (New York: McGraw-Hill, 1956), pp. 3–8.
[19] Truman, op. cit. p. 220.

there cannot be a really serious controversy about them, such as there can be about subsidizing tobacco.

At the other extreme, there are a multitude of matters on which there is no agreement at all. To many of them, some members of the public will give attention and make up their minds pro or con. Some issues may become so important, arouse so much interest, provoke so much discussion, that a clear majority of the electorate will come down on one side or the other. Whether it does or not, *public opinion,* as defined here, *consists of the aggregate of opinions on specific issues.*

Moulding Public Opinion

A good many forces and factors play a role in the formulation, the determination, of public opinion. Sometimes they combine for decisive effect; sometimes one single factor is chiefly responsible for the determination. But given the complex society of our day and the pluralism of democracy, usually a combination of influences rather than a single one shapes public opinion. We have already seen, and shall again, the roles played in the process by legislatures, executives, political parties—government generally—as well as by interest groups. All these forces both mirror *and* manufacture public opinion, for good or evil. The same is true of some important others, which we shall examine briefly.

The Basic Institutions. Home (family), church, and school are generally viewed as the 'basic' institutions in a free society. Each citizen bears allegiance to, and is influenced by—be it negatively or positively—each of these three. The firmness of allegiance and degree of influence differ widely, but these institutions play a definite role—often a crucial one—in the formulation of public opinion. Strongest of them is the home or family, whence come most of man's basic values, mores and predispositions. However, depending upon the individual's tradition, belief, and attitude, the church, too, may well be a mighty factor in the influence it exerts upon its membership. And while the influence of school, no matter what the educational level, may at times be overrated in relation to that of the other two basic institutions, there is little doubt that the lamp of learning often contributes to the light, or darkness, surrounding major issues when public opinion is coming to grips with them.

Media of Communication. In a sense, church and school are media of mass communication (means of conveying information and ideas to the masses), but that term is usually applied to the press (newspapers, magazines, and news agencies), radio and television, books, movies and theaters. In greater or lesser measure, each of these media of communication wields influence upon public opinion; indeed, they have often demonstrated power to color, mould, and create public opinion. All of us are exposed to some, if not all, of the media above, and we adopt points of view from them even as we adopt the opinions of friends, associates, parents, and members of our clubs and fraternities. One or two of the media of communication require more specific attention.

THE PRESS. The press is usually thought of as one of the most influential moulders of opinion in democratic states. But today's press suffers from being essentially 'big business,' with the possible exception of the steadily dwindling small-town dailies and rural weeklies. It may be said that the press has moved from the status of a profession to that of a big business, open only to those with the financial ability to 'make a go of it.' Gone are the days when practically each segment of political, economic, and social thought had a newspaper, however small, dedicated to expressing its views or at least had free access to one. Gone, too, are the days of spirited competition among many local papers. Instead, we have the one-newspaper town, even the one-newspaper city, and large newspaper chains span the country.

This decline of competition among newspapers, and the resultant trend toward concentration and monopoly, especially in Britain and the United States, is a simple matter of economics. To publish a newspaper in the mid-twentieth century is a major financial undertaking. To start even a four- or six-page daily small-town newspaper in the United States today, requires a minimum dollar outlay of six figures. Yet circulation has risen rapidly even as the number of newspapers has declined. At the end of 1962, daily circulation in the United States had reached 59,009,159, almost *triple* the number of readers in 1910; but the number of dailies had declined from the 1910 high of 2202 to 1850 in 1962.[20] Between 1952 and 1962 alone, rising production costs had killed 219 newspapers. Of the cities having daily newspapers, only 4 per cent had more than one at the end of 1962—as compared with 67 per cent in 1910. The chains, the great publishing corporations, such as Hearst, Scripps-Howard, and Newhouse, owned almost half the total number of dailies, and they have reached out to control related and associated

[20] All figures are taken from *N. W. Ayer & Son's Directory* (Philadelphia: N. W. Ayer & Son, 1963).

enterprises as well—e.g. news agencies, magazines, radio and television stations. In Britain, the press has undergone a similar transformation, and has been brought even closer to monopoly control. A few huge corporations control almost all the metropolitan newspapers and the bulk of the newspaper circulation in the country. In France, although circulation has declined, a larger proportion of the dailies remains independently owned and operated. A higher proportion of the French dailies is *avowedly* partisan, however.

The individuals who control and manage the great and near-great publishing corporations are absorbed in the same or similar problems as their counterparts in large industrial, commercial, and financial corporations. They talk one another's language and move in the same social circles, chiefly among bankers, industrialists, and others of the executive class. It would be surprising if their interests and associations did not influence their outlook on many public questions. Moreover, because much the greater part of the income of daily newspapers stems from advertisements, advertisers may exert considerable influence on editorial policy. On the other hand, an often totally different political and editorial attitude is expressed by these newspapers' columnists and reporters. Richard M. Nixon blamed his narrow 1960 election loss to John F. Kennedy on 'biased campaign reporting.'

These factors raise questions about what the press will do to public opinion. How, it may be asked, will readers in the United States, for example, be able to form independent, intelligent views if the wealthy and powerful owners of the increasingly monopolistic press have imposed on their newspapers, as some assert they have, a 'party-line' of 'conservative Republicanism'? There is a threefold reply:

First, increased educational opportunities enable larger segments of the public to evaluate data more carefully and more intelligently than heretofore. Second, while it is true that in national presidential elections in the United States since Woodrow Wilson's time no Democratic candidate has ever had the active support of more than 15 per cent of the press, President F. D. Roosevelt was elected four times by large majorities and President Truman won over Thomas E. Dewey in 1948 in the face of almost unanimous press opposition—he had the support of only two dailies in the entire North and East! [21] The victories of the Labour party in the 1945 and 1950 elections in Britain were likewise won in the face of a predominantly Conservative press.

[21] For a study of how 31 leading newspapers handled the 1952 presidential election campaign, see A. E. Rowse, *Slanted News* (Boston: The Beacon Press, 1957). In the 1956 campaign, Adlai E. Stevenson was backed by not a single newspaper among the dailies in Connecticut, Delaware, the District of Columbia, Maine, North Dakota, Rhode Island, and Utah.

Third, the press is not as close to monopoly control as discussion some-times seems to suggest. The industry is still competitive, although the com-petition is, in the terms of the economist, quite imperfect competition. The competitors are limited in number, protected from the intrusion of outsiders by the large capital requirements for entrance into the industry. But they still struggle—and often struggle fiercely—for their place in the market. They do not engage in price wars, but they do fight for 'scoops' in the news. And they must face outside competition from pamphlets, magazines, movies, theater, radio, and television. As long as this continues, there cannot be anything approaching an organized conspiracy to censor the news.

RADIO AND TELEVISION. In providing entirely new means of communication, radio and television have become highly significant and have helped to main-tain a measure of competition in the distribution of news and formation of opinion. However, the sharply limited number of wave lengths available made this communications industry semimonopolistic from the beginning, and posed at once the problem of controlling it in the public interest—a task that was given to the Federal Communications Commission. Moreover, the need for international agreements to allocate clear channels on an equitable basis has meant that governments have had to retain a much closer contact with radio broadcasting than with the press. Not only do technical factors limit the number of radio and television stations, but the amount of material presented over the air is also restricted within the inflexible boundaries of a twenty-four-hour day. Radio and television, unlike the press, cannot add a few pages to take care of extra material.

Furthermore, despite some hopeful signs to the contrary, radio and tele-vision are still primarily instruments for entertainment rather than for imparting information or formulating opinion. Even in performing the latter function, radio and television must depend on the spoken word and the screen, which, while permitting greater dramatization of events, lack the staying qualities of the written word. An appreciation of this limitation probably accounts for the repetitiveness of modern advertising on radio and television. By constricting reporting of events into brief word-pictures and screen-flashes, radio and television have helped to increase the interest of the public in news but, at the same time, they have undoubtedly strengthened the current trend toward the standardizing of ideas for easy assimilation by busy people. The pace of modern civilization gives us less and less time to sift the material from which we are expected to make decisions on increasingly complex issues. Digests, picture magazines, the radio, and television best fit this new pattern of existence.

Radio and television have been widely regarded as valuable aids to liberal democratic politics. The recent increase in electoral participation at United States presidential elections, for one, has been widely attributed to the use of radio and television in politics, particularly television. The Nixon-Kennedy T.V. debates during the 1960 presidential campaign were viewed by an enormous audience and played a role in the Kennedy victory. The major portion of the budgets of political parties is now devoted to radio broadcasting and to the expensive television. Some observers have even gone so far as to suggest that radio and television have re-established that direct contact between political leaders and followers that characterized Athenian democracy. It is true that leaders can now appeal substantially to the whole people as did the leaders in classical times. But radio and television can only establish a one-way contact: listeners and viewers are passive rather than active participants in the discussion of ideas by their leaders. Citizens' forums, Town Halls of the Air, Round Tables, and the like make possible a limited exchange of ideas on public issues, but this is far from setting up the conditions of Athenian direct democracy. Dictators have taken full advantage of the one-way appeal of radio, and now television, to indoctrinate masses that are in no position to answer back. However, even for dictators, this type of communication is limited because mob hysteria cannot be whipped up easily amongst a scattered radio and television public. The 'fireside chats' of the late President Franklin D. Roosevelt probably exemplified the most effective political use of radio as an instrument of democracy, and the addresses by President Eisenhower and President Kennedy's 'rocking chair' news conferences did the same with television.

RADIO AND TELEVISION IN BRITAIN. Since 1927, radio broadcasting in Britain has been monopolized by the British Broadcasting Corporation, a semi-autonomous government corporation. Financed largely by listeners' fees, the Corporation permits no advertising over its radio and television stations. Regional organization of program service gives a limited range of choice for listeners. The fact that the Corporation can balance its programs and direct them to various groups, regardless of their size and purchasing power, enables it to offer a variety of fare. Opinion differs on whether that variety is comparable to the range of choice provided by sponsors in the United States. An interesting development in this connection is the establishment of a *commer-*

cial television network (I.T.V.) in Britain. It relies on advertisement for revenue and goes in for popular programs. Its long-range effect, if any, upon the present B.B.C. monopoly remains to be seen.

Working through a number of advisory committees, the B.B.C. can place its programs without thought for advertising revenue on the strictly educational value of its offerings. This would suggest that the Corporation is in a better position than broadcasters in the United States to exploit radio and television as instruments of communication and opinion-formation. Hence, cautiousness in using radio and television as positive instruments of political discussion in Britain arises not from a concern for advertising revenues but from a concern for preserving political neutrality. In developing its role as an instrument for the formation of public opinion, the B.B.C. tends to become itself an object of public opinion and partisan criticism.

This indicates the difficulties that a government-operated radio and television system encounters if it tries to stress the media's social or political functions. If it is to remain impartial, such a government-managed system cannot go far in a positive educative role, and in some instances it may be difficult for it to get general acceptance as a neutral channel of communication. The difficulties that arise from charges of political partisanship are not so acute when radio and television are left in private hands subject to governmental regulation. But then radio and television come under the control of a few; they perform such educative functions as advertisers will pay for, and their neutrality comes equally under suspicion.

URGENCY OF FREE RADIO AND TELEVISION AND FREE PRESS. In the liberal democracies, it is not easy to make radio and television—whether under private or public auspices—a positive force in enlightening or focusing public opinion. If radio and television are to assert themselves significantly outside the field of entertainment and the news summary, they require much greater encouragement and backing from an enlightened public. Radio and especially television are still young, and experience with their use and their control is still limited. But, at the moment, it is plausible to say of radio and television, as of the press, that we get the kind we deserve.

Pressure groups, public relations agencies, and propagandists of every kind try to reach the public through all the instruments of mass communications. The breakdown of democracy in continental Europe was accompanied by great blasts of anti-democratic propaganda. As a result, there is considerable demand for the curbing of propaganda. It is by no means clear, however, that the anti-democratic propaganda in Europe would have been at all effective but for the convergence of a number of other favorable conditions. Nor is it at all clear that, given these conditions, any curb on propaganda would have saved the European democracies. Democracy depends on free discussion; it cannot afford to limit discussion except in rare circumstances on clear proof that limits are necessary. Rather it must trust that one brand of propaganda will be counteracted by another. The trust will be misplaced unless we can assure a fair degree of freedom of access to the instruments of communication. That is why a genuinely free press and an impartially administered radio and television system are of such critical importance.

MEASURING PUBLIC OPINION

Many persons and groups, both in and out of public life, seek to use public opinion and to influence it. They need, first of all, to know what it is. If it is favorable to them, they want to be able to urge that it should have its way. If it is found to be unfavorable, they want to take steps to change it. Newspapers first revealed an interest in the measurement of opinion over a century ago when they began to conduct 'straw votes' as a means of predicting election results. It is a far cry from this casual method of measurement to the refined sampling techniques now being developed and applied by some forty private polling organizations in the United States alone.

The Public Opinion Polls. The 'pollsters' divide the population into a number of categories, and select from each category a limited number of persons to be interviewed—usually the national *sample* is between 1500 and 6500 [22]—on the assumption that the opinions expressed by this minuscule sample, drawn from each category, will be a fairly accurate index to the state of opinion in each of the categories as a whole. Then if the samples have been selected properly, the views expressed by this public in miniature presumably come very close to the opinion of the general public—subject to a reasonable margin of error. In making up the representative samples,[23]

[22] In letters to Senator Albert Gore (D-Tenn.) in 1960, George Gallup and Elmo Roper—the two most prominent American pollsters—reported that their average national samples are based on 1500 and 3000 persons in their respective polls. (*The New York Herald Tribune,* February 12, 1960.) Thus, a typical national Gallup survey evidently covers but .0013 of 1 per cent of the nation's current adult population. (In 1934 Gallup had become the first person seriously to apply sampling techniques to political phenomena.)

[23] There are two major types of sampling in *commercial* polling: *stratified-quota* and *random-area*. The former consists of selecting certain factors—e.g. number of voters, age, sex, community-size, economic status, party adherence in the population—and endeavoring to represent these in correct proportion to the sample. In random sampling, on the other hand, interviewers

polling organizations must know the distribution of the population according to region, rural or urban residence, age, sex, education, occupation, race, and economic status. The samples are usually checked against official census data, election statistics, and the like to make sure that each category of the public receives its proper weight.

After the samples have been carefully chosen and weighted, it is necessary to guard against possible distortion of the results at various stages in the polling process. The wording of the questions may be ambiguous or may prompt a particular response from the person polled. This difficulty has been overcome, in part, by careful preparation of test questionnaires, which may be revised a dozen times before the final poll is taken. At the personal interview, the attitude of the questioner, his timing, or the inflection of his voice may affect the response. Careful selection, and even special training, of interviewers avowedly help to guard against error from this source.

CLAIMS OF PROPONENTS. With only about thirty years of experience, the public-opinion polls have established a place for themselves, but it is difficult to assess their usefulness accurately. The nadir of the polls came in 1936, when the *Literary Digest,* using mail ballots, predicted Landon's election by a comfortable margin largely because it had concentrated on people with a telephone listing and/or an automobile registration! When Roosevelt won by 10,500,000 votes, the *Literary Digest* did the decent thing and went out of business! Today's champions of public opinion polls contend that they make it possible to measure opinion more frequently and at the moment most appropriate for particular issues; that opinion on particular issues can be polled in isolation, free from the distracting personal factors and the multiplicity of issues that confuse elections; and that the polls also enable us to inquire whether or not public opinion on an issue like the control of venereal disease, which gets little open public discussion, has crystallized sufficiently to indicate support of government action.

It has also been argued that both legislators and administrators can make use of the polls. Members of the legislature do engage in polling their constituents in quite unscientific ways, often asking the proverbial 'When did you stop beating your wife?' variety of question to support already estab-

---

are assigned certain geographical areas—e.g. a block, section, township, county, city—where he interviews every 'nth' individual located at an assigned position—e.g. the fourth one-family house from the southwest corner of a block, moving west. (See Albig, op. cit., ch. 11, especially pp. 200–208.) For a brief discussion of *private* polling, see the comments on the Michigan Survey Research Center (S.R.C.), *infra,* p. 394.

lished preferences. They might be able to take a firmer stand on public issues if they had a reliable means of testing the claims of the lobbyists to public support. It is sometimes suggested that the standing committees of Congress might use the polls to supplement their public hearings. In the administrative field, the United States Departments of Agriculture and Commerce have made use of polls in the working out of departmental policy as has the United States Information Agency. If public opinion polls came to be widely used by legislators and administrators, they could scarcely be conducted under private auspices. Also, it must be remembered that legislatures claim to be the experts on public opinion, and so are likely to impose sharp limits on the polling of public opinion by government departments.

Adverse Criticisms: QUESTIONABLE ACCURACY. Critics of the polls argue that the basic assumption on which the claim for accuracy in the polls rests is unjustified. They question whether opinion in each of the age, sex, economic, and other categories is homogeneous, whether the opinions expressed by the representative samples can safely be taken to be representative of the opinions held by the public as a whole. They also contend that, as the public concerned varies with each issue, the factors taken into account in making up the sample should vary with each issue.

EQUALIZATION OF OPINIONS. The polls are also criticized for assuming that every man's opinion is of equal importance. Men have equal voting power, it is true, but there is unequal influence on the votes of others in an election, and on the opinions of others in open discussion. Therefore, opinion should be assessed *qualitatively* as well as quantitatively. For example, it is necessary to give additional weight to the opinion of a political leader, although it would be extremely difficult to say how much. Through the use of what are called filter questions, the polling organizations have tried to meet this criticism. Those questions explore the information and knowledge on which individual opinions are based. In this way, some approach to qualitative analysis is presumably made possible.

DIFFICULTIES OF MEASUREMENT. However, in those instances in which the polls are prepared as a commercial product for consumption by the rank and file of newspaper readers, questionnaires normally cover a wide range of topics without going very deeply into the intricacies of any of them. Because of the nature of the market, there is a tendency to select the most recent and lively issues for measurement without sufficient regard for their complexity. For example, in 1956 a national magazine ran a readers' poll on 'who would be the victor in a hypothetical Eisenhower-F. D. Roosevelt election contest today.' (The results gave the victory to the latter.) If the polls are to measure more than the surface drift of the moment, they must use detailed questionnaires that go more deeply into particular issues, as some polling organizations have done. Only in this way is it possible to estimate the grounds on which an opinion is based, and to judge its intensity and stability.

SHALLOWNESS. Critics also urge that, in so far as the questionnaires fail to probe beneath the surface, the polls give a misleading impression of the firmness of opinion on public issues. If a majority appears in the 'yes' column, it is popularly taken to be a matured majority opinion. Possibly, however, it may be the result of a considerable number of unreflective, uninformed judgments, judgments that would be quickly modified by open discussion. How really meaningful *are* the so-called 'closed-end' questions—i.e. those calling for a 'yes,' 'no,' or 'don't know' response? Also, these opinions are generally given by people who will never have to assume direct responsibility for them. How many of them would be prepared to act on the basis of these opinions?

IRRATIONAL ELEMENTS. A frequent criticism is that the polls tend to introduce irrational elements into elections. The desire to be on the winning side is sufficiently strong and pervasive to be a factor of some importance in elections. In so far as polls taken in advance of an election suggest a pronounced drift of opinion, the very fact that the drift is indicated is likely to accentuate it. This point has been much discussed in recent years, in Congress and elsewhere, but without any definite conclusions. It is also urged that the polls tend to undermine the representative system by encouraging the uninformed to make judgments on complex issues, and by suggesting that majorities have made up their minds on such issues.[24] It has already been contended in the preceding chapter that the electorate is not qualified to rule directly on intricate technical matters. Professor Hans J. Morgenthau, a confirmed critic of polls, regards them as 'the curse of democracy. The man in the street doesn't walk around with his head full of foreign-policy alternatives.'[25] But the majority opinion inferred from the results of a poll does not become law, and as long as public officials are dubious of the accuracy of the results, the influence of the polls on governmental action is not likely to be excessive.

[24] For a very hostile evaluation of polling, stressing these particular points, see Lindsay Rogers, *The Pollsters* (New York: Alfred A. Knopf, 1949).
[25] As quoted by *Newsweek*, January 14, 1963.

The 1948 Debacle. The striking failure of the polls to forecast accurately the 1948 presidential election weakened public confidence in the accuracy of public opinion polls but did not destroy it. The episode brought about a searching re-examination of polling techniques by the polling organizations themselves and by other interested persons and bodies. No single explanation of the miscalculations was found. Rather, a number of suggested explanations applicable to one or the other of the polling organizations emerged. They were too confident of the accuracy of their methods. They made errors in sampling and in the interpreting of the data secured by sampling. In particular, they guessed wrong on the voting behavior of the persons who were *undecided* when they were polled, and they underestimated the last-minute changes of mind among those who did state a voting preference. Moreover, while 85 per cent to 90 per cent of those polled stated a voting preference, only about 50 per cent of the electorate actually voted in the election. In their letters to Senator Gore,[26] Messrs. Gallup and Roper agreed that their classic blunder in 1948 resulted from their failure to 'keep checking' until the end of the campaign. But Mr. Roper went on to concede an 'unfortunate secondary influence' of polling on the opinions of convention delegates, and suggested that reassuring prior poll results lulled Republicans into disastrous complacency during the 1948 campaign.

The test of these and other explanations may come as polling organizations continue to refine their techniques. Their forecast in the next three presidential elections, 1952, 1956, and 1960—and in Britain in 1959—did not establish any firm conclusion, however; for while the pollsters proved to be correct in predicting the elections of Presidents Eisenhower and Kennedy and the victory of the British Conservative party, they so hedged their predictions as to make them of questionable value. The accuracy of the polls has improved, but they still provide merely an approximate guide to facts about views and likely courses of action by the populace.

Evaluation. As long as there is any considerable disagreement on the accuracy with which the polls measure opinion, however, they are not likely to be used widely as part of governmental machinery for eliciting the will of the people on critical issues. In the meantime, they help to focus the interest of voters on public questions; make individuals conscious of the opinions

[26] Cf. fn. 23, *supra.* For discussions of the polls on the 1948 presidential elections, see Norman C. Meier and Harold W. Saunders, *The Polls and Public Opinion* (New York: Henry Holt, 1949), and 'The Opinion Polls and the 1948 U.S. Presidential Election: A Symposium,' *International Journal of Opinion and Aptitudes Research,* II (1949), 309–31, 451–591, and III (1949), 1–46, 157–204.

that predominate in groups other than their own; and stimulate the flow of discussion. They have been used with increasing frequency throughout the world, especially in Western Europe—e.g. the British Institute of Public Opinion, a Gallup affiliate. They enable politicians, officials, and others to get some impression of the nature and intensity of opinion on a variety of questions, and to follow trends of opinion over a period of time. As the techniques are further tested and developed, it *may* become possible to estimate public opinion on a specific issue at a given moment, not only with accuracy, but in such a way as to create a general conviction of accuracy. Many observers doubt, however, that such is attainable at all. Indeed, one of them—far from seeing polls as a stimulant of the political process—views them as having a 'constipating effect on the political process. It keeps things from happening. . . . Each poll catches the voter at a moment in time, and fixes him there, like a painting; but the political maturation that is going on in him is a process, and he himself may be largely unaware of it.' [27] Nonetheless, there is little doubt that—whatever the merit of polls and pollsters— the advent of the sample survey in the twentieth century represents a major technical development in the study of politics. It has yielded much previously undiscoverable, or only imperfectly covered, data, and has stimulated considerable new research. Especially praiseworthy has been the work of the well-financed, academically-oriented Survey Research Center at the University of Michigan, which has successfully employed a polling method of interviewing and reinterviewing a 'panel' of the same people, carefully selected to reflect the national electorate.[28]

Whether or not the content of public opinion can be usefully tested and measured, there is no doubt about its existence or its massive political influence in the long run. At a given time and place, public opinion seems amorphous and purposeless, 'like the windy blisters of a troubled water,' as Thomas Hobbes said in another connection. But over a longish period of time, and in a broader perspective set by historical study rather than by contemporary observation, there are surging tides and onrolling waves which at least have direction, if not purpose as well. Some of them beat hard at times on the rugged shores of the community consensus before they recede and change direction. And they do not beat entirely in vain, because the contours of the consensus are gradually changed by their action.

[27] Samuel Grafton, 'Polls and Politics,' *The New York Times Magazine,* February 21, 1960.
[28] Cf. A. Campbell, B. E. Converse, W. E. Miller, D. E. Stokes, *The American Voter* (New York: John Wiley & Sons, Inc., 1960).

The Tides of Opinion. Historians have noted these waves and tides in various countries. In the United States, for example, clearly marked alternating periods of radicalism and conservatism throughout the life of the Republic have been identified. To go no further back than the beginning of the twentieth century, the Theodore Roosevelt-Woodrow Wilson era was one with unmistakable radical and reforming tendencies, the period from Harding to Hoover marked a sharp swing to conservatism, and the reign of Franklin Roosevelt again brought a pronounced rise of radical temper in the electorate. In the first and last of these periods, a certain type of governmental action was encouraged and readily supported by public opinion; in the intervening period, measures of this same type rarely got effective support from public opinion.

Throughout the nineteenth century, and into the maturing twentieth, the tides of radical innovation have receded, to be followed by periods of more or less marked movements towards conservatism. Yet the consensus itself has been significantly modified. On the central issue of *laisser faire versus* government intervention in economic and social relationships, of individualism *versus* collectivism, the consensus has come to tolerate, if not actively to support, collectivist measures by government action in a scale that could not have been contemplated a hundred years ago. The reason for the shift is a widespread conviction, rightly or wrongly held, that, in a complex society, a considerable measure of collectivist action is necessary to enable individuals to live fuller lives.

DEMOCRATIC LEADERSHIP AND PUBLIC OPINION

The relation of political leadership to public opinion requires special attention. We concluded above that, as a practical matter in a democracy, public policy, the decision of what government is to do, always emerges from the competition, clash, and compromise of a great variety of individual and group interests. This might be taken to mean that political leadership is a passive agent which contributes nothing to solutions but waits for the blind jostling of selfish competing interests to reach an equilibrium, out of which the solution emerges automatically. If this were so, we might well despair of political leadership as well as of public opinion. There is, however, an interpretation of democratic politics that assigns important roles to both political leadership and ill-informed, vague, fluctuating public opinion, and rescues them from futility.

The first point to recall is that there is, in a working democracy, a community consensus to which the great bulk of the people subscribe. The consensus does not consist of a set of specific solutions for current problems but rather of a set of beliefs about the ends and purposes that community life should serve. The strongest of these in the democracies in question here is the belief that the community should protect and develop individual personality, and that individual liberty is a highly important means of fostering and expressing personality.

Historically, the general acceptance of the belief in individual liberty has been associated with a related belief in the sanctity of private property as a buttress of individual personality. The latter belief is not as unqualifiedly or as widely held as formerly, but it is still of great significance, as witness the relative infrequency of theft and robbery. True, the criminal law forbids theft and robbery, but its edicts could not be enforced effectively if they did not accord with community sentiment, as witness the American prohibition law.

There is always much going on in social life that seems to flout or contradict the deeper beliefs, and these beliefs give no obvious directions about what to do to bring erring social practice into conformity with them. Massive private property, as represented by present-day capitalist economic organization, seems to limit liberty and dwarf personality for many. How far this is true is not utterly clear, because we do not know what alternative forms of economic organization would do for liberty and personality. Nor is it clear in full detail what restrictions on private property in the form of governmental regulation of economic life will bring a net enlargement of liberty. As Chapter V indicated, the electorates have accepted and governments have incorporated into their activities, substantial restrictions on the freedom of businessmen to do what they like with their property. But the debate about what more and what next still goes on. It could scarcely be otherwise in communities that believe both in individual liberty and the sanctity of private property.

It would be easy to laugh at communities that hold doggedly to contradictory beliefs. The beliefs, however, may not be inherently contradictory. What seems to be going on, at any rate, is a tenacious search for a reconciliation between them which can be incorporated into social and economic practice.

This is only one illustration of several that might be given to show that the consensus, of itself alone, rarely makes clear what to do. The consensus does, however, limit what the interests ranged on either side of the dispute can get—and hold—by pressure on government through political channels. It also limits the choice of solutions for which politicians can hope to get the support of electoral majorities.

Leadership and the Consensus. The purpose of discussion is to search for solutions in harmony with the underlying consensus. The function of competing political parties and political leaders is the same. Democratic political leadership calls for two main qualities, which, of course, the actual leaders do not always possess. It calls for ingenuity and imagination in discovering accommodations between conflicting interests which will be at least tolerable to those concerned on both sides. The political leader needs an extensive knowledge and understanding of the conflict for which he proposes a solution. It calls also for a man who knows by heart the source and course of the deep springs of community belief and feeling, and who can thus perceive what solutions can be floated and supported on the consensus.

Such leadership is genuinely creative. It creates the necessary equilibrium between group interests. It finds the compromise which public opinion rises surely to support. It redeems the politician from being merely a broker and huckster. It is indispensable in the recurring crises of democratic societies.

The democratic leader's search is not for the ideal solution. That may be easy to see in a particular crisis, but it is often impracticable of application by a government based on discussion and consent. Lincoln the statesman knew the ideal solution of the slavery question. Lincoln the politician sought long for an accommodation that would limit the evil of slavery without outraging the belief in the sanctity of property and rending the Union, always hoping that, with time and without violence, the ideal solution could be reached. He failed in part, but no political leadership can cope with sectional and group intransigence which disrupts the underlying consensus.

Public Opinion as the Final Judge. On this interpretation, public opinion is not a sovereign legislator framing specific solutions to specific problems. It is rather a judge who hears the political leaders, the advocates of specific competing solutions, and decides between them. More correctly, it is *the court of last resort,* to which only the more stubbornly contested cases go. The final court of appeal in a judicial system does not render judgment on every dispute. In the same way, the political leaders and permanent officials who make up the government at any given moment make many decisions on which public opinion never renders any perceptible verdict. But just as the lower courts in the judicial system are guided by the precedents and past decisions of the court of last resort, so those who currently control the government are guided by their estimate of what public opinion will stand for or support. Public opinion is always being taken into account, but there is no assurance that the ruling politicians of the moment will not misinterpret it, or even try to circumvent it. Although error may rule perversely in the lower courts for a time, the final tribunal sooner or later brings correction. The democratic hope is that at a certain temperature in public affairs, public opinion will be able to resolve on a judgment that rests squarely and securely on the community consensus.

Although the definition regrettably trails off in vagueness, public opinion is better understood, in the words of Lord Bryce, as something 'impalpable as the wind,' than as a majority will or general will originating and decreeing solutions to particular political issues. When it is thus understood, some of the obstacles in the way of public opinion's performing its function seems less formidable, although they remain too serious to be ignored. The late Raymond Clapper observed with insight: 'Never underestimate the intelligence of the American people; and never overestimate its knowledge of facts.'

Public Opinion and Liberal Democracy. The problem of public opinion can now be stated in summary form. It is widely agreed that public opinion must rule in a democracy. But the facts on which the public must form its judgments are almost innumerable, and hard to discover, sift, and interpret correctly. Because of the limitations of language and the emotional overtones of words, communication is often blocked and distorted. The difficulties of communication are intensified because the possibilities of distortion are deliberately exploited by propaganda in many quarters, because the public is so large and scattered, and because it is hard to persuade large sections of it to attend closely.

The formation of public opinion on the facts, once they are communicated, is a complex process, always influenced by whims and unforeseeable circumstances. The entire public almost never concentrates its thoughts on one specific issue. There is always a movement of individuals in and out of the particular public attending to any one issue. Even among those who give sustained attention over a long period, opinions fluctuate in response to varying moods, the introduction of new facts, and the play of discussion.

Thus it is rarely possible to know whether a majority of the electorate has reached a firm judgment on a question, or what that judgment is. Also, the electorate is unable to formulate satisfactory solutions to many problems in which highly technical considerations have to be taken into account. In such issues, it is generally limited to choosing between alternative solutions proposed to it by political leaders.

If our concepts of democracy and public opinion require that there should be a clear majority decision in every issue, and that the majority should always rule, close study of the actual working of democracy will be disillusioning in the extreme. However, it has been urged here that the substance of democracy as it has been practiced in the countries in question is *a flexible system of adjustment between individuals and groups carried on under ultimate popular control rather than the direct enforcement of a popular will.* Also, it may be doubted whether many of those who subscribe to the majoritarian view of democracy and public opinion really hold it in any strict literal sense. Associated with the demand that public opinion must always decide and rule is the further insistence that democracy desperately needs leadership if it is to survive. Leadership must not become a prisoner of public opinion. To the contrary, public opinion responds to leadership; it has a way of accommodating itself to successful political action.[29] Certainly, if leadership means anything it means something more than automatic registration of a majority will. On the interpretation offered here, it consists of ingenuity and imagination in devising, for the adjustment of conflicting interests, compromises that accord with the deeper community beliefs about the fitness of things. Public opinion does not invent these compromises, but it is the final judge of their adequacy.

PUBLIC OPINION IN THE DICTATORSHIPS

In the dictatorships, open competition in the spread of information and ideas is as intolerable to the leaders as are competing political parties. The one political party settles authoritatively what is to be done in the public interest, and it does not allow its decisions to be shaken by open discussion. But even dictators need co-operation from their citizens, and co-operation depends on a favorable public opinion. Consequently, dictators spare no effort to analyze opinion.[30] Furthermore, since the public interest is paramount, and the actions to be taken in the public interest have been authori-

---

[29] For a strong argument against 'paying undue heed' to public opinion, see Hans J. Morgenthau, 'Is World Public Opinion a Myth?' *The New York Times Magazine,* March 25, 1962.

[30] Thus Mao Tse-tung: 'We must follow wherever the masses go. In no other way can we lead them.' As quoted in William Goodman, *The Two-Party System in the United States,* 2nd ed. (New York: D. Van Nostrand, 1960), p. 459.

tatively settled, it follows that everyone should support these actions. Thus the dictators want unity, and even unanimity, of opinion, and they use every device known to propagandists to secure it, or, at any rate, to create the impression that it has been secured. Governments in the dictatorships control and direct all the media of communication.

Nazi and Fascist Repression. The governments of Fascist Italy and Nazi Germany asserted very effective control over public opinion by a number of methods. First, they enacted laws creating a long list of political crimes. Vigorous criticism of the government and its policies became in both countries crimes, for which extremely severe punishments were imposed under secret and unfair methods of trial. Government spies and secret police were everywhere, and it became extremely dangerous to talk politics freely. Thus free discussion of public affairs was taken out of the sphere of public opinion.

Second, both governments brought the press, radio, motion picture films, and all other media of communication under their direct control. One could not publish a newspaper, or be a working journalist, without first securing a license from the government. Licenses were granted only to persons who could be counted on to give slavish support to the government. All newspapers had to file copies of their output with the government so that their loyalty could be checked. Any failure of support or any criticism of government policy would lead to a cancellation of the license. In this way, the Nazis and Fascists made sure that the newspapers would not discuss forbidden subjects. It was an effective censorship.

Radio was controlled by similar methods. In Germany, the government owned and operated the radio. It subsidized receiving sets with a limited range and organized mass listening groups whom the Nazi leaders then would harangue. Dr. Joseph Goebbels, the propaganda genius of Nazi Germany, whose official title was Minister of Propaganda and Enlightenment, made radio his most effective instrument. In Italy, radio was in the hands of a private monopoly rigorously regulated by the government, which decided both what would be said and what would not be said.

Nazi and Fascist Propaganda. As the use of the radio indicates, the Nazis and Fascists were not satisfied merely to restrict and limit negatively the use made of the media of communication. They wanted to use them positively to indoctrinate the people. So the third method for controlling public opinion was to set up a government agency to drench the public with propaganda. The Ministry of Propaganda in both countries provided the bulk of the news and the ideas that went out over the air waves and into the news-papers and periodicals. Day after day, the newspapers would give the same emphasis in the news and stress identical themes in discussion under the centralized direction of the Ministry of Propaganda.

In addition, the Nazi and Fascist governments carried their propaganda into the schools, into the many youth organizations they fostered, and into every organized group and association that they allowed to exist. In these circumstances, public opinion was no longer distilled by free discussion among the people. It was instead a synthetic nostrum of the Ministry of Propaganda. The highly centralized governmental organization bound the citizen's body and efforts to the tasks set him by the party leaders. The highly centralized propaganda machine tried to shackle his mind as well.

PUBLIC OPINION IN THE SOVIET UNION

Unlike Nazi Germany and Fascist Italy, the Soviet Union has not estab-lished a Ministry of Propaganda. The Soviet press is, however, under the strict control of the state and the Communist party. As in all other spheres of Soviet life, the party exercises its control through organized participation and through the placing of reliable party members in key positions. *Pravda* (Truth), the party's daily, is the most influential Soviet newspaper; its prestige exceeds even that of *Izvestia* (News), the government's organ. As in the Nazi and Fascist dictatorships, and despite the specific guarantees of Article 125 of the Soviet Constitution of 1936, the government controls the press through the device of permitting only the most ardent supporters of the existing regime to hold responsible journalistic jobs, and through the operation of a censorship agency whose task it is to assure that every pub-lication in the Soviet Union meets the requirements of the state. In the case of newspapers this means not only that certain stipulated topics must be ignored, but also that specified other matters *must* be discussed.

As a result of this censorship, the content of the Soviet press is vastly different from that of newspapers in the liberal democracies. News of an economic nature is given the most prominent place, the biggest headline usually proclaiming a victory on the production front. The sensationalism of some sections of the British, French, and American press, which is based on the overemphasis of sexual crimes and on representations of alluring female figures, is paralleled in the Soviet Union by a sensational treatment of political crimes and the printing of bulging production figures. The U.S.S.R. has set up its own 'public opinion poll' system, which is illustrative of the use of poll data for self-fulfilling propaganda.

Criticism—within Limits. It has been suggested above that dictators need the co-operation of their citizens. The Soviet leaders know that enthusiastic co-operation is hard to get without two-way communication between rulers and ruled. Whether in Leningrad or Chicago, individuals like to be consulted, to have a chance to say their say and to vent their criticism. Indeed, the expression of criticism is a safety valve for releasing pent-up annoyances and frustrations. Accordingly, within limits which he is never allowed to forget, the individual citizen is allowed—and even invited—to discuss and make suggestions on public issues. These limits cannot be defined precisely in positive terms, but a fair impression of them can be gained by seeing what matters are placed beyond the realm of free discussion. Generally, there are three broad forbidden areas:

One, basic Communist theory, as defined by the leaders, must not be questioned. Two, the top leaders themselves must not be 'unduly' criticized. Three, once governmental or party policy on some matters has been authoritatively *decided,* its correctness cannot be debated. On the whole, matters not falling in these three categories are left open for public discussion. Since criticism in the realms of high policy is excluded, discussion is largely confined to matters of detail, of the effectiveness with which policies and objectives are being pursued in daily administration. Here it certainly does not lack vigor, often taking the form of vitriolic denunciations of state officials and state agencies that are thought to be falling down on the job. The public thus has a chance to vent its discontent, and the leaders are able to gauge the drift of opinions on various matters and to strain some useful ideas from the flow of criticism.

IN THE PRESS. The Soviet press is one of the most effective media for this kind of Soviet 'self-criticism.' Its contents are mainly composed of government press releases and numerous letters from citizens describing conditions in all parts of the Soviet Union. The amateur journalists, who write these letters or articles, report on the successes or failures of a variety of activities and enterprises. Their stories are usually simply told and are always based on personal experience. The otherwise dull-gray uniformity of the Soviet press is greatly lightened by these personal accounts of Soviet life, and many students of the Soviet press attribute the undoubted popularity of Soviet newspapers to the articles and letters written by these far-flung voluntary correspondents. Another bright spot is the illustrated humor magazine, *Krokodil,* with cartoons that poke fun at certain aspects of Soviet society and government. Moreover, much telling literary criticism of the excesses of the Stalin era was widely popularized and disseminated in the early 1960's.[31]

The Press an Instrument of Government. Despite the measure of freedom accorded the Soviet citizen in expressing his views on a variety of subjects, no assurance is given the correspondent that his contribution will be published. All letters to the editor are subject to 'clearance' in the editorial office of the party-controlled newspaper. The press is closely censored. The censorship determines what the Soviet citizen shall be told about what is going on inside the country, and in the world outside. The Iron Curtain, as it is called, though it has been lifted somewhat for limited travel in the U.S.S.R. by foreign tourists, not only curtails sharply what the Western world can find out about events in the Soviet Union; it also insulates the Soviet citizen from all contact with foreign ideas, and limits his knowledge of facts and events in the outside world to what his leaders tell him. Essentially, the press is a device used by the government for creating consent and selling the official policy to the masses whose sales resistance is low in the absence of any competing commodity.

OTHER MEDIA. The Soviet radio and other media are controlled in much the same manner as the newspapers. The government of the Soviet Union, which, at first, had to deal with an overwhelmingly illiterate population, has relied heavily on public posters and moving pictures for the moulding of opinion. Literature, art, music, and the sciences are all under government censorship or control. Education, which has been notably advanced by the Communist dictatorship, has also been drawn into the service of the party dogma. The rulers see to it that education in Communist doctrine and government policy is not confined to the schools, but is carried on in the professional, recreational, cultural, and occupational associations, and in the armed services.

In this way, the Soviet leaders eliminate all widespread public discussion of ideas and information that challenge or throw doubt on the government. To fill the void thus created, all channels of communication are used to bring to the people the 'facts' they should know and the ideas they must

[31] For example, see the 1962 publications of Yevgeny Yevtushenko's poem accusing Stalin of anti-Semitism and of the sensational autobiographical revelations of life in a Stalin forced labor camp in the 1950's by Alexander Solzhenitsyn, *One Day in the Life of Ivan Denisovich* (New York: E. P. Dutton Co. and Frederick A. Praeger, 1963).

accept. Public opinion, if it can be said to exist at all in the Soviet Union, is not the product of free discussion, nor is it the final judge of the policies of the government.

Suggested References for Further Reading

Albig, W., *Modern Public Opinion* (McGraw-Hill, 1956).
Almond, G. A., *The American People and Foreign Policy,* rev. ed. (Praeger, 1960).
Bean, L. H., *How To Predict Elections* (Knopf, 1948).
Bentley, A. F., *The Process of Government,* 4th ed. (Principia, 1955).
Blaisdell, D. C., *American Democracy Under Pressure* (Ronald, 1957).
Cater, D., *The Fourth Branch of Government* (Houghton Mifflin, 1959).
Chafee, Z., Jr., *Government and Mass Communication* (Chicago, 1947).
The Commission on Freedom of the Press, *A Free and Responsible Press* (Chicago, 1947).
Coons, J. E. (Ed.), *Freedom and Responsibility in Broadcasting* (Northwestern, 1962).
Eckstein, H., *Pressure Group Politics: The Case of the British Medical Association* (Stanford, 1960).
Ehrmann, H. W. (Ed.), *Interest Groups on Four Continents* (U. of Pittsburgh, 1958).
Engler, R., *The Politics of Oil* (Macmillan, 1962).
Fenton, J. M., *In Your Opinion* (Little, Brown, 1960).
Finer, S. E., *Anonymous Empire* (Pall Mall, 1959).
Gallup, G. A., *A Guide to Public Opinion Polls,* 2nd ed. (Princeton, 1948).
Harter, D. L., and J. Sullivan, *Propaganda Handbook* (20th Century Press, 1953).
Inkeles, A., *Public Opinion in Soviet Russia* (Harvard, 1950).
Katz, D., D. Cartwright, S. Eldersveld, and A. Lee, *Public Opinion and Propaganda* (Dryden, 1954).
Kelly, J. K., *Professional Public Relations and Political Power* (Johns Hopkins, 1956).
Key, V. O., Jr., *Public Opinions and American Democracy* (Knopf, 1961).
Lacy, D., *Freedom and Communications* (U. of Illinois, 1961).
Latham, E., *Group Basis of Politics* (Cornell, 1952).
Lippmann, W., *The Public Philosophy* (Little, Brown, 1955).
——, *The Phantom Public* (Macmillan, 1925).
——, *Public Opinion* (Macmillan, 1925).
Matthews, T. H., *The Sugar Pill: An Essay on Newspapers* (Simon & Schuster, 1958).
McPhee, W. N., and W. A. Glaser, *Public Opinion & Congressional Elections* (Free Press, 1962).
Merrill, I. R., and C. H. Proctor, *Political Persuasion by Television* (Michigan State, 1959).
Meynaud, J., *Les Groupes de pression en France* (Armand Colin, 1958).
Milbrath, L., *The Washington Lobbyists* (Rand McNally, 1963).
Mosca, G., *The Ruling Class* (McGraw-Hill, 1961, paper ed.).
Packard, V. O., *The Hidden Persuaders* (McKay, 1958).

————, *The Status Seekers* (McKay, 1959).

Potter, A., *Organized Groups in British National Politics* (Faber & Faber, 1961).

Report of the Royal Commission on the Press, 1947–1949 (H.M. Stationery Office, 1949).

Rogers, L., *The Pollsters* (Knopf, 1949).

Rosenau, J. N., *Public Opinion and Foreign Policy* (Random House, 1961).

Rowse, A. E., *Slanted News* (Beacon, 1957).

Sargant, W. W., *The Battle for the Mind* (Heinemann, 1957).

Schramm, W., *Mass Communications,* 2nd ed. (U. of Illinois, 1960).

Schriftgiesser, K., *The Lobbyists* (Little, Brown, 1951).

Schubert, G. A., *The Public Interest* (Free Press, 1961).

Stepman, F. F., and P. J. McCarthy, *Sampling Opinions* (Wiley, 1958).

Stewart, J. P., *British Pressure Groups* (Oxford, 1958).

Truman, D. B., *The Governmental Process* (Knopf, 1951).

Yevtushenko, Y., *A Precocious Autobiography* (Dutton, 1963).

XI

Representation and Electoral Systems

INTRODUCTORY

Historical Background. To understand what this so-called representation is or can be, it is necessary to recall some history and venture some analysis. The democracies of the ancient world practiced *direct* democracy. The citizens of the city-state *participated directly* in the making of laws and the governing of the city. Lacking the device of representation, the Roman Republic was unable to provide for effective popular participation in government when it expanded too far beyond the confines of the city. Representation is a medieval invention, apparently originating in the practice of the early Christian Church in calling together representative councils to deal with matters affecting the government of Christendom. With the emergence of kings in the feudal societies of Europe, the custom of calling representatives from the communities under their sway developed. Simon de Montfort called representatives of the counties and boroughs to Westminster in 1265 with momentous results, but he did not invent representation. Nor did Edward I who, in 1295, so capably brought together representatives from all the segments of society he considered helpful that the meeting he called has ever since been referred to as the 'Model Parliament.' Representation was already widely used in the medieval world.

EMPHASIS ON THE LOCAL COMMUNITY. In the thirteenth century, and in most instances up to the nineteenth century, the county or borough was a close-knit community with a high degree of economic self-sufficiency in which individuals were bound together by customary relationships. What

406

division of labor and economic specialization there was, was local, not national and international. Without the modern means of communication, there was little movement of individuals from one community to another and little intercourse between communities. People lived and died and found the entire meaning of their lives in a single area. The dialects, which often still differ from county to county, testify to the distinctiveness of the communities that were represented.

They were social unities in much the same sense in which today, rightly or wrongly, we attribute unity to the nation. We have little difficulty in thinking that the government or an ambassador can represent the common interests of the nation in international negotiations. It used to be just as easy, and perhaps easier, to think that a representative could represent the county or borough in the councils of the monarch. He could air the grievances of his community and combine with other representatives in petitioning the monarch to redress them.

EMPHASIS ON INDIVIDUALS. An election district today is not such a community with a distinctive unity of its own which one man can represent. Election districts are now strips of territory in which so many voters live, and their boundaries are always being readjusted so as to contain roughly the same number of voters in each district, and thus to give representation by population. This practice of readjusting the boundaries of election districts gives the clue to the modern theory of representation. It is individuals and not communities which are represented, although for the sake of convenience a territorial basis is customarily employed. This is partly owing to the modern emphasis on individualism. But the older theory could not be maintained today because no longer do local communities possess a distinctive unity. Economic specialization transcends the local community and also the nation. The vital interests of individuals are linked to persons, circumstances, and events far beyond the locality. It should be noted, however, that here practice does not entirely accord with theory. The member of the legislature does represent certain common interests of his constituency, as when he manages to secure a new highway or a new post office.

Modern transport and communications have given extraordinary mobility to the population, making them a nation of transients without deep consciousness of locality. As has already been pointed out, the great ease of communication has facilitated the organization of many communities of interest, economic, social, and cultural, which are at least nation-wide and not connected with any locality. The local undertaker is now likely to be at least as much interested in the shoptalk of the annual embalmers' convention as in the death of his neighbors. The result is that the older social unity based on territory has been broken into a multitude of diverse specialized interests. And governments today are engaged in all sorts of activities that can help or harm these specialized interests, thus inviting people to mix calculations concerning their narrow specialized interests with their opinions about national public policy.

The older localism and the theory of representation appropriate to it have been outmoded. It may help to emphasize the change to point to a remaining vestige of the older theory: The Constitution of the United States gives equal representation to the states in the Senate. The states are still regarded as communities that can be represented, and are thus entitled to be represented as such, not merely as heterogeneous collections of individuals. But even here, the forces just discussed have been at work, and the unity of particular states in the federation is somewhat artificial and pretentious.

EMPHASIS ON THE NATION. The situation today is profoundly different in another respect. As long as the monarch was in reality the government he expressed the general interests of the nation, however defective that expression may have been. Even if he was no more than a leader in war, he made and executed the policy of national defense. The representatives to his councils acknowledged this, although grudgingly. Their function was to act as a check on him, limiting the demands made by the whole on the parts. The monarch and his civil service withstood these pressures, asserting their interpretation of what was needed to maintain the unity and integrity of the country.

When the monarch was reduced to a figurehead or dethroned, the legislature composed of representatives of local interests became supreme. If the members of the legislature represented only their constituencies, who now spoke for the nation? It was a recognition of the inescapable necessity of some body with a unified conception of the national interest which led the framers of the first republican Constitution of France to declare that the deputy—i.e. the member of the legislature—belongs to the nation. He was to represent the nation and speak for it and not for the narrow purposes of his constituency.

The same provision appeared in the Constitution of the Weimar Republic, established in Germany in 1919 at the end of World War I. However, despite some distinguished advocacy of it, this view never caught hold in Britain and especially the United States, where it is the general assumption that the member of the legislature represents the electors of his constituency. Despite this seeming defect in Anglo-American theory, Britain and the United States have not suffered as much from lack of national unity as have continental European countries. The explanation is that theory is of little account unless it is workable in practice, and to say that the deputy belongs to the nation accomplishes nothing unless the deputy and a majority of his fellows can agree on what should be done on behalf of the nation. Until the grim necessities of the atomic age compelled some changes, most Continental democracies—save the Scandinavian countries and Switzerland—never seemed to attain this agreement, being plagued by a multiple-party system, while the two-party system in Anglo-American countries has almost always produced a majority view of the national interest.

Without going into the many factors of history and geography that are responsible for this difference, the short explanation is that most of the democracies on the continent of Europe have always been split by so many deep cleavages that they could never get to the point of agreeing that there were only two important sides to the story. There were always many important sides to the story requiring narration at length by many political parties. Britain and the United States have always had a deeper political unity, a wider acceptance of the liberal democratic political ideals outlined in Chapter II. Partly because of this, they have always been the foremost experts in working out practical procedures for mediating differences. With the possible exceptions stated above, the processes of discussion have always worked more temperately and more fruitfully in the Anglo-American world than anywhere else.

At any rate, the important point for present purposes is that when the monarch lost his power and gave up his function of integrating the parts of the country as a whole, political parties took his place. As we shall explain later, the executive and civil service govern the country; but their ability to do it depends on the support of a political party that has won a majority of the electorate. As has already been argued, political parties in a two-party system are not divisive but unifying influences. In their never-ceasing search for votes they build bridges across local and personal prejudices, sectional and occupational antagonisms. In a democracy, which cannot fall back on some authoritative statement of the national interest but must always manufacture the national interest out of the consent of the people, the unifying function is indispensable. In societies where the ultimate political ideal is the releasing of individual personality in conditions of freedom, the political parties are a procedural device for integrating the inevitable diversity of views into the unity of action that is vital for the running of any government. The burden of European experience shows that where political parties fail to perform this task, dictators arise who do. But, as we have already seen, they do it by destroying spontaneity and stifling diversity—by negating the liberal democratic ideals.

DIRECT DEMOCRACY

The direct democracy, to which we briefly alluded at the beginning of this discussion, is an attempt to get around the problem of representation—to outflank it. Generally, it takes one of three forms today: the *referendum,* the *initiative,* and the *recall.* A fourth, the historic *New England town meeting* (or any other town meeting), while still practiced on a limited scale, is necessarily confined to small local communities and school districts.

The Referendum. Briefly, the referendum—or, as it is still sometimes called, the *plebiscite*—is simply the referral of a question to the electorate on the ballot, usually at the time of a general election. This question may be one of general policy ('Do you favor the sale of alcoholic beverages in your county?'); it may be on a piece of legislation (such as the passage of a soldiers' bonus); it may be on a proposed constitutional amendment (such as the extension of the term of office of the governor of a state); or it may be on a measure initiated by the people (such as appropriations for a new school). Referenda generally become law upon receiving a majority of the votes cast.

A referendum may be either on a part of or on the entire bill. It may be *compulsory* in the sense that the constitution requires the legislature to submit a certain measure or constitutional amendment to the populace, or it may be *voluntary,* whereby the legislative body uses its discretion whether or not to refer the question to the people. In some of the American states a certain number of voters—5 per cent of the registered electorate in Oregon, for example—may *compel* the referral of any question at all. In certain other states some types of legislation are exempt from the referendum process. Thus, in Massachusetts all laws relating to religion, religious institutions, the status of judges, and the establishment or abolition of courts, are constitutionally beyond the pale of referenda.

The Initiative. Under the initiative a certain per cent of the voters—usually between five and ten—will propose a bill, which then may become law in one of two ways: by approval of the legislature or by endorsement in a referendum at a subsequent election. An initiative is customarily confined to proposals for ordinary legislation, but in parts of the United States (e.g. California) and in Switzerland it is also employed for the purpose of proposing constitutional amendments. The initiative is a much severer test of the ingenuity and intelligence of the voter because here he creates and does not simply criticize others. And since it may well be the 'brain child' of a small group of citizens, the initiative represents a possible source of special or minority legislation, which flies in the face of the democratic concept of majority government.

The Recall. In some respects the recall, although employed far less frequently than the other two devices of direct democracy, is not only the most interesting but also the most controversial and most dramatic of the three. The recall, in short, permits the electorate to remove elected public officials from office prior to the expiration of their term, for whatever reason deemed valid by the voters. In view of the gravity of that step, initiation of a recall vote requires the approval of a substantial per cent of the electorate, ordinarily at least 25 per cent of the vote cast in the preceding election. In the recall election itself, a majority of all the votes cast, or sometimes even of all those registered, is necessary to recall the official.

While not used as frequently as the referendum and the initiative, the recall is not merely a theoretical example of direct democracy in the United States. Mayors of Los Angeles, Detroit, and Seattle have been recalled. The Governor, Attorney General, and Secretary of Agriculture of North Dakota were recalled in 1921, although the same electorate proceeded only one year later to elect its just recalled Governor Frazier to the U.S. Senate! A move by the voters of Wisconsin to recall U.S. Senator McCarthy in 1954 failed by a narrow margin. Close to 1000 cities of 10,000 inhabitants and over have provided for the recall. And Oklahoma, at least until World War II, had the interesting record of attempting either to recall or to impeach practically all its governors!

Present Usage. Direct democracy has almost disappeared on the *national* level of government, except in Switzerland. There the intiative and the referendum are still used with some frequency. In April 1963, for example, the Swiss, by a vote of 537,387 to 268,858, rejected a proposed constitutional amendment that would have banned the manufacture, import, transit, use, and storage of atomic weapons. Where direct democracy is used in other countries, it is confined to subordinate levels of government. Thus, in 1963 in the United States, where *direct* democracy is not practiced on the *national* level, twenty-one states provided for the referendum, nineteen for the initiative, and twelve for the recall. In addition to the states, however, a considerable number of local communities has some form of direct democracy.

Evaluation. The advocates of direct democracy attribute the ills of representative democracy to the political parties. They insist that parties get between the electorate and the legislature, and that the legislators forget their pledges and enact bad, or fail to enact good, legislation because the parties that dominate the legislature serve interests other than those of the people. Underlying this analysis is the assumption that the electorate could be counted upon for wisdom and a unified conception of the public good, if only it were enabled to express itself! By authorizing the voters to *by-pass* the parties and the legislature through direct democracy they would be able to participate *directly* in lawmaking.

While the various schemes of direct democracy have never had any serious advocacy in Britain, the experience of many American states with political corruption and boss-controlled legislatures has provided a great temptation for popular intervention. Indeed, direct legislation by the electorate has put some useful legislation in force in some states. It may also be of some use as a standing threat against parties and legislatures that have eluded popular control. However, there are other ways of restoring a measure of popular control. The defects of direct legislation outweigh its merits:

IGNORES THE COMPLEXITY OF LAWMAKING. In the first place, lawmaking in a complex society is not a simple process. For example, to many, the moral issue in proposals for prohibition may be quite clear, to others not. The effectiveness of such legislation if enacted depends on its detailed provisions such as the definition of 'intoxicating,' what is a 'medicinal use,' the apparatus for controlling import and manufacture, and the question whether it is purchase and sale only, or use as well, which are to be prohibited. These are complex questions. And if use is prohibited, enforcement depends on how far the police are to be authorized to search premises and persons on suspicion. Who will say that such interference with the right of privacy is not another and more complex question?

Legislation of this kind and in this detail cannot be placed on the ballot in readily understandable terms, let alone terms enabling the public to discern the deeper issues involved. Complex legislation should only be enacted after extended debate and discussion have eliminated crudities and obscurities, foreseen difficulties and provided for them, and tempered the wind as much as possible to the particular private interests that are to be shorn by the law. Direct legislation requires the voter to take it or leave it in the raw form in which the zealots framed it, without the clarification that comes from discussion and without any modification by minority protests.

ASSUMES A UNIFIED POPULAR WILL. Proposals of this kind assume that the laws that should be made for the common good are simple questions, on which a unified popular will infallibly singles out the correct answer. In fact, the electorate entertains many views shaded in various ways, and a majority opinion has to be created by organization and effort. The parties are professional organizers of opinion and they do not ignore such opportunities. The multiplying of the occasions of voting is not likely to diminish greatly the power of party machines. The special interests that will be directly advanced or prejudiced by the proposed law spend money and pour out propaganda. For example, experience shows that both the temperance and the liquor interests can be counted on for zeal and overstatement, and they will bombard the electorate with biased information and arguments in plebiscites on the liquor question. The influence of parties and special interests is by no means eliminated.

Direct legislation is supposed to educate the citizen and revive his interest in public affairs. But, generally speaking—although some experienced observers emphatically dissent here[1]—experience in the United States does not support this argument. There, roughly half the voters who go to the polls and vote for candidates for office fail to vote by design or oversight, on the laws submitted for their decision on the same ballot. Indeed, numerous measures have been passed or rejected with little more than a quarter of the electorate voting. This suggests that many voters feel themselves more competent to choose men than to make laws. The instinct is sound. If the candidates put forward by the parties are not to their liking, those who feel keenly the need to improve the quality of political life can take more effective steps than resort to direct legislation. Through active participation in party affairs, they can influence the choice of candidates with a smaller expenditure of time and energy than it takes to learn enough to vote wisely on particular measures.

[1] Cf. James K. Pollock, *The Initiative and Referendum in Michigan* (Ann Arbor: University of Michigan Press, 1940).

To revert to the discussion in Chapter IX, it is clear that direct legislation flies in the face of the principle that the political parties take the responsibility for public policy and for administering and enforcing the laws, and that the voters do all they can as voters when they examine the stewardship of the parties at election times. The people cannot directly make the laws and govern the country. Perhaps a prohibtion law cannot be enforced at all. Certainly it cannot be enforced except when the executive, the government of the day, puts great vigor and determination behind it. If the people want the laws enforced, the only way open to them is to concentrate responsibility for the detailed provision of the laws and their administration on the political party that currently enjoys the support of a majority, and then punish it for its failures at election time. Between elections they can warn their parties of their desires and intentions by influence on the local party associations. It is a political axiom that the members of the parties in the legislature are extremely sensitive to clearly expressed opinion.

THE DILEMMAS OF REPRESENTATION

Two major dilemmas present themselves to the student of representation. One is concerned with the already introduced problem 'who or what' is to be represented,[2] the other with 'how' representation is to be made effective. To resolve the latter dilemma, a decision must be made between geographical (territorial) and occupation (functional) representation—i.e. whether representation in the legislative body ought to be based on residence or on occupation. The former dilemma compels a choice between two different concepts of representation: one which places the nation as a whole first on the scale of values, the other which looks upon the local constituency as being of primary importance. These two dilemmas must now be analyzed separately.

THE FIRST DILEMMA

The Meaning of Representation. Mr. Noah Webster, in defining the verb 'to represent,' demonstrated well its enigmatic nature. In one sense it

---

[2] For an interesting, although debatable, assignment of the representative into the roles of 'trustee,' 'delegate,' and 'politico,' see Heinz Eulau, *et al.,* 'The Role of the Representative: Some Empirical Observations on the Theory of Edmund Burke,' *American Political Science Review,* 53 (September 1959), 742.

means 'to serve with *delegated* or *deputed* authority.' In the other, it signifies 'to give *one's own impression and judgments.*' The supplied italics convey the first dilemma: whom or what does the representative represent? That he is intended to be a link between the people and their government is quite clear. But what sort of a link? Is he to be a mere 'servant,' an 'errand-boy,' a faithful mouthpiece for Dogpatch? Little more than a 'tool,' to use a favored American colloquialism? Or is he to be a link who will be free to express his views and cast his vote in accordance with his own analysis and judgments on behalf of his constituents, *but with due regard to the fact that the latter are but one segment of the whole nation?* It is tempting to give a rapid categorical answer in behalf of the second proposition, for it would seem to be the logical and obvious one. It is not!

THE IDEALISTIC VIEW. Although close to two centuries have passed since Edmund Burke delivered his famous speech to his constituents of Bristol, England, the analysis he gave of the duty of a representative still personifies the classic, the ideal, the *national* view:

> Certainly, gentlemen, it ought to be the happiness and the glory of a representative, to live in the strictest union, the closest correspondence, and the most unreserved communication with his constituents. Their wishes ought to have great weight with him; their opinion high respect; their business unremitted attention . . . But his unbiased opinion, his mature judgment, his enlightened conscience, he ought not to sacrifice to you, to any man, or to any set of men living . . . *Your representative owes you, not his industry only, but his judgment; and he betrays instead of serving you if he sacrifices it to your opinion.*[3]

And earlier in his speech, he had lectured his voting public on the proper meaning of a representative assembly:

> Parliament is not a *congress* of ambassadors from different and hostile interests; which interests each must maintain, as an agent and advocate, against other agents and advocates; but parliament is a *deliberative* assembly of *one* nation, with *one* interest, that of the whole; where not local purposes, not local prejudices ought to guide, but the general good resulting from the general reason of the whole.[4]

Clearly this is an idealistic concept of representation—which, in effect, emphasizes the *deliberative* role of the legislature at the expense of its *representative* role. Desirable though its consummation may be, it is clearly

[3] Edmund Burke, *Works,* vol. I (London: Bell and Daldy, 1871), p. 446. (Italics supplied.)
[4] Ibid.

unattainable, given the realities of politics, especially in a country as heterogeneous as the United States. Yet even in the more homogeneous France and the still more closely knit Britain, the Burkean view is hardly a realistic one—although the tight party discipline and attendant governmental machinery in the latter make it more nearly attainable there. Even in the United States, legislators will appear on the political horizon from time to time who can either afford to take the national view because of their 'safe' constituencies, or who are willing to take it at the risk of almost certain defeat—as President Kennedy so ably pointed out in the case studies in his *Profiles in Courage*.[5] But they are exceptions, all too likely to become unsuccessful candidates, such as George M. Abbott, a congressional aspirant from Vermont, who bravely announced:

> The office for which I am a candidate is properly called a United States Representative. I feel that a man holding that office should consider the general welfare of the whole nation above the benefits of certain groups. *If a man holds a United States office, his first loyalty should be to his country.*[6]

Mr. Abbott remained a private citizen.

The Realistic View. Generally, representatives have adopted the parochial view—the attitude of catering to the local constituent interests first, and to those of the nation second; they have found it to be much healthier politically. Thus, U.S. Senator Olin D. Johnston (D.-S.C.):

> I fully realize that my duties in the Senate should be for the best interest of the nation as a whole; however, *my duties and obligations are to the people of South Carolina first of all.*[7]

Others may not state it quite so bluntly, but the quotation above is generally accepted as the norm by the vast majority of the people's representatives. Even such independent legislators as the maverick from Oregon, Wayne Morse—whose political affiliations while in the U.S. Senate have ranged from Republican to Independent to Democrat—when once berated by a questioning student because of his support of the high import duties on Australian wool, retorted, 'If you want me in the U.S. Senate in order to vote for progressive measures, *I've got to remain there,* and I *won't* if I vote against such a major economic interest of my state.'

[5] New York: Harper & Brothers, 1956.
[6] *The New York Times,* July 10, 1950. (Italics supplied.)
[7] Ibid. July 9, 1950. (Italics supplied.)

The first dilemma of representation is thus actually more of a philosophical nature than of a practical one, for as long as geographical representation is used in the democracies the local, or back-home, view will take precedence over the national one, despite protestations for the record to the contrary. The conflict, of course, is often more apparent than real. Genuine national interest consists also of recognition of vital local interests. There is little doubt, however, that every representative would, on occasion, like to follow the example set by U.S. Representative John S. McGroarty, who wrote the following note to one of his California constituents: 'One of the countless drawbacks of being in Congress is that I am compelled to receive impertinent letters from a jackass like you in which you say I promised to have the Sierra Madres mountains reforested and I have been in Congress two months and haven't done it. Will you please take two running jumps and go to hell.' [8]

THE SECOND DILEMMA

The second dilemma, geographical versus occupational representation, has not really presented a serious practical issue. All present-day states that have a representative form of government base representation on territory, sometimes termed the 'political' system. Nor has any country, other than on paper, or in a purely advisory capacity—as will presently be indicated—or as a by-product of dictatorship, ever actually practiced *bona fide* occupational or functional representation, which is also sometimes referred to as 'guild socialism.' Two illustrations of the practice in dictatorships may be noted. One was Mussolini's Corporate State. In 1939, after some thirteen years of preliminary experimentation, Fascist Italy set up the Council of Corporations, chosen by occupational representation, which superseded the already emasculated Chamber of Deputies that had historically been chosen by territorial representation. It never had an opportunity to prove its merit, if any, in action, but it certainly failed to save Italy from its impending fate.[9]

[8] As quoted in John F. Kennedy, 'The Challenge of Political Courage,' *The New York Times Magazine*, December 18, 1955, p. 13.

[9] The *Portuguese* 'benevolent dictatorship,' established by Dr. Salazar in 1928, still resorts to a type of corporate body at the 'parliamentary' level. It consists of representatives of local authorities, industrial committees, and other corporations, including organizations of both employers and employees. The body has no legislative power but, according to the Portuguese Constitution of 1933 which established it, the National Assembly is obliged to submit all bills to it for its 'opinion' ere a final vote on their passage may be taken. In effect, the legislative process in Portugal is often 'in suspense,' with the Government legislating more or less by decree.

Occupational or Functional Representation. The advocates of occupational, or functional—as it is sometimes called—representation contend that specialized economic interests need direct representation, something which the legislator chosen by the geographic method is allegedly not capable of giving adequately. Where farmers, industrial workers, industrial employers, independent tradesmen, and so forth, feel the impact of government action in diverse ways, how—so goes the case—can the member of the legislature who may be a doctor, lawyer, worker, or employer, represent all their interests fairly? In addition to that problem, the proponents of occupational representation allege the inability of the average voter to register an intelligent vote—which, they contend, would also be remedied by the adoption of the proposal.

How It Would Work. Often recommended by its advocates for adoption by democratic Britain, France, Germany, Ireland, and Italy, occupational representation thus abandons the commonly accepted method of representation based upon geography or residence, and substitutes a type of representation based upon vocational or economic activity. Hence it is sometimes referred to as the 'economic' system of representation. Under it, the legislative representatives owe their election and give their allegiance to a particular economic group, such as engineers, carpenters, miners, farmers, physicians, and so forth, rather than to the people at large living in a particular territorial area.

The mere mention of such a system brings to mind its inherent, and probably insuperable, difficulties. Politically and socially divisive, it would almost by definition pit employers against employees and, very likely, the groups would battle among themselves. It would stimulate class consciousness. It would place a premium upon differences in station and activity. And it would render compromise difficult. In addition to these objections, there is the basic and vexatious question of the weight of representation to be given each group. Nevertheless, there has been some dabbling with occupational representation:

FRANCE. As far back as 1925, the French established a *National Economic Council* which, while largely an advisory body, was supposed to be, but did not have to be, consulted on all proposed economic legislation, *except on the budget*. It was continued in revised form under the Fifth Republic as the *Economic and Social Council*. The 229-member body consists of representatives of some twenty-five or thirty groups of workers, employers, farmers, 'economic and social interests overseas,' artisans, co-operatives, family and home associations, among others. They serve for five years; sixty-five appointed by the Government, the balance by the interests. The Council does not initiate legislation, but may advocate social and economic reforms; may be consulted by the executive branch on all social and economic matters; and it must be consulted on 'public economic programs and plans' —again with the exception of the budget. To date the influence of the Economic and Social Council has been slight at best. And we may well ask *how* and *where* the line will be drawn between an 'economic' and a 'non-economic' (or political) proposal. How can the budget be exempted from 'economic' consideration? Something more will be said about the institution in connection with the discussion of the administrative process in Chapter XVII.

GERMANY. The framers of the Weimar Republic attempted to establish functional representation of an even more unusual kind. Article 165 of the 1919 Constitution provided for a special legislative chamber, a 'corporate assembly,' known as the *Reichswirtschaftsrat,* roughly translatable as National Economic Management Advisory Body, which was to advise the lower house of the national legislature, the *Reichstag,* on economic and social matters. Selected by the various interest groups, and appointed by the Minister for Economic Affairs, the *Reichswirtschaftsrat* consisted initially of some three hundred, later two hundred, members. These represented broad occupational groups, such as transportation, agriculture, forestry, the professions, banking, commerce, and industry. Wherever appropriate, employers and employees were accorded equal representation within each of the groups. Both the *Reichstag* and the departments of the executive branch of the government were constitutionally required to consult the *Reichswirtschaftsrat* before introducing legislation of 'fundamental, social and economic importance.'

It is not surprising that the Weimar Republic's attempt to represent functionally was a complete failure. The employers and employees within each occupational group failed to see eye to eye on anything except the most rudimentary measures, thus rendering combined policy all but impossible. Moreover, the *Reichstag,* the political branch, sensing a potential rival, took a dim view of the economic and social branch and did its utmost to render it ineffective and meaningless. It rarely, if ever, consulted the *Reichswirtschaftsrat* as was its constitutional duty—and the ministries pursued a similar course. Thus the *Reichswirtschaftsrat* remained little more than a paper device, denied effective power in the constitution and shorn of influence in practice.

Such has been the general history of occupational representation. However attractive in theory, it is not a workable device. In a democracy, the collective action undertaken by government must put its main emphasis on what unites rather than on what divides. Moreover, pressure or interest groups are quite capable of getting their points of view across to legislators —and executives! Indeed, one of the most notable purposes of the various administrative agencies that make up the bureaucracy is to supply, in some measure, the functional representation which does not *per se* exist in the legislative branch.

ELECTORAL SYSTEMS

Varieties. It is one thing to accept geographical representation as the best method of representation. It is quite another to devise the *type* of representation that will best suit a particular country. Consequently, many different systems have been employed, ranging from the United States' Single Member District system of Plurality Elections for its House of Representatives, to Ireland's Single Member Transferable Vote system of Proportional Representation for its *Dail,* to Australia's mixture of proportional and single member district-preferential systems of election for its Parliament. By and large, however, the chief difference in viewpoint may be boiled down to the two major antagonists: proportional representation (P.R.) *versus* single member district (S.M.D.) representation. There are many different systems of representation—between 1875 and 1963 the French changed their electoral system at least seven times—but they all can be fitted into one or the other of the two categories. Before examining in some detail the diverse mechanics of the several systems, their basic differences should be clarified.

NON-PROPORTIONAL SYSTEMS. The basis for the non-proportional type of elections is the single member district—a geographical area of varying size. From this area *one* person is elected to represent it in the legislature. His election may be based upon a *plurality* vote, as in the case of United States congressional districts, where whoever has the greatest number of votes wins, regardless of the number of candidates running; or it may be based upon an *absolute majority* vote, as in the case of the Australian House of Representatives, where the victor must poll at least one-half plus one of all the votes cast. But in either case the winner takes all in the sense that he will be the sole representative from the area involved—no matter how many other candidates may have participated in the election race.

Hence, the chief objection to the S.M.D., winner-take-all, non-proportional system of representation, is quite clear: It is fundamentally impossible to represent heterogeneous individual opinions and group interests through representatives chosen by a plurality of votes in a single member election district. In a sense, the victor speaks only for that segment of the population which voted for him. The system does not accurately reflect in the legislature, as would proportional representation, the diversity of opinions and interests in the electorate.

PROPORTIONAL SYSTEMS. Diametrically opposed to the S.M.D. concept, P.R. requires a *multiple* member constituency. Here the electoral area is always large, frequently an entire state or region. Each such area sends *several* representatives to the legislature, ranging from four, in parts of Ireland, to as many as 120, in Israel.

This system ensures that each political party or party-group—as has been characteristic of France from time to time—will send representatives to the legislative body *in proportion to its share of the total votes* cast in the electoral area in question. Taking the simplest possible example, let us assume an election in a six-member electoral district, in which a total of 60,000 votes have been cast: 30,000 for Party A, 20,000 for Party B, and 10,000 for Party C. Party A would therefore be entitled to three, B to two, and C to one seat in the legislature. Here the winning party does not, as in the S.M.D. systems, 'take all,' but only his due proportion of the vote. (Of course P.R. is seldom as clear-cut and never so mathematically simple as our example would indicate!)

At first glance, P.R. is obviously the more just and, because minority parties and groups are represented in accordance with their numbers, the more democratic of the two major systems. But is it a workable one? Does it make for stable government? Before trying to answer these questions, we shall discuss the variants of the two systems, beginning with the several forms of non-proportional representation.

NON-PROPORTIONAL REPRESENTATION

(1) *Single Member District System of Plurality Elections.* The 435 members of the U.S. House of Representatives, and the 630 members of the

British House of Commons, are elected by direct popular vote by this system. The two countries are divided into as many districts as there are members in their respective lower houses. Even if a state is entitled to but one congressman, all districts in the United States are designated numerically within each state, e.g. the 'Second Congressional District of Pennsylvania,' which happens to be one of six in Philadelphia. Those in Britain are given geographical designations, such as 'Limehouse,' Earl Attlee's old district in London which he represented for many years while he was a Commoner. As many individuals as care to may run in the election, provided they have met the necessary qualifications. However, there can be only one winner: he who succeeds in obtaining the *plurality* of the votes cast on election day, even if that plurality is only *one* vote, and it does not matter if the winner's plurality happens to be less than a *majority* (one-half of the votes cast plus one) of the total votes.

(2) *'At Large' System of Plurality Elections.* Closely related to (1) is the *at large system.* It signifies elections by plurality from a large constituency, usually an entire state in the United States, with the names of candidates appearing on every ballot in the state. The 'at large' system is employed for the direct election of all U.S. Senators; for the election of the members of the U.S. House of Representatives from the five states—Nevada, Delaware, Wyoming, Alaska, and Vermont—entitled to only one such representative; and, on occasion, for the election of a congressman in a new district which his state, for political or administrative reasons, has not as yet incorporated into the established district system. The representatives in the latter two groups are known as 'U.S. Representatives at Large.'

(3) *'Run-off' or 'Second Ballot' Majority Elections.* In most Southern states of the United States, victory in the direct primary elections of the Democratic party is usually tantamount to election in the general election in November because of no, or merely token, opposition by Republican candidates. Consequently, most of the Southern and Border states use the *Run-off* or *Second Ballot* Majority Election in primaries for both national and local offices.[10] This practice requires the winner of a primary race to obtain an *absolute majority* of all the votes cast. However, if no one thus succeeds, the two top vote-getters must face a Run-off, also known as Second Ballot, against one another, customarily within a month after the

[10] In 1963, there were eleven states with the Run-off: Alabama, Arkansas, Florida, Georgia, Louisiana, Mississippi, North Carolina, Oklahoma, South Carolina, Texas, and Virginia.

initial race—a fairly common occurrence. In Florida, for example, no gubernatorial candidate had ever been elected to office without a Second Ballot until Governor Leroy Collins achieved that goal in the 1956 primary. The result is more often like that of the December 1959 gubernatorial primary election in Louisiana when eleven candidates divided some 1,000,000 votes. No one candidate obtained a majority; New Orleans Mayor de Lesseps S. Morrison and ex-Governor Jimmie H. Davis were the leading vote-getters with 271,816 and 209,765 votes, respectively. Consequently, a month later a Run-off election was held between these two men, which Mr. Davis won by a plurality of 70,000 of the 900,000 votes then cast. Subsequently, Davis easily defeated the Republican candidate.

(4) *Cumulative Vote Elections.* A rather uncommon type of non-proportional voting is the *Cumulative* Vote, which has been used since 1872 by the State of Illinois for the election of the members of the lower house of its legislature. Its purpose is to encourage the election of a minority party candidate through the accumulation of multiple votes. Under the system three members of that branch are chosen from each of the 59 assembly districts of approximately equal population into which the state is divided. Each voter is to cast three votes, which he may distribute in one of three ways: He may cast his three votes for one candidate; split them equally between two; or cast single votes for three. Apparently, the Cumulative Vote in Illinois has indeed produced minority group representation in nearly all districts. It has also evidently encouraged a longer tenure in office than legislators in nearly all other states enjoy.[11] It should be added, however, that there exists some doubt on the part of some experts on constitutional law in Illinois as to the legality of the above-described splitting other than one whole vote for each of three.

(5) *Preferential Vote Majority Election.* The last and most intricate type of non-proportional representation is the *Preferential* or *Alternative* Vote. Because it is often confused with P.R. it needs to be clearly described. It, too, is based upon single member constituencies, but the winner must get an absolute *majority,* and not merely a plurality, of the votes cast. At present, it is best known for its use in Australia to elect the members of the House of Representatives. Under the Preferential or Alternative Vote, *all* candidates running for office in the single member constituency appear on the ballot

[11] For the best work in this field, supported by many statistics, see George S. Blair, *Cumulative Voting* (Urbana: University of Illinois Press, 1960).

in alphabetical order (although determining position by lot is now advocated by many in Australia). Only one person can win, but he must attain an absolute *majority* of all the votes cast.

The voter is required to *rank* the names appearing on the ballot by placing 1, 2, 3, and so forth, according to his preferences among the candidates. He is generally required to mark a preference for each candidate. At the end of the election day, the ballots are examined to determine how many *first* choices each candidate has received. To illustrate, in an Australian Parliamentary election in the 1950's, the total number of 'firsts' cast for the six candidates running was 23,086. They were distributed as follows:

Anderson	6,542
Edwards	4,372
French	942
Jenkins	7,138
Metcalf	2,168
Young	1,924

23,086 = total number of 'firsts'

A *majority* of 'firsts' would have been 11,544 votes, but since no candidate received that many first-place votes, the next step was to consider the transferring of preferences: The candidate with the lowest number of 'firsts,' French, is declared 'not elected'; his 942 ballot papers are then examined, all 'number-*two*-preferences' in them become 'number-one's,' and these 942 are transferred to the candidates entitled to them. If it is assumed that French belonged to the same political party as Young, the bulk of the former's 'number-two-preferences' would normally go to Young, others drifting to the other remaining candidates, with the following results:

	Old Total	From French	New Total
Anderson	6,542	51	6,593
Edwards	4,372	27	4,399
Jenkins	7,138	31	7,169
Metcalf	2,168	102	2,270
Young	1,924	731	2,655

But still no one has received the necessary majority! Consequently, the man with the next lowest number of 'firsts,' Metcalf, is now declared 'not elected,' setting in motion the next step: the *second* preferences of those 2168 voters who gave him their first preference; the *third* preference of the 102 votes he obtained from French; and perhaps the third preference of 'seconds' that Metcalf voters had marked in favor of French, are distributed among the remaining four candidates.

This process of elimination and distribution of preferences to candidates still in the running goes on until one candidate has obtained a clear majority of the votes cast. It is not surprising that sometimes the candidate who is ultimately declared 'elected' as the member from that district, was third or fourth in a field of six at the end of the count of 'first preferences.' (It should be noted, however, that today a more usual number of candidates for most contests for the Australian House of Representatives would be three or four.)

While many varieties of this system exist elsewhere, the above illustration typifies the operation of the Preferential or Alternative vote. Despite its seeming intricacy, particularly so to those unfamiliar with the method, the Australians regard it as satisfactory.

PROPORTIONAL REPRESENTATION

Application. Proportional representation has been widely adopted in the Western democracies. Various versions of this controversial system are presently, or have until recently been, used in national elections—for at least one of the two houses of parliament—in, among others, Sweden, Denmark, Norway, Holland, Belgium, Finland, Ireland, France, Western Germany, Italy, Switzerland, Israel, Australia, New Zealand, and several others. Britain and the United States, devoted to the single member district system, have shunned P.R., although some local communities in the United States have used it from time to time in municipal elections. In 1963 a score of medium-sized cities did so. New York City employed it for ten years, but abandoned it when two Communists continued to be re-elected to its City Council under the system. Cincinnati, an early adherent to P.R., substituted a cumulative system for P.R. in 1957.

Authorship. Although there exists some doubt as to its inventor—certain writers trace it to the days of the French Revolution, others to the Danish statesman, Carl Andrea—P.R. was evidently first spelled out in detail by Thomas Hare, an English barrister, between 1857 and 1859 in two dull books, *The Machinery of Representation* and *Treatise on the Elections of Representatives, Parliamentary and Municipal.* The scheme was embraced by John Stuart Mill, who popularized it in his celebrated *Considerations on Representative Government.* He referred to it as 'one of the very greatest improvements yet made in the theory and practice of government.' A form of the single transferable vote of P.R., as devised by Andrea, was used for the first time in Denmark in 1856. Its application, however, was limited to the election of fifty-five of the eighty members of the then single-chamber *Rigsraad*.

Today many variations of P.R. exist. Generally speaking, however, we may distinguish between two main types: the Hare system, named after its originator, also known as the Single Transferable Vote, present chiefly in English-speaking countries; and the List system, of which there are several variations, used predominantly by continental Europe.

(1) *The Hare System.* The most consistent and devoted user of the Hare system has been Ireland, which employs it to elect the entire membership of its Dail Eireann—although it had a close call in 1959 when its electorate retained it by the narrow margin of 486,989 to 453,322. The Hare system is highly complicated, precise, mathematically intricate, and time-consuming in tabulation. It has, however, the inherent and undeniable virtue of giving weight to every vote.

The ballot resembles that used for the Preferential Vote for the Australian House of Representatives. Of course the vital difference—as outlined above—is that under P.R. the constituency is a multiple one, whereas the Preferential system is a variant of the S.M.D. type.

VOTING. The Irish voter marks his ballot-paper, on which the names of all candidates appear in alphabetical order, by placing the figure 1 opposite the name of the candidate of his first choice. He then places the figure 2 opposite the name of his second choice, 3 opposite that of his third choice, and so forth, until a figure appears opposite as many names as there are seats at stake in the voter's particular constituency. However, there can be only one figure 1 on the ballot, and a ballot-paper which either does not contain such a figure, or has the figure 1 more than once is invalid. Assuming that four seats were to be filled in a constituency, the voter's ballot might look as follows:

Name	Rank
Bragan	
Costello	1
Dwyer	4
Flaherty	
Murphy	2
O'Brien	3

COUNTING THE VOTES. In the first step of the count, all the ballot-papers for the whole constituency are placed into one large pile and arc then *sorted according to the first preferences* recorded for the candidates. All invalid papers are destroyed. After the total number of valid papers has thus been established, the next step is to calculate the *quota* according to the following much-misunderstood formula:

$$\frac{\text{Total Number of Valid Ballots}}{\text{Number of Seats plus 1}} \text{ plus 1} = \text{Quota}$$

Conveniently assuming that 100,000 valid ballot-papers have been cast, and that the total number of seats at stake in that constituency are four, the quota would be established as follows:

$$\frac{100,000}{4 \text{ plus } 1 = 5} = 20,000 \text{ plus } 1 = 20,001, \text{ the Quota}$$

Hence the quota is 20,001 and only four candidates can attain it. It represents the smallest number of 'firsts' that each of four candidates can get out of 100,000 votes.

If, on the first complete count of all valid ballots, no candidate succeeded in obtaining a number of 'firsts' equal to or greater than the quota of 20,001, the candidate with the *lowest* number of 'firsts' is eliminated. His ballots are then transferred to those candidates for whom the 'second' preferences on these ballots are recorded—again very much in the manner described earlier in connection with the Preferential system in Australia.

However, it might happen, especially in the case of a popular candidate, or one with strong party backing, that one of the candidates received a *surplus* of 'firsts,' i.e. *more* than the necessary 20,001. In that case, the successful aspirant for office is declared 'elected,' and his surplus is sorted according to number 2 preferences on the ballot declared surplus; these are transferred appropriately, thus again ensuring that every vote counts at least in some manner. This sorting and shifting, declaring 'elected' and 'not elected,' continues until such time as the required number of places have been filled, if necessary turning to number 3 choices. It is a procedure that has been known to take several weeks.

There is an element of chance in the transfer of the surplus votes because of their re-entry into the remaining count of votes for other candidates. The question usually asked here is 'just *which* ballots in the pile of the candidates having a surplus will be the ones to be transferred?' Assuming, in our example, that candidate Dwyer had received 20,100 'firsts,' 99 of these would be surplusage and thus subject to transfer. Most countries using the Hare system would simply select these 99 papers at random. Ireland attempts to be more scientific about it by re-examining *all* the papers to determine the closest possible relationship between 'first' and 'second' choices of the various voters, so as to do full justice to their intent. In any event, experience has shown—and several mathematicians have so testified—that the element of chance is far more apparent than real, and that no substantial injustice is done.

(2) *The List System.* There are various List systems of P.R. In general, the List system emphasizes a political party's *list* rather than individual candidates—as is true in the case of the Hare system of P.R. Some countries, e.g. Israel, employ the straight party list. West Germany combines the List system of P.R. with a variation of the S.M.D. type for the lower house of its legislature. Denmark does likewise for its unicameral *Folketing,* with at least 60,000 votes necessary for a party to get representation in it. The aim is to keep P.R. from degenerating too much into splinter parties. Others, Belgium, Italy, Sweden, Holland, Finland, and Norway, for instance, use sundry versions of the List system that permit the indication of at least one, and often several, numerical preferences among the names on the party lists. Switzerland uses the *panachage* List system, under which the voter may 'pick and choose' his candidates among *all* the lists on the ballot—he is thus not confined to one party's list. And finally, the Weimar Republic, as well as Czechoslovakia from 1919 to 1938, resorted to a *flexible quota* system, whereby for every 60,000 and 30,000 votes cast, respectively, a political party was entitled to one seat in the lower house of the legislature. The latter's size thus depended on the total turnout of voters.

THE STRAIGHT LIST. Although attacked by Prime Minister Ben-Gurion as 'ridiculous and injurious,' the best current example of the inflexible List system of P.R. is that employed by Israel for its one-house parliament, the 120-seat *Knesset.* Each party prepares one lengthy list for the whole country, incorporating the names of 120 candidates, its favorites appearing at the top. The ballot shows the lists of all political parties; the voter must vote for *one list only.* At the end of election day, the total number of ballots cast is divided by 120—the number of seats available—and the resultant quota becomes the yardstick in the distribution of the seats in the *Knesset.* Any party that receives at least 1 per cent of the total vote is entitled to participate in the distribution of the seats. This particular List system, a rigid and fairly simple arrangement, provides few mathematical problems. But the voter is deprived of the ability to designate which particular candidates on his party's list he may wish to see in the *Knesset*. A premium is thus placed upon party discipline.

THE MIXED LIST. The Mixed List, sometimes known as the *d'Hondt* system after Victor d'Hondt of the University of Ghent, the originator of its 'average quota' computation, is a departure from the Straight List. As used in Belgium, Holland, Denmark, Norway, and Sweden, for example, it permits the voter to indicate on his party's list the, however limited, numerical order in which he wishes to see individuals selected, once the number of available seats have been established by virtue of the votes cast and the quota. This method preserves the concept of the party list, but more or less abridges the party's power to determine the order in which candidates are elected from the list. In Belgium and Denmark, however, the voter's choice is limited to just *one* designation; larger freedom of choice, usually up to three, is available to voters in Italy, Norway, and Sweden. In again other instances, freedom of choice differs between upper and lower houses, e.g. Holland.

These are a few illustrations of the List system of P.R. It is much less complicated than the Hare system, but it also reflects less faithfully the individual voter's choice. Yet both main types of P.R. are far more accurate indications of voter preference than the non-proportional systems. Why, then, has P.R. been unable to replace the single member district system universally?

PRO AND CON P.R.

Arguments Pro. Many of the arguments advanced in favor of P.R. are difficult to refute from a theoretical point of view. Among them are:

1. It is a truly democratic system, for it secures minority representation in the precise ratio of minority votes.
2. Every vote counts; there are no wasted votes, which are inevitable in the winner-take-all systems.
3. It is mathematically accurate.
4. Every politically active group of any size will normally have some representation in the legislature.
5. It provides greater freedom of choice for the voter and thereby raises his interest in the body politic.
6. It tempers the domination of political machines.
7. It eliminates the evils of the *gerrymander*—the practice, so common in the United States, of deliberately dividing election districts to

favor the party in power—since there are no districts to be gerry-mandered.

Arguments Con. While not denying some of the theoretical claims of the advocates of P.R., its opponents base their arguments largely on practical considerations.

1. It creates splinter parties; it balkanizes the party structure.
2. It encourages bloc voting and extremism.
3. It is divisive; it renders compromise extremely difficult, if it does not eliminate it entirely; it encourages 'minority-thinking' and freak candidatures.
4. Majority government—government by a single political party with a majority of the seats in the legislature—is usually impossible or at best difficult to attain under P.R.; hence the latter militates against governmental stability.
5. It centralizes control of political parties by strengthening party machines.
6. It confuses the voter. In the words of Lord Morley, 'a voting system that smacks of decimals and algebra does not strengthen the state.'
7. It weakens the intimate contact with the constituency that is possible under the S.M.D. system.

Many other arguments have been advanced on both sides, but those enumerated represent the main ones.

AN EVALUATION

Any objective evaluation of electoral systems must take into account the particular needs of each country, its form of government, and its political complexion. For example, it does not follow that, just because the Single Member District System of Plurality Elections works well within the framework of the government of the United States, it will be equally suitable for Belgium, Israel, or Switzerland. Conversely, although Proportional Representation has been found highly satisfactory for Sweden, Norway, and Denmark, it may be totally unsuitable for Britain.

The old proverb, that the proof of the pudding is in the eating, is still applicable: P.R. has served the Scandinavian lands very well, indeed, because it has never prevented the formation of stable coalitions, normally composed of the Social Democrats plus one of the small parties, for purposes of governing. West Germany, too, uses a mixed system of P.R., which has to date helped to produce a genuinely stable system of government. On the other hand, it failed to provide a solution for the electoral problems of the Fourth Republic of France, which experimented with two variants of the system. There it brought a splintering of political parties, whose very multiplicity rendered government by coalition ultimately impossible, contributing heavily to the frequent turnover of governments of the day. Yet it would be grossly inaccurate to attribute the fall of the Fourth Republic simply to its electoral systems. (The Fifth Republic adopted a two-ballot 'run-off' type of S.M.D.)

There is no doubt that P.R. reflects accurately the political viewpoints of the various groups that comprise the electorate. Political minorities are represented equitably; their interests cannot be submerged in the same fashion as under the S.M.D. system. Winners do not take all—only their due share. No vote is wasted. The practice of the gerrymander, one of the most objectionable political devices used in the United States—although it came under historic attack by the U.S. Supreme Court in 1962, its effect is as yet undetermined [12]—disappears under P. R. Moreover, although P.R. does tend to splinter parties in several instances, a good case can be made for the contention that in certain countries, France for one, splinter parties would exist with or without P.R. in any free election. Finally, while it would admittedly be more difficult for one party to obtain a working majority in the legislature, such a majority is by no means unattainable, as the experience of the Scandinavian countries proves conclusively. Even in New York City's experiment with P.R., from 1937 to 1947, the Democratic party held a consistent majority in the City Council.

The overriding question that arises, however, is whether the main purpose and object of a legislature, and through it of government, is to reflect the political opinions of the populace in proportion to strength on election day, or whether it is to provide effective responsible government. It is true, of course, that a legislative body ought to represent majority and minority groups of opinion—but it need hardly be based on a precise arithmetic distribution. Majorities have to placate minorities before they can become majorities. It is regrettable when, as has sometimes occurred through the quirks of political accident, a party which gets less than a majority of the popular vote obtains a majority of the seats in a parliament, but it is not necessarily catastrophic. With a two-party system, and without P.R., both the

[12] *Baker v. Carr,* 369 U.S. 186 (1962).

British and American legislatures—whatever other vices they may have—have managed to be reasonably representative.

The primary aim of responsible government ought to be stability. It should put down a deep keel which will respond to the general drift of public opinion, but not to all the choppy waves that agitate its surface. In the West an unresponsive legislature is replaceable by way of the ballot box, although gerrymandered districts may render that much more difficult in the United States than in Great Britain. P.R. was by no means the sole cause for the downfall of the Weimar Republic or the French Fourth Republic—but it was a contributing factor. As has been explained earlier, not once in the history of the struggling Weimar Republic did any political party succeed in obtaining a majority of the seats in the *Reichstag,* thus necessitating constant coalition government, for which the Germans were neither suited temperamentally nor prepared politically. The situation in France was different; but there, too, no political party was ever able to gather a majority of the seats in the National Assembly in the entire twelve-year history of the Fourth Republic. Given the French love for diversity in politics, it may well not be attainable with the new S.M.D. system either, but the Fifth Republic is still too youthful to permit a meaningful judgment.

When all is said and done, however, we must revert to the basic premise that the *legislature must speak for the nation.* Where only two parties are in the field, each knows it must work for a majority in the constituency and in the country. Each knows it must put out bait for the wavering voters, generally the moderates who look at both sides of a question. Each must court significant minorities, and these necessities make for a middle-of-the-road platform and for candidates who have a general appeal. That is to say, minorities are not ignored and they are not entirely unrepresented, because one or other of the party platforms takes their less extreme demands into account.

On the other hand, minority groups of opinion know that their chances of electing members of their own are slim except where they happen to be heavily concentrated in particular constituencies. They tend to swing to one or the other of the two parties, hoping for some consideration in return for support and often bargaining for it. While the middle-of-the-road program may not attract them, it does not positively repel. With reluctance, yet with some minimum of consent, they come into the fold. Extreme views do not construct a party for their propagation unless conditions are such as to encourage them over a long period of time.

This is the party system working at its best. It compels everyone to concentrate on what he shares in common with others, to search for the unifying ideas and policies. It compels everyone either to forget differences or to minimize and compromise them, instead of exaggerating them. And since both parties are competitively engaged in the same task, looking for a basis of unity on which to construct a majority, it draws them closer together rather than forcing them further apart. However, when it becomes electorally possible for minorities to count confidently on getting at least a few seats, they often reject middle-of-the-road programs and set out in full cry to realize their interpretation of the good life. Once a small bloc gets into Parliament, a minority has a forum from which to expound its gospel, and it hopes, as sects always do, to win the world to the obvious truth of its views. Once the core of a party is formed, it tends, as in all organizations, to become important for its own sake as well as for its purposes and thus to perpetuate itself.

When the minorities begin to withdraw their support from the two old parties, these, in turn, change their character. The premium paid for moderation diminishes, and they tend to take more dogmatic positions, hoping to hold a following with strong convictions. As the number of significant parties grows, it becomes unlikely that any one party will get an absolute majority of the seats in the legislature. Not expecting to have the sole responsibility of governing, parties are no longer under the necessity of working out a practicable platform. Since responsibility can no longer be concentrated on them, they cease to feel a sense of responsibility. They devise their programs to attract a fervent following whose particular interests they push, rather than to provide an acceptable policy for the country as a whole.

The Need for Solid Majorities. We come again to some hard realities that were mentioned earlier. Government action is collective action taken on behalf of the whole and, if it is not to be self-defeating, it cannot give expression to all the cross-purposes entertained by particular members and parts of the whole. Presumably, something is to be accomplished by common action and, if it is to be done with consent, it cannot pander to extremes. Also, the immediate effect of much of government policy is to shift burdens from one set of shoulders to another. As long as this is so, there will be disgruntled minorities even though they get direct representation in the legislature. Even if the majority in the legislature agree to do nothing, the minorities that had hoped to shift some of their burdens will be disgruntled.

There is therefore no cure. The best that can be offered is a palliative to be found through government's being limited in its actions in so far as is humanly possible to matters on which something approaching a community of view can be found. Democratic government may not survive unless action is so limited, and unless a sensitive mechanism is available for discovering which policies of action can hope to find a broad base of consent. The two-party system, or the type of P.R. system prevalent in Scandinavia which—to all intents and purposes—operates as a two-party coalition, is the best instrument so far found for this delicate task.

It will be retorted that election by a mere plurality in contests among three of more parties is intolerable. That may be our conclusion if such contests are to become a general and permanent feature of political life. It is not at all clear, however, that degeneration into a multiple-party system is inevitable. All our social institutions must face periodic crises. The sick do not always die and institutions often surmount their crises. An electorate that has had experience of the ease of fixing responsibility under the two-party system and cabinet government is likely to abandon a party that shows, by running third in several successive elections, that it has little chance of gaining a majority. Less rational considerations, such as the desire to be on the winning side, work in the same direction. The excision of such a party may be painful, as all surgical operations are, but those who genuinely cherish democratic government will not shrink from it if it ensures the continued life of the two-party system.

The Problem of Integration. It cannot be repeated too often that the capital problem of politics in a democracy is integration, drawing people into an effective unity on the collective action that government is to undertake in their name, while at the same time cherishing and protecting diversity in their private lives.

Reflection on this fundamental point leads to conclusions applicable to occupational representation as well as to proportional representation. In a democracy, the collective action undertaken by government must put its main emphasis on what unifies rather than on what divides. There is no need, then, for every interest to be specifically represented in political decisions. It is only when the government runs everything and everybody that the demand of every interest for representation becomes legitimate. Within a framework of order firmly maintained by consent because it is in the main limited to those things on which consent, however grudging, can be gained, all sorts of diversities may be permitted self-assertion. Individuals may live rich lives engrossed in a great variety of interests, even though these interests lack direct political representation. The present scheme of representation, through single-member territorial constituencies, in countries that are already well-integrated politically, seems to come closer to giving what is required of a representative system.

Yet it is sufficiently clear that the common interest almost always requires the circumscription or regulation of particular interests or mediation by the government between conflicting interests. In an interdependent society with an advanced technology like ours, this regulation and mediation are always complex questions and, as the argument for occupational representation shows, the interests involved need to be represented in some way. As we pointed out at some length in the preceding chapter, fortunately there are other ways of representing them, and also the minority groups of opinion on whose behalf proportional representation is asked, than by giving them seats in the legislature. Interests know how to organize lobbies to influence the government and the legislature. They can be—and often are—represented on advisory committees attached to the government departments that administer the laws affecting group interests. They even get representation in the administration itself, as when the board enforcing minimum wage laws includes representatives of employers and employees. Participation in government by organized interests and pressure groups is an accomplished fact.

REPRESENTATION AND ELECTIONS IN THE SOVIET UNION

Although the forms of Soviet representation, as manifested in the electoral system, resemble those of the liberal democracies, elections in the Soviet Union and in the Anglo-American countries fulfill completely different functions. In Britain, France, and the United States, elections are devices for asserting control by the people over the government, and therefore representing the will of the people faithfully in the legislature is a central problem in democratic politics. In the Soviet Union, however, elections are instruments used to rally the people behind the policy desired by the leadership of the Communist party. Since the main function of Soviet elections is not to elicit from the public a decision as to who shall represent it in the councils of government, i.e. which party shall temporarily control the state, there really is no genuine problem of representation in Soviet politics.

Electoral practices in the Soviet Union differ radically from those found in non-Communist countries. On the surface, it is true, there are certain similarities. It has already been noted that elections are held at regular intervals, based on a universal, direct, and equal suffrage. The country is divided into electoral areas on the basis of a fixed number of citizens per delegate, except in the case of elections for the 645-member Council of Nationalities— the upper branch of the national legislature—where the number of delegates to be assigned to each of the various national areas is fixed by the Constitution. As in the liberal democracies, Soviet elections pass through three phases: *nominations, campaigns,* and *voting.* The similarity noted thus far ends at the nomination stage. For, in the liberal democracies, it is the last stage, the actual vote, which determines who shall be the people's representatives, whereas *in the Soviet Union, this is decided by the nomination.* Once all candidates have been nominated, the outcome of Soviet elections is a foregone conclusion, for in all electoral districts the candidates bearing the direct or indirect stamp of approval of the Communist party are unopposed.

Nominations. The right to nominate candidates is granted by the Constitution 'to public organizations and societies of the working people.'[13] In practice, this means that almost any organization approved by the state— and there are no others—can nominate a candidate for one of the soviets, whether it be for a village soviet or for the Supreme Soviet of the U.S.S.R. It should be recalled at this stage in the discussion that all approved organizations in the Soviet Union are dominated by the Communist party. No candidate—even if he is not a member of the party—would be out of sympathy with the aims and methods of the party.

Once a number of candidates have been nominated by the various organizations in an electoral district, such as trade unions, Red Army units, and workers on collective farms, the local Communist party unit calls a conference at which delegates from all the nominating organizations in the electoral district meet informally to discuss the nominees. Out of this conference comes an agreement on the best candidate. Once he is picked, the organizations which have nominated the other candidates withdraw their nominations, and only *one candidate remains to be voted on at the forthcoming election.* Thus the local Communist party organization and a few delegates from other organizations really pick the winning candidate, although it is quite clear that 'public organizations' of varied types do exercise considerable initiative in *proposing* candidates for nomination at the local

[13] Constitution of the U.S.S.R., Art. 141.

level. Many of these candidates are members of the party, but there is always a considerable proportion of non-party candidates who are sponsored by what is called the 'Bloc of Communist and non-party people,' the official label under which the 1429 official candidates for the Supreme Soviet seek votes.

The Soviet system of nomination bears some resemblances to the direct primaries in the United States, particularly to most Democratic primaries in the deep South, where the outcome of an election is really decided at the primary stage, because the Republican party is generally too weak to give the Democratic candidate a run for his money—with increasing exceptions in the more industrialized states, however. The difference between the United States primaries and Soviet nominations is that the former *do* provide effectively for wide popular participation in *selecting* a candidate for the impending general election.

Campaigns and Elections. The Soviet nominations are followed by a most intensive election campaign. The purpose of this device is not to convince the public of the relative merits of the contesting parties—for, of course, there is no contest—but to serve purposes of the Soviet State: to explain the policies of the Communist party; to extol its accomplishments; to honor and glorify its loyal servants; to compare the results of Communist rule with that of the czars; to give the government an aura of legitimacy; to explain the economic policies of the Soviet state. In sum, the campaign is designed to educate the masses in Communist doctrine and to whip up their enthusiasm for the Communist cause and the national leaders. All the means of mass propaganda available to the modern totalitarian state are employed in the pre-election drive, and the citizens are subjected to severe social pressure to ensure a large vote on election day, for abstention is viewed as a 'serious neglect of duty.'

Voting, which is carried out in a festive spirit with flags flying and music everywhere, is extremely heavy on election day—one of the few official holidays. In 1958, for instance, 99.7 per cent of the eligible voters went to the polls, and only 500,000 or 0.4 per cent voted against the official candidates, either by crossing out their names on the ballot or by writing in others. Either of these steps is regarded and counted as a negative vote. Such results are widely heralded by the regime as all but unanimous popular approval.

Elections, then, fulfill a different role in Soviet politics than in countries which have the two-party or multi-party systems. They are another expression of the principle of 'democratic centralism,' which assures that all undesirable candidates are prevented by the party from contesting an election, and enables the vast mass of Soviet citizens to take part in the pre-election discussion and in the vote itself. In the light of this function of Soviet elections, the problem of representation is virtually non-existent.

Suggested References for Further Reading

Bird, F. L., and F. M. Ryan, *The Recall of Public Officers* (Macmillan, 1930).

Blair, G., *Cumulative Voting* (U. of Illinois, 1960).

Bonjour, F., *Real Democracy in Action: The Example of Switzerland* (Stokes, 1920).

Burke, E., *Works* (Bell & Daldy, 1871).

Butler, D. E., *The Electoral System in Britain, 1918–1951* (Oxford, 1953).

Butler, D. E. (Ed.), *Election Abroad* (St Martin's, 1959).

Campbell, P., *French Electoral Systems* (Faber, 1958).

Center for the Study of Democratic Institutions, *The Elite and the Electorate: Is Government by the People Possible?* (Fund for the Republic, 1963).

Cole, G. D. H., *Guild Socialism Re-Stated* (Allen & Unwin, 1920).

Crisp, L. F., *The Parliamentary Government of the Commonwealth of Australia* (Yale, 1949).

Crouch, D. D., *The Initiative and Referendum in California* (U. of California, 1950).

DeGrazia, A., *Public and Republic: Political Representation in America* (Knopf, 1951).

Hallett, G. H., and C. G. Hoag, *Proportional Representation—The Key to Democracy*, 3rd ed. (National Home Library, 1940).

Hermens, F. A., *Democracy or Anarchy? A Study of Proportional Representation* (Notre Dame, 1943).

Hogan, J., *Election and Representation* (Blackwell, 1945).

Hollis, C. W., *Can Parliament Survive?* (Hollis and Carter, 1949).

Lakeman, E., and J. D. Lambert, *Voting in Democracies* (Faber, 1959).

Mackenzie, W. J. M., *Free Elections* (Rinehart, 1958).

Millett, J. D., *The Process and Organization of Government Planning* (Columbia, 1951).

Ross, J. F. S., *Elections and Electors: Studies in Democratic Representation* (Eyre & Spottiswoode, 1955).

XII

The Executive–The Mainspring of Government

We have distinguished one of the organs of government as the executive and described its function as executing or carrying out the law. It is now necessary to carry the distinction further and define the function more precisely. In the broadest sense, the executive includes all those engaged in or associated with the active manipulation of men and things in the name of the government. The discussion of the scope of modern government action has indicated the extraordinary range of activity involved.

Who Is It? The executive in this wide sense includes the Chief of State, be he monarch or president. It includes the small group who, through their positions as heads of the great government departments, are in direct command of the manifold activities of government. This is the ministry or cabinet, known in Britain and France as the government, in the sense of (at this writing) Mr. Macmillan's Government and General de Gaulle's Government, and in the United States as the administration, in the sense of Mr. Kennedy's Administration. For convenience of nomenclature, we may call them the *temporary, or political,* executive. The executive also includes the tens, and even hundreds, of thousands of civil servants who may be described as the *permanent* executive because, in the main, they do not now change with a change of government. It also includes the armed forces who, while they cannot be said to carry out the law, do act as agents of the government in whatever they do.

Indeed, it is a gross understatement of the function of the executive to say

439

that it carries out the law. It is often said that the executive carries out the will of the state. If we leave aside the metaphysical question whether the state has an identifiable will, the statement is helpful because it directs attention, not to specific laws that are enforced, but to a complex total of actions of a bewildering variety, many of which are not the execution of laws but discretionary actions that the law permits without commanding. For example, the executive runs the vast household of the modern state, buying rope for the navy and pens, ink, and paper for the civil service, hiring servants, constructing or renting office space, and a thousand other jobs of domestic management. The government provides a great many services that cannot always be described as the carrying out of mandatory laws. There is ordinarily no law requiring the government to conduct geological surveys, maintain diagnostic laboratories or experimental farms. They are lawful because the appropriate legislature, national or state, has granted money for the purpose.

THE EXECUTIVE AS THE MAINSPRING OF GOVERNMENT

In sheer numbers, the executive far outstrips the other two powers. Where judges are numbered by dozens and legislators by hundreds, the executive counts in tens of thousands. Its importance is not merely numerical. In the typical nation-state of today, with a central government exercising a wide authority over an extensive territory and millions of people, the executive is truly the mainspring of government. It makes the wheels go around. Germany and Italy under the Nazi and Fascist dictatorships proved that nation-states can continue in some fashion without a functioning legislature and without a judiciary of significant independence. But when the executive breaks down, as it did in Nazi Germany in the closing days of World War II, the central government collapses.

Its Significance. The reasons for this are quite simple. We know that large business enterprises will not run without the guidance of great executives. Government today, in terms of the scope of its operations, is the largest of all enterprises. It therefore must have leadership. That leadership must be continuous, always devising and revising. It must be informed leadership. It must know the objectives of all the activities carried on. It must also know, or have readily available, detailed information on the problems government is supposed to be solving. Government cannot undertake to improve public health or public education unless it knows in detail what is wrong. It cannot regulate and promote agriculture unless it knows a great deal about agriculture. Even then, the problem is often so complex that trial and error is the only way to approach solutions. So, in order to decide intelligently what to try next, the knowledge gained in the course of administration is indispensable.

There is a steady accumulation of this kind of information in every government department that is effectively organized, and there is often much more of it concentrated there than anywhere else. It is not that the executive necessarily knows best what should be done; often, it does not. But it has a body of information, of expertise that is indispensable in deciding what *can* and what *cannot* be done. The legislature usually does not have it. This explains why so much legislation today is framed by the executive, and why the role of the legislature is increasingly that of criticizing, rejecting, or approving executive proposals, and—at least in the United States—'investigating' their operation once they have become law. Much more will have to be said about this later. For the moment, the point is that if the vast apparatus of present-day government is to perform satisfactorily the tasks laid upon it, there must be continuous initiative by a body that knows the detail of the work and imparts drive and direction. This initiative must come from the executive itself. The legislature is too far away from the complexities of administration; it is not continuously and exclusively absorbed in the study of these matters, and it is always too numerous and often too torn by political battle to give unified and vigorous direction to the daily work of government.

The Roles of Executive and Legislature. The fact is that the emphasis in the literature of the last hundred years on the vital role of the legislature in maintaining democratic control of government has led many to the unwarranted belief that the legislature is the government. Reference to history as well as to current realities should correct this mistaken impression rapidly. Historically, the first origin of central government almost everywhere is in a war leader, or a conqueror, who seizes control of a territory and uses the reserve of force at his command to control the population.

At this stage the executive is everything. The limitations on it are the limitations of nature and the passive or other resistance of the population. There are no internal restraints. To take only one but not an isolated example, the government of William the Conqueror in England was not distinguished from his own personal household. Legislative and judicial institutions emerged later and only slowly became effective brakes on executive action. The essence of government is an executive. It represents the focus of leadership. The legislature and judiciary are merely the instruments for constitutionalizing it.

No matter how fully representative a legislature may be, it cannot govern the country. The great weakness of the Third and Fourth Republics in France, whatever the deeper causes of their collapse, was that the legislatures would not abide a strong executive. Lacking this, no effective leadership existed to prepare the country to meet the Nazi menace, to withstand the shock of military disaster, or to meet the mounting Algerian crisis. The immense concentration of executive power in de Gaulle under the Fifth Republic, and the attendant emaciation of legislative power, followed almost inevitably.

One of the most serious defects of the Articles of Confederation, the first attempt at a national government for the United States, was the failure to provide for distinct organization of the executive power, all powers granted being placed in the hands of the Congress. Similarly, the state constitutions as maintained throughout the nineteenth century did not provide for effective organization of the executive power. While they established the office of Governor, they denied him any substantial authority, dispersing executive power into many hands. The result was a weak executive and a very low level of efficiency in state government. The efficiency of state government did not begin to rise until the movement to reorganize the state executive power was launched in the Midwest in 1917.

To insist on the executive as the essence of government is not a depreciation of the legislature. Rather it reveals the tremendously important and essential role of the legislature as a check, or brake, on an energetic executive. This is vital for the maintenance of constitutionalism, an importance underlined by Lincoln's doubt, whether a government—i.e. an executive—that was strong enough for surmounting emergencies, would not be *too* strong to be kept under effective control by its people. With the aggrandizement of the executive through the great extension of governmental action, and its need for vigor if it is to do efficiently all the tasks assigned to it, the need for checks on the executive is greater than ever before in the history of liberal democratic government.

Executive Leadership. Accepting the necessity for strong executive leadership, it should be clear that that leadership is not provided by the executive defined in the sense of including tens of thousands of civil servants. Leadership is always the function of one or a few. Too many cooks spoil the broth, and what holds for soup holds for government as well. Every numerous body that wants to accomplish anything has to set up an executive committee, and there is ample testimony that if such a committee is to give really vigorous direction to affairs its membership should not exceed ten and had better be five. There is indeed an argument that a plural executive suffers too much from cross-purposes and indecision, and that the executive should be headed by a single person. This argument prevailed in the constitutional convention in Philadelphia in 1787—and in fact, if not in theory, in the de Gaulle Constitution of 1958. Neither the shareholders nor the board of directors of a great business enterprise try to run the daily affairs of the enterprise. They appoint a general manager who is popularly known—and revered and despised by turns—as a 'big executive.'

What It Means. In the preceding paragraph a quite different but commonly used sense of the word 'executive' emerges. *Executive* means commanding men and directing affairs rather than the direct and immediate carrying out of particular objectives in all their detail. This latter aspect of the work of big organizations, be they business or government, is called, by contrast, *administration.* The executive generally means the small group, the cabinet members, who head the great departments of government and thus direct the multifarious efforts of the civil service and who, because they are in command, must supply the initiative and leadership that is necessary. On the one hand, they furnish drive and direction for governmental administration. On the other hand, the civil service funnels to them the continuous stream of information and experience gained in the course of administration from day to day. Using this information to develop their own conception of public needs, and keeping in mind what the legislature wants or will stand for, the executive matures legislative proposals for the consideration of the legislature.

In these functions, the executive is greatly aided by a small group of higher civil servants, their immediate subordinates in the departments, and it is almost impossible to disentangle the separate contributions of the two groups. There are some who say that these few higher civil servants make by far the greater contribution and are the real governors of the modern state. However, because the executive has the *responsible* command, and is always contributing fresh ideas not gleaned from the civil service, it may justly be described as the mainspring. Therefore, the discussion in this chapter will be directed to the executive in the narrow sense.

THE CHIEF OF STATE AND CHIEF EXECUTIVE IN THE UNITED STATES: THE PRESIDENT

The Institution

A frequently quoted old chestnut is Sir Henry Maine's statement that the King of Britain reigns, but does not govern; that the President of the United States governs, but does not reign; that it has been reserved for the President of France neither to reign nor to govern. This assertion can validly still be made solely with respect to the British Chief of State. Since the birth of the Fifth French Republic, the President of France both rules and reigns and, notwithstanding the many congressional, and some latent judicial, checks upon his powers, the mid-twentieth century American President also reigns as well as rules. The latter is, as President Franklin D. Roosevelt once put it, 'King, Prime Minister, party leader—all rolled into one.' And Woodrow Wilson rightly called the President 'the pivot of the whole [American governmental] structure.' He symbolizes the people and he also runs their government. He is both Chief of State and Chief Executive, thus combining functions that are separated in Britain.

It is true that being an elected person, the President arouses antagonism as readily as devotion, and that the Constitution comes closer to being the symbol of unity in the United States than does the President. Since the latter lacks the divinity that hedges a monarch, the Americans have had to find their symbol in an abstraction. The Civil War was fought to preserve the Union, not the kingdom of Abraham Lincoln. Nevertheless, the President represents the focus of democratic leadership in the United States today. He is the one truly national institution—the only national office elected with a national constituency that can truly represent the national interest.

Moreover, as Professor R. E. Neustadt has pointed out so ably,[1] the President has four additional, sometimes overlapping constituencies: (1) the 'governmental' constituency—the public officials who serve under him; (2) the 'partisan' constituency—his party; (3) the 'congressional' constituency—the legislature; and (4) the 'overseas' constituency—foreign states.

The Chief of State. The President is the formal Chief of State who per-

---

[1] Richard E. Neustadt, *Presidential Power: The Politics of Leadership* (New York: John Wiley & Sons, 1960), p. 7.

forms many of the legal and ceremonial functions of the Queen of Britain. He opens public buildings, charity drives, and the baseball season. He chats with delegations which range from the Boy Scouts to the League of Women Voters. He receives ambassadors from, and is the official medium of intercourse with, foreign countries. He is the commander in chief of the armed forces. He gives formal assent to legislation, although his veto may be overridden by a two-thirds vote of both houses of Congress. If he neither assents nor vetoes, the measure automatically becomes law after a lapse of ten days, Sundays excepted, provided Congress is still in session; if it has adjourned in the meantime, the bill is killed by such inaction, known as the 'pocket veto.' The regular sessions of Congress are fixed by law and he cannot change them, just as he cannot prorogue or dissolve Congress, unless its two houses cannot agree on an adjournment date. The principle of the separation of powers limits his interference with Congress to the calling of special sessions in emergent circumstances. He may pardon and reprieve criminals. The formal acts of government are performed in his name.

The Chief Executive. The President also holds the executive power of the United States, and thus he governs within the ambit of power given by the Constitution. It is impossible, in fact, to make any clear distinction between his functions as Chief of State and as Chief Executive. Thus he not merely signs the pardon that frees a convicted criminal; he also decides with the assistance of the Attorney General whether a pardon shall be granted. This latter is a function that in Britain rests not with the monarch but with the Home Secretary. The President not only promulgates ordinances, he decides upon and takes responsibility for their content. His official functions as the executive of the United States are so vast that he cannot begin to give personal attention to the compass of his office. In most matters he accepts the carefully considered and carefully channeled advice of his subordinates.

Selection and Election of the President. Nominated by one of the two major political parties at its national convention, and elected largely through the campaign efforts of that party, the President on attaining office becomes the leader of his party and, presumably, the leader of public opinion. What sort of person is he?

QUALIFICATIONS. According to Article II of the Constitution, anyone who is 'a natural-born citizen,' at least thirty-five years of age, and who has resided in the United States for fourteen years, is eligible for the high office. However, so many unwritten qualifications and customary requirements exist that the proud American claim, 'anyone in the United States can grow up to be

President,' must be viewed in the light of the composite picture of the thirty-five Presidents to date. According to it, the typical American President is:

> fifty-five years old, White, Protestant, male, happily married, of Anglo-Saxon ancestry, with a B.A. college degree, from one of about seven major non-Southern states that have a fairly large electoral vote and are not 'one-party' states, with a brief military or, preferably, more extensive legal and administrative background—and without an easily definable record on major controversial issues.

Not many qualify or are 'available' under these circumstances—yet the election of John F. Kennedy in 1960 proved that no longer is a man's religion necessarily a barrier to the highest office in the land.

TERM OF OFFICE. The President is elected for a four-year term. Until the ratification of the Twenty-second Amendment in 1951 no limit on the number of terms existed, although it had become customary for a President to seek no more than two. Franklin D. Roosevelt, however, ran for and gained a third *and* a fourth term in 1940 and 1944, respectively. Grover Cleveland won the popular vote thrice—in 1884, 1888, and 1892—yet he lost the middle election in the electoral college. Now, however, no President can serve more than two terms, or a maximum of ten years—the latter in the event of a Vice President succeeding to the presidency with two years or less of the old term remaining.

THE ELECTORAL COLLEGE. The President is elected by the absolute majority vote of an 'electoral college' of 538 members to which each of the states contributes a number of electors equal to the total number of senators and representatives to which it is entitled in Congress. These electors, chosen as the laws of the separate states prescribe, meet and ballot for the candidates for the presidency. The ballots are then sent to the capital, and are opened and counted by the President of the Senate in the presence of the entire Congress.

ELECTION MECHANICS. Thus far goes the written Constitution, which intended the electors to exercise their personal judgment in casting their ballots. But the development of two strong political parties has resulted in a complete change in the substance behind these forms. At national conventions called for the purpose, the two parties each choose a party candidate for President. The laws of each state enable each party to nominate a complete slate of candidates—usually prominent party workers or heavy financial contributors—for election to the electoral college. On the day fixed for the presidential election, the electorate in each state in effect votes for either the Democratic or Republican slate of candidates for the electoral college *in that state*. When the electors so chosen meet, they almost always vote for either the Democratic or Republican candidate for the presidency. But since they are pledged from the beginning to vote for the candidate of the party that nominated them, the result is a foregone conclusion as soon as it is known which complexion of electoral slate has been chosen in each state. However, only two states—California and Oregon—require by *law* that the electors heed their pledges. As a result, occasional defections have occurred, the most recent in 1948 and 1956, when electors pledged to Truman and Stevenson, respectively, voted for 'Dixiecrat' candidates, and in 1960, when an elector pledged to Nixon cast his ballot for Senator Harry F. Byrd of Virginia (who was not even a candidate).

The later formalities—the electors' meeting to cast their votes, the dispatch of these ballots to Washington, and the grave proceedings there—are now empty forms whose only justification is the necessity of complying with the precise requirements of the written Constitution. The spirit changes but the letter remains.

In effect, the President is elected by popular vote. This is not quite an accurate statement because it is still the number of electoral votes that counts, and it is possible for a candidate to win a majority of the votes of the electors without having a majority of the popular vote. Presidents Wilson in 1912, Truman in 1948, and Kennedy in 1960 were the last to come to office without a popular majority. But even when he gets a majority of the popular vote it cannot always be said that the President is the popular choice, because the process of nomination often produces presidential candidates whose decisive merit is that they are inoffensive to the important diverse elements in the party—e.g. Warren G. Harding in 1920 and John W. Davis in 1924, both nominated as a result of deadlocks among party leaders, the former on the tenth, the latter on the one hundred and third convention ballot.

DIFFICULTIES. It is also possible, however, that a person who obtains more *popular* votes than his opponent or opponents still loses because he has not received an *absolute majority* of the votes in the electoral college. This happened in 1824, 1876, and 1888. In the first case, Andrew Jackson obtained 50,000 more votes than his closest opponent, John Quincy Adams, but the House of Representatives—where under the Constitution elections are thrown for decision when no candidate has received the necessary majority in the electoral college—chose Adams, for a variety of reasons. In 1876, the famous 'disputed' or 'stolen' election, Democrat Tilden had 250,000 more popular votes than his Republican opponent, Hayes, but lost by one vote in the electoral college—after a stormy, lengthy, politically charged investigation of twenty disputed electoral votes. In 1888 Cleveland defeated Republican Benjamin Harrison by 100,000 votes, but lost the election because Harrison had sixty-five more votes in the electoral college, largely due to the latter's narrow victories in the most populous states, including New York.

REFORM? As a result of some of these inequities, there have been many, and recurring, calls for the abolition or reform of the electoral college. Measures toward that end abound in every session of Congress. None has succeeded to date, chiefly because of the opposition of the small states which fear a resultant loss of power. In 1950, the Lodge-Gossett Resolution, a proposed constitutional amendment which would have divided the electoral vote of the candidates in each state in precise proportion to the popular vote, passed the Senate, but was defeated in the House of Representatives.[2]

Presidential Succession. The Constitution provides for the succession by the Vice President, who is nominated and elected to his office in the same manner as the President, in case of the latter's 'Removal from Office, or of his Death, Resignation or Inability to discharge the Powers and Duties of the said Office.'[3] Seven Vice Presidents have thus succeeded to the presidency, all due to deaths—four by natural causes, three by assassination.[4] A delicate and enigmatic problem is posed by the meaning of the term *inability*. Although history proves that Presidents have indeed been 'inable' 'or disabled' because of illness—e.g. Garfield, Wilson, Eisenhower—the problem has never been tackled really seriously, despite a host of recommendations for remedial legislation. It may well be, as a close student of the inability question has stated it, that the problem 'is quite insoluble . . . [it] will always be a messy situation . . .' even if on the surface it were to yield to overt 'legal' or 'practical solutions.'[5]

In 1947, Congress passed the Presidential Succession Act, which provides for the following order of succession after the Vice President: the Speaker of the House of Representatives, the President *pro tempore* of the Senate, and

[2] For an authoritative treatment of electoral reform, see Lucius Wilmerding, Jr., *The Electoral College* (New Brunswick, N. J.: Rutgers University Pres, 1958).

[3] Article II, sect. I, cl. 5.

[4] Lincoln, Garfield, and McKinley were assassinated; W. H. Harrison, Taylor, Harding, and F. D. Roosevelt died in office.

[5] Clinton Rossiter, *The American Presidency,* rev. ed. (New York: Harcourt, Brace and Co., 1960), pp. 221-2. See also Ruth C. Silva, *Presidential Succession* (Ann Arbor: University of Michigan Press, 1951).

then the heads of the cabinet departments in order of their creation, beginning with the Secretary of State.

The Vice President. The Founding Fathers viewed the office of the Vice President as a spot for the second-best man in the country, perhaps as a step to the top. But partly because of the development of the party system and the niggardly role assigned to the Vice President under the Constitution—as presiding officer of the Senate with a vote only in the very rarely occurring case of a tie—the significance of the office and its incumbents declined rapidly. Indeed, even the first of these, John Adams, referred to it as 'the most insignificant office that ever invention of man contrived.' More often than not occupied by an amiable mediocrity, selected by the national convention as a political 'sop' to disappointed wings of the party, or as a 'balancer' of the presidential ticket, the vice presidency became somewhat of a national joke. Thus Theodore Roosevelt, after having been nominated as Vice President in 1900, wrote General Leonard Wood, '. . . by the time you receive this you will have learned . . . that I have been forced to take the veil.' Wilson's Vice President Marshall likened himself to 'a man in a cataleptic fit' who is aware of all that is going on around him, but incapable of doing anything about it. Wilson himself commented that 'the chief embarrassment in discussing the office is that in explaining how little there is to be said about it one has apparently said all there is to say.' [6] Several early occupants of the office referred to their position as 'His Superfluous Excellency'—a phrase coined by Benjamin Franklin—and Vice President Curtis once suggested that the least the people who curiously stared into his office while on their way to important appointments elsewhere could do was to throw him some nuts.

GROWTH IN IMPORTANCE? Ever since F.D.R.'s time, however, the vice presidency has been accorded a new lease on life. Since the days of Roosevelt's first Vice President, John Nance 'Cactus Jack' Garner, the Vice President regularly attends, and in the absence of the President conducts, cabinet meetings. Beginning with Alben Barkley, affectionately known as the 'Veep' throughout the country—whom Clinton Rossiter has called 'probably the most distinguished man nominated for the office' [7] since Calhoun in 1825—the Vice President was given an important statutory position as a member of the National Security Council. President Eisenhower, more than any other

[6] For a summary of these and other reactions see Arthur Edson, 'L. B. J. Is Third Johnson V.P.,' in *The Philadelphia Sunday Bulletin*, January 22, 1961, Sec. 2, p. 5.

[7] Rossiter, op. cit. p. 138.

President before him, not only delegated many ceremonial and consultative functions to his Vice President, Richard Nixon, but, within limits, made him an active participant in his Administration; a role also delegated to Lyndon Johnson by President Kennedy. Still, Nixon had complained in 1958 that the 'Vice President is a unique official of government. He has access to information in all areas, but power in none.' [8] Nonetheless, at long last the office is the subject of new study and experimentation. Yet there is, concurrently, a gnawing awareness that the establishment of a strong, perhaps independent, Vice President might bring with it a serious undermining of the President's own position.

The President's Cabinet. The framers of the Constitution did not want to create a replica of George III, but they were fully aware that an executive must be able to act with energy and undivided purpose. To that end, they vested the executive power in one man. But one man could not run even the United States government of 1789. Executive assistants had to be provided. From time to time, Congress has created departments of the executive, now ten, each of which is headed by a secretary. These heads of departments early became known collectively as the President's *cabinet*. He has to rely heavily on them for directing the executive work of government for which he alone is responsible. His appointments to the cabinet must be approved by the Senate, but the Senate has to date refused but eight times to ratify his choice —the last time in 1959 by the margin of three votes (49:46) in the case of President Eisenhower's nomination of Lewis L. Strauss to be Secretary of Commerce. It has generally taken the view that the President as the responsible executive should not be restricted in his choice of those on whom he must rely.

SELECTIONS. As far as the Constitution goes the President's selections are limited only by the separation of powers, which prevents a member of Congress from holding an office under the United States. In practice, many political factors influence a President's appointments. He normally, but not always, picks men who are members of his own political party but, with the exception of the post of Postmaster General, which—with an occasional exception—by tradition goes to his successful campaign manager or his party's national chairman, they are not necessarily the principal political leaders of the party. In contrast to the situation in Britain, a political career in the United States is not significantly advanced by elevation to the cabinet.

[8] As quoted by Douglass Cater in *The Reporter*, November 27, 1958, p. 10.

Whether as cause or consequence of this, Presidents tend to consider other qualifications such as executive capacity and experience as being more important than political leadership. President Eisenhower's cabinets contained several successful heads of large business concerns, such as General Motors, Proctor and Gamble, and Eastman-Kodak.[9]

Cabinet posts generally go to men who have been active in party politics without becoming distinguished party leaders. They must be distributed with an eye on the different wings or factions of the party. The great geographical sections of the country and the great economic interests of labor, agriculture, and capital also claim representation, and cannot be entirely denied. The Departments of Agriculture, Commerce, and Labor must generally be headed by men who have the respect, if not the confidence, of agriculture, capital, and labor respectively.

In addition, there are always some more personal considerations. One cannot be elected President without accumulating obligations to staunch lieutenants and supporters. It would be ungracious as well as impolitic to forget these obligations entirely in forming a cabinet. And there is almost always an intimate personal friend or even a relative—e.g. Attorney General Robert Kennedy in his brother's cabinet—whom the President takes into his cabinet. A great many factors have to be considered and balanced in selecting the cabinet.

THE PRESIDENCY AT WORK

Heavy Burdens of the President. The members of the cabinet direct the work of the departments and advise the President on matters coming within his charge. Each has his own department to administer within the generally broad limits laid down by congressional legislation and by the President's decisions on broad questions of policy. When they are held, meetings of the cabinet with the President serve two main purposes. First, they provide a forum for discussion and settlement of questions that affect two or more departments. The scope of present-day government activities ensures that there will always be some interdepartmental questions to be resolved. Second,

[9] President Eisenhower's first Secretary of Labor was Martin Durkin, an ex-plumber and the sole Democrat in the cabinet, who resigned after less than eight months in office. He used to describe himself as a member of 'the Ike Cabinet of eight Millionaires and one Plumber,' and lamented that 'each time I entered a cabinet session during a policy meeting all the other members would stop talking.'

they enable the cabinet to discuss together and advise the President on matters of policy on which he wants advice—a desire that varies widely among Presidents.

All Executive Power Concentrated in the President. Discussions in the cabinet are confidential. Until President Eisenhower introduced his smoothly functioning quasi-military staff-and-command system—quickly scrapped by his successor—no records of these discussions were kept. It still rests with the President what public announcements, if any, are to be made as a result of discussions. The expressed views of members are not executive decisions marking out lines of policy, but merely recommendations to the President. He may, as did President Eisenhower, treat the members of the cabinet as colleagues whose combined judgment he is willing to follow. But there is nothing in the Constitution making them colleagues who share the power and responsibility for decision. Rather, they are his subordinates and subject to his command.

SUBORDINATE POSITION OF CABINET. Accordingly, he may ignore their advice. He may make decisions affecting their departments without consulting them. Indeed, President Kennedy's approach to cabinet meetings provides a sharp break with the formal, almost ritualistic methods of President Eisenhower. Believing meetings of the cabinet quite frankly to be a waste of time, President Kennedy has viewed them as little more than 'pleasant affairs,' has called them but very infrequently, and, in general, has preferred to be in touch with cabinet members individually or in small groups. Often, a President's most confidential advisers are not in the cabinet at all. This was true in the cases of Harry Hopkins, F.D.R.'s intimate co-worker, and Milton Eisenhower, President Eisenhower's brother. Even when the President's entire cabinet votes against his proposal, he may say, as Lincoln did on one occasion when his seven cabinet members opposed something he favored: 'Noes, seven, Ayes, one: the Ayes have it!' President Polk, who insisted on regular cabinet meetings—he called some 400 in his four years in office— nevertheless readily exercised the presidential prerogative of ignoring the collective opposition of his cabinet. Thus he wrote of a measure he had just vetoed, '. . . having made up my mind that I could not sign the Bill under any circumstances, it was unnecessary to consult the Cabinet on the subject.' [10]

The cabinet is not collectively responsible with the President for the deci-

[10] As quoted by Sidney Heyman in 'The Cabinet's Job as Eisenhower Sees It,' *The New York Times Sunday Magazine*, July 20, 1958, p. 38.

sions taken. He is the executive and he alone carries the responsibility. The cabinet, as Professor R. F. Fenno, Jr., its closest modern student has so well observed, is weakest in making direct contributions to policy decisions and in interdepartmental co-ordination; it is strongest in its role of a political sounding board presidential adviser and 'as a forum in which some overall administrative coherence' is obtainable. However, as Professor Fenno goes on to point out, whereas the cabinet *as a group* 'draws its life breath from the President, . . . as individuals the cabinet members are by no means so dependent upon him.' [11]

A MEASURE OF INDEPENDENCE. Thus, acting as individual department heads, members of cabinets have indeed been known to wield a considerable amount of independence of the President—e.g. Jesse Jones as Secretary of Commerce and in other positions close to the business community under President Franklin D. Roosevelt from 1933 to 1944. The possibility of such independence, however limited, is enhanced by the fact that, in addition to policy-making, the cabinet is also a vital sounding board for *public opinion.* The various department heads respond to different sources of such opinion, and a 'popular member'—'popular' with his particular 'constituency'—often serves admirably to draw support to the President; or, as in the case of Jesse Jones (whom the President finally fired when he had enough) to stimulate opposition. Be that as it may, to be a 'strong' cabinet member, the department head must have strong non-presidential 'public' prestige, party following, legislative support, or roots of influence in his own department. This may well mean that, in effect, the member often operates not as a part of the formal body, but independently—and it sometimes means that he will operate to get for his area of responsibility the bigger piece of the pie ere a fellow cabinet-member moves in to do the same for his. In this sense, the political help which the President receives, thus does not come from the cabinet as a group, but from its individual members operating outside the group—and not infrequently with untowardly tenacious individualism (of which examples in addition to the case of Jesse Jones would be F.D.R.'s Secretary of the Interior Harold L. Ickes, President Truman's Secretary of Commerce Charles S. Sawyer, and President Eisenhower's Secretary of the Treasury George M. Humphrey).

SOLE PRESIDENTIAL RESPONSIBILITY. But whatever the roles of the cabinet and his other advisers, there is no doubt whatsoever that the President is very

[11] Richard F. Fenno, Jr., *The President's Cabinet* (New York: Vintage Books, 1959), pp. 155 and 248. (Italics supplied.)

limited in attempts to shift the burdens of his office. No interest of power and consequence is willing to accept a denial of its demands from the head of a department, but insists on having a decision from the President. Because the cabinet cannot compel the President to take account of their views, they often do not give him the blunt, candid criticism he needs, although they are neither irresponsible nor unco-operative. He can dismiss them at will, but it is often politically inexpedient to reveal a rift in the cabinet. There is constant danger that they—and his unofficial advisers—will become sycophants flattering him with too ready confirmation of his views. At any rate, like all men who reach a high pinnacle of authority, the President is likely to be isolated and lonely. President Truman viewed his position—and it was one he loved and respected—as 'the loneliest office in the world.' And after but two weeks in office, President Kennedy wistfully remarked, 'the President is quite alone at the top!'

Help for the President. The steadily growing burdens of the office of President, and the weakness of the cabinet as an advising and deliberating body, led to the establishment of a White House Office under President Roosevelt in 1939. It is a part of the President's personal domain, called the *Executive Office of the President.* In addition to the White House Office, which had 300 employees in 1963, it consists of the National Security Council, the Central Intelligence Agency, the Bureau of the Budget, the Office of Emergency Planning, and the Council of Economic Advisers. All of these report directly to the President. They will be discussed briefly later.

THE WHITE HOUSE OFFICE. As the name implies the White House Office consists of the people deemed essential to the President in his intimate day-to-day operations and comprises his personal staff. Under President Eisenhower, they were headed by the *Assistant to the President,* who in the person of former Governor Sherman Adams of New Hampshire attained a position of immense power and influence. From his assumption of office early in January 1953 until his forced departure from the scene in 1958 as a result of his questionable acceptance of certain gifts from an enterprising private citizen, Mr. Adams—with the full knowledge and consent of the President —exercised more power than any other presidential aide in modern times. Nothing and no one could reach the President without the approval of Adams. Indeed, President Eisenhower quite specifically required that every major document and recommendation reaching his desk bear the marking 'O.K.—S.A.' But Adams's successor, General Wilton B. Persons, was neither given nor did he exercise the degree and scope of authority vested in his predecessor, and the post was summarily abolished by President Kennedy even prior to his inauguration.

Other important members of the White House staff usually are personal presidential assistants for press relations, congressional relations, speechwriting, economic affairs, national defense, foreign affairs, atomic energy affairs, appointments, and others. Then there is the group of personal attendants—military aides, physicians, secretaries, a special legal counsel, and so forth. It must be restated that none of these people reports to any other member of the executive branch except the President.

STAFF WORK. Presidents take different approaches to the work they expect from their staffs. President Eisenhower relied as heavily on the staff system in the White House as he had in the Army—it answered precisely the needs of the military man and national hero, who had little penchant for detail and placed the concept of 'harmony' and 'teamwork' above every other facet of his entourage (quite in contrast to Franklin D. Roosevelt, for one, who delighted in what he saw as the benefits of heady competition and even strife among his immediate subordinates). Thus President Eisenhower also caused the establishment of a cabinet secretariat, headed by an executive secretary, through whom the President endeavored to make of the cabinet an effective co-ordinating board that would produce the teamwork in his Administration which he craved so much. And he relied on the cabinet and his staff for collective advice more than had any of his predecessors—and infinitely more than his successor.

The latter, disdaining and fearing the kind of lofty isolation his predecessor seemed to relish, set out at once to make the White House, his office, the very fountainhead of governmental action. A free-wheeling innovator in the exercise of presidential power, Kennedy has shown a clear preference for the direct, personal approach, a desire to deal with problems from their inception to proposed solution and decision. He has demonstrated an undisguised distaste, if not contempt, for formal agenda and committee and staff meetings. The concept of a Sherman Adams, indeed any so-called 'No. One Assistant' is out—instead President Kennedy surrounded himself with six or eight bright and young associates who work closely *with* him, but never *instead* of him. Under Kennedy, as one close observer of the Washington scene commented with insight, the staff has been shaped to meet the needs of a President with 'abundant stores of restless energy, with a great capacity for assimilating detail, and with a taste for tackling issues before the rough edges are planed away in co-ordination.' [12]

Main Functions of the President. A brief summary cannot give a just impression of the scope of the executive office. The Constitution charges the President to see that the laws are faithfully executed. Today, this means that he must supervise the vast range of regulation and services of the positive state in so far as they are federal and not matters for the separate states. Congress annually piles new duties on the executive, many of which are really of a legislative nature.[13] Whether through delegation by Congress or through the inherent ordinance power of the executive, the President must now make ordinances and regulations which, in sheer bulk, dwarf the output of Congress into insignificance. He must see to the appointment and direction of the officers necessary for the tasks in hand. The Senate shares in some 45,000 appointments to the 'higher' offices, including the federal judiciary, postmasters, military appointments, and the major executive officers. The 'lower' offices are mostly filled by heads of departments under civil service regulations. Yet the President must personally attend, perfunctorily or otherwise, to some 6000 appointments in the course of a year. Subject to certain civil service regulations, he has power to discipline and remove the civil servants of the United States. He has absolute power of removal over 'purely executive' officials, such as members of his cabinet or his Executive Office. Members of the independent regulatory commissions, such as the Interstate Commerce Commission, however, can be removed by him only for specific causes of mal-, mis-, or non-feasance in office. Of course, he has no power of dismissal over the judiciary at all.

He has charge of the conduct of foreign policy, subject to Senate approval of treaties, by a two-thirds vote, and to congressional support by way of necessary appropriations and legislation. While Congress declares war, it is his task to see that the war is fought with energy and intelligence to a successful conclusion. Much discretionary power and heavy responsibility lie with him to deal with all emergencies affecting the nation, whether war or civil disturbance. He must thus keep the peace of the country and ascertain obedience to law and order—as was so dramatically demonstrated by the dispatch of federal troops to Arkansas, Mississippi, and Alabama by Eisenhower in 1957 and Kennedy in 1962 and 1963, respectively, in order to secure com-

---

[12] Joseph Kraft, 'Kennedy's Working Staff,' *Harper's Magazine,* December 1962, p. 30.
[13] The natural query whether this does not violate the separation of powers will be considered later.

pliance with federal court orders that had been deliberately defied by the governors of the three states. In addition, and under present conditions, he must give much of his time to the developing of legislative policy, despite the separation of powers. More will be said on this point later. Finally, the administrative organization of the government of the United States is now so huge that it is a tremendous task to combat its inertia, subdue its internal rivalries, and erase its cross-purposes. Testimony is almost unanimous that the President's burden is too great for any man to carry, despite some of the recent innovations we have just discussed.

AGGRANDIZEMENT. It has already been said that the positive state has everywhere aggrandized the executive. The American presidency is a striking illustration of this truth. The executive must actually perform the tasks of modern government, tasks of such importance to the economy and community life that inefficiency or failure is serious. The President is responsible, and his powers tend to become commensurate with the responsibility. He may need assistance in the exercise of his powers, but he cannot delegate their substance. In any crisis that requires something to be done, almost everyone looks to the President. The country, it is said, needs leadership and knows it. Congress, for reasons that will appear, is peculiarly unfitted to give this leadership, and so it must come from the President. As President Truman put the matter,

> The President, who is Commander in Chief and who represents the interest of all the people, must be able to act at all times to meet any sudden threat to the nation's security. A wise President will always work with Congress, but when Congress fails to act or is unable to act in a crisis, the President under the Constitution, must use his powers to safeguard the nation.[14]

THE NATION'S LEADER. The clearest and most dramatic proof of this comes in the field of foreign affairs. Congress can legislate the country into isolationism, and the Senate can reject all entangling alliances. Yet the President actually conducts foreign policy, and he may take irrevocable steps which in effect commit the country to intervention. While he cannot make treaties, he can make *executive agreements* with foreign states, which often are as effective as treaties. His power to recognize, or to refuse to recognize, newly established governments can be used with decisive effect. In short, his conduct of foreign affairs, as one interpretation of Franklin Roosevelt's policy

[14] *The New York Times*, February 18, 1956.

from 1939 to 1941 would have it, may make war inevitable. And when it comes, the President who has been preparing for it, while Congress has not, is likely to have the major share in deciding how it is to be fought.

President Roosevelt and his advisers, and not Congress, framed the New Deal. It is true this was an emergency like war, but Theodore Roosevelt and Woodrow Wilson exercised similar, if not as great, influence on legislation. The legislation of today is often enacted in general terms. Its detailed application depends more and more on rules and regulations and particular discretionary decisions taken by the executive. The President—or his subordinates over whom he has power of control—exercises these discretionary powers, and the great interests of the country find they must deal with the President as well as with Congress.

At every turn, eyes are focused on the President. His constitutional powers are not at all equal to what he is expected to do. But the fact that everyone listens when he speaks, and that he can reach everybody through the radio, television, and press conferences, often gives him decisive influence where he lacks power. The White House has been called the biggest pulpit in the country. The man who can sway this congregation has something better than formal power. The more serious issue is whether one man can do what is now expected of the President. Be that as it may, it is to him, above all others, that the people look for leadership.

THE EXECUTIVE IN BRITAIN

THE BRITISH CHIEF OF STATE: THE MONARCH

A discussion of the British executive must first take account of the position of the hereditary monarch. In wraith-like legal formalism devoid of substance, the monarch—today Queen Elizabeth II—is the executive. The members of the cabinet are Her Majesty's ministers who tender her advice. While in reality they take all responsibility for actions of the government, legally their acts are the acts of the Queen. Even the judges are Her Majesty's judges, though no monarch since the Stuarts has interfered with the course of justice. The monarch must assent to bills before they become law, but the last refusal was in 1707. The monarch is the head of the state, but it is an office devoid of actual power. The legal rule that the monarch can do no wrong, combined with the conventional rule that he must act on the advice of his ministers, shifts both responsibility and power to the ministers. The legal forms are merely echoes of a time when the monarch had the reality of power.

Surviving Rights. Out of the wreck of his former pre-eminence the monarch has saved what Bagehot called 'the right to be consulted, the right to encourage and the right to warn.' Because his consent, however perfunctory, is required for statutes and many other official acts, he could not well be deprived of all contact with affairs of state. His ministers keep him advised on major issues and they receive in return such counsel and caution as he cares to give them. Governments change and ministers come and go. A monarch who has had many years on the throne has the opportunity for a wide grasp of public affairs. If he joins study and effort to ability, his position obviously enables him to wield great influence. His hand is strengthened by the social popularity with the masses of the people that the monarchy has enjoyed in the present century. Queen Victoria exercised the three rights above to the full and not without effect. But she was the last powerful British monarch. Both she and Edward VII had very substantial influence in foreign policy. Gladstone viewed her as the 'external leader of the opposition party.' George V took a great interest in domestic matters. George VI was a symbol of British determination during World War II, and he had a luncheon-consultation once a week with his Prime Minister, Winston Churchill.

The Monarch's Personal Prerogatives. In addition, the monarch has certain ill-defined personal prerogatives, chiefly relics of the past. The monarch appoints the Prime Minister and is under no *legal* obligation to accept advice as to the choice—although such advice is customarily sought and given. As long as one party has a clear majority in Parliament and that party has an acknowledged leader, the monarch has, in reality, no choice, but must accept that acknowledged leader as Prime Minister. Queen Victoria's selection of Lord Derby in 1858 was probably the last clear-cut case of monarchial preference. However, if the Prime Minister dies or resigns, and the majority party has no acknowledged leader, or if after a three-or-more-cornered election fight no party gets a clear majority, the monarch has the personal responsibility of picking a Prime Minister. This represents power as well as influence, and it may assume critical importance if three or more political parties become a permanent feature. George V is credited with a leading role in the formation of the National Government coalition under Ramsay MacDonald in 1931. Queen Elizabeth II in 1957 was confronted with a choice between Conservatives Macmillan and Butler to succeed the resigned Sir Anthony Eden, because the Conservative party had not selected a leader to replace him. However, the Queen, of course, sought the counsel of the two senior statesmen of the party, Churchill and Lord Salisbury, who evidently advised her to send for Mr. Macmillan.

The monarch has the formal *legal* power to dismiss his ministers, and it is sometimes argued that he may constitutionally dismiss them on his own motion if he believes that the cabinet, while holding the support of the majority in Parliament, has decisively lost the support of the electorate. More accurately, it is suggested that the monarch, if he so believes, may threaten dismissal as a means of securing the consent of the Prime Minister to a dissolution of Parliament, thus bringing on an election to test the matter; and that if the Prime Minister refuses, the monarch may dismiss the cabinet. This is not likely to occur.

Some quarters also maintain that in certain circumstances the monarch may refuse the request of the Prime Minister for a dissolution of the House of Commons, if he has grounds for thinking that an alternative government can get the parliamentary support the Prime Minister has lost. It is contended that the monarch is the guardian of the constitution and that if a government is flouting the will of the people, or is seeking to recoup its fortunes by suddenly springing an unnecessary election on trivial grounds, he may intervene. But this, too, is far more theoretical than real.

All matters touching the relationship of monarch, cabinet, and Parliament are supposed to be settled by the conventions of the constitution, resting on past precedents and practice. Yet on the two points of the monarch's prerogatives above, the precedents are confusing and inconclusive, affording room for difference of opinion. However, royal intervention has far greater dangers for the constitution than those it is intended to meet. If the monarch turns out to be wrong in his judgment and the country supports the government he threatened to dismiss, or if his alternative government gets no parliamentary support and the succeeding election returns to the House of Commons a clear majority supporting the party leader to whom he refused a dissolution, relations between the monarch and that leader's party are bound to be seriously strained. The monarch will be blamed for taking sides, and if the political party that stood to benefit from this intervention does not repudiate his action, it will be turned into a party of the monarch's friends —a return to the days of George III!

Need for Neutrality. In trying to guard the constitution, the monarch may wreck it. If he is to retain his throne in a system of parliamentary government he must, at all costs, retain his neutrality. Of such stuff constitutional monarchy is made. He must bide his time and wait for the *electorate* to say whether the cabinet has lost its sympathy. Even at the expense and confusion of an unnecessary election, he must let the electorate punish an over-crafty cabinet.

Yet the breakdown of the traditional two party system into three or more parties of comparable strength will put an alarming burden on the Chief of State. He has to find a Prime Minister who must be someone who can throw together a coalition. At times it will be tempting, and on rare occasion even legitimate, to try other combinations without resorting to a dissolution and a new election every time a government is defeated in the House. The genuinely important present-day function of the monarch is to stand as a symbol of unity, and there is a natural disposition to hope that the monarch may express that unity at times when the factiousness of numerous parties threatens to make orderly government impossible. No doubt the monarch can appeal to whatever unity underlies party faction and, in so far as it exists, exert a moderating influence and perhaps tide the country over particular crises. The continuity and security of his office should enable him to take an objective view not always reached by the leaders of political parties. But the factiousness of numerous parties is generally symptomatic of a deeper disunity, and if so, the monarch may get little more for his pains than charges of partisanship.

The Monarch as a Symbol of Unity and Continuity. The effectiveness of the monarch as a symbol of unity, to convey a sense of continuity, as long as the duties of his office do not require him to take sides, is not open to question. Steady allegiance to Country, Nation, Community is difficult to obtain because most people are not greatly moved by abstractions. The living figure brings the argument for subordinating our desires to the good of the whole down to the level of common experience. The monarch can call men to arms more effectively than can the Country or the Nation. The good that governments do can be ascribed, through the monarch, to the people; the evil they do can be pinned on the ephemeral government of the day. The opposition which obstructs that government maintains its prestige more easily because it is Her Majesty's Loyal Opposition. It is loyal to the permanent common interests and fundamental aspirations of the British people, while opposed to the audacity of a temporary parliamentary majority.

In fact, the symbol has triumphed over the person. As the case of the abdication of Edward VIII shows, a monarch who does not outwardly conform to the proprieties that move the bulk of the nation must go. Some are disposed to think the symbolism too powerful. The monarch is inevitably a symbol of conservatism, of what has been revered in the nation's past. By nurturing that reverence and projecting it strongly into the present, the monarch may retard necessary social change. The monarch cannot lead in a new attitude toward divorce; he must be a symbol of old attitudes. Yet there is no doubt that in Britain the monarch is identified with the fundamental aspirations of the British people. He is a symbol of the past, present, and future—a personification of British hope. Even the Labour party, which wants to change much in Britain, does not wish to abolish the monarchy. Only the tiny British Communist party does. No monarchy in the world is more secure or more respected than Britain's—to which the present Queen's popularity, after more than eleven years of rule, bears eloquent witness.

The Cabinet as the British Executive

In Britain, the executive, in the narrow sense under consideration here, is the *cabinet*. It consists of the Prime Minister and about twenty colleagues who are the appointed heads of the more important of the roughly thirty-five departments of the government. It has now approximately twice as many members as it had a hundred years ago. As the activities of government expanded, important new departments—labor, education, housing, public works, and so on—were organized, and room had to be found in the cabinet for their heads. It is now admittedly too large for effective discussion and decision, but it is difficult to reduce.

Members of Parliament. The monarch calls on the leader of the majority party in the newly elected House of Commons to be Prime Minister. The Prime Minister is then free to choose his cabinet. The only *constitutional limitation* is that the persons he chooses must either have a seat in Parliament or get one without delay. The linking of the cabinet with Parliament is vital to the British system of fusion of powers and thus differs radically from the American system.

The British Parliament is composed of two chambers, the House of Commons and the House of Lords. While members of the cabinet may be chosen from either House, the great majority are always selected from the House of Commons. The selection of the Earl of Home as Foreign Secretary by Prime Minister Macmillan in 1960 excited sharp attacks from both Labourites and Conservatives. Custom now decrees that the Prime Minister *must* be a Commoner. The last to be chosen from the House of Lords was Lord Salisbury, in 1900. As we shall see later, the House of Lords is not representative of the electorate and has lost most of the powers it once had. The House of Commons does represent the electorate, and only by retaining its confidence can the cabinet retain office. It is said that the cabinet is responsible to Parliament, but it would be more accurate to say it is responsible to the House of Commons.

Selection by the Prime Minister. As a matter of practical politics, the Prime Minister in picking his cabinet has to give weight to roughly the same kind of considerations as affect the President's choice of a cabinet. The Scots and the Welsh and the various sections of England must not be forgotten. Important social and economic interests cannot be passed over. Certain alliances within the party support the Prime Minister's leadership. These must be held together and the bargains on which they are based must be kept. In addition, the Prime Minister's choice is further limited by factors that the President can ignore. Not only must the British cabinet be chosen from Parliament, but certain members of Parliament, particularly of the House of Commons, have special claims to consideration. Members of former cabinets, members who are able parliamentarians and effective critics when the party is in opposition, are difficult to exclude. It may even be necessary for the Prime Minister to include in the cabinet an unsuccessful rival for the leadership of the party, as Macmillan did in choosing Butler as an important member of his first cabinet in 1957. There may be some claimant for cabinet rank whose only recommendation is that it will be safer to have him inside than outside. Many exceedingly delicate decisions must be made, for the Prime Minister, unlike the President, must pick a team of colleagues who will work together and always defend one another in public, who can command the respect of the House of Commons and retain the confidence of the majority therein, who can defend their departments effectively in Parliament as well as direct them efficiently.

MINISTERS OF THE MONARCH. The members of the cabinet are all ministers of the monarch, a body of equals because each is equally commissioned to advise Her Majesty. They need to be united by mutual respect, if not by affection. It is, of course, impossible for twenty men genuinely to agree on all major issues. At the same time, it will not do for foreign policy to commit itself to preparation for war, while financial policy insists on a sharp cut in all government expenditures. Major policy is a unity; the ship of state cannot sail in different directions at one and the same time. Hence the conventions of the constitution, which seek to get from the team the concerted action that a monarch or a President can supply.

Team Work. While each minister is responsible individually to Parliament for the operation of his department, *all members of the cabinet are responsible collectively* for each department and for general policy. This does not mean that all decisions are taken collectively; that is physically impossible today. It does mean that when a minister has taken an important decision on his own initiative, the others must either defend him in the face of parliamentary criticism or throw him to the wolves. As a result, each minister hesitates to take important decisions without prior consultation with the Prime Minister at least, and each takes a personal interest in what the others are doing. Every decision taken in cabinet must be supported by all. A minister who is doubtful of the wisdom of a decision must either conceal his misgivings or part company with his colleagues. The latter course of action was taken, for example, by the Marquess of Salisbury over policy on Cyprus in the Macmillan cabinet in 1957. Lord Melbourne is reported to have told his cabinet on one occasion that he did not much care what decision was taken as long as they all told the same story. Mistakes in policy are not likely to be as immediately disastrous to confidence, in Parliament and in the country, as are evidences of internal disagreement.

COMMON PARTY ALLEGIANCE. It is therefore vitally important for the Prime Minister to pick a good team and hold it together. The greatest single advantage he can have in his selection is to be able to choose it from a single, well-disciplined political party. This ensures, to begin with, a certain similarity of view and temperament, with all members having strong loyalties to the party and hesitating to jeopardize its fortunes by open dissension. Equally important, the political fortunes of each are bound up with those of the party. Each knows that the party will punish revolts, and this disciplines toward agreement. These favorable conditions do not exist when a cabinet is chosen from a coalition of parties (of which contemporary Italy, for one, is a case in point). In 1932, the cabinet of the National Coalition could not agree on tariff policy, and publicly announced an agreement to differ on this question. Such a formula will work only within very narrow limits, and it weakens a government dangerously.

As long as it works within the confines of a two-party system, the British cabinet is a remarkably successful device for combining vigorous and unified direction, joint counsel, and mutual criticism, and for the maturing of decisions through discussion. When working satisfactorily, the cabinet system provides for each of its members desirable frank discussion and blunt criticism. But it will not work satisfactorily when the cabinet has to be pieced together from two or more parties.

The Captain of the Team. Every team needs a captain, and this leadership is accorded to the Prime Minister. It is commonly said that the only significance of the 'prime,' is to make him *primus inter pares,* first among equals. This phrase, however, means nothing unless it means he is something more than an equal. With the coming of the popular franchise and strongly disciplined political parties, it was inevitable that the acknowledged leader of the majority party would have significant pre-eminence in the cabinet. He is a key figure in the central organization of the party, he leads the party in Parliament and in election campaigns, and so has an immense influence on the policy and platforms of the party. Lord Walpole viewed him as the 'political ruler of England.' There is much drama in leadership and little in complex policies, no matter how important they may be for the country. That section of the electorate which is not rigidly frozen in its party allegiance, does not—as indeed one cannot—separate men from measures. Thus general elections have tended to become personal contests between the leaders of the rival parties, and the verdict at the polls to become the choice of a Prime Minister by the people. He has a mandate to lead which his colleagues lack. It is thus fair to say that today the 'P.M.' is no longer *primus* among the *pares* in the cabinet—but *primus,* with the other cabinet ministers acting as responsible and competent team assistants.

HIS PRE-EMINENCE. The Prime Minister's pre-eminence is evident at every turn. He is the channel of communication between the cabinet and the monarch. In sudden emergencies that do not give him time to consult the cabinet, he will act on his own initiative. Particular ministers after consulting him will often take decisions they would not risk on their own judgment. The House of Commons and the country expect him to make all important statements on policy. He is, again in Walpole's words, 'the keystone of the arch.' On advice from him, the monarch will dismiss a minister or force his resignation, e.g. Hugh Dalton, the Chancellor of the Exchequer, in 1947. Most important, it is now settled as a result of the practice of recent years that the decision to advise a dissolution of Parliament rests solely with him. This is a heavy weapon to keep hanging over the heads of a cabinet that cannot make up its mind.

BUT NOT THE CHIEF EXECUTIVE. Yet he remains the captain of a team and has not become Chief Executive for two main reasons. First, the other ministers of the cabinet are equally responsible to Parliament and thus have an equal personal stake in policy. He has to carry them with him. Second, his leadership of the government depends on maintaining control over the House of Commons. He cannot risk frequent resignations and dismissals, nor weak and unconvincing support of policy by his colleagues on the floor of the House, for that will undermine the solidarity of the party majority. The knowledge that they must all hang together or hang separately not only disposes them to earnest effort at agreement, but also limits what the Prime Minister can do with his unquestioned pre-eminence. It ensures the fullness of discussion and candor in criticism that the President of the United States often fails to get in his cabinet even when he solicits it.

The Functions of the British Cabinet. The broad functions of the cabinet can now be stated very briefly. As heads of departments, they furnish direction and drive to the activities of the civil service. They defend the actions of their departments in Parliament, discharging their responsibility to Parliament by answering without demur the most trivial questions in minute detail. No civil servant is ever asked or allowed to defend himself in Parliament. The minister is responsible for every action, and he does not shirk it. Collectively, they must co-ordinate the work of their separate departments, ironing out interdepartmental disputes, and thus integrating the diverse activities of hundreds of thousands of civil servants.

A COMMITTEE OF PARLIAMENT. As an executive committee of Parliament, they must organize the work that the House of Commons particularly is expected to do in a session. They allot the time to be spent on particular matters, prepare the budget and the legislative program that the House is to consider. They pilot government bills through the House, explaining their purpose and meaning and defending them against criticism. Through their pervasive control, they channel the energies of the House, which otherwise would be largely dissipated in discussion, into concrete accomplishments in the form of legislation.

It is through the cabinet that Parliament effects its criticism and surveillance of daily administration. On the other hand, the cabinet brings to Parliament the accumulated knowledge and experience which the civil service collects in the course of administration, and which is a vital ingredient in the making of policy for the future. It brings these data forward not in a heterogeneous mass, but transmuted into either proposed amendments to existing laws or matured plans for new legislation. It almost invariably persuades Parliament to accept its program without substantial modification because it can rely on a disciplined party majority in the House of Commons, fortified in its loyalty by the threat of a dissolution of Parliament. This gives rise to the charge that the cabinet dictates to a subservient House of Commons an indictment that will be considered later. At present, it is sufficient to see why Bagehot described the cabinet as a buckle linking Parliament and the executive— meaning the executive in the broad inclusive sense—and why it can also be described as the mainspring of government.

CO-ORDINATION OF POLICY AND ADMINISTRATION. Directing the work of a department in a government which engages in such a wide range of activities is in itself a heavy burden on a minister, even when he can rely on a number of able senior civil servants. When the tasks of co-ordinating the work of all departments, defending his department and general government policy in Parliament, maturing policy and guiding legislation through Parliament are added, it can be seen why the cabinet is said to be overworked and the job of the Prime Minister to be an exhausting one. The Prime Minister does not normally take on the work of a heavy department, but he has a host of other concerns from which his colleagues are free. There are several posts that are sinecures, such as Lord Privy Seal and Lord President of the Council, and the Prime Minister generally gives these to men whose advice and assistance on general policy are needed, but who do not wish to carry, or do not have time to perform, exacting administrative burdens. Despite this, many devices to ease and simplify the work of the cabinet have had to be introduced.

Easing the Burdens of the Cabinet. PARLIAMENTARY SECRETARIES. For many years, it has been the practice to appoint one or more parliamentary secretaries in each of the important departments of government. The parliamentary secretaries—who are political adherents of the government—are members of the *ministry* but not of the cabinet. Such posts are generally given to promising younger men in the party to keep them satisfied for the moment and train them for higher things. They assist the ministers in administration, and in answering questions and defending their departments in the House.

CABINET COMMITTEES. As the volume of decisions to be taken by the cabinet grew, and as these decisions came to involve more and more considerations, cabinet meetings became more frequent and discussions more prolonged, interfering with the time available for other pressing duties. Some relief has been found in the use of small cabinet committees. Many problems concern two or more departments very closely and others in minor degree or scarcely at all. Small *ad hoc* committees of the cabinet are set up to try for agreement on such issues, thus saving the time of the larger body for more general questions. If the committee can agree, the cabinet as a whole seldom needs to spend time on the matter. Committees are now an established feature of cabinet procedure, even flowering out in subcommittees where the issues are complex. While it does not remove them, this procedure helps to meet the mounting pressures of the positive state.

WAR CABINETS. The cabinet is now about twice as large as it should be for effective discussion and speedy decision—another reason for seeking relief through small committees. The delay involved in reaching decisions becomes quite intolerable in time of war. Lloyd George summed it up by saying you cannot wage war with a Sanhedrin. When he became Prime Minister in World War I, he set up a small War Cabinet of five members (later enlarged). These had no departmental duties and devoted themselves to planning the conduct of the war. As almost every aspect of domestic policy was necessarily subordinated to the dominant aim of winning the war, the War Cabinet was, in effect, *the cabinet*. The use of this small inner cabinet made for more rapid dispatch of business, but the divorce of deliberation on policy from the direction of administration in the several departments proved to be most unsatisfactory.

A war cabinet was again set up by Churchill in World War II. It did not follow the earlier precedent in this respect, but was largely composed of ministers who headed the departments most vitally concerned with prosecuting the war. The best decision on what to do next cannot be made without knowing in detail what is now being done and bringing that experience to bear on the decision. The solution of the problem of the overlarge and overworked cabinet is not to be found in separating the thinking from the doing.

THE PROBLEM OF SIZE. At the end of the war in Europe, the Labour Government came to power. It had a large program which involved much greater government activity and much greater congestion of cabinet business than existed at the outbreak of war. Between 1939 and 1948 six entirely new, and presumably permanent, departments of government concerned with the public interest in food, fuel and power, civil aviation, supply, national insurance, and town and country planning came into existence. The total number of departments increased sharply. On the other hand, Prime Minister Attlee reduced his cabinet to seventeen members. The ministers of the new departments, and some others as well, were not accorded cabinet rank.

This makes necessary still further use of committees. Many weighty questions on which the cabinet must decide will involve departments whose heads are not in the cabinet. These latter are drawn into discussions and decision on matters affecting their departments through membership in appropriate cabinet committees. No device has yet been found to reduce the cabinet to the most effective size of perhaps ten or twelve.

SUPER-MINISTRIES. But the British have been experimenting. In World War II, Prime Minister Churchill created, and occupied with great distinction, the office of Minister of Defence. This office was not an amalgamation of the departments concerned with navy, army, and air force. They remained intact, but Mr. Churchill, as Minister of Defence, took over the strategical conduct of the war with such over-all supervision and co-ordination of the fighting services departments as was required for the purpose.

The Ministry of Defence Act of 1946 aimed to adapt this arrangement for permanent use. It provided for a Minister of Defence, charged with formulating and applying a unified policy for all the armed services of the country. Since his appointment under this Act, the Minister of Defence had been a member of the cabinet, and the First Lord of the Admiralty, the Secretary of State for War, and the Secretary of State for Air had ceased to be members of the cabinet. The Minister of Defence was given supervisory powers over them and their departments. It came as no particular surprise, then, that in July 1963 the government announced the establishment of a unified Ministry of Defence, very much along the lines of the United States Department of Defense, established in 1947. The new British cabinet department was designed to absorb the Admiralty, War Office, and Air Ministry, although the 'separate entities' of the army, navy, and air force are to be maintained.

Here perhaps is the first instance of a new kind of organization, a super-ministry charged with co-ordination of a number of departments whose heads are not in the cabinet and who will almost certainly be subordinated to the super-minister. The cabinet may come some day to be composed largely of such super-ministers. A further tendency in this direction can be detected in the conferring on the Chancellor of the Exchequer of a co-ordinating role in matters of economic policy. Furthermore, although the War Cabinet has disappeared, there is still a small inner group in the cabinet on whom the Prime Minister places special reliance. This may well be a super-ministry in embryo. At any rate, the effective working of the cabinet system under present circumstances seems to require a still further concentration of responsibility and power in the hands of fewer men.

THE CABINET SECRETARIAT. The scope and complexity of cabinet duties is underlined by the establishment of a cabinet office under a secretary to the cabinet. Originally the cabinet was a cabal about whose very existence there was doubt. The doubt has vanished, but the deliberations have remained secret in the highest degree. Throughout the nineteenth century, however, the proceedings of the cabinet were most informal. A minister who wished to raise a matter notified the Prime Minister beforehand and then spoke to the point at the meeting. The agenda was in the Prime Minister's head and the only record of decision was the minute made by the Prime Minister for the purpose of informing the monarch. This gives some indication of the easy tempo of British government in the nineteenth century.

This lack of system became unworkable during World War I. A secretary to the cabinet was appointed in 1917 and has continued ever since. He prepares the agenda for, and keeps the minutes of, cabinet meetings. Except in cases of urgency, a minister who wants to bring a matter to cabinet must first consult the other departments concerned and then prepare a memorandum setting out the matter in detail. The cabinet office then circulates the memorandum several days before the meeting at which it will be raised. Thus all members of the cabinet are apprised in advance of the nature of the question, and those particularly concerned have had time to develop their views on it. A dozen or more higher civil servants will have posted their particular ministers on how the matter affects their departments. Business can be dispatched more rapidly and with a fuller knowledge of what is involved in the decision. Extraordinary precautions are taken to ensure the secrecy of these memoranda and of the minutes of cabinet meetings. Indeed, every cabinet minister takes a solemn oath not to disclose them.

THE CHIEF OF STATE AND CHIEF EXECUTIVE IN FRANCE: THE PRESIDENT OF THE REPUBLIC

THE INSTITUTION: DE GAULLE'S CREATION

Given the traditional French fear of a strong executive, a person who had just emerged from a deep sleep since the dramatic and drastic events of the Spring of 1958 in France would indeed have to ask whether he were in the right country! Few, if any, institutions of democratic government in the history of that philosophy have ever undergone such radical surgery as that inherent in the contrast between the institution of the executive of the Fourth (and Third) and the Fifth Republic of France. What until Charles de Gaulle's return to and re-assumption of power had been little more than a symbol of unity and continuity in the British mould in the case of the old Chief of State, and an insecure, troubled, ineffective, quarrelsome, and short-lived institution of executive power and authority in the case of the old Council of Ministers or cabinet, has been moulded by President de Gaulle into a powerful fountainhead of extraordinary potency and influence. Not perhaps so much as a result of the Constitution of 1958—although, as we saw in Chapter IV, it was drafted by de Gaulle, Michel Debré, and their Gaullist associates and clearly reflects their wishes and governmental creed of a strong executive—but largely because of the decisive, strong, even autocratic personal leadership of General de Gaulle. Coupled with the peculiarly difficult and delicate problems left by the Fourth Republic, notably Algeria, de Gaulle has forged in his person as *le Président de la Cinquième République* the kind of strong and powerful executive that, on a reading of French republican history, would have had to be deemed both impossible and illogical.

Yet the weakness and instability of the Fourth Republic, which featured twenty-five cabinets in the mere dozen years of its existence, and the profound national emergency brought about by the festering sore of the Algerian problem, capped by the military revolt there of May 1958, caused incumbent President René Coty to issue the call that had become an almost foregone conclusion: *de Gaulle au pouvoir!* Emerging from twelve years of self-imposed retirement from active politics, Charles de Gaulle did just that, essentially presenting his countrymen with a choice of 'me-or-chaos.' With his investiture as the twenty-fifth and last *premier* of the moribund Fourth Republic, after having listened to his short seven-minute speech outlining the terms on which he had accepted the call to power, the once proud French Parliament in effect faded away, leaving the Republic to General de Gaulle. The electorate approved the proposed de Gaulle Constitution by a four to one margin in September 1958 and under its provisions—to be described presently—he was elected as the first President of the Fifth Republic by almost 80 per cent of the valid ballots cast three months later, with Michel Debré thereupon becoming the first Prime Minister.

Election: Indirect and Direct. According to the original Article 6 of the de Gaulle Constitution, the President of France is elected for a seven-year term of office (no limits on the number of terms being indicated) by a huge electoral college—numbering 81,761 officials!—consisting of the members of Parliament, local government representatives of metropolitan and overseas departments, members of overseas assemblies and those of the member states of the Community, and—by far the most sizable group—members and delegates of the municipal councils of France and overseas departments. It was this body that elected de Gaulle President. The theory that underlay such an electoral college was the belief that it would be less likely than direct popular election to 'squander' votes among many candidates and that it would be more likely to choose a truly national figure than the ever-bickering, ever-political Parliament—which had thus selected the two Presidents of the Fourth Republic, Vincent Auriol and René Coty.

But in the Summer of 1962 de Gaulle suddenly announced that he would take to the people, in a referendum, the question of whether future presidential elections should be held by popular vote! He was motivated by the conviction that only by such popular approval could a President of less personal stature than he maintain his own executive authority against the assaults of Parliament. As we have seen, the Constitution provides for an orderly amendment procedure, involving consultation with Parliament, prior to submittal of a proposal to the people. But in the face of the nearly unanimous judicial opinion in France that the prescribed Parliamentary channel only was constitutional, the President deliberately determined to bypass Parliament and go directly to the people—a clear indication that he was prepared to subjugate Parliament even more, if possible. The National Assembly did fight back and toppled the first Pompidou Government on the referendum issue by a censure motion, with de Gaulle then immediately exercising his constitutional prerogative of dissolving the Assembly. He proceeded with the referendum, which, after several threats to resign if he were to lose, he won by the rather modest margin of 61.8 per cent of the popular votes cast. Yet, despite dire predictions, he gained a resounding victory in the almost immediately following elections to the new National Assembly, giving him and his party majority control of the lower chamber for the first time in the history of republican France, and thus turning a setback by Parliament and a less-than-enthusiastic referendum endorsement into a victory of major proportions at the polls. 'Again I was right, despite everyone,' the President crowed.

Chief of State and Chief Executive: Powers. Combining certain powers of the British cabinet and the American presidential form of government, but, as will become apparent, being exactly like neither of the two and not the sum of both, the President nonetheless is, in effect, both Chief of State and Chief Executive, with the Prime Minister or Premier cast in the role of his Chief of Staff or, as some would have it, busy Chief Clerk. Briefly summarized, in addition to the obvious ceremonial functions and powers of a Chief of State, his more important constitutional, independent powers are: selecting the Premier; presiding over the Council of Ministers; dissolving the Chamber of Deputies, but no more frequently than once a year and not while Article 16 (see below) is in force (the Senate is not dissolvable at all); vetoing a request for a popular referendum from the legislature or the ministry; submitting legislation directly to the people in a referendum; appointing and removing high officials; negotiating treaties and protocols; commanding the armed forces; sending messages to Parliament; signing laws and decrees; referring matters to the Constitutional Council for a ruling on their constitutionality; pardoning and reprieving. In effect, if not in constitutional theory, the President also selects most of the members of the Council of Ministers. Indeed, he is a powerful crisis executive—a far cry from the reignless, ruleless figurehead of the republics of old. Yet there remains to be discussed an even more potent constitutional provision, Article 16.

ARTICLE 16. This famous emergency power—shades of the Weimar Republic's Article 48—constitutes all but *carte blanche* to the President to assume such power to all intents and purposes at his discretion. For, according to the language of that provision of the Constitution:

> When the institutions of the Republic, the independence of the nation, the integrity of its territory or the fulfillment of its international commitments are threatened in a grave and immediate manner and when the regular functioning of the constitutional governmental authorities is interrupted, the President of the Republic shall take the measures commanded by these circumstances, after official consultation with the Premier, the Presidents of the assemblies and the Constitutional Council.

De Gaulle's insistence upon that provision had its roots in the utter collapse of France's Third Republic when Germany invaded the country in 1940 and, only to a slightly lesser extent, the inability of the leaders of the Fourth Republic to cope with the Algerian situation. On April 23, 1961, de Gaulle invoked the authority thus given to him by the sweeping terms of Article 16 as a result of the abortive attempt of segments of the French Army in Algeria to seize power. He made relatively little use of it and, partly in response to popular criticism, and partly because he had crushed the rebellion, he relinquished it about five months later. It is, of course, intriguing to contemplate the use of this extraordinary power in the hands of one less dedicated to *la patrie* and less proven than the revered first President. To build constitutional safeguards upon personalities is a dangerous governmental game.

THE COUNCIL OF MINISTERS OR CABINET

Powers. Also known as 'the Government,' the Fifth Republic's Council of Ministers, quite unlike those of the preceding republics, functions wholly in the shadow of the strong President, whose creature and executor it is. In the President's image it devises and executes policy; proposes legislation; ratifies ordinances and decrees and supervises their administration and execution. It represents the day-to-day workhorse of the executive branch, presided over by the Premier who is 'the President's man' in name and in fact.

An extraordinarily significant power bestowed by Article 38 of the Constitution upon 'the government' i.e. the Council of Ministers, is that of the making of 'ordinances' or 'decrees' for a limited period in order to 'carry out its program.' It must ask Parliament for an enabling act to invoke this power to supplant 'measures that are normally within the domain of law.' Premier Debré sought, and was given, such emergency power for his cabinet for an entire year and applied it to a host of subjects.

Composition. Theoretically chosen by the Premier, but actually by the President with the active advice and concurrence of the former, the Gaullist cabinets have all reflected the kind of governmental virtues so close to the heart of Charles de Gaulle: non-partisanship; fierce loyalty to duly constituted authority (and de Gaulle); expertise, preferably obtained through long-term apprenticeship in the upper echelons of France's fine civil service; and relative youth—an almost heretical suggestion for cabinet membership in the days gone by! The Constitution of the Fifth Republic eliminated its predecessors' requirements for formal cabinet investiture by the National Assembly, but the Debré cabinet and the cabinets of his successor, Georges Pompidou, were presented to that weakened body as a matter of courtesy— or perhaps as a cynical game.

To date, the cabinets of the Fifth Republic have averaged about twenty-five members, with the second Pompidou cabinet consisting of twenty-nine as of the Autumn of 1963. A majority are inevitably practicing or nominal Gaullists (members of the U.N.R.)—but by design members of other political parties have also been represented, notably those of the Catholic M.R.P.

and the Independents and Peasants. Twenty-one of the members of the above-mentioned Pompidou cabinet had sat in Parliament at one time or another, but the Constitution forbids simultaneous membership in Parliament and the Executive—a radical departure from the Third and Fourth Republics, where it was customary, although not required as in Britain.

Ministerial Responsibility. Under the Third Republic the ministers were responsible to both chambers of the legislature; under the Fourth solely to the lower branch, the National Assembly; under the Fifth Republic, the latter accountability still obtains. Thus the ministers are collectively responsible to the National Assembly and 'individually responsible for their personal actions.' But, as has been pointed out, and will be demonstrated in some detail in the two succeeding chapters, the responsibility is more theoretical than real, given the personal and constitutional umbrella provided by the strong executive and the so markedly weakened power and effectiveness of the legislature. Unlike the members of cabinets of old, which represented a host of coalition government parties, suffered from constant turnovers, and engaged in frequent and prolonged disagreements among themselves, the members of the cabinets of the Fifth Republic function very much like a team—somewhat as the British cabinet does, but without the latter's effective power as the center of gravity of governmental authority.

The Prime Minister or Premier. The personal choice and—to date, certainly—the confrere and loyal servant of the President of the Republic, the Premier is truly the instrument of presidential will, presumably without political or personal ambitions beyond those of serving his President and through him *la France.* Invested with power to initiate legislation, and clothed with the mandates of power from the office of his superior, the Premier thus enjoys infinitely more scope and authority than did his politically embroiled, short-tenured predecessors of the Third and Fourth Republics. In the latter, for example, a Premier was hardly *primus inter pares;* he was fortunate to be *par,* let alone *primus!* Today under the Fifth Republic he is *primus* without question, yet that primacy could easily be exaggerated, for it is not so much his own primacy that causes the smooth functioning of the executive branch, but the primacy of the President who invests his Premier with the necessary tools in addition to those provided by the Constitution. No longer, as was so abidingly true of Premiers of the past, must he, to stay in office, be keen, rugged, intelligent, suave, a bit of a comedian so as to appeal to sixteen political parties at once, with a facility for phrases such as 'we must govern in the center with the aid of the right to reach the goals of the left,' and ever necessarily be ready to leave office.

The Premier of the Fifth Republic is surrounded by advisers and a large personal staff which aid him in research, co-ordination, and execution of policy. Attached to his office also is a regular governmental department known as the 'Services of the Prime Minister,' which in turn has a unit reminiscent of the type of cabinet secretariat and staff favored by President Eisenhower. Moreover, a host of administrative offices and services has direct links with that of the Prime Minister. Although shorn of so much of its power, Parliament's support is both necessary and useful, at least in the domestic sphere, and Premier Debré found it expedient to institute a practice of consulting with and advising influential members of the chief Government party, U.N.R.—a practice that was continued by his successor.

THE DILEMMA

Generally pleased, indeed, with and proud of their national hero-President, who solved the desperate Algerian problem with great determination and personal courage and brought a real measure of order and stability to their governmental process, many a Frenchman—and many a Francophile outside of France—nonetheless does not feel entirely comfortable in the face of the institution he has permitted Charles de Gaulle to create. The memories of past tyrannies die hard; the names of Macmahon and Boulanger—let alone those of Napoleon I and III—are not forgotten and often serve to rekindle the lasting fears of a strong executive. Charles de Gaulle—although he has been called 'autocrat,' 'constitutional dictator,' 'enlightened Bonapartist,' and 'republican royalist'—*bien*, but what of a successor? The haunting doubts and fears are uppermost in the minds of many responsible leaders of public opinion of the nation that is thus still torn between the evident need for governmental stability—a state of affairs that certainly should not be viewed as a luxury—and the fears of old, frequently revived by current drastic government executive action in the name of order and domestic peace.

In striking contrast to the past, Charles de Gaulle has created a President of France with enormous power and prestige and he has brought order and renewed *grandeur* to the House of France. But he has done so largely as a result of the unmistakable stamp of his own inimitable personality upon both domestic and international affairs. Yet after President de Gaulle, not only 'who?' but 'what?'

DICTATORSHIP MAGNIFIES THE EXECUTIVE

The term 'dictatorship,' as we have already noted, is derived from the practice of the ancient Roman Republic in conferring very wide powers on a single man during a serious emergency. Nazi rule in Germany, Fascist rule in Italy, and Communist rule in the Soviet Union have all been called dictatorship because of the enormous power, acknowledged pre-eminence, and carefully fostered adulation of one man. Mussolini was the Duce, the leader. Hitler was the Führer, the leader. Until his massive deflation by Khrushchev, Stalin was, in the Soviet Union, 'our great Stalin,' the leader who was almost deified in the eyes of the masses. These men were the dictators of their respective countries.

Enormous Power. It is not at all clear, in any of these instances, how power has been distributed between the dictator and the small group he gathered round him. It is not necessary for present purposes to decide the difficult question whether all or any of these dictators ever exercised in their own persons supreme and irresponsible power. For it is at least true that, in each instance, enormous power, free of all constitutional limitations, was concentrated in the hands of the leader and the few who shared his confidence. In that sense, Fascist Italy and Nazi Germany were dictatorships, and the Soviet Union is a dictatorship today, despite some of the changes wrought under Khrushchev.

The executive is the one utterly indispensable arm of government. Anyone who wants to wield decisive power must control the executive. The legislature and the judiciary are important mainly to put effective limits on the power of the executive and make it responsible. But when power transcends all limits, the legislature and judiciary become meaningless and the executive is everything. In each of the three countries in question, a small clique got its hands on the executive and then magnified its power.

Rule by Decree. In Italy before Mussolini, and in Germany before Hitler, there had been a parliamentary system—however ineffective—resembling that of Britain, with a cabinet as the executive. The Nazis and Fascists worked their way to control the cabinet. The leading members of the party became the cabinet ministers. Mussolini became Prime Minister. Hitler became Chancellor and President of Germany. Once in control of the executive, they usurped the place of the legislature by making substantially all laws by *executive decree*. Their decrees forbade all other political parties and made the judiciary subservient. Enormous power, free of constitutional checks, was concentrated in the executive, the small clique of leaders of the Fascist and Nazi parties. So it essentially still is in the U.S.S.R. today.

THE EXECUTIVE IN THE SOVIET UNION

It was pointed out in Chapters III and IX that all important decisions in the Soviet Union are reached in the highest councils of the Communist party. This means, in effect, that executive power in the U.S.S.R. is not in the hands of an organ of the government, but is the prerogative of the high functionaries of the Communist party. However, most of the information on which decisions are based comes from the state bureaucracy, which is manned in part by officials who are not members of the party.

The Formal Executive. Formally, the Soviet structure of government provides an executive and a legislature in the sense that these terms are used in Britain, France, and the United States. The Supreme Soviet of the U.S.S.R. is the legislature, and the Council of Ministers of the U.S.S.R. is the executive, theoretically responsible to the Supreme Soviet. *Theoretically,* only the Supreme Soviet can promulgate laws and the Council of Ministers alone can carry them out and supervise their administration. Unlike Britain, France, and the United States, however, the Soviet Union has established a third body which, in practice, combines some of the functions of the legislature and the executive. It is the Presidium of the Supreme Soviet of the U.S.S.R., a committee of some thirty members, appointed by the Supreme Soviet, which in practice is the effective working part of the Supreme Soviet.

THE PRESIDIUM OF THE SUPREME SOVIET. The Presidium issues decrees which have the force of law, and it has no administrative responsibilities; in this sense, it is a legislative body. However, it has a variety of executive functions, such as the appointment of high officials, ordering mobilization of the armed forces, proclaiming martial law, and even declaring war if such declaration has to be made while the Supreme Soviet is not in session. It also has judicial power—but, of course, no effective judicial review—in that it interprets the laws and annuls such decisions of the executive as it finds contrary to law. Finally, it carries out many of the dignified functions of government that are the prerogative of the Chief of State in Britain, France, and the United States. It creates titles of honor, awards decorations, and exercises the right of pardon. Its chairman, who in a sense is 'President of the U.S.S.R.,' signs all decrees of the Presidium and receives foreign ambassadors on behalf of the U.S.S.R. Soviet congratulations to President Kennedy on the occasion of his inauguration were extended by Leonid I. Brezhnev, the Chairman of the Presidium of the Supreme Soviet of the U.S.S.R. The Presidium thus has some share in executive power.

COUNCIL OF MINISTERS. The Council of Ministers—its size has fluctuated between 25 and 65, the latter as of August 1963—which is designated by the Constitution as the executive of the Soviet government, corresponds more closely to the British and French than to the United States cabinet. It is appointed by the Supreme Soviet of the U.S.S.R., and the various ministers introduce proposals for new laws in the Supreme Soviet, which are invariably adopted without change.

Key Position of the Executive. In the Soviet Union, the government directs the whole economic life of the country and exercises far-reaching control over most aspects of social and cultural life. The work that wholesale Soviet socialism puts on the executive of the Soviet Union is enormous and far exceeds that of British Labour cabinets in their efforts at piecemeal socialism. The Council of Ministers is appointed for a four-year term; it consists of a chairman (the Premier), several vice-chairmen, the chairman of GOSPLAN, the State Planning Commission of the U.S.S.R. (a committee of the Council charged with the over-all planning of the Soviet economy), the chairman of the Arts Committee (which supervises and controls the creative arts), and the various ministers of the U.S.S.R. The last group comprises the heads of some fifty administrative departments of the government, which control all aspects of Soviet life. The Soviet ministers have in their charge not only the departments of government common to all countries, such as Foreign Affairs, Defense, Agriculture, and Finance, but many others as well. The names of a few of these ministries will suffice to indicate the wide scope of the Soviet 'cabinet': Aircraft, Power Stations, Cinematography, and Grocery Supplies.

DECENTRALIZATION? However, under the Khrushchev-initiated decentralization of the Soviet Union's industrial empire into forty economic regions, already outlined in Chapter VI, a considerable number of the ministries were abolished, and their tasks transferred to the governments of the various union republics, but under the supervision of the State Planning Commission (GOSPLAN). Nevertheless, economic control over industries of 'obvious national concern' is being retained at the national level—such as the ministries of Aviation, Shipbuilding, Electronics, Chemicals, and Transportation and Medium Machinery.

AN INNER GROUP. In view of its unwieldly size and the realities of the center of gravity of power, dominant control of the Council of Ministers is exercised by its own Presidium. Consisting in 1963 of eight members, it was headed by Khrushchev as Chairman of the full Council, Kosygin and Mikoyan as First Deputy Chairmen, and five other members classified as Deputy Chairmen. This is the group that 'runs the show,' subject to the Party's wishes.

MORE THAN A CABINET. The Council of Ministers of the U.S.S.R. is not only a 'cabinet' in the British sense, but also a board of directors of that super-giant corporation, the Soviet state, which controls and directs economic and social life, turning the vast Soviet Union virtually into a company town. Bearing in mind the central importance of the executive in any enterprise that wants concrete results, it will be realized that the executive in the Soviet Union exercises very wide powers of decision. The decisions and ordinances issued by the Council of Ministers easily outweigh in number and importance the general laws passed by the Supreme Soviet and the decrees issued by its Presidium. One student of Soviet government has summarized the place of the Council as follows: 'The scope and volume of its enactments make it abundantly clear that the Council of Ministers is the greatest producer of obligatory, state-enforced, activity-guiding norms in the Soviet system.' [15]

The Real Executive. On paper, the Council of Ministers is a more powerful body than the British cabinet, but not so in practice. While it is true that the activities of the Council encompass a wider area than those of the British cabinet, and that its activities are rarely, if ever, subjected to severe criticism by the legislature (the Supreme Soviet), it is not as free in formulating basic policy as is the British cabinet. For the Council of Ministers is highly susceptible to control by the Communist party. The basic decisions on what is to be done in the Soviet Union are reached not in the Council of Ministers but in the 'inner cabinet' of the Communist party. The rules of the Communist party state that the party's Central Committee directs the work of the central public organizations through the party groups in them. The party's role in the making of decisions, which have the force of law, is revealed clearly in the fact that many decisions formally made by

[15] Julian Towster, *Political Power in the U.S.S.R., 1917–1947* (New York: Oxford University Press, 1948), pp. 267--7.

the Supreme Soviet or by the Council of Ministers have been first made, announced, *and carried into effect* by the party.

Thus the first Five-Year Plans were prepared by the Communist party, and were actually put into effect before they were formally enacted by the appropriate governmental bodies. Many decrees of the Council of Ministers have been issued jointly by the Communist party *and* the Council of Ministers. The State Defense Committee, the war cabinet of the Soviet Union, for example, was created in 1941 by a joint decree of the Presidium of the Supreme Soviet, the Central Committee of the Communist party, and the Council of Ministers (then known as the Council of People's Commissars). However, it must be recognized that since at least some of the most influential members of the Council of Ministers are usually members of the top echelon of the Communist party as well,[16] a built-in system of interlocking controls exists.

Nevertheless, the lesser Soviet ministers are not, as a rule, men who have spent many years in politics or private pursuits, but are rather experts in particular fields of the Soviet economy. They are successful managers of various sectors of that economy, and as such their strength lies in a familiarity with a particular sector of industry rather than in a deep understanding of the broad issues of public policy. It is the detailed technical information that they supply to the party, which enables the latter to formulate the broad outlines of Soviet policy. The really important decisions in the Soviet Union are made by the leaders of the Communist party who, in the final analysis, control not only policy, but also the personnel who carry it out.

SUGGESTED REFERENCES FOR FURTHER READING

Bernstein, M. H., *The Job of the Federal Executive* (Brookings, 1958).

Binkley, W. E., *The Man in the White House* (Johns Hopkins, 1958).

Carter, B. E., *The Office of Prime Minister* (Princeton, 1956).

Corwin, E. S., *The President: Office and Powers, 1787–1957,* 4th rev. ed. (New York U., 1957).

Coyle, D. C., *Ordeal of the Presidency* (Public Affairs, 1960).

Deutscher, I., *Russia in Transition,* rev. ed. (Grove, 1960).

Duranty, W., *Stalin and Co.: The Politbureau—the Men Who Run Russia* (Sloane, 1949).

Duverger, M., *La Cinquième République,* 2nd ed. (Presses universitaires de France, 1960).

[16] Pertinent examples in 1963 were Khrushchev, Kosygin, and Mikoyan.

Encel, S., *Cabinet Government in Australia* (Cambridge, 1962).
———, *La Quatrième République et le Régime Présidentiel* (Fayard, 1961).
Fenno, R. F., Jr., *The President's Cabinet* (Vintage, 1962).
Fersh, S. H., *The View from the White House: A Study of the Presidential State of the Union Message* (Public Affairs Press, 1961).
Finer, H., *The Presidency: Crisis and Regeneration* (U. of Chicago, 1960).
Geraud, A. (Pertinax), *The Gravediggers of France* (Doubleday, 1944).
Hansen, R. H., *The Year We Had No President* (U. of Nebraska, 1962).
Heller, F., *The Presidency: A Modern Perspective* (Random House, 1960).
Henry, L. L., *Presidential Transition* (Brookings, 1960).
Hobbs, E. H., *Behind the President* (Public Affairs Press, 1954).
Hyman, S., *The American President* (Harper, 1954).
Keith, A. B., *The British Cabinet System, 1830–1938*, 2nd ed. (Stevens, 1952).
Koenig, L. W., *The Invisible Presidency* (Rinehart, 1960).
Kraft, J., *The Struggle for Algeria* (Doubleday, 1961).
Laski, H. J., *The American Presidency* (Harper, 1940).
Longaker, R. P., *The Presidency and Civil Liberties* (Cornell, 1961).
Mackintosh, J. P., *The British Cabinet* (U. of Toronto, 1962).
May, E. R. (Ed.), *The Ultimate Decision: The President as Commander in Chief* (Brazil, 1960).
Meisel, J. H., *The Fall of the Republic: Military Revolt in France* (U. of Michigan, 1962).
Melnik, C., and N. Leites, *The House Without Windows: France Selects a President* (Row, Peterson, 1958).
Milton, G. F., *The Use of Presidential Power* (Little, Brown, 1944).
Moraze, C., *The French and the Republic* (Cornell, 1960).
Morrah, D., *The Work of the Queen* (Kimber, 1958).
Neustadt, R. E., *Presidential Power: The Politics of Leadership* (Wiley, 1960).
Petrie, Sir C., *The Modern British Monarchy* (Eyre & Spottiswoode, 1961).
Rich, B M., *The President and Civil Disorder* (Brookings, 1941).
Rossiter, C., *The American Presidency*, rev. ed. (Harcourt, Brace, 1960).
———, *Constitutional Dictatorship* (Princeton, 1948).
Silva, R. C., *Presidential Succession* (U. of Michigan, 1951).
Smith, J. M., and C. P. Cotter, *Powers of the President During Crises* (Public Affairs Pr., 1960).
Sorensen, Theodore C., *Decision-Making in the White House* (Columbia, 1963).
Taft, W. H., *Our Chief Magistrate and His Powers* (Columbia, 1916).
Tugwell, R. G., *The Enlargement of the Presidency* (Doubleday, 1960).
Waugh, E. W., *Second Consul: The Vice-Presidency—Our Greatest Political Problem* (Bobbs-Merrill, 1956).
Wheare, K. C., *Government by Committee* (Oxford, 1955).
Williams, P. M., and M. Harrison, *De Gaulle's Republic* (Longmans, Green, 1960).
Wilmerding, L., Jr., *The Electoral College* (Rutgers U., 1958).
Wolfe, B. D., *Khrushchev and Stalin's Ghost* (Praeger, 1956).

XIII

The Legislature: Its Functions and Procedure

In the tripartite division of powers, the legislature makes the laws. This function includes the imposing of taxes and the appropriating of money to particular items of expenditure. The legislature is *in theory* the most august authority within the constitution. In the Third and Fourth Republics of France, virtually all effective power was concentrated in the legislature—but those days are gone. In Britain, as we have seen, Parliament has the formal power to amend the constitution, although, of course, the exercise of power is restricted by the conventional requirement of a mandate from the electorate. By making laws and appropriating public money, the legislature sets the tasks of the executive, determines what public services are to be rendered, and within what limits the government is to operate. In democratic theory, the legislature represents the people, or the community; it is supposed to exercise general surveillance over the executive to see that, in its actual administration, government is for the people and not against them. Even in the United States, with an independently elected executive, this is expected of the legislature in some degree. The surveillance works through the cabinet system in Great Britain and Canada, for example. In the United States it operates through the detailed legislative control of finance and administration and, increasingly, through investigations carried out by legislative committees. Under the Fifth Republic of France, however, there is little, if any, meaningful legislative surveillance.

The powerful weapon of impeachment is also potentially available in the

United States. The Constitution authorizes the House of Representatives to bring charges against, and the Senate to try, executive officers from the President down by this method. However, it has been used so rarely that it cannot be said to be a working method of the legislature for controlling the executive. There have been only twelve cases of impeachment proceedings launched under the federal Constitution. Only four of these resulted in convictions, and the convicted parties in every case were federal judges,[1] not members of the executive. It may well become as obsolete as it has in Britain, where the last case of successful impeachment of a minister before the House of Lords was in 1805. Although the House of Lords no longer exercises this power, it has other judicial functions that are still alive. The nine Law Lords in the House of Lords, together with the Lord Chancellor and certain other peers, constitute the final court of appeal for Great Britain and Northern Ireland. These are historical survivals and need no extended comment here. The making of laws and keeping watch over the executive are the significant lawmaking functions today—augmented by such collateral tasks and duties as advising the executive, informing the public and reflecting it, and regulating its internal organization.

SIGNIFICANCE OF THE LAWMAKING FUNCTION

The high significance of the lawmaking function will be made clear by recalling the discussion of liberal democratic ideals of government in Chapter II. The ideal of individual freedom involves the right of private judgment. Democratic ideals, taken as a whole, are phrased in such general terms that when men exercise private judgment there is a wide diversity of opinion on what government should and should not do. The ideal of the rule of law as expressed in constitutional provisions requires governments to act in accordance with law. Individual freedom cannot be abridged except through law. Respect for individual personality requires discussion and debate as a means for composing differences of opinion on what to do to further the ideals. Finally, it is assumed that men are sufficiently rational to undertake discussion and to submit to persuasion on the basis of logic and evidence.

---

[1] U.S. District Court Judge J. Pickering ('insanity,' 1804); U.S. District Court Judge W. H. Humphreys ('support of secession,' 1882); U.S. Commerce Court Judge R. A. Archbald ('taking favors from litigants,' 1913); and U.S. District Court Judge H. L. Ritter ('bringing his Court into scandal and disrepute,' 1936).

The liberal democratic legislature is an institution constructed under the compulsion of these ideals and designed to promote their realization. In a society composed of millions of persons, all cannot meet for discussion. Through the electoral system, these millions elect to the legislature persons who are supposed to represent their views. This representation is admittedly imperfect but it does bring together some kind of cross section of the principal diverse views in the community. If some significant body of opinion is deeply dissatisfied with the existing state of affairs, and fails to get the adjustment it wants through discussion and voluntary action at a lower level, it will sooner or later find a way of proposing a law to the legislature.

The legislature has no magic formula for dealing with such proposals. It is itself representative of diverse views and interests and, therefore, has no agreed view on the matter, in the initial stages at any rate. It can only proceed in patient pedestrian fashion by hearing what is to be said on both sides and collecting as much data as it can on the issue in question. Ultimately, of course, it will have to come to a decision because it is the final authority for composing the clashing demands of private judgment, conscience, and interest. The only appeal beyond its decision is to force and violence, which dishonor and frustrate human personality. So it has to find a solution that will at least be tolerable to almost all concerned. Only rarely will any one course seem both acceptable and right to the legislators who have to decide. Lawmaking is normally a compromise based on debate and majority decision with due regard for minority rights.

The liberal democratic legislature is organized with a view to performing this supreme function. It has a structure of committees for collecting facts and for giving detailed examination to issues. It has rules of debate designed to allow the frankest expression of views and, at the same time, to prevent that unfettered license of expression which destroys mutual respect among the members. In addition to trying to provide the proper atmosphere for rational discussion, the rules of debate aim to guide discussion along orderly lines. The liberal democratic legislature also has rules for compelling, at some point, an end to discussion, and then a decision by majority vote. Finally, as we said in Chapter IX, it has a system of political parties that runs the organized machinery of the legislature, and in the end submerges the private reservations of members in majority decisions. A judgment on how well it now performs these functions will be essayed later—it suffices to note here that the past two generations have witnessed a seemingly unrelenting decline both in its power and its prestige.

CHARACTERISTICS OF THE DEMOCRATIC LEGISLATURE

The British and French Parliaments and the Congress of the United States are *bicameral,* composed of upper (or second) and lower chambers. The lower or popular chamber is in each case made up of representatives of territorial units, or constituencies, chosen by substantially adult suffrage. Attempts are made—rarely with complete success—to so draw the lines of the constituencies that each member represents roughly an equal number of individuals. The lower chamber is 'popular' in the sense that it mirrors the nation, the nation being regarded as a number of collections of individuals resident in particular territorial areas. In the United States, the lower chamber, the 435-member House of Representatives, is chosen for a fixed period of two years, being regularly renewed at the end of that time by a fresh election. In Britain, the maximum life of the 631-member House of Commons is five years, but it may be cut short at any time by a dissolution leading to a general election. In France, the maximum life of the 465-member National Assembly is also five years; but the President of the Republic may, upon consultation with the Premier and the presiding officers of both houses of Parliament, cut its life short at any time, after which no further dissolution may take place for one year.

THE ROLE OF UPPER CHAMBERS

Decline of Upper Chambers. Except for those countries where federalism and bicameralism were logically allied in order to give particular geographical representation to the constituent states or provinces, the advent of the twentieth century saw a marked decline in the power of the upper (or second) [2] chambers in the Western democracies. The extension of the suffrage brought with it a rise of nation-wide political parties, which were prepared to cut across the various special groups and interests in order to

---

[2] 'Upper' is the more precise term, for 'second' is not inevitably tantamount to 'upper'—viz. the 'Second Chamber' of the Estates General (the legislature) in the Netherlands, which is the 'lower,' and more powerful, of the two houses, thus corresponding to the House of Commons, the National Assembly, and the House of Representatives, for example. Hence 'upper' will be used here and throughout the text.

win votes. In fact they were compelled to do so to succeed and survive. The days were soon gone when the two branches of the legislature were afforded the luxury of representing special class interests, and not much else.

The decline in the power of the upper chambers commenced with the *Parliament Act of 1911,* which, as we shall see, struck the British House of Lords a crippling blow. The political children of World War I and World War II subsequently did what the Mother of Parliaments had done—although a reservation will be entered later regarding the West German *Bundesrat.* Today most, but not all, upper chambers have indeed become 'secondary.' If they have not been entirely abandoned, they are little more than chambers of reflection and revision, debating societies, political 'Siberias,' or chambers of protest and delay. However, they are by no means useless. Such weak, or relatively weak, upper houses as the British House of Lords, the French Senate, and the Canadian Senate, at least, perform important functions of polishing and clarifying legislation.

The British House of Lords. The House of Lords antedates the period of deliberate devising of political institutions. It is a relic of the insistence of the feudal barons that they should advise—and control—the monarch, whose centralizing ambitions always threatened to cut down their local perquisites. By the rule of primogeniture, the eldest son of the feudal lord succeeded to his father's estates and to his place on the Great Council advising the monarch. Today the hereditary peerage comprises almost 90 per cent of the House of Lords. Of course, it must be remembered that most of the great feudal houses are long since extinct; the Bohuns, Mortimers, Mowbrays, and DeVeres are 'in the urns and sepulchres of mortality.' The peers are mostly *parvenus,* having been created by royal letters patent since the seventeenth century. There are five ranks or grades of peers: duke, marquis, earl, viscount, and baron.[3]

CHANGING CHARACTER OF PEERAGE. Indeed, the character of the peerage has almost completely changed since the Reform Act of 1832. Most of the existing peerages have been created since that time, almost half of them since 1900. The new peers of the nineteenth century were mostly men who had succeeded in industry and commerce rather than great landlords. And in-

---

[3] However, not all ennobled persons necessarily sit in the House of Lords. For example, there are many *viscounts* whose titles were bestowed on a 'courtesy' basis. Two *other* titled groups, *knights* and *baronets,* are not members of the peerage and do not sit in the House of Lords. In 1963 the following comprised the Lords' membership: 5 Royal Dukes; 27 dukes; 38 marquesses; 203 earls; 138 viscounts; and 523 barons (including, *ex officio,* 2 archbishops and 24 bishops).

creasingly now, peerages are granted for 'political and public services.' Conspicuous service to the state in the civil service, in the armed services, in diplomacy, or in the professions may be rewarded by elevation. Political services meriting a peerage are of various kinds. Politicians may crown their careers by going to the House of Lords. For instance, Labourite ex-Prime Minister Clement Attlee became Earl Attlee in 1955, after twenty years of leadership of his party, and Anthony Eden became the Earl of Avon in 1961. Men of eminence, whose counsel is wanted in the cabinet, but who will not fight elections or undertake departmental responsibilities, may be made peers to give them the necessary qualification for inclusion in the cabinet, as was true of Prime Minister Churchill's controversial wartime adviser on scientific affairs, Lord Cherwell. Of course, it is widely asserted that many are ennobled in return for handsome contributions to party campaign funds. Finally, the ancient barrier against women in the upper house crumbled in 1958 when the Queen named the first four women as life peers—and in the Summer of 1963 the Macmillan Conservative government enacted a Labour party proposal to enable peers to renounce their titles and run for seats in the House of Commons!

Ennoblement is not a personal prerogative of the monarch. The Prime Minister, taking such suggestion and advice as he deems fit, recommends names to Her Majesty. The monarch may object to the inclusion of particular persons, or urge a candidate of his own, and may on occasion win his point. But, generally speaking, peerages are in the gift of the political party in power.

COMPOSITION. In addition to the hereditary peers, the approximately 934-member House of Lords includes princes of royal blood; princes of the church, the twenty-six 'lords spiritual'—the two archbishops and the twenty-four senior bishops of the Church of England; representative Scottish and Irish peers, the latter now almost extinct; nine Lords of Appeal, eminent lawyers and judges who are given life peerages to carry on the judicial work of the Lords; and, since 1958, an increasing number of both male and female *life* peers.

DECLINING POWER OF THE HOUSE OF LORDS. Generally speaking, there is much doubt about the utility of non-elective upper chambers. Once the democratic principle that the will of the majority should prevail was widely accepted, it was inevitable that any forthright challenge of that will by a non-elective upper chamber should be regarded as insolent presumption. So when a trial of strength came in Britain over Liberal Prime Minister

Lloyd George's budget in 1909,[4] the result was the aforementioned Parliament Act of 1911, an ignominious defeat for the House of Lords. By the Act, its power over money bills, which had already been modified by convention, was completely removed—except for a meaningless thirty-day *suspensive veto*. A bill certified by the Speaker of the House of Commons to be a money bill no longer needed the Lords' consent before becoming law. They retained a veto on non-money bills, but this could be overridden if the Commons passed the measure thrice in three successive sessions in a period of not less than two years. The Lords came to have only a suspending power.

Another trial of strength occurred in 1947. The Labour party came to power in 1945, pledged to introduce a large measure of socialism. Fearing that the conservative-minded House of Lords would veto important socialist measures and hold them up for two years, the Labour party majority in the House of Commons passed a bill reducing the period of the suspensive veto of the House of Lords from two years to one. The House of Lords rejected this bill, but the House of Commons passed it again in 1948 and in 1949, thus making it law within the terms of the Parliament Act of 1911. A bill now becomes law over the veto of the House of Lords by being passed twice by the House of Commons in two successive sessions.

Thus the House of Lords is now restricted to very narrow functions. It is sometimes suggested that it can be revivified and made highly useful by making it elective, as is the United States Senate. But if its members are elected at the same time and on the same franchise as the lower house, they are likely to reflect much the same electoral opinion as the lower house and therefore to be superfluous. If they are elected at different times, or on a different franchise, they may represent different popular moods or different general convictions respectively. The result would either be deadlock or, as the experience of the United States suggests, the practical primacy of one house over the other.

REMAINING FUNCTIONS. The alternative reform, which can be accommodated to an almost infinite variety of ways of appointing the upper chambers, is the one adopted in Britain of deliberately reducing the powers of the upper chamber to a mere suspending power. The voice of the people is the voice of God, but God speaks through fallible parties and politicians. The majority in the lower chamber, either in the first flush of victory or in the

---

[4] The Lords had rejected that budget largely because it contained a 20 per cent tax on unearned increments in land—and the landed gentry viewed the land tax as a death blow.

hectic dying hours of a busy session, may well pass measures that, on longer consideration, they would not. So an upper chamber can check such legislative impulses without doing violence to the democratic dogma. Benjamin Franklin likened this process to 'Brother Philip Sober taking care of Brother Philip Drunk.'

Also, the lower chamber in countries with parliamentary government is badly congested because of the enormous grist of legislation, and because it is a forum for criticism of the executive and for party maneuvers, which take up a great deal of time. The upper chamber does not suffer much from these latter distractions. By sheer oversight, bills coming from the lower chamber often lack provisions necessary to their effective administration, or contain clauses involving unnecessary difficulties or hardships for particular groups. The upper chamber has time to spend in trimming and polishing the measures which come rough-hewn from the lower chamber.

These suspending and revising functions are the main functions now performed by the House of Lords. Yet even these are subject to criticism. No major legislative proposal, except in wartime, goes through the lower chamber without being preceded by extensive discussion there and in the country. There is, it is often urged, no justification for permitting the House of Lords to postpone the enactment of such a proposal for a further period.

However, it may be doubted whether any reform is of such immediacy that time spent in broadening consent to it through the slow erosion of opposition is not well spent. For democracy is as much a matter of gaining the consent of minorities as it is of giving effect to the will of the majority. There is much to be said for the suspending function. The revising function also is important—as the Lords proved in forcing a change in the Commons' Suspension of Capital Punishment Bill in 1948 and 1958. There is much to be said for a second chamber which has time for searching inquiry into the confused and complex facts that give rise to proposals for legislation. As we shall see later, one of the chief defects of legislatures today is that they rarely know enough about the facts to frame the laws most effectively. Lord Morrison, who as Herbert Morrison sat as a Labour M.P. in Commons for a third of a century, wrote convincingly that the 'very irrationality of the House of Lords and its quaintness are safeguards for our British democracy. . . . We have a considerable capacity for making the irrational work.'[5]

---

[5] Herbert Morrison, *Government and Parliament: A Survey from the Inside,* 2nd ed. (London: Oxford University Press, 1959), p. 194.

The French Upper House. True bicameralism existed in the Third French Republic. The legislature was divided into two approximately equally powerful branches, the popular house—the Chamber of Deputies—and the *Senate.* The latter owed its creation in 1873 to the demands of the *Orléanistes*, the monarchist faction among the framers of the French Constitution, who agreed to support the Third Republic provided the republicans would support the establishment of a strong second chamber. This was accomplished, and the Senate proved to be a powerful, conservative body indeed—the scourge of many cabinets, which fell at the Senate's pleasure. It was a body of some three hundred members, of whom one-fourth served for life and the balance for a nine-year term, elected indirectly by an electoral college composed of representatives and governmental officials of the various *départements* of France. The Senate, in the words of Léon Gambetta, was 'primarily an assembly of the *communes* of France.'

The Constitution of the Fourth Republic, however, deprived the Senate of much, if not most, of its power, and changed its name to the *Council of the Republic.* The framers of the Constitution, following in the wake of the diminished power of the British House of Lords, deemed it unhealthy for governmental stability to have the French Council of Ministers—the cabinet —serve *two* masters. Hence that upper house was much weaker than the old French Senate, although more powerful than the British House of Lords.

THE SENATE OF THE FIFTH REPUBLIC. No longer the simple advisory body that its predecessor was, the upper house of the Fifth Republic is once again called the *Senate,* and has had some of the powers of its earlier namesake restored. While it lacks the power to overthrow the Government either by a vote of no confidence or by the adoption of a motion of censure, it is once again able to introduce legislation and give to as well as demand from the government opinions and explanations concerning policy. It cannot be dissolved, as can the National Assembly. It can block legislation or tie up bills in which the government is not truly interested by the 'shuttle' method (*la navette*). Here a disputed bill—save financial legislation—may be passed back and forth between the two houses indefinitely, unless and until the Government intervenes and forces it through the Assembly by a compelled vote, usually following an unsuccessful Conference Committee between the two houses. But except for its contingent legislative equality and its effective right to veto any change in its own status, the Senate—despite its renovated prestige—in effect remains a subordinate legislative chamber, for, after all, the Government is not responsible to it.

ELECTION AND COMPOSITION. Members of the Senate are elected indirectly by electoral colleges in each of the *départements,* in some by majority vote, in others by P.R. The 307 senators, of whom about one-fifth come from French overseas territories, serve overlapping nine-year terms; one-third of the Senate is elected at three-year intervals. Gambetta's remark about the location of power in the old Senate is still applicable—for the electoral system continues to emphasize the municipal councils, albeit with diminished emphasis.

A Note on the West German Bundesrat. Although fairly powerful and/or interesting upper chambers exist—e.g. the Swiss *Council of States* and the Senates of Canada, Australia, and Switzerland—a special note, in addition to a discussion of the truly powerful United States Senate, of course, is in order regarding the upper house of West Germany, the unique *Bundesrat.* The Bonn Constitution provided its upper house with a considerable measure of legislative power. Its approval is mandatory for all constitutional amendments as well as for all federal legislation bearing upon the tax, territorial, and administrative 'interests' of the *Laender*—an extensive field, indeed! Moreover, it possesses the authority to scrutinize all government bills before they are submitted to the lower house (the *Bundestag*) and it has a suspensive veto on all legislation. However, its veto may be overridden either by a simple or two-thirds majority of the *Bundestag,* depending upon the veto vote in the upper body. In addition to these powers, the *Bundesrat* also participates in the election of the judges of West Germany's new Constitutional Court. However, on balance, the upper house is clearly subordinate to the lower branch.

Yet what are perhaps more remarkable than any influence and prestige it may be able to wield on the federal level, are its composition and attendant significance as a link between the *Laender* and the central government. The *Bundesrat* is unique in that its membership—a total of forty-one in 1963 based upon a scale geared to the population in the ten states or *Laender*—*consists of delegates appointed by the Laender governments.* These delegates —who are almost always ministers—are required to cast their votes as a unit, regardless of whether the *Land* government 'back home' is a coalition of several political parties. Hence, the *Bundesrat* is not only more of a delegate *cum* representative body than a legislative one, but also a body which necessarily plays down party allegiance in favor of federalist requirements. Whether this intriguing attempt to forestall the natural Germanic tendencies toward centripetal government will succeed in the long run remains to be seen. But it would seem to be a noble effort and, to date, on the whole a successful one.

The United States Senate. In a perceptive study an ardent, although not uncritical, admirer of the United States Senate characterized what he fondly termed the 'Institution,' as the 'one touch of authentic genius in the American political system, apart . . . from the incomparable majesty and decency and felicity of the Constitution itself.'[6] There is little doubt of the prestige and power of this natural habitat of compromise, this Institution, this Club, that 'lives in an unending yesterday where the past is never gone, the present never quite decisive and the future rarely quite visible.'[7] Let us briefly examine this uniquely American phenomenon.

Background. The United States Senate was a deliberate construction with aim and purpose. Sheer imitation of the British system and colonial precedents were factors, but two other considerations were decisive. First, a number of states of greatly unequal size and population were being federated under a national government. Representation in the lower federal chamber was to be on the basis of population, and it was thought that giving the states equal representation in the upper chamber would safeguard the interests of the less populous in the general councils of the nation—a defense which the states still maintain and cherish on many, but not on all, issues.

Second, the American Constitution was formed at the outset of extension of the franchise toward adult suffrage. It was widely feared that the people, and the representatives they chose for the lower chamber, would easily be swayed by gusts of emotion and even moved by the baser passions of envy and cupidity. It was thought to be important for stability, for the security of minorities—propertied and otherwise—that an upper chamber representing more conservative elements, and not chosen by popular vote, should check the vagaries and the envious appetite of the lower chamber. It was for this reason that indirect election was originally chosen as the method of recruitment.

But the House of Representatives has not been nearly so passion-ridden as was feared. It is true that for many years before the change to popular election in the United States, the Senate was a bulwark of the great business interests against regulation by government and was popularly derided as 'a millionaires' club.' But this was owing, perhaps, as much to the general domination of all American political life by big business in that period as to

---

[6] William S. White, *Citadel: The Story of the U.S. Senate* (New York: Harper, 1957), p. ix.
[7] Ibid. p. 2.

the indirect election of senators. Since direct popular election was introduced, the Senate has come increasingly to be moved by the impulses at work within the electorate as a whole.

COMPOSITION. The Senate of the United States has 100 members, two from each state in the Union. The Constitution originally provided for their election by state legislatures. But in 1913, pressure for more direct democratic choice, combined with indignation at the manipulation of state legislatures by would-be senators, forced the Seventeenth Amendment to the Constitution, providing for popular election of the senators in each state for a six-year term; one-third retire every two years and are replaced by new elections, thus combining a degree of continuity with frequent election.

THE POWER AND PRESTIGE OF THE SENATE. The Senate is a very powerful body. The President, who does not find it necessary every day to cater to the lower house, is almost continually compelled to woo the Senate. Even President George Washington had to—though he objected vehemently.[8] For the Senate shares with him in the appointing and treaty-making power, thus gaining prestige and influence. 'Senatorial courtesy' is a well-settled usage of the Constitution by which the Senate—upon the appeal of members of the 'Club' immediately involved—normally refuses to confirm certain presidential appointments[9] unless the President has first consulted the senators of his party from the state concerned. In effect this assures to senators of the President's party control over a considerable number of appointments to government jobs in their respective states, and it may forge for them a powerful connection with the political party machines in the states.

The six-year term frees them from frequent distraction over re-election, from which, by contrast, a member of the House of Representatives, with a two-year term, is scarcely ever free. The continuity of membership afforded by staggered senatorial elections every two years is a great advantage. The fact that the Senate has less than a quarter of the number of members of the lower chamber contributes greatly to the quality and effectiveness of debate, although in the Senate, too, the real work is done in committee rather

---

[8] 'I'll be damned if I ever go to *that* place again,' he declared when the Senate had refused to abide by his wishes for ratification of the Jay Treaty on the spot, during his presence on the floor of the Senate.

[9] However, this concept is actually 'relaxed' when the Senate deals with cabinet nominees, apparently believing that the President, on that level, ought to be able to get the men he wants. From 1789 though 1963 only eight cabinet-designees had been rejected—one each of Presidents Jackson, Johnson, Coolidge, and Eisenhower (Admiral Strauss as Secretary of Commerce), and four of President Tyler.

than on the floor. All these factors, in turn, make the Senate attractive to able men. Members of the House of Representatives aspire to, and frequently achieve, the Senate, thus giving it greater resources of mature political experience.

As a result, the Senate is much more than a check on the lower chamber. Although the Constitution gives both chambers equal powers in *legislation,* except for reserving to the lower chamber the initiation of all revenue bills, the Senate is far more often the dominant partner in legislation. It amends, at will, legislation coming up from the lower chamber, not excluding revenue bills; smothers many such bills in committees; and originates a large share of those finally enacted. When the two chambers disagree on a bill, and a compromise has to be arranged through a conference committee, the Senate generally makes fewer concessions. Thus the widespread doubts about the effectiveness of upper chambers certainly do *not* apply to the Senate of the United States. In prestige and power it has no equal among the liberal democracies.

THE LOWER CHAMBERS

The role and function of the lower chambers of the three leading countries at issue, which we have already seen in relation to political parties in Chapter IX, will be further delineated in conjunction with the discussions on legislative policies, organization and procedures to follow in this chapter and in the next chapter on executive-legislative relations, but a few general observations are in order now. As has become apparent, the center of gravity of legislative power lodges in the lower branches of Parliament in Britain and France. But the noun 'power' must be interpreted with considerable tentativeness in both instances. Especially is this true in the case of the National Assembly of the Fifth Republic, which in fact has practically been shorn of truly meaningful legislative authority, perhaps not so much by the provisions of the de Gaulle Constitution of 1958—although in its Title V it specifically determines and circumscribes its legislative power—as by that document's interpretation by the first President of the Fifth Republic, who has made no secret of his disdain for *le régime des partis.* When the National Assembly did challenge him late in 1962 in connection with his announcement of taking to the people in a referendum the question of direct election of the President, he accepted that challenge readily, and the resultant national elections seemed to prove him correct in his analysis of how far the people would support him—very far!

Britain's House of Commons, operating against the backdrop of a largely unwritten constitution, with its implications of legislative supremacy, does theoretically, at least, possess the kind of overriding residual power once envisaged for legislative bodies as the instrumentality of the popular will. But, as the last chapter has demonstrated, the exigencies of time and the facts of life of the political process have combined to reduce and curtail the effective power of Commons both drastically and dramatically. Commons has been compelled by the facts of party government to abdicate to the cabinet, headed and led by the Prime Minister, who, aided by the superbly disciplined political party in power, in turn reflects the majority opinion of the British electorate. The House of Commons can still bring down the Government, but it does so at the risk of political suicide. Its functions— symptomatic of the decline of legislative bodies everywhere—are now largely those of approving, amending, adjusting, correcting, and legitimating.

Although this conclusion applies broadly also to the House of Representatives in the United States, there are highly significant differences. Independently elected for two-year terms for office, and functioning under a system of separation of powers, the House reflects the federal structure of the American system of government, with its undisciplined party system. It swings its weight, however negative that may be, in the essentially 'no-saying' character of its impact. Almost four and a half times as large as the Senate, and saddled with the necessity to run for office every two years, the House is clearly the less influential of the two bodies; but it does have influence, particularly in financial legislation (see the following chapter), and its veto power over policy-making initiated by the executive is as real as it often proves to be exasperating.

Yet to see a truly powerful lower chamber in a Western liberal democracy, in action, one must look to the House of Representatives in New Zealand— where there is neither a second chamber to restrain it nor a written constitution; where the House does not share powers with a President; and where there are no provincial or state governments. It should be noted, however, that this power structure has existed only since 1950. Prior thereto, for nearly a hundred years, there had been an upper house, the Legislative Council; but it declined in prestige, played an ever diminishing role in government, and was finally abolished.

THE DEMOCRATIC LEGISLATURE AT WORK

THE LEGISLATURE WHEN PARTY LINES ARE DRAWN

In turning now to the organization and working of the more active and more or less powerful chambers of these legislatures, it will be recalled that the members of the United States House of Representatives, the British House of Commons, and the French National Assembly are popularly elected by what is virtually universal suffrage, and that a system of political parties dominates the processes of election in each of these countries. We noted in Chapter IX that the political parties take a commanding role in the working of the legislative processes also. None of these lower chambers, nor the United States Senate, can be understood unless that role is kept constantly in mind. It accounts for many of the features of these legislatures that the public regards with impatience. When party lines are really drawn, the legislature is not the active center of decision where great speeches sway opinion and make history. When party leaders speak, they speak to the country as a whole, or at any rate to groups outside the legislature. Many members do not speak at all; most of them speak but little, and then mostly to their constituencies. When party lines are drawn, they vote in accordance with party considerations. This is a very large part of the explanation of the empty seats—except when the party whips descry an approaching division or roll-call—the seeming triviality of debate, the scant attention, and the almost discourteous lack of overt concern to what is being said.

Power Contest. Parties are arranged against each other in competition for power, for the sweets of office, as well as for the power to carry out the program wanted by the interests in the electorate that support them. The psychological atmosphere thus generated is one of struggle, and when the parties are fully deployed in the legislature they tend to contest every inch of ground, whether or not truth and the public interest are at stake. In these clashes, personal feuds and rivalries tend at times to overshadow issues of principle as inspiration for debate. As long as parties continue to play their present role, legislative proceedings will be deeply affected by them. Yet many people expect legislatures to behave as if political parties did not exist.

ROLE OF THE OPPOSITION. The overshadowing significance of parties, where it exists, must not be taken to mean that the legislature is no more than a

Punch and Judy show in which the puppets move through the unseen manipulations of parties. We should be in a bad situation, indeed, if laws were made and announced by a secret junta. Many men will acquiesce in private to decisions they would not defend in debate. When they know that they must justify their proposals in what is, despite all detraction, the greatest forum in the country, before an opposition that will pounce on the slightest offense to the public sense of decency, a restraining influence of immense weight comes into play. One great service of the opposition lies not in its spoken criticisms, but in the mere fact of its being there.

Moreover, there are always two or more sides to a story, and the majority party has not heard all of the other side until the opposition has had its say. Concession to the arguments of the opposition follows oftener than is generally believed. The public, despite its disillusionment, gets from the dramatic clash of parliamentary debate a grasp of great issues of public policy, which it cannot get in any other way until much larger resources are thrown into political education. Finally, new laws made each year are only a tiny fraction of the old ones that are being administered day by day. Oppressive, wasteful, or neglectful administration will be a black mark against the party that presently controls the executive power if its behavior can be given wide publicity. Questions in the House of Commons in Britain, the mere existence of the National Assembly in France, and investigations by the United States Congress, expose such matters to the public gaze, and the executive proceeds more or less warily. Here again, it is not the actual gleanings of legislative surveillance which are of supreme importance but the ever-present threat of investigation.

Discussion of many matters relevant to a well-rounded account of the place of the legislature in modern government must be postponed to later chapters. Here we are primarily concerned with the legislature as a distinct organ of government, and main emphasis will be on internal organization and procedure and on the role of parties in it. The emphasis will be highly selective and partial and, for Britain and France, will concentrate on the *lower* chambers. The internal workings of each of the legislative bodies under review is a study in itself, and only the briefest sketch designed to bring certain important features into relief can be offered.

LEGISLATIVE COMMITTEES

The growing torrent of legislation that must be enacted to meet demands of the positive state puts increasing pressure on legislatures. Even where party organization formulates almost all of the new legislation and guides it to the statute book, as in Britain, these measures must be explained to the legislature and enacted by it. Time must also be found for debating general policy and examining the trend of administration of the manifold activities of government. It is not only a question of time but also of the sheer size of the legislature. The British House of Commons, the French National Assembly, and the United States House of Representatives are all too large for effective deliberation. Consequently, there is increasing reliance on committees to divide the labor and thus to provide for more effective discussion. Woodrow Wilson stated it well: 'Congress at work is Congress in committee.'

Committees in Congress. In both chambers of the United States Congress a well-developed system of committees antedates the rush of legislation, which has been rising for seventy-five years. This elaborate organization into committees was rendered necessary by the absence there of a general executive committee like the cabinet in Britain. Many permanent *standing committees,* also known as 'subject matter committees,' were formed, each to carry some part of this function of examining proposals for legislation, and deciding which of them should be recommended to the chambers. As the mass of legislative work mounted, these committees came to dominate Congress in somewhat the same fashion that the British cabinet dominates the House of Commons. The standing committees are appointed after each congressional election for a period of two years. In each chamber, there is a standing committee for each of the important recurring subjects of legislation, such as Judiciary, Appropriations, Foreign Affairs, and so forth. The number of standing committees has varied from time to time. The Legislative Reorganization Act of 1946 provided for a sharp reduction in their number, from forty-eight to nineteen in the House of Representatives and from thirty-three to fifteen in the Senate; by 1963 each house had increased its committees by one.

SELECTION. Each party is entitled to membership on each committee roughly proportionate to its strength in the chambers. When the time comes to appoint committees, the members of each party in each chamber meet in party caucus and select a 'Committee on Committees.' Each Committee on Committees then nominates members of its own party to fill the quota to which the party is entitled on the standing committees of the chamber. These nominations are ratified almost as a matter of course by the appropriate party caucuses and the chambers as a whole.

As we shall see later, the standing committees of Congress substantially make the laws. Those who choose the standing committees have a great influence on what laws are made. The Committees on Committees are composed in each case of a rather small group of party leaders or their nominees. For example, the Democratic Committee on Committees in the House of Representatives is composed of Democratic members of the powerful tax-writing Committee on Ways and Means. This gives some indication of the extent to which the party system, if not the majority party, can control Congress. In fact, the majority party can control decisions of the standing committees when it chooses.

SENIORITY. In addition, the chairmanship of each standing committee traditionally goes to the member of the majority party in the chamber who has had the *longest continuous service* on the committee. This is the frequently attacked 'seniority system.' A skillful chairman who has had long experience on a committee, and has accumulated a wide knowledge of the range of matters with which the committee deals, can exercise a powerful influence on its deliberations—for good or evil. The seniority system puts a heavy premium on politically 'safe' election districts. Thus, when the Democrats are in power, between twenty-two and twenty-eight of the thirty-six chairmanships normally go to Southern or Border representatives under this rule by longevity. When the Republicans are in power most of the chairmen come from the Midwest or New England. Chairmanships are gained and retained, once wrote Senator Kefauver (D.—Tenn.), by 'seniority, sectionalism, and senility.' [10] It is hence not surprising that probably no other institutional aspect of Congress is subject to as much outside criticism as the seniority system—and none is less likely to be altered!

STANDING COMMITTEES AT WORK. All bills and proposals for legislation go automatically to standing committees before being considered by the House as a whole. To aid themselves in reaching the recommendations they will make to the House, and/or to publicize their work, the committees hold public and private meetings, where civil servants, disinterested experts, and lobbyists representing the interests concerned are heard pro and con on the subject. Enormous numbers of proposals for legislation are quietly smothered in committee. Less than 10 per cent of those referred to committee ever emerge therefrom. Those not killed or 'pigeonholed' in committee are often subjected to major operations, which remake them in such a way that their sponsors sometimes hardly know them. Of course, the majority party can

[10] Estes Kefauver and Jack Levin, *A Twentieth Century Congress* (New York: Duell, Sloan and Pearce, 1947), p. 267.

theoretically control the committee and, if it is so disposed, compel it by a 'discharge petition'[11] to report to Congress bills that the party is backing, or that the President, provided he is of the same party, urgently wants to go forward—but it is highly reluctant to interfere with committee procedures, and only twice within the past generation has a discharge petition been successfully invoked.

The vital work of the United States Congress is done in these standing committees. With most of the discussions being private, speeches are to the point and not, as on the floor, to the constituencies. Representatives of protesting groups are heard, and they often get some portion of the concessions for which they press. The form in which the bill is finally reported out is generally, but not always, satisfactory to the majority party. Congress rarely makes significant changes in any bill that is positively recommended by the standing committees, although not every bill that emerges necessarily passes. In other words, the committees are performing some of the functions of the British cabinet, but they far less often hew to a party line.

In this way, the labor of the legislature is divided and a bigger harvest of legislation is produced. However, it must be said that in so far as the effective decisions are taken by small committees and sub-committees, ranging in number from twelve to fifty members, the representative character of deliberation on lawmaking is greatly impaired. Attempts are made to distribute membership of committees geographically, but that does little to repair the damage to the representative principle. Also, the system suffers from the nemesis that pursues all divisions of labor—the difficulty of combining the separate specialized efforts into a harmonious whole. Very effective work is done on specific pieces of legislation, but not always with sufficient recognition of their relation to general policy. The British cabinet system, by concentrating responsibility for the formulation of all aspects of policy on a single body, keeps the necessity for integrating the legislative program in the foreground, and the British House of Commons therefore is marked, as Congress is not, for debates of high quality on the general policy of the government. What is true of Britain here applies to France, too, but to a much lesser extent.

JURISDICTION. The legislative work of Congress has been divided among these standing committees in such a way that each committee in each chamber has a well-defined area of jurisdiction corresponding closely to the field

[11] A petition which must be signed by an absolute majority of the members of the house of Congress concerned.

of operations of particular departments and agencies of the executive. Most of the committees divide themselves into sub-committees to enhance efficiency. Staffs of experts assist these committees in their work. These, and other provisions of the Legislative Reorganization Act of 1946, to be referred to later, are improving the effectiveness of the detailed work of standing committees in particular fields of public policy.

OTHER COMMITTEES. In addition to standing committees, *select,* or *ad hoc,* committees are appointed to inquire into *special* issues of concern when they are thought to require it, such as the well-known Kefauver Crime Committee in 1951 and the McClellan Committee on Improper Practices in the Labor or Management Field in 1957. Also, the fact that the two chambers are equal in legislative power often brings them to deadlock on some piece of legislation. Since both chambers must accept a proposal in identical form before it can be sent to the President for his action in the lawmaking process, an acceptable compromise must be found. The usual device is a *conference committee* consisting of a small number of members of both chambers who are familiar with the particular piece of legislation and who search—sometimes long—for a solution, which both houses may accept or reject but may not amend. There are, furthermore, several small but influential *joint committees,* composed of members from both houses of Congress, which deal with matters of an unusually technical or sensitive nature, such as the Joint Congressional Committee on Atomic Energy.

THE HOUSE RULES COMMITTEE. No account of committees in the United States Congress would be complete without reference to the perpetually controversial Committee on Rules of the House of Representatives. (The Senate has a Rules Committee, too, but it is of no comparable significance.) This small, immensely powerful committee of fifteen senior members of the House, ten from the majority party and five from the minority, determines, in effect, when the formal rules of the House are to be temporarily departed from, what priorities are to be observed in the agenda, and the nature of, and time limits on, debate. It is a most important agency of majority party control but it has also been a thorn in the side of the House. 'Rules' is both a traffic manager for and a killer of bills. Its chairman wields authority second only to that of the Speaker and is courted by the President—when indeed he is courtable at all—much the way a foreign dignitary is!

Committees in the House of Commons. The British House of Commons, always averse to standing committees on the ground that, in practical effect, they make inroads on the supremacy of a representative Parliament, managed to avoid any substantial development in this direction until the beginning of the twentieth century. It was able to do so for two reasons: First, the cabinet is largely a committee of the House for framing and guiding legislation. Second, the practice of resolving the whole House into committee for various purposes gave some of the advantages of committee procedure.

'Committee of the Whole,' as it is called, is formed by the Speaker's leaving the chair and giving over his duties to a less exalted chairman of committees. Party reins are slackened and rules of debate are relaxed. For example, members may speak more than once to the point under discussion, and the majority cannot summarily cut off debate by moving that the previous question now be put. All financial proposals, and other bills of unusual importance, still go to Committee of the Whole.

SELECTION. The pressure of work is inexorable and, after some exploratory use of standing committees, they came into general use in 1907. However, there are still only six or seven. Aside from one that specializes in Scottish affairs and one that deals with private members' bills, these are general-purpose committees, designated A, B, C, D, and E. They take whatever assignments are given them by the Speaker on the advice of the Committee of Selection. To provide for expert assistance and specialist interest, the Committee of Selection may add to the normal nucleus of *circa* twenty members another thirty or so temporarily for the purpose of considering a particular bill.

The Committee of Selection is nominated by the party leaders and confirmed by the House at the beginning of each session. The Committee, in turn, nominates the standing committees, taking counsel with the party whips. The chairmen are not necessarily of the majority party, and, while the party whips are not brandished in committee, party persuasion is still within call.

AT WORK. Normally, all public bills (including private members' bills) that are not financial bills are referred to the standing committees *after* second reading in the House of Commons. However, the second reading approves the general principle of the bill, narrowing the scope of discussion in committee to details—in striking contrast to the United States where 'the sky is the limit' on committee action on pending legislation—many of which are of a technical character. Often the decision on these matters of detail will turn on questions of fact or scientific judgment.

Discussion in Commons' committees must be restricted to these details. For example, if the bill in question is one to establish a code of safety and sanitary measures in industrial establishments, the committee cannot debate the issue of whether the law should interfere with the way in which industrial employers run their factories; for that question has already been answered in the affirmative on second reading. The committee must settle down to deciding what particular sanitary and safety measures are necessary to preserve health and prevent accidents.

So there is not so much room for division on party lines and not much temptation to make speeches to the country at large in a small committee whose proceedings get little publicity. Members even of the majority party supporting the government may press for modifications, and within limits the government will concede them, if the argument in committee is cogent or if the debate on second reading has indicated a strong case for some adjustment. But the leaders of the majority party are far from giving the committee its head, and they can apply closure to speed it toward its report. Unlike the practice in the United States, the committees do not provide hearings for private interests concerned. However, while the bill is in committee, private interests may press their views strongly on the cabinet.

LACK OF PRESTIGE. Thus British committees lack the power and prestige of their American counterparts. They can neither smother bills nor make major amendments that cut into the principle of the bill, e.g. they cannot eliminate from the factory bill all requirements for sanitary precautions. On the whole, membership in them is not sought but evaded. Being general-purpose committees, they make no appeal to members with specialized knowledge or interest, and members who go on a committee for the narrow purpose of a single piece of legislation will often ask to be relieved once it has been reported to the House. Professor K. C. Wheare has made the observation that the crucial distinction between the British and American committee systems, in matters of bringing special knowledge and interest to bear on bills, is that in Britain members with special knowledge and interest 'go to the bills' by pursuing them to whatever committee Mr. Speaker has referred them, whereas in the United States the bills 'go to the members' with special knowledge and interest.[12]

The House of Commons is jealous of the committees. Yet it could not do its work without delegating this discussion of detail, and its only alternative is to extend still further the growing practice of limiting legislation to a statement of general principle and delegating the power to fill in details to

---

[12] Kenneth C. Wheare, *Government by Committee: An Essay on the British Constitution* (New York: Oxford University Press, 1955), p. 135.

government departments. The significance of this practice will be taken up later, and it will suffice here to say that it, too, is irksome to the House. So the trend toward greater reliance on committees continues.

SPECIALIZED COMMITTEES? It is often urged that specialized committees should be set up to attract the sustained effort of members according to their interest. To each such committee would be assigned the scrutiny of one of the great government departments. It would consider the legislative proposals and the annual estimates of that department and make a close study of its administrative operations. In this way, Parliament would move toward a better understanding and a more effective control of the complexities of government.

The experience of some of the democratic governments of continental Europe, and the dominant position of committees in Congress in the United States, clearly indicate that such committees would compete with the cabinet for primacy, and it is likely that the party leaders, in order to preserve intact their instrument of unified action, would have to make the practical scope of such committees much narrower than is suggested. There is also the question already noticed, whether concentration on specialized competence in these committees would not detract from the quality of discussion the House of Commons now provides on general policy.

SELECT COMMITTEES. The House of Commons often uses select committees to inquire into particular subjects of great importance, or to give special consideration to particular bills that propose drastic change. Their function is inquiry into complex issues rather than the discussion of legislative detail. Accordingly, they are customarily small committees of fifteen members or less, chosen for their knowledge of or interest in the particular subject matter —such as the 1959 Committee on Procedure. They hold hearings at which interested parties appear and give evidence. When expressly authorized by the House they may compel the attendance of witnesses and require the production of documents. Detailed records of their proceedings are kept and printed along with their formal reports. In short, their function is similar to that of a royal commission of inquiry, although it is performed in a less pretentious manner.

Legislative Committees in France. While there are standing committees, known as *commissions générales parlementaires,* in both chambers of the French Parliament, our concern here is with those in the National Assembly. Structurally, the *commissions*—as we shall call them henceforth—resemble the standing committees of Congress in that they are committees on particular subjects or fields of legislation. Despite this structural similarity, however, a distinct functional difference exists: congressional committees are primarily designed for legislative functions, but the chief task of the French *commissions* is to keep a day by day check on the executive—ineffective as this may be under the Fifth Republic. As a rule, each ministry is under the surveillance of a *commission,* the range and sphere of which encompasses, among several others, its own activities, e.g. Foreign Affairs, Defense, Education, etc. This used to be a striking parallelism, which under the Third and Fourth Republics accorded to the *commissions* a control over policy on a par with that of the ministers themselves, but now no longer in practice under the Fifth.

SELECTION AND COMPOSITION. In 1963 there were six permanent *commissions* in the National Assembly (and the Senate) whereas under the Fourth Republic nineteen special committees existed. With the latter arrangement, much of the work of one often quite naturally overlapped that of another. In some cases the *commissions* were hard put, indeed, to justify their existence. Such a large and specialized group of committees was likewise susceptible to much intensive lobbying and domination by various interest groups.

The reforms of the de Gaulle Constitution sought to eliminate the above evils not only by expanding the *commissions'* fields of jurisdictional subject matter, but by specifically limiting their number to just six new and much larger ones, thus drastically reducing their importance—in addition to the dramatic over-all reduction in power and influence of the legislative body generally. The six *commissions* extant in 1963 and their membership were Culture, Family, and Social Affairs (120), Foreign Affairs (60), National Defense and Armed Forces (90), Finance and Economic Planning (60), Constitutional Laws, Legislation, and General Administration (90), and Production and Exchange (120). When questions of great urgency and/or importance arise, *ad hoc* committees are elected by a majority of the Assembly. There is no set membership size on these committees and they expire when their work has been completed.

Although known as 'permanent' *commissions,* the six units are elected by their fellow legislators for one session, and they, in turn, elect their own chairman. In general, however, the principle of seniority is adhered to. As in Congress, but unlike the House of Commons, the French *commissions* reflect quite closely the strength of the various parties in the Assembly. The standing rules require their selection by P.R., based upon party groups that have thirty or more members. No one may become a member of a *commission* except through membership in such a group.

At Work. All bills are read to the Assembly as they are received from the Government, and may—or may not—be referred to a *commission*. Bills referred to *commissions* must be reported out; 'pigeonholing' is strictly forbidden—as indeed it was under prior republics. Public hearings, such as in America, are unknown to the French *commissions* as information discussed is often considered classified and confidential, yet conferring with proponents and opponents of legislation is customary. But the *commissions* may now administer oaths only if such power is expressly granted by the National Assembly. Outside experts are invited to give their views, as are the ministers concerned. The latter now can no longer be required to appear before a *commission* but, in line with a policy initiated by de Gaulle's first Premier, Michel Debré, they usually do so! The chairman of a *commission*, who bears the lofty title *Monsieur le Président,* is, of course, no longer the influential figure in either the *commission* or the legislative process that he represented in the pre-de Gaulle days.

THE RAPPORTEUR. The key figure in a particular piece of legislation in the past never was the President of the *commission,* but its *rapporteur,* or 're-porter.' While in Britain a government bill is explained, defended, and piloted through Parliament by the appropriate minister, and in Congress by the chairman of the standing committee or one of its sub-committees, in pre-de Gaulle France it was the *rapporteur* who had charge of the bill when it emerged from the *commission*. He was designated as its reporter upon the initial consideration of the bill by the *commission* and, in effect, he eclipsed the minister—who introduced the bill in the first place. As long as *rapporteur* and minister co-operated, the French committee system worked smoothly, but abuse was notorious, and many a *rapporteur* made his minister's life miserable—not surprising in a country that had both a multi-party system and a coalition government. In a sense the *rapporteur* was a quasi-minister. A successful *rapporteur* used his job as a stepping stone to a high governmental position, as the eleven-times Premier Aristide Briand did.

Today, under the Fifth Republic the *rapporteur* still plays a role in the *commission,* but it has become more or less of a mechanical nature, for it is the minister concerned who guides his own bill through Parliament. And inasmuch as the National Assembly must vote on his bill, subject to such amendments as the Government may allow, the once commanding position of *rapporteur* has become decisively subordinate to the minister who has sponsored the legislation—a true reflection of the demise of France's legislature under the new Constitution.

RULES OF PROCEDURE IN THE LEGISLATURE

A glance at the rules of legislative procedure should now enable us to sketch the process of lawmaking in the legislature. Every deliberative body needs rules of procedure to expedite business and also to protect the rights of speech and of protest from abridgment or abuse. Rules against the abuse of the right of speech are particularly required to maintain the equable temper of discussion, without which deliberation cannot be carried on at all.

In the House of Commons. In the long course of its development, the British House of Commons built up an impressive body of *customary* rules of procedure. These remain the basis of its procedure at the present day, but they have been extensively supplemented by deliberately adopted written rules, known as 'standing orders,' covering the order of business, time to be allotted to various kinds of business, stages of debate on measures, and other matters. By majority vote, the House may suspend or repeal any rule of procedure as it sees fit. Thus the majority party controls the procedure of the House. Standing orders give the cabinet about four-fifths of the time of the House, and a session rarely goes by without the cabinet's having to encroach on the limited time left for private members' business.

CLOSURE. By the adoption in standing orders of various forms of *closure* early in this century, the cabinet can use its supporting majority to close discussion at once, or at a definite future hour, and to select which of a number of proposed amendments to a bill shall be discussed and which rejected without discussion. Closure is a drastic power but, as a result of the demand for more and more legislation and government action, the hard choice is between more talk and less completed business, or more business disposed of and less talk. One may sympathize generally with the latter alternative, but it must not be forgotten that the real function of Parliament is to talk reluctant people into consent to measures they dislike. Closure is a necessary instrument under present circumstances, but if not used sparingly and with wisdom it will strangle a deliberative assembly.

In Congress. The colonial legislative assemblies of North America followed the British rules of procedure of the time, and Congress has been deeply influenced by them. Thomas Jefferson, when Vice President, drew up for the Senate a famous *Manual of Parliamentary Practice,* based on the British model. The House of Representatives adopted this manual in 1837. It is still the core of congressional procedure, although it is now surrounded by many modifications and additions. Both the House of Representatives and the Senate can change their rules by majority vote. The two Committees on Rules, dominated by the majority party, propose changes which the chambers accept. The House of Representatives has rules corresponding to the British closure provisions, and they are used not only to limit but at times to strangle debate.

CLOSURE IN THE SENATE. For long, the Senate made no provision in its rules for restricting freedom of debate and recognized the right of minorities to continue talking indefinitely in protest against majority measures. On occasion, senators have turned in prodigious performances, speaking many hours at a stretch, supplementing ideas and arguments with verse and prose, and sometimes with matter of lesser quality. They may work in relays, keeping the house in continuous session around the clock, or *solo,* until they are exhausted. These *filibusters,* as they are called, sometimes accomplish their purpose of wearing out the majority and thereby blocking or defeating the legislation. Sometimes their purpose is merely to call the country's attention to a particular controversy, as Senator Wayne Morse did in his then record solo-filibuster of almost twenty-three hours, without a break, against the Offshore Oil Bill in 1953.

Even under a mild form, as adopted in 1917, closure in the Senate was used only four times. Since the enactment of new closure rules in 1949 and 1959, the former requiring the affirmative vote of two-thirds of the full membership of the Senate, the latter two-thirds of those present and voting (there being a quorum) closure was used just once—on the 'Telstar' bill in 1962. Whatever the influence of the threat of closure may be, it has had no significant influence on debate in the Senate, and filibusters still take place. Of course, the relatively small membership of the Senate reduces somewhat the necessity for restrictive measures, and debate is often held within limits by agreement among the leaders of the parties that a vote shall be taken at a definite future time.

In Britain, the cabinet containing the leaders of the majority party takes the leadership in expediting business within the framework of the rules. It has a program prepared at the opening of every session. It takes up most of the time of the House and sees to it that the important items on its program are dealt with and brought to some conclusion. In the United States, the executive does not *per se* lead in Congress, and its place is taken by the floor leaders, rules committees, and steering committees of the majority party.

In fact, in each chamber, each party has a small steering or policy committee. Naturally, the steering or policy committee of the majority party is the significant one, as the pushing of party measures, the enforcing of the timetable, and changes in the order of business generally originate there. The chairman of the committee is either the floor leader of his party or a very influential member. The floor leader is aided by the *whips,* who herd the members of their party into the chamber for roll-calls. If some members of the party are wavering on an issue that calls for party solidarity, the caucus meets and *tries* to work to a position that all will be willing to support—but, as we have seen, this goal is by no means always attainable in the United States Congress.

In the French National Assembly. Rules of procedure in the Assembly—indeed in both branches of the French Parliament—now resemble those of the House of Commons more than those of Congress. Both members of the ministry and individual legislators may introduce legislation. Government-sponsored bills, known as *projets de loi,* which are invariably introduced by the ministers involved, almost always pass. But only a very few of the private bills, called *propositions de loi,* become law.

In effect, the French ministers, as already indicated, themselves guide the proposed measures through the Assembly. Under the Fifth Republic, it is the French ministry—very much like the British executive—which fixes the legislative agenda, unlike the American executive who must bow to the leadership of the legislature for those vital purposes.

CLOSURE. Standing Orders govern the *clôture* or closure. While closure was attainable even in the Third and Fourth Republics, its use was far more circumscribed than in the House of Commons. Often it was extremely difficult to achieve—since there was no responsible (or other) majority to invoke it. However, the Assembly did rather frequently agree to a form of 'restricted debate' on non-essential bills—a pre-determined classification—under which a limited number of members might speak five minutes each. This practice—which governs under the Fifth Republic—closely resembles that prevalent in the United States House of Representatives. Closure was never a popular or frequent practice in the French legislature, most of whose members preferred to accentuate the French love for individualism—even at the risk of governmental chaos! But now those days, too, are gone, and the Government possesses the weapons to compel legislative action—ultimately on pain of doing without the legislature, if necessary.

Thus in France the Gaullist majority, and in Britain and in the United States the majority party, has procedure within its control and can enforce its will by drastic methods. This is particularly true of Britain and France. In the United States, however, divided majority parties sometimes make 'cracking the whip' difficult. When the chips are really down enough pressure can usually be brought to bear upon the members. But as even the most popular of American Presidents have found out, there comes a point when other loyalties engendered by the federal system obviate those to party.

FORMAL STEPS IN LAWMAKING

Lawmaking in Britain. In Britain, government bills, almost the entire grist of public bills, are drafted by the executive. The department whose special concern a bill is consults with the other departments affected, and civil servants contribute their experience and work out specifications of the technical means required to reach the desired end. When a completed draft of what is wanted has been approved by the cabinet, it goes to the parliamentary counsel to the Treasury, a drafting expert who fits the bill with legal clothing or, more precisely, drafts a bill that will accomplish legally the desired results.

First reading in the House of Commons follows. It is generally reading by title only and never more than notice of motion to bring the bill forward for discussion at a later date. On second reading, the principle of the bill, the general question whether such legislation as this is necessary or desirable, is discussed. While it is not unknown for the government to withdraw a bill after an onslaught on it at second reading, it is extremely rare. After all, the government claims a mandate from the people to pursue its policy, and its bills are the central part of that policy. The bill is passed on second reading and is referred to a standing committee.

As already explained, the committee considers the bill in detail clause by clause, sometimes making amendments at its own behest, but mainly at the government's. When this overhauling is completed, the bill is reported back to the House. At report stage, as it is called, the House considers the bill in detail. But if the time saved in committee is not to be wasted at the report stage, this consideraion must be limited and fewer amendments are moved at report stage than in committee. As soon as report stage is finished, the third reading may be moved. At this final stage, only verbal amendments may be introduced, so that the debate on the third reading tends to rehearse the debate on the second reading. Despite the reservations of the House about standing committees, the really thorough consideration of the bill in detail is given in committee. After passage by the House of Commons, the bill goes to the House of Lords. It may be added that private members draft their own bills, but this is of little import, as such bills have almost no chance of becoming law.

Lawmaking in Congress. In the United States, bills considered desirable by the President may be drafted in the government departments and introduced into one or the other chamber of the legislature by a member of Congress who is of the President's political party. A high proportion of the important measures put before Congress are now initiated in that manner. Congress, however, considers many measures that are not inspired, or even favored, by the executive. Any member may introduce a bill, and the committees often have proposals before them that they wish to put in the form of a bill looking toward legislation. For a long time, Congress had to find its resources of draftsmanship where it could, but some years ago provision was made for the appointment of legislative counsel as officers of Congress to draft bills for its committees and members. In addition, the Legislative Reference Service of the Library of Congress serves as the principal congressional research arm. Special interests, wanting legislation on their behalf, often also draft their own bills and have them presented to Congress. This extensive private enterprise by individual members of Congress and outside groups in introducing bills largely explains why such heavy slaughter of bills occurs in committees.

All bills introduced are given first reading by title only, and are immediately referred to the appropriate committee. In the Senate, first and second readings, both quite perfunctory, are commonly given at the same time before the bill goes to committee. The real deliberative effort, it will be recalled, takes place in committee. The House of Representatives, when a bill is reported to it favorably by committee, generally contents itself with acceptance, rejection, or minor amendment on second reading with little debate. If serious debate and amendment are desired and are acceptable to the steering committee of the majority, the House resolves itself into Committee of the Whole for the purpose. Third reading immediately precedes final passage and occurs without debate.

In the more individualistic Senate, with fewer members, less restrictive rules of procedure, and looser party control, bills favorably reported by committee are likely to get closer examination and more discussion. Amendments are freely offered and debated; whether they have a chance of acceptance depends on whether the measure is one respecting which party lines are drawn. Third reading immediately precedes the final vote on the bill.

Lawmaking in France. We have already seen that bills may be introduced in the French legislature by either private members or ministers. Since there is no legislative or parliamentary counsel, as in Britain and the United States, private members draft their own bills, sometimes with the assistance of members of the Assembly President's legal staff. Bills sponsored by the government are drafted by civil servants who have had some legal training. Often ministers call upon the *Conseil d'Etat* for aid, for this highest administrative court also acts as technical adviser to the government in the drafting of bills and ordinances.

Once introduced by title—its first reading—in the National Assembly, a bill is referred to the appropriate standing *commission,* which cannot bury it but must report it to the Assembly. Upon the report to the floor by the commission's *rapporteur,* a general debate on the measure ensues. This is the second reading. If the bill survives that stage, the Assembly proceeds to a consideration of its various sections; amendments are now in order and are voted upon. Ultimately, the finished bill receives its third reading, and the final vote is taken. Any 'restricted debate,' if previously sanctioned by the Assembly at the commission's behest, occurs at this stage. The completed bill then goes to the Council of the Republic, to be processed in accordance with the procedure described earlier.

In a constitutional regime, all taxation must be approved by legislation, and no expenditure of public money can be made without authorization of the legislature. Taxing and appropriation measures are legislation of vital importance, subject to some special rules. As the course of financial legislation brings out most clearly the working relationship of the executive and the legislature, discussion of it will be postponed to the following chapter, which is devoted to those relationships. For the same reason, discussion of legislative surveillance of administration might be postponed, as some attention will have to be given to it there in any case. On the other hand, a description here of the mechanisms used, and the time available, for inquiring into administration will help to round out discussion of the legislature, and to clear the ground for undivided attention to the essence of legislative-executive relationships.

CONTROL OF ADMINISTRATION BY THE LEGISLATURE

The Methods in the House of Commons. In Britain, the executive is in the legislature and responsible to it. A vote of censure of its administrative performance may cause the downfall of the cabinet just as well as rejection of a government bill. In practice, a motion of censure is rarely successful because the government can generally rely on its majority to preserve it from such disasters, and its demands on the time of the House do not leave much time for the debating of administration. Despite the enormous range of present-day activities of government, the time available for discussing administration in the normal annual session of Parliament is estimated at less than thirty days.

QUESTIONING MINISTERS. A more effective means of criticizing the administration is the right to ask questions of the executive. An hour is set aside each day for oral or written questions addressed by a member to a minister. The questioner may be seeking sheer information, but more often he picks on some incident of administration, perhaps the grievance of one of his constituents against a minor government official or on some unwary remark of a member of the government in the House, or elsewhere, in the hope of forcing the minister into a damaging statement about the policy of the department he is administering. He wants an oral reply, and he needs the right to ask supplementary questions of a minister who is evasive. The question hour is a battle of wits, the minister trying to score off the hecklers and they trying to skewer the minister with a question that cannot be answered without putting him and his department in a bad light. It is an important technique of opposition. Ministers always fear that if there is a chink in their armor, questions on successive days will probe for it until it is found. Civil servants—whom the minister protects loyally in the House, but whom he excoriates afterwards for their mistakes—are extremely wary in what they do. Where thousands of civil servants are dealing daily with hundreds of thousands of citizens, it is important to have a forum where grievances against their conduct can be aired and misdeeds corrected.

The House of Commons would be swamped with questions if each member were not strictly limited in the number to which he can demand oral answers. Only a fraction of the opportunities for grilling the executive for its administrative actions can be followed up. And, of courses, many of the best opportunities are missed even in Britain, because most members of Parliament are not at all conversant with the details of administration. For that matter, the minister himself does not know too much about them, but he is coached by civil servants who know vastly more about these details than anyone else. The actual contest is on unequal terms. The real control is the knowledge that gross maladministration will certainly be exposed on the floor of the House and thus broadcast to the public.

The Methods in Congress. Members of Congress in the United States cannot question the executive on the floor of the legislative chambers, but they do debate administrative action and vote critical resolutions that make specific recommendations. They go further at times and enact detailed laws directing the minutiae of administration. In recent years the congressional committees, particularly the Appropriations Committees, have developed a practice of attaching to their reports to Congress a variety of instructions and limitations, designed to control very closely the expenditure of some portions of the money appropriated.

INVESTIGATIONS AND PUBLICITY. Most important, Congress makes investigations into the conduct of the executive generally through the Committees on Government Operations of the two chambers, but sometimes through special committee set up to investigate some particular aspect of executive stewardship. These committees ask, and often but by no means always, from the executive access to books, papers, and documents· but they can compel the President to surrender them. They frequently require government officials as well as private citizens to appear and testify before them. papers customarily give almost hysterical publicity to these investigations with the unfortunate result that they often become witch-hunts or smears of particular individuals, rather than sober investigations of administration.[13] They are sporadic rather than continuous, and

[13] Space does not permit an over-all discussion of congressional investigating and their practices. They have performed many useful tasks of unearthing facts for the public, but some of their methods have come under considerable fire. The United States Supreme Court ruled, in a case involving the refusal of one Watkins to answer questions put to him by the House Committee on Un-American Affairs regarding the freedoms guaranteed under the First Amendment, that there were limits of Congress to inquire. The Court held 6:1 that there is no general authority to expose the private affairs of individuals without justification; that Congress is not a law or trial agency; and that 'no inquiry is an end in itself; it must be related to one of a legitimate task of Congress.' (*Watkins* v. *U.S.*, 354 U.S. 178). In subsequent decisions the Court retreated somewhat from this holding, requiring it pursue fair procedures (e.g. *Barenblatt* v. *U.S.*, 360 U.S. 109, 1959).

not launched until after the horse has been stolen. Nevertheless, congressional investigations may well be educators of public opinion, and the executive has a well-founded fear of their probings, particularly those of the Senate. They are perhaps as effective as the separation of powers permits them to be. At any rate, they confirm the anticipation of the framers of the Constitution in that they fan the latent hostility between the legislature and the executive.

COMMITTEE OVERSIGHT. Under the Legislative Reorganization Act of 1946, the standing committees are authorized to maintain continuous oversight of administration in the field of public policy assigned to each committee. Thus the committees of the two chambers, which originally studied and reported a particular legislative proposal, are now charged with sustained scrutiny of administration of that legislation. With the aid of sizable, expert, and well-paid staffs, the committees can give closer and steadier attention to the conduct of administration, if they do not indeed try to exercise detailed ervision of it. This may make for closer contact between the legislative ecutive, but not perhaps for more harmonious relationships.

ethods in the French National Assembly. Under the Third and
blics, scrutiny of the French administration by the legislature
g; it was achieved by three devices: the *commissions,* ques-
isters, and *interpellations.* But under the Fifth Republic,
ly subordinated to the executive, these devices are no

pellation used to be the chief legislative threat
ent, and it was keenly feared by all minis-
overnment for information, to which the
minated in serious debate and a vote.
ll. The interpellation was as much
ative weapon, much used for
day, however, with only a
posal—to be explained in
y has been all but stripped
an still topple the Govern-
tory, in the case of the first

nistrative process used to be
he ministers, although oral

questioning—in contrast to interpellation—was always of far less significance in France than the questioning of ministers in Britain. The number of written questions submitted to the ministers annually was about equal in France and Britain—roughly four thousand—but the average number of oral questions in a session of the Fourth Republic's National Assembly was only seventy, while that in the House of Commons averages thirteen thousand. In the Fifth Republic's National Assembly merely the weekly Friday 'question period' remains, when the deputies are free to request responses to certain specific questions and criticize aspects of Government policy in a brief debate.

COMMISSIONS. Probably the most effective immediate supervision over administration used to be imposed by the standing *commissions* and by the special *commissions* of inquiry which were appointed by the Assembly from time to time. They were forever digging into the details of administration. Here again, the French practice was closer to that of the United States than of Britain. The British, conceding the role almost entirely to the cabinet, do not use committees to control or supervise the administration. The French standing *commissions* constantly subjected ministers to questioning, investigations, and general harassment, in effect putting them into the prisoner's box along with the civil servants. Like congressional committees in the United States, they interfered actively in the administrative process, and so wielded a great deal of power that in Britain is primarily exercised by the cabinet. Yet once again, the de Gaulle Constitution, with its strong executive government, has severely reduced what was once a potent weapon of legislative oversight. Nonetheless, despite the already explained downgrading of the role of the *commissions,* which rendered them into six 'big little legislatures' rather than effective parliamentary bodies of executive control and supervision, they can still delay, question, and bargain with the ministers. In that sense only they continue to serve as a check upon administration.

WHAT IS WRONG WITH THE DEMOCRATIC LEGISLATURE

Excessive Burden. Present-day democratic legislatures are ridiculously overworked. Despite the increasing length of sessions, legislatures cannot give careful consideration to many of the laws they enact, and they can find only a limited time in each session to examine the vast administrative machine of the government. Moreover, they could not accomplish what they do if they were not guided and controlled by a relatively small group of men, the leaders of the political parties. Important decisions have to be delegated to committees which are not really representative, and debate has to be curtailed. It is scarcely true nowadays, in more than a formal sense, that legislatures make the law.

Need for Expertise. Yet legislatures are vitally necessary as censures of parties and of administration. There is great need to improve the quality of their work. No doubt their procedure, which is still redolent of more leisurely bygone days, could, and must, be improved. But if the demands of the positive state are to continue to mount, it cannot be emphasized too strongly that the greatest need is to improve the legislators' knowledge of the complexities with which they are asked to deal. The average member does not stand very far above the general standard of the good citizen, often called the man in the street. This is the kind of watchdog of government that a democracy wants, not a walking encyclopedia so devoted to the accumulation of information that he loses the common touch. Unfortunately, it would require a superman without any other distractions to understand what is involved in the present-day range of legislation and administration. And if the legislature does not understand what the government is doing, constitutionalism can only have a precarious existence.

It is often complained that the quality of legislators has declined, that today none can compare with the gigantic figures of the statesmen of the past. Close observers who have tried to measure the stature of the legislators of earlier days are almost unanimous in denying the decline. If the quality of deliberation and legislative action has dropped, the clue is to be found, not in the quality of the legislators but in the extraordinary expectations of what it should be possible to accomplish by legislation. When the accomplishments fall short of the expectations, as they often do, the tendency is to blame the legislators. Rarely is sufficient allowance made for the inherent difficulty of what they are expected to do.

Negativism. Perhaps a far more serious charge is that today's legislatures have primarily become negative bodies. Where they are still able to do so effectively—like the Congress of the United States—they say 'no' not only with relish but with abandon. Rarely, or so the charge goes, does the legislature innovate; it confines itself to saying 'no' to the innovators—i.e. the executive. The oft-quoted characterization of the typical Congressman, in the Al Capp tradition, as 'a gross, groggy creature who woke from his nap only at the sound of the gavel and, after voting an invariable "Nay," immediately went back to sleep,' [14] is unfair because it paints with far too coarse and broad a brush—but it cannot be gainsaid that some of the attitudes of certain legislators would seem to give that impression, at least to the layman.

It is true, however, that the evidently ever-increasing congressional tendency of waiting for the initiative to come from the White House—and the appearance of helplessness until that initiative is forthcoming—represents a serious fact of legislative life today. Time was when Congress, now the sole remaining institution of potential legislative strength among those herein discussed, would advance and further a host of ideas on its own. Whether or not of its own doing, today it confines itself largely to vetoing, approving, adjusting, correcting, amending, and legitimating—which may, of course, merely reflect a dire necessity of government in a time and world of crisis that calls for strong executive leadership. It thus invites the stern evaluative conclusion of so astute an observer as the sometime President of the American Political Association, that:

> Representative bodies, the institutional embodiment of democratic ideology, have by the compelling force of events lost both power and prestige. Their role in the initiation of public policy has been diminished by losses to pressure groups and administrative agencies; their authority to decide many issues has, of necessity, been delegated to the administrative services. They have been driven toward a role of futile and uninformed criticism, at its worst motivated either by partisan or picayune considerations.[15]

There are few signs, if any, that this analysis will stand in need of drastic revision in the foreseeable future.

THE LEGISLATURE UNDER THE DICTATORSHIPS

The executive always governs. The main functions of the legislature are to impose effective constitutional restraints on the executive and to make such laws as the elected representatives of the diverse interests in the electorate can agree to support by majority vote. In the dictatorships, where

[14] See H. H. Wilson, *Congress: Corruption and Compromise* (New York: Rinehart & Co., 1951), p. 2.

[15] V. O. Key, *Politics, Parties, and Pressure Groups*, 4th ed. (New York: Thomas Y. Crowell Co., 1958), p. 368. And one of their own members, Sen. Joseph S. Clark (D.–Pa.), termed them "the greatest menace of the successful operation of the democratic process." (*The New York Herald Tribune*, May 27, 1963.)

constitutional restraints on the executive are repudiated, and the executive makes by decree such laws as it likes, the legislature ceases to be overworked. The German *Reichstag* under Hitler enacted only seven laws in seven years. As we shall see presently, the supreme legislature in the U.S.S.R. meets infrequently. No attempt is made to have it perform the great functions the legislature performs in liberal democratic countries.

Insignificant. In fact, it ceases to be a significant organ of government. Elections to the legislature are carefully controlled by the dictator and his henchmen. In Germany under Hitler, and in the Soviet Union today, only one candidate stands for election for each seat in the legislature. The voters are not given alternative choices. Yet almost all voters go to the polls, and they vote almost unanimously for the 'official' candidate. In Italy, popular election in territorial constituencies was abolished by the Fascist regime in 1939. Thereafter, to the end of the Fascist regime, the legislature was made up of representatives of various occupational groups, as was explained in Chapter XI. However, the Fascist leaders always controlled the choice of representatives by these groups. Thus dictatorships ensure that the legislatures will ever be composed of those who will support the leaders. The legislatures cease to be genuinely and freely representative of the various interests, impulses, and aspirations in the community.

Something will be said presently about the functions of the legislature in the Soviet Union. It is sometimes asked why Mussolini and Hitler bothered to have legislatures at all, and the answer is that they were demagogues anxious to give a convincing demonstration of government by popular consent—a mere front. The carefully rigged elections were occasions for showing, both at home and abroad, how truly popular their regimes were. The legislature itself was one more stage from which these grand-opera dictators and their supporting casts could harangue the nation in interludes between the deafening applause of the members of the legislature. Fascist and Nazi legislatures had nothing in common with Congress and Parliament.

The Legislature in the U.S.S.R.

The formal structure of the Soviet legislature, the *Supreme Soviet of the U.S.S.R.,* resembles that of the major democracies. The Supreme Soviet is elected by universal suffrage for a definite period of four years and consists of two equi-powerful chambers: one, the 784-member *Soviet* (or *Council*) *of the Union,* represents the citizens on the basis of one deputy for 300,000 people; the other, the 645-member *Soviet* (or *Council*) *of the Nationalities,* represents the various union republics, autonomous republics, autonomous regions, and national areas, somewhat as the United States Senate represents the states of the Union. In theory, the Supreme Soviet can be dissolved by the *Presidium of the Supreme Soviet*—the standing committee of the legislature which is almost continuously in session—whenever an irreconcilable disagreement arises between the two branches, but this power of the Presidium has never been used.

According to the Constitution, the Supreme Soviet of the U.S.S.R. is the 'the highest organ of state power in the U.S.S.R.' [16] It appoints the executive authority, the Council of Ministers, who are directly responsible to it. It elects the judges of the highest courts in the Soviet Union. The judges, once appointed, are not responsible to it. However, the Presidium of the Supreme Soviet has the theoretically extremely important power of *interpreting* the laws of the Soviet Union. In the Western world, both the interpreting and the applying of law are reserved to the judiciary. In the Soviet Union, the judiciary is restricted to the applying of the law. There is no such thing as judicial review of legislation and no observance of the separation of powers. Moreover, the Supreme Soviet can change the existing division of powers at any time because it can amend the Constitution by a two-thirds majority vote.[17]

A Rubber Stamp for Executive Decrees. The principal concern here, however, is to see how the Supreme Soviet carries out its function of legislation. It has been noted already that the legislatures in Britain, France, and the United States cannot give adequate time to the consideration of all the laws they enact. If the Supreme Soviet were actually to make all the laws needed in the Soviet Union, where the government directs and controls almost all aspects of life, it would have to be in continuous session day and night the year round. In fact, it usually meets only twice a year and the average length of its sessions is three to eight days, into which it crowds all the formalities observed by Western legislatures, including organization, committee work, the budget, and review of pending legislation!

It is therefore obvious that the Supreme Soviet is not a legislative body like Parliament or Congress, making adjustments between the diverse interests in the electorate through prolonged discussion, and fixing the terms

[16] Constitution of the U.S.S.R., Art. 30.
[17] See Chap. XV, *infra,* for a detailed discussion of the Soviet judiciary.

of the adjustments in new legislation. It is equally obvious that the Supreme Soviet does not hold the Council of Ministers to a strict accounting through careful criticism of administration. Despite its exalted position in the Constitution, it is merely a rubber stamp, giving formal assent to decisions and enactments of its Presidium, the Council of Ministers, and the Secretariat of the Communist party.

A MITIGATING FACTOR. It should not be assumed, however, that the Supreme Soviet has no significant function in the Soviet state. It is an essential part of a peculiar Soviet institution, usually referred to as *democratic centralism.* This often-used term is advanced as 'the guiding principle of the organizational structure of the Party,' and is outlined by *The Rules of the Communist Party of the U.S.S.R.* in a four-point definition, of which the key point is 'the absolutely binding character of the decisions of higher bodies upon lower bodies.'

The main reason for this institution is the belief that the Soviet Union should be administered by a highly centralized government—as is indeed inevitable when the government has to do the over-all economic planning for the nation—but that mass participation should also be elicited in the implementing of decisions. Striving for the appearance of public approval, the Soviet leaders have made numerous concerted efforts to induce a large number of citizens to take part, in one form or another, in discussions about state policy. The most effective method, for this purpose, has been the system of soviets, or councils, of which the Supreme Soviet is merely the highest expression, the summit of a pyramid of soviets.

The Structure of Democratic Centralism. At the base of this structure of councils are the village soviets—of which there are some seventy thousand—and the city soviets, which are usually elected on the basis of one deputy for one hundred inhabitants. Above these local councils are soviets covering a larger administrative area. Above these again are soviets for still larger regions and territories, then the soviets of the union republics, and finally at the top, the Supreme Soviet of the U.S.S.R. Millions of citizens take part in the work of these numerous soviets, work consisting not only of legislation but also, at the lower levels, of the supervision of the state administration. For example, the local soviets have certain limited powers of supervision over the operation of the state-owned factories situated in the local areas. It is almost as if city councils in the United States were given power to supervise some aspects of local post offices.

Each soviet has an executive committee which is responsible not only to the soviet that elects it, but also to the executive committee of the soviet directly above it in the hierarchy. This means, for instance, that the executive committee of the highest soviet in each of the union republics, the Union Republic Council of Ministers, is not only responsible to its own constituting body, the Supreme Soviet of the Union Republic, but also to the executive committee of the Supreme Soviet of the U.S.S.R., which is the U.S.S.R. Council of Ministers. A similar arrangement in the United States would make the state legislatures responsible to the federal cabinet, or perhaps to a committee of Congress.

CRITICIZING METHODS. The hierarchical structure of the soviets, with authority extending downward from the top, as well as the tight party control over the executive committees of all soviets, enable the party leaders to permit mass participation in many of the functions of government without running the risk of seeing their policies defeated by the popularly elected soviets. All decisions of the Supreme Soviet of the U.S.S.R. are binding on the lower soviets, and the inferior councils do not discuss measures that have been decided by a superior soviet. Rather, they criticize the ways in which laws and decrees are carried out in the area over which they have jurisdiction, and they inform the superior soviet of the success with which government policy is carried out. The members of the soviets are particularly well suited to this, for they are all employed in some state enterprise or collective farm, and can consequently judge the effects of government policy from firsthand experience in the Soviet economy.

NO LEGISLATING. The function of the Supreme Soviet, therefore, cannot be compared with that of legislatures in liberal democratic states. It does not make the laws. This function is carried on by its Presidium, and by the executive, the Council of Ministers. It does not criticize and control the executive in any direct or effective fashion. The Supreme Soviet of the U.S.S.R. is important, not as a legislative body but as the summit of a system of soviets, and is designed to realize the ideal of 'democratic centralism.' The soviets, the highest as well as the lowest, are not legislative bodies in the Anglo-American and French sense, but barometers and thermometers enabling the leaders to read the political pressures and temperature of opinion in the Soviet Union. They enable the mass of Soviet citizens to feel that they have a hand in government and, within specific and rigid limits, to air some of their criticism of government action and officials. Whatever the theory behind this system and whatever the meaning given the word 'democratic' in the phrase 'democratic centralism,' the system of soviets in actual practice provides 'an upward stream of political intelligence, suggestion and accounting from the lower organs and a downward stream of laws, decrees, and instructions from the apex, or central organs.' [18]

SUGGESTED REFERENCES FOR FURTHER READING

Bailey, S. K., and H. D. Samuel, *Congress at Work* (Holt, 1952).
Barth, A., *Government by Investigation* (Viking, 1955).
Bromhead, P. A., *The House of Lords in Contemporary Politics* (London, 1959).
Burns, J. M., *Congress on Trial: The Politics of Modern Law-Making* (Harper, 1949).
Codacci-Pisanelli, G., *Parliaments* (Prager, 1963).
Clark, J. S., et al., *The Senate Establishment* (Hill & Wang, 1963).
Farnsworth, D. N., *The Senate Committee on Foreign Relations* (U. of Illinois, 1961).
Galloway, G. B., *The Legislative Process in Congress* (Crowell, 1953).
Gibert, S. P., *The Role of Congress in American Policy* (Random House, 1962).
Gooch, R. K., *The French Parliamentary Committee System* (Appleton-Century, 1935).
Griffith, E. M., *Congress: Its Contemporary Role*, 3rd ed. (New York U., 1961).
Gross, B. M., *The Legislative Struggle* (McGraw-Hill, 1953).
Hansard Society for Parliamentary Government, *Parliamentary Reform 1933–1960* (Oxford, 1961).
Headlam, Sir C. M., and A. D. Cooper, *House of Lords or Senate?* (Rich & Cowan, 1932).
Jennings, Sir W. I., *Parliament,* 3rd ed. (Cambridge, 1959).
Kennedy, J. F., *Profiles in Courage* (Harper, 1956).
Kraines, O., *Congress and the Challenge of Big Government* (Bookman, 1958).
Litterdale, D. W. S., *The Parliament of France* (Hansard, 1951).
Lowi, T. J. (Ed.), *Legislative Politics U.S.A.* (Little, Brown, 1962).
MacKenzie, K., *The English Parliament. A Study of Its Nature and Historic Development* (Penguin, 1950).
Matthews, D. R., *U. S. Senators and Their World* (U. of No. Carolina, 1960).
McNeil, N., *Forge of Democracy: The House of Representatives* (McKay, 1963).
Robinson, J. A., *Congress and Foreign Policy-Making* (Dorsey, 1961).
Rogers, L., *The American Senate* (Knopf, 1926).
Taylor, E., *The House of Commons at Work* (Penguin, 1951).
Taylor T., *Grand Inquest: The Story of Congressional Investigations* (Simon & Schuster, 1955).
Truman, D. B., *The Congressional Party* (Wiley, 1959).
Wahlke, J. C., H. Eulau, W. Buchanan, and L. C. Ferguson, *The Legislative System: Explorations in Legislative Behavior* (Wiley, 1962).
Wallace, R. A., *Congressional Control of Federal Spending* (Wayne State, 1960).
Wheare, K. C., *Legislatures* (Oxford, 1963).
Wilson, H. H., *Congress: Corruption and Compromise* (Rinehart, 1951).
Wilson, W., *Congressional Government* (Houghton Mifflin, 1913).
Young, R., *The British Parliament* (Faber & Faber, 1962).
Young, R. Y., *The American Congress* (Harper, 1958).

[18] Julian Towster, *Political Power in the U.S.S.R., 1917–1947* (New York: Oxford University Press, 1948), pp. 207.

XIV

The Relationship Between the Executive
and the Legislature

The legislative and executive organs in the United States, Britain, and France have been described and their distinct functions have been outlined. Although the legislature has been weakened everywhere, it still makes the laws, levies taxation, appropriates public revenues for the executive to spend, and keeps some check on the activities of the executive. At least in theory, the executive cannot pursue any course of action affecting the rights of citizens except as authorized by, or inferred from, law. The legislature sets the tasks of the executive and is thus superior to it even where the rigid separation of powers makes them co-ordinate organs. The executive runs the household economy of the government, carries out the laws, and supplies the services authorized by legislation.

As we have already seen, however, this is a rank oversimplification. Many of the objects and purposes pursued by governments today are not accomplished merely by making laws. A law and an appropriation of public revenue to the purpose are essential, but the vigor of administration by the executive sets the measure of success. Much legislation in the positive state is to no purpose unless the legislature can transmit to the executive the impulse that put the law on the statute book. The executive, in turn, often finds the laws cannot be made to work with the best economy of effort, or at all, unless they are amended, and the executive must be able to transmit its experience in administration to the legislature. Indeed, the question whether a particular law is workable, or even desirable, may turn on the data and experience accumulated by the executive in trying to enforce it.

As we shall see later, there is even ground for saying that the making of laws and the administration or enforcement of them are not two distinct processes. Most laws enacted nowadays are attempts to correct some social abuse or to ease the tension caused by some conflict of interests. The legislature never knows all the factors involved. It is clear that something should be done, but it is not clear what or how. Accordingly, it often legislates in vague general terms, instructing the executive to exercise a discretion and experiment with possible solutions. The executive makes detailed rules and regulations which are law tentatively, to be modified and recast in the light of the results. Wartime legislation affords the clearest example here. The laws for controlling prices in the United States were not made full-fledged at the time when the fixing of prices was first introduced. Something had to be done. It was not clear what should or could be done, and the general policy was launched with much fear and trembling. The law of price control was developed and refined in great detail in a continuous stream of rules, amendments, and interpretative orders, as experience suggested or compelled. As someone has put it concisely, the law was being made while it was being administered and enforced, and it was being administered while it was being made. The same is true of much of the legislation of the past sixty years.

Of course, it was never possible to separate completely the legislature and executive, and it was never attempted. Today, the scale and importance of governmental action make it imperative to have a very considerable degree of co-ordination between the two organs. It is not enough that they should check one another; everyone expects them to work together as a team to promote the good life. Therefore, the working relationships between them are an important subject of inquiry. The relationships in Britain, France, and the United States are in marked contrast. An examination of these contrasts should illuminate the much-debated question of merits and demerits of presidential and parliamentary systems of government, and give some insight into the workings of democratic government.

LEGISLATURE AND EXECUTIVE IN BRITAIN

Fusion. The British legislature and executive are not separate but are in fact almost entirely fused. The cabinet, as a committee of the legislature, links the administration to the legislature. The impulses that move the legislature move the executive also, and the information and experience gained in administration are readily available to the legislature in its deliberations on policy. This fusion might not be particularly significant if it were not for the fact that both legislature and executive are in the grip of the same political party. Without party control, the executive committee of the House of Commons might be of one view while the majority of the members took another view; or more likely, there would be several factions differing in opinion with the cabinet and among themselves. In reality, *it is the party which links the executive and legislature.* The Prime Minister and his colleagues in the cabinet are the leaders of the majority party in the House of Commons. As we have seen, these leaders have already gained, through the party councils, party adherence to a platform that they themselves had a very large share in making. They come to the House of Commons with a program, a disciplined majority to support it, and a mandate from the electorate to use the majority to push the program.

Power of Dissolution. At bottom, however, parties in a democracy are unstable combinations and the concurrence of a majority with the cabinet would often be uncertain were it not for the power of dissolution. The Prime Minister has the right to ask the monarch for a dissolution of Parliament at any time and the latter—to all intents and purposes—has no choice but to comply. Members of Parliament naturally do not want to face the election that follows a dissolution, because it is expensive, makes heavy demands on energy, and is uncertain in result. The weapon of dissolution is rarely used because the mere fact of its existence generally holds the waverers in line. As long as the political situation gives one party a clear majority in the House of Commons, Parliament lives out the greater part of its allotted span of five years, and during that period the party program is steadily pushed forward under the leadership of the cabinet.

Cabinet Moulds Legislation. The cabinet monopolizes the drafting of legislation, bringing to the task of all the information, experience, and expertness of the civil service. Subject to minor qualifications, the cabinet gets what legislation it wants from Parliament and prevents the enactment of laws it does not want. Indeed, a private member is so limited in the bills he may introduce that the annual total of such measures is normally less than twenty—all of them more or less non-controversial. From 1939 to 1948 private member bills vanished altogether! Thus the cabinet is prepared to enforce vigorously all the laws enacted. The fact that a single body, the cabinet, moulds the legislative program ensures at least a minimum of coherence and unity in that program, so that the administrators are not called on to enforce measures that are contradictory or inconsistent with each other. In so far as modern legislation and administration are inseparable, the British system of government is admirably adjusted to meet the situation.

Party Government versus Parliamentary Government. However, British government is no longer parliamentary government in the classic sense. A hundred years ago, the cabinet was continuously dependent on the will of the legislature, which might be asserted against it at any time. The power of the legislature to deny support to the cabinet, and the power of the cabinet to dissolve the legislature, maintained a balance in which direct responsibility of the executive to the legislature was assured, and frivolous obstruction and irresponsible self-assertion by the legislature were prevented. Both legislature and executive were compelled to estimate closely the temper of the electorate. If the executive found itself hampered by attitudes in the House of Commons that it thought would not get support from the electorate, it would demand a dissolution. If the executive took a line that the House thought the electorate would reject, it would challenge the executive. Government in close correspondence with electoral opinion was assured. Also, predominance in government went to the body best able to estimate electoral opinion. In the absence of strong central party organization to keep it informed, a dozen or so men in the cabinet could not hope to guess as accurately at electoral opinion as could the House of Commons. Government therefore was parliamentary government.

PARTY ASCENDANCY. With the extensions of the franchise, electoral opinion became harder to estimate and easier to mould. Thus central party organization was developed to mould and estimate opinion. With its emergence, leaders of the majority party, who either are in the cabinet or work closely with it, ceased to be inferior to the House of Commons in their guesses at public opinion. At the same time, the central party organizations reached out to influence the choice of candidates and the content of the party program, and to associate candidates and program with the party leadership, until elections came to be primarily contests between the party leaders. There is no great exaggeration in saying that today the Prime Minister is elected by the people and given a popular mandate to carry out the announced policy of the party. The cabinet now has direct relations with the electorate; it is not *merely* a committee of the House of Commons.

In these circumstances, the House of Commons inevitably lost its pre-eminence and British government became party government. In this view of the matter, it has been suggested that the Parliament Act of 1911, which stripped the House of Lords of its powers, was not so much a victory of the House of Commons over the House of Lords as it was the final triumph of party government over parliamentary government.[1] The last obstacle to control of Parliament by the parties was removed. Since 1892 only two governments have fallen through a vote of lack of confidence, and neither of these had the support of a single party with an over-all majority in the House of Commons: the Salisbury Conservative Government in 1892 and the Baldwin Conservative Government in 1923. (The Rosebery Liberal Government, which fell in 1895, is not counted here, for its demise came on a routine motion and a snap division, and was really caused by internal dissension in the Liberal party rather than by the adverse vote in the House.)

Cabinet Dictatorship. Those who focus attention solely on events in the House of Commons see a disciplined party majority invariably supporting the proposals of the cabinet, and they conclude that Britain has been governed for half a century or more by series of approximately four-year cabinet dictatorships. The average member has lost his independence and his influence on legislation, and he is grimly compelled to vote the party line on most occasions. Some even argue that the House of Commons is fast becoming, as the monarch and the House of Lords have already become, a dignified rather than an efficient part of the British constitution.

If we keep in mind some salient points of the preceding chapters, we can make some estimate of this charge of cabinet dictatorship. The executive is the one indispensable element of any government. The more things a government is expected to do, the more important executive leadership becomes, and the widespread activities of present-day governments have everywhere aggrandized the executive. If a government is to be democratic, political parties must organize majorities and find the policies that majorities will support. The party with the majority must rule, and the legislature must register its decisions as long as it holds a majority. Any organization as large in number and as complex in function as a political party becomes a prey to oligarchical tendencies, and the leaders of the party are the active deciding elements in many issues. When the party wins power in an election, the

---

[1] See Don K. Price, 'The Parliamentary and Presidential Systems,' *Public Administration Review*, III (1943), 317–34. This article prompted a critical reply by Harold J. Laski in *Public Administration*, IV (1944), 347–59. See also Don K. Price, 'A Response to Mr. Laski,' ibid. 360–63. The interchange provides an illuminating discussion of the two systems.

party leadership makes or becomes the cabinet. *The executive is undoubtedly the mainspring of the British system of government.*

To estimate whether the cabinet exercises a dictatorship during its period of office, one must look beyond the House of Commons to see who rules the ruling party. The discussion in an earlier chapter indicates that this is not an easy question to answer. The central organization and the parliamentary leadership of the party have enormous leverage on the party. On many matters, they have their way either because the rank and file of the party supporters do not know what is involved, or because they cannot agree on instructions to the leadership. This is far from saying that the leaders can do what they like with impunity. There are always rival would-be leaders in the party who will swim into prominence and power on any strong current of opinion in the party, if the present leaders do not canalize that current by making accommodations for it. Even if they are adept at heading off revolts among the rival would-be party leaders, they always face the danger that disgruntled elements of their popular support, unable to get concessions to their point of view, will transfer their allegiance to the opposition, thus imperiling their party's chances in the next election.

PARTY LEADERS. That is to say, the power of the party leaders, although impressive at a given moment when the party line has been settled, and always effective against individual malcontents, is always contingent on their holding the leadership of the party and securing a majority for the party at the next election. They are therefore responsive to all pronounced trends of opinion in the party or in the electorate; they are anxious, indeed, to anticipate them. The ease or difficulty with which they hold majority support in the House of Commons is the measure of their success. The fact that the party majority always supports the cabinet may not mean much more than that the cabinet has correctly interpreted the will of the majority.

The necessity of running the gauntlet of debate and criticism in the House of Commons always disposes the cabinet to caution and moderation. Not infrequently, bills introduced by the cabinet are modified, or even withdrawn, because of criticism by the opposition and pressure from members of the majority party. Even during World War II, when Britain's desperately critical position might have been expected to bring full acquiescence in cabinet leadership, there were many instances of this kind. Moreover, it is not repeated trials of strength between the horse and the fence that keeps the horse in the pasture, but the fact that the fence is there and the horse knows it. The opposition, as well as the party majority in the House, has an influence over the cabinet that cannot be measured by counting the number of collisions between the cabinet and the House. No simple cliché suffices to describe the relations between the cabinet and the House of Commons.

CO-ORDINATION. Party government in Britain has ensured the co-ordination of legislature and executive necessary to meet the demands of present-day governmental activities. It enables the legislature to enact, and the executive to administer effectively, complicated and far-reaching measures of social and economic adjustment. It is the only method thus far discovered for combining strong vigorous government with democratic control. Of course, it has inevitable costs, and these may become so high as to bankrupt democracy. The consistency and coherence of its public policy, for which the system is praised, involve uniformity of treatment that often cannot take sufficient account of special needs and special circumstances. For example, the British government did not respond effectively to the needs of the depressed industrial areas of the country in the 1920's. The individual members of Parliament for the depressed areas could not escape from the discipline imposed by their parties so as to combine in a bloc for the forcing of special concessions to their constituencies. It may be inevitable, but it is not an unmixed good to have the policy of the country framed in party councils rather than in Parliament. Among other disadvantages, to be considered later, it unfortunately reduces Parliament's prestige in the eyes of the country. Thus, in an issue devoted to 'the sadly diminishing role of Parliament,' the influential *Economist* observed: 'With the single exception of the overthrow of the Chamberlain Government in the supreme crisis of 1940, the great deterrent function that once made Parliament an occasional unmaker of ministries has diminished into a small deterrent function of regular Parliamentary fuss.' [2]

The most serious danger does not arise from the fusion of executive and legislature, but from the fact that it becomes increasingly difficult for the electorate, the rank and file of the party, and even for members of Parliament to understand what is involved in the policies that the party leadership works out in conjunction with the numerous experts in the civil service. This difficulty, however, arises out of the demands for extensive governmental action, rather than out of the form of political organization.

[2] Vol. cxxvi, no. 6104, August 20, 1960, p. 705.

LEGISLATURE AND EXECUTIVE IN THE
UNITED STATES

Separation. In the United States, the executive and legislature are clearly separated. Neither the President nor any member of his cabinet can sit in the legislature. The legislature is cut off from any *direct* access to the information and experience that the executive accumulates, and the executive cannot participate *directly* in the framing and pushing of legislation. The terms of office of each are fixed by the Constitution, and the legislature therefore cannot bring the executive to terms by the threat of a vote of lack of confidence, as in Britain and—now to a much lesser degree—in France. It has to work *indirectly* through its control of appropriations and its ubiquitous committees of investigation, through senatorial refusal to confirm presidential appointments, through refusal to enact or emasculation of proposed legislation desired by the executive, or through enactment of laws in such detail that they confine the executive to exactly prescribed tasks. The executive cannot persuade the legislature to come round to its view, or halfway to that point, by threatening dissolution. It has, of course, a veto power to prevent any legislation that cannot summon a two-thirds majority in Congress, and hints dropped to congressional leaders that it might be used are sometimes effective. The President can always get some leverage on Congress by delaying patronage appointments. He can, as Franklin D. Roosevelt did successfully on occasion, appeal directly to the people over Congress's head.

The Oscillations of Leadership. The formal constitutional relationships work against, rather than for, the co-ordination that has been premised as necessary. The President, who gets some kind of an over-all view from the information flowing to his desk from the administration and from the country, cannot help trying to give a lead in legislation and, as usual, the efforts of one or a few to tell the many what to do cause almost continual tension between him and Congress. As a rule, it takes an emergency, such as war or depression, to secure for the executive the legislative leadership that the British cabinet normally enjoys. The presidential leadership exercised by Abraham Lincoln, Theodore Roosevelt, Woodrow Wilson, and Franklin Roosevelt is explained, in large measure, by certain critical conditions in the period of their rule. There are other instances of less dramatic interest.

CYCLES? In fact, the federal government has oscillated between presidential leadership and congressional leadership with such regularity as to prompt the suggestion that this oscillation, rather than rule by alternating political parties, is the striking feature of American politics. A case can be made for the existence of historical 'cycles' or 'eras' of such oscillation. When Congress leads, it does not lead vigorously in any particular direction, but gives itself over to the play of sectional, local, and group interests. The country periodically tires of the bickering and of the combinations of selfish interest that get their way in Congress. Thus, when a crisis looms, attributable sometimes in part to the lack of political leadership, a President comes to power with a popular mandate for action. With this popular support, an astute President can for a time master the diverse forces in Congress and push a legislative program like the New Deal, unified in purpose if not in all its concrete detail, as F.D.R. did so successfully between 1933 and 1938.

But in the past, at any rate, these periods of effective legislative-executive co-ordination have been short. Many sectional and group interests are inevitably alienated or disappointed, the mood for united action and concentrated leadership passes, and the President's pre-eminence vanishes. At the next election, the country chooses, almost deliberately it would appear, a chief executive who is unfitted by ability and temperament for vigorous leadership, e.g. the choices of Harding and Coolidge after Wilson. One trend, however, is generally discernible in these oscillations. The executive, with the rare exception of a Harding, grows steadily in functions and importance. The authority of the President, when it declines, scarcely, if ever, falls back to the previous low point.

CONGRESSIONAL DEVICES. Much of the time, Congress tries to lead, or leads negatively by obstructionism, and its leadership is divided among its committees. Their chairmanships, or 'fiefs,' as we have noted in the preceding chapter, go by seniority to those of the majority party with the longest continuous service on the respective committees. This puts a premium on *safe* constituencies where opinion changes slowly, and where common sectional or local interests return the same champion to Congress again and again. Thus the most powerful men in Congress are often capricious, aged and stubborn, virtually autonomous, representative of 'back-water' areas of the community, little stirred by changing currents of opinion in the nation as a whole. In these circumstances, there is no unified national leadership, and while a modicum of party discipline, such as it is, generally keeps business moving through Congress, it has comparatively little effect on the content of that business.

Lobbies and sectional interests launch bills in committees and often work up combinations, which generally do not follow party lines, to support them. In the securing of appropriations to be spent for local amenities in the constituencies, members of Congress co-operate in supporting each other just as the pioneer settlers assisted one another in rolling up logs for buildings, or to be burned. This 'logrolling' and its associated device, the 'pork-barrel' —legislation designed to favor the congressman's home district—are always prominent features of congressional leadership in financial and other legislation.

The President, elected by the country as a whole and representing the nation, tries to rally his party in Congress against this kind of legislation and may check the more cynical bargains by his veto. He cannot always prevent the enactment of legislation he dislikes and often cannot get support for legislation he thinks desirable. He may even be required to administer legislation that cannot be made effective, because administrative experience and data were ignored in the framing of it, or because adequate funds were not appropriated for its administration. Congress at times acts irresponsibly, yielding to pressures and enacting legislation it does not genuinely believe in, and counting on the President to take the odium of vetoing it. The worst situations, of course, develop when the President is of one party and the majority in Congress of another, which has been the case during almost one-fifth of the history of the American presidency. But even when the President's party is in a majority, it often turns out either that the leaders of that majority in Congress are not in sympathy with him or that they cannot control their followers. Both of these factors were present during much of President Truman's regime, for example.

Significance of Weak Party Discipline. This suggests that it is not so much the formal constitutional relationship of the legislature and the executive as the character of the party system that determines the real relationship. As already explained elsewhere, the national political parties in the United States are not disciplined parties with a centralized leadership, as are those in Britain. The party platform is a collection of vague resolutions which does not lay down a clear-cut party policy. The national central party organization is a temporary committee for fighting elections every four years, and not for maintaining disciplined party support of a program between elections. Unlike the British central party organizations, it cannot veto the nomination of particular persons as party candidates in the constituencies. Attempts by the President, as the leader of his national party, to influence nominations have generally failed. Thus the choice of candidates is dictated by local and sectional considerations, which ensure that those elected to Congress will reflect local and sectional interests and will be dependent on these interests for re-election. Woodrow Wilson lamented that as a rule the President is not dealing with 'Congress' at all, but with 'the elders of the assembly . . . the dissociated heads of little legislatures.'

SECTIONAL DIVERSITIES. To put it concisely, the national parties are loose federations of state parties which lack unity of purpose. They never have clear-cut programs and, without such a program and a mandate from the electorate to enforce it, there is no strong urge for rigid party discipline. In times of crisis, a President may come to office, as Franklin Roosevelt did more than once, with a mandate from the nation. His ability to execute it comes more from his appeal to the nation over Congress's head than from the disciplined support of his party in Congress. The 'two separate and equal' branches are not acting as partners but as competitors. Even if the executive were fused with, and given power to dissolve, the legislature—as in Britain—executive dominance of the legislature would not necessarily result. This result could be obtained only if the sectional diversities of the United States were overcome by means of unified and disciplined national parties.

LEGISLATURE AND EXECUTIVE IN FRANCE

The Past: Legislative Supremacy. From what has been said in preceding chapters regarding the far-reaching changes evoked by the de Gaulle Constitution and the resultant government reorganization, it will not be a surprise to find a totally altered relationship between executive and legislature in the Fifth Republic when compared with its predecessors. In brief, in the Third and Fourth Republics the legislature was omnipotent and the executive weak, ineffectual, and unstable. Cabinets were little more than a tool of government at the mercy of the legislature. In the Fourth Republic, for one, although the cabinet was responsible only to the National Assembly (it had been responsible to both houses of Parliament in the Third), fully twenty-five cabinets came and went during the brief dozen years of that ill-fated Republic's existence, averaging less than six months in office! The two major reasons for this instability, already alluded to in earlier discussions, were first and foremost, the undisciplined multi-party system—no party ever gaining a majority of the popular vote or seats in Parliament in the history of the pre-Fifth Republics; second, the severe, if not crippling, limitations on the cabinet's power of dissolution. As a result, the fact that the French, like the British, had a government of fusion of powers, with the ministry or cabinet in a sense a committee of Parliament, was all but meaningless in the face of the utter inability of the executive branch to assert itself against the legislature.

LIMITED DISSOLUTION. In the Third Republic, the President had power to dissolve the Chamber of Deputies, provided the Senate concurred. Only one such dissolution took place, however—and it was that of the famous *le seize Mai,* 1877, when Marshal Macmahon, the pro-royalist, authoritarian President, dissolved the strongly republican, progressive Chamber with the consent of a monarchist, conservative Senate. Not only did Macmahon's action backfire and result in his resignation one year later, but, as a direct consequence of his strong-arm technique, no cabinet or President ever again attempted to dissolve the Chamber during the remaining sixty-three years of life of the Third Republic. Moreover—until 1959—the presidency was never again entrusted to a 'strong man.'

Recognizing the ineffectiveness of the provisions for dissolution of the legislature in the Third Republic, the framers of the Fourth Republic attempted unsuccessfully to provide for a stronger method of dissolution without, however, creating a strong executive. The Constitution of 1946 provided for the dissolution of the Assembly by the President of the Republic, but only upon request of the Council of Ministers and the advice of the Assembly's President. Moreover, no dissolution could take place during the *first* eighteen months of the five-year term of the Assembly, and during the remaining forty-two months it could be accomplished only if within a space of any eighteen months during that period *two* cabinets had been toppled from power as a result of either a specific motion of censure or a specific vote of 'no confidence' by an absolute majority vote of the Assembly.

IN PRACTICE. Yet of the first twenty-four ministries that collapsed after the beginning of the Fourth Republic, only two combined to bring about the National Assembly's dissolution. The other twenty-two toppled as a result of internal dissension among the multi-party membership, fell during the first eighteen months, simply resigned, failed to be followed by a legislative vote of censure or 'no confidence' in the cabinet within the necessary span of time, or were forced out of office by less than an *absolute* majority vote. The one historic instance of dissolution took place on December 1,

LIFE SPAN OF PREMIERSHIPS IN THE FOURTH FRENCH REPUBLIC *

Chronological Order	Premier	Number of Months in Office
1	de Gaulle (1946)	2
2	Gouin	4½
3	Bidault	6
4	Blum	1
5	Ramadier	10
6	Schuman	7¾
7	Marie	1
8	Schuman	5 days
9	Queuille	12¾
10	Bidault	8
11	Queuille	2 days
12	Pleven	7½
13	Queuille	4
14	Pleven	4¾
15	Faure	1¼
16	Pinay	9½
17	Mayer	4½
18	Laniel	11½
19	Mendès-France	7½
20	Faure	10¾
21	Mollet	16
22	Bourgès-Maunoury	3½
23	Gaillard	5
24	Pflimlin	19 days
25	de Gaulle † (1958)	7½

* Chart begins after de Gaulle's provisional government and does not include either of the first two provisional regimes.
† Inaugurated as President of the Fifth Republic, Jan. 8, 1959.

1955, in the last six months of life of that Assembly. It occurred as a result of the overthrow of the ministries of Premier Mendès-France on February 5, 1955, followed by that of M. Faure on December 1, 1955—both on absolute majority votes of no confidence that forced the two cabinets out of office. Had either one simply 'resigned,' the provision could not have been invoked. But in the face of strong opposition even among members of his own party, including M. Mendès-France, Prime Minister Faure, with the aid of President Coty, was determined to teach the Assembly a lesson. Hence, for the first time in seventy-eight years—and for the last time until de Gaulle's dissolution of the National Assembly of the Fifth Republic late in 1962—a

French Assembly was sent home by the executive power prior to the completion of its full term of office. Yet the newly elected Assembly predictably reflected precisely the same political division as the dissolved one.

Götterdämmerung. But the time-honored French doctrine of *se débarrasser* (getting rid) of a ministry, at the whim and will of the sovereign legislature, with the tacit approval of the electorate and its representatives under the multi-party system, was doomed. The doctrine that had produced 133 changes in the French executive from 1871 to 1958, in the face of the electorate's practice of returning roughly the same proportion of multi-party legislators to the Assembly election after election—the very same period during which Britain had only twenty-seven executives and the United States seventeen—ended with the dawn of the de Gaulle Republic.

A New Tune

Bearing the stamp of Charles de Gaulle's utter, openly acknowledged, and avowed contempt for parliamentary institutions and the despised regime *des partis politiques,* the Constitution of 1958 provided for a totally revamped relationship between legislature and executive. The aforegoing separate chapters on these two branches have already demonstrated the extreme downgrading of the former and the far-reaching enhancement of the power of the latter. The innovations and surgery brought about and performed as a result of the new basic document and the new climate of executive supremacy are additional proof, if such were needed, of the New Era.

Separation of Power. Where once there was fusion of the powers of the executive and the legislative branches, the new order calls for strict *separation.* Without necessarily going so far in all of its aspects as the separation provided by the Constitution of the United States, that of the Fifth Republic makes clear in its Article 23 that the

> office of member of the Government shall be incompatible with the exercise of any Parliamentary mandate, with the holding of any office at the national level in business, professional or labor organizations, and with any public employment or professional activity.

The organic law that was passed to implement the above provision does permit an 'on leave' status for civil servants who may have been asked to join the cabinet or who may have been elected to Parliament, and it permits simultaneous holding of municipal office. But election to Parliament now definitely *precludes* concurrent membership in the cabinet. Consequently, when ten members of the National Assembly were asked to join the first cabinet of Prime Minister Debré early in 1959, they were compelled to turn over their Assembly seats within a month to ten 'alternate' candidates who had run with them in the 1958 parliamentary elections—a Gaullist innovation consistent with his philosophy of stability and continuity.

Power of Dissolution. Although its application, particularly the frequency thereof, is at best uncertain, it is now readily possible for the President of the Republic to dissolve the National Assembly. Article 12 of the Constitution provides that he may do so after consultation with the Premier and the heads of the two houses of Parliament—although apparently he will not necessarily have to consult the former. New general parliamentary elections must then take place within twenty to forty days, and no further dissolution may be effected for the period of one year. Moreover, the Assembly may not be dissolved while the emergency provisions of Article 16, described in Chapter XII, are in force. Other than these two limitations, however, no barriers are placed into the path of dissolution.

No barriers, however, other than political considerations—which have caused President de Gaulle, for one, to tread very gingerly in this area. For he quite correctly assumed that repeated dissolution might well defeat his basic purposes and both make a martyr out of Parliament and call too much attention to it in the eyes of a nation still somewhat uncomfortable in the knowledge of a President with greater power than anyone since Napoleon III. Thus de Gaulle refused to follow Premier Debré's advice to dissolve the National Assembly after the signing of the Algerian cease-fire agreement and the subsequent referendum that ratified it. Indeed, he refused to dissolve it at all until, with still one year of its five-year term at stake, his hand was forced when on October 5, 1962, an enraged National Assembly defeated the first Pompidou Government on a vote of censure over the presidential referendum issue. But the new elections, following closely upon the heels of de Gaulle's triumph—though one somewhat less than overwhelming—on the referendum question, brought a resounding victory to the Gaullist forces who obtained sufficient seats to form the first majoritarian government in the history of Republican France.

Legislative Weapons. Although they may well prove to be of questionable ultimate potency, the Constitution of 1958 does provide for three methods whereby Parliament may endeavor to enforce Governmental responsibility. In the first place, and most ambiguous of the three, the Premier seems to be

constitutionally obliged to submit his program to the National Assembly
'after deliberation by the Council of Ministers.' However, while he has done
so in each instance to date, and although considerable discussion, even
some walkouts by legislators have ensued on occasion, it is doubtful how
much the provision really means short of a formal motion of censure or
confidence.

CENSURE AND CONFIDENCE. Although a far cry from the powerful weapons
of earlier legislatures, the legislature of the Fifth Republic possesses certain
means of enforcing Governmental responsibility in the two additional
methods of passing a vote of censure—as the National Assembly did in the
instance mentioned above—or by defeating it on a no-confidence vote.

After discussing it with his Council of Ministers, the Premier may thus
designate a policy issue 'a matter of *confidence.*' In the absence of the introduction of a motion of censure by the deputies within twenty-four hours,
the issue is presumed to have been approved by them, *with or without a
vote.* But it is possible, of course, to present such a motion of censure in
accordance with the rules of procedure and the provisions of the Constitution (see below), and this does afford the Assembly an opportunity to hold
the Government responsible. Thus, when in 1959 Premier Michel Debré—
presumably on orders of President de Gaulle—made a matter of confidence
the plan, so dear to the heart of his Government, to establish an independent
nuclear striking force for France, a motion of censure was promptly introduced, quickly signed by the requisite minimum of one-tenth of the deputies.
On the actual vote, however, the Opposition was able to muster but 203
out of 552 votes—a respectable total, but still short of victory by 74 votes. It
represented the third censure test on a matter of confidence faced—and won
—by Premier Debré within one calendar year, and it proved to be the most
dangerous by far. On the two previous occasions the Opposition had been
able to muster but 109 and 122 votes, respectively, against him.

The Constitution of 1958 is quite specific regarding *censure* motions.
Article 49 spells out in considerable detail the procedure to be employed
by the National Assembly. Its chief features are: first, a motion of censure
must be signed by at least 10 per cent of the constitutional membership of
that legislative body; second, the vote on the motion must be taken no
sooner than forty-eight hours after its introduction; third, only those votes
in its *favor* are counted; fourth, it is considered passed only if an absolute
majority votes affirmatively in its favor; and fifth, if it is defeated, its signatories may not introduce another motion during the balance of the legislative

session. (But this latter restriction does not, of course, apply to situations in which the Government has made an issue a matter of confidence, as explained above.)

The first formal censure motion against the Government of the Fifth Republic was filed by the National Assembly late in November 1959 in connection with the 1960 budget. Angry and frustrated, irked by their minor role—made doubly real in the face of restrictions upon the traditional legislative power of the purse—the deputies introduced a censure motion, sponsored by Socialists and radical Socialists. Yet although a clear majority of the Assembly vocally *condemned* the Debré budget—which, among other things, had mandated cuts in war veterans' pensions—only 109 deputies actually voted 'aye' when the question of censure was put to a vote. Since only 'aye' votes count, the fact that far more than a majority abstained was but hollow comfort for the embittered legislators, and Debré had weathered a dangerous storm. The Senate then unanimously (247:0) rejected the budget—but it was a futile act of defiance, since the upper house lacks the power to overthrow the cabinet. All it meant, in effect, was that Premier Debré was compelled to force it through the Assembly once more, which he did after agreeing to some amendments, thus enacting it into law.

However, as already mentioned in passing, the National Assembly did bring down a Government, that of Georges Pompidou, on the presidential referendum issue on October 5, 1962. Charging the President and his regime with a breach of the spirit and letter of his own Constitution, the six-count, severely worded motion of censure carried easily, with 280 members of the now 480-member house voting in its favor—39 more than needed. Highlighting the acrimonious debate was the opening statement by the eighty-four-year-old World War II Premier, Paul Reynaud, initially an ardent de Gaulle supporter, who explained with much emotion why so many of his colleagues were now constrained to turn their backs on the President:

> He has wanted to be George VI and Churchill. He has not accepted the republican concept according to which France exists in its Parliament. He has slid toward personal power . . . The constitution has been violated, Parliament has been despoiled.[3]

Utterly unimpressed with this argument, President de Gaulle—on the following morning—announced his decision to dissolve the National Assembly, and reappoint his defeated Premier who was constitutionally com-

[3] *The New York Times*, October 6, 1962.

pelled to resign after the adverse vote, until a newly elected chamber would assemble. When the results of these elections brought de Gaulle the resounding, aforementioned victory, he redesignated Georges Pompidou his Premier of the third cabinet of the Fifth Republic.

Executive Supremacy. When the third edition of this text went to press in 1957, the weakness of the French executive in relation to the legislature was painfully evident, and had been very well stated in 1954 by Pierre Mendès-France, who at that time was an active member of the Assembly, a cabinet minister, and soon to be Prime Minister. Addressing an Assembly that had forced two cabinets out of office within one month, he commented:

> The Assembly is the judge without appeal of the action of the government. But a government cannot fulfill its mission if it is assailed every day in this body, if its members and its chief are obliged to consecrate their efforts and their time to innumerable discussions so often sterile.
> Parliament legislates, it controls the executive. But the executive ought to be in a position to govern and to administer to meet its responsibilities without any other preoccupation than to realize the program fixed in clear agreement with the National Assembly. It ought not to be arrested in its work by the constant fear of being overthrown. Parliament has the right to withdraw its confidence from the government at any instant; the government ought to be able, at every instant, to act as though it were assured of existing for 20 years.[4]

Three years after Mendès-France had been driven from office, de Gaulle came to power—bringing with him the very embodiment *plus* of the kind of executive power alluded to by the former's words. Yet today one of the President's most eloquent critics—although he had now even lost his seat in Parliament—is Mendès-France! He is not alone. Yet there can be no gainsaying that de Gaulle and his Constitution have brought the kind of stability to France that seemed as impossible of achievement as it was widely deemed desirable. The haunting question whether it has been purchased at too great a price—a prostrate legislature, an all-powerful President—is in the lap of the uncertain future. As these lines are written (Autumn 1963) France and its new Constitution thrive under the stern, dedicated, highly personal direction of the man whom Franklin Roosevelt used to refer to as 'Joan of Arc' and whose proved devotion to *la patrie* is such that he views himself as indistinguishable from it.

[4] Pierre Mendès-France, as quoted by Herman Finer in *Governments of Greater European Powers* (New York: Holt, 1956), p. 441.

FINANCIAL LEGISLATION

In concrete terms, the relationship of the executive and the legislature is best illustrated by the case of financial legislation. He who controls the purse occupies a key position in government, as in other activities. The control of taxation and public expenditure is of high importance for constitutional government, and on this ground, too, financial legislation deserves separate examination. A government required to act in accordance with law, must secure specific laws to justify its imposition of taxes and its expenditure of public revenues.

FINANCIAL LEGISLATION IN BRITAIN

Role of the Treasury. A standing order of the British House of Commons provides that all estimates, i.e. proposals for expenditure of public money, must come from the executive and from it alone. The budget is thus necessarily prepared by the cabinet. In practice, it is prepared by the Treasury, as the department of finance is called (which supervises all the functions normally assumed in the United States by the Treasury Department, the Bureau of the Budget and the Civil Service Commission). By a process of close co-ordination between officials of the Treasury and of other departments, a draft of the annual estimates is worked out and submitted to the Treasury several months in advance of the beginning of the next fiscal year.

The Treasury requires that every increase in a department's estimate be supported by detailed explanation. Since the Chancellor of the Exchequer, the member of the cabinet responsible for finance, must bear the odium of proposing additional taxation, the Treasury is the one department of government unflaggingly devoted to economy. Its attitude toward the estimates submitted by the other departments depends on its forecast of next year's revenues, and on the general policy of the government toward increase or decrease of taxation. In any event, the other departments of the government must justify their estimates to a vigilant Treasury, which may veto any item or insist on a general reduction. A department that thinks it has a grievance may first appeal to the Chancellor of the Exchequer and then to the Prime Minister, or to the cabinet as a whole. Generally speaking, however, the *Treasury has the last word* on the content of the estimates submitted to Parliament.

Role of the House of Commons. Meanwhile, the revenue proposals that are justified or dictated by the estimates are worked out by the Treasury, and after the cabinet has approved them, the Chancellor of the Exchequer presents his budget containing both estimates and revenue proposals to the House on 'Budget Day.' The Chancellor's speech, always eagerly awaited, is inevitably long and detailed—*strict secrecy* having been preserved until his appearance before the House. (An inadvertent advance 'leak' to the press by the then Chancellor of the Exchequer, Hugh Dalton, led to his resignation in 1947.)

The House then resolves itself into the Committees of the Whole House on Supply and on Ways and Means, and considers the financial proposals in terms of departmental policy, since the allotment of a mere twenty-six days for such discussion prohibit detailed analysis of the budget. The thirty-six-member Estimates Committee examines 'such estimates as may seem fit to the committee,' taking different executive departments in turn, so that all of the various estimates get a more thorough screening than the Committee of Supply can accomplish in the time allowed. In practice, the latter's time is taken up in discussing a few groups of expenditures or 'votes,' and the others are rushed through with little or no consideration. Millions upon millions of pounds are always voted in haste at the very end.

A private member *may not move an increase or a shift* in the destination of an item in the estimates, because that would violate the standing order referred to. He may move that particular items be decreased or entirely disallowed. However, except in very trivial matters, the cabinet regards such a motion as one of want of confidence in the government, and party discipline ensures its defeat. Pressure may persuade the government to modify its financial proposals, but it is now unknown for the House openly to force a revision.

The House of Commons accepts these proposals as reported to it and approved by the Committee of the Whole. Since the House of Lords has no power in money matters, other than to delay them for thirty days, the estimates almost invariably emerge from Parliament in an Appropriation Act and the revenue proposals in a Finance Act as true copies of the original proposals of the Chancellor of the Exchequer. The most striking indication of the general expectation that the cabinet will carry its financial proposals unchanged is the law, enacted in 1913, providing that changes in taxation proposed in the Chancellor's budget speech shall come into effect on the day following 'Budget Day.'

EXECUTIVE CONTROL. The system enables the executive, who alone knows in full detail the activities and needs of the various departments of government and the probable yield of the sources of revenue, to draft the financial legislation. It ensures unified responsibility for public expenditure. The appropriations are not arrived at by polling the diverse and unrelated preferences of individual members of Parliament. The executive does not have to countenance raids on the Treasury by blocs of members in order to get support for its main proposals. It surveys the entire field of proposed expenditures and enforces a coherent program. It is unlikely, as has occurred in America, for example, to appropriate funds for the draining of swamps in aid of agriculture and, at the same time, to authorize expenditures on restoration of swamps for the protection of wildlife. The expeditious enactment of financial legislation is also assured.

It is often said that the Chancellor of the Exchequer is the financial boss in Britain. There is much exaggeration in this view. Despite his strong bias for economy, public expenditures have risen sharply and steadily for the past seventy years. The reasons for this are clear and they operate in the United States and France as well. The permanent officials in other departments always see reasons for expanding their activities and extending their establishment. The balance of electoral demand comes down on the side of more government services. The members of Parliament would like to make the best of both worlds, and cut taxes while raising expenditures. Since they cannot, they generally acquiesce in or plump for the latter. From their point of view, the serious thing about cabinet control of finance is not their inability to reduce estimates, but their inability to *raise* them. The cabinet as a whole responds to these inclinations and the Chancellor of the Exchequer is always fighting a rear-guard action on expenditures.

It is, however, a resolute rear-guard action. Incautious department heads, who advance inadequately supported or extravagant proposals, get badly mauled. In another figure sometimes used to depict the situation, the Treasury is the watchdog of the public purse. Within the lines of policy laid down by Parliament, it enforces strict economy, and supervises the household operations of the various departments in aid of efficiency. In this limited sphere, the Chancellor of the Exchequer may be said to be a financial boss. As Parliament does not examine the estimates in full detail, it is necessarily done by an executive agency.

Control of Expenditures. When it comes to the expenditure of the money voted by Parliament, the Treasury, through an accounting officer in each department, sees to it that the money is spent on the purposes for which it was voted. However, Treasury control is not regarded as a sufficient guarantee of probity in such matters. The Comptroller and Auditor General, appointed by the executive for life tenure, but in effect an officer of Parliament, and enjoying the same independence and tenure of office as a judge, audits all the government accounts and reports irregularities to the Treasury. The most important of his duties is to make an annual report to Parliament. This report is a guide to an active select committee of the House of Commons, the Committee of Public Accounts, which examines the use of departmental funds to ascertain that money is spent as the House has directed, and reports to the House on financial irregularities. It is a small committee of fifteen members, with a chairman and a majority of its members *drawn from the opposition*. It probes vigorously in the public accounts, and the government departments take great pains not to incur its censure. It is a very effective instrument of legislative surveillance over the executive.

FINANCIAL LEGISLATION IN THE UNITED STATES

The worst indictment of the separation of powers in the United States is based on the method of enacting financial legislation. Even those who generally approve the separation of powers are unhappy about its consequences in finance. Revenue bills must originate in the House of Representatives, but aside from this unimportant, although emotion-charged, provision—the Senate may, and often does, amend these House-initiated measures at will— each house of Congress has a wide initiative in finance. The President makes a budget and proposes it to Congress, *but Congress does what it likes with his proposals, and when it chooses.*

Before 1921 there was not even the semblance of a unified budget. The government departments worked out their own estimates, and the Secretary of the Treasury submitted them to the House of Representatives along with an estimate of tax revenues for the coming year. The House at once distributed the estimates to its various committees. In these committees, officials of the departments of government, interest groups, and the different sections and localities of the country all clamored for appropriations. Each committee responded to these pressures, and produced a set of appropriations for the sector of government activity with which it was concerned. The budget, as reported to the House by several committees, consisted of several unrelated proposals tied together in a bundle. A similar process went on in the committees of the Senate after the estimates were passed by the House. No single government department or legislative committee ever looked at the budget as a unified whole. Every department and every committee put in its separate demands without too much concern as to what the total was. Thus the President utterly lacked the authority financially to control the executive branch for whose actions and policies he was responsible under the Constitution!

Bureau of the Budget. In 1921, an advance toward British budgetary practice was made. The Budget and Accounting Act passed in that year provided for the establishment of an executive agency, the Bureau of the Budget, headed by a Director appointed by the President without Senate confirmation, and placed under the Treasury Department. The Bureau became responsible to him directly and alone when President Roosevelt, by an executive order in 1939, transferred it into the Executive Office of the President. The Bureau thus came to represent the central controlling authority needed by the President to manage the financial policies of the entire executive branch.

FUNCTIONS. The Director of the Budget's functions resemble those of the Chancellor of the Exchequer, his bias being toward efficiency and economy in the public services. Working with departmental and agency officials, the Bureau of the Budget, which is now located in the Executive Office of the President, goes carefully into the demands of the departments. These must be submitted by October 1 for the fiscal year commencing on the following July 1. The Director cuts and trims what he thinks fitting and, subject to an appeal by the department to the President, he has the last word. The estimates are the amounts that the President and his advisers, on careful consideration, think necessary for the work of the executive. While the estimates are being prepared, the Bureau makes a forecast of the probable receipts from taxation and decides what modification of the taxation system, if any, should be recommended to Congress. When these estimates and calculations have been completed and drawn together in a budget, the President submits it to both houses of Congress. The necessity, under present conditions, of executive drafting of financial legislation has been recognized.

It should also be pointed out that in addition to its budgeting tasks, the Bureau is charged with being a clearing house for legislation; the writing of veto messages; and the general improvement of the organization and management of the executive branch. Its stature has increased constantly.

Appropriations Committees. Under the law of 1921, each house has to set up a Committee on Appropriations to which all estimates must go. The estimates for expenditure go first to the Committee on Appropriations of the House of Representatives. They are considered, often in great detail, by the twenty-one sub-committees of the fifty-member Appropriations Committee—the largest standing committee in Congress—which call officials to explain and justify particular proposals for spending, and hear others who wish to support or oppose particular appropriations. The powerful sub-committees—whose chairmen are frequently as arbitrary and vindictive as they are conscientious and able—often force commitments from officials as to how the administrative work, to be supported by particular appropriations, shall be carried on. In this way, substantial continuous legislative control over administration is secured.

A similar procedure is later followed in the Senate Committee on Appropriations when the appropriations, as passed by the House, are reported to the Senate. Thus all estimates for expenditures must pass through, and be approved by, a single committee of each house of Congress. This, however, is as far as the copying of the British practice of unified responsibility for appropriations goes.

The Appropriations Committee of the House of Representatives reduces some items in the executive proposals and increases others. It may hamstring a particular branch of the administration by cutting its estimates sharply. Through other committees of the House, other legislation, inspired by congressional blocs and not by the President, requiring an appropriation of public money for its execution, will emerge. In this way, large sums may be added by the Appropriations Committee to the proposals of the executive. 'Pork' is still distributed from the pork-barrel!

PIECEMEAL APPROPRIATIONS. Furthermore, the Appropriations Committee of the House of Representatives does not draw all the appropriations it recommends into a single appropriation bill. Rather, it sends forward to the House, one after the other, about a dozen bills endorsing appropriations for the various departments and agencies. The House makes minor, but rarely substantial, changes in these bills without ever considering the appropriations as a whole at a given time.

After appropriation bills pass the House, they are sent to the Senate where further modifications and additions are frequently made by the Senate Committee on Appropriations. Government departments and private interests that were disappointed by the action of the House committees often try their luck again before the Senate committee, ordinarily with considerable success. Again, when the appropriation bills are reported to the Senate for action, members of the Senate may force significant amendments, usually additions.

COMPROMISES. After the Senate has added its thoughts to the estimates, the bills go back to the House for its assent to the changes made by the Senate. If, as often happens, the House refuses to accept these as they stand, a conference committee of the two houses is appointed to find a compromise on which both can agree.[5] When it is found, the bills get their final readings in both houses and are sent to the President to be signed. Two important facts should be noted here in connection with appropriation bills: one, that no appropriation may be made that has not been authorized by previous legislation; and two, that no *authorization* measure can *appropriate* funds itself.

Even in the periods of strong presidential leadership, the action of the legislature may seriously distort the budget as proposed by the President, both by reductions and additions. The appropriations for one of his cherished projects may be cut and his pledges of economy thwarted. Thus Congress *reduced* President Eisenhower's foreign aid request for fiscal 1958 by $900,000,000 but *added* a river and harbor projects bill, a favorite 'porkbarrel.' The President has the power of veto, of course, but Congress rarely gives him a chance to use it. Appropriations known to be obnoxious to him are frequently attached as *riders* to appropriation bills covering vitally important votes of money. Since, unlike some forty governors of the several states, the President cannot veto *particular items* in a bill, but must accept the bill or reject it *as a whole,* he has little choice but to accept. Congress further tightened its hold on the purse strings in 1958 by providing for a ceiling on actual spending of old and new appropriations in any given year, thus giving it more control over actual spending in that year. This would have an effect especially on such areas as national defense, atomic energy, and foreign aid—areas in which much spending is from funds appropriated but unused in previous fiscal years. The unified responsibility of the British system is still lacking.

Ways and Means Committees. The revenue, or tax, side of the budget is similarly handled by the legislature. The revenue-raising proposals of the

---

[5] Until such an agreement—involving also matters of policy and procedure between the two appropriation committees—was finally found after almost four months in July 1962, their feuding octogenarian heads treated the country to an exasperating long-run *opéra-bouffe* that tied up billions of dollars for government payrolls and projects and all but brought the machinery of government to a halt.

Bureau of the Budget go to the Committee on Ways and Means of the House and the Committee on Finance of the Senate. Although the Constitution provides in Article I that revenue bills must originate in the House of Representatives, this does not, in practice, as we have seen, prevent the Senate from introducing new revenue proposals in the guise of amendments to the revenue measure passed by the lower house of Congress. Both houses alter the revenue proposals of the executive as much as they see fit. Officials, representatives of the reluctant taxpayers, and other interests are heard. Logrolling and the push and pull of a great variety of interests are marked features of the framing of tax measures as well as appropriation measures. These practices are found on a grand scale elsewhere, too, particularly in the revisions of the protective tariff, which have always been the scene of unremitting struggle between the various sections and economic interests of the country.

CONGRESS AS BOSS. The President cannot depend on getting the kind of taxes he wants. Nor can he depend on getting tax measures that will bring in the revenues he sees to be necessary to meet governmental expenditures. During World War II, for example, Congress more than once cut his tax recommendations very sharply. Congress has always exercised the right to change, as it sees fit, the appropriations recommended by the President. The executive prepares the budget, but Congress takes it apart and acts on the different parts of it without considering it as a related whole. This is generally agreed to be extremely unsatisfactory.

The Legislative Reorganization Act. The Legislative Reorganization Act of 1946 attempts to meet the situation. It provides that, at the beginning of each session, the four 'money' committees of both houses of Congress shall meet jointly, and, with the President's budget as a guide, prepare and report to Congress on February 15 (or later, if agreed-upon) a proposed 'legislative budget' for the coming year. Spending ceilings were to be established and, if the estimated expenditures exceed the estimated revenues, the resolution introducing the budget in Congress was to contain a clause requiring the public debt to be increased by an amount sufficient to bring the two totals into balance.

It has never been clear how this provision is to be enforced, or how the congressional budget it envisages is to be brought into relation with the budget prepared by the President. The original bill out of which the Act developed contained a provision that, if Congress should later approve appropriations in excess of the total they had adopted earlier in the financial resolution, the President should be authorized to reduce appropriations by the amount necessary to restore balance—i.e. in effect, giving him the item veto. This provision was rejected by Congress, thus limiting the effectiveness that the law is likely to have. The 'legislative budget' was tested in 1948 and 1949, but failed to produce the expected economy. It has not been used since. In 1950, however, an attempt was made to adopt a 'single package' method of introducing all appropriation measures as one bill, much after the method used in the House of Commons. But, like the 'legislative budget,' this plan was quickly abandoned by the House Appropriations Committee.

Most of the provisions of the Legislative Reorganization Act dealing with financial legislation have been ineffective, and pork-barrel legislation has continued to make a properly planned budget impossible. The lack of a presidential item veto, rivalry between the two houses of Congress, and the inability of members of Congress to come to grips with one complete appropriation bill, are some of the more important reasons for failure.

Supervision. The law of 1921 setting up the Bureau of the Budget for the executive branch also provided for the General Accounting Office, headed by the Comptroller General—a type of financial watchdog responsible to Congress. This official is appointed by the President and confirmed by the Senate for one non-renewable fifteen-year term, and he is removable only by impeachment and conviction, or by a joint resolution of both houses of Congress. He has two principal functions. First, he makes decisions whether particular expenditures, proposed by the executive departments, are authorized by the appropriations Congress has made. Second, he investigates and audits all branches of the public accounts to see whether there have been irregularities in the expenditures made, and reports the results of his work to the President and to Congress.

While Congress has not had active standing committees on the public accounts, it should be recalled here that the Legislative Reorganization Act of 1946 directs the standing committees of both houses on expenditures, now known as the Committees on Government Operations, and also the standing committees on particular fields of legislative and executive activity, to maintain continuous surveillance over the work of the executive branch of government, checking on both economy and efficiency. The legislation looks to the abolition of special investigating committees—an unlikely result— and the establishment of more effective checks on all branches of administration.

The Serious Weakness. This account of the enactment of financial legislation points to the greatest weakness of American federal government for present-day purposes. The weakness arises from the impossibility, already noted, of keeping present-day legislation and administration in separate compartments. In an age when governments are expected to enact and administer efficiently a great quantity of complicated and interrelated legislation of the highest importance, it is vital to be able to bring home responsibility for failure. The nation, which elects the President, tends to hold him responsible for failure, but he generally lacks the power to carry his view of what ought to be done. Congress rarely thinks in terms of the whole program, but reacts for and against particular items of it under the stimulus of a great variety of conflicting pressures, intensified by a desire to assert itself against the Administration. Even when it does think in terms of the whole, it lacks the information necessary for fully informed and wise decisions and is, in any event, unable to ensure that administration will be carried on in accordance with its view. Moreover, the means through which the electorate could enforce responsibility on Congress are lacking. Party discipline does not dominate Congress; voting commonly does not follow party lines. The parties do not line up for and against an extensive program in Congress, and nothing therefore would be gained by trying to hold the parties responsible. Where disciplined parties inviting responsibility do not exist, the electorate cannot enforce responsibility. If they did exist, the formal separation of powers probably would not give any great trouble. The parties would see to it that President and Congress became a harmonious team. But for reasons already described at some length, there is little, if any, likelihood of the emergence of major disciplined parties in the United States.

Of course, the present situation is not without advantages. Any threat of executive dictatorship gets short shrift. Policy is not made in secret party councils but in Congress, where the vital forces of the nation find free expression. Effective integration of policy is difficult, but then it is not as important in Washington as it is at Westminster. In Britain, there is no middle term between the national government and the municipalities. Whatever is demanded of government that cannot be done locally by the municipalities must be done by the national government, which has had to respond to the full impact of the great expansion of government activities.

A CONSEQUENCE OF FEDERALISM. In the United States, the states stand as autonomous governments between the national and municipal governments. Much of what we demand of governments today is carried out by numerous state governments and, as long as it is done acceptably there, it does not require such close integration and disciplined action at the national level. Because of the federal system, the national government still retains some of the characteristics of an alliance between states for furthering a limited set of common interests. An alliance of states does not need, and no one expects it to have, the close-knit governmental organization necessary for a unitary state. It is necessary to realize that federalism is an important factor in the workability of the legislative-executive relationship at Washington. The future of that relationship is involved in the fate of federalism.

Changes? For several years there has been a steady flow of proposals for change, some of which advocate bringing legislative-executive relationships somewhat closer to the British pattern. Such proposals indicate widespread current dissatisfaction with the existing relationships. However, if the state governments, as genuinely independent authorities, can carry a large part of total government load, arguments for formal changes designed to secure the efficiency of the British system are not completely convincing.

It is hard to estimate how far formal changes in legislative-executive relationships would be effective. If it is true that the success of the British legislative-executive relationships is largely due to the existence of firmly disciplined political parties, the issue really is whether the national parties of the United States are capable of comparable discipline. If there are forces at work in the party system, and the nation as a whole, fostering more effective party unity on more specific and more coherent programs, formal changes in legislative-executive relationships would aid the development. But if the national parties remain loose combinations of state parties, as they have given every indication of doing, such changes would be likely to have a very limited effect, if any.

FINANCIAL LEGISLATION IN FRANCE

In Britain, the ultimately effective power over financial legislation rests with the cabinet. In the United States it is vested in Congress. In the France of the Fourth Republic, the actual 'boss' of financial legislation was the National Assembly, or more accurately, its *commission* on finance, which was the most powerful of all the French parliamentary *commissions,* i.e. standing committees. The Minister of Finance prepared the annual budget, but his role was only little more than that of an errand boy for the finance *commission* which, as an agent of the National Assembly, and enjoying its strong support, held the fate of all taxation and appropriation measures in its hands. As might be expected, in this area, too, the Fifth Republic has wrought significant and drastic changes.

Executive Preparation. The French budget under the Fifth Republic is prepared annually by the Minister of Finance whose role, in this connection, is somewhat comparable to that of the British Chancellor of the Exchequer or the Director of the Budget in the United States, but the Minister has far less authority to propose reduction or revision. Indeed, his influence in modifying his cabinet colleagues' requests is quite minor unless he obtains vigorous, personal backing from the Premier. Under the Fifth Republic it is the Council of Ministers as an entity that wields decisive influence over revenue-raising proposals. The Minister of Finance subsequently consolidates the various budgetary requests into one national budget of income and expenditures. The finished product is then transmitted to the National Assembly.

In the National Assembly. In the days of old, the Minister would, with considerable trepidation and foreboding, present it to the finance *commission* of the Assembly, which then 'processed' it thoroughly—having *carte blanche* on the budget. The *rapporteur,* appointed by the *commission* to be in general charge, and who might well be a future Minister of Finance, became the key person in the budgetary process—he often referred to it as 'my' budget —and the Government was often constrained to approach him on bended knee. When the *commission* had completed its work, after deliberations lasting several months, it reported the budget, usually in piecemeal fashion, to the floor of the National Assembly, where it was steered through by the *rapporteur.* In thus steering the budget through the Assembly, the *rapporteur* and the *commission* might be friend or foe of the individual deputies as well as the cabinet. The individual deputies, acting for themselves or their constituents, and the Minister of Finance, acting on behalf of the cabinet, both had to coddle, cajole, and plead with the *rapporteur* and his *commission* to adopt, cancel, or restore items. In the absence of party discipline and parliamentary majorities, the budget stage thus frequently proved to be the graveyard of governments. More than one-half of the votes of confidence taken in the Fourth Republic were on the budget.

IN THE FIFTH REPUBLIC. In line with the downgrading of the legislative branch, its power on the budget and financial bills generally was seriously curtailed, of course, under the Constitution of 1958, whose Article 47 specifically deals with the role of Parliament in this sphere. Designed to avoid Parliament's potential delaying tactics as well as to reduce its power and influence, the National Assembly is now required to complete the first reading of the budget in forty days after its receipt. If that time limit is not met, the Government is empowered to send the budget on to the upper house, which is given fifteen days to act on it. If no legislative action has been taken over a span of seventy days, the Government may then apply its provisions 'by ordinance,' i.e. decree. Times have indeed changed! Moreover, if the budget is not presented by the Government in time to ascertain promulgation before the beginning of the new fiscal year, the Constitution authorizes the Government to request the Assembly to sanction taxation and collection powers *by decree,* which may be done in either of two ways: by asking the Assembly ten days prior to the close of its session to vote the parts covering collection of taxes and general expenditures as a matter of 'urgency,' or by asking it two days before the end of the session to authorize the collection of taxes under the assumption that the necessary financial bill will be passed in the next session.

Under the Fifth Republic, as already discussed in connection with the matter of confidence and censure, finance bills must first go to and be voted upon by the National Assembly, but the Senate is not bound by the results of the first vote of the Assembly. This was demonstrated when the Senate rejected the 1960 budget after the Assembly had failed to muster sufficient votes to defeat Premier Debré on a motion of censure. Disagreements between the two houses are resolved by way of conference committees and the Premier's watchful eye—but, failing of agreement, the Senate's authority is nullified if the Government succeeds—as it did in the case of the 1960 budget—in forcing the bill through the Assembly for a second time. Individual deputies have no power to move to raise or lower items in the reported budget; nor may they introduce a resolution whose effect, if it were adopted by the Assembly and accepted by the Government, would be to reduce revenues or increase expenditures. In brief, the sole manner in which the Parliament of the Fifth Republic can effectively assert itself on the budget, if the Government refuses to agree to suggested changes, is to overthrow it on a no-confidence vote or on a successful motion of censure. How difficult this is to do—and of what doubtful political wisdom—we have seen.

Surveillance. Unlike the situation in Britain and the United States, a really effective method of pre-spending audit does not exist in France. However, a post-audit system does operate with a modicum of efficiency. It is concentrated in the Ministry of Finance, backed and checked by the Court of Accounts (*Cour des Comptes*), a fairly effective unit of jurists who are appointed for life and are surrounded by an expert technical staff. Another check of sorts is the interesting group of 250 'Inspectors of Finance,' a small, prestigious elite corps of top civil servants who, like the members of the *Cour des Comptes,* have all been graduated from the excellent *École Nationale d'Administration*—the National School of Administration for civil servants (to be described in Chapter XVI). The Inspectors are the means by which the Ministry of Finance watches over the complex administration of the nation's financial policy. After having undergone rigorous initial examinations, studies, and field work, an Inspector is attached to the Ministry, which at first sends him to the provinces to become familiar with the intricacies of financial administration at the rural, municipal, and departmental levels of government. Ultimately he is given higher posts in the Ministry of Finance—which has proved to be a stepping stone to excellent positions in both government and private business for the holder of the coveted title of Inspector of Finance. But that institution is no substitute for a genuinely effective system of post-audit, and de Gaulle's announcement, early in 1963, of a 'renovation' in that area, as well as many other administrative spheres, was welcome.

Concluding Thoughts

The key to the legislative-executive relationships, indeed the index to the understanding of liberal democratic government, as a whole, is to be found in the state of mind of the electorate—in public opinion, that vaguest and most elusive element in government. All the analysis of the preceding chapters has been leading to this conclusion. The people may not be able to make the laws, but the state of the public mind, in its divisions, diversities, and confusions as well as in the electoral majorities it produces from time to time, has an influence that is decisive *in the long run.* Its influence bears powerfully on the way the constitutions themselves work, as well as on the laws that are made and the manner in which they are administered.

Suggested References for Further Reading

Bailey, S. K., *British Parliamentary Democracy,* 2nd ed. (Houghton Mifflin, 1962).
Beer, S. H., *Treasury Control: The Coordination of Financial and Economic Policy in Great Britain,* 2nd ed. (Oxford, 1957).

Binkley, W. E., *President and Congress*, 3rd rev. ed. (Vintage, 1962).

Brittain, Sir H., *The British Budgetary System* (Macmillan, 1959).

Chamberlain, L. H., *The President, Congress, and Legislation* (Columbia, 1946).

Chester, D. N., and N. Bowring, *Questions in Parliament* (Oxford, 1962).

Dahl, R. A., *Congress and Foreign Policy* (Harcourt, Brace, 1950).

Egger, R., and J. P. Harris, *The President and Congress* (Macmillan, 1963).

Ferguson, J. E., *The Power of the House* (U. of North Carolina, 1961).

Finletter, T. K., *Can Representative Government Do the Job?* (Harcourt, Brace, 1945).

Freeman, J. L., *Executive Bureau–Legislative Committee Relations* (Random House, 1955).

Harris, J. P., *Advice and Consent of the Senate* (U. of California, 1953).

Herring, E. P., *Presidential Leadership* (Farrar, 1940).

Horn, S., *The Cabinet and Congress* (Columbia, 1960).

Jennings, Sir W. I., *Cabinet Government*, 3rd ed. (Cambridge, 1959).

King, J. C., *Generals and Politicians: Conflict between France's High Command, Parliament, and Government* (U. of California, 1951).

Macridis, R. C., and B. E. Brown, *The de Gaulle Republic: Quest for Unity* (Dorsey, 1960).

Millspaugh, A. C., *Toward Efficient Democracy: The Question of Government Organization* (Brookings, 1949).

Morrison, H. S., *Government and Parliament: A Survey from the Inside*, 2nd ed. (Oxford, 1959).

Polsby, N. W., *Congress and the Presidency* (Prentice-Hall, 1963).

Wallace, R. A., *Congressional Control of Federal Spending* (Wayne State, 1960).

Wilson, W., *Constitutional Government in the United States* (Columbia, 1908).

XV

The Judiciary and the Law

We have discussed at some length legislative and executive organs and functions. Attention must now be turned to the judicial power, the third element in the threefold classification. In comparing the judicial organs and their functions in the United States and Britain, more similarity and less contrast will be found than was observed in comparisons of legislatures and executives. The United States has drawn its decisive legal and judicial traditions from Britain. For several reasons, the judiciary is a conservative force in any society, and ordinarily it does not respond to changing fashions and needs as rapidly as other parts of government do. Thus, there is a marked similarity and, in the main, only superficial differences.

However, there is more pointed contrast between the legal and judicial systems of continental Europe, which stem from *Roman* or *civil law,* and what is often called the Anglo-American or *common law* system. France will be briefly treated as an illustration of the former. But even here the differences are often superficial rather than basic, because both systems were moulded by the age-long Western political tradition. The most striking contrast is with the perversions of the civil law system that the Fascists and Nazi dictators set up in Italy and Germany, and with the Soviet legal and judicial system, all shaped by negations of the Western political tradition. Some of the more revealing differences will be noted at particular points.

THE JUDGES

SELECTION AND TENURE

The Rule of Law is one of the strongest elements in the liberal democratic creed. It is designed, however, as a means to a further end, the securing of individual freedom under law. The securing of freedom under law has two distinct aspects or stages. First, the law must mark out, at one and the same time, an area of individual freedom of action and an area of clearly defined prohibitions of individual action, e.g. the criminal law. Further to this, if the law is to provide an equal freedom, it must not deny to some what it concedes to others; it must not establish privilege. Second, the law must rule; it must be made effective through observance and enforcement. Good laws will come to nothing if they can be disobeyed with impunity. To make the Rule of Law effective, there must be a resolute and impartial judiciary devoted to the impartial administration of justice. Appointment and tenure of judges, and the organization of the courts through which they administer justice, are of the highest importance.

Tenure. Reference to Chapter IV will remind us that, in the major British and French courts and in the federal 'constitutional' courts of the United States,[1] the judges are appointed by the executive to hold office during 'good behavior,' and that to all intents and purposes they can be removed only for specific causes, determined in advance, by the Constitution or the legislature. No English judge, for example, has been removed since the Act of Settlement of 1701. In the United States, judges of the federal 'constitutional' courts can be removed only by impeachment of and conviction for 'treason, bribery, or other high crimes and misdemeanors.'[2] Agitations for compulsory retirement of aged justices have been unsuccessful, mainly on the not very convincing ground that this opens the way for political interference

---

[1] Federal *'constitutional'* courts are those created under Article III of the U.S. Constitution, and are hence governed by its tenure safeguards. They comprise the U.S. Supreme Court, the U.S. Circuit Courts of Appeal, the U.S. District Courts, the U.S. Customs Court, the U.S. Court of Customs and Patent Appeals, and the U.S. Court of Claims. The federal *'legislative'* courts are created under Article I of the U.S. Constitution; their judges, not being governed by the tenure requirements of Article III, usually serve from four- to fifteen-year terms, as provided by law. Among these 'legislative' courts are the U.S. Court of Military Appeals and the Territorial Courts. Those in the District of Columbia are both 'legislative' and 'constitutional.'

[2] As of 1963, nine federal jurists, including one Supreme Court Justice (Samuel Chase), had been impeached by the House of Representatives, but only four of these were convicted by the Senate and thus removed from office.

with the independence of judges. Thus their tenure is for life or until voluntary retirement, and they enjoy independence of the executive. Despite the fact that they often make decisions displeasing to the executive and the legislature, there is seldom any responsible suggestion of removing them in the absence of corruption.

This security of tenure is not so fully enjoyed by the lesser magistrates and justices of the peace. In Britain and France, these are appointed and removed by the executive. In the United States, the *state* judges, as distinct from the federal, are elected in most states by popular ballot for relatively short terms. Being dependent on re-election, they cannot enjoy the same assurance of independence. Election of judges is generally considered to be an unwise extension of the democratic principle, but there are only a few states in which election has not been used.

Selection. Appointment of the judges in Britain and France is in the hands of the government of the day; but in France—where since the Fifth Republic prospective judges attend the 'National Center of Judicial Studies' (*Centre National d'Études Judiciaires*) for a four-year course—special competitive examinations are given to the candidates, and standing in these examinations must normally be taken into account. In the United States, the appointment of federal judges is made by the President, with the consent of the Senate, which often insists on a critical investigation of the nominee; it is thus a form of political patronage. In Britain, this patronage is shared by the Lord Chancellor and the Prime Minister. In France today, patronage plays an even lesser role in the appointment of judges. There, the eleven-member High Council of the Judiciary[3] nominates a panel of prospective higher judges, from which the President and the Minister of Justice *must* choose, and it advises the latter on the appointment of lower court judges.

Generally speaking, appointments in Britain and the United States go to persons who have been active supporters of the party in power. As a rule, the capacity and integrity of prospective appointees are also carefully considered, but in each country there have been instances in which it was difficult to see any merit except services to the party. As there are generally equally capable lawyers in each party, there have been few serious abuses. In fact, there are more complaints today about the general outlook of appointees than over their party affiliations, for reasons yet to be discussed. This is seen

[3] This *Conseil Supérieur de la Magistrature* consists of the President of the Republic, as chairman, and the Minister of Justice, as vice-chairman *ex officii*; plus nine appointive members with legal background, selected by the President for a once-renewable term of four years, partly on the recommendation of the *Cour de Cassation* and the *Conseil d'État*.

most clearly in appointments to the Supreme Court of the United States, where the President, at least, is usually more genuinely concerned over the broad political philosophy of his choice—the nominee's so-called 'real politics'—than the party label. Yet many a President has subsequently been grievously disappointed in those 'real politics.'

Limitations. One limitation on choice must be pointed out. The judges in the Anglo-American system must be chosen from the ranks of the legal profession. No matter how able or learned in the law a man may be, he cannot be a judge in a superior court *unless* he is a member of the Bar in good standing. Almost invariably, lawyers in active private practice or public office are appointed, although, in recent years, a number of academic lawyers with distinguished records in teaching and research have been appointed to the Supreme Court and other federal courts of the United States, e.g. Mr. Justice Felix Frankfurter, who was a Professor of Law in Harvard University at the time of his appointment to the Supreme Court by President F. D. Roosevelt in 1939.

BARRISTERS AND SOLICITORS. In Britain, lawyers who aspire to the bench almost always come from the branch of the legal profession known as *barristers,* rather than from the ranks of the *solicitors.* (The British law student initially decides to which class of lawyer he wishes to belong.) The approximately twenty thousand solicitors are, in a sense, the 'office lawyers' of the profession. They comprise the 'workhorses' for minor cases, try cases in the lower courts, do most of the routine legal office work, and deal directly with clients. The little more than two thousand barristers, on the other hand, argue cases in the higher courts, are highly experienced, specialized lawyers, and receive most of their cases from the solicitors rather than from the client direct.

The limitation of judgeships to members of the Bar in Britain and the United States is not thought to be strange, but natural and inevitable. Yet it is in sharp contrast to the practice of continental Europe,[4] where a lawyer who elects private practice [5] abandons all thought of a *judicial* career.

---

[4] The phrase 'continental Europe' as used in this chapter refers principally to Western Europe and does not include the Soviet Union or those countries of East-Central Europe which now have Communist-dominated governments. They are excluded because their practice in legal matters is quite different in many respects from the long established tradition of Western Europe.

[5] The private practitioner of the future will choose among the specialties of *avocat* (roughly similar to the British barrister); *avoué* (the equivalent of the British solicitor); and *notaire* (a lawyer trained especially in the drafting and registration of legal papers). Those who wish to become *public prosecutor* must follow a course similar to that of future judges.

Continental judges are always trained in law, but are chosen from the civil service and not from the lawyers who appear as advocates in the courts. The young French law student of twenty-seven or under, who aspires to be a judge, goes from his university to the National Center of Judicial Studies, whence he is either assigned as a judge to a court, to the high office of the public prosecutor, or to the Ministry of Justice. He may hope within twenty years to rise by promotion step by step up the higher rungs of the judicial ladder. When a judge hopes for promotion from a lower to a higher court, he is exposed to the temptation to please his superiors in the Ministry of Justice, or even politicians who have influence there, although the Council of the Judiciary now serves as a 'check' on politics. By contrast, in the Anglo-American system higher judicial posts are infrequently filled by promotion, although President Eisenhower's appointments of Associate Supreme Court Justices Harlan, Brennan, and Whitaker did represent 'promotion' from state and lower federal courts. The term 'promotion' here does not, however, carry the same connotations as it does in the Continental system.

SIGNIFICANCE OF AN INDEPENDENT JUDICIARY

Complete independence of the judicial power may seem to sort ill with democracy, which means popular control of government. In the nineteenth century this view prevailed in most states of the American Union, bringing popular election of judges for short terms. There have been abuses of the security of tenure of appointed judges, but they have been rare. The law that the judge gives his oath to uphold is a body of relatively certain rules, and as long as he is true to his oath there is not much room for popular control of his actions. Also, he is a member of an ancient profession which has, despite apparent exceptions, a great devotion to the ideal of an impartial law. A judge who obviously abandons impartiality or gives an interpretation of law that lawyers generally think to be obviously wrong, loses caste in the legal profession. Self-respect and the desire to stand well with their professional brethren are powerful controls on the judiciary.

This is a better safeguard of the impartial administration of justice and maintenance of freedom under law than putting judges under direct control of the government. In dictatorships, of course, the primary function of the judiciary is not maintenance of freedom under law, but rather securing of the overriding interests of society, as interpreted by the dictator and the elite he gathers around him. Accordingly, the judiciary is a tool to be manipulated, not a vital institution to be safeguarded from outside influences.

Under the dictatorships the judiciary remains an important institution for settling disputes between private citizens and interpreting the law applicable to such disputes. New judicial functions arise from the revision of the criminal law to include a number of political offenses against the regime, which cover not only overt actions against the state, but also unconstructive attitudes of mind. Generally, special tribunals for defense of the state against its internal enemies are established, but sometimes persons accused of political crimes are tried in the ordinary courts. Great care is taken therefore to ensure that all judges shall have the appropriate attitude toward cases coming before them. In Germany and Italy, the Nazis and Fascists dismissed summarily all judges and court officials who were unsympathetic to them. They thus destroyed the security of tenure of the judges, and they appointed as judges only those who could be counted on for subservience. In the Soviet Union, as we shall see later, the Communist party has exercised effectual control over appointment or election of judges who hold office only for short terms. Finally, in all three dictatorships, the legal profession ceased to be an independently organized profession and came under government control.

THE COURTS

STRUCTURE

Judges do not give authoritative interpretations of the law at their own pleasure, or, as a general rule, at the request of the executive or legislature. They *interpret* the law while sitting in court to settle disputes between parties appearing before them. The Anglo-American courts are just as important a part of the judiciary as the judges. A court is not merely a physical location and a collection of equipment, like stage properties. It is an institution with a set of officials and records, an atmosphere, and an orderly though complex procedure for hearing and deciding disputes.

The courts of continental European countries can be described, for the sake of contrast though not with complete accuracy, as branches of a Ministry of Justice, which is, in turn, an executive department of the central government charged with the administration of justice. Before the coming of dictatorship, at any rate, the judges had security of tenure and independence but they were even then, in a sense, civil servants. The Ministry of Justice organized courts in districts across the country to serve the public somewhat after the fashion of the organization of postal services. Officials of the court are civil servants who keep the records, and make and work the rules of procedures in concert with the judges.

Freedom from Government Control. In England and Wales,[6] the courts were always the King's courts, with their roots in executive decree of the early Norman kings. However, at an early date in English constitutional history, they became practically autonomous and their development was powerfully influenced by the legal profession. The practicing solicitors are still spoken of as officers of the court. For centuries, the judges and officials were paid, not from the general revenues, but from fees collected from litigants. The judges made—and still make—the rules of court procedure, just as they generated the unique atmosphere of decorum which prevails in a court.

The English courts were reorganized on a statutory basis by Parliament in 1873, and many of the anomalies and anachronisms of six hundred years of customary accretion were cut away. The salaries of the judges and the sums needed for maintenance of the courts are now permanent charges on the public revenues, and do not come up for annual appropriation and debate. The executive does not appoint or exercise control over any significant number of the officials of the courts. Appointment of officials is largely in the hands of the Lord Chief Justice, and they do their work under the direction of the judges. There is no Ministry of Justice, as in France. The Lord Chancellor, a member of the House of Lords—he is its Speaker—and of the cabinet as well as a judge, has a small administrative department, but it exercises very little control. The courts are still largely autonomous and in so far as they need to be ruled, they are ruled by the judges.

In colonial days in America, courts modeled on the English type were created by executive order or act of the legislature. Later, in the United States, the state constitutions prescribed the structure of the state courts in considerable detail, and thus limited greatly the power of the state legislatures to modify the judicial systems. The national Constitution, by contrast,

---

[6] For convenience hereafter referred to as England, since Scotland and Northern Ireland, the other two members of the United Kingdom of Great Britain and Northern Ireland, operate separate court systems.

contains only the briefest of provisions on the federal judicial structure,[7] which has been established almost entirely by Congress. One of the first orders of business of the First Congress of the United States was to pass the Judiciary Act of 1789, which created the framework of the American judicial system.

Once established by whatever means, the courts in the United States were given much of the autonomy of English courts in the administration of justice. In the United States, some court officials are elected and some appointed. The Supreme Court of the United States makes the rules of procedure for the federal courts. In some states, the state legislatures, and in others the judges, make the rules of procedure, but there is no general executive supervision of the administration of justice. The federal government has a Department of Justice with a member of the cabinet, the Attorney General, at its head, but it is not a Ministry of Justice in the continental European sense. It is rather the department of the Attorney General, the legal adviser of the government and its attorney in all legal questions, lawsuits or otherwise, in which the government is interested. The courts and the judges are autonomous in the administration of justice—but this has not given them immunity from outside criticism.

The Price of Autonomy. The continental European system has many advantages, particularly in ensuring adequate decentralization of courts for the convenience of local litigants, a simple, inexpensive procedure, and an expeditious handling of cases. Its weakness and dangers are illustrated by the problem of judicial promotions, though as already mentioned, in France this is no longer as serious a problem as it once was. To what extent are impartiality and independence endangered when the executive branch of government participates largely in the administration of justice? The fear of executive interference has always thus far prevented the establishment of Ministries of Justice of the continental European type in Britain and the United States. As a result, there is a confusing multiplicity of courts, each autonomous and separate within the range of matters assigned to it.

In England, the judicial system is centralized in London. Apart from the justices of the peace and the county courts, dealing with petty criminal and civil cases respectively, and the assize circuits, there is no adequate decentralization. When large issues are at stake, they must go as a general rule to the courts sitting in London, and the litigants must go there, too, at great expense, a prohibitive burden on the poor. In the United States, there

[7] The Constitution of the United States, Art. iii and Amendment xi.

is satisfactory decentralization for the trial of most matters in the first instance, but appeals must go to the state capitals or even to the national capital. In continental Europe, on the other hand, the final appeal as well as the original trial is heard in the locality.

In the Anglo-American system, despite many reforms, procedure in the courts is still complicated, adding to cost and often involving delay. It is suited to the convenience and to the sense of professional fitness of the lawyers—every profession tends to develop a distinctive ritual—rather than to the needs of poor litigants. However, it must be said in its defense that it is admirably suited to protect the rights of those who can afford its expense and delay. The same can be said of the two, or three, or even four successive appeals that may be taken from one court to another, contrasted with the single appeal open to the parties in most of continental Europe.[8]

The Anglo-American legal profession never forgets the meddling of the Stuarts in the administration of justice, and resists all proposals that a government department should organize and supervise judicial services on a mass-production basis, as has been done, for example, in employment office and postal services. It takes justifiable pride and satisfaction in saying that genuinely impartial courts are *open to all*. Yet, despite substantial, steady but slow improvements, and a continuing agitation for more, it has no adequate answer to the English judge who retorted, 'So is the Ritz Hotel!'

This question cannot be discussed in detail here. It has been sketched for two reasons: to point to the main features of the problem, and to bring out the significance of the following account of the structure of the courts.

The Judicial Hierarchy

In both the United States and England, the court structure is in the form of a *hierarchy* with its base on the justices of the peace scattered across the country—on the magistrates in the urban areas—and its apex in a final central court of appeal. At the lowest level, the justices of the peace frequently are laymen without legal training, unpaid, or paid only in small fees collected in the course of their work.[9] Their jursidiction is generally limited

---

[8] Before he was finally executed 12 years after sentencing, Caryl Chessman had managed to file 14 appeals in the California courts *and* 28 in the federal courts!

[9] A 1955 study of the minor judiciary in North Carolina showed that *not one* justice of the peace then had a law degree; that 75 per cent had never gone to college; and that 40 per cent had never even attended high school! (Isham Newton, *The Minor Judiciary in North Carolina*. Unpublished Ph.D thesis. University of Pennsylvania, 1956.)

to the trial of lesser crimes and misdemeanors, but it may cover small civil claims as well. In the towns and cities, they are supplemented on the criminal side by police magistrates, who are now usually required to have at least some legal training.

The next tier of courts in England is county or district courts, staffed by judges chosen from the legal profession with permanent tenure, whose jurisdiction is limited to civil claims involving relatively small amounts. Generally speaking, no such tier of courts exists in the United States. In some of the larger cities, there are municipal courts of comparable limited civil and criminal jurisdiction. There are, of course, county and district courts in the states of the United States but, as will be seen below, they are courts with general rather than limited jurisdiction. At the next level in both countries are the courts with general first instance jurisdiction, i.e. courts with authority to try all cases of important civil or criminal consequence. Above this again, there are always courts of appeal to which disappointed litigants have, in most matters, a right of appeal, and there may be, in certain special circumstances, one or even two further appeals to still higher courts. Courts of first instance are generally composed of one judge sitting alone, while courts of appeal have a bench of several judges. This pattern may be set forth briefly for each country.

In Britain. In England and Wales (Scotland and Northern Ireland, as has been pointed out earlier, are distinct areas for the administration of justice) the county courts are limited in authority to small civil claims. The court with general jurisdiction in the first instance is the *High Court of Justice,* which has several divisions, all sitting in London. However, judges of this court periodically go on circuit, holding assizes, or sittings, in the 'assize towns' across the country. The bulk of the assize work is criminal, but civil disputes may be heard there too. The *Court of Criminal Appeal* sits in London, hearing solely appeals from persons convicted of criminal offenses by justices of the peace, stipendiary magistrates, and judges of assize. In *civil* matters, an appeal lies to the *Court of Appeal* in London and thence, in some but rare circumstances, to the *House of Lords,* which is the highest court of appeal in the realm and the sole United Kingdom-wide judicial body. The judicial functions of the House of Lords are performed by the Lord Chancellor, nine Lords of Appeal—eminent lawyers elevated to the House of Lords for this particular purpose—and any peer who has at some time held high judicial office. Only in very special circumstances can an appeal in a *criminal* case be carried to the House of Lords from the Court

THE CRIMINAL AND CIVIL COURTS OF ENGLAND AND WALES

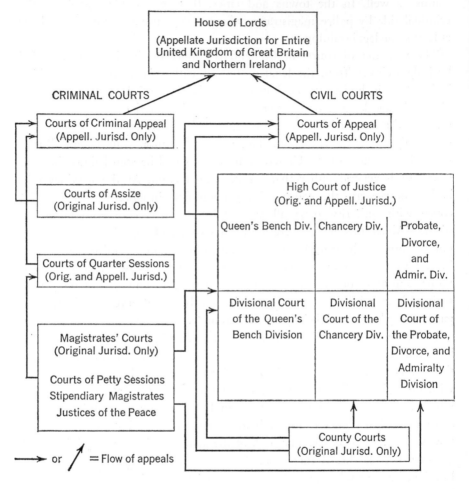

of Criminal Appeal, and lately such appeals have averaged but one a year.[10]

In the United States. Each state in the United States has its own judicial hierarchy, and there are as many systems as there are states. A common pattern, however, can be discerned. Immediately above the level of *justices of the peace,* police magistrates, and municipal courts, such as juvenile courts, family relations courts, and traffic courts, stand the *county or district courts.*

[10] Richard M. Jackson, *The Machinery of Justice in England,* 3rd ed. (Cambridge: Cambridge University Press, 1960), p. 112.

These courts, sitting in the county court houses in the county towns, are courts of first instance for almost all civil cases and for criminal cases of a serious nature. They are therefore not at all comparable to the county courts in England. In some states, the county court system still reveals the defects to be expected from a lack of unified responsibility for the whole system. Generally, the judges can sit only in their own court and can only hear cases arising in their own district. So the judge in one county may be idle while the judge in an adjoining county is overwhelmed with work. However, many states—New Jersey is a praiseworthy example here—have established 'judicial councils' composed of judges, lawyers, state officials, and laymen, which are making progress in meeting this and other defects.

Some states have decentralized district courts of appeal. The presence, or absence, of intermediate courts of appeal depends largely on the density of population and the volume of litigation in the state. Whether they have these courts or not, every state has, at the apex of the hierarchy, *a supreme court,* as it is usually, but not always, called. It constitutes a final court of appeal sitting at the state capital. In cases that involve an interpretation of the national Constitution and a decision whether or not certain rights can be claimed thereunder, there is the possibility of an appeal from it to the Supreme Court of the United States in Washington.

Except where some such question arises, state courts try almost all cases turning on the interpretation of the state constitution and laws. The jurisdiction of the federal courts is set out in section 2 of Article III of the Constitution, as restricted by Amendment XI. It includes a variety of special matters that need not be detailed here. Most of this special jurisdiction of the federal courts turns on the question of the *parties to the dispute* rather than the subject matter. For example, disputes between two or more states, or between a state and a citizen of another state when the state is the plaintiff, must be tried in the federal courts, regardless of the subject matter of the controversy. Where the dispute is between citizens of different states, it may be tried in the federal courts *if* the controversy involves ten thousand dollars or more, but arrangements may be made to handle that type of case in a state court. The main work of the federal courts is to try cases arising under the laws of the United States, principally laws made by Congress. For example, when the mails are used to commit a fraud, the same act may be at once an offense against the law of a particular state *and* *also* an offense against the laws of the United States regulating the use of the post office. For the former offense the culprit would be tried in a state court, for the latter in a federal court.

TWO SEPARATE SETS OF COURTS. Thus, there are in the United States two complete and quite separate sets of courts, *federal and state,* exercising, in each state, jurisdiction over the same people and the same territory. Serious conflicts of jurisdiction are avoided because, generally speaking, the federal courts interpret and apply federal laws, and the state courts interpret and apply the state laws. The jurisdiction of the federal courts is not declared by the Constitution to be an *exclusive* one. As far as the Constitution goes, the cases federal courts are competent to try might be tried and decided in state courts. Congress, however, has provided by statute that in certain types of cases and controversies covered by Article III, the federal courts shall have exclusive jurisdiction, e.g. those dealing with 'domestics or domestic servants' of foreign diplomats.

FEDERAL COURTS. At the lowest level in the federal 'constitutional' court structure stand the *United States District Courts* in some ninety districts across the United States. At the next level are the eleven *United States Courts of Appeal,* one for each of ten circuits and one for the District of Columbia. These courts, commonly called 'Circuit Courts of Appeal,' were established to take from the Supreme Court some of the burden of appeals from the District Courts. There is now *no general right of appeal* from the lower federal and the state courts to the *United States Supreme Court,* except in a few cases specified by law.[11] These cases come to it on what is —somewhat awkwardly—known as a writ of *appeal,* but only if the Supreme Court regards the issue involved to be of a 'substantial federal question.' In all other instances, the Supreme Court decides, on the circumstances of each application for review, whether it will hear the appeal or not. If a minimum of four justices agree to hear an appeal, the Court issues a writ of *certiorari.* The test applied is whether or not, in the opinion of the Court, the case raises a question of 'substantial' constitutional or public importance. In addition to hearing appeals, the United Statees Supreme Court may act as a court of first instance in a very limited number of matters, particularly in disputes involving *foreign* ambassadors, ministers, or consuls, and in certain

[11] Generally speaking, and omitting several of the more technical situations, these are limited to cases in which (a) the highest *state* court has declared a *federal* law or a federal treaty unconstitutional; (b) a *federal* court has declared a *state* law or a provision of a state constitution unconstitutional; and (c) when the highest state court has *upheld* a state law or a provision of a state constitution *against* the challenge that it *conflicts* with the federal constitution, a federal law, a federal treaty, or any provision thereof.

THE JUDICIARY AND THE LAW

disputes in which a state is a party, particularly those between two or more states. But the Court's original jurisdiction has become a very minor fraction of its work.

THE APEX OF POWER. The Supreme Court is, of course, the most dazzling jewel in the judicial crown of the United States. It is the sole court mentioned in the Constitution, all others having been created by statute. It stands at the pinnacle of the judiciary—all others bow before it. In no other liberal democracies do we find a court that is accorded the same power, the same prestige, and the same awe-inspiring reverence as the Supreme Court of the United States. In a very real sense, the Constitution of the United States is what a majority of the members of the Supreme Court say it is at any given time. It is, in Lord Bryce's words, 'the living voice of [the] Constitution.' Indeed, if the concept of Jean-Jacques Rousseau's 'general will' (*la volonté générale*) is to be found on any governmental level in the United States at all, it is in the opinions and decisions of the dignified, learned members of the United States Supreme Court. The Supreme Court is the chief guardian of the Constitution and of the people's liberties—and there are many citizens who rest far more quietly in the knowledge of *that* guardianship than if it were primarily exercised by one of the other two major branches of the government. For the latter are close, indeed, to what Judge Learned Hand once called 'the pressure of public hysteria, public panic, and public greed.'

In France. The French have two entirely separate court systems, the *ordinary,* or regular, courts which concern us here, and the *administrative* courts, to be discussed briefly later.

The de Gaulle judicial reforms of May 1, 1959, dispensed with the tradition of the local justice of the peace, of whom some three thousand used to dispense justice, more or less, in every *canton* of France. Now the lowest ordinary court is the *Court of Instance (Tribunal d'Instance),* one of which is to be found in the capital of every *arrondissement* and has chiefly civil jurisdiction. Each of these 455 tribunals has several trained judges, but decisions are usually rendered by a single judge. At the next higher level is the *Court of Major Instance (Tribunal de Grande Instance).* These 172 tribunals have both original and appellate jurisdiction in civil cases throughout the *département*—the highest administrative subdivision in France. Each case is tried by several judges, with the decision reached by majority vote. Appeals from these courts of instance in civil cases go to one of the twenty-seven *courts of appeal,* each of which has charge of several *départements.*

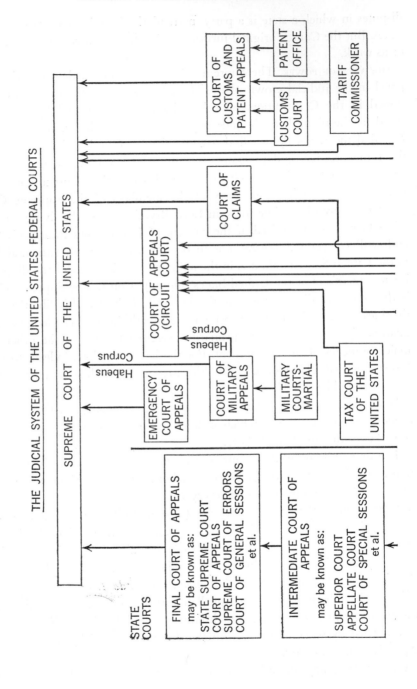

THE JUDICIAL SYSTEM OF THE UNITED STATES FEDERAL COURTS

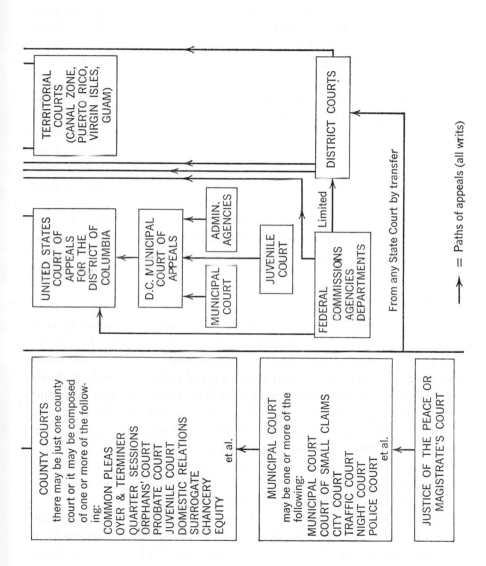

From five to seven judges sit *en banc* here. Appeals in criminal cases go to one of the *assize courts,* which also have original jurisdiction in serious crimes. One such court, with jury, sits in each of the *départements,* and is usually staffed with three judges chosen from the courts of appeal and the courts of major instance.

At the pinnacle of the ordinary courts of France is the *Cour de Cassation.* This is really the Supreme Court of France; it sits in Paris and has eighty-three judges. It is divided into three *chambres,* each presided over by a 'president'—that favorite French term. One *chambre* handles all requests or petitions; one, points of law in civil appeals; the third, points of law in criminal appeals. Unlike the United States Supreme Court, but like the House of Lords, the Court of Cassation has no original jurisdiction and, while it may 'break' (*casser*) decisions of lower courts upon appeal, it is not an appellate court, for it may only 'break' or 'quash' the point of law of the lower court, not its judgment. It cannot *retry* cases. All cases must come to it from lower courts. After the Court of Cassation has broken a point of law in a case, it remands it to the same *level* of court whence it came, but not to the same *court.* And although its procedure resembles, in part, that of the United States Supreme Court, and its prestige is great, the Court of Cassation does not possess the power of judicial review.

THE FUNCTIONS OF THE COURTS

It is somewhat misleading to say that the function of the judiciary is to interpret and to apply the law. The essential primary function of the judiciary is to hear and decide disputes. Sometimes disputes in the courts are entirely concerned with questions of fact, and judges have only to decide the baffling question of which party to believe. Often, however, a dispute involves differing interpretations of the law and, in order to give a decision, the judges may have to determine what is the proper interpretation. But their job is to give a judgment on the dispute, or, at most, a *declaratory judgment,* stating the rights of particular persons arising from a specific set of actual facts, and they generally refuse to give gratuitous opinions on the law that are not necessary for the decision in hand.

Need of a Case or Controversy. The general rule in the Anglo-American system is that the courts cannot be set in motion to grind out interpretations of law in the absence of a dispute between parties with an interest in the result. The courts are always open to hear charges that a particular person

THE REGULAR (ORDINARY) COURTS OF THE FIFTH FRENCH REPUBLIC

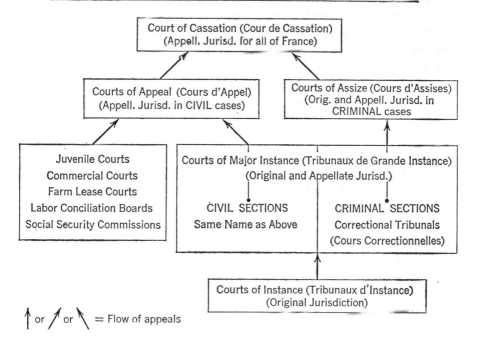

↑ or ╱ or ╲ = Flow of appeals

has committed a crime, or complaints that the civil rights of the complainant have been infringed. The law, however, does not require the courts, or even enable them, to resolve doubtful points that come casually to their attention. Nor does it enable them, except in a few special circumstances, to give advice to perplexed individuals who are in doubt as to what the law requires them to do.

In certain circumstances, through the issue of a *writ of mandamus,* the courts will order a public official to perform a duty specifically imposed on him by law. In certain other limited circumstances, the courts will issue an *injunction,* a writ restraining particular persons, whether officials or not, from performing acts that, if performed, would be infringements of the rights of other specified persons. Normally, however, it is only when an aggrieved person comes forward, asserting that a wrong has been done, and that he should be compensated, or that the culprit should be punished, that the courts are set in motion.

Punishment but not Prevention. It follows that in almost all cases the action of the courts is compensatory or punitive and not preventive. As a general rule, individuals cannot be restrained by judicial action merely on the ground of a plausible suspicion that they are about to commit a wrong against the state or another citizen. Thus, in wartime, the legislature has always been obliged to pass special legislation authorizing the detention of persons who are strongly suspected of seditious aims and traitorous designs not yet put into execution. The abuses to which such powers of detention are always open, and sometimes put, emphasize the importance for individual liberty of restricting very sharply preventive action by the executive or by the courts. Risks of wrongdoing which sometimes would be irreparable are involved, but *the law expresses the liberal democratic faith that individual freedom is worth the risk*. There is also the difficulty of being sure that a man is of an irresistibly vicious state of mind, and the consequent danger of appalling injustice. It has been thought better that the risks should be taken and punishment or compensation provided after the event.

The extreme hesitation of the Anglo-American system to embark on preventive action is not just laziness on the part of the judges or untidy administration of justice. It rests squarely on the beliefs in individual freedom and responsibility. If any confirmation of this is needed, it can be found in the practice of the dictatorships. Since the latter have no strong faith in the individual, and regard him primarily as a means to more important ends, law in their system ceases to be primarily concerned with individual rights and the correlative duties to respect the rights of other individuals. Instead, it puts its main emphasis on the duties of individuals toward the state, and the judges must constantly underline this emphasis in their decisions. If individuals are uncooperative or grudging in their attitudes, there is every reason to make an example of them. The judiciary is an instrument for safeguarding the regime and promoting the conception of the good life entertained by the rulers.

Accordingly, these courts are not concerned merely with acts done, but also with the motives, character, and general attitude of the citizens. In Nazi Germany, for example, the courts often penalized individuals or denied them redress because they had a bad attitude and would no doubt be led into actual transgression, if they were not checked beforehand. The Nazi courts thus had preventive as well as compensatory and punitive functions. Similar instances could be cited for Fascist Italy and the Soviet Union.

Executive Consultation of the Judiciary. In this condition of the law in the United States and Britain, it would seem to follow, too, that neither the

executive nor the legislature can require the judges to give authoritative interpretations of the law or 'advisory opinions' *in the absence of an actual dispute between parties.* Broadly speaking, this is true. In the United States, the
federal Constitution and most state constitutions prevent it in the absence
of constitutional amendment for that purpose. In Britain, the executive is
not permitted to consult the judges on the meaning of particular laws or
on the legality of particular executive action already taken or proposed to
be taken. Of course, the supremacy of Parliament makes it possible for
that body to enact a law at any time requiring the judges to give such
opinions. Suggestions for such legislation have been made in the United
States, but thus far only a few states have passed the enabling constitutional
amendments.[12] However, as already indicated above, all American courts
may give *declaratory judgments* which, while not 'advisory' opinions per
se, do state the rights of particular persons in a controversy *prior* to actual
injury without, however, attaching any consequential or coercive relief to
that judgment—and federal 'legislative' courts (but not the 'constitutional'
courts) may give actual advisory opinions. Such judicial opinions, when
given, are authoritative in the sense that they have the prestige of a considered statement of the court, but ordinarily they are no more than advice
to the executive and do not form precedents binding the courts in later
litigation.

The reason why governments nowadays should want advisory opinions
from the judges before disputes arise is very clear, particularly in federal
states. Much of today's legislation must be actively administered by the
executive, and this often requires the setting up of new offices and employment of hundreds and even thousands of additional civil servants. It often
involves also a very drastic readjustment of their practices by numerous
individuals and businesses. Unfortunately, however, it is not always easy,
in the United States, to be sure legislation is constitutional, and the
decision ultimately rests with the courts. Some eighty-five federal and seven
hundred state laws, or parts thereof, have thus been held *ultra vires.* Important parts—indeed, thirteen separate laws—of President Roosevelt's New
Deal legislation, largely enacted in 1933, were held unconstitutional by the
Supreme Court between 1934 and 1936, after a vast administrative apparatus
to enforce it had been set up and put to work. The purpose of advisory

---

[12] As of 1963, constitutions of ten of the states did permit 'advisory' opinions: Alabama,
Colorado, Delaware, Florida, Massachusetts, Maine, North Carolina, New Hampshire, Rhode
Island, and South Dakota.

opinions by the judges would be to get a settlement of the constitutional issue *before* administrative enforcement of the legislation begins.

In Britain, the judiciary cannot declare legislation unconstitutional, but it must interpret the meaning of legislation when disputes turning on its meaning arise. The judges sometimes give interpretations that surprise and even dismay the executive and upset its program of enforcement of the law. As a result, there has been some agitation for a law that would enable the executive to get judicial interpretations in advance. Such proposals are resisted on the ground that they would unduly strengthen the hand of the executive and tend to knit the executive and judiciary into one. If the executive can get opinions from the judges beforehand, while the individual who resists the intervention of officials in the sphere of his interests cannot, the latter is put at a serious disadvantage.

Judicial Control of Government Officials. The force and bearing of this argument cannot be fully appreciated without looking closely at one of the traditional roles of the Anglo-American judiciary. It was pointed out in Chapter IV that the judiciary has been relied on to enforce the Rule of Law against citizen and government official alike. If government is to be servant and not master, its actions must be limited by predictable rules which are interpreted and applied by some authority independent of the executive. This has been done in the past mainly by the judges of the same courts that settle disputes between citizen and citizen and, in the absence of a law clearly conferring special powers and privileges on the government official, they have required him to observe the standards applicable to private citizens. In this sense, one law interpreted by one set of judges rules everybody. The Rule of Law, or the supremacy of law, as it is generally known in the United States, is a very important principle of Anglo-American constitutions.

So the official who is thought to have exceeded his powers overzealously can be brought before an impartial court on the complaint of the aggrieved person. If the police detain a person on suspicion of crime for any considerable time, without bringing him to trial for a specified offense, his jailer can be compelled to appear in the court on a writ of *habeas corpus* and, if he cannot show that the detention is lawful, an order for release will be made. Equally, if an official seizes an apparatus which he claims is used for making illicit alcohol in violation of the excise law, and which the owner insists is used only for laudable scientific experiment, the owner can have both the fact and the law determined by the judiciary.

IN BEHALF OF PRIVATE RIGHTS. In such disputes, the judges do not normally lean in favor of the official. If they lean at all, it is the other way. For the Anglo-American legal tradition, of which more will be said later, makes the judiciary a champion of private rights and interests against any suggestion of highhanded action by governments. The independence of the executive which the judge enjoys is not always free from antagonism. So the legal profession and the judges regard any suggestion that judges should collaborate with the executive as a threat to individual liberty. The judges, it is said, should not be asked to interpret a law giving powers to the executive until they see, in the actual disputes arising, what use the executive is trying to make of the law in question. The dangers involved in such proposals may be exaggerated. Yet the general rule that judges are to decide disputes over the lawfulness of things already done, and not to foreclose freedom of action by preventive measures or by interpretations of law in advance of action, is an important buttress of constitutionalism.

Today, when great accomplishments are expected of governments, and achievements depend largely on the energy and efficiency of the executive, it is clear why the executive should want to find out from judges in advance what the judges will uphold. This is particularly true when the judges are inclined to be unsympathetic to the executive. And it applies with special force because in the Anglo-American system the official is *personally liable* for damages when he exceeds his powers. The jailer who detains a person unlawfully is liable for heavy damages even though his motives are of the best. Hence when officials are in doubt as to their powers, they are likely to be timid and hesitant in enforcing the law. While this is some protection against executive highhandedness, it also detracts from the vigor of administration. The methods by which constitutionalism has been buttressed are often hindrances to far-reaching governmental action.

Continental European System Contrasted. At this point, it may be useful to introduce a contrast with the European legal and judicial systems which differentiate between their treatment of governmental and private disputes.

FRENCH ADMINISTRATIVE COURTS. In France, for example, the courts that judge between citizen and citizen have no authority to deal with disputes to which the government, or an official of the government as such, is a party. A claim that an official has exceeded his powers in executing his official duties, and has thus committed a wrong against a private citizen, is heard in one of a number of easily accessible special courts known as *administrative courts,* headed by the important *Council of State (conseil d'état).* The *conseil d'état* is a powerful, highly respected body, which has both original and appellate jurisdiction in administrative law and, as we saw in Chapter XIII, acts as a technical adviser in the drafting of bills and ordinances. These courts are very closely connected with the executive, and the judges who sit in them—career personnel, steeped in the law—perform many executive as well as judicial functions. Moreover, the rules of law applied to the settlement of disputes in these courts differ from the rules applied to disputes between citizen and citizen. There is a *special body of law, called administrative law,* which governs in the administrative courts.

The only comparably constituted court known to English history is the *Court of Star Chamber,* which was a branch of the executive and dealt with controversies between the government and the subject. Its memory is infamous because it applied to the officials of the Tudor and Stuart monarchs a different standard from that applicable to the ordinary citizen, and often relied on reasons of state and political expediency to deny redress to citizens in conflict with the Crown. It was abolished three hundred years ago, but even today any suggestion of the creation of administrative courts in the Anglo-American world evokes its image in the minds of the legal profession and others.

It was long thought in these circles that the French administrative courts were similar devices for enabling the executive to escape the restraints of law. In fact, however, since the establishment of the democratic Third Republic in 1870 (whatever may have been true prior to that period), the administrative courts have been impartial and upright, leaning in favor of neither the official nor the citizen, although there has been some criticism that the government has been 'too tough' on itself. They give the average citizen better protection against official over-zealousness and mistakes than does the Anglo-American system. They are easily accessible and have a simple, expeditious, inexpensive procedure. If they find the official at fault, they award immediate compensation to the injured party, which is paid not by the official personally but out of the public treasury. They are quick to detect and to veto abuses of power by officials. In Britain and the United States, on the other hand, until a few years ago, the law generally did not impose on the government and the public treasury any responsibility for official wrongdoing. The official himself has always been liable, but a judgment against him is often worthless because he has not the financial resources to meet it.

LINKING OF JUDICIARY AND EXECUTIVE. Despite the obvious advantages in the French system, Anglo-American opinion clings to the ideal of a judiciary completely independent of the executive and of one law for citizen and official alike. There is a profound suspicion of any judiciary closely connected with the executive and of any special law for testing the validity of governmental action. To the argument that the French administrative courts are, in fact, impartial, it is retorted that what is wanted is not merely justice now, but an assurance of justice in the future.

That assurance is thought to be lacking where the judges are part of the executive, and therefore open to executive pressure. Support for this view is to be found in the experience of Germany and Italy with dictatorship. These two countries had systems of administrative courts on the French model. As soon as the Nazis and Fascists got control of the executive in these two countries, the impartial independence of the administrative courts was overwhelmed, and they became mere tools for consolidating the power of the dictators. So, for that matter, did the French administrative courts under the Vichy regime and under German occupation.

However, Britain and the United States have now recognized the obvious justice of the French system in making the public treasury liable for wrongful acts committed by officials in the course of carrying out their duties. In 1947 and 1946, acts were passed by the British Parliament and the United States Congress, respectively, giving the right to sue the public treasury in some, but not all, of these circumstances. The official, however, remains personally liable as before, and the injured person may elect to sue him instead of, or along with, the state.

Also, as we shall see in detail later, the legislature in adding continuously to the tasks of the executive often gives special powers and privileges to particular officials, and even sets up special administrative tribunals to judge the exercise of these powers. That is to say, the unsympathetic judiciary finds the legislature cutting down materially its function of judging disputes between officials and citizens. The great enlargement of governmental activities in the last seventy years has affected even the judiciary and has made, despite the protests of the legal profession, substantial breaches in the Rule of Law as it used to be understood.

Judging Disputes. The upshot of this discussion of the functions of the judiciary is that its primary function is to judge disputes and to interpret the law as far as is necessary for that purpose. Of course, such interpretations are openly made and furnish guides to the meaning of the law for persons who find themselves in circumstances similar to those in which judges have given decisions. The effect of judicial interpretation in a particular case goes far beyond the particular dispute. How far it goes depends on 'the law,' just as the limits of the judges' power to give interpretations have been said to depend on 'the law.' In fact, throughout this chapter, a number of conclusions have been ascribed to 'the law' and differences between different legal systems have been noted. It is necessary now to inquire what is meant by 'the law.'

THE LAW

The Origin and Nature of Law

It has been said that the function of the legislature is to make the law. In almost all countries in the world, however, there is a great deal of law in force that has never been made by a legislature. Despite their large annual turnout of legislation, present-day legislatures do no more than add to or make minor alterations in a vast body of law that is derived from other sources. Although it lacks the stamp of a legislature, this body of law regulates far more human relationships and is better observed and enforced than are the laws made by legislatures.

Non-Legislature-Made Law. We have here an element of great importance for government and politics, which is not generated by the political and governmental mechanisms we have been describing. To explain the origin and growth of law, and to define its identifying characteristics, would require a large volume; so it must suffice to give summarily some clues as to its origin and nature without attempt at precise definition. The law, in the sense of a body or system of rules, takes form through the ages just as does a language or a literature, or an art like paintaing or sculpture. The current generation builds on the past, rejecting parts of it while maintaining or transforming other parts of it. There is always an interaction between the tradition that is handed down and the needs and desires of the present. Just as the Greeks developed certain canons of art and literature that still command respect, and reappear again and again in many different dresses, so the Romans, for example, developed a body of legal rules, principles, and ideas that still retain authority in various guises in modern systems of law.

CUSTOM. Every civilization and every society in the course of development secrete, by a process of social chemistry which has never been fully explained, a legal system of more or less distinctiveness. It is closely akin to *custom*, which is a set of rules and practices with its roots in the past, and which is always being subtly modified and developed in the present. People living together in a society find out almost subconsciously that certain practices and patterns of behavior are a support, if not a pre-condition, of social life and that other ways of acting are detrimental to or destructive of it. In the most primitive societies, there are always numerous rules to be observed often involving elaborate and intricate ceremonies. At this stage, there may be both law and custom, but it is generally impossible to tell one from the other. Both are enforced by the threat of social ostracism, or worse, and by threats of supernatural punishments.

RELIGION. In these early stages, indeed, it is often impossible to distinguish either law or custom from religion. The priests conduct the ceremonies, interpret the customs, and maintain the authority of the taboos. Sometimes it can be said that the germ of a legal profession is to be found in the priesthood. Legal systems never break entirely free of these early associations. Even today, rules that only recently were no more than custom, now and then become recognized and enforced as rules of law. While no one is now likely to confuse the lawyer and the priest, everyone will have noted how moral and religious feeling help to maintain the authority of the criminal law. Equally, the ideas of justice and fair dealing that find expression in the rules and principles of the law have been impressed on it by moral and religious feeling and by the ethical standards that are honored in the community.

Law Distinguished from Custom and Religion. It is not easy to say at what point a system of law emerges from custom and religion. Somewhat arbitrarily, we can pick the point at which the priest, who is almost always associated with the interpretation and enforcement of rules of social behavior in primitive societies, is able to supplement the sanctions of custom and religion by calling on some reservoir of organized physical force to enforce his decrees. When this happens, we can say that the priest has become a judge and the rules that are enforced in this way are law. Customary rules are obeyed because of habit or fear of censure by one's fellows. The rules of morality are obeyed generally because of a fear of, or a respect and reverence for, divine authority. Most of the law gets support from these sources too. Some even contend that no rule of behavior can be law unless it accords with the community's sense of what is right and fitting.

LAW DEFINED. In any event, all are agreed that what distinguishes law from custom and morality is the additional sanction of sheriffs, bailiffs, police, jails, and armed forces to be called into operation if needed to coerce the stubborn. *So law is defined as the body of rules backed by the organized force of the community.* The government controls this organized force, and thus law has in it a political element lacking in custom and morality. All three are made up of rules for controlling the behavior of men in society, but law alone conjures up the judge-interpreter, the army, and the policeman.

If this is the nature of law, the judges play a double role. They are agents of the government for determining in what circumstances organized political force is to be turned loose on individuals. They are also agents of the community, as distinct from the government, for seeing to it that disputes are settled according to law, i.e. in ways that do not outrage the community sense of right. In fact, the judges in the Anglo-American world do not think of themselves as agents of the government, but as the servants, or high-priests, of the law.

Judges as Servants of a Higher Law. They have been confirmed in this attitude by the persistence of a belief that was first articulated by the Stoic philosophers before the Christian era. As we saw in Chapter II, the Stoics believed in a law of nature, universally binding because it expressed the permanent demands of man's innermost nature. By reflecting on man's essential nature, human reason could unerringly define the right rules for regulating human relationships. Particularly in the United States, lawyers and judges have been deeply influenced by the conception of a law rooted in reason and nature which has a higher validity than the laws made by a legislature. Most of this higher law, they think, is enshrined in the Constitution of the United States, written there by men who had grasped the rational law of nature.[13]

VARIED SOURCES. This is the fundamental significance of the substantial independence that Anglo-American judges enjoy. The *law they interpret is older than the government* and gets much of its support from sources other than the government: custom, morality, reason, and nature. It is on this

---

[13] See, for example, the excellent essay by Professor Edward S. Corwin, *The Higher Law Background of American Constitutional Law* (Ithaca: Cornell University Press, 1929).

ground that judges claim to decide whether or not the acts of the government and its officials are according to law. It is partly on this ground that judges in the United States have made good their power to declare laws made by legislatures void, unconstitutional, as being contrary to a higher law—*the Constitution*. It is on this ground that the judges are sometimes unsympathetic to laws made by the legislature.

Legislation as a Source of Law. However, legislatures do make law, and in ever-growing abundance. In Britain, the law made by the legislature, known as *statutory law,* overrides all other law that may be contradictory to it. Everywhere, law made by the legislature is for the purpose of changing older law in some respect. Law, like constitutions, must always be capable of change to meet changing conditions and new needs and desires. But deliberate, conscious change by legislatures is largely a modern phenomenon. Never before have legislatures undertaken to alter law as radically and as frequently as present-day legislatures do.

Before the Industrial Revolution, law, with its roots in custom, changed slowly as custom changed. Generally, this sufficed because the pace of social change that determines the need for change in the law was very slow. By processes that do not concern us here, law was adjusted almost imperceptibly, just as social change was imperceptible at any given time. But, as everyone knows, the Industrial Revolution and the continuing technological developments it set going have made more changes in the material conditions of life in two hundred years than had occurred in the previous two thousand. These economic and social transformations upset the old customary ways of life and created most of the disorder and maladjustments that legislatures are trying desperately to cure. The law handed down from the past, like the customs by which men lived, fails to maintain order and security in the rapidly changing conditions. Hence the feverish activity of legislatures, trying to patch and improvise by deliberate changes of, and additions to, the law. Most of the new governmental functions outlined in Chapter V involved substantial changes in the law. Statutes add greatly to the bulk of law to be interpreted.

Chapter XVII will explain something of the impact of legislative lawmaking on the inherited legal system and on the work of the judiciary. Here it is important to emphasize that there are inherited legal systems and that, despite their being outmoded in some particulars, they still are of great importance. There are numerous legal *systems,* but we need to comment on only three of them: the *Roman* or civil-law system; the *English* or common-law system; and the new *Soviet* system. Among them, they hold sway over most of the civilized world today.

CIVIL LAW AND COMMON LAW SYSTEMS

Origin and Development of Civil Law. Civil,[14] or Roman, law had its origin in the custom and religion of the tribes that founded the city of Rome. Over a period of a thousand years, the primitive tribal law of Rome was transformed by the slow piecemeal work of priests, judges, and lawyers into the law of a great empire, ruling the then civilized world. It reached its maturity before A.D. 200. When Rome fell, its law fell with it, and the barbarian tribes who overran the Empire brought their own *customary law* with them; among them were the Anglo-Saxons, who moved to Britain. By the end of the Middle Ages several systems of law, owing little to Roman law, had developed in Europe out of the customs of the barbarians, among them the English *common law*.

The Renaissance, which revived the study of ancient art and literature, also aroused great enthusiasm for Roman law, a record of which had happily been preserved. The main reason for this enthusiasm is not far to seek. The Renaissance was marked by beliefs in individualism and human rationality. The Roman jurists, who were most influential in shaping the Roman law in the stages of its highest development, were also Stoic philosophers moved by beliefs in the dignity of the individual, in the brotherhood of man, and in a universal law discoverable by reason. This, by the way, is another instance of the deep roots of the Western political tradition.

ADOPTIONS. Just as the classics became the foundation of the educational system, so Roman law was adopted in most of continental Europe as the main body of law, superseding, for most purposes, native law. In the course of time, the countries of Western Europe framed codes of laws suitable to modern conditions but based on Roman law, e.g. Napoleon's famous *codes*

---

[14] Civil, as used here in connection with *law* or legal *systems*, must not be confused with its meaning in civil *jurisdiction* or civil *action*. As used in connection with the latter two concepts, the term *civil* refers to a case at law between private persons and/or private organizations. There, redress in a personal interest for some right or wrong is sought, such as a breach of contract, a divorce action, or a defamation of character suit against another private person. A *criminal* offense, on the other hand, is brought in the name of the government. It involves an accusation that the defendant has violated some specific prohibition contained in a law for which a penalty has been statutorily provided, such as homicide, espionage, or rape. In the present context, it is the derivation of *civil* from *civis*, meaning citizen. The Romans talked of the *jus civile*, the law applicable to a Roman citizen, whether in his public or private relationships.

in France. The modernized Roman system has been adopted in countries as different as Japan and Turkey, and, of course, it was carried to the colonies of the continental European states. Thus the Canadian province of Quebec, the American state of Louisiana, and most of Latin America have incorpoated into their legal systems varying portions of Roman law.

Scotland went over to the civil law, but England did not, retaining her native system of law. This is just another aspect of the remarkable continuity of English political and social development, without revolutionary breaks with the past. English law by 1500 was more fully developed than any of the native systems of continental Europe. It had called into existence a close-knit legal profession, and at the Inns of Court in London vigorous law schools were maintained, where the native tradition was imparted to each succeeding generation of lawyers. These factors aided in resisting the appeal of the classics in the field of jurisprudence. English law made good its claim to survive and become a rival of Roman law in the modern world.

Origin and Development of Common Law. At the time of the Norman Conquest, custom ruled the land and ruled it variously in different parts of England. The administration of justice was entirely in the hands of local assemblies of neighbors who met to deal with deviations from the customary ways of behavior. The Norman kings pledged themselves to maintain the laws of Edward the Confessor. To help in maintaining order and improving their grip on the kingdom, they gradually took the administration of justice away from the local assemblies and put it into the hands of their officials.

These officials traveled up and down the country on the king's business, dealing with, among other things, disputes brought to their attention. They were often puzzled over what rules to apply to these controversies. The custom in different areas was often conflicting or divergent, and it was difficult to know what the laws of Edward the Confessor were. They did notice, however, that on many matters there was a similarity in custom across the country. They met the difficulty by resolving to apply 'the common custom of the realm.' In this way they came to talk about the *common law*—common because it was generally observed throughout the realm.

MORE THAN CUSTOM. This is the origin of the name and the system of English, or common, law. But it must not be thought that its sole content continued to be common custom. Where customs conflicted, or none could be found, the particular officials who gradually came to specialize in judging disputes relinquished to others the administrative aspects of the king's business, invented new rules, or borrowed from Roman and canon law. To take only one example, the law of property in land came to be perhaps the most distinctive branch of the common law. It was partly based on prevailing custom, but in the main it was developed in great detail by the judges themselves with one dominant purpose in mind: to meet the needs of the feudal system which the Norman kings had brought to England and on which they had to rely for governing the country for two hundred years. The monarch was the overlord and all England was his estate. Everyone who held land held it of the monarch, directly or indirectly. The law of property comprised the rules for the orderly administration of this estate. Many other similar, if not so striking, illustrations could be given. The law is rooted in custom, but it responds through the creative work of the judiciary to the dominant needs of the time.

This law, which was first shaped for the needs of feudal England, survived into the modern world and was made over through the centuries into a system of law adequate for a great commercial and industrial civilization and a world empire. Legislation, i.e. lawmaking by a legislature, played no highly significant part in this development until the second quarter of the nineteenth century. It was the work of succeeding generations of judges who never lost touch with the past, but who also responded more or less slowly to changing needs. The common law was brought to the English colonies on the Atlantic seaboard and there adapted, first to the needs of pioneer America, and then later to the needs of industrial America. All British colonies settled by people of British origin took the common law with them, and so it spread around the world. It was not, however, generally imposed on conquered colonies settled by non-British European stock. South Africa has its Roman-Dutch law, the version of Roman law adopted in Holland, just as Quebec has a version of the French civil law.

The Changing Content of the Common Law. Law must change when new needs can no longer be denied, but its prime function in any given period is to minister to order and stability. For this purpose, the law must have a fair degree of certainty. The sense of security which is the basis of orderly life depends on knowing what others will do or can be held to do in the future. Those who plan for the future must be able to find out what the law permits and requires. As a Lord Chancellor of England has said, 'Amid the cross-currents and shifting sands of public life, the Law is like a great rock upon which a man may set his feet and be safe.' [15] A law that

---

[15] Quoted from Lord Sankey in the *Report of the Committee on Ministers' Powers* (London: His Majesty's Stationery Office, Cond. 4060, 1932), p. 6.

is always changing is uncertain and defeats its own purpose. Moreover, if it is admitted that judges can change the law, people lose confidence in it and in them. Accordingly, judges are sworn to apply the law as they find it. For the best of reasons, and with complete honesty and considerable truth, the judge insists that he does not make law but only interprets it. Nevertheless, in the course of interpreting, he sometimes does make it. Sometimes, when the United States Supreme Court is accused of 'legislating,' the charge has a modicum of truth—yet this is a very subtle and difficult problem. Mr. Justice Holmes put the matter into focus thusly: 'Judges *do and must* legislate . . . [but they] can do so only interstitially; they are confined from molar to molecular motions.' [16]

The explanation of the paradox of certainty and change is that judicial change in the law must be so slow as to be imperceptible, even to judges, unless they have a deep knowledge of history. It can be proved that glaciers flow although casual observers will deny it flatly. Similarly, the movement of law is by a succession of slight shifts in interpretation of some of its rules, the total effect of which will often not be noticed in one generation. As long as social change and economic change were also slow, this method of adaptation of law might suffice. But by the middle of the nineteenth century, the pace of social change was so rapid, its effects so widespread, and the clamor of new needs so insistent, that leadership in the adaptation of law was forced on elected legislatures.

PRIVATE LAW. There is no way of measuring what proportion of the law today is common law and what is statute law made by the legislature. Broadly speaking, the great bulk of *private* law, the law applicable to relationships between private citizens, is still common law, although modified here and there by statutes. This includes the law of *tort* (civil wrongs such as trespass, slander, deceit, assault, and so on); the law of personal relations, such as those between husband and wife, parent and child; and the law relating to property and contract. In Britain and the United States, it includes, in part, the criminal law, but that is increasingly becoming coded.

PUBLIC LAW. Most of the recent legislation concerns *public* law, the law applicable to relationships between government and the individual. Much of public law is still common law, but statute has added to it in recent years, giving new rights and powers to officials and creating new duties and rights for individuals vis-à-vis the government. As we have seen, the great cause of legislation is the extension of government activities. The assumption of these

[16] *Southern Pacific Co.* v. *Jensen*, 244 U.S. 205 (1916), at 221. (Italics supplied.)

new functions always requires some adjustment of the relationship between the government and the individual.

The content of common law is an arduous study in itself and little that is useful can be said about it in a short space. But there are some general characteristics of the system that are important for a study of present-day government and which offer marked contrasts to civil law.

Contrasts between Common Law and Civil Law. The common law is unwritten law in the sense that there is nowhere to be found a compendious set of written rules which authoritatively states that law. Plenty of books have been written on all branches of common law, and they are a great assistance in finding the law. Yet none of them is in any sense binding on the courts, which must always base their decision on some earlier decision of a court, called a precedent.[17]

PRECEDENTS. For hundreds of years, the cases, or judicial decisions, that involved a significant interpretation of law have been collected together in hundreds of volumes, called the law reports. The report of a case contains a statement of the facts of the dispute, the judge's decision, and something of his reason for thinking that the law justified the decision. That is to say, there is in every case, explicit or implicit, a statement of the law applicable to the given facts. To find the law applicable to a dispute arising today, it may be necessary to consult five precedents, or fifty, or even more. Anyone who wishes to master the common law as a whole must master the law reports, 'this codeless myriad of precedent, this wilderness of single instances.'

There was a time when this could be done, but it is past. The accumulation of precedents is now too great. The principal stock-in-trade of the lawyer nowadays is a knowledge of how to use the numerous digests and indices available as guides to the law reports, and a technique for interpreting what he finds there. He collects the cases that are similar to the one he has in hand, noting differences and judging of their significance. He then tries to frame a general rule that will explain these cases. He works inductively from the particular to the general, and applies it to his own case. The judge does the same, remembering that precedents which bind him are decisions in the courts that stand above his court in the hierarchy. Once the highest court of appeal has ruled on a particular question, its decision is binding on itself and all lower courts, until the legislature changes the rules. This, however, is truer of Britain than the United States, where it does not necessarily follow that the *highest* court itself will always follow the rule of *stare*

[17] The rule that precedent should be followed is known as *stare decisis* ('let the decision stand').

decisis. The latter is a 'principle of policy and not a *mechanical formula* of adherence to the latest decision. . . .'[18] The doctrine is relatively flexible in America—and 'requires a careful weighing in each doubtful case of the advantages of adherence to precedent and the necessity for judicially planned social and economic progress to supplement legislative progress.'[19]

CODES. In contrast, the *civil law is written law*. It is always to be found in an authoritative code of general rules which the judge is to apply, and he is not permitted to base his decision on precedent to the neglect of the written code. This is a much neater and less cumbersome system and, on the surface, would seem to leave the layman less at the mercy of the lawyer. However, there is a somewhat esoteric technique for interpreting the provisions of the code and applying it to facts, which only trained lawyers possess. Also, despite the formal ban on precedents, the courts do develop settled practices in applying the code, which come to much the same thing. There is a large body of authoritative doctrine over and above the letter of the code.

INTERPRETATIONS. Both systems have a set of rules for interpreting the meaning of legislation enacted by the legislature. In the civil law, these are few and relatively simple. In the common law, they are much more numerous, having been developed in great detail because every decision of a court interpreting the meaning of some section of a statute is itself a precedent to be followed in later interpretation of the same section. Thus, just as the Supreme Court of the United States has expounded the meaning of the American Constitution at great length, so the Anglo-American judiciary amplifies the meaning of all statutes that come into question in cases before it. The Statute of Frauds, for example, enacted by the English Parliament in 1677, contains only a few hundred words. It now takes a substantial book to explain in detail what the courts over two hundred and fifty years have held it to mean. Almost every word in it has been given a special common-law meaning which may or may not have been present to the minds of the Parliament that enacted it. The statute has been knit into the fabric of the common law.

This is a necessary process because every piece of legislation, whether socially wise and necessary or not, is upsetting to the legal system, as a system. Like the grain of sand in the oyster, it is an irritant until it is well

[18] Mr. Justice Felix Frankfurter, in *Helvering* v. *Hallock,* 309 U.S. 106 (1940), at 119. (Italics supplied.)
[19] Robert A. Sprecher, 'The Development of the Doctrine of Stare Decisis and the Extent to Which It Should Be Applied,' *Journal of the American Bar Association,* 31 (1945), 501–9.

overlaid with precedent. Great pearls of judicial ingenuity—not to say wisdom—are the result. The interpretation of statutes is a creative process adding much to what the legislature has said, and sometimes stultifying its purpose.

The Individualism of the Common Law. Another important characteristic of the common law is its individualism. We have already noticed the tenderness of judges to individuals and individual rights, and their fairly frequent lack of sympathy with certain types of current legislation that restrict in one way or another individual freedom of action. This attitude finds expression in many of the rules and principles of the common law. For example, there is the principle, subject to certain exceptions, that no one should be held liable to pay damages to another unless the injury complained of was due to his personal neglect or fault. To take one instance of this, an employer was not liable for injuries suffered by an employee in the course of his employment, unless they could be shown to be owing to the personal fault or carelessness of the employer. If an employee was injured owing to the fault of a fellow employee, or through his own carelessness, arising perhaps from fatigue, he had no claim on his employer. As already explained, this rule has been changed by legislation.

There are other instances. The common law has always been watchful, since Stuart times, of designs by the government against the property of the subject. Accordingly, legislation imposing taxation is always interpreted strictly, and if the intention of the legislature is not expressed in the clearest of language, the courts are likely to interpret it favorably to the taxpayer and against the government. Ingenious lawyers find loopholes, and the judges insist that it is the duty of the legislature to plug them, if they are to be plugged at all. Similarly, in legislation authorizing the government to regulate business and economic life, restriction of the freedom of businessmen to do as they like with their property is always involved, and no amount of argument on the necessity to protect the public interest will persuade the courts to uphold the actions of the government beyond what the law requires. However, many of these laws are drawn quite broadly.

THE IDEAL. It is sometimes said that the common law has no conception of the public interest but only an ideal of the protection of private rights. It would be more correct to say that the common-law conception of the public interest is the greatest possible freedom for individuals. A famous English judge once said that the highest principle of public policy is that you should not lightly interfere with freedom of contract.[20] The ideal is that everyone should be free to make his own bargains and then be required, as a responsible individual, to make the best of the bad along with the good.

In short, the legal system, which adjusts itself only slowly to changing conditions, to some extent still pays homage to *laisser faire,* which has long been abandoned by public opinion and legislatures as a guide to sound public policy. In many situations, legislation now requires individuals to ensure the safety of others, quite irrespective of the issue of fault. Today's workmen's compensation laws require employers to pay into a fund that compensates injured workmen, even when the accident was the workman's own fault. When legislation provides for minimum wages and maximum hours of work, it interferes with freedom of contract. When the legislature authorizes regulation of public utility industries, it restricts rights of property and limits freedom of contract. In fact, most of the new activities of government, outlined in Chapter V, involve substantial restrictions and limitations of this character. The individualism of the common law and the collectivist measures of present-day legislatures are by no means entirely reconciled to one another.

SAFEGUARDS FOR THE ACCUSED. The temper of the common law on contests between individuals and the state comes out most clearly in criminal trials, where the judge acts, not as an agent of the government bent on getting a conviction, but as an impartial umpire trying to balance the scales of justice evenly. This is one of the consequences of the Anglo-American system of *accusatorial* judicial procedure, whereas under the Roman law system of *inquisitorial* procedure the French judge, for example, is bent upon obtaining a conviction. However, in the latter procedure much careful preliminary investigation by a professional judge, known as the *enquête,* precedes the trial—in a sense a sort of grand jury indictment. If the investigating judge (*juge d'instruction*) is unable to detect any clear evidence of apparent guilt, the case is unlikely to reach the trial stage. He operates in a system which refuses to concede to the contending parties control over the submission of evidence. Thus, in a very real sense, a criminal trial in a French court is an investigation rather than the slugging match between batteries of opposing lawyers so characteristic of courtroom procedure in England and America.

Some of the safeguards available to the accused under the Anglo-American

[20] Sir George Jessel, M.R., in *Printing and Numerical Registering Co.* v. *Sampson,* 19 Equity Cases 462 (1875), at 465.

common law system—several of which have already been discussed in connection with civil liberties in Chapter VIII—may be listed. It must be kept in mind, however, that not *all* of these safeguards necessarily or automatically accrue to the *accused* on *both* the federal and the state level of government in the United States:

1. The writ of *habeas corpus* ensures that the accused will either be tried within a limited time or released. He cannot be kept in a dungeon for years while the police torture him into confession, or wait for Providence to send further evidence against him.
2. At a reasonable time before trial, an *indictment,* or charge, must be laid against him. It must set out a specific offense, alleged to have been committed at a specific date and place. In capital 'or otherwise infamous' criminal cases in the United States, this is usually done by a *grand jury.*
3. He must have ample time to prepare his defense.
4. He is entitled to the expert assistance of a lawyer before and during the trial.
5. He must be tried in open court, normally before a jury of his peers [21] where he confronts his judge face to face. The evidence against him must be sworn to by witnesses *viva voce* in the court, and there must be full opportunity for cross-examination—a powerful weapon in exposing falsehoods. Under certain conditions, this safeguard is tempered by governmental use of confidential data.
6. He cannot be compelled to give evidence that may tend to incriminate him. It is his own choice whether he goes into the witness box at all or not. (However, we have seen that this safeguard has been abridged in the United States in certain cases, e.g. those involving the 'national security,' wherein testimony may now be compelled under the Immunity Act of 1954 in return for immunity from prosecution or jeopardy arising out of incriminating testimony thus compelled.)
7. Any reasonable doubt that is unresolved at the conclusion of the case must tell in favor of the accused.

[21] Space does not permit an extensive discussion of juries, that fascinating and controversial feature of judicial systems. There are various types of juries but, essentially, a jury is simply a group of people that has been assembled by a public official to answer a question. Juries originated in England about eight hundred years ago; they have been alternately praised and attacked ever since. Their use has declined somewhat in Britain and France, but they are still widely employed in the United States. This is particularly true of the *petit,* or *trial,* jury, a twelve-member body of local citizens, who presumably listen impartially to both sides of a case and, upon the conclusion of the trial, armed with the judge's *charge* to it, arrive at a verdict of conviction or acquittal. On the federal level, unanimity is always required; failure to attain it results in a *hung* jury. Some of the American states do not require a unanimous verdict, and some do not always furnish juries, especially not in civil cases.

8. He can appeal against a conviction, but the state—except in a few cases, e.g. Connecticut and Vermont—cannot appeal against an acquittal.

Of course, the habitual criminal thrives on these safeguards. But where they are absent, the contest between the individual and the state may be a very unequal one, and the government can harry its political enemies through criminal law. The contest may also be unequal in civil disputes between the government and private persons or interests, and there is something to be said for the tendency of the judges to lean in favor of the latter. The government, when it takes action in the courts in civil matters, is a resolute litigant, determined to get its pound of flesh!

Reactions against Judicial Individualism. The imperatives of public policy are always paramount, and private interests must be subordinated. The initially unsympathetic attitude of the judiciary to collectivist legislation, along with other considerations to be explained later, provoked a counter-attack by the legislatures in common-law countries. In many instances, they have taken away, or restricted, the power of the judiciary to decide disputes that involve the interpretation of such legislation. To give only one example, in Britain, and in most of the states of the United States, issues concerning a workman's right to compensation for industrial accident are no longer decided by the courts, but by an executive agency, the Workmen's Compensation Board or the Industrial Accidents Commission.

Whether the imperatives of public policy require this kind of action or whether less drastic steps would suffice is not yet settled. A great constitutional controversy has raged over the question for the last four decades in Britain and the United States, and still rages. More will be said about it in discussing the administrative process. It is raised here to show that, as in other fields of government and politics, the growth of governmental functions has had a deeply disturbing effect on the judiciary and the legal system. Under this pressure, long-established techniques for helping to ensure that government shall be servant and not master are being revised.

The characteristics of the Anglo-American judicial system that have been outlined all have an important bearing on government and politics. They make it clear that the independence of the judiciary is not adequately stated by pointing to the fact that the judges cannot be dismissed by the executive. The judges administer justice in courts that are controlled by them and not by civil servants. The greater part of the law they interpret and apply does not depend on the legislature or executive for its authority and vitality. They are the bearers of a legal tradition that dictates impartiality in private disputes and, in disputes in which the government is concerned, an aloofness from the urgencies finding expression in legislative and executive action. The system as a whole is more concerned with the protection of private rights than with the enforcement of the public interest as conceived by the legislature. Legislatures in haste to make many far-reaching adjustments of private rights and interests often find these judicial attitudes irksome. What the outcome will be is far from clear.

JUDICIAL SELF-RESTRAINT. It should be noted, however, that judicial attitudes have shifted perceptibly toward a recognition that the legislature, which presumably expresses public opinion, must be accorded the leadership in the process of social adjustment. For some time now the English courts, in interpreting statutes, have shown more sympathy than formerly with the policy Parliament is trying to enforce. Since the 'court-packing' battle of 1937, American judges, particularly the justices of the United States Supreme Court, who can mount a heavier attack on statutes from the eminences of the Constitution, have—with some notable exceptions—more and more withheld their fire. This is true especially in the realm of economic and social legislation, but the Court has continued to give far closer scrutiny to its responsibility of saying 'no' to government in matters concerning the cultural freedoms—the Bill of Rights. Yet this attitude is not a brand-new phenomenon by any means. Throughout the years, the Supreme Court has reiterated time and again that it is not supposed to serve as a check against inept, unwise, unrepresentative, unfair, or even undemocratic legislators. Thus, Mr. Chief Justice Waite wrote almost a hundred years ago, 'for protection against abuses by legislatures, the people must resort to the polls, not to the courts.' [22] Emphatically, the question is not one of wisdom and fairness, but of constitutionality! No one has stated this fact more pungently than Mr. Justice Holmes in a colloquy with the then sixty-one-year-old Mr. Justice Stone: 'Young man, about 75 years ago I learned that I was not God. And so, when the people . . . want to do something I can't find anything in the Constitution expressly forbidding them to do, I say, whether I like it or not, "Goddamit, let 'em do it." ' [23]

---

[22] *Munn* v. *Illinois,* 94 U.S. 113 (1876).
[23] As quoted by Charles P. Curtis in his *Lions Under the Throne* (Boston: Houghton Mifflin Co., 1947), p. 281.

This self-limitation is called judicial self-restraint.[24] It can be seen even in matters touching the freedoms of the First Amendment to the Constitution, although as we have noted, these have been sporadically viewed as preferred freedoms by varying Court majorities since the end of World War I. In general, the post 1937 Supreme Court—the 'new' or 'Roosevelt' Court—has been loath to interfere with the judgment of legislatures, state as well as federal. Since that time—as of Autumn 1963—only eight provisions of congressional enactments have been held to be *ultra vires* by the Court —all of these because they infringed personal liberties safeguarded under the Constitution [25]—although a considerable number of state laws have been voided by it. When it can reasonably do so, the Court upholds legislative action in all but clear-cut violations of the Constitution. As we have indicated, some justices go further along this line than others—'judges are men, not disembodied spirits,' commented Mr. Justice Frankfurter once—and some are inclined to allow less legislative leeway in the field of freedom of speech, for example, than in that of interstate commerce. Some, as was so characteristic of Justice Frankfurter, are almost always willing to stand by the legislative judgment, no matter how repugnant it may appear to others. Thus, in his 1951 opinion, concurring with the majority of six in upholding the constitutionality of the Smith Act of 1940, he stated this oft-reiterated conviction:

> Even when moving strictly within the limits of constitutional adjudication, judges are concerned with issues that may be said to involve vital finalities. The too easy transition from disapproval of what is undesirable to condemnation as unconstitutional, has led some of the wisest judges to question the wisdom of our scheme in lodging such authority in courts. But it is relevant to remind that in sustaining the power of Congress in a case like this nothing irrevocable is done. *The democratic process at all events is not impaired or restricted. Power and responsibility remain with the people and immediately with their representatives.* All the Court says is that Congress was not forbidden by the Constitution to pass this enactment. . . .[26]

Yet in their dissenting opinions Justices Black and Douglas found that that is precisely what the Constitution does forbid!

[24] For an enumeration of 'The Sixteen Great Maxims of Judicial Self-Restraint' see Henry J. Abraham, *The Judicial Process* (New York: Oxford University Press, 1962), pp. 310–26.
[25] For a listing and explanation of these, see ibid. pp. 253–4.
[26] Mr. Justice Felix Frankfurter, concurring opinion, in *Dennis* v. *U.S.*, 341 U.S. 494 (1951). (Italics supplied.)

THE LAW AND JUDICIARY IN THE SOVIET UNION

The Soviet approach to law, although some of its branches have retained certain of the strong influences of the civil law system of bourgeois continental Europe,[27] is totally different than that of the Anglo-American countries. The Marxist doctrine of economic determinism recognizes law merely as a tool in the hands of the ruling class; in countries where a division of the population into economic classes still persists, the courts and the judiciary are part of the state which exists for the exploitation of the under-privileged by the ruling class. That is to say, legal systems are but reflections of the economic systems within which they operate. According to this view, law, as hitherto known, will disappear when the state withers away.

Law as Instrument of the Ruling Elite. The architects of the Soviet Union realized that a Communist society could not be set up overnight; and consequently, they designed a legal system to meet the requirements of a society in transition from a capitalist to a Communist order. The law became the instrument of the dominant class—the proletariat—in its struggle with the enemies of the new regime. Today, despite the full liquidation of the capitalist class, the regime does not yet feel secure, and law continues to be an instrument for protecting the interests of society as conceived by the ruling group—although a series of mild reforms were adopted in the mid and late 1930's and some more significant ones as recently as 1957-58, when a new penal code was instituted. In contrast to the West, therefore, Soviet law is not conceived of as being impartial and independent arbiter between individuals, and between the state and individuals, but is frankly admitted to be an instrument for supporting and strengthening Communist society. There is nothing individualistic about the Soviet system of law.

It was said in Chapter III that the Communists in the Soviet Union, at present at any rate, hold the individual in low esteem. They believe that the interests of the individual must always be subordinated to the interests of the proletariat as a whole. They believe, moreover, that the Soviet state embodies the interests of all its citizens, since all capitalists have been eliminated and the Soviet Union is an incipient classless Communist society. So when-

[27] See the monumental study edited by Vladimir Gsovski and Kazimierz Grzybowski, *Government, Law, and the Courts in the Soviet Union and Eastern Europe* (New York: Frederick A. Praeger, 1959), which makes this point repeatedly—while concurrently acknowledging that Soviet law is unique.

ever a clash occurs between what the individual claims as a right according to the law, and what the leaders believe to be necessary state policy, the individual's claim is sacrificed to what is held to be the interest of the collectivity, the Soviet Union. Thus, at an international conference in 1948, Andrei Vyshinsky told a Western diplomat: 'I do not accept the contention that policy ends where law begins. Law is an instrument of politics.' [28]

In effect, then, Soviet law is little more than a tool in the hands of the leaders for enforcing conformity to the party line. There is no real separation of powers between the judiciary and the other organs of the state, and in all matters that relate to charges of political crime, the administration of justice is dominated by the group of leaders who form the summits of the party and governmental organizations.

Structure of the Soviet Courts. In conformity with the general pattern of Soviet organization, the structure of the judiciary corresponds to the general structure of the soviets described in Chapter XIII. At the base of the hierarchy of Soviet courts is the '*Comradely Court.*' These courts actually lie outside the judicial system proper and are informal meetings of citizens in factories or apartment houses convoked to settle disputes that arise among their members. There is no prosecutor or defense lawyer, and no rules of evidence are adhered to. The group concerned elects one or more 'judges,' who can reprimand the guilty parties, impose very small fines (up to ten dollars in 1963), and make certain recommendations to the authorities. He has somewhat the same functions as a justice of the peace in the Anglo-American world.

The *People's Court* is the lowest regular court. These courts have original jurisdiction in both civil and criminal cases and are organized on a district basis throughout the Soviet Union. Their judges, who are elected in the districts by universal suffrage for five-year terms, require no legal training in spite of the fact that their jurisdiction covers a wide variety of cases, from disputed alimony to murder. A single judge presides over each court but is joined by two *people's assessors,* or 'juror judges' as they are sometimes called. The people's assessors have equal powers with the judges, are elected in the same manner for two-year terms, and now sit on military as well as civilian courts. The people's courts decide the bulk of criminal and civil cases in the Soviet Union. Their judges and assessors can handle numerous and important cases without the benefit of legal training because Soviet law, unlike Anglo-American law, is not based on precedent. Each case is con-

[28] Quoted in George C. Guins, 'Soviet Law—Terra Incognita,' *Russian Review,* IX (1950), 17.

sidered on its own merits, and in passing judgment the judges and assessors need not consider the decisions made in earlier cases on similar facts.

Above the people's courts stand the successive tiers of the Soviet judicial structure. Each soviet appoints the judges for its respective region, territory, or area. These several courts act as courts of appeal for cases decided in the courts immediately below them in the structure, and also have original jurisdiction in the more serious civil and criminal cases, such, according to the code, as those related to 'counter-revolutionary activities, crimes against administrative orders when they involve particular danger to the state, the pillaging of socialist property, and other important economic crimes.'

Each Union Republic has a Supreme Court, whose five professional judges and the ubiquitous assessors are elected by the Supreme Soviet of the Union Republic for a term of five years. Endowed with both original and appellate jurisdiction, these courts supervise all judicial activities within their respective republics, and act as appeal courts for cases which have been decided in the courts of the tier immediately below them.

Supreme Court. The highest judicial body is the *Supreme Court of the U.S.S.R.* elected by the Supreme Soviet of the U.S.S.R. for a term of five years. The Supreme Court consists of a chairman, two deputy chairmen, nine professional judges, and twenty people's assessors. (Prior to the reforms of 1957, it had seventy-eight judges and thirty-five assessors.) It is divided into three functional divisions or *collegia,* dealing with criminal, civil, and military matters. It is 'charged with the supervision of the judicial activities of all the judicial organs of the U.S.S.R. and of the Union Republics.'[29] Until 1957 it was empowered to hear cases not judged by lower courts, but now it cannot hear such cases unless they have been heard below—i.e. in local courts, regional courts, and supreme courts of regional republics. It lacks the power of judicial review. The Communist party, not the Supreme Court, decides on the constitutionality of legislation or the legality of the actions of the state authorities. Nor can the Supreme Court interpret laws; this function is given by the Constitution to the Presidium of the Supreme Soviet.[30] Its main tasks, in addition to overseeing the judicial system of the Soviet state, are to issue general judicial rules and to act as a court of cassation in important cases.

The Procurator General. The function of supervising the lower soviet courts is shared by the Supreme Court with the Procurator General (*prokuror*) of the U.S.S.R., whose office is one of the highest in the Soviet

[29] Constitution of the U.S.S.R., Art. 104.
[30] Ibid. Art. 49 (c).

Union. (As a matter of historical interest it may be noted that the Soviet procuracy with its function of 'general administrative supervision' is not a creation of the Soviet Union but of Tsar Peter the Great in 1711! It was re-introduced by the Communists in 1922, having lain more or less dormant since 1864.) The meetings of the U.S.S.R. Supreme Court cannot be held without the presence of the Procurator General. He, and not the Supreme Court, is granted 'supreme [general administrative] supervisory power to ensure the strict observance [and execution] of the laws by all Ministries and institutions subordinated to them, as well as by officials and citizens of the U.S.S.R. generally.'[31] Unlike the Attorney General in the United States, the only office in the Anglo-American world that can be compared at all to that of the Procurator General, he is not formally an agent of the executive power but, according to Soviet legal theory, operates independently of it. He is not appointed by the Council of Ministers but by the Supreme Soviet of the U.S.S.R., and his term of office, which is seven years, exceeds that of the Council of Ministers by three years.

The Procurator General personally appoints a procurator, for a five-year term, as his agent at every level of the Soviet structure from the district to the Union Republic. These procurators exercise such powers and functions as are delegated to them by the Procurator General. The powers, often ill-defined, consist generally of investigating the commission of offenses, laying charges against and prosecuting offenders. It was as Procurator General that Andrei Vyshinsky conducted the famous prosecutions for treason against many Soviet leaders in the purges of 1936 and 1937. The courts are subject to extensive supervision by the Procurator General. He has power to bring to the attention of the Supreme Court lower court decisions that he deems too severe or too lenient and he may reopen a completed or closed trial by means of a device known as 'the protest' within a two-year period. If it is asked to whom the Procurator General is responsible, the answer is to the dominant leaders of the Communist party at a given time. Indeed, Vyshinsky described the Procurator General as the 'watchman of socialist legality, the leader of the policy of the Communist party and of Soviet authority, the champion of socialism,'[32] and Nikita Khrushchev—although professing certain doubts about the jurisdictional limits of the procuracy—asserted that it 'must stand guard over the laws of the Soviet Union.'[33]

[31] Ibid. Art. 113.

[32] *The Law of the Soviet State* (New York: The Macmillan Co., 1948), p. 537.

[33] Glenn G. Morgan, *Soviet Administrative Legality: The Role of the Attorney General's Office* (Stanford: Stanford University Press, 1962), p. 249, quoting *Izvestia* of January 25, 1958. Professor Morgan's book is a fine work devoted exclusively to the procuracy.

THE JUDICIARY AND PROCURACY OF THE USSR

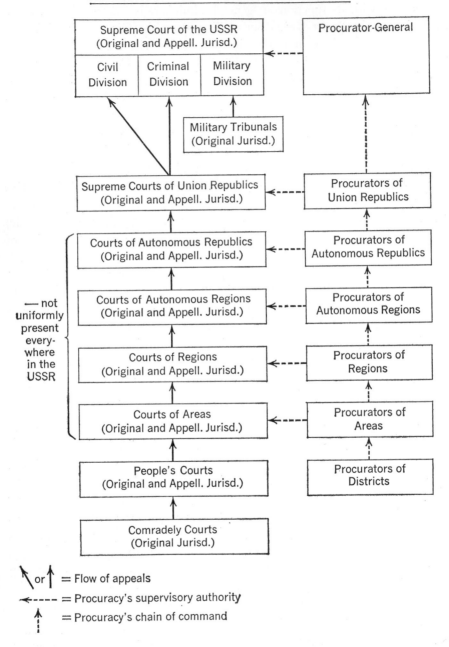

↖ or ↑ = Flow of appeals

←---- = Procuracy's supervisory authority

↑ = Procuracy's chain of command

RECENT CONCERN FOR 'LEGALITY.' Ever since Stalin's death in 1953, and particularly since 1955 under Khrushchev, there has been much talk in U.S.S.R. government and party circles about 'Soviet legality,' and the new law on the judiciary, enacted in 1957–58, stressed the concept of 'Soviet legality.' For example, the official newspapers, *Pravda* and *Izvestia,* have repeatedly stated that 'violations of Soviet legality' will not be tolerated. Talks by Russian leaders have professed concern for the adoption of sundry judicial safeguards. A group of Soviet legal scholars, headed by Professor M. S. Strogovich of the influential Academy of Sciences, issued a public appeal for a liberalized criminal code in 1957 which was adopted late in 1958. This concern may well have arisen out of the demand from the new middle class of bureaucrats, technicians, and factory managers for more protection from capricious arrest and punishment than they have enjoyed. The New Soviet Criminal Code provides *inter alia* a number of rights for the accused, especially during the preliminary investigation, and clearly seems to place the burden of proof on the prosecutors. However, it remains to be seen how much these—and other [34]—ostensible improvements will mean. It is problematical how many, if any, meaningful changes have actually been effected. At any rate, there has been no apparent move to deprive the Communist party of its ability to wield the final power in judicial matters.

Essential Functions of the Soviet Judiciary. To date, the clearest description of the functions of the judiciary in the Soviet Union is still given in a Soviet law of 1938 relating to the judiciary. It is there declared that the general purpose of the courts is 'to educate the citizens of the U.S.S.R. in a spirit of devotion to the fatherland and to the cause of Socialism, in the spirit of an exact and unfaltering performance of Soviet laws, careful attitude towards Socialist property, labor discipline, honest fulfilment of State and public duties, respect towards the rules of the Socialist Commonwealth.' [35] The entire emphasis is on the duties of the citizen, and the first imperative for the courts is to educate the citizen in the socialist way of life in 'Socialist legality,' as the law of 1957 stated it. Soviet jurists have often retorted that the Anglo-American judiciary has also been primarily con-

[34] In May 1957, the Soviet Deputy Procurator-General, P. I. Kudryavtsev, announced that the Soviet Union has released more than 70 per cent of its prisoners and eliminated two-thirds of its labor camps in Siberia in the four years since Stalin's death. (*The New York Times,* May 16, 1957.)

[35] Quoted in James T. Shotwell (ed.), *Governments of Continental Europe,* rev. ed. (New York: Macmillan, 1952), p. 752.

cerned with protecting a way of life, with enforcing the rule of bourgeois capitalism. There is some justice in the retort. It would be nearly accurate *if* it went further and asserted that the Anglo-American judiciary has strived *to maintain the liberal democratic way of life,* including the capitalistic economic system.

A wide sphere of individual liberty involves constant striving and competing which would be destructive of liberty if there were not clear definitions of what the individual is entitled to do, and what he must refrain from doing so as to preserve the rights of others. Accordingly, the judiciary in a liberal democratic system must put a heavy emphasis on individual rights. In a society where other values are supreme, the judiciary must defend those values. In the Soviet Union, the supreme aim is to maintain and strengthen Communist society. Both the law and the judiciary are instruments of this purpose. Their actions are co-ordinated with the Soviet and Party apparatus. Their main functions are to define the duties of the individual to Communist society and to see that he carries them out.

Suggested References for Further Reading

Abraham, Henry J., *The Judicial Process* (Oxford, 1962).

Allen, C. K., *Law in the Making,* 6th ed. (Oxford, 1958).

Archer, P., *The Queen's Courts* (Houghton Mifflin, 1956).

Bedford, S., *The Faces of Justice* (Simon & Schuster, 1961).

Berman, H. J., *Justice in Russia and Interpretation of Soviet Law* (Harvard, 1950).

Bickel, A. M., *The Least Dangerous Branch* (Bobbs-Merrill, 1963).

Blaustein, A. D., and C. O. Porter, *The American Lawyer* (U. of Chicago, 1954).

Bowen, C. D., *The Lion and the Throne* (Little, Brown, 1957).

Cahill, F., *Judicial Legislation* (Ronald, 1952).

Cahn, E. (Ed.), *Supreme Court and Supreme Law* (Indiana U., 1954).

Cardozo, B. N., *The Nature of the Judicial Process* (Yale, 1921).

Corwin, E. S., *The Higher Law Background of American Constitutional Law* (Cornell, 1929).

Curtis, C. P., *Lions Under the Throne* (Houghton Mifflin, 1947).

David, R., and H. P. de Vries, *The French Legal System: An Introduction to Civil Law Systems* (Oceana, 1958).

Douglas, W. O., *We, the Judges* (Doubleday, 1956).

Frank, J., *Courts on Trial* (Princeton, 1949).

Frankfurter, F., *Law and Politics* (Harcourt, Brace, 1939).

Freedeman, C. E., *The Conseil d'État in Modern France* (Columbia, 1961).

Freund, P. A., *The Supreme Court of the United States* (Meridian, 1961).

Friedmann, W., *Law in a Changing Society* (Berkeley, 1959).

Giles, F. T., *The Magistrates' Courts* (Houghton Mifflin, 1955).

Gsovski, V., and K. Grzybowski (Eds.), *Government, Law, and the Courts in the Soviet Union and Eastern Europe* (Praeger, 1959).

Hand, L., *The Bill of Rights* (Harvard, 1958).

Hart, H. L. A., *The Concept of Law* (Oxford, 1961).

Hazard, J. N., *Law and Social Change in the U.S.S.R.* (Stevens, 1953).

Holmes, O. W., Jr., *The Common Law* (Little, Brown, 1881).

Hughes, C. E., *The Supreme Court of the United States* (Columbia, 1928).

Jackson, R. H., *The Supreme Court in the American System of Government* (Harvard, 1955).

Jackson, R. M., *The Machinery of Justice in England,* 3rd ed. (Cambridge, 1960).

Kiralfy, A. K., *The English Legal System,* 3rd ed. (Sweet & Maxwell, 1960).

McClosky, R. G., *The American Supreme Court* (U. of Chicago, 1960).

McWhinney, E., *Judicial Review in the English-Speaking World,* 2nd ed. (Toronto U., 1961).

Mendelson, W., *Justices Black and Frankfurter: Conflict in the Court* (U. of Chicago, 1961).

Morgan, G. G., *Soviet Administrative Legality* (Stanford, 1962).

Peltason, J. W., *Federal Courts in the Political Process* (Doubleday, 1955).

Pound, R., *Justice According to Law* (Yale, 1951).

Rosenblum, V., *Law as a Political Instrument* (Doubleday, 1955).

Rostow, E. V., *The Sovereign Prerogative: The Supreme Court and the Quest for Law* (Yale, 1962).

Schubert, G. A., *Constitutional Politics* (Holt, Rinehart & Winston, 1960).

Seagle, W., *Men of Law. From Hammurabi to Holmes* (Macmillan, 1947).

Vyshinsky, A. Y., *Law of the Soviet State* (Macmillan, 1948).

Warren, C., *The Supreme Court in United States History,* rev. ed. (Little, Brown, 1937).

Wechsler, H., *Principles, Politics, and Fundamental Law* (Harvard, 1961).

XVI

The Civil Service

The threefold classification of governmental powers placed the civil service as a minor branch of the executive. This classification was worked out in a period when central governments had very few functions, and these were carried out or 'executed' by a relatively small number of officials working under close supervision of the Chief of State, or his immediate confidants and advisers. Until the end of the *laisser faire* period, those who expounded the classification were not concerned to improve the efficiency of the central government, but rather to devise effective checks on its action. Accordingly, it was rarely thought worth while to treat the civil service as a separate category or to study its distinctive organization.

Historical Background. Yet wherever a central government has established its sway over a wide territory and large population, there has always been a functioning civil service, by whatever derisive term it may have been called. History tells us much about the great ministers of state, the Cecils and the Richelieus, and the magnitude of their accomplishments. It tells us little about the instruments of their will, always a considerable body of officials. As the Norman and Angevin monarchs strengthened their grip on England, they developed an efficient civil service. Probably the actual order of events was in the reverse: as an effective civil service was developed, the monarchs improved their hold on the country. Certainly the first step was the Domesday Book of 1086, a census and a permanent record enabling William I to see the size and character of the kingdom he had won and to devise instruments of control. The compilation could not have been made without a body of devoted servants, who at the time were still a part of the king's household staff. In this body is to be found the germ of the British civil service, and historians are only now tracing its development through many vicissitudes, but with unbroken continuity, to the present day.

Importance of the Civil Service Today

Historians generally concentrate on those aspects of the past that are connected with the urgencies of the age in which they live. Today, the civil service and the tasks of public administration they perform are seen to occupy a position of central importance. We have noted an enormous expansion in the activities of government, and the voluminous detailed work this involves is performed by the civil service. When governments restrict immigration, impose a tariff on imports, or establish a postal service, it is civil servants in the garb of customs and immigration officials and postmen who do the work. When it is decreed that children's allowances or old-age pensions are to be paid by the government, it takes thousands of officials to make the investigations, keep the records, pay the claims, and supervise the service. We have already seen something of the range of civil service action involved in governmental regulation of various aspects of economic life. At every turn, officials are now expected to do many things which the community wants done quickly and well. The civil service has grown enormously, and it spends or distributes a large portion of the national income. Everyone has a vital interest in what it is doing and how it does it.

The decision by the legislature that the government should undertake a particular service is only the first step. The decision to fight a war will come to nothing unless an effective organization for the purpose can be put together. Some of the laws made nowadays are left entirely to the courts to apply, but most of them, on the analogy of war, require positive action by the government. In effect, the legislature declares war on poverty, ill-health, ignorance, and social injustice as internal enemies of the social order, and it commands mobilization of the civil service to promote health, education, and economic well-being.

Importance of Administration. Whether the specific measures agreed on are done well or ill, or at all, depends on administration, and administration is a difficult art at best. Public administration is greatly complicated in a democracy by the necessary insistence that officials should be kept under control and made responsible to the governed. As we have watched the development of government activities on a large scale, we have come to realize the vital importance of securing efficient organization of and action by the civil service, and at the same time of ensuring effective control of administration on behalf of the governed. It is not at all clear how these two objectives are to be won. This and the succeeding chapter will attempt an introduction to the problem by discussing the organization of the civil service and methods currently used for controlling it.

Size of the Civil Service. Before going on to these matters, it will be well to get some idea of the magnitudes involved. In 1840, Britain had a population of 18 millions, and the central government employed 17,000 civil servants. In 1963, the population had risen to 53 millions, and the civil service was 1.3 millions in number. In 1840, the population of the United States was 17 millions, and there were 23,000 civil servants in the employ of the federal government. By 1963, the population had risen to 185 millions, and the federal government employees numbered 2.5 millions. In 1840 France had a population of 36 millions, and there were already some 135,000 civil service employees. In 1963, France's population had increased to 46 millions, and the civil service rolls had swelled to 1.5 millions.[1]

The figures for the United States do not include the very substantial numbers in the state civil services. For this and several other reasons, such as the inclusion of all public school teachers in France—who are, in fact, employees of the central government—the figures for the three countries are not truly comparable, and they are given here only to show what massive enterprises these governments are. A breakdown of the totals to indicate what these thousands are busied in doing would be significant, but it would introduce complications that would take too much time to explain. As an instance, however, it may be said that in each country about a quarter of the total are post-office employees. A relatively few great government services of this kind account for the bulk of the civil servants.

SIZE OF ADMINISTERED EXPENDITURES. Another useful index to the magnitude and importance of the civil service is the proportion of the national income

---

[1] In 1963 the highest ratio of *all government employees* to citizens was present in New Zealand, which had one of the former for every 25 of the latter. This compared with one for 74 in the United States and one for 102 in Britain.

administered by or distributed through the civil service. In the United States, $90 billion passed through the hands of the federal government in 1963, or about 25 per cent of the estimated national income. In the same year, the British and French central governments handled approximately 35 and 30 per cent, respectively, of the estimated national income for that year. Here again the figures are not strictly comparable because the United States figures do not include the expenditures of state governments; this accounts in part for the lower percentage.

It should also be cautioned that no worth-while judgment about the wisdom of such expenditures can be made without careful attention to the objects on which the expenditure was made. The public gets a variety of services of great, perhaps inestimable, value in return, and only a small portion of the outlay goes to salaries and wages of civil servants. Also, a large proportion of each total consists of what are called 'transfers of income'—sums raised by taxation and distributed to the needy members of the population in the form of social services, such as unemployment aid, old-age pensions, and the like. Nevertheless, the civil service has to be relied on largely for seeing to it that government outlay of whatever kind gets the results aimed at, so there is a vital public interest in its efficiency.

New Dimensions of the Administrative. For these reasons, we must discuss the civil service almost as if it were a separate branch of government. To the legislature, judiciary, and executive we must add the administration, or administrative, as it is often called. Unlike the other three, however, it has no sphere of action in which it can count on going its own way. Formally, as was explained in Chapter XIII, it is under the direction of the executive, the cabinet or the President, and therefore is a part of the executive. In fact, it is now so vast, and its operations so extensive and complex, that neither the President nor the cabinet can give really close supervision and direction to its activities. Officials make every day a multitude of decisions that are not approved in advance by the responsible executive, and often cannot, in practice, be reversed by it. This has led some observers to say that the civil servants are the real governors of the country. One well-known comment on the French civil service is that France is not a democracy but a bureaucracy! This is the substance, such as it is, behind the cries of 'bureaucracy,' which, of course, means government by officialdom. Some attention will be given to this matter in the next chapter after the structure and characteristics of the civil service have been outlined.

STRUCTURE AND CHARACTERISTICS OF THE CIVIL SERVICE

HIERARCHICAL ORGANIZATION

Subject to minor qualifications, civil service organization is *hierarchical.* The old and familiar model to which it can be compared is military organization. At the base are the great mass of private soldiers whose duty is to obey, and at each succeeding higher level wider and wider powers of command are lodged until the commander in chief with over-all authority is reached. The civil service hierarchy can be most easily described by starting at the top and indicating descending levels of decreasing authority. At the apex stands the cabinet, the ministry, or the President; they control the civil service, but are not a part of it since their tenure is temporary and political. The service is divided into a number of departments, each headed by a member of the cabinet who is assisted by a permanent secretary (to use the British structure as an illustration). Each department is divided into a number of divisions headed by an assistant secretary, and each division into a number of sections headed by a principal. The administrative heads of the sections, divisions, and departments are assisted in their work of direction and control by a small number of secretaries and assistants known as the Cadet Corps of Assistant Principals. In the sections are the bulk of the civil servants carrying out the work of the government.

Physically, the civil servant may be located in the central departments in the capital or in one of the branch offices scattered through the country, or even in a foreign country. But wherever he is located, *he is firmly fixed somewhere in the hierarchy.* If he has subordinates, they are directly answerable to him; he in turn answers to his immediate superiors. At each level, a great many routine operations that can be performed without seeking the sanction of higher authority are carefully prescribed. Instructions, requests, or suggestions from the top are sent down the line of authority step by step, and complaints, information, and requests for instructions from the lower levels go up in the same way. One of the great sins against officialdom, just as it is in the military service, is to by-pass furtively an immediate superior in seeking the higher reaches of authority. There are sound reasons for the taboo on such action, but it is clearly one of the reasons for the ponderousness of the government machine when unprecedented situations arise.

Clear Lines of Authority and Responsibility. It is not quite inevitable that civil service organization should take this hierarchical form, but no other form has yet been discovered that fits the requirements of present-day democratic government. The civil servant exists to serve the community in the way in which the community wants to be served. It has already been argued that the only workable criterion of what the community wants is what the majority party insists on or is prepared to support. The only way of ensuring that the spirit of public policy will be made flesh among us, is to have a clear line of authority descending from the political heads of the government to the lowest civil servant. Otherwise, there is no way of galvanizing a civil servant into action at the command of the majority party. Also, it would be impossible for the public to enforce responsibility on the civil service for sins of omission or commission if a search had to be made in every case through the civil service for the particular individuals who acted or failed to act in a given situation. It can be done only if responsibility can invariably be thrown on a few identifiable persons at the top. This necessitates a line of responsibility from the lowest civil servant to the top. Command downward and responsibility upward is the essence of hierarchy. So is loyalty, flowing in *both* directions.

These considerations do not, of themselves, necessitate the interposition of several levels of authority between the mass of civil servants, who do the work, and the head of the department at the top. But other factors do make it necessary. Many of the operations of the civil service are performed at great distance from the capital—fully one-half of the French civil servants, for example, are engaged in local government—and it is physically impossible to consult the minister on every problem of decision that arises locally. More important, each department of government employs hundreds or thousands of civil servants, and it is just as impossible for the secretary at the head of the department to supervise personally the activities of each as it is for the general to command each regiment, company, and platoon in detail. There must be several ascending levels of authority, at each one of which certain problems of discipline and direction arising from below are drawn off and decided, so as to ensure that only the large and vital questions reach the desks of the busy secretary and his immediate aids. In short, much of the work of administration has to be decentralized if it is to be done with any efficiency.

Specialization of Function. Dividing the civil service into departments is partly for the purpose of decentralizing the bulk of decisions that have to be made in running any large organization. It is also for the sake of getting the advantages of specialization, which are vital for the success of any large organization. The clerks in a country general store are generally able to serve at any counter. But the great merchandising units of the large cities are department stores with at least a separate sales staff for each department. In the same way, governments find it necessary to set up separate departments to specialize in the regulation of transport, commerce, and labor matters, in supplying services to agriculture and to war veterans, in supervising public health, education, and so on. Yet these departments cannot be water-tight compartments. The department of education is always having to concern itself with questions of the health of children; the regulation of transport is always raising questions that affect labor and agriculture; and the supplying of services to agriculture bristles with problems of education.

The Problem of Co-ordination. No matter how the work is divided, the work of each department impinges on several other departments. The same is true of the division of work within the divisions and sections of each department. So a great part of the work of heads of sections, divisions, and departments is the co-ordination or integration of the several work units under their control. And perhaps the most vital part of the work of the executive, be he President or cabinet, is the co-ordinating of the work of the separate departments of the governments. The more the advantages of specialization are sought, the more pressing become the task of integration, the settling of disputes between departments, and ensuring that they do not frustrate one another by working at cross-purposes. The hierarchical organization gives the unity of ultimate command necessary for this purpose.

The same problem exists in corporate private enterprise where frequently the work of tens of thousands of employees has to be organized and directed. Although the problems of large-scale public and private enterprise are by no means identical, students of the vitally important art of management are reaching in the study of one kind of enterprise conclusions that can be applied to the other.

PROBLEMS OF SIZE. Unity of command alone does not ensure co-ordination. It is fair to contend that there is a strict limit to the number of departments a chief executive can co-ordinate. Some experts even place a number, such as ten, fifteen, or twenty, on it. The reason is that the number of inter-relationships increases with the number of departments by geometric progression and soon become too numerous for the mind to grasp. Therefore, the administrative answer to continually increasing activities of government is bigger departments with more levels of decentralization within each of them rather than more departments. Co-ordination can only be maintained by increasing the distance from the apex to the base, thus slowing action and decision still more. This implies that there may be a point at which colossal, highly centralized organization breaks down. Certainly present-day governmental organization makes very heavy demands on administrative skill and ingenuity.

One of the devices for co-ordination is to have one or more departments whose main functions are to control and co-ordinate certain aspects of internal management of all other departments. The chief of staff of an army is supported by a staff that is engaged in thinking and planning rather than in active field command. Government also has agencies for this purpose. The most obvious of these is the treasury, or department of finance. We have already seen how this department, through its control over departmental estimates and its power of audit of expenditures, maintains a powerful check on other departments. Sometimes, the treasury, as in Britain, has control over personnel also, thus becoming an efficiency expert for the chief executive and performing for him a great many of the tasks of co-ordination. Other aspects of departmental housekeeping may be similarly centralized.

Such devices make organization still more complex. They are an aid to efficiency and co-ordination only if the administrative skill necessary to operate them is available. For example, a staff agency for planning and co-ordinating the work of the various departments may be attached to the President or cabinet. Rivalry commonly develops between the civil service heads of departments and the staff agency about *who* is to have the ear of the executive in decisions affecting a particular department, and the department may find a major interest in sabotaging the proposals of the staff agency. Administration may be made worse rather than better by this refinement. For instance, there were numerous conflicts of this order between members of President Roosevelt's 'brain trust' and the 'personal staffs' of Presidents Eisenhower and Kennedy and the administrators in the departments.

THE LINKING OF POLITICS AND ADMINISTRATION

In Britain. It would merely be confusing to try to describe and contrast in a brief space the administrative structure of the three governments. It is necessary, however, to see at this stage how the political and administrative are linked together. In the course of this exposition, some concrete indications of the structure may be given. In Britain, the *cabinet* is the link. It is the agency of final co-ordination, and unity of command is ensured by the conventions of unanimity and collective responsibility. The British administration is divided into about thirty-five departments, each headed by a minister. Roughly half of these ministers are not of cabinet rank.

Directly under the minister is a senior civil servant who is the minister's deputy, performing for him most of the work of administering the department. He is appropriately called the permanent secretary of the department because his post, acquired by promotion within the civil service, gives him security of tenure. Many of the notable accomplishments of British administration are largely due to the teamwork of the amateur minister and his *parliamentary secretary* (described earlier)—who are, after all, politicians and not administrators—and the expert permanent civil servant in the direction of the department. It is through their collaboration that public policy as indicated by elections and party majorities is reconciled with what is administratively possible or inevitable.

ADMINISTRATIVE CLASS. The department is divided into divisions, and divisions are sub-divided into sections, each headed by *permanent* civil servants—assistant secretaries and principals, respectively. These and their secretaries and immediate assistants, and the permanent secretary and his assistants, form what is known in Britain as the *administrative class* of civil servants. They are occupied not in performing the services that their department provides for the public, but in administering the departments. They see to it that legislation and other political decisions that come down from above are turned into action. Whether or not the department is an effective working unit depends on the quality of the direction they give. They funnel up to the cabinet all those problems of administration that have political implications, whether they are internal problems of administration or concern the relation of the department to the public. These problems are not sent up in the raw form in which they arise. It is the function of the administrative class to collect all the available data that may bear on the decision in the direction of the department, to submit memoranda outlining the alternative courses open, and to explain in detail what the consequences of the alternative choices are likely to be.

The minister and the cabinet, who are always having to decide grave questions about people they have never seen and about situations they have never examined at first hand, rely on the administrative class to supply them with every fact and argument that may have a bearing on the decision, except, of course, political expediency, in which they themselves are the experts. This circulation up and down through the administrative class sets the tone and temper of the department, determining whether its performance will be mediocre or distinguished. When we come to consider the methods of recruiting civil servants, special attention will have to be given to the selection of the administrative class—a small, highly qualified, dedicated group.

In the United States. The President stands at the apex of authority and responsibility. The members of his cabinet are his subordinates for controlling the departments and keeping him in touch with administration. With the exception of the Postmaster General and the Attorney General, members of the cabinet carry the title of Secretary. Each is the political head of one of the ten executive departments. In addition, there are some forty-five other executive agencies outside the departments, which are neither under the supervision of any member of the cabinet nor under the direct control of the President. Most of these agencies have developed since the turn of the century as a direct consequence of the rapid growth of the activities of the federal government. For example, depression in the 1930's and war in the 1940's each brought a great expansion in the activities of the federal government and a new lash of these more or less independent executive agencies. Indeed, at the peak of World War II, they totaled almost a hundred. The dismantling of the war organization and executive reorganization have reduced them to their present number.

INDEPENDENT AGENCIES. The character of these executive agencies, the purposes for which they were created, their rise and fall, and their permutations and combinations are a distinct province of knowledge. Generally speaking, most of them have arisen as a result of the rapid expansion of activities of the federal government over the last seventy years. The Interstate Commerce Commission and the Federal Trade Commission, briefly noticed in Chapter V, now have a long history—close to eighty and fifty years, respectively—as agencies for regulating certain aspects of economic life. Others, such as the Securities and Exchange Commission and the National Labor Relations Board, were established for similar purposes in the economic confusion of the 1930's. Again others, like the now defunct Reconstruction Finance Corporation, and those now drawn together under the Federal Housing and Home Finance Agency, were creations of the depression period to provide services for certain groups in the community rather than to apply coercive regulation. Others of earlier creation are the

Bureau of the Budget and the Civil Service Commission, set up to assist in the internal housekeeping of the national administration. After World War II, the Atomic Energy Commission and the Economic Co-operation Administration were created to deal with urgent post-war problems affecting the security of the United States. These are merely illustrations to show the range and importance of independent agencies.

In the next chapter, attention will be drawn to some of the reasons which were thought to justify giving these agencies independent status outside the regular departments. Meanwhile, it should be noted that in recent years there has been much severe criticism, however varied, of the wisdom of maintaining this welter of independent executive agencies. Their conduct of administration often has been unsatisfactory. Their conceptions of their particular functions often have been out of harmony with the general policies the President as the responsible chief executive is trying to enforce. The President has not had the power to direct co-ordinating control of them, with the result a lack of consistency even to the point of cross-purposes in the administration as a whole. Moreover, even if he had such power as a matter of law, expert judgment is unanimous in saying that the co-ordination of the work of the ten departments and the many executive agencies would be an impossible burden on the President.

REORGANIZATION. Separate official investigating bodies, e.g. the President's Committee on Administrative Management in 1937, the two Hoover Commissions on Organization of the Executive Branch of Government in 1949 and 1955, and others repeatedly since, have recommended a sharp reduction in the number of independent agencies. In pursuance of some of these recommendations, several successive *Reorganization Acts* were passed by Congress after 1933, the most recent one in 1963, giving the President power to reduce, consolidate, and reorganize most, but not all, of the numerous executive agencies, subject to a variety of resolutions of disapproval by Congress. Considerable executive reorganization has already been accomplished under these Acts—70 per cent of the recommendations of the first Hoover Commission had been adopted by the end of 1957. Further reduction of the number of independent agencies may be hoped for, but it is not certain. Many of these agencies—the Interstate Commerce Commission, for example—have proved to be all but politically 'untouchable.'

DEPARTMENTAL STRUCTURE. To return to the internal structure of the ten regular departments, none of them has an official corresponding to the permanent secretary in Britain. There is no administrative chief of the department linking it as a whole to the political head. In almost all departments, there is an undersecretary, acting as a deputy for the secretary, and also several assistant secretaries, all political and temporary, almost certain to go when the secretary goes. Each department is divided and subdivided in a way difficult to describe because there are no standardized terms of description—despite repeated recommendations to that end by the Hoover Commissions. But each department is divided into bureaus, offices, or services —corresponding to the British division—and each of these is headed by a bureau chief, or director, under the surveillance of an assistant secretary. As a rule, each assistant secretary gives some over-all supervision to several bureaus or offices within the department.

The bureaus are divided into divisions—corresponding to the British sections—and headed by assistant bureau chiefs. In some departments, these divisions are still further divided into branches, and the branches into sections. Similar division and subdivision are found within the larger of the independent executive agencies. The bureau chiefs, assistant bureau chiefs, and their immediate assistants are the key administrators. With ever lessening exceptions, these are career civil servants who survive changes of government.

This structure as described does not provide adequately for departmental integration and, in recognition of this in recent years, the secretaries of the departments have been surrounding themselves with assistants who help them in planning and co-ordinating the work of the department, and one of whom often acts as its 'general manager,' with most of the duties, but not the acknowledged position, of the permanent secretary in British departments. Administrative-political collaboration goes on at the bureau level between the bureau chief and the assistant secretary, and also at the top between the secretary of the department and his acting 'general manager.'

In France. While the members of the Council of Ministers determine the over-all administrative policy and must assume the responsibility for it, the permanent civil servants—the *fonctionnaires*—constitute an integral and powerful component of French administration. Their strong position has always been largely attributable to their permanence in office. Prior to the days of the Fifth Republic, ministries came and went at an average of two per year, but the *fonctionnaires* continued their tasks unmoved by, if not oblivious to, the changes at the top of the political structure. Under de Gaulle, who drew the most important ministers from the ranks of the higher civil servants because he mistrusted 'politicians,' the *fonctionnaires* were provided not only with a stable, centralized executive authority but also with welcome direction and co-ordination. This has not, however, served to diminish their importance, and it still remains true that to a greater degree than in Britain, and to a *much* greater degree than in the United States, the French permanent civil servant influences and makes policy.

MINISTERIAL STRUCTURE. A minister, the political chief, heads each of the roughly twenty-five departments of the French executive branch. The departments are organized along strictly hierarchical lines. Each *minister* surrounds himself with a more or less personal *cabinet* of appointees and an *undersecretary,* who is either a political ally or a *civil administrator,* i.e. a member of the highest level of the French civil service on leave of absence. Each ministerial department is sub-divided into *services, bureaus,* and *sections,* each headed by chiefs and staffed by civil servants of definite classification and rank. The vast majority of these civil servants hold permanent appointments, based upon special schooling or competitive examinations, to be described subsequently.

CLOSE LINK TO PARLIAMENT. As already indicated, the instability of French cabinets of the past and the frequent interdepartmental shifting of ministers served to emphasize and perpetuate the power, prestige, and influence of the *fonctionnaires*—a situation which has not been changed by the stable Fifth Republic. Moreover, since French civil servants are not expected to embody the strict political neutrality of the British, or even the less pervasive neutrality of the American civil servants, a link may exist between many members of the French Parliament and the civil servants. Indeed, deputies may be civil servants 'on leave'—a permissible practice under French law even in the Fifth Republic—and subsequently return to their position in the executive branch! On the other hand, the drastic decline of legislative power under the de Gaulle Constitution has robbed parliamentary membership of much of its erstwhile attractiveness. But it remains true that more than any other democratic civil servant the French *fonctionnaire* bridges politics and administration.

COMMON FEATURES OF CIVIL SERVICES

With this brief glance at the hierarchical structure, and what it involves, it should be possible to understand some of the characteristics of a civil service, or, to use the terminology of contempt, a bureaucracy. The features to be considered appear in more or less exaggerated form in every large-scale organization where many persons work together to make a common product, or to achieve a common result, in which the contribution of each is not easily, if at all, distinguishable. They appear in large industrial and commercial corporations, and also in the bureaucracies of the dictatorships. Those selected for discussion are found in more marked degree perhaps in the civil services of democratic states than anywhere else.

That they are so found is mainly because of the fact that the civil service in a democracy works under very peculiar conditions. The control exercised over it from the top is both more lax and more severe than in other bureaucracies. Because of conflicting and unreconciled interests in the electorate, in the legislature, and in the political parties, direction of the civil service is often vacillating and lacking in vigor. Many groups think it better to let sleeping dogs lie and do not want to rouse the civil service into unwonted activity. There are always influences tending to let the civil service go slack. On the other hand, because the civil service deals so much with the private interests of groups and individuals whose rights must be respected to the letter, except in so far as legislation authorizes interference, there is very rigid control of the actions of the service from the top. There is more reliance on the bit and the tight rein than on the spur. The sphere in which the civil service is free to act imaginatively and to explore the way to new pinnacles of achievement is very small, although this is probably less true of the French civil service for reasons indicated above.

No Objective Test of Efficiency. One characteristic has important consequences in all directions. Government usually has an unchallenged monopoly of the activities it carries on. This is obvious in the case of the postal services, but no less true in most other things. Government is mainly occupied in doing the things that it has been decided, rightly or wrongly, we will not or cannot do effectively for ourselves, either individually or by voluntary co-operation. This is just as true of the regulation of business as it is of the provision of social security.

The existence of a monopoly means that there is no direct and automatic test of efficiency. Postal rates may be too high, but it cannot be proved by pointing to a competitor who provides the same service at lower rates. Those who are convinced they are being overcharged cannot bring the government to terms by transferring their account to a competitor. Government never has to face the hard choice of increasing the efficiency of its staff or going out of business because more efficient producers are underselling it on the market. As a result, government is sometimes viewed as an easy-going employer, satisfied with short hours, a modest pace of work, and easy discipline. Some civil servants may be dismissed for overt or covert political activity, or for certain other reasons, to be described presently, but rarely for slackness or incompetence. (Of course, the same may today be said for certain areas of private employment.)

In time of war, however, the relative calm of the civil service gives way to bustle and feverish activity. Those at the top drive harder because they have a goal that challenges all their powers. Conflicts of interest within the community are set aside while the one supreme aim is being pursued. Also many, if not all, civil servants find an incentive that is sometimes lacking in peace. Where the individual applies himself to a task he has set himself and masters it, there is a savor both to the challenge and the accomplishment. In any large organization, by contrast, it is extremely difficult for any one person in it to grasp the objectives at which the organization is aiming, or to see the relation of his duties to that objective. Moreover, we have seen that it is hard to get agreed definitions of the public interest, and civil servants are sometimes lukewarm about the goals at which they are expected to be aiming. Powerful incentives for the rank and file in a large organization are hard to find. Where the public interest can be objectified in the winning of a war, the difficulty is in part overcome. Democracies have not yet found how to give a comparable crystallization of the public interest in time of peace. This helps to explain the frequent criticism that the rank and file of the civil service is stolid, unimaginative, and lackadaisical. The rank and file lack a sense of mission.

Impersonal Character. Another feature of large organization is its impersonal character. The owner and operator of the country store comes into direct contact every day with his customers and employees. This is not true either of the manager of the department store or of the Postmaster General. When a service is on a mass-production basis, it must be conducted on the assembly-line principle, relying to a great extent on highly standardized and invariable procedures. In addition, those in control in central governments rarely see the persons or situations on which they may have to give final decisions. There are generally several levels of authority between those who make final decisions and those who carry them out.

So the private citizen cannot see those who finally decide unless he can invoke political influence, and the civil servants whom he can see, and with whom he has to deal, are obliged to treat him distantly and impersonally. They cannot respond to individual cases and appeals as their instinct or reason suggests. They are acting under precise orders or under rules that limit their authority. The relation of the civil servant to his immediate superiors is also impersonal, because they too are not free agents but must answer to those above them.

PAPER WORK. The best index to the impersonal quality of civil service relationships is the pervasiveness of paper work. The standardized procedures by which departments are run, the rules and regulations which are at once the guide and protection of all subordinates, are only the beginning of the written work. All significant decisions made and actions taken are recorded as permanent evidence of what has been done, and as a guide for the future. Much of the discussion within a department as to what can or ought to be done goes on paper. The complaints, suggestions, and requests for instructions made by subordinates are recorded. If their immediate superior thinks he cannot or should not deal with the issue raised, he records his views and sends the file on. Like a snowball, it picks up comments, suggestions, queries as it moves along.

Busy heads of departments have not time to go through all this information, and they may require an assistant to prepare a *précis* or a memorandum on it. At any stage, the responsible official to whose desk a matter has come may think more information is needed, and someone is detailed to collect it and to comment on what he finds—more material added to a growing file. In the same way, complaints from aggrieved members of the public or questions raised in the legislature set going the procession of files from one desk to another. Most of the administrators deal far more with papers than with persons or concrete situations. There is constant danger that they will identify reality with what they see, that they will regard this paper world as the real world and keeping their desks clean as the acme of accomplishment.

Impersonality and paper work are characteristic of large organization in general. Governments that are strictly responsible to the governed suffer from them in a marked degree. They are expected to act and act vigorously in many matters. It is also insisted that they should do what is right and shun injustice and wrongdoing. It is not easy to combine these virtues because such governments always act under limited authority. Beyond the margins of that authority, they come at once into collision with the vested rights and interests of individuals and groups.

Reliance on Rules and Precedents. Even where they have clear discretionary power, there is an insistent demand that they act justly. In the public mind, justice means, among other things, equality of treatment. There is not necessarily a great outcry when a merchant treats one customer differently from another. But if one recipient of unemployment relief or an old-age pension is treated differently from another, the government is likely to be called upon to justify it. A fierce light beats on constitutional governments as well as on thrones. Under the cabinet system, at any rate, political responsibility is concentrated on the political heads of the civil service, and they know that careless action may cost them dearly at the next election.

They therefore tend to limit very narrowly what can be done by their subordinates on their own discretion, and to insist that doubtful matters shall be referred to superiors for decision. They likewise tend to insist that where a discretionary power is to be exercised, the past practice should be consulted to see what has been done in similar cases, and that doubts about whether the past practice covers the present circumstances should also be referred to superiors. The civil servant at the lower levels of authority, however, who deals with living persons and concrete situations, is immersed in rules, precedents, and instructions. It requires great circumspection to obey them all, and his caution may make him almost immobile. It is not easy to see how else he can keep out of trouble with his superiors, or the political heads can know what is being done in their names in distant places. The civil servant who will not stay in the rut of routine lives dangerously. In the rut, there is safety and peace.

Red Tape. There is no need to search further for the explanation of 'red tape.' The term originally gained currency through the fact that the British government departments tied up their files with a red binding tape. It is now used as a compendious description of the way these files are built up. To the citizen, red tape means the perverse insistence on the letter of rules and regulations, the completion of inquisitive forms and seemingly irrelevant questionnaires, the non-committal and evasive letters of civil servants relying on the security of their routine, the 'passing of the buck' to superiors and to other bureaus and other departments. It is infuriating to all who suffer delay or denial in their urgent affairs. In its more extreme forms, it is due to faulty or inefficient organization, or to the stupidity or unnecessary timidity of officials, and therefore can be cured.

But for much of the red tape there is good and sufficient reason not apparent on the surface. It is the necessary concomitant of large organization and constitutional government. Large organization demands departmentalized division of labor, standardized procedures, and routine. Constitutional government demands hierarchical structure with its concentration of authority and responsibility, and extreme caution in exploring the boundary between public duty and private right.

Classification of Personnel. Another common feature of large organization is standardized procedures for dealing with personnel. This is really an aspect of the impersonality already noted, but it deserves separate comment. Effective financial control requires standardization. Financial control has to be worked through a budget of expenditures prepared in advance and adhered to in execution. Budgeting is not possible if each head of a department is free to make what bargains he likes with his subordinates about pay. The only way to prevent this and to stick to a budget is to *classify* all the positions in the department and assign a fixed rate of pay for each class.

There is another imperative reason for classification. It has already been pointed out that, in a large organization, there is no indisputable criterion of what the services of particular persons are worth. So the employee who works in a niche, unseen by the heads of the department, has no effective way of bringing his worth forcibly to the attention of his superiors, and no assurance that favoritism among his superiors will not prefer the less deserving in matters of pay and promotion. While he cannot be assured of exact justice, he can be protected against the grosser kinds of injustice, and his morale consequently strengthened, by a classification of the positions in the entire service to the end that there should be no discrimination between employees in the same class—that there should be equal pay for equal work.

There is, of course, plenty of heartache in any classification that seeks to reduce tens of thousands of positions to a relatively small number of categories, because few positions can be exactly equated. Some measure of rough justice can be had by careful allotting of similar jobs to one class, assigning to each class a scale of pay and increases, and fixing the terms of promotion, transfer, vacation, and retirement allowances, if any. Some measure of equity in these matters is a necessity. Most civil servants get little chance for self-expression and little of the satisfaction of personal achievement in their work. The most concrete of the substitutes open to them are pay increases, promotions, and other perquisites. Their concern with equity on such points may become an obsession and have a most serious effect on the *esprit de corps* of the organization.[2] The proof of these assertions is to

[2] The discussion above of common features of civil services relies heavily on Herman Finer, *The Theory and Practice of Modern Government*, rev. ed. (New York: Holt, 1949), ch. xxvii.

be found in the importance now attached by large enterprises, whether public or private, to the growing art of personnel management.

CLASSIFICATION, TENURE, AND RECRUITMENNT OF THE CIVIL SERVICE

Classification of a civil service is important for still another reason. It is a prerequisite to recruiting the civil service by any other method than political patronage and spoils, a condition of selecting the man for the job instead of the job for the man. If posts are to be filled by merit rather than by political preferment, it is necessary to know what kind of merit is required. Positions must be classified according to the general nature of the work done, and to the qualifications necessary for doing it, so as to arrive at methods of testing the fitness of applicants. This brings up one of the large issues of democratic government, the method of recruiting the civil service. We have seen that large organization, and particularly a civil service, has a number of peculiar characteristics. All these create serious problems of securing and maintaining efficiency. The first step in meeting these problems is to secure a high quality of the personnel. There are also important principles of organization and administration to be observed, but these cannot make the service better than the personnel of which it is composed.

Fivefold Classification. Before turning to methods of recruitment in Britain, the United States, and France, something should be said generally about classifications. In each country, there are hundreds of classes of positions and the plans on which they are based vary considerably. Yet from the point of view of the kind of work performed rather than of the precise range of duties in each case, a civil service can be divided into *five quite distinct grades or classes.* It is useful for preliminary appreciation of the make-up of a civil service to set them out:

1. *Administrative*—the work of general management such as organizing, directing, planning, and co-ordinating.
2. *Professional*—the class of experts such as doctors, lawyers, economists, entomologists, engineers, and a whole range of scientists concerned with public health, fisheries, forestry, agriculture, and the like.
3. *Clerical*—all the office workers who, working under supervision, are engaged in the voluminous paper work of the government, including

the immediate supervisors concerned with the detail of office manment.

4. *Skilled industrial workers*—engaged in maintenance, printing, and government enterprises such as the mint and the arsenals.

5. *Unskilled workers*—employed on various tasks at roughly the level of skill of day labor.

There are a number of civil servants whom it would be difficult to fit into any of these classes, but they are only a small fraction of the total.

Defects of Recruitment by Party Patronage. In 1850, when *laisser faire* was at its peak, civil services were the playthings of politics. With the exception of Prussia, which had had for a long time a career service recruited by merit and enjoying security of tenure, those who controlled the governments in most Western countries disposed of civil servants and their posts as they saw fit. Democracy inherited rather than invented political patronage. The favorites of monarchs and ruling cliques were succeeded in government posts by the favorites of politicians. Although the United States for a time rivaled the excesses of the older regimes, the significant fact is that civil service reform almost everywhere has been carried through under democratic auspices. The zeal of reformers has found enough support in public opinion to make steady advances in the methods of recruiting for the public service.

At the same time, the changing role of government has played an important part. As long as central governments did little but maintain internal order and security from foreign aggression, there was no urgent need for a highly efficient civil service. When governments undertook to regulate many aspects of social and economic life, and to provide a wide variety of essential services, the tasks to be performed became too complex and too important to be left in the hands of a civil service haphazardly recruited by patronage. In 1855, when civil service reform began in Britain, it had already been recognized that the central government had to do something about the social confusion caused by the Industrial Revolution. The first legislation in the United States came as a result of the assassination of President Garfield by a disappointed office-seeker in 1881, when Congress, urged on by President Arthur, passed the Pendleton Act of 1883. It established a Civil Service Commission of three members and provided for open competitive examinations, forbidding discrimination for political reasons.

Extensions of the merit system have, on the whole, kept pace with the expansion of activities of government. Government's role of regulator and dispenser of services began later, and for a considerable time developed more slowly in the United States and France than in Britain. Broadly speaking then, civil service reform has followed closely the growing importance of government in the everyday life of the community. In France, on the other hand, no comprehensive civil service law was passed until 1945-46. However, reform-movements had begun to take place as long ago as the days of Napoleon Bonaparte, and many series of orders and decrees, handed down by cabinets and individual ministers, helped to bring about an early, though piecemeal, merit system.

As long as the spoils of office went to the victor in the last election, it was difficult to attract competent persons to temporary insecure service with the government. Even if able men did come to it by chance, a reversal of party fortunes in a few years often put them out just as they were mastering their jobs. *Esprit de corps,* the indispensable condition of efficiency in a large organization, could not be had in these circumstances. Moreover, party politicians had not the necessary techniques, even if they had had the will to select the many kinds of expert and highly specialized talent that governmental activities now require. Without some recognition of the merit principle, governments could not do the things they do today. This consideration brings us to the important matter of the civil servant's tenure of office.

Tenure of Office. Without security of tenure, the merit system of appointment would mean practically nothing. Consequently, while dismissal is possible, of course, for certain specified reasons, such as malfeasance in office, serious misconduct or unauthorized political activity—although, as we shall presently see, the latter category does not entirely apply to France— the merit-appointed civil servant enjoys what is, in effect, life tenure. Government administrators frequently feel hampered and frustrated because of the barriers to dismissal, but they must face the fact that secure tenure is one of the more attractive compensations of government employment. Actually, there are several ways and means of bringing pressure to bear on an 'undesirable' employee—for example, transferring him to another position. But the requirements, in all three countries, that the employee be supplied with some sort of a written notice of charges and given an opportunity for a hearing before some kind of review board or commission, serve as effective checks against wrongful suspension or dismissal.

LOYALTY AND SECURITY. About 1940, however, a new and vexatious issue arose in the realm of dismissal of civil servants, namely what to do about government employees who were allegedly 'disloyal' or 'security risks.' Rightly or wrongly, the problem has been of particular concern to the United States, where it reached a peak in the years following World War II. The French initially viewed the matter as merely a passing phase, exaggerated out of all proportion by the Americans for domestic political reasons; consequently, they generally chose to ignore it more or less until the days of the Algerian crisis during the de Gaulle regime, when widespread attempts at subversion, chiefly led by adherents to the armed forces, also brushed members of the civil service. The British, with considerable distaste, began to show concern as a result of the revelations of defections to the Soviet Union, early in the 1950's, by some highly placed civil servants heretofore thought thoroughly loyal. A security program was then instituted, but it is one heavily weighted on the side of protecting the individual, and it has been carried out with great circumspection and without any fanfare or publicity.

Even before the entry of the United States into World War II, a series of statutes and executive decrees called for the exclusion of Communists, Nazis, and Fascists from government employment. Until approximately 1947, this took chiefly the form of 'security checks' by the Federal Bureau of Investigation of prospective civil servants. Anyone whose 'loyalty' was deemed to be open to a 'reasonable doubt' by the personnel officer of the hiring agency was removed from the list of eligibles. Moreover, from 1942 on the heads of certain 'sensitive' executive departments and agencies were authorized to dismiss summarily any employee whose dismissal was deemed by the former to be 'warranted by the demands of national security.'

Early in 1947, the intensification of the 'cold war,' a growing congressional pre-occupation with the whole issue of 'loyalty,' and an increasing national concern about internal security—based partly upon several well-publicized instances of past or present pro-Communist activities by some government employees—combined to cause President Truman to issue a 'loyalty order.' This order, which culminated in an intensive loyalty investigation of *all* government employees, provided for the removal from employment of, and the refusal of employment to, a particular person if 'on all the evidence, *reasonable grounds* exist for belief that the person involved is disloyal.' This terminology was made more rigid in 1951 by changing 'reasonable grounds' to *reasonable doubt*.[3] It was rendered still more rigid by an executive order

[3] Seth Richardson, then Chairman of the Loyalty Review Board (established under the security program), commented that the purpose of this change in the standard was to *lessen* the degree of proof; it is easier to justify a doubt than to support a positive finding. ('The Federal Employee Loyalty Program,' *Columbia Law Review*, 51, May 1951, 555.)

by President Eisenhower in 1953 which established as the test of acceptability or retention the concept that a person's employment by government 'shall be clearly consistent with the interests of national security.' And Congress gave statutory authority to the heads of certain 'sensitive' agencies—e.g. the State and Defense Departments, the Atomic Energy Commission—to dismiss summarily any employee as a 'poor security risk.' [4]

THE DILEMMA. The loyalty-security program has been steeped in almost constant controversy. On the one hand, the government assuredly has a right and a duty to ascertain the loyalty of its employees, and the Supreme Court has held repeatedly that government employment is a *privilege* and not a *right*.[5] On the other hand, some of the procedures to which the government resorted in the administration of the program have been widely condemned —such as the denial of the right to confront adverse witnesses or to be told their identity and the acceptance of the idea of 'guilt by association,' based either on a list of private organizations viewed as subversive by the Attorney General, or on personal associations with 'suspect' persons (even if these were close relatives, as parent or spouse).

In one important test, the *Bailey* case,[6] in which both horns of the dilemma were in evidence, the procedures of the federal loyalty-security program were upheld by an equally divided (4:4) United States Supreme Court. The four justices who voted to side with the ruling of the—also divided—lower court, which upheld the program, did so on the basis of that tribunal's judgment that the President, lacking congressional restrictions, may remove from government service any person of whose loyalty he is not completely convinced. But on another occasion, Justices Black and Douglas, speaking as two of the four dissenters in *Bailey,* and expressly referring to it, voiced the concern of those who are deeply disturbed by some of the characteristics of the program. The jurists warned that 'the entire loyalty program grossly deprives government employees of the benefits of constitutional safeguards' (Black), and that it is 'a subversive influence of our own design that destroys us from within' (Douglas).[7] Although it has never met the *constitutional* issue of the programs, the Court, as of 1956, employing statutory interpretations as its weapon, began to make clear to the executive branch

---

[4] Of some 5 million federal employees investigated by 1963, some 5,000 (or 0.1 per cent) either left the service voluntarily or were dismissed on loyalty-security grounds, the latter accounting for roughly one-tenth of the total. (These figures do not include those adjudged 'poor risks' for other reasons.)

[5] See *United Public Workers* v. *Mitchell,* 330 U.S. 75 (1947), for example.

[6] *Bailey* v. *Richardson,* 341 U.S. 918 (1951).

[7] *Joint Anti-Fascist Refugee Committee* v. *McGrath,* 341 U.S. 123 (1951).

that it was expected to proceed strictly within the limits of the law. Thus it ruled 6:3 that, by the language inserted into a 1950 statute, Congress had intended to limit the program to *sensitive* positions.[8] In 1955 it held 7:2 that in the dismissal of a Dr. John Peters, the Loyalty Review Board had exceeded its statutory authority.[9] In 1957 the Court held 8:1 that former Secretary of State Acheson had violated the regulations of his own department and wrongfully discharged an employee as a security risk.[10] And in 1959, continuing its increasingly firm insistence upon proper procedural safeguards, the Supreme Court ruled that if a department endeavored to dismiss an employee under its loyalty-security program, it must live up to its rules, even if the employee is not under the civil service laws.[11]

A special twelve-member Commission on Government Security appointed jointly by President Eisenhower and Congress in 1955 was asked to investigate the entire security program. It submitted its report in 1957 and recommended a long-range, thorough overhauling. It reported that its study had shown the loyalty-security programs in force for government employees to be a 'hodge-podge, sorely trying public confidence, and causing fear and unrest in Government ranks.'[12] The 800-page report urged prompt action, but to date (Autumn 1963) Congress has not been disposed to enact remedial legislation—although several government agencies have quietly modified their procedures in order to meet the standards prescribed by the Supreme Court's decisions.

RECRUITMENT IN BRITAIN

The scope and methods of appointment by merit may now be considered. In Britain, the *entire* civil service has been withdrawn from political patronage. Appointments are under the control of the Civil Service Commission, a board of three members, experienced public servants usually, who are appointed by the Crown but enjoy substantial independence. The chief functions of the Commission are to determine qualifications for entrance and to test applicants for the possession of these qualities. (Questions of pay, promotion, discipline, and working conditions are the province of the Treasury.) Once certified by the Commission, candidates at the top of the list are appointed as positions open up.

---

[8] *Cole* v. *Young*, 351 U.S. 356 (1956).
[9] *Peters* v. *Hobby*, 349 U.S. 341 (1955).
[10] *Service* v. *Dulles*, 354 U.S. 363 (1957).
[11] *Vitarelli* v. *Seaton*, 359 U.S. 535 (1959).
[12] Summary of Recommendation of the Commission on Government Security, as reported in *The New York Times*, June 23, 1957.

Competitive Examinations. Generally speaking, the tests are made by open competitive examination. The largest exceptions to this rule are the skilled and unskilled handworkers, who are recruited through the employment exchanges and certified by interview only. No satisfactory examination has been found to test a janitor's handiness with a coal scuttle, and even manual skills do not lend themselves easily to testing. Professional and scientific workers are chosen by competitive interview from among those who are already members of the professions or holders of scientific degrees. The clerical group are chosen by open competitive examinations of great variety combined with interviews. The examinations for this group are partly tests of special aptitude and partly tests of general knowledge and intelligence, with the emphasis strongly on the latter. The administrative class are chosen by *competitive written general examinations,* usually covering eight academic subjects including social sciences, humanities and natural sciences, but also extending to some technical ones. Since the adoption of certain testing revisions in 1947–57, increasing importance—some contend the main emphasis—is now placed on oral interviews, consisting of a battery of sharply challenging individual and group interviews. No attempt is made to test their aptitude for or knowledge about the particular duties to which they will be assigned. It is sought rather to discover those who have the imagination and intellect, the industry and self-discipline necessary to master a number of fields of academic study.

PROMOTIONS. It must not be thought that all posts are filled by appointment from the outside as they fall vacant. Indeed, almost all the recruiting from the outside in the administrative and clerical classes is from the sixteen to twenty-four years of age group for posts at the bottom of the particular class for which they are chosen. Almost all the higher posts are filled by promotion. In some instances, promotion is made to depend on the results of a competitive examination among a selected group of candidates, and opportunities for promotion within any one grade or class are closely related to the type of examination given. One that tests special aptitude for a particular task may give no clue at all to capacity to rise. On the other hand, examinations that test general knowledge and intelligence are likely to discover a civil servant who will quickly learn to master a routine instead of letting the routine master him. He is likely to be able to deal with novel situations and therefore to be worthy of promotion. This kind of ability is of great importance for those in the higher clerical positions, sometimes called the executive class, who have to do with office management and supervision.

The Administrative Class. General intelligence and adaptability are most needed, however, in the administrative class of roughly 3200 men and 300 women. We have already seen that this class occupies the key positions in governmental administration. There is a most intimate relationship between the capacities of this group and the effective execution of laws passed by the legislature. It largely depends on them whether the lessons to be learned in administration of particular laws are brought to the attention of the political heads of the government as material for deciding on changes and amendments. They are concerned with policy as well as administration, and consequently need breadth of mind and interests as well as mastery of routine. These considerations led in Britain to the adoption of the *highly academic written and oral examinations* already described. Experience has more than justified the decision. The most serious criticism made of the method of recruiting the administrative class is that for practical purposes the nature of the qualifying examinations—with their stress on broad cultural training in the liberal arts—almost limits membership of the administrative class to top graduates of Oxford and Cambridge.

It is not so much that the examinations are so difficult, as they are more or less based on the course of studies followed and the life in the ancient universities. So the key group in the civil service is almost exclusively drawn from the upper middle-class, who alone in the past have enjoyed any considerable access to these educational advantages. The Labour party in Britain regards this situation as a criticism of the class structure and the educational system rather than of the method of choosing the administrative class. Therefore, in addition to supporting a widening of the basis of recruitment, they are trying in a variety of ways to widen the avenues to higher education, so that more and more able sons of the working class can go to the universities and thus become eligible for appointment to the administrative class.

RECRUITMENT IN THE UNITED STATES

The federal Civil Service Commission in the United States is a board of three members appointed by and responsible to the President, subject to confirmation by the Senate but carrying on its work relatively free of political interference and control. Its chairman serves as chief administrative officer. Its main work is to examine and certify candidates for entrance to the federal civil service. The Commission has broader functions than its British counterpart. It is charged with working out the details of classifications of positions within a general plan adopted by Congress; participates in the establishing and working of schemes for rating the efficiency of civil servants; and has power to investigate the fairness of disciplinary measures such as suspension, dismissal, and demotion. Thus it has a partial responsibility for personnel management within the service.

Merit and Spoils. On the other hand, the scope of its control of appointments is *not as wide* as that of the British Commission, for it rests with Congress to say what posts shall be filled by competitive tests or other scrutiny of qualifications made by the Commission. In 1963 there were still 200,000 permanent posts in the service not yet under the merit system.[13] Even within the *classified service,* i.e. positions to be filled by merit, numerous exceptions are specified by Congress or by presidential orders, based upon statutory authority. Under such authority, for example, President Eisenhower was able to 'declassify' some fifteen hundred top-ranking civil service jobs between 1954 and 1957, thereby enabling their replacement with patronage appointments. The positions in question were viewed as being of a 'confidential or policy-determining nature.' The practice of making and continuing temporary appointments, sometimes for years, also makes holes in the merit system even within the classified service. It is to be noted, too, that none of the higher administrative officials whose appointments must be confirmed by the Senate comes within the jurisdiction of the Commission. These are still a substantial group, and include a goodly number of the extremely important bureau chiefs already referred to. Much room for patronage appointments still remains, and these are generally used according to the exigencies of party politics. There is still considerable support in the United States for the argument that government jobs are a form of reward. An illustration of this contention is the so-called Veterans Preference Act, whereby five points are automatically added to the examination scores of all ex-service men. Disabled veterans, their wives, and widows are accorded even more favorable treatment when applying for a government job. While special job consideration for war veterans is not peculiar to the United States, it is nowhere as extreme and costly.

Examinations. Within the classified or merit service, appointments are almost all made on the basis of competitive tests, which may or may not consist of written examinations. Generally speaking, written tests are used to test applicants for the more subordinate positions requiring clerical, man-

[13] Among these were attorneys, chaplains, intelligence specialists, policy-determining positions, part-time 'professional experts,' and 'key positions which involve close personal relationships between incumbents and the head of agency or his key officials.'

ual, or other operative skill to be applied under the close direction of superiors. Applicants for posts requiring professional or scientific knowledge and attainments are usually rated by interview, and by evidence of their knowledge and experience derived from sources other than a formal written examination.

GREATER SPECIALIZATION. The types of examinations given differ—although not as markedly as formerly—from those used in Britain. The civil service examinations in Britain are accommodated to the educational system, and try to draw some of the best products of the system into the civil service at an early age with little regard for specialized skills. In the United States, most examinations have always been drafted with an eye to the posts to be filled, and are therefore *framed to test technical competence*. Also, they are open to older age groups than in Britain. There is a much greater variety of examinations, and while they provide a good test of capacity for a particular job, they do not as a rule test capacity for other work to which the civil servant may be promoted.

Selection of Key Administrators. Unlike Britain, the United States has not adopted an academic examination on a wide variety of subjects for selecting general administrative capacity, with the welcome exception of the Federal Service Entrance Examination. This examination, which is *general* in scope, is now administered annually to prospective college graduates, and has become a fertile source for recruitment. But the Civil Service Commission does not recognize a distinct administrative class. Probably this is in part due to an equalitarian philosophy which dislikes fencing off higher posts as a preserve for those who have enjoyed superior educational advantages. It is partly owing to the fact that quite a few of the higher posts are subject to senatorial confirmation and so remain actively political. There is, of necessity, an administrative class, but its ranks are filled either by promotion from other classes in the service or, more rarely, by appointments from outside the service.

The undersecretaries and assistant secretaries are political appointments and change when a new President comes into office, if not before. They, and the bureau chiefs and assistant bureau chiefs, are the key administrators. As already noted, a substantial number of the bureau chiefs are still in the *unclassified service* and open, as far as the law goes, to political pressure and appointment. However, there is a growing practice to fill these posts by promotion, even when they are unclassified, and to give the holders of them security of tenure. That is to say, higher administrative work, at least in part, is becoming a career in the United States just as it is in Britain. Nothing more clearly reveals the changing attitudes towards the civil service arising from the necessities of present-day government. The efficient conduct of public administration is now so important to the community, and makes such demands on skill and knowledge, that it cannot be left to amateur partisans who come and go. It is being recognized that the men who run a department must not only understand it but must also feel themselves to be a part of it. It is not easy otherwise to account for the self-restraint of politicians in the face of plums of such size and succulence.

Expansion of Career Service? It is believed by many in the United States that this tendency must go further, and that all high administrative posts in a department below the rank of assistant secretary must be brought into a career service. Also, it is urged that special attention be paid to the recruiting of an administrative class. It is not enough that posts should be filled by promotion. It is necessary to ensure that there shall be in the service a sufficient number of able men with administrative talent who will look forward to, and deserve, promotion to the highest posts. As matters now stand, most of those who are promoted to be chiefs of bureaus were originally brought into the service as specialists of one kind or another and not as administrators. What is true of them is true also of their immediate assistants and of heads of the divisions into which each bureau is divided. No one would think of recruiting bomber pilots solely by promotion of ground crew who proved themselves handy. In its own way, a government department is just as sensitive an engine with just as close a relation between skillful handling and distinguished performance. On these grounds, it is argued that the British method of recruiting the administrative class should be adopted. In evaluating the over-all problem, Professor Max Beloff, a long-time British observer of the American scene, was moved to comment: 'The *damnosa hereditas* of Jacksonian democracy, the view that one man is as good as another, that any literate citizen can do almost any job, and that a Democracy can do without an administrative (and military) élite must be eliminated once and for all.' [14]

Expert opinion in the United States, however, is not of one mind on the point. For example, it is contended that in Britain there is scant possibility of promotion from the clerical class into the administrative class, and therefore administrative work has so far been very largely a career for the talents of those lucky enough to be well-born and well-educated. An unstratified

[14] *The American Federal Government* (New York: Oxford University Press, 1959), p. 204.

society cannot make such a discrimination but must keep clear the road from the bottom to the top. The office boy who becomes chief of a bureau will bring with him an experience that is a surer guide in departmental matters than the knowledge British administrators get from books and memoranda. Whether or not this contention is sound, it is clear that the contrast between Britain and the United States on this point goes beneath the surface and is founded on still deeply rooted marked differences in social outlook and social conditions. There are signs, however, that some of these differences have begun to lessen.

HOOVER COMMISSION RECOMMENDATIONS. In its 1955 Report, the Second Hoover Commission, expressing deep concern with the civil service, declared the 'greatest weakness in government today' was the need for improved expert management, ranging downward from the political appointees and career administrators. It recommended the creation of a 'senior civil service group,' of non-partisan, well-paid administrators of exceptional skill and experience (i.e. an administrative class) whose competence and integrity had been demonstrated in government service.

It also called for more politically appointed executives to take over much of the partisan work, concern for which has threatened the usefulness of many career executives who had become embroiled in political battles. The report of the Commission further urged higher pay for top managers, better training programs, and greater use of merit pay increases. This, it said, would attract more able men and women to government service, and stem the costly employee turnover which has averaged 25 per cent annually for the past twenty years. Responding to the Commission's call for a career service, and in the absence of any action by Congress, President Eisenhower, by Executive Order, established machinery for 'A Career Executive Service' in 1957. But the Presidential board of five members, established under it to administer the service, never properly functioned, Congress refused to support it, and the program has remained a paper tiger.

The question of how to organize and co-ordinate the work of hundreds of thousands of civil servants is of immense importance, especially in the United States, because of the headlong growth of the federal administration in the present century, and particularly in the last three decades. As we have already seen in connection with the Executive Office of the President, for instance, a considerable overhauling has been under way for the past few years, largely as a result of the searching inquiries by the Committee on Administrative Management and the two Hoover Commissions on Organization of the Executive Branch of the Government. Much remains to be done, however, in order to bring about more effective administrative organization of the federal government—not to mention the state governments—of which the civil service is but one vital arm. The general matter of administration will be given consideration in the succeeding chapter.

RECRUITMENT IN FRANCE

In view of the extreme centralization of the French system of government, and the frequent change of ministries prior to the de Gaulle Fifth Republic, the French civil service—especially the *fonctionnaires,* the permanent civil servants—has long commanded considerably more power in government than those of Britain and the United States. But France lagged far behind the latter two countries in establishing a uniform, national civil service system. It was not until 1945–46 that the Civil Service Directorate (*Direction de la Fonction Politique*) was established in the General Secretariat of the Premier. The Directorate is a central personnel office charged with the unification and classification of the merit system, which heretofore had been scattered over more than 125 different statutes covering recruitment and classification in the various ministries. While the French civil service never suffered from the extremes of the 'spoils system' that was prevalent for so long in the United States, personal patronage by and on behalf of the ministers and members of Parliament was very common. The statutes finally adopted in 1945–46, however, have combined to bring about many commendable reforms. Today, while not entirely free from patronage and favoritism, the French civil service is largely based upon a unified, classified merit system. The department heads may still select their subordinates, but these must have previously met the entrance requirements of the service and have been classified by the *Direction* according to their ability.

Classification. France has the simplest classification system in Europe. A civil servant is in class A, B, C, or D in accordance with his academic ability and his vocational training. In class A are the *civil administrators,* who are practically identical with the British administrative class. Responsible for top-echelon policy decisions in the highest ranks of the civil service—e.g. the *grand corps* of the diplomatic service, the Council of State, the Court of Accounts, and the Inspectorate of Finance (all described elsewhere in these pages)—they are recruited through the *École Nationale d'Administration,* the National School of Administration, to be described below.

At the next highest level, class B, are the *secretaries of administration,* the office managers, accountants, and translators, who are 'in charge of the execution of current operations' and, according to the law of 1945, 'execute certain specialized functions which require sound administrative knowledge and experience.' Into class C fall the clerks and typists, and into class D the skilled and unskilled workers. (Only class A requires a degree from a school of higher learning.)

Selection and Examinations. The new French civil service system adopted the British emphasis on examinations, testing broad educational ability rather than the American emphasis on specialized, practical experience. The secretaries of administration and the lower classes are thus generally recruited by competitive examinations, geared to various levels of secondary education, although in most cases of older persons a certain number of years of public service may be substituted for formal schooling. But the members of the small, powerful class of civil administrators are now all recruited through the National School of Administration (E.N.A.).

THE ÉCOLE NATIONALE D'ADMINISTRATION. Established in 1945, this unique institution graduates from eighty to ninety civil administrators annually, all of whom are guaranteed high positions in the ministries and other top-level executive agencies. There are at most 140 openings for admissions to the school annually, and as many as 1500 applications for these are usually received. To be eligible, applicants must either have had five years of experience in the public service, usually in class B, *or* they must have been graduated from the Institutes of Political and Social Sciences of the several universities. The total number of vacancies is equally divided between the two groups. To be admitted, they must pass stiff competitive examinations geared to their previous public service field or to their academic background. These oral and written examinations test not only areas of general knowledge of the fields the administrators might enter, but also their ability to make 'command decisions.' The course at the school lasts three years, and it embraces concentrated academic studies in one of four fields—General Administration, Economic and Financial Administration, Social Administration, External Affairs—as well as a considerable amount of practical on-the-job training in public agencies in Paris and in the provinces. The courses are taught by leading social scientists and public servants. Neither Britain nor the United States has a civil service training institution akin to the valuable and interesting French *École Nationale d'Administration.*

Prerogatives. The statute of 1946 also provided for a comprehensive series of rules and regulations for all civil servants, i.e. the *fonctionnaires*. Differences between various departments and agencies, and provisions for exceptions to rules, are subject to approval of a 'watch-dog committee,' the statutorily established Superior Council of the Civil Service. Civil servants have the right to appeal any disciplinary action or policy to this body. With few exceptions, civil servants are not permitted to have other remunerative jobs simultaneously, and they are forbidden to be members of organizations that might compromise their 'independence.'

The *fonctionnaires* may belong to civil service unions—but not to others—and many, although not all, are permitted to strike. While their union membership is permitted in Britain and the United States, strikes by government employees are forbidden in the latter and considered an unacceptable practice in the former. Contrary to the British and American prohibition on political activity, French civil servants are not only permitted to run for partisan political office while holding their jobs but, as noted earlier, they may also obtain a 'leave of absence' from their civil service position if they gain an elective or appointive office. Promotions are based on merit and seniority. Salary scales compare unfavorably with the other two countries, but allowances and other benefits are very liberal, and all classes or grades enjoy a comfortable degree of protection against unwarranted dismissal or suspension.

The French civil servants today possess legally stipulated privileges that exceed both in kind and extent those of their British and American colleagues. But their responsibilities are greater, too: not infrequently they have the burden of steering a foundering ship of state through stormy water. They must be professionals in every sense of the word.

Conclusion. We come back to the principal emphasis of the chapter—the problem of over-all governmental management. Without defending every enterprise in which present-day governments engage, it is clear that a host of their complex interrelated activities are vital to the stability and well-being of the society. These activities must be planned intelligently, skillfully coordinated, and effectively executed. To ensure this, the civil service itself must be made a highly efficient machine. As the discussion in this chapter shows, considerably more attention has been paid in recent years to invigorating the administration than to improving the performance of either the legislature or the judiciary.

The executive branch of government, occupying, as it does, a strategic position, will, with the backing of a superior civil service, strengthen itself still further vis-à-vis the other organs of government and the electorate. Without unduly hampering the administration in its efforts to perform its vital functions quickly, surely, and well, how are we to ensure that it does not oppress the governed? An introduction to this burning issue will now be essayed.

Suggested References for Further Reading

Appleby, P. H., *Big Democracy* (Knopf, 1945).

Ashton-Gwatkin, F. T. A., *The British Foreign Service* (Syracuse, 1950).

Association of the Bar of the City of New York, *The Federal Loyalty-Security Program* (Dodd, Mead, 1956).

Beer, S. H., *Treasury Control,* 2nd ed. (Oxford, 1957).

Blau, P. M., *The Dynamics of Bureaucracy* (U. of Chicago, 1955).

Campbell, G. A., *The Civil Service in Britain* (Penguin, 1955).

Carpenter, W. S., *The Unfinished Business of Civil Service Reform* (Princeton, 1952).

Chapman, B., *The Profession of Government: The Public Service in Europe* (Macmillan, 1959).

Corson, J. J., *Executives for the Federal Service* (Columbia, 1952).

Crough, W. W., *The Responsibilities of a Civil Service Commissioner* (Public Res. Assn., 1959).

Greaves, H. R. G., *The Civil Service in the Changing State* (Oxford, 1947).

Hoogenboom, A., *Outlawing the Spoils* (U. of Illinois, 1962).

Kelsall, R. K., *The Higher Civil Service of Britain* (Routledge, 1955).

Lasswell, H., *Psychopathology and Politics* (U. of Chicago, 1930).

McLean, J. E. (Ed.), *The Public Service and University Education* (Princeton, 1949).

Macmahon, A. W., and J. D. Millett, *Federal Administrators* (Columbia, 1939).

Mann, D. E., *Federal Political Executives* (Brookings, 1964).

Parkison, C. N., *Parkinson's Law* (Houghton Mifflin, 1957).

Report of the President's Committee on Administrative Management, *Administrative Management in the Government of the United States* (U.S. Government Printing Office, 1937).

Reports of the two (Hoover) Commissions on the Organization of the Executive Branch of the Government, *Task Force Reports on Personnel and Civil Service* (U.S. Government Printing Office, 1949 and 1955).

Robson, W. A. (Ed.), *The Civil Service in Britain and France* (Macmillan, 1956).

Sayre, W. S., *The Federal Government Service: Its Character, Prestige and Problems* (American Assembly, 1958).

Selznick, P., *Leadership in Administration: A Sociological Interpretation* (Row, Peterson, 1958).

Stahl, O. G., *Public Personnel Administration,* 5th ed. (Harper & Row, 1962).

Strauss, E., *The Ruling Servants* (Praeger, 1961).

Taylor, Sir H., *The Statesman,* new ed. (Heffer, 1957).

Van Riper, P. P., *History of the United States Civil Service* (Row, Peterson, 1958).

Yarmolinsky, A. (Ed.), *Case Studies in Personnel Security* (Bureau of National Affairs, 1955).

XVII

The Administrative Process

The last chapter dealt mainly with internal aspects of the civil service. Here attention is to be focused on the external relations of the civil service—its connections with and its impact on members of the public. These are of great variety. Almost all the activities of government recounted in Chapter V involve action by civil servants affecting some or all members of the public. Sometimes the government provides a *service* such as the post office or the employment exchange. Sometimes it is *mixed service and regulation* as in public health activities. The government maintains diagnostic clinics and laboratories for analysis, and also enforces pure-food regulations and a minimum of sanitary measures on municipalities and individuals. Sometimes it is *purely regulation,* as when employers are required to pay minimum wages and maintain safety devices, and when public utilities are required to provide certain standards of service at fixed rates.

Where a service only is being supplied to the public with or without charge, the public wants little more than efficiency, courtesy, and equality of treatment from the civil servant. If he knows his job, the public is satisfied with good manners from the post-office clerk, and with sympathetic understanding of the plight of the unemployed from the clerk in the employment exchange. But when civil servants are engaged in regulating our lives, other considerations enter. Here the official has power to require us to do or not to do something *and* he is backed by the organized power of the government. He must act firmly and without fear, favor, or discrimination, because he is expected to enforce the public interest even if it is at the expense of private interests. Of course, his firmness will be less galling if it is gloved in courtesy. We do—and should—resent any unnecessary brusqueness by sanitary inspectors, customs officials, and highway police.

The Need for Limits. Beyond all this, however, is the prime need of good assurance that there will be a limit to the regulating. There must be some way of ensuring that the sanitary inspector sticks to the sanitary code, the customs official to the tariff schedule, and the highway police to the traffic regulations. They cannot be permitted to follow intuition and impose their own personal conceptions of what ought to be done in the public interest. It is true that their superiors control them and surround them with instructions they must obey. This is small comfort to those whose protests against official action are met by the answer that 'orders are orders and must be carried out.' The difficulty is that the officials with whom the citizen has to deal directly rarely make the decisions that affect him, and he cannot get face to face with those who do.

This fact complicates greatly the problem of controlling the administrative actions of government. On the one hand, men will often make decisions they would not make if they had also the painful duty of imposing those decisions on protesting individuals. On the other hand, men will enforce without question drastic decisions made by others, decisions they themselves would shrink from making if they had to explain and justify them to those affected. So, where regulation enters, the vital question is a very ancient one: *quis custodiet ipsos custodes*—how to control the controllers, how to permeate the entire civil service with a sense of responsibility.

A hundred years ago, the short—and, on the whole, adequate—answer was that official action was bounded everywhere by the law and that no one could be required to do, or refrain from doing, any act except as required by the letter of the law. The law—either common law or statute law —defined in fairly precise detail what burdens or restrictions government could impose, and the courts were available to punish any official who overstepped or commanded his subordinates to overstep the limits set by law. Of course, it has never been possible to reduce government to an automaton carrying out the dictates of clearly defined laws. There were even then in the hands of the governments in question some discretionary powers not sharply bounded by law. But such powers were few, and they did not affect deeply the character of economic and social life, the terms on which individuals and groups live together in the community.

Modern Requirements. This short answer is by no means a complete answer today. We have noted that the present-day legislature cannot enact all the laws in all the detail necessary, and that it delegates a good deal of lawmaking power to the executive. We have also seen that the power of the courts to sit in judgment on official action has been progressively limited by legislation in the past seventy years—with some notable exceptions, as will be seen in the Administrative Procedure Act of 1946 in the United States. There is a widening sphere of action open to the executive which the courts are not permitted to control. In a broad sense, officials are still bound by the law; but the difficulty is that, over a substantial part of the field of government, the law gives them a *discretionary power* to make rules and regulations, and then to decide what burdens and restrictions the rules and regulations justify them in imposing on individuals in concrete situations.

DISCRETIONARY POWERS AND SUBORDINATE LEGISLATION

THE DISCRETIONARY POWERS OF THE ADMINISTRATIVE

The discretionary powers just referred to are conferred by the legislature on the executive. The executive in the narrow sense, the President or cabinet, cannot itself exercise this authority. The decisions to be taken are so numerous, and so often require long study and expert knowledge, that they are of necessity taken by members of the civil service, the administrators. It is always possible, of course, for the President or cabinet to intervene, but it is not common, and in France this is unlikely. The manner of exercise of discretionary powers by officials is often described as the *administrative process.* Good manners and courtesy in dealing with the public are, as we have seen, highly desirable qualities in a civil service, but the success or failure of a government in its public relations does not necessarily raise constitutional or serious political questions. However, the rapidly growing importance of the administrative process does raise important political and constitutional questions which must be discussed.

The Debate on Administrative Discretion. In the period between the two World Wars, the controversy over delegation of legislative and judicial powers to the executive overshadowed all other constitutional discussion in Britain and the United States. France, with a well-established tradition of such delegation as a matter of practical need for purposes of governing, and a smoothly functioning system of administrative courts and administrative law, already explained in Chapter XV, did not engage in such discussions. The French administrative system and experience were, however, much debated by British and American writers—a debate that produced a large, and sometimes acrimonious, literature. The practice of delegation was attacked as undermining the very foundations of constitutional government. According to this view, the legislature, whose function it is to make whatever laws are needed and to control the executive, abdicates *pro tanto* when it confers lawmaking powers on the executive. The representatives of the people betray the trust reposed in them when they let an unrepresentative civil service define what the public interest requires. The rule of law, which subjects official action to scrutiny by independent courts, has been a vital safeguard of individual liberty. In so far as the judging of disputes between the government and citizens is taken away from the courts, a most salutary external check on the government is weakened. To allow a government official to judge finally in such disputes is to make the government a judge in its own cause—a violation of the elementary canons of justice. In short, it was argued that the well-tried methods of ensuring that government should be servant and not master are being abandoned.

NECESSITY? The practice of delegation was supported, however, on the ground of necessity. Legislatures, it was said, have neither the time nor the technical knowledge to make in full detail all the laws the public now expects them to make. Democratic legislatures would have been completely overwhelmed and discredited long ago had they not had the wit to limit themselves in many matters to the discussion and settlement of general principles of legislation, leaving the voluminous details to be filled in by the executive with rules and regulations. For several reasons the common-law courts—in contrast with the French administrative courts—are quite unsuitable tribunals for deciding disputes that arise out of much present-day legislation: Sometimes it is the sheer number of disputes that the judiciary with its present organization and procedure could not begin to handle expeditiously. Sometimes it is the highly technical issues that arise, calling for expert knowledge which the judges do not possess. Sometimes it is the judges' lack of sympathy with the purposes of the legislation—purposes the public wants carried out whether the judges approve of them or not. In short, according to this contention, nineteenth-century machinery of government will not meet twentieth-century needs. Cautious experimenting over the last seventy years has produced the administrative process as a partial answer to the new needs.

The debate subsided with the outbreak of war and the need to concentrate all energies on military objectives. It was resumed on the return of peace with many new arguments made available to both sides by the experience of war organization. In organizing for total war, the democratic governments relied heavily on the administrative process, and developed it at a fantastic rate to a point far beyond its peacetime scope. The legislatures, while reserving to themselves the decision on a few great matters of principle, delegated the planning and management of the war to the executive. The laws that assigned to the population their several duties and responsibilities in the common effort were almost entirely made by the executive through rules and regulations and orders-in-council. Very few of the innumerable disputes that arose between governments and private interests in the war organization ever came before the courts. They were settled either by negotiation or by orders and directives emerging from the executive or from one of the many administrative boards and alphabet agencies that the executive established to aid in the task of winning the war.

DANGERS? This experience lends support to the view that the administrative process is the inevitable instrument of large-scale governmental operations. At the same time, it is far from refuting the contention that the administrative process has grave dangers for liberal democracy. Indications were not lacking during the war that government by administrative order and decision can easily get out of hand. The debate has become sharper than ever. In the United States, for example, a score of big government agencies underwent a long siege of investigation and criticism in the late 1950's and early 1960's—with rather mixed and uncertain results, however.

The place to be accorded to the administrative is one of the big issues facing democratic government. The time has not come to suggest a conclusion. It is much more important at present to try to understand *what is involved*. Some appreciation of its scope must be gotten. Its character, whether virtuous or vicious, must be estimated and that can only be done by seeing what it does and how it does it. Finally, it cannot be judged at all without some understanding of its causes.

Why Administrative Discretions Are Given. Its causes can be suggested at once, leaving fuller verification to emerge from a discussion of its scope and character. The administrative process is the result of the great expansion in the activities of governments in the last seventy years. In Chapter V, a distinction was made between the negative state of the nineteenth century and the positive state of the twentieth, and some of the sweeping social and economic changes contributing to the shift were indicated. In the *negative* state, *laisser faire* was the ideal. Within a framework of order provided by government, each person was expected to take care of himself, either by his own efforts or in voluntary co-operation with others. Little was expected of governments. The legislature could itself make whatever small supplementary additions to or modifications of the common law were required. The laws, whether common law or statute, were adequately enforced by the courts' punishing those who broke them and thus deterring the bulk of the population from infringing them. The technique, if not the aim, of government was negative. It contented itself, in the main, with saying, 'Thou shalt not.'

CONSEQUENCE OF THE POSITIVE STATE. In the *positive* state, government ceases to be merely an umpire calling fouls and retiring offending players to the cooler. It becomes a schoolmaster of the old school, setting lessons that the citizens positively must learn. The aim of the teaching is to get people to do the things necessary to ensure minimum standards of health, education, safety, and economic well-being for all. The materials set out in Chapter V show how numerous are the fields in which government is pushing the realization of one or other of these standards. The attaining of these standards is regarded as so important that, wherever possible, government defines in great and precise detail the rules of deportment for well-behaved citizens in a complex society. For the same reason, government takes vigorous steps to enforce observance of rules and standards. It is not regarded as sufficient in many instances to have courts punish those who disobey; they must be made to obey. So government gets into a great deal of inquisitorial and supervisory activity after the fashion of schoolmasters. We are in the era of the positive state because the state is now concerned to get positive results. It says, 'thou shalt,' and maintains a great inspectorial and enforcement staff to enforce its commands.

The executive is the only branch of government equipped to put energy into getting concrete results. Wars, for example, are directed by the executive and not by legislatures and courts. So the growth of government activities and the shift in the role government is expected to play have aggrandized the executive. The legislature sets the broad objectives of public policy. The executive uses its administrative establishment to expound those objectives in innumerable rules and regulations and to enforce their observance. The way in which this enlarges the discretionary power of officials will be made clear by concrete illustrations that are actual instances of discretionary powers generally found in the United States or Britain. France, as already noted, falls into a separate category in the administrative process. Some of the United States illustrations are drawn from the state rather than the federal sphere, because government action in the former is often more closely related to common experience and therefore should be easier to understand. The purpose is to indicate the *nature* of a common development and not to measure its scope in either one of the governments under consideration.

The Special Case of France. In line with the practice characteristic of other Continental states, administrative discretion has always been considerably greater in France than in either Britain or the United States. In administrative matters, centralized France thus gives the state a much wider latitude. The French ministers, individually as well as collectively, either by virtue of delegation of power or by departmental policy, are authorized to issue a variety of *decrees*—rules and regulations that have the force of law, but that are *not regarded as law* (except as authorized by Parliament under the emergency-decree procedure of Article 38 of the de Gaulle Constitution).

As a rule, decrees cannot formally be law for the reason that if a decree were to be regarded as *law*, it could not be effectively contested in the administrative courts, since the French separation of powers forbids judicial interference with legislation, other than via the extra-judicial Constitutional Council, which cannot 'interfere' with ordinary legislation unless it is asked to do so by the President, the Premier, or the presiding officers of the two houses of the legislature. Therefore, because it is *not* regarded as law, a minister's decree-making power is subject to check by the system of administrative courts, headed by the Council of State (*conseil d'état*). That system, as we saw in Chapter XV, provides redress to the injured citizen far more expeditiously, more simply, and more inexpensively than is available under the common-law system.

DELEGATION OF LEGISLATIVE POWER TO THE EXECUTIVE

The giving of discretionary power to the executive to make rules of law may be looked at first. In most present-day legislation, the legislature does not attempt to make the law in all its concrete detail. It sketches in outline broad general principles and delegates power to fill in details. Sometimes in Britain, as in the emergency legislation authorizing the executive to fight the war, the power delegated is very wide. In the United States, certain constitutional restrictions, and a natural desire of Congress to limit the executive, have, on the whole, prevented the grant of extremely wide legislative powers.

Usually, the power given is limited to making rules under one particular statute such as the pure-food law or the law regulating the issue and sale of corporate securities. Even here, the power is sometimes stated generally, 'to make such rules and regulations as may be necessary for the operation of this Act,' and is not limited to making rules on certain specified and narrowly limited matters.

Scope of Subordinate Legislation. Sometimes in Britain the power is delegated to the cabinet. Such delegations can be readily identified as they are always exercised by order-in-council. Sometimes it is given to a minister of a particular department, or to a board or commission outside the departmental structure such as the Railway Commission. In either case, rules and regulations so made are generally known as delegated, or subordinate, legislation. In the United States, the rule-making power may be conferred on the President, on one of the members of the cabinet, or on one of the many independent boards and commissions such as the Federal Communications Commission or the Securities and Exchange Commission.

It will be recalled that the separation of powers imposed by the Constitution of the United States reserves the exercise of legislative power to Congress. This might be thought to prevent all delegation to executive agencies of power to make rules and regulations. It does prevent the grant of *extremely wide general powers* of legislation such as are occasionally given by the legislature to the executive in Britain. But the Supreme Court has always upheld the validity of the delegation of *clearly defined and limited powers* to make detailed regulations. In this way, room has been made within the Constitution for extensive subordinate legislation by the executive.

It is impossible to give, in a short space, any accurate impression of the scope and extent of the practice of subordinate legislation. Half the statutes of the British Parliament enacted in the 1920's gave such power to the executive. The proportion is now much higher. In sheer bulk, the annual output of subordinate legislation greatly exceeds the annual output of the legislature.

Even in what are called normal times, the number of pages of orders-in-council, rules, and regulations put out by the executive under a statute generally far exceeds the number of pages covered by the statute itself. In periods of emergency, legislative lawmaking is completely dwarfed by executive rule making. The rules made in one year under the Agricultural

Adjustment Act, one of the Roosevelt New Deal measures for meeting the great depression in the United States, covered more pages than all the laws relating to agriculture passed by Congress since the founding of the Republic. The rules made under the National Industrial Recovery Act, another of these measures, filled 10,000 pages in the two years of its existence. The emergency of war carried this development to hitherto unimagined lengths. In 1946, immediately after the war, some nineteen hundred federal statutory provisions either authorized or required executive agencies to make rules and regulations. Many of these were of minor importance, but the figure gives some idea of the reliance on subordinate legislation.

Reasons for Subordinate Legislation

Lack of Time. Obviously, no legislature could begin to debate and enact a fraction of the rules that emergencies call for. But even in the normal activities of present-day governments, the legislature cannot find time for much of the detailed lawmaking. The terms on which the citizen can use facilities of the post office, for example, depend much more on regulations made by the Postmaster General than on laws made by the legislature. These regulations fix the size and weight of packages and determine what matter shall enjoy mailing privileges at particular rates. They provide for determining, within the context of the general law on the subject, what is dangerous, immoral, or fraudulent matter, and for prohibiting transmission of such matter through the mails. They also fix, among other things, conditions of the issue of money orders and postal notes, of registration of letters, and of insuring of parcels.

The exact scope of the rule-making power relating to the post office varies from country to country, but postal regulations generally cover a very wide field. The legislature could take time to make these rules, but only at the expense of deliberation on other matters. The upshot is that in many fields of legislation, the legislature debates and fixes the general policy, and the administration makes most of the detailed rules thought necessary to carry out that policy.

Many of the questions to be decided in making post-office regulations require special knowledge. The size and weight of parcels and the scope of insurance and special-delivery facilities, among other things, can only be fixed by those who have had considerable experience in the post-office business and know the general conditions in which it is to be conducted. Whatever regulations are made must be approved and issued by the Postmaster General, but they are not made by him. They are made by the permanent civil servants who do the work of running the post office.

Need for Detailed Expert Knowledge. Often the question what the details of the law should be depends on expert technical or scientific knowledge. Legislatures are not chosen for their scientific attainments; hence experts in the civil service must be relied on. The details of legislation prescribing safety measures in factories and other work places must be adjusted to the conditions of a great variety of industrial establishments. In some instances, it may be enough to require the fencing and covering of exposed machinery. But if protection is to be afforded against physical injury from such risks as explosions, and against industrial diseases in the more complicated industrial processes, measures must be worked out through careful study of the different kinds of risks, and of the kinds of provisions that will combat them, in all types of establishments and processes. Expert engineering and other scientific knowledge is vital to success. In one state after another, the fixing of details of the safety code has been delegated to an administrative agency. Scientific knowledge has been applied, in one way and another, in most spheres of economic and social life, and when government intervenes in these spheres, it must master the elements of science involved as well as take account of economic and political considerations.

Moreover, when government undertakes to regulate economic matters, it must bring a wide knowledge of economic facts to its decisions. A legislature may decide, for example, that employers of labor must pay at least a minimum wage and be content with a maximum number of hours of work per week from each employee. But the minima and maxima must be related to the cost of living and to the state of the labor market. Also, conditions vary so widely in different industries that a single standard of minimum wages and maximum hours often cannot be set for all industries and employments affected by the law, although the United States Congress has repeatedly endeavored to do so. So there is a practice in some jurisdictions to leave it to an administrative agency to make orders prescribing, within certain broad limits laid down by the legislature, the exact minima and maxima for different employments. The proportion of apprentices and learners to be allowed in each trade, the minimum scale of payment to them and to handicapped or partially disabled workers, are often similarly fixed.

Reliance on copious subordinate lawmaking in this particular field has gone considerably further in Britain than in the United States, where

Supreme Court decisions holding minimum-wage and maximum-hour laws to be unconstitutional delayed for a long period extensive experimenting with this kind of legislation. Not until 1938 did the Congress succeed in passing a comprehensive federal wage and hour law, the Fair Labor Standards Act, which, upon challenge, was held constitutional by the Supreme Court three years later.[1] But it does afford a simple illustration of what occurs nowadays in many fields. The complexity of industry and economic life is such that the legislature, after deciding on a broad policy of regulation, has to leave much of the necessary rule making to the administrative.

Frequent Changes in the Rules. The intricate regulations that we have seen to be necessary in one sphere of government activity after another, can hardly ever be laid down once for all. In some instances, it is by no means clear what should be done, and the regulations must be tentative and experimental. In other instances, such as the minimum-wage laws, the interests being regulated discover loopholes in the regulations, and these must be plugged by changes in and additions to the regulations. In any field of regulation, new circumstances and new conditions not contemplated when the law was made emerge from time to time, and the rules must be adjusted to them. That is to say, much of present-day legislation is continually in a process of adjustment and change. Adjustment can be made best by a body that can act quickly at any time and that is close to the experience gained in trying to make the law effective. This is another reason for lodging powers of subordinate legislation with the administration.

It is clear that the political executive, the cabinet or President, is no more able to make all these regulations than is the legislature. Subordinate legislation frequently issues in their name and, because the civil service is under their command, they can modify or veto proposed regulations at any time. If an influential body of opinion is aroused over a piece of subordinate legislation, it will be able to get the political executive to examine carefully the content of the rules and regulations and perhaps to modify it. Short of insistent and convincing external pressure, the political executive accepts without much question what its informed and expert advisers propose on the details of subordinate legislation. Keeping this qualification in mind, it will be convenient henceforth to speak of subordinate legislation as being made by the administration, meaning civil servants in government departments or in independent boards and commissions sometimes set up to assist in the administrative process.

[1] *United States* v. *Darby,* 312 U.S. 100 (1941).

CONTROL OF SUBORDINATE LEGISLATION

Because it is often left to civil servants to say how the general principles declared by the legislature shall be applied to concrete situations, they have a substantial discretionary power to determine how the law shall bear on individuals and groups. In fact, it is often impossible to say who will be affected in what ways and how much, until regulations have been framed and issued. So lobbies and pressure groups are almost as much concerned with the deliberations of the administration in framing regulations as they are with the deliberations of the legislature. With a vital interest in the way civil servants exercise their discretion, the pressure groups likely to be affected are always seeking access to the administration to present their suggestions and protests.

For example, when regulations are to be made under the minimum-wage law, a large number of employers' organizations and several trade unions are likely to ask to be heard. For every exercise of a power of subordinate legislation, there is a cluster of interests with representations to make. They try to persuade the civil servants, or the political executive, or both, how the discretion should be exercised. The legislature, the representatives of the people, has no direct part in the making of these rules. What then ensures that the civil servants will exercise their discretion conformably to the public interest or the will of the legislature?

Legal Limits on Rule-Making Power. In the first place, the legislature sets limits to rule-making power and any rules that go beyond the power granted are invalid. If the minimum-wage board, which is authorized to fix minimum wages, presumes to fix maximum wages as well, no one need obey the maxima so set. In the Anglo-American system, it is always possible to refuse to obey subordinate legislation on the ground that the legislature never gave the necessary power to make it, and the courts are open to test such a contention. In this way, subordinate legislation can be kept within the limits laid down by the legislature.

The effectiveness of such a check depends on how clearly the legislature has specified the limits. We have already noticed the power given to the post-office department to make rules on certain specific matters. If the grant of power is thus limited to particular specified matters, there are reasonably clear limits set to administrative rule-making powers. But often the statute goes on to give the administrative authority in question power 'to make such rules and regulations as may be necessary to carry out the provisions of this act.' Where this is done, the courts find it considerably harder to say what the precise limits of the rule-making power are. If the legislature wants to impose sharp control, it should be chary of the use of general phrases. But the frequency of such phrases in grants of rule-making power suggests that the legislature is impressed with the need for flexible grants of power.

Review of Rules by Legislature. Second, the legislature can require that subordinate legislation shall be 'laid on the table' in the legislature within a stated time after it is made. In this way the legislature knows what regulations have been made and can find opportunities of debating those it does not like. It can, if it so desires, enact a law repealing any or all subordinate legislation. It can go further and repeal the delegation, taking all rule-making power away from a particular administrative agency.

In the United States, Congress has not made any significant use of the device of requiring subordinate legislation to be tabled. In France, the executive's power to issue decrees without specific legislative authority obviates such a requirement without, however, negating the—now sometimes theoretical—parliamentary power of intervention in its prescribed spheres of authority. In Britain, Parliament often but not invariably inserts such a requirement in particular statutes delegating legislative power. But in practice, little use was made of the opportunity for a long time, and regulations were rarely taken off the table. There are so many of them and their subject matter is so complicated and technical that busy members of the legislature preferred to allot their time to matters that paid larger dividends in public attention. In 1944, however, a select committee of the House of Commons was established to give sustained scrutiny to the subordinate legislation tabled in the House and to report to the House on particular rules and regulations that seemed to merit special consideration. As a result of the work of this committee, Parliament passed an act in 1946 standardizing some of the procedures for enacting, tabling, and publishing subordinate legislation. These checks are proving to be reasonably effective. If outrageous regulations are made, they will be debated in the House, and someone will have to answer for them. So the administration always keeps the House in mind when framing subordinate legislation.

Control by Political Executive. Third, the political executive that controls the civil service is the instrument of the ruling political party, and the parties are responsive to electoral opinion. Therefore the cabinet or President is concerned with the content of subordinate legislation. Proposed regulations which, if enacted, might rouse significant sections of opinion, are likely to get careful scrutiny by or on behalf of the political executive. In some respects, this scrutiny is closer in Britain than in the United States. As we shall see later, many of the powers of subordinate legislation granted by Congress are placed in the hands of the independent executive agencies of the national government. In their daily work, these agencies are all more or less independent of the President and he generally has no effective power to check their rule-making activities.

Consultation of Interest Groups. Fourth, one of the best indications of what reactions to subordinate legislation can be expected is the attitude of the interest groups concerned. There are, therefore, varying degrees of consultation in all three countries between the executive and interest groups when controversial regulations are being framed or amended, which provides the most continuous check on subordinate legislation. The nature of this consultation will be considered more fully at a later point in this chapter. It should be noted here, however, that Congress often lays down in the statute itself certain requirements as to how the rule-making authority is to proceed in making rules. In recent years, there has been a growing legislative tendency to require particular administrative authorities to hold a hearing, at which interested persons and groups are entitled to appear, *before* regulations are made. In 1946, Congress thus passed the Administrative Procedure Act, which requires, as a general rule, that almost all administrative rule making shall be preceded by a formal hearing. The procedure to be followed at the hearing is specified in some detail and resembles that followed in judicial trials.

Constitutional Limitations. A fifth kind of check on subordinate legislation, peculiar to the United States, is of *occasional* importance. It arises from the fact that its Constitution establishes the separation of powers and also certain guarantees of private rights which no governmental agency is entitled to override. If Congress delegates to the executive or to an administrative agency an *unfettered discretion* to make rules without imposing, at the same time, standards or principles to control and limit the exercise of the discretion, the courts may in due course hold this to be an unconstitutional delegation of legislative power to the executive. This occurred notably in the case of one of the most famous and most controversial of the New Deal measures, the National Industrial Recovery Act of 1933. Two years after its enactment, the United States Supreme Court declared it to be unconstitutional as an illegal delegation of legislative power by Congress to the President. 'This is delegation running riot,' wrote Mr. Justice Cardozo. 'No such plenitude of power is susceptible of transfer.'[2] However, no federal law has fallen since 1935 on the grounds of illegal delegation of legislative power to the executive. In certain limited circumstances, the procedure followed by the administrative authority in fixing its rules and regulations or the content of the rules themselves may be held by the courts to violate due process of law. If so, the rules in question are invalid.

In Britain and France, where the same constitutional provisions do not exist, subordinate legislation is not open to attack on these grounds. The courts can only inquire whether the legislature has manifestly authorized the rule-making body to do what it has done, but in France the administrative courts provide a convenient source of redress to the injured citizen.

ADMINISTRATIVE ENFORCEMENT OF THE LAW

When subordinate legislation, enacted under the powers given in a particular statute, has defined with some exactness what individuals are to do or refrain from doing, the executive is ready to enforce the general policy laid down by the statute. As already explained, the requirements of the positive state often cannot be met merely by having courts impose fines or imprisonment on those who infringe the regulations. The framers of the general policy are not so much concerned to punish offenders as to ensure that regulations will be obeyed and thus achieve positive results. Accordingly, the legislature often arms the executive with still further powers.

License and Inspection. In many of the functions of government outlined in Chapter V, the administration is authorized to employ inspectors with power to enter premises and conduct investigations to see whether the law is being obeyed. Where particular trades and businesses are being extensively regulated, the legislature often authorizes the administration to require individuals or corporations engaged in one of these businesses to take out a license or permit. If inspection shows serious infringement of the law, the license may be cancelled or suspended and the right to engage in that

---

[2] *Schechter Poultry Corporation* v. *United States,* 295 U.S. 495 (1935). A section of the N.I.R.A. had already been declared unconstitutional earlier that year in *Panama Refining Co.* v. *Ryan,* 293 U.S. 388.

particular business taken away. These are powerful weapons for compelling obedience.

For example, in enforcing certain portions of the pure-food laws, the government does not wait until the poisoned consumer of canned meat starts an action in the courts against the manufacturer. It establishes a permit system, and sends inspectors into the factories to see that the legal conditions on which the permit is issued are being obeyed. If not, it may suspend the permit, or, in some circumstances, refuse to allow the manufacturer to use approved labels, until he takes adequate steps to comply with the law. However, in enacting such an inspection system, the legislature must guard against 'undue statutory vagueness' lest it run the risk of a declaration of unconstitutionality, as occurred with a section of a pure-food law in 1952 in the United States.[3]

Preventive Justice. License and inspection and similar techniques have a very wide application. It is not now regarded as satisfactory that those who carelessly allow disastrous fires to break out should be punished after the event. The victims can sue the culprit for damages, but too often this is just the old case of locking the stable after the horse is stolen, and often the culprit has not the means to make good the damage he has caused. The community is reaching for an enforced standard of safety, and the legislature authorizes the government to employ fire inspectors to enter premises and insist on a minimum of precautions against fire. Minimum standards of sanitation are not sufficiently enforced by keeping the courts open to punish those who ignore the sanitary code. Medical health officers are authorized to inspect premises and to placard those they find are not reasonably fit for human habitation. Similar illustrations could be found in many fields of government activity.

This is what is called *administrative,* as distinct from judicial, *enforcement of the law.* In discussing the Anglo-American judicial system we saw that judicial enforcement of the law is, by long tradition, punitive and compensatory rather than preventive. It punishes wrong and does not try directly to compel people to do right. Administrative enforcement does try to prevent wrongdoing. It is no exaggeration to say that this can be a colossal task if it is undertaken in many branches of human affairs. In part, it explains why the negative state could get along numbering its judges in dozens, while the positive state must count its civil servants in thousands or even millions.

[3] *United States* v. *Cardiff,* 344 U.S. 174.

It also goes far to explain the increasing inroads on the constitutional principle of the rule of law, referred to in earlier chapters. This principle was explained as ensuring that government officials could not impose burdens on the citizens by their own decision, but could only do so through the decision of a court that the law justified the burden. With few exceptions, this principle ruled in the era of the negative state.

The Administration Decides. In the last seventy years, the exceptions have eaten deeply into the principle. The owner of premises may find them closed without the courts' having first decided the issue whether they are fit for human habitation or not. The Securities and Exchange Commission in the United States, in its regulation of brokers and stock exchanges, has power in specified circumstances to revoke licenses of brokers and to cancel the registration of securities, thus preventing trading in these securities on a national stock exchange. Commercial disputes over the correct grade of particular lots of grain are settled with virtual finality by officials of the federal Department of Agriculture in the United States. Foreigners who enter the United States unlawfully may be expelled without being able to get their case before a court. These are but a few instances drawn from widely different fields in which the legislature has conferred on administrative authorities the power of deciding issues and/or enforcing the law. The agencies or officials who possess such powers are often called *administrative tribunals.*

SOME COURT REVIEW. It must not be thought that the courts are excluded from all consideration of the exercise of powers of the kind just described. Sometimes, the statute that grants such powers to administrative agencies expressly provides for a limited appeal from the decision of the agency to the courts which have a varying power to review most kinds of administrative action. The scope of judicial review will be considered later. It is sufficient here to remember that it does exist, and that it is considerably broader in the United States than in Britain, again remembering that the case of France is a special one because of its system of administrative courts.

It may be that some of these instances of administrative power should be approved and others rejected. It is not the present purpose to suggest whether particular inroads on the authority of the courts to settle disputes are justifiable or not. The purpose rather is to examine the nature of the administrative process and see the main reasons for its increasing use. This can only be done by considering still further instances of its use.

ADMINISTRATION AND THE RULE OF LAW

ADMINISTRATIVE ADJUDICATION

We have seen that the legislature often cannot make the law in detail for lack of knowledge of all the circumstances to which the law is to be applied. It lays down a general policy in terms of a standard of health or safety that it desires to be achieved. In a significant numbers of instances, it is recognized that the administration, for the same reasons, cannot make precise rules and regulations, and the legislature makes the best of it by authorizing the administration to apply the standard to particular cases as they arise. For example, it has long been found necessary to have laws regulating railways and other public utilities because of their monopoly position. Such enterprises, if unregulated, always produce a variety of abuses. They charge exorbitant rates, discriminate between their customers, and give poor service with a take-it-or-leave-it attitude. It is clear enough, to take the case of railways, that the law should require them to act *reasonably*. But to define in advance *what* would be *reasonable* in all the possible circumstances of railway operation is an impossible task. Thus, on these vital points, the legislature merely says that railways must charge reasonable rates, provide reasonable facilities, avoid unreasonable delay in transporting commodities, and refrain from favoring one shipper over another. It then authorizes an administrative agency, the Interstate Commerce Commission in the United States, the Railway and Canal Commission and the Railway Rates Tribunal in Britain, to apply these standards to particular complaints as they arise, and, in the case of rates, to fix certain standard rates of charges for the future.

Application of Vague Standards. In one sense, the commission *judges* disputes between the railways and their customers, interpreting the law as stated in the standard of reasonableness set by the legislature. In another sense, the commission *makes law,* not by general rules, but by a special order for each case as it comes up. In fact, the experts on legal theory are not agreed as to whether many of the activities of these commissions are legislative or judicial. For present purposes, it does not matter which is the correct view. The essential point is that any body authorized to take all the circumstances of a particular case into account has important discretionary power to affect the rights of those who appear before it.

In the United States for many years, attempts were made to regulate railways by minute rules of law interpreted and applied by the judiciary. They were not effective. In Britain for many years, the function of applying to particular cases the vague standards mentioned above was left to the courts. This too was unsatisfactory and was abandoned. The body that is to enforce these standards on railway companies must know the technical ramifications of railway management and engineering as well as the part played by railway transportation in a diversified economy. The courts do not possess this expert knowledge. In the end, in both countries, the legislature delegated the power of regulating railways to a specialized administrative agency which devotes most, if not all, of its time and energy to railway regulation, and which can draw on the necessary expert talent.

There are a great many other instances, always increasing in number, in which the legislature has authorized administrative agencies to apply vague standards to particular cases and thus to modify the rights and liabilities of citizens. Such instances are most commonly found where regulation of some aspect of economic life is being undertaken. The legislature has a view of the desired result, which it embodies in a standard. At the same time, it recognizes the impossibility of visualizing in advance the almost infinite number of different combinations of circumstances that may arise, and of making precise rules of law to cover them.

PROBLEMS OF REGULATION. In fact, law is not at all a suitable technique for regulating the innermost intricacies of human relationships. Regulation by fixed rules of law is only workable where you can specify particular kinds of conduct as undesirable and forbid them. It is one thing to enact a law that makes wife-beating a criminal offense. It is an entirely different thing to lay down a complete code of fair and sympathetic treatment of wives, by following which a man would fully honor the standard of conduct set by his marriage vows. If comprehensive regulation of marital enterprise ever becomes necessary, it will have to be done by an administrative agency with power to decide according to the particular circumstances of each case.

Law can regulate the margins but not the minutiae of conduct. If the minutiae must be closely regulated, the appropriate technique is military discipline, with every hour and every movement of the soldier subject to command. So where government regulation of a trade or business becomes very extensive, there are at least plausible arguments for government ownership and operation where the necessary discipline can be imposed. Administrative regulation of economic life of the order outlined in Chapter V is a halfway house between free private enterprise subject to general rules of law, on the one hand, and state ownership where the government gives all the orders, on the other. It is not yet clear whether the halfway house can be made a permanent stopping place.

LAW OR DISCRETION? Thus there is today a large sphere where the courts no longer judge disputes because there is no law for them to apply. The judgments to be made in many fields of governmental activity involve *discretion,* and the exercise of discretion requires a judgment on what public policy should be. In a democracy, the legislature and the majority party are the authorities on public policy for the time being. Therefore, discretion in the hands of administrative agencies has to be controlled either by the legislature or by the political executive, which, in turn, is responsible through the legislature and/or the political parties to the electorate. In this way, the discretionary decisions made by administrative agencies can be kept in touch with the policy that the authorities on public policy want to enforce.

Expert and Rapid Decision. Also, the discretion can only be exercised satisfactorily in many instances by those with expert knowledge. An administrative tribunal, such as the Interstate Commerce Commission or the Railway Commission, generally specializes in one type of problem and can be staffed with experts. The judiciary has to deal with all sort of disputes and cannot be expected to have a wide range of expertness in railways, sanitary engineering and so on.

THE EXAMPLE OF SOCIAL SECURITY. There is still another class of modern legislation which confers the power of settling disputes on administrative agencies to the exclusion of the courts. This is the legislation making provision for social security. Where it is decided that the government should make certain payments to those persons who suffer from particular types of misfortune, it is necessary, either by statute or by subordinate legislation, to define carefully the conditions on which persons can claim such payments. For example, old-age pensions are payable only to those who can show that they belong to a certain category of age, residence, need, etc. A claim for a pension, or an application for cancellation of one now being given, will raise issues that one might expect to be settled by the judiciary. However, almost invariably, an administrative agency, such as an old-age pensions board, is given power to decide whether a pension should be granted or canceled, reduced or increased in amount.

The reasons for taking claims to social security payments away from the courts are several. Claims for and disputes over pensions, unemployment-insurance benefits, and the like are very numerous. The judicial system with its cumbrous, if not dilatory, procedure could not begin to handle all the claims and disputes that arise, and delays would amount to denials of justice. Most people who make such claims are needy persons and can afford neither delay nor expense. Accordingly, such cases commonly go to administrative tribunals, which use a summary procedure adapted to the kind of cases arising and settle all disputes without significant cost to the claimants.

The Demands of the Positive State. Encroachment of the administrative on the preserves of the judiciary is going on in many fields. It is everywhere related to the assumption of positive tasks by government. It is a response to the demands of the positive state for *preventive rather than punitive action,* for close collaboration between the making of law and the interpreting and enforcing of law, for expert knowledge, sympathetic interpretation, flexible procedure, and rapid decision in settling claims and disputes. It is impossible to give any meaningful statement of the extent of the encroachment beyond saying that there are scores of administrative agencies with powers of this kind in each of the countries under study here. The significance of the development can be stated most clearly by saying that the more complex the functions assigned to government, the more specialized administrative tribunals must be used to settle the arising disputes.

The Scandinavian Ombudsman. An intriguing institution, designed to provide simple redress for grievances wrought by administrative action, is the Scandinavian Parliamentary Commissioner or *ombudsman.* This tribune of the people, which originated in Sweden in 1809, has become increasingly popular and, especially since its adoption, and highly successful operation, by Denmark in 1955, has found increasing favor particularly among the smaller states. Thus, by August of 1963, the institution was in use in varying degree and with varying impact in Sweden, Denmark, Norway, Finland, West Germany, New Zealand, and the Philippines, with several others, including Britain, the State of Connecticut, and the City of Philadelphia giving it more or less serious consideration.[4]

Not designed to replace judicial procedure *per se,* the *ombudsman* (using the Danish one as an illustration here) is a legislatively appointed administrative watchdog whose duty it is to publicize and thus help ferret out any

---

[4] For a comprehensive view of the *ombudsman* see, for example, the Symposium on *Ombudsmen,* 109 *University of Pennsylvania Law Review* 1057–126 (June 1961).

cases of mis-, mal,- and/or non-feasance by members of the executive—in Sweden even the judicial—branch of the government. In his investigatory position he remains detached from the other branches, thus side-stepping political intervention; he is allowed a free hand to look into the deeds and records of any executive-administrative official or department. Anyone at all, be he a private citizen or a public official, may without cost register a complaint with the *ombudsman* who, if he deems the complaint to be properly within his jurisdiction and worthy of investigation, will proceed with dispatch and thoroughness. The result of the investigation will either be exoneration or an official 'criticism' of the administrative action or practice by the *ombudsman*.

Normally, the public criticism will suffice to bring about remedial action, but if no such action is taken the *ombudsman* is empowered to 'instruct' the public prosecutor to take the matter to court. As of this writing the latter action has never been necessary under the Danish system, whose first *ombudsman*, the Professor of Criminal Law at the University of Copenhagen, Stephan Hurwitz—unanimously elected and re-elected by Parliament —has proved to be a great success both institutionally and personally. His judicious and statesmanlike handling of the office has given him a universally excellent press and has prompted inquiries and invitations from all over the world.

But the question arises whether the *ombudsman*—however successful the institution has proved to be in a small, thoroughly homogeneous land, blessed with a united, politically alert, and knowledgeable electorate, such as Denmark—is not to a large degree a palliative of decreasing value as the size of the state involved increases. It may well be the better part of wisdom for the states under discussion in this text to try harder to make the traditional controls work, and to labor on the refining of additional procedural practices and attitudes from the inside.

JUDICAL REVIEW OF ADMINISTRATIVE ADJUDICATION

On Constitutionality. The question arises how can the administrative encroach on the sphere of the judiciary in the United States, in view of the prominent place occupied by the separation of powers in the American Constitution? Article III of the Constitution clearly vests the judicial power of the United States in the federal judiciary. Many of the powers to make discretionary decisions that Congress confers on administrative agencies have been held not to involve exercise of the judicial power. Numerous other such powers, however, contain undoubted judicial elements. Article III, as interpreted, does not forbid Congress to give the initial exercise of judicial power to an administrative agency, but it does prevent Congress from making such an administrative adjudication final and conclusive. That is to say, where specifically judicial power is so delegated, the decisions made are always open to fairly extensive judicial review by the courts.

LIMITING THE SCOPE OF ADMINISTRATIVE ADJUDICATION. The separation of powers thus limits the scope of administrative adjudication in the United States. We have already noted above that the National Industrial Recovery Act of 1933, for example, was declared unconstitutional by the United States Supreme Court as constituting an illegal delegation of legislative power by Congress to the executive. In Britain, where the separation of powers is not written into the constitution, and in France, where it is applied differently, the legislature may make any administrative adjudication final and conclusive if it wishes.

Apart altogether from the question of the separation of powers, the judiciary in both the United States and Britain retains significant power to review administrative decisions that affect the rights of citizens, whether these decisions are specifically judical or not. This power may arise from the terms of the particular statute conferring administrative powers, or from accepted principles of the common law, supplemented in the United States by the due process clauses of the Constitution. For example, as alluded to earlier in this chapter, in 1952 the Supreme Court struck down 8:1 a section of the Federal Food, Drug and Cosmetic Act, dealing with factory inspection, as 'lacking in *due process* because of vagueness.' In its broadest outlines, which alone can be discussed in brief space here, this power of judicial review is much the same in both countries. In France, however, the presence of the administrative court system all but obviates the need for that particular power.

On Excess of Power. It is for the legislature to say, within the limits, if any, imposed by the constitution, how far administrative adjudication is to go. In many statutes that give the administration power to decide particular issues, provision is made for an appeal to the courts on questions of interpretation of the law. In addition, each such statute always limits the matters that the official is empowered to decide. If the latter presumes to decide questions the statute does not authorize him to decide, his decision has no validity, and the courts, on application to them, will so hold. For example, an administrative order was made some time ago by the United States Department of Justice under the immigration laws for the deportation of one Ng Fung Ho, then a resident in America, as an undesirable alien. Ng Fung Ho, however, claimed to be a citizen by birth and could thus get the judiciary to decide this question of citizenship. For, held the Supreme Court, while the administration has power to deport aliens, it has no power to deport natural-born citizens. 'Jurisdiction in the executive to order deportation exists only if the person arrested is an alien. The claim of citizenship is thus a denial of an essential jurisdictional fact.'[5] Nor, as that same tribunal had occasion to rule in 1962, did the Federal Power Commission have power to approve a merger of two natural gas pipelines while an anti-trust suit challenging the merger was before the courts.[6] Every power of administrative decision is subject to limits, and the courts can always be invoked to see that these limits are not transgressed.

On Fairness of Procedure. The courts also retain power to examine the fairness of the procedure of administrative agencies. For example, if the agency fails to give a party notice of proceedings being taken against him or an opportunity to tell his side of the story, the courts will, on request, set aside the decision against him. Also, if the decision is obviously and scandalously wrong, as when there was no substantial evidence to support the finding of fact on which the decision is based, it is possible for the courts to intervene.

In Britain, the power of the courts to review the procedure followed by an administrative agency rests mainly on the common law and so can be modified or removed by an act of the legislature. In the United States, in the absence of a statute imposing more stringent procedural requirements, it rests on the due process clauses of the Constitution and therefore is beyond the power of Congress. Also, the effect of the due process clauses is to extend the scope of judicial review of administrative decisions considerably further in the United States than in Britain.

Prescribing Procedure by Law. The legislature may, if it sees fit, prescribe in detail the procedure that administrative agencies are to follow in making decisions. This is rarely done in Britain and France, but, in recent years, Congress has frequently specified the procedure to be followed by particular agencies.

[5] *Ng Fung Ho v. White,* 250 U.S. 276 (1922).
[6] *California v. Federal Power Commission,* 369 U.S. 482.

THE ADMINISTRATIVE PROCEDURE ACT OF 1946. Moreover, the Administrative Procedure Act of 1946, already referred to, lays down uniform rules of procedure for almost all administrative agencies of the federal government. It also enlarges the possibilities of judicial review of administrative action. It subjects to judicial review a number of agencies hitherto exempt from it and opens to judicial review some kinds of administrative action which, prior to the Act, were not subject to scrutiny by the courts.[7]

The Act is an attempt to recapture for the judiciary much of the ground it has lost through the rise of the administrative process. It is worth noting that the Act was sponsored by the American Bar Association, and thus represents another stage in the determined struggle of the organized legal profession against recent trends in administration. The New Deal and World War II brought a great advance in the use of the administrative process in the United States. The Administrative Procedure Act of 1946 was designed as a major counter-offensive. Yet the American Bar Association, still disturbed by the range and extent of administrative discretion, in the spring of 1955—and at least twice since—officially petitioned Congress to strip such federal agencies as the Federal Trade Commission and the National Labor Relations Board of their quasi-judicial authority, and to establish separate administrative courts to assume these judicial functions. The Second Hoover Commission made a similar recommendation for an Administrative Court of the United States, to consist of three sections having jurisdiction, respectively, in the fields of taxation, regulation, and labor.

Limited Judicial Review on Merits. One other important characteristic of judicial review of administrative action in the United States should be kept in mind. In the absence of express authorization by the legislature, judicial review does not entitle the courts to try the *merits* of the case and render a decision settling the issue between the parties. It merely entitles them to *quash* the administrative decision for some specified defect and, in effect, require the agency to retry the case as the courts of appeals have had occasion to do repeatedly in connection with F.C.C. awards of T.V. channels, for example. The reason for this limitation is clear enough. The courts are experts on matters of law and fair play. But the substance of the issue decided by the administrative agency is often a highly technical question as, for example, in railway or airline regulation. Thus in 1957, the

[7] For example, the Act provides that every executive agency give full publicity to its formal procedures; that ample notice of contemplated adoption of rules be given; that persons compelled to appear be permitted counsel; that employees or officials engaged in investigating cases have no part in deciding them.

United States Supreme Court denied to four airlines a review of a Civil Aeronautics Board order revoking their licenses to operate as *irregular* carriers. The administrative agency rather than the courts is the competent expert on the substance of the matter to be decided by it. As one judge put it in a private interview: 'The courts can try to keep the game clean. But the public should be made to understand that they [the courts] do not have the responsibility for administrative decisions.' [8]

Another important limitation arises out of the fact that, in practice, judicial review can be brought into operation only in a mere fraction of the great numbers of issues dealt with by the administrative agencies. In any case, the problem of the scope of judicial review of administrative constructions of statutes is part of the difficult and broader problem of the review of questions of law and 'mixed' questions of law and fact.

SPECIAL ADMINISTRATIVE UNITS

The Independent Regulatory Boards and Commissions

We should now be able to understand the current discussions about the role of boards and commissions in present-day government. The powers of subordinate legislation, administrative adjudication, and administrative enforcement of the law discussed in this chapter are conferred on the executive. In Britain and France, they are, in almost all cases, conferred on one or another of the existing departments of government and the minister at the head of the department is responsible to Parliament for their exercise. Or— as will be shown shortly—a *government corporation* is established. But in the United States, boards or commissions outside the regular departments are often—although not always—set up to exercise such powers, particularly when powers to hear and settle claims and disputes are involved. These are known as the *independent regulatory commissions*. Here, too, sometimes, as in the case of the Tennessee Valley Authority (T.V.A.), for example, the device of the government corporation, an autonomous unit whose stock is wholly owned by the government and financed by congressional appropriations, is employed.

In the United States. In setting up independent boards, the legislature takes the view that since the functions to be exercised resemble judicial functions, they should be exercised by bodies with some independence of

[8] As reported by Anthony Lewis in *The New York Times,* March 15, 1958.

the government of the day. Accordingly, these agencies are kept outside the departmental structure and they are not directly under the control of the President or the cabinet. While the commissioners are appointed for specific terms of office by the President, subject to approval by the Senate, they are removable only for certain causes, as spelled out by Congress in the statute creating the commissions—e.g. 'inefficiency, neglect in office or malfeasance.' Ordinarily, no more than a bare majority of the commissioners may belong to the same political party. In their everyday operations, the commissions are more or less independent of both the executive and the legislature. They are often called 'the fourth branch of government.' Some of the more famous in the United States are the Interstate Commerce Commission, the Federal Trade Commission, the Federal Reserve Board, the Securities and Exchange Commission, the Federal Communications Commission, the National Labor Relations Board, and the Federal Power Commission.

POWERS AND ACTIVITIES. There is widespread, vigorous criticism of the powers and activities of these boards and commissions. In part, the criticism is aimed at their independence. They are not judges, members of an ancient profession sworn to uphold the law, yet they have independence of a kind accorded to judges. They are instruments for enforcing the policy of the legislature and the dominant political party, yet they are, to some degree, independent of both legislature and executive. The essence of the criticism, however, is that each of them is a government in miniature, violating the doctrine of the separation of powers. For most, if not all, of these boards and commissions also have powers of subordinate legislation—they make rules and regulations. Moreover, they possess powers of inspection and investigation, thus performing executive functions. They are authorized to launch and carry through prosecutions of offenders against the laws they are administering. In many matters, they are themselves the judges of whether individuals are meeting the requirements of the laws and vague general standards they are administering.

COMBINED POWERS. So a board is often, at one and the same time, *lawmaker, detective, prosecutor, judge, and jury*. Those who make the law also interpret and enforce it. The board is likely to be biased in favor of the policy it is trying to enforce. Allowing a board or government department or anyone else to be judge of his own case leaves something to be desired. It is easy to point to instances of capricious, if not oppressive, use of this panoply of powers—abuses which advocates of the separation of powers have always feared.

On the other hand, it is argued that this combination of quasi-legislative, quasi-executive, and quasi-judicial powers in the hands of a board or commission is not likely to be seriously abused as long as the legislature has—as it undoubtedly has—the authority to take back from these bodies the powers it has given them. Up to a point, this argument is correct. It is correct only in so far as the legislature has a genuine alternative. If it is necessary that we should rely ever more heavily on government to perform complex functions, and if these functions can only be performed through the use of wide administrative discretions, the legislature has not a genuine alternative. It cannot abolish administrative agencies and powers; it can merely re-shuffle them.

Attacks on the Independence of the Commissions. The independent regulatory boards and commissions of the federal government in the United States are under heavy fire. Some of these attacks have come from high-level, responsible groups created by the Congress and/or the President to study the problem.[9] The attacks, covering a wide range, have aimed at two major objectives: first, that almost all boards and commissions be brought into one or the other of the ten great departments, where their work would be subject to direction by the President. Second, that the judicial functions of these agencies be separated, and be performed by officers substantially independent of both President and Congress.

The first recommendation is based upon the conviction that the President should be the over-all co-ordinator of all administrative policy, in order to bring it into line with general governmental policy. Such a step would open the work these independent regulatory boards and commissions have been performing to direct political influence, but it would also ensure clear lines of responsibility, culminating in the President, who, in turn, is responsible to the electorate for his conduct of administration. Moreover, there has been mounting criticism of the commissions as being easy prey to the wishes of the industries they are supposed to regulate, and their incorporation into the regular governmental departments is viewed as an ameliorative step in that connection.[10]

---

[9] See the reports by the President's Committee on Administrative Management (1937); the Attorney General's Committee on Administrative Procedure (1939); the (First Hoover) Commission on Organization of the Executive Branch (1947); the Second Hoover Commission (1953); and the Harris Committee of the House of Representatives (1958 ff.).

[10] 'A subtle malady which is apparently institutional rather than personal in its incidence is the tendency of the independent regulatory commissions not to die, but to fade away; with advancing age they tend to *become the servants rather than the governors of the industries which they regulate,* and attain a sort of dignified stability far from the objectives which they originally sought.' (Report of a Subcommittee of the Senate Committee on Labor and Public Welfare, 82nd Cong., 1st Sess., 1951, p. 60. Italics supplied.)

The second point is strongly supported by an important segment of the legal profession, which contends that administrative bodies should not be allowed to perform essentially judicial functions. The already-mentioned specific recommendation of the Second Hoover Commission here was the establishment of one large administrative court with branches having specialized jurisdiction.

With the exception of some relatively minor reshuffling as the result of the first recommendation, no really significant action has been taken on these two areas of dispute. Legislators are prone to view these agencies as 'arms of Congress' and hence their business. There is the greatest diversity of counsel on what to do about independent boards and commissions and the administrative process. The most prevalent view, however, is clearly that reform, not abolition, of the agencies is the wiser course. As one of his very first actions, the then still President-elect Kennedy appointed ex-Harvard Law School Dean James M. Landis to issue a report on the regulatory agencies. The remedies suggested by Landis emphasized centralized planning, rather than segregating functions. But, not surprisingly, only some of the Landis Report's recommendations were accepted by Congress in 1961. In order to keep the over-all matter of improving the workings of federal regulatory agencies alive, the President then created the eighty-six-member *Administrative Conference of the United States*. Paralleling the well-established *Judicial Conference of the United States,* representing the federal courts, which had in fact recommended the creation of such an administrative group, the new body immediately embarked upon a series of important and timely recommendations.

The Case of Britain. The problem of keeping administrative discretion adequately under control remains acute even though the powers are always housed in a government department. Although the device of independent boards and commissions is little used in Britain, the same arguments are broadly applicable to the British situation. The same combination of discretionary powers is widely used there. The principal difference is that they are generally given to government departments rather than to independent boards and commissions. This difference has one important consequence. In Britain, anyone who is dissatisfied with the treatment he has received at the hands of the administration can use what influence he has to get redress through political means. He may get members of Parliament to air his grievance in the House of Commons or he can seek direct access to the minister in charge of the department concerned.

This may mean much or little in the cases of particular individuals. It does mean that discretionary administrative powers are always exercised in accordance with the views of the government of the day. Those who can move the ruling political party can influence the use made of the kind of powers we are considering here. Yet where the powers are in the hands of independent boards, there is no assurance that they will be so immediately responsive to the political pressures that can be exerted on the government through the ruling political party. But it would be wrong to suppose that they are sheltered from all external pressure in the way in which judges are. Whether effective or not, pressure may be applied either through political channels or by representations made directly to the heads of the administrative board. The *Crichel Down* case illustrates both aspects:

THE CRICHEL DOWN CASE. Briefly, this *cause célèbre,* which occupied headlines in Britain for months, if not years, derives its name from a three-part farm in Dorset, converted to Air Force Ministry use in 1937. The land, which was needed for a bombing range and was appropriated much against the wishes of the several owners and tenants, was transferred to the Ministry of Agriculture in 1949, which equipped the farm at considerable expense as a single-unit model farm. Despite considerable public criticism, and the clamor of former owners to be permitted to buy back or rent the land at prices higher than their erstwhile compensation, the Ministry proceeded with its project—ultimately renting it to a tenant wholly unrelated to the original owners over the latter's violent protests, augmented by similar protests by their legislative representatives. Believing itself to be driven into a corner, the Ministry then persisted in what a number of papers called 'bull-headed bureaucratic obstinacy.'

Spearheaded by the dogged efforts of one Lt. Commander Marten, one of the interested, ignored, and 'bullied' unsuccessful applicants for the land, the case resulted in 1954 in a full-dress debate in the House of Commons; an official public inquiry; the voluntary resignation of Sir Thomas Dugdale, the Minister of Agriculture, although he had been unaware of all the facts in the case and was fully trusted by the House; and the proffered resignation, rejected by Prime Minister Winston Churchill, of the two junior ministers more directly involved. The official investigation by Sir Andrew Clark, Q.C., appointed by Sir Thomas, had found that although there was no trace of 'anything in the nature of bribery, corruption, or personal dishonesty,' there was gross ineptness and arrogance on the part of the bureaucrats involved, proving that 'the public official can be as stupid, as inaccurate, as wrong-headed, as selfish, as mendacious, as obstinate as if he were in private employment.' Pointing out that this was essentially a matter of the position of the civil servant toward his minister, Sir Andrew's report concluded that too many inexperienced junior officials had been permitted to participate in important decisions; that the attitude of the bureaucrats had been one of 'the public be damned'; that the case involved serious interdepartmental 'tanglements and botches, leaving the right hand not knowing what the left is up to'; and that the decisions taken were either made without knowledge why they were made or wrongly made on the basis of incorrect data. If it did little else, the *Crichel Down* case served to focus a glaring spotlight upon the administrative process and its personnel and became a considerable object lesson for both.

The Franks Committee Report. The Crichel Down case and others like it led indirectly to general dissatisfaction with the piecemeal system of administrative tribunals and boards of enquiry. As a result, in 1957 Parliament established the Committee on Tribunals and Enquiries, under the chairmanship of Sir Oliver Franks, whose terms of reference included examination of 'an important part of the relationship between the individual and authority.' Its report stressed the basic desire to balance the rights inherent in that relationship. Observing that a thorough revamping was needed in the then existing system of organizing the diverse rules of procedure that characterized each new tribunal and board, the Franks Committee charged that Parliament had created an immense system of 'judicature piecemeal,' and called for common grounds of procedure for all. The Committee asked that all hearings be open to the public; that if a citizen could not, or did not choose to, be represented by legal counsel, the administrative agency involved likewise should not have counsel; that 'a statement of reasons' behind all decisions made be filed; and that all investigating reports be made part of the public record.

THE COUNCIL ON TRIBUNALS. But, the most important recommendation of the Franks Committee was its proposal for the creation of the Council on Tribunals. Since instituted, this Council enjoys general supervision over all administrative tribunals. Its members visit the hearings to study methods of procedure; it is consulted ere new tribunals are established; and it advises on rules of procedure before a tribunal begins to operate. To a degree, the Council on Tribunals contains some of the elements of the Danish *ombudsman,* especially in its capacity of receiving and investigating complaints against tribunals coming to it from aggrieved citizens. But as presently constituted, its powers and stature fall considerably short of that of the Scandinavian institution. Nonetheless, as H. W. N. Wade has observed, the Council's aim 'is not to conquer new territory, but to promote peace, order and good government in the territory already won.' [11]

The Public Corporation in Britain. It should be mentioned that in one very important field of administration, the operation of the nationalized industries, Britain relies increasingly on agencies outside the government departments and beyond the detailed control of the cabinet. When an industry or business is nationalized, it is not operated under a regular government department but is put in the hands of a public corporation, like the British Broadcasting Corporation or the National Coal Board.

These corporations—which are not confined to Britain but are used widely in France and, as we have seen, sometimes in the United States as well— have the same kind of structure as a private corporation except that the shares are publicly owned and the boards of directors are appointed for a fixed term by the government of the day. Once appointed, a board has a wide independence of action in determining policy for the industry and in administering its detailed operation. The statutes creating these corporations generally give one or other of the ministers in the cabinet power to give directions to the public corporation on matters of broad general policy, but they preserve him from any responsibility for short-run policy and day-to-day management.

CONTROL AND AUTONOMY. Control of the public corporation by the public on whose behalf it operates is therefore intermittent and indirect. At infrequent fixed intervals, the corporation must come to Parliament to have its charter renewed. It is required to submit annual reports and financial statements to the minister and to Parliament, and these can be debated. Borrowing for capital purposes requires the consent of the Treasury, and directives on general policy issue from the political executive from time to time.

The public corporation in Britain has an autonomy comparable to that of the regulatory boards and commissions in the United States. It is therefore a very significant exception to the general British insistence that officials who work out and apply public policy must be subject to direct control by a responsible minister. The reason given for the exception is that when the government goes into business, it must apply business methods rather than civil service methods, and must be free of the normal political control and meddling imposed through Parliament and the cabinet.

[11] 'The Council on Tribunals,' Public Law 351 (1960).

The wide use of the public corporation in Britain today raises sharply a problem mentioned before: how is a government that does so many things for us to be kept under popular control? British experience with the public corporation over a period of time is likely to throw important light on this question.

ADMINISTRATION AND THE PUBLIC

INTEREST GROUPS AND ADMINISTRATION

Legislative and judicial control of the administrative process are not of themselves sufficient for keeping the administration from getting out of hand. From the point of view of the interests concerned in any particular aspect of administration, the legislature and courts are too remote and the methods of control too roundabout. Thus, they always want to have direct access to the administration to press their views and protests on the President or cabinet, or on the officials themselves. We have already seen that there is always a cluster of pressure groups wanting to be heard when subordinate legislation is being framed. Similarly, various interests always want to be heard when the administration has a discretionary power of making decisions in particular cases.

The Case for Consulting Interest Groups. Despite its employment of numerous experts in various subjects, the government is always conscious of inadequate knowledge about the complex matters it is undertaking to regulate. For example, in the framing and amending of standards for use in the grading of grain, the United States Department of Agriculture has always consulted representatives of producers, shippers, traders, and processors of the grains in question. The government also knows that it is much easier to enforce its regulations if it can get the co-operation of the interests concerned. But this co-operation is not likely to be had unless the government takes the interests into its confidence, listens to their representations, and makes adjustments here and there in deference to them.

Accordingly, the government generally welcomes the approach of the interests. The administration of many of the more complex activities of government today is carried on by close and continuous collaboration between the political executive, the administrative officials, and the various interests concerned. Generally speaking, there is as much collaboration of this kind where the administration is organized under an independent board as where it is housed in a government department. For example, the Federal Trade Commission in the United States encourages the *Trade Practice Conference*. This is a conference of the members of one industry, profession, or trade to adopt self-imposed 'codes of fair procedure,' which are to serve as guides to all concerned members, and which are frequently adopted by the Commission itself.

GROUP ORGANIZATION. It has been said that administration sets the measure of a law. Certainly the decisions taken nowadays by the administration under its discretionary powers are often the vital decisions as far as the individuals and corporations affected are concerned. It follows that in so far as pressure groups find the administration accessible and responsive, they are better represented in government that if they had been allowed to elect representatives to the legislature. More than that, the influences that mould administrative action are often decisive in determining the content of a particular government activity. Interests that are well-organized and recognized by the government get deference and consideration, while unorganized interests do not. In administration, as in legislation, the importance of group organization emerges clearly. Interests must be effectively organized if they wish to make their weight felt in present-day government.

There is a body of opinion that looks for salvation in a fuller organization of all significant interests in the community. It doubts whether democratic control of administration can be made effective through the legislature and the judiciary. It wants to develop direct connections between the branches of administration enforcing particular laws and the various sections of the public interested in those laws. In relation to any particular law or government activity, some interests will want more vigorous administration and more extended application, while others will want less. Under their pressure and counter-pressure, the administration can shape its action to a form that all the interests will accept and will co-operate in making effective. Democratic government in this way will shed most of its coercive aspects, and become a great co-operative enterprise in which all groups share in the administration of those activities which concern them.

Interests versus the Public Interest. This proposal should not be too hastily branded as utopian. Trying to approach the administration via the political party, the legislature, and the political executive may involve a long and hazardous detour. There is little doubt that organs of direct consultation will increase in number and importance. Yet there are two problems to be considered. First, the experience of the United States with this kind of consultation is not wholly reassuring. Because of the number of independent boards and commissions, and the inability of the President in recent years to co-ordinate and maintain control of all branches of the administration, administrators in the United States in many of their activities have had more freedom to respond to group pressures and to negotiate with the interests concerned than have administrators in Britain. In too many cases, the result has been that the most powerful interests concerned with a branch of the administration have gained a predominant influence over the administration for a time and diverted it to their purposes. At various times and under various circumstances, as we noted earlier, this has been true.

The influence of the railroads with the Interstate Commerce Commission, of the American Farm Bureau Federation with the Department of Agriculture, and of the American Legion with the Veterans Administration are well-known illustrations. Congress may be swayed by one interest, now by another; but the administrative agencies, so long as their functions remain unchanged, are always concerned exclusively with the same general interests. These pressures upon agency commissioners are 'almost inconceivable' in the words of one Washington expert. After their appointment 'they live in a world somewhat akin to [the late] Marilyn Monroe's, since everybody who sees them from then on has something on his mind.' [12]

Second, the interests immediately and consciously concerned with a particular field of government action are not the only interests with a stake in the matter. It is often thought that the only interests concerned with the fixing of minimum wages and maximum hours of work are employers and employees. In fact, everyone who is concerned with the level of prices for goods or with health or education has a lively interest in the matter. It is almost impossible to get all the interests with a stake in administrative decisions fairly represented. For this reason, control through the political parties, the legislature, and the political executive, which alone represent the broad general and unorganized interests, is extremely important.

If administrative discretion is to be kept under control, a combination of the older, more indirect, methods of control through the legislature and the political executive and the newer, more direct, consultation between administration and interests affected must be used. The means by which the legislature, and the cabinet or President, control administration have been described in earlier chapters. It remains to indicate briefly how the interested sections of the public make contact with the administration.

[12] William C. Burt, as quoted by Alan F. Westin (Ed.), *The Uses of Power* (New York: Harcourt, Brace and World, Inc., 1962), p. 225.

Methods of Consulting Interests. In Britain, the United States, and France, when subordinate legislation is to be framed it is standard practice for the department or administrative agency that has the matter in hand to consult the organized interests. Copies of the proposed regulations are circulated to the associations and their comments are invited. In the United States it is common, even where not required by statute, to arrange a conference or public hearing where all sides can make representations. In this way, the administration gets expert knowledge of the complexities it is expected to regulate. It may learn that certain of the proposed regulations are really unworkable, that others rouse violent opposition and attract little support. It hears all the objections before it acts, and decides what concessions or modifications it can afford to make. On the other hand, the fact that the interests are consulted disposes them to co-operate even when the decision goes against them. And after the regulations have been enacted and put into effect, the interests keep in touch with the administration with complaints and suggestions. When a considerable experience of their operation has accumulated, discussions looking to their revision may be held. There is here a complex interaction between rulers and ruled.

In a less formal way through correspondence and interview with officials, pressure groups make representations about administrative decisions in particular cases. In the United States, officials often attend meetings and conventions of the various associations, addressing them on the policy and work of their department or agency. This is rarely done in Britain, where officials are subject to closer check by the political executive and generally refuse to discuss matters of policy in public. In France, on the other hand, the multiparty system is made to order for powerful interest groups, which exploit the presence of weak, undisciplined, relatively small political parties to put sharp pressure on deputies and administrators alike. Nowhere among the liberal democracies was the immediate influence of pressure groups as obvious and as constant as during the Third and Fourth Republics in France. The presence of the National Economic Council, to be discussed briefly below, partly contributes to that influence.

The Use of Advisory Committees and Bodies

Wherever possible, the methods used by pressure groups to influence the legislature are used to urge their views on the administration. These methods are mostly informal and have not yet hardened into a well-established practice. There is, however, one recurring pattern of consultation that is widely used—the advisory committee. This device has been described optimistically as the democratic answer to the challenge of the corporate state. The corporate state meets the problem discussed in this chapter by formally turning over the functions of government to associations or corporations directly representative of interests, as Fascist Italy, for one, purported to do. In the process, democracy disappears. The advisory committee, it is alleged, meets the need for giving representation to and getting co-operation from the interest groups without destroying democracy. How is this accomplished?

Meeting a Need. When the government is faced with a complex and arduous task of administration aimed at realizing some objective of the positive state, it can set up a committee representative of the interests affected to advise the administrators. In so far as the interests are organized in active associations, persons who play leading roles in the associations can be put on the committee. Interests that are not organized effectively can also be given representation. A number of persons can be appointed to the committee to speak for consumers or for the general public. For example, the Advisory Council on Social Security, attached to the Social Security Administration in the United States Department of Health, Education and Welfare, is composed of representatives of employers, labor unions, and the general public. And consumers at large were given an 'official voice' by President Kennedy in 1962 with his establishment of the Consumers Advisory Council—representing the fulfillment of a 1960 campaign pledge. Such committees, like the British monarch, have influence but no power to say what the administration shall do. They have the right to advise, to be consulted, and to warn. If they do their job, administration will be carried on under the watchful eye of representatives of those directly interested in what is being done.

The French National Economic Council. While by no means to be viewed as a substitute for the activities of interest groups—which independently engage in efforts to influence administrators—the Economic Council serves, in a sense, as a constitutionally created gathering place for pressure groups in government. Designed as an advisory body at the legislative level, this 229-member unit is composed of representatives from some twenty-five or thirty 'economic and social interest groups.' It must be remembered, however, that its power is chiefly *advisory:* it may not initiate legislation, but may advocate social and economic reforms; may be consulted by the executive branch on all social and economic matters *except* the budget, and in drafting of departmental rules and regulations concerning the 'national economy';

and it *must* be consulted in the compiling of rules of administrative procedure for *those* laws on which it had previously been asked for official advice and on 'public economic programs and plans'—again with the exception of the budget. As was already explained in Chapter XI, the influence of the Economic Council has been spotty, at best. The members and their respective interests are often in bitter disagreement; it meets irregularly; and there is much absenteeism and abstention from voting. It has been of some definitely constructive value to the government on certain important national questions, such as labor policy, price and wage problems, tariff matters, and the Schuman Plan—but it cannot be relied upon as a permanent source of solid advice and support. Moreover, it is regarded with considerable suspicion by many, if not most, legislators, and it is frequently ignored by them. Individual pressure groups are also highly suspicious of the Council.

Advantages. Through advisory committees, the administration can get quickly and in advance the reactions of various sections of the public on what it proposes to do. It can tap the practical experience and expert knowledge which are essential to making governmental regulation of complex affairs practicable. By consultation and discussion it can also explain to the representatives of various groups what ends and purposes the government is trying to accomplish. In so far as it succeeds in educating these representatives they, in turn, will carry the explanations to their membership, and the chances of getting co-operation from those who are to be regulated are increased. While the member of the legislature, among other duties, maintains liaison between the government and a territorial constituency, the member of the advisory committee maintains liaison between the government and a functional constituency.

The positive state cannot accomplish what it is trying to do unless it gets widespread co-operation as well as general acquiescence from the public. The advisory committee is calculated to improve the quality of administration, to foster an atmosphere of co-operation, and to make possible continuous scrutiny of the exercise of discretionary administrative powers. It is on these grounds that the advisory committee is sometimes put forward as the democratic answer to the corporate state.

Defects. Advisory committees are now widely used as instruments of the administrative process in Britain and the United States, and—on a somewhat different basis—through the National Economic Council in France, and reliance on them is increasing. Generally, they are designed to give representation to interests, organized or unorganized. However, particular persons are often appointed solely because they possess knowledge that the government hopes to be able to use. Advisory committees are useful for the purposes indicated, but they cannot be regarded as an adequate solution for the problems raised in this chapter. In practice, there is continual difficulty in getting able persons to accept membership and take an active interest in the work of the committee. This arises mainly from the fact that the committees are advisory only; they have no power to insist that their recommendations be accepted, and interest therefore tends to lag. It can be maintained, perhaps, if the administration shows itself willing to accept any unanimous recommendation. But any such practice would turn the substance of power over to the advisory committee, and this the administration cannot do. It takes great skill on the part of the administration to get useful results from advisory committees.

The truth is that the organized interests want power and not merely influence in the matters that affect them. If provision is made by the legislature for the government to intervene in the struggle of conflicting group interests, those group interests want to have some share in the control of the administrative agency that tries to regulate the conflict. They have met with some success in this claim. For example, it is not uncommon for administrative agencies that regulate employer-employee relations to be composed of equal numbers of representatives of employers and employees, with or without provision for a neutral chairman or other members to represent general public interests. Where the government undertakes to confer benefits on particular organized interests, those interests want a share in administration. So when the legislature provides for compulsory marketing of agricultural produce through a marketing board, the compulsory powers, which only the legislature can confer, are often delegated, in part at least, to boards composed of producers, or of producers, dealers, and processors, of the particular product concerned. The powerful interests want to participate directly in administration and bend the administrative process to their purposes.

THE SIGNIFICANCE OF THE ADMINISTRATIVE PROCESS

This is not necessarily objectionable where the interests that get control are the only interests with a stake in the matter. However, this can only rarely be true. As we have already seen, there are generally wider interests involved. The existence of wider interests, which are likely to be prejudiced when administration is diverted to serve narrow and immediate interests, is the reason for insisting on primacy of control through political parties, the legislature, and the political executive. It is also the reason for the demand, so insistent in the nineteenth century, that civil servants should be neutral tools obeying the hand of the legislature and political executive. The legislature and executive, it was contended, expressed adequately the common good and the national interest, and there was no place for the imaginative civil servant with ideas of his own. Today, by contrast, there is a wide demand that civil servants have a positive constructive attitude toward their work, putting energy and even passion into the accomplishment of great tasks.

The Importance of the Civil Servant. This reversal of attitude toward the civil servant is the clearest possible indication of the great change wrought by the rapid growth of governmental functions and the development of the administrative process. Legislatures and executives can no longer express the full content of public policy. The officials are given discretion to expound it in detail. They need, therefore, knowledge, imagination, and a strong will if much is to be accomplished. Yet when civil servants give a marked display of these qualities in their daily work, they are accused in many quarters of despotic ambitions. The question remains acute how civil servants can be genuinely creative and still kept under control. The administrative process, as sketched here, is the result of tentative groping in the last forty years for an answer to this question.

It must be remembered, of course, that the civil servants who have a substantial discretion to exercise, and who are expected to be genuinely creative, are very few in number. They are generally senior officials standing close to the top of the hierarchy in each department. The vast majority of civil servants are, as the last chapter indicates, cogs in an impersonal organization, firmly clamped in a restricting routine with little chance to follow their inclinations or sympathies in their work. Indeed, it seems to be a general tendency in large-scale organization to impose a confining discipline on the many and to make overwhelming demands on a few for creative thought and action. The discretionary powers lodged with a few administrators merit the attention given to them here, because the decisions they are expected to make are vitally important decisions. More and more, the decisions taken in the course of administration affect the character of community life and the basic terms on which economic and social groups in the community live together.

Ultimate Responsibility. Accordingly, we often hear the charge that the higher officials of the civil service really govern the country. There is no doubt that the political executive relies considerably on these officials for suggestions on policy, on what to do in the public interest. But final decisions must always rest with the political executive, which is ultimately responsible to the electorate. The political executive must retain the support of a political party and it must take account of views of organized pressure groups. The civil service is drawing closer to the formulation of policy, but it is still a long way from governing the country. It is, however, undoubtedly true that if government is to be all things to all men, the executive—in the broad sense including President or cabinet and civil service—must be vigorous, imaginative, and possessed of wide powers. The unsolved problem is how to maintain a powerful executive and at the same time to ensure its continued responsibility to the governed.

A Consequence of the Positive State. Most of the previous exposition and discussion in this book has been meant to converge on this point. At the beginning, it was stated that the essence of liberal democracy is a determination that government shall be servant and not master. Constitutions were framed for that purpose in a day when little was expected of governments. It was explained that the fundamental role of political parties is to enable the governed to change their rulers peaceably, to keep power contingent on their approval, and to construct electoral majorities that will support certain general lines of governmental action.

The great expansion in governmental functions in the last seventy years was sketched and asserted to have imposed great strain on the constitutions under consideration. In particular, it was seen that the tasks of the legislature and executive have been complicated immensely by the new burdens. A legal and judicial system, whose procedures and traditions were firmly fixed before the great expansion in governmental functions, and designed to support a negative rather than a positive conception of government, was seen to be unsuited on a number of points for meeting present-day demands. The rise of pressure groups, some of the divisive tendencies within the political parties, and the widespread dissatisfaction with the present system of representation were traced to the same source. The principal, although not the sole, effort to adjust these constitutions to the radically changed conception of the appropriate functions of government has been the development of the administrative process.

Suggested References for Further Reading

Appleby, P. A., *Morality and Administration in Democratic Government* (Louisiana State U., 1952).

The Attorney General's Committee on Administrative Procedure, *Final Report* (U. S. Government Printing Office, 1941).

Cushman, R. E., *The Independent Regulatory Commissions* (Oxford, 1941).

Freedeman, C. E., *The Conseil d'État in Modern France* (Columbia, 1961).

Friendly, H. J., *The Federal Administrative Agencies* (Harvard, 1962).

Gaus, J. M., *Reflections on Public Administration* (U. of Alabama, 1947).

Hyneman, C. S., *Bureaucracy in a Democracy* (Harper, 1950).

Karl, B. D., *Executive Reorganization and Reform in the New Deal* (Harvard, 1963).

Mackenzie, W. J. M., and J. W. Grove, *Central Administration in Britain* (Longmans, Green, 1957).

Mailick, S., and E. H. Van Ness, *Concepts and Issues in Administrative Behavior* (Prentice-Hall, 1962).

Marx, F. M., *The Administrative State* (U. of Chicago, 1958).

Meyer, P., *Administrative Organization* (Stevens, 1957).

Millett, J. D., *Management in the Public Service* (McGraw-Hill, 1954).

Nash, B. D., and C. Lynde, *A Hook in Leviathan. A Critical Interpretation of the Hoover Commission Report* (Macmillan, 1950).

Pennock, J. R., *Administration and the Rule of Law* (Rinehart, 1941).

Pfiffner, J. M., and R. V. Presthus, *Public Administration*, 2nd ed. (Ronald, 1960).

Pollard, R. S. W. (Ed.), *Administrative Tribunals at Work* (Stevens, 1950).

Robson, W. A., *Justice and Administrative Law*, 2nd ed. (Stevens, 1947).

Rowat, D. C. (Ed.), *Basic Issues in Public Administration* (Macmillan, 1961).

Schwartz, B., *French Administrative Law and the Common Law World* (New York U., 1954).

———, *The Professor and the Commissions* (Knopf, 1959).

Selznick, P., *Leadership in Administration* (Row, Peterson, 1957).

Sieghart, M. A., *Government by Decree, A Comparative Study of the History of the Ordinance in English and French Law* (Praeger, 1950).

Simon, H., *Administrative Behavior* (Macmillan, 1947).

Thompson, V. A., *Modern Organization* (Knopf, 1961).

Wade, H. W. R., *Administrative Law* (Oxford, 1961).

Waldo, D., *The Administrative State* (Ronald, 1948).

White, L. D., *Introduction to the Study of Public Administration*, 4th ed. (Macmillan, 1955).

Woll, P., *American Bureaucracy* (Norton, 1963).

XVIII

Democratic Trends

The preceding chapters have outlined and compared in a general way the main features of the structure and working of government in the United States, Britain, and France. The striking contrast offered by the government of the Soviet Union has been presented at several points. The description given falls far short of what would be necessary to explain the complex operations of these four governments as going concerns. No one will know them well unless he observes them at work and reads widely in books that give detailed exposition. The caution given at the beginning may be repeated; the working of any system of government is the study of a lifetime.

No system of government can be understood even in an elementary way without some reference to the ends it is designed to serve. For this reason, the discussion began with a consideration of ideals of government. The basic structure and much of the actual working of government in the United States, Britain, and France are a response to liberal democratic ideals. Similarly, the practical implications of the Communist ideals explain the essential character of government in the Soviet Union. The practice of the Nazi and Fascist dictatorships becomes more intelligible when related to their rejection of democratic ideals. Although the hostility and bitterness between the United States and its allies on the one hand, and the Soviet Union and its allies on the other, are to be explained partly on the ground of a clash of material interests, they also spring from sharply different conceptions of social, economic, and political organization.

The clash between the Soviet Union and the liberal democratic societies of the United States, Britain, and France is the central political fact in the world today. In the United States and Britain, there are small but vigorous minorities crusading for Communist ideals; in postwar France, the Communist minority has usually been able to poll between one fifth and one-quarter of the popular vote. These minorities insist that liberal democratic ideals are shams, and that liberal democratic government is merely a cloak for exploitation of the masses. Democracy is subject to challenge from within. It is also subject to challenge from without. It is impossible to say at what moment citizens of Britain, the United States, and France may be required to risk their lives in what is essentially a struggle over social and political ideals.

In still larger perspective, there are the confusions and doubts within the ranks of the liberal democrats themselves. While holding firmly to the value of individual personality as the ultimate ideal, they are much more perplexed than they were seventy years ago on the appropriate means of serving that ideal. Specifically, there is disagreement on how far we can permit the government to go in organizing our lives without making it our master. The collapse of democracy under internal strains in many countries in Europe in the last generation or so shows that democratic government is not impregnable, that there are conditions in which it will not work. There is no generally accepted explanation of why it has failed in these instances. This adds to the perplexity. So at every point we are compelled to go beyond an examination of the structure and working of particular governments and ask what purposes they are designed to serve, and how their structure and operation are related to those purposes. It is important to grasp the essential features of democratic beliefs and to see their implications for government and politics. When this has been done, one is better able to estimate the significance of changing trends in democratic government.

For these reasons, description has been limited to the main outlines of the governments of the United States, Britain, and France, and to contrasting sketches of the principal features of government in the Soviet Union, thus reserving a good deal of space for elementary analysis of the significance of what has been described. It was pointed out at the beginning that liberal democratic government is expected to serve two principal related ends or purposes. First, democracy, defined as government by, of, and for the people, seeks to ensure a close correspondence between what the people want and what the government does. For government is an instrument for the purposes of the men associated together in the state. Second, a democracy that is liberal seeks adequate guarantees of a large sphere of freedom of thought and action for individuals as the indispensable means of serving the claims of individual personality.

The manner and degree in which the main institutions of government in the United States, Britain, and France contribute to these ends have been discussed. An attempt has been made to explain the essential functions that the different organs of government are expected to perform and the nature of the difficulties in the way of a satisfactory performance. By way of contrast, it has been pointed out that government in the Soviet Union is organized differently and works differently because it has been designed for quite different ends. The same point was made briefly with respect to the Fascist dictatorship in Italy and the Nazi dictatorship in Germany. There is immensely more to be said on all these matters, and many students of the subject would question some of the explanations suggested here. Yet there is no doubt that these are matters of vital import, and there is little use in the study of government and politics unless it contributes to an understanding of them.

Summary of Trends in Democratic Government

New Activities of Government. We have seen that the main institutions of government do not remain unchanged from one generation to another. They have been considerably modified in the last two generations in the United States, Britain, and perhaps somewhat less so in France. The modification has come about in response to the rapidly expanding activities of government. The new activities have not only added greatly to the total of government business, but they have also made the conduct of that business much more complicated and difficult. It is no longer possible to make a clear-cut classification of the powers of government into legislative, executive, and judicial. It was shown that in many fields nowadays the law is being made in the course of its administration, or execution, and that it is being administered while it is being made. Not only is it clear that the judges sometimes make law while they are interpreting it and applying it to particular cases, but also that the administration often exercises judicial functions when it rules on claims and disputes in the course of administration.

Rise of the Administrative. The fact is that the administration has become in some measure a government within a government. It makes a great deal of law by rules and regulations, orders-in-council, and decrees; it executes and enforces the law generally; and it exercises substantial powers of a judicial nature. Some students of the subject urge that if analysis is to be realistic we must add a fourth power, the administrative, to the traditional classification of the three powers of government. It is at least clear that the older classification does not sufficiently explain the facts.

If the tripartite classification of the powers of government is now inadequate, the doctrine of the separation of powers that rests on this classification is also defective. Whether or not the separation of powers is necessary to protect the liberties of the citizen against the government—a point on which liberal democrats are in disagreement among themselves—there is no doubt that governments cannot perform efficiently their present-day tasks if they are bound by rigid separation of powers. This is conceded even in the United States, where the separation of powers is written into the Constitution, and much thought is being given to ways and means of greater legislative-executive collaboration. In all three countries, it is still generally and strongly believed that the judiciary should be independent of both legislature and executive. Judicial independence has been maintained, but at the cost of taking the power to adjudicate on numerous matters away from the judiciary and reposing it with the administrative. This is particularly true in France—whose de Gaulle Constitution of 1958 theoretically resuscitates a system of separation of powers. Indeed, the clear proof that strict adherence to the separation of powers interferes with the performance of the present-day tasks of government is the rise of the administrative, in which are frequently joined powers of legislating, of executing, and of judging.

It does not necessarily follow, of course, that the administrative will swallow the other powers. The legislature—with the exception of France under the Fifth Republic—still fixes the broad objectives and methods of administrative action and the judiciary still applies certain canons of legality to administrative discretion. It may be possible to limit the mingling of legislative, executive, and judicial powers to certain areas of governmental activity. New and better devices of control may be devised. Much depends on whether the functions of government continue for an indefinite period to grow more numerous and complex.

Aggrandizement of the Executive. Frequent reference has been made to the aggrandizement of the executive. The rise of the administrative is the most striking aspect of that aggrandizement, for the administrative is always under the control and direction of the executive. The administrative is a part of the executive, and they have been treated separately here only for purposes of exposition. Another important factor in the strengthening of the executive is its indispensability in lawmaking. The legislature cannot make effective laws on most subjects without constant reliance on the data and experience gathered by the executive in the course of administration. In Britain and France the executive has gained an almost unchallenged initiative in legislation, and even in the United States the trend is clearly in that direction.

The members of the legislature, coming from all walks of life and having a short tenure of office that frequently is not renewed by the electorate, are the amateurs in government. They have an advantage in being closer to the currents of public opinion than the civil service, but even the most intelligent of them are at a decided disadvantage in technical matters when ranged against expert civil servants with permanence of tenure. The legislatures have not taken adequate steps to adjust their procedure to the increased tempo and growing complexity of government. So they are becoming much more dependent on the executive to invent policies for them to approve. Moreover, governmental administration has so wide a range and so many ramifications, which can only be understood after long, patient, and skilled investigation, that legislatures are steadily becoming less effective critics of administration. They criticize, but they often do not know what to criticize, or what to regard as a satisfactory answer to their criticisms. Perhaps the most serious aspect of the aggrandizement of the executive is that the intricacies of the administrative machine and of the operations it is performing leave the legislature in a state of bewilderment and frustration.

Dilemma of Political Parties. In theory, at least, the legislature still makes the decisions on ultimate policy, fixing the general line that government is to take. But the legislature does what the ruling political party or political bloc wants it to do. Although the authority of the majority party is not so extensive in the United States Congress, it now controls the legislature both in Britain and France. If the legislature is weak, it is partly because the political parties have not established secretariats to help them to formulate policy, to explore ways of putting their policies into practice, and to study administration in detail to see how the policies of the opposing party work out in practice. In fact, the parties have brought vote-gathering to a fine art, but they have not taken comparable pains to study public policy and its administration. By and large, the parties have not adapted themselves to the great expansion of governmental functions.

Whatever the weakness of a two-party system, it is an improvement on the shifting coalitions of a multiple-party system, except as it is seen in Scandinavia. Government is expected to do every day so many things of vital importance that it must act vigorously and consistently if the tasks are to be accomplished. These requirements are not likely to be met unless one party has a clear majority in the legislature. However, the great range of governmental action and the consequent rise of numerous pressure groups which seek to influence or control governmental action, are making it difficult to secure or maintain a *vigorous* two-party system.

One of the most significant features of American politics is the internal weakness of the national parties. Blocs in Congress often act like splinter parties. As already noted, part of the alarm over the activities of pressure groups in Washington is justified because of the weakness of the discipline maintained by the majority party in Congress. Britain has the better disciplined two-party system. However, even there, divisive influences must not be overlooked. Firmness, vigor, and coherence in public policy are needed as never before, but there is some doubt whether the well-disciplined majorities, which alone can impregnate public policy with these qualities, will be forthcoming—especially in Washington.

Questionable Scope of Court Authority. The courts have maintained their independence, but the scope of their authority is being narrowed and the discretionary powers of government officials correspondingly increased. How greatly the rule of law is threatened by this development depends on how far it goes. An essential safeguard of liberal democracy would be lost if a numerous officialdom with wide powers were completely free from control by the judiciary. On the other hand, the judges cannot—and never could— supervise all governmental action. Today, they are not entirely satisfactory interpreters of much of the legislation under which officials hold their powers. The truth is that the judges are best fitted, by tradition and training, to interpret and apply the common law. The common law with its roots in custom has been largely made up of general rules of conduct applicable to all, rules that are observed in most instances because they accord with the community sense of right. In those relatively few instances in which common law rules were not obeyed voluntarily, the loose organization and the dilatory procedure of the Anglo-American judicial system sufficed for a long time to enforce obedience.

The rapid economic and social changes of the last hundred years have upset habitual and customary ways of life, causing much insecurity. The common law has not been able to adapt itself to these changes. Attempts are therefore made to adapt the law by legislation. But, as we have seen, much of the legislation now being passed does not make law in the sense of establishing general rules of conduct for all. Rather it authorizes administrators to make different orders for different situations, and to enforce them. In many human relationships, law is being superseded by discretionary administration. The scope of the judicial power narrows, because judges are not administrators but interpreters of law. Yet, withal, in the United States a disturbing tendency has developed of 'passing the buck' to the courts—especially the Supreme Court—on major policy matters that the executive and the legislature have been unwilling and/or unable to tackle, e.g. the racial problem and equitable redistributing of legislative constituencies.

Trend Toward Centralization. The great growth in the functions of government has not merely modified the relationship of the legislative, executive, and judicial powers; it has also altered the relationship between the different levels of government. When government is required to do many things, and when everything it does has numerous effects on other aspects of life which in turn may have to be regulated, the advantage goes to the government with the longest reach because it can control more of the factors involved. Thus local government loses authority to the senior government and comes under its direct and detailed supervision. In a federal system, the state governments lose powers to the national government. They become less able to fend for themselves, and their autonomy within the federal system is restricted, if not threatened with extinction. The trend toward centralization has been a marked feature of the last seventy years.

SIGNIFICANCE OF THE TRENDS

In summary form, these are the trends that can be observed in liberal democratic government. If we were to summarize the outstanding characteristics of modern dictatorship generally, we should find that they were rejection of the separation of powers and the rule of law, atrophy of the legislature, subordination of the judiciary, unchallenged dominance of the executive, and centralization of all power in the senior government at the expense of local and state autonomy. All these features look like projections of the recent trends in democratic government.

Modern one-party dictatorships are marked by an utter concentration of power in the hands of government. The uses made of this concentrated power confirm the democratic fears of all-powerful governments and democratic arguments for limiting and controlling sharply the powers of government. The individual becomes a means to the ends thought good by the leaders and ceases to be an end in himself. The most alarming thing is that once government escapes from confining checks, it is immensely difficult, if not impossible, to restore them.

The situation in the dictatorship makes this crystal clear. Power concentrated in the hands of a small clique of leaders is not checked in any way by judicial institutions, and is no longer contingent on the party winning the next election. For the one party takes no chances on losing the next election. The only way to break its rule is by revolution. And revolution is almost impossible because all unofficial organizations that might become centers of opposition are stamped out. The secret police are everywhere, and every meeting that lacks official blessing meets in the shadow of the forced labor camp.

The recent trends in democratic government are mainly the result of great increases in functions of government in the last seventy years. These functions continue to grow and the trends are being projected further along the same lines. Some liberal democrats think the trends are approaching the point, if they have not already passed it, where it will be impossible to maintain popular control of the government, and government will become master and not servant. They think the liberal democracies are thus traveling the totalitarian road.

Other liberal democrats, particularly the democratic socialists, have more confidence in the resources available for popular control of a powerful government. Of course, governments get out of hand when liberal democratic ideals are rejected or when faith in them declines seriously. They insist, however, that if we hold fast to liberal democratic ideals, we have standards for controlling government action. Even more important, we will elect to power in government men who are themselves loyal to these ideals, men who will direct the work of government to enlarging the possibilities for individual personality. There is no serious danger, they say, until the electorate begins to elect imperious men of dictatorial temperament. As long as we elect good men, we will get good results.

The liberal democrats who fear the constant expansion of the power of government reply that we are, in fact, losing our faith in the liberal democratic ideals. Growing government activities are, in almost all cases, responses to popular demand for greater social equality and more social security at

the expense of individual freedom. Precious qualities of individual personality can only be preserved and developed through a large measure of
freedom and a willing acceptance of the risks and responsibilities that freedom
entails. According to this view, if we go on wanting to exchange freedom
and responsibility for security provided by government, we shall have lost
the essence of the democratic ideal and also the means of keeping government under control.

As as been noted from time to time in this book, these issues are being
debated at length in the United States, Britain, France, and the other liberal
democracies with a great range of data and arguments being brought into
the discussion. The data and arguments cannot be rehearsed here, and therefore no judgment on the debate should be offered.

CONCLUSION

A few points can be stated by way of conclusion. It is clear enough that
liberal democracy cannot survive where power is concentrated as it has been
in the modern dictatorships. Yet the democracies are still a long way from
such a concentration of power, and it is open to them to halt the trends
described here before they present us with the monolithic state. There is now
much more concentration of power in democratic governmental structure
than there was in 1900, and this is not without its alarming aspects. But it is
not necessarily beyond human ingenuity to find improved methods of control as counterpoises to the aggrandizement of the executive and the growing
predominance of national over local and state governments.

This is the crux of the matter. If government is going to perform many
positive services for the community, there must be greater concentration and
less dispersion of power than that which marked the age of *laisser faire*.
But wherever power is lodged, devices are needed to ensure that it can be
called to account. The more power is concentrated, the more nicely calculated the means of controlling it must be. The elaboration of new and more
effective controls has not kept pace with the growing concentration of
power. More thought must be given to such controls in the immediate
future. And it is not going too far to say that some caution will have to be
exercised in adding still further to the positive functions of government. If
the democratic ideal of the supreme importance of individual personality
is clearly understood and firmly held by the bulk of the people, and if enough
persons with an informed intelligence participate actively in democratic poli-

tics, there is little doubt that the needed controls will be devised and the required caution will be exercised.

Suggested References for Further Reading

Appleby, P. H., *Citizens as Sovereigns* (Syracuse U., 1962).

Berle, A. A., *The 20th Century Capitalist Revolution* (Harcourt, Brace, 1954).

Brecht, A., *Political Theory: The Foundations of Twentieth-Century Political Thought* (Princeton, 1959).

Breymer, H. F. (Ed.), *Challenges of the Sixties* (U.S. Dept. of Agriculture, 1963).

Brogan, D. W., *The Free State* (Hamilton, 1945).

Brown, H., J. Bonner, and J. Weir, *The Next Hundred Years* (Viking, 1957).

Cahn, E., *The Predicament of Democratic Man* (Macmillan, 1961).

Center for the Study of Democratic Institutions, *The Elite and the Electorate: Is Government by the People Possible?* (Fund for the Republic, 1963).

Dewhurst, J. F., *et al., America's Needs and Resources: A New Survey* (20th Century Fund, 1955).

Dupre, J. S., and S. A. Lakoff, *Science and the Nation: Policy and Politics* (Prentice-Hall, 1962).

Friedrich, C., *The New Belief in the Common Man* (Little, Brown, 1942).

Gardner, J. W., *Excellence* (Harper, 1961).

Harrison, G. R., *What Man May Be* (Morrow, 1957).

Jessup, J. K. (Ed.), *The National Purpose* (Holt, Rinehart & Winston, 1960).

Kohn, H., *The Twentieth Century* (Macmillan, 1949).

Lapp, R. E., *Atoms and People* (Harper, 1956).

Lippmann, W., *Essays in the Public Philosophy* (Mentor, 1956).

MacIver, R. M., *The Ramparts We Guard* (Macmillan, 1950).

Mills, C. W., *The Power Elite* (Oxford, 1956).

Morgenthau, H. J., *The Purpose of American Politics* (Knopf, 1960).

Packard, V., *The Status Seekers* (McKay, 1959).

Perkins, D., *The American Way* (Cornell, 1957).

President's Commission on National Goals, *Goals for Americans* (Prentice-Hall, 1960).

Riesman, D., *et al., The Lonely Crowd* (Yale, 1952).

Roelofs, H. M., *The Tension of Citizenship* (Rinehart, 1957).

Rossiter, C., *Conservatism in America,* 2nd ed. rev. (Random House, 1962).

Tussman, J., *Obligation and the Body Politic* (Oxford, 1961).

Whyte, W. H., *The Organization Man* (Simon & Schuster, 1957).

Willmore, J. N. (Ed.), *Critical Issues and Decisions* (U.S. Dept. of Agriculture, 1963).

XIX

International Politics

The world is divided into a number of separate, independent states. There were some 118 to 125 in 1963, depending on what is reckoned to constitute independence. Each of these is ruled by a separate government whose prime objective is to safeguard the independence of its particular state. Some, the liberal democratic governments, want independence so that their people will be free to pursue the good life within the national framework of order already firmly established. Others, like the old Nazi and Fascist dictatorships, wanted freedom for the state so that it could pursue its mission in the world. The Soviet Union wants to maintain its independence in order to show the world, and particularly the new states, by a variety of methods, how communism will settle its problems. But for whatever reason, each government still regards its freedom of action vis-à-vis the outside world as the highest law. It acknowledges no political superior from whom it accepts orders.

Of course, particular states often have something in common with some of the other states. Twice in twenty-five years, Britain, France, and the United States found a common interest in resisting German designs in Europe. The United States and Great Britain have always shared a common language and a large element of common tradition. Since the nineteenth century, they have both adhered to substantially the same ideal of government. In general, they have shared a desire to maintain the *status quo,* i.e. the preservation of the existing distribution of power and status in the world. For these reasons, war between them is most unlikely, if not unthinkable. Bismarck, the realistic German statesman of the nineteenth century, said the most important fact about international politics was that the United States spoke the English language. Later German statesmen failed to see the significance of this, to the sorrow of their country. It would not be easy to find two other states with anything like as much in common, with the possible exception of some of the members of the Commonwealth. Most of them have much less, and many of them seem to have nothing.

INTERNATIONAL POLITICS VERSUS DOMESTIC POLITICS

Although they are primarily self-regarding, states do not exist in isolation. Each has relationships with some or all of the others. Those that have common boundaries have line-fence disputes. Several may covet the resources of undeveloped areas of the world and thus get into a scramble for spheres of influence of one sort or another. Each has raw materials, finished products, or skills that some of the others need. Commercial intercourse and international exchange of goods and services develop. When the means of transport and communication reach into the furthest corners of the world, intercourse between states is on a world-wide scale. As a result, every state is brought into relationships with almost all the others. What happens between North Korea and South Korea profoundly affects the relationships of the United States to other states. These relationships between states are the content of international politics.

Different Politics. Politics within a single state is concerned with the adjusting and ordering of the relationships between individuals and groups within that state. International politics has to do with the adjustment of relationships between separate states. There is a deep difference between international politics and domestic politics within the household of a particular state. The individuals and groups involved in domestic politics are all subject to one superior authority, the government, which makes and enforces law, preserves order, and keeps them all in check. The separate states, whose relationships are the stuff of international politics, acknowledge no superior authority or common lawmaking body, and reserve the right to be disorderly if they wish. Hence, while we can talk about international politics, we cannot talk about international government, for there is no such thing, although some would consider the U.N. a step in that direction.

There is another and deeper difference between international politics and the domestic politics of liberal democratic states in particular. Individuals in the liberal democratic state are united by habit and custom, the innumerable ties that come from living together in peace and security over a long period of time. They are also united by widespread allegiance to liberal democratic ideals. There is a voluntary cohesion out of which, as we have seen, an unmistakable public opinion arises from time to time.

Different Climate and Environment. The people of the United States, Britain, and France are governed by public opinion as well as by the restraint of superior force in the hands of the government. In the community of states, or the family of nations as it is sometimes called, there is little or no community or family feeling. The several states have not lived together in peace and security, but rather in fear intensified by recurring wars. There is no unifying ideal held by all the people of all the nations. Consequently, there is no voluntary cohesion that unites people across national boundaries, no international public opinion that puts restraints on the actions of particular states in the way in which public opinion in the United States or Britain or France operates as a restraint on the actions of individuals and groups.

At most, there are widely shared aspirations for world peace, dreams of world order without any genuine agreement across boundaries on ways and means, terms, and conditions. So far at any rate, each of the powerful states wants peace and order on its own terms, consistent with its own independence and security. So international politics works in an entirely different climate and environment from liberal democratic politics.

The principles and procedures of liberal democratic domestic politics do not operate in international politics. The analysis that explains the former does not apply in any significant way to the latter. The techniques of adjustment that settle conflicts and maintain order in the former—discussion, compromise, the making and enforcing of new laws, the impartial judiciary, settling disputes in accordance with accepted law—cannot be transferred bodily to the latter. That is why prescriptions for world order and peace originating from liberal democratic sources have failed to work. The lack of a common unifying ideal, and of an unquestioned common superior authority in the latter case, makes such transfer improbable.

Distinct Subject of Study. International politics therefore is a distinct and separate subject of study. Not only are the facts entirely different; the postulates and assumptions from which analysis must start are different. A separate book, and not merely a chapter, is needed to give an adequate introduction to the subject. There are, however, two important reasons for looking at international politics in a book on liberal democratic government.

First, the continuance of liberal democratic government in any country depends on some minimum of stability and order in international relations. Liberal democracy does not thrive on war, because war exalts the authoritarian elements and personalities in a society, and increases tremendously the social dislocations and maladjustments. Continual war or threat of war may burden the processes of discussion and compromise beyond what they can bear and compel reliance on authoritarian methods and personalities. Most important, liberal democratic ideals claim a universal validity, and must seek the allegiance of all men. They aim at peace, harmony, and mutual respect among men, and hope in them may well be abandoned if they are continually frustrated by war. It is important to see something of the conditions on which their continuance and their projection on a world scale must be estimated.

Second, the contrast with international politics should help to clarify still further the principal characteristics and conditions of democratic politics. Both kinds of politics are made of the same basic human nature and the same psychological drives. Presumably, there is nothing in human nature as such which prevents lawlessness, violence, and insecurity *within* national boundaries yet at the same time manifests itself *across* national boundaries. Men have had to learn the secret of political unity and to work out the institutions and procedures that secure internal peace. We forget them at our peril, and a contrast that sharpens their outlines improves our grip on them. By the same token, there is reason to hope. For presumably there is nothing in nature that prevents the establishment of world order and peace if the appropriate conditions for it are brought into existence. But a universal wish for it is not enough.

A SYSTEM OF STATES

The situation that confronts us is a system of states, or a state system, the members of which cannot live in isolation from one another. They are continually enmeshed in relationships that affect one another's interests, effective power, and security; as an entity, they have not been able to establish these relationships on a permanently peaceful basis. The term, *state system,* is justified despite the disorderliness of their relationships. For these relationships show a recurring pattern of aggrandizement, diplomacy, war, peace treaties, alliances, counter-alliances, and so on. The modern state system emerged in Western Europe in the sixteenth century, at the end of the

Middle Ages. It has now expanded to embrace all the states in the world and we are living in the advanced stages of its tribulations. However, it is by no means the first state system known to human history and exhibiting these characteristics.

Older State Systems

Some of those which are a part of the history of the Western world may be noted. For several thousand years before Christ there were successive state systems in what is now called the Middle East, where repeatedly a number of separate, independent states contended with one another after the fashion mentioned. In the millennium before Christ, the numerous Greek city-states composed a state system of their own. Despite common language, common gods, and common culture, they were unable to live together permanently at peace. The disastrous Peloponnesian War between Athens and Sparta found most of them ranged on one side or the other. In the five hundred years before Christ, expanding maritime intercourse in the Mediterranean drew the states that lined its shores into a state system which culminated in the death struggle between Rome and Carthage.

In the later Middle Ages the city-states of the Italian peninsula, Florence, Genoa, Pisa, Milan, Venice, and so on, participated in a state system. It was as a diplomat in the service of the city of Florence that Niccolò Machiavelli got his experience of the methods necessary for survival in such a system, and which he immortalized in his famous book *The Prince.* These methods consisted so largely of fraud, treachery, and violence that the record has shocked the civilized world ever since and has made 'Machiavellian' a term of reproach.[1]

Their Usual Fate. The usual fate of such state systems at some time or other in their history has been the loss of independence of the several states and their subjugation by the strongest one among them. They were brought into a political unity, or at any rate some kind of peace, by conquest. The Babylonian, Assyrian, and Persian Empires successively swallowed up the ancient state systems of the Middle East. The Greek city-states were subdued by Philip of Macedon; and his son, Alexander the Great, incorporated them into his short-lived empire that stretched from the Greek peninsula to the borders of India. After the destruction of Carthage, Rome made herself mis-

---

[1] For the contention that Machiavelli himself was not really a 'Machiavellian,' see Henry J. Abraham, 'Was Machiavelli a Machiavellian?' *Social Science,* xxviii (1953), 25–30.

tress not only of the Mediterranean basin but also of the then-known world. The Roman Empire established the *pax Romana,* the Roman peace, and held it steadily for hundreds of years, partly through the power of its legions, and partly through an effective system of law and administration. In most of the state systems of the past, the price of prolonged peace has been forcible unification by a single great power.

The Roman Empire collapsed completely in Europe about A.D. 400, but the memory of the peace and security it provided in its best days has never quite died from the minds of Europeans. With the revival of Europe in the Middle Ages—roughly from A.D. 900 to 1500—attempts were made to restore the universal empire under the joint auspices of the Papacy and the Holy Roman Empire. In this period Europe had a tenuous sort of unity. Its people had a religious unity under the Catholic (universal) Church, which moderated the tensions among them. The Holy Roman Empire, under the leadership of an elected Emperor, claimed to be the heir of the old Roman Empire, and tried with indifferent success to exercise a loose dominion over Europe. The desire for political unity was there, but it was mostly ineffective.

Europe was far from enjoying universal peace during the Middle Ages. However, the effective units of power were mostly small feudal principalities. Subsistence agriculture, which was the prevailing mode of production, could not sustain prolonged or extensive wars. The difficulties of transportation and the state of technology in general were also limiting factors. The conditions for a full-fledged state system did not exist.

THE MODERN STATE SYSTEM

The modern state system emerged in Western Europe after the close of the Middle Ages. From small beginnings, a number of feudal lords and their successors managed over long periods of time to consolidate large territories under their control, in much the same way that land-hungry farmers expand, and to set themselves up as kings. Large areas, France, England, Spain, Austria, and Holland, roughly as we now know them, became united under a single political control. These kingdoms rejected the overlordship of the Holy Roman Empire. Each asserted the right to consider only its own interests in its dealings with the others.

Its Development in Europe. The term 'sovereignty' came into use in the sixteenth century to denote the status of a ruler who was supreme in his own territory and acknowledged no superior external political authority above him. His might became right. At about the same time, the Reformation broke the religious unity of Europe, severing the bonds that might have helped to unite people across frontiers. Britain and Holland became Protestant; Spain, France, and Austria remained officially Catholic. From about 1650 to 1750 Europe was rent by religious wars, sometimes civil wars, but increasingly wars between what we now call nation-states.

The process of development into separate independent states was at the same time a process of division. The prince who established order and security firmly within his boundaries helped to enthrone anarchy on his frontiers. The double process went on from the sixteenth century to the twentieth century. As communications improved and trade, wealth, and population grew, more and more states were drawn into the European state system. As the Napoleonic wars show, Russia had been drawn into it by the end of the eighteenth century. Germany and Italy were not unified until after the middle of the nineteenth century, but they rapidly became great powers. After the readjustments in the peace treaties at the end of World War I, there were twenty-six separate, independent states in Europe, each devoted to maintaining its independence.

Its Expansion on a World Scale. However, as World War I clearly showed, the European state system had become world-wide. The War of 1914–18 began in Europe but the whole world was drawn into the conflagration. The participation—however reluctant—by the United States, for example, showed that it had a vital stake in the results of the conflict. World War II also began in Europe, but decisive battles in it were fought in Africa, Asia, and even on the borders of Australia and in the oceans of America. All the states in the world have become neighbors in the sense that what happens between any two of them may affect decisively *all* the others.

At the same time, the states, or powers, that really count are becoming fewer and bigger. At the outbreak of World War II the Great Powers, those that dwarfed all the others in military power, numbered eight: Germany, the Soviet Union, Britain, France, Italy, the United States, Japan, and China. In 1963 there were just two of these, the United States and the Soviet Union, but with Communist China a potential third—and, as we shall see, a growing pluralism in the offing on the international horizon generally. The vital decisions are no longer exclusively being taken in European chancelleries. The European states, excluding the Soviet Union, are today little more than pawns in a bigger game. They are reaping the fruits of their inability to keep Europe from wasting her strength in exhausting wars.

The world as a whole is having to come to terms with the consequences of the European state system with the present situation growing out of its history. The pattern of intercourse between states is largely that developed in the experience of European states in dealing with one another. All the means and devices for trying to maintain peace have been thought out primarily for application to the European state system. Hence, any discussion of international politics still requires close attention to it.

The Rise of Nationalism

The European states that emerged at the end of the Middle Ages were first dynastic states. They were ruled by monarchs whose power stayed in the family and was passed on to their descendants, the Tudors, the Stuarts, the Bourbons, Hapsburgs, and Hohenzollerns. However, they all developed, or divided, sooner or later, into nation-states. A *dynastic state* is one in which the bond of union among the people is common subjection to a monarch, who is not quite a god but who claims the awe and reverence of a god. The European dynasties each claimed to rule by Divine Right. A *nation-state* is one in which the bond of union among the people is the feeling of a common nationality, or nationalism. The feeling of loyalty and reverence is transferred from the monarch to the nation. The nation is deified and its welfare and interests are the highest law. The sovereignty of the monarch, already referred to, becomes the sovereignty of the nation.

Exclusiveness of Nationalism. The unification of the separate European states laid the foundations of modern nationalism. The more or less diverse people, who were held together in peace in these kingdoms, gradually developed a common consciousness. They became Englishmen or Frenchmen. As the sense of national fellowship grew, it was accompanied by a sense of national exclusiveness. Finding out what they had in common was accompanied by a discovery of how different and superior they were to other national groups. National pride and national exclusiveness went hand in hand. In the Middle Ages, the universal Church taught the brotherhood of all men and sought to secure for itself the highest loyalty of all men. For modern nationalism, it can almost be said that the brotherhood of man stops at the national frontier. The widest loyalty that now attracts the masses of men is the nation-state. Millions fought, suffered, and died for it in both world wars.

Napoleon scourged Europe not only by his military genius, but by exploiting the passion of French national feeling. Hitler desolated Europe in the name of the world-mission of the German people. The ferment in the Far East and Africa against domination by the white race has been, in part at least, due to the stirrings of nationalism. The Soviet Union, which claims to have a universal message of hope for all men, has not hesitated in recent years to stimulate Russian nationalism and to turn czars and czarist generals into national heroes.

Liberal democratic ideals are stated in universal terms and those who hold them assert their universal validity. Yet these ideals have been principally effective in the modern world in strengthening national cohesion in the countries where they are held. When it is proposed to feed the starving peoples of other countries, it has to be explained or 'sold' in large part at any rate—especially in the United States—as a measure for our own security. Nationalist feeling and loyalty are almost everywhere an obstacle to wider loyalties.

Nationalism and Total War. Even after the sovereign states of Europe arose, the memories of the cultural and religious unity of Europe in the Middle Ages lingered on. In the eighteenth century, educated people could still think of themselves as Europeans, and eighteenth-century wars were gentlemen's games played according to rules, by professional soldiers for limited stakes. When peace was made, the victors did not try to humiliate the vanquished. They made peace coolly with an eye to their own self-interest but without vindictiveness. Twentieth-century wars are fought by entire populations roused to the highest pitch of passion by their governments. Less and less attention is paid to the rules of the game. Nazi Germany, the archetype of this strident nationalism, did not even show its opponents the courtesy of declaring war, but struck without warning. So did Japan. When nations are convinced that they are fighting for their existence, they will use almost any methods, and they make peace vindictively, which rouses a passion for revenge. Twentieth-century wars are total wars, and nationalism is one of the main factors making them so.

Yet it will not do merely to condemn nationalism. The good life requires order and security. The existing nation-states provide the only order and security that is effective in the world today. On the basis of national feeling, the nation-states have provided a more civilized order over wider areas than any previously known political organization.

WIDER LOYALTIES. It is true that wider loyalties are necessary for the effective establishment of world peace in our day. But the tragic difficulty is that it has never been clear how these wider loyalties are to be focused and nourished. One can give loyalty to the idea of world peace, and most people do. Ideas alone, however, will not secure peace. That requires the establishment of the institutions of world government as a focus for loyalty. Until they take concrete and promising form, few are prepared to compromise the substance of order and security on a national basis for the shadowy possibility of a world order.

Perhaps what is needed in terms of institutions is to duplicate the achievement of the United States on a world scale. This was not easy to do, and even then it did not preclude a fierce civil war. It is infinitely harder to do on a world scale amid the confusion of tongues, cultures, and passionate nationalisms, although the United Nations and various regional arrangements, both to be discussed later, have tried to point the way.

The Implications of a State System

To understand the nature of the problem and its difficulties, it is necessary to look very closely at the motives that move states in a state system. Each state cherishes its freedom, and knows that the others cherish their independence. Freedom, whether for individuals or for states, leads to self-expression, the trying out of one's powers and capacities in the environment. As innate powers and capacities, whether of individual men or of groups of men associated together in a state, are tested and developed, they call for a larger arena in which to test and express them still further.

Power-Drives of Men and States. When men learned to fly, they were not content with showing that a heavier-than-air machine could be kept in the air. There began a competition to see who could fly farthest, fastest, highest, and longest. Even yet, no limit has been set to these ambitions. As long as the contest is directed to conquest of a material environment, it does not raise directly any political question. However, the environment in which self-expression takes place is social as well as material. For many, the intoxication of directing and controlling other people is greater than that of mastering the purely material environment. It is not true of all persons, nor are all states always seeking to exercise power over their neighbors. But it is always true of enough persons and enough states to make it a dominating factor in both domestic and international politics.

If self-expression through power-seeking is not checked, it comes to regard the sky as the limit, 'the restless search of power after power that ceaseth only in death,' as Hobbes expressed it in his *Leviathan*. It becomes imperialism in one form or another. This is why every political system which accepts freedom as a value to be protected must be concerned to check and limit the power of individuals, organized groups, and governments as well. This is why every political system that does not accept freedom as a value is likely to end in the arbitrary power of a few over the many.

CURBS. There are several ways of checking imperialistic self-expression. Ideals which inculcate respect for the claims of others to freedom and self-realization are the strongest check, because they operate directly on motivation. In the Anglo-American world, while there have been some embarrassing exceptions, we see relatively little evidence of power-thirst in ourselves or our neighbors, and this has at times made it difficult there to appreciate the essential character of international politics. Another way is to persuade power-seekers that particular ambitions are inherently incapable of realization. For a long time, men put little effort into trying to fly because it seemed to be out of the question. Switzerland and Denmark do not want to conquer the world. One state will not try to conquer all the others if on any careful estimate successful conquest seems to be impossible. If one state seeking to dominate is always confronted by an effective combination of states against it, its imperialistic ambitions will be checked. Finally, there is the check of a superior political authority which is found in the government in domestic politics, but does not exist in international politics.

URGES. The urges to imperialistic self-expression that move individuals move states also, the drive for power in the latter case being much more complex in motivation. Just as the farmer covets the next piece of land to round out his holdings, so some states want to extend their boundaries to their 'natural' frontiers, e.g. Germany's demand for Danzig and the Polish 'Corridor' before World War II. The feudal lords of Europe before the sixteenth century and the monarchs after that time were literally land-hungry farmers. From 1650 to 1750, the monarchs of Europe were also moved by religious imperialism, the desire to further a particular religious cause. At other times, as in the late nineteenth century, it is colonial imperialism, a search for raw materials, markets, and fields of investment for an expanding capitalism. Or it may be a Mussolini-inspired Italian dream for a *mare nostrum* and a Greater Italy abroad. Whatever the motivations, when the state expresses in international politics deep desires of its millions of people, it is a massive phenomenon. When millions of Germans and Japanese are convinced, as they were before World War II, that Germany and Japan are suffocating for want of *Lebensraum* for their people, an explosive force of terrifying power is built up.

Fear Provokes Security Measures. In a state system in which each state is sovereign, considerations of power, of the organized force needed for security or for realizing ambitions, must always be dominant. While some states may be satisfied and content with the *status quo,* it is almost unthinkable that they should all be. Even those content with the *status quo* cannot feel secure and must live in fear, unless they are satisfied that all other states are equally content, and will continue to be so content. This is a far-reaching statement because it really says that no state in a state system can ever feel secure. Yet it must be true for a very simple reason:

The decisive motivation in a state system is the desire of each state to preserve its freedom now and in the future. If this desire were removed, there might be a voluntary political unification as in the Thirteen Colonies in 1789, and the separate state system might come to an end. For each to be able to preserve its freedom in the future, it must be alert to the power its neighbors now possess, or are likely to possess in the near future. Even if these neighbors are now pacific in demeanor and devoted to the arts of peace—increasing their industrial potential—a new set of statesmen may arise there at any time who will decide to use this power for imperialistic designs. So, even if all states in a state system were presently content with the *status quo,* considerations of power would still take priority in the calculations of statesmen, and each state would feel compelled to take measures for its own security. Of course, the people and the statesmen of particular states may forget that this is true. The democratic world did forget it between the two World Wars with almost fatal consequences.

Security Measures Provoke Fear. Most states remember most of the time. Each is thus disposed to take such steps now as it can to protect itself in the future. But when a state increases its armaments, or seeks an expansion of territory to the natural defense line of a sea or range of mountains, it is likely to provoke fear in some or all of the other states, because they lack any assurance about the purposes to which this increase of power will be put. Fear then is likely to provoke counter-preparation by other states. Almost before they know it, the strong powers in a state system may slide insensibly into an armament race, and thence into open war.

Even when one state has outdistanced all the others in its effective power, it still does not feel secure. It knows itself to be the object of widespread fear, envy, and suspicion by the other states. Alliances are formed, or may be formed, against it. So its disposition is to take still further anxious and alarming measures to protect itself. It may even come to the point of thinking that security requires the subjection of all the others. Small, weak states have to resign themselves to seeking the protection of a stronger state. But the stronger they become in relative terms, the more do they have to attend to considerations of power.

To explain international rivalry and power-seeking leading to repeated wars, it is not necessary to postulate imperialistic ambitions as a primary motive. It is enough to postulate a tendency on the part of human organization to seek to extend and to use power. If this is assumed to be an inherent tendency, then each state must be on guard constantly against the possibility that the enlarging power of other states is becoming the instrument of imperialistic designs. In particular instances, the possibility may or may not be a reality. The existing rivalry between the United States and the Soviet Union may not be due to a determination by the Soviet Union to dominate the world. The leaders of the Soviet Union may be convinced that the inherent character of capitalism is driving the United States inevitably to war against communism as represented by the Soviet Union, and their whole policy since 1945 may be primarily defensive in purpose. For all we know with utter certainty, this *may* be true. But equally, for all we know with utter certainty, it may *not* be true.

The Risks of a Trusting Policy. The critical questions are these: who is prepared to make, and act on, the assumption that current Soviet policy is really defensive, caused by fear; who is prepared to take the responsibility and risk of stopping all military preparations that might add to that fear? It is not merely that the assumption might be mistaken, but also that the consequences of acting on mistaken assumption in this situation are likely to be irretrievable. No responsible statesman will take the risk.

If we take up again the contrast with domestic politics it will help to make the situation in international politics clear. While there are struggles for power in domestic politics, they are moderated by various factors. There is at least some mutual trust based on widespread adherence to common ideals. The conflicting ideals of the United States and the Soviet Union heighten enormously their mutual distrust. Mutual trust within the United States and Britain is greatly strengthened by two other considerations.

First, there is the knowledge that others, while they may wish us ill, are restrained in their designs on us by fear of the law and of the government which exists to enforce general security. Second, the consequences of misplaced trust are not nearly so likely to be irretrievable, and risks can be taken with a lighter heart. For, even if we are mistaken in trusting our fellows and they wrong us, we can still seek redress through the force of public opinion, through the award of damages or punishment against the wrongdoer by the courts, and through physical coercion of him by the government if necessary. States that take wide risks for peace in international politics and guess wrong have no such recourse to retrieve their position. They must retrieve their position, if at all, by their own efforts. This gives a desperate character to gambling in international politics. Yet, as the King of Siam sang in a Broadway musical, 'unless somebody trusts somebody, there will be nothing left on earth excepting fishes!' Perhaps not even they, given modern radiation-polluted waters.

The Old and New Balance of Power

When several sovereign states face one another in a state system, even the most pacific is driven to try to amass enough power to persuade others not to attack it. If the power of two states between which tension exists appears approximately equal, each is likely to feel that the outcome of a war is too uncertain to risk it. As long as this conviction is general among the several states, there is equilibrium, or balance, of power, and peace, although essentially an unstable peace.[2] However, the different states in the modern state system have almost always been unequal in power, in populalation, resources, skill, and organizing capacity. Generally, there have been a few great powers with a larger number of smaller powers in descending order to the point of insignificance.

Alliance and Counter-Alliance. In this situation, varieties of maneuvers are possible for trying to maintain a balance of power. The most frequent historical pattern has been systems of alliances. This was certainly the case until the appearance of the two super-powers, and the consequent introduction of a bipolar or two-bloc system of strength that, of course is potentially tempered by the de Gaulle-conceived (perhaps wishfully) 'third force' of the Old World or even the Afro-Asian bloc. For example, before World War I, there was the Triple Alliance of Germany, Austria-Hungary, and Italy, the last proving unreliable in the event. Facing it was the Triple Entente of France, Russia, and Britain, the last not firmly attached till the last minute. Every particular historical effort at balance is too complex for brief description. A simplified model will help to give some inkling of the mechanics of the classic balance of power.

[2] For an interesting dissenting viewpoint, see A. F. K. Organski, *World Politics* (New York: Alfred A. Knopf, 1958), ch. 11.

Assume a situation in which State A is clearly greater in power than any other single state. Because of that power there are doubts, justified or not, about its pacific intentions. Or State B, the next of the lower order of powers, may want to gain for itself by maneuver the advantages of A's position. Each of the lesser powers standing alone, B included, is outweighed by A. But B and C, which have a common interest in checking A, might in firm alliance together so balance the power of A as to give a feeling of considerable security against attack or severe diplomatic pressure by A.

This technique of alliance, once applied, cuts both ways. If A now thinks there is a preponderance of power against it threatening its security, it may seek a counter-alliance with State D, which thinks it has reason to fear the ambitions of B or C, or both. The tendency then is for all states of significant power to be drawn into alliance on one side or other of the scale. If that happens, and the alliances and counter-alliances hold firm, all the resources of the technique of balance of power have been exploited. The balance is never likely to be exactly even, and events in any one or other of the states concerned may tip it sharply one way or the other. If an occasion for war arises, war is likely to be the result.

The Need for a Balancer. More delicate adjustments and more effective use of the balance of power were possible, if one of the stronger states in the system felt sufficiently secure and sufficiently satisfied with the *status quo* to afford some detachment from the struggle for security that engrossed the others. Given sufficient diplomatic skill and coolness, it could act as a balancer, standing in the middle, and throwing its weight, now on one side of the scale and now on the other, to redress dangerous tips of the balance.

The balancer could not make any permanent alliance. It had to keep both sides in doubt about its policy so that they would always be courting its favor, and it could award its temporary support only on conditions that tended to preserve the balance. This accomplished, it could use its greater freedom of action to pursue policies for its own advantage. As long as the balance worked, of course, the balancer not only maintained its own freedom but also the independence of the other states and general peace as well.

Britain as Balancer. For a long time, Great Britain was this balancer in the European balance of power. Her insular position made her secure from attack, at least as long as Europe was divided into a number of competing powers. From the sixteenth century on, her primary interests were not in Europe, but in her maritime empire. She looked with detachment on the

European scene. Her interests in continental Europe were of a very limited character as long as a balance of power was maintained. Her one constant aim was to prevent the political consolidation of Europe under a single power, to prevent any drastic alteration of the *status quo*.

She never committed herself permanently to any one ally or set of allies. Successively, she supported coalitions against Spain, France, and Germany precisely *because* these states in turn became so strong as to threaten the balance of power. From the seventeenth to the nineteenth centuries, France was the power to be feared—witness the long British struggle against Napoleon. The unification of Germany in 1870 soon made it the greatest European power. So Britain moved to the side of France—witness the two successive struggles against Germany in the twentieth century.

PAX BRITANNICA. Freed from hampering commitments on the Continent of Europe, Britain enjoyed great freedom in the rest of the world. In the nineteenth century particularly, when her naval supremacy and economic leadership were unquestioned, she maintained throughout the world what might be called *pax Britannica*. She herself profited immensely from this situation. But so also did many other non-European states. For example, the *pax Britannica,* in large measure, provided security for the states of the Western Hemisphere without requiring them to expend significant resources on military and naval establishments until the twentieth century. It was the *pax Britannica,* rather than the breadth of the oceans, which enabled North American isolationism to continue into the twentieth century. It was only when British power declined and ceased to be an effective balancer that its significance became clear.

Precariousness of Balance of Power. This balance of power, even if it responded to the diplomacy of a skillful balancer, did not always prevent wars. It did not ensure permanent peace. There were recurring wars throughout the history of the efforts to maintain a European balance of power. Its primary purpose was not to ensure peace but to ensure the continued freedom and independence of the states within a state system. States that wanted to preserve their freedom within a state system were compelled to play power politics with the balancing technique. The most that can be said for the above-described balance of power is that it tended to make war less frequent and on occasion brought long periods of peace. What peace it did bring was inherently precarious.

Reasons. It was and is inevitably so for several reasons. First, power cannot be exactly weighed. God is not always on the side of the biggest battalions.

The morale of the soldier counts too. So does the morale of the civilian population in this age of 'total wars,' when states throw the whole of their industrial power into the fight. So neither available raw materials nor industrial potential can be overlooked in any consideration of power. It is extremely difficult to know when there is a 'balance,' and different statesmen will make different estimates and draw different conclusions about the likely outcome of a war. What is needed is not only approximate balance in fact but also a general belief that it does exist.

Second, the larger powers are rarely content with a balance, or static equilibrium, that limits their freedom of movement and action. Each of them wants for itself something of an edge, a preponderance of power on its side to enable it to demand and get what it wants. Even though each wants to maintain the balance, each wants to get a favored position in it. The struggle for advantage is constantly threatening to upset the balance. This is certainly true in the case of the 'bipolar' balance of power between the two post-World War II colossi, the United States and the Soviet Union.

Third, this balance of power will only work when the most that any state can objectively hope to do is to maintain its freedom and check the designs of others on it. As long as ambition beyond this point seems incapable of realization, each state accepts the balance as the least of evils and works in its own, and no doubt often misguided, way to maintain it. In these circumstances, the states have a common interest in the balance, if in nothing else.

Ambitions for Domination. However, there is always danger that one state may attain such power that its ambitions shift from attempts to get the most favorable position within a balance to an attempt to destroy the balance by decisive domination of all the others. Then the game ceases to be played for limited stakes within a balance and wars cease to be fought for limited objectives. The very existence of the several states is at stake, and wars are likely to become total wars.

Because the complete domination of Europe became an element in German calculations in World War I, her enemies were not content to check her but imposed a humiliating peace. The result was a second desperate effort by Germany to make herself mistress of Europe, a total war for mastery and not for freedom within a balance. The probability that the Soviet Union has conceived an even more grandiose ambition for mastery gives an especially desperate character to international politics today. Even if Britain or an incipient European or other federation were strong enough to contemplate the role of balancer between the United States and the Soviet Union, there would be no point in redressing the balance in favor of a power which, as far as outward actions go, shows no disposition at all to be content with balance.

A 'New' Balance of Power? This brings us to a crucial development concerning these considerations: The entire concept of the 'balance of power' underwent a dramatic and radical transformation in the years following the end of World War II. The power of the United States and the Soviet Union became so overriding vis-à-vis their allies or satellites, that these two, in their new role as super-powers, determined the balance of power between them. In the words of Professor Hans J. Morgenthau, '. . . the balance of power has been transformed from a multipolar into a bipolar one.'[3] What we have in the early 1960's is, to all intents and purposes, a two-bloc system, whatever the possibilities of the various incipient 'third forces' may be.

As we have already seen, other factors, such as nationalism, have contributed to the emergence of total war in the twentieth century. It is enough at present to see that—whatever its modern form—the technique of balance of power, to which has now been added *the balance of nuclear terror,* does not prevent war, and is unlikely to be workable at all in the immediate future unless there are presently unforeseeable changes in the relations of the United States and the Soviet Union and the rest of the world. One further point may be added. Where there are half a dozen great powers and a number of lesser but still important powers, a great many different combinations are possible. The diplomatic maneuvers needed to explore them take time, and peace prevails at least for longish intervals. But where two super-powers dwarf all the rest, the resources of diplomacy are painfully few, and the situation is likely to move to a climax much faster.

INTERNATIONAL LAW AND ORGANIZATION

International Law

Attention will now be turned to international law and organization. *International law* is another approach to the regulation of relationships between sovereign states—i.e. between governments or between the government of one state and the subjects of another. It merits attention because

---

[3] For a penetrating discussion of the balance of power, which has been much relied upon in these pages, see his *Politics Among Nations,* 3rd ed. (New York: Alfred A. Knopf, Inc., 1960), parts IV and VII.

some have thought it could be developed into a system of rules capable of ensuring peace between states, on the analogy of the role law plays in maintaining peace and order between individuals within the state.

The emergence in Europe in the sixteenth century of independent, sovereign states that acknowledged no superior authority above them, was followed by savage wars among them in the first half of the seventeenth century. The absence of all rule and measure in these collisions shocked civilized Europeans, and in their midst, Hugo Grotius (1583–1645), a Dutch jurist, wrote a book entitled *The Law of War and Peace*. In it, he assembled a body of rules and principles for governing the relations of sovereign states with one another.

Grotius's Rules. Although he built on the work of many predecessors, he is regarded as the founder of modern international law. He made a coherent system of the rules, and he gave cogent reasons for states accepting them as unconditionally binding on them. As his title indicates, he did not conceive international law as forbidding war. He tried rather to formulate laws that would regulate the peaceful intercourse of states and thus reduce the occasions for war. He also tried to establish laws of war that would help to isolate and confine the conflict and regulate the actual course of hostilities after the fashion of the rules of a game.

Although there were conferences and multilateral treaties, there existed, of course, no international legislature to make these into laws. The sovereign states had just rejected the notion of any political authority superior to themselves. Grotius did not assume to make rules out of whole cloth, nor did he ask for them to be accepted on his authority. In part, his work was a collection of customary rules that had been widely observed in the intercourse and mutual dealings of different political authorities for hundreds of years. In part, it consisted of an appeal to the law of nature both as a source of rules and as proof of their binding obligation on states.

The law of nature, it will be recalled, was a product of Stoic philosophy. There are, it was contended, certain rules binding mankind generally because these rules express the minimum conditions on which men can live together. For example, the law of nature requires all men to keep their covenants, to keep faith in what they have promised. If such a rule is unconditionally binding on all men, it should equally be binding on all states, which are, after all, only instruments of human purposes. Accordingly, it was argued, states are under an obligation to abide loyally by the treaties and engagements entered into with other states.

Development of the System. The first attempt to regulate directly the relations of the modern sovereign states was through a system of international law. From the seventeenth century to the twentieth century the system was steadily developed and refined by the writings of jurists, the establishment of new customary patterns of behavior, the decisions of judicial tribunals, and the elaboration of a great network of treaties. Some of these treaties were bilateral only, regulating the relations of the signatory states on some specific subject. Increasingly after 1850, treaties were multilateral, signed by almost all the powers of consequence and intended to declare law that would be binding on all states. The first of these was the Declaration of Paris in 1856, laying down certain rules relating to war at sea.

The Hague Peace Conferences of 1899 and 1907 were great international assemblies, called for the express purpose of making international law on a great many subjects. A third such assembly was projected for 1914, and these periodic assemblies might have developed into a continuing international legislature *if* their machinery had not been too weak to prevent the great world-wide wars that intervened. These wars revealed new and unsuspected dimensions and terrors in the conflicts of sovereign states, and they led to entirely new departures in trying to regulate international relations.

Range and Effectiveness. Before the outbreak of World War I, there was a system of rules and principles covering most of the typical relationships that arise between states in times of peace. Procedures were defined for settling disputes between states by peaceful methods: *mediation or conciliation* (inviting a disinterested party or parties to *suggest* settlement of a dispute, without a binding commitment of its acceptance by either party to the dispute); *arbitration* (settlement of a dispute by a neutral party or parties, which both sides commit themselves to accept); and submission to *judicial determination.* The laws of peace were reasonably well observed and procedures for peaceful settlement were used to dissipate many tensions. The laws of war and of neutrality defined the rights of belligerents and of neutrals. The laws of war laid down many rules of the game for actual hostilities and increasingly tried to outlaw the more horrible weapons. They also laid down rules designed to protect non-combatants from injuries unrelated to the pursuit of strictly military objectives, and to ensure fair treatment—in the Geneva Convention, for example—to prisoners of war and to the sick and wounded. Despite glaring examples to the contrary, the laws of war have by no means been universally ignored, even in the last two World Wars. (Crime makes news while law-abiding conduct does not.) The most widespread and persistent violations have probably been in the laws protecting neutrality and non-combatants, and these largely because the conditions in which a genuine neutrality or non-combatant status is possible are ceasing to exist.

Never Successfully Outlawed War. While international law does have large achievements to its credit, it has not been able to prevent the deterioration of international relations into world-wide wars, where neutrality is almost impossible and little distinction is made between combatants and non-combatants. Of course, international law has never purported to prevent wars, but only to minimize their risks and to moderate their conduct. In recognition of this, it has many loopholes. A treaty ceases to be binding on the parties to it when there is an essential change in the circumstances contemplated by them at the time of signing it. A great many of the disputes arising between states are not 'justiciable.' That is to say, political issues are raised on which there is no rule or principle of law to be interpreted or applied by a judicial tribunal. In certain ill-defined circumstances of a grave threat to the safety of the forces under his command, a military commander is entitled to disregard some of the laws of war. Each state, of course, interprets qualifications of this kind in its own interests.

Moreover, as domestic politics prove only too well, it is hardly possible to settle every issue by law. Politics frequently intervenes. The problems of resolving conflicting legal and political questions are enormous—witness the bitter segregation controversy in the United States. On the other hand, in domestic politics within a given state the chief function of law has been to prevent violence through severe punishment, putting the incorrigibly lawless behind bars and deterring all the others from violent action. The disruptive violence of war has always been one of the chief enemies of civilized society. Since World War I there has been no doubt that war on its modern scale threatens the very existence of civilized society. Why did international law not forbid and prevent it?

LACK OF AN EFFECTIVE COMMON SUPERIOR. It is scarcely necessary to state the answer. Within a given state, the individuals who are its members all owe allegiance to a common superior, the government. Laws lay down their rights and duties, and forbid everyone to take the law into his own hands. Law and government ultimately compel everyone to submit his disputes to judicial determination in a court. When that court pronounces its decision, the government possesses overwhelming force to enforce acceptance of the decision. More than that, in any well-ordered state with prospects for continuance, the great majority of individuals support the government in the application of whatever force is necessary to enforce the law.

These conditions do not exist in the society of states. By definition, the states in a state system are each independent and sovereign. There is no effective common superior standing above them possessed of sufficient force to coerce them. Since the end of the Middle Ages there has not even been the fiction of such a superior above the separate states of Europe. In the world today the United States and the Soviet Union, and probably Communist China, can each overawe any other lesser power. But where is the international authority backed by the necessary power to compel them to submit their differences to judicial determination and abide the result (leaving the United Nations aside for later discussion)? If one of them has its rights infringed by the other, what alternatives has it to suffering the wrong in silence or taking the law into its own hands?

ENFORCED BY SELF-HELP. International law lacks the sanction of dependable legalized coercion applied by an acknowledged superior authority. The coercive sanctions actually available for its enforcement have to be applied by the party seeking redress. A state that thinks its rights under international law have been violated is entitled to apply pressure for their recognition by the offender. A variety of reprisals, as they are called, could be, and have been, used for this purpose: occupation of territory of the offending state, seizure and destruction of property belonging to it or its citizens, and the blockade of its ports.

The state applying the pressure decides what is sufficient provocation for reprisals, and the severity of them. As a rule, reprisals are used only by strong states against weak ones. Used against a strong state, they are likely to be regarded as acts of war. Used by one citizen against another within a state, they would be unlawful acts, a form of self-help that is always outlawed in the early stages of political development. But self-help is the only readily available sanction of international law, and if reprisals are thought inappropriate or fail when applied, the next stage is war to impose retribution on the offender.

WEAKNESS OF THE MORAL SANCTION. In Chapter XV, law was defined as the body of rules backed by the organized force of the community. It was noted that there are in any society many customary and moral rules that lack this backing and yet are widely observed. International law bears a greater resemblance to such customary and moral rules than it does to the law of a given state, strictly defined. Much of it is based on the established custom of states in their relationships with one another, and has, therefore, the sanction of custom. Many of its rules make a moral claim on states; they ought to be obeyed because they are right, because they accord with the Christian and Stoic traditions of Western civilization. International law has depended for its authority very largely on the sanctions of custom and morality. Unfortunately, these sanctions are weak and uncertain because modern men, under the influence of nationalism, have tended to think that the safety of their own nation comes first and makes the highest moral claim on them.[4]

PEACEFUL SETTLEMENT OF INTERNATIONAL DISPUTES

Until the total wars of the twentieth century, it was widely believed that the sanctions of custom and morality were very strong, that states really wanted to live together in peace under international law. The frequency of war was attributed in large part to inadequate machinery for settling disputes that arise between states.

Disputes are inevitable in human relationships under the conditions of freedom, as is shown by their frequency in the United States, France, and Britain. The success of public order in these countries depends largely on procedures, a judiciary, and a system of courts for dealing with disputes. If there were not an impartial arbiter readily available, disputes would frequently degenerate into violence. In the belief that this reasoning applied to the relations between states, much effort was put into the development of peaceful procedures of settlement in the late nineteenth and early twentieth centuries.

Mediation or conciliation and arbitration had long been accepted and fairly well-defined methods for trying to settle disputes between states. States in controversy would on occasion accept the good offices of another state as mediator or refer the controversy to some impartial body for conciliatory suggestions based on fairness or compromise. A celebrated example here is the successful effort of President Theodore Roosevelt to settle the Russo-Japanese conflict with the Treaty of Portsmouth in 1905. But mediation or conciliation procedures never involved any obligation on the disputants and were advisory only. Nor has international law, apart from special arrange-

---

[4] See J. L. Brierly, *The Law of Nations,* 6th ed (Oxford: The Clarendon Press, 1963) for an illuminating account of the nature, principles, and prospects of international law.

ments by treaty, ever asserted a legal obligation on states to submit their disputes to arbitration.

Machinery for Arbitration. Arbitration has always involved an agreement between states to submit a particular dispute, or class of dispute, between them to the decision of a board of arbitrators named by them. The arbitrators make an award in which they are guided by the rights of the parties according to international law, but they are entitled to take other non-legal factors into consideration. Once the award is made, international law does impose an obligation on the parties to abide loyally by its terms.

TREATIES. During the nineteenth century there was a steady increase in the number of disputes submitted to arbitration by special agreement—an example being the settlement of the *Alabama* claims case between the United States and Britain in 1872. At the end of the century arbitration treaties between particular states specifying in advance the kinds of disputes they agreed to submit to arbitration became common. The United States made such treaties with a dozen states in 1908. The Hague Peace Conferences of 1900 and 1907 declared in favor of the principle of compulsory arbitration, but it failed to put in the Convention for the Pacific Settlement of International Disputes any binding obligation to that effect. The Conference of 1899 did establish what is called the *Permanent Court of Arbitration.* Rules of procedure were laid down and a permanent secretariat established at The Hague. It did not appoint a permanent body of judges, or arbitrators, but merely provided a panel from which signatory states could choose arbitrators for a dispute. It was not a court in any real sense, although it did facilitate the submission of disputes to arbitration. The Hague tribunal has not been used since 1940, although there have been renewed recent calls for an arbitral convention.

Despite the growth of arbitration and arbitral machinery, it has done little to lessen the serious threats of war in international relations. No general treaty imposing on states a legal obligation to submit disputes to arbitration has ever been signed. Special arbitration treaties have generally been limited in application to disputes involving legal questions. Even then, most of them expressly exclude from arbitration disputes that affect the vital interests, the independence, or the honor of the states signing the treaty. These are precisely the issues on which states go to war. Arbitration treaties and arbitral awards have been quite faithfully observed by states for the simple reason that they refuse to submit to arbitration those issues which are of vital importance to them.

THE INTERNATIONAL COURT

To supplement the machinery for arbitration, The Hague Peace Conference of 1907 proposed the creation of a *genuine international court,* to be called the *Judicial Arbitration Court.* It was to be a permanent body, composed of jurists of high reputation and available for the deciding of all disputes between states that raised questions of law. Its conclusions would not be arbitral awards based partly on compromise and other non-legal factors, but rather judgments according to the letter of the law. It was thought that states would welcome the opportunity to get such justice, and that the court's decisions would rapidly build up a body of authoritative interpretations of international law. The project came to nothing, because a number of states insisted on the unacceptable condition that each state should have the right to nominate a judge. The establishment of such a court was postponed until after the end of World War I.

The attempts made since World War I to improve the machinery for settlement of international disputes will be considered in the discussion of the League of Nations and the United Nations. It will be convenient here, however, to follow through the efforts to set up an international court. Under the auspices of the League of Nations, the *Permanent Court of International Justice* was established in 1921. Under the auspices of the United Nations, it has been continued as the fifteen-member *International Court of Justice,* with its Constitution substantially unchanged. The seat of the new Court, like that of the old one, is in the impressive Carnegie Peace Palace at The Hague.

Jurisdiction of the Court. Proposals to make *compulsory* the reference of disputes to it were rejected. It was given power to decide only those cases which the parties to a dispute referred to it. However, an *optional clause* was inserted in the Statute of the Court enabling a state to submit itself to the compulsory jurisdiction of the Court. By doing so, a state acknowledged the jurisdiction of the Court to decide any dispute between it and any other state similarly submitting itself to compulsory jurisdiction, in so far as the dispute raised legal questions or justiciable issues.

About fifty states signed the optional clause of the old Permanent Court. In 1963, thirty-nine had accepted compulsory jurisdiction of the International Court, but many have so hedged their signatures with special reservations that they have almost denied the very compulsory jurisdiction to which they have voluntarily submitted. For example, by virtue of the so-called Connally

Amendment,[5] the United States has expressly excluded disputes on matters which are 'essentially within [its] domestic jurisdiction,' the term 'domestic' to be determined by the United States! In substance, the jurisdiction of to-day's International Court of Justice depends on the consent of states, and it covers, at most, disputes in which some *legal issue* is involved. For instance, in 1949 the Court ordered Albania to pay £2,363,051 to Britain as compensation for damages to British destroyers resulting from Albania's illegal mining of the Corfu Channel in 1946.[6] Many disputes raise issues not covered by the rules of international law, and it is not easy to say when a non-legal issue is, or is not, involved. This opens the door for evasion by states which think a decision of the Court will likely go against them. In the absence of an effective and powerful international authority enforcement of a decision of the International Court of Justice depends on voluntary obedience by the losing state. More significant, of course, is the fact that no state can be compelled to come before the Court—all of which, in the words of Walter Lippmann, reduces it to a small side show.

The domestic judicial system within a given state belongs to a different world. There, individuals must submit their disputes to judicial decision. All issues are, or become, legal issues when the essentials of public order are at stake. The sovereign state does not want to submit its vital interests wholly to law and judicial decision. In these circumstances, international law will not ensure peace, no matter how well developed the rules of international law may be or how good the judicial machinery for applying them.

THE LEAGUE OF NATIONS

Almost every large-scale war since the sixteenth century has inspired one or more proposals for some kind of union of states to preserve peace on the ground that war is the common enemy of all states and that there is a common interest in abolishing it. Almost invariably, these schemes proposed an international assembly representative of states to make laws governing international relations, and some mechanism for settling international disputes. The Quaker William Penn, the German and French philosophers Kant and Rousseau, and the English legal reformer Bentham all made such plans. The

[5] Named after Democratic Senator Tom Connally of Texas, then Chairman of the Senate Committee on Foreign Relations.
[6] For a short résumé of other cases in which the Court rendered judgments, see Stephen S. Goodspeed, *The Nature and Function of International Organization* (New York: Oxford University Press, 1959), pp. 322–7.

only plan of this kind that ever took concrete form prior to the League of Nations was the Holy Alliance, formed in 1815 by the monarchs of Russia, Austria, and Prussia and designed to protect the peace against a recurrence of the wars that followed the French Revolution. It was effective for only a very limited period of time. It was succeeded by the Concert of Europe, which consisted of a general understanding between the Great Powers of nineteenth-century Europe that they should, when occasion demanded, take concerted measures to preserve peace. The Concert of Europe failed, of course, to prevent World War I.

The Need and the Hope. The notion of united action by the several states to prevent war was not at all new when World War I led everybody to reflect still more earnestly on how to preserve peace. Before the end of the war, numerous plans were put forward, particularly in Britain and the United States. It was urged more strongly than ever that war is the universal enemy, that all states have a vital, common interest in eliminating it, and that they have a common purpose to achieve collective security guaranteed by all states to each state. What is needed, it was thought, are institutions and procedures through which this community of purpose can express itself. States should therefore agree among themselves to create these institutions and procedures. Once created and set going, the good faith and community of interest of states would be sufficient to maintain peace. French proposals went beyond this to the establishment of a military force under international authority to coerce lawbreakers, but they were rejected in the final event.

The Treaty of Versailles in 1919 set the terms of the settlement of World War I. The first twenty-six articles constituted the Covenant of the League of Nations. The terms of the Covenant were a synthesis of the main British and American views on how to secure peace, with a faint recognition of French views.

It is not necessary for present purposes to describe in detail the structure of the League of Nations, or of the several auxiliary organizations created under it, to deal with such matters as the treatment of labor throughout the world and the administration of colonial territories. The important questions at this distance are the essential organization it provided for ensuring peace and the reasons for its failure.

The Essence of the League. The League of Nations was a covenant, or treaty, between the forty-two sovereign states who became its original members. They obligated themselves only to the strict terms of the covenant and no further. The aim of the League was to secure international peace and collective security through peaceful settlement of disputes. The core of the Covenant was Article 10, in which the member states undertook 'to respect and preserve as against external aggression the territorial integrity and existing political independence of all members of the League.' It was thus committed to maintenance of the *status quo* of the Treaty of Versailles, which, in turn, was founded on the principle, only imperfectly honored in its express terms, of the *self-determination of all nations* including the principle of peaceful change. In effect, the Covenant was a guarantee of the sovereignty and independence of the then existing states.

The Organs of the League. The organs of the League, the institutions through which the will for peace was to be made effective, were an Assembly, a Council, and a Secretariat. The *Secretariat* comprised the permanent staff of officials of the League, working under the direction of the Assembly and Council. The *Assembly* was framed on the model of a legislature, each member state being represented in it, and each state having one vote. It was to meet periodically to deal with any matter affecting the peace of the world. Essentially a deliberative body with power to advise and recommend, it lacked power to make laws which would extend the obligations of member states beyond the terms of the Covenant. Generally speaking, its decisions relating to issues of peace and war had to be by *unanimous vote*, exclusive of the votes of representatives of the parties to a dispute.

The *Council* was, in substance, a small executive committee of the Assembly in which the Great Powers had permanent seats, and a number of nonpermanent seats were rotated among the other powers. It met at least four times annually. Like the Assembly, it could deal with any matter affecting the peace of the world. Its principal functions, in the present focus of interest, were the settlement of international disputes. Intractable disputes requiring attention by the League were to be referred, in the first instance, to the Council. The Council, in turn, might refer them to the Assembly, and the Assembly had power to deal with them, but the Council had the main responsibility for devising settlement. Like the Assembly, its critical decisions had to be *unanimous* except for the representatives of the parties to the dispute in question.

Obligations of the Covenant. Each member of the League agreed to undertake four principal obligations designed to ensure peaceful settlement of disputes: First, to submit any dispute with another member that was likely to lead to war to arbitration, judicial settlement, or inquiry by the Council, and not to resort to war until three months after the award, judicial decision, or report of the Council; second, to abide loyally by any award or judicial decision, and not to make war against any member state that complied with its terms; third, that, if the Council made a unanimous—subject, of course, to the exception of the representatives of the parties to the dispute—report on a dispute referred to it, members of the League would not go to war against any complying party; and fourth, if any member resorted to war in disregard of its covenanted promises, it would be deemed to have committed an act of war against all the other members, who undertook in that event to break off all relations and intercourse with the offending state, and to lend assistance of specific kinds to those who were disciplining the offender.

Sanctions of the Covenant. The aims of these four promises were to ensure a cooling-off period for hot tempers, to isolate an offender by refusing to fight on his side, and to bring him to his senses by denying to him the society of all other members. The sanction for enforcing these obligations was ostracism, and the Covenant further provided for canceling the membership of an offender by a vote of the Council. These are the sanctions of a gentlemen's club. It was ignored that the members of this particular club were sovereign states, compelled by circumstances of their relationships to think in terms of power, and that effective sanctions would have to speak in those terms.

A SERIOUS GAP. It is true that Article 16, as a gesture to French proposals, authorized the Council 'to recommend to the several governments concerned what effective military, naval, or air force the members of the League shall severally contribute to the armed forces to be used to protect the covenants of the League.' This vague clause could not be read as compelling a state to go to war in support of the sanctions of the League. Moreover, if the Council failed to bring in a unanimous report on a dispute, all members regained full freedom of action. War was not categorically forbidden. The Covenant was binding only on members, but although it made provision for dealing with disputes involving non-members, the Covenant at best did not compel stronger measures against non-members than the members. And while it is further true that, between 1928 and 1930, all the great powers and almost all the significant lesser powers signed the Pact of Paris, renouncing war 'as an instrument of national policy' in their relations with one another; but the Pact contained no sanctions of its own. No means were provided for enforcing it against a signatory that violated it. It filled a gap in the Covenant of the League with another piece of paper.

The League was successful in settling many minor disputes in which lesser states were involved, yet was never able to settle a dispute which concerned the vital interests of one of the great powers. It did not take effective action when Japan invaded China in 1931. When Italy attacked Ethiopia in 1935, and economic sanctions under the League were actually applied, it was soon discovered: (1) that Mussolini was not a gentleman; (2) that the members of the League could not co-operate effectively in applying the full force of the voted economic sanctions—partly because that might turn a little war into a big one; and (3) that members would not contemplate the military sanction of superior force against Italy. After this disaster, the futility of the League was generally recognized, and no attempt was made to use its machinery to prevent Germany's reoccupation of the Rhineland in 1936 and her seizure of Austria in 1938 and of Czechoslovakia in 1939. The sovereign states thus rushed headlong into World War II.

REASONS FOR FAILURE OF THE LEAGUE

Non-Membership of Major Powers. Many explanations of the failure of the League have been offered. For example, much has been made of the fact that the United States was *never* a member, and that the Soviet Union did not become one until 1934, two years after Japan's and Germany's withdrawal —when the League had already substantially failed. No doubt the absence of these two great powers from the League in the critical post-war reconstruction period of the 1920's was a serious defect. Indeed, at any time during its existence, at least two of the then major powers were not members of the League.

Attachment to the Status Quo. Further, the League was committed from the beginning to maintain the *status quo* of the Treaty of Versailles with no specific provision for its alteration. This too was a serious defect. For reasons that cannot be discussed here, Germany, Italy, and Japan were each deeply dissatisfied with it; they came to a fierce determination to change it, and to do so at the expense of other members of the League.

However, peace must always stand from moment to moment on a *status quo* of some kind; otherwise there can be no peace or security at all. Whether or not peace can be maintained among sovereign states depends on whether tolerable revisions of an intolerable *status quo* can be negotiated by consent. Even if both the United States and the Soviet Union had been members from the beginning, Germany, Italy, and Japan would still have demanded the same changes in the *status quo*. Of course, with the United States and the

Soviet Union actively participating in the councils of the nations, the course of events might have been vastly different. For example, France might have been less fearful, and concessions to Germany might have been worked out that would have kept Hitler an obscure agitator and demagogue.

Lack of a Superior Enforcing Authority. But the effectiveness of negotiation and concession would still have depended on the will of the states concerned to accept them. If the will was there, wise diplomacy would suffice. (The forum for discussion provided by the League would perhaps have been an aid to diplomacy.) If the will was lacking, then the League had nothing essentially new to add to diplomacy in maintaining peace, because it had no means of coercing by force those who broke its covenants. Three hundred years before the collapse of the League of Nations, Thomas Hobbes wrote its epitaph: 'Covenants without the sword are but words and of no force to bind a man at all.'

This judgment on the League of Nations is not too severe, but a word of further explanation must be added. No scheme which leaves full sovereignty in the several states will ensure permanent peace. A superior authority with adequate coercive power is necessary. That alone, however, is not enough. Individuals within the state are restrained from law-breaking by the fact of the sword in the hands of the government. Yet we know from experience that if the *status quo* which the government maintains becomes intolerable to large groups within the state, there will be rebellion and even revolution.

The reason dissatisfied groups within the state accept the *status quo* is that they hope to be able to negotiate a change in it by peaceful political means; and having negotiated it, they count on the coercive machinery of the government to compel the acceptance of the change by those who might otherwise resist it. Moreover, there is a general disposition to appease minority groups because the government exists to set limits to their demands. Germany, Italy, and Japan could not count on this process of peaceful change through the League. By the same token, the states that did try to appease them late in the game found there were no limits to their demands. There was no superior authority able to compel Germany, Italy, and Japan to accept limited concessions as final.

THE UNITED NATIONS

The alliance of states that fought World War II against Germany, Italy, Japan, and their satellites came in the course of the conflict to call themselves the United Nations. The representatives of these victorious powers met at

San Francisco in 1945, at the close of the European phase of the war, and agreed on the Charter of the United Nations as the basic constitution of a new world organization to maintain peace. With the lessons of the failure of the League of Nations before them, they improved on the Covenant in a number of particulars, but they did not, as indeed they could not in any practical way, curtail their own sovereign power by conferring it on a superior political authority, despite some language to the contrary in Article 25. They did not create a super-state, nor did they return to the League system of an organization of all states to preserve peace. Setting aside the form of the Charter and looking at substance alone, the new organization for world peace still reveals many aspects of a gentlemen's club.

Improvements over the League. However, in addition to the victorious powers, membership is open to 'all other peaceloving states.' By 1963 virtually all of the states in the world, the old and the new, the significant—except Communist China—and the not-so-significant, and *including the defeated powers of World War II,* except Germany, had been admitted to membership —totaling more than 112. Their association together is expressly based on the formal principle of 'the sovereign equality of all members.'

The central principles and obligations of membership are more rigorous and clear cut than they were in the Covenant. Under Article 2, all agree to the principle of peaceful settlement of their international disputes, and to refrain from 'the threat or use of force against the territorial integrity or political independence of any state. . . .' In substance, this is a renunciation of war for any purpose except temporary self-defense against armed attack until the United Nations takes effective measures against that attack. This right of self-defense is expressly provided by Article 51. As we shall see later, there are much sharper sanctions in the Charter for compelling obedience to these principles than there were in the Covenant. Also, there is a clear obligation on the member states to provide the necessary means to make military and other sanctions effective against aggressors, when called upon to do so by the Security Council of the United Nations. And, as will be demonstrated, the United Nations has a number of genuine achievements on its record.

Furthermore, the League had just two power centers, London and Paris; the U.N. has any number—including New Delhi and Cairo as well as Moscow and Washington. Whereas any but a British or French Secretary-General was unthinkable under the League, the three first Secretaries-General of the U.N. were a Norwegian, a Swede, and a Burmese. Indeed, any but a 'small' or 'neutralist' nation Secretary-General would be unthinkable for the United Nations.

Organs of the United Nations. Like the Covenant of the League, the Charter provides for a General Assembly, a Security Council, a Secretariat, and a number of auxiliary organizations, such as the eighteen-member Economic and Social Council and the fourteen-member Trusteeship Council. There are also several specialized agencies.[7]

THE ASSEMBLY. The *General Assembly* is composed of representatives of all the member states, each member state having one vote. The requirement of unanimity in decisions of the Assembly of the League has not been imported into the procedure of the General Assembly under the Charter. Instead, votes relating to important issues of peace and war are taken by a *two-thirds majority*. Some see in this distinct advance, a recognition that an otherwise sovereign state can be bound without its own consent. But, in fact, the General Assembly has no effective power to make decisions binding on any state, whereas the League Assembly had in formal terms power to make any decision that the Covenant authorized to be made.

According to the terms of the Charter, the United Nations Assembly was empowered only to discuss, investigate, and recommend. By Article 24, the members of the United Nations 'confer on the Security Council primary responsibility for the maintenance of international peace and security and agree that in carrying out its duties under this responsibility, the Security Council acts on their behalf.' And, under Article 12, when the Security Council is exercising this function in respect of a dispute or troubled situation, the Assembly could not even make recommendations unless requested to do so by the Security Council. Experience with the League showed clearly that whatever lesser powers might decide to do, effective action depended on the Great Powers. They alone had the power to act, and the U.N. Charter placed responsibility where the power lies by denying the General Assembly any decisive voice in relation to the enforcement of the Charter. However, as will be explained below, with its Uniting for Peace Resolution of 1950 the General Assembly gained an increase in its power, not envisaged by the authors of the Charter.

THE SECURITY COUNCIL. *The Security Council* is a small body of eleven members. Five of its seats are permanently allotted to China, France, the Soviet Union, Britain, and the United States, the Great Powers according to 1945 standards. The other six seats are rotated among members of the General Assembly representing various agreed-upon sections of the world,

[7] Among the more important and generally quite successful of these specialized agencies are the: Food and Agriculture Organization, International Bank for Reconstruction and Development, World Health Organization, International Civil Aviation Organization, and United Nations Educational, Scientific and Cultural Organization (UNESCO).

chosen by election for a period of two years. Each member on the Council has one representative and one vote. By Article 27, decisions on all 'procedural' matters are by majority vote of seven out of the eleven members. Again, the rule of unanimity is dropped. However, Article 27 goes on to provide that 'on all other matters' *the affirmative vote of seven must include the concurring vote of all five of the permanent members.* That is to say the Great Powers can never be outvoted by the non-permanent members; and furthermore, no critical decision can be taken by the Security Council without the concurrence of such of the five Great Powers on the Council as are present and actually vote on the decision.[8] In other words, *each of them can impose a veto on any proposal for coercive measures.*

The Security Council is not an executive committee of the General Assembly. As we have noted, the framers of the Charter envisaged the General Assembly as a deliberating and not a deciding body, with the Security Council as the effective organ of the United Nations, and the Assembly advisory to it. The powers and functions of the Security Council represent the major contribution of the Charter to the political problems of international peace and security.

THE SECRETARY-GENERAL. Preceding editions of this book did not dwell upon the Secretary-General, who heads the 4000-employee Secretariat which, through its core of international civil servants, services the various organs of the United Nations, but the increased importance of the office calls for some comment. He is empowered to call the Security Council's attention to any matter which he believes to be a threat to the peace and security of the world. The initial occupant of the office, Trygve Lie of Norway, after first moving gingerly, quickly endeavored to use the prestige of his office to settle international disputes, and thus incurred the enmity of the Soviet Union, which denounced him for supporting the U.N. intervention in Korea and compelled his resignation in 1953. His successor, Dag Hammarskjold, reputed to be 'softer' than his predecessor, soon proved himself to be a master of the art of compromise in private negotiations. With the skilled diplomacy of his forebears in Sweden, he intervened in major crises without precipitating undue controversy—such as his mission in 1955 to Communist China, where he caused the release of eleven American prisoners of war, and his endeavors to strengthen the Arab-Israeli armistice in the Middle East in 1956. He played a major role in the settlement of the Suez Canal crisis later

[8] As will be seen later, the Soviet Union was boycotting the Council during the time of the Korean crisis of 1950, and her absence was interpreted as precluding any consideration of her vote.

that year, during which he took the floor in the Security Council and roundly denounced the invasion. When he was given a second five-year term of office in 1958, he announced that he would continue to use his agency as an independent force for peace. Soon he found himself at odds with the Russians, who declared that they would not support him again, and instead called for the creation of a 'troika' of secretaries-general, to be composed of one 'Western,' one 'Eastern,' and one 'Neutral' member.

But Dag Hammarskjold continued his efforts, capped in a sense by the 1960 Congo intervention, which directly resulted in his death in 1961. He worked always to enhance the effectiveness of the United Nations and in the process, in the words of one of the many glowing obituaries, he built himself and his office into one of the great hopes for world peace. His successor, U Thant of Burma, less assertive and more acceptable to the Eastern bloc, nonetheless evidently resolved to continue the office of the Secretary-General in the spirit and tradition of his predecessor.

Obligations and Sanctions of the United Nations. In Articles 33–37, members undertake to submit their disputes to settlement by mediation or conciliation, arbitration, judicial decision, or some other peaceful means. If these methods fail to settle a dispute, the members agree that it shall be referred to the Security Council. Articles 36 and 37 authorize the Security Council to intervene at any stage of a dispute with recommendations on procedure, methods of adjustment, and terms of settlement. By Articles 41 and 42, the Security Council has power to decide what sanctions of an economic, military, or other character shall be applied to enforce its decisions.

Articles 43–47 provide the machinery for organizing and applying economic and military sanctions. No international army or police force is contemplated: rather, the members of the United Nations undertake to supply contingents on call from the Security Council. A Military Staff Committee composed of the military chiefs of staff of the permanent members of the Security Council is to advise and assist the Security Council in the planning and execution of military sanctions. As we have already seen, the members agree that the Security Council acts for them in maintaining international peace and security. Finally, by Article 25, the members agree 'to accept and carry out the decisions of the Security Council.'

Lesser Powers Firmly Bound. These provisions go much further than the Covenant of the League. Members agree to accept the decision of the Security Council in a dispute concerning them. That is to say, they agree to keep the peace against their own will. They agree to take orders from the Security Council in support of military sanctions, which may amount to war. If mem bers live up to the Charter, they have subjected themselves to a superior authority, the Security Council.

In assessing this last statement, it is necessary to remember the voting procedure in the Security Council, which is the key to everything else. Decisions require the *affirmative vote of seven* of the eleven members, *including the concurrence of all the permanent members* present at the time of the decision and voting. If all permanent members, i.e. the five Great Powers, are in agreement on an issue, they can always be sure of getting two of the remaining votes necessary for an effective majority. Great powers have many ways of securing the assent of lesser powers. In these circumstances, the lesser powers are clearly subject to coercion from above under the Charter. But this really is nothing new. Sovereign equality of large and small states has always been a pretense. The small ones have aways had to submit to the big ones. The vital issues of war and peace arise out of the disorderliness and quarrels of the Great Powers.

Great Powers Able To Veto. Under the Charter, the Great Powers, like all the rest, promise to submit their intractable disputes to the Security Council, and to abide by its decisions. But all the Great Powers have seats on the Security Council, and *each has a veto on decisions affecting coercive action against it.* There is no diminution of sovereignty here. As far as compelling the Great Powers to keep the peace is concerned, the United Nations is no advance at all on the League of Nations.

The basic assumption underlying the Covenant of the League of Nations was that almost all nations wanted peace more than anything else and could agree on the measures to secure it. The basic assumption underlying the Charter of the United Nations was that the nations that stuck together to win World War II would sick together to enforce peace on the world. Both assumptions have been proved wrong in the event. From the date of the signing of the Charter, the Soviet Union and the United States drew rapidly apart, exhibiting the mutual fear and suspicion that is the constantly recurring, if not the normal, condition of the two greatest powers in a system of independent states.

Dominant Position of the Super-Powers. These two are still so dominant that when they are in agreement—as they seemed to be, for practical purposes, during the Suez Canal crisis in 1956—Britain and France, theoretically also 'great powers' under the Charter, had no choice but to acquiesce. So the workability of the Charter really depends on the ability of the United States and the Soviet Union to pull together. If they were able to do so, world peace would be assured. If they cannot, the Charter does not provide any truly effective means to restrain them from war. However, deliberations of the Assembly and the Council may have some deterrent effect on them. The discussion of vital international questions by these bodies registers with some accuracy what the other states in the United Nations think of the policies pursued by the super-powers and, as the Cuba crisis of 1962 proved, they serve to keep channels of communication between the principal powers open. In so far as there is any international public opinion, it is brought to bear persuasively on the super-powers in this way. Moreover, within the obvious limitations of the realities of power, there is no question of the growing importance and moderating influence of the smaller states, the so-called 'neutralist' ones, and the new blocs, e.g. the Afro-Asian bloc—which defeated the older and greater powers in the Algerian vote in 1961, for one.

There has been much criticism of the veto of the Great Powers in the Security Council as the fatal weakness of the United Nations. It is urged that no power should have a right to vote in a decision on a dispute to which it is a party. Two comments must be made on this argument: First, as things still stand, the United States and the Soviet Union are parties to every significant international dispute in any corner of the world in the sense that each considers that it has a vital interest in its outcome. Certainly the Soviet Union can foment disputes in many corners of the world which bear very directly on the security of the United States. Effective removal of the veto would almost require the forbidding of the two super-powers to vote on decisions for compulsory settlement of any dispute.

VETO POWER REFLECTS REALITIES. Second, the veto is a recognition of realities which cannot be changed merely by altering voting procedures. If the United States and the Soviet Union cannot settle their outstanding differences by peaceful negotiation and compromise, it is wildly improbable that both of them would accept a settlement determined on by the unanimous decision of all other members of the Security Council. (Indeed, both might refuse.) If either super-power refused, how could the Security Council impose effective military sanctions on it without relying almost entirely on the military forces of the other super-power party to the dispute? The Great Power veto in the Security Council does not weaken the Charter of the United Nations. *It is weakened rather by the fundamental realities of power politics in a system of sovereign states.* What the veto does is to prevent the world from forgetting these realities.

A Major Test: Korea. The foregoing analysis of the United Nations provides little comfort for anyone. There would be profound relief and thankfulness if logic and the unfolding of events should prove it wrong. In fact,

the analysis given here is supported rather than refuted by the Korean incident of 1950–51, the first major open test of the workability of the United
Nations Charter. It precipitated the greatest international crisis since the end
of World War II.

When the attack on South Korea by North Korea came before the Security
Council at the request of the United States on June 25, 1950, one day after
the invasion, the Soviet Union was still on a boycott of that body which it
had begun that January against the presence of Nationalist China. The
Security Council requested—although it did not command—the imposition
of sanctions by a 9:0 vote,[9] and the United States immediately threw in its
weight to enforce them. The United Nations appealed to the other member
states to contribute military forces. Only sixteen promised to do so, but forty-
three others pledged moral support. The very limited response to this appeal
made it clear that if the United Nations' decision was to be enforced in
Korea, the power of the United States would be the decisive force—especially
since its occupation troops were readily available in sizable numbers in Japan
and other nearby bases.

Despite active military intervention in Korea by the Chinese Communists
on November 5, 1950, there could be no doubt of the ability of the United
States to punish North Korean aggression over a period of time, at least if
the Soviet Union did not intervene actively on the other side. In short, what
took place in Korea under the form of action by the United Nations was an
incident in the power struggle between the Soviet Union and the United
States.

PEACE EFFORTS. Nevertheless, member states in the United Nations did
swing into action to attempt to restore peace. Twelve Arab-Asian states,
under India's leadership, succeeded in establishing a Cease-Fire Commission
under the sponsorship of the General Assembly. Communist China's non-
membership status complicated matters, and long debates ensued in the
Security Council as well as the Assembly. Prospects for peace seemed dim,
although the fighting, after many advances and retreats, had become localized
around the 38th parallel in the spring of 1951. The main obstacle to a negotiated peace now appeared to be Communist China, and more than fifty
member and thirteen non-member states complied with a General Assembly
suggestion for an embargo on war material shipments to the Chinese main-
land.

Finally, it was pressure by the Soviet Union in the summer of 1951 that

[9] Yugoslavia abstained; those voting in favor were Nationalist China, Cuba, Ecuador, Egypt,
France, India, Norway, the United Kingdom, and the United States.

prompted the North Koreans and Chinese to agree to discuss a cease-fire and an armistice. Lengthy negotiations commenced, aided by a Neutral Nations Repatriations Commission, but not until July 1953 was an armistice agreement concluded at Panmunjom. The agreement is still in force—but Korea is also still a divided country. Nevertheless, the Korean episode must be recorded as a major, and at least partly successful, effort of the United Nations, whose forces still patrol the 38th parallel.

Other Achievements. Whatever its weaknesses, the United Nations organization has recorded several achievements in settling political disputes: In 1946, after a long Security Council debate, the Soviet Union withdrew its forces from Northern Iran. In 1949, in response to Security Council appeals to stop the fighting in Kashmir between India and Pakistan, a cease-fire went into effect, and U.N. observers began to police the demarcation lines. Also in 1949, the Security Council adopted a resolution calling for a cease-fire between Netherlands and Indonesian forces, and the grant of independence to Indonesia—which the Dutch conceded one year later. Still later in 1949, various armistice agreements were signed between United Nations-created Israel and the several Arab states who had warred against Israel upon its establishment in 1948. The armistice agreements were completed in accordance with Security Council resolutions, and with the help of Dr. Ralph J. Bunche, the United Nations mediator. At the end of busy 1949, the Big Four found themselves unable to reach agreement on the disposition of the Italian colonial possessions in Africa, and they referred their problems to the General Assembly. The latter adopted a resolution setting up Libya as an independent state, and making other provisions for Italian Somaliland and Eritrea. The Soviet blockade of Berlin of 1948–49, while settled by direct negotiations among the Big Four, was before the Security Council and the General Assembly throughout that time. In 1958 a fifteen-nation U.N. observer unit was sent to Lebanon to ensure its territorial integrity against Syria, and another U.N. mission provided on-the-spot mediators for Jordan.

THE SUEZ CANAL. The two most dangerous problems to come before the United Nations since Korea concern the Suez Canal and Congo crises. The Suez Canal crisis occurred in October 1956 with its invasion—as a result of at least some Egyptian provocation—by Israel, Britain, and France. Strong pressure, both inside and outside of the U.N., from the United States and the Soviet Union—for once on the same side of the fence, albeit for different reasons—prompted the three invading states to withdraw. A United Nations Emergency Force, composed of 6000 troops from several small neutral member states, such as Denmark and Yugoslavia, moved almost immediately into the border zones between Egypt and Israel to keep the two antagonists apart. The prestige of the United Nations had reached a high point, and the debates raging in the General Assembly were heard by millions who heretofore had had but little interest in, and regard for, the world organization.

THE CONGO. Belgium's abrupt granting of independence to the Congo in June 1960, was too much for this ill-prepared, strife-torn, ill-led land. Chaos ensued, and the Belgian troops returned to protect Belgian lives and property. Acting upon the appeal of the Congo's new Prime Minister, the pro-Russian Patrice Lumumba, the U.N. Security Council, with Secretary-General Hammarskjold acting with determined rapidity and efficiency, sent ultimately 18,000 troops and observers from twenty-seven small and neutralist countries, chiefly from Asia and Africa. Internal order was partly restored. But the subsequent secession of the rich province of Katanga, under the pro-Belgian President Moise Tshombe, continued to keep the new 'nation' in turmoil. Congo reunification became the goal of the United Nations and its forces, under the authority of Security Council resolutions requiring them to keep the peace, rid Katanga of foreign mercenaries, and promote but not dictate Congo unity. It proved to be an involved and frustrating task, not only of peace-keeping but also of nation-building. During its course—one that was still far from complete late in 1963—Lumumba was murdered; Congolese leaders came, went, and arrested each other; the Soviet Union and the United States accused each other of intervention—and Dag Hammarskjold lost his life in a Congo plane crash in this major U.N. effort to maintain peace. Whatever its ultimate outcome, the U.N. learned much from the Congo operation, diplomatically, militarily, and organizationally. Walter Lippmann might well call the U.N. program in the Congo the world's most sophisticated example of international co-operation.[10]

Expanded Role of the General Assembly. Late in 1950—as already indicated—the United Nations General Assembly, taking matters into its own hands, set up new machinery, designed to deprive aggressors of the possible protection afforded them by the veto in the Security Council. In the *Uniting for Peace Resolution*, adopted by an overwhelming majority, provision was made for convening the Assembly on twenty-four hours notice to discuss and recommend on the advisability of taking some action that had already been blocked by exercise of the veto in the Security Council. The Assembly, it will be recalled, is empowered to make recommendations on critical issues by a two-thirds majority of those present and voting. Although the Assembly is

[10] As quoted by Clark Eichelberger, 'Anarchy or a Monument to Cooperation?' *Saturday Review*, July 14, 1962, p. 12.

limited to making recommendations, and has no power under the Charter to order the member states to take action, the new plan proposed that the Assembly should give leadership in organizing sanctions against an aggressor, sanctions which may then be imposed despite the veto in the Security Council.

Aside from any question of the constitutionality of this resolution under the United Nations Charter, its adoption is a revolutionary move, striking at the central provisions of the Charter, which relied on Great Power unanimity to keep the peace. While the new plan may enable the United Nations to escape the hampering effects of the veto, it has two serious defects. First, the Assembly can merely recommend. The several member states are left free to decide whether to act on the recommendation. Second, there is the danger that a majority made up of small states without effective military power will try to push the Great Powers to punitive action, which may start a general war. In deciding whether to undertake punitive action laden with these risks, each Great Power will consider whether its own vital interests call for such action. If the conclusion is in the negative, it is almost unthinkable that it should allow its judgment to be overcome by a vote of the United Nations Assembly. Those on whom the burden and responsibility of action falls cannot thus easily be deprived of the power of deciding when action is to be taken.

However, it is a fact that since the passage of the Uniting for Peace Resolution and the Korean War the political role of the General Assembly has expanded materially at the expense of the Security Council. Moreover, when it was unable to do more than pass general resolutions, it resorted to the device of delegating authority to the Secretary-General to implement them. These developments have altered the character of the United Nations. The General Assembly may still only be able to recommend, but its recommendations now carry considerable weight. It possesses considerable residual power.

Evaluation. Despite its spotty and often disheartening record, the United Nations is thus far from a useless organization. Modern transport and communications have unified the world in a physical sense, and the effect is to multiply relationships between states. There are thus many international problems besides the critical ones of peace and war. Many of these can be dealt with by international co-operation, and the solving of them may ease tensions that would otherwise intensify into occasions for war. The Economic and Social Council, the Trusteeship Council, and the other specialized agencies of the United Nations, which have been alluded to earlier but cannot be discussed here, can do and have already done important work of social amelioration. Among their achievements are the programs of technical assistance to underdeveloped nations, capital development, and aid in dealing with problems of health, housing, literacy, child welfare, labor standards, and development of industry. And much has been done to assist a host of United Nations-administered trust territories to achieve independence and self-government. It can be hoped that the habit of international consultation will grow with practice. It is no small achievement to create a forum for discussion where the statesmen of the world can meet to enlarge their mutual understanding, and improve their mutual respect in so far as there is a will on all sides to do so. This is an essential first step even if it does not take us far toward the elimination of war. Moreover, the educative effect of the deliberations of the United Nations on the people of the world should not be underestimated. But to date, at least, it remains nonetheless true that the United Nations cannot maintain peace between the super-powers if one of them is resolved to break it.

CONDITIONS NEEDED FOR A WORKABLE WORLD-STATE

The Soviet Union and the United States cannot be coerced except by an acknowledged superior authority—a world-state. However, even a world-state would be an empty shell unless it drew to itself immediately the primary loyalty of the great bulk of the people of the United States, the Soviet Union, and all other important states. In a sense, the problem is to duplicate the founding of the United States of America on a world scale. As far as forms and machinery are concerned, we already know how to do it. The main features of the Constitution of the United States are a model ready made for the architects of world federation.[11] But constitution makers cannot supply everything necessary to make a constitution work. The people of the Thirteen Colonies on the Atlantic seaboard in 1789 had something the peoples of the world lack today.

Common Feeling and Common Ideals. Despite the differences in habits, outlook, and interests in the several colonies at that time, the people living in them had already a considerable degree of unity. They had just thrown off a common allegiance to the British Crown, but that common subjection had given them the habit of living in peace and consultation together. They were predominantly of one ethnic stock and they had a common language. They had essentially similar views in religion, and a common political tradition

[11] See G. A. Borgese, *Preliminary Draft of a World Constitution* (Chicago: University of Chicago Press, 1948) for a draft on the main lines of the United States Constitution.

derived from Britain, which was rapidly taking shape as one of the main expressions of the wider liberal democratic tradition. Finally, they had the clearest of common interests in keeping all European powers out of the North American continent. They understood, respected, and within limits trusted one another, even though they did not always agree. Such peoples are ripe for political unification.

It is scarcely necessary to point out how far the diverse peoples of the world are from such ripeness. For example, there would have to be some measure of agreement on the aims and purposes of the single world order into whose care and keeping the security and welfare of all was being submitted. What common ideals of government would there be to justify such trust and submission? Would it be the liberal democratic ideals or the Communist ideals? The bitterness of the clash between these two sets of ideas is now so great as to threaten to tear the world apart. On this ground alone, voluntary world federation is out of the question at present, although many thoughtful plans have been advanced—notable among them that by two eminent American legal minds, Grenville Clark and Louis B. Sohn.[12]

Adjustments in the Status Quo. To come down from the level of ideals to mundane interests, a world government would have to take the necessary steps to prevent civil war. There is no point in exchanging wars between sovereign states for recurring civil wars. And it must be remembered that the people of the United States, with all they had in common, nevertheless incurred a terrible civil war. To prevent civil war, the world government would have to make major political adjustments to ensure tolerable conditions for the various peoples of the world. Tariffs would have to be lowered to allow goods from countries with low standards of living and low costs of production to compete in Britain, the United States, Canada, and so on, with goods produced by workers with high standards of living. Even more challenging, the world government would have to take measures to relieve the pressure of population in badly crowded areas of the world. Among the principal outlets for such surplus population are the empty spaces of the United States, Canada, and Australia.

Nothing is said here about the wisdom or effectiveness of such measures. The pressure of native colored peoples with low standards of living and

[12] See their remarkable work, *World Peace Through World Law,* 2nd ed. rev. (Cambridge: Harvard University Press, 1960). To maintain peace, and using the present organs of the U.N. as a base, they advocate a world legislature with a carefully worked-out system of Proportional Representation; an executive council chosen by and responsible to the legislature; a world police force composed of volunteers, selected by quota to obviate any state's or bloc exerting undue influence; international courts and other tribunals to deal with all disputes between nations; and a reliable world revenue system with funds collected from all states.

restricted living space on a genuinely democratic world federation would be immense. To refuse to yield to it might cause civil war. To pass such measures and try to enforce them would also cause civil war in the present climate of opinion. Accordingly, when it is said that the peoples of the world do not want war, the statement is undoubtedly true. It is necessary, however, to add that peoples often want to get or to keep things that cannot be got or kept without war. There is but little evidence amid the rampant nationalism of our time of common international ideals, of the mutual respect and spirit of accommodation necessary to found and maintain a world federation.

Subordination of National Interests. The limited project of a federation of Western European states has been discussed continually since the end of World War II. In 1957, the heads of the governments of France, West Germany, Italy, Belgium, the Netherlands, and Luxembourg—already joined in a common market for coal and steel—agreed to pool their atomic resources and to merge their economies in a common tariff-free market. It was henceforth to be known as the *European Economic Community* or simply *Common Market,* and has already been described.[13] A political union was held out as a future possibility. There is at least a possibility that a stable, solid federation of Western Europe, which made a new great power approaching that of the two super-powers, might do more than anything else to relieve tension between the United States and the Soviet Union, and give the world a breathing spell. There are the most cogent reasons for Britain to take a strong lead in this movement, for the British people are unusually intelligent and accommodating in political matters. Yet for reasons noted earlier,[14] after having long been reluctant even to consider entering such a federation, their application to enter the Common Market as a full partner in 1962 was rebuffed by France—although perhaps not irrevocably. The core of the matter still remains: national interests are the solid ones, and there is little or no disposition to subordinate them to international welfare.

Conclusion

The main elements of a somber situation may now be recapitulated, or recalled from common knowledge. Physically, the world has been unified by modern transport and communication. High economic productivity enables the world to employ great numbers of men and many resources entirely in destruction. The range and destructiveness of the new weapons make destruc-

[13] Cf. Chapter V, pp. 127 ff.
[14] Ibid.

tion of civilization more than an idle speculation. The passions of nationalism turn wars into struggles by entire populations. The technical possibilities of total war are fully employed by nationalistic feeling. There is no assurance of escape from recurring total wars except a world state.

The Vicious Circle. A world state cannot be willed, created, and maintained without a substantial consensus on a world scale, a widely accepted international ideal of government, a world public opinion. An exclusive nationalism monopolizes the political loyalties of men and keeps them continually fighting one another. We cannot have a world-state because we need first to create a consciousness of the world community. We cannot have a consciousness of a world community because we do not have a world state to keep peace while the different nations learn to live together on a basis of mutual respect and mutual concession. This is the vicious circle in which the world finds itself.

The discussion in this chapter is intended as a background for the understanding of the dilemma. To go on and discuss the international politics of the present day in any revealing way would require too much space. In any case, the situation is so fluid, new and unforeseen events follow one another so quickly, that any analysis of the current situation is soon outdated.

Several considerations bearing on current events should, however, be stated. First, a long period of confusion in the wake of World War II was inevitable. The disruption was so extreme that order in many parts of the world still rests on military force, although it is not entirely fanciful to hope for more settled conditions as efforts toward recovery from the war continue briskly. Second, international tension is inevitably heightened where there are only two super-powers that really count.

Third, there are now hopeful signs that the recovery of Western Europe will be followed by close economic and political integration, thus producing in time a powerful make-weight between the Soviet Union and the United States. Fourth, the emergence of Communist China as a very powerful state, and the growing tension between her and the Soviet Union, tempers Soviet truculence toward the West. It may be hazarded now that Soviet fears of China are roughly of the same order as her fears of the United States. As long as the United States maintains 'second-strike capability,' the Soviet Union knows that a nuclear attack on the United States would bring prostrating retaliation and expose a shattered world to Chinese domination. The Soviet Union knows well that her present consequence in the world is a legacy from the internecine wars that exhausted Western Europe. The Soviet leaders strongly desire to weaken the United States but not, as one may guess, at a cost that would deliver the Soviet Union as well as the rest of the world to China. For the time being then, the balance of nuclear terror does work, and so maintains an uneasy peace.

SUGGESTED REFERENCES FOR FURTHER READING

Bailey, S. D., *The General Assembly of the United Nations* (Praeger, 1960).

Ball, M. M., *NATO and the European Movement* (Praeger, 1959).

Beloff, M., *Foreign Policy and the Democratic Process* (Johns Hopkins, 1955).

Bloomfield, L. P., *The United Nations and U.S. Foreign Policy* (Little, Brown, 1961).

Brennan, D. G. (Ed.), *Arms Control, Disarmament, and National Security* (Braziller, 1961).

Brierly, J. L., *The Law of Nations,* 6th ed. (Oxford, 1963).

Brzezinski, Z., *The Soviet Bloc: Unity and Conflict* (Harvard, 1960).

Carr, E. H., *The Twenty Years' Crisis 1919–1939* (Macmillan, 1946).

——, *Nationalism and After* (Macmillan, 1945).

Churchill, W. S., *The Second World War* (Houghton Mifflin, 1948–53).

Clark, G., and L. B. Sohn, *World Peace through World Law,* 2nd ed. rev. (Harvard, 1960).

Claude, I. L., Jr., *Swords into Plowshares: The Problems and Progress of International Organization,* 2nd ed. (Random House, 1959).

Cohen, B. V., *The United Nations: Constitutional Development, Growth, and Possibilities* (Harvard, 1961).

Cousins, N., *In Place of Folly* (Harper, 1961).

Coyle, D. C., *The United Nations and How It Works,* rev. ed. (Columbia,, 1961).

Dallin, D. J., *Soviet Foreign Policy after Stalin* (Lippincott, 1961).

Etzioni, A., *The Hard Way to Peace: A New Strategy* (Collier, 1962).

Feis, H., *Churchill, Roosevelt, Stalin* (Princeton, 1957).

Frank, J., *The European Common Market* (Praeger, 1961).

Frye, W. R., *A United Nations Peace Force* (Oceana, 1957).

Gross, E. A., *The United Nations: Structure for Peace* (Harper & Row, 1962).

Haas, E. B., *The Uniting of Europe* (Stanford, 1958).

Haines, C. G. (Ed.), *European Integration* (Johns Hopkins, 1957).

Hayes, C. J. H., *Nationalism: A Religion* (Macmillan, 1960).

Hemleben, S. J., *Plans for World Peace Through Six Centuries* (Chicago, 1943).

Henkin, L. (Ed.), *Arms Control: Issues for the Public* (Prentice-Hall, 1961).

Herter, C. A., *Toward an Atlantic Community* (Harper & Row, 1963)

Herz, J. H., *International Politics in the Atomic Age* (Columbia, 1959).

Hoffmann, S. H. (Ed.), *Contemporary Theory in International Relations* (Prentice-Hall, 1960).

Horwitz, I. L., *The War Games: Studies of the New Civilian Militarists* (Ballantine, 1963).

Kahn, H., *On Thermonuclear War* (Princeton, 1960).

Kennan, G. F., *American Diplomacy, 1900–1950* (U. of Chicago, 1951).

Kissinger, H. A., *Nuclear Weapons and Foreign Policy* (Doubleday, 1958).

Kohn, H., *The Idea of Nationalism* (Macmillan, 1946).

Kraft, J., *The Grand Design: From Common Market to Atlantic Partnership* (Harper & Row, 1962).

Lash, J. P., *Dag Hammarskjold: Custodian of the Brushfire Place* (Doubleday, 1958).

Lawson, R. C., *Constitutional Foundations of International Regional Organizations* (Praeger, 1962).

Lefever, E. W. (Ed.), *Arms and Arms Control* (Praeger, 1962).

Lerner, M., *The Age of Overkill: A Preface to World Politics* (Simon & Schuster, 1963).

Lie, T. H., *In the Cause of Peace* (Macmillan, 1954).

Lippmann, W., *Western Unity and the Common Market* (Little, Brown, 1962).

Liska, G., *Nations in Alliance: The Limits of Interdependence* (Johns Hopkins, 1962).

Lissitzyn, O. J., *The International Court of Justice* (Carnegie Endowment, 1951).

Macridis, R. C., *Foreign Policy in World Politics,* 2nd ed. (Prentice-Hall, 1962).

Middleton, D., *The Supreme Choice: Britain and Europe* (Knopf, 1963).

Millikan, M. F., and D. L. M. Blackmer, *The Emerging Nations: Their Growth and United States Policy* (Little, Brown, 1962).

Millis, W., and J. Real, *The Abolition of War* (Macmillan, 1963).

Morgenthau, H. J., *Politics Among the Nations,* 3rd ed. (Knopf, 1960).

Nathan, O., and H. Norden (Eds.), *Einstein on Peace* (Simon & Schuster, 1962).

Nicholas, H. G., *The United Nations as a Political Institution* (Oxford, 1959).

Nicolson, Sir H. G., *Diplomacy,* 3rd ed. (Oxford, 1963).

Organski, K., and A. F. K. Organski, *Population and World Power* (Knopf, 1962).

Osgood, R. E., *NATO: The Entangling Alliance* (U. of Chicago, 1962).

Palmer, N. D., and H. C. Perkins, *International Relations,* 2nd ed. (Houghton Mifflin, 1957).

Preston, R. A., S. F. Wise, and H. O. Werner, *Men in Arms: A History of Warfare and Its Interrelationships with Western Society,* rev. ed. (Praeger, 1962).

Robertson, A. H., *The Council of Europe,* 2nd ed. (Praeger, 1961).

Rosecrance, *Action and Reaction in World Politics* (Little, Brown, 1963).

Rosenne, S., *The World Court: What It Is and How It Works* (Oceana, 1962).

Rostow, W. W., *The United States in the World Arena* (Harper, 1960).

Schmitt, H. A., *The Path to European Union* (Louisiana State U., 1963).

Schuman, F. L., *The Cold War: Retrospect and Prospect* (Louisiana State U., 1962).

Singer, J. D., *Deterrence, Arms Control, and Disarmament* (Ohio State U., 1963).

Spanier, J. W., *American Foreign Policy Since World War II* (Praeger, 1961).

—— and J. L. Nogee, *The Politics of Disarmament: A Study in Soviet-American Gamesmanship* (Praeger, 1963).

Strachey, J., *On the Prevention of War* (St. Martin's 1963).

Strausz-Hupé, R., *et al., The Protracted Conflict* (Harper, 1959).

Streit, C. K., *Union Now* (Harper, 1949).

Stuart, G. H., *American Diplomatic and Consular Practice,* 2nd ed. (Macmillan, 1952).

Vandenbosch, A., and W. N. Hogan, *Toward World Order* (McGraw-Hill, 1963).

Wadsworth, J. J., *The Price of Peace* (Praeger, 1961).

Walters, F. P., *A History of the League of Nations,* rev. ed. (Oxford, 1961).

Westerfield, H. B., *The Instruments of American Foreign Policy* (Crowell, 1963).

Wright, Q., *A Study of War* (Chicago, 1942).

Zurcher, A. J., *The Struggle To Unite Europe, 1940–1958* (New York U., 1958).

Selected Basic Bibliographical References

In a book of this scope, certain broad, basic texts may properly be listed repeatedly as basic references for many, if not most, of its nineteen chapters. Not having attempted to do so in the body of the text, we shall enumerate some of these 'staples' here. A few will be designated *general works* in view of their wide range; others are listed here under the four countries with which they, and our work, deal. The balance of the suggested references for further reading appear at the end of each appropriate chapter.

I. General Works

Almond, G. A., and J. S. Coleman, *The Politics of the Developing Areas* (Princeton, 1960).

Beer, S. H., and A. Ulam (Eds.), *Patterns of Government: The Major Political Systems of Europe,* 2nd ed. (Random House, 1962).

Brogan, D. W., and D. V. Verney, *Political Patterns in Today's World* (Harcourt, Brace & World, 1963).

Bryce, J., *Modern Democracies* (Macmillan, 1921).

Carter, G. M., and J. H. Herz, *Major Foreign Powers,* 4th ed. (Harcourt, Brace & World, 1962).

Cole, T. (Ed.), *European Political Systems,* 2nd ed. (Knopf, 1958).

Corry, J. A., and J. E. Hodgetts, *Democratic Government & Politics,* 3rd rev. ed. (Toronto U., 1959).

Eckstein, H., and D. E. Apter (Eds.), *Comparative Politics: A Reader* (Free Press, 1962).

Finer, H., *Major Governments of Modern Europe* (Holt, 1960).

——, *The Theory and Practice of Modern Government,* abbrev. Br. ed. (Methuen, 1954).

Friedrich, J., *Constitutional Government and Democracy,* 3rd ed. (Ginn, 1964).
Heckscher, G., *The Study of Comparative Government and Politics* (Allen & Unwin, 1957).
Loewenstein, K., *Political Power & the Governmental Process* (Cambridge, 1958).
Macridis, R., and B. E. Brown, *Comparative Politics: Notes and Readings* (Dorsey, 1961).
Morgenthau, H. J., *Politics in the Twentieth Century* (U. of Chicago, 1963).
Neumann, R. G., *European and Comparative Government,* 3rd ed. (McGraw-Hill, 1960).
Peaslee, A. J., *Constitutions of the Nations,* 2nd ed. (Rinnford, 1956).
Shils, E., *Political Development in the New States,* 3rd ed. (Praeger, 1962).
Spiro, H., *Government by Constitution* (Random House, 1959).
Stewart, M., *Modern Forms of Government: A Comparative Study* (Praeger, 1961).
Strong, C. F., *Modern Political Constitutions,* 5th ed. rev. (Sidgwick & Jackson, 1958).
UNESCO, *Contemporary Political Science* (UNESCO, 1950).
Verney, D. V., *The Analysis of Political Systems* (Routledge, 1959).
Zink, H., *Modern Governments,* 2nd ed. (Van Nostrand, 1962).

II. The United States

Beard, C. A., *The Republic* (Viking, 1946).
Binkley, W. E., and M. C. Moos, *A Grammar of American Politics* (Knopf, 1949).
Brogan, D. W., *Politics in America* (Doubleday, 1960).
Bruckberger, R. L., *Image of America* (Viking, 1959).
Bryce, J., *The American Commonwealth,* 2nd ed. rev. (Commonwealth Publ. Co., 1908).
Burns, J. M., and J. W. Peltason, *Government by the People,* 5th ed. (Prentice-Hall, 1963).
Calhoun, J. C., *A Disquisition on Government* (Poli. Sci. Classics, 1947).
Carr, R. K., M. H. Bernstein, W. F. Murphy, *American Democracy in Theory and Practice,* 4th ed. (Holt, Rinehart & Winston, 1963).
Dimock, M. E., *Business and Government,* 4th ed. (Holt, Rinehart & Winston, 1961).
Eliot, T. H., *Governing America* (Dodd, Mead, 1960).
Ferguson, J. H., and D. E. McHenry, *The American Federal Government,* 7th ed. (McGraw-Hill, 1963).
Griffith, E. S. *The American System of Government,* 3rd ed. (Praeger, 1962).
Hamilton, Jay, and Madison, *The Federalist* (Random House ed., 1937).
Irish, M. D. (Ed.), *Continuing Crisis in American Politics* (Prentice-Hall, 1963).
Junz, A. J. (Ed.), *Present Trends in American National Government* (Praeger, 1961).
Laski, H., *The American Democracy* (Viking, 1948).
Morgenthau, H. J., *The Purpose of American Politics* (Knopf, 1960).
Schmeckebier, L. F., and R. B. Eastin, *Government Publications and Their Use* (Brookings, 1961).
Westin, A. (Ed.), *The Uses of Power: 7 Cases in American Politics* (Harcourt, Brace & World, 1962).
Young, W. H. (Ed.), *Ogg and Ray's Introduction to American Government,* 12th ed. (Appleton-Century-Crofts, 1962).

III. Britain

Attlee, Earl, *Empire into Commonwealth* (Oxford, 1961).

Beloff, M., *The Tasks of Government* (Oxford, 1958).

Cole, G. D. H., *The Post-War Condition of Britain* (Praeger, 1958).

Derry, T. K., *The United Kingdom: A Survey of British Institutions Today* (New York U., 1963).

Eckles, R. B., and R. W. Hale, *Britain, Her Peoples, and the Commonwealth* (McGraw-Hill, 1955).

Harrison, W., *The Government of Britain,* 6th ed. (Hutchinson, 1958).

Harvey, J., and K. Hood, *The British State* (Lawrence & Wishart, 1958).

Jennings, Sir W. I., *Problems of the New Commonwealth* (Duke, 1958).

Keir, Sir D. L., *The Constitutional History of Modern Britain, 1485–1951,* 6th ed. (Black, 1960).

Laski, A. J., *Parliamentary Government in England: A Commentary* (Viking, 1938).

Lowell, A. L., *The Government of England* (Macmillan, 1920).

Mathiot, A., *The British Political System* (Stanford, 1959).

Middleton, D., *These Are the British* (Knopf, 1957).

Moodie, G. C., *The Government of Great Britain* (Crowell, 1961).

Sampson, A., *Anatomy of Britain* (Harper & Row, 1962).

Smellie, K. B., *The British Way of Life* (Allen & Unwin, 1955).

Somervell, D. C., *British Politics Since 1900* (Oxford, 1950).

Stout, H. M., *British Government* (Oxford, 1953).

White, L. W., and W. D. Hussey, *Government in Great Britain, the Empire, and the Commonwealth* (Cambridge, 1958).

IV. France

Aron, R., *France: Steadfast & Changing* (Harvard, 1960).

Brogan, D. W., *The Development of Modern France* (Hamilton, 1949).

Dutourd, J., *The Taxis of the Marne* (Simon & Schuster, 1957).

Duverger, M., *The French Political System* (U. of Chicago, 1958).

Earle, E. M. (Ed.), *Modern France* (Princeton, 1951).

Fauvet, J., *La IVe République* (Fayard, 1960).

Furniss, E. S., Jr., *France, Troubled Ally* (Harper, 1960).

Goguel, F., *France under the Fourth Republic* (Cornell, 1952).

Hoffman, S., et al., *In Search of France* (Harvard, 1962).

Kohn, H., *Making of the Modern French Mind* (Van Nostrand, 1955).

Laponce, J. A., *The Government of the Fourth Republic* (Methuen, 1955).

Luethy, H., *France Against Herself* (Praeger, 1955).

Maurois, A., *A History of France* (Farrar, Straus and Cudahy, 1957).

Pickles, D. M., *The Fifth French Republic,* rev. ed. (Praeger, 1962).

Schoenbrun, D., *As France Goes* (Harper, 1957).

Tannenbaum, E., *The New France* (U. of Chicago, 1961).

Thomson, D., *Democracy in France,* 3rd ed. (Oxford, 1958).

Werth, A., *The Twilight of France* (Harper, 1942).

V. The Soviet Union

Barghoorn, F. C., *The Soviet Cultural Offensive* (Princeton, 1960).

Brzezinski, Z., *Ideology and Power in Soviet Politics* (Praeger, 1961).

Clarkson, J. D., *A History of Russia* (Random House, 1961).

Crankshaw, E., *Khrushchev's Russia* (Houghton Mifflin, 1959).

Dallin, D. I., *Soviet Foreign Policy after Stalin* (Lippincott, 1961).

Deutscher, I., *Russia in Transition* (Grove, 1960).

Fainsod, M., *How Russia Is Ruled,* 2nd ed. (Harvard, 1963).

Fischer, L., *Russia Revisited* (Doubleday, 1957).

Florinsky, M. T., *Russia: A History and an Interpretation* (Macmillan, 1953).

Gripp, R. C., *Soviet Government and Politics* (Dorsey, 1963).

Hazard, J. N., *The Soviet System of Government,* 2nd ed. (Chicago, 1960).

Hendel, S. (Ed.), *The Soviet Crucible: Soviet Government in Theory and Practice,* 2nd ed. (Van Nostrand, 1963).

Inkeles, A. and Geiger, K. (Eds.), *Soviet Society: A Book of Readings* (Houghton Mifflin, 1961).

Kennan, G. C., *Russia and the West under Lenin and Stalin* (Little, Brown, 1961).

Marcuse, H., *Soviet Marxism: A Critical Analysis* (Columbia, 1960).

McCloskey, H. and Turner, N. E., *The Soviet Dictatorship* (McGraw-Hill, 1959).

Mackintosh, J. M., *Strategy and Tactics of Soviet Foreign Policy* (Oxford, 1963).

McNeal, R. H. (Ed.), *The Bolshevik Tradition: Lenin, Stalin, and Khrushchev* (Prentice-Hall, 1962).

Mosley, P. E. (Ed.), *The Soviet Union, 1922–1962* (Praeger, 1963).

Pethybridge, R., *Key to Soviet Politics: The Crisis of the 'Anti-Party' Group* (British Book Center, 1963).

Reschetar, J. S., *Problems of Analyzing and Predicting Soviet Behavior* (Doubleday, 1955).

Riasanovsky, N. V., *A History of Russia* (Oxford, 1963).

Rubinstein, A. Z. (Ed.), *The Foreign Policy of the Soviet Union* (Random House, 1960).

Schuman, F. L., *Government in the Soviet Union* (Crowell, 1961).

Schwartz, H., *The Red Phoenix: Russia Since World War II* (Praeger, 1961).

Simmons, E. J. (Ed.), *Continuity and Change in Russian and Soviet Thought* (Harvard, 1955).

Towster, J., *Political Power in the U.S.S.R., 1917–1947* (Oxford, 1948).

Triska, J. F. (Ed.), *Soviet Communism Programs and Rules* (Chandler, 1962).

Ulam, A. B., *The New Face of Soviet Totalitarianism* (Harvard, 1963).

Whitney, T. P. (Ed.), *Khrushchev Speaks* (U. of Michigan, 1963).

APPENDICES

The Constitution of the United States

We the people of the United States, in Order to form a more perfect Union, establish Justice, insure domestic Tranquility, provide for the common defence, promote the general Welfare, and secure the Blessings of Liberty to ourselves and our Posterity, do ordain and establish this Constitution for the United States of America.

ARTICLE I

SECTION 1. All legislative Powers herein granted shall be vested in a Congress of the United States, which shall consist of a Senate and House of Representatives.

SECTION 2. The House of Representatives shall be composed of Members chosen every second Year by the People of the several States, and the Electors in each State shall have the Qualifications requisite for Electors of the most numerous Branch of the State Legislature.

No Person shall be a Representative who shall not have attained to the Age of twenty-five Years, and been seven Years a Citizen of the United States, and who shall not, when elected, be an Inhabitant of that State in which he shall be chosen.

Representatives and direct Taxes shall be apportioned among the several States which may be included within this Union, according to their respective Numbers, *which shall be determined by adding to the whole Number of free Persons, including those bound to Service for a Term of Years,*[1] and excluding Indians not taxed, *three fifths of all other Persons.*[2] The actual Enumeration shall be made within three Years after the first Meeting of the Congress of the United States, and within every subsequent Term of ten Years, in such Manner as they shall by Law direct. The Number of Representatives shall not exceed one for every thirty Thousand, but each State shall have at Least one Representative; *and until such enumeration shall be made, the State of New Hampshire shall be entitled to chuse three, Massachusetts eight, Rhode-Island and Providence*

[1] Altered by the Fourteenth Amendment.
[2] Rescinded by the Fourteenth Amendment.

Plantations one, Connecticut five, New-York six, New Jersey four, Pennsylvania eight, Delaware one, Maryland six, Virginia ten, North Carolina five, South Carolina five, and Georgia three.[3]

When vacancies happen in the Representation from any State, the Executive Authority thereof shall issue Writs of Election to fill such Vacancies.

The House of Representatives shall chuse their Speaker and other Officers; and shall have the sole Power of Impeachment.

SECTION 3. The Senate of the United States shall be composed of two Senators from each State, *chosen by the Legislature thereof,*[4] for six Years; and each Senator shall have one Vote.

Immediately after they shall be assembled in Consequence of the first Election, they shall be divided as equally as may be into three Classes. The Seats of the Senators of the first Class shall be vacated at the Expiration of the second Year, of the second Class at the Expiration of the fourth Year, and of the third Class at the Expiration of the sixth Year, so that one third may be chosen every second Year; *and if Vacancies happen by Resignation, or otherwise, during the Recess of the Legislature of any State, the Executive thereof may make temporary Appointments until the next Meeting of the Legislature, which shall then fill such Vacancies.*[5]

No Person shall be a Senator who shall not have attained to the Age of thirty Years, and been nine Years a Citizen of the United States, and who shall not, when elected, be an Inhabitant of that State for which he shall be chosen.

The Vice President of the United States shall be President of the Senate, but shall have no Vote, unless they be equally divided.

The Senate shall chuse their other Officers, and also a President pro tempore, in the Absence of the Vice President, or when he shall exercise the Office of the President of the United States.

The Senate shall have the sole Power to try all Impeachments. When sitting for that Purpose, they shall be on Oath or Affirmation. When the President of the United States is tried, the Chief Justice shall preside: And no Person shall be convicted without the Concurrence of two thirds of the Members present.

Judgment in Cases of Impeachment shall not extend further than to removal from Office, and disqualification to hold and enjoy any Office of honor, Trust or Profit under the United States: but the Party convicted shall nevertheless be liable and subject to Indictment, Trial, Judgment and Punishment, according to Law.

SECTION 4. The Times, Places and Manner of holding Elections for Senators and Representatives, shall be prescribed in each State by the Legislature thereof, but the Congress may at any time by Law make or alter such Regulations, except as to the Places of chusing Senators.

The Congress shall assemble at least once in every year, and such Meeting shall be on the first Monday in December, unless they shall by Law appoint a different day.[6]

SECTION 5. Each House shall be the Judge of the Elections, Returns and Qualifications of its own Members, and a Majority of each shall constitute a Quorum to do Business; but a smaller Number may adjourn from day to day, and may be authorized to compel

[3] Temporary provision.
[4] Modified by the Seventeenth Amendment.
[5] Modified by the Seventeenth Amendment.
[6] Superseded by the Twentieth Amendment.

the Attendance of absent Members, in such manner, and under such Penalties as each House may provide.

Each House may determine the Rules of its Proceedings, punish its Members for disorderly Behaviour, and, with the Concurrence of two thirds, expel a Member.

Each House shall keep a Journal of its Proceedings, and from time to time publish the same, excepting such Parts as may in their Judgment require Secrecy; and the Yeas and Nays of the Members of either House on any question shall, at the Desire of one fifth of those Present, be entered on the Journal.

Neither House, during the Session of Congress, shall, without the Consent of the other, adjourn for more than three days, nor to any other Place than that in which the two Houses shall be sitting.

SECTION 6. The Senators and Representatives shall receive a Compensation for their Services, to be ascertained by Law, and paid out of the Treasury of the United States. They shall in all Cases, except Treason, Felony and Breach of the Peace, be privileged from Arrest during their Attendance at the Session of their respective Houses, and in going to and returning from the same; and for any Speech or Debate in either House, they shall not be questioned in any other Place.

No Senator or Representative shall, during the Time for which he was elected, be appointed to any civil Office under the Authority of the United States, which shall have been created, or the Emoluments whereof shall have been increased during such time; and no Person holding any Office under the United States, shall be a Member of either House during his Continuance in Office.

SECTION 7. All Bills for raising Revenue shall originate in the House of Representatives; but the Senate may propose or concur with Amendments as on other Bills.

Every Bill which shall have passed the House of Representatives and the Senate shall, before it become a Law, be presented to the President of the United States; If he approve he shall sign it, but if not he shall return it, with his Objections to that House in which it shall have originated, who shall enter the Objections at large on their Journal, and proceed to reconsider it. If after such Reconsideration two thirds of that House shall agree to pass the Bill, it shall be sent, together with the Objections, to the other House, by which it shall likewise be reconsidered, and if approved by two thirds of that House, it shall become a Law. But in all such Cases the Votes of both Houses shall be determined by yeas and Nays, and the Names of the Persons voting for and against the Bill shall be entered on the Journal of each House respectively. If any Bill shall not be returned by the President within ten Days (Sundays excepted) after it shall have been presented to him, the Same shall be a Law, in like Manner as if he had signed it, unless the Congress by their Adjournment prevent its Return, in which Case it shall not be a Law.

Every Order, Resolution or Vote to which the Concurrence of the Senate and House of Representatives may be necessary (except on a question of Adjournment) shall be presented to the President of the United States; and before the Same shall take Effect, shall be approved by him, or being disapproved by him, shall be repassed by two thirds of the Senate and House of Representatives, according to the Rules and Limitations prescribed in the Case of a Bill.

SECTION 8. The Congress shall have Power To lay and collect Taxes, Duties, Imposts and Excises, to pay the Debts and provide for the common Defence and general

Welfare of the United States; but all Duties, Imposts and Excises shall be uniform throughout the United States;

To borrow Money on the credit of the United States;

To regulate Commerce with foreign Nations, and among the several States, and with the Indian Tribes;

To establish an uniform Rule of Naturalization, and uniform Laws on the subject of Bankruptcies throughout the United States;

To coin Money, regulate the Value thereof, and of foreign Coin, and fix the Standard of Weights and Measures;

To provide for the Punishment of counterfeiting the Securities and current Coin of the United States;

To establish Post Offices and post Roads;

To promote the Progress of Science and useful Arts, by securing for limited Times to Authors and Inventors the exclusive Right to their respective Writings and Discoveries;

To constitute Tribunals inferior to the supreme Court;

To define and punish Piracies and Felonies committed on the high Seas, and Offences against the Law of Nations;

To declare War, grant Letters of Marque and Reprisal, and make Rules concerning Captures on Land and Water;

To raise and support Armies, but no Appropriation of Money to that Use shall be for a longer Term than two Years;

To provide and maintain a Navy;

To make Rules for the Government and Regulation of the land and naval Forces;

To provide for calling forth the Militia to execute the Laws of the Union, suppress Insurrection and repel Invasions;

To provide for organizing, arming, and disciplining, the Militia, and for governing such Part of them as may be employed in the Service of the United States, reserving to the States respectively, the Appointment of the Officers, and the Authority of training the Militia according to the discipline prescribed by Congress;

To exercise exclusive Legislation in all Cases whatsoever, over such District (not exceeding ten Miles square) as may, by Cession of particular States, and the Acceptance of Congress, become the Seat of the Government of the United States, and to exercise like Authority over all Places purchased by the Consent of the Legislature of the State in which the Same shall be, for the Erection of Forts, Magazines, Arsenals, dock-Yards, and other needful Buildings; —And

To make all Laws which shall be necessary and proper for carrying into Execution the foregoing Powers, and all other Powers vested by this Constitution in the Government of the United States, or in any Department or Officer thereof.

SECTION 9. *The Migration or Importation of such Persons as any of the States now existing shall think proper to admit, shall not be prohibited by the Congress prior to the Year one thousand eight hundred and eight, but a Tax or duty may be imposed on such Importation, not exceeding ten dollars for each Person.*[7]

The Privilege of the Writ of Habeas Corpus shall not be suspended, unless when in Cases of Rebellion or Invasion the public Safety may require it.

No Bill of Attainder or ex post facto Law shall be passed.

No Capitation, or other direct, Tax shall be laid, unless in Proportion to the Census or Enumeration herein before directed to be taken.

[7] Temporary provision.

No tax or Duty shall be laid on Articles exported from any State.

No Preference shall be given by any Regulation of Commerce or Revenue to the Ports of one State over those of another; nor shall Vessels bound to, or from, one State, be obliged to enter, clear, or pay Duties in another.

No Money shall be drawn from the Treasury, but in Consequence of Appropriations made by Law, and a regular Statement and Account of the Receipts and Expenditures of all public Money shall be published from time to time.

No Title of Nobility shall be granted by the United States: And no Person holding any Office of Profit or Trust under them, shall, without the Consent of the Congress, accept of any present, Emolument, Office, or Title, of any kind whatever, from any King, Prince, or foreign State.

SECTION 10. No State shall enter into any Treaty, Alliance, or Confederation; grant Letters of Marque and Reprisal; coin Money; emit Bills of Credit; make any Thing but gold and silver Coin a Tender in Payment of Debts; pass any Bill of Attainder, ex post facto Law, or Law impairing the Obligation of Contracts, or grant any Title of Nobility.

No State shall, without the Consent of the Congress, lay any Imposts or Duties on Imports or Exports, except what may be absolutely necessary for executing its inspection Laws: and the net Produce of all Duties and Imposts, laid by any State on Imports or Exports, shall be for the Use of the Treasury of the United States; and all such Laws shall be subject to the Revision and Controul of the Congress.

No State shall, without the Consent of Congress, lay any Duty of Tonnage, keep troops, or Ships of War in time of Peace, enter into any Agreement or Compact with another State, or with a foreign Power, or engage in War, unless actually invaded, or in such imminent Danger as will not admit of delay.

ARTICLE II

SECTION 1. The Executive Power shall be vested in a President of the United States of America. *He shall hold his Office during the Term of four Years,*[8] and, together with the Vice President, chosen for the same Term, be elected, as follows:

Each State shall appoint, in such Manner as the Legislature thereof may direct, a Number of Electors, equal to the whole Number of Senators and Representatives to which the State may be entitled in the Congress: but no Senator or Representative, or Person holding an Office of Trust or Profit under the United States, shall be appointed an Elector.

The Electors shall meet in their respective States, and vote by Ballot for two persons, of whom one at least shall not be an Inhabitant of the same State with themselves. And they shall make a List of all the Persons voted for, and of the Number of Votes for each; which List they shall sign and certify, and transmit sealed to the Seat of the Government of the United States, directed to the President of the Senate. The President of the Senate shall, in the Presence of the Senate and House of Representatives, open all the Certificates, and the Votes shall then be counted. The Person having the greatest Number of Votes shall be the President, if such Number be a Majority of the whole Number of Electors appointed; and if there be more than one who have such Majority, and have an equal Number of Votes, then the House of Representatives shall immediately chuse by Ballot one of them for President; and if no Person have a Majority, then from the five highest on the List the said House shall in like Manner chuse the

[8] Modified by the Twenty-second Amendment.

President. But in chusing the President, the Votes sall be taken by States, the Repre-
sentation from each State having one Vote; A quorum for this Purpose shall consist
of a Member or Members from two thirds of the States, and a Majority of all the
States shall be necessary to a Choice. In every Case, after the Choice of the President,
the Person having the greatest Number of Votes of the Electors shall be the Vice Presi-
dent. But if there should remain two or more who have equal Votes, the Senate shall
chuse from them by Ballot the Vice President.[9]

The Congress may determine the Time of chusing the Electors, and the Day on which they shall give their Votes; which Day shall be the same throughout the United States.

No Person except a natural born Citizen, or a Citizen of the United States, at the time of the Adoption of the Constitution, shall be eligible to the Office of President, neither shall any Person be eligible to that Office who shall not have attained to the Age of thirty-five Years, and been fourteen Years a Resident within the United States.

In Case of the Removal of the President from Office, or of his Death, Resignation, or Inability to discharge the Powers and Duties of the said Office, the Same shall de-volve on the Vice President, and the Congress may by Law provide for the Case of Removal, Death, Resignation or Inability, both of the President and Vice President, declaring what Officer shall then act as President, and such Officer shall act accordingly, until the Disability be removed, or a President shall be elected.

The President shall, at stated Times, receive for his Services, a Compensation, which shall neither be increased nor diminished during the Period for which he shall have been elected, and he shall not receive within that Period any other Emolument from the United States, or any of them.

Before he enter on the Execution of his Office, he shall take the following Oath or Affirmation:— "I do solemnly swear (or affirm) that I will faithfully execute the Office of President of the United States, and will to the best of my Ability, preserve, protect and defend the Constitution of the United States."

Section 2. The President shall be Commander in Chief of the Army and Navy of the United States, and of the Militia of the several states, when called into the actual Service of the United States; he may require the Opinion, in writing, of the principal Officer in each of the executive Departments, upon any Subject relating to the Duties of their respective Offices, and he shall have Power to grant Reprieves and Pardons for Offences against the United States, except in Cases of Impeachment.

He shall have Power, by and with the Advice and Consent of the Senate, to make Treaties, provided two thirds of the Senators present concur; and he shall nominate, and by and with the Advice and Consent of the Senate, shall appoint Ambassadors, other public Ministers and Consuls, Judges of the supreme Court, and all other Officers of the United States, whose Appointments are not herein otherwise provided for, and which shall be established by Law; but the Congress may by Law vest the Appoint-ment of such inferior Officers, as they think proper, in the President alone, in the Courts of Law, or in the Heads of Departments.

The President shall have Power to fill up all Vacancies that may happen during the Recess of the Senate, by granting Commissions which shall expire at the End of their next Session.

Section 3. He shall from time to time give to the Congress Information of the State of the Union, and recommend to their Consideration such Measures as he shall judge

[9] Superseded by the Twelfth Amendment.

necessary and expedient; he may, on extraordinary Occasions, convene both Houses, or either of them, and in Case of Disagreement between them, with Respect to the Time of Adjournment, he may adjourn them to such Time as he shall think proper; he shall receive Ambassadors and other public Ministers; he shall take Care that the Laws be faithfully executed, and shall Commission all the Officers of the United States.

SECTION 4. The President, Vice President and all civil Officers of the United States, shall be removed from Office on Impeachment for, and Conviction of, Treason, Bribery, or other high Crimes and Misdemeanors.

ARTICLE III

SECTION 1. The judicial Power of the United States, shall be vested in one supreme Court, and in such inferior Courts as the Congress may from time to time ordain and establish. The Judges, both of the supreme and inferior courts, shall hold their Offices during good Behaviour, and shall, at stated Times, receive for their Services, a Compensation, which shall not be diminished during their Continuance in Office.

SECTION 2. The judicial Power shall extend to all Cases, in Law and Equity, arising under this Constitution, the Laws of the United States, and Treaties made, or which shall be made, under their Authority;—to all Cases affecting Ambassadors, other public Ministers and Consuls;—to all Cases of admiralty and maritime Jurisdiction:—to Controversies to which the United States shall be a Party;—to Controversies between two or more States;—*between a State and Citizens of another State;* [10]—between Citizens of different States,—between Citizens of the same State claiming Lands under Grants of different States, and *between a State, or the Citizens thereof, and foreign States, Citizens or Subjects.*[10]

In all Cases affecting Ambassadors, other public Ministers and Consuls, and those in which a State shall be Party, the supreme Court shall have original Jurisdiction. In all the other Cases before mentioned, the supreme Court shall have appellate Jurisdiction, both as to Law and Fact, with such Exceptions, and under such Regulations as the Congress shall make.

The Trial of all Crimes, except in Cases of Impeachment, shall be by Jury; and such Trial shall be held in the State where the said Crimes shall have been committed; but when not committed within any State, the Trial shall be at such Place or Places as the Congress may by Law have directed.

SECTION 3. Treason against the United States, shall consist only in levying War against them, or in adhering to their Enemies, giving them Aid and Comfort. No Person shall be convicted of Treason unless on the Testimony of two Witnesses to the same overt Act, or on Confession in open Court.

The Congress shall have Power to declare the Punishment of Treason, but no Attainder of Treason shall work Corruption of Blood, or Forfeiture except during the Life of the Person attainted.

ARTICLE IV

SECTION 1. Full Faith and Credit shall be given in each State to the public Acts, Records, and judicial Proceedings of every other State. And the Congress may by general Laws prescribe the Manner in which such Acts, Records and Proceedings shall be proved, and the Effect thereof.

[10] Restricted by the Eleventh Amendment.

SECTION 2. *The Citizens of each State shall be entitled to all Privileges and Immunities of Citizens in the several States.*[11]

A Person charged in any State with Treason, Felony, or other Crime, who shall flee from Justice, and be found in another State, shall on Demand of the executive Authority of the State from which he fled, be delivered up, to be removed to the State having jurisdiction of the Crime.

No Person held to Service or Labour in one State, under the Laws thereof, escaping into another, shall, in Consequence of any Law or Regulation therein, be discharged from such Service or Labour, but shall be delivered up on Claim of the Party to whom such Service or Labour may be due.[12]

SECTION 3. New States may be admitted by the Congress into this Union; but no new State shall be formed or erected within the Jurisdiction of any other State; nor any State be formed by the Junction of two or more States, or Parts of States, without the Consent of the Legislatures of the States concerned as well as of the Congress.

The Congress shall have Power to dispose of and make all needful Rules and Regulations respecting the Territory or other Property belonging to the United States; and nothing in this Constitution shall be so construed as to Prejudice any Claims of the United States, or of any particular State.

SECTION 4. The United States shall guarantee to every State in this Union a Republican Form of Government, and shall protect each of them against Invasion; and on Application of the Legislature, or of the Executive (when the Legislature cannot be convened) against domestic Violence.

ARTICLE V

The Congress, wherever two thirds of both Houses shall deem it necessary, shall propose Amendments to this Constitution, or, on the Application of the Legislatures of two thirds of the several States, shall call a Convention for proposing Amendments, which, in either Case, shall be valid to all Intents and Purposes, as Part of this Constitution, when ratified by the Legislatures of three fourths of the several States, or by Conventions in three fourths thereof, as the one or the other Mode of Ratification may be proposed by the Congress; *Provided that no Amendment which may be made prior to the Year One thousand eight hundred and eight shall in any Manner affect the first and fourth Clauses in the Ninth Section of the first Article;* [13] and that no State, without its Consent, shall be deprived of its equal Suffrage in the Senate.

ARTICLE VI

All Debts contracted and Engagements entered into, before the Adoption of this Constitution, shall be as valid against the United States under this Constitution, as under the Confederation.[14]

This Constitution, and the Laws of the United States which shall be made in Pursuance therof; and all Treaties made, or which shall be made, under the Authority of the United States, shall be the supreme Law of the Land; and the Judges in every

---

[11] Made more explicit by the Fourteenth Amendment.
[12] Superseded by the Thirteenth Amendment in so far as pertaining to slaves.
[13] Temporary clause.
[14] Extended by the Fourteenth Amendment.

State shall be bound thereby, any Thing in the Constitution or Laws of any State to the Contrary notwithstanding.

The Senators and Representatives before mentioned, and the Members of the several State Legislatures, and all executive and judicial Officers, both of the United States and of the several States, shall be bound by Oath or Affirmation, to support this Constitution; but no religious Test shall ever be required as a Qualification to any Office or public Trust under the United States.

ARTICLE VII

The Ratification of the Conventions of nine States, shall be sufficient for the Establishment of this Constitution between the States so ratifying the Same.

Done in Convention by the Unanimous Consent of the States present the Seventeenth Day of September in the Year of our Lord one thousand seven hundred and Eighty seven and of the Independence of the United States of America the Twelfth. In witness whereof We have hereunto subscribed our Names,

G° WASHINGTON—Pres^t
and deputy from Virginia

New Hampshire { John Langdon / Nicholas Gilman

Massachusetts { Nathaniel Gorham / Rufus King

Connecticut { Wm Saml Johnson / Roger Sherman

New York { Alexander Hamilton

New Jersey { Wil: Livingston / David A. Brearley. / Wm Paterson. / Jona: Dayton

Pennsylvania { B Franklin / Thomas Mifflin / Robt Morris / Geo. Clymer / Thos FitzSimons / Jared Ingersoll / James Wilson / Gouv Morris

Delaware { Geo: Read / Gunning Bedford jun / John Dickinson / Richard Bassett / Jaco: Broom

Maryland { James McHenry / Dan of St Thos Jenifer / Danl Carroll

Virginia { John Blair— / James Madison Jr.

North Carolina { Wm Blount / Richd Dobbs Spaight. / Hu Williamson

South Carolina { J. Rutledge / Charles Cotesworth Pinckney / Charles Pinckney / Pierce Butler.

Georgia { William Few / Abr Baldwin

AMENDMENTS TO THE CONSTITUTION

Articles in addition to, and Amendment of the Constitution of the United States of America, proposed by Congress, and ratified by the Legislatures of the several States, pursuant to the fifth Article of the original Constitution.

ARTICLE I

[The First Ten Articles Proposed 25 September 1789; Declared
in Force 15 December 1791]

Congress shall make no law respecting an establishment of religion, or prohibiting the free exercise thereof; or abridging the freedom of speech, or of the press; or the right of the people peaceably to assemble, and to petition the Government for a redress of grievances.

ARTICLE II

A well regulated Militia, being necessary to the security of a free State, the right of the people to keep and bear Arms, shall not be infringed.

ARTICLE III

No Soldier shall, in time of peace be quartered in any house, without the consent of the Owner, nor in time of war, but in a manner to be prescribed by law.

ARTICLE IV

The right of the people to be secure in their persons, houses, papers, and effects, against unreasonable searches and seizures, shall not be violated, and no Warrants shall issue, but upon probable cause, supported by Oath or affirmation, and particularly describing the place to be searched, and the persons or things to be seized.

ARTICLE V

No person shall be held to answer for a capital, or otherwise infamous crime, unless on a presentment or indictment of a Grand Jury, except in cases arising in the land or naval forces, or in the Militia, when in actual service in time of War or public danger; nor shall any person be subject for the same offence to be twice put in jeopardy of life or limb; nor shall be compelled in any criminal case to be a witness against himself, nor be deprived of life, liberty, or property, without due process of law; nor shall private property be taken for public use, without just compensation.

ARTICLE VI

In all criminal prosecutions, the accused shall enjoy the right to a speedy and public trial, by an impartial jury of the State and district wherein the crime shall have been committed, which district shall have been previously ascertained by law, and to be informed of the nature and cause of the accusation; to be confronted with the witnesses against him; to have compulsory process for obtaining witnesses in his favor, and to have the Assistance of Counsel for his defence.

ARTICLE VII

In Suits at common law, where the value in controversy shall exceed twenty dollars, the right of trial by jury shall be preserved, and no fact tried by a jury, shall be otherwise re-examined in any Court of the United States, than according to the rules of the common law.

ARTICLE VIII

Excessive bail shall not be required, nor excessive fines imposed, nor cruel and unusual punishments inflicted.

ARTICLE IX

The enumeration in the Constitution, of certain rights, shall not be construed to deny or disparage others retained by the people.

ARTICLE X

The powers not delegated to the United States by the Constitution, nor prohibited by it to the States, are reserved to the States respectively, or to the people.

ARTICLE XI

[Proposed 5 March 1794; Declared Ratified 8 January 1798]

The Judicial power of the United States shall not be construed to extend to any suit in law or equity, commenced or prosecuted against one of the United States by Citizens of another State, or by Citizens or Subjects of any Foreign State.

ARTICLE XII

[Proposed 12 December 1803; Declared Ratified 25 September 1804]

The Electors shall meet in their respective states and vote by ballot for President and Vice-President, one of whom, at least, shall not be an inhabitant of the same state with themselves; they shall name in their ballots the person voted for as President, and in distinct ballots the person voted for as Vice-President, and they shall make distinct lists of all persons voted for as President, and of all persons voted for as Vice-President, and of the number of votes for each, which lists they shall sign and certify, and transmit sealed to the seat of the government of the United States, directed to the President of the Senate;—The President of the Senate shall, in presence of the Senate and House of Representatives, open all the certificates and the votes shall then be counted;—The person having the greatest number of votes for the President, shall be the President, if such number be a majority of the whole number of Electors appointed; and if no person have such majority, then from the persons having the highest numbers not exceeding three on the list of those voted for as President, the House of Representatives shall choose immediately, by ballot, the President. But in choosing the President, the votes shall be taken by states, the representation from each state having one vote; a quorum for this purpose shall consist of a member or members from two-thirds of the states, and a majority of all the states shall be necessary to a choice. And if the House of Representatives shall not choose a President whenever the right of choice shall devolve upon them, before the *fourth day of March* [15] next following, then the Vice-President shall act as President, as in the case of the death or other constitutional disability of the President.—The Person having the greatest number of votes as Vice-President, shall be the Vice-President, if such number be a majority of the whole number of Electors appointed, and if no person have a majority, then from the two highest numbers on the list, the Senate shall choose the Vice-President; a quorum for the

[15] Superseded by the Twentieth Amendment.

purpose shall consist of two-thirds of the whole number of Senators, and a majority of the whole number shall be necessary to a choice. But no person constitutionally ineligible to the office of President shall be eligible to that of Vice-President of the United States.

ARTICLE XIII

[Proposed 1 February 1865; Declared Ratified 18 December 1866]

SECTION 1. Neither slavery nor involuntary servitude, except as a punishment for crime whereof the party shall have been duly convicted, shall exist within the United States, or any place subject to their jurisdiction.

SECTION 2. Congress shall have power to enforce this article by appropriate legislation.

ARTICLE XIV

[Proposed 16 June 1866; Declared Ratified 28 July 1868]

SECTION 1. All persons born or naturalized in the United States, and subject to the jurisdiction thereof, are citizens of the United States and of the State wherein they reside. No State shall make or enforce any law which shall abridge the privileges or immunities of citizens of the United States; nor shall any State deprive any person of life, liberty, or property, without due process of law; nor deny to any person within its jurisdiction the equal protection of the laws.

SECTION 2. Representatives shall be apportioned among the several States according to their respective numbers, counting the whole number of persons in each State, excluding Indians not taxed. But when the right to vote at any election for the choice of electors for President and Vice-President of the United States, Representatives in Congress, the Executive and Judicial officers of a State, or the members of the Legislature thereof, is denied to any of the male inhabitants of such State, being twenty-one years of age, and citizens of the United States, or in any way abridged, except for participation in rebellion, or other crime, the basis of representation therein shall be reduced in the proportion which the number of such male citizens shall bear to the whole number of male citizens twenty-one years of age in such State.

SECTION 3. No person shall be a Senator or Representative in Congress, or elector of President and Vice-President, or hold any office, civil or military, under the United States, or under any State, who, having previously taken an oath, as a member of Congress, or as an officer of the United States, or as a member of any State legislature, or as an executive or judicial officer of any State, to support the Constitution of the United States, shall have engaged in insurrection or rebellion against the same, or given aid or comfort to the enemies thereof. But Congress may by a vote of two-thirds of each House, remove such disability.

SECTION 4. The validity of the public debt of the United States, authorized by law, including debts incurred for payment of pensions and bounties for services in suppressing insurrection or rebellion, shall not be questioned. But neither the United States nor any State shall assume or pay any debt or obligation incurred in aid of insurrection or rebellion against the United States, or any claim for the loss or emancipation of any slave; but all such debts, obligations and claims shall be held illegal and void.

Section 5. The Congress shall have power to enforce, by appropriate legislation, the provision of this article.

ARTICLE XV

[Proposed 27 February 1869; Declared Ratified 30 March 1870]

Section 1. The right of citizens of the United States to vote shall not be denied or abridged by the United States or by any State on account of race, color, or previous condition of servitude—

Section 2. The Congress shall have power to enforce this article by appropriate legislation.—

ARTICLE XVI

[Proposed 12 July 1909; Declared Ratified 25 February 1913]

The Congress shall have power to lay and collect taxes on incomes, from whatever source derived, without apportionment among the several States, and without regard to any census or enumeration.

ARTICLE XVII

[Proposed 16 May 1912; Declared Ratified 31 May 1913]

The Senate of the United States shall be composed of two Senators from each State, elected by the people thereof, for six years; and each Senator shall have one vote. The electors in each State shall have the qualifications requisite for electors of the most numerous branch of the State legislatures.

When vacancies happen in the representation of any State in the Senate, the executive authority of such State shall issue writs of election to fill such vacancies: *Provided,* That the legislature of any State may empower the executive thereof to make temporary appointments until the people fill the vacancies by election as the legislature may direct.

This amendment shall not be so construed as to affect the election or term of any Senator chosen before it becomes valid as part of the Constitution.

ARTICLE XVIII

[Proposed 18 December 1917; Declared Ratified 29 January 1919]

Section 1. *After one year from the ratification of this article the manufacture, sale, or transportation of intoxicating liquors within, the importation thereof into, or the exportation thereof from the United States and all territory subject to the jurisdiction thereof for beverage purposes is hereby prohibited.*

Section 2. *The Congress and the several States shall have concurrent power to enforce this article by appropriate legislation.*

Section 3. *This article shall be inoperative unless it shall have been ratified as an amendment to the Constitution by the legislatures of the several States, as provided in the Constitution, within seven years from the date of the submission thereof to the States by the Congress.*[16]

[16] Rescinded by the Twenty-first Amendment.

ARTICLE XIX

[Proposed 4 June 1919; Declared Ratified 26 August 1920]

The right of citizens of the United States to vote shall not be denied or abridged by the United States or by any State on account of sex.

The Congress shall have power by appropriate legislation to enforce the Provisions of this article.

ARTICLE XX

[Proposed 2 March 1932; Declared Ratified 6 February 1933]

SECTION 1. The terms of the President and Vice-President shall end at noon on the twentieth day of January, and the terms of Senators and Representatives at noon on the third day of January, of the years in which such terms would have ended if this article had not been ratified; and the terms of their successors shall then begin.

SECTION 2. The Congress shall assemble at least once in every year, and such meeting shall begin at noon on the third day of January, unless they shall by law appoint a different day.

SECTION 3. If, at the time fixed for the beginning of the term of the President, the President-elect shall have died, the Vice-President-elect shall become President. If a President shall not have been chosen before the time fixed for the beginning of his term, or if the President-elect shall have failed to qualify, then the Vice-President-elect shall act as President until a President shall have qualified; and the Congress may by law provide for the case wherein neither a President-elect nor a Vice-President-elect shall have qualified, declaring who shall then act as President, or the manner in which one who is to act shall be selected, and such person shall act accordingly until a President or Vice-President shall have qualified.

SECTION 4. The Congress may by law provide for the case of the death of any of the persons from whom the House of Representatives may choose a President whenever the right of choice shall have devolved upon them, and for the case of the death of any of the persons from whom the Senate may choose a Vice-President whenever the right of choice shall have devolved upon them.

SECTION 5. SECTIONS 1 and 2 shall take effect on the 15th day of October following the ratification of this article.

SECTION 6. This article shall be inoperative unless it shall have been ratified as an amendment to the Constitution by the legislatures of three-fourths of the several States within seven years from the date of its submission.

ARTICLE XXI

[Proposed 20 February 1933; Adopted 5 December 1933]

SECTION 1. The eighteenth article of amendment to the Constitution of the United States is hereby repealed.

Section 2. The transportation or importation into any State, Territory, or possession of the United States for delivery or use therein of intoxicating liquors, in violation of the laws thereof, is hereby prohibited.

Section 3. This article shall be inoperative unless it shall have been ratified as an amendment to the Constitution by conventions in the several States, as provided in the Constitution, within seven years from the date of the submission thereof to the States by the Congress.

ARTICLE XXII

[Proposed 24 March 1947; Adopted 26 February 1951]

Section 1. No person shall be elected to the office of the President more than twice, and no person who has held the office of President, or acted as President, for more than two years of a term to which some other person was elected President shall be elected to the office of the President more than once. But this Article shall not apply to any person holding the office of President when this Article was proposed by Congress, and shall not prevent any person who may be holding the office of President, or acting as President, during the term within which this Article becomes operative from holding the office of President or acting as President during the remainder of such term.

Section 2. The article shall be inoperative unless it shall have been ratified as an amendment to the Constitution by the legislatures of three-fourths of the several States within seven years from the date of its submission to the States by the Congress.

ARTICLE XXIII

[Proposed 6 January 1960; Adopted 3 April 1961]

Section 1. The District constituting the seat of Government of the United States shall appoint in such manner as the Congress may direct:

A number of electors of President and Vice President equal to the whole number of Senators and Representatives in Congress to which the District would be entitled if it were a State, but in no event more than the least populous State; they shall be in addition to those appointed by the States, but they shall be considered, for the purposes of the election of President and Vice President, to be electors appointed by a State; and they shall meet in the District and perform such duties as provided by the twelfth article of amendment.

Section 2. The Congress shall have power to enforce this article by appropriate legislation.

ARTICLE XXIV

[Proposed 27 August 1962; Adopted 24 January 1964]

Section 1. The right of citizens of the United States to vote in any primary or other election for President or Vice President, or for Senator or Representative in Congress, shall not be denied or abridged by the United States or any State by reason of failure to pay any poll tax or other tax.

Section 2. The Congress shall have power to enforce this article by appropriate legislation.

The French Constitution

Adopted by the Referendum of September 28, 1958, and Promulgated on October 4, 1958

PREAMBLE

The French people hereby solemnly proclaims its attachment to the Rights of Man and the principles of national sovereignty as defined by the Declaration of 1789, reaffirmed and complemented by the Preamble of the Constitution of 1946.

By virtue of these principles and that of the free determination of peoples, the Republic hereby offers to the Overseas Territories that express the desire to adhere to them, new institutions based on the common ideal of liberty, equality and fraternity and conceived with a view to their democratic evolution.

ARTICLE I

The Republic and the peoples of the Overseas Territories who, by an act of free determination, adopt the present Constitution thereby institute a Community.

The Community shall be based on the equality and the solidarity of the peoples composing it.

TITLE I

ON SOVEREIGNTY

ARTICLE 2

France is a Republic, indivisible, secular, democratic and social. It shall ensure the equality of all citizens before the law, without distinction of origin, race or religion. It shall respect all beliefs.

The national emblem is the tricolor flag, blue, white and red.
The national anthem is the 'Marseillaise.'
The motto of the Republic is 'Liberty, Equality, Fraternity.'
Its principle is government of the people, by the people and for the people.

ARTICLE 3

National sovereignty belongs to the people, which shall exercise this sovereignty through its representatives and by means of referendums.

No section of the people, nor any individual, may attribute to themselves or himself the exercise thereof.

Suffrage may be direct or indirect under the conditions stipulated by the Constitution. It shall always be universal, equal and secret.

All French citizens of both sexes who have reached their majority and who enjoy civil and political rights may vote under the conditions to be determined by law.

ARTICLE 4

Political parties and groups shall be instrumental in the expression of the suffrage. They shall be formed freely and shall carry on their activities freely. They must respect the principles of national sovereignty and democracy.

TITLE II

THE PRESIDENT OF THE REPUBLIC

ARTICLE 5

The President of the Republic shall see that the Constitution is respected. He shall ensure, by his arbitration, the regular functioning of the governmental authorities, as well as the continuance of the State.

He shall be the guarantor of national independence, of the integrity of the territory, and of respect for Community agreements and treaties.

ARTICLE 6 [1]

The President of the Republic shall be elected for seven years by direct universal suffrage.

The procedures implementing the present article shall be determined by an organic law.

ARTICLE 7 [1]

The President of the Republic shall be elected by an absolute majority of the votes cast. If this is not obtained on the first ballot, there shall be a second ballot on the second Sunday following. Only the two candidates who have received the greatest number of votes on the first ballot shall present themselves, taking into account the possible withdrawal of more favored candidates.

[1] Amendments: Adopted by popular referendum October 28, 1962.

The voting shall begin at the summons of the Government.

The election of the new President shall take place twenty days at the least and thirty-five days at the most before the expiration of the powers of the President in office.

In the event that the Presidency of the Republic has been vacated, for any cause whatsoever, or impeded in its functioning as officially noted by the Constitutional Council, to which the matter has been referred by the Government, and which shall rule by an absolute majority of its members, the functions of the President of the Republic, with the exception of those provided for by Articles 11 and 12 below, shall be temporarily exercised by the President of the Senate and, if the latter is in his turn impeded in the exercise of these functions, by the Government.

In the case of a vacancy, or when the impediment is declared definitive by the Constitutional Council, the voting for the election of a new President shall take place, except in case of *force majeure* officially noted by the Constitutional Council, twenty days at the least and thirty-five days at the most after the beginning of the vacancy or the declaration of the definitive character of the impediment.

There may be no application of either Articles 49 and 50 or of Article 89 of the Constitution during the vacancy of the Presidency of the Republic or during the period that elapses between the declaration of the definitive character of the impediment of the President of the Republic and the election of his successor.

ARTICLE 8

The President of the Republic shall appoint the Premier. He shall terminate the functions of the Premier when the latter presents the resignation of the Government.

On the proposal of the Premier, he shall appoint the other members of the Government and shall terminate their functions.

ARTICLE 9

The President of the Republic shall preside over the Council of Ministers.

ARTICLE 10

The President of the Republic shall promulgate the laws within fifteen days following the transmission to the Government of the finally adopted law.

He may, before the expiration of this time limit, ask Parliament for a reconsideration of the law or of certain of its articles. This reconsideration may not be refused.

ARTICLE 11

The President of the Republic, on the proposal of the Government during [Parliamentary] sessions, or on joint motion of the two assemblies, published in the *Journal Officiel,* may submit to a referendum any bill dealing with the organization of the governmental authorities, entailing approval of a Community agreement, or providing for authorization to ratify a treaty that, without being contrary to the Constitution, might affect the functioning of [existing] institutions.

When the referendum decides in favor of the bill, the President of the Republic shall promulgate it within the time limit stipulated in the preceding article.

ARTICLE 12

The President of the Republic may, after consultation with the Premier and the Presidents of the Assemblies, declare the dissolution of the National Assembly.

General elections shall take place twenty days at the least and forty days at the most after the dissolution.

The National Assembly shall convene by right on the second Thursday following its election. If this meeting takes place between the periods provided for ordinary sessions, a session shall, by right, be held for a fifteen-day period.

There may be no further dissolution within a year following these elections.

ARTICLE 13

The President of the Republic shall sign the ordinances and decrees decided upon in the Council of Ministers.

He shall make appointments to the civil and military posts of the State.

Councillors of State, the Grand Chancellor of the Legion of Honor, Ambassadors and envoys extraordinary, Master Councillors of the Audit Office, prefects, representatives of the Government in the Overseas Territories, general officers, rectors of academies [regional divisions of the public educational system] and directors of central administrations shall be appointed in meetings of the Council of Ministers.

An organic law shall determine the other posts to be filled in meetings of the Council of Ministers, as well as the conditions under which the power of the President of the Republic to make appointments to office may be delegated by him and exercised in his name.

ARTICLE 14

The President of the Republic shall accredit Ambassadors and envoys extraordinary to foreign powers; foreign Ambassadors and envoys extraordinary shall be accredited to him.

ARTICLE 15

The President of the Republic shall be commander of the armed forces. He shall preside over the higher councils and committees of national defense.

ARTICLE 16

When the institutions of the Republic, the independence of the nation, the integrity of its territory or the fulfillment of its international commitments are threatened in a grave and immediate manner and when the regular functioning of the constitutional governmental authorities is interrupted, the President of the Republic shall take the measures commanded by these circumstances, after official consultation with the Premier, the Presidents of the assemblies and the Constitutional Council.

He shall inform the nation of these measures in a message.

These measures must be prompted by the desire to ensure to the constitutional governmental authorities, in the shortest possible time, the means of fulfilling their assigned functions. The Constitutional Council shall be consulted with regard to such measures.

Parliament shall meet by right.

The National Assembly may not be dissolved during the exercise of emergency powers [by the President].

ARTICLE 17

The President of the Republic shall have the right of pardon.

ARTICLE 18

The President of the Republic shall communicate with the two assemblies of Parliament by means of messages, which he shall cause to be read, and which shall not be followed by any debate.

Between sessions, Parliament shall be convened especially for this purpose.

ARTICLE 19

The acts of the President of the Republic, other than those provided for under Articles 8 (first paragraph), 11, 12, 16, 18, 54, 56 and 61, shall be countersigned by the Premier and, should circumstances so require, by the appropriate ministers.

TITLE III

THE GOVERNMENT

ARTICLE 20

The Government shall determine and direct the policy of the nation.

It shall have at its disposal the administration and the armed forces.

It shall be responsible to Parliament under the conditions and according to the procedures stipulated in Articles 49 and 50.

ARTICLE 21

The Premier shall direct the operation of the Government. He shall be responsible for national defense. He shall ensure the execution of the laws. Subject to the provisions of Article 13, he shall have regulatory powers and shall make appointments to civil and military posts.

He may delegate certain of his powers to the ministers.

He shall replace, should the occasion arise, the President of the Republic as chairman of the councils and committees provided for under Article 15.

He may, in exceptional instances, replace him as chairman of a meeting of the Council of Ministers by virtue of an explicit delegation and for a specific agenda.

ARTICLE 22

The acts of the Premier shall be countersigned, when circumstances so require, by the ministers responsible for their execution.

ARTICLE 23

The office of member of the Government shall be incompatible with the exercise of any Parliamentary mandate, with the holding of any office at the national level in business, professional or labor organizations, and with any public employment or professional activity.

An organic law shall determine the conditions under which the holders of such mandates, functions or employments shall be replaced.

The replacement of members of Parliament shall take place in accordance with the provisions of Article 25.

TITLE IV

THE PARLIAMENT

ARTICLE 24

The Parliament shall comprise the National Assembly and the Senate.

The deputies to the National Assembly shall be elected by direct suffrage.

The Senate shall be elected by indirect suffrage. It shall ensure the representation of the territorial units of the Republic. Frenchmen living outside France shall be represented in the Senate.

ARTICLE 25

An organic law shall determine the term for which each assembly is elected, the number of its members, their emoluments, the conditions of eligibility and ineligibility and the offices incompatible with membership in the assemblies.

It shall likewise determine the conditions under which, in the case of a vacancy in either assembly, persons shall be elected to replace the deputy or senator whose seat has been vacated until the holding of new complete or partial elections to the assembly concerned.

ARTICLE 26

No member of Parliament may be prosecuted, sought, arrested, detained or tried as a result of the opinions or votes expressed by him in the exercise of his functions.

No member of Parliament may, during Parliamentary sessions, be prosecuted or arrested for criminal or minor offenses without the authorization of the assembly of which he is a member except in the case of *flagrante delicto.*

When Parliament is not in session, no member of Parliament may be arrested without the authorization of the Secretariat of the assembly of which he is a member, except in the case of *flagrante delicto,* of authorized prosecution or of final conviction.

The detention or prosecution of a member of Parliament shall be suspended if the assembly of which he is a member so demands.

ARTICLE 27

All binding instructions [upon members of Parliament] shall be null and void.

The right to vote of the members of Parliament shall be personal.

An organic law may, under exceptional circumstances, authorize the delegation of a vote. In this case, no member may be delegated more than one vote.

ARTICLE 28

Parliament shall convene, by right, in two ordinary sessions a year.

The first session shall begin on the first Tuesday of October and shall end on the third Friday of December.

The second session shall open on the last Tuesday of April; it may not last longer than three months.

ARTICLE 29

Parliament shall convene in extraordinary session at the request of the Premier, or of the majority of the members comprising the National Assembly, to consider a specific agenda.

When an extraordinary session is held at the request of the members of the National Assembly, the closure decree shall take effect as soon as the Parliament has exhausted the agenda for which it was called, and at the latest twelve days from the date of its meeting.

Only the Premier may ask for a new session before the end of the month following the closure decree.

ARTICLE 30

Apart from cases in which Parliament meets by right, extraordinary sessions shall be opened and closed by decree of the President of the Republic.

ARTICLE 31

The members of the Government shall have access to the two assemblies. They shall be heard when they so request.

They may call for the assistance of commissioners of the government.

ARTICLE 32

The President of the National Assembly shall be elected for the duration of the legislature. The President of the Senate shall be elected after each partial re-election [of the Senate].

ARTICLE 33

The meetings of the two assemblies shall be public. An *in extenso* report of the debates shall be published in the *Journal Officiel*.

Each assembly may sit in secret committee at the request of the Premier or of one tenth of its members.

TITLE V

ON RELATIONS BETWEEN PARLIAMENT
AND THE GOVERNMENT

ARTICLE 34

All laws shall be passed by Parliament.

Laws shall establish the regulations concerning:

— civil rights and the fundamental guarantees granted to the citizens for the exercise of their public liberties; the obligations imposed by the national defense upon the persons and property of citizens;

— nationality, status and legal capacity of persons, marriage contracts, inheritance and gifts;

— determination of crimes and misdemeanors as well as the penalties imposed therefor; criminal procedure; amnesty; the creation of new juridical systems and the status of magistrates;

— the basis, the rate and the methods of collecting taxes of all types; the issuance of currency.

Laws shall likewise determine the regulations concerning:

— the electoral system of the Parliamentary assemblies and the local assemblies;

— the establishment of categories of public institutions;

— the fundamental guarantees granted to civil and military personnel employed by the State;

— the nationalization of enterprises and the transfer of the property of enterprises from the public to the private sector.

Laws shall determine the fundamental principles of:

— the general organization of national defense;

— the free administration of local communities, the extent of their jurisdiction and their resources;

— education;

— property rights, civil and commercial obligations;

— legislation pertaining to employment, unions and social security.

The financial laws shall determine the financial resources and obligations of the State under the conditions and with the reservations to be provided for by an organic law.

Laws pertaining to national planning shall determine the objectives of the economic and social action of the State.

The provisions of the present article may be developed in detail and amplified by an organic law.

ARTICLE 35

Parliament shall authorize the declaration of war.

ARTICLE 36

Martial law shall be decreed in a meeting of the Council of Ministers.

Its prorogation beyond twelve days may be authorized only by Parliament.

ARTICLE 37

Matters other than those that fall within the domain of law shall be of a regulatory character.

Legislative texts concerning these matters may be modified by decrees issued after consultation with the Council of State. Those legislative texts which may be passed after the present Constitution has become operative shall be modified by decree, only if the Constitutional Council has stated that they have a regulatory character as defined in the preceding paragraph.

ARTICLE 38

The Government may, in order to carry out its program, ask Parliament to authorize it, for a limited period, to take through ordinances measures that are normally within the domain of law.

The ordinances shall be enacted in meetings of the Council of Ministers after consultation with the Council of State. They shall come into force upon their publication, but shall become null and void if the bill for their ratification is not submitted to Parliament before the date set by the enabling act.

At the expiration of the time limit referred to in the first paragraph of the present article, the ordinances may be modified only by law in those matters which are within the legislative domain.

ARTICLE 39

The Premier and the members of Parliament alike shall have the right to initiate legislation.

Government bills shall be discussed in the Council of Ministers after consultation with the Council of State and shall be filed with the Secretariat of one of the two assemblies. Finance bills shall be submitted first to the National Assembly.

ARTICLE 40

Bills and amendments introduced by members of Parliament shall not be considered when their adoption would have as a consequence either a diminution of public financial resources, or the creation or increase of public expenditures.

ARTICLE 41

If it appears in the course of the legislative procedure that a Parliamentary bill or an amendment is not within the domain of law or is contrary to a delegation [of authority] granted by virtue of Article 38, the Government may declare its inadmissibility.

In case of disagreement between the Government and the President of the assembly concerned, the Constitutional Council, upon the request of either party, shall rule within a time limit of eight days.

ARTICLE 42

The discussion of Government bills shall pertain, in the first assembly to which they have been referred, to the text presented by the Government.

An assembly, given a text passed by the other assembly, shall deliberate on the text that is transmitted to it.

ARTICLE 43

Government and Parliamentary bills shall, at the request of the Government or of the assembly concerned, be sent for study to committees especially designated for this purpose.

Government and Parliamentary bills for which such a request has not been made shall be sent to one of the permanent committees, the number of which shall be limited to six in each assembly.

ARTICLE 44

Members of Parliament and of the Government shall have the right of amendment.

After the opening of the debate, the Government may oppose the examination of any amendment which has not previously been submitted to committee.

If the Government so requests, the assembly concerned shall decide, by a single vote, on all or part of the text under discussion, retaining only the amendments proposed or accepted by the Government.

ARTICLE 45

Every Government or Parliamentary bill shall be examined successively in the assemblies of Parliament with a view to the adoption of an identical text.

When, as a result of disagreement between the two assemblies, it has become impossible to adopt a Government or Parliamentary bill after two readings by each assembly, or, if the Government has declared the matter urgent, after a single reading by each of them, the Premier shall have the right to have a joint committee meet, composed of an equal number from both assemblies and instructed to offer for consideration a text on the matters still under discussion.

The text prepared by the joint committee may be submitted by the Government for approval of the two assemblies. No amendment shall be admissible except by agreement with the Government.

If the joint committee fails to approve a common text, or if this text is not adopted under the conditions set forth in the preceding paragraph, the Government may, after a new reading by the National Assembly and by the Senate, ask the National Assembly to rule definitively. In this case, the National Assembly may reconsider either the text prepared by the joint committee or the last text adopted [by the National Assembly], modified, when circumstances so require, by one or several of the amendments adopted by the Senate.

ARTICLE 46

The laws that the Constitution characterizes as organic shall be passed and amended under the following conditions:

A Government or Parliamentary bill shall be submitted to the deliberation and to the vote of the first assembly to which it is submitted only at the expiration of a period of fifteen days following its introduction.

The procedure of Article 45 shall be applicable. Nevertheless, lacking an agreement between the two assemblies, the text may be adopted by the National Assembly on final reading only by an absolute majority of its members.

The organic laws relative to the Senate must be passed in the same manner by the two assemblies.

Organic laws may be promulgated only after a declaration by the Constitutional Council on their constitutionality.

ARTICLE 47

Parliament shall pass finance bills under the conditions to be stipulated by an organic law.

Should the National Assembly fail to reach a decision on first reading within a time limit of forty days after a bill has been filed, the Government shall refer it to the Senate, which must rule within a time limit of fifteen days. The procedure set forth in Article 45 shall then be followed.

Should Parliament fail to reach a decision within a time limit of seventy days, the provisions of the bill may be enforced by ordinance.

Should the finance bill establishing the resources and expenditures of a fiscal year not be filed in time for it to be promulgated before the beginning of that fiscal year, the Government shall immediately request Parliament for the authorization to collect the taxes and shall make available by decree the funds needed to meet the Government commitments already voted.

The time limits stipulated in the present article shall be suspended when Parliament is not in session.

The Audit Office shall assist Parliament and the Government in supervising the implementation of the finance laws.

ARTICLE 48

The discussion of the bills filed or agreed upon by the Government shall have priority on the agenda of the assemblies in the order set by the Government.

One meeting a week shall be reserved, by priority, for questions asked by members of Parliament and for answers by the Government.

ARTICLE 49

The Premier, after deliberation by the Council of Ministers, may pledge the responsibility of the Government to the National Assembly with regard to the program of the Government, or with regard to a declaration of general policy, as the case may be.

The National Assembly may question the responsibility of the Government by the vote of a motion of censure. Such a motion shall be admissible only if it is signed by at least one tenth of the members of the National Assembly. The vote may only take place forty-eight hours after the motion has been filed; the only votes counted shall be those favorable to the motion of censure, which may be adopted only by a majority of the members comprising the Assembly. Should the motion of censure be rejected, its signatories may not introduce another motion in the course of the same session, except in the case provided for in the paragraph below.

The Premier may, after deliberation by the Council of Ministers, pledge the Government's responsibility to the National Assembly on the vote of a text. In this case, the text shall be considered as adopted, unless a motion of censure, filed in the succeeding twenty-four hours, is voted under the conditions laid down in the previous paragraph.

The Premier shall be entitled to ask the Senate for approval of a general policy declaration.

ARTICLE 50

When the National Assembly adopts a motion of censure, or when it disapproves the program or a declaration of general policy of the Government, the Premier must submit the resignation of the Government to the President of the Republic.

ARTICLE 51

The closure of ordinary or extraordinary sessions shall by right be delayed, should the occasion arise, in order to permit the application of the provisions of Article 49.

TITLE VI

ON TREATIES AND INTERNATIONAL AGREEMENTS

ARTICLE 52

The President of the Republic shall negotiate and ratify treaties.

He shall be informed of all negotiations leading to the conclusion of an international agreement not subject to ratification.

ARTICLE 53

Peace treaties, commercial treaties, treaties or agreements relative to international organization, those that imply a commitment for the finances of the State, those that modify provisions of a legislative nature, those relative to the status of persons, those that call for the cession, exchange or addition of territory may be ratified or approved only by a law.

They shall go into effect only after having been ratified or approved.

No cession, no exchange, no addition of territory shall be valid without the consent of the populations concerned.

ARTICLE 54

If the Constitutional Council, the matter having been referred to it by the President of the Republic, by the Premier, or by the President of one or the other assembly, shall declare that an international commitment contains a clause contrary to the Constitution, the authorization to ratify or approve this commitment may be given only after amendment of the Constitution.

ARTICLE 55

Treaties or agreements duly ratified or approved shall, upon their publication, have an authority superior to that of laws, subject, for each agreement or treaty, to its application by the other party.

Title VII

THE CONSTITUTIONAL COUNCIL

ARTICLE 56

The Constitutional Council shall consist of nine members, whose term of office shall last nine years and shall not be renewable. One third of the membership of the Constitutional Council shall be renewed every three years. Three of its members shall be appointed by the President of the Republic, three by the President of the National Assembly, three by the President of the Senate.

In addition to the nine members provided for above, former Presidents of the Republic shall be members ex officio for life of the Constitutional Council.

The President shall be appointed by the President of the Republic. He shall have the deciding vote in case of a tie.

ARTICLE 57

The office of member of the Constitutional Council shall be incompatible with that of minister or member of Parliament. Other incompatibilities shall be determined by an organic law.

ARTICLE 58

The Constitutional Council shall ensure the regularity of the election of the President of the Republic.

It shall examine complaints and shall announce the results of the vote.

ARTICLE 59

The Constitutional Council shall rule, in the case of disagreement, on the regularity of the election of deputies and senators.

ARTICLE 60

The Constitutional Council shall ensure the regularity of referendum procedures and shall announce the results thereof.

ARTICLE 61

Organic laws, before their promulgation, and regulations of the Parliamentary assemblies, before they come into application, must be submitted to the Constitutional Council, which shall rule on their constitutionality.

To the same end, laws may be submitted to the Constitutional Council, before their promulgation, by the President of the Republic, the Premier or the President of one or the other assembly.

In the cases provided for by the two preceding paragraphs, the Constitutional Council must make its ruling within a time limit of one month. Nevertheless, at the request of the Government, in case of emergency, this period shall be reduced to eight days.

In these same cases, referral to the Constitutional Council shall suspend the time limit for promulgation.

ARTICLE 62

A provision declared unconstitutional may not be promulgated or implemented.

The decisions of the Constitutional Council may not be appealed to any jurisdiction whatsoever. They must be recognized by the governmental authorities and by all administrative and juridical authorities.

ARTICLE 63

An organic law shall determine the rules of organization and functioning of the Constitutional Council, the procedure to be followed before it, and in particular the periods of time allowed for laying disputes before it.

TITLE VIII

ON JUDICIAL AUTHORITY

ARTICLE 64

The President of the Republic shall be the guarantor of the independence of the judicial authority.

He shall be assisted by the High Council of the Judiciary.

An organic law shall determine the status of magistrates.

Magistrates may not be removed from office.

ARTICLE 65

The High Council of the Judiciary shall be presided over by the President of the Republic. The Minister of Justice shall be its Vice President ex officio. He may preside in place of the President of the Republic.

The High Council shall, in addition, include nine members appointed by the President of the Republic in conformity with the conditions to be determined by an organic law.

The High Council of the Judiciary shall present nominations for judges of the Court of Cassation [Supreme Court of Appeal] and for First Presidents of Courts of Appeal. It shall give its opinion, under the conditions to be determined by an organic law, on proposals of the Minister of Justice relative to the nomination of the other judges. It shall be consulted on questions of pardon under conditions to be determined by an organic law.

The High Council of the Judiciary shall act as a disciplinary council for judges. In such cases, it shall be presided over by the First President of the Court of Cassation.

ARTICLE 66

No one may be arbitrarily detained.

The judicial authority, guardian of individual liberty, shall ensure respect for this principle under the conditions stipulated by law.

TITLE IX

THE HIGH COURT OF JUSTICE

ARTICLE 67

A High Court of Justice shall be instituted.

It shall be composed of members [of Parliament] elected, in equal number, by the National Assembly and the Senate after each general or partial election to these assemblies. It shall elect its President from among its members.

An organic law shall determine the composition of the High Court, its rules, and also the procedure to be followed before it.

ARTICLE 68

The President of the Republic shall not be held accountable for actions performed in the exercise of his office except in the case of high treason. He may be indicted only by the two assemblies ruling by identical vote in open balloting and by an absolute majority of the members of said assemblies. He shall be tried by the High Court of Justice.

The members of the Government shall be criminally liable for actions performed in the exercise of their office and deemed to be crimes or misdemeanors at the time they were committed. The procedure defined above shall be applied to them, as well as their accomplices, in case of a conspiracy against the security of the State. In the cases provided for by the present paragraph, the High Court shall be bound by the definition of crimes and misdemeanors, as well as by the determination of penalties, as they are established by the criminal laws in force when the acts are committed.

TITLE X

THE ECONOMIC AND SOCIAL COUNCIL

ARTICLE 69

The Economic and Social Council, whenever the Government calls upon it, shall give its opinion on the Government bills, ordinances and decrees, as well as on the Parliamentary bills submitted to it.

A member of the Economic and Social Council may be designated by the latter to present, before the Parliamentary assemblies, the opinion of the Council on the Government or Parliamentary bills that have been submitted to it.

ARTICLE 70

The Economic and Social Council may likewise be consulted by the Government on any problem of an economic or social character of interest to the Republic or to the Community. Any plan, or any bill dealing with a plan, of an economic or social character shall be submitted to it for its advice.

The composition of the Economic and Social Council and its rules of procedure shall be determined by an organic law.

TITLE XI

ON TERRITORIAL UNITS

ARTICLE 72

The territorial units of the Republic are the communes, the Departments, the Overseas Territories. Other territorial units may be created by law.

These units shall be free to govern themselves through elected councils and under the conditions stipulated by law.

In the departments and the territories, the Delegate of the Government shall be responsible for the national interests, for administrative supervision, and for seeing that the laws are respected.

ARTICLE 73

Measures of adjustment required by the particular situation of the Overseas Departments may be taken with regard to their legislative system and administrative organization.

ARTICLE 74

The Overseas Territories of the Republic shall have a special organization, which takes into account their own interests within the general interests of the Republic. This organization shall be defined and modified by law after consultation with the Territorial Assembly concerned.

ARTICLE 75

Citizens of the Republic who do not have ordinary civil status, the only status referred to in Article 34, may keep their personal status as long as they have not renounced it.

ARTICLE 76

The Overseas Territories may retain their status within the Republic.

If they express the desire to do so by a decision of their Territorial Assemblies taken within the time limit set in the first paragraph of Article 91, they shall become Overseas Departments of the Republic or member States of the Community, either in groups or as single units.

TITLE XII

ON THE COMMUNITY

ARTICLE 77

In the Community instituted by the present Constitution, the States shall enjoy autonomy; they shall administer themselves and manage their own affairs democratically and freely.

There shall be only one citizenship in the Community.

All citizens shall be equal before the law, whatever their origin, their race and their religion. They shall have the same duties.

ARTICLE 78

The Community's jurisdiction shall extend over foreign policy, defense, currency, common economic and financial policy, as well as over policy on strategic raw materials.

It shall include, in addition, except in the case of specific agreements, the supervision of the tribunals, higher education, the general organization of external transportation and transportation within the Community, as well as of telecommunications.

Special agreements may create other common jurisdictions or regulate any transfer of jurisdiction from the Community to one of its members.

ARTICLE 79

The member States shall benefit from the provisions of Article 77 as soon as they have exercised the choice provided for in Article 76.

Until the measures required for implementation of the present title go into force, matters within the common jurisdiction shall be regulated by the Republic.

ARTICLE 80

The President of the Republic shall preside over and represent the Community.

The institutional organs of the Community shall be an Executive Council, a Senate and a Court of Arbitration.

ARTICLE 81

The member States of the Community shall participate in the election of the President according to the conditions stipulated in Article 6.

The President of the Republic, in his capacity as President of the Community, shall be represented in each State of the Community.

ARTICLE 82

The Executive Council of the Community shall be presided over by the President of the Community. It shall consist of the Premier of the Republic, the heads of Government of each of the member States of the Community, and the ministers responsible for the common affairs of the Community.

The Executive Council shall organize the cooperation of members of the Community at Government and administrative levels.

The organization and procedure of the Executive Council shall be determined by an organic law.

ARTICLE 83

The Senate of the Community shall be composed of delegates whom the Parliament of the Republic and the legislative assemblies of the other members of the Community shall choose from among their own membership. The number of delegates of each State shall be determined according to its population and the responsibilities it assumes in the Community.

The Senate of the Community shall hold two sessions a year, which shall be opened and closed by the President of the Community and may not last longer than one month each.

The Senate of the Community, when called upon by the President of the Community, shall deliberate on the common economic and financial policy before laws on these matters are voted upon by the Parliament of the Republic and, should circumstances so require, by the legislative assemblies of the other members of the Community.

The Senate of the Community shall examine the acts and treaties or international agreements, which are specified in Articles 35 and 53, and which commit the Community.

The Senate of the Community shall make executory decisions in the domains in which it has received delegation of power from the legislative assemblies of the members of the Community. These decisions shall be promulgated in the same form as the law in the territory of each of the States concerned.

An organic law shall determine the composition of the Senate and its rules of procedure.

ARTICLE 84

A Court of Arbitration of the Community shall rule on litigations occurring among members of the Community.

Its composition and its jurisdiction shall be determined by an organic law.

ARTICLE 85 [2]

By derogation from the procedure provided for in Article 89, the provisions of the present title that concern the functioning of the common institutions shall be amendable by identical laws passed by the Parliament of the Republic and by the Senate of the Community.

The provisions of the present title may also be amended by agreements concluded between all the States of the Community; the new provisions shall be put into force under the conditions required by the Constitution of each State.

ARTICLE 86 [3]

A change of status of a member State of the Community may be requested, either

[2] Second paragraph is an Amendment: Adopted by Parliament, May 18, 1960.

[3] Last three paragraphs constitute an Amendment: Adopted by Parliament, May 18, 1960.

by the Republic, or by a resolution of the legislative assembly of the State concerned confirmed by a local referendum, the organization and supervision of which shall be ensured by the institutions of the Community. The procedures governing this change shall be determined by an agreement approved by the Parliament of the Republic and the legislative assembly concerned.

Under the same conditions, a member State of the Community may become independent. It shall thereby cease to belong to the Community.

A member State of the Community may also, by means of agreements, become independent without thereby ceasing to belong to the Community.

An independent State not a member of the Community may, by means of agreements, join the Community without ceasing to be independent.

The position of these States within the Community shall be determined by agreements concluded to this end, in particular the agreements mentioned in the preceding paragraphs as well as, should the occasion arise, the agreements provided for in the second paragraph of Article 85.

ARTICLE 87

The special agreements made for the implementation of the present title shall be approved by the Parliament of the Republic and the legislative assembly concerned.

TITLE XIII

ON AGREEMENTS OF ASSOCIATION

ARTICLE 88

The Republic or the Community may make agreements with States that wish to associate themselves with the Community in order to develop their own civilizations.

TITLE XIV

ON AMENDMENT

ARTICLE 89

The initiative for amending the Constitution shall belong both to the President of the Republic on the proposal of the Premier and to the members of Parliament.

The Government or Parliamentary bill for amendment must be passed by the two assemblies in identical terms. The amendment shall become definitive after approval by a referendum.

Nevertheless, the proposed amendment shall not be submitted to a referendum when the President of the Republic decides to submit it to Parliament convened in Congress; in this case, the proposed amendment shall be approved only if it is accepted by a three-fifths majority of the votes cast. The Secretariat of the Congress shall be that of the National Assembly.

No amendment procedure may be undertaken or followed when the integrity of the territory is in jeopardy.

The republican form of government shall not be subject to amendment.

TITLE XV

TEMPORARY PROVISIONS

ARTICLE 90

The ordinary session of Parliament is suspended. The mandate of the members of the present National Assembly shall expire on the day that the Assembly elected under the present Constitution convenes.

Until this meeting, the Government alone shall have the authority to convene Parliament.

The mandate of the members of the Assembly of the French Union shall expire at the same time as the mandate of the members of the present National Assembly.

ARTICLE 91

The institutions of the Republic, provided for by the present Constitution, shall be established within four months after its promulgation.

This time limit shall be extended to six months for the institutions of the Community.

The powers of the President of the Republic now in office shall expire only when the results of the election provided for in Articles 6 and 7 of the present Constitution are proclaimed.

The member States of the Community shall participate in this first election under the conditions derived from their status at the date of the promulgation of the Constitution. The established authorities shall continue to exercise their functions in these States according to the laws and regulations applicable when the Constitution becomes operative, until the authorities provided for by their new regimes are set up.

Until it is definitively constituted, the Senate shall consist of the present members of the Council of the Republic. The organic laws that determine the definitive composition of the Senate must be passed before July 31, 1959.

The powers conferred on the Constitutional Council by Articles 58 and 59 of the Constitution shall be exercised, until this Council is set up, by a committee composed of the Vice President of the Council of State, as chairman, the First President of the Court of Cassation, and the First President of the Audit Office.

The peoples of the member States of the Community shall continue to be represented in Parliament until the measures necessary to the implementation of Title XII have been put into effect.

ARTICLE 92

The legislative measures necessary for the setting up of the institutions and, until they are set up, for the functioning of the governmental authorities, shall be taken in meetings of the Council of Ministers, after consultation with the Council of State, in the form of ordinances having the force of law.

During the time limit set in the first paragraph of Article 91, the Government shall be authorized to determine, by ordinances having the force of law and passed in the same way, the system of elections to the assemblies provided for by the Constitution.

During the same period and under the same conditions, the Government may also adopt measures, in all matters, which it may deem necessary to the life of the nation, the protection of citizens or the safeguarding of liberties.

Constitution of
the Union of Soviet Socialist Republics, 1936
(As Amended)

CHAPTER I—THE SOCIAL STRUCTURE

ART. 1—The Union of Soviet Socialist Republics is a socialist state of workers and peasants.

ART. 2—The political foundation of the U.S.S.R. is the Soviets of Working People's Deputies, which grew and became strong as a result of the overthrow of the power of the landlords and capitalists and the conquest of the dictatorship of the proletariat.

ART. 3—All power in the U.S.S.R. belongs to the working people of town and country as represented by the Soviets of Working People's Deputies.

ART. 4—The economic foundation of the U.S.S.R. is the socialist system of economy and the socialist ownership of the instruments and means of production, firmly established as a result of the liquidation of the capitalist system of economy, the abolition of private ownership of the instruments and means of production, and the elimination of the exploitation of man by man.

ART. 5—Socialist property in the U.S.S.R. exists either in the form of state property (belonging to the whole people) or in the form of co-operative and collective-farm property (property of collective farms, property of co-operative societies).

ART. 6—The land, its mineral wealth, waters, forests, mills, factories, mines, rail, water and air transport, banks, communications, large state-organized agricultural enterprises (state farms, machine and tractor stations and the like), as well as municipal enterprises and the bulk of the dwelling-houses in the cities and industrial localities, are state property, that is, belong to the whole people.

ART. 7—The common enterprises of collective farms and co-operative organizations, with their live-stock and implements, the products of the collective farms and co-operative organizations, as well as their common buildings, constitute the common, socialist property of the collective farms and co-operative organizations.

Every household in a collective farm, in addition to its basic income from the common collective-farm enterprise, has for its personal use a small plot of household land and, as its personal property, a subsidiary husbandry on the plot, a dwelling-house, livestock, poultry and minor agricultural implements—in accordance with the rules of the agricultural artel.

ART. 8—The land occupied by collective farms is secured to them for their use free of charge and for an unlimited time, that is, in perpetuity.

ART. 9—Alongside the socialist system of economy, which is the predominant form of economy in the U.S.S.R., the law permits the small private economy of individual peasants and handicraftsmen based on their own labor and precluding the exploitation of the labor of others.

ART. 10—The personal property right of citizens in their incomes and savings from work, in their dwelling-houses and subsidiary husbandries, in articles of domestic economy and use and articles of personal use and convenience, as well as the right of citizens to inherit personal property, is protected by law.

ART. 11—The economic life of the U.S.S.R. is determined and directed by the state national-economic plan, with the aim of increasing the public wealth, of steadily raising the material and cultural standards of the working people, of consolidating the independence of the U.S.S.R. and strengthening its defensive capacity.

ART. 12—Work in the U.S.S.R. is a duty and a matter of honor for every able-bodied citizen, in accordance with the principle: "He who does not work, neither shall he eat."

The principle applied in the U.S.S.R. is that of socialism: "From each according to his ability, to each according to his work."

Chapter II—The State Structure

ART. 13 The Union of Soviet Socialist Republics is a federal state, formed on the basis of a voluntary union of equal Soviet Socialist Republics, namely: The Russian Soviet Federative Socialist Republic, the Ukrainian Soviet Socialist Republic, the Byelorussian Soviet Socialist Republic, the Uzbek Soviet Socialist Republic, the Kazakh Soviet Socialist Republic, the Georgian Soviet Socialist Republic, the Azerbaijan Soviet Socialist Republic, the Lithuanian Soviet Socialist Republic, the Moldavian Soviet Socialist Republic, the Latvian Soviet Socialist Republic, the Kirghiz Soviet Socialist Republic, the Tajik Soviet Socialist Republic, the Armenian Soviet Socialist Republic, the Turkmen Soviet Socialist Republic [and] the Estonian Soviet Socialist Republic.

ART. 14—The jurisdiction of the Union of Soviet Socialist Republics, as represented by its higher organs of state power and organs of state administration, embraces:

a) Representation of the U.S.S.R. in international relations, conclusion, ratification and denunciation of treaties of the U.S.S.R. with other states, establishment of general procedure governing the relations of Union Republics with foreign states;

b) Questions of war and peace;

c) Admission of new republics into the U.S.S.R.;

d) Control over the observance of the Constitution of the U.S.S.R., and ensuring conformity of the Constitutions of the Union Republics with the Constitution of the U.S.S.R.;

e) Confirmation of alterations of boundaries between Union Republics;

f) Confirmation of the formation of new Territories and Regions and also of new Autonomous Republics and Autonomous Regions within Union Republics;

g) Organization of the defense of the U.S.S.R., direction of all the Armed Forces of the U.S.S.R., determination of directing principles governing the organization of the military formations of the Union Republics;

h) Foreign trade on the basis of state monopoly;

i) Safeguarding the security of the state;

j) Determination of the national-economic plans of the U.S.S.R.;

k) Approval of the consolidated state budget of the U.S.S.R. and of the report on its fulfillment; determination of the taxes and revenues which go to the Union, the Republican and the local budgets;

l) Administration of the banks, industrial and agricultural institutions and enterprises and also trading enterprises of all-Union importance; the general guidance of industry and construction of Union-Republican importance;

m) Administration of transport and communications;

n) Direction of the monetary and credit system;

o) Organization of state insurance;

p) Contracting and granting of loans;

q) Determination of the basic principles of land tenure and of the use of mineral wealth, forests and waters;

r) Determination of the basic principles in the spheres of education and public health;

s) Organization of a uniform system of national-economic statistics;

t) Determination of the principles of labor legislation;

u) Legislation concerning the judicial system and judicial procedure; criminal and civil codes;

v) Legislation concerning Union citizenship; legislation concerning rights of foreigners;

w) Determination of the principles of legislation concerning marriage and family;

x) Issuing of all-Union acts of amnesty.

ART. 15—The sovereignty of the Union Republics is limited only in the spheres defined in article 14 of the Constitution of the U.S.S.R. Outside of these spheres each Union Republic exercises state authority independently. The U.S.S.R. protects the sovereign rights of the Union Republics.

ART. 16—Each Union Republic has its own Constitution, which takes account of the specific features of the Republic and is drawn up in full conformity with the Constitution of the U.S.S.R.

ART. 17—The right freely to secede from the U.S.S.R. is reserved to every Union Republic.

ART. 18—The territory of a Union Republic may not be altered without its consent.

ART. 18a—Each Union Republic has the right to enter into direct relations with foreign states and to conclude agreements and exchange diplomatic and consular representatives with them.

ART. 18b—Each Union Republic has its own Republican military formations.

ART. 19—The laws of the U.S.S.R. have the same force within the territory of every Union Republic.

ART. 20—In the event of divergence between a law of a Union Republic and a law of the Union, the Union law prevails.

ART. 21—Uniform Union citizenship is established for citizens of the U.S.S.R.

Every citizen of a Union Republic is a citizen of the U.S.S.R.

ART. 22—The Russian Soviet Federative Socialist Republic includes the Bashkirian, Buryat-Mongolian, Daghestan, Kabardinian-Balkar, Karelian, Komi, Mari, Mordovian,

North Ossetian, Tatar, Udmurt, Checheno-Ingush, Chuvash and Yakut Autonomous Soviet Socialist Republics; and the Adygei, Gorny Altai, Jewish, Kalmyk, Karachayevo-Cherkess Tuva and Khakass Autonomous Regions.

ART. 23—Repealed.

ART. 24—The Azerbaijan Soviet Socialist Republic includes the Nakhichevan Autonomous Soviet Socialist Republic and the Nagorny Karabakh Autonomous Region.

ART. 25—The Georgian Soviet Socialist Republic includes the Abkhazian Autonomous Soviet Socialist Republic, the Ajarian Autonomous Soviet Socialist Republic and the South Ossetian Autonomous Region.

ART. 26—The Uzbek Soviet Socialist Republic includes the Kara-Kalpak Autonomous Soviet Socialist Republic.

ART. 27—The Tajik Soviet Socialist Republic includes the Gorny Badakhshan Autonomous Region.

ART. 28—The solution of problems pertaining to the administrative-territorial structure of the regions and territories of the Union Republics comes within the jurisdiction of the Union Republics.

ART. 29—Repealed.

CHAPTER III—THE HIGHER ORGANS OF STATE POWER IN THE UNION OF SOVIET SOCIALIST REPUBLICS

ART. 30—The highest organ of state power in the U.S.S.R. is the Supreme Soviet of the U.S.S.R.

ART. 31—The Supreme Soviet of the U.S.S.R. exercises all rights vested in the Union of Soviet Socialist Republics in accordance with Article 14 of the Constitution, in so far as they do not, by virtue of the Constitution, come within the jurisdiction of organs of the U.S.S.R. that are accountable to the Supreme Soviet of the U.S.S.R., that is, the Presidium of the Supreme Soviet of the U.S.S.R., the Council of Ministers of the U.S.S.R., and the Ministries of the U.S.S.R.

ART. 32—The legislative power of the U.S.S.R. is exercised exclusively by the Supreme Soviet of the U.S.S.R.

ART. 33—The Supreme Soviet of the U.S.S.R. consists of two Chambers: the Soviet of the Union and the Soviet of Nationalities.

ART. 34—The Soviet of the Union is elected by the citizens of the U.S.S.R. voting by election districts on the basis of one deputy for every 300,000 of the population.

ART. 35—The Soviet of Nationalities is elected by the citizens of the U.S.S.R. voting by Union Republics, Autonomous Republics, Autonomous Regions, and National Areas on the basis of 25 deputies from each Union Republic, 11 deputies from each Autonomous Republic, 5 deputies from each Autonomous Region and one deputy from each National Area.

ART. 36—The Supreme Soviet of the U.S.S.R. is elected for a term of four years.

ART. 37—The two Chambers of the Supreme Soviet of the U.S.S.R., the Soviet of the Union and the Soviet of Nationalities, have equal rights.

ART. 38—The Soviet of the Union and the Soviet of Nationalities have equal powers to initiate legislation.

ART. 39—A law is considered adopted if passed by both Chambers of the Supreme Soviet of the U.S.S.R. by a simple majority vote in each.

ART. 40—Laws passed by the Supreme Soviet of the U.S.S.R. are published in the languages of the Union Republics over the signatures of the President and Secretary of the Presidium of the Supreme Soviet of the U.S.S.R.

ART. 41—Sessions of the Soviet of the Union and of the Soviet of Nationalities begin and terminate simultaneously.

ART. 42—The Soviet of the Union elects a Chairman of the Soviet of the Union and four Vice-Chairmen.

ART. 43—The Soviet of Nationalities elects a Chairman of the Soviet of Nationalities and four Vice-Chairmen.

ART. 44—The Chairmen of the Soviet of the Union and the Soviet of Nationalities preside at the sittings of the respective Chambers and have charge of the conduct of their business and proceedings.

ART. 45—Joint sittings of the two Chambers of the Supreme Soviet of the U.S.S.R. are presided over alternately by the Chairman of the Soviet of the Union and the Chairman of the Soviet of Nationalities.

ART. 46—Sessions of the Supreme Soviet of the U.S.S.R. are convened by the Presidium of the Supreme Soviet of the U.S.S.R. twice a year.

Extraordinary sessions are convened by the Presidium of the Supreme Soviet of the U.S.S.R. at its discretion or on the demand of one of the Union Republics.

ART. 47—In the event of disagreement between the Soviet of the Union and the Soviet of Nationalities, the question is referred for settlement to a conciliation commission formed by the Chambers on a parity basis. If the conciliation commission fails to arrive at an agreement or if its decision fails to satisfy one of the Chambers, the question is considered for a second time by the Chambers. Failing agreement between the two Chambers, the Presidium of the Supreme Soviet of the U.S.S.R. dissolves the Supreme Soviet of the U.S.S.R. and orders new elections.

ART. 48—The Supreme Soviet of the U.S.S.R. at a joint sitting of the two Chambers elects the Presidium of the Supreme Soviet of the U.S.S.R., consisting of a President of the Presidium of the Supreme Soviet of the U.S.S.R., fifteen Vice-Presidents—one from each Union Republic—a Secretary of the Presidium and sixteen members of the Presidium of the Supreme Soviet of the U.S.S.R.

The Presidium of the Supreme Soviet of the U.S.S.R. is accountable to the Supreme Soviet of the U.S.S.R. for all its activities.

ART. 49—The Presidium of the Supreme Soviet of the U.S.S.R.:

a) Convenes the sessions of the Supreme Soviet of the U.S.S.R.;

b) Issues decrees;

c) Gives interpretations of the laws of the U.S.S.R. in operation;

d) Dissolves the Supreme Soviet of the U.S.S.R. in conformity with Article 47 of the Constitution of the U.S.S.R. and orders new elections;

e) Conducts nation-wide polls (referendums) on its own initiative or on the demand of one of the Union Republics;

f) Annuls decisions and orders of the Council of Ministers of the U.S.S.R. and of the Councils of Ministers of the Union Republics if they do not conform to law;

g) In the intervals between sessions of the Supreme Soviet of the U.S.S.R., releases and appoints Ministers of the U.S.S.R. on the recommendation of the Chairman of the Council of Ministers of the U.S.S.R., subject to subsequent confirmation by the Supreme Soviet of the U.S.S.R.;

h) Institutes decorations (Orders and Medals) and titles of honor of the U.S.S.R.;

i) Awards Orders and Medals and confers titles of honor of the U.S.S.R.;

j) Exercises the right of pardon;

k) Institutes military titles, diplomatic ranks and other special titles;

l) Appoints and removes the high command of the Armed Forces of the U.S.S.R.;

m) In the intervals between sessions of the Supreme Soviet of the U.S.S.R., proclaims a state of war in the event of military attack on the U.S.S.R., or when necessary to fulfill international treaty obligations concerning mutual defense against aggression;

n) Orders general or partial mobilization;

o) Ratifies and denounces international treaties of the U.S.S.R.;

p) Appoints and recalls plenipotentiary representatives of the U.S.S.R. to foreign states;

q) Receives the letters of credence and recall of diplomatic representatives accredited to it by foreign states;

r) Proclaims martial law in separate localities or throughout the U.S.S.R. in the interests of the defense of the U.S.S.R. or of the maintenance of public order and the security of the state.

ART. 50—The Soviet of the Union and the Soviet of Nationalities elect Credentials Committees to verify the credentials of the members of the respective Chambers.

On the report of the Credentials Committees, the Chambers decide whether to recognize the credentials of deputies or to annul their election.

ART. 51—The Supreme Soviet of the U.S.S.R., when it deems necessary, appoints commissions of investigation and audit on any matter.

It is the duty of all institutions and officials to comply with the demands of such commissions and to submit to them all necessary materials and documents.

ART. 52—A member of the Supreme Soviet of the U.S.S.R. may not be prosecuted or arrested without the consent of the Supreme Soviet of the U.S.S.R., or, when the Supreme Soviet of the U.S.S.R. is not in session, without the consent of the Presidium of the Supreme Soviet of the U.S.S.R.

ART. 53—On the expiration of the term of office of the Supreme Soviet of the U.S.S.R., or on its dissolution prior to the expiration of its term of office, the Presidium of the Supreme Soviet of the U.S.S.R. retains its powers until the newly-elected Supreme Soviet of the U.S.S.R. shall have formed a new Presidium of the Supreme Soviet of the U.S.S.R.

ART. 54—On the expiration of the term of office of the Supreme Soviet of the U.S.S.R., or in the event of its dissolution prior to the expiration of its term of office, the Presidium of the Supreme Soviet of the U.S.S.R. orders new elections to be held within a period not exceeding two months from the date of expiration of the term of office or dissolution of the Supreme Soviet of the U.S.S.R.

ART. 55—The newly-elected Supreme Soviet of the U.S.S.R. is convened by the outgoing Presidium of the Supreme Soviet of the U.S.S.R. not later than three months after the elections.

ART. 56—The Supreme Soviet of the U.S.S.R., at a joint sitting of the two Chambers, appoints the Government of the U.S.S.R., namely, the Council of Ministers of the U.S.S.R.

CHAPTER IV—THE HIGHER ORGANS OF STATE POWER IN THE UNION REPUBLICS

ART. 57—The highest organ of state power in a Union Republic is the Supreme Soviet of the Union Republic.

ART. 58—The Supreme Soviet of a Union Republic is elected by the citizens of the Republic for a term of four years.

The basis of representation is established by the Constitution of the Union Republic.

ART. 59—The Supreme Soviet of a Union Republic is the sole legislative organ of the Republic.

ART. 60—The Supreme Soviet of a Union Republic:

a) Adopts the Constitution of the Republic and amends it in conformity with Article 16 of the Constitution of the U.S.S.R.;

b) Confirms the Constitutions of the Autonomous Republics forming part of it and defines the boundaries of their territories;

c) Approves the national-economic plan and the budget of the Republic, and constitutes the economic administrative areas;

d) Exercises the right of amnesty and pardon of citizens sentenced by the judicial organs of the Union Republic;

e) Decides questions of representation of the Union Republic in its international relations;

f) Determines the manner of organizing the Republic's military formations.

ART. 61—The Supreme Soviet of a Union Republic elects the Presidium of the Supreme Soviet of the Union Republic, consisting of a President of the Presidium of the Supreme Soviet of the Union Republic, Vice-Presidents, a Secretary of the Presidium and members of the Presidium of the Supreme Soviet of the Union Republic.

The powers of the Presidium of the Supreme Soviet of a Union Republic are defined by the Constitution of the Union Republic.

ART. 62—The Supreme Soviet of a Union Republic elects a Chairman and Vice-Chairmen to conduct its sittings.

ART. 63—The Supreme Soviet of a Union Republic appoints the Government of the Union Republic, namely, the Council of Ministers of the Union Republic.

Chapter V—The Organs of State Administration of the Union of Soviet Socialist Republics

ART. 64—The highest executive and administrative organ of the state power of the Union of Soviet Socialist Republics is the Council of Ministers of the U.S.S.R.

ART. 65—The Council of Ministers of the U.S.S.R. is responsible and accountable to the Supreme Soviet of the U.S.S.R. or, in the intervals between sessions of the Supreme Soviet, to the Presidium of the Supreme Soviet of the U.S.S.R.

ART. 66—The Council of Ministers of the U.S.S.R. issues decisions and orders on the basis and in pursuance of the laws in operation, and verifies their execution.

ART. 67—Decisions and orders of the Council of Ministers of the U.S.S.R. are binding throughout the territory of the U.S.S.R.

ART. 68—The Council of Ministers of the U.S.S.R.:

a) Co-ordinates and directs the work of the all-Union and Union-Republican Ministries of the U.S.S.R. and of other institutions under its jurisdiction and governs the republic economic councils and the economic councils of the economic administrative areas through the Councils of Ministers of the Union Republics;

b) Adopts measures to carry out the national-economic plan and the state budget, and to strengthen the credit and monetary system;

c) Adopts measures for the maintenance of public order, for the protection of the interests of the state, and for the safeguarding of the rights of citizens;

d) Exercises general guidance in the sphere of relations with foreign states;

e) Fixes the annual contingent of citizens to be called up for military service and directs the general organization of the Armed Forces of the country;

f) Sets up, whenever necessary, special Committees and Central Administrations under the Council of Ministers of the U.S.S.R. for economic and cultural affairs and defense.

ART. 69—The Council of Ministers of the U.S.S.R. has the right, in respect of those branches of administration and economy which come within the jurisdiction of the U.S.S.R., to suspend decisions and orders of the Councils of Ministers of the Union Republics, of republic economic councils, and of the economic councils of the economic administrative areas, and to annul orders and instructions of Ministers of the U.S.S.R.

ART. 70—The Council of Ministers of the U.S.S.R. is appointed by the Supreme Soviet of the U.S.S.R. and consists of: the Chairman of the Council of Ministers of the U.S.S.R.; the First Vice-Chairmen of the Council of Ministers of the U.S.S.R.; the Vice-Chairmen of the Council of Ministers of the U.S.S.R.; the Ministers of the U.S.S.R.; the Chairman of the State Planning Committee of the Council of Ministers of the U.S.S.R.; the Chairman of the Commission of Soviet Control of the Council of Ministers of the U.S.S.R.; the Chairman of the State Vocational and Technical Education Committee of the Council of Ministers of the U.S.S.R.; the Chairman of the State Labor and Wages Committee of the Council of Ministers of the U.S.S.R.; the Chairman of the State Automation and Machine Building Committee of the Council of Ministers of the U.S.S.R.; the Chairman of the State Scientific and Technical Committee of the Council of Ministers of the U.S.S.R.; the Chairman of the State Aviation Technology Committee of the Council of Ministers of the U.S.S.R.; the Chairman of the State Defense Technology Committee of the Council of Ministers of the U.S.S.R.; the Chairman of the State Radio Electronics Committee of the Council of Ministers of the U.S.S.R.; the Chairman of the State Shipbuilding Committee of the Council of Ministers of the U.S.S.R.; the Chairman of the State Chemistry Committee of the Council of Ministers of the U.S.S.R.; the Chairman of the State Construction Committee of the Council of Ministers of the U.S.S.R.; the Chairman of the State Grain Products Committee of the Council of Ministers of the U.S.S.R.; the Chairman of the State Foreign Economic Relations Committee of the Council of Ministers of the U.S.S.R.; the Chairman of the Committee of State Security of the Council of Ministers of the U.S.S.R.; the Chairman of the Board of the State Bank of the U.S.S.R.; the Director of the Central Statistical Administration of the Council of Ministers of the U.S.S.R.; the Chairman of the State Scientific Economic Council of the Council of Ministers of the U.S.S.R.

The Council of Ministers of the U.S.S.R. includes the Chairmen of the Councils of Ministers of the Union Republics as ex officio members.

ART. 71—The Government of the U.S.S.R. or a Minister of the U.S.S.R. to whom a question of a member of the Supreme Soviet of the U.S.S.R. is addressed must give a verbal or written reply in the respective Chamber within a period not exceeding three days.

ART. 72—The Ministers of the U.S.S.R. direct the branches of state administration which come within the jurisdiction of the U.S.S.R.

ART. 73—The Ministers of the U.S.S.R., within the limits of the jurisdiction of their respective Ministries, issue orders and instructions on the basis and in pursuance of the laws in operation, and also of decisions and orders of the Council of Ministers of the U.S.S.R., and verify their execution.

ART. 74—The Ministries of the U.S.S.R. are either all-Union or Union-Republican Ministries.

ART. 75—Each all-Union Ministry directs the branch of state administration entrusted to it throughout the territory of the U.S.S.R. either directly or through bodies appointed by it.

ART. 76—The Union-Republican Ministries, as a rule, direct the branches of state administration entrusted to them through corresponding Ministries of the Union Republics; they administer directly only a definite and limited number of enterprises according to a list confirmed by the Presidium of the Supreme Soviet of the U.S.S.R.

ART. 77—The following Ministries are all-Union Ministries:

The Ministry of Foreign Trade; the Ministry of Merchant Marine; the Ministry of Railways; the Ministry of Medium Machine Building; the Ministry of Transport Construction; the Ministry of Construction of Electric Power Stations.

ART. 78—The following Ministries are Union-Republican Ministries:

The Ministry of Higher and Specialized Secondary Education; the Ministry of Geology and Conservation of Mineral Resources; the Ministry of Public Health; the Ministry of Foreign Affairs; the Ministry of Culture; the Ministry of Defense; the Ministry of Communications; the Ministry of Agriculture; the Ministry of Finance.

CHAPTER VI—THE ORGANS OF STATE ADMINISTRATION OF THE UNION REPUBLICS

ART. 79—The highest executive and administrative organ of the state power of a Union Republic is the Council of Ministers of the Union Republic.

ART. 80—The Council of Ministers of a Union Republic is responsible and accountable to the Supreme Soviet of the Union Republic, or, in the intervals between sessions of the Supreme Soviet of the Union Republic, to the Presidium of the Supreme Soviet of the Union Republic.

ART. 81—The Council of Ministers of a Union Republic issues decisions and orders on the basis and in pursuance of the laws in operation of the U.S.S.R. and of the Union Republic, and of the decisions and orders of the Council of Ministers of the U.S.S.R., and verifies their execution.

ART. 82—The Council of Ministers of a Union Republic has the right to suspend decisions and orders of the Councils of Ministers of its Autonomous Republics and to annul decisions and orders of the Executive Committees of the Soviets of Working People's Deputies of its Territories, Regions and Autonomous Regions, and also the decisions and orders of the republic economic councils and the economic councils of the economic administrative areas.

ART. 83—The Council of Ministers of a Union Republic is appointed by the Supreme Soviet of the Union Republic and consists of:

The Chairman of the Council of Ministers of the Union Republic; the Vice-Chairmen of the Council of Ministers; the Ministers; the Chairmen of the state committees and commissions and directors of other agencies of the Council of Ministers set up by the Supreme Soviet of the Union Republic in accordance with the constitution of the Union Republic.

ART. 84—The Ministers of a Union Republic direct the branches of state administration which come within the jurisdiction of the Union Republic.

ART. 85—The Ministers of a Union Republic, within the limits of the jurisdiction of their respective Ministries, issue orders and instructions on the basis and in pursuance of the laws of the U.S.S.R. and of the Union Republic, of the decisions and orders of the Council of Ministers of the U.S.S.R. and the Council of Ministers of the Union Republic, and of the orders and instructions of the Union-Republican Ministries of the U.S.S.R.

ART. 86—The Ministries of a Union Republic are either Union-Republican or Republican Ministries.

ART. 87—Each Union-Republican Ministry directs the branch of state administration entrusted to it, and is subordinate both to the Council of Ministers of the Union Republic and to the corresponding Union-Republican Ministry of the U.S.S.R.

ART. 88—Each Republican Ministry directs the branch of state administration entrusted to it and is directly subordinate to the Council of Ministers of the Union Republic.

ART. 88a—The economic councils of the economic administrative areas direct the branches of economic activity entrusted to them and are directly subordinate to the Council of Ministers of the Union Republic.

In Union Republics where republic economic councils are formed, the economic councils of economic administrative regions are subordinate in their activities to both the Councils of Ministers of the Union Republics and the republic economic council.

The economic councils of the economic administrative areas, within the limits of their jurisdiction, issue orders and instructions on the basis and in pursuance of the laws of the U.S.S.R. and of the Union Republic, and of the decisions and orders of the Council of Ministers of the U.S.S.R. and the Council of Ministers of the Union Republic.

ART. 88b—The republic economic council coordinates the economic activity of the economic councils of economic administrative regions and is directly subordinate to the Council of Ministers of the Union Republic.

The republic economic council, within the bounds of its competence, issues resolutions and directives on the basis and in execution of the laws of the U.S.S.R. and the Union Republic and of the resolutions and directives of the Council of Ministers of the U.S.S.R. and the Council of Ministers of the Union Republic.

The republic economic council has the right to suspend the resolutions and directives of the economic councils of economic administrative regions.

CHAPTER VII—THE HIGHER ORGANS OF STATE POWER
IN THE AUTONOMOUS SOVIET SOCIALIST REPUBLICS

ART. 89—The highest organ of state power in an Autonomous Republic is the Supreme Soviet of the Autonomous Republic.

ART. 90—The Supreme Soviet of an Autonomous Republic is elected by the citizens of the Republic for a term of four years on a basis of representation established by the Constitution of the Autonomous Republic.

ART. 91—The Supreme Soviet of an Autonomous Republic is the sole legislative organ of the Autonomous Republic.

ART. 92—Each Autonomous Republic has its own Constitution, which takes account of the specific features of the Autonomous Republic and is drawn up in full conformity with the Constitution of the Union Republic.

ART. 93—The Supreme Soviet of an Autonomous Republic elects the Presidium of the Supreme Soviet of the Autonomous Republic and appoints the Council of Ministers of the Autonomous Republic, in accordance with its Constitution.

Chapter VIII—The Local Organs of State Power

Art. 94—The organs of state power in Territories, Regions, Autonomous Regions, Areas, Districts, cities and rural localities (stanitsas, villages, hamlets, kishlaks, auls) are the Soviets of Working People's Deputies.

Art. 95—The Soviets of Working People's Deputies of Territories, Regions, Autonomous Regions, Areas, Districts, cities and rural localities (stanitsas, villages, hamlets, kishlaks, auls) are elected by the working people of the respective Territories, Regions, Autonomous Regions, Areas, Districts, cities or rural localities for a term of two years.

Art. 96—The basis of representation for Soviets of Working People's Deputies is determined by the Constitutions of the Union Republics.

Art. 97—The Soviets of Working People's Deputies direct the work of the organs of administration subordinate to them, ensure the maintenance of public order, the observance of the laws and the protection of the rights of citizens, direct local economic and cultural affairs and draw up the local budgets.

Art. 98—The Soviets of Working People's Deputies adopt decisions and issue orders within the limits of the powers vested in them by the laws of the U.S.S.R. and of the Union Republic.

Art. 99—The executive and administrative organ of the Soviet of Working People's Deputies of a Territory, Region, Autonomous Region, Area, District, city or rural locality is the Executive Committee elected by it, consisting of a Chairman, Vice-Chairmen, a Secretary and members.

Art. 100—The executive and administrative organ of the Soviet of Working People's Deputies in a small locality, in accordance with the Constitution of the Union Republic, is the Chairman, the Vice-Chairman and the Secretary elected by the Soviet of Working People's Deputies.

Art. 101—The executive organs of the Soviets of Working People's Deputies are directly accountable both to the Soviets of Working People's Deputies which elected them and to the executive organ of the superior Soviet of Working People's Deputies.

Chapter IX—The Courts and the Procurator's Office

Art. 102—In the U.S.S.R. justice is administered by the Supreme Court of the U.S.S.R., the Supreme Courts of the Union Republics, the Courts of the Territories, Regions, Autonomous Republics, Autonomous Regions and Areas, the Special Courts of the U.S.S.R. established by decision of the Supreme Soviet of the U.S.S.R., and the People's Courts.

Art. 103—In all Courts cases are tried with the participation of people's assessors except in cases specially provided for by law.

Art. 104—The Supreme Court of the U.S.S.R. is the highest judicial organ. The Supreme Court of the U.S.S.R. is charged with the supervision of the judicial activities of all the judicial organs of the U.S.S.R. and of the Union Republics within the limits established by law.

Art. 105—The Supreme Court of the U.S.S.R. is elected by the Supreme Soviet of the U.S.S.R. for a term of five years. The Supreme Court of the U.S.S.R. includes the Chief Justices of the Supreme Courts of the Union Republics, ex officio.

Art. 106—The Supreme Courts of the Union Republics are elected by the Supreme Soviets of the Union Republics for a term of five years.

Art. 107—The Supreme Courts of the Autonomous Republics are elected by the Supreme Soviets of the Autonomous Republics for a term of five years.

Art. 108—The Courts of Territories, Regions, Autonomous Regions and Areas are elected by the Soviets of Working People's Deputies of the respective Territories, Regions, Autonomous Regions or Areas for a term of five years.

Art. 109—The People's Judges of the District People's Courts are elected by the citizens of the districts on the basis of universal, direct and equal suffrage by secret ballot for a term of five years.

The People's Assessors of the district People's Courts are elected by general meetings of workers, office employees and peasants at their places of work or residence, and of servicemen at military units, for a term of two years.

Art. 110—Judicial proceedings are conducted in the language of the Union Republic, Autonomous Republic or Autonomous Region, persons not knowing this language being guaranteed the opportunity of fully acquainting themselves with the material of the case through an interpreter and likewise the right to use their own language in court.

Art. 111—In all Courts of the U.S.S.R. cases are heard in public, unless otherwise provided for by law, and the accused is guaranteed the right to defense.

Art. 112—Judges are independent and subject only to the law.

Art. 113—Supreme supervisory power to ensure the strict observance of the law by all Ministries and institutions subordinated to them, as well as by officials and citizens of the U.S.S.R. generally, is vested in the Procurator-General of the U.S.S.R.

Art. 114—The Procurator-General of the U.S.S.R. is appointed by the Supreme Soviet of the U.S.S.R. for a term of seven years.

Art. 115—Procurators of Republics, Territories, Regions, Autonomous Republics and Autonomous Regions are appointed by the Procurator-General of the U.S.S.R. for a term of five years.

Art. 116—Area, district and city procurators are appointed by the Procurators of the Union Republics, subject to the approval of the Procurator-General of the U.S.S.R., for a term of five years.

Art. 117—The organs of the Procurator's Office perform their functions independently of any local organs whatsoever, being subordinate solely to the Procurator-General of the U.S.S.R.

Chapter X—Fundamental Rights and Duties of Citizens

Art. 118—Citizens of the U.S.S.R. have the right to work, that is, the right to guaranteed employment and payment for their work in accordance with its quantity and quality.

The right to work is ensured by the socialist organization of the national economy, the steady growth of the productive forces of Soviet society, the elimination of the possibility of economic crises, and the abolition of unemployment.

Art. 119—Citizens of the U.S.S.R. have the right to rest and leisure.

The right to rest and leisure is ensured by the establishment of a seven-hour day for industrial, office, and professional workers, the reduction of the working day to six hours for arduous trades and to four hours in shops where conditions of work are particularly arduous; by the institution of annual vacations with full pay for industrial, office, and professional workers, and by the provision of a wide network of sanatoria, holiday homes and clubs for the accommodation of the working people .

ART. 120—Citizens of the U.S.S.R. have the right to maintenance in old age and also in case of sickness or disability.

This right is ensured by the extensive development of social insurance of industrial, office, and professional workers at state expense, free medical service for the working people, and the provision of a wide network of health resorts for the use of the working people.

ART. 121—Citizens of the U.S.S.R. have the right to education.

This right is ensured by universal and compulsory eight-year education; by the extensive development of secondary general polytechnical education, technical vocational education, and specialized secondary and higher education on the basis of a link between training and life and production; by the comprehensive development of evening and correspondence education; by free education in all types of schools; by a system of state stipends; by instruction in the schools of the native languages; and by the organization at plants and state and collective farms of free vocational, technical, and agronomic training for the working people.

ART. 122—Women in the U.S.S.R. are accorded equal rights with men in all spheres of economic, government, cultural, political and other public activity.

The possibility of exercising these rights is ensured by women being accorded an equal right with men to work, payment for work, rest and leisure, social insurance and education, and by state protection of the interest of mother and child, state aid to mothers of large families and unmarried mothers, maternity leave with full pay, and the provision of a wide network of maternity homes, nurseries and kindergartens.

ART. 123—Equality of rights of citizens of the U.S.S.R., irrespective of their nationality or race, in all spheres of economic, government, cultural, political and other public activity, is an indefeasible law.

Any direct or indirect restriction of the rights of, or, conversely, the establishment of any direct or indirect privileges for, citizens on account of their race or nationality, as well as any advocacy of racial or national exclusiveness or hatred and contempt, are punishable by law.

ART. 124—In order to ensure to citizens freedom of conscience, the church in the U.S.S.R. is separated from the state, and the school from the church. Freedom of religious worship and freedom of anti-religious propaganda is recognized for all citizens.

ART. 125—In conformity with the interests of the working people, and in order to strengthen the socialist system, the citizens of the U.S.S.R. are guaranteed by law:

a) freedom of speech;
b) freedom of the press;
c) freedom of assembly, including the holding of mass meetings;
d) freedom of street processions and demonstrations.

These civil rights are ensured by placing at the disposal of the working people and their organizations printing presses, stocks of paper, public buildings, the streets, communications facilities, and other material requisites for the exercise of these rights.

ART. 126—In conformity with the interests of the working people, and in order to develop the organizational initiative and political activity of the masses of the people, citizens of the U.S.S.R. are guaranteed the right to unite in public organizations; trade unions, co-operative societies, youth organizations, sport and defense organizations, cultural, technical and scientific societies; and the most active and politically-conscious citizens in the ranks of the working class, working peasants and working intelligentsia voluntarily unite in the Communist Party of the Soviet Union, which is the vanguard of the working people in their struggle to build a communist society and is the leading core of all organizations of the working people, both public and state.

Art. 127—Citizens of the U.S.S.R. are guaranteed inviolability of the person. No person may be placed under arrest except by decision of a court or with the sanction of a procurator.

Art. 128—The inviolability of the homes of citizens and privacy of correspondence are protected by law.

Art. 129—The U.S.S.R. affords the right of asylum to foreign citizens persecuted for defending the interests of the working people, or for scientific activities, or for struggling for national liberation.

Art. 130—It is the duty of every citizen of the U.S.S.R. to abide by the Constitution of the Union of Soviet Socialist Republics, to observe the laws, to maintain labor discipline, honestly to perform public duties, and to respect the rules of socialist intercourse.

Art. 131—It is the duty of every citizen of the U.S.S.R. to safeguard and fortify public, socialist property as the sacred and inviolable foundation of the Soviety system, as the source of the wealth and might of the country, as the source of the prosperity and culture of all the working people.

Persons committing offenses against public, socialist property are enemies of the people.

Art. 132—Universal military service is law.

Military service in the Armed Forces of the U.S.S.R. is an honorable duty of the citizens of the U.S.S.R.

Art. 133—To defend the country is the sacred duty of every citizen of the U.S.S.R. Treason to the Motherland—violation of the oath of allegiance, desertion to the enemy, impairing the military power of the state, espionage—is punishable with all the severity of the law as the most heinous of crimes.

Chapter XI—The Electoral System

Art. 134—Members of all Soviets of Working People's Deputies—of the Supreme Soviet of the U.S.S.R., the Supreme Soviets of the Union Republics, the Soviets of Working People's Deputies of the Territories and Regions, the Supreme Soviets of the Autonomous Republics, the Soviets of Working People's Deputies of the Autonomous Regions, and the Area, District, City and rural (stanitsa, village, hamlet, kishlak, aul) Soviets of Working People's Deputies—are chosen by the electors on the basis of universal, equal and direct suffrage by secret ballot.

Art. 135—Elections of deputies are universal: all citizens of the U.S.S.R. who have reached the age of eighteen, irrespective of race or nationality, sex, religion, education, domicile, social origin, property status or past activities, have the right to vote in the election of deputies, with the exception of insane persons.

Every citizen of the U.S.S.R. who has reached the age of twenty-three is eligible for election to the Supreme Soviet of the U.S.S.R., irrespective of race or nationality, sex, religion, education, domicile, social origin, property status or past activities.

Art. 136—Elections of deputies are equal: each citizen has one vote; all citizens participate in elections on an equal footing.

Art. 137—Women have the right to elect and be elected on equal terms with men.

Art. 138—Citizens serving in the Armed Forces of the U.S.S.R. have the right to elect and be elected on equal terms with all other citizens.

Art. 139—Elections of deputies are direct: all Soviets of Working People's Deputies, from rural and city Soviets of Working People's Deputies to the Supreme Soviet of the U.S.S.R., are elected by the citizens by direct vote.

Art. 140—Voting at elections of deputies is secret.

Art. 141—Candidates are nominated by election districts.

The right to nominate candidates is secured to public organizations and societies of the working people: Communist Party organizations, trade unions, co-operatives, youth organizations and cultural societies.

Art. 142—It is the duty of every deputy to report to his electors on his work and on the work of his Soviet of Working People's Deputies, and he may be recalled at any time upon decision of a majority of the electors in the manner established by law.

Chapter XII—Arms, Flag, Capital

Art. 143—The arms of the Union of Soviet Socialist Republics are a sickle and hammer against a globe depicted in the rays of the sun and surrounded by ears of grain, with the inscription "Workers of All Countries, Unite!" in the languages of the Union Republics. At the top of the arms is a five-pointed star.

Art. 144—The state flag of the Union of Soviet Socialist Republics is of red cloth with the sickle and hammer depicted in gold in the upper corner near the staff and above them a five-pointed red star bordered in gold. The ratio of the width to the length is 1:2.

Art. 145—The Capital of the Union of Soviet Socialist Republics is the City of Moscow.

Chapter XIII—Procedure for Amending the Constitution

Art. 146—The Constitution of the U.S.S.R. may be amended only by decision of the Supreme Soviet of the U.S.S.R. adopted by a majority of not less than two-thirds of the votes in each of its Chambers.

Index